W9-CAX-007

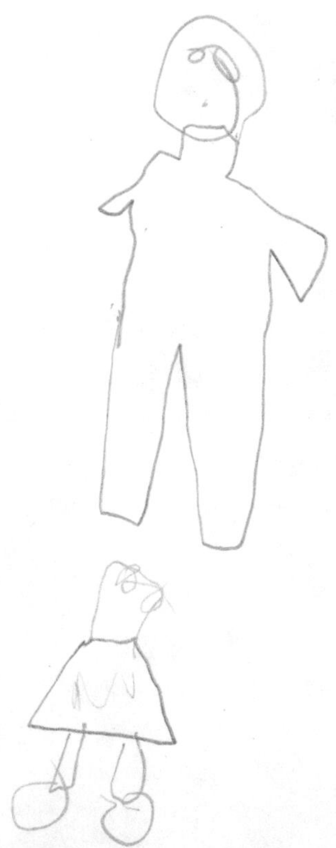

VOLUME 19 Meyer to Naval Rank

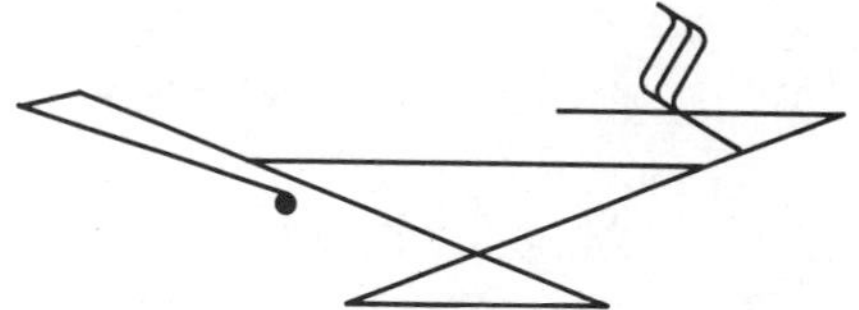

THE ENCYCLOPEDIA AMERICANA

INTERNATIONAL EDITION

COMPLETE IN THIRTY VOLUMES FIRST PUBLISHED IN 1829

AMERICANA CORPORATION International Headquarters: 575 Lexington Avenue, New York, New York 10022

Library of Congress Cataloging in Publication Data
Main entry under title:

THE ENCYCLOPEDIA AMERICANA.

Published 1829–58 under title: Encyclopaedia
Americana; 1907–12: The Americana.
Includes bibliographical references.
1. Encyclopedias and dictionaries.
AE5.E333 1976 031 75–1443
ISBN 0–7172–0107–4

MANUFACTURED IN THE U.S.A.

J. Allan Cash from Rapho Guillumette

MODERN ARCHITECTURE: The U.S. Embassy at New Delhi, India, by Edward D. Stone.

MEYER, mī′ẽr, **Adolf,** American psychiatrist and neurologist: b. Niederweningen, Switzerland, Sept. 13, 1866; d. Baltimore, Md., March 17, 1950. After passing a Swiss examination for the practice of medicine in 1890, Meyer spent two years in postgraduate studies at Paris, London, Edinburgh, Berlin, and Zurich, and received his M.D. at the University of Zurich in 1892. He then set out for the United States, where he served as docent in neurology, University of Chicago (1892–1895); pathologist to the Illinois Eastern Hospital for the Insane, Kankakee (1893–1895); pathologist, and later director of clinical and laboratory work, Worcester (Mass.) Insane Hospital, and docent in psychiatry, Clark University (1895–1902); director of the Pathological Institute, New York State Hospitals (1902–1910); and professor of psychiatry, Cornell University Medical School (1904–1909). In 1910 he went to Johns Hopkins University, where he served as professor of psychiatry and director of the Henry Phipps Psychiatric Clinic until his retirement in 1941.

Meyer, who was influenced by both Sigmund Freud, founder of psychoanalysis, and the physiologist Ivan Petrovich Pavlov, combined the principles of psychology and physiology in an approach which he called psychobiological, in which he attempted to evaluate the patient's personality from several points of view—"the whole individual in action." He introduced into American psychiatry the practice of compiling case histories, including data on hereditary and environmental, constitutional, social and economic, conscious and unconscious, factors. Together with Clifford Whittingham Beers he began the mental hygiene movement, which had as its aim the prevention of psychopathological ills by corrective social and individual measures. Meyer published extensively on neurology, pathology, psychiatry, and mental hygiene, and received many honors for his contributions in these fields.

MEYER, Conrad Ferdinand, Swiss poet and novelist: b. Zurich, Switzerland, Oct. 11, 1825; d. Kilchberg near Zurich, Nov. 28, 1898. He grew up in a home of cultured refinement. After studying law he became a recluse, a man without a mission, and oblivious to the immediate present, he sought to wrest the meaning of life from history. For years he wavered between painting and literature, between French and German. The Franco-German War of 1870 forced him to decide. In 1871 Meyer published *Huttens letzte Tage,* a heroic epic. In a series of dramatic monologues the hero records in terse couplets the events of his last days and his heroic life's struggles. Thus Meyer objectifies his own inner combat. The decades of reflective brooding now began to produce a rich harvest. In 1874 Meyer completed *Jürg Jenatsch,* a historical novel set in Graubünden (Grisons), Switzerland, during the Thirty Years' War, in which overweening pride leads to guilt and tragedy.

Feeling an affinity for the drama, Meyer turned to the dramatic, compact historical *Novelle.* The finest of his *Novellen,* in all of which Meyer avoids a happy ending, are: *Der Heilige* (1880), the tragedy of Thomas à Becket; *Gustav Adolfs Page* (1882), the tragedy of a young girl's hero worship; *Die Leiden eines Knaben* (1883); *Die Hochzeit des Mönchs* (1884), in which Dante is the narrator; *Die Richterin* (1885), the tragic tale of a heroic woman in the days of Charlemagne; and *Die Versuchung des Pescara* (1887).

Die Leiden eines Knaben is unique in Meyer's work and the literature of the day. A decade before Henrik Ibsen and Gerhart Hauptmann, Meyer made a helpless child the center of a tragedy. He had gained the needed insight from memories of his own childhood, but to free the story from every trace of subjectivity Meyer laid the scene in the days of Louis XIV and made the king's physician the narrator. Meyer chose his narrators with great skill. In his finest comic novel, *Plautus im Nonnenkloster* (1882), the narrator is a former cleric, now an adroit diplomat and collector of facetiae. Thus a subtle humor reigns supreme in a somewhat crude and boisterous plot.

Meyer had great lyric as well as great narrative gifts. In 1882 he published *Gedichte,* a rigorous selection of his poems of high quality, arranged in a sequence which is in itself a work of art. Warmly welcomed by Gottfried Keller and Theodor Storm, both lyrists in their own right, *Gedichte* soon won wide approval, and by 1892 five editions had been published. Since Meyer's lyric verse is the product of his mature years, a note of mellow quiet prevails, and many of his short and concise lyrics have the chaste self-restraint of a marble statue.

Meyer the poet, just like Meyer the novelist, seeks to attain the maximum of objectivity, and prefers a general objective statement to the more personal subjective confession. He loved life's exuberant fullness, however. The opening poem *Fülle* presents a picture of the riotous overflowing abundance of autumn. Here the human heart can satisfy its deepest needs and the poetic spirit take sustenance. The objective cast of the poem intensifies its passion. A number of fine ballads of great variety and a series of dramatic monologues, some of utmost intensity, further enrich the volume. All his work bears the imprint of consummate artistry.

Consult Maync, Harry, *Conrad Ferdinand Meyer und sein Werk* (Frauenfeld, Switz., 1925); Burkhard, Arthur, *Conrad Ferdinand Meyer, the Style and the Man* (Cambridge, Mass., 1932).

FRIEDRICH BRUNS,
Professor of German, Emeritus, University of Wisconsin.

MEYER, Eduard, German historian: b. Hamburg, Germany, Jan. 25, 1855; d. Berlin, Aug. 31, 1930. Meyer early became interested in ancient history, and had acquired a thorough background in Greek, Latin, Hebrew, and Arabic before he entered the university at Bonn when he was 17. After a year there he went to Leipzig, where he studied Egyptian and wrote his doctoral thesis on the Egyptian god Set-Typhon (1875). He spent a year as tutor in an English family in Constantinople (Istanbul), where he began his *Geschichte Troas* (1877). In 1879 he went to the University of Leipzig as lecturer; in 1885 he became professor of ancient history at Breslau; in 1889 at Halle; and in 1902 at Berlin, where he remained until his retirement in 1923.

Meyer had a particularly strong background in Egyptology, and his *Geschichte des alten Aegyptens* (1887) was the first detailed, integrated history of Egypt published. His particular interests were in the fields of economic history and religion. A universal historian in a day when it was still possible for one individual to control all the available material in an area extending from the Mediterranean to the Iranian Plateau, Meyer is known especially for his *Geschichte des Altertums,* first published in five volumes between 1884 and 1902, which has the unity of antiquity as its integrating theme. Because of the wealth of new archaeological material being discovered, Meyer began to revise this work in 1907 and continued revisions for the rest of his life. After his death revisions were continued by Hans Erich Stier.

Among Meyer's other works are: *Zur Theorie und Methodik der Geschichte* (1902); *Aegyptische Chronologie* (1904 and 1907); and *Ursprung und Anfänge des Christentums,* 4 vols. (1921–1924).

MEYER, Eugene, American banker, government official, and newspaper executive: b. Los Angeles, Calif., Oct. 31, 1875; d. Washington, D.C., July 17, 1959. The son of a banker, Meyer graduated from Yale University in 1895, then spent two years in European banking houses learning the fundamentals of economics and international finance. After four years in the New York office of a great international bank, he established in 1901 his own investment banking house, Eugene Meyer, Jr., and Company. In 1917, after a highly successful career in this field, he dissolved the firm and entered government service as a dollar-a-year man. Among the many positions held in the following years were those as director of the War Finance Corporation (1918–1927); member of the Farm Loan Board (1927–1929); governor of the Federal Reserve Bank (1930–1933); and first chairman of the board of the Reconstruction Finance Corporation (1932).

In 1933, Meyer turned to another career, buying at auction the Washington *Post,* which had gone into receivership. As publisher (1933–1946) and editor (1940–1946), he built the *Post* into one of the foremost newspapers in the United States. In addition to his publishing activities, Meyer found time to serve in a number of organizations. He was president of the National Committee on Mental Hygiene (1944–1946) and of the Washington Criminal Justice Association (1936–1945), for example, and in 1946 he became the first president of the International Bank for Reconstruction and Development.

MEYER, George von Lengerke, American diplomat and cabinet officer: b. Boston, Mass., June 24, 1858; d. March 9, 1918. Born into a wealthy Beacon Hill family, he graduated from Harvard College in 1879 and entered local politics as a Republican. From 1894 to 1897 he was speaker of the state House of Representatives. In 1900 President William McKinley named him ambassador to Italy, where Meyer won the personal confidence of the newly crowned King Victor Emmanuel III and also of Emperor William II of Germany. When President Theodore Roosevelt wanted an effective advocate for his proposals to mediate the Russo-Japanese War, he shifted Meyer to the embassy at St. Petersburg (1905), with notable success. Two years later Meyer became postmaster general in Roosevelt's cabinet. In the administration of President William Howard Taft, he was secretary of the navy (1909–1913) and contributed significantly to the fighting efficiency of the fleet, especially in the improvement of gunnery and engineering operations.

MEYER, Hans, German explorer and publisher: b. Hildburghausen, Germany, March 22, 1858; d. Leipzig, July 5, 1929. The son of Herrmann Julius Meyer (see JOSEPH MEYER), he studied political and natural science and made a trip around the world (1881–1882) before becoming a partner (1884) in the Bibliographisches Institut, the family publishing house. He made a number of expeditions to East Africa, and was the first (in 1889 with L. Purtscheller) to ascend to the high Kibo summit of Mount Kilimanjaro. In 1894 he visited the Canary Islands and in 1903 studied volcanoes and glaciation in the mountains of Ecuador. In 1911 he explored Ruanda-Urundi, then a part of German East Africa. He became a member of the German colonial council in 1901. After resigning the directorship of the Bibliographisches Institut in 1914, Meyer served as professor of colonial geography at Leipzig from 1915 to 1928. His many publications include *Ostafrikanische Gletscherfahrten* (1890; *Across East African Glaciers,* 1891); *Der Kilimandscharo* (1900); and *Das Deutsche Kolonialreich,* 2 vols. (1909–1910).

MEYER, Hans Heinrich, Swiss painter and writer on art: b. Zurich, Switzerland, March 16, 1760; d. Jena, Germany, Oct. 11, 1832. After studying painting in Zurich, he spent five years, from 1784 to 1789, studying art in Rome. There he met Goethe, and together they began to study the historical aspect of art. Although he became Goethe's counselor in matters of art, he was primarily a follower. His moment of glory came when he was asked to write the history of 18th century art for *Winckelmann und sein Jahrhundert* (1805), to which Goethe himself contributed a notable study of Johann Joachim Winckelmann. As a representative of pure classical doctrine in the arts, Meyer fulminated against the romantics. In 1824 he began a lengthy, dogma-ridden treatise on Greek and Roman sculpture. In his own day he was often called Goethe-Meyer, not always in token of admiration.

MEYER, Joseph, German publisher and industrialist: b. Gotha, Germany, May 9, 1796; d. Hildburghausen, June 27, 1856. After unsuccessful ventures in trade and industry, he made a translation of Shakespeare's works. He also began publishing a *Correspondenzblatt für Kaufleute* which was so successful that he started an English literary review, *Meyer's British Chronicle.* In 1826 he established a publishing house, the Bibliographisches Institut, in Gotha, moving it two years later to Hildburghausen. Meyer had the idea of making the classics available at popular prices; the resulting *Bibliothek der Deutschen Classiken* ran to 150 volumes and 4 printings. Other publications included *Meyers British Classics; Our Globe,* a weekly published in Philadelphia, Pa., from 1832 to 1837; and *Meyer's Universum,* a historical-geographic periodical (1835–1860) and yearbook (1860–1862), published in 12 languages and with 80,000 subscribers. An illustrated encyclopedia, *Das grosse Konversations-Lexikon,* was published in 46 volumes in 1839–1852 with 6 supplements appearing between 1853 and 1855. Meyer himself contributed to many of these publications.

In 1830 Meyer's interests turned to industry, and he built up a network of holdings which included a railroad, foundries, and mines. He suffered financial reverses as a consequence of the 1848 revolution, however, and at the time of his death his enterprises were in bankruptcy. The Bibliographische Institut was saved by his son, Hermann Julius Meyer, who had fled to New York City after the revolution but had returned in 1854. The Bibliographische Institut continued under Meyer's son Hermann Julius and his grandsons Hans and Hermann, and *Meyers Lexikon* continued to be published, its 7th edition appearing in 12 volumes in 1924–1930.

MEYER, (Julius) Lothar, German chemist: b. Varel, Oldenburg, Germany, Aug. 19, 1830; d. Tübingen, April 11, 1895. He studied medicine at Zurich and Würzburg, later specializing in physiological chemistry at Heidelberg, and in mathematical physics at Königsberg. He received his degree at Breslau in 1858 and lectured there the following year. After lecturing at Eberswalde (1866–1868) and at Karlsruhe (1868–1876), he became professor of chemistry at Tübingen in 1870. Meyer's early research was on the physiology of respiration, and in 1857 he recognized that the oxygen breathed was held in the blood by some sort of chemical union. Later he turned to a classification of the chemical elements and, independently of Dmitri Ivanovich Mendeleyev, worked out the periodic law (q.v.), publishing his results in the same year (1869) as Mendeleyev. Meyer's *Die modernen Theorien der Chemie* (1864), which discusses the relations between atomic weights and the properties of elements, went through a number of editions and was translated into English (1888).

MEYER, (Marie) Paul (Hyacinthe), French philologist: b. Paris, France, Jan. 17, 1840; d. Saint-Mandé, Sept. 7, 1917. Educated at the École des Chartes, he first specialized in Provençal, later in Old French. He was employed as archivist in Tarascon and at the Bibliothèque Nationale before returning to the École des Chartes as professor (1869) and director (1882). In 1876 he was appointed professor of Romance languages at the Collège de France, and in 1884 he became a member of the Académie des inscriptions et belles-lettres. With Gaston Paris he founded the *Revue critique* (1866) and *Romania* (1872). Meyer was a leader in developing a rigorous method in the field of Romance philology. He edited a number of Provençal and Old French texts, many of which were published by the Société de l'histoire de France and the Société des anciens textes français. Other publications include *Recueil d'anciens textes bas-latins, provençaux et français,* 2 vols. (1874–1877) and *Documents linguistiques du midi de la France* (1909).

MEYER, Viktor, German chemist: b. Berlin, Germany, Sept. 8, 1848; d. Heidelberg, Aug. 8, 1897. He studied at Heidelberg under Robert Wilhelm Bunsen from 1865 to 1868, then went to Berlin as assistant to Adolf Baeyer. After a year at Württemberg he became professor of chemistry at the Zurich Polytechnic in 1872; went to Göttingen in 1885, and in 1889 returned to Heidelberg to occupy the chair of his former professor, Bunsen. In spite of ill health he was a brilliant teacher as well as a tireless research scientist. His career was cut short by suicide.

Meyer's is one of the important names in the history of chemistry. In 1874 he discovered the nitrocompounds of the aliphatic series, the investigation of which occupied him and his students for the following 20 years. In 1877 he described his method for determining vapor densities which, later refined so that densities at high temperatures could be determined, became known as the Meyer method. In 1882 he discovered the series of organic compounds known as oximes, and this began a fruitful study of isomerism of the oximes, and to his coining of the term stereochemistry. An accident during a lecture demonstration, in which a supply of pure benzene failed to give the expected reaction, led to the discovery in 1883 of a new substance, thiophene, a sulphur compound which had been present in the coal-tar benzene normally used in the demonstration. In 1891 Meyer carried out a series of experiments on the ignition temperatures of explosive gas mixtures, and in 1892 he began investigation of the iodoso compounds. From 1894 until his death Meyer and his students studied the phenomenon to which he gave the name steric hindrance, the influence exerted on a reacting group by the spatial arrangement of neighboring atoms.

Meyer's publications include *Pyrochemische Untersuchungen* (1885), a collection of his studies on the vapor densities of inorganic substances; *Die Thiophengruppe* (1888), on the thiophene compounds; and *Lehrbuch der organischen Chemie* (1893–1896; 2d ed., 1922–1929), a two-volume textbook prepared by Meyer in collaboration with Paul Jacobson.

MEYER-LÜBKE, mī'ẽr-lüp'kĕ, **Wilhelm,** Swiss philologist: b. Dübendorf, Switzerland, Jan. 30, 1861; d. Bonn, Germany, Oct. 4, 1936. After studying Romance and Indo-Germanic philology at the universities of Zurich, Berlin, and Paris, he became professor of Romance philology at Jena (1887), Vienna (1890), and Bonn (1915). His systematic comparative studies of the Romance languages, and of the Vulgar Latin from which they evolved, made his publications essential reference works for scholars in the field of Romance philology, and many of them were translated into various Romance languages. In addition to his classic etymological dictionary, *Romani-*

sches etymologisches Wörterbuch (1911–1920; 3d ed., 1930–1935), his chief works were the *Grammatik der romanischen Sprachen,* 4 vols. (1890–1902); *Italienische Grammatik* (1890); *Einführung in das Studium der romanischen Sprachwissenschaft* (1901; 3d ed., 1920); *Historische Grammatik der französischen Sprache,* 2 vols. (1908–1921); and *Das Katalanische* (1925). In his later years there was some feeling that his methodology was overrigid, and that he had failed to keep up with new developments in linguistic science.

MEYERBEER, mī'ēr-bār, **Giacomo** (real name JACOB LIEBMANN BEER), German composer: b. Berlin, Germany, Sept. 5, 1791; d. Paris, France, May 2, 1864. Born into a family of Jewish bankers, he became a prodigious pianist before his tenth birthday. After studies in Berlin and Darmstadt, Meyerbeer heard his oratorio *Gott und die Natur* sung at Berlin in 1811, and his first opera—*Jephthas Gelübde*—at Munich in 1812. Neither of these was successful, but *Wirt und Gast,* his second opera (Stuttgart 1813), was received well enough to have been heard in Vienna, Prague, and Dresden by 1820. When Antonio Salieri, the noted court conductor at Vienna, advised Meyerbeer to go to Italy for further study, he did so, first visiting Venice in 1815. After having acquainted himself with the ways of Italian opera and Italian singing, he composed to Italian librettos six operas much influenced by those of Gioacchino Antonio Rossini. The last of these—*Il Crociato in Egitto* (Venice 1824)—was a resounding triumph. Meyerbeer then spent some years in Paris perfecting his knowledge of French opera, the French language, and, above all, French declamation. The first fruit of this devotion was the opera *Robert le Diable,* produced at the Paris Opéra in Nov. 21, 1831. One of the greatest of all operatic successes, this spectacular work set the French (later international) taste for the grandest grand opera.

Giacomo Meyerbeer

The Bettmann Archive

Robert le Diable was followed by Meyerbeer's masterpiece, *Les Huguenots* (Opéra 1836), which, though coolly received at first, became even more popular. When it was staged at Berlin in 1842, Friedrich Wilhelm IV of Prussia appointed Meyerbeer general music director there, and he thereafter divided his time between Berlin and Paris. His German opera *Ein Feldlager in Schlesien* (1844) was a comparative failure until, in 1847, Jenny Lind won audiences as its heroine, Vielka. *Le Prophète,* the third of Meyerbeer's French grand operas, was sung at the Paris Opéra in 1849. Five years later, the Opéra-Comique staged his *L'Étoile du nord,* parts of the score of which he had taken over from *Ein Feldlager in Schlesien.* The Opéra-Comique also produced his *Le Pardon de Ploërmel,* soon better known as *Dinorah,* in 1859. *L'Africaine,* the opera on which Meyerbeer had worked intermittently from 1838 on, was in rehearsal when he died; it was triumphantly staged at the Opéra on April 28, 1865, one year after his death.

Meyerbeer's purely musical gifts were notable, if eclectic; his mastery of technique was complete. But his long, almost unparalleled domination of the world of opera depended upon his unique ability to create—with the help of the expert librettist Augustin Eugène Scribe (1791–1861)—musical stage spectacles of ardent theatrical vitality which were also vehicles for great singers. All the most renowned stars of the second half of the 19th century delighted to perform in his operas, to the applause of eager audiences everywhere. Early in the 20th century, however, Meyerbeer's operas fell into disuse. None of them, for example, was sung at the Metropolitan Opera House in New York between the 1933–1934 season and 1960, and any revival of them would require huge expenditures for staging and the special training of casts of phenomenally agile and expressive singers.

Meyerbeer's nonoperatic music, much of it lacking vitality, is no longer played, although his incidental music for *Struensee* (1846), a tragic drama by his brother Michael Beer, has been considered one of his best works.

Consult Dauriac, L., *Meyerbeer,* 2d ed. (Paris 1930); Becker, H., *Der Fall Heine-Meyerbeer* (Kassel 1958).

HERBERT WEINSTOCK.

MEYERHOF, mī'ēr-hōf, **Otto,** German physiologist and biochemist: b. Hannover, Germany, April 12, 1884; d. Philadelphia, Pa., Oct. 6, 1951. Graduated in 1909 at the University of Heidelberg as a doctor of medicine, he developed an early interest in psychology and philosophy. His meeting with Otto Warburg at the Heidelberg Medical Clinic stimulated Meyerhof's interest in what was going to be his life work. He joined the Department of Physiology at Kiel University in 1918 and in 1924 became director of the Physiology Division at the Kaiser Wilhelm Institute for Biology in Berlin-Dahlem. In 1929 he became director of the Physiology Division of the Kaiser Wilhelm Institute for Medical Research at Heidelberg. Meyerhof's pioneer work threw considerable light upon the chemistry and thermodynamics of muscular contraction, intermediate enzymatic steps of carbohydrate metabolism in muscle and yeast, and cellular oxidations in general. He was awarded the 1922 Nobel Prize in Medicine (with Archibald Vivian Hill) for his discovery of the origin and fate of lactic acid in muscle. In 1930 he published his now classical monograph *Die Chemischen Vorgänge in Muskel . . .* (The Chemical Processes in Muscle . . .). In 1938–1940 he worked at the Institute of Physiochemical Biology in Paris, and subsequently continued his research activities at the School of Medicine of the University of Pennsylvania. He became an American citizen in 1948. Among many other honors he was a foreign fellow of the Royal Society (London) and a member of the United States National Academy of Sciences.

SEVERO OCHOA,
Department of Biochemistry, New York University College of Medicine.

MEYERHOLD, mī′ər-hōlt, **Vsevolod Emilievich** (1874–1942), Russian stage director and actor. He was born in Paris, France, on Feb. 9, 1874 (Jan. 1, Old Style). He was a student of Vladimir Nemirovich-Danchenko, the cofounder with Konstantin Stanislavsky of the Moscow Art Theatre, at the Musical-Dramatic School of the Moscow Philharmonic Society. As a result of this apprenticeship he was invited to join the just-formed Moscow Art Theatre Company in 1898. He acted in the naturalistic stage convention of Stanislavsky until 1902, when he left to work in the provinces. He founded a group called the Society of New Drama, in which he was actor, artistic director, dramaturgist, and teacher. He showed so much capability in the latter category that in 1905, Stanislavsky invited him to head a newly organized studio of the parent Moscow Art Theatre, where his flair for symbolism was given free rein.

In the fashion of Russian acting studios, he rehearsed Maeterlinck's *La Mort de Tintagiles* for months although it was never shown to the public. Probably on the strength of this production, Vera Kommisarjevskaya in 1906 invited him to direct her in her theater in St. Petersburg. There he put into practice the symbolism and stylization he had been practicing in the Moscow Art Theatre studio. In his "abstract" theater he reduced the actor to the role of a puppet, thus anticipating Gordon Craig's conception of the actor as a "super-marionette," dispensing with the human element entirely. Meyerhold's dehumanization of the actor led to his inevitable break with Kommisarjevskaya. Between 1913 and 1917 he staged some brilliant productions at the Imperial playhouses in St. Petersburg (now Leningrad), the Aleksandrinsky (now the Pushkin), and the Mariinsky (now the Kirov), notable of which was Lermontov's *Masquerade* in March 1917 on the night of the opening of the first, or moderate, revolution.

Encouraged by Anatoli V. Lunarcharsky, who was appointed commissar of education in charge of theaters after the October, or Bolshevik, Revolution, Meyerhold joined the Communist party in 1918 and for nearly 20 years was the favored director and *regisseur*. His downfall came in 1938 when his theater in Moscow (opened in 1920) was dissolved because of his deviation from the party line. He was accused of dropping Soviet plays from his repertoire and of having offered no new production at all in two years. He was arrested in 1939 and disappeared, and his wife, the actress Zinaida Raikh, subsequently was found stabbed to death in their apartment. His own death was reported to have taken place on March 17, 1942.

George Freedley, *Former Curator Theatre Collection, New York Public Library*

Further Reading: Cole, Toby, and Chinoy, H. K., eds., *Actors on Acting* (Crown 1949); Lyons, Eugene, "Red Propaganda, Oxonian Style," *Theatre Arts*, vol. 39, pp. 26–27, August 1955; Symons, James M., *Meyerhold's Theatre of the Grotesque: The Post-Revolutionary Productions, 1920–1932* (Univ. of Miami Press 1971).

MEYNELL, mĕn′l, **Alice Christiana Gertrude** (née Thompson), English poet and essayist: b. Barnes, Surrey, England, Sept. 22, 1847; d. London, Nov. 27, 1922. She spent much of her childhood in Italy, and was educated by her father. About 1872 she became a Catholic, following the conversion of her mother, a concert pianist. Alfred Lord Tennyson encouraged her to publish, and his own publisher brought out her first volume of poems, *Preludes* (1875), which was illustrated by her sister Elizabeth, Lady Butler. In 1877 she married Wilfrid Meynell, by whom she had eight children.

Dependent on journalism for a livelihood, the Meynells edited briefly (1880) *The Pen*, which published essays by Tennyson, Browning, Rossetti, and Ruskin; the Catholic *Weekly Register* (1881–1895); and a monthly, *Merry England* (1883–1895). In addition to writing for these, Mrs. Meynell contributed to the *Dublin Review* (1906–1922), the *Scots Observer*, later the *National Observer* (1889–1894), and the *Pall Mall Gazette*, for which she wrote a weekly column (1894). Most of her volumes of prose were collections of essays first published in periodicals. Among these are *The Rhythm of Life* (1893); *The Colour of Life* (1896); *The Children* (1897); *The Spirit of Place* (1899); *Ceres' Runaway* (1909); *Hearts of Controversy* (1917); and *Second Person Singular* (1921). *John Ruskin* (1900), commissioned by a publisher, was written as a book. *Poems*, published posthumously in 1923, brought together the verse which had appeared in several earlier volumes.

The sensitive perception, freshness, and strength of her writing brought Alice Meynell many friends (Wilfrid Meynell asked to be introduced to her after reading one of her poems), and the Meynell home was a meeting place for the most celebrated writers in London. George Meredith was a close friend, and on the death of Lord Tennyson, Coventry Patmore proposed her for the laureateship of England. Her poetry reveals the same delicacy, the same mystic searching for the unseen world of the soul, that characterize the poems of her idols, Elizabeth Barrett Browning and Christina Rossetti.

Further Reading: Meynell, Alice, *Alice Meynell, a Memoir* (1929; reprint, R. West 1973).

MEZZO-SOPRANO, met-sō-sə-pran′ō, the female singing voice intermediate between the contralto and the soprano voices. The mezzo-soprano voice usually has a range of about two octaves—from G below the staff to A above the staff in the treble clef. The tonal quality of the mezzo-soprano voice is somewhat darker than that of the soprano voice, and it usually is throatier and less brilliant.

MEZZOTINT, met′sō-tint, a kind of print, and the intaglio printing technique to produce it, achieving gradations of tone. The surface of a copper plate is evenly roughened by drawing a rocker, a sort of comb with metal teeth, over it in all directions to raise a burr. At this point, the plate, covered with tiny barbs and depressions, which hold ink, would print entirely a rich deep black. The design is made, working from dark to light, by scraping off and polishing the plate in areas to be light so that they will print in shades of gray or sharp white. Areas may be roughened again with a roulette, a small wheel with incised lines, and linear effects may be achieved by etching or engraving.

Mezzotint was invented about 1640 by Ludwig von Siegen, who probably trained another early practitioner, Prince Rupert of Bavaria. The process was popular from the 17th to the 19th century for making prints of oil paintings. No longer a commercial procedure, it is used by artists in combination with other techniques.

GEORG GERSTER, FROM RAPHO GUILLUMETTE

Downtown Miami (*foreground*), with Port of Miami terminal in Biscayne Bay. Across the bay is Miami Beach resort.

MIAMI, mī-am′ē, is a city in southeastern Florida, the most southerly major city in the continental United States. It is located on the Atlantic coast, some 2° north of the Tropic of Cancer, and has a warm subtropical marine climate, with an average annual temperature of about 75° F (24° C). Because of its mild weather, ocean setting, and extensive resort facilities, Miami, together with its environs, is one of the great tourist centers of the world.

Miami and Environs. Miami, with an area of 54 square miles (140 sq km), fronts on Biscayne Bay, an arm of the Atlantic Ocean created by islands that constitute the northern reaches of the Florida Keys. The Miami River, which is connected by canal with Lake Okeechobee to the northwest, bisects the city. Miami is divided into four parts—Northwest, Northeast, Southwest, and Southeast—formed by the intersection of Flagler Street, running east and west, and Miami Avenue, running north and south.

Miami is the seat of Dade county, with which the Miami metropolitan area (Greater Miami) is coextensive. Greater Miami consists of 27 independent municipalities and of large unincorporated areas, some of which are heavily populated. Among the communities north of Miami are North Miami Beach, North Miami, and Miami Shores. Hialeah and Miami Springs are to the west, and Coral Gables, South Miami, and Homestead are to the south. On islands offshore, east of Miami across Biscayne Bay, are the luxurious resorts of Miami Beach, Surfside, and Bal Harbour. These communities, as well as fashionable Key Biscayne to the south, connect with the mainland by causeways.

Dade county covers 2,408 square miles (6,237 sq km), of which 354 square miles (917 sq km) is water. The western half of the county forms part of the Everglades National Park, one of the nation's most extensive wilderness preserves.

People. Greater Miami is predominantly white. About 15% is nonwhite, mostly Negro, with a sprinkling of other races. More than a quarter of a million persons of Cuban origin live in and around Miami. This group, which introduced its Latin-Caribbean culture to the area, greatly expanded from an influx of refugees after the Castro regime came to power in Cuba in 1959. Another large segment of the population—about 14% of the total—consists of people 65 years of age or older, many of whom retired to Florida from the northern United States. In Miami Beach nearly half the residents are in this age group.

The city of Miami had a population of 1,681 in 1900. By 1960 it had increased to 291,688, and by 1970 to 334,859. Greater Miami increased from 935,047 in 1960 to 1,267,792 in 1970.

Sports and Recreation. Few places offer such a variety of sports, both professional and nonprofessional, as the Miami area. There are extensive opportunities for aquatic activities—swimming, water skiing, skindiving, fishing, and boating—as well as for golf (over 40 courses), tennis, shuffleboard, bowling, and other participant sports.

Among professional sports there are Thoroughbred racing (at Hialeah and Calder tracks and at Gulfstream track in Hallandale, just north of the Dade county line), dog racing, and jai alai. Miami is the home of the Dolphins, a professional football team, which plays in the Orange Bowl stadium. The stadium is also the site of the Orange Bowl Classic, a championship intercollegiate football game, held annually on New Year's Day, and the North-South College All-Star game. Another important sports facility is Marine Stadium, on Rickenbacker Causeway leading to Key Biscayne, for spectators of powerboat racing and regattas in Biscayne Bay.

Miami has a professional symphony orchestra and ballet company, which perform in the Dade County Auditorium. Various concert series feature visiting artists from the United States and abroad. There are also professional theater, at the Coconut Grove Playhouse, and amateur theatrical productions. Nightlife abounds, principally in Miami Beach, where many of the major hotels have supper clubs with variety entertainment and dancing.

Places of Interest. Greater Miami has a number of art museums. Villa Vizcaya, an Italian Renaissance-style palazzo built by industrialist James Deering, houses the Dade County Art Museum.

On the campus of the University of Miami at Coral Gables is the Lowe Art Museum, with paintings from the Kress Collection. The Bass Museum is in Miami Beach. Specialized museums include the Historical Museum of Southern Florida, the Holbrook Antique Arms and Gun Museum, and the Museum of Science, with a planetarium.

There are numerous attractions devoted to nature. The Everglades National Park offers a unique opportunity to observe the flora and fauna of an unspoiled wilderness, as does the Grossman Hammock State Park, near Homestead. Organized animal refuges include the Crandon Park Zoo, on Key Biscayne; Monkey Jungle and Parrot Jungle, both south of Coral Gables; and the Seaquarium, with marine shows, on Rickenbacker Causeway. Tropical plants and flowers are featured at the Miami Beach Garden Center and Conservatory; Orchid Jungle and the Redland Fruit and Spice Park, in the Homestead area; and the Fairchild Tropical Gardens, in south Coral Gables. There are also many public parks with a profusion of trees and flowers. Some of these have facilities for camping and various sports activities.

Economy. Tourists—over 10 million per year—generate more than 60% of the Miami area's economic activity. To serve these visitors, nearly 10% of the work force is employed by hotels and motels, restaurants, and recreational facilities. Various other industries, such as construction and wholesale and retail suppliers, greatly depend, directly or indirectly, on the tourist trade. Military installations, including the Homestead Air Force Base, also contribute to the economy.

Greater Miami has considerable light manufacturing, notably in the garment industry. It is also an important agricultural region, producing tomatoes, avocados, mangoes, and beans. Although Dade county is south of Florida's great citrus belt, there is a large lime crop.

Transportation. Miami is a major transportation center. There are a number of airports in the area, of which the most important is the Miami International Airport, on the western edge of the city, with flights to Latin America and Europe, as well as to cities in the United States. Direct passenger rail service is available to the northeast and midwest United States. Interstate bus lines also serve the city, which is connected with the Florida turnpike and the interstate highway system.

Miami, situated on the Atlantic Intracoastal Waterway, is a major seaport for both cargo and cruise lines. In 1960 the Port of Miami, administered by the Dade County Seaport Commission, began the long-range development of a deep-water marine terminal in Biscayne Bay. In addition to extensive cargo and passenger facilities, the terminal is used as a base by the National Oceanic and Atmospheric Administration and the Rosenstiel School of Marine and Atmospheric Sciences of the University of Miami.

Education. The Dade county public school system is the sixth largest in the United States, with about 250,000 pupils and more than 10,000 teachers. There are also many nonpublic schools, with an enrollment of some 43,000.

The leading institution of higher learning in Greater Miami is the University of Miami, whose main campus is at Coral Gables. The Miami-Dade Junior College has three campuses —one in downtown Miami and two outside the city proper, north and south. Among other colleges in the area are the state-supported Florida International University and Barry College and Biscayne College, both Roman Catholic. Florida Memorial College is a Baptist-affiliated school.

Government. The city of Miami has a council-manager form of government. Dade county is administered by a county manager, appointed by a nine-member county commission, whose chairman is a directly elected county mayor.

History. The name Miami probably derived from *Mayami,* an Indian word meaning "Big Water." Maps of the 16th century show an Indian village at what is now Bayfront Park in downtown Miami. Fort Dallas, near the mouth of the Miami River, was built in 1836, during the Seminole Indian wars. In 1896, Henry M. Flagler, through the urging of the pioneer settler Julia Tuttle, extended the East Coast Railroad to Miami. The city was incorporated that year, and visitors began to flock to the area. Miami Beach was incorporated in 1915.

During the early 1920's, Miami was the scene of a great land boom. However, in 1926, as a result of a severe hurricane and financial panic, the boom collapsed, leaving real estate interests with acres of swampland and no buyers. Despite this setback the region continued to grow, as land was drained and streets and parks laid out. After World War II there was a phenomenal increase in hotel building, and the Miami area became the great metropolitan and tourist center it is today.

MIAMI, mī-am'ē, a city in northeastern Oklahoma, in Ottawa county, is 75 miles (121 km) northeast of Tulsa. Tires, building stone and brick, clothing, and wood products are manufactured here. Northeastern Oklahoma Agricultural & Mechanical College is a two-year junior college.

The Neosho River flows through Miami and empties into the Grand Lake of the Cherokees southeast of town. The lake has been developed for recreation and fishing.

The city, then in Indian Territory, was settled in 1891 and called Richardville. The city charter was approved by the governor in 1910. Miami has a mayor-council form of government. Population: 13,880.

MIAMI, University of, mī-am'ē, a private coeducational institution of higher learning in Coral Gables, Fla. It was chartered in 1925 and opened in 1926. The university consists of the college of arts and sciences; schools of graduate studies, business administration, education, engineering, music, nursing, medicine, law, and marine and atmospheric sciences; and the center for advanced international studies. Bachelor's, master's, and doctor's degrees are given. There are a summer session and a continuing education division, which offers an intensive English course especially useful to Latin American immigrants. The medical school and continuing education division are in Miami. The Institute of Marine Science is on Virginia Key.

The university library has special collections of Russian and Soviet material, works by Colombian authors, and material on Florida, the West Indies, and contemporary Cuba. The university has a press and publishes various journals, including the *Bulletin of Marine Science of the Gulf and Caribbean* and the *Journal of Inter-American Studies.* Total enrollment in the 1970's exceeded 15,000.

MIAMI BEACH, mī-am′ē, is one of the leading resort cities in the United States. It is situated on the Atlantic Ocean, in southeast Florida, in Dade county. Miami Beach comprises a number of islands lying parallel to the city of Miami on the mainland, from which it is separated on the west by Biscayne Bay. Four causeways for automotive traffic connect it with Miami, where air, rail, and bus terminals are located.

Because of its subtropical marine climate and its extensive tourist and recreational facilities, Miami Beach is a popular vacation center for visitors from the northern United States and Canada. It offers abundant opportunities for swimming, fishing, boating, golfing, tennis, and other warm-weather sports. Professional sports in the Greater Miami area include football, jai alai, horse racing, and dog racing. Within easy reach of the city are the Everglades National Park, the Florida Keys, and Lake Okeechobee.

Parks and golf courses are interspersed throughout Miami Beach. Collins Avenue, the main thoroughfare, runs north and south along the ocean. The major hotels and motels, with their nightclubs and luxurious accommodations, line the avenue. To the west, on the many islands that form the city, are the residential areas, with tropical gardens and Spanish-Mediterranean architecture. Many fashionable stores and shops are located on Lincoln Road, most of which has been made into a pedestrian mall. Other points of interest in Miami Beach proper include the Bass Art Museum, the Miami Beach Garden Center and Conservatory, and the Miami Beach Auditorium and Convention Hall.

Originally, Miami Beach was a desolate stretch of sand and mangrove swamp. However, in the early decades of the 20th century, largely through the efforts of John S. Collins and Carl G. Fisher, the area was cleared, and fill was pumped from Biscayne Bay to create new land. The city was incorporated in 1915, and, through careful planning and restrictive sales and building codes, it rapidly expanded into the tourist wonderland it is today. It is governed by a mayor, city council, and city manager. Population: 87,072.

MIAMI INDIANS, mī-am′ē, an Algonkian tribe whose earliest range was in Wisconsin, northern Illinois, and Indiana. They later expanded to Ohio. They were active in Indian wars and in the War of 1812. Gradually, they surrendered their land to the United States in a series of treaties, and in 1840 agreed to move to land assigned to them west of the Mississippi River. They first settled in Kansas and then moved to Indian Territory, now Oklahoma. In 1867 the Miami and Peoria tribes agreed on a treaty of confederation. In the 1960's about 300 Miami lived on the Quapaw reservation in Oklahoma, and a small number lived in the vicinity of Peru, Ind.

MIAMI RIVER, mī-am′ē, in Ohio, about 160 miles (257 km) long. It is also called the Great Miami River to distinguish it from the Little Miami. The Miami River rises in Hardin county and flows south and southwest to enter the Ohio River in the southwest corner of the state. It furnishes extensive hydroelectric power for manufacturing. The Miami Canal, which paralleled the river for some 80 miles (129 km), was closed in 1895.

MIAMI SHORES, mī-am′ē, is a village in southeastern Florida, in Dade county. Part of the Greater Miami area, it is situated between Miami to the south and North Miami to the north. Primarily a residential community, it fronts on Biscayne Bay, across from northern Miami Beach and Surfside. Miami Shores is the site of the Biscayne Kennel Club. Separated from Miami proper in 1932, it has a council-manager form of government. Population: 9,425.

MIAMI SPRINGS, mī-am′ē, is a town in southeastern Florida, in Dade county, west of Miami and south of Hialeah. It is bounded on the south by the Miami International Airport and on the northeast and west by canals. Primarily residential, Miami Springs has five lakes within its confines, fed by springs underlying the city that supply much of the fresh water that is used in the Greater Miami area. Incorporated in 1926, it has a mayor-council form of government. Population: 13,279.

MIAMI UNIVERSITY, mī-am′ē, is a coeducational state institution of higher learning in Oxford, Ohio. Endowed with federal land leased to Ohio, it was chartered in 1809 and opened in 1824. The university has branches at Hamilton for a junior college program and at Middleton for freshmen and sophomores. It offers bachelor's, master's, and doctor's degrees.

The university consists of six schools: arts and sciences, business administration, education, fine arts, applied science, and graduate studies. Special programs with other institutions lead to joint degrees—in engineering with the Massachusetts Institute of Technology, Columbia University, and Case Western Reserve University; in medical technology with University Hospital in Cleveland and in Columbus, Ohio State University, and Mercy Hospital, Hamilton; in physical therapy with Northwestern University and the D. T. Watson School of Physiatrics; and in forestry with Duke University. There are also a cooperative doctoral program with Ohio State and summer programs in geology and archaeology. Enrollment in the 1970's exceeded 15,000.

MIAMISBURG, mī-am′ēz-bûrg, a city in Ohio, in Montgomery county, on the Miami River, is 9 miles (14.5 km) south of Dayton. Paper, boats, castings, and tools are manufactured. Tobacco is shipped from Miamisburg, which is in the center of the state's richest tobacco-growing region.

Miamisburg was settled about 1800 by Zachariah Hole and was known for some years as Hole's Station. It was incorporated as a village in 1832 and made a city in 1930. Miamisburg Mound State Memorial, to the southeast, preserves Ohio's largest mound built by prehistoric Indians. Miamisburg has a council-manager form of government. Population: 14,797.

MIANTONOMO, mī-an-tō-nō′mō (died 1643), was an American Indian chief. He was a sachem of the Narragansett tribe of Rhode Island, and he shared power with his uncle, Canonicus. In 1637 he helped the Massachusetts settlers in their war with the Pequot Indians. The English authorities accused him several times of plotting against them, but he was cleared of the charges. In 1643 his tribe was attacked by Uncas, a Mohegan sachem and his bitter rival. Miantonomo was captured and turned over to the English in Hartford, Conn. Still distrusted by the whites, he was tried, found guilty, condemned to death, and turned over to Uncas, who killed him near Norwich, Conn. He was buried there, and a monument was placed over the spot in 1841.

MIAO, myou, a non-Chinese people dwelling in southwest China in Kweichow and Yunnan provinces and the Kwangsi-Chuang Autonomous Region; and in northern Laos and Vietnam, where they are known as Meo. In the 1950's the Miao, who speak a distinct language related to Chinese, numbered about 2.5 million. They live on mountain slopes between 3,000 and 6,000 feet in altitude in villages of plank or bamboo houses, and raise buckwheat, maize (corn), rice, beans, and peas in fields which are abandoned when the soil becomes exhausted. At intervals the whole village moves to another hill slope. Cows and water buffalo are used to draw the plow, and most families keep chickens, ducks, geese, and a pig or two. Only the prosperous have riding horses, which they treasure. Miao from different localities are distinguished by the clothing of the women, and are known by such names as the Red Miao, the Short-skirted Black Miao, and Miao Who Wear Cowrie Shells.

MIAOULES or **MIAULIS,** mē-ou'lyēs, **Andreas Vokos,** Greek admiral: b. Euboea, Greece, 1768?; d. Athens, June 11, 1835. He grew up in the Aegean Islands and was a wealthy merchant captain at the outbreak of the Greek war of independence in 1821. Made admiral of the Greek fleet of small insurgent vessels which he organized, he was the terror of the Turks at sea until 1827, when an Anglo-French-Russian naval force destroyed the Turkish-Egyptian fleet at Navarino. At the end of the war he retired to the island of Hydra, where he opposed the pro-Russian Ioannes Antonios Kapodistrias, who had been elected president of independent Greece. Miaoules took part in the insurrection of 1831 during which Kapodistrias was assassinated, and in 1832 was a member of the deputation that offered the Greek crown to the Bavarian prince who ascended the throne as Otto I.

MIASKOVSKY, myȧs-kôf'skĭ, **Nikolai Yakovlevich** (also spelled MYASKOVSKI), Russian composer: b. Novogeorgievsk (now Modlin), near Warsaw, Poland, April 20, 1881; d. Moscow, USSR, Aug. 9, 1950. Although his musical gifts were precocious, he reluctantly allowed his father, a military engineer who ultimately became a general, to map out a military engineering career for him. After his term of army service ended in 1907, he devoted himself exclusively to music, graduating in 1911 from the St. Petersburg Conservatory, where Anatol Liadov taught him composition and also helped him financially by assigning some of his own pupils to him. A copious composer, Miaskovsky quickly exhibited a wide eclecticism that served to make his compositions acceptable to all but the radical. Yet his tapping of such diverse sources as Frédéric Chopin and Peter Ilich Tchaikovsky, Modest Musorgski and Alexander Scriabin, was balanced by an ability to put ideas together in an unquestionably personal way. He served creditably in World War I and easily transferred his allegiance to the Soviet regime. In 1921 he became professor of composition at the Moscow Conservatory and was widely influential in forwarding a brand of musical optimism that endeared him to the official spokesmen. He wrote more symphonies than any other modern composer: of the 27, only one appears to have remained unperformed.

WALLACE BROCKWAY.

MICA, mī'kȧ, a term applied to certain silicate minerals with a very characteristic platy basal cleavage, which is an effect of their crystal structure. As in other silicates, their structure is built around SiO_4 tetrahedrons, having a central silicon atom surrounded by four oxygen atoms at the corners of an imaginary tetrahedron. Micas have a sheet structure of planar layers of these SiO_4 tetrahedrons. In addition, there are layers of magnesium (Mg), iron (Fe) and hydroxyl (OH), or aluminum (Al) and hydroxyl, arranged in octahedral form, one octahedral layer sandwiched between two SiO_4 layers; these three-layer units are loosely joined to similar layers above and below by cations such as potassium (K) or sodium (Na). Micas have a strong tendency to cleave into plates parallel to the sheets in their structure. The plates are elastic. Micas are monoclinic, with hardness of 2.5 to 3.0.

Micas are distinguished chemically by a silicon to oxygen ratio of 2:5, related to their sheet structure. Commonly one or more aluminum atoms substitute for silicon atoms in this ratio. Micas also contain two hydroxyls. They are placed in two divisions depending on whether magnesium, iron, or aluminum occupies their octahedral layers. The principal micas are:

Muscovite $KAl_2\ (AlSi_3O_{10})\ (OH)_2$
Paragonite $NaAl_2\ (AlSi_3O_{10})\ (OH)_2$
Lepidolite $KLi_2Al\ (Si_4O_{10})\ (OH)_2$
Margarite $CaAl_2\ (Al_2Si_2O_{10})\ (OH)_2$
Phlogopite $KMg_3\ (AlSi_3O_{10})\ (OH)_2$
Biotite $K(Mg,Fe)_3\ (AlSi_3O_{10})\ (OH)_2$
Clintonite $CaMg_3\ (Al_2Si_2O_{10})\ (OH)_2$.

Margarite and clintonite, the calcium micas, are generally referred to as brittle micas, as they are harder and more brittle than the others, and their cleavage is less perfect, because calcium (Ca) exerts a stronger binding force between structural layers than potassium or sodium. The mineral talc, $Mg_3Si_4O_{10}\ (OH)_2$, is closely related

Sorting mica sheets into standard sizes, Tanganyika.

Camera Press-Pix, Inc.

to the micas; it has the same silicon to oxygen ratio of 2:5 and a similar layered structure and platy basal cleavage, but it is less cohesive through lack of a cation such as potassium or sodium to bind the layers closely. Talc has a greasy feel and a hardness of 1. Chlorite $(Mg,Fe)_5$ Al $(AlSi_3O_{10})$ $(OH)_8$, is also closely related to the mica group, having the same silicon to oxygen ratio, platy cleavage, and similar hardness.

Muscovite is generally considered to be the most common mica. It is colorless or pale green or brown, and transparent in thin sheets. It occurs in siliceous igneous rocks, often in large sheets in pegmatites, and in metamorphic and sedimentary rocks. Roscoelite is a variety of muscovite having considerable vanadium replacing aluminum; it is a source of vanadium in the United States.

Paragonite is similar to muscovite in appearance. It is a product of alteration of highly sodic minerals such as nepheline and albite, and is found in metamorphic rocks. Lepidolite is a lilac or colorless mica commonly found in pegmatites. Phlogopite has a submetallic luster, is bronze to colorless, and often shows asterism. It is found in metamorphic rocks. Biotite is a very common black, brown, or green mica, the color darkening as the iron content increases. It is an important constituent of many metamorphic and igneous rocks.

Although the United States consumes a large part of the world's mica production, only a small part of the supply is of domestic origin, most being imported from India, Canada, and Madagascar. North Carolina, South Dakota, Georgia, Maine, New Hampshire, and Connecticut are producing states.

Sheet mica is used in electrical insulation, in the manufacture of motors, dynamos, lamp sockets, and high-voltage induction apparatus; it comes from pegmatite dikes. Scrap mica, in smaller pieces, is ground and used in roofing, paints, rubber, wallpaper, lubricants, and plastics. Of diminishing importance is the use in stove and lamp chimneys. Muscovite is the principal commercial mica; biotite is of little use.

See also BIOTITE; LEPIDOLITE; ROSCOELITE.

MARSHALL KAY,
Professor of Geology, Columbia University.

MICA SCHIST, shĭst, a rock having schistosity, the parallel arrangement of platy minerals, particularly of mica, a mineral that cleaves readily in parallel sheets, giving the rock a foliate or layered structure. Mica schists result from the regional metamorphism of argillaceous rocks, shale changing to mica schist under increased temperature and pressure in metamorphism. With increasing temperatures, a succession of minerals is formed. Low-grade mica schists, the least metamorphosed, contain muscovite, quartz, and some chlorite; with higher metamorphism, biotite appears and chlorite tends to disappear; as metamorphism intensifies, the schists, still with muscovite, quartz, and biotite, also have progressively garnet, kyanite (cyanite), staurolite, and sillimanite. See also MICA; SCHIST.

MARSHALL KAY.

MICAH, mī'kȧ (in Douay Bible, MICHEAS), one of the great prophets of Israel and Judah in the 8th century B.C. Reliable information about him is limited to a portion of the prophecy which bears his name (Micah 1–3), to a brief reference in Jeremiah (26:17–19), and to general information about the reign of Hezekiah found in II Kings 18–20 and in the prophecy of Isaiah, which falls in the same period. Micah lived in Moresheth, a small village near Gath, the large fortified city commanding the southern approach to the coastal plains of Palestine. There is no reliable evidence, internal or external, as to his trade or work. His name means "Who is like Yahweh?"

Although the opening verse of the Book of Micah asserts that the prophecies were made in the days of Jotham, Ahaz, and Hezekiah, which would give a possible time span of 737–686 B.C., it is believed that this verse was added by a later editor, and that Jeremiah's statement that Micah "prophesied in the days of Hezekiah" (Jeremiah 26:18)—that is, between 715 and 686 B.C.—is more acceptable. While some scholars would place the first prophecies before the capture of Samaria by the Assyrian King Sargon II in 721 B.C., others would date Micah 1:6 as spoken about 713, after the fall of Samaria and not long before Sargon's invasion of Ashdod to the south. The last prophecies were probably made in 701, just before the Assyrian armies of King Sennacherib invaded Judah.

Micah was called to prophetic activity by international and domestic dangers. Assyria was in the ascendancy, having crushed Syria in 732 B.C. and the Northern Kingdom (Israel) in 721. With the fall of Samaria in 721, the Southern Kingdom (Judah) cast her lot with Assyria and began payment of a large tribute to guarantee immunity from the Assyrian armies. In 715, King Hezekiah sought to free himself from Assyria, and dread rumor soon brought word that the Assyrian army was marching on Jerusalem.

The internal situation, as Micah viewed it, was no less dangerous. Corruption had vitiated the royal court, the priesthood, and the judicial system, as well as the established prophets of the land. Jerusalem was the symbol of immorality, idolatry, and every other form of evil.

Micah, like his prophetic predecessors, saw a profound connection between the sins of Jerusalem and the advancing Assyrians. God was about to bring His judgment upon His people for their disloyalty to Him. Hence the authentic portions of Micah ring with prophecies of judgment and destruction on Jerusalem and her leaders. His prophecy (1–3) consists of oracles spoken during the two periods when Assyria was threatening Jerusalem (713 and 701 B.C.). In each case, he attributes Israel's punishment to her sins: disobedience to God; oppression of the poor; and corruption in the Temple, civil courts, and royal palace.

The only clue to the reception of Micah's message is the term of respect which characterizes the reference to it made a century later in Jerusalem and recorded in Jeremiah 26:17–19.

See also MICAH, THE BOOK OF.

HAROLD A. BOSLEY,
Minister, First Methodist Church, Evanston, Ill.

MICAH, The Book of, the 6th among the Twelve Minor Prophets in the Hebrew and English Bibles. "Minor" refers to the length of the book, not the value of the prophecy. Micah consists of three general divisions which have different authors and come from widely separated periods in Hebrew history. Chapters 1–3 are attributed to Micah and were spoken and recorded at the end of the 8th century. (See MICAH.)

Chapters 4 and 5 (with the possible exception of 5:10–15, which may belong to Micah) are from unknown authors living in Israel in post-Exilic days (after 538 B.C.). Chapters 6 and 7 (some scholars would attribute 6:9–7:16 to Micah) come from another writer or writers living in a still later period. There are no reliable clues as to how and when these three writings came to be a part of the one book which bears the name of Micah today.

The entire book is in poetic form. Though scholars have been forced to engage in extensive reconstruction of the damaged text in order to get meaning from it, there is general agreement on the main divisions in the text and the central emphases of the entire book.

Chapters 1–3, from Micah himself, are prophecy in the grand manner. The prophet sees the Lord bringing His people to judgment and punishment, and hears Him pleading the justice of what He is doing to the peoples of the earth. The judgment goes through Israel like a fine-toothed comb, missing none who have sinned against God. Micah excoriates the self-righteous attitude of the leaders who assume "the Lord [is] in the midst of us" (3:11; Revised Standard Version text). When ordered to keep quiet (2:6–8), he indignantly refuses and asserts his need to speak and his right to be heard (3:8–10).

Chapters 4 and 5 reflect a different situation, one most readily identified as the post-Exilic period in Hebrew history. Destruction is no longer feared because it has already been endured. Restoration rather than judgment is the key word in this section. The enemies of Israel are to be destroyed, and she will reign supreme on earth. Israel is promised a divine deliverer who is to come from Bethlehem and will bring victory and peace to his people.

Chapters 6 and 7 come from a period when trouble is again threatening Israel's life. God charges Israel with forgetting Him and falling once more into evil ways; her worship is without ethical content. God's requirement is simple enough: "to do justice, and to love kindness, and to walk humbly with your God" (6:8; R.S.V. text).

Throughout the book the main themes of prophecy are stressed: the supremacy of God in life and history; the moral requirements of obedience to Him; the inescapable judgment He pronounces upon sin and sinners; and His use of historical events as the means of expressing His favor and pronouncing His judgments

Consult "The Book of Micah," introduction and exegesis by Rolland E. Wolfe, exposition by Harold A. Bosley, in *The Interpreter's Bible,* vol. 6, pp. 895–949 (New York 1956).

HAROLD A. BOSLEY.

MICAWBER, mĭ-kô′bẽr, **Mr. Wilkins,** one of the principal characters in Charles Dickens' *David Copperfield* (1849–50, q.v.). Alternating between periods of depression and high spirits, of temporary financial embarrassment and an optimistic belief that "something will turn up," the character was inspired by Dickens' father, as that of the devoted Mrs. Micawber was inspired by his mother.

MICHAEL, mī′kĕl, one of the four archangels recognized in ancient Judaism (Daniel 10:13, 21; 12:1; Enoch 9:1–11:1). The name means "Who is like God?" Michael was believed to be specially charged to guard and defend the Jewish people as their heavenly "prince" or champion. Many legendary ideas gathered about his name, especially in connection with his duty as heavenly protector. In Jude 9 he is said to have disputed with the devil about (the location of?) the body of Moses, the whereabouts of which remained a great mystery for later generations (Deuteronomy 34:6). In Revelation 12:7 he and his angels fought a war in heaven, conquered the "dragon" (Satan), and cast it down from the skies. This ancient mythological feature is undoubtedly an allegory of the coming struggle between good and evil, God and Satan, light and darkness, Christianity and paganism, and foretells its outcome. In Dante and John Milton, as in Thomas Aquinas, Michael is the first of the seven archangels recognized by the Christian religion. Many churches have been dedicated to him, especially on high hills or islands—such as Mont St. Michel on the coast of France—to provide the heavenly warrior with the best possible vantage point for attacking his enemies, including plague, drought, famine, and tempest.

FREDERICK C. GRANT.

MICHAEL, the name of nine emperors of the Eastern Roman Empire.

MICHAEL I RHANGABE: d. 845. The son-in-law of Emperor Nicephorus I, he became emperor in 811 following the death of Nicephorus' son Stauracius (r. 811), during the war against the Bulgarians. Michael antagonized the army, and also the iconoclasts in the heated controversy of the period over religious images (see ICONOCLAST). Following his defeat at Versinicia (near Adrianople, in Thrace) by the Bulgarians in 813, Michael was deposed by one of his generals, Leo the Armenian, who succeeded him on the throne as Leo V and banished Michael to a convent.

MICHAEL II (called THE AMORIAN or THE STAMMERER): d. October 829. A native of Amorium in Phrygia, he rose from private to commander of the guards in the Byzantine Army. Imprisoned and sentenced to death for treason by Leo V, he was rescued by adherents who assassinated Leo and raised Michael to the throne in 820. At first tolerant of both iconoclasm and orthodoxy, he later supported the iconoclasts. During his reign, in 827, Muslim forces first invaded Byzantine Sicily.

MICHAEL III (called THE DRUNKARD): b. 838; d. Sept. 23, 867. A grandson of Michael II, in 842 he succeeded his father Theophilus (r. 829–842). Under the regency of his mother, Empress Theodora, the iconoclastic controversy was ended in favor of orthodoxy. In 856, Theodora's brother Bardas seized the regency and ruled for 10 years as Caesar Bardas. During his reign the Muslims were strengthening their hold on Crete and Sicily, but Byzantine influence was spread in the north through the propagation of the Greek Orthodox faith. In 865, after an invasion led by Bardas, Boris I of Bulgaria was baptized and made Christianity compulsory in his kingdom. Michael, a drunken and capricious emperor, raised his favorite, the Macedonian peasant Basil, to high office, and in 866 they murdered Bardas. The following year Basil assassinated Michael and mounted the throne as Basil I, first of the Macedonian dynasty.

MICHAEL IV (called THE PAPHLAGONIAN): d. Dec. 10, 1041. The low-born paramour of Zoë, daughter of Emperor Constantine VIII and wife of Emperor Romanus III, Michael plotted with her the murder of Romanus in 1034 and thereupon became emperor and husband of Zoë. An epileptic, Michael left the affairs of government largely to his brother John.

MICHAEL V (called CALAPHATES, the Calker). A nephew of Michael IV, he was adopted by Zoë and succeeded his uncle in December 1041. His banishment of Empress Zoë and his uncle John led to a popular revolt during which he was blinded and sent into exile in April 1042. He was succeeded by Zoë and her sister Theodora.

MICHAEL VI (called STRATIOTICUS, the Warrior). He was raised to the throne by palace officials following the death of Empress Theodora in 1056. In June 1057 there was a revolt of aristocratic generals, encouraged by the Orthodox patriarch and led by Isaac Comnenus; on Aug. 31, Stratioticus abdicated and retreated to a monastery where he died.

MICHAEL VII DUCAS. The eldest son of Constantine X, Michael ruled under the regency of his stepfather Romanus IV and his mother Eudocia (1067–1071). When Romanus IV was captured in battle with the Turkish Army of Alp Arslan, Michael seized the throne in his own name and had Romanus killed when the latter was released by the Turks. Ineffectual in controlling the turbulent unrest within the empire, he was unable to stop a massive Turkish encroachment on its eastern borders; in the West also the last Italian holdings of Byzantium fell to the Normans in 1071. In 1078, Michael was deposed by Nicephorus III Botaniates who, supported by Turkish arms, usurped the throne and married Michael's wife, Maria.

MICHAEL VIII PALAEOLOGUS: b. 1224/1225; d. Dec. 11, 1282. A general of aristocratic family in the army of the Greek Orthodox emperor of Nicaea, Michael managed by intrigue to become regent (1258) of the boy emperor, John IV Lascaris, and in 1259 set himself up as co-emperor with John. When Constantinople, which had been under a Latin ruler from 1204, was taken by the Greeks in 1261, Michael blinded and deposed John and became sole emperor of a renewed Byzantine Empire. Much of his reign was devoted to diplomatic maneuvers to protect the empire from Bulgaria and Serbia on the north and from the Latin rulers who still held much of the western part of the old Byzantine Empire. For a time he gained papal support by promises of uniting the Greek with the Latin church, and in the Second Council of Lyon (1274) he submitted completely to the papacy. The Greek people and clergy rejected this, however, and Pope Martin IV denounced the agreement in 1281. On his death in 1282, Michael was succeeded by his son Andronicus II.

MICHAEL IX PALAEOLOGUS: d. 1320. The grandson of Michael VIII, he ruled with his father Andronicus II from 1295 to 1320.

MICHAEL (Rum. MIHAI), king of Rumania: b. Sinaia, Rumania, Oct. 25, 1921. Son of Crown Prince Carol of Rumania and Princess Helen of Greece, Michael became crown prince when his father renounced his rights to the Rumanian throne in 1925 and went into exile. When King Ferdinand I, Michael's grandfather, died on July 20, 1927, Michael became king under a regency, but in 1930 Carol returned to Rumania and relieved his son of the crown. In 1940, when Carol was forced to abdicate by the pro-German faction in Rumania, Michael again became king, but was little more than a figurehead until 1944, when he asserted himself and led his country to shift its support from the Axis to the Allies. In 1947 he was forced by the Communists to abdicate and went to Switzerland. The next year he married Princess Anne of Bourbon-Parma. In 1956 he became the director of an American school of advanced aircraft instrument training in Geneva. See also RUMANIA—*History*.

MICHAEL (Russ. MIKHAIL FYODOROVICH), czar of Russia and founder of the Romanov dynasty: b. 1596; d. July 23, 1645. A descendant of Rurik, reputed founder of the Russian empire, and a grandnephew of Anastasia, wife of Czar Ivan IV (Ivan the Terrible) and mother of Czar Fyodor I, Michael was elected and crowned czar of Russia in 1613 at the end of the Time of Troubles. He was chosen by a representative assembly, the Zemski Sobor, from a number of candidates. The eminence of his family pleased the conservatives; the fact that his father had been patriarch of Rostov made him acceptable to the Cossacks; and his youth appealed to Muscovite leaders, who hoped to manipulate him for their own aims. Michael was not only young but a weakling brought up by a domineering mother. The Zemski Sobor met regularly between 1613 and 1622, and his mother, Xenia Chestov, together with her numerous relatives, dominated the government during the early years of Michael's reign. When his father, known as Philaret, was released from a Polish prison in 1619, he was made patriarch of Moscow. In addition he was officially recognized as coruler with Michael and in effect ruled Russia until his death in 1633.

Michael's reign marked the signing of peace treaties with Sweden (1617) and Poland (1634). In 1637 the first Russian pioneers reached the shores of the Pacific Ocean, only 56 years after the conquest of Siberia began. Internally there was a strong development of autocratic centralized government. The regional self-governing bodies (zemstvo) of provinces and cities were gradually supplanted by centrally appointed governors (*voevoda*). Districts (*uezd*) were consolidated into larger administrative units (*razryad*). The mounting tax burden caused many peasants to flee beyond the borders of effective Muscovite rule. In 1619 the Zemski Sobor ordered that runaway peasants be searched out and returned to the communities from which they had fled, and a census taken in 1627–1628 thereafter was used as evidence of the legal residence of peasants and their descendants. Michael was succeeded by his son, Alexis I.

MICHAEL, Serbian prince: b. Kragujevac, Serbia, Sept. 4, 1823; d. Belgrade, June 10, 1868. The son of Miloš, founder of the Obrenovich dynasty, Michael succeeded his brother Milan as ruling prince of Serbia in 1839 but was deposed in 1842 by the constitutional faction. The leader of this faction, Alexander Karageorgevich, ruled until 1858, when Michael's father Miloš was restored to the throne with Russian and Turkish support. On Miloš' death in 1860, Michael again became the ruler. Well educated and widely traveled, Michael sought to unite the Balkans against Turkey. With the support of the great powers he obtained the withdrawal of all Turkish troops from Serbia in 1867 and established alliances with Montenegro, Rumania, and Greece, aimed at securing complete independence from

Turkey. In 1868 he was assassinated by members of the faction which sought to restore Alexander Karageorgevich. The assassins were arrested, however, and a grandson of Miloš' younger brother was placed on the throne (Milan I). See also SERBIA—*History* (The Fight for Independence).

MICHAELIS, mĭ-kä-ā'lĭs, **Adolf,** German archaeologist: b. Kiel, Germany, June 22, 1835; d. Strasbourg, Aug. 12, 1910. He was educated at Berlin, Leipzig, and Kiel universities, was professor of archaeology at Strasbourg after 1872, and was a member of the German Central Archaeological Institute at Rome after 1874. He was the author of numerous works on classical archaeology, notably *Der Parthenon* (1871), *Ancient Marbles in Great Britain* (1882), and *Kunstgeschichte des Altertum* (*History of the Art of Ancient Times,* 1898). He edited successive issues of volume 1 of Anton Springer's *Handbuch der Kunstgeschichte* after Springer's death in 1891.

MICHAELIS, Georg, German statesman: b. Haynau, Germany, Sept. 8, 1857; d. Bad Saarow, July 24, 1936. He entered the Prussian civil service in 1879, held various administrative posts in the German Imperial government after 1915, and in 1917 succeeded Theobald von Bethmann-Hollweg as chancellor of the German Empire. As chancellor he tried unsuccessfully to reconcile demands for peace with moderate nationalistic aims. He was dismissed by Emperor William II in November 1917, because, it is said, he failed to take a decisive stand on the question of peace with the Allies. He was the author of an autobiography, *Für Staat und Volk: Eine Lebensgeschichte* (1922) and a book of travel essays, *Weltreisegedanken* (1923).

MICHAELIS, Johann David, German Biblical scholar: b. Halle, Germany, Feb. 27, 1717; d. Göttingen, Aug. 22, 1791. He studied at the University of Halle, traveled in Great Britain and the Netherlands, and subsequently joined the faculty of the University of Göttingen, where he was professor of philosophy (after 1746) and of Oriental languages (after 1750). He was the author of numerous works on the structure of Hebrew and other Near Eastern languages and on the social and cultural background of the Bible. He is considered the founder of modern Biblical studies in Germany. Michaelis was the editor of *Orientalische und exegetische Bibliothek,* 24 vols. (1771–1779) and 8 vols. (new ser., 1786–1791).

Consult Smend, Rudolf, *Johann David Michaelis* (Göttingen 1898).

MICHAELIS, mê-kȧ-ē'lês, **Karin** (or MICHAELIS-STANGELAND, -stȧng'ĕ-lȧn), Danish author: b. Randers, Denmark, March 20, 1872; d. Copenhagen, Jan. 11, 1950. Privately educated, she turned from an early interest in music to literature and social problems, working and writing on behalf of the underprivileged and the rights of women. She wrote pro-German stories and novels in World War I, but in World War II was active in the anti-German Free Danish movement in the United States. Twice-married, in 1895 to Sophus Michaelis (q.v.), from whom she was divorced, and in 1912 to Charles Emil Stangeland, an American diplomat, she advocated trial marriage and insurance policies to protect women from the financial difficulties of divorce or perpetual maidenhood. Her novel *The Dangerous Age* (1910), dealing with the emotional problems of a woman of 45, created a sensation, was translated into 20 languages, and sold a million copies. Her other works include *The Child* (1902), *The Governor* (1913), *The Girl with the Flowerpot* (1925), *Mother* (1935), and an autobiography, *Little Troll* (1946).

MICHAELIS, mĭ-kä-ā'lĭs, **Leonor,** German-American physical chemist: b. Berlin, Germany, Jan. 16, 1875; d. New York, N. Y., Oct. 9, 1949. He received a doctorate in medicine from the University of Berlin in 1896, and subsequently studied at the University of Freiburg and again in Berlin under Paul Ehrlich, discoverer of the Salvarsan treatment for syphilis. At the Ehrlich laboratories he discovered the histologic staining properties of Janus green, useful in preparing certain cell structures (mitochondria) for microscopic examination. Michaelis also worked at the Berlin Institute of Cancer Research (1902–1906), the Berlin Municipal Hospital (1906–1922), the Medical School, Nagoya, Japan (1922–1926), the Johns Hopkins University (1926–1929), and the Rockefeller Institute for Medical Research (1929–1940). He made important contributions to knowledge concerning the properties of enzymes and proteins and the nature of metabolic oxidation and reduction. His discovery that keratin, a protein of the hair is soluble in thioglycolic acid, made possible cold-permanent-wave coiffures for women.

MICHAELIS, mê-kȧ-ē'lês, **Sophus,** Danish author: b. Odense, Denmark, May 14, 1865; d. Copenhagen, Jan. 28, 1932. He was the author of numerous works of fiction, poetry, and drama, *Sirenen* (*Siren,* 1898), and *Das Fest des Lebens* (*Festival of Life,* 1902), *Die Palmen* (*Palms,* 1904), volumes of verse; the novel *Äebelö* (1895), and the dramas *Revolutionsbryllup* (*The Revolutionary Wedding,* 1906), and *Den evige Sövn* (*The Eternal Sleep,* 1912). He was celebrated for his translations of Goethe's *Faust* and novels by Gustave Flaubert.

MICHAELIUS, mê-kā'lĭ-ŭs, **Jonas,** first minister of the Dutch Reformed Church at New Amsterdam: b. Grootebroek, the Netherlands, 1584; d. the Netherlands, after 1637. Educated at the Latin school of Hoorn, near Grootebroek, and at the Theological College, Leiden, he was a minister of the Dutch Reformed Church in Brabant and Holland between 1605 and 1624. In 1628 he emigrated with his family to New Amsterdam, where he organized a church that subsequently became the Collegiate Church of New York City. He quarreled with Director General Peter Minuit and his council, whom he accused of fraud, immorality, and oppression. The directors of the Dutch West India Company, who controlled New Amsterdam, refused to hear his charges and prevented his reappointment to the ministry at New Amsterdam after 1637. Michaelius returned to the Netherlands, probably permanently, in 1633. Three of his letters are extant, including one in Latin containing a hostile account of Minuit and his council.

Consult Eekhof, Albert, *Jonas Michaelius, Founder of the Church in New Netherland* (Leiden 1926).

MICHAELMAS, mĭk'ĕl-mȧs, or MICHAELMAS DAY, a feast honoring St. Michael and all the angels, celebrated annually on September 29 by the Roman Catholic Church and the churches of the Anglican Communion.

In England, Michaelmas is one of four traditional quarter-days (q.v.), and its name designates a quarterly court term (October 12 to December 21) and academic terms at Oxford (October 1 to December 17) and Cambridge (October 1 to December 19). Formerly, English civil magistrates were elected at Michaelmas, perhaps in allusion to St. Michael as the prince of guardian angels. Another Michaelmas custom in England is the eating of roast goose, traditional since the 15th century or earlier. According to an old English proverb, one who eats goose on Michaelmas Day will not lack money all the year.

MICHAELMAS DAISY. See ASTER.

MICHAL, mī'kĕl, in the Old Testament, a daughter of Saul (I Samuel 14:49; 18:20). Michal was offered by Saul to David on condition that he kill 100 Philistines. The offer was intended as a snare, but the feat was accomplished, and Saul in jealousy sent soldiers to kill David. Michal contrived David's escape (I Samuel 19:11-17). Subsequently Saul gave her to Phalti who was eventually compelled to relinquish her to David (I Samuel 25:44; II Samuel 3:13-16). Michal and David became estranged when she rebuked him for immodest dancing before the Ark in celebration of its restoration to Jerusalem (II Samuel 6:16-23).

MICHALAKOPOULOS, mē-kä-lä-kô'pōō-lôs, **Andreas,** Greek statesman: b. Patras, Greece, 1875; d. Athens, March 27, 1938. A lawyer, he entered politics as a Liberal, was elected deputy for Patras in the national assembly of 1910, and held several posts (1912–1916) in cabinets formed by Elutherios Venizelos, whose pro-Allied policy in World War I Michalakopoulos supported. He became prime minister of Greece in 1924, and subsequently was also minister of foreign affairs; but in 1925 he was overthrown by Gen. Theodoros Pangalos and exiled. His later career was marked by successive returns to office as foreign minister (1926, 1932, 1933). He was again exiled, shortly before his death, by Gen. Ioannes Metaxas.

MICHAUD, mē-shō', **Joseph François,** French journalist and historian: b. Albens, France, June 19, 1767; d. Passy, Sept. 30, 1839. He was a journalist in Paris, where, he edited the royalist periodical *La Quotidienne* (1796). His monarchist writings caused him in 1795 to be sentenced to death by a tribunal of the First French Republic, but the sentence was revoked and he escaped to Switzerland. He soon returned to Paris, produced several political satires and historical works, and in 1815, when the Bourbon monarchy was restored, resumed publication of *La Quotidienne.* After 1813 he was a member of the Académie Française.

Michaud's writings include *Adieux à Bonaparte* (1799); *Histoire des progrès et de la chute de l'empire de Mysore sous Hider Aly et Tippov-Saëb* (1801); *Histoire des croisades,* 7 vols. (1812–1822); *Histoire des quinze semaines ou le dernier règne de Bonaparte* (1815). With Jean Joseph François Poujoulat he edited *Collection de mémoires pour servir à l'histoire de France depuis le XIIIe siècle,* 32 vols. (1836–1839). With his brother, LOUIS GABRIEL MICHAUD (1773–1858), he compiled *Biographie Universelle,* 52 vols. (1811–1828), a standard reference work, several times reprinted and sometimes called *Biographie Michaud.* Louis Gabriel Michaud was the author of several independent biographies, notably of Louis Philippe (1849) and of Charles Maurice de Talleyrand-Périgord (1853).

MICHAULT, mē-shō', **Pierre,** French poet and rhetorician: b. in Franche-Comté; d. c.1467. He was a retainer of Charles the Bold, comte de Charolais and duc de Bourgogne. He composed an allegorical satire called, variously in successive editions, *Le doctrinal du temps présent* (1466) or *Le doctrinal de court, par lequel on peut estre clerc sans aller à l'escole* (1522). In mingled prose and verse, it tells how the author was conducted by Merit (*Vertu*) through various schools in which the students were graded according to their vices. Michault also composed *La danse des aveugles* (1506), a kind of satiric drama, in prose and verse, the principal characters of which include Fortune, Love, and Death, three blind persons "before whom everyone must dance." He may have collaborated in the writing of *Cent nouvelles nouvelles* (q.v.), a collection of tales which was later used as source material by Jean de La Fontaine for his *Fables.*

MICHAUX, mē-shō', **André,** French botanist: b. near Versailles, France, March 7, 1746; d. in Madagascar, Nov. 16, 1802. He studied under the French botanist Bernard de Jussieu and subsequently visited England, Persia, and the United States, collecting specimens and data for botanical studies. He was the author of *Histoire des chenes . . . de l'Amerique septentrionale* (1801) and *Flora boreali-americana . . .* (1803).

His son, FRANÇOIS ANDRÉ MICHAUX (1770–1855), collaborated with him in botanical researches in the United States and was the author of *Histoire des arbres forestiers de l'Amérique septentrionale* (3 vols., 1810–1813; trans. as *The North American Sylva*).

MICHAUX, Henri, French poet and painter: b. Namur, Belgium, May 24, 1899. His poems, in mingled verse and prose, exhibit a surrealistic play of fantasy and a great variety of prosodic effects. He is the author of *Un certain plume* (1930), *Un barbare en Asie* (1947; trans. *A Barbarian in Asia,* 1949), *Epreuves, exorcismes 1940–1944* (1945), and *Arriver a se reveiller* (1950).

MICHEL, Claude. See CLODION.

MICHEL, mĭch'ĕl, DAN (Middle English "sir," "master"), or **MICHEL OF NORTHGATE,** English monk and translator: fl. 1340. A brother in the cloister of St. Augustine of Canterbury, he is remembered for his translation of a French moral treatise by Laurentius Gallus entitled *La somme des vices et des vertues* (1279). Dan Michel's translation, in the Kentish dialect of Middle English, is called *The Ayenbite of Inwit* (that is, *The Remorse of Conscience*). A manuscript bearing the autograph of Dan Michel and dated 1340 is preserved in the British Museum, London. The poem is valued by scholars as a dated specimen of the Kentish dialect spoken in the middle of the 14th century, but it did not receive wide circulation at the time of writing. The standard modern edition is that by Richard Morris for the Early English Text Society (London 1866).

MICHEL, mē-shĕl′, **Louise** (full name Clémence Louise Michel), French revolutionist: b. Haute-Marne, France, May 29, 1830; d. Marseille, Jan. 9, 1905. Educated to be a teacher, she opened a school in Paris in 1860 and there expounded anarchist philosophies. In the Franco-Prussian War she ministered to the wounded and took part in armed sorties from Paris. After fighting at the barricades during the uprising of the Commune in 1871, she was sentenced to deportation for life and was exiled to New Caledonia, but was pardoned under the general amnesty of 1880. Returning to Paris, she edited *La révolution sociale,* was twice imprisoned (1883 and 1886), lived for some time in London, and spent the last ten years of her life propagandizing for the anarchist cause throughout France. She published her *Mémoires* (1866) and a number of political and social tracts.

MICHELANGELO, mī-kĕl-ăn′jĕ-lō, Ital. mē-kâl-än′jâ-lō, or **MICHAEL ANGELO,** mī′-kĕl ăn′jĕ-lō (full Ital. name Michelangelo Buonarroti, mē-kâl-än′jâ-lō bwô-när-rô′tē; the commonest Renaissance spelling is Michelagnolo); Italian sculptor, painter, architect, and poet: b. Caprese, Tuscany, Italy, March 6, 1475; d. Rome, Feb. 18, 1564. A Florentine, he was active mainly in Florence and Rome.

Although he was briefly apprenticed to the painters Ghirlandaio (1488/1489), from the first the young Michelangelo felt a kinship not with the elegant craftsmen of the later 15th century but rather with the titans of earlier Tuscan art. His first extant works are drawings after the frescoes of Giotto and Masaccio. Soon he began to work as a sculptor in a kind of free art academy maintained in the Medici gardens and supervised by Donatello's follower, the sculptor Bertoldo di Giovanni. Lorenzo de' Medici (Lorenzo the Magnificent) took him into his household (1490–1492), where he became acquainted with the finest intellects of the time, such as the poet Politian, and absorbed the Neo-Platonism with which his art is saturated. His earliest surviving sculpture is the relief, the *Madonna of the Stairs* (c. 1490–1492; Florence, Casa Buonarroti), a disconcertingly unyouthful work for a boy in his teens. Here he looks back past all the charming Madonna compositions of the later 15th century and finds inspiration in the grander tragedy of Donatello's reliefs. The twisting, muscular forms of the heroic Christ Child and the struggling youths in the background, prophetic of the expressive figure style of Michelangelo's later years, are a foil for the towering, impassive profile of the Madonna. Soon afterward, this style was considerably developed in the tumultuous tangle of nude bodies that fill the relief, the *Battle of the Centaurs* and *Lapiths* (c. 1492; Casa Buonarroti). Here already is the essence of Michelangelo's art. The exclusive vehicle of his communication is the human body. But Michelangelo, far from accepting the harmonious reconciliation of spirit and flesh attained by his contemporaries of the High Renaissance, felt a torturing ambivalence toward the body. He loved it with the passionate intensity which would permit his skill to master its representation as never before, and would make his genius create definitive paragons of human perfection. Yet to the Christian mystic in him, the body was "the earthly prison of the soul" (a phrase from his own poetry); its perfections are of no avail, and serve Michelangelo only in the delineation of its doom. Even in this early relief, though the heroic forms are marvelously beautiful, their furious struggle seems curiously inconclusive and unavailing, and the tragic figures of the falling and the fallen, in which Michelangelo achieves unforgettable images of despair, already adumbrate the devastating pessimism of his maturity.

In Rome (1496–1501) the rapidly developing Michelangelo produced monumental marble statues: the *Bacchus* (Florence, Museo Nazionale), inspired by the antique, the subtle unbalance and trancelike appearance of which tactfully suggest a state of release through wine, as in the mystic rites of ancient Dionysiac cults; and the beautiful *Pietà,* or *Madonna with the Dead Christ* (Rome, St. Peter's), two interlocking curved figures composed with all the clarity and logic of the classic art of the High Renaissance, and with its characteristic idealism, its amplitude of forms, and its harmonious calm; but Michelangelo's deep melancholy repudiates the predominant optimism of the period. This classic phase of Michelangelo's art is continued in the marble *Madonna of Bruges,* Belgium (c. 1501; except for two models, all of his extant sculpture is in marble), and in three circular compositions in which, as a typical artist of the High Renaissance, he eloquently orders equilibrated masses within a round frame: two Madonna reliefs (c. 1504–1506; Museo Nazionale and London, Royal Academy) and the *Doni Madonna* (c. 1504; Florence, Uffizi), his only painting that has survived except for his frescoes.

This classic phase is culminated in the colossal *David,* a splendid nude figure 14 feet high (1501–1504; Florence, Accademia), which established Michelangelo in the opinion of his contemporaries as the greatest artist who had ever lived. In it he provided the modern Occident with a new standard of physical beauty. The familiar "at ease" pose of antique sculpture, with weight primarily on one leg and with the whole figure therefore pleasingly relaxed yet securely balanced, produces, as in ancient statuary, a composition in which a single view, the front, is wholly predominant. But now Michelangelo begins to complicate the simple clarity of classic art, since the observer must then move to a compositionally very secondary view in order to read the meaning of the work, the furious defiance that flames forth from the heroic face. The dramatic contrast of posture suggesting external calm and physiognomy suggesting internal turmoil, developed from Donatello, is also at odds with the principles of classic art.

Michelangelo's next statue, the unfinished *St. Matthew* (1506; Accademia), constitutes a violent rejection of classic art. The pose that had traditionally expressed balanced repose, as still in the *David,* is now wrenched into the violent torsion called *contrapposto,* which expresses the opposite extreme, a painful and frustrating tension. Now Michelangelesque tragedy has its protagonist.

These were the heroic forms and expressive powers which Michelangelo brought to the superhuman task now imposed upon the unwilling sculptor by the great pope of the High Renaissance, Julius II: the frescoing of the Sistine Chapel ceiling (133 by 45 feet; 1508–1512). The program of the earlier frescoes on the walls below, which had opposed equivalent episodes of the lives of Moses and Christ, surmounted by figures of the early popes, was now to be made universal by Michelangelo's additions of the essentials of the Old Testament, and eventually, by Raphael's tapestries of later New Testament material and by Michelangelo's *Last Judgment* on the altar wall. The ceiling frescoes reduce Genesis to nine scenes of the Creation and of Noah and the Flood; at the sides are colossal Hebrew prophets and gentile sibyls who foretold the Coming, such proto-saviors as David and Esther, and the ancestors of Christ. Even in Michelangelo's painting, everything is concentrated in the human body, and here, in astounding variety and quantity, its expressive possibilities were infinitely multiplied. Landscape and even space itself are reduced to an unprecedented minimum. Michelangelo is more interested in massive three-dimensional form than in the color which serves primarily for the further clarification of this form. It is appropriate that the text which says God created man in His own image should occasion Michelangelo's most sublime figure, the *Adam* whose human beauty thus partakes of the divine—a concise visual epitome of the Renaissance; yet Adam, doomed by his own iniquities, is also the archetype of Michelangelesque tragedy. The immense accomplishment of the Sistine Chapel expanded the scope of art to incalculably broader dimensions.

As early as 1505 Michelangelo had conceived as his principal masterpiece a great tomb project for Julius II, the 40 huge figures of which would have constituted a compendium of Christianity and its church. A reduced form, undertaken only after the pope's death in 1513, was to have included the so-called *Bound* and *Dying Captives* (Paris, Louvre), which illustrate the terrible intensity of the fully developed Michelangelesque *contrapposto.* Ultimately the tomb was cut down to pitiful dimensions (completed 1545; Rome, San Pietro in Vincoli) that seem scarcely adequate to contain the titanic seated figure of Moses (c. 1515).

The Medici Tombs in Florence (mainly 1520–1534; San Lorenzo, New Sacristy) were planned under the Medici pope, Leo X, as an unprecedented unity of architecture, sculpture, and painting by a single artist (the frescoes were abandoned). The wholly idealized figures of the Medici dukes, which are rather representatives of mankind than portraits, are conceived as liberated by death from the bonds of place (to have been symbolized by bronze river gods) and of time (symbolized by four anguished nude figures of *Night, Day, Morning,* and *Evening*), and turning from their tombs at the sides of the room to their holy intercessors on the end wall (two patron saints by assistants, and the Madonna), they seek unity with the divine (the Christ Child). The Medici tombs are the complete fulfillment of Renaissance Neo-Platonism—a creative synthesis of pagan antiquity and Christianity. Meanwhile, in an independent statue of *Apollo* (c. 1530; Museo Nazionale), Michelangelo indicated a solution to the problem of the free-standing statue with multiple views by disposing the body in a spiral that impels the observer to follow the continuity of views around the figure.

Revolutionary innovations abound in Michelangelo's architecture for the tombs, and, especially, in the Medici's Laurentian Library (mainly 1524–1534; San Lorenzo). Here the traditional antique forms with which the High Renaissance had sought to make architecture a rational and objective art are now given a radically subjective reinterpretation. In Michelangelo's hands, architecture becomes an expressive medium no less intensely personal than any other art. An elaborate, oppressive vestibule hall is almost filled with confusingly intricate curved steps, and its walls are broken into so many different planes that as one approaches them their mass seems to disintegrate. Great columns, which would traditionally represent structural support, are sunk so deeply into the walls that they appear engulfed and impotent. Michelangelo has emphasized the forceful three-dimensionality of these contentious forms so that, when one moves up into the library hall, one is astounded by the suddenly contrasting calm and austerity of its flat, calculatedly monotonous architecture.

In 1534 Michelangelo returned to Rome, never to leave. Increasingly preoccupied with religion, he devoted his life to the service of his church and its pope. Paul III had him complete the Sistine Chapel by frescoing the whole altar wall with the vast and terrible *Last Judgment* (1534–1541). Its disheartening images, gigantically muscular yet curiously powerless, drift in clustering hordes about a vague and shifting space that has been subtly deranged by ambiguous variations in figure scale. In his last paintings, the frescoed *Conversion of St. Paul* and *Crucifixion of St. Peter* in the same pope's Cappella Paolina (1542–1550), Michelangelo is even more despondent. The aged ascetic ventures the deliberately unpleasing—the visual equivalent of the mortification of the flesh. In these strange, bewildered people, the artist who had infinitely enlarged the variety of figure composition cultivates a disturbing monotony. The depths of his pessimism were plumbed in these last frescoes.

The troubled old man withdrew increasingly to the abstraction of architecture. The Roman Capitol, or Campidoglio (begun 1546?), with its separate buildings combined by a graduation of forms into an integrated unity, is a milestone in urban design, prefiguring the 17th century. With characteristic unorthodoxy, Michelangelo decided to exploit the fortuitous existing trapezoidal plan of a site upon which the preceding generation would have imposed rectangularity; but the pavement is patterned in an ellipse. Michelangelo's new colossal orders, which abolish the implied human scale of earlier Renaissance architectural members, here took the form in which they remained as an indispensable feature of post-Renaissance architecture. Most of St. Peter's (excluding the later nave and façade) is by Michelangelo, who simplified and clarified the designs of his predecessors, impressing them with an austere and overwhelming monumentality. The low, brooding dome he had proposed was given instead a lighter, springing verticality. The most mysterious of Michelangelo's works is his last building, the fascinating Porta Pia, a Roman gate undertaken in 1561. Here the fantastic detail, freely improvised in complete emancipation from tradition, is spare and brittle in the lateral parts of the façade, but burgeons climactically in the harsh angularities and the volutes of the great portal.

In Michelangelo's last sculptures the now deeply devout old artist turned again to the theme

Ewing Galloway

MICHELANGELO: "Moses" (1513–1516) by Michelangelo, in the church of San Pietro in Vincoli, in Rome.

New York Public Library

The "Delphic Sibyl" (1508–1512) by Michelangelo, painted on the ceiling of the Sistine Chapel in the Vatican in Rome.

Ewing Galloway, N.Y.

"Lorenzo de' Medici" (1524–1533) by Michelangelo, on Lorenzo's tomb in the Medici Chapel of San Lorenzo, Florence.

of the Pietà. During the very years (c. 1550–1555) when Michelangelo was working on the four-figure group planned for his own modest tomb (but placed in the cathedral of Florence), Michelangelo had written a beautiful sonnet ending with the lines, "Neither painting nor sculpture can now quiet the soul turned to that Divine Love which spread arms out wide to take us, on the Cross," a poetic image which he translated into a series of moving drawings of the Crucifixion (especially the example in the British Museum). The terrible despair, the torturing ambivalences, seem at last to have been dispelled by the power of this Divine Love; and in the same spirit, Michelangelo has carved his self-portrait in the figure of Nicodemus, who tenderly lowers the broken body of Christ into the Madonna's embrace. In the two-figure *Rondanini Pietà* (Milan, Castello), probably begun soon after the group in Florence, the theme is the tender intimacy of Mother and Son, expressed in a soaringly vertical composition of frailer forms; but shortly before his death at almost 90, he began to revise it radically, making them very much frailer still—wraithlike forms that recall the art of the Middle Ages. And though even today the heroic physical ideal of the Occident has remained the one formulated by Michelangelo, the old man himself had at last renounced it and "turned to that Divine Love."

Bibliography.—Grimm, Herman, *Das Leben Michelangelos* (1860), tr. by Fanny Bunnett, *Life of Michel Angelo* (London 1865); Condivi, Ascanio, *Vita di Michel agnolo Buonarroti* (1553), tr. by Charles Holroyd, *Michael Angelo Buonarroti,* 2d ed. (London 1911); de Tolnay, Charles, *Michelangelo,* 6 vols. (Princeton 1943–); Vasari, Giorgio, *Le vite de' più eccellenti pittori, scultori, et architetti* (1568), tr. by Betty Burroughs, *Lives of the Artists* (New York 1959); Tusiani, Joseph, ed., *Complete Poems of Michelangelo* (New York 1960); Ackerman, James S., *The Architecture of Michelangelo,* 2 vols. (New York 1961); Goldscheider, Ludwig, *Michelangelo: Paintings, Sculptures, Architecture,* 4th ed. (New York 1962); Ramsden, E. H., ed., *The Letters of Michelangelo,* 2 vols. (Stanford, Calif., 1963); Goldscheider, Ludwig, *Michelangelo Drawings,* 2d ed. (New York 1966).

JAMES HOLDERBAUM,
Princeton, University.

MICHELET, mĕsh-lĕ′, **Jules,** French historian: b. Paris, France, Aug. 21, 1798; d. Hyères, Feb. 9, 1874. Michelet's youth, as the son of a printer, was one of intermittent poverty, but he was able to enter the Collège Charlemagne, and graduated as one of its most brilliant students. In 1821 he became professor of history at the Collège Rollin and in 1827 lecturer at the École Normale, publishing, in the latter year, an abstract of modern history. After the Revolution of 1830 he was appointed director of the historical section of the national archives, and in 1838 became professor of history at the Collège de France, where he began a series of anticlerical lectures and published such works as *Étude sur les jésuites* (1843); *Le prêtre, la femme et la famille* (1844); and *Le peuple* (1844). He lost his offices in 1851 by his refusal to take an oath of allegiance to Louis Napoleon (later Emperor Napoleon III) and thereafter devoted himself wholly to his writings.

Michelet's multivolume *Histoire de France* (1833–67) is among the monumental productions of historical composition. Its descriptions of life in the Middle Ages are beyond compare, and the work as a whole is of sufficient merit to place its author in the front rank of French historians. His *Histoire de la révolution française* (1847–53), though a splendid specimen of the eloquent use of language, is less highly regarded as history, being marred by an excessive political bias. Michelet, who identified himself strongly with the oppressed masses, at times subordinated historical accuracy to dramatic effect. A byproduct of his interest in style, however, was a series of vividly recorded impressions under such titles as *L'oiseau* (1856), *L'amour* (1859), and *La montagne* (1868). While at work on his history of France, he published *Origines du droit français* (1837); *Histoire romaine: république* (1839); *Légendes démocratiques du nord* (1854); *Les femmes de la révolution* (1854); and many other books. At the time of his death he had completed several volumes of an ambitious *Histoire du XIXe siècle* (1873–74).

MICHELL, mĭch′ĕl, **John,** English physicist, geologist, and astronomer: b. in England, 1724; d. Thornhill, Yorkshire, April 21, 1793. He was educated at Queen's College, Cambridge, became a fellow of the college, and in 1762 was made professor of geology. From 1767 until his death he was rector at Thornhill. He was the original inventor of the torsion balance (which Charles Augustin de Coulomb developed independently in France) and, shortly before his death, proposed a means of using this device to determine the mean density of the earth, an experiment carried out by his friend Henry Cavendish (q.v.) in 1798. Considered one of the founders of seismology, Michell also made valuable contributions to astronomy and published numerous scientific papers, one of the most important of which was *A Treatise of Artificial Magnets, in which is shown an easy and expeditious method of making them superior to the best natural ones* (1750).

MICHELOZZO, mē-kä-lôt′tsō, or **MICHELOZZI,** -tsē (full name MICHELOZZO DI BARTOLOMMEO), Italian architect, sculptor, and goldsmith: b. Florence, Italy, probably in 1396; buried there, Oct. 7, 1472. He studied sculpture under Donatello and architecture under Brunelleschi, and was a protégé of Cosimo de' Medici. As a sculptor, he worked in silver, bronze, and marble. His known statues include one of St. John, in silver, in the Duomo, Florence, and another of that saint, in bronze, at the Bargello. Much of his sculpture however was executed in collaboration with Donatello and is difficult to identify.

Michelozzo's fame rests principally upon his achievements in architecture, his name ranking among the foremost of the famous Florentine architects of the 15th century. He designed the library of San Giorgio Maggiore at Venice, as well as other buildings there, during the period when he shared the exile of his patron, Cosimo de' Medici (c. 1433). He designed the Riccardi Palace in Florence for the Medici (c. 1444) and repaired and partially rebuilt the Palazzo Vecchio, which was falling to ruin. He also undertook the repairs and remodeling of the monastery of San Marco at Florence. He designed the Medici summer villa at Careggi, the Medici palace at Fiesole, and many other buildings. His mature style is notable for its successful combination of early Italian Gothic and classical elements, without sacrifice of dignity or unity of effect.

MICHELSEN, mĭk′kĕl-sĕn, **Christian** (full name PETER CHRISTIAN HERSLEB KJERSCHOW

MICHELSEN), Norwegian statesman and philanthropist: b. Bergen, Norway, Mar. 15, 1857; d. near Bergen, June 29, 1925. He was elected to the Storting (Parliament) in 1891, his country being, at that time, politically united with Sweden. A persuasive advocate of both international conciliation and the independence movement, he headed, in 1895, a coalition government which attempted to establish a separate Norwegian consular service, and ten years later led a delegation in negotiations which secured Swedish agreement to the restoration of the independent kingdom of Norway. He then served for two years as its first prime minister, retiring from political life in 1907. The greater part of his fortune was bequeathed to the Christian Michelsen Institute of Science and Intellectual Freedom, whose charter received royal confirmation in 1929. Situated at Bergen, the institute has sponsored scientific research and has endeavored to promote studies contributing to understanding and tolerance in international affairs.

MICHELSON, mī'kĕl-s'n, **Albert Abraham,** American physicist: b. Strelno, Prussia, Dec. 19, 1852; d. Pasadena, Calif., May 9, 1931. He was an infant when his parents moved to America. In 1873 he was graduated at the United States Naval Academy, served as science instructor there in 1875–1879, took graduate courses in physics in Berlin, Heidelberg, and Paris, and in 1883, having resigned from the navy, became professor of physics at the Case School of Applied Science in Cleveland, Ohio. From 1889 to 1892 he was professor of physics at Clark University, and from 1892 until shortly before his death in 1931 headed the department of physics of the University of Chicago. As a young instructor at Annapolis, he improved an apparatus invented by J. B. Léon Foucault (q.v.) and in 1879 announced new figures for the velocity of light in a vacuum. Shortly afterwards he developed his interferometer (q.v.), which established the wave length of light as a practical unit of measure. At Sèvres, France, in 1892, he measured the standard meter, expressing his results in units based on the wave length of the red spectrum in the light emitted by a cadmium arc (1,553,163½ units). He also developed the echelon spectroscope, making possible the first accurate measurement of the diameter of a star in 1920. A new figure expressing the speed of light (186,270 miles per second), announced in 1933, after Michelson's death, was made possible largely by a new series of experiments which he began in 1926 and in which he used a one-mile-long vacuum pipe equipped with mirrors.

The best known of Michelson's experiments was first performed in 1881, conducted on a more elaborate scale in 1887 in collaboration with Edward William Morley (1838–1923), and subsequently repeated and refined by these and other scientists. Called the Michelson-Morley experiment, it was designed to measure the "drag" exerted on the passage of light by a hypothetical, stationary medium known as the "luminiferous ether," in the hope of fixing the absolute speed at which the earth moved through space. By its negative results, the experiment eliminated the concept of a motionless, measurable ether and cleared the way for the development of the theory of relativity. (See also RELATIVITY—*Absolute Motion.*) Michelson was the first American scientist to win a Nobel Prize, being granted the award in physics in 1907. He published *Velocity of Light* (1902), *Light Waves and Their Uses* (1903), *Studies in Optics* (1927), and some 75 scientific papers.

MICHENER, mĭch'ĕn-ẽr, **James Albert,** American writer and educator: b. New York, N.Y., Feb. 3, 1907. Raised in Doylestown, Pa., he attended Swarthmore College, graduating with honors in 1929. He spent some years in Europe on a research grant, returning to teach at the George School in Pennsylvania (1933–1936). Subsequently he studied at several major universities, was associate professor at the Colorado State College of Education (1936–1939), and visiting professor at Harvard (1940–1941). He also published numerous articles in the field of education and in 1940 edited *The Future of Social Studies* for the National Education Association.

Michener was an associate editor at the Macmillan Company at the time of the attack on Pearl Harbor. While on active duty as a naval reserve officer in the Pacific island area (1944–1945) he gathered the material for his *Tales of the South Pacific.* Published in 1947, the work earned the Pulitzer Prize for fiction in the following year, and was the basis of one of the most popular of modern Broadway musical plays, *South Pacific* (1949). Later works included *The Fires of Spring* (1949); *Return to Paradise* (1951); *The Voice of Asia* (1951); *The Bridges at Toko-ri* (1953); *Sayonara* (1954); and *The Bridge at Andau* (1957). Several of these have been adapted into feature-length motion pictures.

MICHIGAN, mĭsh'ĭ-găn, one of the east north central states of the United States, lying within the region of the Great Lakes. It is composed of two peninsulas, a southern and a northern, separated by the Straits of Mackinac. The Upper Peninsula is bounded on the north by Lake Superior; on the east by Lake Superior, Whitefish Bay, Lake Huron, and St. Marys River, which separates Michigan from the Province of Ontario, Canada; on the south by Lake Huron, the Straits of Mackinac, which separate the two peninsulas, and Lake Michigan; and on the southwest and west by Wisconsin. The Lower Peninsula is bounded on the north by Lake Huron, the Straits of Mackinac, and Lake Michigan; on the east by Lake Huron, the St. Clair River, Lake St. Clair, the Detroit River, and Lake Erie (the rivers separating the state from Ontario, Canada); on the south by Ohio and Indiana; and on the west by Lake Michigan.

State flag
(adopted April 29, 1911)
(Colors: blue background upon which is delineated the state coat of arms.)

Total area	58,216 square miles
Land area	57,022 square miles
Water area (inland)	1,194 square miles
Upper Peninsula (approx., land)	16,538 square miles
Lower Peninsula (approx., land)	40,484 square miles
Latitude	41° 41′–47° 30′ N.
Longitude	82° 26′–90° 31′ W.
Altitude	578 feet to 2,023 feet
Population (1970)	8,875,083
Capital—Lansing, population	131,546
Admitted to Union as 26th state	Jan. 26, 1837
Bird (adopted 1931)	Robin
Flower (adopted 1897)	Apple blossom
Motto	*Si Quaeris Peninsulam Amoenam Circumspice* (*If You Seek a Pleasant Peninsula, Look Around You*)
Nicknames	Auto State; Water Wonderland; Lake State; Wolverine State
Song	*Michigan, My Michigan* (Douglas Malloch)
Tree (adopted 1955)	White pine

The material in this article is arranged under the following main headings:

State seal
(adopted June 2, 1835)

It is the view of many authorities that the name "Michigan" is a simplification of Indian syllables which together mean "monstrous lake" or "vast body of water." Perry F. Powers states that the name first appeared in the congressional proceedings of 1804.

1. PHYSICAL FEATURES

Geology.—The western half of the Upper Peninsula is a part of the Laurentian upland area of North America. Upon a foundation of ancient Archean rocks are laid old sedimentary formations of limestone and sandstone containing iron and copper deposits. The eastern half of the Upper Peninsula and the entire Lower Peninsula are composed of more recent sedimentary formations. These occur one above the other like a nest of shallow dishes filling a structural basin, the rim of which is represented by the Archean rocks of the western half of the Upper Peninsula. Glacial ice made the exact outlines of the state. The structural basin of Lake Superior was deepened, and glacial tongues dug the present depressions occupied by Lakes Michigan, Huron, and Erie. Retreating ice spread a mantle of glacial drift over all of the state except the higher parts of the western half of the Upper Peninsula. These higher areas were reshaped by the ice fronts into hilly belts, rolling plains, and uplands. The retreating ice blocked the previous drainage channels and left thousands of undrained depressions, thereby making Michigan a state of many lakes, swamps, and marshes. In the southern half of the Lower Peninsula the glacial mantle formed fairly rich loamy soils, but over most of the northern parts it resulted in sandy and poorer soils. This difference in soil material between the southern part of the Lower Peninsula and the remainder of the state divides Michigan into a southern part which is agriculturally well developed and prosperous and a northern part where farming is successful only in some localities.

Topography.—The southern half of the Lower Peninsula reveals a level to gently rolling surface, the most conspicuous features of which are chains of low glacial hills. The highest points of these hilly chains reach altitudes between 1,000 and 1,200 feet above sea level. The northern half of the Lower Peninsula is composed largely of a tableland capped by hilly belts of glacial origin attaining elevations of between 1,200 and 1,700 feet. This tableland is the water divide between the rivers flowing westward, northward, and eastward into the bordering Great Lakes. The eastern half of the Upper Peninsula is fairly level—nowhere exceeding 400 feet above the surrounding lake levels—and contains considerable areas of swampy land. The western half is higher and more rugged with successions of rocky ridges, sandy plains, and wet shallow valleys. The highest elevations in the state occur along the Lake Superior shore on rocky, almost mountainous, ridges called the Huron Mountains (elevation 1,980 feet) in Marquette and Baraga counties, and the Porcupine Mountains (elevation 2,023 feet) in Ontonagon County.

Rivers and Lakes.—Approximately 70 per cent of the surface of the state is drained by 34 primary river systems; the remaining 30 per cent drains directly into the lakes by smaller streams. The Saginaw and its tributaries, the Shiawassee, the Tittabawassee, and the Cass, form the largest river system, draining approximately 6,500 square miles into Lake Huron. Other principal rivers of the Lower Peninsula which empty into Lakes Huron or Erie are the Raisin, the Huron, the Au Sable, the Thunder Bay, and the Cheboygan. Drainage into Lake Michigan is accomplished principally by the Kalamazoo, the Grand, the Muskegon, the Manistee, and the Boardman. The Upper Peninsula rivers flowing into Lakes Michigan and Huron are the Menominee, the Escanaba, the Whitefish, the Manistique, and the St. Marys, a stream that forms part of the international boundary with Canada. The north-flowing rivers of the Upper Peninsula are the Montreal, which forms part of the boundary with Wisconsin, and the Ontonagon, the Sturgeon, and the Tahquamenon.

There are more than 11,000 lakes in the state, of which 6,454 are large enough to be listed in the *Michigan Lakes and Streams Directory*. Houghton Lake in Roscommon County is the largest of these, with 31 square miles of surface. The length of the courses of the major rivers is 5,499 miles; in addition there are an estimated 30,000 miles of tributaries. The state has 3,177 miles of shoreline, more than that of any other state in the Union; of the total, 120 miles are accounted for by harbors.

Climate.—Michigan is characterized by marked seasonal differences in temperature and by an even yearly distribution of rainfall, which is

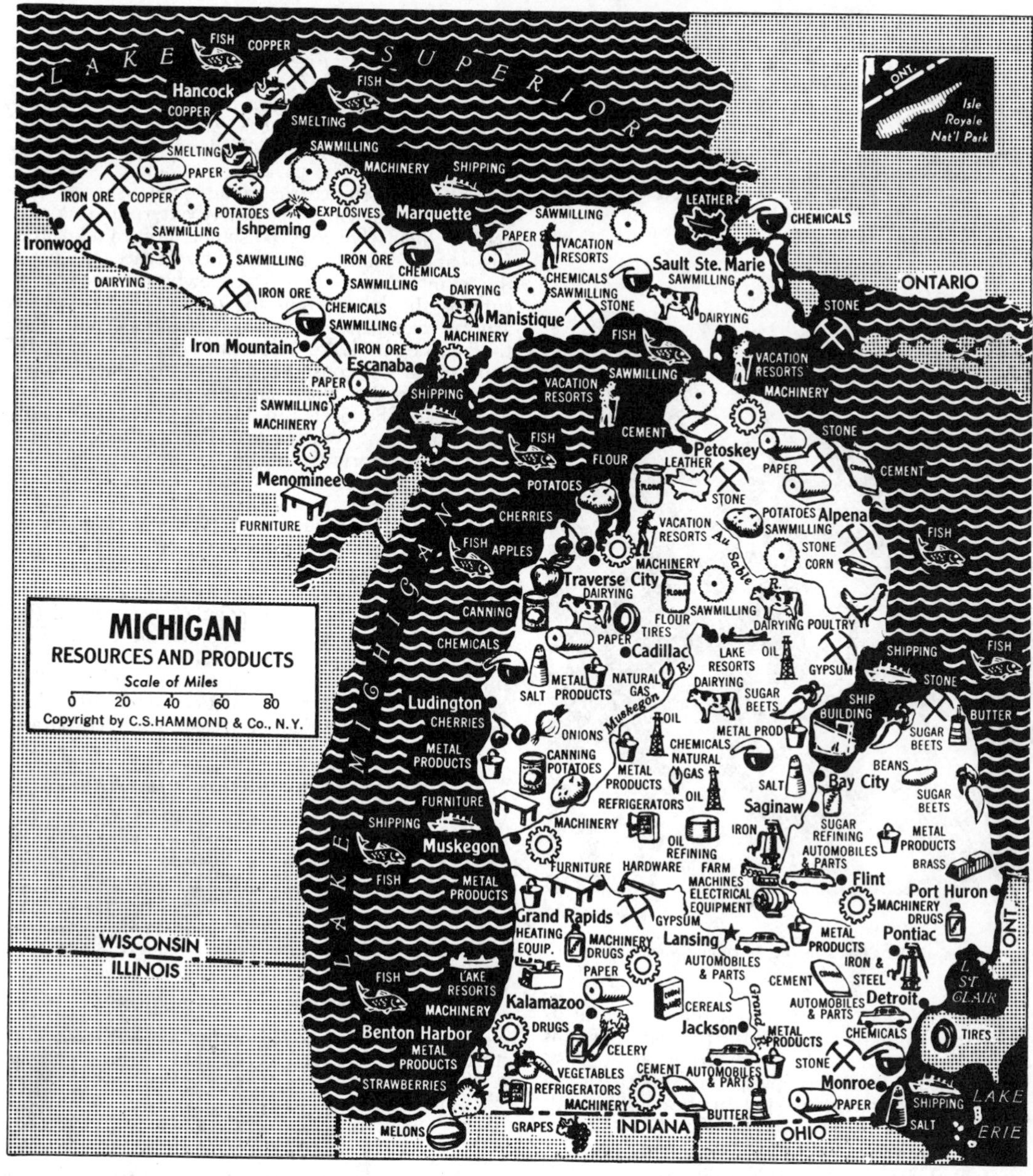

abundant but not excessive. Winters are cool to cold, with minimum monthly temperatures ranging from 11°F. along the northern coast of the Upper Peninsula to 27°F. in the southwestern and southeastern corners of the Lower Peninsula. Summers are warm to hot, with maximum monthly temperatures in the same localities ranging from below 60°F. to over 70°F. In any season there is a difference of about 10°F. between the extreme northern and southern parts of the state. The growing season for crops varies considerably with latitude and extent of exposure. In the Upper Peninsula, it may be as long as 150 days along the coast, while inland and at higher locations there may be only 70 growing days. In the Lower Peninsula, similar locations may have a growing season of 70 to 170 days. The stabilizing effect of the lake waters is important, especially in a narrow band along the Lake Michigan shore where retardation of both early growing temperatures and early frosts form a climatic setting for the Fruit Belt. Precipitation is everywhere adequate for agriculture and is fairly evenly distributed from place to place. The state as a whole averages approximately 30 inches a year within a range of some 10 inches from year to year. In general, one day in three is rainy, one in two is cloudy. The northern lake shores receive heavy snows in winter.

Flora.—Michigan abounds in plant species. Hardwoods such as elm, oak, maple, and hickory are pre-eminent in the southern part of the Lower Peninsula. In the northern part of the Lower Peninsula, jack pine, white birch, and aspen are predominant. Scattered throughout the state are numerous varieties of deciduous and coniferous trees.

There are several hundred species of wild flowering plants. A few of those that bloom in the early spring are the bloodroot, dicentra, adder's-tongue, cress, hepatica, buttercup, trillium, and mandrake. At a later date the blue lupine, iris, pink phlox, orange milkweed, shooting stars, and tiger lilies make their appearance. Still later, sunflowers, rudbeckia, eupatorium, asters, and goldenrod burst forth. Many of the vines that grow in the forest have edible fruits. There are numerous varieties of blackberry, raspberry, blueberry, and gooseberry, and wild grapes sometimes attain great size.

Devaney Inc.

Lake of the Clouds in the Porcupine Mountains.

Animals.—Michigan is well represented in its stock of fish, game, and birds. Its many streams and lakes are abundant with trout, pike, bass, perch, smelt, sunfish, crappies, and catfish. Among its more important game and fur-bearing animals are the deer, black bear, rabbit, hare, beaver, wolf, coyote, muskrat, weasel, mink, otter, marten, raccoon, opossum, red fox, and badger. Most of the birds are migratory, although a considerable number remain all year. Pheasant, woodcock, partridge, and wild geese and ducks are the more important game birds.

Conservation.—Dedication of the large area of cut-over land in the north to public ownership and recreational development has led the state Department of Conservation into an outstanding program of research and operations. The pioneer work of its Institute for Fisheries Research in improvement of lakes and streams for fishing produced nationally accepted remedial procedures. Experimental work in controlled fish population, selective fishing, and extended seasons has made notable changes in recreational angling. The management of Michigan's deer herd in the interests of 600,000 deer hunters has been a continuing problem for both biologists and law enforcement officers.

The Land Economic Survey devoted more than a decade to inventorying the character and value of the statelands; and from the findings came an enlightened policy for land disposition and development. Fires have ceased to be a large scale hazard to forest growth.

Several related conservation problems arose from the linking of the Great Lakes with the Atlantic Ocean by the Welland Canal around Niagara Falls. The parasitic sea lamprey entered the lakes and ruined the commercial fisheries for lake trout and whitefish, nearly exterminating the species themselves. A poisoning program of the Fish and Wildlife Service has greatly reduced the number of lampreys. Alewives, which also entered the lakes from the ocean, die and wash ashore each summer in great numbers, polluting the beaches of Lake Michigan resorts. The state department of conservation has introduced coho salmon into the lakes, partially as a check to the alewives. The first full fishing year (1967) of these salmon produced excellent results, which may revive sports fishing in the Great Lakes.

2. POPULATION

Population Characteristics.—Michigan was the seventh most populous state in the Union in 1970 and, except for the period 1890–1910, has grown faster than the nation as a whole.

After 1910, the urban population exceeded the rural population, and by 1970 the state was 73.8 per cent urban (according to the new urban definition of the federal Bureau of the Census). The growth of the rural population since 1930 has been largely in residential areas outside corporate city limits.

GROWTH OF POPULATION SINCE 1840

Year	Population	Year	Population
1840	212,267	1930	4,842,325
1860	749,113	1940	5,256,106
1880	1,636,937	1950	6,371,766
1900	2,420,982	1960	7,823,194
1920	3,668,412	1970	8,875,083

Gain, 1960–1970: 13.4% (U. S. gain, 13.3%). **Density,** 1970: 155.6 persons per square mile (U.S. density, 56.2).

URBAN-RURAL DISTRIBUTION

Year	Percent urban	Percent rural
1920	61.1 (U.S., 51.2)	38.9
1930	68.2 (U.S., 56.2)	31.8
1940	65.7 (U.S., 56.6)	34.3
1950	70.7 (U.S., 64.0)	29.3
1960	73.4 (U.S., 69.9)	26.6
1970	73.8 (U.S., 73.5)	26.2

LARGEST CENTERS OF POPULATION

City or Metropolitan area[1]	1970	1960	1950
Detroit (city)	1,513,601	1,670,144	1,849,568
Metropolitan area	4,199,931	3,762,360	3,016,197
Grand Rapids (city)	197,649	177,313	176,515
Metropolitan area	539,225	363,187	288,292
Flint (city)	193,317	196,940	163,143
Metropolitan area	496,658	374,313	270,963
Warren	179,260	89,246	727
Lansing (city)	131,546	107,807	92,129
Metropolitan area	378,423	298,949	244,159
Livonia	110,109	66,702	17,534
Dearborn	104,199	112,007	94,994
Ann Arbor (city)	99,797	67,340	48,251
Metropolitan area	234,103	172,440	134,606
Saginaw (city)	91,849	98,265	92,918
Metropolitan area	219,743	190,752	153,515
St. Clair Shores	88,093	76,657	19,823
Westland	86,749	...	...
Kalamazoo (city)	85,555	82,089	57,704
Metropolitan area	201,550	169,712	126,707
Royal Oak	86,238	80,612	46,889
Pontiac	85,279	82,233	73,681
Dearborn Heights	80,069	...	...
Taylor	70,020	...	...

[1] Standard metropolitan statistical area.

Immigrants have always made up a large segment of Michigan's population. During the period from 1860 to 1900, lumbering and mining operations drew into the state Swedes, Norwegians, Finns, Italians, and large numbers of Canadians. About 1910, Detroit provided employment opportunities for the unskilled immigrants who began to arrive in large numbers from Poland, Italy, Russia, Austria-Hungary, and many other European countries. More than 500,000 persons are of foreign birth, with the largest numbers having been born in Canada, Poland, Germany, England and Wales, Italy, and the USSR.

During World Wars I and II the need for industrial manpower brought to Detroit and other Michigan cities an influx of Negroes from the Southern states. In 1910, Michigan had 17,115 Negroes and in 1930, 169,453. By 1970 the number of Negroes had increased to 991,066, representing 11 per cent of the total population.

Cities.—In 1970 there were seven standard metropolitan areas whose city populations exceeded 50,000. Detroit is the fifth-largest city and one of the leading industrial centers in the United States. The Detroit metropolitan area, including Macomb, Oakland, and Wayne counties, has almost one half the total population of the state. Warren, Livonia, and Dearborn are separate incorporated cities forming part of the metropolitan area. In Pontiac, which also is in the Detroit metropolitan area, there are large automobile manufacturing plants.

Grand Rapids, a manufacturing center in the west central part of the state, is the second-largest city. Lansing, the capital city, is the principal trading center for central Michigan. A large proportion of the people within its metropolitan area are engaged in the city's automobile and parts plants. Flint, in east central Michigan, is second to Detroit in the manufacture of automobiles.

Ann Arbor, situated in the southern part of the state, is the seat of the University of Michigan. Saginaw is the center of the agriculturally rich Saginaw Valley. Formerly a lumber center, it has diversified manufacturing, sugar-beet refining, and food processing activities. Kalamazoo, situated in the south central part of the state, is noted for its drug and paper industries.

Counties.—Of the 83 counties, 68 are in the Lower Peninsula and 15 in the Upper Peninsula. Marquette is the largest county and Benzie the smallest. Wayne, which contains the city of Detroit, is the most populous, and Keweenaw has the fewest people. A list of the counties with their county seats follows:

UPPER PENINSULA

County	County Seat	County	County Seat
Alger	Munising	Keweenaw	Eagle River
Baraga	L'Anse	Luce	Newberry
Chippewa	Sault Ste. Marie	Mackinac	St. Ignace
Delta	Escanaba	Marquette	Marquette
Dickinson	Iron Mountain	Menominee	Menominee
Gogebic	Bessemer	Ontonagon	Ontonagon
Houghton	Houghton	Schoolcraft	Manistique
Iron	Crystal Falls		

LOWER PENINSULA

County	County Seat	County	County Seat
Alcona	Harrisville	Berrien	St. Joseph
Allegan	Allegan	Branch	Coldwater
Alpena	Alpena	Calhoun	Marshall
Antrim	Bellaire	Cass	Cassopolis
Arenac	Standish	Charlevoix	Charlevoix
Barry	Hastings	Cheboygan	Cheboygan
Bay	Bay City	Clare	Harrison
Benzie	Beulah	Clinton	St. Johns
Crawford	Grayling	Midland	Midland
Eaton	Charlotte	Missaukee	Lake City
Emmet	Petoskey	Monroe	Monroe
Genessee	Flint	Montcalm	Stanton
Gladwin	Gladwin	Montmorency	Atlanta
Grand Traverse	Traverse City	Muskegon	Muskegon
Gratiot	Ithaca	Newaygo	White Cloud
Hillsdale	Hillsdale	Oakland	Pontiac
Huron	Bad Axe	Oceana	Hart
Ingham	Mason	Ogemaw	West Branch
Ionia	Ionia	Osceola	Reed City
Iosco	Tawas City	Oscoda	Mio
Isabella	Mount Pleasant	Otsego	Gaylord
Jackson	Jackson	Ottawa	Grand Haven
Kalamazoo	Kalamazoo	Presque Isle	Rogers City
Kalkaska	Kalkaska	Roscommon	Roscommon
Kent	Grand Rapids	Saginaw	Saginaw
Lake	Baldwin	St. Clair	Port Huron
Lapeer	Lapeer	St. Joseph	Centerville
Leelanau	Leland	Sanilac	Sandusky
Lenawee	Adrian	Shiawassee	Corunna
Livingston	Howell	Tuscola	Caro
Macomb	Mount Clemens	Van Buren	Paw Paw
Manistee	Manistee	Washtenaw	Ann Arbor
Mason	Ludington	Wayne	Detroit
Mecosta	Big Rapids	Wexford	Cadillac

3. GOVERNMENT

State Constitution.—Michigan's first constitution was adopted in 1835, two years before the state was admitted to the Union. The first revision went into effect in 1850. Two later attempts at revision were rejected by the voters.

Michigan Tourist Council Photo

State capitol building, Lansing.

The constitution of 1908 was in effect until the present (1963) constitution became effective on Jan. 1, 1964. The constitution contains a bill of rights; provides for the division of state government into legislative, executive, and judicial branches; sets forth the bases of local government, public education, taxation, and education; and provides for initiative, referendum, and amendment by petition. In 1978 and every 16 years thereafter the question of constitutional revision must be submitted to the voters.

Suffrage requirements are United States citizenship, six months of residence in the state, and eligibility under local regulations. The state has two senators and 19 representatives in the Congress of the United States.

Executive.—The constitution of 1963 provides for the election of the governor and lieutenant governor (on the same party ticket), the secretary of state, and the attorney general to 4-year terms.

The executive branch is organized into 19 departments, each supervised by the governor. Except for constitutionally elected officials and board members, the director of each department is appointed by the governor, with the advice and consent of the senate. A bipartisan civil rights commission appointed by the governor is required by the constitution.

The governor holds the usual powers of a chief executive. He may call special sessions of the state legislature on extraordinary occasions to consider only the items mentioned in his call. He must submit to the legislature a balanced budget and has veto power over individual items in appropriations bills.

Most state employees in Michigan work under a civil service system.

GOVERNORS

Name	Party	Term
UNDER FRENCH DOMINION		
Samuel Champlain		1622–1635
M. de Montmagny		1636–1647
M. d'Aillebout		1648–1650
M. de Lauson		1651–1656
M. de Lauson (Jr.)		1656–1657
M. d'Aillebout		1657–1658
M. d'Argenson		1658–1660
Baron d'Avangour		1661–1663
M. de Mesey		1663–1665
M. de Courcelles		1665–1672
Count de Frontenac		1672–1682
M. de la Barre		1682–1685
M. de Nonville		1685–1689
Count de Frontenac		1689–1698
M. de Callieres		1699–1703
M. de Vaudreuil		1703–1725
M. de Beauharnois		1726–1747
M. de Galissoniere		1747–1749
M. de la Jonquiere		1749–1752
M. Duquesne		1752–1755
M. de Vaudreuil de Cavagnac		1755–1763
UNDER BRITISH DOMINION		
James Murray		1763–1767
Guy Carleton		1768–1777
Frederick Haldimand		1777–1785
Henry Hamilton		1785–1786
Lord Dorchester		1786–1796
UNDER NORTHWEST TERRITORY		
Arthur St. Clair		1796–1800
INDIANA TERRITORY		
William Henry Harrison		1800–1805
MICHIGAN TERRITORY		
William Hull		1805–1813
Lewis Cass		1813–1831
John T. Mason (acting)		1831
George B. Porter		1831–1834
Stevens T. Mason (*ex officio*)		1834–1835
STATE		
Stevens T. Mason	Democrat	1835–1840
Edward Mundy (acting)	"	1838
William Woodbridge	Whig	1840–1841
James W. Gordon (acting)	"	1841–1842
John S. Barry	Democrat	1842–1846
Alpheus Felch	"	1846–1847
William L. Greenly (acting)	"	1847–1848
Epaphroditus Ransom	"	1848–1850
John S. Barry	"	1850–1851
Robert McClelland	"	1851–1853
Andrew Parsons (acting)	"	1853–1855
Kinsley S. Bingham	Republican	1855–1859
Moses Wisner	"	1859–1861
Austin Blair	"	1861–1865
Henry H. Crapo	"	1865–1869
Henry P. Baldwin	"	1869–1873
John J. Bagley	"	1873–1877
Charles M. Croswell	"	1877–1881
David H. Jerome	"	1881–1883
Josiah W. Begole	Democrat and Greenback	1883–1885
Russell A. Alger	Republican	1885–1887
Cyrus G. Luce	"	1887–1891
Edwin B. Winans	Democrat	1891–1893
John T. Rich	Republican	1893–1897
Hazen S. Pingree	"	1897–1901
Aaron T. Bliss	"	1901–1905
Fred M. Warner	"	1905–1911
Chase S. Osborn	"	1911–1913
Woodbridge N. Ferris	Democrat	1913–1917
Albert E. Sleeper	Republican	1917–1921
Alexander J. Groesbeck	"	1921–1927
Fred W. Green	"	1927–1931
Wilber M. Brucker	"	1931–1933
William A. Comstock	Democrat	1933–1935
Frank D. Fitzgerald	Republican	1935–1937
Frank Murphy	Democrat	1937–1939
Frank D. Fitzgerald	Republican	1939 (died 1939)
Luren D. Dickinson	"	1939–1941
Murray D. Van Wagoner	Democrat	1941–1943
Harry F. Kelly	Republican	1943–1947
Kim Sigler	"	1947–1949
G. Mennen Williams	Democrat	1949–1961
John B. Swainson	"	1961–1963
George W. Romney	Republican	1963–1969
William G. Milliken	Republican	1969–

Legislature.—The Michigan legislature is a bicameral body consisting of a senate and a house of representatives. The 34 senators are elected to 4-year terms from senatorial districts defined on a population basis. The 110 representatives are elected to 2-year terms from districts also drawn on a population basis. The constitution provides for a bipartisan commission to reapportion the state after each decennial census. The legislature meets on the first Wednesday in January for a session of indeterminate length. With the exception of appropriation bills which require a two-thirds vote, bills passed by a majority vote of the members of both houses and signed by the governor became law. A two-thirds majority of each house is required to override a gubernatorial veto.

Judiciary.—The judicial system is divided into five parts. The state supreme court consists of seven members elected on nonpartisan ballots to 8-year terms. The court selects a chief justice from its members. The court of appeals consists of nine judges selected in nonpartisan elections from districts as nearly as possible of equal population. This court may sit in various places and in sections of not less than three judges as directed by the supreme court.

The state is divided into judicial circuits drawn along county lines. Each circuit has one or more judges and must hold court at least four times each year. Probate courts are established in counties or combinations of counties, and the office of probate judge may be combined with any other office of limited jurisdiction. Justices of the peace are being replaced by such local courts as are created by the legislature.

Taxation and Revenue System.—The Michigan government is supported primarily by taxes levied in the state. Principal sources of revenue are the 4 percent sales tax, and taxes on gasoline, motor vehicles, cigarettes, and liquor. In 1966 the legislature added income taxes of 2.6 percent on personal incomes, 5 percent on corporate profits, and 7 percent on banks and other financial institutions. Other income is derived from regulatory fees, patient and ward payments, licenses, and miscellaneous sources.

In fiscal 1965, total revenues collected by the state were $2,419,986,000, and total expenditures were $2,053,768,000. General fund revenues totaled $1,959,333,000, of which about two thirds was derived from taxes. General expenditures were $1,782,086,000, of which approximately one half was for education, one fifth for highways, one tenth for public welfare, and smaller proportions for other public services.

The gross outstanding indebtedness of the state in 1965 was $952 million. Of the total, a substantial amount was for highways and the Straits of Mackinac Bridge. Other indebtedness represented costs of hospitals, educational buildings, and veterans' bonuses.

The state department of revenue is the chief tax collection agency in Michigan. It determines the amount of tax that is due the state and is responsible for the collection of taxes under its jurisdiction.

4. EDUCATION, HEALTH, AND WELFARE

Educational System.—Leadership and general supervision of all public education, with the exception of institutions granting baccalaureate degrees, is vested in a state board of education consisting of eight members elected to terms of eight years. The board appoints a superintendent of public instruction, administers certain state schools, and grants teachers' certificates.

Education in Michigan is free for all students over 5 years of age and is compulsory for those between the ages of 6 and 16.

In 1966–1967 there were an estimated 895 school districts in the state. The number of districts has been steadily decreasing through the process of consolidation. At the same time there were 2,053,000 pupils and 75,000 teachers in the state's public elementary and secondary schools, and 368,400 pupils and 11,320 teachers in nonpublic schools.

Higher Education.—There are 11 public coeducational colleges or universities in the state, each under a constitutionally organized board of direction. These are, with their 1966 enrollments: Central Michigan University, Mt. Pleasant (7,929); Eastern Michigan University, Ypsilanti (12,000); Ferris State College, Big Rapids (5,787); Grand Valley State College, Grand Rapids (1,003); Michigan Technological University, East Lansing (41,-782); Northern Michigan University, Marquette (5,661); University of Michigan, Ann Arbor (34,-453); Wayne State University, Detroit (26,542); and Western Michigan University, Kalamazoo (15,242). Saginaw Valley College at University Center opened in 1968.

There are also 21 private colleges in the state. Among those with a liberal arts character are Adrian College at Adrian, Albion College at Albion, Alma College at Alma, Aquinas College at Grand Rapids, Calvin College at Grand Rapids, Hillsdale College at Hillsdale, Kalamazoo College at Kalamazoo, Olivet College at Olivet, and the University of Detroit. All are 4-year coeducational institutions. Fourteen professional institutions and three with a technical character are located in the state. Among the larger of these are the Detroit Institute of Technology, Detroit College of Law, General Motors Institute, and the Lawrence Institute of Technology.

In 1965 there were 270,918 students enrolled in Michigan's colleges and universities.

Libraries.—Michigan has outstanding technical libraries. Many of the manufacturing companies such as the Ford Motor Company in Dearborn, General Motors in Detroit, Parke, Davis and Company in Detroit, and the Dow Chemical Company in Midland maintain libraries of considerable size, and some of these permit interlibrary loans. The state university libraries are very extensive and specialize in law, government, and local history. By 1965 the University of Michigan library at Ann Arbor had 33 branches and approximately 3,370,000 volumes. Michigan State University library contains approximately 1,146,000 volumes. The Detroit Public Library in 1965 had more than 2,000,000 volumes, including the Burton historical collections of local history. The Hackley Public Library at Muskegon has notable collections on lumbering and local history. Michigan State Library (1828), the state government library, includes the State Law Library and one for the blind.

Ewing Galloway

At Detour, mountains of crushed dolomite await shipment to steel mills.

Health, Welfare, and Penal Institutions.—The Department of Health, headed by the state health commissioner, is responsible for the enforcement of the public health laws and for the establishment of rules and regulations pertaining to statewide health practices. The Department of Mental Health has jurisdiction over state hospitals for the mentally ill at Kalamazoo, Newberry, Pontiac, Traverse City, and Ypsilanti. For mentally deficient people there are state homes and training schools at Coldwater, Lapeer, Mount Pleasant, and Northville. The Department of Mental Health also maintains a state hospital for the criminally insane at Ionia, and another hospital for epileptics situated near Caro. The state maintains a school for the blind at Lansing, and a school for the deaf at Flint.

The Department of Corrections maintains the following institutions: the state prison of southern Michigan, located in Jackson County; the State House of Corrections and Branch Prison, a maximum security institution located at Marquette; the Cassidy Lake Technical School at Chelsea, a minimum security unit for youthful first offenders; and the Michigan Reformatory at Ionia for males through 25 years of age. In addition,

Philip Gendreau

The vast Ford Motor Company plant at River Rouge, adjacent to Detroit.

the state has two schools for socially maladjusted boys and girls—for boys at Lansing, and for girls at Adrian.

5. ECONOMIC ACTIVITIES

Manufacturing is the most important economic activity in the state. Since the beginning of the 20th century population increase has centered in the industrial cities which have provided the greatest economic opportunities for individuals in addition to furnishing markets for agricultural products.

There are approximately 3.2 million employed persons in the state. More than 36 percent of these are engaged in manufacturing, 17 percent in trade, and 15 percent in state and government activities. Other important categories of employment are construction, transportation, and public utilities. Agricultural employment has declined in the number of persons engaged and, in the late 1960's, was between 2 and 3 percent of the state's labor force.

In 1966, total personal income in Michigan exceeded $27 billion. Average per capita income was $3,269 compared with $3,132 in the nation as a whole.

Manufacturing.—Michigan ranks fifth among the states in the value added by its manufactured products. The value of manufactures, more than $13 billion annually, is more than twelve times the annual value of all crops sold or of recreational income in the state. Although manufacturing is widely distributed in the southern part of Michigan, there are three principal districts in that region: the Detroit metropolitan area and adjoining counties, which produce automobiles, machinery, chemicals, drugs, and numerous other products; the Lansing-Grand Rapids-Muskegon area which produces automobiles, furniture, household appliances, engines, and many light products; and the Battle Creek-Kalamazoo-Jackson area, which produces automobile parts, paper, drugs, food, and other products. Between 1945 and 1965 the number of manufacturing plants in the state increased by more than 50 percent and spread to many of the smaller cities and towns. The diffusion in manufacturing is brought about in part by highway trucking, which enables industries in central locations to establish branch plants or to purchase parts from suppliers in outlying areas.

The state is the world's leading automobile maker, and more than one third of its manufacturing value is derived from automobile production. Other important categories of manufacturing are, in order of value, machinery, primary metals, fabricated metals, paper, food products, and metal working machines. Michigan ranks first in the country in the production of machine tools, hardware, metal office furniture, nonferrous castings, and industrial patterns. The presence of industrial research is important in the state. Several industrial companies and governmental agencies have research branches in and around Ann Arbor. In 1967, following racial riots in Detroit, job training programs were accelerated by public agencies, and automobile manufacturers offered to train and employ several thousand disadvantaged persons.

Forestry Production.—In its original condition the state was almost completely forested. During the early periods of settlement the southern hardwoods were removed in the process of converting the land to agriculture. Beginning about 1860, large-scale lumbering operations cut the pine timber in the northern part of the state. For some years during the late 19th century, Michigan was the leading lumber-producing state in the nation. Almost one half of the state is still considered to be commercial forest land, which in 1963 contained an estimated 20.0 billion board feet of hardwood and 7.4 billion of softwood saw timber.

Fisheries.—Before the parasitic sea lamprey invaded the Great Lakes, Michigan was noted for its catches of lake trout and whitefish. Fishing for these species, both regarded as table delicacies, has been practically abandoned, and a federal program to control the lamprey is in progress. In the late 1960's the fishing industry produced about $2.7 million per year from such species as chubs, herring, smelt, and yellow perch. In 1965 the commercial catch in the state was 19,747,651 pounds. Among the lake states, Michigan ranks first in the value of fisheries.

Agriculture.—About 50 percent of the state is classified as farmland, and some 40 percent is in farms. There are 94,000 farms with an average size of about 145 acres. While there has been a steady decline in the number of farms and farmers, the size of individual farms is rising. Approximately one half of the farms sell less than $10,000 in products per year. Some of these are "retirement" farms, that is, farms on which the operator works part time in other employment. In 1966 the number of farm operators in Michigan was 71,700.

All of the state except a strip along the southern border is in the hay and dairy belt of the United States. The southern strip lies within the corn belt. Agriculture is concentrated in the southern part of the Lower Peninsula where more than 60 percent of the land is in farms. Some counties in the south have as much as 80 percent of the land in farms. North of the latitude of Saginaw Bay and in the Upper Peninsula a much smaller percentage of land is in farms, and less of the farmland is in crops.

The agricultural emphasis in the state as a whole is on the production of crops for animal food, and the principal source of farm income is from the sale of animals and animal products. About 50 percent of the income from animals is in the form of dairy products. The importance of dairying is the result of good pasture conditions and markets provided by the industrial cities, which consume most of the dairy production as whole milk. In the corn belt counties, beef cattle and hogs are the chief products. Hay crops occupy some 30 percent of harvested land, and corn, oats, and winter wheat are the principal grains. Notable agricultural specialties are field beans, sugar beets, and fruits. In 1966 cash receipts for livestock and products amounted to $424 million, and for all crops, $364 million.

Mining.—Until the latter part of the 19th century Michigan was the leading copper and iron-ore producing state in the nation. After nearly 100 years of production the copper mines of the Upper Peninsula are deep and expensive to operate. In competition with cheaper western ores, Michigan copper production has dropped to sixth in the nation. The iron ores, also in the Upper Peninsula, lie for the most part deep underground and are more costly to mine than those in Minnesota. They suffer in competition with high-grade foreign ores. Exploitation of lower grade, but more cheaply mined, deposits of both copper and iron is being carried out.

Petroleum and natural gas occur in several places in the Lower Peninsula. The fields are relatively shallow and unattractive to large operators, although smaller independent companies continue their exploitation. There are more than 4,000 wells in the state. In 1965 oil production

Michigan Tourist Council Photo

A Lake Michigan fisherman mends his nets.

exceeded 14,000 barrels with a value of $41 million.

There are extensive deposits of salt in the Michigan basin, and the state has ranked high in salt production for many years. At Midland, Manistee, Saginaw, Bay City, and Ludington, salt is produced by evaporating natural and artificial brines. Rock salt is mined by deep-shaft methods at Detroit. Products from the salt deposits are the raw materials for much of the chemical industry of the state.

There are many deposits of limestone in the state, the most important being near Alpena, where the rock can be quarried cheaply and shipped by lake freighters. More than half of it is used for blast-furnace flux and for chemical purposes. Limestone deposits also support cement plants at several locations in the state. The mantle of glacial deposit contains substantial supplies of sand and gravel used in construction

Michigan Tourist Council Photo

A good day's hunting in northern Michigan.

and highway building. Gypsum deposits in the central part of the state are mined for plasterboard production.

The total mineral production value for 1966 was $565 million. Leading minerals, in order of their value, were iron ore, cement, petroleum, sand and gravel, copper, and salt.

Electric Power.—In 1965 the installed capacity of all generating units operating in the state was 8,278,000 kilowatts. Actual output totaled 47.4 billion kilowatt-hours, of which 41.7 billion were produced by privately and publicly owned utilities and 5.7 billion by industrial plants.

Banking and Insurance.—The financial institutions bureau of the state department of commerce has general responsibility for administering laws relating to banking, financial institutions, savings and loan associations, and credit unions. In 1966 there were 354 commercial and stock banks with assets of more than $15 billion and deposits of approximately $14.5 billion.

In 1966, Michigan ranked 7th among the states in the number of life insurance policies in force, with a total of more than 15.5 million policies carrying protection of $47.8 billion. In the same year, 89.1 percent of the state's population was covered by hospital insurance, 85.6 percent by surgical insurance, and 73.4 percent was covered by medical insurance.

Trade.—The commerce of the state centers around its manufactured products. Detroit is the chief area of trade and the main gateway for United States-Canadian shipments. Its port facilities extend for 36 miles along the Detroit and Rouge rivers and embrace 151 docks and wharves. In 1965 more than $3.6 billion in exports and imports cleared through the Michigan customs district, and more than 32.7 million tons passed through the port, which ranks 12th in tonnage and second in export-import value in the United States. The bulk of the tonnage was composed of such industrial materials as ore, coal, limestone, cement, sand, and scrap iron, but much of the value lies in shipments of automobiles, machinery, and parts.

The rapid increase in the amount of wholesale and retail trade sales since 1948 is indicative of Michigan's expanding economy. Wholesale trade sales in 1963 amounted to $14,054,572,000, an increase of almost $3 billion over the 1958 figure. In both years the Detroit metropolitan area accounted for more than two thirds of the sales. From 1958 to 1963 retail sales throughout the state rose from $8,898,000,000 in the former year to $10,855,000,000 in the latter.

Recreation and Tourism.—It is estimated that 11 million people spend some of their vacation time in Michigan each year and that the tourist business produces approximately $1 billion in annual revenue. The basis for this business is the dense industrial population of southern Michigan and adjoining states together with the great amount of woods and waters areas in the north. There are some 4,000 commercial resorts in the state together with thousands of summer homes, and hunting and fishing cottages. Through the Department of Conservation an active program of research and development in forestry, game, and fish is maintained.

6. TRANSPORTATION AND COMMUNICATIONS

Transportation.—The southern border of Michigan lies somewhat north of the principal communication lines between the Atlantic coast and the Midwest, but the importance of Detroit and other industrial cities draws transportation into the state. In 1966 there were 112,912 miles of federal, state, and local roads, of which 93,290 were surfaced. There were 789 miles of Interstate highways open to travel. The highway system carries approximately 75 percent of the goods and supplies consumed in the state. About 6,400 miles of railroad track are in operation, and several car ferries carry trains across the Great Lakes. There are 115 commercial and municipal airports, of which 22 have scheduled services. More than 4,300,000 motor vehicles are registered in the state of Michigan.

The Great Lakes are important routes for bulk cargoes of iron ore, coal, and limestone. Detroit receives more tonnage than any other lake port, and its connection with the St. Lawrence Seaway permits direct importation of ship cargoes from Europe. The Detroit River, one of the world's busiest waterways during the shipping season, and the Sault Sainte Marie Canals (q.v.) give the state a strategic position in waterborne traffic.

Communications.—In 1966 there were 116 commercial radio stations in the state together with 22 television stations. More than 4,000,000 telephones were in operation.

Detroit's two large newspapers, the Detroit *Free Press* and the Detroit *News,* have a combined daily circulation of about 1,300,000. In 1966 there were 53 daily newspapers with a circulation of 2,353,100 and 299 weeklies and semiweeklies with a total circulation of 1,267,517.

MICHIGAN

COUNTIES

Alcona, 7,113 F 4
Alger, 8,568 C 2
Allegan, 66,575 D 6
Alpena, 30,708 F 4
Antrim, 12,612 D 3
Arenac, 11,149 F 4
Baraga, 7,789 A 2
Barry, 38,166 D 6
Bay, 117,339 E 5
Benzie, 8,593 C 4
Berrien, 163,875 C 7
Branch, 37,906 D 7
Calhoun, 141,963 D 6
Cass, 43,312 C 7
Charlevoix, 16,541 D 3
Cheboygan, 16,573 E 3
Chippewa, 32,412 E 2
Clare, 16,695 E 5
Clinton, 48,492 E 6
Crawford, 6,482 E 4
Delta, 35,924 C 2
Dickinson, 23,753 B 2
Eaton, 68,892 E 6
Emmet, 18,331 E 3
Genesee, 444,341 F 5
Gladwin, 13,471 E 4
Gogebic, 20,676 F 2
Grand Traverse, 39,175 D 4
Gratiot, 39,246 E 5
Hillsdale, 37,171 E 7
Houghton, 34,652 G 1
Huron, 34,083 F 5
Ingham, 261,039 E 6
Ionia, 45,848 D 6
Iosco, 24,905 F 4
Iron, 13,813 G 2
Isabella, 44,594 E 5
Jackson, 143,274 E 6
Kalamazoo, 201,550 D 6
Kalkaska, 5,272 D 4
Kent, 411,044 D 5
Keweenaw, 2,264 A 1
Lake, 5,661 D 5
Lapeer, 52,317 F 5
Leelanau, 10,872 D 4
Lenawee, 81,609 E 7
Livingston, 58,967 F 6
Luce, 6,789 D 2
Mackinac, 9,660 D 2
Macomb, 625,309 G 6
Manistee, 20,094 C 4
Marquette, 64,686 B 2
Mason, 22,612 C 4
Mecosta, 27,992 D 5
Menominee, 24,587 B 3
Midland, 63,769 E 5
Missaukee, 7,126 D 4
Monroe, 118,479 F 7
Montcalm, 39,660 D 5
Montmorency, 5,247 E 3
Muskegon, 157,246 C 5
Newaygo, 27,992 D 5
Oakland, 907,871 F 6
Oceana, 17,984 C 5
Ogemaw, 11,903 E 4
Ontonagon, 10,548 F 1
Osceola, 14,838 D 5
Oscoda, 4,726 E 4
Otsego, 10,422 E 3
Ottawa, 128,181 C 6
Presque Isle, 12,836 F 3
Roscommon, 9,892 E 4
Saginaw, 219,743 E 5
Saint Clair, 120,175 G 6
Saint Joseph, 47,392 D 7
Sanilac, 34,889 G 5
Schoolcraft, 8,226 C 2
Shiawassee, 63,075 E 6
Tuscola, 48,603 F 5
Van Buren, 56,173 C 6
Washtenaw, 234,103 F 6
Wayne, 2,666,751 F 6
Wexford, 19,717 D 4

CITIES and TOWNS

Addison, 595 E 7
Adrian⊙, 20,382 F 7
Akron, 525 F 5
Alabaster, 46 F 4
Alanson, 362 E 3
Albion, 12,112 E 6
Algonac, 3,684 G 6
Allegan⊙, 4,516 D 6
Allen, 385 E 7
Allen Park, 40,747 B 7
Alma, 9,790 E 5
Almont, 1,634 F 6
Alpena⊙, 13,805 F 3
Amasa, 450 G 2
Anchor Bay Gardens■, 2,272 G 6
Anchorville, 440 G 6
Ann Arbor⊙, 99,797 F 6
Ann Arbor, ‡234,103 F 6
Antrim, 475 D 4
Arcadia, 350 C 4
Argyle, 800 G 5
Armada, 1,352 G 6
Ashley, 521 E 5
Athens, 996 D 6
Atlanta⊙, 475 E 3
Atlantic Mine, 785 G 1
Auburn, 1,919 F 5
Auburn Heights, 7,500 F 6
Au Gres, 564 F 4
Augusta, 1,025 D 6
Au Sable-Oscoda, 3,475 F 4
Averill, 800 E 5
Bad Axe⊙, 2,999 G 5
Baldwin⊙, 612 D 5
Bancroft, 724 E 6
Bangor, 2,050 C 6
Bannister, 379 E 5
Baraga, 1,116 G 1
Barbeau, 400 E 2
Bark River, 550 B 3
Baroda, 439 C 7
Barryton, 368 D 5
Bath, 600 E 6
Battle Creek, 38,931 D 6
Bay City⊙, 49,449 F 5
Bay City, ‡117,339 F 5
Bay Port, 600 F 5
Bayport Park-Lakeside■, 2,101 F 6
Bay View, 500 E 3
Bear Lake, 376 C 4
Beaverton, 954 E 5
Bedford, 450 D 6
Beechwood, 2,714 C 6
Belding, 5,121 D 5
Bellaire⊙, 897 D 4
Belleville, 2,406 F 6
Bellevue, 1,297 E 6
Benton Harbor, 16,481 C 6
Benton Heights, 8,067 C 6
Benzonia, 412 D 4
Bergland, 635 F 1
Berkley, 22,618 B 6
Berrien Springs, 1,951 C 7
Bessemer⊙, 2,805 F 2
Beulah⊙, 461 C 4
Beverly Hills■, 13,598 B 6
Big Rapids⊙, 11,995 D 5
Bingham Farms■, 566 B 6
Birch Run, 932 F 5
Birmingham, 26,170 B 6
Bitely, 350 D 5
Blanchard, 350 D 5
Blissfield, 2,753 F 7
Bloomfield Hills, 3,672 B 6
Bloomingdale, 496 C 6
Boyne City, 2,969 E 3
Breckenridge, 1,257 E 5
Bridgeport, 1,900 F 5
Bridgman, 1,621 C 7
Brighton, 2,457 F 6
Brimley, 490 E 2
Britton, 697 F 6
Bronson, 2,390 D 7
Brooklyn, 1,112 E 6
Brown City, 1,142 G 5
Brownlee Park■, 2,985 D 6
Brutus, 431 E 3
Buchanan, 4,645 C 7
Bunny Run■, 1,391 F 6
Burnips, 725 D 6
Burr Oak, 873 D 7
Byron, 655 E 6
Byron Center, 900 D 6
Cadillac⊙, 9,990 D 4
Caledonia, 716 D 6
Calumet, 1,007 A 1
Camden, 405 E 7
Capac, 1,279 G 5
Carleton, 1,503 F 6
Caro⊙, 3,701 F 5
Carp Lake, 375 E 3
Carrollton, 7,300 E 5
Carson City, 1,217 E 5
Carsonville, 621 G 5
Caseville, 607 F 5
Casnovia, 403 D 5
Caspian, 1,165 G 2
Cass City, 1,974 F 5
Cassopolis⊙, 2,108 C 7
Castle Park, 500 C 6
Cedar Springs, 1,807 D 5
Cedarville, 800 E 2
Cement City, 531 E 6
Center Line, 10,379 B 6
Central Lake, 741 D 3
Centreville⊙, 1,044 D 7
Champion, 550 B 2
Channing, 550 B 2
Charlevoix⊙, 3,519 D 3
Charlotte⊙, 8,244 E 6
Chase, 534 D 5
Cheboygan⊙, 5,553 E 3
Chelsea, 3,858 E 6
Chesaning, 2,876 E 5
Clair Haven■, 2,177 B 6
Clare, 2,639 E 5
Clarklake, 500 E 6
Clarkston, 1,034 F 6
Clawson, 17,617 B 6
Clayton, 505 E 7
Clifford, 472 F 5
Climax, 594 D 6
Clinton, 1,677 F 6
Clio, 2,357 F 5
Coldwater⊙, 9,099 D 7
Coleman, 1,295 E 5
Coloma, 1,814 C 6
Colon, 1,172 D 7
Columbiaville, 935 F 5
Comstock, 5,003 D 6
Comstock Park■, 5,766 D 5
Concord, 983 E 6
Constantine, 1,733 D 7
Conway, 560 E 3
Coopersville, 2,129 C 5
Cornell, 640 B 3
Corunna⊙, 2,829 E 6
Covert, 650 C 6
Croswell, 1,954 G 5
Crystal, 649 E 5
Crystal Falls⊙, 2,000 A 2
Curtis, 350 D 2
Cutlerville, 6,267 D 6
Daggett, 366 B 3
Dalton, 400 C 5
Dansville, 486 E 6
Davison, 5,259 F 5
Dearborn, 104,199 B 7
Dearborn Heights, 80,069 B 7
Decatur, 1,764 C 6
Deckerville, 817 G 5
Deerfield, 834 F 7
Delton, 350 D 6
De Tour Village, 494 E 3
Detroit⊙, 1,511,482 B 7
Detroit, ‡4,199,931 B 7
Detroit Beach, 2,053 F 7
De Witt, 1,829 E 6
Dexter, 1,729 F 6
Dimondale, 970 E 6
Dollar Bay, 950 G 1
Dorr, 550 D 6
Douglas, 813 C 6
Dowagiac, 6,583 C 6
Drayton Plains, 16,462 F 6
Drummond Island, 700 F 3
Dryden, 654 F 6
Dundee, 2,472 F 7
Durand, 3,678 E 6
Eagle River⊙, 36 A 1
East Detroit, 45,920 B 6
East Grand Rapids, 12,565 D 6
East Jordan, 2,041 D 3
East Kingsford, 1,155 A 3
Eastlake, 512 C 4
East Lansing, 47,540 E 6
East Tawas, 2,372 F 4
Eastwood, 9,682 D 6
Eaton Rapids, 4,494 E 6
Eau Claire, 527 C 6
Eben Junction, 380 B 2
Ecorse, 17,515 B 7
Edenville, 700 E 5
Edmore, 1,149 E 5
Edwardsburg, 1,107 C 7
Elba, 460 F 5
Elberta, 542 C 4
Elk Rapids, 1,249 D 4
Elkton, 973 F 5
Ellsworth, 362 D 3
Elsie, 988 E 5
Elwell, 350 E 5
Empire, 409 C 4
Engadine, 500 D 2
Erie, 975 F 7
Escanaba⊙, 15,368 C 3
Essexville, 4,990 F 5
Estral Beach, 419 F 7
Evart, 1,707 D 5
Ewen, 600 F 2
Fairgrove, 629 F 5
Fair Haven, 550 G 6
Fair Plain, 3,680 C 6
Fairview, 600 F 4
Falmouth, 350 E 4
Farmington, 13,337 F 6
Farwell, 777 E 5
Fennville, 811 C 6
Fenton, 8,284 F 6
Ferndale, 30,850 B 6
Ferrysburg, 2,196 C 5
Flat Rock, 5,643 F 6
Flint⊙, 193,317 F 6
Flint, ‡496,658 F 6
Flushing, 7,190 F 5
Fowler, 1,020 E 5
Fowlerville, 1,978 F 6
Frankenmuth, 2,834 F 5
Frankfort, 1,660 C 4
Franklin, 3,344 B 6
Fraser, 11,868 B 6
Frederic, 350 E 4
Freeland, 1,303 E 5
Freeport, 501 D 6
Fremont, 3,465 D 5
Fruitport, 1,409 C 5
Fulton, 500 D 6
Gaastra, 479 G 2
Gagetown, 408 F 5
Gaines, 408 F 6
Galesburg, 1,355 D 6
Galien, 691 C 7
Garden City■, 41,864 B 7
Gaylord⊙, 3,012 E 3
Genesee, 950 F 5
Germfask, 750 C 2
Gibraltar, 3,325 F 6
Gladstone, 5,237 C 3
Gladwin⊙, 2,071 E 5
Gobles, 801 D 6
Good Hart, 500 D 3
Goodrich, 774 F 6
Gowen, 400 D 5
Grand Blanc, 5,132 F 6
Grand Haven⊙, 11,884 C 5
Grand Junction, 400 C 6
Grand Ledge, 6,032 E 6
Grand Marais, 650 D 2
Grand Rapids⊙, 197,649 D 5
Grand Rapids, ‡539,225 D 5
Grandville, 10,764 D 6
Grant, 772 D 5
Grass Lake, 1,061 E 6
Grayling⊙, 2,143 E 4
Greenbush, 650 F 4
Greenville, 7,493 D 5
Gregory, 400 E 6
Grosse Ile, 7,799 B 7
Grosse Pointe, 6,637 B 7
Grosse Pointe Farms, 11,701 B 6
Grosse Pointe Park, 15,585 B 7
Grosse Pointe Shores, 3,042 B 6
Grosse Pointe Woods, 21,878 B 6
Gulliver, 962 D 2
Gwinn, 1,054 B 2
Hale, 500 F 4
Hamburg, 500 F 6
Hamilton, 950 C 6
Hamtramck, 27,245 B 6
Hancock, 4,820 G 1
Hanover, 513 E 6
Harbor Beach, 2,134 G 5
Harbor Springs, 1,662 D 3
Harper Woods, 20,186 B 6
Harrison⊙, 1,460 E 4
Harrisville⊙, 541 F 4
Harsens Island, 750 G 6
Hart⊙, 2,139 C 5
Hartford, 2,508 C 6
Haslett, 3,492 E 6
Hastings⊙, 6,501 D 6
Hazel Park, 23,784 B 6
Hemlock, 900 E 5
Henderson, 600 E 5
Hermansville, 950 B 3
Herron, 950 F 3
Hesperia, 877 D 5
Hessel, 500 E 2
Higgins Lake, 400 E 4
Highland Park, 35,444 B 6
Hillman, 366 F 3
Hillsdale⊙, 7,728 E 7
Holland, 26,337 C 6
Holly, 4,355 F 6
Holt, 6,980 E 6
Holton, 500 C 5
Homer, 1,617 E 6
Hopkins, 566 D 6
Horton, 375 E 6
Houghton⊙, 6,067 G 1
Houghton Lake, 500 E 4
Houghton Lake Heights, 1,252 E 4
Howard City, 1,060 D 5
Howell⊙, 5,224 E 6
Hubbardston, 403 E 5
Hubbell, 1,251 A 1
Hudson, 2,618 E 7
Hudsonville, 3,523 D 6
Huntington Woods■, 8,536 B 6
Ida, 970 F 7
Idlewild, 800 D 5
Imlay City, 1,980 F 5
Indian River, 950 E 3
Inkster, 38,595 B 7
Interlochen, 800 D 4
Ionia⊙, 6,361 D 6
Iron Mountain⊙, 8,702 B 3
Iron River, 2,684 G 2
Ironwood, 8,711 F 2
Ishpeming, 8,245 B 2
Ithaca⊙, 2,749 E 5
Jackson⊙, 45,484 E 6
Jackson, ‡143,274 E 6
Jasper, 400 E 7
Jenison, 11,266 D 6
Jones, 420 D 7
Jonesville, 2,081 E 6
Kalamazoo⊙, 85,555 D 6
Kalamazoo, ‡201,550 D 6
Kaleva, 377 C 4
Kalkaska⊙, 1,475 D 4
Kawkawlin, 450 F 5
Keego Harbor, 3,092 F 6
Kent City, 686 D 5
Kentwood, 20,310 D 6
Kinde, 618 G 5
Kingsford, 5,276 A 3
Kingsley, 632 D 4
Kingston, 464 F 5
Laingsburg, 1,159 E 6
Lake, 600 E 5
Lake Angelus■, 573 F 6
Lake City⊙, 704 D 4
Lakeland, 720 F 6
Lake Leelanau, 350 D 4
Lake Linden, 1,214 A 1
Lake Michigan Beach, 1,201 C 6
Lake Odessa, 1,924 D 6
Lake Orion Heights■, 2,556 F 6
Lakeview, 1,198 D 5
Lakeview■, 11,391 D 6
Lakewood Club, 590 C 5
Lambertville, 5,721 F 7
L'Anse⊙, 2,538 G 1
Lansing (cap.), 131,546 E 6
Lansing, ‡378,423 E 6
Lapeer⊙, 6,270 F 5
Lapeer Heights■, 7,130 F 6
Lathrup Village■, 1,429 B 6
Laurium, 2,868 A 1
Lawrence, 790 C 6
Lawton, 1,358 D 6
Leland⊙, 776 D 3
Leonard, 378 F 6
Leslie, 1,894 E 6
Level Park-Oak Park■, 3,080 D 6
Levering, 967 E 3
Lewiston, 750 E 4
Lexington, 834 G 5
Lincoln, 371 F 4
Lincoln Park, 52,984 B 7
Linden, 1,546 F 6
Linwood, 950 F 5
Litchfield, 1,167 E 6
Little Lake, 950 B 2
Livonia, 110,109 F 6
Long Lake, 900 F 4
Lowell, 3,068 D 6
Ludington⊙, 9,021 C 5
Luna Pier, 1,418 F 7
Lyons, 758 E 6
Mackinac Island, 517 E 3
Mackinaw City, 810 E 3
Madison Heights, 38,599 F 6
Mancelona, 1,255 E 4
Manchester, 1,650 E 6
Manistee⊙, 7,723 C 4
Manistique⊙, 4,324 C 3
Manitou Beach-Devils Lake■, 1,892 E 7
Manton, 1,107 D 4
Maple Rapids, 683 E 5
Marcellus, 1,139 D 6
Marenisco, 865 F 2
Marine City, 4,567 G 6
Marion, 891 D 4
Marlette, 1,706 G 5
Marne, 950 D 5
Marquette⊙, 21,967 B 2
Marshall⊙, 7,253 E 6

⊙ County seat. ‡ Population of metropolitan area. ■ Name not shown on map.

All figures available from 1970 final census are supplemented by local official estimates.

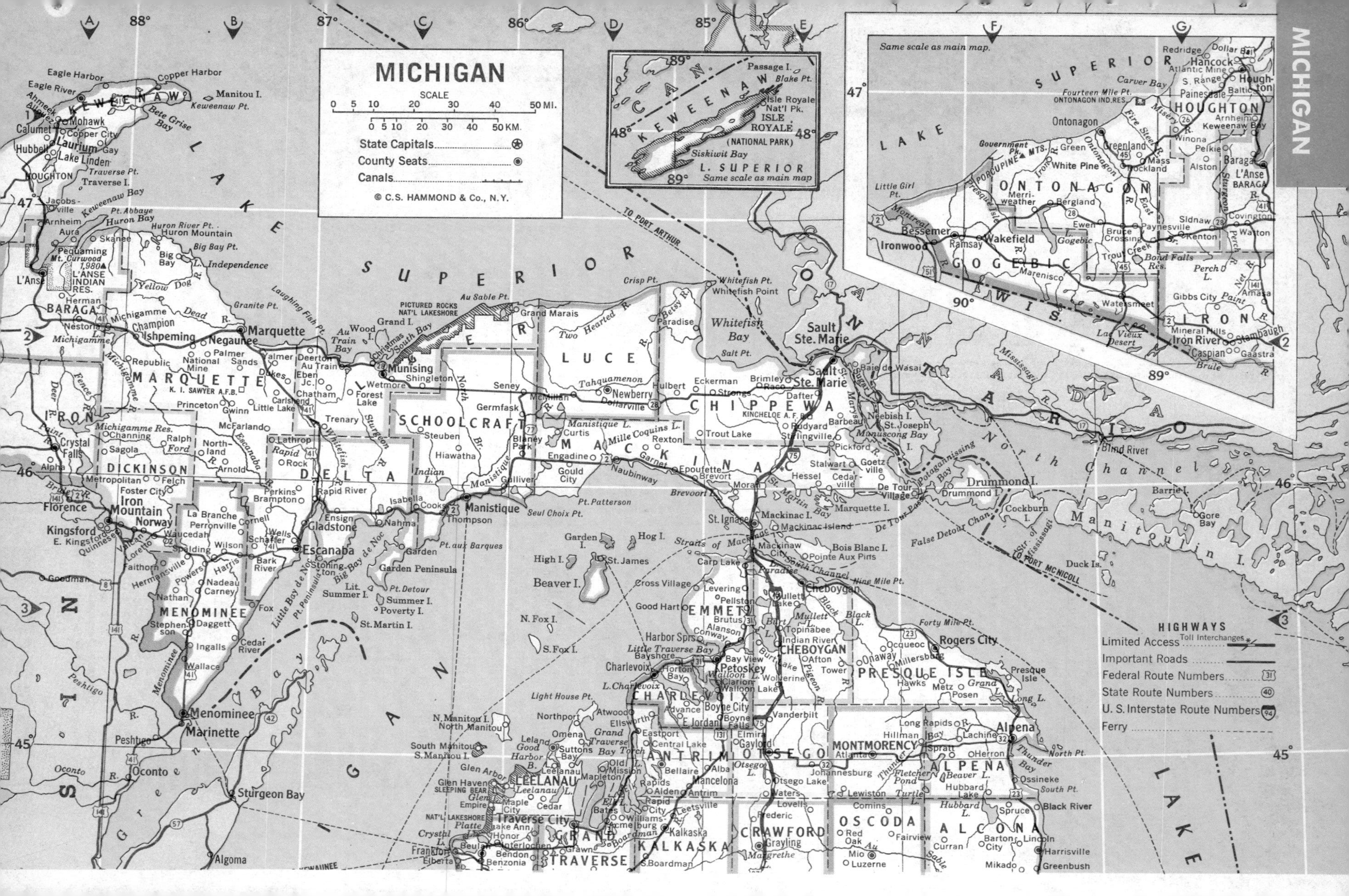
MICHIGAN
MICHIGAN
SCALE
0 5 10 20 30 40 50 MI.
0 5 10 20 30 40 50 KM.
State Capitals
County Seats
Canals
© C.S. HAMMOND & Co., N.Y.
ISLE ROYALE
(NATIONAL PARK)
L. SUPERIOR
Same scale as main map
Same scale as main map.
HIGHWAYS
Limited Access
Toll Interchanges
Important Roads
Federal Route Numbers
State Route Numbers
U. S. Interstate Route Numbers
Ferry
LAKE SUPERIOR
LAKE MICHIGAN
ONTARIO
WISCONSIN
North Channel
Manitoulin I.
KEWEENAW
HOUGHTON
BARAGA
MARQUETTE
IRON
DICKINSON
MENOMINEE
DELTA
SCHOOLCRAFT
LUCE
CHIPPEWA
MACKINAC
EMMET
CHEBOYGAN
PRESQUE ISLE
CHARLEVOIX
ANTRIM
OTSEGO
MONTMORENCY
ALPENA
LEELANAU
GRAND TRAVERSE
KALKASKA
CRAWFORD
OSCODA
ALCONA
ONTONAGON
GOGEBIC
Marquette
Sault Ste. Marie
Escanaba
Manistique
Menominee
Marinette
Petoskey
Cheboygan
Alpena
Traverse City
Iron Mountain
Ironwood
Houghton
Hancock
TO PORT ARTHUR
TO PORT McNICOLL

HURON
LAKE MICHIGAN
LAKE ERIE
LAKE ST. CLAIR
WISCONSIN
INDIANA
OHIO
ONTARIO
MILWAUKEE
GRAND RAPIDS
DETROIT
WINDSOR
TOLEDO
FLINT
Lansing
Saginaw
Bay City
Kalamazoo
Battle Creek
Ann Arbor
Jackson
Muskegon
Ludington
Sheboygan
Two Rivers
Manitowoc
Racine
Kenosha
Green Bay
SOUTH BEND
Port Huron
Sarnia
West of Greenwich
Longitude

MICHIGAN

Martin, 502 D 6
Marysville, 5,610 G 6
Mason⊙, 5,468 E 6
Mass, 850 G 1
Mattawan, 1,569 D 6
Maybee, 485 F 6
Mayville, 872 F 5
McBain, 520 D 4
Mears, 400 C 5
Mecosta, 396 D 5
Melvindale, 13,862 B 7
Memphis, 1,121 G 6
Mendon, 949 D 7
Menominee⊙, 10,748 B 3
Merrill, 961 E 5
Mesick, 376 D 4
Metamora, 468 F 6
Metz, 495 F 3
Michigan Center, 4,900 E 6
Middleton, 500 E 5
Middleville, 1,865 D 6
Midland⊙, 35,176 E 5
Milan, 4,533 F 6
Milford, 4,699 F 6
Millington, 1,099 F 5
Mio⊙, 975 E 4
Mohawk, 800 A 1
Moline, 750 D 6
Monroe⊙, 23,894 F 7
Montague, 2,396 C 5
Montgomery, 404 E 7
Montrose, 1,789 F 5
Morenci, 2,132 E 7
Morley, 481 D 5
Morrice, 734 E 6
Mount Clemens⊙, 20,476 G 6
Mount Morris, 3,778 F 5
Mount Pleasant⊙, 20,504 E 5
Muir, 617 D 5
Mulliken, 454 E 6
Munger, 432 F 5
Munising⊙, 3,677 C 2
Munith, 360 E 6
Muskegon⊙, 44,631 C 5
Muskegon-Muskegon Heights, ‡157,426 C 5
Muskegon Heights, 17,304 C 5
Napoleon, 950 E 6
Nashville, 1,558 D 6
National Mine, 565 B 2
Naubinway, 350 D 2
Negaunee, 5,248 B 2
Newaygo, 1,381 D 5
New Baltimore, 4,132 G 6
Newberry⊙, 2,334 D 2
New Boston, 800 F 6
New Buffalo, 2,784 C 7
New Era, 466 C 5
New Haven, 1,855 G 6
New Lothrop, 596 F 5
New Troy, 430 C 7
Niles, 12,988 C 7
North Adams, 574 E 7
North Branch, 932 F 5
North Muskegon, 4,243 C 5
Northport, 594 D 3
North Star, 350 E 5
Northville, 5,400 F 6
Norton Shores, 22,271 C 5
Norway, 3,033 B 3
Novi, 9,668 F 6
Oakley, 418 E 5
Oak Park, 36,762 B 6
Ocqueoc, 500 F 3
Okemos, 7,770 E 6
Olivet, 1,629 E 6
Omer, 366 F 4
Onaway, 1,262 E 3
Onekama, 638 C 4
Onsted, 555 E 6
Ontonagon⊙, 2,432 F 1
Orchard Lake, 1,487 F 6
Ortonville, 983 F 6
Oscoda-Au Sable, 3,475 F 4
Osseo, 400 E 7
Otisville, 724 F 5
Otsego, 3,957 D 6
Otsego Lake, 500 E 4
Otter Lake, 551 F 5
Ovid, 1,650 E 5
Owosso, 17,179 E 5
Oxford, 2,536 F 6
Painesdale, 600 G 1
Palmer, 950 B 2
Palmyra, 600 E 7
Palo, 350 E 5
Parchment, 2,027 D 6
Parma, 880 E 6
Patterson Gardens■, 2,169 F 7
Paw Paw⊙, 3,160 D 6
Paw Paw Lake, 3,726 C 6
Pearl Beach, 1,744 G 6
Peck, 580 G 5
Pellston, 469 E 3
Pentwater, 993 C 5
Perkins, 400 B 3
Perrinton, 489 E 5
Perry, 1,531 E 6
Petersburg, 1,227 F 7
Petoskey⊙, 6,342 E 3
Pewamo, 498 E 5
Pickford, 800 E 2
Pigeon, 1,174 F 5
Pinckney, 921 F 6
Pinconning, 1,320 F 5
Pittsford, 610 E 7
Plainwell, 3,195 D 6
Pleasant Ridge, 3,989 B 6
Plymouth, 11,758 F 6
Pontiac⊙, 85,279 F 6
Portage, 33,590 D 6
Port Austin, 883 F 4
Port Hope, 377 G 5
Port Huron⊙, 35,794 G 6
Portland, 3,817 E 6
Port Sanilac, 493 G 5
Potterville, 1,280 E 6
Powers, 560 B 3
Prudenville, 500 E 4
Pullman, 375 C 6
Quakertown■, 837 F 6
Quincy, 1,540 E 7
Quinnesec, 770 A 3
Ramsay, 1,068 F 2
Rapid City, 450 D 4
Rapid River, 950 C 3
Ravenna, 1,048 D 5
Reading, 1,125 E 7
Reed City⊙, 2,286 D 5
Reese, 1,050 F 5
Remus, 425 D 5
Republic, 900 B 2
Richland, 728 D 6
Richmond, 3,234 G 6
Richville, 650 F 5
Riverdale, 380 E 5
River Rouge, 15,947 B 7
Riverside, 650 C 6
Riverview, 11,342 B 7
Rives Junction, 350 E 6
Rochester, 7,054 F 6
Rock, 400 B 2
Rockford, 2,428 D 5
Rockland, 450 G 1
Rockwood, 3,119 F 6
Rogers City⊙, 4,275 F 3
Romeo, 4,012 F 6
Romulus, 3,900 F 6
Roosevelt Park, 4,176 C 5
Roscommon⊙, 810 E 4
Rosebush, 439 E 5
Rose City, 530 E 4
Roseville, 60,529 G 6
Rothbury, 394 C 5
Royal Oak, 85,499 B 6
Rudyard, 950 E 2
Saginaw⊙, 91,849 F 5
Saginaw, ‡219,743 F 5
Saint Charles, 2,046 E 5
Saint Clair, 4,770 G 6
Saint Clair Shores, 88,093 G 6
Saint Helen, 700 E 4
Saint Ignace⊙, 2,892 E 3
Saint Johns⊙, 6,672 E 6
Saint Joseph⊙, 11,042 C 6
Saint Louis, 4,101 E 5
Saline, 4,811 F 6
Sand Lake, 380 D 5
Sandusky⊙, 2,071 G 5
Sanford, 818 E 5
Saranac, 1,223 D 6
Saugatuck, 1,022 C 6
Sault Sainte Marie⊙, 15,136 E 2
Sawyer, 650 C 7
Schoolcraft, 1,277 D 6
Scottville, 1,202 C 5
Sebewaing, 2,053 F 5
Selfridge-Capehart■, 1,694 G 6
Shelby, 1,703 C 5
Shepherd, 1,416 E 5
Sheridan, 653 D 5
Sherwood, 400 D 6
Shoreham, 666 C 6
Shorewood Hills, 1,629 C 7
Sister Lakes, 700 C 6
Six Lakes, 350 D 5
Snover, 400 G 5
Southfield, 69,285 F 6
Southgate, 33,909 F 6
South Haven, 6,471 C 6
South Lyon, 2,675 F 6
South Monroe, 3,012 F 7
South Range, 898 G 1
South Rockwood, 1,477 F 7
Spalding, 600 B 3
Sparlingville, 1,845 G 6
Sparta, 3,094 D 5
Spring Arbor, 1,832 E 6
Springfield, 3,994 D 6
Springfield Place■, 4,831 D 6
Spring Lake, 3,034 C 5
Springport, 723 E 6
Stambaugh, 1,458 G 2
Standish⊙, 1,184 F 5
Stanton⊙, 1,089 D 5
Stephenson, 800 B 3
Sterling, 507 E 4
Sterling Heights, 61,365 B 6
Stevensville, 1,107 C 6
Stockbridge, 1,190 E 6
Stony Point■, 1,370 F 7
Stronach, 500 C 4
Strongs, 450 E 2
Sturgis, 9,295 D 7
Sunfield, 497 D 6
Sunrise Heights■, 1,626 D 6
Suttons Bay, 522 D 3
Swartz Creek, 4,928 F 6
Sylvan Lake, 2,219 F 6
Tawas City⊙, 1,666 F 4
Taylor, 70,020 B 7
Tecumseh, 7,120 E 7
Tekonsha, 739 E 6
Temperance, 2,900 F 7
Three Oaks, 1,750 C 7
Three Rivers, 7,355 D 7
Topinabee, 350 E 3
Tower, 425 E 3
Traverse City⊙, 18,048 D 4
Trenary, 360 C 2
Trenton, 24,127 B 7
Troy, 39,419 B 6
Trufant, 600 D 5
Ubly, 899 G 5
Union City, 1,740 D 6
Union Pier, 900 C 7
Unionville, 647 F 5
Utica, 3,504 F 6
Vandalia, 427 D 7
Vanderbilt, 522 E 3
Vassar, 2,802 F 5
Vermontville, 857 E 6
Vernon, 818 F 6
Verona Park■, 2,107 D 6
Vestaburg, 680 E 5
Vicksburg, 2,139 D 6
Vulcan, 975 B 3
Wakefield, 2,757 F 2
Waldron, 564 E 7
Walker, 11,492 D 6
Walled Lake, 3,759 F 6
Walloon Lake, 550 E 3
Warren, 179,260 B 6
Washington■, 1,563 F 6
Watersmeet, 700 G 2
Watervliet, 2,059 C 6
Wayland, 2,054 D 6
Wayne, 21,054 F 6
Webberville, 1,251 E 6
Weidman, 450 D 5
Wells, 1,085 B 3
West Branch⊙, 1,912 E 4
Westland, 86,749 F 6
Westphalia, 806 E 6
Westwood■, 9,143 D 6
White Cloud⊙, 1,044 D 5
Whitehall, 3,017 C 5
White Lake-Seven Harbors■, 4,504 F 6
White Pigeon, 1,455 D 7
White Pine, 1,218 F 1
Whitmore Lake, 2,763 F 6
Whittaker, 500 F 6
Whittemore, 460 F 4
Williamston, 2,600 E 6
Willis, 500 F 6
Wilson, 500 B 3
Winn, 600 E 5
Wixom, 2,010 F 6
Wolf Lake, 2,258 D 5
Wolverine Lake■, 4,301 F 6
Wood Creek Farms■, 1,090 F 6
Woodhaven, 3,330 F 6
Woodland, 473 D 6
Woodland Beach■, 2,249 F 7
Wyandotte, 41,061 B 7
Wyoming, 56,560 D 6
Yale, 1,505 G 5
Ypsilanti, 29,538 F 6
Zeeland, 4,734 D 6
Zilwaukee, 2,072 F 5

OTHER FEATURES

Abbaye (pt.) B 2
Au Sable (pt.) C 2
Au Sable (pt.) F 4
Au Sable (riv.) E 4
Au Train (bay) C 2
Bad (riv.) E 5
Barques (pt.) C 3
Beaver (lake) F 4
Beaver (isl.), 219 D 3
Belle (riv.) G 6
Bete Grise (bay) B 1
Betsy (riv.) D 2
Big Bay (pt.) B 2
Big Bay de Noc (bay) C 3
Big Sable (pt.) C 4
Big Sable (riv.) C 4
Big Star (lake) C 5
Black (lake) E 3
Black (riv.) E 3
Black (riv.) G 5
Blake (pt.) E 1
Boardman (riv.) D 4
Bois Blanc (isl.), 28 E 3
Bond Falls (res.) G 2
Brevoort (lake) D 3
Brule (riv.) A 3
Burt (lake) E 3
Carver (bay) G 1
Cass (riv.) F 5
Cedar (lake) F 4
Charlevoix (lake) D 3
Chippewa (riv.) E 5
Crisp (pt.) D 2
Crystal (lake) C 4
Curwood (mt.) A 2
Dead (riv.) B 2
Deer (riv.) A 2
De Tour (passg.) E 3
Detour (pt.) C 3
Detroit (riv.) B 7
Drummond (isl.), 479 F 2
Duck (lake) F 4
Elk (lake) D 4
Erie (lake) G 7
Escanaba (riv.) B 2
False Detour (chan.) F 3
Fawn (riv.) D 7
Fence (riv.) A 2
Fire Steel (riv.) G 1
Fletcher (pond) F 4
Flint (riv.) F 5
Ford (riv.) B 2
Forty Mile (pt.) F 3
Fourteen Mile (pt.) F 1
Garden (isl.) D 3
Garden (pen.) C 3
Glen (lake) C 4
Gogebic (lake) F 2
Good Harbor (bay) D 3
Government (peak) F 1
Grand (isl.), 32 C 2
Grand (lake) F 3
Grand (riv.) D 6
Grand Traverse (bay) D 3
Granite (pt.) B 2
Green (bay) B 4
Gun (lake) D 6
Hamlin (lake) C 4
Higgins (lake) E 4
High (isl.) D 3
Hog (isl.) D 3
Houghton (lake) E 4
Hubbard (lake) F 4
Huron (bay) A 2
Huron (lake) G 4
Huron (riv.) F 6
Huron River (pt.) B 2
Independence (lake) B 2
Indian (lake) C 2
Iron (riv.) F 1
Isle Royale Nat'l Park E 1
Kalamazoo (riv.) C 6
Keweenaw (bay) A 1
Keweenaw (pt.) B 1
Kincheloe A.F.B., 6,331 E 2
K.I. Sawyer A.F.B., 6,679 B 2
L'Anse Ind. Res., 508 A 2
Laughing Fish (pt.) B 2
Leelanau (lake) D 4
Light House (pt.) D 3
Little Bay de Noc (bay) B 3
Little Girl (pt.) E 1
Little Sable (pt.) C 5
Little Summer (isl.) C 3
Little Traverse (bay) D 3
Long (lake) F 3
Lookingglass (riv.) E 6
Mackinac (isl.), 517 E 3
Mackinac (str.) E 3
Manistee (riv.) C 4
Manistique (lake) D 2
Manistique (riv.) C 2
Manitou (isl.) B 1
Maple (riv.) E 5
Margrethe (lake) E 4
Marquette (isl.) E 3
Maumee (bay) F 7
Menominee (riv.) B 3
Michigamme (lake) A 2
Michigamme (res.) B 2
Michigamme (riv.) A 2
Michigan (lake) B 5
Mill (creek) G 5
Mille Coquins (lake) D 2
Misery (riv.) G 1
Montreal (riv.) F 1
Mullett (lake) E 3
Munuscong (bay) E 2
Muskegon (riv.) C 5
Neebish (isl.) E 2
Net (riv.) G 2
Nine Mile (pt.) E 3
North (chan.) F 2
North (pt.) F 3
North Fox (isl.) D 3
North Manitou (isl.), 4 C 3
Oak (pt.) F 5
Ontonagon (riv.) G 1
Ontonagon Ind. Res. F 1
Otsego (lake) E 4
Paint (riv.) A 2
Paradise (lake) E 3
Passage (isl.) E 1
Patterson (pt.) D 3
Paw Paw (riv.) C 6
Peninsula (pt.) C 3
Perch (lake) G 2
Perch (riv.) G 2
Pere Marquette (riv.) D 5
Pictured Rocks (cliff) C 2
Pictured Rocks Nat'l Lakeshore C 2
Pigeon (riv.) D 7
Pigeon (riv.) E 3
Pine (lake) F 4
Pine (riv.) D 4
Pine (riv.) E 5
Platte (lake) C 4
Porcupine (mts.) F 1
Potagannissing (bay) F 2
Poverty (isl.) C 3
Prairie (riv.) D 7
Presque Isle (riv.) F 1
Rabbit (riv.) D 6
Raisin (riv.) F 7
Rapid (riv.) B 2
Reedsburg (res.) E 4
Rifle (riv.) E 4
Royale (isl.) E 1
Saginaw (bay) F 5
Saginaw (riv.) F 5
Saint Clair (lake) G 6
Saint Clair (riv.) G 6
Saint Joseph (riv.) C 7
Saint Martin (bay) E 3
Saint Martin (isl.) C 3
Saint Marys (riv.) E 2
Salt (pt.) E 2
Sand (pt.) F 5
Selfridge A.F.B., 1,614 G 6
Seul Choix (pt.) D 3
Shiawassee (riv.) E 5
Siskiwit (bay) E 1
Sleeping Bear Nat'l Lakeshore C 4
South (bay) C 2
South (chan.) E 3
South (pt.) F 4
South Fox (isl.) D 3
South Manitou (isl.), 12 C 3
Sturgeon (riv.) C 2
Sugar (isl.), 237 E 2
Summer (isl.) C 3
Superior (lake) C 2
Tahquamenon (riv.) D 2
Tawas (lake) F 4
Tawas (pt.) F 4
Thunder (bay) F 4
Thunder Bay (riv.) F 3
Tittabawassee (riv.) E 5
Torch (lake) D 3
Traverse (isl.) A 1
Traverse (pt.) A 1
Turtle (lake) F 4
Two Hearted (riv.) D 2
Vieux Desert (lake) G 2
Walloon (lake) E 3
White (riv.) C 5
Whitefish (bay) E 2
Whitefish (pt.) E 2
Whitefish (riv.) C 2
Wood (isl.) C 2
Wurtsmith A.F.B., 6,932 F 4
Yellow Dog (riv.) B 2

Michigan Tourist Council Photo

A quiet street scene on Mackinac Island, in the Straits of Mackinac.

7. CULTURAL LIFE

There is not one but three ways of life in Michigan. In the northern vacation lands the legends of Hiawatha and the giant lumberman, Paul Bunyan, are ever present. Woods and waters are the setting and outdoor life the mode. The rural and agricultural parts draw their backgrounds from New England and New York from whence came the pioneer farmers. Two story frame houses, steepled churches, and quiet towns mark the landscape; independence and community spirit characterize the people. The tenor of the industrial cities may be expressed by "know how": the men, the machinery, the technology to make almost anything rapidly, cheaply, and in great amount. These three ways of life are contained within the state rather than blended together; from the deep waters of Isle Royale to the blast furnaces of River Rouge it is farther in cultural separation than it is in miles.

Navigation of the Great Lakes and the lumbering period furnish a body of lore that is seldom used by able writers. The National Music Camp at Interlochen is a superb combination of summer outdoor life and musical instruction. The May Festival and Drama Season at Ann Arbor are widely known for distinguished artists and performances. Exhibitions at the Detroit Institute of Arts bring into the state masterpieces of the world's art. The Hopwood Awards for creative writing at the University of Michigan have attracted scores of aspiring authors and produced many successful works.

Industries the world over send their representatives to Michigan to learn the technologies and the developments of dynamic production. In the research and testing centers of the automobile industry are developed the cars that will be on the road a decade hence. The research facilities of the University of Michigan and Michigan State University are heavily engaged in many kinds of projects, including atomic, some of them sponsored by government or industry.

From the earliest days, religion has been important in the state. French settlers around Detroit were almost all Roman Catholics. St. Anne's in that city is the second oldest continuously operated parish in the country. Later European immigration reinforced this nucleus and added to it Greek Orthodox and several eastern church congregations. Dutch settlers on the West Coast came to Michigan from the schism of the state church in Holland and have continued their determination to "make the colony Christian". The Christian Reformed Church was founded in Michigan in 1890 by a further division of these people. For 48 years the Seventh Day Adventists had their national headquarters in Battle Creek. The contribution of church-related schools to education in the state is substantial and in these days of crowded facilities is critical.

The history of the state is assiduously collected and preserved. The Michigan Historical Commission, an official body, publishes the quarterly journal *Michigan History* and through the Historical Society of Michigan encourages and correlates the many county historical groups. The *Historical Collections* number 40 volumes. At the university, the Michigan historical collections hold some 30,000 bound items and more than a million other papers.

8. PLACES OF INTEREST

Detroit has many attractions in addition to its automobile factories. The Ambassador Bridge with a span of 1,850 feet and the Detroit and Windsor Fleetway Tunnel connect Detroit with Canada. The Detroit Institute of Arts is internationally noted for its collections of paintings and sculpture, and the Detroit Zoological Park is

Michigan Tourist Council Photo

Tulip time in Holland, Michigan.

one of the nation's largest and most modern zoos. Ten miles west of Detroit at Dearborn is the Henry Ford Museum containing replicas of Independence Hall and Congress Hall in Philadelphia, together with many other replicas of historic buildings. Located at the museum is the laboratory of Thomas Edison and an industrial arts exhibit featuring the history of progress in agriculture, manufacturing, and transportation. Adjoining the Henry Ford Museum is Greenfield Village, representing a typical American village of the 1800's with many authentic historic buildings which have been moved to the site and reconstructed.

At Cranbrook, 20 miles north of Detroit, is a cultural center containing the Cranbrook Academy of Art and the Cranbrook Institute of Science. The buildings are the work of Eliel Saarinen (1873–1950), the Finnish-American architect, and much of the statuary and fountains are by the noted sculptor Carl Milles (1875–1955). The University of Michigan at Ann Arbor is the home of the William L. Clements Library with its famous collection of rare Americana. The 53-bell Charles Baird Carillon located in the Burton Memorial Tower is one of the largest in the United States. The Museums Building houses anthropological and paleontological collections as well as a herbarium and a museum of zoology. The lecture and concert series and the May Festival, a week of musical presentations, attract outstanding artists and large audiences. At Holland, the tulip festival in May of each year draws thousands to see the colorful flowers and the old Dutch costumes and dances. At Traverse City the annual Cherry Festival celebrates the harvesting of the crop with a colorful parade and other festivities. At Sault Ste. Marie, the northeastern tip of the state, the "Soo Locks" (St. Marys Falls Ship Canal) is a great attraction for visitors. This is the world's busiest canal, passing annually during its nine-month ice-free period some 113 million tons, more than the Panama and Suez canals combined. Connecting the Lower with the Upper Peninsula at Mackinaw City is the Mackinac Straits Bridge, built at a cost of $100 million and opened in 1957. Its total length is five miles, and its 3,800-foot center span makes it the second longest suspension bridge in the world. For additional places of interest, see separate articles on the leading cities of the state.

Parks and Forests.—A large amount of the cutover land of the north was of low quality for agriculture and came into state ownership through tax abandonment. This public domain has been organized primarily for recreational use rather than forestry. There are 23 state forests and 4 national forests, which together contain more than 7,000,000 acres of state and federal land. About 176,000 acres of choice recreational land including much waterfront purchased by the state, has been organized into 79 state parks and recreation areas with developed facilities for public use. Isle Royale, an isolated island in Lake Superior, is a national park noted for its scenery and wildlife, including Michigan's only moose herd.

9. FAMOUS MEN AND WOMEN

In the field of government and politics, Michigan numbers among her sons Henry Hastings Sibley (Detroit, 1811–1891), fur trader and later governor of Minnesota; William Lawrence Penfield (Dover, 1846–1909), jurist; Truman Handy Newberry (Detroit, 1864–1945), businessman and political leader; and Frank Murphy (Harbor Beach, 1890–1949), governor, United States attorney general, and associate justice of the United States Supreme Court; and Thomas E. Dewey (Owosso, 1902–1971), governor of New York.

Outstanding industrialists include Robert Hawley Ingersoll (Delta, 1859–1928), manufacturer of the famous Ingersoll $1 watch; Martin Antoine Ryerson (Grand Rapids, 1856–1932), capitalist, philanthropist, and art collector; Roy Dikeman Chapin (Lansing, 1880–1936), industrialist; and Henry Ford (Dearborn Township, 1863–1947), automobile manufacturer.

In the field of science and education, there are Alfred Noble (Livonia, 1844–1914), civil engineer; Calvin Thomas (Lapeer, 1854–1919), Goethe scholar and educator; William James Beal (Adrian, 1833–1924), botanist and educator; Alfred Hulse Brooks (Ann Arbor, 1871–1924), geologist and geographer; William Albert Locy (Troy, 1857–1924), zoologist, teacher, and historian of biological science; Robert Simpson Woodward (Rochester, 1849–1924), engineer, mathematical physicist, and teacher; Max Levy (Detroit, 1857–1926), photoengraver and inventor of the hemocytometer; Jeremiah Whipple Jenks (St. Clair, 1856–1929), political economist, teacher, and author; Henry Rogers Seager (Lansing, 1870–1930), economist and teacher; Claude Halstead Van Tyne (Tecumseh, 1869–1930), historian and teacher; James William Toumey (Lawrence, 1865–1932), forester and teacher; and Paul de Kruif (Zeeland, 1890–1971), bacteriologist and author.

Among those who have won fame in music, art, and literature are Brownson Crocker Howard (Detroit, 1842–1908), playwright; Frederick Russell Burton (Jonesville, 1861–1909), composer and student of Indian music; Will (William McKendree) Carleton (near Hudson, 1845–1912), poet; Henry Edward Krehbiel (Ann Arbor, 1854–1923), music critic, historian, author, and lecturer; Frederick Stuart Church (Grand Rapids, 1842–1924), painter; James Oliver Curwood (Owosso, 1878–1927), novelist; Julius Rolshoven (Detroit, 1858–1930), painter; John Albert Macy (Detroit, 1877–1932), author, literary critic, poet, and socialist; (Julius) Gari Melchers (Detroit, 1860–1932), painter; and Stewart Edward White (Grand Rapids, 1873–1947), fiction writer.

Other native-born sons include Charles Michel De Langlade (Mackinac, 1729–c. 1801), the French half-breed who became known as "Father of Wisconsin" and to the Western tribesmen as Akewaugeketauso; Leonard Bacon (Detroit, 1802–1881), clergyman; James Anthony Bailey (Detroit, 1847–1906), showman who went into partnership with P. T. Barnum in 1881; Olympia Brown (Prairie Ronde, 1835–1926), minister and suffragist; Cressy Livingston Wilbur (Hillsdale, 1865–1928), vital statistician; Delos Franklin Wilcox (near Ida, 1873–1928), franchise and public-utility expert; and Milton Alexander McRae (Detroit, 1858–1930), newspaper publisher.

Other prominent citizens whose fame is linked with the history of the state are Douglass Houghton (Troy, N.Y., 1809–1845), geologist; Henry Rowe Schoolcraft (Albany County, N.Y., 1793–1864), explorer and ethnologist; Lewis Cass (Exeter, N.H., 1782–1866), lawyer and governor of Michigan Territory, soldier, and statesman; George A. Custer (New Rumley, Ohio, 1839–1876), headed Michigan brigade in the Civil War; Zachariah Chandler (Bedford, N.H., 1813–1879), United States senator and Republican Party leader in Michigan; Robert McClelland (Greencastle, Pa., 1807–1880), lawyer, congressman, and governor of Michigan; Thomas McIntyre Cooley (near Attica, N.Y., 1824–1898), jurist and writer on constitutional law; Russell Alexander Alger (Lafayette, Ohio, 1836–1907), governor of Michigan and United States secretary of war; Henry Billings Brown (South Lee, Mass., 1836–1913), jurist and associate justice of the United States Supreme Court; James Burrill Angell (near Scituate, R.I., 1829–1916), president of the University of Michigan (1871–1909) and diplomat; Donald McDonald Dickinson (Port Ontario, N.Y., 1846–1917), lawyer and United States postmaster general; Eliza Maria Mosher (Cayuga County, N.Y., 1846–1928), physician, educator, and civic worker; Edwin Denby (Evansville, Ind., 1870–1929), political leader and United States secretary of the navy; and Edgar Albert Guest (Birmingham, Eng., 1881–1959), poet.

10. HISTORY

Indian Period.—The Ottawa and Potawatomie tribes occupied the Lake Michigan shore of the Lower Peninsula, and the Ojibway (Chippewa) the Upper Peninsula and some of the northern parts of the Lower Peninsula. In the area between Saginaw Bay and Detroit were the minor tribes, the Hurons, the Sacs, and the Foxes. These tribes lived by garden agriculture, hunting, fishing, and gathering. Their villages were located near water bodies, along the shores of the Great Lakes or on the larger rivers and lakes of the forested interior. When white men provided guns and traps and when furs acquired a commercial value, the tribes scattered into smaller groups and families.

French Occupation: 1634–1763.—French explorers, traders, and missionaries entered Michigan from Canada and made it a part of the great fur-producing empire centering on Montreal. In 1634, Jean Nicolet, an agent of Gov. Samuel de Champlain, passed through the Straits of Mackinac in search for a water passage to the South Seas. As early as 1616 traders visited Sault Ste. Marie, and in 1641 the Jesuit fathers Charles Raymbault and Isaac Jogues had established a mission there. For 70 years thereafter the French established missions, settlements, and forts to secure the northern part of their great line of outposts extending from Canada to New Orleans by way of the Mississippi. The first permanent settlements were made at Sault Ste. Marie in 1668 and at Michilimackinac, now St. Ignace, in 1671. In 1701, Antoine de la Mothe Cadillac founded Fort Pontchartrain at the narrows (*de troit*) of the river connecting Lake Huron with Lake Erie by way of Lake St. Clair. This fort became the city of Detroit. In 1763 the Treaty of Paris transferred to the British all of Canada and the Great Lakes area, but not the loyalties of the Indians.

British Control: 1763–1796.—The British immediately assumed control of the fur trade in Michigan and, like the French, discouraged settlement and restricted land acquisition. The Indians, hoping for French support, attempted to drive the British out of the lake country. In 1763, under the leadership of the great Ottawa chief, Pontiac, they made simultaneous attacks on the British posts from the Straits of Mackinac to western New York. Detroit was besieged for five months but was not taken.

During the Revolutionary War the British posts in Michigan were used as bases for the frontier war against the settlements in Ohio and western Pennsylvania. The Peace of Paris in 1783 ended the war, but the British were not eager to relinquish their control over the area north of the Ohio River. In 1794 a United States force under Gen. Anthony Wayne defeated the Indians at Fallen Timbers, near the present city of Toledo, Ohio, and this ended the Indian troubles. The British garrison evacuated Detroit on July 11, 1796, according to the terms of the Jay Treaty concluded with Great Britain a year earlier.

Michigan Tourist Council Photo

On the Au Sable River, to the northeast of Tawas City, stands this memorial to Michigan's lumbermen.

Territorial Status.—The Ordinance of 1787 provided for the organization and government of the Northwest Territory, which included Michigan, and in 1800 the western half of the Lower Peninsula and the eastern part of the Upper Peninsula became a part of the newly formed Territory of Indiana. The remainder of both peninsulas was added in 1802, and on July 1, 1805, the Territory of Michigan was separated from that of Indiana. Detroit was the capital city and William Hull, an aging officer of the Revolutionary War, was appointed the first governor. In 1810 there were 4,762 white people within the territory, of whom 1,650 resided in Detroit.

The declaration of war against Great Britain on July 18, 1812, found Michigan helpless. On July 17 the fort on Mackinac Island was taken without a shot being fired, and the Michigan

Indians openly joined the British. When British forces under Gen. Isaac Brock arrived before Detroit, Governor Hull surrendered the city on August 16, believing that he had prevented the massacre of its inhabitants. The surrender of Detroit gave Michigan to the British and permitted their Indian allies to commit outrages against the settlements. On Aug. 23, 1813, the garrison at Frenchtown, on the Raisin River, was massacred by the Indians. Oliver H. Perry's victory on Lake Erie in 1813, however, opened the way for Gen. William Henry Harrison's troops to reoccupy Detroit on September 29, and the defeat of the British at the Battle of the Thames River in Canada on Oct. 5, 1813, broke the British hold on Michigan, scattered their Indian allies, and restored the territory to American control.

Devaney Inc.

Greenfield Village, a museum of the American past.

Lewis Cass was now appointed governor of the territory, serving until 1831; under his able direction the region progressed rapidly. Cass negotiated treaties with the Indians in 1819 and 1821 which transferred to the United States title to almost half of the Lower Peninsula. In 1818 steamship navigation was established on the Great Lakes, and the completion of the Erie Canal in 1825 turned some of the westward migration into Michigan.

Statehood.—In 1834 the territorial legislature petitioned Congress for permission to form a state. A state convention assembled at Detroit and formulated a constitution. This was ratified by the electorate in 1835, and a complete set of state officers was elected. The admission of Michigan was opposed by the Southern senators, who disliked the formation of another free state, and by the State of Ohio, which had a boundary dispute with Michigan. The first of these objections was compromised by promising the admission of Arkansas as a slave state simultaneously, and the second by awarding the Toledo strip to Ohio and giving Michigan the Upper Peninsula, which had been part of the Territory of Wisconsin. A Convention of Assent to these proposals met in Ann Arbor on Sept. 26, 1836, but would not accept the compromise. In December 1836 the Democrats assembled another Convention of Assent which accepted the federal proposal, and on Jan. 26, 1837, Michigan was admitted as a state in the Union.

The development of the state was rapid after 1837. An extensive program of internal development, including roads and water transportation, brought great numbers of settlers into the southern part of the state. The discovery and exploitation of copper and iron deposits in the Upper Peninsula led to a demand for a ship canal around the rapids of the St. Marys River. The project was begun in 1853 and completed in 1855. In 1847 the state legislature fixed the location of the capital at Lansing, a recognition of increased interior settlement.

Civil War and After.—Michigan was a center of antislavery agitation, and Jackson, Mich., is sometimes claimed to be the official birthplace of the Republican Party, established in 1854. During the Civil War, the state put nearly 100,000 troops into the field. Commanding the Michigan Cavalry Brigade was George A. Custer, who later (1876) was killed with his entire company at the well-known Battle of the Little Big Horn in Montana.

After the war, the Granger movement was organized by the farmers to protect their interests. The farmers' demand for cheap money in the form of "greenbacks" led to a Greenback and Democratic Party fusion ticket, which captured the governorship in 1882.

The 20th Century.—The turn of the century witnessed the beginnings of a dramatic transformation in the economic activity of the state from agriculture, mining, and lumbering to manufacturing, particularly the manufacturing of motor vehicles. By 1904, after several years of experimentation, Henry Ford of Dearborn had developed a practical and cheap car that could be mass produced. By 1914 his conveyor-belt type of assembly and his announcement of $5 wages for an eight-hour day had placed him in the forefront of automobile manufacture. In 1908, William C. Durant had formed the organization that was to become the General Motors Corporation, and a reorganization of the Maxwell Motor Car Company by Walter P. Chrysler led, in 1923, to the formation of the Chrysler Corporation. By 1928, Ford, General Motors, and Chrysler, all centering in the Detroit metropolitan area, were the three largest producers of automobiles in the nation.

During World War I Michigan industry provided great quantities of shells, trucks, and Liberty engines for the nation's war effort. Despite a short break in the early 1920's the economic expansion and industrial prosperity stimulated by the war continued and, in addition, attracted great numbers of foreign immigrants, Negroes, and farmers from outlying areas into Michigan's manufacturing centers. Detroit's population grew from 285,704 in 1900 to 1,568,622 in 1930. In

1900, Michigan was 60.7 per cent rural, but by 1930 the state was 68.2 per cent urban.

During the crisis years following 1929, Michigan was hard hit. In Detroit, by April 1930, 76,018 people able to work were out of a job and 15,979 were on layoff. By January 1931 these figures had risen to 174,527 and 49,041 respectively, or 32 per cent of the working population of Detroit. Unable to collect real estate taxes, the state was forced to enact a 3 per cent sales tax in order to obtain its revenue. In 1932 a strike among tool and die workers in Detroit was followed by a damaging raid upon Detroit factories and offices by men in 300 automobiles. In the same year a riot among people clamoring for work at the Ford plant left four dead. The unrest throughout Michigan was further exemplified by the uncovering of a secret night-riding terrorist organization known as the Black Legion, and Father Charles E. Coughlin of Royal Oak was inferentially condemned by William Cardinal O'Connell of Boston for attempting to create uprisings among the poor.

Unionism.—Spurred by the discontent among the workers and by the National Labor Relations Act of 1935, which required employers to bargain collectively with unions, the United Automobile Workers of the Congress of Industrial Organizations (UAW-CIO) began a drive to organize the auto workers. In 1937 a sit-down strike took place at the Fisher Body Company (General Motors) in Flint. Through Gov. Frank Murphy's mediation, violence was avoided, and General Motors eventually recognized the UAW-CIO. Chrysler Corporation soon followed suit, but it was not until 1941 that the Ford Motor Company recognized the union and began collective bargaining.

World War II and After.—The entrance of the United States into World War II brought renewed expansion and unprecedented prosperity throughout the state's industrial areas. From 1940 to 1943 the population of the Detroit metropolitan area increased from 2,373,823 to 2,612,115. After a further economic rise due to the Korean War in the early 1950's, unemployment and fiscal problems beset the state late in the decade. In 1948, a Democrat, G. Mennen Williams, was elected governor, beginning a record six terms in office. He declined to run in 1960 and Lieut. Gov. John B. Swainson was elected his successor. In 1962 he lost to Republican George Romney, who was reelected in 1964 and 1966. Romney resigned in 1969 to become U.S. secretary of housing and urban development and was succeeded by Lieut. Gov. William G. Milliken, who was elected in 1970 to a full term.

CHARLES M. DAVIS, *University of Michigan*

11. BIBLIOGRAPHY

Russell, Nelson V., *The British Regime in Michigan and the Old Northwest, 1760–1796* (Northfield, Minn., 1939); Goodrich, Calvin, *The First Michigan Frontier* (Ann Arbor 1940); Florer, Warren W., *Early Michigan Settlements* (Ann Arbor 1941); Works Progress Administration, *Michigan, a Guide to the Wolverine State* (New York 1941); Quaife, Milo M., and Glazer, Sidney, *Michigan, from Primitive Wilderness to Industrial Commonwealth* (New York 1948); Fasquelle, Ethel, *When Michigan Was Young* (Grand Rapids 1950); Quaife, Milo M., ed., *This Is Detroit: 1701–1951, Two Hundred and Fifty Years in Pictures* (Detroit 1951); Bald, Frederick C., *Michigan in Four Centuries* (New York 1954); Nevins, Allan, *Ford: the Times, the Man, the Company* (New York 1954); Dunbar, Willis F., *Michigan Through the Centuries,* 4 vols. (New York 1955); Library of Congress, *Michigan, Sesquicentennial of the Territory* (Washington 1955); Dunbar, Willis F., *Michigan, a History of the Wolverine State* (Grand Rapids 1965).

MICHIGAN, Lake. One of the five Great Lakes (q.v.), and by far the largest body of fresh water lying wholly within the United States, though somewhat smaller than Lakes Superior and Huron. It extends some 325 miles from north to south, and is more than 60 miles wide throughout most of its length. Records kept since 1860 reveal an extreme surface variation from 578.3 to 583.4 feet above sea level, with a mean elevation of about 581 feet. At its northeasterly end the lake empties into Lake Huron through the Straits of Mackinac, several miles wide. Lake Michigan has an area of 22,400 square miles. The maximum depth of 870 feet in the north diminishes to about 200 feet off Chicago in the south.

Throughout its southern 200 miles the shoreline is remarkably regular, with no natural harbors. The northern portion of the shoreline is considerably indented, and in this section there are numerous islands and many good harbors. By far the major indentation is Green Bay, over 100 miles long and up to 20 miles wide. The other major indentations are Grand Traverse and Little Traverse bays, on the eastern side of Lake Michigan. The principal island groups are the Fox, the Manitou, the Beavers, and the chain of islands extending across the entrance of Green Bay. The largest single island is Big Beaver, 14 miles long and up to 6 miles wide. In the mid-19th century it was for several years the seat of the fantastic Mormon Kingdom of St. James. Its prophet and king, James J. Strang, who was killed by his subjects in 1856, claimed to be the divinely-appointed successor to Joseph Smith as head of the Church of Latter Day Saints. (See also BEAVER ISLAND.)

The Lake Michigan drainage basin is but twice the area of the lake itself, and the numerous rivers that flow into it are necessarily comparatively short. The major rivers are the Fox and the Menominee on the western side of the lake and the Muskegon, Pere Marquette, Grand, and St. Joseph on the eastern side. Sand dunes border the lake for hundreds of miles, especially on its eastern and southern sides. A lake current flows southward on the western side and northward on the eastern, clogging the river mouths with sand and in numerous instances causing the rivers near their outlets to expand into more or less extensive lakes. The harbors throughout the southerly 200 miles of the lake are all artificial, created either by constructing breakwaters in the open lake or by opening and stabilizing the river mouths.

The white discoverer of Lake Michigan, probably in 1634, was Jean Nicolet, sent from Quebec by Samuel de Champlain in search of a route to the Oriental kingdom of Marco Polo's narrative. Active French penetration of the upper lakes area, however, was delayed for a generation. Then by an amazing burst of commercial and geographical achievement the entire Great Lakes and Mississippi Valley areas were explored and added to France. Around Lake Michigan flourishing missionary and trading centers were established at such points as Chicago, Green Bay, St. Ignace, and Niles before the close of the 17th century. Until 1763 the country remained wholly French, and the influence of the French occupation is still felt. Although British rule supplanted the French in 1763 and American rule superseded the British in 1796, when the Jay Treaty of 1794 became effective, the region tributary to Lake Michigan remained inaccessible to American settlers until the second quarter of the 19th century. Then such developments as the construction of the Erie Canal and the coming of the steamboat to the Great Lakes and the western rivers produced a flood of settlement which quickly occupied southern Michigan and northern Indiana, and swept onward over northern Illinois and southern Wisconsin. Chicago, a tiny wilderness hamlet in 1830, was the metropolis of the West and one of the wonders of the world a generation later. Because of the lake's situation, all overland travel between East and West during the period of settlement diverged southward around it, while travelers by water found easy access on it to the heart of the continent.

Until the close of the 19th century, fishing and the transportation of lumber and grain were important factors in the commerce of Lake Michigan, and during most of the period the volume of passenger travel on the lake was important. By the mid-20th century all save the grain trade had shrunk to insignificant dimensions. In their stead an almost constant procession of huge freighters carries the iron ore of Lake Superior and the Upper Michigan Peninsula downward to the mills which line the southerly shore of Lake Michigan, and coal, grain and other staples in the opposite direction. A development in which Lake Michigan leads the world is the extensive employment of car ferries, by whose use the railroads have in effect leaped the lake from east to west.

With its wealth of forests and fisheries depleted, the northerly shore of Lake Michigan is but sparsely populated and possesses but slight industrial importance. The contrast, both of climate and of industrial development, with the populous and busy southern end of the lake is striking indeed. Nature has provided another marked contact between the eastern and western shores. The prevailing continental wind is from west to east and the vast reservoir of water in Lake Michigan is less susceptible to changes of temperature than is the surrounding land. Thus the lake air conditions the winds that blow over it, absorbing their extremes of summer heat and winter cold and giving the east coast freedom from freezing temperatures in late spring and early autumn. Along practically the entire 300-mile eastern shore, one of the nation's richest fruit belts has developed. Orchards of apples, peaches, plums, and cherries vie with vineyards and fields of berries to claim the attention of visitors and fatten the pocketbooks of those who till the soil. Because of its climatic attractions, too, the entire east coast from the Straits of Mackinac to the Indiana line has become a vast summer playground for the teeming millions of interior America.

The Ordinance of 1787, which created the first American government in the region lying between the Ohio and Mississippi rivers and the Great Lakes, fixed an east and west line through the southern extreme of Lake Michigan as the boundary between the three southern states of the old Northwest Territory (Ohio, Indiana, and Illinois), and the two northern ones (Michigan and Wisconsin). Although the proviso was subsequently violated in every instance, Lake Michigan figured prominently in determining the boundaries of the five states. Both the center of population and the industrial heart of the United States lie close to Lake Michigan's southern end. The wealth of human and material resources gathered in this region are of tremendous importance to the vigor and continuing economic development of the nation.

MILO M. QUAIFE,
Editor, "The Lakeside Classics Series," and "The American Lakes Series"; Author, "Lake Michigan," and "The Flag of the United States."

MICHIGAN, University of, a state-supported coeducational university located in Ann Arbor, Mich. Created in 1817 by the government of Michigan Territory, it was first named the Catholepistemiad, or University of Michigania. Adopting its present name in 1821, it remained for 20 years in Detroit, where it comprised only grade schools and a classical academy, supported by sale of federal land grants. In 1837, when Michigan became a state, the university's board of regents (appointed by the governor) accepted a gift of land in Ann Arbor for a campus. Construction was undertaken immediately, and in 1841 instruction on the college level was begun.

In 1850 a new state constitution provided for direct election of the regents, thus increasing the university's independence of the state government. The regents and faculty retained exclusive control of the university until 1852, when Henry P. Tappan was appointed president. During his 11-year administration Tappan inaugurated the lecture system, enlarged the facilities of the university, and instituted a scientific curriculum in addition to the old classical course. Graduate study was offered, and faculty members were expected to do research. The excitement of learning increased enrollment, and for four years following the Civil War the university was the nation's largest. In 1869 the state legislature adopted a mill tax to begin state aid and ensure the university's autonomy. The regents admitted women students for the first time in 1870 and began a program of upgrading state high schools.

In 1871, James B. Angell began his 38-year tenure as president. More buildings were erected, and new colleges were organized. Other state universities looked to Michigan for leadership because of its size and independence. World War I was followed by a decade of further building and modern administrative reforms.

Alexander G. Ruthven, president from 1929 to 1951, guided the university through the Depression. During World War II it rendered distinguished service to the war effort without jeopardizing its educational identity. Under Harlan Hatcher, president from 1951 to 1967, a second Ann Arbor campus was developed and senior college branches were opened in Flint and Dearborn; enrollment doubled to 33,000 in residence, while university control of student conduct diminished; a trimester system was adopted; and governmental and industrial research flourished. In 1967 the total university budget passed $200 million. Robben Fleming became the university's tenth president in 1968.

In the late 1960's the university comprised 15 schools and colleges, organized as such in the years indicated below: Literature, Science, and the Arts (1841); Medicine (1849); Law (1859); Dentistry (1875); Pharmacy (1876); Engineering (1895); Graduate School (1912); Architecture and Design (1913); Education (1921); Business Administration (1924); Natural Resources (1927); Music (1929); Nursing (1940); Public Health (1941); and Social Work (1951). The university libraries held more than 3 million volumes. The university also maintains a renowned teaching hospital, a cyclotron and an atomic reactor, a radio telescope, and a research fleet on the Great Lakes.

HOWARD H. PECKHAM, *Director Clements Library, University of Michigan*

MICHIGAN CITY, city, Indiana, LaPorte County, situated on the south shore of Lake Michigan at an altitude of 600 feet and 35 miles west of South Bend. Its transportation facilities include the Chesapeake and Ohio, the New York Central, the Chicago, Indianapolis and Louisville, the New York, Chicago and St. Louis, and the Chicago South Shore and South Bend (electric) railroads. A diversified industrial center, the city has foundries and railroad shops, and manufactures railway cars, industrial machinery, wire, furniture, building materials, clothing, sports equipment, and numerous other products. With its large harbor and yacht basin, Michigan City is a noted vacation resort. It is the site of the International Friendship Gardens, a permanent exposition of the flower gardens of the world consisting of 100 acres of rolling land where Father Marquette preached to the Potawatomi Indians in 1675. The city was settled in 1832 and incorporated in 1836. Government is by a mayor and council. Pop. 39,369.

MICHIGAN STATE UNIVERSITY, a coeducational land-grant institution of higher education located in East Lansing. It is financed and controlled by the state of Michigan. Founded in 1855 and opened in 1857 as the Agricultural College of the State of Michigan, it was the first state agricultural college in America and served as a model for the Morrill Land-Grant Act of 1862. After changing its name several times the university adopted its present name in 1964.

Michigan State University includes colleges of agriculture, arts and letters, business, communication arts, education, engineering, home economics, human medicine, natural science, social science, and veterinary medicine; Justin Morrill and University colleges; and a school for advanced graduate studies. With Oakland University, its branch in Rochester, Mich., the university had in the late 1960's an enrollment of about 40,000, making it one of the largest universities in the United States. Its library held well over one million volumes.

MICHIGAN TECHNOLOGICAL UNIVERSITY, a coeducational state technological institution located in Houghton. Founded in 1885 as the Michigan Mining School, it was successively renamed Michigan College of Mines in 1897 and Michigan College of Mining and Technology in 1927, receiving its present name in 1964. In 1946 the university established a junior college branch, Lake Superior State College, in Sault Ste. Marie.

The university offers undergraduate courses of study in various fields of engineering and science and in forestry, business administration, engineering administration, and medical technology. There are also premedical and predental programs. Graduate work is offered in many fields, and doctorates are available in chemistry, geology, metallurgical engineering, and engineering mechanics. The university, which had about 4,000 students in the late 1960's, maintains 5 research agencies, including Ford Forestry Center.

MICHILIMACKINAC, mĭsh-ĭ-lĭ-măk'ĭ-nô. See MACKINAC ISLAND.

MICHIPICOTEN, mĭsh-ĭ-pĭ-kō't'n, a bay, island and river, Canada, situated in the western part of the Province of Ontario. Michipicoten Bay is an arm of Lake Superior, on the northeast shore, located 110 miles north of Sault Sainte Marie. Michipicoten Island, which is 17 miles long and varies in width from three to six miles, lies at the entrance to the bay. Michipicoten River has its source in lakes on the south side of the height of land dividing the waters of Hudson Bay and Lake Superior and flows 70 miles in a generally southwest direction into Michipicoten Bay.

MICHOACAN, mē-chô-ä-kän', Mexico, a state of 23,202 square miles bounded on the north by the state of Guanajuato, on the northwest by Jalisco and Colima, on the east by Mexico, on the south by Guerrero, and on the west by the Pacific Ocean. Michoacán is mountainous except for a narrow coastal strip and some flat lands in the north and south. Its largest drainage streams are the Lerma River on the north boundary and the Río de las Balsas on the south border. The climate is cold in the mountains, temperate on the north plateau, and tropical in the southern valleys and on the coast. There is considerable volcanic activity; a new volcano, Paricutín, erupted near Uruapan in 1943. The principal inhabitants are Tarascan Indians and mestizos. In 1951 the United Nations and Mexico sponsored the first regional fundamental education center to train leaders for Latin America on the eastern shore of Lake Patzcuaro. Some sheep and cattle are raised but the economy is mainly agricultural. The leading products are sugar, rice, cereals, fruit, coffee, and tobacco. Valuable minerals are found here, and silver, lead, copper and iron are mined. The capital is Morelia (q.v.). Pop. (1960) 1,851,876.

MICHURINISM or MICHURIN SCIENCE, a set of biological doctrines named for Ivan Vladimirovich Michurin (1855–1935), a Russian nurseryman who also imported and hybridized plants. Michurin, who is credited with having developed numerous hardy varieties of fruit trees, was reputedly discovered by Nikolai Lenin and later was made into an authority by Joseph Stalin. In August 1948, the Communist authorities outlawed Mendelian genetics and put "Michurin science" in its place and thereby gave the doctrine an official status. The Soviet Michurinists thereupon assumed control of all agricultural and genetic research in the USSR.

Michurin's biological ideology is post-Darwinian but pre-Weismannian. It is almost identical with the Communist biological line set by Karl Marx and Friedrich Engels in the 1870's. Michurinists accept the theory of evolution and attempt to improve domestic plants and animals by artificial selection but they also accept the Lamarckian doctrine of the inheritance of acquired characters. Michurin himself added little to the biological theories of his time. He claimed to be able to cross-pollinate distant species by the technique of using a "mentor;" that is, one of the species to be hybridized would be grafted on the other until the two species—the stock and the scion—had learned to be compatible, whereupon the cross-pollination supposedly would take and a viable hybrid would be produced. Michurin's scientific and experimental procedures have been questioned by Western geneticists, such as the practice he described in his *Selected Works,* p. 207, "In dealing with interspecific crosses definitely known to be difficult, I have often achieved success by adding a very small amount of the pollen of the maternal parent to the pollen of the male parent." This practice would explain (1) why Western geneticists could not repeat his species crosses, and (2) why his hybrids all came within the seedling range of the maternal species. Wherever biologists are free to reject Michurinism they have done so.

Michurinism was elaborated in considerable detail after it displaced genetics in the USSR. Its chief doctrines may be summarized as follows: Important economic characteristics of plants are controlled by limiting factors which are not Mendelian genes. The worse limiting factor is always neutralized by the better one—the one which encourages the most appropriate course of development—so that consequently, in hybrids, the dominance or recessiveness of any particular character can be predicted because the best characters, those most suited to local conditions, are always dominant. Inbred lines deteriorate but they can be rejuvenated by hybridization. This is accomplished by a selective fertilization since the ovum is able to select the pollen grains from which the best adapted offspring will come. Heredity is defined as the capacity of the living body to react in a definite way to any given set of conditions. Hereditary characteristics thus are merely the environmental conditions that have been assimilated during the preceding generations. All organisms absorb nutrients from their environments and convert them into their own living substance. Their constitutions remain unaltered in an optimum environment, however, because an organism always absorbs the nutriments to which it is best adapted. By regulating the quality of the nutrients, the breeder may produce new and desirable types at will. Any segregation of types that may appear superficially to be Mendelian is caused by local difference in the nutrition supplied to the reproductive cells. Graft chimeras are regarded as true vegetative hybrids.

Michurin and his followers rejected Mendelian heredity and modern genetics. The most extreme exponent of the doctrine was Soviet agriculturist T. D. Lysenko, a scientific power in Stalinist Russia. Since Stalin's death, Michurin science has been discredited in the Soviet Union.

CONWAY ZIRKLE,
Professor of Botany, University of Pennsylvania.

MICKIEWICZ, mêts-kyĕ'vêch, **Adam Bernard,** Polish poet: b. Nowogrodek, Lithuania, Dec. 24, 1798; d. Constantinople, Nov. 26, 1855. He studied at the University of Wilno and then attracted national attention with his first volume of poetry in 1822. Because of his association with a group of young Polish patriots who protested Russian control of their country, he was exiled to Russia in 1824. After five years he was allowed to leave and eventually traveled to Paris where he became professor of Slavonic languages and literature at the Collège de France in 1840, but his espousal of the mystical and political doctrines of André Towianski (1799–1878) caused his dismissal from the college in 1844. In 1848 he attempted unsuccessfully to enlist Polish regiments in the Italian struggle against Austria. He died while trying to raise Polish armies in Turkey. A lifelong patriot who glorified the romantic traditions of Poland in his poetry, Mickiewicz was the greatest Polish poet of his age. *Pan Tadeusz* (q.v., 1834), a humorous epic of Polish country life in the early 19th century, is considered his masterpiece, and his other noteworthy works include *Grazyna* (1823), *Crimean Sonnets* (1826), *Conrad Wallenrod* (1828), and *The Books of the Polish Nation and of the Polish Pilgrimage* (1832).

MICMACS, mĭk'măks, a tribe of Algonquian Indians found in Newfoundland and the Maritime provinces of Canada. Historically they were friendly to the French settlers and hostile to the British. Their population of about 3,500 is surprisingly much the same as their estimated number during the 17th century. The Micmacs hunt and fish for a living, and are one of the few Indian tribes to remain virtually intact after prolonged contact with the white race.

MICROANALYSIS. See CHEMICAL ANALYSIS.

MICROBE, mī'krōb, a microscopic organism; applied particularly to bacteria, and more especially to the forms that cause disease. See also BACTERIA AND BACTERIOLOGY; PROTOZOA.

MICROBIOLOGY, mī-krô-bī-ŏl-ô-jĭ, the science dealing with the structure, classification, physiology, and distribution of microorganisms, and with their technical and medical significance. The term microorganism is applied to the unicellular and structurally closely related simple representatives of the plant and animal kingdoms. With few exceptions, the unicellular organisms are invisible to the naked eye and generally have dimensions between a fraction of a micron and 200 microns (1 micron = 1/25,400 inch).

Principal Types of Microorganisms.—In its broadest sense, microbiology deals with the biology of the Protozoa, the Algae, the Fungi, the Bacteria, the *Rickettsiae,* and the viruses.

Protozoa.—These are unicellular organisms generally placed in the animal kingdom, although some of the photosynthetic species are, with equal justification, often considered to be plants (green Algae). All Protozoa have distinct nuclei and generally reproduce by cell division. Many exhibit a sexual process known as conjugation, which is analogous to the sexual phenomena in higher plants and animals. The nutrition of the Protozoa is varied: some are holophytic and lead a plant-like existence; others are holozoic and prey on other microorganisms; a few are parasitic.

Algae.—The simple forms of Algae, which are microscopic, unicellular and simply organized, filamentous and colonial, are found mainly among the green Algae (Chlorophyceae), the yellow Algae (Chrysophyceae), and the blue-green Algae (Cyanophyceae). In general, the Algae have a photosynthetic mode of nutrition and produce cell material and oxygen from carbon dioxide and water. The energy used in this process is derived from sunlight, which is absorbed by the green plant pigments known as chlorophylls. Most Algae have a distinct nucleus and show sexual behavior as well as cell division. Unlike other Algae, the blue-green Algae do not have chloroplasts and are not known to have a sexual cycle. Their nucleus is not distinct, although nuclear bodies have been shown to be present. If they are motile, the blue-green Algae have a creeping movement and never swim by whip-like processes known as flagella, which occur in other Algae and some Protozoa. In addition to chlorophyll, they contain a blue pigment, phycocyanine, which gives them their characteristic color.

Fungi.—The true Fungi, which, like the Algae, are generally considered to be primitive plants, differ from the Algae in being non-photosynthetic and in not depositing cellulose in their cell walls. This group includes the yeasts, the molds, the rusts, the mushrooms, and related organisms. True Fungi possess distinct nuclei and, with some exceptions, a sexual reproductive mechanism. The yeasts are unicellular Fungi and generally reproduce by budding or fission, while the molds are filamentous (mycelial) organisms, which often show a certain degree of differentiation of the various portions of the plant body (mycelium) into special sexual or asexual reproductive structures. Being incapable of photosynthesis, the Fungi are saprophytic or parasitic in their nutrition.

Bacteria.—The Bacteria, or Schizomycetes, which are usually classified as a group of Fungi, differ from most of the true Fungi in being smaller and simpler in structure. No sexual reproduction comparable to that found in the true Fungi has been proved for Bacteria. Although nucleus-like bodies have been demonstrated in many Bacteria, their nature and behavior have not been entirely established, perhaps mainly because of their small size. While most Bacteria are saprophytic or parasitic, like the true Fungi, some or photosynthetic. Bacterial photosyntheses, however, differ from green plant photosynthesis in that oxygen is never produced and in that the bacterial chlorophylls, which are diffused in the cells, differ slightly both in chemical structure and in absorption spectrum from green plant chlorophylls. Bacteria are unicellular or mycelial in structure and may be either rigid or flexible. Many possess a swimming motility, generally achieved by flagella, while some show a creeping motility similar to that of the blue-green Algae. In general, the group known as Bacteria appears to be a somewhat heterogeneous and poorly defined collection of organisms, some of which may be more closely related to the blue-green Algae than to Fungi. Because of the small size, the lack of distinct characters, the absence of sexuality, and the variability of Bacteria, their classification is difficult and admittedly unsound.

Rickettsiae.—These are small, bacterium-like organisms, which are found as parasites in arthropods and occasionally in warm-blooded animals. They are obligately parasitic and, while they can be grown in living tissues, they do not generally yield to cultivation in lifeless, artificial media.

Viruses.—The filterable viruses are the smallest known entities possessing certain characteristics of living organisms. They pass through bacteriological filters which retain Bacteria and *Rickettsiae.* The viruses are obligately parasitic in the tissues of plants or animals and cannot be grown in lifeless artificial media. While the larger viruses may well be thought of as organisms, some of the smaller ones can be crystallized and appear to be nucleoprotein molecules or aggregates.

Microbiological Methods.—The success of experimental laboratory work and of the medical and large-scale industrial applications of microbiology is based mainly on the techniques of sterilization, aseptic manipulation, and propagation of pure cultures.

Sterilization.—This is the complete destruction of all germs in an environment or in a medium wherein microorganisms are cultivated. This is usually accomplished by prolonged exposure to dry heat (160° to 180° C. for 90 to 150 minutes) or to steam under pressure (15 to 20 pounds pressure from 15 to 60 minutes).

Aseptic Technique.—This implies the manipulation of sterile media and pure cultures without their contamination with foreign germs, which are present everywhere in soil and water, on the human body, and on dust particles in the air. Protection against dust is commonly effected by the use of sterile cotton plugs, which act as air filters, and by the use of a gas flame, with which dust particles are burned before they can enter sterilized receptacles.

Pure Cultures.—These are populations of cells derived from the multiplication of a single cell of a microorganism and, therefore, the progeny of one individual. They are usually obtained by the isolation of individual cells on a sterile, nutrient, solid medium, on which their progenies accumulate as segregated masses, known as colonies.

Physiology and Nutrition of Microorganisms.—Because of their availability and their enormous rates of growth and metabolism, the microorganisms have served as excellent material for studies of nutrition and physiology. Some of the greatest contributions to the understanding of the physiology and biochemistry of higher plants and animals have come from experiments on yeasts, unicellular Algae, and Bacteria. The Fungi, and particularly the Bacteria, which occur in a great variety of natural habitats, exhibit a remarkable multiplicity of nutritional requirements and physiological processes. The autotrophic organisms are those which can grow in entirely inorganic environments, synthesizing their cell material from carbon dioxide and inorganic salts, such as nitrates, sulphates, phosphates, etc. The photoautotrophs use the radiant energy of sunlight as a source of energy for their life processes. Thus, the Algae carry out the type of photosynthesis characteristic of all green plants, while the green and the purple sulphur Bacteria make their organic compounds by the reduction of carbon dioxide with hydrogen sulphide or sulphur. The chemoautotrophic or chemosynthetic organisms are also capable of growing in environments containing only inorganic compounds, but do not possess chlorophylls and are incapable of photosynthesis. They derive their energy from energy-yielding oxidation-reduction reactions involving inorganic compounds. The colorless sulphur Bacteria use oxygen to oxidize sulphides to sulphur, which they store in the cells and which they subsequently oxidize to sulphates. Some nitrifying Bacteria obtain their energy from the aerobic oxidation of ammonia to nitrites, while others oxidize nitrites to nitrates. The hydrogen Bacteria can oxidize molecular hydrogen to water, while the iron bacteria, which are found in iron springs, oxidize ferrous iron salts to ferric hydroxide, which they deposit outside the cell body.

The heterotrophic organisms use organic compounds in their nutrition and are, therefore, ultimately dependent on the autotrophs for their livelihood. They obtain organic compounds either as saprophytes, by decomposing dead organisms or the waste products of living ones, or as parasites or symbionts living in or with other living organisms. Certain Bacteria are photoheterotrophic, using organic compounds in their nutrition, but obtaining their energy from sunlight. All the Fungi and most of the Bacteria, on the other hand, are chemoheterotrophic. They depend on organic nutrients as a source of carbon for making protoplasm and obtain their energy from oxidation-reduction reactions involving organic compounds. Some chemoheterotrophs can grow with a single organic compound, while others need more than one. Many Protozoa, Fungi, and Bacteria require minute amounts of special organic compounds, known as nutrilites, for growth. These compounds are in many cases identical with the vitamins needed by higher animals.

Aerobic or respiratory organisms obtain their energy by oxidizing organic compounds with molecular oxygen. While complete oxidation leads to the production of carbon dioxide, incomplete oxidations may lead to partially oxidized products. The vinegar Bacteria, for instance, transform alcohol into acetic acid. While many organisms require air, many others can use anaerobic oxidations as a source of energy. The obligate anaerobes are restricted to this type of metabolism and are inhibited or even killed by contact with air. Anaerobic oxidations involve oxidizing agents other than oxygen. Thus, some Bacteria oxidize organic compounds with nitrates, which they reduce to nitrites, nitrogen gas, or ammonia. Others use sulphates as oxidizing agents and produce sulphides. Still others can oxidize organic compounds with carbon dioxide, which they reduce to methane, or marsh gas. Fermentations are oxidation-reduction reactions involving only organic compounds or portions of organic compounds. The products of fermentation vary with different organisms and include such compounds as ethyl and butyl alcohol; formic, acetic, propionic, butyric, and caproic acids; lactic acid; acetone; glycerine; carbon dioxide; hydrogen gas; etc.

Significance of Microorganisms and Practical Applications of Microbiology.—The universal distribution and the varied physiological activities of microorganisms make them extremely important in the economy of nature. It is estimated that about 90 per cent of the decomposition of organic compounds, which is necessary for the continuation of plant and animal life, is carried out by microbes. In soil and in water microorganisms are responsible for the transformations of carbon and nitrogen compounds, through which the fertility of the soil and, indirectly, the composition of the earth's atmosphere are maintained. (See BACTERIA AND BACTERIOLOGY.)

The variety of technological uses to which microorganisms are put is enormous. In brewing and baking, the alcohol and carbon dioxide produced in fermentation by yeasts are utilized. Bacterial fermentations are used industrially to produce organic acids and solvents. In food manufacture, microorganisms are used for the production of vinegar, the preservation of olives, sauerkraut, and pickles, for the souring of cream in making butter, for the ripening of cheese, and for the curing of tea and tobacco. The control of undesirable microorganisms is the principal aim of canning, pasteurization, and other methods of preservation of food.

Since Protozoa, Fungi, Bacteria, *Rickettsiae,* and viruses are the causes of almost all infectious diseases of plants and animals, the control of these parasitic microorganisms is one of the main aspects of both preventive and therapeutic medicine. The sciences of pathology, immunology, and epidemiology are concerned with the medical aspects of the microbes in their relation to the hosts which they invade.

Certain microorganisms produce antibiotic substances which are destructive of or inhibitory to other microbes. Some of these substances have great therapeutic value in the treatment of disease and are produced on a large commercial scale. Of the many antibiotics which have been described, the most important are the penicillins, which are produced by Fungi, and the bacterial antibiotics, streptomycin and tyrothricin. See also BACTERIA AND BACTERIOLOGY; FUNGI; PROTOZOA; YEAST.

Bibliography.—Ainsworth, G. C., and Sneath, R. H. A., *Microbial Classification* (New York 1962); Dubos, René, *The Unseen World* (New York 1962); Sistrom, W. R., *Microbial Life* (New York 1962); Brieger, E. M., *Structure and Ultrastructure of Microorganisms* (New York 1963); Brock, Thomas D., *Principles of Microbial Ecology* (New York 1966); Kudo, Richard, *Protozoology,* 5th ed. (Springfield, Ill., 1966); Wedberg, E. E. *Introduction to Microbiology* (New York 1966); Andrewes, C. H., *The Natural History of Viruses* (New York 1967); Carpenter, P. L., *Microbiology,* 2d ed. (Philadelphia 1967); Waksman, Selman A., *Actinomycetes* (New York 1967).

MICHAEL DOUDOROFF,
Associate Professor of Bacteriology, University of California.

MICROCEPHALUS, mī-krô-sef'ȧ-lŭs, in *pathology,* the condition of having an abnormally small head, further marked by a peculiarly shaped cranium. The forehead is small and receding and the vertex somewhat pointed. The condition results in mental deficiency, amounting in some cases to idiocy.

MICROCLINE, mī'krô-klīn, a feldspar identical in composition with orthoclase, but crystallizing in the triclinic system. Thin sections examined in polarized light frequently show a grating-like structure, due to double twinning. The color varies from white to yellow and, occasionally, red or green.

MICROCONODON, mī-krō-kŏn'ō-dŏn, a fossil Upper Triassic animal of North America, of interest chiefly in reference to the structure of its teeth as indicating the subsequently developed mammalian type. *Microconodon* was for a long time doubtfully placed among the Protodonta, or most primitive of Mammalia, but the animal is now considered to be one of the later mammal-like reptiles.

MICROCOSM, mī'krô-kŏz'm, **AND MACROCOSM,** măk'rô-kŏz'm. Among the ancients a belief prevailed that the world or cosmos was animated, or had a soul. This theory led to the notion that the parts and members of organic beings must have their counterparts in the members of the cosmos. The natural philosophers of the 16th century took up this theory in a somewhat modified shape, and considered the world as a human organism on the large scale, and man as a world, or cosmos, in miniature; hence they called man a microcosm (Greek, "little world") and the universe itself the macrocosm ("great world"). Heylin gave the title *Microcosmus* to a work on cosmography in 1621.

MICROFICHE. See INFORMATION STORAGE AND RETRIEVAL.

MICROFILM. See INFORMATION STORAGE AND RETRIEVAL; LIBRARY—*New Technology* (Effects on Acquisitions—Photocopies and Microforms).

MICROFORM. See LIBRARY—*New Technology.*

MICROGROOVE RECORDS. See SOUND RECORDING AND REPRODUCTION—*Disc Recording.*

MICROMETER, mī-krŏm'ē-tẽr, mī'krō-mē-tẽr (in micrometer caliper), an instrument using a highly accurate screw for determining minute measurements. This screw has a fine, uniform pitch, measuring 0.025 inch in American machinists' micrometer calipers and 1 millimeter in instruments employing the metric scale. It is turned by a head marked in equal divisions. A reading of scales on the head and shaft gives the distance through which the screw has traveled. The micrometer was invented about 1638 by William Gascoigne, an English astronomer, as an improvement on the vernier (q.v.) for use in measuring the diameter of the sun, moon, and planets. The principle is now an essential adjunct of instruments used by astronomers, engineers, and machinists.

The filar micrometer is an attachment placed at the eye end of a telescope to aid in measuring distances between stars, the direction of one star from another, the diameters of planets, the positions of comets and asteroids, and other astronomical phenomena. In addition to the screw mechanism, it contains one or more fixed fine wires or threads and one or more that are movable, so that the two sets can be aligned with the objects viewed and give the observer the required measurements. It has come to be employed more frequently in studying distances on astrographic plates than in making measurements by eye. This device is essentially a comparator whose carriage moves on a micrometer screw. It is used also for measuring distances through a microscope and between the lines taken by a spectrograph.

The micrometer is also employed by physicists, as in a comparator for measuring polarized light and in the adjustment of the movable mirror in an interferometer for separating a beam of light into two or more parts. It is an essential mechanism in the adjustable leg of a spherometer for measuring either convex or concave curvatures, and is particularly useful in the grinding of lenses. Civil engineers use an attachment at the eyepiece of transits similar to that on telescopes and microscopes.

Perhaps the most familiar micrometer is the machinist's micrometer caliper. This is an extremely accurate measuring device, capable of readings to within 0.0001 inch. It consists of a slide caliper, resembling an ordinary screw clamp in shape and having a fixed contact or anvil and a movable contact or spindle. These contacts are adjusted by a precision screw provided with graduations that can be read in hundredths of a millimeter or in thousandths of an inch. When the contacts are closed, the scales read zero; when they are open and closed again on a thin plate or wire, the reading gives the thickness. Most micrometer calipers in use in the United States have screws with 40 threads per inch; thus each turn of the screw represents a distance of 0.025 inch. The head or thimble is graduated from 0 to 25, and the sleeve through which the spindle moves is graduated with marks 0.025 inch apart, every fourth mark representing one tenth of an inch. Many of these micrometers are equipped with a ratchet stop that prevents further turning when a given pressure is applied. There are inside as well as outside micrometers.

FRANK DORR,
Associate Editor, "Popular Science Monthly."

MICRON, mī'krŏn (also called MICROMETER), a unit of length equal to the millionth part of a meter or the 25,640th part of an inch. The Greek letter μ is used as its symbol. Thus 47μ is read "47 microns."

MICRONESIA, mī-krō-nē'zhȧ (Gr. *mikros,* small + *nēsos,* island), the northwestern of the three great divisions of the Pacific islands (see OCEANIA), located north of Melanesia and separated from Polynesia (qq.v.) by the international date line. The designation "little islands" is apt, for the 2,250 islands and islets of Micronesia have a combined land area of only about 1,100 square miles. Many of the islets are low and sandy, lying along a rim of reefs, most of which enclose shallow lagoons and form atolls. All of the Marshall Islands and the Gilbert Islands (except Ocean Island) are of this low type. In the Caroline Islands there are 5 assemblages of "high" islands, from east to west: Kusaie, Ponape, Truk, Yap, and Palau. The other 43 island units in the group are low and sandy. The 15 Mariana Islands lie along the southern third of the Mariana Ridge, an arc of submerged mountains extending north from Guam to near Tokyo. The northern Marianas are recent volcanic peaks; those from Saipan to Guam are of older volcanic material mixed with raised reef rock.

Most of the islands of Micronesia lie outside the typhoon belt, but some of them are visited at intervals by destructive gales of this type. Although the islands are entirely within the tropics, cool breezes and the wide expanse of surrounding ocean prevent excessively high temperatures. Rainfall is moderately heavy on the high islands and on the atolls nearest the equator, providing enough water for drinking even in the absence of streams and fresh ground water, as on atolls, and for cultivation of subsistence crops of breadfruit, bananas, taro, yams, sweet potatoes, and coconuts. On the low islands farther north rainfall decreases, there are fewer edible plants, and between rains the only drinking water is from shallow, brackish wells. The chief export of the low islands is copra. Some livestock are raised, and fish and other marine products are harvested for local consumption.

In addition to the four main island groups, a few nearby single islands fall within Micronesia: Wake Island, north of the Marshalls; Marcus Island, northeast of the Marianas; the independent island of Nauru; and Ocean Island, of the Gilberts. The Gilbert Islands are administered by Britain as part of the Gilbert and Ellice Islands Colony. The other three island groups (except Guam) form the Trust Territory of the Pacific Islands, administered by the United States since World War II, and Guam itself is a United States possession.

Although the term "Micronesian" is applied to the peoples of all these island groups, they are not as unified as the Polynesians, whom they resemble. Local groupings show distinct differences in physical characteristics, language, and customs, merging eastward into Polynesia. Among the peoples of the Carolines, Mongoloid-type characters seem to be more emphasized, while the peoples of the Marshalls and Gilberts are more Caucasoid and closer to Polynesians. Descendants of the Chamorros of the Marianas have intermixed with Spanish, Filipinos, Germans, Americans, and Japanese to such an extent that the original type is hard to determine. It is now preferable to refer to Gilbertese, Carolinian, and the like than to lump all the people as Micronesian. As of 1958, the population of the larger groups was estimated as follows: Trust Territory, 70,594; Guam, 40,000; Gilbert and Ellice Islands, 35,919.

EDWIN H. BRYAN, JR.,
Manager, Pacific Scientific Information Center.

MICROORGANISMS. See MICROBIOLOGY.

MICROPHONE, mī'krō-fōn, a device that changes sound energy into electrical energy and, though relatively simple, forms the basis of all voice communication, enabling sound to be transmitted and recorded by electronic means. There are four basic types of microphones in use.

The *carbon microphone,* the oldest and most widely used type, is familiar as the telephone transmitter. Credit for the invention of the microphone can therefore be attributed to Alexander Graham Bell (q.v.) as an indirect achievement of his pioneer work on the telephone. Though restricted in sound quality, the carbon microphone provides high intelligibility for accurate voice communication, can be manufactured at low cost, and is rugged in nature. It consists of a metal diaphragm placed against an insulated cup that contains loosely packed carbon granules. Sound vibrations striking the diaphragm alternately increase and decrease pressure on the granules, producing a variation in the current because of a proportional change in resistance of the mass of granules. This variation in current corresponds to variations in sound applied to the diaphragm, and the resulting alternating voltage may be amplified and used to provide the signal necessary for the desired communication.

The *crystal microphone,* which is widely used in public-address systems and home recording work, depends for its action on the piezoelectric effect of certain crystals, most commonly Rochelle salts. The term "piezoelectric" refers to the fact that when pressure (in this instance, sound waves) is applied to the crystal in the proper direction, a proportionately varying voltage is produced between opposite faces of the crystal. The advantages of the crystal microphone are its relatively high output voltage, good sound quality, and low cost. Crystal microphones are quite sensitive to extremes of heat and humidity, however, and they do not tolerate rough handling or severe mechanical shock.

The third basic type of microphone, which depends on magnetism for the translation of sound energy into electrical energy, includes the dynamic microphone and the velocity or ribbon microphone. The *dynamic microphone* closely resembles the dynamic loudspeaker, found in all radio and television receivers, in principle. In fact, a two- or three-inch dynamic speaker will make a satisfactory microphone for such limited-quality use as intercommunication systems and is frequently so employed. The dynamic microphone consists of a number of turns of wire wound in what is called a voice coil and rigidly attached to a diaphragm. This coil is suspended between the poles of a permanent magnet. Sound causes the diaphragm to vibrate, moving the coil back and forth between the poles and producing an alternating voltage proportional to the applied sound. The *velocity microphone,* a high-quality device widely used in commercial broadcasting and recording, is similar in principle. A thin, corrugated metallic ribbon is suspended between the poles of a permanent magnet. When vibrated by sound, the ribbon cuts the lines of force between the poles in alternating directions, generating an alternating voltage across the length of the ribbon. Since the voltage generated by both dynamic and velocity microphones is very small, much greater amplification is necessary for practical use than in the case of carbon and crystal microphones.

The fourth general variety of microphone in use is the *condenser microphone,* in which a tightly stretched metal disk or diaphragm is very closely positioned to a heavy, fixed metal disk. A direct current potential is applied between the disks (which are actually the plates of the condenser) through a high resistance. Any changes in capacitance, such as are caused by applied sound energy, develop charging and discharging currents through the series resistance, generating the alternating voltage output of the microphone. Condenser microphones, particularly those of European manufacture, are among the highest-quality units available, and are almost universally used in the most exacting broadcasting and recording work.

ROBERT E. SHENTON,
Recording Engineer, National Broadcasting Company.

MICROPHOTOMETER, mī-krō-fō-tŏm'ē-tẽr, an instrument for the measurement of light on small areas and light of low value. It is used in determining exposure time in both black-and-white and color photomicrography and in studying the structure of metals through a microscope. The device consists essentially of a photoelectric cell in a search unit, an electronic amplifier, and a galvanometer to indicate intensity. The photocell of one type is self-generating, requires no battery or power connection, and is about 20 times more sensitive than ordinary pocket-type exposure meters. Other photocells, still more sensitive, operate on line current.

FRANK DORR.

MICROSCOPE, mī'krō-skōp, an optical instrument used to augment the power of the eye to see small objects and distinguish fine detail. For small objects to be seen, they must be made to appear larger by a process of magnification, but simple magnification furnishes no additional information unless the instrument is capable of sufficient resolution to distinguish the individual units of fine detail which the eye cannot separate. Moreover, resolution and magnification may be adequate and the object still remain invisible because insufficient contrast is provided to set off the object or its structural detail from its immediate surroundings. These three functions of the microscope—resolution of fine detail, magnification to bring the resolved detail within the resolution of the eye, and contrast control—are manifested in the microscopical image. Accordingly, the design and construction of a microscope are directed primarily toward the perfection of the instrument's ability to produce an image that will be a faithful likeness of the object or will contain information not available to the unaided eye, and secondarily toward the facilitation of the observation of the image.

Microscopical images are formed in two principal ways. In the most usual method, radiation (light, electrons, or other) from a suitable source, directed through the object or reflected from its surface, is collected by a system of lenses or mirrors that brings it to a focus in the image plane. A less common method involves radiation from a point source directed through the object to form a "shadow" image.

Microscopes are named for the kind of radiation employed for image formation. In the *light microscope* images are formed in visible light by lenses constructed usually of glass. The visible light portion of the electromagnetic spectrum, measured in angstrom units (A), extends from a wavelength of about 4000 A to one of about 7500 A. Glass lenses are also used in the *ultraviolet microscope* to focus the near ultraviolet radiation—that is, invisible radiation just beyond the short wavelength end of the visible spectrum, from about 4000 A down to about 3000 A. Below 3000 A glass is no longer transparent to ultraviolet radiation, and quartz lenses are required for use between 2500 and 3000 A. At the other end of the visible spectrum glass lenses transmit the very near infrared radiation, from 7500 to 12,000 A, and the *infrared microscope* is used for image formation in this region. Microscopes using reflecting optics—that is, concave mirrors with aluminum reflecting surfaces instead of refracting lenses—can operate over a wide spectral range. A *reflecting microscope* of this construction will form images at wavelengths from 2500 A in the ultraviolet, through the visible spectrum, to nearly 1 micron in the infrared.

Microscopes utilizing X-rays for image formation are of two principal types. The *reflection X-ray microscope* focuses X-rays by reflection from a system of concave mirrors with platinum or gold reflecting surfaces. In the *projection X-ray microscope,* X-rays emanating from a point source pass through the object and form an enlarged shadow image. The *electron microscope* (q.v.) is analogous to the light microscope in optical principles except for the fact that electrons rather than light waves form the image.

Simple Light Microscope.—At any arbitrary distance an object of a given size subtends a certain angle at the eye and is imaged over a certain area of the retina. If the object is moved closer to the eye, the *visual angle* (as subtended angle is called) increases in size, and the image covers a larger area of the retina. The object consequently appears larger, and the eye is able to distinguish finer detail. The normal eye cannot accommodate to an object closer than about 25 centimeters, however, and cannot resolve the discrete units of fine structure even at this distance if the units are closer together than about 0.1 millimeter. The size that any object appears when positioned at 25 centimeters from the eye is arbitrarily taken as unit magnification, and this distance is called the normal distance of clearest vision.

The simple microscope permits the eye to focus clearly on objects held closer than 25 centimeters, thus effectively increasing both the visual angle and the size of the retinal image. When a converging lens of short focal length is placed close to the eye and an object is held at or just within the focal point of the lens, the eye sees an erect virtual image that appears to be at the normal distance of clearest vision. When so used, the magnification of the lens or simple microscope is $M = \frac{25}{f}$, f being the focal length in centimeters. For magnification to occur, therefore, the focal length must be less than 25 centimeters. Moreover, it is apparent that, for magnifications greater than about 50 diameters, the distance at which the object must be placed in order to be at or within the focal point becomes inconveniently small. For most uses the magnification of the simple microscope does not exceed 30 diameters. A single lens can also form a real image on a screen or photographic film. This is the principle of the camera.

The simple microscope may consist of a single converging lens or of a lens combination which performs optically as a single lens. Since a single lens has inherent spherical and chromatic aberrations which make it unsuitable as a magnifier for any but the lowest magnifications, various combinations of lenses designed to correct these aberrations partially or completely are used for hand lenses and simple microscopes of better quality.

Compound Light Microscope.—In principle, the compound microscope consists of two simple microscopes in series. The first of these, the objective lens, is positioned close to the object and forms a magnified real image in the primary image plane (Fig. 1). This image then becomes the object for the second lens, the eyepiece or ocular, which can either form a virtual image with the eye at the normal distance of clearest vision or project a real image on a screen. This arrangement permits much greater resolution and magnification than is possible with a single simple microscope.

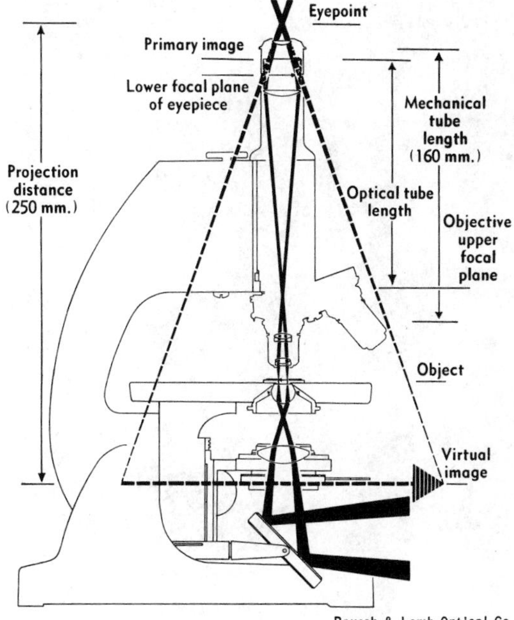

Bausch & Lomb Optical Co.

Fig. 1. Ray paths and image formation in the compound microscope.

Microscope objectives are lens combinations in which the front lens, which does most of the magnifying, is small and of short focal length to enable it to get close to the object, while the remaining lenses correct the aberrations of the small front lens. The objective lens is the most important component in the microscope optical system, since it controls resolution and image quality. Achromatic objectives are corrected for spherical aberrations at one wavelength and for chromatic aberrations at two wavelengths. Apochromatic objectives are corrected for spherical aberrations at two wavelengths and for chromatic aberration at three wavelengths. Immersion objectives are designed for use with an immersion oil, of refractive index equal to that of glass, filling the space between the front lens and the cover glass over the object. This increases the numerical aperture.

The concept of numerical aperture is important, since it provides a way of determining and comparing the resolving power of objective lenses. It is expressed as N.A. $= \eta \sin u$, where η is the refractive index of the medium between the object and objective front lens and u is one half the aperture angle—that is, the largest angle which the objective front lens can take in from a single point in the object.

The eyepiece commonly used with achromatic objectives is the negative or Huygenian ocular. With apochromatic objectives a compensating eyepiece is required to compensate for the slight residual color at the edges of the field.

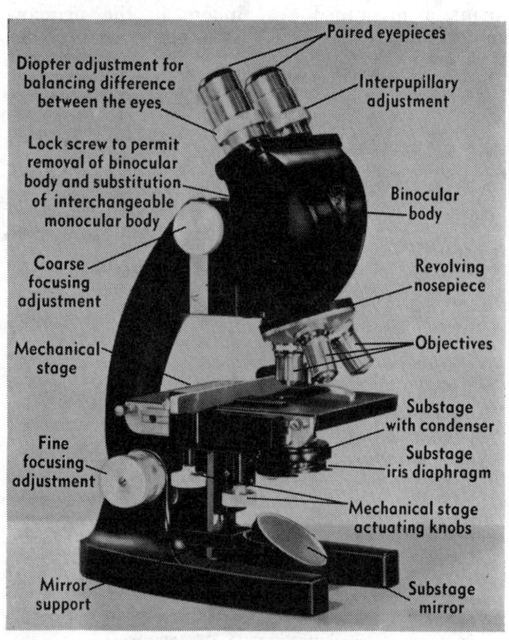

Bausch & Lomb Optical Co.

Fig. 2. Compound microscope.

Although it has no role in image formation, the substage condenser is an essential part of the optical system of the microscope. Its function is to furnish adequate brilliance for viewing by concentrating the incident light on the object and, with high powers especially, to provide strongly convergent light so that the full resolving power of the objective lens may be realized.

The stand of the conventional compound microscope (Fig. 2) serves to hold the optical parts in alignment and to support the object. A sturdy base carries the rest of the instrument on an inclination joint. The body tube, with objectives on a revolving nosepiece at its lower end and either monocular or binocular eyepiece provision at its upper end, works on a rack-and-pinion coarse focusing adjustment which articulates it with the arm. A fine focusing adjustment enables focusing to be controlled precisely. The stage holds the object, which is normally mounted on a 1-inch by 3-inch glass slide and is covered by a thin cover glass.

Special Microscopes.—Several varieties of light microscope are designed either for observation of special kinds of objects or for utilization of special ways of illuminating an object. The *stereoscopic binocular microscope,* often referred to as the Greenough type, comprises two low-power compound microscopes mounted to converge on a single object, thereby giving stereoscopic vision. A *dark-field microscope* is a light microscope fitted with a special type of substage condenser which directs a hollow cone of illumination to the object at a very oblique angle so that none of the direct rays enter the objective. Against a dark background the object appears self-luminous from the light it reflects, refracts, or diffracts into the objective lens. An *ultramicroscope* (q.v.) is a special type of dark-field instrument which utilizes an intense beam of light directed onto the object from one side. Particles of colloidal size (about 10^{-6} to 10^{-3} millimeters) are revealed by the light they scatter even though they are generally far too small for the light microscope to resolve. In the *fluorescence microscope* ultraviolet radiation is converged on the object with a quartz condenser, the object becoming self-luminous and the fluorescence being viewed with regular glass optics. Metals and other opaque materials require a special type of illumination with vertical reflected light. Light is directed into the side of the microscope tube, above the objective, where it is reflected downward through the objective lens, which acts as a condenser to concentrate light on the surface under observation. Light reflected back from the object is collected by the objective, which now forms an image in the usual way. An inverted type of *metallurgical microscope,* as this arrangement is called, combined with a bellows camera is a *metallograph.*

The eye responds only to differences of brightness and differences of color. Colorless objects often have other properties which are undetected unless they can be converted to brightness or color differences. The *polarizing microscope* gives color images of doubly refracting materials and permits crystallographic properties to be determined. The *phase microscope* converts optical path differences, which result in phase changes of the light, into brightness contrast by an interference method. The *interference microscope* converts optical path differences to brightness or color differences by a different interference method.

History.—While the magnifying property of crude lenses was known to the ancient Greeks and Romans, lenses were not used for spectacles until the 13th century, and it was not until the early 17th century that small lenses were made with the precision required for use as simple microscopes. The simple microscope was exploited to great advantage by Anton van Leeuwenhoek (1632–1723). The origins of the compound microscope are obscure, but credit for its invention is usually given to Hans and Zacharias Janssen, Dutch spectaclemakers of Middleburg, who about

1590 succeeded in combining a convex objective lens with a concave eye lens in such a manner that it served as both microscope and telescope. In 1611, Johannes Kepler (1571–1630) demonstrated the advantages of a form of microscope having both the objective lens and the eye lens convex. This became the dominant form of microscope and was later improved by the addition of a third lens, the field lens. An ocular designed by Christian Huygens (1629–1695), which incorporated both eye and field lenses in a single mount, was quickly adopted as the standard eyepiece for microscopical viewing. The microscopes designed and used by Robert Hooke (1635–1703) were mostly of this three-lens type.

The uncorrected lenses in the early microscopes were a serious limitation on usable resolution. Sir Isaac Newton (1642–1727) held that construction of an achromatic lens was impossible, but a Swedish physicist, Samuel Klingenstierna (1698–1765), performed experiments to show that Newton was in error. Inspired by Klingenstierna's demonstrations, John Dollond (1706–1761) succeeded in producing a partially achromatic combination, but much of the credit for achromatizing and reducing the other aberrations in the compound microscope belongs to Joseph Jackson Lister (1786–1869). The work of Giovanni Battista Amici (1786–1863) on immersion objectives opened the way for improvements, which culminated in the perfection of homogeneous oil immersion systems by Ernst Abbe (1840–1905).

Improvements in the compound microscope since about 1870 have been made mostly in the design of the stand, with minor improvements in optics. Since 1930 the phase and interference microscopes, electron microscope, and X-ray microscope, all embodying new principles of image formation, have become firmly established as research instruments.

See also MICROSCOPY.

Bibliography.—Hale, Arthur J., *The Interference Microscope in Biological Research* (Edinburgh 1958); Disraeli, Robert, *New World Through the Microscope,* rev. ed. (New York 1960); Duddington, C. L., *Practical Microscopy* (New York 1960); Clark, George L., *Encyclopedia of Microscopy* (New York 1961); Riemer, Marvin F., *The Microscope and the World of Science* (Boston 1964); Anderson, M. D., *Through the Microscope: Man Looks at Unseen World* (Garden City, N.Y., 1965); Barron, A. L. E., *Using the Microscope,* 3d ed. (New York 1965); Cosslett, V. E., *Advances in Optical and Electron Microscopy* (New York 1966); id., *Modern Microscopy or Seeing the Very Small* (Ithaca, N.Y., 1966); Jacker, Corinne, *Window on the Unknown: A History of the Microscope* (New York 1966); White, G. W., *An Introduction to Microscopy* (New York 1966).

GLENN COVEN,
Microscopist, American Cyanamid Co.

MICROSCOPIUM, mī-krō-skō′pĭ-ŭm, one of the 14 constellations which Nicholas Louis de Lacaille (1713–1762) added to the knowledge of the heavens in connection with his work at the Cape of Good Hope. It is located south of Capricornus and is very inconspicuous, its brightest star being of only the 4th magnitude.

MICROSCOPY, mī-krŏs′kô-pĭ or mī′krō-skō-pĭ, the investigation and interpretation of the images produced by microscope optical systems. The attainment of proficiency in microscopy presupposes a knowledge of microscope optical principles, correct manipulation of the instrument, specimen preparation techniques, and application of microscopical methods to one or more fields. In placing the emphasis on the microscopical image, we recognize the important fact that what the eye sees, or the photographic film records, is an optical effect resulting from interaction between the object under observation and the radiation (light, electrons, or other) which it intercepts. Light passing through an object may be reflected, refracted, diffracted, scattered, selectively absorbed, or polarized, suffer phase changes, or undergo interference. One or more of these effects contribute to the formation of the image, and image quality is no better than the ability of the optical system of the microscope to reproduce faithfully the changes impressed on the radiation by the object.

The ability of any optical system to image a faithful likeness is impaired by lens aberrations and improved in direct proportion to the degree of correction given to the lenses. Most optical systems are a compromise, for it is rarely possible to correct fully for a series of aberrations without either introducing other aberrations or sacrificing such desirable attributes as numerical aperture or depth of field. The microscopical image can never duplicate the object exactly because of the limits placed on resolving power by (1) the finite wavelength of light (or other radiation) and (2) the impossibility of realizing theoretically attainable numerical aperture. The finite wavelength of light introduces diffraction effects which cause a point in the object to be imaged not as a point but as a diffraction disk called the Airy disk. The realization of theoretically attainable numerical aperture would demand an optical system capable of collecting radiation from a point in the object through an angle of 180°—an impracticable design problem. The type of illumination used and the manner in which it is directed onto the object also greatly affect image quality.

Microscopical Images.—Depending on the nature of the object, the type of illumination used, and the optical design of the microscope, a number of different images are possible. In the ordinary transmission light microscope the image of objects which are not completely transparent is an *absorption image,* visible as a pattern of brighter or darker areas due to differential absorption of white light, or as a color pattern due to selective absorption of different wavelengths. Completely transparent objects become visible by refraction or reflection of light from their surfaces and from internal reflections at fissures, inclusions, and the like. This causes the addition or subtraction of light intensity, resulting in a *refraction image.* Objects completely transparent in visible light frequently have pronounced absorption images when illuminated with ultraviolet or infrared radiation, or with an electron beam in the electron microscope (q.v.). When the object consists of very small particles or of fine detail close to the limit of resolution, diffraction effects become prominent, especially with dark-field illumination. The *diffraction image* must be recognized in order to avoid grave misinterpretations of appearances.

An opaque object viewed in reflected light presents a *reflection image,* which may result from selective absorption, in which case it is analogous to the absorption image, or from the differential scattering of light from surfaces of varying roughness, in which case it is analogous to the refraction image. Other images produced by special illumination techniques or optical systems are the *fluorescence image,* formed from a self-luminous object excited to fluorescence by ultraviolet illumination; the *polarization image,* formed in polarized light by a doubly refractive object; and the phase image, of phase and interference microscopes.

Specimen Preparation.—Almost all specimens and materials destined for microscopical study are subjected to a preparation procedure. They may need to be ground, teased apart, coagulated, sliced, stained, mounted in an artificial medium, or desiccated before they are suitable for observation. These treatments may alter the original appearance and structure or create artifacts which confuse interpretation of the image.

Applications.—The microscope is one of the most valuable tools for extending man's visual perception. It is used in biology, mineralogy, petrography, metallography, chemical analysis, and many other sciences and technologies.

Biology.—The microscope is a useful tool in almost every phase of biology, and the study of cytology, histology, and bacteriology could hardly exist without it. In particular, the electron microscope is responsible for rapid strides in many areas. Viruses, for example, which can be seen only indistinctly if at all with the light microscope, are seen in some detail with the electron microscope. The phase microscope reveals structure in living cells which cannot readily be seen in the ordinary light microscope.

Microscopic anatomy was founded by Marcello Malpighi (1628–1694), who made extensive discoveries in plant and animal structures. Anton van Leeuwenhoek (1632–1723) observed all manner of living things with his simple microscope and made many discoveries of fundamental importance; he was probably the first to see bacteria. After these early successes little progress was made until the advent of the achromatic light microscope. The modern science of bacteriology was founded by Ferdinand Julius Cohn (1828–1898).

Because most biological tissues are soft and subject to decomposition, they are not easily studied without special techniques. Histological techniques consist of fixing the tissue in order to coagulate its proteins and harden it sufficiently to allow thin sections to be made, and of dehydrating, sectioning, and mounting the sections in a suitable medium on a microscope slide. Just before the final mounting the sections are customarily stained with dyes that are selective for certain classes of tissue or cell components. Entire pieces of tissue or whole small organisms can be sectioned serially, supplying material from which a faithful three-dimensional reconstruction of internal structure can be fashioned.

Mineralogy, Petrography, and Metallography.—The microscope has played a dominant role in the study of minerals and rocks. As early as 1663, Robert Boyle (1627–1691) examined inclusions in a diamond. Rocks were crushed and the grains examined under the microscope by Déodat de Gratet de Dolomieu (1750–1801) and others. This was the method of study until William Nicol (1768?–1851) prepared thin sections of minerals for observation in polarized light. The first systematic use of thin sections for the study of rocks and rock minerals was made by Henry Clifton Sorby (1826–1908). Later workers raised the study of minerals in thin sections to a highly developed tool. Sections are made by sawing thin wafers, which are then ground to a uniform thickness, often less than 0.001 inch. In sections this thin many minerals are transparent and can be observed in polarized light. Others remain opaque and must be studied in reflected light. For this purpose the specimen is ground flat on one side and given a high polish to prepare it for viewing in vertical reflected illumination. Both thin-section and polished-section petrographic techniques are also applicable to the study of artificial cements and ceramics.

Because metals are opaque even in thin sections, they require the use of vertical reflecting illumination. A flat surface of the metal or alloy is ground on successively finer abrasives and finally polished to a scratch-free, mirrorlike finish. It is then etched with a reagent to convert the structureless mirror into a visible pattern revealing the various constituents, the crystal pattern, and the grain boundaries.

Chemical Analysis.—The microscope was introduced into chemical investigations by Andreas Sigismund Marggraf (1709–1782), who used it to observe the crystals he obtained from sugar beets. In 1833, François Vincent Raspail (1794–1878) published what is probably the first book on chemical microscopy. Later, Heinrich Behrens (1842–1905) developed a system of microscopical qualitative analysis, and Émile Monnin Chamot (1868–1950) systematized analytical procedures for the identification of chemical substances with the microscope.

Chemical analysis with the microscope involves two approaches to the identification of unknown materials. In one approach the chemical reactions which result in crystalline precipitates are carried out on a microscope slide, using very small amounts of sample. If well-formed crystals appear, they may be recognized and identified by their morphology, or they may have their optical constants determined with the polarizing microscope. In the second approach the polarizing microscope is used on the original material to determine the optical crystallographic properties of crystalline solids.

Bibliography.—McClung, Clarence E., ed., *Handbook of Microscopical Technique,* 3d ed., rev. and enl. (New York 1950); Martin, Louis C., and Johnson, Benjamin K., *Practical Microscopy,* 2d ed. (New York 1951); Insley, Herbert, and Fréchette, Van Derck, *Microscopy of Ceramics and Cements* (New York 1955); Vickers, Arthur E. J., ed., *Modern Methods of Microscopy* (London 1956); Smith, Herbert G., *Minerals and the Microscope,* 4th ed. (London 1956); Wallis, Thomas E., *Analytical Microscopy,* 2d ed. (Boston 1957); Chamot, Émile M., and Mason, Clyde W., *Handbook of Chemical Microscopy,* 2 vols.: Vol. 1, 3d ed. (New York 1958); Vol. 2, 2d ed. (New York 1940); Hartshorne, Norman H., and Stuart, Alan, *Crystals and the Polarising Microscope,* 3d ed. (London 1960).

GLENN COVEN,
Microscopist, American Cyanamid Co.

MICROTOME, mī'krō-tōm, an instrument designed for cutting thin sections of plant and animal tissues for study under the microscope by means of transmitted light. It may be small and simply designed or very large with extremely complex mechanisms, but the principle is the same in all cases. The three essential parts are a means of supporting rigidly the tissue material to be cut; a knife honed to razor sharpness, held rigidly in the proper position for making the cut, and movable across the tissue in the plane of the cut; and a means of advancing the position of the knife with respect to the tissue by a definite, predetermined, and uniform amount for each cut.

Since the microscope, especially when high magnifications are involved, has a minute depth of focus, and since some materials are relatively opaque, a microtome must be able to cut sections within the range of useful thickness. The more elaborate instruments are susceptible of adjustment to cut any desired thickness between 1 and 60 microns (a micron is approximately 1/25,000 of an inch). The usual thickness employed for histological and pathological tissues is from 5 to 10 microns. Advances in the use of the electron microscope for studying sections have required refinements in the design of microtomes for this purpose so as to make them cut sections as thin as 1/10 of a micron (1/250,000 of an inch).

Microtomes may be grouped into three types —simple hand models, sliding microtomes, and rotary microtomes. In the sliding types the object being cut is usually stationary, the knife moving horizontally over it on sliding tracks. Rotary microtomes have a vertical stationary knife with the object moving up and down across it. In both types the object is advanced after each cut to give the desired thickness.

For the technique of preparing specimens for sectioning and mounting see MICROSCOPY—*Specimen Preparation.*

ROY MORRIS ALLEN,
Author of "The Microscope."

MICROWAVE. See ELECTRONICS—*Microwave Electronics;* RADAR; RADIO—*2. Commercial Applications of Radiotelephony* (Broad-Band Microwave Radio Relay); TELEPHONE—*Radio Relay.*

MIDAS, mī′dăs, in classical mythology, a legendary king of Phrygia (q.v.). Because he befriended Silenus, Dionysius offered to grant any wish he would name. Midas asked that all he touched be turned into gold, but when he found that food and drink were included, he begged Dionysius to take back the gift. This was accomplished by bathing in the Pactolus River, which thereafter was full of gold-bearing sand.

Ass' ears were given Midas by Apollo to punish him for declaring Pan's pipes more musical than Apollo's lyre. By wearing a Phrygian cap, the king concealed his deformity from everyone but his barber, who whispered the secret into a hole in the ground. There reeds grew up to spread the story in the wind.

MIDBRAIN. See BRAIN—*2. Major Divisions of the Brain* (Midbrain).

MIDDELBURG, mĭd″l-bûrg, commune, Netherlands, capital of Zeeland Province, situated on Walcheren Island, 4 miles north-northeast of Vlissingen (Flushing). A market town, it has establishments processing food and manufacturing pianos, furniture, wood and brass products, and textiles. In the Middle Ages, Middelburg enjoyed a flourishing foreign trade as a member of the Hanseatic League. Among its many old buildings are a 12th century abbey with an 18th century tower 289 feet high and a 16th century Gothic town hall. Damaged by fire and bombardment in 1940, they were restored after World War II. The town is the seat of the Museum of the Zeeland Society of Sciences. Pop. (1957) 21,968.

MIDDLE AGES, the term commonly applied to the period of European history between ancient and modern times. Although the period cannot be precisely dated, the fall of the Western Roman Empire (476 A.D.) is often used as a starting point. The first centuries of the Middle Ages are sometimes called the Dark Ages. The whole period is now divided into early medieval history, extending to about 1000; and late medieval history, from 1000 to about 1450 or 1500. See also articles on the 5th through the 15th centuries.

MIDDLE EAST, the region situated mainly in southwestern Asia and northeastern Africa, predominantly Muslim in religion, which may be broadly described as forming the bridge between Europe, Asia, and Africa. For the purposes of this series of articles the term "Middle East" includes the following: *in Europe,* Turkey in Europe; *in Asia,* Turkey in Asia, Iran, Iraq, Israel, Jordan, Lebanon, Syria, Saudi Arabia, Yemen, South Yemen, Muscat and Oman, the Trucial Coast (frequently called Trucial Oman), Qatar, Kuwait, and Bahrain; and *in Africa,* the United Arab Republic (UAR), also known as Egypt, and Sudan. Various adjacent areas could be included in the Middle East, and are from time to time alluded to, but they are formally excluded because of geographic, cultural, or other divergences. These areas include the following: *in Europe,* Greece, other Balkan states, Cyprus, and the Crimea; *in Asia,* Afghanistan, West Pakistan, the Caucasus region, and Turkestan; and *in Africa,* Morocco, Algeria, Tunisia, Libya, Ethiopia, the French Territory of the Afar and Issa (French Somaliland), and Somalia.

The term "Middle East" as here used replaces the older terms "Near East," which applied to the Balkan states plus or minus southwestern Asia, and "Levant," which designated wide areas in the eastern Mediterranean region, although the latter is still useful to designate Israel, Jordan, Lebanon, and Syria. While the term "Middle East" did not become popular until World War II, when it was used extensively by the British Army, it has almost eliminated the older terms.

The total area of the Middle East is 3,509,284 square miles, and the population (1967) is estimated at 140,333,000. Distribution is very uneven. Whereas the Nile Delta has one of the highest population densities in the world, the desert or steppe areas of Egypt, Arabia, Iran, eastern Syria, and western Iraq and parts of Anatolia are almost vacant. Perhaps 90 to 93 per cent of the people are Muslims, 6 to 9 per cent are Christians, less than 1 per cent are Jews, and less than 1 per cent are pagans. The largest city in the region is Cairo, Egypt. The other major centers are Teheran, Iran; Alexandria, Egypt; Istanbul, Turkey; Baghdad, Iraq; Beirut, Lebanon; Ankara, Turkey; Damascus, Syria; Aleppo, Syria; Tel Aviv-Jaffa, Israel; Tabriz, Iran; Izmir (formerly Smyrna), Turkey; and Isfahan, Iran.

Politically, the Middle East is composed of two more or less successful Western-style republics (Lebanon and Israel), two nominal constitutional monarchies (Jordan and Iran), six nominal republics under military control (Iraq, the Sudan, Turkey, Syria, the UAR, and Yemen), and two older forms of monarchy with the ruler limited by custom and religious law (Saudi Arabia and the Sultanate of Muscat and Oman). In addition, there is the republic of South Yemen, formed in 1967 from the former British colony of Aden and the former British protectorate of South Arabia. The sheikdoms of the Persian Gulf are independent but, except for Kuwait, they are under British protection; following an announcement in 1968 that all British troops would be withdrawn from the area by 1971, Bahrain, Qatar, and the Trucial Coast agreed to form a union. Kuwait retains its independence. The small neutral zones northeast of Saudi Arabia are under the individual joint rule of that country and of Iraq of Kuwait. The Gaza Strip, part of the former British mandate of Palestine, was under Egyptian administration until the Israeli-Arab War of 1967; it was then occupied by Israel, together with that part of Jordan west of the Jordan River (including Old Jerusalem), the Sinai Peninsula (part of Egypt), and a small portion of Syria.

The Middle East is strategically the most important geographical area in the world, joining as it does three continents and being integrally related to some of the world's most strategic waterways, especially the Dardanelles and the Suez Canal. The area is washed by the Mediterranean, Red, Black, and Caspian seas, by the Persian Gulf, and by the Indian Ocean. It looks by water in as many directions as it looks by land, and since the dawn of history its geostrategic uniqueness has been recognized by world powers. In modern times two new factors have arisen to accentuate the importance of the Middle East: air communications and oil. The first of these is a mere extension and confirmation of the geostrategic uniqueness of the area. The second is an unexpected new development which by itself would have been sufficient to project the area into the forefront of the world scene. Proved oil reserves constitute almost two thirds of the world's known reserves. Access to these vast reserves is essential to the industrial plant of western Europe and to the growing industries of free Asia and Africa.

In addition to the religion of Islam, the area is characterized in varying degrees by a number of common features. Among them are aridity and a hot climate; the extended family; the presence of nomadic elements; low socioeconomic levels with primary economic dependence on agriculture, but with increasing industrialization; the concentration of leadership in the urban upper and middle classes, which also have been the main channels for modernization; a strong intellectual tradition coupled with low but rising literacy rates; recent exposure to European colonial or quasicolonial rule; and hothouse nationalism. The people of the region also share a pride in the great past of the Middle East, which was the scene of the most dramatic and decisive episodes in the history of mankind. There metals were first worked, animals first domesticated, plants first cultivated, and the wheel invented. The magic symbols which have made mankind's intellectual voyage possible—the letters of the alphabet—also had their first home in the Middle East. Art, architecture, and natural science all flourished there first. The world's great monotheistic religions, Judaism, Christianity, and Islam, all sprang from this soil. In culture as well as in geostrategy the position of the Middle East has been central.

R. BAYLY WINDER, *Princeton University. Revised by the Editors.*

The development of the Middle East, particularly in its ethnic, economic, artistic, intellectual, sociological, and historical aspects, is treated under the following headings:

1. The Land
2. The People
3. Economic Life
4. Cultural Life
5. History
6. Chronology
7. Bibliography

1. THE LAND

The Middle East is composed geographically of six regions: (1) the Nile Valley, (2) the eastern Mediterranean or Levant states, (3) the Tigris-Euphrates Valley, (4) the Arabian Peninsula, (5) Anatolia, and (6) the Iranian plateau. The Nile Valley region[1] is relatively flat in the west and has low mountains paralleling the Red Sea coast on the east. The Levant states are marked by a coastal plain and by two parallel ranges of mountains with a valley between them, and then by a gradual slope down to the Tigris-Euphrates Valley. Except for its mountainous northeastern section, Iraq consists generally of low, flat land. If the Red Sea plain and the mountains of Oman (geologically an extension of the Zagros Mountains of Iran) are disregarded, the Arabian Peninsula may aptly be likened to a limp playing card tilted up from its southwest corner, where the mountains that parallel the coastal plain attain a height of 12,336 feet. On its three water sides, Anatolia also has a coastal strip and parallel mountains, although in some areas the mountains reach the sea; its treeless plateau is somewhat lower than the rim mountains. Eastern Turkey, adjoining Iran, is very mountainous; Mount Ararat (Büyük Ağri Daği) rises to 16,945 feet. Northwestern Iran also is mountainous, and the central Iranian plateau is ringed by mountains—the Zagros on the south and west, the Elburz Mountains on the north, and the mountains of Afghanistan on the east. A fertile plain borders the Caspian Sea, and a barren one the Persian Gulf. Much of the plateau itself is desolate desert.

Geology[2].—While the geology of the Middle East as a whole is both complex and insufficiently studied in detail, its broad features may be outlined. The southern and western areas—the foreland, composed of Egypt and Arabia—consist of plateaus formed by later sediments on a rigid basement of ancient crystalline rocks (the so-called Gondwana land), which resisted folding but occasionally gave way by rifting, especially in early Tertiary times (the Red Sea was a result). Volcanic activity followed this major rift, particularly in the east (the Hejaz). Additional localized faulting and differential erosion have helped to vary the landscape.

North of Gondwana land was a sea called Tethys, in which calcareous sedimentation occurred, forming extensive limestone and chalk. Since the basement of Tethys was less resistant than Gondwana land, in the north and east (Turkey and Iran) earth movements beginning in Cretaceous and ending in Pliocene times produced extensive fold mountains. This folded zone probably resulted from pressure from inner Asia, with Gondwana land providing counterpressure, and the folds are therefore toward the south. In Turkey other factors seem to have been at work, for the folds there are not nearly as parallel as in Iran. The origin of the central Iranian plateau is not clear, but it may be an ancient hard mass—a small-scale Gondwana land.

Between the foreland and this folded zone is an intermediate zone, called the Fertile Cres-

---

[1] In much of this discussion the southern Sudan is disregarded.

[2] This subsection and those on climate, soils, vegetation, and hydrography are largely based on William B. Fisher, *The Middle East: A Physical, Social and Regional Geography*, 3d ed., rev. (Methuen & Co., Ltd., London 1956).

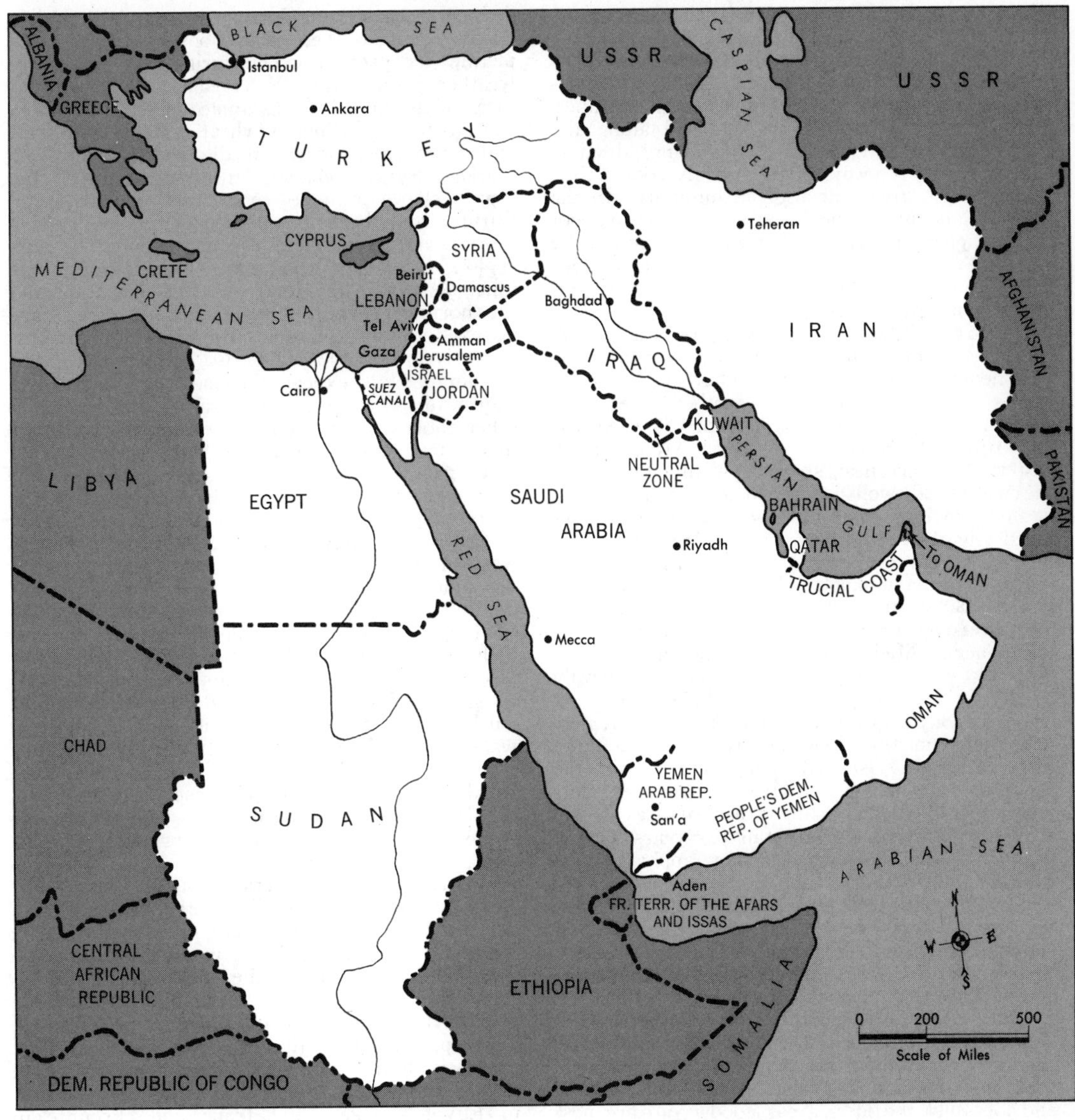

Map showing the area of the Middle East.

cent, where the simple structure of the south gives way to a more diverse topography, but one that is less difficult than the folded mountains to the north. One of the distinctive features in the western part of this zone is the northeastern extension of the Red Sea fault from the Gulf of Aqaba through the Dead Sea and the Jordan Valley. From the upper Jordan the valley veers a little farther east into Lebanon and western Syria. It is no longer a mere continuation of the rift, for it is defined by a fault line in the west only, the eastern side (the Anti-Lebanon) being steeply inclined but not faulted. Volcanic activity has occurred east of the trough, especially in Hauran (Ḥawrān). There has been east-west faulting between Tripoli (Ṭarābulus) and Homs (Ḥimṣ) and at the plain of Esdraelon (Jezreel), producing corridors leading inland from the Mediterranean. The mountains and highlands of the intermediate zone are all anticlinal, and folding has not been abrupt. This folding continues in an arc around the northern part of the Arabian foreland, but the hills are lower and more open in Iraq. It is in the eastern wing of this zone that the great oil deposits are found.

Calcareous strata, including limestone, chalk, and marl, are by far the most numerous rock types. The marls are especially significant because water can penetrate them, and in an arid land human settlement long depended on surface water. The same permeability is found in such rocks as basalts. Igneous rocks are important because of the possible association of metallic deposits; these layers are commonest in Turkey. The sedimentaries carry oil, salts, coal, and gypsum.

Climate.—Temperatures in the Middle East are marked by regularity. July is generally the hottest month (in the coastal regions the sea delays maximum temperatures until August), and January the coldest. The cold weather lasts through February, but thereafter the temperature rises quickly. In Iran and Turkey continental influences are more marked than in the Arabic-speaking countries. In the former winter temperatures are extreme: the January average minimum in Erzurum, Turkey, for example, is −17° F. The Persian Gulf region is probably the hottest area: in Basra (al-Baṣrah) the mean daily maximum in July is 111°. Diurnal variations are likewise extreme, especially in summer, although this feature is less marked along the coasts than inland, where blistering daytime temperatures give way to surprisingly cool nights. There is also great variation in humidity. In the interior humidity is very low in summer and not much higher in winter, but on the coasts the parallel ranges prevent the humid sea breezes from spreading inland, resulting in high humidities and great discomfort.

In most of the Middle East there is a regular pattern of summer drought and winter rain. The first heavy rains begin late in October, but rainfall is spasmodic until late December, when winter really begins. (The same word is used for both *rain* and *winter* in the spoken Arabic of the eastern Mediterranean shores.) While January is the wettest as well as the coldest month in the western regions, maximum precipitation is delayed slightly in the east, and in Iran March is often the rainiest month. By mid-June rain ceases entirely in much of the area for about 12 weeks. Since in most places rain originates in moisture-laden winds from the Atlantic, the westward-facing Mediterranean coastal areas, particularly the mountainous sections, generally attract the greatest precipitation. When the westerlies do not pass over a large body of water, they lose their moisture long before they reach the Middle East. Eastward-facing slopes and the lowlands behind them receive progressively less precipitation, and in many areas of Egypt and Arabia no rain at all may fall for years. These generalizations, however, do not apply to two regions: the Black and Caspian seacoasts, which are influenced by a different climatic system and receive heavy precipitation, including summer rain; and the mountains of southwestern Arabia, where the influence of the monsoons causes heavy summer rains.

Soils.—Depending on climatic conditions, Middle Eastern soils have been classified into arid, semiarid, semihumid, and humid types. The arid soils consist of sand, gravel, saline desert marls, and loess. In the loess areas good crops are possible with irrigation. There are two semiarid types: loamy soils, which when irrigated can sustain intensive cultivation; and dune sands, which offer little scope to agriculture. The semihumid areas are characterized by brown and reddish earths with a hard crust close to the surface. This crust results from a relatively heavy rainfall followed by hot, dry summers, and is formed by chemical action. While shallow-rooted plants may be grown successfully, for trees the crust must be broken to reach the subsoil. In the humid areas is found the characteristic terra rossa of the Mediterranean Basin, which results from the combination of heavy rainfall in winter and drought in summer. Its bright red color is caused by a low humus and high iron content. This soil supports cereals well and, when deep enough, fruit trees, but it is easily eroded. Besides these types directly connected with climatic conditions, there are alluvial soils in various basins and valleys. These soils are heavy, contain humus, and are most suitable for agriculture.

Vegetation.—The Middle East has a wide variety of plants ranging from alpine to desert types, but distribution and types are both sharply defined by aridity and summer heat. Plant life adapts itself to these conditions either by completing its growth cycle during the cool, wet weather (for example, cereals), or by structural adaptation (for example, vines). Mediterranean plants, including wheat, grapes, and fruit and olive trees, grow in the coastal plains of Turkey, Syria, Lebanon, and Israel and on the lower slopes of the mountains behind them. Shrubs and herbs, bulbs, poplar trees, scrub thorns, and evergreen oaks also flourish in this region. A steppe vegetation is characteristic of inner Anatolia, large parts of western Iran, and the northern Fertile Crescent. There trees are nonexistent, but seasonal grasses are numerous. In early spring there are also many flowers, but in summer all except the hardiest bushes and thorns die. In the desert areas the tamarisk and other thorns are the commonest plants, but even in the true desert there is a brief spring period when grasses flower. The mountainous areas are characterized by forest or alpine types of vegetation. One forest type, found in southeastern Turkey, the Zagros Mountains, Lebanon, and western Syria, features mixed coniferous and deciduous trees, among them the celebrated cedars of Lebanon. Another forest type, characteristic of the Caspian side of the Elburz Mountains, includes oak, hazel, alder, maple, and wild fruit trees, as well as dense brambles and creepers. A similar forest type, found east of Sinop in Turkey, also features an indigenous beech tree, walnuts, and rhododendrons. In the higher mountains, there is a limited bush or grass vegetation. Finally, in the river valleys, especially those of the Nile, Tigris, and Euphrates, there are date palms, alders, poplars, and willows, together with lotus, papyrus, and reeds.

Minerals.—The mineral resources of the Middle East are unevenly distributed, undiversified, and, on balance, meager. Oil, the most valuable mineral, is concentrated in Kuwait, Saudi Arabia, Iraq, and Iran, with smaller fields in Egypt, Israel, Syria, and Turkey. Among other fuel resources are the coalfields of northern Turkey, which produce more than 5 million metric tons of coal and lignite annually. Iran also has small deposits of coal. Metallic minerals include iron in Egypt, Turkey, and Iran; and chromite in Iran and Turkey, which is second only to the Philippines in its production. There is some gold in Egypt and Turkey, and Turkey and Iran share deposits of lead, antimony, and copper. Other Turkish metals are zinc, silver, manganese, mercury, and molybdenum. Nonmetallic minerals include phosphates (Egypt), potash and bromine (Dead Sea), gypsum (Iraq), and alum, arsenic, asbestos, emery, sulphur, and meerschaum (Turkey). Various salts are produced by evaporation in most places.

Hydrography.—A striking feature of the Middle East is the absence of perennially flowing rivers in an area that includes Arabia, central Iran, central Syria, western Iraq, and, with the exception of the Nile, Egypt and the northern Sudan. In this vast area ravines called wadies (Ar. *wādī*) are characteristic. When rain falls, these ravines quickly but briefly fill, and not infrequently there are flash floods. Perennial rivers occur in the rainier mountainous areas of Turkey, Iran, and the Levant. The largest of them, the Tigris, Euphrates, and Nile, rise in areas other than those with which they are historically associated. Most of the others are short and steep, and few of them are navigable. Largely because of the coastal ranges, inland drainage is common. This phenomenon is most widespread on the Iranian plateau, but it exists on a smaller scale in Turkey and in Syria east of the mountains. The most famous of the streams whose waters do not reach the ocean is the Jordan, which terminates in the Dead Sea. Like the Dead Sea, most of the closed basins are saline.

See also sections on the land in articles on the various countries of the Middle East.

R. BAYLY WINDER,
Associate Professor of Oriental Studies, Princeton University.

2. THE PEOPLE

The people of the Middle East can be classified into constituent groups according to four basic criteria: (1) physical types; (2) languages; (3) religions; and (4) way of living, based on ecology and occupation. Of these, the first classification is the least important in the consciousness of the Middle Eastern peoples themselves. Though aware of the presence of widely different physical characteristics, they tend to disregard these, and social distance or affinity is felt to be determined by linguistic criteria, religious affiliation, and ecological grouping.

Physical Types.—The great majority of the peoples of the Middle East belong either to the Mediterranean or the Alpine race (which, jointly with the Nordic race, form the white or Caucasoid stock of the human species) or exhibit a mixture of these two physical types. The former, as its name indicates, is found principally around the Mediterranean Sea, and is the predominant physical type on the north shore (Spain, Portugal, southern Italy, and Greece) as well as on the south shore (northern Morocco, Algeria, northern Tunisia, northern Libya, and Egypt) and among the nomads of the Arabian Peninsula. The Mediterranean physical type is characterized by small to medium stature, a slight or moderate build, a long head (cephalic index lower than 75), wavy brown to black hair, brown to black eyes, and light brown to brown skin.

Intermingled everywhere with this type are one or more varieties of the Alpine race, characterized by medium stature, a heavier build, a broad head (cephalic index higher than 80), wavy (occasionally frizzly) light brown to brown hair, light brown to brown eyes, and light to light brown skin. The Armenoid subvariety of the Alpine type—with the strongly curved nose that is often misnamed Semitic or Jewish, and the flat occiput (back of the head)—is found in Armenia and, intermixed with the Mediterranean type, in western Anatolia (Turkey), on the Levant coast (Syria and Lebanon), and in Iraq. In Iran, in addition to the Armenoid type, there is another subvariety of the Alpine race which is occasionally referred to as the Iranian or Scythian type; it differs from the Armenoid chiefly in a somewhat longer head and lighter coloring.

To make the picture more complex, a Nordic strain appears among the Alpines of North Africa (the Berbers) and among some ethnic groups inhabiting the Iranian plateau, adding a percentage of individuals with higher stature and lighter skin and even with bluish eyes and blondish hair. The occasional Nordic type found in Syria, Lebanon, and Jordan can be attributed partly at least to the influx of Nordic strains during the Crusades.

Nigel Watt from Pix, Inc.

Aerial view of Aden, chief port of Southern Yemen.

An infusion of the two other great racial stocks can be observed on the outskirts of the Middle East. Mongoloid elements occur on the northeastern frontier of the area (in Iran and Afghanistan as well as in Turkey), while in the southwestern borderland (in the Sahara, the Sudan, and occasionally in the Mediterranean area and in the Arabian Peninsula) a Negroid intermixture is evident. As one would expect in an area which for thousands of years was exposed to many different ethnic influences, the racial intermingling is considerable in all parts of the Middle East with the exception of some very isolated regions, such as the interiors of deserts.

The Jews of Israel, most of whom settled there after 1948, exhibit many different physical types which show considerable affinity with those predominant in the countries whence they emigrated.

See also ARABS; ASIA—*5. Races;* BERBERS.

Languages.—The Middle East was the historical birthplace of the Semitic languages, and the central part of the area still is inhabited almost exclusively by Semitic-speaking peoples. Arabic, the chief surviving Semitic tongue, is spoken by 80 million persons in the Arabian Peninsula, Iraq, Syria, Lebanon, Jordan, Israel, Egypt, the Sudan, Libya, Tunisia, Algeria, Morocco, and elsewhere. From the Arabian Peninsula, its motherland, it spread all over the Middle East with the Arab conquest following the rise of Islam. As a result of isolation and illiteracy, local Arabic dialects almost unintelligible to outsiders developed everywhere. A Syrian Arab, for example, has difficulty in understanding the speech of a Yemenite Arab or of a Moroccan

Arab and vice versa. The literary Arabic language, which is taught in the schools, is uniform all over the area, however, and is used in books, newspapers, and magazines and partly also in radio broadcasts, theatrical plays, and motion pictures. Arabic is still spreading and continuing to replace other languages which survived in the Arab lands and in North Africa. This is true especially of Tunisia, Algeria, and Morocco, where the older Berber-speaking population is caught in a process of Arabization.

Two other Semitic languages are spoken by small groups. Aramaic or Syriac, once the lingua franca of the Middle East, is spoken only by the Christians (Nestorians) and Jews of Kurdistan (a border area divided among Iran, Iraq, Turkey, and Syria) and in a few villages near Damascus (Dimashq). Hebrew, reintroduced into the Middle East as a result of Zionist settlement in Palestine in the early 20th century, is the chief official language of Israel.

Despite its conquest by Arabs, Iran retained its ancient language, Persian. An Indo-European language with a close affinity to European tongues, Persian borrowed for its script the Arabic alphabet with minor modifications. Persian or Persian dialects are also spoken by almost half of the people of Afghanistan; most of the other inhabitants of that country speak Pushtu (Pashto), a related Iranian language. A third Iranian language, Kurdish, is spoken by the Muslim Kurds, who form the majority of the people of Kurdistan.

Turkish, the chief member of the Turkic family of languages, is the language of Turkey, although it has not completely replaced the other local tongues, such as Greek, Armenian, Kurdish, and the Caucasian dialects of Circassian, Laz, and Mingrelian. Like the Persians, the Turks borrowed the Arabic alphabet for their language, but by government decree they changed to the Latin alphabet in 1928.

A considerable proportion of the population of the Sudan speaks Hamitic and Nubian dialects.

See also ARAB CIVILIZATION—*2. Language;* ARAMAIC LANGUAGE; HEBREW LANGUAGE AND LITERATURE; KURDISTAN; SEMITIC LANGUAGES; TURKISH LANGUAGE.

Religions.—The Middle East is a predominantly Muslim area, with nine tenths or more of the people belonging to one or another sect of Islam. Founded by the Arabian Prophet Mohammed (q.v., Muḥammad, 570/571–632), Islam spread all over the Middle East and beyond it within a century after his death. It soon broke up into major and minor sects, of which the Sunnites (Ar. Sunnī) and Shi'ites (Ar. Shī'ī) have remained the most important. The Sunnites follow the sunnah, the practice of the Prophet as handed down by hadith (Ar. *ḥadīth,* oral tradition), while the Shi'ites regard Mohammed's son-in-law, 'Ali ('Alī), and his descendants as the legitimate successors of the Prophet. Most of the Arab countries and Afghanistan adhere to Sunnite or orthodox Islam, while about half of the population of Iraq and of Yemen and almost all Iranians are followers of one or another sect of Shi'ite Islam.

The common basis of all Muslim sects is the Koran (q.v., Ar. *Qur'ān*), regarded as the word of Allah (Allāh, God) as revealed to Mohammed and containing distinct Jewish and, to a slightly lesser extent, Christian influences. In the Koran, as well as in subsequent Muslim religious literature and doctrine, great emphasis is placed on strict monotheism, in contrast to Christian Trinitarian theology.

An important characteristic of Islam is the absence of a priesthood. Every person is enjoined in an equal measure to fulfill the commandments of the faith, and no appointed or consecrated intermediaries between the common man and God are recognized. The interpretation of the Koran and the application of its law to new problems arising out of the changing everyday life are in the hands of the ulema (Ar. *'ulamā',* singular *'ālim,* the learned ones). Some ulema act as muftis (literally, deciders), who give *fatwas* (decisions) on legal or doctrinary issues. Others function as qadis (cadis; Ar. *qāḍī*), religious judges whose task is to administer the traditional Muslim religious law, the shari'ah (sharia; Ar. *sharī'ah*), which deals not only with ritual and belief, but also with civil, criminal, and constitutional matters. The shari'ah had not yet completely eliminated the older *'urf* (local customary law), which survived in tribes and villages, when it had to begin to give way to modern law adopted from the West by one Muslim country after another.

All Muslims recognize the five pillars of the faith as the quintessence of their religious duties. These are (1) the pronunciation of the oneness of God in the formula "There is no god but Allah, and Mohammed is the prophet of Allah"; (2) fasting during the month of Ramadan, q.v. (Ar. *Ramaḍān*); (3) the recitation of prayers five times a day; (4) the giving of prescribed alms to the poor; and (5) the performance of the pilgrimage to Mecca (Makkah) and Medina (al-Madīnah), the two holiest cities of Islam.

In addition, Islam enjoins on its followers holy war against infidel idolators but commands toleration of those who believe in one God, notably the Jews and Christians. Ethnic groups adhering to these religions were enabled to maintain themselves within the "house of Islam" as protected peoples (*dhimmīs*), and were recognized as distinct minority groups (millets) allowed to regulate their own personal and communal lives in accordance with the tenets of their faiths. Thus, Jewish communities survived in practically all Middle Eastern countries, Zoroastrian (Parsi) groups in Iran, and some two dozen Christian churches in Lebanon, Syria, Iraq, Egypt, and elsewhere.

The Middle Eastern Christian churches fall into two main categories: (1) the Eastern churches organized under their independent patriarchs (the Orthodox Eastern or Greek Orthodox Church, the Coptic Church in Egypt, the Jacobite or Syrian Monophysite Church, the Armenian Church, and the Nestorian or Assyrian Church; and (2) the Eastern Rite (Uniat) churches, which are autonomous but are affiliated with Rome and recognize the pope's supremacy (the Greek Catholic Church, the Syrian Catholic Church, the Armenian Catholic Church, the Chaldean Catholic Church, the Coptic Catholic Church, and the Maronite Church). In addition, the Roman Catholic (Latin) Church and the Anglican and other Protestant churches also have groups of adherents in various Middle Eastern countries.

Outside the three major monotheistic faiths, but close to Islam in their general orientation, are the extremist or heretical sects (from the point of view of Islam, from which they branched off) of the Isma'ilis (Ar. Ismā'īlī), the Druses (Druzes), the 'Alawites (Ar. 'Alawī), the Ahl-i-haqq, the Kharijites (Ar. Khārijī), and the Yazidis (Ar. Yazīdī). The Mandaeans or Sabaeans (so-called Christians of St. John) of Iraq are Gnostics.

Finally, in the southern Sudan and in the northeastern corner of Afghanistan are found the last remnants of old pagan tribes.

Despite considerable differences in doctrine and practice, all religions in the Middle East share a number of common characteristics. Religion is everywhere the central normative force, regulating all action and behavior. Psychologically, it is a powerful sustaining influence. Its great promise to followers is twofold: good life on this earth and rich rewards in the Beyond. While it is intolerant of deviations and of other creeds, it tolerates on the popular level beliefs in demons and spirits and all kinds of superhuman forces side by side with the established principle of monotheism.

See also ARMENIAN CHURCH; COPTIC CHURCH; DRUZE; EASTERN CHURCHES, CATHOLIC; ISLAM; JACOBITES; MARONITES; MOSLEM SECTS; NESTORIANISM; ORTHODOX EASTERN CHURCH; SYRIAN CHURCHES.

Way of Living.—Man made fundamentally different ecological adjustments to the two basic geographical land types of the Middle East. In the nine tenths of the area consisting of deserts with very little rainfall or none at all he developed a pastoral economy based on animal husbandry, while in the smaller, better-watered areas around the deserts or scattered through them he developed an agricultural way of life. The typical inhabitant of the deserts is the nomad whose life depends on the camel. The nomadic camel-herding tribes, especially those of the Syrian and Arabian deserts and the Sahara, pasture their animals in the dry summer season near the cultivable land which receives more rain, and in the winter far out in the desert. The camel provides them with food (meat and milk), clothing and shelter (the hair), and is used as a mount and a beast of burden. On the outskirts of the deserts are the smaller tribal wandering territories of the sheep and goat nomads, some of whom (for example, in Iran and Morocco) practice transhumance—that is, they lead their animals up into high mountain pastures in the summer and down into the warmer valleys in the winter. The characteristic social organization of all nomadic and seminomadic groups is the tribal structure, each tribe comprising families related to one another in the male line. In the Arabian Desert and in the Sahara there are both noble and vassal tribes.

About nine tenths of the people of the Middle East are sedentary, living either in villages or in towns and cities. The villagers, who comprise two thirds of the total population, are mostly cultivators with a narrow subsistence economy. Agriculture ranges from the extensive cultivation of semiarid fields yielding one crop in two or even three years, as in Syria, Iraq, and Iran, to intensively irrigated lands yielding two or even three crops annually, as in Egypt. The village itself is usually a highly nucleated structure with small one- or two-story houses built of mud or adobe in the plains, of stone in the mountains, of palm leaves and fronds in the far south, and of reed mats in the marshes of southern Iraq. Two local developments deserve special mention: the beehive houses in some villages in

Inge Morath from Magnum

Interior of the Church of the Holy Sepulchre, Jerusalem.

northern Syria; and the villages or towns in Yemen and the Hadhramaut of southern Arabia, with their houses of four, five, and even more stories. The life of the villagers revolves around three focal interests: the land, the family, and religion. In all parts of the area the unequal distribution of landed property, with a few large landowners at one end of the scale and many landless cultivators at the other, has created an increasingly serious problem to which more and more attention has been paid by Middle Eastern governments in the form of land reforms and other measures.

Traditionally, the townspeople were either merchants, artisans, administrators, or religious functionaries. To these have been added many modern occupations in the wake of Westernization and industrialization since the beginning of the 20th century. Another outcome of these processes of modernization is urbanization, with such desirable features as an increase in literacy and social benefits and such deplorable ones as a growth of slums.

Wherever traditional forms have been preserved, the people of the Middle East live in large, extended families, often three generations under one roof and under patriarchal rule. The preferred marriage mates in these families are cousins. Under the impact of Westernization this traditional family structure tends to break down, however, and the old forms of personal contact to be replaced by a new, impersonal frame of existence. The emancipation of women is spreading from the Mediterranean shoreline into the interior, together with a decline of polygyny (the marriage of one man and several women) and with such other Western cultural features as general education, sanitation, medicine, and social benefits. Demographically, the Middle East is one of the world's highest fertility areas, with an annual birth rate as high as 50 or even more per 1,000 population. In the underdeveloped regions of the area this high birth rate has been offset traditionally by a similarly high death rate, resulting in no marked natural increase. One of the results of Westernization is the reduction of the death rate, and especially of the rate of infant mortality, without a corresponding reduction of the birth rate. This produces a sudden population increase, which in turn creates considerable economic pressure in some countries, notably Egypt.

RAPHAEL PATAI
Director of Research, Theodor Herzl Institute

3. ECONOMIC LIFE

The development of economic life in the Middle East in the 20th century is the story of a people, long dormant, suddenly awaking to the fact that they have fallen considerably behind in the march of modernization. Their desire to catch up has thrust upon them a difficult struggle against a hard natural environment on the one hand and against a restraining institutional and cultural heritage on the other. This story can best be told by: (1) a description of the limitation to development set by environment and tradition; (2) an account of the deliberate efforts exerted to mitigate these disabilities; and (3) an assessment of results achieved in improving organization, expanding production, and promoting welfare.

Basic Structure.—Economic life is influenced considerably by physical endowments. The physical feature which is most dominant in the Middle East is the desert. Out of a total area of 3,509,284 square miles, only about 223,000 square miles, or approximately 6 per cent, is cultivated. For some countries the percentage is considerably lower. In the United Arab Republic, for instance, not more than 2.5 per cent of the total area was under cultivation before the completion of the Aswan High Dam project in the 1960's. The dam raised the cultivable area to 3.25 per cent. In Saudi Arabia the proportion of the cultivated area is much lower still, amounting to less than 1 per cent. Nevertheless, agriculture is the largest economic activity in most of the countries of the region. Aside from exceptional countries—like Israel, where agriculture is a relatively minor sector; Lebanon, where income from trade and financial services predominates; and Persian Gulf countries, which derive most of their income from oil—agriculture occupies between 50 and 80 per cent of the population and generates one third to one half of the national income.

Since World War II the populations of most Middle Eastern countries have grown at average annual rates of over 20 per 1,000. This rapid growth has resulted generally in great pressure on the land, although the density of population varies considerably from country to country. It is highest in the United Arab Republic, where agricultural land amounts to one fifth of an acre per head of population, while approximately 60 per cent of the working population is engaged in agriculture. This makes the ratio of agricultural population to cultivable land in the United Arab Republic one of the highest in the world. Other densely populated countries of the region, like Lebanon, with one third of an acre, and Israel, with one acre of agricultural land per head of population, do not suffer the same pressure on agricultural resources, since those engaged in agriculture form only one third of the working population in the former and only 12 per cent in the latter. The pressure, although increasing, is much less in countries like Syria, Iraq, and the Sudan, where agricultural land per head of population is about five to six acres.

Barring radical changes in known technology, such as the devising of commercial methods for watering the desert, cultivable area can not be expected to expand to much more than 10 per cent of the total. Even then there will not be much relief from population pressure in the areas where such relief is most needed, since the potentially cultivable lands lie largely in countries with relatively low population pressures, such as Syria, Iraq, Iran, and the Sudan. On the other hand, in the United Arab Republic, where density is high, the increase in cultivable area or in its productivity is very difficult and costly to achieve. Cultivation is already intensive; practically the entire arable land has been brought under perennial irrigation. Furthermore, the strict pursuit of crop rotation and the lavish use of fertilizer and pesticides have raised land yields to exceptionally high levels, thus imposing serious constraints on further rises in productivity.

Another dampener on land yield has been the pattern of land distribution. Before the land reform legislation of 1952 in the United Arab Republic, less than 0.5 per cent of the proprietors owned more than one third of the cultivated land, while three fourths of those engaged in agriculture did not own as much as one acre each. On the other hand, in less populated countries like Syria and Iraq, improvement in land productivity was hampered by absentee large holders and by a system of sharecropping which discouraged, to a certain extent, capital expenditure and modernization of cultivation methods. Land reform legislation was introduced in the UAR in 1952; and in Syria and Iraq in 1958. These reform measures have not been very effective in the latter two countries, but in the UAR, where the redistribution of land was accompanied by other reform measures, including rent control, regulation of tenure, consolidation of fragmented holdings, and the promotion of cooperatives, they have resulted in improved land productivity. Since the redistribution of land covered only about one sixth of the total area, the pattern of holding has not been substantially altered. Almost half of the total area is owned by 4.5 per cent of the owners, but while 0.5 per cent owned more than one third of the total area before the reforms, now they own less than one fifth, and their average holding has declined from 180 to 70 acres per owner. Nevertheless, the fundamental land problem remains one of overall scarcity rather than deficient distribution.

The basic structure of the Middle East's economy, characterized thus by a limited cultivable area, an unequal distribution of land ownership, a predominance of agriculture and pastoralism, and a rapidly growing population, has resulted in low productivity, depressed standards of living, and extremes of wealth and poverty, with the virtual absence of a middle class except in Israel and Lebanon. Since World War II, however, these economic ills have been consciously combated throughout the region with varying degrees of success. The chief forces contributing to success in this struggle against environment and tradition have been the assumption of responsibility for their own destiny by a large proportion of the inhabitants of the region, whose countries became politically independent only after the war; the growing consciousness of the importance of material welfare; the growing drive towards the modernization of techniques; the spectacular expansion of the petroleum industry, which, in the first two postwar decades, poured some $20 billion into the public coffers of the producing countries, and continues to feed government treasuries at an annual rate of more than $2 billion; and the vast spread of education and the marked advance in the levels of technical skills. The chief deterrents to economic and social progress have been political instability, the unbalanced distribution of capital and skilled manpower, inefficient public administration, market limitation, and managerial and institutional deficiencies.

Development Programs.—The conflict of environment and tradition with a rapidly intensifying desire for greater material welfare has generated a common popular belief throughout the region that it is primarily the duty of government to promote economic development. As a consequence, most governments have responded by promulgating programs of public investment. In some instances, these efforts have resulted in the establishment of special planning and development organizations and have taken the form of integrated overall development plans covering a wide range of activity and extending for several years, as in the case of the 5-year plans of Iraq and the 7-year plans of Iran. In other instances, as in Jordan and Lebanon, although special planning organizations have been created, development has not followed long-term comprehensive plans, but has been conducted rather on an ad hoc project basis. In still other instances, as in Israel and Turkey, no special organizations have been created, but public investment has been decided as part of annual budgets and has been effected through existing channels.

The fields to which public investment is applied and the sources of financing it have a direct bearing on the needs and endowments of the countries concerned. In most cases, the two largest categories of development expenditure have been agriculture (including irrigation) and transportation. A concern with irrigation is to be expected, since water is the most precious resource in desert-ridden economies that are overwhelmingly agricultural and pastoral. The discovery of freshwater sources, the conservation and regularization of water flows, the piping of potable water, the extension of irrigation systems, the generation of hydroelectric power, and the control of floods have been the chief targets of public investment in most countries of the region. In the UAR, for instance, the development project overshadowing all others has been that of the Aswan High Dam, with a storage capacity of 130 billion cubic meters of water, an irrigation potential of 2 million acres—adding about 30 per cent to total cultivable area—and an electric power capacity for generating some 10 billion kilowatt-hours a year. Similarly, the most important projects in Iraq have been the Wadi Tharthar and the Habbaniya (Habbānīyyah) schemes for flood control and for the expansion of irrigation. The Litani (al-Līṭānī) project of Lebanon, the Ghāb project of Syria, and the Yarmūk project of Jordan are other instances of the dominance of water in development programs.

Because of greater regularity of rainfall in Turkey and Iran, the paucity of water does not constitute as acute a problem there as it does elsewhere, and their development programs have not been as heavily charged with agricultural projects as those of neighboring countries. On the other hand, because of the existence in these two countries of great expanses and of mountainous areas with poor communications, road construction has figured heavily.

While agriculture and transportation have absorbed the greater part of public investment, a tendency to change the emphasis to industry and the services can be discerned. In the majority of the countries the percentage of the national product generated in the sectors of manufacturing and mining has been growing steadily. Moreover, technical education, health, social services, and scientific research are receiving an increasing share of public investment. As major agricultural and transportation projects get under way, attention is expected to shift increasingly toward the expansion of national industry.

The sources of financing development vary. In the oil-producing countries, development has been financed almost wholly from oil revenue. In Iraq, for example, the government authorizes the use of 70 per cent of its oil revenue for development purposes. Since actual development expenditures have consistently fallen considerably below allocations, it has not been necessary to look for a source of finance other than the oil revenue. In Kuwait, about one third of oil revenue has been ample to cover all development expenditure, one third has been used for ordinary government expenditure, and one third for a reserve fund. In Saudi Arabia, where development has been on an ad hoc project basis, oil revenue has been the sole source of finance.

Transit and terminal fees accruing to the three transit countries—Jordan, Lebanon, and Syria—have been less than 3 per cent of the oil revenue received by the producing countries. Thus the contribution of oil revenue to the financing of development programs in the transit countries has not been very significant. In Syria and Lebanon, the biggest portion of development funds has come from tax revenues. In addition, Syria received substantial development loans from the Soviet Union, and Lebanon contracted a loan of $27 million from the International Bank for Reconstruction and Development applicable to the Litani River project. Until 1956–1957, Jordan received a regular annual subsidy from the British government. Thereafter, the United States augmented considerably its financial assistance, which by the end of 1966 amounted to a cumulative total of $436 million. For many years foreign aid to Jordan has consistently exceeded the portion of its public revenue raised domestically.

The financing of development in other countries varies in source and magnitude. The chief source of domestic finance for most of these countries is tax revenue. Domestic borrowing is not utilized to as wide an extent as in some Western industrial countries. In most Middle Eastern countries, outstanding domestic debts are a fraction rather than a multiple of annual public expenditures. The United Arab Republic, Iran, and Israel have the highest outstanding public debts.

Foreign loans and grants, although a much smaller component of development finance than taxes and royalties, have played a more significant role than domestic loans, and have been an

Inge Morath from Magnum

An arcaded market in Teheran, capital of Iran.

important means of easing pressure on the price level and relieving balance of payments stresses. Turkey, which participated in the Marshall Plan and is a member of OECD, NATO, and CENTO, has been the recipient of the greatest amount of foreign aid. In the two decades following the end of World War II, it received $1,740,000,000 in United States grants and credits alone. This compares with $604 million of United States aid to Iran, $513 million to Israel, $436 million to Jordan, and $172 million to the United Arab Republic. The UAR, Syria, Iraq, Yemen, and the Sudan received substantial Soviet and other Communist aid. By far the largest share of this assistance, reaching a cumulative total of over $1.5 billion by 1967, has gone to the UAR. In addition, the UAR has had two other sources of foreign exchange: a large accumulation of war balances in sterling, which had been frozen and released periodically; and dues from the Suez Canal, which had augmented substantially after the nationalization of the canal in 1956 and had reached the annual level of $200 million before the closure of the canal in 1967.

The various development programs have constituted the response of the governments to the environmental and institutional challenge facing the Middle East. In addition to promoting programs of economic development, most of the governments have attempted social and administrative reforms. Marked strides were made in the direction of reducing graft and corruption in the various civil services and increasing their technical competence and efficiency. A good advance was also registered by both government and private efforts in the spheres of education, public health, social welfare, labor legislation, rural cooperation, and other social relations.

Growth of the Economy.—The public and private development efforts described above have resulted in a substantial growth of the natural product of most countries of the region. The gross national product for the whole region has grown at an annual average of over 6 per cent during the decade of 1957 to 1966, forming a per capita increase of 3.7 per cent. This compares quite favorably with development in other regions, such as South Asia, with a per capita product increase of 1.8 per cent, or Africa, with an increase of 2.5 per cent. This overall growth has been fairly well distributed over the various sectors of economic activity.

Agriculture.—During World War II, agricultural production in the region as a whole declined because of soil depletion and shortages of fertilizers and insecticides, but after the war it picked up and soon surpassed prewar levels. In the first two postwar decades, agricultural output for the whole region more than doubled. The increase is attributable to irrigation, increased use of chemicals, seed selection, the adoption of better methods of cultivation, and the resort to greater mechanization.

The rise in output was confined largely to existing products. From the standpoint of acreage and output, the principal crops are wheat, barley, and cotton. Other important products are rice, dates, beets, sugarcane, olives, and citrus and other fruits. The products registering the greatest postwar expansion were wheat, barley, cotton, and fruits. Turkey and Syria became substantial cotton growers after the war, and Lebanon registered a great increase in the output of fruits, particularly apples and peaches.

Industry.—Before World War I, industrial production in the region was conducted almost wholly under a handicraft system. Thereafter, handicraft production gradually gave way to factory production, although in most countries one still finds in and around towns thriving handicrafts in metalwork, textiles, weaving, rugs, embroidery, and other articles. A modest growth in factory production, mainly in food processing, textiles, and such building materials as cement and tiles took place in the interwar period. During World War II, when the sea lanes were no longer free for trade and imports dropped, industry had a strong stimulus for expansion, and production increased by about 50 per cent. Some of the new industries went out of existence after the war, and others had to undergo drastic adjustments to survive. Despite the reappearance of foreign competition, however, the wartime rate of expansion was maintained and surpassed in the postwar period. Not only were many existing industries considerably expanded, but a good number of new industries were established. The latter included the assembling of motor cars, tractors, radios, and refrigerators; the manufacture of chemicals, pharmaceuticals, electrical appliances, plastics, metal products, and tools; diamond cutting and polishing; shipbuilding and ship repairing; and steel production. Expansion was greatest in Israel, the UAR, and Turkey.

Several forces have contributed to the development of industry in the region. The most important have been the growth of economic nationalism, manifesting itself in state capitalism, as in Turkey and Iran, or in the protection of domestic industry, as in the UAR; the expenditure of oil revenue for industrial development, as in Iraq and Iran; the increase in local demand resulting from agricultural expansion; and the extension of foreign technical and financial assistance.

Although industry has become more important in the economies of the Middle East than at any previous period, it still plays a relatively subordinate role. The contribution of the industrial sector (petroleum excluded) to the national product is as low as 6 per cent in a country like the Sudan, and as high as 18, 19, and 24 per cent respectively in Turkey, the UAR, and Israel. But for the majority of the countries in the region, it ranges between 12 and 14 per cent. The chief hindrances to rapid growth have been the small size of home markets, the shortage of capital in some countries, and the general deficiency in skill and organization. These forces in turn have contributed to the inability of Middle Eastern industrial products to compete in world markets on the basis of price and quality, resulting in a further check to industrial expansion.

Petroleum.—The most vigorous industry is the petroleum industry. Since the early 1930's, petroleum investment is estimated to have gone well over $4 billion. In the postwar period, crude oil production grew spectacularly, rising from 430.4 million barrels in 1948 to 7,938 million barrels in 1973. Middle East production thus amounted to more than a quarter of the world total, and Middle East proved reserves are about 56% of world reserves.

Most of the petroleum extracted in the Middle East is exported. Less than a quarter of the regional production is refined in the region. A good portion of the refined product and almost all the crude are exported. About 15 per cent of the crude exports flow through pipelines to Mediterranean terminals, and the rest is transported by tankers. Petroleum shipments constitute over three fourths of total Middle East exports. By far the greatest part is shipped to western Europe, which receives over 70 per cent of its oil supplies from the Middle East.

Refining increased substantially in the postwar period, rising from about 190 million barrels in 1946 to over 929 million in 1973. During the 1960's there was a notable growth of new large-scale export-oriented petrochemical industries. Ammonia, urea, sulfate, and other chemicals are being produced in different countries of the region.

Trade.—Foreign trade in the region declined to very low levels during World War II, but postwar recovery was rapid and prewar levels were soon recaptured and surpassed. From 1948–1965, exports increased by more than four times and imports by more than three times. Without petroleum exports, imports would have resulted in trade deficits for most of the countries. Of course, imports in the oil-producing countries have expanded rapidly because of the enormous expansion in petroleum exports. On the whole, these countries have had no shortages of foreign exchange and no serious balance of payments problems, except on rare occasions, as when the flow of oil revenue was interrupted in the early 1950's in Iran, or levelled off in the early 1960's in Saudi Arabia. Other countries of the region faced serious shortages of foreign exchange at various times, particularly when their development programs were stepped up in volume and pace. Import surpluses in these countries have been counterbalanced mainly by foreign loans and grants or, in addition, by drawing down their accumulated war balances as in the case of the UAR throughout the 1950's.

Before the war, the bulk of the foreign trade of the Middle East was with western Europe. European trade declined to very low levels during the war, but intraregional trade and trade with Asian countries expanded. While the trade with Europe revived after the war, for the first several years, when Europe was in the process of reconstruction, the United States became the dominant exporter to the Middle East. In the 1950's, western Europe regained its ascendancy and became once again the chief source of Middle Eastern imports, a position which it continues to maintain. Western Europe is also the chief market of Middle Eastern exports, if petroleum is included among the exports. Exclusive of petroleum, however, there is a clear shift in the direction of trade towards eastern Europe. Until the mid-1950's, Middle Eastern exports to Communist countries were negligible. In one decade, countries like Syria and the UAR increased their exports to Communist countries from almost nothing to about one third of total exports in the case of the former and about one half in the case of the latter. Even a country like Jordan, which had not revolved politically in the Soviet orbit, increased its exports to the Communist bloc in the decade from the mid-1950's to the mid-1960's from zero to some 15 per cent.

The composition of exports did not change very much after the war. Agricultural products, chiefly cotton, wheat, barley, dates, and tobacco continued to constitute between 80 and 90 per cent of all exports other than petroleum. There

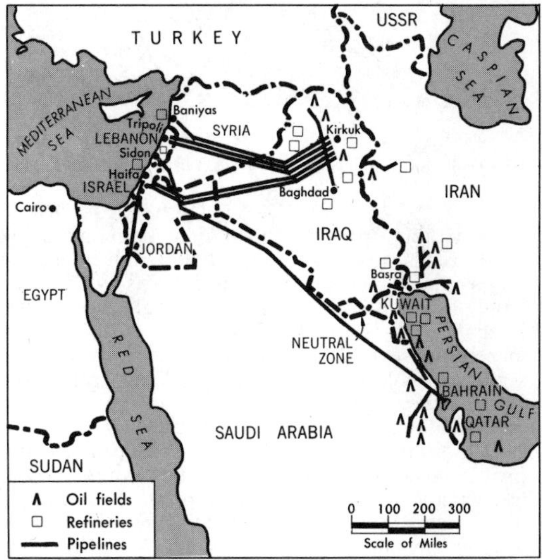

The major oil-producing areas of the Middle East.

were, however, notable changes in the composition of imports. With the spread of local industry the importation of manufactured goods declined, but that of capital goods, including metal products, chemicals, machinery, and transportation equipment expanded considerably. There was also some expansion in food imports, attributable mainly to the increase in population and to the rise in levels of income and consumption.

The terms of trade for the region as a whole registered some improvement during the first decade after the war because of the rise in world prices of cotton and other raw materials brought about by the vigorous program of reconstruction in western Europe and accentuated by the Korean

War. In the second decade, however, the terms of trade moved against the countries of the Middle East. In the period 1956 to 1965 the export-import price index deteriorated by some 10 per cent, placing particular hardship on countries whose exports were dominated by one or two products.

Transportation.—The postwar period marked great activity in the field of transportation, with the main emphasis on roads and airports. There is a continuous growth in the number of passenger and commercial vehicles in every country.

Iraq Petroleum Co., Ltd.

Manifold controlling oil flow from Basra to Fao in Iraq.

Considerable attention has also been given to local roads for facilitating the movement of crops and for connecting rural areas with cities. Civil aviation expanded at a high rate, with international traffic at Middle Eastern airports increasing severalfold. While little railway construction took place except in Saudi Arabia and Iran, large sums were devoted to the improvement and expansion of port facilities.

Finance.—Financial systems have been improved in several countries, and banking activity has expanded throughout the region. New central banks were founded in countries which did not have them, and in most countries agricultural and industrial banks, partly or wholly owned by governments, were established, and existing banks were enlarged. A regional development bank was established by the Kuwait government in 1961 and has extended loans for financing several development projects in various Arab countries. Perhaps one of the most spectacular occurrences in the financial sphere is the development of Beirut, Lebanon, into an international financial center. There are, for instance, over 80 banks registered in Beirut, including branches of American, Russian, and other European and Asian financial establishments of international renown.

ALBERT Y. BADRE, *Professor of Economics Southern Illinois University*

4. CULTURAL LIFE

Many Westerners have the impression that the Middle East is largely a land of shifting sand dunes inhabited by turbaned nomads. While nomads exist, they form only about one tenth of the total population, and in most places their importance is less than commensurate with their numbers. Agriculturalists living in villages constitute two thirds of the population, and the limited role they play in such fields as politics and artistic and intellectual life is therefore even more striking than that of the nomads, whose numbers are after all small. Although this phenomenon is historical to a considerable degree, for the Middle East has in the past typically consisted of a mute mass and an educated elite, this tendency has been reinforced in the 20th century by the fact that modernization has primarily affected the cities. It is the urban fourth of the population that sets the tone of the society.

The purpose of this section is to examine selected facets of the more modernized urban segments of Middle Eastern society. It may be noted that Israel is more modernized than its neighbors because a large proportion of its population consists of persons who emigrated from Europe after World War II. In general, the great variations from medieval Yemen to sophisticated Beirut (Bayrūt) should be borne in mind.

EDUCATION AND LAW

Education.—A prerequisite of a modern society is modern-style education. In the 20th century it has moved forward with relatively giant strides, although many parts of the region, particularly the Arabian Peninsula, still have very few modern educational facilities. Development in education has been especially marked following the withdrawal of colonial or semicolonial regimes in such countries as Egypt and Syria. Naturally, conditions reflect the resultant of financial, historical, and other forces in a given country, but in general it may be observed that Middle Eastern educational systems are highly centralized with little local responsibility, that foreign institutions, once dominant, have receded in importance, that the growth of nationalism is directly related to the growth of modern education, that Middle Eastern scientists have as yet made few real contributions to man's control over his environment (Israel, as often, excepted), and that teacher shortages are endemic.

One of the most remarkable cases of educational progress is that of oil-rich Kuwait, where in 1940 there were no modern-style public schools, but by 1957–1958 there were 44 boys' schools, 38 girls' schools, and 4 kindergartens, with a combined enrollment of 30,000 out of a total population (1957 census) of 206,177, and housed in magnificent plants. A very different pattern is provided by Egypt, which has an illustrious educational tradition going back several millenniums and a modern educational tradition going back into the early 19th century. Although the law nominally compelling free primary education between the ages of 6 and 12 was enacted in 1933, it was still only about half implemented by 1960. In that year, however, Egypt boasted six universities with a combined enrollment of well over 100,000 men and women.

Lebanon and Israel present the most diversified educational systems. The former still relies heavily on foreign institutions at all levels. Of its three universities only one, and that the newest, is Lebanese; the other two are, respectively, American and French. In Israel diversification is of a somewhat different variety. State education, which has been growing, is secular, but provides special religious schools for Jews and Arabic-language schools for Arabs. The Agudat Israel ultraorthodox religious schools and the various schools for young immigrants constitute the main body of private schools. Israel has four universities.

Law.—The legal scene mirrors the transition through which Middle Eastern societies are passing. Before 1800 there had been little change for centuries. In theory, shari'ah (sharia; Ar. *sharī'ah*) or Islamic law ruled, although in practice a set of noncanonical regulations had been followed in certain spheres. Legal reform began in the 19th century in Ottoman Turkey and in its nominal vassal, Egypt. The reforms, both in law and in court systems, resulted from external pressures applied by European powers and from internal pressures of a general modernizing type.

In the 20th century there have been three intertwined legal schools of thought: secularists who have advocated the wholesale substitution of Western law for shari'ah; modernists who have promoted the adaptation of shari'ah to evolving conditions; and traditionalists who would adhere literally to sacred law in its medieval form. In broad terms, secularism has won in Turkey; an amalgam of secularism and modernism is found in the Fertile Crescent and Egypt; and traditionalism still rules, but less strongly, in Arabia.

The early reforms, up to 1915, resulted in (1) a clean break between shari'ah and secular courts; (2) the promulgation of criminal and commercial codes "received" from the *Code Napoléon;* (3) the corollary that judges trained in Western rather than in Muslim traditions could apply the new law; (4) an authoritative codification of shari'ah (*al-Majallah,* 1876); and (5) courts with mixed European and native judges to try civil and commercial cases involving foreigners. Criminally charged foreigners were tried by their consular courts under the capitulations (see CAPITULATION). In 1915 reform also began in a sphere previously reserved everywhere to shari'ah—that of marriage, divorce, and inheritance. The Ottoman law of family rights was promulgated in 1917, and still survives partially in Israel and Lebanon. These reforms were minor, however, in comparison with those of Mustafa Kemal, which revolutionized law in Turkey. In 1926 the Swiss civil code and the Italian penal code were adopted and added to the Turkish commercial code of 1850, itself adapted from the French code. The legal system of Iran was almost as radically changed in the mid-1920's.

In the Fertile Crescent and Egypt the situation has been more complex. In family matters cumulative Egyptian reforms have given wives the right to judicial divorce, restricted the Muslim husband's right to divorce, regulated testamentary matters, and, in 1956, abolished both Muslim and non-Muslim religious courts. Other Arab countries have gone further: in Syria, for example, a law of 1953 empowered courts to refuse a second marriage to a man who could not support two wives and to order a husband to pay alimony where divorce was unjustified and the wife would suffer poverty. Reforms have also continued in civil law. In Egypt a new civil code was drafted in 1948–1949 under the guidance of 'Abd al-Razzaq al-Sanhuri ('Abd al-Razzāq al-Sanhūrī); it was almost wholly adopted by Syria in 1949. Al-Sanhuri also chaired the commission which drafted the new civil code for Iraq in 1951. Both of these codes drew on shari'ah to some extent. The Iraqi code, which was more dependent on shari'ah, was designed as a model for a unified Arab civil code which would mediate between the Westernism of some Arab codes and the conservatism of others.

The Arabian Peninsula is at the other end of the spectrum, for there shari'ah generally rules. In Saudi Arabia, however, some changes have appeared. An ordinance based on the Turkish commercial code of 1850 has been promulgated, and a merchants' council has been established in Jidda (Juddah) to deal with commercial disputes.

JOURNALISM AND LITERATURE

The first Arabic printing press in the world was that of Fano, Italy (1514), and the first in the Arab world was that of Aleppo (Ḥalab, 1702), which was followed by those of al-Shuwayr (1733), Beirut (1751), and Cairo (al-Qāhirah, 1798). The first Turkish press was that of Constantinople (now İstanbul, 1728); the first Persian press, that of Tabriz (Tabrīz, 1816). The press was the indispensable instrument for the spread of mass education, journalism, and literature.

Journalism.—Arabic journalism began in Beirut and matured in Cairo. In both cities, Christian Lebanese directed most of the early periodical ventures. The first private paper in Arabic was founded in Beirut in 1858. The first daily, *al-Junaynah* (The Garden), also was founded there, in 1871. Around 1875 a migration of Lebanese Christian journalists and intellectuals to Cairo transplanted the new medium to Egypt, where the original immigrants and their descendants have continued to be leading journalists and publishers though now eclipsed by their Muslim colleagues. The most distinguished paper is *al-Ahrām* (The Pyramids), which was founded by the Lebanese brothers Salim (Salīm) and Bisharah (Bishārah) Taqla in Alexandria (al-Iskandarīyah) in 1875, moved to Cairo in 1892, and continued under the

G. A. Johnson from Pix, Inc.

A mosaic globe is the focal point of Kuwait's new university. In the background is the university's mosque.

Taqla family until the Egyptian revolution of 1952, when it came under government control. In format and coverage, *al-Ahrām* and other leading dailies in the more mature Middle Eastern countries compare favorably with the leading papers of Europe. The largest circulation reported from the area is that of the İstanbul daily *Hürriyet* (Freedom): 220,000.

In fact, the press in the Middle East has had both a prodigious development and great influence. A 1959 survey reported, for example, 27 dailies in Egypt (in 5 languages), 24 in Israel (in 10 languages), 30 in Lebanon (in 4 languages), 12 in Iran (in 3 languages), and 35 in Turkey (in 4 languages). Comparable figures could be cited for weeklies and other serial publications ranging from comics to scientific journals. Aside from elite productions of the journalistic world, however, many of these papers and magazines are of inferior quality and have very small circulations (a number of them under 5,000), and many are the subsidized organs of regimes, parties, or individuals. Advertising is not yet a major factor.

The importance of the press has transcended its informational aspect, for journalism has been the chief medium for modernizing the various languages, transforming them from their flowery, imprecise, medieval state at the beginning of the 19th century into instruments capable of serving mid-20th century needs. In the 19th and early 20th centuries the press was also the major vehicle for popular education and for the emerging new Western-type literatures.

Literature.—While modern Middle Eastern literature should be considered in terms of the various languages of the region, certain general tendencies may be discerned. The most important is the massive impact of European prose literature, chiefly English and French, on the somnolent, ossified local traditions—an impact so great as to destroy any but a learned interest in the medieval literatures. Initially, Western literary forms came to the Middle East via outright translations or thinly disguised adaptations. Only gradually did they integrate themselves into the local scenes and thereby become simply facets of world literature.

The Western impact made itself felt in the areas of genre, subject matter, and style. The new genres included particularly the short story, the novel (more precisely, the novelette), the drama, and the essay, but ranged beyond them to comprise biography, autobiography, and social and political literature of Western inspiration. Western literary trends from romanticism to existentialism appeared in Middle Eastern literature. In the realm of subject matter the most striking feature was the movement away from medieval court literature to a secular concern for the common man and for everyday problems. The literature of revolutionary protest became commonplace. The development of a modern, comprehensible style was essential if writers wanted to reach anyone but the handful of euphuists who carried on the old tradition. Poetry remained much more conservative than prose, however, and much modern poetry still clings to traditional forms even where it deals with contemporary subject matter.

In distinguishing the separate literatures two general points should be made. First, the chronology of acceptance of the new literature was uneven, with the Turks perhaps a generation ahead of the Arabs, and the Arabs a generation ahead of the Iranians. Second, Israeli literature fits awkwardly into the general scheme, although its problems may not be as dissimilar to those of Arabic literature as appears at first glance. In any case, Israeli authors of the older generation, like Samuel Joseph Agnon (1888–) and Hayim Hazaz (1897–), or younger luminaries like Moshe Shamir (1921–) have either original or translated works in English. Hazaz, especially, has dealt with Arabic subject matter.

In Turkish literature, three writers might be singled out. Ziya Gökalp (1875–1924), who held high positions of state, was the leading nationalistic writer and the intellectual leader of Mustafa Kemal's Turkism. Both his poetry and his prose glorified Turkey, and his *Türkçülük Esasları* (1923; Principles of Turkism) became the bible of Turkish nationalism. A woman writer, Halidé Edib Adivar (1884–), symbolized her sex's rise to literary prominence and established an international reputation. Her works in English include *The Shirt of Flame* (1924), *Memoirs of Halidé Edib* (1926), *The Turkish Ordeal* (1928), *Turkey Faces West* (1930), *The Clown and His Daughter* (1935), and *Inside India* (1937). A new writer, perhaps the first from the whole area who began life as a simple peasant, is Mahmut Makal (1931–). His *Bizim Köy* (Our Village) and *Köyümden Haber* (News from Our Village) have been combined and translated as *A Village in Anatolia* (1954), and the former has also been translated into Russian.

In Arabic literature the Egyptian Tawfiq al-Hakim (Tawfīq al-Ḥakīm, 1902–) is outstanding both as a novelist and a dramatist. One of his works, *Yawmīyāt Nā'ib fī al-Aryāf* (1937; The Diaries of a Country Magistrate), has appeared in English as *Maze of Justice* (1947). Ostensibly a murder mystery, this novelette is also a witty and satirical picture of Egyptian rural society, showing the serious problems which arise when a foreign legal system is imposed on traditional society. The picture of the judge, who commutes to the village from Cairo and signs sentences on the step of the train, is remarkably vivid. Al-Hakim's plays are usually modern symbolic interpretations of older themes—Greek, Christian, Japanese, Arab. Another important figure is the blind Taha Husayn (Ṭāhā Ḥusayn, 1889–), whose autobiography, *Al-Ayyām* (1929–1939), translated in two volumes as *An Egyptian Childhood* (1932) and *The Stream of Days: A Student at the Azhar* (1943), simply but movingly tells the story of the blind country boy confronting his rapidly changing environment. Husayn has also written fiction and important works on literary criticism and cultural problems, some of which have been translated.

The most important modern Persian writer is Sadiq Hidayat (Ṣādiq Hidāyat, 1902–1951), whose *Būf-i Kūr* (1936), written in the manner of Franz Kafka, has been translated into French and English. The latter version is called *The Blind Owl* (1957).

See also ARABIC LITERATURE; HEBREW LANGUAGE AND LITERATURE; PERSIAN LITERATURE; TURKISH LITERATURE.

PERFORMING ARTS

Drama.—No art form represents more of an innovation in the Middle East than does the drama, for even at its height medieval Islamic culture turned a deaf ear to drama as a high art form. At a popular level, marionette theaters, shadow plays (*karagöz* in Turkish), religious recitals, and the Persian *lūṭī*, or Turkish *meddah*, comic buffoons existed and provided vehicles for social criticism, satire, and humor. None had any influence on the contemporary theater, however, for drama in the modern sense was purely a result of Western influence. As in other literary forms, translation came first, with Molière and William Shakespeare especially favored, and adaptations and original works followed successively. The specific inspiration for the early European-style performances was the presence of foreign troupes, particularly Italian.

Under the aegis of the Christian Marun al-Naqqash (Mārūn al-Naqqāsh, 1815–1855), who invited local notables and resident foreigners to his adaptation of Molière's *L'avare* in 1848, Beirut became the first center of the modern Arab theater. From al-Naqqash's death until the opening of the Suez Canal in 1869, however, lack of interest and religious opposition caused a hiatus. Egypt then took the lead, with the construction of the Cairo Opera House for the canal opening by Khedive Ismail (Ismā'īl), who also subsidized actors and playwrights. The range and depth of theatrical performances in the Arab world increased considerably after 1918. Professionalization went on apace, and women, disregarding older taboos, appeared on the stage. Nevertheless, many plays, including some excellent ones, are still written mainly to be read. Melodrama remains the most popular type actually performed, and full emancipation from Western ties has not been achieved.

In Iran the situation is roughly similar to that in the Arab world, one marked difference being that Russia provided much of the early stimulation. After World War II plays glorifying the nation increased in popularity. Prominent theaters in Teheran (Ṭihrān) include the Deghan Theater, which has an attached school of dramatics; the Firdawsi Theater; the Sa'di Theater, specializing in plays by Iranian authors; and the Barbud Theater.

Turkish drama is of the same pattern, although its stages precede the Iranian. Namık Kemal (1840–1888) stands out as a reformist playwright: his patriotic play *Vatan yahut Silistre* (1872; Fatherland or Silistria) caused his arrest and exile. In fact, political oppression retarded the Turkish theater in the late 19th and early 20th centuries. The most celebrated modern writers are Reşat Nuri Güntekin (1892–1957) and Cevat Fehmi Başkut. The most prominent company is the Sehir Tiyatrosu (City Theater) of İstanbul.

The Hebrew theater had initially a unique problem: namely, Hebrew was not a spoken language. Nevertheless, young Jews in Moscow founded in 1918 a Hebrew theater company, Habimah (The Stage). Because it was an aspect of a deeply emotional national feeling, and because its leader, Eugene V. Vaghtangov, was an artist, Habimah succeded. The company toured Palestine in 1928 and later settled there. Now a permanent part of the Israeli scene, Habimah retains as its classic *Haddybbuk*, the Yiddish play of S. Ansky (pseudonym of Salomon Rappaport, 1863–1920), which was translated into Hebrew by Chaim Bialik (1873–1934). Other Israeli companies include Ohel (Tent), whose founder had been with Habimah; Kameri (Chamber Theater), corresponding roughly to American off-Broadway companies; and Matate (Broom), the satirical theater. Amateur theatricals also are numerous.

Cinema.—The cinema, imported or local, is undoubtedly the most popular entertainment medium in the Middle East (it is still barred on religious grounds in much of Arabia), and cinematography has developed strikingly in one country, Egypt, although infant industries exist elsewhere. The first direct Egyptian contact with the medium was via Pathé silent films before World War I. The first Arabic film was made during the war, and studios appeared in the 1930's. The industry has been successful commercially, for Egyptian films, some in color, are shown not only throughout the Arab world, but also in Iran, Israel, the Soviet Union, France, the United States, and South America. Arab films have appeared at international festivals. One of the best of these films, shown in Venice in 1951, is *Ibn al-Nīl* (Son of the Nile), which portrays the corruption of an innocent peasant in the big city.

Language is a problem in films as on the stage. Generally, historical films are in classical Arabic, but other types, such as comedies and melodramas, are in the vernacular. Frequently comic effects are introduced by playing on a Lebanese dialect. A special feature is the emphasis on singing. A post-World War II trend is to make the industry serve propaganda purposes. While censorship is routine, the government has also aided cinematography by sending young people abroad for training and by awarding prizes for quality films. The star system functions as in Hollywood, but there is much less specialization, and individuals sometimes star, write, and produce simultaneously.

Broadcasting and Music.—Radio, which in almost all of the countries is state owned, plays an important role in popular education and entertainment and also in propaganda warfare. While television exists in Baghdad (Baghdād), Beirut, Cairo, Teheran, and Dharan (al-Ẓahrān), its impact has been limited.

Radio is the chief source of Western classical music—a field in which Israel, with its famous Israel Philharmonic Orchestra and its generally creative musical life, holds pre-eminence. Iran maintains a state ballet and a symphony orchestra, and in Turkey there are the Presidential Philharmonic Orchestra and the State Opera. Lebanon maintains the vigorous Lebanese Academy of Fine Arts and the National Conservatory of Music. Moreover, its annual, week-long Baalbek Festival, featuring both local and visiting performers, is one of the artistic highlights of the Fertile Crescent.

R. Bayly Winder,
Associate Professor of Oriental Studies, Princeton University.

ISLAMIC ART

The earliest appearance of a true Islamic art coincided with the formation of an organized and fairly secure Muslim empire in the ancient lands of the Middle East. Very little in this art can be related to the traditions of the Arabian population which made the conquest; most of it finds its origin in the art of the Christian and Zoroastrian empires of Byzantium and Iran, whose artists and artisans simply adapted the techniques, styles, and iconographies of their former patrons to the needs and the taste of the new masters of the Middle East. In this sense, Islamic art is but the last of a long succession of Middle Eastern arts.

Nevertheless, the history of the Muslim world,

as well as specific features pertaining to the faith and culture of Islam, led to many transformations in the earlier styles and types and to the creation of an art which acquired, with regional variations, certain identifiable characteristics. These transformations took place quite rapidly; as early as the 8th century A.D., there was a fully formed Muslim art. The greatest moments of this art occurred between the 8th and the 17th centuries, for by the early 1600's Muslim art as well as Muslim culture in general had lost much of its vigor and originality. In its greatest phases, therefore, Islamic art is a medieval art.

It must first be pointed out that, in contradistinction to what happened in contemporary Christian countries, the main patronage of artists did not come from religious institutions, but from the secular power in its various aspects. The reasons for this are many, but the most important one was that the Muslim doctrine objected, at times even in the strongest terms (although Muslim theologians have never been unanimous on this subject, and the commonly found assertion that the Koran was opposed to images is incorrect), to representations of living beings, especially of men. With a few late exceptions, there are no Islamic counterparts to the illustrated Bibles of Christianity or to the sculptures of cathedrals. Only in one area can one distinguish the direct impact of the faith, and that is in the importance given to calligraphy, whether in beautifully written and illuminated pages of the Koran (Ar. *Qur'ān*) or in splendidly carved inscriptions on tombs or buildings, or else in majestic and elegant holy quotations painted on the tiles of mosques. But, while the central position of calligraphy is no doubt an important characteristic of Islamic art, its effect was comparatively limited.

Islamic secular art, on the other hand, had two primary aims. First, it was supposed to surround the princes and those who imitated princes with beauty and luxury. For this reason, Islamic artists (most often artisans transformed into artists because of the quality of their market) fully developed all the techniques pertaining to what may be called the arts of luxury: ceramics, metalwork, glass, textiles, carpets, and stucco and wood sculpture. In all of these media, Muslim artists made significant contributions, including luster and improved firing techniques in ceramics, better inlays in metalwork, and new methods of weaving in textiles, all of which provided the artist with splendid tools to show his virtuosity and further to enhance the richness of his designs. The second purpose of works of art made for princes was to reflect their actual or imaginary life. It is in miniatures, especially Persian ones, that this side of Islamic art is best expressed, although many examples exist in other media as well, especially in metalwork. Enthroned princes in brilliant palaces or in gardens in bloom, hunting scenes, battle scenes, and love scenes are the commonest themes used to illustrate at the same time traditional subjects of Persian epic or lyric poetry and the splendor of contemporary Muslim life.

The second general point which should be made about Islamic art as a whole pertains to the characteristics of its styles. As a general rule, the Muslim artist was concerned mostly with decorative values. Whether it be the page of a manuscript or the surface of an object or of a wall, the aim of the designer was to create a pleasing and exciting combination of forms and colors. At times the subject matter is subordinated to formal considerations, and the Muslim artist did not hesitate either to create purely artificial spaces on golden backgrounds, with many colored rocks and impossible relations between man and landscape, or to combine in his designs geometric, animal, vegetal, written, and even human elements into endless variations on a few themes. The rules of perspective or attempts at realism are not totally absent from Islamic art, but they are almost always overshadowed by formal considerations pertaining to decorative designs. Among the many features which illustrate the Islamic fascination with decorative values is the arabesque, which combines a denaturalization of vegetal forms with a rhythmic alternation of movement and the filling of the whole area with ornament, and which appeared as early as the 8th century. Each medium developed its own means and techniques, but the striking feature of Islamic art is that in all media the same decorative tendencies are apparent.

In the 17th century the artistic activities of the Islamic world ceased to be creative. Here and there, especially in Muslim India and Turkey, interesting features still appeared, but comparatively little occurred which was entirely new. In the 19th century many stylistic and iconographic traditions previously connected with the royal courts came down to the folk level and became endlessly repeated on objects made in series in bazaars. Certain techniques, especially in ceramics, disappeared completely.

Two major changes have taken place in the 20th century. First, under the impact of western European painting, schools of design were created in several Middle Eastern cities, and the various styles of Western art were transmitted to the Orient. The results, while not by any means negligible, suffer from being too little related to the taste and traditions of the contemporary Muslim world. Second, in a number of countries, especially Iran, a conscious effort has been made to revive the artisan traditions of old and to instill a new life into the techniques which were the glory of the Middle East in the past. The difficulty of such revivals is to create a meaningful vocabulary for these new attempts and to avoid an artificial folklorism. In either case, the trends on contemporary arts in the Middle East are still young for proper appreciation.

See also DECORATIVE ART—*Minor Decorative Arts;* GLASS—*Historical Background* (Mohammedan Near East); ISLAMIC ART AND ARCHITECTURE; LACQUER AND LACQUERWORK—*Near and Middle East;* PAINTING—*Persian Painting;* PERSIAN ART; RUGS, ORIENTAL; TEXTILE FABRICS—*History.*

OLEG GRABAR,
Associate Professor of Near Eastern Art and Near Eastern Studies, University of Michigan.

ISLAMIC REVIVALIST MOVEMENTS

The first noteworthy attempt to rethink Islam in the light of modern developments and to revivify its decadent spirit—an attempt which, in the Middle East at least, was centered in the Arab world—dates back to the mid-18th century, when Mohammed ibn-'Abd-al-Wahhab (Muḥammad ibn-'Abd-al-Wahhāb, 1703–1792) returned to his home in the Nejd from a sojourn in Syria impressed with the idea that Islam as practiced had deviated markedly from the orthodox path. What disturbed the young man in particular were such innovations as the cult of saints, veneration of shrines, and use of the rosary, all savoring of idolatry. In this the influence of the Syrian theologian Ahmad ibn-Taymiyah (Aḥmad ibn-Taymīyah, 1263–1328), whom he had studied in Damascus (Dimashq), and the earlier conservative Ahmad ibn-Hanbal (Aḥmad ibn-Ḥanbal, 780–855) is apparent. Ibn-'Abd-al-Wahhab was also disturbed by the loose application of the shari'ah (sharia; Ar. *sharī'ah*) to such offenses as drunkenness, adultery, and breaking the fast. He felt a call to purify the faith and to restore the majesty of the law. His followers were known as Muwahhidun (Ar. Muwaḥḥidūn, unitarians). While his cause, thanks to its espousal by the Saudi rulers, ultimately achieved success in the peninsula, outside Arabia its only marked traces were in the Senusi (Ar. Sanūsī) order of Libya and the Ikhwan al-Muslimun (Ar. al-Ikhwān al-Muslimūn, Muslim Brotherhood) of Egypt.

The Senusi order derives its name from Mohammed ibn-'Ali ibn-al-Sanusi (Muḥammad ibn-'Alī ibn-al-Sanūsī, 1787–1859), an Algerian who had sojourned in the Hejaz and won a reputation for holiness and wisdom. The system he established was a syncretistic compromise between Sufi North African schools and Sunni Islam. Less puritanical than Wahhabism, it forbade the use of tobacco and coffee but allowed tea and fine clothes. It was also less mystical than Sufism. Before the end of the century its missionary zeal had planted fraternities (*zāwiyahs*) from Fez (Fās) to Damascus and from Constantinople to India, despite opposition from the Turks in Tripolitania and Cyrenaica on political grounds and from al-Azhar sheikhs on religious grounds. Its transformation from a call to reform Islam by peaceful means to a militant organization was conditioned by its contact with the French in the interior and with the Italians, who after 1911 were in occupation of Libya. The king of Libya, Idris I (Muḥammad Idrīs al-Sanūsī, r. 1951–), is head of the order.

The Ikhwan movement was begun in 1928 by a teacher in Ismailia (al-Ismā'īlīyah), Hasan al-Banna' (Hasan al-Bannā', 1906–1949). As a new defense against external attacks on Islam and as a remedy for internal decay, it was timely and effective. Its evolution was conditioned by a spirit of inflamed nationalism in a disturbed period in which British occupation was becoming more irksome to Egyptians and Zionism more aggravating in Palestine. While emphasizing a personal approach to religion and its social aspects, al-Banna' exhorted his followers to return to the teachings of the Koran (Ar. *Qur'ān*) and the practices of the Prophet and his companions. The Ikhwan ideal was the building of a new society on the basis of old Islamic principles and of modern ideas of justice and humanity. Under its dynamic politico-religious leader its membership swelled with disciplined, devoted believers who acted with determination, energy, and singleness of purpose. The program of social welfare and agricultural cooperatives which characterized the early stage of Ikhwan development was later put aside in favor of the struggle against foreign domination. The daring feats of the Ikhwan units in Palestine attracted new admirers, and by the end of World War II the movement could claim a mass following of 500,000 members with branches in Palestine, Syria, and Iraq. Nevertheless, the writings of Sayed Kotb (Sayyid Quṭb), author of *Social Justice in Islam* (1953), and of other Ikhwan spokesmen revealed no thorough insight of the problems involved in creating a social order on the basis of justice and human equality.

Before long the militant revolutionary spirit thus engendered was turned against local political leaders and the government of King Faruk (Fārūq) I. In 1948–1949, following the assassination of the chief of police of Cairo (al-Qāhirah), suppressive measures were taken against the movement, but the coup d'état which forced the king to abdicate in July 1952 gave the Ikhwan a temporary revival. Gen. Mohammed Naguib (Muḥammad Najīb), who became president in 1953, and other officers were members or sympathizers. In 1954, however, the successor of al-Banna' as supreme guide, Hasan al-Hudaybi (Ḥasan al-Hudaybī), was sentenced to life imprisonment, and six others were hanged for complicity in an attempt on the life of Premier Gamal Abdel Nasser (Jamāl 'Abd-al-Nāṣir).

Quite different from ibn-'Abd-al-Wahhab and al-Banna' was the Egyptian reformer Mohammed 'Abduh (Muḥammed 'Abduh, 1849–1905). Born to a peasant family in Lower Egypt, he rose to the two highest religious positions in his country: the rectorship of al-Azhar and the muftiship of Egypt. It was his good fortune to study at al-Azhar under Jamal-ad-Din al-Afghani (Jamāl-al-Dīn al-Afghānī, 1839–1897), the first effective agent of modernism in Islam. Starting from the same premises as al-Afghani and ibn-'Abd-al-Wahhab—the unhealthy condition of Islam and the need for its revivification—'Abduh arrived at different conclusions as to treatment. In his youth he was moderately nationalist, opposed excessive Europeanization under Khedive Ismail (Ismā'īl), and after the collapse of the rebellion of 1882 was exiled to Syria. Later he went to Paris, where he edited an Arabic paper with al-Afghani. 'Abduh kept his writings free from xenophobia. By insisting on both intellectual and spiritual rejuvenation of Islam and by extending a measure of hospitality to the products of scientific research, this liberal scholar contributed more than any of his contemporaries to the cracking of the scholastic shell that had encased Islam. He stood for the separation of religious and political issues; deprecated the resort to violence as a means of reform; and favored a flexible interpretation of the Koran. He wanted to purify Islam not only by eradicating distortions in its teachings, but by fighting vices in Muslim lives.

Such liberal writers as Qasim Amin (Qāsim Amīn, 1865–1908), who ventured to attack polygyny, divorce, and the practice of veiling, owed a clear debt to Mohammed 'Abduh. On the whole, however, 'Abduh's influence was not as widespread as expected. Conservatives, of course, rejected him, and modernists failed to understand him. His biographer, commentator, and disciple, Mohammed Rashid Rida (Muḥammad Rashīd Riḍā, d. 1935), went off on a tangent and initiated a more conservative trend. By the mid-20th century, Muslim thinkers in Pakistan, India, and Turkey had taken longer steps on the path of reconciling the precepts of Islam with the requirements of modern life than their Arab counterparts, but nowhere had the work been completed.

See also MOSLEM SECTS; WAHHABISM.

PHILIP K. HITTI,
Professor Emeritus of Semitic Literature, Princeton University.

5. HISTORY

The history of the Middle East may be divided into five broad periods: (1) from the earliest times to the rise of Islam, (2) the period of the rise of Islam and the Arabs, (3) that of the domination of the Ottoman Turks and the Safavid Persians, (4) the period of growing contacts between East and West, and (5) that of the modernization of the region.

FROM THE EARLIEST TIMES TO THE RISE OF ISLAM

Recorded history had its dawn in what is now called the Middle East, and for 5,000 years its light illumines our path in the region. No other area can display such a record. This is the region in which Western civilization was cradled, nurtured, and developed. With no predecessors to serve as guides, Middle Easterners lifted themselves from the savage state to the highest level of culture attained in antiquity and raised other peoples with them. Enduring elements of their culture—material, intellectual, and spiritual—have become part of mankind's heritage.

By about 3000 B.C., both the Sumerians of Mesopotamia and the Hamites of Egypt had evolved adequate systems of writing, the earliest in history, and had developed urban settlements. The cities developed into city-states, and these in turn coalesced by force or by persuasion to form larger political units. The ground was thus laid for kingdoms and dynasties. By the early part of the 3d pre-Christian millennium, Egypt had established itself on a firm dynastic basis. Outstanding among its early pharaohs were Khufu (Cheops, r. 2590–2568 B.C.), who was responsible for the Great Pyramid at Giza; and Khafre, in whose reign (which began about 2556 B.C.) was carved from the living rock nearby the spectacular Sphinx which still gazes mutely at the sands of the surrounding desert.

See also CUNEIFORM WRITING; EGYPTIAN LANGUAGE AND WRITING; HIEROGLYPHICS, EGYPTIAN.

Imperial Age.—Lower Mesopotamia, more exposed than Egypt to invasion, was not able to achieve nominal unity until about 2360 B.C., under Sargon I of Accad (Akkad), the first empire builder in history. Sargon was part of the Semitic migration which had brought settlers from nomadic Arabia to the Tigris-Euphrates Valley. There the Semites absorbed many elements of Sumerian culture but imposed their own language and rule on the land. Sargon destroyed Sumerian power, consolidated the Mesopotamian realm, and undertook campaigns westward into northern Syria, evidently prompted by a need for the copper, stone, and coniferous trees in which his alluvial land was deficient.

Even more distinguished than the Sargonid (Accadian) line was another Semitic dynasty founded in Babylon, which later gave its name to the entire country. Its sixth monarch, Hammurabi (r. 1728–1686 B.C.), compiled the earliest existing code of laws (see HAMMURABI, THE CODE OF), which he—Moses-like—received from his god, a sun deity called Shamash. In several particulars his code bears a striking resemblance to Mosaic law, which it antedated by half a millennium.

In about 1530, Hittites from Carchemish, on the Euphrates River near the modern Syrian-Turkish border, moved against Babylon, sacked the city, and put an end to the ruling dynasty. The peoples loosely styled Hittites were a mixture of Indo-Europeans and Armenoids, who from their headquarters at Khattusas (now Boğazköy), 95 miles east of Ankara, dominated Asia Minor between 1800 and 1200 B.C., and for a time competed with Egypt for control of the Middle East.

Egypt did not embark on its imperial career until Ahmose, founder of the 18th dynasty (r. 1570–1545 B.C.), pursued the Hyksos invaders to their homeland in Syria. More militarily brilliant was Thutmose III (r. 1490–1436), who incorporated the Syrian-Phoenician coast and the northern part of Nubia into his rising empire. This was the earliest extensive empire of antiquity. Its capital, Thebes, became the most opulent and cultivated city of the day: the renowned remains of the temples, palaces, and tombs at Luxor and Karnak give only a faint idea of its bygone splendor. Especially glittering were the imperial treasures buried with Tutankhamen (r. 1352–1343 B.C.), whose discovery in 1922 dazzled the world.

By the late 12th century, Babylonia and Egypt had declined and the Hittite nation had vanished as world powers—a development which gave Assyria, in the upper reaches of the Tigris River, its chance. The Assyrians were Semites, cousins of the Babylonians. Their essays at imperialism achieved no enduring success until the 9th and 8th centuries B.C., when Aramaean Syria, centered in Damascus (Dimashq), and the Kingdom of Israel, whose capital was Samaria, were conquered. The zenith of Assyrian power was reached under Esarhaddon (r. 681–669 B.C.) and his son Ashurbanipal (r. 668–631), when Upper Egypt was added to the empire. Only 19 years after Ashurbanipal's death, however, the proud capital of Nineveh was wiped out of existence under a joint onslaught of Medes and neo-Babylonians (Chaldeans). The neo-Babylonians were Semites, whose King Nebuchadnezzar II (r. 605–562) checked the advance of Egypt in Syria and destroyed Jerusalem, capital of the Kingdom of Judah, in 587. He adorned his capital, Babylon, with palaces, temples, and gardens, and enriched his land by means of irrigation canals and caravan roads.

See also ASSYRIA; BABYLONIA; CIVILIZATION, HISTORY OF—*Early Civilizations to 1000 B.C.*; EGYPT—*10. History*; HITTITES.

Persian Empire.—The neo-Babylonian dynasty was short lived. A new people, Indo-European in speech and Zoroastrian in religion, was emerging under a great leader, Cyrus (r. 559–529 B.C.), who united the Medes and Persians under his scepter and, in 546, led his army victoriously as far as Sardis in western Asia Minor. In 539 he captured Babylon itself. His son Cambyses II (r. 529–522) added Egypt to the empire. A Persian emperor now "reigned, from India even unto Ethiopia" (Esther 1:1).

A revolt of Ionian Greeks under Cyrus' successor, Darius I (r. 522–486 B.C.), led to a prolonged conflict with the European Greeks, culminating in the battles of Marathon (490), Thermopylae (480), and Salamis (480). The last two battles were fought under Xerxes I (r. 486–465), often identified as the Biblical Ahasuerus. The Greeks construed their victory to imply the survival of liberty against Oriental despotism, an interpretation that cannot be squared with the fact that much of Persian culture, particularly religion, was then higher than its Greek counterpart. In theology and morality, Zoroastrianism yielded to no systems of the ancient world except Judaism and Christianity.

See also ACHAEMENIDS; IRAN—*History* (The Achaemenids).

Legacy of the Ancient East.—Curiously enough, the two most significant contributions of the region were not made by the empire states but by relatively petty countries: Palestine, which gave us monotheism; and Phoenicia, which gave us the alphabet. The Hebrew prophets, who taught the belief in one God, were also hitherto unexcelled moral teachers. Their Phoenician neighbors and relatives developed and disseminated the 22 signs from which all alphabetic systems, Eastern and Western, originated.

The Mesopotamians evolved such early stories as those relating to the creation of man and the world and to the deluge, which through Hebrew channels have become part of the literary heritage of the West. From the same people were derived the sexagesimal and duodecimal systems still used in dividing, for example, the hour into 60 minutes and the day into 12 hours. Sunday is so named because early Semites dedicated the first day of the week to the worship of the sun; Monday was dedicated to the worship of the moon, and Saturday to that of Saturn. Babylonian mathematics and astronomy served as fountainheads for their Greek counterparts, but it was from Egypt that the solar calendar was introduced into the West by Julius Caesar. Galen and other early Greek physicians went to that country to specialize in medicine, in which Egyptians excelled partly because of their interest in mummification. Of all peoples of antiquity, none manifested such a keen interest in life after death, an interest to which the 35 major pyramids and numberless mummies extant bear witness. The *Book of the Dead* (see BOOK OF THE DEAD, THE) survives as the chief literary monument of this firm belief in a future life.

In art as in religion and science, Babylonia and Egypt rose to unprecedented heights, and Persia joined them in this field to form a matchless trio. Surviving specimens of their metalwork, glassware, and sculpture have exercised their fascination on generations of onlookers.

See also ALPHABET; BIBLE—6. *Old Testament History, Including Archaeology and Chronology;* CALENDAR; EGYPTIAN ARCHITECTURE; EGYPTIAN ARTS; EGYPTIAN CIVILIZATION; EGYPTIAN LITERATURE; PALESTINE—*History;* PYRAMID.

Alexander and His Successors.—The meteoric rise and fall of Alexander the Great, who in four years (334–330 B.C.) carried Macedonian arms triumphantly through the Persian Empire from the Hellespont to its eastern provinces and southward into Egypt, forced the course of Middle Eastern history into new channels. The entire area was ushered into the European politico-cultural sphere—first Macedonian and Greek, then Roman and Byzantine. There in large part it remained for 1,000 years. Even after the rise of Islam, Graeco-Roman strands stayed woven in the fabric of Middle Eastern society.

In his advance through Asia Minor the Macedonian invader encountered faint resistance. His victory over Darius III (r. 336–330 B.C.) at Issus (333) opened the way through Syria into Egypt, where his foundation of the city named for him (332) perpetuated his foresight. His second victory over the Persian army, at Gaugamela (Arbela, 331), laid Persia and its capital, Persepolis, at his feet. The Macedonian victor, who claimed to be the legitimate successor of Darius, endeavored to bring East and West together by intermarriage and by the settlement of his troops in Eastern cities.

After Alexander's untimely death at Babylon (323), his generals contended over his empire. The shrewdest of them, Seleucus I Nicator (r. 321–280 B.C.), took the lion's share, extending from the Hellespont to India. Following Alexander's precedent, he built cities, chief among which was Antioch, which became the capital of his dynasty. Ptolemy I Soter (r. 323–283) held Egypt, and with his successors contested southern Syria with the Seleucids. Gradually the Syrian kings lost their hold over Persia, where the Parthians (c. 250 B.C.—c. 226 A.D.) and the Sassanids (c. 226–641 A.D.) established their kingdoms; and over Asia Minor, which was lost to the Romans, the new empire builders of the West. Incompetence, corruption, and intrigue, combined with pressure from Armenians and Arabian tribes, undermined the house of Seleucus, and the *coup de grâce* was administered by Roman legions under Pompey the Great in 64 B.C. Meanwhile, the Ptolemaic kingdom had also come under Roman domination, and in 30 B.C. was incorporated as a province in the Roman Empire.

See also GREECE—2. *Ancient History and Culture: To 330 A.D.;* PARTHIA—*History;* SELEUCIDS; SYRIA—9. *History.*

Hellenism.—The Seleucids and Ptolemies came and went, but the stream of Hellenistic culture, an interweaving of Greek and Semitic elements, continued to flow. It was fed by the scores of Greek cities planted throughout the region. The country folk persisted in the use of their native tongues and in the pursuit of their traditional way of life, but Greek became the lingua franca. It was the language in which Christ's teachings, delivered in Aramaic, were preserved. Alexandria (al-Iskandarīyah) with its library and museum attracted such renowned scholars as the geometrician Euclid (fl. c. 300 B.C.) and the geographer Eratosthenes (c. 275–194). While Hellenism did not strike as deep roots in Persia as in Egypt, Parthian kings inscribed Greek on their coins, and some took pride in entitling themselves Philhellenes. In Asia Minor the ruling houses adopted the tongue and manners of the Greeks and founded and protected Greek cities. In Pergamum (modern Bergama), Smyrna (modern Izmir), and Ephesus the torch of Hellenism continued to burn with a bright flame throughout the Roman period, as it did in Antioch and Alexandria.

See also ALEXANDRIAN LIBRARY; HELLENISM.

Roman Rule.—The eastward march of Roman arms, which began in Asia Minor in 190 B.C. and culminated in the conquest of Syria and Egypt, was checked by the Parthians on their western frontiers. Therewith the center of political gravity shifted from Asia to Europe, where it remained until the rise of the Arab caliphate. For the first time, the Roman, Greek, and Middle Eastern areas were brought under one scepter, and the dream of Alexander was realized by the first Roman emperor, Augustus Caesar.

Under Augustus (r. 27 B.C.–14 A.D.) and his successors a conscious, sustained effort was made to unite the varied parts of their vast domain by building and repairing roads, promoting a postal service, promulgating uniform laws, granting Roman citizenship generously, and spreading the

Pax Romana. The framework of local administrations and trained local officials were generally maintained under Roman provincial governors. Protection from external enemies, immunity from internal strife, and the opening of an imperial market produced an era of prosperity and rising population. Ephesus, Sardis, Smyrna, and Pergamum served as the main commercial outlets for the hinterland and as connecting links with Greece and Italy. In renown and luxury the Syrian capital, Antioch, yielded only to Rome, and in population it vied with the Egyptian capital, Alexandria, for second place. While Egypt was almost a one-city country, Syria had Heliopolis (classical Ar. Ba'labakk; anglicized Baalbek), Berytus (Bayrūt; anglicized Beirut), and other centers on which Roman colonial status had been bestowed.

In the great Heliopolitan temple, built largely by Caracalla (r. 211–217 A.D.) and other members of the Syrian dynasty in Rome, the Semitic Baal-Hadad was identified and worshiped with Jupiter. At about the same time, Berytus became the seat of a school of Roman law which until the mid-6th century drew to the city the best minds of the region. Two of the school's professors, Papinian (d. 212) and Ulpian (170?–228), bequeathed to Justinian's *Digesta* the bulk of its material.

See also ROME—*History of Rome, City and State;* ROMAN LAW.

Rise of Christianity.—The birth and spread of Christianity was one of the most pregnant events in the history of the Middle East under Roman rule. Starting as a Semitic religion, Christianity had to incorporate Greek elements (mainly neo-Platonic) before it became acceptable to the Roman world. This process was begun by St. Paul, a Roman citizen, and was carried on by the Greek fathers of the church in Alexandria. It was the Alexandrian school, headed first by Clement of Alexandria (190–202) and then by Origen (c. 211–231), which developed what became orthodox Christian theology. A later head of the school, St. Athanasius (c. 296–373), had much to do with the formulation of the Nicene creed.

A series of persecutions inflicted on members of the new church, which began with Nero in 64 A.D. and culminated with Diocletian and his successors in 303–313, seems to have had the opposite effect. Christianity was accorded a tolerated, even a favored position by Constantine the Great (r., as sole emperor, 324–337), and it became the official religion of the empire in 380. By then it had established a give-and-take relationship with neo-Platonism and Stoicism, the then dominant systems of Graeco-Roman philosophy, both of which had been deeply influenced by Middle Eastern thought.

See also BIBLE—*14. New Testament History, Including Archaeology and Chronology;* CHRISTIANITY.

Byzantine Empire.—Constantine the Great deserved his epithet not only for his support of Christianity, but also for his choice of Byzantium, situated at the entrances of two seas and the gateways of two continents, as the site of his new capital, Constantinople, inaugurated in 330. This choice recognized the fact that the center of the empire had shifted eastward and foreshadowed its final division. As Rome itself declined, the new Rome on the Bosporus rose, and in 395 one son of Theodosius the Great, Honorius, succeeded him as emperor of the Western Roman Empire, and another, Arcadius, as emperor of the Eastern.

The Eastern Roman or Byzantine Empire was Greek in language, Christian in religion, and partly Eastern in culture. Its power was based in Asia Minor, whose population had been almost entirely Greek in language and orthodox in faith, but most of the Syrians, Mesopotamians, and Egyptians adhered to their vernaculars and developed their own theology, particularly as it related to the nature of Christ. In Arianism, Monophysitism, and Nestorianism (considered heresies by Byzantium), they found a channel for expressing their opposition to imperial rule.

Meanwhile, Persia, rejuvenated under the Sassanids (c. 226–641 A.D.), again aspired to ascendancy in the Middle East and challenged the domination of the West. Syria was overrun more than once, and even Egypt was occupied. Under Khosrau II (r. 590–628), Persian forces penetrated Asia Minor, seized Caesarea, and, in 617, sent a detachment as far as Chalcedon (modern Kadiköy), opposite Constantinople. Because of these protracted wars, Persia and Byzantium so weakened themselves that a hitherto unheralded people was able to emerge and in a short time destroy the one and shake the other to its foundations. These newcomers were the Arabians under the banner of Islam.

See also ARCHAEOLOGY—*Old World;* BYZANTINE EMPIRE; ORIENTAL ARCHAEOLOGY (NEAR EAST); SASSANIDS.

ISLAM AND THE ARABS

The man who founded Islam and initiated the movement that united the Arabians into one nation and launched them on their career as world conquerors was the son of a camel driver of the Quraysh tribe born in Mecca (Makkah) in 570/571. With Mohammed, q.v. (Muḥammad), the Middle East began a new chapter in its history, one in which not only was its existing political structure (except in Asia Minor) replaced by another, but its Christian and Zoroastrian religions gave way before Islam and its dominant languages yielded to Arabic. The practices and beliefs which Mohammed established under the name of Islam constitute a monotheistic system with close affinities to both Judaism and Christianity. This system is based on the Koran, q.v. (Ar. *Qur'ān*), which was revealed by the Angel Gabriel to the Arabian prophet, considered by his followers to be the last and greatest of all prophets. The Koran itself is the earliest and still the most important work in Arabic literature.

When Mohammed died at Medina (al-Madīnah) in 632, he was succeeded by his father-in-law, Abu-Bakr (r. 632–634), who ushered in the series of four caliphs styled orthodox (632–661). All of them were Qurayshites intimately associated with the Prophet. This was the patriarchal period of the caliphate. Its achievements included the subjugation and consolidation of the Arabian Peninsula, the conquest of the Fertile Crescent, Egypt, and Persia, and the compilation and codification of the Koran.

The removal of the capital to Damascus by Mu'awiyah (Mu'āwiyah) I (r. 661–680), also a Qurayshite, ushered in a new caliphate, the Umayyad (661–750), which was more secular and oriented farther to the West than its predecessor. Mu'awiyah behaved like a Byzantine king rather than an Arab tribal chief. Introducing the hereditary principle, he nominated his son Yazid (Yazīd) I (r. 680–683) as his successor. With a well-organized army and a newly created navy he repeatedly attempted to conquer Asia Minor and on two occasions reached Constantinople. The Byzantine capital resisted all Muslim attacks, however, until the advent of the Ottoman Turks. Under 'Abd-al-Malik (r. 685–705) and Walid I (al-Walīd, r. 705–715), the Umayyad caliphate reached the height of its power. By then all of North Africa, almost all of Spain, and parts of Turkestan and India had been incorporated in its territory. Three of the architectural monuments of these two caliphs—the Umayyad Mosque in Damascus and the Dome of the Rock, q.v. (Qubbat al-Ṣakhrah) and the Aqsa Mosque (al-Masjid al-Aqṣā) in Jerusalem—still rank among the finest in Islam.

See also ARABIA—*History;* UMAYYADS.

Abbasid Caliphate.—In 750 the Umayyad caliphate was superseded by the Abbasid (Ar. 'Abbāsid), likewise of Qurayshite origin, which established a new capital at Baghdad (Baghdād) in 762. This was the longest-lived caliphate (750–1258) and, thanks to the glamorous court of Harun al-Rashid (Hārūn al-Rashīd, r. 786–809) and stories about it in *The Thousand Nights and a Night* (*Alf Laylah wa-Laylah;* see ARABIAN NIGHTS, THE), the most celebrated. Under the patronage of Harun and his son al-Ma'mun (al-Ma'mūn, r. 813–833), Arabic, hitherto a language of poetry and religion, came to possess the chief works of Aristotle in philosophy, the masterpieces of Hippocrates and Galen in medicine, and the major treatises of Euclid and Archimedes in mathematics. Other translations were made from Persian. The translators were mostly Syrians, whose normal procedure was to translate first from Greek into Syriac. Through these acquisitions, Islam became a cosharer with Christianity and Judaism of the classical heritage and was to that extent alienated from its desert traditions. The translators were followed by research workers of Persian, Syrian, Egyptian, and other nationalities who made distinct contributions in Arabic. Geber (Jābir ibn-Ḥayyān, fl. late 8th century) of Iraq was the father of alchemy (from Ar. *al-kīmiyā*). A Persian, al-Khwarizmi (al-Khwārizmī, 780–?850), produced in Baghdad (c. 830) a mathematical work whose title included the word *al-jabr,* whence *algebra* is derived. When translated into Latin in Spain, al-Khwarizmi's works introduced Arabic numerals to the West. (The Arabs themselves had received them from India and therefore called them Hindi.) Another Persian, Avicenna (ibn-Sīnā, 980–1037) of Bukhara (Bukhārā), wrote a medical compendium used as a textbook for years in its Latin rendition. A Damascene, ibn-al-Nafis (ibn-al-Nafīs, d. 1288/1289), had an elementary conception of the pulmonary circulation of the blood centuries before the Europeans were credited with that discovery. Many of the Arabic works were rendered into Latin in the 12th century in Toledo and so contributed to the intellectual awakening of Europe.

What we call Arab science was basically Greek science expressed through the medium of Arabic and enriched by the contributions of scholars of varied nationalities living under Islam. The Muslim Arabians started with no science, philosophy, or art of their own. Their transmission of Greek philosophy into Europe was accompanied by commentaries that clarified the texts and made them more palatable. The master commentator was Averroës (ibn-Rushd, 1126–1198) of Spain, whose works in their Latin versions were used as textbooks until the end of the 16th century. What we call Muslim or Arab art was likewise the art of Persians, Syrians, and Egyptians developed in the Islamic period and adapted to the needs and tastes of Muslims. In it the representation of animate objects was held to a minimum, and multicolor was stressed.

The Abbasid caliphate began to decline in the 10th century. Seljuk and other Turks, Persians, and Bedouin Arabians began to build their own states at its expense. Originally nomadic tribesmen from Central Asia, the Seljuks first infiltrated Persia and Mesopotamia, where they were Islamized, and then spilled over into Asia Minor. The Battle of Manzikert (now Malazgirt, 1071), in which their sultan, Alp Arslan, decisively defeated the Byzantine emperor, Romanus IV Diogenes, opened the door for their settlement and colonization of Anatolia. Meanwhile, two mighty caliphates, one Sunnite (Ar. Sunnī) in Córdoba (929–1031) and the other extreme Shi'ite (Ar. Shī'ī) in Tunisia and Egypt, shared with the Abbasids pre-eminence in Islam. That of Tunisia and Egypt, called Fatimid (Ar. Fāṭimī), endured from 909 to 1171, when it was destroyed by Saladin (Ṣalāḥ-al-Dīn). It figured in the annals of the Crusades, as did the Ayyubids (Ar. Ayyūbī, 1171–1250) and Mamluks (Mamelukes; Ar. Mamlūks, 1250–1517), who succeeded it.

The Shi'ites (partisans, that is, of 'Ali) believed that God through Mohammed had designated his son-in-law, 'Ali ('Alī), as his successor (*khalīfah,* caliph), and that successorship was hereditary, limited to 'Ali's progeny. Accordingly, they considered the Umayyads and the Abbasids usurpers and took advantage of every opportunity to harass or fight them. In general, the Shi'ites were nonconformists and split into numerous sects, but the orthodox Sunnites presented a unified front. While the bulk of the Muslim community maintained its Sunnite creed, there were times, as under the Fatimids, when the political ascendancy of that community was seriously threatened.

See also ABBASIDS; ARAB PHILOSOPHY; ARABIC LITERATURE; AYYUBID or AYUBITE; CALIPHATE; CRUSADES; FATIMIDS; SCIENCE, HISTORY OF—*Brief Outline;* SELJUKS.

Mamluks.—The destruction in 1258 of the Abbasid caliphate and with it Baghdad by the Mongol Hulagu resulted in the further fragmentation of political Islam. Mongols superseded Seljuks in Persia and Mesopotamia; Mamluks had already replaced Ayyubids in Egypt and Syria. The Mamluks (1250–1517), as the word indicates, were originally slaves, Turkish and Circassian, who had usurped power and held it by force. Their successful resistance to the repeated attacks of Tatar and Mongol hordes in the 13th century saved Syria and Egypt, and their military campaigns against the Crusaders cleared the land of the last Franks. Though mostly greedy, cruel, and uncultured, if not illiterate, the Mamluk sultans left a number of mosques and schools in which the Egyptians still take pride. It was in the Mamluk period that *The Arabian Nights* took its final form.

In 1516–1517, Mamluk power was overthrown by Selim (Salīm) I, the Ottoman sultan. Originally Central Asian tribesmen, the Ottoman Turks had gradually infiltrated the westernmost part of Asia. They had adopted Islam before their arrival in Anatolia, where they built on foundations laid by the Seljuks. Their name was derived from their ancestor chief Osman (Othman; Ar. 'Uthmān) I (r. 1288–1326). Half a century later his successors invaded Europe. By capturing Adrianople (modern Edirne) in 1361, they outflanked the Byzantine capital, cut it off from its Balkan hinterland, and isolated it from its potential supporters, the Slavs. By the time of Selim, the Ottomans were already firmly established in Asia Minor and the land opposite it in Europe. Constantinople itself had been conquered by Mohammed (Muḥammad) II in 1453 and had become the Ottoman capital; this marked the end of the Byzantine Empire. Before attacking the Mamluk domain, Selim had battled the Safavid (Ar. Ṣafawī) shah, Ismail (Ismā'īl) I, of Persia and, in 1514, had wrested from him a large part of Mesopotamia. The Turks had acquired the use of firearms in Europe, and against Selim's troops, armed with muskets and supported by 300 cannon, the Persian cavalry had no chance. These weapons were equally effective against the Mamluks. By decisively defeating Mamluk forces in northern Syria (1516) and capturing Cairo (al-Qāhirah, 1517), Selim brought Syria, Egypt, and western Arabia under the ascendant Ottoman crescent. The acquisition of the holy cities of the Hejaz raised his prestige throughout the Islamic world. With that the last vestiges of Arab power vanished, and the Ottoman Turks and Safavid Persians assumed the leadership of Islam.

See also ARCHITECTURE—*Islamic;* ISLAMIC ART AND ARCHITECTURE; ISLAMIC LITERATURE; MAMELUKES.

OTTOMAN TURKS AND SAFAVID PERSIANS

During the 16th century the coast of North Africa as far as the eastern border of Morocco was overrun and held by Turkish agents. This conquest was made possible by the development of the Turkish navy to first-rate rank under Selim's son Suleiman (Sulaymān) I (r. 1520–1566), generally considered the greatest of the sultans. No small share of the credit for his success belonged to his grand vizier, Ibrahim (Ibrāhīm) Pasha, the son of a Greek. In Europe even Vienna was attacked (1529), and the sultan's realm extended from Budapest to Baghdad and from the Crimea to the First Cataract of the Nile.

Ottoman Empire.—The empire founded by Mohammed II and enlarged by Selim I and Suleiman I was the mightiest Muslim state of modern times and the most enduring. The dynasty counted 3 emirs and 36 sultans, all in the direct male line of Osman, the last being Mohammed (Muḥammad) VI, deposed in 1922. In territory the empire was the heir of Byzantium and of the successor states of the Arab caliphate. In due course, the sultans claimed to be the legitimate caliphs and were so recognized.

Suleiman, known as al-Qanuni (al-Qānūnī, the lawgiver) to his people, and as the Magnificent to Europeans, codified a system of laws, based on the sacred law of Islam, the shari'ah (sharia; Ar. *sharī'ah*), that remained standard until the reforms of the 19th century. His court was magnificent, and so was his capital, which he adorned with mosques, palaces, and other public works, mostly undertaken by his chief architect, Sinan (Sinān), originally a Christian slave. Sinan's masterpiece was the exquisite Suleiman Mosque (Sulaymānīyah), which was designed to eclipse Hagia Sophia. Its mosaics and faiënce decorations were in the Persian style. Tiles, patterned on Seljuk models, reached the height of their artistry. Previously blue and white had been the popular colors, but now a brilliant scarlet was used in combination with emerald green and turquoise. The predominant flower pattern was the tulip, carnation, and rose. Other cities also benefited from Suleiman's munificence, Jerusalem and Mecca, for example, having their water supply improved.

The culture developed under the sultans blended Turkish, Persian, Arab, and Byzantine elements. From the Arabs the Turks acquired their religion, their science, and the Arabic alphabet, which remained in use until it was replaced by Latin characters in 1928. The thousands of Arabic words embedded in the Turkish language, relating to theology, law, medicine, science, philosophy, and art, testify to the intellectual debt the Turks owe the Arabs.

The Ottoman Empire was basically military and dynastic. Its subjects, a conglomeration of Turks, Arabs, Kurds, Armenians, Slavs, Greeks, and Albanians, were held together by the sword of Osman. There is no doubt that the empire furnished stability to a large area of the Middle East and maintained it for centuries. While the Ottomans constituted a class by themselves, they accepted anyone who adopted Sunnite Islam and their style of Turkish and generally conformed to the social pattern considered correct by Ottoman high society. In this they resembled the Umayyads and the Abbasids in their attitudes toward non-Arabians. The Turkish-speaking element remained a minority, however, and it could not colonize any area in Asia except Anatolia. Early in their imperial career the Ottoman sultans imposed on their Christian subjects a levy of boys, who were drawn to the capital to be Islamized, Turkicized, trained, and pressed into service as government officials or soldiers. The dreaded corps of Janizaries (q.v.), responsible for many a Turkish victory, was recruited from this levy. More than one prime minister, vizier, admiral, and general were once slaves and so remained, at least in theory. They held their positions, property, and even their lives at the pleasure of the sultan-caliph.

As the Ottomans pushed the boundaries of their empire eastward, the Persians under a new and energetic dynasty, the Safavid, were pushing their frontiers westward. This struggle involved more than Mesopotamia: the stake was supremacy in the Middle East, with the Turks replacing the Romans.

Safavid Dynasty.—In the Safavids (1502–1736) the Persians acquired their first national dynasty in eight centuries. Since the time of the Sassanids they had been almost always under alien rule. Just as the Sassanids had been inspired by a revival of Zoroastrianism, so the Safavids, who traced their descent from 'Ali, were inspired by Shi'ite Islam. Proclaiming Shi'ism as the state religion, they became alienated from the Sunnite Turks. Ismail I (r. 1502–1524), founder of the dynasty, started the country on its fresh career of progress and expansion. His defeat at the hands of Selim I in 1514 served to rally his people around his throne with intensified loyalty.

The successive defeats of his successor, Tahmasp I (r. 1524–1576), by Suleiman I had the same effect.

The most highly esteemed of the Safavids was 'Abbas ('Abbās) I the Great (r. 1587–1629), who recovered several western provinces from the Ottomans, reorganized the army, cultivated the arts and literature, fostered trade, and pursued an enlightened foreign policy that involved diplomatic relations with his European contemporaries. His public works included new roads, caravansaries, and schools. The palaces, mosques, and public baths that he built in his capital, Isfahan (Isfahān), made it a wonder of the world.

Safavid power began to fade after 'Abbas and was finally extinguished by the Afghans in 1722. The eclipse was brief, however, and Persia soon found a new leader in Nadir Shah (Nādir Shāh, r. 1736–1747), chief of the Afsharid (Turk. Afshārī) Turkish tribe, who freed the country and restored its unity. He also attempted unsuccessfully to make the Persians renounce Shi'ism in favor of Sunnism. Nadir embarked on a military campaign which added Afghanistan to his domain and carried him as far as Delhi, which he sacked in 1739. The spoils of the Mughul (Mogul) capital included the Koh-i-Noor, the famous diamond now among the British crown jewels; and the Peacock Throne, still used by the Iranian shahs. Once again the Persian Empire extended from the Indus to the Caucasus, but Nadir's conquests were of short duration.

Artistic and Literary Developments.—The political revival under the Safavids was reflected in the arts. The entire period was one of architectural development, in which color, polychrome, and mosaic faïence were emphasized. 'Abbas I brought from China 300 potters, whose influence is manifest in the delicate coloring and refined designs of Safavid porcelain. Metalwork continued in the classical pattern. Carpet weaving, with Isfahan, Tabriz (Tabrīz), Kashan (Kāshān), Kerman (Kirmān), and Herat (Harāt) as principal centers, became and remained the outstanding medium for expressing the Persian feeling for decoration. With carpets went textiles—silk, satin, and brocades—featuring themes from nature, particularly flowering gardens.

Curiously enough, the impetus given political and artistic life in this era had little effect on literature. The last of the classical poets, Jami (Jāmī), had died in 1492. He had dominated the 15th century poetically, as Hafiz (Ḥāfiẓ) had dominated the 14th, and Sa'di (Sa'dī) the 13th. Later poetry and prose generally lacked originality. Subordinating content to form, Persian writers used ornate similes and inflated figures of speech.

Nonetheless, the influence of the Persian language and literature transcended the limits of the empire. In India, Persian poetry was the dominant genre at the Mughul court. In Turkey, which had a scant native literary heritage, Ottoman writers used Persian (and Arabic) works as models. As in Persia, an artificial style became prominent in Turkish literature. Moreover, many Turkish writers composed poetry in Persian, among them Selim I, who left a divan (Per. *dīwān*) of Persian odes. Outstanding among the Turkish poets of the period was Fuzuli (Fuẓūlī, d. 1555/1556 or 1562), who sang the glories of love, which, as a mystic, he considered more than a profane emotion. Turkish Islam was tinged with a mysticism of its own, and Sufi orders throve in Anatolia. For a time, even Ottoman historians preferred to write in Persian. The most distinguished of the official historiographers was Na'imah (Na'īmah, d. 1716), whose work, covering the reigns of Selim and Suleiman, displays a high standard of accuracy and thoroughness. One of the most renowned men of letters Turkey produced, Hajji Khalifah (Ḥājjī Khalīfah, 1600?–1658), wrote his bibliographical masterpiece, *Kashf al-Zunūn,* in Arabic. In this work, which is still widely used, he arranged alphabetically the titles of all works in Arabic, Turkish, and Persian of whose existence he was aware. In the 17th century, which saw the beginning of political decay, Turkish literary activity continued its normal course, although there was a substantial increase in the numbers of books dealing with religion and mysticism. With the impact of Western thought in the 18th century, Persianizing and Arabicizing tendencies faded away.

See also DECORATIVE ART—*Minor Decorative Arts;* PAINTING—*Persian Painting;* PERSIAN ART; PERSIAN LITERATURE; RUGS, ORIENTAL; TEXTILE FABRICS—*History;* TURKISH LITERATURE.

Political Decline.—The Ottoman state began to decline early in the 17th century, and the Persian state followed it a century and a half later. While the continuity of the house of Osman for more than six centuries gave a measure of unity and stability to the Turkish Empire, it deprived it of the advantage of reinvigoration through new blood which Persia had had. The basic weakness in the Ottoman structure was its reliance generally on force rather than on commerce and diplomacy. Persia presented a more compact geographical unit and a more homogeneous ethnic and religious grouping. Linguistically, too, it was less diversified. Moreover, its greater distance from Europe mitigated the effect of disrupting Westernizing forces. In contrast, Turkey not only was fitfully engaged in war against Persia, but had to contend with European foes and subjects as well.

The Afsharid series of rulers inaugurated by the energetic Nadir Shah numbered only four; before it came to an end in 1796, the country was in a state of anarchy, with petty dynasties of Persians, Afghans, and Turks rising all over the land. In the struggle for power a eunuch of the Turkish Kajar, q.v. (Ar. Qājār) tribe, Agha Mohammed Khan (Agha Muḥammad Khān), seized Teheran (Tihrān), which he made his capital in 1785, and gradually gained control of the entire country. He became shah in 1796, but was murdered in the following year. Agha Mohammed's castration as a boy by political enemies of his family had made him a pathological figure with a sadistic lust for domination. His Kajar dynasty lasted until 1925.

The Ottoman state had more destructive elements inherent in its structure than the Persian. Degeneracy among the sultans, the growth of corruption and of harem influence, and the inevitable decline of the military undermined central authority. Among the empire's subjects the line of cleavage was sharply marked not only between Muslims and Christians, but also between Muslim Turks and Muslim Arabs and between one Christian sect and another. The millet system recognized the right of each religious community to a considerable measure of self-rule. Cases relating to marriage, divorce, inheritance, and other problems of personal status were left to the ecclesiastical heads of each community. Fragmentary loyalties were thus promoted and maintained. Other elements of weakness were embedded in the political structure of a state organized primarily for warfare rather than the welfare of the people. Chief among these was the centralization of authority in the hands of one man, the sultan-caliph. Under him power was divided between the military (the viziers generally belonged to this class), representing force; and the ulema (Ar. *'ulamā',* learned theologians), representing religion.

The general run of sultans after Suleiman and Selim was mediocre. Ambiguity in the right of succession to the throne provided ambitious members of the house of Osman with opportunities to seek the throne, resulting in endless intrigue and civil strife. To ensure succession to his son, the ruling sultan often murdered his brothers. Suleiman's grandson Murad (Murād) III (r. 1574–1595), for example, opened his reign by killing 5 of his brothers, and the latter's son Mohammed (Muḥammad) III (r. 1595–1603) murdered 15 of his. With this went another practice, that of confining the heir apparent in a carefully guarded kiosk in the seraglio, which often resulted in arresting his growth. Abdul Hamid ('Abd-al-Ḥamīd) I (r. 1774–1789) was kept in such a cage for 43 years, an experience which left him weak in mind.

Provincial Government.—Misrule, corruption, and decay in the central government were reflected in the provincial government of the Ottoman Empire. The concern of the typical provincial official was to provide the treasury in Constantinople with all possible revenue and the military with manpower, while ensuring his own future by compensating himself in an office that he usually had bought. Taxes were therefore farmed out to the highest bidder, and little heed was paid to the improvement of agricultural or industrial methods, to say nothing of exploiting the natural resources of the land. Without certainty of tenure the viceroy or pasha could ill afford to lose time in replenishing his own purse. In Syria's first 184 years as an Ottoman province, 133 pashas succeeded each other in Damascus, and Egypt's record was worse. Moreover, as the central authority declined, respect for its representatives in the provinces decreased proportionately and the aspirations of local chiefs increased. Some provinces lapsed into anarchy or passed under native control, which was not always an improvement over Ottoman rule. By the mid-18th century, the Syrian area between Aleppo (Ḥalab) and the Euphrates, once fertile and sufficiently irrigated to support kingdoms, had become a desert. By the end of that century the population of Syria-Palestine, which may have reached 5 million in Roman days, had dwindled to an estimated 500,000.

Mountainous Druse (Druze)-Maronite Lebanon fared better. Local authority was in the hands of feudal lords, first the Ma'ns and then the Shihabs (Ar. Shihābs), under whom the country enjoyed a measure of security and progress that its neighbors did not experience. The feudal lords did not furnish troops to the Sublime Porte, and they exercised the power of life and death over their subjects. One of the Ma'ns, Fakhr-al-Din (Fakhr-al-Dīn) II (r. 1590–1635), carved a principality which embraced western Syria and northern Palestine. In 1608 he negotiated with Ferdinand I de' Medici, grand duke of Tuscany, a treaty containing a military article directed against his sovereign. One of the Shihabs, Bashir (Bashīr) II (r. 1788–1840), allied himself with Ibrahim Pasha of Egypt in the conquest of Syria. After prolonged civil disturbances, culminating in the Christian massacre of 1860, Lebanon was granted in the following year an autonomy recognized by the great powers of Europe. It was placed under a Christian governor nominated by the Porte, but it paid no imperial taxes and offered no troops. The progress that it made in this period of self-rule, which was abrogated during World War I, had no parallel in any other Ottoman province.

In Mesopotamia, Ottoman pashas contended with Mamluks and local chiefs while the people suffered. The situation was made worse by the periodic attacks of Bedouin tribes. The land of ancient renown under Nebuchadnezzar and of medieval splendor under Harun al-Rashid faded under the Ottomans to a degree probably unmatched in its long history. Since Mesopotamia lay between the two major powers of the Middle East, parts or all of it changed hands repeatedly in the 16th and 17th centuries. The Turko-Persian wars adversely affected the economy of the land and interfered with pilgrimage to its shrines, the holiest in Shi'ism. From 1747 to 1830 the country was in the grip of a Mamluk oligarchy composed mostly of imported Circassian slaves.

Egypt was the unhappiest province of all. For a time, the theme was the recurring conflict between pashas from Constantinople and Mamluks from different lands, while the natives sank deeper into poverty. Some of the Mamluks had the advantage of having been acclimatized in Egypt and of having acquired some of its language, but on the whole they were less cultured and more oppressive than the Ottoman officials whom they superseded. Pestilence and famine worked havoc: in 1619 the plague carried away about 500,000 persons, and in 1643 it left 230 villages desolate. The country, whose population had reached 8 million in Roman days, had by the end of the 18th century about 2.5 million inhabitants.

In 1769 one Mamluk took the logical step of proclaiming himself independent. Reportedly the son of a Christian priest from the Caucasus, he came to Egypt as a slave and took the name of 'Ali ('Alī) Bey. Not content with nominal independence, he assumed the title of sultan and struck coins in his own name. For ally he chose a Bedouin sheikh of Palestine, Zahir al-'Umar (Ẓāhir al-'Umar), who had expelled all Ottoman officials from his province, made Acre ('Akkā) the seat of his government, and revived it as a port for the export of silk and cotton. Both usurpers were disposed of by bloody rivals, 'Ali in 1773 and Zahir two years later.

In western Arabia, Ottoman sovereignty was from the outset more nominal than real. The Hejaz was under the control of the sherifs (Ar. *sharīfs*) of Mecca, descendants of the Prophet, and Shi'ite Yemen was mostly ruled by native imams. Neither was mindful of what was going on in the empire. In the mid-18th century signs of new life became manifest in the Nejd, where Mohammed ibn-'Abd-al-Wahhab (Muḥammad ibn-'Abd-al-Wahhāb, 1703–1792) initiated a puritanical revival. The new prophet found in a Nejdi (Ar. Najdi) chieftain, Mohammed ibn-

Saud (Muḥammad ibn-Su'ūd, d. 1765), an ally and son-in-law. This marriage between religion and the sword, a recurring theme in Islam, resulted in the spread of Wahhabism (q.v.) through central and eastern Arabia. In 1803–1804, Mecca and Medina fell into the hands of Wahhabi (Ar. Wahhābī)-Saudis, who purged them of what they considered idolatrous innovations, such as saints' shrines and venerated tombs. In 1805, Wahhabi hordes invaded Syria and Iraq, bringing their state to a height unattained in the peninsula since the orthodox caliphate, but between 1811 and 1818 they were crushed by Mohammed 'Ali of Egypt.

See also IRAN—*History;* TURKEY—*History: The Ottoman Empire.*

EAST AND WEST

Military Contacts with the Ottoman Empire.—The Ottoman state was established at the expense of a European power; it embraced the Balkans and Hungary, and for centuries the keynote of its contacts with eastern and central Europe was warfare. Geographically, it was partly European, but culturally it was almost entirely Asian. In the 17th century it warred repeatedly against Spain because of Tunisia; against Venice because of Crete, Cyprus, and navigation rights; and against Russia because of the Ukraine, Azov, and trading rights on the Black Sea. The struggle against Russia and Venice was carried on into the 18th century. As late as 1683, almost 400 years after its birth, the Ottoman state was on the aggressive vis-à-vis Europe. The restoration of its striking power under the Kuprili (Köprülü) viziers culminated in a full-scale siege of Vienna, stronghold of its major European enemy. This was the last high-water mark of the Ottoman military tide, and the failure of the siege marked the reversal of Turkey's position.

Meanwhile, a new enemy loomed in the north. Under Peter the Great, Russia drove southward in quest of warm-water ports. In 1696, Peter took Azov from the Turks, and from 1768 to 1774 Catherine the Great warred against them. Her troops invaded the Ottoman-ruled principalities of Moldavia and Walachia; conquered the Crimea; and, on July 21, 1774, exacted from the Porte an especially humiliating treaty, that of Kuchuk Kainarji (modern Kainardzha). By this treaty not only did Russia require its enemy to pay a large indemnity and to recognize its right to free navigation in Turkish waters, but it also acquired the right to protect the Greek Orthodox Christians of the Ottoman Empire. This last provision furnished Russia with the opportunity of interfering in Turkish internal affairs, and Russian influence virtually replaced French influence at Constantinople. Russian claims for the protection of the holy places in Palestine, to which France also had a claim, were a cause of the Crimean War (1853–1856), in which Great Britain and France were allied with Turkey. Neither of these powers wished to see Russia installed on the Bosporus, and this international rivalry gave Turkey a new lease on life.

The Treaty of Kuchuk Kainarji was the first political manifestation of what became known as the Eastern question, but was actually a Western question that involved the carving of spheres of influence in a decadent Eastern empire by the rival great powers of Europe. Two of the four imperialist contenders, Austria-Hungary and Russia, were interested in territorial annexation. The two others, Great Britain and France, with their worldwide trade and colonies, were interested in the area both for its own sake and for its strategic position athwart their imperial life lines. Once the terror of Europe, the Turk had become its sick man.

See also EASTERN QUESTION; RUSSO-TURKISH WARS.

Commercial and Political Contacts with Persia.—It was in the Safavid period that western Europe first discovered Persia. The contacts were primarily economic, derived from the British presence in India and that of the Portuguese in the Persian Gulf, but commercial relations often led to political complications and entailed military action.

Only two years after Vasco da Gama's return (1499) from the first all-sea journey to India, Portuguese ships and fleets were ready to do business in the subcontinent. In 1515 the Portuguese began trade relations with Persia, and in 1561 the English followed suit. Under 'Abbas I, in 1616, the East India Company began to penetrate the Persian market. The resentment of Portuguese traders led to a conflict in which, in 1622, the Persians, aided by the forces of the company, captured Hormuz, the leading mart on the Persian Gulf, which the Portuguese had held since 1515. Thereafter, British influence outweighed that of other countries in the shah's court and in the gulf. English merchants received special privileges in Hormuz, whose exports included carpets, cotton, wool, fruits, and gum. Nearby Bandar Abbas (Bandar 'Abbās), founded by the shah in 1623, subsequently became the center of international trade in the gulf. In 1763 the English established a factory at Bushire (Būshihr).

Early in the 18th century a new influence made itself felt in Persia, when the urge that had impelled Russia southward through Turkey also became effective farther east. Peter the Great invaded Persia and seized Baku and other cities in 1722–1723, and in 1724 he entered into an agreement with Turkey for the dismemberment of Persia, with Turkey retaining the right to hold Tabriz and other cities which it seized that year. Only 11 years later, however, Russia relinquished its acquisitions in Persia and joined in an alliance with Nadir Shah against their common enemy, Turkey.

Ottoman Attempts at Reform.—Until the 18th century almost all Turkish importations from Europe had been conditioned by military considerations. Beginning with gunpowder in the 14th century, they included shipbuilding, navigation, artillery, and military engineering. (In the nonmilitary field mention may be made of the Italianate style of architecture.) The introduction of a printing press in 1728 was not due to Turkish initiative. Nevertheless, there was a new awareness on the part of certain Turkish leaders that Europe had far outstripped the Turks in all fields, and that their own traditional synthesis of faith, state, and sword had become inadequate to meet the challenge of a changed and changing world. That Europe was coalescing into new nationalist states, supported by unprecedented industrial and economic development and an expansion of trade and political influence to the remotest parts of the world and armed by swift striking power to defend their interests, was realized only slowly and tardily. Three bold sultans endeavored to cope with a desperate situation, but their efforts lacked adequate implementation and were on the whole ineffective.

Selim (Salīm) III (r. 1789–1807) established military schools on European lines, with compulsory French instruction. He also promulgated regulations for the revision of the tax system, which were opposed by corrupt officials, and for the reorganization of the military system, which were opposed by the Janizaries. Deposed by rebellious Janizaries in 1807, he was murdered in the following year.

Selim's nephew and disciple Mahmud (Maḥmūd) II (r. 1808–1839) was fully occupied with wars in the Balkans, which resulted in the independence of Greece (1830) and the rise of Egypt under Mohammed 'Ali, but he did remove a huge obstacle in the path of national progress when, in June 1826, he had the artillery of a new loyal corps turn its guns on the Janizaries' barracks and left the mob to do the rest. An estimated 6,000 to 10,000 Janizaries were massacred. Once the shield of the state, the corps had for years been its scourge. Under Mahmud the study of French became more widespread. Introduced to implement a military program, the new language became a key to unlock a treasury of all kinds of thought—political, social, economic, scientific, philosophical—some of which were more effective than physical weapons. For the first time, Western institutions and ideas began to make serious inroads. The belief in the perfection of the Ottoman way of life, which national pride, fostered by centuries of phenomenal success, had engendered, was being shaken.

The regulations of Abdul Medjid ('Abd-al-Majīd) I (r. 1839–1861) aimed at removing the disabilities under which non-Muslim subjects labored by guaranteeing the lives, property, and honor of all subjects and by considering all of them, regardless of race or religion, as equal before the law. Influential ulema did not approve of the new measures, however, and foreigners with extraterritorial rights derived from capitulations did not like them. The capitulations, which originated with the Venetians under Suleiman I, had later been extended to French (1535), English (1580), and other European residents.

In any event, it was too late for reforms to redeem the situation. The independence of Greece was followed by that of Rumania, Serbia, and Montenegro, all of which were recognized by the Treaty of San Stefano in 1878. At that time, Bulgaria also was given autonomy, leading to its final detachment from the Porte in 1908. Of the Arab lands, North Africa was the first to be lost. Algeria was occupied by the French beginning in 1830, Tunisia followed in 1881, and the British occupied Egypt in 1882.

Abdul Aziz ('Abd-al-'Azīz, r. 1861–1876) followed in the footsteps of his brother Abdul Medjid, whom he succeeded. His interest in Western civilization led him to visit the Paris Universal Exposition of 1867 and to include London and Vienna in his tour. He was the first sultan to travel abroad. In 1868, after his return to Turkey, the French *lycée* of Galata Serai was founded, and in 1870 the University of Constantinople was reorganized, and its school of law established. Law was one of the fields which Ottoman scholars cultivated and in which they were specialists.

See also CAPITULATION.

Reaction in Turkey.—The flow of liberal ideas from the West was checked by the long, reactionary reign of Abdul Hamid II ('Abd-al-Ḥamīd, 1876–1909), one of Turkey's most oppressive sultans. He began his reign with a liberal-minded grand vizier, Midhat (Midhat) Pasha, who had drafted a national constitution modeled on those of France and Belgium. The first of its kind in the Ottoman Empire, the constitution acknowledged Islam as the state religion but declared all subjects to be personally free and to be known as Ottomans. It guaranteed freedom of the press and provided for a bicameral Parliament with deputies elected for four-year terms to represent constituencies of 50,000 each. The sultan proclaimed the constitution on Dec. 23, 1876, but it remained in effect only until Feb. 13, 1878, when he dismissed Parliament. Meanwhile, in February 1877, he had banished Midhat. As a means of reorienting the country toward Asia, he adopted the idea of reviving Pan-Islam as a political power and of placing himself at its head as caliph. To this end, he elaborated the fiction that the Abbasid caliphate had passed to the Ottoman sultans through a puppet caliph, al-Mutawakkil, whom Selim I had found in Syria in 1516. All Westernizing elements were repressed by the sultan-caliph, who forbade Turkish Muslims to attend Robert College, which had been founded in Constantinople in 1863 as an American missionary enterprise. Rather than appease threatening Western powers, Abdul Hamid endeavored to wield as a club his pretended leadership of the Muslim world. In pursuance of his Pan-Islamic dream he completed in 1908 the Hejaz Railway, linking his capital with the holy cities of Islam.

Meanwhile, Germany had won a place for itself among the imperialist powers of the West. Its rapidly increasing population, remarkable industrial development, and quest for foreign markets, combined with its naval inferiority, dictated a new policy of *Drang nach Osten* (thrust toward the East), which soon made its influence preponderant at the Porte. In 1898, William II visited Constantinople, Jerusalem, Beirut, and Damascus, where at the tomb of Saladin he pledged eternal friendship to the sultan and his Muslim followers. A concession for the Baghdad Railway (q.v.) was given to a German company in 1899, and German officers were used to train a new Turkish army. Britain construed the railway, which when completed would connect Berlin with the Turkish provinces, as a threat to its favored position in the Middle East and in India.

Opposition to Abdul Hamid, begun by the Young Ottomans, who were inspired by Midhat, was continued by the Young Turks, whose striking force was the Committee of Union and Progress, a secretly organized society whose headquarters were at first in Geneva and later in Paris. Gathering strength, the committee engineered a successful military coup on July 24, 1908. Abdul Hamid immediately proclaimed the abolition of espionage and of censorship, the release of all political prisoners, and the restoration of the constitution of 1876. He had no more intention of preserving the constitution in 1908 than in 1876, however, and when he was discovered to be intriguing with other reactionaries, he was replaced by his doddering brother, Mohammed (Muḥammad) V (r. 1909–1918). Real authority remained in the hands of the Young Turks, whose rise to power was a turning point in the life of the Ottoman state.

Foreign Influences in Persia.—Persia was drawn into the orbit of great power politics not long after Turkey, but it revolved therein at a much quicker pace. With the death of 'Abbas I in 1629, it ceased to be an important power, and in succeeding years it passed through more than one chaotic period. Nevertheless, it did not fully realize its inadequacy to meet the challenge posed by its foreign relations until the early 19th century. As in the case of Turkey, Persian interest in Western civilization was circumscribed at first by military needs, but those needs could not be met adequately without the study of a European language. Once the language barrier had been broken, the people became exposed to modern nationalistic, democratic, and other dynamic ideas. Moreover, the Persians were soon to realize, as the Turks had done before them, that military development was only one aspect of national life, and that it could not be achieved without a corresponding development of economic, social, and other spheres.

At this time, corruption was the rule in Persian administration, and prodigality in court life. Especially wasteful was the court of the second Kajar shah, Fath 'Ali (Fatḥ 'Alī, r. 1797–1834), with its large harem and countless favorites. Fath 'Ali thought his opportunity had come in 1807, when Napoleon, who had failed in his Egyptian campaign to carry out his scheme of striking at the British Empire through India, negotiated an alliance under whose terms France agreed to send officers to train and equip a Persian army for the invasion of India. Heretofore the Persians had relied on cavalry recruited mainly from nomadic tribes, and Fath 'Ali welcomed the opportunity to use a modernized army against Russia. As in the case of Turkey, however, the new developments came too late to save the day. The French military mission (1807–1808) was succeeded in 1810 by the British; others from other countries followed. The role of Persian politicians was reduced to playing one power off against another. Great Britain persisted in its view that Persia lay on its imperial life line, while Russia considered the annexation of Persia essential to its designs in Central Asia. Russia's fresh advance through the Caucasus was concluded with the Treaty of Turkmanchai (now Turkman, 1828), by which Persia paid a heavy indemnity, waived its right to the largest Caucasian provinces, and even granted its powerful enemy extraterritorial rights patterned after those exacted under the Turkish capitulations. These rights later were claimed by other European consuls and residents, and the independence of the country and the sovereignty of its government were thereby seriously impaired.

During the long reign of Nasir-al-Din (Nāṣir-al-Dīn, 1848–1896), foreign influences grew in importance. More or less forced concessions, including the Imperial Bank of Persia, telegraph lines, and a railway system, were granted to the British, while the cultivation and trade of tobacco were transferred to European capitalists. The shah, who was only 16 years old at his accession, showed a genuine interest in Western civilization. He visited Europe three times, founded the first modern college in his capital, and sent young Persians to France to acquire not only military training but education for other professions. Agitation in favor of a new order became more articulate. A brilliant writer, Jamal-al-Din al-Afghani (Jamāl-al-Dīn al-Afghānī), exposed corruption in high places and demanded reforms, but as a Pan-Islamist he found a more congenial atmosphere in Abdul Hamid's court. One of his disciples assassinated the shah.

Meanwhile, the state religion of Shi'ite Islam was affected by the rise of a new sect called Babism. Its founder was 'Ali Mohammed ('Alī Muḥammad), a Shi'ite Sufi of Shiraz (Shīrāz), who proclaimed himself the Bab (Ar. *bāb*, door), the gateway to esoteric knowledge of divine truth. As such he arrogated to himself the means of communication between believers and the hidden imam (Ar. *imām*), eagerly awaited by Twelver Shi'ites. He favored equality of the sexes, cessation of the obligation of veiling, and the abolition of circumcision and of ritual ablutions. In neo-Pythagorean style, he attached a hidden significance to numbers, especially 19. The prescribed annual fast was reduced to 19 days, and the daily reading of his book, containing his reforms, to 19 verses. The Bab was executed at Tabriz in 1850, and about 40,000 of his followers were massacred two years later.

A disciple successor, Mirza Husayn 'Ali (Mirza Ḥusayn 'Alī), adopting the title of Baha'ullah (Bahā' Allāh, splendor of God), assumed the mission of revising the Bab's system. In reality, he started a new system. Following an attempt on the shah's life, Baha'ullah was exiled to Baghdad in 1852 and later was interned by the Ottoman government in Adrianople and Acre. Meanwhile, he had proclaimed himself the manifestation of the divinity and the apostle of the final revelation not only to Islam but to all mankind. In his exile he had absorbed certain Christian doctrines and liberal ideas current in Europe, which he combined with his mystical Shi'ite heritage to create Baha'ism. He condemned war, preached human brotherhood, and advocated a universal language. His eldest son, 'Abbas ('Abbās) Effendi, who succeeded him in 1892 and was known as Abdul Baha' ('Abd-al-Bahā', slave of Bahā'), stressed the pacifist, humanitarian, and cosmopolitan elements of the Baha'i (Ar. Bahā'ī) system, which aspired to become a universal religion. The success of the movement in the United States, which he visited in 1912, encouraged its propagation in Germany and other European countries. In Persia itself, however, Baha'i proselytizing activity was met with hostility by the Muslim majority.

See also BABISM; BAHA'I FAITH.

Anglo-Russian Rivalry in Persia.—In the fashion of his father, Muzaffar-al-Din (Muẓaffar-al-Dīn, r. 1896–1907) undertook European trips at great cost to the treasury, which, with the added drain of the expenses of his courtiers and favorites, was unable at times to pay officials' salaries. Loans from Russia did not provide a satisfactory solution. As the shah led his country toward bankruptcy, the constitutional movement passed from the hands of the few Western-educated youths to the merchant class and even to the theologians. Finally, in December 1906, the shah signed a parliamentary constitution, which marked the nominal transition of the country from an absolute to a constitutional monarchy. Muzaffar-al-Din died in January 1907, and was succeeded by his son Mohammed 'Ali (Muḥammad 'Alī, r. 1907–1909), who with Russian support endeavored to abolish the constitution despite his repeated oaths to preserve it. On June 23, 1908, he bombarded the Parliament building, provoking a revolution which forced him, in July 1909, to seek refuge in the Russian legation, abdicate, and flee the country. Meanwhile, Russia and Great Britain, determined to present a common front against German penetration of the Ottoman Empire, temporarily put aside traditional rivalries and agreed to divide Persia between them. The Anglo-Russian Convention of 1907 opened with a solemn declaration to respect "the strict independence and integrity of Persia," but the Persians took the declaration to be the tribute which hypocrisy pays to sincerity. They stood helpless under Russian domination in the north and center and that of Britain in the south.

Conditions continued to deteriorate under Ahmad Shah (Aḥmad Shāh, r. 1909–1925). The Anglo-Persian Oil Company (later, Anglo-Iranian Oil Company) was formed in 1909 on the basis of a 1901 concession to an Englishman, William Knox D'Arcy. Expecting only exploitation from European powers, the Persian government turned to the United States for aid and advice. In 1911, William Morgan Shuster was appointed on the recommendation of Washington to reorganize the country's finances, but his services were terminated under Russian pressure in December of that year. On Nov. 1, 1914, Persia declared its neutrality in World War I, but its soil soon became a hotbed of international intrigue and its frontiers a battleground of British and Russian against Turkish and German forces. After the war, in 1921, the new Bolshevist regime in Russia renounced by treaty the claims and privileges inherited from the czarist era.

Literary Developments.—Turkish response to Western intellectual stimuli was slower than the response to military stimuli. Although the French language was studied in Turkey by the first decades of the 19th century, translations did not appear until 1859, when a student returned from Paris, Ibrahim (Ibrāhīm) Shinasi, rendered into Turkish selections from French poets. Before long the Turkish reader could sample works by Molière, Victor Hugo, Alphonse de Lamartine, and Jean Jacques Rousseau. These and other writers opened a window onto a different philosophy of life. Meanwhile, the Turkish writer discovered that he could free his idiom from pomposity and artificiality, adapt it to scientific thought, and make it comprehensible to the public. Young writers favored the new, simple style and realized that the old Persian school had outlived its usefulness.

In Persia itself writers since 1500 had added little in form or content to the inherited store of accepted subjects and styles. The 18th century was almost barren in the field of poetry, which hitherto had always flourished on Persian soil. One reason was the general lack of royal patronage. Fath 'Ali, himself a versifier, sought, though unsuccessfully, to attract writers and scholars to his court, but the imitation which his poet laureate, Fath 'Ali Khan Saba (Fath 'Alī Khān Sabā), composed of the classic of Firdawsi (Firdawsī) was not especially meritorious. The printing press, even in its lithographic form, did not reach Persia until about 1816, and it was not until the 1850's that channels for transmitting Western thought became effective. In 1852 a vizier founded a polytechnic institute, the Dar al-Funun (Dār al-Funūn), and staffed it partly with Austrian professors. Young students were sent to Europe to prepare them for teaching in the institute, around which schools of law, medicine, agriculture, and other professions later were gathered to form the University of Teheran (1935). The institute's first director, Riza Quli Khan (1800–1871), published historical, geographical, and biographical works which helped disseminate knowledge. Modern educated men began to make their contributions to the simplification and clarification of the mother tongue and to the popularization and spread of knowledge. The shah himself, Nasir-al-Din, wrote an account of his three European trips in simple Persian. The deviation from the classical style was accelerated by the rise of journalism in the last decades of the 19th century. Early in Nasir-ad-Din's reign an official newspaper had appeared; it was followed by other, nonofficial Persian papers in India and Turkey. Newspapers and magazines became the chief media for the ideas of young Western-educated writers.

Arab intellectual activity in the Ottoman period was marked by sterility and paucity. Cut off from world currents of thought and suffering under adverse political and economic conditions, the Arabic-speaking peoples produced no works of distinction in literature, history, science, or philosophy. Until the second half of the 19th century, when the shackles of tradition and uncritical reverence for the past were finally loosened, compilers, commentators, biographers, and chroniclers were the dominant writers. Mystic literature was exemplified by an Egyptian, 'Abd-al-Wahhab al-Sha'rani ('Abd-al-Wahhāb al-Sha'rānī, d. 1565), whose extensive work on Sufis and saints achieved a measure of popularity. Another Egyptian, Murtada al-Zabidi (Murtaḍa al-Zabīdī, 1732–1791), wrote commentaries on the celebrated lexicon of al-Firuzabadi (al-Fīrūzābādī) and the classic *Iḥyā'* of al-Ghazzali (al-Ghazzālī). Among Egyptian chroniclers, mention should be made of 'Abd-al-Rahman al-Jabarti ('Abd-al-Raḥmān al-Jabartī, 1754–1822), a professor at al-Ahzar whom Napoleon appointed to the council through which the French invader hoped to rule the land. The outstanding Lebanese chronicler was Istifan (Iṣṭifān) al-Duwayhi (1630–1704), a Maronite patriarch and graduate of the seminary established in Rome in 1584 for the training of Maronite clergy. Using Syriac and Arabic documents, he compiled a history of the Maronite sect. The most distinguished graduate of the seminary was Giuseppe Simone Assemani (Yūsuf Sam'ān al-Sam'ānī, 1687–1768), through whose scholarly activity Oriental studies, especially in their relation to the Christian churches of the East, were first popularized in Europe. Assemani helped to build up the Oriental collection of the Vatican Library and compiled a voluminous work, *Bibliotheca Orientalis,* embodying his researches in Syriac, Arabic, Hebrew, Persian, Turkish, Armenian, and Ethiopic. In Syria a Damascene, Mohammed al-Muhibbi (Muḥammad al-Muḥibbī, 1651–1699), typified the literary spirit of the age. His principal work was a collection of 1,290 biographies of celebrities who died in the 11th Muslim century (1591–1688).

For literary developments in the 20th century, see *4. Cultural Life.*

MODERNIZATION

The growing contact with the West in the 20th century accelerated the modernization not only of Persia and Turkey, but also of the former Turkish provinces—the new nations of the

Arab world in the Middle East.

Persia (Iran).—World War I left Persia impoverished economically, politically, and intellectually. The time was ripe for a radical change, and an officer named Reza Khan Pahlavi made his way into the cabinet as minister of war (1921) and prime minister (1923), and finally onto the throne. In 1925 he deposed Ahmad, last of the Kajars (Ahmad had been in Europe since 1923), and started a new line, which he called Pahlavi in honor of his birthplace in northeastern Persia. Under the Pahlavis the modernization of Persia was carried out as a conscious, sustained effort.

Reza Shah (r. 1925–1941), a dictator and an admirer of his Turkish contemporary, Mustafa Kemal, began by modernizing the army and building up the police force. The unruly tribesmen were disarmed, and state monopolies were imposed on industry. In the process the shah amassed a large fortune. In 1928 the government abolished the capitulations, and five years later it renewed the concession of the Anglo-Persian Oil Company under more favorable terms. Polygyny was discouraged, the veil was ordered removed, and the privileges of the ulema and theologians were curtailed, but popular response to such radical social reforms, especially as they impinged on religion, was much less favorable than in Turkey. Persia possessed no comparable class of experienced administrative officials and no equally long tradition of contact with the West. In 1935 the country's name was officially changed to Iran. Its major project, the Trans-Iranian Railway from the Persian Gulf to the Caspian Sea, was opened in 1939 after 12 years of construction supported entirely by Persian capital.

In World War II, Iran was no more able to maintain its neutrality than in World War I. The advance of German troops through the Ukraine threatened the entire Caucasian region and constituted a menace to the British position in the Middle East. Moreover, there were the oilfields to protect and the important supply route across Iran to the Soviet Union to keep open and secure. In August 1941, the USSR occupied the northern half of the country, while Britain occupied the southern half. Impressed by German military might and distrustful of the Allies, Reza Shah had leaned toward the Axis. He was now forced to abdicate in favor of his son, Mohammed (Muḥammad) Reza Pahlavi.

After 16 years of dictatorial rule the pendulum swung in the opposite direction. On his accession the young shah took steps to turn over most of his father's fortune to philanthropic institutions and to divide his cultivated property for sale among the tillers on a long-term installment plan. In 1943, Iran declared war on Germany and took its position in the Allied camp. Turning to the United States, the Iranian government engaged for the second time the services of Dr. Arthur Chester Millspaugh as financial adviser. Meanwhile, in 1942, Col. H. Norman Schwarzkopf of the New Jersey State Police had become organizer and director of the Iranian Gendarmerie.

In accordance with a treaty signed on Jan. 29, 1942, the British withdrew their forces from Iran in March 1946, and the Russians in the following May, leaving behind valuable electrical and other installations and an enlarged and improved system of communications. The Russians also left behind a leftist movement which had crystallized into a vigorous party called Tudeh. In 1945, Tudeh activity had resulted in a serious rebellion in Azerbaijan. Four years later, following an attempt on the life of the shah, the party was outlawed. In the ensuing cold war, Iran adhered to the democratic camp. The shah, who visited the United States in 1949, received loans and generous grants. Expected investment of American capital did not materialize, however, and economic conditions worsened, especially after the National Assembly (Majlis) nationalized the oil industry in 1951. After three years of depleted national income the government and an international consortium of eight oil companies reached agreement, and production continued to increase thereafter. In 1955, Iran defied the USSR by signing the Baghdad Pact (later, Central Treaty Organization), in which it joined Turkey, Iraq, Pakistan, and Britain for mutual defense. Between the end of World War II and June 1962, Iran received $1,205 million in net grants and credits from the United States. In 1959 the two countries signed a treaty whereby the United States agreed to take appropriate action in case of aggression against Iran.

Turkey.—The liberal movement in Turkey in the 20th century was directed first by the Young Turks and then by Mustafa Kemal. With good intentions, patriotic zeal, and enthusiasm, but with little experience and no cooperation from neighboring countries and the constituent nationalities of the Ottoman Empire, the Young Turks tackled the task of transforming a decrepit, antiquated state into a modern one. Three months after their successful coup of July 1908, Austria annexed Bosnia and Hercegovina, and Bulgaria declared its independence. In 1911, Italy sent its troops against Tripoli (Ṭarābulus) and Benghazi (Banghāzī), and in 1912–1913, in the First Balkan War, the alliance of Greece, Serbia, Montenegro, and Bulgaria deprived Turkey of most of its remaining possessions in Europe. Meanwhile, with a view to strengthening their position at home, the Young Turks projected a policy of Ottomanism that aimed at welding the diverse communities in the empire into a common nation based on loyalty to the sultan and the constitution and united by the Turkish language under Turkish leadership. The immediate result was the stimulation of separatist movements and the encouragement of local nationalist loyalties among Greeks, Arabs, Armenians, and others. As a countermeasure, the Constantinople regime evolved a policy of Pan-Turanism, which aimed at enlisting the support of the large groups of Turkish speakers on the Volga River, in Persia, and in Central Asia, but it remained academic. When both Ottomanism and Pan-Turanism failed, resort was had to Pan-Islam, which had already been tried and found wanting by Abdul Hamid. His successor, Mohammed V, declared a holy war on Nov. 14, 1914, after Turkey entered World War I on the side of the Central Powers, but the declaration fell on deaf ears insofar as non-Turkish Muslims were concerned. By entering the war, the Young Turks lost the opportunity of pursuing any policies of their own. By entering it on the side of Germany, they threw themselves into the arms of the one power which they thought could help them against the Russian enemy.

Despite its unpreparedness and weakened condition, Turkey rendered real service to its allies in the war. Its troops tied up large British forces in Egypt and Iraq and put up a surprisingly obstinate defense of the Dardanelles that prevented contact between the Western powers and their Russian ally. But the civil population, especially the Arabic speakers, was subjected to unprecedented privation, and four years of desperate defensive warfare crippled Turkey's will and ability to fight. By Oct. 31, 1918, when an armistice went into effect, British and French troops, with the aid of Arab nationalists, had occupied Syria and Iraq, and Husayn (Hussein; Ar. Ḥusayn) of the Hejaz had declared himself king of the Arabs (1916). The leaders of the Young Turks fled the country, leaving it in a state of anarchy and at the mercy of the victors.

Black Starr

Near Ankara, capital of Turkey, huge modern machines as well as horses are used to build new roads.

One mistake the victors made: under the protection of their naval guns a Greek contingent landed in Smyrna on May 14, 1919. Indignation at this invasion of the homeland aroused Anatolia. Turkish nationalism, which hitherto had been limited to a few officers and intellectuals, spread among the masses of the population, and a leader emerged in the person of an officer who had fought in the losing war, Mustafa Kemal. Rather than transform a dying into a living empire, the new leader proposed to erect a modern, secular, one-nation state on the remains of a medieval, Islamic, and multinational state. The new state was to be coterminous with the Turkish homeland of Anatolia, which was to be retained intact. By September 1922, the Greeks had been driven from Smyrna, and Allied designs to partition Turkey had been frustrated. In the following year, Ankara was made the capital of the new state, and the Grand National Assembly proclaimed the government a republic and elected Mustafa Kemal its first president. The Treaty of Lausanne (1923) recognized the independence of Turkey within its own ethnic frontiers. In March 1924, Abdul Medjid ('Abd-al-Majīd) II, who had become caliph in 1922, was sent into exile, and the caliphate was abolished. Religion and the state were separated.

The way was now clear to resume the process of modernization. During World War I the Young Turks had abolished the capitulations, begun to secularize education, extended the facilities of the restored University of Constantinople (which then opened its doors to women), reformed the laws of marriage and divorce, and placed the religious courts under the Ministry of Justice. President of the republic in name and dictator in fact, Mustafa Kemal in 1925 suppressed the religious orders, for no radical social reforms could succeed while they functioned, and replaced the fez with the hat as an outward expression of identification with European culture. In the following year, he dethroned the shari'ah, replacing it with civil codes based on Swiss and other European systems. Women were subsequently given equal legal rights with men, and in March 1935, 17 of them were elected to the Grand National Assembly.

A complete rupture with the past was effected in 1928, when the Arabic alphabet was replaced by Latin characters and the use of loan words from the Arabic language was discouraged. Even the Koran was translated into Turkish for the first time (1931), and the muezzin's call to prayer was heard in the vernacular. In 1930, Constantinople became İstanbul, and Smyrna was renamed İzmir. A law of 1934 made Turkish family surnames obligatory for Turks after Jan. 1, 1935; after passing it, the assembly bestowed on the president the title of Atatürk (father of the Turks).

Kemal Atatürk's policies were continued at a slower pace under his collaborator and successor, İsmet İnönü, who served as president from 1938 to 1950. The situation was complicated by World War II, in which Turkey maintained an armed neutrality favorable to the Allies. The country declared war on Germany and Japan on Feb. 23, 1945, only in order to be admitted to the United Nations organization meeting at San Francisco. Nevertheless, the European war subjected the economy to a severe strain, and martial law and censorship of the press were strictly enforced. In 1945 the single-party system was abandoned. Beginning in 1947, loans and subsidies were received from the United States on an increasing scale. Civil and military aid strengthened domestic stability and the will to resist Soviet advances and threats. Besides training young Turks for military service, the United States made available experts in agriculture, industry, education, and transportation. In 1952, at its request, Turkey was accepted in the North Atlantic Treaty Organization (NATO).

Under Mahmud Celâl Bayar, who became president in 1950, policy remained steadfast in support of the West. His administration inaugurated a more liberal policy toward the opposition and the press. Evidently these changes were not considered adequate by students and liberal thinkers. Unrest spread into the army, which in 1960 overthrew the civilian regime. The revolutionary government, headed by Gen. Cemal Gürsel, condemned Bayar and his premier, Adnan Menderes, to death and drafted a new constitution. Menderes and other officials were executed, but Bayar's sentence was commuted to life imprisonment. In 1961, Gürsel was elected president, and İsmet İnönü formed a new cabinet.

See also Balkan Wars; World War I—

11. Turkish Campaigns.

Arab World.—Following the grant of extraterritorial rights by the Ottoman government in the 16th century, France and Great Britain established trading centers and consular posts in Syria and Egypt. Relations remained largely commercial, with no attempt to control natural resources and means of communication or to interfere with local administration, until 1798, when Napoleon Bonaparte occupied Egypt. Thereafter, not only did the economic relationship become more intimate, but the way was opened for social and intellectual contact, resulting in political entanglements.

Beginnings in Egypt.—Mohammed 'Ali (Muḥammad 'Alī), a young officer in the Turkish Army, which had helped the British to drive the French invader from the country, worked his way into a position of mastery, although he remained under the nominal suzerainty of the sultan as pasha of Egypt (1805–1848). He annihilated his Mamluk predecessors (1811), practically confiscated all landholdings in private hands, and monopolized the chief products of the country. An illiterate Turkish-speaking man of Albanian parentage, he nevertheless established the first Arabic press in Egypt (not counting the special one brought by Napoleon), founded the first schools of medicine and engineering, and sent military and academic student missions to France. He also employed French officers to reorganize the army and to build a navy. After crushing the Wahhabi uprising between 1811 and 1818, he annexed the Sudan (1820–1822), and in the Greek War of Independence he sent land and naval forces to support the Ottoman troops. As a reward, he demanded Syria, and when the Porte rebuffed him, his son Ibrahim (Ibrāhīm) Pasha conquered it (1832) and would probably have dealt a final blow to the Ottoman Empire itself had it not been for the intervention of Russia, Great Britain, and France. In 1840 these powers forced the Egyptian troops to evacuate the entire area.

Mohammed 'Ali set his country on the path toward modernization. An English steamship company began regular service to Egypt and Syria in 1836; the first Egyptian railway, from Cairo to Alexandria, was completed by a British company in 1856; and in 1869 the Suez Canal was opened by a French company. By giving world communications the international Egypt-Red Sea route, the canal restored the ancient strategic importance of the country.

Western Influences in Syria and Lebanon.—The measure of security enjoyed in the 1830's by Syria under the relatively tolerant and liberal Egyptian regime and by Lebanon under Bashir II encouraged Westerners to undertake commercial, industrial, and educational enterprises in both lands on an unprecedented scale. The Christians, especially in Lebanon, where they predominated, were naturally more hospitable to Western ideas and institutions than their fellow countrymen. The Jesuits, who had operated in Lebanon before 1773, returned with renewed vigor, and British and American Protestant missions struck deep roots in the land. In Beirut an Arabic printing press was established by the Americans in 1835, and another by the French in 1853. The Bible and other religious works were translated into neoclassical Arabic. The Druse-Maronite wars (1841–1860) aroused sympathetic interest in Britain, France, Germany, and the United States, resulting in greater philanthropic and educational activity.

In 1866 the Americans founded what is now the American University of Beirut, and in 1875 the Jesuits established the Université St.-Joseph on the other side of the city. Some of the area's most influential men of letters and political leaders received their education in these two institutions, whose graduates in medicine and other professions attained the first rank in their respective fields. Before long, indigenous schools, presses, and learned societies and publications, all modeled on Western ones, made their appearance. Two Christian Lebanese graduates of the American University founded in Cairo the earliest scientific-literary magazine, *al-Muqtaṭaf,* and one of the earliest and most influential newspapers, *al-Muqaṭṭam.* Another Christian Lebanese and former student of the university established in Cairo in 1892 a historical-literary magazine, *al-Hilāl,* which has remained one of the most flourishing Arabic periodicals. For the first time, the Arabic reader had access to the treasures of English and French literature, science, and technology in an idiom that he could understand, and for the first time he had a clear idea of the literary treasures of his own heritage and of the glory that was once Arab. Like other minds stretched by new ideas, Arab minds could not resume their former dimensions.

Growth of Arab Nationalism.—The Arab intellectual awakening was bound to bring political awakening in its wake. Most of the pioneers in the nationalist movement were Western-educated Lebanese Christians who had found in Egypt under the khedives, and after 1882 under the British, a congenial climate for their activity. They coined the technical phraseology of such concepts as patriotism, nationalism, and democracy in their modern connotations.

For a half century after its beginnings in the 1860's the Arab nationalist movement was a purely intellectual activity limited to a few writers and thinkers. Starting from the wide base of Pan-Arabism, it made language, literature, and history, rather than religion, its focal point. In this it was in conflict with Pan-Islam, which recognized no linguistic, geographical, or ethnic boundaries, but made faith the common denominator. Clearly the Arab brand of nationalism was a Western importation that had to be domesticated in Islamic culture before it could be accepted. In its negative form it represented a reaction to Ottoman domination and fed on opposition to it, but it did not envisage a complete rupture with the Porte until World War I. When the Young Turks made their promising start in 1908, Arab nationalist leaders assumed that they could collaborate with them. They immediately organized at Constantinople the Arab-Ottoman Fraternal Society (Jam'īyat al-Ikhā' al-'Arabī al-'Uthmānī), but in the following year the authorities banned all societies of non-Turkish groups. The movement then went underground. In 1911 students in Paris founded the Young Arab Society (al-Jam'īyah al-'Arabīyah al-Fatāt), which in 1913 organized a six-day congress attended by 24 delegates (mostly Syrians and Iraqis), of whom 11 were Christians.

It was the extreme suffering endured by the Arab subjects of the Ottoman Empire in World War I that sharpened their discontent and brought a growing number of recruits from the lower classes to the nationalist cause. By this time, the liberalizing influence of Lebanese and Syrian emigrants, especially in the United States, had begun to take effect. Through publications impregnated with ideas of patriotism, democracy, and nationalism, Arabic writers abroad contributed immeasurably to the intellectual and political awakening of the Middle East. Some conception of their effectiveness may be gained from the large number of editors and writers condemned to death *in absentia* by the Hamidian regime.

Development of the Independent Arab States.—With the institution of the mandatory system after World War I, Arab nationalism took on a new aspect: opposition to the British in Egypt, Palestine, and Iraq and to the French in Syria and Lebanon. None of the peoples in the mandated areas had demanded the mandate or had acquiesced in it after its imposition. While many Lebanese, especially the Christians among them, were at first amenable to French rule, they later turned against it.

As Pan-Arabism passed from the theoretical to the practical, it was on its way to fragmentation. In Egypt it was confronted with a major local obstacle, British occupation, and had to concentrate on its removal. Opposition to British rule became the touchstone of patriotism, and for the first time the Egyptian realized that he was an Egyptian. Egyptian nationalism was born and soon parted company with Pan-Arabism. The local movement produced its first leader in Ahmad 'Arabi (Aḥmad 'Arābī) Pasha, whose revolt against the British sent him to exile in Ceylon in 1882; and its second in Sa'd Zaghlul (Sa'd Zaghlūl) Pasha, who in 1919 also was sent into exile. While Egyptian control increased after the establishment of the Kingdom of Egypt in 1922, Britain continued to maintain troops in the Suez Canal Zone until 1956. Descendants of Mohammed 'Ali occupied the throne until 1952, when Faruk (Fārūq) I was deposed by a military coup that brought to power Lt. Col. Gamal Abdel Nasser (Jamāl 'Abd-al-Nāṣir). Nasser developed into a national and Pan-Arab hero in 1956, when the attack on his country by Israel, France, and Britain failed to achieve its purpose.

A new printing plant near Jidda, on the road to Islam's holy city of Mecca, in Saudi Arabia.

Waagenaar from Pix, Inc.

In 1958, Egypt and Syria joined to form the United Arab Republic (UAR), with the expectation that the new state would serve as a nucleus for an expanded Arab republic, but Syria seceded from the union in September 1961. An agreement proposing a new union, including Iraq as well, was signed in April 1963, but proved ineffective.

The mandates over Syria, Lebanon, and Iraq were supposedly held as trusts under the League of Nations, pending the training of their peoples for independence. The situation in Palestine was complicated by the Balfour Declaration of Nov. 2, 1917, which promised the Jews "a national home" in Palestine with a clear reservation in favor of the rights of the people of the land. The discrepancy between mandatory theory and practice was so flagrant as to provoke uprisings, one after another, beginning in the 1920's in both Iraq and Syria. Meanwhile, Palestine remained in a state of turmoil, the people recognizing neither the mandate nor its national home appendage. Syria became the hotbed of Arab intrigue. In March 1920, in defiance of the French mandatory power, a Syrian congress was hurriedly held in Damascus and elected Faysal (Faisal; Fayṣal), son of King Husayn of the Hejaz, king of a greater Syria. Four months later, the French high commissioner, Gen. Henri Gouraud, sent troops against Damascus, and Faysal was forced to leave the land, only to be crowned in 1921 as ruler of the new Kingdom of Iraq. The dynasty he founded was terminated by an army coup in July 1958. The new regime, headed by Abdul Karim Kassim ('Abd-al-Karīm Qāsim), destroyed the monarchy and set up a republic with leftist leanings, which in turn was overthrown in February 1963 by an ex-deputy of Kassim, Abdul Salam Arif ('Abd-al-Salām 'Ārif).

In Syria the French persisted in repressive measures against nationalist leaders, imprisoning some and banishing others. Nevertheless, the colossal task confronting the mandatory power should not be underestimated. It involved the creation of administrative and judicial organs, the introduction of modern codes of civil procedure, the establishment of departments of education and public health, and the construction or repair of ports, roads, and other means of communication. On the whole, however, both government and people devoted their energies to the political problem to the detriment of the socioeconomic situation. The local currency was linked to the depreciated French franc, and French was promoted at the expense of the native tongue. By the end of 1943, however, complete independence had been achieved by Syria and Lebanon, and at the beginning of the following year both began to exercise their full responsibilities as sovereign states. Both countries set up republican forms of government, but Syria's government has been extremely unstable. Most of its numerous presidents have been deposed by military coups.

Lebanon pursued a pro-Western policy, accepting aid from the United States and giving no encouragement to the Soviet Union. By its prompt and unreserved adoption of the Eisenhower Doctrine in 1957, it alienated a considerable element in its population as well as two of its neighbors, Syria and Egypt. In essence, the doctrine promised military and economic aid to any country in the Middle East that sought it against international Communist encroachment. This was one of the factors leading to the uprising of 1958, which ended after American Marines had landed in Beirut at the request of the Lebanese government. The uprising brought to power a more neutral, but still pro-Western regime under the presidency of Gen. Fouad Chehab (Fu'ād Shihāb), who upheld his country's democratic procedures.

In 1923 the British amputated Transjordan from the body of Palestine, constituted it an emirate, and installed Faysal's elder brother 'Abdullah ('Abdullāh) as ruler. The emir declared himself king in 1946; three years later, he became head of the Hashemite Kingdom of Jordan. The expansion of the kingdom westward from the Jordan River was accomplished in the course of the joint Arab war against the Zionists that ended with the birth of Israel in 1948. Until his assassination in 1951, 'Abdullah worked for his pet project of uniting Syria with his kingdom. His young grandson, Husayn (Hussein; Ḥusayn) I, ascended the throne in 1952. Jordan's throne has been repeatedly threatened, chiefly by Palestinians seeking union with Egypt, but has managed to maintain itself under Husayn.

Created by the West, particularly the United States, and supported by it thereafter, Israel became a major source of alienation between Arabs and Westerners. After 1948 the neighboring Arab states, which though joined together in the Arab League had many disagreements among themselves, remained united in their wholehearted hostility to Israel. The formation of the league in 1945, with Cairo as headquarters and an Egyptian as secretary general, constituted a conscious step toward the realization of the Pan-Arab ideal. Through its committees the league strove thereafter to standardize educational procedures and textbooks, to remove economic barriers, and to produce concerted action in foreign policy and defense. Nevertheless, differences between the states were accentuated in the 1950's. After the attack on Egypt in October 1956 by Israel, Britain, and France, the Soviet Union strengthened its economic relations with Egypt and Syria, thus driving a wedge between these two countries on the one hand and Lebanon and Iraq on the other.

See also ARAB LEAGUE.

Arabian Peninsula.—Arabia proper remained in a class by itself, distinct from Egypt and North Africa as well as from the Fertile Crescent. In the mid-20th century it was still medieval in outlook, Islamic in culture, and entirely Arabic in its spoken and literary language. Only three countries, Saudi Arabia, Yemen, and Kuwait, are fully independent, the states of the southern and eastern coastal regions being under British protection. Oil-rich Kuwait, at the western corner of the Persian Gulf, terminated its 62-year-old agreement with Britain in 1961 and became a fully independent state.

Saudi Arabia was created by ibn-Saud ('Abd-al-'Azīz ibn-Su'ūd, r. 1932–1953), who in the 1890's was a political refugee in Kuwait from his native Nejd. At the head of his Wahhabi tribesmen, he overthrew the pro-Ottoman ibn-Rashids (ibn-Rashīds) at Hail (Ḥā'il, 1921), consolidated his possessions in the Nejd, and then fought against King Husayn. In 1924–1925 he wrested from him Mecca, Medina, and the rest of the country, and in 1926 himself became king of the Hejaz. Six years later he proclaimed himself king of Saudi Arabia, a country extending from the Persian Gulf to the Red Sea across the northern and central portion of the Arabian Peninsula.

The granting of the first oil concession to an American company in 1933 marked the beginning of a new era in Arabia. Exploration and exploitation thereafter revealed the peninsula to contain some of the world's richest oilfields. The huge royalties that accrued to the royal house and the abrupt changes which they effected in the standard of living recalled episodes in *The Arabian Nights*. Before the discovery of oil, Arabia had been insulated against Western influences and unmindful of the progress of its neighbors to the north. Mecca and Medina and their environs had always been forbidden areas to non-Muslims. Despite opposition from conservatives and theologians, ibn-Saud succeeded in modernizing means of communication, introducing hospitals and schools, and generally setting his people on the road to progress. The country was firm in its opposition to international communism, and it remained steadfast in its friendship with the United States despite dissatisfaction with American policy toward Israel. Expression was given to common Arabian-American interests by the visit of King Saud (Su'ūd, r. 1953–), ibn-Saud's son and successor, to the United States in 1957. The visit aroused opposition among his subjects, especially the pro-Egyptian ones, however, and led in 1958 to the delegation of much of his authority to Crown Prince Faysal (Faisal, Fayṣal), the king's younger brother, as prime minister and minister of foreign affairs.

Though strictly not a part of the holy land of Islam, Yemen remained as self-contained as the Hejaz, if not more so, for it lacked the annual stream of pilgrims from all over the Muslim world. While it was the first country in Arabia to achieve a high measure of civilization in ancient times, with the rise of Islam it was eclipsed by its northern neighbor and thereafter did not figure prominently in international affairs. Nominally under Ottoman suzerainty until the end of World War I, Yemen was administered by native imams, descendants of 'Ali, who combined spiritual and temporal authority in their persons. The sacred law of Islam remained the law of the land, but the people adhered to Zaydi Shi'ism, whereas the Hejazis (Ḥijāzī) and Nejdis were Sunnites. Yemen's complete independence was achieved under Imam Yahya (Yaḥyā), who was assassinated in 1948 and was succeeded by his son Ahmad (Aḥmad). In the 1950's the country's common frontier with the Aden Protectorate became the cause of armed conflict with British forces and of hostility to the West. In 1958, after the declaration of the union between Syria and Egypt, Yemen associated itself with the UAR in the United Arab States. The association was, however, terminated in 1961. On Ahmad's death in 1962, his son Mohammed (Muḥammad) al-Badr succeeded but was soon overthrown by a military coup headed by Brig. Abdullah al-Salal ('Abdullāh al-Salāl). Al-Salal set up a republic, with himself as president, and received financial and military support from Egypt, while the royalists were aided by Saudi Arabia.

See also sections on history in articles on the modern Middle Eastern countries; biographies of the chief historical figures; WORLD WAR II.

PHILIP K. HITTI,
Professor Emeritus of Semitic Literature, Princeton University.

6. CHRONOLOGY

622—Islamic era begins (July 16); Mohammed's hegira from Mecca to Medina (September).
632—Mohammed dies after unifying Arabia (June 8).
632–661—Orthodox caliphate.
634–650—Arabs conquer Byzantine Palestine, Syria, Egypt; Sassanid Iraq, Persia.
c. 653—Establishment of sacred text of Koran.
661—Assassination of 'Ali, Mohammed's son-in-law; Mu'awiyah founds Umayyad caliphate at Damascus.
680—'Ali's son Husayn killed at Karbala' (Oct. 10).
747–750—Abbasids and Shi'ites revolt in Khurasan; take Persia, Iraq, Syria; slay Umayyads.
750–1258—Abbasid caliphs shift Islamic center to Iraq, where Baghdad becomes capital (762).
786–809—Caliphate of Harun al-Rashid.
820–872—Taharids of Khurasan, first rivals in east.
867–902—Saffarids and others divide Persia.
868–905—Tulunids rule Egypt, (from 877) Syria, Hejaz.
874–999—Samanids rule northeast Persia.
899—Qarmatian sect starts revolt in northeast Arabia; takes Mecca; sacks the Ka'bah (930).
909–1171—Shi'ite Fatimid caliphs in Tunisia, then Egypt, Syria, Hejaz; found Cairo (969), capital from 972.
929–1031—Hamdanids in Iraq and (944–1003) Syria.
932–1055—Buwayhids of Persia dominate caliphs.
935–969—Ikhshidids rule Egypt, Syria, Hejaz.
994–1149—Ghaznavids in Persia.
1037–1194—Seljuk Turks conquer and rule Persia.
1052—Banu-Hilal Arabs devastate North Africa.
1055—Seljuks conquer Iraq, dominate caliphs.
1071—Seljuks rout Byzantines at Manzikert (Aug. 26).
1077–1300—Seljuks dominate Anatolia.
1090–1256—Isma'ili Assassins at Alamut in Persia.
1096–1099—First Crusade wins Edessa, Antioch, Jerusalem; Frankish Kingdom of Jerusalem (1100).
1127–1146—Zangi leads countercrusade, takes Edessa.
1138–1221—Khwarizm shahs hold northeast Persia.
1146–1174—Zangi's son Nur-al-Din leads countercrusade.
1147–1149—Second Crusade accomplishes nothing.
1149–1215—Ghurids replace Ghaznavids in east.
1171–1193—Saladin, Kurdish general, leads countercrusade; founds Ayyubid dynasty, replacing Fatimids in Egypt, Syria, Arabia.
1187—Saladin vanquishes Franks at Hattin (July 4); Jerusalem falls (Oct. 2), kingdom crumbles.
1189–1192—Third Crusade restores coast to Franks.
1202–1204—Fourth Crusade diverted, takes Constantinople; Latin empire of Constantinople (1204–1261).
1218–1221—Fifth Crusade, against Nile Delta, fails.
1220—Mongols under Genghis Khan overrun Persia.
1229–1244—Jerusalem regained by Frederick II.
1248–1250—Crusade of Louis IX in Nile Delta fails.
1250–1517—Mamluks rule Egypt, Syria, Hejaz.
1258—Hulagu ends caliphate, sacks Baghdad (Feb. 10).
1260–1335—Il-Khanid Mongols rule Persia (adopt Islam).
1260—Mamluks defeat Mongols at 'Ayn Jalut (Sept. 3).
1261—Byzantines retake Constantinople (July 25).
1268—Antioch falls to Mamluk Baybars I (May 21).
1291—Mamluks clear Syria of Franks.
1299–1922—Ottoman sultans: major empire.
1326–1393—Ottomans conquer Anatolian Turks, Greeks.
1354–1461—Ottomans conquer Balkan Greeks, Slavs.
1365—Alexandria sacked by Crusaders (October).
1381–1402—Mongols under Timur overrun Persia, Iraq, Syria, Anatolia.
1396—Ottomans rout Crusaders at Nicopolis (Sept. 25).
1402—Timur overthrows Ottomans at Ankara (July 20).
1405–1471—Ottomans retake Anatolia.
1453—Constantinople falls to Mohammed II (May 29), becomes Ottoman capital.
1461—Ottomans take Trebizond, last Byzantine city.
1502–1736—Shi'ite Safavids rule Persia.
1507–1650—Portuguese in Persian Gulf.
1516—Ottomans under Selim I conquer Mamluk Syria (August) and Egypt (January 1517); kill Mamluks.
1520–1566—Suleiman I the Magnificent, Ottoman sultan.
1534—Ottomans take Baghdad from Safavids (November).
1587–1629—'Abbas I the Great, Persian shah.
1622—British begin to dominate Persian Gulf commerce.
1699—Treaty of Karlowitz (Jan. 26): Ottoman defeat.
1718—Treaty of Passarowitz (July 21): Ottoman defeat.
1736–1747—Afsharid Nadir Shah supplants Safavids.
1750–1794—Zands of Shiraz supplant Afsharids.
1757—Rise of Wahhabi sect in central Arabia.
1774—Treaty of Kuchuk Kainarji: Ottoman defeat.
1789–1807—Selim III, Ottoman sultan; efforts to modernize fail.
1796–1925—Kajar dynasty of Persian shahs.
1798–1801—Napoleon in Egypt, Syria.
1803–1813—Wahhabis occupy Hejaz; expelled by Egyptians.
1805–1848—Mohammed 'Ali, pasha of Egypt.
1811—Mamluks massacred by Egyptian Army (March 1).
1821–1830—Revolt frees Greece from Ottoman rule.
1826—Janizaries massacred by Mahmud II (June 15).
1832–1840—Ottoman Syria occupied by Egyptians.
1839—Aden captured by British (Jan. 20).
1859–1869—Suez Canal constructed by French firm.
1860–1861—French intervene after Christian massacre in Lebanon, which is then given autonomy.
1878—Treaty of San Stefano: Ottomans lose Balkan areas.
1881–1898—Mahdist revolt in Sudan; quelled by British.
1882–1936—British in Egypt (protectorate, 1914–1922).
1884–1907—Acute Anglo-Russian rivalry in Persia.
1902–1953—Ibn-Saud unites and rules most of Arabia.
1902—Aswan Dam on Nile completed.
1907—Persia divided into British and Russian spheres separated by neutral zone (Aug. 31).
1908—Young Turk revolt (July 24); Ottomans lose Bulgaria, Bosnia, Hercegovina (October).
1909—Sultan Abdul Hamid deposed (April 27); Shah Mohammed 'Ali likewise deposed (July 16).
1912–1913—First Balkan War; Ottomans defeated and lose remaining Balkan possessions.
1913—Young Turk coup (Jan. 23).
1914—Turkey enters war against Allies (Oct. 29).
1915–1916—British-Anzac attack on Gallipoli fails.
1916—Hejaz revolts against Ottomans (June 5); Sherif Husayn of Mecca made king (Oct. 29).
1917—British take Baghdad from Ottomans (March 11); Balfour Declaration aids Zionism (Nov. 2); Gen. Edmund Allenby enters Jerusalem (Dec. 11).
1919–1922—Anatolia invaded by Greeks, Italians, French.
1920—French assigned mandates over Syria, Lebanon; British, over Iraq, Palestine, Transjordan.
1921—Reza Khan Pahlavi's coup succeeds in Persia (Feb. 21); Faysal made king of Iraq (Aug. 23).
1922—Fuad I proclaimed king of Egypt (March 15); Ottoman sultanate abolished (Nov. 1).
1923—Treaty of Lausanne (July 24); Turkey a republic under Mustafa Kemal (Atatürk), Oct. 29.
1924—Ottoman caliphate abolished (March 3).
1924–1925—Ibn-Saud conquers and annexes Hejaz.
1932—Saudi Arabia proclaimed a kingdom (Sept. 22); Iraq independent of British (Oct. 3).
1935—Persia officially renamed Iran (March 21).
1939—Turkey annexes Hatay in Syria (June 23).
1941—Axis coup in Iraq (April 4) thwarted (May); Reza Shah of Iran abdicates (Sept. 16).
1941–1946—Iran occupied by British and Russians.
1942—German invasion of Egypt repelled.
1944—Syria and Lebanon legally sovereign (Jan. 1).
1945—Arab League founded (March 17).
1946—French leave Syria (April) and Lebanon (December); Jordan a kingdom under 'Abdullah (May 25); Communist revolt in Azerbaijan fails (December).
1947—Truman Doctrine: aid to Turkey, Greece (March 12); UN votes to partition Palestine (Nov. 29).
1948—British leave Palestine; Israel a republic (May).
1948–1949—Arab-Israeli war, ended by armistice agreements under United Nations auspices.
1950—Jordan annexes eastern Palestine (April 24).
1951—Iran nationalizes oil industry (May 2).
1952—Turkey joins North Atlantic Treaty Organization (Feb. 18); King Faruk of Egypt ousted (July 26).
1953—Egypt a republic under Mohammed Naguib (June 18); Shah Mohammed Reza Pahlavi of Iran overthrows dictator Mohammed Mossadegh (Aug. 19).
1954—Gamal Abdel Nasser supplants Naguib (Nov. 14).
1955—Baghdad Pact (Turkey, Iraq, United Kingdom, Pakistan, Iran).
1956—Egypt nationalizes Suez Canal (July 26); Israel, United Kingdom, France attack Egypt (October).
1958—Egypt and Syria form United Arab Republic (UAR), Feb. 21; Faysal II slain in Iraq revolt, republic formed (July); U.S. Marines land in Lebanon (July) but do not engage in fighting during Lebanese insurrection. Order restored by September.
1960—Aswan High Dam begun (Jan. 9); Turkish Army overthrows Menderes regime (May 27).
1961—Kuwait becomes independent (June 19); Syria leaves UAR (Sept. 28–29).
1962—Yemen's monarchy overthrown, republic established (Sept. 26–27); civil war ensues.
1963—Iraq's government overthrown by Army and Baathist coalition (Feb.); agreement for UAR-Syria-Iraq union (April) suspended by UAR (July 22); proposed Syria-Iraq union (Sept. 2) upset by overthrow of Iraq Baathists (Nov. 18).
1967—Israel defeats Arabs in brief war (June 5–10), occupies parts of UAR, Jordan, and Syria; Aden and Aden Protectorate become independent, form People's Republic of South Yemen (Nov. 30).
1970—UAR and Israel begin (August 7) cease-fire along Suez Canal; Civil war flares in Jordan between government troops and Palestinian guerrillas (Sept. 16–27); UAR President Nasser dies in Cairo (Sept. 28) and is succeeded by Anwar Sadat.
1971—Bahrain (Aug. 14) and Qatar (Sept. 1) declare their independence after being under British protection since 1820.
1973—Egypt and Syria attack Israel (Oct. 6), initiating 4th Arab-Israeli war. U.S. Secretary of State Kissinger later negotiates troop disengagements.
1973–1974—Arab oil-producing states embargo oil sales to some nations deemed friendly to Israel.

7. BIBLIOGRAPHY

BIBLIOGRAPHICAL WORKS: Hill, Richard L., comp., *A Bibliography of the Anglo-Egyptian Sudan* (London 1939); Thomsen, Peter, *Systematische Bibliographie der Palästina-Literatur,* vols. 1–6 (Leipzig 1908–39); Birge, John K., *A Guide to Turkish Area Study* (Washington 1949); Şabā, Moḥsen, *Bibliographie française de l'Irān,* 2d ed., rev. and enl. (Teheran 1951); United States Library of Congress, Orientalia Division, *The Arabian Peninsula* (Washington 1951); Elwell-Sutton, Laurence P., *A Guide to Iranian Area Study* (Washington 1952); Field, Henry, *Anthropogeographical Bibliography of the Persian Gulf Area* (Washington 1952); *Türkiye bibliyoğrafyasi* (İstanbul 1934–52; Ankara 1953–); Ettinghausen, Richard, ed., *A Selected and Annotated Bibliography of Books and Periodicals in Western Languages Dealing with the Near and Middle East* (Washington 1952; supplement 1954); American University of Beirut, Economic Research Institute, *A Selected and Annotated Bibliography of Economic Literature on the Arabic Speaking Countries of the Middle East, 1938–1952* (Beirut 1954; supplements 1955–); Burke, Jean T., *An Annotated Bibliography of Books and Periodicals in English Dealing with Human Relations in the Arab States of the Middle East* (Beirut 1956); Field, Henry, *Bibliography on Southwestern Asia,* 5 vols. (Coral Gables, Fla., 1953–58); Pearson, James D., and Ashton, Julia F., *Index Islamicus, 1906–1955* (Cambridge, Eng., 1958); Storey, Charles A., *Persian Literature: a Bio-Bibliographical Survey,* vol. 1, vol. 2 (part 1) (London 1927–58).

PERIODICALS: *Journal asiatique* (Paris 1822–); *Journal of the Royal Asiatic Society of Great Britain and Ireland* (London 1834–); *Journal of the American Oriental Society* (Boston, New Haven, Baltimore 1843–); *Zeitschrift der deutschen morgenländischen Gesellschaft* (Leipzig Wiesbaden 1847–); *Der Islam* (Strasbourg, Berlin 1910–); *Muslim World* (London, Hartford 1911–); Royal Central Asian Society, *Journal* (London 1914–); London University, School of Oriental and African Studies, *Bulletin* (London 1917–); *Oriento moderno* (Rome 1921–); *Islamic Culture* (Hyderabad, India, 1927–); *Revue des études islamiques* (Paris 1927–); *Journal of Near Eastern Studies* (Chicago 1942–); *Middle East Journal* (Washington 1947–); *Oriens* (Leiden 1948–); *Middle Eastern Affairs* (New York 1950–); *Cahiers de l'Orient contemporain* (Paris 1951–); *Studia Islamica* (Paris 1953–); *Arabica* (Leiden 1954–).

THE LAND; THE PEOPLE: Coon, Carleton S., *Caravan* (New York 1951); Patai, Raphael, *Israel Between East and West* (Philadelphia 1953); Fisher, William B., *The Middle East,* 3d ed., rev. (London 1956); Lerner, Daniel, *The Passing of Traditional Society* (Glencoe, Ill., 1958); Cressey, George B., *Crossroads: Land and Life in Southwest Asia* (Philadelphia 1960).

ISLAM: Guillaume, Alfred, *The Traditions of Islam* (Oxford 1924); Arberry, Arthur J., *An Introduction to the History of Ṣūfism* (New York 1943); Gibb, Sir Hamilton A. R., *Modern Trends in Islam* (Chicago 1947); id., *Mohammedanism,* 2d ed. (London 1953); Khalid, Khalid Muhammad, *From Here We Start,* tr. from the Arabic by Isma'il R. el Faruqi (Washington 1953); Watt, William Montgomery, *Muhammad at Mecca* (Oxford 1953); Guillaume, Alfred, *Islam* (Harmondsworth, Eng., 1954); Arberry, Arthur J., tr., *The Koran Interpreted,* 2 vols. (New York 1955); Ibn Hishām, 'Abd al-Malik, *The Life of Muhammad,* tr. from the Arabic by Alfred Guillaume (New York 1955); Cragg, Kenneth, *The Call of the Minaret* (New York 1956); Watt, William Montgomery, *Muhammad at Medina* (Oxford 1956); Smith, Wilfred C., *Islam in Modern History* (Princeton 1957); Daniel, Norman, *Islam and the West* (Edinburgh 1960); Hitti, Philip K., *Islam and the West* (Princeton 1962).

ECONOMIC LIFE: Siddiqi, Shujaat A., *Public Finance in Islam* (Lahore 1948); Overseas Consultants, Inc., *Report on Seven Year Development Plan for the Plan Organization of the Imperial Government of Iran,* 5 vols. (New York 1949); International Bank for Reconstruction and Development, *The Economy of Turkey* (Washington 1951); Lambton, Ann K. S., *Landlord and Peasant in Persia* (New York 1953); Issawi, Charles P., *Egypt at Mid-Century* (New York 1954); International Bank for Reconstruction and Development, *The Economic Development of Syria* (Baltimore 1955); Salter, 1st Baron, *The Development of Iraq* (London 1955); Stanford Research Institute, *Industrial Economy of Israel,* final report, by Jessie Knight Allen and others (Menlo Park, Calif., 1955); International Bank for Reconstruction and Development, *The Economic Development of Jordan* (Baltimore 1957); Warriner, Doreen, *Land Reform and Development in the Middle East* (New York 1957); Bullard, Sir Reader, ed., *The Middle East,* 3d ed. (New York 1958); Finnie, David H., *Desert Enterprise: The Middle East Oil Industry in Its Local Environment* (Cambridge, Mass., 1958); Meyer, Albert J., Jr., *Middle Eastern Capitalism* (Cambridge, Mass., 1959).

CULTURAL LIFE: Gibb, Elias J. W., *A History of Ottoman Poetry,* 6 vols. (London 1900–09); Levy, Reuben, *Persian Literature* (London 1923); Gibb, Sir Hamilton A. R., *Arabic Literature* (London 1926); Arnold, Sir Thomas W., *Painting in Islam* (Oxford 1928); Browne, Edward G., *A Literary History of Persia,* 4 vols. (Cambridge, Eng., 1928); Nicholson, Reynold A., *A Literary History of the Arabs,* 2d ed., rev. (Cambridge, Eng., 1930); Martinovitch, Nicholas N., *The Turkish Theatre* (New York 1933); Pope, Arthur U., and Ackerman, Phyllis, eds., *A Survey of Persian Art from Prehistoric Times to the Present,* 7 vols. (New York 1938–39); Creswell, Keppel A. C., *Early Muslim Architecture,* 2 vols. (Oxford 1932–40); Dimand, Maurice S., *A Handbook of Muhammadan Art,* 2d ed., rev. and enl. (New York 1944); Fyzee, Asaf A. A., *Outlines of Muhammadan Law* (New York 1950); Schacht, Joseph, *The Origins of Muhammadan Jurisprudence* (Oxford 1950); Khadduri, Majid, *War and Peace in the Law of Islam,* 3d ed. (Baltimore 1955); Landau, Jacob M., *Studies in the Arab Theater and Cinema* (Philadelphia 1958); Anderson, James N. D., *Islamic Law in the Modern World* (New York 1959); Creswell, Keppel A. C., *The Muslim Architecture of Egypt,* 2 vols. (Oxford 1952–59).

HISTORY; CHRONOLOGY: Longrigg, Stephen H., *Four Centuries of Modern Iraq* (Oxford 1925); Sykes, Sir Percy M., *A History of Persia,* 3d ed., rev. and enl., 2 vols. (London 1930); Arnold, Sir Thomas W., and Guillaume, Alfred, eds., *The Legacy of Islam* (Oxford 1931); Barthold, Vasilii V., *Mussulman Culture,* tr. from the Russian by Shahid Suhrawardy (Calcutta 1934); Wittek, Paul, *The Rise of the Ottoman Empire* (London 1938); Poliak, A. N., *Feudalism in Egypt, Syria, Palestine and the Lebanon, 1250–1900* (London 1939); Marriott, Sir John A. R., *The Eastern Question,* 4th ed. (Oxford 1940); Antonius, George, *The Arab Awakening* (London 1946); Hourani, Albert H., *Syria and Lebanon* (London 1946); Rifaat, Mohammed, *The Awakening of Modern Egypt* (London 1947); Lenczowski, George, *Russia and the West in Iran, 1918–1948* (Ithaca, N.Y., 1949); Hurewitz, Jacob C., *The Struggle for Palestine* (New York 1950); id., ed., *Documents in Near East Diplomatic History* (New York 1951); Thomas, Lewis V., and Frye, Richard N., *The United States and Turkey and Iran* (Cambridge, Mass., 1951); Mekki, Abbas, *The Sudan Question* (London 1952); Grunebaum, Gustave E. von, *Medieval Islam,* 2d ed. (Chicago 1953); Longrigg, Stephen H., *Iraq, 1900–1950* (London 1953); *The Encyclopaedia of Islām,* 4 vols. and supplement in 5 parts (Leiden 1913–38); new ed. in fascicles (Leiden 1954–); Hazard, Harry W., comp., *Atlas of Islamic History,* 3d ed., rev. (Princeton 1954); Philby, Harry St. John B., *Sa'udi Arabia* (London 1955); Laqueur, Walter Z., *Communism and Nationalism in the Middle East* (New York 1956); Lenczowski, George, *The Middle East in World Affairs,* 2d ed. (Ithaca, N.Y., 1956); Lewis, Bernard, *The Arabs in History,* 3d ed. (London 1956); Bernstein, Marver H., *The Politics of Israel* (Princeton 1957); Gibb, Sir Hamilton A. R., and Bowen, Harold, *Islamic Society and the West,* vol. 1, parts 1 and 2 (London 1950–57); Hitti, Philip K., *History of Syria,* 2d ed. (New York 1957); id., *Lebanon in History* (New York 1957); Ibn Khaldun, *The Muqaddimah,* tr. from the Arabic by Franz Rosenthal, 3 vols. (New York 1958); Longrigg, Stephen H., *Syria and Lebanon Under French Mandate* (New York 1958); Patai, Raphael, *The Kingdom of Jordan* (Princeton 1958); Twitchell, Karl S., and others, *Saudi Arabia,* 3d ed. (Princeton 1958); Wilber, Donald N., *Iran Past and Present,* 4th ed. (Princeton 1958); Yale, William, *The Near East: a Modern History* (Ann Arbor, Mich., 1958); Fisher, Sydney N., *The Middle East* (New York 1959); Kirk, George E., *A Short History of the Middle East,* 5th ed., rev. (New York 1959); Hitti, Philip K., *History of the Arabs,* 8th ed. (London 1963); id., *Lebanon in History,* 2d ed. (London 1963); id., *The Near East in History,* 3d printing (Princeton 1963).

R. BAYLY WINDER,
Princeton University.

NOTE: The foregoing articles on the Middle East were prepared under the joint direction of the editors of THE ENCYCLOPEDIA AMERICANA and Dr. R. Bayly Winder, associate professor of Oriental studies, Princeton University.

MIDDLE ENGLISH. See ENGLISH LANGUAGE; ENGLISH LITERATURE—*1. Middle English Literature: 1066–1500.*

MIDDLE FORK, river, Oregon, flowing approximately 115 miles northwestward across Lane County. With Coast Fork it forms the Willamette River near Eugene. Lookout Point Reservoir, with a dam 250 feet high, is above Eugene.

MIDDLE TEMPLE. See INNS OF COURT; LONDON.

MIDDLEBORO (officially MIDDLEBOROUGH), unincorporated village, Massachusetts, situated in Plymouth County, at an altitude of 110 feet, 35 miles south of Boston, on the New York, New Haven and Hartford Railroad. It is in a cranberry-growing area. Manufactures of importance are shoes, hospital supplies, varnishes, fire apparatus, brass products, plastics, and caskets. The village has a high school and a public library.

Middleboro forms part of the town of Middleboro, settled in 1660 and incorporated in 1669. One of the oldest towns in the county, it was called Nemasket by the Indians, who were friendly toward the townspeople until the outbreak of King Philip's War in 1675. Burned by the Indians, it was soon rebuilt. An excellent supply of water power favored the growth of industries in the 19th century. Pop. 13,607.

MIDDLEBURY, town, Connecticut, situated in New Haven County, six miles west-southwest of Waterbury. The town is largely residential but has some dairy farms and a plant manufacturing watches and clocks. To the west is Quassapaug Pond. In the town are the Westover School for Girls and the Chauncey Judd House, scene of an incident in the American Revolution. Middlebury was settled early in the 18th century and incorporated in 1807 on land taken from Waterbury, Woodbury, and Southbury. Pop. 5,542.

MIDDLEBURY, village, Vermont, seat of Addison County, on the Rutland Railway, 33 miles north-northwest of Rutland. Located in the town of Middlebury at an altitude of 365 feet on both sides of Otter Creek and under the shelter of Chipman Hill, it is a noted cultural center, the seat of Middlebury College (q.v.), famed as a foreign language study center.

Among its historic buildings are the Wainwright House (1807), the Congregational Church (1806–1809), the Community House (1816) and the Sheldon Art Museum (1829). The village is also the center of a winter and summer resort region.

Midway between Salisbury and New Haven, Vt., Middlebury received its name and charter in 1761 as one of the New Hampshire Grants (q.v.). By edict of George III, it became part of New York in 1764, and for some 20 years its town meetings were held in Salisbury, Conn., home of most of the early proprietors. The first land was cleared in 1766, with settlements undertaken in 1773 and 1778 and renewed, after Indian Tory raids, in 1783. The town was organized in the independent state of Vermont in 1786, and the village was incorporated in 1832. Middlebury College was founded here in 1800. In 1807, Emma Hart (later Emma Willard) of Connecticut, author of *Rocked in the Cradle of the Deep*, began here a pioneer project for women's education; in 1814 she opened the Middlebury Female Seminary as a private institution to demonstrate the capacity of women to master subjects studied by men.

Early industrial developments at Middlebury include the discovery (1799) of a practical method of welding cast steel; development of the use of sand, water, and toothless saws in quarrying marble, and the invention of the first machine for manufacturing doors and window sashes. Paper, cotton, woolen, and lumber mills were established in the 19th century. Dairying, poultry raising, and fruit growing are the chief farming activities. Pop. 6,532.

MIDDLEBURY COLLEGE, a nonsectarian, coeducational institution of higher education located in Middlebury, Vt. A private liberal arts college chartered and opened in 1800, it is the oldest college in the state. Admission to the college was restricted to men until 1883, when the school became coeducational. In 1915 the college acquired more than 30,000 acres of land at nearby Bread Loaf, Vt., and on this site the Bread Loaf School of English was opened in 1920. The Bread Loaf Writers' Conference has been held there annually since 1926. In the late 1960's the college's total enrollment was about 1,400, and the faculty numbered more than 100.

Middlebury College is famous as a center for the study of foreign languages. In 1915 it instituted a series of foreign-language summer schools, which contributed importantly to the development of language studies in the United States. Beginning in 1949 it established graduate schools abroad in various languages: in French at Paris (1949), in Spanish at Madrid (1951), in German at Mainz (1959), and in Italian at Florence (1960). Middlebury's summer schools teach these four languages and also Russian and Chinese.

In addition to B.A. and M.A. degrees in the modern languages, Middlebury offers B.A. degrees in various fields of the humanities and in the natural and social sciences, and M.A. degrees in biology, chemistry, and English. It also offers a doctorate of modern languages. In addition, the college maintains a five-year engineering program in conjunction with several technical schools.

MIDDLEMARCH (in full MIDDLEMARCH, A STUDY OF PROVINCIAL LIFE), a novel by George Eliot (q.v.), first published in 1871–1872. To many critics, *Middlemarch* is the greatest novel George Eliot ever wrote. Its scope, its variety, its maturity and insight are indubitable. Yet to others it lacks something of the charm and spontaneity of the author's earlier works, and its very inclusiveness and scope lead to a certain confusion of plan and blurring of outline that mark it as artistically imperfect. Whichever view is correct, the novel is admittedly great. Written late in George Eliot's career, it is at once weighty with her considered evaluation of the essential factors in life and rich in her observation and experience of human nature. The plot is the most involved of any that the author presented, and the characters are numerous even for a Victorian three-decker. In general there are two main groups of characters, not, it must be confessed, as closely interrelated as artistically they should be. Dorothea Brooke may be regarded as the center of one group, and Dr. Lydgate of the other. Both represent the tragedy of high aims that fail to take fully into account the actualities of life. Dorothea sentimentally pines to be the helpmate of a genius; but as the wife of the Rev. Edward Casaubon, who is writing a *Key to All Mythologies,* she is disillusioned, and her misery is ended only by the death of her husband. Dr. Lydgate comes to Middlemarch with excellent training, determined to push forward in biological research. However, he marries the attractive but unpractical Rosamond Vincy, is overwhelmed in debts, and his possible career fades into nothingness. But George Eliot's view of life is not distortedly pessimistic. Over against the somber recognition of the inadequacies and weaknesses of humanity must be placed her portrayal of the fine and strong elements. Dorothea herself is genuine and charming fundamentally; the Garths are sterling, and full of vitality. For all its wavering and crowded plot, *Middlemarch* is permanently valuable because it represents a realism that endeavors to reflect in just proportions the good and bad in life; a realism, moreover, that does not content itself merely with presenting life, but does not shrink from the task of interpretation and evaluation.

MIDDLEPORT, village, Ohio, situated in Meigs County, at an altitude of 565 feet, on the Ohio River, 51 miles southwest of Marietta. It has freight service via the Chesapeake & Ohio and the New York Central railroads. There are coal mines and gas and oil wells in the vicinity, and the village has railroad shops and plants processing food and manufacturing cement blocks. After a disastrous flood in 1937, Middleport was moved back from the river front. Pop. 2,784.

MIDDLESBOROUGH or **MIDDLESBORO,** city, Kentucky, situated in Bell County, at an altitude of 1,135 feet, near Cumberland Gap, 110 miles southeast of Lexington. It is served by the Louisville & Nashville and the Southern railroads. In a coal and iron mining region, it produces mining equipment, foundry and machine shop products, leather, elastic webbing, coke, wood products, and overalls. Just south of the city is Fern Lake, and nearby are the ruins of Fort Lyon. Middlesborough was founded in 1889 by English interests and named for the English town of Middlesborough. Incorporated as a city in 1892, it is governed by a commission and owns its airport. It is a popular summer resort. Pop. 11,844.

MIDDLESBROUGH, mĭd"lz-brŭ, county borough, England, situated in the North Riding of Yorkshire, on the south bank of the Tees River, 34 miles south of Newcastle. It dates from 1829–1830, with the development of the coal and iron mines of the neighboring Cleveland Hills and Durham fields. It is distinguished for its municipal enterprises; it has handsome public buildings, including a fine Roman Catholic cathedral; and extensive and commodious docks. Its chief industries are connected with iron manufactures. It has numerous blast furnaces and rolling mills, foundries, engineering works, potteries, chemical works, and shipyards; salt is extensively worked.

The borough was incorporated in 1853 and received a county charter in 1888. One member is returned to the House of Commons. The chief public utilities are municipally owned. Pop. (1961) 157,308.

MIDDLESEX, mĭd"l-sĕks, county, England, located in the Thames basin, adjoining London; bounded on the north by Hertfordshire, on the south by Surrey, on the east by Essex and London, and on the west by Buckinghamshire. The chief towns are Brentford (the capital) and Chiswick, Willesden, Uxbridge, Ealing, Hornsey, Harrow, Tottenham, and Hampton. The county is drained by the Thames, Colne, and Lea rivers. It is chiefly residential, with market gardening. The area is 232 square miles.

Middlesex, so named because it was between the east and the west Saxons, is one of the older English counties. Pop. (1961) 2,230,093.

MIDDLETON, mĭd"l-tŭn, **Arthur,** American colonist: b. Charleston, South Carolina, 1681; d. Sept. 7, 1737. He was conspicuously engaged in public affairs as a member of the council as early as 1712; and exerted his political influence in favor of popular claims, opposing the lords proprietors, and finally heading the revolution which threw off the whole proprietary government and placed the colony under the immediate protection of the Crown (1719). In 1725 he succeeded Gen. Francis Nicholson as acting governor of the colony, which office he held till 1731, when the royal governor arrived; he then retained his position in the governor's council. His administration as governor was partly occupied by war and negotiations with the Spaniards of Florida and the French of Louisiana.

MIDDLETON, Arthur, American patriot, signer of the Declaration of Independence: b. Middleton Place, near Charleston, South Carolina, June 26, 1742; d. Goose Creek, South Carolina, Jan. 1, 1787. He was educated in England at the University of Cambridge, then returned to South Carolina for a time and was a member of the legislature, but went abroad again for two years' travel on the Continent. On his final return to America, he established himself as a planter, and soon became one of the leaders of the Revolutionary party. He was one of the most efficient members of the first council of safety, and in 1775 was sent to the Provincial Congress. In 1776 he was sent as a delegate of the state to the Continental Congress, and as such affixed his signature to the Declaration of Independence. He held his seat in Congress until 1777, declined the governorship of South Carolina in 1778, and took the field for the defense of Charleston in 1779. His plantation was devastated by the British and he was made a prisoner after the fall of Charleston in 1780, and was one of the leading citizens who were kept in confinement as hostages. His estate was sequestered, and he was shipped to the castle of St. Augustine, and thence transferred to the *Jersey* prison ship. Exchanged in the latter part of 1780, he served until the close of the war as a delegate in the Continental Congress, and was afterward elected to the state senate. He was a skillful stenographer, and reported many of the debates in which he participated.

MIDDLETON, Conyers, English divine: b. York, or Richmond, Yorkshire, Dec. 27, 1683; d. Hildersham, near Cambridge, July 28, 1750. He was educated at Cambridge and was elected a fellow there in 1706. He married soon afterward, thus losing his fellowship, and for a short time was rector of Coveney in the Isle of Ely, a rectory in the gift of his wealthy wife. He received his D.D. at Cambridge in 1717. He was appointed university librarian in 1721, and was in Italy in 1724–1725. His *Letter from Rome* (1729) dealt at some length upon the adaptation of pagan beliefs and ceremonies in the Roman Catholic Church and was highly praised by the orthodox English clergy, and occasioned great indignation among the Catholics. His controversy with Daniel Waterland, in which he urged the then heretical theory that theologians should not attempt to maintain the historical accuracy of the Bible in all instances, brought a storm of criticism and he was obliged to make some qualifications regarding his statements in order to retain his Cambridge degrees. He next engaged upon a life of Cicero, which to a great extent was related in the statesman's own words, and which gained a high reputation as a model of style, but was later found to be largely plagiarism from a rare book of William Bellenden's *De tribus luminibus Romanorum.* He then returned to the field of theological controversy, publishing his *Introductory Discourse* (1747), and his *Free Inquiry* (1748), attacking the miraculous powers supposed to have been inherent in the Church from early times. While this controversy was in progress Middleton died.

MIDDLETON, George, American playwright: b. Paterson, New Jersey, Oct. 27, 1880. After receiving his A.B. degree at Columbia University in 1902 he embarked on a literary career. The same year his first play, *The Cavalier,* written in collaboration with Paul Kester, was produced. Other successful play collaborations were *The Sinner,* with L. Westervelt (1907); *Hit-the-Trail-Holliday,* with George M. Cohan and Guy Bolton (1915); *Polly with a Past,* with Bolton (1917); *Accused,* with E. H. Southern (1925); and *The Big Pond,* with A. E. Thomas (1929). He was also sole author of several other plays including *Rosalind at the Gate* (1910) and *The Prodigal Judge* (1913).

In 1911 Middleton married Fola La Follette and the following year became literary editor of *La Follette's Weekly Magazine.* After serving as president of the Dramatists Guild of the Authors' League of America (1927–1929), he was for two years an associate producer of Fox Film Corporation. In 1942 he joined the staff of the Alien Property Custodian as a copyright expert. He died in Washington, D.C., on Dec. 23, 1967.

MIDDLETON, Henry, American patriot, son of Arthur Middleton (1681–1737, q.v.): b. South Carolina, 1717; d. Charleston, South Carolina, June 13, 1784. He was elected to the South Carolina House of Commons and in 1745–1747 was its speaker. Appointed commissioner of Indian Affairs in 1755, he also served as a member of the council in 1755–1770. Elected a delegate to the Continental Congress in 1774, he was its president from October 1774 to May 1775. He was president of the Provincial Congress of South Carolina in 1775–1776. Re-elected to the Continental Congress in 1776, ill health obliged him to surrender his seat to his son Arthur (1742–1787, q.v.).

MIDDLETON, Henry, American politician and diplomat: b. London, England, Sept. 28, 1770; d. Charleston, South Carolina, June 14, 1846. Elected to the South Carolina legislature in 1801, he served until 1810, when he began a two-year term as governor of the state. A vigorous supporter of the war policy in 1812, he was elected to Congress in 1815 and served for four years. In 1820 he was appointed minister to Russia, in which capacity he negotiated a treaty regulating trade and fisheries in the Pacific (1824). After his return to the United States in 1830 he retired from public life.

MIDDLETON, Thomas, English dramatist: b. probably in London, England, 1570?; d. Newington Butts, England, July 1627. Little is known of his life, but his writings testify to the excellence of his education before his entry at Gray's Inn in 1593 or 1596.

Several minor prose works preceded what seems to be his first play, *Old Law* (1599), written with William Rowley. From that time on he wrote constantly for the stage, now alone, now with Rowley, Philip Massinger, or Thomas Dekker. Among these works are several masques, of which the best and most dramatic is *The World Lost at Tennis* (1620). Middleton's *The Witch* (1778) is his best known work. His most successful play was *A Game at Chess* (1624), which satirized the wooing of the Spanish Infanta and was stopped by the Privy Council; it packed the playhouses because of its political and Protestant tone.

Among his other plays are *Michaelmas Terme* (1607), *A Trick to Catch the Old-One* (1608), *The Roaring Girle* (1611), *The Spanish Gipsie* (1653), and *Women Beware Women* (1657).

His works were edited by Alexander Dyce, 5 vols. (1840), and by A. H. Bullen, 8 vols. (1885).

MIDDLETON, municipal borough, England, in Lancashire, 5 miles northeast of Manchester. Its industrial establishments include cotton and silk factories, dye and print works, ironworks, chemical works, and aircraft plants. Coal is extensively mined in the vicinity.

The Church of St. Leonard dates from the 12th to the 16th century; the grammar school was founded in 1572. Gas and electric lighting plants are municipally owned. Pop. (1961) 56,674.

MIDDLETOWN, city, Connecticut, Middlesex County seat, on the Connecticut River, altitude 50 feet, about 14 miles south of Hartford, on the New York, New Haven and Hartford Railroad, and modern highways.

The city is the business center of a rich agricultural region producing tobacco, fruits, and dairy products. Manufactures include metal products, elastic webbing, textiles, hardware, automobile parts, asbestos, chemicals, machinery, cigars, and rubber goods.

It is the seat of Wesleyan University (q.v.), founded in 1831. Two state institutions, Connecticut State Hospital for the insane, and Long Lane Farm, an industrial school for girls, are located here.

The town was settled in 1650 by colonists from Hartford and Wethersfield, and was incorporated in 1651 under its Indian name of Mattabeseck. In 1653 it was given the name Middletown because of its location midway between Hartford and Saybrook. A company recruited here by Col. Return Jonathan Meigs, at the outbreak of the Revolutionary War, fought at Bunker Hill and was cited for bravery by Washington. During the latter half of the 18th century it was one of the most prosperous towns in the state and is still a thriving industrial, commercial, and educational community. It was once a port of entry and carried on a flourishing trade with the West Indies in lumber and farm products. Silver and lead were mined in the vicinity, gold was found there, and valuable deposits of freestone, feldspar, and columbite became commercially important.

Incorporated as a city in 1784, it obtained a new charter in 1882 providing for a mayor and council. The water supply is municipally owned. Pop. 36,924.

MIDDLETOWN, city, New York, in Orange County, on the Walkill River; altitude 559 feet; about 21 miles southwest of Newburgh on the Erie; New York, Ontario and Western; Middletown and New Jersey railroads; and state and federal highways.

It is the business and industrial center of a fertile agricultural region in the foothills of the beautiful Shawangunk Mountains, producing poultry, fruit and garden truck, onions, celery, and potatoes. The city has railroad shops, foundries, a tannery, and silk mills, and manufactures of saws, shirts, leather goods, footwear, underwear, wrapping and printing machinery, hats, handbags, and fur. The Orange County Community College was opened here in 1950.

The town was settled in 1796, and named as a halfway point on the Minisink trail from New York City to western New York. Incorporated as a village in 1848, it obtained a city charter in 1888. It has mayor and council, and municipally owned water supply. Pop. 22,607.

MIDDLETOWN, city, Ohio, in Butler County; altitude 666 feet; on the Great Miami River, about 33 miles north of Cincinnati; on the Baltimore and Ohio; Big Four; and Pennsylvania railroads; state and federal highways.

In the heart of the rich Miami Valley, it is the industrial center of a fertile agricultural region producing wheat, corn, hay, and oats. Manufactures include sheet and corrugated steel, paper, paper bags, boxes, and steel paper-making machinery.

The town was laid out in 1802 and named for its location midway between the mouth of the Great Miami River and its most northern navigable point. On one of Ohio's early canals, it was a shipping point for hogs during the mid-19th century. Later it turned to the manufacture of paper and tobacco. During World War I it grew in importance for the manufacture of steel.

Middletown was incorporated as a city in 1833, and adopted the commission type of municipal government in 1913. In 1949 the city charter was amended to provide for the commission-manager type of government. It has municipally owned water supply, and an airport. Pop. 48,767.

MIDDLETOWN, borough, Pennsylvania, in Dauphin County; altitude 355 feet; on the Susquehanna River; about 8 miles southeast of Harrisburg; on the Reading and the Pennsylvania railroads.

Founded in 1755 on the site of an Indian village, Middletown was incorporated in 1828. A market center for a farming region its principal local manufactures are infant's shoes, work clothing, boilers and stoves. A boat-building center during the Revolutionary War, it was one of the first towns in the United States to make steel. During the early 19th century it was a canal shipping center. Nearby is Emaus Orphanage, founded in 1837, one of the oldest orphanages in the United States. St. Peter's Lutheran Church was built here in 1767. Olmsted Air Force Base is located here. Pop. 9,080.

MIDDLETOWN, town, Rhode Island, in Newport County, 5 miles north of Newport, on Narragansett Bay. It is on the New York, New Haven, and Hartford Railroad (for freight only), and on state highways. Predominantly agricultural, it is also a resort town. St. George's School, a private boys' school, is located here. The town was incorporated in 1743; government is by town meeting. Pop. 29,621.

MIDEWIN, mĭ-dā'wĕn, or **MIDEWIWIN,** mĭ-dā'wĕ-wĕn, or **MIDE,** mē'dĕ, or **MEDA SOCIETY,** a secret religious organization of the Ojibway Indians and neighboring tribes. The aim of the society was to prolong life by the use of herbs and magic.

MIDGARD, mĭd'gärd, in Scandinavian mythology, the dwelling place of the human race, formed from the eyebrows of Ymir, one of the first giants, and joined to Asgard, the abode of the gods, by the rainbow bridge.

MIDGE. See GNAT.

MIDGLEY, mĭj'lĭ, **Thomas, Jr.,** American research chemist: b. Beaver Falls, Pennsylvania, May 18, 1889; d. near Columbus, Ohio, Nov. 2, 1944. He was educated at Cornell University, and received his M.E. in 1911. From 1912 to 1914 he did research work on automobile tires, and from 1914 to 1916 he was superintendent of the Midgley Tire and Rubber Company of Lancaster, Ohio. He worked with Charles F. Kettering and the General Motors Research Corporation until 1923 when he was appointed vice president of the Ethyl Corporation, a position he retained until his death. He was a vice president of Kinetics Chemical, Inc. from 1930, and director of Ethyl-Dow Chemical Company from 1933. From 1940 he was vice president of the Ohio State University Research Foundation, and vice chairman of the National Inventors Council.

His most noteworthy contribution to science was the discovery of tetraethyl lead as a gasoline anti-knock compound; also certain organic fluoride compounds for refrigerants which are noninflammable and nontoxic.

He was awarded the Nichols Medal of the American Chemical Society in 1923, the Perkins Medal in 1937, the Longstreth Medal of the Franklin Institute in 1925, the Priestly Medal of the American Chemical Society in 1941, and the Willard Gibbs Medal in 1942.

MIDHAT PASHA, mĭd-hät'pä-shä', Turkish statesman: b. Constantinople, 1822; d. Arabia, May 8, 1884. He entered the Turkish government service, was made pasha in 1860, was governor successively of Uskup, Bulgaria and Salonica, and distinguished himself by his wise administration. In 1873 he was for a short time grand vizier. He aided in deposing the sultans Abdul-Aziz and Murad V in 1876, was grand vizier under Abdul-Hamid (Dec. 1876-Feb. 1877), and was then banished by the suspicious monarch. Later, however, he was governor of Smyrna, then of Syria. He was tried with other pashas for the murder of Abdul-Aziz, was found guilty and was sentenced to death; but this sentence was commuted to life imprisonment.

MIDIANITES, mĭd'ĭ-ăn-ītz, an Arab tribe, descended, according to Scripture, from Midian, the son of Abraham by Keturah. They occupied most of the country between the Arabian Gulf and the Plains of Moab. The Midianites were very troublesome neighbors to the Israelites till Gideon's victory over them. Midian ceased to be Egyptian and became Turkish in 1887. It is now part of Saudi Arabia.

MIDLAND, city, Michigan, and Midland County seat; altitude 620 feet; on the Chippewa and Tittabawassee rivers; 19 miles west of Bay City; served by the New York Central and Chesapeake and Ohio railroads. It is the home of one of the nation's largest chemical companies; it also derives revenue from petroleum wells in the vicinity. Midland was incorporated as a village in 1869, and as a city in 1887. Government is by a city manager and council. Pop. 35,176.

MIDLAND, town, Province of Ontario, Canada, in Simcoe County, on Georgian Bay, about 90 miles north of Toronto by Canadian National and Canadian Pacific railway lines. It is in a good farming district and has a fine harbor which is a port of call for shipping on the upper lakes. With its elevators of a total capacity of 12,800,000 bushels, the town's main industrial activities are flour milling and three large shipbuilding and repair yards. Lumber, planing and woolen mills, foundry and machine shops are located there. Hydroelectric power is obtained from the Severn River to the east. There are five public schools and a collegiate institute, a weekly newspaper, a public library, a fine park, a hospital, and three banks. Midland is annually visited by many pilgrims to the shrine of the Jesuit martyrs of early Canada nearby. Population: 10,992.

MIDLAND, borough, Pennsylvania, in Beaver County, 28 miles west-northwest of Pittsburgh, on the Ohio River; served by the Pennsylvania Railroad. Manufactures include coke by-products, steel and iron. Settled around 1820, the borough has a mayor-council form of government. Pop. 5,271.

MIDLAND, town, Texas, Midland County seat; 20 miles north of Odessa, and midway between Fort Worth and El Paso; altitude 2,760 feet; on the Texas and Pacific Railroad, with bus service, and three airlines; on federal and state highways.

Situated in the center of the vast Permian Basin oilfields of western Texas and southeastern New Mexico, Midland is the headquarters of more than 300 oil companies and affiliate offices operating in the area. It is also an important center of the cattle industry in a region comprising the greater part of 12 counties of Texas and New Mexico. In the vicinity, cotton, grain sorghum, fruits and vegetables are the leading crops. Business enterprises include carbon black plants, natural gasoline and extraction plants, refineries, and numerous pipeline companies.

History.—A cow town on the trail from Pecos to Fort Worth in the late 19th and early 20th century, as recently as 1921 Midland had only 1,400 inhabitants. The oil strike made that year brought sudden wealth to the townsfolk and ranchers, also a rapid increase in the population. The unsightly oil derricks which mar the appearance of so many oil towns are not in evidence, the city fathers having decreed that no well may be drilled within the city limits. Though trees do not grow easily here, the Chinese elm, with its feathery leaves, lines the streets and open spaces.

The town has a theater and a music association, a branch of the American Association of University Women, a chapter of the League of Women Voters, and the Petroleum Club.

Settled in 1885, Midland was incorporated in 1906. Pop. 59,463.

MIDLOTHIAN, mĭd-lō'thĭ-ăn (formerly EDINBURGH or EDINBURGHSHIRE), county, Scotland, on the south shore of the Firth of Forth. The northern portion is flat; the Pentland Hills cross the county from the southwest, and the Moorfoot Hills are in the southeast. The Gala, Esk, Almond, and Tyne rivers flow through the county. Agriculture, livestock raising, dairying, fisheries, shipbuilding, manufactures of paper, iron products, and carpets, and distilling of whiskey are carried on. Edinburgh is the capital city. Area of county 366 square miles; pop. (1961) 580,332.

MIDNAPUR, mid'nə-poor, is a city in eastern India. It is situated in the state of West Bengal, about 70 miles west of Calcutta. Midnapur (formerly Midnapore) is a center of indigo and silk industries and also has manufactures of brass and copper goods. It is the administrative headquarters of Midnapur district (area 5,258 square miles) in the southern part of West Bengal. Population (1961): city, 59,532; district, 4,341,855.

MIDNIGHT JUDGES, or **APPOINTMENTS,** a term applied to executive appointments or nominations made by President John Adams, the last night of his administration. Congress had passed a bill authorizing the appointment of 18 new United States judges, and Adams with the consent of the Senate appointed judges to fill these newly created vacancies. They were known as Adams Midnight Judges. The new law was repealed early in Jefferson's term and the judges lost their offices. The suit of one of these judges, William Marbury, resulted in an important legal decision. See also MARBURY v. MADISON.

MIDNIGHT SUN, is the appearance of the sun above the horizon at midnight. It may be witnessed at any point on the Arctic Circle on June 21, and on the Antarctic Circle on December 21. Within these circles the length of time the sun is in the sky without setting gradually increases, being 65 days in latitude 70°, and 134 days in latitude 80°, while the sun does not set for six months at the poles. Tourists visit the north of Norway about midsummer to witness the phenomenon. This phenomenon of the midnight sun is due to the inclination of the earth's axis, and to the fact that the axis points in the same direction during the whole period of the earth's yearly revolution round the sun.

MIDRASH (Hebrew, from *darash,* to make research), among the Jews, is the general name given to the exposition or exegesis of the

Scriptures. When such writings first arose is not known, but the most flourishing period of midrashic exegesis was from about 100 B.C. to 200 A.D. The term midrash expressed "any and every ancient exposition on the law, psalms and prophets, disquisitions that took the form of allegorical illustration, homiletics or practical commentary." Thus in its most general meaning it expressed the whole uncanonical Jewish literature, including the Talmud, down to the compilation of the book Jalkuth in the 13th century, since which time the term gradually ceased to be applied to rabbinical writings.

MIDRIFF (A.-S. *mid,* middle; *hrif,* abdomen), the diaphragm (q.v.).

MIDSHIPMAN, in the United States Navy, is the designation of a student taking the four-year course of study at the U.S. Naval Academy, Annapolis, Md.; upon graduation he is commissioned ensign. In the British Navy, a midshipman holds the intermediate rank between a naval cadet and a sublieutenant.

MIDSHIPMAN, a California coast-fish of the genus *Porichthys.*

MIDSHIPMAN EASY, Mr. See **MR. MIDSHIPMAN EASY.**

MIDSHIPMAN'S HITCH. See KNOTTING AND SPLICING.

MIDSUMMER NIGHT'S DREAM, A, is a comedy by William Shakespeare, first printed in 1600. Probably written in 1594, or even earlier, it was doubtless written for some wedding festival as it has many of the characteristics of a masque. The incidents connected with Theseus and Hippolyta were taken from Plutarch's *Life of Theseus* and perhaps Chaucer's *Knights Tale,* while the fairy story which makes up such a large part of the play was Shakespeare's transformation of the somewhat crude elements of mediaeval folklore. The first and last acts take place in Athens at the palace of Theseus, and the other three acts in the forest near Athens. Theseus and his queen fit into the story insofar as they celebrate their nuptials, and as they are interested in the love affairs of Demetrius and Helena, Lysander and Hermia; they are brought into the forest only by their love of the chase, which is realistically portrayed. The well-known words of Theseus upon "the lunatic, the lover, and the poet, as of imagination all compact," are in striking contrast with the fantastic fairies that really dominate the play. Even further removed from fairyland are the prosaic mechanics who represent, with all the characteristics of low comedy, the story of Pyramus and Thisbe. By their rehearsal in the forest they are caught for a moment in the magic web of Oberon, Titania, and Puck. Under the same influences fall the Athenian lovers, who after unfortunate experiences are brought to the happy conclusion of their dreams. The title of the play, as indeed the major part of the story and the background, suggest the tone, the atmosphere, of the play. It is the magical midsummer night with the moon in the sky that forms the appropriate setting of the mystery, the fantasy, and the unreason of fairyland. Oberon, Titania, and Puck, along with the other incarnations of the beauty and magic of nature, have fixed in the popular imagination the principal elements of fairyland. The fact that they were represented by boys on the Elizabethean stage gave to these creations the spirit of childhood that has been lost in the modern stage representation. No analysis can suggest the delicacy, or the beauty, or the charm of these airy nothings to which Shakespeare has given a local habitation and a name.

The comedy was also the inspiration for an overture, and music to accompany the play, composed in 1826 and 1843, respectively, by Felix Mendelssohn-Bartholdy. This work, incorporating one of the composer's most celebrated scherzos, beautifully recreates the elfin delicacy of Shakespeare's fairyland.

MIDWAY ISLANDS, a coral atoll in the North Pacific, a possession of the United States. Situated 1,300 miles northwest of Honolulu, the atoll, some six miles in diameter, contains two coral islands—on the western side Sand Island (1¾ miles long and ¾ miles wide, with an average elevation of 8 to 10 feet); and Eastern Island (1¼ miles long and ½ mile wide, with an elevation of 6 to 12 feet). The total area of the atoll is about 28 square miles, and the population in 1958 numbered 200. Both islands are partly covered with coarse grass and bushes, and are a breeding ground of the tern. Fish of many varieties, turtles, crabs, and crawfish, abound in the lagoon. Good water is obtained by sinking wells.

Midway was known as Brooks for several years after its discovery in 1859 by N. C. Brooks, commander of the Hawaiian vessel *Gambia,* who found it uninhabited. During 1887–1889 a shipwrecked crew lived on the atoll for 14 months; several of the men died from scurvy before rescue came. By Executive Order No. 199A, of Jan. 20, 1903, administration of Midway was made a responsibility of the United States Navy Department, and the same year it became a station site of the transpacific cable system. In 1935 the atoll became a stopping point on the Pan American Airways service between Honolulu and the Philippines, a hostel and other facilities being erected on the north side of Sand Island; and in 1939, on the eve of World War II, the United States government commenced construction of submarine and air bases on Eastern Island. In 1941 Midway was proclaimed a national defense area, and when Japan entered the war on December 7 her warships shelled the American installations on Eastern Island the same day. Thereafter the Japanese made occasional air attacks, and on June 7-8, 1942, an air battle was fought between American and Japanese large carriers some 700 miles west of Midway; this engagement, known in history as the Battle of Midway, resulted in a severe defeat for Japan and proved to be one of the decisive naval victories of the war.

MIDWIFE TOAD, a European representative (*Alytes obstetricans*) of the family Discoglossidae, noteworthy on account of its unusual breeding habits. Pairing of this widely distributed species occurs throughout spring and summer, the female being capable of spawning from two to four times during the year. When she is ready to lay, the male, approaching from behind, grasps her about the waist and aids in the extrusion of the yellow ova. These, numbering from 50 to 100 and strung together by elastic filaments, are expelled explosively into a receptacle formed by the mother's closely pressed hind limbs, bound behind and beneath by the feet of the male. At the moment of extrusion the male shifts his hold to a point in advance of the fore-limbs and proceeds to fertilize the eggs. After this is accomplished he repeatedly thrusts his feet into the sticky mass until the strings of eggs are wound about, and adhering to, his thighs. Releasing his mate, the male midwife toad slowly hops or crawls away to the retreat where he is accustomed to spend the day. When he emerges in search of food, nocturnal dews assist in keeping the eggs moist; during exceptionally dry weather, the male may resort to brief immersions. During the 20 or more days it takes for the larvae to develop, they are nourished by the large yolks of their eggs. Toward the end of this period, the male parent seeks out a pool, in which he remains until the young burst through their envelopes and take up life in the water.

MIDWIFERY. See OBSTETRICS.

MIELATZ, mē'läts, **Charles Frederick William,** American etcher: b. Breddin, Germany, May 24, 1860; d. New York, N. Y., June 2, 1919. Taken to the United States in childhood, he studied drawing at the Chicago, Ill., School of Design and Painting; from 1903 he maintained his studio in New York City. He was an instructor at the National Academy of Design, in that city, and became widely known for his etchings, dry points, aquatints, and lithographs. He is best known for his large number of views of New York, but he also executed rural, woodland, and marine scenes.

MIERES, myā'râs, town, Spain, located in Oviedo Province, 9 miles south-southeast from Oviedo, on the Lena or Caudal River. It is situated in a mountainous region with heavy forests and fertile land. The center of an important industrial area, it has coal, iron, sulfur, and cinnabar mines, and iron and chemical works. Pop. (1960) 75,388.

MIEREVELT or **MIEREVELD,** mē'rĕ-vĕlt, **Michiel Janszoon van,** Dutch portrait painter: b. Delft, Netherlands, May 1, 1567; d. there, June 27, 1641. As court painter to the house of Orange he did portraits of William of Orange and other princes of that house and of Nassau. He worked mainly in his native city and at The Hague.

His son PIETER VAN MIEREVELT (b. Delft Oct. 5, 1596; d. there, Jan. 11, 1623) followed his father's style and devoted himself similarly to portraits.

MIES VAN DER ROHE, mēs' van dər rō'ə, **Ludwig,** German-American architect and industrial designer: b. Aachen, Germany, March 27, 1886. Together with Walter Gropius and Le Corbusier, Mies was one of the three major exponents of the International style that dominated architecture during the first half of the 20th century. "Less is more"—Mies' summary of his own architectural aesthetic—became the credo of architectural functionalism, but the spare elegance of his buildings achieves a classic grace that transcends the merely functional.

He was born Ludwig Mies. (He later added "van der Rohe," his mother's surname, to his own.) After ending his formal education at the age of 15, Mies worked for five years as a designer of stucco architectural ornaments. In 1905 he went to Berlin, where he worked first for the decorator and furniture designer Bruno Paul. From 1908 to 1911 he was an apprentice in the office of the architect Peter Behrens, with whom both Gropius and Le Corbusier had been associated for some time.

Mies' early works include the Riehl house (1907) in Berlin and the Glass Industry Exhibit for the Deutsche Werkbund exposition in Stuttgart (1927). He also designed a series of daring projects, such as a Glass Skyscraper (1921), that became widely known but were never carried out.

The two masterpieces of Mies' career in Europe were the German Pavilion at the International Exposition in Barcelona (1929, later destroyed), and the Tugendhat house (1930), in Brno, Czechoslovakia. He also designed the furniture for both buildings, and his "Barcelona chair" became a classic of 20th century design.

From 1930 until the victory of the Nazi movement in 1933, Mies was director of Germany's famous Bauhaus (q.v.). He moved to the United States in 1937, becoming a citizen in 1944, and headed the school of architecture at the Illinois Institute of Technology in Chicago until 1958. His designs in Chicago include the twin 26-story apartment towers at 860 Lakeshore Drive (1951), Crown Hall on the ITT campus (1955), and the Chicago Federal Center (1964). In New York, in association with Philip Johnson, he designed the Seagram building (1958). Other notable buildings include the Schaefer Museum in Schweinfurt, West Germany (1962) and the National Gallery in Berlin (1968). He died in Chicago on Aug. 18, 1969.

Further Reading: Blake, Peter, *Mies van der Rohe* (Baltimore 1964); Blaser, Werner, *Mies van der Rohe* (New York 1965); Drexler, Arthur, *Ludwig Mies van der Rohe* (New York 1960); Hilberseimer, Ludwig, *Mies van der Rohe* (Chicago 1956).

MIESZKO I, myĕsh'kô, Polish ruler: b. ?921; d. 992. Duke of Poland from 962 until his death, he is considered the historic head of the Piast dynasty. Uniting a number of principalities, he began their conversion to Christianity in 963 (or 966, according to some authorities). About this time, threatened by German encroachment, he signed a pact with Otto I, king of Germany and Holy Roman emperor. Under Mieszko I the Christian faith spread through Poland, and he has become known as the founder of the Polish state. His eldest son Boleslav I (q.v.), who succeeded him, was the first king of Poland.

MIESZKO II, king of Poland: b. 990; d. May 10, 1034. The son of Boleslav I, he was assailed by neighbors on all sides and ruled amid strife for less than 10 years (1025–1034), part of that time under the sovereignty of the German emperor. He was followed by his son, Casimir I (q.v.).

MIFFLIN, Thomas, American Revolutionary officer and politician: b. Philadelphia, Pa., Jan. 10, 1744; d. Lancaster, Jan. 20, 1800. He was by birth a Quaker; was graduated at Philadelphia College in 1760; entered public life in 1772 as a member of the Pennsylvania assembly; and in 1774 was elected a delegate to the Continental Congress. In 1775 he entered the army with the rank of major, and as colonel and first aide-de-camp to George Washington accompanied him to Cambridge, Mass. He subsequently held the appointment of adjutant general, and in the spring of 1776 was commissioned as brigadier general. He fought in the Battle of Long Island, and by his energy succeeded in the latter part of 1776 in raising considerable reinforcements in Pennsylvania to recruit Washington's army. He was present at the Battle of Trenton, and did good service in driving back the enemy's line of cantonments from the Delaware. In 1777 he was made a major general, and in the same year became an active member of the faction organized for the purpose of placing Horatio Gates instead of Washington at the head of the Continental Army, and known in history as the Conway Cabal (q.v.). The project failing, he resigned his commission, and in 1782 was elected to Congress, of which body he became president during the following year. In this capacity he received from Washington the resignation of his commission as commander in chief. In 1785 he became speaker of the Pennsylvania legislature, and in 1787 was a delegate to the Constitutional Convention. In October 1788, he succeeded Benjamin Franklin as president of the Supreme Executive Council of Pennsylvania, which position he filled for two years; and from 1790 to 1799 he was governor of the state. In 1794, while holding this office, he rendered important assistance to Washington in quelling the Whisky Rebellion (q.v.).

MIFFLIN, Warner, Quaker reformer: b. Accomac County, Va., Oct. 21, 1745; d. Camden, Del., Oct. 16, 1798. For many years he worked for the abolition of slavery, manumitting his own slaves in 1774–1775. Because of Quaker principles, he refused to support the Revolutionary War, and was consequently dubbed a Tory.

MIFFLIN, Fort. See FORT MIFFLIN.

MIGDOL, mĭg'dōl (Hebrew, a tower), Biblical place mentioned in Jeremiah 44:1; 46:14, as in lower Egypt; in Ezekiel 29:10; 30:6, as the northeastern limit of the country; and in Exodus 14:2 and Numbers 33:7 as a station on the route of the Israelites to the Red Sea.

MIGNARD, mē-nyȧr', **Pierre,** French painter and engraver: b. Troyes, France, Nov. 1610; d. Paris, May 1695. In his middle twenties he went to Italy, working mostly in Rome, whence his surname "the Roman." He painted likenesses of Popes Urban VIII and Alexander VII and of other Roman notables. In 1654 he went to Venice where his success as a portrait painter continued. Summoned to Paris by Louis XIV, he did portraits of the young king, of ladies of the court, and of Cardinal Mazarin, and afterward decorated the cupola of the church of Val-de-Grace with over 200 figures of prophets, martyrs, etc. He subsequently produced some paintings for the palace of Versailles and was made court painter and director (1690) of the Gobelin tapestry works.

His brother, NICOLAS MIGNARD (b. Troyes, 1606; d. Paris, 1668), also was a noted portraitist. He did paintings of Louis and other court dignitaries, and decorations for the Tuileries.

MIGNE, mēn'y', **Jacques Paul,** French Roman Catholic priest and publisher: b. Saint-Flour, France, Oct. 25, 1800; d. Paris, Oct. 24, 1875. He was educated at Orleans, was ordained in 1824, and in 1833 went to Paris and founded *L'Univers religieux,* which later became *L'Univers.* In 1836 he disposed of his interest in that publication and established a publishing house for the production of religious books in inexpensive editions. Perhaps most important was the *Patrology,* published as *Patrologiae cursus completus* (Latin series, 221 vols., 1844–1864; Greek series, in Latin, 81 vols., 1856–1861; Greek series, with Greek text and Latin trans., 166 vols. 1857–1866).

MIGNET, mē-nyĕ', **François Auguste Marie,** French historian: b. Aix, France, May 8, 1796; d. Paris, March 24, 1884. He was educated at Avignon; studied law in Aix and was admitted to the bar in 1818; went to Paris in 1822 after winning a prize for his essay on French institutions of the 13th century. In 1830, with Armand Carrel and his lifelong friend Louis Adolphe Thiers, he founded the liberal, anti-Bourbon journal *Le National.* He was elected to the Academy in 1836; and after the Revolution of 1848 lost the place he had held for 18 years as archivist of the Foreign Office. His most important work was *Histoire de la Révolution française* (1824). Besides this he wrote biographies of Benjamin Franklin (1848), of Mary Stuart (1851), and of Charles V (1854).

MIGNON, mē-nyôɴ', **Abraham,** Dutch painter: b. Frankfurt am Main, Germany, 1640; d. there or at Wetzlar, ?1679. Going to Holland when he was about 20, he studied under Jan Davidsz de Heem, the still-life artist whose style he followed. With a delicate touch, Mignon concentrated on flowers, fruits, birds and other small animals, achieving great finish in his work.

MIGNON, French term of endearment (darling, favorite, pet), sometimes used as a given name. 1. The elflike Italian girl, daughter of an aged harpist, who dies in despair through unrequited love in Goethe's *Wilhelm Meister's Apprenticeship.* 2. Opera by Ambroise Thomas, founded on *Wilhelm Meister,* with words by Michel Carré and Jules Barbier, first produced in Paris in 1866, in London in 1870, and in New York in 1871. 3. A term of opprobrium applied to certain favorites of Henry III of France, youths of frivolous habits and effeminately fashionable dress, popularly charged with dissolute morals and generally hated because of the king's lavish generosity to them.

MIGNONETTE, mĭn-yŭn-ĕt', a genus (*Reseda*) of annual and perennial herbs of the family Resedaceae. The species, of which there are about 50, are natives of western Asia and the Mediterranean region. They have simple or compound leaves, and terminal spikes of small, pale, usually greenish flowers. Less than half a dozen species are cultivated, the most important being the common mignonette (*R. odorata*), a universal favorite both in gardens and in greenhouses because of its fragrant flowers. It is a branching annual herb of decumbent habit when in its prime, and will thrive in any cool, moist, fairly rich soil, when partly shaded from the noonday sun. For outdoor blooming the seeds are sown successionally from early spring to midsummer, and for winter blossoming from that time forward at intervals of three or four weeks.

MIGRAINE, mī'grān (from Lat. *hemicrania,* referring to half of the skull), a disease featured by periodic attacks of headache, usually one-sided, accompanied by other symptoms referable to the nervous system such as vertigo, nausea, and partial loss of vision. Migraine usually takes onset in adolescence; attacks of cyclic vomiting in childhood may be a precursor. Headaches are recurrent, the interval between seizures being of varying length in days, weeks, or months. Head pain begins in the eye or frontotemporal region and soon involves one half of the head, or sometimes the whole cranium. Striking its victim frequently during a state of well-being and lasting proverbially "from sunup to sundown," an attack of migraine leaves the exhausted sufferer to sleep for hours, and upon awakening he may feel unusually healthy. "Migraine equivalents" or substitute seizures include bouts of pain in the face, chest, abdomen, or extremities, diffuse edema, or fever without other explanation.

The excruciating headache which is the most prominent symptom of migraine is the result of paroxysmal enlargement of the branches of the external carotid artery, particularly the vessels in the soft tissues of the temple and also the middle meningeal artery, which supplies the intercranial dura mater (membrane). Neurologic phenomena which precede, accompany, or replace headache in many individuals are due to spasm of the intracranial blood vessels. In other words, in a typical migraine attack arteries of the head outside the brain dilate, while arteries of the brain itself constrict—a paradox which is yet to be solved. "Fireworks" in one visual field are due to contraction of the ophthalmic artery; evanescent loss of half the field of vision in both eyes is caused by spasm of the opposite posterior cerebral artery; temporary hemiplegia (paralysis on one side) is the result of constriction of one middle cerebral artery.

Causes.—Migraine is one of the most common functional diseases of civilized people and is a particular affliction of "brain workers." The cause or causes of the condition are variable with the individual. Heredity plays such a definite role that the diagnosis is suspect if there is not a family history of similar periodic headaches. Stressful situations may precipitate attacks, or in many cases food allergy appears to be almost solely causative. Hormonal influences are often contributory in women, who are affected twice as often as men. Personality characteristics of the typically migrainous patient include meticulous personal habits, obsessive thinking, suppressed aggressive drives, perfectionism, rigidity, and fear of failure.

Treatment.—Migraine treatment is directed largely at control of headache. If such ordinary analgesics as acetylsalicylic acid alone or in combination with caffeine or codeine are ineffective, medication containing ergotamine is in order. Rarely, surgical procedures which divide arteries or remove nerves in the soft tissues of the cranium are necessary. They are successful only if headache always recurs in one area of the head.

JAMES PETER MURPHY, M.D.

MIGRATION, mī-grā'shŭn, **Human,** a coordinated voluntary movement of a considerable number of people from an accustomed habitat to a new one. The outcome of a migration depends upon the possibility of gaining a foothold in the region entered. Neither the wanderings of nomads nor venturesome exploration by individuals constitutes migration, nor does the term apply to rhythmic changes of base by pastoral peoples who move their herds seasonally within a familiar region. The term is often loosely used, however, to denote any considerable movement of a large number of people. For instance, population movements often result from failure of natural resources—notably from lack of water. In the 1930 decade protracted drought forced thousands of farmers to leave the "dust bowl" of Oklahoma and adjacent districts, chiefly for California. Similar tragic flights have recurred throughout history—most frequently in expanding desert areas such as the Sahara borderlands, the margins of the Asian and Australian deserts, and the arid portions of North America. Exhaustion of mineral deposits also has occasioned an exodus of miners from a district. Such abandonment of a place by unorganized individuals, however, does not constitute true migration.

For at least 3,000 years the widening deserts of central Asia have witnessed genuine tribal migrations. Archaeological evidence indicates prehistoric movements to China, to Europe, and to the Fertile Crescent. Central Asian peoples usually are nomads. When the desert expanded, these tent dwellers were organized to move as units with their herds and beasts of burden. For example, the fierce Hsiung-nu tribes repeatedly invaded China as early as the 3d century B.C.; their armed incursions stimulated the Chinese to build the Great Wall. Repulsed from China, they turned westward. In the 5th century A.D. the Hūṇa (White Huns or Ephthalites) invaded India via the passes of the Hindu Kush. In the same century other groups of Hun stock invaded the Germanic countries and drove the Ostrogoths, Visigoths, and Vandals into the crumbling Roman Empire. The successes of the Huns and the Vandals were the result of their social organization; they were organized for war and entered new territory as conquerors. Less organized peoples come as straggling refugees powerless to establish themselves; of such character were many African tribal migrations, few of which have been recorded.

Another type of migration is the organized exodus of surplus population from sharply limited territory. Islanders in particular are able to appraise overpopulation, because their resources are limited visibly. As numbers increase, organized groups of young men seek new homes elsewhere. Such migrations have been typical in Oceania. For example, the Maori of New Zealand are descended from people of central Polynesia who migrated according to plan in the 14th century A.D.; their exploring ancestors had discovered New Zealand in the 12th century.

On a larger scale, the Pallavas of south India began to establish colonies in Oceania in the 1st century B.C., partly to relieve population pressure and partly to escape repeated invasions by hostile Indian states. By the 5th century A.D. there were typical south Indian cities in Cambodia, Sumatra, Java, Borneo, and the southern Malay Peninsula—areas previously underpopulated. Subsequent empires such as Srivijaya, Madjapahit, and Cambodia all manifested their Indian cultural background, as does modern Indonesia.

Politically motivated migrations, frequent in modern times, probably have occurred ever since the earliest development of empires powerful enough to suppress minorities. The Old Testament contains a detailed example, the flight of the Jews from Egypt to seek living space in the Promised Land. In the 20th century Jews fled from Europe to the same Promised Land. Perhaps the most dramatic migration of this type was the flight of the Torgot or Kalmyk (q.v.) people from Russia to China in the 18th century. A central Asian tribe of Lamaist faith, in the early 17th century they had worked westward and settled on the banks of the Volga River. In January 1771, impelled by fear of the Russians and by the intrigues of their own nobles, over 300,000 out of the 400,000 Torgot suddenly burned their homes and started eastward with their goods, cattle, and camels. They were attacked repeatedly by Cossacks, Bashkirs, and Kirghiz, while thousands died in the winter cold and the summer heat of the desert. The remnant were rescued from annihilation at the hands of Bashkirs and Kirghiz by the timely arrival of Chinese troops at Lake Balkhash. Approximately 250,000 perished in the long trek of seven months. The Manchu emperor allotted the survivors lands, herds, and equipment, and their descendants still live in the Sinkiang region southeast of Lake Balkhash.

In 1950, some 15,000 Kazakhs fled from Sinkiang before the Chinese Communists, across Tibet into Kashmir. About 12,600 were killed, captured, or dispersed by the Communist forces; still others died fighting their way across Tibet. The 350 survivors who reached Kashmir were eventually settled in Turkey among people who speak an allied language.

In the course of migration wandering herdsmen and seafarers often amalgamate with settled agriculturalists. Roving bands of fighters sometimes conquer sedentary farmers, and come to rest in the process. The anthropologist Richard Thurnwald (1869–1954) emphasized the frequency of voluntary peaceful amalgamation of wanderers with settled agriculturalists. The newcomers contributed meat or fish to the formerly limited diet, and provided skill in war and in organization; the agriculturalists contributed grain and vegetables and taught the newcomers to build permanent dwellings. (Consult Thurnwald's *Der Mensch geringer Naturbeherrschung,* Berlin 1950.)

Formerly historians and anthropologists explained cultural similarities of geographically separated peoples by hypothetical prehistoric migrations. Scholars have become cautious, however, in postulating migrations to account for cultural resemblances that could have occurred by contacts of travel, trade, or war. The folklore of many peoples includes tales of wanderings of their remote ancestors; such tales are now regarded skeptically. Wholesale migrations have occurred and still occur, but legends of past migrations should not be taken seriously unless verified by historical or archaeological evidence.

In the modern world, tribal migrations happen less frequently as tribal organizations disappear in the sweep of nationalism. Under conditions of civil society, individuals may now move to other countries without involving an entire people. This relatively modern phenomenon, from the point of view of the vacated area, is called emigration, and from the point of view of the area entered, immigration (see sections on population and immigration in such articles as AUSTRALIA; CANADA; NEW ZEALAND; UNITED STATES). Immigration on the part of individuals and families has become the contemporary mode of population transfer. In addition, totalitarian states of today make a practice of moving large groups of population to accommodate the plans of their ruling oligarchies.

Bibliography.—CHINA AND THE HSIUNG-NU: Eberhard, Wolfram, *Chinas Geschichte* (Bern 1948), tr. by E. W. Dickes as *A History of China,* pp. 68 ff. (Berkeley, Calif., 1950). HŪNA: Rawlinson, Hugh George, *India, a Short Cultural History,* pp. 110–111, 199–200, 243 (London 1937). MAORI: Buck, Peter Henry, *Vikings of the Sunrise,* chap. 19 (New York 1938). PALLAVAS: Steiger, George Nye, and others, *A History of the Orient,* chaps. 5, 9 (Boston 1926). TORGOT: Hedin, Sven Anders, *Jehol, kejsarstaden* (Stockholm 1931), tr. by E. G. Nash as *Jehol, City of Emperors,* chap. 3 (London 1932). KAZAKHS: Clark, Milton, J., "How the Kazakhs Fled to Freedom," *National Geographic Magazine,* vol. 106, pp. 621–640 (Washington 1954). CHINESE IN MANCHURIA: Pelzer, Karl Josef, *Population and Land Utilization,* Part I of *An Economic Survey of the Pacific Area,* pp. 23–28 (New York 1941).

DOUGLAS G. HARING,
Professor of Sociology and Anthropology, Syracuse University.

MIGRATION OF ANIMALS, a term often used to refer to any movement of animals from one locality to another, but preferably confined to rhythmic movements which involve a journey from one place to another and back again. Such movements can usually be correlated with environmental periodicities or with internal physiological rhythms, and are in some way controlled by the animal. While a single animal usually completes the round trip, among some forms the return trip is made by a different generation. In general, it appears that migrations are genetically controlled rhythms transmitted from generation to generation through complex genes.

Animal populations which move from place to place but do not return are described by terms such as "mass movements," "emigration," or "dispersal." Such movements as that of the lemming of Lapland and Scandinavia are emigrations, for the animals move from their normal range when conditions become too crowded. Sporadic eruptions of grasshoppers, cicadas, and locusts also cannot be considered true migratory movements.

Four types of migratory movements are recognized. These are: daily, lunar, seasonal, and cyclic. All these migrations are made in response to a stimulus which may be either external or internal.

Daily Migration.—Many animals make daily movements from a "home base" in response to such daily events as light and darkness or temperature changes. In lakes and oceans, the vast numbers of planktonic animals tend to move toward the surface at night and down to deeper levels in the daytime. For example, the movements of the copepod, *Calanus,* in the Firth of Clyde, Scotland, were shown to correlate with the differences in the time of sunset and sunrise and the intensity of the noon sun. The scattering layer of the open ocean consists of hordes of planktonic forms as well as larger animals; it has been shown by the use of underwater acoustical equipment that there are wide ranges in the depth at which this layer is located during various times of the day.

Among terrestrial animals, similar daily movements have been shown. Opilionids often descend from tree trunks to the forest floor as evening approaches, then ascend toward morning. Many birds also make daily migrations from their nesting sites out to feeding areas. The house sparrow, which does not undertake long migrations, moves out of permanent colonies for feeding; the European starling makes similar flights. Even among parasites daily migrations can be observed. The nematode parasite (*Wuchereria bancrofti*) which causes elephantiasis in man moves to the surface blood vessels at night when the mosquito which transmits it is flying.

Lunar Migration.—Movements made in response to the cycle of the moon have been observed since very early times. Many organisms, particularly marine ones, show a correlation between their reproductive cycle and the moon cycle. The most spectacular of these responses are found among the polychaete worms. The palolo worm (*Eunice viridis*), found in the waters around the islands of the South Pacific, comes to the surface of the ocean in swarms on the first day of the last quarter after the October–November full moon. The worms produce a luminescence and discharge their eggs and sperm into the water.

The reproductive rhythm of the California smelt or grunion (*Leuresthes tenuis*) is even more remarkable. During the full of the moon from March to July and when the tides are running high at night, thousands of these fish ride onto the beach in the waves. The females quickly burrow into the sand, the males curve about them, and the eggs and sperm are discharged. About two weeks later, when the high tides of the dark of the moon are running, the eggs hatch and the young are washed out to sea.

Seasonal Migration.—Migrations of animals in response to seasonal changes are very common. In tropical or subtropical areas, they occur at the beginning or end of the dry season. In temperate areas, the movements are more likely to be in response to temperature changes. Monarch butterflies (*Danaus plexippus*) gather in flocks in late summer and fall, then migrate south. After an inactive period from November to March, they start northward, moving as their milkweed host plant becomes suitable for egg laying. As the young larvae become adults, they continue the northward movement.

Among both amphibians and reptiles migratory movements have been observed. Aquatic salamanders such as the hellbender and northern mud puppy may move from one part of a lake or stream to another. The desert tortoise (*Gopherus agassizi*) congregate in dens in the winter, move out in the spring, and return to their dens in the fall. Some snakes make similar seasonal local migrations, and bats have a habit of concentrating in caves for hibernation in the winter and spreading out over the adjacent territory for the summer.

Some aquatic animals illustrate a type of seasonal migration termed *vertical migration*. Many fish, lobsters, crabs, prawns, and squids rise to the surface of the water in summer and descend into deeper waters for the winter. A large number of fish move from deep water into shallow coastal areas for breeding.

Larger mammals such as the caribou and reindeer also have seasonal migratory movements which are associated with their searching for food. The movements of birds which nest in the temperate and frigid zones, go to warmer areas for the winter, then return to the breeding area the following spring represent typical migrations. Such migrations are known in Europe, North America, and Asia. They are best known in the northern hemisphere which has such a tremendous land mass, temperate and frigid zones, and great changes of the environment, but migration of birds in the southern hemisphere does occur. Some birds of South America, for example, move north during their winter season, then return south for nesting.

In some of our western mountains, birds make an *altitudinal migration* in response to seasonal changes. As winter approaches, such birds as the chickadees, kinglets, jays, and nuthatches move down the mountain in search of better shelter and food. They obtain temperature effects similar to those obtained by birds which have a latitudinal migration, but in a much more limited area.

Some birds move only short distances. Thus populations of the common robin, which migrates southward from its nesting sites, may be present in any one area throughout the year, but the winter group will comprise different individuals from the summer group. Other birds such as the blue jay may be present throughout the year, but tend to move out of the more northern portions of their range in winter. Many summer residents, however, make long flights southward as winter approaches. Some birds such as the tree sparrow and slate-colored junco summer in Canada and move into the United States for the winter. Others, including the chipping sparrow, red-winged blackbird, and many ducks nest in the northern part of the United States and in southern Canada, then move south to areas on the Gulf of Mexico. Species such as the olive-backed thrush, the barn swallow, and many warblers and nighthawks make a longer flight into South America, the West Indies, or Central America from their nesting sites in Canada or the United States. The champion migrators are the water and shore birds (snipes, plovers, and others). Several of these nest north of the Arctic Circle and winter in southern South America. The farthest traveler of our hemisphere is the Arctic tern. It nests far north (up to 7° 30′ south of the North Pole), then migrates to the Antarctic, 11,000 miles away.

Migrating birds follow definite routes or flyways, of which there are four in the United States: the Atlantic, the Mississippi, the central, and the Pacific. Usually birds follow the same flyway for both portions of their round trip, but some go one way on one route and return on another.

Cyclic Migration.—Some animal migrations are not seasonal, but do recur at irregular intervals. Grasshoppers have been shown to make migrations of this type; the return trip is usually made by the next generation, the one derived from eggs that have been laid by the last migrating generation.

Fish, such as many salmon, illustrate this kind of migration. The young hatch in small fresh-water streams at the heads of large rivers, then move down into the ocean for a stay of from one to three years. As adults, they return to the rivers in which they were spawned, lay their eggs, and then die. These migrations usually occur every year, but it takes any one individual several years to mature.

The eels of the Atlantic Ocean reverse this process. The young hatch in the deep water of the mid-Atlantic, then make their way over a period of one to three years toward either North America or Europe. The females ascend fresh-water streams, spend many years developing there, and finally return to their birthplace for spawning.

The occasional migrations of the snowy owl into the United States in the winter is apparently dependent upon the three- to five-year lemming cycle. As lemmings constitute the chief food of the snowy owl, the owl must move southward when the lemming population is low.

Problems of Long Migration.—When an animal migrates from one place to another, it is better able to use areas that are not equally valuable at all times. For instance, foods such as berries and insects vary in abundance with the seasons, and climatic conditions tend to be less favorable in winter. By moving, an animal has optimum conditions for a greater part of the year.

A long migration, however, involves a tremendous effort. It might well be questioned whether or not the advantages gained are worth the effort. During a long migration, an animal may go through a great variety of climatic conditions; there are long flights, an uncertain food supply, often unfavorable winds, storms, and predators. Some animals have special problems: eels and salmon must find the mouths of rivers, monarch butterflies must find special plants on which to feed. Once the migrant arrives at its destination, it must compete with the resident forms for food and places in which to rest.

How Animals Find Their Way.—There are many stages or degrees of migratory behavior, and the manner in which animals learn to follow their routes varies. The mule deer of western North America migrates relatively short distances. Such migrations are made over areas familiar to the older animals, and the young learn the way by following the herd. Among other forms, however, the young must find their way without help from the adults. For example, the young of the migratory gulls begin their migration before the adults; thus they must depend entirely upon themselves. Those butterflies which migrate annually have a life cycle of but one year, and each generation must find its own way. Experimental evidence has resulted in a greater understanding of the environmental factors used by animals as well as a greater understanding of what they are capable of doing.

While studying ants in the deserts of North Africa, Felix Santschi observed in 1923 that the ants were able to use the sun's position for orienting themselves toward their nests. Further observations disclosed that these ants could orient themselves correctly if they could see only a portion of the blue sky, even though the sun was not visible to them. Karl Von Frisch, while studying the behavior of bees, noted that the bees also needed to see only a portion of the blue sky to orient themselves, and he showed further that the bees used the polarization of the light for their orientation. (Polarization is an optical feature of light from a blue sky, but not from the light which penetrates a cloud cover. See also POLARIZED LIGHT—*Uses of Linear Polarization.*) Since then other investigators have demonstrated that a wide variety of animals including *Limulus,* the horseshoe crab, and *Daphnia,* the water flea, can use polarized light for orientation. It has also been shown that underwater light is polarized; thus marine and freshwater animals may well respond to light in a manner similar to that of terrestrial forms.

Gustav Kramer demonstrated in 1952 the most definite response by birds to polarized light. His experiments with starlings showed that they used polarized light to orient themselves for both homing and food finding. Not only did they respond to the direction of the light, but they were able to adjust for the differences in time of day. Thus a starling trained to find food in a certain direction in the morning would unerringly go in that direction in the afternoon. This "time sense" also appears to be present among many different animals. Donald Redfield Griffin suggested in 1953 that the pecten, a fanlike structure in the eyeball of birds, may function as a built-in sextant by which the bird is able to gauge the angular distance of the sun above the horizon.

Those salmon which migrate back to their birthplace to spawn must often travel 800 to 900 miles. The manner in which they are able to accomplish this amazing feat has long puzzled scientists. Arthur Davis Hasler and James A. Larsen announced in 1955 a series of experiments indicating the possible method which these salmon use to find tiny streams often hundreds of miles from the open ocean in which they have grown to maturity. Apparently the salmon are able to detect very small amounts of chemicals, and small differences in the organic contents of various streams may be sufficient to attract them back to their birthplace.

Bibliography.—Lincoln, F. X., *Migration of Birds* (New York 1952); Clarke, George Leonard, *Elements of Ecology* (New York 1954); Woodbury, Angus Munn, *Principles of General Ecology* (New York 1954); Wallace, George John, *An Introduction to Ornithology* (New York 1955); Reid, Leslie, *Earth's Company* (London 1958); Welty, Joel Carl, *The Life of Birds* (Philadelphia 1962); Farb, Peter, and the editors of "Life," *Ecology* (New York 1963); Marshall, N. B., *The Life of Fishes* (New York 1966).

CLARENCE J. GOODNIGHT,
Professor of Biological Sciences, Purdue University.

MIGRATORY LABOR. See LABOR, MIGRATORY.

MIGUEL, mê-gĕl' (full name MIGUEL MARIA EVARISTO DE BRAGANÇA, often called DOM MIGUEL), Portuguese usurper: b. Lisbon, Portugal, Oct. 26, 1802; d. Bronnbach Castle near Wertheim, Germany, Nov. 14, 1866. He was a son of John VI of Portugal, who fled with his family to Brazil when France invaded Portugal (1807). After the return of John in 1821, Miguel and his mother attempted a reactionary revolution against him. On John's death (1826), Miguel's elder brother, Pedro I of Brazil, succeeded to the throne of Portugal, but he conditionally abdicated his Portuguese rights in favor of a seven-year-old daughter, Maria da Gloria (Maria II, q.v.), with Miguel as regent. Pedro's conditions were that Miguel would accept Pedro's liberal constitutional charter and marry Maria when she should reach 18. Reactionaries supported Miguel for absolute power, but he accepted the charter and became regent. In 1828 he chose new ministers, and by continuous political pressure and acts of terror they raised him to the throne, a Cortes composed of reactionaries declaring him to be the rightful king in June 1828. Various liberal uprisings followed, with the aid of English mercenaries, and a full-scale civil war developed. An English fleet destroyed the Miguelite fleet on July 5, 1833, and the Quadruple Alliance of France, Great Britain, Spain, and Portugal against him spelled his downfall. On May 26, 1834, Miguel abdicated. He has been characterized by the faction hostile to him as ignorant, vicious, and drunken, but his coreligionists make him a model prince.

MIHAJLOVIC, mē-hī'lō-vēt'y', **Draža,** Balkan guerrilla leader, b. Shumadija, near Belgrade, Serbia, 1893; d. by execution, Belgrade, July 17, 1946. He fought in both Balkan Wars and World War I, attended staff schools and became colonel in 1940. When the Nazis overran Yugoslavia the next year, Mihajlović retreated to mountains near Belgrade, picking up stragglers whom he organized into *chetniks,* guerrillas in the old Serb tradition. He was effective against the invader and was made war minister by King Peter II in 1942. But his Serbs fell into conflict with the Croat and Communist forces of Joseph Broz, or Tito (q.v.); they and their leader were accused of collaboration with the Axis against their countrymen. The *chetniks* were deprived of Allied support, Mihajlović himself being dismissed as minister of war in May 1944. His following diminished to a handful before Tito captured him in hiding, March 13, 1946. His subsequent trial for treason and collaboration was widely condemned by world opinion as political.

MIKADO (Japanese *Mi,* exalted, *Kado,* gate), an ancient and poetic title of the Japanese emperor, similar to the Sublime Porte title of the Ottomans; probably transferred to the ruler and judge from the gateway to his palace, where he did justice. It was never a separate title for a spiritual ruler; this incorrect idea results from the historical fact that much of the mikado's or emperor's temporal power was usurped before 1867 by shoguns or generals, who, however, always admitted that they derived their power from him. The present mikado, Emperor Hirohito (r. Dec. 25, 1926–) is the 124th of his line, which legend dates back to 660 B.C.; of him the title mikado, essentially a foreign solecism, is much less used than *Dai Nippon Teikoku Tennō,* "Imperial Son of Heaven of Great Japan." *Tennō* corresponds to the English word emperor.

MIKADO, The, or **THE TOWN OF TITIPU,** a comic opera in two acts, libretto by W. S. Gilbert, music by Sir Arthur Sullivan; first production, Savoy Theatre, London, March 14, 1885; first American performance at the Museum, Chicago, July 6, 1885. The plot is simple burlesque, without the infusion of any Eastern imagery. The Mikado, a highly moral ruler, has issued an edict condemning to death every man found guilty of flirtation "unless connubially linked." To evade this stern sentence the citizens of Titipu appoint one thus condemned (Ko-Ko the tailor) to the office of executioner, with the result that he could not behead the next man until he had first executed himself. It being necessary eventually to execute someone, Ko-Ko, who is engaged to Yum-Yum and is also first on the list of the condemned, finds a substitute in Nanki-Poo, (the Mikado's son in disguise), who had gone into temporary hiding to avoid marrying the elderly Katisha. Nanki-Poo agrees to suffer execution in a month provided he can be married to Yum-Yum for that period. In the end Nanki-Poo is forgiven and weds Yum-Yum, and Ko-Ko saves himself by marrying Katisha. An amusing character is Poo-Bah, "Lord High Everything Else."

MIKANIA (also known as WILLUGBAEYA; both neo-Latin from the names of J. C. or J. G. Mikan and Francis Willughby respectively), a genus of composite plants of the tribe *Eupatorieae* and the subtribe *Ageratеae.* It is widespread throughout tropical and temperate America and grows either in an erect shrub or in twining vines. The genus numbers about 150 recognized varieties, all natives of the warmer regions of America, except one species which grows in Asia and tropical Africa. The plant is characterized by opposite leaves, heart-shaped or triangular, toothed at the base and with petioles. The flowers are small and white, pinkish or yellowish. The tropical types, *M. amara, M. cordifolia* and *M. guaco* have a high reputation in South America as snakebite cures.

MIKI, Takeo (1907–), Japanese public official, who became president of the Liberal Democratic party and prime minister of Japan. He was born in Tokushima prefecture, the son of a farmer. After attending the schools of law and commerce at Meiji University, in Tokyo, he entered politics at the age of 30 and was elected to the Japanese House of Representatives in 1937. In 1939 he organized the Japanese-U. S. Friendship Association, hoping to prevent war between Japan and the United States. Miki became minister of communications (1947–1948) and of transport (1954–1955). His party, originally the People's Cooperative party, was reorganized in 1952 to form the Progressive party. This merged with the Democratic party in 1954 to form the Japan Democratic party, which again merged with the Liberal party in 1955 to form the Liberal Democratic party, of which Miki became president.

In the ensuing years, Miki served as director of the Economic Planning Agency (1958–1959) and of the Science and Technology Agency (1961–1962), minister of international trade and industry (1965–1966) and foreign minister (1966–1968). He served as deputy prime minister from 1972 until July 1974, and had been director-general of the Environment Agency since 1972, when he was designated prime minister, succeeding Tanaka Kakuei, on Dec. 9, 1974, by the House of Representatives and the House of Councillors in plenary session.

MIKKELSEN, Ejnar, Danish polar explorer: b. Vester Brønderslev, Jutland, Dec. 23, 1880; d. Copenhagen, Denmark, May 3, 1971. He was on the Amdrup expedition to Christian XI Land, East Greenland, in 1900, and in 1901–1902 served with the Baldwin-Ziegler expedition to Franz Josef Land. With Ernest de K. Leffingwell he organized an Anglo-American expedition to the north of Alaska and determined the position of the continental shelf of the Arctic Ocean (1906–1908). His expedition to the north coast of Greenland in 1909–1912 resulted in his recovery of the records of the lost explorers Mylius-Erichsen and Höeg-Hagens. In 1925 he led an experimental fishing cruise to West Greenland. In 1933 he became inspector general of East Greenland, retiring in 1951. Governor of the Arctic Institute of North America in 1948, he was made chairman of the Danish Arctic Institute in 1954.

MILAN, mĭ-lăn (Ital. MILANO mē-lä'-nō), province, Lombardy Region, north Italy, comprising part of the fertile Po plain, between the Adda and Ticino rivers. Area, 1,065 square miles.

The province is the most highly industrialized in Italy, as not only its capital, Milan, but also such centers as Monza, Sesto San Giovanni, Legnano, Rho, and Abbiategrasso have a variety of industries: textiles, machinery, metallurgical products, chemicals, shoes and furniture are among the province's products. The chief crops are cereals, rice, fruit and vegetables. Silkworms are grown and stockraising is also important. Lodi and Gorgonzola are the centers of a flourishing dairy and sausage manufacturing industry. Pop. (1951) 2,500,228.

MILAN (ancient MEDIOLANUM), city and commune, northern Italy, the capital of Milan Province and of the region of Lombardy, is located in the fertile Po plain, midway between the Po River and the Alpine foothills, 300 miles northwest of Rome. The second city of Italy in population and the country's chief industrial, financial and commercial center, it is the seat of an archdiocese. The climate is continental, with cold winters and hot summers; fogs are frequent in winter and fall.

Economic and Cultural Life.—The importance of Milan is largely due to its geographic situation, at the intersection of communication lines connecting all parts of Europe and the Mediterranean. Highways, rails and airlines radiate in all directions from the city and canals connect it with the Po. Milan is the headquarters of great import and export firms, and for the major industries and banks of the country; its stock exchange is the leading one in Italy. The commercial fair held in April is one of the most important in Europe. The chief industries are textiles (Milan being, with Lyon, the leading European silk manufactory), machinery and metal products (aircraft, automobiles, railroad equipment, agricultural machinery), printing and publishing (especially music), electrical appliances, chemicals, pharmaceuticals, furniture and food products. Recently it has also become a world fashion center. The most progressive city in Italy, it has long been the center of the trade union movement.

The cultural traditions of Milan are ancient. It is the seat of many societies such as the *Istituto lombardo di scienze e lettere,* founded in 1797, and the *Accademia scientifico letteraria.* Art exhibitions are held in the modern Palazzo dell'Arte, including the Triennale of decorative arts. Milan is also a music and drama center with numerous theaters and concert halls including the famous La Scala Opera. Educational facilities are excellent: the main institutions of higher learning are one state and one Catholic university, the Luigi Bocconi school of commerce, an engineering school, the Brera Academy of Fine Arts and the Giuseppe Verdi Conservatory of Music. There are also important libraries, especially the Ambrosiana. Besides the museums mentioned below there are the Poldi-Pezzoli Museum, one of the finest art collections in Europe, the Natural History Museum, a numismatic collection in the Castello and a gallery of modern art. In the Brera Palace is the astronomical observatory (1763).

The City.—The general appearance of Milan is that of a modern metropolis. The rise after World War I was spectacular both in the economy and in population. The same expansion took place after World War II; despite very heavy damage from Allied air raids, especially in 1943, the city

Ewing Galloway
The Duomo or cathedral of Milan.

recovered swiftly. Whole quarters have been redeveloped and others planned. The old part of the city, polygonal in shape, still has many narrow winding streets but the main thoroughfares have been enlarged to handle the increasing traffic. The center of the city is the Piazza del Duomo, from which radiate a number of streets leading to the suburbs; Milan has spread well beyond its former walls and new residential and industrial quarters are expanding in every direction. The most notable structure is the cathedral on the east side of the Piazza del Duomo, the most important Gothic structure in Italy. Started by an unknown architect in 1386, who was inspired by the Gothic cathedrals of northern Europe, it was continued by French, German, and Italian master masons; although consecrated by St. Charles Borromeo in 1577 it was completed in the 19th century. The exterior is adorned with a profusion of pinnacles, statues, and other ornaments, and the highest pinnacle (354 feet) is topped by a gold-covered statue of the Madonna. On the north side of the Piazza is the Galleria Vittorio Emanuele, lined with cafés and elegant shops, which leads to the Piazza della Scala, with its world-renowned La Scala Theater built by Piermarini in 1778. Damaged during the war, it was modernized and reopened in 1946. Opposite is the Palazzo Marino, seat of the municipal government, which also suffered severely in World War II. West of the Piazza del Duomo is the Piazza dei Mercanti, medieval center of Milan, surrounded by old buildings including the Palazzo della Ragione (1223–1238) and the Loggia degli Osii (1316). Farther west is the Ambrosiana Palace (1603–1609) containing the library, an art gallery with works of the Lombard school, and a special exhibition dedicated to Leonardo da Vinci who lived and worked in Milan for several years. One of his most famous paintings, *The Last Supper,* is in the refectory adjacent to the Church of Santa Maria delle Grazie. The fresco is now undergoing a delicate work of restoration. In the Brera Palace, also war-damaged, is one of the finest art collections of Italy, recently reorganized and modernized: among its treasures are the *Marriage of the Virgin* by Raphael and the *Dead Christ* by Mantegna. Northwest of the Piazza del Duomo is the Castello Sforzesco, an imposing Renaissance moated castle, built by Francesco I Sforza in 1450 as the residence and fortress of the lords of Milan. It was enriched by Leonardo and Bramante but later became a barracks. It now contains a number of collections and libraries. In the ducal chapel is Michelangelo's uncompleted *Pietà*

Rondanini. The other great Renaissance structure of Milan was the Ospedale Maggiore, founded in 1456. Virtually destroyed in World War II, it is being rebuilt. Milan's oldest church is the Basilica di Sant'Ambrogio, founded in 386 by St. Ambrose, the bishop of Milan and its patron saint, who is buried in the crypt. Rebuilt early in the 12th century, it is one of the most typical examples of Romanesque-Lombard architecture; the main altarpiece is a splendid example of medieval goldsmithing. The Basilica of San Lorenzo Maggiore, originally of the 6th century, was restored in the 16th. Also worthy of mention are San Satiro, designed by Donato d'Agnolo Bramante (1476–1514) and Sant' Eustorgio, with a fine Renaissance chapel (1462–1468).

History.—Originally a Celtic settlement, Milan was seized by Rome in 222 B.C. Diocletian made it an imperial residence and in the 4th century A.D. it became a religious center; the Edict of Milan, granting religious tolerance to all sects throughout the empire, was issued in 313 A.D. by Constantine. Ambrose was bishop from 374 to 397. In the 12th century it was a free commune, and although sacked by Frederick I in 1158 and 1162, it rose again and contributed with the Lombard League cities to Frederick's defeat at Legnano in 1176. At the Peace of Constance (1183) the emperor recognized Milanese independence; in spite of internal strife between Guelphs and Ghibellines (q.v.) and struggles with neighboring cities Milan continued to grow. The Torriani, leaders of the popular party, gained control, and Martino della Torre became lord of Milan in 1259, but one of his successors was beaten in 1277 by the aristocratic leaders, the Visconti (q.v.).

Ottone Visconti, archbishop since 1262, became lord of Milan in 1277 and Matteo Visconti imperial vicar in 1311. Under Gian Galeazzo Visconti, made duke of Milan in 1395 by Emperor Wenceslas, the family reached its peak. When in 1447 Filippo Maria Visconti died without male issue, the Ambrosian Republic was proclaimed, but three years later Francesco Sforza, husband of Filippo's daughter Bianca Maria Visconti, succeeded in gaining power. Under the Sforza (q.v.) the Duchy of Milan became one of the most powerful states in Italy, playing a leading role in the peninsula's politics. Rival claims to Milan, however, brought Louis XII of France to Italy in 1499.

Milan changed hands several times, a pawn in the rivalry between France and Spain. After the death of Francesco II Sforza in 1535, Milan came under Spanish domination. Ruled by incompetent Spanish governors, the city had a long period of decline, but at the end of the War of the Spanish Succession, the Treaty of Utrecht (1713) assigned it to Austria, and a recovery took place. It fell to the troops of Napoleon in 1796, as described in Stendhal's *The Charterhouse of Parma,* and was part of Napoleon's puppet Italian republics and kingdom (1797–1814). In 1805 Napoleon was crowned with the Iron Crown of Lombardy in Milan Cathedral. Austrian rule was restored in 1815, but political repression soon became intolerable. In 1848, during the Risorgimento, the people chased the Austrians from the city, but they returned a few months later. Only in 1859 was Milan liberated from foreign rule and incorporated in the kingdom of Sardinia, which in 1861 became the kingdom of Italy. Milan has prospered ever since. After World War I it was the center of the Fascist movement; Benito Mussolini left Milan for Rome in 1922 to assume the premiership. Pop. of the commune (1951) 1,268,994.

MILAN, town, Tennessee, in Gibson County, altitude 420 feet; 21 miles north of Jackson; on the Louisville and Nashville and the Illinois Central railroads. It is in a diversified farming area. Manufactures include fruit and vegetable containers and cottonseed oil. There is a United States arsenal here. Incorporated in 1868, Milan has a mayor and council government. Pop. 7,313.

MILAN DECREE, an order issued by Napoleon I from Milan, Italy, on Dec. 17, 1807, to check British use of neutral shipping; the British were thus attempting to get their goods onto the continental market, from which Napoleon's Berlin Decree (Nov. 21, 1806) and other edicts had nominally barred them. The Milan Decree fell with particular force on American shipping. (See CONTINENTAL SYSTEM.)

MILAN OBRENOVICH IV and **I**, ô-brĕn'ô-vĭch, prince and king of Serbia: b. Jassy, Rumania, Aug. 22, 1854; d. Vienna, Feb. 11, 1901. He was cousin to Michael Obrenovich III, prince of Serbia, by whom he was adopted on the death of his parents. He was educated in Paris at the Lycée Louis-le-Grand and upon the assassination of Michael in 1868 he succeeded him as Milan Obrenovich IV, prince of Serbia, under a regency headed by Ristić. In 1872, aged 18, he took over the government, retaining, however, the services of Ristić. He carefully balanced political relations between Serbia and Austria and Russia, so strengthening his position that after the Russo-Turkish War (1877–1878) he was able to have Serbia's independence declared and himself proclaimed as Milan Obrenovich I, king of Serbia (1882). He then entered a secret pact with Austria, which increasingly influenced affairs in Serbia, to the rage of the patriots gathering about Milan's hereditary rivals, the Karageorgevich (q.v.) family. He tried to modernize Serbia, but taxes, burdensome conscription laws, the failure of his attack on Bulgaria (1885) turned the public against him, as did his private life and quarrels with Queen Natalie. On March 6, 1889, he abdicated and lived in Paris (1889–1894), his son Alexander succeeding under a regency. Milan returned to Serbia, without resuming the throne, in 1894; officially reunited to the queen, he was given the army as his special charge, and was commander in chief from 1897 to 1900, when his son's marriage to the commoner Draga Mašin caused an estrangement between them. Milan resigned his army post, left the country, and died in Vienna.

MILANES Y FUENTES, mē-lä-nās' ē fwän'tās, **José Jacinto**, Cuban poet: b. Matanzas, Aug. 16, 1814; d. there, Nov. 14, 1863. He was self-taught, working as a clerk and blacksmith's helper; his tragedy *El Conde Alarcos* (1838) made him famous. His best play was probably *Una Intriga Paternal*. He broke down as a result of early hardships and a long tour in 1848–1849 failed to help him. In his last years he showed only flashes of lucidity. Milanes was the best Cuban writer of his time, with José Maria de Heredia (q.v.).

MILAZZO, mê-lät'tsô (ancient MYLAE), city and commune, Italy, in Messina Province, northern Sicily, about 17 miles west of Messina, on the Tyrrhenian Sea. A wine trade center exporting wine, olive oil, and citrus fruit, it also produces flour, macaroni, chemicals, soap, glass; has tunny fishing; and has steamer service to the Lipari Islands. Founded in 716 B.C. by colonists from Zancle (Messina), Milazzo was conquered by the Athenians in 426 B.C. In its harbor in 260 B.C. the Romans, using grappling irons and boarding bridges for the first time, won the great naval victory over the Carthaginians which was the beginning of Rome's sea power. At Milazzo, in 1860, Giuseppi Garibaldi defeated the Bourbons and liberated Sicily. Pop. (1951) 16,129 (city), 22,013 (commune).

MILAZZO, Gulf of, inlet, Tyrrhenian Sea, on the northeast coast of Sicily. The port of Milazzo (q.v.) is at the western end, on Cape Milazzo. Cape Rasocolmo is on the east. Tunny fishing is the major enterprise in the waters of the gulf.

MILBANK, mĭl'băngk, **Joseph,** American financier and philanthropist: b. New York, N.Y., March 24, 1848; d. there, Sept. 7, 1914. The son of Jeremiah Milbank (1818–1884), organizer and builder of the Chicago, Milwaukee and St. Paul Railroad, he became a director of the railroad at an early age, and with his sister, Mrs. Elizabeth Milbank Anderson (1850–1921), inherited a large fortune which he increased by his own efforts in banking and railroad enterprises. In memory of their parents, he and his sister gave the Milbank Memorial Chapel to Teachers College, Columbia University, and Milbank Memorial Hall to Barnard College. They also gave $650,000 to found a Social Welfare Bureau and contributed $500,000 to the Children's Aid Society. In 1905, with a gift of more than $9 million, Mrs. Anderson established the Memorial Fund Association (later known as the Milbank Memorial Fund) for charitable and benevolent purposes. By 1959 the fund had increased in value to about $17 million, and in recent years has sponsored scientific research in public health and demography.

MILBURN, mĭl'bẽrn, **Devereux,** American sportsman: b. Buffalo, N.Y., 1881; d. Westbury, L.I., N.Y., Aug. 15, 1942. He was educated at Oxford University and Harvard Law School, and became internationally known as a polo player, playing on American international teams from 1909 to 1927 and as captain from 1921 to 1927. He was rated a 10-goal player. The most sensational back known to the sport, he radically changed the tactics of that position, making it one of attack as well as defense.

MILCH, mĭlk, **Erhard,** German aviator: b. Wilhelmshaven, March 30, 1892; d. Luneburg, Jan. 25, 1972. He served as an army pilot in World War I, then became a civilian flyer and, in 1926, a director of Lufthansa. In 1933 he was appointed secretary of state for aeronautics. He successively attained the ranks of lieutenant general (1935), general (1936), colonel general (1938), and air field marshal in Tunisia (1942). The international war crimes tribunal sentenced him to life imprisonment in 1947, but the sentence was commuted to 15 years in 1951, and in July 1954 he was released.

MILDEW, mĭl'dū, a term generally referring to parasitic fungi that cause certain plant diseases, or to saprophytic fungi that grow on clothing, canvas, and other such materials. The term is also frequently used with reference to the diseases themselves or to the general effects produced by the fungi. The two main groups of parasitic mildew fungi are the Erysiphaceae, called powdery or true mildews, and the Peronosporaceae or downy mildews.

The powdery mildews affect many different host plants, primarily in the temperate zones. On the surfaces of the diseased leaves and stems, they produce large numbers of conidia, which are powdery white in appearance. These spores are disseminated by wind and cause reinfections. The fungal threads penetrate the host cells by means of knoblike absorbing organs called haustoria. In late summer and early fall, tiny, dark, globose fruiting bodies appear, and these contain the ascospores, which are primarily responsible for new infections in the spring. Some of the better-known examples are the powdery mildews of cereals, grape, apple, rose, and lilac. The best control practice is to avoid varieties of plants that are highly susceptible to these parasites.

The downy mildew fungi, like the foregoing group, cause destructive diseases of higher plants, including many of considerable economic importance. The fungus imparts a fuzzy or downy appearance to the infected parts, mainly leaves and stems, which is caused by the presence of large numbers of sporangiophores bearing sporangia. The sporangia, which are readily detached and blown about by the wind, cause reinfection. The fungal threads penetrate the host tissue, passing between the cells and sending haustoria into them. Downy mildews overwinter primarily by means of sexually produced, thick-walled cells (oöspores). Some of the more important examples of this group are the downy mildews of grape, tobacco, cabbage and related plants, onion, and lettuce. Late blight of potato is sometimes included here. Some of the more useful sprays for controlling these parasites are Bordeaux mixture, captan, and nabam-zinc sulphate mixture.

Mildew of clothing and other fabrics is caused by a variety of saprophytic fungi (*Chaetomium, Aspergillus, Penicillium,* and others). These fungi impart a musty odor and often cause a discoloration of the material, which they weaken by their action. They can be controlled by keeping the material clean and dry. Effective antiseptics for use on fabrics such as canvas are zinc chloride, copper sulfate, paranitrophenol, and anilide of salicylic acid. See also FUNGICIDE; FUNGUS.

LINDSAY S. OLIVE
University of North Carolina

MILDMAY, mīld'mā, SIR **Walter,** English chancellor of the exchequer and founder of Emmanuel College, Cambridge University: b. Chelmsford, England, about 1520; d. Hackney, London, May 31, 1589. He was educated at Christ's College, Cambridge University, later studied law at Gray's Inn, and in 1545 became surveyor general in the court of augmentation (established in 1537 to control the properties which the crown took from the monasteries), of which his father, Sir Thomas Mildmay, was auditor. Sir Walter was knighted on Feb. 22, 1546 or 1547. A skillful financier, he received many grants of land for his services to the crown. He established a large estate at Apethorpe, Northamptonshire, and from 1557 represented Northamptonshire in Parliament. When Elizabeth I came to the throne, he was made treasurer of her household, and in 1566 succeeded Sir Richard Sackville as chancellor of the exchequer. In 1583 he bought land in Cambridge on which he built Emmanuel College, dedicated in 1588. He also established scholarships and a Greek lectureship at Christ's College. He was one of the special commissioners in the trial of Mary Queen of Scots in 1586.

MILDURA, mĭl-dūr'ȧ, municipality, Australia, in northwestern Victoria. It is located about 300 miles northwest of Melbourne, on the Murray River, about 15 miles east of its junction with the Darling, near the New South Wales border. It is a hydroelectric power center and the commercial and irrigation center for a sheep-ranching and fruit-raising agricultural area, trading in wool, butter, dried fruit, and wheat. Local industries include a flour mill, brickyards, and fruit and vegetable canneries. Modern irrigation methods were introduced by George and W. B. Chaffey who emigrated from the United States to Australia in the 1880s. They had been irrigation pioneers in California. Pop. (1954) 10,971.

MILE, mīl (Lat. *milia,* pl. of *mille,* a thousand), a measure of length or distance. It comes from the old Roman mile of 1,000 paces (*milia passuum*), or 5,000 feet, each pace being a double step measuring about 5 feet. By an act of 1593, Parliament established the English statute mile as measuring "8 furlongs of 40 perches of 16½ feet each," that is, 1,760 yards measuring 3 feet each, or 5,280 feet. This is the standard land mile also in use in the United States. While many countries have their own standard lengths for the mile, most countries, other than the United States and the British Commonwealth, have adopted the kilometer as standard (the kilometer measuring 3,280.8 feet, or about five eighths of a mile, or 0.6214 statute miles). The following are some of the standards of miles or leagues which are or have been in use in European countries:

Kilometer	1,093.6	yards
Ancient Roman mile	1,614	"
Modern Roman mile	1,628	"
English statute mile	1,760	"
Tuscan mile	1,808	"
Ancient Scottish mile	1,984	"
Geographical mile	2,028.4	"
Italian mile	2,028.4	"
Irish mile	2,240	"
French posting league	4,263	"
Spanish league (judicial)	4,635	"
French league	4,860	"
Portuguese league	6,760	"
German short mile	6,859	"
Flanders league	6,864	"
Spanish league (common)	7,416	"
German geographical mile	8,113.6	"
German (new imperial)	8,202	"
Old Prussian mile	8,237	"
Danish mile	8,244	"
Swiss mile	9,153	"
German long mile	10,126	"
Swedish mile	11,700	"

The International Nautical Mile of 1,852 meters (6,076.10333 . . . feet)—determined by the International Hydrographic Bureau and adopted by many countries in 1929—was adopted for use by the United States on July 1, 1954, replacing the United States Nautical Mile of 1,853.248 meters (6,080.20 feet) formerly used. The knot, the unit of speed used in navigation, equals one nautical mile an hour; hence a ship traveling 10 nautical miles an hour has a speed of 10 knots. The British admiralty knot is 6,080 feet per hour. See also WEIGHTS AND MEASURES—*Unit Standards.*

MILES, mīlz, **Eustace,** English athlete: b. West End House, Hampstead, London, England, Sept. 22, 1868; d. Dec. 20, 1948. He was educated at King's College, Cambridge University, was assistant master at Rugby School, and became prominent as an amateur tennis champion both in England and the United States. He was deeply interested in physical culture and diet as health factors, and established the Eustace Miles Restaurants, Ltd., the Eustace Miles Foods, Ltd., and was principal of the Normal Physical School. He published a number of books on tennis, physical culture, food and diet.

MILES, Nelson Appleton, American soldier: b. Westminster, Mass., Aug. 8, 1839; d. Washington, D.C., May 15, 1925. He attended district school and the local academy in Westminster, and at 17 went to work in a Boston store and attended night school. At the outbreak of the Civil War in 1861, he raised a company of volunteers and entered the army as a lieutenant in the 22d Massachusetts Regiment. In 1862 he was promoted to the rank of colonel, commanding the 61st New York Regiment. He fought in the battles of the Peninsula, before Richmond and at Anteitam, and in every battle of the Army of the Potomac, with one exception, until the surrender of Gen. Robert E. Lee at Appomattox Court House. He was distinguished in the battles of Chancellorsville, Wilderness, Spottsylvania Court House, Reams Station, Richmond campaign of 1864, and many other important battles of the war; and at one time, at the age of 25, was in command of the Second Army corps, numbering 25,000 men. He was wounded four times, most severely at the Battle of Chancellorsville. In May 1864 he was promoted brigadier general and in 1865 major general of volunteers.

At the close of the war Miles entered the regular army, was commissioned colonel of the 40th United States Infantry, and attained the rank of brigadier general in 1880 and of major general in 1890. He successfully conducted several important campaigns against the Indians and did much to open up for civilization large portions of the West. In 1874 and 1875 he defeated the Cheyennes, Kiowas, and Comanches in the Staked Plains country; he also subjugated the hostile Sioux and other Indians in Montana, driving Sitting Bull across the frontier and breaking up the bands that were led by him and other chiefs. In December 1877, after a forced march over a distance of more than 160 miles, he captured Chief Joseph and his tribe of Nez Perces after a hard-fought battle of four days in northern Montana; in 1878 he intercepted and captured Elk Horn and his band on the edge of Yellowstone Park. In 1886 he subjugated and forced to surrender Geronimo, Nahche, and the band of Chiricahua Apaches that had made much of the Southwest uninhabitable, thus restoring peace and prosperity to Arizona and New Mexico. For his services up to this time he received the thanks of the legislatures of Kansas, Montana, New Mexico, and Arizona. Later he settled the Indian troubles in the Dakotas, saving the country from a serious war that had threatened it for years. In 1894 he was in command of the United States troops sent to Chicago at the time of the railroad strike; and in October 1895 succeeded to the command of the United States Army. In 1898 he conducted the brief campaign in Puerto Rico with ability, taking possession of the island with trifling loss, and in 1901 was promoted to the rank of lieutenant general. In December 1901 he was officially reprimanded for publicly expressing his approval of Adm. George Dewey's report on the charges against Adm. Winfield S. Schley. In 1902 he made a tour of inspection to the Philippines and on his return filed a report which called forth considerable controversy by its denunciation of some of the abuses he had found in the conduct of military affairs there. In August 1903 he was retired from active service. He wrote *Personal Recollections and Observations of General Nelson A. Miles* (1896); *Military Europe* (1898); *Serving the Republic* (1911).

MILES CITY, city, Montana, and Custer County seat, situated on the Yellowstone River, at the mouth of the Tongue River, at an altitude of 2,364 feet, 140 miles east-northeast of Billings, and served by the Northern Pacific and the Chicago, Milwaukee, St. Paul and Pacific railroads and a municipal airport. Formerly a rough cow country center, the city still carries on an extensive trade in cattle, sheep, and horses. It has gas wells nearby and manufactures flour, leather goods, and saddles.

It has a Carnegie library, and a small museum with relics of range days. Fort Keogh, rebuilt in 1877 and now used as a livestock experimental station, is nearby. Settled and incorporated in 1876–1878, the city was named for Gen. Nelson A. Miles. Pop. 9,023.

MILES GLORIOSUS, mī'lēz glō-rĭ-ō'sŭs (Lat., braggart soldier). (1) A comedy by Titus Maccius Plautus. (2) The name slyly applied by Ferdinand I of Bulgaria at a banquet when toasting Kaiser Wilhelm II of Germany who mistook it for a compliment.

MILESIAN TALES, a form of anecdotal satire current in Miletus and Asia Minor about one hundred years B.C. The original tales were written by Antonius Diogenes and were of an erotic and obscene character. They are important in so far as they form a link in the chain of the development of satirical romance, exemplified in Gaius Petronius' *Trimalchio's Supper* and Lucius Apuleius' *Story of Cupid and Psyche.* Six volumes of the tales were collected by Aristides of Miletus and were later translated into Latin by Lucius Cornelius Sisenna (120?–67 B.C.), but of these only fragments remain. They have been compared to the French *fabliaux* and the tales of Giovanni Boccaccio

Bibliography—Müller, Theodore, *Fragmenta Historicum Graecorum,* vol. 4 (Paris 1841–51); Bücheler, Franz, his small edition of Petronius (Berlin 1882); Peck, Harry T., tr. Petronius' *Trimalchio's Dinner* (New York 1913).

MILESIANS, mī-lē'shănz, (1) the inhabitants of Miletus; (2) *in Irish mythology,* the early colonists of Ireland, a portion of whose inhabitants, according to Irish tradition or legend, are descended from Mileadh, a fabulous king of Spain, whose three sons, Heremon, Heber, and Ir, conquered the island about four hundred years before Christ, establishing a new nobility. This was the fourth and last of the traditional prehistoric colonizations of Ireland.

MILETUS, mī-lē'tŭs, ruined city, Asia Minor, now in the vilayet of Aydın, opposite the mouth of the Menderes on the Latmic Gulf. The Ionians are said to have taken forcible possession of the town about 1100 B.C., massacred the Carians living there and taken the women as their wives. The extent of the four harbors of Miletus, one of which could contain a large fleet, soon raised the town in the hands of the Ionians, to a place of importance, and it became one of the first cities and republics of the 12 Ionian Cities, in Asia Minor. Its commerce covered the Mediterranean and extended to the Atlantic. It had upward of 75 colonies, most of which were on the approaches to the Black Sea. It was also distinguished as a seat of literature.

On the rise of the Lydian kingdom repeated attempts were made to conquer Miletus. It finally recognized the sovereignty of Croesus, and paid tribute. A similar arrangement was made with Cyrus in 546 B.C., which saved it the calamities of a contest with the Persians. The city revolted against the Persians in 499 B.C., and was taken by storm five years later, plundered, and the inhabitants massacred or transported. It recovered its independence in 479 B.C., after the Persian defeat at the Battle of Mycale. It yielded for a time to the supremacy of Athens but ultimately threw off the yoke in 412 B.C., only to fall under the Persians again.

Miletus was conquered by Alexander the Great in 334 B.C., but he did not interfere with its government. From the time of its subjugation by the Persians it had never recovered its early importance, but it still continued to enjoy some commercial prosperity under the Romans until the time of St. Paul, who visited it during its final decline, as recorded in Acts 20:17 and II Timothy 4:20. It was finally taken and destroyed by the Turks.

MILFOIL. See YARROW.

MILFORD, mĭl'fẽrd, town, Connecticut, in New Haven County, at an altitude of 10 feet, on the Housatonic River and Long Island Sound, about 9 miles southwest of New Haven, served by the New York, New Haven and Hartford Railroad and state and federal highways. The town is in an agricultural area engaged in oyster growing, seed raising, and dairy, poultry, and truck farming, and has manufactures of brass fittings, automobile and boat hardware, electric motors, garters, suspenders, earmuffs, rubber substitutes, locks and novelty jewelry, rivets, screws, and machine products. Known since the 17th century for its shellfish, it has thousands of acres of undersea oyster beds. The site was purchased from the Indians and settled in 1639, and the town was incorporated in 1640. It has council-manager type of government. Pop. 50,858.

MILFORD, city, Delaware, in Kent and Sussex Counties, situated on the Mispillion River at an altitude of 20 feet, 18 miles south of Dover, on the Pennsylvania Railroad and modern highways. It is in a fertile truck and fruit farming area, has canneries, a poultry processing plant, boat yards, and manufactures of dental supplies, fertilizers, bricks, wood products, and woolen yarns. The town was established in 1787 on the site of plantations settled in 1680 and was incorporated in 1867. It has a mayor, council and city manager. Pop. 5,314.

MILFORD, town, Massachusetts, in Worcester County, at an altitude of 257 feet, 16 miles east-southeast of Worcester, on the Boston and Albany and the New York, New Haven and Hartford railroads. It is in an agricultural region, but has industrial interests. There are shoe factories here, and granite quarries are located nearby. The local pink granite has been used in the Boston Public Library, the Corcoran Art Gallery in Washington, and the Grand Central and Pennsylvania stations in New York City.

Milford was originally settled in the 1660's and was part of the town of Mendon. In 1780 it was separated from Mendon and incorporated as a municipality. Town meetings, held usually twice a year, administer the government. Pop. 19,352.

MILFORD, town, New Hampshire, in Hillsboro County, situated on the Souhegan River at an altitude of 271 feet, 11 miles west-northwest of Nashua, and served by the Boston and Maine Railroad. It is in a fertile agricultural region producing apples, peaches, grain, timber, and granite. It has woodworking and stonecutting plants, and manufactures woolen goods, cotton and jute, and paints. There are granite quarries nearby. The district was settled in 1738 and the town was incorporated in 1794. It was formed from tracts ceded by several other towns in its vicinity. Its government is by a board of selectmen. Pop. 6,622.

MILFORD, borough, Pennsylvania, seat of Pike County, situated on the Delaware River at an altitude of 503 feet, 47 miles east of Scranton and 7 miles southwest of Port Jervis, N. Y., where it is served by the Erie Railroad. It is located in a portion of the Delaware Valley noted for its beautiful and picturesque scenery, with mountains, woods, and river. First settlement on the site was made in 1733 by Tom Quick. Some years later Quick was killed by an Indian in sight of his son, who spent the rest of his life avenging his father's death, killing indiscriminately a total of 99 Indians. There is a monument to Tom Quick in Milford. The town was laid out in 1796 and incorporated in 1874. Its government is administered by a borough council. Pop. 1,190.

MILFORD, Engagements at. Milford, Va., on the east bank of the south branch of the Shenandoah, was the scene of several skirmishes and three cavalry engagements during the Civil War. On June 24, 1862, detachments of the First Maine and First Michigan cavalry attacked about 300 mounted Confederate infantry at the place, without decisive result, and withdrew.

When Gen. Philip N. Sheridan, after the Battle of the Opequon, followed Gen. Jubal Early up the valley, he ordered Gen. Alfred T. A. Torbert, commanding the cavalry, up the Luray Valley, to get past Early's right and cut off his retreat. Gen. James H. Wilson's division advanced and on Sept. 21, 1864, attacked Gen. Williams C. Wickham's cavalry division of two brigades and drove it from Front Royal (q.v.) and up the valley to Milford, where Wickham took up a strong defensive position on the south side of Milford Creek. When Torbert came up on the 22d he concluded that the position was too strong to be attacked, and fell back to near McCoy's Ferry, again advancing, and on the 23d occupying Milford, which had been abandoned by Wickham. Sheridan was greatly disappointed by Torbert's failure to carry the place on the 22d.

After the battle of Cedar Creek (q.v.), Oct. 19, 1864, Milford was occupied by Gen. Lunsford L. Lomax's Confederate cavalry division, and its defenses strengthened. On October 24, Gen. William H. Powell's cavalry division, two brigades of about 1,100 men, with six guns, moved up the Luray Valley to reconnoiter. Powell skirmished with Lomax's outposts on the 25th, and on the morning of the 26th attacked Lomax in position at Milford, using his artillery freely, and continuing the contest until 2 P.M. when, finding the defense so stubborn and the position too strong to be carried, he withdrew.

MILFORD HAVEN, MARQUIS OF. See BATTENBERG, LOUIS ALEXANDER.

MILFORD HAVEN, urban district and seaport, Wales, in Pembrokeshire on the celebrated Milford Haven, one of the safest, deepest, and most capacious harbors in Britain, forming a deep indentation in the southwest coast of Wales. The haven stretches about 12 miles from east to west, with a breadth of from one to two miles, and branches off into numerous bays, creeks, and reaches. The largest vessels can enter and put to sea in any wind or at any tide more expeditiously than from almost any other large harbor in Great Britain, and it has long been proposed to make Milford the eastern seat of the transatlantic trade, as bringing London nearer by several hours. The haven is defended by fortifications.

Henry II embarked at Milford Haven in 1172 on his way to the conquest of Ireland, and here Henry Tudor (later Henry VII) landed in 1485 in his successful effort to dethrone Richard III. The town of Milford Haven on the north shore, eight miles northwest of Pembroke and six miles from the mouth of the haven, has extensive modern docks. It is a fish-curing station, and the headquarters of a trawler fleet. Pop. (1961) 12,802.

MILHAUD, mē-yō′, **Darius,** French composer: b. Aix-en-Provence, Sept. 4, 1892; d. Geneva, Switzerland, June 22, 1974. In 1910 he entered the Paris Conservatory, where he studied with Vincent d'Indy. As a student he won prizes in violin, counterpoint, and the fugue, composed numerous pieces for a string quartet, sonatas, ballet, incidental music to the *Orestes* trilogy of Aeschylus, and a musical novel, *La Brebis Égarée,* with the text by Francis Jammes. In 1917–1919, as an attaché in the French legation at Rio de Janeiro, he made the acquaintance of the poet Paul Claudel, who later was the librettist of most of his operas. Milhaud returned to Paris in 1919 and there associated with Arthur Honegger and others who came to be called "Les Six." He came to the United States in 1922 where he gave recitals and lectured at Harvard, Columbia, and Princeton. In 1940, after the fall of France, he came to the United States again and taught at Mills College, Oakland, Calif. In 1947 he was made professor of the Conservatory of Paris.

A prolific composer, Milhaud has used numerous thematic motifs in his work, achieving effects through the use of jazz and South American rhythms, and through polytonal passages. His works, though brilliant, are uneven, some being too purely intellectual in approach and others too trivial for critical appreciation. A prolific writer, Milhaud is skilled in polytonal writing and an expermentalist in musical forms and in instrumental combinations. His works, with dates of first performance, include the ballets *Le boeuf sur le toit,* or *The Nothing-Doing Bar* (1920, ballet by Jean Cocteau), *La création du monde* (1923), *Jeux de printemps* (1944), and *The Bells* (1946, after Edgar Allan Poe); and the operas *Le pauvre matelot* (1927; composed 1916), *Les choéphores* (first concert performance, 1919; first stage performance, 1935); *Les malheurs d'Orphée* (1926); *Christophe Colombe* (1930, libretto by Paul Claudel), and *David* (1954). He also wrote three *opéras-à-la-minute,* a type of music drama of his own creation; *L'enlèvement d'Europe* (1927), *L'abandon d'Ariane,* and *La délivrance de Thésée* (1928). His orchestral works include symphonies for small orchestras and large orchestras (the eighth large-orchestra symphony, *Rhodanienne,* was performed in 1958); *Saudades do Brasil* (1920); and concertos for piano, violin, cello, harp, clarinet, and other, more exotic solo instruments such as the marimba, the vibraphone, and the harmonica. He has also written music for ensemble (including the popular *Cheminée du roi René,* 1942), for piano, and for voice.

MILIARIA, mĭl-ĭ-âr'ĭ-ȧ (PRICKLY HEAT or HEAT RASH), an acute inflammation of the sweat glands brought on by excessive heat over prolonged periods, as in the tropics, where high temperatures, high humidity, and profuse sweating prevail. The clinical picture is characterized by an elevated rash at the sweat gland orifices, accompanied by intense itching and burning. Such areas are prone to infection if the individual scratches or if skin sanitation is not promptly restored. The folds of the body are most susceptible, particularly in young children. Essentially, the condition is a benign irritative dermatitis which responds promptly to alleviation of the conditions which produce it. The typical skin picture is the multiple occurrence of minute papules and vesicles corresponding to the orifices of the sweat glands. Treatment is concentrated on cleanliness, dusting powders, and antibiotics if secondary infection occurs. Air conditioning and the maintenance of skin hygiene have done much to reduce the incidence of miliaria.

REAUMUR S. DONNALLY, M.D.

MILIČ, mĭ'lēch, **Jan** (known as MILIČ OF KREMSIER), Moravian reformer: b. Kroměříž (Kremsier), Moravia; d. Avignon, France, June 29, 1374. A priest who held various offices in the chancery of Emperor Charles IV and was a canon of the Prague Cathedral, Milič resigned all his offices and preferments in 1363 to embrace an ascetic life, denouncing the worldliness of both clergy and laity. Preaching in the Czech language to the common people, and thus appealing to their growing sense of national identity, he warned that the Antichrist would appear in 1365 and that the church must repent and reform immediately. Once, while preaching before Charles IV, he pointed at the emperor and denounced him as the Antichrist. In 1367, having gone to Rome, he was imprisoned by the Inquisition, but was later released and received by Urban V. While in prison, he wrote the *Libellus de Antichristo,* in which he recommended that an ecumenical council be called to cleanse the church of corruption. Upon his return to Prague he resumed his preaching, but in 1372 he was denounced as a heretic by the mendicants, whom he had attacked for their lapsed way of life, and by the parish priests. He chose to defend himself before the papal court at Avignon, was allowed to preach before the cardinals there, and was ultimately cleared of the charge of heresy, though he died before the suit was concluded. In his emphasis on reform and his appeal to the national consciousness of the people, though not on doctrinal grounds, he is considered a forerunner of Jan Hus.

MILITARISM, mĭl'ĭ-tȧ-rĭz'm, a term applied to the policy of giving exceptional emphasis to military preparedness, exalting the military virtues, and relying on force in international relations. Preparation for war encourages the growth of the militaristic spirit to strengthen the combatants for battle. However, militarism frequently outlasts the threat of war. In some cases, a government may manufacture crises, both internal and external, so that there is an apparent justification for allowing military considerations to overrule civilian concerns. In other cases, rival countries may find themselves in conflict in so many areas that each adopts aggressive militaristic policies in anticipation of open conflict. Militarism of either kind is usually evidenced by ever-increasing armament production and by direct or indirect military control of governmental operations. Carried to its extreme, militarism develops into the theory that only in war can a nation properly fulfill its destiny.

Consult Vagts, Alfred, *History of Militarism,* rev. ed. (New York 1959).

MILITARY ACADEMY, United States. See UNITED STATES MILITARY ACADEMY.

MILITARY AERONAUTICS, mĭl'ĭ-tĕr-ĭ ā-ĕr-ō-nô'tĭks. Advances in weapons and military mobility have fashioned the art and science of warfare throughout the ages. In the 20th century, aeronautics—the science of flight through air space—came to dominate the military scene. After two world wars, aeronautics had created a revolution in warfare. In 1949, Sir Winston Churchill summarized the importance of air power in this way: "For good or ill, air mastery is today the supreme expression of military power, and fleets and navies, however necessary and important, must accept subordinate rank. This is a memorable milestone in the march of mankind."

The use of balloons for observation or wind-blown transport was the first military application of aeronautics. Balloons were employed by Napoleon, the Union Army in the American Civil War, and besieged Parisians in the Franco-Prussian War. With the invention of the airplane, the impact of aeronautics upon warfare was swift and widespread; the period from the pioneering achievement of the Wright brothers at Kitty Hawk, N.C., in 1903, to the destruction of Hiroshima, Japan, by one atomic bomb dropped from a single airplane in 1945, was a relatively short one. As aircraft and their weapons were improved in World Wars I and II, the leaders of nations were forced to grapple with sweeping changes in the problems of national defense. The story of military aeronautics is, therefore, one largely studded with bitter controversies among military professionals—soldiers, sailors, and airmen—on the proper role of the air forces in warfare: whether they should be independently and strategically employed, or employed in tactical conjunc-

Above: The British Vickers-Vimy bomber, designed to bomb Berlin but unfinished in November, 1918, when World War I ended.

Top left: The Royal Air Force's de Havilland DH-4 bomber.

Top right: A German biplane, the Albatros two-seater, type C5.

MILITARY AERONAUTICS

AIRPLANES OF WORLD WAR I

Center left: A French single-seat monoplane, the Morane 27.

Left: The Curtiss JN-4 ("Jenny"), an American training plane.

Bottom left: The Spad 13, a product of Blériot's great factory.

Bottom right: An S.I.A.-7B biplane, flown by the Italians.

British Information Services; The Institute of the Aeronautical Sciences, Inc.

tion with army and naval forces. World War II demonstrated that superiority in the air (a condition in which air forces can be employed with negligible enemy opposition) was the hinge of victory. The total defeat of Germany and Japan, and the first use of atomic bombs, ended most arguments among military thinkers about the primacy of air power in military affairs. But the revolution in warfare brought about by aeronautics must be traced more carefully to appreciate its great significance in this day of global-legged jet bombers, intercontinental ballistic missiles, earth satellites, and spatial glide bombers. No end is yet in sight for the future military use of the latter-day offspring of aeronautical progress.

Early Years.—Prior to World War I, the future of military aeronautics was not clearly seen in the high commands of armies and navies of any nation. The United States was the first nation in the world to possess a military airplane: a Wright Flyer was bought for the Signal Corps of the United States Army in 1908. But aviation was not considered seriously as a potential weapon in the United States until the outbreak of war in 1914.

The birth of military aeronautics was as slow in Europe as in the United States. But the European vision of the future was clearer. When Alberto Santos-Dumont became the first to fly off the soil of Europe in a heavier-than-air craft in 1906, the English newspaper publisher, Baron (later Viscount) Northcliffe, said, "The news is not that man can fly, but that England is no longer an island." No nation had aerial shores from that time on, as later events were to prove. In 1908, H. G. Wells wrote *The War in the Air,* in which he clearly foresaw that the air power of nations would revolutionize the conduct of war, for it would bring the cities, industry, and population of nations onto the battlefields of the future. And in Italy, an obscure army major, Giulio Douhet, wrote in 1909, "It must seem strange that the sky, too, is about to become another battlefield no less important than the battlefields on land and sea. But from now on we had better get accustomed to this idea and prepare ourselves for the new conflicts to come."

World War I.—World War I in Europe witnessed the first military use of aircraft on any appreciable scale. While each nation glamorized its aerial combat heroes, known as aces (those with five or more air victories), air operations during the entire war had little direct influence upon the course of the fighting. German Zeppelins and Gotha bombers demonstrated with bombs to the residents of London that England was no longer an island. French and German Rhineland cities also suffered air attack. Over the trenches on the western front, stretching from Switzerland to the Atlantic, aerial spotting for artillery fire and the use of bombing aircraft gave rise to air combat, which assumed embryonic significance when by 1916 machine guns were synchronized to fire forward through the arc of propellers. Specialized aircraft—single-seater pursuit fighters, bombers, and observation aircraft—performed missions suited to their speed, maneuverability, or load-carrying characteristics. Lighter-than-air ships and balloons proved hopelessly vulnerable. Such aircraft as were employed could not break the deadlock in the trenches, any more than concentrated artillery barrages, waves of human flesh in the form of massive infantry attacks, or the naval blockade of Germany could. In the closing months of the war, the Western Allies created an

North American Aviation, Inc.

Three generations of fighter aircraft: the Spad, flown during World War I (bottom); the F-51 Mustang of World War II (right); and the F-86 Sabre of the Korean War.

Independent Air Force under the command of Sir Hugh M. Trenchard for the purpose of combining all available bombers for strategic operations directly against targets in Germany. The armistice intervened before this air force had had a chance to develop.

Aerial operations thus had only minor importance in World War I. Only in Great Britain did the need for defense against German air attacks prompt the creation of an independent air force. All other nations subordinated their air units to their respective armies. The Magna Carta of Britain's Royal Air Force (RAF) was a report of a cabinet committee on Home Defence headed by Field Marshal Jan Christiaan Smuts. This report stated (October 1917): "The day may not be far off when aerial operations may become the principal operations of war to which the older forms of military and naval operations may become secondary and subordinate. Air supremacy may in the long run become as important a factor in the defence of the Empire as sea supremacy."

Before the United States entered World War I in 1917, Alexander Graham Bell had told the national convention of the Navy League in 1916: "We must realize that we are only in the infancy of aerial locomotion. If you will allow your mind to look ahead you can see that land power and sea power will ultimately be secondary in importance to air power." Not until 1947, 30 years after the creation of the RAF and a world war later, did the United States Air Force (USAF) come into being as an autonomous military arm.

Emergence of the Doctrine of Air Power.—The theory that air power would one day be decisive in military strategy was entertained by a few gifted airmen of World War I. Best known of these early champions of air power were Air Chief Marshal Sir Hugh (later 1st Viscount) Trenchard of Great Britain, Gen. Giulio Douhet of Italy, and Brig. Gen. William (Billy) Mitchell of the United States. Their views stood the test of time and were taken up by the outstanding spokesmen of air power before World War II.

Mitchell, Douhet, and Trenchard were one in believing that strategic bombing of the German homeland would have shortened World War I. They maintained that by reason of an air force's mobility and speed, it was inherently more powerful than any surface force and could not be defeated by armies and navies. Hence, in a future war, air forces were indispensable weapons not only for the destruction of the enemy's air force but for the defeat of his army and navy as well. Further, they believed that an enemy nation could probably be beaten to its knees by strategic air attack upon its air forces, then on its industries and cities. In other words, the air advocates held that an air force should be much more than long-range artillery, tactically tethered to army and naval forces on the surface of the earth. Douhet was court-martialed in 1916 for his views, Mitchell in 1925. Trenchard was more fortunate and commanded the RAF during its shaky first decade after World War I.

Perhaps because he did not set forth his views in writing, Trenchard is ignored by many students of military strategy. Yet Trenchard schooled the generation of British airmen who won the Battle of Britain, the turning point of World War II. These airmen, such as air chief marshals Sir Charles Portal, Sir Hugh Dowding, Sir Arthur Tedder, Sir Arthur Coningham, Sir Robert Saundby, Sir John Slessor, and others, animated Anglo-American air operations through World War II.

Billy Mitchell had a global view of American security in the air age, pointing out the importance of Alaska and predicting the attack on Pearl Harbor. From the moment his squadron sank a former German warship, the *Ostfriesland,* during bombing exercises off the Virginia capes in 1921, he held that battleships were obsolete. Although he wrote several books and many articles in support of an independent air force, he failed to win his fight for it during his lifetime. In spirit if not always in doctrine, his latter-day disciples have included the Amercan generals Henry H. Arnold, Carl A. Spaatz, and Orvil A. Anderson. Among the most notable of his intellectual offspring has been Maj. Alexander P. de Seversky, who has written and spoken widely on American air power.

Douhet, the Italian exponent of air power, wrote *Il dominio dell'aria* (1921; Eng. tr., *Command of the Air,* 1942), the first classic statement on the application of aeronautics to the art of warfare. It was widely studied and debated during the European "cold war" of the 1930's, and during and even after World War II. The principles enunciated by Douhet first appeared to come to life during the operations of the Japanese Air Force against China in 1931 and 1937, the bombing of Ethiopia by Italy in 1935 and 1936, and the operations of German and Russian air units in the Spanish Civil War of 1936–1939. Fear of the German Luftwaffe was an important influence in the appeasement of Adolf Hitler during the Munich crisis of 1938. While Douhet, Mitchell, and Trenchard may have exaggerated the decisiveness of air forces in warfare in their own time, technical progress was to bear out the substance of their theories during World War II and after.

World War II.—While both Germany and Japan made effective use of their air forces at the beginning of World War II, their leaders did not fully understand the dynamics of air warfare. In Europe, the war began in September 1939 with the German blitzkrieg, or "lightning war," upon Poland. Exploiting tactical surprise, Hitler's Luftwaffe gained complete air superiority at the outset. Stukas (dive bombers) then cleared the way for tank formations which spearheaded the swift advances of the German Army. Prewar army textbooks had become worthless almost overnight. Denmark, Norway, the Netherlands, Belgium, and France also succumbed to the blitzkrieg form of warfare by May 1940. Tactical air support of the German Army also worked well in the Balkan campaigns of 1941 and in the first summer and fall campaigns of the Germans in Russia, when they swept almost to Moscow.

The Battle of Britain in the late summer of 1940, however, was the turning point of World War II. Fighting alone, Britain stood off the German efforts to knock her out of the war by air attack. For the first time in history, air warfare was pivotal to strategic victory. The German Luftwaffe failed to achieve daylight air superiority over the RAF, a necessary condition for either an amphibious invasion of England, a successful air-sea blockade, or a decisive bombing campaign. For the first time, the German Air Force fought a first-rate opponent, and it was beaten. The fact that the Luftwaffe had lost the first strategic air battle was not recognized by Hitler and his generals until it was too late. England survived as a launching base for Anglo-American bombers to carry the air war to German skies. Germany lost the air battle over North Africa and eventually over Germany itself.

In the summer of 1944, over 8,000 German V-1 missiles were launched against Britain. In the fall of that year, a ballistic rocket missile, the V-2, bombarded Britain in a German attempt to regain the decision in the air. But this decision had already been lost to the day and night strategic air offensive (around-the-clock bombing) by the RAF and the United States Army Air Forces (USAAF) on German supply lines, industries, and cities, from which there was no recovery after March 1944. The Germans also introduced to combat a superior jet fighter, the Me-262, but it appeared too late. In the Normandy invasion and in the occupation of Germany by Allied ground forces, a condition of absolute Allied air superiority prevailed.

For the United States, World War II began with the Japanese air attack on Pearl Harbor. Although the continental United States was spared bombing in World War II, the Pacific campaigns demonstrated that the range and firepower of military aircraft had extended the radii of battlefields. Battleships were no longer capital ships. Sea battles, such as Midway and the Coral Sea, were fought by aircraft flown from carriers. Aircraft carriers had extended the range of Japanese aircraft for their attack on Pearl Harbor, they were used in Gen. James H. Doolittle's raid on Tokyo in April 1942, and they helped to establish air superiority over the island steppingstones leading to Japan itself. The strategic "bomber line" advanced slowly in the Pacific while Japan's leaders, like Germany's, failed to appreciate the dynamic progress in aeronautics soon enough to take corrective action. Eventually the Superfortress B-29's, four-engine bombers developed after the war had started, brought Japan itself under the bombsights. Japan surrendered without being invaded by surface forces.

After the Japanese cities of Hiroshima and Nagasaki were struck by atomic bombs in August 1945, the revolution in warfare wrought by aeronautics was even more complete. The mobility, speed, and directness of air attack was now wedded to a massive concentration of firepower. Air superiority emerged from World War II as the prerequisite for successful strategic action. The ruins of German and Japanese cities attested to the fact that the strongest nation could not survive in modern warfare without a superior air force. Tactical air operations—direct support of surface forces by air forces destroying the enemy lines of supply, wearing down his combat forces, and providing airlift for troops and supplies—had likewise radically altered the tactics of surface forces on land and sea.

Peace, Korea, and the Race for Air Superiority.—Gen. Henry H. Arnold, commander in chief of the USAAF, said in his final report in 1946: "The weapons of today are the museum pieces of tomorrow." Technical progress in military aeronautics was extremely rapid in the decade after World War II, largely as a result of the global conflict growing out of the postwar ambitions of the Soviet Union in areas weakened by the war. The Berlin airlift (1948–1949) and the Korean War (1950–1953) saw American air power remobilized. Propeller-driven aircraft were superseded by supersonic jet fighters and long-range heavy jet bombers which, with aerial refueling, could attack any target on the earth. The technical race for air superiority proved a key factor in the struggle for a balance of power in a world split between the United States and its allies on the one hand, and the Soviet Union and its allies and satellites on the other.

In 1949 the Soviet Union acquired its first atomic bomb. In the Korean War, the Soviet MIG-15 fighter proved a match for the best American fighter, the F-86. By 1955 the Soviet Union also possessed thermonuclear bombs a thousand times more powerful than the Nagasaki bomb, and had turned out an intercontinental jet bomber, the Bison, equal in performance to the American B-52.

Intercontinental ballistic missiles were developed. In 1957 the Soviet Union launched the first artificial earth satellite; the United States sent up a satellite of its own in the following year. Both nations since those days have carried out an ambitious program to explore space with unmanned scientific and military satellites and also with manned satellites, having a moon landing as their ultimate objective.

Significance of Military Aeronautics.—The most significant effect of military aeronautics on human affairs has been the rise of total war. No nation has geographic barriers that can prevent the penetration of its air space in the sense that mountains, oceans, rivers, and deserts restrict surface mobility. Because of military aeronautics, no nation is immune from the range of enemy air action. Everyone lives on a potential battlefield. The survival of a nation at war is dependent upon its ability to exploit air space. Technical progress is the key, then, to air supremacy.

Air vehicles are global in range, and men can now fly faster than bullets, and beyond the earth's atmosphere. One aircraft or missile can deliver more explosive power on an enemy target than has been released in all wars since the invention of gunpowder. Nuclear-powered submarines, such as the *Nautilus,* can also serve as underwater launching platforms for strategic missiles, just as nuclear-powered bombers may one day serve as launching platforms while orbiting around the earth in outer space. Some experts even predict that there will be military bases on the moon in the near future; others envision air forces that will act as a world police force. The dynamic pace of progress in aeronautics and astronautics makes it certain that there will continue to be extremely significant and interesting developments in the future.

See also AEROSPACE INDUSTRY; AIR FORCE, DEPARTMENT OF THE; AIR TRANSPORTATION; ASTRONAUTICS; LIGHTER-THAN-AIR CRAFT; NAVAL AVIATION; ROCKETS; WORLD WAR I—*14. The War in the Air;* WORLD WAR II.

U.S. Air Force Photographs

Heavy bombers of the modern United States Air Force: the Boeing B-52 Stratofortress (top), and an artist's conception of the delta-winged, supersonic B-70 Valkyrie.

Bibliography.—Hoeppner, Ernst von, *Deutschlands Krieg in der Luft* (Leipzig 1921); Mitchell, William, *Our Air Force* (New York 1921); id., *Winged Defense* (New York 1925); Vauthier, Paul, *La doctrine de guerre du général Douhet* (Paris 1935); Rohden, Herhudt von, *Vom Luftkriege* (Berlin 1938); de Seversky, Alexander P., *Victory Through Air Power* (New York 1942); Douhet, Giulio, *Command of the Air,* tr. by D. Ferrari (New York 1942); Lee, Asher, *The German Air Force* (New York 1946); Tedder, 1st Baron Arthur; *Air Power in War* (New York 1948); Arnold, Henry H., *Global Mission* (New York 1949); de Seversky, Alexander P., *Air Power: Key to Survival* (New York 1950); Holley, Irving B., *Ideas and Weapons* (New Haven 1953); Richards, Denis, and Saunders, H. St. George, *Royal Air Force,* 3 vols. (London 1953–54); Stockwell, Richard E., *Soviet Air Power* (New York 1956); Goldberg, Alfred, ed., *A History of the United States Air Force, 1907–1957* (Princeton 1957); Slessor, Sir John C., *Central Blue* (New York 1957); Stewart, James T., ed., *Airpower: the Decisive Force in Korea* (Princeton 1957); Craven, Wesley, and Cate, James, eds., *The Army Air Forces in World War II,* 6 vols. (Chicago 1948–58); Emme, Eugene M., *The Impact of Air Power* (Princeton 1958); Garthoff, Raymond L., *Soviet Strategy in the Nuclear Age* (New York 1958); Levine, Isaac D., *Mitchell: Pioneer of Air Power,* rev. ed. (New York 1958); Emme, Eugene M., *The Impact of Air Power* (Princeton 1959); id., *Aeronautics and Astronautics* (Washington 1961); id., *History of Space Flight* (New York 1965).

EUGENE M. EMME,
Historian, National Aeronautics and Space Administration.

MILITARY ARREST. See COURT MARTIAL.

MILITARY CAMPS, groups of tents, huts, or other temporary shelters set up for troops; temporary military posts. Early Egyptian and

Assyrian inscriptions show military camps, frequently fortified and possessing at least rudimentary interior organization. Persian, Greek, and Macedonian armies followed the same general system. The Romans, with their willingness to work as well as fight, fortified all of their camps—even those occupied only overnight—with a ditch and wall. The interior organization of their camps was uniform and well planned, each unit having its assigned area. These strongholds, which as formidable an opponent as Hannibal regarded with respect, were key factors in the Roman art of warfare. From them, the legions marched out to battle, fresh and rested; within them, a defeated Roman force could hold out until a relief column arrived. In contrast, medieval camps were generally noted for their disorder and squalor; but professional interest in castrametation (q.v.), as the art of laying out camps was termed, gradually revived thereafter. Camps played an important part in the comparatively slow and formal warfare characteristic of the 16th, 17th, and 18th centuries. Frederick the Great of Prussia considered skill in choosing suitable camp sites to be one of the requisite qualities of a good general. The camp of this period was seldom fortified, but prudent commanders were careful to take advantage of favorable terrain and to encamp so that they could rapidly draw up their troops in order of battle. A great variety of camps (such as offensive, defensive, and foraging camps) were mentioned in the military writings of the day. A curious variety was the so-called *flying camp,* which was actually a strong, mobile force used to screen friendly positions and to harass the enemy. Large *entrenched camps,* extensive enough to shelter an entire army with its trains and supplies, were frequently used to dominate strategic areas and to serve as pivots around which the armies might maneuver. The more aggressive warfare of the French Revolutionary and Napoleonic wars, along with the more powerful artillery of the 19th century, reduced the value of these entrenched camps. The term continued to be used, however, up to World War I when the defensive area set up around the French capital was referred to as the "entrenched camp of Paris."

During Napoleonic times the term "camp" came to mean an orderly encampment of huts or tents, used only in peacetime for training, or during armistices. Troops in the field in wartime might be "billeted" in the houses of the local inhabitants, but would usually "bivouac" in the open without shelter. (American and British soldiers continued to speak of "camping" overnight, rather than bivouacing, and this common expression continued in use at least until World War I.)

In modern United States military terminology, a camp is a temporary military post, as compared to a fort, which is a permanent one. Most of the present camps in the United States were constructed during World Wars I and II as troop training centers, staging areas, and prisoner-of-war enclosures. The problems involved in their construction were complicated: modern armored and artillery units required large training areas, frequently in excess of 100,000 acres; each camp needed water and fuel supplies and sewage disposal facilities roughly equivalent to those necessary for a city of from 10,000 to 70,000 persons; many camps of necessity were built in areas where the supply of local labor and building materials was insufficient; and occasionally there was the danger that firing on the camp's ranges would interfere with air traffic or other activities in the area. Military authorities met the problems by developing rigid criteria to guide survey teams in their selection of camp sites, and by careful site planning to provide the most compact and economical layout consistent with operational efficiency. In order to make the best use of available training time, camps were planned so that traffic jams were avoided and travel from housing to training areas within the camp was kept to a minimum. A large number of these camps are still in use; others have been placed on caretaker status against future emergencies.

In a theater of war, a preselected area generally out of direct contact with the enemy, where a command rests and prepares for further action, is now called a *bivouac.* A satisfactory bivouac is roomy enough to permit normal dispersion of vehicles and weapons, and offers concealment from enemy air and ground observation. Areas that are boggy or easily flooded, and areas that must be entered through defiles which the enemy might block, are avoided.

JOHN R. ELTING,
Lieutenant Colonel, United States Army; Department of Military Art and Engineering, United States Military Academy.

MILITARY COLORS. See COLORS, MILITARY.

MILITARY COMMUNICATIONS. Since man first bore arms against his neighbor, military communications have been an essential element of warfare. They are the commander's means of exercising control over his forces on the battlefield and of maintaining contact with key forces and agencies not on the battlefield. Just as civil transportation has frequently been used for military purposes in times of war, so also have civil communications been utilized for military communications, mainly off the field of battle. Long-range military communications from the seat of government or from key forces and agencies not located upon the battlefield may be referred to as *strategic military communications,* whereas those military communications employed on the battlefield may be referred to as *tactical military communications.* Both categories have existed since earliest times.

Antiquity.—Undoubtedly the earliest means of military communications were the voice and runner, but they were supplemented at a very early date by bugles and trumpets, drums, signal fires and smoke, pigeons, flags, and mounted messengers. Ancient historians relate how early in the 5th century B.C. the Persian King Darius, father of Xerxes, established "voice relay" systems, which were capable of transmitting messages in one day over a distance comparable to a 30 days' march by placing soldiers with unusual vocal capacities in a relay system operating from hilltop to hilltop. A similar system was employed by the Gauls in the time of Caesar. From the ancient Greeks we learn of Pheidippides, who covered 150 miles in two days to solicit Spartan aid when the Persians landed in Greece in 490 B.C.; he also reputedly ran from Marathon to Athens to announce the Greek victory, though he died of the strain shortly thereafter. Elaborate relays by mounted messengers were developed by such great military captains of antiquity as Alexander, Hannibal, and Caesar. The Greek writer Aeschylus tells how the news of the fall of Troy was transmitted from Troy to Greece by means of a series of signal fires on mountaintops. Both the ancient Greeks and the Romans devised means of signaling with torches at night and with smoke during daylight. The American Indian transmitted messages over great distances by means of smoke signals, while African natives use drums to send messages through the dense jungles. Messages have been sent by homing pigeons since the days of the ancient Egyptians; they were used in relays by Genghis Khan (c. 1162–1227). All of the foregoing ancient means of communication may be classified as strategic, since they generally operated over long distances, off the battlefield.

Tactical military communications were provided for the battlefield commander in ancient times by the runner and mounted messenger, the trumpet and bugle, the kettledrum and snare drum, flags and pennants, and the warrior's shield. The kettledrum was used by the ancient Persians both to control their own cavalry formations and to frighten their enemies. Alexander the Great controlled his phalanx by means of trumpets, fifes, standards, or simply by an upraised weapon, while the Mongol cavalry of Genghis Khan was directed by pennants and bugles by day, and lanterns and fires by night. Genghis Khan's Mongols had ingenious devices for tactical communications, such as whistling arrows, capable of producing three different tones, and naphtha bombs. At sea, messages were transmitted between ships by voice, by the display and movement of a gilded shield on the admiral's galley, by torches at night, or by a profusion of flags in the daylight. Herodotus also relates how the Persians, after their defeat at the Battle of Marathon, received a message from the Greek mainland by means of the sun's reflection upon a burnished shield, urging them to sail southward and attack undefended Athens.

Frederick the Great to Napoleon.—With the advent of gunpowder in Europe in the 13th century, a new means of tactical communication was introduced on both land and sea. Frederick the Great, in the Seven Years' War, relied upon the distant cannonading from his secondary attack to initiate his attack upon the Austrians in the Battle of Torgau (1760). He also established an excellent military post system to link his scattered forces in central Europe.

With the invention of the telescope (c. 1608), the ranges of visual signaling systems on both land and sea were increased, contributing significantly to the success of the mechanical telegraph system constructed by a Frenchman, Claude Chappe, between Paris and Lille in 1794. The Chappe telegraph system consisted of a series of posts, each 30 feet high, with a movable crossbar at the top and a movable 6-foot indicator at either end of the crossbar. By manipulating the crossbar and indicators by means of ropes and pulleys at the base of the post, 196 different signals could be formed. The posts were established some 8 to 12 miles apart and could transmit a signal over a distance of 130 miles in 2 minutes under favorable weather conditions. Napoleon Bonaparte employed and extended Chappe's telegraph system throughout his empire for strategic military communications, linking Paris with such key cities as Brussels, Boulogne, and the Italian cities of Milan, Venice, and Mantua. At night, lanterns were attached to the crossbar and indicators to permit communication. The system was adopted and used for both civil and strategic military communications by all of the major European powers for 50 years, and provided the most dependable and reliable means of long-range communications before the advent of the electric telegraph.

In addition to Chappe's mechanical telegraph, Napoleon established an excellent military post system of mounted messengers, comparable to the American Pony Express, to serve his armies throughout Europe. He also used a field relay system with red, white, and black flags to extend the mechanical telegraph. On the Napoleonic battlefield, the trumpet and the unit standard were the primary means of controlling the cavalry, while the snare drum was to Napoleon's infantry what the portable radio is to the troops of today. A staff of aides and orderlies generally provided Napoleon himself with an immediate means of communication with his troops both on and off the battlefield. Rockets and signal shells were employed for communication at night, and the British even sent messages by plugging them inside cannon balls. Both the British and the French experimented with balloons for purposes of transporting military messages. Meanwhile, during the Revolutionary War in America, an unusual semaphore was devised. It consisted of a mast, similar to the one used in the Chappe telegraph, to which could be attached a barrel, a flag, and a basket. By shifting the positions of these three unusual items on the mast, a limited number of prearranged messages could be transmitted.

Electric Telegraph.—Although the electric telegraph was conceived by Samuel F. B. Morse in 1832, patented in 1837, and successfully demonstrated with the Morse code of dots and dashes in 1844, it served no military purpose until the Crimean War in 1854 and then only for strategic communications by the British. Three years later, in 1857, the British used the electric telegraph again, during the Indian Mutiny, for military communications between their headquarters in Calcutta and their scattered military outposts throughout India. It was adopted by the Prussian, French, and Spanish armies before the beginning of the American Civil War.

Although Albert J. Myer was commissioned as "Signal Officer with the rank of Major" and head of the Signal Department of the Union Army on June 21, 1860, the United States Army Signal Corps was not officially created by Congress as an independent signal service until March 3, 1863. Meanwhile, the Confederate Signal Service, which was in full operation by the First Battle of Bull Run, July 21, 1861, was created as the first independent Signal Corps by the Confederate Congress on April 19, 1862 and was organized as a distinct branch of the Confederate Army on May 29, 1862 under Maj. William Norris. The Confederate and Union Signal corps were the first corps of officers and men within any army whose sole mission was communications. Strategic telegraph communications, however, were provided for both armies during the early years of the Civil War by civilian telegraphers who were exempted from conscription and hired by the War Department, but remained free from military control.

The first tactical wire communications were established by a special military field signal detachment with Gen. George B. McClellan's army during the Peninsular Campaign, using the new portable Beardslee magnetoelectric telegraph instrument. The same system was used by the Union Army to provide telegraph communications across the Rappahannock River on the Fredericksburg, Va., battlefield.

As a result of the success of this tactical telegraph system operated by military personnel, intense rivalry, not unlike the interservice rivalries of today, arose between the newly established Union Army Signal Corps and the Military Telegraph Service. Secretary of War Edwin M. Stanton, a former director of the Atlantic and Ohio Telegraph Company, directed Colonel Myer to turn over all telegraph equipment to the civilian Military Telegraph Service. Consequently, all tactical as well as strategic telegraph communications for the Union Army were provided by civilian telegraphers without military status; in all, some 15,000 miles of wire were laid by the Military Telegraph Service. The Union Signal Corps was forced to confine its activities to the use of such visual signaling devices as flags, torches, disks, lanterns, semaphores, candlebombs, rockets, and smoke—both off and on the battlefield. The same visual means were generally adopted by the Union Navy for ship-to-shore and ship-to-ship communications. Forerunner of military ground-to-air communications, as well as aerial observation, was the operation of the telegraph from a balloon by Professor Thaddeus S. C. Lowe on June 17, 1861. Codes or ciphers were also developed by both Union and Confederate forces to provide secure communications during the Civil War.

U.S. Army Photograph

Flag signaling during the Philippines campaign of 1898.

The Prussians capitalized on the use of the electric telegraph in the war with Denmark in 1864, the Austro-Prussian War of 1866, and the Franco-Prussian War of 1870–1871, for purposes of controlling the movements of their armies in the field. Balloons and pigeons were again utilized as means of military communications by the French during the siege of Paris in the Franco-Prussian War. A large measure of the success of the British Army in the Abyssinian Campaign of 1867–1868 was attributed to the effective military application of the telegraph, as well as visual signaling, in maintaining contact with Sir Robert Napier's expeditionary force. The heliograph, or mirror telegraph, was employed with great success by the British Army during the Jowaki Afridi Expedition of 1877–1878 in India, as well as by the United States Army during the campaigns against the Indians on the sunny southwestern frontier of the United States, but its application was limited because of its dependence on the sun. A strategic Anglo-American link was created by the completion of the first continuously successful transatlantic cables in 1865 and 1866.

Telephone.—In 1876, Alexander Graham Bell successfully demonstrated and patented the instrument that has become the mainstay of both the military and the civil communications system—the talking telegraph, or telephone. Civil as well as military application of the telephone was painfully slow in the latter portion of the 19th century, and its use for military communications in the Spanish-American War of 1898 and the South African War of 1899–1902 was very limited. During the attack of United States forces upon Manila in the Philippines during August 1898, ship-to-shore communications were maintained between Adm. George Dewey's fleet in Manila Bay and the United States Army on shore by means of signal flags, or wigwag. A telegraph or telephone line was established to Manila by a Signal Corps party with the advance elements of the Army. Meanwhile, in Cuba, a captive balloon equipped with an air-to-ground telephone circuit was used by two enterprising United States Army officers for aerial observation.

With the advent of trench warfare in the Russo-Japanese War of 1904–1905, use of the telephone on the battlefield became quite common; telephone communications were generally employed from the army headquarters toward the front and telegraph communications toward the rear. The ever-increasing lethal power of the bullet and the artillery shell on the battlefield was making visual means of signaling, which exposed the signal personnel to the enemy's fire, extremely hazardous and impracticable.

Radio.—Meanwhile, in 1896 an Italian, Guglielmo Marconi, had obtained a British patent for the first practical wireless telegraph, or radio. Unlike the slow development of the telephone for military as well as civil communications, the development of the radio for military purposes was extremely rapid. As early as 1899, an experimental, 12-mile ship-to-shore radio circuit was operated by the United States Army Signal Corps in the vicinity of New York City. In December 1901, strategic communications took another significant step forward with the transmission of the first wireless signal across the Atlantic Ocean. The South African War saw the use of several radio sets in the field, while during the Russo-Japanese War strategic radio communications were established between the Far East and England. The radio quickly became the backbone of the joint military-civil communications system which Congress authorized the United States Army Signal Corps to establish and operate to and inside the territory of Alaska in 1900—a system now known as the Alaska Communication System and still operated by the Signal Corps.

With the Wright brothers' successful flight in 1903, air-to-ground communications became a problem; but by 1912 the United States Army Signal Corps, to which the operation of aircraft was assigned, had successfully adapted the radio

U.S. Army Photograph

Pigeons carry messages to the front lines in Korea, 1953

with the Morse code for air-to-ground communications. Thus, at the beginning of World War I, all of the major powers involved were equipped to various degrees with such modern means of military communication as the telephone, with its switchboards and wire lines, the telegraph, and the radio, both aerial and ground.

World War I.—The impact of these new means of military communications upon the conduct of World War I became apparent in the concurrent and decisive battles of Tannenberg and the Marne in 1914. During the former battle, the lack of wire communications in the Russian armies operating in East Prussia led to the use of the radio, but without codes or ciphers for security. As a result, the eagerly listening German Army in East Prussia intercepted the Russian broadcasts and, armed with this information, achieved a modern Cannae. Meanwhile, on the western front, the lack of adequate wire communications between Gen. Helmuth von Moltke's general headquarters and the German armies sweeping through Belgium and northern France, and the interference with or jamming of German radio communications by the French atop the Eiffel Tower, contributed heavily to the failure of von Moltke's modified Schlieffen Plan and the repulse of the German armies along the Marne River. Thereafter, the war on the western front degenerated into a trench stalemate with such heavy emphasis upon the use of telephones that the United States Army alone had strung more than 100,000 miles of wire and operated 282 telephone exchanges in France by the end of the war.

In 1915, vocal communication was established by radiotelephone between Paris, France, and Arlington, Va. Two years later the Army Signal Corps developed the aerial radiotelephone, permitting air-to-ground and air-to-air communication by voice, and it was quickly adopted by both the British and French. Panels of black and white cloth were also placed on the ground in various patterns for ground-to-air communication. Other tactical signaling devices employed by both the Allied and Central powers were electric signal lamps, smoke, pyrotechnics in the form of rockets and the Very pistol, pigeons such as Cher Ami of "Lost Battalion" fame, war dogs, sirens and gongs to warn of a gas attack, and aircraft itself. Within the American infantry division in the field, radio and wire communications were provided from division headquarters down to the infantry battalions by a field signal battalion.

At sea, the Navy was quick to adapt the radio for its communications, though hoisted flags, wigwag flags, semaphore flags, blinker lights, and pyrotechnics still played major roles. The telephone was adapted to use on shipboard. Even portable radios which could be packed into 4 haversacks each weighing 20 pounds were developed for marine landings. During World War I, the phonetic alphabet was introduced for voice communications, and the forerunners of present-day signal security and electronic warfare agencies made their appearance in the form of radio, telegraph, and telephone intercept, monitoring, and direction-finding operations.

World War II.—Following World War I, the complexity and multiplicity of military communications equipment rapidly increased in response to the many specialized requirements of the infantry, artillery, cavalry, Marines, Air Corps, Signal Corps, and worldwide military communications. The years between the wars saw the development of engine-driven, truck-mounted wire reels; rugged field telephones; sound-powered telephones; more durable field wire; smaller field switchboards; families of special infantry, artillery, cavalry, and Air Corps radios including vehicular, manpack, and handcarry sets of both AM and FM varieties; a mechanical cipher machine; an improved panel system; teletypewriters; facsimile equipment; and the highly secret radar for antiaircraft target detection and gun laying. Therefore, at the outset of World War II, although military communications still used essentially the same equipment as had emerged from World War

Radio equipment in a United States Army airborne communications center. The center is designed to aid in the control of troops which, under modern conditions of war, may be widely dispersed in small, highly mobile units.

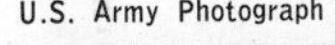

U.S. Army Photograph

I (with the exception of radar), the equipment had been vastly improved and augmented. Within the United States infantry division, as the result of an Army reorganization in 1920, communications below the division-headquarters level were provided by infantry and artillery personnel; a signal company provided communications between the division headquarters and the infantry regiments assigned to it.

U.S. Army Photograph

The DIANA radar "dish" in New Jersey bounces signals off the moon to help check out satellite-tracking devices.

The importance of military communications in the United States armed forces during World War II at all levels from the squad to national defense headquarters in Washington, D.C., and in every type of operation, cannot be over overstated. New communications equipment and procedures were developed for airborne, amphibious, and mechanized operations, and multichannel, automatic radioteletypewriter circuits emanating from the War and Navy departments in Washington, D.C., girdled the globe. The Army Communications Service with a traffic-handling capacity of some 100 million words per day was the greatest military communications system ever developed. Special teletypewriter circuits with display facilities made conferences possible between key military leaders around the world. In the field, newly developed radio relay and carrier equipment began to supplement telephone wire circuits, particularly in rapidly moving operations. Other wartime developments included extralightweight assault wire in disposable containers, teletype switchboards, light rubber-covered telephone cable, and wire-laying techniques by light aircraft, bazooka shell, or rifle grenade. Outstanding achievements in the field of strategic wire communications were construction of the 2,060-mile Alaska Highway telephone and telegraph lines between the United States and Alaska, and construction of the 2,000-mile India-China line between Calcutta and Kunming. The development and growth of integrated tactical and strategic communications systems both within and between the various services permitted an easier transition to the unified commands and joint operations which followed the Japanese attack upon Pearl Harbor.

Since World War II.—Since World War II and particularly since the Korean War, military communications have become communications electronics, with transistors replacing tubes and printed circuits replacing conventional wiring. The Korean War saw the introduction of a new series of vehicular, pack, and hand radios for tactical communications, and ever-increasing reliance upon multichannel, highly directional, very high frequency (VHF) radio relay to supplement and replace vulnerable, time-consuming land lines.

The atomic explosions which terminated World War II affected the organization, tactics, and equipment of all United States military forces. The concept of widely dispersed, highly mobile, self-sustained battle groups operating on an expanded field of combat led to the development of a flexible, multiaxis, mobile grid communications system to replace the highly vulnerable single-axis, echelon-to-echelon communications system of World Wars I and II and the Korean War. Ionospheric and tropospheric scatter techniques have been developed to permit long-distance, over-the-horizon radio communications where conventional high frequency radio communications are not feasible. The exploitation of the jet-powered aircraft and missiles introduced by the Germans at the end of World War II has led to a demand for communications systems capable of transmitting early warning, target acquisition, and weapons control data in a matter of seconds. To satisfy this requirement, automatic data transmission systems using digital code and multiplexing equipment have already been made available in such air defense systems as the Army's Missile Master and the Air Force's Semiautomatic Ground Environ-

Canadian soldier in helmet with built-in radio receiver.

Annan Photo Features

Annan Photo Features

Artillery radar unit can map terrain, spot moving troops.

ment (SAGE). The missiles and jet-powered aircraft themselves are largely dependent upon ground and organic communications systems for control.

The need to be able to locate targets for destruction by the new arsenal of atomic and thermonuclear warheads delivered by artillery shell, missiles, and aircraft has led to the development of a combat surveillance system using such means of reconnaissance and surveillance as infrared, radar, sound, television, and photography, again placing primary reliance upon high-speed, high-capacity data transmission and processing equipment. The evolution of light Army artillery-spotting aircraft into a variety of fixed- and rotary-wing aircraft for increased combat mobility, control, and logistic support of Army forces has necessitated the development of an air traffic control and navigation system, again relying primarily upon communications. In light of the great reliance placed upon communications in the new weapons systems, increasing emphasis has been placed upon an electronic warfare system capable of denying or reducing the enemy's use of the electromagnetic spectrum while ensuring maximum utilization of the spectrum by one's own electronic communications equipment.

Over-all control of the foregoing elements of warfare on the battlefield will be provided for the nuclear missile and satellite age field commander in the form of a tactical operations center, a master communications-electronics system in itself. Even the individual soldier has been provided with a helmet radio and microphone by means of which he may receive instructions and transmit information on the battlefield without exposure to fire.

The spectacular advent of the space satellite and the inevitability of space travel has introduced new problems in military communications electronics related to outerspace communications. The Army Signal Corps' gigantic DIANA radar, which bounces signals off the moon, is but one step in the solution of these new problems. It is apparent that the most efficient utilization and control of the electromagnetic spectrum is the fundamental objective of military communications electronics in the future.

See also NAVAL COMMUNICATIONS; RADAR; SIGNALS AND SIGNALING.

Bibliography.—Plum, William R., *The Military Telegraph During the Civil War,* 2 vols. (Chicago 1882); Bernhardi, Friedrich A. J., *The War of the Future in the Light of the Lessons of the World War,* tr. by F. A. Holt (New York 1921); Lavine, Abraham L., *Circuits of Victory* (New York 1921); Portway, Donald, *Military Science Today* (London and New York 1940); Koenig, Duane, "Telegraphs and Telegrams in Revolutionary France," *Scientific Monthly,* vol. 59, pp. 431–437 (Washington 1944); Still, Alfred, *Communication Through the Ages* (New York 1946); Thompson, George R., "Civil War Signals," *Military Affairs,* vol. 18, pp. 188–201 (Washington 1955); U.S. Signal Office, *Report of the Chief Signal Officer, May 1951–April 1955* (Washington 1955); Terrett, Dulany, *The Signal Corps: the Emergency* (Washington 1956); U.S. Signal School, *History of the Signal Corps,* rev. ed. (Fort Monmouth, N.J., 1956); Thompson, George R., Harris, Dixie R., Oakes, Pauline M., Terrett, Dulany, *The Signal Corps: the Test* (Washington 1957); U.S. Department of Defense, Armed Forces Information and Education Division, *Getting the Word, Military Communications,* DOD Pamphlet 1–8 (Washington 1957).

REX D. MINCKLER,
Lieutenant Colonel, United States Army; Signal Officer, United States Military Academy.

MILITARY CONSCRIPTION. See ARMY; ARMY RESERVE; CONSCRIPTION; MILITARY MANPOWER; NAVAL RESERVE.

MILITARY COURTS-MARTIAL, military tribunals established under military law for the trial of persons in, and in some instances connected with, a military establishment.

The ancient Greeks and Romans had no written code of military law. Punishment of wrongdoers was left almost entirely to the discretion of the military commander in the field, who had complete and unrestricted power of life and death over members within his command. Even then the need for disciplinary control over those who fought in battle was recognized. Commanders realized that disciplinary control was required to ensure that orders were promptly and unfailingly carried out, that soldiers were present for duty when needed, and that certain standards of conduct were followed. Not until the 12th or 13th century, however, did written military codes providing for military tribunals appear in the European armies.

United States.—A system of courts-martial came into existence in the present United States in 1775 at the outbreak of the Revolutionary War. British Army courts-martial were established under the Mutiny Act and the British Articles of War, and this system was well known to the colonists. The Continental Congress therefore used it as a guide in preparing the American Articles of War. These articles remained virtually unchanged until shortly after World War I, when Congress enacted legislation designed to remove the operation of military justice from the control of line officers and place it under the supervision of the judge advocate general. As a result of further dissatisfaction with so-called "command influence" during World War II, Congress adopted further changes in the Articles of War (passed in 1948; effective 1949), and finally in 1951 the Uniform Code of Military Justice replaced the old Articles of War. The code created for the first time a single courts-martial system for all of the armed services and guaranteed to the accused many procedural safeguards not known under the Articles of War.

Types of Courts.—The Uniform Code of Military Justice authorizes the imposition of non-judicial punishment by a commanding officer for minor offenses, and provides for three types of courts known as general, special, and summary courts-martial, in descending order of importance. Certain officers derive the authority to convene a particular type of court directly from the code by virtue of their military position; others are specially given that authority by the secretary of their military department. Commanding generals of armies, corps, and divisions, among others, have statutory authority to convene general courts-martial. Commanding officers of brigades, regiments, and detached battalions, among others, have statutory authority to convene special courts-martial. The authority to convene a particular type of court includes the authority to convene lesser courts.

General courts-martial are composed of not less than five members, who make all findings of fact, determine the guilt or innocence of the accused, and, if he is guilty, decide upon his sentence. They also include a qualified law officer who acts in a manner generally similar to the judge in a civilian jury trial. The court may adjudge any punishment within specified maximums for each offense, including the death penalty in the gravest cases. Special courts-martial, consisting of at least three members, and summary courts-martial, consisting of one officer, are courts of limited power and are commonly referred to as inferior courts. They are designed for the consideration of alleged offenses of less than the most serious nature and do not include a law officer.

The Uniform Code of Military Justice requires a prompt, thorough, and impartial investigation of charges before they can be referred to a general court-martial for trial. The accused is entitled to qualified legal counsel both at the investigation and during trial by general court-martial, and he may refuse to say anything which may tend to incriminate him concerning the offenses with which he is charged. The accused must be apprised of these rights prior to the time any statement is taken from him, and he is again advised during trial that he may refuse to testify and that his silence may not be considered by the court as evidence of his guilt. Enlisted persons may demand that at least one third of the court members be enlisted personnel.

Appellate Review.—The Uniform Code of Military Justice provides for a system of appellate review after the accused has been convicted by a general court-martial. The convening authority who appointed the court must review the record of trial prior to taking action on the findings and sentence of the court. If the sentence imposed upon the accused extends to a punitive discharge or confinement for one year or more, the record of trial is reviewed by a board of review in the office of the Judge Advocate General of the armed force to which the accused belongs. Finally, in certain cases, the record is reviewed by a civilian appellate court known as the United States Court of Military Appeals, which has jurisdiction to review records of trial from each of the armed forces. An accused whose record of trial has been reviewed and whose sentence has been affirmed by a board of review may petition to this court for a review of his case. In cases tried by special and summary courts-martial, the review is conducted by the officer who appointed the court and by the staff judge advocate (a qualified lawyer) of the command having supervisory authority over the officer who convened the court.

Persons subject to the Uniform Code of Military Justice may be tried by a court-martial for offenses of a military nature such as absence without leave, desertion, disobedience of orders, and misbehavior before the enemy, as well as for offenses common to both civil and military law such as murder, rape, arson, burglary, larceny, and forgery.

Other Countries.—The American system of military law is in many respects similar to that of other countries. Every military code provides for the trial and punishment of persons who commit military offenses. However, in certain countries, France for example, a soldier who commits an offense not purely military in nature is tried by a civilian tribunal. Most military codes provide that in serious cases the accused is entitled to representation by legal counsel. Similarly, nearly every military code makes provision for appellate review of the decision of the trial court. In Russian military law, some decisions may be appealed directly to the Supreme Court of the USSR. There is a similar provision in French military law, which allows the accused in certain cases to appeal directly to the French court comparable to the Supreme Court of the United States. No such provision is found in the United States military legal system, although some cases eventually are reviewed by the Supreme Court after they have been brought into the federal court system by means of habeas corpus proceedings (an inquiry into the lawfulness of restraint of a person who has been deprived of his liberty). Generally, the federal courts in the United States will review a court-martial only when a question of jurisdiction has been raised.

In the United States and Great Britain, courts-martial are convened on an *ad hoc* basis by the appropriate military commander. In France, Germany, and Switzerland, however, the judges are qualified lawyers who are part of a permanent panel and sit on all cases, rather than being picked for a particular case by the military commander. In Switzerland, the judges are selected by the Federal Council (cabinet). Under the French system, the court-martial is made up of both civilian judges and military personnel; in Germany and Switzerland, the members are judges exclusively. In Great Britain, all the members of the court-martial must be officers, whereas the Court-Martial Appeal Court, which was instituted in 1951, is composed of judges of the regular High Court of Justice.

Procedure.—Court-martial procedure is usually patterned after the civilian legal system of the country in question. Thus in France the civil law largely determines the form of court-martial procedure. Frequently these procedures are alien to Anglo-American common law principles. Under the civil law system the accused is the first witness to appear in the trial. He is asked whether he is guilty or not, and although he may remain silent, the court may infer guilt from his silence. Under French law, the counsel of the accused may not be heard until after this questioning.

One characteristic of Soviet military law not generally found in other systems is that in cases of espionage, terrorist acts, wrecking, and other subversive acts, the ordinary legal procedures are not applicable. In cases of this sort the procedure is summary in form, with the accused having no right of counsel or appeal. In fact the case may be tried without the participation of the accused at all. In other respects the Soviet system appears to provide basic legal safeguards for accused persons characteristic of other systems of military justice.

One distinct feature found in many military codes, including the French and the British, is that a different procedure is followed in time of war than in time of peace. Even then, however, there are usually safeguards for the protection of the accused. The German Army, under the Adolf Hitler regime in World War II, adopted a summary form of military justice in which the accused was provided with few of the fundamental rights; but the new German code again provides basic protections for the accused. Likewise, in Soviet Russia during World War II, courts-martial proceedings were largely summary in nature.

During the 20th century, more and more of the protections afforded to an accused in civilian courts have been extended to the accused tried by military courts. This trend is not restricted to the United States but is to be found in many of the countries with large standing armies. It is yet to be determined, however, what effect on disciplinary control these changes will have in the event of a full-scale war.

See also ARTICLES OF WAR; MILITARY LAW.

Bibliography.—Winthrop, William, *Military Law and Precedents,* 2d ed., rev. (Washington 1920); Lawson, W. J., "Canadian Military Law," *Canadian Bar Review,* vol. 29, pp. 241–255 (Ottawa 1951); Gaynor, J. K., "The French Code of Military Justice," *George Washington Law Review,* vol. 23, pp. 318–336 (Washington 1954); Berman, Harold J., and Kerner, Miroslav, *Soviet Military Law and Administration* (Cambridge, Mass., 1955); Rheinstein, Max, "Comparative Military Justice," *Federal Bar Journal,* vol. 15, pp. 276–285 (Federalsburg, Md., 1955); The War Office, *Manual of Military Law,* 9th ed. (London 1956); *Manual for Courts-Martial, United States, 1951,* with supplement (Washington 1960).

GEORGE W. HICKMAN, JR.,
Major General, United States Army, Retired.

MILITARY CUSTOMS AND COURTESIES, a body of both unwritten and written rules governing relations among persons in military service. While the distinctions are not rigidly defined, military customs—or "customs of the service"—are best described as the unwritten or common law of the armies, navies, and air forces of national armed services, whereas military courtesy is the written, officially prescribed code of personal deportment.

Official Customs.—In official, as distinguished from social or off-duty relationships, there are a number of well-established customs in the United States service. For example, the wish or desire of the commander is an order; if an officer says to a subordinate, "I would like you to do such and such," this statement carries just as much authority as if he had said, "I order you to do such and such." It is a violation of military custom to reprimand a man in the presence of his subordinates. A commander should not bypass subordinate leaders and give orders directly to men under the latter's command. If the urgency of the situation demands such direct action, custom prescribes that the superior notify the intermediate commanders of his action as soon as possible. It is improper for a subordinate to bypass an intermediate commander and deal with a superior. To guard against favoritism or persecution, a leader does not permit a familiar or personal relationship to develop with subordinates. A lessening of formality on the part of a superior (for example, the use of the first name in address) does not give the subordinate the privilege of adopting a familiar manner toward that superior unless specifically asked to do so.

Rank has its privileges (RHIP) in military as well as in civilian life; however, the privileges of military rank are more clearly defined, particularly at the lower and intermediate levels of the hierarchy. A recruit in barracks, for example, is expected to perform more of the menial chores of military housekeeping than fellow privates who have more service. A noncommissioned officer is not normally required to perform kitchen police or fatigue duty. An enlisted man should not be required to perform personal services for an officer, unless he consents to do so and unless performance of these personal services does not interfere with his official duties. It is customary for officers to pay enlisted men when such services are rendered. It is an old custom of the service for a subordinate not to thank a superior for an official action or decision which benefits him (for example, the award of a decoration, a promotion, or the approval of a leave request), since such thanks would imply personal favor rather than recognition of official rights or good performance of duty.

European military customs are older and more complex than American. French army officers, for example, are addressed by their subordinates with the word *mon* in connection with their titles of military rank, as *"mon capitaine"*; naval officers, on the other hand, are addressed simply by title, as *"capitaine."* However, marshals and admirals are addressed as *"monsieur le maréchal"* and *"monsieur l'amiral."* In the British service it is customary to drink to the health of the sovereign, a vestige of the days when response to such a toast was an important loyalty check. Some British regiments, however, do not observe this custom, having been given a special dispensation. While the British Army drinks this toast standing, it is drunk seated by the Navy.

Social Customs.—Military life is governed by social customs extending to such matters as visiting and the off-duty etiquette of military personnel and their families. It would be improper, for example, if an officer used his official rank to settle a personal dispute. A man in uniform should not carry an umbrella. Guests should not leave a formal social function ahead of the senior officer present. Officers do not normally mix socially with enlisted men. In wearing civilian clothes, officers are expected to display conservative good taste.

Many practices formerly prescribed only by custom have now been written into the official regulations; for example, the etiquette of social visits, the prohibition against accepting personal gifts from subordinates or from civilians with whom a military person deals in official matters. Other customs fall into disuse when social changes make them no longer practicable; for example, since few officers now have personal servants, it is no longer considered improper for an officer to carry large bundles in the street or to push a baby carriage. In the United States Army it is no longer customary to address lieutenants socially as "mister"; in the Navy, on the other hand, officers through the grade of lieutenant commander should be addressed as "mister."

Military Courtesy.—Military courtesy is prescribed by official regulations. The hand salute is the most distinctive feature of military courtesy; common to all armed forces of the world as the gesture of recognition and mutual respect among military persons, it is executed by raising the right hand to the cap visor. This form of salute is used also as a token of respect to the national flag and anthem. A body of troops in formation salutes when ordered to "Present arms!" Gun salutes of a prescribed number of shots are fired to honor high civil and military officials. Other forms are the rifle salute, sword salute, and the dipping of flags. Military courtesy prescribes that a junior address a superior as "sir," that he walk or sit to the superior's left, and that he show the same deference observed by socially correct civilians toward persons to whom respect is due. The main difference between military and civilian courtesy is that service personnel are required to know and practice proper form and are subject to disciplinary action for ignorance or violation of military courtesy, whereas a lack of courtesy in civilian relationships may do no more than deprive the offender of social acceptance.

See also SALUTES AND HONORS.

Bibliography.—Moss, James A., *Officers' Manual,* 8th ed. rev. (Menasha, Wis., 1941); Edwards, Thomas J., *Military Customs,* 4th ed. (Aldershot, England, 1954); Boatner, Mark M., III, *Military Customs and Traditions* (New York 1956).

MARK M. BOATNER, III,
Lieutenant Colonel, United States Army; Author of "Military Customs and Traditions" and "The Civil War Dictionary."

MILITARY EDUCATION AND TRAINING. When soldiers are not fighting, they are undergoing military education and training. Even during hostilities, these are major activities as new units are created, newcomers are incorporated into existing organizations, and old units are retrained in new methods or in the handling of new equipment.

History.—Although the great captains of Greece and Macedon had established the value of organized military training in their victories over more numerous but less well-trained adversaries, the art of such training was largely lost in the West after the fall of the Roman Empire. With the emergence of strong national monarchies in the 14th and 15th centuries, large-scale military training reappeared. The emerging pattern, exemplified by the renowned Spanish infantry, called for tightly disciplined and highly maneuverable ranks. This system reached its zenith in the 18th century with the armies of Prussia's Frederick II, in which the soldier was converted into an automaton. It was adapted to short-range, inaccurate weapons, which had to be volley fired to gain maximum effect, and was suited primarily to professional armies, which could be drilled and trained interminably. It therefore ultimately gave way in the face of political and technological change.

In capitalizing on the French Revolution's principle of the "nation in arms" to create the first well-trained army with mass national support, Napoleon established a new political base for warfare. The spectacular improvement of weapons and the flood of output made possible by industrial mobilization further combined to eliminate small professional armies with their packed formations and paradelike maneuvers. The changed character of war became apparent first in the American Civil War and again, shortly afterward, in Prussia's wars for German unification. However, it did not become fully apparent until the outbreak of World War I, when mass conscript armies were put in the field by all the major belligerents, equipped with highly destructive weapons and supported by corps of signal, chemical, engineer, and other military technicians, and by a mobilized home front. The era of total war included unrestricted sea (and undersea) warfare and the birth of military aviation. The educational and training requirements posed by such military developments were prodigious.

World War II demanded even more in the way of skilled manpower. Airplanes, tanks, and radar are but a few examples of the materiel requiring skilled operators and repairmen. Officers who had never commanded units of more than a few hundred men, nor dealt with supplies in quantity, were required to lead whole armies, air forces, and fleets and to direct a flow of hundreds of millions of tons of supplies. Since World War II, the development of missiles and nuclear weapons has given further importance to military education and training.

Enlisted Personnel.—The response to these requirements has been similar in most military forces. Military organizations seek, first, to enlist bright individuals and to screen all incoming personnel for intelligence and special aptitudes. Basic training in the skills of the individual soldier is conducted in either a regular military unit or a training center. After basic training, individuals with the requisite aptitudes are sent to various specialist or technical schools for courses varying in length from a few weeks to a year or more. The high cost of training the modern soldier and the possibility that in another crisis the decision may be reached before large-scale training can become effective now argue for emphasis on a well-trained professional army.

After individual training, soldiers are placed in units to learn the teamwork on which military effectiveness depends. Unit training proceeds through successively larger units until, in such major powers as the United States and the USSR, whole armies, air forces, and fleets conduct realistic training exercises. Such large-scale maneuvers generally bring together a nation's land, sea, and air units and often involve the forces of several nations. To ensure adequate standards and uniformity, supervision of military training is generally centralized in three respects: training directives or programs are centrally directed; actual training is inspected by officers from central headquarters; and proficiency tests for each phase of training are conducted by headquarters teams.

Officers.—Parallel with the training of enlisted men and units sketched above, each military power has a system for educating and training the officers who direct its forces. In many cases, this system begins with a military academy devoted exclusively to the preparation of young men for the profession of arms. In others, officer material is derived mainly from the graduates of the nation's colleges or universities, young men who have had some basic military education as a part of their collegiate training. In still others, officers are commissioned directly from the enlisted ranks, usually after a careful selection process and a short schooling period. The United States military forces use all three methods of choosing officers.

Besides the United States Air Force, Military, and Naval academies, leading academies in various countries are:

Brazil.—Academia Militar das Agulhas Negras (Resende); Escola de Aeronautica (Rio de Janeiro); Escola Naval (Rio de Janeiro).
Canada.—Royal Military College of Canada (Kingston, Ontario).

Above: Instructor and pupil prepare for a training flight at the famous Royal Air Force College in Cranwell, England.

Above: U.S. Army trainees at Fort Dix, N.J., make the "confidence climb" on an obstacle course.

Above: During a U.S. Army training exercise, a tank which has been subjected to a simulated gas attack is decontaminated.

MILITARY EDUCATION

Center right: At the Royal Naval College in Dartmouth, England, cadets study seamanship with the aid of ships' models.

Right: A personnel and barracks inspection is conducted at the U.S. Military Academy Preparatory School, Fort Belvoir, Va.

France.—École Speciale Militaire Interarmes de Saint-Cyr (Coëtquidan, near Guer); École Navale (Brest); École de l'Air (Salon-de-Provence).
Great Britain.—Royal Military Academy (Sandhurst); Royal Air Force College (Cranwell); Royal Navy College (Dartmouth).
India.—National Defence Academy (Khadakavasla, near Poona).
Japan.—Defense Academy (Yokosuka).
Mexico.—Heróico Colegio Militar (Popotla, Federal District); Escuela del Aire (Base Aerea de Zapopan, Jalisco); Escuela Naval Militar (Antón Lizardo, Veracruz).

The Soviet Union and the Federal Republic of Germany do not have military academies of this type.

In addition to the basic military education afforded new officers, progressive military forces return their officers to school frequently during their careers to apprise them of changing weapons and military concepts and to train them for wider responsibilities. In the United States, for instance, all officers attend schools that teach them to use the arms of their particular service and the techniques of employing small military formations. A large proportion of officers also attend staff colleges that teach the skills of higher staff officers and commanders. A selected few proceed to the highest level schools, such as the war colleges and the Industrial College of the Armed Forces, where they examine questions of national power and strategy.

Extension or correspondence courses on every conceivable military subject are also generally available to both reserve and regular officers. Since an average American officer may spend about one third of his career as either a pupil or instructor in such schools, and since a significant proportion also attend civilian universities for graduate study, senior military officers are likely to be at least as well educated as their civilian colleagues and superiors.

Wartime Training.—In time of war, the tempo and scope of military education and training have increased greatly. Some schools, particularly the higher level ones, have closed altogether, but others have increased their facilities or shortened their courses in order to handle more students, and all training activities have been accelerated and expanded, with the opening of officer candidate schools and mass training camps for enlisted men. The complexities of a modern military force are such that unless a war can be consummated with the forces on hand at its outbreak, it is necessary to expand the educational and training establishment despite the diversion of resources that it entails.

In the past, the difficulties of wartime education and training have been partly mitigated by the existence of partially trained reserve or militia-type units at the outbreak of hostilities. Thus, in the United States, when the National Guard's 18 divisions, comprising 300,000 men, were ordered to active service in World War II, they doubled the size of the then-existing Army. Similarly, although the Reserve Officers Training Corps (ROTC) furnished only 12 per cent of the officers in the United States Army in World War II, a high proportion of them were available in the first critical months of mobilization. The extent to which these historic patterns will apply in the future will depend on the nature and duration of conflicts.

USSR and Asia.—Other major military powers have systems of military education and training similar to that of the United States. In the characteristic pattern of totalitarian states, the Soviet Union starts the military indoctrination of its populace earlier and pursues it longer than do more liberal states. The famous Suvorov military academies enroll 9- and 10-year-old students. Even in ordinary secondary schools, pupils start military training in the eighth grade as a part of their normal studies. Apart from these differences and the greater stress on discipline, political education, and physical endurance in Soviet training, the variations from the general pattern are relatively minor. In Asia, Western-style training methods are also in vogue, India and Red China patterning theirs after Britain and the Soviet Union respectively, and Korea, Nationalist China, and Japan after the United States.

Exchange Students and Military Missions.—Leading military institutions the world over have always been a Mecca for career officers bent on rising to the top of their profession. For centuries, allies have exchanged student officers. More recently, officer candidates have been entered as cadets in foreign countries. As of March 1960, for example, the roster of the United States Military Academy included 13 foreign cadets, 10 of them from Latin America. At the same time, foreign officers and enlisted men by the thousands were enrolled in the military schools of the three armed services in the United States. In turn, a number of United States officers are sent abroad for study.

Another long-standing practice is the assignment of military missions from one nation to other friendly nations to help improve their common defenses. As of 1959, for example, United States military missions or advisory teams were stationed in more than 40 foreign nations. At the same time, Soviet officers were directing the military efforts of their satellites, and military training and advisory teams were functioning in such friendly nations as the United Arab Republic and Afghanistan.

NATO.—The most complex international training system on record is the effort to blend the North Atlantic Treaty Organization (NATO) military units into a fully integrated force. The NATO Defense College in Paris trains selected staff officers and civilians in NATO strategy and its military implementation. At NATO headquarters, on-the-job training continues this program. The attempt to adopt certain common procedures and equipment requires international training crews in various tactical units. Field tests and maneuvers further this combined training to an extent thought impossible a few decades ago.

See also ARMY, NAVY, AND AIR FORCE MANEUVERS; ARMY SERVICE SCHOOLS; NAVAL EDUCATION; NAVAL WAR COLLEGE, UNITED STATES; UNITED STATES AIR FORCE ACADEMY; UNITED STATES MILITARY ACADEMY; UNITED STATES NAVAL ACADEMY.

Bibliography.—Up-to-date information about military education and training is best obtained in official publications of the various ministries of defense and the service journals of the respective armed forces. Among the most useful of these are: Air Force Association, *Air Force* (Washington, monthly); Association of the United States Army, *Army* (Washington, monthly); *Brassey's Annual* (London and New York, yearly); Ministère de la Défense Nationale, *Revue militaire d'information* (Paris, monthly); *Soldat und Technik* (Frankfurt am Main, monthly); *Truppenpraxis* (Darmstadt, monthly); U.S. Army Command and General Staff College, *Military Review* (Fort Leavenworth, Kans., monthly); U.S. Naval Institute, *Proceedings* (Annapolis, Md., monthly).

AMOS A. JORDAN,
Lieutenant Colonel, United States Army; Professor of Social Sciences, United States Military Academy.

MILITARY ENGINEERING, the application of the basic fundamentals and principles of the engineering sciences to the specific requirements of military forces. It originated in the need for the construction of fortifications (q.v.), the bridging of obstacles, and the making of maps. Military engineering in support of military forces has kept pace with advances in the engineering sciences, the development of modern civil and military equipment, and the evolution of the methods of modern warfare.

Modern military engineering has the prime objective of maintaining and increasing the combat effectiveness of military forces by facilitating the movement and supply of friendly forces, impeding hostile movement and supply, and providing such other engineering services as may be required to further combat operations.

Military engineering facilitates the movement and supply of friendly forces by: (1) engineer reconnaissance of defensive positions, roads, railways, bridges, tunnels, and sites for command and logistical installations; (2) construction, rehabilitation, and maintenance of roads and railways; (3) furnishing troops and equipment during assault river-crossing operations, including assistance in the transport of infantry elements across the water barrier, erection and operation of rafts and ferries, and erection and maintenance of tactical floating bridging; (4) removing obstacles and furnishing assistance to other combat arms in overcoming obstacles to the forward movement of friendly forces; (5) the production or procurement and distribution of military maps or map substitutes; and (6) issuing items of engineer supply, and producing and distributing potable water in the forward areas.

Military engineering impedes hostile movement and supply by (1) increasing natural obstacles, erecting artificial obstacles, and demolishing structures to create a barrier between enemy and friendly forces; (2) furnishing technical personnel, equipment, and field-fortifications supplies for the purpose of assisting other combat units in organizing, developing, and camouflaging defensive positions; and (3) constructing other defensive structures such as command posts, communication centers, and alternate defensive positions.

Other military engineering services include (1) the construction of ports, wharves, supply depots, hospitals, and other logistical installations; (2) the receipt, storage, and issue of all engineer items of supply, including maintenance (other than organizational) of such items of supply; (3) the furnishing, maintenance, and fire protection of all utilities, except signal items, for all installations; (4) the acquisition and disposal of real estate; and (5) the construction of airfields and other airbase facilities.

Military engineering practices differ from those of civilian engineering in several ways: (1) the controlling economic factors are time, manpower, materials, and monetary cost, but in military engineering the last is usually of less importance in times of military urgency; (2) the life expectancies of military engineering accomplishments are comparatively short, so that safety factors are reduced, absolute minimum standards are adhered to, and all but the most essential items are eliminated; (3) the shortage of technically qualified personnel during periods of national mobilization requires maximum use of standard plans, rules of thumb, and brief but easily understood graphs, charts, and guides; (4) the relatively low priorities given engineering construction materials, as compared with more essential military items, make the maximum use of local, often inferior, materials of the utmost importance; (5) the enemy's ability to destroy and to interrupt projects, combined with the lowered construction standards, make the provision of more complete and continuous maintenance an absolute necessity.

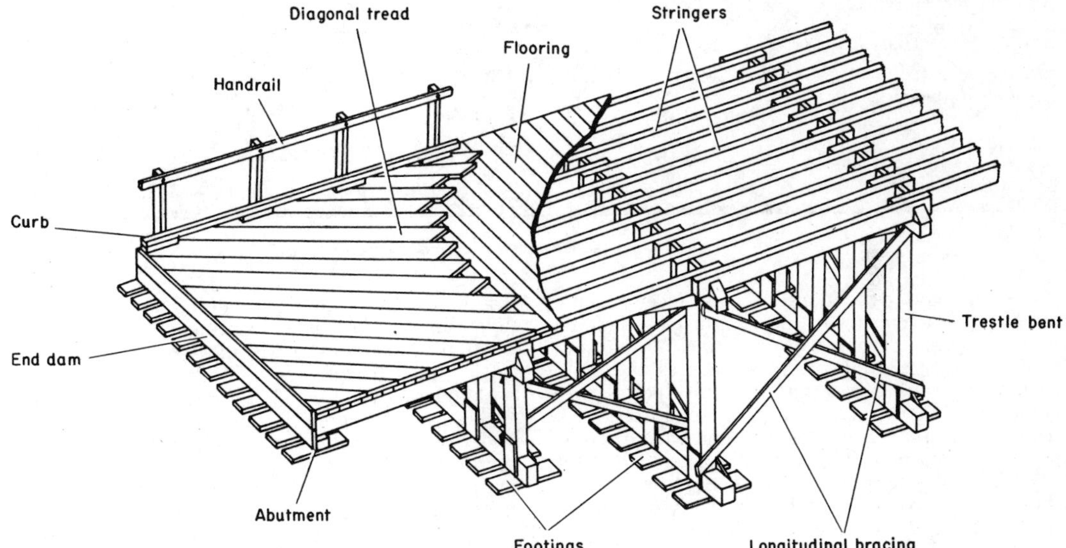

Fig. 1. Timber trestle bridge.

The elements of military engineering that support combat operations are discussed in the following sections.

Demolitions.—Military demolitions impede the enemy and facilitate the movement of friendly troops. They are used to destroy, or to make unusable, roads, bridges, airfields, and important items of abandoned equipment, and to destroy or to breach enemy obstacles. Demolition is usually accomplished by fire, water, mechanical means, artillery fire, aerial bombing, or hand-placed explosive charges. In general, the last-named method is the most rapid, the most certain, the most effective, and the most economical.

Demolitions may be either *deliberate* or *hasty*. Deliberate demolition is carried out when there is time for careful reconnaissance and preparation; it is carried out to the extent that it will be more economical for the enemy to replace the object than to repair it. Hasty demolition is employed when time is limited and speed is more important than making the most economical use of explosives. All demolitions are planned to produce only the destruction required to gain the necessary tactical advantage or delay. Destruction beyond this, particularly in bridge destruction, is usually not necessary or desirable. Long-range plans may call for the recovery of the ground and reconstruction of the destroyed structure.

The shaped charge is cylindrical, with a conical top and a conical recess in the base. It is shaped so that the energy of the explosive is concentrated in a small area, creating a small tubular hole in the object against which it is placed. One standard shaped charge containing 30 pounds of explosive will perforate 60 inches of reinforced concrete or 20 inches of armor plate. The bangalore torpedo is a long demolition made up of connected elements of steel pipe filled with explosive; it is used primarily to clear paths through barbed wire entanglements.

Military Bridging.—Military bridging is classified as *fixed* or *floating*. In general, floating bridging is used in the forward combat area to cross water barriers. As the combat area moves forward, the floating equipment is replaced by fixed bridging. This replacement is necessary since floating equipment is usually an item of critical supply and needed for further operations as the field of battle moves forward. Moreover, it is de-

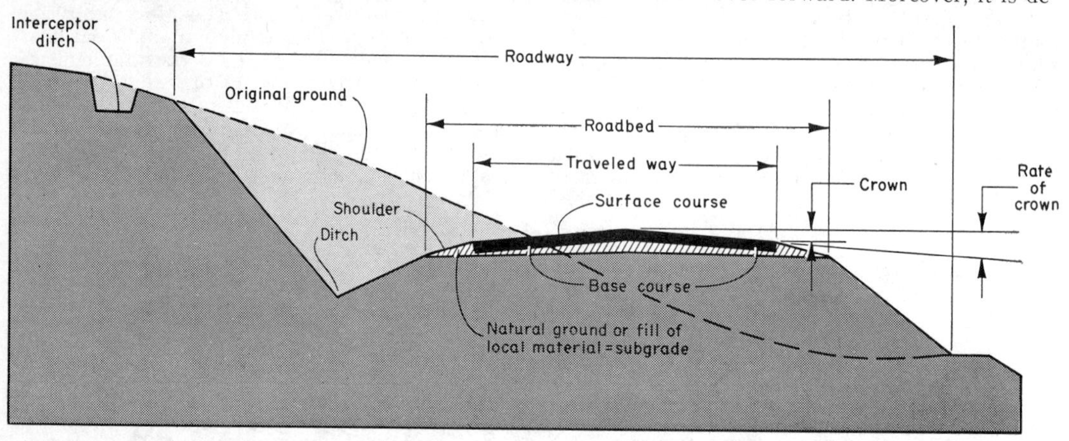

Fig. 2. Typical cross section illustrating road nomenclature.

Commercial dynamite does not meet normal military requirements in that it must be handled with caution, is subject to relatively rapid deterioration, freezes at low temperatures and must be thawed prior to use, and requires special surveillance. The primary military explosives are trinitrotoluene (TNT), tetrytol, and various composition explosives. The last can be molded to fit any shape desired. All of these explosives have the common property of a high velocity of detonation (TNT: 21,000 feet per second), since the desired result is to produce a shattering effect. Military dynamites are used for both blasting and quarrying operations.

Military explosive charges are computed by formulas derived from experience and experiment. Demolition cards quickly give formulas for: (1) steel-cutting charges; (2) timber-cutting charges; (3) pressure charges, effective against concrete bridges which, by an overloading effect caused by the explosion, break at mid-span and pull free from the piers or abutments; (4) breaching charges, used to breach walls, bridge piers, and bridge abutments, and to blow holes in concrete slabs or roadways; (5) cratering charges for creating obstacles too wide to be spanned by track-laying vehicles and too deep and steep-sided to allow vehicles to pass through them.

Military demolitions are also used in the form of fixed, special-purpose charges. Among these are the shaped charge and the bangalore torpedo.

sirable to replace floating bridging as early as possible since it requires continuous maintenance when in use. The more distant the site is from the battle area, therefore, the more permanent the bridging becomes.

Floating bridging is designed as mobile, and to be used primarily for crossing rivers in assault operations. The bridges are made of standardized equipment and consist in general of flotation units or pontons (pontoons) to which the deck structure is attached by means of saddle arrangements. The deck is usually of lightweight metal and is fabricated in sections, which in turn are fastened together, supported by pontons, and pushed out until the stream has been crossed. All of the component parts are designed so that the entire load of bridging can be readily broken down into specific truck loads for transportation to the bridge site.

The erection of the floating bridge involves the following operations: preparation of entrance to and exit from the crossing site; placing of anchor cables or other anchoring means to keep the floating structure aligned since it is not designed to withstand such lateral forces as wind and current; erection of a fixed or trestle span built out to the point where sufficient depth of water will permit the use of the pontons; erection and alignment of the floating portion of the bridge. In addition, certain protective devices must be installed, such as booms to intercept and detonate floating mines, and booms to intercept large floating debris which might damage the structure. Floating bridges must be kept under continuous inspection and maintenance, pontons reinflated as necessary, the structure freed of debris, and damaged equipment replaced.

Floating bridges range from footbridges to the heavier vehicular bridges. The equipment for the latter may be assembled into rafts and ferries and used to transport combat vehicles and tanks to the far shore prior to the erection of the vehicular bridge. In a typical river-crossing operation, the footbridge and rafts are put into service as soon as small arms fire has been eliminated from the crossing site. The vehicular bridge is erected as soon as observed artillery fire has been eliminated from the crossing site.

bent bridge or pier bridge, with the cap of the bent or pier serving as the floor beam upon which systems of stringers and decking are applied. (See Fig. 1.) Bents require adequate bottom footing. Spans are determined usually by the materials available for the stringers. Designs in both timber and steel are common, large rolled-steel beams being used generally in railway bridges.

Stream crossings may be effected by fords as well as by bridging. Fords are, however, often unreliable in that they are subject to sudden increases in depth and deteriorate quickly under heavy traffic. The maximum depths for military usage are as follows: infantry on foot, 3½ feet; trucks, 2 feet; light tanks, 1 to 3 feet; medium tanks, 2 to 4 feet; and heavy tanks, 4 to 6 feet.

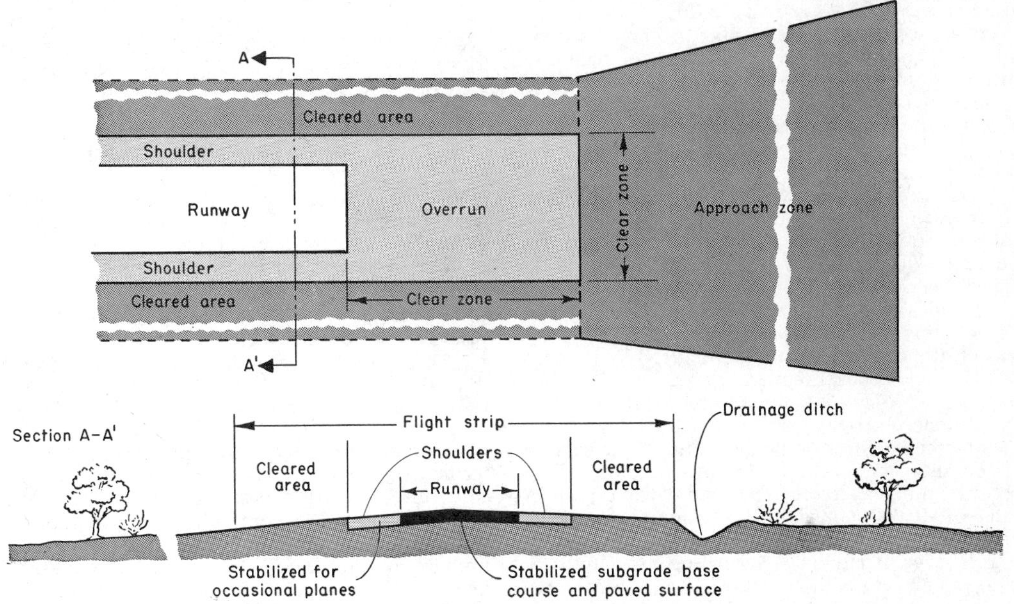

Fig. 3. Plan and cross section of flight strip.

Fixed bridging may be erected from standard fixed-bridge sets or constructed from local or imported timber or steel materials. In general, fixed bridging from standard sets is used in, or immediately behind, the combat area, the bridges farther to the rear being especially designed for the kind of loads they must bear. The standard fixed bridges consist of shallow trusses made up of short panels connected to give the desired length. The trusses are connected by standard floor-beam components together with a stringer decking component and the necessary lateral bracing. All components are designed to be transported as mobile loads. The load-carrying capacity of the bridge is predetermined for various span lengths. Nonstandard fixed bridging is designed and constructed in the field according to the loads to be carried and the materials available. In general, military engineering practice follows civil engineering practice here, except that the factor of safety is reduced through the use of increased working stresses in the materials used. Civil practice uses a factor of safety of 4 to 6 for timber and 2.2 for steel. Military practice uses 3 for timber and 1.75 for steel. These reduced factors of safety are permissible because the military structures are not permanent.

The most common type of nonstandard fixed bridge used in military operations is the trestle-

The above rules apply to continuous traffic crossings and the general situation, but individual crossings can be made at greater depths. When a body of water is frozen, crossings can be made with the following thicknesses of sound ice in contact with water: troops in single file at a 2-pace distance, 3 inches; ¼-ton trucks, 6 inches; 2½-ton trucks, 10 inches; light tanks, 14 inches; 20-ton vehicles, 16 inches; 45-ton vehicles, 24 inches. Whenever possible, test loadings should be made to determine the actual load capacity of ice, and the ice should be reinforced to spread the load application over as large an area as possible.

Military Roads.—A good road network is essential to the success of combat operations. The road net, though it supplements the rail and air nets, must be capable of carrying the entire supply load and must be kept open at all times. It must ensure the continuous flow of supplies to the front, evacuation to the rear, and maximum mobility in the movement of combat elements laterally, to the front, and to the rear. Though military vehicles can move cross-country, such movement is slow and increases the wear and tear on the vehicles. Therefore, cross-country movement is used by combat vehicles only where necessary in the immediate battle area.

Roads in the combat zone are designed to meet

the pressing needs resulting from military urgency. They are characterized by rough, hasty work, and though location is determined by military necessity, alignment is planned to avoid conditions requiring the expenditure of large amounts of manpower and materials. High-grade road surfacing is usually not employed, and materials are limited where possible to those locally available. Waterproof surfaces are often too costly in time and materials to be practicable; therefore, drainage is essential in building all-weather roads. Roads behind the combat zone may vary from hastily built roads to first-class roads, depending on the uses to which they are put.

Military roads are classified with respect to location and use as follows: *axial road,* a road leading to the front and generally perpendicular thereto; *main supply road* (MSR), an axial road designated as the principal traffic artery of a division or higher unit; *belt road,* a road generally parallel to the front, also known as a *lateral road; reserved road,* a road reserved by competent authority for designated traffic; *restricted road,* a road on which traffic is controlled as to character, speed, loads, or time of use.

Specifications that will satisfy most military requirements are as follows (see Fig. 2): (1) width of traveled way, 12 feet for one-way roads and 22 feet for two-way roads; (2) crown, ¼ to ¾ inch per foot depending on the type of surface; (3) shoulders, minimum of 4 feet on each side with minimum slope of ¾ inch per foot; (4) vertical clearance, 14 feet minimum; (5) alignment suitable for speeds ranging from 25 to 35 miles per hour; (6) grades, maximum of 10 per cent except under extreme conditions (desirable grades are 6 per cent or less on tangents and 4 per cent or less on sharp curves); (7) radius of curves, 150 feet minimum desirable; (8) load capacity, wheel loads of 10,000 pounds; (9) volume of traffic, 2,000 vehicles per day.

Military Airfields.—According to military usage, an airfield is that portion of an airbase prepared for the accommodation, landing, and take-off of military aircraft. From an engineering point of view, it includes runways, taxiways, parking aprons, and hardstands, all of which ordinarily consist of a pavement placed on a stabilized or compacted subgrade; shoulders and clear zones, normally composed of materials which are already there; and approach zones and lateral safety zones, within which only clearing and the removal of obstructions above the prescribed glide angle and safety angle are required. (See Figs. 3 and 4.) The term "pavement" includes both the base course or courses and the surface or wearing course, if provided. The airfield, together with shelter for personnel and facilities for the supply and repair of aircraft, is termed an airbase.

Military airfields are designed for the largest aircraft they are to accommodate. They vary from fields for small numbers of aircraft operating for short periods to fields from which large aircraft will operate for long periods. In the former case, portable surfaces (landing mats) may be placed on a poor base or subgrade of low supporting value; in the latter, heavy-duty pavements must be used.

The construction of military airfields in the theater of operations requires a proportionately large share of the military engineering capability available. Time is usually limited, and the utmost economy of manpower and materials must be attained. To this end, great emphasis is placed on airfield reconnaissance. Commensurate with operational and tactical requirements, site selection must be based upon a ground conformation ensuring adequate drainage and requiring minimum earthwork. Construction materials of sufficiently high bearing capacity must be available. If the general site area is still in the hands of the enemy, detailed ground reconnaissance is replaced by aerial reconnaissance and the study of technical reports and

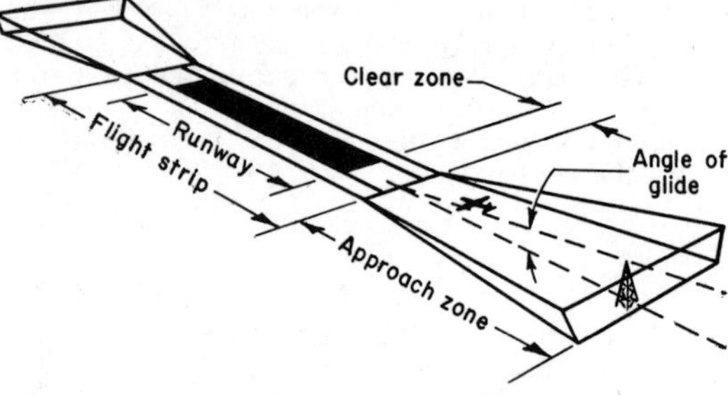

Fig. 4. Flight strip and approach zones.

other data. This will usually indicate a site meeting the requirements, with last-minute verification by ground reconnaissance performed later.

The design of pavement for military airfields is facilitated by the use of available design curves, which take into consideration the type of pavement to be constructed, the type of landing gear of the aircraft, tire pressures, wheel loads, bearing capacity of materials (California Bearing Ratio, CBR), and the operational condition of the field. Operational conditions are classified as *full operational, minimum operational,* or *emergency.* These terms apply only to pavement thickness and indicate full-design thickness, 80 per cent full-design thickness, or 50 per cent full-design thickness, respectively. Included in these classifications are limitations on the amount of traffic and its frequency; there is also the consideration that less than full-design thicknesses require increased maintenance. The types of pavement used are *flexible* or *rigid.* Flexible pavements normally consist of the subgrade, base course, and wearing surface, the last usually a bituminous treatment or a bituminous pavement. Rigid pavements are of unreinforced concrete. Portable surfaces (landing mats) are used only when lack of time, materials, or other important considerations preclude the use of a more suitable surface, since their use results in increased airfield maintenance, higher accident rate, and excessive damage to electronic gear and aircraft tires.

Military Pipelines.—Military pipelines are the most reliable, rapid, and efficient means of delivering overland, in bulk, the immense quantities of liquid fuels required in modern warfare. These fuels make up over half the total tonnage moving into the theater of operations. The military pipeline system usually consists of: (1) ship-to-shore tanker unloading lines or dockside unloading facilities; (2) bulk-storage tank farms; (3) trunk and branch pipelines; (4) pumping stations. The design of military pipeline equipment has been adapted from the most portable items used in civilian oilfield practice. Shipping volume of the equipment is kept to a minimum so that it can be transported in standard military cargo vehicles and aircraft, and can be installed without heavy construction equipment. The major items are: (1) standard lightweight tubing with standard-gauge steel nipples furnished in lengths of 20 feet and in diameters from 4 inches to 12 inches; (2) split-ring groove couplings designed to seal both under pressure and with a vacuum; (3) gasoline-driven pumps; (4) bolted metal and fabric storage tanks; (5) accessory equipment. Single or multiple 4-, 6-, and 8-inch lines can be quickly laid above the ground by trained personnel.

Military Engineering Personnel.—The planning and execution of engineering tasks may be done by the engineer staff of the commander, engineer troop units, troop units of other arms, indigenous civilian labor, or by contractual arrangements. Engineer staffs, troop units, and technical personnel are assigned as integral parts of larger units for direct combat-support missions, or they are assigned, as required, for general engineer support missions. Engineer troop units are also organized and trained to serve as infantry in combat.

J. A. Betts,
Lieutenant Colonel, United States Army; Former Associate Professor, Department of Military Art and Engineering, United States Military Academy.

MILITARY ETIQUETTE. See Military Customs and Courtesies; Salutes and Honors.

MILITARY FORTIFICATIONS. See Castles and Chateaux; Fortifications.

MILITARY GOVERNMENT. See Military Law—*Military Government;* War, Laws of.

MILITARY HONORS. See Military Customs and Courtesies; Decorations and Orders; Salutes and Honors.

MILITARY HOSPITALS. See Hospital—*Military Hospitals;* Medical Services in the Armed Forces.

MILITARY INSIGNIA. See Insignia of Rank, Armed Forces.

MILITARY INTELLIGENCE, information concerning an actual or possible enemy, immediately or potentially valuable for military planning. The complete process by which military intelligence is produced includes the *collection* of raw (unverified or fragmentary) information; *evaluation* of its pertinence, creditability, and accuracy; and *analysis* to determine its probable significance in the light of intelligence already available. Once this processing is complete, the resulting military intelligence must be promptly disseminated to those commanders or officials who will use it.

The principal subdivisions of military intelligence are *combat intelligence, strategic intelligence,* and *counterintelligence.* Combat intelligence is a wartime product; its purpose is to determine how and to what extent the enemy, the terrain, and the weather may be able to affect the operations of troops in the field. It forms the basis for the combat orders of military commanders. Strategic intelligence is concerned with the capabilities, vulnerabilities, and probable courses of action of foreign nations. It is used by those high-level military and civil authorities who are charged with the planning and execution of major national security measures in time of peace and with the conduct of large-scale military operations in war. The knowledge which it provides is a major factor in guiding foreign relations. Counterintelligence covers all security control measures designed for protection against espionage, sabotage, or subversion by foreign powers or discontented domestic groups.

Military intelligence has played its part in warfare since the beginnings of civilization. Moses sent spies into the land of Canaan (Numbers 13); Hannibal infiltrated agents into northern Italy long before he began his first campaign against Rome in the 3d century B.C. Gustavus Adolphus of Sweden (r. 1611–1632) added a "chief of scouts" to his staff; while Frederick the Great of Prussia (r. 1740–1786) employed spies methodically and in large numbers. Napoleon's campaigns were always preceded by the collection and study of all available information, and the march of his Grande Armée was covered by a cavalry screen, which both concealed its maneuvers and searched out the enemy. In the United States, prior to 1917 every war saw the painful development of an intelligence agency—and its prompt dissolution as soon as hostilities ended. Thus, in 1846, the War Department had no information as to whether Mexican roads were good enough to permit the use of wagons by the invading United States Army. In 1861, Gen. George B. McClellan's advance on Richmond, Va., was crippled from the start by a complete ignorance of the topography of eastern Virginia and a wildly inflated estimate of the strength of the Confederate Army.

An intelligence section normally forms one of the major staff sections in every military headquarters, beginning with that of a battalion (or equivalent unit). Special military intelligence units, often employing highly technical equipment, are at the disposal of higher headquarters; the military attachés at embassies abroad function primarily as accredited intelligence officers.

Enemy Capabilities and Intentions.—The modern concept of total war has increased and complicated the work of the intelligence officer. The development of modern nuclear weapons and long-range bombers and missiles has made the detection of any possible surprise attack literally a matter of life and death, requiring a constant state of alert. Concurrently, the importance of strategic intelligence, as a means of predicting future problems, has steadily increased. Strategic intelligence requires consideration of both the present status and future development of such factors as enemy industry, agriculture, natural resources, education, communications, leadership, and public opinion—the sum of which is the enemy capability, and possible intention, to wage war.

It is usually far easier to determine enemy capabilities (what he can do) than enemy intentions (what he will do). This is especially true in combat intelligence, where decisions must be made under pressure and a mistake means heavy casualties, if not defeat. Consequently, military commanders in action base their plans and orders on available military intelligence as to enemy capabilities. Strategic intelligence, on the other hand, being concerned with future problems and policies, must attempt to estimate the intentions, or probable courses of action, of foreign nations. Usually more time and information are available for such a study, since a nation's long-range intentions may be hard to hide, involving as they do the whole orientation of its industry and foreign policy.

Sources of Information.—In peacetime, the major source of information is a systematic study of all available foreign publications, including government bulletins, technical reviews, and newspapers and magazines of all kinds. Military or trade journals are especially valuable. Such material usually can be acquired legally and with relative ease. Other sources are diplomatic reports, fugitives and defectors from hostile foreign countries, intelligence furnished by allied governments, and the material collected by the various military and civilian intelligence agencies in their normal peacetime work.

In wartime, additional information is secured from prisoners, deserters, local inhabitants, captured documents, weapons and equipment, air reconnaissance and photography, ground reconnaissance and observation, and from intercepted enemy signal communications. Spies are still an important source of information. Normally they operate under the disguise of peaceful civilians going about their legitimate and unsensational daily business. Rebellious elements in the enemy population may be used as a source of information or to assist agents. Even the most apparently insignificant items of information may be of value. During World War II, the first evidence that the Germans were developing guided missiles came from pictures taken in 1942 by a British aviator on a routine photographic mission.

Problems and Application.—Military intelligence, especially combat intelligence, is seldom complete, and is always subject to unexpected change. Bad weather may handicap ground and air observers; hostile native populations refuse information; enemy feints and ruses conceal true strengths and positions; radio silence or the use of code messages thwart efforts to intercept the enemy's communications. Ground or air reconnaissance can be smothered by stronger enemy forces. Likewise, strategic intelligence is handicapped by the difficulty of obtaining reliable information concerning nations which, like the Soviet Union, maintain a strict counterintelligence program. Publications in such countries may be heavily censored; statistics and economic data may be released only in fragmentary form and sometimes deliberately falsified; military preparations may be carried out under the strictest secrecy. Though new methods and instruments have been developed for gathering information, some of these have been canceled out by equally effective technical countermeasures, while others have become relatively useless because of the increasing speed of operations in modern warfare. Under such circumstances, the intelligence officer must make full use of all available information, then form the best possible estimate of the facts he does not have and their significance. Without being an irresponsible alarmist, he must be alert to any changes in enemy capabilities, since these normally must be countered by corresponding changes in his commander's plans.

The guiding principles by which military intelligence is judged are usefulness and timeliness. But the production of accurate and timely intelligence cannot, in itself, guarantee either military success or national survival. To do this, it must be *used;* military intelligence can be effective only when it leads to prompt and correct decisions followed by resolute action.

See also ESPIONAGE AND COUNTERESPIONAGE; NAVAL INTELLIGENCE.

Bibliography.—de Chilly, Numa, *L'Espionnage* (Paris 1888); Furse, George A., *Information in War* (London 1895); Lanoir, Paul, *L'Espionnage allemand en France* (Paris 1908); Bywater, Hector C., and Ferraby, Hubert C., *Strange Intelligence* (London 1931); Hittle, James D., *The Military Staff* (Harrisburg, Pa., 1944); Chandler, Stedman, and Robb, Robert W., *Front-Line Intelligence* (Washington 1946); Renault-Roulier, Gilbert (pseudonym Rémy), *Mémoires d'un agent secret de la France libre, juin 1940–juin 1942* (Paris 1946), Eng. tr. by Lancelot C. Sheppard, *Memoirs of a Secret Agent of Free France* (New York 1948); Dewavrin, André (pseudonym Colonel Passy), *Souvenirs,* 2 vols. (Monte Carlo 1947); id., *Missions secrètes en France, novembre 1942–juin 1943* (Paris 1951); Farago, Ladislas, *War of Wits* (New York 1954); Townsend, Elias C., *Risks* (Harrisburg, Pa., 1955); Platt, Washington, *Strategic Intelligence Production* (New York, 1957); Babington-Smith, Constance, *Air Spy* (New York 1957).

JOHN R. ELTING,
Lieutenant Colonel, United States Army; Department of Military Art and Engineering, United States Military Academy.

MILITARY LAW, a separate system of jurisprudence providing for the government and regulation of the military forces, and of civilian communities under military rule. Narrowly defined, it refers to the rules of conduct by which the military force, existing as a distinct and separate entity within the over-all community of a nation, is governed; in this sense it is identical with *military justice.* Broadly defined, it extends to that body of law which establishes the relationship of the military force of any nation to the civilian community and is encompassed within the broader jurisprudences of constitutional law and international law (q.v.). Included in this broad concept are *military government,* which is the exercise of military jurisdiction by a belligerent occupying enemy territory; *martial law,* which is the exercise of military jurisdiction by a government temporarily governing the civil population of a locality through its military forces as necessity may require, without the authority of written law; and finally, the exercise of military jurisdiction over troops stationed in a friendly foreign territory in time of peace.

Military Justice in the Armed Forces of the United States.—The Constitution empowers Congress to make rules for the government and regulation of the land and naval forces, and exempts military trials from the guaranty of trial by jury in criminal prosecutions. Congress, in the exercise of its power, enacted the Uniform Code of Military Justice, which prescribes both the substantive and the procedural law governing military justice and its administration in all of the armed forces. The Uniform Code, which went into effect in 1951, superseded the Articles of War, the Articles for the Government of the Navy, and the Disciplinary Laws of the Coast Guard, and provided for the first time in the history of the United States a single law for the administration of military justice in the armed forces. It is the sole statutory authority for: (1) the imposition of limited disciplinary penalties for minor offenses without judicial action; (2) the establishment of pretrial and trial procedure; (3) the creation and constitution of three types of courts-martial; (4) the eligibility and qualifications of personnel for each type of court-martial; (5) the review of findings and of sentences, and the creation and constitution of the reviewing tribunals; and (6) the listing and definition of offenses.

The Uniform Code is historically a descendant of the British Articles of War, but incorporates many of the methods of the civilian courts, and offers a number of protections not available in civilian jurisdictions. All members of the armed services are subject to the jurisdiction of the code, as are certain categories of civilians who are within the constitutional grant of power with respect to the exercise of court-martial jurisdiction. The Uniform Code is implemented by a presidential executive order promulgated in the *Manual for Courts-Martial, United States, 1951,* and various service regulations promulgated by the secretaries of the military departments. See also MILITARY COURTS-MARTIAL.

Law of War.—Military law in the narrow sense relates to the government of the military forces at all times, in peace as well as in war. In the broader sense it includes the law of war, which is operative only during a time of war or similar emergency, and which regulates the actions of belligerents. The law of war is a branch of international law and encompasses that part of the law of nations which prescribes the conduct of war and the status, rights, and duties of enemy and neutral nations as well as individuals. It is designed to diminish the evils of war by protecting both combatants and noncombatants from unnecessary suffering; safeguarding certain fundamental rights of persons who fall into the hands of the enemy, particularly prisoners of war, the wounded and sick, and civilians; and facilitating the restoration of peace. The law of war requires that belligerents refrain from employing any kind or degree of violence not actually necessary for military purposes, and that they conduct hostilities with regard for the recognized principles of humanity. The authority for the establishment and administration of military government and, to some extent, martial law is found in the law of war. See also WAR, LAWS OF.

Military Government.—Military government is the exercise of sovereignty by a belligerent, through force of arms, over the occupied territory and civilian population of the enemy. Whether administered directly by the army of the belligerent, or indirectly through civilians left in office or appointed by the occupying power, it is the government of and for all of the inhabitants, both native and foreign, superseding so far as may be deemed necessary and expedient the local civil authority. The military commander has the duty not only to repel and defeat the enemy but, as an adjunct to the law of war, to furnish the inhabitants of an occupied country with a system of law and courts pending the re-establishment of a civil government. Wherever practicable, however, the local civil and criminal laws are permitted to remain in effect.

Military commissions and occupation courts are the usual tribunals utilized in the administration of justice under a military government. The jurisdiction of the military commission, which is derived primarily from the law of war, extends generally to two classes of offenses: (1) crimes committed against the civil population which are made punishable by the criminal codes of all civilized nations and are included within the so-called common law of war (for example, murder, larceny, arson, robbery, and rape); and (2) offenses condemned by local statute which cannot otherwise be tried, insofar as the civil authority has been superseded by the military.

Under the Constitution of the United States, the president, as commander in chief, may in time of war establish and prescribe the jurisdiction and procedures of military commissions in occupied territories, and this authority may survive the cessation of hostilities, as in the military government of Germany after World War II. In addition, those persons who commit acts of cruelty, perfidy, or vandalism forbidden by the rules or laws of war may likewise be tried by a military commission either during or after the war. Such war crimes include mistreatment of the wounded or sick, violation of an armistice, massacre or mistreatment of nonresisting civilians, or abuse of flags of truce.

Martial Law.—Martial law, sometimes referred to as martial rule, is the assumption of the function of the domestic government by the military forces of that government in an effort to preserve order and ensure the public safety during a period of emergency. It is called into being in times of insurrection or invasion within domestic areas where the ordinary law can no longer function adequately. The occasion and justification for martial law is public necessity as indicated by the circumstances. Its ultimate purpose is to restore law and order so that re-establishment of the civil authority may be accomplished as expeditiously as the situation warrants. Where it becomes necessary to establish military tribunals to punish violators of lawful rules and regulations or of local law, military commissions or provost courts are generally utilized. In the United States, martial law may be proclaimed by the president or by the governor of a state, depending upon the general or local nature of the cause. The duty of the executive to enforce the law is considered to vest in him the discretionary power to determine whether an exigency requiring military aid for that purpose has arisen. This power, however, can never bestow a license upon the military commander to perform unwarranted acts of violence or oppression, and a military commander acting under cover of martial law does so at his peril and may be subsequently held civilly, or even criminally, liable for such unwarranted acts. Inasmuch as martial law is a temporary expedient, it is to be continued only so long as the exigency giving rise to its creation prevails. Once the emergency has ceased to exist, or within a reasonable time thereafter, martial law can be deemed to have lapsed, even in the absence of a formal declaration to that effect. See also MARTIAL LAW.

Status of Forces Stationed in Friendly Countries.—The stationing of American troops in friendly countries pursuant to the North Atlantic Treaty Organization (NATO) Status of Forces Agreement (1951) and the Security Treaty with Japan brought into focus the problem of the exercise of criminal jurisdiction by a host country over offenses committed by members of the visiting forces. Under military government or martial law, discussed above, the commander of the military forces has the supreme authority, and the continuing efficacy of the laws of the civil jurisdiction in which his troops are stationed is dependent solely upon his discretion. However, in the instances of the NATO countries and Japan, American troops were stationed in sovereign countries in peacetime; and it is a fundamental principle of international law that, with few exceptions, a sovereign nation has exclusive jurisdiction to punish offenses against its laws committed within its borders, unless it expressly or impliedly consents to surrender its jurisdiction. The above mentioned treaties, taking cognizance of these established principles, provide generally that each state has exclusive criminal jurisdiction over personnel of the visiting forces with respect to offenses punishable by its law but not by the law of the other state. In all other cases, jurisdiction is concurrent; but the military authorities of the sending state have the primary right to exercise jurisdiction over its personnel for offenses against the security or property of the sending state, for offenses solely against other personnel of the sending state and their property and for offenses arising out of the performance of official duty, while the authorities of the receiving state have primary jurisdiction in all other cases. The receiving state may waive its primary right and has done so in the great majority of cases.

Relationship of Military Law to the Civilian Community.—***United States.***—In any country this relationship is a manifestation of the country's concept of the role of the military in society as a whole. In the United States, military law is administered by the military, but the source of authority is the Constitution, which empowers the Congress to enact the necessary legislation. Decisions of military tribunals alleged to have gone beyond the authority of such tribunals may be tested in civilian courts through habeas corpus proceedings. The Uniform Code of Military Justice provides for a Court of Military Appeals, composed of three civilian judges, as the highest military appellate tribunal. It requires the approval of the president before a death sentence may be carried out, and requires the approval of the secretary of a military department before an officer may be dismissed from the service.

Great Britain.—In the United Kingdom, a Courts-Martial Appeal Court has been established. This court is composed of judges of the regular civilian court, the High Court of Justice, and is presided over by the lord chief justice of England. There also exists the possibility of a limited second appeal to the House of Lords. The legal provisions concerning military justice are contained in the Naval Discipline Act, the Army Act, and the Air Force Act.

Canada.—Canadian military law has traditionally been closely associated with that of the United Kingdom. Until 1944, the provisions of the Army Act, the Naval Discipline Act, and the Air Force Act of the United Kingdom were incorporated by reference into the laws for the government of the armed forces of Canada. In 1944 a code of discipline was established for the Canadian Navy. However, not until 1950, with the passage of the National Defense Act, was there promulgated a complete Canadian code independent of the laws of the United Kingdom. In addition to establishing a uniform law for all branches of the Canadian armed forces, the act provided that the administration of military law was to be subject to review by a civilian court of appeals, and, under certain conditions, by the Supreme Court of Canada.

France.—In France, the extent of civilian controls on military law differs in peace and war. In peacetime, a civilian judge serves as presiding officer of the trial court. In time of war, courts-martial are composed entirely of military personnel. The French soldier may appeal a judgment rendered by a military tribunal in time of peace to the Cour de Cassation (the French Supreme Court), but in time of war appeals go to a permanent military review court. French military law is contained in a comprehensive military code enacted on March 9, 1928.

Soviet Union.—The Soviet Union's system of military law and administration reflects a greater interdependence of military and civil authority than exists in England or the United States. The minister of defense promulgates a disciplinary code which is administered by professional judges and administrators. This fusion of military and nonmilitary criminal law results in the subordination of the former to the general system of criminal law set forth in the Soviet criminal code, and is exemplified by the fact that the office appears within the various units of the armed forces. Supervision over the military courts is exercised by the Supreme Court of the USSR, the Ministry of Justice of the USSR, and the Office of the Procurator-General of the USSR.

For bibliography, see MILITARY COURTS-MARTIAL.

GEORGE W. HICKMAN, JR.,
Major General, United States Army, Retired.

MILITARY LIBRARIES. See LIBRARIES—*4. United States Government Libraries* (Military Libraries).

MILITARY MANPOWER, a term used variously to describe (1) the number of men under arms in active military formations; (2) the number actively under arms plus those trained reserves that may be readily mobilized; (3) those under arms plus all who have ever received military training; or (4) all men in the population between certain arbitrary age limits, such as 18 to 45, regardless of prior training. The term "military manpower pool" usually refers to the fourth category.

Numbers alone will not give an accurate comparison of the manpower resources of nations. The quality of manpower resources is as important as the quantity; and the totality of modern warfare relates military demands to the total demands of other sectors of the economy such as essential industry, agriculture, education, and science. Like other national resources, the national military manpower pool has fixed limits, set by the birth rate 18 to 45 years before.

Military Manpower and Industry.—Until the Industrial Revolution, the term "military manpower" was used to describe either the size of forces a ruler had under arms, or the number of able-bodied men available in his domain. Weapons were simple and resembled those used by civilians. Training emphasized discipline rather than weaponry. Home protection and production was left to women, children, invalids, and old men. Subsistence and supply for men under arms was provided locally or captured from the enemy. There was a minimum of reliance on supply lines of communication.

The coming of industry, the technological revolution, and the growing complexity of weapons systems gave emphasis to the pretraining of soldiery and the necessity of an industrial base and supply lines to furnish ammunition and replace weapons consumed in combat. Thus, in a war effort requiring extensive mobilization, limits appeared on the percentage of the male population that could be used for battle, in comparison with the proportion required to man the supporting industrial machine. The complex nature of the soldier's weapons has steadily imposed more exacting, and hence more limiting, requirements with respect to age and education.

The modern industrial nation is confronted with the dilemma of a wartime military machine and an industrial base which are competitors for the same sort of people. For that reason it will never be able to reach the theoretically optimum limits on strictly military manpower for any extended period. Except in those rare cases of countries which can maintain military forces with volunteers, most modern nations adopt some form of conscription to decide who shall fill military manpower needs. (See CONSCRIPTION.) In World War II such nations as Great Britain, Soviet Russia, Germany, and Japan were forced to adopt a form of national service which carried the conscription principle over into the industrial area.

Although the United States has resorted to conscription to fill its military ranks in every major war, it was always assumed that its manpower was sufficient to meet military needs while still allowing adequate manpower for industrial labor. World War I was within six months of its end before the first "Work or Fight" order was issued. It took World War II to make the country realize that its military manpower was a scarce resource. The War Manpower Commission (WMC) was not established until April 1942, four months after Pearl Harbor, and even then only indirect compulsion was used to control civilian labor. The Korean War was a conflict of limited scale; yet the United States was forced to tap the same military manpower as was used in World War II. The Reserve Forces Act of 1955 was an attempt to adjust this inequity, which put trained men in double jeopardy while excusing the untrained.

Age Distribution.—An important factor in assessing a constantly changing manpower situation is the relative distribution of ages. In the 7 years after World War II, the population of the United States increased by over 10 per cent, yet the percentage increase of males between 18 and 64 for the same period was not even 2 per cent. The Department of Labor estimated that whereas the United States was able to raise a military force of 12 million for World War II, the country would not be able to raise such a force again until 1960, given the same deferment standards. Because of the terrible casualties of World War II and the reduced birth rate, Soviet Russia entered a period during which her military manpower pool temporarily declined, despite an increasing population. The problems of present day France are often attributed to the bloodletting at Verdun over 40 years ago.

Effect of Thermonuclear Weapons.—The new technology has dissolved the time-distance cushion of protection behind which some countries, including the United States, traditionally mobilized their military manpower. The advent of intercontinental ballistic missiles has opened all continents to direct and unannounced attack. At the same time, thermonuclear weapons and their destructive capacity have made more vital the problem of protecting industry and recuperating from attack; hence new demands will be made on the traditional military manpower pool. Under such circumstances the United States, like other nations, will be forced to adopt effective manpower controls in a general war which lasts beyond the initial exchange of thermonuclear blows.

In a thermonuclear war, distinctions between military and civilian manpower become blurred. Flexibility of movement between the two categories may become essential, and with that need, adequate authority to make such switches. The War Manpower Commission of World War II dealt only indirectly with the problem in the United States and never possessed congressionally granted powers of the scope now envisaged. The Office of Defense Mobilization (created 1950; reorganized 1953) absorbed the residual powers of the WMC, but its powers are untried. In any general war, the effective utilization of military manpower may mark the distinction between success and defeat.

See also ARMY RESERVE; MILITIA; NATIONAL GUARD; NAVAL RESERVE.

Consult Lincoln, George A., *Economics of National Security* (New York 1954).

WILLIAM A. KNOWLTON,
Lieutenant Colonel, United States Army; Associate Professor of Social Sciences, United States Military Academy.

MILITARY MINING. See MILITARY ENGINEERING—*Demolition.*

MILITARY MUSIC. The earliest surviving pictorial, sculptured, and written records show musical or quasimusical instruments employed in connection with military activity—for signaling in encampments, during parades, and in combat. Because the sounds most often were produced in the open air, the instruments have tended to be of the easily audible brass and percussion families. Oriental, Egyptian, Greek, Roman, Amerindian, and other chronicles and pictorial remains show trumpets and drums of many varieties allied to soldiers and battles. Few, if any, records can survive, however, of what music or protomusic was played on instruments before the development of decipherable musical notation. This limitation of sensible discussion also occurs in connection with military (and other) instruments discovered among primitive peoples in Africa, Asia, America, and elsewhere during historic times.

In Europe, military music developed importantly in the late 15th and early 16th centuries, largely as used by mercenary armies. The battles of Marignano (1515) and Pavia (1525) between such troops, fighting for Francis I of France and (at Pavia) for Holy Roman Emperor Charles V, became notorious for the din created by trumpets and kettledrums, used to give new spirit to flagging troops and to terrify the enemy. Somewhat later, the men who produced these complex calls, rolls, and signals formed organizations that were accorded special privileges to distinguish them from nonmilitary musicians. The ritualistic gestures evolved by their drummers have lasted into our own time; they can be seen modified in the posturings of drum majors and majorettes, as well as in the motions of parade drummers.

The Battle of Marignano led directly to the variety of programmatic music, intended for nonmilitary entertainment, known as the *battaglia;* in 1529, Clément Janequin (1485?–?1560) wrote a vocal battle piece called *La guerre,* and it fathered a line of *battaglie* in France, Germany, Italy, and England, by such composers as William Byrd (1543–1623), Adriano Banchieri (1568–1634), Johann Kaspar Kerll (1627–1693), and Franz Kotzwara (1730–1791). Gunshots were often used for added realism in these imitations of the supposed sounds of actual battle. The most renowned of the later, more elaborate examples of this genre were Kotzwara's *The Battle of Prague* (1788) and Ludwig van Beethoven's *Wellington's Victory or the Battle of Vitoria* (Opus 91, 1813), the latter originally composed for a mechanical instrument, the panharmonicon.

In the 18th century, especially in Germany and France, military bands began to absorb melody-producing instruments—oboes, bassoons, clarinets, piccolos, serpents, French horns, and others—and to perform carefully scored marches and pseudo-symphonic compositions. Toward the end of the century, the spread of "Janizary" music, an imitation of that played by the musical bodyguards of the Turkish sultans, affected both military and nonmilitary music throughout Europe. Introducing large drums, cymbals, triangles, glockenspiels, and Turkish ("Chinese") crescents, "Janizary" music was echoed in Wolfgang Amadeus Mozart's opera *The Abduction from the Seraglio* (1782), and in the *Turkish March* in his Piano Sonata in A Major (K. 331, 1778), and in incidental music (Opus 113, 1811) that Beethoven composed for the German author August von Kotzebue's play *The Ruins of Athens.*

The 19th century saw the greatest spread and evolution of military music and music of military provenance. In 1838 Friedrich Wilhelm Wieprecht, musical supervisor of the Prussian Army, honored Czar Nicholas I's visit to Berlin by conducting the combined bands of 32 regiments (1,000 wind instruments and 200 drums). Many renowned 19th century composers wrote pseudo-military music, especially familiar examples being Franz Schubert's D-major *Marche militaire* for two pianos (published 1826), Franz Liszt's *Hunnenschlacht* (1856), Hector Berlioz's *Symphonie funèbre et triomphale* for military band, strings, and chorus (1840), and Peter Ilich Tchaikovsky's *1812 Overture* (1880); this last, representing the opposed French and Russian armies by their respective national anthems, is often punctuated by rhythmically placed cannon shots. Less music of this variety has been composed in the 20th century, but Ottorino Respighi's *The Pines of Rome* (1924) concludes with a noisy vision of Caesarean legions ascending the Capitoline Hill.

In the mid-19th century the Belgian Adolphe Sax (1814–1894) began the alteration of military and other instruments by substituting valve mechanisms for keys, thus influencing the make-up of French military bands and incidentally evolving the saxhorns and saxophones. In the United States, military music was much influenced by Patrick Sarsfield Gilmore (1829–1892), a Civil War army bandmaster who later toured Europe with the highly efficient brass band of the 22d New York Regiment. He was followed by John Philip Sousa (1854–1932, q.v.), whose bands probably represented the acme of this evolution, and whose marches became world famous.

One instrument has remained almost exclusively military. This is the bugle, a brass instrument related to the trumpet, but generally limited to calls and signals, though it has at times been equipped with valves and keys to make it more versatile. The melodies of the traditional bugle calls of all nations frequently have been incorporated into concert, operatic, and other nonmilitary music. Modern military bands often include sousaphones (a variety of tuba), trombones, horns, baritones (a variety of horn), euphoniums, cornets, trumpets, clarinets, saxhorns, saxophones, helicons, piccolos, fifes (a variety of flute), several sorts of drums, cymbals, triangles, and other percussion. In recent times, military and near-military bands have flourished throughout Latin America, as well as in England (bands of the Coldstream and Grenadier Guards). In the United States, a farther removal from military origins is indicated, for example, by the Goldman Band of New York City, which is in effect a specially constituted outdoor concert orchestra for playing mostly nonmilitary music.

HERBERT WEINSTOCK,
Author of "Music as an Art."

MILITARY OATH. See OATH, MILITARY.

MILITARY OCCUPATION. See MILITARY LAW—*Military Government;* WAR, LAWS OF.

MILITARY ORDERS. See DECORATIONS AND ORDERS.

MILITARY OUTPOSTS. See OUTPOSTS, MILITARY.

MILITARY PENSIONS. See PENSION OR RETIREMENT SYSTEM—*Governmental Systems* (Military Pensions and Compensation).

MILITARY POLICE, soldiers who guard property, prevent crime, arrest offenders, enforce laws and regulations, and perform other duties within the army similar to those of civilian police. They appear in military history as early as the campaigns of Alexander the Great (r. 336–323 B.C.). Officers responsible for such duty in the Middle Ages came to be called *provosts.* Usually these officers had to depend on troops temporarily detailed to assist them as *provost guards,* though a few commanders designated permanent personnel for such duty. During the French Revolution, the government began the custom of assigning a small unit of its newly organized National Gendarmerie to each division of its army to serve as military police. Under Napoleon Bonaparte, these units functioned in thoroughly modern style. The 1st duke of Wellington was so impressed with their effectiveness that he organized a unit of "Staff Corps Cavalry" to discharge the same duties for his army.

Prior to 1941, the United States Army had no regularly constituted corps of military police. George Washington appointed a "Provost Martial" in 1776; in 1778, Congress ordered the establishment of a "Provost Company," armed and equipped as light dragoons. This unit, frequently referred to as "the Marechaussée corps," served until 1783. In 1862, a provost marshal general was appointed for the duration of the Civil War, with the primary function of enforcing the draft law. He also was responsible for apprehending deserters, spies, and disloyal persons. An Invalid Corps (later the Veteran Reserve Corps) was likewise established in 1862 to assist in maintaining internal security.

During World War I, a provost marshal general and the Military Police Corps formed part of the American Expeditionary Force (AEF), but they were demobilized at the end of hostilities. Between wars, military police duties were performed by individuals or units designated for that purpose at the various military installations. In 1941, the Office of the Provost Marshal General and the Corps of Military Police were again established; both have since become parts of the permanent military establishment of the United States.

Military police units are of two general types. The first are regularly assigned to divisions, corps, and larger units; their special functions include maintaining discipline, controlling traffic, handling prisoners of war, and the prevention of straggling. Units of the second type operate in the zone of the interior and the communications zone of a theater of operations and have the responsibility of maintaining internal security, guarding supplies in transit, maintaining discipline among military personnel in civilian communities and on public carriers, and controlling civilian refugees and interned enemy nationals. The police force of the United States Navy is the Shore Patrol; that of the Air Force is the Air Police.

See also PROVOST MARSHAL.

JOHN R. ELTING,
Lieutenant Colonel, United States Army; Department of Military Art and Engineering, United States Military Academy.

MILITARY PRISONERS. See PRISONERS OF WAR; WAR, LAWS OF—*Prisoners of War.*

MILITARY PRISONS. Early prisons for military offenders were almost entirely punitive institutions. The modern concept of rehabilitation appeared with Napoleon Bonaparte's special regiments for refractory conscripts, in which picked officers carefully trained their unwilling charges into good soldiers. Military correctional institutions today have the mission of rehabilitating their inmates, with the purpose of fitting them either for restoration to honorable duty or for a successful return to civilian life. In the United States, minor military offenders are confined in the guardhouse or "stockade" of the post where they are stationed or of the organization to which they are assigned. Prisoners convicted of serious offenses by a general court-martial are incarcerated at a United States Disciplinary Barracks. (The term "military prison" has not been used in the United States since 1915.) The eldest of these installations is at Fort Leavenworth, Kans. Another is presently located at New Cumberland, Pa. Corresponding United States Navy installations are the Naval Retraining Commands at Portsmouth N.H., and Camp Elliott, Calif. Military personnel found guilty of especially serious crimes may be sent to one of the federal penitentiaries. During World War II, this system was supplemented by the establishment, both overseas and in the United States, of various types of rehabilitation centers (sometimes called disciplinary training centers or detention centers) designed to retrain military offenders so that they could be returned to combat duty.

JOHN R. ELTING.

MILITARY PUNISHMENTS. See ARREST, MILITARY; MILITARY COURTS-MARTIAL; MILITARY LAW.

MILITARY RANK. See INSIGNIA OF RANK, ARMED FORCES; RANK.

MILITARY RESERVE. See ARMY RESERVE; MILITIA; NATIONAL GUARD; NAVAL RESERVE.

MILITARY SCIENCE, that branch of study of military and related affairs that has as its object the discovery of the principles and rules that govern military operations. The utilization of these rules to solve military problems and to achieve military goals is the art of war. Thus, warfare is both science and art.

Insofar as military science is based on understanding men and their actions, it faces the same difficulties as are confronted by all the social and psychological sciences. These difficulties are compounded for military science by the fact that it cannot experiment with men at war in the same sense that natural scientists can experiment with the objects of their studies. The strengths and weaknesses of weapons and equipment can be tested in maneuvers along with ideas about organization and tactics. But maneuvers can never reproduce faithfully the conditions of war. The battlefield is the only true testing ground. Yet nations do not engage in war simply to evaluate strategy, tactics, training, weapons, and equipment under the impact of battle.

There remains as a field for study and analysis by military science the conduct of battles and campaigns in the past. However, there are difficulties encountered even here. No two battles or campaigns are ever the same. The morale, condition, discipline, and competence of men, the efficiency of their leaders, weather, terrain, weapons, and other factors, all differ from battle to battle. Still another obstacle in studying battles of the past is that the accounts may not accurately present the realities. Interpretation is mixed in with every account, and the stress and excitement of the times are likely to prevent objective reporting.

Thus, military science cannot be an exact science, but despite these inherent complexities, it has synthesized its main conclusions into a series of generalizations known as the principles of war (see STRATEGY, MILITARY). These are few in number, but their truth has been demonstrated throughout the history of warfare. More than half of the present day principles were postulated in the 6th century B.C. by the Chinese philosopher Sun Tzu. These principles and the few added later have remained unaltered, but their application has undergone successive changes due to military and scientific developments. The wheel, the catapult, the crossbow, gunpowder, the rifle, artillery, field fortifications, the railroad, signal communications, mass production, motor transportation, chemical agents, the tank, the airplane, guided missiles, and finally atomic weapons, each in turn caused modifications in military theory and practice and in the practical application of the principles of war. Stubbornness in adhering to tradition and failure to recognize the true military potentialities of technical developments have caused many military reverses. Blind, rigid adherence to the principles of war also has produced disastrous results at times, for these are useful tools of the military art only when applied with a true appreciation of the circumstances affecting the conduct of a given conflict: the virtues and defects of the weapons and equipment of the day, psychological and geographic considerations, time and space, and other factors.

Since World War II, groups of scientists from many different fields have been organized in the military services to study military operations, tests, trials, and maneuvers scientifically, quantitatively and qualitatively, with a view to improving future strategy, tactics, and weapons. Actual operations in Korea were subjected to on-the-spot study and analysis by such groups. Their activities are known variously as operations research, operational research, operations evaluation, or operations analysis. In the highest echelons similar studies are made of entire weapons systems of the separate services and their relationships. In the United States these studies are conducted by the Weapons Systems Evaluation Group of the Department of Defense.

See also NAVAL STRATEGY AND TACTICS; OPERATIONS RESEARCH; TACTICS.

MILITARY STRATEGY. See NAVAL STRATEGY AND TACTICS—*Strategy;* STRATEGY, MILITARY.

MILITARY TACTICS. See NAVAL STRATEGY AND TACTICS—*Tactics;* TACTICS.

MILITARY TERMS. From the thousands of military terms in use, the following have been selected as those most generally used by commentators on military subjects. Although each term has been chosen for its military significance, many may also be used in a general sense.

Abatis.—Obstacle formed of felled trees, or of bent down small trees, often interlaced with barbed wire. The former is called a dead abatis and the latter a live abatis. See also separate article ABATIS.

Absent Without Leave.—Failure to be at the proper place at the proper time, but without intending to desert the military service. The absentee may be unaware that his absence is not authorized. Abbreviation AWOL.

Accrued Leave.—Total amount of leave of absence due an individual in the military service at any given time.

Action Station.—Place to be occupied and duties to be performed by an individual in the event of an attack.

Activate.—To put a military unit on the active list by assigning personnel and equipment thereto with which it can operate as a distinctive organization.

Active Duty.—Military service performed by those on the active list.

Adjustable-pitch Propeller.—A propeller with blades that can be pitched at different angles while the propeller is not in motion.

Advance by Bounds.—To move forward in a series of separate advances, usually from one concealed position to another, or from one point of observation to another.

Advance Guard.—Force sent out ahead of the main body to protect it from surprise attacks and to ensure its uninterrupted advance by removing obstacles and wiping out enemy resistance where possible. See also separate article ADVANCE GUARDS.

Aerial Torpedo.—Large explosive projectile driven by its own motor, and usually launched from low-flying aircraft at water-borne targets.

Aid Station.—First medical establishment to which the wounded are brought on the route of evacuation from the fighting zone. The wounded are given first aid treatment and separated into groups according to the kind of treatment needed. Those needing further care are sent to the rear.

Air Superiority.—Greater number or superior types of military aircraft possessed by one force, preventing effective opposition by enemy aircraft to air or ground operations in a particular area.

Airborne.—Transported by air or in the air. Airborne troops are soldiers specially organized, trained, and equipped for transportation into combat by air. They usually land by parachute or glider.

Aircraft-warning Service.—System established for informing air defenses of the movement of aircraft. The system includes observers, filter centers, and communications.

Alert.—Warning signal of a real or threatened danger, usually an air attack; time during which troops are on the lookout for danger; condition of aircraft prepared to perform a mission.

Alignment or Alinement.—Formation in a straight line; the line so formed; straight line on which several elements are formed; the dressing of individuals or units upon a straight line.

All-around Traverse.—Terms describing gun, radar, or other equipment capable of being turned by its traversing mechanism in a complete circle in a horizontal plane.

All-clear Signal.—Signal to indicate that danger, usually an air attack, has passed.

Allotment.—Portion of their pay that military personnel may authorize to be paid directly to another person, as a dependent, or to an institution, as a bank or insurance company.

Allowance.—Prescribed amount of rations, supplies, or equipment allotted to an organization or to an individual. Monetary remuneration in addition to the prescribed pay, such as travel, quarters, subsistence, and clothing allowances.

Alternate Position.—Location assigned to a unit, weapon, or piece of equipment from which the same mission can be accomplished as when it is located at the main position. The alternate position is occupied when the main position becomes untenable.

Angle of Approach.—In gunnery, the angle between the line along which the gun is pointed and the line along which the target is traveling.

Antipersonnel.—Explosive charges, such as antipersonnel mines and antipersonnel bombs, designed to be used against individuals rather than against materiel.

Antitank.—Explosive charges, weapons, and other devices, such as antitank bombs, antitank mines, antitank grenades, antitank rockets, antitank guns, and antitank ditches, designed to be used against tanks and other armored vehicles. See also separate article ANTITANK WEAPONS.

Area Target.—Target for gunfire or bombing covering a considerable space. It differs from a point target in that the latter is a particular point or structure.

Armor-piercing.—Term describing bombs, shells, rockets, and grenades designed to pierce armor. See also separate article ARMOR-PIERCING PROJECTILES.

Armored Car.—Motor vehicle protected by light armor and provided with machine guns or small caliber cannon. Used chiefly for scouting, but also as self-propelled mounts for antiaircraft artillery and as personnel and ammunition carriers. See also separate article ARMORED CARS.

Articles of War.—Laws governing the conduct of military personnel and others temporarily attached to the armed services. See also separate article ARTICLES OF WAR.

Artificial Moonlight.—Illumination provided by searchlights for ground operations carried out during the hours of darkness.

Assault.—Final phase of an attack; closing with the enemy in close combat. It may be made by dismounted, mounted, mechanized, or armored units.

Assembly Area.—Location in which parts of a command are assembled in preparation for further action. Also called assembly point, and assembly position.

Assign.—To place an individual, unit, or item of equipment in a military organization so as to make it an integral part thereof.

Atomic Energy.—Energy resulting from nuclear fission or fusion. See also separate article ATOMIC ENERGY.

Attach.—To place an individual, unit, or item of equipment in a military organization temporarily.

Attack.—Offensive action against an enemy. Usually involves an advance combined with firing and fighting at close range.

Automatic Fire.—Fire from an automatic weapon which continues until the ammunition is exhausted or until the pressure on the trigger is released.

Axis.—Route of advance or supply toward the enemy or route of evacuation of personnel and materiel to the rear.

Azimuth Deviation.—In gunnery, the difference between the azimuth from gun to target and the azimuth from the gun to the point where the projectile strikes.

Bail Out.—To make an emergency jump, with a parachute, from an aircraft in flight.

Ball Turret.—Ball-shaped projection on aircraft containing guns power-driven to enable them to be quickly aimed in various directions.

Ballistic.—Pertaining to the motion of projectiles, as ballistic curve and ballistic wind. See also separate article BALLISTICS.

Balloon Barrage.—Protective screen of balloons anchored to the ground or to ships, to hinder flights by aircraft at low levels over a certain area or point.

Band of Fire.—Belt of fire, at least part of which grazes the ground; usually fired from more than one automatic weapon.

Bangalore Torpedo.—Metal tube containing a high explosive; principally used for clearing a path through a mine field or barbed wire.

Barrage.—Prearranged concentration of artillery or automatic weapons fire on one or more lines. Often used to isolate a portion of the front to prevent its reinforcement or attack. See also separate article BARRAGE.

Base.—Installation from which a military force operates and from which it obtains its supplies.

Base Angle.—Angle between the line from the gun to its principal target and the line from the gun to the visible reference point, from which angles to other targets are measured.

Bazooka.—Portable launching tube for rocket projectile. Two men usually carry the ammunition and launcher and serve as the firing crew. It is used chiefly against armored vehicles. See also separate article ROCKETS.

Billet.—Shelter for military personnel consisting of buildings other than barracks. See also separate article BILLETING OF SOLDIERS.

Biological Warfare.—Employment of bacteria, fungi, viruses, rickettsiae, and toxic agents derived from living organisms to produce death or disease in humans, animals, or growing plants.

Bivouac.—Temporary camp in the field. It may have no overhead cover, or only natural cover, shelter tents, or cover made from available material.

Black Out.—To obscure in darkness, as by extinguishing all lights, as a protective measure against enemy observation.

Blast Effect.—Destruction or damage to the works of man or vegetation caused by the force of an explosion on or slightly above the surface of the ground or water.

Blitzkrieg.—German word meaning "lightning war." Violent surprise offensive by coordinated air, armored, and ground units, designed to crush all enemy resistance quickly. See also separate article BLITZKRIEG.

Blockade.—Shutting off of a place or enemy troops by the use of troops, warships, or both, to prevent ingress and egress; force maintaining a blockade. See also separate article BLOCKADE.

Blowback.—Gases forced to the rear of a gun when a projectile is discharged. Blowback is a necessary part of the firing action in some automatic weapons. In other weapons it is usually the result of faulty ammunition.

Bomb.—Receptacle, usually of metal and streamlined in shape, containing a chemical agent, explosive charge, or both. Explosive bombs are usually demolition bombs for the destruction of heavy material; fragmentation bombs are used to cause casualties among personnel. Chemical bombs include incendiary, gas, and smoke bombs. See also separate article BOMB.

Bomb Bay.—Portion of the interior of an airplane designed for carrying large bombs. Bombs are carried in a device known as a bomb rack, and are dropped from the plane when the bomb door is opened and the bomb release mechanism is actuated.

Bombing.—Act of dropping bombs from an aircraft. Bombing is classified as skip, dive, or glide bombing, according to the performance of the plane at the time of release. Bombing is further classified as area, pattern, or precision bombing according to the method used in hitting the target.

Bracket.—In gunnery, space between two shots or groups of shots, one of which is over the target and the other short of it. Normally, the third shot or group should be very close to the target.

Breakthrough.—Penetrating into and beyond an enemy defensive position with a force sufficiently large to continue for a considerable distance.

Bridgehead.—Position on the enemy's side of a stream or other body of water, established by the leading elements of a force to protect the crossing of the remainder of the troops. Also used for any advanced position without reference to a water crossing. See also separate entry BRIDGEHEAD.

Briefing.—Concise instruction given to participants of an air, ground, or sea mission immediately prior to departure.

Burst Interval.—Distance between the target and the point of explosion of a shell.

Cadence.—Uniform length of step and time in marching. Number of steps marched per minute.

Call Sign.—Signal used for identifying a radio station or military unit.

Camouflage.—Disguise or concealment by the use of nets, burlap, paint, foliage, and the like. It also includes the placing of dummy targets. See also separate entry CAMOUFLAGE.

Capital Ship.—Large warship mounting guns of more than 8-inch caliber; battleship or battle cruiser. An aircraft carrier is not classified as a capital ship.

Cartel.—Written agreement between opposing nations, usually for the exchange of prisoners or the passage of mail and supplies through a blockade.

Ceiling.—Top limit of visibility for flying as determined by a cloud bank or fog. Highest altitude an aircraft can attain under certain conditions. See also separate article CEILING.

Censorship.—Act of inspecting and, if necessary, deleting all or part of written and printed matter; telegraph, telephone, and radio messages; radio and television broadcasts; still and motion pictures; tape recordings. The purpose is to prevent military information from reaching the enemy. See also separate article CENSORSHIP.

Center of Resistance.—Location in the main defensive position at which troops are concentrated to repel enemy attacks. Centers of resistance are part of a system of mutually supporting defense areas or fortified tactical localities.

Central Fire Control.—System of fire control of weapons from a central location, often used by antiaircraft batteries.

Chain of Command.—Series of military officers and noncommissioned officers through which orders or other instructions must be transmitted.

Chemical Agent.—Chemical substance used in combat, such as poison gases, incendiaries, and screening smokes.

Chemical Warfare.—Use of chemical agents in combat. Bombs, shells, grenades, smoke generators, and flame throwers are used to spread chemical agents. Gas masks, special clothing, and decontaminants are used to neutralize their effects. See also separate article CHEMICAL WARFARE.

Chief of Staff.—Senior staff officers in a unit as large as, or larger than, a division. He is in charge of coordinating the duties of all staff sections and is an adviser to the commanding general.

Classified.—Pertaining to the security restriction placed on military letters, messages, maps, publications, photographs, drawings, tape recordings, and motion pictures. The classifications, in order of importance, are top secret, secret, confidential, restricted, and unclassified.

Close-order Drill.—Formations and movements usually performed in drill, marching, and parades at normal or at close interval.

Coastal Force.—Naval force operating in a certain area as an aid in situations where the local naval defense forces are not sufficiently strong.

Coastal Frontier.—Geographical division of a coast to ensure effective coordination between the armed forces of the nation defending the coastal area.

Color or Colors.—Flag of a nation; also the flag of a military unit comparable in size to a regiment. When both are carried together they are called the colors. See also separate article COLORS, MILITARY.

Combat Drill.—Drill formations and movements designed to train small units for combat.

Combat Troops.—Soldiers specially trained and equipped for actual fighting, as distinguished from service troops who provide supply, transportation, communication, evacuation, maintenance, construction, and other services for combat units.

Combat Zone.—Area where fighting is actually taking place; forward part of the theater of operations.

Combined Operations.—Military action carried out by two or more nations in concert. Military action by army and naval forces acting together is called joint operations.

Combined Training.—Maneuvers of two or more branches of the army that normally fight together, such as infantry, artillery, engineers, armor, and air units.

Command Net.—Electrical means of communication over which orders are sent from the headquarters of a command to subordinate units. These means include radio, telegraph, and telephone.

Command Post.—Headquarters of a military unit; location of the commander. In combat the command post is often divided into a forward and a rear echelon.

Commando.—Soldier specially trained to make surprise raids in small groups. This is the British term; the corresponding United States term is Ranger. See also separate article COMMANDO.

Compartment of Terrain.—Separate division or section of the ground bounded on at least two sides by features such as woods, ridges, or villages which limit observation and observed fire into the area from points outside.

Cone of Dispersion.—The cone-shaped space outlined by shots fired from a gun with one sight setting. The cone-shaped dispersion is caused by vibration, ammunition variances, and other factors.

Correspondent.—Writer, photographer, artist, radio, or television broadcaster authorized to collect and disseminate information in a theater of operations.

Corridor.—Compartment of terrain, the longer axis of which extends in the direction of advance, or is parallel thereto.

Corvette.—Small war vessel used to protect convoys from submarines. See also separate article CORVETTE.

Counterattack.—Attack made in reprisal for an enemy's attack. It is mostly a defensive action and differs from a counteroffensive, which is aggressive action on a large scale.

Counterbattery Fire.—Artillery fire intended to destroy the enemy's artillery.

Counteroffensive.—Aggressive action on a large scale to seize the initiative from the enemy. It differs from a counterattack in that the latter is a small local action.

Court-martial.—Military court. The three kinds, in order of importance, are general, special, and summary. See also separate article MILITARY COURTS-MARTIAL.

Cover Position.—Location immediately in rear of a firing position in which personnel and materiel are protected from enemy fire.

Cross Compartment.—Compartment of terrain the longer axis of which is oblique or perpendicular to the direction of advance.

Danger Space.—Space in the trajectory of bullets fired from small arms which is not higher than the height of an average man.

D-day.—Day on which a previously planned attack or operation is initiated.

Debark.—To unload troops and equipment from a vessel or aircraft.

Decontaminate.—To remove chemical, radiological, or biological contamination so as to make an area safe for unprotected personnel or equipment.

Defend.—To attempt to hold an area against enemy opposition.

Defense.—Means used as protection against an attack. An active defense is carried out by counterattacking. A passive defense is carried out by attempting merely to hold the area.

Deflection.—In gunnery, the horizontal angle between the line of sight and the axis of the bore of a gun when the gun is pointed for firing.

Delaying Action.—Defensive battle used to slow the enemy's advance and to gain time without becoming closely engaged, characteristic of the actions of a rear guard in a retreat.

Demobilize.—To disband troops, as at the end of a war.

Deployment.—Act of spreading out a body of troops, as for combat. The extension may be made in width, or depth, or both.

Desertion.—Leaving a military post or duty with the intention of not returning, or of avoiding hazardous duty. See also separate article DESERTER.

Develop.—To make more apparent, as to develop the enemy's position. To break up a body of troops into smaller groups in preparation for combat.

Dumdum Bullet.—Bullet that expands upon impact. It usually has a soft lead nose. Its use is prohibited by The Hague Convention. See also separate article DUMDUM BULLET.

Dummy Installations.—False targets, such as dummy artillery guns, used to deceive the enemy.

Echelon.—Arrangement of individuals, units, or equipment, each slightly to the right or left of the one immediately in front, like a series of stairsteps. Also, an arrangement of aircraft in which each unit or group flies above or below another unit or group, and frequently to the right or left of it. A grade of command in a chain of command. Subdivision of a unit, as the forward echelon and rear echelon of a headquarters. See also separate article ECHELON.

Element.—Smaller part of a military organization or maneuver. It may be an individual, platoon, crew, or any unit that is part of a larger group.

Elevation.—In gunnery, the vertical angle between the line of sight and the axis of the bore of a gun when the gun is pointed for firing.

Embark.—To load troops and equipment on a vessel or aircraft.

Embrasure.—Opening, with sides flaring outward, in the wall of a parapet or a fortification, through which weapons are fired.

Emplacement.—Position prepared for heavy guns or other weapons or equipment, from which their missions may be executed. Usually there is side and overhead protection against hostile firing and bombing.

Enfilade.—To rake a line with fire along its entire length. Gunfire which sweeps a line in the direction of its length is known as enfilade fire.

Envelopment.—Attack made around one or both of the enemy's flanks, usually coordinated with an attack on his front; enveloping attack.

Expeditionary Force.—Military force for invading or fighting in a foreign country.

Field.—Terrain over which battles are fought or maneuvers are conducted.

Fifth Column.—Sympathizers and supporters of the enemy secretly engaged in espionage, sabotage, and other subversive activities behind the battle lines of a military force. See also separate article FIFTH COLUMN.

Fire Control.—In gunnery, the operations required to prepare data on firing and to place fire on a target. Ability of a commander to open fire, adjust fire upon the target, shift fire to other targets, and cease firing as required.

Fire Discipline.—Obedience of personnel to the orders of a commander in delivering fire on designated targets.

Fire Superiority.—Fire of greater accuracy and volume than that of the enemy. Fire superiority enables troops to advance against the enemy without unduly heavy losses.

Fixed Gun.—Firearm mounted in an airplane or vehicle in such a manner that it cannot be aimed except by maneuvering the plane or vehicle.

Flare.—Very bright light, designed primarily for illumination. Flares are a form of pyrotechnic and may be fired from weapons, dropped from aircraft, suspended from small parachutes, or burned on the ground.

Flash and Sound Ranging.—Method of locating the position of an enemy gun by observing the flash and by calculations based on the time intervals between the reception of the sound at previously oriented microphone stations.

Flexible Gun.—Firearm mounted in such a manner that it can be swung in any direction.

Flight Deck.—Upper deck of an aircraft carrier designed and constructed for the landing and taking off of aircraft.

Forced Crossing.—A stream crossing made against enemy opposition.

Forced Landing.—Aircraft landing due to adverse mechanical or weather conditions. Landing troops on a shore in opposition to the enemy.

Forced March.—Distance march during which the rate of march is increased above normal or the time for rest is reduced below normal, in order that troops may arrive at their destination in less than the usual time.

Foxhole.—Small pit used for the protection of one or two men against firing or bombing. It is usually constructed so that an occupant can fire from it.

Garrison.—Military post at which troops are stationed. To station troops at a military post or in a fortification.

Gas.—Chemical agent used for casualty effect in combat. To use such an agent. See also separate article CHEMICAL WARFARE.

General Staff.—Group of officers in a unit as large as, or larger than, a division who assist the commanding general. The general staff is usually divided into four sections: personnel, intelligence, operations and training, and supply and evacuation.

Grade.—Rank in the military service; applies to both officers and enlisted personnel. See also INSIGNIA OF RANK, ARMED FORCES.

Grenade.—Small bomb, containing explosives or chemicals, thrown by hand or fired from a weapon. The two most widely used types are hand grenades and rifle grenades. See also separate article GRENADE.

Guerrilla Warfare.—Irregular operations carried on by small independent bands, usually in connection with a regular war, for the purpose of harassing the enemy. See also separate article GUERRILLA WARFARE.

Guided Missile.—Projectile which contains a mechanism governing its speed or direction, or both, in response to built-in data or signals received while in flight. See also separate article GUIDED MISSILES.

Gunnery Officer.—Officer who is especially qualified in the practical handling of guns and the technical problems involved in firing. He supervises the preparation of all data required for effective control of the fire.

H-hour.—Hour at which an attack or operation, previously planned, is initiated; zero hour.

Height of Burst.—Vertical distance from the target to the bursting point of a projectile.

Helmet.—Hat made of steel and worn as protection against small arms bullets, shell and bomb fragments.

High Explosive.—Any explosive that burns with extreme rapidity and has a shattering effect. A high explosive is used as a bursting charge in projectiles and bombs, whereas a low explosive is used as a propelling charge in guns and for blasting. See also separate article EXPLOSIVES.

Holding Attack.—Attack for the purpose of containing the enemy in one part of the field, thus preventing him from reinforcing his troops along the line of main attack; secondary attack.

Howitzer.—Artillery piece with a medium length barrel, designed to deliver high angle fire with shells of a medium muzzle velocity. The high angle of fire enables this weapon to hit targets that cannot be reached by flat trajectory guns.

Incendiary.—Any chemical agent which generates sufficient heat to ignite usually noninflammable material. The incendiary material may be contained in shells, bombs, or grenades, and be ignited at the bursting of the container.

Indirect Fire.—Gunfire delivered at a target that cannot be seen from the gun position. The gun is aimed by sighting at a fixed object, called the aiming point, or by using a means of pointing other than the sight.

Inshore Patrol.—Part of the local naval defense forces operating in the inner areas of navigable coastal waters. It consists of naval vessels and aircraft, and it controls shipping within a defensive sea area.

Insignia.—Distinguishing badges, bars, medals, chevrons, and other marks, worn on the uniform to show rank, branch, service, and honors. See also INSIGNIA OF RANK, ARMED FORCES.

Intelligence.—Collected, evaluated, and interpreted military information concerning a possible or actual enemy or theater of operation. See also separate articles ESPIONAGE AND COUNTERESPIONAGE; MILITARY INTELLIGENCE; NAVAL INTELLIGENCE.

Jeep.—Four-wheel motor vehicle, capable of carrying ¼-ton of cargo or 3 passengers, in addition to the driver. It has great cross-country and hill-climbing ability. Its many uses include reconnaissance, towing small cannon and cargo trailers, and transporting stretchers.

Jet Propulsion.—Type of reaction propulsion in which the propelling unit obtains oxygen from the air, as distinguished from rocket propulsion in which the unit carries its own oxygen-producing material. In aircraft propulsion, a turbine jet unit, employing gasoline or other fuel, discharges hot gas through a tail pipe and nozzle, causing a thrust which propels the aircraft. See also separate article JET PROPULSION.

Joint Operations.—Military action carried out by army and naval forces acting together. Military action by two or more nations in concert is called combined operations.

Journal.—Daily record of principal events, messages received and dispatched, visits of superior officers, and absences of the commander from the headquarters. It is kept by a unit or staff section in the field.

Kamikaze.—Japanese word meaning "divine wind," applied to a kind of suicide corps. It refers to the Japanese pilots in World War II who attempted to destroy enemy ships by flying into them and exploding their planes' bomb loads on impact. See also separate article KAMIKAZE.

Landing Area.—Area for the landing of all units of an airborne or amphibious force. Usually it contains several regimental or battalion parachute-drop zones and glider-landing zones or landing beaches.

Landing Party.—A detachment of marines, sailors, or soldiers debarked from a vessel onto a foreign shore to protect the lives and property of citizens of their own country.

Launcher.—Device for firing rockets, grenades, ballistic missiles, or guided missiles; also for catapulting an airplane.

Liaison.—Contact and coordination between a commander and his subordinates or between adjacent units. It is often maintained by an exchange of personnel between the headquarters concerned.

Line of Communication.—Network of roads, navigable waters, and airplane-landing and rail facilities over which supplies are transported and combat movements made.

Loran.—Short for "long-range navigation," a system by which a receiver can fix his ship's or aircraft's position. The receiver picks up and interprets signals sent out by radio stations broadcasting from several different points.

Mach Number.—The ratio of the speed of an object to the velocity of sound in the medium in which the object is moving. Principally used in discussing the performance of aircraft and guided missiles. See also separate article MACH NUMBER.

Magazine.—Container which can be attached to a gun to hold a supply of ammunition. The cartridges are fed into the gun from the magazine.

Maginot Line.—Line of defensive fortifications built by France, after World War I, to protect her eastern frontier. Named for André Maginot (1877–1932), French minister of war.

Main Attack.—Attack carried out by the larger portion of a commander's troops with the mission of securing the chief objective or key point.

Main Line of Resistance.—Line joining the forward edges of the principal centers of resistance. A determined effort is made to prevent the enemy from penetrating this line.

Maneuvers.—Tactical exercises; war games carried out in the field by large bodies of troops for instruction of military personnel and tests of matériel. See also separate article ARMY, NAVY, AND AIR FORCE MANEUVERS.

Matériel or Materiel.—Equipment, apparatus, and supplies used in combat.

Mechanize.—To provide a unit with armored motor vehicles such as tanks and weapons such as self-propelled guns, with which the unit both travels and fights.

Meeting Engagement.—Encounter in the field between opposing forces, neither of which is fully deployed for combat.

Military Government.—Government by military forces over occupied foreign territory or over domestic territory regained from insurgents.

Mine.—Container with explosive or chemical agents fired at will by a control device or upon contact. Mines may be submerged, laid on the ground, or buried. They are used to cause casualties among ships, vehicles, and troops. See also MINES AND MINING, MILITARY; SUBMARINE MINES, MINE SWEEPERS, AND COUNTERMEASURES.

Morale.—Mental attitude of military personnel toward their duties and to army life and its associations.

Mortar.—Short-barreled, muzzle-loading weapon, usually with a smooth bore. It has a shorter range and a higher angle of fire than a howitzer.

Motorize.—To provide a unit with motor vehicles for transportation. The unit normally dismounts from the vehicles to fight.

Mule.—Low silhouette four-wheel motor vehicle able to carry one half ton of cargo or 5 passengers besides driver. Used for reconnaissance, towing or carrying cannon, etc.

Muzzle Brake.—Device on the muzzle of a gun barrel which utilizes the escaping gases to reduce the recoil.

Napalm.—Substance for thickening gasoline to be used in flame throwers and incendiary bombs. See also separate article CHEMICAL WARFARE—*Incendiaries* (Napalm).

Neutralize.—To render harmless or wipe out enemy troops and equipment by the use of gunfire, bombs, or chemicals. To decontaminate a chemical agent.

Nissen Hut.—Quickly erected, arched shelter of corrugated iron.

Objective.—Military goal, such as a place that a unit has been ordered to occupy, or an enemy force that it has been ordered to overcome.

Offense.—Act of attacking; assault.

Operation.—Military action; combination of all the details of planning and executing a phase of combat.

Order of Battle.—The arrangement of troops, aircraft, or vessels in preparation for attack. The way a military unit is prepared, equipped, and disposed for battle.

Ordnance.—Military equipment, such as weapons, ammunition, combat and special purpose vehicles, and repair tools and machinery.

Outpost.—Security detachment sent out some distance by a halted command or defensive position to protect against surprise, observation, and annoyance by enemy ground forces. See also separate article OUTPOSTS, MILITARY.

Pack Transportation.—Animals, with the required equipment and personnel, used for carrying weapons, ammunition, and supplies on their backs. Pack transportation finds its greatest use in mountainous terrain.

Panzer.—German word meaning "armor." When combined with nouns it means armored, as panzer division, a mechanized, armored offensive force employed specially for attack in coordination with attack aviation.

Parachute.—Folding umbrellalike contrivance, usually of light fabric, which opens and catches the air, retarding the speed of a falling body attached to it. It is used to enable personnel and supplies to be dropped from an aircraft in flight without injury or damage. See also separate article PARACHUTE.

Patrol.—Small group of troops, vehicles, aircraft, or ships assigned to provide security for, or to gain information for, a larger force. See also separate article PATROL, MILITARY.

Pillbox.—Low fortification, containing one or more machine guns or antitank weapons, used to strengthen a defensive line. It is usually constructed of concrete, steel, or filled sandbags.

Ponton Bridge or Pontoon Bridge.—Temporary floating bridge supported by boats, metal cylinders, or other buoyant objects. See also separate article BRIDGE—*10. Movable Bridges* (Pontoon Bridges).

Position in Readiness.—Location in which troops trained and equipped for battle are held ready for instant action, especially when the exact place in battle they will be required has not been determined.

Pyrotechnics.—Flame- or smoke-producing devices used for signaling, illumination, display, or igniting. They may be dropped from aircraft or fired from the ground or vessels. See also separate article PYROTECHNICS.

Quartering.—Assigning shelter for troops, headquarters, establishments, and supplies.

Quartermaster Corps.—Branch of the army responsible for providing food, clothing, shelter, and some types of equipment. See also separate articles QUARTERMASTER; QUARTERMASTER CORPS.

Radar.—Short for radio detection and ranging equipment. Electrical apparatus with which the range, elevation, and direction of movement of objects are detected. The radar transmits radio waves that are reflected by the target back to the receiving apparatus. See also separate article RADAR.

Radio Direction Finder.—Aircraft instrument that receives direction signals from radio stations. By this means the position of the aircraft can be determined.

Raid.—Sudden attack or invasion by troops, aircraft, or naval vessels for the purpose of securing information, harassing or deceiving the enemy. Usually there is no intention of holding the territory invaded.

Railhead (Truckhead, Navigationhead, or Airhead).—Point at which supplies are unloaded, and from which they are distributed or forwarded, usually by another means of transportation.

Range.—Distance from the gun to the target; elevation of a gun necessary to hit a certain target; operating limit, such as the range of a gun or an airplane. Also, area equipped for practice shooting at targets, called target range.

Ration.—Fixed daily allowance of provisions for one soldier. To supply with food. See also separate article, RATIONING.

Recoilless Weapon.—Weapon characterized by a lack of backward movement when fired. It differs from a rocket launcher in that the propelling charge is burned in the chamber of the weapon instead of in an attachment to, or a part of, the projectile. See also PROJECTILES—*Recoilless Rifle Projectiles.*

Reconnaissance.—Examination of an area to gain military information. Reconnaissance may be made from the air, water, or ground. See also separate article RECONNAISSANCE.

Revetment.—Retaining wall of filled sandbags, boards, wire mesh, brush, to prevent steep earthen slopes or other materials from giving way. Often used in fortifications.

Ricochet.—Glancing rebound or skipping of a projectile.

Road Block.—Obstacle to prevent the movement of vehicles along a road. It is usually guarded or covered by fire to prevent its unauthorized removal.

Rocket.—Projectile which is self-propelled by the escape of gases from the rear of the combustion chamber.

Single rockets are fired from the bazooka and other hand-carried rocket launchers. Multiple rockets are fired from launchers mounted on aircraft, ships, tanks, trucks, and trailers. See also separate article ROCKETS.

Roger.—Word used in radiotelephone conversation meaning received. In the phonetic alphabet, it is also the letter *R*.

Sabotage.—Destruction of, or damage to, installations and facilities by agents acting surreptitiously in an attempt to impede the enemy's war effort. See also separate article SABOTAGE.

Salient.—Outwardly projecting part of a battle line or fortification. The corresponding dent in the opposing line is called a re-entrant.

Salvage.—Collection of property (condemned, abandoned, or captured) for reclaiming or scrapping. See also separate article SALVAGE.

Salvo.—Group of shots fired at the same time by a battery, or a group of bombs dropped at the same time by an airplane. One round per gun, in a battery, fired in a prescribed order with a prescribed time interval between shots.

Screen.—Protection from enemy ground reconnaissance or observation, and sometimes from enemy fire. A body of troops, camouflage, smoke, or a feature of the terrain may serve as a screen.

Sector.—Clearly defined subdivision of a defensive position which a given unit, weapon, or individual protects or covers. Sometimes only the areas held by regiments or large units are called sectors.

Security.—Measures taken to prevent the enemy from gaining information. They include the placing of troops to protect against attack and the steps taken to ensure that messages are genuine and that the meaning of the codes and ciphers is not known to the enemy.

Self-propelled Gun.—Artillery piece mounted on a motor vehicle, usually on a track-laying vehicle similar to a tank.

Service.—Military duty. Branch of the army primarily concerned with administration, supply, transportation, or medical care. A combatant branch is called an arm.

Shaped Charge.—Explosive material molded with a cone-shaped depression so that the explosive energy is concentrated in one direction. The shaped charge has great penetrating qualities and is able to blast holes in steel and concrete.

Shock Troops.—Troops specially organized, trained, and equipped for attack and hand-to-hand combat.

Situation Map.—Map showing the tactical and/or administrative situation of a unit at any time. It also shows the known enemy situation.

Small Arms.—Firearms carried on the person and used in the hands. See also separate article SMALL ARMS.

Sniper.—Rifleman, often camouflaged, who fires from a concealed position at detached enemy individuals, frequently at long range using a telescopic sight.

Snooperscope.—Portable device using infrared rays to enable an operator to see in the dark.

Sonar.—Short for sound navigation ranging. A method using high frequency sound waves for the detection and location of moving or stationary objects under water.

Spearhead.—The leading assault troops in an offensive operation. To hold the most advanced position in an attack.

Standing Operating Procedure.—Previously prescribed instructions regarding the procedures to be followed when certain normal conditions exist or situations arise. Abbreviation SOP.

Strafe.—To shell or bombard vigorously, especially to machine-gun and bomb enemy ground positions from low-flying aircraft

Strategy.—Science and art of employing the strength of a nation in gaining and keeping the advantage over the enemy in combat operations, or in winning the most from defeat. Strategy involves planning on a large scale; tactics involves the operations necessary to carry out these plans. See also separate article STRATEGY, MILITARY; TACTICS.

Support.—Assistance or protection given by one element or unit to another, as artillery fire used to support infantry troops. Unit which assists another in combat.

Sweep.—To pass a mine detector over the ground to locate buried mines. To drag the water to locate submerged mines. To cover an area with gunfire. Swift flight of a group of aircraft over enemy territory. The trace produced on the screen of a radar.

Tactics.—Science and art of maneuvering troops and ships in battle. Tactics differs from strategy which refers to the broad plan of a nation at war. See also separate article TACTICS.

Task Force.—Temporary grouping of several units (such as air, infantry, artillery, armor, and engineers) under one commander to perform a specific combat mission.

Terrain.—Area of ground considered in terms of its natural features for use in a military operation.

Theater of Operations.—Combat area, including that portion of the adjacent districts necessary for administration and supply pertaining to combat operations.

Thermite.—Incendiary agent used in projectiles, consisting of powdered aluminum and the oxide of another metal, usually iron. When ignited thermite produces hot molten metal.

Ultimatum.—Final proposition or condition offered by one nation or military force to another, carrying with it a threat of military action if the demands are not met.

Unconditional Surrender.—Act of giving up without reservations or terms.

Unit.—Military organization. A unit may vary in size from a squad of a few men to an army of millions.

Variable-pitch Propeller.—Propeller with blades that can be pitched at different angles while the propeller is in motion.

VT Fuze.—Short for variable-time fuze. Fuze on a shell or a bomb containing a device, normally a small radio, which causes the fuze to operate when it comes within a certain distance of the ground or any object. Used against targets in the air as well as against targets on the ground and water.

War Dog.—Dog trained to perform such special tasks as guard duty, scouting, carrying messages, and searching for the wounded.

War of Masses.—Warfare in which the large number of men involved, rather than the quantity and quality of their equipment, is the deciding factor.

War of Movement.—Mobile warfare characterized by maneuver, initiative, and the seizure of key terrain features.

War of Position.—Warfare characterized by lack of movement and aimed principally at denying strategic areas to the enemy.

Westwall.—Line of defensive fortifications near the western boundary of Germany before and during World War II; Siegfried Line.

Window.—Metallic strips scattered in the air by aircraft, rocket, or shell for the purpose of deceiving a radar operator as to the actual number and location of aircraft in the area.

Y Gun.—Antisubmarine gun, shaped like the letter Y, and usually mounted near the stern of a vessel. It is used to throw depth charges into the water.

Zero Hour.—Hour at which a previously planned attack or operation is initiated; H-hour.

Zone of Operations.—Ground, sea, and air area containing the routes by which an army advances from its base toward its objective.

See also AERONAUTICS—*11. Aeronautics Glossary.*

RICHARD G. THOMAS, JR.,
Colonel, United States Army (Retired).

MILITARY TRAINING. See MILITARY EDUCATION AND TRAINING.

MILITARY TRANSPORTATION. See ARMY TRANSPORTATION SERVICE; LOGISTICS, MILITARY.

MILITARY UNIFORMS. See UNIFORMS, ARMED FORCES.

MILITIA, mĭ-lĭsh'ȧ, a Latin word meaning "military service," first used in English about 1590. It now is applied to a military force composed of citizens available for service in emergencies. The basic concept of the militia—that every free man has the right and duty to bear arms in defense of national freedom, law, and order—is practically universal. Among primitive peoples, the tribal fighting force of necessity included all able-bodied males. From this developed the concept of linked political and military responsibility and privilege. In the city-states of Greece, among the Germanic and Celtic tribes, and in early Rome, youths were admitted to manhood by qualifying as fighting men. The whole population of free men met to vote on the question of peace or war. If they chose war, they formed themselves into the army that fought it. Consequently, the militia was from the beginning a democratic institution, in contrast to the professional armies of monarchies.

Such a force, however capable for home defense, always proved unsatisfactory during long wars, especially those involving operations against distant enemies. Such campaigns kept the citizen-soldier absent from his farm or trade for ruinously long periods; they also demanded a higher level of military competence and specialization than the citizen-soldier could offer. As a result, the long-service professional gradually replaced the Greek and Roman citizen-soldier, and the average civilian generally lost what interest and competence in military matters he once had.

England.—The collapse of Rome led to the revival of European militias. In England by 605 A.D., this appeared in the fyrd, a levy of all able-bodied freemen, locally organized and controlled. By 894, an increasing population made it possible to leave half of the fyrd to work the farms while the other half campaigned. After the Norman Conquest (1066), the fyrd, or general levy, was replaced by the feudal levy, a form of militia based on tenure of land and mutual obligation between lord and vassal. The English kings, however, appreciated the value of a general levy as a counterweight to a turbulent nobility. King Henry II's Assize of Arms (1181) and Edward I's Statute of Winchester (1285) ruled that all free men must provide themselves with arms and armor "for to keep the peace," though it was eventually established that this levy, as such, could not be required to serve outside the kingdom.

From the 12th century to the 16th century, the organization of the militia was slowly improved. "Trained bands" or "train bands" were organized in each county, under the supervision of a royal officer, later titled a "lord lieutenant." By the time of the Spanish Armada (1588), the decay of England's feudal system had left this militia the only armed force available for the land defense of the kingdom. Fortunately, English sailors stood between it and the Spanish veterans. During the English Civil War (1642–1649), only the London train bands proved of much value; but so strong was popular feeling against standing armies following the Restoration (1660) that many Englishmen wished to rely upon the militia alone for national defense. Since both officers and men of the militia were locally selected and paid, the militia was considered a safeguard against possible royal despotism.

A series of foreign wars, plus the militia's poor showing in 1745 against Bonnie Prince Charlie, the Stuart pretender to the throne, made a professional army again necessary. After 1757, service in the militia was determined by lot. The Napoleonic Wars led to the use of the militia as a source of replacements for the Regular Army, the old general levy being reinstituted in 1808 for home defense. After 1815, the English militia was gradually replaced by various volunteer formations, and control was increasingly invested in the crown. Almost disregarded during and after World War I, it reappeared during World War II in the form of the Home Guard and various civil defense services; the latter may be regarded as a new type of militia made necessary by changing conditions of warfare. Present English military policy appears to be continuing this specialization.

Western Europe, Communist China, and Soviet Russia.—In continental Europe, the militia system largely disappeared during the Middle Ages, though the burgher militia of the Low Countries and Lombardy, organized around the trade guilds, and the Swiss general levies established themselves as formidable fighting forces. In France, Louis VI (r. 1108–1137) organized a burgher militia to defeat his nobles. The militia finally developed by the 18th century into provincial units, resembling the British militia. The French Revolution produced the National Guard, which Napoleon I reorganized into a general militia.

During the 19th century, compulsory military service generally replaced the militia system throughout Europe. Only Switzerland has continued to rely upon a citizen-militia for defense, and even in Switzerland the system is becoming outmoded as longer periods of active service are necessitated by the increasing complexity of modern weapons. Communist China maintains a loosely organized militia, comprising all politically reliable, able-bodied citizens, to ensure internal security. In Soviet Russia, the term "militia" is now applied to the civil police.

American Colonies.—In North America, early colonists—whether English, French, or Dutch—were continually threatened by Indian attack and famine. The only chance for survival was for every male colonist to be both soldier and settler. Consequently, the traditional general levy, now beginning to be called militia, was revived. The 1611 codification of laws for Virginia set forth the detailed organization of this militia, warning the governor to harden his men by daily exercise in armor. By 1634, the Virginia organization was fully developed after the English model, the colony being divided into counties, each of which was supervised by a "lieutenant." Other Southern colonies adopted the same system, but in New England and New York the towns, rather than the counties, were the basic units of militia organization. In 1636, Massachusetts grouped its town train bands into three regiments. One of these, the old North Regiment, exists today as the 182d Infantry Regiment.

The growing population of the colonies led to a gradual change in the military system. Universal service was found only on the frontier. Colonial troops for service against the French (1689–1763) were normally raised by ordinary recruiting, though the legal obligation for universal militia service remained in force, and local musters for review, inspection, and drill, were still held. On the approach of the American Revolution, the patriots gained control of the militia. If its conduct in battle was often poor, at least it was available for smothering Loyalist movements, reinforcing the Continental Army in emergencies, and harassing British detachments.

United States.—Following the revolution, Congress reduced its Army to 80 men, since they held it to be "dangerous to the liberties of a free people." In 1792, it enacted that all free, able-bodied white male citizens between 18 and 45 were to be enrolled in the militia by local authorities and organized into brigades and divisions by the state governors. Militiamen were to provide their own weapons and equipment. Although this militia was capable of overawing domestic disturbances like Shays' Rebellion (1786–1787) and the Whiskey Insurrection (1794), it proved relatively useless in frontier fighting and had to be largely replaced there by regular troops. The 1792 law was largely unenforced; annual musters were frequently farcical. Except when led by officers like Andrew Jackson and Jacob Brown, militia units performed poorly during the War of 1812, sometimes refusing to serve outside their state or to cross the Canadian frontier.

Thereafter, militia service tended to become

voluntary. Local groups organized themselves into military units with little or no assistance from state authorities. Many of them were from the socially elite and wealthy; others represented immigrant groups, particularly Irish and Germans. Their political influence was considerable; some, like the Richmond Light Infantry Blues and the New York 7th Regiment, have become part of American military tradition. In 1840, Massachusetts abolished all of its militia establishment except for these volunteers. Other states soon followed. This volunteer militia played a very minor part in the Mexican War, but its units increased in number through the years preceding the Civil War. Haphazard as their instruction might be, such units provided the cadre of many Civil War regiments for both North and South, and furnished many partially trained officers. Except for Abraham Lincoln's initial call for 75,000 militia for three months' service, however, all Civil War levies were for individuals, either as volunteers or drafted men. The militia units continued to exist, were useful for internal security duty, but did no fighting except when called up to supplement the field armies in emergencies such as the invasion of Pennsylvania by the Confederates under Robert E. Lee in 1863.

Demobilization after the Civil War left the volunteer militia (soon to be termed the National Guard) the nation's only available reserve force. Its failures during the 1877 railroad strike led to the establishment of the National Guard Association. Most National Guard units volunteered for Spanish-American War service, but a few (notably the New York 7th Regiment) refused. These refusals and the lack of efficiency of many of the willing units resulted in the repeal (1903) of the Militia Act of 1792. The volunteer National Guard became the "organized militia," organized, trained, and equipped in the same manner as the Regular Army. In 1916, it was made subject to federal standards of efficiency and to federal control for any type of emergency, the federal government in turn assuming responsibility for the Guard's drill pay. The beginnings of an officers' and an enlisted men's reserve were authorized. In 1917, the National Guard regiments lost their historic state designations; in 1933, the Guard was definitely given the additional status of a reserve component of the Army.

The Reserve Forces Act of 1955 set up a United States Reserve Force of seven components: Army National Guard, Army Reserve, Naval Reserve, Marine Corps Reserve, Air National Guard, Air Force Reserve, and Coast Guard Reserve. The Reserve elements are completely federal forces, but the National Guard, when not on active federal service, is under the control of the respective states in which it is organized. These units maintain the American militia tradition; otherwise the former functions of the fyrd levy have been replaced by selective service.

See also CONSCRIPTION; NATIONAL GUARD.

Consult Oman, Charles, *Art of War in the Middle Ages, A.D. 378–1485*, rev. ed. (New York 1924); Spaulding, Oliver L., Nickerson, Hoffman, and Wright, John W., *Warfare to 1790* (Washington 1937); Ganoe, William A., *History of the United States Army*, rev. ed. (New York 1942); Jacobs, James R., *Beginning of the U.S. Army, 1783–1812* (Princeton 1947); Millis, Walter, *Arms and Men* (New York 1956).

JOHN R. ELTING,
Lieutenant Colonel, United States Army; Department of Military Art and Engineering, United States Military Academy.

MILITIA, Canadian. See CANADA—*24. Defense*.

MILITIA, Naval. See NAVAL RESERVE.

MILIUM, mĭl'ĭ-ŭm, a skin disease caused by the retention of the secretion of the sebaceous glands, resulting in small, white or yellowish-white globules the size of a pinhead or less, constituting a minute tumor. It usually forms around the eyes, on the cheeks or forehead, although it also occurs on other parts of the body. The tiny tumor, lying just beneath the skin and slightly raised above its surface, may undergo calcification, but at no time in the process of its formation nor in its continued presence is there inflammation. In some cases it disappears in the course of the continuous change in the cuticle.

MILK, mĭlk, the normal secretion by the mammary glands of female mammals for the nourishment of their young. It is a whitish liquid consisting of small globules of fat suspended in a watery solution containing proteins, sugar, and minerals.

The milk of various mammals differs in composition and there is no legal definition of milk. Because of its value commercially, cow's milk, however, is generally meant. The suggested definition of the United States Food and Drug Administration states: "Milk is the whole fresh lacteal secretion obtained by the complete milking of one or more healthy cows, excluding that obtained 15 days before and 5 days after calving, or such longer period as may be necessary to render the milk practically colostrum (first milk after calving) free."

Milk is important economically. In the United States, dairying ranks first as a source of farm income; more than one seventh of the cash receipts of farmers is obtained from milk alone. Milk accounts for about one eighth of the cash income of Canadian farmers. Some other countries are even more dependent upon milk and milk products as a source of farm income. Finland so obtains one half of its farm income, and Norway about three eighths. Milk supplies about one third of the farmer's income in Denmark, New Zealand, and Sweden, and one quarter of the return to farmers in Ireland and the Netherlands.

Production of milk on United States farms averaged over 120 billion pounds annually in the 1960's, of which more than 110 billion pounds were sold. The average per capita consumption of fluid milk and cream in the United States in the same period was over 300 pounds yearly.

Constituents of Milk.—Milk is the first food of the newborn mammal. Man's use of the milk of other animals precedes written history. Fresh milk is highly palatable and its constituents easily digestible. It requires no preparation for use as a food, except for some slight modification and sterilizing for infants.

The nutrients of cow's milk are designed to supply a calf with the necessary food for its rapid growth, yet it contains some fraction of most of the food requirements of humans. According to the National Research Council, a quart of milk supplies about one fifth of the calories required daily by an average-weight man and one half the protein; about one quarter of the vitamin A and thiamine requirements are met and 80 per cent of the riboflavin. A quart of milk contains more than a sufficient amount of calcium to meet the daily intake needed.

Like most foods, milk is largely water; about 87.65 per cent of cow's milk is no different from drinking water. The water serves to hold in solution the soluble contents of milk.

The fat in milk, called milk fat or butterfat, is commercially the most valuable constituent of milk. It is the fat which imparts to milk much of its palatability and agreeable flavor. Milk fat also is responsible for much of the food energy and nutritive value of milk. The fat content averages 3.70 per cent.

Milk fat is not a simple compound, but is a variable mixture of several different glycerides. Each glyceride is an ester, or formation caused by a joining of glycerol with an organic acid. There are at least 10 fatty acids in milk and there may be more. Butyric acid gives butter its characteristic taste and is largely responsible for the flavor of cream.

Proteins are the most complex of chemical substances and their precise composition is not yet known. They contain carbon, hydrogen, oxygen, and nitrogen; sulphur and phosphorus are also present in small amounts. Protein is an indispensable food of man and animals. Several proteins in varying amounts account for 3.20 per cent of the milk. The principal protein is casein, accounting for about 80 per cent of all milk protein material. No other natural protein is similar to casein; in milk it is found in combination with calcium. In addition to its high value as food, casein is also important industrially.

Lactalbumin is another protein. It resembles blood albumin, but is not of the same composition. Most albumin has a high sulphur content. A third protein, lactoglobulin, formerly thought to be an independent substance, is now believed to be a component of albumin. The nutritive value of these three proteins together is greater than the total separately. They are, in fact, complementary.

There are small amounts of other proteins in milk, although not all have been identified. Enzymes are substances of a protein nature in milk and are important as catalysts.

A substance found only in milk is lactose, or milk sugar. Unlike other sugars it is practically tasteless. Simply, lactose can be said to be made up of one molecule of glucose, a sugar found in the blood, and one molecule of galactose. Lactose comprises 4.75 per cent of the milk and has a high nutritional value. It is also the only source of galactose, a substance found in brain and nerve tissue. A primary commercial use of lactose is in the preparation of baby foods.

About 0.70 per cent of milk is composed of minerals or salts of milk (sometimes designated as ash). They are the same as are found in the body, although not in the same proportion. Milk is deficient in iron, but the other minerals make milk a premier source of supply of minerals for humans.

Of the minor constituents of milk, enzymes have already been mentioned. Others are phospholipids, fat-like substances containing phosphoric acid; cholesterol, a sterol (naturally occurring solid alcohol) which helps maintain the stability of the fat emulsion; pigments; gases and nitrogenous materials which are not proteins or vitamins. Among the vitamins in milk are A, B, B_2, B_5, C, D, E, K and niacin and pantothenic acid.

Milk Secretion.—Milk is a glandular material produced by myriads of cells which make up the mammary glands. In the cow there are four glands grouped together in a structure called the udder. Each of the four glands is separated from the others in a section called a quarter; each quarter has a teat for the removal of milk.

Two large arteries, one on each side, run to the udder. The arteries branch into continually smaller tubes as they carry blood from the heart to all parts of the udder. As it passes through the udder, the blood bathes the cells which form into billions of pear-shaped, hollow structures, the alveoli, and the major constituents of milk —the fat, casein, and lactose—are synthesized and manufactured into milk. The alveoli, when full, discharge the milk into an inner cavity. The teat is below each of these milk cisterns and the milk, which is present in these cistern cavities, the ducts, the alveoli, and the individual cells themselves, is withdrawn through the teat during each complete milking.

Experimental work has established that hormones, special chemical messengers carried by the blood, are responsible for the growth of the udder and the duct and alveoli systems. The udder itself grows normally, as any other organ, as a dairy calf grows older. As the animal passes into the young adult stage with the beginning of the estrous cycle, a profound change is made in the udder in the development of the ducts. With pregnancy the udder begins to assume its definite form. The tube growth is completed and the alveoli evolve from the duct end buds of the immature gland. During the latter part of pregnancy the secretory function of the alveoli cells is begun, but extensive lactation does not start until after the birth of the calf.

The exact physiological mechanism controlling the start of milk secretion is not known although several theories have been advanced on the release of the hormone prolactin which initiates lactation. After birth of the calf, milk is maintained by the stimulus of the suckling of the calf and the washing of the udder preparatory to milking which apparently release a "let down" hormone causing the alveoli to initiate the flow of milk.

Breeds of Milk Cows.—The dairy cow is a most efficient converter of plants to food, but there are differences in the abilities between cows and between breeds.

Among the main dairy breeds are the Ayrshire, Brown Swiss, Guernsey, Holstein, and Jersey. In addition, there are several minor breeds and some dual-purpose cattle, those developed for meat and milk production.

The Ayrshire cow is white and red, the white predominating, and reaches an average weight of 1,200 pounds. The cow is a full-bodied animal and has a regular conformation. The udder of the Ayrshire is rated highly for balance, uniformity, and teat placement. A mature cow should yield annually 10,000 pounds of milk with a butterfat content of 4 per cent.

The Brown Swiss is large bodied, and mature cows may often reach 1,500 pounds. The average yearly yield is approximately 11,000 pounds of 4 per cent butterfat milk.

The Guernsey, a lemon or orange fawn cattle, is known for its adaptability to extremes of climate and for the rich butterfat of the milk. The butterfat content of Guernsey milk is about 5 per cent in the yield of 6,000 to 7,000 pounds of milk given per year.

The Holstein-Friesan, with its nonblending black and white markings, is the most popular breed of dairy cattle in the United States. Mature cows average over 1,300 pounds and some may weigh as much as 1,600 pounds. The Holstein cow is a large and efficient user of roughage and is the heaviest milk producer, although the milk fat content is about 3.5 per cent. Herd Improvement Registry data show annual average yields of 11,500 pounds. The record high single year yield of over 38,500 pounds is held by a Holstein.

Jersey cattle have solid colors with black points. The breed is the smallest of the major dairy types, being somewhat smaller than the Guernsey; a mature cow seldom exceeds 1,000 pounds in weight. She has the ideal dairy wedge-shape conformation, a large barrel, and a well-developed udder. A Jersey cow is a very efficient converter of feed to milk. She is an easily kept cow if properly cared for, but is inclined to nervousness and low yield if carelessly handled. A yearly milk yield of 6,500 pounds is average and a fat content of over 5 per cent is not unusual.

Among the minor breeds, the Dutch Belted cow is probably descended from the original Holland Holsteins. The French-Canadian breed is a native of Normandy and closely related to the Guernsey and Jersey breeds. The Kerry and Dexter breeds originated in Ireland and are the smallest of dairy cattle. The Devon is a small but hardy and strong dairy animal from Britain. The Red Danish breed was first imported by the United States Department of Agriculture in 1935.

A dual-purpose cow produces a fair amount of milk for a dairy cow and will fatten readily and sell at a fair price for a beef animal. The Milking Shorthorn, of English origin, and the Red Poll breed, a hornless variety, are popular in areas where fattening out grains are produced. See also CATTLE—*1. The Cattle Family.*

Dairy Farms.—Since the turn of the century dairying has developed from a family cow business to a highly specialized industry. The degree of specialization is often due to physical as well as economic factors. The climate, topography, soil, the type and location of markets are all important in determining the type of farm operation.

Regardless of size, in order to ensure quality milk production, proper management (husbandry) practices must be followed. The barn area must be well planned and well equipped and efficiently maintained to ensure a healthy herd. Adequate fresh water must be available. Palatable feed and roughage, supplemented by concentrates, should be fed in balanced rations. Hay and silage space must be available for crops which should be harvested and stored to maintain the optimum nutrient values.

Two general housing methods are the stall barn and the loose-housing system. In the stall method cows are maintained in individual areas, usually with stanchion arrangements. Here, during inclement weather, they are rested, fed, watered, and possibly milked. In the loose-housing procedure, the cows are free to move about in either open or closed type structures.

In the latter type of accommodations, a separate milking shed or milking parlor must be provided. Such a structure is also preferable to stall milking; in some instances local health codes require separate milking facilities regardless of the housing. An adjacent milk room should be available for the straining, cooling, and storing of the milk until delivery to the plant. The room may also serve for the cleaning and storing of utensils and the milking machine.

In the industrialized countries, the milking machine is gradually replacing the milking of cows by hand. The cow's udder is first cleaned and a small amount of milk is "stripped" from the teat. Teat cups are connected to each teat and the milk drawn by vacuum suction through the action of pulsators operated electrically. With a machine, a cow may be milked in 3 minutes. In some instances each cow's milk is drawn separately into a pail, but in large dairy farms the milk from each of several machines goes di-

Diagram shows the principal parts of a dairy stall barn. Pen shown is for the youngest calves; other young stock would be housed separately.

Hoard's Dairyman

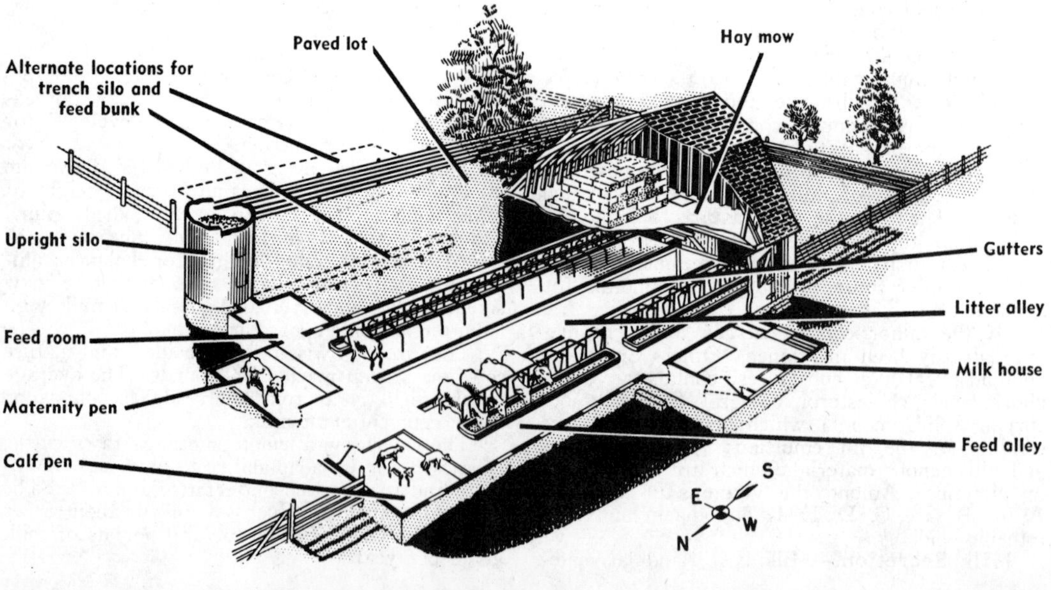

rectly to the cooler or refrigeration tank through a milk pipeline. This bulk handling has improved quality and greatly reduced the labor involved.

Mechanical feeders and field chopping machines also have cut labor time. New insecticides for the control of flies and pests reduce the possibility of contamination of milk and the spread of disease among the cattle.

Standards and Tests.—Milk is a highly perishable item and its distribution and sale is subject to regulations from local, state, and national governments. Milk delivered in cities is subject to local and state regulations in which the emphasis is on sanitary requirements in production and handling; state authorities also set general standards on quality of milk products. Milk and milk products entering interstate commerce are subject to regulation by the United States Public Health Service, and to the Food and Drug Administration of the United States Department of Health, Education, and Welfare. In addition, plants manufacturing dairy products establish conditions to be met for milk delivered for processing; while not always as stringent as government regulations, these measures provide for a good quality milk.

Marketing can be said to begin even before the milk has been produced. The first requirement is healthy cows. The cows must be clean and milked in clean surroundings, which often are required to be buildings separate from the barn or lot areas. All utensils must be of approved construction and must be properly cleaned and sterilized. Filters should be discarded after one use. Milk should be immediately cooled to 60° F. or less and this temperature maintained until pickup or delivery. To ensure compliance with these principal requirements and the more stringent modifications which may be imposed, particularly for milk for fluid consumption, the farms are liable to rigid inspections.

The milk is subject to various tests for quality. A butterfat test is made to determine the fat content. The test invented by Dr. Stephen M. Babcock of Wisconsin in 1890 is performed by treating milk with sulphuric acid to dissolve the nonfat solids that are in suspension and to liquefy the fat. The solution is then centrifuged to separate the milk fat.

A sediment (cleanliness) test is made by filtering a pint sample of milk through a cotton disk which is then dried and observed for sediment. Milk quality in regard to bacteria count may be determined by adding methylene blue and noting the time necessary to decolorize the sample; the longer the time required, the less the chemical activities of the microorganisms and the better the quality of the milk. Another microorganism test measures the number of the colonies. In this plate count test a small amount of milk is mixed with liquefied agar at 115° F. and spread on a sterile glass slide and allowed to harden for three hours or more. The plate is cooled, stained with methylene blue, and the colonies counted under a microscope.

The acidity of milk is determined by measuring the amount of sodium hydroxide required to neutralize the acid-reacting substances in a given amount of a milk sample. Fresh milk is very slightly acid and the amount of sodium hydroxide needed to neutralize this slight acid content is a measure of the apparent acidity. Any increase beyond this amount is a result of fermentation.

The total solids content of milk is obtained by combining lactometer and fat test results. The lactometer, a cylindrical instrument, is based on the principle that a floating body is pushed upward by a force equal to the weight of the displaced liquid. The measurement is a comparison with the specific gravity of pure water, which is 1.0. The specific gravity of normal, fresh milk is 1.032.

Courtesy Carnation Company

A laboratory worker tests butterfat content in a delicate balance capable of weighing a pencil's dot.

The Dairy Plant.—The great bulk of milk is handled and processed through various types of dairy plants. The plant which handles market milk (milk which is intended for fluid consumption) also uses some of the surplus in the manufacture of dairy products. Its main activity, however, is concerned with the receiving, processing, bottling, and sale of milk.

Milk is delivered to the plant receiving room where it is weighed and sampled for quality and milk fat content before being passed to a cooler. Since not all milk is of the same milk fat content, the first step in processing is the blending, often termed standardizing, of the milk to the desired composition. The milk is then passed to another room for pasteurization.

Pasteurization improves the keeping quality by destroying most of the microorganisms affecting the composition or palatability of the milk. It is performed by two general methods. In the holding process, milk is heated to 143° F. and held at this temperature for at least 30 minutes. In the other method, the milk is heated to 161° F. and, because of the higher temperature, needs to be so heated for only 16 seconds. In either procedure the milk is transferred immediately to coolers to inhibit the growth of microorganisms not affected by the heat.

Some consumers are content merely with pasteurized milk, while others want the milk fortified with vitamin D; still other buyers may demand that the milk also be homogenized. The volume of the dairy milk receipts that a market milk dealer moves through each of these processes depends on his estimate of the demand.

The homogenizer is a high pressure pump of

Courtesy Carnation Company

In spray-dryers, hot air converts liquid milk into powder.

one or more cylinders. The milk is drawn by suction through an inlet valve and forced out under pressure through a small discharge valve against a metal plate. The fat clumps are thus broken up and the size of the fat globules reduced. This dispersion of the fat increases the viscosity of the milk and makes a more stable emulsion. Milk may be fortified with vitamin D by subjecting thin films of milk to ultraviolet light, but vitamin D is now usually added as an oil emulsion.

When processing has been completed, the milk is delivered to the bottling or packaging room where it is machine measured into containers which are then sealed or capped automatically. The use of paper containers has found widespread consumer acceptance, primarily because there is no problem of bottle returns. The paper container is more expensive since it can be used only once while glass bottles are re-used many times. At one time there was a considerable sale of milk in pint containers; now consumer preference is for the quart and two quart sizes. In some markets, gallon containers are popular.

Grades and Types of Milk and Fluid Milk Products.—In order to extend his service and to sell more of his milk at market milk levels or above, the dealer may also provide certain grades of milk and other fluid milk products. Among the refinements in market milk is that of certified milk. In 1892, Dr. Henry L. Coit, a New Jersey physician, demanded a superior quality milk. He, and other physicians, selected a dairyman who agreed to follow rigid sanitation practices. The term "certified milk" has since been registered in the United States Patent Office. Certified milk commands a higher price than other market milk.

In addition to the various types and grades of market milk, the dealer handles specialty milk—the most common of which is cream. Cream is the sweet, fatty liquid in the milk and is obtained by centrifugal separation. Market cream usually tests between 18 and 40 per cent milk fat, with the heavier cream being used for whipping. Recently, cereal cream, or "half and half," has become a popular market milk item.

Since nonfat, or skim, milk contains all the nutrients except the milk fat, it has become a popular dairy beverage. Often a flavor is added and the nonfat milk is sold under such names as strawberry milk drink and chocolate milk drink. (Flavoring may also be added to whole milk.) The chocolate drink, for example, contains about one part chocolate sirup to 9 parts nonfat milk. A stabilizer, like gelatin, is used to raise the viscosity of the milk and to hold the sirup in suspension.

Cottage cheese is a soft product made from nonfat milk. Creamed cottage cheese has had homogenized cream added so the fat content is 4 per cent by weight of the finished product.

Buttermilk is a byproduct of buttermaking. It contains about 8.5 per cent or more of the nonfat solids and a small part of the fat lost in the churning process. A cultured buttermilk is also an item of market milk. It is prepared principally from fresh skim milk by the addition of bacteria which will produce the desired flavor and quantity of lactic acid. To imitate more closely natural buttermilk, small amounts of melted butter or butterfat particles are added.

Fermented milk beverages have long been known. Under primitive conditions and lacking refrigeration, milk was often highly contaminated with many microorganisms and fermentation took place in the milk. The beverages obtained by accident are today duplicated under sanitary conditions. The acid-type fermentations, such as cultured buttermilk, cause part of the lactose to change to lactic acid. The other is a combined gas and acid fermentation, forming acid and alcohol from the lactose and breaking down a portion of the protein. Bulgaricus milk and leban are examples of the former type, while kumiss and yogurt (yoghurt) are fermented beverages. Acidophilus milk is the product of a friendly culture (*Lactobacillus acidophilus*). Low sodium milk, for those on special diets, is available. These days, in urban communities, unpasteurized milk itself has become a "specialty" milk for those that prefer it.

Ice cream is no longer considered a luxury product, but is looked upon as a staple food item. While technically classed as a manufactured dairy product, it is an important item in the market milk industry. Ice cream may contain a variety of ingredients, but it is essentially a "frozen" product made from cream and sugar with (or without) a natural flavoring and a stabilizer. There are various state standards for ice cream, but generally the fat content is 10 per cent or more.

Manufacturing Milk.—Since many farms are not within market milkshed areas or cannot qualify for fluid milk deliveries, their milk must be sent to processing plants for manufacture into dairy products. Most of the milk for processing is sold for the making of butter. Over one third of the milk produced in 18 of the major dairying countries is used for buttermaking.

Formerly a large part of the milk fat for buttermaking was delivered as farm-separated cream, with farmers retaining the skim milk for feeding purposes. With the recognition of the nutritive value of skim milk, more of the nonfat solids are being used for human consumption and more of the receipts at creameries are in the form of whole milk. The creamery operator separates the milk, using the cream for butter and either processing the skim milk at the creamery or selling it to special plants.

Milk which has been machine skimmed contains very little milk fat. Water comprises over 90 per cent, proteins about 3.75 per cent, lactose slightly less than 5 per cent, and mineral matter about 0.8 per cent. There are numerous products which can be made from skim milk. As mentioned previously, some food items are cottage cheese, cultured buttermilk, flavored milk drinks, and certain skim milk cheeses. Among industrial items are casein products, paint, plastics, and bristles.

Skimmed milk is also processed by drying. This process has become increasingly used since World War II. In the United States, for example, on the basis of nonfat solids only, about one eighth of the milk supplied is processed by drying. The products are becoming increasingly popular for home use where reconstitution by adding water gives a palatable, nutritive beverage. Bakeries, confectioneries, and meat processors are large users of dry milk. About one eighth of the milk production of 18 of the major dairy countries goes to the manufacture of cheese. A wide variety of cheeses is produced. See also CHEESE AND CHEESE MAKING.

Canned milk is the term given to sweetened condensed and evaporated milks because they are sold to consumers in small cans. Evaporated milk is made by reducing the water content of milk by about one half, homogenizing, and then sterilizing. Sweetened condensed milk is similarly treated except that it is not sterilized and sugar is added as a preservative.

Whole milk is also dried. Much of the United States production has been exported. Lately this market has been declining because of the increased competition of other suppliers and the development of the milk industry in the importing countries.

Milk Pricing in the United States.—Milk for manufacturing purposes can be considered a competitive product in that it may easily be shifted from one type plant to another if the stronger market for the product of the second plant is such as to cause the operators to raise their prices in order to obtain more milk. There is, however, a floor beneath which prices cannot go without the federal government supporting the market by buying certain dairy products at previously announced prices.

The farmer selling market milk knows what the prices for fluid milk and manufacturing milk are in his particular market, but he does not know what his return per hundredweight will be because his return is determined by the use to which his milk is put. This system, called classified pricing, is weighted average pricing.

There are generally two classes of milk in the market areas (there may be more or there may be subdivisions within classes). If only two classes, the first class is that used as market milk—fluid milk and cream, and certain specialty milk products—and usually commands a premium of $2 or more per hundredweight, depending on the market. The other class is usually priced at the general level of prices being obtained for manufacturing milk. If the milk supply at any given time is divided equally between class uses, the price the farmer receives is an average midway between the two class prices. During the flush production months when milk supplies are large and a larger proportion goes to manufacture, the average price is closer to the manufacturing level; the opposite is true in times of reduced production.

Some dealers in any given market at any given time may have a larger amount of their

The Rotolactor holds 50 cows, takes 10 minutes to make a revolution, and milks 275 cows an hour.

Walker-Gordon Laboratory Co.

Courtesy Pure-Pak Division of the Excello Corporation

In today's plants, the glass milk bottle has been replaced by a wax-impregnated paper carton.

receipts directed toward fluid milk than do other dealers. To prevent switching of dealers to obtain the highest average price, the pricing mechanism called the market pool may be established. The pool is a method of arranging a classified price by the market rather than by individual dealers. The total milk of all dealers going to fluid use and manufacture is used as determinants of the average or blend price received by every farmer. An equalization fund is set up to facilitate the payment of the market blend price in an equitable manner. A dealer who sold more milk as fluid milk than the market average would owe the fund, while a dealer putting most of his milk to manufacture during the period would have a fund credit.

The marketing of milk through stores or home delivery has been a dealer problem since the 1930's. Since a dealer can deliver milk to stores in large quantities, the price to the store may be from 3 to 4 cents less than the price for a single unit delivered at homes; chain stores may be granted additional quantity discounts. If the store's margin is not much over 2 cents a quart, the price at the store can be kept under the home-delivered price. There is, however, a matter of competition in that stores usually handle only two or possibly three different brands of milk and the use of home delivery service is a means of maintaining sales and obtaining brand name recognition.

Milk Around the World.—Asia presents the extremes in the use of milk. In China, there is a cultural aversion to milk. In India the only source of animal proteins to many is milk and the need far exceeds the supply. Milk which is not consumed at once is processed into ghee, a dehydrated butter, and khoa, buffalo milk concentrated by boiling and stirring, and which is often allowed to dry into a powder.

In the New Hebrides, milk is not used at all. In Tanganyika, women are forbidden to touch milk and in neighboring Uganda the men of the tribes must abstain. The desert nomad people of Asia and Africa are fond of milk although the supply is extremely limited. Milk boiled with rice and flour makes a favorite dish of the desert Bedouin.

In the Far North, the Laplanders obtain from their reindeer a milk high in fat. The summer's supply of milk is made into a rich, crumbly cheese to be eaten during the long winter. In mountainous northern China, the yak cow also gives a rich milk. It is seldom, if ever, drunk by the tribesmen, but is made into butter and the buttermilk is boiled and dried in the sun before it is used as a food.

In ancient times, milk which was not consumed immediately was allowed to ferment. In many parts of the world today milk is allowed to ferment. In parts of Mongolia mare's milk is used to make an alcoholic fermented beverage called airak, or kumiss. In the Carpathian Mountains, the people make cheese and ferment the whey; the product, shuta, is quite alcoholic. The most popular fermented drink is yogurt, particularly in the Middle East and the Balkans. It is prepared by reducing the volume of milk as much as one half by boiling. After cooling, a starter is added and the product set aside for 12 hours. Yogurt is nonalcoholic and is found extensively around the world under different names.

In the Western Hemisphere, since milk from animals is of relatively recent origin, fermented milks are little known. Surplus milk in Latin American countries is utilized primarily in the manufacture of indigenous soft cheeses.

For the history of milk see DAIRY INDUSTRY; also see separate articles on the various milk products.

Bibliography.—Eckles, Clarence H., Combs, W. B., and Macy, H. W., *Milk and Milk Products,* 4th ed. (New York 1951); Espe, D., and Smith, V. R., *Secretion of Milk,* 4th ed. (Ames, Iowa, 1952); Petersen, W. E., and Field, A. M., *Dairy Farming* (New York 1953); Davis, John G., *A Dictionary of Dairying,* 2d ed. rev. and enl. (London 1955); McCabe, Terrence W., *The Pattern of World Milk Production,* Foreign Agricultural Service, U.S. Dept. of Agriculture (Washington 1955); *Farmers and Farm Production in the U.S.,* vol. 3, part 9, chap. 5, U.S. Departments of Commerce and Agriculture (Washington 1956); Frandsen, Julius H., ed., *Dairy Handbook and Dictionary* (Amherst, Mass., 1958); *Milk Production on Farms and Statistics of Dairy Plants, 1958,* Agricultural Marketing Service, U.S. Dept. of Agriculture (Washington 1959); *The Dairy Situation,* Agricultural Marketing Service, U.S. Dept. of Agriculture (bimonthly, Washington 1958 and 1959).

TERRENCE W. MCCABE,
Agricultural Economist and Dairy Marketing Specialist, Foreign Agricultural Service, United States Dept. of Agriculture.

MILK FEVER, a fever occurring in females at the time of lactation. In veterinary medicine, it is a curable disease occurring in dairy cattle upon parturition, not to be confused with milk sickness (q.v.).

MILK IN SYMBOLISM AND FOLKLORE. Since milk holds a primary position among the natural foods of man, it is not surprising to find that it has played a variety of roles in his religions, folk legends, and superstitions. Man's first use of milk from domesticated animals began in prehistoric times, and by the time written testimony appears, the production of milk and milk products was already a well-developed home industry, as is evidenced by Homer's description (*Odyssey* IX; 248f.) of goat milking in the cave of Polyphemus. However, in spite of its economic importance throughout the ages, milk probably owes its manifold symbolism more to the marvel of its origin and life-nourishing function than to man's dependence on it as food.

In the religion of the primitive Toda tribes of southern India, milk forms the most sacred element; the dairy is the most important tribal organization, and the gods assist in its operation. At their death rites, milk is fed to the dying, and after death the body is placed in the dairy. The Hereros of western Africa also use milk as an important element in their rites for the dead, at which it is consecrated and after which a small amount is left near the grave. Numerous milk superstitions are found among other primitive tribes: the Bahima and the Masai of East Africa believe that the cattle will die if their milk is boiled; the Zulus believe a wounded man must be purified before he may drink milk; among the Hottentots, the milk containers and the rams are touched by a pubescent girl for good luck; and the Gallas of East Africa rub their sacred trees with blood, butter, and milk to keep them from decaying.

In some ancient civilizations milk became the symbol for nourishment. In Egypt, the sky goddess was depicted either as a full-breasted woman or a cow, and milk was the food she gave to the deified kings as they entered their celestial childhood; but it was otherwise of little importance in Egyptian mythology. In Indian Vedic literature, the earth is spoken of as a mother who pours forth milk to her worshipers (Athar Veda IX: iii, 16) and ritual offerings combine both milk and honey (Rig Veda VIII: iv, 8); both the latter, however, were subordinate to soma, the sacred drink of the Hindus, just as the same combination seems to have been subordinate to wine in Graeco-Roman rites. How this combined use of milk and honey originated is not known; it is found in several traditions, representing either the best and purest in food, or, in its Biblical use (Exodus 3:8 and elsewhere), fertility, as the fertility of Palestine.

The early Hebrews were forbidden to boil a kid in its mother's milk (Exodus 23:19) and from this scriptural prohibition sprang complicated dietary laws regarding milk. See JEWISH HISTORY AND SOCIETY—*Religious Traditions and Customs* (Dietary Laws). Also in the Semitic tradition there is evidence that leban, or curdled milk, was used to drive away illness from the body and was extolled for its purity, a frequent attribute of milk. In the Persian Avesta, milk was known as a purifier of women who had given birth to a still-born child (Vendidad V: 52; VII: 67).

Graeco-Roman World.—Milk played a part in the symbolism of classical antiquity from the earliest times, perhaps even more than in later times when it was replaced by wine in religious rites. There is evidence that its use in ritual goes back to the Phrygian cult of the Magna Mater, and, by the time of Homer, mixtures of milk, honey, and wine were often employed in rites for the dead. In Euripides' *Orestes,* Helen instructs Hermione to "pour round Clytemnestra's tomb a mingled cup of honey, milk, and frothing wine" (115). Aeschylus describes a similar death offering in *The Persians* (1. 611), in which Atossa's libations at the tomb of Darius include milk and honey. As in other ancient civilizations, milk was usually associated with honey, and when combined, the mixture was called *melicration* (*μελίχρχτου*) by the Greeks.

The symbolical use of milk survived a long time in Greek pastoral religions, as evidenced in a poem of the bucolic poet, Theocritus (fl. c. 275 B.C.), and was also an important factor in the Greek mystery cults. Featured in the Dionysiac rites in lower Italy were the enigmatic words *ἔριφος ἐς γαλ ἔπετου*, found on a small gold plate of the 3d or 4th century B.C. In this rite, milk was a symbol of immortality and the medium for the baptizing or bathing of a baby goat. In the worship of Cybele in the Attis mysteries, its use is described by the Platonist Sallustius as a symbol of regeneration (*Concerning the Gods and the Universe,* ed. A. D. Nock, Cambridge 1926, p. 9). Later, milk symbolizing the first nourishment of man was included in elaborate Pythagorean cosmologies by the neo-Platonists, Porphyry (*De antro nympharum,* 28) and Macrobius (*Commentarii in somnium Scipionis,* I:12). According to the latter, "Pythagoras thinks that Pluto's empire extends from the Milky Way downward, because the souls, having fallen from there, seem already to have lost their celestial attributes. On that account, he said, milk was the first nourishment offered to the newly born, because, by means of milk, the first motion of those souls falling into their terrestrial bodies was induced." From the number of references to the Milky Circle or Way in classical literature, it is evident that its "milky" attribute goes far back: Aristotle records various theories regarding its nature and origin (*Meteorologica* I:8) and later Ovid tells us "There is a high way easily seen when the sky is clear. 'Tis called the Milky Way, famed for its shining whiteness. By this way the gods fare to the halls and royal dwelling of the mighty Thunderer" (*Metamorphoses* I:168–172).

Like the Greeks, the Romans used milk in the rites of their pastoral worship. It played an important part in the cult of the Roman gods Rumina and Cumina, whose worshipers, according to Marcus Terentius Varro (*Rerum rusticarum* II:11, 4), were accustomed to offer sacrifices with milk instead of wine, and Virgil, in his 7th Eclogue (33), mentions a milk offering made to the garden god, Priapus. Milk instead of wine was used for the libation at the *ferae Latinae,* the rites to Jupiter Latiaris, which were held yearly on the Alban mount outside Rome. The Romans even had gods called *Lacturcia* or *Lacturnus* who were the special protectors of grain steeped in milk (*frumenta lactentia*). The evidence of the symbolical use of milk in Roman times is abundant, and many practices and superstitions regarding it were prevalent, as, for instance, the Roman women calling the wine libation made to the *bona dea* milk, and their drinking a mixture of milk, crushed poppies, and honey as a philter at the festival of *Fortuna virilis.*

The Christian Era.—Several legends have been preserved regarding the milk of the Virgin Mary. A Milk Grotto in Bethlehem, originally a shrine of Ashtoreth, was supposedly the refuge of the nursing Virgin, a drop of whose milk fell to the floor, and since has been thought to promote the flow of female milk and to cure barrenness. Also according to legend, the small white limestone pebbles found around Bethlehem were miraculously formed by a drop of Mary's milk falling onto a rock. In several early Christian catacomb paintings a milk pail is depicted near the Good Shepherd carrying a lamb; these allusions to milk in this context have been interpreted as symbolic of the joys of heaven.

Milk and wine were used in the early Christian Agape ceremonies in honor of the dead, and in some early baptismal rites, a mixture of milk and honey was given to the neophyte to taste. This practice was described by Tertullian as forming a part of the baptismal ceremonies of the Christians in Africa; in the West, the ceremonial tasting of milk and honey often accompanied the baptism of infants as late as the 9th century. Officially, however, its use in baptisms was banned by the Trullan Council of 692.

With the development of Christian dogma, the use of *lacticinia* (milk and milk products) was prohibited during fast days because of their fleshly origin. A Russian sect called the Molokani (milk-drinkers) were thus known because they opposed the Orthodox ban; in the West, it became customary, especially in Germany, for the church to award exemptions from this prohibition, called *Butterbriefe,* in return for some specific beneficence. From such revenues a steeple of the Rouen Cathedral, formerly known as the Butter Tower, was financed.

Proverbs and sayings regarding milk in modern times are too numerous to mention. Some of them are rooted in superstition and others are derived from ancient symbols and associations. An example of a modern holdover of ancient symbolism is found in the German wine, *Liebfraumilch,* which comes from the vineyards surrounding the *Liebfrauenkirke* (Church of Our Beloved Lady) outside of Worms.

Bibliography.—Consult articles and references in Hastings, James, ed., *Encyclopedia of Religion and Ethics* (New York 1928); Pauly, A., Wissowa, G., and Kroll, W., eds., *Real-Encyclopädie der klassischen Altertumswissenschaft,* vol. 15 (Stuttgart 1931); and Leach, Maria, ed., *Dictionary of Folklore, Mythology, and Legend* (New York 1949).

HOWARD ISHAM.

MILK SICKNESS (also TREMBLES). This disease, which is a poisoning and commonly called milk sickness in man and trembles in livestock, was formerly attributed to a bacillus organism. However, the cause has been definitely established as a toxic substance called tremetol, which is found in the white snakeroot (*Eupatorium urticaefolium*) and rayless goldenrod or jimmyweed (*Aplopappus heterophyllus*). The livestock contract the disease by eating the plants and in turn cause the condition to occur in humans through milk and milk products. The disease occurs at the same time the animals are in pasture, usually the latter part of the summer and the beginning of autumn. Clinical signs of this condition are headache, loss of appetite, fatigue, nausea, excessive thirst, constipation, and foul breath. While the prognosis is generally favorable, death may occur in a few days preceded by convulsions, then coma. The duration of the disease in man and lower animals is from a few days to several weeks.

Affected animals should be isolated and treated. No milk or milk product should be used from these affected animals, either for human or animal use. Treatment consists of saline laxatives, parenteral solutions of physiological salt solution, and glucose and sodium thiosulfate.

MILK SNAKE, the name given to a group of snakes (*Lampropeltis triangulum*) deriving their name from the unproven belief that they drink the milk of cows in pasture. Of moderate size, they are covered with reddish-brown, black-edged blotches on the body and tail, whose ground color is grey or light brown above and white with black spots underneath. The milk snake feeds on rodents, birds, and slugs, is nonpoisonous, and is found throughout the eastern United States and southeastern Canada. It is also known as house snake, spotted adder, or checkered adder.

MILK TREE, any of various tropical trees yielding a milky, wholesome sap. See COW TREE.

MILKWEED. See ASCLEPIAS.

MILKWORT, the common name for plants of the genus *Polygala* (q.v.), widely distributed in the temperate and tropical zones.

MILKY WAY, The, or **THE GALAXY** (from Greek *galaktos,* milk), a nebulous band of faint stars, extending entirely around the celestial sphere. This band of luminosity is the result of an edge-on view from the earth through a disk-shaped aggregation of stars (Galactic System) in which the earth and sun occupy a position well out from the center. The greater number of stars seen looking outward through the flat portion of the disk accounts for the diffuse belt of luminosity in this plane. Since the Milky Way is inclined 62° to the celestial equator, its appearance is variable with the seasons, the time of night, and the observer's latitude. Its brightest portions are in Cygnus, Aquila, Scorpius, and Sagittarius, where many bright star clouds exist. The apparent width of the Milky Way is irregular and its length is interrupted by rifts and superimposed dark nebulae, such as the northern and southern Coal Sacks. An imaginary line passing roughly central along the Milky Way and projected on the celestial sphere forms the galactic circle, from which galactic latitude is reckoned. See also STARS—*The Milky Way.*

MILL, mĭl, **Hugh Robert,** Scottish geographer: b. Thurso, Caithness, Scotland, May 28, 1861; d. East Grinstead, near London, England, April 5, 1950. Educated at the University of Edinburgh, he became physicist and chemist to the Scottish Marine Station in 1884 and, three years later, a University Extension lecturer. He served on several study boards and associations, including the British Rainfall Association, of which he was the director from 1901 until it was taken over by the Meteorological Office. He also edited *British Rainfall* and *Symons's Meteorological Magazine* and wrote *The Realm of Nature* (1892); *The Clyde Sea Area* (1895); *The Siege of the South Pole* (1905); "Historical Introduction" to Sir Ernest Shackleton's *Heart of the Antarctic* (1909); *The Life of Sir Ernest Shackleton* (1923); and *Life Interests of a Geographer* (1945), his autobiography, privately printed; and edited *Report of the Sixth International Geographical Congress* (1896); and *The International Geography* (new ed. 1911).

MILL, James, English historian, economist, and philosopher: b. Northwater Bridge, Forfarshire, Scotland, April 6, 1773; d. Kensington, London, June 23, 1836. The eldest son of a shoemaker named James Milne, or Mill, he was encouraged in his education by his mother. He was sent to the parish school, transferred to Montrose Academy, and was recommended to a resident of the parish, Sir John Stuart, who wished to educate poor young men for the ministry. Mill entered Edinburgh University in 1790, became an outstanding Greek scholar, and in 1794 began his studies in divinity. He was licensed to preach in 1798 and delivered some sermons in his own district, but apparently he was too intellectual for the cottage folk, for when he was 30 he still had no parish. He decided then to seek a literary career.

Sir John took him to London, and after working on several periodicals Mill became editor of the *St. James's Chronicle.* He married (1805) the daughter of a well-to-do widow (who managed a lunatic asylum); his first child, born May 20, 1806, was named after Mill's benefactor, John Stuart Mill (q.v.). At this time Mill began his imposing literary monument, his *History of India.* He had never been to India and he expected to write the book in only three years; it actually took him 12 years to write it. Despite the fact that it criticized many prominent men and the administration of the East India Company, the *History* brought him a position with the India House (1819) and there he remained, becoming head of the office in 1830.

In the meantime, Mill had made the acquaintance (1808) of Jeremy Bentham, the utilitarian philosopher, and promptly became his lieutenant and chief propagandist. The two men worked together the remainder of their lives, Bentham supplying most of the theories and Mill publicizing them. By this time Mill was writing for and editing several periodicals. In 1821 he published his *Elements of Political Economy,* the first English textbook on economics, in which he expounded the theories of the Philosophical Radicals. He pointed out that reform must aim at the limitation of population, that the value of a thing depends on the amount of labor put into it, and that the unearned increment of real estate should be taxable. In 1829 his *Analysis of the Phenomena of the Human Mind* appeared, a psychological interpretation of the utilitarian philosophy of Bentham and an elaboration of David Hartley's theory that all the activities of the rational consciousness are resolvable into "three grand classes of phenomena": sensations, ideas, and trains of ideas. A year before his death Mill wrote his last work, *Fragment on Mackintosh,* a rejoinder to an attack on the utilitarians.

Mill was not an original thinker but he had indomitable Scottish devotion to what he believed to be the truth, a lucid mind, and a perspicuous literary style. He was able to give resolution and clarity to the dicta of his friends and under his leadership there arose the most efficient group of political reformers modern Europe had known.

HENRY HUMPHREY,
Staff Editor, "The Encyclopedia Americana."

MILL, John, English Biblical scholar (known until 1673 as MILNE): b. Hardendale, Westmoreland, England, in 1645; d. probably at Canterbury, June 23, 1707. The son of a weaver, he entered Queen's College, Oxford, at the age of 16; distinguished himself in the classics; took the degrees B.A. (1666), M.A. (1669), B.D. (1680), and D.D. (1681). He was elected fellow of his college in 1670; became prebendary of Exeter in 1677; and in 1681 became rector of Bletchington and chaplain in ordinary to Charles II. In 1684 he married Priscilla, the daughter of Sir William Palmer of Warden, Bedfordshire. He had retired from his fellowship in 1682, and in 1685 became principal of St. Edmund Hall, Oxford. Becoming fourth prebend at Canterbury in August 1704, he resigned his Exeter prebend a year later.

Mill is especially noted for his scholarly work on the New Testament, on which he expended 30 years of labor. It was published on June 9, 1707, just two weeks before his death. He used the 1550 Greek text of Robert Stephanus (q.v.), leaving the text unchanged and giving the various readings at the bottom of the page. For this he used collations of the principal European manuscripts, and he, himself, collated the most important ones in England. He also prepared the three-part prefix treating each book of the New Testament, giving a history of the text from the time of the Apostles, and reviewing his own work on it. He was the first editor of the New Testament to draw up a genealogy of the various editions of the Greek text and to describe accurately and clearly the manuscripts used. The work was dedicated to Queen Anne, and although it met with considerable adverse criticism, it is considered a masterpiece, and was the most beautiful edition produced up to that time. It was republished in Rotterdam and Amsterdam in 1710, again in Amsterdam in 1746, and in Leipzig in 1723. A copy of Mill's original text with his manuscript additions is in the Bodleian Library at Oxford, and the library at Queen's College, Oxford, has a large number of his notes for the work and much of his correspondence with eminent men of the day. George Vertue (q.v.) made an engraving of Mill presenting his Greek Testament to Queen Anne, which was reproduced in the Oxford Almanack for 1747.

MILL, John Stuart, English economist, philosopher, and radical reformer; b. London, May 20, 1806; d. Avignon, France, May 8, 1873. Best known of his works are his *Autobiography* (1873), his writings on logic, utilitarianism, and political philosophy, and his restatement of classical economics. Though he had a commanding intellectual position in his day, most of his ideas no longer are thought valid, and his enduring interest comes from the exceptional qualities of his mind.

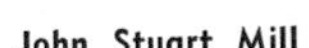

John Stuart Mill

Brown Brothers

His father was James Mill (q.v.), an eclectic and reformer, the intimate of Jeremy Bentham, celebrated utilitarian philosopher; of David Ricardo, whose *Principles of Political Economy* was written at his prompting; and the mentor and hector of others engaged in the radical politics of the early 19th century. A man of strong views and an energy equal to them, James

Mill himself undertook the education of his son, who at 13 had been taught more than most people are in their lives, showing, John later recorded, what so ordinary a mind as his own could achieve under proper instruction. His interests were austere until at about the age of 25, after an extended emotional disturbance, he became more objective about his father and acquired an interest in romantic poetry and the humanitarian ideas of Continental socialists. He spent 14 months in France, 1820–1821, and on his return studied for the law but did not complete the course. Instead he entered the examiner's office of the East India Company, a trading monopoly with political authority over India, as a junior clerk under his father. He eventually attained the position of chief examiner and was retired in 1856.

At 15, Mill became familiar with Bentham's ideas and these had a decisive influence on him. The next year he formed the first of three discussion groups, enlisting a number of young men who later became important in Victorian politics and letters. From one of these groups came the Philosophical Radicals whose ideas were advanced enough to shock the public but sound enough to gain its respect as well.

Starting from Bentham's principle that the good of society lies in that which brings the greatest benefit to the largest number, the Philosophical Radicals agitated for repeal of the grain tariff, removal of the causes of overpopulation, extensive free education, prison reform, religious liberty, freedom of labor unions, extension of the vote and other parliamentary reforms, cheap and efficient local government, and the improvement of working conditions in factories. Despite initial ridicule and then fierce opposition, they in time attained some of their objectives entirely and toward the others made noticeable progress. Mill himself did not approve of all of them, because he opposed extensive government control of the economy, but they were a reasonable application of the utilitarian principle he took from Bentham.

In economics, Mill's most influential work was *The Principles of Political Economy* (1848). It restates the classical idea that the quantities of labor-time required to produce goods determine their exchange value, that a country's total production is limited by the extent of its land, that population tends to increase faster than production, and that therefore the standard of living can rise only if population growth is slowed down. Mill believed his contribution was to distinguish between laws of production, which he said were unalterable, and distribution of the product which, he said, can be done in any way a country chooses. Later economists have found his most valuable contribution to be the detailed explanation of the principles which should guide the government in its control of the economy. The book is not Mill's most notable work. He had, uncharacteristically, neglected to notice what his contemporaries were adding to the theory of price and business cycles. In later editions, upon the urgings of his wife, he changed his opposition to socialism into a restrained approval.

The distinctive feature of Mill's *A System of Logic . . .* (1843) was the idea that the rules of reasoning are obtained from experience, as opposed to the traditional view that they are a part of the mind's construction, or of the universe. A statement, he said, asserts either the existence of a fact or the relations between facts, which may be those of coexistence, sequence, resemblance, or causality. Its truth is tested by its correspondence with the reality we perceive by our senses or by reasoning inductively from the perception, that is, from the particular to the general. In stating that logic is the method of testing the factual validity of statements, Mill was the forerunner of the scientific method. To utilitarian ethics, he contributed the idea, taken from associationist psychology, that men are prompted to do good initially to serve themselves, in circumstances in which by helping others they help themselves; but in time virtue becomes a habit and they serve others even when there is no gain to themselves. Happiness is the goal of all conduct, according to Mill, and consists of pleasures of the mind, not senses, because the former endure and the latter quickly perish. Applied to politics, utilitarianism argued for measures which benefited more people than they injured; for instance, the repeal of the grain tariff which added more to the purchasing power of the masses by lowering bread prices than it took from the landlord by lowering rents. The principle of utility was the premise of Mill's essay *On Liberty* (1854) and *Considerations on Representative Government* (1861). He argued that freedom requires people to exercise their judgment and to accept its consequences. By making them more self-reliant, it makes them better men and women. He opposed despotism, even if efficient and benign, because it asks nothing of people but obedience.

After most of his important books were written, Mill was a member of the House of Commons (1865–1868) where he stood with the radicals, principally on the extension of the right to vote. He independently proposed woman suffrage, proportional representation, land reform in Ireland, the payment of the national debt before British coal reserves were exhausted, and he conducted a memorable and unsuccessful campaign to indict the British governor of Jamaica whom he believed responsible for the cruel suppression of a native rebellion.

Throughout his adult life, he was helped, ministered to, and supported in ways for which he was profusely grateful, by Harriet Taylor whom he met in 1830 and married in 1851 after the death of her husband. She died in 1858, and her daughter, Helen, remained with Mill to the end of his life. Though called, respectfully, the saint of rationalism, Mill was a man of feeling, great kindness, and affection. No thinker of the century was as knowledgeable about the ideas of those who disagreed with him, or treated them as fairly, or showed as much generosity. He was friendly with Thomas Carlyle, Auguste Comte, and Herbert Spencer, who disagreed with him, sometimes fiercely and with invective; to all of them he paid tribute and made personal benefactions. Although originality was not the outstanding quality of his mind, it was remarkably analytic, fair, and thorough, capable of synthesizing views in opposition to his own as well as those in agreement, and had a facility with abstract ideas which was unique among the English. To all of this, Mill joined a writing ability which makes his prose memorable even in an age distinguished for its use of English. See also MILL, AUTOBIOGRAPHY OF JOHN STEWART.

Bibliography.—In addition to those noted above,

Mill's principal works are: *The Rationale of Judicial Evidence,* from the MSS. of Jeremy Bentham, ed. by Mill, 5 vols. (London 1827); *Essays on Some Unsettled Questions of Political Economy* (London 1844); *Thoughts on Parliamentary Reform* (London 1859); *Dissertations and Discussions,* 4 vols. (London 1859–1876); *Utilitarianism* (London 1863); *An Examination of Sir William Hamilton's Philosophy* (London 1865); *The Subjection of Women* (London 1869); *The Spirit of the Age* (Chicago 1942).

About Mill: Bain, Alexander, *John Stuart Mill* (London 1882); Green, Thomas Hill, "The Logic of J. S. Mill" in Green's *Works,* vol. 2 (London 1886); Stephen, Leslie, *The English Utilitarians,* vol. 3 (New York 1900); Neff, Emery E., *Carlyle and Mill* (New York 1926); Hayek, Friedrich A., *John Stuart Mill and Harriet Taylor* (Chicago 1951); Halévy, Élie, *The Growth of Philosophic Radicalism* (London 1953); Packe, Michael St. John, *The Life of John Stuart Mill* (New York 1954).

WILLIAM D. GRAMPP,
Professor of Economics, University of Illinois.

MILL, the common name for a machine for grinding or crushing grain or other substances, as corn, coffee, ore, sugarcane; also any of various machines which produce a manufactured product by the continuous repetition of some simple mechanical action, as a sawmill. The term may also refer to the building or buildings in which certain processes of manufacture are carried on, as a cotton mill, a steel mill, a flour mill; or it may be attached to a word indicating the source or power, as a windmill.

MILL, Autobiography of John Stuart. The *Autobiography* of John Stuart Mill, published in 1873, has been called the history of an education, showing what may be accomplished in forming a boy's mind both for good and ill. Mill's teacher was his father, whose ardor in the task was stimulated by the facility of his pupil. He began Greek at three; Latin at seven; by 12 he knew most of the best in both languages, besides reading in English "chiefly histories," and composing one book in continuation of Pope's *Iliad.* At 12 he began logic; at 13, political economy; at 17 he was writing articles for the *Westminster Review.* But such forcing of the faculties must be paid for. It was impossible that Mill's education should not produce a distinguished mind; it was equally impossible that it should produce a joyous one. His boyhood lacked games and youthful companionship. At 20, a not unnatural reaction caused a sudden collapse in his whole intellectual outlook, resulting in profound depression, when this brilliant boy "seemed to have nothing left to live for."

From this state of "dry, heavy dejection," Mill was roused by the discovery of beauty, art, music and poetry, all of which had been omitted from the system of the elder Mill. Thus he came to perceive the value of feeling and emotion, and was brought back to hope and enjoyment by pleasure in William Wordsworth's poetry and the *Memoirs* of Jean François Marmontel. Admirable as all this is, not less so is his account of "that friendship which has been the honor and chief blessing of my existence," his marriage with Harriet Taylor in 1851. Mill's intellectual isolation made the experience a vital one; and the words in which he draws his wife's character and their companionship in work and thought are among the most impressive of their kind.

Much of the *Autobiography* is taken up with an account of the genesis and growth of Mill's chief works and with a discussion of his father's character and opinions and of the philosophy of Sir William Hamilton and of Auguste Comte. But the book, while primarily intellectual, is not without humanity and warmth, even apart from the glowing passages devoted to the author's wife. Mill's friends, John Austin, Frederick Denison Maurice, John Sterling, Thomas Carlyle (qq.v.) and others, come into the human picture as well. The style is admirable for the purpose, clear, dispassionate and not unduly restrained; and the attitude of sane analysis, of modesty and of thoughtful discrimination has never been surpassed in any autobiography. The world has taken the earlier portion of the book—the story of the growth of the boy's mind and character—as its unique contribution to the literature of autobiography; but scarcely less valuable are Mill's pictures of his contemporaries and his analysis of the thought and the social movements of his time.

ANNA ROBESON BURR.

MILL ON THE FLOSS, The, a novel by George Eliot (q.v.), published in 1860. The scene of the story is 19th century England.

Tom and Maggie Tulliver are the children of the miller of Dorlcote Mill, near St. Ogg's on the river Floss. Tom is unimaginative, domineering, and self-righteous; Maggie is intelligent, sensitive, and something of a tomboy. She yearns for fellowship with her brother, but is usually repulsed. In Philip Wakem, the hunchback son of a local lawyer, she finds the intellectual and emotional understanding she needs. But her father, a headstrong and ignorant man, starts an ill-advised lawsuit over water rights, in which Philip's father represents the other side. Tulliver loses, and is bankrupted. Blaming all his misfortunes on Wakem, he forbids Maggie to have any further association with Philip. Tom concurs in his father's admonition, and Maggie obeys meekly.

After several years of struggle the Tullivers clear all their debts. Just when it seems that Maggie may look forward to some happiness, a brief infatuation with Stephen Guest, fiancé of her cousin, Lucy Deane, involves her in a highly compromising, though actually innocent, situation. St. Ogg's society condemns her, and Tom disowns her. But when the Floss rises in flood, Maggie, at peril of her life, saves Tom from the mill just before it is washed away. Tom at last recognizes his sister's worth, but almost in the moment of recognition their boat is overturned and both are drowned.

The ending is artificial and unconvincing, as are many of Maggie's sufferings. For a girl as intelligent and courageous as Maggie is represented to be, she is browbeaten too easily and too often. The best parts of the story are the brilliant studies of provincial types, such as Bob Jakin, the shrewd young packman, and the whole family album of Maggie's aunts and uncles, who have little to do with the main action. Maggie, like most of George Eliot's heroines, is an idealized self-portrait; her struggles for an education, and her relations with a narrow-minded and uncomprehending brother, are almost literal autobiography.

DELANCEY FERGUSON.

MILL SPRINGS, Battle of. In the American Civil War, the Battle of Mill Springs marked the opening of the Kentucky-Tennessee campaign of 1862. It was also known as the Battle of Fishing Creek and the Battle of Logan Cross

Roads. It was the first important Union victory in the west.

At the close of 1861 the Confederate line extended from Columbus, Ky., on the Mississippi, through Fort Henry on the Tennessee, Fort Donelson on the Cumberland, Clarksville, Tenn., and Bowling Green, Ky., to Mill Springs on the Cumberland. Gen. Albert Sidney Johnston was in chief command. Gen. Dan Carlos Buell was the opposing Union commander. Gen. Felix K. Zollicoffer established the Confederate right at Mill Springs early in December. Gen. George B. Crittenden took general command there at the middle of the month, with the brigades of Zollicoffer and W. H. Carroll under him. Gen. Leonidas Polk held the Confederate left at Columbus, Gen. J. B. Floyd reached Fort Donelson on January 13, and had under him Generals Pillow, Buckner and Bushrod Johnson. Gen. A. S. Johnston was at Bowling Green, the center, Gen. George H. Thomas was on the Union left, with Gen. Albin F. Schoepf immediately opposed to Zollicoffer, while General Buell, with headquarters at Louisville, was in close communication with the Union center, which threatened Bowling Green and Nashville.

Gen. Zollicoffer having crossed from Mill Springs to the north bank of the Cumberland from which he threatened central Kentucky, General Thomas was sent against his forces, now commanded by General Crittenden, from the direction of Lebanon. On January 18 General Thomas reached Logan's Cross Roads about 10 miles from Crittenden's entrenchments. The latter officer, with the purpose of attacking before Thomas could concentrate his forces, marched at midnight of the 18th with Zollicoffer's and Carroll's brigades, consisting of eight regiments of infantry, six guns and four battalions of cavalry, and attacked General Thomas soon after daylight of January 19.

The Union troops, consisting of six infantry regiments, one battery and a portion of a cavalry regiment, were brought rapidly into action, both sides fighting with spirit. Finally, when three fresh Union regiments fell on the Confederate right, and the 2d Minnesota was pouring a galling fire upon the center, the 9th Ohio (German Turners) made a brilliant bayonet charge completely turning the Confederate left, resulting in the Confederate lines breaking and retiring in confusion. At this point General Schoepf's brigade from Somerset reached the field, and the whole force continued in pursuit, reaching the Confederate entrenchments during the night, and forming to assault them at daylight. During the night the Confederates succeeded in crossing their men, leaving artillery, cavalry, horses, mules, wagons, camp equipage, and private baggage. The Confederate right wing was effectually broken and largely dispersed.

MILL VALLEY, town, California, in Marin County, eight miles north of San Francisco on a branch of the Northwestern Pacific Railroad providing freight service only. Altitude 57 feet. It is a residential suburb of San Francisco located at the foot of Mount Tamalpais. Nearby is the Muir Woods National Monument.

In 1834 John Reed (Reid or Read) built a sawmill here, whence the place became locally known as Mill Valley. On a map of 1873, the site was designated as Read. The town was not established, however, until the Tamalpais Land and Water Company acquired the land and built a branch of the North Pacific Coast Railroad to it. The community was incorporated in 1900 and has a council-manager form of government. Pop. 12,942.

MILLAIS, mĭ-lā′, Sir **John Everett,** English painter: b. Southampton, England, June 8, 1829; d. London, Aug. 13, 1896. His earliest years were spent in Jersey and at Dinan in France, and at the age of nine he was sent to study art under Henry Sass in London. In 1840 he became a student in the Royal Academy, and in 1846 he exhibited his *Pizarro seizing the Inca of Peru.* Next year the gold medal of the Academy was awarded to his *Young Men of Benjamin seizing their Brides.*

In 1848, along with Holman Hunt, Dante G. Rossetti, and others, Millais founded the Pre-Raphaelite Brotherhood. Among the chief works of this period are *A Huguenot, The Order of Release* and the *Proscribed Royalist.* In 1853 he was elected an associate of the Royal Academy, and 10 years later Academician. For a few years thereafter his pictures were still influenced by the Pre-Raphaelite principles, which he gradually abandoned. He developed into a splendid colorist, a master of technique and altogether a great modern master.

Numerous honors fell to him; he was decorated with the Legion of Honor in 1878, elected a member of the Académie des Beaux-Arts in 1882, created a baronet in 1885 and elected to succeed Lord Leighton as president of the Royal Academy in 1896; but he only held this last position about six months, dying in August of the same year. He was most successful in figure pieces and portraits, but he also produced a certain number of landscapes, one of the finest being *Chill October* (1871). He painted portraits of some of the foremost men of the day, including Mr. Gladstone, Lord Beaconsfield, Lord Salisbury, Mr. Ruskin, Lord Tennyson and others.

His son, John Guille Millais (1865–1931), was an artist and author who traveled extensively in Africa, Norway, Iceland, and the North American continent. He was known for his collection of birds, mostly of the British Isles, and his illustrations of books on sporting and natural history.

MILLAR, mĭl′ẽr, **Andrew,** British publisher: b. Scotland, 1707; d. London, June 8, 1768. He established his shop in London in 1729 and soon carried on a flourishing business. Among the books published by his firm were *Sophonisba* (1729), *Spring* (1729), and the *Seasons* (1738) by James Thomson; and *Joseph Andrews* (1742), *Tom Jones* (1749), and *Amelia* (1751) by Henry Fielding. He also published the historical works of David Hume and William Robertson. His most notable undertaking, however, was the *Dictionary* of Dr. Samuel Johnson, who cherished a high opinion of his publisher.

In 1765 Thomas Cadell became Millar's partner and two years later took over the business, when Millar retired to Kew Green.

MILLARDET, mē-yȧr-dĕ′, **Alexis,** French botanist: b. Montmirey-la-ville (department of Jura), Dec. 13, 1838; d. Bordeaux, Dec. 15, 1902. He taught botany at the universities in Nancy, Strasbourg, and Bordeaux, and is noted for his plan of hybridization of French and American grapevines. He also worked out a treatment for grapevines against mildew by using copper compounds. Among his writings are *Le Prothalle Mâle des Crytogames Vasculaires* (1869) and *La Question des Vignes Américaines au Point du Vue Théoretique et Pratique* (1877).

MILLAU, mē-yō', (also MILHAU; the ancient AEMILIANUM, ē-mĭl-ĭ-ā'nŭm), town, France, in the department of Aveyron, 30 miles southeast of Rodez, at the confluence of the Tarn and Dourbie rivers. It is a glove manufacturing center with industries including tanneries, furniture, and woolen textiles. Roquefort cheese is also marketed. The seat of a viscounty in the Middle Ages, Millau has a Romanesque church of Notre Dame, restored in the 16th century, and a modern church of St. François. Pop. (1962) 19,215.

MILLAY, mĭ-lā', **Edna St. Vincent,** American poet and writer: b. Rockland, Me., Feb. 22, 1892; d. Austerlitz, N. Y., Oct. 19, 1950. One of the most popular poets America has produced, Miss Millay gained her reputation by voicing the spirit of rebellion and emancipation of the 1920's, and throughout her life her poetry, while in some respects conventional, reflected an individual and genuinely poetic talent.

She began writing verses in her childhood and her first poem to be published was "Renascence," which appeared in *The Lyric Year* for 1912. Graduating from Vassar in 1917, she published her first volume of poems in the same year. After several years of bohemian living in Greenwich Village, New York City, where she wrote short stories under the name of Nancy Boyd, Miss Millay married Eugen Jan Boissevain, with whom she moved to a farm in upper New York, and in 1923 received the Pulitzer Prize for her poem *The Harp Weaver.*

In later years her poetry revealed an increasing social consciousness. Besides her lyric and satiric verse, her works included verse plays such as *The King's Henchman,* made into an opera by Deems Taylor (1927), and a translation, with George Dillon, of Baudelaire's *Flowers of Evil* (1936). She was a member of the American Academy of Arts and Letters and in 1943 the Poetry Society of America awarded her a medal for her contribution to the humanities. First editions of her volumes of poems have commanded high prices and become collectors items. Among her many published works are *Figs from Thistles* (1920); *Second April* (1921); *The Harp Weaver and Other Poems* (1923); *Wine from These Grapes* (1934); *Conversation at Midnight* (1937); *There Are No Islands Any More* (1940); *Collected Sonnets* (1941); *The Murder of Lidice* (1942); and *Collected Lyrics* (1943).

MILLBRAE, mĭl'brā, city, California, in San Mateo County, 13 miles south of San Francisco on U.S. Highway 101 and the Southern Pacific Railroad; altitude 18 feet. Chiefly a residential community, Millbrae has only local industries, including dairies and wholesale flower growing.

In 1850 an American by the name of Perry Jones settled in this area, which was originally part of Rancho Buri Buri, granted by Mexico to Jose Sanchez. A large part of this ranch was purchased by Darius Ogden Mills in the 1860's, the name Millbrae then applying only to a railroad station there. In 1867 Millbrae was the name of a postoffice and three years later Mills built his own residence south of the townsite. Although there were only six families in Millbrae in 1905, the community has developed rapidly since then. It was incorporated in 1948 and government is administered by a mayor and council. Pop. 20,781.

MILLBURY, mĭl'bĕr-ĭ, town, Massachusetts, in Worcester County, six miles south-southeast of Worcester on the Blackstone River, State Highway 122A, and the New York, New Haven, and Hartford Railroad; altitude 407 feet. Located in an industrial area, Millbury is a manufacturing town producing woolens and felt. Other manufactures are textile supplies, wire, tools, and castings. The New England Power Company which distributes electric power throughout central New England is located here. Nearby many Indian relics have been found.

Settled in 1716, Millbury was incorporated as a town in 1813. It developed rapidly after the opening of the Blackstone Canal in 1828, and on its closing 20 years later, transportation for Millbury's growing textile industry was provided by the Providence and Worcester Railroad. The town includes the village of West Millbury and government is administered by a board of selectmen. Pop. 11,987.

MILLE, mēl, **Pierre,** French journalist and fiction writer: b. Choisy-le-Roi, near Paris, Nov. 27, 1864; d. Paris, Jan. 15(?), 1941. Receiving his baccalaureate degree from the Collège Rollin in 1885, he entered the Law School and the School of Political Sciences at the University of Paris, where he completed his studies in those subjects. He traveled extensively as a member of expeditions to West Africa, the Congo, Indo-China, and India, and served as a war correspondent for the *Journal des Débats* during the Greco-Turkish War (1897). From 1901 to 1932 he contributed the column *En Passant* to the Paris newspaper *Le Temps.*

Among his many published writings, including novels and short stories, are *Le Congo Léopoldien* (1903); *Barnaveaux et Quelques Femmes* (1908); *L'Ange du Bizarre* (1921); *Christine et Lui* (1926); *Mes Trônes et mes Dominations* (1930); *Chez les Hommes de l'Ombre et du Soleil* (1932).

MILLEDGE, mĭl'ĭj, **John,** American soldier and politician: b. Savannah, Ga., 1757; d. Feb. 9, 1818. At the dawn of the Revolution he was one of Joseph Habersham's party which captured the colonial government of Savannah. When the British took Savannah Milledge fled to South Carolina. He was at the sieges of Savannah (1779) and of Augusta, and rendered good service in the patriot army.

Appointed attorney-general of Georgia in 1780, Milledge later served in the Legislature, was representative in Congress 1792–1802, twice governor of the State 1802–1806 and United States senator 1806–1809. He is remembered for his donation of land to the University of Georgia and was honored by having Milledgeville, the first capital of Georgia, named after him.

MILLEDGEVILLE, mĭl'ĭj-vĭl, city, Georgia, seat of Baldwin County, 29 miles northeast of Macon on the Oconee River, state and federal highways, and the Georgia and the Central of Georgia railroads. It is also served by an airport with airline facilities. At an altitude of 325 feet, Milledgeville is situated in a rich agricultural region for which it is an important trade center. Nearby clay deposits and forests have contributed to the growth of the clay products and lumber industries in the city. Manufactures include tile, brick, clothing, candy, and lumber. Other important industries are dairying, cattle raising, and cotton ginning.

In addition to its public school system, Milledgeville has the Georgia Military College and the Georgia State College for Women. From 1835 to the Civil War, and for a few years after the war, Milledgeville was the seat of the original Oglethorpe University, a name that was revived, in 1913, for the present college near Atlanta. Besides the college libraries, there is a county library in the city, and the State College for Women supports a museum, with collections of manuscripts and documents bearing upon the history of the South.

Milledgeville was laid out by state surveyors in 1803 as a site for a state capital, and named for John Milledge, the revolutionary soldier who was then governor. It was incorporated in 1836 and in 1868 the capital of the state was moved to Atlanta. A mayor and council administer the government. Pop. 11,601.

MILLENNIUM, mĭ-lĕn'ĭ-ŭm, (Lat. *mille,* 1,000, and *annus,* a year), a period of 1,000 years. Hence it is a term applied to the period during which, according to some, Jesus Christ will return to reign on earth before the end of the world. This premillennial appearance of Christ will be signalized by a first or particular resurrection of the just, who are to reign with Him on earth, and by the destruction of Antichrist. Those who hold such views are called millenarians or chiliasts, and their tenet chiliasm (Gr. χίλιοι, 1,000). It is admitted on all sides that these views were, if not general, at least very common in the ancient church. The belief was generally founded on Psalms xc, 4, according to which 1,000 years are before the Lord as one day, compared with the account of the creation as given by Moses. The six days of creation are taken as designating 6,000 years of toil, and the subsequent sabbath as designating 1,000 years of rest and happiness. The millennium was to be the sabbath rest of the new creation of mankind in Christ. Besides these passages, Revelation 21:1-6, is especially quoted by chiliasts in support of their views.

Chiliasm prevailed chiefly among the Jewish Christians, who retained after their conversion the hope that they would rule over all other nations under a royal Messiah (q.v.). The Ebionites, the Nazarenes and Cerinthians all advocated it and Montanus, and the sect which was called after him, regarded it as a fundamental doctrine of the Christian religion. Some early fathers of the Church also declared themselves generally in favor of the doctrine; Papias, Irenaeus and Tertullian were chiliasts; and Papias appealed in support of his view to apostolic traditions. On the other hand, however, the epistles of Clement of Rome and Ignatius of Antioch are silent about it.

Justin Martyr who wrote in the 2d century was a believer in the millennium. "I and all Christians whose belief is in every respect correct," he says, "know that there will be both a resurrection of the flesh and a thousand years in Jerusalem, which will then be rebuilt, adorned and enlarged, as the prophets Ezekiel, Isaiah and others declare." This view was opposed by the whole Alexandrian school, especially by Origen, who believed in a spiritual supramundane interpretation of Revelations. Still it continued to find advocates during the 3d century, among whom Tertullian, Nepos, bishop of Arsinoe, and Methodius, bishop of Tyre, were prominent.

In the 4th century, Jerome, who did not believe in it himself, did not dare to condemn it, in consideration of the many pious and learned advocates it had found in former centuries. Soon after it began to die out; it was temporarily revived toward the close of the 10th century, by the popular belief in the approaching end of the world, but it never regained great strength.

The reformation of the 16th century gave a new impulse to chiliasm. Fanatical opinion identified the Pope with Antichrist, and regarded the anticipated downfall of the Roman Catholic Church as foreshadowing the approach of the millennium. But when the Anabaptists undertook in 1534 to erect the New Zion, both the Lutheran and Reformed churches declared themselves against this reversion of the old doctrine. Yet it was preached by many sectarians and theologians of the 16th and 17th centuries, among whom were Weigel and the Moravian bishop Comenius in Germany, Jurieu in France, the Labadists in the Netherlands, and Joseph Mede and Jane Lead (d. 1704) in England.

A third period in the history of chiliasm may be commenced with the writings of the esteemed exegete and New Testament commentator, Johann Albrecht Bengel. He practically reintroduced it into Protestant theology, where it has ever since been advocated by a number of prominent theologians. The ingenious prelate Friedrich Christoph Oetinger (d. 1782) brought it into connection with his favorite theosophic views. August Hahn (the founder of a pietistic sect in Württemberg), Johann Heinrich Jung-Stilling, and Johann Kaspar Lavater gave it a wide circulation among the lower classes of the people in Germany and Switzerland. In opposition to the "spiritualism" of modern exegesis, it was advocated, with exegetical arguments, by Hoffmann, Franz Delitzsch, Johann Heinrich Kurtz, and others; while Heinrich Thiersch, Karl Emanuel Nitzsch, Johann Peter Lange and August Ebrard supported it from a dogmatical as well as an exegetical standpoint. Swedenborg taught that the last judgment took place in 1757, and that the New Church or church of the New Jerusalem had actually been formed both in heaven and on earth.

After Germany, England and America have been the chief fields of modern chiliasm. The "Catholic Apostolic Church," organized by Edward Irving, laid great stress on the belief that the kingdom of glory was very near. Chiliasm lies at the foundation of Mormonism, whose adherents call themselves Latter Day Saints in reference to the near approach of the last day.

In the United States great excitement was caused by the preaching of William Miller (q.v.) who sought to prove from the Scriptures that the second advent of Christ would take place about 1843. He not only met with numerous chiliasts in most denominations, but he also founded the sect of Adventists (q.v.).

Chiliasm has been seriously taken in declarations of doctrine formulated by several churches. The Augsburg Confession implicitly repudiates it, speaking of "the last days foreshown in Holy Scripture, in which the world is to become ever more and more degenerate and mankind more sinful and weak." Later in the 16th century, the Council of Trent declared that "the Scriptures also inform us that the General Judgment shall be preceded by the preaching of the Gospel throughout the world, a defection from the faith and the coming of Antichrist."

Another sense of "millenium" was of some importance during the 19th century, when the term often referred to a virtually perfect state or condition of mankind to be achieved within a foreseeable future through natural human progress. Exponents of this philosophy, if they did not discount the supernatural altogether, at least denied religion a role as the prime agency in renovating the world. They anticipated instead a moral growth of the individual and an approach to the ultimate in human well-being as a result of the material improvement of man's environment, the elimination of the causes of social maladjustment, the eradication of diseases, and other such blessings earned by enlightened human effort. (See PROGRESS.) World War I and its legacy of violence and suffering shattered the illusions of many for whom this doctrine had assumed the force of inevitable natural law. Thereafter, "millenium" was largely replaced in secular usage by other terms, especially by "utopia" (q.v.), implying a far more distant and fanciful ideal.

See also ESCHATOLOGY.

MILLEPEDE or **MILLIPEDE,** mĭl'ē-pēd, the popular name of any of the myriapods of the class Diplopoda. The millepede is a small, many-legged, cylindrical land animal somewhat resembling a worm and having some of the characteristics of an insect, though it belongs to neither group. Unlike the closely related centipede (q.v.), it lacks poison fangs and each of its many body segments, except for a few front joints, bears two pairs of legs instead of one pair. Each of these four-legged segments in the adult represents a fusion of two embryonic segments. The total number of legs may exceed 200, although never approaching the 1,000 implied in the name "millepede." The most common species are brownish, averaging a little more than an inch in length, and are found in damp places, concealed under stones, under the bark of trees, or under decaying leaves. The body usually consists of from 30 to 55 joints, protected by a horny "skin." When irritated or at rest, the millepede coils up for protection. Rotting vegetable matter constitutes the major part of its diet, but it occasionally becomes a garden pest by feeding on live roots, the mouth being equipped with a pair of strong jaws or "mandibles." The antennae consist of six or seven joints. See also MYRIAPODA.

MILLEPORE, mĭl'ē-pōr, the name of a marine organism, a type of colonial coelenterate (order Milleporina) in which the minute polyps occupy pores in a massive calcareous skeleton which may form upright leaflike growths reaching a height of one to two feet or may encrust corals or other objects. The polyps are of two sorts: short feeding polyps, occupying the larger pores; and taller protective polyps armed with stinging capsules, occupying the smaller pores. The sting is painful to man. Sexual reproduction occurs by the giving off of tiny medusae that shed sex cells into the sea. The millepores are restricted to tropical and subtropical seas in shallow waters. They are regular components of coral reefs, to whose formation they contribute. As in the case of corals, living polyps are found only at the surface of the calcareous mass to which past generations of polyps have contributed.

L. H. HYMAN.

MILLER, mĭl'ẽr, **Alice Duer,** American novelist and poet: b. New York, N.Y., July 28, 1874; d. there, Aug. 22, 1942. After graduating from Barnard College in 1899, she married Henry Wise Miller, with whom she lived in poverty for many years on a Costa Rica plantation and in New York City. Later her husband succeeded as a stock broker and Mrs. Miller as a writer of fiction. Her stories usually appeared in national magazines, after which they were often published as novels and dramatized for the stage. In the latter category were *Come Out of the Kitchen* (1916) and *The Charm School* (1919). Her *Gowns by Roberta* (1933) provided the materials for the musical comedy *Roberta.* In 1940 she published the long, sentimental narrative poem, *The White Cliffs,* eulogizing the spirit of embattled Great Britain.

MILLER, Arthur, American playwright: b. New York, N.Y., Oct. 17, 1915. He was educated in New York public schools, worked for two years to earn college tuition, and entered the University of Michigan. While there, he won the Theater Guild National Award with the play *The Grass Still Grows* (1936). After graduating in 1938, he joined the Federal Theater Project in New York, but the organization dissolved before his first play could be produced. He then turned to radio writing. His excellent source book on army life, *Situation Normal* (1944), was the by-product of an assignment as a researcher for the producers of the film *The Story of GI Joe.* In 1945 he published a novel, *Focus,* dealing with anti-Semitism. His first Broadway-produced play, *The Man Who Had All the Luck,* failed in 1944, but his second, *All My Sons* (1947), received the Drama Critics' Circle Award and had a long run.

Miller's most famous play, *Death of a Salesman* (1949), won the Critics' Award, the Pulitzer Prize, and the Antoinette Perry Award. *The Crucible* (1953), concerning witchcraft in Salem, received mixed reviews but was successfully revived in the late 1950's, and *A View from the Bridge* (1955) created much interest both at home and abroad. *All My Sons* and *Death of a Salesman* were produced as motion pictures, and a Jean-Paul Sartre adaption of *The Crucible* was filmed in France. Miller has been ranked with the more prolific Tennessee Williams as the most important in the post-World War II generation of American playwrights. His unfailingly serious subject matter often gains dramatic intensity from conflicts within individuals, in which enobling visions of personal integrity may be pitted against human weaknesses and outside pressures, either social, political, or economic.

MILLER, Cincinnatus Hiner or **Heine** (pen name JOAQUIN MILLER), American poet: b. Liberty, Ind., March 10, 1839; d. Oakland, Calif., Feb. 17, 1913. The son of Hulings Miller, a Quaker schoolmaster, he accompanied his parents to Oregon in 1852, but at 17 left home and worked for a time in a California mining camp, later accompanying the adventurer William Walker on his filibustering expeditions in Nicaragua. He lived among the Digger Indians near Mount Shasta, Calif., between 1857 and 1859, and subsequently returned to Oregon, leaving behind an Indian wife and a young daughter. He then briefly attended Columbia College in Eugene, Oreg., studied law in his spare time while teaching school at Clarke, in the Washington Territory, and was admitted to the bar in Portland, Oreg., in 1861. He did not practice, but founded a pony express route, and in 1863 bought the Eugene *Democratic Register,* which was soon suppressed by the United States government because of its pro-Confederate tendency.

Miller removed to Canyon City, Oreg., where, after winning favor by leading a posse against hostile Indians, he was elected judge of the Grant County court in 1866. He published two volumes of verse, *Specimens* (1868) and *Joaquin et al* (1869), which brought him to the attention of literary circles and enabled him to become acquainted with prominent authors in San Francisco, notably Bret Harte. Subsequently he visited England and became a London celebrity with the publication of his *Pacific Poems* (1870). He was lionized as a romantic figure of the American West by the literary circle of William Michael Rossetti, and a revision of *Pacific Poems,* issued as *Songs of the Sierras* (1871), was praised by British reviewers.

He returned to the United States in 1872 but subsequently visited Europe, South America, and possibly the Near East, meanwhile continuing to write and publish. After residing for brief periods in New York and other eastern cities, he settled in Oakland, Calif., in 1887. He was a special correspondent in the Klondike for the New York *Journal* in 1897–1898.

Miller's many published writings included *Songs of the Sun-lands* (1873); *Life Amongst the Modocs* (1873); *The Ship in the Desert* (1875); *The Baroness of New York,* a novel (1877); *Songs of Italy* (1878); *Shadows of Shasta* (1881), a prose romance; *The Danites in the Sierras* (1882), a drama; *The Destruction of Gotham* (1886), a novel; and *The Building of the City Beautiful* (1893), a Utopian essay. *The Complete Poetical Works of Joaquin Miller* appeared in 1897 (rev. ed., 1902), followed by *Joaquin Miller's Poems* (6 vols., 1909–1910).

Consult Peterson, Martin S., *Joaquin Miller, Literary Frontiersman* (Palo Alto, Calif., 1937).

MILLER, Dayton Clarence, American physicist and musicologist: b. Strongsville, Ohio, March 13, 1866; d. Cleveland, Ohio, Feb. 22, 1941. He received a doctorate in physics from Princeton University in 1890, and was professor of physics from 1893 at the Case School of Applied Science (now Case Institute of Technology) in Cleveland, Ohio. Among his major scientific contributions were studies of the relative motion of the earth and ether, and the photographing of sound waves. He was the author of *Sound Waves, Shape and Speed* (1937); *Sparks, Lightning, Cosmic Rays* (1939); and of several works on music, notably *Boehm on the Flute and Flute-Playing* (1908); *The Science of Musical Sounds* (1916); and *An Anecdotal History of Sound* (1935).

MILLER, Edward, American physician: b. near Dover, Del., May 9, 1760; d. New York, N. Y., March 17, 1812. He began to study medicine with a physician at Dover, was a surgeon's mate in the Revolutionary War, and subsequently practiced at various places in Delaware and Maryland, meanwhile studying intermittently at the University of Pennsylvania, where he received a doctorate in medicine in 1789.

Miller settled in New York City in 1796, and there joined in founding the first medical periodical in the United States, the *Medical Repository* (August 1797). He served as physician to the Port of New York from 1803, and helped to start the College of Physicians and Surgeons (1807). An authority on yellow fever, he recognized that it was not communicated from person to person. He studied the epidemic in New York in 1805, and wrote a celebrated report on it, entitled *Report on the Malignant Disease which Prevailed in the City of New York in the Autumn of 1805: Addressed to the Governor of New York* (1806).

MILLER, Ferdinand von, German bronze founder: b. Fürstenfeldbruck, Germany, Oct. 18, 1813; d. Munich, Feb. 11, 1887. He studied bronze founding and sculpture in Munich under his uncle, Johann Baptist Stiglmayer, whom he succeeded as director of the Royal Bavarian Foundry in 1844. He cast many celebrated bronzes, notably a statue representing Bavaria, in Munich, and the bronze door of the Capitol at Washington, D.C.

Baron Ferdinand von Miller (b. Munich, Germany, June 8, 1842; d. there, Dec. 19, 1929), his son and pupil, became director of the Bavarian Academy of Fine Arts in 1900 and received the title of baron in 1912. He cast statues of Shakespeare and Columbus in St. Louis, Mo.; figures for a fountain in Cincinnati, Ohio, and for the Soldiers' Monument in Charleston, S. C.; and an equestrian statue of Emperor William I at Metz, in Lorraine.

Oskar von Miller (b. Munich, Germany, May 7, 1855; d. there, April 9, 1934), another son of the elder Ferdinand, was an electrical engineer. He organized the first German electrical exposition, at Munich (1881), and was a co-founder and director (1884–1890), with Emil Rathenau, of the Allgemeine Elektrizitäts-Gesellschaft (General Electric Company) in Berlin. He was also president of the International Electrical Exhibition at Frankfurt (1891), where he demonstrated the practicability of high-tension alternating current transmission over long distances. In 1903 he founded the Deutsches Museum, devoted to science and technology, in Munich.

MILLER, Frieda Segelke, American public official: b. La Crosse, Wis., April 16, 1889. A lifelong champion of improved working conditions, especially for women, she was educated at Milwaukee-Downer College and the University of Chicago, and in 1918 became secretary of the Women's Trade Union League in Philadelphia, serving until 1923. In 1929 she was appointed director of the women's division of the New York State Department of Labor and, after nine years in that position, was made industrial commissioner of New York State, the second woman to occupy the office. Miss Miller improved the administration of the state's unemployment insurance laws and re-employment services, and worked to eliminate racial and religious discrimination in employment. She resigned at the end of 1942, and in the summer of 1944 was chosen by President Franklin D. Roosevelt to head the Women's Bureau of the United States Department of Labor, remaining in office until November 1953.

Miss Miller also represented the United States at many meetings of the International Labour Organisation and various organs of the United Nations.

MILLER, Harriet Mann (pen name OLIVE THORNE MILLER), American author: b. Auburn, N. Y., June 25, 1831; d. Los Angeles, Calif., Dec. 25, 1918. She was educated at private schools in Ohio and, after her marriage in 1854 to Watts Todd Miller, went to live in Chicago. Here, pursuing a life-long interest, she began to write and lecture about birds and their habits. A children's book, *Little Folks in Feathers and Fur, and Others in Neither* (1875), was well received. It was followed by *Queer Pets at Marcy's* (1880), *Bird-Ways* (1885), *A Bird-Lover in the West* (1894), *The First Book of Birds* (1899), *True Bird-Stories from My Note-book* (1903), and *The Children's Book of Birds* (1915). Her extensive knowledge of birds, founded on personal observation rather than scientific research, and the unaffected charm of her writing have given her books a lasting appeal for adults as well as children.

MILLER, Henry, American author: b. New York, N. Y., Dec. 26, 1891. He attended the College of the City of New York and subsequently resided in Paris, where his first books were published. His fiction became well known for its experimental style, its surrealistic fantasy, its frank treatment of sex and morals, and its pictures of life in the Bohemias of New York and Paris. Several of his works were banned as obscene in the United States and Britain. Miller is the author of *Tropic of Cancer* (1934), *Tropic of Capricorn* (1938), *The Cosmological Eye* (1939), *The Colossus of Maroussi* (1941), *The Air-Conditioned Nightmare* (1945), and *The Smile at the Foot of the Ladder* (1948).

MILLER, Henry (John), American actor and theater manager: b. London, England, Feb. 1, 1860; d. New York, N. Y., April 9, 1926. He accompanied his parents to Toronto, Canada, at an early age, became interested in the theater, and made his debut as an actor before he was 19. Coming to the United States, he played supporting roles opposite several stars, notably Helena Modjeska, Adelaide Neilson, Clara Morris, Fanny Janauschek, and Minnie Maddern, and gained valuable experience as a member of a celebrated troupe managed by Dion Boucicault in New York Ctiy.

Miller was leading man of the Empire Theatre Stock Company, under Charles Frohman, after 1890, and was an established star after 1896. He scored a triumph with his own production of *The Great Divide,* by William Vaughn Moody, at the Princess Theatre, in New York in 1906. Subsequently he produced and acted in numerous successful plays, including *The Havoc* (1911), *Daddy Long Legs* (1913), *La Tendresse* (1922), and *The Changelings* (1923). After 1918, his productions appeared in New York at Henry Miller's Theatre, designed and built under his supervision.

MILLER, Hugh, Scottish geologist and author: b. Cromarty, Scotland, Oct. 10, 1802; d. Portobello, near Edinburgh, Dec. 23, 1856. Apprenticed to a stone mason at 17, he was prompted to a life-long interest in geology by the sight of some ripple marks in the bed of a quarry. While working as a journeyman mason between 1822 and 1834 he read widely, studied geological formations in various parts of Scotland, formed friendships with persons of literary interests, and began to write verse and essays.

His *Poems Written in the Leisure Hours of a Journeyman Mason* (1829) received the praise of prominent critics, and his *Letters on the Herring Fishery* (1829), originally published in the *Inverness Courier,* gained him a local reputation.

He became an accountant in a bank at Cromarty in 1834 and continued to pursue various literary, religious, and scientific interests. His *Scenes and Legends of the North of Scotland* (1835), containing a chapter on geology, broadened his reputation, and in 1840 he became editor of *The Witness,* a periodical established at Edinburgh by leaders of the Scottish Free Church movement to advocate popular control of the Church of Scotland. In this publication he first brought out the articles subsequently collected as *The Old Red Sandstone, or New Walks in Old Fields* (1841), his most important geological work, illustrated with his own drawings of rocks and fossils, which first drew attention to the importance of this formation as a source of fossil remains.

A devout Christian, Miller defended the doctrine of special creation and maintained that the Bible, rightly interpreted, was not contradicted by geological discoveries. He believed that the six days of creation mentioned in Genesis correspond to six geological eras, of which he found evidence in rock formations. This theory he set forth in *The Footprints of the Creator, or the Asterolepsis of Stromness* (1847), and in *The Testimony of the Rocks* (1857). *My Schools and Schoolmasters,* an autobiography, appeared in 1852.

MILLER, (David) Hunter, American lawyer and government official: b. New York, N. Y., Jan. 2, 1875; d. Washington, D.C., 1932. He graduated from the New York Law School in 1910, was admitted to the bar in 1911, and subsequently practiced law in New York City.

An authority on legal and other problems of international relations, he became a special assistant in the State Department in June 1917, and helped prepare data used at the Peace Conference at the end of World War I. He was legal adviser to the American commission to the conference (1918–1919); co-author, with Sir Cecil Hurst, of the final draft of the League of Nations Covenant; and a member of the delegation that submitted the American disarmament plan to the League (1924). Subsequently he returned to the State Department as treaties editor (1929) and historical adviser (1931). He was the author of numerous articles and books on international affairs, notably *My Diary at the Conference of Paris, with Documents,* 21 vols. (1924–1926); *The Drafting of the Covenant,* 2 vols. (1928), and *The Peace Pact of Paris* (1928).

MILLER, James Russell, American Presbyterian clergyman and author: b. Harshaville, Pa., March 20, 1840; d. Philadelphia, July 2, 1912. He was educated at Westminster College, New Wilmington, Pa., and the Allegheny Theological Seminary of the United Presbyterian Church, where he graduated in 1867 and was ordained a minister. He was editorial superintendent of the Presbyterian Board of Publication in Philadelphia from 1887 until his death, and was the author of more than 60 devotional books, notably *Devotional Hours with the Bible,* 8 vols. (1909–1913), which sold more than two million copies.

MILLER, Joaquin. See MILLER, CINCINNATUS HINER.

MILLER, Johann Martin, German novelist and poet: b. Ulm, Germany, Dec. 3, 1750; d. there, June 21, 1814. He studied theology at Göttingen and subsequently was a clergyman at Ulm. He was the author of sentimental novels in the manner of *Die Leiden des jungen Werthers* by Johann Wolfgang von Goethe. Among them were *Siegwart, eine Klostergeschichte* (1776); *Beitrag zur Geschichte der Zärtlichkeit* (1776); *Briefwechsel dreier akademischer Freunde* (1776–1777); and *Geschichte Karls von Burgheim und Emiliens von Rosenau* (1778–1779). His lyric poem, *Was frag ich viel nach Geld und Gut,* became widely known.

MILLER, John Henry (Ger. JOHANN HEINRICH MILLER or JOHANN HENRICH MILLER), German-American printer, editor, and publisher: b. Rheden, Germany, March 12, 1702; d. Bethlehem, Pa., March 31, 1782. He was apprenticed in 1715 to a printer at Basel, Switzerland, and subsequently published a newspaper at Zurich. In 1741–1742 he visited Philadelphia and for a short period worked in the printing shop of Benjamin Franklin. Returning to America in 1751, he joined Samuel Holland in founding a bilingual newspaper, *Die Lancastersche Zeitung,* in Lancaster, Pa. After another sojourn in Europe (1754–1760), Miller took up residence in Philadelphia, where in 1762 he established a newspaper, *Der Wöchentliche Staatsbote,* which continued to appear under various titles until 1779. As a patriotic gesture, he suspended it in protest against the Stamp Act, from Oct. 31 to Nov. 18, 1765. He also published a yearly almanac in German and other books in German and English, notably Thomas Godfrey's *Juvenile Poems* (1765), which contained *The Prince of Parthia,* the first play by an American to be produced professionally in America.

Henrich Miller's Pennsylvanische Staatsbote was the first newspaper to announce the adoption of the Declaration of Independence, carrying the news on July 5, 1776. The paper was again suspended in September 1777 because of the occupation of Philadelphia by British troops. It was reestablished in August 1778, but Miller retired from business the next year and removed to Bethlehem, Pa.

MILLER, John Peter, German-American Protestant clergyman: b. Zweikirchen, Germany, Dec. 25, 1709; d. Ephrata, Pa., Sept. 25, 1796. He attended the University of Heidelberg and in 1730 emigrated to Philadelphia, where he was ordained and engaged as a minister by various German Reformed congregations. Influenced by Johann Conrad Beissel (q.v.) to adopt a life of ascetic rigor, he renounced the Reformed Church in 1735 and retired to the Seventh Day Baptist cloister at Ephrata, where he remained until his death. He succeeded Beissel as head of the Ephrata Community in July 1768.

Miller edited various books published by the Seventh Day Baptist press at Ephrata, corresponded with Benjamin Franklin, George Washington, and other prominent men, and became widely known for his learning. He was chosen by the Continental Congress to translate the Declaration of Independence into various European languages.

MILLER, Joseph or **Josias** (known as JOE MILLER), English comic actor: b. 1684; d. London, England, Aug. 16, 1738. He first appeared at the Drury Lane Theatre in London in 1709 and from 1714 was a regular member of the company there, playing comic roles in all the popular favorites of the day. He is remembered chiefly because of the title of a book, *Joe Miller's Jests, or the Wit's Vade Mecum,* a collection of 247 jests compiled by John Mottley, which appeared in 1739. Three of the jests are told of Miller; but he had no other connection with the volume. It was reissued in so many revised and enlarged editions that any stale joke came to be called "a Joe Miller."

MILLER, Kenneth Hayes, American painter and etcher: b. Oneida Community, Oneida, N. Y., March 11, 1876; d. New York, N. Y., Jan. 1, 1952. He attended the Art Students' League and the New York School of Art in New York City, and subsequently studied in Europe. He taught drawing and painting at the New York School of Art between 1899 and 1911 and at the Art Students' League between 1911 and 1936 and again in 1943. Miller was awarded the gold medal for painting by the National Academy of Design in 1943 and the Ada S. Garrett prize at the Chicago Art Institute annual American painters' exhibit in 1945. His works, characteristically scenes of life in New York City, are represented in numerous collections, notably in the Museum of Modern Art, the Whitney Museum, and the Metropolitan Museum, New York City.

MILLER, Lewis, American inventor and philanthropist; b. Greentown, Ohio, July 24, 1829; d. New York, N. Y., Feb. 17, 1899. He worked as a machinist for the Ball brothers, manufacturers of reapers and mowing machines in Greentown, and in 1852 became a partner in Ball, Aultman & Company, which established its plant in Canton. When another plant was founded in Akron in 1863, Miller became its manager. He made several improvements in the design of mowing machines and binders.

In 1874, at Chautauqua Lake, N. Y., Miller and John H. Vincent organized the first Chautauqua Assembly, which became a regular annual summer event thereafter, providing educational and recreational activities for tens of thousands of adult visitors (see CHAUTAUQUA MOVEMENT). He remained active as a director of the institution until his death. Miller's daughter, Mina, became the wife of Thomas Alva Edison in 1886.

MILLER, Max, American author: b. Traverse City, Mich., Feb. 9, 1899; d. La Jolla, Calif., Dec. 27, 1967. He served in the Navy in World War I, attended the University of Washington, and after traveling in the South Pacific settled in San Diego as a reporter. Miller's first book, *I Cover the Waterfront* (1932), a volume of vivid reportage on the lives of San Diego maritime workers, scored an immediate success and was made into a motion picture. It was followed by *The Great Trek* (1935) and

Fog and Men on Bering Sea (1936), accounts of life in Alaska, and *Mexico Around Me* (1937), an unusual travel book dealing mainly with the southernmost part of the country. Miller's first novel, *A Stranger Came to Port* (1938), tells the story of a business executive who escapes for a year from his respectable surroundings to live on a houseboat among waterfront characters. During World War II, Miller again served in the navy and wrote several books based on his experiences.

MILLER, Olive Thorne. See MILLER, HARRIET MANN.

MILLER, Patrick, Scottish inventor: b. Glasgow, Scotland, 1731; d. Dalswinton, Dumfriesshire, Dec. 9, 1815. He was engaged in business as a merchant and banker in Edinburgh from 1760, became a director of the Bank of Scotland in 1767, and was deputy governor of the bank from 1790 until his death. He was also an important stockholder in the Carron Iron Company, manufacturers of ordnance, and participated in experiments for improving the naval cannon produced by the concern.

In October 1788, he demonstrated the practicability of steam navigation by sailing an experimental boat, with paddle wheels powered by a steam engine, on a lake at his estate of Dalswinton, Dumfriesshire, where he resided after 1785. In his old age he introduced the cultivation of fiorin grass into Scotland. Miller was for a time the landlord of the poet Robert Burns, and was occasionally his benefactor.

MILLER, Samuel Freeman, American jurist: b. Richmond, Ky., April 5, 1816; d. Washington, D.C., Oct. 13, 1890. He received a doctorate in medicine from Transylvania University in Lexington, Ky., in 1838, and subsequently practiced in the neighborhood of Barbourville, Knox County. Here he became a justice of the peace and a member of the county court. In 1847, after studying law privately, he abandoned medicine to become an attorney.

An antislavery Whig, Miller in 1850 removed to Keokuk, Iowa, hoping to find a community congenial to his moderate abolitionism. He established a successful law practice and, following the decay of the Whig Party, helped to organize the Republican Party in the state. In 1862 he was nominated by President Abraham Lincoln to succeed Peter V. Daniels as associate justice of the United States Supreme Court. The nomination was unanimously confirmed in the Senate because of the strong support of Republican politicians in Iowa and other Western states.

Miller soon became a prominent figure on the Supreme Court bench. His decisions were based on his view of what best served the national interest, with due regard to states' rights, rather than on legal and historical precedents. He admitted that he lacked scholarly training in the law, but regarded a sense of justice and a concern for the national well-being as more important than historical arguments concerning the meaning of the Constitution.

While a member of the Supreme Court, Miller wrote more than 600 majority decisions. In the so-called Slaughterhouse Cases (q.v.), he rendered the first important interpretation of the 14th Amendment, ruling that its guarantees apply only to rights and privileges held under federal, and not under state, law. He was a Republican member of the Electoral Commission of 1877, and voted with the majority that decided the disputed presidential election of 1876 in favor of Rutherford B. Hayes.

MILLER, William, American religious leader: b. Pittsfield, Mass., Feb. 15, 1782; d. Hampton, N. Y., Dec. 20, 1849. He had little formal schooling, but read widely in books borrowed from educated neighbors at Hampton, N. Y., where he spent his childhood and youth. After some years as a farmer at Poultney, Vt., he fought in the War of 1812, and then returned to Hampton to resume farming. During these early years Miller was a deist, but in 1816 he underwent a religious conversion. Minute study of the Bible for the next 15 years convinced him that various passages prophesied the second coming of Jesus and the end of the world in 1843. He began to preach the second coming publicly in 1831, attracting large audiences and gaining many adherents.

In 1836 he published a volume of lectures entitled *Evidence from Scripture and History of the Second Coming of Christ, about the Year 1843*. His teachings were given wide circulation after 1839 in publications issued by one of his disciples, Joshua Vaughan Himes, whose activities as a publicist for Miller led to the formation of a nation-wide Adventist movement. Miller traveled from town to town conducting revival meetings in which he preached the second coming and urged his hearers to prepare for the fatal day.

The Adventists, or Millerites as they were sometimes called, finding that the second coming did not take place in 1843, fixed on Oct. 22, 1844, as the prophetic date. As the day approached, thousands abandoned their occupations in expectation of the world's end. Disappointed a second time, Miller did not lose faith, but thenceforth refrained from trying to predict the date of the advent.

Up to this time, Miller's adherents had retained their membership in the established Protestant churches, but in 1845 rising dissension between his followers and other Protestants led to the formation of a separate Adventist Church. Miller soon retired from active leadership, but his disciples carried on his teachings, which in essentials formed the basis of several successor denominations that stemmed from the Adventist Church. See also ADVENTISTS.

MILLER, William, English soldier: b. Wingham, Kent, England, Dec. 2, 1795; d. Callao, Peru, Oct. 31, 1861. He entered the supply department of the British Royal Artillery in 1811, served under the 1st duke of Wellington in campaigns against Napoleon in the Iberian Peninsula and southern France (1811–1814), and accompanied British expeditionary forces to the United States towards the end of the War of 1812. After two years of travel in Europe, he joined the forces of Gen. Bernardo O'Higgins in the Chilean war for independence. Miller was commandant of marines aboard the flagship of the Chilean fleet in 1818, defeated a Spanish garrison at Pisco, Peru, in August 1821, and subsequently was made governor of the Peruvian Province of Ica. He became general of a brigade in the Peruvian Army in 1823, and later the same year was promoted by the Peruvian commander in chief, Simón Bolívar, to the rank of commander in chief of cavalry. At the decisive Battle of Ayacucho, July

1824, he distinguished himself by leading a brilliant cavalry charge.

After a four years' visit to Europe, Miller returned to Peru in 1830 and held important civil and military posts there until 1839, when changes in political control caused his banishment. He became British consul general in the Pacific in 1843 and died while on a mission to the Peruvian government.

MILLER, William, Scottish poet: b. Glasgow, Scotland, August 1810; d. there, Aug. 20, 1872. He became a wood turner or maker of wooden vessels at an early age, and worked at the trade until a few months before his death. He contributed verse regularly to the Scottish miscellany *Whistle Binkie,* and was especially well known for his nursery rhymes, notably *Wee Willie Winkie.* A collection of his verse, *Scottish Nursery Songs and Other Poems,* was published in 1863.

MILLER, William Allen, English chemist: b. Ipswich, England, Dec. 17, 1817; d. Liverpool, Sept. 30, 1870. At the age of 15 he became a surgical apprentice to his uncle, Bowyer Vaux, at Birmingham General Hospital, and later studied medicine at King's College, London, receiving a doctorate in 1842; but his major interest was chemical research. He became assistant lecturer in chemistry at King's College in 1841 and professor of chemistry there in 1845.

Miller devised new methods for using spectrum analysis to determine the chemical identity of substances, demonstrating in 1862, by means of photographs, the existence of characteristic differences in the spectra of 25 metals. Subsequently, with Sir William Huggins (q.v.), he made photospectroscopic analyses of the light of various stars and obtained the first reliable detailed information about solar and stellar chemistry.

MILLER, William Edward was the unsuccessful Republican candidate for Vice-President of the United States in 1964. Miller and Barry Goldwater, the Republican presidential candidate, were defeated by President Lyndon Johnson and his running-mate Sen. Hubert Humphrey.

Miller was born in Lockport, N.Y., on Mar. 22, 1914. Reared a Roman Catholic, he graduated from Notre Dame in 1935, and from Union University Law School in Albany, N.Y., in 1938. He enlisted in the U.S. Army in 1942, and the next year married Stephanie Wagner. Assigned to military intelligence, he rose to the rank of lieutenant before his discharge in 1946.

After serving as district attorney for New York's Niagara County from 1948 to 1950, Miller was elected to Congress in 1950. A political conservative, he was returned to Congress in each succeeding election until 1964, when he ran for the vice-presidency. He also served as national chairman of the Republican Party from 1961 to 1964.

Shortly after Goldwater received the 1964 Republican nomination for the presidency, he announced that Miller would be his running mate. He told friends that he had picked Miller because "he drives President Johnson nuts."

Miller conducted an extensive and hard-hitting campaign, particularly against Democratic vice-presidential candidate Hubert Humphrey. A skilled speaker, Miller drew large crowds on his campaign tour.

MILLER, William Henry Harrison, American jurist: b. Augusta, N. Y., Sept. 6, 1840; d. Indianapolis, Ind., May 25, 1917. He graduated from Hamilton College in 1861, served briefly in the 84th Ohio Infantry in the Civil War, and subsequently studied law privately in Toledo, Ohio, and Peru, Ind. He was admitted to the bar in 1865 and eventually, in Indianapolis, became a law partner of Benjamin Harrison, 23d president of the United States. When Harrison assumed office in 1889, Miller became attorney general in his cabinet and one of his closest political advisers. As attorney general, Miller was known for his impartiality and his refusal to bow to political influences.

MILLER, Willoughby Dayton, American dentist and bacteriologist: b. near Alexandria, Ohio, Aug. 1, 1853; d. Newark, July 27, 1907. He graduated from the University of Michigan in 1875 and subsequently studied chemistry, physics, and mathematics at the University of Berlin. In 1877, after working on a research project with F. P. Abbot, an American dentist in Berlin, Miller decided to adopt dentistry as his profession. He received a doctorate in dental surgery from the University of Pennsylvania in 1879, returned to Berlin, and began to practice with Abbot. In 1884 he was appointed professor of dentistry at the University of Berlin, and received a doctorate in medicine there in 1887.

Miller made important contributions to the knowledge of the chemical and bacterial causes of dental and oral disease. Using extracted teeth, he demonstrated in the laboratory that decay is the result of the acids formed by bacteria in the human mouth. His researches and his skill as a dentist brought him numerous honors. In 1894 he was appointed professor extraordinary on the medical faculty of the University of Berlin, one of the few foreigners and the first dentist to receive such an appointment. He was president of the National Dental Association of Germany and personal medical councilor to Emperor William II. He returned to the United States in 1907 to become dean of the dental college of the University of Michigan, but died before he could assume his post. He was the author of numerous articles on dentistry and of *The Micro-Organisms of the Human Mouth* (1890).

MILLER, the popular name for any moth whose wings appear to be covered with a dust or powder resembling the flour on a miller's clothes. By many entomologists, however, the name is restricted to members of the family Noctuidae—medium to large, hairy moths, with long antennae and strong wings, which are found all over the world, most abundantly in forests and plains. The family comprises about 500 genera and 20,000 species. The larvae of many species, known commonly as cutworms or army worms, are destructive pests.

MILLERAND, mēl-rän′, **Alexandre,** French statesman: b. Paris, France, Feb. 10, 1859; d. Versailles, April 6, 1943. He studied law at the University of Paris, became an attorney in 1881, and the following year began to contribute articles to the periodical *Justice,* founded in 1880 by Georges Clemenceau. He entered the Chamber of Deputies in 1885 as a Socialist, and in 1889 founded the newspaper *Voix* to advocate socialism.

Millerand assumed management of the Socialist periodical *La Petite République* jointly with

René Viviani in 1893, but in 1899 broke with the majority of Socialists, led by the Marxists Jules Guesde and Jean Jaurès, to become minister of commerce in a coalition cabinet of moderates and liberals under René Waldeck-Rousseau. He was instrumental in securing the enactment of far-reaching social legislation limiting hours of labor and providing for old age pensions, the latter adopted in 1905, after he had left office.

While minister of public works under Aristide Briand (1909–1910), Millerand broke a general strike of railroad workers in October 1910 by temporarily drafting them into the French Army. He was minister of war in the cabinet headed by Raymond Poincaré (1912–1913) and again during World War I under Viviani (1914–1915), and served simultaneously as premier and foreign minister from January to September 1920, when he was elected president of the French Republic. His repeated attempts to intervene in the conduct of affairs, however, led to his downfall. In 1924 Édouard Herriot refused to assume the premiership while Millerand was president, and he was forced to resign. He remained in public life as a senator from 1925 to 1940.

MILLEROVO, mĭl-ĕ-rō'vō, Russ. myĭl-lyĕ-rô'vŭ, city, USSR, located in Rostov Oblast, Russian Soviet Federated Socialist Republic, 120 miles northeast of Rostov. It is an important rail junction on the Moscow-Rostov line and a distributing and industrial center, with flour and oilseed mills, machine manufacturing plants, and railroad repair shops. In World War II, it was taken by German troops in July 1942 and recaptured, after a four weeks' siege, by the Red Army in January 1943. Pop. (1959) 30,005.

MILLER'S TALE, The, one of the *Canterbury Tales,* by Geoffrey Chaucer (qq.v.). It concerns the deception practiced on an old husband, a carpenter of Oxford, by his young wife and a clerk who lodges with them. The source of the tale is unknown. It was composed about 1390.

MILLER'S-THUMB, a common English and American name for several species of small, fresh-water fish of the genus *Cottus.* They are smooth skinned, and are remarkable for their disproportionately large heads, flattened like the proverbial miller's thumb. They feed on insects, small crustaceans, algae, and the eggs of other fishes.

C. gobio, common in streams in England, northern Europe, and northern Asia, seldom grows more than 4 or 5 inches long; it is brownish above and whitish beneath. *C. bairdii* and *C. cognatus,* common in clear, rocky streams in North America east of Missouri, grow up to 5 or 6 inches long. Olive green, or brownish mottled with darker brown, they readily blend with the appearance of stream bottoms or tangles of pondweed. The spawning season of these small fishes is from April to July. The eggs, which are about an eighth of an inch in diameter, are laid in pinkish clusters, each cluster containing from one hundred to two hundred eggs.

Miller's-thumbs have also been given the name of bullheads. They differ from the bullheads of the common American catfish family (see BULLHEAD).

MILLERSBURG, mĭl'ẽrz-bûrg, village, Ohio, county seat of Holmes County, in the central part of the state, 32 miles southwest of Canton. It is a market and distributing point for an adjoining agricultural region, with some manufacturing (furniture, concrete burial vaults). Nearby are coal mines, sandstone quarries, and gravel pits. The village was settled in 1816. Pop. 2,979.

MILLERSBURG, borough, Pennsylvania, located in the central part of the state, on the Susquehanna River, in Dauphin County, 20 miles north of Harrisburg. Metal products, shoes, and clothing are manufactured here. The borough was laid out in 1807 and incorporated in 1850. Pop. 3,074.

MILLERSVILLE, mĭl'ẽrz-vĭl, borough, Pennsylvania, located in the southeastern part of the state, in Lancaster County, four miles southwest of Lancaster. A state teachers college is located here. The borough was incorporated in 1932 and is named for John Miller, who settled here in 1761. Pop. 6,396.

MILLES, mĭl'lĕs, **Carl** (originally WILHELM CARL EMIL ANDERSON), Swedish-American sculptor: b. Lagga, Sweden, June 23, 1875; d. Lidingö, near Stockholm, Sept. 19, 1955. After receiving his first instruction in carving and modeling at the Technical School in Stockholm, he attended the École des Beaux-Arts in Paris between 1898 and 1900. His work received praise from the celebrated sculptor Auguste Rodin, in whose studio Milles worked for several months, and in 1900 he was awarded an honorable mention for a marble sculpture at the Salon des Artistes Français and a silver medal for a figure at the Paris World Exposition.

His artistic reputation thereafter steadily widened, and by 1914 he was considered by many the foremost Swedish sculptor. In 1920 he was appointed professor of modeling at the Royal Academy of Art, Stockholm, but his artistic development ran counter to prevailing tendencies at the academy, and in 1929 he accepted a position in the sculpture department of the Cranbrook Academy of Art, Bloomfield Hills, Mich. He became a naturalized citizen of the United States in 1945.

Milles executed more than 100 major works, including numerous monumental sculptures for public buildings, parks, and gardens in Europe and the United States. Notable among his sculptures in the United States are *The Meeting of the Waters* in St. Louis, Mo., a group of 19 heroic nude figures representing mythologically the meeting of the Missouri and Mississippi rivers; a wood-carved mural for the Time and Life Building, Rockefeller Center, New York City; the *Fountain of Faith* at Falls Church, Va.; and bronze figures for the courtyards of the Chicago Art Institute and the Des Moines (Iowa) Art Center.

Milles was the recipient of numerous honors, including the decoration of the French Légion d'Honneur and honorary doctorates from universities in Europe and the United States.

Consult Rogers, Meyric R., *Carl Milles: an Interpretation of His Work* (New Haven 1940).

MILLES, Ruth Anna Maria (original surname ANDERSON), Swedish sculptor: b. Vallentuna, Sweden, April 10, 1873; d. Rome, Italy, Feb. 11, 1941. Sister of Carl Milles (q.v.), she was known for the delicate elegance of her work.

Unlike her brother, she avoided large subjects and specialized in statues and figurines of women and children. She is represented in Stockholm in the Thielska Gallery and in the National Museum, whose collection includes *The Mother, Farmer's Wife,* and *The Little Cripple.* Her *Windy Weather* and *Girl with a Bouquet* are in Rome. She was also a well-known illustrator of children's books.

MILLET, mē-lĕ', **Aimé,** French sculptor: b. Paris, France, Sept. 28, 1819; d. there, Jan. 14, 1891. Unsuccessful as a painter, he turned to sculpture, which he studied with Pierre Jean David (David d'Angers) and Eugène Viollet-le-Duc. He was commissioned to make statues for many public buildings in Paris, including the marble figure *Mercury* for the Louvre Museum and *Civil Justice* for the town hall of the first *arrondissement.* His best-known works are *Apollo* on the façade of the Opéra in Paris and the colossal bronze *Vercingetorix,* which Napoleon III had erected on Mont Auxois near Dijon.

MILLET, mĭl'ĕt, **Francis Davis,** American painter and author: b. Mattapoisett, Mass., Nov. 3, 1846; d. at sea, April 15, 1912. After serving briefly as a drummer in the Union forces during the Civil War, he completed his education at Harvard (1869) and studied art at the Royal Academy in Antwerp, Belgium (1871–1872). As a correspondent for the New York *Herald* and the London *Daily News* he covered the Russo-Turkish War of 1877–1878. Later, *Harper's Magazine* commissioned him to travel through eastern Europe (1891), a trip which he described in *The Danube* (1893). Millet's articles on the action in the Philippines during the Spanish-American War, for *The Times,* London, and the New York *Sun,* were collected in *The Expedition to the Philippines* (1899). He also published a translation of Count Leo Tolstoy's *Sebastopol* (1887) and a collection of short stories, *A Capillary Crime and Other Stories* (1892).

Millet exhibited his paintings widely in the United States and Europe, including the Paris Salon and the British Royal Academy, and in 1885 became a member of the National Academy of Design. Examples of his work as a genre painter are *The Cosy Corner* (The Metropolitan Museum of Art, New York City) and *Between Two Fires* (Tate Gallery, London). Later he became well known as a muralist, executing commissions in such public buildings as the Essex County Courthouse in Newark, N.J., the Federal Building in Cleveland, Ohio, and the Minnesota State Capitol at St. Paul. His murals in the customhouse in Baltimore, depicting the evolution of navigation, were considered especially fine. He was director of decorations for the World's Columbian Exposition in Chicago (1893), and in 1911 became director of the American Academy in Rome. He died in the sinking of the *Titanic.*

Consult American Federation of Arts, *Francis Davis Millet: Memorial Meeting* (Washington, D.C., 1912).

MILLET, mē-lĕ', **Jean François,** French painter, a founder of the Barbizon school of painting: b. Gruchy, near Cherbourg, France, Oct. 4, 1814; d. Barbizon, Jan. 20, 1875. Millet was born of peasant stock, of which he was proud. Much later, when his scenes of country life were acknowledged as masterly achievements, he declared: "I am a peasant, and only a peasant." His father recognized his son's talents when Millet was still a boy and encouraged him to study with such masters as he could find in Cherbourg. There for two years (1834–1836) he worked with a pupil of Antoine Jean Gros, Lucien Langlois de Chèvreville, who persuaded the municipal council to award Millet a scholarship for study in Paris.

Early Career.—Millet arrived in the capital in January 1837 and entered the studio of a fashionable academic painter, Paul Delaroche. His powerful but still clumsy style annoyed his master, and after a difficult time for both, Millet left the studio to spend long hours in the Louvre Museum studying the works of the old masters. He particularly admired Nicolas Poussin's classic style and Francisco Goya's realistic technique. From 1840 he exhibited in the Salon, but his contributions went unnoticed until 1844 when a pastel, *The Riding Lesson,* attracted the enthusiastic attention of such painters as N. V. Diaz (Narcisse Virgile Diaz de la Peña) and Théodore Rousseau. During these years Millet supported himself and his young wife, Pauline Ono, whom he had married in 1841, by painting small pictures in the style of such 18th century masters as François Boucher. In the worst of times he was reduced to painting signboards.

After the death of Mme. Millet in 1844, the artist returned to Cherbourg and Le Havre, where he gained some reputation as a portrait painter. The *Naval Officer* (Rouen Museum) is a fine example of his strong portrait style. He returned to Paris in 1845 with his second wife, Catherine Lemaire, and two years later had his first success at the Salon with *Oedipus Taken from the Tree,* a classic subject chosen to demonstrate his ability in painting the nude but created in a vigorously realistic manner. It was thought crude and ugly by many critics but was strongly defended by two influential writers, Théophile Gautier and Théophile Thoré, who were acute judges of new painting.

Barbizon Period.—During the revolutionary days of 1848 and 1849, Millet and his growing family knew financial hardships when prices rose and purchasers disappeared. Finally, in June 1849, Millet and the landscape and animal painter, Charles Jacque, left Paris and settled with their families in the small village of Barbizon, near the Forest of Fontainebleau, where they were later joined by Diaz, Rousseau, Jules Dupré, and other artists. In these rural surroundings Millet turned from the classic and nude subjects which he had worked on in Paris to scenes of peasant life. His understanding of the hard lot of the farm laborer found perfect expression in his choice of subject and natural inclination toward powerful but simple drawing and coloring.

When Millet's Barbizon paintings were first exhibited in Paris, the critics complained that the subjects were vulgar and the treatment subversive, but gradually his sincerity and artistic mastery were better understood. His first great success, *The Gleaners* (Louvre Museum), was shown at the Salon of 1857 and praised by Edmond About, who hailed "the arrival of a great painter treading the footsteps of Michelangelo and Le Sueur."

Critical controversy broke out again in 1863 when Millet exhibited his *Man with a Hoe,* which was condemned as dangerously socialistic. Millet's reply to his critics in a letter to his friend, Alfred Sensier, was a succinct statement of his artistic principles: "They say that I deny the charms of the countryside. I find much more there than

Museum of Fine Arts, Boston

"The Potato Planters" by Jean François Millet.

charm: I find infinite splendor. . . . I see it in the work-horses sweating in the fields, and again, in a rocky place where a man, totally exhausted, whose labored breathing we have heard since morning, tries to straighten up for a moment to get his breath. . . . My critics are men of taste and learning, I suppose, but I cannot put myself in their shoes; and since I have never seen anything but the country, I try to tell, as best I can, what I saw and felt when I worked there."

At the Universal Exposition of 1867, Millet finally was recognized as one of the masters of modern French painting. Nine important works were shown, and he received a first medal. The following year he was awarded the Legion of Honor. During the Franco-Prussian War (1870–1871) he took refuge with his family in his native village, where he painted splendid landscapes and views of the Norman coast. His last years in Barbizon were clouded by illness, but he had the satisfaction of receiving a government commission to decorate a chapel in the Panthéon in Paris. Unfortunately he did not live to undertake the work.

Reputation.—Although at his death and for a quarter of a century afterward Millet's art was highly prized by collectors and the public, it fell into neglect early in the 20th century. His palette of earth colors, often discolored and darkened by later varnish, seemed dull to eyes accustomed to the brighter hues of impressionist painting, and his peasant subjects were scorned in a period dominated by the aesthetic of nonrepresentational art. With time, however, his true qualities are re-emerging. He was a master of figural composition, organizing a few elements in a truly monumental way and eliminating all unnecessary and sentimental details. His colors, which are found to be fresh and delicate when his paintings are cleaned, are the unassuming complement to his design. In black and white, whether in his etchings or in the usually ungrateful medium of charcoal, he organized his masses in terms of the poetics of light and dark in a way equaled only later in the century by Odilon Redon and Georges Seurat. Unfortunately, the popularity of a few of his works, such as the *Angelus* and the *Sower,* long obscured the more majestic structure of such paintings as *The Potato Planters* (Museum of Fine Arts, Boston) and the *Newborn Calf* (Art Institute of Chicago).

Millet's art was much admired by American collectors, through whose generosity several important groups of his work can be studied in the United States, notably in the museums of Boston, New York City, Chicago, and in the Walters Art Gallery, Baltimore. See also BARBIZON PAINTERS.

Bibliography.—Sensier, Alfred, *Jean-Francois Millet* (Boston 1881); Ady, Julia (Cartwright), *Jean François Millet, His Life and Letters* (London and New York 1896); Rolland, Romain, *Millet* (New York 1902); Holme, Charles, ed., *Corot and Millet* (New York 1903); Tomson, Arthur, *Jean-François Millet and the Barbizon School* (London 1903); Moreau-Nélaton, Etienne, *Millet raconté par lui-même* (Paris 1921).

GEORGE HEARD HAMILTON,
Professor of the History of Art, Yale University.

MILLET, mĭl'ĕt, a common name applied to a variety of cultivated grasses with small seeds. In the United States several are used for hay or pastures, for stock and birdseed, and as supplementary crops in drought areas. In other parts of the world, however, especially in regions of arid climate and poor soils in China, India, and Africa, millets are staples in the human diet. In the Middle Ages they were also important grains in Europe, and they are still common in eastern Europe for making porridges, flat breads, and beer.

Foxtail millet (*Setaria italica*), the best known in North America, is extensively grown in Japan, China, India and Pakistan, the East Indies, and temperate Europe. It is probably of eastern Asian origin and was one of China's five sacred plants as early as 2700 B.C. It has dense bristly spikes, in some varieties long and drooping, in others short and erect. It reaches maturity in 6 to 10 weeks, and may be planted as a catch crop after the failure of an earlier crop.

The true millet of the Romans was the bread or proso millet (*Panicum miliaceum*), probably a native of India or the eastern Mediterranean and also long in cultivation. It has branching compact or one-sided heads with variously colored grains, which have a high protein content and provide valuable food for man and his animals. It is now most commonly grown in central Asia and southern Europe but finds some use in drier parts of North America.

A third millet sometimes cultivated in the United States is the Japanese or barnyard millet (*Echinochloa crusgalli*). It is an erect species with awnless spikes, turgid purple seed, and a large leaf area. Eight forage crops may be harvested annually. In the Orient it is an important grain and may be made into porridge or mixed with rice. Several other species of *Echinochloa* are also important in India and in central Africa.

Pearl or cattail millet (*Pennisetum glaucum*) is grown in arid western India, Pakistan, Egypt, and other parts of Africa as a wet-season crop and does well in high temperatures. It reaches 6 to 15 feet in height, has several compact heads of white seeds with high food value, and produces large quantities of foliage.

Ragi or African or finger millet (*Eleusine coracana*) favors a moist climate, producing a large crop even on poor soil in either upland or irrigated situations. It is most grown in India, Indonesia, and North Africa. The grain stores well and is made into cakes, puddings, and fermented drinks.

RICHARD M. STRAW,
Assistant Professor of Botany, Los Angeles State College.

MILLIGAN, Ex Parte, mĭl'ĭ-găn, a legal case decided in 1866 by the Supreme Court of the United States, which ruled that civilians may not be tried by military tribunals except where civil courts have ceased to function because of invasion or disorder. In 1863, President Abraham Lincoln (with the authorization of Congress) suspended the writ of habeus corpus in cases where civilians were taken into custody by military authorities for crimes against the armed forces. At this point during the Civil War some of the antiwar activities of pacifists and Copperheads (q.v.) were considered treasonable. Lambdin P. Milligan, who lived in Indiana and had participated in such activities, was arrested by military officers in 1864. He was charged with conspiracy against the United States, with aiding and comforting the enemy, and with fomenting rebellion. When tried by a court-martial, he was found guilty and was sentenced to death.

In a federal circuit court his counsel claimed that Milligan had been deprived of his constitutional right to trial by jury and attempted to have the military trial declared illegal. The case eventually reached the Supreme Court, which considered it from the point of view of the limitations of martial law. The court ruled in Milligan's favor. It held that although the United States was at war, the court-martial did not have jurisdiction in this case since Milligan was not a member of the armed forces and should have been tried in the civil courts in Indiana, which were still functioning normally. Milligan was then set free, having been in custody for 18 months. When this decision was interpreted by some to imply that the postwar military governments set up in defeated Southern states were illegal, the Supreme Court was widely attacked, especially by Radical Republicans.

Consult Klaus, Samuel, ed., *The Milligan Case* (New York 1929).

MILLIGAN COLLEGE, a coeducational institution near Johnson City, Tenn., connected with the Christian Churches (Disciples of Christ). Immediately following the Civil War, Wilson Barker developed the old Cave Springs School into an academy named the Buffalo Male and Female Institute. In 1867, Joshua Williams donated land for a permanent building, and the institute was chartered as an educational corporation. The program was raised to collegiate rank in 1881, and the name was changed to Milligan College, in memory of Robert Milligan (1814–1875), a prominent leader of the Disciples of Christ, who had been president of Kentucky University and the College of the Bible. Josephus Hopwood became the first president.

Instruction leads to bachelor's degrees in the arts and sciences, and there is preprofessional training for education, the ministry, medicine, and law. Courses in business and management are also offered. A traditional feature of the curriculum is the inclusion of relevant Biblical data as integral to the understanding of each area of learning.

MILLIGRAM, the thousandth part of a gram. See METRIC SYSTEM.

MILLIKAN, mĭl'ĭ-kăn, **Robert Andrews,** American physicist: b. Morrison, Ill., March 22, 1868; d. San Marino, Calif., Dec. 19, 1953. He studied at Oberlin College (B.A., 1891), Columbia University (Ph.D., 1895), and later also in Germany, and in 1896 joined the faculty of the University of Chicago, where he had a distinguished career as a teacher for the next 25 years. Millikan simplified methods of teaching elementary physics, and textbooks that he wrote about 1903 were still being used in revised editions at the time of his death. In 1921 he was named chairman of the executive council of the California Institute of Technology and director of its Norman Bridge Laboratory, and served in these capacities until his retirement in 1945.

Millikan made significant contributions to the 20th century revolution in physics. He did original research on X-rays and the free expansion of gases, and in 1923 received the Nobel Prize for isolating the electron and measuring its electric charge and for his work on the photoelectric effect (the electricity which light generates in certain metals). Important as these and other contributions were, he was best known for his research on cosmic rays, which he named; the results of the many years of investigation that he devoted to the subject are described in *Electrons (+ and*

California Institute of Technology

Bust of Dr. Robert A. Millikan.

—), Protons, Photons, Neutrons, Mesotrons, and Cosmic Rays (1947; enl. ed. of *The Electron,* 1917). In his opinion, cosmic rays originate in outer space, may serve as a rebuilding force in the universe, and are evidence that "the Creator is still on the job."

The son of a Congregational minister, Millikan was intensely interested in the reconciliation of science and religion, which he regarded as complementary. This philosophy is seen in some of his works, such as *Science and Life* (1924), *Evolution in Science and Religion* (1927), and *Science and the New Civilization* (1930). Besides many technical writings, he published an *Autobiography* (1950).

During World War I, Millikan served as scientific adviser to the United States government, and he received the Presidential Medal of Merit for his work on rockets and jet propulsion during World War II. See also COSMIC RADIATION; ELECTRON.

MILLIKIN UNIVERSITY, mĭl'ĭ-kĭn, a private coeducational institution of liberal arts and music in Decatur, Ill., affiliated with the Presbyterian Church. The school was founded in 1901 as the result of a generous endowment of land and funds by the Decatur banker James Millikin (1834–1909), absorbing the former Decatur College and Industrial School; instruction began in 1903. The name was changed to its present form from James Millikin University in 1953. Undergraduate curriculums include an engineering course, and master's degrees are granted in education and music. A special feature is training for radio and television work, in which local commercial stations cooperate.

MILLIN, mĭl'ĭn, **Sarah Gertrude** (nee LIEBSON), South African author: b. Barkley West, South Africa, March 19, 1889; d. Johannesburg, July 6, 1968. She began writing at 16, and by 1920 had published *The Dark River,* first of many novels dealing with South African colonial and racial issues. The most successful of them was a story of the Cape Colored people, *God's Stepchildren* (1924; new ed., 1951). Others are *Three Men Die* (1934), *King of the Bastards* (1949), and *Two Bucks Without Hair* (1958). Mrs. Millin's publications also include excellent biographies of Cecil John Rhodes (*Rhodes: a Life,* 1933; new ed., 1952) and Jan Christiaan Smuts (*General Smuts,* 1936). Her history of South Africa, *The South Africans* (1926; rev. eds., 1934, 1951), is a definitive work, and she is generally regarded as one of the most successful of South African writers in interpreting her country to the rest of the world. *The Night is Long* (1941) and *The Measure of My Days* (1955) are autobiographical.

MILLINGTON, mĭl'ĭng-tŭn, town, Tennessee, in Shelby County, in the southwestern part of the state, 15 miles northeast of Memphis. At an altitude of 270 feet, it is located on the Illinois Central Railroad and a federal highway. It is the banking town for the surrounding agricultural district, which is devoted to dairying and the production of livestock and cotton. Manufactures include wire, hats, and wood products. Pop. 21,106.

MILLINOCKET, mĭl-ĭ-nŏk'ĕt, town, Maine, in Penobscot County, in the central part of the state about 55 miles north of Bangor, on the West Branch of the Penobscot River. To be near the forests which supply its raw materials, the Great Northern Paper Company chose this site for a newsprint plant, completed in 1900. The town grew up rapidly around the mill, which became one of the largest of its kind in the United States. It was incorporated in 1901, and municipal government is of the council-manager type. At an altitude of 360 feet, it is on a state highway and is served by the Bangor and Aroostook Railroad. Millinocket Lake is north of the town, and northwest is Mount Katahdin (5,268 feet), the highest peak in the state, in Baxter State Park. Pop. 7,558.

MILLOCKER, mĭl'ûk-ĕr, **Karl,** Austrian composer: b. Vienna, Austria, May 29, 1842; d. Baden, near Vienna, Dec. 31, 1899. He was educated in Vienna and began his career as a conductor in Graz in 1864. Returning to Vienna, he served from 1869 to 1883 as conductor and composer at the historic Theater an der Wien, where most of his many operettas were first produced. Among these were *Wechselbrief und Briefwechsel* (1872), *Gräfin Dubarry* (1879), and *Der arme Jonathan* (1890). Light, melodious works of the type composed by Johann Strauss, they were highly popular in Germany and Austria and are still produced there. Most of Millöcker's operettas were performed in the United States soon after their European premières. *Der Bettelstudent* (1882), his most successful work, was especially well received in New York City when it was presented in 1883 in an English translation called *The Student Beggar.*

MILLS, mĭlz, **Benjamin Fay,** American clergyman: b. Rahway, N.J., June 4, 1857; d. Grand Rapids, Mich., May 1, 1916. Ordained to the Congregational ministry in 1878, he gave up his pastorate in 1886 to travel as an interdenominational evangelist. In 1897 he withdrew from the Congregational Church and held independent religious meetings in Boston. He was then minister (1899–1903) of the First Unitarian Church in Oakland, Calif., founder and minister (1904–1911) of the Los Angeles Fellowship, and founder and leader (1911–1914) of the Chicago Fellowship. In 1915 he was received into the Chicago Presbytery and became active in interdenominational evangelistic work, advocating broad principles of religious faith rather than dogmas or creeds. Among his books are *Power from on High* (1890); *Victory Through Surrender* (1892); *God's World, and Other Sermons* (1894); *Twentieth Century Religion* (1898); and *The Divine Adventure* (1905).

MILLS, Clark, American sculptor and bronze founder: b. Onondago County, N.Y., Dec. 13, 1810; d. Washington, D.C., Jan. 12, 1883. After learning the trades of cabinetmaker and millwright, he became a worker in stucco in Charleston, S.C. In 1835 he became interested in modeling busts in clay and devised a means of taking casts from the living face. Next he studied marble-cutting and in 1845 completed a bust of John C. Calhoun, which was bought by the Charleston city council. Encouraged to devote himself to sculpture, Mills went to Washington to study the statues there and was offered an opportunity in 1848 to design an equestrian statue of Andrew Jackson. He accepted a contract for $12,000, prepared a full-scale plaster model, and set about to cast it in bronze. He was obliged to learn casting, for no foundry was then prepared to handle such work. Congress appropriated an additional $20,000 for the sculptor, and this first American equestrian statue was placed in Lafayette Square, across from the White House, in 1853; copies of the statue were purchased for New Orleans and for Nashville. Congress then commissioned Mills to make an equestrian statue of George Washington, which was unveiled in Washington on Feb. 22, 1860; and also ordered from the sculptor a bronze casting of Thomas Crawford's colossal statue representing Freedom or armed Liberty, which was placed on the dome of the Capitol in 1863. Mills made many portrait busts, and took a life mask of Abraham Lincoln shortly before the president's death. The sculptor's last work was a design for an elaborate Lincoln memorial, to contain at least 36 heroic statues, but none of the plans materialized.

MILLS, Darius Ogden, American financier and philanthropist: b. North Salem, N.Y., Sept. 5, 1825; d. Millbrae, Calif., Jan. 4, 1910. At 22, he became cashier and partner in the Merchants' Bank of Erie County at Buffalo, N.Y., and in 1848 he set out for California to establish a trading and banking agency. In 1850 he founded the Bank of D. O. Mills & Company at Sacramento, accumulating a large fortune in the succeeding decade. He helped organize the Bank of California at San Francisco in 1864, serving as its president until 1873. When the bank failed two years later, he resumed the presidency for a year and re-established its finances, then removed permanently in 1878 to New York to engage in other financial, railroad, and industrial activities. His philanthropies included the University of California, the Lick Observatory, the San Francisco Protestant Orphan Asylum, and the Metropolitan Museum of Art; but most notable perhaps were the hotels he built for the inexpensive accommodation of people of limited means.

MILLS, Enos Abijah, American naturalist and writer: b. near Kansas City, Kans., April 22, 1870; d. near Estes Park, Colo., Sept. 21, 1922. Known as the Father of the Rocky Mountain National Park, he spent his adult life exploring nature, chiefly in the Rockies of Colorado, and writing or lecturing on his observations. In 1886 he settled in a log cabin near Long's Peak, Colo., and guided visitors to the peak. He traveled in the mountains in all seasons, making photographs which he used to illustrate his books and articles. He was a lecturer on forestry for the federal government from 1907 to 1909, and in the same period was a snow observer for the state of Colorado. Mills' long agitation for the creation of a national park in Colorado led to the establishment of the Rocky Mountain National Park in 1915. Many of his magazine articles were reprinted in such collections as *Wild Life in the Rockies* (1909) and *The Adventures of a Nature Guide* (1919). His other works included *In Beaver World* (1913); *Rocky Mountain Wonderland* (1915); and *The Grizzly, Our Greatest Wild Animal* (1918).

MILLS, John, English translator and writer on agriculture: d. about 1784. He translated (1745) into French, with the assistance of Gottfried Sellius, the English *Cyclopaedia* (1728) of Ephraim Chambers. Mills was cheated out of his rights to the work by the bookseller, André François Lebreton, who ultimately turned the editorial labors over to Denis Diderot and others and formed of it the famous *Encyclopédie* (1776–1777). Mills wrote many books on agriculture, the chief one being *A New System of Practical Husbandry,* 5 vols. (1767). This was the earliest complete treatise on the subject and brought together the observations of many agriculturists.

MILLS, Lawrence Heyworth, American Orientalist: b. New York, N.Y., 1837; d. Oxford, England, Jan. 29, 1918. He was graduated from the University of the City of New York in 1858 and from the Protestant Episcopal Theological Seminary in Alexandria, Va., in 1861. He preached until 1870 in Brooklyn, N.Y., and in Hartford, Conn., and from 1873 until 1877 in the American Episcopal Church in Florence, Italy. After 1877 he devoted himself to the study of Vedic and Iranian literature. Having established his reputation as an authority on the Zend-Avesta, the sacred writings of Zoroastrianism, he was invited by Friedrich Max Müller to complete the translation of the texts left unfinished by the French Orientalist James Darmesteter. These were published in 1887 as volume 31 of Max Müller's *Sacred Books of the East.* Mills became professor of Zend philology at Oxford in 1897. His many publications include *A Study of the Five Zarathushtrian Gâthâs, with Texts and Translations* (1894); *The Creed of Zarathushtra* (1916); and *The Vital Necessity of Persian Theology to All Biblical Study* (1916).

MILLS, Ogden Livingston, American lawyer and politician: b. Newport, R.I., Aug. 23, 1884; d. New York, N.Y., Oct. 11, 1937. A grandson of Darius Ogden Mills (q.v.), he was educated at Harvard University and the Harvard School of Law, graduating from the latter in 1907. He was admitted to the New York bar in 1908. He became active in Republican political affairs, was defeated as a candidate for Congress in 1912, but was elected to the New York Senate in 1914 and again in 1916. In 1921 he was elected to Congress as representative from New York, continuing through three terms. He was appointed undersecretary of the treasury in 1927, then succeeded Andrew Mellon as secretary of the treasury in 1932 and served until the administration terminated a year later. An expert on finance and taxation, Mills was highly critical of New Deal policies. His views were expressed in *What of Tomorrow?* (1935) and in *The Seventeen Million* (1937), the latter an effort to guide those who voted against the New Deal in 1936.

MILLS, Robert, American architect and engineer: b. Charleston, S.C., Aug. 12, 1781; d. Washington, D.C., March 3, 1855. The first native American professional architect to study exclusively in the United States, Mills served his apprenticeship under James Hoban, Thomas Jefferson, and Benjamin Latrobe. He established himself as an architect in Philadelphia in 1808 and in 1817 moved to Baltimore, his work including the Washington monument in Baltimore (1815–1829), as well as many churches and other public buildings. He was state engineer and architect of South Carolina from 1820 to 1830 and designed some of the state's most important public structures. From 1836 until his retirement in 1851, Mills was United States architect of public buildings in Washington, D.C. He designed and built the Treasury, Post Office, and Patent Office buildings in the national capital, as well as customhouses, hospitals, penitentiaries, and other structures throughout the United States. His most memorable work is the Washington Monument (1848–1885); his design for it included a circular colonnade at the base, but this was omitted from the completed structure. Among his books are *Internal Improvement of South Carolina* (1822) and *The American Pharos, or Lighthouse Guide* (1832).

Consult Gallagher, Helen, *Robert Mills, Architect of the Washington Monument, 1781–1855* (New York 1935).

MILLS, Susan Lincoln Tolman, American missionary and educator: b. Enosburg, Vt., Nov. 18, 1826; d. Oakland, Calif., Dec. 12, 1912. After graduating from Mount Holyoke Seminary in 1845 and teaching there three years, she married Cyrus Taggart Mills and went with him as a missionary to Ceylon. They spent six years there at Batticotta Seminary, then from 1860 to 1864 were at Oahu College, in the Hawaiian Islands, where Mrs. Mills taught English and natural science. In 1865 the Millses bought a girls' seminary at Benicia, Calif., and moved it to Oakland in 1871. It developed into what is now Mills College. Mrs. Mills, succeeding her husband as trustee upon his death in 1884, is recognized as the college's founder.

MILLS, Wilbur Daigh, American political leader: b. Kensett, Ark., May 24, 1909. He graduated from Hendrix College, Conway, Ark., in 1930. Three years later he received a law degree from Harvard and was admitted to the Arkansas bar. He began practice in Searcy, and from 1934 to 1938 he served as county and probate judge of White county. A Democrat, Mills was first elected to Congress in 1938.

Assigned first to the House Banking and Currency Committee and then, in 1943, to the House Ways and Means Committee, Mills became an expert on internal revenue. His general voting record reflected his basically—but not inflexibly—conservative stance. On bills concerning segregation and civil rights he voted with the Southern bloc. Rising to the chairmanship of the Ways and Means Committee in 1958, Mills thereby gained great influence on the tax, Social Security, tariff, and welfare legislation that the committee guides through Congress. He was widely recognized as brilliant and diligent, with an immense knowledge of tax law and other fiscal matters. Originally an opponent of "medicare" for the aged, Mills backed the measure when it became clear it could pass without his support. His ability to be independent of the executive was illustrated in 1967 when he held up action for almost a year on a surtax measure requested by President Johnson. Mills supported President Nixon's welfare-reform plan in 1970 but subsequently opposed the President's program for sharing federal revenues with the states. Despite prolonged hearings in 1972, his committee failed to report out a national health insurance bill.

In the early 1970's, Mills was considered the single most powerful person in Congress. He entered the presidential nomination race in 1972, but withdrew before the balloting at the Democratic National Convention. In November 1972 and 1974 he was reelected to Congress.

By late 1974, however, Mills' career and reputation had suffered seriously as press reports linked him with an Argentine striptease dancer named Fanne Foxe. He was discovered with her in an auto accident in Washington in October, then appeared on stage with her in Boston in November. By early December the House Democratic caucus had approved major reforms in committee assignments and procedures, notably affecting Mills' Ways and Means Committee. On Dec. 3, 1974, Mills entered Bethesda (Md.) Naval Medical Center for treatment.

Under pressure from his Democratic colleagues, he resigned the chairmanship of the Ways and Means Committee on December 10. On December 30 he announced that he was suffering from alcoholism and that he had had blackouts in which he did not know what he was doing. He pledged himself to "total abstinence," and reaffirmed his intention to return to Congress. (He did so in May 1975.) Meanwhile, Rep. Al Ullman (D-Oreg.) had become chairman of the Ways and Means Committee.

MILLSPAUGH, Charles Frederick, American botanist: b. Ithaca, N.Y., June 20, 1854; d. Chicago, Ill., Sept. 15, 1923. He was graduated from the New York Homeopathic Medical College in 1881 and practiced medicine at Binghamton and Waverly, N.Y., for 10 years before devoting himself chiefly to botany. His interest lay in the application of botanical knowledge to medicine and to economics. In 1891 he became professor of botany at the University of West Virginia, and from 1893 until his death was curator of the department of botany at the Field Museum of Natural History, Chicago. Here he developed the herbarium and was noted for his lectures and exhibits. He was also a professor of botany at the University of Chicago and at the Chicago Homeopathic Medical College. An explorer of and authority on plant life, Millspaugh wrote *American Medicinal Plants,* 2 vols. (1887).

MILLSTONE, either of the two cylindrical stones used to grind grain into flour. The best rock for the purpose is buhrstone. The lower stone is usually fixed; the upper is the "runner." Each stone is deeply scored with furrows, which lead the milled grist away from the center; the intervals are styled "land"; and the hole in the center is called the "eye." A depression about the eye is the "bosom." The scheme for scoring the stone varies greatly. In the United States, millstones have been almost entirely superseded by steel rollers in the manufacture of flour.

MILLSTONE GRIT, a hard, siliceous conglomerate (q.v.) found, in the United States, at the base of the Pennsylvania coal measures series of the Carboniferous (q.v.) system. The formation occurs practically throughout the Appalachian Range. In Pennsylvania the beds are coarse and over 1,200 feet thick; the rock is light in color and is called Pottsville conglomerate. It is interstratified with some sandstone, thin beds of carbonaceous shells, and thin beds of coal.

MILLTOWN, borough, New Jersey, in Middlesex County; altitude 50 feet; 3 miles south of New Brunswick. Manufactures include textiles, clothing, furniture polish, cables, and paper products. Vegetables, fruit, cattle, and poultry are raised in the area. It was incorporated in 1889. Government is by mayor and council. Pop. 6,470.

MILLVALE, borough, Pennsylvania, in Allegheny County; altitude 900 feet; on the Allegheny River, opposite Pittsburgh; served by the Pennsylvania Railroad. It has a meat-packing plant and manufactures iron and steel products. It was incorporated as a borough in 1868. Pop. 5,815.

MILLVILLE, city, New Jersey, in Cumberland County; altitude 35 feet; at the head of tidewater on the Maurice River, 10 miles southeast of Bridgeton, on the Pennsylvania-Reading Seashore Lines Railroad. There are river fisheries, and manufactures include glass, textiles, bricks, concrete products, and fertilizers. When first settled in 1720 it was important as a market for sea fish. In 1806 German glassmakers established a glass factory here. Millville was incorporated as a town in 1801 and received its city charter in 1866. Government is by a commission. Pop. 21,366.

MILMAN, Henry Hart, English historian and divine: b. London, Feb. 10, 1791; d. near Ascot, Sept. 24, 1868. He graduated at Brasenose College, Oxford University in 1814, and was professor of poetry at Oxford from 1821 to 1831. Ordained in 1816, in 1835 he was made rector of St. Margaret's and canon of Westminster; and he was dean of St. Paul's from 1849 until his death. He wrote dramas, epic poems, and hymns, but was best known for his historical works. His *History of the Jews* (1830) gave offense by his treatment of Jewish history from the secular point of view. He wrote *A History of Christianity to the Abolition of Paganism in the Roman Empire* (1840). His greatest work was *A History of Latin Christianity down to the Death of Pope Nicholas V* (1855). In 1838 he edited *The Decline and Fall of the Roman Empire,* by Edward Gibbon and wrote a *Life of Gibbon* (1839). One of his best-known hymns is *When Our Heads Are Bowed with Woe.*

MILMORE, Martin, American sculptor: b. Sligo, Ireland, Sept. 14, 1844; d. Roxbury Highlands, Boston, Mass., July 21, 1883. He moved to Boston in 1851 and in 1860 began studying sculpture under Thomas Ball. Later he studied in Rome where he made a bust of Pope Pius IX. His Soldiers' and Sailors' Monument on Boston Common, generally regarded as his greatest work, was dedicated in 1877. He also executed the Soldiers' Monument at Forest Hills Cemetery, Roxbury, Mass. His portrait bust of Charles Sumner was placed in the Metropolitan Museum, New York City; that of George Ticknor, in the Boston Public Library; and a bronze copy of that of Wendell Phillips is also in the Boston Library, to which it was presented by the Phillips Memorial Association in 1900. One of his best-known works (made in collaboration with his brother Joseph) was the huge granite Sphinx in Mount Auburn Cemetery, Cambridge, Mass.

MILNE, miln, **A.A.,** was an English playwright, essayist, and poet who achieved world fame with his books of verse and prose for children. Among them were *When We Were Very Young* (1924), *Winnie-the-Pooh* (1926), *Now We are Six* (1927), and *The House at Pooh Corner* (1928).

Alan Alexander Milne was born in London, on Jan. 18, 1882. He went to Cambridge University, where he edited the student magazine, the *Granta.* He was assistant editor of *Punch* from 1906 to 1914. A collection of his contributions to *Punch* was published as *Those Were the Days* (1929).

Among his adult prose works are *The Day's Play* (1910); *Once on a Time* (1917); *The Red House Mystery* (1921); *Two People* (1931); *Four Days' Wonder* (1933); *It's Too Late Now* (1939); *Behind the Lines* (1940); *Birthday Party* (1949); *A Table Near the Band* (1950).

His comedies, successful on both the New York and London stages, include: *Belinda* (1918); *Mr. Pim Passes By* (1919); *The Romantic Age* (1920); *The Truth About Blayds* (1921); *The Ivory Door* (1927); *Michael and Mary* (1930); *Toad of Toad Hall* (1930); *Miss Elizabeth Bennet* (1936); *Sarah Simple* (1937); *Gentleman Unknown* (1938). Milne died at Hartfield, Sussex, on Jan. 31, 1956.

MILNE, John, English geologist and seismologist: b. Liverpool, Dec. 30, 1850; d. Isle of Wight, July 30, 1913. He was educated at King's College and the Royal School of Mines, London, and practiced as a mining engineer in Cornwall, Lancashire, central Europe, and Newfoundland, besides accompanying an expedition to Arabia as geologist. In 1875 he was appointed by the Japanese government to the chair of geology and mining in the Imperial College of Engineering at Tokyo, where he married a Japanese lady and remained nearly 20 years. In 1880 he founded the Seismological Society of Japan from which hundreds of observing stations sprang up all over the country—a land subject to perhaps a thousand earthquake shocks a year. With the assistance of English colleagues, Milne was the first to devise instruments for recording these shocks, and his investigations led to the precision now obtaining in the science of seismology. Shortly before leaving Japan his residence was destroyed by fire; all his books, instruments and 2,000 volumes of the *Transactions of the Seismological Society of Japan* were lost. Returning to England in 1895, Milne and his wife settled in the Isle of Wight, where he erected a famed seismological observatory and equipped it with instruments that recorded shocks in any part of the globe. His principal works, *Earthquakes* (1883) and *Seismology* (1898) became standard textbooks.

MILNE-EDWARDS, Henri, French zoologist: b. Bruges, Belgium, Oct. 23, 1800; d. Paris, July 29, 1885. His parents were English. He studied medicine in Paris, taking his degree in 1823. Soon he turned his attention to zoology. After teaching for several years in the Collège de Henri IV, he was elected in 1838 a member of the Académie de Sciences. His *Recherches anatomiques sur les crustacés,* published in 1828, attracted attention, and from that time until his death he published books and essays on his specialty. He taught natural history, and became a noted educator, as well as an original investigator. In 1837 he became editor of the zoological department of the *Annales des sciences naturelles,* which he held for 50 years, and to which he was a contributor. In 1841 he became professor of entomology in the Jardin des Plantes (Museum of Natural History), Paris, where, 21 years later, he succeeded Étienne Geoffroy Saint-Hilaire (q.v.) in the chair of zoology. In 1864 he became director of that famous institution. The Royal Society of England honored him in 1850 with the Copley Medal for his zoological work. Milne-Edwards was the first to describe the important biological principle of the physiological division of labor. Although a contemporary of Charles Robert Darwin and Thomas Henry Huxley, Milne-Edwards was little influenced by those men of science and held to the doctrine of special creations instead of the evolution theory. In the work of his latest years he was assisted by his son, ALPHONSE (1835–1900), who was a specialist in the study of fossil birds and deep-sea exploration. Milne-Edwards published *Éléments de zoölogie ou leçons sur l'anatomie, la physiologie, la classification, etc., des animaux* (1834–35), which had an enormous circulation, and was much used as a basis for manuals of zoology; a revision of Lamarck's *L'histoire naturelle des animaux sans vertèbres* (1836–45), and with Dehayes *Leçons sur la physiologie et l'anatomie comparées de l'homme et des animaux* (1855–84); *Histoire naturelle des crustaces* (1834–40) and *Histoire naturelle des corallinaires* (1857–60) were noteworthy. His *Lectures on the Physiology and Comparative Anatomy of Man and the Animals* (14 vols., 1857–81) were valued for their great fund of information and ample references. He also published *Natural History of the French Coasts* (1832–45) and *Natural History of the Mammalia* (1871).

MILNER, Alfred, 1ST VISCOUNT MILNER, British statesman and colonial administrator: b. Giessen, Germany, March 23, 1854; d. Canterbury, Kent, May 13, 1925. He studied in Germany, where his father was instructor in English at the University of Tübingen, and at King's College, London, before entering Balliol College, Oxford University. Graduating in 1877, he was elected to a fellowship at New College, Oxford, and in 1881 he was called to the bar at Inner Temple. In 1886, after five years on the editorial staff of the *Pall Mall Gazette,* he became private secretary to George Joachim (later Viscount) Goschen (q.v.), and in 1889 he was appointed undersecretary of finance in Egypt. His *England in Egypt* (1892), published following his return to Britain, was an important account of the occupation of the country. During 1892–1897 he served as chairman of the board of inland revenue, in 1895 receiving a knighthood for his services. In 1897 he was sent to South Africa as governor of the colony of the Cape of Good Hope and high commissioner for South Africa, and in the latter capacity he was the principal British representative in negotiations with the government of the South African Republic (Transvaal) respecting the demand of the Uitlanders (q.v.) for the franchise in that country. The discussions culminated in a conference at Bloemfontein, in June 1899, between Sir Alfred Milner and President Paul (Stephanus Johannes Paulus) Kruger (q.v.), and with its failure the South African War (q.v.) ensued. With British annexation of the Transvaal and the Orange Free State in 1901, he relinquished the governorship of the Cape of Good Hope to become administrator of the two states, and when the war ended the next year he drafted the terms of surrender which were signed at Pretoria on May 31. Created a viscount, he served as governor of the Orange River Colony and the Transvaal until December 1905, laying the groundwork for the self-government which they secured two years later. In the years that followed he took a prominent part in advocating an imperial federation, tariff reform, and compulsory national service. When David Lloyd George became prime minister of Great Britain in December 1915, in the midst of World War I, he chose Lord Milner, for long a bitter political opponent, to be a member of his small War Cabinet; appointed secretary of state for war in April 1918, he continued to hold office until victory had been achieved. After the general election in December 1918, he became colonial secretary; in this capacity, during 1919, he attended the Paris Peace Conference and was a signatory to the Treaty of Versailles, and late in the year he headed a special mission to Egypt which reported in favor of granting that country's independence. When he retired from public life in 1921, the Order of the Garter was conferred upon him. Although possessed of high administrative gifts, a certain reserve, sometimes called harshness, prevented Lord Milner from ever becoming a popular figure. He was accused of being a bureaucrat of the Prussian type, while with equal unreason he was regarded as opposed to progress of all kinds. His death was due to sleeping sickness, contracted while on a visit to South Africa. His *Credo* (1925), found among his papers, was published posthumously. Consult Headlam, C., *The Milner Papers* (London 1931–33).

MILNES, Richard Monckton. See HOUGHTON, RICHARD MONCKTON MILNES.

MILO, mī'lō, or **MILON,** ancient Greek athlete of late 6th century B.C. He was a native of Crotona, in Magna Graecia, Italy, and celebrated for his great strength. He bore off the prize six times in the Olympic games, and on an equal number of occasions at the Pythian. Many anecdotes are related of him. He once carried a heifer of four years to the sacrifice on his shoulders, killed it with a blow of his fist, and afterward, it is added, ate the whole of it on one day. His death is characteristically related. When enfeebled by age, he attempted to rend open the trunk of a tree partially split by woodcutters, but the wood, closing on his hands, held him fast, and he was attacked and devoured by wolves.

MILO, Titus Annius Papianus, Roman tribune and political leader: b. Lanuvium 95 B.C.; d. district of Thurii, 48 B.C. In 57 B.C., when tribune of the plebs, his quarrel with Publius Clodius (q.v.) began. Seeking preferment in the state, he became the ally of Gnaeus Pompey, urging the recall of Cicero from exile, whither he had been sent at the instance of Clodius, as a pretext for their acts. Bands of gladiators in the employ of Milo and of Clodius kept Rome in constant terror by their skirmishes. Finally, in a clash at Bovillae, on the Appian Way, Clodius was murdered Jan. 20, 52 B.C. Milo was impeached for acts of violence in occupying public places and going about under arms, and for bribery in his canvass for the consulship. His trial began April 4, 52 B.C., Cicero undertaking his defense, but the hostility of the Clodius faction was so marked that his speech was not delivered. In a revised and enlarged form it was sent by Cicero to Milo at Massilia (Marseilles), whither he had gone into exile upon his condemnation under the first count. In 48 B.C., Milo returned to Italy and joined Marcus Caelius in rebellion against Julius Caesar.

MILO, or MILOS. See MELOS.

MILORADOVICH, myĭ-lŭ-rȧ'dŭ-vyĭch, **Mikhail Andreevich,** Russian army officer: b. 1771; d. St. Petersburg (later Leningrad), Dec. 26, 1825. He fought in the wars against Turkey (1787–1791), Poland (1793), and Italy and Switzerland (1799); and in 1805, as a lieutenant general, he commanded a division at Austerlitz. In 1812 he was in command of a corps at the indecisive Battle of Borodino, and in the subsequent retreat of Napoleon's Grand Army from Moscow he was active in destroying the rearguards. In 1819 he was appointed military governor of St. Petersburg, and he met his death there while attempting to put down the rising of the Decembrists (q.v.).

MILOS, mē'lôsh, prince of Serbia, founder of the Obrenovich dynasty: b. 1780; d. Belgrade, Sept. 27, 1860. In early life a herdsman, he became a leader of the opposition to the Karageorgevich faction. Although given an official post by the Turks, he turned against them because of their cruelties and in 1815 conducted the Serbian war of liberation. In 1817 he made himself ruler of Serbia; a national assembly, in 1827, proclaimed him hereditary prince, and this was formally recognized by the Turks in 1830. The people revolted because of his tyrannical methods, and forced his abdication in 1839. He was succeeded by his son, Milan, who died the same year; a second son, Michael, then ruled until 1842, being followed by Alexander, son of Karageorge, who was deposed by the national assembly in 1858. Milos was then recalled to power, but did not live long to exercise it.

MILOVANOVIC, mē'lȯ-vä'nȯ-vĭch, **Milovan,** Serbian jurist and statesman: b. Belgrade, March 2, 1863; d. there, July 1, 1912. The first Serb to obtain a doctorate of law at the University of Paris, he was appointed professor of international law at Belgrade University. He had a considerable share in drafting the Serbian Constitution of 1888, and became minister to Rome in 1901; despite the overthrow of the Obrenovich dynasty in 1903, he retained his diplomatic post, continuing as minister until 1907. In that year he represented Serbia at the Second Hague Conference, and was named a member of the Permanent Court of Arbitration, and in 1908 he became minister of foreign affairs. He guided the country through the crisis which followed annexation of Bosnia and Hercegovina (q.v.) by Austria-Hungary in the fall of that year. From 1911 until his death he served as prime minister; he concluded a treaty with Bulgaria which paved the way for creation of the Balkan League (q.v.).

MILREIS, mĭl'rās, formerly the monetary unit of Portugal, and also of Brazil. The word *milreis* is Portuguese for thousand reis, name of an earlier monetary unit displaced because of its depreciation. The Portuguese milreis was replaced by the escudo in 1911; and the cruzeiro was substituted for the Brazilian milreis in 1942.

MILTIADES, mĭl-tī'ȧ-dēz, Athenian general: b. ? 540 B.C.; d. ? 489 B.C. He was a descendant of the Philaïdes and, after being archon at Athens in 524, inherited a minor principality in the Chersonese in 518. He governed well there; accompanied Darius against the Scythians in 515, and being left at the bridge across the Danube, urged its destruction in order that Greece might thus be rid of a possible Persian enemy. This plan was vetoed by Histiaeus, another Greek tyrant. In 493 he left his kingdom for fear of the Persians, and upon their invasion of Greece in 490 became one of the 10 generals of the Athenian Army. Each of the other generals retired in Miltiades' favor, but he refused to lead the army until his own day of command came. Then he won the great Battle of Marathon, routing the Persian land forces. The victorious general in the next year asked the state of Athens for a fleet of 70 ships, and got his request, but did not explain that he wished to punish the people of Paros from motives of private revenge; when his expedition failed and its purpose became known, he was impeached, fined 50 talents, and imprisoned for lack of ability to pay. He died in prison of a wound received at Paros.

MILTIADES, Saint (also called MELCHIADES), pope or bishop of Rome from c. 310 to 314. He is best known as having sat as presiding officer at a synod held at Rome in 313, by desire of the Emperor Constantine, to hear a petition from the Traditones or Catholics in North Africa who had, on demand of the Emperor Diocletian, given up their sacred books and thus, in the opinion of those who resisted the demand, forfeited the rights and privileges of church membership. The action of the Traditones split the church into two bitter factions, a condition that continued for more than a century. Nothing is known of the early life of Miltiades, save that he was born in Africa, and the date of his death is uncertain. See also DONATISTS.

MILTO. See ASPASIA THE YOUNGER.

MILTON, John, American politician: b. Jefferson County, Ga., April 20, 1807; d. near Marianna, Fla., April 1, 1865. He was educated in Louisville, Ga., where he studied law and, following his admission to the bar, practiced for two years. He practiced law in Columbus, Ga., Mobile, Ala., and New Orleans, La., until 1846, when he settled in Florida on a plantation near Marianna. In 1849 he was elected to the state Senate, and in 1861 became governor. As chief executive of Florida during the Civil War, he did not always agree with the Confederate military authorities as to the best means of defending the state, but he raised, outfitted, and dispatched troops for the Confederate Army, provided hospital supplies, and met Confederate requisitions for money promptly. As the war drew to an end, he became mentally ill at the prospect of the defeat of the South and committed suicide.

MILTON, John, English poet: b. London, England, Dec. 9, 1608; d. there, Nov. 8, 1674. He was the son of John Milton (1563?–1647), who had come up to London from his ancestral home at Stanton St. John near Oxford and risen to prosperity as a scrivener or law writer. Richard Milton, the poet's grandfather, was a Roman Catholic and is said to have disinherited his son for deserting the ancient faith. The elder Milton, like other scriveners, was also a money broker. We have records of his career in the form of lawsuits growing out of this activity. Milton himself inherited investments and was involved to some extent in legal matters. He was later to thank his father for not forcing him to go into law or business, but encouraging him rather in his propensity for the pursuit of humane letters. It is an important fact of Milton's early environment that his father was an accomplished musician, having perhaps been educated as a chorister at Christ Church College, Oxford. He was associated with some of the outstanding composers of the day in the publication of both secular and religious part songs and is said to have been honored by Continental patrons. A number of his compositions remain in manuscript. The poet himself pursued music as an avocation throughout his life. He was afterward to speak of his father as a fellow artist and to have as an early friend and collaborator Henry Lawes, the chief successor of the great Elizabethan and Jacobean school of madrigalists, whom it is natural to suppose he had met as one of his father's younger associates.

Milton's mother, Sarah Jeffrey, was the daughter of a merchant tailor. Of her personality we learn only that she was a woman of "incomparable virtue and goodness," and that she was known throughout the parish for her charities. The poet had an elder sister, Anne, who married when he was 15, and a younger brother, Christopher, born in 1615 after the deaths of two earlier children. The usual opinion that the Milton home was Puritan rests on plausible conjecture. The house in Bread Street, where Milton was born, was in the parish of All Hallows. The minister, Richard Stock, was an eminent member of the preaching brotherhood who were in the poet's early life laying the foundations for church reform. The choice of Young, a minister of Presbyterian leanings, as Milton's tutor and of Cambridge, where the Puritan tradition was strong, as his university, is also evidence of the affiliation of the family with the rising movement.

Education.—Milton's education was very carefully looked after. He was sent to St. Paul's School, perhaps as early as the usual age of 7, but the fact that he was some two years older than the average student at the time of his graduation suggests either that he began late or that his schooling was interrupted. Thomas Young, the Puritan minister already mentioned, was certainly his tutor at some time. There is every evidence that Milton was an eager and proficient student. He says of himself that from his twelfth year he rarely went from his lessons to bed before midnight, and adds that this was the first cause of injury to his eyes. He speaks also of a great enthusiasm for the study and imitation of the Roman poets and the early discovery by his elders of a genius for composition in prose or verse. The biographer John Aubrey says that Milton was already a poet by the age of 10. Milton maintained a companionship in Latin poetry with Alexander Gill, son of the headmaster and himself an instructor in the school. His other great friend there was Charles Diodati, whose father was a distinguished physician of Protestant Italian ancestry.

John Milton, from a portrait dated 1670.

Milton took up residence at Christ's College, Cambridge, in the spring of 1625 at the age of 16. He is said by Aubrey on the authority of Christopher Milton to have quarreled with his first tutor, William Chappell, and to have received corporal punishment. There seems to be an allusion to this event in the first Latin elegy, written perhaps toward the end of his second year, in which he speaks of being about to go back to his forbidden college room, but the incident is a rather shadowy one. He was thereafter transferred to another tutor, and there is no evidence of further trouble. Cambridge was at that time already the scene of ideological contention. Milton belonged to the more progressive humanistic group, and his letters and college exercises record disapproval of scholastic study and of those students who devoted themselves to shallow disputation at the expense of solid learning in the ancient authors. Milton was intending at this time to go into the ministry and would naturally have shared the rivalry between the Anglican and Puritan groups. His deepest interest, however, was in literature and learning. He distinguished himself in Latin poetry, writing Ovidian elegies and other imitations, including a poem in hexameters on the Gunpowder Plot, and in the academic orations which were the test of proficiency in rhetoric and logic. In one of these orations he breaks off his Latin to deliver himself of an apostrophe to his mother tongue written in English couplets, and to declare his intention of composing an epic poem on some lofty theme. At about the same time, in 1628, he wrote an English elegy on the death of his sister's child. These two compositions definitely mark the beginning of his career as an English poet. The great ode *On the Morning of Christ's Nativity* followed in December 1629. In an epistle to Charles Diodati, *Elegy VI,* written at the same time, he declares that he is done with lighter themes and intends henceforth to devote himself to the heroic muse.

Milton continued at the university for three years after taking his B.A. in March 1624, and received his M.A. in July 1632, still intending, so far as we know, to enter the church. The literary work of this period includes the lines on William Shakespeare prefixed to the Second Folio, two humorous epitaphs in octosyllabic couplets on the death of the marchioness of Winchester, and perhaps the famous companion lyrics, *L'Allegro* and *Il Penseroso.* Nothing in this late university writing matches the *Nativity* in high Miltonic seriousness, but the poetry exhibits increasing versatility and skill. There are evidently various literary influences at work in Milton, notably that of the Spenserian school represented by Giles and Phineas Fletcher and that of the more classical Ben Jonson. He was already deeply interested also in Italian poetry and had written a group of sonnets in imitation of Petrarch. There is a strong erotic vein in Milton's poetry written before *Elegy VI* and the *Nativity* ode. According to his own account, enthusiasm for the sensual Romans gave way to an appreciation of the idealism of Dante, Petrarch, and Edmund Spenser, then to an interest in the Platonic philosophy of love in the *Symposium,* and finally to the religious ecstasy of the mystic marriage in the Book of Revelation. To what extent the record of his own affairs of the heart in the elegies and Italian sonnets is autobiographical must remain a question.

Residence at Horton.—On his graduation from Cambridge, Milton went into residence at his father's recently acquired house in Horton, Buckinghamshire, and remained there for almost six years. The reasons for his doing this are given in a letter to an anonymous friend who had expostulated with him about the apparent idleness of his way of life. He says that it is not mere love of study which kept him from entering upon the active duties of life, but the desire to be better prepared for them. He speaks as if he were still intending to enter the church, and he confesses that he has noted a certain belatedness in his own development. The conscientious earnestness of his attitude is confirmed by a sonnet written apparently on his twenty-fourth birthday and expressive of his sense of a lack of inward ripeness and of his acceptance of God's will concerning the seasons of his service. At some time during the Horton period he must have definitely given up the church as a career. A Latin epistle to his father, written probably somewhat later than the sonnet, implies that his dedication is to poetry. It is an expression of gratitude for the indulgence which has thus far been accorded him and a plea for its continuance. The elder Milton was by this time retired from business. The poet says he is but following his father's example in his devotion to the arts. In commenting later on his decision, Milton says that to enter the establishment was to subscribe himself slave, and he speaks of himself as being "church-outed by the prelates." William Laud had been made archbishop of Canterbury in 1633 and was rigorously enforcing conformity on the clergy. That Milton's sympathies were strongly on the side of men like Young is evident. He was in the process of working out for himself another kind of ministry, the nature of which remained to be defined by circumstances.

Milton's actual occupations during this period of studious leisure are pretty well established. He devoted himself, he tells us, to the study of Greek and Latin authors, visiting London occasionally to buy books or to learn something new in music or mathematics. Volumes which have survived from his library contain elaborate and minute scholarly annotations of classical texts, as if he were preparing editions of these authors. A notebook of his readings shows that he pursued a systematic course of historical study from the downfall of the Roman Empire to modern times. The emphasis on ecclesiastical history and the church fathers suggests that he was concerned with the religious issues of the time.

While engaged in these serious studies, with whatever end or ends in view, Milton continued to write English poetry as he had done in his later college years. The two masterpieces of his youthful art, *Comus* and *Lycidas* (qq.v.), were written in the years 1634 and 1637, respectively. The first of these pieces is a masque, composed for performance at the inauguration of John Egerton, 1st earl of Bridgewater, as lord president of Wales. This nobleman's stepmother, the countess dowager of Derby, had her estate at Harefield only a few miles from Milton's residence. Both her family and her stepson's were patrons of the musician Henry Lawes, and it was doubtless at his suggestion that the poet was invited to supply the text for an entertainment of which he himself was the producer. An earlier experiment in this collaboration was *Arcades,* a pastoral presentation acted by members of the countess' household. *Comus,* a much more elaborate affair, was performed at Ludlow Castle, the principal parts being taken by Lawes himself and three of the earl's children, Lord Brackley, Lady Alice, and Thomas Egerton. It is not known whether Milton himself was present, nor can we be sure how close a social relationship he may have had with these great families. The masque, besides being a work of delicacy and charm, contains Milton's most serious moral and religious convictions and is everywhere stamped with his personality. The theme is the security of the virtuous mind under divine protection against all the powers of evil. More specifically, it is the virtue of chastity. There was nothing surprising in any poet taking this for a motif, but biographers and critics have attached special and personal significance to it in the case of Milton. They remember that he was called the Lady at Christ's College and was later said to have been thought prudish by his acquaintances in Italy. There is data also regarding Milton's ascetic inclinations and ideals in both the poetry and the prose: *Elegy VI,* for example, and the long personal defense in the *Apology for Smectymnuus* against Bishop Joseph Hall's charge of immorality. The interpretation of such material in its relation to Milton's personality is always open to question, and the suggestion that too much has been made of it is worth pondering. What is very clear and certain is that Milton's convictions regarding love and purity were both strong and individual, and that he found the interfusion of Christian and Platonic ideas which characterizes the philosophy of *Comus* an inspiring theme of poetic eloquence.

There is apparently a gap in Milton's literary activity between *Comus* and *Lycidas,* the last published work of the Horton period. This elegy, by general agreement the finest in the English language, was prompted by the death of a college classmate, Edward King, in whose memory an anthology of tributes, including Milton's poem, appeared in 1638. The author makes the cutting off of one who was both a fellow of the college and a brother poet the occasion for a seemingly very personal meditation on fate, fame, and immortality, as well as for the expression of tenderness and sorrow. An invective against the corrupt clergy, prompted by King's clerical status or perhaps by Milton's own decision against taking orders, is the poet's first great utterance of this kind.

Continental Travel.—Milton's mother died in 1637, and his brother Christopher, now married and a lawyer, settled with his new wife at Horton. In the following April the poet left England for a year and three months of foreign travel. The experience, though brief, was ever memorable to him. He went rather as a mature man of letters than as a pupil, seeking contact with outstanding personalities in the international community of scholars and actually participating in the intellectual and cultural activities of which they were the leaders. His itinerary led him first to Paris, where he was introduced by the English ambassador to Hugo Grotius, the great Dutch jurist and statesman, and then to Florence, where he was at once accepted by a congenial group of scholars, writers, poets, and patrons of the arts, most of whom were members of the Accademia degli Svogliati, one of the numerous cultural organizations which flourished in Italy at that time. On two occasions, Milton was invited to read poems at meetings of this organization, and with one of its younger members, Carlo Roberto Dati, he formed a lasting friendship. The dramatic episode of the Florentine visit was an interview with Galileo, then confined to his house by order of the Inquisition and much restricted in his intercourse, particularly with foreigners. Milton himself mentions this episode in *Areopagitica,* but for some reason omits it in his detailed account of the Italian journey in the *Defensio Secunda.* There are references to Galileo's telescope in *Paradise Lost,* and Milton shows acquaintance with the new system of astronomy, though he taught the old in his school and used it as the cosmological basis of his epic.

After two months in Florence, Milton went on south to Rome and thence to Naples, where he was entertained by a well-known patron of letters, Giambattista Manso, whose distinction and hospitality he celebrated in a Latin poem. This and some epigrams in praise of the Italian singer Leonora Baroni are the only compositions known to have been written during the period of foreign travel. In Naples he received news from home which interrupted his plan for going on to Sicily and Greece. "I thought it base to be travelling for amusement abroad," he wrote afterward, "while my fellow citizens were fighting for liberty at home."

Journeying northward, he stopped again at Rome, this time to make the acquaintance of the papal librarian, Lukas Holste, and through his influence that also of Francesco Cardinal Barberini, in whose palace he attended a brilliant operatic performance. After a second stay of two months at Florence and one month in Venice, he crossed the Alps to Geneva, where he was entertained in the house of Giovanni Diodati (uncle of Charles), one of the most distinguished Calvinist theologians of the day. He arrived in England in the summer of 1639, amidst the turmoil of Charles I's efforts to force obedience on the Covenanting Scots and a little over a year before the king was compelled to summon the Long Parliament. At some time during his absence, Milton had learned of the death of his friend Charles Diodati; he commemorated this event after his return in a beautiful Latin elegy, *Epitaphium Damonis,* similar in form to *Lycidas* but more concretely personal. Milton had already in the poem on Manso spoken of his plan of writing an epic on the legendary history of Britain culminating in the reign of Arthur. Now in the *Epitaphium* he says that he has begun such a poem but found his pastoral style inadequate for its requirements. A set of manuscript notes, drawn up within a year or so after his return to England, shows that the subject of the fall of man, now conceived as a drama, was beginning to claim his interest.

Teaching and Public Affairs.—Milton had already embarked on activities which were to carry him far from poetry for many years. Taking a house in London, he set up a school with his two nephews, Edward and John Phillips, and a few others as pupils, and at the same time began to contribute pamphlets to the great controversy which was then raging over the abolition of episcopacy. Between May 1641 and April 1642, he published five tracts against the bishops and in favor of the Presbyterian system. The first and fourth of these, *Of Reformation Touching Church-Discipline in England* and *The Reason of Church Government Urg'd Against Prelaty,* are the longest and the most weighty. The last, *An Apology Against a Pamphlet Call'd a Modest Confutation of the Animadversions upon the Remonstrant Against Smectymnuus* (*Apology for Smectymnuus*), was written after a personal attack by Bishop Hall, a defender of episcopacy, whom Milton himself had ridiculed in the third tract, *Animadversions upon the Remonstrants Defence, Against Smectymnuus.* The controversy became highly vituperative on both sides.

At the conclusion of this controversy, in the spring of 1642, Milton married Mary, the 17-year-old daughter of Sir Richard Powell, an Oxfordshire squire of Royalist sympathies who was in debt to the poet's family. The disparity of age, politics, and probably of temperament and education was not the best basis for a happy marriage, and there was almost immediate trouble. Mary sought relief from the sobriety of Milton's household by returning to her parents for a visit and staying beyond her appointed time. War had already broken out, and Oxford had become a royal camp. What complications there may have been in the situation we do not know, but the story of the early biographers is that Milton was very angry at what he interpreted as desertion and began to pay court to another woman. A new outburst of pamphlet writing followed on the subject of divorce. Without alluding in any specific way to his own case, Milton attacks the canon law which admitted divorce only for adultery, setting forth a spiritual ideal of marriage and insisting, with much use of scriptural and other authority, that incompatibility, because it defeats these higher ends, should be admitted as a sufficient ground.

This crusade against the law of divorce, unlike Milton's earlier campaign against episcopacy, was a purely individual affair, but he carried it on with even greater energy. *The Doctrine and Discipline of Divorce,* originally issued in 1643, was amplified the next year to a length almost twice as great as any of the ecclesiastical pamphlets. Three other pamphlets on the subject followed: *The Judgement of Martin Bucer, Concerning Divorce* in 1644; and *Tetrachordon* and *Colasterion,* a reply to an anonymous writer who had taken issue with the first tract, in 1645. In maintaining the doctrine of divorce, Milton had written himself heretic from the point of view of the Presbyterians whose cause he had defended. He was indignant at the opposition which arose against him and from now on his role was that of an Independent, combating the new tyranny which was endeavoring to maintain its hold on the affairs of church and state. The passing of a licensing law by Parliament in 1643 was to him a reactionary step, threatening the very liberty for which the English people had engaged in battle with their king, and Milton paused in the middle of the divorce argument to write *Areopagitica* (published November 1644, q.v.) in defense of freedom of the press. This eloquent oration is the most notable of his prose works, or at least the one which best represents his moral and political philosophy to the modern mind. Though it fell on deaf ears in its own time, the arguments have proved to be of perennial validity, and the work is universally regarded as one of the great charters of democratic thought. In 1644 also he published a treatise in the form of a letter to Samuel Hartlib setting forth a very thorough and liberal program of humanistic education.

After the publication of the last divorce tracts, Milton desisted from pamphlet writing for nearly four years. His wife returned to him in the summer of 1645, and his eldest daughter, Anne, was born a year later. With the surrender of Oxford to the forces of Parliament in 1646, the Powell family took refuge for a time in Milton's household. On the death of his father in 1647, the poet gave up his school and moved to a smaller house. A second child, Mary, was born in 1648. His intellectual activity in this period included work on a history of Britain which remained unpublished until 1670. The publication of his poems in 1645 and the writing of a half dozen sonnets, together with a series of Psalm translations, in the three years following suggest a renewal of his creative interests.

Commonwealth Service.—The trial and execution of Charles I in 1649 brought Milton again into action as a publicist and is a major turning point in his career. Before the judgment was delivered, he wrote *The Tenure of Kings and Magistrates,* maintaining the theoretical right of the people to bring their governors to account and, after due trial, to depose and even to execute a monarch who has become a tyrant. The exercise of this right belongs, he declares, "to any who have the power." The treatise is therefore a justification of extralegal revolution. Milton does not deal directly with the case of Charles, but in one passage inveighs against the Presbyterians, who, having taken arms against the king, now protest against the talk of bringing him to justice. The pamphlet was published in February 1649, just after the execution. As an immediate result, Milton was appointed Latin secretary (secretary for foreign tongues) to the Council of State, an office which he was to continue to exercise until the Restoration. The regular duties of this office consisted in drafting the foreign correspondence, translating, and communicating in person with envoys, but Milton was expected also to defend the new regime by propaganda. Thus he prepared and published *Eikonoklastes,* the first of a new series of prose works, on order of the council within seven months after his appointment. This was a severe indictment of the personality and career of Charles I in answer to *Eikon Basilike* (q.v.), a work of powerful appeal to popular feeling purporting to have been written by the king's own hand.

The next year saw the beginning of the greatest literary battle of Milton's career. Again by order, he undertook to answer the French scholar Claudius Salmasius (Claude de Saumaise), who had become the official spokesman of the royal cause on the Continent. *Pro Populo Anglicano Defensio Contra Claudii Anonymi, Alias Salmasii Defensionem Regiam* appeared early in 1651, addressing itself to the court of learned opinion throughout Europe and containing, besides the already familiar political arguments of *The Tenure of Kings and Magistrates* and *Eikonoklastes,* a wealth of personal abuse of his opponent. Salmasius, discredited and disgraced, as rumor had it, by Milton's scathing treatment of his work and character, retired temporarily from the arena, but his cause was vigorously taken up in Peter du Moulin's *Regii Sanguinis Clamor ad Coelum Adversus Parricidas Anglicanos* (1652), in which Milton himself is made a victim.

The poet's answer to this work was delayed nearly two years, perhaps by a series of crises in his own life. A third child and only son, named John, was born to him in 1651, but died within a few months. A year later, Mary Powell herself died, three days after giving birth to a third daughter, Deborah. Milton was thus left alone with three young children. He was, moreover, burdened at this time by sickness and by increasing trouble with his eyes. His sight had been failing for some time, and he had been warned by his physicians of the danger of continuing to work on the first *Defensio.* Blindness became complete early in 1652. In December of that year, he speaks in a letter of "what is now an almost perpetual enemy of mine, ill health." Further evidence of relative incapacity is afforded by his increasing absences from council meetings, by the appointment of an assistant to him in office, and a little later (1655) by the reduction of his salary and further relief from responsibility. By this time, however, Milton had apparently recovered much of his energy. He published the monumental *Pro Populo Anglicano Defensio Secunda* in May 1654, castigating the personality of Alexander More, whom he supposed to be the author of the *Clamor,* setting forth the ideals which had governed his own career and paying noble tribute to the great leaders of the revolution. He had celebrated Oliver Cromwell and Sir Henry Vane in sonnets written in 1652, and there is a new outburst of utterance in this form in 1655, notably the sonnet on the massacre of the Waldenses in Piedmont and one at least of the two sonnets on his blindness, in which Milton speaks of his personal tragedy with noble pride and resolution. A long personal statement in the *Defensio Secunda* reveals his thought and feeling on this subject even more deeply. He was convinced that his great affliction was not, as his enemies had intimated, a judgment of God against him, but rather a trial of faith—something which set him apart from other men and entitled him to special favor from on high. In taking away his outward sight, God had vouchsafed him an inner illumination of the spirit. It was his duty to cherish this gift by spiritual communion with the divine and at the same time to persevere in the daily tasks appointed him.

Though his great day as the defender of English liberty was now over, he continued to carry on foreign correspondence in Cromwell's name throughout the protectorate and, as we shall see, to rally his forces for further controversial writing in the moment of defeat.

The true inwardness of Milton's domestic life in this period is something we really know very little about. He was not friendly with his mother-in-law, to whom he might naturally have turned for assistance with the children after Mary's death. There is little evidence of intimacy with his brother Christopher, who was now in London trying to make composition as a Royalist for his sequestered estate. On the other hand, Milton was rich in devoted friends and felt very warmly towards them. His greatest intimacy was with Cyriac Skinner, a former pupil to whom two of the sonnets of 1655 are addressed.

On Nov. 12, 1656, Milton contracted a second marriage, with Katherine Woodcock, who lived only a year and four months, giving birth to a daughter on Oct. 19, 1657, and dying, with the child, early in the following winter. It is generally believed, though positive evidence is wanting, that the beautiful sonnet to his deceased wife which stands last in the series of sonnets in the Trinity manuscript and in the published poems was addressed to her, and on the basis of this description rests the assumption that this marriage was romantically happy. According to the authority of Edward Phillips and Aubrey, Milton again took up work on *Paradise Lost* at about this time (1658). He had now decided that the material could best be handled in epic form. How far he proceeded with it while still occupied in the secretaryship is a matter of conjecture.

With the death of Oliver Cromwell in 1658, Milton again undertook to exert an influence on politics by addressing himself to Parliament in behalf of religious liberty. *A Treatise of Civil Power in Ecclesiastical Causes,* holding that it is unlawful for a magistrate to enforce conformity of belief, and *Considerations Touching the Likeliest Means to Remove Hirelings out of the Church,* advocating a voluntary and unpaid clergy, appeared in 1659. Finally, in 1660, amidst the political confusion of the last days of the Puritan regime, he drafted a plan of republican government in *The Ready and Easy Way to Establish a Free Commonwealth,* proposing the establishment of a self-perpetuating Parliament and protesting with all his eloquence against the movement, now inevitable, toward the restoration of the house of Stuart. A month after the appearance of a second edition of the work, Charles II landed in England, and Milton's public career was at an end.

Post-Restoration Period.—The effects of the Restoration on Milton's personal fortunes, as well as his hopes for England, were little short of ruinous. Losing not only his salary of £200 a year, but a considerable investment in government securities, he became almost overnight a relatively poor man. More than that, he was henceforth the relic of a treasonable cause, which every possible means was employed to discredit and root out. Many of the men with whom he had been most closely associated were exiled or put to death, and Milton's name, so far as he was noticed publicly at all, was mentioned only with execration. Except for a brief imprisonment and the burning of *Eikonklastes* and the first *Defensio,* he himself escaped punishment. He lived quietly and simply thereafter, industriously engaged in literary work of many kinds, but finding his deepest satisfaction in his devotion to poetry. His own activity in the composition of *Paradise Lost* was essentially religious. The muse who inspired him was none other than the spirit of the Almighty, and his meditations on the truth revealed to him by Scripture were a continuous prayer.

In February 1663, he married for the third time, his bride, Elizabeth Minshull, being but 24 years old. She evidently proved a good wife to him and lived to cherish his memory and to report to John Aubrey many details of his later life. The daughters of his first marriage, at least the two elder ones, seem to have been unfriendly. Milton is described by Phillips as trying without success to make them read and write for him in languages which they did not understand and finally apprenticing them to the trade of lace-making. There was a controversy after Milton's death between the children of his first marriage and his widow respecting his property. The poet's brother and a former maidservant testified to the effect that the girls had exhibited great hostility to their father and that he had intended to disinherit them. Though the picture may be somewhat overdrawn, there can be little doubt that relations were strained, particularly after the third marriage. The youngest daughter, Deborah, nevertheless professed great affection for her father when she was interviewed about him in the 18th century, and he may have had satisfaction in her society in his later years. Anne, the eldest daughter, was a cripple and whether for this or some other reason was, according to Phillips, excused from service as an amanuensis. The other two were 12 and 8 years old, respectively, at the Restoration and may have come to be of some assistance before they left the household.

In this last period of his life, Milton, after changing residences many times, was finally established in a house near Bunhill Fields on the eastern edge of London. He corresponded with foreign scholars and continued to enjoy the friendship of such old associates as Andrew Marvell, and from time to time exchanged instruction with young men for the literary assistance he so sorely needed. In this respect, his chief dependence was probably on the elder of his two nephews, Edward Phillips, who became his literary executor.

Paradise Lost was completed about 1665 and published two years later by Samuel Simmons. The original contract, which still exists, provided for a payment of £5 down and a second £5 when the first impression of 1,500 copies should have been sold. This second payment was made in 1669. All rights to the poem were ultimately sold by Milton's widow for £8. In its final form as an epic, *Paradise Lost* is cosmological in its scope, an epic of creation and the wonders of the universe, as well as of the fall and the regeneration of mankind. In this respect, it has much in common with the type of Biblical paraphrase known as hexaemeron, which takes the first chapter of Genesis and Scripture generally as a basis for the exposition of scientific and philosophical lore of every sort. The most popular work of this kind in England was the translation of a Huguenot poem, *La Semaine,* **by Guillaume de Salluste,** seigneur du Bartas. Milton had been familiar with this from youth and was undoubtedly much influenced by it. His version of the world system is, however, both more artistic and more individual than its English predecessor. Many years of study and meditation had gone into it, and it reflects the whole of its author's experience of life. In the invocations, Milton speaks of his long devotion to the subject, of the difficulties imposed upon him by his loss of sight, and of the assurance given him by the divine spirit whose aid he implores. Other less tangible biographical elements have been found in the poem, particularly in the portrayal of the relations of Adam and Eve, and Milton's psychological attitudes with reference to his imaginative projection have been complexly explored. There is, however, no agreement in such matters. Reflections of his politics, on the other hand, as in his reading of the history of the Christian Church, are obvious enough. Theologically, Milton rejected the Calvinistic view of predestination and the dogma of the Trinity in its orthodox form. His anti-Trinitarian position, set forth explicitly elsewhere, is obscured in *Paradise Lost,* and the doctrine of the poem has been generally acceptable to Protestant readers. (See also PARADISE LOST.)

Milton's last two poetical works appeared in 1671 in a single volume bearing the title *Paradise Regain'd. A Poem. In IV Books. To Which is added Samson Agonistes.* No positive evidence of the date of their composition is available. The natural inference that *Paradise Regained,* being as it is a kind of sequel to *Paradise Lost,* would have followed it immediately, is supported by Thomas Ellwood's account of the part which he himself played in suggesting it. The story of Milton's acquaintance with this Quaker boy is famous in literary history and deserves special notice as giving the only intimate view we have of the poet in the moment of fulfillment of his most cherished literary hopes. Ellwood had sought Milton's instruction in 1662 and been admitted through the mediation of Dr. Nathan Paget "not as a servant, which at that time he needed not, nor to be in the house with him, but only to have the liberty of coming to his house at certain hours when I would and to read to him what books he should appoint me." As commonly happened with Milton and his pupils, the two became warm friends. In the summer of 1665, when the poet was living at Chalfont St. Giles to escape the plague, Ellwood was allowed to read the manuscript of *Paradise Lost,* returning it with the remark: "Thou hast said much of Paradise lost, but what hast thou to say of Paradise found?" When the new poem was handed him at some later time in London, Ellwood reports Milton as declaring: "This is owing to you; for you put it in my head by the question you put to me at Chalfont, which before I had not thought of." It would appear from this plausible account by a person of unquestionable veracity that Milton went on immediately from the poem of highest inspiration and hardest achievement, which had been meditated for so many years, to one which was an afterthought. *Paradise Regained* is, indeed, a beautiful and serene work by no means unworthy of its author, but in one sense it is little more than an amplification of a theme already incorporated in the other. Milton is prolonging the kind of poetic meditation represented in the more didactic passages of the earlier work, and his imagination is much less deeply engaged. (See also PARADISE REGAINED.)

The origin and significance of *Samson Agonistes* (q.v.) is something different. The common view is that it represents a new and final creative moment in Milton's poetic history and is, like *Paradise Lost* itself, the fulfillment of a long-cherished purpose. Subjects from the life of Samson had been included in the early literary plans for tragedies, and the Hebrew champion had come to be for Milton an important symbol. His own blindness and the failure of his cause, together with his abiding faith in God's ultimate triumph, make it difficult for us to dissociate his treatment of the Biblical story from his personal experience. The analogy, of course, is not complete. Samson's weaknesses are those of England rather than of Milton himself, and his great vindication represents something which the poet could hardly expect to witness. Whatever its validity as a biographical document, *Samson Agonistes* is a work of great imaginative intensity, and if it was actually written after *Paradise Regained* it shows that Milton's poetic powers were still undiminished.

Last Years.—In the years which remained to him after the composition of his major poems, Milton continued busy with a variety of literary tasks. He published his *History of Britain* in 1670, an early work on logic in 1672, a second edition of the minor poems with the addition of earlier and later lyrics in 1673, and a volume of his college exercises and Latin letters and the second edition of *Paradise Lost* in 12 books in 1674. He was at work also on a Latin dictionary and on the final revision of a great theological manuscript which remained unpublished until the 19th century.

More surprising than any of these evidences of the persistence of Milton's energies and purposes is his return at this eleventh hour to his old role as a publicist. He did so in a pamphlet entitled *Of True Religion, Heresy, Schism, Toleration, and What Best Means May Be Used*

Against the Growth of Popery, which appeared in 1673 amid the storm of popular opposition to Charles II's efforts to secure favor for the English Roman Catholics. Its announced purpose was to lend a hand to the efforts of those who, alarmed at the growth of Catholicism, were exhorting the public to "beware the growth of this Popish weed." The proposition is that Catholicism, "false religion," can be stopped only by true religion and that, in rallying their forces to oppose the common enemy, Protestants must need tolerate each other. The essential thing is not that the sects should hold the same beliefs but that they should jointly have the moral force to regenerate a people which had fallen into the bondage of sin, and was not unlikely as a consequence to lose even the remaining vestiges of its liberty.

Milton died of gout in 1674 and was buried in St. Giles, Cripplegate, beside his father. Had he lived long enough to witness the outcome of the new struggle against the Stuart autocracy, he would have seen his name restored to honor as a party hero. His real work had, however, been accomplished in another form. He once said that in prose he had the use, as it were, only of his left hand. It is fortunate for mankind that enforced retirement from the heat and dust of politics enabled him to fulfill the aspiration of his early life by leaving something so written to later times that they would not willingly let it die. Yet the greater achievement includes the lesser. Milton believed that he who would speak worthily of worthy things must himself be a man of lofty virtue. He could not have written the great poems without having done what he conceived to be his duty as a servant of the will of God. What that duty was he never doubted, and this is at once his weakness and his strength. Though he was a man of singular urbanity and charm, not lacking even in a sense of humor, there were in him elements of harshness and egocentricity which have not been spared by some biographers. On the other hand, he exemplified the moral discipline and the spiritual elevation of the Puritan character in so enlightened and humane a form that many admirers are loath to admit even his obvious imperfections.

JAMES H. HANFORD,
Author, "John Milton, Englishman."

Bibliography

The Works of John Milton, complete, was edited by F. A. Patterson, 20 vols. (New York 1931–1940).
Bush, Douglas, *John Milton* (New York 1966).
Daiches, David, *Milton* (New York 1957).
Darbishire, Helen, ed., *Early Lives of Milton* (London 1932).
Fixler, Michael, *Milton and the Kingdoms of God* (Evanston, Ill., 1966).
French, Joseph Milton, *Life Records of John Milton,* 5 vols. (New York 1949–1958).
Hanford, James H., *A Milton Handbook,* 4th ed. (New York 1946).
Hanford, James H., *John Milton, Englishman* (New York 1949).
Masson, David, *Life of John Milton,* 6 vols. (London 1859–1894).
Saurat, Denis, *Milton, Man and Thinker,* rev. ed. (London 1944).
Sensabaugh, George A., *That Grand Whig, Milton* (New York 1952).
Tillyard, E. M. W., *Milton,* rev. ed. (New York 1965).
Tillyard, E. M. W., *The Miltonic Setting* (New York 1938).
Tillyard, E. M. W., *Studies in Milton* (New York 1951).

MILTON, town, Massachusetts, in Norfolk County, 6 miles south of Boston. It manufactures chocolate, crackers, and metal products. On Great Blue Hill (625 feet) fires were kindled on the news of the repeal of the Stamp Act; of the adoption of the Declaration of Independence; and on the surrender of Gen. John Burgoyne and Gen. Charles Cornwallis. Beacon fires burned here during the Revolutionary War. At an early date an observatory for tourists was erected on Great Blue Hill and in 1885 the Blue Hill Observatory for meteorological investigations was established by Abbott Lawrence Rotch (1861), who made important investigations regarding clouds. Milton Academy was founded in 1798 and a public library was opened in 1871. Milton owns two granite quarries and two public parks: Cunningham Park and Hutchinson Field, the latter on a portion of the estate of Thomas Hutchinson, a colonial governor of Massachusetts.

Milton was settled in 1640. It was originally a part of Dorchester and was called Uncataquisett. The town was separated in 1662 and incorporated. It owes its name either to Milton Abbey, Dorset, from which members of the Tucker family emigrated, or to the number of mills established here—Mill Town. It was the residence of two colonial governors—Jonathan Belcher and Thomas Hutchinson. In 1712 the Blue Hill lands were divided between Milton and Braintree. In 1868 part of Milton was given to the new township of Hyde Park. Milton now includes the village of East Milton and Milton Lower Mills. Milton was brought into political importance during the early days of the Revolution by the passage of the famous "Suffolk Resolves." These bold resolutions were passed on Sept. 9, 1774, at a meeting of the citizens held in the house of Daniel Vose, these men having adjourned from Dedham. The "Suffolk Resolves" declared that a sovereign who breaks his contract with his subjects forfeits their allegiance; that the repressive measures of Parliament were unconstitutional; that tax collectors should not pay over money to the royal treasury; that the towns should choose public officers from the patriot party; that they would obey the Continental Congress; that they favored a provincial congress; that they would seize Crown officers as hostages for any political prisoners arrested by the governor; and they recommended that all persons in the colony should abstain from lawlessness. Pop. 27,190.

MILTON (formerly MILTON WEST) a town in Ontario Province, Canada, and capital of Halton County, is situated 29 miles southwest of Toronto, on the Canadian Pacific and Canadian National railways. Its manufactures include lumber, flour, butter, pressed brick, crushed stone and lime, screws, rivets, and rugs. There is also a spinning mill which makes sweaters, socks, and other knit goods. The town has two parks, waterworks and electric lighting. Population: 7,018.

MILTON, borough, Pa., Northumberland County, is located on the West Branch of the Susquehanna River, the Pennsylvania and the Reading railroads, 11 miles northeast of Sunbury. Products of its industrial plants are railroad tank cars, bolts and bars, nails and nuts, hosiery, chemicals, food products, shirts, silk, and wooden articles. The old Pennsylvania Canal ran past the town. Milton was partly destroyed by fire in 1880. The town is four miles from Bucknell University, at Lewisburg. Settled shortly after the Revolutionary War, Milton was incorporated in 1817. In 1880 it suffered a disastrous fire, and in 1890 it received a revised charter. Government is of the council-manager type. Pop. 7,723.

MILVIAN BRIDGE, mĭl'vĭ-ăn (Lat. PONS MULVIUS; Ital. PONTE MILVIO), bridge, Rome, Italy, erected in 109 B.C. by Marcus Aemilius Scaurus, then censor, on the site of an earlier bridge first mentioned in 207 B.C. It forms part of the Flaminian Way. Here Marcus Tullius Cicero had the ambassadors of the Allobroges, who had conspired with Catiline, arrested in 63 B.C.; and here Maxentius was drowned after his defeat by Constantine I on Oct. 28, 312 A.D. The bridge was restored in 1815 by Pope Pius VII.

MILWAUKEE, mĭl-wô'kē, city, Wisconsin, seat of Milwaukee County, situated on the west shore of Lake Michigan at the meeting place of the Milwaukee, Menomonee, and Kinnickinnic rivers, about 80 miles directly north-northwest of Chicago. The meaning of its name, which is an Anglicized Indian word, has been disputed, but "beautiful land" is generally accepted. The principal city of Wisconsin and the eleventh largest city in the United States, Milwaukee is one of the nation's great industrial communities and a major Great Lakes port. It is the center of a 795-square-mile metropolitan area comprising Milwaukee and Waukesha counties.

Physical Features.—The city, which covers an area of 91.1 square miles approximately, lies 581 feet above sea level on a crescent-shaped bay of Lake Michigan. Its shoreline is 8.18 miles long. A short distance inland, bluffs rise from 85 to nearly 150 feet above the lake. While the bluffs to the north and south are still steep, the terrain in the central part of the city now slopes gradually to the valleys of the Milwaukee, Menomonee, and Kinnickinnic rivers. In these valleys and along the lake shore, where the original swamps and marshes have been filled in, are the principal business sections. There are residential areas on the higher land between the valleys as well as in such nearby suburbs as Shorewood, Whitefish Bay, Fox Point, River Hills, and Wauwatosa.

Because of its proximity to Lake Michigan, Milwaukee has a more moderate climate than inland Wisconsin communities. The average January temperature is 21° F., and that in July is 69°, the annual average being about 45°. Total annual precipitation averages nearly 30 inches, distributed fairly evenly throughout the year, and the annual fall of sleet and snow averages more than 40 inches.

Population.—The earliest settlers of Wisconsin were French Canadians, but the first wave of immigration, from New England and upper New York State, lent the community a Yankee flavor. After 1840 occurred the first great foreign influx, which gave Milwaukee a reputation for an Old World atmosphere that it has never relinquished. By 1850, 64 percent of the city's population was of foreign birth, principally German. Later, Polish, Irish, Italian, and Bohemian peoples also played prominent roles in Milwaukee's development. As early as 1870, however, natives of the United States accounted for 53 percent of the population, and by 1950 they totaled 90 percent. The foreign immigrants, especially the Germans, strongly influenced the city's character, affecting its architecture, eating and drinking habits, music, theater, recreation, and education.

The 1840 census showed 1,712 persons in Milwaukee. By 1850 the population had risen to 20,061, or by 1,071.8 percent, the largest increase recorded. As might be expected, the second largest increase coincided with a wave of immigration. Between 1880 and 1890 a 76.9 percent increase occurred, raising the city's population from 115,587 to 204,468. In comparison with some other American cities, Milwaukee became a sizable community early in its history. It reached the 100,000 mark in 1875, at a time when Minneapolis had fewer than 40,000 inhabitants and Los Angeles fewer than 10,000. Up to 1900 and the advent of the automobile, Milwaukee and Detroit were of about the same size. Since then, Milwaukee has experienced the more measured growth associated with maturity, and its population in 1970 totaled 717,099 (that of its metropolitan area, 1,403,688).

Economic Life.—The Milwaukee metropolitan area is one of the leading producers of durable and capital goods in the United States. The chief industry groups, in order of value added by manufacture, are machinery (nonelectrical), electrical machinery, food and kindred products, primary metal industries, fabricated metal products, transportation equipment, printing and publishing, and instruments and related products. Milwaukee County is the nation's third largest user of steel, and it leads the world in the manufacture of construction and roadbuilding equipment, diesel and gasoline engines, outboard motors, motorcycles, tractors, wheelbarrows, padlocks, and malt beer. It is also the world's largest veal-packing center and barley market. It leads the United States in the production of electrical generators, transmission and distribution apparatus, work shoes, and saw and flour mill equipment. A major producer of machinery, castings, and forgings, it is also a center of the graphic arts trade and of the manufacture of junior dresses, sport clothes, and other apparel.

The City of Milwaukee has a well-equipped port, handling between 8,500,000 and 9,250,000 tons of material annually. Besides the facilities available to shippers, there are modern passenger and municipal piers. As of 1962, the city was served by more than 40 international steamship lines. While sizable shipments are made to overseas markets, however, the bulk of the port's trade consists of domestic Great Lakes commerce; coal, petroleum, iron and steel, and package freight are the principal commodities involved. The port is served by the car ferry lines of the Chesapeake and Ohio and the Grand Trunk railways. Passenger and automobile service is also furnished by the Wisconsin & Michigan Steamship Company.

Transportation and Communications.—In addition to its port facilities, Milwaukee has extensive systems of land and air transportation. Numerous highways, including a major interstate route, connect in the city, and in 1962 Milwaukee County completed the first section of a 50-mile expressway system. The Chicago, Milwaukee, St. Paul, and Pacific Railroad (Milwaukee Road), the Chicago and North Western Railway, the Chesapeake and Ohio Railway, the Grand Trunk Railway, and the Chicago North Shore & Milwaukee Railway maintain freight and passenger service to and from Milwaukee; the Minneapolis, St. Paul & Sault Ste. Marie Railroad (Soo Line) has freight service only. The county airport,

Ewing Galloway

Kilbourn Avenue passes Milwaukee's new municipal building and St. Mary's Church near the heart of the city.

General Mitchell Field, located 6.5 miles south of the city's business district, is served by six scheduled airlines.

Two large daily newspapers serve Milwaukee: the morning Milwaukee *Sentinel,* founded in 1837; and the evening Milwaukee *Journal,* founded in 1882. Ownership of the *Sentinel* was acquired by the *Journal* in 1962. Two other daily papers, 18 weeklies, 2 semiweeklies, and 1 monthly are distributed in the Milwaukee area. As of 1962, there were 12 radio stations, including 3 FM stations, and 1 educational and 4 commercial television stations.

Education and Cultural Life.—The Milwaukee public school system is administered by a School Board of 15 members, who are elected at large for six-year terms. There are some 24 junior and senior high schools. In addition, many children attend private or Roman Catholic and Lutheran parochial schools. The Milwaukee Vocational School, which is administered by the Board of Vocational and Adult Education, is strongly supported by local industry and labor organizations. Also under the board is the Milwaukee Institute of Technology.

Marquette University, located in downtown Milwaukee, is the largest university in the area. A coeducational Roman Catholic institution opened in 1881, it has schools and colleges of Business Administration, Dentistry, Engineering, Journalism, Law, Liberal Arts, Medicine, Nursing, and Speech and a Graduate School. The University of Wisconsin-Milwaukee, formed in 1955 by the amalgamation of the University of Wisconsin Extension Center in Milwaukee and Wisconsin State College, Milwaukee, offers a four-year liberal arts program as well as graduate work in a limited number of fields. Among other institutions of higher learning in the city are Milwaukee-Downer College, a nonsectarian college for women; three Roman Catholic colleges for women—Mount Mary College, Alverno College, and Cardinal Stritch College; St. Francis Seminary, for men; Concordia College, a Lutheran junior college for men; the Layton School of Art; the Wisconsin Conservatory; and the Milwaukee School of Engineering.

The Milwaukee Public Library system consists of a central library, 15 neighborhood libraries, the Charles Allis Art Library, and the Municipal Reference Library at City Hall. A large addition was made to the central library in 1956. As part of a local library building program, the Finney Neighborhood Library was completed in 1953, and the Atkinson Neighborhood Library in 1960. The central library contains numerous special collections, including one on trans-Mississippi frontier history.

The Milwaukee Public Museum, one of the four largest natural history museums in the United States, is municipally owned and operated. The Milwaukee Art Center, successor to the Milwaukee Art Institute and Layton Art Gallery, is housed in the War Memorial Center, designed by Eero Saarinen and completed in 1957. Its notable resources include the Layton Collection of late 19th and 20th century painting and sculpture. The Charles Allis Art Library of the Milwaukee Public Library system has an outstanding collection of American and European paintings, Oriental ceramics and rugs, Italian bronzes, and French silver. The Milwaukee County Historical Society operates a historical museum in the County Courthouse and also administers the Terrace Avenue Museum at the former Falk home.

Milwaukee has four legitimate theaters, the Pabst Theater, built in 1895 in the heyday of the

German theater, and the Fred Miller, Swan, and Skylight theaters. The first accommodates touring companies, while the others offer semipermanent companies, frequently with guest stars. A number of small theatrical companies, including an outstanding group at Marquette University, operate throughout the Milwaukee area.

The Milwaukee Symphony offers a full program of adult concerts each winter as well as special concerts for young people. In summer the Music Under the Stars Concerts are presented under the auspices of the Milwaukee County Park Commission at the Blatz Temple of Music in Washington Park. Among other notable contributors to music in the city are the Civic Orchestra, the Milwaukee Catholic Symphony, the Lutheran Symphonic Band, the Civic Symphonic Band, and such groups as the Civic Light Opera Company, the Florentine Opera Chorus, and various German choral societies.

Milwaukee is the seat of a Roman Catholic archdiocese and a Protestant Episcopal bishopric. Some 500 churches and synagogues are to be found in the city and its environs. Roman Catholic communicants slightly outnumber the Lutherans, who, due mainly to heavy German immigration during the mid-19th century, have the largest membership of any Protestant sect.

Ewing Galloway

The Milwaukee County War Memorial Center in Juneau Park—a striking example of modern architecture.

Places of Interest.—Milwaukee County has 92 parks, varying in size from 620-acre Whitnall Park to small neighborhood green spots. Also under the direction of the Milwaukee County Park Commission is the Milwaukee County Zoo. One of the city's show places is the 3.5-mile drive along the lake front, starting at the War Memorial Center. The Milwaukee Public Library and Public Museum buildings, the War Memorial, and the City Hall Annex offer interesting tours to visitors, and the landscaped Civic Center contains the Auditorium-Arena, the municipal convention and exposition building. The Milwaukee County Stadium is the home field of the Milwaukee Braves baseball team (which planned to move to Atlanta, Ga., in 1966) and is the site of some of the Green Bay Packers' football games.

Government.—Milwaukee has a mayor-council form of government. The city is divided into 20 wards, each electing an alderman for a four-year term to the Common Council, which is presided over by a president elected from the body of aldermen by his colleagues. In addition to the mayor, the city comptroller, city treasurer, and city attorney are elected at large for terms of four years. The major appointive positions are the commissioners of public works, health, and taxation and the building inspector, all of whom are appointed by the mayor with Common Council confirmation. The council chooses the city clerk.

There are also a number of boards and commissions responsible for administering various specialized activities. Members of these bodies are appointed by the mayor, some without confirmation by the council, as in the case of the City Service Commission and the Library Board, and others with confirmation, as in the case of the Harbor and the Fire and Police commissions. It is not unusual, and in some cases it is mandatory, for aldermen to serve on boards and commissions.

Some local governmental functions are not directly controlled by the city's administration. The School Board, for example, has its own taxing and administrative powers. Sewage disposal for the city and most of the county is handled by the Metropolitan Sewerage Commission, which also enjoys taxing powers. The parks located in the city are managed by the Milwaukee County Park Commission, which administers most of the parks in the county and is responsible to the Milwaukee County Board.

The record of Milwaukee for good government is evidenced by the awards won by its health, traffic, police, and fire services, as well as by its A-1 credit rating. The city's debt-free status vanished under the pressure of post-World War II needs, but it has continued to pursue a cautious financial policy, and its bonded indebtedness, which, even including self-liquidating revenue issues, did not exceed $200 million in 1962, was low for a city of its size.

History.—Because of Milwaukee's setting, with three rivers meeting and running into Lake Michigan at the site of a natural harbor, it served as a meeting place for Indians long before white men arrived. It is probable that Father Jacques Marquette stopped at Milwaukee in 1674 on his way to the Illinois country. Certainly, Father Zenobius Membré, a member of the expedition of René Robert Cavelier, sieur de La Salle, visited the area in 1679. Subsequently, many French Canadian fur traders came there to barter with the Indians. Jacques Vieau, the most important of the early traders, arrived in approximately 1795 as an employee of the North West Company (later of the American Fur Company). His son-in-law, Solomon Laurent Juneau, who came in 1818, is generally credited with being the first permanent white settler and founder of Milwaukee. Three other men who, with Juneau, were responsible for Milwaukee's growth were Morgan L. Martin, a Green Bay land speculator and Juneau's partner; Byron Kilbourn, a Yankee promoter; and George H. Walker. These individuals, sometimes together but mostly in rivalry, founded settlements on both sides of the Milwaukee River and vied for supremacy. On March 11, 1839, the Village of Milwaukee was incorporated, bringing the quarreling communities together, though much of the rivalry remained. Milwaukee was incorporated as a city on Jan. 31, 1846, more than two years before the Territory of Wisconsin became a state.

Early economic activity was restricted to speculation in land and the beginnings of crude industries that exploited the raw materials of the region. After an early boom and panic, Milwaukee settled down to steady growth, as the hinterland filled with settlers who were transported through the city, which equipped and supplied them. The development of railroads was fundamental to this growth, and the Chicago and North Western Railway and the Milwaukee Road emerged from a welter of small lines to become the forerunners of the two large systems that now serve Wisconsin.

Until 1870, Milwaukee had primarily a market economy, with wheat and hogs as leading products. Indeed, by 1862 the city had become the largest primary wheat market in the world. Thereafter manufacturing began to assume more importance: in 1879 the annual value of manufactured products totaled nearly $100 million, and by 1909 it exceeded $200 million. Meanwhile, wheat shipments declined from 16 million bushels in 1870 to less than 2 million in 1890. By 1918, Milwaukee's industrial complex was well established, and by 1940 the city, then thirteenth in population, ranked as the fourth largest concentration of industry in the country. World War II both stimulated and added to its size and reputation, and the boom period after the war gave new impetus to the durable goods industry, particularly in the instruments and related products field. By 1960 the annual value of manufactured products in Milwaukee County was close to the $3.5 billion mark.

Though local elections are nonpartisan, Milwaukee was and remained a Democratic stronghold despite Republican inroads at various times. The city had Socialist mayors in three periods: Emil Seidel, from 1910 to 1912; Daniel W. Hoan, from 1916 to 1940; and Frank P. Zeidler, from 1948 to 1960, when he retired. Zeidler was succeeded by Henry W. Maier, long identified with the Democratic Party. Socialists were seldom in full control of the city government, however, and the Milwaukee brand of socialism, while deeply humanitarian, was quite conservative in financial matters.

Municipal politics were often agitated by national issues, but such local problems as internal improvements, railroad promotion, debt, and reform were the principal issues in the early period. The new Republican Party made sizable gains in the election of 1860 and throughout the Civil War, but it was unable to capture the city government. Post-Civil War politics were concerned largely with the increasing participation of labor in local affairs, and with the emergence of the Socialist Party under Victor Berger and its capture of parts of the city government, beginning with the election of Seidel in 1910. It is generally conceded that the Milwaukee Socialists contributed largely to decent, thrifty, efficient local government, but that the basic elements of socialism, such as public ownership, received little advancement. A good deal of Milwaukee's reputation as one of the best-governed American cities rests on the people of the city, whose respect for law and order and whose demand for clean government became proverbial.

Bibliography.—Bruce, William G., *History of Milwaukee City and County,* 3 vols. (Milwaukee 1931); Gregory, John G., *History of Milwaukee, Wisconsin,* 4 vols. (Chicago 1931); Austin, H. Russell, *The Milwaukee Story* (Milwaukee 1946); Still, Bayrd, *Milwaukee: the History of a City* (Madison, Wis., 1948); Milwaukee Public Library, *Milwaukee, City and County: a Statistical History* (Milwaukee 1958).

RICHARD E. KRUG,
City Librarian, Milwaukee Public Library.

MILWAUKEE-DOWNER COLLEGE, an independent liberal arts college for women, situated in Milwaukee, Wis. It confers the B.A. degree in languages and literature, social science, natural science, and the fine arts, and the B.S. degree in occupational therapy and home economics. The 40-acre wooded campus contains 14 buildings, including 3 residence halls, the large Ellen C. Sabin Science Hall, and the Chapman Memorial Library.

Founded in 1851 as Milwaukee College (it adopted its present name in 1895 after uniting with Downer College), the college is old enough to have developed traditions: step singing, a freshman hat hunt, crew races in the spring, and Colors Day—a sequence of red, green, yellow, and purple class banners under the Downer royal blue. It is also young enough to initiate new courses and to adopt new patterns in independent study, advanced placement, and proficiency evaluation; and small enough (average enrollment, 200) to help each student plan a program suited to her needs and capacities. There is a chapter of Phi Beta Kappa at the college.

GERTRUDE B. JUPP,
Director of Public Relations.

MILWAUKEE INSTITUTE OF TECHNOLOGY, a coeducational municipal institution of higher education, situated in Milwaukee, Wis. It was established in 1951 by the Milwaukee Board of Vocational and Adult Education. The degree of associate in applied science is conferred in the various fields of technology. Two-year terminal technical programs are offered in business and distributive education, secretarial science, graphic and applied arts, air conditioning and refrigeration, and automotive, chemical and metallurgical, diesel, electrical (including electronic), mechanical, structural, and technical engineering. Other two-year programs train medical assistants and persons planning careers in restaurant and hotel cookery and in telecasting. In addition, an associate of arts degree is awarded in the General Education Division, and a diploma in the one-year practical nursing program. The institute, which is accredited by the North Central Association of Colleges and Secondary Schools, is well equipped with laboratories and shops. Annual enrollment averages 4,900.

GEORGE A. PARKINSON,
Director.

MILWAUKEE SCHOOL OF ENGINEERING, a private, nonprofit institution of higher education for men, situated in Milwaukee, Wis. It was founded in 1903. The school is governed by a 63-member Corporation and Board of Regents representing industry, commerce, engineering, and education. Laboratories and classrooms are housed in 10 buildings, including the Allen-Bradley Hall of Science (1960). The school's College of Engineering offers four-year programs leading to bachelor of science degrees in electrical and mechanical engineering. Two-year programs offered by its Technical Institute lead to associate in applied science degrees in computer, electrical power, electronic communications, air-conditioning, internal combustion engine, chemical production, industrial, and metallurgical technology.

The four-year and two-year programs have a common first year of study, at the end of which the student chooses his educational objective. An extended freshman-year curriculum is available for students who must augment their secondary school education in preparation for further college-level study in the Technical Institute or the College of Engineering. All programs are offered the year around in four 12-week quarters, the summer quarter being optional. Industrial scholarships, cooperative programs, and other financial aids, including national defense student loans, are available to qualified students. Eighteen fraternities, student branches of professional societies, and social clubs offer extracurricular activities. The annual cumulative student enrollment is about 2,000.

MILWAUKIE, mĭl-wô'kē, city, Oregon, situated in Clackamas County, on the Willamette River, 7 miles south of the center of Portland. The city of Milwaukie was mainly residential until 1950, when the site of a war housing project was cleared and became Milwaukie Industrial Park. Located in the park are warehouses and air-conditioning, quick-freezing, and sheet metal plants, while elsewhere in the city there are woolen mills and plants engaged in woodworking and toolmaking

The first fruit tree nursery in Oregon was established in 1847 on the site of Milwaukie by Henderson Luelling, who brought an assortment of rootings with him across the plains from Iowa. The city itself was founded the next year by Lon Whitcomb, who built and launched a power-driven boat on the Willamette in 1850. For a short time, Milwaukie claimed to be the head of deep-sea navigation, but it was soon superseded by Portland. Milwaukie was incorporated as a city in 1903 and put the council-manager form of government into effect in 1945. Pop. 16,379.

MILYUKOV, myĭ-lyo͝o-kôf', **Pavel Nikolayevich,** Russian historian and political leader: b. Moscow, Russia, Jan. 27, 1859; d. Aix-les-Bains, France, March 31, 1943. In 1877 he entered the Faculty of Letters of the University of Moscow. Taking a moderate position in the rebellious student activities, Milyukov was jailed and suspended briefly but returned to complete his studies and become a professor at the university. He gave courses in aspects of historiography and history, embarking at the same time on a notable study of Russian political economy in the time of Peter the Great. Exiled to Ryazan for his liberal enthusiasm, he there prepared *Glavniye techeniya russkoi intelligentsii* (1898; Main Currents of Russian Historical Thought), as well as his most famous and influential work, *Ocherki po istorii russkoi kultury* (3 vols., 1896–1903; Eng. tr., *The Outlines of Russian Culture,* 1942). In 1895, given a choice of police exile in Ufa or of leaving the country, he accepted a chair in history at the University of Sofia. His sojourn in Bulgaria (1897–1899) led him to study the history of the Slavs and made him an outstanding authority in the field.

Returning to Russia in 1899, Milyukov again fell under official supervision. Nevertheless, he helped to establish a journal, *Osvobozhdenie* (Liberation), which, published abroad starting in 1902, became the organ of the zemstvo liberals. Another prison term was followed by his acceptance of an invitation to teach a course in Russian history at the University of Chicago (1903–1904). The revolution of 1905 brought him back to Russia and plunged him into political activity. He organized a union of writers and scholars and then, associating that union with other professional unions, formed the so-called Union of Unions. Thus he became the leader of the Constitutional Democratic (Kadet) Party. After the czar's reluctant granting of a constitutional regime, Milyukov, who had been kept out of the first two Dumas by governmental machinations, served in the 3d and 4th Dumas as the leader of the Kadets, the party that more than any other sought to make the constitutional monarchy work, resisting encroachments against a government of law from left- as well as right-wing elements.

World War I, accompanied as it was by military disasters and the incompetence of the czar's ministers, caused Milyukov's star to shine the brightest. Organizing a patriotic Progressive Bloc of Duma factions, he called on Nicholas II to change the course of affairs that was leading Russia to ruin. Always the legalist, however, he halted before a call to revolution, and the Romanov regime was allowed to drift to its doom. For some weeks after the revolution of March 1917, Milyukov stood out as the foreign minister of the Kadet-centered first provisional government, but riots on May 3–4 forced his resignation. His note of May 1 to the Allied governments, in which he referred to Russia's claim to Constantinople, had made him appear the champion of imperialism, by that time a word of shame in Russia. After the Bolshevik coup d'état in November, he took refuge in German-occupied Kiev, and soon after the end of the war he left Russia for good. He ended his days as an editor of a Russian émigré journal in Paris.

STANLEY W. PAGE,
Associate Professor of History, City College of the City University of New York.

MIMANSA. See INDIA—*13. Religion and Philosophy* (Religion and Philosophy of Indian Origin): Formal Philosophies.

MIME, mīm (Lat. *mimus,* from Gr. *mimos*), a dramatic entertainment popular in the ancient Greek and Roman world, particularly in Sicily and Magna Graecia, in which scenes from everyday life or from mythology were enacted with elaborate gestures. It seems to have originated in the performances of strolling acrobats and jugglers, some of whom were gifted mimics. Originally performed in public squares on festival days, it was developed into a literary form in the 5th century B.C. by Sophron of Syracuse, who wrote in a rhythmic prose. In the 3d century B.C., the Greek satirist Herodas (q.v.) used the form to present portraits of typical contemporary characters in choliambic meter; eight of his mimes survive.

The Romans adopted the mime in its popular form as early as the 3d century B.C., but it was not until the 1st century B.C. that it won a place in Latin literature at the hands of Decimus Laberius and Publilius Syrus, fragmants of whose works survive. As an afterpiece and later as an independent performance, it was as popular as it was indecent in words and action.

MIMICO, mĭm'ĭ-kō, town, Ontario, Canada, in York County on the shore of Lake Ontario, immediately west of Toronto, with which it is connected by the Canadian National and Canadian Pacific railways and by the services of the Toronto Transportation Commission. Primarily a residential suburb, Mimico has a growing number of small industrial establishments. The site of a provincial reformatory, it has two banks and a chamber of commerce. Pop. 19,431.

MIMICRY, mĭm'ĭk-rĭ, a special form of adaptive coloration in animals, serving as a protective mechanism to ensure the better survival of the species.

The colors of animals are often of an adaptive nature, effecting concealment, disguise, or conspicuousness, and serving to protect the animal from enemies or predators. Protective coloration constitutes the camouflage of an animal by its close resemblance to its general background or to some inanimate object that is of no interest to its enemies.

A horned toad in its natural habitat is concealed by the wonderful resemblance of the creature to its background of sand and rock. Its gray color pattern so closely resembles the interplay of light and shadow on a small rock that only its movement attracts attention. The majority of desert animals are concealed against their natural sun-bleached background by their possession of gray and beige coloration. Tropical regions abound with green colored insects and animals which blend in with the lush growth of trees and vines. Similarly, the Arctic regions are the only areas supporting a great number of white forms.

Some animals, notably those with unpalatable or dangerous qualities, achieve protection from enemies by their conspicuousness. Such warning coloration is flaunted by its possessors in bold patterns of bright or contrasting colors.

The brilliant stripes of the coral snake, the black and white pattern of the skunk, and the innumerable intricate patterns of stripes and spots in contrasting colors of black, red, yellow, and white displayed by numerous insects all serve to advertise their undesirable qualities to enemies.

That predators do learn to associate the color patterns of unpalatable or noxious prey has been experimentally proved. Both lizard and bird predators presented with warningly colored and unpalatable insect prey quickly learn to recognize certain conspicuous color patterns as representing distasteful prey, and distinguish these from palatable prey. The warning coloration may advertise a noxious odor (certain moth larvae exude formic acid or other repellent juices), barbed hairs which are irritating to the predator's mouth, a bitter or otherwise unpleasant taste, or poisonous qualities. Protection from predators is assured by the warning coloration.

Protective mimicry provides a warning to predators. Thus a species without warning coloration simulates another species which is warningly colored, and attains protection by living on the reputation of the latter. The former is known as the *mimic,* the latter as the *model.* The mimic makes use of the warning coloration of the model.

A classical example of mimicry is provided by two well known North American butterflies, *Danaus plexippus,* the monarch, and *Limenitis archippus,* the viceroy. The wide ranging and unpalatable model, the monarch, is mimicked by the more restricted and palatable viceroy. Experimental evidence indicates that bird predators which have had no previous experience with the monarch, will eat the viceroy. If first confronted with the unpalatable monarch, the bird predators will associate the color pattern common to both model and mimic with a distasteful prey, and will not touch the palatable viceroy. Mimicry, in this case, was proved to be effective under the experimental conditions. It was further shown that the effectiveness of the mimicry is dependent upon the learning of the predators that the color pattern of the model represented an unpalatable prey, and that the relative scarcity of the mimic as compared to the model facilitates rapid learning on the part of the predators.

Two general types of mimicry are recognized. In the first type, the model is protected from predators by an unpleasant taste or odor or by the possession of stingers or irritating hairs, and the mimic is not so protected, but escapes predation by its deceivingly detailed resemblance to the model. This is called Batesian mimicry.

Fritz Müller (1821–1897), German zoologist, described a second scheme of mimicry after encountering a complex of mimetic species of butterflies in South America which did not fit into the Batesian pattern. Müllerian mimicry involves a number of different species, uniform in appearance and unpalatable. All possess warning coloration, and through the pooling of the advertisement of their undesirable qualities, the education of their enemies is assured without undue detriment in number to any one species.

The striking yellow and black banding exhibited by variously distantly related wasps is an example of Müllerian mimicry.

A survey of the habits and attributes of mimics reveals several general principles concerning the relationship of mimic to model. First and foremost, the geographic distribution of the mimic must fall within that of the model for the operation of the mimicry to be effective.

Model and mimic are further seen to exploit the same environment and to display similar habits. The genus *Hemaris* consists of hawk moths which mimic bumblebees. However, unlike most hawk moths, the clearwings fly by day, possess transparent wings and a black and yellow body, make a whirring noise as they fly, and are of relatively small size. In these characteristics they definitely resemble bumblebees. The superficial nature of the resemblances is readily observed in the method by which the moths achieve the clear wings of their models. Upon emergence from the pupa, the wings of the moth are opaque due to their covering of colored scales. However, the first vibration of the wings results in the dropping off of the loosely attached scales, leaving the transparent wing membrane characteristic of the bees.

Mimics of Hymenopterous insects simulate their wasp-waisted models by various optical devices. Thus the grasshopper, *Myrmecophana fallax,* displays antlike contours through the superimposing of a constricted waist and swollen abdomen in back pigment on its own stout, contrastingly light-colored body.

A mimic may even resemble its model in behavior. *Myrmarachne,* an ant-mimicking spider, copies its model in gait. Undisturbed, it progresses in the steady and determined fashion of worker ants searching for food. But when alarmed, it rushes about excitedly exactly as do its models.

The relative numbers of model and mimic must be limited for the effective operation of Batesian mimicry. Here, the model must remain more numerous than the mimic, for otherwise predators would not learn to associate a certain coloration with nauseous or undesirable qualities. With Müllerian mimicry, no limitation is placed on the proportions of model and mimic.

Mimicry often involves species distantly related phylogenetically, and the mimic may be widely divergent from its congeners in appearance as well as habit. Thus the viceroy butterfly (*Limenitis archippus*), which mimics the monarch, is entirely different in appearance from most members of the genus *Limenitis.*

The similarities between model and mimic are clearly of an adaptive nature and affect only visible characters. Their resemblances are independent of life history, environment, or anatomy, and are due to many independent modifications producing similar appearances by diverse methods. Thus the red markings of *Papilio polytes romulus* and its model, *Papilio hector,* two species of swallowtail butterfly, are due to chemically distinct pigments. Lepidopterous forms mimicking bees achieve the characteristic transparent wings of the latter by various methods. Some shed their colored scales, others attain the optical effects of transparency by various structural devices such as reduction in scale size or modifications in scale shape.

Although mimicry usually involves model and mimic of distantly related species, in the European yellowtail moth, *Euproctis chrysorrhoea,* the male mimics the female of the same species. The female is well protected from enemies by its possession of numerous irritating barbed spicules attached at the tip of its yellow abdomen. This protective mechanism is clearly adapted to the female's role in egg laying, for upon depositing a sticky pile of eggs, she fans her tail over the eggs whereupon a number of the spicules adhere to the egg mass, covering it with a protective layer of barbed spicules. The male, having no such similar adaptation, closely resembles the female in color pattern, and thus gains protection from her reputation.

Many species of butterflies which exhibit Batesian mimicry are polymorphic, that is, the population contains several different alternative mimicking forms. It will be recalled that under Batesian mimicry a mimic must be much less frequent than its model for the mimicry to be effective. The mimicking species can, however, increase in numbers by copying two or more different models. Polymorphism is the device by which this is accomplished.

The Oriental butterfly, *Papilio polytes,* exhibits four different polymorphic forms. The male is represented by a single phase, whereas the female displays three different phases. These latter are *cyrus,* a nonmimetic form resembling the male in appearance; *polytes,* a mimic of another butterfly, *Polydorus artistolochiae;* and *romulus,* a mimic of *Polydorus hector.* A single dominant sex-controlled gene governs the difference between *cyrus* and *polytes,* and a second gene that between *polytes* and *romulus.*

Polymorphism of egg color increases the number of host species available for the breeding parasitism of the European cuckoo, *Cuculus canorus.* Different strains lay their eggs in the nests of robins, warblers, sparrows, crows, and wrens. Upon hatching the young cuckoo ejects his foster brothers from the nest and is raised alone by his host parents. Here the mimetic scheme is operative only in the critical egg stage, and the coloration of the cuckoo eggs varies according to that of the host species, the mimicry becoming more perfect in the nests of more selective hosts. Polymorphism of egg color is attained in some of the widely distributed cuckoo strains, thus permitting one species to parasitize the nests of several host species. The mimetic phenomena of insects are thus closely paralleled by the breeding parasitism of the cuckoo.

As we have seen, mimics resemble their models in a complex of characters including details of color, pattern, and habit, and are often widely divergent in appearance from their congeners. Such striking changes in appearance are the result of evolutionary changes brought about by natural selection.

Thus we might postulate the gradual formation of a Batesian mimic as starting with a mutation (or simple hereditary change) altering the appearance of an individual within a species. Now, if this genetic difference resulted in an individual which somewhat resembled a species with warning coloration, the mutant might gain an advantage in survival. And if this mutant were better protected from predators than its siblings, the mutant gene could be transmitted to progeny generation after generation and could increase in frequency within the population. Natural selection would tend to preserve those individuals more perfectly resembling the model, and eliminate the less perfect forms. Thus, step by step, a Batesian mimic could gradually evolve through the preserving and modifying action of natural selection.

Mimicry and protective resemblance are closely allied and intergrading aspects of adaptive coloration. The concealment or disguise afforded by the resemblances of a spider to a piece of bark or lichen, an insect or larva to a leaf or twig, fish to seaweed or gravel, are adaptations for protection. Protective resemblance concerns the concealment of an organism by its similarity to an object which is of no interest to predators. Mimetic resemblance provides protection in that an organism becomes conspicuous through its similarity to an object avoided by predators.

Mimicry is thus a special type of adaptive coloration in animals which has attained its most specialized form in the insects and spiders. As a means of protection for the mimic, the phenomenon has reached its greatest frequency, at least in the Lepidoptera, in the crowded conditions of insect life prevalent in tropic and subtropic regions. The false warning of the Batesian mimic and the combined warning of the Müllerian mimics aid in the perpetuation of the species. Slight genetic differences may provide the basis from which mimicry may evolve with the directive aid of natural selection. Genetic variability and natural selection work in balance to bring about the phenomenon of mimicry, where it benefits the species.

See also COLORATION IN ANIMALS; NATURAL SELECTION; POLYMORPHISM.

Consult Ford, Edmund B., *Moths* (New York and London 1955); Cott, Hugh B., *Adaptive Coloration in Animals* (London 1957).

VERNE GRANT,
Biosystematist, Rancho Santa Ana Botanic Garden of the Native Plants of California.

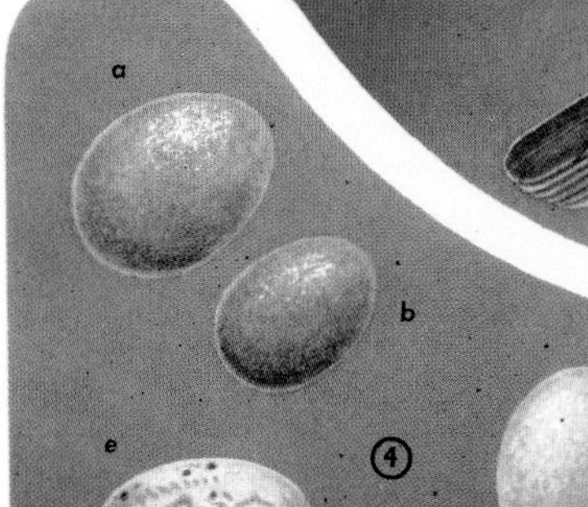

MIMICRY

(1) The viceroy butterfly, *b*, is protected by its close resemblance to the monarch, *a*, which is unpalatable to birds and other enemies. (2) Clearwing moth, *a*, and hover fly, *b*, are both mimics of a hornet. (3) The oriole, *a*, on the island of Ceram, Indonesia, mimics the honey eater, *b*. (4) The European cuckoo, well known for its parasitic nesting habits, lays eggs that sometimes very closely resemble those of the host species. Here *a*, *c*, and e are cuckoo eggs imitating those of *b*, sedge warbler; *d*, whinchat; and *f*, tree pipit. (5) The tarantula hawk wasp, *a*, is a model for the mimicry of the robber fly, *b*, also called assassin fly, and *c*, mydas fly. (6) The male European yellowtail moth, *a*, mimics the barbed spicule-protected female, *b*, of the same species. (7) In this example, a bumblebee, *a*, is the model, and a robber fly, *b*, is its mimic.

Painted for "THE ENCYCLOPEDIA AMERICANA" by A. Seidel

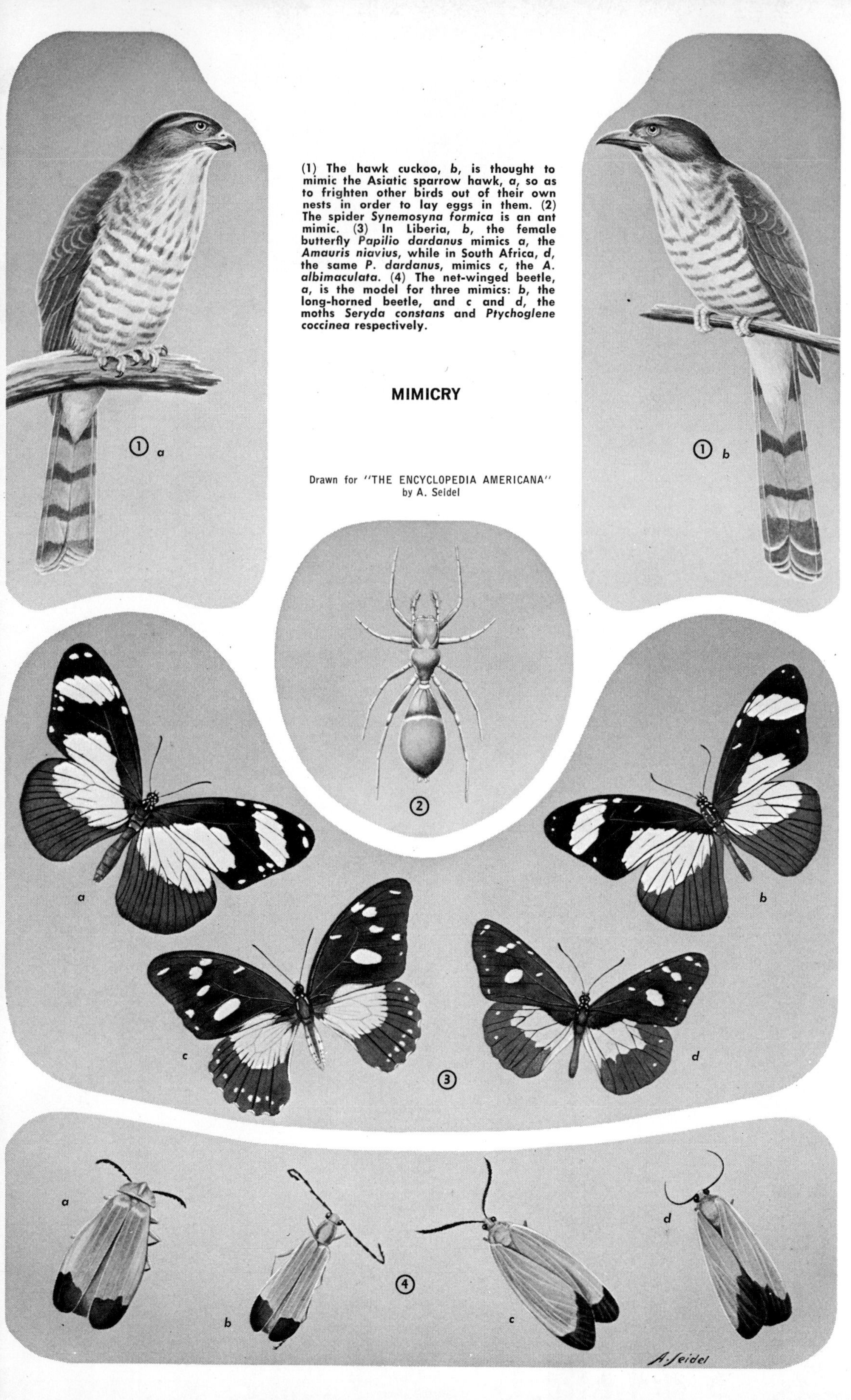

(1) The hawk cuckoo, *b*, is thought to mimic the Asiatic sparrow hawk, *a*, so as to frighten other birds out of their own nests in order to lay eggs in them. (2) The spider *Synemosyna formica* is an ant mimic. (3) In Liberia, *b*, the female butterfly *Papilio dardanus* mimics *a*, the *Amauris niavius*, while in South Africa, *d*, the same *P. dardanus*, mimics *c*, the *A. albimaculata*. (4) The net-winged beetle, *a*, is the model for three mimics: *b*, the long-horned beetle, and *c* and *d*, the moths *Seryda constans* and *Ptychoglene coccinea* respectively.

MIMICRY

Drawn for "THE ENCYCLOPEDIA AMERICANA"
by A. Seidel

MIMIR, mē′mêr, a figure in Norse mythology, usually described as a giant, the son of Aegir (or Hler, god of the calm sea) and Ran (goddess of the stormy sea), but in one saga he is a dwarf master smith. As a giant, Mimir was associated with the open sea (Mimir's Well), by drinking from which he possessed a magical insight into all things, past and future; and he is therefore sometimes called the god of wisdom.

MIMNERMUS, mĭm-nûr′mŭs, Greek poet and musician: fl. late 7th century B.C. He lived in Colophon and Smyrna (now İzmir), Asia Minor, where he gained repute as a flutist and even more as an elegiac poet. Mimnermus' elegies—some of which he set to music—were collected into two books, of which one was called *Nanno* after a flute girl whom he loved in vain. The 24 extant fragments, totaling about 90 lines, treat historical, military, mythological, and (particularly) erotic themes.

The best Greek text with English version is in John M. Edmonds, *Elegy and Iambus,* vol. 1, pp. 88–103 (Cambridge, Mass., 1931; reprinted 1954).

P. R. COLEMAN-NORTON.

MIMOSA, mĭ-mō′så, a genus of the pea family (Leguminosae) with some 250 species of herbs, shrubs, or small trees, many of them spiny, native mostly to tropical America but with some species also in east and tropical Africa. It is the typical genus of the subfamily Mimosoideae (or the separate family Mimosaceae of some authorities) in which the calyx and corolla are nearly regular and very small. The tiny flowers, which are gathered into dense globose or cylindrical clusters, are conspicuous only because of the longer red, purple, or white stamen filaments. The fruit is a flat pod (legume) that breaks into one-seeded segments at maturity. The leaves are twice pinnate, and many respond to a touch by folding the pinnae downward, as in the sensitive plant, *M. pudica,* and others. The florists' mimosa is usually a species of *Acacia* (q.v.).

RICHARD M. STRAW.

MIN, mĭn, in the religion of ancient Egypt, the god of virility and procreation. Personifying the generative force in nature, he was the chief deity worshiped in harvest festivals. While his cult was widespread, the chief centers were Panopolis (or Chemmis, now Akhmîm) and Coptos (now Qift). Identified with Amon-Ra by later Egyptians and with Pan by the Greeks, he is represented in art by the figure of an ithyphallic man, holding a whip in his right hand and wearing a headdress of two enormous feathers with a long streamer descending from its back. The chief animal sacred to Min was the Ram.

Consult Gauthier, Henri, *Les fêtes du dieu Min* (Cairo 1931); Černý, Jaroslav, *Ancient Egyptian Religion* (London 1952).

P. R. COLEMAN-NORTON.

MINA, mē′nä, **Francisco Javier,** Spanish guerrilla leader and revolutionary: b. Ydozin, Spain, 1789; d. Mexico City, Mexico, Nov. 11, 1817. When Napoleon invaded Spain in 1808, beginning the Peninsular War (q.v.), Mina, a student at the University of Saragossa, joined the resistance movement and until his capture in 1810 opposed the French with some success. Imprisoned in France from 1810 until 1814, he returned to Spain upon his release and took part in a revolutionary attempt against the autocratic Ferdinand VII. When the rebellion was put down he fled to France, ultimately reaching the United States, where he organized an expedition to support Mexican insurgents against the Spanish rule. Arriving at Galveston, Texas, with 200 volunteers in November 1816, he sailed to the Mexican border state of Tamaulipas in April 1817, and, with about 100 additional recruits from New Orleans, marched into the interior. Although he succeeded in taking the towns of León and Guanajuato, with the fortress of Sombrero, most of his followers soon deserted him; and on October 17, Mina was captured by a greatly superior Spanish force, taken to Mexico City, and shot after a brief trial. See also MEXICO—*26. Mexico from 1810 to 1910* (Morelos).

MINA, monetary unit of ancient Greece. See DRACHMA.

MINA-BIRD, mē′nä bûrd, or **MYNA,** one of several species of starlings native to southeastern Asia. Mynas are noisy, bold, and heavily built birds varying from about 10 to 15 inches in size with powerful bills and big feet. They inhabit forests or open regions and some species show no fear of man and can be easily tamed. The best known is probably the talking myna (*Gracula religiosa*) which is very popular as a cage bird. It is a handsome and very self-confident bird with a black plumage glossed with purple and green, relieved by bold white patches in the wing and curious bright yellow wattles attached below the eye and on the nape. The bill is orange and the legs yellow. It can be taught to whistle and to talk remarkably well. Other mynas are white, or various shades of gray and brown and some have long graceful crests. Mynas have been introduced as pets in many countries and some have escaped to breed freely, such as the crested myna (*Acridotheres cristatellus*) in British Columbia near Vancouver.

CHARLES VAURIE.

MINAEANS, mĭ-nē′ăns, a group of people, akin to the Sabaeans, Qatabanians (Katabanians), and Himyarites, who flourished in ancient southwestern Arabia. The name is derived from their leading city Ma'ān (modern Arabic Ma'īn, spring water), related to Biblical Mā'ōn, Me'ūn, Me'īn (Joshua 5:55; I Samuel 23:24; 25:2; Numbers 32:38; compare Judges 10:12; II Chronicles 20:8; Ezra 2:50). The name survives in present-day Ma'ān, southern Jordan. The site of the Minaean capital was identified by the French Orientalist Joseph Halévy (1827–1917) who visited it in 1870 and located it in al-Jawf (depression) southeast of Sanaa, capital of modern Yemen. The remains are visible on a hilltop surrounded by a well-preserved wall. While the city owed its origin to a spring of water, its prosperity it owed to its location astride the southern extremity of the famous "incense route" followed by the caravans which transported frankincense, spices, myrrh, and other products of South Arabia, east Africa, and southern India into the Mediterranean ports. From these ports the products were distributed all over the Fertile Crescent and the Graeco-Roman world. The caravans passed through Mecca and Medina and stopped at stations built and colonized by South Arabians. Dedan, later al-'Ula in north Hejaz, was a famous Minaean station. A 3d century inscription found in Egypt tells of a Minaean merchant who exported Egyptian goods to South Arabia in his own merchant ship.

The Minaeans shared with the Sabaeans and Himyarites the early Semitic religious beliefs, basically planetary astral. At the head of the pantheon stood the moon god called by the Minaeans Wadd (love or lover, father). His consort was Shams, the sun, over whom he took precedence. From the union came 'Athtart (Babylonian Ishtar, associated with the planet Venus), the third member of the trinity. Other heavenly bodies sprang from the celestial pair. In addition there was an indeterminate number of local deities.

The language of the Minaeans, like their religion, belonged to the Semitic family and differed only dialectally from Sabaean, Qatabanian, and Himyarite. It was a sister of North Arabic, which became the language of the Koran and Islam and is today Arabic par excellence. South Arabic was written in alphabetic script, generally known as Himyarite, and was derived probably from the Sinaitic, from which the Phoenician script originated. The probable date of the earliest known Himyarite inscriptions is the 9th pre-Christian century. The language and script were used until the 7th Christian century when superseded by the North Arabic as a result of the advent of Islam. Since 1870 thousands of Himyarite inscriptions have been found and deciphered. The last expedition into the area was that of the American Foundation for the Study of Man, 1950 to 1951. The records indicate that the Minaeans developed a kingdom around 700 B.C. which lasted for about four centuries, after which it was absorbed by its neighbors.

In the late Ptolemaic or early Roman period, Greeks or Romans in Egypt, realizing for the first time that the products in which South Arabians traded and on which they prospered were not all of Arabic origin, began to invade the market and break the monopoly. This marked the beginning of the decay of South Arabia.

Bibliography.—Ryckmans, Jacques, *L'institution monarchique en Arabie méridionale avant l'Islam* (Louvain 1951); Fakhry, Ahmed, *An Archaeological Journey in Yemen* (Cairo 1952); Phillips, Wendell, *Qataban and Sheba* (New York 1955); Hitti, Philip K., *History of the Arabs,* 6th ed. (New York and London 1956); Bowen, R. LeBaron, Jr., and Albright, Frank P., *Archaeological Discoveries in South Arabia* (Baltimore 1958).

PHILIP K. HITTI.

MINARET, mĭn-ȧ-rĕt' (from Arab. *manar,* "place where there is a light," probably because of formal analogy between minarets and lighthouses), a tall structure found in or by almost every Muslim religious building for the primary purpose of calling the faithful to prayer. At the beginning of Islam there were no minarets and the call to prayer (*adhān*) was made from the roof of the mosque or of a nearby house. The earliest known references to minarets are found in the description of the rebuilding of the mosque of Fusṭāṭ (Egypt) in 673 A.D. From this time on minarets became a permanent fixture of all mosques. In each region, different models were used for minarets, square in Syria and in western Islamic countries, round in Persia, spiral in a group of Mesopotamian minarets, but in all cases we are dealing with a structure which towers above all the buildings of a city. Very soon, however, minarets began to play more than a purely functional role in Islamic architecture. They became an essential feature in the aesthetics of religious buildings. In Persia they acquired an elaborate decoration and were used to heighten the main part of the sanctuary. In India their massive bases received handsome balconies. The great minarets of Cairo built between the 13th and the 16th centuries became articulated in combining square, circular, and polygonal forms to make up the main feature of the Cairene skyline. But it is perhaps the Ottoman minarets of Istanbul and Edirne which were most successfully used in groups of four and even six to frame the large Turkish mosques and to add vertical lines to the curves of the domes.

OLEG GRABAR.

MINAS, mē'näz, city, Uruguay. About 60 miles northeast of Montevideo, with which it is connected by rail and highway, Minas is the capital of the Department of Lavalleja and a trade center for the surrounding agricultural region. Marble and granite are quarried near the city, and there is a small rock-crushing industry. Minas dates from colonial times (founded 1783). Pop. (1959 est.) 30,000.

MINAS DE RIOTINTO, mē'näz thȧ rē-ō-tēn'tō, town, Spain. In the province of Huelva in southwestern Spain, about 40 miles northeast of the city of Huelva, with which it is connected by rail and highway, Minas de Riotinto has extensive deposits of iron and copper pyrites. Worked in antiquity by the Phoenicians and Romans, the copper mines of the region are still productive. Industries include the milling of copper ore and the manufacture of sulphuric acid. Pop. (1950) 7,072.

MINAS GERAIS, mē'nȧ zhȃ-rīs' (Port., general mines), state, Brazil. With an area of about 226,000 square miles (not including the 3,900-square-mile Serra dos Aimorés zone, disputed between Minas and Espírito Santo), Minas is Brazil's most mountainous state and foremost mining zone. Consisting largely of a hilly upland averaging about 2,500 feet in elevation, the state has many mountain ranges (mostly low), including the Serra do Espinhaço, ranging north and south in east central Minas, and the Serra da Mantiqueira, along the southern border. Brazil's highest peak, Pico da Bandeira (9,462 feet), is in the Serra do Caparaó on the Minas-Espírito Santo border. The state's largest river is the 1,800-mile-long São Francisco, which rises in central Minas and flows north to Bahia. Other important rivers include the Paraopeba and Rio das Velhas, tributaries of the São Francisco; the Jequitinhonha and the Doce, on the eastern watershed of the Serra do Espinhaço; and the Grande and the Paranaíba, headwaters of the Paraná, which enclose the triangular protrusion of western Minas known as the Triángulo Mineiro.

A mild highland tropical climate prevails in most of the state, with occasional frosts in the higher mountain ranges. Rainfall, averaging 40 to 60 inches yearly, occurs chiefly in the summer (October to March). The chief vegetational zones are the southern and eastern semideciduous forests, the savannas of the southwest and the Triángulo Mineiro, the evergreen tropical rain forest of the Rio Doce valley, and the scrub forests of the São Francisco basin and the Serra do Espinhaço. Much of the scrub forest has been cut or burned—either to provide pastures for cattle, or, in the south, to supply charcoal as fuel for the iron and steel industry.

Europeans first penetrated the Minas region in 1553, via the Rio São Francisco; and in 1560, Braz Cubas (founder of Santos) crossed the area from São Paulo, going down the São Francisco and back by the same route. In 1576 emeralds were discovered, in 1694 gold was found in the southern Serra do Espinhaço, and in 1728 diamonds were found at Tijuco (now Diamantina). During the gold rush, towns such as Mariana (1696), Villa Rica (1698, later named Ouro Preto), and Sabará (1712) sprang up near the most profitable placer sites. During the gold period (about 1700 to 1800) Minas produced some 44 per cent of the world's gold. The Portuguese crown claimed one fifth (the "quinto") of the gold and a monopoly of the diamond production. In 1720, Minas, previously a part of the São Paulo captaincy, became a separate political entity. In 1789 a conspiracy, the "Inconfidência Mineira," was put down in Ouro Preto. One of the leaders of the conspiracy, Joaquim José da Silva Xavier (known as Tiradentes—the "toothpuller"), was executed in 1792, becoming one of the first martyrs to Brazil's independence from Portugal.

Described as having "a heart of gold in a breast of iron," Minas is one of the world's chief depositories of mineral wealth. It is estimated that 16,250 million tons of high purity, high iron content ore—about one fifth of the world's reserves—can be quarried. The production in 1953 was 3,597,979 tons, less than half of which was exported from Brazil. Substantial quantities of manganese are mined, along with tin, tungsten, and graphite; and the state is the non-Communist world's only commercial source of industrial quartz crystals. Bauxite reserves are estimated at 100 million tons; promising reserves of thorium have been discovered; and there are substantial deposits of mica, zinc, and nickel. Minas also produces substantial quantities of gold, along with diamonds, emeralds, and semiprecious stones. The 9,000-foot Morro Velho gold mine at Nova Lima, in continuous operation since 1834, is the world's deepest mine.

Inadequate fuel supplies and poor transportation facilities have inhibited the development of manufacturing in Minas. Steel is produced domestically at Sabará and Monlevade, but most of Minas' ore is either exported or shipped to the large Volta Redonda steel mill in the neighboring state of Rio de Janeiro. Numerous local textile mills use Minas-grown cotton, and other plants are for the most part small agricultural processing establishments.

With about 12,000,000 head of cattle, Minas is a major source of Brazil's meat and dairy products. The state ranks first in production of beans, corn, and garlic; second in coffee, tea, rice, bananas, and oranges; and third in sugar and tobacco. Cotton is grown in quantity, especially in the São Francisco basin.

The rail network of Minas, with 5,385 miles of track, is plagued by steep grades and worn equipment. The São Francisco is navigable by river barge from the north central railhead of Pirapora to Juàzeiro, Bahia, where commodities are transshipped by rail to Salvador on the coast. There are 5,210 miles of state roads and 1,265 miles of federal roads, including a paved highway from Belo Horizonte to Rio de Janeiro. Minas has many airports, and air transportation is an important supplement to its inadequate road and rail systems.

The *mineiros* (inhabitants of Minas), comprising about 15 per cent of Brazil's total population, are mostly concentrated in the southeast along the rail and road links to Rio de Janeiro and São Paulo, the chief outlets for Minas' mineral and agricultural products. The state is divided into nearly 390 *municípios* (city-county political units), of which the largest is the state capital, Belo Horizonte (1957 est. pop., 508,000). Laid out in 1897 on a plan similar to that of Washington, D.C., the capital is an agricultural, air, and rail center boasting many handsome modern buildings. In the southeast Juiz de Fora (1950 pop., 126,989) and Barbacena (1950 pop., 68,285) are manufacturing centers. Other important cities include Uberaba and Uberlândia, in the Triángulo Mineiro cattle region, and Teófilo Otôni and Montes Claros. Southwestern Minas is noted for its thermal spas, including Araxá, Caxambú, Lambarí, Poços de Caldas, and São Lourenço. The colonial capital Ouro Preto, now preserved as a national monument, is a veritable museum, noted for the 18th century sculptures of Antonio Francisco Lisboa (known as Aleijadinho—"little cripple"), a mulatto leper who carved wood and sandstone statues, medallions, and altars with tools strapped to his arms. Works of Aleijadinho are found also in other colonial mining towns—among them Congonhas do Campo, São João del Rei, and Sabará.

At Belo Horizonte are the University of Minas Gerais (founded in 1927) and a state veterinary school. There are schools of pharmacy at Alfinas, Juiz de Fora, and Ouro Preto (which also has an excellent mining school); agricultural schools at Lavras and Viçosa; and a technical school at Itajubá. Pop. (1950) 7,717,792.

Bibliography.—Sainte-Hilaire, Augustin de, *Voyages dans les provinces de Rio de Janeiro et de Minas Geraes*, 2 vols. (Paris 1831); Kidder, Daniel P., and Fletcher, J. C., *Brazil and the Brazilians*, 9th ed. (Boston 1879); Santos, Lúcio José dos, *Historia de Minas Geraes* (São Paulo 1926); Calogeras, João P., *A History of Brazil*, tr. and ed. by Percy A. Martin (Chapel Hill, N.C., 1939); Amoroso Lima, Alceu, *Voz de Minas*, 2d rev. ed. (Rio de Janeiro 1946); James, Preston E., *Brazil* (New York 1946); Azevedo, Fernando de, *Brazilian Culture*, tr. by William R. Crawford (New York 1950); Almeida, Lúcia Machado de, *Passeio a Sabará* (São Paulo 1952); Smith, Thomas Lynn, *Brazil: People and Institutions* (Baton Rouge, La., 1954).

KARNA S. WILGUS.

MINBU, mĭn'bo͞o', town, Burma. The capital of the district of the same name, Minbu is in Magwe Division, about 145 miles southwest of Mandalay. It is situated on the right bank of the Irrawaddy River, across from the town of Magwe. Nearby are mud volcanoes, a productive oil field, and forest reserves containing large stands of teak. Fishing on the Irrawaddy is an important local industry. Because Central Burma is cut off from the southwest monsoon by the Arakan Yoma range, the climate of the region is relatively dry; but rice, millet, legumes, sesame, and tobacco are grown with the aid of irrigation. Transportation is chiefly by means of river steamers on the Irrawaddy, normally three miles wide at Minbu. Pop. (1953) 9,096.

MINCH, The, or **NORTH MINCH,** mĭnch, strait, Atlantic Ocean, separating Scotland from the northern part of the Outer Hebrides. From 25 to 45 miles wide, it is connected with the Sea of the Hebrides on the south by The Little Minch

(15 to 20 miles wide), the channel between the Isle of Skye and the middle Outer Hebrides.

MINCIO, mēn'chô (the MINCIUS of ancient Rome), river, Italy. From its source at Peschiera del Garda on the southeastern end of Lago di-Garda in northern Italy, the Mincio flows 41 miles south and east to the Po River. Its course lies almost entirely within the fertile lowlands of the Po Basin. At Mantua, 10 miles northwest of its junction with the Po, the Mincio widens to form three small lakes (Superiore, di Mezzo, and Inferiore) which bound the city on the northwest and east. Lago di Garda, 32 miles in length, is fed at its northern end by the 47-mile-long Sarca River, which rises in the Adamello group of the Italian Alps and may be considered as the upper course of the Mincio.

MIND, in ordinary usage, is contrasted with *body,* but the defining characteristics of mind and body, and the nature of the relationship between them, are matters of long-standing philosophical investigation and controversy—so much so that it is impossible to furnish a philosophically neutral characterization of mind. Nonetheless, dreams, feelings, sensations, and thoughts are generally regarded as typical mental phenomena; and all these states are felt by many philosophers to share certain distinctive features: (1) Each individual is so related to his mental states that he knows them directly and without inference. (2) Mental states are privately owned, so to speak; an individual has direct access only to his own mental states, while he can know the mental states of another individual only indirectly and by inference—either from the behavior of that individual, or by analogy with his own mental states. (3) Each individual is absolutely certain regarding the occurrence and conscious content of his own mental states, and is never to this degree certain regarding the occurrence or content of mental states in any other individual. (4) Mental states are nonspatial, and are not located in space—it would not be reasonable to ask where a thought, for example, is located. (5) Mental states have a special quality of "aboutness"—a thought is always *of* something, as are feelings, beliefs, and other mental phenomena. Not every philosopher accepts all of these criteria, and few philosophers will accept any of them without further qualification. Even if all of the criteria are valid, it does not follow necessarily that minds are irreducibly different from, or cannot be explicitly defined in terms of, bodily properties; but many philosophers nonetheless maintain the doctrine—known as mind-body dualism—that bodies and minds *are* irreducibly different.

Historically, the most important dualist was René Descartes (q.v.), who claimed that the world is constituted of two wholly different substances, *res extensa* (extended thing) and *res cogitans* (thinking thing). Each of us is made up of these two substances, according to Descartes, but the manner of their conjunction and the nature of their mutual influence proved extremely difficult to define. Few dualists in the mid-20th century wish to regard mind and body as distinct substances, but so long as the two are regarded as irreducibly different, the problem of their connection and of their causal interrelationships—the so-called mind-body problem—remains. There are three main views: (1) that mind and body are not causally related—parallelism; (2) that they causally interact—interactionism; and (3) that bodily changes cause mental changes, but not conversely—epiphenomenalism.

Substance was traditionally so defined that no two substances could interact causally. It immediately follows from Descartes' theory that mind and body are separate substances, therefore, that there can be no causal relationship between body and mind. Yet events in the mind seem correlated with events in the body, and vice versa, in such a manner that mind and body appear as two parallel series of events which correspond in a peculiarly intimate way with each other. The bodily event of stubbing one's toe, for example, is accompanied by a pain in the series of mental events. Some of Descartes' followers—the occasionalists—regarded each such tandem occurrence as due to the direct intervention of God. Leibniz (q.v.), on the other hand, proposed a "pre-established harmony" and suggested, among other explanatory metaphors, that mind and body are like two synchronous clocks, coordinated from eternity. Few philosophers, however, are prepared to accept such vast metaphysical conjectures, and once the notion of substance is given up (as it has by many philosophers), what reason remains for not supposing the correspondences to be due to causal interaction?

Both science and common sense support the interactionist's belief that mental states cause and are caused by bodily states. Thus, electric changes in the brain seem to be accompanied by changes in mental activity; while mental states, such as fear, seem to cause shivering, perspiration, or other bodily states. More familiarly, one feels pain when burnt and moves one's arm when one chooses to do so. Yet, interactionism, also, is liable to certain objections. First, the mechanisms of causation are hard to visualize. How can a spaceless, weightless thought trigger a nerve, so causing an arm to move? How does the last impulse in a series of nerve impulses get transformed into a sensation, so different in quality from a nervous impulse? Secondly, it is sometimes alleged that interactionism violates the principle of conservation of energy; bodies should lose or gain energy as they respectively act upon, or are acted upon by, minds, but no such gains or losses of energy have been discerned. Interactionists have replied that inability to visualize a causal connection is no disproof of the proposed relationship; and the second difficulty, they argue, is itself based upon the questionable premise that whenever *A* acts causally upon *B*, *A* loses and *B* gains energy.

According to the epiphenomalist's view, bodily phenomena are efficacious while mental phenomena are causally inoperative. Mental states are held to be the effects of bodily causes, and no two mental states are causally related to one another; they are supposed to succeed each other as their corresponding bodily states do, the *latter* being related in terms of cause and effect. However, epiphenomenalists have not produced convincing reasons against the possible causal efficacy of mental on bodily states. They tend to support their position by advancing certain propositions regarding matter which are at least as speculative as those of the parallelists; and they offend the common-sense view, from which interactionism draws its main strength, that thoughts can change the face of the world.

Many philosophers deny the existence of irreducible differences between mind and body, and repudiate dualism by insisting that the world is all of a piece. Such philosophers, known as monists, fall into three main camps. Materialists, such as Thomas Hobbes (q.v.), have held that mental phenomena are really bodily phenomena—that sensations and other mental states are nothing more than brain states. At the other extreme, idealists, such as George Berkeley (q.v.), have held that *only* mental phenomena are real, and that bodies (including brains) are ideas in some mind. Intermediate between these two groups are the neutral monists, such as William James (q.v.), who have held that both mental and bodily phenomena are but different modes, aspects, or arrangements of some neutral stuff.

See also IDEALISM; MATERIALISM; MONISM; PHILOSOPHY—*Metaphysics*.

Consult Broad, C. D., *The Mind and Its Place in Nature* (London 1925); Morris, Charles W., *Six Theories of Mind* (Chicago 1932); Ryle, Gilbert, *The Concept of Mind* (New York 1949).

ARTHUR C. DANTO,
Department of Philosophy, Columbia University.

MINDANAO, mĭn-dȧ-nä'ô, island, Philippines, bounded by the Pacific Ocean on the east, the Celebes Sea on the south, the Sulu Sea on the west, and the Mindanao Sea on the north. It is the southernmost major island of the Philippine Archipelago and the second largest in area (about 36,500 square miles). Mindanao has an irregular coastline with numerous peninsulas and bays, some of which are very large. Much of the island consists of mountains, high plains, and upland plateaus, of which the Bukidnon and Lanao plateaus are the largest and best known. Mount Apo (9,690 feet), the highest mountain in the Philippines, is a volcanic peak in the southeast, near Davao; and Mount Katanglad is an impressive mountain farther north. The principal rivers are the Rio Grande de Mindanao, which flows in a general southerly and westerly direction from the western slopes of the principal mountain range of the island; and the Agusan, which flows in a general northerly direction across a large alluvial valley between the same mountain range and the east coast. Both streams are navigable for small river craft, the Agusan for a distance of about 160 miles (or a distance of 20 miles for boats of six-foot draft).

Since the island is within 10° of the equator, its climate is definitely tropical; but because of its insular and upland character temperatures are not as high as in many tropical areas, being moderated both by altitude and by ocean winds. Precipitation is heavy and reasonably uniform along the east coast and at most highland stations, averaging about 100 inches annually. The western side of the island is drier, particularly at Zamboanga (43 inches), the driest of the Philippine regions in which weather records have been kept over a reasonably long period of time, and in the interior lowlands of Cotabato Province.

The island's economy is largely agricultural, with rice, corn, coconuts, and abacá (manila hemp) the principal products. Other crops include coffee, pineapples, cassava, peanuts, ramie, tobacco, rubber, and various tropical fruits and vegetables. Cotton, cacao, and pepper and other spices have been grown experimentally or on a small-scale commercial basis. Lumbering is an important industry, especially along the east and north coasts, and some of the larger sawmills in the Far East are on Mindanao and nearby Basilan Island. Minerals include gold and a large body of nickel-bearing iron ore, both in Surigao Province; a small amount of chromite in Misamis Oriental Province; and the Malangas coal field in Zamboanga del Sur—the largest coal deposit in the Philippines. Maria Cristina Falls, on the Agus River between Lake Lanao and the north coast, is the best natural power site in the Philippine Republic; and a hydroelectric station which began operating there in 1953 supplies energy for a fertilizer plant, a small steel mill, a carbide plant, and the city of Iligan. The larger industrial plants on the island are the government-owned fertilizer plant at Iligan, a modern pineapple cannery at Bugo, in Misamis Oriental, and a large sawmill and hardboard plant at Nasipit, Agusan Province. A cultivated pearl industry has been undertaken in Davao Gulf.

Mindanao is one of the frontier areas of the Philippines. Traditionally, settlements have been along the coast, in most cases at or near the mouth of a river or at the head of a bay. Since 1950, however, many new roads have been built, and settlers have followed the roads into the interior. The world's attention was drawn to these interior lands in 1954 by the amnesty plan of the late President Ramón Magsaysay (q.v.), whereby members of the Hukbalahaps (a dissident group on Luzon Island) who surrendered voluntarily were given land in Mindanao. Most of the settlers, however, are Cebuanos from the densely populated island of Cebu in the Central Philippines. They have settled primarily along the northern and eastern coasts, the Bukidnon Plateau, and in the interior valleys.

At least a third and probably one half of the residents of Mindanao are Christian Filipinos. The other large group is the Moros, racially no different from other Filipinos, but Moslem in religion. The principal Moslem area is the Marawi (formerly Dansalan) region in the Province of Lanao, while Zamboanga Peninsula is the next most important Moslem region. The interior mountains and parts of the Bukidnon Plateau are peopled in part by various pagan groups, of which the Manobos and Bukidnons are the most numerous and the best known.

The principal cities (normally each Philippine city or municipality includes a number of neighboring *barrios* or villages), with their populations according to the 1960 census, are: Davao, 225,712; Zamboanga, 131,489; Butuan, 82,485; Cagayan de Oro, 68,270; Iligan, 58,433; Ozamiz, 44,091; Cotabato, 37,499; Marawi, 27,049; Pagadian, 17,865; Surigao, 15,661, and Dipolog, 15,102. Pop. of the island (1960) 4,699,475.

See also PHILIPPINES, REPUBLIC OF THE.

ALDEN CUTSHALL,
Undergraduate Division, University of Illinois.

MINDEN, mĭn'dĕn, city, Louisiana, in the northwestern part of the state 28 miles east of Shreveport; altitude, 194 feet. The capital of Webster Parish, Minden is governed by a mayor and council. The town is served by the Louisiana and Arkansas Railway, and is on both state and federal highways. It is a commercial center for the surrounding agricultural area and a shipping terminal for regional produce, including cotton, corn, and potatoes. Among the local industries are plants for processing raw cotton and extracting cottonseed oil, lumber mills, sand and gravel plants, and nearby oil wells. Fishing and recreational areas in the vicinity include the 16-mile-long Lake Bistineau and the Mississippi River. Minden was incorporated as a town in 1850, and as a city in 1928. Pop. 13,996.

MINDEN, town, West Germany, in the north central part of the country about 40 miles west of Hannover. Situated on the left bank of the Weser River, at the junction of the Ems-Weser and the Weser-Elbe canals, the town is a busy river and canal port as well as rail junction. Industries include iron foundries and forging and rolling mills, dockyards, sawmills and associated woodworking industries, brewing and distilling plants, and glass and chemical factories. Two of the town's most celebrated buildings, a town hall (13th–17th century) and a fine Gothic cathedral (11th–13th century), were destroyed during World War II. Local cultural centers include a state theater and a museum devoted to water transport.

Originally founded in 798 under the name of Mimda, Minden is one of the oldest towns in Germany. About 803 it was made the seat of a bishopric by Charlemagne, during the 13th century it became a member city of the Hanseatic League, and by the Peace of Westphalia (1648) it passed into the possession of Brandenburgh. During the Seven Years' War, on Aug. 1, 1759, the combined British and Hannoverian armies defeated the French here at the Battle of Minden. Pop. (1957) 44,000.

MINDORO, mĭn-dō'rō, island, Philippines, lying south of the main part of Luzon and a little north of the center of the Philippine Archipelago. Except for a western projection at the northern end of the island its shape is somewhat oval, with the longer axis (100 miles in length) extended in a northwest-southeast direction. The island's area is 3,759 square miles (or, including nearby dependencies, 3,891 square miles).

Separated from Luzon by Verde Island Passage, Mindoro is geologically more closely related to Palawan than to the rest of the Philippines. It has a mountainous core that ranges from west to east in the north, then from north to south through the center of the island. The highest peaks are Mount Halcon (8,484 feet) in the north and Mount Baco (8,161 feet) in the south central area. A coastal plain of varying width, including many tidal swamps, extends along the northern and eastern shores and occurs on some parts of the western shore; most of the coastal region is under cultivation. Lake Naujan, on the eastern plain, is the fourth largest lake in the Philippines. Between the coastal lowlands and the mountainous core are variable uplands that include low mountains, eroded hills, and small upland plains. The uplands to the east of the mountain crest are covered predominately with tropical forest, and on the western uplands there is a mixture of secondary forest, parkland areas, and grassy interfluves. Probably 40 to 50 per cent of the western upland suffers from soil erosion. The island has numerous small rivers but no general river system. The largest streams are the Magaswangtubig in the northeast, the Bongabong in the southeast, and the Bugsanga in the southwest. Among the native fauna is the timarau, a small species of water buffalo found only in interior Mindoro.

Between 12° and 14° from the equator, Mindoro has a tropical monsoon climate characterized by high temperatures throughout the year, high relative humidity, and abundant precipitation, subject to some seasonal fluctuation. Average rainfall at the island's 10 weather-recording stations varies from 85 inches at Calapan to 125 inches at San Jose. The southwestern coast is the wettest; it has fewer rainy days (102 at San Jose), with a distinct dry season from December or January until May, but it is exposed to the southwest monsoon from June until November. The eastern and northern coasts have a more uniform rainfall, with February and March the period of least rain. The western coast, in contrast with the rest of the island, has inadequate precipitation. The entire island has experienced destructive typhoons, but only the northern third is within the region where serious damage has occurred with frequency.

When the Philippines were a Spanish possession, before the decay of Spain's monarchy, the rice yield was said to be so abundant that Mindoro was called the "granary of the Philippines." Partly because of the once frequent attacks of Moro pirates, partly because of an increased population on the island, and possibly for other reasons, the region as a whole is now a rice-deficit area, although the east coast still produces a considerable quantity of the grain. Sugarcane was important on the San Jose Plain from about 1915 until 1941, but it has not been commercially significant since World War II, primarily because of an infestation of rats. Cotton has been grown experimentally on these prewar sugar lands. Bananas for the Manila market are grown on the plains and rolling hills to the south of Calapan, and coconut culture, for sun-dried copra, is widespread on the well-drained lands at low elevation. Minor agricultural products, largely in the interior uplands, are coffee, abacá (Manila hemp), sweet potatoes, beans, and corn. Agriculture is less well developed than on most other major islands of the republic—probably less than 300 square miles are under cultivation. About two thirds of the farms are owner operated, and there is much shifting cultivation (*kaingin*) in the interior uplands. Copper, gold, and coal have been found, but none of them are of commercial quality and quantity. Philippine hardwoods, both lumber and logs, are shipped to Manila and foreign ports, and rattan is shipped to Manila. Tortoise shells and other marine products are of minor importance.

The principal highway runs along the coast from Calapan southward to Bongabong and westward to Puerto Galera, where the University of the Philippines maintains a small marine biological station. There is regular ferry service from Calapan to Batangas, on Luzon. Philippine Air-lines connects Calapan, San Jose, and Mamburao with each other and with Manila.

In June 1902 civil government was extended to Mindoro and its adjacent islands, and it was detached from the Province of Cavite and made a subprovince of Marinduque. Subsequently becoming a separate island province, in 1950 it was divided into two provinces: Oriental Mindoro and Occidental Mindoro, the latter including the smaller island of Lubang to the northwest. During World War II, United States forces landed on Japanese-held Mindoro on Dec. 15, 1944.

The population (1960) was: Oriental Mindoro 227,100; Occidental Mindoro 84,300. Calapan, capital of Oriental Mindoro, and Mamburao, the capital of Occidental Mindoro, had populations (including residents of neighboring *barrios* or villages) of 32,989 and 5,832, respectively. The inhabitants are principally Tagalogs who have settled along the northern and eastern coasts, and secondarily Visayans who have migrated to the southern plains and nearby hills. The interior is peopled by primitive tribes, among them the Manguianes (about 15,000 in number) and the Hanuóo (about 6,000).

See also PHILIPPINES, REPUBLIC OF THE.

ALDEN CUTSHALL,
Undergraduate Division, University of Illinois.

MINDSZENTY, mĭnd′zĕn-tē, **József** (originally József Pehm), Hungarian cardinal: b. Csehimindszent, Austria-Hungary, March 29, 1892. One of six children of János and Borbála Pehm, a prominent farming family in Csehimindszent, the young József helped with the chores on the family's farm while carrying on the studies which led to his ordainment as a priest on June 12, 1915. In 1919, when the short-lived communist government of Bela Kun came into power, Father Pehm was teaching religion at the Zalaegerszeg high school. Because of his opposition to the Communists he was imprisoned briefly and lated exiled to his native village; but after the fall of the Kun regime in July 1919 he returned to Zalaegerszeg where he was appointed administrator, becoming parish priest and rural dean of the district in 1922. With the rise of German-inspired fascism in Hungary in the mid-1930's, Father József renounced his German surname in favor of "Mindszenty" (derived from the name of his birthplace) and joined the Small Holders' Party which was opposed to the fascistic Arrow Cross movement. Appointed a Papal prelate in 1937, he was consecrated bishop of Veszprém on March 29, 1944, 10 days after the invasion of Hungary by German troops. In November 1944, after the Arrow Cross Party had seized power, the bishop—who had spoken out against the persecution of Jews—was imprisoned on a charge of treason, and held until April 1945—two months after the capture of Budapest by Russian forces. In October of the same year he was appointed archbishop of Esztergom, prince primate of Hungary, and on Feb. 20, 1946, he received the cardinal's red hat.

Because of his steadfast opposition to the Communists—particularly to their campaign to secularize schools, Mindszenty had by early 1946 aroused the hostility of government leaders, and a campaign was launched to convince the Hungarian people that the cardinal was reactionary and anti-Semitic. On Dec. 26, 1948 he was arrested in Esztergom and charged with plotting against the government, spying, treason, and black-market dealings in currency. When brought to trial on Feb. 3, 1949, the cardinal confessed to many of the acts he was charged with, and he was sentenced on February 9 to life imprisonment. Before his arrest the cardinal—anticipating his trial and conviction—had written that any confession he might make would be forced and not genuine; and during his trial observers noted that his appearance was haggard and his behavior strange, as if he had been subjected to torture or brainwashing. Released from prison on Oct. 30, 1956, as a concession to the Hungarian rebels, he took refuge in the U.S. legation in Budapest when Soviet troops reentered the city on November 4. He was unable to be present at the elections of Pope John XXIII and Pope Paul VI, but on Sept. 29, 1971, he was permitted to leave Hungary, never to return. After visiting the Vatican, he retired to a college in Vienna, where he was relieved of the primacy of Hungary by Pope Paul on Feb. 5, 1974, and died on May 6, 1975.

MINE, in military and naval warfare, an explosive device designed to disrupt or impede enemy movements. Naval, or submarine, mines are employed to destroy or damage enemy ships in either friendly or enemy coastal waters, in harbors, and in sea lanes. Land mines are laid in the path of enemy tanks, artillery, or troops, and they are also used to destroy bridges and to cut railway lines.

Submarine mines consist of a case containing a heavy charge of a powerful explosive, usually TNT (trinitrotoluene) or a combination of TNT and another explosive, of sufficient force to sink the largest ship if detonated directly under its hull. The fuzes which set them off are usually coupled to an intermediate, highly sensitive booster charge, or detonator, which fires the main charge of explosive. Activation may be by direct contact with a ship; by contact with an antenna wire connected to the mine, closing an electrical circuit which fires the charge; by electrical remote control from the shore, in a coastal-defense system;

Stages in laying a submarine mine, from launching from surface craft to automatic anchoring.

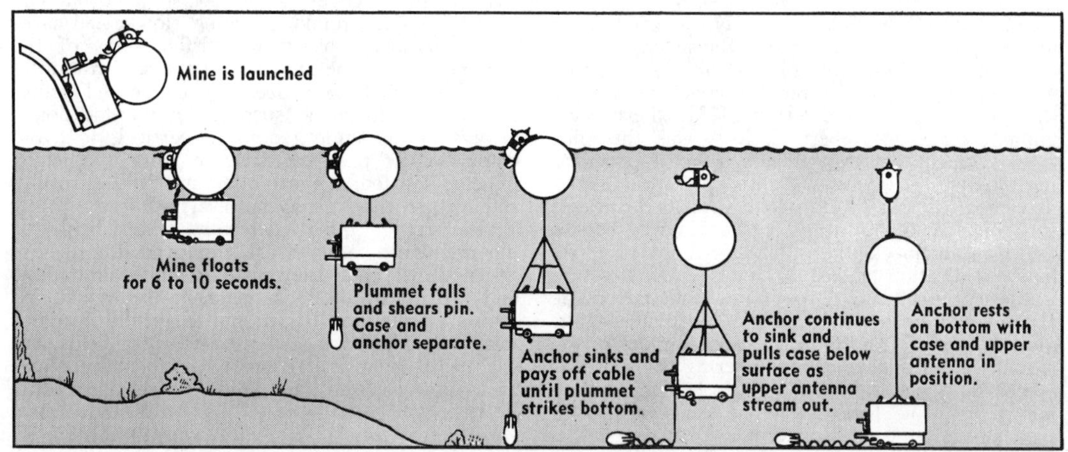

or by a ship passing in the proximity of a so-called influence mine. Influence mines include magnetic mines, which are fired by a disturbance in the magnetic field; acoustic mines, activated by the sound of a ship's propeller; and pressure mines, sensitive to the change in water pressure caused by a passing ship. The mine may be designed to lie on the bottom in shallow water, or, anchored to the bottom, to float at a predetermined depth. Some buoyant mines are allowed to drift, but this practice may endanger friendly as well as enemy vessels. Mines may be laid by specially fitted surface ships, by submarines, or by aircraft.

See also MINE SWEEPING AND MINE CLEARING; SUBMARINE; SUBMARINE MINES, MINELAYING, AND MINE COUNTERMEASURES.

Land mines are of two general types: antipersonnel mines and antitank mines. Both are designed primarily to delay or to restrict enemy movement in the field, with casualties and destruction of secondary importance. Most land mines are set off by means of a fuze and a detonator, the antipersonnel devices being triggered by light pressure on a trip wire or booby trap, while a heavier pressure is needed to explode the antitank mines. The two types differ chiefly in the amount of explosive contained in the metal or plastic cases. Often they are planted together in mine fields devised to delay breaching by antimine personnel. Land mines are usually buried by hand, but mechanical planters have also been developed. *Disabling* antitank mines are designed to halt tanks by damaging their tracks and immobilizing them, so that other weapons can destroy them. *Tank-killing* mines explode under the belly of the vehicle. Antipersonnel mines kill or wound by concussion, by fragmentation, or by spreading toxic chemicals or incendiary fuel. Some have small charges that propel them a few feet into the air so that the explosion may affect a larger area; and others control the direction of fragmentation to increase their effectiveness. See also ARMS—*Grenades and Mines.*

Besides the ordinary submarine and land mines other types have been designed for special purposes, including those intended to hinder amphibious or airborne landings, floating mines to destroy or damage bridge piers and ferries, railroad mines to destroy roadbeds and rolling stock, and harmless dummy mines which serve to confuse the enemy.

FRANK DORR,
Associate Editor, "Popular Science Monthly."

MINE RUN CAMPAIGN, a Civil War military operation. After the Battle of Gettysburg in July 1863, the Mine Run Campaign—involving the Army of the Potomac under Gen. George Meade and the Army of Northern Virginia under Gen. Robert E. Lee—was the only Civil War military engagement of any importance until General Grant inaugurated his great series of campaigns in 1864. On Nov. 7–8, 1863, Meade, with his 70,000-man army forced his way across the Rappahannock at Kelly's Ford and Rappahannock Station about 20 miles northwest of Fredericksburg, Va., and set up headquarters at Brandy Station. On November 26, Meade again moved, crossing the Rapidan River without opposition, while Lee's troops—numbering about 50,000—took up a well-defended position behind a brook known as Mine Run. Early in the morning of November 29, Gen. Gouverneur Warren led a part of the northern troops in a flanking operation around Lee's right, and on the night of November 29 Gen. John Sedgwick began a similar attempt against the poorly entrenched right flank of the Southern army. Both Warren and Sedgwick were ordered to attack at 8 o'clock on the morning of November 30 after preliminary artillery bombardments, but Warren found himself opposed by a heavily fortified position and refused to close with the enemy. Because of Warren's refusal, Meade ordered Sedgwick to suspend his attack, and on December 1 the Army of the Potomac retired across the Rapidan.

MINE SWEEPING AND MINE CLEARING, any of several methods of clearing sea and land mine fields in order to permit the safe passage of friendly ships and troops.

Naval mine sweeping includes the clearing of coastal waters in which an enemy has laid mines, opening sea lanes for fleets and convoys, and the removal of unexploded mines after a war. It is a dangerous mission, and many mine sweepers have been lost—sunk by the mines they sought to disarm. Anchored mines are usually swept by vessels in pairs towing a serrated wire rope between them to cut the mooring line. When the mine bobs to the surface, it is destroyed by rifle fire. Magnetic mines can be exploded by pulses of electricity sent through towed cables, while acoustic mines may be set off by noisemakers towed or pushed by the sweeper.

Four types of mine sweepers were used by Great Britain and the United States in World War II to precede fleet movements into enemy waters. In the van were destroyers—too old for regular duty, but still fast and powerful—converted for sweeping service. These were followed by specially built mine sweepers, resembling ocean tugs, of a type developed during World War I. Next came shallow-draft, wooden-hulled, diesel-powered sweepers; and, finally, small motorboats for close inshore work. During both world wars, the British employed trawlers and other fishing vessels as mine sweepers in home waters. See also SUBMARINE MINES, MINELAYING, AND MINE COUNTERMEASURES.

In land warfare, buried mines in captured mine fields must be cleared to make the ground safe for friendly troops and equipment, as well as for civilians. Removal of land mines requires a careful visual and tactile inspection of the ground combined with cautious probing by specially trained personnel. Each member of a mine-clearing squad covers a narrow strip (about one yard wide) of ground, crawling slowly and carefully forward, looking for visible signs of the presence of a mine and feeling the soil cautiously with his hands. A probe may be pushed gently into the earth at a suspected mine location—always at an angle from the vertical, to avoid detonating a pressure-sensitive mine. When a mine is located, the earth around it is carefully removed so that it may be disarmed.

Electronic mine detectors, hand-held or mounted on a vehicle, are employed to help discover mines, but they have definite limitations and are used only to supplement the visual and tactile methods of inspection. Specially designed mine exploders are also used to clear fields, but such equipment is frequently disabled by blasts from powerful antitank mines. See also MINE.

FRANK DORR,
Associate Editor, "Popular Science Monthly."

MINEOLA, mĭn-ē-ō'lȧ, village, New York, on Long Island about 20 miles east of New York City; altitude, 106 feet above sea level. Incorporated as a village in 1906, Mineola is the seat of Nassau County and is governed by a mayor and board of trustees. Situated at the junction of the main line and the Oyster Bay branch of the Long Island Rail Road, and having excellent highway connections with other Long Island points, and with New York City, the town is one of the major commercial distribution centers on Long Island. Local manufactures include clothing, radio and electronic equipment, light machinery, meat products, and wood and metal products. Mitchel Air Force Base (named for John Purroy Mitchel, mayor of New York City from 1914 to 1917, who was killed in an airplane accident in 1918) and Roosevelt Field are nearby. Pop. 21,845.

MINEOLA, city, Texas, in Wood County about 80 miles east of Dallas; altitude, 414 feet above sea level. It is served by the Texas and Pacific, the Missouri-Kansas & Texas, and the Missouri Pacific railroads. Situated on federal and state highways, Mineola is a busy transportation, trading, and produce marketing center for the surrounding area. Manufactures include lumber products, cement blocks, mattresses, dairy and agricultural products, and clothing. The town has an active youth foundation which has developed a 63-acre plot for outdoor sports. Founded in 1873, it was incorporated in 1913, and has a mayor-alderman form of government. Pop. 3,926.

MINER, mīn'ẽr, **Jack** (JOHN THOMAS MINER), Canadian naturalist, author, and lecturer; b. Dover Center, Ohio, April 10, 1865; d. Kingsville, Ontario, Canada, Nov. 3, 1944. In 1878 he moved to Canada with his parents to settle in Essex County, Ontario. On his farm at Kingsville, Ontario, Miner established a bird sanctuary in 1904 which soon achieved worldwide fame, and he became known as one of the chief bird conservationists of North America. During the course of his life he lectured on conservation of bird life in every town and city of Canada with a population of 2,000 or more. In 1931 his friends, in appreciation of his pioneering work, established the Jack Miner Migratory Bird Foundation for the purpose of continuing the work of his bird sanctuary. Among his publications were *Jack Miner and the Birds* (Kingsville 1923) and *Jack Miner on Current Topics* (Toronto 1932).

MINERAL OIL, mĭn'ẽr-ăl oil, any oily liquid of mineral origin, as distinguished from oils of animal or vegetable derivation. Aside from the so-called essential oils, which are of varied composition and are largely employed as flavors, animal and vegetable oils are primarily glycerine esters of fatty acids. (See also BIOCHEMISTRY; ESSENTIAL OILS; FAT; OIL.)

In the broad sense of the term, mineral oil includes oils derived from the distillation of coal, which are highly reactive chemically and serve as neither fuels nor lubricants, as well as petroleum and oil-shale derivatives. In the narrow sense of the term, only those oils obtained from the distillation of petroleum and oil shale are classed as mineral oils. In the early years of the petroleum industry light oils were known as kerosine oil, but the term "oil" is now applied only to the higher boiling-point hydrocarbons from petroleum. Gas oils and diesel oils are used as fuels; and the higher distillates, from which crystalline paraffins have been removed, are lubricants of various grades. They are made up largely of saturated hydrocarbons.

In the pharmaceutical industry, the term "mineral oil" is applied to a highly refined liquid which is colorless, tasteless, completely transparent, and practically free of the fluorescence which characterizes lubricating oils. Also called liquid petrolatum, paraffin oil, and Russian oil, its specific gravity is between 0.860 and 0.905; its minimum boiling point is 360° C.; its viscosity at 100° F. is around 177 Saybolt seconds, or about 38 centistokes; and it must show no paraffin at 0° C. In addition to its place as a medicinal, oil of this grade has considerable use in industry in sprays, paints, varnishes and lacquers, and as a solvent.

W. T. READ,
Chemistry Consultant.

MINERAL WATERS, those natural waters, usually obtained from springs, which have dissolved an appreciable quantity of salts and gases from the rocks and soil of their underground course. From the physiological point of view, mineral waters must contain a sufficient amount of inorganic salts, with or without dissolved gases, to enable them to exert a physiological effect.

Natural spring mineral waters derive their solid and gaseous components solely from their passage through soil and rocks, and not from artificially added substances; but it is sometimes necessary to treat them in order to remove excess iron, and to adjust the salt and carbon dioxide content to give the physiological effect desired. Waters which have been treated by adding salts and by charging with carbon dioxide are usually called artificial or imitation mineral waters.

History.—The discovery of mineral waters, and their application for medicinal uses, probably occurred before the beginning of recorded history, for it is known that mineral waters were used for remedial purposes from the earliest days of Greece and Rome. About 400 B.C. the Greek physician Hippocrates wrote a book entitled *Airs, Waters, and Places,* in which the watering places of his time were described; and some 500 years later, in 77 A.D., Pliny wrote about the mineral springs in various parts of Europe. The Romans discovered the thermal springs of Italy, and as the empire expanded, they found many other celebrated European springs, including the hot sulphur springs of Aachen (Aix-la-Chapelle) and Baden-Baden, in West Germany; possibly at Spa, in Belgium; and those at Bath, in England. The sulphurous thermal springs at Tiberias in Lower Galilee have been used by invalids since Biblical times. Many well-known resorts—even cities—have been built around mineral springs; and some of these waters, including Seltzer and Vichy water, have achieved such worldwide renown that their names have been adopted for common use.

In the United States, Rock Spring at Saratoga, N.Y., among many other springs, was known to the Indians, and friendly Mohawks brought Sir William Johnson to bathe here in 1776. White Sulphur Springs, W.Va., was first used by white men in 1778. In the late 19th century, the spots for taking mineral water became very fashionable, with elaborate facilities set up to amuse the patrons, the waters usually being but an accessory to the social life. In general, American mineral springs have been much less extensively developed than those of Europe, and scientific research into the properties of these waters has been relatively neglected in the United States, although such research has had a definite place in European medicine. The State of New York, however, which purchased the spring area of Saratoga Springs and made it a state reservation, set up a research institute in balneology there in 1935. In 1921, Arkansas Hot Springs, believed by some to have been the "Fountain of Youth" which Ponce de Leon sought, was made a national park.

Among the first to produce mineral water artificially was the physician of the Elector of Brandenburgh, Leonhard Thurneisser, who prepared a sulphur water about 1572. In the United States the production of imitation mineral waters, made by the addition of salts or carbon dioxide gas to plain water, has become, along with the bottling of natural waters, a thriving industry.

Occurrence.—The majority of the commercial springs of the United States are located in the older parts of the country east of the Mississippi. It has been estimated that there are about 8,800 mineral springs in the United States in about 2,700 separate areas, of which over 400 are used commercially. Wyoming, California, Virginia, Texas, Missouri, Colorado, and New York have the greatest number of springs. New York leads in the commercial exploitation of mineral waters. In the South, Kentucky, Tennessee, and Arkansas are the chief producers of mineral waters.

Among the best known United States waters are those of Saratoga Springs in New York State and several of the springs in Virginia and West Virginia. Among the better known European mineral springs are those of England, at Bath and Harrogate; the German springs at Baden-Baden, Bad Pyrmont, Aachen, Ems, and Wiesbaden; the celebrated waters of Vichy and Dax in France; and those of Baden, Switzerland, and Carlsbad, Czechoslovakia.

The mineral waters at Gettysburg, Pa., and some at Saratoga, as well as those at Vichy and Ems, are generally cold and alkaline. Those of Nieder-Selters (Seltzer) and Bad Pyrmont, and the type known as Apollinaris, are carbonated. Alkaline-saline waters, also, are found at Saratoga. White Sulphur Springs and Salt Sulphur Springs, in Virginia, have sulphuretted waters, and Harrogate is a European spring of the same type. The geysers along Gardiner River and in Firehole Basin, in Yellowstone National Park, and the hot springs of Iceland are examples of siliceous mineral waters.

Physical Characteristics.—Although they sometimes have a greenish opalescent hue attributable to their content of various substances, mineral waters are generally clear. Occasionally they are whitish because of suspended calcium carbonate or free sulphur; some waters are slightly bluish because of suspended clay or slate; and others have a reddish tint due to a suspension of particles of red iron oxide or to the presence of reddish-colored algae.

Mineral waters containing hydrogen sulphide have the penetrating and unpleasant odor characteristic of this gas. A bitter taste in a mineral water is generally attributable to the presence of magnesium sulphate or sodium sulphate. Salty tastes are due to the presence of sodium chloride, and alkaline waters have a smooth feel and the characteristic brackish alkaline taste. Ferruginous waters have a definite styptic taste.

Classification.—Mineral waters are classified in several ways, usually in terms of temperature at the source, utilization, chemical composition, and geographical origin. The classification based on chemical composition is most important; that based on geographical origin will not be discussed here.

Temperature.—With respect to temperature at the source, mineral waters fall into four major groups: cold or nonthermal, with temperatures below 70° F.; tepid or thermal tepid, with temperatures between 70° and 98° F.; thermal, with temperatures from 98° to 107° F.; and hyperthermal, with temperatures above 107° F. Well-known examples of each of the groups include the cold springs of Sharon, N.Y.; the tepid springs at Warm Springs, Ga. (70° to 90°) and at Lebanon Springs, N.Y. (75°); the thermal springs of Hot Springs, Ark.; and the hyperthermal springs at San Bernardino, Calif. (108° to 172°), and at Steamboat Springs, Colo. (212°, with the water escaping as steam).

Utilization.—With respect to their use, mineral waters may be classified into two principal groups: waters for table and for beverage use, and those for medicinal or therapeutic use. Medicinal waters include those taken internally as laxatives and for other purposes, and those administered externally. The use of mineral waters for therapeutic purposes is known as balneotherapy.

With respect to their osmotic influence on the tissues of the body and the blood, waters for medicinal use which have an osmotic pressure less than that of the blood are called *hypotonic;* those which have an osmotic pressure equal to that of the blood are known as *isotonic;* while waters which have an osmotic pressure greater than that of the blood are called *hypertonic.*

The use of mineral waters for therapeutic purposes should be undertaken only upon the prescription of a physician, and then only for the specified length of time.

Composition.—With respect to their chemical make-up, waters may be conveniently considered in terms of their principal constituents other than water itself: gases and salts.

Gas Content.—From the standpoint of gas content, mineral waters may be classified as carbonated, or containing carbon dioxide; sulphuretted, or containing hydrogen sulphide; nitrogen-bearing; carburetted, or containing methane; oxygenated; and nongaseous. The first two groups are the most important.

Effervescent waters: In terms of carbon dioxide content, mineral waters fall into two groups: sparkling (effervescent) waters, which contain carbon dioxide; and nonsparkling (noneffervescent) waters, from which the gas is absent. When carbon dioxide escapes quickly from a mineral water, it is said to be free; and when it escapes slowly, it is said to be dissolved. In the former case, the carbon dioxide is under pressure when the water leaves the ground, and in the latter it is dissolved at a pressure only slightly above that of the atmosphere. The carbon dioxide may also be present as "half-bound," in the form of bicarbonate.

Sulphuretted waters: The characteristic gaseous component of sulphuretted mineral waters is hydrogen sulphide which has an odor resembling that of rotten eggs. These waters—among the first to be known and used—were long esteemed for their curative powers. Some of the waters in Europe are those of Aachen; Baden, of metallic sulphides. The most important sulphur waters in Europe are those of Aachen; Baden, Austria; and Barèges, France. There are hundreds of such sulphur-bearing springs in the United States, including Richardson Springs, Calif., and White Sulphur Springs.

Salt Content.—With respect to type and concentration of salts, mineral waters are classed as saline, alkaline, alkaline-saline, alkaline-earth, ferruginous, and siliceous.

Saline: Saline mineral waters usually contain sodium ions for the most part, along with some potassium, magnesium, and calcium cations, and with chloride and sulphate anions; but at times iodide or bromide are present as well. When sodium chloride (common salt) is a principal ingredient, the water is sometimes termed *muriated.* Important springs with muriated waters are those at Wiesbaden and Baden-Baden. The so-called *bitter waters,* which act as purgatives, have as their principal components sodium chloride, magnesium sulphate (Epsom salts), and sodium sulphate (Glauber's salts). Well-known springs of this group include those of Bad Kissingen, Bavaria; Cherry Rock, in Gloucestershire, England; and Mount Clemens, Mich.

Alkaline: The alkaline mineral waters usually have sodium bicarbonate and sodium carbonate as their principal components, and sodium chloride and sodium sulphate are usually present also. Important springs of this class include the thermal springs of Las Vegas, N.Mex., and the cold springs of Sharon, N.Y.

Alkaline-saline: The mineral waters of the alkaline-saline group usually contain salts characteristic of each of the preceding groups. A typical alkaline-saline mineral water containing both sodium sulphate and sodium bicarbonate is that obtained from the warm springs of Carlsbad.

Alkaline-earth: Mineral waters of this group, also known as earthy waters, contain calcium sulphate and calcium carbonate, commonly termed sulphate and carbonate of lime. Such waters are found at Bad Wildungen, Germany, and at Leuk, Switzerland.

Ferruginous or chalybeate: Ferruginous waters contain ferrous iron as a component, normally in the form of the bicarbonate or sulphate; and usually sodium carbonate, sulphate, and chloride are also present. Two examples of ferruginous springs are at Chalybeate Springs, N.C., and at Chalybeate Springs, Ga. The majority of mineral springs in the New England region belong to the chalybeate group.

Siliceous: The siliceous mineral waters contain alkaline silicates as a principal component of the mixture of salts.

Special Waters.—In addition to the mineral waters with the relatively common components discussed above, there are a number of special types of waters. Those containing the radioactive gas radon are known as *radium waters;* those containing lithium are known as *lithiated waters;* and other special waters contain strontium, arsenic, and iodine. These waters should never be used except by order of a physician.

Bibliography.—Haywood, John K., and Smith, Bernard H., *Mineral Water of the United States,* Bulletin No. 91, U.S. Chemistry Bureau (Washington 1905); Walter, Erich, *Manuel for the Essence Industry* (New York 1916); Chambers, Alfred A., "Comparison of American and European Mineral Waters," in *Production of Mineral Waters,* U.S. Geological Survey (Washington 1918); Fitch, William E., *Mineral Waters of the United States and American Spas* (Philadelphia 1927); Goldberger, J., "Physiological Fundamentals of Spa Therapy," *Archives of Physical Medicine,* 26:558–566 (1945); Kühles, R., *Handbuch der Mineralwasser-Industrie* (Lübeck 1947); Gübeli-Litscher, O., *Chemische Untersuchung von Mineralwassern* (Innsbruck 1948); Osol, Arthur, and Farrar, George E., *The Dispensatory of the United States of America* (Philadelphia 1955).

Morris B. Jacobs,
Consulting Chemist and Chemical Engineer.

MINERAL WEALTH OF THE WORLD. See articles on the various minerals, such as Coal—*3. World Coal Resources;* Copper—*5. Modern Copper Industry;* also articles on various countries, such as: Australia—*2. The Land and Natural Resources* (Minerals); Canada—*12. Mining;* United States—*4. Minerals.* For latest production statistics, see the article *Mining* in the Americana Annual.

For the study of minerals, see Mineralogy; and for the processes of extracting minerals, see Mining.

MINERAL WELLS, city, Texas, in Palo Pinto County of north central Texas, about 45 miles west of Fort Worth; altitude, 925 feet above sea level. In the midst of a grain and livestock area, the town is situated on federal highways and is served by the Weatherford, Mineral Wells and Northwestern Railroad (in the Texas and Pacific system) and by Continental Air Lines. The mineral waters of the vicinity attract thousands of visitors annually, making the town a popular health and pleasure resort. The chief industries of Mineral Wells are dairying and the manufacture of bricks, ceramics, and nylon hose; and several smaller plants are devoted to metal fabrication, production of kitchen cabinets, and electronic development. Points of interest in or near the town include Hexagon House, an architectural curiosity erected in 1897; Lake Mineral Wells, a reservoir created by a dam in Rock Creek; and Possum Kingdom Lake, a 32-square mile body of water formed by Possum Kingdom Dam in the Brazos River 18 miles west northwest of the town. Founded in 1872 and incorporated in 1891, the town is governed by a three-member commission, elected for two years. Pop. 18,411.

MINERAL WOOL, also known as Rock Wool, Slag Wool, and Glass Wool, is a light, fluffy, vitreous fiber, used principally for insulation, soundproofing, and filtering. Its fine, intermingled fibers form an excellent trap to prevent the passage of heat, sound waves, dust in the air, or solid particles in a liquid or gas. The basic manufacturing process consists of shredding a stream of molten mineral into fine fibers by the action of jets of high-pressure steam. The fibers are produced in the form of a loose wool; in batts, blankets, blocks, boards, tiles, and pads; and as granulated pellets which can be blown into the walls and floors of existing buildings. Mineral wool is used as a covering or lining to insulate pipes, boilers, refrigerators, and ovens. Some glass wools with extremely fine fibers are used extensively as insulation in the automotive, aircraft, and refrigeration industries, and as a filling for naval life preservers.

Rock wool was discovered in 1836 as a natural

volcanic product of Kilauea Crater in Hawaii, where it was called Pele's hair by the natives after the goddess of volcanoes. Commercial rock wool is made from natural rock or a combination of minerals. Slag wool, first produced in 1840, is commonly manufactured from iron, copper, lead, and blast-furnace slags; and glass wool, which has been manufactured since 1931, is made from conventional glass batch materials. (See GLASSMAKING.) In addition, several mineral wools with special characteristics are manufactured for military and other purposes.

FRANK DORR,
Associate Editor, "Popular Science Monthly."

MINERALOGRAPHY. See MINERALOGY—*Optical Mineralogy.*

MINERALOGY, mĭn-ĕr-ăl′ō-jĭ, is the science which deals with minerals. It is especially concerned with their chemical composition and their physical characteristics, including the crystal form and structure. Mineralogy considers the origin and occurrence of minerals in the earth's crust, their geographical distribution and their utilization.

The science is closely related to several others, such as geology, chemistry, physics, and mathematics. The rocks studied by the geologist are made up of minerals. Their identification and classification depend upon their mineral composition. The study of the crystal forms and atomic patterns of minerals is a branch of solid geometry. Chemical methods must be used to establish the composition of minerals, and many chemical tests are used in their identification. The processes of mineral formation and alteration are chemical reactions. Important discoveries in physics, especially in optics, have been made through the study and use of mineral crystals. The recovery of minerals from the earth involves mining engineering, while the extraction of useful metals and compounds involves metallurgical and chemical engineering.

A mineral is a homogeneous substance with a composition which may be expressed by a chemical formula, and which occurs in nature and is not the direct product of life. Most minerals are crystalline. Many minerals may be duplicated by man, but are then termed synthetic or artificial, as synthetic ruby and sapphire, and artificial ice. The term mineral is not restricted to terrestrial objects, but is also applied to the components of meteorites, which in general are similar to minerals found on earth.

Among the members of the mineral kingdom which do not fully qualify as minerals are asphalt and petroleum, because they are complex mixtures, and volcanic glass, formed when lava cools too quickly to allow individual mineral constituents to crystallize. A pearl is the direct product of an organism and does not change after formation, hence is not called a mineral. Shells, which definitely belong in the animal kingdom, may lose their organic material, and be broken, compacted, and cemented to form limestone, which is composed of calcite, a mineral. Likewise, vegetation may form peat, and then soft coal, hard coal, and sometimes graphite. The last is definitely a mineral. The coals and certain other natural hydrocarbons clearly belong to the mineral kingdom, but because of variable compositions do not fully qualify as minerals.

Mineralogy as a science is comparatively modern. While the ancients utilized a very considerable number of minerals, some for the metals they contained, others as pigments, ornaments, charms and talismans, and still others in medicine and the arts, they knew little as to their composition. They classified them, but in an unscientific way. There is still extant part of a work *On Stones,* written by Theophrastus before 287 B.C., while Pliny in his great work on natural history, in the year 77 A.D., devoted five books to "earths, metals, stones, and gems."

As chemical knowledge increased, the compositions of minerals were gradually determined and became the basis of classification. The recognition of the importance of the crystal form in mineral determination followed the invention of the reflecting goniometer by William Hyde Wollaston in 1812. This made possible a study of the relation of crystal form to chemical composition in groups of isomorphous minerals. With the development of modern optics and the recognition of the unique optical properties of crystals, there developed techniques for mineral identification by the determination of their optical properties. X-ray methods make possible the determination of the atomic positions in minerals.

Thus the modern classification and description of a mineral includes not only the chemical composition and ordinary physical properties, but also the crystallographic and optical constants, and the data concerning the size of the unit cell and the location of the individual atoms.

Mineralogy may be conveniently considered under the following headings:

Crystallography
Physical Mineralogy
Chemical Mineralogy
Optical Mineralogy
Crystal Structure
Formation and Occurrence
Uses
Descriptive Mineralogy
Determinative Mineralogy

Crystallography.—This is a limited phase of solid geometry, being restricted to those geometric forms which result from crystal growth. Since the crystal form is of great value in identifying minerals, the subject has been developed largely by mineralogists, and has its own nomenclature, its own type of projections and drawing, and its own methods of calculation. See CRYSTALLOGRAPHY; and CHEMICAL CRYSTALLOGRAPHY.

Physical Mineralogy.—Physical mineralogy considers the physical properties of minerals. Some of these are directly related to the crystal structure, and are discussed separately in the articles on CRYSTALLOGRAPHY, and CLEAVAGE. Other physical properties, which are either not dependent on or not so closely related to crystal structure, are here discussed.

Luster, as used in the mineralogical sense, is difficult to define precisely. It includes the *degree* of brilliancy, as indicated by the use of such terms as dull, shining and splendent, but is more concerned with the *kind* of brilliancy. For mineral descriptions, luster is divided into metallic and nonmetallic. The former is further described as iron black, steel gray, tin white, golden yellow, etc. The nonmetallic lusters include vitreous, adamantine, pearly, resinous, silky, waxy, greasy, pitchy, etc.

Color depends upon the ability of a mineral to absorb in different proportions the various wave lengths which make up the incident light. A white or colorless substance transmits or reflects all colors equally.

Some minerals have a constant color, such as gold, malachite and sulphur, and are said to be

Ektachromes by Willard R. Culver © N.G.S. Reproduced by Special Permission from "National Geographic Magazine"

Age of these specimens varies from a few centuries to nearly a billion years. ***Upper left and clockwise:*** **Sulphur crystals; wulfenite crystals; malachite; rhodonite, a manganese silicate, created some 800 million years ago.**

MINERALOGY

Barite.

Quartz crystal.

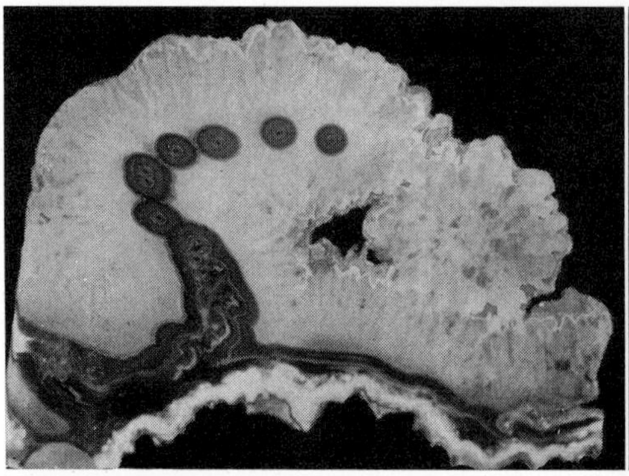

Agate-quartz radiating from agate nuclei.

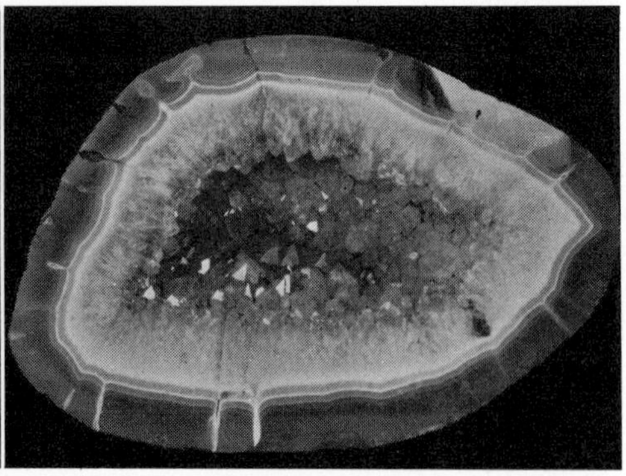

Quartz agate geode.

Calcite group.

Hematite.

Pyrolusite and magnetite.

Fluorite.

Courtesy of The American Museum of Natural History

idiochromatic. The color in this case is inherent in the substance itself, and is always evident unless the mineral is so admixed with impurities that the color is diluted or masked. Other minerals may be colorless or white when pure, but show colors when impurities are present. These are said to be allochromatic. The color may be due to dissolved impurities, as in the case of ruby and sapphire, or to colored inclusions. For example, quartz may be red or yellow, due to disseminated particles of iron oxide, or green, due to scales of chlorite.

Other color or optical effects are known as play of colors, opalescence, tarnish, dichroism, asterism, etc.

Streak is the color of the fine powder of the mineral. It is usually obtained by rubbing the mineral on a piece of unglazed porcelain. If the mineral is softer than the porcelain, it leaves a streak whose color is readily apparent. In some cases the streak is markedly different from the color of the original specimen. Thus hematite and goethite, both occurring in black fibrous masses, give red-brown and yellow-brown streaks, respectively, and may be easily distinguished. Minerals too hard to rub off on the streak plate are said to have colorless streaks.

Hardness is defined by the mineralogist as resistance to scratching or abrasion. A harder mineral will scratch a softer one. An arbitrary scale of minerals was devised by the mineralogist Friedrich Mohs, and is used to designate degrees of hardness. It consists of ten minerals, beginning with (1) talc (softest); (2) gypsum; (3) calcite; (4) fluorite; (5) apatite; (6) feldspar; (7) quartz; (8) topaz; (9) corundum; (10) diamond (hardest). Each mineral in the scale will scratch all of the preceding ones, hence there is a progressive increase in hardness. However, this increase is not uniform. There is an especially large gap between (9) and (10). Moreover, no mathematical ratio is implied. A mineral with a hardness of four is not twice as hard as one with a hardness of two. The hardness is not expressed in specific units, but merely by comparison with the hardness of certain minerals selected as standards.

If two minerals both scratch each other, or if neither scratches the other, they have the same hardness. A mineral may be intermediate between two adjacent minerals in the scale. For example, if a mineral will scratch calcite (3), but is scratched by fluorite (4), it is said to have a hardness of 3½. No fractional values other than ½ are used. The approximate hardness can be determined by reference to other standards if the minerals of the scale are not available. For example, the fingernail is 2½; a copper coin is 3; window glass, 5½; hard steel file, 6½. The hardness of a crystal varies with different directions. Although the diamond is said to have a hardness of 10, some directions are harder than others. It is only because of this variation that it is possible to use diamond powder to grind and polish diamonds. Harder directions in the powder will act on softer directions of the stone being shaped. Usually these variations in hardness for a given mineral are small in comparison with the divisions of the scale. Thus both the hardest and softest directions of calcite are considered as hardness 3. The mineral kyanite is an exception. It occurs in long bladed crystals, and across the blades the hardness is 7; parallel to them it is 4.

Specific gravity is defined as the weight of a substance compared with the weight of an equal volume of distilled water at 4°C. It is numerically equal to density, if the latter is expressed in grams per cubic centimeter. The specific gravity of a pure crystallized substance is practically constant, but as indicated in the later section on Chemical Mineralogy, most minerals contain at least traces of other substances and hence may have variable specific gravities.

Various methods are used to measure specific gravity. Many are based on the fact that when an object is immersed in water it weighs less than when weighed in air. The loss in weight is equal to the weight of the water it displaces. Obviously it displaces its own volume of water, hence by definition specific gravity =

$$\frac{\text{wt. in air}}{\text{wt. of equal volume of water}} = \frac{\text{wt. in air}}{\text{loss of wt. in water}}$$

There are various other properties which may be of value in mineral identification. The fracture surface is described by such terms as even, uneven, conchoidal, splintery and hackly. Substances may be described as elastic or as flexible. Tenacity is expressed as brittle, sectile, malleable, ductile or tough. The feel is described as smooth, rough, slippery or soapy. A few minerals have a characteristic taste or odor. Although many minerals will respond to a powerful electromagnetic field, only a few will be attracted by a simple horseshoe magnet.

When minerals do not occur in crystals they are said to be massive. Even without the crystal form there are many characteristic appearances which may be helpful in identification. Minerals may occur in fine or coarse granular aggregates. They may be in needles or fibers, which may be interlaced, parallel, or in radiating or divergent groups. They may be in small rounded particles or in larger rounded masses, termed in order of increasing size, oolitic, pisolitic, botryoidal, mammillary and reniform. Numerous other descriptive terms are used for various structural features, including columnar, tabular, foliated, platy, spongy, cellular, arborescent and dendritic.

Variations in physical properties without any basic change in composition or structure give rise to what are known as varieties of a mineral. The mineral quartz has several varieties based on color, as rose quartz, citrine, amethyst, and carnelian. Ruby and sapphire are colored varieties of the mineral corundum. Gypsum, when occurring in white, fine-grained form, is called alabaster, while a fibrous form is satin spar. Calcite occurring in sharp scalenohedral crystals is known as dog-tooth spar. Brilliant black hematite is specular iron ore, while the red earthy type is called red ocher.

Chemical Mineralogy.—A few minerals occur as elements, such as sulphur, copper, silver and gold, but the great majority are chemical compounds. The chemical composition of a mineral is its most important feature as far as classification is concerned, and is of prime importance in identification. Standard chemical procedures are used in mineral analysis. The results of such an analysis for the mineral beryl show how the formula is calculated.

	Percentage composition		Molecular weights			Ratio
BeO	14.01	÷	25.02	=	0.560	3
Al_2O_3	19.26	÷	101.94	=	0.189	1
SiO_2	66.37	÷	60.06	=	1.105	6

The formula may thus be written $3BeO.Al_2O_3.6SiO_2$, or $Be_3Al_2Si_6O_{18}$.

In addition to the regular chemical methods for making a complete analysis, many qualitative tests for particular elements are useful in mineral identification. The so-called "blowpipe methods" include colored sublimates on charcoal and plaster tablets, colored beads made by dissolving minute amounts of the mineral in molten drops of borax and other salts, and colored flames produced by the volatilization of certain compounds or elements.

The chemical classification of minerals is described in section (*8*) *Descriptive Mineralogy*. Within the major divisions, whenever possible, minerals are placed in isomorphous groups, which are based on analogous chemical composition and similar crystal forms. An example of isomorphism is the well known calcite group, which consists of the minerals calcite, magnesite, siderite, rhodochrosite and smithsonite. They all crystallize in the same symmetry class, all have high double refraction, and all have rhombohedral cleavage. In a series of this kind, if the atomic dimensions are close, it is possible for one element to proxy for another in the structure. This is known as isomorphous replacement. Thus in siderite, $FeCO_3$, any proportion of the iron (Fe) atoms may be replaced by manganese (Mn) atoms, giving a continuous solid solution series from pure $FeCO_3$ to $MnCO_3$. For intermediate members the formulas may be written as $(Fe,Mn)CO_3$ or $(Mn,Fe)CO_3$, depending upon which element predominates.

Optical Mineralogy.—Crystallized substances have unique optical properties. With the exception of those in the cubic system, all are double refracting, that is, in passing through them ordinary light is broken up into two plane polarized rays which travel with different velocities and are refracted at different angles. Cubic substances have only one index of refraction, but hexagonal and tetragonal substances have two indices, and those in the remaining systems, orthorhombic, monoclinic and triclinic, have three indices of refraction. The determination of these indices alone may be sufficient for identification. Such determination can be made even on microscopic grains, by use of the petrographic microscope, which differs from the ordinary microscope by its use of plane polarized light. Because of the different velocities with which the rays travel, various interference colors and figures may also be obtained, and make possible a complete method of identification.

Opaque ore minerals may be studied by the use of reflected light with the microscope. Variations in color, reflectivity and response to various etching agents provide a means of identification of opaque minerals. This field is known as mineralography.

Crystal Structure.—The determination of the actual atomic arrangement in a mineral by X-ray methods may be of importance in several ways. (a) In minerals with complex compositions the exact formula may be impossible to deduce without a knowledge of the structure. (b) The structure offers a more precise way of establishing isomorphism. Thus a long used classification of the barite group included $CaSO_4$, $SrSO_4$, $BaSO_4$ and $PbSO_4$. However, the arrangement of the Ca and the SO_4 group in $CaSO_4$ is quite different from that in the others, and it is not isomorphous with them. (c) A knowledge of the structure may make possible a correlation between the atomic positions and certain physical properties. (d) An X-ray powder diffraction photograph, even when not utilized in deducing the atomic arrangement, is a precise and indisputable method of mineral identification. It can be used on an extremely small amount of material, and has the advantage of not consuming the sample, as does a chemical analysis.

Formation and Occurrence.—The processes by which minerals are formed follow the same laws which govern reactions in the laboratory. However, there are important differences in degree with respect to pressure, temperature, and time. Man so far has not produced simultaneously the temperatures and pressures which are required for certain types of mineral formation, nor does he have available the almost unlimited time which nature has used to produce some minerals.

The origin of some minerals is very obvious, as in the simple deposition of rock salt and gypsum from evaporating sea water, as has occurred in past geological periods. In other cases the origin is complex and not entirely understood. The possible methods of formation may be summarized as follows:

Formation from Gases: Sublimation.—The most common example of this process is the formation of snowflakes from water vapor. Direct deposition from hot gases may occur in connection with volcanic activity. A related process, known as pneumatolysis, refers to the interaction of two gases, or that of a gas with the country rock adjacent to igneous intrusions.

Formation from Liquids.—These liquids may be either molten rock, magmatic water, or ground water. Molten rock reaching the earth's surface is called lava, while beneath the surface it is known as magma. A magma is formed by the melting of previously existing rocks at moderate depths. The resulting liquid tends to migrate toward the earth's surface. If it reaches the surface as a lava flow or volcanic eruption, the resulting "extrusive" rocks are fine grained or glassy, because of the rapid cooling. If the magma does not reach the surface, cooling may be very slow, resulting in coarser grained "intrusive" rocks. Certain characteristic minerals, including feldspars, quartz, pyroxenes, amphiboles and micas make up the great bulk of these igneous rocks, while a number of so-called accessory minerals may be present in minor amounts. The composition of the magma corresponds to that of the rocks which produced it. It contains, even at a high temperature, certain volatile constituents such as water, chlorine, fluorine, sulphur and boron compounds called mineralizers. These are retained in the magma because of the high pressure, and materially affect the fluidity and the chemical activity of the magma. They do not enter appreciably into the major crystallization products of the magma, and eventually form a residue, which is a hot concentrated aqueous solution called magmatic water, in contrast to the cool and dilute water solutions at or near the earth's surface known as ground water. The magmatic water produces important mineral deposits known as pegmatite dikes and plays an important part in the production of many ore deposits. The dissolved gases in the magma and in the magmatic water are involved in the pneumatolytic reactions mentioned under sublimation.

Ground water is the surface water in oceans, lakes and streams, as well as that in the porous strata near the surface of the earth. Many characteristic reactions are brought about by the action of ground water. Minerals are dissolved, transported, altered and redeposited, and new minerals may be formed. Some common methods of this type of formation are (1) evaporation of ocean water to form salt; (2) decrease in temperature and pressure of water from geysers and hot springs, allowing their mineral content to be deposited; (3) bacterial action, and the action of organisms which extract mineral matter from the water and then secrete it to form shells and skeletons which may ultimately give rise to deposits of limestone, chalk, or tripolite; (4) the action of ground water containing CO_2 in dissolving limestone to form channels and caverns, and the reverse of this process, in which the dissolved material may again be deposited to form stalactites, stalagmites and other cave and stream deposits. Many other chemical reactions occur in ground water, including oxidation, reduction, hydration and carbonation.

Formation by Metamorphism.—This includes the production of new minerals or new varieties of old ones, chiefly through the action of heat and pressure, but the presence of water and other mineralizers may be important. In the movements of the earth's crust resulting in warping and folding of rock strata, various changes occur in which pressure is the predominating factor. These include the change from soft to hard coal, and the recrystallization of limestone to form marble. This process is known as regional or dynamic metamorphism, and may occur over large areas. When a large body of molten rock, magma, is working its way upward through the earth's crust, marked changes may occur in the country rock adjacent to the intrusion. This is known as local or contact metamorphism. Heat and pressure are both important, as well as the chemical action of mineralizers in the magma.

Occurrence of Minerals.—Minerals may occur in large rock formations, such as beds of salt, gypsum and limestone. One mineral may be disseminated in another. Minerals may be deposited in cracks and fissures to form veins and in a similar way cavities may be filled to form geodes. The occurrences of calcite in various types of cave deposits is well known. When mineral fragments are transported by water, sorting may occur, giving rise to placer deposits of the heavier, more durable constituents and stream and beach deposits of sand, which may be composed almost entirely of quartz, or may contain concentrations of other minerals as well.

Uses.—The ore minerals which furnish our metals are of enormous importance, but many non-metallic minerals are likewise essential to our civilization.

A great number of the raw materials of chemistry and industry are directly of mineral origin. And of course, all vegetable and animal products are derived indirectly from soil and water, both of the mineral kingdom. Some minerals are used in their original state, as building materials like limestone, marble, granite, sand and gravel. Others go directly into ceramic products, such as pottery, porcelain and glass. Others are processed into cements, plasters, plastics, artificial abrasives, fertilizers, pigments, etc. Chemistry finds important uses for sulphur, for sodium and chlorine derived from salt, for phosphates, borax, and many others. Numerous organic compounds are derived from coal and petroleum. Sources are not limited to mineral deposits. Salt has always been obtained in warm climates by evaporation of sea water, and the modern production of bromine and the light metal magnesium is from this same source. One important element, nitrogen, is obtained only in small amounts from mineral sources—the greater proportion is obtained from the atmosphere. See also MINERAL PRODUCTION OF THE UNITED STATES.

Descriptive Mineralogy.—This branch of mineralogy sums up the results of the study of minerals, as already outlined, into orderly form for each mineral species, and classifies the different species so that related minerals will be grouped together. The classification for inorganic compounds is as follows:

1. Elements
2. Sulphides and sulpho minerals
3. Oxides and hydrated oxides
4. Haloids
5. Nitrates, carbonates and borates
6. Sulphates, chromates, molybdates and tungstates
7. Phosphates, arsenates, and vanadates
8. Silicates

Within these major divisions, the chemical composition and crystal form are used to group those minerals which are isomorphous, or which are most similar.

Determinative Mineralogy.—Determinative mineralogy deals with the identification of minerals. When a new mineral is found, a chemical analysis must be made to establish its formula, the crystallographic and optical data must be determined, and the various physical properties noted. These data constitute the description of the mineral. Previously described minerals, however, are usually identified by much simpler methods. Sight recognition may be possible if there is some obvious feature, such as a unique color, definite crystal form, recognizable cleavage or characteristic structure. With experience in handling and testing minerals, it becomes possible to identify many minerals in this way. The more general methods of determinative mineralogy make use of tables in which the minerals are arranged in some systematic order. Two or more major divisions are used, based on some easily determined property. These are divided into smaller groups by using a second property, and these in turn are subdivided, and so on. By noting these same properties on an unknown mineral, it is placed first in the proper major division, and then successively in the smaller and smaller groups. Finally the possibilities are restricted to such a small number of minerals that the individual differences between the members are readily recognized, and the final decision can be made. Obviously, the mineral in question must be among those listed in the table.

Tables of this kind may be based solely on (1) physical properties; or (2) a combination of chemical tests and physical properties. In addition to these, there are special tables based on (3) optical properties; (4) mineralographic tests; and (5) X-ray data.

Physical Property Tables.—Most of the tables used are modifications of the original tables prepared by Albin Weisbach in 1866. One set in common use has two major divisions based on (1) metallic luster; and (2) nonmetallic luster. Each of these is divided into five color groups, and each color group subdivided according to streak.

In each of these smallest groups the minerals are arranged in order of increasing hardness. Another set of tables likewise makes the initial division into metallic and nonmetallic lusters, with the latter subdivided into (a) streak colored; and (b) streak colorless. Further subdivision is according to hardness, combined with the presence or absence of a prominent cleavage. Some tables begin with divisions based on streak, followed by subdivision into color groups.

Chemical and Physical Tables.—The chemical tests are chiefly those called "blowpipe tests" as described in the section on *Chemical Mineralogy.* Most tables of this kind are modifications of Franz von Kobell's tables, first published in 1833. The initial division is into minerals with metallic and nonmetallic lusters. The former are divided into (1) fusible, with specific tests for As, Sb, and S; and (2) infusible, with tests for Fe and Mn. The nonmetallics are divided into (1) volatile or combustible; (2) fusible, with subdivisions: (a) metal globules when fused on charcoal with soda; (b) magnetic after heating in reducing flame; (c) those not included in (a) and (b), separated according to behavior in HCl, alkaline reaction after intense ignition, solubility in water, etc.; (3) infusible, with subdivisions similar to (2c). Final identification in many cases is made by specific tests for elements or radicals. As an example, a specimen of olivine would be placed successively in the following divisions and subdivisions:

Nonmetallic luster.
Infusible.
Dissolves in HCl, leaving gelatinous residue of silica or evaporation.
Gives test for Mg.
Contains no water.
Gives test for Fe. Therefore olivine.

This identification is confirmed by the green, glassy, granular appearance of the specimen, which is typical of olivine.

Optical Properties.—The determination of the optical properties is very important in the identification of very small crystals and fine-grained material. Substances are classified either as (1) isotropic (with one index of refraction); or (2) anisotropic, including (a) uniaxial (two refractive indices) and (b) biaxial (three refractive indices). The uniaxial and biaxial groups are further divided according to their positive or negative character. Tables are available with divisions, corresponding to these groups, in which the minerals are arranged in order of increasing refractive indices. Additional optical observations can be made, such as color, pleochroism, optic angle, extinction angle, dispersion, and the orientation of the optical directions with respect to crystallographic directions.

Mineralographic Tests.—For opaque minerals, the microscopic examination of polished surfaces with reflected light is very useful in identification. Minerals may have a distinctive color or varying shades of gray which can be compared with standards. Various reagents applied as tiny drops may produce effervescence, staining, a precipitate, or reveal a structure or texture. There are determinative tables for opaque minerals based on such tests.

X-Ray Identification.—X-rays can be reflected from the internal atomic planes of crystallized substances, and various X-ray methods have been developed for determining the arrangement of the atoms. The so-called "powder method" not only furnishes data from which the crystal structure may be deduced, but also provides an extremely useful method of identification. An X-ray powder photograph consists of a pattern of lines whose positions and intensities are dependent upon the atomic arrangement. To the extent that no two different substances may have identical atomic arrangements, no two substances may have identical X-ray powder patterns. Positive identification of a mineral may be made by measuring the positions and intensities of the lines of its powder photograph, and by then checking the results of these findings against published data for known materials.

See also section on Minerals in articles on countries, states of the United States, and provinces of Canada.

Bibliography.—Following is a partial list of comparatively recent works. See also the bibliography following the article CRYSTALLOGRAPHY.

DESCRIPTIVE MINERALOGY: Dana, James Dwight, *System of Mineralogy,* enlarged by Charles Palache, Harry Berman, and Clifford Frondel, 7th ed., vols. 1 and 2 (New York 1944, 1951); vol. 3 in preparation (1960).

TEXTBOOKS: Miers, Sir Henry A., and Bowman, Herbert L., *Mineralogy,* 2d ed. (New York 1929); Dana, Edward S., and Ford, William E., *Textbook of Mineralogy,* 4th ed. (New York 1932); Rogers, Austin F., *Introduction to the Study of Minerals,* 3d ed. (New York 1937); Read, Herbert H., *Rutley's Elements of Mineralogy,* 25th ed. (New York 1953); Kraus, Edward H., Hunt, Walter F., and Ramsdell, L. S., *Mineralogy,* 5th ed. (New York 1959); Hurlbut, Cornelius S., Jr., ed., *Dana's Manual of Mineralogy,* 17th ed. (New York 1959).

OPTICAL MINERALOGY: Winchell, Alexander N., *Elements of Optical Mineralogy,* Part 1, 5th ed. (New York 1937); Part 2, 4th ed. (New York 1951); Wahlstrom, Ernest E., *Optical Crystallography,* 2d ed. (New York 1951); Rogers, Austin F., and Kerr, Paul F., *Optical Mineralogy,* 3d ed. (New York 1959).

GEMS AND PRECIOUS STONES: Spencer, Leonard J., *Key to Precious Stones* (New York 1937); Webster, Robert, *Practical Gemmology* (London 1940); Kraus, Edward H., and Slawson, Chester B., *Gems and Gem Materials,* 5th ed. (New York 1947); Pearl, Richard M., *Popular Gemology* (New York 1948); Smith, George Frederick H., *Gemstones,* 13th ed., rev. by F. C. Phillips (New York 1958).

ROCK MINERALS: Kemp, James F., and Grout, Frank F., *Handbook of Rocks,* 6th ed. (New York 1940); Pirsson, Louis V., and Knopf, Adolph, *Rocks and Rock Minerals,* 3d ed. (New York 1947).

USES AND PRODUCTION: United States Bureau of Mines and Geological Survey, *Mineral Resources of the United States* (Washington 1948); American Institute of Mining Engineers, *Industrial Minerals and Rocks,* 2d ed. (New York 1949); United States Department of the Interior, *Minerals Yearbook* (Washington, annual); *Engineering and Mining Journal* (New York, annual review issue).

DETERMINATIVE MINERALOGY: Kraus, Ernest H., and Hunt, Walter F., *Tables for the Determination of Minerals,* 2d ed. (New York 1930); Lewis, Joseph V., and Hawkins, Alfred C., *Manual of Determinative Mineralogy,* 4th ed. (New York 1931); Larsen, E. S., and Berman, H., "Microscopic Determination of Non-opaque Minerals," 2d ed., United States Geological Survey *Bulletin 848* (Washington 1934); Eakle, Arthur S., and Pabst, Adolf, *Mineral Tables,* 3d ed. (New York 1938); Short, M., "Microscopic Determination of Ore Minerals," United States Geological Survey *Bulletin 914* (Washington 1940); Winchell, Alexander N., *Elements of Optical Mineralogy,* Part 3, "Determinative Tables," 2d ed., rev. (New York 1940); American Society for Testing Materials, Card Index of Powder Diffraction Data, sponsored by American Crystallographic Association (Philadelphia 1949); Smith, Orsino C., *Identification and Qualitative Chemical Analysis of Minerals,* 2d ed. (New York 1953); Donnay, J. D. H., and Nowacki, W., "Crystal Data: Determinative Tables Based on X-ray Data," *Memoir 60,* Geological Society of America (New York 1954).

MISCELLANEOUS: Honess, Arthur P., *Nature, Origin and Interpretation of the Etch Figures of Crystals* (New York 1927); Bragg, William L., *Atomic Structure of Minerals* (Ithaca, N.Y., 1937); Hey, Max H., *Index of Mineral Species and Varieties Arranged Chemically,* 2d ed. (London 1956).

LEWIS S. RAMSDELL,
Professor of Mineralogy and Chairman of the Department of Mineralogy, University of Michigan.

MINERALS. See MINERAL WEALTH OF THE WORLD; MINERALOGY; and individual articles on the minerals.

MINER'S INCH. See WEIGHTS AND MEASURES—*Unit Standards.*

MINERS' LETTUCE, mīn'ẽrz lĕt'ĭs, a common name for *Montia perfoliata,* a succulent annual herb of the purslane family (Portulacaceae), native to moist areas of western North America from northern Mexico to British Columbia, and most common toward the coast. It is a highly variable species over its wide range. The plants are commonly rather coarse, with numerous simple stems rising a foot or more from the base. The many basal leaves have long petioles and broadly rhombic to narrowly linear blades. Each stem has a pair of opposite leaves united into a cup or disk around the stem that may be as much as two inches across. From the cup grows the raceme of whitish or pinkish flowers, which mature into small capsules with black shiny seeds. The plants are typically green but become reddish with age. The common name refers to its purported use by miners (and others) as a salad green. It is rarely cultivated in America, and is established locally and somewhat cultivated in Europe for the same use. It is also known as winter purslane, and sometimes by the scientific name, *Claytonia perfoliata.*

RICHARD M. STRAW.

MINERSVILLE, mīn'ẽrz-vĭl, borough, Pennsylvania, in Schuylkill County, 3 miles north-northwest of Pottsville. It lies in an anthracite coal region at an altitude of 697 feet, on the Schuylkill River and on a state highway; railroad service (freight only) is provided by the Pennsylvania and Reading systems. Besides mining and coal shipping, its industries include manufacture of pajamas, shirts, and other clothing. It has a burgess and council form of government. First settled in 1793 by Thomas Reed, who built a tavern, sawmill, and distillery on the site, it was incorporated in 1831. Pop. 6,012.

MINERVA, mĭ-nûr'vȧ, in Roman mythology, an Italian goddess of handicrafts, but eventually, as the Roman goddess of wisdom, identified with the Greek goddess Athena (q.v.). Her name, originally Menerva, doubtless is derived from the Latin root *men,* whence come such words as *mens* (mind), *mentio* (mention), and *meminisse* (to remember), and suggests her characteristic as the personification of the thinking, calculating, inventing power of the intellect. Lucius Tarquinius (surnamed Priscus), the first Etruscan king of Rome (r. 616–578 B.C.), introduced the worship of Minerva as one of the Capitoline Triad (so called because their cult was on the Capitoline Hill), whose other members were her father Jupiter and his sister-wife Juno. Minerva was a virgin deity, to whom calves were sacrificed. Her special worshipers were all who desired to distinguish themselves in any art or craft, such as painting, literature (especially poetry), teaching, medicine, dyeing, spinning, weaving, sewing. To her was ascribed the invention of numbers and of musical instruments. Minerva was also patroness of warriors who won victory through cunning, prudence, courage, and perseverance. Hence in art she often was portrayed with helmet, shield, armor, and spear. Her festival, called the *Quinquatrus,* because it began on the fifth day after the ides of March, lasted five days (March 19–23).

P. R. COLEMAN-NORTON.

MINERVA, village, Ohio, situated on the line between Stark and Carroll counties, on the Sandy River at an altitude of 1,050 feet, 15 miles east-southeast of Canton. It is on the Lincoln Highway and a state highway and is served (freight only) by the New York Central, Pennsylvania, and Nickel Plate railroads. It lies in a farm area and manufactures ceramic tile, electric switches, road machinery, wax-paper products, aluminum storm windows and doors, and vacuum metal ingots. It was founded in 1835. Pop. 4,359.

MINES, in military and naval warfare. See MINE; MINE SWEEPING AND MINE CLEARING.

MINES, mīnz, **Bureau of,** an agency of the United States Department of the Interior, established in 1910 by act of Congress to conduct research and educational campaigns aimed at promoting efficiency, conservation, and healthful working conditions in the nation's mineral industries. One of the bureau's first programs was research in the use of rock dust (powdered limestone) to make bituminous coal dust nonexplosive. This led to regular rock dusting of all modern bituminous coal mines in the United States. The bureau developed a series of rigid standards, based on fundamental research, concerning the use in coal mines of safer equipment and materials, such as electric cap lamps, gas-testing devices, explosives, mining machines, and respiratory protective devices. In 1941, Congress authorized the bureau to make safety inspections of all coal mines and to make its findings public, while in 1952 another federal law made certain safety recommendations in larger coal mines mandatory. The effect of these laws was seen in sharp reductions in deaths and injuries in coal mine accidents.

Among the bureau's other accomplishments and programs are: promotion of the use of roof bolts to replace or supplement conventional timbering and thus curb roof-fall accidents, the leading cause of death and injuries in coal mines; control of fires in coal seams; development of efficient milling methods used by many companies in processing uranium; large-scale continuous production of nonflammable helium gas; extensive research and demonstrations in producing gasoline, diesel fuel, and other products from coal and oil shale; development of efficient ventilation practices, since adopted in many railroad and vehicular tunnels; creation of commercially used processes for making metallic zirconium and titanium; promotion of more efficient methods of burning coal; development of a method for extracting radium from Colorado and Utah carnotite ores; discovery of valuable commercial-grade domestic mineral deposits, including copper, tungsten, potash, and chromite; promotion of secondary recovery methods and development of other techniques aimed at increasing the ultimate recovery of petroleum; development of new and improved devices for mining coal and other minerals.

With headquarters in Washington, D.C., the bureau operates numerous research stations and field plants, reports regularly on statistical studies of leading mineral commodities, and issues a wide range of technical publications on mining methods, safety, metallurgical techniques, explosives testing, mineral-dressing studies, and other research endeavors. It issues the annual *Minerals Yearbook* as a complete volume and in separate commodity and area chapters.

MARLING J. ANKENY,
Director, United States Bureau of Mines.

MING DYNASTY. See CHINA—*8. History* (The Ming, 1368–1644 A.D.), also the sections in CHINA on literature, drama, art, and ceramics; also ORIENTAL THEATER—*China;* PAINTING—*Eastern Art* (Ming Dynasty); POTTERY—*Vitreous Pottery* and *History.*

MINGHETTI, mĕng-găt'tē, **Marco,** Italian statesman and writer: b. Bologna, Italy, Nov. 8, 1818; d. Rome, Dec. 10, 1886. Called to Rome in 1846, he became a member of the state council summoned by Pope Pius IX to prepare a constitution for the papal territories; he was appointed minister of public works in 1848 but resigned after the pope's allocution against the Italian war of independence and joined the Piedmontese Army of Charles Albert, king of Sardinia, in the conflict with Austria. In 1859 he became Sardinian secretary of state for foreign affairs in the cabinet of Conte Camillo Benso di Cavour; he served as Cavour's minister of the interior in 1860–1861, became minister of finance under Luigi Carlo Farini in 1862–1863 and, as successor to Farini, was premier of the conservative cabinet of 1863–1864. As premier, he was instrumental in concluding the convention with France (September 1864) under which Napoleon III agreed to evacuate Rome and the Italian capital was moved from Turin to Florence. After serving as ambassador to Great Britain (1868), minister of agriculture (1869), and envoy to Austria (1870–1873), he became premier of united Italy in 1873; in this office he fostered rapprochement with Austria and balanced the budget but was defeated in 1876 on the issues of the flour tax and railway nationalization. He wrote *Dell'economia pubblica* . . . (1859), *Stato e Chiesa* (1878), and other works including a biography of Raphael Santi (1885).

Consult Smith, Dennis Mack, *Italy, A Modern History* (Ann Arbor 1959).

MINGO JUNCTION, mĭng'gō jŭngk'shŭn, city, Ohio, in Jefferson County, on the Ohio River, four miles south of Steubenville, on a state highway. Its altitude is 662 feet. Forming part of Steubenville township, it has large steelworks and neighboring coal mines, and is served (freight only) by the Pennsylvania, the Nickel Plate, and the Pittsburgh and West Virginia railroads. It is also a center for fruit and truck farming. Once the site of a Mingo Indian village, the city was settled in 1809 and incorporated in 1882. Near its Potter's Spring section George Washington and his party camped in 1770 while exploring the Ohio River. Pop. 5,278.

MINGRELIA, mĭn-grē'lĭ-ȧ, historic region of the Georgian Soviet Socialist Republic, USSR, on the Black Sea. In ancient times the region was known as Colchis, famous in Greek mythology as the home of Medea and the Golden Fleece, the goal of the Argonauts. To the Greeks the area was famous as the seat of Dioscurias (modern Sukhumi), a colony of Miletus, noted for its wines and fruits. The region was conquered by the Romans in the 1st century B.C. and was known as a center of culture in the 4th century A.D. Mingrelia was part of a united Georgian state in the 11th to 13th centuries. After the rule of Timur, or Tamerlane (1386–1403), Mingrelia became a separate principality. It passed to Russia in 1803. Modern produce of the area includes tea and grapes. Its chief city, Zugdidi, has a Mingrelian museum and lies near a large pulp and paper mill on the Ingur River. Its chief port is Poti.

THEODORE SHABAD.

MINHOW, China. See FOOCHOW.

MINIATURE PAINTING, mĭn'ĭ-ȧ-tûr (from the Latin *minium,* "red lead"), a painting on a very small scale. The word has its origin in the practice of embellishing books, in which the principal pigment used was red lead. Hence the Low Latin verb *miniare,* to color with red lead, was applied to the art, and those who practiced it came to be known as *miniatori.* (See ILLUMINATED MANUSCRIPTS.) Eventually the word was applied to all works of art of "miniature" size. Its principal meaning today is that of a very small portrait painting.

The early artists painted on vellum, and used body colors—for example, colors mixed with white or other opaque pigments—and this was continued until the 17th century when thin leaves of ivory were substituted. Ivory was adapted to richer and more varied coloring; transparent colors were employed on faces and hands, while opaque ones were used for other textures. Another technique was that in oil on thin copper. From the use of miniature on boxes, watches, jewelry, and similar objects, enamel came into favor too.

Illuminated manuscripts often contained portraits of authors or owners; suitable persons were represented on manuscript diplomas and other such documents. Late illuminators like Hans Müelich (1516–1573) and Giulio Clovio (1498–1578) painted portrait miniatures. But most of the early work of this kind was done by great portraitists like Hans Holbein the Younger (1497?–1543), Lucas Cranach the Elder (1472–1553), Agnolo Bronzino (1503–1572); and great portraitists ever since occasionally have worked in miniature scale.

In *England* the tradition started by Holbein was continued by Nicholas Hilliard (1537–1619) who wrote a treatise on the *Art of Limning* (ed., P. Norman, Walpole Society, 1911–1912) and Isaac Oliver (1556–1617). The transition to a new style, influenced by Sir Anthony van Dyck (1599–1641), is made by John Hoskins the Elder (1620–1664); the style is fully developed by the brothers Cooper, Alexander (1605?–1660) and Samuel (1609–1672) by whom we have the likeness of Oliver Cromwell. Then follow Lawrence Crosse (1650?–1724) and Bernard Lens (1682–1740). A new impetus came with the prince of English miniature painting, Richard Cosway (1742–1821) who combined English sentiment with French refinement. Followers of his were: Andrew Plimer (1763–1837) and John Smart (1741?–1811); a rival who preferred a more sober style was the court painter George Engleheart (1752–1829). Into early Victorian times reach the Scot, Andrew Robertson (1777–1845) and the court miniaturist of Queen Victoria, Sir William Charles Ross (1794–1860).

The *United States* is best represented by the portrait painters, John Singleton Copley (1738–1815), Gilbert Stuart (1755–1828), and James

Right: Man in a Red Cap, early miniature in oils on a wooden panel, painted by the great portraitist Hans Holbein the Younger.

MINIATURE PAINTING

Courtesy of The Metropolitan Museum of Art

Below: Figures in a Renaissance Porch, by the Flemish miniaturist Hendrik van Steenwyck II, painted in oils on thin copper.

Below: Balloon Ascension, an 18th century miniature executed in gouache on cardboard, probably by Louis Nicholas van Blarenberghe.

Right: Vertumnus and Pomona, painted on paper by J. le Febvre, an artist of the 17th century French school of miniaturists.

MINIATURE PAINTING

Courtesy of The Metropolitan Museum of Art

Above: The actor Pierre Louis Dubus, water color on ivory, attributed to Jean Fragonard.

Above: Jérôme Bonaparte, water color on ivory, painted by the Italian artist Andreoli.

Above: Portrait of Lady Sophia Boyle by the foremost English miniaturist, Richard Cosway.

Below: Self-portrait of Edward Greene Malbone, the first great American miniaturist.

Below: A fine portrait of Augusta Temple Prime by Jean Baptiste Isabey.

Peale (1749–1831). Edward Greene Malbone (1777–1807), however, was the first great American miniaturist. Charles Fraser (1782–1860) and John Trumbull, his contemporaries, and later George Freeman (1789–1868) deserve mention.

In *France,* one of the earliest examples is the self-portrait by Jean Fouquet (1416?–1480), in enamel, and this technique remained in favor there and elsewhere: Léonard Limosin the Elder, at Limoges (1505?–1577?); Jean Petitot of Geneva (1607–1691) and his son, Jean Louis Petitot (1653–1699), who both also worked in England, and many others in the 17th and 18th centuries. Small portraiture, almost miniaturelike, was practiced in the 16th century in the workshops of the Clouet family and of Corneille de Lyon (d. 1575). Typical of the 16th–17th century miniaturist is Louis Du Guernier the Elder (1550–c. 1620). Among the many miniaturists of the 18th century must be mentioned: Jean Baptiste Massé (1687–1767), Ignace Jean Victor Campana (d. 1786), Hubert Drouais (1699–1767), and the greatest of them, the Swede Peter Adolf Hall (1739–1793). The finest flowering of the art came in the period from Louis XVI to the Restoration with Jean Baptiste Isabey (1767–1855), one of the most famous miniaturists of all ages, and his contemporaries J. B. J. Augustin (1759–1832), Jean Urbain Guérin (1760–1836), Ferdinando Quaglia (1780–1853), Jean Baptiste Singry (1782–1824), Louis Sicard (Sicardy, 1746–1825), and François Dumont (1751–1831).

In *Germany* and *Austria* the art was practiced by Ismael Israel Mengs (1688–1764), Martin van Meytens (1695–1770), J. H. Hurter (1734–1799), active also in England, and above all the Viennese Heinrich Friedrich Füger (1751–1818) who followed English taste. Popular was Moritz Michael Daffinger (1790–1849).

In *Italy* only Rosalba Carriera (1675–1757) gained international fame.

The *Netherlands,* just as Italy, produced too many great portraitists to leave much room for this minor art, which was practiced by lesser men, for example P. Fruytiers (1607?–1660), and J. B. van Deynum (1620–1668).

Sweden, besides Peter Adolf Hall, had many good miniaturists—Arvid Karlsten (1647–1718), who also was a medalist; Erik Utterhjelm (1662–1717); the learned Elias Brenner (1647–1717), who wrote a Latin treatise on the technique (Stockholm 1680); Niclas Lafrensen, father and son (1698–1756; 1737–1807) who were famous in Paris; and Jacob Axel Gillberg (1769–1845).

In *Russia* many foreigners were active: the two Swiss, H. F. G. Viollier (1750–1829) and N. Soret (1759–1830), the Italian D. Bossi (1765–1853), and others.

Except for miniatures in oil, which mostly look like regular portraits reduced in size, miniature painting has a distinct style which is characterized by a brilliant coloring in a light key, suggested by the technique, and by a minute execution of highest precision, required by the scale. The tastes of the late 17th, 18th, and the early 19th centuries were susceptible to such qualities; and this accounts for the flowering of the art at this time. Such periods of refinement could savor to the fullest the elegance, preciousness, and intimacy of this art; miniatures, often in precious settings on boxes, and other objects, then played a more vital part in everyday life.

The invention of photography meant the end of miniature portraiture as a well-defined art. It was still practiced, but either became a slave to photographic likeness, losing all style, or went to the other extreme by indulging in stylistic experiments not suited to the medium and purpose.

Miniature portraits in low relief, in wax (often elaborately colored), terra cotta, Wedgwood ware, on coins and medals are akin to the painted ones, as are countless small portrait drawings, in black on parchment (for example, Vischer the Younger, Haarlem [1618/29–1658/62]) or in red and black on paper (Louis Carmontelle or Louis Carrogis; 1717–1806), and similar engravings (Charles Nicholas Cochin, 1715–1790).

In miniature scale, in the same techniques, many other subjects were painted: devotional subjects and mythologies (Joseph Werner II, 1637–1710; K. G. Klingstet of Riga, 1657–1734; Pierre Antoine Baudouin, 1723–1769); landscapes (Hans Bol, 1534–1593); animals and flowers, often as scientific illustrations (Maria Sybilla Merian, 1647–1717; Catherine Perrot, c. 1680, from whom there is also a treatise on the technique); battle scene (Louis Nicholas van Blarenberghe, 1716?–1794); copies after famous pictures (S. F. Dinglinger, 1739–1791).

A special branch of miniature painting, technically related to enamel, is that on porcelain which developed during the 18th century in such factories as Meissen, Sèvres, Chelsea, and Capodimonte. Tableware was decorated with miniature landscapes, pastoral and other scenes, flowers, birds, and other subjects; a great deal of imagination was spent on porcelain snuffboxes. Toward the end of the century and in the beginning of the 19th century these decorations became increasingly like real miniature pictures, and on cups, for example, even portraits became the fashion. In the *Near East,* particularly in Persia and in India, portrait miniatures are found beginning with the 16th century. They have their origin in the rich secular book illustration of these countries and they were actually painted by the great miniaturists themselves. It is not always quite easy, however, to tell the borderline between illustration and portraiture, especially in Persia. Among the known painters there Ali Rizā Abbāsi (c. 1598–1643) should be remembered, for to him are ascribed some of the finest examples known. In greater numbers portrait miniatures existed at the court of the Mogul emperors in India (16th–18th centuries), particularly those of the emperors themselves. They are true portraits and differ little in general character from their Western contemporaries.

Bibliography.—Propert, John L., *History of Miniature Art* (London 1887); Foster, Joshua J., *Miniature Painters, British and Foreign,* 2 vols. (New York 1903); Williamson, George C., *The History of Portrait Miniatures,* 2 vols. (London 1904); Bouchot, Henri F. X. M., *La Miniature Française* (Paris 1907); Williamson, George C., *Portrait Miniatures,* ed. Charles Holme (London 1910); Lemberger, Ernst, *Meisterminiaturen aus fünf Jahrhunderten* (Stuttgart 1911); Norgate, Edward, *Miniatura,* ed. Martin Hardie (Oxford 1919); Clouzot, Henri, *Dictionnaire des Miniaturistes sur L'Email* (Paris 1924); Foster, Joshua J., *A Dictionary of Painters of Miniatures, 1525–1850* (London 1926); Williamson, George C., and Buckman, Percy, *Art of the Miniature Painter* (New York 1926); Darmon, J. E., *Dictionnaire des Peintres Miniaturistes sur Vélin, Parchemin, Ivoire et Ecaille* (Paris 1927); Wehle, Harry B., and Bolton, Theodore, *American Miniatures, 1730–1850,* new ed. (New York 1937); Metropolitan Museum of Art, *Persian Miniatures,* 2d ed. (New York 1944); Lister, Raymond, *British Miniature* (New York 1951); Reynolds, Graham, *English Portrait Miniatures* (New York 1953); Colding, Torben Holck, *Aspects of Miniature Painting; Its Origins and Development* (New York 1954); Salmi, Mario, *Italian Miniatures,* tr. by Elisabeth Borgese-Mann, 2d ed., rev. (New York 1956); Lillys, William, ed., *Persian*

Miniatures (Rutland, Vt., 1958); Reiff, Robert, ed., *Indian Miniatures* (Rutland, Vt., 1959); and the catalogues of museum, university, and private collections.

U. MIDDELDORF.

MINIATURE SCHNAUZER. See DOG —*Terrier Group.*

MINIMUM WAGE, mĭn′ĭ-mŭm, the lowest wage permitted to be paid to workers by legislative authority. The minimum wage may apply to a nation, a state or other political subdivision, or to an industry or trade. Historically, governmental minimum wage setting has been directed at the elimination of oppressive wages and sweatshop conditions, particularly as they affected female and child workers. By mid-20th century, a secondary purpose developed in terms of governmental interest in all workers receiving a fair wage or reasonable value for the work performed.

While there were instances of governmental minimum wage regulations in France and England as early as the 13th and 14th centuries, the modern concept of minimum wage by legislative fiat dates from the late 19th century. The first significant experience was in Australasia, where New Zealand in 1894 and the colony (later state) of Victoria, Australia, in 1896 adopted minimum wage regulations. In 1910, England followed the Victorian example by authorizing the establishment of trade boards to fix minimum wages in any trade in which the prevailing rate was "exceptionally low as compared with other employments." The first minimum wage legislation in the United States was passed in Massachusetts in 1912, to be followed shortly by similar legislation in 14 other states and the District of Columbia, and for Puerto Rico. It was not until 1937 that the constitutionality of these state laws was finally established by the Supreme Court of the United States. The minimum wage movement also spread to Canada, the European continent, South America, Mexico, and South Africa. It is also subject matter considered by the International Labour Organization.

In the United States an experiment in wage regulation of a rather novel character was part of the New Deal legislative program in the 1930's. The National Industrial Recovery Act of 1933 included a provision for industry codes for minimum wages to be paid in certain industries in an effort to shore up the economy by increasing the amount of purchasing power in the hands of the consumer. The NIRA was declared unconstitutional in 1935, so the results of this experiment were inconclusive. Minimum wages for work performed on contracts with the United States government for construction, alteration, or repair of public buildings or public works were established by the Davis-Bacon Act of 1931 and on government contracts of all kinds in excess of $10,000 by the Walsh-Healey Public Contracts Act of 1936. The Fair Labor Standards Act of 1938 firmly established the federal government as a regulator of wages in the United States by establishing a minimum hourly wage for all employees engaged in interstate commerce or in the production of goods for interstate commerce. The minimum wage was 25 cents an hour in 1938, and was increased over the years. In 1966, new legislation raised the minimum to $1.60 in 1968 for workers already covered. For most workers newly covered, the minimum was to rise to $1.60 in 1971.

Minimum wage legislation uses two basic approaches in the establishment of wage rates: (1) the setting of a flat rate in the law which applies to all covered industries in the particular political jurisdiction, or (2) the establishment of wage boards or commissions consisting of representatives of the employers, employees, and the public, to conduct investigations and recommend minimum wages in a particular trade or industry to an administrator, whose responsibility it is to act on the recommendations of the board or commission.

See also FEDERAL WAGE AND HOUR LAW; LABOR LEGISLATION; WAGES.

ROBERT L. STUTZ, *University of Connecticut.*

MINING, mīn′ĭng, the process of extracting from the earth natural inorganic elements or compounds which can be made useful to man. The etymology of the word is uncertain, although its relationship to an old French verb *mineor,* to excavate, appears to be close. The range of activities which mining includes is impressive, for the mine may be a clay pit or a stone quarry, worked from the top; it may be an underground complex of shafts, levels, crosscuts, and other tunnels extending thousands of feet below the surface; it may be a hole bored into the ground through which liquid sulphur is drawn; or it may be a well from which liquid or gaseous minerals are pumped to the surface. The raising of gold-bearing gravel by a bucket chain or a suction pump is also a mining operation, as is the dissolving of salt underground in order to pump it in solution. The product may therefore be solid, liquid, or gaseous, so long as it is obtained from the earth's crust and is procured for economic or technical advantage.

In this article, mining is reviewed under five main headings:

1. MINING PRODUCTS

Minerals are of two kinds: metallic and nonmetallic. Of the metals, iron has been and still is the most useful. In fact, discovery of iron in prehistoric times has been called by Thomas A. Rickard, an American mining authority, "the most portentous event in the development of human industry." Iron can be processed very cheaply; it can be hammered, cast, rolled, welded, or drawn into wire. As the principal component of modern steel, it occupies an unrivaled position as an industrial material.

Copper, useful from the earliest times for utensils and in association with tin and zinc to form bronze and brass, respectively, has become more important through its use in the electrical industry. Lead, also known from remote times, has become important in the electrical, shipbuilding, automobile, munitions, and atomic energy industries. Zinc, found in close combination with lead, serves industry in the preparation of brass products, electrical equipment, roofing materials, rubber tires, and chemicals. Lead and zinc oxides yield valuable pigments for paints, as do the rarer metals, titanium and strontium. Nickel, beryllium, chromium, cobalt, tungsten, molybdenum, and vanadium are valuable alloys, particularly of steel.

Aluminum, one of the newest important industrial metals, is more prevalent in the earth's crust than any other, is light, corrosion resistant, and a good conductor of heat; these qualities make it useful in the aircraft, automobile, railroad, and household utensil industries. Magnesium and titanium have still more recently followed the pattern established by aluminum as useful light metals. Thorium and uranium have valuable radioactive qualities and are intimately connected with the production of atomic energy.

Of all the nonmetallics, the most valuable are the mineral fuels: coal, petroleum, and natural gas. The production of these in vast quantities is vital to the processing of all the other minerals and to the movement of all transport.

While metals and fuels are the most valuable and necessary of mine products, many other nonmetallics are indispensable. The chemical industry uses great quantities of sulphur, chlorine, iodine, bromine, and fluorine. Equally important are the fertilizers: nitrogen, calcium, phosphate, and potassium. Asbestos serves as a fireproofing and insulation material. Graphite is used in the paint, lubricant, and electrical industries. The construction work of the world requires immense supplies of sand, gravel, gypsum, cement, and building stone.

COURTNEY ROBERT HALL,
Professor of History, Queens College, New York.

2. MINING OPERATIONS

The following discussion of mining operations covers the broad field of solid materials, usually mined as ores, and is divided into sections on prospecting and exploration, surface mining, underground mining, mineral ore dressing, the mine plant, personnel, and mine administration. For a detailed discussion of petroleum and natural gas extraction, see the separate article on PETROLEUM, especially section *5. Drilling and Production Methods.*

PROSPECTING AND EXPLORATION

When people are looking for a mineral deposit, they are *prospecting;* when they have found a deposit and examine it more closely to determine its size, shape, and mineral content, they are *exploring* the deposit.

Prospecting requires only that a person recognize the mineral he finds and know whether or not it is valuable. Early prospectors sometimes did not recognize minerals other than gold and silver, or they failed to understand the value of a large lead or copper deposit if they did know these ores. On the other hand, they sometimes mistook mica or iron pyrite for gold and wasted much time and energy mining these minerals only to learn later that they were relatively worthless.

A skilled modern prospector, however, has a wide knowledge of minerals—what they look like, what their physical properties are, and where they are usually found. He also knows why ores are found in one place and not another, and what different ores are worth. Such a prospector may be a geologist who will use theories, clues, and techniques in his search for ore in much the same way that a detective solves a mystery.

The prospector usually limits his search to an area he can cover in a predetermined length of time. He begins by making an accurate survey and map of the area. If there are no holes in the ground, he must limit his search to the surface. If the area has wells, pits, or existing mines, he will make use of these to discover what is beneath the surface. If he or his company can afford it, they may drill a hole or excavate a small pit or trench to aid in the underground analysis.

By relating rocks he finds in different places, the prospector can determine the area's structure. That is, he will know how beds, layers, and masses of rock are related to each other not only on the surface but thousands of feet underground. If the number of rock outcrops is small and he does not believe he has enough information to make the correlations, he will have holes drilled through bedrock in selected locations, and will examine the rock extracted from the holes. He also examines "float," or scattered fragments of rock, and determines their composition and origin.

The prospector next determines specific places where ore minerals are likely to be found. He does this by noting how the different rocks in the area were formed, what their positions are to one another, and how they are physically and chemically associated. He may use paleontology and radioactive minerals to determine the age and history of formation of the rocks. He carefully locates all faults (breaks in the earth's crust) and fractures and other structural areas where minerals may be deposited.

He knows that mineral deposits may be formed by (1) segregation of rising liquid rock (magma); (2) precipitation from gaseous or liquid solutions; (3) chemical alteration and concentration caused by heat and pressure on existing rock; (4) precipitation and concentration from materials in surface waters; or (5) concentration and segregation resulting from erosion and transportation of rock on land. By associating the possible methods of origin with rock structures favorable to each type of origin, he isolates specific places where mineral deposits are likely to be found.

Use of Geophysics.—The prospector is now ready to examine the smaller areas more carefully and he can use geophysics to aid in the continuing search and exploration of mineral deposits. At any point in the process, he may find a deposit but will continue to explore it in order to determine all of its physical properties. The same techniques used for prospecting may thus be used for exploration and vice versa.

By using geophysics, the prospector can measure differences in the physical properties of rocks and minerals. The properties he measures are (1) gravity, (2) elasticity, (3) magnetic susceptibility, and (4) electrical conductivity. In addition he may measure (5) heat conductivity and (6) radioactivity. For example, iron has magnetic susceptibility which can be measured by a magnetometer.

Since most minerals are heavier or lighter than the surrounding rock, they cause slight differences in gravity which can be measured by a gravimeter or a torsion balance. Differences in elasticity are measured by seismographs that record waves caused by blasts or impacts on the earth's surface. Electrical measuring devices consist of galvanometers, microammeters, and other instruments. The geiger counter is an instrument that measures radioactivity. Heat conductivity is measured by thermometers and thermocouples.

Each of these methods (gravimetric, seismic, magnetic, electric, geothermic, and radioactive) tells the geophysicist or prospector something about what, where, and how much of a mineral lies below the surface. The methods also tell him more about the structure below ground. However, there is no such thing as an instrument that will tell him exactly what lies beneath the surface. He must interpret the information he receives from his instruments and make an intelligent guess based on his knowledge and experience. See also GEO-

PHYSICAL EXPLORATION; GEOPHYSICS.

When a prospector has discovered a mineral deposit by any of the above methods, he usually knows something about its size, shape, and mineral content. However, any mine operation depends upon continued exploration so that the operator can ascertain how much ore he can plan to mine over a given period of time. Consequently, the process of exploration continues after the mine begins production.

Depending on the shape and size of the deposit, and how deeply it is buried beneath material (waste) that is not ore, the methods used in extracting the ore are those of surface mining or underground mining.

SURFACE MINING

Deposits that are at or near the surface may be mined by surface methods which include (1) open-pit mining or quarrying, and (2) alluvial mining. Other mining methods that have been under development include (3) mining by nuclear blasts and (4) deep-sea mining. In conventional surface mining, open-pit mining is the more general term and can refer to any type of open excavation. Quarrying refers to the mining of a bedded rock such as limestone, marble, or slate.

The Anaconda Company

A typical open-pit mine is terraced with shelves, or benches, to permit ease of working and ore removal.

Open-Pit Mining.—Open-pit mining is begun by breaking ore or waste into small pieces. If the ore deposit is buried, the waste rock on top (overburden) must be removed first. Ore is usually broken by drilling holes in the surface of a bench, or shelf, near the edge, loading the holes with an explosive, and blasting onto the bench below. The ore is then loaded by power shovels into trucks, railroad cars, or conveyor belts for transport from the mine. In deep pits, a skip (a railroad-type car pulled by a cable up steeply inclined tracks) is sometimes used to haul the ore directly from the extraction areas up the pit sides to the surface.

The greatest advance in rock breaking in modern times was the development of an explosive consisting largely of low-cost ammonium nitrate. Because the use of ammonium nitrate explosives lowered the cost of rock breaking, mines could be profitably worked to greater depths and lower-grade ores could be mined.

If the rock is soft enough, it may be broken by rippers mounted on crawler tractors (a technique similar to plowing) and loaded by scrapers. Draglines, instead of power shovels, are sometimes used to strip overburden or to excavate soft materials when the pit is not deep. Also, an instrument of more recent conception that breaks rocks by electromagnetic waves offers possibilities for some types of rock.

When the material to be mined is too soft to require blasting, bucket-wheel excavators, capable of removing up to 13,000 cubic yards per hour, are sometimes used. A bucket-wheel excavator, for example, was selected to mine oil sands in Alberta, Canada.

"Glory hole" mining is a form of open-pit mining where material is allowed to fall down surface craters to underground tunnels. The ore is then transported from the tunnels.

Strip mining refers to shallow open pits where layered material such as coal is mined. Often it is necessary to remove a layer of overburden before mining the coal or ore.

Alluvial Mining.—Alluvial mining is done in surface deposits of silt, sand, and gravel that contain valuable mineral particles. Since the valuable minerals are usually heavy, they can be gravity separated by mixing the material with water in a mechanical device.

The simplest form of alluvial mining is panning. The miner scoops sand and gravel into a pan about the size of a wash basin, mixes it with water, and shakes the pan. Heavy minerals such as gold settle to the bottom and the miner can remove the upper sands a little at a time and pick the gold from the bottom.

Larger devices, such as sluice boxes, washing pans, and jigs use the same principle, but they are filled by hand shovels, scrapers, or dragline excavators. Water is introduced separately.

The floating dredge is one of the most advanced alluvial-mining machines. A large dredge has the appearance of a three-story houseboat and floats on natural or artificial pools. The dredge scoops the material from under the water by a chain of buckets. The material is washed in the dredge, the ore and waste separated, and the waste deposited at the side or rear. Dredges are also used to remove overburden and water from ore deposits that lie beneath lakes, such as at Steep Rock Lake, Ontario, Canada.

Hydraulic mining is the breaking and transporting of sand and gravel by a high-pressure stream of water. The stream is directed against a bank of material. The force of the water breaks the bank and the water carries the particles down to a sluice box or other separation device.

Nuclear Blasts.—Nuclear blasts would remove overburden by blasting it away from the ore deposit. The blasts might also be used to break all the ore at once. However, much study needs to be done before such methods can be adopted, since obviously it would be unwise to experiment with valuable deposits until there is assurance that nuclear methods will be economical.

Deep-Sea Mining.—Deep-sea mining of man-

Above: One of the world's largest bucket-wheel excavators in operation in West Germany's Fortuna mine. Twelve buckets in the rotary head dig into the walls of an open-pit mine and conveyor belts transfer the load to waiting railroad cars.

MINING

Photos courtesy Engineering and Mining Journal

Above: Two teeth-like plows at the rear of this ripper tear up the surface of an open-pit mine. This method is less costly than drilling and blasting and is particularly good where rock is soft.

Left: Electrically-powered trucks with motors on all four wheels, like this 64-ton Lectra Haul model, are effective in open-pit mines.

Left: **In this open-stope lead mine pillars of unmined rock have been left as supports; little trolley cars are used to move ore and waste.**

St. Joseph Lead Co.

MINING

Below: **Mucking out a drift in a Utah lead-zinc mine with a small power shovel. Broken rock is dumped into the car in tunnel behind workman.**

Eimco Corp.

Left: **Several, or many, drills to prepare holes for blasting may be mounted together on mobile trucks; these are known as drilling jumbos.**

Joy Mfg. Co.

ganese and phosphorite nodules was proposed by John Mero of the Institute of Marine Resources, University of California. These rich deposits cover many thousands of square miles of the ocean floor and could be mined by dredges.

UNDERGROUND MINING

Access to mineral deposits in underground mines is provided by shafts, tunnels, levels, drifts, inclines, crosscuts, winzes, and raises. All have the form of tunnels but are given different names to indicate their position and direction.

The Anaconda Company

Underground mines have headframes above vertical shafts, and horizontal tunnels penetrate the deposit of ore.

Shafts are vertical tunnels driven from the surface. If the deposit can be reached from the side of a mountain, a horizontal tunnel (also called an adit) is driven to the area. Levels are in all cases horizontal tunnels driven at any given elevation; they include drifts and crosscuts that connect drifts. Winzes are vertical or steeply inclined shafts sunk from levels; raises are vertical tunnels driven upward. Inclines are tunnels that are neither vertical nor horizontal.

In addition, underground mines contain stopes, which are larger openings from which ore is mined. The stopes may be just large enough to allow men and machines to work in them or they may be about as large as a five-story building. Their size depends on the strength of the ground and the mining method. Stopes occupy the space between levels.

Working in an underground mine is different from working on the surface. First, there is a total absence of natural light as well as a total absence of natural fresh air. Then, too, the miner must usually work in a small, confined area where the temperature may be below freezing or near boiling. Generally, the deeper the mine, the higher the temperature becomes. Sometimes the mines are dry; often, however, much water seeps through the rock into the mine openings. Always there is the danger that the ground may cave or that pieces of rock may fall on the miner. Poisonous gases and poisonous minerals such as arsenic and lead add to the problems of working underground. Also there is the danger that an explosion may occur, either from the accumulation of gas or from the misuse of explosives.

Therefore, before any mining can be done, the mine must be made as safe and as comfortable as possible for the men who work there. (See the following subsection on *Safety*.) Fresh air must be pumped into the mine and circulated to every opening. The miner must have a light to carry with him. Well-traveled areas and dangerous ones require additional lights. Where water seeps into the mine, it must be drained off and pumped to the surface. To keep the rock from falling, various types of supports such as timber and rock bolts are required. To protect him, the miner needs special clothing and equipment. Only after these things are provided, can the miner proceed to the stope to begin breaking the ore.

The miner usually breaks the rock in a stope by drilling holes into the rock, loading the holes with an explosive, and blasting. The holes are about an inch in diameter and usually 4 to 8 feet long. He may proceed in any direction—up, down, or straight ahead. In some mines, the rock is so soft that machines can rip it from the deposit. In other mines, special methods are used to cause the rock to cave and break by itself.

The broken ore is then loaded by mechanical devices, such as mucking machines and shovels, into railroad cars or trucks, or onto conveyor belts, for transport to the main haulage shaft or to an adit. Usually, only a few levels in a mine are used for haulage while ore from other levels is allowed to fall down chutes to the main haulage levels. The ore is then hoisted up a shaft in a container (skip) and dumped into a storage bin on the surface. The shaft arrangement resembles an elevator in a building.

Classification of Underground Mines.—Underground mines may be classified according to the method used to mine them. However, it is difficult to distinguish mines in this manner because each mine operator develops individual methods and practices that depend solely on the deposit being mined, and no two deposits are exactly alike. Consequently, how to classify methods has been a subject of controversy among miners. In this discussion, as a matter of convenience, we shall adopt the classification suggested by Dr. Bohuslav Stočes, a Czechoslovakian mining engineer and teacher. He classifies all underground mining, according to the method used, as follows: (1) open stopes; (2) timbered stopes; (3) filled stopes; (4) shrinkage stopes; and (5) caving methods. This classification is based on the fact that most ore is broken in a stope or caved to a level. If possible, waste is left underground and only ore brought aboveground. Since the deposit determines the method used, not all methods can be used in any particular mine.

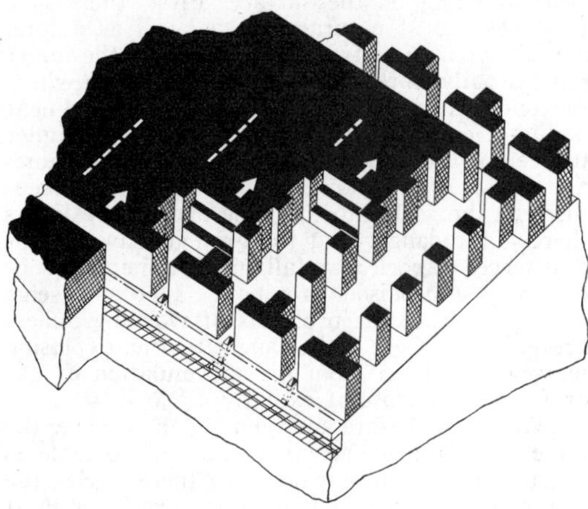

From "Introduction to Mining" by Bohuslav Stočes (Lange, Maxwell & Springer, publishers)

Excavating open stopes by breast-and-bench mining (in direction of arrows), with pillars left for support.

Open stopes are used where the working area does not have to be supported by timber or loose rock. This means that the ground will support its own weight. One way to mine an open stope is to leave pillars of unmined rock between the stopes; another is to leave unmined walls of rock between successive stopes, or chambers. If the ground is strong enough, the miner can proceed directly from a lower level to an upper level (overhand stoping) or from the upper to the lower (underhand stoping). If he proceeds in a horizontal direction, it is termed breast stoping; if he uses benches, he is mining by bench and breast stoping. In rill stoping the miner proceeds along an incline and the ore is broken so as to fall downward. Open stopes also include underground glory holes similar to those used in surface mining.

Timbered stopes have posts, or stulls, supporting platforms for miners; the broken ore drops to the floor.

"Introduction to Mining"

Timbered stopes are those in which timber is used to support the ground and prevent caving. Stulls (props or posts) may be used in overhand stoping when the stope is narrow and the ground moderately strong. They are usually placed in a nearly horizontal position and keep the walls of the stope apart. The ore is allowed to fall down to a lower level or is scraped to a chute by machines. A rectangular framework of timbers, called square sets, is used in larger stopes where the ground is weaker. After a small section is mined, a square set is wedged in the open area. Mining proceeds in both horizontal and vertical directions.

Filled stopes are filled with waste after being mined in small sections. To prevent wall caving, the open space is usually filled as soon as possible. In overhand stoping, a space is left between the waste pile and the roof of the stope so that the miner may stand on the waste to reach the roof. Chutes extend through the waste for the broken ore to fall through. This method permits the miner to sort the ore from the waste and leave the waste in the stope, although all the material is sometimes brought to the surface for sorting. Another technique in filled stopes is to divide the stope into horizontal sections and scrape the ore to a chute. Each section, or layer, is then filled. Timber may be used for temporary support. The waste rock used for fill may come in part from the stope, from other underground excavations, or from the surface.

When the stope proceeds against the long side of a narrow stope, it is termed longwall mining (comparable to mining all along a side of a tunnel). This roof is allowed to cave behind the working area as mining progresses, or the back area is filled—sometimes with a plastic material, such as a mixture of sand and water, brought from the surface in pipes.

Shrinkage stopes are mined by leaving the ore in the stope after blasting. Because ore expands about one third upon breaking, this expanded proportion of the material must be removed immediately. A whole section between two levels is broken, with the miner proceeding overhand by standing on the ore pile. Another method is to drill long holes into the section and blast only part of the ore body at one time. After the section has been blasted, the accumulated ore is removed and the mined-out room is filled with waste or left to cave.

Caving methods are used where possible because they eliminate much of the expense of breaking the ore and supporting the stopes. Rock, in this method, caves naturally into previously mined-out rooms from which it is removed and transported to the surface. The three caving methods, top slicing, sublevel caving, and block caving, differ from each other in size. In top slicing, the miner proceeds underhand a layer at a time, and scrapes the ore to chutes. In sublevel caving, he removes larger layers, and in block caving he removes the whole volume of rock between levels in one continuous operation.

Other underground methods include dissolving the broken ore in stopes with water, and pumping the water to treatment plants (leaching). Sulphur may be mined by dissolving the deposit in hot water.

MINERAL ORE DRESSING

Many ores contain only small percentages of metal. Copper, for example, can be economically

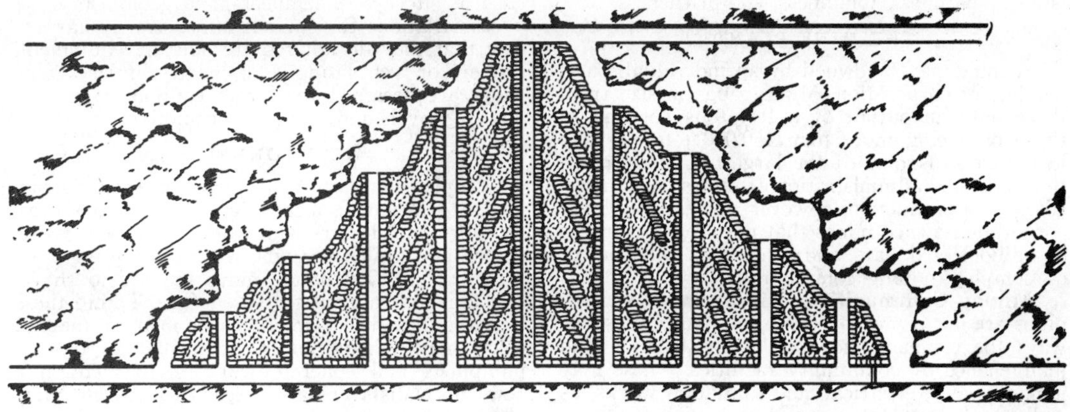

"Introduction to Mining"

In filled stopes miners start from central shaft and work overhead, standing on waste; chutes convey ore to bottom.

extracted from rocks containing less than 1 per cent of the metal. However, low-grade ores cannot be shipped many miles to a smelter because transportation costs would soon exceed the value of the metal. Then, too, smelters are not usually designed to process low-grade ores. Therefore, the percentage of metal in the rock that is shipped must be high enough to offset the transportation costs and high enough for the smelter to handle. To make this possible, ore-dressing plants are constructed at or near the mine. Ore dressing is the partial separation and concentration of valuable minerals from worthless minerals by physical means.

The first step in separating and concentrating ore is to crush and grind the material. The material is then sorted and sized by screens and sizing machines. Separation of the particles then takes place by a variety of methods, depending on the physical properties of the ore. The simplest method is to sort the material by hand. However, machines have been built that separate the material by gravity, magnetism, electrical conductivity, flotation, or amalgamation, or according to such character-

In shrinkage stopes a whole section between two levels is blasted, the ore removed and replaced with waste.

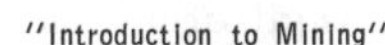

"Introduction to Mining"

Chutes at the bottom level carry off rock broken by the block-caving method, a relatively inexpensive practice.

The Anaconda Company

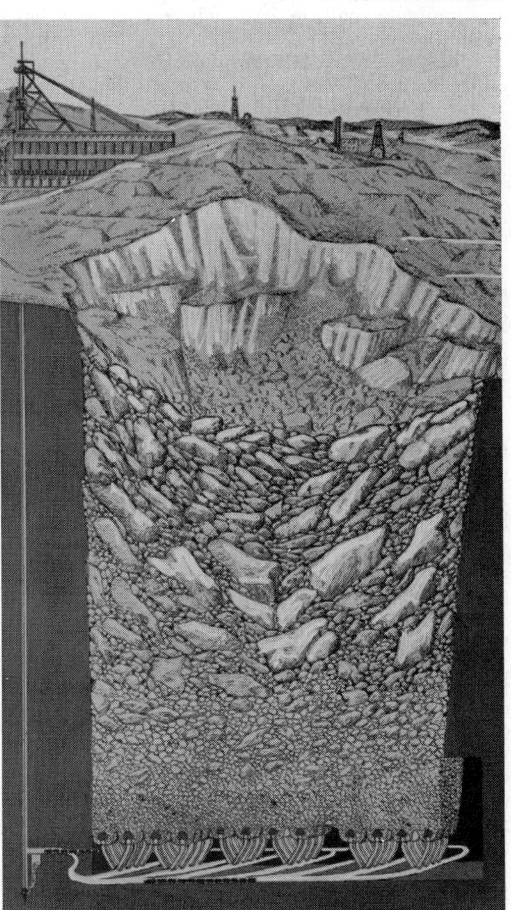

istics as hardness, toughness, and brittleness.

THE MINE PLANT

A mine may be owned by an individual, partnership, or corporation. Mines range in size from those with an output of a few tons per day to those producing more than 150,000 tons per day in the case of some of the largest. Consequently, the plants and administration of mines vary markedly. Most production, however, comes from large corporation-owned mines that require investments of millions of dollars, and often the establishment of complete mining communities.

Mining Communities.—Most mining communities are not owned by companies but almost always the company aids in the construction and maintenance of community facilities. These may include water, electrical, and sanitation works, as well as a hospital, stores, and recreation facilities. In addition, many installations must be built for the operation of the mine.

Because mining communities are usually in remote areas, especially in underdeveloped countries, the company often generates its own electricity. Usually a steam generator is built, but a water turbine may be used if conditions are favorable. The generator is constructed at a place best suited for its operation (near a water or coal source), which may be distant from the mine. High-voltage lines are then built to the mine and the power distributed where needed.

Roads and railroads are required to connect the mine area with the rest of the world, and to provide a transportation route for incoming supplies and outgoing ore. The company must build and maintain roads in areas where none may have existed previously.

Surface Installations.—For an underground mine, surface installations include a shaft headframe, workshops, warehouses, storage bins, and buildings to house special machinery. Administration buildings and buildings for the welfare of the miners are also erected.

First, a headframe must be constructed above the shaft opening. The purpose of the headframe is to support the cables that raise and lower the skips in the shaft. One end of the cable is connected to the skip and the other end to a hoist motor located in a house near the shaft opening. The cable rides over a pulley installed near the top of the headframe. Storage bins are located so that the ore may be dumped into them from a skip on the headframe.

Workshops are provided for mechanics, electricians, and other artisans to repair the equipment used underground and to sharpen drill bits. Extra parts and equipment are stored in warehouses.

A special building is erected to house compressors that supply the mine with air for ventilation and power for some mine equipment. Drilling machines, mucking machines, and winches are normally powered by compressed air. Storage yards for timber, rail, pipe, and other supplies are built near shops which process them. To handle excess water in the mine and to provide water for drilling and drinking, special pump houses are installed on the surface.

Usually a first-aid room is built near the shaft to provide emergency service for injured miners and to house safety equipment. Buildings where miners can change their clothing and bathe are also provided. Finally, offices must be built for the administration staff and technical workers such as surveyors, engineers, and geologists.

Installations for surface mines are similar except that they do not require hoisting equipment, timber, or ventilating equipment. Surface mine shops are designed for larger equipment such as power shovels and full size locomotives.

PERSONNEL

People who work in mines are specialists. There are powdermen who handle explosives, muckers and drillers who work in the benches or stopes, and timbermen who work to keep the mine from caving. Trammers move the ore to shafts and hoisters carry it to the surface. To aid these men are pipe fitters, maintenance men, mechanics, electricians, blacksmiths, carpenters, masons, pumpmen, and concrete workers, to mention a few. Specialists are also needed to operate mine machines, such as locomotives, trucks, shovels, and loaders.

The complete mine organization also includes mining, mechanical, electrical, and civil engineers; surveyors, draftsmen, geologists, and supervisors. Accountants, lawyers, personnel experts, buyers, sellers, and public relations men are also necessary. If the company owns the community buildings, additional people are hired to care for these.

MINE ADMINISTRATION

Generally the complete mine is under the supervision of a general manager who heads the various departments connected with the mining operation. A large mine that employs several thousand men might divide the departments as follows: (1) managerial, (2) operations, (3) accounting, (4) engineering, (5) geology, (6) personnel, (7) legal, (8) medical, (9) supply, (10) transportation, (11) maintenance, (12) safety, (13) power, and (14) assay. A smaller mine would have fewer departments and greater consolidation of activities. In a very small mine, one man would be expected to do the work of several of the departments listed above.

The *managerial* department consists of the general manager and his assistants, whose job it is to coordinate the work of the other departments. Work is assigned to the various departments so that there is no duplication of effort. This department is directly responsible to the board of directors for the entire mine operation.

The *operations* department is in charge of mine production and is generally headed by the mine superintendent. He must see that the men and machines are in their proper places. The mine superintendent has a number of foremen, subforemen, and shift bosses to assist him.

The *accounting* department is responsible for keeping the records of the mine. Purchasing equipment and supplies and selling ore are functions of the department. A chief accountant heads this department that must also handle the mine payroll.

The *engineering* department plans the future development of the mine, in addition to making continual surveys and maps of current operations. The chief engineer also has charge of new construction. Another department function is to measure the advance in the mine, the size of the stopes, and to estimate how much ore is left in the deposit. Mine ventilation and mine drainage are included in problems handled by this department.

The *geology* department searches for new ore and explores the deposit being mined. The chief geologist tries to ensure that there will be enough

General Electric Company

Above: **A 2,500-horsepower ore hoist (foreground) and a 1,000-horsepower service hoist (background) move men and materials in a midwestern mine shaft.**

MINING

Right: **These skips, or cars, in a Kellogg, Idaho, lead mine run in a shaft inclined at a 50-degree angle to 3,600 feet below the main haulage level.**

The Bunker Hill Company

Below: **Headframes support the cables attached to the skips, which are raised or lowered in the mine shaft by the motors shown at the top of the page.**

Engineering and Mining Journal

ore to keep the company in business for a long time. By determining the structure of the deposit being mined, he is able to tell the general manager the exact location and grades of ore.

The *personnel* department has charge of hiring and firing personnel as well as attending to their welfare. If the company owns the community associated with the mine, the personnel manager must see that facilities, including recreation, are provided.

The *legal* department advises the company about ownership rights of the mineral deposits and laws related to mining. The head lawyer and his staff defend the company in suits brought against it by workmen or others. If the company is operating in foreign countries, the legal department informs the company of its rights, privileges, and obligations in that country. The department also calculates tax and tariff obligations.

The *medical* department is charged with the health of the workmen and community. The head doctor and his staff treat miners for accidents or illness. Usually the workmen are charged for the service or belong to a medical insurance plan in which the company participates.

The *supply* department sees that the warehouses are stocked with sufficient parts and equipment to keep the mine operating.

The *transportation* department coordinates traffic in and out of the mine. The chief dispatcher assigns vehicles ranging from automobiles to heavy trucks to the places they are needed, to transport either people, supplies, ore, or waste. If the mine has a railroad, he must also direct rail traffic.

The *maintenance* department makes all repairs on machinery and mine plants. The head of this department is also charged with the care and proper use of equipment.

The *safety* department ensures that safe practices are being followed in the mine. All accidents are reported to the safety supervisor, who makes an investigation of the cause and recommends measures to prevent similar accidents.

The *power* department is in charge of the electric generators and transmission lines to the mine. Its job includes provision of alternate power sources to ensure uninterrupted service in case of failure of the main generators.

The *assay* department keeps a close check on the grade of ore being mined. The chief assayer has samples taken from various areas in the mine and from mine cars and storage bins. He then makes a chemical analysis to detemine the mineral content.

SAFETY

Mining is a dangerous occupation because miners are subject to hazards not normally encountered in other fields. These hazards can cause either accidents or illness, sometimes minor but often fatal.

Causes of Accidents and Illness.—Accidents are caused chiefly by explosions, falling material, poisonous gas, and foul air. Illness is caused chiefly by dust and lowered body resistance to some types of disease.

Mine explosions are the result of improper handling of explosives or of accidental igniting of air laden with methane gas, often found in mines. Many fatalities, sometimes hundreds at a time, have occurred from mine explosions, especially in coal mines. In addition to injuries caused by falling material, large-scale caving can bury the miner or seal him from the surface. A miner may fall down a shaft or incline and be seriously injured or killed. Gas and foul air are caused by improper ventilation, or by fires and explosions. Some of the harmful gases produced are carbon monoxide and the oxides of nitrogen.

Silicosis is a mining disease caused by inhaling very fine particles of quartz. The particles, which are produced by drilling and blasting, cause laceration of the lung tissue. Over a period of time, enough lacerations may occur to kill the miner. Mineral poisoning may occur in mines where lead, mercury, or arsenic are found. Because the poisoning affects some people more than others, not everyone can work in these mines. Usually the poisoning is not fatal. Finally, the miner is subject to conditions of darkness and dampness that are conducive to diseases such as tuberculosis, pneumonia, and rheumatism.

Prevention of Accidents and Illness.—Accident prevention in mines is accomplished by safety training and practices, dust control, and the use of safety equipment.

Perhaps the most important step toward reducing mine accidents is the proper training of miners in safe practices. Usually a new man is never allowed to work by himself and is placed under the supervision of an experienced miner. Mine owners have long recognized that the legal, medical, and lost-time expense of accidents is greater than the cost of providing safety programs. Mine unions also consider safe practices essential to the welfare of their members. Therefore a safety education program is conducted and statistical analysis made of the cause of accidents. Responsibility is thus fixed on both the worker and mine management.

Dust control, essential to prevent silicosis, is effected by screens in the ventilation system and by the use of water in drilling and blasting. Since most dust originates in drilling and blasting operations, water is sprayed in places where these operations are conducted. A water line is connected to the drilling machine and water is sprayed through the bit.

Safety equipment is used to prevent accidents by protecting the miner. Such equipment consists of hard hats, goggles, respirators, safety belts, gloves, hard-toed boots, ear plugs, and first-aid kits. Sometimes special equipment is needed, such as rubber suits for wet mines and wool hat liners for cold mines. Additional devices that check the gas content of the air and the amount of static electricity present are also essential to the operation.

See also COAL—*6. Mining;* COPPER—*4. Mining;* GOLD, MINING OF; IRON—*10. Mining and Handling of Iron Ore;* QUARRYING; SILVER AND SILVER MINING.

BERNARD R. HENDERSON,
Assistant Editor, "Engineering and Mining Journal."

3. MINING HISTORY

Men of the Old Stone Age were miners. Using stone hammers and picks of deerhorn, they scraped their way down to chalk or limestone beds, where the hard flint material for their weapons was to be found. Later cultural ages were designated "bronze" and "iron," as the primitive humans learned to mine and use copper, tin, and iron, at various periods in Europe and Asia. The Egyptians had important copper and turquoise mines in the Sinai Peninsula during the

6th dynasty (c. 2300 B.C.) and great rock quarries in the upper Nile. Their methods of washing gold particles by pouring the impure mixture down inclined planes and of crushing lumps of ore by use of fire were skillful operations.

The Phoenicians were the first extensive dealers in metal; from their extensive colonies in the western Mediterranean—and even, it is thought, from Britain—they secured tin, copper, gold, and silver (c. 1200 B.C.). The Hittites, who flourished about 1500 B.C., found extensive iron deposits in northern Asia Minor, and first distributed that metal to other countries. The Greeks did not have extensive metallic resources; their most valuable minerals were the marbles from Paros Island and from the mainland mountain areas and the fine potter's clay which helped to develop the finest ceramic industry in the ancient world (5th century B.C.). The Romans were not great miners, but they improved and stimulated mining in all the areas they conquered in the last two centuries B.C. Having introduced enormous numbers of slave workers into the mines, the Romans increased their wealth to a high degree by devoting to purposes of the state the mineral production of Britain, Gaul, Spain, North Africa, and the Near East.

By the 5th century A.D., the long-continued pressure of barbarians on the Roman frontiers put an end to operations in most of the imperial mines, even salt becoming difficult to obtain. During the so-called Dark Ages which followed, the search for metals went on. Small amounts of gold were washed from the sands of rivers such as the Po, the Rhone, and the Rhine. The gold and silver mines of Spain were reopened by the Moors in the 8th century. Charlemagne (r. 768–814) began an extensive renovation of the Roman mines in his new empire, using hordes of war captives as labor; when this western European state collapsed in the late 9th century, mining fell into the hands of a multitude of feudal barons and ecclesiastical rulers. In eastern Europe it was much the same, as war and pestilence interfered with the efforts to restore to production the old mines of Hungary and Germany. In the former, silver in a lead ore had been mined from the 6th century, also some gold in the region of Körmöcbánya (Ger. Kremnitz; modern Kremnica, Czechoslovakia). The greatest mineral discovery in Germany in the Middle Ages was the gold strike in the Harz mountain area in 965.

As early as 1201, strong organizations of miners were protected from outside interference by the king of England; his decrees applied especially to the tin mines of Devon and Cornwall, and only royal officials (the wardens of the stannaries) could reverse the legal and judicial acts of the workers' groups. In France, Philip IV (r. 1285–1314) freed the serfs, which ended all forced labor in French mines. An early forerunner of the modern joint-stock company appeared in the 13th century in Genoa, Italy, where shares in German mining ventures were sold. By the 16th century a considerable share of the large fortune of the Fugger family (q.v.) of Germany was invested in silver and copper ventures in the Tyrol, Austria, and in Hungarian copper, silver, and lead mines.

Very little was known about mining or minerals until the *De re metallica* of Georgius Agricola (1494–1555), a German scientist, was published in 1556. This became the great classic in the literature of mining. The author related how even in 16th century Germany the miners had a five-day week, could break down the hardest rock by "firesetting," and had elaborate windlasses to hoist the ore from below. There were water pumps to dry the mines, ventilators, and oil lamps to light the dark channels.

By the 15th century European commercial leaders were hampered by an increasing lack of precious metals with which to balance their transactions with the East. Spain and Portugal led the great movement to secure more direct routes of trade and also to procure, by discovery or conquest, more extensive stocks of precious metals. Spain was more immediately successful through her seizure of vast stores of gold and silver in Mexico and Peru; Portugal later exploited effectively, beginning in 1721, the gold and diamonds of Brazil.

Far more important in the development of modern mining than the increase in the world's stock of precious metals, however, was the discovery of the usefulness of coal, and its byproduct coke, in the processing of iron, by Abraham Darby (1677–1717), an English Quaker, in the early 18th century. Henry Cort (1740–1800), an English industrialist, produced in the 1780's a malleable wrought iron by the puddling process and at about the same time evolved the process of rolling iron into plates. In the middle of the 19th century Henry Bessemer (1813–1898) invented the converter which first provided a cheap steel for the great industrial age which had already begun. Thus the coal in plentiful supply in Great Britain, western Europe, and the United States assumed great importance as the chief industrial fuel, and its marriage to iron, the most useful industrial material, was firmly established.

In America, the hopes of English settlers in Virginia and other coastal settlements to find valuable minerals proved, with a few minor exceptions, vain; not until the discovery of gold in California (Jan. 24, 1848) did it become evident that the United States was exceedingly rich in these materials. Other rich strikes soon followed: silver in Nevada; gold in Colorado and the Dakotas; copper in Montana and Arizona; petroleum in Pennsylvania and in widely scattered areas of the West and Southwest; iron in enormous quantities in the Lake Superior district. All these discoveries and many others pushed the United States into an important position among world producers by the end of the 19th century.

The second half of the 19th century brought great discoveries in other areas also. Vast new gold fields were found in Victoria, Australia, in 1851; great resources of silver, nickel, and cobalt were tapped some 300 miles north of Toronto, Canada, and gold was discovered in the Yukon, in the Canadian northwest. The old silver and copper mines of the South American Andes were expanded. Rhodesia and the Belgian Congo became important sources of copper ore, and near the century's end the world's most extensive gold and diamond area was found in South Africa.

In Asia, meanwhile, large coal areas were prospected in China, Siberia, Manchuria, and in the island of Sakhalin. Several Far Eastern countries were found to possess major deposits of tin, antimony, and tungsten. China produces from one third to two fifths of the world supply of tungsten. Malaysia, China, Thailand, and Indonesia provide far more than one half of the world's supply of tin. Except for these metals and for coal, however, in none of the Far Eastern countries have minerals been produced in anything like the massive quantities as have been dug in Europe, Africa, and the Western Hemisphere. Most significant in the modern history of mineral production and processing, however, has been the swift rise of the Soviet Union. It leads the world in iron ore and manganese production and is second only to the United States in steel production.

4. MINING IN THE MODERN WORLD

The history of mining before the mid-19th century was mostly a prologue to the almost fantastic changes that were to occur in the following century. Mining in the modern world has become a highly mechanized and a very large-scale productive operation. Great corporations with millions of capital have replaced the guilds of workers and the small-scale individual operators. The engineer and the financier have become the central figures of the process. The mining worker has become the operator of a machine.

Mineral exploration on the Colorado plateau: removing core samples by means of a truck-mounted diamond drill.

Sprague & Henwood

As the 20th century advanced, coal and iron continued to be important, but the mining economy became more varied, as new minerals were discovered and found their place in industry. The steel, electrical, petroleum, and chemical industries registered great growth, and placed increasing demands upon mining. The coming of the automotive and aviation industries created entirely new demands, particularly in the fields of light metals and fuels. World Wars I and II revolutionized mining, as almost everything else, by stepping up the demand for mineral products (34 new minerals came into industrial use between the wars), and they made the factor of speed in extraction most vital; the two conflicts also helped to raise the specter of exhaustion of some mineral reserves. Mining in the mid-20th century therefore emphasized the expansion of prospecting, improvement in the techniques of mineral extraction, and the integration of new mineral products into industry.

Mining in the 20th century has thus been marked by a striking expansion of areas already under production and the discovery of new ones in many parts of the world. For generations before World War II, the world output of minerals had been doubling every 20 years. With continued expansion in the postwar period, the traditional sources of minerals were no longer sufficient to assure an adequate future supply of metals and fuels, though much could be done by more effective exploitation of low-grade ores, such as iron-bearing taconite. But additional sources of iron ore have been sought by American steel companies, for example, in newer areas such as Liberia, Venezuela, and Quebec Province, Canada. Oil companies were drilling deeper (even as deep as five miles), and were exploiting the resources beneath the ocean floor; still they were continually hunting for new areas. Chemical companies began to pump sodium and bromine from offshore waters, hinting that the ocean itself might well be one of the greatest sources of valuable minerals. Teams of prospectors were at work constantly in remote corners of the world, hoping to locate new sources of copper, lead, zinc, titanium, aluminum, petroleum, uranium, and other vital minerals.

Mining was thus a dynamic activity, for there was no absolute certainty that demands or available supplies would continue at existing rates. Historically, the industrial economy had depended almost exclusively on coal for its energy requirements; this condition had now changed largely to dependence on petroleum and natural gas. These two types of fuel, according to the National Planning Association, now supply most of the energy consumed in the United States. If the trend were to continue, much of the productive capacity in coal might have to be curtailed, or new markets for it found, perhaps in the field of coal chemicals. Yet the growing dependence on petroleum and natural gas as sources of energy was not a comfortable one, for reserves in petroleum were strictly limited, and were computed in decades, compared to those of coal, which might be adequate for several centuries. Furthermore, energy demands were constantly increasing.

Between 1957 and 1965, total U.S. energy production increased by 19 per cent, whereas consumption increased by 34 per cent. This trend poses a problem that can not be met by known sources of gas or petroleum. The solution might be found in mining more fissionable materials that could be processed to expand, by atomic means, the total supply of energy.

Mining is basic to industrial progress because it alone furnishes the means, in both energy and materials, for carrying on any sort of advanced industrial operations. It follows therefore that to possess military strength, a nation must possess or have ready access to extensive mineral wealth. In the world situation which has existed since the 1950's, much emphasis has been placed upon "self-sufficiency"; this desirable condition might be partially achieved by Western nations through a large and growing mining economy, and the careful stockpiling of critical materials for defense purposes.

See also METALLURGY; METALS; MINERALOGY.

COURTNEY ROBERT HALL,
Professor of History, Queens College, New York.

5. BIBLIOGRAPHY

Rickard, Thomas A., *Man and Metals*, 2 vols. (New York 1932); Read, Thomas T., *Our Mineral Civilization* (Baltimore 1932); Lindgren, Waldemar, *Mineral Deposits* (New York 1933); Witcombe, Wallace H., *All About Mining* (New York 1937); Lahee, Frederic H., *Field Geology*, 4th ed., rev. (New York 1941); Young, George J., *Elements of Mining*, 4th ed. (New York 1946); Staley, William W., *Mine Plant Design*, 2d ed. (New York 1949); Taggart, Arthur F., *Elements of Ore Dressing* (New York 1951); Shimkin, Demetri B., *Minerals: A Key to Soviet Power* (Cambridge, Mass., 1953); Woytinsky, Wladimir S., and Woytinsky, Emma S., *World Population and Production* (New York 1953); Stočes, Bohuslav, *Introduction to Mining*, 2 vols. (London 1954); United States Bureau of the Census, *Census of Mineral Industries*, 2 vols. (Washington 1954); Organization for European Economic Cooperation, *Industrial Statistics, 1900–1955* (Paris 1956); United States Atomic Energy Commission and United States Geological Survey, *Prospecting for Uranium* (Washington 1957); United Nations, Department of Economic and Social Affairs, *World Economic Survey 1957* (New York 1958); Teitelbaum, Perry D., *Nuclear Energy and the U.S. Fuel Economy, 1955–1980* (Washington 1958); United States Department of the Interior, Bureau of Mines, *Minerals Yearbook* (annual).

MINING ENGINEERING, mīn'ĭng, that branch of engineering concerned with the efficient extraction of useful mineral substances from the earth's crust. It is one of several of the specialized branches of engineering that constitute the general class, *mineral engineering*, others being petroleum, geological, geophysical, and metallurgical engineering. The fields of interest of these branches are not mutually exclusive; the work of a mining engineer may include many aspects of each, as well as of civil, chemical, electrical, and mechanical engineering. The scope of mining engineering ranges from the searching for and exploration of new ore bodies, through planning their exploitation by suitable methods and guiding the production of the mineral substance, to the processing of the newly mined mineral material into commercially acceptable forms.

Need for Specialization.—As is true in every other branch of engineering, mining engineers tend to specialize in one or other aspects of the field—exploration, surface or underground exploitation, engineering and design, production, or beneficiation. In addition to the knowledge of mathematics, physics, chemistry, and engineering sciences commonly required of all engineers, mining engineers must have a good understanding of mineralogy, geology, rock mechanics, beneficiation practice, principles of management, and of the economic factors inherent in the evaluation of real or potential mining enterprises. The training of a mining engineer in the United States commonly requires from four to five years of college work for the bachelor of science or mining engineer degrees; students undertaking advanced studies work one to three or more additional years for the master of science or doctor of science degrees.

All branches of engineering, including mining engineering, have become more specialized. As the demand for mineral products increases under the impact of improving technology, rising standards of living, and increasing populations, the necessity of finding new ore bodies and of profitably exploiting those of lower grade become more acute. In response to this need, new techniques of discovery and exploitation are constantly being developed and advances in other fields are being adapted to mining requirements. From the complexity of these changes the need for specialists arises.

As an example, the growing science of rock mechanics may be cited. Before any science can develop it is necessary to observe in detail the behavior of suitable subject matter under measurable stress over a wide range of conditions. From these observations the laws governing its behavior can be deduced or confirmed, and from these laws and their application a myriad of new developments arise.

The difficulty of developing a science of rock mechanics, from which mining engineers could logically plan new extractive operations on a scientific basis, has been that there has been no way of measuring accurately the total and incremental stresses in the rock masses or of determining their structure in the undisturbed condition. The problem is complicated by the fact that rock masses are not commonly homogeneous and massive—they are made up of several rock types and are divided by fractures, joints, faults, and bedding planes into fragments of various size. These are acted upon by the forces of weathering, ground water movements and pressures, and gravity. They react in quite a different fashion from the small isolated specimen under conventional test.

However, new methods have been developed for measuring these stresses, as well as for the direct examination of the rock structure in place. To an increasing extent, therefore, it will be possible to measure the engineering properties of a rock mass and to use these properties in the design of more efficient methods of mineral exploitation.

Production, Drilling, and Blasting.—All mining involves the movement of quantities of ore and waste; therefore it is not surprising that much of the work of a mining engineer is concerned with the problems of materials handling, nor that there have been many changes in this field, all in the direction of more rapid, lower-cost movement of ore and waste. These, in turn, make possible, and may necessitate, changes in mining methods. The mining engineer must be searching constantly for more efficient, lower-cost methods of mineral production.

Drilling and blasting is another phase of mining that absorbs much of the mining engineer's interest. The use of the machine drill dates only from the second half of the 19th century as does the use of dynamite. Modern drills and explosives are vastly superior to those in earlier use and research is constantly under way on the problems of increasing their efficiencies still further. The development of the tungsten-carbide-tipped drill bit revolutionized drilling practices. A similar revolution in blasting has resulted from the discovery that suitable admixtures of prilled ammonium nitrate and fuel oil make an excellent blasting compound. Research into the chemistry of explosives and their physical influence on the surrounding rock suggests many practical applications.

One of the most challenging avenues for mining engineering research lies in the adaptation of nuclear explosives to mining operations. There are many ore bodies of low grade and value but of large size to which nuclear explosives might profitably be applied, but entirely new methods of development and extraction will be required.

One of these possibilities is the leaching of the ore in place after the nuclear explosives have thoroughly broken it up. Many problems must first be solved before this becomes practical, among them those of controlling the distribution of the leaching fluids to achieve as nearly perfect extraction as possible. Bacterial leaching is one possible solution that merits attention; certain organisms are capable of converting insoluble minerals into soluble forms. However, the techniques and conditions of profitable application of this method have yet to be determined.

Charles O. Frush,
Associate Professor of Mining Engineering, Colorado School of Mines.

MINISTER, mĭn′ĭs-tẽr, in diplomacy, a diplomatic agent who serves abroad as a representative of a state. A minister ranks below an ambassador and does not possess an ambassador's special status as personal representative of a head of state. Of the two classes of minister recognized in international diplomacy, the higher ranking is that of envoy extraordinary and minister plenipotentiary; the lower ranking is that of minister resident. See also Ambassador; Consul; Envoy; Foreign Service, United States.

MINISTER, in government, a high officer of state who serves as the head of a government department or, in the case of a prime minister, as head of the government. In many countries, especially in Europe, the ministers of a government are called, collectively, the ministry, and a number of the ministers comprise the cabinet, or chief executive body. However, in Great Britain the heads of government departments are called by various designations, chiefly secretaries—for example, secretary of state for foreign affairs—and ministers. In the United States the term minister is not used for government department heads; instead, the designation secretary—for example, secretary of state—is most generally used. See also Cabinet and Cabinet Government; Minister, in diplomacy.

MINISTER, in religion, a person authorized or licensed to conduct Christian worship, preach the gospel, administer the sacraments, and perform other sacerdotal duties; a clergyman or pastor. Specifically, in the Roman Catholic Church, one who performs sacramental functions, such as a priest at Mass.

MINK, mĭngk, a species of weasel (family Mustelidae), with habitat extending into the circumpolar regions, especially valuable as a fur bearer. It is known in North America as *Mustela vison* and in Europe and Asia as *M. lutreola,* although both are essentially the same animal. It belongs to the marten, otter, and skunk family. Carnivorous, it has 34 teeth, the same number as the weasel, but differing from the marten (American sable) with 38. It is generally the size of the marten being 20 to 28 inches in length, with a rather long, bushy tail and stouter body form, often with a white spot on the throat. Males weigh about 2 pounds, being much larger than females. Minks differ from both weasels and martens, but, just as their mode of life is similar, they display similar characteristics in half-webbed hind toes, short ears, and a close-set, bristly, glistening pelage. The color ranges from dull russet brown to a rich dark chocolate-brown and does not turn white in winter. The pelage consists of a dense, soft, matted underfur, mixed with long, stiff, lustrous hairs on all parts of the body and bristly hairs on the tail. Animals in the colder regions have fine hair coats, but their tussling, burrowing, and scampering habits damage the fur so that only pelts taken in early winter yield full value to the trapper. Both sexes can be extremely odorous. They secrete a fetid musky scent from small perineal sacs on each side of the anus; the secretion is powerful, penetrating, and persistent, and is under voluntary control but cannot be sprayed. The odor probably attracts the opposite sex and is used by trappers to scent their traps.

Minks occur in abundance but remain secretive in even thickly populated areas. They abound near coasts, around large lakes, along rivers, marshes, tidal flats and islands, and along most streams. They are mainly aquatic but take to the land and even forage in trees. They cling to the water courses where they find plentiful food in the form of meadow mice, frogs, mussels, fish (such as brook trout and eels), insects, and earthworms. When hungry or in a competitive mood they attack larger animals such as muskrats which fight courageously, stir mud into the water for concealment, but end up second best to the cunning and lightning-fast mink which severs the main blood vessels of its victim's neck. They are known to attack rabbits, partridge, and ducks, and sometimes destroy dozens of chickens. They search stream banks in solitary fashion mainly at night, diving, swimming long distances, scurrying under loose ice and snow, climbing rough-barked trees, and penetrating crevices and hollows so that little is safe from their inquisitive ferocity. They scream, spit, hiss, and often emit their powerful musk when cornered. In winter they wander over frozen marshes and streams.

Their homes in burrows or natural cavities are found littered with pieces of fur, bones, and whole carcasses. Often their tunnels open onto the bank of a stream. Rutting begins about mid-February and the female brings forth an average litter of five young 42 to 60 days after mating, although the length of gestation is still debatable. The female guards its young against all enemies including the male, which may attack and eat the young. The kittens play like otters but in an almost savage way. When the kittens can fend for themselves, the family disbands.

Fur Farming.—Mink fur is beautiful and durable and provides abundant income for experienced trappers and ranchers. Early in the century about 650,000 minks were trapped yearly throughout the world. In spite of overzealous trapping, the population of fur bearers has remained high, so that fur farmers the world over receive approximately $16,500,000 a year for silver fox and mink pelts. Of this, about one sixth goes to fur ranchers of silver foxes and minks. A good dark mink pelt may fetch $75 while a pale blue mutation could return as much as $125. Fur farming in the United States and Canada has existed since 1895. Mink ranches can be run in three ways—by using an extensive natural range and trapping the animals, by raising colonies with a runway connected to a creek, or by penning each animal separately with a running-water supply. One male serves for five females. After mating, the females are kept in separate pens. One daily feeding consists of bread and sweet milk or corn mush and milk plus occasional chunks of meat; there should be ample fresh water. Fish is fed to minks twice a week. Recommended pens are about six feet square on bare ground with a small dark nesting box attached containing fine straw or hay.

Consult Audubon, John J., and Bachman, John, *The Viviparous Quadrupeds of North America,* 3 vols. (New York 1845–48); Coues, Elliott, *Fur-bearing Animals* (Washington 1877); Hollister, Neal, *A Synopsis of American Minks* (Washington 1913); Ashbrook, Frank G., *Fur Farming for Profit,* rev. ed. (New York 1948); Palmer, Ralph S., *The Mammal Guide* (Garden City, N.Y., 1954).

ALFRED NOVAK,
Department of Natural Science, Michigan State University.

MINNA VON BARNHELM, mĭn′ä fôn bä′rn-hĕlm, or **THE SOLDIER'S FORTUNE,** a prose comedy in five acts by Gotthold Ephraim Lessing (1729–1781), written in 1763 and first produced in 1767. Its importance lies in the fact that it ranks as the beginning of German national drama—a work in which the author skillfully combines several purposes: the reflection of great national events in the theater, the reduction of hatred between Prussia and Saxony after the Seven Years' War (1756–1763), the exposure of the rulers' indifference toward soldiers who fought in the war, and the emancipation of German theater from French influences. The events take place in a Berlin hotel about six months after the end of the war. The Prussian Major von Tellheim, motivated by an extreme sense of honor and by chagrin at his discharge from the army and by a slight wound and financial reverses that have made him "a cripple and a beggar," decides to break off his engagement to Minna von Barnhelm, a rich and beautiful young Saxon lady. However, Minna seeks him out and, in a series of delightful and witty sequences, subjects him, with the aid of her maid, Franziska, to artifices designed to prove that true love transcends even extreme honor. She prevails. And at the last minute a letter from Frederick the Great clears von Tellheim's name and restores his fortunes, so that all ends happily.

Consult Goethe, Johann Wolfgang von, *Aus meinum Leben: Dichtung und Wahrheit* (Book 7); von Stockmayr, K. H., *Das deutsche Soldatenstück des 18. Jahrhunderts seit Lessings Minna von Barnhelm* (Weimar 1898); Leopold, Werner F., and Goedsche, Curt R., eds., *Minna von Barnhelm* (New York 1937); also the English translation in the Harvard Classics, vol. 26.

MINNEAPOLIS, mĭn-ē-ăp′ô-lĭs; ăp′lĭs, the largest city in Minnesota, seat of Hennepin County, situated at an altitude of 828 feet at the Falls of Saint Anthony on the Mississippi River, approximately 350 miles northwest of Chicago. With its twin city, St. Paul, contiguous on the southeast, it is the center of a standard metropolitan area of five counties (Anoka, Dakota, Hennepin, Ramsey, and Washington). Lying on both sides of the river, it spreads over the gently rolling plain to the west, north, and south to join its principal suburbs (Bloomington, Brooklyn Center, Brooklyn Park, Columbia Heights, Crystal, Edina, Golden Valley, Hopkins, Morningside, Richfield, Robbinsdale, St. Anthony, St. Louis Park, Deephaven, Excelsior, Island Park, Minnetonka, Mound, Shorewood, Tonka Bay, and Wayzata). Approximately 12 miles to the west lies Lake Minnetonka, 12 miles long with 110 miles of irregular shore line along which are located 8 residential communities. Minnehaha Creek, flowing eastward from the lake along a deeply wooded boulevard, drops over picturesque Minnehaha Falls (q.v.) in the southern part of the city into the Mississippi. Within the city boundaries are 22 lakes and lagoons. The city's climate shows wide seasonal variations, with winter temperatures often down to —20° F. and summer temperatures about 90° F., the average mean levels being 16° F. in winter and 70° F. in summer. Annual average precipitation is approximately 27 inches, about half of which falls during May, June, July, and August.

History.—Father Louis Hennepin, exploring the Mississippi in 1680, was the first white man to see the Falls of Saint Anthony, which lie today in the heart of the city's milling district. He named them for his patron saint. In 1766, Jonathan Carver, an Englishman noted for his travels in North America, visited the falls and later described them in glowing terms in his book of travels. In 1820, a fort which was first called Fort Saint Anthony and later Fort Snelling was built by the American government for the protection of the fur trade at the nearby confluence of the Minnesota and Mississippi rivers. Its round tower is still a historic landmark in the area. Soldiers from the fort ground flour in a mill which they built at the Falls of Saint Anthony in 1821, but settlers in the city of Saint Anthony, laid out in 1849 on the east side of the falls and incorporated in 1855, first used the power of the falls commercially to turn their sawmills. Across the river another town grew up which was named Minneapolis (from the Sioux Indian, *minne,* water and the Greek *polis,* city) in 1852; it was incorporated in 1856. Settlers, largely from the New England and other Eastern states poured in, and in 1872 the two towns with a population of approximately 20,000 were united as Minneapolis by act of the legislature. A near calamity marked the growth of the industrial community: in 1869 the falls collapsed when their soft supporting limestone was undermined by a tunnel dug by citizens who were overly eager to obtain power for their own mill. With the help of federal funds, a concrete apron was finally finished in 1875 and continued water power was assured.

Logs floated downstream from the great forests of the North supplied the booms and mills of Minneapolis and brought the lumber business to its peak in the 1890's. The two previous decades, however, had seen the city growing as the center of a great flour-milling industry thriving on the burgeoning wheat crops of the Northwest. The invention in the 1870's of a process known as the middlings purifier (see MINNESOTA—5. *Economic Activities:* Foundations of the Economy) made possible the use of spring wheat on an expanded scale and Minneapolis by 1885 was known as the

"Flour City of the World." Tragedy struck the city when the explosion of one of its major mills in 1878 caused the death of scores of workmen and the destruction of many buildings. Research in dust control eventually prevented similar disasters.

Population.—The population of Minneapolis more than trebled during the decade of 1880–1890, and after that the dominant group of European-born immigrants were Swedes, followed by Norwegians and Germans. After 1900, people from southern and eastern Europe came in greater numbers and, though a small group proportionately, have added a cosmopolitan flavor to the city. Between 1900 and 1940 the population rose from 202,718 to 492,370. There was an increase in the subsequent decade to 521,718 in 1950 and a decrease to 482,872 in 1960 and to 434,400 in 1970. The city's population in 1970 included 406,414 whites, 19,005 Negroes, and 8,981 of other races.

Government.—Under its home rule charter, adopted in 1920, the city's elected officials include the mayor, city treasurer, comptroller, a council (composed of aldermen elected by wards), the 7 members of the Board of Education, 10 members of the Board of Park Commissioners, 6 members of the Library Board, and 2 members of the Board of Estimate and Taxation. The Department of Public Welfare, the Planning Commission, and the Long Range Capital Improvements Committee are composed of appointed members.

Industry, Finance, and Transportation.—The milling industry flourished on favorable freight rates after the 1880's (in 1888 a connection was completed with the East through Sault Ste. Marie via the Minneapolis, St. Paul and Sault Ste. Marie), but after World War I a change in rates shifted the center of the export trade to Buffalo. Minneapolis remains the headquarters of the world's five largest wheat-flour-milling companies. The Minneapolis Grain Exchange, a nonprofit association, is the world's largest cash grain market. Manufacture of linseed oil from the flax crops of the surrounding country began in the 1880's and has continued to be a leading industry, together with its associated products, paint and industrial finishes. Precision instruments are also a famous Minneapolis product, along with farm machinery, printing and publishing, fabricated metal products, paper, apparel, and electric machinery. In 1917 the ninth Federal Reserve District Bank was established in Minneapolis. The wholesale trade area of Minneapolis covers Minnesota, North and South Dakota, most of Montana, the northern third of Iowa, and western Wisconsin. The Twin City Metropolitan Area, designated locally by a planning commission in 1958 for purposes of mutual community services, includes seven counties (Anoka, Ramsey, Washington, Hennepin, Carver, Scott, and Dakota).

Ten railroads serve Minneapolis and six major airlines enter Wold Chamberlain International Airport. The barge traffic on the Mississippi is served by the municipal docks below the falls, though the Upper Harbor Project, begun in 1948 by the federal government, has as its purpose the accommodation of barges above the falls. City planning for downtown Minneapolis includes a new civic center, of which the first building, the public library, opened in 1961. The Foshay Tower, an office building designed as a monumental shaft 477 feet tall has been a landmark since 1929, when it was built by a utilities baron, Wilbur Burton Foshay, but newer and more functional buildings have since approached it in height. Nicollet Avenue, named for Joseph Nicolas Nicollet (1786–1843), famous French geographer, is known as the Fifth Avenue of the Midwest, while Marquette and Hennepin avenues, the two other main arteries, are respectively the banking and amusement thoroughfares.

Educational and Cultural Activities.—Educational institutions include Augsburg College and Theological Seminary (Lutheran), the MacPhail College of Music, the Minneapolis School of Fine Arts, and Dunwoody Institute, a privately endowed, world-famous trade school. The public school system of 99 elementary, junior and senior high, and vocational schools, had in 1960 a total professional staff of 2,800. The University of Minnesota, situated mainly on the river in southeast Minneapolis, provides many cultural advantages to the metropolitan area. Northrop Memorial Auditorium on the campus is the home of the Minnesota Orchestra (formerly the Minneapolis Symphony Orchestra) and a concert and lecture center. A university radio station (KUOM) broadcasts educational programs. Minneapolis in 1960 also had 10 commercial radio stations, as well as 5 FM stations and an educational television station, community supported; there were also 4 commercial television stations serving the area. Its two daily newspapers are the *Star* (evening) and *Tribune* (morning).

Minneapolis enjoys professional theater through a circuit of Broadway plays. The Walker Art Center, founded by private endowment in 1879, occupied a new building in 1971. The center, noted for its collection of jade, has fine exhibits of contemporary art. The Minneapolis Institute of Arts, supported by the city and private subscriptions, houses its collection of tapestries, paintings, and sculpture in a building owned and operated by the Minneapolis Society of Fine Arts, incorporated in 1883. The American Swedish Institute, established in 1929 and housed in the Victorian mansion of its founder, Swan T. Turnblad, a Swedish-American newspaper editor and philanthropist, specializes in domestic and decorative arts. The public library opened its new functional main building in 1961 as a part of a future civic center. Its large central collection is augmented by the endowment of the Minneapolis Athenaeum, a subscription library founded in 1859 and merged with the public library in 1885. The Science Museum and Planetarium are housed in the public library and are under its administration. The suburbs and county are served by the Hennepin County Library and its branches.

General Points of Interest.—Minneapolis is a city of churches, many of which exhibit striking contemporary design in architecture. Though the Lutheran faith predominates, all denominations and many evangelistic sects are represented. Among the 19 major hospitals, the Elizabeth Kenny Institute, founded by the Australian nurse on the invitation of the city, pioneered in the treatment of poliomyelitis. The Metropolitan Sports Area Stadium, in the suburb of Bloomington, is the home of the Minnesota Vikings of the National Football League and of the Minnesota Twins baseball team of the American League. The stadium, which has been greatly enlarged, also features starlight concerts. Among the famous annual events is the Minneapolis Aquatennial, a summer festival marked by a parade of floats and many aquatic events. The Minneapolis Park

Board, created by the state legislature in 1883, has developed the natural beauty of the lakes and streams through a justly famous system of 152 parks and nearly 63 miles of parkways. Summer concerts are held in a lakeside shell, and community centers, day camps, bathing beaches, skating rinks, and ski jumps encourage the Minneapolitan's genuine enthusiasm for the out-of-doors. The many neighboring lakes and the great northern recreational area of the state are the mecca of fishermen. Lake Minnetonka, in the 1880's a famous and fashionable summer resort, is now a part of the suburban area. Always a city of homeowners, the tradition of homes and yards has been carried into the rapidly expanding suburbs which have attracted also many light industries, offices, and shopping districts, conveniently joined to the city by a system of highways.

Bibliography.—Atwater, Isaac, *History of the City of Minneapolis*, 2 vols. (New York 1893); Hudson, Horace B., ed., *A Half Century of Minneapolis* (Minneapolis 1908); Shutter, Marion D., *History of Minneapolis* (Minneapolis 1923), Hartsough, Mildred, *Twin Cities as a Metropolitan Market* (Minneapolis 1925); Schmid, Calvin, *Social Saga of Two Cities* (Minneapolis 1937); Minnesota Historical Society, *Minnesota under Four Flags* (St. Paul 1946); Humphrey, Hubert H., Jr., *Territory of Minnesota* (U.S. Government Printing Office, Washington 1949); Federal Writer's Project of the Works Progress Administration, *Minnesota*, rev. ed. (New York 1954); *Story of Minneapolis* (Minneapolis 1954); *Minneapolis, City of Opportunity*, official centenary commemorative book (Minneapolis 1956).

MARTHA BRAY.

MINNEAPOLIS SYMPHONY ORCHESTRA. An orchestra founded in 1903 as an outgrowth of the Philharmonic (choral) Club, Minneapolis. Emil Oberhoffer, leader of that organization, became conductor of the new orchestra which gave its first concert on Nov. 5, 1903. A guarantee fund of $75,000 was raised, and an auditorium was built in 1904 by the National Life Insurance Company. Oberhoffer continued as conductor until 1921. After a season of guest conductors, Henri Verbrugghen directed the orchestra from 1922 to 1931. He was succeeded by Eugene Ormandy who conducted from 1931 to 1935. The 1935–1936 season was led by guest conductors and in 1936 Dimitri Mitropoulos became conductor. He was followed by Antal Dorati from 1949 to 1960 and then by Stanislow Skrowaczewski. The orchestra is officially called the Minnesota Orchestra.

MINNEDOSA, mĭn-ĕ-dō'să, town, Manitoba Province, Canada, 142 miles west of Winnipeg, on the Minnedosa River, the Canadian Pacific Railway, and a provincial highway. The name is derived from two Sioux Indian words: *minne* (water) and *duza* (rapid). Settlement developed around a stopping place and ford across the Little Saskatchewan (now Minnedosa) River used by the Red River cart brigades on the Fort Garry to Fort Edmonton route. In 1880, after the arrival of settlers from Ontario, the settlement, first known as Tanner's Crossing, after John Tanner, who had established a store and post office, was renamed Minnedosa; it was reached by a railway in 1883 and incorporated the same year. In the late 1890's and early 1900's Scandinavian and Ukrainian settlers arrived. An important trading center, it lies in a good mixed-farming and grain-farming district. A dam built by the Prairie Farm Rehabilitation Administration in 1950 provided for better stock-watering facilities for the district; a municipal waterworks was completed in 1954. The area's butter-making industry supplies both the local and Winnipeg markets; woodworking is also important. Population: 2,621.

MINNEHAHA, Falls of, mĭn'ē-hä'hä (from the Sioux Indian *minne,* water, and *haha,* waterfall, often romantically mistranslated as "laughing water"), a cascade more than 50 feet high in Minnehaha Creek, Minnehaha Park, Minneapolis, Minn. It is situated in a picturesque ravine which extends to the Mississippi River. A stone arch bridge below the falls affords a fine view; however, only in spring is the water flow abundant. The name has become world-famous through its use in Henry Wadsworth Longfellow's *The Song of Hiawatha.*

MINNESINGER, mĭn'ĕ-sĭng-ẽr, or **MĬNNESÄNGER,** mĭn'ĕ-zĕng-ẽr, the name given to those German medieval poets who, in the 12th and 13th centuries, created a body of impressive and sophisticated poetry which had as its ostensible topic the chivalric, if platonic, love of a knight for a married lady and which reflects a highly cultivated, idealistic, and Christian sensibility. Its sources are both literary and religious: the formal intricacies of the southern French troubadour poetry had become fashionable in northern France and Holland and, toward the middle of the 12th century, began to influence poets in the area of the Danube and Rhine, in Austria and Switzerland, and later in Saxony and Silesia. Some of these poets were minstrels who performed in the service of the nobility, but the more distinguished of them belonged to the higher aristocracy. Poems by more than 160 of these minnesingers are extant; while their subject matter is not confined to love they are essentially concerned with the complicated medieval code of thought, feeling, and behavior that was implied in the term *minne* (love). Originally conveying the joys and sorrows of a spontaneous love relationship, the minnesingers soon developed a set of poetic conventions of subject matter and form that may seem to us artificial but that required of the minnesinger not only great formal discipline but a profound understanding of the social and religious convictions of the age. The minnesinger was not, as far as we know, a spontaneous and, in the modern sense, inspired poet, but a craftsman who reiterated and varied accepted forms of idealism. Among the poetic assumptions which he accepted were the secrecy of "minne," the reluctance to name the beloved, or even to suggest that the woman was aware of the singer's love; indeed, unrequited love and the willingness of the knight to serve and glorify his lady without her response or gratitude point to the abstract idealism that seems frequently divorced from any reality of experience. As this absorption in poetic play became more and more refined, and as the social role of the chivalric aristocracy declined, a counteremphasis upon what was called "lower" minne gave increasing scope and popularity to less cultivated poets from the middle classes whose view of minne poetry became increasingly personal, direct, and exuberant, and who now dealt with political and historical subjects as well. By the 14th century, power and cultural domination had passed from the princes, nobles, and prelates to the burghers and artisans whose literary interests are represented by the Meistersinger (q.v.).

The minnesingers, by actually singing, though

not usually themselves writing down, their works, represent the flowering not only of German poetry but of medieval music; their notation was similar to that used in the church; their melodies came from the French troubadours and from popular sources, as well as from the tradition of the Gregorian chant. Many of the minnesongs are preserved in splendid medieval manuscripts; the best known among them is the Heidelberg collection which is said to have been gathered by Rüdiger Manesse (d. 1325) and which was first published in 1838 by Friedrich Heinrich von der Hagen. The song *(Lied)* itself was carefully constructed of a definite number of lines and stanzas which suggest by their intricate rhyme schemes a public well trained and sensitive to rhythmic qualities.

The earliest minnesingers are the Austrian der von Kürenberg (q.v.) or der Kürenberger (12th century) whose *Falconsong (Das Falkenlied)* is one of his 15 extant poems, and Dietmar von Aist (Eist) (d. about 1171), author of the first German *aubade* (the lovers' awakening at dawn).

Heinrich von Veldeke (fl. late 12th century) and Friedrich von Hausen (d. 1190) developed certain troubadour forms, and in the work of Heinrich von Morungen (d. 1222) and Reinmar von Hagenau (d. about 1210; q.v.) minnesong achieves its indubitable perfection. Wolfram von Eschenbach (c. 1170–c. 1220; q.v.) and especially Walther von der Vogelweide (c. 1170?–?1230; q.v.) enrich the subject matter of their craft by a more personal involvement and by a more critical view of their predecessors. In Ulrich von Lichtenstein (c. 1199–1276; q.v.), Neidhart von Reuenthal (fl. early 13th century; q.v.), and Tannhäuser (c. 1205–c. 1270; q.v.) the original identity of faith and discipline turns into artifice and sentimentality. Oswald von Wolkenstein (1377–1445) and Hugo von Montford (1357–1423) are commonly considered the last of the minnesingers.

Bibliography.—The work of the earliest group of minnesingers was first published by Karl Konrad F. W. Lachmann and Moriz Haupt under the titles *Des Minnesangs Frühling* (1857; 30th ed., Carl von Kraus, ed., Leipzig 1950); further collections are by Max Wehrli, ed., *Minnesang vom Kürenberger bis Wolfram* (Bern 1946), and Carl von Kraus, ed., *Deutsche Liederdichter des 13. Jahrhunderts,* 2 vols. (Tübingen 1952–58). Also consult Burdach, Konrad, *Über den Ursprung des mittelalterlichen Minnesangs* (Munich 1918); Brinkmann, Hennig, *Entstehungsgeschichte des Minnesangs* (Halle 1926); Gennrich, Friedrich, Das Formproblem des Minnesangs, *Deutsche Vierteljahrschrift,* Vol. IX, pp. 285–347 (Berlin 1931); Kraus, Carl von, *Walther von der Vogelweide* (Berlin 1935); Richey, Margaret F., *Essays on the Medieval German Love Lyric* (New York 1942); Frings, Theodor, *Minnesinger und Troubadours* (Berlin 1949).

VICTOR LANGE,
Chairman, Department of German Languages and Literatures, Princeton University.

MINNESOTA, mĭn-ĕ-sō′tȧ, one of the north central states of the United States. It is bounded on the east by Wisconsin and Lake Superior, on the north by the Canadian provinces of Ontario and Manitoba, on the west by North and South Dakota, and on the south by Iowa. The extreme length (north-south) of the state is 406 miles, the greatest width (east-west) is 358 miles; the average width, however, is 225 miles. The name of the state is derived from the two Dakota Indian words *minne,* meaning water, and *sota,* interpreted variously as "clouded," "turbid," "clear," and "the peculiar appearance of the sky on certain days"—hence the widely accepted translation of the name as "sky-tinted water." The state motto, *L'Etoile du Nord* (Star of the North), points up the fact that Minnesota includes the northernmost tip of land in the United States, Alaska excepted, the Northwest Angle lying on the western shore of the Lake of the Woods.

The common stereotype of Minnesota as a land of wilderness and farms, of lonely lakes and waving fields of grain, chiefly wheat, overlooks the variety of economic and social life that distinguishes the state. A complex and diversified industrial structure contributes as largely to the state's economy as does the once dominant agriculture, which itself has become broadly diversified since the 1860's when wheat was king. The virgin lakes and woods that draw devotees of primitive living to the far north country are balanced by a cosmopolitan metropolis (the Twin Cities of Minneapolis-St. Paul and their suburbs) of more than a million population and a score of smaller communities with urban interests and pursuits, as well as roots in the agricultural hinterland. Variety in modes of life, as well as in scenery, is perhaps the salient characteristic of the state.

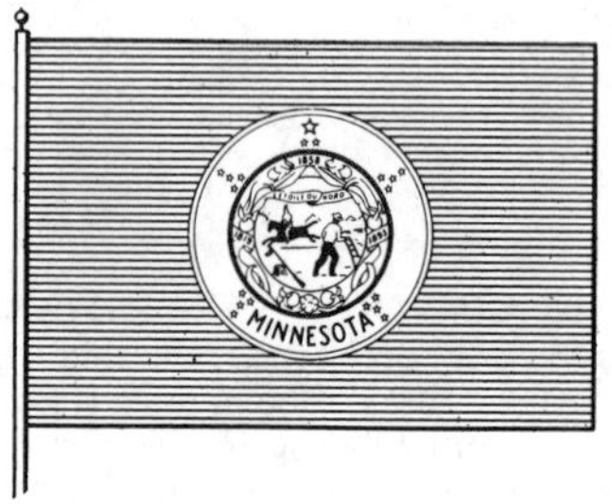

State flag

Total area	84,068 square miles
Land area	80,009 square miles
Water area	4,059 square miles
Latitude	43° 34′–49° 23′ N.
Longitude	89° 34′–97° 12′ W.
Altitude (average)	1,000–1,500 feet
High point, Misquah Hills	2,230 feet
Low point, Lake Superior	602 feet
Population (1970)	3,805,069
Capital city—St. Paul; population (1970)	309,980
Admitted to Union as the 32d state	May 11, 1858
State motto	*L'Etoile du Nord* (Star of the North)
State bird (adopted March 1961)	Loon
State flower (adopted February 1902)	Pink and white lady's-slipper
State tree (adopted February 1953)	Red or Norway pine
State song (adopted April 1945)	*Hail! Minnesota*
State nicknames	Gopher State; North Star State; Bread and Butter State; Land of Sky-Blue Waters; Land of Ten Thousand Lakes; Theater of Seasons

State seal

A detailed discussion of the geography, government, economic and social life, and history of Minnesota is presented under the following headings:

1. PHYSICAL FEATURES

Topography.—The four great glaciers of the ice age that, one after another, spread over all but the southeastern tip of Minnesota molded the land into patterns of lake and rolling plain, river and deep valley. Covering almost half the state is the central hill and lake region. Here low hills abound, along with lakes, streams, and marshes. Here too the old Laurentian highland survives as a divide from which originate three of the continent's great river systems: one draining northward through the Red River to Hudson Bay; one eastward by way of the Great Lakes and the St. Lawrence River to the Atlantic Ocean; and one southward by way of the Mississippi River to the Gulf of Mexico. To the northeast, in a section shaped like the tip of an arrow, rocky ridges and deep lakes make up the Arrowhead country; the highest and lowest points in Minnesota are found here. Across the southern reaches of the state are rolling plains, interspersed in the southeast with deep river valleys. In the bed of glacial Lake Agassiz lies the fourth distinct region, the flat plain of the northwest. Once 700 miles long and 200 wide, Lake Agassiz drained away to the north as the last of the rivers of ice receded, but it left behind traces of its lowering beach lines in many flat sandy ridges. It was finally reduced to Lake Winnipeg, Manitoba, and its level, fertile bottom became the valley of the Red River of the North.

Much of Minnesota's boundary is outlined by natural waterways, and the interior of the state is laced by navigable rivers and their numerous good-sized tributaries. The Mississippi is fed by the Crow Wing, Rum, Minnesota, St. Croix, Cannon, Zumbro, and Root; the Minnesota by the Blue Earth, Cottonwood, Redwood, Chippewa, Pomme de Terre, and Lac qui Parle; the Red by the Red Lake and Wild Rice; the Rainy by the Vermilion, Big Fork, and Little Fork; the St. Croix by the Kettle and the Snake.

The lakes of Minnesota number about five thousand more than the 10,000 of legend. They range in size from a few acres to the 440 square miles of Red Lake and the 200 square miles each of Leech Lake and Mille Lacs. Perhaps the most famous is Lake Itasca, principal source of the Mississippi River.

The glaciers which gouged out hollows later filled by lakes, and which furrowed paths for rivers, also determined the character of the soil and contributed to the mineral resources of the state. Glacial drift—boulders, sand, and clay carried by the sheets of ice and then dropped as they melted—formed the parent material for almost all the soil of Minnesota. Acted upon by wind and water, the drift was varied in texture and composition, ranging from fine, sandy silt to clayey till. The resulting soils determined the vegetational regions of the state: the pine forests in the northeast, the deciduous wood strip from northwest to southeast, and the prairies in west and south.

The great iron ranges of Minnesota—Vermilion, Mesabi, and Cuyuna, stretching from Lake County southwest to Morrison County—were formed slowly, over geologic ages, of lava, seas, and erosion. Finally, the glaciers cut deeply into the rock above the iron beds and, as they retreated, left at Mesabi and Cuyuna only a thin layer of drift over soft ores. The topographic face of northern Minnesota is pocked with the open pits from which this ore has been scooped.

Climate.—Minnesota has a dramatic round of seasons, with extremes of temperature and rapid changes characteristic of both summer and winter. The winters are often severe, the summers marked by sudden intense heat waves. Indian summer, in October, is a season of exceptional beauty and charm. The annual mean temperature is 44° F., but in some counties the range may be from 35° below zero to 108° above.

The growing season is longest (160 days) in the south central and southeastern sections; in the northern counties it is much shorter, in some places only 100 days. Rainfall varies from 32 inches along the central and southeastern boundary to 20 inches in the northwest. In most of the state the prevailing winds are from the northwest. There has never been a general crop failure due to the weather.

Plant Life.—At one time the most important of Minnesota's plant resources was the timber which covered more than two thirds of the state. The great coniferous forests, spread over the entire northern section as far as the Red River, accounted for most of Minnesota's 38 million acres of virgin timber. Including some hardwoods, the species in this vast wooded expanse were white, Norway, and jack pine, white and black spruce, tamarack, cedar, balsam, yellow and paper birch, aspen, balm of Gilead, green and black ash, basswood, elm, red and hard maple, ironwood, and pin cherry. Only about half this area remains forested, and in that half little is left of the virgin timber. The new growth is in jack pine, white birch, aspen, and pin cherry.

In the broad diagonal band of deciduous hardwoods that stretched south of the coniferous forests, the trees were principally sugar maple, basswood, white and slippery elm, red and green ash, butternut, and bur and white oak, with tamarack and black spruce in swamp openings. In the southeast black oak, black walnut, and river birch were added to the northern species. Little of this forest remains.

The prairies that formed the original vegetation area in the west and southwest were treeless except along the rivers; there the willows, cottonwoods, box elders, and sugar maples still grow. Flowers in many varieties are found, and clover and other grasses are widespread.

Animal Life.—Of the big game that once roamed the prairies and forests of Minnesota, only the white-tailed deer survives in numbers. Still abundant despite large hunting kills, the deer makes its home chiefly in the second-growth forests of the north. Bison, most important of the mammals in the early days, disappeared about 1880, and elk followed a few decades later. Moose and caribou are found only in small herds in the far north swamps. The furbearing animals have shown adaptability and tenacity in holding their own. The beaver, after a period of protection, has been re-established; muskrat, mink, fox, and raccoon are among the smaller animals also found.

The shallow lakes and marshes of the northern counties make good feeding and breeding grounds for waterfowl; ducks in 25 species and several kinds of geese are found in Minnesota's waters. Partridge, sharp-tailed grouse, and the ring-necked pheasant also draw hunters. The most valuable game fish is the northern pike. Also common are largemouthed and smallmouthed bass, brook and rainbow trout, crappies, perch, sunfish, bluegills, whitefish, and the walleyed pike, for which more than half the state's fishing waters are managed. State hatcheries stock the lakes and streams with millions of fry and fingerlings yearly, balancing the enormous catch by fishermen in both summer and winter.

Conservation.—Minnesota pioneers, one commentator has said, "created with one hand and destroyed with the other." The bounty of nature seemed unlimited; ruthless felling of pine trees, slaughter of game and fish, and exhausting of the soil—all appeared justified by the demands of advancing civilization. In 1876 a forestry association to protect timber resources was founded, the first of a long line of groups that gave increasing though sporadic and haphazard attention to the conserving of the state's natural resources. Finally in 1931 the state Department of Conservation was established. It developed a systematic program for the preservation and wise use of the state's forest, game and fish, soil and mineral, and water resources. It plants millions of new trees yearly, supervises the activities of more than a million fishermen and some half a million hunters, and watches over the park system of the state.

In the 1950's there were increasing demands for a comprehensive water-use program. Mismanagement of land, reduction of storage areas through indiscriminate drainage, and pollution of water posed a serious threat to the state's waters at the same time that industrial water requirements were growing. Floods, causing damage of $5 million a year on the average, were also a matter of grave concern. In 1955 the Water Resources Board was created to set state policy and establish watershed districts.

2. POPULATION AND POLITICAL DIVISIONS

Population Characteristics.—The population growth of Minnesota in the first decades after its organization as a territory was explosive. In the census of 1850, 6,077 residents were reported; in 1860, two years after Minnesota became a state, her people numbered 172,023. Very rapid increase continued through the rest of the century. By 1900 Minnesota boasted a population of 1,751,394.

Much of this phenomenal increase was due to the influx of immigrants from Europe, but, although the earliest pioneers included French, English, Scots, Swiss, and French Canadians, the first large wave of settlers was made up chiefly of Yankees. Then, needing more people to till the land and fell the trees, these enterprising folk reached out to sell the idea of Minnesota, through personal agents and glowing campaign literature, to the oppressed, ambitious, and discontented of Europe. The first rush of immigration in response was made up principally of Germans, Irish, Norwegians, and Swedes. By 1890 there were 467,356 foreign-born living in Minnesota and of these all but 30,000 were Germans, Scandinavians, or immigrants from English-speaking countries. Germany led all nations in numbers sent to Minnesota until 1910; then Sweden took first place.

During the 1880's and 1890's the earlier trickle of Czechs, Slovaks, and Poles swelled rapidly; now the iron mines, as well as the lumber industry, needed laborers. The Finns, however, soon became the largest group in this so-called new immigration. Also, in smaller numbers, came Slovenes, Russians, Icelanders, Italians, Greeks, and Mexicans.

After the turn of the century, although each decade saw a growth in population, the rate of increase declined markedly. A drastic reduction in immigration and a declining birth rate were largely responsible, but there was also a fairly heavy migration of Minnesotans out of the state—exceeding in some years those moving in. By the 1940's Minnesota was apparently rapidly approaching a stabilized population. Then a sudden sharp upturn in the birth rate helped turn the trend.

Two important shifts in the character of Minnesota's population became strongly evident by the mid-20th century: the rising age level of the people and the increase of urban residents over rural. In 1880 the age group over 45 made up 14.7 per cent of the total population; by 1950 the proportion had increased to 30.4. Although the proportion of urban population in the state increased steadily after the 1860's (when fewer than 10 per cent of the people lived in cities), not until 1950 did urban dwellers exceed rural residents, with 54.5 per cent of the total population. Meanwhile, the strictly farm population declined in absolute numbers as well as proportionately.

The distribution of Minnesota's nonfarm population is in some respects unusual. The Twin Cities metropolis of Minneapolis-St. Paul and their suburbs contain almost half of the state's population, forming a standard metropolitan area that in 1970 ranked 15th among such areas in the country. Only one other city, Duluth, had a population of more than 100,000 in 1970, while all other cities were relatively small.

Of the 1970 population, almost 99 per cent were white. Negroes made up less than 1 per cent of the population. Although Asians have never accounted for much as 1 per cent of the Minnesota population, their number did increase during World War II when a body of Japanese Americans moved from the west coast. The foreign-born make up less than 10 per cent of the population, but the ethnic strains one or two generations removed are still clear. These are dominantly Swedish, Norwegian, and German, with Polish, Finnish, and Czech also significant.

Cities.—Minneapolis is the state's largest city; St. Paul ranks second. The intense rivalry of early years between the twin cities on the

GROWTH OF POPULATION SINCE 1860

Year	Population	Year	Population
1860	172,023	1940	2,792,300
1880	780,773	1950	2,982,483
1900	1,751,394	1960	3,413,864
1920	2,387,125	1970	3,805,069

Gain, 1960–1970: 11.5% (U.S. gain, 13.3%). **Density,** 1970: 47.6 persons per square mile (U.S. density, 56.2).

URBAN-RURAL DISTRIBUTION

Year	Percent urban	Percent rural
1920	44.1 (U.S., 51.2)	55.9
1930	49.0 (U.S., 56.2)	51.0
1940	49.8 (U.S., 56.6)	50.2
1950	54.5 (U.S., 64.0)	45.5
1960	62.1 (U.S., 69.9)	37.9
1970	66.4 (U.S., 73.5)	33.6

MINNESOTA

COUNTIES

Aitkin, 11,403 .... E 4
Anoka, 154,556 .... E 5
Becker, 24,372 .... C 4
Beltrami, 26,373 .... C 2
Benton, 20,841 .... D 5
Big Stone, 7,941 .... B 5
Blue Earth, 52,322 .... D 6
Brown, 28,887 .... D 6
Carlton, 28,072 .... F 4
Carver, 28,310 .... E 6
Cass, 17,323 .... D 4
Chippewa, 15,109 .... C 5
Chisago, 17,492 .... F 5
Clay, 46,585 .... B 4
Clearwater, 8,013 .... C 3
Cook, 3,423 .... H 3
Cottonwood, 14,887 .... C 6
Crow Wing, 34,826 .... D 4
Dakota, 139,808 .... E 6
Dodge, 13,037 .... F 7
Douglas, 22,892 .... C 5
Faribault, 20,896 .... D 7
Fillmore, 21,916 .... F 7
Freeborn, 38,064 .... E 7
Goodhue, 34,763 .... F 6
Grant, 7,462 .... B 5
Hennepin, 960,080 .... E 5
Houston, 17,556 .... G 7
Hubbard, 10,583 .... D 3
Isanti, 16,560 .... E 5
Itasca, 35,530 .... E 3
Jackson, 14,352 .... C 7
Kanabec, 9,775 .... E 5
Kandiyohi, 30,548 .... C 5
Kittson, 6,853 .... B 2
Koochiching, 17,731 .... E 2
Lac qui Parle, 11,164 .... B 6
Lake, 13,351 .... G 3
Lake of the Woods, 3,987 .... D 2
Le Sueur, 21,332 .... E 6
Lincoln, 8,143 .... B 6
Lyon, 24,273 .... C 6
Mahnomen, 5,638 .... C 3
Marshall, 13,060 .... B 2
Martin, 24,316 .... D 7
McLeod, 27,662 .... D 6
Meeker, 18,810 .... D 5
Mille Lacs, 15,703 .... E 5
Morrison, 26,949 .... D 4
Mower, 43,783 .... F 7
Murray, 12,508 .... C 6
Nicollet, 24,518 .... D 6
Nobles, 23,208 .... C 7
Norman, 10,008 .... B 3
Olmsted, 84,104 .... F 7
Otter Tail, 46,097 .... C 4
Pennington, 13,266 .... B 2
Pine, 16,821 .... F 4
Pipestone, 12,791 .... B 6
Polk, 34,435 .... B 3
Pope, 11,107 .... C 5
Ramsey, 476,255 .... E 5
Red Lake, 5,388 .... B 3
Redwood, 20,024 .... C 6
Renville, 21,139 .... C 6
Rice, 41,582 .... E 6
Rock, 11,346 .... B 7
Roseau, 11,569 .... C 2
Saint Louis, 220,693 .... F 3
Scott, 32,423 .... E 6
Sherburne, 18,344 .... E 5
Sibley, 15,845 .... D 6
Stearns, 95,400 .... D 5
Steele, 26,931 .... E 7
Stevens, 11,218 .... B 5
Swift, 13,177 .... C 5
Todd, 22,114 .... D 4
Traverse, 6,254 .... B 5
Wabasha, 17,224 .... F 6
Wadena, 12,412 .... D 4
Waseca, 16,663 .... E 6
Washington, 82,948 .... F 5
Watonwan, 13,298 .... D 7
Wilkin, 9,389 .... B 4
Winona, 44,409 .... G 6
Wright, 38,933 .... D 5
Yellow Medicine, 14,418 .... B 6

CITIES and TOWNS

Ada⊙, 2,076 .... B 3
Adams, 771 .... F 7
Adrian, 1,350 .... C 7
Afton, 248 .... F 6
Ah-Gwah-Ching, 500 .... D 3
Aitkin⊙, 1,553 .... E 4
Akeley, 468 .... D 3
Albany, 1,599 .... D 5
Albert Lea⊙, 19,418 .... E 7
Albertville, 451 .... E 5
Alden, 713 .... E 7
Alexandria⊙, 6,973 .... C 5
Altura, 334 .... G 6
Alvarado, 302 .... B 2
Amboy, 571 .... D 7
Angora, 287 .... F 3
Annandale, 1,234 .... D 5
Anoka⊙, 13,489 .... E 5
Appleton, 1,789 .... C 5
Apple Valley, 8,502 .... G 6
Arden Hills■, 5,628 .... G 5
Argyle, 739 .... B 2
Arlington, 1,823 .... D 6
Arnold, 750 .... F 4
Ashby, 415 .... C 4
Askov, 287 .... F 4
Atwater, 956 .... D 5
Audubon, 297 .... C 4
Aurora, 2,531 .... F 3
Austin⊙, 25,074 .... E 7
Avoca, 203 .... C 7
Avon, 725 .... D 5
Babbitt, 3,076 .... G 3
Backus, 257 .... D 4
Badger, 327 .... B 2
Bagley⊙, 1,314 .... C 3
Balaton, 649 .... C 6
Barnesville, 1,782 .... B 4
Barnum, 382 .... F 4
Barrett, 342 .... B 5
Battle Lake, 772 .... C 4
Baudette⊙, 1,547 .... D 2
Baxter, 1,556 .... D 4
Bay Lake, 250 .... E 4
Bayport, 2,987 .... F 5
Beardsley, 366 .... B 5
Bear River, 250 .... E 3
Beaver Bay, 362 .... G 3
Beaver Creek, 235 .... B 7
Becker, 365 .... E 5
Belgrade, 713 .... C 5
Bellechester, 199 .... F 6
Belle Plaine, 2,328 .... E 6
Bellingham, 263 .... B 5
Belview, 429 .... C 6
Bemidji⊙, 11,490 .... D 3
Benson⊙, 3,484 .... C 5
Bertha, 512 .... C 4
Bethel■, 311 .... E 5
Bigelow, 262 .... C 7
Big Falls, 534 .... E 2
Bigfork, 399 .... E 3
Big Lake, 1,015 .... E 5
Bingham Lake, 214 .... C 7
Birchwood■, 926 .... F 5
Bird Island, 1,309 .... D 6
Biwabik, 1,483 .... F 3
Blackduck, 595 .... D 3
Blaine, 20,640 .... G 5
Blooming Prairie, 1,804 .... E 7
Bloomington, 81,970 .... G 6
Blue Earth⊙, 3,965 .... D 7
Bluffton, 195 .... C 4
Bovey, 858 .... E 3
Bowlus, 268 .... D 5
Boyd, 311 .... C 6
Braham, 744 .... E 5
Brainerd⊙, 11,667 .... D 4
Branch, 880 .... F 5
Brandon, 414 .... C 5
Breckenridge⊙, 4,200 .... B 4
Breezy Point Village, 233 .... D 4
Brewster, 563 .... C 7
Bricelyn, 470 .... E 7
Brooklyn Center, 35,173 .... G 5
Brooklyn Park, 26,230 .... G 5
Brooten, 615 .... C 5
Browerville, 665 .... D 4
Brownsdale, 625 .... F 7
Browns Valley, 906 .... B 5
Brownsville, 417 .... G 7
Brownton, 688 .... D 6
Buffalo⊙, 3,275 .... E 5
Buffalo Lake, 758 .... D 6
Buhl, 1,303 .... F 3
Burnsville, 19,940 .... E 6
Butterfield, 619 .... D 7
Bygland, 475 .... B 3
Byron, 1,419 .... F 6
Caledonia⊙, 2,619 .... G 7
Callaway, 233 .... C 3
Calumet, 460 .... E 3
Cambridge⊙, 3,467 .... E 5
Campbell, 339 .... B 4
Canby, 2,081 .... B 6
Cannon Falls, 2,072 .... F 6
Canton, 391 .... F 7
Carlos, 260 .... C 5
Carlton⊙, 884 .... F 4
Carver, 669 .... E 6
Cass Lake, 1,317 .... D 3
Center City⊙, 324 .... F 5
Centerville, 534 .... E 5
Ceylon, 487 .... D 7
Champlin, 2,275 .... G 5
Chandler, 319 .... C 7
Chanhassen, 4,879 .... F 6
Chaska⊙, 4,352 .... F 6
Chatfield, 1,885 .... F 7
Chisago City, 1,068 .... E 5
Chisholm, 5,913 .... E 3
Chokio, 455 .... B 5
Circle Pines, 3,918 .... G 5
Clara City, 1,491 .... C 6
Claremont, 520 .... E 6
Clarissa, 599 .... C 4
Clarkfield, 1,084 .... C 6
Clarks Grove, 480 .... E 7
Clearbrook, 599 .... C 3
Clear Lake, 280 .... E 5
Clearwater, 282 .... D 5
Clements, 252 .... D 6
Cleveland, 492 .... E 6
Climax, 255 .... B 3
Clinton, 608 .... B 5
Cloquet, 8,699 .... F 4
Coates■, 212 .... E 6
Cohasset, 536 .... E 3
Cokato, 1,735 .... D 5
Cold Spring, 2,006 .... D 5
Coleraine, 1,086 .... E 3
Collegeville, 1,600 .... D 5
Cologne, 518 .... E 6
Columbia Heights, 23,997 .... G 5
Comfrey, 525 .... D 6
Cook, 687 .... F 3
Coon Rapids, 30,505 .... G 5
Corcoran, 1,656 .... F 5
Cosmos, 570 .... D 6
Cottage Grove, 13,419 .... F 6
Cotton, 350 .... F 3
Cottonwood, 794 .... C 6
Courtland, 360 .... D 6
Crane Lake, 350 .... F 2
Crookston⊙, 8,312 .... B 3
Crosby, 2,241 .... D 4
Crosslake, 358 .... E 4
Crown, 200 .... E 5
Crystal, 30,925 .... G 5
Crystal Bay, 6,787 .... F 5
Currie, 368 .... C 6
Cyrus, 289 .... C 5
Dakota, 369 .... G 7
Dalton, 221 .... C 4
Danube, 497 .... C 6
Darwin, 224 .... D 5
Dassel, 1,058 .... D 5
Dawson, 1,699 .... B 6
Dayton, 517 .... E 5
Deephaven, 3,853 .... G 5
Deer Creek, 287 .... C 4
Deer River, 815 .... E 3
Deerwood, 448 .... E 4
De Graff, 195 .... C 5
Delano, 1,851 .... E 5
Delavan, 281 .... D 7
Dellwood, 514 .... F 5
Detroit Lakes⊙, 5,797 .... C 4
Dexter, 252 .... F 7
Dilworth, 2,321 .... B 4
Dodge Center, 1,603 .... F 6
Donnelly, 252 .... B 5
Dover, 321 .... F 7
Dresbach, 250 .... G 7
Duluth⊙, 100,578 .... F 4
Duluth-Superior, ‡265,350 .... F 4
Dumont, 204 .... B 5
Dundas, 460 .... E 6
Dunnell, 237 .... D 7
Eagle Bend, 557 .... D 4
Eagle Lake, 839 .... E 6
East Bethel, 2,586 .... E 5
East Grand Forks, 7,607 .... B 3
East Gull Lake, 440 .... D 4
Easton, 352 .... E 7
Echo, 356 .... C 6
Eden Prairie, 6,938 .... G 6
Eden Valley, 776 .... D 5
Edgerton, 1,119 .... B 7
Edina, 44,046 .... G 5
Eitzen, 208 .... G 7
Elbow Lake⊙, 1,484 .... B 5
Elgin, 580 .... F 6
Elizabeth, 188 .... B 4
Elk River⊙, 2,252 .... E 5
Ellendale, 569 .... E 7
Ellsworth, 588 .... C 7
Elmore, 910 .... D 7
Elrosa, 203 .... C 5
Ely, 4,904 .... G 3
Elysian, 445 .... E 6
Embarrass, 195 .... F 3
Emily, 386 .... E 4
Emmons, 412 .... E 7
Erhard, 748 .... B 4
Ericsburg, 300 .... E 2
Erskine, 571 .... B 3
Esko, 500 .... F 4
Evansville, 553 .... C 4
Eveleth, 4,721 .... F 3
Excelsior, 2,563 .... E 6
Eyota, 639 .... F 7
Fairfax, 1,432 .... D 6
Fairmont⊙, 10,751 .... D 7
Falcon Heights, 5,507 .... G 5
Faribault⊙, 16,595 .... E 6
Farmington, 3,104 .... E 6
Felton, 232 .... B 3
Fergus Falls⊙, 12,443 .... B 4
Fertile, 955 .... B 3
Finland, 300 .... G 3
Finlayson, 192 .... F 4
Fisher, 383 .... B 3
Flensburg, 259 .... D 5
Floodwood, 650 .... E 4
Florenton, 635 .... F 3
Foley⊙, 1,271 .... D 5
Forbes, 225 .... F 3
Forest Lake, 3,207 .... F 5
Foreston, 273 .... E 5
Fosston, 1,684 .... C 3
Fountain, 347 .... F 7
Foxhome, 185 .... B 4
Franklin, 557 .... D 6
Frazee, 1,015 .... C 4
Freeborn, 296 .... E 7
Freeport, 593 .... D 5
French River, 200 .... G 4
Fridley, 29,233 .... G 5
Frontenac, 223 .... F 6
Frost, 290 .... D 7
Fulda, 1,226 .... C 7
Garden City, 270 .... D 6
Garfield, 198 .... C 5
Garvin, 201 .... C 6
Gary, 265 .... B 3
Gaylord⊙, 1,720 .... D 6
Gem Lake■, 216 .... G 5
Geneva, 358 .... E 7
Ghent, 301 .... C 6
Gibbon, 877 .... D 6
Gilbert, 2,287 .... F 3
Glencoe⊙, 4,217 .... D 6
Glenville, 740 .... E 7
Glenwood⊙, 2,584 .... C 5
Glyndon, 674 .... B 4
Golden Valley, 24,246 .... G 5
Gonvick, 344 .... C 3
Goodhue, 539 .... F 6
Good Thunder, 489 .... D 6
Goodview, 1,829 .... G 6
Graceville, 735 .... B 5
Granada, 381 .... D 7
Grand Marais⊙, 1,301 .... G 2
Grand Meadow, 869 .... F 7
Grand Rapids⊙, 7,247 .... E 3
Granite Falls⊙, 3,225 .... C 6
Greenbush, 787 .... B 2
Greenfield, 977 .... F 5
Green Isle, 363 .... E 6
Greenwald, 244 .... D 5
Greenwood■, 587 .... F 5
Grey Eagle, 325 .... D 5
Grove City, 502 .... D 5
Grygla, 211 .... C 2
Hackensack, 220 .... D 4
Hallock⊙, 1,477 .... A 2
Halstad, 598 .... B 3
Hamburg, 377 .... D 6
Hamel, 2,396 .... F 5
Hampton, 369 .... E 6
Hancock, 806 .... C 5
Hanley Falls, 265 .... C 6
Hanover, 365 .... E 5
Hanska, 442 .... D 6
Hardwick, 274 .... B 7
Harmony, 1,130 .... F 7
Harris, 559 .... F 5
Hartland, 331 .... E 7
Hassan, 778 .... E 5
Hastings⊙, 12,195 .... F 6
Hawley, 1,371 .... B 4
Hayfield, 939 .... F 7
Hayward, 261 .... E 7
Hector, 1,178 .... D 6
Henderson, 730 .... E 6
Hendricks, 712 .... B 6
Hendrum, 311 .... B 3
Henning, 850 .... C 4
Herman, 619 .... B 5
Heron Lake, 777 .... C 7
Hewitt, 198 .... C 4
Hibbing, 16,104 .... F 3
Hill City, 357 .... E 4
Hills, 571 .... B 7
Hilltop■, 1,015 .... G 5
Hinckley, 885 .... E 4
Hoffman, 627 .... C 5
Hokah, 697 .... G 7
Holdingford, 551 .... D 5
Holland, 263 .... B 6
Hollandale, 287 .... E 7
Holyoke, 190 .... F 4
Hopkins, 13,428 .... G 5
Houston, 1,090 .... G 7
Howard Lake, 1,162 .... D 5
Hoyt Lakes, 3,634 .... F 3
Hugo, 751 .... E 5
Hutchinson, 8,031 .... D 6
Independence, 1,993 .... F 5
International Falls⊙, 6,439 .... E 2
Inver Grove Heights, 12,148 .... E 6
Iona, 260 .... C 7
Ironton, 562 .... D 4
Isanti, 679 .... E 5
Isle, 551 .... E 4
Ivanhoe⊙, 738 .... B 6
Jackson⊙, 3,550 .... C 7
Jacobson, 225 .... E 4
Janesville, 1,557 .... E 6
Jasper, 754 .... B 7
Jeffers, 436 .... C 6
Jordan, 1,836 .... E 6
Kandiyohi, 295 .... D 5
Karlstad, 727 .... B 2
Kasota, 732 .... D 6
Kasson, 1,883 .... F 6
Keewatin, 1,382 .... E 3
Kelliher, 289 .... D 3
Kellogg, 403 .... G 6
Kelly Lake, 950 .... F 3
Kennedy, 424 .... B 2
Kensington, 308 .... C 5
Kenyon, 1,575 .... E 6
Kerkhoven, 641 .... C 5
Kiester, 681 .... E 7
Kimball, 567 .... D 5
Kinney, 325 .... F 3
Knife River, 350 .... G 4
La Crescent, 3,142 .... G 7
Lafayette, 498 .... D 6
Lake Benton, 759 .... B 6
Lake Bronson, 325 .... B 2
Lake City, 3,594 .... F 6
Lake Crystal, 1,807 .... D 6
Lake Elmo, 4,032 .... F 6
Lakefield, 1,820 .... C 7
Lake Fremont (Zimmerman), 495 .... E 5
Lake George, 200 .... D 3
Lakeland, 962 .... F 6
Lake Lillian, 316 .... C 6
Lake Park, 658 .... B 4
Lake Saint Croix Beach, 1,111 .... F 6
Lake Shore, 410 .... D 4
Lakeville, 7,556 .... E 6
Lake Wilson, 378 .... B 7
Lamberton, 962 .... C 6
Lancaster, 382 .... B 2
Landfall■, 671 .... F 6
Lanesboro, 850 .... G 7
Lansing, 300 .... F 7
La Prairie, 413 .... E 3
Lauderdale, 2,419 .... G 5
Le Center⊙, 1,890 .... E 6
Leota, 285 .... C 7
Le Roy, 870 .... F 7
Lester Prairie, 1,162 .... D 6
Le Sueur, 3,745 .... E 6
Lewiston, 1,000 .... G 7
Lewisville, 291 .... D 7
Lexington, 1,926 .... G 5
Lilydale, 664 .... G 5
Lindstrom, 1,260 .... F 5
Lino Lakes, 3,692 .... G 5
Lismore, 323 .... B 7
Litchfield⊙, 5,262 .... D 5
Little Canada■, 3,481 .... G 5
Little Falls⊙, 7,467 .... D 5
Littlefork, 824 .... E 2
Long Beach, 219 .... C 5
Long Lake, 1,506 .... F 5
Long Prairie⊙, 2,416 .... D 5
Lonsdale, 622 .... E 6
Loretto, 340 .... F 5
Lowry, 257 .... C 5
Lucan, 254 .... C 6
Lutsen, 620 .... F 2
Luverne⊙, 4,703 .... B 7
Lyle, 522 .... F 7
Lynd, 267 .... C 6

⊙ County seat. ■ Name not shown on map. ‡ Population of metropolitan area.

All figures available from 1970 final census are supplemented by local official estimates.

HIGHWAYS
Limited Access
Toll Interchanges
Important Roads
Federal Route Numbers
State Route Numbers
U.S. Interstate Route Numbers
NORTHEASTERN PART OF MINNESOTA
Same scale as main map
CANADA
MANITOBA
ONTARIO
DAKOTA
KITTSON
ROSEAU
LAKE OF THE WOODS
MARSHALL
PENNINGTON
RED LAKE
POLK
NORMAN
MAHNOMEN
CLAY
BECKER
CLEARWATER
BELTRAMI
HUBBARD
CASS
ITASCA
KOOCHICHING
SAINT LOUIS
LAKE
COOK
AITKIN
CARLTON
CROW WING
WADENA
OTTER TAIL
WILKIN
LAKE SUPERIOR
RED LAKE INDIAN RES.
NETT LAKE IND. RES.
LEECH LAKE IND. RES.
WHITE EARTH INDIAN RESERVATION
FOND DU LAC IND. RES.
RED CLIFF IND. RES.
Upper Red Lake
Lower Red Lake
Lake of the Woods
Rainy River
Fort Frances
International Falls
South International Falls
Baudette
Roseau
Warren
Thief River Falls
Crookston
East Grand Forks
Grand Forks
Fargo
Moorhead
Detroit Lakes
Bemidji
Park Rapids
Grand Rapids
Hibbing
Virginia
Eveleth
Chisholm
Aurora
Hoyt Lakes
Babbitt
Ely
Cloquet
Proctor
Duluth
Superior
Two Harbors
Silver Bay
Washburn
Wadena
Aitkin

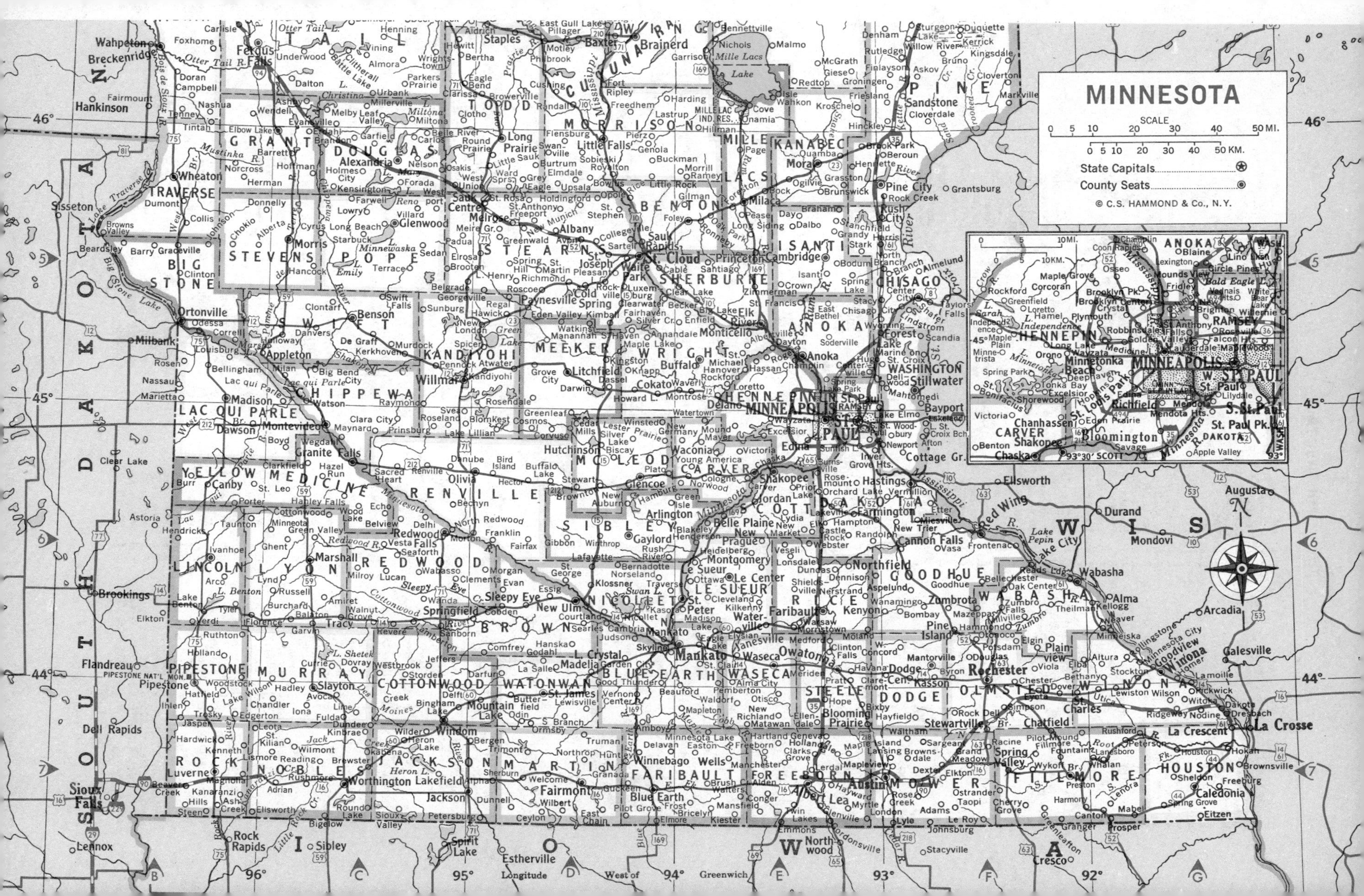
MINNESOTA
SCALE
0 5 10 20 30 40 50 MI.
0 5 10 20 30 40 50 KM.
State Capitals
County Seats
© C.S. HAMMOND & Co., N.Y.

MINNESOTA

Place	Key
Mabel, 888	G 7
Madelia, 2,316	D 6
Madison⊙, 2,242	B 5
Madison Lake, 587	E 6
Magnolia, 233	B 7
Mahnomen⊙, 1,313	C 3
Mahtomedi, 2,640	F 5
Mankato⊙, 30,895	E 6
Mantorville⊙, 479	F 6
Maple Grove, 6,275	F 5
Maple Lake, 1,124	D 5
Maple Plain, 1,169	F 5
Mapleton, 1,307	E 7
Mapleview, 328	E 7
Maplewood, 25,222	G 5
Marble, 682	E 3
Marcell, 350	E 3
Marietta, 264	B 5
Marine on Saint Croix, 513	F 5
Marshall⊙, 9,886	C 6
Mayer, 325	E 6
Maynard, 455	C 6
Mazeppa, 498	F 6
McGregor, 331	E 4
McIntosh, 753	C 3
McKinley, 317	F 3
Medford, 690	E 6
Medicine Lake, 930	G 5
Medina (Hamel), 2,396	F 5
Melrose, 2,273	D 5
Menahga, 835	C 4
Mendota, 327	G 5
Mendota Heights, 6,165	G 6
Mentor, 236	B 3
Merrifield, 300	D 4
Middle River, 369	B 2
Miesville, 192	F 6
Milaca⊙, 1,940	E 5
Milan, 427	C 5
Milroy, 247	C 6
Minneapolis⊙, 434,400	G 5
Minneapolis-Saint Paul, ‡1,813,647	G 5
Minneota, 1,320	C 6
Minnesota City, 301	G 6
Minnesota Lake, 738	E 7
Minnetonka, 35,776	G 5
Minnetonka Beach■, 586	F 5
Minnetrista, 2,878	F 5
Montevideo⊙, 5,661	C 6
Montgomery, 2,281	E 6
Monticello, 1,636	E 5
Montrose, 379	E 5
Moorhead⊙, 29,687	B 4
Moorhead-Fargo, ‡120,238	B 4
Moose Lake, 1,400	F 4
Mora⊙, 2,582	E 5
Morgan, 972	D 6
Morris⊙, 5,366	C 5
Morristown, 659	E 6
Morton, 591	C 6
Motley, 351	D 4
Mound, 7,572	E 6
Mounds View, 9,988	G 5
Mountain Iron, 1,698	F 3
Mountain Lake, 1,986	D 7
Murdock, 358	C 5
Nashwauk, 1,341	E 3
Naytahwaush, 350	C 3
Nerstrand, 231	E 6
Nett Lake, 470	E 2
Nevis, 308	D 4
New Auburn, 274	D 6
New Brighton, 19,507	G 5
Newfolden, 390	B 2
New Germany, 303	E 6
New Hope■, 23,180	G 5
New London, 736	C 5
New Market, 215	E 6
New Munich, 307	D 5
Newport, 2,922	F 6
New Prague, 2,680	E 6
New Richland, 1,113	E 7
New Ulm⊙, 13,051	D 6
New York Mills, 791	C 4
Nicollet, 618	D 6
Nisswa, 1,011	D 4
Nopeming, 268	F 4
North Branch, 1,106	F 5
North Crosslake, 362	D 4
Northfield, 10,235	E 6
North Mankato, 7,347	D 6
North Oaks■, 2,002	G 5
Northome, 351	D 3
Northrop, 188	D 7
North Saint Paul, 11,950	E 5
Norwood, 1,058	E 6
Oakdale■, 7,304	F 5
Oak Park Heights■, 1,238	F 5
Odessa, 194	B 5
Ogema, 236	C 3
Ogilvie, 384	E 5
Okabena, 237	C 7
Oklee, 536	C 3
Olivia⊙, 2,553	C 6
Onamia, 670	E 4
Orchard Lake, 200	E 6
Ormsby, 199	D 7
Orono (Crystal Bay), 6,787	F 5
Oronoco, 564	F 6
Orr, 315	F 2
Ortonville⊙, 2,665	B 5
Osakis, 1,306	C 5
Oslo, 417	A 2
Osseo, 2,908	G 5
Ostrander, 216	F 7
Outing, 425	E 4
Owatonna⊙, 15,341	E 6
Parkers Prairie, 882	C 4
Park Rapids⊙, 2,772	D 4
Paynesville, 1,920	D 5
Pease, 187	E 5
Pelican Lakes (Breezy Point Village), 233	D 4
Pelican Rapids, 1,835	B 4
Pengilly, 625	E 3
Pennock, 255	C 5
Pequot Lakes, 499	D 4
Perham, 1,933	C 4
Peterson, 269	G 7
Pierz, 893	D 5
Pillager, 374	D 4
Pine City⊙, 2,143	F 5
Pine Island, 1,640	F 6
Pine River, 803	D 4
Pipestone⊙, 5,328	B 7
Plainview, 2,093	F 6
Plato, 303	D 6
Plummer, 285	B 3
Plymouth, 17,593	G 5
Ponemah, 531	D 2
Porter, 207	B 6
Preston⊙, 1,413	F 7
Princeton, 2,531	E 5
Prinsburg, 448	C 6
Prior Lake, 1,114	E 6
Proctor, 3,123	F 4
Racine, 197	F 7
Randall, 536	D 4
Randolph, 350	E 6
Ranier, 255	E 2
Ray, 200	E 2
Raymond, 589	C 5
Redby, 475	D 3
Redlake, 300	C 3
Red Lake Falls⊙, 1,740	B 3
Red Wing⊙, 10,441	F 6
Redwood Falls⊙, 4,774	C 6
Remer, 403	E 3
Renville, 1,252	C 6
Rice, 366	D 5
Richfield, 47,231	G 6
Richmond, 866	D 5
Robbinsdale, 16,845	G 5
Rochester⊙, 53,766	F 6
Rochester, ‡84,104	F 6
Rock Creek, 805	F 5
Rockford, 730	F 5
Rockville, 302	D 5
Rogers, 544	E 5
Rollingstone, 450	G 6
Roscoe, 195	D 5
Roseau⊙, 2,552	C 2
Rose Creek, 390	F 7
Rosemount, 1,337	E 6
Roseville, 34,518	G 5
Rothsay, 448	B 4
Round Lake, 506	C 7
Royalton, 534	D 5
Rush City, 1,130	F 5
Rushford, 1,318	G 7
Rushford (vill.)■, 601	G 7
Rushmore, 394	C 7
Russell, 398	C 6
Ruthton, 405	B 6
Sabin, 333	B 4
Sacred Heart, 707	C 6
Saginaw, 407	F 4
Saint Anthony Falls, 9,239	G 5
Saint Bonifacius, 685	F 5
Saint Charles, 1,942	F 7
Saint Clair, 488	E 6
Saint Cloud⊙, 39,691	D 5
Saint Francis, 897	E 5
Saint Hilaire, 337	B 2
Saint James⊙, 4,027	D 7
Saint Joseph, 1,786	D 5
Saint Louis Park, 48,883	G 5
Saint Martin, 188	D 5
Saint Marys Point■, 319	F 6
Saint Michael, 1,021	E 5
Saint Paul (cap.)⊙, 309,980	G 6
Saint Paul Park, 5,587	G 6
Saint Peter⊙, 8,339	E 6
Saint Stephen, 331	D 5
Sanborn, 505	C 6
Sandstone, 1,641	F 4
Sartell, 1,323	D 5
Sauk Centre, 3,750	C 5
Sauk Rapids, 5,051	D 5
Savage, 3,611	G 6
Sawyer, 200	F 4
Scandia, 200	F 5
Scanlon, 1,132	F 4
Schroeder, 550	G 3
Sebeka, 668	C 4
Shakopee⊙, 6,876	F 6
Shelly, 260	B 3
Sherburn, 1,190	D 7
Shevlin, 185	C 3
Shoreview■, 11,034	G 5
Shorewood, 4,223	F 5
Silver Bay, 3,504	G 3
Silver Lake, 694	D 6
Skyline, 400	D 6
Slayton⊙, 2,351	C 7
Sleepy Eye, 3,461	D 6
Sobieski, 189	D 5
Soudan, 900	F 3
South Haven, 238	D 5
South International Falls, 2,116	E 2
South Saint Paul, 25,016	G 6
Spicer, 586	C 5
Springfield, 2,530	C 6
Spring Grove, 1,290	G 7
Spring Lake Park, 6,417	E 5
Spring Park, 1,087	F 5
Spring Valley, 2,572	F 7
Stacy, 278	E 5
Staples, 2,657	D 4
Starbuck, 1,138	C 5
Steen, 191	B 7
Stephen, 904	A 2
Stewart, 666	D 6
Stewartville, 2,802	F 7
Stillwater⊙, 10,191	F 5
Stockton, 346	G 6
Storden, 364	C 6
Sunfish Lake, 269	E 6
Swanville, 300	D 5
Swatara, 250	E 4
Taconite, 352	E 3
Taunton, 195	B 6
Taylors Falls, 587	F 5
Thief River Falls⊙, 8,618	B 2
Tofte, 400	H 3
Tonka Bay, 1,397	F 5
Tower, 699	F 3
Tracy, 2,516	C 6
Trimont, 835	D 7
Truman, 1,137	D 7
Twin Lakes, 230	E 7
Twin Valley, 868	B 3
Two Harbors⊙, 4,437	G 3
Tyler, 1,069	B 6
Ulen, 486	B 3
Underwood, 278	C 4
Upsala, 312	D 5
Utica, 240	G 7
Vadnais Heights, 3,391	G 5
Vergas, 281	C 4
Vermillion, 359	F 6
Verndale, 570	C 4
Vernon Center, 347	D 7
Vesta, 330	C 6
Victoria, 850	F 6
Villard, 221	C 5
Virginia, 12,450	F 3
Wabasha⊙, 2,371	G 6
Wabasso, 738	C 6
Waconia, 2,445	E 6
Wadena⊙, 4,640	C 4
Wahkon, 208	E 4
Waite Park, 2,824	D 5
Waldorf, 285	E 7
Walker⊙, 2,073	D 3
Walnut Grove, 756	C 6
Waltham, 189	F 7
Wanamingo, 574	F 6
Warren⊙, 1,999	B 2
Warroad, 1,086	C 2
Warsaw, 200	E 6
Waseca⊙, 6,789	E 6
Watertown, 1,390	E 6
Waterville, 1,539	E 6
Watkins, 785	D 5
Watson, 228	C 5
Waubun, 345	C 3
Waverly, 546	E 5
Wayzata, 3,700	G 5
Welcome, 694	D 7
Wells, 2,791	E 7
Wendell, 247	B 4
Westbrook, 990	C 6
West Concord, 718	F 6
West Saint Paul, 18,799	G 5
Wheaton⊙, 2,029	B 5
White Bear Lake, 23,313	G 5
Willernie, 697	G 5
Williams, 220	D 2
Willmar⊙, 12,869	C 5
Willow River, 331	F 4
Wilmont, 390	C 7
Windom⊙, 3,952	C 7
Winger, 228	B 3
Winnebago, 1,791	D 7
Winona⊙, 26,438	G 6
Winsted, 1,266	D 6
Winthrop, 1,391	D 6
Winton, 193	G 3
Woodbury, 6,184	F 6
Wood Lake, 418	C 6
Woodland■, 544	F 5
Woodstock, 217	B 7
Worthington⊙, 9,825	C 7
Wykoff, 450	F 7
Wyoming, 695	F 5
Young America, 611	E 6
Zim, 608	F 3
Zimmerman, 495	E 5
Zumbro Falls, 203	F 6
Zumbrota, 1,929	F 6

OTHER FEATURES

Feature	Key
Ash (riv.)	F 2
Bald Eagle (lake)	G 3
Bald Eagle (lake)	G 5
Basswood (lake)	G 2
Battle (riv.)	D 3
Baudette (riv.)	D 2
Bear (riv.)	E 3
Bemidji (lake)	D 3
Benton (lake)	B 6
Big Fork (riv.)	E 2
Big Sandy (lake)	E 4
Big Stone (lake)	B 5
Birch (lake)	G 3
Black (riv.)	D 2
Blue Earth (riv.)	D 7
Bois de Sioux (riv.)	B 4
Bowstring (lake)	E 3
Buffalo (riv.)	B 4
Burntside (lake)	F 3
Cass (lake)	D 3
Cedar (riv.)	F 7
Chippewa (riv.)	C 5
Christina (lake)	C 4
Clearwater (riv.)	C 3
Cloquet (riv.)	F 4
Cobb (riv.)	E 7
Cottonwood (riv.)	C 6
Crooked (lake)	G 2
Crow (riv.)	F 5
Crow Wing (riv.)	D 4
Cuyuna (range)	D 4
Dead (lake)	C 4
Deer (lake)	E 3
Des Moines (riv.)	C 7
Eagle (mt.)	G 2
East Swan (riv.)	F 3
Elbow (lake)	C 3
Emily (lake)	C 5
Fond du Lac Ind. Res., 850	F 4
Grand Portage Ind. Res., 335	G 2
Grand Portage Nat'l Mon.	G 2
Green (lake)	D 5
Greenwood (lake)	G 3
Gull (lake)	D 4
Heron (lake)	C 7
Hill (riv.)	C 3
Independence (lake)	F 5
Isabella (lake)	G 3
Isabella (riv.)	G 3
Itasca (lake)	C 3
Kabetogama (lake)	E 2
Kanaranzi (creek)	C 7
Kettle (riv.)	F 4
Knife (lake)	G 2
La Croix (lake)	F 2
Lac qui Parle (lake)	C 5
Lac qui Parle (riv.)	B 6
Lake of the Woods (lake)	D 1
Leaf (riv.)	C 4
Leech (lake)	D 3
Leech Lake Ind Res., 2,750	D 3
Lida (lake)	C 4
Little Rock (creek)	C 7
Long (lake)	D 4
Long (lake)	F 3
Long Prairie (riv.)	D 4
Lost (riv.)	C 3
Lower Red (lake)	C 3
Maple (lake)	B 3
Maple (riv.)	E 7
Marsh (lake)	B 5
Mary (lake)	C 5
Mesabi (range)	E 3
Middle (riv.)	B 2
Mille Lac Ind. Res., 820	E 4
Mille Lacs (lake)	E 4
Miltona (lake)	C 4
Minneapolis-Saint Paul Airport	G 5
Minnesota (riv.)	E 6
Minnetonka (lake)	F 5
Minnewaska (lake)	C 5
Misquah (hills)	F 2
Mississippi (riv.)	D 4
Moose (riv.)	C 2
Mud (lake)	C 2
Mud (riv.)	C 2
Muskeg (bay)	C 2
Mustinka (riv.)	B 5
Nemadji (riv.)	F 4
Nett (lake)	E 2
Nett Lake Ind. Res., 665	E 2
North (lake)	F 1
Otter Tail (lake)	C 4
Otter Tail (riv.)	B 4
Partridge (riv.)	G 3
Pelican (lake)	C 4
Pelican (lake)	D 4
Pelican (lake)	F 2
Pelican (riv.)	B 4
Pelican (riv.)	F 2
Pepin (lake)	F 6
Pigeon (riv.)	G 1
Pike (riv.)	F 3
Pipestone Nat'l Mon.	B 6
Pokegama (lake)	E 3
Pomme de Terre (riv.)	C 5
Poplar (riv.)	C 3
Prairie (riv.)	E 3
Rainy (lake)	E 2
Rainy (riv.)	D 2
Rapid (riv.)	D 2
Redeye (riv.)	D 4
Red Lake (riv.)	B 2
Red Lake Ind. Res., 3,200	C 2
Red River of the North (riv.)	A 2
Redwood (riv.)	C 6
Reno (lake)	C 5
Rice (lake)	E 4
Rock (riv.)	B 7
Root (riv.)	G 7
Roseau (riv.)	B 2
Rum (riv.)	E 5
Saganaga (lake)	H 2
Saint Croix (riv.)	F 5
Saint Louis (riv.)	F 4
Sand Hill (riv.)	B 3
Sarah (lake)	F 5
Schoolcraft (riv.)	C 3
Shakopee (creek)	C 5
Shell (riv.)	C 4
Shetek (lake)	C 6
Sleepy Eye (creek)	C 6
Snake (riv.)	A 2
Snake (riv.)	E 4
South Fowl (lake)	G 1
Star (lake)	C 4
Sturgeon (riv.)	F 3
Superior (lake)	G 3
Swan (lake)	D 6
Tamarac (riv.)	A 2
Tamarack (riv.)	D 2
Thief (lake)	C 2
Thief (riv.)	B 2
Traverse (lake)	B 5
Trout (lake)	F 2
Two Rivers (riv.)	A 1
Upper Red (lake)	D 2
Vermilion (lake)	F 3
Vermilion (range)	F 3
Vermilion (riv.)	F 2
Wabatawangang (lake)	D 3
West Swan (riv.)	F 3
White Earth Ind. Res., 2,550	C 3
Whiteface (riv.)	F 3
Whitefish (lake)	D 4
White Iron (lake)	G 3
Wild Rice (lake)	F 4
Wild Rice (riv.)	B 3
Willow (riv.)	E 4
Winnibigoshish (lake)	D 3
Woods (lake)	D 1
Zumbro (riv.)	F 6

LARGEST CENTERS OF POPULATION

City or Metropolitan area[1]	1970	1960	1950
Minneapolis (city)	434,400	482,872	521,718
Minneapolis-St. Paul metropolitan area	1,813,647	1,482,030	1,151,053
St. Paul	309,980	313,411	311,349
Duluth (city)	100,578	106,884	104,511
Duluth-Superior (Minn.-Wis.) metropolitan area (Minn. portion)	220,693	...	...
Bloomington	81,970	50,498	11,118
Rochester (city)	53,766	40,663	29,885
Metropolitan area	84,104	...	...
St. Louis Park	48,883	43,310	22,644
Richfield	47,231	42,523	17,502
Edina	44,046	28,501	9,744
St. Cloud	39,691	33,815	28,410
Minnetonka	35,776	25,037	...
Brooklyn Center	35,173	24,356	4,284
Roseville	34,518	23,997	6,437
Crystal	30,925	24,283	5,713
Mankato	30,895	23,797	18,809
Coon Rapids	30,505	14,931	...

[1] Standard metropolitan statistical area.

Mississippi survives in large part only in athletic competitions and occasional press agentry. Physically they have grown so close that the visitor and often the resident cannot tell when he leaves one and enters the other. Although the two remain distinct in government, general characteristics, and to some extent economic activities, they share many facilities and have many interests in common. The increasing interdependence of the Twin Cities and their suburbs was recognized by the 1957 legislature which created a metropolitan planning commission to study the problems of the governmental units in the areas.

Duluth, in St. Louis County, the state's third city in size and economic importance, was founded on the lumbering industry. Later it grew rapidly with the development of iron mining when, because of its strategic site at the head of the Great Lakes, it became a great shipping center. It also developed a considerable list of manufactures and became a distributing center for a wide area reaching westward into the Dakotas.

Although most of the smaller cities of the state have traditionally been "agricultural service stations," that is, centers of trade and social life for the farming areas immediately surrounding them, many have sought to develop new economic interests. Some Minnesota communities have achieved special prominence. For example, Rochester as the home of the Mayo Clinic and Foundation is a world-famous medical center; South St. Paul and Austin are nationally known meatpacking centers; Red Wing manufactures pottery from Minnesota clays; Brainerd and Bemidji make a lucrative business of being gateways to the Paul Bunyan country for tourists; Northfield is a college town, the seat of both St. Olaf College and Carleton College; St. Cloud is well known to American architects for its fine granite.

Counties.—There are great variations in area and population among Minnesota's 87 counties. Ramsey County is the smallest in size and St. Louis the largest. In population, Hennepin, containing Minneapolis, is the largest. The least populous is Cook.

County	County Seat
Aitkin	Aitkin
Anoka	Anoka
Becker	Detroit Lakes
Beltrami	Bemidji
Benton	Foley
Big Stone	Ortonville
Blue Earth	Mankato
Brown	New Ulm
Carlton	Carlton
Carver	Chaska
Cass	Walker
Chippewa	Montevideo
Chisago	Center City
Clay	Moorhead
Clearwater	Bagley
Cook	Grand Marais
Cottonwood	Windom
Crow Wing	Brainerd
Dakota	Hastings
Dodge	Mantorville
Douglas	Alexandria
Faribault	Blue Earth
Fillmore	Preston
Freeborn	Albert Lea
Goodhue	Red Wing
Grant	Elbow Lake
Hennepin	Minneapolis
Houston	Caledonia
Hubbard	Park Rapids
Isanti	Cambridge
Itasca	Grand Rapids
Jackson	Jackson
Kanabec	Mora
Kandiyohi	Willmar
Kittson	Hallock
Koochiching	International Falls
Lac qui Parle	Madison
Lake	Two Harbors
Lake of the Woods	Baudette
Le Sueur	Le Center
Lincoln	Ivanhoe
Lyon	Marshall
McLeod	Glencoe
Mahnomen	Mahnomen
Marshall	Warren
Martin	Fairmont
Meeker	Litchfield
Mille Lacs	Milaca
Morrison	Little Falls
Mower	Austin
Murray	Slayton
Nicollet	St. Peter
Nobles	Worthington
Norman	Ada
Olmsted	Rochester
Otter Tail	Fergus Falls
Pennington	Thief River Falls
Pine	Pine City
Pipestone	Pipestone
Polk	Crookston
Pope	Glenwood
Ramsey	St. Paul
Red Lake	Red Lake Falls
Redwood	Redwood Falls
Renville	Olivia
Rice	Faribault
Rock	Luverne
Roseau	Roseau
St. Louis	Duluth
Scott	Shakopee
Sherburne	Elk River
Sibley	Gaylord
Stearns	St. Cloud
Steele	Owatonna
Stevens	Morris
Swift	Benson
Todd	Long Prairie
Traverse	Wheaton
Wabasha	Wabasha
Wadena	Wadena
Waseca	Waseca
Washington	Stillwater
Watonwan	St. James
Wilkin	Breckenridge
Winona	Winona
Wright	Buffalo
Yellow Medicine	Granite Falls

3. GOVERNMENT

State Constitution.—The political climate in the Territory of Minnesota was so intensely partisan in July 1857 that the Republicans and Democrats, elected in about equal numbers as delegates to the constitutional convention, refused to sit down together in one room. The two parties met separately for a month and a half, but through the good offices of a conference committee, composed of leaders from both factions, the same constitution was approved by each body. The Democratic delegates signed one copy of the document (on blue paper), the Republicans another (on white paper), giving Minnesota the distinction of two constitutions. Since they were substantially identical, however, no legal difficulty ensued. The voters of the territory accepted the constitution on Oct. 13, 1857, and it went into effect the following year when Minnesota became a state.

The state capitol, at St. Paul.

A. Devaney

The document thus issuing from bitter factional cleavage proved workable and generally adaptable to meet the state's needs. Although amended 87 times since adoption, it has not undergone fundamental revision. The most frequently amended article is that concerned with the finances of the state; a 1906 amendment enlarging taxing powers had far-reaching influence. An important series of amendments had the effect of permitting the state to engage in internal improvements through the provision of a state road and bridge fund (1898); the encouragement of good roads (1906); the establishment of a state trunk highway system (1920); and the authorization of a system of airport development on a statewide basis (1944).

The procedure for amendment requires that proposals be approved by a majority of both houses of the legislature and submitted to the voters at a general election. Only if a majority of all those voting at the election approve the amendment does it become valid. The constitution also permits revision by convention, but none has ever been held.

Elections.—The right to vote is granted to all those 18 years and older who have been United States citizens for at least 3 months, residents of the state for 6 months, and residents of a precinct for 30 days. (A constitutional amendment adopted in 1960 gives the legislature the right to protect the franchise of Minnesotans who move from one precinct to another within 30 days of an election.)

Minnesota was the first state in the Union to enact a limited statewide compulsory primary law, in 1901. It now has an open primary system. Voters cannot split their ballots (they must select among candidates running under only one party label) but they vote on a consolidated ballot without having to declare party preference in advance.

In addition to its two senators, Minnesota has eight representatives in the United States Congress. The present number of representatives, determined on the basis of the 1960 census, is one less than the nine apportioned after the 1950 census.

Executive.—The executive department is headed by six constitutional officers: governor, lieutenant governor, secretary of state, auditor, treasurer, and attorney general. Since 1962, all have been elected for four-year terms.

In the years following statehood, the administrative functions of the executive branch became more complex. It therefore became necessary to set up a number of specialized boards and commissions to take care of these new duties. In time the authority of these agencies overlapped. In 1939 a thorough reorganization integrated these functions in a more orderly arrangement of agencies. In 1968 there were 37 administrative agencies. The Department of Administration, created in 1939, supervises budgeting and fiscal and business affairs; all state departments, except the legislature, the judiciary, the university, and certain licensing boards, are subject to it. The Civil Service Department is the central personnel agency for all of the state's classified employees. Most of the administrative heads of departments are appointed by the governor and are responsible to him. An exception is the Railway and Warehouse Commission whose three members are elected for six-year terms by the voters; they regulate the rates and practices of railways, bus and truck companies, and telephone companies.

GOVERNORS OF MINNESOTA

Territorial		
Alexander Ramsey		1849–1853
Willis A. Gorman		1853–1857
Samuel Medary		1857–1858
State		
Henry H. Sibley	Democrat	1858–1860
Alexander Ramsey	Republican	1860–1863
Henry A. Swift	Republican	1863–1864
Stephen Miller	Republican	1864–1866
William R. Marshall	Republican	1866–1870
Horace Austin	Republican	1870–1874
Cushman K. Davis	Republican	1874–1876
John S. Pillsbury	Republican	1876–1882
Lucius F. Hubbard	Republican	1882–1887
Andrew R. McGill	Republican	1887–1889
William R. Merriam	Republican	1889–1893
Knute Nelson	Republican	1893–1895
David M. Clough	Republican	1895–1899
John Lind	Democrat	1899–1901
Samuel R. Van Sant	Republican	1901–1905
John A. Johnson[1]	Democrat	1905–1909
Adolph O. Eberhart	Republican	1909–1915
Winfield S. Hammond[1]	Democrat	1915
Joseph A. A. Burnquist	Republican	1915–1921
Jacob A. O. Preus	Republican	1921–1925
Theodore Christianson	Republican	1925–1931
Floyd B. Olson[1]	Farmer-Labor	1931–1936
Hjalmar Petersen	Farmer-Labor	1936–1937
Elmer A. Benson	Farmer-Labor	1937–1939
Harold E. Stassen	Republican	1939–1943
Edward J. Thye	Republican	1943–1947
Luther W. Youngdahl	Republican	1947–1951
C. Elmer Anderson	Republican	1951–1955
Orville L. Freeman	Democrat-Farmer-Labor	1955–1961
Elmer L. Andersen	Republican	1961–1963
Karl Rolvaag	Democrat	1963–1967
Harold LeVander	Republican	1967–1971
Wendell R. Anderson	Democrat	1971–

[1] Died in office.

Legislature.—Although the constitution establishes population as the basis of representation, the legislative districts in 1960 remained the same as in 1913, the last year of reapportionment. In the decades following 1913, as the population shifted to urban centers, the problem of finding an equitable balance between urban and rural representation had faced each legislature but had not been solved. Finally, in 1966, the governor signed a bill reapportioning both houses of the legislature on a population basis. The bill did not change the number of legislators in either house, but it gave the Minneapolis-St. Paul urban area 11 more House seats and 5½ more Senate seats.

The legislature meets in odd-numbered years for 120 legislative days (excluding Sundays and holidays) beginning the Tuesday after the first Monday in January. The complex problems facing the legislature have made it increasingly difficult for the body to finish its work in the prescribed period, and extra sessions are frequently found necessary.

The 135 members of the House of Representatives are elected for two-year terms; the 67 senators serve for four years. All members of the legislature are elected without party designation, but the houses are organized by caucuses of so-called liberal and conservative factions.

Judiciary.—The judicial branch of the state government is composed of the Supreme Court, the District Court, the Probate Court, municipal courts, and justices of the peace. The system is headed by the Supreme Court, the state's court of last resort, made up of a chief judge and six associate judges, elected for six-year terms on a nonpartisan ballot.

Reform of the judicial procedures in the lower courts began in 1948 and continued in 1956 when a constitutional amendment was adopted authorizing reorganization of the state court system. Under it the chief judge of the Supreme Court supervises and coordinates the work of the state District Court. The three or more judges for each district are elected for six-year terms, also on a nonpartisan ballot.

Minnesota is part of the Eighth Judicial Circuit served by a United States Court of Appeals.

Taxation and Revenue.—Minnesota entered the Union with a generous land endowment from the federal government, and it continued to receive additional lands for schools, railroads, and other internal improvements. Only Florida has received more public land. The state has guarded well this patrimony: the permanent funds based on these grants amount to more than $300 million. The capital sum in each of the funds is invested, and only the interest may be expended on current public services.

In the early years of statehood Minnesota's taxing resources were constitutionally limited to the property tax. As the state began to assume direct responsibility for governmental functions like education and road construction, it needed more revenue to pay for its increasing activities. When the so-called wide-open tax amendment of 1906 removed most controls from the legislature's taxing power, the state was free to broaden its base of taxation and to develop its present well-diversified revenue system. The chief sources of the state's revenue are taxes on income (personal and corporate), gasoline, motor vehicles, iron ore, gross earnings of railroads and communication companies, property, liquor, and cigarettes. In 1967 the legislature enacted a highly controversial state sales tax, levying a 3 per cent tax on all items purchased at retail except food, medicines, clothing, and gasoline. Tax administration in Minnesota is centralized in the Department of Taxation. Other income derives from United States grants-in-aid, department earnings, and interest.

In the first half of the 20th century state and local expenditures together increased ninefold, but the balance between the state and local shares shifted markedly. In 1911 the state spent only 15 per cent of the total; 40 years later it spent more than 27 per cent. Local governments remained restricted to one major source of revenue, the property tax. At the same time grants of state funds to local governments increased tremendously after 1900, both absolutely and in proportion to other expenditures. This has been especially true in three major fields—education, highways, and public welfare—and to some extent also in health and hospitals. School districts and counties have fared better in the sharing of state funds than cities, villages, and towns. With growing urbanization, the needs of the latter three classifications for general revenue were increasing.

Local Government.—Minnesota's counties are governed by boards of five elected commissioners each, except Ramsey County, which has six, and St. Louis, which has seven. The usual county officers (elective) are auditor, treasurer, register of deeds, sheriff, attorney, surveyor, coroner, clerk of court, judge of probate, and superintendent of schools.

Of the 111 communities classed as cities in 1968, all but 19 operated under home-rule charters. The great majority of the cities have adopted a mayor-council form of government; some have a council-manager; a few operate under the commission form. The most common form of government in the 735 communities classified as villages is the mayor-council.

4. EDUCATION, HEALTH, AND WELFARE

Education.—In 1849 the territorial legislature passed an act to "establish and maintain common schools"; and in 1858 the state constitution proclaimed firmly the responsibility of the legislature to "establish a general and uniform system of public schools." But the evolution from the scattered early mission schools to a comprehensive educational system was necessarily slow. In 1858 there were only 72 organized school districts in the state and in 1870 only 17 communities had high schools. Not until 1878 was a state high school board created and state aid provided to public high schools from general funds. State support was extended to grade schools in 1895.

Local school districts retained responsibility for raising a large share of the necessary funds, and authority for the management and operation of schools through school boards elected by the people. But as the state legislature became increasingly concerned with encouraging and guaranteeing proper standards, it created and supported state administrative agencies to see that legislative policies were carried out. A seven-man state Board of Education appointed by the governor formulates general policy and appoints a commissioner as head of the state Department of Education, which has broad powers for administration and supervision of the public school system.

Enrollment in elementary schools increased from 386,405 in 1900 to 454,537 in 1920, and then flattened out and declined to 365,000 in 1940; in the 1965–1966 school year the enrollment was 464,000. Secondary school enrollment, only 12,802 in 1900, showed a continuous growth to 1940, reaching 147,355 in that year; then after a sharp dip during the war years it began to climb again, to 361,000 in 1965–1966.

Per capita support of public education increased more than tenfold in the half century after 1900 and remained consistently above the national average. In 1900 per capita expenditure on public education amounted to $3.21; it rose to $14.97 in 1920, to $20.13 in 1930, and to $36.90 in 1950. In 1967, Minnesota ranked 11th nationally in per capita expenditure, with $174. In 1930, Minnesota ranked 14th among the states in expenditure per pupil in average daily attendance, with $101; in 1967 it ranked 12th with $634.

State support to the schools—amounting to about 40 per cent of the total cost of maintenance —is derived from four sources: (1) An endowment fund consisting of income from the permanent school trust fund and half the income from the swampland fund. The funds comprise all money derived from the sale or lease of the lands granted to the new Territory of Minnesota by a generous Congress, which set aside two sections in each township instead of the usual one. Since some of the lands have turned out to be rich in timber and iron ore, the funds exceeded $250 million in the 1960's. The income from the funds is apportioned to school districts on the basis of school attendance. (2) An occupation tax fund consisting of income from 40 per cent of the occupation tax on iron ore. (3) Income tax receipts, dedicated by law to school use. The legislature allocates state aid from these funds biennially. (4) A foundation program that aims at equalizing in some measure educational quality and opportunity among the several counties, which vary widely in per capita wealth. Established by the legislature in 1957, the foundation program allocates state aid (a minimum of $87 per pupil unit) with the purpose of guaranteeing a basic standard of education to all children regardless of what part of the state they live in. Education is free for all young people from 5 to 21 and compulsory from 7 to 16 inclusive.

More than a third of the students attending institutions of higher learning in Minnesota enroll at the state university; almost a third are students at the 14 junior colleges and 5 state colleges. The rest attend the state's 16 private colleges. College enrollment increased from 4,821 in 1900, to 17,210 in 1920, and 24,186 in 1930. After a sharp decline during World War II the number of college students again turned upward, with a rapid spurt in the 1960's. Enrollment in the fall of 1965 was 118,533.

Chartered in 1851, the University of Minnesota has become one of the three largest in the nation. In a real sense the university is statewide: it grants degrees on four campuses (the main campus in Minneapolis, the agricultural campus in St. Paul, and the branches in Duluth and Morris), offers specialized instruction at Crookston and Rochester, and has research and experimental units scattered around the state.

The state colleges trace their beginnings to 1858, when the first state legislature authorized normal schools. Five were later established—at Winona, Bemidji, Mankato, Moorhead, and St. Cloud. Historically they have emphasized teacher preparation, but the increasing importance of their liberal arts programs was recognized by the 1957 legislature which changed their name from teachers colleges to state colleges. The junior colleges were largely supported by local funds until 1957 when, for the first time, state aid was granted by the legislature. In 1963 this aid amounted to $350 per pupil.

Private collegiate institutions date back to the territorial period when Hamline in 1854 and St. John's in 1857 were established. Later, among others, Gustavus Adolphus, Carleton, St. Olaf's, and Macalester were founded.

Libraries.—About 75 per cent of the state's population is served by public libraries. The public system began in 1858 when the first public library association was formed in Northfield, and it developed steadily. A public library commission was established in 1899 (later becoming a division in the state Department of Education). In 1957 the legislature granted its first state aid to libraries, in the Rural Aid to Public Libraries Act.

One of the special collections of importance is the James Jerome Hill Reference Library in St. Paul. It has a very fine collection of Americana. The University of Minnesota Library, with more than 2 million volumes, ranks among the most notable research libraries in the United States. Its chemistry library is exceptionally complete, with books and treatises published as early as 1673, and its law library possesses one of the largest collections of Commonwealth of Nations legal material in the United States, as well as an outstanding collection of laws of Indian tribes. The Mayo Clinic Library in Rochester has many interesting old medical works. The library of the Minnesota Historical Society, official depository of all state documents, has one of the largest historical collections in the Northwest, including thousands of manuscripts.

Public Health.—Minnesota was fourth among the states to establish a Board of Health. This was in 1872. The naming of Dr. Charles N. Hewitt as professor of public health at the state university in that same year was the first such appointment in the United States.

The state Board of Health, consisting of nine members appointed by the governor for three-year terms, is the official state agency charged with the protection, preservation, and promotion of the public health. Its policies are executed by the state Department of Health.

Control of contagious diseases was one of the earliest functions of the board and this continues as a major concern with emphasis on prevention. A laboratory for virus diseases, set up in 1937, carries on an extensive testing program. Newer developments include a statewide blood donor program and a poison information center. One of Minnesota's remarkable achievements has been the virtual eradication of brucellosis in the state.

Public Welfare.—The state Department of Public Welfare is charged with responsibility for service and financial aid to about 190,000 dependent Minnesotans; it also operates the 20 state institutions for the handicapped and the mentally ill and retarded, with an average of 13,000 patients. The bulk of the child welfare services and financial aid programs are administered locally by the 87 county welfare boards. In general, local government authorities in Minnesota retain considerable administrative power in welfare functions, but the state department oversees and coordinates their activities.

Services to children have traditionally been well developed in Minnesota. It was the first state in the Union to treat crippled children at public expense; and it continues to serve the physically handicapped through the Gillette State Hospital for Crippled Children in St. Paul, and the School for the Deaf and the Braille and Sightsaving School, both at Faribault. The Children's Center was formally established in 1953 to serve emotionally disturbed youngsters. Although institutional care is still maintained at a high level, the child welfare program in the state is characterized by emphasis on service to children in their own homes so far as possible.

Along with continued concern for young people, the state has shown increasing attention to programs for senior citizens and for the mentally ill and retarded of all ages. Beginning in 1949 the state's mental health program was expanded substantially with an emphasis on research as well as added staff and facilities for institutions. In 1957 state aid was granted to local communities to encourage the establishment of local mental health clinics. The oldest of the state's seven mental hospitals is located at St. Peter (established 1866). There are seven hospitals for the mentally retarded or epileptic, the oldest being at Faribault; all provide training and an opportunity for return to society to those who can be trained, as well as long-term custodial care.

Corrections.—The program of custody, treatment, and training for criminal offenders committed to the state prison at Stillwater, the state reformatory for men at St. Cloud, and the state reformatory for women at Shakopee was until 1959 administered for a division of the Department of Welfare. In that year a separate Department of Corrections was established. Rehabilitation and vocational training are stressed in all three institutions. The state prison has long maintained one of the most active prison industries programs in the country, with twine, rope, and farm

machinery the chief manufactures.

With the creation of the Youth Conservation Commission in 1947, the state recognized a special responsibility to young people in trouble. The commission became a division of the Department of Corrections in 1959. All those under 21 who are judged to require custody or rehabilitation must be committed to the division, which maintains seven institutions. The division also carries on a vigorous program aimed at preventing delinquency.

5. ECONOMIC ACTIVITIES

Furs, northern pines, wheat, and iron ore—these were the dominant forces that shaped Minnesota's economy. The promise of unbounded riches in beaver, muskrat, and mink pelts lured first French, then British, and finally American fur traders to the old Northwest. For more than a century their posts were centers of economic and social life in the area. Then, about 1837, as fur animals became scarce and a panic forced prices down, Minnesota fur trade began to decline, although it never died out completely.

The logger was next on the scene. Logging and milling began in the St. Croix valley in 1839 and moved northward through the stands of high-quality white and Norway pine. Growth in size of operations was spectacular, in key with the legend of Paul Bunyan, which it spawned; in two years, from 1850 to 1852, the value of the industry jumped from $57,800 to $2,500,000. The high point was reached in 1902 when 2.5 billion board feet of lumber were processed. But the careless prodigality of the industry had taken its toll, and lumbering declined as rapidly as it had grown. It has been estimated that during the golden age of lumbering 100 billion board feet of pine were harvested—and that in addition 50 to 100 billion board feet were wasted by destructive logging practices and by forest fires, many of them set intentionally to clear the land.

Waves of settlers followed the logger into Minnesota and welcomed the rapid clearing of the forest land. These were the farmers who were to dominate the economic life of Minnesota for a century. By 1860 wheat had become the major—and virtually only—crop. Two million bushels were harvested in 1860; 19 million in 1870. In the rich Red River valley, the famous "bonanza" farms, thousands of acres each, became literally farm factories with the use of the new agricultural machinery. But one-crop farming exhausted the soil quickly, and gradually farming became diversified. Wheat gave way to corn as the leading crop; dairying and livestock took on increasing importance.

The early emphasis on wheat growing made flour milling a natural development as Minnesota's first important manufacturing industry. Utilizing revolutionary technical developments like the middlings purifier—a device for blowing off the fine bran particles from the middlings and hence enhancing the quality of the finished flour—and rollers for grinding, Minnesota mills, most of them in Minneapolis, quickly forged ahead of all competitors. By 1895, Minnesota flour was acknowledged to be the best made, flour was the state's leading manufactured product, and Minneapolis was the world's foremost milling center. The mills continued to increase their output to a peak of 29,389,889 barrels in 1916. Their advertising slogans, such as that for Gold Medal flour—"Eventually, Why Not Now?"—and the answering "Because Pillsbury's Best," became household words. But after 1916 the Minnesota mills gradually lost their pre-eminence. Like agriculture itself, the giant milling firms that remained in Minneapolis began to diversify their product and activities.

Not until 1890 did iron mining join lumbering, agriculture, and milling in the big four of Minnesota's economy. Leonidas Merritt and his six brothers found the "buried iron giant" at Mesabi and developed the open-pit method of mining. By 1901 the range was producing 9 million tons of ore annually. Before World War II the annual output of all Minnesota mines was between 40 and 50 million tons. Under wartime pressure, production jumped to 75 million tons in 1942, almost 70 per cent of the national total. Even before the war, however, there had been signs that the mining industry in Minnesota was approaching a turning point, and this was accelerated by the wartime demands that hastened depletion of the rich ores which had given Minnesota its advantage over other mining areas.

By the middle of the 20th century Minnesota had depleted much of its virgin resources—in timber, ore, and even soil—but it had developed a diversified economy dependent as much upon the technical and managerial skill of its people as upon natural resources. Manufacturing displaced farming as the major source of income in the state in 1952, but agricultural produce of many kinds remained a vital element in the economy, as did iron ore (both the remaining rich ores and those of lower grade) and new forest products.

In the 1950's the state Department of Business Development, in cooperation with local communities, encouraged the growth of new industries through the formation of local industrial development corporations. Nearly 200 such community corporations have been established.

Agriculture.—Minnesota ranks fifth (after Iowa, California, Illinois, and Texas) among the states in agricultural importance. Its farms account for about 4 per cent of national cash farm marketings, their earnings averaging over $1.5 billion annually. Between one fourth and one third of this income is derived from cash crops, the balance from livestock and its products.

There are four major farming regions in the state: the rich corn belt in the south-central and southwest; the main dairy region in the central and southeast; the cash crop belt in the Red River valley; and a broad transitional zone running from northwest to southeast in which production of dairy goods, corn, and cash crops fluctuates in response to demand. The northeastern section is largely limited to hay. Although three fourths of Minnesota's land is covered by farm fields and pasture, agricultural conditions vary widely—from a marginal area in the northeast where only a small fraction of 1 per cent of the land area is in farming, to the south central section where harvested crops occupy more than 80 per cent of the land area.

The most important trend in agriculture has been the continuing northern migration of corn and soybeans. Corn has been the number one crop since 1900; new hybrids have permitted expanded planting. Introduced in 1930, soybean production rocketed from 1 million bushels in 1941 to a record 81 million bushels in 1966. Among the states in 1966 Minnesota ranked first in the production of oats, and among the leaders in soybeans, turkeys, corn, chickens, eggs, milk, barley, rye, sugar beets, flaxseed, and hay. Livestock products are dominant in all agricultural areas except the Red River valley.

Manufacturing.—Minnesota's manufacturing industries, while relatively modest compared with those of the great industrial states, have shown sharp expansion in common with the national trend. The state ranks 20th in manufacturing output, accounting for about 1½ per cent of the value added to goods by manufacture throughout the nation. In 1964, this contribution amounted to more than $3 billion.

Food and kindred products form the major industry in Minnesota, accounting for about a fourth of the manufacturing employment. Meat products make up the largest segment; South St. Paul is the second largest packing center in the nation. Processing of poultry is also important. In dairy products, of which 80 per cent are shipped to other states, Minnesota ranks first nationally in the production of butter as well as dry milk, and fourth in American cheese. In vegetable processing, freezing has gained in importance; the state has long been a major producer of canned corn and peas. Minnesota firms still rank high nationally in flour milling, but they have greatly expanded their interests in developing new products such as cake mixes.

Machinery is the state's second most important manufacturing industry; farm equipment has a major place in this field. Pulp and paper and their products also rank high among manufactures. By the grace of technology, in the form of new processes, the jack pine, aspen, and other hardwoods growing on the cutover forest lands have become the backbone of the pulp and paper industry. Lumber and its products, such as cedar poles, fence posts, railway ties, and window- and door-

Above: Grain elevators and railroad yards at Duluth, an important port on Lake Superior. It is the third largest city in the state.

Right: A lumberman prepares logs for the sawmill. Lumber and other wood products are important to the economy of Minnesota.

MINNESOTA

(Above) H. Armstrong Roberts; (right center) A. Devaney; (below) Minnesota Division of Publicity; (others) Louis Goldman, Rapho-Guillumette.

Right: A project for processing taconite, an iron-bearing rock. Iron ore accounts for 90 per cent of the state's mineral output.

Above: A turkey ranch in southwestern Minnesota. In turkey production Minnesota ranks among the top five states in the country.

Right: Related to Minnesota's large production of wood pulp and paper, printing has become one of the state's notable industries.

frames, are also important. Ironically, however, although its forests today bring in more wealth than in the boom at the turn of the century, Minnesota must import more than three fourths of its lumber needs. Quality lumber is scarce; low-quality lumber is in excess supply. Christmas trees, mostly for export to the south and east, are a fairly new element in the forest industry.

Printing and publishing, chemicals and their products, metals and metal products, transportation equipment, clay and glass products, and apparel are other notable industries. In general, manufacturing is well diversified, ranging from thermostats and research balloons to plastic tape and electronics equipment.

Mineral Industries.—Iron ore has for many years kept Minnesota among the top 15 states in value of mineral production; it accounts for approximately 70 per cent of the state's mineral output, valued at over $500 million annually in the mid-1960's.

From 1882 to 1950, the Mesabi range alone contributed 1.5 billion tons of high-grade ore. It still supplies between 40 and 50 per cent of the nation's ore needs. Although direct shipping ores are by no means exhausted (reserves were calculated at 400 million tons in 1960), iron ore concentrates, produced by beneficiation of low-grade ores, have become the foundation of the industry's future.

Beneficiation was introduced in 1907 when the first commercial concentration plant was built on the Mesabi range and the iron-mining industry began experimenting with upgrading regular ore at the same time that high-grade ore was being shipped out. In the late 1940's the successful processing of taconite—a low-grade iron-bearing rock—was a significant step forward in the industry's battle to keep up with the yawning iron furnaces. After decades of experimentation, Edward W. Davis of the University of Minnesota Mines Experiment Station developed a method for doing in a few minutes what nature had taken millions of years to accomplish. In 1955, 1 million tons of taconite pellets were shipped; in 1965, 15.8 million tons. In 1968 the total capacity of the taconite plants in operation was 33.3 million tons. One estimate placed the amount of taconite available in Minnesota at 5 billion tons. A "taconite amendment" to the state constitution, adopted in 1964, guaranteed tax equity to the taconite industry for a period of 25 years. This amendment spurred the construction of new and expanded facilities; by 1968 more than $411 million had been invested.

Besides iron ore, mineral products include manganiferous ore, sand, and gravel. Since 1880, the state has also ranked high in production of building stones, particularly granite. Many of the 40-odd varieties of Minnesota stone are well known to architects—for example, Lasota limestone, Winona travertine, and Kettle River sandstone.

Power.—In expansion of its electrical power resources, Minnesota, since World War II, has kept pace with the national rate of growth, both the installed capacity and production of its electrical utilities having more than tripled between 1945 and 1965. The vast bulk of the state's electricity plants are fuel-powered (of total capacity in 1965 of 3,542,000 kilowatts, including electrical utilities and industrial plants, only 183,000 kilowatts, or 5 per cent, was hydropowered); and almost all fuel supplies—coal, oil, and natural gas—must be imported over long distances.

Tourism.—The early boast of "cascades and pine forests and cooling breezes" brought vacationers to Minnesota even before the Civil War and they continued in the later years of the century to luxuriate at fashionable Lake Minnetonka and rough it in the northern wilds. By the mid-20th century tourism had become big business.

Trade.—Historically, the state's major market has extended westward. Although developments in transportation have lessened the early heavy dependence of the Dakotas and Montana on Minnesota distributing centers, the Twin Cities and Duluth remain the principal economic capitals of this northwest empire. Its trade keeps Minnesota's wholesale sales substantially above its retail sales. Minneapolis dominates the state's wholesale business. The Twin Cities together rank as the ninth largest wholesale center in the United States.

Banking and Insurance.—The Twin Cities have grown rapidly in importance as a financial center. Their many financial institutions include the Minneapolis Federal Reserve Bank for the ninth district, a federal land bank, a federal intermediate credit bank, a bank for cooperatives, large commercial banks, trust departments, a mutual savings bank, 3 of the nation's 25 largest savings and loan associations, life and casualty insurance companies, and investment houses.

Banking began on a small scale in Minnesota, often as a sideline of real estate men and lumber dealers. By 1900, however, there were 267 banks in the state and by 1911, 997. After the agricultural depression of the 1920's sharply reduced the number of banks, particularly in the rural areas, two major group banking systems developed, Northwest Bancorporation and First Bank Stock Corporation, with headquarters in Minneapolis. The Twin Cities rank seventh among the nation's insurance centers. The oldest of the companies was founded in St. Paul in 1853 to insure river traffic. Life insurance companies followed in the 1880's.

Cooperatives.—Minnesota has long been known for the strength and scope of its cooperative movement—an activity in which it was an early leader, partly perhaps because its Danish and Finnish settlers were schooled in cooperative principles and methods in Europe. The movement has also benefited from sound management policies that are enforced by state laws enacted to protect and encourage cooperatives.

Though the major cooperative associations are rural in membership and deal in agricultural products, the thousands of cooperatives, large and small, in operation in the state cover marketing, processing, and consumption in many fields—grain marketing, butter production, milk and oil distribution, fire insurance, rural electrification, dry cleaning, and book buying, to name only a few. The total volume of business handled by Minnesota farmers' cooperatives rose from $228.5 million in 1936 to over $984 million in 1965.

Labor Force.—Minnesota's labor force has traditionally been characterized by high productivity and good labor relations. The trade union movement began before Minnesota was a state, with the chartering of the St. Paul Typographical Union in 1858. In 1890 the Minnesota State Federation of Labor was formed. But until 1934 employers were able to maintain the open shop. In that year Minneapolis truck drivers staged a dramatic and effective strike. Most of labor's gains in Minnesota, however, have been won through political action and the ballot box. Important steps were laws regulating factory working conditions (1893) and child labor (1895), providing workman's compensation (1913), and setting up an industrial commission to exercise state supervision and protection for labor (1921). Trade union membership in 1964 was 33 per cent of the nonagricultural workers in the state, compared with 24.8 per cent in 1929. Minnesota ranked thirteenth in the nation in 1964 in percentage of organized workers.

In 1966, out of a total labor force of 1,389,700 there were 227,000 agricultural workers. The breakdown of the nonagricultural force, in major classifications and the percentage employed in each, was as follows: manufacturing, 24; wholesale and retail trade, 23; local, state, and federal government, 17; service industries, 15; transportation, communication, and public utilities, 7; construction, 5; finance, insurance, and real estate, 4; mining and quarrying, 1.

Personal Income.—Until the 1920's annual personal income in the state was above average. With more rapid industrialization in other areas, personal income then began to drop, reaching 18 per cent below the national average in 1932. It remained low through World War II but subsequently began to climb. In 1966, at $2,904, it was 7 per cent below the national average.

For further statistics, see THE AMERICANA ANNUAL.

6 TRANSPORTATION AND COMMUNICATIONS

Transportation.—White men first arrived in Minnesota by way of river and lake and for two centuries—in canoe, keelboat, and steamer—continued to depend heavily on the watercourses that had long been the main highways of their predecessors, the Indians. The steamboat reached its heyday in the 1850's as the most important means of transportation in the upper Mississippi River area. Overland the creaking Red River carts and rumbling stagecoaches were a familiar sight from the late 1840's until the 1860's. The advent of railroads in the 1860's brought a new era in transportation and within a few decades they advanced to national prominence the first of three Minnesotans to contribute dramatically to modern transportation growth—James J. Hill, who made St. Paul the capital of the rail empire he pushed westward to the Pacific. The others were C. Eric Wickman, whose jitney service for iron range miners, begun at Hibbing in 1914, grew into the continental Greyhound bus system; and Charles A. Lindbergh, Jr., of Little Falls, who opened a new age of air travel in 1927 with his nonstop transatlantic flight.

As its population grew, Minnesota seized promptly on new developments in transportation to provide a varied system of high caliber in road, rail, air, and water transport in order to offset, as far as possible, its handicap of long distance from markets and certain raw materials. Its roads became the backbone of the system. State motorists travel in 2,212,500 vehicles on 126,385 miles of roads and streets (1966). Rural roads, making up about 90 per cent of the total mileage, are for the most part well surfaced, the trunk highway system, for example, being nine-tenths concrete and bituminous.

The 10-mile track from St. Paul to St. Anthony that introduced railroads to Minnesota in 1862 grew to 6,943 miles by 1900 and to a maximum of 9,114 in 1920. In 1967 there were 8,046 line miles of railway track in the state. Although 90 per cent of the rail business is freight, the dome-topped passenger streamliners linking the Twin Cities daily with Chicago and the West Coast are the pride of the major lines.

The Mississippi River, with the Twin Cities at the head of navigation, and the Great Lakes, with Duluth as the westernmost port, remain important water highways for the state in the transport of bulky goods. In fact, Duluth and its twin port Superior (Wisconsin) rank, among the nation's ports, second only to New York City in tonnage, even though they have only an eight-month shipping season. Between 1871 and the mid-1960's more than 2.5 billion tons of commerce were handled there; the record shipment was 70.4 million tons in 1953. The completion of the St. Lawrence Seaway in 1959 made Duluth a world port, with more than 250 oceangoing vessels arriving annually by the mid-1960's.

Air traffic in constantly increasing volume, both in passengers and freight, is centered at Wold-Chamberlain Field in Minneapolis. The first commercial flight from Minnesota was made in 1926 from Minneapolis to Chicago; in 1960 there were 500 flights a week in and out of the Twin Cities including regular service to Alaska, Honolulu, and Tokyo, and frequent flights every day to Chicago, Washington, D.C., and New York.

Communications.—Minnesota's first newspaper, the Minnesota *Pioneer,* was launched before its territorial officers arrived, on April 28, 1849. Its flamboyant editor, James M. Goodhue, was an early and vigorous promoter of Minnesota's beauties. In the territorial period 88 other newspapers were established including the St. Cloud *Visitor,* edited by the fiery antislavery crusader Jane Grey Swisshelm. In the mid-1960's, there were 30 daily and almost 400 weekly and other newspapers in the state, serving more than 1.5 million readers. The state was also served by 107 radio stations and 17 television channels, representing all major national networks.

7. CULTURAL LIFE

The cultural, intellectual, and social scene in Minnesota reflects the rich pattern of racial strains in its people, the long tradition of sturdily self-reliant family farming, and the pressures of climate and geographical location. In meeting the challenges of rapid transformation from rough frontier to civilized complexity, adaptable and independent Minnesotans sometimes have retained —with respect and affection—the ways of the Old World and the American East, sometimes have broken new paths through experimentation and ingenuity.

In no area has this readiness to experiment been more clearly demonstrated than in agricultural, industrial, and medical research. The University of Minnesota is a leader in such research. Its scientists have developed rust-resistant wheat, corn hybrids, and new varieties of fruit adapted to the northern climate; they have made possible the commercial utilization of taconite; they have pioneered in the conquest of plant and animal diseases like brucellosis.

The conquering of stubborn human ills has been a steady preoccupation since Dr. William Worrall Mayo, father of the famed Doctors Wil-

Left: **Called the Land of Ten Thousand Lakes, Minnesota has many fine resorts.**

MINNESOTA

Above: **The round tower at Fort Snelling, where Dred Scott was married, now contains various historical exhibits.**

Left: **A gallery of the Walker Art Center in Minneapolis. It is one of the state's chief cultural institutions.**

(Top left) Minnesota Division of Publicity; (left) Louis Goldman from Rapho-Guillumette; (below left) Minnneapolis Institute of Arts; (others) George Waters, Rapho-Guillumette.

Below: **Students on the campus of the University of Minnesota, one of the three largest in the United States.**

Left: **Affiliated with the University of Minnesota, the internationally renowned Mayo Clinic is in Rochester, Minn.**

Above: At its source in Itasca State Park, the mighty Mississippi River is shallow enough for a child to cross.

Above right: The National Outdoor Ice Skating Races, a popular winter sporting event which is held at St. Paul.

MINNESOTA

(Above) Louis Goldman, Rapho-Guillumette; (right) Minnesota Division of Publicity; (others) George Waters, Rapho-Guillumette.

Below: A modernistic Lutheran church, the Church of the Good Shepherd, which is located in a suburb of Minneapolis.

Right: Split Rock Lighthouse on Lake Superior, near Duluth, warns mariners on the Great Lakes of dangerous reefs.

liam J. and Charles H. Mayo, opened his Rochester Clinic in 1889. The Mayo Clinic and its partner, the Mayo Foundation, affiliated with the University of Minnesota, have become internationally renowned for their contributions to medical science. In 1954 a team of university doctors scored a significant breakthrough with the development of the cross-circulation method of open-heart surgery. The Variety Club Heart Hospital on the university campus was noteworthy as the only hospital in the United States devoted exclusively to research in techniques of surgery and treatment for chronic heart patients.

The arts in Minnesota have partaken rather less of the spirit of experimentation and independence. The literary products of Minnesotans who have achieved wide attention have, however, discernible roots in the frequently rebellious mood, most marked in politics, of the state's citizens. Ole Rölvaag's *Giants in the Earth,* Sinclair Lewis' *Main Street* and *Babbitt,* and F. Scott Fitzgerald's novels of youthful despair each in some measure mirrors the values and problems of the region and its people.

Music in the state owes much to early German and Scandinavian pioneers. Numerous German instrumental groups were formed in the first decades of statehood; out of them in 1903 came the Minneapolis Symphony Orchestra (q.v.), brought to world fame under the batons of Eugene Ormandy and Dimitri Mitropoulos. The sacred choral music of the Scandinavians reached a high point in the St. Olaf College Choir at Northfield, led for many years by F. Melius Christiansen.

Architecture, sculpture, and painting in Minnesota have, for the most part, followed the prevailing conventional mode. The precisely geometric grain elevators that rise uncompromisingly against the sky are the state's one original contribution to functional architecture. Except for Indian survivals that are somewhat artificially cultivated, there is no real folk art in the state; machine products followed pioneers too quickly. But there is a developing tradition in leisure-time practice and appreciation of the arts. The Institute of Arts, the Walker Art Center, and the American Swedish Institute, all in Minneapolis, are centers of lively activity. In drama and the dance many amateur and semiprofessional groups give regular performances. The University Theatre's touring company performs before midwestern high schools and occasionally abroad. The Tyrone Guthrie Theatre opened in Minneapolis in 1963, with a repertory company. In St. Paul the Arts and Sciences Center houses an art gallery, a theater, and a science museum.

Other organizations devoted to intellectual pursuits are numerous. The oldest institution in the state is the Minnesota Historical Society, incorporated in 1849. Its library and museum galleries in St. Paul preserve important historical resources in records and goods; its publications department has produced more than 100 volumes and issues two periodicals.

The James Ford Bell Museum of Natural History on the Minneapolis campus of the University of Minnesota provides exhibits, lecture programs, and occasional publications for its patrons, including large numbers of school children.

Religion.—The early religious history of the state reflected both the racial backgrounds and the cheerfully independent leanings of Minnesota pioneers. The first rush of immigration in the 1850's brought Irish and German Catholics in force, particularly to St. Paul, and a little later Scandinavian arrivals established numerous Lutheran congregations. Later immigrants founded, in lesser numbers, churches of other denominations. The various Protestant bodies, even within a single denomination, showed a disinclination to unite, and by 1870 there were 877 organized churches in the state; by 1900, 4,000. Consolidation became more marked in the 20th century.

The early dominance of Catholics and Lutherans carried over into the 20th century, as the two remained Minnesota's strongest religious groups.

8. PLACES OF INTEREST

Visitor and resident alike are drawn to Minnesota state parks and state and national forests by their unusual natural beauty. The state park system, begun in 1889 and greatly expanded during the 1930's, includes 86 recreational areas comprising more than 150,000 acres. Among the well-known parks are Itasca, including within its boundaries the headwaters of the Mississippi; Interstate, with the famed Dalles of the St. Croix rock formations; and the ruggedly primitive Scenic. The 54 forests in the state system cover 8,186,299 acres. Superior National Forest, largest in continental United States, lies in the Arrowhead region. Here the Echo and Gunflint trails wind through impressive wilderness. The entire Arrowhead country is a center of resort activity.

Minnesota's two national monuments lie at opposite corners of the state. In the northeast is the Grand Portage National Historic Site, an 18th century trading post which has been restored; and in the southwest Pipestone National Monument preserves the quarries from which the Indians obtained material for their peace pipes. Other scenic and historic sites are the Round Tower of Fort Snelling (St. Paul); the largest open pit mine in the world (Hibbing); the North Shore Drive and Split Rock Lighthouse, tallest in the nation (Duluth-Lake Superior); and Minnehaha Falls (Minneapolis), inspiration for Henry W. Longfellow's *Hiawatha.*

Throughout the year carnivals and festivals are numerous and varied. The Twin Cities celebrate the extremes of climate: St. Paul with its Winter Carnival in January and Minneapolis with its aquatennial in July. Both offer parades, pageantry, and sports of the season. Lumbering legend and history are annually revived by Bemidji and Brainerd in their Paul Bunyan carnivals, and by Stillwater in its lumberjack day; Montevideo bows to its South American namesake in a July fiesta; Dan Patch days in Savage honor the famous champion horse.

The varied national make-up of the state's people is dramatized every three years by the International Institute of St. Paul in its Festival of Nations, at which the foreign-born of the community and their descendants display their Old World heritage in craft and food, song and dance. St. Paul is also the home of the annual Minnesota State Fair, a gargantuan mélange of agricultural displays, art exhibits, and sporting events, which attracts more than a million visitors on Labor Day and the nine days preceding.

9. FAMOUS MEN AND WOMEN

Many Minnesotans (by birth or residence) have achieved national distinction. They include the following:

Politics and Government.—Ignatius Donnelly (1831–1901), political crusader and philosopher; John Albert Johnson (1861–1909) and Floyd B. Olson (1891–1936), governors; Harold Edward Stassen (1907–), governor and disarmament adviser to President Dwight D. Eisenhower; Frank Billings Kellogg (1856–1937), secretary of state under President Calvin Coolidge; Pierce Butler (1866–1939), associate justice of the United States Supreme Court; Hubert Horatio Humphrey, Jr. (1911–), senator and vice president under President Lyndon B. Johnson; Orville Lothrop Freeman (1918–), governor and secretary of agriculture under President John F. Kennedy and Lyndon B. Johnson; Walter Wolfgang Heller (1915–), chairman of the Council of Economic Advisers under Presidents Kennedy and Johnson; Eugene Joseph McCarthy (1916–), senator.

Business and Industry.—John Sargent Pillsbury (1828–1901), Charles Alfred Pillsbury (1842–1899), Cadwallader Colden Washburn (1818–1882), and John Crosby (1829–1887) in flour milling; Frederick Weyerhaeuser (1834–1914) in lumbering; Leonidas Merritt (1844–1926) and Edward W. Davis (1888–) in mining; James Jerome Hill (1838–1936) in railroad building; Charles Augustus Lindbergh (1902–) in aviation.

Agriculture.—Oliver H. Kelley (1826–1913), founder of the National Grange.

The Professions.—William J. Mayo (1861–1939) and Charles H. Mayo (1865–1939), surgeons; Lotus Delta Coffman (1875–1938) and George Edgar Vincent (1864–1941), university presidents; Thorstein Bunde Veblen (1857–1929), economist and philosopher.

Military.—Lauris Norstad (1907–) supreme Allied commander, Europe (NATO).

Religion.—Henry Benjamin Whipple (1822–1901), Episcopal bishop; John Ireland (1838–1918), Roman Catholic archbishop.

Arts and Letters.—Sinclair Lewis (1885–1951), F. Scott Fitzgerald (1896–1940), and Ole Edvart Rölvaag (1876–1931), novelists; Cameron Booth (1892–) and Adolf Arthur Dehn (1895–), painters; Paul Manship (1885–1966), sculptor; Cass Gilbert (1859–1934), architect; Wanda Gág (1893–1946), writer and illustrator; F. Melius Christiansen (1871–1955), choral conductor and composer.

10. HISTORY

About 20,000 years ago a Pleistocene epoch people roamed the lands that are now Minnesota. The skeleton of one, known as Minnesota Man, was found near Pelican Rapids in 1931. Much later, Indian inhabitants left evidence of their activities in abandoned village sites and in mounds. But probably the most popularly known, and certainly the most controversial, of Minnesota's archaeological remains is one of unproved authenticity, the Kensington Rune Stone, discovered in 1898, which purports to record a visit of Vikings to the area in 1362.

Exploration.—Continuous recorded history begins with the intrepid sons of New France, who came seeking a route to the Pacific and on to Cathay. Pushing westward from their settlements on the lower St. Lawrence they discovered the Great Lakes one after another, and then, drawn on by the Indian tales of a great river "called the Mechasipi" and of a western sea "whose waters are not fit to drink," they followed the river routes from Lakes Michigan and Superior into the upper Mississippi Valley. They did not find the passage to the East they sought, but the wealth of furs to be exploited and of Indian souls to be won brought trader and missionary to join the explorer. Participating, directly or indirectly, in the opening of Minnesota country were such figures of the French regime in American history as Robert Cavelier, sieur de La Salle; Samuel de Champlain; Jacques Marquette and Louis Jolliet; Jean Nicolet; Pierre Esprit Radisson and Médart Chouart, sieur des Groseilliers; Father Louis Hennepin; Daniel Greysolon, sieur Duluth (Du Lhut); and Pierre Gaultier de Varennes, sieur de La Vérendrye. Through their efforts the great northern wilderness was claimed as part of the French Empire in America.

Thus it remained for a century. But when France yielded to Great Britain in the Treaty of Paris, 1763, the Union Jack replaced the flag of France in the Minnesota country east of the Mississippi. The area west of the Mississippi came under the sovereignty of Spain, but in actuality British traders and trading companies were in control of the entire upper Mississippi Valley. With the successful conclusion of the American Revolution, Minnesota East passed into possession of the United States. It was joined by Minnesota West as a part of the Louisiana Purchase. The British, however, remained in control of the region and its trade until well after the War of 1812.

Settlement.—The earliest effective step toward American occupation of the Minnesota country was the building of Fort Anthony in 1819–1820 (renamed Fort Snelling in 1825) at the junction of the Mississippi and Minnesota rivers. The fort served not only as a military center on the frontier, but even more as a base for further exploration of the wilderness and as a nucleus for settlement. Here the soldiers made rudimentary beginnings in the economic activities that would later characterize the state—agriculture, flour milling, lumbering.

Actual settlement got really under way with the government's purchase from the Indians, in 1837, of the triangle of land between the St. Croix and the Mississippi rivers. Once the land had been bought and opened to settlers, the pioneer lumbermen, farmers, artisans, townsite speculators, storekeepers, doctors, and teachers began to arrive.

During this early period of settlement the Minnesota country was, in succession, a part of Michigan, Iowa, and Wisconsin territories. Finally, in 1849, settlement had progressed far enough for Congress to authorize the organization of Minnesota Territory. When, two years later, the federal government took over from the Indians the bulk of territorial lands west of the Mississippi, the influx of settlers, both from older communities to the east and from Europe, began in earnest. Towns sprang up, some actually and some on paper only, stagecoach lines provided regular service, railroads were chartered, hotels, churches, and schools were built, newspapers multiplied. In 1858 Minnesota was admitted to the Union as the 32d state.

Two years later, when the Civil War broke out, the infant commonwealth responded to President Lincoln's call by being the first state to offer troops to the Union cause. Its soldiers, 22,000 in all, served throughout the war, distinguishing themselves with special gallantry at Gettysburg. But within its own borders the state faced an even greater crisis, the Sioux outbreak of 1862, one of the worst Indian uprisings in the history of the nation. When the French entered Minnesota country about 1669, they found the Dakotan Sioux in possession of most of the land. But during the following two centuries the Sioux fell on hard times; not only did the advancing white man take, by force or scarcely more honorable treaty, their ancient lands, but they were also constantly harassed and steadily pushed back by the Chippewa (or Ojibway) Indians. They made their final bloody protest in 1862, but at the end the result was their complete and final expulsion from Minnesota.

The decade of the 1870's further tested the young state—with the great snowstorm of 1873, the panic of that same year, the "grasshopper" plague of 1873–1878, and the Minneapolis flour mill explosion of 1878. Although war and disaster had their temporary effects, the rapid growth of the state was not deterred.

Maturity.—Minnesota remained a pioneer community for some years in its western and northern reaches, but in its older areas it soon began its development toward maturity. Most of the important aspects of this development have been touched on in foregoing sections: the change from a predominantly rural society to one marked by industrialization and urbanization; the shift from exploitation to conservation of natural resources; the conversion from one-crop farming to a diversified agriculture and from a simple to a complex economy; the growth of cooperatives; the increasing assumption by the state of responsibility for the public welfare; the participation in cultural and intellectual pursuits. To these should be added the gradual replacement of frontier preoccupation with the interests of the local community by a growing sense of oneness with the nation and, more recently, with the world.

Politics.—Minnesota political history has been marked by a tradition of mild intransigency. Although the Republican Party has, over the years, dominated the state government—as shown concretely in the list of state governors—it has been under almost constant challenge from a succession of third-party movements expressing political protest. These groups have had more influence in governmental policies and legislative developments than their relatively few victories at the polls would indicate.

Minnesota has been the center of what historians call "the agrarian crusade," and for many decades the farmers were considerably more important than labor in the protest groups; organized labor was slower to resort to direct political action as a means of achieving its goals. Nonetheless, labor has been represented to some degree in virtually all the phases of the protest movement: the Anti-Monopoly Party and Greenback Party of the 1870's, the Farmers' Alliance Party of the 1880's, the Populist Party of the 1890's, and the Nonpartisan League of the 1910's. But the full-fledged union of the two forces came only with the organization of the Farmer-Labor Party and its election of Henrik Shipstead and Magnus Johnson to Congress in 1922 and 1923. The Farmer-Labor Party achieved control of the state in the 1930's with the election of Floyd B. Olson as governor for three terms and Elmer Benson as governor for one term.

The Democrats were until the 1950's for the most part an "also ran" group in Minnesota. They gained strength through the state's consistent support of Franklin D. Roosevelt from 1932 to 1944 and of Harry S Truman in 1948. (President Roosevelt was the first Democratic presidential candidate ever to win Minnesota's vote.) After joining forces in 1944 with the Farmer-Laborites in the Democratic-Farmer-Labor Party, they developed young and vigorous leaders, and elected Hubert H. Humphrey to the United States Senate in 1948 and most of their candidates to state office, including the governorship, in 1954, 1956, and 1958. At the same time, however, the presidential vote in 1952 and 1956 went to the Republicans. In 1960 the Democratic candidate for president and the Republican candidate for governor were the voters' choices. The state's first contest for a 4-year gubernatorial term, in 1962, saw the Democratic-Farmer-Labor candidate defeat the Republican incumbent by the margin of 91 votes out of more than 1.25 million ballots cast—the closest election for governor in the state's history. However, after supporting Democrat Lyndon B. Johnson for president by an overwhelming majority in 1964 (when Minnesota's Senator Hubert H. Humphrey was his running mate), the state's voters elected a Republican governor in 1966. Four years later a Democrat was elected.

That Minnesota in recent decades has so often given its presidential vote to one party and its vote for state officers to the other major party is evidence of a vital fact in its politics: its voters have become more than usually independent about following party lines. It is perhaps the persistence of a third party group in one form or another, causing shifting alliances and allegiances, that has made Minnesota voters independent.

11. BIBLIOGRAPHY

General: Federal Writers' Project of the Works Progress Administration, *Minnesota: A State Guide,* rev. ed. (New York 1954); Szarkowski, John, *The Face of Minnesota* (Minneapolis 1958); Poatgieter, A. Hermina, and Dunn, James T., eds., *Gopher Reader: Minnesota's Story in Words and Pictures* (St. Paul 1958); Brings, Lawrence M., ed., *Minnesota Heritage* (Minneapolis 1960).

Physical Features: Roberts, Thomas S., *Birds of Minnesota,* 2 vols. (Minneapolis 1936); Eddy, Samuel, and Surber, T., *Northern Fishes* (Minneapolis 1943); Gunderson, Harvey L., and Beer, J. R., *The Mammals of Minnesota* (Minneapolis 1953); Schwartz, George M., and Thiel, G. A., *Minnesota's Rocks and Waters: a Geological Story* (Minneapolis 1954); Rosendahl, Carl O., *Trees and Shrubs of the Upper Midwest* (Minneapolis 1955); Borchert, John R., *Minnesota's Changing Geography* (Minneapolis 1959).

Population: Sickles, Alice L., *Around the World in St. Paul* (Minneapolis 1945); Nelson, Lowry, Ramsey, C. E., and Toews, J., *A Century of Population Growth in Minnesota* (Minneapolis 1954); Nelson, Lowry, *The Minnesota Community: Country and Town in Transition* (Minneapolis 1960).

Government: *The Minnesota Manual* (St. Paul, biennially); Anderson, William, and Weidner, Edward W., eds., *Intergovernmental Relations in the United States as Observed in the State of Minnesota,* monographs, 10 vols. (Minneapolis 1950–1960).

Economic Factors: De Kruif, Paul H., *Seven Iron Men* (New York 1929); Jarchow, Merrill E., *The Earth Brought Forth: A History of Minnesota Agriculture to 1885* (St. Paul 1949); Larson, Agnes M., *History of the White Pine Industry in Minnesota* (Minneapolis 1949); Storck, John, and Teague, W. D., *Flour for Man's Bread: A History of Milling* (Minneapolis 1952).

Education and Health: Minnesota Commission on Higher Education, *Higher Education in Minnesota* (Minneapolis 1950); Gray, James, *The University of Minnesota, 1851–1951* (Minneapolis 1951); Jordan, Philip D., *The People's Health* (St. Paul 1953); Clapesattle, Helen, *The Doctors Mayo* (Minneapolis 1941; abridged ed., 1954).

Cultural Life: O'Connor, William Van, ed., *A History of the Arts in Minnesota* (Minneapolis 1958).

History and Politics: Folwell, William W., *History of Minnesota,* 4 vols. (St. Paul 1921–1930); Hicks, John D., *The Populist Revolt* (Minneapolis 1931); Hartsough, Mildred L., *From Canoe to Steel Barge on the Upper Mississippi* (Minneapolis 1934); Stephenson,

George M., *John Lind of Minnesota* (Minneapolis 1935); Blegen, Theodore C., *Building Minnesota* (New York 1938); id., *Grass Roots History* (Minneapolis 1947); id., *The Land Lies Open* (Minneapolis 1949); Blegen, Theodore C., and Jordan, P. D., eds., *With Various Voices* (St. Paul 1949); Helmes, Winifred G., *John A. Johnson, the People's Governor* (Minneapolis 1949); Mayer, George H., *The Political Career of Floyd B. Olson* (Minneapolis 1950); Nute, Grace L., *The Voyageur* (New York 1931; St. Paul 1955); Heilbron, Bertha L., *The Thirty-Second State: A Pictorial History of Minnesota* (St. Paul 1958); Blegen, Theodore C., and Nydahl, Theodore L., *Minnesota History: A Guide to Reading and Study* (Minneapolis 1960); Mitau, G. Theodore, *Politics in Minnesota* (Minneapolis 1960); Blegen, Theodore C., *Minnesota: A History of the State* (Minneapolis 1963); Minnesota Historical Society, *Minnesota History* (St. Paul, 4 issues yearly); id., *The Gopher Historian* (St. Paul, 3 issues yearly).

JEANNE SINNEN, *Senior Editor, University Press, University of Minnesota.*

MINNESOTA, University of, a coeducational state institution of higher learning, with campuses at Minneapolis, St. Paul, Duluth, and Morris. It was established by an act of the territorial legislature in 1851 and confirmed by the state constitution adopted in 1857. The present charter was adopted in 1868 and the first collegiate work began the next year. The university is governed by a board of 12 regents elected by the legislature for six-year terms, 4 members being elected at each biennial session.

The university's colleges or schools granting degrees of bachelor or higher comprise those of Science, Literature, and the Arts (known as the Arts College); Engineering, Architecture, Chemistry, Mines and Metallurgy, and Physics (grouped in the Institute of Technology); Agriculture, Forestry, and Home Economics; Education; Dentistry; Medical, providing medical, medical technology, physical therapy, and occupational therapy curriculums; Nursing; Public Health; Business Administration; Law; Pharmacy; Veterinary Medicine; University College, providing special study programs to fit individual needs; and the Graduate School. Periods of college preparation required for entry into the professional schools include one year for Pharmacy, two years for Dentistry, Veterinary Medicine, Education, and Business Administration, and three years for Law and Medicine. The Duluth campus, which became part of the university in 1947, offers courses leading to the bachelor degree in elementary teaching and liberal arts, as well as numerous preprofessional courses. The Morris campus opened and enrolled its first freshman class in the fall of 1960. In addition, two-year courses leading to the associate in arts degree are provided by the General College and the Duluth Branch, while the Arts College grants two-year associate in liberal arts degrees. Shorter courses leading to certificates in certain specialized subjects such as dental assisting and practical nursing are also offered. Other divisions include the Summer Session, organized for two terms of five weeks each, and the General Extension division, offering late afternoon and evening extension classes in Minneapolis and St. Paul, Duluth, and elsewhere (this division also operates the university's 5,000-watt radio station KUOM).

The university offers a wide range of student services, including loans and scholarships, a library system with nearly 2 million volumes, the University Theater dramatic group, and many sports, musical, and other activities. The Minneapolis Symphony Orchestra presents its concerts in the Northrop Memorial Auditorium on the Minneapolis campus, while the Metropolitan Opera Association of New York presents a spring season in the same auditorium.

MALCOLM M. WILLEY.

MINNESOTA HISTORICAL SOCIETY, a society organized in 1849 to collect and preserve materials relating to Minnesota history. It is located in St. Paul, Minn., has 3,000 members, and is supported mainly by legislative appropriation. Its collections, comprising one of the largest historical libraries in the Northwest, include books, pamphlets, and state and federal documents; manuscripts; paintings, photographs, and prints; and a vast collection of newspapers published in the state since 1849. The society's museum, with its four large galleries, depicts the story of the Minnesota country from prehistoric to modern times. The society publishes a quarterly magazine, *Minnesota History,* a junior magazine, *The Gopher Historian* (issued periodically), and books on various aspects of the state's history. It holds an annual meeting, conducts tours to historic sites, assists the state's 87 county historical societies, and gives reference service on all phases of Minnesota history. The society's undertakings include the restoration of Fort Snelling, Fort Ridgely, and the homes of Charles A. Lindbergh in Little Falls, Morrison County, and the Civil War general, William Gates Le Duc, in Hastings, Dakota County; and the development of the Mille Lacs Museum (a state Indian museum) at Kathio, site of a decisive battle between the Sioux and Chippewa Indians around 1750.

RUSSELL W. FRIDLEY, *Director.*

MINNESOTA RIVER, river, rising in Big Stone Lake, on the Minnesota-South Dakota border. It flows southeast 224 miles to Mankato, where it is joined by the Blue Earth River, then 108 miles northeast to the Mississippi River at Mendota, opposite St. Paul. Its total length is 232 miles, and it drains a rich agricultural region. The Minnesota follows the valley of the prehistoric River Warren, southern outlet of Lake Agassiz. It was formerly called the St. Peter or St. Pierre, and was an important route for explorers and fur traders. At its mouth is Fort Snelling.

MINNETONKA, Lake, mĭn'ĕ-tŏng'kȧ, lake, Minnesota, mostly in Hennepin County, 12 miles west of Minneapolis. It is 10 miles long, and has a maximum width of 2.5 miles, an area of 23 square miles, a deeply indented, wooded shoreline, and several small islands. It drains eastward through Minnehaha Creek into the Mississippi River. Once famous for its luxurious, multidecked excursion steamers, it later became a playground for sailboats and speedboats, and has many resorts and summer homes. Its natural beauty is celebrated in the songs *By the Waters of Minnetonka* by Thurlow Lieurance and *From the Land of the Sky-Blue Water* by Charles Wakefield Cadman.

MINNOW, mĭn'ō, a name used for many of the smaller members of the carp family (Cyprinidae, q.v.) whose numerous genera and species are dominant in the fresh waters of the northern continents, and numerous in the East Indies, but do not reach Australia.

Fishes of their order, the Ostariophysi, share a unique feature called the Weberian mechanism.

This is a chain of small ossicles formed by modification of the first four vertebrae behind the skull and connecting the air bladder and the spaces surrounding the inner ear. The mechanism appears to be a sense organ.

Cyprinidae have pharyngeal but no jaw teeth. There is a single dorsal fin, usually of soft rays only; the head is naked and the body densely scaled in most species. The groups are distinguished from each other by scale and fin counts, color pattern, and the structure of the air bladder.

Some of the species are vegetarian; others eat insects or their larvae, or smaller fishes. They spawn in large schools in shallows in spring and summer, the females depositing four or five hundred eggs which are immediately fertilized by the males. There is no parental care. At this time the males develop small tubercles on head or body; these are lost immediately after spawning.

C. W. COATES.

MINO DA FIESOLE, mē'nô dä fyâ'zô-lā, Italian sculptor: b. Poppi, Italy, c. 1431; d. Florence, 1484. He is said to have been a pupil of Desiderio da Settignano, whom he resembles in style, although his work is more uneven in quality. Except for sojourns in Rome in 1454 and 1463, and from about 1473 to 1480, he spent his life in Florence, and there and in nearby Fiesole are a number of his best works. Among them are the tomb of Bishop Leonardo Salutati and the altarpiece in Fiesole Cathedral; the tombs of Bernardo Giugni and Hugo, margrave of Tuscany, and the altarpiece in the Badia, Florence; a tabernacle in Sant' Ambrogio, and busts of Piero de' Medici, Giovanni de' Medici, and Rinaldo della Luna in the Bargello, Florence. In Rome he collaborated with Giovanni Dalmata on the tomb of Pope Paul II (of which fragments remain in the museum of St. Peter's), and with Andrea Bregno in that of Cristoforo della Rovere in Santa Maria del Popolo. Among other Roman works are the monument of Niccolò Cardinal Forteguerri in Santa Cecilia in Trastevere and that of Pietro Cardinal Riario in Santi Apostoli (in collaboration with Dalmata and Bregno). The National Gallery of Art in Washington, D.C., has several of his pieces, including a bust of Astorgio Manfredi, a *Madonna and Child* (bas-relief), and two figures, *Faith* and *Charity,* all in marble.

MIÑO RIVER, mē'nyô (Port. MINHO, mē'nyōō; ancient MINIUS), river of northwestern Spain and northernmost Portugal. It rises in northern Lugo Province, Spain, flows southward through the Galician mountains past Lugo to its juncture with the Sil River, its chief tributary, then turns southwestward past Orense, and for its last 47 miles forms the Spanish-Portuguese boundary. It empties into the Atlantic at Caminha, Portugal. With a total length of 210 miles, the Miño is navigable from Monção, Portugal, to its mouth, a distance of 28 miles. Its valley and that of the Sil are noted for vineyards.

MINOAN CIVILIZATION. See ARCHAEOLOGY—*Old World* (Neolithic and Later); CHRONOLOGY—*Minoan Chronology;* CRETE; GREECE—*2. Ancient History and Culture: To 330 A.D.* (Prehistoric Greece [To c. 1000 B.C.]); HISTORY, ANCIENT.

MINOR, mī'nẽr, in law, a person who has not reached the age at which the law recognizes a general contractual capacity and at which full civil rights are accorded. In England and generally in the United States, a minor is one under 21 years of age; however, in some states of the United States females become of age at the end of the 18th year, while some states make all persons adults upon their marriage. Among legal disabilities generally applicable to minors are inability to make a binding contract or a will, or to vote. In modern societies, minors benefit from laws designed to safeguard them from want or neglect, to protect them against certain criminal acts, and to mitigate, in some degree, criminal culpability. See INFANT.

MINOR, in music, a term applied to intervals and scales. The interval between one note and another of the diatonic scale is named according to the number of tones between them (both notes included), but some intervals—thirds, for example—have four semitones, and some only three. The former is a major interval or major third; the latter, a minor interval or minor third (see also INTERVAL). A minor scale differs from a major scale in that it has a minor third. When descending, it may also have a flatted seventh and sixth (melodic minor scale), or, both ascending and descending, a flatted sixth (harmonic minor scale).

MINOR ARTS. See DECORATIVE ART—*Minor Decorative Arts;* also EMBROIDERY; ENAMELS AND ENAMELING; FURNITURE; GLASS; LACQUER AND LACQUERWORK; METALWORK; POTTERY; TEXTILE FABRICS.

MINOR FRIARS or FRIARS MINOR. See FRANCISCANS.

MINORCA. See MENORCA.

MINORITIES, mĭ-nŏr'ĭ-tĭz. The treaties and declarations made under the auspices of the League of Nations provided protection for "racial, religious or linguistic minorities," but in practice these words were found to be imperfectly descriptive of the groups whose protection was intended. Some sociologists have referred to minority groups of distinctive national and cultural characteristics, while others have given greater emphasis to the subjective element of national consciousness which might characterize minorities not distinguished from the rest of the population by obvious features of language, dress, habits, or physique. Without some easily recognizable characteristic associated by both the minority and the majority with stereotyped traits, a minority is likely to be rapidly absorbed and lose its identity. The term "minority" is not usually applied to groups when such absorption is not resisted by either the minority itself or the majority of the population.

At the World Congress of Sociology held in Zurich, Switzerland, in September 1950, Professor Louis Wirth of the University of Chicago emphasized the inferior status of minorities by defining them as "groups distinguished from the rest of society by racial or cultural characteristics [which have] become the objects of differential and inferior treatment, and [have] develop[ed] a consciousness of their inferior status" (*International Social Science Bulletin,* vol. 3, p. 410, Paris 1951). The United Nations Subcommission on Prevention of Discrimination and

Protection of Minorities, however, excluded the ideas both of race and of inferiority from its definition, which included as minorities "only those non-dominant groups in a population which possess and wish to preserve stable ethnic, religious or linguistic traditions or characteristics markedly different from those of the rest of the population" (*Yearbook on Human Rights for 1950,* p. 490, New York 1952). The subcommission also insisted that the minority must include a number of persons sufficient by themselves to develop these characteristics, and that its members must be loyal to the country of which they may be nationals.

Origin and Character of Minorities.—The movements of peoples, ideologies, and political boundaries have meant that distinctive minorities have been common phenomena throughout history. This was true of the Samaritans in ancient Palestine, of Christians in the early Roman Empire, and of Jews and heretical sects like the Albigenses in medieval Christendom. This development has, however, been accentuated by the rise of nationalism in the post-Renaissance period and especially since the French Revolution. Under the influence of Giuseppe Mazzini and other advocates of the principle of nationality, the conception that political boundaries should conform to the national characteristics of the people became a political movement and stimulated governments and other groups to mold people by education, propaganda, and political and legal action to the national stereotype in the minds of the leaders of the movement. Minorities were groups that resisted such efforts at assimilation or that were so different from the majority that the latter did not wish to assimilate them. They remained distinctive groups in the nation and were considered an unfortunate derogation from the principle of nationality.

In the New World immigrant groups in general wished to be assimilated, and usually were after a generation or two. They consequently did not constitute minorities, although the Indians, Negroes, and Asians, as well as the French Canadians, manifest some characteristics of minorities.

In Buddhist, Confucian, and Hindu Asia the spirit of nationality developed much later, and the religious ideas in this area tended to minimize cultural differences as a foundation for political opposition, although the caste system in India may manifest the subordination of the Dravidian majority to the invading Aryan minority in the 2d millennium B.C. In this area converts to missionary religions such as Islam and Christianity also have some of the characteristics of minorities.

In Africa, European minorities have sought to dominate the natives as the Aryans did in ancient India, but such dominant groups are not usually considered minorities. In southern and eastern Africa the development of large Indian populations has presented a minority problem. In the Union of South Africa the white population, itself divided between English- and Afrikaans-speaking groups, attempts to treat both the Indian minority and the native African majority as minorities.

The Soviet Union, with some 150 distinct nationalities, has claimed to be a multinational state, according each group cultural autonomy, and those occupying large areas political autonomy. The dominant Great Russian nationality controlling the central organs of the monolithic Communist Party has, however, tended to develop minority problems among some of the smaller nationalities both within the USSR and in its surrounding satellite areas.

In western Europe, on the breakup of the medieval system, strong states governed by dynamic monarchs arose before the idea of nationalism had developed. By means of the printing press, education, and propaganda, their governments, integrated populations into nations based largely on distinctiveness of language. The Scots and Welsh in Great Britain, the Bretons and Provençals in France, the Catalans, Andalusians, and Basques in Spain, and the Sicilians and Neapolitans in Italy can hardly be called minorities. Whether Italian- and French-speaking Swiss and Flemish-speaking Belgians are minorities is a more debatable question. In the Scandinavian countries there were few groups that could be called minorities. In the German Empire there were French, Polish, Danish, and Jewish minorities. The minority status of the last named, proceeding from religious and cultural distinctiveness, dates from the Middle Ages, and is typical of minorities in that the Jews usually wished to maintain their distinctiveness and were sporadically persecuted.

In eastern Europe and the Middle East the minority problem has been of major importance. Apart from Jews and gypsies who live in small groups throughout much of this area, Poles, Balts, Ukrainians (Ruthenians), Czechs, Slovaks, Yugoslavs, Hungarians, Greeks, Armenians, Syrians, and Arabs were minorities in the German, Russian, Austro-Hungarian, and Turkish empires before World War I. After the war most of these groups established independent countries in which they formed the majority, but it was impossible to devise boundaries which would exclude all minorities. In the 14 countries bound by minority treaties or declarations in 1930, which had a combined population of 130 million, minorities were estimated at about 30 million persons, of whom about half were divided equally among Jews, Germans, and Ruthenians, and the other half among some 22 other nationalities. The minorities therefore constituted about 23 per cent of the total population of these countries, ranging from over 30 per cent in Czechoslovakia and Poland to less than 10 per cent in Austria and Greece.

World War II, with its unparalleled persecutions, displacement of populations, and changes of boundaries, resulting in an extraordinary development of national, ideological, and political intolerance, greatly augmented the seriousness of the minority problem in eastern and central Europe, and extended the problem to Asia and Africa and even to the Americas.

The Minority Problem.—The rise of the principle of nationality and the practical propaganda of nationalism have created the general opinion that minorities are undesirable. Resistance to this principle by the Habsburg empire contributed to its demise after World War I. The theory of some liberals like the 1st Baron Acton, who opposed the principle of nationality and drew attention to the stimulating influence of many nationalities under a common government, has generally been discarded, although some advocates of this opinion can still be found in the United States and Great Britain, and it is the official doctrine of the Soviet Union. Advocates of this theory, at least in the West, believe that it can be realized only if education and propaganda are devoted to encouraging a spirit of tolerance and individual freedom, and if constitutional and legal guarantees support principles of human equality and freedom. Such methods, which had considerable influence in the 19th century in moderating the sentiment of nationalism have declined in influence with the spread of international tensions and ideological conflicts characteristic of the 20th century.

Efforts to realize the principle of nationality, on the other hand, have led to demands for boundary changes which restore irredentas or which permit subject nationalities to become national states. Many such changes were effected after World War I, often as a result of plebiscites. Another possible solution is the conversion of minorities to the national way of life by means of education, propaganda, and legal pressure. Nearly all countries have at times indulged in such Germanization, Italianization, Americanization, or other assimilation movements. Treaties between Poland and Czechoslovakia in 1925 and between Germany and Poland in 1937 reciprocally forbade such denationalization efforts. Still another method of solving the problem is through an exchange of populations, such as those which took place between Greece and Bulgaria in 1919, between Greece and Turkey in 1923, and in the Tyrol (Tirol) in 1939 by agreement between Benito Mussolini and Adolf Hitler after the German seizure of Austria.

The more barbarous method of expulsion or extermination of populations to assure national uniformity in the existing area of a country was initiated by Turkey in the case of Armenians even before World War I, and was carried out on a larger scale by Nazi Germany, involving the extermination of some 6 million members of Jewish and other minorities and the driving of many others into exile. Soviet Russia exterminated many Poles and deported or exterminated a considerable proportion of the Balts from Estonia, Latvia, and Lithuania. Poland and Czechoslovakia ejected millions of Germans from their territories after World War II, and the formation of the new state of Israel resulted in the migration of 800,000 to 900,000 Arab refugees. The separation of India and Pakistan displaced at least 6 million persons and cost the lives of hundreds of thousands.

These methods of realizing the principle of nationality, which was advanced in the early 19th century as a doctrine of liberalism, progressively increased intolerance and barbarity and raised a serious question as to the validity of the principle altogether.

Protection by the League of Nations.—The regime of minority protection as established under the League of Nations was a political rather than a legal device. It was based on a compromise between the principles of nationality and of liberalism which had been insisted upon by the great powers in treaty provisions intended to protect minorities in the Netherlands (1814), Greece (1830), and Turkey and the Balkans (1856, 1878). It was formally established through the acceptance of concrete obligations in treaties or declarations by the countries in which the problem was most serious, either as a condition of their recognition as independent countries or as a requirement for the establishment of peace in the case of countries which had been defeated in World War I. Such treaties were made after the war with Poland, Yugoslavia, Czechoslovakia, Rumania, and Greece, and minority protection provisions were included in the peace treaties with Austria, Bulgaria, Hungary, and Turkey. No such provisions were included in the peace treaty with Germany, but they were included in the conventions on Upper Silesia and Memel. Declarations accepting obligations similar to those in these treaties were made by Albania, Estonia, Latvia, Lithuania, and Iraq, and by Finland in regard to the Åland Islands. Each of these countries undertook to protect the lives, liberty, and religious freedom of all inhabitants without distinction of birth, nationality, language, race, or religion; to admit the inhabitants of newly acquired territories to its nationality with a right of option for another nationality within a year; to assure civil liberties and linguistic rights to all nationals; to assure special educational and cultural facilities to all nationals who constituted racial, religious, or linguistic minorities; and to accept the League of Nations guarantee of these provisions.

In order to maintain these provisions the League received petitions from individuals residing in the countries concerned. The petitions were screened by the Secretariat and, if found receivable, were considered by a committee of the League of Nations Council. The council would consider the situation indicated by the petition only if it was sponsored by a member of the League. This procedure indicated that the rights assured by the treaty were individual rather than group rights, and the encouragement of separatist movements among the minorities was thus avoided. It was assumed that the minorities were peaceful inhabitants of the country, or loyal citizens whose object was to remedy abuses and not to disrupt the existing political order. Out of respect for the domestic jurisdiction of the country concerned, petitions were not considered to initiate a legal procedure, but were regarded merely as information which might provide the basis on which some country interested in the minority could initiate a procedure in the council for enforcement of the obligation of the country bound by a minority treaty or declaration. The tendency of the League was conservative. The effort was to protect minority rights without preventing reasonable efforts of the country to assimilate the minorities if it desired to do so.

The concepts of civil liberties for minority individuals, of cultural self-determination for minority groups, and of national solidarity for the country concerned were difficult to reconcile. Minorities themselves usually felt that the protection given by the system was inadequate, often attributing this inadequacy to the political nature of the process and suggesting the establishment of an impartial minorities commission like the Permanent Mandates Commission under the League of Nations. This was not done, but in a few cases opinions were obtained from the Permanent Court of International Justice that were more satisfactory to the minorities than were the council's recommendations. A relatively small number of the petitions sent to the League by members of minorities were considered, and only a small number of those considered resulted in formal action by the council criticizing the country involved. The countries bound by minority agreements resented the discrimination between them and other countries with minorities that were not so bound, and urged that the minority principle either be made universal or be abandoned. They also believed that the system encouraged disloyalty, separatism, and irredentist movements and impeded assimilation.

The United Nations and Minorities.—The United Nations, established in 1945 when the world was slowly recovering from the shock of Hitler's massacres of Jews and other minorities, sought to meet the problem in a more general and more legalistic manner than had the League of Nations. The preamble of the United Nations Charter reaffirmed "faith in fundamental human rights, in the dignity and worth of the human person, in the equal rights of men and women and of nations, large and small," and member nations expressed their determination "to practice tolerance and live together in peace with one another as good neighbors. . . ." These ideas were reasserted as purposes in Article 1, in which are included "respect for the principle of equal rights and self-determination of peoples" and "international cooperation . . . in promoting and encouraging respect for human rights and for fundamental freedoms for all without distinction as to race, sex, language, or religion." These purposes are implemented in various articles of the charter, most concretely in Article 56, by which members "pledge themselves to take joint and separate action in cooperation with the Organization for the achievement of the purposes set forth in Article 55," which include "promotion of universal respect for, and observance of, human rights and fundamental freedoms for all without distinction as to race, sex, language, or religion." Here, as under the League of Nations system, there is a compromise between the ideas of individual rights and group self-determination, but emphasis is placed on individual rights to a greater degree than under the League of Nations system.

To implement these provisions of the charter the United Nations General Assembly approved without dissent a Universal Declaration of Human Rights in 1948, and the United Nations Human Rights Commission has drafted covenants of human rights which would define these rights as formal treaty obligations and provide procedures for their implementation. No such covenant has been approved by the General Assembly, and on April 6, 1953, United States Secretary of State John Foster Dulles, urged by Senate opposition to treaties which might encroach on domestic jurisdiction, said that it would not be the policy of the United States to approve such treaties. This attitude may have been influenced in part by the insistence of the General Assembly, under pressure by Soviet bloc and Asian states, that covenants should be drafted not only on civil liberties, but also on social and economic rights. Articles defining the right of self-determination of peoples were also drafted by the Human Rights Commission. Such provisions looking toward the welfare state and the self-government of subject nationalities and dependent peoples were more disturbing to the West than were provisions setting standards for the protection of civil liberties.

The Subcommission on Prevention of Discrimination and Protection of Minorities, set up under the Human Rights Commission, has studied various minority problems and prepared drafts on the subject for inclusion in the covenants on human rights. Many petitions on human rights were sent to the commission, and those dealing specifically with minority problems were transmitted to the subcommission, but neither body was given power to investigate or act on them.

Despite the many allusions to human rights in the charter and the great efforts of United Nations organs and private groups in the field, the United Nations has no procedure for dealing with minority problems. If the broad obligations of the charter binding members to respect human rights were observed, they would prevent discrimination against minorities, but no means of effective implementation has been devised. Discrimination against and persecution of minorities continue in many parts of the world. The proportion of the world's population suffering because of the failure of governments to respect and protect human and minority rights has probably never been greater in human history. Because the traditions of international law and the modern concept of national sovereignty have treated minority matters as within the domestic jurisdiction of a country, international action to remedy mistreatment is exceptionally difficult. Doubtless little can be done unless international tensions can be reduced, intense nationalism moderated, and a spirit of tolerance and respect for human dignity re-established. This is a problem involving education, political action, legislation, and adjudication, both national and international. Until the general atmosphere is changed, it is doubtful whether effective international procedures for protecting either human or minority rights will be widely accepted.

QUINCY WRIGHT,
Professor of Foreign Affairs, University of Virginia.

Bibliography.—Mair, L. P., *The Protection of Minorities* (New York 1928); Yarmolinsky, Avrahm, *The Jews and Other Minor Nationalities Under the Soviets* (New York 1928); Ladas, Stephen P., *The Exchange of Minorities: Bulgaria, Greece and Turkey* (New York 1932); Stone, Julius, *International Guarantees of Minority Rights* (New York 1932); Robinson, Jacob, and others, *Were the Minority Treaties a Failure?*, Institute of Jewish Affairs (New York 1943); Azcárate y Flórez, Pablo de, *The League of Nations and National Minorities*, tr. from the Spanish by Eileen E. Brooke (Washington 1945); Lauterpacht, Hersch, *International Law and Human Rights* (New York 1950); "Joint Roundtable on the Role of Minorities in International Affairs," *International Social Science Bulletin*, vol. 3, pp. 409–20 (Paris 1951); Claude, Inis L., Jr., *National Minorities, an International Problem* (Cambridge 1955); La Ponce J. A., *The Protection of Minorities* (Berkeley 1960); Barron, Milton, ed., *Minorities in a Changing World* (New York 1967); United Nations, *Yearbook of the United Nations;* United Nations, *Yearbook on Human Rights.*

MINORITY AND PROPORTIONAL REPRESENTATION. The election of a representative from a single-member district falls to the candidate receiving the highest vote. There is no representation for groups supporting other candidates, except insofar as the person elected gives voice to the wishes of such groups. Hence, direct representation is not afforded minority groups. To give them such representation, various European countries, with Norway taking the lead in its Constitution of 1814, have provided for systems of proportional representation, which necessarily operate in plural-member districts. If, for example, seven persons are to be elected to a city council, or from an election area to a larger legislative body, proportional representation among several parties may be accomplished by having three members come from one party with 42 per cent of the total vote, two from another party with about 30 per cent, and one each from two other parties sharing equally the remaining number of votes.

Many plans for voting have been devised, ranging all the way from a single vote per voter (regardless of the number of places to be filled) to a complicated preferential-and-transfer arrangement. If a single vote is allowed each voter, with election falling to the persons with the highest totals of votes, large factions may get no more representation than other groups winning seats. Through such methods as the limited vote, cumulative voting, and preferential voting, however, relative strength may be reflected.

Limited and Cumulative Voting.—Under the limited-vote method the voter casts his ballot for fewer than the number of persons to be elected—for example, he votes for five when nine are to be chosen. This plan permits at least one minority party to share seats with the leading party, preventing the winner-take-all result that characterizes some electoral systems.

In Illinois, under its 1870 constitution, cumulative voting for the House of Representatives is allowed for each of the state's 59 legislative districts. Three representatives are chosen to the legislature from each district, the voter casting all three votes for his favorite candidate, one and one-half votes for each of two candidates, or one vote for each of three different candidates. This plan has no counterpart in other states. The practical workings of the Illinois system have led the two major parties to offer two candidates each, thereby assuring two seats to the stronger party in a district and the third seat to the weaker party. But understandings in advance may lead simply to the running of two candidates by the admittedly stronger group and one candidate by the weaker, thus leaving no real choice to the voters unless there are strong competing minor parties or independent candidates.

List System of Proportional Representation.—Proportional representation operates according to the list system in several European countries. Under this system voters designate their party rather than the candidates of a party, and seats are assigned to the parties in proportion to their total vote. If, for example, 20 persons are to be elected and one party gets 55 per cent of the votes cast, it elects 11; the other party or parties with 45 per cent elect the remaining 9. Actually, more splintering than this takes place, and no party is likely to get more than 30 or 40 per cent of the vote. A party with 5 per cent of the total vote will receive 1 seat in 20. In countries not having the individual vote, party leaders name the sequence of candidates on the list, and those at the top are elected to the number of seats the party gets. A variation of the plan (as in France) allows the voter to indicate his preference as to candidates within each party, as well as to vote for a party list. Those candidates having the highest votes in a list are elected to the number of seats that the party is entitled to by proportional representation.

Under the Weimar Republic (1919–1933) the quota to elect a representative to the German Reichstag was 60,000. A party with 125,000 votes in a district elected two members and had a surplus of 5,000 votes. Surpluses in several districts could accumulate 60,000 votes and thus entitle the party to an additional member for the whole region. The Constitution of the Federal Republic of Germany (1949) provided for a single-member district system for three fifths of each state's representation in the Bundestag and proportional representation for election of the remaining two fifths. (In 1953 the Bundestag adopted a new combination election system.)

Americans often associate the weakness of the Weimar Republic and the Third and Fourth French republics with the multiparty systems of Germany and France, and therefore condemn proportional representation, which encourages the splintering of parties. Essential differences are revealed in the operation of two-party and multiparty systems. In a two-party system the factions of a party generally adjust their differences before an election campaign, but in a multiparty system adjustments are constantly taking place within Parliament after the election. The political pattern of France reflects a highly individualistic people.

Hare System of Proportional Representation.—Under this system, which is named for the English political reformer Thomas Hare (1806–1891) and is used in some United States cities, the voter marks first, second, third, and other choices. Election is based on a quota determined by the following formula: The total vote cast is divided by the number of seats to be filled plus one, and one is added to the quotient. If 100,000 votes are cast and 4 seats are to be filled, divide by 5 to get a quotient of 20,000, then add 1 to get 20,001, which is the quota. A candidate receiving the quota of first-choice votes is elected. Surplus votes are counted for second choices, thus adding to the totals of other candidates. When other candidates reach the quota, their surpluses are distributed to later choices. The next calculation is to drop the lowest candidate and distribute his votes to the next choices marked. When the required number reach the quota, the counting terminates.

A party with a very popular candidate does not, under this system, waste votes beyond his quota, for the excess votes are distributed—probably to others in his party. Votes far down the scale are not wasted because the successive elimination of party members allows one man to be elected provided the total concentration reaches the quota. While this system provides for the single transferable preference vote, it must be distinguished from various forms of preferential voting, such as a plan for adding all second choices to all first choices or a plan for presidential preference primary voting.

In the United States the two most notable experiments with proportional representation have been in New York City (from 1936 to 1947, when it was abandoned largely because of distrust of Communist representation in the city council) and Cincinnati (adopted in 1924, abandoned in 1957). Of the score of cities which have used the system only a few have continued its operation. See also REPRESENTATION.

Consult Hoag, Clarence G., and Hallett, George H., *Proportional Representation* (New York 1926); Hermens, Ferdinand A., *Democracy or Anarchy?* (South Bend, Ind., 1941); Carter, Gwendolen M., Ranney, John C., and Herz, John H., *Major Foreign Powers*, 3d ed. (New York 1957); Bromage, Arthur W., *Introduction to Municipal Government and Administration*, 2d ed. (New York 1957); Key, Valdimer O., *Politics, Parties, and Pressure Groups*, 4th ed. (New York 1958); also *The National Civic Review* (formerly *The National Municipal Review;* New York, monthly).

SPENCER D. ALBRIGHT,
University of Richmond.

MINOS, mī′nŏs, in classical mythology, a king of Crete. Ancient authors confuse two Cretan kings of this name: one the grandfather of the other. Most legends make the grandson a wise legislator in life and a judge in the underworld after death. He was the son of Zeus and Europa, the brother of Rhadamanthus and Sarpedon, the husband of Pasiphaë, who bore him Ariadne, Phaedra, and four other less noted children, and the seducer of various women, by whom he fathered numerous children.

Minos persuaded Poseidon, the sea god, to send him a bull from the sea as a sign of sovereignty in his contest for the Cretan kingship, and promised to sacrifice it in the deity's honor. Crete prospered under Minos, who conquered the islands of the Aegean Sea, suppressed piracy, and successfully warred in Greece against Athens and Megara. Minos died by treachery in Sicily during his vengeful pursuit of Daedalus, who had helped Pasiphaë to gratify her unnatural passion for Poseidon's bull (which Minos had considered too handsome to kill) and thus to become the mother of the monstrous Minotaur.

Scholars suspect that Minos was a dynastic title for several Cretan rulers and apply its adjectival form, Minoan, to the culture of Crete during the Bronze Age.

See ARIADNE; DAEDALUS; MINOTAUR; PASIPHAË; SCYLLA; THESEUS.

Consult Graves, Robert, *The Greek Myths,* vol. 1, pp. 292–331 (Baltimore 1955).

P. R. COLEMAN-NORTON,
Princeton University.

MINOT, mī'nŭt, **Charles Sedgwick,** American biologist and educator: b. West Roxbury, Mass., Dec. 23, 1852; d. Boston, Nov. 19, 1914. After graduating from Massachusetts Institute of Technology (1872) and studying abroad, he gained a D.Sc. from Harvard in 1878, and from 1880 until his death taught embryology and comparative anatomy at Harvard Medical School, becoming professor in 1892. Known chiefly as an embryologist, he invented improved forms of the sledge microtome, designed the rotary form that attained general use, and made valuable anatomical studies, especially on the placenta. He wrote *Human Embryology* (1892), *Laboratory Textbook of Embryology* (1903; 2d ed. 1910), and *The Problem of Age, Growth and Death* (1908), a study of senility.

MINOT, George Richards, American physician and hematologist and joint winner of the Nobel prize for medicine and physiology: b. Boston, Mass., Dec. 2, 1885; d. Brookline, Feb. 25, 1950. He was educated at Harvard (M.D., 1912) and was prominently associated with several Boston hospitals, including Massachusetts General, Peter Bent Brigham, and Boston City. He was professor of medicine at Harvard from 1928 to 1948 and was director of the Thorndike Memorial Laboratory of Boston City Hospital at the university. Minot specialized in diseases of the blood, his greatest achievement being his discovery with William Parry Murphy (1892–), a Harvard associate, that pernicious anemia, a hitherto uniformly fatal disease, could be consistently held in abeyance by feeding sufficient amounts of liver. Together, in 1926, they introduced the Minot-Murphy diet for pernicious anemia, with beef liver as a major constituent. For their work in this field, Minot, Murphy, and George Hoyt Whipple (1878–), of Rochester, N.Y., were awarded the Nobel prize in 1934. Minot's chief published work was his *Pathological Physiology and Clinical Description of the Anemias* (with William B. Castle, 1936).

MINOT, Laurence, English lyric poet: b. 1300?; d. ?1352. Nothing is known of his life, but from the detailed descriptions in his 11 extant poems it is believed that he accompanied Edward III on some of his campaigns. Reflecting the dialect of the English northeast midlands, the poems are written in a rhymed, alliterative, and high-spirited style, each being headed by a couplet—for example, "Herkins how King Edward lay/ With his men bifor Tournay." The first poem glorifies the battle of Halidon Hill, England (1333) and the last the capture of Guînes, France (1352). Other subjects are the battle of Crécy (1346) and the siege of Calais (1347). The poems are contained in a 15th century manuscript in the British Museum and have appeared in several paintings.

Consult Douglas C. Stedman, ed., *The War Ballads of Laurence Minot* (Dublin 1917).

MINOT, city, North Dakota, seat of Ward County, situated at an altitude of 1,557 feet on the Souris (Mouse) River, 110 miles northwest of Bismarck. It is on three federal highways and on main lines of the Great Northern and Soo Line railroads. Minot is an important distribution point for a wheat-growing, livestock, dairying, and oil-producing region, and has flour-milling, poultry- and dairy goods-processing industries, railroad shops, and a large freight classification yard. Vast lignite coal fields are nearby. With three hospitals, including a federal veterans' institution, it is a medical center for northwest North Dakota. It is the site of a state teachers college, the state's largest indoor auditorium (the scene of championship rodeos), and 450 acres of parks, including Roosevelt Park with a fine zoo. There is a large airport and a Strategic Air Force jet interceptor base. Incorporated in 1887, the city has a council and city manager form of government. Pop. 32,290.

MINOTAUR, mĭn'ō-tôr (from Gr. *Minotauros,* from *Minos,* Minos + *tauros,* bull), in classical mythology, the monstrous (half man, half bull) offspring of a bull and Pasiphaë, wife of Minos, king of Crete. This creature was confined in a labyrinth, constructed by Daedalus, under the palace of Knossos, Crete. At stated intervals it fed on seven youths and seven maids, who were sent to Minos as tribute from Athens, Greece. Theseus, son of King Aegeus of Athens, eventually volunteered to be one of the victims. Aided by Ariadne, Minos' daughter, who had fallen in love with him, he penetrated the labyrinth, slew the Minotaur with a magic sword, retraced his path by following the thread unwound from a skein by him in his passage into the maze, eloped with Ariadne, and thus freed Athens from the tribute. See ARIADNE; DAEDALUS; LABYRINTH; MINOS; PASIPHAË; THESEUS.

Consult Graves, Robert, *The Greek Myths,* vol. 1, pp. 293–94, 297–98, 336–40, 345–47 (Baltimore 1955).

P. R. COLEMAN-NORTON.

MINOTS LEDGE, mī'nŭts, or **COHASSET ROCKS,** kō-hăs'ĕt, a reef in Massachusetts Bay, Mass., about 2½ miles off Cohasset and 17 miles southeast of Boston. It is the site of a 114-foot-high granite lighthouse built in 1860.

MINSK, mĭnsk; Russ. myēnsk, oblast, USSR, in central Belorussian Soviet Socialist Republic. Its area is 8,500 square miles, and its capital is the city of Minsk. Lying in the Lithuanian-Belorussian upland, it is drained by the Berezina, upper Ptich, and Svisloch rivers. Its economy, chiefly agricultural, includes production of flax and dairy products in the northeast, potatoes and hogs in the east, and grains (mainly rye, oats, barley, buckwheat) in the west. The chief industrial centers are Minsk (q.v.) and Borisov, the latter with match, wood-distillation, glassworking, musical instrument, enamelware, and food product industries. The oblast was formed in 1938. Pop. (1959) 1,728,000.

MINSK, city, USSR, capital of the Belorussian Soviet Socialist Republic, and of Minsk Oblast. It is situated in European Russia, on the Svisloch River (a tributary of the Berezina River) and 400 miles west-southwest of Moscow. Minsk is the leading industrial and cultural center of Belorussia. Its industries include the manufacturing of trucks, tractors, bicycles, machine tools, and radios; woodworking; and food processing. Minsk is the seat of the Belorussian State University, the Belorussian Academy of Sciences, and several other higher educational institutions. It publishes books and periodicals in the Belorussian language. Among the city's noteworthy buildings are the modern Government Building and the Communist party headquarters, forming the core of a modern civic center, and the Theater of Opera and Ballet. Minsk was first mentioned in chronicles as of 1066. As the capital of a separate principality after the 12th century, it was conquered in 1326 by Lithuania. The city remained under Lithuanian and later Polish rule until the second partition of Poland in 1793. Under Russian rule, Minsk developed as a commercial center, especially after the 1870's when it became the crossing of two trunk railroads, one linking Moscow with Warsaw, and the other linking Liepaja, on the Baltic Sea, with Gomel, in southeastern Belorussia. The city's population reached 105,000 by 1912, but its industrial development was limited to small consumer goods enterprises and handicrafts. Until World War II, when Minsk was held by the Germans from 1941 to 1944, the city's population was 40 per cent Jewish. Its industrial development was speeded during the postwar period, when the city repaired its heavy wartime damage and expanded into new industrial and residential suburbs. Pop. (1959) 509,000.

THEODORE SHABAD.

MINSTER, mĭn'stẽr (Anglo-Saxon, *mynster,* from Lat. *monasterium*), an old English term for monastery, applied particularly to a monastery's church. The term is often retained by the church after disappearance of the monastery (or convent); it is also sometimes applied to large churches or cathedrals of nonmonastic origin. Thus it is found in Westminster Abbey, a monastic foundation; and it is applied to York, Lincoln, Ripon, Southwell, and other cathedrals of nonmonastic origin. Two small towns in Kent County, England—Minster-in-Thanet and Minster-in-Sheppey—once contained convents and have churches dating back to these institutions.

MINSTREL, mĭn'strĕl, from the Latin *minister* or servant, a term designating primarily the order of musicians of the Middle Ages who were in the employ of noblemen. Minstrels are referred to by various names in medieval literature. In France the term *jongleur* was used until the end of the 13th century when *ménestral* came into more general usage; in Germany, *gaukler* was used; and in England, minstrel and juggler. Minstrels were held in high regard and rewarded handsomely by the noblemen in whose castles they performed. During the 12th and 13th centuries they were accomplished musicians who sang and played with great skill. Afterward, the field became so generalized that all manner of jugglers, acrobats, storytellers, dancers, and sleight-of-hand performers were known as minstrels. They were found at fairs, in village squares, and in taverns.

Because of the rewards they received from the nobility, minstrels flocked to royal households in such numbers that measures were occasionally taken to curb their activities. In 1315, Edward II, king of England, issued a proclamation regulating the number that might enter a household and curtailing their demands for remuneration. Indeed, it is in medieval English literature that one finds most references to their activities. In 1469, during the reign of Edward IV, a guild was set up whereby the competence of those who exercised the minstrel profession might be judged according to certain standards.

In spite of such attempts to elevate the profession, it continued to degenerate, and during the reign of Elizabeth I rogues, vagabonds, and "minstrels wandering abroad" were severely punished. In reality true minstrelsy had ceased to exist by the end of the Middle Ages. During the Commonwealth an ordinance was finally passed (1656) which might be said to have put an end to the minstrel profession. It declared that "any person or persons, commonly called Fidlers or Minstrels . . . taken playing, fidling, and making music at any inn, alehouse, or tavern . . . shall be adjudged and declared to be rogues, vagabonds, and sturdy beggars." See also BARD; MINNESINGER; PROVENÇAL LITERATURE; SKALD.

Bibliography.—Chambers, Sir Edward K., *The Mediaeval Stage,* 2 vols. (London 1903); Percy, Thomas, "An Essay on The Ancient Minstrels in England" and "Notes and Illustrations Referred to in the Foregoing Essay," *Reliques of Ancient English Poetry* (London 1767; Astor ed., J. V. Prichard, ed., New York 1906); Duncan, Edmondstoune, *The Story of Minstrelsy* (New York 1907).

ROBERT H. PERRIN.

MINSTREL SHOW, an indigenous American theatrical entertainment which flourished in the 19th century. It consisted of a series of farcical Negro impersonations by a "band" of white musicians in blackface. The Virginia Minstrels (comprising fiddler Dan Emmit or Emmett, a banjoist, bone player, and tambourine player) gave the first such organized show, an "Ethiopan Concert," on March 7, 1843, at the Masonic Temple in Boston, Mass. Dressed in the ragged costume of earlier representations of the Southern Negro, they sat in a semicircle on the stage, bones and tambourine at either side, and played, sang, and acted out current minstrel ditties in a comically exaggerated plantation manner. They also interspersed their scenes with dialogues, conundrums, and a stump speech.

The numerous troupes which originated during the 1840's largely preserved the pattern of performance of the Virginia Minstrels. However, into the opening section of their show they introduced the Northern urbanized Negro, a dandy in tails (known from earlier solo acts); they enlivened the finale with an exuberant solo or ensemble dance and made the middleman of the band the interlocutor. At times they used the jawbone (of a horse, ox, sheep, or ass), whose teeth were rattled, scraped, or struck, and the triangle. (These, like the original four instruments, were closely associated with the plantation slave.) They also used the accordion. During the 1850's and 1860's the first part of the show favored the polished or sentimental minstrel song (the kind Stephen Collins Foster wrote for Edwin P. Christy's Minstrels), and even popular "ballads" in ordinary English. The second part, the "olio," featured musical virtuoso acts, topical burlesques, and parodies of plays and of Italian opera, while the finale included a skit or a "Plantation Festival," such as "Dixie," in which all members of the company sang and danced a "walk-around." In keeping with the backwoods humor of the minstrel show, female characters were impersonated by men.

Although the minstrel band steadily increased in size, it always kept banjo, bones, and tambourine as a nucleus. During the 1840's it consisted of 4, 5, or 6 musicians and in the late 1850's of about 12; after the 1860's it grew in size more quickly, and more frequently admitted conventional orchestral instruments. The primitive Negro character of the show began to pale as early as the 1850's but was revived by the Bryant's Minstrels, whose heyday was between 1857 and 1866. From then on, despite a few individuals who preserved the original style, the minstrel show developed into a series of flashy, standardized variety acts using in the 1880's as many as 100 performers. The interlocutor often appeared in white face with elegantly dressed collaborators suggesting Negroes in little more than make-up. Professional minstrel companies existed up to the second decade of the 20th century though they resembled but faintly those of ante-bellum days.

Bibliography.—Paskman, Dailey, and Spaeth, Sigmund G., *Gentlemen, Be Seated!* (New York 1928), a popular, illustrated survey; Wittke, Carl, *Tambo and Bones* (Durham, N.C., 1930), a professional historian's account; Nathan, Hans, "The First Negro Minstrel Band and Its Origins," *Southern Folklore Quarterly,* vol. 16, no. 2, pp. 132–44 (1952); Chase, Gilbert, "The Ethiopian Business," *America's Music* (New York 1955); Nathan, Hans, *Dan Emmett and Early American Negro Minstrelsy* (Norman 1961).

HANS NATHAN.

MINT, mĭnt, any plant in the genus *Mentha,* or, in a broader sense, any plant in the mint family, Labiatae. Mints are mostly herbaceous, with square stems, opposite, simple leaves, usually aromatic. The flowers are commonly irregular, with a two-lipped corolla, four stamens, and a four-lobed ovary which ripens into four nutlets, each with one seed. The genus *Mentha* consists of probably not more than 15 true species, but with numerous transitional forms, so that several hundred species have been described. All are native of Eurasia or of Australia, except *M. arvensis,* which is widely distributed in the northern hemisphere. The two best-known forms are *M. spicata,* the spearmint, with narrow, interrupted spikes of pink to pale violet flowers and sessile leaves, native of Europe, and *M. piperita,* the peppermint, with thicker spikes of purplish flowers and petioled leaves; this is probably a hybrid, of European origin. Both of these species, and a number of others, have escaped in North America. Peppermint oil is distilled from the dried, upper portions of plants of *M. piperita,* grown in Europe and, in the United States, especially in rich moist soils in northern Indiana and southern Michigan. It consists largely of menthol, and is used medicinally, and in flavoring confections, chewing gum, and tooth paste. Japanese peppermint oil is extracted from *M. arvensis* var. *piperascens,* grown mostly in northern Japan; it is utilized for liniments, nasal sprays, and cough drops. Spearmint oil, containing carvone, is derived from *M. spicata,* or from one of its hybrids, *M. Cardiaca.* It serves in flavoring mint sauce, and the shoots form a garnish for lamb and mint juleps. Various other genera in the Labiatae are also called mint, such as *Pycnanthemum,* the mountain mint, *Monarda,* the horse mint and lemon mint, *Blephilia,* the wood mint, and *Cunila,* the stone mint. All of these are American genera. See also BASIL; MENTHOL; PEPPERMINT; SPEARMINT.

EDWIN B. MATZKE.

MINT, a place where coins are manufactured, usually operated by a national government or with governmental authority. The term is derived from the Latin *moneta,* a surname of Juno, the principal goddess of the Romans and, as Juno Moneta, also goddess of money. While major nations of the world maintain their own mints, most smaller countries have their coins minted on contract by others.

The first known mint was established in ancient Lydia, in Asia Minor, near the end of the 8th century B.C. Shortly afterward, the coinage of silver was originated on the island of Aegina, Greece. Until the 16th century A.D., minting of coins was accomplished by hammering engraved dies together by hand, although the Romans cast some of their large copper coins. In 1553, however, machines for producing coins were introduced at the mint in Paris, France.

United States Mints.—In the United States, the first official mint was created at Philadelphia by act of Congress on April 2, 1792. Prior to that time, private contractors had minted the so-called Franklin cent on authority of the Congress. The Philadelphia mint still supplies the major portion of the coins minted in the United States. In addition, the Denver mint has operated as a coinage mint since 1906, after serving as an assay office from 1862. Other United States coinage mints have been located at Carson City, Nev. (1870–1893); Charlotte, N.C. (1838–1861); Dahlonega, Ga. (1838–1861); New Orleans, La. (1838–1861, 1879–1909); and San Francisco, Calif. (1854–1955).

Mints in the United States are operated by the Bureau of the Mint. Originally placed under the secretary of state, the bureau has been in the Treasury Department since 1795. The act of 1792 authorized a mint for only five years. Several attempts were made to abolish the mint, and one such resolution actually passed the House of Representatives. However, the mint was saved for successive five-year periods until 1828, when legislation was passed to continue a mint in Philadelphia until specifically abolished by law.

The mints of the United States have produced only minor silver, nickel, and copper coins since 1934, when coinage of gold was suspended. In addition to regular coins for circulation, commemorative coins are minted when authorized by Congress. All the expenses of minting are borne by the sponsoring body. Specially selected and polished coins, called mint issues, are also prepared as collectors' items at the Philadelphia mint.

The United States Bureau of the Mint also

has supervision over the assay offices, which test ore and bullion, and which also check weight and quality of coins. Once a year, the presidentially appointed Assay Commission meets in Washington to evaluate newly minted coins selected at random from all coinage production. The bureau also has charge of the gold bullion depository at Fort Knox, Ky., and the silver bullion depository at West Point, N.Y. All acquisitions and refining of gold and silver bullion are handled by the bureau, as well as coinage for many Latin American, Asian, and African nations.

Mints of Other Nations.—Major mints are operated in Great Britain, France, Italy, West Germany, Communist China, Russia, and Japan, among others. The Chinese originated and developed coinage independently of Western nations, and spread the idea of the mint throughout Asia. In the Western world, the mint in London, England, is perhaps most influential, supplying coin for all nations of the Commonwealth of Nations except Australia and Canada, which maintain their own mints.

Brassage and Seigniorage.—Mints derive their income from fees charged for assaying, refining, and coining monetary metals. When the charges just cover the expenses involved, it is termed brassage. When a profit is made on the transaction, particularly when the monetary value of coins exceeds their bullion value, it is called seigniorage. Between 1180 and 1850 in England, private contractors minted coins at great personal profit derived from seigniorage. This system was abolished in 1850.

Coins are regularly tested for uniformity of weight and quality in assay offices. In England in the Middle Ages, minting of deficient coins was considered treason. Although such minting is no longer a capital offense, great care is taken to avoid the loss of confidence and acceptability that result from deficient coins.

Increased ease of communication and expanded use of credit in commercial transactions have diminished the need for a multiplicity of mints throughout the world. Counterfeiting has become more difficult and paper money has become the major medium of exchange for large denomination cash. This is indicated by the fact that shortly after the Norman Conquest (1066), there were more mints in England (70) than there are in the entire world today.

See also ASSAYING; COINAGE OF THE UNITED STATES.

WILLIAM N. KINNARD, JR.,
University of Connecticut.

MINTO. See ELLIOTT, SIR GILBERT, 3D BARONET OF MINTO; ELLIOT-MURRAY-KYNYNMOUND, SIR GILBERT, 1ST EARL OF MINTO; ELLIOT-MURRAY-KYNYNMOUND, GILBERT JOHN, 4TH EARL OF MINTO.

MINTON, mĭn′t'n, **Herbert,** English potter: b. Stoke-upon-Trent, England, Feb. 4, 1793; d. Torquay, April 1, 1858. Son of Thomas Minton (q.v.), he became a partner in his father's business in 1817, and following his father's death greatly expanded the business, employing artists and inventors and extending the range of products from largely earthenware and soft porcelain to many other types. The added wares included hard porcelain, Parian ware, encaustic tiles, *azulejos* or colored enamel tiles, mosaics, majolica, and products after Della Robbia and Palissy ware.

MINTON, Thomas, English potter: b. Shropshire, England, 1765; d. 1836. After learning engraving and pottery making, he settled in Stoke-upon-Trent and in 1791 founded a business that became noted for beautiful Minton products, especially under his son, Herbert Minton (q.v.). He first engraved the famous willow pottery pattern, and is honored by a window in St. Peter's church, Stoke-upon-Trent.

MINUCIUS FELIX, mĭ-nū′shĭ-ŭs fē′lĭks, **Marcus,** Latin Christian apologist: fl. 2d or 3d century. While Minucius probably was African in origin and apparently practiced law in Rome, Italy, yet no agreement on his *floruit* has been attained. Most investigators place it before 185, but some scholars set it after 200 and as late as 250. The divergence stems from the problem whether Tertullian (Quintus Septimius Florens Tertullianus) based his *Apologeticus* (written c. 197) on Minucius' *Octavius* or Minucius was indebted to Tertullian, since both treatises, though vastly different in style, defend Christianity by many similar arguments and often identical illustrations.

The *Octavius* with graceful rhetoric presents its author at Ostia, Italy, moderating an informal debate between Octavius Januarius, a Christian convert, and Caecilius Natalis, his pagan friend, on the validity of Christian and pagan beliefs. Caecilius arraigns Christianity with philosophical and pagan arguments against the new religion. Octavius answers these allegations and eventually elicits from his antagonist the admission that Christianity is superior to paganism.

Bibliography.—The best Latin text with English translation is in the joint work by Terrot R. Glover and Gerald H. Rendall, *Tertullian: Apology, De Spectaculis,* tr. by Glover, and *Minucius Felix,* tr. by Rendall (New York 1931). Consult also Baylis, Harry J., *Minucius Felix and His Place Among the Early Fathers of the Christian Church* (New York 1928); Axelson, Bertil, *Das Prioritätsproblem Tertullian-Minucius Felix* (Lund, Sweden, 1941); Quasten, Johannes, *Patrology,* vol. 2, pp. 155–63 (Westminster, Md., 1953).

P. R. COLEMAN-NORTON,
Princeton University.

MINUET, mĭn′ū-ĕt, a French dance and the music connected with it. The word is derived either from *menu* (small) or from the name of an earlier dance, the *branle à mener.* Apparently imported from country districts, the minuet was introduced in mid-17th century into Louis XIV's court. Having superseded most other dances there, it was soon carried throughout Europe. Jean-Baptiste Lully (1632–1687), the French composer, introduced it into suites, ballets, and operas; German composers were quick to adapt the new musical pattern to their own purposes. The sinfonie (overtures) preceding the operas of Alessandro Scarlatti and of other composers active about 1700 frequently end with a minuet.

Originally a slow dance in three-quarter time (and usually employing melodic phrases three measures long), the minuet gradually increased in speed and complexity. By the time of its use in symphonies by Franz Joseph Haydn and Wolfgang Amadeus Mozart, it had acquired the joking, jovial character that Ludwig von Beethoven was to put into his scherzos.

Early minuets in dance suites from about 1700 already show the ABA pattern (minuet 1—minuet 2—minuet 1) that evolved into the minuet-trio-minuet form familiar in later symphonies, the intervening trio deriving its name from being performed by three soloistic instruments. The minuet showed remarkable adaptability: when the baroque suite declined about 1750, the minuet alone, of all the dance forms that had gone to make up the typical suites, did not decline too. On the contrary it went on to become important in the architecture of many sorts of sonatas, including the symphony. The most famous of all classical minuets is that played and danced in Act I of Mozart's opera *Don Giovanni.*

HERBERT WEINSTOCK.

MINUIT, mē-nwē'; mĭn'ū-ĭt, or **MINNEWIT,** mĭn'ĕ-wĭt, **Peter,** colonial governor in the Dutch and Swedish services: b. Wesel, duchy of Cleves, 1580; d. St. Christopher, West Indies, 1638. Of French or Walloon family, he pronounced his name like the French *minuit* (midnight) and his coat of arms displayed midnight's emblem, the bat; but the Dutch spelled and pronounced the name Minnewit. A member of the council of Willem (William) Verhulst, director of New Netherland at Manhattan in 1625, Minuit returned to Holland and, on Dec. 19, 1625, was commissioned Verhulst's successor. With his private secretary Leonard Kool and the new secretary of the province, Isaac de Rasière, he sailed from Amsterdam aboard the *Het Meeuwtje* (*The Sea Mew*) which anchored at Manhattan May 4, 1626; but he did not, however, replace Verhulst until September 23, then assuming office as first of the province's directors general. Minuit immediately legalized the years of settlement on Manhattan by executing with local Indian sachems a deed of purchase of the island, estimated at 11,000 morgens (22,000 acres) in area, for trinkets valued at 60 guilders ($24). He also began construction of Fort Amsterdam. When regular church services were inaugurated at the fort in 1628 by the Rev. Jonas Michaëlius, he served as an elder.

An energetic governor, successful in his dealings with the Indians, whom he treated with tact and kindness, Minuit was inclined to act domineeringly with his fellow colonists and made enemies—among them de Rasière and the latter's successor Johan van Remunde, also Pastor Michaëlius. His recall to Holland in 1631 and dismissal from the West India Company's service was due mainly, however, to a bitter internecine conflict among the company directors over the extent of privileges accorded the patroons. That Samuel Blommaert, one of the most active and influential members of the company's Amsterdam chamber, thought Minuit had been badly used is evidenced by the glowing recommendation he gave him in an application to the Swedish chancellor, Axel Oxenstierna, for the post of governor of a Swedish settlement in America.

Minuit was accepted by the Swedes. In the spring of 1638 he bought from the Indians a tract on the South (Delaware) River where he built Fort Christina on the site of Wilmington, Del., founding the colony of New Sweden. Later that year he left Måns Kling in charge and sailed to St. Christopher, there exchanging his cargo for tobacco. While visiting the captain of a Dutch ship, a hurricane struck the island; the ship foundered and he was drowned.

DRAKE DE KAY.

MINUTE, mĭn'ĭt, a unit of time or of angular measurement. *In time,* the 1440th part of a mean solar day, or the 60th part of an hour. The minute is divided into 60 seconds. *In angular measurement,* the 60th part of a degree (a degree being the 360th part of the circumference of a circle), or a *minute of arc,* which again is divided into 60 seconds. The symbol for a minute of arc is an acute accent ('), and for a second of arc a double accent ("). Hence, in geography, we have such designations as 10°30' 45", or 10 degrees, 30 minutes, and 45 seconds, latitude or longitude. A minute of a great circle of the earth's surface is a geographical or nautical mile.

MINUTEMEN, mĭn'ĭt-mĕn, in the American Revolutionary War, militiamen who were ready to turn out for service "at a minute's warning." They originated in Worcester and other Massachusetts counties as part of the voluntary reorganization of the old militia to eliminate Tory influences. On Oct. 26, 1774, the Provincial Congress directed that the process be extended throughout the colony but this was never done because of the early outbreak of hostilities. In the opening engagements at Lexington and Concord, Mass., on April 19, 1775, minutemen were among the patriots who fought the British. Later, other colonies organized minutemen on the recommendation of the Continental Congress (July 18, 1775), Maryland, New Hampshire, and Connecticut being on record as accepting the plan. There are statues to minutemen at Lexington and Concord, and at Westport, Conn.

MINYA, mĭn'yȧ (Ar. AL MINYA; also spelled MINIA), province, in the Upper Egypt region of the United Arab Republic, in the Nile River valley, bounded on the north by Beni Suef Province, on the east by the Arabian Desert, on the south by Asyut Province, and on the west by the Libyan Desert. Its area is 782 square miles and its capital Minya (q.v.); other important cities include Beni Mazar, Maghagha, El Fashn, Abu Qurqas, and Samalut. All are served by the Cairo-El Shallal railroad. The chief agricultural products are cotton, sugarcane, and cereals, for which there are processing industries; imported wool is woven. The province contains the archaeological sites of Beni Hassan and Oxyrhyncus. Pop. (1947) 1,056,466.

MINYA (Ar. AL MINYA; also spelled MINIA or MINIEH), city, Egypt, United Arab Republic, capital of Minya Province (q.v.), on the Nile River, 140 miles south-southwest of Cairo. It is an important port and center of trade and agriculture (cotton, sugarcane, cereals), and has cotton gins and sugar and wool mills. Pop. (1947) 69,667.

MINYA KONKA, mĭn'yȧ kŏng'kȧ, or **MINYA GONGKAR** (Chin. KUNGKA SHAN), highest peak (24,900 feet) of the Tahsuëh Mountains, forming an extension of the Tibetan plateau in Szechwan Province, China. It is situated about 25 miles south-southwest of Kangting. It was climbed for the first time in October–November 1932 by three American youths—Richard L. Burdsall of Port Chester, N.Y., Terris Moore of Philadelphia, Pa., and Theodore Young, a Chinese born in Honolulu.

Consult Burdsall, Richard L., and Emmons, Arthur B., *Men Against the Clouds* (New York 1935).

MINYAS, mĭn'ĭ-ăs, in Greek mythology, founder and king of the ancient Boeotian city of Orchomenus. He was reputed to be the ancestor of Jason and other of the Argonauts, who were frequently called Minyae or Minyans, and may have been the hero of a lost epic, *Minyas.* His three daughters Alcithoë, Leucippe, and Arsippe were said to have been driven mad and changed into bats by the god Dionysus for refusing to join in the revels connected with his worship; another version of the legend has the god Hermes changing them into birds.

MIOCENE, mī'ô-sēn, in geology, the fourth epoch of the Tertiary period, spanning a period variously estimated at from 10 million to 18 million years. It follows the Oligocene epoch and precedes the Pliocene. The name, derived from two Greek words meaning "less" and "recent," was suggested in 1833 by Sir Charles Lyell on the basis of studies made in France and Italy which showed that the rocks of the epoch contained fewer fossil species than the more recent Pliocene. During the Miocene epoch the seas first transgressed and then receded, and it was a period of great sedimentation and of volcanic activity. The Alps were severely deformed and raised, as were the Apennines, Caucasus, Himalayas, and Andes. Areas of the Coast Range in the western United States rose, and marine sediments more than a mile thick were deposited. Marine rocks along the coast of Oregon and Washington adjoined plains of contemporaneous lava flows extending eastward to Yellowstone Park.

The climate was milder and more uniform than in the succeeding epochs, even in the Arctic and Antarctic regions. Plant life came to resemble that of today. There was considerable reduction of forest land, which gave way to grassy plains that were important in the development of herbivorous mammals. The epoch marked important steps in the evolution of the horse and the ape; camels and rhinoceroses were plentiful on the grasslands of western North America, and there were numerous carnivores, including the oreodonts, doglike mammals which became extinct before the close of the epoch. Mastodons, raccoons, and weasels made their appearance. Most of the fossil marine invertebrates belong to genera that are found today. See also GEOLOGY—*Geologic Time Scale;* PALEOBOTANY—*Flora of the Tertiary Period* (Miocene Epoch); PALEONTOLOGY—*Cenozoic Era.*

MIOHIPPUS. See HORSE—*The Evolution of the Horse.*

MIQUELON. See SAINT PIERRE AND MIQUELON.

MIR, mēr, in czarist Russia, a rural commune of one or more villages. As a community, the inhabitants owned the surrounding land and were mutually liable to the central government for the taxes. From time to time the land was redistributed as desirable among the members. The mir was self-governing as a community, with elective officers, but was subject to higher control; it coordinated and controlled farming activities by prescribing what crops were to be raised and the dates for sowing and harvesting.

MIRA, mī'rȧ (from Lat. *mirus,* wonderful), in astronomy, the variable star Omicron Ceti, situated in the neck of the constellation Cetus, the Whale. It was discovered in 1596 by David Fabricius, and its variability was apparently first noticed in 1638. The period of this star, which is irregular, averages about 330 days. During the greater part of this time the star remains at about 9th magnitude, but during about 100 days it rises to a maximum which may vary from the 2d to the 5th magnitude, remains there for a week or 10 days, then sinks to its minimum again. When shining at 2d magnitude brightness, it gives out more than 600 times as much light as when at the 9th magnitude.

Mira's greatest recorded variation occurred between the years 1779 and 1783 when, after attaining a brightness equal to that of the 1st magnitude star Aldebaran, it sank so low that it was invisible even in telescopes showing stars of the 10th magnitude. The period of its changes is also irregular, sometimes varying to the extent of two months. Thus neither the times of greatest brightness nor the amount of the brightening can be accurately predicted. As the time of greatest brightness approaches, the spectrum gives evidence of powerful disturbance. The outburst comes from the depths of the main body of the star, the outlying strata of vapors remaining comparatively cool. This periodical surging or pulsation is so widespread as to amount to a real bodily distortion rather than to a mere tide, but its cause is not known. Thus, Mira's diameter of about 260 million miles varies over 30 million miles from maximum to minimum. See also STARS—*Variable Stars.*

Consult Campbell, Leon, and Jacchia, Luigi G., *The Story of Variable Stars* (Cambridge 1951).

MIRABEAU, mē-rȧ-bō', Anglicized mĭr'ȧ-bō, COMTE DE (HONORÉ GABRIEL RIQUETI): French orator and revolutionary leader: b. Bignon, near Nemours, France, March 9, 1749; d. Paris, April 2, 1791. This scion of a noble French family of Provence (his father was the MARQUIS DE MIRABEAU, q.v.) had a tempestuous youth. His choleric and erratic character alienated even parental affection, of which there was little enough for a small boy scarred by smallpox. To make matters worse, his parents detested each other. Soon their ugly son became a gambler and a debauchee. In 1767 he entered the Berry cavalry regiment as a gentleman volunteer, and in due course was commissioned second lieutenant. A successful rival to his colonel for the favors of a local beauty, he was imprisoned on the island of Ré until March 1769. He then joined an expedition to Corsica, was commissioned a captain of dragoons in 1771, and in 1772 was married to the daughter of the marquis de Marignane.

In 1774, owing to debts and quarrels with his wife and his father (a stern unloving man), Mirabeau was imprisoned in the Château d'If, Marseilles, and later in the castle of Joux near Pontarlier. There he fell in love with the young wife of the septuagenarian marquis de Monnier—"Sophie," as he called her. Trouble ensued. He escaped to Switzerland, where he was joined by his mistress, and in October 1776 they settled in Amsterdam. In May 1777, however, they were arrested and brought to Paris, where Mirabeau was imprisoned again for three and a half years. It was at this time that he wrote his famous erotic letters to Sophie.

During this and other imprisonments Mirabeau was able to read and write enormously, and became one of the most enlightened minds of his time. Having secured the revocation of the death sentence imposed on him for Sophie's seduction, and being legally separated from his wife (1783), he left France for a few months. Upon his return, having abandoned Sophie, who some years later committed suicide, he began an intimacy with Henrietta van Haren, known as Mme. de Nehra; her influence was undoubtedly exerted to his great benefit. In August 1784 he fled to London to allow more trouble to blow over; while there he wrote the *Considérations sur l'ordre de Cincinnatus* (1785). At about this time, he began to devote himself completely to French politics, and in 1786 was entrusted by Louis XVI's comptroller general, Charles Alexandre de Calonne, with a secret mission to Prussia. As a result of this and a subsequent mission there, he published *De la monarchie prussienne sous Frédéric le Grand* (1788) and *Histoire secrète de la cour de Berlin* (1789).

Brown Brothers

Honoré Gabriel Riqueti, Comte de Mirabeau.

A candidate for election to the States-General in 1789, he was rejected by the nobility; but his attacks against the privileged orders eventually made him well enough known to the third estate (the bourgeoisie) to be elected by the town of Aix as its representative to the States-General. He had the ambition to play a great part and the means to play that part: a powerful, lucid, realistic intelligence; a lack of scruples; a great oratorical talent. Mme. de Staël said of him that his speech was "like a powerful hammer, wielded by a skillful artist, and fashioning men to his will."

Mirabeau's speeches, however, were not altogether his own—a group of friends united to supply him with outlines, and these he filled in, suffusing and ennobling the completed work with his genius. He eclipsed all other orators of the National Assembly and became the center around which gathered all the men of greatest mark and force in the third estate. He was soon famous because of his resistance to the king's demand, after the royal sitting of June 23, 1789, that the third estate should vote separately from the other two orders (the clergy and the nobility).

Both before and after this occasion, Mirabeau delivered many speeches of such eloquence as to earn him the title of the "French Demosthenes." Among the most remarkable of these are his address to the king demanding the removal of his troops encamped at Versailles, and speeches on the national bankruptcy, the civil constitution of the clergy, the royal sanction, and peace and war.

After having shown himself a bold reformer and the most dangerous adversary of the court, Mirabeau ended by offering his support to the throne. The king paid his debts, amounting to 208,000 francs, and gave him a monthly pension of 60,000 francs. Though he had not scrupled to accept the royal retainer, he maintained the independence of his political principles, and only mitigated his opposition to the court. This new attitude began approximately in May 1790. Mirabeau acted partly from ambition (he wanted to lead the king and the revolution), partly from conviction, foreseeing the imminence of national catastrophe which he wanted to avert if possible. The revolution, he argued, should end with establishment of a constitutional monarchy somewhat like that of England. Though his tolerant attitude toward the monarchy and the fact that he was receiving a royal subvention earned him enemies, he was still extremely popular. On Jan. 16, 1791, he was elected member for the Paris department, and on January 29 president of the National Assembly. He died suddenly on April 2 of that year. His death was felt as a national loss. His remains were buried with great pomp in the church of Ste. Geneviève in Paris (the Pantheon), but three years later they were exhumed to make room for those of Jean Paul Marat.

Bibliography.—A good bibliography can be found in the translation of Louis Barthou's *Mirabeau* (New York 1913). Other important works are Aulard, F. Alphonse, *Les orateurs de l'assemblée constituante* (Paris 1882); Jouvenel, Henry de, *The Stormy Life of Mirabeau* (Boston 1929); Chevallier, Jean Jacques, *Mirabeau* (Paris 1947); Lefebvre, Georges, *La revolution française* (Paris 1951).

PIERRE BRODIN,
Director of Studies, Lycée Français de New-York.

MIRABEAU, COMTESSE DE (MARIE DE GONNEVILLE), French writer: b. Nancy, France, 1827; d. Cossesseville, 1914. Under various pseudonyms —Vicomte de Flagy, de Chut, Nick, Jack Frank, Shocking, Zut—she wrote much light fiction and contributed to the periodicals *Le Figaro, La mode,* and *La vie parisienne.* Among her novels are *Les jeunes filles pauvres* (1863), *Hélène de Gardannes* (1868), *Jane et Germaine* (1875), *Chut!!!* (1880), and *Coeur d'or* (1896). She was married to Comte Arundel-Joseph de Mirabeau (d. 1860) and was the mother of the popular novelist Comtesse de Martel de Janville (who wrote under the pseudonym of Gyp).

MIRABEAU, MARQUIS DE (VICTOR RIQUETI), French political economist: b. Pertuis, Vaucluse Department, France, Oct. 14, 1715; d. Argenteuil, July 11, 1789. He entered the army in 1728, but had little interest in a military career and rose only to a captaincy. After leaving the army, he wrote *Testament politique* (1747) and *L'utilité des états provinciaux* (1750). His *L'ami des hommes, ou traité de la population* (1756) shows clearly the influence of François Quesnay and the physiocrats (q.v.), and to promote physiocratic views he bought the *Journal de l'agriculture, du commerce et des finances.* His *Théorie de l'impôt* (1760), in which he severely criticized the farmers-general of the taxes, caused his exile to his estate at Bignon, which then became the center of the physiocratic school. He was the father of COMTE DE MIRABEAU (q.v.), famous leader of the French Revolution, and of ANDRÉ

Boniface Louis Riqueti (1754–1792), vicomte de Mirabeau, who served in the American Army from 1780 to 1785, was elected to the States-General in 1789, and after 1790 lived in Austria as an *émigré* because of his royalist sympathies.

MIRABILITE, mĭ-răb'ĭ-līt, a native hydrous sodium sulphate $Na_2SO_4 \cdot 10\ H_2O$, called Glauber's salt. It is found in saline lakes and in arid regions, and is used principally in the making of pulp for kraft paper by the sulphate process.

Lewis S. Ramsdell.

MIRACLE, mĭr'ȧ-k'l, an event which may be briefly defined as supernatural. The basic meaning of the word is derived from the Latin noun *miraculum,* from the verb *mirari,* to admire, marvel, or wonder. A miracle is more fully defined as an event which apparently contravenes the established laws of nature and can be explained only as the direct result of divine intervention or as a consequence of the operation of laws which are (at least at present) beyond human comprehension. But for God, of course, all law is natural, and so are His acts; nothing is accidental or contrary to His will or permission. As St. Augustine said (*City of God,* book xxi, chap. 8), "The will of God is the nature of things." Compare Thomas Aquinas, *Summa theologica,* part 1, question 110, 4th article; also Mark 10:27, "With God all things are possible." (Also compare Mark 9:23; Zechariah 8:6.)

From the more distinctively religious or theological viewpoint, therefore, a still more accurate definition may be attempted: a miracle is an event in the physical or historical order which produces awe or wonder and makes those who experience it aware of the power, the presence, or the purpose of God. Such a definition can be illustrated both from the Old Testament and the New, from the accounts of ecclesiastical miracles (that is, those which are reliably attested), and also from those reported in other religions (that is, those with valid evidence). As a matter of fact, miracles have been reported from all ages and all parts of the world. Some ages, and some peoples, have reported more miracles than have others; but from the point of view of general history and also that of the history of religions, there is no sharp dividing line between Biblical and ecclesiastical miracles, or between Jewish or Christian and others.

The "ages of faith" (Middle Ages) produced many more accounts of miracles than the ages of rational inquiry or of modern science; and yet religion, under all circumstances and conditions, has continued to produce and to cherish such accounts. The explanation offered in one age has sometimes differed from that in another. For example, the sun and the moon standing still in Gibeon and Ajalon (Joshua 10:12–14) or the crossing of the Red Sea on dry ground (Exodus 14:21–31) could have been due to an optical illusion, in the first case, or to a failure to realize the lapse of time (a whole day "crowded into one hour"); the second case may have been the natural effect of a powerful sirocco blowing in from the desert—the water at this point was shallow. But such explanations do not touch the heart of the story. For the ancient world, except for a few natural scientists in Greece and Rome, there was no order of natural law which would stand in the way of any supernatural event; the only problem was the evidence, and after that was established, the interpretation of the significance of the event, whether portent, prodigy, sign, or manifestation of divine favor or purpose.

To understand the miracle stories, as they were understood by those who believed in them and reported them, we must simply forget our modern scientific view of the world. Even skeptics such as Lucian, the 2d century satirist (as in his *Lover of Lies*) did not question the remarkable results obtained, for example, at the shrines of Asclepius (or Aesculapius, q.v.), where the sick really recovered. Such a view as that given classic expression by David Hume (*Dialogues on Natural Religion,* 1779), "Miracles do not happen," may be true in a purely scientific or purely secular world—though there are still many unexplained mysteries in modern science—but it does not touch the religious understanding and appreciation of miracles, which are believed not solely on the basis of evidence but because of the meaning they convey to those who accept them.

In the New Testament, the miracles of Jesus are chiefly exorcisms of demons, and other cures; such miracles as the multiplying of broken bits of bread and fish, or walking on the water, or restoring the dead to life again, are most rare and unusual. His own resurrection from among the dead (which is what the Greek of the New Testament means), as viewed by the early church, was the supreme example of a supernatural event (compare I Corinthians 15:3–11; Romans 1:4, 6:9), and at the same time was most natural, for He was the Son of God who had fought the battle with death and overcome it "for all believers."

All the miracles of the New Testament, including those of the apostles, have an eschatological meaning; that is, they are signs of the oncoming power of the reign of God, evidence of the immediate arrival of the messianic age and the beginning of the great transformation of this world into the world to come (Revelation 11:17). They are "the powers of the age to come" (Hebrews 6:5), already manifested in this present age which is now drawing to a close. As Jesus said, "If it is by the finger of God that I cast out demons, then the Kingdom of God has come upon you" (from the oldest gospel source, Q; Luke 11:20; compare Matthew 12:28). The miracles of the apostles accompanied their preaching as signs confirming the truth and authority of their message (compare Mark 16:20).

Bibliography.—Micklem, Edward R., *Miracles and the New Psychology* (New York 1922); Fenner, Friedrich, *Die Krankheit im Neuen Testament* (Leipzig 1930); Dibelius, Martin, *From Tradition to Gospel,* tr. by B. L. Woolf (New York 1935); Richardson, Alan, *Miracle-Stories of the Gospels* (New York 1942); McGinley, Laurence J., *Form-Criticism of the Synoptic Healing Narratives* (Woodstock, Md., 1944); Dibelius, Martin, *Jesus,* tr. by C. B. Hedrick and Frederick C. Grant (Philadelphia 1949); Grant, Frederick C., *An Introduction to New Testament Thought* (New York 1950); McCasland, Selby V., *By the Finger of God* (New York 1951); Bornkamm, Günther, *Jesus von Nazareth* (Stuttgart 1956).

Frederick C. Grant,
Professor of Biblical Theology, Union Theological Seminary.

MIRACLE AND MYSTERY PLAYS, the religious drama which had its beginning in the church of the Middle Ages. The term miracle play, though sometimes used for both miracle and mystery play, is properly restricted to drama based upon the life or miraculous deeds of Christian saints. The mystery play, on the other hand, presents Old and New Testament narratives.

Religious drama came into being during the early Middle Ages when the essential elements of dialogue, impersonation, and action were combined in an elaboration of the liturgical service of the church. In a 10th century manuscript these elements occur together in a simple *"Quem quaeritis"* trope which was sung during the Easter service. From this modest beginning of the three Marys visiting the sepulchre of Christ, other Biblical narratives were dramatized, especially those associated with the Passion and the Nativity of Christ. These mystery plays were performed in Latin and by members of the clergy (at first the choir) in order to instruct the congregation. They became so popular and expanded to such proportions, especially during the 13th century, that it became more practicable to move them outside the church and eventually to turn them over to secular authorities. By this time elaborate cycles of Biblical plays had developed, purporting to give a complete history of the world from Creation or the Fall of Lucifer to Doomsday.

Beginning with the early 14th century these mystery cycles were commonly performed as a part of the newly instituted Feast of Corpus Christi adopted at the Council of Vienna in 1311. Plays and processions became a main feature of the festival throughout most of the countries of Western Europe. The Corpus Christi play cycles achieved special prominence in the north and east of England. Four complete cycles in English have been preserved in addition to individual plays and fragments of other cycles.

Illustration Research Service, London

A play of the Corpus Christi cycle as staged in England.

The Chester group is the best preserved of the English plays and apparently the oldest, containing 24 pageants or individual plays. Unlike other English cycles, however, it seems to be derived from French originals, translations or redactions by Ranulf Higden about 1328. After the mid-15th century this cycle was shifted from Corpus Christi Day performance to Whitsuntide.

Illustration Research Service, London

Engraving depicting the performance of a *Mystère de la Passion* in the nave of a French cathedral in the 15th century.

The plays were acted on heavy vehicles which were moved from one station to another about the city. The next or York cycle contains 48 plays in a manuscript dated about 1430–1440 with a few omissions from the original group. York had from 12 to 16 playing stations located about the city. The third cycle or Towneley plays were performed at Wakefield. This group was originally based upon the York cycle. There are 32 plays preserved and some of these contain revisions by the so-called "Wakefield Master," a writer with special talent for realism and farce. The fourth cycle or Hegge plays (falsely called *Ludus Coventriae* or Coventry plays) were possibly performed at Lincoln. There are 42 plays in a manuscript dated about 1468. These four cycles and numerous records concerning the production of these and other English cycles give a great deal of information about the Corpus Christi plays. Each play in the cycle was generally assigned to one of the trade guilds of the town. The bakers, for instance, would probably do the play of the Last Supper, the watermen or shipwrights the play of Noah's Ark, and so on. Plays of the Nativity, the Passion, the Resurrection, and subjects from the Acts of the Apostles were included in the panorama of biblical history. Also comparable to the English Corpus Christi plays is the French *mystère du Viel Testament.*

In London and southern England the Passion play (q.v.) was more popular than the Corpus Christi play, and the same was true in many areas of Europe. But manuscripts and records of the Passion play are not so well preserved. The same is true of the miracle plays. There are references to many of them in England and on the continent, especially in France, but only St. Nicholas plays are extant in Latin and there remain relatively few other examples in the vernacular. In English *The Play of the Sacrament,* late 15th century, is the only typical miracle play which is well preserved.

Bibliography.—Chambers, E. K., *The Medieval Stage,* 2 vols. (Oxford 1903); Adams, J. Q., *Chief Pre-Shakespearean Dramas* (Boston 1924); Young, Karl, *The Drama of the Medieval Church,* 2 vols. (Oxford 1933); Frank, Grace, *The Medieval French Drama* (Oxford 1954); Craig, Hardin, *English Religious Drama of the Middle Ages* (Oxford 1955).

WILLIAM BRACY.

MIRAFLORES LAKE. See PANAMA CANAL—*The Existing Panama Canal and Canal Zone* (Features of the Canal).

MIRAGE, mĭ-räzh′, an optical illusion produced in the atmosphere by an unusual refraction (q.v.) of light rays. The illusion may result in the appearance of a distant object floating in midair, or projected transparently against a ground or sea surface where the object does not physically exist. Often, complex inversions and distortions of the mirage image cause it to assume weird shapes (see FATA MORGANA).

The basic cause of a mirage is the bending of light rays from a distant object as they pass the boundary or interface between two layers of air having sensibly different densities. The difference in density is usually caused by an unequal distribution of temperature, as when the layer of the atmosphere closest to the ground is heated from below by intense reradiation of the sun's rays from the ground. For this reason, mirages are more frequently seen over deserts and wherever temperature inversions are found. Stratification of the atmosphere is necessary for a mirage to occur.

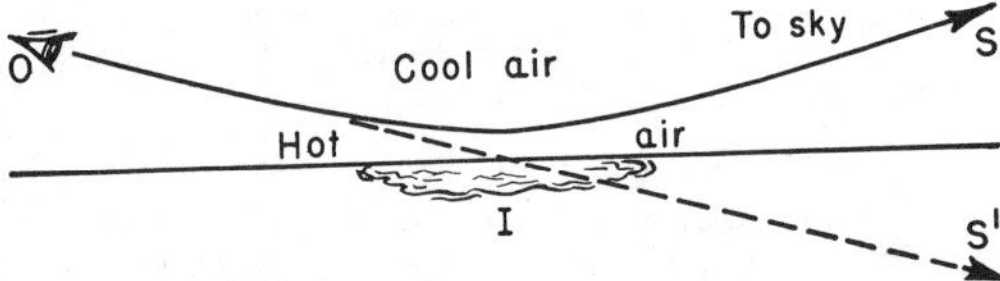

Fig. 1. Inferior mirage.

Since light rays are bent upward in entering obliquely into a stratum of air of lesser density, the image of an object seen under these conditions is in an inverted position below and apparently in front of the object. This is known as an *inferior* mirage. The appearance of a spurious lake on the desert, or an incongruous film of water over a portion of the highway ahead on a clear hot day, are typical examples of inferior mirages. These phenomena occur only under conditions where, in the lowest few feet of the atmosphere, the air is superheated and substantially less dense than the air above it. The apparent pool of water is but a refracted and shimmering image of the clear sky above (see Fig. 1). Light rays from a point *S* in the sky are curved upward by refraction so that an image of a patch of the sky is formed at a point directly beneath, and seems to originate in a point *S′* below the ground. The glistening, waterlike image of the sky thus appears as if reflected from the ground at a point *I*, where the line of sight from the observer *O* intersects the ground in front of the apparent source *S′*.

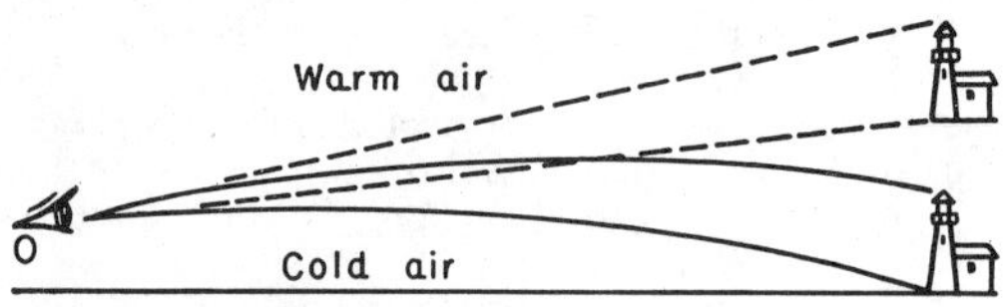

Fig. 2. Superior mirage.

Conversely, if the light rays from a distant object are refracted downward on entering a cold air mass having greater density, the apparent position of the object is elevated above its actual position (see Fig. 2). If the density transition is marked, the image of an object on the ground may be projected upward against the sky in a phenomenon known as a *superior* mirage ("looming"). When a strong temperature inversion occurs some 30 feet above the surface, as is common over quiet bodies of water, a superior mirage is frequently formed. Because of this stratum of abnormally warm air overlying a stratum of cold air, many complex refractions resulting in both erect and inverted images, and fragments thereof, are possible, depending upon the height of the observer and his angle of vision with respect to the refracting layer.

As an optically real, though physically illusory phenomenon, a mirage can be photographed.

FERGUS J. WOOD.

MIRAMICHI, mĭr-ȧ-mĭ-shē′ (Indian "happy retreat"), river, New Brunswick, Canada, formed by several streams flowing east or northeast and joining to enter Miramichi Bay on the Gulf of St. Lawrence. The main stream, the Southwest Miramichi, is 135 miles long. Newcastle and Chatham are the chief towns on the lower river.

MIRAMON, mē-rä-môn′, **Miguel,** Mexican soldier and politician: b. Mexico City, Mexico, Sept. 29, 1832; d. Querétaro, June 19, 1867. Educated at a military school in Chapultepec, Miramón fought in the Mexican Army against the United States in 1847, and by 1855 had risen to the rank of colonel. The next year he took part in two unsuccessful revolts at Puebla against the moderate liberal provisional president, Ignacio Comonfort. When the War of the Reform began in 1858, he joined Gen. Félix Zuloaga as leader of the Conservative faction against the Liberals, led by Benito Juárez. Miramón was chosen by the Conservative junta to succeed Zuloaga as president in February 1859, but was defeated at Capulálpam (Dec. 22, 1860) by Jesús González Ortéga, Juárez' general, and fled to Cuba and then to Europe. There he became involved in Napoleon III's plans to invade Mexico, and returned to his native land with Maximilian in 1862 as a grand marshal. From 1864 to 1866 he served as minister to Berlin. When Maximilian's army was finally defeated by Juárez at Querétaro (May 14, 1867), Miramón was taken prisoner and later shot, along with the emperor.

MIRANDA, mē-rän′dä, **Francisco de,** Venezuelan precursor of South American independence: b. Caracas, Venezuela, March 28, 1750; d. Cádiz, Spain, July 14, 1816. As an officer in the Spanish Army he fought in North Africa and then volunteered for service in the Western Hemisphere, where he played a part in the American Revolution. Miranda received the surrender of the British at Pensacola, Fla.; cooperated in the capture of New Providence in the Bahamas; and after Admiral François de Grasse had captured Tobago (1781), helped him re-equip and provision his fleet for the voyage to Chesapeake Bay, thus contributing to the decisive Franco-American victory at Yorktown. Angered at the arrogant attitude of the Peninsular Spaniards toward colonials, Miranda sailed to the United States. It was in New York (1784) that, according to his own testimony, he formed "a project for the liberty of the entire Spanish-American Continent with the cooperation of England." By this time he had made the acquaintance of almost every important United States leader.

After 18 months in North America, the Venezuelan patriot sailed for England. During a six-month stay in London he made friends, heard debates in the House of Commons, and wrote articles about the prospects for freedom in South America. Then, to complete his "imperfect education," he also traveled widely on the Continent. In Russia he became so much a favorite of Catherine II that, after his return to London, he was granted the protection of the Russian embassy there. At a conference with Prime Minister William Pitt, plans were discussed for liberation of the Spanish colonies in America. In 1792, however, Miranda became interested in the French Revolution and in September 1793, as a general of division, served under Charles François Dumouriez on the historic field of Valmy. Another victory, this time at Antwerp, was followed by a debacle of the Republic's armies at Neerwinden. Tried on charges of treachery for this defeat, the Venezuelan was acquitted triumphantly. When Napoleon won control of France, however, Miranda returned to London and, renewing his friendship with Pitt, maintained contact with numerous agents in the Americas. In 1806 his first expedition to Venezuela, organized in New York with the alleged connivance of American authorities, ended in complete failure.

Napoleon's invasion of the Iberian Peninsula (1810) set the stage for uprisings in Hispanic America. On April 19, the patriotic forces in Venezuela decided to disown the distant Madrid regency. This was the signal for Miranda to return to his own land. After eloquent speeches by Miranda and Simón Bolívar, the first republic in South America was proclaimed in Caracas on July 5, 1811. When royalist armies threatened to destroy the young republic, Don Francisco was elected generalissimo and virtual dictator; but due to disunity and the fall of the fortress of Puerto Cabello, the Venezuelan leader was forced to capitulate, July 25, 1812. Trapped by the Spaniards in the port of La Guaira, Miranda was transported a prisoner to Cádiz where he died on the anniversary of the fall of the Bastille.

Consult Robertson, William S., *The Life of Miranda* (Chapel Hill, N.C., 1929); Thorning, Joseph F., *Miranda: World Citizen* (Gainesville, Fla., 1952).

JOSEPH F. THORNING,
Advisory Editor of "The Americas."

MIRANDA, state, Venezuela, on the Caribbean coast, south and east of the Federal District. The area is 3,069 square miles; the capital, Los Teques. The terrain is mountainous except for the lower valley of the Tuy River, which crosses the state from west to east. The chief occupation is agriculture (coffee, cacao, sugarcane, and other crops). Extensive mineral deposits are mostly undeveloped. Pop. (1950) 276,273.

MIRANDOLA, mē-rän'dô-lä, commune, Italy, in Modena Province, Emilia-Romagna Region, 18 miles northeast of Modena. Its records go back to 1102, when the first fort was probably built. Until 1710 it was the seat of the Pico family, of which the humanist, Count Giovanni Pico della Mirandola, was the most famous member. It is a cathedral town and a rail terminus, and manufactures canned goods, macaroni, hemp products, shoes, and chassis trucks. Pop. (1961) 22,528.

MIRBEAU, mĕr-bō', **Octave (Henri Marie),** French novelist and playwright: b. Trévières, Calvados, France, Feb. 16, 1850; d. Paris, Feb. 16, 1917. Educated at a Jesuit school at Vannes, of which he later wrote bitterly in *Sébastien Roch* (1890), Mirbeau became dramatic critic on *L'ordre,* and a founder of the satirical paper *Les grimaces.* His political ideas were often unpopular, but he was influential in attracting favorable attention to contemporary painters and writers, and was an early defender of Capt. Alfred Dreyfus (q.v.). His stories of the peasants of Normandy, where he was born, were well received in 1886, and he published several novels. In 1897 his *Les mauvais bergers,* a five-act drama, was played by Sarah Bernhardt. His most successful play, *Les affaires sont les affaires* (1903), was produced in New York as *Business is Business* (1905).

MIRFIELD, mûr'fēld, urban district, England, in the West Riding of Yorkshire, on the Calder River and canal, four miles northeast of Huddersfield. It is a railroad junction, and an important cotton and woolen milling town, making carpets and blankets. Pop. (1961) 12,289.

MIRIAM, mĭr'ĭ-ăm, in Biblical history, the sister of Moses and Aaron, first mentioned (Exodus 2:4–10) as being stationed by her mother to watch her brother Moses' cradle among the rushes on the riverbank. In Exodus 15:20–21, Miriam is called "the prophetess," and leads the women in a song of rejoicing over the safe crossing of the Red Sea. Later (Numbers 12) she rebuked Moses for his marriage with an Ethiopian woman, and for this was stricken with leprosy, but the curse was removed. She died after the wandering in the desert, and was buried in Kadesh.

MIRKHOND, mĕr-kŏnd' (Pers. MIRKHVAND; Ar. MUḤAMMAD IBN-KHAVAND SHAH IBN-MAḤMUD), Persian historian: b. 1433; d. at Herat (now in Afghanistan) June 22, 1498. His father was a native of Bokhara who migrated to Balkh; Mirkhond spent most of his life in Herat, which was then a flourishing center of the arts. Mirkhond compiled a monumental history, the *Rauḍat-al-Ṣafā'* (*Garden of Purity*), which in seven huge volumes recounted the history of the known world, from the Creation through the time of patriarchs, prophets, and pre-Muslim kings of Iran, up to his own time. The seventh volume was continued by another hand, probably that of his grandson Khvandamir, to the year 1507.

Mirkhond drew on a vast number of earlier works, and in the first volume listed all the Persian and Arabic historical works known to him, but by modern standards the *Garden of Purity* is often tedious and uncritical. It was for a long time the chief history of Persia known to European scholars, however, and between the 17th and 19th centuries parts of it were edited and translated into Spanish, French, German, and English. The last two volumes, dealing with Mirkhond's own time, were valuable historical documents on the Timurid period, and the fifth volume contains some material on Mongol history not found in other sources. In Persia Mirkhond's work was so highly esteemed that in the mid-19th century a Persian historian added a supplement bringing the history up to his own time.

Mirkhond's style, remarkable for its florid verbosity, was greatly admired by non-Persians writing in the Persian language, and was emulated by 16th century writers attached to the court of the Mughul emperors of India.

MIRÓ, mē-rō′, **Joan,** Spanish artist: b. Montroig, Catalonia, Spain, April 20, 1893. Miró's education in painting began at the age of 14 in the School of Fine Arts of Barcelona under Modesto Urgell and José Pascó. In 1912 he studied at the Gali Academy, where Miró's interest in the allied arts was stimulated by Francesco Gali.

Miró's early works show the influence of Cézanne, Van Gogh, and the Fauves, whose works had been known in Barcelona through José Dalmau, who organized Miró's first one-man show in Barcelona in 1918. Miró went to Paris in 1919 where he met Picasso and responded to the innocent honesty of the Douanier Henri Rousseau (1844–1910). He synthesized these opposing influences in the next few years in work containing all the germs of his later style. After 1921 surrealism predominated over cubism in Miró's work, a surrealism of lines, circles, and cones distributed in a readable symbolism. The moustache appearing with the regularity and intensity of a psychological fixation, the sex symbols recurring up to the 1950's, and the rich colors and shapes of black and white which became typical of his work, were released by his contact with Dadism and the surrealist movement.

Miró collaborated with Max Ernst in designing the sets and costumes for *Romeo and Juliet* (1927) of the *Ballets Russes* of Sergei Pavlovich Diaghilev, and in 1928 he made a trip to Holland which resulted in his *Dutch Interior* (1928). He also turned to collages and constructions at this time, and painted a series of imaginary portraits. With the advent of the Spanish Civil War (1936–1939) his work became increasingly abstract and forbidding.

During World War II, Miró stayed at Palma de Mallorca where he painted a series of gouaches called "constellations" from the multitude of correlated shapes on their surfaces. The myriad details in black generate tension; yet the works are as witty and charming outwardly as any of his deeply possessed painting. Reacting from the "constellations," Miró produced a number of looser, opener works which herald the mellowness of his later painting.

In 1944 Miró began his association with José Artigas, the ceramist. In this field Miró's designs are logical extensions of the arbitrary shapes supplied by Artigas. A second burst of ceramic creativity culminated in the decorative walls commissioned for the UNESCO headquarters building in Paris (1955–1958). In 1947 he painted a mural for a restaurant in Cincinnati, Ohio, and from 1950 to 1951 he worked on another mural for the Harvard University Graduate Center. Lush areas of diaphanous colors appear in most of his work from 1950 to 1960.

HERBERT D. HALE, JR.

An 84-inch telescope mirror blank, designed for the National Observatory, Kitt Peak, Ariz. Ribbing of the back face provides great strength and rigidity at minimum weight.

Corning Glass Works

MIRÓ FERRER, Gabriel (GABRIEL MIRÓ). See SPAIN—*11. Literature* (The 20th Century).

MIRROR, mĭr′ẽr, any bright, smooth, surface used for reflecting light or an image. The surface may be of glass, of metal, or of metal-coated glass, depending on its purpose, and it may be flat, concave, or convex.

Common household mirrors or looking glasses are customarily made of flat glass, such as plate glass, backed on one side by silver. Metal mirrors or reflectors are often employed in searchlights, in solar furnaces, and where there is need for a surface that will not crack when subjected to violent temperature changes. Optical mirrors, such as those used in telescopes, cameras, and the like, are usually made of optically correct glass coated with silver or some other metallic substance.

History.—Highly polished mirrors, usually of bronze, were used by Egyptian women in the 3d millennium B.C. Mirrors are mentioned in the Pentateuch (Exodus 38:8), and thin metal disks with handles, similar to those of the ancient Egyptians, were employed by the Greeks, Etruscans, and Romans, and were made by Celtic craftsmen in western Europe. In the Middle Ages pocket mirrors of polished steel or silver were used. Glass mirrors were made in Venice as early as 1300 A.D., and in Nürnberg in 1373, but it was not until the 17th century that Venetian glassmakers were imported to France and England to make sheets of plate glass for use in wall mirrors such as those in the Hall of Mirrors at Versailles. The usual backing for glass mirrors, introduced by the Venetians and in general use until the 19th century, was tin foil amalgamated with mercury. In 1835, Baron Justus von Liebig (1803–1873), a German chemist, observed that upon heating aldehyde with an ammoniacal solution of nitrate of silver in a glass vessel, a brilliant deposit of metallic silver was formed on the surface of the glass. To this observation the more recent process of silvering glass may be largely credited.

Coating Materials.—The chemical deposition of silver on glass became by far the most common treatment. Silvering preparations in use in the mid-20th century consisted in part of an ammoniacal solution of silver nitrate and potassium hydroxide, plus a reducing solution which converts the ammoniacal silver to metallic form. Other metals used in coating processes include platinum, gold, palladium, ruthenium, rhodium, iridium, and copper. Rhodium plate on a metallic base is also used in the manufacture of mirrors, and evaporated aluminum on glass is sometimes employed to make mirrors for telescopes. Also used in telescopes is speculum metal, an alloy of copper and tin, sometimes with a little arsenic, antimony, or zinc added to make it whiter. It is capable of taking a brilliant polish. Thiourea is used as a backing for nonglare mirrors.

Types of Mirrors.—Mirrors are spoken of as first-surface or second-surface mirrors, according to whether the light is reflected directly without passing through glass or is reflected from a backing after passing through glass. Ordinary looking glasses are second-surface mirrors, but where there is an advantage, as in precise optical work, in having a pure reflection with no refraction, first-surface mirrors are used.

Half-silvering is a method of putting on a mirror a thinner than normal coating which reflects a percentage of the light and lets the remainder pass through. A half-silvered glass placed between a darkened room and a lighted room will appear as a reflecting surface to anyone in the lighted room but will be transparent to someone viewing it from the darkened side.

In addition to the familiar flat surface, there are mirrors which are convex, concave, and even spherical and paraboloid in shape. Of special importance are concave mirrors, which produce real images of distant objects and are used in place of objective lenses for large astronomical telescopes in order to obtain greater distance. For example, the 200-inch mirror of the Hale telescope on Mount Palomar, by catching more light, permits the observation of stars twice as far away as the 100-inch mirror on Mount Wilson. See also Observatory—*Mount Wilson and Palomar Observatories;* Telescope—*The Reflecting Telescope.*

Frank Dorr,
Associate Editor, "Popular Science Monthly."

MIRROR CARP. See Carp.

MIRROR FOR MAGISTRATES, A, one of the popular collections of early Elizabethan narrative poetry. The term mirror emphasizes the didactic purpose of the book—the edification of persons having special responsibilities of office and public leadership. Each example is a verse narrative of the life of someone prominent in early English history and a victim of misfortune.

The idea and model for such a book is medieval. Giovanni Boccaccio had written verse "tragedies" about the downfall of illustrious persons in *De Casibus Virorum Illustrium,* which Geoffrey Chaucer made use of for *The Monk's Tale* and John Lydgate adapted and expanded as *The Fall of Princes* (c. 1430).

For a new edition of the Lydgate work about 1555, the publisher John Wayland engaged the services of William Baldwin, George Ferrers, and other poets to write poems about the misfortunes of prominent Englishmen, but Queen Mary's chancellor stopped the publication of these modern examples. After Elizabeth I came to the throne the new poems were published as *A Mirror for Magistrates* (1559), 19 narrative "tragedies" of the period from the reign of Richard II through that of Edward IV (1377–1483).

The next edition (1563) is of even greater significance in the development of English poetry. Eight new biographical poems were added including two of special literary merit—Thomas Sackville's *Complaint of Henry Duke of Buckingham* with an "induction," which has been called the greatest English poem between Chaucer and Edmund Spenser; and Thomas Churchyard's *Shore's Wife.*

Numerous editions continued to appear as late as 1610, with a great deal of new material added to cater to the popular thirst for sentimental and didactic narrative poetry.

William Bracy.

MIRROR OF PERFECTION, The, an intimate and illuminating account of St. Francis of Assisi. The volume, of about 50,000 words, was written by Leo of Assisi, who is often spoken of as the beloved disciple of St. Francis. "Brother Leo was not merely a fellow-townsman, 'companion,' disciple, and dear friend of Francis of Assisi. He was also his sicknurse, secretary and confessor during the last six years of his life. None knew Francis so intimately, or remembered him so well. None could be more scrupulously conscientious in recording what he believed to be the exact truth about the not yet canonized Saint." It is the oldest life of St. Francis, and was completed, according to a note at the end of the volume, "this fifth of the Ides of May in the year of Our Lord 1228." St. Francis died Oct. 3, 1226. The significance of the title is disclosed in these words of the author: "Here endeth the Mirror of Perfection of a brother Minor; to wit, of the Blessed Francis, wherein we may most sufficiently behold as in a glass the perfection of his calling and profession."

The style in which the book is written is in keeping with the spirit and character of the subject, and of the type of life he represented—simple, direct, shorn of all scholarly vanities and conceits, as the life of the subject was shorn of all worldly comforts. There is a charm and power of revelation to this narrative that is simple and homely almost to the point of bluntness. It is hardly a disinterested biography. Some of it has been written with the distinct purpose of showing not only what kind of man St. Francis was and the kind of life he lived, but what principles and rules he laid down as the foundation of the famous order which takes its name from him; it is plainly also the purpose to show that obedience to these principles is the true path of the perfect Christian. Sometimes Brother Leo becomes controversial, taking vigorous issue with those who "desired to ignore certain of the wishes and to modify certain of the injunctions of Francis in what they believed to be the interests of the Order." All this, however, does not lessen the value of the book as a carefully drawn and reliable picture of the founder of the order of Franciscans. Leo recounts instances showing with what unswerving zeal St. Francis carried out to the limit of perfect example his ideals of absolute poverty in all things, of humility, charity, compassion, and condescension. There may be much more to the life of St. Francis than is here given, but the author has pictured Francis in the fashion in which he most desired to appear before his fellow men.

MIRZA, mēr′-zä, a Persian title, derived from the Persian *mīr-zāda,* with the original meaning of "born of a prince." The title came also to be applied to noblemen, and in the early 18th century its use was further extended to men of education other than religious scholars. Both in Iran and western India and Pakistan "Mirza" placed before a given name is roughly the equivalent of "Mr." When it occurs after the given name it has the meaning of "prince."

MIRZAPUR, mĭr′zä-pŏŏr, the name of a district and a city in India. The district, which has an area of 4,322 square miles, is situated in southeastern Uttar Pradesh south of the Ganges River. It is crossed from east to west by the Vindhya Range. The section north of the mountains is highly cultivable, yielding crops of rice, wheat, corn, sugarcane, linseed, rape, and mustard, but the rest of the district consists of gorges and sparsely populated forests. This land once made up a large proportion of the hereditary domains of the maharaja of Banaras (Benares). Pop. (1951) 1,017,289.

The city of MIRZAPUR, capital of the district, is located on the right bank of the Ganges, 35 miles west-southwest of Banaras. Once the largest market on the river for grain and cotton, it is still a commercial center of some importance. There are fine sandstone quarries nearby, and Mirzapur is famous for its brass industry, lac factories, and handmade woolen carpets and rugs dyed with traditional permanent vegetable colorings. The river front which is lined with stone ghats or flights of stairs (Pukka Ghat, especially), temples, mosques, and homes of wealthy merchants, is attractive, but the interior of the city is composed to a great extent of mud huts. Within the municipal limits is Vindhyachal (Bindhyachal), which is an important center of pilgrimage famous for a shrine to Vindhyeshwari, meaning "Our Lady of the Vindhyas," a form of Kali whose temple here was once a rendezvous of the Thugs (see THUG). Pop. (1941) 70,944.

RODERICK MARSHALL.

MISAMIS OCCIDENTAL, mê-sä′mês ôk-sê-thân-täl′, province, Philippines, situated in Mindanao, bounded on the north by the Mindanao Sea, on the east by Iligan Bay, on the west by Zamboanga del Norte and Zamboanga del Sur, and on the south by Lanao. Its area of 802 square miles is largely mountainous; Mount Malindang (7,956 feet) is the highest peak. Corn, coconuts, and hemp are the chief products. The principal towns are Oroquieta (the capital), Ozamiz (formerly Misamis), Plaridel, and Tangub. Until 1939, Misamis Occidental formed with Misamis Oriental the single province of Misamis. Pop. (1948) 207,575; (1957 est.) 244,870.

MISAMIS ORIENTAL, mê-sä′mês ō-ryân-täl′, province, Philippines, situated in Mindanao, bounded on the north by the Mindanao Sea, on the east by Agusan, on the west by Iligan Bay, and on the south by Bukidnon and Lanao. Included within its 1,512 square miles is Camiguin Island. The chief products are hemp, coconuts, corn, rice, and tobacco. The principal towns are Cagayan (the capital), Gingoog, and Balingasag. Misamis Oriental was formed in 1939 from a part of the former province of Misamis. Pop. (1948) 369,671; (1957 est.) 436,080.

MISANTHROPE, mē-zäN-trôp′, **Le,** a five-act comedy in verse by Molière (q.v.), produced at the Théâtre du Palais-Royal, Paris, on June 4, 1666, when the author was 44 years old. It is Molière's most realistic and most serious work, a comedy of character and manners, a parlor comedy; or perhaps not, in the modern sense, a comedy at all, but a drama. The central character is Alceste, a gentleman who tries to conduct his life on a basis of honesty, sincerity, and truth telling. But he is a misanthrope, because he hates mankind's mean compromises and convenient falsities. His foil is his friend Philinte, who accepts the world, finding its ways amusing rather than hateful, and who represents enlightened common sense. Alceste loves Célimène, a charming coquette, avid for attention and adoration. The action is slight. Alceste's angry efforts for total sincerity involve him in a series of misfortunes as the world takes its revenge for his excess of virtue. Through five acts he seeks a resolution with Célimène; in the end, defeated, he flees to a country solitude, and Célimène refuses to accompany him.

Le misanthrope is Molières most original, most profound play. The sources lie in his own experience. The play was written during a dreadful year, when Molière was constantly harried, ill, and overworked, when his theatrical ventures went awry, when he discovered his wife's unfaithfulness. Alceste is a transposition of Molière's own misanthropic mood, as Philinte is a transposition of the happier side of Molière's character. The role of Célimène, played by Molière's wife, Armande, is written to display her charm and with a painful awareness of her faults.

The play has been interpreted in various ways. Jean Jacques Rousseau called it an immoral attack on nobility of character. Others have praised its lesson of the golden mean. Still others see Alceste as a tragic hero, a King Lear undone by a wicked world. And some say there is no problem; the play is just a stage play, with characters who have no significance beyond the necessities of the performance. Well, if a work of art can hold a content of mystery, to puzzle and fascinate three centuries, that work can be called great. Alceste, on the stage or in print, continues to live and change and enter our own quiet thought. *Le misanthrope* is Molière's *Hamlet.*

There are modern verse translations by Richard Wilbur, *The Misanthrope* (1955), and by Morris Bishop, *Eight Plays by Molière* (1957).

MORRIS BISHOP.

MISCARRIAGE, mĭs-kăr′ĭj, *in medical jurisprudence,* a term employed in the sense of abortion (q.v.). *In law,* a miscarriage of justice is a failure of the law to attain its ends, as in cases in which a party's rights are prejudiced.

MISDEMEANOR, mĭs-dê-mēn′ẽr, in law, an act committed or omitted in violation of public law. In the classification of crimes a misdemeanor is a relatively minor offense, as distinguished from a felony (q.v.). Generally misdemeanors are offenses punishable by fine or imprisonment other than in a penitentiary. Infractions of municipal ordinances, such as minor traffic violations, are not considered misdemeanors. Whether a particular crime is a felony or a misdemeanor is ordinarily determined by the maximum sentence possible under the controlling statute rather than by the actual extent of the punishment awarded by the judge or jury. Some courts, however, have declared that where a crime may be punished either as a misdemeanor or as a felony, it will be considered to be only a misdemeanor. The practical significance of the distinction is that an arraignment (q.v.) is almost universally considered essential in felony cases, but there is a difference of opinion as to whether it is necessary in prosecutions for misdemeanors.

In a broader sense, the term "misdemeanor" may denote misconduct or misbehavior, such as malpractice by a lawyer or maladministration by a public official.

See also CRIME.

RICHARD L. HIRSHBERG.

MISENO, mê-zâ'nô, **Cape,** promontory, Italy, situated between the Bay of Naples and the Gulf of Gaeta. It is marked by a lighthouse. At its foot are the ruins of Misenum, a resort town in Roman times. In 31 B.C., Marcus Vipsanius Agrippa, later son-in-law of Augustus, constructed a naval station there which became one of the chief bases of the Roman fleet. The town was destroyed by the Saracens in 890 A.D., and only the remains of a reservoir and a theater are still extant.

MISERABLES, mē-zâ-rȧ'bl', **Les,** the greatest work of Victor Hugo (q.v.), published in 10 volumes in 1862 while the author was in exile in Guernsey. The action covers the years 1815 to 1833.

Jean Valjean, a poor peasant of Brie, is sent to the galleys for stealing a loaf of bread for his sister's starving children. Attempts to escape lengthen his term to 19 years; on his release in 1815 he finds every door shut against him. He finally is sheltered by the saintly Bishop Myriel, whose silver dishes he steals. Caught with the goods by a suspicious policeman, he faces return to the galleys until the bishop, called to identify his property, says that the dishes were a gift and adds to them his silver candlesticks. The bishop's act changes Valjean's life. Under the assumed name of Madeleine he prospers for 8 years, becomes noted for his charities, and is chosen mayor of his town. Only Javert, the police inspector, eyes him askance, observing his likeness to the convict he had once known. Then word comes that a petty thief at Champmathieu has been identified as Jean Valjean and faces a life sentence for another theft the real Valjean had committed 8 years before. After a terrible struggle with his conscience, Valjean gives himself up and receives the life sentence. Escaping, he finds sanctuary as a convent gardener in Paris.

One of the needy he had helped in his prosperous days was Fantine, a Parisian grisette deserted by her lover. She was struggling to support her little daughter, Cosette, whom she had entrusted to Thénardier, a villainous innkeeper at Montfermeil. Valjean had promised the dying Fantine to care for Cosette, and kept his promise after his escape, though with Javert on his track it added to the risk of recapture.

Meanwhile in Paris, Marius Pontmercy, son of a Napoleonic officer, had quarreled with his royalist grandfather and joined a revolutionary organization seeking to restore the republic. He and Cosette meet and fall in love. When street fighting breaks out in 1832, Valjean saves Marius, unconscious and desperately wounded, by carrying him for miles through the Paris sewers, having previously saved Javert's life when he was in the hands of the revolutionaries. Javert, torn between his debt to Valjean and his duty as a policeman, can find no way out of the dilemma except in suicide. Marius recovers, is reconciled with his grandfather, and marries Cosette. Valjean, having revealed his past to Marius, pines away with grief at losing Cosette, but dies happy in the knowledge that both the young people love and reverence him the more for his sufferings.

The book is filled with moral disquisitions, and with such rhetorical set pieces as the description of the Battle of Waterloo and the historical essay on the sewers of Paris. Hugo is always positive, whether his facts are right or not. Coincidence is endemic; wherever they go, Valjean, Javert, and the Thénardiers run into each other. Passages of wild melodrama, reminiscent of the Gothic romances, alternate with episodes of grim realism. But the very copiousness of the writing and the geographical exactness of the settings give the book a vitality which overrides all the mechanical contrivances of its plot. Primarily a study of the redemption of a soul through voluntary expiation, *Les misérables* is also an epic of democratic idealism and a realistic novel. It even contains elements of autobiography, for the character of young Marius is a somewhat glorified portrait of young Victor Hugo.

DELANCEY FERGUSON.

MISERERE, mĭz-ĕ-rē'rê or mĭz-ĕ-rē' rā (Lat. "have mercy"), the name (taken from its first word) by which the 50th Psalm in the Vulgate edition of the Bible is known, corresponding to the 51st Psalm of the Authorized Version. The fourth of the seven penitential Psalms, it forms part of certain liturgies and has been set to music by many composers. The Miserere of Gregorio Allegri (q.v.) is particularly famous.

In architecture, misereres are projections on the undersides of the seats of the stalls of medieval churches and chapels. Usually they are elaborately carved. When the seats are folded up, the misereres serve as supports to standing worshipers. See also STALL.

MISFEASANCE. See LEGAL TERMS.

MISHAWAKA, mĭsh-ȧ-wô'kȧ, city, Indiana, situated in St. Joseph County, at the head of navigation of the St. Joseph River, at an altitude of 725 feet, on the Grand Trunk and New York Central railroads, 4 miles east of South Bend. The surrounding district raises corn, wheat, oats, and rye, and power generated by dams in the river above the city has been used in the local industries. Mishawaka's varied products include clothing, rubber and leather footwear, foundry equipment, upholstery, bedding, furniture, plastics, structural steel, drop forgings, brass and bronze castings, machinery, and guided missiles. The city has a public library, a high school, and six parks.

The name Mishawaka was that of an Indian village which once occupied the site. White settlement began as early as 1828, and in the early 1830's the St. Joseph Iron Works was established on the south side of the river and Indiana City was laid out on the north side. In 1839 the two villages were combined as the town of Mishawaka, and incorporation as a city was effected in 1899. Government is administered by a mayor and council. Pop. 35,517.

MISHMIS, mĭsh′mēz, members of a Mongoloid tribe living north of the upper Brahmaputra River in Assam, India. A primitive, short-statured people speaking a Tibeto-Burman language, they derive their livelihood from agriculture and grazing. The Mishmis are divided into four groups, all of which practice polygamy and engage in blood feuds.

MISHNAH or **MISHNA,** mĭsh′nȧ, the first part or text of the Talmud, consisting of oral traditions and glosses on the Pentateuch, compiled by Judah (Jehudah) called ha-Nasi or ha-Kadosh (q.v.) about 210 A.D., and based in part on earlier compilations. The second part of the Talmud, known as the Gemara, is a commentary on the Mishnah, rendered necessary because of the extreme terseness of the style in which the latter is composed. The Mishnah, which is divided into six orders, is written in Hebrew, but it contains a number of Greek, Latin, and Aramaic words, as well as traces of Aramaic idioms. The traditions set down in the Mishnah were held by the Pharisees to be of equal authority with the written law of Moses, and were supposed to constitute an oral law delivered to Moses by God and by Moses delivered to Joshua, by Joshua to the elders, by the elders to the prophets, and by the prophets to the men of the Great Synagogue. The Sadducees rejected this doctrine, although in many cases they followed the oral traditions with great fidelity. See also HEBREW LANGUAGE AND LITERATURE—*Hebrew Literature* (Biblical and Post-Biblical Writing): The Mishnah; JEWISH HISTORY AND SOCIETY—*6. World of the Talmud.*

MISIONES, mê-syō′nâs, province, Argentina, bounded on the north by the Iguassú River, which separates it from Brazil; on the east and southeast by Brazil, from which it is separated in part by the Uruguay River; on the southwest by Corrientes Province; and on the west by the Paraná River, which divides it from Paraguay. It has an area of 11,749 square miles, most of which is forested. Three low mountain chains radiate from the center of the province. Besides timber and dyewoods, the chief products are cotton, sugarcane, corn, rice, tobacco, yerba maté, and tung oil. There are interesting remains of 17th century Jesuit missions, and the Iguassú Falls on the Brazilian border, which average 200 feet in height, attract many visitors. The capital is Posadas, on the Paraná opposite Encarnación, Paraguay. Formerly a territory, Misiones became a province in 1953. Pop. (1947 census) 246,396; (est. 1955) 327,578.

MISKOLC, mĭsh′kôlts, city, Hungary, situated on the Sajó River, at the foot of the Bükk Mountains, 85 miles northeast of Budapest, with which it is connected by air and rail. Second in industrial importance to Budapest, it also carries on a substantial trade in grain, tobacco, wine, and fruit. Its varied manufactures include iron and steel, motor vehicles, locomotives, textiles, furniture, shoes, paper, flour and other food products, lumber, bricks, and soap. There are large lignite mines nearby.

The city has a 13th century Gothic church, a law school, a technical university, and a museum noted for its Scythian remains. On nearby Mount Avas are government-owned vineyards, and 4 miles southwest of the city is Tapolca, with its warm springs and baths. Miskolc suffered destruction by the Mongols in the 13th century, and by the Turks in the 16th and 17th centuries. Pop. (1960) 143,400.

MISPICKEL. See ARSENOPYRITE.

MISPRISION, mĭs-prĭsh′ŭn, a legal term applied to certain types of misconduct. Negative misprision consists in the failure to inform the proper authorities of some wrongdoing of which one has knowledge. Positive misprision consists in a contempt of the sovereign or the maladministration of high office. The terms "misprision of felony" and "misprision of treason" are used to denote concealment of these crimes by one who has knowledge of them.

MISRULE, mĭs-ro͞ol′, **Lord of,** the title given to the leader of the Christmas revels in the Middle Ages in England. He was probably a descendant of the king of the ancient Roman Saturnalia, who impersonated Saturn. In *A Survay of London . . .* (1598–1603), John Stow gives the following account of him: "In the feast of Christmas there was in the king's house, wheresoever he lodged, a Lord of Misrule or Master of Merry Disports, and the like had ye in the house of every nobleman of honor or good worship. The mayor of London and the sheriffs had their several Lords of Misrule ever contending without quarrel or offence, who should make the rarest pastime to delight the beholders. These lords beginning their rūle at Allhallows Eve continued the same till the morrow after Candlemas Day, in which space there were fine and subtle disguisings, masks and mummeries, with playing at cards for counters in every house, more for pastimes than for gain." In Cambridge and Oxford universities the functions of the lord of misrule were performed by a master of arts who was elected to superintend the annual reproduction of Latin plays by the students, besides taking charge of their diversions during the Christmas season. The ceremonies attending the lord of misrule at the Inns of Court in London were particularly splendid. In Scotland a similar function was performed by the abbot of unreason.

MISSAL, mĭs′ăl (Medieval Latin *Missale,* from *Missa,* Mass), in the Roman Catholic Church, the book which in its modern form contains all the prayers (including special blessings connected with the Mass) and rubrics required by the priest for celebrating Mass throughout the ecclesiastical year. In antiquity and in the early Middle Ages the priest employed a Sacramentary, a book containing only what he had to say himself. Portions of the Mass sung by the choir and the Epistle and Gospel were in separate books: Antiphonary, Gradual, Lectionary or Epistolary, Evangeliary or Evangelistary. An Ordo or Directorium, an annual calendar containing directions for the Mass of each day during the year, was also needed.

The first step toward amalgamating these separate books into one was taken by early Irish missionaries with the *Libelli Missae,* little books containing only two or three Masses, but including all parts of the Mass. The *Missale plenarium* (complete Missal) began to take shape in the late

10th century but did not reach its full development or come into general use before the second half of the 13th century. While the Canon of the Mass was the same everywhere, medieval missals exhibited a wide variety, corresponding to local uses or to those of the older religious orders: Ambrosian rite, Sarum use, Lyon use, and Carmelite, Carthusian, Dominican, and other uses. The *Missale plenarium* developed by the Franciscans was adopted by the Roman Curia under Pope Clement V (r. 1305–1314). This *Missale secundum consuetudinem Romanae Curiae* (first edition, 1474) and those of other uses were widely disseminated after the invention of printing.

A thorough revision of the *Missale Romanum,* entrusted to the pope by the Council of Trent, was published under Pius V (1570) with an accompanying bull requiring its exclusive employment except in the case of uses which could show a prescription of 200 years. The new Missal was subsequently revised under Clement VIII (1604), Urban VIII (1634), Leo XIII (1884), and Pius X (ordered in 1911, but completed under Benedict XV in 1920).

Many of the extant medieval missals are masterpieces of calligraphy, illumination, and bookbinding.

MARTIN R. P. MCGUIRE,
Professor of Greek, Latin and Ancient History, The Catholic University of America.

MISSI DOMINICI, mĭs′ī dŏ-mĭn′ĭ-sī, special envoys sent out by the Carolingian rulers. They were instituted by Charles Martel (689?–741) and Pepin the Short (r. 751–768) and were made a regular part of the administration by Charlemagne (r. 768–814). Every year, Charlemagne sent into each district two or three missi dominici, of whom one was always a prelate. It was their business to hold court, hear complaints, redress grievances, and make full reports to the emperor. By this means, Charlemagne controlled the courts and centralized the government of his vast empire. The missi dominici disappeared from France and Germany in the 9th century and from Italy in the 10th century.

MISSILE RANGES, mĭs′ĭl rān′jĕz, areas with testing facilities, launching complexes, and networks of tracking and control stations developed primarily for the launching of all types of single stage or multistage rockets, such as the missiles which propel warheads or other payloads in guided or ballistic trajectories toward their targets and the space carriers which inject satellites into terrestrial orbits or send space vehicles off toward the moon or other bodies in the solar system.

EVOLUTION OF RANGES

Missile ranges evolved from simple open spaces, in which the rockets or missiles could be fired and recovered over short distances, to today's complex, costly, and extensive ranges which must also track and receive information from the vehicles during flight. Modern ranges reflect modern rocket systems: each rocket costs up to several million dollars and contains thousands of parts; the larger rockets can reach any point on earth as well as some nearer bodies in space. Proving the accuracy and reliability of such vehicles requires elaborate step-by-step testing programs which involve many test flights. Almost as many things can go wrong in a rocket as it has parts. When failure occurs, and failure must always be expected in developing a new system, engineers must know precisely what part failed and when and why it failed, in order to correct for the next attempt. Therefore ranges must be equipped not only with the multitude of facilities necessary to launch modern rockets—assembly shops, checkout equipment, fueling stations, launch pads, control centers in blockhouses, and central control stations—but also with instruments to photograph, track with radar and radio, and receive data and transmit commands during the rocket's brief lifetime between roaring blast-off and silent orbit, flight through space, or fiery impact.

Early Rocket Ranges.—The first rocket-powered missiles were developed as a result of the invention of gunpowder. Missiles propelled by burning gunpowder helped the Chinese repel invading Mongols at the siege of Kaifeng in 1232 A.D. Before their use, these missiles were tested presumably at the world's first missile range. Similar rocket-driven missiles were employed in later battles in Europe, India, and the United States. Again, these missiles must have been tested. The ranges were probably the same as those used to test other weapons, such as artillery, consisting only of enough open area for safety during launching and for determining the accuracy of the weapons at their maximum range.

The rocket pioneer, Robert H. Goddard (q.v.), an American physicist, used his aunt's farm in Auburn, south of Worcester, Mass., to launch the first liquid-fuel rocket in 1926. The fire marshal took a dim view of the experiments, however. Goddard also felt hampered by the cold New England weather which prevented year-round work. He moved to the Mescalero Ranch near Roswell, in southeastern New Mexico, to continue his experiments in a milder climate with more powerful rockets which required greater range. Here the first range designed specifically for testing rockets took shape. Goddard built a workshop to make and assemble the rockets for firing, a tower from which to launch them, and cameras to photograph them during takeoff and flight. This in-flight information provided by the cameras helped him develop, among other things, methods to stabilize the vehicle in flight. The first rocket was launched at the Mescalero range on Dec. 30, 1930.

Missile flights were being conducted in Germany meanwhile. These led to the first long-range missile, the V-2, which could span 190 miles at maximum speeds of greater than 3,000 miles an hour. To develop the V-2, Germany established a missile range near Peenemünde on Usedom Island in the Baltic Sea, beginning in 1937. Shops were built to assemble and inspect the missiles, check guidance instruments, test engines, fuel and launch missiles, and photograph their flights.

The United States recognized the emerging value of rockets during World War II. In 1944, the Army established the White Sands Proving Grounds in south-central New Mexico, coincidentally only 100 miles from Goddard's range at Mescalero Ranch. White Sands was chosen because it occupied a sparsely inhabited region, its climate allowed year-round operation, it was accessible by air and rail to transport missiles and technicians, and it did not lie under a major airline route. The first important United States research on rockets was conducted there, resulting in the WAC-Corporal, a scientific research rocket launched for the first time from White Sands in 1945. Flights of captured V-2's and the first large

American missile, the Navy's Viking, followed. From White Sands in 1949 rose the first two-stage United States vehicle, a WAC-Corporal second stage boosted by a first-stage V-2, to send instruments 244 miles high and begin the era of space exploration.

Range Growth.—White Sands had intolerable size limitations, however. To officials searching for a larger site, as early as 1946, it was obvious that only the ocean offered the necessary uninhabited area, so the launching site was to be on the seashore. Cape Kennedy (until Nov. 28, 1963, Cape Canaveral), Fla., for the launching area, and the string of islands stretching southeast thousands of miles for tracking stations, seemed ideal, and the range was established in 1949. Eventually, ships were employed to fill the gaps between islands in the South Atlantic Ocean. Ships were also employed to extend the Atlantic Missile Range (AMR), as it is now called, beyond the tip of South Africa into the Indian Ocean, 9,000 miles from Cape Kennedy.

Cape Kennedy soon ran out of land on which to build the launching pads and support facilities for the variety of rocket types being developed. Each type requires its unique pad and associated equipment. After another search, the Pacific Missile Range (PMR) was established in 1957 with headquarters at Point Mugu, Calif. Its area extends west to the mid-Pacific and south to Antarctica. This ability to launch due south is important for putting satellites into polar orbits from which they, unlike satellites launched from Cape Kennedy, pass effectively over all parts of the earth.

AMERICAN MISSILE RANGES

Atlantic Missile Range.—When the nation began to develop the Atlantic Missile Range (AMR) in 1949, Cape Kennedy, located about 60 miles south of Daytona Beach, Fla., was an inhospitable stretch of sand, shrub, swamp, and more than an occasional rattlesnake and alligator. It was first called the Long-Range Missile Proving Ground; in 1950 the Air Force was given responsibility for its operation. An abandoned naval air station 15 miles south of Cape Kennedy was reactivated as Patrick Air Force Base, headquarters of the Air Force Missile Test Center. The Missile Test Annex was created to launch the missiles.

The first missile launched from the site was a combination of a WAC-Corporal and a V-2, fired on July 24, 1950. A few tents, some sand trenches, and an old Sherman tank attended the firing, along with an uninvited 10-foot alligator. In subsequent years, 15,000 acres of Cape Kennedy were turned into a complex of roads, buildings, blockhouses, launch pads, and the giant gantry towers that have become the signatures of modern rocket sites. A deepwater port was dredged to handle tracking ships from down range and Polaris-firing submarines. Scores of computers, one as large as a basketball court, and an elaborate communication station were built at Patrick Air Force Base.

Over 20,000 persons work at the mainland and tracking stations of the Atlantic Missile Range, which contains more than $1.4 billion worth of equipment and land. About 150 major firings are conducted at Kennedy each year. The construction by the National Aeronautics and Space Administration (NASA) of enormous manned spaceflight launching facilities at the adjacent 88,000-acre Merritt Island, which lies just north and west of Cape Kennedy, has almost doubled the national investment in the range. See also CAPE KENNEDY; NATIONAL AERONAUTICS AND SPACE ADMINISTRATION.

Preparation for Launchings.—Rockets arrive at the cape by rail, truck, barge, or air. They go first to the industrial area of 19 large, hangar-like structures with their associated service buildings. There, rocket contractors inspect the vehicles for any damage during shipment and test the components. The first stages of large rockets are erected on the launching pads and upper stages are mated to them. Electrical systems, guidance systems, flight control systems, and other major networks in the vehicles are operated to make certain they do not interfere with each other. At least one complete countdown is performed, with the vehicle held down to earth while the engine is ignited. Small rockets have dry launching pads; the large ones have wet pads which contain a hollow core through which the exhaust flames are funneled down and off to one side while, at the same time, millions of gallons of water are pumped into the rushing exhaust to cool it. Without the piping away of the exhaust, the flames would bounce up and consume the rocket.

Launch Complexes.— Twenty-four launch complexes line the ocean side of Cape Kennedy. Each complex consists of a launching pad, a blockhouse from which the countdown is directed, a gantry service tower which envelops the upright vehicle until a few minutes before blast-off, fueling facilities, and instrumentation to record the early portion of the flight. The large complexes cost up to $10 million to build and equip.

Complex 34 and Complex 37 are the largest on the cape. These handle the giant Saturn I space carriers. Their dome-shaped blockhouses have walls of reinforced concrete 13 feet thick, with 2-foot-thick steel doors that weight 23 tons. Fueling facilities can pump 750,000 pounds of fluid into a rocket's tanks in one hour. Complex 37 has two launching pads three fourths of a mile apart, with a mobile gantry tower that services both on rails connecting the pads. The gantry stands 37 stories high and weighs 3,500 tons. Two fixed towers stand on the pads for last minute servicing and for providing electric power to the missiles after the gantry has moved away. Each tower is 268 feet tall.

Launch Complex 39, the site from which manned Apollo missions are sent into space, is on Merritt Island. The giant Apollo/Saturn 5 vehicles, instead of being constructed on the launching pad, are built one at a time in the protected environment of the 525-foot-high Vehicle Assembly Building, about 3½ miles away. The building consists of an upper bay that houses the upright rocket and a lower bay that contains servicing shops and equipment. The Saturn/Apollo is assembled atop a mobile launcher, and the completed assembly—which weighs more than 11 million pounds—is then transported to the launch pad by giant tracked vehicles that move on four crawlers, each one 10 feet high and 40 feet long. Launchings from this facility are run by NASA, although the Air Force is responsible for tracking the vehicles in the early part of their flights.

Launch Operations.—When a rocket is ready to be fired at Cape Kennedy, over-all direction for the test transfers from the blockhouse to the central control coordinating operation housed in a distant building. Here it is made certain that the tracking stations are ready, the weather is

Above: A U.S. Air Force tactical range ballistic missile of the MACE B type undergoing test launching from a hard site at Cape Kennedy, Florida. *Right:* Small Vernier side rockets correct the attitude of an Atlas D intercontinental ballistic missile as it ascends on its 9,000-mile southeastward journey from Florida to the Indian Ocean.

Authenticated News

good, the range is cleared of airliners and ships, and once the rocket is launched, that it is traveling in the proper trajectory. Should an unmanned rocket veer off course, the range safety officer sends a radio signal to the vehicle which sets off an explosive charge inside of it to end its flight.

Twenty cameras photograph the rocket, each for a specific portion of the flight, from the beginning of the firing sequence to a 5,000-foot altitude. Cameras taking pictures of the early part of the flight stand only 6 feet from the rocket exhaust. Some operate at speeds of 8,400 frames a second. Theodolites, which are telescopes designed to determine the direction the rocket is taking, provide the control center with data on the position, velocity, and acceleration of the vehicle as its engine burns out and separates and subsequent stages ignite at distances up to 100 miles from the launching pad. Finally, ballistic plate cameras photograph a flashing light aboard the vehicle to plot its trajectory against the background of dark space and brilliant stars. The high-speed cameras are extremely valuable devices for detecting the origin of explosions or other malfunctions in the rocket. A high-precision tracking system for coverage of launchings up to 20,000 feet is being developed, as well as a launch and reentry infrared tracking system to help determine the efficiency of rocket engines.

High-precision radars are most important for determining this early trajectory of the rocket. Eight Azusa systems, housed in pressurized radomes, collect data on the speed and position of the rocket. The data is fed into a high-speed digital computer and displayed automatically on a plotting board in central control. This information provides officials with continuous predictions of the rocket's impact point if its fuel were cut off at any given instant. Tracking radars which lock onto a rocket when it rises above 15 miles follow it throughout the flight. These units are so accurate that they could call a ball fair or foul when located 88 miles from the ball park.

While optical and radar instruments are critical, data radioed back from the rocket systems account for 75 percent of the information on a rocket flight. As many as 250,000 bits of data are sent back on as many as 175 different functions going on within the rocket. These bits are recorded on magnetic tape to be analyzed later by engineers. After the flight has ended, the engineers can refly the rocket at any time on computers to determine its altitude, attitude, battery voltage, temperature, vibration, acceleration, valve operation, fuel-pump rate, stage separation, stage ignition, and a host of other factors at any given instant during its short life.

Range Stations.—Much of this telemetered information is recorded at the down-range tracking stations that stretch southeast from Cape Kennedy. There are 13 stations on land, plus a variable number of stations aboard ships, in the missile range. The first station is at Cape Kennedy, the second at Jupiter Inlet, Fla., 100 miles south of the cape. Station No. 3 is on Grand Bahama Island. Stations 4 through 9 are on Eleuthera Island, San Salvador (Watling) Island, Mayaguana and Grand Turk Islands, the Dominican Republic, and Puerto Rico, respectively. Station 9.1 is on Antigua Island and Station 10 on St. Lucia Island. Next is Fernando de Noronha, a Brazilian island about 225 miles northeast of Cap São Roque on the Brazilian bulge of South America and 4,100 miles from Cape Kennedy. Last is Station No. 12 on Ascension Island, midway between South America and Africa and more than 5,000 miles from the cape.

A typical down-range island station is dominated by its white radome and communications building. Rain usually provides the drinking water. Supplies for the technicians, who number between 30 and 160, must be shipped in, as well as parts for the complex instruments at the station.

A fleet of tracking aircraft equipped with electronic and optical gear supplements the ground and ship stations. Thanks to the impact predictor system at Kennedy, the aircraft can be at the impact area well in advance to photograph the reentering vehicle and locate it for recovery.

To communicate between Cape Kennedy and the down-range stations, the AMR has an extensive telephone, cable, radio, and microwave system. The submarine cable is of greatest importance, providing channels of multiple voice, teletype, tracking, and timing-data signals. The mass of information, which may run to 15,000 feet of film and 10,000 feet of magnetic tape from a single missile flight, is sent to Patrick Air Force Base. At the data reduction laboratory there, the raw data is translated by electronic machines into permanent printed records of the flight. This test flight report, sometimes totaling 28,000 pages of numbers, is the end product of the costly, laborious, and exciting test.

Pacific Missile Range.—The Pacific Missile Range (PMR) was authorized in 1957 when Cape Kennedy threatened to become overloaded soon and a range was needed at which military personnel could be trained to operate missiles which had been developed through testing at the Atlantic Missile Range. AMR also was limited in the direction in which rockets could be fired without passing over populated areas. Unless the rocket was "doglegged" (turned at an angle) during its powered flight, with an attendant waste of rocket energy, it could not be launched due north or south into polar orbit.

Range Centers.—In establishing the PMR, the Navy began by converting the Naval Air Missile Test center at Point Mugu, Calif., 56 miles up the coast from Los Angeles, into the Naval Missile Center which became the headquarters of the new range. The site was already equipped with some missile instruments, its personnel had experience, and nearby islands provided good locations for tracking stations. An Army firing range at Camp Cooke, 100 miles farther up the coast, was then taken over, partly by the Air Force to establish Vandenberg Air Force Base, and partly by the Navy to establish the Naval Missile Facility at Point Arguello, which late in 1963 was ordered transferred to the Air Force.

Communication facilities, optical-, radar-, and radio-tracking instruments, missile-assembly buildings, launching pads, and the host of associated equipment were built at the sites, following for the most part the pattern set by AMR. The Pacific Missile Range was commissioned in June 1958. Six months later, the first missile, a Thor intermediate-range weapon, was launched from Vandenberg.

Range Stations.—Tracking stations were established at Point Arguello, on Santa Cruz and San Nicolas islands, and at Point Sur and Pillar Point (Half Moon Bay) on the mainland. A half-dozen instrumented ships provide tracking facilities out to Hawaii where four stations are located on the islands of Kauai and Oahu and one on Hawaii Island. Beyond Hawaii are stations on Midway, Wake, Johnston, Eniwetok, Kwajalein, and Canton islands. The Canton station, the Kokee Park station on Kauai, and Point Arguello provide facilities for tracking Mercury manned space vehicles. The South Point station on Hawaii Island is instrumented for tracking deep-space probes. The Pacific tracking stations were also ordered transferred to the Air Force in 1963.

Subranges.—PMR has facilities for tactical Navy missiles as well as long-range Air Force and

PACIFIC MISSILE RANGE SECTOR

DASH LINES SHOW TYPICAL GROUND TRACKS FOR SOUTHWARD LAUNCH FROM PMR

ATLANTIC MISSILE RANGE SECTOR

DASH LINES SHOW TYPICAL GROUND TRACKS FOR EASTWARD LAUNCH FROM AMR

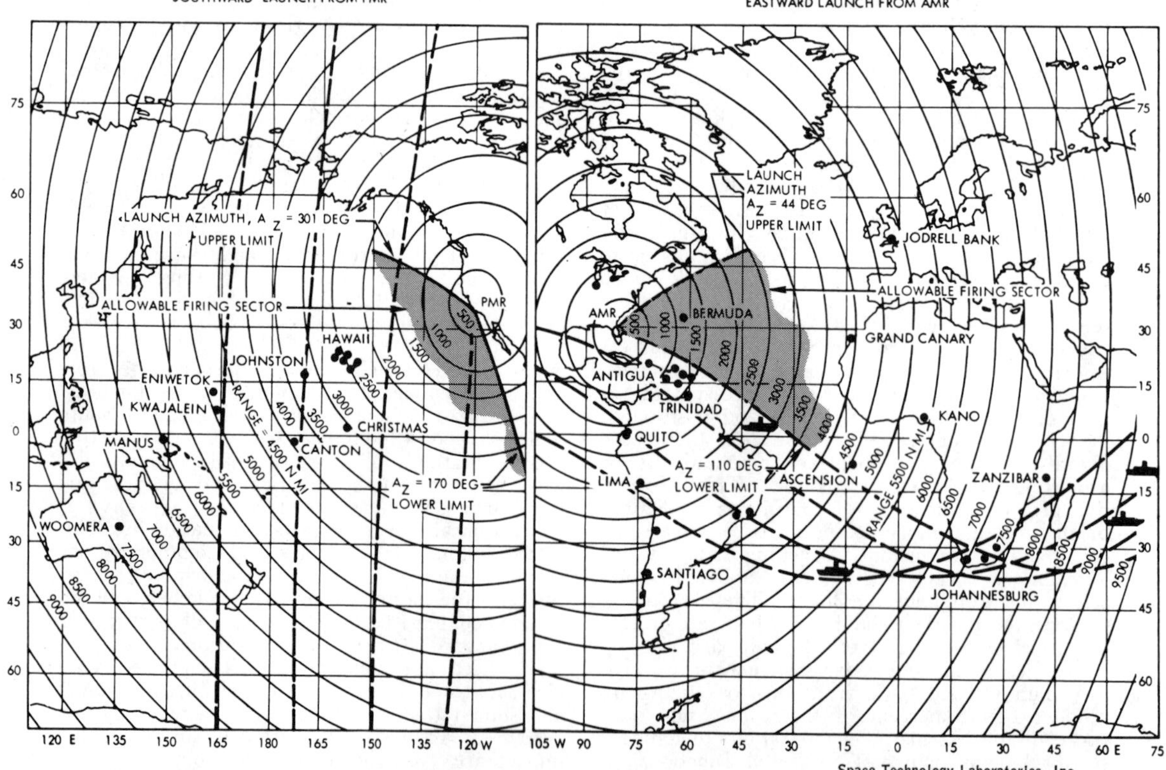

Space Technology Laboratories, Inc.

The U.S. Pacific Missile Range (*left*), centered in California, extends over some 9,000 nautical miles to Antarctica and the Indian Ocean, complementing the Atlantic Missile Range (*right*) centered at Cape Kennedy, Florida.

Navy weapons. Missiles which can be handled include surface-to-surface vehicles, surface-to-air (antiaircraft), air-to-air (fired from aircraft against other aircraft), air-to-surface, and underwater missiles, as well as rockets which launch satellites.

Four subranges make up the over-all PMR system. The Sea-Test Range extends 500 miles parallel to the California coast, roughly northwest from Los Angeles to San Francisco, and 250 miles seaward. The Ballistic Missile Range accommodates 1,200-mile intermediate and 6,000-mile intercontinental weapons. For intermediate weapons such as the Polaris missile, the impact area is midway between the mainland and the Hawaiian Islands. For the ICBM's, such as the Atlas, Titan, and Minuteman, the impact zone lies between Midway and Eniwetok islands in the Mid-Pacific Ocean. The Satellite Range permits firing over water all the way to Antarctica. It is ideal for launching polar satellites that can scrutinize the Soviet Union from space. The Anti-Missile Missile Range has its launching site on Kwajalein Island. Such anti-missile missiles as the Nike Zeus can be fired from the island to intercept ICBM's launched from Vandenberg.

Range Functions.—The Pacific Missile Range is manned by over 11,000 military, civil service, and contractor personnel. The total national investment in the range is about $500 million. Because much of PMR's operation is essentially military in nature, less is known about the details of the range than about Cape Kennedy. Three operational Atlas ICBM's are always on their pads and ready to fire at an enemy from Vandenberg Air Force Base, and essentially all of the satellite launchings at PMR are related to military needs.

Helical and dish radar antennae at a tracking station downrange on the U.S. Pacific Missile Range are used for scanning the area of expected trajectory.

Official U.S. Navy photograph

Authenticated News

On White Sands Missile Range in New Mexico, a Nike-Zeus radar receiver operates inside its "golf ball" housing; in the foreground is pattern measurements equipment.

White Sands Missile Range.—The White Sands Proving Ground, as the site was originally called, has grown from a meager beginning into the busiest missile range in the nation. The launching sites for the larger, spectacular rockets have eclipsed the New Mexico range in the eyes of the public, but it remains the key testing ground for the host of smaller weapons that complete the nation's missile arsenal. At the White Sands Missile Range, as it has been known since 1958, engineers have developed and tested the Navy Viking and Aerobee research vehicles, the Air Force Mace, the Army Corporal, and many other missiles. The 100 by 40 mile range, incidentally, includes the site of the first atomic bomb test, now a desolate fenced-off area with empty instrument bunkers and green glass created out of the sand by the fiery blast.

From the handful of men and rudimentary equipment used to develop the Aerobee and Viking rockets and test the captured German V-2's, there has grown a complex which, through the Army, Navy, Air Force, and their contractors, employs over 15,000 persons. The $100 million range, operated by the Army, stretches from north of El Paso, Texas, to south of Albuquerque, N.Mex. Since 1957 the range has averaged 2,000 test firings a year. Two radar vans were brought in to track the V-2's; there are now 640 stations for optical instruments, radar, telemetry, and electronic trajectory equipment, and timing, communications, and control facilities.

Range Facilities.—The range includes facilities for firing and recovering remote-controlled target planes for testing antiaircraft missiles, chase aircraft to accompany balloon flights and help track missiles, and meteorological stations to predict the weather. The Army's Test and Evaluation Directorate supports contractors who are developing missiles for the Army, and also evaluates a missile's performance, decides whether the weapon is practicable for use by troops in the field, and tests how well it stands up to the various environments in which it might be operated around the world.

The Navy test area contains a striking anomaly: a landlocked simulated ship (designated LLS-1) in the midst of desert and sagebrush. Inside are special missile launchers that simulate the roll of waves and facilities like those aboard real ships to test-fire weapons under conditions as close as possible to actual shipboard life.

The Air Force facility is located at Holloman Air Force Base on the east side of the range. It is one of the service's most complete and up-to-date research posts, with facilities that run from drawing board to actual testing of new missile systems. Here too are conducted experiments on the dangers to man of aerospace flight and the phenomena of near space (space in the vicinity of the earth). For many experiments balloons are used. Balloons from Holloman have risen to search for cosmic-ray effects and make other studies on the fringes of space, and to carry men high up in the atmosphere, some of them to return by parachute from 20 miles above the earth. At the Aero-Medical Laboratories at the station, the famed rocket-sled rides of Col. John Stapp were conducted, and the space chimps, Ham and Enos, were trained.

Once the missiles have been developed and thoroughly tested at missile ranges, they become operational at the locations for which they have been designed, in large launching complexes, on shipboard, or in aircraft or submarines; they may also be employed for further research and development, and missile stages may be used as carriers for satellites or space vehicles. See also WARSHIPS —*Changes of the Postwar Period*.

Eglin Gulf Test Range.—Eglin Air Force Base Aerospace Facility is a small missile range with a launching station on Santa Rosa Island, about halfway between Panama City and Pensacola, Fla. Small rockets for testing weapon components and for space research projects are launched into the 400-mile Eglin Gulf test range running south in the Gulf of Mexico, with five tracking stations along Florida's west coast.

Wallops Island Station.—The Wallops Island complex was established in 1945 by the National Advisory Committee for Aeronautics (NACA), the predecessor of the National Aeronautics and Space Administration (NASA), as the Pilotless Aircraft Research Station. Its function then was to supplement wind tunnel and laboratory studies into the problems of flight, particularly those beyond the sound barrier. When NACA was absorbed into NASA with the latter's establishment in 1958, the facility became the Wallops Island Station.

Station Centers.—This station, on the eastern shore of Virginia (Delmarva Peninsula) about 40 miles south of Salisbury, Md., consists of three areas covering a total of 4,335 acres. First, the main base houses administrative offices, technical service support shops, and such facilities as the range control center, a prototype of a Mercury manned spacecraft tracking station which is used for engineering tests and training purposes, a main telemetry building, and the prime command and data acquisition station for the Tiros weather satellites, the other station for these being located at the Pacific Missile Range. Second, Wallops Island is the range launch site, located about 7 miles southeast of the main base and separated from the mainland by 2 miles of marsh and inland waterway. About 5 miles long and up to ½ mile wide, the island contains the launching pads, assembly shops, blockhouses, rocket storage buildings, and related facilities. Third, Wallops Mainland is a ½-mile strip of land opposite the island on which are located the long-range radar and optical tracking stations. The capital value of the facility is almost $25 million and it employs more than 400 persons.

Types of Launches.—The NASA facility launches experimental vehicles designed to gather information on the flight characteristics of aircraft and rockets, and scientific data on the upper atmosphere and space. About 300 launchings are conducted each year, with the vehicles ranging from small rockets to four-stage Scout rockets which can put small payloads into earth orbit. For the most part, well-proved rockets are employed in the experiments; the station does not develop rockets, as such, although sometimes small tests are conducted there on components of major rocket systems. The physics of objects reentering the earth's atmosphere from space at 25,000 miles an hour—as may the Apollo manned moon capsule if retrofiring is not used—have been studied at Wallops. The escape and recovery systems built into the Mercury manned spacecraft were tested at the station. Inflatable balloons have been launched from Wallops into suborbital flights, and experiments with vapor trails to determine winds at high altitudes have been conducted there. Several small Explorer-series satellites have been fired into orbit from Wallops by the Scout vehicle.

RANGES OF OTHER COUNTRIES

Woomera Missile Range.—The Australian missile range near Woomera, a town in central south Australia, 110 miles northwest of Port Augusta, has been used for testing British missiles, firing scientific rockets into the upper atmosphere, and tracking United States satellites. Woomera lies on a vast and empty plain — the roads warn of crossing kangaroos. Once a sheep station, it has grown to a town of 5,000 because of the missile range. Missiles fired from Woomera have the advantage of great overland travel — 1,250 miles to the continent's northwest coast. When necessary, the range can be extended 2,000 miles into the Indian Ocean.

A Baker-Nunn astronomical camera is used at the Woomera Rocket Range in South Australia. Ideal for tracking satellites, it could photograph a tennis ball 1,000 miles away.

Australian News and Information Bureau

Russian Missile Ranges.—The locations of the Russian missile ranges have not been made public. The launching area is believed to be slightly northeast of the Caspian Sea–Aral Sea region, the missiles traveling northeast over central Siberia. One missile test range is reported near Kapustin Yar, a town northeast of the Caspian Sea, 60 miles east-southeast of Volgograd (formerly Stalingrad). Another is reported to be located near the town of Tyuratam, 100 miles east of the Aral Sea, and it is believed there are others. When the Russians exhaust their overland range, they fire into the Pacific Ocean, with impact zones south of the Hawaiian Islands near the Palmyra Islands, some 8,000 miles from the launching sites. Soviet naval vessels, usually trawlers, stand off the impact area to collect data on the reentering vehicles. Soviet satellites and manned space vehicles are believed to communicate with trawlers, which serve as tracking stations outside Soviet territory.

Other Ranges.—Egypt, France, Israel, and Japan have missile ranges of varying complexity and extent. The Japanese have launched two-stage, 33-foot-tall research rockets from Michikawa Beach in northern Japan, 250 miles from Tokyo, since 1960. Another range, in southern Japan, was contemplated to fire rockets over the Pacific Ocean.

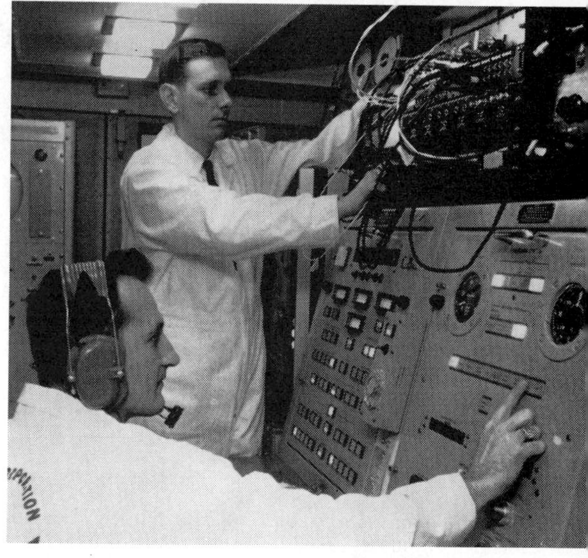

The Bendix Corporation

A U.S. Army satellite communications control center in radio telephone and teletype contact with a SYNCOM satellite in synchronized orbit 22,300 miles from earth.

TRACKING AND DATA ACQUISITION

The success of a space vehicle depends largely on the success with which it communicates with the ground. Unless data is obtained on the vehicle's position, performance, and observations—whether it contains a man or instruments—the experiment is a failure.

Intercommunication. — The communication system is called tracking and data acquisition. It links the earth and the vehicle—whether it be a research sounding rocket, a missile, an earth satellite, or a deep-space probe—to make possible the transfer of information via radio signals. In addition to radio voice communication with the astronauts on manned vehicles, tracking and data acquisition systems fall into four general functions: tracking, telemetry, command, and control.

Tracking provides data on the location and trajectory or orbit of the vehicle. Where it is at any given time is as important as the observations it makes at that time and place. The spacecraft's location must also be known to evaluate the accuracy of its guidance system and to correct any errors, to determine when and where the vehicle will reenter the earth's atmosphere and be recovered, and to analyze its findings.

Telemetry is the transmitting to earth of data ranging from the astronaut's blood pressure to radiation levels in deep space and the temperature of Venus. Sensing devices aboard a spacecraft react to the environment; these reactions are encoded in number systems, translated into radio signals, and sent back to earth to be recorded, decoded, and evaluated.

The command function is the use of a ground radio transmitter to order a spacecraft to perform maneuvers, take pictures, or make measurements expected of it on its mission.

Control is coordinating the space vehicle and the ground networks toward achieving success of the vehicle's mission, whether it be correctly predicting the landing point of a manned flight or radioing recorded data within the satellite to ground stations capable of receiving it.

The National Aeronautics and Space Administration (NASA) has two basic networks to serve its spacecraft: the minitrack and the manned space flight systems. These are complemented by three stations for supporting deep-space probes and flights to planets, and a 12-station optical tracking network.

Minitrack Network.—The minitrack network, devised for unmanned satellites, consists of 15 stations around the world. Each has instruments which can receive the signals from an earth satellite's radio transmitter only if the satellite is passing through a narrow area, or fan, overhead. These stations provide precise data on the satellite's location in space and time. The data is then transmitted to the communications center (known as SPACON for its call letters) at NASA's Goddard Space Flight Center in Greenbelt, Md. There the data is fed into computers to determine the orbit of the satellite over the course of many hours involving three or four revolutions. The minitrack stations are located at Blossom Point, Md.; Rosman, N.C.; Fort Myers, Fla.; Quito, Ecuador; Lima, Peru; Antofagasta, Chile; Santiago, Chile; Woomera, Australia; Johannesburg, Republic of South Africa; Goldstone, in Camp Irwin, Calif.; St. Johns, Newfoundland; East Grand Forks, Minn.; College and Fairbanks, Alaska; and Winkfield, Berkshire, England.

Manned Space Flight Tracking Network.—This network is much faster than minitrack. Engineers need immediate information on a manned space vehicle to determine if it is functioning properly. With a life at stake, they cannot wait on the slow pace of the minitrack system. The manned space flight network also differs in station locations and technical equipment. It uses a combination of radio listening devices, radar, astronaut communication links, and radio-telemetry equipment capable of commanding the space ship. It was built to meet strict requirements. It must be in communication with the space vehicle or astronaut one third of the flight time. It must be able to determine quickly whether the vehicle, launched from Cape Kennedy, will go into a suc-

Authenticated News

The U.S. Pacific Missile Range fleet includes USNS *Range Tracker*, a converted Victory Ship manned by civilians and mounted with complex radar antennae and automatic missile tracking and telemetry equipment.

cessful orbit; if this is doubtful, the spacecraft must be brought to earth before it reaches the African jungles. And the system must provide that all the data from the 16 tracking and telemetry stations around the world be displayed immediately (in technical jargon, in "real time") at the control center for manned space flight at Cape Kennedy. All stations have telemetry equipment and voice communication with the astronaut. Eleven stations have tracking radars. Seven stations have the capability of transmitting commands to the space ship. The 16 stations include 2 instrumented ships which are assigned to the mid-Atlantic and Indian Ocean areas.

The 14 fixed ground stations are located as follows: Guaymas, Mexico; Point Arguello, Calif.; Corpus Christi, Texas; White Sands, N. Mex.; Eglin Air Force Base, Fla.; Cape Canaveral, Fla.; Bermuda; Grand Canary Island; Kano, Nigeria; Zanzibar, East Africa; Muchea, Australia; Woomera, Australia; Canton Island; and Kauai Island, Hawaii. A fifteenth station is planned at Carnavon in western Australia.

Deep-Space Instrumentation Network.—This network for the support of lunar and planetary missions consists of three stations, each with an 85-foot-diameter, parabolic radio antenna. The stations are at Goldstone (Camp Irwin), Calif., Woomera, Australia, and near Johannesburg, Republic of South Africa. A fourth is planned near Canberra, Australia. Their antennas are mounted to receive data from a spacecraft and determine the vehicle's location in space. The stations are so placed that at least one will have line-of-sight communication with a spacecraft despite the earth's rotation. The network is operated by the Jet Propulsion Laboratory of California Institute of Technology under a NASA contract.

In 1962 the Goldstone antenna commanded actions by the historic Mariner II space probe, first in a mid-course trajectory correction, and then when it was near Venus, 36 million miles from earth. Two more 85-foot, parabolic-disc antennas are planned, although they will not be primarily for deep-space probes, but for more sensitive reception of data from closer satellites; and a 210-foot dish is being developed with an anticipated pointing accuracy of approximately 0.01° for improved reception from future lunar and planetary probes.

Optical-Tracking Network.—This network is intended to provide optical data, like the radio data of the minitrack network, on the location of earth satellites. It consists of 12 specially designed (Baker-Nunn) tracking cameras which can be pointed in any direction above the horizon. The cameras photograph the satellite against a known star background, and the angles between the stars and the satellite are measured to fix the latter in time and space. The position data from the cameras is more accurate than the minitrack data; but satellites are visible only during dawn and dusk in clear weather, so the cameras have limited value, unless the satellites carry lights such as those of the flashing Anna geodetic vehicle.

The Baker-Nunn cameras are located at Hobe Sound, Fla.; Curaçao, Netherlands Antilles; Arequipa, Peru; Villa Dolores, Argentina; Olifantsfontein, Republic of South Africa; Cádiz, Spain; Shiraz, Iran; Naini Tal, India; Woomera, Australia; Mitaka, Japan; Haleakala, Hawaii; and White Sands, N.Mex. The optical network is supplemented by 200 volunteer groups, called moonwatch observer teams, around the Western World. These teams use simple telescopes to sight satellites and provide guidance information for the Baker-Nunn cameras.

Space Surveillance System.—Like the Distant Early Warning (DEW) Line to detect aircraft and the Ballistics Missile Early Warning System (BMEWS) for missiles (see also RADAR—2. *Uses and Types:* Military Radar), the space surveillance system (Spasur) was built to discover, identify, and predict the path of satellites that cross United States territory. The seven stations of the network are placed along the 33° north latitude from the east to the west coasts. Three of the stations send continuous radio waves into space, creating an invisible fence through which orbiting vehicles must pass. The other four stations receive signals bounced off the satellites which pass through the fence. The network alternates receiving stations with transmitting stations across the continent in a leapfrog arrangement which makes most efficient use of the transmitters. For the eastern three and western three stations, the receivers are 500 miles apart with 50,000-watt transmitters between them.

In the east, the receivers are located at Silver Lake, Miss., and Fort Stewart, Ga., with the transmitter between them at Jordan Lake, Ala. In the west, a receiving station is placed at San Diego, Calif., a transmitting station at Gila River, Ariz., and a receiving station at Truth or Consequences, N.Mex. At the center of the system is a 560,000-watt transmitter at Archer City, Texas, said to be one of the largest radio transmitters in the world.

Spasur, begun in 1958, is managed by the Navy. It includes a computer facility at the Naval Weapons Laboratory at Dahlgren, Va., to analyze data from the system and predict the orbits of detected objects. Data is fed to the laboratory by cable direct from the four receiving stations. Supplementing Spasur's responsibilities is the National Space Surveillance Control Center, called Spacetrack, which is run by the Air Force at Cambridge, Mass. Its purpose is to catalog the orbital data of all satellites supplied by Spasur and other sources. Both Spacetrack and Spasur are under the direction of the North American Air Defense Command.

Large Radio Telescopes.—The world's largest steerable radio telescope is the Jodrell Bank instrument of the University of Manchester, located at Macclesfield, Cheshire, England. It is a 250-foot-diameter, disc-shaped reflector which was built to listen to radio noise coming from natural phenomena in the distant universe. However, its sensitivity has made it very useful for tracking deep-space probes of the United States and the Soviet Union.

Australia, lying in the Southern Hemisphere, is slated to become an important site for radio telescopes probing the southern skies. Under construction is the largest fixed radio telescope in the world—an array of wires laid out along the ground in New South Wales to form a great cross, each arm of which is a mile long and 40 feet wide. A steerable, 210-foot-diameter, disc-shaped telescope, located near Parkes, New South Wales, about 200 miles west of Sidney, has been completed. With these and other facilities, Australia will be able to track deep-space probes launched from the United States.

See also GUIDED MISSILES; RADAR; ROCKETS; SATELLITES, ARTIFICIAL; SPACE EXPLORATION; TELESCOPE—*Radio Telescopes.*

ROBERT C. TOTH,
National Science Correspondent, Los Angeles "Times."

MISSILES. See GUIDED MISSILES; BALLISTICS; MISSILE RANGES; PROJECTILES; ROCKETS.

MISSINAIBI RIVER, mĭs-ĭ-nī′bĭ, river, Ontario, Canada, rising in Missinaibi Lake and flowing for 265 miles north and northeast. With the Mattagami, 50 miles southwest of Moosonee, it forms the Moose River, which empties into James Bay.

MISSION, mĭsh′ŭn, city, Texas, situated in Hidalgo County, near the Rio Grande River, 55 miles west-northwest of Brownsville. The trading and processing center of a district raising grapefruit, tomatoes, cabbages, and cotton, Mission has fruit and vegetable canneries, as well as plants producing bricks, tiles, and concrete pipe. A Citrus Fiesta is held annually. A mission was founded nearby in 1824, but the city was not settled until 1908. Incorporated two years later, it has been governed by a city manager and council since 1928. Pop. 13,043.

MISSION ARCHITECTURE. See ARCHITECTURE—*Early American;* UNITED STATES—*37. Art and Architecture* (Colonial Period).

MISSION CITY, town, British Columbia, Canada, on the Fraser River, 42 miles east of Vancouver. The trading and processing center of a district with fruit, vegetable, and dairy farms, it has canneries as well as lumber mills. Founded about 1860 as an Indian mission, the village was incorporated in 1922. Population: 3,412.

MISSION INDIANS, a general term applied to the Indians of southern and central California who were Christianized by Spanish Franciscan missionaries beginning in 1769, when the mission at San Diego was founded. Totaling at their peak some 40,000 individuals, they included many tribal families and dialects, but originally inhabited the coastal region from San Diego to San Francisco.

Father Junípero Serra (q.v.) and succeeding friars brought the Indians in from their scattered villages to live in the mission communities, taught them European customs and trades, and forced them to abandon their aboriginal customs in favor of agricultural pursuits. Discipline was severe, and although there was individual affection for many of the friars, the Indians tended to seek escape where possible. Actually, the system amounted to a form of benevolent servitude, and although cattle, lands, and crops theoretically belonged to the natives, held in trust for them by the Franciscans, rarely did they have an opportunity to profit by this wealth. Spanish rule was overthrown in California in 1822 and in 1833–1834 the Mexican government confiscated the mission properties, exiled the friars, and secularized the missions, dividing all mission property among the newly freed Indians. Almost immediately the Indians, inexperienced in property ownership, either were easily deprived of their holdings or squandered them. This situation persisted until after the publication of *A Century of Dishonor* (1881) by Helen Hunt Jackson (q.v.), who almost singlehandedly forced the United States government to examine the plight of these people. As a result, some 30 small reservations totaling 180,000 acres were established to accommodate the remaining 3,000 natives. Slowly these groups intermingled; by the 1950's few of the original Mission Indian tribes existed as such. The major tribes making up this group are the Chumash, Costanoan, Diegueño, Fernandeño, Gabrielino, Juaneño, Luiseño.

See also CALIFORNIA—*7. History;* SHOSHONEAN INDIANS.

FREDERICK J. DOCKSTADER.

MISSIONARY MOVEMENTS. The term "missionary," which is derived from the Latin verb *mittere* (to send), refers to one who is sent forth on an errand. Since the middle of the 17th century the word has been used to describe those men and women who are sent forth by religious bodies for the purpose of spreading their faith. Missionary movements constitute only one of many ways that have been used to spread religion, and in the history of the world as a whole they seem to have been a relatively minor way. Military conquests, political privileges, and general cultural contacts have all been important means whereby people have been converted to a new religion, and taken together these other ways account for a far larger proportion of conversions than do missionary movements. Nevertheless, missionary movements have always been the most truly religious way of spreading a religion. The sending out of men who by their preaching and their own conviction carry conviction to the hearts of others is in accord with the very nature of religion, which is essentially a matter of internal conviction and can never be simply a matter of external conformity. Considered in succession are Zoroastrian, Jewish, Buddhist, Muslim, and Hindu missions and, finally, Christian missions in their successive periods.

ZOROASTRIAN MISSIONS

One of the two earliest religions to engage in missionary activity was Zoroastrianism. The early Persian religion had been completely nonmissionary, but when Zoroaster (Zarathustra) initiated his movement about the 6th century B.C., he proclaimed it as his desire to "convert all men living." In that early period, in addition to priests who stayed at home, there were itinerant priests who proclaimed their beliefs from place to place, and missionaries are said to have gone even to foreign lands. We have no clear knowledge of missionary activity, however, until we come to the revival of Zoroastrianism as the official faith of the new Persian empire which arose under the Sassanids (226–641 A.D.). In an attempt to revive the past glories of Persia and the Persian religion, the Sassanids zealously fostered conversions. It was said in those days that every Zoroastrian tried to propagate his religion. Emperor Shapur (Sapor) II (r. 309–379) is the most famous for his proselytizing labors, which he carried out with the help of his priest Ādarbād.

When the Arabs conquered the Sassanids and Islam came to rule in the area, Zoroastrianism was deprived of its missionary dynamic. It survived as an encysted minority in Persia and on the west coast of India, building walls around itself for protection rather than reaching out to mankind. Among its modern adherents even the possibility of conversions is questioned.

See also PARSIS; ZOROASTRIANISM.

JEWISH MISSIONS

The ancient religion of Israel was usually conceived of as the faith of a particular people, and consequently it made no effort at missionary preaching. Some of the prophets and later writers of the Old Testament recognized that the God whom Israel worshiped was the God of all the world, however, and in some places, such as the Book of Jonah, the inevitable missionary consequences of that recognition are made clear. As Jews spread over the ancient world in the Hellenistic and Roman periods, missionary activity must have developed on a fairly wide scale. The number of Jews in the early Roman Empire comprised about one tenth of the population, a figure whose size can be explained only on the basis of much successful missionary work. In addition to the full proselytes who kept the Jewish law, there were large numbers of God-fearers who accepted the Jewish teachings about the one true God and the rejection of all idols, and who therefore counted themselves religiously as adherents of the Jewish faith. The appeal of Judaism was chiefly to educated people, to whom it was presented by such writers as Philo Judaeus (fl. late 1st century B.C.—early 1st century A.D.) and Flavius Josephus (37–?100 A.D.) as the philosophic religion equipped with the oldest book in the world. Hillel (fl. 30 B.C.–9 A.D.) and Gamaliel (d. about 50 A.D.) were teachers of this mission-minded Judaism. After the destruction of Jerusalem in 70 A.D., and the terrible blows which the Jewish community suffered in that period, however, missionary work seems to have disappeared permanently.

See also JEWISH HISTORY AND SOCIETY—*5. Expansion of Judaism.*

BUDDHIST MISSIONS

South Asia.—Buddhism has been one of the first and one of the most active missionary religions. Into country after country the message of Buddhism has been carried primarily by monks. The Buddha himself (563?–?483 B.C.) sent out monks as the first missionaries to spread his teaching. We know very little about their missions, however, until the time of the great Indian Emperor Aśoka (r. about 274–237 B.C.), who launched Buddhism on an international missionary expansion. On the advice of the president of the Third Buddhist Council, he sent messengers of his religion to all the countries around India. Aśoka's own son (or, possibly, brother) went to Ceylon and there converted King Tissa, and a short time later his sister joined him in his missionary labors and instituted the order of Buddhist nuns in Ceylon. Within a generation the island had become a strong center of Buddhist belief.

Aśoka's messengers are said traditionally to have preached also in Lower Burma. Certainly that area had many contacts with India, and from Aśoka's time on these contacts brought a knowledge of Buddhism. The spread of Buddhist teachings in Burma was slow, however, until the rise of a great Buddhist center in Conjeeveram in south India where men could be trained in the religion and sent out as missionaries.

The impulse from south India was felt not only in Burma, but also in Siam (now Thailand), Cambodia, Java, Borneo, and Malaya. For many centuries this area surrounding the South China Sea was a kind of Farther India, ruled by Indian princes, filled with Indian traders, and led by Indian religious men. Buddhism spread widely through the area, but after the extinction of the Indian connections it disappeared generally except in Siam and Cambodia.

China.—To the north also, Aśoka's messengers penetrated, and contacts were made with China in the following years. The first official introduction of Buddhism into China came in 67 A.D., when an expedition sent by the Emperor Ming returned with two Indian Buddhist monks, Kāśyapa Mātaṅga and Dharmarakṣa. Their arrival was followed by mass conversions, and a continuous stream of Indian and Central Asian monks reached China by the overland trade routes. For the most part, these missionaries devoted themselves to the translation of the Buddhist scriptures. Changan (modern Sian), Loyang, and Nanking developed as their chief centers. Later, through monks who came by the sea route from India and Ceylon, Buddhism also penetrated south China.

Among the famous Buddhist missionaries who came to China were Fou-t'u-têng (232–349), who reached Loyang in 310 and worked as a healer and translator; Kumārajīva (344–413), who became the most famous preacher in Changan; Guṇavarman, who came from Ceylon to Canton in 424 and founded two monasteries where his influence was continued; and Bodhidharma (d. about 530), who came from India in 520 and founded a school of meditation known as Ch'an. After the 11th century, however, as Indian Buddhism declined, this flow of monks from the west came to an end.

Korea.—Meanwhile, China had taken up the missionary concern. Chinese monks moved first into Korea, where, in 374, two monks named Atao and Shuntao were invited. Others followed, and Korea soon became a stronghold of Buddhism. At first the work was carried on only in the north, with the modern Pyongyang as an important center, but in the middle of the 5th century missionaries reached the southern extremity of the peninsula and converted its rulers.

Japan.—South Korea then became the staging area for the entrance of Buddhism into Japan. In 552 (or, possibly, 538) the king of Paekche sent a delegation to the emperor of Japan to inform him of the truth of this new religion and to present him with some of its symbols. A struggle ensued in the Japanese court between those who favored the new beliefs and those who opposed them. Korean missionaries continued to flow into the country and spread their teachings and finally, in 587, the opposition fell. Under Shōtoku Taishi, prince regent from 593 to 621/622, Buddhism became the official religion of the country, and Shōtoku has been called the Constantine of Japan. As Christianity was used after Constantine in an attempt to unify the Roman Empire, so in Japan Buddhism became part of the imperial effort to unify the country, and the spread of Buddhist teachers and Buddhist temples grew out of and supported the spread of the centralizing power. At first, Buddhist strength had been confined largely to the capital city, but now it reached out to all the pronvinces. Nuns from Korea played a significant part in its propagation.

The work of the missionaries to Japan was not that of making translations of the Buddhist books, which had been the chief concern of the Chinese missionaries. Since Japan was still backward, no need was felt to put the scriptures into the local language, as had been necessary in the high civilization of China. The missionaries to Japan concentrated on preaching and healing, and the temples that were built often had attached to them a hospital, dispensary, and asylum. Especially in the 8th century, combined bands of monks and physicians were dispatched to the provinces, and by the end of that century the whole country had been converted.

20th Century.—In later times Buddhism lost its missionary concern, and only in the 20th century did it begin slowly to revive its missionary nature. The leadership in this movement was taken by the lands of southern Buddhism, especially Ceylon and Burma. In 1946 a Buddhist mission to the Burma hill districts was organized to reach the more primitive inhabitants of the country, among whom Christianity had made great progress. Within a few years this mission had established 29 centers and gained thousands of converts. The Buddhist Sansana Council for the Union of Burma, founded by the government in 1950, included a Propagation Committee in charge of missionary activity within and without Burma. In the same year, Ceylon organized the first world Buddhist conference, of which a succession were held thereafter in various countries. These conferences constitute ecumenical gatherings attended by strong delegations of Buddhists from Eastern countries and by some representatives of small Buddhist groups in the West. They have led to the creation of a World Fellowship of Buddhists, which has the avowed purpose of carrying out a mission to all mankind. Also interested in this purpose are the International Buddhist Association, with headquarters in Burma, and the World Buddhist Mission. Moreover, many thousands of converts to Buddhism have been reported among the depressed classes of India since the death in 1956 of the depressed-class leader, Dr. B. R. Ambedkar, who himself had become a Buddhist. The Sixth Buddhist Council, held in Rangoon from 1954 to 1956, further stimulated the missionary revival, so that contemporary Buddhism was clearly regaining the right to be called a missionary religion.

See also BUDDHA AND BUDDHISM; CEYLON—*2. The People* (Religion); INDIA—*13. Religion and Philosophy* (Buddhism).

MUSLIM MISSIONS

What monks have been to the expansion of Buddhism, traders and merchants have been to that of Islam. The faith of the Prophet Mohammed (570–632) makes no provision for an ordained clerical or monastic body which could assume the main responsibility for missions, as is the case with Christianity and Buddhism. Rather, the missionary task has fallen to the lot of the ordinary believer, and, perhaps by consequence, he has generally been more effective in this work than have his counterparts in other religions.

Beginnings.—Mohammed himself set the example by his preaching, and he instructed his disciples in missionary responsibility. "Summon thou to the way of thy Lord with wisdom and with kindly warning," he said, and he sent one of his early converts, Mūṣ'ab ibn-'Umair, to spread the faith in Medina at a time when Mecca was proving hostile. In the early centuries of Islamic rule, however, we find little evidence of conscious missionary effort. When Muslim power came to dominate North Africa and western Asia, the inhabitants of these areas gradually adopted the ruling faith, but this does not seem to have been done because missionaries were sent to them. In general, the same absence of real missionary effort applies to Central Asia, though in this region, especially in connection with the conversion of the Mongol rulers, we hear of occasional saints with a missionary concern. The Mongol ruler of Kashgar, Tūqluq Tīmūr Khan (r. 1347–1363), for example, was converted by a Persian holy man, Jamāl al-Dīn, whom he met one day while out hunting. The spread of Islam to China was accomplished largely by the immigration of merchants, tradesmen, and officials in connection with the Yüan (Mongol) dynasty (1260–1368).

India.—The first, and probably the greatest, area of Muslim missionary preaching was India. In addition to conquering armies, there came to that land a long succession of Muslim saints who moved about or settled down among the people and made thousands of converts. Among the very early ones was Sheikh Ismā'īl of Bukhara, who began work in Lahore in 1005 as the first preacher of Islam in that city. Late in the 11th century missionaries of the Ismā'īlites arrived in western India and laid the foundations for the importance of their community in that area. Nūr-al-Dīn (also known as Nūr Satāgar) is still revered as the first missionary of the Khoja sect to come from Ismā'īlite headquarters to work in western India.

Farther north, in Ajmer, lived one of the greatest saints of Indian Islam, Khwājah Mu'īn al-Dīn Chishtī, who came from Persia and made many converts before his death in 1236. The most successful missionary worker in western India is said to have been Shah Muhammad Ṣādiq Sarmast Ḥusaynī, who came from Medina in 1568 and finally settled in Nasik. But the scene of Islam's greatest missionary success in India was not in the west but far to the east in Bengal, where Sheikh Jalāl-al-Dīn Tabrīzī initiated the work in the first half of the 13th century. The large masses of Bengali Muslims who are obviously derived from the tribal and depressed peoples of that area provide continuing evidence of the effective work of the sheikh and of the preachers who followed him.

Southeast Asia.—The Muslim creed was carried by merchants and traders from India east to Malaya and Indonesia, and through their activities Islam gradually spread throughout southeast Asia. At times, however, the preaching was done by men who came primarily with a missionary purpose. In Java, for example, Mawlana Mālik Ibrāhīm (d. 1419) is venerated as the first Muslim missionary to the island. He arrived late in the 14th century and established himself on the north coast opposite Madura. The early centers of missionary effort in Java were concentrated on the north coast, and from there Islam moved slowly southward and covered the land, so that Java became the greatest Muslim stronghold of the East Indies.

Africa.—In Africa, scene of the most recent triumphs of Islam, missionary work has again been done largely by traders, but there more than anywhere else the work of such men has been supplemented by the activity of religious orders with a missionary purpose. Sometimes these orders have added forceful conquest to peaceful proclamation. 'Abdallāh ibn-Yāsīn (d. 1058?) came at the invitation of a Berber chieftain to preach among the Berber tribes of the Sahara but, on meeting indifference and hostility, retired to an island in the Senegal River, where he gathered a large number of devoted converts. After organizing them into a military band, the famous Almoravides, he proceeded to attack those tribes that refused to accept his preaching and to force them to become Muslims.

The religious orders are by no means all of the military missionary type. The most widespread order has been that of the Qādirites, who have been inspired not by military exploits but by the love and concern for men of their founder, 'Abd-al-Qādir al-Jīlāni (1077–1166). The Qādirites entered western Africa in the 15th century and established schools widely. In fact, until the middle of the 19th century the majority of the schools of the Sudan were under their auspices. As a result of their work, individual converts and then groups were gathered around the centers they established, and the most promising members of the groups were often sent to Qādirite training centers or to the leading Muslim universities for further study.

19th and 20th Centuries.—The 19th and 20th centuries have seen considerable intensification and conscious organization of Muslim missions. The preachers of the Wahhābi reform reaching out from Arabia made their approach to non-Muslims as well as to Muslims. In northern Africa the Senusi (Sanūsi) order, founded in 1837, spread across the continent and with its women's work and other activities greatly aided the peaceful advance of Islam. Toward the end of the 19th century societies for the support of continuous mission work were established on the Christian pattern. Many of the cities of India began to have their *anjumans,* as these societies were commonly called, and regular missionary preaching was maintained in the bazaars.

The most visible missionary activity to come out of Islam in this period was the work of what are commonly regarded as heretical offshoots of the faith. One of these, the Baha'i, was founded by the Persian Bahaullah (1817–1892), who taught that the divine command for this age is to unify mankind in one faith and one order. True to this message, his disciples have tried to reach men of many lands. His son, Abdul Baha, visited Egypt, Europe, and the United States before 1914 in an effort to establish peace and to unify men. Other representatives worked in other areas, so that Baha'i communities came into existence in over 40 countries.

Another missionary offshoot of Islam, and one which has remained closer to the parent body, is the Ahmadiyah movement, founded about 1879 by Mirza Ghulam Aḥmad. He came from a small town in the Punjab, and the chief strength of the movement continues to be in West Pakistan, although members maintain active missionary centers in many of the principal cities of Europe, the United States, southeast Asia, and West Africa. In most of these places, Ahmadiyah centers are the dominant and often the only representatives of Muslim missions.

Through their activities and through the work of merchants and religious orders, Islam continues to win large numbers of converts. Particularly in Africa its advance is widespread and rapid.

See also BAHAI FAITH; ISLAM; MOSLEM SECTS.

HINDU MISSIONS

Traditionally, Hinduism has not been a missionary religion. It has been the religious expression of the people of India, and only those who were born in it could belong to it. In the medieval period, it is true, Hinduism expanded overseas into large areas of southeast Asia. But this was the consequence of the emigration of Indians who set up Hindu kingdoms and dominated the commercial life of that area. After the kingdoms disappeared, Hinduism also gradually vanished, and Hindus generally continued to think of their religion in nonmissionary terms.

The principal leader who caused much of Hinduism to abandon the traditional attitude was Swami Vivekanada (1863–1902). He was a disciple of the great Rāmakrishna Paramahaṅsa (1834–1886), and when his master died, he came out of his retreat in the Himalayas and toured India and the United States, creating great interest and winning many followers. He established ashramas (Sanskrit *āśramas*) as centers for the training of missionaries and developed missions for the preaching of Vedantism and for educational and social work in India and in the United States. The movement which he initiated has carried on such work in those areas and in Europe as well.

Vigorous missionary work among non-Hindus in India has also been carried on by the Ārya Samaj, a reform movement founded by Dayanand (Dayānanda) Sarasvatī (1824/1825–1883) in 1875. Preaching by both paid and volunteer preachers, schools and colleges, tract societies, orphanages, and work among the depressed classes have all been carried on by this group.

See HINDUISM; INDIA—*13. Religion and Philosophy* (of Indian Origin [Modern Hinduism and Brahmanism; Reformed Hinduism]).

ANCIENT AND MEDIEVAL CHRISTIAN MISSIONS

Christianity has been the most consciously missionary of all religions. The Christian faith began within Judaism, and Jesus Himself had no intention of going outside Jewish boundaries in His own ministry, but His message was concerned with the love of God for all men and the mission which He initiated soon burst those boundaries. The New Testament mentions a number of early missionaries—Philip, Barnabas, Mark, Silas, Apollos, and, greatest of them, Paul. It was Paul who did the most to prepare the way for Gentiles to become Christians without conforming to Jewish law, and his missionary journeys resulted in the establishment of churches in much of Asia Minor and Greece.

In the succeeding period the mission was carried on, apparently, by teachers and writers, such as the apologists whose works have come down to us, though little is known of their activities. As the office of bishop increased its importance in the church, it became increasingly the center of missionary leadership. The most famous of the ancient bishops for his achievements in Christianizing an entire area was Gregory Thaumaturgos (213?–?270), bishop of Neocaesarea from about 240 until his death. He was responsible for the development in Pontus of the first great mass movement to Christianity. Later, in the declining days of the Roman Empire, the greatest missionary bishop was Martin of Tours (315?–?399), who regularly led his monks on expeditions to confront the pagans of the countryside.

Through the labors of such men, and perhaps even more through natural contacts of ordinary Christians, the Christian faith spread throughout the Roman Empire. At the same time, it was extended beyond the Roman borders. Gregory the Illuminator (257?–332), member of a noble family of Armenia, brought the faith to his homeland and was responsible for making it the first Christian country in the world. Arabia and India were the scene of early Christian churches founded by merchants or missionaries. Ulfilas (311?–381), an Arian Christian of the 4th century, labored with considerable success among the Gothic tribes on the Danubian border. Frumentius (d. about 380), who is said to have been held as a captive in Ethiopia, established there an enduring Christian faith.

Western Europe.—In the West also, Christian missionaries carried their faith beyond the borders of Roman rule and, as that rule collapsed under the impact of Germanic tribes, proceeded to convert the barbaric conquerors. For this endeavor the British Isles produced the greatest succession of missionaries that the world has known. First there was Ninian (d. 432?), who developed the Christianity of the west coast of Great Britain and possibly of Ireland. Then came Patrick, who was born in Britain in the first quarter of the 5th century, when Roman power was declining. He was carried as a captive to Ireland and later, after escaping, returned to that land to spread Christianity among its inhabitants. He died about 492. The Irish church, which reached the height of its fame and learning during the confused times which followed, was noted for its wandering ascetics, the *peregrini*. Men like Columban (543–615) and Gall (550?–?645) traveled through Scotland, France, Germany, Switzerland, and Italy, often engaging in missionary preaching.

In 563 the most famous of these Irish missionaries, Columba (521–597), established a monastery on the island of Iona off the coast of Scotland as a center from which to carry on the conversion of that country. The Ionan succession moved beyond Scotland into England. Aidan (d. 651), who also was Irish, went from there to the island of Lindisfarne off the coast of Northumbria and took the lead in the conversion of that northern English kingdom. Finan (d. 661), his successor, did the most for the conversion of Mercia and Essex, and Wilfrid (634–709), also from Lindisfarne, converted the South Saxons and moved on to the Isle of Wight. Meanwhile, in 596, in one of the most celebrated missionary episodes of history, Augustine (d. 604) led a band under orders from Pope Gregory I (r. 590–604) and accomplished the conversion of the rulers of Kent.

The newly established English church immediately undertook the missionary task on the Continent. Wilfrid himself went from the Isle of Wight to begin work in Frisia, where he was soon followed by his disciple, Willibrord (657?–?738), the Apostle of the Frisians. Then came the most famous man in the whole succession, Winfrid or Boniface (680?–754), who began work under Willibrord and then moved southward and established the church firmly in central Germany. He was killed on a mission to the Frisians.

Central and Eastern Europe.—Nowhere else does the medieval church display such a series of missionaries. In most of the other areas conversions were accomplished through the influence of powerful kings, although often they brought in foreign priests to assist them in their efforts. So, for example, the most famous missionaries of the Greek Church, Cyril (Constantine, 827–869) and Methodius (826–885), were called in 862 by the ruler of Moravia to help him carry out the conversion of his country. They made one of the most successful efforts on record to present Christianity in indigenous forms, developing a script for the Slavonic tongue of the country and creating a Slavonic liturgy.

The principal effort in central Europe was made by the German church as part of the German expansion toward the east. Magdeburg and Salzburg were the chief headquarters for this missionary effort, the former being concerned principally with the north Slavs and the latter with the south Slavs. Among the German missionaries was Adalbert (955?–997), who in 983 became the second bishop of Prague, was active in the Christianization of Bohemia, and later died in an attempt to carry the Gospel to the Prussians. Otto of Bamberg (1060?–1139), another missionary, undertook the difficult and dangerous mission to the Pomeranians with remarkable success. Another side of this German expansion is seen in the military orders, the Teutonic Knights and the Knights of the Sword, which in the early 13th century undertook the Christianization of Prussia and the Baltic lands. Their method was that of conquest and colonization, not unlike that of some of the Muslim religious orders in North Africa, however, and whether such efforts can rightly be termed missionary is open to question.

To the north, among the Scandinavian peoples, Christianity was established somewhat earlier, usually under royal pressure. The one great missionary of that area was Anschar (801–865), who devoted his life to bringing the Christian message to the Norsemen. In 857 he was made archbishop of Hamburg-Bremen with a commission from the pope to reach Scandinavia. Anschar went repeatedly to the rulers of the Scandinavian lands and sent others on missions, but the destructiveness of the Viking raids defeated his efforts, and the conversion of the Norsemen awaited a later generation, when the kings themselves took up the task.

In the East, Russian Christianity spread by missionary work from its original center in Kiev, where it had been established by royal decision. Starting at the end of the 10th century, missionaries and bishops went to the Dnieper and Volga areas, and in later centuries they reached as far north as the White Sea and as far east as the Urals, carrying their message. The Eastern missionaries, like the Western, were usually monks. In their desire to retire from contacts with their fellow men, they continually moved out into sparsely populated and backward areas where Christianity had not penetrated. Thus, by a strange development, it happened that monasticism, which because of its emphasis on retirement from the world would seem to be a completely nonmissionary movement, became in both Eastern and Western churches the mainstay of missions.

Asia and North Africa.—In the late Middle Ages, when the conversion of Europe had been practically completed, a new force appeared with a new missionary dynamic. This was the movement of the Dominicans and Franciscans. In contrast with the earlier monks, these friars made it their major concern to preach to men, and they took the lead in reaching beyond Europe to Asia and North Africa. Francis of Assisi (1182–1226) himself engaged in three missionary journeys to the Muslims, and Dominic (1170–1221) declared that his commission was to make the Gospel known to all mankind. The two orders established a chain of monasteries across the Middle East and North Africa. The great advocate and exemplar of missions to the Muslims was Raymond Lully (Ramón Lull, 1235?–1315), who developed a program for schools for missionaries and a presentation of the significance of Christ for Islam. Lully also undertook several missionary trips, on the last of which he was stoned to death outside Bougie.

During this same period, while the empire of the Mongols created some safety of movement across Asia, a series of intrepid missionaries penetrated India, Central Asia, and China. Even earlier, Nestorian Christian traders and missionaries had spread their faith from their centers in Mesopotamia among the mercantile community of that same area. Nestorian bishops had sent representatives to work with some of the tribes of Central Asia, and in 635 one of them, Alopen (Olopan), had brought Christianity to China, where it flourished for a time. This Nestorian expansion remained tied to the Syriac culture whence it emanated, however, and it was limited generally to the traders and tradesmen of the cities, never taking real root in the countries to which it spread. Nestorianism remained a religion of foreigners, and when the Chinese government attacked it in 845, it disappeared. (See also NESTORIANISM.) The 14th century effort from Europe was no more lasting in its effects. John of Montecorvino (1246–1328) made his way to the Chinese capital and won some 6,000 converts. Others followed him, and the Christian work was appreciated and subsidized by the Mongol rulers of the land. Some of the Central Asian peoples, notably the Keraits, were Christianized, and there was hope for a time that through their marriages and other contacts with the Mongol princes Christianity might be established from Persia to China. With the collapse of the Mongol dynasty in China in 1368, however, the church again rapidly disappeared from that country, and the Muslim environment won over the Mongol rulers of western Asia. By the end of the Middle Ages, Christianity was in full retreat from all of its Asian extensions.

MODERN CHRISTIAN MISSIONS

The new zeal for the faith that arose in the 16th century, combined with the new contacts with non-Christian peoples, brought a surge of fresh life to the Christian missions. The leadership was taken by Spain and Portugal, which were the first to be involved in the new contacts and were centers of much new religious life. The monarchs of both countries were committed strongly to the missionary enterprise and made it their particular responsibility to support missionary work. This proved a considerable asset in the beginning, but in later years tight royal control was a great handicap.

At the same time, the reformed papacy developed a new interest in missions. In 1622 there was founded at Rome the Congregatio de Propaganda Fide (Congregation of Propagation of the Faith), which was responsible under the pope for the supervision and guidance of the missionary enterprise. Ever since then the Propaganda has been the headquarters of Roman Catholic missions, a focus of worldwide information and worldwide concern. Another mark of the new interest was the formation in 1663 of the Société des Missions Étrangères (Foreign Missionary Society) of Paris. The first organization in the Christian Church to be devoted purely to missions among non-Christians, it thereafter maintained work in many parts of the world. Even more important was the formation in 1540 of the Jesuit Order, which soon took the lead in missionary work all over the world. The pioneer of Jesuit missions, and one of the greatest missionaries of all time, was Francis Xavier (1506–1552), who was sent to the East in 1541. His whole missionary career lasted only 10 years, but in that brief period he blazed a path into south India, Ceylon, Malaya, Indonesia, and Japan, and he died in an attempt to reach China. By the time of his death the Jesuits were embarked on a mission to the entire Orient.

Early Asian Missions.—In India the Jesuits not only worked with the older orders along the west coast, but also dispatched a series of missions to the court of the Mogul emperors. Under Akbar (r. 1556–1605) and his successors they were received with honor, and at one time several princes of the court were baptized. In south India the Jesuit Roberto De Nobili (1577–1656) carried out in Madura what must be regarded as the most remarkable and peculiar mission in the history of Christianity. He renounced all contact with Europeans and established himself as a Brahman ascetic, living the life of a Hindu holy man, teaching about a new Hindu holy book ("the fifth Veda"), and allowing his Brahman converts —who came in considerable numbers—to keep their full caste status. Objections from other orders and trouble with his superiors greatly damaged his mission, but this Hinduized type of work continued for another century.

No less determined to fit Christianity into the culture of the land were the leaders of the Jesuit enterprise in China. In 1582, Matteo Ricci (1552–1610), the chief figure in the mission, was sent to China. Settling there in the following year, he accepted the ceremonies for the veneration of Confucius and those honoring ancestors which dominated Chinese academic and family life. Because of their scientific knowledge, Ricci and his successors were given high position by the emperors, but as in India complaints by other Christians led to a century-long rites controversy and to the final prohibition of the liberal practices of the Jesuits. Christianity in China then passed through a period of persecutions and of decline.

In Japan the course of the mission was even more meteoric. Within 30 years of Xavier's visit, 1 per cent of the people, or twice the percentage of Christians in 20th century Japan, had been converted. The baptisms continued rapidly and a number of feudal lords were won, so that Christianity bade fair to become a great power in the country with strongholds chiefly in the extreme southwest. This very possibility turned the rulers against it, however, and a series of bloody persecutions starting in 1596 drove the missionaries from the land and almost exterminated all the Christians.

Only in the Philippines did Christian missionaries find an Eastern country where their work bore continuing fruit. There nearly the entire population was converted.

Early American Missions.—While these remarkable experiments were being undertaken in the East, other missionaries were achieving far larger results in the Western Hemisphere. There, following the Spanish conquests, came the most rapid mass movements to Christianity that have ever taken place. Mexico was the scene of the largest achievement. In 17 years from the time of Hernán Cortés' arrival in 1519 some 9 million to 10 million persons are said to have been baptized. This was not primarily due to enforced conversion, such as was sometimes practiced in the West Indies, but was probably to a greater extent the result of the long training in submissiveness which the Indian tribes had received under Aztec rule. The Indians proved not only docile but eager to accept the religion of their new rulers. One missionary reported as many as 14,000 baptisms in a single day. By the end of the 16th century the peoples of the Aztec and Inca empires, together with the more civilized tribes of Colombia, had all been baptized.

The greatest missionary of that period in the Americas was Bartolomé de las Casas (1474–1566), who spent his long life championing the cause of the Indians against the colonial Spaniards. Las Casas was appointed protector general of the Indians (1516) and later secured royal laws in their favor (1542). He thus typified the long struggle which missionaries have waged against their fellow countrymen in the interests of the people to whom they have gone.

In most of this early work the Franciscans took the lead. It was they, too, who led the missionary advance north of Mexico in the 17th century, although the Jesuit Eusebio Francisco Kino (1645?–1711) was important there. In the 18th century the Franciscans pushed into Texas and California. In California, under the inspiring leadership of Junípero Serra (1713–1784), they eventually established 21 missions. The Franciscans were given full control over the Indians whom they baptized, and their method was to bring the nomadic indigenous people together in settlements around each mission and to teach them agriculture and handicrafts. (See also MISSION INDIANS.)

A much wider application of this method was made in Venezuela and Paraguay. There large ranches or industrial settlements were founded by the missionaries. In Paraguay particularly, the settlements were brought together into a kind of national government exercised by the Jesuits, with an army organized to defend the communities against Spanish and Portuguese slave raiders. With the suppression of the Jesuits in 1773, however, most of the work collapsed. In other areas, such as Central America and Brazil, the missions progressed more slowly, and their effectiveness was much less, so that considerable areas remained untouched as late as the 19th and 20th centuries.

The other great American missions were those of the French Roman Catholics across the far-flung French possessions. The period of their greatest activity was the 17th century, when they pressed up the St. Lawrence River, along the entire length of the Great Lakes, and then down the Mississippi, following the trail of the missionary explorer Jacques Marquette (1637–1675). For the most part, it was a widely scattered work which left little continuing effect once the French power had been overthrown. Its largest success was achieved in the mission to the Hurons, who rapidly became Christian under Jesuit leadership. In 1650, however, the tribe was almost anihilated by the powerful Iroquois.

Protestant Beginnings.—North America was also the scene of the first Protestant missions. The English settlers there represented the first Protestant group to come into continuing contact with non-Christians. John Eliot (1604–1690), the most famous of the Puritan missionaries to the Indians, began his work outside Boston in 1646. There were some 2,500 converts gathered in settlements in New England 30 years later, but the ravages of disease and, particularly, of war destroyed their communities. In the 18th century the work was continued by men like David Brainerd (1718–1747), whose brief and painful life of missionary service became an inspiration to later generations in many lands. Various missionary organizations in Great Britain, such as the Society for the Propagation of the Gospel in Foreign Parts (1701) and the Society for Promoting Christian Knowledge (1699), which are still in existence, grew out of the efforts to aid such work.

It was not until the rise of Pietism and the spread of the evangelical revival that Protestantism generally began to take seriously its missionary responsibility. The Pietist center at Halle in Germany became the source of the first Protestant mission in Asia, established by Bartholomäus Ziegenbalg (1683–1719) in 1706 in the small Danish possession of Tranquebar in south India. The most famous member of this mission was Christian Friedrich Schwartz (1726–1798), whose sympathy and integrity won him the respect and love of the rulers and people of the whole area. The first denomination to become dominated by Pietism was the Moravian Church, which gave itself completely to missionary work, sending its few members across the face of the earth from

Pennsylvania and Greenland to Africa and Ceylon in the latter half of the 18th century. Moravian missions have continued on a small scale to the mid-20th century, and in relation to its size there is no church that has contributed as much heroism and sacrifice to the Christian mission.

When the evangelical revival, which was closely related to Pietism, spread over England, it stirred the beginnings of a widespread interest in missions. Important missionary societies began to be organized, the first of these being the Baptist Missionary Society, which was formed in 1792 under the inspiration of William Carey (1761–1834). Carey, the father of modern Protestant missions, was a humble shoemaker and part-time Baptist preacher who became convinced of the worldwide missionary responsibility of the church and in 1793 went himself as a missionary to India. Following his initiative, an interdenominational group formed the London Missionary Society in 1795, and the evangelical wing of the Church of England established the Church Missionary Society in 1799. These bodies, together with those begun a century earlier, have provided most of the missionary work originating in England.

The interest in establishing missionary societies soon spread to the Continent, where the Netherlands Missionary Society (1797) and the Basel Missionary Institute (1815) were the first of a considerable number of large and effective bodies that appeared all over Germany and Scandinavia as well as in the Netherlands, Switzerland, and France. The same movement reached the United States, and as a result of the interest of a student group in New England the American Board of Commissioners for Foreign Missions was formed in 1810. On the American scene, however, independent societies following the European pattern soon gave way to official church boards entrusted with the missionary concern of a whole church. Most American denominations eventually established such boards.

The first area of large success found by the early missionary societies was the South Pacific. In 1797 the London Missionary Society started work in Tahiti. After early years of great difficulty, a sudden change came with the conversion of the king, Pomare II, who, beginning in 1815, led his whole people into the church. The same sort of thing happened in the Tonga Islands as a result of the work of the Methodists. Under the leadership of the Tongan king, the Methodist Church was established as the state church and won over the bulk of the population. Missionaries from Tonga and the urging of the Tongan king led in 1854 to the conversion of the ruler of Fiji, which put an end to cannibalism and reduced the tribal warfare that had ravaged those islands. Samoa was won to Christianity partly by Tongans and to an even greater degree by Tahitian missionaries under the leadership of John Williams (1796–1839), an intrepid missionary of the London Missionary Society, who started work in many of the Pacific islands. Williams himself was killed in an effort to introduce Christianity in the New Hebrides. In most of the New Hebrides and the rest of Melanesia the bulk of the population was not converted until the 20th century. The Hawaiian Islands, however, like the other principal Polynesian centers, were converted early. There, as a result of the work of American Congregationalists, a mass movement started in 1836 which rapidly brought the whole population into the church.

Although in no other area did modern Christian missions achieve such complete success as in the Pacific islands, there are some sections of other lands where nearly the whole people were converted. The Karens of Burma, the Hovas of Madagascar, and the Bataks of Sumatra are the outstanding examples of such peoples. The conversion of the Karens grew out of the efforts of Adoniram Judson (1788–1850), the first foreign missionary of the American Baptists. Judson, laboring under great difficulties and dangers, established a mission in Burma which in other men's hands developed a large Baptist denomination among the Karens. The conversion of the Hovas, the ruling people of Madagascar, was primarily the result of London Missionary Society efforts beginning in 1818. The Hova church had to undergo a long period of persecutions under an anti-Christian queen who had Christians speared, thrown over cliffs, and otherwise done to death, but the church survived and by 1890 included most of the Hovas and nearly 10 per cent of all the people of Madagascar. The Bataks became Christian considerably later. Their remote and dangerous territory was not entered successfully until 1861, when the Rhenish Missionary Society started work among them. The leader of that work, Ludwig Ingwer Nommensen (1834–1918), lived to see the day when he was accepted as the "grandfather" of the Batak people, who became overwhelmingly Christian.

Later Asian Missions.—In other parts of the East Indies, Dutch missionaries carried on a thorough and persistent work, achieving their greatest success in the Moluccas and in adjacent islands. The church in the Moluccas, which had begun in the period of Portuguese trade in the East, had its strong centers on such islands as Amboina, Ternate, and Halmahera. By far the largest church that arose out of the Dutch work was that of Minahassa, the long northern peninsula of Celebes, but there were other important churches among the Torajas in central Celebes and on the islands of Timor, Sangihe, and Talaud. In Java there developed the largest number of converts from Islam to be found in any country, and Roman Catholic missionaries developed a strong church in the Lesser Sunda Islands. The result is that over 3 million Indonesians are Christian, constituting one of the strongest churches of the East.

In nearby Indochina another strong church was developed chiefly by the work of the Foreign Missionary Society of Paris. To an even greater degree than that of the Hovas, this church had to undergo severe persecutions and thousands of martyrdoms before it was finally established. It numbers about 1.5 million Roman Catholics.

Quite different has been the story of Christian missions in the major countries of Asia: India, China, and Japan. In none of them has the church grown to more than 1 or 2 per cent of the population. India has by far the largest church, mission work having been re-established there considerably earlier than in the other two countries. At the beginning of the 19th century, Protestant societies began to enter the country, and soon thereafter Roman Catholic work was revived. At first the British authorities were extremely hostile and would allow no missionaries in their territory. William Carey established himself in a Danish enclave, and Henry

Martyn (1781–1812), the most famous evangelist to Muslims, came as a chaplain to Britishers. After 1813, however, British policy softened, and Christian work spread over the country. From the beginning, Carey regarded the work in broader terms than had been known before. He led missions into higher education, social reform, and agricultural service as well as into translation and publication. Education soon became the major missionary contribution to the country, hundreds of schools and dozens of colleges being scattered throughout the land. The great pioneer and advocate of educational missions was Alexander Duff (1806–1878) of Scotland, and since his day the Scottish churches have been deeply involved in educational work. Duff led Christians in an approach to the higher castes, but to the surprise of the missionaries the great surge toward Christianity came from the very lowest castes and from the tribal peoples. First in the Tinnevelly District in the extreme south in the 1840's, then in southern Travancore and Andhra in the 1870's, even more in Chota Nagpur in the 1880's and later in Assam, the United Provinces (now Uttar Pradesh), and the Punjab, great numbers of such people entered the church in mass movements. The result was that by the mid-20th century there were some 10 million Christians in India, about equally divided between Roman Catholics and Protestants and including a large body of Syrians. Among Protestants the largest numerical success has been won by the Anglican Church, with the American Methodists and Baptists close behind.

China missions began much later. Not until about 1860 were missionaries allowed into the country, although five ports had been opened to them by the Treaty of Nanking (1842). Robert Morrison (1782–1834), who began the Protestant work, was able to stay in China only because he served as translator for the East India Company. Through most of the 19th century the position of missionaries remained uncertain. The predominance among Protestants, which in India belonged to the Anglicans, in China was with the Calvinist groups: Presbyterian, Congregational, and Reformed, who early established themselves along the coast. Among Roman Catholics the predominance was with the Foreign Missionary Society of Paris, which covered the largest part of the country; the Lazarists in the Peking area, who had the largest number of Christians under their care; and the Jesuits. Special mention must be made of the China Inland Mission, a body established in 1865 by James Hudson Taylor (1832–1905) of England, which grew to be by far the largest single mission in China. Working on a nondenominational basis with a strongly conservative and strictly evangelistic emphasis, it left social service and church development largely aside. It was the forerunner of an increasing number of such missions in many countries in the 20th century.

In the closing years of the 19th century the picture in China suddenly changed. The people awoke to the need of modernization and turned to the missionaries to lead the way. Great Christian educational and medical institutions sprang up. Outstanding Protestant missionaries like Timothy Richard (1845–1919) and William Martin (1827–1916), the first president of the Imperial University, acquired wide influence in the country. The Boxer Rebellion, though it inflicted massive casualties among the Christians, only slightly delayed this process. Such leaders of the new China as Sun Yat-sen, Chiang Kai-shek, and the C. J. Soong family were converted. The Roman Catholics generally stayed outside this national movement, but they developed a church several times larger than that of the Protestants. The triumph of the Communist Party finally put an end to this wide Christian influence and to the Christian institutions on the mainland. The church remained, though with only half the numerical strength of that of India.

Japan remained tightly closed to Christian missions until 1859, and the Japanese church has always remained small. It grew most rapidly as a result of the work of American Protestant missionaries in the 1880's, when the samurai and other upper-class groups were widely attracted to Christianity. This beginning gave the church the independent and highly educated character which it has always maintained. Japan is the one country where an effective foreign mission of the Russian Orthodox Church was established (1861), and a considerable group of converts won. The Roman Catholic work received a great stimulus when, in 1865, about 100,000 secret Christians were discovered in the rural areas, remnants of the 17th century church.

In neighboring Korea the church was started by natives who had come in contact with Roman Catholics in Peking. All through the 19th century, in the face of strict prohibitions and severe persecutions, attempts were made by Roman Catholics to keep the church alive. Finally, in 1884, the land was opened to Christian missions. At first growth was slow, but by the mid-20th century the Korean church had become one of the fastest growing in the world, claiming 5 per cent of the population. Over half of the Christians are Presbyterians.

Of the other Asian lands, Ceylon has a large church (nearly 10 per cent of the people, mostly Roman Catholics) and much missionary activity. Western Asia, the homeland of Islam, has been the scene of patient efforts and widespread Christian service, particularly through outstanding colleges, schools, and hospitals, but not of a growing church.

Africa.—It was not hostile governments but hostile climate and terrain and disease which held back Christian missions from Africa. In the early 19th century, when the missions were starting, it was not unusual for half or more of a party of missionaries to die within a few years of their arrival. The first attempts were made along the West African coast, the so-called white man's grave. Here missions were founded in connection with the colonies of freed slaves which had been begun in relation to the missionary movement. Some of the ex-slaves, such as the powerful Samuel Adjai Crowther (1809?–1891), returned to their people as missionaries, and out of these beginnings there developed a large church in West Africa. Crowther himself started the large Anglican Church of Nigeria. At about the same time, work was begun in South Africa under the leadership of the London Missionary Society. Robert Moffat (1795–1883) became the society's great pioneer, pushing north to the Bechuanas and Matabeles. He was succeeded by his son-in-law, the great pioneer David Livingstone (1813–1873). Starting in 1841, Livingstone opened up the route north across the Kalahari Desert, and then proceeded to cross the continent twice and to spend long years exploring the lake region of central Africa. In the same period, the Scottish church pioneered in education for the natives of South Africa, and the Paris Evangelical Missionary Society founded what came to be practically the national church of Basutoland.

Livingstone's reports on central Africa stirred great interest in England, and several societies followed him there, notably the Universities Mission to Central Africa. In 1878 the first Roman Catholic society to take seriously the needs of Africa, the Society of African Missioners (White Fathers) founded by Bishop Charles Martial Allemand-Lavigerie (1825–1892), also entered the lake region and began what became the largest church of that area. The White Fathers were joined by the Congregation of the Holy Ghost (Holy Ghost Fathers), who were second only to them in the size of the Christian community they established and who also developed the principal group of Christians in Angola. An entrance into Uganda was effected by the White Fathers in 1879 and by the Anglicans in 1877 with remarkable effectiveness. For a time the country fell into civil war among Roman Catholic, Protestant, and Muslim chieftains, but by 1895 order had been established and the church grew rapidly. Even more successful was the mission in the Belgian Congo, where in the 20th century Christianity made its most massive advance. The Congregation of the Immaculate Heart of Mary (Scheutveld Fathers) from Belgium took the lead there, but the White Fathers, Holy Ghost Fathers, and several Protestant groups also worked effectively. By the middle of the 20th century, Christianity had been established throughout Africa below the Sahara, with its greatest centers of strength in the Congo, South Africa, Madagascar, and Uganda. In each of these areas between one fourth and one half of the people were Christians.

Later American Missions.—The greatest numerical success of Christian missions in the 19th century was achieved among the Negroes of North America. Through natural contacts and persistent missionary work the proportion of Christians among the Negroes increased from 7 per cent at the beginning of the 19th century to the great majority of the Negro population in the 20th century. Two thirds of the Negroes were Baptist, and nearly one third Methodist. The chief programs for Negro education were carried on first by the Presbyterians and then by the Congregationalists, who did the largest amount of this work in the development of schools and colleges following the Civil War. Through most of the 19th century, Negro education was primarily a task of Christian missions.

American missions also had to be directed toward the frontier settlements as they moved across the continent, and toward the masses of immigrants. Both groups were effectively kept in the church. Beyond the frontier there were the Indians, who were approached by such heroic missionaries as David Zeisberger (1721–1808) of the Moravians and Pierre Jean De Smet (1801–1873) of the Roman Catholics. Indian work was carried on under great difficulties while the whites were despoiling and demoralizing the red men, but eventually the majority (in Canada, the great majority) of that people were won to the faith.

In South America the 19th century was largely a time of quiescence in missions, but in the 20th century Protestant groups, particularly of the more emotional type, began to move in with much effectiveness. Roman Catholics also greatly strengthened their work in order to reach the untouched elements of the population.

20th Century Conditions.—In the 20th century, Christian missions have met new difficulties in nationalism, communism, and the widespread reaction against Western domination, all evidenced most sharply in the expulsion of missionaries from China by the Communist regime in the 1950's. The growth of anti-Christian movements in the West has led to a recognition that the former homelands of Christianity must be treated as the objects of missionary concern, and, as a result, vital new movements in home missions have developed. Christian churches as a whole have put far more effort into home missions than into foreign missions, but the latter have also been greatly expanded in the 20th century. The number of Roman Catholic foreign missionaries increased from 22,000 in 1925 to double that number in 1950, and that of Protestant foreign missionaries from 15,000 in 1903 to 34,000 in 1956. In general the proportion of Europeans declined because of the effects of war on European countries, and the proportion of Americans increased; among Protestants, Americans accounted for two thirds of the total. The increase from American Roman Catholics was due very largely to the work of the Catholic Foreign Mission Society of America (Maryknoll Fathers), founded in 1911.

The 20th century has been primarily one of the growth and strengthening of the churches founded by 19th century missions. The churches developed by Protestant missions increased in size from 6 million members in 1925 to 36 million in 1952. Roman Catholics in mission areas increased, in the same period, from 33 million to 50 million (including 17 million in the Philippines). The training and strengthening of national leaders for these churches has come to be regarded as the first priority in missionary work. Pope Pius XI (r. 1922–1939) signalized the new day when, in 1926, he consecrated six Chinese priests to the episcopate at a special service in Rome. Since then members of the indigenous church have been raised to the episcopate in India, Japan, China, Indochina, Madagascar, and Africa. Protestants have followed the same policy in their leadership. The new churches have also become increasingly indigenous in their art and music, their types of worship and of evangelism, and their sense of responsibility toward the countries in which they exist.

Christian missions have branched out into many new forms of service, adding to educational and medical work such types of activity as agricultural improvement, rural development and cooperatives, adult literacy training and literacy campaigns, urban social work, medical education, nursing and midwifery education, and technical and scientific services of various kinds. The Bible has been translated into 1,100 languages, making it available in all the major and many minor tongues. For the first time in history the Christian Church has become truly worldwide, being established by the late 1950's in every country of the world except Outer Mongolia.

See also CANADA—*28. Protestant Churches; 29. Roman Catholic Church;* CATHOLIC CHURCH, ROMAN—*3. History; 5. Missions;* CHRISTIANITY; LATIN AMERICA—*9. Religion;* MIDDLE EAST—*5. History;* ORTHODOX EASTERN CHURCH; THEOLOG-

ICAL EDUCATION; articles on the various Protestant churches; sections on religion in articles on the various countries; and the biographies of the leading missionaries.

Bibliography.—An introductory book on Christian missions is Basil J. Mathews' *Disciples of All Nations: The Story of Christian Expansion* (London 1952). The standard work in the field is Kenneth Scott Latourette's *History of the Expansion of Christianity,* 7 vols. (New York 1937–45). The standard work on Muslim missions has long been Sir Thomas Walker Arnold's *Preaching of Islam: A History of the Propagation of the Muslim Faith,* 2d ed. (New York 1913); a description of Buddhism is found in August Karl Reischauer's chapter "Buddhism," in *The Great Religions of the Modern World,* ed. by Edward J. Jurji (Princeton 1946). Further bibliographical guidance can be obtained from these works.

CHARLES W. FORMAN,
Professor of Missions, Yale University.

MISSIONARY RIDGE. See CHATTANOOGA CAMPAIGN.

MISSISSAUGA, mis-i-sô'gȧ, a town in Peel county, Ontario, Canada, is a western suburb of Toronto. It was incorporated as a town on Jan. 1, 1968, and named for the Mississauga Indians, an Algonkian tribe that had signed a treaty with the British crown in August 1805 by which it agreed to sell for £1,000 the tract of land on which Mississauga stands. It was first called the Township of Toronto, and its first settler, Philip Cody, was deeded 200 acres (81 hectares) on May 27, 1807. By 1851 the township had a population of 7,539.

When it was incorporated in 1968, Mississauga covered 71,040 acres (28,700 hectares) and included the former communities of Cooksville, Clarkson, Malton, Churchville, and others. The most important of Mississauga's many industries is aircraft construction. The Toronto International Airport is here.

Mississauga is governed by a mayor, a reeve, a deputy reeve, and a council. Population: 156,070.

MISSISSINEWA, mĭs-ĭ-sĭn'ĕ-wä, **Battle of,** a skirmish which took place on the Mississinewa River in Grant County, Indiana, on Dec. 18, 1812. Since it had become evident to Gen. William Henry Harrison that the Miami Indians were being incited by the British, he sent Col. John B. Campbell to attack and destroy their villages. After destroying several Indian settlements, Campbell's troops moved up the Mississinewa to Jalapa, planning to continue their destruction until they reached its junction with the Wabash. Their camp was surrounded before daylight by 300 Miamis, however, and in the ensuing battle Campbell sustained casualties of 8 killed and 48 wounded, while about 30 Indians were killed. As a result, Campbell decided to return to Ohio, but his campaign had accomplished its purpose, for the Miamis took no further part in the War of 1812.

MISSISSIPPI, mĭs-ĭ-sĭp'ĭ, South Central state, United States, bounded on the north by Tennessee, on the east by Alabama, on the south by the Gulf of Mexico and Louisiana, and on the west by the Mississippi River, which separates it from Louisiana and Arkansas. Along the gulf coast the state claims all islands "within six leagues of the shore." The greatest length north and south is 330 miles; the greatest breadth east and west, 180 miles. Mississippi's name is taken from the river which forms its western boundary.

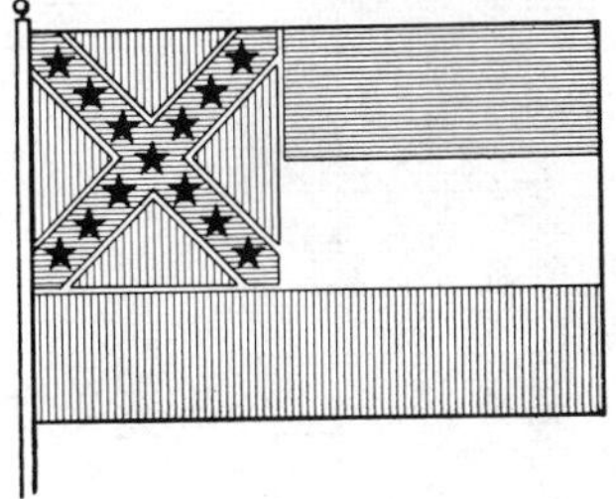

State flag.

Total area	47,716 square miles
Land area	47,248 square miles
Water area	468 square miles
Latitude	30° 13′—35°N.
Longitude	88° 7′—91° 41′W.
Altitude (average)	300 feet
High point, Woodall Mountain, near Iuka	806 feet
Low point, Gulf of Mexico	Sea level
Population (1970)	2,216,912
Capital city—Jackson; population	153,968
Admitted as the 20th state	Dec. 10, 1817
State bird (adopted in 1929)	Mockingbird
State flower (adopted in 1900)	Magnolia
State tree	*Magnolia grandiflora*
State song (unofficial)	*Mississippi*
State motto	*Virtute et Armis* (By valor and arms)
State nicknames	Magnolia State; Bayou State

State seal.

A discussion of Mississippi's geography, government, social and economic life, and history is presented under the following headings:

1. Physical Features
2. Population and Political Divisions
3. Government
4. Education, Health, and Welfare
5. Economic Activities
6. Transportation and Communications
7. Cultural Life
8. Places of Interest
9. Famous Men and Women
10. History
11. Bibliography

1. PHYSICAL FEATURES

Topography.—Mississippi may be divided into 10 physiographic areas, which conform generally to the geologic structure of the state:

(1) The low, fertile, productive delta lies between the Yazoo and Mississippi rivers.

(2) The loess bluffs, beginning at Memphis, Tenn., stretch around the eastern border of the delta to Natchez. These rugged hills quickly erode and become impossible to cultivate.

(3) Along the Gulf of Mexico lie the coastal terraces, a narrow strip of low, level, sandy soil unsuited for agriculture. The Mississippi coastline is 44 miles long.

(4) Immediately above these plains and reaching northward almost to Jackson and Meridian lie the piney woods. This portion developed

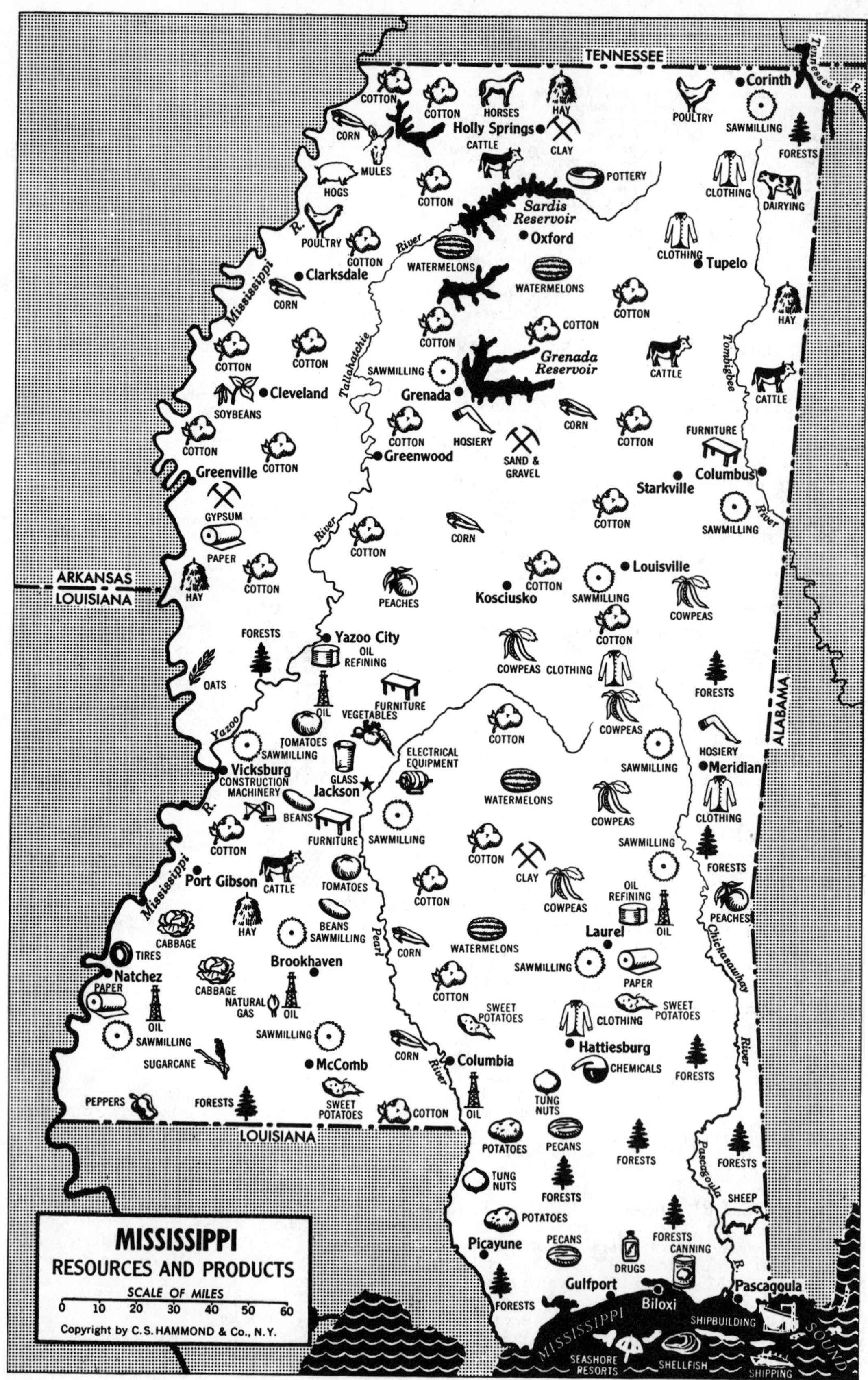
TENNESSEE
Tennessee R.
Corinth
COTTON
COTTON
HORSES
HAY
POULTRY
SAWMILLING
Holly Springs
CORN
CATTLE
CLAY
FORESTS
MULES
HOGS
POTTERY
CLOTHING
DAIRYING
COTTON
Sardis Reservoir
Oxford
Mississippi R.
POULTRY
COTTON
River
WATERMELONS
CLOTHING
Tupelo
Clarksdale
WATERMELONS
CORN
COTTON
HAY
Tallahatchie
COTTON
COTTON
COTTON
COTTON
COTTON
Grenada Reservoir
Tombigbee
CATTLE
SAWMILLING
CATTLE
Cleveland
Grenada
SOYBEANS
CORN
COTTON
HOSIERY
COTTON
COTTON
FURNITURE
Greenwood
SAND & GRAVEL
Greenville
COTTON
Columbus
Starkville
GYPSUM
COTTON
River
River
CORN
SAWMILLING
PAPER
COTTON
ARKANSAS
LOUISIANA
Louisville
COTTON
HAY
COTTON
Kosciusko
SAWMILLING
PEACHES
COWPEAS
FORESTS
Yazoo City
COTTON
OIL REFINING
COWPEAS
CLOTHING
OATS
FORESTS
OIL
FURNITURE
ALABAMA
VEGETABLES
Yazoo
COTTON
COWPEAS
HOSIERY
TOMATOES
SAWMILLING
ELECTRICAL EQUIPMENT
SAWMILLING
Meridian
Vicksburg
CONSTRUCTION MACHINERY
GLASS
Jackson
WATERMELONS
R.
BEANS
COWPEAS
CLOTHING
FURNITURE
SAWMILLING
SAWMILLING
COTTON
Mississippi
COTTON
FORESTS
Port Gibson
CATTLE
TOMATOES
CLAY
COTTON
OIL REFINING
COWPEAS
PEACHES
HAY
BEANS
SAWMILLING
Pearl
OIL
CABBAGE
Laurel
TIRES
CORN
WATERMELONS
Chickasawhay
Brookhaven
SAWMILLING
Natchez
CABBAGE
PAPER
COTTON
PAPER
NATURAL GAS
OIL
SWEET POTATOES
SWEET POTATOES
OIL
CLOTHING
SAWMILLING
SAWMILLING
CORN
Columbia
Hattiesburg
SUGARCANE
McComb
River
CHEMICALS
FORESTS
River
PEPPERS
FORESTS
SWEET POTATOES
COTTON
OIL
TUNG NUTS
LOUISIANA
POTATOES
PECANS
FORESTS
FORESTS
Pascagoula
TUNG NUTS
FORESTS
SHEEP
POTATOES
FORESTS
CANNING
Picayune
PECANS
DRUGS
R.
Gulfport
Pascagoula
FORESTS
Biloxi
MISSISSIPPI SOUND
SHIPBUILDING
SEASHORE RESORTS
SHELLFISH
SHIPPING
MISSISSIPPI
RESOURCES AND PRODUCTS
SCALE OF MILES
0 10 20 30 40 50 60
Copyright by C.S. HAMMOND & Co., N.Y.

slowly until the commercial value of the longleaf pine forests was realized.

(5) A narrow prairie belt stretches from Vicksburg to the Alabama line. This gently rolling area yields some of the state's highest agricultural profits.

(6) The most rugged and highest section consists of the fall-line hills near the Tennessee River in the extreme northeastern part of the state. Its red, sandy hills are very poorly suited to cultivation.

(7) Around the western border of these hills lies the black prairie belt. Its rolling, fertile surface has become a center for livestock.

(8) The long, narrow, wedge-shaped district known as the Pontotoc Ridge enters the state from the northeast and moves south along the western edge of the black prairie. The soil erodes easily, but it originally grew a diversity of crops.

(9) Then comes a strip of low-lying land, the flatwoods, which skirts the western and southern edges of the Pontotoc Ridge and black prairie belt. This area is important only as a source of forest products.

(10) The remaining section, called the north central highlands, lies between the flatwoods and the loess bluffs. Its soil is a yellowish brown loam adaptable to a number of crops.

A number of rivers drain the state. In the southwest the Big Black and Homochitto flow into the Mississippi, and the west and northwest are drained by the Yazoo and its tributaries, which flow into the Mississippi near Vicksburg. In the northeast are the Tombigbee, which flows through Alabama into Mobile Bay, and the Tennessee, which turns northward and empties into the Ohio. In the southeast the Leaf and the Chickasawhay come together to form the Pascagoula, which ultimately passes into the Gulf of Mexico. The longest river of Mississippi is the Pearl, which drains the central portion of the state and flows into the gulf. The only area where drainage is a serious problem is the delta. There a system of canals and levees has been built to protect the land against inundation. There are also large earthen dams across the Tallahatchie near Sardis, the Yazoo near Enid, and the Yalobusha near Grenada, to help control flood waters.

Climate.—The climate of Mississippi is semitropical, the average annual mean temperature over a 30-year period at Jackson being 65.4° F. The average for January is 48.3°, and that for July is 82.1°. The extended period of warm weather permits long growing seasons and pasturage. In general, rainfall is abundant, with more occurring along the coast than in the north. The annual average for Jackson over a 30-year period is 50.86 inches.

Plant Life.—Deserving special mention among Mississippi's flowers are the azalea, the camellia, and the poinsettia, all of which grow without protection in the south. More than 100 species of trees are found, including numerous varieties of oak. The section known as the piney woods is noted for its longleaf pine. Particularly colorful are the live oaks laden with Spanish moss in the south, the mountain laurel and sycamore in the north, and the holly and yaupon, which are distributed fairly evenly but occur more frequently in the central portion.

Forests cover 16,473,000 acres, or 54 per cent of the total area of the state. Commercial forests account for 16,440,000 acres, of which 1,245,000 acres are under federal control, 473,000 acres are under state, county, or municipal jurisdiction, and 14,722,000 acres are privately owned. The gross area of the national forests in the state is 2,861,773 acres, of which 1,134,106 acres are actually under Forest Service administration. The first national forest to be established in Mississippi, the Homochitto National Forest, lies in the southwestern corner of the state. The De Soto National Forest, a dense growth of pine, is located in the southeast just north of the gulf. There are also the Chickasawhay, Bienville, and Delta national forests and, in the extreme north, the Holly Springs National Forest.

Animal Life.—Few of the larger wild animals formerly abundant in the state remain there. The chief game animals are the rabbit, squirrel, raccoon, and opossum, although occasionally one may find a deer or a fox. In the Bayou Pierre swamp and elsewhere there are alligators. One can catch almost any kind of freshwater fish in Mississippi, including bass, catfish, bream, and perch. The greatest numbers of birds are found on the coast, where many kinds are plentiful. The mockingbird is common to all sections.

Conservation.—The importance of the soil and its resources is indicated by the fact that over half of the state's labor force is employed in agriculture and related occupations. The soil was never unusually rich, however, and it is poor in organic material. The topsoil is thin, in places only a foot deep, and erosion works constantly against this layer. A large share of the public administration of natural resources is therefore concerned with conservation and utilization of the land. In 1934 only 34 per cent of the total land area showed negligible erosion, but impressive accomplishments were achieved thereafter, and by 1945 the United States Soil Conservation Service estimated that 80 per cent of the land area was slightly or moderately eroded, while only 20 per cent was severely eroded. In 1968 there were 74 soil conservation districts, comprising 30,231,000 acres, or almost the entire area of Mississippi.

The state has a supply of ground water pure enough and available in sufficient quantity for domestic uses. For a long time no statutes were in force to prevent needless waste, but in the 1950's some water conservation measures were adopted. Water pollution has taken on new importance with the increase of industry, but control has been mainly negative in character.

Water problems are concerned primarily with the control and disposition of rivers and streams. The resources of federal and local agencies are sometimes taxed in meeting the problems of flood control, land reclamation, and stream alignment. These problems have been solved largely by the erection of levees, the construction of reservoirs to control the headwaters of tributaries of the Mississippi, and the maintenance of the present channels.

2. POPULATION AND POLITICAL DIVISIONS

Population Characteristics.—The population of Mississippi is overwhelmingly native born.

Only about 1 per cent of the state's total resident population is foreign-born. The greatest numbers of the original settlers were Scotch Irish from the Atlantic seaboard states, although the leaders generally came from New England and New York and were of English origin.

In the late 19th century there was an infiltration of Germanic, Slavic, and Latin peoples from New Orleans following the Illinois Central Railroad, but they were quickly absorbed. In the delta there are small settlements of Chinese. A small number of Indians also live in the state.

Until 1940, Mississippi had a numerical preponderance of Negroes. Then, for the first time since 1840, the census showed a slight majority of whites. By 1970 there were 1,393,283 whites to 815,770 Negroes. Blacks are concentrated largely in the delta counties, in many of which they constitute two thirds to three fourths of the population.

Cities.—In the central section of the state the most important city is Jackson, the capital. Others are Meridian, a leading industrial city; Hattiesburg, near which was located Camp Shelby in World Wars I and II; and Laurel, a center of the lumber industry. The outstanding delta communities are Greenville, Greenwood, and Clarksdale, all of which are centers of cotton growing and trading.

David W. Corson from A. Devaney Inc.

A corner on Main Street, Natchez, Mississippi.

GROWTH OF POPULATION SINCE 1820

Year	Population	Year	Population
1820	75,448	1920	1,790,618
1840	375,651	1940	2,183,796
1860	791,305	1950	2,178,914
1880	1,131,597	1960	2,178,141
1900	1,551,270	1970	2,216,912

Gain, 1960–1970: 1.8% (U.S. gain, 13.3%). **Density,** 1970: 46.9 persons per square mile (U.S. density, 56.2).

URBAN-RURAL DISTRIBUTION

Year	Percent urban	Percent rural
1920	13.4 (U.S., 51.2)	86.6
1930	16.9 (U.S., 56.2)	83.1
1940	19.8 (U.S., 56.6)	80.2
1950	27.9 (U.S., 64.0)	72.1
1960	37.7 (U.S., 69.9)	62.3
1970	44.5 (U.S., 73.5)	55.5

LARGEST CENTERS OF POPULATION

City or Metropolitan area[1]	1970	1960	1950
Jackson (city)	153,968	144,422	98,271
Metropolitan area	258,906	147,480	142,164
Biloxi (city)	48,486	44,053	37,425
Biloxi-Gulfport met. area	134,582	...	...
Meridian	45,083	49,374	41,893
Gulfport	40,791	30,204	22,659
Greenville	39,648	41,502	29,936
Hattiesburg	38,277	34,989	29,474
Pascagoula	27,264	17,155	10,805
Columbus	25,795	24,771	17,172
Vicksburg	25,478	29,143	27,948
Laurel	24,145	27,889	25,038
Greenwood	22,400	20,436	18,061
Clarksdale	21,673	21,105	16,539
Tupelo	20,471	17,221	11,527
Natchez	19,704	23,791	22,740
Moss Point	19,321	6,631	3,782

[1] Standard metropolitan statistical area.

The gulf coast is represented by Biloxi and Gulfport. Biloxi, the state's second largest city, is a shipbuilding and fishing center. Gulfport is a major recreational center with an artificial harbor for shipping.

The old South still lives at Vicksburg and Natchez, on the Mississippi River, and at Columbus, on the Tombigbee River. The new South is the spirit of Tupelo, which negotiated the first contract for the purchase of electric power from the Tennessee Valley Authority. (See also section on *Places of Interest.*)

Municipal charters fall into two broad types: those specifically tailored by the legislature for a given municipality; and those following the code, a general legislative enactment for municipalities. The constitution of 1890 required general legislation for municipal incorporations, and in 1892 the legislature approved a general municipal code to govern all municipalities unless within one year municipalities so desiring voted to retain their old charters. Only 22 voted to do so.

Counties.—Mississippi's 82 counties, with their county seats, are as follows:

County	County Seat
Adams	Natchez
Alcorn	Corinth
Amite	Liberty
Attala	Kosciusko
Benton	Ashland
Bolivar	Cleveland Rosedale
Calhoun	Pittsboro
Carroll	Carrollton Vaiden
Chickasaw	Houston Okolona
Choctaw	Ackerman
Claiborne	Port Gibson
Clarke	Quitman
Clay	West Point
Coahoma	Clarksdale
Copiah	Hazlehurst
Covington	Collins
De Soto	Hernando
Forrest	Hattiesburg
Franklin	Meadville
George	Lucedale
Greene	Leakesville
Grenada	Grenada
Hancock	Bay St. Louis
Harrison	Gulfport
Hinds	Jackson Raymond
Holmes	Lexington
Humphreys	Belzoni
Issaquena	Mayersville
Itawamba	Fulton
Jackson	Pascagoula
Jasper	Bay Springs Paulding
Jefferson	Fayette
Jefferson Davis	Prentiss
Jones	Ellisville Laurel
Kemper	De Kalb

County	County Seat
Lafayette	Oxford
Lamar	Purvis
Lauderdale	Meridian
Lawrence	Monticello
Leake	Carthage
Lee	Tupelo
Leflore	Greenwood
Lincoln	Brookhaven
Lowndes	Columbus
Madison	Canton
Marion	Columbia
Marshall	Holly Springs
Monroe	Aberdeen
Montgomery	Winona
Neshoba	Philadelphia
Newton	Decatur
Noxubee	Macon
Oktibbeha	Starkville
Panola	Batesville Sardis
Pearl River	Poplarville
Perry	New Augusta
Pike	Magnolia
Pontotoc	Pontotoc
Prentiss	Booneville
Quitman	Marks
Rankin	Brandon
Scott	Forest
Sharkey	Rolling Fork
Simpson	Mendenhall
Smith	Raleigh
Stone	Wiggins
Sunflower	Indianola
Tallahatchie	Charleston Sumner
Tate	Senatobia
Tippah	Ripley
Tishomingo	Iuka
Tunica	Tunica
Union	New Albany
Walthall	Tylertown

MISSISSIPPI

Courtesy Mississippi Agricultural and Industrial Board

The Mississippi state capitol at Jackson.

Courtesy Mississippi Agricultural and Industrial Board

Melrose, a pre-Civil War home at Natchez.

MISSISSIPPI

Courtesy Mississippi Agricultural and Industrial Board

Tung trees in blossom. From the nuts of these trees is obtained the tung oil used in paints and varnishes.

Photograph by A. V. Ragusin

Lighthouse at Biloxi, with the flags the city has flown.

Photograph by A. V. Ragusin

An oyster schooner unloading at Biloxi on the Gulf Coast.

Courtesy Mississippi Agricultural and Industrial Board

Part of Mississippi's great cotton crop after baling.

Warren	Vicksburg	Winston	Louisville
Washington	Greenville	Yalobusha	Coffeeville, Water Valley
Wayne	Waynesboro		
Webster	Walthall	Yazoo	Yazoo City
Wilkinson	Woodville		

Walthall is the smallest county, with only 403 square miles, while Yazoo is the largest, covering an area of 938 square miles. In terms of population, Issaquena is the smallest, with only 2,737 people, and Hinds the largest, with 214,973.

3. GOVERNMENT

Constitution and Elections.—The basic law of the state is the constitution of 1890 with subsequent amendments. Mississippi's first constitution was adopted in convention in 1817, the second in 1832, the third in 1869, and the fourth in 1890; proposed constitutions were rejected in 1851 and 1865. Of those adopted, only the 1869 constitution was submitted to the people for approval. That of 1832 was modified slightly in 1861, when the state joined the Confederacy.

The 1890 document made no provision for calling a constitutional convention, but it is assumed that such a call is within the inherent powers of the legislature. To amend the constitution a proposed amendment must pass both houses of the legislature by a two-thirds majority vote on "three several days," and then be approved by a simple majority of the electors voting. At the next succeeding session of the legislature the approved amendment must be inserted as part of the constitution. By 1968, the constitution had been amended more than 50 times.

Voting is by secret ballot. A voter must be 18 years old, must have had legal residence in the state for two years and in the election district for one year, must not have been convicted of certain crimes, and must be of good moral character.

Voter registration is for life. A voter need not renew his registration unless he changes his place of residence. A voter may, however, be asked to read, to demonstrate an understanding of, or even to interpret, a section of the state constitution in order to register. Officials are nominated by party primaries, the costs of which are borne by the party. Normally, nomination in a Democratic primary is tantamount to election. The state sends two senators and five representatives to the U.S. Congress.

Executive.—The governor and more than 100 agencies, departments, boards, and commissions form the executive branch of the government. Elective officers include the governor, lieutenant governor, treasurer, superintendent of public education, attorney general, auditor, commissioner of agriculture and commerce, commissioner of insurance, highway commissioners, public service commissioners, secretary of state, and land commissioner. The governor is elected every four years and may not immediately succeed himself.

GOVERNORS OF MISSISSIPPI

Name	Party	Term
TERRITORIAL		
Winthrop Sargent		1798–1801
William C. C. Claiborne		1801–1805
Robert Williams		1805–1809
David Holmes		1809–1817
STATE		
David Holmes	Democratic Republican	1817–1820
George Poindexter	Democrat	1820–1822
Walter Leake[1]	"	1822–1825
Gerard C. Brandon[2]	"	1825–1826
David Holmes[3]	"	1826
Gerard C. Brandon[4]	"	1826–1832
Abram M. Scott[1]	"	1832–1833
Charles Lynch[5]	"	1833
Hiram G. Runnels[3]	"	1833–1835
John A. Quitman[5]	Whig	1835–1836
Charles Lynch	Democrat	1836–1838
Alexander G. McNutt	"	1838–1842
Tilghman M. Tucker	"	1842–1844
Albert G. Brown	"	1844–1848
Joseph W. Matthews	"	1848–1850
John A. Quitman[3]	"	1850–1851
John I. Guion[5]	"	1851
James Whitfield[5]	"	1851–1852
Henry S. Foote[3]	Union Democrat	1852–1854
John J. Pettus[5]	Democrat	1854
John J. McRae	"	1854–1857
William McWillie	"	1857–1859
John J. Pettus	"	1859–1863
Charles Clark[6]	"	1863–1865
William L. Sharkey	Provisional	1865
Benjamin G. Humphreys[6]	Democrat	1865–1868
Adelbert Ames	Provisional (military)	1868–1870
James L. Alcorn[3]	Republican	1870–1871
Ridgley C. Powers[2]	"	1871–1874
Adelbert Ames[3]	"	1874–1876
John M. Stone[7]	Democrat	1876–1882
Robert Lowry	"	1882–1890
John M. Stone	"	1890–1896
Anselm J. McLaurin	"	1896–1900
Andrew H. Longino	"	1900–1904
James K. Vardaman	"	1904–1908
Edmund F. Noel	"	1908–1912
Earl L. Brewer	"	1912–1916
Theodore G. Bilbo	"	1916–1920
Lee M. Russell	"	1920–1924
Henry L. Whitfield[1]	"	1924–1927
Dennis Murphree[2]	"	1927–1928
Theodore G. Bilbo	"	1928–1932
Martin Sennett Conner	"	1932–1936
Hugh L. White	"	1936–1940
Paul B. Johnson[1]	"	1940–1943
Dennis Murphree[2]	"	1943–1944
Thomas L. Bailey[1]	"	1944–1946
Fielding L. Wright[8]	"	1946–1952
Hugh L. White	"	1952–1956
James P. Coleman	"	1956–1960
Ross R. Barnett	"	1960–1964
Paul B. Johnson	"	1964–1968
John Bell Williams	"	1968–1972
William Waller	"	1972–

[1]Died in office. [2]Succeeded as lieutenant governor. [3]Resigned. [4]Succeeded as lieutenant governor; elected to governorship for term beginning in 1828. [5]Succeeded as president of the Senate. [6]Removed from office. [7]Succeeded as president of the Senate; elected to governorship for term beginning in 1878. [8]Succeeded as lieutenant governor; elected to governorship for term beginning in 1948.

Legislature.—The legislature, composed of a 57-member Senate and a 127-member House of Representatives, convenes regularly in even-numbered years on the first Tuesday after the first Monday in January. The governor may call special sessions at any time when the legislature is not in session. Such sessions are generally called in even-numbered years. No restrictions of a statutory or constitutional character limit the length of the regular or special sessions.

The makeup of the legislature is based on a constitutional amendment reapportioning both houses. It came into force in 1963. Adoption of the amendment followed a decision of the United States Supreme Court in 1962, upholding a complaint by voters in Tennessee against the distribution of legislative seats in their state. Before this decision, the Mississippi legislature had not been reapportioned since 1890.

Judiciary.—The hierarchy of courts runs from justices of the peace and 15 county courts, to chancery and circuit courts, and finally the state supreme court. The 18 chancery and 19 circuit courts have equal dignity. The supreme court consists of nine members selected from three supreme court districts for terms of eight years. All judges are elected, except police justices in cities with populations of 10,000 or more.

Revenue and Expenditure.—Over 90 per cent

of the state's revenue is collected by three agencies: (1) the state tax commission, the most important, which collects the 3 per cent sales tax, income and estate taxes, timber and oil and gas severance taxes, and property and other taxes; (2) the motor vehicle comptroller, who collects the tax on fuel use and motor vehicle fees; and (3) the alcoholic beverage control board, which collects the tax on sales of alcoholic beverages. The financial condition of the state government appears to be excellent. As of June 30, 1967, Mississippi had $123,495,000 full faith and credit bonded indebtedness and $97,514,000 outstanding in highway revenue bonds.

4. EDUCATION, HEALTH, AND WELFARE

Education.—Although the first general school law in the state was passed in 1846, education in Mississippi before the War Between the States was largely in the hands of academies operated under private or church auspices. The first Negro schools were established in 1862, and a uniform public education system was inaugurated in 1870. Beginning in 1910 a system of county agricultural high schools was created, and in 1918 a compulsory attendance law was enacted (this law was repealed in 1956). Between 1900 and the school year 1963–1964 enrollment in public elementary and secondary schools increased from 387,507 to 585,000. The latter figure included 356,000 pupils in 899 elementary schools and 229,000 students in 525 secondary schools. In addition, there were in 1963–1964 more than 25,000 pupils enrolled in 108 private and parochial schools.

The elective state superintendent of public education is the executive head of the public school system. With the attorney general and the secretary of state, he forms the three-member Board of Education. Handicapped children are trained under a program of the Vocational Rehabilitation and Crippled Children's Service.

A new day dawned for public education in Mississippi with the passage by the legislature of a new school code in 1953. This code provides for an allotment of $12 for each pupil in average daily attendance and an additional $3 for each Negro child in average daily attendance to assist in the construction of schools for Negroes. Supplanting the former equalization fund, a minimum foundation plan was created to guarantee that every child, regardless of race or residence, would have at least the opportunity to secure a minimum education. This minimum consists of an eight-month school year, which may be lengthened by local districts; payment to teachers of at least the salaries designated in a statewide schedule; free transportation for children living one mile or more from an attendance center; and administrative funds for the maintenance of school buildings.

While the plan represents additional recognition by the state of its responsibility for public education, it is financed cooperatively by the state, counties, and local districts. A six-member Educational Finance Commission was created to approve plans for school district reorganization and to allocate state aid for school construction. State aid is given where the children are, and local jurisdictions contribute to the cost on the basis of their ability to pay, according to an economic index of six factors. The plan involved one of the most progressive revisions in school district organization ever undertaken by any state. The counties and school districts were given until July 1, 1957, to prepare plans for the reconstitution of districts, on pain of disqualification from full participation in the distribution of funds.

Between 1900 and the academic year 1964–1965 enrollment in Mississippi's institutions of higher education increased from 3,493 to about 54,000. In 1968 there were 5 public and 6 private senior colleges and 14 public and 4 private junior colleges that were predominantly white or in various stages of integration. There were 3 public and 3 private senior colleges and 3 public and 4 private junior colleges that were predominantly Negro in administration, faculty, and student body composition. The 4-year colleges and universities are administered by the Board of Trustees of Institutions of Higher Learning. These are the University of Mississippi (near Oxford), Mississippi State University (near Starkville), the University of Southern Mississippi (Hattiesburg), Mississippi State College for Women (Columbus), Delta State College (Cleveland), and three institutions founded for Negroes: Alcorn A. and M. College (Lorman), Jackson State College, and Mississippi Valley State College (Itta Bena). Blue Mountain College is a Baptist women's college. Private coeducational colleges include Millsaps College (Methodist) and Belhaven College (Presbyterian) in Jackson, Mississippi College (Baptist) in Clinton, William Carey College (Baptist) in Hattiesburg, and three colleges that were founded for Negroes: Rust College and Mississippi Industrial College (both Methodist) in Holly Springs, and Tougaloo Southern Christian College. The Roman Catholic bishop of Natchez holds an endowment fund for the education of young men for the priesthood, and at Bay St. Louis there is a major seminary, St. Augustine's, for the training of Negro priests.

Libraries.—The 1950's and 1960's witnessed a rapid expansion of library facilities in the state. By 1965 there were 30 municipalities operating libraries, and there were 74 county and 14 regional libraries. Only 7 counties reported no public library facilities.

The library of the Mississippi Department of Archives and History in Jackson, which has special collections of Mississippi and American history, is excellent for research. The University of Mississippi library, also well equipped, has special collections of Mississippiana, political science, and international law, and there are good libraries at Mississippi State and other colleges. The United States Waterways Experiment Station at Vicksburg has a fine technical collection.

Public Health and Welfare.—State health and welfare institutions include hospitals for the mentally ill at Meridian and Brandon, a school for the mentally deficient and the epileptic at Ellisville, a tuberculosis sanitarium near Magee, and schools for the blind and the deaf at Jackson. The state health program has been so successful that it has been acclaimed by national authorities. The state Board of Health, established in 1877, is composed of 10 members, of whom 8 are physicians, 1 is a dentist, and 1 is an executive officer appointed by the other 9, who are themselves gubernatorial appointees. Field work is accomplished largely through county health departments, and since 1953 all 82 counties have provided health services. Besides seven essential services rendered by all county departments—sanitation, chronic disease prevention and control, maternal and child health, laboratory work, vital statistics, health education, and communicable disease control and prevention—expanded programs are in operation in the larger counties, and other programs are maintained by the state department. The Mississippi Commission on Hospital Care inspects, regulates, and licenses hospitals, while the state Hospital Commission oversees the operation of hospitals receiving charity funds.

The federal-state public welfare program is administered through the Department of Public Welfare, which is responsible to a state Board of Public Welfare composed of three members chosen by the governor from the Supreme Court districts. The board in turn selects a commissioner of public welfare to serve as head of the department, and the commissioner appoints county welfare agents to administer public welfare programs on the local level. Old-age assistance is by far the most expensive responsibility of the department, consuming approximately three fourths of all welfare expenditures. Aid to dependent children is the next largest program, and aid to the blind is in third place. Among other programs of note are child welfare, foster care, and services to the blind and the disabled. A Children's Code Commission was created by the legislature in 1946 to study legislation pertaining to children and to recommend programs for the advancement of child welfare.

A state Veterans' Affairs Board was established in 1948 to assist veterans or their dependents in obtaining the benefits and privileges to which they are entitled. The Mississippi Employment Security Commission, whose three members are chosen by the governor from the Supreme Court districts, administers the federal-state employment security program. A full-time executive director, appointed by the commission, supervises its two principal divisions, the state Employment Service and the state Unemployment Compensation Commission. The former matches jobs and those who seek them, and the latter makes benefit payments to the eligible unemployed. Mississippi, the last state to do so, adopted a workmen's compensation law in 1948. The program is administered by the Workmen's Compensation Commission, a three-member body selected by the governor. In 1952 a public employees' retirement system was established with authorization to bring state employees under the federal social security program. All public employees, including teachers, are covered by the joint retirement plan.

Public Safety.—The Mississippi National Guard dates from 1798, when Winthrop Sargent was territorial governor. He created the first regiment of the Mississippi Militia, which later became the 155th Infantry Regiment, the seventh oldest in the United States. In the Korean War, 95 per cent of the Mississippi National Guard units were called up for service (less than 50 per cent of the National Guard of the United States as a whole was inducted at that time). In 1953 the Air National Guard established a permanent training site at the Gulfport Municipal Airport. The Mississippi National Guard complement consists of 48 units of the 31st Division, 89 nondivisional units, and 16 Air National Guard units. In addition, the state conducts a civil defense program in which most of Mississippi's cities participate.

The Mississippi Highway Safety Patrol has its headquarters in Jackson and maintains nine substations operating within its nine patrol districts. About 6,000,000 miles of state and federal highways are patrolled monthly by more than 180 patrolmen. Nine district inspectors are primarily responsible for making investigations of crimes originating on state and federal roads. The patrol may also be called on to assist in the apprehension of fugitives attempting to escape over Mississippi highways. In addition, it files about 25,000 accident reports annually, investigates all thefts of livestock and other farm products, maintains identification and automobile theft bureaus, administers a safety education and public relations program, and operates a police radio system which covers the state, keeps in touch with neighboring states, and services the Civil Defense Council's emergency communications center. The state penitentiary is located at Parchman, and there are reformatories at Columbia and Oakley.

A. Devaney Inc.

Illinois Memorial in Vicksburg National Cemetery for Civil War dead.

5. ECONOMIC ACTIVITIES

Agriculture has always been the most important branch of Mississippi's economy. Since the 1930's, however, the state has made a strong effort to attract manufactures in order to reduce its dependence on one economic activity. Total personal income rose from $474 million in 1940 to $2,018 million in 1955, and to $4,100 million in 1966. Nevertheless, per capita income in Mississippi in 1966 was still only $1,777, the lowest of any state in the United States (the national average being $2,963).

Labor Force.—Of the 798,100 persons in the state's civilian labor force in 1968, less than 18 per cent were earning their wages in agriculture. In 1968, nonagricultural employment totaled 656,-376, divided as follows: mining, 1.1 per cent;

contract construction, 6.0 per cent; manufacturing, 31.9 per cent; transportation and utilities, 5.2 per cent; wholesale and retail trade, 18.8 per cent; finance, insurance, and real estate, 3.4 per cent; service and miscellaneous, 11.6 per cent; and government, 22.0 per cent. Between 1939 and 1966, trade union membership rose from 13,000 persons, or 6.5 per cent of those in nonagricultural employment, to 53,000, or 8.1 per cent, a proportion that was far below the national average.

R. Gates from Frederic Lewis

Cotton gins at Inverness, Mississippi.

Agriculture.—Agriculture was first practiced seriously in the Natchez area, where, in addition to subsistence crops, tobacco and indigo were raised for export. Around 1800, however, cotton became the big money crop, and it has held this position ever since. The finest cotton is grown in the delta, but the plant is cultivated in most other parts of the state, although in some areas it has been supplanted by dairying, stock raising, and grain and truck farming.

Cotton production increased from an annual average of 1,649,000 bales in the period 1946–1957 to one of 1,845,000 bales in 1960–1964, but the combined value of lint cotton and cottonseed has declined to less than one half of that of all crops. Other leading crops, in order of value, are soybeans, corn, oats, rice, pecans, tung nuts, hay, and sweet potatoes. More than a fourth of the state's agricultural income is derived from livestock and livestock products. While holding its own in the dairy industry, Mississippi is rapidly becoming a major livestock center. The total cattle population in the state increased from 1,140,000 in 1940 to 1,569,000 in 1950, and to 2,351,000 in 1964. The raising of commercial broilers has also become important, numbers rising from 17,005,000 in 1950 to 167,867,000 in 1965.

The number of farms declined from 313,000 in 1930 to 291,000 in 1940 and to 251,000 in 1950. By 1964, the number had plunged to 109,141. In that year there were 64,557 full owners, 18,542 part owners, 408 managers, and 25,634 tenants. The number of tenant farmers (sharecroppers) had been nearly four times as great 10 years earlier. The high rate of farm mechanization contributed to a rapid reduction in the number of farms and to the displacement of large numbers of unskilled farm laborers during the 1950's and 1960's. See COTTON—*5. Production, Supplies, and International Trade* (Qualities of Cotton Produced): United States—*7. Economic Problems.*

Mining.—Mississippi ranks twenty-second among the states in the value of mineral production, which rose from $21,370,000 in 1945 to $220,194,000 in 1963. Except for petroleum and natural gas, however, its mineral resources are not extensive. Common brick clay and crude sandstone overlay nearly all the geologic structures of the state. A small quantity of iron ore adaptable for paint pigments has been found, and there is a large untapped supply of bauxite. In addition, there are deposits of bentonite, fuller's earth, and lignite.

The most spectacular development in mineral extraction has taken place in petroleum and natural gas. The search for commercial fields began as early as 1903, and new impetus was given to the industry with the discovery of the Jackson gas field in 1930. The Tinsley petroleum field in Yazoo County began producing in 1939. From their discovery through 1966, the state's oil and gas fields produced a total of 968 million barrels of petroleum and 3,058,573 million cubic feet of natural gas.

Lumbering and Fishing.—The importance of lumbering in Mississippi's economy can be gauged from the fact that pulp, paper, and products and lumber and wood products are the two most important branches of manufacturing in the state, accounting together for almost a third of the value added by manufacture. Production of wood pulp alone more than doubled between 1947 and 1955 and exceeded 150 million cords a year in the 1960's. Of the estimated 26,364 million board feet of live sawtimber in the state, 17,111 million board feet consist of softwood.

Some 70,000 private ponds and lakes and innumerable streams stocked with game fish, as well as saltwater fishing along the gulf coast, attract sportsmen from other states. In addition, commercial fishing along the coast has become a profitable enterprise, the total catch of fish and shellfish increasing from 70,787,000 pounds in 1945 to 195,165,000 pounds in 1956 and to 331,898,000 pounds in 1964.

Manufacturing.—In 1936 the legislature passed a bill to "balance agriculture with industry," which empowered communities to offer land, buildings, and a five-year exemption from taxes as a special inducement to out-of-state capital. Then, in 1944, an Agriculture and Industrial Board was established to assist in industrialization. The program, which the state advertised effectively, succeeded in attracting new manufacturing facilities to most areas of the state. Value added by manufacture rose from $72,661,000 in 1939 to over half a billion dollars in 1955. By 1963, the total had climbed to $1,016,262,000. In order of value, the most important branches

David W. Corson from A. Devaney Inc.

An old Mississippi River stern-wheeler now houses the Vicksburg Yacht Club.

are pulp, paper, and products; lumber and wood products; apparel and related products; food and kindred products; and chemicals and allied products.

Power.—Mississippi's hydroelectric power resources are estimated at 410,000 kilowatts, but they have not been developed, and steam plants accounted for the 2,639,000 kilowatts of installed capacity in 1964. Power is provided primarily through the Mississippi Power and Light Company, which covers an area of about 22,000 square miles; the Mississippi Power Company, which covers 11,500 square miles; the Tennessee Valley Authority, which covers 16,000 square miles; and the Rural Electrification Administration (REA), which distributes its power through REA cooperatives (formed to extend electrification to rural areas) and through municipalities.

Banking and Insurance.—There were 196 commercial banks in the state in 1965, 168 credit unions, and 89 savings and loan associations. Mississippians held 2,445,000 life insurance policies, a rise of nearly a million in 10 years. About 1,290,000 people, or more than half of the population, were covered by hospitalization policies, 1,192,000 had surgical insurance, and 780,000 had medical insurance.

Trade.—Three principal distribution areas trifurcate Mississippi from east to west: a northern area, which is served by the greater Memphis trade area; a central area, served by Jackson; and a southern area, served largely by New Orleans and Mobile. Besides Jackson, Gulfport, Biloxi, Meridian, Hattiesburg, Greenville, and Vicksburg are the largest commercial centers within the state. In the 20 years from 1946 to 1966, total indicated sales in Mississippi more than tripled, rising from $1,390 million to $4,762 million, to which wholesale trade contributed $1,507 million, retail trade $3,075 million, and service sales $180 million.

For additional statistics on industry, agriculture, labor, and other economic aspects, see THE AMERICANA ANNUAL.

6. TRANSPORTATION AND COMMUNICATIONS

Although the first settlers traveled mainly by water, roads such as the celebrated Natchez Trace (see section on *History*) soon became important in Mississippi's economy. The construction of modern highways dates from 1910 and, particularly, from the passage of the Federal-Aid Road Act of 1916. The network of surfaced roads in the state grew from 2,164 miles in 1923 to 55,778 miles by 1964. The number of registered motor vehicles, including passenger cars, buses, and trucks, increased from 186,000 in 1935, to 263,000 in 1945, to 623,329 in 1957, and to 928,000 by 1964. Continental Trailways and Greyhound Bus Lines provide intrastate and interstate passenger service.

Railroad building began on a small scale in 1831, but during the War Between the States the railways were destroyed, and a new period of construction was inaugurated in 1880, when there were only 1,127 miles of main-line track in the state. By 1889 there were 2,366 miles, and by 1920, 4,369 miles. The decline in main-line mileage to 3,632 miles by 1965 was due to the expanding motor truck industry. Of the 18 railway companies operating in Mississippi, the Illinois Central Railroad and the Gulf, Mobile and Ohio Railroad play the most important part as carriers of the state's traffic.

Water transportation in Mississippi is less important than it was before the War Between the States, when it was one of the chief modes of transport and travel. The Mississippi River was of particular consequence, but the Tombigbee, Pearl, and other streams were also used. Ports along the gulf coast and the Mississippi still do a modest business.

There are 66 public and 83 private airports and airfields in the state, including one airport that is owned and operated by the University of Mississippi. The ownership of private airplanes increased greatly in the 1950's and 1960's, as it did elsewhere. Delta Air Lines serves Jackson, Meridian, Greenwood, and Hattiesburg; Southern Airways stops at nine cities; and Gulfport and Biloxi are also served by National Airlines.

Mississippi was served in 1968 by 128 radio stations, of which 93 were AM and 35 were FM stations. Television stations included 8 VHF and 5 UHF facilities. As of Jan. 1, 1966, there were 574,000 telephones, of which 550,000 were owned by the Southern Bell Telephone Company. Exclusive of stations, approximately 515 post offices are located in the state.

In the late 1960's, Mississippi was supporting 22 daily newspapers and more than 100 weekly, semiweekly, and monthly newspapers. The most widely circulated papers were the *Clarion Ledger* and *Jackson Daily News* of Jackson. The oldest was the Woodville *Republican* (1824). In addition, the Memphis *Commercial Appeal,* New Orleans *Times-Picayune,* and Birmingham *News* cater successfully to Mississippi readers.

7. CULTURAL LIFE

There are four aspects under which culture in Mississippi may be subsumed. The first is the obvious literary and artistic phase. For a state which is deemed backward in many ways, Mississippi has produced far more than its share of writers and artists, some of whom, such as William Faulkner, have attained universal fame.

The second aspect is the less tangible but nonetheless real and prevalent way of life. There is even in the mid-20th century a leisureliness, an easygoing quality, that is not successfully duplicated elsewhere in the United States. This may, of course, be accounted for in part by climatic conditions, in particular the long-lasting warmth of spring, summer, and autumn, and by the fact that most of the land is relatively low.

The third aspect is the deliberate effort to preserve an elder culture. This becomes quite patent in the annual Natchez pilgrimage in March, a movement imitated by such other ante-bellum cities as Holly Springs and Columbus, and also in the annual promotional recognition of a hospitality month when tourists are treated to a taste of an older way of living.

The fourth aspect is the widespread practice of forming clubs for the diffusion of knowledge and information. Mississippi is a land of clubs. Indeed, one of the facetious and flippant remarks often made by natives is that "Mississippi is not a state; it is a club."

The state government itself has also engaged in promoting a phase of cultural life by providing beautiful historical markers for places of interest and by maintaining a state museum in addition to its Department of Archives and History.

A more detailed treatment of some phases of Mississippi's cultural life will be found in the sections on *Education, Health, and Welfare; Places of Interest; Famous Men and Women;* and *History.*

8. PLACES OF INTEREST

Mississippi's beautiful gulf coast, ante-bellum houses, parks, and natural scenic beauty attract many visitors. In February, Mardi Gras celebrations take place in Biloxi, and field trials for hunting dogs are held in Holly Springs. In the spring there are historical tours of Vicksburg, held in March; an Azalea Trail and Spring Festival, which takes place in March along the gulf coast; and garden and estate pilgrimages in Natchez and other cities, in March and April. In summer there are regattas and fishing rodeos at Biloxi, Gulfport, and Pass Christian, in July; a ceremony of blessing the shrimp fleet, held in Biloxi in August; and a cotton festival, which takes place in Clarksdale in August or September. State fairs are held in Meridian and Jackson in October.

The National Park Service administers the Vicksburg National Military Park and Cemetery (1899); the Brices Cross Roads and Tupelo national battlefield sites of the War Between the States (1929); and the Ackia Battleground National Monument (1938), which preserves the site where the Chickasaws defeated the French in 1736. In addition, it participates with Mississippi, Alabama, and Tennessee in the restoration of the Natchez Trace.

In 1934, Mississippi had no state parks, but beginning in the following year 11 were created. The parks are administered by the Mississippi Board of Park Supervisors. There are two small bird sanctuaries in the state, one in Livingston Park, Jackson, the other on the grounds of the University of Southern Mississippi, Hattiesburg. The Choctaw Indian Agency in Philadelphia, established in 1918, supervises a settlement of the descendants of those Indians who chose to remain after the Treaty of Dancing Rabbit Creek (1830).

Reminders of the French, the first white settlers in Mississippi, include the site of Fort Maurepas (1699), at Ocean Springs near Biloxi; and the fortress erroneously called the Old Spanish Fort (1718), at Pascagoula. Authentic Spanish remains include the Conti House (before 1788) in Natchez. The Anglo-American settlers, as their way of life became well established in the decades before the War Between the States, built mansions and public buildings in the Greek Revival style, as well as less formal homes in the indigenous Southern Planter style. Natchez and its environs in particular are known for their beautiful and historic homes, among them Linden (1788–1825); Auburn (1812); the Briars (1815), home of Varina Howell, who married Jefferson Davis; and Dunleith (1847). In Biloxi is Beauvoir (1852–1854), where the Davises lived; for many years a Confederate home, it is now a museum. The Old Capitol in Jackson was built in 1842, as was the handsome Governor's Mansion.

In the New Capitol (1903) in Jackson are a museum and a hall of fame. Other museums in the state include the Historical Museum of the Vicksburg National Military Park and the Lauren Rogers Library and Museum of Art in Laurel. Paintings are also exhibited in the Municipal Clubhouse Art Gallery in Jackson, and there are Indian relics in the Carnegie Public Library in Clarksdale.

9. FAMOUS MEN AND WOMEN

Mississippians have won renown in politics, in art, and in literature. Famous natives of the state in public life include Gerard C. Brandon (near Natchez, 1788–1850), Benjamin G. Humphreys (Claiborne County, 1808–1882), and Anselm J. McLaurin (Brandon, 1848-1909), governors of the state; George Earle Chamberlain (near Natchez, 1854–1928), governor of Oregon and United States senator; Hernando De Soto Money (Holmes County, 1839–1912), Francis Griffith Newlands (Natchez, 1848–1917), and Pat Harrison (Crystal Springs, 1881–1941),

MISSISSIPPI

COUNTIES

Adams, 37,293 B 8
Alcorn, 27,179 G 1
Amite, 13,763 C 8
Attala, 19,570 E 4
Benton, 7,505 F 1
Bolivar, 49,409 C 3
Calhoun, 14,623 F 3
Carroll, 9,397 E 4
Chickasaw, 16,805 G 3
Choctaw, 8,440 F 4
Claiborne, 10,086 C 7
Clarke, 15,049 G 6
Clay, 18,840 G 3
Coahoma, 40,447 C 2
Copiah, 24,749 D 7
Covington, 14,002 E 7
De Soto, 35,885 E 1
Forrest, 57,849 F 8
Franklin, 8,011 C 8
George, 12,459 G 9
Greene, 8,545 G 8
Grenada, 19,854 E 3
Hancock, 17,387 E 10
Harrison, 134,582 F 10
Hinds, 214,973 D 6
Holmes, 23,120 D 4
Humphreys, 14,601 C 4
Issaquena, 2,737 B 5
Itawamba, 16,847 H 2
Jackson, 87,975 G 9
Jasper, 15,994 F 6
Jefferson, 9,295 B 7
Jefferson Davis, 12,936 E 7
Jones, 56,357 F 7
Kemper, 10,233 G 5
Lafayette, 24,181 E 2
Lamar, 15,209 E 8
Lauderdale, 67,087 G 6
Lawrence, 11,137 D 7
Leake, 17,085 E 5
Lee, 46,148 G 2
Leflore, 42,111 D 3
Lincoln, 26,198 D 8
Lowndes, 49,700 H 4
Madison, 29,737 D 5
Marion, 22,871 E 8
Marshall, 24,027 E 1
Monroe, 34,043 H 3
Montgomery, 12,918 E 4
Neshoba, 20,802 F 5
Newton, 18,983 F 6
Noxubee, 14,288 G 4
Oktibbeha, 28,752 G 4
Panola, 26,829 E 2
Pearl River, 27,802 E 9
Perry, 9,065 G 8
Pike, 31,756 D 8
Pontotoc, 17,363 F 2
Prentiss, 20,133 G 1
Quitman, 15,888 D 2
Rankin, 43,933 E 6
Scott, 21,369 E 6
Sharkey, 8,937 C 5
Simpson, 19,947 E 7
Smith, 13,561 E 6
Stone, 8,101 F 9
Sunflower, 37,047 C 3
Tallahatchie, 19,338 D 3
Tate, 18,544 E 1
Tippah, 15,852 G 1
Tishomingo, 14,940 H 1
Tunica, 11,854 D 1
Union, 19,096 F 2
Walthall, 12,500 D 8
Warren, 44,981 C 6
Washington, 70,581 C 4
Wayne, 16,650 G 7
Webster, 10,047 F 3
Wilkinson, 11,099 B 8
Winston, 18,406 F 4
Yalobusha, 11,915 E 2
Yazoo, 27,304 D 5

CITIES and TOWNS

Abbeville, 600 F 2
Aberdeen⊙, 6,157 H 3
Ackerman⊙, 1,502 F 4
Acona, 200 D 4
Agricola, 200 G 9
Alcorn College, 2,380 B 7
Algoma, 150 G 2
Allen, 80 C 7
Alligator, 280 C 2
Amory, 7,236 H 3
Anding, 50 D 5
Anguilla, 612 C 5
Arcola, 517 C 4
Arkabutla, 195 D 1
Artesia, 444 G 4
Ashland⊙, 348 F 1
Askew, 200 D 1
Auburn, 500 C 8
Avalon, 275 D 3
Avera, 150 G 8
Avon, 400 B 4
Bailey, 320 G 6
Baird, 212 C 4
Baldwyn, 2,366 G 2
Ballardsville, 105 H 2
Ballground, 25 C 5
Banks, 100 D 1
Banner, 200 F 2
Barlow, 80 C 7
Barnett, 50 G 7
Basic, 75 G 6
Bassfield, 354 E 8
Batesville⊙, 3,796 E 2
Baxter, 225 F 6
Baxterville, 100 E 8
Bay Saint Louis⊙, 6,752 F 10
Bay Springs⊙, 1,801 F 7
Beaumont, 1,061 G 8
Beauregard, 199 D 7
Becker, 450 G 3
Belden, 241 G 2
Belen, 500 D 2
Bellefontaine, 360 F 3
Belmont, 968 H 1
Belzoni⊙, 3,146 C 4
Benndale, 500 G 9
Benoit, 473 C 3
Benton, 500 D 5
Bentonia, 544 D 5
Bethlehem, 210 F 1
Beulah, 443 B 3
Bexley, 130 G 9
Bigbee Valley, 370 H 4
Big Creek, 148 F 3
Bigpoint, 100 H 9
Biloxi, 48,486 G 10
Biloxi-Gulfport, ‡ 134,582 G 10
Black Hawk, 100 E 4
Blaine, 75 C 3
Blue Mountain, 677 G 1
Blue Springs, 125 G 2
Bobo, 200 C 2
Bogue Chitto, 658 D 8
Bolatusha, 87 E 5
Bolton, 787 D 6
Bond, 350 F 9
Bonita, 300 G 6
Booneville⊙, 5,895 G 1
Bothwell, 100 G 8
Bourbon, 350 C 4
Bovina, 70 C 6
Boyle, 861 C 3
Bradley, 61 G 4
Brandon⊙, 2,685 E 6
Braxton, 180 D 6
Brazil, 229 D 2
Brody, 50 F 1
Brookhaven⊙, 10,700 C 7
Brooklyn, 750 F 8
Brooksville, 978 G 4
Brownfield, 300 G 1
Brownsville, 200 D 6
Brozville, 150 D 4
Bruce, 2,033 F 3
Brunswick, 90 C 5
Buckatunna, 500 G 7
Bude, 1,146 C 8
Buena Vista, 75 G 3
Burns, 100 E 6
Burnside, 75 F 5
Burnsville, 435 H 1
Byhalia, 702 E 1
Byram, 250 D 6
Caesar, 80 E 9
Caile, 350 C 4
Caledonia, 245 H 3
Calhoun City, 1,847 F 3
Camden, 248 E 5
Canaan, 200 F 1
Cannonsburg, 240 B 7
Canton⊙, 10,503 D 5
Carlisle, 350 C 7
Carmichael, 150 G 7
Carnes, 50 F 8
Carpenter, 60 C 6
Carriere, 900 E 9
Carrollton⊙, 295 E 4
Carson, 285 E 7
Carthage⊙, 3,031 E 5
Cary, 517 C 5
Cascilla, 150 D 3
Cedarbluff, 180 G 3
Centreville, 1,819 B 8
Chalybeate, 350 G 1
Charleston⊙, 2,821 D 2
Chatawa, 300 D 8
Chatham, 40 B 4
Cheraw, 100 E 8
Chester, 60 F 4
Chicora, 50 G 7
Chunky, 280 G 6
Church Hill, 31 B 7
Clara, 400 G 7
Clarksdale⊙, 21,673 D 2
Clarkson, 100 F 3
Clayton, 35 D 1
Clermont Harbor, 200 F 10
Cleveland⊙, 13,327 C 3
Cliftonville, 280 H 4
Clinton, 7,246 D 6
Coahoma, 350 C 2
Cockrum, 75 E 1
Coffeeville⊙, 1,024 E 3
Coila, 75 E 4
Coldwater, 1,450 E 1
Coles, 195 C 8
College Hill, 175 E 2
Collins⊙, 1,934 E 7
Collinsville, 700 G 6
Columbia⊙, 7,587 E 8
Columbus⊙, 25,795 H 3
Como, 1,003 E 1
Conehatta, 50 F 6
Conway, 125 E 5
Cooksville, 78 H 5
Corinth⊙, 11,581 G 1
Cornersville, 235 F 1
Courtland, 316 E 2
Coxburg, 300 D 5
Cranfield, 100 B 7
Crawford, 391 G 4
Crenshaw, 1,271 D 2
Crosby, 491 B 8
Crowder, 815 D 2
Cruger, 415 D 4
Crystal Springs, 4,180 D 7
Cuevas, 200 F 10
Curtis Station, 200 D 2
Daleville, 65 G 5
Dancy, 116 F 3
Darbun, 100 D 8
Darling, 250 D 2
Decatur⊙, 1,311 F 6
Deerbrook, 60 G 4
Deeson, 75 C 2
De Kalb⊙, 1,072 G 5
De Lisle, 450 F 10
Delta City, 300 C 4
Denmark, 50 F 2
Dennis, 175 H 1
Dentville, 50 C 7
Derby, 189 E 9
Derma, 660 F 3
De Soto, 150 G 7
D'Iberville, 7,288 G 10
Dixon, 125 F 5
D'Lo, 485 E 7
Doddsville, 276 C 3
Dorsey, 100 H 2
Dossville, 50 F 5
Drew, 2,574 C 3
Dubbs, 20 D 1
Dublin, 385 C 2
Duck Hill, 809 E 3
Duffee, 100 G 6
Dumas, 200 G 1
Duncan, 599 C 2
Dundee, 80 D 1
Dunleith, 140 C 4
Durant, 2,752 E 4
Eastabuchie, 200 F 8
Ebenezer, 150 D 5
Ecru, 417 F 2
Eddiceton, 175 C 8
Eden, 152 D 5
Edinburg, 200 F 5
Edwards, 1,236 C 6
Egypt, 100 G 3
Eldorado, 25 C 5
Electric Mills, 200 G 5
Elizabeth, 540 C 4
Elliott, 200 E 3
Ellisville⊙, 4,643 F 7
Enid, 80 E 2
Enterprise, 458 G 6
Errata, 85 F 7
Escatawpa, 1,579 G 10
Estill, 100 C 4
Ethel, 560 F 4
Etta, 100 F 2
Eucutta, 75 G 7
Eudora, 200 D 1
Eupora, 1,792 F 3
Evansville, 34 D 1
Falcon, 230 D 2
Falkner, 500 G 1
Fannin, 250 E 6
Farmhaven, 50 E 5
Farrell, 400 C 2
Fayette⊙, 1,725 B 7
Fearns Springs, 50 G 4
Fernwood, 600 D 8
Fitler, 800 B 5
Flora, 987 D 5
Florence, 404 D 6
Flowood, 352 D 6
Forest⊙, 4,085 F 6
Forkville, 180 E 6
Fort Adams, 129 B 8
Foxworth, 950 E 8
French Camp, 174 F 4
Friars Point, 1,177 C 2
Fruitland Park, 75 F 9
Fulton⊙, 2,899 H 2
Gallman, 75 D 7
Garlandville, 150 F 6
Gattman, 175 H 3
Gautier, 2,087 G 10
Georgetown, 339 D 7
Germania, 60 C 5
Gholson, 40 G 5
Gibson, 30 G 3
Gillsburg, 75 C 8
Glancy, 120 C 7
Glen, 250 H 1
Glen Allan, 400 B 4
Glendora, 201 D 3
Gloster, 1,401 B 8
Gluckstadt, 150 D 5
Golden, 115 H 2
Good Hope, 125 E 5
Goodman, 1,194 E 5
Gore Springs, 120 E 3
Goshen Springs, 100 E 6
Goss, 100 E 8
Grace, 325 C 5
Grand Gulf, 50 B 6
Grapeland, 200 B 3
Greenville⊙, 39,648 B 4
Greenwood⊙, 22,400 D 4
Greenwood Springs, 170 H 3
Grenada⊙, 9,944 E 3
Gulfport⊙, 40,791 F 10
Gunnison, 545 C 3
Guntown, 304 G 2
Hamburg, 50 B 7
Hamilton, 350 H 3
Hampton, 200 B 4
Hardee, 100 C 5
Hardy, 50 E 3
Harperville, 260 E 6
Harriston, 500 C 7
Harrisville, 500 D 7
Hatley, 500 H 3
Hattiesburg⊙, 38,277 F 8
Hazlehurst⊙, 4,577 D 7
Heidelberg, 1,112 F 7
Helm, 80 C 4
Hermanville, 500 C 7
Hernando⊙, 2,499 E 1
Hesterville, 100 E 4
Hickory, 570 F 6
Hickory Flat, 354 F 1
Highpoint, 50 F 4
Hillhouse, 50 C 2
Hillsboro, 350 E 6
Hinchcliff, 125 D 2
Hintonville, 100 F 8
Hinze, 140 F 4
Hiwannee, 250 G 7
Hohenlinden, 96 F 3
Holcomb, 50 D 3
Hollandale, 3,260 C 4
Holly Bluff, 250 C 5
Holly Ridge, 375 C 4
Holly Springs⊙, 5,728 E 1
Hollywood, 125 D 1
Holmesville, 200 D 8
Homewood, 75 E 6
Hopewell, 300 D 7
Horn Lake, 850 D 1
Houlka, 646 G 2
Houston⊙, 2,720 G 3
Howison, 15 F 9
Hub, 80 E 8
Hurley, 500 H 9
Hushpuckena, 100 C 2
Independence, 150 E 1
Indianola⊙, 8,947 C 4
Ingomar, 150 F 2
Inverness, 1,119 C 4
Isola, 458 C 4
Itta Bena, 2,489 D 4
Iuka⊙, 2,389 H 1
Jacinto, 150 H 1
Jackson (cap.)⊙, 153,968 D 6
Jackson, ‡258,906 D 6
James, 100 B 4
Jamestown, 75 E 8
Jayess, 150 D 8
Johns, 90 E 6
Johnstons Station, 53 D 8
Jonestown, 1,110 D 2
Keirn, 50 D 4
Kewanee, 100 H 6
Kilmichael, 543 E 4
Kiln, 750 F 10
Kirkville, 200 H 2
Knoxville, 100 B 8
Kokomo, 150 E 8
Kolola Springs, 150 H 3
Kosciusko⊙, 7,266 E 4
Kossuth, 227 G 1
Lafayette Springs, 80 F 2
Lake, 441 F 6
Lake Como, 150 F 7
Lake Cormorant, 300 D 1
Lakeshore, 550 F 10
Lake View, 125 D 1
Lamar, 135 F 1
Lambert, 1,511 D 2
Lamont, 450 B 3
Langford, 100 E 6
Lauderdale, 600 G 5
Laurel⊙, 24,145 F 7
Lawrence, 200 F 6
Leaf, 350 G 8
Leakesville⊙, 1,090 G 8
Learned, 116 C 6
Leesburg, 50 E 6
Leesdale, 18 B 7
Le Flore, 99 D 3
Leland, 6,000 C 4
Lemon, 90 E 6
Lena, 233 E 5
Lessley, 100 B 8
Lexie, 270 D 8
Lexington⊙, 2,756 D 4

⊙ County seat. ‡ Population of metropolitan area. ■ Name not shown on map.

All figures available from 1970 final census are supplemented by local official estimates.

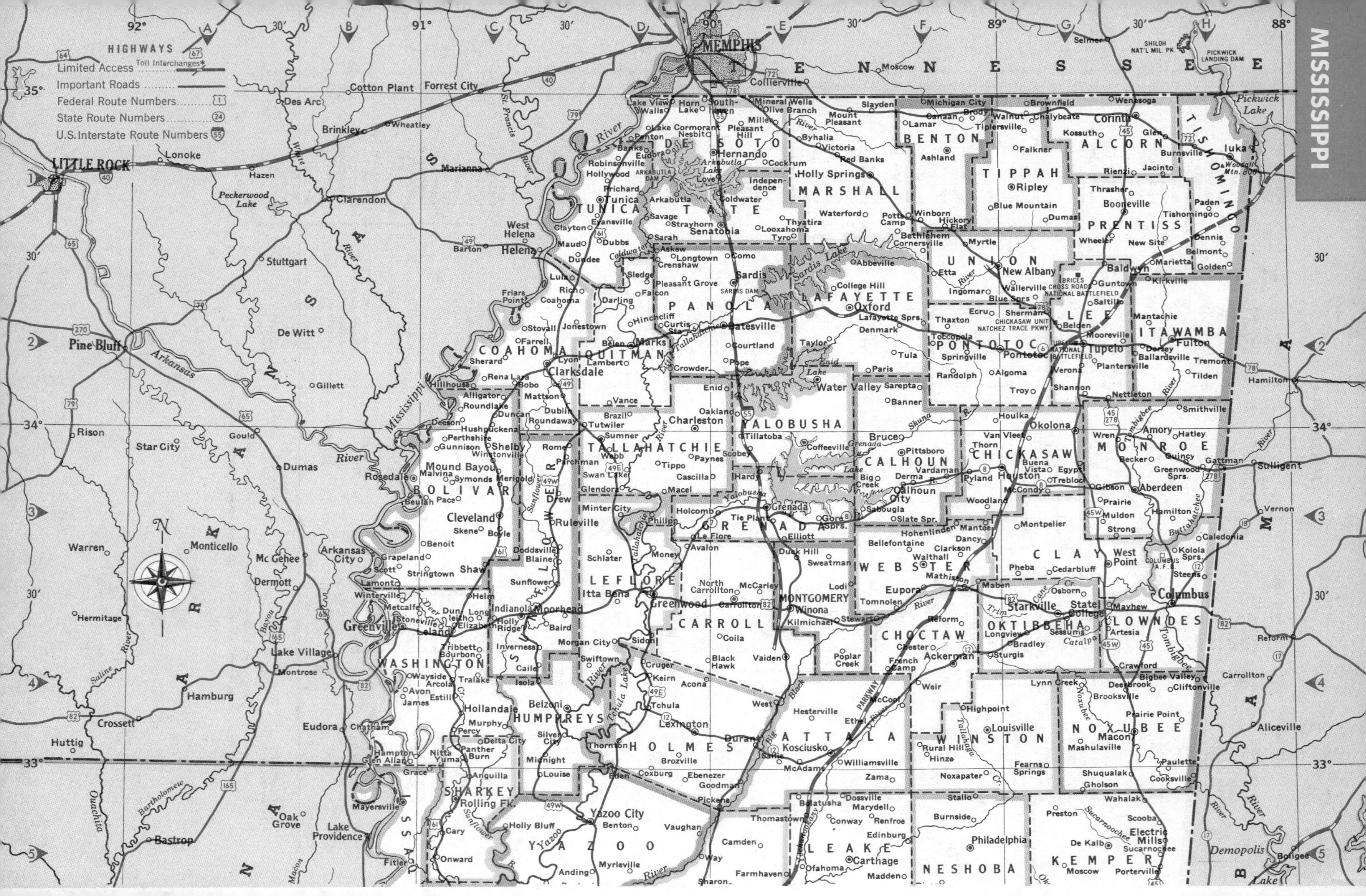
HIGHWAYS
Limited Access
Toll Interchanges*
Important Roads
Federal Route Numbers
State Route Numbers
U.S. Interstate Route Numbers
TENNESSEE
ARKANSAS
ALABAMA
LOUISIANA
MEMPHIS
LITTLE ROCK
Pine Bluff
Greenville
Clarksdale
Oxford
Tupelo
Columbus
Greenwood
Yazoo City
Corinth
TISHOMINGO
ALCORN
TIPPAH
BENTON
MARSHALL
DE SOTO
TUNICA
TATE
PANOLA
LAFAYETTE
UNION
PRENTISS
LEE
ITAWAMBA
PONTOTOC
MONROE
CHICKASAW
CALHOUN
YALOBUSHA
QUITMAN
COAHOMA
TALLAHATCHIE
GRENADA
BOLIVAR
SUNFLOWER
LEFLORE
CARROLL
MONTGOMERY
WEBSTER
CLAY
OKTIBBEHA
LOWNDES
CHOCTAW
WASHINGTON
HUMPHREYS
HOLMES
ATTALA
WINSTON
NOXUBEE
SHARKEY
YAZOO
LEAKE
NESHOBA
KEMPER
ISSAQUENA

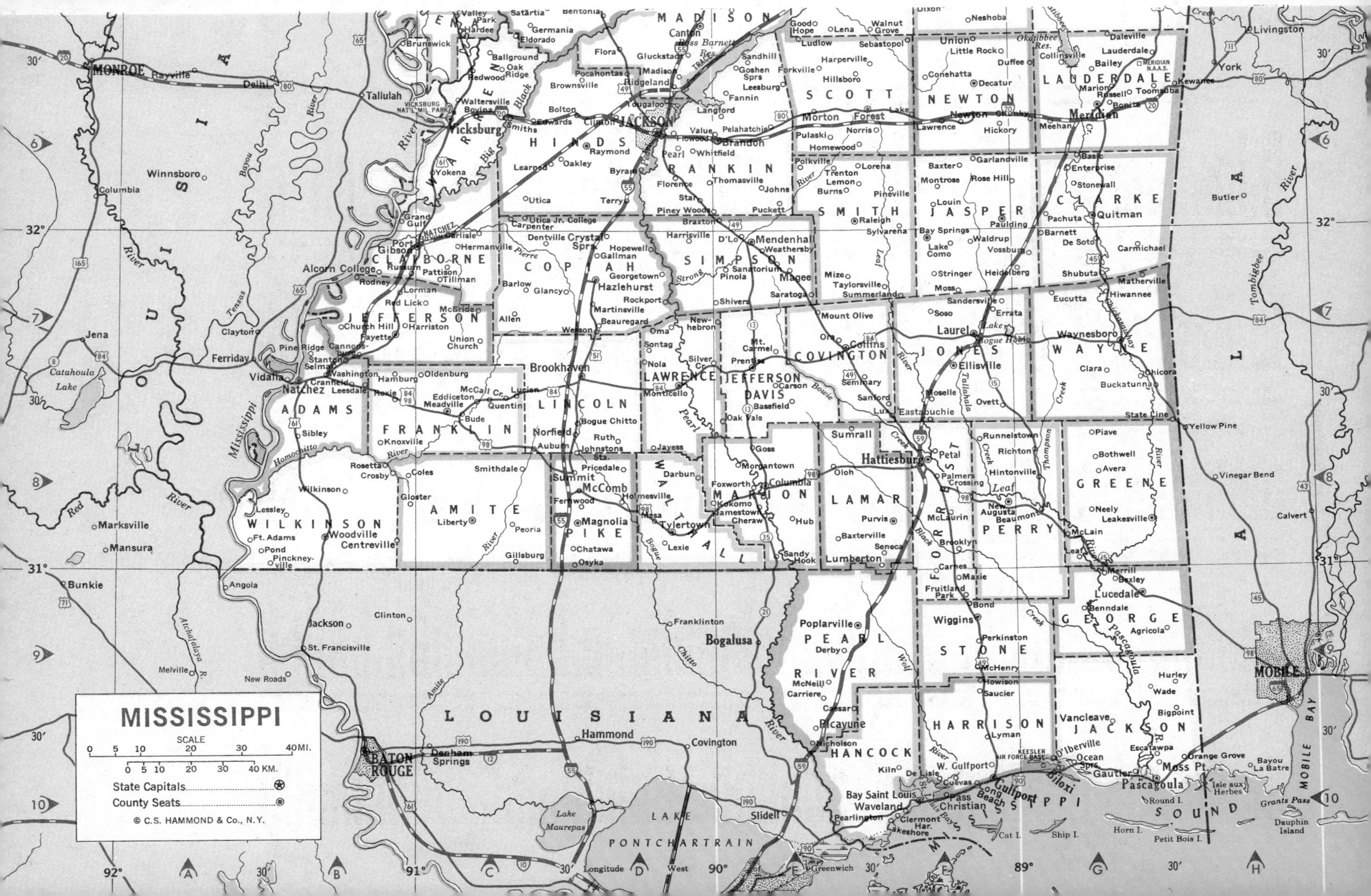
MISSISSIPPI
SCALE
0 5 10 20 30 40 MI.
0 5 10 20 30 40 KM.
State Capitals
County Seats
© C.S. HAMMOND & Co., N.Y.
MADISON
SCOTT
NEWTON
LAUDERDALE
HINDS
RANKIN
SMITH
JASPER
CLARKE
COPIAH
SIMPSON
CLAIBORNE
JEFFERSON
ADAMS
FRANKLIN
LINCOLN
LAWRENCE
JEFFERSON DAVIS
COVINGTON
JONES
WAYNE
WILKINSON
AMITE
PIKE
WALTHALL
MARION
LAMAR
FORREST
PERRY
GREENE
PEARL RIVER
STONE
GEORGE
HANCOCK
HARRISON
JACKSON
LOUISIANA
MISSISSIPPI SOUND
LAKE PONTCHARTRAIN
Lake Maurepas
Catahoula Lake
MOBILE BAY
Jackson
Vicksburg
Natchez
Meridian
Hattiesburg
Laurel
Gulfport
Biloxi
Pascagoula
McComb
Brookhaven
MOBILE
BATON ROUGE
MONROE
Bogalusa
Hammond
Covington
Slidell
Ferriday
Vidalia
Tallulah
Delhi
Rayville
Winnsboro
Columbia
Jena
Marksville
Mansura
Bunkie
Angola
St. Francisville
New Roads
Melville
Clinton
Livingston
York
Butler
Vinegar Bend
Yellow Pine
Calvert
Longitude West of Greenwich
92°
91°
90°
89°
32°
31°
30′

MISSISSIPPI

senators from Mississippi; Maj. Gen. Earl Van Dorn of the Confederate Army (Port Gibson, 1820–1863); Varina Howell Davis (near Natchez, 1826–1906), wife of Confederate President Jefferson Davis, himself a resident of the state for most of his life; and Jacob McGavock Dickinson (Columbus, 1851–1928), United States secretary of war. In the field of art, the sculptor Arthur Putnam (Waveland, 1873–1930) and the painter John McCrady (Canton, 1911–) have done outstanding work. Besides the historian John Francis Hamtramck Claiborne (near Natchez, 1807–1884) and the philologist James Albert Harrison (Pass Christian, 1848–1911), Mississippians who have made notable contributions to the world of letters include Catherine Ann Ware Warfield (near Natchez, 1816–1877), Katherine Sherwood MacDowell (Holly Springs, 1849–1883), the poet Irwin Russell (Port Gibson, 1853–1879), Stark Young (Como, 1881-1963), William A. Percy (1885–1942), David L. Cohn (Greenville, 1896–), the Nobel laureate William Faulkner (New Albany, 1897–1962), James Street (Lumberton, 1903–1954), and Eudora Welty (Jackson, 1909–).

10. HISTORY

Before Mississippi was known to Europeans, and for some time thereafter, it was inhabited by Indians. The Chickasaws lived in the north, and the Choctaws in the central portion and in the south. In the southwest were the aristocratic Natchez, who were related to the highly civilized Indians of Mexico. There were also other smaller tribes.

The first Europeans appeared in December 1540, when Hernando de Soto and his followers entered the area. They spent the winter of 1540–1541 in northeastern Mississippi before discovering the river on May 8, 1541. The next (1673) were the French priest and trader Jacques Marquette and Louis Jolliet, who had some contact with the Chickasaws but did not remain long. French interest was continued by Robert Cavelier, sieur de La Salle, who reached the mouth of the river and claimed the valley for Louis XIV, naming it Louisiana in his honor. Father Zenobius Membré celebrated for this party, near the site of Fort Adams on Easter Sunday, 1682, the first Mass in Mississippi. Other explorers followed but no permanent settlement was made until 1699.

In that year, Pierre le Moyne, sieur d'Iberville, established Fort Maurepas near the site of Biloxi. From then until 1763, Mississippi was part of the French colony of Louisiana, ruled first from Mobile, then from Biloxi, and after 1722 from New Orleans. The second settlement, Fort Rosalie (Natchez), was made in 1716, and others soon followed. Women were brought from France as wives for the colonists, and successful companies were formed to promote immigration. The Scottish adventurer John Law aroused great European interest in 1717 with his speculative Mississippi Company, which three years later fell into disrepute as the Mississippi Bubble (q.v.).

British ambition was aroused, and, as a result of the Seven Years' War and the Treaty of Paris (1763), the country came under British domination as West Florida, which was governed from Pensacola. Many Anglo-Americans who received land as payment for military services moved in from the Atlantic seaboard. With France out of the way, they faced the Spaniards, who meanwhile had acquired New Orleans and Louisiana west of the Mississippi River.

During the American Revolution the Natchez region was relatively neutral and indifferent to the conflict. The Spanish, taking advantage of the situation, moved in (1779) and took Fort Rosalie, which was called Fort Panmure by the British. The American settlers were at first amenable to the change and took oaths of allegiance to Spain. Except for a short-lived rebellion of the British colonists in 1781–1782, the territory remained in Spanish hands officially until 1795 and virtually until 1798.

Max Hunn from Frederic Lewis

The Old Spanish Fort at Pascagoula, said to be the oldest building in the Mississippi valley.

By the Treaty of Paris (1783), Great Britain relinquished its claims north of latitude 31° to the United States, but Spain refused to recognize this transfer. The situation was further confused when Georgia laid claim to the territory, erected it as Bourbon County (1785–1788), and later (1795), sold the land. Ultimately the federal government had to redeem the claims obtained in the notorious Yazoo fraud (see YAZOO FRAUD, THE).

The issue between the United States and Spain was adjudicated in the Treaty of San Lorenzo (1795), by which Spain relinquished the land north of latitude 31°. There was considerable delay in running the line of demarcation. The American surveyor Andrew Ellicott finally arrived in Natchez in February 1797, but then the Spanish governor delayed, and the government was not surrendered until March 1798.

On April 7, 1798, the federal government created the Territory of Mississippi. The land problem was made chaotic by conflicting claims based on French, British, Spanish, and Georgian grants, and the intrigues of Aaron Burr and James Wilkinson kept the territory in confusion. Troubles with the Indians continued until defeats were inflicted on them by Andrew Jackson at Econochaca (Holy Ground) in 1813 and at Horseshoe Bend in 1814. Meanwhile, the country was at war again with Britain (1812–1815), ending with the success of Jackson at the Battle of New Orleans. Statehood was finally achieved for the western part of the territory on Dec. 10, 1817, the eastern part forming the Territory of Alabama.

Mississippi was now a fast-growing frontier region. The population increased from 40,352 in 1810 to 75,448 in 1820, and the state capital was located at Jackson in 1822. Two thirds of the area was still in Indian hands, but the Indians gradually ceded their lands to the state and were removed. This period was the heyday of the famous bandits of the Natchez Trace: Joseph Thompson Hare, Samuel Mason, James Murrell, the Harpe brothers, and others. It was also characterized by the flush times of land grabbing, financial speculation, panic, and repudiation in a raw, new country. A great deal of this rambunctious energy went into the support of Texan independence, the Mexican War, and filibustering in Cuba, but much also was devoted to national politics, the discussion of nullification, and the extension of slavery. By 1850, however, the forces of law and order had gradually made themselves felt. A latently aristocratic and feudal society was beginning to take shape in the more settled communities of the state. It did not last long.

The question of secession could not be suppressed. The election of Abraham Lincoln to the presidency in 1860 and the action of South Carolina were quickly followed by the dissolution of Mississippi's relation with the Union, on Jan. 9, 1861. Jefferson Davis, who represented Mississippi in the United States Senate, became president of the Confederate States of America. The census of 1860 showed 70,295 white men between the ages of 18 and 45 in Mississippi, but the number of enlistments of Mississippians in the Confederate Army has been estimated at 78,000. The major operations of the Union forces in the state were the capture of Corinth (1862), the campaign for Vicksburg culminating in its surrender on July 4, 1863, and the destruction of Jackson and Meridian. Resistance ended on May 4, 1865. (See also CIVIL WAR IN AMERICA—*The War in 1862* [War in the West]; *The War in 1863* [Vicksburg Campaign]; *The War in 1864* [Other Actions].)

By presidential proclamation, Judge William L. Sharkey was made provisional governor of Mississippi. A new constitution was adopted, under which Benjamin G. Humphreys was elected governor. Congress declined to accept the mild presidential reconstruction, however, and a military government was established. In 1868, Humphreys was ejected from the executive mansion, and Gen. Adelbert Ames became military governor. A reign of extravagance and corruption produced another constitution, which was at first defeated by the people. By a process of concession and pressure it was finally accepted in 1869, and James L. Alcorn, a former Confederate general, was elected governor. In February 1870, Mississippi was readmitted to the Union as a state, and in March Alcorn took office. He resigned in 1871 and was succeeded by Ridgley C. Powers. Disagreement arose between two Republican factions, led, respectively, by Ames and Alcorn, and Ames became governor again in 1874. Under him Negro power reached its zenith, and the lieutenant governor, A. K. Davis, and other prominent officials were Negroes. Rioting broke out in Meridian, Vicksburg, and Clinton in consequence.

The election of 1875 was a veritable revolution, returning a majority of Democrats to the legislature. In January 1876, that body set itself the task of removing the radical officials. Davis was impeached and removed from office, Ames resigned under fire, and the reconstruction era came to an end. From 1876 to the late 1960's, the state government was Democratic.

Back in power, the Democrats developed a tension never quite amounting to a split in the party. Two vaguely defined groups resulted, the old, established group on the one hand, and the poorer farmers and plain people on the other. The common man increased his influence during the administrations of Governors James K. Vardaman (1904–1908), Edmund F. Noel (1908–1912), Theodore G. Bilbo (1916–1920 and 1928–1932), and Paul B. Johnson (1940–1943).

Mississippi contributed its share in the Spanish-American War and in World Wars I and II. During World War II one of the largest induction centers was Camp Shelby, near Hattiesburg, where at the height of its service 120,000 soldiers were stationed.

The mid-20th century has seen a number of significant economic and social developments in the state. The diversification and mechanization of agriculture have freed Mississippi's economy from the bonds of King Cotton and the use of inefficient field labor. Industrialization has improved the utilization of labor and natural resources and brought a higher standard of living to all citizens. The civil rights movement was at first met with a stand of massive resistance that resulted in mass arrests of sit-in and freedom rider demonstrators. The state's image was marred by a number of fire bombings, a few sensational killings, and riots at the University of Mississippi in 1962. More recently the attitude of the state's officials and a majority of its citizens has become one of compliance with the law and maintenance of order.

See also separate biographies of the leading figures in Mississippi's history.

11. BIBLIOGRAPHY

Rowland, Dunbar, *History of Mississippi: The Heart of the South,* 4 vols. (Indianapolis 1925); Federal Writers' Project, *Mississippi: A Guide to the Magnolia State* (New York 1938); Sydnor, Charles S., *A Gentleman of the Old Natchez Region: Benjamin L. C. Wailes* (Durham, N.C., 1938); Cabaniss, Allen, *Life and Thought of a Country Preacher: C. W. Grafton* (Richmond 1942); Welty, Eudora, *The Robber Bridegroom* (New York 1942); Bettersworth, John K., *Confederate Mississippi* (Baton Rouge 1943); McLemore, Richard A., and McLemore, Nannie P., *Mississippi Through Four Centuries* (Atlanta 1945); Highsaw, Robert B., *Mississippi's Wealth* (University, Miss., 1947); Cabaniss, Allen, *A History of the University of Mississippi* (University, Miss., 1949); Kirwan, Albert D., *Revolt of the Rednecks* (Lexington, Ky., 1951); Bettersworth, John K., *People's College: A History of Mississippi State* (University, Ala., 1953); Highsaw, Robert B., and Fortenberry, Charles N., *The Government and Administration of Mississippi* (New York 1954); Hobbs, Edward H., "County Government Structure in Mississippi," *Public Administration Survey* (University, Miss., July 1955); id., *A Manual of Mississippi Municipal Government* (University, Miss., 1955); id., *Legislative Apportionment in Mississippi* (University, Miss., 1956); McKinney, David, *Income Payments to Mississippians: County Estimates, 1939 and 1947* (University, Miss., 1952), brought up to date by "Personal Income in Mississippi Counties" and "Income Structure of Mississippi Counties," *Mississippi's Business* (August and October 1957); Mississippi, Secretary of State, *Mississippi Blue Book* (Jackson, quadrennially).

EDWARD H. HOBBS,
Professor of Political Science,
The University of Mississippi.
Revised by EDGAR W. WOOD,
Professor of Economics,
The University of Mississippi.

MISSISSIPPI, mĭs-ĭ-sĭp'ĭ, river, United States, is the great river of North America, and with its far-reaching tributaries embraces one of the major river systems of the world. Long ago, Ojibway Indians, roaming the forests of Wisconsin, called it Missi Sipi, which in their musical language meant the Great River. In the lower valley, where the impetuous current swollen in flood time overflows its banks to convert millions of acres of fertile land into a moving sea, other tribes termed it the Father of Waters. Both names were appropriate, for the scope and volume of this vast stream has made it almost a synonym for great rivers everywhere: even the Volga has been termed the Russian Mississippi, and by a more doubtful comparison, the Murray-Darling, has been called the Mississippi of Australia.

An excursion into Recent geological time reveals a different Mississippi, although one quite as interesting. What is now its lower basin was once a prolongation of the Gulf of Mexico, and Cape Girardeau in Missouri then deserved its name, for it was a bluff promontory overlooking a prehistoric sea. This gulf eventually became filled with wind-swept glacial dust which in places accumulated to a depth of several hundred feet, together with the silt borne downward from the eroded uplands by the turbulent waters.

Meanwhile, the upper branches of the river were undergoing an even more extensive transformation. As the continental ice field, which had crossed the valley of the Ohio, slowly retreated before an increasing climatic warmth, its formidable ramparts still dammed up all northward egress, so that its melting waters were forced to seek an outlet to the south. How extensive were these waters may be inferred from the fact that several of the Great Lakes became united in one superlake, while another vast expanse called Lake Agassiz, nearly four times as extensive as Superior, sprawled across Minnesota into North Dakota and reached far upward into Canada. Meanwhile, the Missouri, the major branch of the Mississippi system, seems to have gone wandering off on its own to empty into Hudson Bay. Before the Great Lakes subsided into something like their present shorelines, two of them, Superior and Michigan, flowed for a time into the Mississippi. So also did Agassiz until much of its volume had drained away. Eventually its major remnants—the Lake of the Woods and Lakes Winnipeg, Winnipegosis, and Manitoba in Canada—were captured by the Saskatchewan, while Superior and Michigan turned eastward to join their kindred Great Lakes in the valley of the St. Lawrence. Many smaller remnants of huge Agassiz, however, which still dot Minnesota forests, remained within the original system, and among them the upper Mississippi still finds its source. To compensate partially for the loss of its big lakes in this period of changing watersheds, the Missouri turned eastward and the entire system began to assume something of its present form and magnitude.

If we view a map of North America with all man-made boundaries eliminated, we shall observe that the Mississippi system seems to cut an enormous wedge out of the heart of the continent, a wedge comprising 1,243,000 square miles. Southward it narrows to the State of Louisiana and becomes still more restricted as it pours its waters through the several mouths of its narrow delta into the Gulf of Mexico. But to the northwest its remotest tributaries drain the mountainous borderland between Idaho and Montana, while to the northeast the Allegheny branch of the Ohio taps the water sources of western New York. Although it penetrates into the Rockies to the west and courses the wooded valleys of the Appalachians, the Mississippi system primarily drains the alluvial grain belt of the Middle West and that vast area known as the Great Plains. The watery surplus from 31 states and two Canadian provinces swells its current. Of its hundreds of tributaries no fewer than 45 are navigable for at least 50 miles of their course, providing a combined system of waterways which exceeds 15,000 miles.

More than most rivers, the Mississippi has suffered from a mistaken nomenclature. The main trunk is formed by the union of three great branches, and of these the upper Mississippi, which has given its name to the entire system, is the least impressive. There was a time when it drained the vast lakes of the melting ice fields that it deserved such major rating. But when it lost those lakes to the predatory Saskatchewan and St. Lawrence it also lost its priority; for it yields to the Missouri in length and the extent of its drainage basin, and it yields to the Ohio both in drainage basin and the volume of its waters. This fact is recognized in measuring the length of the system which is always reckoned from the headwaters of the Missouri.

A glance at some statistics will illustrate this comparison. The upper Mississippi to its juncture with the Missouri drains an area of 171,500 square miles. In contrast, the Missouri, longer by nearly 1,600 miles, drains an area more than three times as extensive, or approximately 530,000 square miles. Even the drainage basin of the Ohio is 202,000 square miles. The upper branch of the great river was merely the first to come to the attention of exploring white men. A similar situation has occurred elsewhere, which emphasizes the fact that while river systems are geographical, their names are merely historical and subject to confusion and error.

The source of the upper Mississippi is usually given as Lake Itasca in northern Minnesota. More accurate surveys, however, have traced its ultimate beginnings to Elk Lake and one or two lesser bodies of water which empty into Itasca. The region abounds with glacial relics where river stability is still emerging from the confusion following the ice age. From this elevation of 1,670 feet above the sea, the river winds through swamps and forests, descending by numerous rapids and gaining volume from the spillways of other lakes. At one point it approaches fairly close to the St. Louis River which marks the headwaters of the St. Lawrence. From the Falls of St. Anthony, where the river falls 65 feet in three quarters of a mile—a series of rapids which are broken by a sheer drop of 18 feet—it emerges as a navigable stream all the way to the sea.

As it descends from the continental plateau with its ancient rock formations and relatively thin covering of soil, the Mississippi presents much varied and pleasing scenery. At times it broadens into such lakes as Pepin; other times it is flanked by precipitous heights called bluffs that may rise 300 feet or more. At several places the current is interrupted by other series of rapids. Above Rock Island there is a descent of some 22 feet; the mouth of the Des Moines River is marked by another of 24 feet; while over a 12-mile stretch approaching Keokuk the river again descends 24 feet.

Geographically, the true source of the Mississippi, however, lies far away on the western borders of Montana. There three considerable streams, the Madison, the Jefferson and the Gallatin, unite to form the Missouri. Fed by the melting snows and gushing springs of the Rockies in the tangled watershed which separates Montana from Idaho, it sweeps on through the wide open spaces of the great Northwest, its branches adding picturesque touches to some of the grandest scenery on the continent. One of these tributaries is the Yellowstone which courses among the geysers, hot springs, and painted gorges of a scenic wonderland. Arching northward, the Missouri sends other branches across the border into the two Canadian provinces of Alberta and Saskatchewan. Bending southward, it meets such tributaries as the Platte, often choked with sand bars. Since much of the territory through which it passes has an annual rainfall of 20 inches or less, the volume of the Missouri varies enormously. In times of flood it discharges more than 800,000 cubic feet a second; in times of excessive drought, it has shrunk to barely 13,000 cubic feet. Such violent aberrations make it one of the most ungovernable of rivers, but its normal volume exceeds the smaller but steadier flow of the upper Mississippi. Where the two rivers unite, they maintain their individuality to a singular degree for more than a hundred miles, the yellow waters of the Missouri being distinguishable as they flow beside the clear waters of the upper Mississippi. Eventually, however, the shifting of the channel from one side of its bed to the other mingles these discordant elements.

Some 200 miles to the south the great twin rivers of the north unite with their eastern branch, the Ohio. This river, formed by the junction of the Allegheny and the Monongahela, is nearly 1,000 miles in length. From Olean, N. Y., on the Allegheny, a river steamer may proceed all the way to Great Falls, Mont., on the Missouri, 4,000 miles from east to west, a distance which nearly spans the continent. The Ohio and its many tributaries drain the ridges and valleys of the Appalachian Mountains where the scenery, though less grand than along the upper Missouri, is less empty and desolate. Here the rainfall exceeds 40 inches annually, or more than twice that in the larger basin of the Missouri, so that the Ohio pours a greater volume of water into the Mississippi system than either of the other main branches. Among its many contributing streams the Tennessee, the Wabash, and the Cumberland are noteworthy.

Farther south the Mississippi attracts other tributaries. Chief among these is the Arkansas whose drainage basin, 187,000 square miles, is larger than that of the upper Mississippi itself. Another considerable affluent approaching from the west is the Red River with a drainage area of 93,000 square miles.

Some 30 miles above the junction of the Ohio and the Mississippi, the topography changes decidedly Here the upland plateau terminates and the river enters an alluvial valley largely of its own creation, through which it meanders for some 1,100 miles to the sea. Through this valley it advances in a series of broad loops and horseshoe bends necessitating a frequent diversion of the current from one side to the other, forming shifting mud bars and frequent changes in the channel. In its lower course these horseshoe bends are sometimes cut through leaving semicircular lakes or lagoons. Meanwhile, new curves and horseshoe bends which the restless waters gouge out of the yielding soil are continually forming. The entrance of the Red River presents a picture even more confusing. This river once flowed into the Atchafalaya which roughly paralleled the lower Mississippi. But the old mouth silted up and the Red River opened its present outlet to the Mississippi. From this point all the way to the Gulf of Mexico the river in flood loses itself in a maze of cross channels called bayous, characteristic in newly made land formed of recently deposited silt. All this region might properly be termed delta since it fills the original oceanic trough; but the obvious delta extends far into the sea in a crowfoot formation of quaking mud and marshland. Here, during the past century and a half, some 50 square miles of land have been added to the State of Louisiana.

The head of this advancing formation is broken by five distinct outlets to the sea. These are known respectively as Southwest, South, Southeast, Northeast and North passes. The main volume of waters pours through Southwest Pass, but more accessible South Pass is the channel usually preferred by ocean shipping.

The volume discharged by the Mississippi varies greatly. The maximum reported by the Mississippi River Commission occurred on April 28, 1927, a total of 1,557,000 cubic feet a second. The minimum recorded on Nov. 1, 1939, had shrunk to 49,200. The mean annual output is given as 513,000 cubic feet a second, about one third the maximum, but more than ten times the minimum.

From the Ohio River to the Gulf of Mexico the width of the Mississippi, though occasionally broadening to a mile and a half, usually ranges between 800 and 1,500 yards. Below its juncture with the Red River it narrows to 300 yards for a considerable distance. Although this width compares unfavorably with the expansive shorelines of the great Siberian rivers and with the oceanic horizons of the Amazon, the Mississippi is quite deep, its channel ranging usually from 50 to 100 feet or more.

The length of the Mississippi has long been a theme for argument. Most atlases give this as 4,200 miles, and add that it is the longest river in the world. The Mississippi River Commission, however, reduces this figure to a more moderate and more exact 3,986 miles from the farthest headwaters of the Missouri to the delta outlet at the sea. This is topped slightly by recent reports which give the extreme length of the Nile, including its lake interruptions, as 4,053. Moreover, the length of the Mississippi continues to be a variable factor. Horseshoe loops are cut through, reducing the figure which swells again by the creation of new loops as the river meanders down its lower valley. How considerable such variations may be is shown by the fact that within recent years a series of such cutoffs has reduced one stretch of river channel from 330 to 210 miles.

History.—Early explorations in the Mississippi Valley are of historic interest. It is believed by some that Columbus' sailors may have sighted the river, for its mouth is indicated on the admiral's map of the region made in 1507. Hernando de Soto, however, is usually credited with its discovery. Advancing all the way from the Atlantic seaboard, de Soto and his band of adventurers reached the banks of the river somewhere in the present State of Mississippi in the year 1541. Disappointed in the quest for gold which lured the conquistadors to incredible hardships, de Soto died there and was buried, and the river remained for over a century little more than a legend and a name on the distorted and almost formless maps of the New World.

In 1673 the French missionary explorers Father Jacques Marquette and Louis Jolliet, venturing westward from Lake Michigan, voyaged down the Mississippi for 300 miles or more, passing the mouth of the Missouri. In 1682, René Robert Cavalier, sieur de La Salle completed this voyage of discovery by sailing down the river to the sea. Naming the present area of Louisiana for his sovereign, Louis XIV of France, he dreamed of founding a vast French empire in the wilderness, but his ambitious schemes were cut short in 1687, when, during a second trip to the mouth of the Mississippi, he was murdered by his mutinous followers. Under his instructions Michel Accault had also ascended the upper Mississippi to the Falls of St. Anthony.

That picturesque character, Pierre Radisson, whose highly colored stories of the wealth of the Canadian wilderness led to the organization of the Hudson's Bay Company, may have sighted the Missouri while on an expedition to the Lake Superior region. At least he may have heard of the river through Indian traders from what he termed the land of "the beef" where great herds of bison ranged. But the honor of discovery is usually conferred upon Pierre Gaultier de Varennes, sieur de La Vérendrye, and his sons, who carried French arms and civilization into the western forests, although they are better remembered for the fort which they established on the shores of the Lake of the Woods and as founders of the city of Winnipeg. In 1797, David Thompson, exploring for the North West Company of Canada, descended a stretch of the Missouri, but it was Meriwether Lewis and William Clark, on their expedition to the Pacific coast during the years 1804–1806, who really introduced the river to the outside world. They ascended it for long distances, then changing their operations to the Columbia, followed that river to the sea.

It would be difficult to exaggerate the influence of the Mississippi upon the development of the United States. Basically, it is the drainage system of more than one third of the country, carrying the surplus rainfall of that semicontinent to the Gulf of Mexico. In the formative period of the country, its waterways provided the major means of transportation. The canoes of the Indians were gradually supplanted by every conceivable type of craft that the ingenuity of the pioneer could devise. Of these the simplest was the log raft. For decades northern timber was thus ferried to the South, usually bearing cargoes of merchantable produce. A voyage to New Orleans on such a raft gave Abraham Lincoln an insight into human slavery which was destined to have momentous consequences. Such one-way traffic was soon followed by the era of the river steamboat, a romantic period dramatized by Mark Twain, himself a river pilot, who adopted his pen name from the leadsman's cry of "by the mark twain," or a two-fathom depth across some shoaling sand bar.

The first river steamboat to follow the route of La Salle left Pittsburgh for New Orleans in 1811. Among the hazards of the voyage, it seems to have become involved in the earthquake disturbance which changed the bed of the river at one point and created Reelfoot Lake. By the year 1857 when this type of navigation reached its height, no fewer than 1,100 river steamers called at St. Paul, while the number on all the tributaries was estimated to swell that total to 3,000 or more. In voyages up the Missouri, pilot houses were made bullet proof, as roving bands of Pawnees or Sioux sometimes resented this intrusion of the white man. A colorful development of the period was the show boat which carried theatrical entertainments to settlements along the shores.

Steamers still ply the Mississippi, but the day of their supremacy has passed. Not a few old favorites were broken up and transferred half way around the world, to be reassembled on other rivers, such as the Congo and the Irrawaddy.

The lower reaches of the Mississippi remain a busy thoroughfare and ocean liners from all parts of the world still assemble at New Orleans. The importance of the river and its principal tributaries as arteries of commerce is well illustrated by the great cities that have sprung up along their banks. Among these the most populous is St. Louis, but there are many others, including New Orleans, Memphis, Minneapolis, St. Paul, Kansas City, Pittsburgh, Cincinnati, Louisville, and Nashville.

Floods and Erosion.—While the great river has conferred benefits that are well-nigh incalculable, there is a darker side to the picture. Its waters sweep away a precious and irreplaceable fortune in soil erosion. In this work of depletion the Missouri has well earned its name of Big Muddy. On an average day, 275,000 tons of topsoil go swirling past the city of Omaha. In flood time a cubic foot of water may contain up to 42 pounds of silt. Disconsolate farmers viewing the ruin remark that this mixture is "too thick to drink, too thin to plow." The annual loss of soil through this one great branch alone is estimated at 240 million tons.

Such wastage is emulated in lesser degree by other tributaries, so that through its yawning mouths, according to the Soil Conservation Service, the Mississippi in flood sweeps away the equivalent of a 40-acre farm every minute.

The historian Garcilaso de la Vega (1539–1616), who described De Soto's expedition in his *La Florida del Ynca* (1605), has given us the first description of one of these episodes: "The flood was forty days in reaching its crest, which came on the twentieth of April. And it was a most magnificent spectacle to behold. That which previously had been forests and fields was converted now into a sea, for from each bank the water extended across more than twenty leagues of terrain." [Tr. by J. and J.

Varner (Austin 1951), p. 554.] This description is based on the account of one of De Soto's companions. Father Marquette in his voyage of 1673 was, however, less favorably impressed. "I have seen nothing more frightful," he wrote. "A mass of large trees . . . real floating islands. They came rushing so impetuously that we could not, without great danger, expose ourselves to pass across."

Several such floods have rated among national calamities. Perhaps the greatest of recorded times began in the autumn of 1926 and extended through the following spring. Another almost as disastrous occurred ten years later, in 1937. Heavy rains had deluged the valley of the Mississippi with an estimated 250 cubic miles of water, or nearly one quarter the content of Lake Erie. At Cairo, Ill., the river rose 56 feet. The lower valley became a lake nearly as extensive as Superior. The city of New Orelans was saved only by dynamiting the dikes and permitting some of the swollen waters to surge across the lowlands to the gulf. Meanwhile, three quarters of a million people were made temporarily homeless and property loss rose above $350,000,000.

While the lower valley has always been the chief sufferer from such inundations, the railroad station at Cincinnati has sometimes been buried beneath 30 feet of water, and the 1951 flood in the Missouri caused enormous damage to Kansas City.

Flood Control and Navigation.—The control of the Mississippi poses a major problem. Two methods for its solution have been suggested, both simple in principle but difficult of application. The first would deepen the channel by employing the erosive force of the waters themselves, or, in other words, divert the vast energies of the river from agents of destruction to useful factors. Below the Missouri, hurdles of piles and brush extending from the banks have caught the sediment of that turbulent stream, restricted the width of the channel, and actually made new land.

Such methods, however, have proved less practicable farther south until the delta region is reached. There through South Pass the current, confined by side obstructions or jetties, has plowed out a channel 31 feet deep across shoals that once showed a depth of only 8 feet. For 20 miles Southwest Pass has been constricted between similar jetties to a width of 1,000 feet, later reduced to 600 feet, and a depth of 35 feet maintained. Through these outlets the furious current in flood has gouged out pockets 104 feet deep.

While jetties have proved their value in limited areas, a more effective method of flood control has been that long since developed in the Netherlands, where the encroaching sea has been thrust back and kept in bounds by dikes. To a degree the Mississippi raises its own dikes. As the river bed fills with silt, the banks are built up in a similar manner by the deposit of sediment from overflows, so that the surface of the water may be higher than the surrounding country. In the cemeteries of New Orleans tombs are built above the water-logged earth.

The first artificial dike, or levee as it is called, was erected at New Orleans in 1717 and the system gradually extended at intervals for 2,130 miles. Along exposed stretches of the upper river, dikes from 8 to 14 feet in height have sufficed, but along the lower river these rise to 24 feet, which is about as great a height as their unstable bases will support. That such shackles of the unruly river are at best precarious is recorded in reports of the late 1880's which show that the dikes were broken through in 712 places.

Along the Missouri where farmers watch acre after acre of rich soil caving into the muddy current, willow mats have been utilized to protect the crumbling banks. Modern engineering has supplemented these devices with articulated concrete mattresses of jointed concrete matting sometimes coated with asphalt. Salt has been strewn beneath to prevent the growth of water vegetation, and points of particular danger have been reinforced with stone riprap.

As far back as 1789 the federal government seems to have made its first appropriation for Mississippi River control, and that initial venture has broadened ever since. In 1879 Congress appointed the Mississippi River Commission, under whose supervision the river and its branches have been more thoroughly studied and investigated than any other waterway of comparable area. At first, governmental appropriations were largely devoted to the maintenance of a minimum depth of channel for navigation purposes, and this was achieved by dredging operations. But it is now recognized that the only practicable method of control is to envisage the entire system as a unit, for a sudden influx of waters from any one of the major branches would upset the normal balance. Harnessing the Tennessee, a particularly unruly member of the Ohio system, has been accomplished through the construction of more than a score of dams, while a similar series of barrages impedes the current of the upper Mississippi. Even more ambitious are plans to tame the Missouri by a series of no fewer than 105 dams designed to cost well over a billion dollars.

Meanwhile, river gages established at strategic points record fluctuations in current and volume that foretell well in advance any serious flood menace.

Although flood control has become a paramount issue, the loss of precious water through mad torrents that rush seaward spreading nothing but havoc has seemed to arid regions of the Far West a tragic waste. Water shortages in many localities have aroused a public consciousness of the extent to which our expanding civilization depends upon an adequate water supply. The building of dams conserves surplus water in artificial lakes which become reservoirs for irrigation projects. A certain dependability in the normal flow of the Missouri should supersede the chaotic era of alternate flood and sand bar.

The development of hydroelectric power is also an issue. Such natural power gave the upper Mississippi its prominence long ago when the Falls of St. Anthony attracted the first settlements at Minneapolis and St. Paul and made possible the great flour mills which brought early prosperity to those cities. Dams, though artificial, are quite as effective as natural waterfalls, and the energy which they develop (called by the Italians white coal), unlike most natural resources, is never dissipated.

In these extensive remodelings of a vast system of waterways, their original function as a means of navigation has not been neglected. The dams of the upper Mississippi tend to maintain a more even depth of current and are bypassed by canals so that steamers ascend readily to St. Paul. In fact, plans have been outlined for greatly increasing the scope of river navigation. The city of Chicago has repeatedly sought legislation permitting the deepening of the channel through canal and river which would reunite Lake Michigan with the Mississippi, and link the vast commerce of the Great Lakes area with the central United States and the Gulf of Mexico. This reversal to conditions which prevailed during the waning of the ice age is opposed by other cities—Detroit, Cleveland, and Buffalo—which fear that the diversion of any great amount of water would lower the lake surfaces and imperil their own costly harbor facilities.

Quite as intriguing, though less likely to be realized, is the suggestion that a canal little more than a mile in length between Big Stone Lake on the Little Minnesota and Lake Traverse draining into the Red River of the North would provide an uninterrupted water route through the Saskatchewan system from the Gulf of Mexico to Hudson Bay.

In volume and in drainage basin the Mississippi ranks far below the Amazon or the Congo. Its commerce is but a tithe of that of the St. Lawrence with its fabulous empire of the Great Lakes. One might even draw unfavorable comparisons with the La Plata-Paraná of South America, with the giant rivers of Siberia, or with the Yangtze Kiang, the life line of China. But the Mississippi, both in magnitude and importance, remains one of the greatest of world systems, and to Americans it will always be what Algonquian tribes first termed it—the Missi Sipi or Great River.

Bibliography.—Clemens, Samuel L. (Mark Twain), *Life on the Mississippi* (New York 1883); Anderson, A. D., *The Mississippi and Its Forty-four Navigable Tributaries* (Washington 1890); Ockerson, J. A., *The Mississippi River; Some of Its Physical Characteristics* (Paris 1900); Parkman, Francis, *La Salle and the Discovery of the Great West* (Boston 1907); Mathews, J. L., *Remaking the Mississippi* (New York 1909); Chambers, J., *The Mississippi River and Its Wonderful Valley* (New York 1910); Humphreys, B. G., *Floods and Levees of the Mississippi River* (Washington 1914); Lane, F. C., *Earth's Grandest Rivers* (New York 1949); Reports of the Mississippi River Commission, Chief of Engineers, U.S. Army.

FERDINAND C. LANE,
Author of "Earth's Grandest Rivers."

MISSISSIPPI, University of, at University, Miss., near Oxford, was chartered Feb. 23, 1844, and opened for its first session Nov. 6, 1848, with four faculty members and 80 students, under George Frederick Holmes as president; since that time it has operated continuously except for the four years of the Civil War, and since 1882 it has been coeducational. Maintained by the State of Mississippi, the university is governed by a board of trustees, made up of the governor of the state and 13 other members. The institution is a fully accredited member of the Southern Association of Colleges. In addition to the original College of Liberal Arts, the university now comprises, in the order of their establishment, schools of law, engineering, education, medicine, pharmacy, and commerce and business administration, and a graduate school. There are also an extension division and departments of music, home economics, and military science and tactics.

More recent additions are the departments of journalism and office administration. The engineering curriculum has been modernized and bureaus of business research and educational research established. The university library has several thousands of volumes and documents of Mississippiana and the Gardner Collection of Political Science. The 60-acre campus forms part of the 640 acre tract of wooded hills. The University also owns some 23,400 acres elsewhere. The average yearly enrollment is 2,700.

MISSISSIPPI BUBBLE, The, an historical novel by Emerson Hough, published in 1902, and centered around one John Law of Lauriston, adventurer, gambler, and financier. More than one writer has woven his tale around this intriguing hero. Mr. Hough has followed history fairly closely. John Law, penniless and on foot, journeys to London, begging a ride for the last few miles in a coach occupied by two women. These two women greatly influenced his life, as is shown in the book's subtitle, "How the star of good fortune rose and set and rose again, by a woman's grace for one John Law of Lauriston."

The review in *The Bookman,* from which we quote, was published in June 1902, and concerns itself with Law the gambler, the soldier of fortune. "History records the unfortunate duel which destroyed Law's prospects at the outset, his imprisonment in Newgate, his escape, and his reappearance many years later in France as the founder of the famous 'system' and promoter of the 'Mississippi scheme' which, bursting, left a wreckage unparalleled in the annals of finance. Mr. Hough's bold innovation consists in accounting for the intervening years by making Law, a fugitive from justice, bury himself in the wilds of America, joining a band of intrepid voyageurs and pushing on westward and southward to the unknown lands beyond the Mississippi. Here Law beholds the boundless expanse of rolling prairie, of a fertility never yet put to the test; he sees some acres of maize, thinly sown by Indian women, a plant never yet seen by European eyes, and his far-seeing mind of economist and financier grasps at a bound the limitless possibilities of wealth spreading out before him—a drama since realized, of the West converted into a vast granary, rolling its flood of golden grain across the Continent and across the ocean to bring renewed prosperity to European nations. This is the dream which the John Law of Mr. Hough's imagination carries back with him to France; it is this on which he bases his 'system' and his Mississippi Company and all the rest of the financial schemes which ended so disastrously. According to the author's conception, Law was an economist far in advance of his time; his methods were sound and should have been successful, had not the Regent, in defiance of his advice, flooded the market with worthless paper and precipitated a panic." See also LAW, JOHN; MISSISSIPPI BUBBLE (financial scheme).

MISSISSIPPI BUBBLE, a celebrated financial scheme, projected by John Law (q.v.) at Paris in 1717. Law issued shares for a vast company to be called the Compagnie d'Occident, and to be engaged in the colonization and cultivation of the banks of the Mississippi. Reports skillfully spread as to gold and silver mines discovered in these parts raised in the people the hope of great gains. The company soon absorbed those of the Senegal and the East Indies, and took the new title Compagnie des Indes. Such were the hopes raised by this undertaking that the shares originally issued at $100 were sold at 10, 20, 30, and 40 times their value. Law had promised to the regent that he would extinguish the public debt. To keep his word he required that the shares in this company should be paid for one fourth in coin and three fourths in *billets d'état* or public securities, which rapidly rose in value on account of the foolish demand which was created for them. In October 1719 the shares mounted as high as $4,000. The state took advantage of the popular frenzy to issue increased quantities of paper money, which was readily accepted by the public creditors and invested in shares of the Compagnie des Indes. This went on until the value of the paper money in circulation was more than three milliards, while the value of coined money was no more than 700 millions. Before this stage was reached Law himself who had originated the idea of paper money had endeavored to check the issue but his efforts were unavailing. A catastrophe was now inevitable. About the end of 1719 the more prudent speculators began to sell out. In payment of their shares they received, of course, in great part, *billets d'état,* and with these bought gold, silver, diamonds, lands or anything else having a real value. As the *billets* became depreciated such articles as tallow, soap, etc., were often bought at fabulous prices. Law struggled desperately against the fall in the value of these shares, but all his devices to check their downward course were futile or had only a temporary success, and when the state finally declared that it would receive no further payments in paper, he perceived that all attempts to bolster up the scheme were in vain, and made his escape from France (December 1720). The affairs of the company were wound up by the state acknowledging itself debtor to the creditors of the company to the amount of $340,000,000. The public debt was augmented by $2,600,000 of "annual rentes."

MISSISSIPPI COLLEGE, at Clinton, Mississippi. A private coeducational institution, it was founded as Hampstead Academy under charter of the state legislature in 1826. Renamed Mississippi Academy in 1827, it assumed its present name in 1830. After more than a decade of municipal management, control of the college was assumed by the Clinton Presbytery in 1842; its present owners, the Mississippi Baptist Convention acquired it in 1850. The convention controls its policies through a board of 15 trustees, elected for three-year terms.

The college's 30 buildings, including the Old Chapel (1859) and a new administration and classroom building, are situated on a 300-acre campus. Undergraduate degrees conferred are the B.A., B.S. in Ed., and B.M. An M.A. is given in education. Preprofessional training is given to students planning careers in medicine, dentistry, nursing, law, teaching, engineering, and theology. The college endeavors to develop in students the highest standards of scholarship and Christian character. It has full accreditation including membership in the National Commission on Accrediting and Southern Association of Colleges and Secondary Schools. Student enrollment in the late 1960's averaged over 2,000.

MISSISSIPPI SCHEME. See Mississippi Bubble.

MISSISSIPPI SOUND, an arm of the Gulf of Mexico, extending along the coasts of Mississippi and Alabama from Bay St. Louis on the east to Mobile Bay on the west and connecting with the latter by Grants Pass. It is about 100 miles long, from 7 to 15 miles wide, from 6 to 10 feet deep, and is formed by a chain of low, narrow, sandy islands, chief of which are Dauphin, Petit Bois, Horn, Ship, and Cat. It is traversed by steamers and coasting vessels trading between New Orleans and Mobile.

MISSISSIPPI STATE UNIVERSITY, a coeducational state university and land-grant college located near Starkville, Miss. Founded as the Mississippi Agricultural and Mechanical College in 1878, it was renamed Mississippi State College in 1932 and received its present name in 1958. The university comprises colleges of arts and sciences, business and industry, agriculture, education, and engineering; a school of forest resources; and a graduate school. Doctoral programs are offered in many areas. During the late 1960's the university's enrollment averaged about 7,000 students, and the faculty numbered more than 400.

MISSISSIPPIAN. See Carboniferous.

MISSOLONGHI, mĭs-ô-lông'gĭ, or **MESOLONGION,** mâ-sô-lông'gyôn, city, Greece, capital of Acarnania nome, on the marshy site on the north side of the Gulf of Patras, 24 miles west of Návpaktos (Lepanto) and the seat of an archbishopric. Missolonghi is the most important strategical point of western Greece and is famous for the sieges it has undergone. In 1804 it came under the rule of Ali Pasha of Janina. In the Greek revolt against the Turkish conquerors in 1821 it was brilliantly defended by 400 men against a Turkish army of 14,000 for two months; when reinforced, they again for over a year resisted the Turks, who raised the siege Jan. 6, 1823. The town was hastily fortified, and from September to December 1823 was again besieged by the Turks, who were defeated by a small Greek force under Marco Bozzaris (Markos Botzaris), but with the loss of their patriotic general. In 1825–1826 it stood a long siege by the Turks. A body of its defenders cut their way through the Turkish force and escaped; the remainder determined to sell their lives as dearly as possible, and when the Turks forced their way in, the powder magazine was exploded, thus overwhelming besiegers and besieged in one common catastrophe. Lord Byron, who went to Missolonghi Jan. 5, 1824 to aid the Greeks, died there April 19, 1824; his heart was interred in the Church of St. Spyridion, and a monument erected by the Greeks in his honor. Here also is the tomb of Bozzaris. Pop. (1961) 11,266.

MISSON, mĭ-sôn', **François Maximilien,** French traveler and author: b. Lyon, about 1650; d. London, England, Jan. 12, 1722. He was a councillor in the Parlement of Paris, but at the revocation of the Edict of Nantes, as a Protestant, fled to England. There, in 1685, he became tutor to Charles Butler, afterward earl of Arran, whom he accompanied on his travels. In 1691 he published *Nouveau Voyage d'Italie,* in which his comments on the customs of the Roman Catholic Church led to a celebrated controversy with Father Freschot. In 1698 he published a volume of *Mémoires et Observations,* which constitutes a humorous descriptive dictionary of London life in Queen Anne's reign. His other chief work is *Théâtre sacré des Cévennes* (1707).

MISSOULA, mĭ-zōō'lȧ, city, Montana, and Missoula County seat; altitude 3,223 feet; on the Pacific slope of the Rocky Mountains; and the Clark Fork of the Columbia River (locally called the Missoula); 120 miles northwest of Butte; served by the Northern Pacific; and Chicago, Milwaukee, St. Paul and Pacific railroads. The city is built on both banks of the river at the mouth of Hell Gate Canyon, and is the marketing center for four fertile valleys: Flathead, Bitterroot, Blackfoot and Missoula. Major industries are flour milling and sugar refining. There are also lumber mills, a brewery, meatpacking plant, and several creameries. Gold, lead and copper are mined nearby. It is the seat of Montana State University and headquarters of the Lolo National Forest. First settled in 1860, it was called Missoula Mills. Fort Missoula, southwest of the city, was established in 1877. The city was incorporated in 1885. Pop. 29,497.

MISSOURI, mĭ-zōōr'ĭ, one of the West North Central states of the United States, is bounded on the north by Iowa, on the east by Illinois, Kentucky, and Tennessee, on the south by Arkansas, and on the west by Nebraska, Kansas, and Oklahoma. The Mississippi River flows along the eastern boundary and the Missouri forms the western boundary from the northwest corner to its junction with the Kansas River at Kansas City. The Des Moines River in the extreme northeast and the St. Francis on the western side of the "boot heel" in the southeast are also boundary streams. The name Missouri is of Indian origin and probably means "the town of the big canoes."

State flag of Missouri
(Officially adopted, March 13, 1913)

(Colors, from top to bottom: single red, white, and blue stripes of equal width, with centered circular band of blue enclosing coat of arms.)

State seal of Missouri
(Adopted Jan. 11, 1822)

Total area	69,686 square miles
Land area	68,995 square miles
Water area	1,392 square miles
Latitude	36° to 40°35′N.
Longitude	89°6′ to 95°42′W.
Altitude	230 to 1,772 feet
Population (1970)	4,677,399
Capital—Jefferson City; population (1970)	32,407
Admitted to Union as 24th state	Aug. 10, 1821
State motto	*Salus Populi Suprema Lex Esto* (Let the welfare of the people be the supreme law)
State bird (approved March 30, 1927)	Bluebird
State flower (approved March 16, 1923)	Hawthorn
State tree (approved June 20, 1955)	Flowering dogwood
State song (approved June 30, 1949)	The Missouri Waltz
State nickname	"'Show Me' State"

A discussion of Missouri's geography, government, social and economic life, and history is presented under the following headings:

1. Physical Features and Resources
2. Population and Political Divisions
3. Government and Politics
4. Education and Welfare
5. Economic Activities
6. Places of Interest
7. Famous Men and Women
8. History

1. PHYSICAL FEATURES AND RESOURCES

Topography.—Missouri's topography is varied because the state is located where three physiographical regions converge. Most of the land north of the Missouri River and in a triangular region south and west of the center of the state is prairie with rolling hills interspersed along streams. Generally, this area resembles the prairies of Illinois and Iowa, but parts are like the Great Plains. The Ozark uplift, low and ancient mountains of only 1,200 to 1,700 feet above sea level, runs southwest from the region near St. Louis to the southern and southwestern boundaries of the state. The crest of the Ozarks is relatively level, but the edges are eroded with sharp ridges and deep valleys. Between the Ozark border and the prairies are regions of rough hills. In the extreme southeast is a flat alluvial area of river plains that is like the Mississippi Delta. Before it was drained about the turn of the century, it was a swampy region. Along the Mississippi, Missouri, and some of the smaller rivers are flat bottomlands that are largely alluvial flood plains.

Climate.—The average annual temperature for the entire state is about 55°F., ranging from a January average of 31°F. to a July average of 77.5°F. The variations are considerable and often abrupt, but seldom fall below −10°F. or rise much over 100°F. The frost-free period averages from mid-April to mid-October. The average annual precipitation is 30 to 40 inches in the northwest and from 40 to 50 inches in the southeast, with a maximum in May and June, the most important months of the growing season.

Soils.—The soils of Missouri are of infinite variety in geological origin, physical properties, texture, depth, color, and fertility. Five different soil regions further subdivided into 16 areas have been designated, but in each of these there is great variation. The soils in the Ozark region are geologically much older than those of the northern prairies. Weathering and leaching through the centuries have made the Ozark soils relatively less fertile. The presence of large amounts of chert makes these soils less valuable for farming. In prehistoric times, the soils of the northern Missouri prairies were covered by glaciers. Through the action of the wind, during later geological periods, much of it was covered by loessial deposit. Thus, the prairie region is deeper, more uniform in texture, darker, and more fertile than the Ozark soils. In the northwest section is an area of loess that is deep and very fertile. In the southeast lowlands and along the rivers are deep alluvial bottoms that are rich and productive. In the southeast lowlands there is also a ridge of loess. The triangular prairie region south of the Missouri and toward the western boundary has a great variety of soils. Much of it is a brown, stony limestone soil that is excellent for grass and hay. In any region the soils will differ in tilth, depth, color, and fertility.

Erosion, the removal of timber, and overcropping have depleted much of the soil resources. Since the mid-1930's the balanced farming program of the Agricultural Extension Service of the College of Agriculture of the University of Missouri and the effective work of the various federal soil districts have led to the building of terraces, the conservation of timber and grasses, and the use of fertilizers that make production on the best areas much more abundant.

Water Resources.—There are 11,500 miles of permanently flowing streams in the state, of which 1,060 miles are classified as navigable, and of these nearly all are on the Mississippi and Missouri rivers. Tributaries of the Mississippi north of the Missouri are small, the Salt River being the largest. South of the Missouri the Meramec, St. Francis, Current, and Black rivers are in the Mississippi watershed and are much longer than the northern rivers. These, with the White River in the southwest, throw much of the Ozarks into the Mississippi drainage system. Into the Missouri from the south flow the Gasconade, draining the northern Ozarks, and the Osage, draining the western Ozarks and the southern plains. From the north the Missouri's tributaries are the Tarkio, Platte, Grand, and Chariton.

The rivers and flowing streams furnish over half the people of the state with a bountiful water supply for industrial and domestic use. The problems of flood control and navigation have been troublesome ones because of the uneven flow due to alternating periods of drought and heavy rainfall. The construction of dams and canals on the Mississippi and its eastern tributaries has brought to that river an enormous expansion in navigation since the late 1930's. Although there are dams on the upper Missouri and the river has a 6- to 9-foot channel from its mouth to Sioux City, Iowa, navigation has not developed to any great extent. In 1944, the Pick-Sloan Plan was authorized by Congress for the purpose of building dams on the Missouri and its tributaries, in order to improve navigation on the Missouri, minimize the effects of floods, and promote irrigation and power development throughout the whole Missouri Valley. See also DAMS.

By 1968 the state's developed hydroelectric generating capacity totaled about 782,000 kilowatts, 16 per cent of the state's electric power capacity. The potential supply, chiefly in the

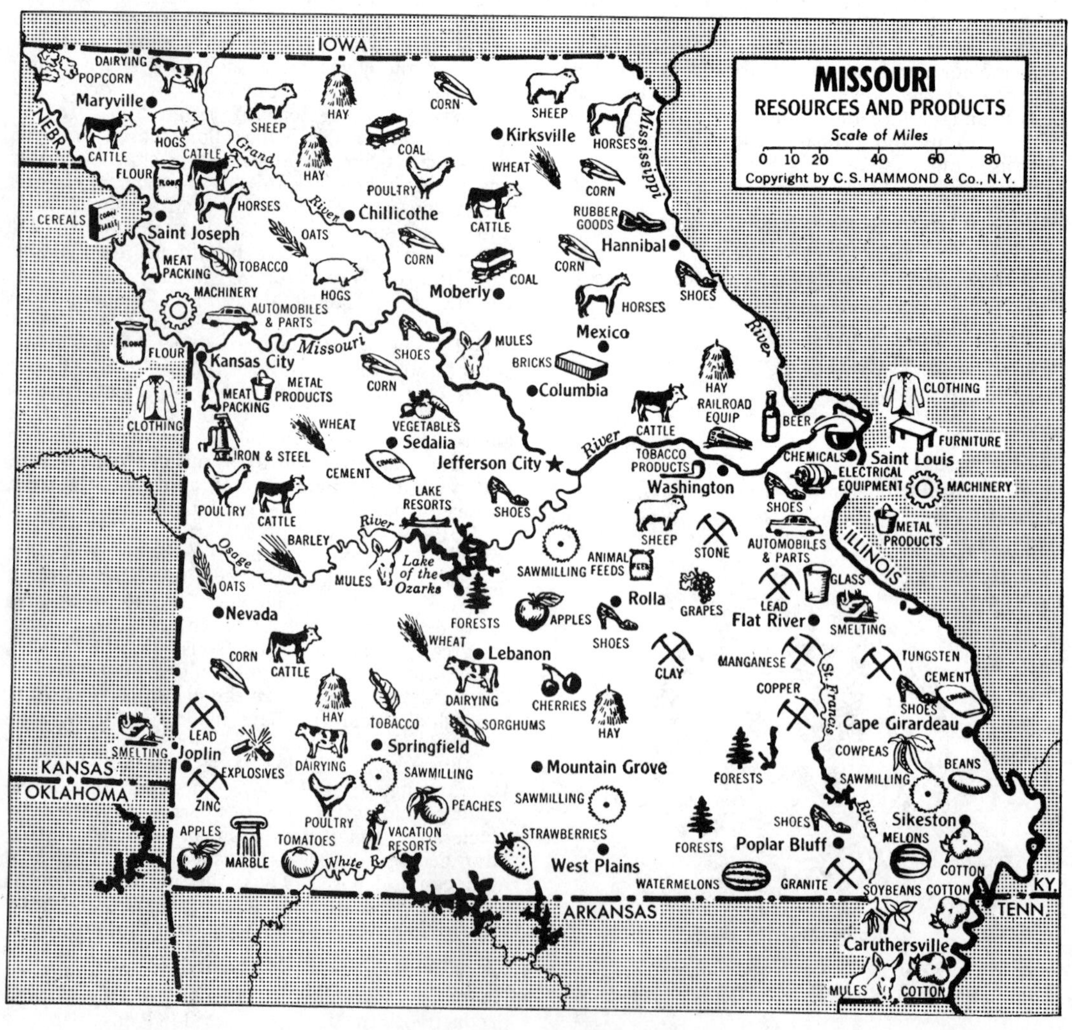

Ozarks, is another 100,000 kilowatts. There are no reservoirs for irrigation projects in the state, but many farmers are using water from streams, small lakes, and wells for supplementary irrigation in limited areas.

Missouri has eight large artificial lakes and a number of smaller ones formed by dams. They include Lakes Taneycomo and Table Rock on the White River in the southwest and the Lake of the Ozarks on the Osage above Bagnell. The latter is one of the largest artificial lakes in the world, covering an area of 65,000 acres with 1,672 miles of shoreline. Wappapello Reservoir on the St. Francis and Clearwater Lake on the Black River in the southeast are federal flood control projects. Lake Norfolk on the Arkansas line is formed by Norfolk Dam in Arkansas on the north fork of the White River and is a combination power and flood control reservoir. Bull Shoals Dam (power and flood control) on the White River in Arkansas, creates Bull Shoals Lake, which extends into Missouri. A similar project is Thomas Hill Dam on the Chariton. Under construction are Clarence Cannon on the Salt and Kaysinger and Pomme de Terre on the upper Osage system.

The Missouri Ozarks have over 10,000 springs, some of which rank among the largest in the world. There are 159 large springs, 98 of which have a flow of over a million gallons a day. Big Springs in Carter County is the largest and has had a daily measured flow of 840 million gallons. Double Spring in Ozark County, Bennett Spring in Dallas, Alley Springs in Shannon, Blue Spring in Oregon, Blue Spring in Shannon, Cave Spring in Shannon, Greer Spring in Oregon, Hahatonka Spring in Camden, Meramec Spring in Phelps, and Montauk Spring in Phelps are all large.

Minerals.—Missouri has a wide variety of mineral resources. The lead area in the southeast, chiefly in the St. Francis River Valley, at one time led the world in production, and Missouri has always been a leading U.S. producer of lead. Discovery of a rich vein in the southeast has caused an expansion in production. Missouri's extreme southwest, with adjacent sections of Kansas and Oklahoma, is in the Tri-State zinc area, which leads nationally in production. Discoveries of rich iron ore deposits in the southeast have spurred rapid development. Missouri is the chief U.S. producer of cobalt. Small amounts of nickel have been produced from complex ores at Fredrickstown. Cadmium, germanium, pyrites, copper, and silver are also found in small quantities throughout the state. Bituminous coal is widely distributed throughout the prairie areas, with the heaviest concentration of production occurring in the west-central counties. Missouri is a leading producer of barite. Other minerals produced in increasing quantities include cement, clays, lime, sand and gravel, and stone.

Plant Life.—At the time of Missouri's settlement, nearly two thirds of the area of the state was covered with virgin timber. The native trees were short-leaf pine. hickory, elm, maple, walnut, cedar, sweet gum, cottonwood, black tupelo, sassafras, hornbeam, redbud, service-berry, persimmon, and many varieties of oak.

Missouri's virgin forests succumbed quickly to modern industry, so that most first-class lumber was soon depleted. The acreage of forests has declined from its original 31 million acres to 15 million.

The short-leaf pine was an important species on more than 4 million acres and could be found interspersed with other trees on 2½ million additional acres. At present, little of this acreage is left. Most of the forested area is covered with second-growth oak and hickory of relatively small size. Present forest areas are concentrated heavily in the Ozarks and the Missouri River counties from Howard County eastward. In recent years two national forests (Clark and Mark Twain) have been established in the Ozarks.

Missouri abounds with numerous varieties of well-known wild plants and flowers, such as May apple, sweet William, jack-in-the-pulpit, and goldenrod, as well as verbena, columbine, white bloodroot, and snakeroot. The Ozark region, because of its unusual geological history, contains the most complex and varied flora in the state.

Animal Life.—The settling of the state, the plowing up of the prairies, and the removal of the forests have changed the availability of wildlife in the state. Big game such as elk, bear, bison, and antelope have vanished, and wild turkey and deer have almost disappeared. The passenger pigeon, Louisiana paroquet, ivory-billed woodpecker, and Eskimo curlew are extinct. But other birds and animals have found modern Missouri attractive. Today the bobwhite quail, red fox, crow, and fox squirrel thrive where once the prairie chicken, ruffed grouse, gray fox, raven, and gray squirrel held sway. The coyote has taken the place of the gray wolf. Rabbits, opossums, skunks, racoons, and muskrats are common. Native to the state are the mourning dove, bluebird, bullfinch, cardinal, and woodpecker.

Aquatic life has been affected more adversely than has animal and bird life. Fish life has been depleted in some streams because of poor drainage, land erosion, untreated sewage, the emptying of industrial waste into streams, the damming of rivers, and the lowering of the water table. In the Ozark streams and in many of the lakes are to be found crappie and large- and small-mouth bass. The cold Ozark streams have been stocked with trout. In the slow-flowing and turbid streams of northern Missouri, channel and flathead catfish abound, and bluegill and green sunfish are not uncommon. The Grand, Meramec and St. Francis rivers are the homes of carp, buffalo, drum, shad, sucker, gar, river sturgeon, and spoonbill, as well as the channel, blue, and flathead catfish.

2. POPULATION AND POLITICAL DIVISIONS

Population Characteristics.—Missouri's population grew rapidly from 1820 to 1900, while there was still vacant land in the state and while the cities were still absorbing large numbers of people. The state's population rose at a slower rate in the 20th century.

After the Civil War, Missourians began emigrating to the new frontiers of the Great Plains and the Far West. In recent decades the cities of the Middle West, as well as those of the Far West and Southwest, have attracted many Missourians. As a result, Missouri has sent more of its people to other states than it has received. Also, there has been a shift of population within the state from rural areas to the cities, and since 1910 there has been an absolute decline in the rural population. In some areas the rural population has fallen very sharply as families have become smaller and farms much larger.

The state's population is heavily native American. Up to the Civil War, Kentucky, Tennessee,

Virginia, and North Carolina furnished the bulk of immigrants. From 1830 to 1860 large numbers of Germans, Irish, and English emigrated to St. Louis and surrounding areas. Southern and eastern European immigrants did not migrate to Missouri in great numbers between 1870 and 1920, the years when the greatest number of these immigrants went to the United States.

The Negro population is concentrated in St. Louis, Kansas City, the southeast lowlands, and in some cities along the Missouri. Since 1910, due to migrations from the South, Negroes have increased both in total numbers and as a percentage of the population. In 1970, Negroes made up about 10 per cent of the population.

GROWTH OF POPULATION SINCE 1820

Year	Population	Year	Population
1820	66,586	1920	3,404,055
1840	383,702	1940	3,784,664
1860	1,182,012	1950	3,954,653
1880	2,168,380	1960	4,319,813
1900	3,106,665	1970	4,677,399

Gain, 1960–1970: 8.3% (U.S. gain, 13.3%). **Density,** 1970: 67.6 persons per square mile (U.S. density, 56.2).

URBAN-RURAL DISTRIBUTION

Year	Percent urban	Percent rural
1920	46.6 (U.S., 51.2)	53.4
1930	51.2 (U.S., 56.2)	48.8
1940	51.8 (U.S., 56.6)	48.2
1950	61.5 (U.S., 64.0)	38.5
1960	66.6 (U.S., 69.9)	33.4
1970	70.1 (U.S., 73.5)	29.9

LARGEST CENTERS OF POPULATION

City or Metropolitan area[1]	1970	1960	1950
St. Louis (city)	622,236	750,026	856,796
Metropolitan area (Mo. portion)	1,826,907	...	...
Kansas City (city)	507,087	475,539	456,622
Metropolitan area (Mo. portion)	849,409	...	...
Springfield (city)	120,096	95,865	66,731
Metropolitan area	152,929	126,276	...
Independence	111,662	62,328	36,963
St. Joseph	72,691	79,673	78,588
Florissant	65,908	38,166	3,737
Columbia	58,804	36,650	31,974
University City	46,309	51,249	39,892
Lemay (U)	40,115	...	...
Joplin	39,256	38,958	38,711
Fort Leonard Wood (U)	33,799	...	...
Raytown	33,632	17,083	...
Jefferson City	32,407	28,228	25,099
Kirkwood	31,890	29,421	18,640
St. Charles	31,834	21,189	14,314
Cape Girardeau	31,282	24,947	21,578

[1] Standard metropolitan statistical area. (U) Unincorporated as of 1970 Census.

Political Divisions.—Missouri is divided into 114 counties and the City of St. Louis. The county is the principal division of local government, although some counties have organized township governments, with limited duties in the hands of township officers.

St. Louis, in the eastern part of the state, and Kansas City, in the west, are by far the largest cities. St. Joseph and Springfield are centers of smaller metropolitan areas. Jefferson City, the state capital, is the chief city of central Missouri.

The state's counties and their county seats are as follows:

County	County Seat	County	County Seat
Adair	Kirksville	Livingston	Chillicothe
Andrew	Savannah	McDonald	Pineville
Atchison	Rockport	Macon	Macon
Audrain	Mexico	Madison	Fredericktown
Barry	Cassville	Maries	Vienna
Barton	Lamar	Marion	Palmyra
Bates	Butler	Mercer	Princeton
Benton	Warsaw	Miller	Tuscumbia
Bollinger	Marble Hill	Mississippi	Charleston
Boone	Columbia	Moniteau	California
Buchanan	St. Joseph	Monroe	Paris
Butler	Poplar Bluff	Montgomery	Montgomery City
Caldwell	Kingston	Morgan	Versailles
Callaway	Fulton	New Madrid	New Madrid
Camden	Camdenton	Newton	Neosho
Cape Girardeau	Jackson	Nodaway	Maryville
Carroll	Carrollton	Oregon	Alton
Carter	Van Buren	Osage	Linn
Cass	Harrisonville	Ozark	Gainesville
Cedar	Stockton	Pemiscot	Caruthersville
Chariton	Keytesville	Perry	Perryville
Christian	Ozark	Pettis	Sedalia
Clark	Kahoka	Phelps	Rolla
Clay	Liberty	Pike	Bowling Green
Clinton	Plattsburg	Platte	Platte City
Cole	Jefferson City	Polk	Bolivar
Cooper	Boonville	Pulaski	Waynesville
Crawford	Steelville	Putnam	Unionville
Dade	Greenfield	Ralls	New London
Dallas	Buffalo	Randolph	Huntsville
Daviess	Galatin	Ray	Richmond
DeKalb	Maysville	Reynolds	Centerville
Dent	Salem	Ripley	Doniphan
Douglas	Ava	St. Charles	St. Charles
Dunklin	Kennett	St. Clair	Osceola
Franklin	Union	St. Francois	Farmington
Gasconade	Hermann	Ste. Genevieve	Ste. Genevieve
Gentry	Albany	St. Louis	Clayton
Greene	Springfield	Saline	Marshall
Grundy	Trenton	Schuyler	Lancaster
Harrison	Bethany	Scotland	Memphis
Henry	Clinton	Scott	Benton
Hickory	Hermitage	Shannon	Eminence
Holt	Oregon	Shelby	Shelbyville
Howard	Fayette	Stoddard	Bloomfield
Howell	West Plains	Stone	Galena
Iron	Ironton	Sullivan	Milan
Jackson	Independence	Taney	Forsyth
Jasper	Carthage	Texas	Houston
Jefferson	Hillsboro	Vernon	Nevada
Johnson	Warrensburg	Warren	Warrenton
Knox	Edina	Washington	Potosi
Laclede	Lebanon	Wayne	Greenville
Lafayette	Lexington	Webster	Marshfield
Lawrence	Mt. Vernon	Worth	Grant City
Lewis	Monticello	Wright	Hartville
Lincoln	Troy		
Linn	Linneus		

3. GOVERNMENT AND POLITICS

Constitution.—The first constitution of the state was put into effect in 1820. This document, although amended several times, lasted until 1865. In that year the Radical Republicans submitted a constitution that was adopted. This fundamental law did away with slavery, disfranchised Southern sympathizers, and reformed the governmental structure in a number of ways. By 1875 the Southern element had recaptured the government, and the Liberal Republican Party was strong in the state. As a result, a new constitution of 1875 was adopted. This constitution reflected the impact of the Panic of 1873 and mounting heavy state and local debts, as well as reaction against the Radical Republican rule of the 1860's. Many of its provisions were restrictive and conservative, and in the years following World War I constituted a barrier to economic and social progress. Its archaic character was illustrated by the fact that by 1940 a total of 167 amendments had been submitted and 56 had been adopted. Between 1920 and 1940, amendments were approved that provided for a state highway system financed by gasoline taxes, a social welfare system, tighter budgetary control by the governor with the power of item veto, a bipartisan conservation commission, and a plan for the selection of certain judges without regard to partisan politics.

In 1942 the voters provided for a new constitutional convention. In 1945 the constitution submitted by this body was ratified by the voters and put into operation. The convention's objectives were clearly a frame of government to increase efficiency with sufficient flexibility to meet modern problems. The bicameral system was retained, but a plan was introduced to force a reorganization of the senatorial districts through a bipartisan commission after each decennial census. In 1966 the constitution was changed to provide for the same method of redistricting for the House.

Many of the most restrictive provisions on legislation were relaxed. The assembly was not to be restricted to short sessions and it was provided with power to set up a legislative reference service, now known as the Committee on Legislative Research.

The constitution can be amended only by a majority of the popular vote in a regular or special election. Amendments may be submitted by an initiative petition signed by 8 per cent of the legal voters in two thirds of the congressional districts, or by a majority vote of both houses of the General Assembly.

Executive.—The governor, elected for four years, is the state's chief executive officer. A 1966 constitutional amendment makes it possible for him to serve two consecutive terms. The voters also elect a lieutenant governor, secretary of state, attorney general, state treasurer, and state auditor. These officers are strictly limited by the constitution to functions germane to their offices. The executive branch must be organized into not more than 15 departments. The governor appoints the heads of these departments with the advice and consent of the Senate. In the cases of the highway, conservation, and educational departments, the control of their functions lies with bipartisan commissions. Other executive departments are headed by single officials.

The constitution provides for a Department of Revenue that collects all taxes and fees, pre-audits all accounts, and prepares the budget for the governor. The governor has the power of item veto in appropriation bills.

GOVERNORS

TERRITORIAL PERIOD

William C.C. Claiborne	Acting governor general and intendant of Louisiana	1803–1804
Amos Stoddard	First civil commandant of Upper Louisiana	1804
William Henry Harrison (Gov. of Indiana Terr.)	Governor, District of Louisiana	1804–1805
James Wilkinson	Governor, Territory of Louisiana	1805–1807
Joseph Browne	Acting governor	1807
Frederick Bates	" "	1807
Meriwether Lewis	Governor	1807–1809
Frederick Bates	Acting governor	1809–1810
Benjamin Howard	Governor	1810–1812
Frederick Bates	Acting governor, Territory of Missouri	1812–1813
William Clark	Governor	1813–1820

STATE

Alexander McNair	Democrat	1820–1824
Frederick Bates[1]	"	1824–1825
Abraham J. Williams[2]	"	1825
John Miller	"	1825–1832
Daniel Dunklin	"	1832–1836
Lillburn W. Boggs	"	1836–1840
Thomas Reynolds[1]	"	1840–1844
M. M. Marmaduke[2]	"	1844
John C. Edwards	"	1844–1848
Austin A. King	"	1848–1852
Sterling Price	"	1852–1856
Trusten Polk[3]	"	1856–1857
Hancock Jackson[2]	"	1857
Robert M. Stewart	"	1857–1861
Claiborne F. Jackson[4]	"	1861
Hamilton R. Gamble[5]	Unionist	1861–1864
Willard P. Hall[2]	Unionist	1864–1865
Thomas C. Fletcher	Republican	1865–1869
Joseph W. McClurg	"	1869–1871
B. Gratz Brown	Liberal	1871–1873
Silas Woodson	Democrat	1873–1875
Charles H. Hardin	"	1875–1877
John S. Phelps	"	1877–1881
Thomas T. Crittenden	"	1881–1885
John S. Marmaduke[1]	"	1885–1887
Albert P. Morehouse[2]	"	1887–1889
David R. Francis	"	1889–1893
William Joel Stone	"	1893–1897
Lon V. Stephens	"	1897–1901
Alexander M. Dockery	"	1901–1905
Joseph W. Folk	"	1905–1909
Herbert S. Hadley	Republican	1909–1913
Elliot W. Major	Democrat	1913–1917
Frederick D. Gardner	"	1917–1921
Arthur M. Hyde	Republican	1921–1925
Sam A. Baker	"	1925–1929
Henry S. Caulfield	"	1929–1933
Guy B. Park	Democrat	1933–1937
Lloyd C. Stark	"	1937–1941
Forrest C. Donnell	Republican	1941–1945
Phil M. Donnelly	Democrat	1945–1949
Forrest Smith	"	1949–1953
Phil M. Donnelly	"	1953–1957
James T. Blair, Jr.	"	1957–1961
John M. Dalton	"	1961–1965
Warren E. Hearnes	"	1965–1973
Christopher S. Bond	Republican	1973–

[1]Died in office. [2]Acting. [3]Resigned. [4]Expelled by convention. [5]Appointed by convention.

Legislature.—The legislature, legally known as the General Assembly, is composed of a House of Representatives of 163 members and a Senate of 34. Representatives are elected for two-year terms; senators for four. The courts ruled in 1966 that the lower house be redistricted in terms of "one man, one vote," with each district substantially equal in population. The 1966 revision removed the county as the principal unit of representation. The General Assembly meets on the first Wednesday after the first day of January in odd-numbered years, and adjourns no later than July 15. The governor may at any time call an extraordinary session, limited to 60 days, to consider subjects he recommends.

Judiciary.—The system of courts is made up of a Supreme Court of 7 judges, 3 courts of appeals, and more than 40 circuit courts. In each county there is a magistrate court to hear cases of first instance, and a probate judge. Supreme Court and appellate court judges serve for 12 years, circuit court judges for 6 years, and probate judges and magistrates for 4 years. For the selection of Supreme Court judges, appellate court judges, judges of the circuit and probate courts of St. Louis City and Jackson County, and judges of the St. Louis courts of criminal corrections, a nonpartisan court plan, adopted in 1940 and retained in the constitution of 1945, is used. In case of a vacancy the governor makes his appointment from among three nominations presented by a nonpartisan judicial commission. After a year's service the name of the appointee is submitted to a popular vote if he desires to continue in office, but no one can run against the incumbent and there is no political designation on the ballot. A similar ballot is provided for a judge whose term is expiring and who wishes to remain in office. The judges in other parts of the state are elected by the voters on a general party ballot. The Supreme Court has the power to make rules of procedure for all courts and to transfer judges temporarily from one court to another. It has extensive power to review opinions of the appellate courts.

Special Government Bodies.—In 1949, the legislatures of Missouri and Illinois created a bistate development agency for the metropolitan

Massie-Missouri Resources Division

Missouri State Capitol, Jefferson City.

area around St. Louis. The agency is empowered to carry on activities in transportation, sanitation, water works, recreational projects, and civil defense. The Missouri-Tennessee Bridge Commission manages the bridges across the Mississippi at the mouth of the Ohio.

Taxation and Revenue.—The Department of Revenue, headed by a director, is the chief fiscal agent of the state. This department collects all fees, licenses, and taxes due the state, except taxes on tangible property. The latter are collected by the county or township collectors in the units of local government. The Division of the Budget is also in the Department of Revenue and collects budget data and prepares budget estimates for the governor. The Department of Revenue must also pre-approve all claims and accounts against the state before payment. All pre-audits are performed by the comptroller and all post-audits are done by the state auditor. All accounts are deposited with the state treasurer.

For the fiscal year 1967–1968 the state's receipts from taxes was $619,963,000. The sales tax brought in $267,000,000; income taxes, $132,000,000; motor vehicles, $67,550,000; motor fuel, $108,336,000, and cigarette taxes, $25,250,000. The remaining receipts came from liquor, corporation franchise and inheritance taxes, drivers' licenses, and earnings on deposits. Federal funds for highway construction and support of various welfare, insurance, and educational functions amounted to $365,287,000. The total expenditures were about $1,200,000,000. The remainder of the state's funds came from permanent accounts.

Suffrage and Elections.—The general election is held on the first Tuesday after the first Monday in November in even-numbered years, and the primary is held on the first Tuesday in August of the same years. To vote, a citizen must have lived in the state a year and in the county and district 60 days before an election. The constitution provides that a bill passed by the General Assembly and signed by the governor can be submitted to the people by referendum if 5 per cent of the legal voters in each of two thirds of the congressional districts sign a petition asking that the law be referred. In the case of either a referendum or initiative a majority of those voting is required for passage.

Although Missouri is considered a politically unpredictable state, the Democratic Party is generally the majority party. In each presidential election since 1904, Missouri voted for the national winner, with the exception of 1956 when the Democrats carried the state for Adlai Stevenson. However, in four of these elections the major party that lost the national election carried the governorship. Missouri is represented in Congress by 2 senators and 10 representatives.

4. EDUCATION AND WELFARE

School Administration.—The supervision of the State Department of Education is lodged in a bipartisan State Board of Education of eight members appointed by the governor and approved by the Senate for eight-year terms. The executive officer of the state department is the commissioner of education, appointed by the state board and serving at its pleasure. For higher education there are boards of curators for the University of Missouri, for Lincoln University, and for each of the seven state colleges. The State Board of Education has broad powers of supervision of the public schools and governs the schools for the deaf and the blind. The board allocates state and federal appropriations to local districts, supervises and classifies school systems for accreditation, issues teaching certificates to teachers, collects and publishes information on the schools, and directly regulates many educational functions.

Elementary and Secondary Schools.—Missouri's schools are growing in size and scope. Expenditures for public education increased sharply during the 1950's and 1960's. In 1955 there were 724,750 pupils enrolled in Missouri public schools; in 1967–1968 the enrollment was 1,002,449. In 1957 there were 26,245 teachers; in 1967–1968, 40,224. Total revenue for education from all sources rose from $198,304,000 in 1955 to $632,381,000 in 1967–1968. Direct state support of public schools increased from $56,500,000 in 1955 to $164,420,000 in 1967–1968. Church supported schools enroll over 100,000 pupils.

Higher Education.—Missouri has 7 universities, 14 four-year colleges of arts and science, 7 state colleges, 20 junior colleges, of which 12 are public, 8 theological seminaries, 2 colleges of music, 1 college of art, 2 colleges of pharmacy, and 2 osteopathic schools.

The University of Missouri (q.v.) at Columbia, Kansas City, Rolla, and St. Louis, chartered in 1838 and opened in 1841, is the oldest state university west of the Mississippi. Other institutions of higher education include Avila College (Catholic), Kansas City; Central Methodist, Fayette; Culver-Stockton (Disciples of Christ), Canton; Drury College (Congregational), Springfield; Cardinal Glennon (Catholic), St. Louis; Evangel (Assemblies of God), Springfield; Fontbonne (Catholic), St. Louis; Lincoln University (state), Jefferson City; Lindenwood for Women (Presbyterian), St. Charles; Maryville of Sacred Heart (Catholic), St. Louis; Marillac (Catholic), St. Louis; Missouri School of Religion, Columbia; Missouri Valley (Presbyterian), Marshall; Notre Dame (Catholic), St. Louis; Park (Presbyterian), Parkville; Rockhurst (Catholic), Kansas City; Southwest Baptist, Bolivar; School of the Ozarks (Presbyterian), Point Lookout; St. Louis University (Catholic), St. Louis; Stephens (private), Columbia; Tarkio (United Presbyterian), Tarkio; Washington University (private), St. Louis; Westminster (Presbyterian), Fulton; William Jewell (Baptist), Liberty; William Woods (Disciples of Christ), Fulton; Webster College (Catholic), Webster Groves.

In the fall of 1967 the combined enrollment of these institutions was 112,609 full-time and 38,164 part-time students. Public institutions enrolled 100,773; private, about 51,000 full-time students. By 1970 enrollment is expected to reach 120,000. To meet this rapid growth the state's colleges and universities have been seeking funds for expansion and support. Plans under way in 1957 were expected to expand existing facilities to accommodate a total of 85,000 students. St. Louis University, Washington University, the University of Missouri, and the state colleges and Lincoln University have launched extensive building programs, and church-related colleges have been working together to encourage industry and business to support their expansion.

Libraries.—The constitution of 1945 provided for the promotion and support of public libraries by state as well as by local taxation. As a result of the small appropriations made under the provision, the number of public libraries receiving state support came to 113 in 1968. A bookmobile service has been instituted for areas remote from regular libraries. Expenditures for buildings, expansion, and support have grown in recent years.

Special libraries of note in the state are the library of the University of Missouri and the State Historical Society of Missouri at Columbia, the libraries of Washington University and of St. Louis University in St. Louis, the Linda Hall Library in Kansas City, the Missouri Historical Society Library in St. Louis, and the St. Louis Mercantile Library. The Linda Hall Library has one of the best collections in science and technology in the Middle West. St. Louis University, soon to contain the microfilm records of the Vatican Library, is one of the finest libraries on religion in the world. The University of Missouri Library at Columbia, which also houses the State Historical Society Library of Missouri and the Western Historical Manuscripts Collection, is a superior library in American history and agriculture. At Independence, the Harry S. Truman Library and Museum contains 3,500,000 documents and numerous mementos of President Truman's administration.

Public Health and Welfare.—The State Department of Public Health and Welfare is one of the principal administrative units of the state government. The Division of Health within this department is the central health authority of the state and exercises its powers through such bureaus as those of Vital Statistics, Laboratories, Communicable Diseases, Food and Drug Inspection, Child Hygiene and Maternity Care, and Tuberculosis Control. The department directly administers the Missouri State Tuberculosis Sanatorium at Mt. Vernon, the Ellis Fischel Cancer Hospital at Columbia, and the Trachoma Hospital at Rolla. Its laboratories are at Jefferson City, Sikeston, and Springfield. The Division of Mental Diseases maintains state hospitals at St. Louis, Fulton, St. Joseph, Nevada, and Farmington, and the state schools for the feeble-minded at St. Louis, Marshall, Carrollton, and Higginsville.

Missouri maintains, through its Division of Welfare, programs of old-age assistance, aid to dependent children, general relief, aid to the permanently and totally disabled, and aid to the blind. The division also places qualified welfare workers in the field to help take care of children, accepts the guardianship of neglected children, and inspects child-caring institutions. In recent years, the annual budget for all the services of the division has reached the $200,000,000 level.

The Division of Employment Security administers the cooperative unemployment compensation system of the state and federal government and maintains a system of public employment offices. Reserves in the unemployment insurance fund were over $200,000,000 by 1955. The Division of Workmen's Compensation enforces the workmen's compensation law, an optional statute covering protection of workers on any job.

Public Safety.—The Missouri National Guard is composed of approximately 10,000 officers and men with home stations in 60 communities. It has infantry, artillery, antiaircraft, and air wing components.

The state Highway Patrol is composed of about 350 patrolmen and officers. The patrol has an identification bureau for the detection of crime and the identification of criminals. An auto theft and information bureau and a crime detection laboratory are maintained.

The state has a maximum security penitentiary at Jefferson City, which was opened in 1836 and is one of the largest in the nation. The Algoa Farms near Jefferson City is an intermediate reformatory for young men and has a minimum security unit. The Church Farm unit, also near Jefferson City, is a minimum security unit for prisoners about to be released. An appropriation of $15,000,000 has been made to construct a medium security prison to be built near Moberly.

5. ECONOMIC ACTIVITIES

In 1965 the per capita income in Missouri was $2,845, which was slightly above the national average. Missourians derived this income from a wide variety of occupations. By August 1966, Missouri's labor force totaled 1,713,200 persons, of whom 195,500 were agricultural workers. Persons employed in nonagricultural establishments numbered 1,517,700, of whom 28.6 per cent were engaged in manufacturing, 22.3 per cent in wholesale and retail trade, and 15.6 per cent in government (including local, state, and federal governments). The remainder were engaged in service industries; in transportation, communication, and other public utilities; in construction; in finance, insurance, and real estate; and in mining and quarrying.

Agriculture.—Historically, agriculture has been Missouri's chief industry, but in recent years manufacturing has surpassed it both in value of production and in the number of persons employed. Nevertheless, the state ranks in the upper ten in the total value of farm products.

Missouri's agriculture is built heavily around its livestock industry, with over 70 per cent of cash income being derived from meat animals, dairy, and poultry. About 11,392,000 acres are planted each year to harvested crops, accounting for almost 35 per cent of the total acreage in farms. In 1965 the total value of farm property was estimated at about $2.9 billion, and the value of all farm products sold, including livestock, totaled $1,383,000,000. Because of a diversity of agricultural products, ranging from corn and wheat to cotton and tobacco, the state's crop production is widely varied. Hay production amounts to 4.8 million short tons per year. In excess of 4 million acres are planted to corn each year, with a production of about 175 million bushels. Corn and hay are used on the farm for feed, with little reaching the central markets. Wheat and soybeans are the leading cash crops, wheat bringing in about $70 million and soybeans, more than $160 million.

Mining.—In recent years, Missouri's diversified mineral production has ranked the state between 21st and 23d among the states. The state has led in lead output for many years (125,412 short tons in 1955 valued at $37,422,941), and is usually first or second in barite production (363,-692 short tons in 1955 valued at $4,003,842). Other leading minerals include cement, 12,255,346 short tons ($34,912,186); lime, 1,464,828 ($14,-408,279); coal, 3,232,485 ($12,771,570); and zinc, silver, sand and gravel, copper, native asphalt, natural gas, and nickel.

Manufacturing.—Missouri ranks among the top 12 states in manufacturing. In the 1950's and 1960's it made rapid advances in the manufacture of airplanes, missiles, and jet engines. However, production is varied, since the state has 319 of the 446 types of manufactures listed by the Bureau of the Census. The types of industry that rank high in the state are transportation equipment, motor vehicles, food products, beverages, chemicals, fabricated metal products, leather and leather goods, printing and publishing, electric machinery, apparel, and stone, clay, and glass products.

The state is a leader in some industry specialties because of its natural resources: for example, firebrick is an important industry in east central Missouri because fireclay is prevalent, and glass is made in an area just south of St. Louis because fine silica sand is abundant there. The Portland cement industry and the high production of limestone and marble are due to the abundance of limestone in many sections of the state and marble in the southwest near Carthage. Other specialties such as beer, shoes, clothing, and automobiles have been important in Missouri because of early development, local resources, and central location.

Manufacturing is Missouri's most important economic activity, and it has continued to expand more rapidly in recent years than has agriculture. In 1953, 368,000 Missourians were employed in manufacturing, while 382,021 were employed in 1963. The earnings of persons engaged in manufacturing advanced from $1,420,000,000 to $2,065,-877,000 in this 10-year period. The value added by manufacturing also increased, from $2,727,266,-000 to $4,296,000,000, in this same period.

Banking.—As of June 30, 1966, the banking facilities of the state were supplied by 554 state-chartered banks and 96 national banks with combined assets of $9,498,525,211. Missouri has two Federal Reserve banks, one in St. Louis and the other in Kansas City. Each serves the large trade territory of which the home city is the center.

Trade.—Wholesale trade in the state totaled $12,307,000,000 in 1963, with most of the trade centering in St. Louis ($6,582,000,000) and Kansas City ($5,070,000,000). In St. Louis, the leading wholesale businesses were those handling groceries, drugs, chemicals and allied products, farm products, electrical appliances, and machinery equipment. In recent decades, the women's apparel trade has achieved a vigorous growth in St. Louis.

Retail sales throughout the state in 1963 amounted to $5,946,184,000, with the St. Louis metropolitan area ranking 10th among all metropolitan areas as a retail market in the United States. Between 1948 and 1963 retail sales in the St. Louis area climbed from $1,539,391,000 to $2,427,460,000; this was an increase of about 55 percent.

The Kansas City metropolitan area, which is dominated to a great extent by the grain and livestock area to the west, is also a major distribution center for farm machinery, automobiles and parts, and construction materials consumed by the Southwest and the Great Plains areas. Its retail trade sales increased from $977,244,000 in 1948 to $1,682,724,000 in 1963. In the latter year the Kansas City metropolitan area ranked 15th in retail sales in the nation.

Tourism.—Since the development of state parks and power dams in Ozark regions, Missouri has had a very rapidly developing recreational and tourist business. In recent years the State Division of Resources and Development, the official agency that promotes recreation, has reported that annual recreation income amounts to approximately $250,000,000 or four times the amount of recreation income in 1938.

Transportation.—The location of Missouri at the crossroads of the nation makes the state a major unit in the transportation and communication fields. The state has 11,202 miles of railroad track (8,147 line miles), and both St. Louis and Kansas City are great railroad terminals served by 22 trunk line systems. Also, St. Louis has 275 truck carriers providing daily freight service to 45 states and Canada.

Both metropolitan cities have large air terminals served by nine major airlines that connect directly with the major cities of the continent. A new Kansas City air terminal was nearing completion in 1968, at a cost of $150 million. When completed, it will be one of the largest terminals in the center of the United States. The largest jets will be able to land. Adjacent to the terminal are the TWA shops for the repair and servicing of large jets.

All highways in the state total 74,777 miles, about 60,000 miles of which are surfaced. The state maintains over 31,000 miles of the surfaced roads: 8,283 miles are primary roads, 22,653 miles are supplementary roads, and 650 miles are interstate highways. The total cost of the state system was $1,879,804,950.

Communications.—In 1968 the state was served by 128 commercial broadcasting stations, of which 89 were AM, 20 were FM, and 19 were television stations. Over 95 percent of all Missouri families owned radios. There were 2,228,-617 telephones in use in Missouri, of which 607,162 were business phones. The state is served by 1,292 post offices whose annual gross receipts amount to $100,000,000.

There were 388 weekly newspapers and 55 daily newspapers published in the state in 1968. Total circulation (combined daily and Sunday) ran above 3 million. The St. Louis *Post-Dispatch,* the St. Louis *Globe-Democrat,* and the Kansas City *Star* are dailies of outstanding reputation and influence.

6. PLACES OF INTEREST

Parks.—Of the more than 20 state parks, ranging in size from 16,148 acres (Lake of the Ozarks) to 34 acres (Arrow Rock State Park), 9 are in the Ozarks. Several of these include big springs, and most of them are in good fishing areas and have camping facilities. Three are of historical interest, two containing the birthplaces of Mark Twain (Florida) and of Gen. John J. Pershing (Laclede), and the third including Arrow Rock Tavern, a meeting place for men significant in the early history of the West. Mention should be made also of the private

MISSOURI

COUNTIES

Adair, 22,472 G 2
Andrew, 11,913 C 3
Atchison, 9,240 B 2
Audrain, 25,362 J 4
Barry, 19,597 E 9
Barton, 10,431 D 7
Bates, 15,468 D 6
Benton, 9,695 F 6
Bollinger, 8,820 M 8
Boone, 80,911 H 4
Buchanan, 86,915 C 3
Butler, 33,529 M 9
Caldwell, 8,351 E 3
Callaway, 25,850 J 5
Camden, 13,315 G 6
Cape Girardeau, 49,350 N 8
Carroll, 12,565 F 4
Carter, 3,878 L 9
Cass, 39,448 D 5
Cedar, 9,424 E 7
Chariton, 11,084 F 3
Christian, 15,124 F 9
Clark, 8,260 J 2
Clay, 123,322 D 4
Clinton, 12,462 D 3
Cole, 46,228 H 6
Cooper, 14,732 G 5
Crawford, 14,828 K 7
Dade, 6,850 E 8
Dallas, 10,054 F 7
Daviess, 8,420 E 3
De Kalb, 7,305 D 3
Dent, 11,457 J 7
Douglas, 9,268 G 9
Dunklin, 33,742 M10
Franklin, 55,116 K 6
Gasconade, 11,878 J 6
Gentry, 8,060 D 2
Greene, 152,929 F 8
Grundy, 11,819 E 2
Harrison, 10,257 E 2
Henry, 18,451 E 6
Hickory, 4,481 F 7
Holt, 6,654 B 2
Howard, 10,561 G 4
Howell, 23,521 J 9
Iron, 9,529 L 7
Jackson, 654,558 D 5
Jasper, 79,852 D 8
Jefferson, 105,248 L 6
Johnson, 34,172 E 5
Knox, 5,692 H 2
Laclede, 19,944 G 7
Lafayette, 26,626 E 4
Lawrence, 24,585 E 8
Lewis, 10,993 J 2
Lincoln, 18,041 L 4
Linn, 15,125 F 3
Livingston, 15,368 E 3
Macon, 15,432 G 3
Madison, 8,641 M 8
Maries, 6,851 J 6
Marion, 28,121 J 3
McDonald, 12,357 D 9
Mercer, 4,910 E 2
Miller, 15,026 H 6
Mississippi, 16,647 O 9
Moniteau, 10,742 G 5
Monroe, 9,542 H 3
Montgomery, 11,000 K 5
Morgan, 10,068 G 6
New Madrid, 23,420 N 9
Newton, 32,901 D 9
Nodaway, 22,467 C 2
Oregon, 9,180 K 9
Osage, 10,994 J 6
Ozark, 6,226 H 9
Pemiscot, 26,373 N10
Perry, 14,393 N 7
Pettis, 34,137 F 5
Phelps, 29,481 J 7
Pike, 16,928 K 4
Platte, 32,081 C 4
Polk, 15,415 F 7
Pulaski, 53,781 H 7
Putnam, 5,916 F 2
Ralls, 7,764 J 3
Randolph, 22,434 G 3
Ray, 17,599 E 4
Reynolds, 6,106 L 8
Ripley, 9,803 L 9
Saint Charles, 92,954 L 5
Saint Clair, 7,667 E 6
Sainte Genevieve, 12,867 M 7
Saint Francois, 36,818 M 7
Saint Louis, 951,353 M 5
Saint Louis (city county), 622,236 M 5
Saline, 24,633 F 4
Schuyler, 4,665 G 2
Scotland, 5,499 H 2
Scott, 33,250 N 8
Shannon, 7,196 K 8
Shelby, 7,906 H 3
Stoddard, 25,771 N 9
Stone, 9,921 F 9
Sullivan, 7,572 F 2
Taney, 13,023 F 9
Texas, 18,320 J 8
Vernon, 19,065 D 7
Warren, 9,699 K 5
Washington, 15,086 L 7
Wayne, 8,546 L 8
Webster, 15,562 G 8
Worth, 3,359 D 2
Wright, 13,667 H 8

CITIES and TOWNS

Adrian, 1,259 D 6
Advance, 903 N 8
Affton, 24,067 P 3
Airport Drive, 300 C 8
Alba, 365 D 8
Albany⊙, 1,804 D 2
Alexandria, 453 K 2
Allenton, 800 N 3
Alma, 380 E 4
Altamont, 225 D 3
Altenburg, 277 O 7
Alton⊙, 715 K 9
Amazonia, 326 C 3
Amoret, 219 C 6
Anderson, 1,065 D 9
Annapolis, 330 L 8
Anniston, 515 O 9
Appleton City, 1,058 D 6
Arbor Terrace■, 1,440 P 3
Arbyrd, 575 M10
Arcadia, 627 L 7
Archie, 525 D 5
Argyle, 262 J 6
Armstrong, 354 G 4
Arnold, 1,950 P 4
Asbury, 201 C 8
Ash Grove, 934 E 8
Ashland, 769 H 5
Atlanta, 377 H 3
Augusta, 259 M 3
Aurora, 5,359 E 9
Auxvasse, 808 J 4
Ava⊙, 2,504 G 9
Avondale, 748 P 5
Ballwin, 10,656 O 3
Baring, 206 H 2
Barnard, 206 C 2
Barnett, 167 G 6
Bates City, 229 E 5
Battlefield, 291 F 8
Belgrade, 349 L 7
Bella Villa■, 1,419 P 3
Bell City, 424 N 8
Belle, 1,133 J 6
Bellefontaine Neighbors, 13,987 R 2
Bellerive■, 437 P 3
Belleview, 225 L 7
Bellflower, 360 K 4
Bel-Nor■, 2,085 P 3
Bel-Ridge■, 5,561 P 2
Belton, 9,783 C 5
Benton⊙, 640 O 8
Berdell Hills■, 449 P 3
Berger, 226 K 5
Berkeley, 19,743 P 2
Bernie, 1,641 M 9
Bertrand, 604 O 9
Bethany⊙, 2,914 E 2
Beulah, 160 J 7
Beverly Hills■, 846 P 3
Bevier, 806 G 3
Billings, 760 F 8
Birch Tree, 573 K 9
Birmingham, 266 P 5
Bismarck, 1,387 L 7
Blackburn, 294 F 4
Black Jack, 3,500 P 2
Blackwater, 249 G 5
Blairstown, 161 E 5
Bland, 621 J 6
Blodgett, 220 O 8
Bloomfield⊙, 1,584 M 9
Bloomsdale, 411 M 6
Blue Springs, 6,779 R 6
Blue Summit, 1,283 R 5
Blythedale, 213 E 2
Bogard, 294 E 4
Bois D'Arc, 250 F 8
Bolckow, 225 C 2
Bolivar⊙, 4,769 F 7
Bonne Terre, 3,622 L 7
Bonnots Mill, 210 J 5
Boonville⊙, 7,514 G 5
Boss, 180 K 7
Bosworth, 386 F 4
Bourbon, 955 K 6
Bowling Green⊙, 2,936 K 4
Braggadocio, 285 N10
Bragg City, 210 N10
Branson, 2,175 F 9
Brashear, 316 H 2
Braymer, 919 E 3
Breckenridge, 598 E 3
Breckenridge Hills, 7,011 O 2
Brentwood, 11,248 P 3
Bridgeton, 19,992 O 2
Bridgeton Terrace■, 332 P 2
Bronaugh, 203 C 7
Brookfield, 5,491 F 3
Browning, 412 F 2
Brunswick, 1,370 F 4
Bucklin, 654 G 3
Buckner, 1,695 R 5
Buffalo⊙, 1,915 F 7
Bunceton, 437 G 5
Bunker, 447 K 8
Burlington Junction, 634 B 2
Butler⊙, 3,984 D 6
Cabool, 1,848 H 8
Cadet, 300 L 6
Cainsville, 454 E 2
Cairo, 248 H 4
Calhoun, 360 E 6
California⊙, 3,105 H 5
Callao, 373 G 3
Calverton Park■, 2,025 P 2
Camden, 286 D 4
Camden Point, 192 C 4
Camdenton⊙, 1,636 G 6
Cameron, 3,960 D 3
Campbell, 1,979 M 9
Canalou, 358 N 9
Canton, 2,680 J 2
Cape Girardeau, 31,282 O 8
Cardwell, 859 M10
Carl Junction, 1,661 C 8
Carrollton⊙, 4,847 E 4
Carterville, 1,716 D 8
Carthage⊙, 11,035 D 8
Caruthersville⊙, 7,350 N10
Cassville⊙, 1,910 E 9
Catawissa, 250 N 4
Cedar City, 454 H 5
Cedar Hill, 500 L 6
Center, 588 J 3
Centertown, 277 H 5
Centerview, 234 E 5
Centerville⊙, 209 L 8
Centralia, 3,618 H 4
Chaffee, 2,793 N 8
Chamois, 615 J 5
Charlack■, 1,872 P 3
Charleston⊙, 5,131 O 9
Chesterfield, 2,350 O 3
Chilhowee, 297 E 5
Chillicothe⊙, 9,519 E 3
Chula, 244 F 3
Clarence, 1,050 H 3
Clark, 271 H 4
Clarksburg, 343 G 5
Clarksdale, 248 D 3
Clarkson Valley, 157 N 3
Clarksville, 668 K 4
Clarkton, 1,177 M10
Claycomo, 1,841 P 5
Clayton⊙, 16,222 P 3
Clearmont, 226 C 1
Cleveland, 256 C 5
Clever, 430 F 8
Clifton Hill, 174 G 4
Clinton⊙, 7,504 E 6
Clyde, 158 C 2
Cobalt City■, 238 M 7
Coffey, 157 E 2
Cole Camp, 1,038 F 6
Columbia⊙, 58,804 H 5
Columbia, ‡80,911 H 5
Commerce, 234 O 8
Conception Junction, 237 C 2
Concord■, 21,217 P 3
Concordia, 1,854 E 5
Conway, 547 G 7
Cool Valley■, 1,291 P 2
Cooter, 414 N10
Corder, 476 E 4
Cottleville, 275 N 2
Country Club Hills■, 1,644 P 3
Country Club Village, 221 C 3
Cowgill, 232 E 3
Craig, 369 B 2
Crane, 1,003 E 9
Creighton, 294 D 6
Crescent, 425 N 3
Crestwood, 15,398 O 3
Creve Coeur, 8,967 O 3
Crocker, 814 H 7
Cross Timbers, 204 F 6
Crystal City, 3,898 M 6
Crystal Lake Park■, 356 P 3
Cuba, 2,070 K 6
Curryville, 337 K 4
Darlington, 164 D 2
Dawn, 176 E 3
Dearborn, 543 C 3
Deepwater, 565 E 6
Deerfield, 200 D 7
De Kalb, 287 C 3
Dellwood■, 7,137 P 2
Delta, 462 N 8
Des Arc, 222 L 8
Desloge, 2,818 M 7
De Soto, 5,984 M 6
Des Peres, 5,333 O 3
Dexter, 6,024 N 9
Diamond, 554 D 9
Diehlstadt, 155 N 9
Dixon, 1,387 H 6
Doe Run, 900 M 7
Doniphan⊙, 1,850 L 9
Doolittle, 509 J 7
Dorena, 500 O 9
Downing, 406 H 2
Drexel, 723 C 6
Dudley, 248 M 9
Duenweg, 656 D 8
Duquesne, 738 D 8
Durham, 160 J 3
Eagleville, 388 D 2
East Lynne, 255 D 5
Easton, 183 C 3
East Prairie, 3,275 O 9
Edgar Springs, 450 J 7
Edgerton, 477 C 4
Edina⊙, 1,574 H 2
Edmundson■, 1,608 P 2
Eldon, 3,520 G 6
El Dorado Springs, 3,300 E 7
Elkland, 196 F 8
Ellington, 1,094 L 8
Ellisville, 4,681 N 3
Ellsinore, 342 L 9
Elmer, 193 G 3
Elmo, 199 B 1
Elsberry, 1,398 L 4
Elvins, 1,603 L 7
Eminence⊙, 520 K 8
Emma, 224 F 5
Eolia, 321 L 4
Essex, 493 N 9
Esther, 1,040 M 7
Ethel, 162 G 3
Eugene, 163 H 6
Eureka, 2,384 N 3
Everton, 264 E 8
Ewing, 330 J 2
Excelsior Springs, 9,411 R 4
Exeter, 434 D 9
Fairfax, 835 B 2
Fair Grove, 431 F 8
Fair Play, 328 E 7
Fairview, 263 D 9
Farber, 470 J 4
Farley, 174 O 4
Farmington⊙, 6,590 M 7
Faucett, 190 C 3
Fayette⊙, 3,520 G 4
Fenton, 2,275 P 3
Ferguson, 28,915 P 2
Festus, 7,530 M 6
Fidelity■, 191 D 8
Fillmore, 251 C 2
Fisk, 503 M 9
Flat River, 4,550 M 7
Fletcher, 200 L 6
Flordell Hills■, 989 P 2
Florissant, 65,908 P 2
Foley, 224 L 4
Fordland, 399 G 8
Forest City, 365 B 3
Foristell, 273 M 2
Forsyth⊙, 803 F 9
Fortuna, 175 G 5
Foster, 178 D 6
Frankford, 472 K 4
Franklin, 252 G 4
Fredericktown⊙, 3,799 M 7
Freeburg, 577 J 6
Freeman, 417 C 5
Frohna, 225 N 7
Frontenac, 3,920 O 3
Fulton⊙, 12,148 J 5
Gainesville⊙, 627 G 9
Galena⊙, 391 F 9
Gallatin⊙, 1,833 E 3
Galt, 261 F 2
Garden City, 633 D 5
Gasconade, 235 J 5
Gerald, 762 K 6
Gideon, 1,112 N10
Gilliam, 248 F 4
Gilman City, 376 D 2
Gladstone, 23,128 P 5
Glasgow, 1,336 G 4
Glenaire, 505 R 5
Glencoe, 2,500 N 3
Glendale, 6,891 P 3
Glenwood, 184 G 1
Golden City, 810 D 8
Goodfellow Terrace■, 744 P 3
Goodman, 565 C 9
Gorin, 220 H 2
Gower, 758 C 3
Graham, 213 C 2
Grain Valley, 709 S 6
Granby, 1,678 D 9
Grandin, 243 L 9
Grandview, 17,456 P 6
Graniteville, 375 L 7
Grant City⊙, 1,095 D 2
Grantwood■, 994 P 3
Gravois Mills, 34 G 6
Grayridge, 300 N 9
Gray Summit, 950 M 3
Green Castle, 235 G 2
Green City, 629 F 2
Greendale■, 972 P 3
Greenfield⊙, 1,172 E 8
Green Ridge, 403 F 5
Greentop, 351 H 2
Greenville⊙, 328 M 8
Greenwood, 925 R 6
Grover, 550 O 3
Hale, 461 F 3
Half Way, 200 F 7
Hallsville, 790 H 4
Hamilton, 1,645 E 3
Hanley Hills■, 2,104 P 3
Hannibal, 18,609 K 3
Hardin, 683 E 4
Harris, 174 F 2
Harrisonville⊙, 4,928 D 5
Hartville⊙, 524 G 8
Harviell, 160 M 9
Hawk Point, 354 K 5
Hayti, 3,841 N10
Haywood City■, 420 N 8
Hazelwood, 14,082 P 2
Hematite, 300 L 6
Hemple, 350 D 3
Henrietta, 466 E 4
Herculaneum, 1,885 M 6
Hermann⊙, 2,658 K 5
Hermitage⊙, 284 F 7
Higbee, 641 H 4
Higginsville, 4,318 E 4
High Hill, 192 K 5
High Ridge, 350 O 4
Hillsboro⊙, 432 L 6
Hillsdale■, 2,599 P 3
Holcomb, 593 N10
Holden, 2,089 E 5
Holland, 329 N10
Holliday, 167 H 3
Hollister, 906 F 9
Holt, 319 D 4
Homestown■, 273 N10
Hopkins, 656 C 1
Horine, 850 M 6
Hornersville, 693 M10
House Springs, 500 O 4
Houston⊙, 2,178 J 8
Houstonia, 312 F 5
Houston Lake■, 338 O 5
Howardville■, 500 N 9
Humansville, 825 E 7
Hume, 350 C 6
Hunnewell, 304 J 3
Huntleigh■, 714 P 3
Huntsville⊙, 1,442 H 4
Hurdland, 225 H 2
Hurricane Deck, 169 G 6
Iantha, 165 D 8
Iberia, 741 H 6
Illmo, 1,232 O 8
Imperial, 900 P 4
Independence⊙, 111,662 R 5
Irondale, 319 L 7
Iron Gates■, 367 D 8
Ironton⊙, 1,452 L 7
Jackson⊙, 5,896 N 8
Jameson, 172 E 2
Jamesport, 614 E 3
Jamestown, 243 G 5

⊙ County seat. ‡ Population of metropolitan area. ■ Name not shown on map.

All figures available from 1970 final census are supplemented by local official estimates.

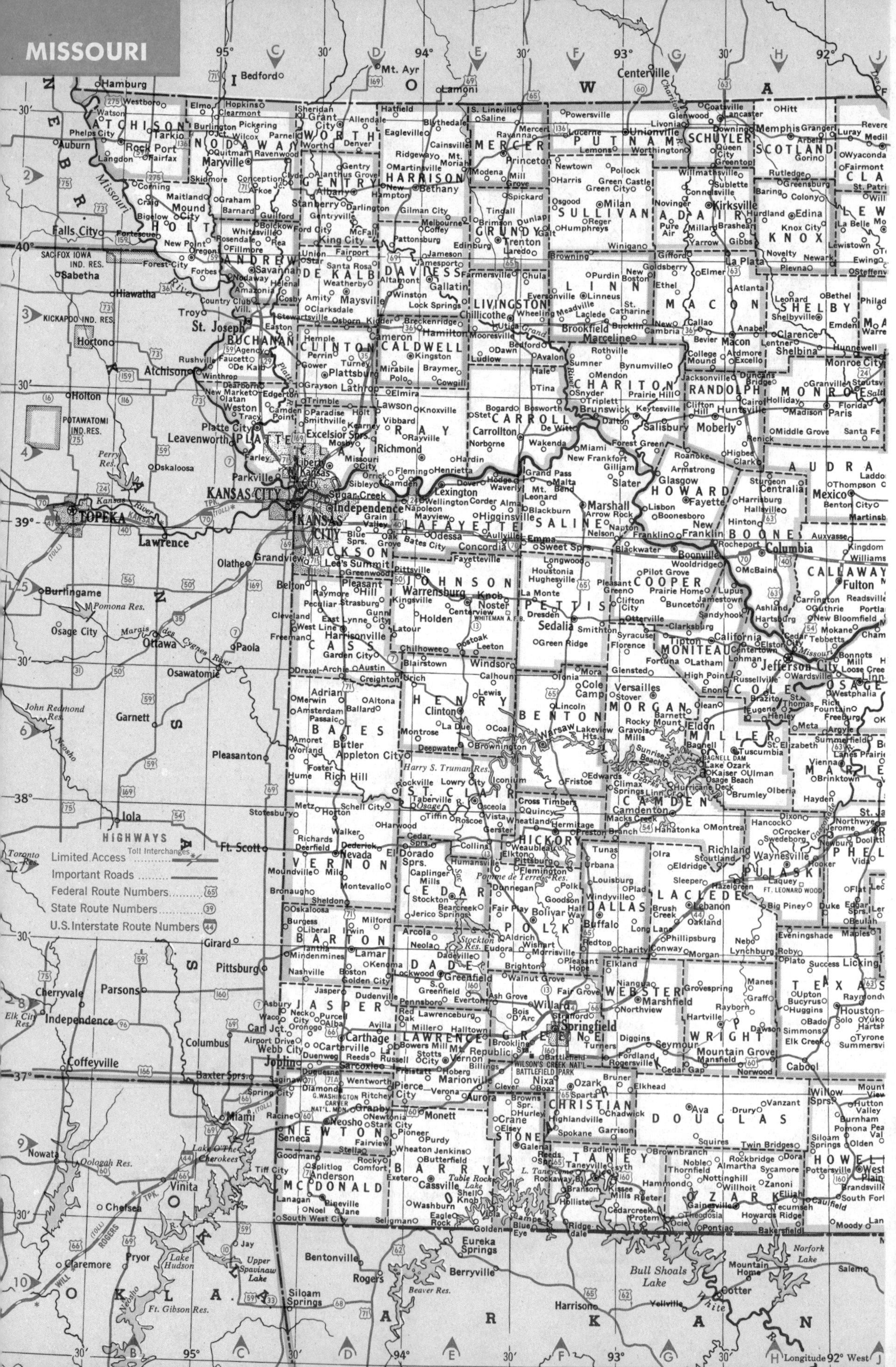
MISSOURI
HIGHWAYS
Limited Access
Toll Interchanges
Important Roads
Federal Route Numbers
State Route Numbers
U.S. Interstate Route Numbers
Longitude 92° West
IOWA
NEBRASKA
KANSAS
OKLAHOMA
ARKANSAS
ATCHISON
NODAWAY
WORTH
HARRISON
MERCER
PUTNAM
SCHUYLER
SCOTLAND
HOLT
GENTRY
GRUNDY
SULLIVAN
ADAIR
KNOX
ANDREW
DE KALB
DAVIESS
LINN
MACON
SHELBY
BUCHANAN
CLINTON
CALDWELL
LIVINGSTON
CHARITON
RANDOLPH
MONROE
PLATTE
CLAY
RAY
CARROLL
HOWARD
AUDRAIN
JACKSON
LAFAYETTE
SALINE
BOONE
CALLAWAY
CASS
JOHNSON
PETTIS
COOPER
MONITEAU
COLE
OSAGE
BATES
HENRY
BENTON
MORGAN
MILLER
MARIES
ST. CLAIR
HICKORY
CAMDEN
PULASKI
PHELPS
VERNON
CEDAR
POLK
DALLAS
LACLEDE
BARTON
DADE
WEBSTER
WRIGHT
TEXAS
JASPER
LAWRENCE
GREENE
CHRISTIAN
DOUGLAS
HOWELL
NEWTON
BARRY
STONE
TANEY
OZARK
McDONALD
Kansas City
St. Joseph
Springfield
Jefferson City
Columbia
Joplin
Sedalia
Topeka

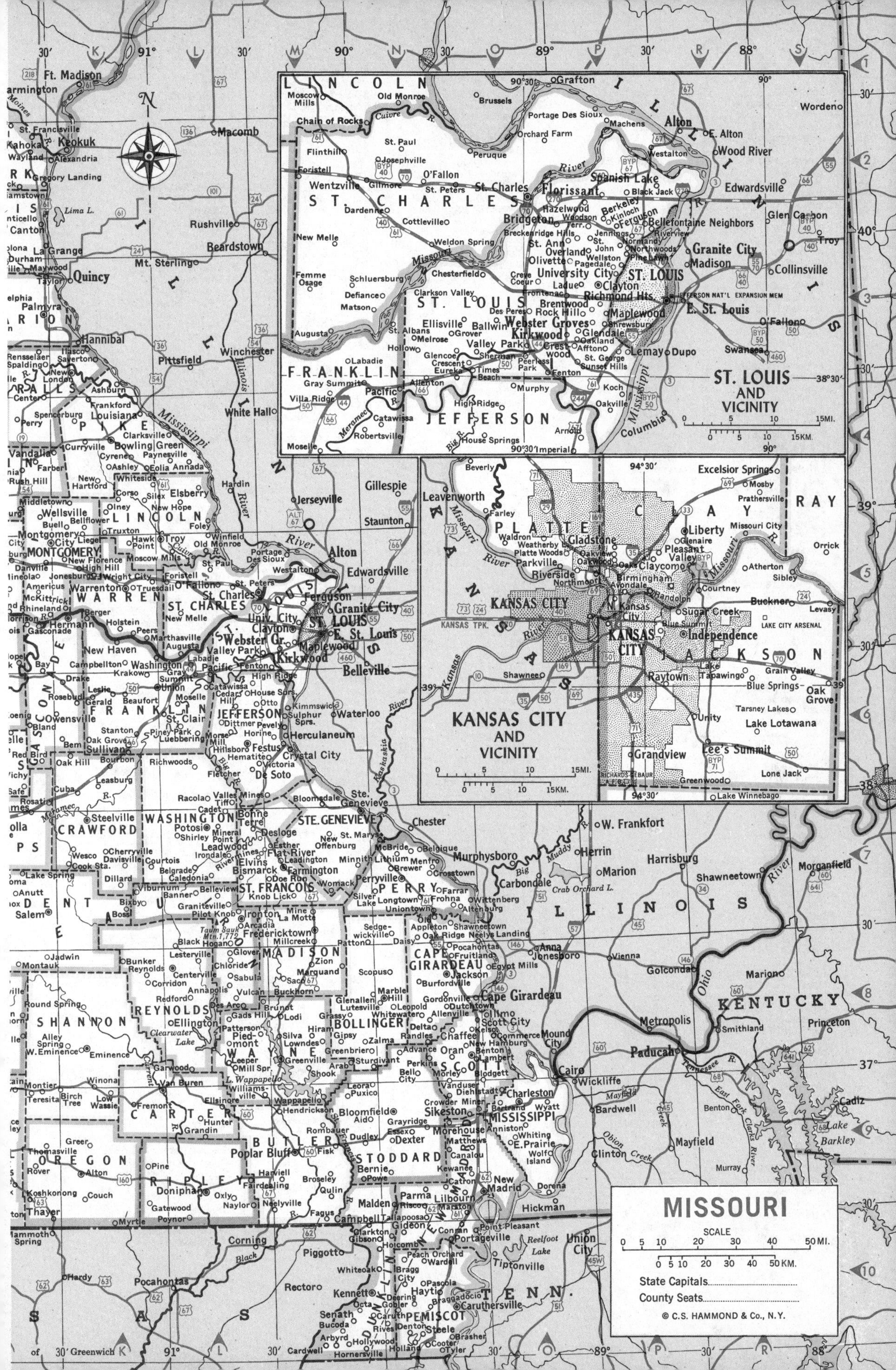
MISSOURI
SCALE
0 5 10 20 30 40 50 MI.
0 5 10 20 30 40 50 KM.
State Capitals
County Seats
© C.S. HAMMOND & Co., N.Y.
ST. LOUIS AND VICINITY
0 5 10 15 MI.
0 5 10 15 KM.
KANSAS CITY AND VICINITY
0 5 10 15 MI.
0 5 10 15 KM.
ILLINOIS
KENTUCKY
TENN.
ST. LOUIS
KANSAS CITY
Ohio River
Mississippi
Missouri River

MISSOURI

Jasper, 796 D 8
Jefferson City (cap.)⊙, 32,407 H 5
Jennings, 19,379 P 2
Jerico Springs, 188 E 7
Jerome, 200 J 7
Jonesburg, 479 K 5
Joplin, 39,256 C 8
Josephville, 250 N 2
Junction City■, 166 M 7
Kahoka⊙, 2,207 J 2
Kansas City, 507,087 P 5
Kansas City, ‡1,253,916 P 5
Kearney, 984 D 4
Kelso, 401 O 8
Kennett⊙, 9,852 M 10
Kewanee, 160 N 9
Keytesville⊙, 730 G 4
Kidder, 231 D 3
Kimmswick, 268 M 6
King City, 1,023 D 2
Kingston⊙, 291 E 3
Kingsville, 284 D 5
Kinloch, 5,629 P 2
Kirksville⊙, 15,560 H 2
Kirkwood, 31,890 O 3
Knob Lick, 200 M 7
Knob Noster, 2,264 E 5
Knox City, 284 H 2
Koch, 600 P 4
Koshkonong, 216 J 9
Krakow, 300 K 6
Labadie, 350 N 3
La Belle, 848 J 2
Laclede, 430 F 3
Laddonia, 745 J 4
Ladue, 10,491 P 3
La Grange, 1,237 K 2
Lake Lotawana, 1,786 R 6
Lake Ozark, 507 G 6
Lakeshire■, 1,186 P 3
Lake Tapawingo, 867 R 6
Lake Waukomis■, 1,105 P 5
Lake Winnebago, 432 R 6
Lamar⊙, 3,760 D 8
La Monte, 814 F 5
Lanagan, 374 C 9
Lancaster⊙, 821 H 1
La Plata, 1,377 H 2
Laredo, 383 E 2
Lathrop, 1,268 D 3
Lawson, 1,034 D 4
Leadington, 299 M 7
Leadwood, 1,397 L 7
Leasburg, 218 K 6
Leawood■, 174 D 8
Lebanon⊙, 8,616 G 7
Lee's Summit, 16,230 R 6
Leeton, 425 E 5
Lemay, 40,115 P 3
Lesterville, 275 L 8
Levasy, 283 S 5
Lewistown, 615 J 2
Lexington⊙, 5,388 E 4
Liberal, 644 D 7
Liberty⊙, 13,679 R 5
Licking, 1,002 J 8
Lilbourn, 1,152 N 9
Lincoln, 574 F 6
Linn⊙, 1,289 J 5
Linn Creek, 268 G 6
Linneus⊙, 400 F 3
Lockwood, 887 E 8
Loose Creek, 370 J 5
Louisiana, 4,533 K 4
Lowry City, 520 E 6
Ludlow, 175 E 3
Lutesville, 626 M 8
Mackenzie■, 1,392 P 3
Macon⊙, 5,301 H 3
Madison, 540 H 4
Maitland, 319 B 2
Malden, 5,374 M 9
Malta Bend, 342 F 4
Manchester■, 5,031 O 3
Mansfield, 1,056 G 8
Maplewood, 12,785 P 3
Marble Hill⊙, 589 N 8
Marceline, 2,622 F 3
Margona Village■, 321 P 3
Marionville, 1,496 E 8
Marlborough■, 1,459 P 3
Marquand, 400 M 8
Marshall⊙, 11,847 F 4
Marshfield⊙, 2,961 G 8
Marston, 666 N 9
Marthasville, 415 L 5
Martinsburg, 318 J 4
Maryland Heights■, 8,805 P 3
Mary Ridge■, 602 P 2
Maryville⊙, 9,970 C 2
Matthews, 538 N 9
Maysville⊙, 1,045 D 3
Mayview, 330 E 4
Maywood, 176 J 3
McFall, 203 D 2
Meadville, 409 F 3
Memphis⊙, 2,081 H 2
Mendon, 289 F 3
Mercer, 364 F 2
Meta, 387 H 6
Mexico⊙, 11,807 J 4
Miami, 205 F 4
Middletown, 235 J 4
Midway■, 234 D 9
Milan⊙, 1,794 F 2
Miller, 676 E 8
Mill Spring, 207 L 8
Mindenmines, 279 D 8
Mine La Motte, 200 M 7
Miner, 640 N 9
Mineral Point, 369 L 7
Missouri City, 375 R 5
Moberly, 12,988 G 4
Mokane, 398 J 5
Moline Acres■, 3,722 P 2
Monett, 5,937 E 9
Monroe City, 2,456 J 3
Montgomery City⊙, 2,187 K 5
Monticello⊙, 157 J 2
Montrose, 531 E 6
Morehouse, 1,332 N 9
Morley, 528 N 8
Morrison, 234 J 5
Morrisville, 256 F 8
Morse Mill, 200 L 6
Mosby, 337 R 4
Moscow Mills, 399 M 1
Mound City, 1,202 B 2
Mountain Grove, 3,377 H 8
Mountain View, 1,320 J 8
Mount Moriah, 165 E 2
Mount Vernon⊙, 2,600 E 8
Murphy, 900 O 4
Myrtle, 188 K 9
Napoleon, 263 E 4
Naylor, 586 L 9
Neelyville, 231 M 9
Nelson, 230 F 4
Neosho⊙, 7,517 D 9
Nevada⊙, 9,736 D 7
New Bloomfield, 427 J 5
Newburg, 806 J 7
New Cambria, 260 G 3
New Florence, 635 K 5
New Franklin, 1,122 G 4
New Hamburg, 185 O 8
New Hampton, 327 D 2
New Haven, 1,474 K 5
New London⊙, 967 K 3
New Madrid⊙, 2,719 O 9
New Melle, 225 M 2
Newtonia, 182 D 9
Newtown, 211 F 2
Niangua, 309 G 8
Nixa, 1,636 F 8
Noel, 924 D 9
Norborne, 950 E 4
Normandy, 6,306 P 3
North Kansas City, 5,183 P 5
North Lilbourn■, 334 N 9
Northmoor, 562 P 5
Northview, 200 G 8
Northwoods, 4,611 P 2
Norwood, 294 H 8
Novelty, 156 H 2
Novinger, 547 G 2
Oak Grove, 2,025 S 6
Oak Grove, 340 K 6
Oakland, 1,609 P 3
Oakland Park■, 156 D 8
Oak Ridge, 181 N 7
Oaks, 162 P 5
Oakview, 541 P 5
Oakville, 2,400 P 4
Oakwood, 163 P 5
Oakwood Manor■, 170 P 5
Oakwood Park■, 196 P 5
Odessa, 2,839 E 5
O'Fallon, 7,018 N 2
Old Monroe, 330 N 1
Olivette, 9,341 P 3
Oran, 1,226 N 8
Oregon⊙, 789 B 2
Oronogo, 492 D 8
Orrick, 883 D 4
Osage Beach, 1,091 G 6
Osborn, 338 D 3
Osceola⊙, 874 E 6
Otterville, 440 G 5
Overland, 24,949 P 3
Owensville, 2,416 K 6
Ozark⊙, 2,384 F 8
Pacific, 3,247 N 4
Pagedale, 5,571 P 3
Palmyra⊙, 3,188 J 3
Paradise, 200 D 4
Paris⊙, 1,442 J 4
Parkdale■, 836 L 6
Parkville, 1,253 O 5
Parkway■, 233 L 6
Parma, 1,051 N 9
Parnell, 232 C 2
Pasadena Hills■, 1,019 P 2
Pasadena Park■, 760 P 3
Pascola, 180 N 10
Patterson, 175 L 8
Patton, 195 M 7
Pattonsburg, 540 D 2
Peculiar, 705 D 5
Perry, 839 J 4
Perryville⊙, 5,149 N 7
Pevely, 517 M 6
Philadelphia, 200 J 3
Phillipsburg, 173 G 7
Pickering, 245 C 2
Piedmont, 1,906 L 8
Pierce City, 1,097 E 8
Pilot Grove, 701 G 5
Pilot Knob, 582 L 7
Pine Lawn, 5,773 P 3
Pineville⊙, 444 D 9
Platte City⊙, 2,022 C 4
Platte Woods, 484 O 5
Plattsburg⊙, 1,832 D 3
Pleasant Hill, 3,396 D 5
Pleasant Hope, 265 F 8
Pleasant Valley, 1,535 R 5
Pocahontas, 604 N 8
Polo, 438 D 3
Pomona, 250 J 9
Poplar Bluff⊙, 16,653 L 9
Portage Des Sioux, 509 P 2
Portageville, 3,117 N 10
Portland, 250 J 5
Potosi⊙, 2,761 L 7
Prairie Home, 231 G 5
Prathersville, 153 R 4
Princeton⊙, 1,328 E 2
Purcell, 325 D 8
Purdin, 236 F 3
Purdy, 588 E 9
Puxico, 759 M 9
Queen City, 588 H 2
Qulin, 496 M 9
Racine, 274 C 9
Randles, 170 N 8
Ravenwood, 336 C 2
Raymondville, 284 J 8
Raymore, 587 D 5
Raytown, 33,632 P 6
Rayville, 202 E 4
Redings Mill■, 179 D 8
Reeds Spring, 286 F 9
Renick, 188 H 4
Republic, 2,411 E 8
Revere, 184 J 2
Reynolds, 175 K 8
Rhineland, 190 J 5
Rich Fountain, 200 J 6
Rich Hill, 1,661 D 6
Richland, 1,783 H 7
Richmond⊙, 4,948 D 4
Richmond Heights, 13,802 P 3
Ridgeway, 469 D 2
Risco, 412 N 9
Rivermines, 402 L 7
Riverside, 2,123 O 5
Riverview, 3,741 R 2
Robertsville, 200 N 4
Roby, 175 H 7
Rocheport, 307 H 5
Rockaway Beach, 195 F 9
Rock Hill, 7,275 P 3
Rock Port⊙, 1,575 B 2
Rockville, 203 D 6
Rogersville, 574 G 8
Rolla⊙, 13,245 J 6
Rombauer, 200 M 9
Rosebud, 305 K 6
Rosendale, 245 C 2
Rushville, 300 B 3
Russellville, 557 H 6
Saginaw, 185 C 8
Saint Ann, 18,215 O 2
Saint Charles⊙, 31,834 O 2
Saint Clair, 2,978 L 6
Sainte Genevieve⊙, 4,468 M 6
Saint Elizabeth, 287 H 6
Saint George, 1,806 P 3
Saint James, 2,787 J 6
Saint John, 8,960 P 2
Saint Joseph⊙, 72,691 C 3
Saint Joseph, ‡86,915 C 3
Saint Jude Acres■, 246 M 7
Saint Louis⊙, 622,236 P 3
Saint Louis, ‡2,363,017 P 3
Saint Marys, 645 M 7
Saint Peters, 486 N 2
Saint Robert■, 1,279 H 7
Salem⊙, 4,363 J 7
Salisbury, 1,960 G 4
Sappington■, 10,603 P 3
Sarcoxie, 1,175 D 8
Savannah⊙, 3,324 C 3
Saverton, 160 K 3
Schell City, 367 D 6
Schuermann Heights■, 290 P 2
Scott City, 2,464 O 8
Sedalia⊙, 22,847 F 5
Seligman, 424 D 9
Senath, 1,484 M 10
Seneca, 1,577 C 9
Seymour, 1,208 G 8
Shelbina, 2,060 H 3
Shelbyville⊙, 601 H 3
Sheldon, 498 D 7
Sheridan, 251 C 1
Sherman, 200 O 3
Shoal Creek Drive■, 329 D 8
Shrewsbury, 5,896 P 3
Sibley, 279 S 5
Sikeston, 14,699 N 9
Silex, 306 K 4
Silver Creek■, 410 D 9
Skidmore, 440 B 2
Slater, 2,576 G 4
Smithton, 402 F 5
Smithville, 1,785 D 4
South West City, 453 D 9
Spanish Lake, 15,647 P 2
Sparta, 380 F 9
Spickard, 408 F 2
Springfield⊙, 120,096 F 8
Springfield, ‡152,929 F 8
Stanberry, 1,479 C 2
Stanton, 350 K 6
Steele, 2,107 N 10
Steelville⊙, 1,392 K 7
Stella, 197 D 9
Stewartsville, 634 C 3
Stockton⊙, 1,063 E 7
Stotts City, 203 E 8
Stoutland, 205 G 7
Stover, 849 G 6
Strafford, 491 F 8
Strasburg, 181 D 5
Sturgeon, 787 H 4
Sugar Creek, 4,755 R 5
Sullivan, 5,100 K 6
Summersville, 435 J 8
Sumner, 178 F 3
Sunnyvale■, 311 D 9
Sunset Hills, 3,728 P 3
Swedeborg, 175 H 7
Sweet Springs, 1,716 F 5
Sycamore Hills■, 821 P 3
Syracuse, 199 G 5
Tallapoosa, 200 N 9
Taneyville, 157 F 9
Tarkio, 2,517 B 2
Tarsney Lakes, 401 D 5
Thayer, 1,609 J 9
Times Beach, 1,265 O 3
Tina, 167 F 3
Tipton, 1,914 G 5
Town and Country■, 2,645 O 3
Tracy, 252 C 4
Trenton⊙, 6,063 E 2
Trimble, 206 D 4
Triplett, 191 F 4
Troy⊙, 2,538 L 5
Truesdail, 262 K 5
Tuscumbia⊙, 256 H 6
Ulman, 200 H 6
Union⊙, 5,183 L 6
Union Star, 417 C 2
Unionville⊙, 2,075 G 2
Unity, 242 R 6
University City, 46,309 P 3
Uplands Park■, 695 P 3
Urbana, 369 F 7
Urich, 433 E 6
Utica, 275 E 3
Valles Mines, 200 L 6
Valley Park, 3,662 O 3
Van Buren⊙, 714 L 8
Vandalia, 3,160 J 4
Vanduser, 306 N 9
Velda■, 2,134 P 3
Velda Village Hills■, 1,157 P 3
Verona, 515 E 9
Versailles⊙, 2,244 G 6
Viburnum, 520 K 7
Vichy, 250 J 6
Victoria, 250 M 6
Vida, 300 J 7
Vienna⊙, 505 H 6
Villa Ridge, 200 M 4
Vinita Park■, 3,684 P 3
Vinita Terrace■, 363 P 3
Vulcan, 200 L 8
Walker, 227 D 7
Walnut Grove, 442 F 8
Wappapello, 254 M 9
Wardell, 275 N 10
Wardsville, 460 H 5
Warrensburg⊙, 13,125 E 5
Warrenton⊙, 2,057 K 5
Warsaw⊙, 1,423 F 6
Warson Woods■, 2,544 P 3
Washburn, 250 E 9
Washington, 8,499 K 5
Watson, 164 A 1
Waverly, 827 E 4
Wayland, 467 J 2
Waynesville⊙, 3,375 H 7
Weatherby Lake, 832 O 5
Weaubleau, 343 F 7
Webb City, 6,811 C 8
Webster Groves, 26,995 P 3
Wellington, 720 E 4
Wellston, 7,050 P 3
Wellsville, 1,565 K 4
Wentzville, 3,223 M 2
Westalton, 435 R 2
Westboro, 234 B 1
Weston, 1,267 C 4
Westphalia, 332 J 6
West Plains⊙, 6,893 J 9
Westwood■, 311 P 3
Wheatland, 317 F 7
Wheaton, 360 E 9
Wheeling, 268 F 3
Wilbur Park■, 289 P 3
Willard, 1,018 F 8
Williamsville, 398 L 9
Willow Springs, 2,045 H 9
Wilson City■, 295 O 9
Winchester■, 2,329 O 3
Windsor, 2,734 E 5
Winfield, 620 L 5
Winona, 973 K 8
Winston, 189 D 3
Woods Heights■, 362 S 4
Woodson Terrace, 5,936 P 2
Wright City, 943 K 5
Wyaconda, 356 J 2
Wyatt, 562 O 9

OTHER FEATURES

Bagnell (dam) G 6
Big (riv.) L 6
Black (riv.) L 10
Bull Shoals (lake) G 10
Chariton (riv.) G 1
Clearwater (lake) L 8
Cuivre (riv.) N 2
Current (riv.) K 8
Des Moines (riv.) J 1
Fort Leonard Wood, 33,799 H 7
Gasconade (riv.) H 7
George Washington Carver Nat'l Mon. D 9
Grand (riv.) F 3
Jefferson Nat'l Expansion Mem. R 3
Lake City Arsenal R 5
Meramec (riv.) M 4
Mississippi (riv.) L 4
Missouri (riv.) H 5
Norfork (lake) H 10
Osage (riv.) E 6
Ozark (plat.) F 9
Ozarks (lake) G 6
Platte (riv.) C 3
Pomme de Terre (res.) E 7
Richards Gebaur A.F.B. P 6
Sac (riv.) E 7
Saint Francis (riv.) M 9
Salt (riv.) J 3
Stockton (res.) E 7
Table Rock (res.) E 9
Taneycomo (lake) F 9
Taum Sauk (mt.) L 7
Wappapello (lake) L 8
White (riv.) G 10
Whiteman A.F.B., 5,040 E 5
Wilson's Creek Nat'l Battlefield Park F 8

recreational centers on Lake Taneycomo and especially around the Lake of the Ozarks.

Memorials.—Jefferson National Expansion Memorial in St. Louis is a newly developed park along the river front. It contains various city landmarks, including the Old Rock House, built in 1818 for the Missouri Fur Company, the Old Court House, and the old Cathedral of Saint Louis. Also at St. Louis is the Soldiers' Memorial Building dedicated to St. Louis soldiers who died in World War I. The new Gateway Arch, the highest monument in the United States, is in the park and signifies that early St. Louis was the gateway to the West. Harry S Truman's birthplace at Lamar is now state owned and a historical monument.

Wildlife Refuges.—There are nearly 50 wildlife refuges, public and private, of which 3 are federal, 20 are located in state parks, and 10 are under the control of the state Department of Conservation. This agency has done excellent work in restocking the rivers and in restoring wildlife in game areas, particularly deer and wild turkeys.

Other Points of Interest.—Hannibal, the home of Mark Twain, is full of interest to anyone who enjoys reading about Huckleberry Finn or Tom Sawyer. St. Louis, aside from its many points of historical interest, has many beautiful modern sights to offer. Near the Union Station stands Carl Milles' fountain, *The Meeting of the Waters.* On Government Drive is the Polychrome Electric Fountain, a terraced limestone formation, illuminated by colored lights at night. The St. Louis Zoological Garden is famous for its large collections of animals and birds and many rare specimens. The Missouri Botanical Garden contains more than 12,000 species of trees and plants and is nationally known for its flower shows.

Cultural Activities.—St. Louis provides educational and cultural facilities, such as the City Art Museum and the Auditorium Opera House, in which are given concerts of the nationally known St. Louis Symphony Orchestra and presentations of the Grand Opera Association. The St. Louis Playgoers Association, the Light Opera Guild, and the St. Louis Artists Guild are other cultural organizations.

Kansas City boasts a philharmonic orchestra in addition to the William Rockhill Nelson Gallery of Art, the Mary Atkins Museum of Fine Arts, and the Kansas City Museum. See also KANSAS CITY; SAINT LOUIS; and articles on other Missouri cities.

7. FAMOUS MEN AND WOMEN

Among political leaders may be mentioned Thomas Hart Benton (1782–1858), born in North Carolina, who represented Missouri in the United States Senate for 30 years, and Francis Preston Blair (1821–1875), who, though born in Kentucky, lived in St. Louis and practiced law there. He organized the Free Soil Party, opposed slavery, and supported the Union during the Civil War. Missouri placed his statue in the United States Capitol. Richard Parks Bland (1835–1899), Kentucky-born lawyer who was a United States representative from Missouri for 24 years, was the leader of the free silver bloc and coauthor of the Bland-Allison Act remonetizing silver. Champ (James Beauchamp) Clark (1850–1921), born in Kentucky, was a United States representative from Missouri for many years and speaker of the House for eight years. Harry S Truman (1884–), born in Lamar, Mo., served as president of the United States from 1945 to 1953.

In the military field, Missouri is represented by two citizens of outstanding importance. John Joseph Pershing (1860–1948), born in Linn County, Mo., became a full general and commanded the American Expeditionary Force in World War I, and became army chief of staff in 1921; and Omar Nelson Bradley (1893–), born in Clark, Mo., became chief of staff, United States Army, in 1948, and served as chairman, Joint Chiefs of Staff, 1949–1953.

In science, Missouri is represented by William Pope McArthur (1814–1850), born in Ste. Genevieve, Mo., a naval officer and hydrographer who was the first surveyor of the Pacific Coast; George Washington Carver (c. 1864–1943), born near Diamond, Mo., an agricultural chemist known especially for his research on the industrial use of the peanut; and Harlow Shapley (1885–), astronomer, born in Nashville, Mo., director of Harvard College Observatory (1921–1952).

Literature and the arts have been favored by several very well-known natives of Missouri. These include Samuel Langhorne Clemens (Mark Twain, 1835–1910), humorist and author, born in Florida, Mo., and lived in Hannibal; Eugene Field (1850–1895), poet and journalist, born in St. Louis; Rupert Hughes (1872–1956), author, born in Lancaster, Mo., prolific writer of both fiction and plays; Sara Teasdale (1884–1933), poet, born in St. Louis; Zoë Akins (1886–1958), poet and playwright, born in Humansville, Mo., winner of the Pulitzer drama prize for 1934–1935; Thomas Stearns Eliot (1888–1965), poet and essayist, born in St. Louis; Augustus Thomas (1857–1934), playwright, born in St. Louis; James Carroll Beckwith (1852–1917), portrait painter, born in Hannibal, Mo.; Gladys Swarthout (1904–), soprano, born in Deepwater, Mo.; Helen Traubel (1903–), operatic and

Massie-Missouri Resources Division

The boyhood home of Mark Twain in Hannibal, and the whitewashed fence immortalized in "Tom Sawyer."

concert soprano, born in St. Louis, Mo.; and Thomas Hart Benton (1889–), artist, born in Neosho, Mo., painter of many famous murals.

Others of note include Susan Elizabeth Blow (1843–1916), educator, born in St. Louis, where she opened the first public kindergarten in the United States (1873); and Bernarr Macfadden (1868–1955), physical culturist and publisher, born near Mill Springs, Mo.

8. HISTORY

Early Settlement.—Missouri, with her role as the gateway to the West for the fur traders and Forty-niners and for settlers of Oregon, California, and Texas, and her tragic division of opinion as a border slave state in the 1860's, has had an unusually colorful history. White occupation began around 1700 with the establishment of French-Canadian villages just across the Mississippi. Young men on hunting trips up the Missouri began to mine lead in the St. Francis Valley. The state's first permanent settlement was made around 1735 at Ste. Genevieve, at the crossing to the lead country. After Illinois and the eastern half of the great Mississippi Valley were ceded by France to England in 1763, many French Canadians moved across the river. St. Louis, founded in the winter of 1763–1764 as a fur trading post, became a prosperous little town. Under the Spanish, to whom France had ceded the western Mississippi Valley, absolute government continued, and little trace of French influence remained in Missouri.

By the time of the Louisiana Purchase of 1803, settlers from east of the Mississippi constituted the majority of Missouri's population. Until 1815, the growth of population was slow, but after 1815, pioneers poured into Missouri, especially into lands along the Missouri and Mississippi rivers. By 1820 the population of Missouri Territory, which had been granted an elective legislature in 1812 and 1816, was over 66,000. St. Louis, Ste. Genevieve, and Franklin were the leading towns.

Statehood.—The admission of Missouri to statehood, for which she applied in 1818, precipitated the first clear-cut clash between Northern and Southern interests, when the House of Representatives at Washington proposed the exclusion of slavery from the new state. The result was the well-known Missouri Compromise (q.v.) of 1820, by which Missouri was admitted without restriction, but by which slavery was prohibited elsewhere in the Louisiana Purchase north of 36°30′, the southern boundary of the state. Due to a secondary dispute over free Negroes, Missouri was actually admitted by presidential proclamation on Aug. 10, 1821. Meanwhile, in 1820, Missouri had drawn up a constitution and had elected and organized a state government 10 months before her actual admission.

Devaney Inc.

A sternwheeler on the Mississippi at St. Louis.

Expansion and Trade.—The most important activity in the next three decades was the extension of settled areas and the conquest of the wilderness. The spread of settlement was chiefly in the plains areas. The dates of occupation and the emergence of more mature economic and social conditions in the different areas depended partly on the relative fertility of the soil but more significantly on the availability of river transportation. A considerable number of blue-grass Kentuckians, cashing in on increased land values, moved into Missouri with capital and slaves, and became the ruling class along the Missouri and Mississippi rivers. A similar society developed in the Platte Purchase, the northwestern corner (the original western boundary was a straight line) that was added to the state in 1837. Steamboats, the first of which reached St. Louis in 1817 and Franklin in 1819, were supplementing the rafts and flatboats, and stage lines of a sort were running from St. Louis to the western border of the state. Settlers were taking up the narrow fertile valleys in the Ozarks, but the real settlement of the rougher country awaited the 1850's.

The upper Missouri River fur trade and the Santa Fe trade provided romance and adventure. William Henry Ashley made a fortune in the fur trade from the area north of the Great Salt Lake. His Rocky Mountain Fur Company did not have fixed trading posts or hired hunters. The furs were gathered by the "mountain men," such as Jim Bridger and Jedediah Smith, who along with others took their furs each year to an agreed-upon rendezvous and got their supplies. In the 1830's the American Fur Company, managed by men from St. Louis and backed with capital from John Jacob Astor, forced out all competition. By the 1840's, the institutionalizing of the fur trade, the killing off of the beaver, and the coming of the silk hat were factors responsible for the decline of the fur trade and of the romance and adventure associated with it.

Furs from the southern Rockies went to St. Louis by the overland route from Santa Fe. The trade that grew up was carried on chiefly by individual adventurers who outfitted at western Missouri River towns, and rendezvoused for the annual caravan in southern Kansas. In their covered wagons they took out manufactured goods, especially textiles, and brought back fur, gold and silver bullion, horses, and jacks, sires of the Missouri mule. Individuals and small groups suffered severely from the Indians but caravans were seldom attacked. The trade was profitable, often netting 50 per cent, and took into Missouri as much as $200,000 in bullion in one year.

The hunters and fur traders were followed in the 1840's by an increasing migration of Missourians who settled in Oregon and California before the arrival of the Forty-niners. Missourians also were prominent in early Texas history, and Missouri volunteers under Col. Alexander Doniphan and Gen. Stephen W. Kearny had a key role in the conquering of New Mexico and California.

The Mormons furnished another colorful incident in Missouri's history. In 1831 their leader, Joseph Smith, went to Independence, declared it to be the future Zion of his church, and dedicated the temple site. After Smith's return east, the Mormons arrived at Independence in increasing numbers, and friction with the "gentiles" developed until mob violence, turning into guerrilla warfare, necessitated the calling out of the state militia. Eventually, the Mormons agreed to withdraw to Nauvoo, Ill., their last station before the long trek to Utah. Their combination of church and state, the fear that they would secure political control and their opposition to slavery caused concern. A Mormon faction still owns the temple site at Independence, which is also headquarters for the Reorganized Church of Jesus Christ of the Latter-day Saints.

Economic and Social Changes.—The economic and social changes of the 1850's transformed the state. Overland traffic developed with the gold rush to California in 1849 and to Colorado in 1859. From St. Louis, goods went by steamer to St. Joseph, then westward by ox and mule. St. Joseph was, in 1861, starting point of the Pony

Devaney Inc.

The skyline of Kansas City, with Union Depot in the foreground.

Express to California. The rapid development of the upper Mississippi Valley and the growing Southern market, because of its increasing specialization in cotton, were added stimuli to trade and to the growth of St. Louis. The coming of the railroads was the outstanding change. In addition to the need for better transportation within the state was the conviction, shared by Missouri's outstanding political leader, Senator Thomas Hart Benton, and St. Louis interests, that a railroad across the state would inevitably make St. Louis the eastern terminus of the proposed transcontinental railroad. Liquid capital for construction was lacking, however, and in 1851 the state lent $2,000,000 in state bonds to the proposed Pacific road to Kansas. Despite additional loans and state and federal land grants, the great expectations of railroad enthusiasts were not realized. But a beginning had been made, and clearly a new economic era was dawning.

In 1860, Missouri topped the million mark in population. More than half were natives of Missouri. Of the total white population, 15 per cent were born in free states, chiefly Ohio, Indiana, and Illinois, and about 15 per cent were foreign born, chiefly German and Irish. More than half of these were in St. Louis and constituted more than half of that city's population of 190,500. That is, nearly a third of the total population and nearly two thirds of the population of St. Louis were born in free states or abroad. In people, as in economics, the earlier Southern coloring was fading out. The institution of slavery itself was losing ground; the percentage of slaves in the total population, steadily declining since 1830, had dropped to about 9 per cent in 1860. The institution was holding its own only in some 20 of the older, richer river counties, in a few of which the percentage was over 25. Slaveholdings for the most part were small, and the majority of slaves were household or personal servants. Slave labor was used, however, in raising tobacco and hemp and even more for general farming.

The Civil War.—The political downfall of Thomas Hart Benton who, as Missouri's United States senator from 1821, had been one of the dominant leaders of the Democratic Party during the Jacksonian period, and the breakup of the Whig Party during the decade of the 1850's confused party politics in Missouri. Benton was never reconciled to the growing dominance of the Southern wing within the Democratic Party. His arrogance toward local party leaders and his failure to build up a personal machine were responsible for his defeat in the election of 1850. His defeat was a portent of the division that was to take place in ante-bellum Missouri politics. Benton's strong nationalism and anti-Southern views forced the victorious anti-Benton leaders generally into a close alliance with the Southern wing of the Democratic Party. In the presidential election of 1860, however, the rank and file of the party compelled them reluctantly to support Stephen A. Douglas, who just barely carried the state. In addition, troubles on the Missouri-Kansas border, having their origin in the Kansas-Nebraska Act, and agitated by the Border Ruffians, a collection of frontier roughnecks and ne'er-do-wells, further divided the state's politics.

The secession of South Carolina presented Missouri and the border slave states with a most difficult choice. Except for the Southern market, Missouri's economic interests were clearly Northern and Western. Consequently, there was increasing feeling for a strong federal government that would support Missouri's interest in westward expansion. On the other hand, the pro-Southern and well-to-do ruling groups in the older sections of Missouri looked eastward to Kentucky and Virginia as their original homelands, regarded the Southerners as kinsfolk, and therefore had strong states' rights feelings. Most Missourians hoped desperately for compromise and the avoidance of civil war. A convention meeting in March 1861 to determine Missouri's allegiance did not include a single advocate of immediate secession. It defeated the attempt of the pro-Southern minority to pledge Missouri to secession if compromise failed, and by a two-thirds majority pledged the state's support to any peaceful settlement.

When Governor Claiborne F. Jackson surreptitiously tried to push Missouri into the Confederacy by gathering a group of militia into a camp just outside St. Louis, federal forces under Nathaniel Lyon broke it up. On the militia's return, Lyon's forces fired into a civilian mob and the state was in an uproar. The governor called for 50,000 vounteers for a state army, but Lyon occupied Jefferson City, and the officials fled to the southwest. This federal interference and the unfortunate Camp Jackson affair certainly drove thousands of Missourians into Jackson's militia and eventually into the Confederate Army. In October 1861, Jackson convened a rump of the legislature at Neosho, which passed an ordinance of secession, and Missouri was formally admitted to the Confederacy. However, the decisive defeat of the Confederate Army early in 1862 at the Battle of Pea Ridge in Arkansas ended any chance of establishing a Confederate state government by force.

The old convention, controlled by the conservative Unionists, reconvened and appointed Hamilton R. Gamble, an old-line Whig, as provisional governor, and authorized him to borrow money and organize a militia. This loyal state government was recognized by Lincoln, who aided Gamble to equip his militia. Gamble and the convention—it did not dissolve until 1863—were moderate and conciliatory and won the acceptance if not the too active support of the great majority. Throughout 1862 and most of 1863, local government broke down over much of Missouri. There were local civil wars and guerrilla raids, accompanied by much destruction of public and private property. During 1864 law and order were slowly restored.

Reconstruction.—Meanwhile there was a steadily rising Radical opposition to the Gamble regime. Originally unconditional Unionists, the Radicals by 1863 were demanding immediate abolition of slavery and more drastic treatment of Confederate sympathizers. They won the election of 1864, which restored a regular state government and, in the Constitutional Convention of 1865, abolished slavery immediately and without compensation. Through the use of "ironclad" test oaths they sought to disfranchise and to exclude from the professions even passive sympathizers with the Confederacy. The new constitution was ratified by a narrow plurality, which had been provided by the absentee soldier vote.

The unpopularity of the Radicals was increased by their activities with the railroads. All the state-aided roads, except the Hannibal and St. Joseph, were hopelessly in arrears on the interest on the bonds lent to them. Their rolling stock was worn out, and rights of way were seriously damaged. The state finally foreclosed on most of the roads and sold them, recovering a little over $6,000,000 of an overall investment of more than $31,000,000. An important condition of the sale was the completion of the roads by the new owners. This was accomplished by 1872. Unverifiable stories of graft and favoritism, and numerous unsuccessful or fraudulent local railroad promotions added to the popular dissatisfaction with the Radical rule. The reorganized Democratic Party was hopelessly handicapped by the test oaths. However, a large minority of the Republicans had accepted the test oaths with reluctance. They regarded them as a temporary measure and demanded their repeal after the 15th Amendment in 1869 had given the Negro the vote. They demanded "universal suffrage and universal amnesty." Under the leadership of Carl Schurz these Liberal Republicans nominated a separate ticket in 1870, and with the aid of the Democrats elected B. Gratz Brown as governor. In the same election the voters repealed the test oaths and the Radical regime was over. The new constitution of 1875, therefore, was a reaction to the Radical Reconstruction rule. The attempt to make this coalition of Liberal Republicans and Democrats nationwide was defeated in the presidential campaign of 1872, and the local Liberals drifted back to the regular parties.

Later 19th Century Developments.—The last three decades of the century were a period of recovery and readjustment. Economically the state had suffered severely as a result of the war. Railroads were destroyed and bankrupt, the emancipated slaves had been worth at least $40,000,000, and, more important, Missouri had lost its chance of continuing as the single gateway to the Far West. By 1870 Chicago had surpassed St. Louis in population and influence and was emerging as the railroad, distribution, and meat-packing center of the upper Mississippi Valley, as well as the connecting link with the Far West. Nevertheless, the rapid spread of railroads across the state and into the Great Plains gave St. Louis and the emerging metropolis of Kansas City a new but restricted trading area, and both cities grew rapidly.

The farmer was passing through a period of falling prices and difficult transition from subsistence farming to a money economy. Dissatisfaction with railroads, low prices, and a restricted currency drove him into Grange politics in the 1870's and the Farmers' Alliance in the 1880's, but the state Democratic Party supported free silver, so that the Greenback and Populist parties never gained ascendancy. Conservatism in politics was manifest by a program of low taxes, economy, and a refusal to expand governmental activities and services. The Democratic Party was dominant after 1872, although its plurality was often small.

20th Century Politics.—The younger generation's growing impatience with conservatism was shown in the popularity of William Jennings Bryan, who carried the state in 1896 and 1900. In 1904, Theodore Roosevelt swept the state into the Republican column for the first time since Reconstruction days. As a result of the leadership of two reform governors, Joseph W. Folk and Herbert S. Hadley, Missouri adopted many progressive measures, such as the direct primary, stricter control of railroads, a pure food law, and the initiative and the referendum. After 1904, Missouri became a politically doubtful state, usually voting with the party that carried the nation. Missouri had its most spectacular intraparty struggle in 1939 when Governor Lloyd C. Stark broke with the Democratic organization of Thomas J. Pendergast in Kansas City and, with the assistance of United States District Attorney Maurice M. Milligan, convicted Boss Pendergast of income tax evasion.

This conflict within the Democratic Party, combined with the disgrace shed upon the Democrats by the uncovering of frauds in the election of 1936, broke the preponderance of Democratic strength and paved the way for Republicans to win the governorship in 1940 despite the victory

Mural entitled *Independence and the Opening of the West* adorns the rotunda of the Harry S. Truman Library at Independence, Mo. The painting is by Thomas Hart Benton, a native son of Missouri.

HARRY S. TRUMAN LIBRARY

of Democrats nationally. With the election of Missouri's Sen. Harry S. Truman as vice president of the United States and his subsequent elevation to the presidency following the death of Franklin D. Roosevelt in 1945, Missouri Democrats slowly began to rebuild their strength. From 1948 on, they again were the dominant party in state politics. In 1972 the Republicans elected their first governor, Christopher S. Bond, in 32 years, but Democrats still controlled both houses of the legislature and held nine of the state's ten congressional seats.

20th Century Social and Economic Changes. More important than party politics were the rapid social and economic changes that took place. After 1920, Missouri had moved into an era of expanded state services. The state highway system was planned and started in the 1920's. After that time, with the added help of federal funds, the highway system was constantly improved. The extension of the highway system opened the isolated sections and greatly altered the pattern of rural and urban life.

During the Depression of the 1930's, legislation was passed for the relief of the handicapped, the blind, and the unemployed. In 1937 a state social security commission, administering old-age benefits, and a state unemployment commission were organized. Despite these innovations, it soon became evident, in the face of demands for more social and economic legislation, that the constitution of 1875 was too restrictive and that a new constitution would have to replace the old. In order to keep pace with the increasingly popular philosophy of more governmental involvement in economic and social affairs, a new constitution embodying this principle was adopted in 1945.

The growth of high schools, both in number and enrollment, accelerated after 1920. The state budget for education rose constantly following World War II. In a 20-year period ending in the mid-1970's, the state budget increased 8½ times to a total of nearly $2 billion, of which more than 40 percent was earmarked for education. In 1950 the voters approved a constitutional amendment that would make it easier for school districts to raise levies for school support. Missouri faithfully complied with the U. S. Supreme Court ruling of 1954 outlawing segregation in public schools, and by 1956 the process of integration was almost completed.

Public and higher education in Missouri was reorganized between 1940 and the late 1960's. The one-room rural school disappeared as the number of districts was reduced sharply. Expenditures for education rose as new services increased. The system of higher education was expanded with the launching of the four-campus university system in 1963, and a state-supported public junior college program was authorized. In the following ten-year period, state college and university enrollment increased by 86 percent.

Missouri's economic growth was steady in the decades following World War II. Population grew moderately, and the metropolitan areas of St. Louis and Kansas City continued to spread. Manufacturing continued to increase in the two cities, with St. Louis becoming a center for airplane and missile production. Some manufacturing of specialties arose in the smaller cities. Farming continued to be a leading occupation, but it was distinctly second to manufacturing.

W. FRANCIS ENGLISH, *University of Missouri*

Bibliography

Atherton, Lewis, *Main Street on the Middle Border* (Ind. Univ. Press 1954).

Chambers, William N., *Old Bullion Benton, Senator from the New West* (Little 1956).

Federal Writers' Project, *Missouri: A Guide to the "Show Me" State* (1941; reprint, Scholarly Press 1972).

Geiger, Louis G., *Joseph W. Folk of Missouri* (Univ. of Mo. Press 1953).

Gist, Noel P., and others, *Missouri, Its Resources, People and Institutions* (Univ. of Mo. Press 1950).

Houck, Louis, *A History of Missouri from the Earliest Explorations . . . Until the Admission of the State into the Union* (1908; reprint, Arno Press 1971).

Karsch, Robert F., *The Missouri Citizen: History, Institutions and Constitution of the State* (Univ. of Mo. Press 1960).

March, David D., *The History of Missouri,* 4 vols. (Lewis Historical Pub. Co. 1967).

Missouri Sesquicentennial History Series: *A History of Missouri:* Vol. 1, *1673–1820,* by William E. Foley; Vol. 2, *1820–1860,* by Perry McCandless; Vol. 3, *1860–1875,* by William E. Parrish (Univ. of Mo. Press 1971–).

Mott, Frank L., ed., *The Missouri Reader* (Univ. of Mo. Press 1964).

Shoemaker, Floyd, *Missouri and Missourians: Land of Contrasts and People of Achievements,* 5 vols. (1943).

Stevens, Walter, *Centennial History of Missouri: One Hundred Years in the Union, 1820–1921,* 6 vols. (1921).

MISSOURI, University of, mi-zo͝or′ē, a state-controlled, coeducational institution of higher learning, with four branches, at Columbia, Kansas City, Rolla, and St. Louis. The system is under the control of a nine-member governing board, called the Curators of the University of Missouri, appointed by the governor with the approval of the state senate. A president administers the system, and each of the components is headed by a chancellor. All branches of the university grant undergraduate and graduate degrees. The total enrollment in all branches in the mid-1970's exceeded 50,000.

University of Missouri–Columbia. The branch at Columbia has curriculums in arts and sciences, agriculture, business and public administration, education, engineering, forestry, home economics, journalism, nursing, social and community services, law, medicine, veterinary medicine, and library and information science. On the graduate level, special research centers in the social sciences include the Center in Research in Social Behavior, the Research Center of the School of Business and Public Administration, and the Freedom of Information Center; in the physical and biological sciences, the Space Sciences Research Center, the Sinclair Research Farm, the University Research Reactor, and Research Farms of the College of Agriculture and School of Veterinary Medicine.

The University of Missouri–Columbia was the nucleus of the state system. It was established by an act of the Missouri General Assembly in 1839 and began instruction in 1841. Women were first admitted in 1869. In the mid-1970's about 24,000 students were enrolled.

University of Missouri–Kansas City. The Kansas City branch of the university offers degrees in arts and sciences, administration, education, music, pharmacy, dentistry, law, and medicine. The branch was incorporated as the private University of Kansas City in 1929, and instruction began in 1933. It became part of the state system in 1963, when it adopted its present name. The enrollment in this branch exceeded 10,000 in the mid-1970's.

University of Missouri–Rolla. The branch of the university at Rolla offers degrees in arts and sciences, engineering, and mines and metallurgy. It also administers the St. Louis Graduate Engineering Center, for evening students, which grants master's degrees in engineering as well as in related fields.

The University of Missouri–Rolla was established as the University of Missouri School of Mines and Metallurgy in 1870, with instruction beginning in 1871. It became a campus of the University of Missouri in 1964, when it received its present name. The enrollment in the mid-1970's was in excess of 5,000.

University of Missouri–St. Louis. The University of Missouri–St. Louis includes the College of Arts and Science, the School of Business Administration, and the School of Education. This branch of the university also operates an evening college that gives undergraduate instruction leading to bachelor's degrees in business administration and education.

The St. Louis branch was established in 1960 as the Normandy Residence Center of the University of Missouri. It became a four-year institution in 1963 and began graduate instruction. The branch had an enrollment of more than 11,000 in the mid-1970's.

MISSOURI COMPROMISE, the name given to legislation passed by the U. S. Congress in March 1820 with the object of ending the dispute resulting from the attempt of Northern congressmen to insert an antislavery amendment in the bill providing for Missouri's admission to statehood. Although not popular at the time of its enactment, the compromise contributed greatly to the stability and harmony of the nation for more than three decades.

Origin of the Controversy. In February 1819, when the House of Representatives had under consideration a bill to enable Missouri to form a state government, James Tallmadge (N. Y.) introduced an amendment providing for the gradual abolition of slavery in the proposed state. Accepted by the House, where representatives from the free states had a substantial majority, the amendment was defeated in the Senate, where the slave states presented a united front and received aid from Northern allies.

After Congress adjourned in March 1819, leaving the fate of Missouri in doubt, most Americans seemed indifferent toward the Tallmadge amendment until a series of public meetings, arranged by Elias Boudinot and other philanthropists, aroused the free states to awareness of the importance of the slavery question. Slavery, however, was not the only issue at stake. Northerners resented the South's political power, and there was increasing sectional disagreement over the tariff and other matters.

Provisions of the Compromise. The passage of a compromise was made easier by an application for statehood from Maine, because the joint admission of a slave and a free state would preserve the sectional balance in the U. S. Senate. The Missouri Compromise, adroitly piloted through the House by Speaker Henry Clay, consisted of an act of March 3, 1820, admitting Maine to the Union and an act of March 6 enabling Missouri to organize a state government without slavery restrictions. Included in the enabling act was a proviso, introduced by Sen. Jesse Thomas (Ill.), prohibiting slavery in the remainder of the Louisiana Purchase north of 36° 30′. Most Northern members of Congress opposed the compromise, but it was generally accepted by the South as the lesser of two evils.

Later Developments. The controversy was revived when Missouri drew up a constitution that not only protected slavery but also directed the legislature to prevent the migration of free blacks to the state. Blacks were citizens in some states, and Congress, before granting final admission to Missouri, enacted a second compromise (March 2, 1821) requiring the state to promise that the citizens of other states would not be denied their constitutional rights. The Thomas proviso of the compromise of 1820, prohibiting slavery in the territories north of 36° 30′, was repealed in 1854 by the Kansas-Nebraska Act and declared unconstitutional by the U. S. Supreme Court in 1857 in the Dred Scott case. By 1854 the compromise had become sacrosanct in the eyes of many Americans, and the bitterness created by its repeal greatly hastened the coming of the Civil War.

GLOVER MOORE
Mississippi State University

Further Reading: Moore, Glover, *The Missouri Controversy, 1819–1821* (1953; reprint, Smith, P. 1967); Shoemaker, Floyd C., *Missouri's Struggle for Statehood, 1804–1821* (1916; reprint, Russell & Russell 1969).

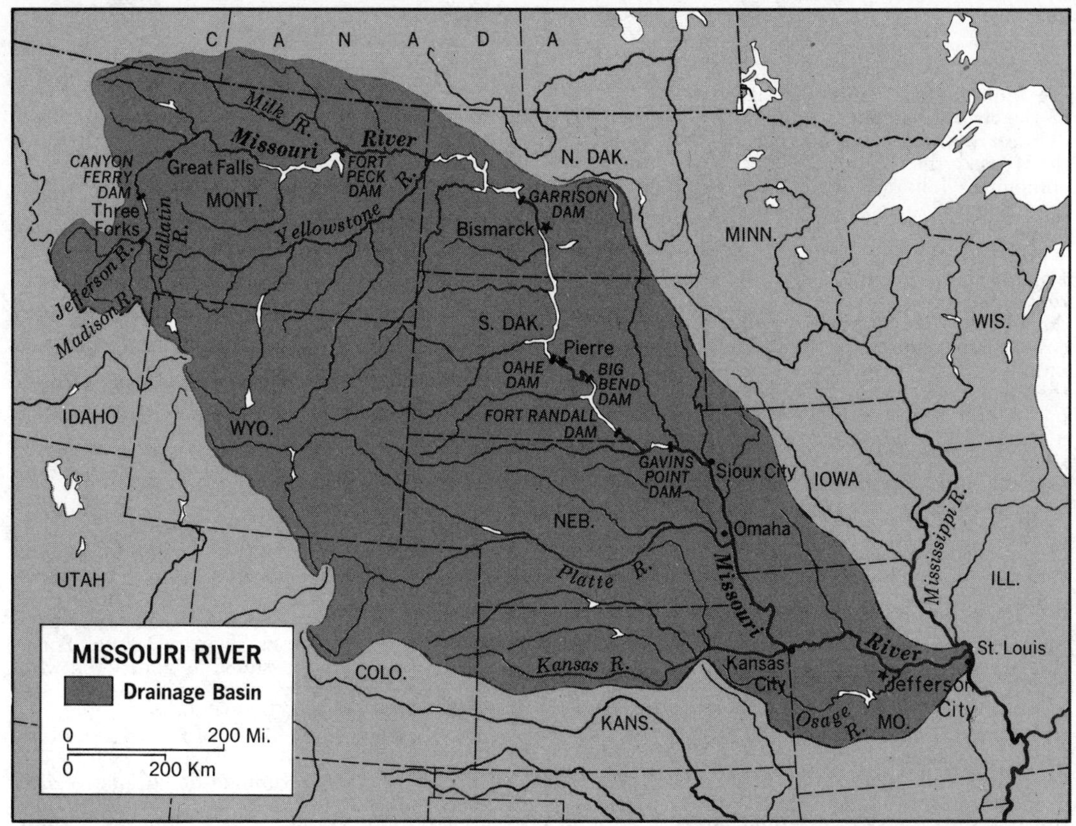

MISSOURI RIVER, mi-zo͝or′ē, the second-longest river in the United States. Its length from its source near Three Forks, Mont., to its mouth near St. Louis, Mo., is 2,315 miles (3,725 km), making it 33 miles (53 km) shorter than the Mississippi River. However, the Red Rock, Beaverhead, and Jefferson rivers form a continuous river path to the source of the Missouri, and the combined length of this river path and the Missouri is 2,564 miles (4,125 km).

From source to mouth, the Missouri traverses seven states. Over its course it typically is a broad, silt-laden river, giving rise to its nickname "Big Muddy." Tons of silt are carried into the river as the Yellowstone River and other tributaries join it.

The Missouri has many tributaries. They extend over midwestern and Rocky Mountain states and parts of Canada. The vast drainage basin of the Missouri and its tributaries covers an area of about 530,000 square miles (1,372,000 sq km). (See accompanying map.)

Course. The Missouri River begins where the Jefferson, Madison, and Gallatin rivers come together near Three Forks, Mont., at an elevation of about 4,000 feet (1,220 meters). In the first part of its course, the river flows northward, passing the Canyon Ferry Dam near Helena, Mont., and then flowing through a deep gorge called Gates of the Mountains. Further on near Great Falls, Mont., the river drops more than 400 feet (122 meters) in 12 miles (19 km) in a series of cataracts. Turning eastward, the river broadens at the huge reservoir above Fort Peck Dam in northeastern Montana. The Missouri is joined near the Montana–North Dakota border by the Yellowstone River, its biggest tributary.

Downstream, the Missouri flows southeast through South Dakota, broadening at the reservoir of the big Garrison Dam and passing by Bismarck, the state capital. Through South Dakota, the river flows south and southeast, passing the state capital of Pierre and providing the waters for the reservoirs of the big Oahe, Big Bend, Fort Randall, and Gavins Point dams. Further downstream, the river forms part of the boundary line between South Dakota and Nebraska, Nebraska and Iowa, and Kansas and Missouri. At Kansas City, Mo., the largest city on its banks, the river turns eastward, flowing past Jefferson City, the capital of Missouri, and emptying into the Mississippi River at Missouri Point, about 15 miles (24 km) north of St. Louis, at an elevation of about 400 feet (122 meters).

Major Tributaries. Major tributaries of the Missouri River include the Marias, Milk, Musselshell, and Yellowstone rivers in Montana; the Little Missouri in North Dakota; the Cheyenne, White, and James rivers in South Dakota; the Niobrara and Platte rivers in Nebraska; the Big Sioux and Little Sioux rivers in Iowa; the Kansas River in Kansas; and the Osage River in Missouri.

Principal Cities. The main cities on the Missouri are Great Falls, Mont.; Bismarck, N. Dak.; Pierre, S. Dak.; Sioux City and Council Bluffs, Iowa; Omaha, Nebr.; Kansas City, Kans.; and Kansas City and Jefferson City, Mo. The city of St. Charles, Mo., about 20 miles (32 km) northwest of St. Louis, is the oldest permanent white settlement on the Missouri. It was first settled by French pioneers in 1769.

Commerce. Transportation on the 760-mile (1,225-km) stretch of river between Sioux City, Iowa, and the river's mouth was greatly increased by the development of navigational facilities after World War II. Tugboats commonly push strings of barges hauling grain, steel, oil, and other commodities. North of Sioux City, the big multipurpose dams are dominant in the use of the river's waters.

History. Before the coming of white men, Indians used the Missouri River as an artery of commerce. They plied its waters in dugout canoes and bullboats. The bullboat was a basket made of willow sticks covered with buffalo skin.

The French explorers Jacques Marquette and Louis Jolliet were the first white men to see and report on the Missouri River. While journeying down the Mississippi River in 1673, they discovered the mouth of the Missouri, where its muddy and debris-laden waters discharged into the clearer waters of the Mississippi. The upper part of the Missouri was first reached by white men in 1738 when Pierre Gaultier de Varennes, sieur de la Vérendrye, led a party down from Canada and visited an Indian village on the river in what is now North Dakota.

By the end of the 18th century the lower part of the Missouri had become well known to fur traders, but the upper part of the river was virtually unexplored. However, immediately after the Louisiana Purchase in 1803 a party under Meriwether Lewis and William Clark explored the Missouri River from its mouth to its headwaters in an expedition that took them all the way to the Pacific coast and back to the mouth of the river during the years 1804–1806. See also LEWIS AND CLARK EXPEDITION.

Lewis and Clark and other early travelers used oar-powered keelboats to haul supplies up the Missouri. In 1819 the *Independence* became the first steamboat used on the Missouri. Its trip on the lower Missouri showed that such boats could navigate the river. Its success was followed by the steamboat *Yellowstone,* which traveled upstream to the mouth of the Yellowstone River in 1832, and the steamboat *Chippewa,* which reached Fort Benton (Montana) on a record-setting upstream trip in 1859. For a few decades the steamboat played a major role on the Missouri, carrying such freight as fur, lumber, paper, wheat, coal, and gravel. Freight hauled by steamboat peaked in 1858 but later declined because of competition from the railroads.

During the 1840's and 1850's the Missouri had an even more important role—moving people westward. Pioneers heading for California and Oregon traveled on the river across the present-day state of Missouri and then proceeded overland. The Mormons followed the same river path on their way to Utah in 1846 and 1847. After the Civil War, the Missouri was important in settling Kansas and Nebraska.

Until about 1940 little was done to improve navigation on the Missouri River or meet the needs for flood control, irrigation, and hydroelectric power. Flood control was particularly important because floods periodically caused great destruction to homes, farmlands, and population centers along the river banks, notably in 1844, 1881, 1903, 1908, 1915, 1927, 1937, 1947, and 1952. During a flood the river sometimes rose more than 30 feet (9 meters), covered as much as 3 million acres (1,215,000 hectares) of land, and discharged as much as 900,000 cubic feet (25,500 cu meters) of water per second at its mouth. In 1940 the federal government completed the first big dam on the river, the Fort Peck Dam in Montana. This dam provides flood control, hydroelectric power, and water for irrigation. See also FORT PECK DAM.

Under the Missouri River Basin Project authorized by Congress in 1944, other big dams also were built on the upper Missouri for flood control, hydroelectric power, and irrigation. They include Canyon Ferry Dam (1954) in Montana, Garrison Dam (1956) in North Dakota, and the Oahe (1963), Big Bend (1967), Fort Randall (1956), and Gavins Point (1956) dams in South Dakota.

Bibliography

Anderson, John, *Mackinaws Down the Missouri* (Utah State Univ. Press 1973).
De Voto, Bernard, *Across the Wide Missouri* (Houghton 1947).
De Voto, Bernard, *Journals of Lewis and Clark* (Houghton 1953).
Sunder, John E., *Fur Trade on the Upper Missouri, 1840–1865* (Univ. of Oklahoma Press 1965).
Terral, Rufus, *Missouri Valley* (Kennikat 1970).
Vestal, Stanley, *The Missouri* (Univ. of Nebraska Press 1964).

MISSOURI RIVER BASIN PROGRAM, a federal project to control floods, irrigate farmlands, develop hydroelectric power, and improve navigation in the Missouri River basin. The project affects Colorado, Iowa, Kansas, Minnesota, Missouri, Montana, Nebraska, North Dakota, South Dakota, and Wyoming—states in which the Missouri and its tributaries drain an area of about 525,000 square miles (1,360,000 sq km).

The Missouri River Basin project was authorized by the Flood Control Act of 1944. The major part of the multibillion-dollar plan called for the construction of some 103 major dams and reservoirs by 1980 to irrigate about 4 million acres (1.6 million hectares) of farmland, generate about 13 billion kilowatt-hours of electricity per year, control floods, and improve navigation on the lower Missouri River. Beginning in 1944, the U. S. Army Corps of Engineers and the Bureau of Reclamation have completed more than 35 dams. The overall project, now called the Pick-Sloan Missouri Basin Program, will extend beyond 1980.

Dams. Major dams built on the Missouri River include the Canyon Ferry Dam (1954) in Montana, the Garrison Dam (1956) in North Dakota, and the Oahe (1963), Big Bend (1967), Fort Randall (1956), and Gavins Point (1956) dams in South Dakota. Dams built on tributaries of the Missouri include the Yellowtail Dam (1966) in Montana, the Keyhole Dam (1952) in Wyoming, the Bonny Dam (1951) in Colorado, the Jamestown Dam (1953) in North Dakota, the Shadehill Dam (1951) in South Dakota, the Harlan County Dam (1952) in Nebraska, the Tuttle Creek Dam (1962) in Kansas, and the Pomme de Terre Dam (1962) in Missouri.

Irrigation and Flood Control. Throughout the Missouri basin, reservoir waters must be carefully controlled to satisfy conflicting demands, such as providing irrigation water in upstream areas and maintaining proper depths for navigation in downstream areas.

Regions that receive irrigation waters include lands along major rivers in Montana, the Big Horn basin in Wyoming, northern Colorado, and lands along the North and South Platte rivers in Nebraska.

Flood control by dams has been largely successful. Since the early 1950's the Missouri River basin has had only a few major floods, notably one in Missouri in 1973.

MIST. See FOG; METEOROLOGY—*Visibility*.

MISTASSINI, mis-tə-sē′nē, is the name of the largest lake in the province of Quebec, of a tributary of the Saguenay River in Quebec, and of a town on the Mistassibi River in Quebec. The lake is about 100 miles (160 km) long and has an area of 840 square miles (2,175 sq km). The river, which is 185 miles (298 km) long, flows south into Lac Saint Jean. Population of the town: 3,601.

MISTER ROBERTS is a novel by the American author Thomas Heggen, published in 1946. Heggen committed suicide in 1949, and *Mister Roberts,* a bestseller with considerable literary merit, is his only book.

The title character is Lt. Douglas Roberts, an officer aboard the *Reluctant,* a U. S. Navy supply ship in the Pacific during World War II. The *Reluctant* has never seen action, and boredom has destroyed morale. Captain Morton, the ship's skipper, is a petty, unreasonable man, who has aroused the hostility of the crew. Led by Mister Roberts, officers and seamen spend their time and energy in harassing the hated captain. In the end, Mister Roberts, who had sought an active role in the war, is transferred to a destroyer, where he is killed. The book, filled with humorous, almost farcical incidents, was made into a successful play (1948) and motion picture (1955).

MR., MRS. Articles on literary works beginning with *Mr.* and *Mrs.,* such as *Mr. Britling Sees it Through* and *Mrs. Dalloway,* are found later in this volume, following MOZART.

MISTI, El, mēs′tē, a volcano in the Andes of southern Peru, 10 miles (16 km) northeast of Arequipa. Noted for the beauty of its perfect snow-covered cone, El Misti has long figured in Peruvian folklore and poetry. It appears to have had religious significance for the Incas.

El Misti stands between two other volcanoes, Chachani and Pichu Pichu. Officially named Volcán Misti, and also called Volcán de Arequipa, it has an elevation of 19,101 feet (5,822 meters).

MISTINGUETT, mē-staɴ-get′, was the stage name of Jeanne Bourgeois (1875–1956), French music-hall performer. She was born in Enghien-les-Bains, France, and made her Paris debut in 1895. Although she occasionally appeared on the legitimate stage and in films, she had her greatest success as a star of the lavish spectacles mounted at the Folies-Bergère, the Casino de Paris, and the Moulin-Rouge. Among the many great partners of this accomplished singer-dancer was Maurice Chevalier, whom she discovered and whom she introduced into her act at the Folies-Bergère in 1905.

As an actress, Mistinguett specialized in portraying lower-class Parisian women, but as the acknowledged queen of revue she set styles in high fashion. Her legs, reputedly the most beautiful in the world, were certainly the most highly insured. Mistinguett died in Bougival, France, on Jan. 5, 1956.

MISTLETOE, mis′əl-tō, any of various parasitic shrubs in the family Loranthaceae. The mistletoe usually referred to in European literature is *Viscum album,* a parasite on various trees, including apples, poplars, maples, and lindens, but rarely oak. It was regarded as a sacred plant by the ancient druids—especially when found on oak trees.

ROBERT H. WRIGHT, FROM NATIONAL AUDUBON SOCIETY

American mistletoe (*Phoradendron flavescens*)

Growing throughout most of Europe, it is an evergreen shrub with opposite, oblong, leathery leaves. The inconspicuous male and female flowers occur on separate plants. The mistletoe is propagated from tree to tree by its sticky white berries, some of which cling to the beaks of birds that feed on them.

In the United States the name mistletoe is most often applied to species of *Phoradendron,* especially *P. flavescens,* a parasite of deciduous trees that ranges through the eastern states from New Jersey to Florida and as far west as New Mexico. Except for its smaller berries and shorter, broader leaves, it closely resembles the European species. Other species of *Phoradendron* occur on the Pacific coast.

MISTRA, mēs′trä, is a historical site 4 miles (6 km) west of Sparta, Greece. The remains of Mistra are chiefly of the 14th–15th century Byzantine city.

Guillaume de Villehardouin, whose father, Geoffroy, had established himself as the Frankish prince of Achaea in 1209, built a castle on the heights of Mistra in 1248–1249. The Byzantine emperor Michael VIII Paleologus, whose brother had captured Guillaume in 1259, received Mistra as part of Guillaume's ransom. In 1348 the despotate of Mistra was established under Manuel Cantacuzenus, son of the Byzantine emperor John VI.

Mistra became the cultural and political center of the Peloponnesus. It fell to the Turks in 1460, was held by the Venetians from 1686 to 1715, and then was retaken by the Turks. It was abandoned in the 19th century.

The remains provide fine examples of Byzantine painting and architecture, especially in the Peribleptos Church, the Metropolitan Church, the former monastery of Brontochion, and the Pantanassa, which was built as a church and now is a nunnery. The Despot's Palace is a composite of 14th and 15th century styles. Villehardouin's castle, which stands at the summit, was largely reconstructed by the Turks.

MISTRAL, mēs-träl′, **Frédéric** (1830–1914), French poet, who was a leader of the Félibrige movement, which sought to restore Provençal as a living language and create a literary renaissance in that tongue. He received the Nobel Prize in literature in 1904.

Mistral, the son of a landowner, was born near the village of Maillane, northeast of Arles, in southern France. He studied in Avignon under Joseph Roumanille, who inspired him to cultivate Provençal, the regional language. He also met Anselme Mathieu, another student of Roumanille, and, together, the three men formed the nucleus of the Félibrige.

Mistral's poetry first appeared in *Li Prouvençalo* (1852), a collection of Provençal texts. Shortly, the group, now grown to seven, brought out the *Provençal Almanach,* the journal of the movement, under Mistral's direction.

Mistral's first major work, *Mirèio,* a 12-part pastoral poem, was published in 1859. This was followed by *Calendal* (1867), in the epic style of medieval Provençal literature; *Lis Isclo d'Or* (1875), a collection of lyrics; and *Le Rhône,* another epic, about the Rhône Valley. Mistral published his *Memoirs* in 1906 (Eng. tr., 1907), and in 1910 he completed his translation of the Psalms into Provençal, a project he had begun in his school days. He died in Maillane on March 25, 1914.

Further Reading: Aldington, Richard, *Introduction to Mistral* (Southern Ill. Univ. Press 1960).

MISTRAL, mēs-träl′, **Gabriela** (1889–1957), Chilean poet, whose real name was Lucila Godoy Alcayaga. One of Latin America's leading literary figures, she won the Nobel Prize in literature in 1945. Her pen name was taken from the names of two poets, Gabriele D'Annunzio of Italy and Frédéric Mistral of France.

She was born in Vicuña, Chile, on April 7, 1899. She attended a teachers college in Santiago and taught for several years. She rose to important posts in the Chilean educational system and helped reorganize the rural schools of Mexico in 1922–1924. She also served as Chilean consul in European and American cities. She died in Hempstead, N. Y., on Jan. 10, 1957.

Gabriela Mistral began writing poetry after a tragic love affair. Her first important book, *La voz de Elqui,* was published in 1908, followed by *Sonetos de la Muerte* (1914), *Ternura* (1925), *Preguntas* (1930), *La oración de la maestra,* and *Tala* (1938). Her poems are passionate and direct and express a deeply religious nature. A selection was translated into English by Langston Hughes and published in 1957.

Further Reading: Arce De Vasquez, Margot, *Gabriela Mistral* (N. Y. Univ. Press 1964).

MISTRAL, mis′trəl, a dry, cold wind that blows down from the mountains of southeastern France, southward through the lower Rhône River valley, and over the southern coast of France along the Mediterranean Sea. The mistral is especially strong during the winter and spring, often lasting for several days and sometimes reaching a velocity of 85 miles (135 km) per hour. Coastal villages commonly have windbreaks to protect fields and gardens from the mistral, which increases in intensity as it blows down from the mountainous interior.

The southward flow of the mistral results from a high atmospheric pressure over the mountainous interior and a low atmospheric pressure over the Mediterranean coast, with the Rhône Valley forming a corridor for the winds. In addition, the mistral flows southward because of the fall of cold heavy air from higher to lower elevations.

MISTRIAL, in law, an erroneous or invalid trial, or a case in which the jury is discharged without having reached a verdict. In legal effect, it is equivalent to no trial at all. A mistrial is declared because of some circumstance indicating that justice may not be done if the trial continues. It may be granted only as a result of a fundamental error or shortcoming vitiating the whole proceedings rather than merely for an erroneous ruling on a point of law. Since a mistrial is a failure of trial, it is not a judgment or order in favor of one of the parties.

In a civil proceeding, a mistrial may be declared when necessary to further justice as, for example, in cases of surprise, an unexpected act. A mistrial may also be granted because of improper remarks or conduct of counsel, misconduct of jurors, introduction of improper evidence, or emotional demonstration by a litigant. In criminal cases, the prevailing view is that the court may declare a mistrial when necessity or the ends of public justice require it, even without the consent of the accused. A trial judge has broad, but not absolute, discretion in determining whether or not to declare a mistrial.

RICHARD L. HIRSHBERG, *Attorney-at-Law*

MITANNI, mi-tan′ē, was a kingdom of the ancient Middle East. At its height during the 15th century B. C., it controlled a territory extending from the Zagros Mountains westward across northern Mesopotamia and Syria to the Mediterranean Sea. Its capital was Waššuggani, in the Khabur River region of Mesopotamia.

The founders of Mitanni were Indo-Iranians from the northwest, one of several groups of tribesmen that overran the centers of Middle Eastern civilization between 1700 and 1500 B. C. Masters of chariot warfare, the Mitannians subjugated the Hurrians of northern Mesopotamia. They adopted Hurrian speech and ruled as a warrior aristocracy.

Expanding in the 15th century, Mitanni came into conflict with Egypt over Syria and was defeated by Thutmose III. The marriage of a Mitannian princess to Thutmose IV established peaceful relations between the two powers. Around 1380 the Hittites took Waššuggani, subsequently reducing Mitanni to vassalage. Assyria, which had been a Mitannian vassal, then gained its independence. The Assyrians finally destroyed and annexed Mitanni about 1260.

MITCHEL, John Purroy (1879–1918), American public official, who was a reform mayor of New York City. He was born in Fordham (now part of New York City), N. Y., on July 19, 1879. After graduating from Columbia University (1899) and the New York Law School (1901), he began the practice of law in New York City.

As a special counsel to the city in 1906 and as commissioner of accounts from 1907 to 1909, Mitchel exposed dishonest practices of the borough presidents of the Bronx and Manhattan, leading to their removal from office. Elected president of the Board of Aldermen in 1909, he also served briefly as acting mayor in 1910.

Running on a Fusion ticket, Mitchel was elected mayor in November 1913, the youngest in the city's history. During his term he instituted a program of tax relief for the city, opposed an increase in the funded debt, raised a small relief fund, and established workshops for the unemployed. But his administration became increasingly unpopular, primarily due to an official investigation of religious charities and the discovery that the police department was tapping private telephone lines. He was defeated for reelection in 1917. He joined the Army aviation corps, but was killed during a training flight near Lake Charles, La., on July 6, 1918.

MITCHELL, Billy, American army officer and aviator. See MITCHELL, WILLIAM.

MITCHELL, Donald Grant (1822–1908), American author, who wrote under the pseudonym *Ik Marvel.* He was born in Norwich, Conn., on April 22, 1822. After study at Yale University, he worked in the American consulate in Liverpool, England, from 1844 to 1845, when ill health forced him to resign. After returning to the United States in 1846, he began writing for a New York newspaper. His first book, *Fresh Gleanings,* about travel in Europe, appeared in 1847.

Mitchell's most popular books were *Reveries of a Bachelor* (1850) and *Dream Life* (1851)—collections of essays. Later books, based on life at his Connecticut farm, included *My Farm at Edgewood* (1863) and *Wet Days at Edgewood* (1865). He died in New Haven, Conn., on Dec. 15, 1908.

MITCHELL, James Paul (1900–1964), American government official. He was born in Elizabeth, N. J., on Nov. 12, 1900. After pursuing various occupations, he served as head of labor relations in the New York City division of the Works Progress Administration (1936–1940). After World War II he was a department-store executive.

In the Eisenhower administration, Mitchell, a Republican, was assistant secretary of the Army in 1953 and secretary of labor from 1953 to 1961. He supported a higher minimum wage and more jobs for blacks and migrant workers. He opposed a federal right-to-work law, which would have rendered illegal all contracts that make employment conditional on union membership. Mitchell ran unsuccessfully for governor of New Jersey in 1961. He died in New York City on Oct. 19, 1964.

MITCHELL, John (1870–1919), American labor leader, who was president of the United Mine Workers from 1898 to 1908. He was born in Braidwood, Ill., on Feb. 4, 1870. He went to work in the coal mines at the age of 12 and joined the Knights of Labor in 1885. In 1890 he became a member of the newly organized United Mine Workers (UMW).

Mitchell was dismissed from his job in 1894 after taking part in a UMW strike. Rising through the ranks of the union to an important position of leadership, he played an active part in the first successful national strike called by the UMW in 1897. The following year he became president of the union. Mitchell won nationwide attention of 1902 when he organized a strike of 150,000 immigrant miners in the anthracite coal mines of Pennsylvania. After a five-month strike the miners won better wages and shorter working hours.

Mitchell was head of the trade agreement department of the National Civic Federation from 1908 to 1911. He was chairman of the New York State Industrial Commission from 1915 until his death in New York City on Sept. 9, 1919. He was the author of *Organized Labor* (1903) and *The Wage Earner and His Problems* (1913).

MITCHELL, John Newton (1913–   ), American lawyer, who was U. S. attorney general under President Richard Nixon. Mitchell was later sentenced to prison for his role in the Watergate scandal.

Mitchell was born in Detroit on Sept. 5, 1913. He received a law degree from Fordham University in 1938. For the next 30 years, except for service in the Navy in World War II, Mitchell practiced law in New York City. He was a leading authority on state and municipal bonding.

In 1967, Mitchell's firm merged with that of Richard Nixon. He became a close confidant of Nixon and managed his campaign for president in 1968. After his election, Nixon named Mitchell attorney general.

Professing a strong commitment to fighting crime, Mitchell approved the use of wiretaps in "national security" cases without obtaining court authorization until the Supreme Court held the practice unconstitutional. He advocated preventive detention of suspects and "no-knock" police entries. He initiated conspiracy trials against critics of the Vietnam War but obtained few convictions. He proposed conservatives for judgeships, but two of his selections for the U. S. Supreme Court were rejected by the Senate as unqualified.

Mitchell left the cabinet in 1972 to direct the Committee for the Reelection of the President. Three times he discussed with other officials a plan that included the break-in at the headquarters of the Democratic National Committee. On July 1, two weeks after the break-in, Mitchell resigned. In 1974 he was indicted on charges that he had approved the break-in and had helped to cover it up. In 1975 he was found guilty of conspiracy, obstruction of justice, and perjury, and was sentenced to two and one-half to eight years in prison. He appealed. See also WATERGATE AFFAIR.

In 1974, Mitchell was acquitted of charges that he had conspired to impede the investigation of a financial supporter of President Nixon.

Mitchell's second wife, Martha, was an outspoken defender of her husband until their marriage crumbled under the strain of scandal. They separated in 1973.

MITCHELL, Margaret (1900–1949), American novelist, whose book *Gone with the Wind* was one of the most successful bestsellers ever written. She was born in Atlanta, Ga., on Nov. 8, 1900. The daughter of the president of the Atlanta Historical Society, she was reared in a family deeply concerned with local history. She attended Smith College in 1918–1919, after which, on the death of her mother, she returned to Atlanta to keep house for her father and brother.

The stories of the Civil War and the reconstruction era that she had heard in childhood from her family and household servants were translated during the next decade into a rambling, colorful historical novel of more than a thousand pages and finally published as *Gone with the Wind* (1936). This work, her only novel, was awarded the 1937 Pulitzer Prize for fiction and in 1939 made into a motion picture which set new attendance records. The book itself was a phenomenal best seller, reaching a sales record of 50,000 copies in one day and about a million and a half copies the first year. It has been a popular success throughout the world. Her death was caused by injuries received when she was accidentally struck by a speeding automobile.

See also GONE WITH THE WIND.

MITCHELL, Margaret Julia (known as MAGGIE MITCHELL), American actress: b. New York, N.Y., June 14, 1837; d. there, March 22, 1918. She grew up in New York City, where she made her first stage appearance at the age of 14 as little Julia in a play by Andrew Cherry, *The Soldier's Daughter.* This performance led to an engagement at the Bowery Theatre, where she danced and played boy parts, doing the role of Oliver Twist with great success. Soon she had become a popular comedienne and dancer and toured the country with great acclaim, especially the South.

Her most perfect role was that of the elfin child in *Fanchon the Cricket,* adapted from George Sand's *La petite Fadette.* It opened in New Orleans in 1860, reached New York in 1862, and was continually revived during the next 20 years. She played other famous roles such as Jane Eyre and Mignon with success, but it was the role of Fanchon which endeared her to the American public.

MITCHELL, Maria, American astronomer and educator: b. Nantucket, Mass., Aug. 1, 1818; d. Lynn, June 28, 1889. The daughter of William Mitchell (1791–1869), a noted amateur astronomer, she early became her father's assistant in mathematical calculations. For 20 years she was librarian in the Nantucket Athenaeum, using her leisure time for reading and astronomical observations. In October 1847 she discovered a telescopic comet, in recognition for which she received a gold medal from the king of Denmark. In 1848 she was elected a member of the American Academy of Arts and Sciences, the first woman so honored, and in 1850 she was unanimously elected a member of the American Association for the Advancement of Science.

When Vassar College was opened for instruction in 1865, Miss Mitchell became professor of astronomy and director of the college observatory, a post she held until her retirement in 1888. Well known at home and abroad for her scientific observations and her efforts on behalf of education for women, she received many honors during her lifetime. After her death a Maria Mitchell chair in astronomy was endowed at Vassar. She was elected to the Hall of Fame, New York University, in 1905, and a bronze bust of her was placed there in 1922.

Consult Wright, Helen, *Sweeper in the Sky: the Life of Maria Mitchell, First Woman Astronomer in America* (New York 1949).

MITCHELL, Peter, Canadian statesman: b. Newcastle, New Brunswick (now a part of Canada), Jan. 24, 1834; d. Montreal, Quebec, Oct. 25, 1899. After studying law he was admitted to the New Brunswick bar in 1848 and practiced law in Newcastle. Elected to the New Brunswick provincial assembly in 1856, he became a cabinet minister a few years later and was appointed to the Legislative Council. At the Quebec conference on federation of the British North American provinces (1864), Mitchell took part in drawing up plans for union. He became premier and president of the council of New Brunswick in 1866, and as such made final arrangements for the entrance of the province into the confederation, attending the Westminster (London) conference during that year. After the Dominion of Canada became a reality on July 1, 1867, Mitchell became a member of the first cabinet as minister of marine and fisheries and also a member of the Senate. As minister he was active in settling disputed fishing rights with the United States. Under his influence provisions were made in the Washington Treaty of 1871 for opening Canadian waters to United States fishing fleets. Resigning from the Senate in 1872, he was elected to the House of Commons, where he served as an independent Liberal from 1872 to 1878 and from 1882 to 1891. He lived in Montreal from 1873 on, becoming editor of the Montreal *Herald* in 1873 and proprietor in 1885.

MITCHELL, S(ilas) Weir, American physician, poet, and novelist: b. Philadelphia, Pa., Feb. 15, 1829; d. there, Jan. 4, 1914. He was graduated in 1850 from the Jefferson Medical College and spent a year of study abroad. After his return he practiced medicine but also did medical research. In "Researches upon the Venom of the Rattlesnake . . . ," appearing in 1860 as part of the volume *Smithsonian Contributions to Knowledge,* he was the first to state that snake venom is a double rather than a single poison. As a Civil War surgeon he studied nerve wounds and diseases and prepared, with two other doctors, *Gunshot Wounds and Other Injuries of the Nerves* (1864), reissued in amplified form as *Injuries of Nerves and Their Consequences* (1872), an important contribution to knowledge of the peripheral nerves.

In *Wear and Tear, or Hints for the Overworked* (1871) and in *Fat and Blood* (1877) he pointed out the relation of nervous disorders to the inability to rest or play, describing the "rest cure" and other methods of treatment in the latter work. He was the first to give a satisfactory description of the rare neurosis, erythromelalgia (1878), sometimes called Weir Mitchell's disease. In all, he wrote about 170 papers on medical and neurological subjects. Beginning in the early 1870's, he served on the staff of the Philadelphia Orthopaedic Hospital and Infirmary for Nervous Diseases for some 40 years.

In literature Mitchell distinguished himself both in poetry and fiction. *The Hill of Stones and Other Poems* (1882) was his first published poetry collection. Among later volumes were *Francis Drake, a Tragedy of the Sea* (1893) and *Pearl* (1906), a metrical adaptation of the Middle English poem. *The Complete Poems of S. Weir Mitchell* appeared in 1914.

His first work of fiction was a short story appearing in the *Atlantic Monthly* for July 1866, entitled *The Case of George Dedlow,* a satire on spiritualism. This story foreshadows Mitchell's later success in writing psychological novels and popular historical romances. His first novel, *In War Time,* appeared in the *Atlantic Monthly* during 1884 and was published separately in 1885. A number of novels followed, many of which were first published in magazines. His second novel, *Roland Blake* (1886), combines the psychological portrayal of character with historical romance. The central character, Octopia Darnell, is the first of the neurotic women so successfully portrayed by Mitchell.

He depicted the period of the American Revolution in his masterpiece of historical romance and his best-selling work, *Hugh Wynne, Free Quaker* (1897), and the French Revolution in *The Adventures of François* (first published in *Century Magazine* in 1898). Returning to the psychological novel, Mitchell gave an account of dual consciousness in *Dr. North and His Friends* (1900), and in *Constance Trescot* (1905) he portrayed the revenge of a pathological woman. *The Red City* (1907) is a novel of Philadelphia as national capital during the administration of George Washington. For his last novel, *Westways* (1913), the author-physician returned to the Civil War period.

Mitchell's novels attained great popularity. His psychological fiction provides special historical and scholarly interest with its probing into psychiatric problems and careful delineation of character. It was in the historical romance, however, that he achieved his greatest literary success.

Consult Earnest, Ernest Penney, *S. Weir Mitchell, Novelist and Physician* (Philadelphia 1950); Rein, David M., *S. Weir Mitchell as a Psychiatric Novelist* (New York 1952).

MITCHELL, Samuel Alfred, Canadian-American astronomer: b. Kingston, Ontario, Canada, April 29, 1874; d. Bloomington, Ind., Feb. 22, 1960. Graduated (1894) from Queen's University, Kingston, he took his Ph.D. at Johns Hopkins (1898) and taught at Columbia until 1913, when he became professor of astronomy and director of the Leander McCormick Observatory at the University of Virginia, retiring in 1945. A pioneer in the use of high-speed photography in astronomical observations, he calculated the distances of some 1,000 stars. He also played a leading part in the observation and study of solar eclipses, publishing *Eclipses of the Sun* (1923; 5th ed., 1951). He received the Watson Gold Medal of the National Academy of Sciences for 1948.

MITCHELL, Samuel Augustus, American geographer and publisher: b. Bristol, Conn., March 20, 1792; d. Philadelphia, Pa., Dec. 18, 1868. A teacher during his youth, Mitchell became dissatisfied with the treatment of geography in contemporary textbooks and determined to furnish more satisfactory materials. For 40 years he prepared and published in Philadelphia maps, atlases, textbooks, and geographical manuals, most of which went through many editions. At one time over 400,000 copies of his works were sold annually. His *New American Atlas* appeared in 1831, and in the next year he published *Mitchell's Traveller's Guide Through the United States,* containing current information on stage, canal, and steamboat routes. The guide was revised annually for over 20 years. To meet the need for up-to-date information on the expanding nation, he prepared many maps of the United States and separate maps of the states and territories, as well as various general atlases. His *Map of the United States and Territories* (1861) included information on the fortifications then existing. Mitchell also conceived the idea of a graded school geography series, including *Mitchell's School Geography* . . . (1839), *Mitchell's Primary Geography* (1840), and others. Some of these were issued in revised form as late as the 20th century.

MITCHELL, Sir **Thomas Livingstone,** Australian explorer: b. Craigend, Stirlingshire, Scotland, June 15, 1792; d. Sydney, Australia, Oct. 5, 1855. He served in the British Army for many years, gaining experience in surveying while on duty in Spain during the Napoleonic Wars. In 1827 he was appointed deputy surveyor of the colony of New South Wales, Australia, and the next year became surveyor general. His duties included making maps and laying out towns and roads. In 1835 he published a survey of the entire colony.

Mitchell is remembered chiefly for his exploring expeditions, beginning in 1831 with the search for a navigable river to the north coast. He failed to find such a river, but explored the Macintyre River (1832) and other headstreams of the Darling River. In 1835 and 1836 his explorations southwest of Sydney proved that the Darling River emptied into the Murray, and they were influential in encouraging settlement of what is now Victoria. In 1839 Mitchell was knighted. His fourth expedition, in the years 1845–1847, searched for an overland route from New South Wales northward to the Gulf of Carpentaria. Believing that a river valley would constitute the best route, he followed the broad Barcoo River in a northwesterly direction, but turned back without realizing that the river would make a great final turn to the southwest.

Two Australian rivers, both discovered by others during the 1840's, were named for Mitchell. One, in Queensland, flows 350 miles west-northwest into the Gulf of Carpentaria. The other, in Victoria, is formed by the confluence of the Wonangatta and Dargo rivers, flowing southeast to the Gippsland Lakes on the coast. Another Mitchell River in New South Wales may have been named for the explorer.

Mitchell's books include *Three Expeditions into the Interior of Eastern Australia* (1838) and *Journal of an Expedition into the Interior of Tropical Australia* (1848).

Consult Cumpston, John H. L., *Thomas Mitchell, Surveyor General and Explorer* (London 1954).

MITCHELL, Wesley Clair, American economist and educator: b. Rushville, Ill., Aug. 5, 1874; d. New York, N.Y., Oct. 29, 1948. After teaching at the universities of Chicago, California, Harvard, and Columbia and spending a few years at the newly founded New School for Social Research, he returned to Columbia as professor of economics from 1922 to 1944. He had a special interest in research and helped to organize the National Bureau of Economic Research in 1920, serving as its research director until 1945. Many of his books are publications of that organization. He served as chairman of the Social Science Research Council from 1927 to 1930 and was active on many government boards, including President Herbert Hoover's Research Committee on Social Trends and the National Resources Board.

Mitchell was a leading economist and tried to bring the evidence of human behavior to bear on the analysis of economic institutions. Among his works are *A History of the Greenbacks* (1903);

Gold, Prices, and Wages under the Greenback Standard (1908); *Business Cycles* (1913; 2d ed. *Business Cycles: The Problem and Its Setting,* 1927); and *The Backward Art of Spending Money* (1937).

Consult Burns, Arthur Frank, ed., *Wesley Clair Mitchell, the Economic Scientist* (New York 1952); Mitchell, Lucy Sprague, *Two Lives, the Story of Wesley Clair Mitchell and Myself* (New York 1953).

MITCHELL, William (commonly called BILLY MITCHELL), American army officer and aviator: b. Nice, France, Dec. 29, 1879; d. New York, N.Y., Feb. 19, 1936. The son of Senator John Lendrum Mitchell, he was brought up in Milwaukee, Wis. At the beginning of the war with Spain (1898), Mitchell left his studies at Columbian (now George Washington) University and enlisted as an army private, soon obtaining a commission in the Signal Corps. He served in Cuba and later in the Philippine Insurrection. In 1901 he was assigned to the establishment of the telegraph system between the United States and Alaska. He rose rapidly through the ranks, graduating from the Army Staff College in 1909, and in 1912 he became the youngest officer ever appointed to the General Staff.

William (Billy) Mitchell

The Bettmann Archive

Early in his career Mitchell became interested in aeronautics, fired by the enthusiasm of his superior, Gen. Adolphus Washington Greely. When the Army Signal Corps began to acquire a few planes, beginning in 1908, Mitchell began to urge the importance of military aviation. He himself learned to fly during 1915–1916, eventually becoming a pilot of superlative skill. During 1917 he planned the very modest American Expeditionary Force aviation program, while continuing to appeal for more aviators and more and better planes. In World War I Mitchell commanded the aviation branches of several army units in succession. He himself was the first United States officer to fly over enemy lines, and he continued to fly his own plane in battle. In September 1918 he directed a mass of 1,481 Allied planes, less than half of them American, against the St. Mihiel salient. Returning home a much-decorated hero in March 1919, he was made assistant chief of air service. In 1920 he became brigadier general on a permanent basis.

During the early 1920's, though only assistant air chief, Mitchell was the foremost champion of air power, while his more conservative superiors and a budget-conscious government combined to keep air strength at a minimum. The World War I ace was also battling to secure greater independence for the air forces, either through a separate air arm or through a single defense department with coordinated air, sea, and ground forces. He publicized his message in numerous speeches and magazine articles and claimed further that the airplane had rendered the battleship no longer effective in war. On three occasions his aviators proved that in bomb-carrying planes they could sink battleships—the German *Ostfriesland* (July 1921), the obsolete United States warship *Alabama* (September 1921), and the obsolete *New Jersey* and *Virginia* (September 1923). Mitchell began to warn of Japan's air strength and the likelihood that she would attack without warning. In 1925, as a result of his continued agitation, he was transferred, with the rank of colonel, to a minor post at San Antonio, Texas. After the destruction of the navy dirigible *Shenandoah* (September 1925), Mitchell charged the war and navy departments with "incompetency, criminal negligence, and almost treasonable administration of the national defense." For these statements he was court-martialed at Washington, D.C., beginning on October 25. Mitchell endeavored with some success to use the trial as a sounding board for his opinions. However, the court-martial on December 17 found him guilty of making statements to the prejudice of good order and military discipline. Although the ballot was secret, wide circulation was given to the rumor that one member of the court, Gen. Douglas MacArthur, voted not guilty. Mitchell was sentenced to five years' suspension from the service, with loss of pay and allowances, although half of these were later restored. He resigned from the army in February 1926 to become a stock farmer in Virginia.

In books and periodicals Mitchell continued to fight for a strong, autonomous air force, and he continued to warn against Japanese aggression, emphasizing also the strategic importance of Alaska in the air age. The Army Air Corps was formed in 1926 as a slight concession to his views, but with the Pearl Harbor attack and United States entry into World War II (1941, almost six years after his death), Billy Mitchell's warnings struck home. On Jan. 12, 1942, the Senate passed a bill raising Mitchell posthumously to the rank of major general, but the change of rank was never officially made. On July 25, 1946, Congress voted him a special medal of honor. A more lasting vindication came in 1947, with the establishment of the Department of Defense, consisting of separate coordinated departments of the army, navy, and air force. In 1958, however, Air Force Secretary James H. Douglas rejected a recommendation to reverse the court-martial made by the Air Force Board for the Correction of Military Records on the ground that Mitchell had violated military law in attacking his superiors.

Among Mitchell's writings are *Our Air Force, the Keystone of National Defense* (1921); *Winged Defense* (1925); *Skyways, a Book on Modern Aeronautics* (1930); and *General Greely, the Story of a Great American* (1936).

Consult Levine, Isaac Don, *Mitchell, Pioneer of Air Power* (New York 1943); Burlingame, Roger, *General Billy Mitchell, Champion of Air Defense* (New York 1952); and Mitchell, Ruth, *My Brother Bill* (New York 1953).

MITCHELL, William DeWitt, American lawyer and public official: b. Winona, Minn., Sept. 9, 1874; d. Syosset, N.Y., Aug. 24, 1955. After receiving his law degree from the University of Minnesota (1896), he practiced law in St. Paul for almost 30 years, with interruptions occasioned by service in the Spanish-American War and World War I. Under President Calvin Coolidge he was United States solicitor general (1925–1929) and then was appointed attorney general (1929–1933) by President Herbert Hoover. Resuming private practice in New York City, he was made chairman of the Supreme Court's advisory committee on federal rules of procedure in 1935, retaining the post until his death. In September 1945 he was selected chief counsel for the congressional committee investigating the circumstances of the Japanese attack on Pearl Harbor, but resigned in December because he believed some members of the committee were obstructing its work. He served in 1952 on the international legal panel which recommended that the United Nations secretary general discharge any staff employee found to belong to the Communist Party of the United States or to be guilty of subversion or espionage against the United States.

MITCHELL, city, Indiana, in Lawrence County 9 miles south of Bedford, lying at an altitude of 687 feet. Fruit and grain are grown in the area, and limestone is quarried. Each year Mitchell holds a persimmon festival. The city's manufactures include school bus bodies, clothing, brass valves, processed gypsum, and cement. Nearby is Spring Mill State Park, with caves and a restored pioneer village. Pop. 4,092.

MITCHELL, town, Ontario, Canada, located on the Thames River in Perth County, 12 miles northwest of Stratford. Served by Canadian National Railways, the town is also a highway junction. It produces flax, knit goods, flour, lumber, canned milk, and farm implements, and there are cold storage plants and grain elevators. The first permanent settler arrived here in 1836. Incorporated as a village in 1857, Mitchell became a town in 1874. Population: 2,545.

MITCHELL, city, South Dakota, the seat of Davison County, located 70 miles west-northwest of Sioux Falls, near the James River, at an altitude of 1,300 feet. Mitchell's basic industry is processing foods, and it is a trading and shipping point for the grain, meat, poultry, and dairy products of the area. An agricultural festival is held annually in Mitchell's Corn Palace. Transportation is provided by Braniff Airways, the Chicago, Milwaukee, St. Paul, and Pacific Railroad, and the Chicago and North Western System (freight only). The city is the home of Dakota Wesleyan University, a Methodist coeducational institution chartered in 1883. Laid out in 1879 and chartered in 1883, Mitchell is governed by a mayor and council. Pop. 13,425.

MITCHELL, Mount, mountain, North Carolina, in Yancey County near the western border of the state, altitude 6,684 feet. It is the highest United States peak east of the Mississippi River. Mount Mitchell is part of the Black Mountains, a northern spur of the Blue Ridge Mountains of the Appalachian chain. The mountain slopes contain dense forests of hardwood and pine in the lower altitudes and a continuous expanse of evergreens in the higher altitudes. There is heavy undergrowth, especially in the lower areas, and a tremendous variety of plant and animal life. At the summit is Mount Mitchell State Park, including recreational facilities. On the north side of the mountain is a 32,000-acre state game refuge area. A hard-surface road gives easy access to the top of the mountain.

The peak was named for Elisha Mitchell (q.v.), a professor of geology and related sciences at the University of North Carolina. He measured the altitude of the mountain for the first time in 1835 and discovered that it was higher than Mount Washington, N.H., which had been considered up to that time the highest peak east of the Mississippi.

MITCHELL RIVER, river, Australia, in northern Queensland, on the Cape York Peninsula. It rises in the Great Dividing Range along the east coast and flows 350 miles northwest across the peninsula into the Gulf of Carpentaria. It was named after Sir Thomas Livingstone Mitchell (q.v.).

MITCHILL, mĭch'ĭl, **Samuel Latham,** American physician, scientist, and legislator: b. North Hempstead, N.Y., Aug. 20, 1764; d. New York, Sept. 7, 1831. After taking his M.D. degree at the University of Edinburgh (1786), he was licensed to practice medicine in New York. He then studied law and served in the New York legislature in 1791 (also in 1798 and 1810). From 1792 to 1801 Mitchill was a science professor at Columbia College. He introduced a system of nomenclature based upon Antoine Laurent Lavoisier's work and in 1797 became a founder and chief editor of *Medical Repository,* a quarterly devoted to medicine and other sciences.

Mitchill resigned from Columbia in 1801 to enter the United States Congress, where he sat as representative (1801–1804; 1810–1813) and as senator (1804–1809). He was appointed a professor at the New York College of Physicians and Surgeons in 1807 and taught there until 1826, when, with several of his colleagues, he founded Rutgers Medical College.

Mitchill was a scientific investigator throughout his life. He exerted strong influence in the promotion of scientific research and made contributions to the industrial preparation of soap, gunpowder, and disinfectants. He published papers on the American Indian and wrote articles on fishes, American animals, minerals, and botanical specimens. He was especially interested in the mineralogy of New York State and was an organizer and first president of the Lyceum of Natural History (1817), precursor of the New York Academy of Sciences.

Consult Hall, Courtney Robert, *A Scientist in the Early Republic, Samuel Latham Mitchill* (New York 1934).

MITES AND TICKS, mītz ănd tĭkz, arthropods of the order Acari (or Acarina), class Arachnida, including the smallest members of the class. Of all arachnids they are the most numerous and widely distributed, the most diversified in form and habits, and the most important from the medical and economic standpoint. The tiniest are gall mites one tenth of a millimeter long, the largest are female ticks engorged to nearly a full inch, but the average length for the whole group is probably only one millimeter. Among them are predators, herbivores, scavengers, and types which practice many degrees of symbiosis in roles from commensals to obligatory parasites. Much of the diversity in habits and body forms of mites may be attributed to the effects of the parasitic habit which has developed to different degrees along several distinct lines. The free living types, also numerous and varied, account for at least half of all mites and include many that, even though they may be found attached to insects, are not true parasites. Often only one stage lives as a parasite. A most unusual adaptation, for which no adequate explanation seems to have been advanced, is the possession of only three pairs of legs by the larval stage, whereas succeeding stages have the normal eight. An analogous six-legged stage is found in the Ricinulei, arachnids only distantly related to mites.

The ubiquitous mites occupy almost every conceivable habitat on the land areas of the world, occur in northern Greenland (83°N.) and other Arctic regions, and even are found on the Antarctic continent (77°S.). Common even at high altitudes, some live in the wool of mountain sheep at 15,000 feet above sea level. The land forms live in the soil and its detritus, on plants of all types, where many cause galls, spots and blemishes on the foliage, and on and in the bodies of both vertebrate and invertebrate hosts. *Acarapis woodi* inhabits the tracheal system of the domestic honeybee and is the causative agent of the well-known Isle of Wight disease which results in paralysis of the flight muscles. In the United States, *Locustacarus trachealis,* a strange species which retains only six legs in adults of both sexes, lives in the tracheae of grasshoppers, sucking the blood of the host through incisions in the tracheal wall and, when in numbers large enough to act as an obstruction, causing pathological changes in the vital organs. Others live in ant and termite nests, in the feathers of birds, in the tracheal passages of seals, in the lungs of monkeys, and in the skin of man. In favorable situations millions of individuals swarm within the limits of a few cubic inches. A large fauna lives in fresh waters and a modest number have become adapted for life in the seas.

The parasitic mites are of particular interest because of the annoyance and misery they deal out to man and his domestic animals. Some acarologists believe that an intensive survey would reveal that parasitic mites far outnumber the free living types. Furthermore some free living types seem even now to be becoming parasites. Many of our deadliest human diseases are transmitted by mites and ticks, and every year more species are being identified as important vectors. Furthermore, many are becoming established in new localities and bringing with them important diseases. Noteworthy is the fact that disease organisms (viruses, Rickettsiae, bacteria, protozoa, etc.) may be transferred casually from host to host, or may be a hereditary residue lying viable in dormant stages and then transmitted by an active, feeding stage to another victim at a much later date.

The small size of mites make them difficult subjects for study but admirable ones for dispersal. They float as aerial plankton at high altitudes, at 10,000 feet up and probably even higher, and are carried about by birds and flying insects. The term "phoresy" is applied to the habit of certain mites of clinging to the bodies of insects, notably the beetles, while they are transported by these active vehicles. The larva of *Uropoda* glues itself to the host by means of an adhesive cord of excrement. The strange nymphal stage of cheese mites known as the hypopus is also concerned with distribution. After transforming into a mouthless, quiescent creature, it attaches itself by means of ventral suckers to an insect, usually a fly, and is carried to a favorable breeding place, where it again assumes the form of a normal nymph.

Structure.—The body of mites is typically saclike with the cephalothorax and abdomen broadly joined and intimately coalesced. Almost all evidence of the original segmentation is absent except in a few primitive forms. In some the posterior legs are virtually terminal, indicating that the abdominal segments have assumed a very different location in the animal. The cephalothorax bears one or several pairs of small, simple eyes on each side, but they may be absent. The normal six pairs of appendages are present but they are often much changed. The pedipalpi, chelicerae, and accessory mouthparts are often formed into a distinct division called the beak or capitulum, which is sometimes completely retracted into a chamber known as the camerostoma. The mouthparts are adapted for piercing, sucking, biting and sawing. The legs are normally four pairs; but the first active stage is a six-legged larva. In *Locustacarus* the adults have only three pairs of legs; and in the Tetrapoli only two pairs are retained by all stages, including the adults. The body and appendages, in many hardened and grotesquely ornamented, are provided with setae of many types, often pointed, hooked, plumose, flattened, or modified into diverse forms.

Respiration is effected by breathing oxygen directly through the thin integument or by tubular tracheae which open through more or less distinct spiracles. Coxal glands opening on the cephalothorax, and Malpighian tubules opening into the gut are the excretory organs. The circulatory system is the usual open one of arachnids, consisting of a tubular heart and arteries which ramify and empty the blood into sinuses between the organs. Copulation is usually accomplished by direct apposition of the genital openings, which in typical arachnids open ventrally on the second abdominal somite in both sexes. The position is variable in mites even in the same species and in many the males have copulatory organs. That of the male *Demodex* is situated on the dorsal surface of the cephalothorax. The orifice of the female ticks is located far forward between the coxae in a position behind the mouth. Some water mites (Hydrachnidae) exhibit a curious mode of pairing analogous to that of the Ricinuleids. The third legs of the males are somewhat modified and used as hands to transfer the spermatophores to the genital opening of the female. Other members use the chelicerae in much the same way to effect the transfer as in the solpugids. In still another group of mites (Gamasidae) the pedipalp is used, a procedure analogous to that of spiders.

The development of mites is accompanied by a marked metamorphosis during which, depending on the group, five or even more distinct stages are undergone, each marked by the shedding of membranes. The major stages are egg, larva, nymph, and adult. In general, oviparity is the rule but ovoviviparity is credited to some (Oribatidae) which retain the developing egg within the body until an advanced stage is reached. Some mites develop parthenogenetically. The eggs may be few, laid singly or in small groups, but in some (the ticks) the oviposition is a lengthy routine during which hundreds or thousands are laid in one batch, after which the female dies. In many only a single egg is matured and laid before the chorion is developed over the succeeding one. After a few days the egg shell breaks and reveals a developing embryonic stage called the deutovum, from which later hatches a hexapod larva. The six-legged larval stage is an active one during which many species find a suitable host, attach and engorge, and then drop off to change into the next stage. There then follows a quiescent period during which the body of the nymph develops within the changed, engorged larva, and then the nymph appears. This, the first eight-legged stage which resembles the adult except for smaller size and sexual immaturity, is an active one which feeds before changing to the final sexually active adult stage. The adults are active and, in the parasitic forms, voracious types that again attach to the host to feed, during which copulation often takes place. The length of life of adult stages is ordinarily not longer than a month or so. However, many mites and ticks are extremely resistant to desiccation and starvation and, particularly in the nymphal stages, are able to withstand their effects for very long periods, as long as two or three years in ticks which ordinarily live a much shorter total life span.

The mites are most closely allied to the harvestmen (order Opiliones) and differ in their respective primitive forms principally in having the abdomen distinctly segmented, in the position of the quite similar chelicerae, and in numerous minor details. More distant relatives are other broad waisted arachnids, such as the scorpions and solpugids. The oldest fossil mites come from the Old Red Sandstone of Scotland, which is of Devonian Age. They also occur in the Carboniferous where all the other arachnids are also represented and are known from numerous examples in Baltic amber and a few other deposits of Oligocene age.

The Kinds of Mites.—It is not possible to mention here more than a few of the principal groups of mites, which are divided by recent students into hundreds of families assigned to six principal suborders. The suborder Notostigmata is represented by a small group of brightly colored primitive mites with well marked segmentation of the abdomen as in ancestral forms. Another small group is the suborder Holothyroidea, comprising some of the largest of known mites, often exceeding one fourth inch, known only from Papua.

Some of the most atypical of all are the gall mites of the suborder Tetrapoli. These minute forms with elongate, annulate abdomens have only four legs in all stages and are responsible for galls on leaves of plants. These galls differ from those of insects in that there is an opening through which the young mites escape, whereas insect larvae are usually completely imprisoned.

The suborder Sarcoptiformes includes the beetle mites (Oribatidae), common, often shining black forms of little economic importance which live in soil detritus and feed on vegetable matter, and most of the parasitic atracheate mites (superfamily Sarcoptoidea). Most are parasitic during their whole life on the same host, where they infest the feathers, hairs or skin. The feather mites (family Analgesidae) are small, flattened types which frequent the feathers of birds. Itch mites (Sarcoptidae) live on the hoofs of horses, producing a disease known as foot-mange, infest the head, eyes and ears of dogs and cats, cause a disease of chickens called scaly-leg, and are responsible for serious and widespread scab diseases of sheep, cattle and rabbits. The various scabies mites (genus *Sarcoptes*) infest many domestic animals and include among them the itch mite of man (*Sarcoptes scabiei*). They burrow into the skin, usually between the fingers and toes, and cause distressing symptoms, but they have become a rarity in the United States and some other countries. The cheese mites and their allies are for the most part free living but a few are parasitic, sometimes causing mysterious outbreaks of dermatitis in houses and factories. Species of *Tyroglyphus* may be found in cheeses, grains, sugar and hay and on occasion are responsible for conjunctivitis and various itches in those who handle these products. This suborder also includes the curious *Acarapis*, previously mentioned as causing the Isle of Wight disease of bees.

The suborder Trombidiformes is another tremendous assemblage of mites, including many that are free living but others of great biologic interest and pressing medical importance. The louse mite (*Pediculoides ventricosus*) is remarkable in that it acts freely either as predator, scavenger, or parasite during its life history. An important pest on corn and crops, it also produces severe skin eruptions on hands and arms of workers. The numerous red spider mites (family Tetranychidae) are among the greatest enemies of the gardener, attack tomatoes, cucumbers and similar crops, defoliate fruit trees, and do serious damage to grass and clover crops. One of them (*Bryobia pratensis*) often enters houses in the fall, much to the distress of the housewife. A relatively innocuous member of this subfamily is *Demodex folliculorum* which lives in the hair follicles of man and is said to be quite common in the blackheads which form on his face. An elongate creature with tapering abdomen, *Demodex,* is harmless in man and extremely rare in the United States. Related species are more important, and one causes the red mange of dogs, a serious dermatitis. Living in freshwater ponds and streams, often in great numbers, are the extremely varied and beautiful water mites (family Hydrachnidae), forms of which are gaily dressed in bright reds and greens and which swim through the water with the aid of long hairs on the legs. The larval forms are sometimes parasitic on the gills of mollusks but the predaceous adults feed largely on minute aquatic creatures. The less common water mites of the family Halacaridae live in the sea. Among the most pestiferous of all mites are the six-legged larval forms of the harvest mites (Trombidiidae) well known to Americans as redbugs or chiggers. These tiny creatures attack a great variety of small hosts, such as birds, rabbits, snakes, turtles, and similar creatures. They swarm in grassland in the moist hot tropics and cause violent itching and irritation when they attack man. *Eutrombicula akamushi* is the vector of a Rickettsia organism which causes a febrile disease, frequently fatal to man in Japan and over much of the Oriental region and the major Pacific islands. In the United States, *Eutrombicula alfreddugesi* is the offensive species and causes a severe dermatitis following attachment to the skin by means of their hooked chelicerae. They do not burrow in as often believed but the effects of even temporary attachment is burning and intolerable itching. Effective repellents are now available as a prophylaxis.

The final suborder, the Parasitiformes, includes the generalized gamasid mites (group Parasitoidea) and the ticks (Ixodoidea). Among the former are two tropical rat mites (*Liponyssus bacoti*), an Egyptian species now widely distributed over the world and the United States, which frequently attacks man, and *Allodermanyssus sanguineus,* the vector of a recently described new febrile disease of the United States. Most important of all the mites from the standpoint of human health are the ticks. As a source of annoyance in tropical countries they rank with the red bugs because of their vast numbers and their persistence in crawling over the body of man. Although they do not often cause serious local injury, many are known to carry deadly diseases. All are ectoparasites which suck blood during their active life stages. The ticks of the family Argasidae, which lack dorsal shields and have the capitulum ventral, are long lived and lurk in the nests and habitats of their hosts, feeding intermittently and then retreating to a hiding place. The spinose ear-tick of the American Southwest infests the ears of horses and occasionally attacks man. Species of *Ornithodorus,* some of which are essentially human parasites, live in native huts and around camp sites and transmit spirochaetes which cause relapsing fevers in Africa and the Orient. The ticks of the family Ixodidae, which have a dorsal scutum and terminal capitulum, are specialized parasites which may be limited to a single host but more often use several different ones to complete their life history. They feed slowly and when engorged drop off the host to change into the next stage. Important diseases transmitted by Ixodid ticks are Texas fever of cattle and Rocky Mountain Spotted Fever, a serious and widespread Rickettsial disease of man.

Bibliography.—Baker, E. W., and others, *A Manual of Parasitic Mites of Medical Importance* (New York 1956); Herms, W. B., *Medical Entomology,* 5th ed. (New York 1961); Arthur, Don R., *Ticks and Diseases* (New York 1962); Savory, T.H., *Arachnida* (New York 1964).

WILLIS J. GERTSCH,
Associate Curator, Department of Insects and Spiders, The American Museum of Natural History.

MITFORD, John, English clergyman and writer, friend of Charles Lamb and Samuel Rogers: b. Aug. 13, 1781; d. Benhall, Suffolk, April 27, 1859. He graduated from Oriel College, Oxford in 1804, and five years later he took orders in the English church. He was the editor of, and contributor to, *Gentleman's Magazine* (1834–1850).

In 1814 he edited the first accurate edition of the *Poems of Thomas Gray, with Critical Notes, a Life of the Author, and an Essay on his Poetry* and in 1816, he embodied this material into two large volumes which contained important additions to the published letters of the poet.

MITFORD, mĭt'fōrd, **Mary Russell,** English writer: b. Alresford, Hampshire, England, Dec. 16, 1787; d. Swallowfield, near Reading, Berkshire, Jan. 10, 1855. Her education was obtained largely through her very wide reading. She won a lottery prize of £20,000 when three years old, with which her spendthrift father built a house at Reading. Owing to his extravagance, the family had to move to a laborer's cottage, and she to earning by her pen. Her first published work was *Miscellaneous Poems* (1810). With the sketches *Our Village,* descriptive of English rural life (first appeared in *Lady's Magazine,* 1819; collected 1824, 1826, 1828, 1830, 1832), she may be said to have originated a branch of literature. Among her dramatic works, five in number, *Rienzi* (1828) was most successful; in America it became popular with Charlotte Cushman as Claudia. Included in her further writings are *Recollections of a Literary Life* (1852), and the works of fiction *Belford Regis* (1835) and *Atherton* (1854), the latter highly praised by Ruskin. Her correspondence (published 1870) has been by some ranked almost with her books. Consult the *Life* by L'Estrange (1870); id., *The Friends of Mary Mitford as Revealed in Letters from her Literary Correspondents* (1882); the correspondence with Boner and Ruskin, edited by Elizabeth Lee (1915).

MITFORD, William, English historian: b. London, Feb. 10, 1744; d. Exbury, Feb. 10, 1827. He was educated at Oxford, and obtained a commission in the Hampshire militia, of which he became colonel. His early fondness for Greek led him to the study of Greek historians, and he was induced, partly through the advice of Gibbon, a fellow-officer in the same regiment, to undertake a *History of Greece.* The first volume appeared in 1784, the fifth and last, bringing the narrative down to the death of Alexander the Great, in 1818. With considerable critical acumen and diligent research he elucidated many obscure points, and until the appearance of the works of Thirlwall and Grote, his history was considered of the highest authority. A strong prejudice against democracy leads him to speak of the Athenians as a horde of treacherous miscreants, of Demosthenes as a malignant demagogue and of Philip as a perfect statesman, and warrior. Mitford was professor of ancient history in the Royal Academy, and member of Parliament for three boroughs in succession 1785–1818. Besides his principal work he published an *Essay on the Harmony of Language* (1774) and lesser works.

MITHRAS, mĭth'ras, in Perso-Iranic divinity, first the god of the heavenly light and the lord of all countries, afterward the sun, or the genius of the sun, which was worshiped as a deity by the Persians, and at a later period also in Rome. Mithras stands as a mediator between Ormuzd and the world, and was involved in the struggle with Ahriman, the evil power. He is commonly represented as a handsome youth, wearing the Phrygian cap, tunic and cloak, and kneeling on a bull, into whose throat he is plunging the sacrificial knife. The bull is at the same time attacked by a dog, a serpent and a scorpion. As the monuments of this worship were destroyed during the Mohammedan conquests, knowledge of its doctrines and rites is necessarily vague and uncertain; but it had some remarkable resemblances to Christianity. The worship of Mithras was formally suppressed in the 4th century. In Germany many tokens of its former existence are still to be found, as the monuments at

Heddernheim and other places.

MITHRIDATES, mĭth-rĭ-dā'tēz, or **MITHRADATES,** mĭth-rȧ-dā'tēz, **VI EUPATOR,** ū'pȧ-tôr (sometimes called MITHRIDATES VI THE GREAT), king of Pontus: b. Sinope, about 132 B.C.; d. Pantacapaeum, 63 B.C. The last of six kings of Pontus named Mithridates, he ruled his small kingdom on the south shore of the Black Sea from 120 B.C. until his death. He early extended his rule southward in Asia Minor where he encountered Roman opposition in 88 B.C. and was defeated by Sulla in a war lasting four years. Mithridates bested the Romans during another campaign in 83–81 B.C., but was then pursued by the Roman legions of Lucullus into Armenia where he was given refuge by Tigranes I. He succeeded in reconquering his kingdom by 67 B.C., but the following year Pompey routed his army. The king fled to Bosporus (the Crimea), where his troops mutinied under the leadership of his son Pharnaces, and Mithridates killed himself. He was considered by Rome its most formidable enemy.

MITLA, mē'tlä, village, Mexico, situated in the state of Oaxaca, on the Mixtecapán Plateau, 26 miles southeast of Oaxaca. The altitude is 5,413 feet. Mitla (meaning "the place of the dead") is celebrated for its extensive ancient ruins of the Zapotec civilization which date from the 13th century and comprise five great groups of temples, palaces, and other edifices covering an area of 1,640 feet by 984 feet. See also MEXICO—*18. Architecture* (Valley of Oaxaca): Mitla. Pop. (1950) 2,865.

MITO, mē-tô, city, Japan, capital of the prefecture of Ibaraki on Honshu Island. It is located on the Naka River, seven miles from the east coast and 73 miles by rail northeast of Tokyo. Chief products include tobacco, coal, raw silk, cloth, cigarettes, and paper. Mito became the residence of a main branch of the important Tokugawa family in the early 17th century. The city was damaged by Allied bombing in 1945. Pop. (1960) 139,389.

MITOSIS, mĭ-tō'sĭs (also called KARYOKINESIS), the characteristic manner of reproduction of the cell nucleus in plants and animals. The term was originated in 1882 by the German anatomist Walther Flemming. Sometimes mitosis is used to designate the whole of cell reproduction including mitotic nuclear division and division of the cytoplasm (cytokinesis). Mitosis assures the accurate duplication and distribution of the chromosomes (the carriers of the genetic factors), so that each daughter cell obtains an exact duplicate of the chromosome set and therefore of the genetic determiners typical of an animal or plant species. Mitosis includes the following steps: chromosome reproduction, chromosome coiling (prophase), chromosome movements (metaphase and anaphase), and reconstruction of nuclei (telophase). Chromosome duplication occurs before any morphological indications of impending cell division are visible. It is recognized by the behavior of the specific chromosomal substance desoxyribose nucleic acid (DNA), now thought to be the gene substance. New DNA is made only during chromosome duplication and the amount per chromosome exactly doubles at that time. Just how the daughter chromosomes are made from the parent chromosome, however, is not known. Later the doubled threadlike chromosomes coil into short rodlike structures. The chromosome halves are now clearly visible and with the help of special cell structures, the mitotic apparatus, they are separated and moved to opposite sides of the cell. The two groups of daughter chromosomes develop into the daughter nuclei. The cytoplasm then constricts in between, pinching the cell in two. Thus two new cells with identical nuclei are formed from the parent cell.

The mitotic cycle is the life cycle of multiplying cells. The accompanying diagram shows the subdivisions of the mitotic cycle in chick embryo cells grown in tissue culture. The mitotic cycle may be interrupted at various points in certain cells, or, experimentally through *mitotic poisons,*

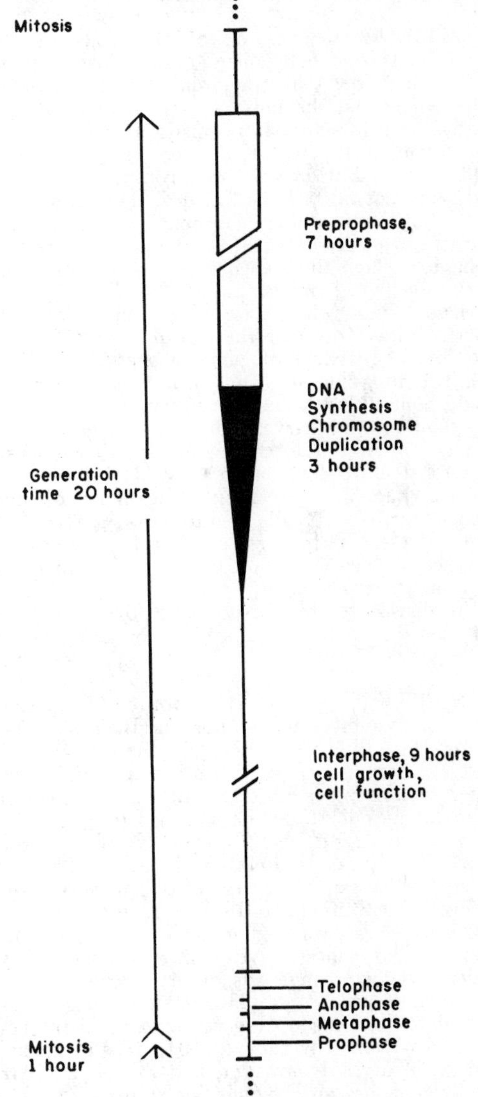

Mitotic cycle in an animal cell (after Firket, 1958).

substances that interfere specifically with one or another step of mitosis. Most commonly found is chromosome reproduction without separation of daughter chromosomes and cell division: *endomitosis.* The result is cells with doubled chromosome numbers (polyploidy). Mitosis is a major factor in the growth of organisms from the egg cell to the many-celled adult. In many tissues of the adult, worn-out cells are constantly replaced through mitosis. The *mitotic index* (percentage of cells in mitosis) of a tissue indicates the rate of new cell formation. Certain as yet not-understood changes in cells can upset the delicate control of cell function and cell reproduction; cell reproduction may run wild and produce destructive tumors. See also CELL, THE—*Cell Division;* CYTOLOGY—*Cell Reproduction.*

Consult Ris, Hans, "Cell Division," *Analysis of Development,* ed. by Benjamin H. Willier, Paul A. Weiss, and Viktor Hamburger, chap. 3, pp. 91–125 (Philadelphia 1955); Swann, M. M., "The Control of Cell Division: a Review," *Cancer Research,* vol. 17, pp. 727–757 (Chicago 1957), vol. 18, pp. 1118–1160 (1958).

HANS RIS,
Professor of Zoology, University of Wisconsin.

MITRA, mē′trȧ, one of the gods of the Aryan invaders of ancient India, closely allied to Varuna (q.v.) as coguardian of the laws by which men and the universe are maintained and nature and human nature made fruitful. Only one hymn of the *Rig Veda* (book 3, no. 59) is addressed to Mitra alone, and from it his individuality cannot be fully established. However, it is clear that he was a god of light, connected with the sun, who promoted life and joy and punished behavior which threatened these values. In Sanskrit the word *mitra* meant "ally" and later "friend," and Mitra, like his Iranian counterpart Mithras (q.v.) of the *Avesta,* was above all the divine guardian of punctual good faith. In this role he guided the sun so that its movements could be used by the farmer to measure the times of planting and harvest, and he guided human hearts so that the community might flourish through truth-telling and fidelity. His distinctive epithet *Yātayaj-jana* meant "Bestirrer of the People" or he who calls men to work, prayer, and truthfulness. The worship of Mitra seems to have been given up soon after the Aryans arrived in India, perhaps because no god of humble agriculturalists, preaching truth and love, could be retained by warriors in the flush of victory.

RODERICK MARSHALL.

MITRE, mē′trā, **Bartolomé,** Argentine statesman, soldier, and author: b. Buenos Aires, Argentina, June 26, 1821; d. there, Jan. 18, 1906. After 15 years in exile in Uruguay and other countries as an opponent of the dictator Juan Manuel de Rosas, he returned to Argentina with the army of Justo José de Urquiza, which overthrew Rosas in February 1852. Mitre and other Buenos Aires leaders refused to accept the federal constitution of 1853, and the province organized a separate government, in which he held various offices. After a provincial army under his command was defeated by federal forces at Cepeda (Oct. 23, 1859), Buenos Aires agreed to join the confederation, and Mitre became provincial governor (1860). Hostilities began again in 1861, however, and this time Mitre was victorious, at Pavón (September 17). He assumed the presidency of the whole country, was regularly elected the following year, and served until 1868. Under his administration Argentina was finally united, and considerable internal progress was made. In alliance with Brazil and Uruguay, he commanded the forces that defeated Paraguay (1865–1870). Mitre founded the famous newspaper *La Nación* in 1870. He also won distinction as a biographer and historian for his *Historia de Belgrano . . .* (1858; 4th ed., rev., 3 vols., 1887) and *Historia de San Martín . . .* (3 vols., 1888–89; Eng. tr., in part, *The Emancipation of South America,* 1893). See also ARGENTINA—*12. History* (National Government).

MITROPOULOS, mê-trô′pōō-lôs, **Dimitri,** Greek-American pianist and conductor: b. Athens, Greece, Feb. 18, 1896; d. Milan, Italy, Nov. 2, 1960. He studied at the Athens Conservatory, where his opera *Soeur Béatrice* was performed in 1919, and later with Ferruccio Busoni in Berlin, where he was assistant conductor of the Staatsoper (1921–1924). After serving as conductor of the Athens Conservatory orchestra (1924–1930), Mitropoulos made musical headlines in 1930 when he substituted at the last moment for Egon Petri as piano soloist in a Prokofiev concerto with the Berlin Philharmonic, conducting the orchestra from the keyboard. Following a guest appearance with the Boston Symphony (1936), he succeeded Eugene Ormandy as conductor of the Minneapolis Symphony (1937–1949) and then became musical director of the New York Philharmonic (1950–1958). In his last years he devoted himself mostly to opera, with the Metropolitan in New York City, and elsewhere. He became an American citizen in 1946. Mitropoulos, who had a remarkable memory and conducted without a score, was a musician of great emotional intensity as well as technical brilliance. He took a special interest in contemporary music and was known for his interpretations of such composers as Arnold Schoenberg and Alban Berg. He died while conducting a symphony rehearsal at La Scala.

MITROVICA or **SREMSKA MITROVICA,** srĕm′skä mē′trô-vê-tsä, town, Yugoslavia, in the autonomous province of Vojvodina, 42 miles west-northwest of Belgrade. It is an important port on the Sava River and serves as the commercial center of a livestock-raising and fruit- and grain-growing area. The ruins of the ancient Roman city of Sirmium are here. Pop. (1953) 15,416.

MITSCHER, mĭch′ẽr, **Marc Andrew,** American naval officer: b. Hillsboro, Wis., Jan. 26, 1887; d. Norfolk, Va., Feb 3, 1947. He graduated in 1910 from the United States Naval Academy and received his wings at the Naval Air Station, Pensacola, Fla., in 1917. After serving as executive officer of the *Langley* and the *Saratoga,* and with the Navy's Bureau of Aeronautics, he was promoted rear admiral (1941) and commanded the aircraft carrier *Hornet,* from which United States planes under Maj. Gen. James Doolittle took off to bomb Japan (April 18, 1942). In the spring of 1943 he was air commander on Guadalcanal, where his forces gained air supremacy over the Japanese. Mitscher directed the operations of the massive Task Force 58 in most of the major sea and air battles of the Pacific during 1944–1945. Promoted admiral in 1945, he was commander of the Atlantic Fleet at his death.

MITSCHERLICH, mĭch′ẽr-lĭĸ, **Eilhard,** German chemist: b. Neuende, Germany, Jan. 7, 1794; d. Berlin, Aug. 28, 1863. In 1811 he moved to Heidelberg, where he devoted himself to philology and more particularly to Persian. In 1813 he went to Paris, hoping to obtain permission to join the embassy which Napoleon I was about to send to Persia. Political changes frustrated this plan, and Mitscherlich determined to study medicine in order to have the privileges accorded to physicians traveling in the East. For this purpose he went to Göttingen, and while there compiled a history of Persia from manuscripts in the university library. Entitled *Mirchondi historia Thaheridarum historicis nostris huiusque incognitorum Persiae principum,* it was published in 1814 in both Latin and Persian.

While studying medicine at Göttingen, his attention was attracted to geology, chemistry, and physics, and he moved to Berlin in 1818 to work in the laboratory of the botanist Heinrich Friedrich Link. There his researches led him, in 1819, to the discovery of the principle of isomorphism (q.v.). He studied with Jöns Jakob Berzelius in Stockholm, Sweden, in 1820–1821 and then returned to Berlin to lecture in chemistry at the university. He later discovered the double crystalline form of sulphur, one of the first observed cases of dimorphism. His investigations in the production of artificial minerals, his paper on benzene and the formation of ether, and his discovery of permanganic and selenic acids were also important. His principal work is *Lehrbuch der Chemie* (2 vols., 1829–1830; 4th ed., 1844–1847). Shortly after his death in 1863, many of his previously unpublished notes and papers were recorded in the *Memoirs* of the Berlin Academy.

MITSUI, mē-tsōō-ē, and **MITSUBISHI,** mē-tsōō-bē-shē, Japanese financial and industrial combines. Before and during World War II, these two industrial trusts were the first and second respectively of the *zaibatsu,* the powerful, centralized Japanese commercial investment houses. Though in competition with each other and with other *zaibatsu* concerns, they collectively exercised a considerable measure of control over the economic life of Japan and were largely responsible for the country's quick rise to a position of competitive strength in the world market after the Meiji Restoration of 1868. They also provided the financial backbone of the nation's military might in the 1930's and 1940's.

The Mitsui organization, founded by Takatoshi Mitsui in the 17th century, had a long tradition of successful commercial and banking activity behind it when the government, attempting to industrialize Japan in the 1870's, began to shower the firm with subsidies, loans, and special privileges. The company expanded and prospered to the point at which its net worth was conservatively estimated in 1940 at a billion yen, but it remained primarily a family or clan-owned concern. Though in its later development it owed much to a succession of managers developed within the organization, many of these were absorbed into the Mitsui family by marriage or by adoption.

The *zaibatsu* firms were often able to influence the government and were sometimes represented in the cabinet itself. In 1932 the Mitsubishi concern aided financially in the creation of the Manchukuo government and was rewarded with lucrative business concessions in the conquered territories. There were close ties between the Mitsui concern and the Seiyukai Party, and between the house of Mitsubishi and the only other major political party, the Minseito. After World War II, the Allies ordered the dissolution of all the *zaibatsu* concerns in an effort to democratize the control and ownership of Japanese economic resources. In August 1955, however, a revival of the parent Mitsui Bussan Co., Ltd. was brought about by a merger of two of its most powerful subsidiaries.

MITTAG-LEFFLER, mĭt'täg lef'lẽr, **Magnus Gösta,** Swedish mathematician: b. Stockholm, Sweden, March 16, 1846; d. Djursholm, near Stockholm, July 7, 1927. From 1877 to 1881 he was professor of mathematics in Helsingfors (now Helsinki), Finland, and then went to the University of Stockholm where he taught mathematics until 1911, serving as rector of the university in 1886, 1891, and 1893. Shortly after his arrival in Stockholm he founded the journal *Acta Mathematica,* which became internationally known. In 1916 he and his wife founded a mathematical library at Uppsala. Among his contributions to mathematical theory is the theorem, which has since come to be identified with his name, on the one-valued function. See also COMPLEX VARIABLE.

MITTEN, mĭt''n, **Thomas Eugene,** American business executive: b. Brighton, Sussex, England, March 31, 1864; d. near Milford, Pa., Oct. 1, 1929. In 1877 he left England with his parents, who settled near Goodland, Ind. After working for several railroads, he began his connection with the street-railway business in 1896, first as an assistant superintendent at Milwaukee, Wis. By 1905 he was president of the Chicago City Railway Company, resigning in 1911 to become president of the Philadelphia Rapid Transit Company. There he established a cooperative plan which gave his employees a voice in all matters from general policy to wages and working conditions. He resigned as president in 1923, serving as chairman of the board until 1929. In the latter year the mayor of the city ordered an audit of the company's books because of its failure to submit annual reports to the city comptroller. This study showed that the company had incurred unjustifiably heavy expenses, and the comptroller filed suit on Dec. 1, 1929, for a financial accounting. Two months earlier, however, Mitten had drowned in a pond on his estate. In 1931 his company was ordered into receivership, and his management severely condemned.

MITTERRAND, mĕt-räɴ', **François** French political leader: b. Jarnac, France, Oct. 26, 1916. After obtaining degrees in law, literature, and political science, he became a lawyer. From 1944 he occupied several important government posts, including secretary to the presidency of the council, minister of the interior, and minister of justice. Mitterrand was a member of the National Assembly from 1946, except when he served as a senator from 1959 to 1961. In 1965 he was the candidate of the left in the presidential election; although defeated by Gen. Charles de Gaulle, he did unexpectedly well. His Federation of the Democratic and Socialist Left formed a tactical coalition with the Communists in the 1967 parliamentary elections, thereby gaining impressive results; later that year, Mitterrand led an unsuccessful fight against the granting of special powers to the government.

SERGIO BARZANTI,
Fairleigh Dickinson University.

MITTIMUS, mĭt'ĭ-mŭs (Lat. we send), a written warrant issued after a criminal conviction by a court or magistrate, directing a proper officer to convey the body of a prisoner to jail, and ordering the jailer to keep the individual in custody until legal provision is made for his release.

MITTWEIDA, mĭt-vī'dä, town, eastern Germany, in Saxony, 11 miles north-northeast of Chemnitz and 34 miles south-southeast of Leipzig, on the river Zschopau. It manufactures a wide range of products, including paper and cotton, machines, precision instruments, glass, clothing, cigars, and leather. The town has a fine 15th century church, now Protestant. Pop. (1946) 22,794.

MITYLENE. See LESBOS.

MITZVAH, mĭts'vä, a Jewish religious commandment; also, more loosely, a good deed. The Torah contains over 600 *mitzvoth,* both positive and negative. Their varying importance and number were established by Maimonides (q.v.) and other scholars and rabbis.

MIVART, mī'värt, **St. George Jackson,** English biologist: b. London, England, Nov. 30, 1827; d. there, April 1, 1900. A prosperous hotelkeeper's son, he was educated at Harrow and King's College, London. Having been converted to the Roman Catholic Church in 1844, he was barred from attending Oxford, and received his higher academic training at St. Mary's College, Oscott. In 1851 he was called to the bar at Lincoln's Inn, but the possession of ample means enabled him to gratify his taste for natural history. He was appointed lecturer in comparative anatomy at St. Mary's Hospital medical school in 1862, and from 1874 until 1877 was professor of biology at University College, a Roman Catholic institution which functioned briefly in Kensington, London. On the invitation of the Belgian episcopate he served from 1890 to 1893 as professor of the philosophy of natural history in the University of Louvain. He was vice president of the Zoological Society twice, and secretary and vice president of the Linnaean Society. In 1876 Pope Pius IX awarded him a Ph.D.

Mivart's scientific specialties were the insectivora and carnivora, but he was drawn into controversy by the warfare raging over the evolutionary theories of Charles R. Darwin, a struggle which, as a Catholic, he felt acutely. In *The Genesis of Species* (1871), he admitted organic evolution, but argued against Darwin's theory of natural selection and tried to explain the production of new species as due to an innate plastic power of "individuation"; he also rigidly differentiated between human and animal mental faculties. Gradually his views estranged him from Darwin and Thomas Huxley, while his articles on religion and science, between which he had been anxious to play the role of mediator, brought the disfavor of his religious superiors. Articles by Mivart appearing in 1892 and 1893 were placed on the Index; further magazine articles appearing in January 1900 resulted in his excommunication by Cardinal Herbert Vaughan on Jan. 18, 1900. He died shortly thereafter, unreconciled to the church; but in 1904, persuaded that his final illness had unbalanced his judgment, Catholic authorities allowed Mivart's reburial in consecrated ground. Mivart's evolutionary stand is summed up in *Lessons from Nature* (1876) and *Contemporary Evolution* (1876); his greatest single monograph is probably *The Cat: an Introduction to the Study of Backboned Animals, especially Mammals* (1881).

MIWOK. See MOQUELUMNAN.

MIXCOATL, mēks'kô-ā-t'l, in Aztec mythology, the Cloud Serpent, a star god and the god of the hunt; sometimes also identified with the god of war (Camaxtli), and the god of the wind (Tezcatlipoca). As Camaxtli, he was counted among the four gods who made the world. He created fire from sticks shortly before the creation of man. At the feast of Quecholli, an annual fall festival in his honor, a ceremonial hunt was conducted. It is possible his name was suggested by the Milky Way, but his star was a morning star, usually the planet Venus.

MIXE, mē'hā, a tribe of Mexican Indians dwelling on the Tehuantepec Isthmus, southern Mexico. They speak the Zoquean language. The Mixe were conquered by Pedro de Alvarado in 1521–1524 and proselytized by missionaries from 1526; however, they remained religious conservatives until very recent times. They are good farmers, and their women are capable weavers and potters. In 1940 there were 51,261 Mixe, including bilinguals; in 1950 there remained 21,005 who spoke only Zoquean.

MIXED MARRIAGE, *in theology,* a marriage between a Catholic and Protestant, or, more loosely, any non-Catholic. Anglicans also employ the term. The Roman Catholic Church insists that the non-Catholic partner agree in writing before the marriage that the worship of the Catholic spouse shall not be interfered with; that children be reared as Catholics; and that no non-Catholic wedding ceremony be performed. On acceptance of these conditions, and the granting of a dispensation, a valid ceremony may be performed by a priest.

In American law mixed marriage means marriage of a Caucasian to a person of designated colored race or races. Such marriages were in 1955 illegal in 29 states, in some of which these laws were reinforced by criminal sanctions. Judges in state courts generally sustained antimiscegenation laws against challenges as to their constitutionality.

MIXED PROPERTY, neither real property such as a house and land, nor personal property such as clothing, but having the nature of both. Heirlooms, house keys, tombs, and title deeds, among other articles, are in law mixed property.

MIXITE, mĭk'sīt, in mineralogy, a green-to-whitish basic copper bismuth arsenate, named for A. Mixa, inspector of mines in Bohemia. Chemically it is Cu_2O,As_2O_3,xH_2O with 13 per cent Bi_2O_3.

MIXODECTES, mĭk-sô-dĕk'tēs, in paleontology, a genus of insectivores with very large incisors analogous to those of rodents, found in the Paleocene and Eocene of North America. It is the type of the family Mixodectidae.

MIXOSAURUS, mĭk-sô-sô'rŭs, a genus of

small fish-lizards (*Ichthyosauria*) from the Triassic formations of Europe, differing from typical ichthyosaurs by their much straighter tail and some minor characters.

MIXTEC, mĭs'tĕk ("cloud people"), an Indian people of southwestern Mexico inhabiting Oaxaca and part of Guerrero. They comprise one of the most important Indian groups of that country. Prior to the arrival of the Toltecs (q.v.) on the plateau of central Mexico in the late 7th century A.D., the Mixtec and Olmec appear to have been the representatives of the Highland culture. About the year 900 the Mixtec struck southward into the valley of Oaxaca and seized from the Zapotec their towns of Monte Albán and Mitla. This aggression initiated a period of warfare between the two peoples which continued until the end of the 15th century, when they temporarily united in a campaign against the Aztecs. That war terminating successfully for the allies, they again became enemies, the Zapotec forming an alliance with the Aztecs. In the early 16th century the Zapotec king concluded an alliance with the Spaniards of Hernán Cortés; but the Mixtec fought the white invaders until subdued by Pedro de Alvarado. The culture of the ancient Mixtec represents one of the high spots in Mexican Indian civilization; their present-day descendants are highly skilled in agriculture and are noted for their pottery and textiles.

FREDERICK J. DOCKSTADER.

MIXTURE, mĭks'tūr, an organ stop compounded of the higher-sounding and therefore shorter members of the foundation and mutation classes of stops, combined or mixed and arranged to draw together. At certain points in their ascending range, mixtures return to a rank of a lower octave. This return is called a break, and the stop is said to break back. See also ORGAN—*Early Christian Organ.*

MIYAZAKI, mē-yä-zä-kē, city, Japan, capital of Miyazaki Prefecture, southeastern Kyushu Island. Situated in an agricultural region on the Pacific coast, near the mouth of Oyodo River, the city is a port of call for coastal trading vessels, and is the site of the great Miyazaki-jingu Shinto shrine and museum. Chinaware and trays are manufactured, and fishing is locally important. Pop. (1960) 158,328.

MIZAR, mī'zär, the second-magnitude star ζ (Zeta) in the constellation Ursa Major (q.v.), familiar as the bright star at the bend of the handle of the Big Dipper. Near it is the fourth-magnitude star Alcor. In 1650 the Italian astronomer Giovanni Battista Riccioli, viewing Mizar through his telescope, saw that it consisted of two stars; Mizar thus became the first star discovered to be a double star. It was also the first double star to be successfully studied photographically when, in 1857, George Phillips Bond at Harvard College Observatory obtained measurable photographic images of both its components. Then, in 1889, Mizar became the first spectroscopic binary to be discovered, when Edward C. Pickering, director of Harvard Observatory, found by means of the spectroscope that the brighter of Mizar's two components is composed of two stars revolving around each other. In 1908, Edwin B. Frost, director of Yerkes Observatory, discovered that Mizar's fainter component is also a binary, and at the same time found that Mizar's near neighbor Alcor is a double star. Thus, Mizar is actually four stars, and with Alcor makes six stars at the middle of the handle of the Big Dipper. For further discussion of double stars or binaries see ASTRONOMICAL TERMS—*Terms of Descriptive Astronomy* (Star); DOUBLE STARS; STARS—*Double Stars.*

MIZPAH, mĭz'pä, or **MIZPEH,** mĭz'pĕ, the name of several Palestine localities mentioned in the Old Testament. It means watchtower in Hebrew. The Mizpah of Genesis 31:45–54 is the place in the highlands of ancient Gilead (now in the Hashemite Kingdom of Jordan) overlooking the Jabbok River (Wadi Zerqa'), where Jacob set up a pillar to mark his covenant with Laban when he left Laban's domain for Canaan. Here Laban pronounced the "Mizpah benediction": "The Lord watch between me and thee, when we are absent one from another." Jacob also called the site Galeed (Genesis 31:47). The exact spot is not known, but a group of rough stones is pointed out in the village of Suf as the traditional place of covenant.

Archaeologists do not agree as to the site of Mizpeh mentioned in Joshua 18:26 as one of the cities of the tribe of Benjamin. Some place it at Tell en-Naṣbeh, a mound eight miles north of Jerusalem; others at Nebī Samwîl, a height four miles southwest of Tell en-Naṣbeh and overlooking Jerusalem. Archaeological remains uncovered at Tell en-Naṣbeh show the place to have been a strongly fortified walled town with a 9th century B.C. city gate. Its latest occupation dates from about 300 B.C. Nebī Samwîl, according to Muslim tradition the burial place of Samuel, may have been the Mizpeh of Judges 20:1, 3, the Maspha of I Machabees (Maccabees) 3:46, a sanctuary or place of prayer for the Jews when Antiochus IV Epiphanes stopped their Temple worship in Jerusalem.

The Mizpeh of Judah (Joshua 15:38), near Lachish, is identified by some with a village in the cliffs of the Shephelah (Sephelah in I Machabees 12:38), perhaps the Tell es-Safiyeh, seven miles north of Beit Jibrin and about 20 miles south of Jerusalem, but others consider this to be the site of Gath.

The Mizpeh of Moab (I Samuel 22:3), whose king gave sanctuary to David's parents while David was in hiding from Saul, has not been identified. Other Old Testament localities called Mizpah or Mizpeh include an area in present-day Syria at the foot of Mount Hermon, possibly near Banias (Baniyas) to the west, occupied by Hivites in the days of Joshua (Joshua 11:3); and the home of Jephtha (Judges 11:29, 34), which may be the same as the Mizpah of Hosea 5:1, but the site is uncertain.

MJOSA, Lake, myû'sä (Nor. MJØSA), lake in southeastern Norway, in Opland and Hedmark counties, in the Gudbrandsdal. Norway's largest lake, it is 65 miles long, from one to nine miles wide, has an area of 141 square miles, and is up to 1,453 feet deep. It contains the small island of Helgoy (Nor. Helgøy). Cities on its shores are Lillehammer (north), Gjovik (west), and Hamar (east). The Vorma River flows out of the southern end into the Glomma.

MLAVA, mlä'vä, river, Yugoslavia, in east Serbia. It rises on the slopes of the Crni Vrh near Zagubica and flows about 60 miles north-northwest past Petrovac, entering an arm of the Danube north of Kostolac.

MLAWA, mwä'vä (Pol. MŁAWA), town, Poland, in Warszawa Province, northeast central Poland, 65 miles north-northwest of Warsaw. It has manufactures of cement, candy, and thread. Founded in 1429, it had become a wealthy city by the mid-17th century when, like so many other Polish cities, it was devastated by the Swedish invasion. Occupied by the Germans in both world wars, during World War II it was under East Prussia's administration and was called Mielau. Pop. (1946) 13,817.

MLJET, 'm-lyĕt (Ital. MELEDA, ancient MELITA), island, Yugoslavia, off the Dalmatian coast and in the Adriatic Sea, about 65 miles southeast of Split. Narrow and mountainous, it stretches for about 25 miles and covers an area of 38 square miles. It is believed by some to be identical with the Melita on which St. Paul was shipwrecked, though he probably was stranded on Malta.

MNASON OF CYPRUS, mentioned in Acts 21:16 as one who entertained Paul and his companions on their journey from Caesarea to Jerusalem. The Greek admits of two constructions to the passage rendered in the King James version of the Bible as "and brought with them one Mnason of Cyprus, an old disciple, with whom we should lodge." It may mean "brought with them one Mnason," or "bringing us to Mnason." Probably the home of this "old disciple" was in some village on the road between Caesarea and Jerusalem, and the distance of 60 or 70 miles made it convenient to break the journey there.

MNEME, nē'mē (Gr. Μνήμη, Memory), in Greek mythology the goddess of Memory and one of the three muses worshipped in early times on Mount Helicon in Boeotia, her sister muses being Aoide (Song) and Melete (Meditation). Later mythology increased the number of the muses to seven, and then to nine.

MNEMONICS, nē-mŏn'ĭks, a system of artificial aids for assisting the memory. Such methods have been in use for many years. They consist in the main of some mechanical scheme or framework which, by association, is linked with what one desires to memorize. One of the oldest forms of verbal mnemonics is contained in the familiar lines, "Thirty days hath September, April, June and November"; and many similar devices are known. The medical student has an unlimited number of mnemonic aids whereby to remember the names of the muscles, to call to mind the relation of important viscera and to determine accurately the order of the cranial nerves. Students of logic have for years made use of mnemotechnic devices to remember the parts of the syllogism. (See LOGIC.) Some of these devices are based on topical association, whereas others depend on number and letter relations, and a great many which have been in vogue in recent years are based upon sound and rhyme relations. A general criticism that can be made of most of these memory-schemes is that the processes are purely mechanical, and that one of the fundamental features in memory, that is, memorizing for the sake of idea-relation, is given up for the sake of word-relation. For certain classes of students and for certain lines of work these mechanical schemes may be of much service; for salesmen, for instance, who need to bear in mind immense quantities of goods with their wholesale, retail and discount prices. But as a process of general culture, improving mind-facilities, so called, mnemotechnics are mechanical. See also MEMORY AND ITS DISORDERS.

MNEMOSYNE, nē-mŏs'ĭ-nē, in Greek mythology, the goddess of memory; the mother of the nine muses of Zeus. She was a daughter of Uranus.

MNESICLES, nē'sĭ-klēz, Athenian artist of the age of Pericles. He was the architect of the gate-porches, called "Propylaea," to the Acropolis, which required five years for their construction (437–433 B.C.). Attic legend tells that he fell from the top of the Propylaea and was mortally injured. That night in a dream Athena came to Pericles and showed him an herb which would cure his artist; and the following day Mnesicles was restored to health.

MNESITHEUS, Athenian physician, probably of the 4th century B.C. Very little is known of him, but Galen and other early physicians often speak of him in praise. The comic poet Alexis quotes him.

MNESTER, celebrated Roman pantomime actor: d. 48 A.D. He attained his reputation as a mime in the reigns of Caligula and Claudius. When he failed to respond to the advances of Messalina she complained to Claudius that he had disobeyed her orders. The emperor had him flogged, and sternly commanded that he never again disobey the empress. Subsequently charged with participating in Messalina's orgies, he vainly pleaded that he had only obeyed the imperial command. He was executed.

MNEUIS, or **MNEVIS**, the name of Egypt's sacred bull worshipped at Heliopolis in the temple of Ra. His cult closely resembled that of Apis at Memphis where both cults were combined in the temple.

MNICHOVO HRADISTE, 'm-nyĭ'kô-vô hrä'dyĭsh-tyĕ, town, Czechoslovakia, in northern Bohemia, nine miles north-northeast of Mlada Boleslav, on the left bank of the Jizera River. Its industries include manufactures of footwear and textiles. Here the convention of Münchengrätz met on Sept. 28, 1833, and representatives of Austria, Prussia and Russia agreed to guarantee the integrity of the Turkish Empire. During the Austro-Prussian War of 1866 it was the scene of a Prussian victory over the allied Austrians and Saxons on June 28, 1866. Pop. (1947) 3,733.

MOA, one of a race of extinct ratite flightless birds of New Zealand, forming the family Dinornithidae and composed of several genera (see DINORNITHES) ranked between the apteryx and the epiornis. They had comparatively small heads, small eyes, bills of varied form, great legs, wings almost or quite wanting, and the head and neck bare. The feathers of the body were rounded, loose in part, downy, with great aftershafts. Some of the feathers were black with red-brown bases and white, others blackish brown or yellowish. They varied in size from that of a turkey (*Anomalopteryx parva*) to that of the huge *Dinornis robustus*, 12 feet in height. The remains of these birds are found in dunes, bogs, caves and places where the aborigines had fed upon their flesh. Not only bones, but pieces of skin, ligaments, feathers and eggs have been recovered. It is probable, indeed, that these birds became extinct only four or five centuries ago. The Maori traditions recount the wars of extermination which their early ancestors waged against the moa; and the natives profess to show the spot where the last one was killed. Clearer traditions say that the habits of the birds were sluggish, but their disposition fierce. They lived in pairs, fed upon green shoots and fern roots and made rude nests on the ground. Their anatomy was first elaborately described by Sir Richard Owen, the great English comparative anatomist, in 1879. It is quite possible that the larger species of the moa gave rise to the legend of the roc, the monstrous mythical bird of the *Arabian Nights* stories.

MOAB, mō'ăb, the name of an ancient Semitic people who occupied a rugged tableland between the Dead Sea and the Arabian desert, about 3,000 feet above sea level, now forming the southwestern part of the Hashemite Kingdom of the Jordan. Their land was also called Moab. The Dead Sea and the Jordan River formed its boundary on the west, while its other boundaries varied with the successes or defeats of the Moabites in wars with other nations. The "plains of Moab" spoken of in the Bible (Numbers 22:1) are the hot plains of the Jordan valley. The origin and meaning of the name is not known. Some authorities accept Moab, the son of Lot, as the ancestor of the Moabites (Genesis 19:37); others maintain that the expression "children of Lot" (Deuteronomy 2:9, 19) comes from the earliest known name of the land, which was Lotan, or Lot. Some authorities believe the Moabites settled there as early as the 13th century B.C. They had reached a high degree of civilization by the 9th century B.C.

The Moabites were a pastoral people and their country was noted for its rich pasturage and its wine. The institution of monarchy was established among them much earlier than among the Israelites, but their language, religion, and customs were similar to those of the Israelites, who regarded them as kinsmen. Their supreme god was Chemosh, who held among them much the same position as Jehovah among the Hebrews. Moab was for a time tributary to Israel under David and Solomon, but regained its independence either during the latter part of Solomon's reign or during the subsequent reign of Rehoboam. Later the Moabites paid tribute to the Assyrians. They were eventually invaded by tribes from the Arabian desert and their national existence came to an end in the 6th century B.C.

MOAB, town, Utah, county seat of Grand County, on the Colorado River; altitude 4,000 feet; 100 miles southeast of Price. It is on federal and state highways. The town is an important trading center for the livestock, fruit, and agricultural products raised in the area. Vanadium and uranium mines are nearby. To the north is the Arches National Monument and to the east La Sal National Forest, both tourist attractions. Pop. 4,793.

MOABITE STONE, a block of black basalt, about 3 feet 8½ inches high, and 2 feet 3½ inches wide, and 1 foot 1¾ inches thick, with rounded top but square base, on which there is an inscription of 34 lines in Hebrew-Phoenician characters, discovered in 1868 by the Reverend F. A. Klein at Dhiban, the Dibon of ancient Moab, just north of the river Arnon. An attempt made to purchase it led to a quarrel among the Arabs of the district, who thought to make more money out of it by selling it in pieces, and the stone was destroyed partially by being heated and then by throwing water upon it, which caused it to break into three large and several small pieces. The larger pieces were secured for the Louvre by Charles Clermont-Ganneau, a French Orientalist, who was also fortunate in obtaining a paper impression of the inscription before the stone was broken. The inscription dates about 850 B.C., and is the oldest known in the Hebrew-Phoenician form of writing. It was erected by Mesha, king of Moab, and is a record of his wars with Omri, king of Israel, and his successors. The narrative also treats of Mesha's wars against the Edomites.

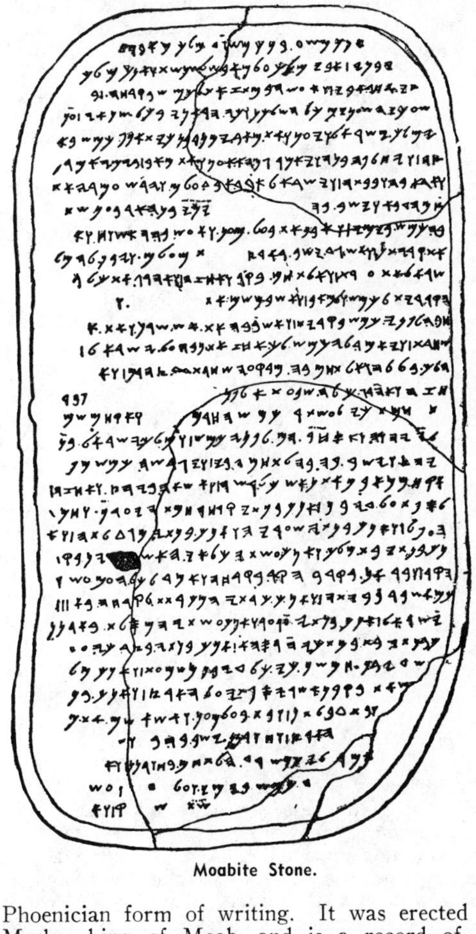

Moabite Stone.

Consult Ginsburg, Christian David, *The Moabite Stone* (London 1871), and Bennett, W. H., *The Moabite Stone* (Edinburgh 1911).

MO'ALLAQAT, or **MU'ALLAQAT.** See ARABIC LITERATURE.

MOAT. See FORTIFICATIONS.

MOBANGI. See UBANGI.

MOBERLY, mō'bẽr-lĭ, **George,** English prelate: b. St. Petersburg (now Leningrad), Russia, Oct. 10, 1803; d. Salisbury, Eng., July 6, 1885. He was educated at Winchester and Oxford. He was consecrated Bishop of Salisbury in 1869, and in 1872 urged omission of the damnatory clauses from the Athanasian Creed.

MOBERLY, Robert Campbell, English theologian: b. Winchester, July 26, 1845; d. Oxford, June 8, 1903. He was the son of George Moberly (q.v.). He was educated at Winchester and Oxford, and became regius professor of pastoral theology at Oxford in 1892. He was honorary chaplain to Queen Victoria (1898–1901) and chaplain in ordinary to Edward VII in 1902.

MOBERLY, city, Missouri, Randolph County, altitude 872 feet, is located 34 miles north of Columbia, on the Missouri, Kansas and Texas, and the Wabash railroads, in a grain-growing and dairy-farming region. Valuable deposits of fire clay and coal are nearby. The Wabash Railroad has machine and car repair shops here. Manufactured products include syrups, dairy products, shoes, hosiery, and farm implements and equipment. Moberly Junior College, coeducational, is here. Platted in 1866, on the watershed between the Missouri and Mississippi rivers, Moberly received a city charter in 1873. Pop. 12,988.

MOBILE, mô-bēl', city, Alabama, county seat of Mobile County, is situated in the southwestern part of the state on Mobile River at its entrance to Mobile Bay, 31 miles from the Gulf of Mexico, 179 miles from Montgomery, the capital of Alabama, and 139 miles by rail from New Orleans. The city is built on a level, sandy plain from six to 35 feet above the river and rising gradually to the tablelands, 200 to 300 feet above sea level, six miles west of the river.

Transportation Facilities.—Mobile is served by the Alabama; Tennessee and Northern; Frisco; Gulf, Mobile and Ohio; Louisville and Nashville; and the Southern railroads. Daily air service is provided by major air lines operating between New York and New Orleans, La., with connections for cities east, west and north of Mobile; and between Mobile and Jacksonville, Fla., with connections for the West Indies, Central and South America. The Port of Mobile has one of the largest and most complete systems of warehouses and docks on the Gulf of Mexico, and ocean-going vessels provide adequate service to all ports of the world as well as to ports on the Atlantic and Pacific coasts. The Alabama, the Tombigbee, the Black Warrior rivers and the Intracoastal Canal provide inland water routes over which barge lines are operated between Mobile and Demopolis, Selma, Montgomery and Birmingham. There is also an inland waterway between Mobile and West Florida cities, and to Louisiana and Texas ports. The ship channel is maintained by the United States Government at a minimum depth of 32 feet, and a minimum width of 300 feet. Across the outer bar the channel is 36 feet deep and 450 feet wide. Bates Field, the municipal airport, embraces 163 acres, and here too is the Army's Southeast Air Depot, Brookley Air Force Base.

Education.—Mobile and Mobile County jointly operate an excellent public school system. In 1950 there were 48 schools for white children in Mobile and Mobile County, with over 30,223 pupils enrolled, and 32 schools for colored children with about 13,827 pupils enrolled. The school buildings are of modern construction, most of them being built of brick or concrete and tile. One of the noteworthy buildings of the Mobile school system, from a historic standpoint, is Barton Academy, the first public school erected in the State of Alabama. It was completed in 1836. The building has been remodeled and is in use as an elementary school. Spring Hill College, established in 1830, is a senior college of arts and sciences offering courses leading to the degrees of bachelor of arts, bachelor of science, and bachelor of science in Commerce. Courses in law, medicine, and engineering also are offered.

Religion.—When the first settlement was established by the French in 1711, the "Church" was one of the original buildings, and one of the present churches stands nearly on the same site. There are in the city more than 150 churches for white and colored persons. They represent practically all religious denominations.

Public Parks.—Mobile has 13 public parks, including famous Bienville Square, in the heart of the city. In addition, there are several private parks that are open to visitors.

Places of Interest.—There are numerous attractions for tourists in Mobile. One of these is the home of Joseph Jefferson, famous actor, who created the role, *Rip Van Winkle*. Seasonal attractions include Azalea Trail, a 17-mile flower-lined drive over city and suburban streets, passing Bellingrath Gardens in Mobile County, one of the famous beauty spots of the South. The flowers along the Trail bloom in late winter and early spring and each year attract thousands of visitors. Another seasonal attraction is the Mardi Gras festival, observed each year for 10 days prior to Ash Wednesday, or the beginning of Lent. It was in Mobile that the first Mardi Gras was celebrated in this country. Another annual attraction is the Alabama Deep Sea Fishing Rodeo, held in the waters of lower Mobile Bay and the Gulf of Mexico. It attracts fishermen from all parts of America.

Mobile was the home of Admiral Raphael Semmes, Confederate naval officer; of Gen. Braxton Bragg of the Confederate Army; of Gen. William C. Gorgas, U.S.A., who rid the Panama Canal Zone of yellow fever; of William A. Alexander, who designed and built a submarine during the Civil War; of Rufus W. King, Vice-President of the United States, 1853–1857, and before that United States senator and minister to France.

Industries.—Mobile has experienced a remarkable industrial development within recent years. The city was selected by the federal government as a site for a United States Army air depot, which was constructed at an initial cost of $8,000,000. The output of Mobile factories in 1950 exceeded in value $250,000,000.

The leading industries include shipbuilding and repairing, the manufacture of paper and pulp, the reduction of bauxite, cotton manufactures, lumber, timber and related products, oil refining, clothing, the mixing of fertilizers, naval stores extraction, processing of food products, paint manufacture, steel fabrication, and the manufacture of asphalt and asbestos roofing The pulp and paper industry includes a large kraft paper mill, bag plants, a plant for the manufacture of insulation board, and a boxboard plant. The textile industry operates two cotton cloth mills and a garment factory. There are hardwood lumber mills, pine wood saw mills, creosoting plants, veneer plants, millwork plants, and cabinet, cooperage, box, plywood, and panel plants.

Mobile is also the center of a large wholesale and retail business. In 1950, the jobbing business alone amounted to about $50,000,000 a year, and the retail business was estimated at $140,000,000 a year.

Commerce.—Mobile is one of the leading cotton markets and shipping points of the country, the natural center of the Alabama-Tombigbee cotton region, the nearest tidewater shipping port for the soft coal, iron, cement, lime, lumber, turpentine, resin and agricultural products of the southern, central and northern sections of Alabama and large amounts from upper Mississippi and lower Tennessee. It is the third largest tropical importing city in the United States; has steamship connection with Europe, Cuba, Central America, Mexico, Windward and all Caribbean Sea islands, Brazil, the Pacific Coast of the United States, western coast of South America, Australia, New Zealand, Hawaiian Islands, Japan and China, via the Panama Canal, to which Mobile is the nearest, deep, fresh water railroad-connected city in the United States. In 1928 the Alabama State Docks Commission completed a State ocean terminal occupying a site of 550 acres on the west bank of the harbor at a cost of $12,000,000. The accommodations of this ocean terminal are open to all shippers, shipping lines, and railroads. The principal units of the terminal are four piers, several cotton warehouses, a coal and bulk material handling plant, a terminal railway, and an industrial canal.

Mobile's commerce was further facilitated by the completion in 1927 at a cost of $2,500,000 of the Cochrane Bridge, stretching 10½ miles across the headwaters of Mobile Bay and spanning the widest gap on the entire route of the Old Spanish Trail (U.S. 90) from Florida to California. The one-half mile Bankhead tunnel under Mobile River, completed in 1941, the first underwater vehicular tunnel in the south, shortened the distance across the bay by nine miles. The Florida-Midwest, and federal highways No. 31, 43 and 45 also converge at Mobile.

Commerce statistics for the city of Mobile include for exports cotton and subsidiary products, coal, coal oil, crude oil and by-products, iron, iron pipe, cement and cement products, lime, whiting, fuller's earth, lumber and allied products, tar, turpentine, resin, livestock, canned foods and other canned products, flour, lard, salted and pickled pork, salt, soap, cotton goods and notions, gun shells and other ordnance stores, general foundry and machineshop products, agricultural and mill machinery, belting and other mill supplies, fire and burglar-proof safes, scales, typewriting, computing and other machines; also store and office furniture and fixtures, electrical supplies, hardware, cordage and ship supplies, hay, grain, garden, flower and field seed, household furniture, sewing machines, musical instruments. Among its imports, are Cuban magnetic iron ore, zinc, ammonia sulphate, sulphur ore, iron pyrites, sodium nitrate, fire brick, tropical fruits and other products, coffee, molasses, sugar, sisal grass, chicle gum, mahogany logs and lumber, iron, satin, sandal, lignum vitae woods, dye woods, cork, cigars, Cuban tobacco, Peruvian bark, opium and other drug materials, camphor, sponges, bird lime, dried bone, phosphate rock, asphalt, lemons, limes, olives and olive oil, raisins, currants, nuts, prunes, matting, bamboo poles and rods, together with a miscellaneous line of embroideries, laces, rugs, and toys. The importation of Cuban molasses or black strap, used in the making of stock feed and explosives, has increased to a greater extent than any other article of late years.

Hospitals.—There are six hospitals in Mobile, including City Hospital, operated by the Sisters of Charity for the city, and the United States Marine Hospital. Two new hospitals costing $4,000,000 each replaced Mobile Infirmary and Providence Hospital in 1951.

Government.—Mobile has a commissioner form of government, with three commissioners, including a mayor. One commissioner is elected every two years for a term of six years, and while in office each commissioner serves for two terms of one year each as mayor. All departments of the municipal government, except the Police and Fire departments, are housed in the City Hall, which was the Confederate Armory in Mobile during the Civil War, and which recently was remodeled. The County Court House, housing the offices of the county government, stands directly across the street from the City Hall.

Population.—In 1930 Mobile's population was 68,202 In 1940 it was 78,720 with about 101,000 in the metropolitan area. In 1970 the incorporated city of Mobile had a population of 190,026 with 376,690 in the metropolitan area. Sixty-one per cent of the population come within the classification of "native-born whites"; 3 per cent are foreign born; 36 per cent are colored.

Federal Buildings and Services.—The federal government has a court house and office building in Mobile. Besides the courts and the post office, the federal services maintained in the city include the Gulf Division headquarters of the United States Coast Guard; the district office of the Army Engineers; Customs Office; lighthouse depot for the Gulf Coast; a bureau of the Department of Commerce; an Immigration Bureau; Weather Bureau; branch of the Social Security Board; an Employment Service Office; Internal Revenue Office; Public Health Service Station; branch of the Steamboat Inspection Service, and other agencies.

Water Supply.—The water supply of Mobile is municipally owned and operated, and comes from springs, unfiltered, with gravity flow into the city. The total capacity is 20,000,000 gallons daily. There are two reservoirs with a capacity of 10,000,000 gallons each. The daily water consumption of the city is between 13 and 18 million gallons. A $7,000,000 industrial water supply system provides up to 50,000,000 gallons a day.

Utilities.—Natural gas is piped to Mobile from the Louisiana and Mississippi fields in high-pressure mains having a capacity of 160,000,000 cubic feet a day. Electricity is supplied by the Alabama Power Company.

History.—Twenty-seven years after Columbus discovered America, Spanish explorers mapped Mobile Bay, but it was not until 1699, nearly two centuries later, that adventurous Frenchmen under the leadership of Le Moyne d'Iberville landed on Dauphin Island at the entrance to the bay with the first colonial enterprise ever attempted on the shores of the Gulf of Mexico. In 1711, after many vicissitudes, Jean Baptiste Le Moyne, Sieur de Bienville, the younger brother of d'Iberville, established a permanent colony on the present site of Mobile under the name of Fort Louis de la Mobile—the first part of the name honoring le Grande Monarque Louis XIV and the last part for the Mauvilla tribe of Indians who lived in the vicinity. France ceded Mobile and the territory east of the Mississippi to Great Britain in 1763. The practical British explored the rivers and sounded the bay, leaving excellent maps for historians. They improved the fort and built up a good trade with the Indians.

In 1779 Spain declared war on Great Britain. Hostilities spread to the American Colonies. The Spanish under young Bernardo Galvez captured the fort at Mobile after burning a large part of the town and the banner of St. George was lowered. The colony remained under the rule of Spain for 33 years, and enjoyed a good trade with Europe. During this period the Spanish king favored many of his subjects with large grants of land and consequently many titles to property in Mobile today date back to the Spanish occupation.

In 1800 Napoleon forced Spain to cede to France the province of Louisiana, then in 1803 President Thomas Jefferson purchased Louisiana from France. The treaties were not clear and although the United States from then on claimed Mobile, Spain insisted that Mobile was in Florida and not in Louisiana and Spanish officers remained in authority. The population in 1803 was 810 people.

When the war of 1812 broke out between the United States and England, the Spanish ports were being used by the English. President James Madison directed General James Wilkinson to capture Mobile, and the community came under the American flag in April, 1813. Gen. Andrew Jackson made his headquarters in Mobile in several of his Indian campaigns and for a large part of the time during the war with England in 1812 and 1813.

After the War of 1812 was over, the community grew rapidly and was incorporated as a city in 1819. The first newspaper was published in 1812; Spring Hill College was built in 1830. America's first Mardi Gras was staged here in 1830. Gas lighting was introduced in 1835. Barton Academy was completed in 1836. In 1836 the Cedar Point Railroad was started to parallel the bay to Dog River. In 1848 a charter was granted for building a railroad from Mobile to the Ohio River. Construction of the Custom House was started in 1852. Street railways were laid in 1861. The population of Mobile at that time was nearly 15,000 people.

When the clouds of civil war gathered over the Nation, Alabama seceded from the Union and in January, 1861 the flag of the Republic of Alabama was unfurled over the state capitol.

Alabama became one of the Confederate States of America in March, 1861. Mobile was one of the most important Confederate ports and one of the famous naval battles of American history was fought in Mobile Bay by Federal and Confederate fleets in August, 1864. In that battle Federal forces took command of Mobile Bay but the city did not fall into the hands of the Union troops until April 12, 1865, three days after General Robert E. Lee surrendered at Appomattox.

Then followed the difficult reconstruction period, but the city soon renewed its march of progress. Railroads pushed their lines into the city, the harbor was further improved and in 1870 an appropriation of $50,000 was made to survey the channel from Mobile to deep water. The first project was for a channel 13 feet deep and 200 feet wide. The present channel is 32 feet deep by 300 feet wide and 31½ miles long.

Mobile is Alabama's only seaport. Through the years its harbor has received massive infusions of federal and state funds to improve its dock facilities. During both world wars Mobile was a busy port, and it has become an important shipping center for goods traveling between Latin America and the United States.

MOBILE, river, Alabama, the name given to the western stream or mouth of the river formed by the junction of the Alabama and Tombigbee rivers. The eastern stream or mouth is called the Tensaw. From this junction of the rivers to the head of Mobile Bay is, in direct line, about 25 miles, but the winding of the stream makes its course about 50 miles long. The Mobile and Tensaw communicate at several points, but the two streams enter Mobile Bay at the city of Mobile by the same delta. With its tributaries the Mobile River drains an area of about 42,300 square miles. There is a large river traffic between Mobile and the Birmingham area via the Black Warrior River, and with Montgomery via the Alabama River.

MOBILE BAY, a bay on the southwest coast of Alabama, forming an estuary into which, through the deltaic mouths of the Mobile and Tensaw branches, flow the waters of the Tombigbee and the Alabama rivers. That part of the estuary to which the name of Mobile Bay is applied is about 30 miles long and from 9 to 12 miles wide. At the entrance to the bay are long narrow strips of land, almost obstructing the entrance. On the east, at Mobile Point, is Fort Morgan and a revolving light; to the West on Dauphin Island is Fort Gaines. Between Dauphin and the mainland is Grant's Pass, a strait connecting Mobile Bay with Mississippi Sound. The United States government has improved the harbor, and from a shallow entrance, which was a hindrance to navigation, there is now a channel through which vessels drawing 30 feet and over can enter and ascend to the wharves of Mobile city.

MOBILE BAY, Battle of, a battle of the Civil War fought Aug. 5, 1864. Mobile Bay is divided from the Gulf of Mexico by Mobile Point east and Dauphin Island west, about three miles apart; but the ship channel of less than 2,000 yards, narrowing to 750 outside, closely skirts Mobile Point. The latter was defended by Fort Morgan; the island by Fort Gaines, too far from the channels to be very formidable. Between them stretched a line of piles and torpedoes, but leaving a narrow channel for blockade-runners. Within was the Confederacy's most powerful ram, the *Tennessee,* and three small unarmored paddle-wheel gunboats. Commander David Farragut's Federal fleet comprised the monitors *Tecumseh, Manhattan, Winnebago* and *Chickasaw,* forming an inshore column; and the wooden sloops of war *Brooklyn, Hartford* (flagship), *Richmond, Lackawanna, Monongahela, Ossipee* and *Oneida,* forming an outer one, each with a smaller mate lashed to the port side, to ensure passage through if the starboard vessel's machinery should be disabled. Farragut would have led in the *Hartford,* but the *Brooklyn* had machinery for picking up torpedoes. The advance began at 5.30 A.M., and firing at 7.05; the instructions were to keep east of the red buoy, but the *Tecumseh* went west and was sunk by a torpedo. The *Brooklyn* stopped in fear of a like disaster, and the *Hartford* with Farragut passed her and led the fleet into the bay. Each vessel received much damage from Fort Morgan, but they silenced its guns by destructive fire, and all succeeded in anchoring three miles up. One Confederate gunboat was then sunk, one was captured, and one took refuge next the fort; the *Tennessee* was to be attacked after dark, but itself assailed the flagship, and after a desperate fight was disabled, and surrendered. The *Lackawanna* collided with the *Hartford* and nearly sank her. The Union fleet lost 52 killed, 170 wounded, and 113 drowned in the *Tecumseh;* the Confederates 10 killed, 16 wounded, and 280 prisoners, besides the casualties in the fort. Both forts surrendered a few days later. The Union fleet carried 159 guns, and the officers and crews numbered 3,000 men. The Confederate fleet carried 22 guns and 470 officers and men.

MOBILES, mō'bēlz, in art, three-dimensional abstract compositions made of metal, wood, plastic, glass, cardboard, wire, thread, or any combination of these. The composition is essentially a combination of two-dimensional shapes, together with the light and space between them. The mobile differs from abstract sculpture, first, in that it is not a continuous solid form, although the work of some modern sculptors like Henry Moore resembles the mobile in this respect; and, second, in that it is intended to move in certain predetermined ways. Its characteristic movement is, in fact, the most distinctive feature of the mobile (hence the name).

In order that the construction may move, it must be suspended freely in space. This is generally done by hanging it from a ceiling, although some mobiles are mounted on pedestals or stands in such a way as to allow freedom of movement. The possibility of movement is derived from the fact that the component parts of the composition are held together by thin wire (or thread), which allows them to swing in response to the circulation of air, the only motive force involved.

Aesthetically as well as mechanically, the most important element in a mobile is balance. Although the composition moves, it must also be in dynamic equilibrium. Balance is secured by the skillful handling of shapes and space relationships, and by the proper use of color, which can add to or reduce the apparent massiveness of the component forms. The artistic problem is to secure balance without sacrificing variety or complexity of design.

Although mobiles are usually composed of abstract shapes, realistic forms like leaves, fish, or birds are sometimes employed as well, without necessarily being combined to constitute a realistic whole. A related art form called the *stabile* retains the airy spatial quality of the mobile but lacks its power of movement.

The mobile as an art form is a very modern development. Its creator is Alexander Calder (1898-), an American artist, who began working in wire sculpture about 1930 and had his first one-man show in Paris in 1931. From the beginning, his aim was to suggest movement in his abstract constructions; not satisfied with this, he went on to install mechanisms and motors which actually moved the parts. The next step was the creation of forms that would move "naturally," without mechanical aids—that is, mobiles.

Since their origin in the 1930's, mobiles have won widespread acceptance as genuine art forms, and the work of Calder and others in this genre has received international recognition. Mobiles have become increasingly popular as decorations in homes and places of business. They have also been put to more pragmatic use as a means of displaying small articles of merchandise in shop windows and on counters. Since no elaborate technical training is required, the creation of original mobiles has become a popular hobby as well. Schools have found them an excellent way to introduce children to the excitement of artistic creation.

Consult Sweeney, James J., *Alexander Calder,* rev. ed. (New York 1951); Lynch, John, *How to Make Mobiles* (New York 1953); id., *Mobile Design* (New York 1955).

MOBILIER, Crédit. See CRÉDIT MOBILIER OF AMERICA.

MOBIUS, mû'bĭ-o͞os, **August Ferdinand,** German mathematician: b. Schulpforte, Germany, Nov. 17, 1790; d. Leipzig, Sept. 26, 1868. He was educated at Leipzig University, and became professor of astronomy there in 1816. He also studied at Göttingen under the eminent mathematician and astronomer Karl Friedrich Gauss. From 1844 Möbius was director of the Leipzig observatory. His writings in pure mathematics —and in particular his chief work *Der barycentrische Kalkul* (1827)—were of importance to the development of analytic projective geometry, especially in the use of homogeneous equations and the geometric principle of duality (of which he was an independent discoverer).

MOBUTU SESE SEKO, Zairian general and political leader: b. Lisala, Belgian Congo (now Zaire), Oct. 30, 1930. Joseph Désiré Mobutu, who changed his name to Mobutu Sese Seko in 1972, was educated at missionary schools in the Congo. From 1949 to 1956 he served in the Belgian-controlled colonial army, rising to sergeant major, the highest rank then open to Africans. After his discharge from the army he became a journalist.

Mobutu developed an increasing interest in politics and in 1958 he joined Patrice Lumumba's Congolese National Movement. In January 1960 he was a delegate to the Brussels Round Table Conference on Congo. After Congo achieved independence on June 30, 1960, Mobutu was named secretary of state for national defense. When the army mutinied in July he was reappointed to the army as chief of staff.

Conditions in Congo continued to deteriorate and, in September, Mobutu suspended Premier Lumumba and President Joseph Kasavubu; he instituted a College of High Commissioners to run the country. In February 1961, Mobutu returned control of the government to President Kasavubu and was named commander in chief of the army with the rank of major general. Thereafter he attempted to modernize and retrain the army.

On Nov. 25, 1965, Mobutu again seized power and declared himself president for five years. He introduced a new constitution consolidating power in the presidency and founded a new party, the Popular Movement of the Revolution.

L. GRAY COWAN, *Columbia University*

MOBY-DICK, mō'bĭ dĭk, Herman Melville's greatest novel, was published in London and New York in 1851. The English edition, somewhat bowdlerized, appeared under the title of *The Whale* and was presented to the public ostensibly as a description of whales and the whale fisheries. The work is really made up of three elements. One of these is a fairly full and accurate account of American whaling customs in the 1840's and the natural history of the sperm whale. The second is an exciting narrative depicting the hunt for a particular white whale, Moby-Dick, by mad Captain Ahab, who has previously lost one leg to its ferocious jaws. The third element is philosophical commentary upon human life and fate. This last has been variously interpreted. Some find the book an involved allegory representing the revolt of Satanic Ahab against his God. To others the white whale symbolizes evil, and Ahab is a Promethean figure who courageously struggles against it. Melville, however, leaves little doubt of his intention to show Ahab as a rebel protesting against fate and as one who considers the individual capable of warring against the forces of nature which limit his powers. Whatever he symbolizes, Ahab's final failure reveals the tragedy of unconquerable pride. So rich in symbolism is the style of the book that every reader can interpret the underlying philosophy according to his own prejudices. Some even read the book as pure adventure, though there can be no question of its author's desire to present moral and philosophical ideas as well as entertainment. *Moby-Dick* has been called "the one undoubted classic" of American literature.

TYRUS HILLWAY,
Associate Professor, Colorado State College of Education.

MOCCASIN, mŏk'ȧ-sĭn, among American Indians (the word is of Algonquian origin), a one-piece, heelless shoe formed of undressed soft leather, usually deerskin, seamed at the instep and heel. The Plains Indians added a hard sole of rawhide. Moccasins were decorated with porcupine quills until white traders made beads available. Sturdy and comfortable, moccasins have become popular as house shoes in soft leather and as outdoor shoes in heavy leather. The usual type has the vamp gathered to the edge of a U-shaped tongue over the instep. They are often lined.

MOCCASIN (snake). See WATER MOCCASIN.

MOCCASIN-FLOWER. See LADY'S-SLIPPER.

MOCHA, mō'kȧ (Arabian MUKHA, mōō-KÄ'), town, Yemen, in Taiz Province, on the Red Sea, 45 miles north of Bab el Mandeb Strait and 105 miles south of Hodeida. During the 16th and 17th centuries it was a flourishing port from which was shipped the fine Arabian coffee that became known by its name. The town declined steadily in the 19th century. Pop. (1959) 600.

MOCK ORANGE, a name commonly applied to any shrub of the genus *Philadelphus,* family Saxifragaceae (saxifrage). In the United States the name is also applied to the southern buckthorn (*Bumelia lyciodes*), the cherry laurel, the Osage orange, and several other shrubs and trees. In Australia it is the common name for the native laurel (*Pittosporum undulatum*). See also SYRINGA.

MOCKINGBIRD, mŏk'ĭng-bûrd, an American bird, *Mimus polyglottos polyglottos,* the eastern species in the United States ranging from Maryland through Ohio, Illinois, Iowa, Nebraska, and south to the Gulf of Mexico, with a few found as far north as Massachusetts and the Great Lakes; the western species ranging through central California south to Vera Cruz, Mexico. The bird is about the size of a robin, though more slender. Its average adult length is about 10 inches, with a wing spread to 15 inches. Its plumage is a pale brownish gray above, grayish white below, with white wing and tail patches. It has a beautiful and exuberant song of its own, a long sequence of notes in great variety, each phrase repeated several times in succession, and it is also able to imitate the calls of many other birds. The mockingbird often sings at night, especially on bright moonlight nights. In the South, it begins to sing in February and continues singing throughout the spring. It makes its nest of coarse twigs lined with roots and grasses, in thickets and low trees; its eggs, 3 to 6, are pale bluish green in color, flecked with brown, and take 14 days to hatch. There are two or three annual broods. The bird shows great courage in defending its nest from enemies, especially snakes. During the spring and summer its food consists largely of insects, such as grasshoppers, ants, flies, boll weevils, wasps, even spiders and caterpillars. In autumn it eats the berries of wild trees and shrubs, such as sumac, wild grape, Virginia creeper, barberry, and bittersweet. It is the state bird of Arkansas, Florida, Mississippi, Tennessee, and Texas.

Allan D. Cruickshank from National Audubon Society

A mockingbird at her nest.

MODDER RIVER, mod'ər, in the Republic of South Africa, in Orange Free State and Cape provinces. The river rises to the northeast of Bloemfontein and flows westward for 225 miles to join the Riet River, a tributary of the Vaal, 22 miles southwest of Kimberley. It came into considerable prominence during the South African War of 1899–1902. Along its banks at Magersfontein the British were driven back with great loss (especially in the night attack of Dec. 11, 1899), and at Paardeberg the Boer general, Piet Arnoldus Cronjé, surrendered on Feb. 28, 1900.

MODE, mōd, in statistics, that value, if it exists, which occurs most frequently in a set of statistical data. Thus, in the series 2, 6, 8, 9, 9, 9, 13, 14, the mode is 9. Given a finite number of values, each of which occurs equally frequently, there is no mode according to this definition. Thus, the series 1, 2, 3, 4, 5, 6, 7, 8, 9, has no mode. However, when data are grouped into a frequency distribution, there will usually be one class or interval which has maximum frequency, and the mode is said to be contained within this modal class. Disadvantages of the mode as a measure of location or central tendencies for empirical data are that it is dependent upon the particular grouping selected, and that for ungrouped data it may not exist or may not be unique.

Basically, the mode is a concept associated with continuous theoretical distributions. Given a random variable X with frequency function $f(X)$, the mode is that value of X for which $f(X)$ has a maximum point, that is, the point about which the concentration of random values of X is greatest. A distribution is unimodal or multimodal according to whether it has a single maximum point or two or more maximum points. Thus, the series 1, 2, 3, 3, 3, 3, 4, 5, 6, 7, 7, 7, 7, 8, 9, has two maximum points of concentration, and is multimodal. When the distribution of a series is symmetrical, the mean (average value of the series), median (middle point in the series), and mode are identical. If the distribution is unimodal and only moderately asymmetrical, the approximate relationship

$$\text{Mode} = 3(\text{Median}) - 2(\text{Mean})$$

seems to hold. See also STATISTICS—*Descriptive Statistics.*

D. V. HUNTSBERGER,
Statistical Laboratory, Iowa State College.

MODELS AND MODELMAKING, mŏd"lz, mŏd"l-māk-ĭng. Models play an important part in modern civilization. They are used for a great variety of purposes by industry, governmental agencies, and many professions. Modelmaking has become a recognized vocation which calls for specialized precision techniques. Models are used to instruct and entertain, and to advertise, sell, plan, manufacture, and test products. New uses for models are constantly being developed.

People often think of models as small versions of the things they represent. This is not necessarily so; a model may be smaller than its prototype, or considerably larger. The size or scale to which a model is built depends entirely upon the purpose for which it has been designed.

HISTORY

Fetishes.—Models have been used since early prehistoric times; no one knows when they were first employed. Primitive people have always made fetishes, carved figures, and other handmade objects which were worshiped as having supernatural powers. Many, particularly those made by African natives, were modeled after people or animals. Fetishes were used for various purposes. Primitive sorcerers cast spells over their enemies by fashioning small models or figures of their intended victims. After the appropriate magic had been performed with the model, the person it represented was supposed to die.

In some societies, small manikins were used in treating sickness. The shaman or witch doctor undertook to drive the illness from the body of the sufferer. The demons or evil spirits which were thought to be responsible for the patient's illness were presumably frightened into leaving his body; they were then supposed to inhabit the manikin.

Tomb Figures.—The earliest known models of which we have definite records are those which were made by the ancient Egyptians about 4000 B.C. These were tomb models, miniatures carved of wood, which depicted scenes of everyday life. They were placed in the tombs of deceased nobles and kings. The ancient Egyptians believed that the *ka,* or spirit, would one day return to the body. For this reason, bodies were carefully preserved by mummification. The models, which showed almost all phases of Egyptian life, were placed in the tombs so that the deceased would have aid, comfort, and the use of all his worldly goods in the spirit world, awaiting the day when the *ka* would return.

These burial models were not simply crude carvings of individual figures, but skillfully fashioned miniatures. In most cases they represented scenes involving many figures. They showed sailors and their boats, servants performing their daily tasks, artisans at work, soldiers, and domesticated animals. They were constructed with careful attention to details. We know exactly how their ships were rigged, their horses were harnessed, and their clothing fastened in place. Because of this, burial models have given us a firsthand record of the dress, customs, and everyday activities of the ancient Egyptians. Egyptian tomb models have been carefully preserved in museums all over the world. (See also EGYPTIAN ARTS.)

The Egyptians were not the only people who made use of burial figures. This practice was also carried on by the ancient Chinese. Beautiful ceramic figures have been found in the tombs of wealthy Chinese. Among these are representations of horses, servants, musicians and dancers. It is believed these figures were placed in the tombs in order that they might serve the dead. See also CHINA—*14. Art* (Sculpture); *15. Ceramics.*

Ship Models.—Models have played an important part in the development of ship design. Throughout the ages, sailors had idled away hours aboard ship by constructing small models of ships upon which they had served. These were regarded as curiosities and were purely decorative in purpose.

In the early days of shipbuilding, designs for ships were planned by master shipbuilders; new ideas were incorporated by improvisation. In France in 1679, Jean Baptiste Colbert, Louis XIV's minister of marine, ordered the superintendents of all royal navy yards to make a scale model of every ship they built. The idea was to construct a set of models which would serve as precise standards for any ships built in the future. During the years that followed, thousands of exquisite scale models were built. Many of these found their way into the curio collections of noblemen and members of the French court. Early in the 19th century, the French government established a maritime museum, in which many of these models were displayed. The museum still functions. Not only are early ship models displayed, but beautiful, precise scale models are also constructed by a staff of highly skilled craftsmen. All types of ships are represented; they furnish invaluable, accurate data for historical research.

Musée de la Marine, Paris

Model of an 18th century warship, said to have been a gift to Louis XV of France when a child.

Ship models also served another purpose. With the development of worldwide commerce, large numbers of ships were needed to carry on trade with other countries. Most of these were built by wealthy companies of merchants. Single trading ships were often built by speculators. Funds for their construction and operation were raised by selling shares. Carefully built scale models were exhibited to show prospective shareholders exactly how the finished ship would look.

HOW MODELS ARE USED

Advertising.—Models are used widely in advertising. Window displays often contain dioramas, three-dimensional backgrounds against which products are exhibited, and the products are often shown as scale models. A travel agency display may feature models of ships or trains, placed against appropriate scenic backgrounds. Small products may be shown by oversized models; packages, containers, and bottles can be scaled up in size for dramatic presentation.

Outdoor signs may be very elaborate, particularly in large cities. Some of these incorporate animated models, or models with moving parts; the models seem to be performing the functions for which the products they represent were designed. For example, an oversized coffee percolator may be made to give off a visible vapor, which would suggest hot coffee to the observer.

Models are frequently used in store counter displays. Containers of products are usually featured, their size depending upon the setting in which they are placed.

Television Commercials.—With the advent of television advertising, a new field was opened for the use of models. Since most television commercial presentations are filmed, all the tricks of the movie industry are utilized to make them interesting. Models can be made to move, speak, dance, or change their shapes in a variety of ways.

This is made possible by a process known as stop-motion photography. In order to understand how this is done, one must first understand how a movie camera works. A movie camera exposes a series of individual pictures, or frames. A film sequence of a person smiling may consist of four or five frames. The first may show the mouth completely relaxed; the second may show the beginning of a smile; the third, fourth, and fifth frames may show the smile becoming progressively larger. When the film is run through a projector, the sequence of frames appears on the screen as a smooth, unbroken action.

The same smile can be duplicated with models. Five separate models will be needed, one for each frame in the film sequence; the models are identical, except for the shape of the mouth. The first model may show the mouth relaxed, and the others a progressively larger smile. Each model is photographed on a single frame. After one is photographed it is removed, and the next one in sequence photographed in the identical position. When the completed film is run off on the screen, it is seen as a smooth action, exactly like the one of the person smiling. For further information on photographing models, see section on *Theater and Motion Pictures*.

Aircraft and Automobile Design.—Model airplane building is not only an interesting hobby, but also an essential part of the procedure used in developing new aircraft designs. A new airplane is first planned on paper. The next step is to build a scale model, so that the designer can see how the plane looks in three dimensions. Solid, miniature scale models are built from the designer's plans, and tested in wind tunnels. This is a very important aspect of plane design, as it shows up any aerodynamic faults the plane may have. Since the scale model will behave exactly the same way as a full-sized plane, corrections in design can be worked out at this time. When the scale model has passed the wind-tunnel test, it is reproduced as a *mock-up,* a full-sized model made of wood. The mock-up is subjected to further design refinements, after which a *prototype* is made. This is a handmade, full-sized model complete in all details, which is actually tested for performance. Prototypes are made by master mechanics, and are fully powered. These are the planes that are flown by test pilots.

The automobile industry also makes use of models to a great extent. Preliminary sketches for automobile designs are first drawn on paper. Acceptable designs are then constructed as small clay models, usually one fourth the actual size

B. Altman & Co.

Above: The Christmas window display of a department store on New York's Fifth Avenue. Its animated models of children and animals move about in a setting of yesteryear.

KLM Photo

Above: The ticket office of an intercontinental airline features a 10-foot-high model of the world.

Westinghouse Broadcasting Company

Above: Models of the *Monitor* and the *Merrimac*, built to re-enact the Civil War naval battle for television audiences.

Jan Scott

Above: Scaled set models are often used by television producers in planning the movement of cameras, microphones, and actors.

MODELS AND MODELMAKING

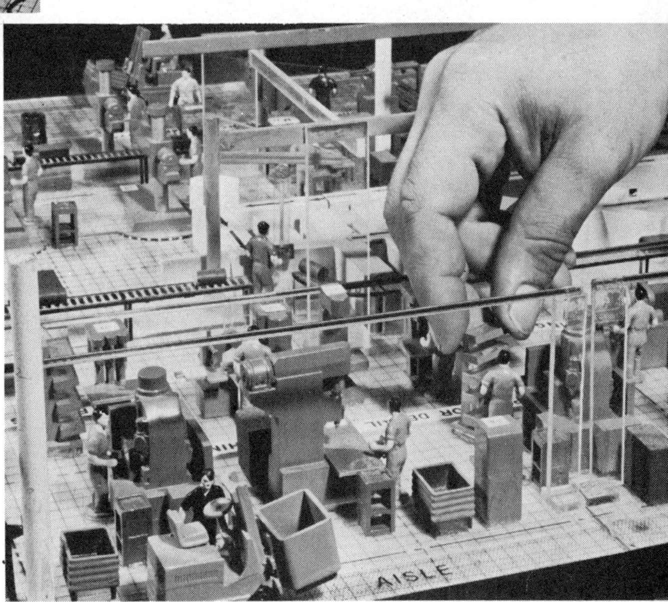

Right: Three-dimensional model of the interior of a factory, carefully scaled to show the exact placement of workers, machinery, and equipment.

Westinghouse Electric Corporation

of the automobile. The best model is enlarged to full scale as a wooden mock-up upon which all details are carefully worked out. Finally, skilled metal workers fashion an automobile by hand; this model is subjected to exhaustive road tests and then put into production.

Factory Design.—Factories and other industrial plants must be designed for greatest efficiency. Ideas for factory layout are first planned through the use of models. Tiny, accurate scale models of machines and other equipment are arranged on scaled-down floor layouts by engineers who specialize in plant construction. Space must be allotted for various plant functions such as storage and routing of raw materials, manufacturing processes, storage, packing and shipping of finished merchandise, and safety factors.

Scale models are often used to visualize proposed improvements in existing factories. Large organizations with extensive modernization programs usually employ modelmakers on a full-time basis.

Some industries maintain traveling exhibits of plant structures and operations which are shown through civic organizations, schools, and museums. They build good public relations by acquainting people with the basic functions of industry, as well as with some of the specific manufacturing processes involved.

Architecture and Community Planning.—Architects use models to show their clients how a finished building will look. All types of buildings are shown as models, from simple, one-family dwellings to immense skyscrapers.

Architectural models are built directly from architects' plans to exact scale. Some are made very simply, merely showing the outer form of the building they represent. Others are very complicated and show every detail of construction. Models of large buildings may incorporate such features as working doors, lights, and elevators. Small buildings are sometimes made with removable roofs which can be lifted off to show interior construction. Realism is often carried to the point of adding scaled-down room furnishings, complete with electric lights and miniature paintings on the walls. House models are often placed on landscaped plots showing driveways, lawns, and plantings.

In the old days cities just grew, usually expanding outward from business centers. Buildings were often erected haphazardly, resulting in crowding and other undesirable conditions. Zoning laws were put into effect after slums had already been created. Modern communities are scientifically planned. This is easily done through the use of models. All aspects of community life are taken into consideration: traffic problems, street arrangements, and locations of schools, churches, parks, playgrounds, and community recreation centers. Zoning requirements are respected. Everything is arranged so that residents in such areas will have easy access to shopping and business centers while living in desirable areas.

Civil Engineering.—Engineers have found that in general, a model has practically the same characteristics as the structure it represents. Models serve a dual purpose: (1) proposed structures can be visualized in three dimensions; and (2) models can be tested under conditions similar to those to be endured by their prototypes.

Scale models of bridges and dams are set up in scaled-down surroundings in which every topographical feature is duplicated. Models are subjected to conditions of wind, heat, cold, pressure, humidity, and anything else needed for test purposes. This enables the design engineer to discover structural faults and make needed corrections.

Topographical models of large areas are used in planning flood control measures. A scale model has been built of the entire Mississippi Basin, upon which proposed dams and other structures are shown.

The United States Corps of Engineers has constructed a scale model of the entire San Francisco Bay area. It covers an area of concrete and represents 550 square miles of tidal waters. Artificial tides and currents, which duplicate those found in nature, are created by pumping water through specially regulated valves and pipes. A carefully controlled amount of sediment is introduced into the water so that silt deposits are formed. This enables engineers to study the formation of similar deposits in the bay itself. The primary purpose of the model is to study plans for controlling the bay's waters. As each of the plans is tested on the model, engineers determine its effects on the underfloor surfaces.

Ship Design.—Scale models of ship hulls are tested in special tanks known as ship model basins. Shippers, shipbuilders, and naval architects receive valuable data concerning the behavior of hull designs under controlled test conditions.

Model hulls are constructed of balsa wood, laminated hardwood, or a mixture of paraffin and beeswax. Electronic equipment is used to measure data such as speed and propeller revolutions,

An engineer inspects a section of the concrete reproduction of the San Francisco Bay area, one of the largest working hydraulic models in the world. The model covers a paved area of 29,000 square feet.

U.S. Army Photograph

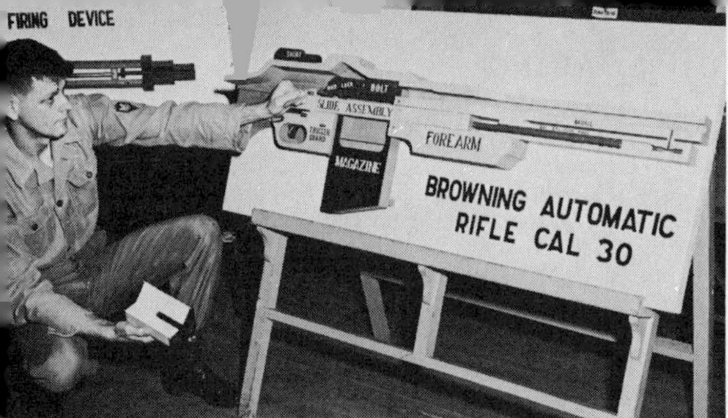

MODELS AND MODELMAKING

Above: An oversized demonstration model of an automatic rifle, used in the training of United States Army personnel.

Right: Midship section model of a warship of the early 19th century, showng the vessel's internal structure and decks.

Left: **Dr. Walter R. Guild of Yale University sits at a table covered with models of the basic molecules which make up living cells. The models were designed to assist researchers in discovering how nucleic acid contributes to the changing of normal cells into cancer cells.**

(Upper left) U.S. Army Photograph; (upper right) British Crown Copyright, Science Museum, London; (center) American Cancer Society; (lower left) Museum of the City of New York; (lower right) The American Museum of Natural History

Right: The blood vessels, bones, and internal organs of the human body are clearly displayed in a life-sized model called the "Transparent Woman."

Below: New Amsterdam, 1659. In a finely-detailed miniature group by Ned J. Burns, a Manhattan street is depicted as it looked in Dutch colonial days.

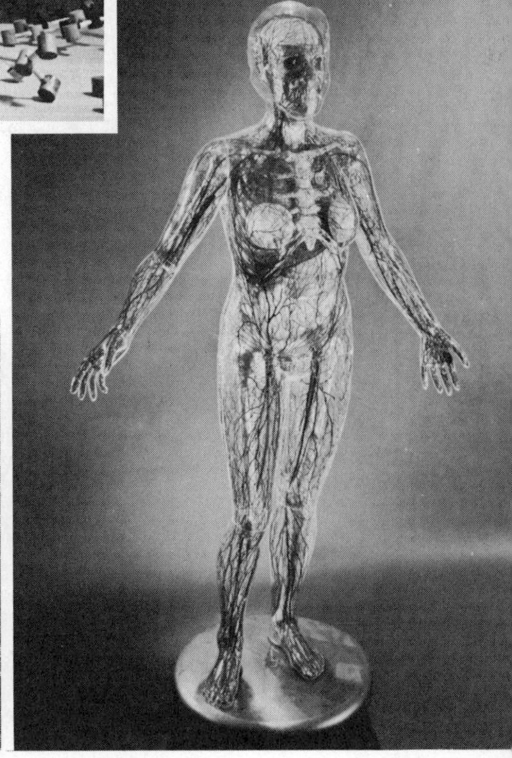

pitching, rolling, heaving, displacement, and thrust. Special machinery is used to generate winds of any desired velocity, as well as waves of different types. Hydrodynamic research of this type determines the effects of winds and waves on specific hull designs.

Military Uses.—Models have important military applications. The armed services have developed highly effective instructional techniques, which make use of models. Scale models are used to train personnel in the operation of weapons, scientific instruments, and other specialized equipment.

Topographical scale models are used in planning military strategy and tactics. An entire area can be visualized, showing the disposition of naval, air, and ground forces. Special problems involving various types of terrain can be solved before an operation is undertaken. During World War II the invasion of Europe was planned through the use of scale topographical models; assault tactics were worked out in minute detail. Full-scale models of streets and even complete villages were used to train Commandos and Rangers in house-to-house fighting tactics.

Models are also used to review military operations. Battles are refought in miniature, and carefully analyzed by strategists.

National Film Board Photograph

A Canadian model maker adds a finishing detail to his replica of Newfoundland's historic Fort Townshend.

Educational Uses.—Models are important educational aids. They are used a great deal in teaching the sciences. Various types of models are used. Some, like topographical models, are simply scaled-down replicas of larger forms. Others, like engines and machines of different types, may be shown as *working models,* which have moving parts like their prototypes.

Cutaway models are often used to show internal constructional details. Models of this type have had sections sliced away so that their inner workings are exposed. In others, part of the model has been cut away and replaced with clear plastic so that the inside is visible.

Sectional models are designed so that they can be taken apart, either in sections or in layers. These also show internal construction, and are used widely in teaching subjects such as biology and anatomy. Medical schools use sectional models of human figures which may be disassembled to show musculature and arrangements of internal organs.

Models are a particularly effective means of illustrating scientific laws and concepts. They can show phenomena which we cannot see because they exist on such a vast scale. For example, studies of the movement of the earth in space are made interesting and meaningful when illustrated by a working model of the solar system. Conversely, enlarged models of many types are invaluable aids in illustrating microscopic details. In teaching biology, large models of transparent plastic can show how a cell is constructed. This is a three-dimensional concept; a microscope shows cells in only two dimensions. Models showing arrangements of atoms and molecules are often used in physics and chemistry classrooms. Students can see three-dimensional visualizations of the structure of matter on a tremendously enlarged scale.

Museums.—Museums use models of every description. Dioramas, three-dimensional backgrounds, are used as settings for special displays. They may be full sized, or scaled down. Natural history groups can be created in which animals can be exhibited in authentic surroundings. A series of models is frequently employed to show a progression of ideas or an evolutionary development. The story of transportation may include models of vehicles of all types, from oxcarts to diesel trains.

Almost anything can be shown in miniature. An entire village, representing a cultural group of the past, can be recreated by using models. This makes it possible to present an authentic picture of a situation which no longer exists.

Theater and Motion Pictures.—In the theater, a stage setting is first designed on paper, then executed as a scale model. This is then set up on a scale-model stage. Details relevant to lighting, color harmonies, set changing, and entrances and exits of actors can all be worked out before the full-sized sets are constructed.

Models are very important to the motion picture industry. They are used to show trains, ships, buildings, and other structures that could not be reproduced in their actual size without great cost or inconvenience. Many other things seen on the screen are actually ingenious illusions. Movie modelmakers go to incredible lengths to achieve realism. Dozens of highly skilled technicians contribute their efforts to obtain special screen effects.

Ship Scenes.—Let us examine a typical scene in which a model of a full-rigged clipper ship is being photographed. Motion picture models are not necessarily small; this model is 27 feet long. It is large enough to show every minute detail of construction. The ship is floated in a large, shallow tank. It is photographed against a canvas background about 50 feet high, upon which the sky and clouds are painted. The water in the tank is dyed blue, enhancing the effect of realism. As the ship moves through the water, it looks exactly like the real thing. Its auxiliary engine puffs smoke and steam, but that is all it does; the ship is towed by an underwater cable. The smoke is produced by special cartridges hidden in the engine stack. Small figures which move about on the deck of the ship are models, powered by tiny battery-operated motors. Realistic bow and stern waves are produced by shooting jets of water from hidden underwater pumps. Special machines are used to produce ocean waves and swells. Wind machines create moving air of any desired velocity, from a gentle breeze to a hurricane. They fill the ship's sails very realistically and impart just the right degree of chop to the surface of the water. When seen on the screen, the picture is one of absolute, convincing realism. The illusion is helped by shooting the scene from a low camera angle.

Train Scenes.—Motion pictures sometimes show train wrecks. These are usually models, too. Scale-model trains are made to have scale-model accidents in scaled-down surroundings. Meticulous attention is paid to all details so that the picture of reality is maintained. Motion pictures of real train wrecks are studied by technicians, who build exact scale models in order to simulate disaster.

A moving picture may show a wooden trestle bridge. If possible, a real bridge is photographed; otherwise a model must be constructed. It is usually necessary to build not only the bridge, but also the surroundings in which it is set. Such a setting is actually constructed from the ground up. It may be built in a studio, where hills and gullies are made of canvas reinforced with plaster of Paris, or an outdoor setting may be employed. This is usually a small area which is cleared of all vegetation. Since the trestle is to be a scale model, everything else in the setting must be built to scale. The presence of one full-scale plant would otherwise immediately identify the scene as a model shot. Forests of miniature trees must be planted. Each tree may consist of a single stalk, into which small branches have been inserted. These are set into the ground. Underbrush is also built to scale. Rock formations may be those found in nature, or shaped from plaster of paris and canvas. The finished setting is then painted by scenic artists, who spray it with nonreflecting paint.

The miniature canyon may have a mountain torrent rushing through it. Water may be supplied from a small dam or a series of pipes; water pressure is adjusted to produce exactly the right effect. If the trestle is to be blown up, it must be built so that it can be demolished on cue. Hidden wires pull down specially weakened timbers. Small charges of black powder are set off at exactly the right moment so that they are synchronized with the structure's collapse.

Other Uses.—Motion pictures make use of models in another important way. Moving picture scenes are shot against backgrounds or *sets*. Sometimes these are natural settings found outdoors. In most cases picturemakers improve upon nature by building full-sized backgrounds which fit the specific actions called for by the script. In order to be certain that a set is exactly what is needed, it is first constructed as a scale model. The model is used to work out problems of lighting, color, camera angles, and action or movement of actors. Model sets are also used in planning shooting schedules.

Law.—Models of machinery, streets, railroads, traffic conditions, and buildings are commonly used as legal aids. They provide simple visualizations of complex situations which might otherwise be difficult to explain, and help to determine the legal issue of negligence and other points of law.

Official U.S. Navy Photograph

A full-size operating model of a ground-skimming vehicle built by the Navy will aid engineers in determining the behavior of the perfected craft.

With the development of modern patent offices, devices which were to be protected had at first to be uniformly submitted for adoption. Those which were too large for actual submission were presented as working scale models. At present, the United States Patent Office requires a model only if the idea or device that is to be patented cannot be described in another way.

HOW MODELS ARE MADE

Buildings.—Small buildings are usually made of illustrator's board, a type of smooth-surfaced cardboard used by artists. It may be cut with a razor blade or a modelmaker's knife. Pieces are glued together with model airplane cement.

Simple models may merely be painted with show-card colors. A more realistic effect can be obtained by simulating the material which is used on the sides and roof of the house represented by the model. In order to do this it is necessary to duplicate the textures of the real materials in miniature. Clapboards and shingles are usually cut from thin cardboard and glued on exactly like real siding.

Fieldstone can be simulated by mixing a thin solution of plaster of paris, and painting it on the sides of the house. The plaster is permitted to form a small pool, which represents a piece of stone. Just before each spot of plaster dries, it is roughened slightly by going over it with the edge of a piece of wire screening or a stiff, dry brush. It is then painted with show-card colors. Spaces between stones are tinted to represent mortar joints.

The texture of brick may be duplicated by using a fine grade of sandpaper. This is given a thin wash of show-card color, tinted to match the brick used in the construction of the house. Mortar lines can be shown by scratching through the paint with a sharp metal awl or any pointed metal tool. This exposes the sandpaper underneath the paint, which looks like real mortar. The prepared sandpaper is cut to size, then glued over the outside walls of the model.

Window sash and trim is cut from strips of balsa wood, soft pine, or thin cardboard such as artists' Bristol board. An entire cardboard window can be cut in one piece, backed with a piece of thin, transparent plastic, and glued in place. The plastic must be handled with care, otherwise it will wrinkle.

Large buildings are usually more complicated. Many are made of plastics and metal. Special cements are used to join plastics such as Lucite and Plexiglas; when properly used, no joint is visible. Tiny motors, similar to those used in scale-model trains, furnish power for moving parts such as working elevators. Extra thin neon tubes may be built in to simulate fluorescent lights. In some cases it may be necessary to install a small blower system in order to carry off the heat developed by the lighting system.

Scale-model furniture is usually made of mahogany or other hardwood. Completed pieces are carefully sanded, stained, and finished like real furniture.

Other Forms.—Bridges and other wooden structures in which individual members are shown are made of scale-model timbers, cut from soft pine or balsa wood. The pieces are joined together exactly like the timbers in the real thing. Although the model timbers may be glued together in order to give strength to the model, scaled-down nails, bolts and other fastenings must be added to the structure. This adds to the effect of realism.

Large ship models are usually built very meticulously. Some are constructed from scale-model timbers and planks, and are built up exactly like real ships. It has been estimated that it takes as long to build some of these models as it would to construct a full-sized ship. Models are authentically rigged, and are complete in every detail. Each part must be specially made by hand. Even the anchor line is sometimes constructed to scale, containing the same number of twisted strands as the one on the ship it represents.

Many scientific models, particularly those used in the study of botany and biology, were formerly made of intricately blown glass. These have been largely supplanted by models made of transparent plastics, which are cheaper and stronger.

Models which simply show form without many details, such as those used in factory planning, may be made of solid plastics or wood. Duplicates of such pieces are cast in rubber molds. Liquid latex is sprayed or brushed over a model. When it dries, it is simply peeled off; this is the mold. Plaster of paris is mixed with water to the proper consistency and poured into the mold. After the plaster has hardened, the mold is stripped off to be used again as many times as necessary.

Landscapes.—Small models of rocks and earth formations can be modeled from a putty made of asbestos fiber and water. Models of larger formations are first shaped out of wire window screening. The wire forms may be strengthened by tacking them to wooden supports. They are then covered with either plaster of paris or texture paint. Texture plaint has a water base; it may be mixed so that it is thick enough to be applied with a spatula, or thinned out so that it can be applied with a brush. After the paint has become partially dry, it can be modeled like soft clay. Thin mixtures of oil colors in turpentine are brushed over the texture paint while it is still damp. Dry surfaces may be retouched with show-card colors.

Model trees and shrubs can be made from bits of natural sponge or foam latex rubber, cemented to twisted wire tree trunks. Realistic-looking trees can be cut from bits of ordinary weeds. These look exactly like real trees without leaves. Masses of leaves can be added by cementing on pieces of sponge. Finished trees can be sprayed or brushed with show-card colors. Model airplane cement is generally used to fasten model trees and shrubs in place.

See also HOBBIES—*Creative Hobbies* and *Bibliography;* AUDIO-VISUAL EDUCATION.

Bibliography.—Grimwood, Victor Redmond, *American Ship Models and How to Build Them* (New York 1943); Wickham, Peter Raymond, *Commercial Model Making: . . . Industrial Purposes, Exhibitions, General Advertising Display* (London 1945); Forman, Robert, *Architectural Models* (New York 1946); Johnson, Gene, *Airplane Model Building* (Cambridge, Md., 1946); Ahern, John, *Miniature Building Construction* (London 1947); Maginley, C. J., *Historic Models of Early America, and How to Make Them* (New York 1947); Bayley, Thomas, *The Craft of Model Making* (Leicester, England, 1950); Ahern, John Henry, *Miniature Landscape Modelling* (London 1951); Bartley, Richard F. C., *Models in Bottles* (London 1951); Hopwood, Robert R., *Science Model Making* (London 1951); Johnson, Gene, *Ship Model Building,* 2d ed. (Toronto, Ont., 1953); Zarchy, Harry, *Model Railroading* (New York 1955); Museiano, Walter A., *Building and Operating Model Cars* (New York 1956); Gilmore, Horace Herman, *Model Planes for Beginners,* rev. ed. (New York 1957); Winter, William John, *Model Aircraft Handbook,* 4th ed. (New York 1957).

HARRY ZARCHY.

MODENA, mô'dâ-nä, province, Italy, in Emilia-Romagna Region, in the north central part of the peninsula. The province extends between the Secchia and Panaro rivers from the watershed line of the Apennines to the Po plain. Half of its 1,038 square miles is mountainous and hilly, while the other half is part of the fertile Po Valley. Most of the population is occupied in agriculture: wheat, corn, hemp, sugar beets, and fruits and vegetables are the main crops; cattle, pigs, and sheep are also raised. Pork sausages made in the province are shipped to the rest of Italy and abroad. Manufacturing, mostly processing of local farm products, is carried on on a relatively small scale in Modena (the provincial capital), Mirandola, Sassuolo, and Carpi. Pop. (1951) 498,146.

MODENA, commune and city, Italy, capital of Modena Province in the Region of Emilia-Romagna, in the north central part of the peninsula. It is an agricultural trade center in the fertile Po plain near the foothills of the Apennines, lying on the Aemilian Way. The city is an archiepiscopal see. Agricultural machinery, fertilizers, vegetable oils, macaroni, and pork sausages are the chief products.

A characteristic feature of the old part of the city of Modena is its narrow arcaded streets, reminiscent of nearby Bologna. The most important building is the cathedral, a fine example of Romanesque architecture, started in 1099 and completed in the 14th century. The adjoining bell tower, called La Ghirlandina, is Lombard-Gothic in style, and consists of six stories. The tower stands slightly off-center. The ducal palace, former residence of the Este (q.v.) family, is an imposing structure begun in 1643, now housing a military school and historical museum. Another building, the Palace of the Museums, contains the famous Este Library, transferred from Ferrara to Modena in 1598, which includes many priceless manuscripts, among them the 15th century Bible of Borso d'Este with 1,200 illuminated pages. Other parts of the palace also contain the Galleria Estense, housing the famous Este art collection; the Este medals collection;

and the municipal museum. Noteworthy also are the Campori art collection and the Church of San Pietro. The origins of the University of Modena may be traced to the 12th century; it now has schools of law, medicine, science, and pharmacy.

First inhabited by Ligurians and Etruscans, the area around Modena was held by the Gauls when it was conquered by the Romans in 183 B.C. Called Mutina by the Romans, the town acquired some importance because of its location on the Aemilian Way. After the free commune was established in the 12th century A.D., Modena, like many Italian towns, soon found itself not only in conflict with its neighbors, of which Bologna was the most powerful, but also torn by internal struggles between Guelph and Ghibelline factions. The lordship of the Este family, rulers of Ferrara, was first established in 1288. In 1452, Borso d'Este received the title of duke of Modena and Reggio from the Holy Roman emperor. When, in 1598, Cesare d'Este was forced to relinquish Ferrara to the popes, he moved his court to Modena, which remained the seat of the Este until Ercole III was driven out by the French in 1796. In 1814, his grandson, the Austrian archduke Francis, recovered the duchy and ruled as Francis I. He put down with great cruelty the insurrections of 1821 and 1831, and in the latter year had the local leader of Italian independence, Ciro Menotti, hanged. In the war of Italian independence of 1859, the people expelled the last duke, Francis V, and Modena was included in the Kingdom of Sardinia (from 1861, the Kingdom of Italy). Pop. (1951) city 82,180; commune 111,364.

MODERN ARCHITECTURE, mŏd'ẽrn är'kĭ-tĕk-tûr. The origins of modern architecture extend back to the 18th century and are associated with the romantic movement in England and the Enlightenment in France. On the other hand, the popularly recognizable forms of modern architecture, especially in their revolutionary manifestations, belong to the 20th century. Viewed historically, the evolution of these new architectural styles may be divided into three distinct phases. The first phase comprises the two decades prior to World War I; the second, commonly known as the International style, occupies the interwar period of the 1920's and 1930's; the third begins after 1945.

First Phase: to 1920.—Preceding the initial stage of 20th century architecture, there was a complex series of developments, theoretical and technological as well as stylistic, which made possible the characteristic forms of today. The introduction of industrial techniques and new factory-produced materials revolutionized the building industry in the course of the 19th century. Iron, steel, and reinforced concrete prompted new structural systems. Meanwhile the architectural profession was contributing to this rapid expansion of knowledge through an extensive study and reuse of past styles, ancient and medieval, a tendency which was responsible for the numerous "revivals" characteristic of 19th century building.

Various individual attempts to synthesize and master this vast body of new technological and historical knowledge, to combine the rapidly diverging professions of architect and engineer, never met with complete success. By 1900 a crisis was reached which called forth drastic solutions and, on the surface, a well-advertised rejection of the revival styles and their associative values. In their place appeared new forms superficially less dependent upon precedent and tradition, and frequently based upon some of the more conspicuous aspects of structural technology.

In spite of vigorous activity in Europe at the turn of the century, an American, Frank Lloyd Wright (1869–1959), emerged as the first master of 20th century forms. A champion of what he called "organic architecture," dwellings conceived in harmony with their particular landscapes, he rejected the historical modes current in 1900. He began his own practice in 1893 and by 1910 had not only evolved his personal style but was recognized as a master and leader in the profession, especially by the younger generation of European architects. In the Ward Willitts House, Highland Park, Ill. (1902), and the Robie House, Chicago (1909), Wright created a style that avoided the entanglements of revivalism and emphasized more fundamental aspects of architectural vocabulary: interlocking forms of dramatically contrasting textures and colors. These and other designs by Wright were published and widely admired in Europe.

Architectural Record

The first independent work of the architect Walter Gropius: the Fagus Factory (1910), at Alfeld, Germany.

Monumental public architecture in America and Europe around 1900 was following a hesitant, conservative course. Leading the academic wing of the profession was the firm of McKim, Mead, and White (Boston Public Library, 1888–1892; Pennsylvania Station, New York City, 1906–1910). In Europe this official style was likewise a tradition inherited from the previous century and, with minor local variants, could be found in every Continental capital.

Before World War I there were numerous

Museum of Modern Art

Tugendhat House (1930–1931), in Brno, Czechoslovakia, designed in the International style by Mies van der Rohe.

signs of dissatisfaction with these traditional and official styles. Auguste Perret (1874–1954) in Paris, Peter Behrens (1868–1940) in Germany, Josef Hoffmann (1870–1956) and Adolf Loos (1870–1933) in Vienna were leaders in the development of a radical and original style. Some pioneered in the use of reinforced concrete structures; some championed the total elimination of ornament, traditional or original, to achieve more fundamental geometric effects; others were concerned with low-cost public-housing projects.

With the design of a model factory at the Cologne Werkbund Exhibition of 1914, Walter Gropius (1883–1969), a student of Behrens and an admirer of Wright, emerged as the leader of the younger generation. Gropius combined Wright-derived forms with the use of glass walls on a large scale, thus opening the way to an entirely new conception of architectural volume, in which the building's skin is either transparent or, alternately, a hard mirrorlike reflecting surface. This achievement marked the culmination of the first phase of modern architecture and ushered in the second phase, the International style.

Second Phase: International Style.—Gropius developed his revolutionary conception of the wall in an even more daring fashion in the Bauhaus, Dessau, Germany (1926), where the glass-enclosed forms were detached from the ground by set-back foundations. In all probability Gropius had, at this stage of his career, been influenced by recent developments in Holland, where the movement called de Stijl (literally, the Style) had been founded in 1917 by a painter, Theo van Doesburg.

The works of Gropius and his contemporaries, Ludwig Mies van der Rohe (1886–1969) and Le Corbusier (pseudonym of Charles Édouard Jeanneret-Gris, 1887–1965), are usually grouped together as the International style. This term has obtained a degree of popular acceptance for nearly all unconventional manifestations of modern architecture. However, in its strictest application the term refers to the 1920's and early 1930's. This style is characterized by an exploitation of glass-enclosed volumes, thin walls independent of the structural frame, and the concomitant manipulation of seemingly insubstantial horizontal and vertical planes, without direct visual correlation with the normal demands of structural stability or the laws of gravity.

This new architecture was institutionalized at Gropius' art school, the Bauhaus, established at Weimar in 1919 and transferred to Dessau in 1925. Gropius was succeeded in the directorship, after a brief interval, by Mies van der Rohe in 1929, the latter holding the post until the Nazis closed the school in 1933. Subsequently both Gropius and Mies left Germany, ultimately settling in the United States. Gropius became director of the School of Architecture at Harvard; Mies undertook a similar post at Illinois Institute of Technology, Chicago. Thus the center of gravity of modern architecture shifted away from Europe.

Mies had been as well known as Gropius for his contributions to the International style. By accident his finest early works were built not in Germany but in Spain (Barcelona Pavilion, 1929) and Czechoslovakia (Tugendhat House, Brno, 1930–1931). To the already well-established new style Mies brought a sense of elegant proportion and a love of polished, mirrorlike surface finishes, adding chrome and marble facings to the crystalline glass forms already introduced by Gropius. Mies' later American works, the new campus of Illinois Institute of Technology, Chicago (planned 1940), and the Seagram Building, New York City (1956–1958, in collaboration with Philip Johnson), are properly a part of the third and most recent phase of modern architecture, although they are closely related to the earlier International style. The shapes of these buildings were subjected to an austere simplification, and the active interlocking forms so characteristic of the 1920's were suppressed.

Third Phase: from 1945.—The simplified glass and metal structures of the International style had a far-reaching influence on American commercial architecture after 1945, while in the field of domestic architecture Frank Lloyd Wright, almost paradoxically, reasserted the leadership that he had held a quarter of a century earlier. Though often critical of the boxlike appearance of the International style, he in turn learned much from it, and in the Kaufmann House, Bear Run, Pa. (1937–1939), he successfully fused the severe qualities of the European mode with his own organic architecture. Later, in the Jacobs House, Middleton, Wis. (1948), he combined modern themes with the romantic American tradition. Southern California houses by the Viennese-trained Richard Neutra (1892–1970) favor the International style modified by the tendencies of Wright, with whom he had worked in the 1920's.

Paralleling the dominance of Gropius, Mies, and Wright in American building during the third phase of modern architecture was the worldwide influence of the French-Swiss master, Le Corbusier, whose boldly modeled forms in reinforced concrete were admired especially in tropical and subtropical areas. His career began with a group of houses in and around Paris, dating from 1922 to 1931; all display the recognized qualities of the International style. His early masterpieces, the Stein Villa, Garches (1928), and the Savoye Villa, Poissy (1929–1930), represent the synthesis of many interests. Le Corbusier, who combined painting with his other activities, had a profound attachment to the stark geometrical form of ancient Greek and Roman architecture, and was likewise affected by forms spontaneously

Right: The spiraling ramp of New York's Guggenheim Museum, in which Frank Lloyd Wright attempted to achieve "the atmosphere of an unbroken wave."

MODERN ARCHITECTURE

Below: Louis I. Kahn employs straight lines and a hexagonal motif in the AFL-CIO Medical Center in Philadelphia.

(Upper right) George Cserna; (center) John Ebstel; (lower left) René Burri, from Magnum; (lower right) Ezra Stoller

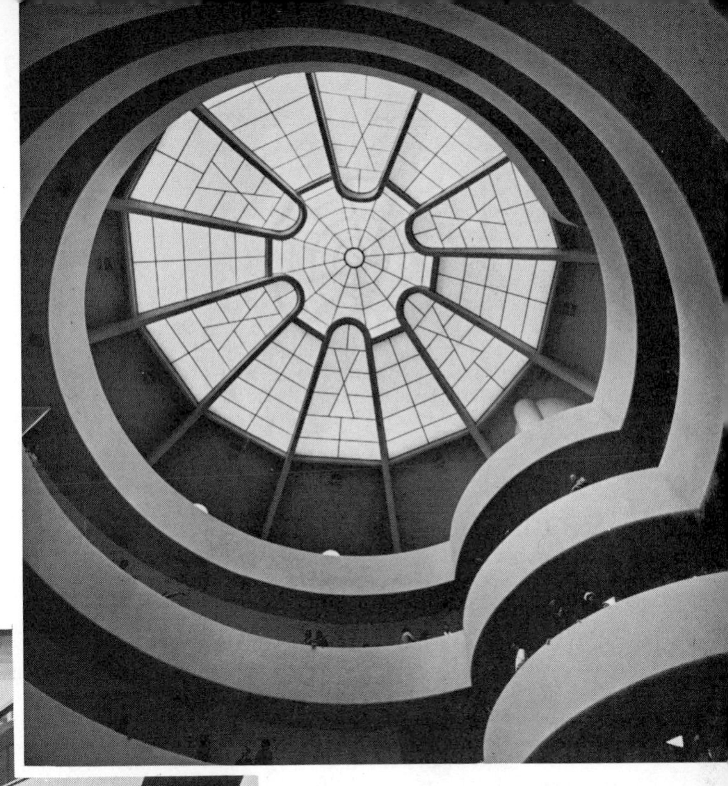

Below: The Seagram Building in New York, by Mies van der Rohe and Philip Johnson.

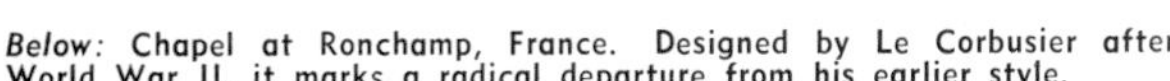

Below: Chapel at Ronchamp, France. Designed by Le Corbusier after World War II, it marks a radical departure from his earlier style.

engendered by modern industry: factories, grain elevators, automobiles, airplanes, and ocean liners. This repertoire of forms was integrated into his own personal variant of the International style, particularly in the Savoye Villa. The latter, taken together with Mies van der Rohe's Barcelona Pavilion of the same year (1929), represents the culmination of the entire movement.

If the styles of Mies and Le Corbusier were converging in the late 1920's, their subsequent developments seem markedly opposed. The spontaneous undulating contours of Le Corbusier's chapel at Ronchamp, France (1950–1954) and the richly modeled lines of the government buildings at Chandigarh, India (begun 1950)—forms that were latent but not obvious in his earlier work—contrast with the calculated simplicity and regularity of Mies' later designs. Hints of Le Corbusier's explosive postwar style are evident in his Swiss Pavilion, Paris (1930–1932) and in Latin American works done by disciples under his direct influence, such as the Ministry of Education and Health, Rio de Janeiro, Brazil (1937–1943), by Lúcio Costa (1902–), Oscar Niemeyer (1907–), and others. Subsequent designs of Costa and Niemeyer reveal some of the most provocative developments following the example of Le Corbusier. In Mexico the works of architect-mosaicist Juan O'Gorman (1905–) and engineer Félix Candela (1910–), have a distinctive, sometimes even aboriginal quality.

The Finn Alvar Aalto (1898–) from the early 1930's also made striking contributions to the growing variety of modern forms. Italian architecture, after adopting the International style, engaged in similar tendencies after World War II. Its most conspicuous and very nearly its best achievement was the completion (1950) of the Termini Station, Rome, by Eugenio Montuori (1907–) and others, featuring a dramatically curved roof over a glass-enclosed entrance hall. The leading figure in Italy was the engineer Pierluigi Nervi (1891–), whose Sports Palace, Rome (c. 1957), is a highly original domical structure.

After 1955, the leadership in American architecture slipped gradually away from the older generation, although large firms, such as Skidmore, Owings & Merrill turned to Mies for inspiration, as in Lever House, New York City (1952), and the Air Force Academy, Colorado Springs, Colo. (1957–1959). Perhaps the most widely publicized architect of this period was Edward D. Stone (1902–). After a sophisticated International style design for the Museum of Modern Art, New York City (1939, with Philip L. Goodwin), he turned to a more traditional mode. His United States Embassy, New Delhi, India (1957), the United States Pavilion at the World's Fair, Brussels, Belgium (1958), and the controversial Gallery of Modern Art, New York City (designed 1959), all represent successful efforts to dress up contemporary buildings in fashionably modernized period costumes.

Philip Johnson (1906–), sometime collaborator with Mies van der Rohe, also had recourse to traditional forms in the Port Chester Synagogue (1956), without compromising his devotion to the spirit and appearance of post-International style building. Another approach to new design problems is found in the work of Paul Rudolph (1918–), whose Mary Cooper Jewett Art Center, Wellesley College (completed 1958), features nervous intricate detailing with jagged edges and surfaces. By way of contrast, sober, straightforward effects were produced by Louis I. Kahn (1901–) in the Yale Art Gallery, New Haven, Conn. (1952–1954) and the AFL-CIO Medical Center, Philadelphia, Pa. (finished 1957). By abstaining from the more eye-catching affectations that had grown in popularity since 1950, Kahn's work seems to preserve much of the fresh vitality of the earlier modern styles.

Western European countries, especially Germany and France, which were leaders of the original International style, produced little of pioneering significance after the mid-1930's, beyond the efforts of already established personalities like Le Corbusier. Leadership in architecture by the 1950's had passed to the Western Hemisphere and to a lesser extent to underdeveloped countries like India, where European architects were afforded some of their most splendid opportunities.

See also ARCHITECTURE—*Ancestry and Character of the International Style;* LATIN AMERICA—*14. Modern Architecture, Housing, and City Planning;* sections on architecture in articles on the various countries; and biographies of leading architects mentioned.

Bibliography.—Giedion, Sigfried, *Space, Time and Architecture,* 3d ed. (Cambridge, Mass., 1954); Hitchcock, Henry Russell, *Architecture, Nineteenth and Twentieth Centuries* (Baltimore 1958).

JOHN M. JACOBUS, JR.,
Department of Art and Archaeology, Princeton University.

MODERN ART, a term used to distinguish the experimental and dynamic currents of 20th century painting and sculpture from more conservative attitudes. In their search for new forms expressive of the new spiritual and social conditions of the age, modern artists have tended to reject traditional solutions to problems of technique, composition, subject matter, and expression. In the process, modern art has, on the whole, become more and more abstract in the sense of nonrepresentational and consequently less dependent upon the description of the visual world in terms of easily or immediately recognizable images. Despite the many varieties of modern expression and the many movements within which it has developed chronologically, this abstract quality is fundamental to almost all modern art, and not only constitutes a new artistic epoch, but requires a new aesthetic justification.

Basic Concepts.—As early as 1890 the French symbolist painter, Maurice Denis (1870–1943), indicated the direction the new art and aesthetic would take when he declared that "a picture—before being a battle horse, a nude woman, or some anecdote—is essentially a plane surface covered with colors assembled in a certain order." Much later the Alsatian painter and sculptor Hans (Jean) Arp (1888–) expressed the same concept in a more poetic and humorous form: "Art is a fruit that grows in man, like a fruit on a plant, or a child in its mother's womb. But whereas the fruit of the plant, the fruit of the animal, the fruit in the mother's womb assume autonomous and natural forms, art, the spiritual fruit of man, usually shows an absurd resemblance to the aspect of something else . . . . I like nature, but not its substitutes" (1932).

Since works of art are no longer created in imitation of natural appearances, they can no

National Gallery of Art, Chester Dale Collection

Museum of Modern Art

Above: Still Life: Apples on Pink Tablecloth by Henri Matisse, who is often ranked with Picasso as the greatest of 20th century painters.

Above right: Ernst Kirchner's *Dunes at Fehmarn* (1912) reveals a boldness and angularity typical of German expressionist art.

Right: Improvisation, executed in 1915 by the pioneer of nonrepresentational (or "nonobjective") painting, Wassily Kandinsky.

MODERN ART

Below: Card Players (1913–1914), by Pablo Picasso. The canvas belongs to the period when the artist was experimenting with cubism.

Below right: In *The Cow,* Theo van Doesburg at once creates a balanced design and expresses the impassive solidity of his subject.

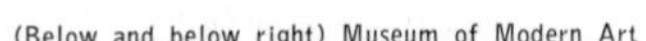

(Below and below right) Museum of Modern Art

Museum of Modern Art

longer be judged in terms of their fidelity to such appearances. They are to be criticized and enjoyed as manifestations of artistic impulse fulfilled in the manipulation of the physical elements and psychological effects of the work of art itself. A painting is first of all a series of relationships of color and shape, of texture and composition; a sculpture is to be understood as an arrangement of volumes in relation to the surrounding space. References to natural objects and familiar human situations may be present or not; their absence will not diminish the essential artistic character of the work. With the disappearance of the outer objective world of appearances, the attention of artist and spectator has been turned to the inner world of feeling, of psychological experience. More and more it has become apparent that nonrepresentational colors and forms are not just capricious exercises in the principles of design, but are visual projections of interior emotions and experiences.

Simple as these concepts may seem in retrospect, it was far from easy to discover the inherent artistic properties of color, form, line, texture, volume, and composition, and to present them in works wherein subject matter in the literal sense was minimized, distorted, or suppressed entirely. The research engaged the creative energies of the finest artistic minds of the early period of modern art, just as its elucidation required the formulation of the keenest critical insights. Necessarily, much of this work by both artist and critic was experimental and is now of more historical than artistic interest; but at their best the paintings and sculptures by the pioneers of the modern movement are now recognized as masterpieces, just as the best critics have succeeded in defining and establishing the new aesthetic situation.

"Romantic" and "Classic" in Modern Art.—Exchanges of position and overlappings of intention are so frequent that it often is difficult to follow the chronological sequence of movements, at times formally organized but more often only temporary groupings of artists sharing similar points of view. The greatest artists, of the stature of Pablo Picasso (1881–1973), for example, continue to defy the arbitrary classifications of the historian, just as they themselves reject the misleading descriptions which so often have been accidentally applied to their work. In general terms, however, it is possible to observe an alternation between two opposite but complementary poles of activity, depending upon whether the artist, in his conception and execution, has emphasized the expression of emotion or an intellectual order. For convenience these might be described as "romantic" and "classic" modes of creativity. Thus, where a surrealist artist sought imagery for the "psychic necessity" of dreams and discovered the techniques of accident and automatic expression, the constructivist planned all the details of his work in advance in order that in execution it might be revealed as a complete and self-sufficient artistic concept. These positions, of course, represent only the extremes of the creative process. Between them may be found all varieties of expression and intention, and it is possible to maintain that even the most accidental effects, such as the random spattering of paint and sand upon a canvas, nonetheless have been foreseen and thus willed by the artist, just as the most strictly controlled formal order cannot be entirely devoid of feeling.

Schools of Painting.—The first manifestation of the revolutionary implications of the new aesthetic in theory and in fact occurred early in the 20th century in Paris, the city which until World War II was pre-eminently the artistic center of Western culture. Indeed, much of the work produced there has been characterized as of the "school of Paris," although the diversity is such that no single current predominates to the exclusion of all others. Young artists from every country found in Paris an atmosphere sympathetic to freedom of action and discussion.

Fauvism.—At the Salon d'Automne, in the fall of 1905, the vivid antinaturalistic color and simplified drawing in the works of Henri Matisse (1869–1954), André Derain (1880–1954), Georges Braque (1882–1963), and others suggested to one critic the work of wild beasts (in French, *fauves*). Their subject matter, whether still life, landscape, or portraiture, was scarcely radical and indeed had long been familiar in the work of the impressionists; but the individual departures from naturalistic representation announced a new kind of art based upon the exploitation of feeling. Although the Fauve episode as such was short-lived and most of the artists developed in other directions, Henri Matisse, the greatest of the Fauves, continued to explore the expressive possibilities of color and flattened forms throughout his long life. See also FAUVISM.

Expressionism.—Such art is, perhaps, best described as expressionist, but the term is specifically associated with the work of the German painters of the same period, principally Ernst Ludwig Kirchner (1880–1938), Erich Heckel (1883–1970), and Karl Schmidt-Rottluff (1884–), who founded in Dresden in 1905 the movement known as Die Brücke (The Bridge) to bring together everyone "who portrays directly, without qualification, the creative impulse." Their drawing was more violently distorted than the Fauves', and their colors were often startlingly harsh; but at their best these masters painted with impressive power.

In Munich, only a few years later, the Russian painter Wassily Kandinsky (1866–1944) was led by his study of the expressive properties of color to create the first completely nonrepresentational paintings. Their generic title of "Improvisation" suggests how the free association of colors in the palette and canvas were intended to provoke corresponding states of mind in the spectator. Kandinsky's treatise *Uber das Geistige in der Kunst . . .* (1912; Eng. tr. *Concerning the Spiritual in Art,* 1947) is the first and still one of the most important arguments for abstract art.

Cubism and Its Offspring.—Meanwhile, in Paris, the Spanish painter Pablo Picasso and the French artist Georges Braque, influenced to some extent by their study of African sculpture, had begun by 1908 their exhaustive analysis of the properties of form in space. By combining several views of the same object within a single canvas they created a new type of design in which multiple perspectives create an ambiguously situated, constantly shifting space; the essential planes to which the object has been reduced interpenetrate and overlap according to the requirements of the composition as a whole. The pseudo-geometrical appearance of their first works in this manner suggested the title "cubist," although cubes as such had nothing to do with their program.

The geometrical implications of cubism were

Museum of Modern Art

Three works in the tradition of Dada and surrealism, by (left to right) Marcel Duchamp, Hans Arp, and Joan Miró.

carried by others to the extremes of nonobjectivity. In Russia, before 1914, Kasimir Malevich (1878–1935) had developed a point of view he described as "suprematist," in which the ultimate or supreme pictorial elements were defined as the circle and the square. In Holland, during World War I, the Dutch artists Theo van Doesburg (1883–1931) and Piet Mondrian (Pieter Cornelis Mondriaan, 1872–1944), founded the "de Stijl" movement as an attempt to produce a kind of design appropriate for all aspects of modern living. Their insistence upon using only straight lines, right angles and the three primary colors, plus black and white, was most skillfully expressed in Mondrian's extraordinarily austere paintings of the 1930's. See also CUBISM.

Dadaism and Surrealism.—During World War I the Dada movement, as much a reaction against the rigors of such analytical work as a protest against the debacle of European culture, appeared simultaneously in Europe and America. Led by Hans Arp in Zurich, by Marcel Duchamp (1887–1968) and Man Ray (1890–) in New York, and later by Max Ernst (1891–) and Kurt Schwitters (1887–1948) in Germany, the Dadas systematically created antiartistic objects apparently devoid of meaning, but actually imbued with profoundly satirical intentions. Their exploitation of automatism and accident soon suggested the possibility of expressing psychological experience through dream imagery and the sensations evoked by the accidental juxtaposition of unrelated objects and events. This point of view, known as "superrealism" or more usually "surrealism," from the artists' desire to present "the more real than real world of reality," was announced by André Breton (1896–1966) in his first Surrealist Manifesto (1928). The earlier works of the Catalan artist Salvador Dali (1904–) are among the most convincing demonstrations of this point of view. The surrealist mood of psychic urgency also helped to enlarge the emotional potentials of more abstract work, to be seen in the organic and biomorphic forms of the constructions of Hans Arp and the paintings of the Spaniard Joan Miró (1893–). See also DADAISM; SURREALISM.

Modern Sculpture.—The poles of "classic" order and "romantic" subjectivity characterize the different developments of modern sculpture. As early as 1901 the French sculptor Aristide Maillol (1861–1944) stated his rejection of the idealistic expressiveness of his master, Auguste

***Mother and Child*, an early marble by Jacob Epstein.**

Museum of Modern Art

Rodin (1840–1917), in his own contemplative seated figure called *Mediterranean.* His investigation of large simple masses was carried further by the Rumanian sculptor Constantin Brancuşi (1876–1957), who reduced natural appearances to a series of variations upon ovoid and elliptical forms. In Germany and England, Wilhelm Lehmbruck (1881–1919) and Jacob Epstein (1880–1959) developed their diverse but very individual styles in a series of elongated figures in cast stone and a number of remarkably powerful portraits in bronze.

The career of the Polish sculptor Jacques Lipchitz (1891–1973), long resident in Paris but later an American citizen, spans the whole modern movement in sculpture. In his earlier work he achieved perhaps the most successful translation into stone and metal of certain aspects of cubist painting; in the 1930's he turned to monumental figural sculpture, often charged with surrealist emotion. Elsewhere the Russian constructivists Antoine Pevsner (1886–) in Paris and his younger brother, Naum Gabo (1890–), in England and the United States, have continued their distinguished nonobjective work. Surrealism has affected, often indirectly, much work in metal, from the highly abstract but menacing constructions of Julio Gonzalez (1876–1942) to the attenuated figures of Alberto Giacometti (1901–1966) and the more recent American sculptors, David Smith (1906–1965), Herbert Ferber (1906–), Seymour Lipton (1903–), and Theodore Roszak (1907–).

American Developments.—Until 1913 most Americans, except for the very few who had studied abroad, were unaware of European developments. In that year a considerable number of advanced works were seen in New York City at the large international exhibition of modern art which has become known as the Armory Show. Public reaction, on the whole, was hostile, but once the modern works were available their influence could not be stemmed. After World War I many artists went to Europe to study, and European art was brought to the United States in increasing quantity. The foundation of the Society of Independent Artists in 1917, of the Collection of the Société Anonyme in 1920 (now at Yale University), and of the Museum of Modern Art in New York City in 1929 are landmarks in the recognition and establishment of progressive art in the United States. Painters such as John Marin (1870–1953), Max Weber (1881–1961), Marsden Hartley (1877–1943), and Stuart Davis (1894–1964) returned from abroad and interpreted American life in forms and techniques closely related to contemporary abstract art, but with an unmistakably native accent. The influence of abstract design can even be seen in the work of such men as Charles Burchfield (1893–1967), Charles Sheeler (1883–1965), Edward Hopper (1882–1967), and Ben Shahn (1898–1969), who continued the earlier American realist tradition.

Museum of Modern Art

***Number 12* (1949), by the American, Jackson Pollock.**

***Wild Roses* (1942), an oil painting by Marsden Hartley.**

Phillips Collection, Washington

Tachisme.—In New York City, toward the close of World War II, a new direction was given to American art, and eventually to the abstract movement as a whole, by such painters as Willem de Kooning (1904–), Robert Motherwell (1915–), Franz Kline (1910–1962), and Jackson Pollock (1912–1956). Although they are usually described as "abstract expressionists," their works are alike only in that each artist has stressed the artistic significance of the actual activity of painting. Each brush stroke is in itself an essential element in the total visual image rather than submerged in the final effect. Sir Herbert Read has described such works as "automatic registers of the dimensions of the soul," a phrase which suggests not only the intentional suppression of preconceived design but also the expression in each work of a psychic experience continuing and developing in the course of creation. The movement has, for the first time in American history, been influential abroad. In England it is known as "action painting," and in France as *tachisme* (from *tache,* spot, in the sense of brush stroke). The highly emotional qualities of abstract expressionism continue to inspire many of the most gifted of the youngest generation of American sculptors and painters.

See also PAINTING—*Modern Painting;* SCULPTURE—*History* (The 20th Century); biographies of individual artists mentioned; and sections on art and architecture in articles on the various countries and LATIN AMERICA.

GEORGE HEARD HAMILTON,
Yale University.

Bibliography.—Bell, Clive, *Art* (New York 1914); Wilenski, Reginald H., *The Modern Movement in Art* (New York 1927); Rothschild, Edward F., *The Meaning of Unintelligibility in Modern Art* (Chicago 1934); Sweeney, James Johnson, *Plastic Redirections in 20th Century Painting* (Chicago 1934); Barr, Alfred H., Jr., *Cubism and Abstract Art* (New York 1936); Read, Herbert E., ed., *Surrealism* (New York 1937); Barr, Alfred H., Jr., *Picasso, Fifty Years of His Art* (New York 1946); id., ed., *Fantastic Art, Dada, Surrealism,* 3d ed. (New York 1947); Kandinsky, Wassily, *Concerning the Spiritual in Art and Painting in Particular,* tr. by Michael Sadlier (New York 1947); Klee, Paul, *On Modern Art* (London 1948); Blanshard, Frances Bradshaw, *Retreat from Likeness in the Theory of Painting,* 2d ed. (New York 1949); Soby, James Thrall, and Barr, Alfred H., Jr., *Twentieth-Century Italian Art* (New York 1949); Barr, Alfred H., Jr., *Matisse; His Art and His Public* (New York 1951); Motherwell, Robert B., ed., *The Dada Painters and Poets; an Anthology* (New York 1951); Gray, Christopher, *Cubist Aesthetic Theories* (Baltimore 1953); Read, Herbert E., *The Philosophy of Modern Art* (New York 1953); Barr, Alfred H., Jr., ed., *Masters of Modern Art* (New York 1954); Giedion-Welcker, Carola, *Contemporary Sculpture, an Evolution in Volume and Space* (New York 1955); Seuphor, Michel (Ferdinand Louis Berckelaers), *Piet Mondrian: Life and Work* (New York 1956); Myers, Bernard S., *The German Expressionists; a Generation in Revolt* (New York 1957); Baur, J. I. H., *New Art in America* (New York 1957); Ritchie, Andrew C., ed., *German Art of the Twentieth Century* (New York 1957); Selz, Peter, *German Expressionist Painting* (Berkeley, Calif., 1957); Brion, M., and others, *Art Since 1945* (New York 1959); Goodrich, Lloyd, and Baur, John I., *American Art of Our Century* (New York 1961); Selz, Peter, *Seven Decades, 1895–1965: Crosscurrents in Modern Art* (New York 1966).

MODERN COMEDY, A, a group of three novels by John Galsworthy, constituting the second half of the Forsyte Chronicles. It is the counterpart of *The Forsyte Saga,* that series of brilliant pictures of English upper-class life which lifted Galsworthy to the front rank of novelists in his time. While the *Saga* dealt with established Victorian attitudes and the morals of a relatively sedate and ordered era, *A Modern Comedy* depicts the doings and misdoings of the next generation, the young people who came to maturity—or retained their immaturity—after World War I. The three novels composing the *Comedy* cover the postwar years to 1926. The first book, *The White Monkey,* appeared in 1924; the second, *The Silver Spoon,* in 1926; the third, *Swan Song,* in 1928; and the trilogy under the single title, *A Modern Comedy,* in 1929.

The whole triptych is a moral analysis of "that tenth or so of the population whose eyes are above the property line." To this youthful "advanced" set, the manners and morals of their elders appear stuffy; the new goal is freedom for the passions in an atmosphere of self-questioning and doubts about a future life. Shocked by the horrors of war, these men and women have few illusions and little respect for settled conventions, principles, or ideals. They have one foot in the air, Galsworthy tells us, and the other in a racing motorcar.

Against the fixed, solid qualities of Soames Forsyte, Sir Lawrence Mont, and other stalwarts of the old order, we follow the affairs and love affairs of the younger group—Fleur and Michael in their first married years; Wilfred Desert in his hopeless passion for Fleur; Jon and his wife from the American South, and her brother Francis Wilmot; Marjorie Ferrar, the actress, whose characterization of Fleur as a snob precipitates a scandalous trial for libel; and a host of others. Despite the spectacle of a generation chasing the happiness of which it feels it has been cheated, the conclusion of the work suggests that the traditional values will again prevail.

Galsworthy's chronicle of a floundering generation gripped the interest of all England, so close was the story to the realities of the life it projected.

EDWARD YORDAN.

MODERN DRAMA. See DRAMA; SCHOOLS OF DRAMA, MODERN; THEATER; and sections on drama or theater in articles on the various countries or literatures and LATIN AMERICA.—*17. Theater.*

MODERN INSTANCE, A, a novel by William Dean Howells, published in 1882. The action takes place during the 1870's in Maine and Boston, with one scene in Indiana. The plot portrays domestic infelicity and traces the gradual coarsening, morally and physically, of the husband, Bartley Hubbard—one of Howell's most original character delineations. The social and business life of a small New England town in the late 19th century, and the everyday experiences of a provincial couple embarking on life in the big city—Boston—are presented with the author's characteristic realism, and save the book from morbidity. The fate of two of the chief characters—Bartley's widow, Marcia, portrayed realistically with all her shortcomings, and her chastely correct gentleman admirer, Halleck—is left unsettled. Howells' photographic reproduction of the little things of contemporary life and his insight into social conditions place this novel among his best.

MODERN LANGUAGE ASSOCIATION OF AMERICA, a society for the advancement of the study of modern languages and their literatures through the promotion of friendly relations among scholars, the presentation and discussion of papers at annual meetings, and the publication of results of research by members. It was incorporated in Baltimore, Md., in 1883. Four regional associations—the Rocky Mountain, the South Atlantic, the South Central, and the Philological Association of the Pacific Coast—are affiliated with it. The association belongs to the American Council on Education, the American Council of Learned Societies, and the International Federation for Modern Languages and Literatures. It issues the periodical *PMLA* in quarterly installments with two yearly supplements—a directory issue and an international bibliography of current scholarship in the field of modern languages and literature. Membership, which is open to all who are interested, includes college and university professors in both hemispheres, graduate students, and others.

GEORGE WINCHESTER STONE, JR.

MODERN LITERATURE. See AMERICAN LITERATURE—*4. The 20th Century;* ENGLISH LITERATURE—*5. The 20th Century;* LATIN

AMERICA—*10. Literature* (Modern Movements); and sections on literature in articles on the various countries.

MODERN LOVE, a poem by George Meredith published in 1862. In 50 sonnetlike stanzas of 16 lines each, it records the failure of a marriage.

Insofar as the stanzas are dramatic, the husband is the speaker. Besides the wife ("Madam"), a third and fourth character are obliquely suggested—the wife's lover, and "my Lady," the other woman from whom the husband seeks the love which no longer exists in his marriage. At intervals both husband and wife struggle to resume their old affection; but the purity is gone—each effort ends in revulsion:

We two have taken up a lifeless vow
To rob a living passion . . .

The impasse apparently ends in the wife's suicide. The often quoted lines of stanza 43 state the central theme:

. . . In tragic life, God wot
No villain need be! Passions spin the plot.
We are betrayed by what is false within.

The poem is autobiographical. In 1849, Meredith married Mary Peacock Nicolls, widowed daughter of Thomas Love Peacock, a woman of keen intellect and remarkable beauty. The poet's son, William M. Meredith, thus summed up the marriage: "Two highly strung temperaments—man and wife—each imaginative, emotional, quick to anger, cuttingly satirical in dispute, could not find domestic content within the narrow bounds of poverty and lodgings."[1] They separated in 1858; Mary Meredith ran off to the Continent with another man and died three years later. The identity of her supposed lover, referred to in the poem, is uncertain; "my Lady," on the other hand, may be Janet Anne (Duff Gordon) Ross (q.v.), though she gave Meredith only friendship, not love, and married another man in 1860.

Modern Love is frequently obscure, but in its deep psychological probing of the complexities of emotion and motivation it is unique among Victorian poems.

DELANCEY FERGUSON.

MODERN MACCABEES, Knights of the. See MACCABEES, THE.

MODERN MUSIC. See MUSIC—*The Modern Age;* and sections on music in articles on the various countries and LATIN AMERICA.

MODERN PAINTERS, five volumes of studies in art criticism by John Ruskin, published at intervals from 1843 to 1860. The first two volumes (1843, 1846) at first came out anonymously because of the youth of the author, who was then in his mid-twenties. Volumes 3 and 4 (1856) and volume 5 (1860) appeared when Ruskin was well established in the world of letters. The work became a bible for the Pre-Raphaelite school of artists (see Pre-Raphaelites), who championed a romantic naturalism against the academic formalism of the time.

The original plan of the work is stated in the subtitle to volume 1: *Modern Painters: Their Superiority in the Art of Landscape Painting to all the Ancient Masters, proved by Examples of the True, the Beautiful, and the Intellectual from the Works of Modern Artists, especially from those of J. M. W. Turner, Esq., R.A.* The first volume is in fact a prolonged eulogy of Joseph M. W. Turner (1775–1851), the English landscape painter, whose work Ruskin attempts to judge by two essentially incompatible standards, one scientific, the other moral. By the first, Ruskin holds painting to be great insofar as it accurately renders such physical facts as vegetation and rock structure; by the second, he holds that no picture is complete if it contains "a single space . . . where I can crowd in another thought."

In volume 2, Ruskin undertook to define beauty. "I wholly deny," he wrote, "that the impressions of beauty are in any way sensual; they are neither sensual nor intellectual, but moral." On this, Ruskin's biographer, Joan Evans, comments: "The whole book is profoundly pious. Like a medieval treatise it finds the ultimate origin of every kind of beauty in some aspect of the divine." Volumes 3 and 4 develop still further the ideas of anthropocentric theology and a conscious artistic purpose in nature, while a major section of volume 5 also deals with the relation of art to God and man.

Ruskin's weakness as a critic of art is this constant intrusion of science and ethics into the field of aesthetics. The abiding value of *Modern Painters* is not in its judgments of art and artists, which are personal, temperamental, and sometimes based on incomplete knowledge, but in the poetic prose of the author's own descriptions of scenery and other subjects.

Consult Evans, Joan, *John Ruskin* (London 1954).

DELANCEY FERGUSON,
Author and Critic.

MODERNISM, mŏd′ẽr-nĭz'm, in religion, any outlook based on the conviction that modern scholarship and scientific advance require a fundamental restatement of traditional doctrine; the term is widely used in Protestantism to describe liberal movements and tendencies, but more specifically it applies to a Roman Catholic movement of the late 19th and early 20th centuries.

The 19th century stress on science and the application of scientific methods to Biblical scholarship seemed to many to raise serious problems for traditional articles of faith. The Modernists in the Roman Catholic Church sought to retain the letter of church doctrine by reinterpreting it in the light of modern knowledge; in so doing, they showed the influence of current evolutionary philosophies. Dogmas, for example, were not thought to be exact and authoritative formulations of truths revealed by God and fixed for all time, but rather statements of the religious feelings and experiences of men of a given historical epoch. Religious truths, therefore, were thought to be subject to a constant evolutionary process as part of the progressive experience of mankind; consequently new and more advanced concepts were required to express modern thought and progress. Although there were many differences among individual Modernists, they tended in their thought to be personal and pragmatic rather than universal and abstract. Abandoning scholastic philosophy, some Modernists were led to stress action and the will instead of reason, to follow the actionist philosophy of Maurice Blondel (1861–1949), to be receptive to the intuitionism of Henri Bergson (1859–1941), and to respond to the pragmatism of William James (1842–1910). Revela-

[1] *Letters of George Meredith,* ed. by William M. Meredith, 2 vols. (London 1912).

tion itself, to the Modernist, was a concrete personal experience of the truth about God, rather than an objective communication of universal truth from God.

Leading Modernists included Alfred Loisy (1857–1940), Lucien Laberthonnière (1860–1932), and Blondel in France; Romolo Murri (1870–1944) and Antonio Fogazzaro (1842–1911) in Italy; and George Tyrrell (1861–1909), and Baron Friedrich von Hügel (1852–1925) in Great Britain. They believed that the church could progress through their program—furthering social reform and developing new ideas—thus reclaiming true leadership in the modern world. The church, however, regarded the movement as an attack on true religion that was deeply rooted in agnosticism and immanentism, and considered it a misinterpretation of scholarly and scientific findings. It was condemned by Pope Pius X in 1907 as a "synthesis of all the heresies," and within a short time Modernism was ended as a Catholic movement.

Modernism, in Protestant churches, is not an organized movement but an approach to religion; sometimes the term is used interchangeably with liberalism. The Modern Churchmen's Union was founded in 1898 for the advancement of liberal thought, chiefly in the Church of England. It undertook to spread new liberal and scholarly views of the Bible, theology, the psychology of religion, and related subjects. William R. Inge (1860–1954), Hastings Rashdall (1858–1924), and Kirsopp Lake (1872–1946) were among those who gave the movement considerable intellectual prominence, especially in the years before World War II. In the United States, the term "Modernism" is sometimes used among Protestants as the opposite of Fundamentalism (q.v.). Harry Emerson Fosdick (1878–1969), a liberal, played a leading part in this conflict during the 1920's when it was at its height. Modernism has been challenged by neo-orthodox theologians who believe that the crises of 20th century life and thought are best understood in terms of traditional theology. Modernists agree that their doctrines are open to revision in the light of changing times and of advances in knowledge, but consider this to be a source of strength, not of weakness.

Bibliography.—Lilley, A. L., *Modernism: a Record and a Review* (London 1908); Vidler Alexander R., *The Modernist Movement in the Roman Church* (Cambridge, Eng., 1934); Nash, Arnold S., ed., *Protestant Thought in the 20th Century* (New York 1951); Anne Freemantle, ed., *The Papal Encyclicals in Their Historical Context* (New York 1956).

MODES, mōdz, in music, rows of selected tones, ascending or descending, from which basic tonal fabric is regarded as derived. The 13th century *rhythmic modes,* however, were repetitive patterns of rhythm. Post-Renaissance Western music has been regarded as built on seven-step (diatonic) octave scales in which each tone exists in relation to one chief tone, the tonic, an assumption less applicable to much recent music, and inapplicable to "atonal" music. The modes or scales of the post-Renaissance system are *major* and *minor* (the latter having natural, harmonic, and melodic forms). The only difference between one major scale and another, or one minor scale of a specified sort and another of the same sort, is in pitch.

In medieval music, basic tonal fabric is derived from eight-tone scales of another character, Oriental and Greek in origin. The ancient Greek modes, each regarded as having an ethical tendency, remain extremely theoretical; learned quarrels about them continue to embarass the discipline of musicology. The ecclesiastical or Gregorian modal system is based on scales that may differ in overall pitch; most importantly, one ecclesiastical mode differs from another as any modern major scale differs from a minor scale, each such mode being a different arrangement of intervals at whatever pitch.

The term "modes" is thus most commonly employed in three connections: (1) with the seven ancient Greek modes (Dorian, Phrygian, Lydian, mixolydian, hypodorian, hypophrygian, and hypolydian); (2) the more numerous ecclesiastical or Gregorian modes, which confusingly perpetuate Greek names; and (3) the modern major and minor modes.

HERBERT WEINSTOCK.

MODESTO, mô-dĕs'tō, city, California, county seat of Stanislaus County, on the Tuolumne River at an altitude of 90 feet, about 78 miles east of San Francisco. It is served by the Southern Pacific, Tidewater Southern, and Modesto and Empire Traction railroads, and United Airlines.

Modesto is primarily an agricultural and trading center. Manufacturing is concentrated in food processing with 60 per cent of the plants and 80 per cent of the workers so engaged. Several frozen-food processing companies and a large refrigeration plant handle meat, poultry, and dairy products. Food is also canned and packaged by other local firms. Nonfood industries include the manufacture of printed business forms, crates, chemicals, glass containers, electrical goods, television parts, floor wax, poultry equipment, cabinets, and fabricated metals.

The city was first settled in 1870, became the county seat in 1871, and was incorporated in 1884. It has a council-manager form of government. Modesto Junior College is located here. Pop. 61,712.

MODICA, mô'dê-kä (ancient MOTYCA), commune and city, Italy, in Ragusa Province on the island of Sicily, five miles south-southeast of the city of Ragusa. The city, whose site is commanded by a medieval castle, has a beautiful 17th century church dating from the days of quasi independence under Spanish rule, and a monastery with 15th century ruins. Five miles to the east is the Cava d'Ispica, a limestone ravine which is one of the most important archaeological sites in Italy. Numerous grottoes containing prehistoric cemeteries and early Christian tombs have been discovered here.

The economic profile of modern Modica is chiefly agricultural. Commercial products include olive oil, wine, cheese, macaroni, and candy. Pop. (1951) city 27,730; commune 40,421.

MODIGLIANI, mō-dē-lyä'nē, **Amedeo,** Italian painter and sculptor: b. Livorno (Leghorn), Italy, July 12, 1884; d. Paris, France, Jan. 25, 1920. The son of Jewish parents of moderate means, he obtained a rather haphazard art education at the Florentine Academy of Fine Arts and at Venice, Rome, and Capri. In Rome he carefully studied the work of Michelangelo; Modigliani's maturing painting, somewhat like that of the Italian Renaissance masters, is an art of delicate line distorted for emotional effect, chiefly through elongation, in an early modernist style.

In 1906, Modigliani arrived in Paris, where he soon sank into a life of dissipation and became addicted to drink and narcotics, often without settled lodgings. His brother, the prominent Italian Socialist political leader and deputy, Giuseppe Emanuele Modigliani, occasionally sent him money, which he consumed on various excesses. His art, however, was rated highly by well-known contemporaries of the Paris school, although it was largely unknown to the general public.

In Paris, Modigliani met Pablo Picasso, and his own art, particularly his sculpture, shows the influence of cubism. More especially, his sculpture was influenced by African Negro primitivism with its unspoiled naïveté and simple formalism. This primitivism soon manifested itself in Modigliani's oil paintings, including his nudes, with their long oval faces, slanted eyes, and flaring nostrils.

His health undermined by dissipation, Modigliani died of tuberculosis at the age of 36 and was interred in Père Lachaise cemetery. After his death, his works began to find their market, rising steadily in popular esteem. They may now be seen in nearly all museums of modern art.

Consult Craven, Thomas, *Modern Art; the Men, the Movements, the Meaning,* rev. ed. pp. 193–203 (New York 1940); Douglas, Charles, *Artist Quarter; Reminiscences of Montmartre and Montparnasse in the First Two Decades of the Twentieth Century* (Toronto 1941); Roy, Claude, *Modigliani,* tr. from the French by James Emmons and Stuart Gilbert, with color plates of his work (New York 1958).

MODJESKA, mô-jĕs'kȧ, **Helena** (nee Opid), Polish-American actress: b. Kraków, Poland, Oct. 12, 1840; d. Bay Island, East Newport, Calif., April 8, 1909. Her father, Michael Opid, a music master from the Tatra Mountains of Galicia, died young, leaving a large and impoverished family. Helena early showed dramatic ability. While still in her teens, she married her guardian, Gustav Modrzejewski, a small-town concert impresario many years her senior, by whom she had a son who became the noted American bridge designer, Ralph Modjeski (q.v.). Before Modrzejewski died in 1868, his young wife had already become the rising Polish national tragedienne. Later in 1868, she married a scion of the Polish aristocracy, Count Charles Bozenta Chlapowski, who throughout her subsequent career acted as her manager. Both were temperamentally idealists, passionately devoted to Polish independence, and completely lacking in business acumen.

After the actress reigned at the Imperial Theater in Warsaw for a number of years, the couple's anti-Russian sentiments made it advisable to leave Poland. In 1876, they went to America with a group of fellow Poles who had ambitions of transforming a ranch in California into a utopian colony. This scheme soon failed, and Mme. Modjeska (the Anglicized form of her first married name, which she retained for professional purposes) went back on the stage in 1877 at the urging of Edwin Booth, having learned English in six months. She made her American debut in San Francisco in the French tragedy, *Adrienne Lecouvreur.* Thereafter she played for many years with great success in the United States, in London, and even occasionally again in Poland, where she was finally barred in 1893 after making an anti-Russian speech at the Chicago World's Fair.

Mme. Modjeska was noted for, and preferred, Shakespearean roles although she also did such well-known feminine parts as Alexandre Dumas fils' Camille and Friedrich Schiller's Maria Stuart, and in 1883 unsuccessfully tried to introduce Henrik Ibsen's work to America in a revised version of *A Doll's House,* called *Nora.* Her style was that demanded by the canons of Victorian romanticism—romantically tragic womanhood, graceful and pure. Within the limits of this genre, she was highly effective. Despite the large sums of money she earned, she died in relative poverty. Her husband was allowed to bury her in Polish soil at Kraków.

MODJESKI, mô-jĕs'kĭ, **Ralph** (originally Rudolphe Modrzejewski), Polish-American civil engineer and bridge designer: b. Kraków, Poland, Jan. 27, 1861; d. Los Angeles, Calif., June 28, 1940. He was the son of the famous tragedienne, Helena Modjeska, and her first husband, Gustav Modrzejewski. Like his mother, he Anglicized his name when he went to the United States in 1876. He later became a naturalized citizen. As a boy, Modjeski hesitated between engineering and music. He took lessons in Poland from the celebrated pianist, Casimir Hofmann, and kept the piano as an avocation all his life. However, in 1878, he settled on engineering, and after graduating with high honors in Paris at the École des Ponts et Chaussées, he returned to the United States and became one of the country's leading bridge engineers, opening his own offices in Chicago in 1893. Among the many spans which he built were several beautiful suspension bridges, including the Delaware River Bridge (completed 1926) between Philadelphia, Pa., and Camden, N.J., and the Mid-Hudson Bridge (completed 1930) at Poughkeepsie, N.Y. Shortly before his death, he developed the preliminary plans for the huge San Francisco-Oakland Bay Bridge. Modjeski's work was marked by grandiosity in conception, and by innovations such as the use of new steel alloys and stronger cables. His firm also trained a number of leading younger bridge architects.

MODLING, mûd'lĭng, district, Vienna, Austria, on the extreme southern edge of the metropolis, about nine miles from the city's center, on the western slope of the famous Vienna Woods (Wiener Wald). The nucleus of the district is the old town of Mödling, at the entrance to the beautiful Brühl Valley. To this in 1938 the Nazi authorities added several surrounding towns, including Brunn and Wiener Neudorf, and attached the whole to the city of Vienna as a new district. These boundaries have been retained. From 1945 to 1955 the district was in the sector of Vienna occupied by the Russians. It is essentially an industrial suburb of the Austrian capital, producing shoes, iron products, paints, and chemicals.

The old town of Mödling contains the early Gothic Roman Catholic Church of St. Othmar, dating from 1454, with a Romanesque baptistry. The town is less industralized than some other components of the district, and has something of a resort character. There are chalybeate baths and a sanatorium, and some wine is grown on the Brühl slopes. An agricultural school has a curriculum which includes brewing and horticulture. Pop. (1951) district 49,799.

MODOC, mō'dŏk (Indian *móatokni,* southerners), a tribe of northern California Indians belonging to the Shapwailutan linguistic family; together with the Klamath (q.v.) they form the Lutuamnian division of that stock. They originally inhabited the Lost River, Tule Lake, and Lower Klamath Lake area, calling themselves *Maklak* (the people). Always warlike, they bitterly resisted white invasion of their country, and under Chief Kintpuash (Captain Jack) waged one of the most remarkable Indian defensive campaigns in American history (see MODOC WAR). In 1864 they ceded their territory to the United States and were settled on the Klamath Reservation in Oregon, where 334 individuals lived in 1959. They are noted for their basketry and the use of obsidian (q.v.), which they supplied to the neighboring Yurok and Karok tribes.

Consult Miller, Joaquín, *Life Amongst the Modocs* (London 1873); and Spier, Leslie, *Klamath Ethnography* (Berkeley, Calif., 1930).

FREDERICK J. DOCKSTADER.

MODOC WAR, one of the costliest Indian campaigns in the history of the settlement of the West. Although the causes were little understood at the time, and are not well remembered today, the war captured nationwide attention for several years.

Following the opening of the Modoc country in California, frequent clashes between whites and Indians resulted in a treaty in 1864 by which the Klamaths and Modocs ceded their lands and were removed to a new reservation in Oregon. The more numerous Klamaths continually harassed their traditional enemies, and the Indian agent refused to intervene. In 1870, made desperate by this situation and aggravated by continued government neglect, a large band of Modocs under the leadership of Kintpuash, a subchief (called Captain Jack by the whites), fled from the reservation.

For two years the Modoc band lived quietly in northern California, passively resisting efforts to return them to their reservation. In a foolhardy attempt at force, a United States Army unit was sent against the Modoc camp, resulting in losses on both sides. Kintpuash retreated to the nearby lava beds (now Lava Beds National Monument) south of Tule Lake, where his band successfully held off all attempts to dislodge them from January to April 1873.

In April a peace commission was attacked while trying to negotiate an end to the hostilities, and Gen. Edward R. S. Canby and the Reverend Eleazer Thomas were treacherously murdered, bringing on an all-out effort to finish the campaign. It was not until the Modocs quarreled among themselves, split up, and left the protection of the lava beds that they were finally overcome. With the surrender of Kintpuash on June 1, the Modoc War ended; he and three other leaders were hanged at Fort Klamath on Oct. 3, 1873. The hostiles were taken to the Quapaw Reservation in Oklahoma, while the rest of the tribe was returned to the Klamath Reservation in Oregon.

The campaign engaged more than 1,000 Regular Army soldiers, about 80 Indian scouts, and a company of Oregon volunteers. These were opposed by about 75 Modoc warriors and their families. In all, the cost to the United States was 65 killed and 67 wounded, plus $500,000. The Modocs lost 11 warriors killed or executed, plus an unknown number of women and children.

Consult Dunn, Jacob Piatt, Jr., *Massacres of the Mountains* (New York 1886); Riddle, Jeff C. Davis, *The Indian History of the Modoc War and the Causes That Led to It* (San Francisco 1914); Schmitt, Martin F., and Brown, Dee, *Fighting Indians of the West* (New York 1948).

FREDERICK J. DOCKSTADER,
Assistant Director, Museum of the American Indian.

MODULATION, mŏd-ŭ-lā'shŭn, in music, a shift within a composition from one key to another. A key is established by the felt presence of a "tonic" tone; modulation entails either the transient or the final establishment of a new tonic. Modulation most commonly is made to a new key in which the dominant or subdominant tone (fifth or fourth degree) of the existing key becomes the new tonic; and to a key in the minor mode (if the existing key is major) or in the major mode (if the existing key is minor) having the same tonic as the existing key (for example, from C major to C minor).

A *diatonic* modulation makes pivotal use of a chord consisting of tones native to both keys; a *chromatic* modulation, of a chord consisting in part of tones not native to one key or the other; an *enharmonic* modulation, of a chord in which at least one tone is given a new function without being actually changed (for example, when C sharp is regarded as D flat). The term "modulation," widely restricted to a change of key without break in melodic line or chordal progression, may also be applied (as is frequent in harmonic analysis of the music of Franz Schubert) to the arbitrary replacement of one key by another without the use of any diatonic, chromatic, or enharmonic pivot chord. See also HARMONY; KEY; MUSICAL ELEMENTS AND TERMS.

HERBERT WEINSTOCK.

MODULE, mŏd'ūl (from Lat. *modulus,* a small measure), in architecture, a unit of measurement used especially in classical and Renaissance times for plotting the size and harmonious proportions of a building. Historically the use of the module sprang up in connection with the five classic orders of architecture—Doric, Ionic, Corinthian, Tuscan, and Composite. These were named from the type of column peculiar to each, and the unit of measurement taken as a module was usually the diameter or semidiameter of one of the columns just above its base, although infrequently a fraction of the entire height of the column was used. The module itself was divided into parts or minutes (degrees), and a building can thus be said to be so many modules and a fraction or so many modules and minutes in height. Since the column of each order differed in circumference and height, there were also five individual modules and various standardized modules covering some or all of the orders. In modern times, when the module is used as a measuring device, it is usually the semidiameter of whatever type of column, classical or modern, is used in construction of the building.

MODULUS, mŏd'ŭ-lŭs, in mathematics, a constant, referring to properties of matter in certain equations. As stress is proportional to strain within the elastic limits, some constant quantity may be introduced making this proportionality into an equality. In strength of materials, such a constant is called a modulus. Thus in Hooke's law, which says that extension, as of a bar, is proportional to the extending force, the constant which converts this proportionality into an equality is called the modulus of elasticity, or Young's modulus, and is denoted by E. Where the elastic limits are not exceeded, the transverse strain—the contraction per unit of transverse dimension—is from one third to one fourth the longitudinal strain. The symbol denoting the modulus of elasticity of bulk is K. It denotes the lessening of bulk per unit cube, usually per cubic inch, under hydrostatic stress. See also ELASTICITY; STRENGTH OF MATERIALS—*Laws of Elasticity.*

MOE, mō'ė, **Jørgen Engebretsen,** Norwegian poet: b. Hole, Ringerike, Norway, April 4, 1813; d. Kristiansand, March 27, 1882. Though a clergyman and eventually bishop of Kristiansand, he is best known for his collection of Norse folklore made in collaboration with Peter Christian Asbjørnsen and published as *Norske folkeeventyr* (1842–1844; 1852; 1871). English translations of these tales were made by Sir George Dasent and others. Some of Moe's poems and children's stories have become Norwegian classics. His works other than the folk stories were published in a two-volume collection, *Samlede skrifter,* in 1877.

His son (INGEBRET) MOLTKE MOE (1859–1913) was also a folklorist, edited collections of folk songs and tales made by his father and Asbjørnsen, and from 1899 was professor at Oslo University.

MOELLER, mûl'ẽr, **Henry,** American Roman Catholic prelate: b. Cincinnati, Ohio, Dec. 11, 1849; d. there, Jan. 5, 1925. His elementary studies were pursued at St. Joseph's parochial school and he afterward attended St. Francis Xavier's College. In 1869 he went to the American College at Rome, where he followed a seven years' course in philosophy and theology. He was ordained priest in the church of St. John Lateran, Rome, June 10, 1876, and after his return to Cincinnati was assigned to St. Patrick's Church, Bellfontaine, Ohio, and later appointed to a profesorship in Mount St. Mary's Seminary, remaining there until 1879. In 1880 Archbishop William Henry Elder named him chancellor of the diocese of Cincinnati, and on Aug. 25, 1900, he was consecrated bishop of Columbus, Ohio. On April 27, 1903 the Holy See appointed him titular archbishop of Areopolis and coadjutor archbishop of Cincinnati with right of succession, and on the death of Archbishop Elder, Oct. 31, 1904, he assumed charge of the archdiocese, the pallium being conferred upon him by Cardinal Gibbons Feb. 15, 1905.

MOELLER, Louis Charles, American genre painter: b. New York, N. Y., Aug. 5, 1855; d. Weehawken, N. J., Nov. 11, 1930. He worked for three years with his father, a decorative painter, studied art at Cooper Institute and the National Academy of Design, New York, and in Munich, Germany, with Frank Duveneck. In 1883 he established his studio in New York. He received First Hallgarten Prize (1884), and was elected associate (1894) and member (1895) of the National Academy. He is represented at the Corcoran Gallery, Washington, D.C., by the painting *Disagreement.*

MOELLER VAN DEN BRUCK, mûl'ẽr fän dĕn bro͝ok', **Arthur,** German writer: b. Solingen, Germany, April 23, 1876; d. 1925. He edited the works of Edgar Allen Poe in German (1901–1904), and was coeditor with Dmitri Merezhkovsky of the first German edition of the works of Fyodor Mikhailovich Dostoyevsky (1906–1915). The Nazis took their name for Germany, the Third Reich, from his book *Das Dritte Reich.*

MOERIS, Lake, mē'rĭs, Egypt, an ancient artificial body of water which formerly lay north of El Faiyum, and was described by Herodotus as constructed entirely by human industry. He reported it to be 350 miles in circumference and more than 250 feet deep, and said that the fishing was important and profitable. Moeris was connected by canal with the natural lake of Birket Qârûn and also by canal with the Nile. At the site of ancient Crocodilopolis (site of modern El Faiyum), near the entrance to the latter canal, two huge statues (mentioned by Herodotus) were unearthed late in the 19th century.

MOERITHERIUM, mē-rĭ-thē'rĭ-ŭm, a genus of primitive proboscidean mammals occurring in the Upper Eocene and early Oligocene of Egypt. Their remains have been found in the vicinity of ancient Lake Moeris. These mammals were about the size of tapirs and had a short proboscis and simple mastodont teeth. Later specializations led to the mastodons and elephants. See also ELEPHANT.

MOESIA, mē'shĭ-ȧ, a province of the ancient Roman Empire lying north of Thrace and Macedonia, extending to the Danube and the Black Sea, and corresponding in the main to modern Serbia and Bulgaria. Strabo described its original inhabitants as Thracians. The Romans first invaded it in 75 B.C., penetrating as far as the Danube, but it was not until 29 B.C., that it was finally subjugated.

MOFFAT, mŏf'ăt, **David Halliday,** American capitalist: b. Washingtonville, N. Y., July 22, 1839; d. en route to New York, N. Y., March 18, 1911. He began work in 1854 as messenger for the New York Exchange Bank, and in 1855 went to Des Moines, Iowa, to join his brother. He worked for a year there as clerk in the bank of A. J. Stevens and Company, then became teller of the Bank of Nebraska at Omaha. After that bank closed in 1860, he joined a partner in operating a stationery and general store in Denver, Colo. The store also contained the post office and was the agency for the Western Union Telegraph Company. In 1861 Moffat returned East to marry his boyhood sweetheart Fannie A. Buckhout of Mechanicsville, N. Y., and with her made his permanent home in Denver. He became cashier of the First National Bank there in 1865, and later its president. He was closely identified with the development of Denver and with the mining and railroad interests of Colorado. He was president of the Denver and Rio Grande Railroad in 1884–1891, financed the building of the Florence and Cripple Creek line, and promoted building of the Denver, Northwestern and Pacific (later the Denver and Salt Lake), still known as "the Moffat road." He died while on a trip to New York to finance its building. Moffat Tunnel under James Peak in the Rockies is named for him.

MOFFAT, mŏf'ăt, **Robert,** Scottish Congregationalist missionary to South Africa: b. Ormiston, Haddingtonshire, Dec. 21, 1795; d. Leigh, near Tunbridge Wells, Kent, Aug. 8, 1883. In early life a gardener, the London Missionary Society sent him in 1816 to Namaqualand, where he converted a local chief. At Capetown, in 1819, he married Mary Smith, daughter of a former employer, who aided him in establishing a mission station at Kuruman, in Bechuanaland, in 1825. He visited England during 1839–1843, and returned there for good in 1870. Besides pursuing his work in Bechuanaland, he frequently journeyed northward to visit the Matabele and other tribes. He translated the Bible, many hymns, and *Pilgrim's Progress* into Sechuana, the language of the Bechuanas, and wrote the notable *Missionary Labours and Scenes in South Africa* (1842). One of his daughters married David Livingstone (q.v.). John S. Moffat, a son, published *The Lives of Robert and Mary Moffat* (1885).

MOFFATT, James, Scottish theologian: b. Glasgow, July 4, 1870; d. New York City, June 27, 1944. He was educated at Glasgow University, and from 1896 to 1912 he was a minister of the United Free Church of Scotland. During 1911–1915 he served as Yates professor of Greek at Mansfield College, Oxford University, then returning to Glasgow to become professor of church history at the United Free Church College. In 1927 he relinquished this chair to go to the United States to assume the post of Washburn professor of church history at Union Theological Seminary, New York City. He made a notable translation of the Bible which bears his name. His numerous books include *Historical New Testament* (1901); *The Bible in Scots Literature* (1925); *Presbyterianism* (1928); *The Books of the Prophets* (1939).

MOGADISHU, mŏg-à-dĭsh'o͞o, capital of the republic of Somalia. It is situated on the Indian Ocean, on the Benadir coast of Somalia, and is the country's chief seaport. Mogadishu has a modern airport, and is connected by road with Bosaso, on the Gulf of Aden, and with Ethiopia and Kenya. Oilseed pressing, sawmilling, and the manufacture of ice are the chief industries. The city has several mosques dating from the 1200's. Its old fort, which was restored in 1933–1934, now serves as a museum.

Mogadishu was formerly the capital of Italian Somaliland, and became the capital of Somali when the latter was formed by a merger of British Somaliland and Italian Somaliland in 1960. The area had been conquered in 1871 by the sultan of Zanzibar, who leased it (1892) and then sold it (1905) to Italy. Mogadishu was one of Italy's chief supply bases during the conquest of Ethiopia in 1936. The Italian spelling of the city's name was Mogadiscio. Pop. (1964) 180,000.

MOGADOR, mŏg-à-dôr' (Essaouira), city, Morocco, on the Atlantic Ocean, 100 miles west of Marrakech. Its sheltered harbor is used mainly for coastwise shipping. The beaches are popular as bathing resorts. Mogador's chief industries are fish processing, tanning, sugar refining, and palm-fiber working. Handicraft products include inlaid furniture, jewelry, and copper utensils. The city was founded in the 1760's by Sultan Mohammed XVI of Morocco and was formerly a caravan terminus. Pop. (1961) 26,392.

MOGILEV, mŭ-gĭ-lyôf', city, USSR, capital of Mogilev Oblast in the Belorussian Soviet republic. Situated on the Dnepr River, 110 miles east of Minsk, Mogilev is a railroad and highway junction and a manufacturing center. Its industries include foundries, smelters, and tanneries, and plants that manufacture machinery, apparel, and tobacco products.

Mogilev grew up around a castle built in the late 1200's. It was ruled successively by the Poles, Lithuanians, and Swedes until 1772, when it was acquired by Russia. Pop. of the oblast (1961) 1,182,000; of the city (1962) 139,000.

MOGILEV-PODOLSKI, mŭ-gĭ-lyôf' pŭ-dôl'y'-ski, city, USSR, in Vinnitsa Oblast, in the Ukrainian Soviet republic. It is situated on the Dnestr River, 60 miles southwest of Vinnitsa. The leading industries are machinery manufacture, lumber milling, limestone quarrying, tanning, distilling, flour milling, and canning.

In the Middle Ages, Mogilev-Podolski was a center of the caravan trade between the Ukraine and Moldavia. Russia annexed it from Poland in 1793. Pop. (1960) 19,000.

MOGOLLON MESA, mō'gô-yŏn, the southern edge of the high plateau of Arizona, in the extreme south of Coconino County. The average altitude is some 8,000 feet. The mesa, which consists of limestone in part covered by lava, bears considerable pine forest.

MOGOLLON MOUNTAINS, a range in the southern part of Catron County, N. Mex., constituting the divide between the San Francisco and Gila rivers. It is over 30 miles long. The highest summits are Whitewater Baldy (10,892 feet), Mogollon Peak (10,778 feet), and Grouse Mountain (10,132 feet). The range consists of a thick succession of Tertiary volcanic rocks. Veins of silver and other ores are mined. It is largely forested, and has been included in Gila National Forest.

MOGUL, mô-gŭl, or **MUGHUL,** mo͝o'go͞ol, name applied to the dynasty of Mongol rulers of India. It was founded in 1526 by Baber (Babur, Babar), a descendant of Tamerlane and Genghis Khan. Under his grandson, Akbar the Great, the Mogul empire embraced central and northern India, and much of Afghanistan. On the death of Aurangzeb in 1707 the empire declined; and Bahadur Shah II, last of the Mogul emperors, was deposed by the British in 1857.

MOHÁCS, mô'häch, city, Hungary, on the Danube River, near the Yugoslav border. It is situated in Baranya County, 23 miles southeast of Pécs. Mohács is a rail terminus and river port, and since 1950 has become a center of Hungary's metallurgical industry. Other manufactures are hemp, textiles, and leather goods.

Mohács was the scene of a crucial battle in 1526, when the Turks crushed the Hungarians and proceeded to conquer the country. In 1687 the Turks were defeated nearby in one of their last attempts to hold Hungary. Pop. (1960) 18,015.

MOHAIR, mō'hâr, the common commercial name of the fleece of the Angora goat. The word comes to the English through the Old French *mohere,* from the Arabic *mukhayyar,* meaning mohair cloth. In color mohair is pure white, except in rare cases, and grows in ringlets. The hairs composing a fleece are of varying lengths, but the average annual growth of the long hairs, which largely predominate, is about 10 inches. The hairs are not composed of epithelia, as is the case with wool, and therefore the felting property characteristic of wool is wanting. In fineness, mohair is variable with the individual animals, and is placed between the fine and coarse wools; in luster, durability, and strength it has no equal among fibers.

The only vitiating feature of mohair as it comes from the animal is the intermixture of an undercoat of lusterless, chalky white hairs; the hairs vary in length from one to three inches, and vary in total amount according to the breeding of the animal. This undercoat is known technically as "kemp," and the principal objection to it is that it does not take the fast dyes. It becomes necessary, therefore, to remove the kemp from the mohair used in the finest fabrics, and this work is done by a comb which, in removing the kemp, also takes out every mohair fiber of equal length or shorter than the kemp. This entails a loss ranging from 10 to 30 per cent, but the average loss lessens as better goats are developed.

The luster of mohair is very pronounced, and no amount of washing, dyeing, or other manipulation will dull it. Its durability is remarkable, and because of this fact it enters largely into goods of fine quality which are subjected to hard usage. Fast dyes have such an affinity for it that sunshine and storms have no effect on its brilliancy.

The uses of mohair are many. It is used in the manufacture of plush, and enters into such fabrics as alpaca, cashmere, and astrakhan. A high grade of mohair is derived from the goat ranches of Turkey, South Africa, and the southwestern United States.

MOHAIR GOAT, the Angora goat. See Goat, Domestic.

MOHAMMED. Mohammed was the founder of a religious system of belief, Islam (q.v.), which is now professed by some 300 million people scattered all over Asia, Africa, and southeastern Europe. Though born within the full light of history, his early life is but dimly known. The earliest record of it was not composed until over a century after his death and has not been preserved except in a recension, that of ibn-Hisham, who died two centuries after Mohammed. The exact date of Mohammed's birth is not certain; it must have fallen sometime between 570 and 571 A.D. Even of the name his mother gave him we cannot be positively sure. The one by which he is universally known, *Muḥammad* (highly praised), sounds like an honorific one. Once in the Koran (61:6) it takes another form, *Aḥmad* (more praiseworthy). His fellow citizens at times called him *al-Amīn* (the trustworthy).

Early Career.—From casual references in the Koran, however, and from a critical study of the traditional material that has accumulated around the name of Mohammed, we can arrive at a number of reasonably certain facts in his career prior to the call to prophecy. His birthplace was Mecca, located in the words of the Koran (14:40) in "an uncultivable valley." The tribe to which he belonged was the Koreish (Quraysh), a noble tribe in charge of the sanctuary in that city and interested in caravan trade; but the immediate family of the boy was humble. His father, Abdullah, died before his birth; his mother, Aminah, when he was about six years old. Tradition asserts that as an infant he was entrusted to the care of a Bedouin family in which he found a foster mother. The Koran has preserved a clear reference to Mohammed's lowly childhood: "Did He not find thee an orphan and protect thee?" etc. (93:6-8).

The fatherless and motherless boy found home with his parental grandfather, Abd-al-Muttalib, who died two years later leaving a son, abu-Talib, in charge of his protégé. The story that at the age of 12 Mohammed accompanied his uncle to Syria with a trade caravan has been embellished with so many legends as to cast doubt on its veracity. Besides, no passage in the Koran suggests any familiarity on the part of Mohammed with Syria. One of those legends is that on his Syrian trip Mohammed met at Busra, south of Damascus, a Christian monk Bahira, who recognized in him the future great prophet and identified on his body certain significant signs, including the seal of the prophetic office between his shoulders.

His Call.—At the age of 25 Mohammed married a wealthy, energetic, and resolute widow of the Koreish, named Khadija, who was 15 years his senior. Before she became his wife the lady merchant was his employer. That the marriage proved successful may be inferred from the fact that only after her death in 620 did Mohammed practice polygamy and gradually increased the number of his wives to about a dozen. By Khadija he had the only child who survived, Fatima, who married his cousin Ali and became the mother of all those descended from the Prophet.

With the greater economic competence which came through his first marriage, Mohammed was now able to pursue his own tastes. He was then often seen in solitude, wandering on mountain paths and seeking opportunities for contemplation in out-of-the-way places and ravines. He must have been inoculated with certain effective ideas of Judaeo-Christian sources relating to God, man, and their interrelationship. Evidently he had been impressed by the fact he observed that the few Jews and Christians with whom he had come in contact had a "book" and were prosperous and advanced, whereas his own people, the heathen of Arabia, had no "book" and were backward.

It was supposedly in the course of one of these contemplative moods in a cave outside of Mecca, called Hira, that Mohammed one day heard a strange voice commanding: "Read in the name of thy Lord, who created." Puzzled, the unlettered Mohammed hesitated. But the assuring voice reiterated: "Read, for thy Lord is the most bounteous, who teacheth man that which he knew not" (96:1-5). Then and there the Prophet received his first call. The exact time of the occasion was later fixed toward the end of the fasting month of Ramadan, year 610. The night was named "the night of power" (97:1) and is still celebrated in Turkey and other parts of the Moslem world with deep reverence and special ritual. The voice which to Mohammed first sounded like the "reverberating of bells" was soon identified as that of Gabriel.

The Message.—The early utterances of Mohammed as a prophet took the form of rhymed prose, the type used by oracles, soothsayers, and pagan priests. The fact that he, an *ummi* (unschooled man), could produce such exquisite prose was adduced by him and his followers as the only proof of his prophethood. He performed no other miracles and claimed none. His first teachings revolved around the unity of God, his attributes, and future life. The doctrine of a judgment day involving reward for the righteous and punishment for the iniquitous was stressed as people failed to respond, and was used as an inducement or deterrent depending upon the nature of the response.

Early Followers.—His early followers, as to be expected from the nature of his message, largely came from the socially insignificant and economically discontent. On the higher level, the first to believe in him were his wife, Khadija, his cousin Ali (son of abu-Talib), and his future successor, abu-Bakr. All these were of the Koreish, but the bulk of the tribe were not only hesitant but actually hostile. That their hostility had economic motivation cannot be doubted. As custodians of the Kaaba, the pagan shrine and pilgrimage object, they could not afford to be indifferent to the inroads of a new faith.

About 615 some of the small band of Mohammed's followers fled the country to Christian Abyssinia (Ethiopia) because of persecution. Their choice of place of refuge shows that they looked upon Christianity as the religion most closely related to their own. A deputation sent by the Meccans to demand the extradition of the refugees returned empty handed. Meantime Mohammed and those who stayed with him were practically put under siege in a Meccan quarter with the expectation of being starved to submission. It was at this juncture that a revelation came acknowledging the genuineness of the three Meccan goddesses—together with Allah, who had hitherto been declared as the only one—and the siege was thereupon raised. The exiles returned, and Mohammed later withdrew the revelation as coming from the devil. The verses were expunged from the Koranic text.

The Hegira.—The truce between the Prophet and his aristocratic kinsmen was but a temporary one. After a brief sojourn in Taif (al-Tā'if), an oasis in the mountains southeast of Mecca, Mohammed sought a more secure abode in a farther place, Yathrib. Some citizens of this town had met Mohammed at a pilgrimage festival outside of Mecca and evidently encouraged him in the belief that Yathribites would be predisposed to receive him as a prophet because some of them were Jews, expecting the advent of such a leader. A number of Mohammed's followers preceded him to Yathrib, on July 16, 622. He himself, accompanied by Abu-Bakr, followed, arriving there September 24, 622. Yathrib was hence called Medina (al-Madīnah, the city [of the Prophet]). The migration was termed Hegira (*hijrah*). It constituted a turning point in the career of Mohammed, indeed in the history of Islam.

This date, July 16, 622, became the earliest fixed point in Moslem chronology, and was chosen as the starting point of the new calendar. According to this calendar the Moslem year is a lunar one, consisting of six months of 29 days each and six other months of 30 days each. This makes the entire year 354 days, with a discrepancy amounting to a little over three years in a century.

Medinese Period.—With the Hegira, the Medinese period in Mohammed's career begins. In Medina he entered upon a period of success which made him more of a politician and less of a prophet. Here he contracted many marriages, some for political purposes, others with a view to having an heir, including one with the infant Aisha (A'ishah), daughter of abu-Bakr, and Hafsah, daughter of Umar. Gifted with ambition and astuteness, Aisha maintained her influence over her husband and priority over all other wives. Many of the traditions ascribed to him were transmitted through her.

Battle of Badr.—Mohammed felt the responsibility for providing sustenance for his followers from Mecca, now called Emigrants (*muhājirūn*), as well as for the new converts in Medina, termed Helpers (*anṣār*). Under the pressure of this new necessity he considered it legitimate to intercept a Meccan caravan led by abu-Sufyan of the Koreish, on its way back from Syria in 624, and that in Ramadan, a holy month in which fighting was prohibited. On the battlefield Badr, some 20 miles southwest of Medina, the Moslem army of 300 encountered the Meccan reinforcement of 1,000 rushing to the aid of the caravan. The outcome was a complete victory for the Prophet and, in the eyes of his followers, a divine sanction of his new creed. This victory of Badr laid the basis of the temporal power of Islam. Ever since then Islam has remained a militant polity.

The following year (625) at another encounter with the Meccans, at Uhud, abu-Sufyan won the day. The Prophet himself suffered a wound, but his prestige was not impaired. Two years later he successfully defended Medina, by digging a trench around it, against a more serious attack on the part of Meccans, Bedouins, and other confederates. This trench method of warfare, said to have been suggested by a Persian in Mohammed's camp, was an innovation the like of which the Arabians never saw before. His converts increased in direct proportion to his victories.

Mohammed hereafter felt secure in the leadership of Medina. Having failed in his attempt to secure alliance with the Jews of Medina, he turned against them and chased them from their plantations. Gradually he divorced his system from both Judaism and Christianity, and Arabicized it. Thereby Islam's independence was asserted. Mohammed ordered his followers henceforth to turn their faces toward Mecca and not Jerusalem as before (2:139). The Kaaba, the cube-like sanctuary which housed the heathen idols in the city, became the new kiblah (*qiblah*). Pilgrimage to Mecca was authorized, and so was the kissing of the Black Stone in the Kaaba. The religious laws governing fasting, almsgiving, and prayer were enjoined and incorporated in the Koran. Social and political ordinances relating to marriage, divorce, inheritance, and treatment of slaves and prisoners of war were likewise promulgated in this period.

The laws for the small Medinese congregation became the laws of Islam as a world religion and a world empire. From Medina the Islamic theocracy spread into the rest of Arabia, and thence into the rest of the world. The congregation was conceived of as a religious brotherhood: "The believers are naught else but brothers" (49:10). The extraordinary subsequent conquests of Moslem arms testify to the success the Arabian Prophet had in welding his unwieldy followers into a unified, devoted organization.

Mecca, Religious Capital.—In 628 Mohammed made a truce with his Meccan adversaries guaranteeing for his followers the right of performing the pilgrimage. Mecca thus became the religious capital, while Medina remained the political capital. In the course of the pilgrimage in the following year, Khalid ibn-al-Walid and Amr ibn-al-As, both of the Koreish and destined to play brilliant roles in the military career of Islam, were recruited to the new cause.

Early in 630 Mohammed found an excuse for attacking Mecca. He entered it as a conqueror, and with his own hands smashed the 360 idols in its sanctuary exclaiming: "Truth hath come and falsehood hath vanished." Scarcely was there another victor who exploited his victory with more restraint and moderation. Only ten of his old Meccan enemies were proscribed. It was about that time that Mohammed proclaimed the territory around the Kaaba *ḥaram* (forbidden, sacred). The passage itself is not very clear: "O ye who believe! The idolaters are certainly unclean. So let them not come near the forbidden Mosque after this their year" (9:28). The early Moslems, however, put a generous interpretation on it, extended the forbidden area to include both Mecca and Medina with their environs, and considered even Christians and Jews as intended in the prohibition. Since then no non-Moslem could enter the sacred area and escape with his life. The few Christian-born Europeans who managed to do so professed Islam and practiced it while there.

Mohammed's Death.—On June 8, 632, Mohammed fell suddenly ill, and passed away complaining of a severe headache. He was buried where he died in the apartment of his favorite wife Aisha, later annexed to an adjoining mosque and made an object of pilgrimage to all future Moslem generations. The man, whose main strength lay in his unwavering belief that he was called in person by God to execute His will, had succeeded in establishing a religion, creating a nation, and laying the foundations of an empire. All members of his politico-religious community were to be brothers with no distinction among them except in their degree of piety (9:11; 49:13). Two years before his death he had dispatched an expedition against Syria which proved to be the first act in a struggle that did not cease until the empire of Islam had encompassed a large part of the then civilized world.

The traditional description of Mohammed makes him a man of medium height, with a large head, large eyes, heavy eyelashes, thick beard, broad shoulders, and hair neither straight nor curly. While his physical features may not be exactly known, his mental traits are clear. The impact of his personality, the trust he engendered in his followers, the enthusiasm he awakened in those with whom he came in contact, are all unmistakable. The devotion and loyalty of such unusually able men as abu-Bakr, Umar, and others indicate a strong character. Even at the height of his glory Mohammed lived a simple, unpretentious life. His behavior has been imitated by millions upon millions of men and women, in different places and times, who looked upon him as the perfect man.

Bibliography.—Buhl, Fr., "Muhammad," *Encyclopaedia of Islām;* Grimme, Hubert, *Mohammed,* 2 vols. (Münster 1892–95); Margoliouth, David S., *Mohammed and the Rise of Islam* (New York 1905); Muir, William, *The Life of Mohammad,* ed. by T. H. Weir (Glasgow 1923); Andrae, Tor, *Mohammed: The Man and His Faith,* tr. by Theophil Menzel (New York 1936).

PHILIP K. HITTI,
Professor Emeritus of Oriental Languages and Literature, Princeton University.

MOHAMMED, the name of six sultans of Turkey:

MOHAMMED I (b. 1387; d. 1421), son of Bajazet I, succeeded Prince Musa in 1413. He extended Turkey's boundaries to the Danube, established friendly relations with Greece, and fostered literature, arts, and sciences.

MOHAMMED II (b. Adrianople, 1430; d. 1481) succeeded his father, Murad II, in 1451. Styled "the Conqueror" or "the Great," he captured Constantinople in 1453, making it his capital; conquered Serbia in 1456–1458; and took Scutari from the Venetians and Kaffa from the Genoese. He also acquired the Crimea, and in 1481 seized Otranto with a view to making war on Naples.

MOHAMMED III (b. 1566; d. 1603) succeeded his father, Murad III, in 1595, executing 19 brothers to assure himself the throne. In 1596 he captured Erlau, in Hungary, but his campaign against Abbas I, shah of Persia, proved unsuccessful.

MOHAMMED IV (b. 1641; d. 1691) succeeded his father, Ibrahim, in 1648, the nominal regency of his grandmother soon being exchanged for actual control by the Kuprili (grand viziers). The Turks were defeated before Vienna in 1683, and subsequently met many reverses inflicted by a league of Poland, Russia, Venice, and Leopold I, Holy Roman emperor. Seized and imprisoned by the Turkish Army in 1687, he was succeeded by his brother, Suleiman II (or III), and languished in chains until his death.

MOHAMMED V (b. Topqapu, Nov. 3, 1844; d. Yildiz, July 3, 1918). A son of Abdul-Medjid I, in 1909 he succeeded Abdul-Hamid II, his brother, who was deposed and exiled. Until placed on the throne at the age of 65, he had been held a state prisoner in close palace confinement. Poorly educated and ignorant of the world, he was a quiescent tool of the leaders of the Committee of Union and Progress. These men involved the country in World War I as ally of Germany, and he died as Turkish resistance was collapsing.

MOHAMMED VI (b. Constantinople, Jan. 12, 1861; d. San Remo, Italy, May 16, 1926), brother of his three immediate predecessors, found the country exhausted from war when he succeeded in 1918. He opposed the reforms sought by the Turkish Nationalists led by Mustafa Kemal (later, Kemal Atatürk). The latter organized a provisional government, and after they defeated the Greeks in Asia Minor in 1922 they deposed Mohammed. He fled to Malta aboard a British battleship, and thence went into exile in Italy.

MOHAMMED AHMED, mo͝o-hăm′măd ă′măd (called the *Mahdi,* mä′dē), Sudanese agitator: b. Dongola, 1843?; d. Omdurman, June 22, 1885. A leader of the Moslems in the Sudan, about 1880 he proclaimed himself the mahdi (guided one), the messiah who would free the people from their oppressors. At the head of thousands of his followers, he defeated an Egyptian army in Kordofan in 1882, and the next year, at Kashgil, an Anglo-Egyptian force led by Gen. William Hicks (Hicks Pasha), who was killed. In 1884 he routed another Anglo-Egyptian force commanded by Gen. Valentine Baker (Baker

Pasha), and in 1885 he besieged and captured Khartoum, where Gen. Charles George Gordon was killed. He died five months later.

MOHAMMED ALI, mô-hăm′ĕd ä-lī′ (Arab. MUHAMMAD 'ALI; Turk. MEHMET ALI), viceroy of Egypt: b. Rumelia, then part of the Turkish Empire, about 1769; d. Cairo, Egypt, Aug. 2, 1849. Reputedly the son of an Albanian farmer—though the date and place of his birth are not certainly known—he grew up in Kavala, Macedonia, and because of his admiration for Napoleon, always claimed the same birth date. He became an officer (1798) in the Turkish army recruited to help drive Napoleon out of Egypt, was saved by the British in the Turkish defeat at Abukir, July 25, 1799, and in 1801 returned in command of his regiment to be present when the French finally withdrew from Egypt in September of that year. He rapidly made himself a figure of importance in the political world of Cairo, supporting first one side and then the other in the struggle for power between the Mamelukes (Mamlūks) of Egypt and the Turks. After he was chosen by the sheikhs of Cairo to be pasha (1805), his authority as viceroy was confirmed by an imperial Turkish edict (1806). His dynasty has come down to our own times, its latest representatives being King Farouk I, who abdicated July 26, 1952, and his infant son, King Ahmed Fu'ād II whom Farouk vainly named to succeed him.

Mehmet Ali displayed great initiative, energy, and vision, and remade the face of Egypt with new canals and methods of agriculture and industry while he was reshaping her institutions. Although illiterate himself, he started a ministry of education, founded the first school of engineering, and the first school of medicine. To rebuild Egypt's military power he called in a French colonel to reorganize the army and a French naval engineer to build up an Egyptian Navy. Then in 1811 he undertook a war against the Wahhabis in Arabia who had occupied the holy cities, Mecca and Medina. When the first troops left for Arabia, Mehmet Ali gave a reception at the citadel in Cairo to which he invited, among other guests, 470 Mameluke leaders. As the Mamelukes, who had held, or contested, the power in Egypt for more than 600 years, departed through a narrow passage leading to the gate, their host directed an attack against them. Very few escaped the massacre.

The war against the Wahhabis did not end until 1818. Two years later Mehmet Ali moved into the eastern Sudan, and in 1823 he founded the city of Khartum. In the meantime, in 1822, he had been drawn into the Greek War of Independence, joining forces with his suzerain, the Turkish Sultan Mahmud II, against Greece and her allies, Britain, France, and Russia. In the naval Battle of Navarino, Oct. 20, 1827, the Turko-Egyptian fleet lost all but 29 out of 782 vessels. When Mahmud was unable to give him Syria, as promised, Mehmet Ali sent his son Ibrahim Pasha (q.v.) with an army to conquer Syria in 1831. After 10 years' occupation of the country, in the course of which he reduced Anatolia and threatened Constantinople, he was forced by the European powers to withdraw within Egyptian borders. In 1841 the Porte made the pashalik of Egypt hereditary in Mehmet Ali's family and gave him government of the Sudan. He himself became senile and power passed to Ibrahim in 1848. The latter, dying nine months before his father, was succeeded by his nephew, Abbas I. See also EGYPT—*History* (Mehmet Ali).

MOHAMMEDAN or **ISLAMIC ART.** See MIDDLE EAST—*21. The Arts: Reaction Against Hellenism* (Islamic Art).

MOHAMMEDAN SECTS, the numerous schisms and schools of thought which arose in Islam. See MOSLEM SECTS.

MOHAMMEDANISM, a system of belief founded by Mohammed, the Arabian prophet. See ISLAM.

MOHAVE DESERT. See MOJAVE DESERT.

MOHAVE INDIANS. See MOJAVE INDIANS.

MOHAWK, mō′hôk, a river whose headwaters rise in Mohawk Hill, in the southern part of Lewis County, N.Y. It flows south to Rome, where, east by south, with many curves, it continues to the Hudson River, which it enters at Cohoes, nine miles above Albany. It is about 175 miles long, and is the largest tributary of the Hudson. In several places along the route there are rapids and falls, as at Little Falls in Herkimer County and Oriskany in Oneida County, all of which are noted for manufacturing. The falls of the Mohawk River (Cohoes Falls) 70 feet high are near Cohoes, where in a glacial pothole the complete skeleton of a mastodon was discovered in 1883. The bed of the Mohawk River was once much wider than the present channel through which the water passes; in some places the distances between the old banks are from a mile to nearly three miles. The Mohawk Valley is noted for its beauty and the fertility of its soil. The Barge Canal (q.v.) of New York State is parallel with the river to Rome, as are two railroads, the New York Central and the West Shore. A number of pretty villages and thriving manufacturing towns are on its banks, chief of which from west to east are Rome and Utica in Oneida County; Ilion, Herkimer, and Little Falls in Herkimer County; Fort Plain, Canajoharie, Fonda, and Amsterdam in Montgomery County; Schenectady in Schenectady County; and Mechanicville in Saratoga County.

In the early history of the United States, the Mohawk Valley was the main highway from the eastern colonies to the Great Lakes. It was the home of the most warlike Indians, the Five Nations, and much of the early period is connected with their relations to Sir William Johnson (q.v.), who lived there from 1738 to 1774. His death in that year removed a conciliatory power from the councils of the Tories, just at the crucial beginning of the revolution. Johnson's sons and their friends lacked his humanity and his wisdom, and the union between British and Indians resulted in the massacres of Cherry Creek and Schoharie, and the burning of many homes and taking of many lives. Gen. John Burgoyne realized the valley's strategic value, and thought he could hold it, since the Tories outnumbered the patriots and were allied with the Indians. However, Barry St. Leger's defeat at Oriskany by men under Nicholas Herkimer on Aug. 6, 1777, saved the valley for the revolution and greatly increased the enthusiasm and confidence of the patriots.

MOHAWK INDIANS, a tribe of North American Indians, the easternmost of the Six Nations, named collectively by the French, the Iroquois. According to their own tradition, confirmed by those of other tribes, they were the eldest people in the confederacy of the Six Nations and styled themselves Kaniengehaga, "people of the place of the flint." They believed that they were liberated from subterranean confinement by Tareya-wagon, who guided them into the valley of the Mohawk; thence they passed to the Hudson and to the sea. The valley in which they at first established themsleves was the seat of their power from the discovery of the country until the American Revolution. Their dominion extended from Lake Champlain to the headwaters of the Susquehanna and the Delaware. A warlike tribe, they inflicted great tortures on their prisoners and practiced cannibalism. With the introduction of firearms by Dutch traders they became renowned above all the other nations for their skill as warriors, and carried terror wherever they went. Their forays extended as far as the Connecticut River, and their influence prevailed among the small independent tribes about the region of the present city of New York.

During the French and Indian War, the Mohawk aided Sir William Johnson in the British victories at Lake George (1755) and Fort Niagara (1759). After Johnson's death in 1774, they transferred their allegiance to his family, and sided with the British during the American Revolution. After the Revolution, they were forced to flee from their ancestral home to Canada. They received lands on the Grand River and on the Bay of Quinte in Ontario, where they still reside. There are some Mohawk in Quebec Province. They are descended from a minority who emigrated there after the French converted them to Roman Catholicism in the mid-1700's.

See also IROQUOIS LEAGUE; SIX NATIONS OF THE IROQUOIS.

MOHEGAN, mō-hē′gän, **INDIANS,** a tribe of North American Indians of the Algonquian (Mahican) family, who formerly lived on the Thames River in eastern Connecticut. They were at one time united with the Pequots and after the death of Sassacus, the Pequot leader, the remainder of the tribe came to the camp of the Mohegan chief. After the death of King Philip (Metacomet) in 1676, the Mohegan tribe was the only important one in that region.

The Mohegan seem to have been the eastern branch of that group of closely connected tribes that spread to the farther side of the Hudson River. As the white settlements extended the Mohegan sold most of their lands and confined themselves to a reservation on the Thames River in New London County, Conn. Their village, also called Mohegan, was on the site of the present town of that name. They rapidly dwindled away when surrounded by the whites. Many joined the Scaticook but in 1788 a still larger number, under the leadership of Occom, joined the Brotherton Indians in New York. The rest of the tribe continued to reside in the vicinity of Mohegan or Norwich, Conn.

MOHILEV. See MOGILEV.

MOHL, mōl, **Hugo von,** German botanist: b. Stuttgart, April 8, 1805; d. Tübingen, April 1, 1872. He studied at the universities of Tübingen and Munich, and from 1832 he held the professorship of botany at Tübingen. His researches into the physiology of higher plant forms was of major importance. He suggested use of the term protoplasm to indicate the substance of the cell body, and may be considered the founder of the cell theory. His *Die Vegetabilische Zelle* (1851) was translated into English by H. Henfrey under the title *Principles of the Anatomy and Physiology of the Vegetable Cell* (1852). *Vermischte Schriften botanischen Inhalts* (1845) was a collections of his most important papers. He was the brother of Julius von Mohl (q.v.).

MOHL, Julius von, German Orientalist: b. Stuttgart, Oct. 25, 1800; d. Paris, France, Jan. 3, 1876. He was the brother of Hugo von Mohl (q.v.). In 1823, after studying theology for five years at Tübingen, he went to Paris to devote himself to Oriental languages and history. Although holding the assistant professorship of Oriental literature at Tübingen from 1826 to 1833, he spent most of that period in research in London and Oxford. The French government commissioned him in 1826 to prepare a translation of *Shah Namah* (Book of Kings), the great epic of Firdausi (Firdusi), the Persian poet, and this task was his major preoccupation until his death. Six folio volumes of the work were published in Paris between 1838 and 1866, the seventh being completed by Barbier de Meynard. In 1847 he was appointed professor of Persian at the Collège de France; and he became secretary and subsequently president of the Société Asiatique. He published *Lettres de M. Botta sur les découvertes à Khorsabad* (1845), concerning the search for Assyrian antiquities near Khorsabad by Paul Émile Botta; and in collaboration with Justus Olshausen he wrote *Fragments relatifs à la religion de Zoroaster* (1829). His valuable reports to the Société Asiatique between 1840 and 1867 were collectively published after his death by his widow, Mary (daughter of Charles Clarke), under the title *Vingt-sept ans d'histoire des études orientales* (1879–1880). Consult, Simpson, M. C. M., *Letters and Recollections of Julius and Mary Mohl* (London 1887).

MOHLER, mû′lẽr, **Johann Adam,** German Roman Catholic theologian: b. Igersheim, Württemberg, May 6, 1796; d. Munich, April 12, 1838. He studied theology at the University of Tübingen, and after entering the priesthood taught there, becoming tutor in 1822 and full professor in 1828. He was an able doctrinal exponent, distinguished alike intellectually and spiritually, doing much to arouse the Roman Catholic Church in Germany to new vigor. His writings at this period included *Die Einheit in der Kirche* (1825), *Athanasius der Grosse* (1827), and *Symbolik* (1832). The last, of which an English translation was published by J. B. Robertson in 1843, was an exposition of the doctrinal differences between Protestants and Catholics. It attracted considerable attention, and provoked works in rebuttal by Ferdinand Christian Baur (also a professor at Tübingen), Philipp Marheineke, Karl Immanuel Nitzsch, and others. In reply to their writings, he published *Neue Untersuchungen der Lehrgegensätze zwischen den Katholiken und Protestanten* (1834). In 1835 he was given a professorial post at the University of Munich. Consult Friedrich, J., *J. A. Möhler* (Munich 1894).

MOHOLE PROJECT, mō'hōl, a research project sponsored by the U.S. government, the aim of which was to drill through the several miles of the earth's crust and reach the mantle below. Initiated in 1961, it achieved some success before it was abandoned in 1966.

Objectives. The mantle makes up the greater bulk of the earth's mass, and knowledge of its composition would help scientists to reconstruct the early geological history of the earth and the manner in which the crust was generated. Because many geologists thought, until recently, that the ocean floors are relatively ancient features, it was hoped that the single long core derived from the drilling would contain an extensive layer-by-layer fossil-bearing record of the earth's history. Scientists also wanted to investigate the nature of the region of contact between the crust and the mantle—the *Mohorovicic discontinuity* from which the project drew its name.

Achievements. Early drilling tests took place off the California coast in 1961, and the Mohole project succeeded in test-drilling the rock called *serpentine* from the oceanic crust near Puerto Rico in 1964. Another test, near Uvalde, Texas, demonstrated the feasibility of new drilling methods devised for hard rock. After drilling such test holes for six months, work was to begin on the Mohole itself. An ocean site near Hawaii was chosen where the crust is only 17,000 feet (5,000 meters) thick.

The drilling was planned to proceed from a self-stabilizing floating platform, and was to take 2½ to 3 years at a cost of about $47 million. As the drill bits wore out rapidly in the hard rock, the core was to be withdrawn at intervals and the bit replaced. However, the tremendous cost of the Vietnam War in 1965–1966 drained off both the available money for the project and congressional enthusiasm for expensive research. In addition there was an upward revision of the original cost estimate to $127 million. As a result the House of Representatives, in the spring of 1966, cut off the funds necessary to complete the construction of the drilling platform. Further appeals to Congress for funds failed.

Further Projects. In 1965–1966 research scientists discovered that new areas of the ocean floor are formed by the welling up of magma along the world-encircling mid-ocean ridge. Thus the molten material rises to the surface, congeals to basalt, and is carried away in opposite directions from the central axis of the ridge crest. This process is called *sea-floor spreading.* Because this exciting discovery proved that oceans are dynamic and actively evolving systems, hope faded that "ancient" areas of ocean basin could be found for obtaining a continuous fossil record.

Interest turned, instead, to the softer unconsolidated and semiconsolidated sediments in which the more youthful history of the oceans is recorded. Thus, the plans of the U.S. JOIDES (Joint Oceanographic Institution for Deep Earth Sampling) program, developed for the study of sea-floor spreading, include the drilling of about 60 long cores in sediment layers in the sea floors of the Atlantic and Pacific oceans. And, with the new technical information thus obtained about deep drilling and the use of stabilized platforms, an easing of economic pressures could revive the abandoned Mohole project.

BRUCE C. HEEZEN
WILLIAM F. RUDDIMAN
Lamont Geological Observatory

MOHOLY-NAGY, mô'hôl-y nŏd'y', **László** (or **Ladislaus**), Hungarian painter and designer: b. Borsod, Hungary, July 20, 1895; d. Chicago, Ill., Nov. 24, 1946. First identified with constructivism in Budapest, Moholy-Nagy later designed stage sets, painted, and made use of many materials and forms of art. Forced by the Nazis in 1935 to leave Germany, where in 1923–1928 he had been professor of constructive, texture, and photographic technique at the Bauhaus school in Weimar, he went to London, where he designed the sets for H. G. Wells' motion picture, *The Shape of Things to Come.* In 1937 he founded the Bauhaus School of Design in Chicago, which failed, but as head of the Chicago Institute of Design in 1939 he won backing from important industrial firms for his theories of art in the machine age. He was the author of *The New Vision* (Eng. tr. 1932) and *Vision in Motion* (1947).

MOHR, Joseph, Austrian Catholic priest and poet: b. Salzburg, Dec. 11, 1792; d. Wagrein, Dec. 4, 1848. As curé of the newly established parish of Obendorf he wrote a poem entitled *Stille Nacht, heilige Nacht* (*Silent Night, Holy Night*) which, on Dec. 24, 1818, he asked the village schoolmaster and organist, Franz Xaver Gruber (1787–1863), as the latter recalled, "to set to suitable music, for two solo voices, chorus and guitar accompaniment." The organist composed the simple melody in a few hours, and brought it to Father Mohr. The same evening it was sung with great success at the Christmas Eve service, the priest and organist singing the solo parts. A guitar accompaniment had been stipulated because the church organ had broken down. In a few years this nostalgically tender Christmas carol had attained so wide a popularity that it was translated into most modern tongues and became perhaps the best known of all Christmas carols.

MOHS, mōs, **Friedrich,** German mineralogist: b. Gernrode, Anhalt, Germany, Jan. 29, 1773; d. Agordo, near Belluno (now in Italy), Sept. 29, 1839. Successively professor at Graz (1811), Freiberg (1816), and Vienna (from 1826), and the author of several books on mineralogy, he is best remembered for the Mohs' scale, named for him, which he proposed in 1822 to classify the hardness of minerals. See HARDNESS, SCALE OF.

MOHUN, mōōn, **Charles,** 4TH BARON MOHUN, English duelist: b. ?1675; d. London, England, Nov. 15, 1712. The diaries and records of the period in which Mohun flourished show him as a high-spirited and uncontrollable young man, playing tricks with Edward Rich, earl of Warwick, arrested at the age of 17 for murder, but acquitted before a jury of his peers, and dueling at every opportunity. He occasionally took his seat in the House of Lords, and was a Whig, supporting William III. His final duel with James Douglas, 4th duke of Hamilton, in which both men were killed, arose from a quarrel over estates, but was interpreted by the Tory Party to have been a Whig plot against Hamilton. An account of the duel occurs in W. M. Thackeray's *Henry Esmond.*

MOHUN, Michael, English actor: b. about 1620–1625; d. London, England, October 1684. Before the Civil Wars he acted at the Cockpit in

Drury Lane. Fighting for King Charles I, he attained a captaincy; in Flanders he was promoted major. At the Restoration he returned to England to resume his stage career. Pepys seeing him for the first time in the *Beggar's Bush* (Beaumont and Fletcher) reported the consensus that he was "the best actor in the world." He was the original Beamont in Dryden's *Amboyna,* and Ventidius in *All for Love, or the World Well Lost,* as well as the original Pinchwife in Wycherley's *Country Wife.*

MOIDORE, moi'dōr (Port. *moeda d'ouro,* coin of gold), a gold coin of 4.93 grains of fine gold worth about $3.27 when in use as formerly in Portugal and Brazil (1640–1732). A double moidore was also minted.

MOIRA, MOIRAI, or **MOERAE,** moi'rȧ, in Greek mythology, the Fates, corresponding to the Roman Parcae. Homer speaks of a single divinity who assigns to every man his lot *(moira)*; Homer's Moira is the personification of Fate, directing the consequences of man's actions at the behest of the gods; only once does he speak of Fates (Moirai). Hesiod develops the personification of several Fates, identifying the Moirai as three daughters of Zeus and Themis: Clotho, the spinner; Lachesis, the disposer of lots; and Atropos, the inevitable. The first spins the thread of life, the second assigns to man his fate, and the third severs the thread. Like the Parcae, the Latin Tria Fata were assimilated to the Greek Moirai. See also FATES.

MOIRÉ, mwȧ-rā', a French name for watered silks. Though made in the same way as ordinary silks, these are of double width and must be of a stout substantial make. They should also be folded in such a way that the air contained between the folds should not be able to escape easily. They are subjected to an enormous pressure, of from 60 to 100 tons, generally in a hydraulic machine, and the air, in trying to escape, drives before it the small quantity of moisture that is used, and so produces the permanent marking called watering, which is for the most part in curious waved lines. The finest kinds of watered silks are known as *moirés antiques.* Woolen fabrics to which the same process has been applied are called *moreen.*

MOISE, moi'sē, **Penina,** American poet: b. Charleston, S. C., April 23, 1797; d. there, Sept. 13, 1880. A personality of much charm, she was born of French parents of Hebrew extraction, who came originally from the island of St. Eustatius. She contributed to many of the magazines and newspapers of her day, and a collection of her poems was published as *Fancy's Sketch Book* (1833). Her best known work is contained in *Hymns Written for the Use of Hebrew Congregations* (1856). Despite blindness in later years, she continued to write poems, and her home was a place of pilgrimage to her admirers.

MOISSAN, mwȧ-sȧɴ', **Henri,** French chemist: b. Paris, France, Sept. 28, 1852; d. there, Feb. 20, 1907. Educated at the Museum d'Histoire Naturelle and at the School of Pharmacy in Paris, he taught in the latter from 1879 to 1883, in 1886–1899 was professor of toxicology and inorganic chemistry there, and in 1900 became professor of general chemistry at the Sorbonne. He isolated and liquefied fluorine, winning in 1887 the Lacaze Prize from the Academy of Sciences. He won great fame by his important experiments and achievements with the electric arc furnace. In 1892 he made the manufacture of acetylene simple and commercially profitable by his discovery that if carbon and lime are fused in the electric arc furnace, pure calcium is formed, which makes the liberation of acetylene an easy matter. Much more spectacular was his formation of artificial diamonds in 1893. In 1906 he received the Nobel Prize in chemistry. He wrote *Reproduction du diamant* (1893); *Étude complète des carbones amorphes et des graphites* (1898); and *Traité de chimie minerale,* in 5 vols. (1904–1906).

MOJAVE DESERT, mô-hä'vê (also MOHAVE), arid basin, California, mainly in San Bernardino County. Part of the Great Basin, it lies south of Death Valley and the southern end of the Sierra Nevada and is bordered on the west and southwest principally by the Tehachapi, San Gabriel, and San Bernardino Mountains, meeting the Colorado Desert on the southeast.

Thomas Hollyman from Photo Researchers

Calico, ghost town in the Mojave Desert near Daggett. In the 1880's it was a busy silver-mining center.

The Mojave River, an intermittent stream, rises in the San Bernardino Mountains near Lake Arrowhead and flows generally northeastward, disappearing into the sand at Soda Lake, about 90 miles distant. The desert is about 15,000 square miles in extent. Elevations vary from 2,000 to 5,000 feet. Deposits of minerals, including gold, silver, tungsten, iron, manganese, clay, perlite, talc, salines, and boron lend the Mojave considerable economic importance.

The area is one of low humidity and very

scanty annual rainfall, no part ordinarily receiving more than 5 inches annually. Temperatures are moderately high in winter, very high in summer, with a wide daily range. Before noon the winds begin to blow down the mountainsides, frequently attaining gale proportions on the desert floor. The velocity increases until about midnight, when it lessens, and calm prevails before dawn. On the higher edges of the area are found weird forests of California, or desert, juniper (*Juniperus californica*) and Joshua trees (*Yucca brevifolia*). The latter reach heights of 30 feet, and present sentinel-like silhouettes against the sky. Various U. S. military installations and the Joshua Tree National Monument (established 1936) are located in the desert.

JOHN H. JONTE
Formerly, University of the Pacific

MOJAVE INDIANS, mō-hä'vē, an American Indian tribe, formerly the most populous and warlike of the Yuman linguistic stock. Mojave (also, Mohave) means "three mountains," a reference to needlelike formations in western Arizona. Mainly an Arizonan tribe, they still live in their old homeland on both sides of the Colorado River, from the Needles to Black Canyon, near Needles, Calif.

The Mojave are farmers who grow corn, melons, and beans on the bottom lands, relying on periodic inundations for moisture. Their low, brush huts are widely scattered along the river banks, and are well suited to the environment in which they live. The Mojave women make a poor grade of pottery and some beadwork that they sell to tourists. From a population of 3,000 estimated by Father Francisco Tomas Garcés in 1775, they declined to approximately 1,200 in 1975.

FREDERICK J. DOCKSTADER, *Director, Museum of the American Indian, Heye Foundation*

MOJI. See KITAKYUSHU.

MOKI. See HOPI INDIANS.

MOKPO, môk'pō, is a city in Korea, on the Yellow Sea, about 190 miles (305 km) south of Seoul. It is a major port for the densely populated rice-paddy region of southwestern Korea. Its major industries are fishing, food processing, and cotton ginning.

Mokpo is noted for the many small islands that surround its harbor. The first successful cultivation of American cottonseeds in Korea took place on one of these islands in 1904. The city has air and steamer connections with the large island of Cheju, 90 miles (145 km) to the south. Population: (1970) 177,801.

SOON-WON LEE, *Muhlenberg College*

MOKSHA RIVER, môk'shə, a river in the central European part of the Russian republic, USSR. It rises about 20 miles (32 km) west-northwest of Penza and flows north and west through the Mordva (Mordvinian) ASSR. It joins the Oka River below Murom. The Moksha is about 430 miles (690 km) long but is navigable only in its lower course.

MOLASSES is any of various thick brownish syrups obtained as a by-product in manufacturing sugar. Most of the world's molasses is produced from sugarcane grown in countries with warm climates, notably Cuba, Brazil, and India. Beet molasses is produced mainly in the Soviet Union, the United States, West Germany, France, and other countries with temperate climates.

Cane Molasses. Generally, rotating machines called centrifuges separate cane molasses from sugar crystals at three stages in the manufacture of raw sugar from sugarcane. The first extraction provides a molasses that is lighter in color and contains more sucrose than succeeding extractions. The third and usually final extraction provides blackstrap, a thick, dark, strong-tasting molasses from which all the sugar that can be recovered economically by crystallization has been removed. Refiner's blackstrap is a by-product in a later step in refining raw sugar.

Light molasses consists of about 65% carbohydrates, 24% water, 6% ash, and small percentages of minerals and vitamins in the B family. Blackstrap consists of about 55% carbohydrates, 24% water, and larger percentages of ash, minerals, and vitamins than does light molasses. It is more nutritious than the lighter types.

The lighter molasses are used in many baked foods, in candies, and in making rum. Blackstrap is a major raw material for feeds for cattle, sheep, and horses. In industry, cane molasses is used in making yeast, alcohol, and some organic chemicals.

Beet Molasses. Centrifuges are used to separate by-product beet molasses from the sugar crystals formed by evaporating the syrupy juice of sugar beets. Beet molasses has fewer vitamins and a less desirable taste than cane molasses. It is used mainly in animal feeds and in making yeast and alcoholic beverages.

See also SUGAR.

MOLASSES ACT, a British law placing a prohibitive tax on molasses, sugar, and rum imported from non-British islands in the Caribbean to the North American colonies. It was passed by Parliament in 1733 following British West Indian pressure for protection from competition by the more fertile French and Dutch islands.

The planters of the British islands complained that American trade with the foreign West Indies was threatening to destroy the British sugar industry. The American colonists were outraged, claiming that the British West Indies could not meet their demand for molasses. The Molasses Act was one of a series of navigation and trade acts passed by Parliament in an effort to make the British Empire self-sustaining and to ensure the dependence of the colonies on Britain.

The high tax threatened to destroy the lucrative New England rum industry, an integral part of the "triangular trade" between the American colonies, Africa, and the West Indies. The Molasses Act was largely nullified by wide-spread smuggling, and Parliament made little effort to enforce it. In 1764 it was replaced by the Sugar Act, which was designed to raise revenue. Although the duties imposed were lower than those charged under the Molasses Act, the Sugar Act duties were enforced by a reorganized British customs service.

MOLAY, mô-lā', **Jacques de** (c. 1243–1314), last grand master of the Knights Templar. He was born in Molay, in the Jura, France, and died in Paris in March 1314. He entered the Order of the Templars in 1265 and fought in Syria. He was elected grand master of the Order in 1298. In 1306, after the Templars had been driven from

Palestine, and while he was in Cyprus busied about raising new troops against the Saracens, he was summoned to France by Pope Clement V, who was determined to end the feuds between the Templars and the Knights of St. John. King Philip IV of France fearing, it is alleged, the power of the order, seized de Molay and all the knights then resident in France, after receiving them with the greatest kindness, charged the order with heresy, tried them before a packed court and found them guilty. Molay was imprisoned and ill-used for more than five years, then, after recanting certain admissions of guilt he had made, was burned at the stake as a relapsed heretic. The guilt of the Templars is still a disputed historical question.

Consult Viollet, P. M., *Les Interrogatoires de Jacques de Molay* (Paris 1910).

MOLDAU. See VLTAVA.

MOLDAVIA, mol-dā-vē-ə, a historic region in eastern Rumania, separated from the Moldavian Soviet Socialist Republic of the USSR by the Prut River on the east, and from Transylvania in the west by the Carpathian Mountains. The Ukraine is on its northern border, Walachia on the south. It has extensive forests and raises grain, fruit, and livestock. Founded in the 14th century as a principality, it suffered in wars between rulers and countries, under Turkey, Russia, and Austria. The union of Moldavia and Walachia (1861) began the nation of Rumania.

MOLDAVIAN SOVIET SOCIALIST REPUBLIC, a constituent republic, European USSR, in the southwest, in the center of the former province of Bessarabia. On its west is the Prut River and Rumania; the Ukraine surrounds its other borders. A very fertile region, though very rainy, with poor roads, its industries are mainly agricultural. Several railways cross it. In 1918, after World War I, Rumania annexed all of Bessarabia. In 1924 the USSR established the Moldavian Autonomous SSR of the Ukraine; in 1940, when the USSR reannexed Bessarabia, the Moldavian Autonomous SSR was merged with the Rumanian-speaking districts of Bessarabia to form the present Moldavian SSR, and the Ukrainian-speaking districts were merged with the Ukrainian SSR. The capital of the Moldavian SSR is Kishinev (formerly Chişinau). Pop. (1965) 3,300,000.

MOLDENKE, mōl-dĕn'kė, **Charles Edward,** American Egyptologist: b. Lyck, East Prussia, Oct. 10, 1860; d. Watchung, N. J., July 18, 1935. Moldenke was taken to the United States when a year old by his father, a Lutheran clergyman. He was educated at Columbia University and at the Lutheran Seminary in Philadelphia, after which he traveled and studied abroad, earning a Ph.D. from Strasbourg University in 1885. Until 1900 he was a practicing minister, after which he devoted his time to the study of botany and archaeology. He published *The Egyptian Origin of Our Alphabet* (1886); *The Trees of Ancient Egypt* (1886); *Egyptian Classics* (1900).

MOLE, mô-lā', COMTE **Louis Mathieu,** French statesman: b. Paris, France, Jan. 24, 1781; d. Château Champlâtreux, Seine-et-Oise, Nov. 23, 1855. His early years were spent abroad, but after his return to France he became an adherent of Napoleon Bonaparte, who gave him several important offices. In November 1813 Molé was made minister of justice, and held the same office during the Hundred Days. After the Restoration, Louis XVIII appointed him minister of marine (1817–1818). In 1830 he became minister of foreign affairs and in 1836 premier, resigning in 1839, but continued to sit in the Constituent Assembly (1848) and the Legislative Assembly (1849), where he opposed the coup d'état of 1851 which brought Louis Napoleon (Napoleon III) to French dictatorship and retired to private life.

MOLE, mô-lā', **Mathieu,** French jurist and politician: b. Paris, France, 1584; d. there, Jan. 3, 1656. Entering politics at an early age, he became procureur général in 1614. Molé's insistence on law and justice in the case of political prisoners brought him into conflict with his superiors. From 1641 to 1653 he was president of the Parlement, having been appointed by Cardinal Richelieu. During the first Fronde (1648–1649, q.v.), although often threatened with violence, he attempted to mediate between monarchy and Parlement, succeeding in negotiating the temporary peace of Rueil (1649). In 1651 he became keeper of the great seal, retiring from active politics. His *Mémoires,* in 4 volumes, were published in 1855.

MOLE, mōl, a small, fossorial (digging) velvety-furred mammal of the family Talpidae. The several species are distributed throughout the temperate zones of the Northern Hemisphere in North America, Europe, and Asia. Moles are the size of common rats, but their tails are usually very short; sometimes more or less equal to the length of the head and body. The body is thick and cylindrical; head, in the more highly specialized fossorial species, placed well between the shoulders; neck short; pectoral muscles bulky; snout elongated and either pointed, trumpet-shaped, or "star-nosed"; eyes small, in some species hidden beneath the skin; external ears small, generally without pinna, and nearly always completely hidden by the fur. The limbs are short, with five digits each, and in most species adapted for digging. The forefeet are especially large, powerfully built, and spadelike in form and function. The coat is thick, soft, usually velvety in texture, and often has a silky sheen. Females are provided with three or four pairs of mammae. There are 9 to 11 teeth on each side of the upper jaw, 8 to 11 in the lower jaw.

Most moles are strictly fossorial; some may be semiaquatic as well. The so-called shrew moles of the Old World, though classified with typical moles in the family Talpidae, do little or no digging. The almizclero and desman are other nonfossorial members of the family.

The typical fossorial species and type of the family is the common European mole (*Talpa europea*). This species occurs in all European countries south of 59° north latitude, except Ireland and Portugal. It is very like the North American eastern mole in size, appearance, and habits. Other species of moles of the genus *Talpa* are found in Europe, and in northern, eastern, and extreme southwestern Asia.

The common eastern mole (*Scalopus aquaticus*) of the eastern United States is from four and a half to six and a half inches in head and body length. The tail is from one to one and a half inches long. This mole spends practically its whole life underground. It tunnels just beneath the surface by pushing its way through loose dirt in search of food, which consists of earthworms, insects, and grubs. Its subterranean runways appear on the surface as ridges of broken ground. For nesting purposes, the eastern mole makes burrows from 6 to 25 inches below the surface. Despite its Latin name, the eastern mole is not aquatic.

The starnose mole (*Condylura cristata*) of the eastern United States is fond of water and swims as proficiently as it burrows. It is somewhat smaller than the eastern mole, but has a longer tail proportionately. Its eyes are functional and exposed to the surface. The principal distinction of the starnose mole is the presence of a starlike ring of 22 fleshy tentacles around the tip of its nose.

The hairytale mole (*Parascalops breweri*), the smallest of the eastern American moles, measures about four and a half inches in head and body length. The distinctly haired tail is little more than an inch long. Its nose, as in the eastern mole, is naked and without tentacles. It further resembles the eastern mole by its degenerate eyes, which are covered with a membrane, and its fused eyelids.

Star-nosed mole.

The four moles that occur along the west coast of the United States include the smallest and largest American species. The Townsend mole (*Scapanus townsendi*) of Washington and Oregon, is the largest, with its head and body six to seven inches long, tail about two inches and slightly hairy. The California mole (*Scapanus latimanus*), an inch shorter, but otherwise similar, ranges along the coast from southern Oregon to northern Lower California. The Pacific mole (*Scapanus orarius*) of Washington, Oregon, and northern California is slightly smaller than the preceding, but otherwise hardly distinguishable. The fourth Pacific coast species, the American shrew mole (*Neurotrichus gibbsi*), is the smallest, measuring less than four inches in head and body length. Its small eyes are visible at the surface, and functional. Its tail is hairy. This species is found on the humid northwest coast from the northern half of California into southern British Columbia.

Closely related to and closely resembling the moles of the western United States are the Japanese hairytale mole (*Urotrichus talpoides* and *pilirostris*), the Kansu mole (*Scapanulus oweni*) of China, and the long-tailed mole (*Scaptonyx fusicaudus*) of China and Burma.

American shrew mole.

PHILIP HERSHKOVITZ,
Curator, Division of Mammals, Chicago Natural History Museum.

MOLE, a long pier or breakwater built of masonry and extending into the sea, at times to a distance of a mile or more.

MOLE CRICKET, any insect of the family Gryllotalpidae, order Orthoptera. Mole crickets differ from other members of the Orthoptera in having the front legs modified for digging in the soil. Their tunnels are inconspicuous, unlike the tunnels of moles. The day is spent underground. While mole crickets appear to be sluggish creatures, they are able to fly with considerable speed. The front wings are short, the hind wings protrude behind them like a pair of tails. The tarsi usually have three segments, as in the true crickets, the ovipositor is inconspicuous, and the unsegmented cerci are short.

The commonest European species, *Gryllotalpa gryllotalpa,* which is about two inches long, has become established in the United States. The most widespread American species is *G. hexadactyla,* which occurs over most of the United States and Central and South America. The eggs are laid in the burrows, some of which may extend a foot or more below the surface of the ground. The young resemble the adults except for the absence of wings. When numerous, mole crickets may cause damage to cultivated crops. Poisoned baits are used to control them. Members of the South American and Australian genus, *Cylindrachaeta,* are quite slender, and burrow into the stems of plants.

CHARLES HOWARD CURRAN,
Curator, Department of Insects and Spiders, The American Museum of Natural History.

MOLECH. See MOLOCH.

MOLECULAR THEORY, in physics and chemistry, asserts that the properties of ordinary pieces of matter are the properties of an aggregate of very small particles, called molecules. The distinction between molecular theory and atomic theory is that whereas a molecule is generally defined as the smallest particle of a chemical substance that is capable of independent existence, an atom is defined as the smallest amount of any chemical element that can take part in chemical combination. (See ELEMENT.) Until the 19th century it was not possible to distinguish between atoms and molecules, and even today the names are sometimes used interchangeably. The early Greek philosophers of the atomistic school used the term atom in much the same way that we now use the word molecule.

The distinction between atoms and molecules may be illustrated by considering the substance *water.* If we imagine ourselves taking a progressively smaller and smaller amount of this substance there comes a time when we can no longer subdivide the material without destroying its character as being water. At this stage we are dealing with one molecule. But this molecule may be broken into fragments by an electrical discharge or by other means, and it yields three atoms, two of hydrogen and one of oxygen. For that reason the molecule of water is said to be triatomic, and is written H_2O. A molecule such as sodium chloride (common salt) is diatomic, and is written NaCl (Na for sodium, after the Latin *natrium,* Cl for chlorine). Ethyl alcohol (the normal alcohol in spirits) is C_2H_6O, and is said to be polyatomic, though for reasons to appear later it is more usual to write it C_2H_5OH. Thus molecules vary in size from the monatomic elements helium, neon, argon—which contain only one atom and are therefore both atoms and molecules according to our definition—through diatomic and triatomic molecules to huge assemblies such as a protein molecule (see PROTEINS) containing many thousands of atoms. There are even grounds for believing that each of the 10 to 20,000 genes (see GENETICS) which control the hereditary characteristics that we inherit from our two parents, is essentially one large molecule.

The distinction between atoms and molecules may be seen in a slightly different way if we compare two solids, solid hydrogen and solid copper. Hydrogen, which is a gas under normal conditions, becomes a solid at very low temperatures. Solid hydrogen consists of diatomic molecules (written H_2) arranged in a regular fashion. The individual molecules may be free to turn round about, and even to vibrate to and fro in a limited fashion; but they remain individual molecules, and on allowing the temperature to rise, the solid evaporates to become a gas of H_2 molecules. In solid copper, however, there is again a regular arrangement of atoms which can vibrate to and fro around their mean centers of position. But the unit is the separate atom, and there is no tendency to form clusters of atoms of any definite size. Solid hydrogen may therefore be called a molecular crystal, solid copper is an atomic crystal.

STATES OF AGGREGATION

Gases.—Molecules may exist in three states of aggregation—gaseous, liquid, and solid. In the gaseous state the molecules are well separated from each other, and fly about in all directions with a wide range of velocities, occasionally colliding with each other, or with the walls of the container, and then bouncing off. Except during the relatively short time of collision the molecules may be regarded as distinct and isolated. Their behavior is described by the kinetic theory of gases (see GASES, KINETIC THEORY OF) which accounts in a satisfactory way for the pressure which they appear to exert on the container as a result of their incessant collisions with it, and for the heat energy which they possess as a result both of their random velocities and also of their internal motion. A molecule of water, for example, which we write as H_2O, is not entirely rigid; but the three atoms can make small vibrations, or oscillations, relative to each other. These internal vibrations and rotations occur with very great frequency, but the distances moved by the atoms away from their mean positions are very small, so that these internal motions do not at any stage destroy the triatomic character of the molecule.

Liquids.—In the liquid state the molecules are much closer together, but they do not have fixed, or even nearly fixed, centers of position, and can drift—or, more strictly, diffuse—from one part of the liquid to another. The rate of this diffusion depends on the temperature, since at higher temperatures it is supposed that the molecules have more energy of motion than at lower temperatures, and are therefore better able to overcome any restraining forces that tend to confine them to any one region. The rate of diffusion is measured by the diffusion coefficient, and the variation of this coefficient with the temperature allows us to estimate the magnitude of the forces tending to confine the molecule. Thus according to this picture any one molecule in a liquid is always surrounded by other molecules, almost filling the available space, and in continual oscillatory motion; from time to time a small gap appears momentarily in the surrounding sheath of molecules (molecule *C* in Fig. 1), and if the central molecule has sufficient energy, it may break through this gap and thus move one unit of distance away from its starting point. The energy *E* necessary to break through in this fashion is called the activation energy for molecular diffusion, and the diffusion coefficient varies with the temperature according to an exponential law $e^{-E/kT}$. (*T* is the absolute temperature and *k* is Boltzmann's constant $1 \cdot 371 \times 10^{-16}$ ergs per degree.)

The process of evaporation of a liquid is a particular case of this phenomenon, for it corresponds to a molecule of the liquid breaking completely away from its neighbors and becoming a gas molecule. The fact that in order to evaporate any large quantity of liquid it is necessary to heat it, and thereby to give the molecules more energy, shows us that in the liquid state molecules attract each other. These attractive forces have to be overcome when a molecule evaporates. It also follows that a molecule (*A* in Fig. 1) in the body of a liquid is being attracted by its neighbors on all sides, and therefore experiences no mean force in any particular direction. But a molecule at the edge of a liquid (*B* in Fig. 1) is attracted towards the body of the liquid by those adjacent molecules which lie inside the liquid, and there are no corresponding forces to balance this, since there are effectively no adjacent molecules outside the boundary. Thus there is an apparent force tending to pull the liquid into as compact a volume as possible. Another way of putting this is to say that the liquid appears to be always trying to reduce its surface area. In this way we see how intermolecular forces give rise to the phenomenon of surface tension. (See SURFACE TENSION.) The stronger these forces of attraction the larger is the surface tension.

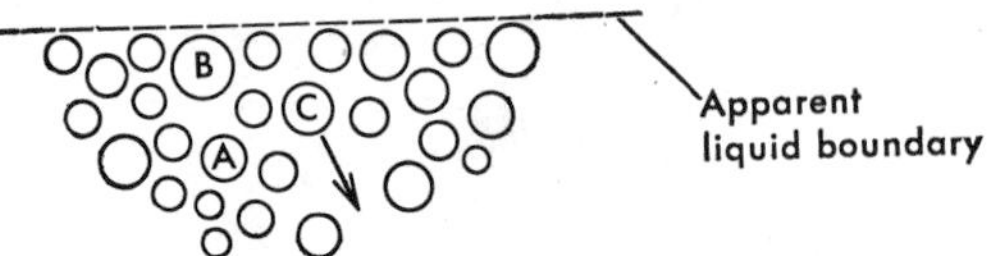

Fig. 1. The boundary of a molecular liquid. Notice the fairly close type of packing of the molecules. A molecule *A* experiences forces in all directions and these effectively cancel each other out. A molecule *B* is attracted towards the interior of the liquid, and can evaporate from the liquid only if sufficient energy is given to it. A molecule *C* finds itself with a momentary gap in the sheath of surrounding molecules, and, if it has sufficient energy, can diffuse to a neighboring position, as shown by the arrow.

Molecular Layers.—A particularly interesting and important application of this occurs in the common use of soap. A good foam, or lather, can be obtained if the surface tension is sufficiently low. Water has a rather high surface tension, but this value is considerably reduced by the use of soap. The important part of the soap for this purpose is a molecule called sodium stearate.

This is a long molecule similar in shape to a match, and having for the "stick" a relatively inert tail composed of carbon atoms and hydrogen atoms. The "head" is a much more chemically active group (actually CO_2Na) which rapidly embeds itself in the water, so that a layer of molecules is soon formed (see Fig. 2) with the "matches" all parallel to each other and sticking out of the water. The forces of attraction between these hydrocarbon tails which form the new surface are so much smaller than those between molecules of water that the surface tension is drastically reduced, and a good lather is easily formed. The existence of this layer of sodium stearate molecules, which, if it is only one molecule thick, is called a monomolecular layer, has been verified by an ingenious technique due to J. W. McBain, whereby the top layer of the liquid can be skimmed off. The change in surface tension when a small amount of soap is dissolved in the water is clearly demonstrated.

Molecular Distribution Function in Liquids.—According to our earlier description of a liquid, the constituent molecules are quite close together, as in Fig. 1, but in a somewhat irregular fashion. This description can be verified experimentally by the use of X-rays. For if we let a beam of X-rays fall upon a liquid and think of the beam as if it were a stream of bullets (sometimes called photons), then we can see that there will be

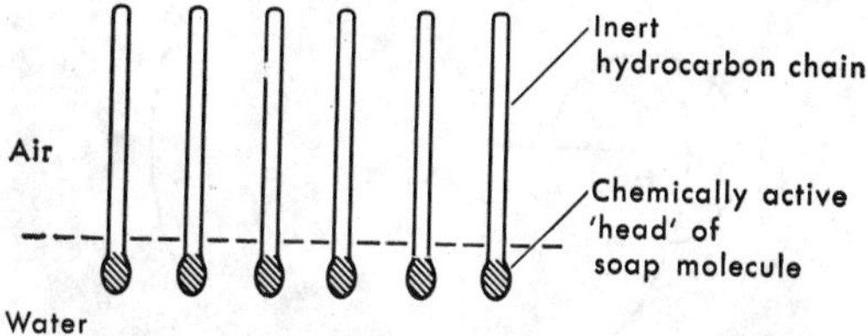

Fig. 2. A monomolecular layer of soap (sodium stearate) on the surface of water, which reduces the surface tension and makes foaming and lathering much easier.

collisions of these photons with the molecules of the liquid. Consequently many of the photons will emerge from the liquid in directions different from their line of incidence. It was shown by F. Zernicke and J. Prins in 1927, and more fully by P. Debye and H. Menke in 1932, that from a careful study of the way in which the number of photons scattered through a certain angle depended on the angle, it was possible to calculate the distribution of neighbors around any given molecule. This distribution, which is called the molecular distribution function, is an average taken over all the molecules. Thus, in the case of liquid water at room temperature it appears that on the average each H_2O molecule is surrounded by a first shell of between 4 and 5 neighbors, though none of these ever gets closer than about 2.3 angstrom units of length (1 angstrom is 10^{-8} cms). This, incidentally, tells us something about the size of the water molecule, though there are better ways for measuring these sizes, as will be shown later. Other details of the molecular distribution are found in the same way, such as that outside the first coordination shell there is a tendency to form a second shell at a distance of 4.8 angstroms. However, on account of the diffusion and other motion of the molecules these distances are only mean or average distances. What this analysis shows most clearly is that in a liquid there does not exist the rigid and highly regular type of molecular arrangement which is typical of a solid. It also shows that as the temperature is increased the various coordination shells become more and more blurred, as a result of the molecules acquiring more heat energy, and oscillating backwards and forwards through larger and larger distances.

Molecular Solids.—The distinction between a liquid and a solid is that although both are compact, without much space being wasted between the component molecules, the arrangement in the solid is regular and, relatively, fixed. A particular example will show what this means. Let us consider the molecules of methane—the chief constituent gas which bubbles up in muddy water containing decaying vegetation, when it is disturbed. Each molecule of methane consists of one carbon atom and four hydrogen atoms, and is written as CH_4. Its shape (see later) is roughly spherical. If the temperature is sufficiently low methane becomes liquid: the molecules remain intact, but fit quite close together in the fluctuating sort of manner illustrated in Fig. 1. Now let the temperature be lowered still further. Eventually the liquid freezes, that is, solidifies, and in this state each molecule takes up a definite position, or center, around which it moves with a vibrational motion of relatively small amplitude. These regularly arranged positions form what is called a face-centered-cubic lattice. This means that if an array of similar cubes are stacked corner to corner, there is a molecule of methane at every corner of each such cube, and another molecule in the center of each face. These molecules are rotating and vibrating but only very occasionally does one leave its lattice site and diffuse to some other lattice site. If the temperature is now lowered still further, there comes a moment when the molecules cease to spin around their centers. But they still vibrate and retain their molecular identity.

There are other forms of crystal packing with molecules of a different shape from that of methane. All of them may be identified by X-ray analysis, using methods analogous to those previously described for liquids. However, the analysis of solids, particularly monatomic solids such as copper, had been developed much earlier than the analysis of liquids, and dates from the discovery by Max von Laue in 1912 of the scattering of X-rays by a crystal. Molecules such as methane, whose chemical valence (see later) is fully satisfied, do not exert very great forces on each other, and consequently they tend to fit into a crystal lattice in such a way that they pack as closely together as possible. Generally this implies a large number of neighbors which may be said to be almost touching each other. (In the case of methane each molecule has 12 close neighbors.) The essential problem in this field of chemical crystallography is two-fold: first, to discover the type of lattice at whose lattice points the molecules are centered; second, to discover the way in which the molecules orientate themselves relative to these lattice points. With nearly spherical molecules such as methane there is very little tendency to orient the molecules except at exceedingly low temperatures. But with less symmetrical shapes the elucidation of the orientation of the molecules is a matter of great complexity. Benzene, for example, is a molecule with the chemical formula C_6H_6. Its shape is that of a rather thin flat disk. Fig. 3 shows the appearance of crystalline benzene. The molecules arrange themselves in such a way that, when looked at end-on, they fit together in this unexpected manner. Each molecule has 12 nearest neighbors, four of which, unshaded, lie with their centers in the plane of the paper, and four, shaded, in each of two parallel planes above and below the original plane. By virtue of the two directions in which the planes of the molecules lie, it is found that a closer packing is possible than if all the disks were placed parallel to each other.

Forces Between Molecules.—Two questions immediately arise out of this discussion. First, are molecules in the gaseous, liquid and solid states identical, or does the state of aggregation modify them in any way? Second, what is the nature of the forces that act between molecules, and determine both the temperatures at which the changes occur from one state to another, and the way in which molecular packing occurs?

The answer to the first question is that in most cases the molecule is scarcely affected by a change of state. Two examples will illustrate this. The iodine molecule is diatomic, and written I_2. Each molecule, when isolated, consists of two atoms held together at a distance of about 2.65 angstroms. But when the molecular crystal is formed, this distance is increased to about 2.70 angstroms. Such a small change shows that each I_2 molecule is almost unchanged in going from the gas phase to the solid phase. Our second example is benzene, already referred to in connection with crystal packing. It can be shown from infrared spectroscopy that a benzene molecule performs a variety of internal vibrations in which its shape is distorted in a rhythmical fashion. These vibrations can be studied in the gaseous, liquid, and solid states. It is found that the time taken for a typical vibration changes by only one third of one per cent on going from the gas to the crystal. We conclude that in most cases the molecules suffer very little deformation in these phase changes. It is this near-invariable character of a molecule that makes a thoroughgoing molecular theory possible.

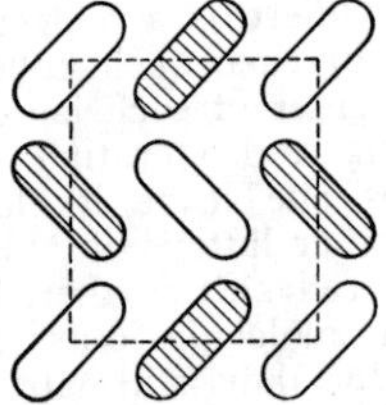

Fig. 3. Solid benzene. Each disc, shown in profile, represents one molecule. Unshaded molecules have their centers in the same plane as the central molecule. Shaded ones have their centers in parallel planes above and below the plane of the paper.

For the sake of completeness it must be added that this invariable character of a molecule does break down sometimes. The most interesting examples are referred to as molecular complexes. In such complexes pairs of molecules—usually of different species—are able to exert sufficiently strong forces on one another that, for example, their color is profoundly modified. A familiar illustration is a combination of benzene (C_6H_6) and iodine (I_2) which forms a molecular complex with one molecule of I_2 attached strongly to one molecule of C_6H_6. In this close association the properties of both molecules are much more modified than in liquid benzene or liquid iodine. But even now it is interesting to notice that if the complex is broken up, as will occur on heating, the components split off as normal molecules of iodine and benzene.

The second question—concerning the forces between molecules—is more difficult to answer. It is evident that they are of great importance in understanding both the transitions from one state of aggregation to another, and also the type of crystal packing in the solid. Two facts about these so-called intermolecular forces are well established. When two molecules are well separated from each other—by a distance more than 2 to 3 times the size of the molecule—it seems that they will almost always attract each other. The only serious exceptions to this rule arise when the molecules carry net electrical charges, and then, on account of the inevitable forces of repulsion between like charges, the molecules will repel each other. The other well-established fact is that if we attempt to bring two molecules close together, there comes a stage when, instead of attracting each other, they exert forces of repulsion. The interpretation of these repulsion forces is that they come into play when the molecules begin to overlap each other. We shall see in later paragraphs that there is no rigorously defined boundary of a molecule, so that the moment at which the overlap begins is itself not clearly defined. We may say that the repulsive forces are ineffective until the separation between the molecules is decreased below a certain value, but that then the magnitude of these forces increases very rapidly. As a result the combination of attractive and repulsive forces leads to a net attractive force at large distances of separation, and a net repulsive force at small distances. If the molecules are not very symmetrical (compare benzene whose shape is like a thin disk) then there is a complicated variation of the repulsive force with the mutual orientation of the molecules, as well as with their mutual separation. It appears that a good description of this situation is obtained if we suppose that we draw an imaginary surface round each atom of a molecule; the radii of these spherical surfaces are sometimes called the van der Waals' radii of the atoms, in honor of J. D. van der Waals, the Dutch scientist whose early observations of the pressure of a gas, in his doctoral dissertation at Leiden in 1873, initiated much of the later study of intermolecular forces. Fig. 4 shows the van der Waals' spheres round the diatomic molecule hydrogen chloride (HCl). Experience now shows that in the solid state it is exceedingly rare to

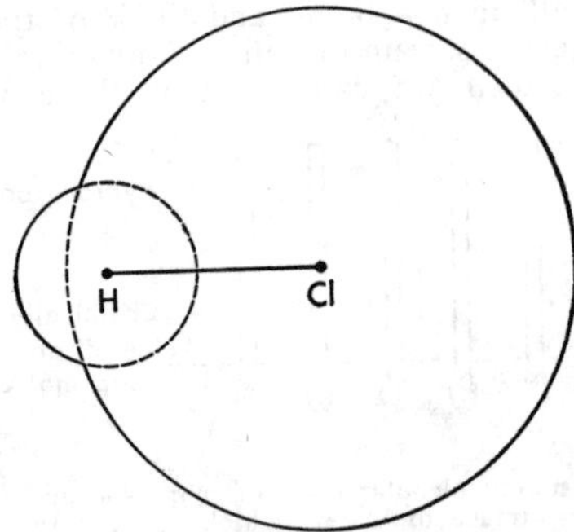

Fig. 4. Van der Waals' surfaces around the hydrogen and chlorine atoms in a molecule HCl. The outer contour, which is symmetrical around the axis joining H and Cl, gives the distance of closest approach of any other molecule.

find atoms in adjacent molecules closer together than the sum of their van der Waals' radii. This is because as soon as the van der Waals' surfaces of two molecules begin to overlap, the forces of repulsion grow rapidly, and the system is no longer stable.

An example will show how this notion is applied in practice. Molecular iodine is diatomic, written I_2. In the solid it crystallizes as shown in Fig. 5, where any one I_2 molecule lies surrounded by six others in the same plane, and eight more in parallel planes above and below it. The diagram shows that the packing is such that all iodine—iodine distances between neighbor molecules are approximately equal, with a value 3.54 angstroms. Thus we may infer that the van der Waals' radius of an iodine atom is $\frac{1}{2} \times 3.54$, i.e. 1.77 angstroms. In passing we may notice that this radius is considerably greater than one-half of the distance between iodine atoms in the same molecule ($\frac{1}{2} \times 2.65 = 1.33$ angstroms). This shows that the forces responsible for holding the atoms together to form the molecule are of a different nature from those which one complete molecule exerts on another complete molecule.

At this stage it may be asked why, if each pair of molecules attract each other at reasonably large distances apart, they do not always come together and form liquid or solid aggregates.

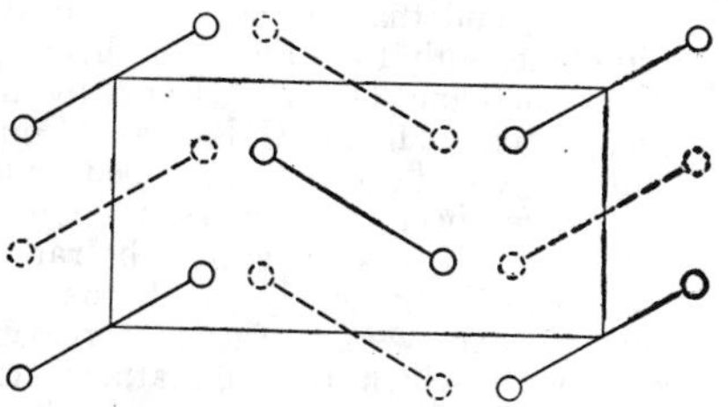

Fig. 5. The crystal of molecular iodine I_2. The thick molecules lie in the plane of the paper, the dotted ones lie above and below the plane of the first group.

For by doing this they would appear to lower their total energy, that is, become more stable. The explanation of this apparent paradox is that at temperature T° (measured on the absolute scale of temperature) each molecule possesses an energy of motion, called kinetic energy, whose magnitude is $\frac{3}{2}$ kT where k, as before, is Boltzmann's constant. Unless T is fairly small this kinetic energy of motion will be sufficient to overcome the gain in potential energy when the two molecules are kept near each other, and the system behaves as a gas. On cooling the gas, however, the kinetic energy term $\frac{3}{2}$ kT decreases until eventually the potential energy forces dominate, and first a liquid (where the molecules are close together but still can move about) and then a solid (when they can no longer move about so easily) are formed.

Origin of the Attractive Forces.—We have seen that the origin of the repulsive forces between molecules lies in the compressive distortion of each when they are held too close together. The origin of the attractive forces which are so important in the gaseous and liquid phases, is more complex. Following the pioneer work of W. H. Keesom (1912), P. Debye (1920) and F. London (1930) it is now recognized that at least three effects all contribute to these attractive forces. The first of these, identified by Keesom, is called the orientation force (some-

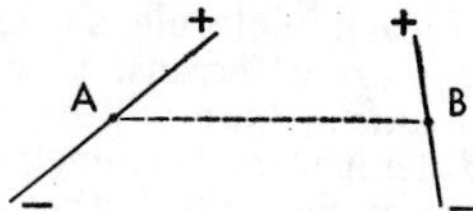

Fig. 6. Two molecules *A*, *B*, with permanent dipole moments. The interaction of the + and – charges on these molecules gives rise to the orientation force of attractions.

times alignment force); the second, identified by Debye, is called the induction force; the third, whose development had to wait for the growth of wave mechanics, since it has no simple model in classical theories, was identified by London, and is called the dispersion force. These three forces may be briefly described as follows:

Suppose (Fig. 6) that we have two molecules *A* and *B*, in which the electric charge possesses an asymmetry, with the result that the mean center of the positive charges does not coincide with the mean center of the negative charges in each molecule. These mean positions are labeled + and – in the figure. The molecules are electrically neutral, because the total amounts of positive and negative charge are equal. But they are said to possess a dipole moment. We may suppose that these dipole moments are of fixed magnitude, but as the molecules spin around their respective centers, the direction of each dipole moment is continually changing. The energy of interaction of the two molecules is the same as the energy of interaction of the pair of + and – charges. Evidently this depends on the directions in which the dipoles are instantaneously pointing. But when proper allowance is taken for all positions, it turns out that there is a mean energy of attraction; and this energy varies inversely as the sixth power of the distance between the molecular centers. This corresponds to a force of attraction varying as the inverse seventh power. This force is called the orientation force because it arises from the mutual orientation of the molecules. With symmetrical (homonuclear) molecules such as H_2 or I_2, it is evidently zero, since by symmetry the centers of positive and negative charge coincide and there is no dipole moment.

The induction force has a related origin. For if, as in Fig. 7, the molecule *A* has a fixed dipole moment, but *B* does not, it will, notwithstanding, acquire one as a result of the electric field due to *A*. We may say that the asymmetry of charge in *A* induces an asymmetry in *B*. Once this happens there will be a net force of attraction just exactly as in the case of two fixed dipole moments. Its variation with distance is also of the same type. In the above account we have explicitly assumed that *B* had no permanent dipole moment. This, however, is an unnecessary assumption. All that happens in that eventuality is that an additional moment is induced; this adds on to the original permanent moment, leading to an induction force superposed upon an orientation force.

The dispersion force can best be understood

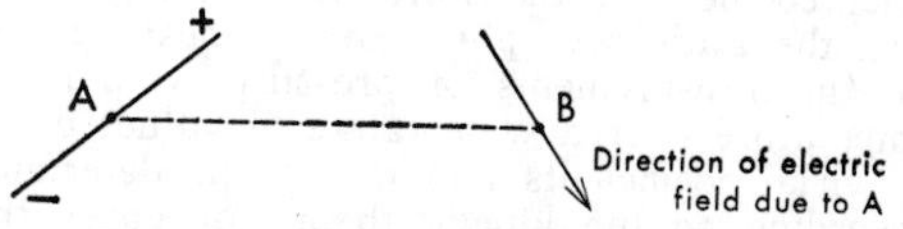

Fig. 7. Two molecules *A*, *B*, of which *A* has a permanent dipole moment. The electric field due to this, shown by the arrow at *B*, induces in *B* a new dipole moment, which then interacts with the original one on *A* to give the induction force.

if we think of each molecule as a system containing one or more electrons, in continual motion. At any moment there will be, in both molecules *A* and *B*, temporary asymmetries of charge. These asymmetries fluctuate with extreme rapidity, but they interact with each other and when averaged over their fluctuations give rise to an attractive force. The reason for the name dispersion forces lies in the fact that the electrons responsible for the fluctuating dipole moments are precisely the same as the electrons which are responsible for the scattering, or dispersion, of light according to the theories of H. A. Lorenz and, later, H. A. Kramers and W. Heisenberg (1925).

The most interesting and important fact concerning the three contributions to the attractive forces is that all of them correspond to a potential energy of interaction which varies as the inverse sixth power of the distance. This implies a force varying as the inverse seventh power. The orientation force is inversely proportional to the temperature, and becomes of less importance as the temperature rises. The other two contributions are independent of temperature. This group of three forces is often known collectively as the van der Waals' force between the two molecules. Generally the induction forces are the smallest of the three, the orientation forces (at room temperature) being greater than the dispersion forces if the dipole moments are large (as in water) and smaller if the dipole moments are not large (as in HCl). With molecules such as H_2 and CH_4, which possess no permanent dipole moment, only the dispersion forces exist.

The most simple mathematical expression of these forces is due to J. E. Lennard-Jones (1924). He suggested that the potential energy be used, rather than the force; this is the sum of a term b/r^6 due to the attractions, where b is a constant and r is the intermolecular separation; and a term often taken to be a/r^{12}, to represent the repulsion. Since the attraction gives negative potential energy, the total energy of interaction is the so-called Lennard-Jones potential $a/r^{12} - b/r^6$.

Virial Coefficients.—This account which has just been given of the forces between two molecules is largely a theoretical one. Experimental measurements are almost wholly confined to applications of the kinetic theory of gases. If a gas consists of molecules which are quite rigid and exert absolutely no forces on one another, the pressure p and volume V are related to the number of molecules N and the absolute temperature T by Boyle's and Charles' law: $pV = NkT$ (k is Boltzmann's constant). However, if the molecules do exert forces on each other this equation of state is no longer valid, and may be replaced by a more general equation:

$$pV = NkT\ \{1 + B/V + C/V^2 + \ldots\}$$

where the coefficients B, C, are functions of the temperature. They are called the second, third, virial coefficients, the word virial being derived from the Latin *vis* (plural *vires*) meaning force. Careful measurements of pressure, volume, and temperature over a wide range of values enables the virial coefficients B and C to be determined. According to the kinetic theory of gases these are simply related to the forces between the molecules. By this means it has become possible to infer the law of force, and, if the Lennard-Jones potential is being used to represent it, to estimate the values of the unknown parameters a and b.

An alternative line of approach to the study of molecular interactions is by careful measurement of the transport properties—thermal conductivity, viscosity, electrical conductivity. Yet another approach is to shoot a stream of molecules with known speed into a gas of the same molecules. There will be collisions, so that the original molecules are scattered. From a study of the number scattered through any given angle it is, in principle, possible to calculate the law of force. At present these methods have not proved so easy to handle, or so fruitful, as the earlier virial expansion methods.

STRUCTURE OF MOLECULES

We now pass from an account of the forces between molecules and the way they pack together in liquids and solids, to consider the structure of an individual molecule. In early days there was no point in asking the questions: what is the size and what is the shape of a molecule? For there were no ways of effectively answering such questions. The only kind of question which it was possible to ask was: how many atoms of one kind will combine with an atom of another kind? Considerable progress was made in this latter direction. It was found, for example, that atoms of hydrogen always formed a diatomic molecule (H_2), and that one atom of carbon was able to combine with four atoms of hydrogen in the form of methane (CH_4). But why no one could ever isolate H_3 or CH_3 was a question whose answer could not be provided until the advent of wave mechanics in 1926. Until that time the atom itself was thought to be rather like a billiard ball of extremely small size around whose surface there were attractive forces, rather like hooks, with which it could attach itself to other atoms. The number of such hooks measured the number of atoms with which it could simultaneously enter into chemical combination. It was usually called the valence of the atom. Thus hydrogen was monovalent, carbon tetravalent. For light atoms the combining ratio was usually a constant for any pair of atoms (for example C and H, giving CH_4). But for heavier atoms, particularly the so-called transition elements of the periodic table (see PERIODIC LAW) and the rare earth atoms, many different valences were found to exist for the same atom, and the idea of a definite valence for an atom is less satisfactory. As long ago as 1860 (W. Odling) and 1861 (A. Kekulé) it became the custom to represent the bonding together of two atoms in a molecule by a line. Thus H_2 would be written

H—H and CH_4 would be written

```
   H
   |
H—C—H,
   |
   H
```

to represent the mutual satisfying of all the valency demands of each of the atoms in the molecule. This representation provides some sort of basis for understanding our inability to isolate any CH_3, since not all the valency demands of the carbon atom would be satisfied. (Incidentally, we now have very good grounds for believing that CH_3—the methyl radical—does exist, for minute periods of time, and plays a central part in many chemical reactions. But it cannot be isolated, and can at best be called an unstable molecule.)

In cases such as those of molecular hydrogen and methane, in which the valency demands were all met by the drawing of a single line between pairs of atoms, it became usual to speak of a saturated molecule, and the bonds were called single bonds. But there were other cases, such as carbon dioxide (a chief constituent of soda water), where, to preserve the valence numbers of the atoms, it was necessary to draw two lines between some of the atoms—for example O=C=O. These bonds were called double bonds, and the molecules were said to be unsaturated. In acetylene, whose formula was simply C_2H_2 it was necessary to introduce triple bonds H—C≡C—H. To a very large degree, however these diagrams were formal; for they did not say whether the three atoms in CO_2 were in a line, as in fact they are, or whether the two C=O directions make an angle with each other. The matter is not at all obvious or clear-cut, for although both O=C=O and H—C≡C—H are linear, neither water (H—O—H) nor hydrogen peroxide (H—O—O—H) is linear. Nor do such diagrams give any indication of the size or length of the bonds. Historically their value was, first, that by concentrating on the valence number of an atom they interpreted the familiar combining ratios and showed, for example, that methane could only have the structural relationship expressed by

```
    H
    |
H—C—H
    |
    H
```

all other possibilities such as H—H—C—H—H, which were not excluded by the chemical formula CH_4, being excluded by their failure to saturate all the atomic valences. This, incidentally, is the reason why, a little earlier, we said that ethyl alcohol was written C_2H_5OH rather than C_2H_6O. For C_2H_5OH shows that its structural formula must be

```
H    H
 \   |
H—C—C—O—H.
 /   |
H    H
```

In this way it is distinguished from the known molecule dimethyl ether, which has the same overall formula, but the different structural formula

```
 H       H
  \     /
H—C—O—C—H.
  /     \
 H       H
```

Molecules with the same overall formula, but different relative structural arrangement of the atoms, are called isomers. Secondly, these structural formulae focused attention on the mutual orientation of the atoms, and led to further work, both theoretical and experimental, which established the stereochemistry of a molecule (that is, spatial relationship of the atoms) and its size and shape (that is, distance apart of the atoms). In the solving of these problems, mathematics, physics and chemistry have now almost merged into one another.

Experimental Molecular Structure.—Questions about the size of a molecule are essentially physical questions, and so physical ideas and experiments are needed to answer them. But questions about the shape of a molecule are both physical and chemical. The strictly chemical type of reasoning is less clear-cut than the physical, but until the 1920's it had progressed much farther.

In methane the structural formula

```
    H
    |
H—C—H
    |
    H
```

suggests, as was found experimentally, that all four C—H bonds are equivalent, so that there is only one type of molecule CH_3X, where X is some other monovalent atom which has replaced one of the H atoms. But the original CH_4 molecule might be planar; or it might be a prism with the four H atoms as base and the C atom as vertex; or it might be a tetrahedron with the C atom at the center and the H atoms at the vertices (see Fig. 8); and there are other alternatives also. The chemical fact that it has only been found possible to obtain one di-substituted methane of type CH_2X_2 makes it almost certain that the tetrahedral shape is the correct one. Arguments of this kind were used by J. H. van't Hoff and J. A. Le Bel to establish the tetrahedral character of carbon in a large number of saturated systems, and led to the idea of definite valency angles. But quite evidently the number of cases where such arguments are applicable, is limited, and the arguments themselves are not rigorous. Thus the nonexistence of more than one type of molecule CH_2X_2 may mean nothing more than that one of the various alternatives is so much more stable than the others that we always form it and not the others. We should not therefore be led unequivocally to a tetrahedral carbon atom.

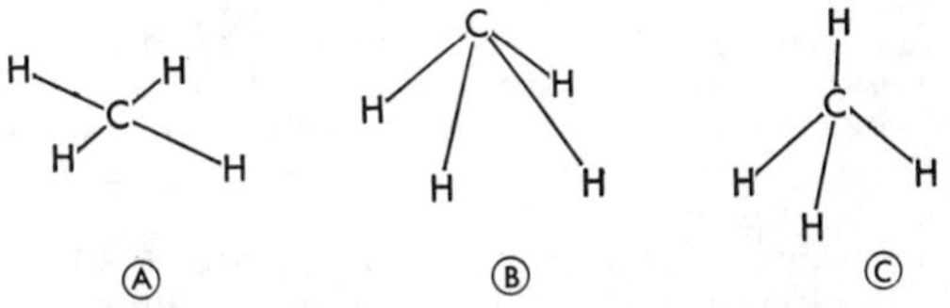

Fig. 8. Conceivable shapes for the methane molecule CH_4. (A) is planar, (B) is pyramidal and (C) is tetrahedral. Only (C) is correct.

Physical Approach.—The more physical lines of approach to this problem may be classified under the main headings (a) electron diffraction, (b) X-ray diffraction, (c) spectroscopic.

Electron diffraction: In electron diffraction a beam of electrons is fired into a container filled with a gas containing the molecules under investigation. The electrons are scattered in all directions, chiefly by the nuclei of the atoms. These electrons, on emerging from the gas, fall on a photographic plate, or other measuring system. From a careful analysis of the way in which the number of electrons at any angle varies with the angle of scatter, it is possible to infer the relative positions of the atoms of the scattering molecules. This technique has been much used, particularly in America, to study small molecules in the gas phase. In the early 1950's, however, modifications of the method, particularly in the USSR, have allowed crystalline solids to be studied also.

We have already discussed X-ray diffraction methods in our earlier account of solids. In early days this method was widely used for nonmolecular solids. The reason for excluding molecular solids was that in each repeating unit, or unit cell, of the solid there might be a quite large number of atoms, so that immense calculations would be needed to establish the detailed shape of each molecule. But the advent of electronic computers has changed this situation. Professor R. Peipinsky of Pittsburgh University has developed a machine of this kind (XRAC) which will make the necessary calculations in what is often less than one per cent of the previous time. As a result it is now practicable to deal with molecules of 30 or 40 atoms; and there is every reason to suppose that eventually some of the very large systems like proteins will be understood in their molecular architecture.

There is one important difference between electron diffraction and X-ray diffraction so far as the study of molecules is concerned. A beam of electrons is scattered chiefly by the nuclei of the atoms, a beam of X-rays chiefly by the electrons of which the atoms are composed. So it would be more accurate to say that electron diffraction tells us where the nuclei are, X-ray diffraction tells us the charge-cloud density at all points of the molecule. We shall see later that the electrons in a molecule may be represented by a kind of cloud of negative charge. It is the density of this cloud that may be inferred from X-ray observations. With heavy atoms the density is exceedingly great in the immediate vicinity of the nucleus, so that there is no difference between conclusions from the two types of experiment. But with light atoms, and particularly with hydrogen, which only carries one electron, the electron diffraction technique has advantages over the X-ray technique. In the year 1955 the relative status of the two methods was that except for the location of hydrogen atoms, X-ray analysis (in the solid) was distinctly more accurate than electron diffraction (in the gas). Since World War II a beam of neutrons (see NEUTRONS) has been used instead of X-rays. These particles are greatly scattered by hydrogen atoms, so that a new approach to molecular structure determination has begun, complementary to the other two.

However, there can be little doubt but that, where it can be applied, spectroscopy gives the greatest accuracy. Conventional spectroscopic measurements yield what are effectively principal moments of inertia. Now each molecule has three such moments, though a planar molecule is such that the greatest moment of inertia is exactly equal to the sum of the other two. A linear molecule has one moment of inertia zero and the other two equal. In the case of a diatomic molecule consisting of two masses m and M a distance l apart, the moment of inertia, measured relative to the center of mass as origin, is $mMl^2/(m+M)$. If the value of this quantity is known, then l is soon calculated. With polyatomic molecules the corresponding formulae are more complex, but not fundamentally more difficult to obtain. With three atoms, for example, they involve not only the three atomic masses, but also the two bond lengths and one valence angle. The experimental measurement of one moment of inertia does not therefore immediately yield one bond length or one valence angle, but a relation between them. As there are in general three independent moments of inertia it follows that by careful analysis of the rotation-vibration spectrum three independent relations between the molecular constants can be obtained. By themselves these may not be sufficient to specify all the parameters—such as bond lengths and bond angles—which define the shape and size of the molecule. But the number may not infrequently be increased by supposing that in related molecules (such as CH_4, $H_3C—CH_3$) certain parameters (such as C—H bond length) remain invariant. The number may also be increased by the device of replacing one or more atoms by isotopes (see ISOTOPES) which are chemically entirely equivalent to the original atoms, but which differ by having a different mass. This new mass affects the moments of inertia, and so alters the spectrum. The most important such isotopic replacement is of hydrogen (H) by deuterium (D), that is, heavy hydrogen, for which the mass is twice as large. But carbon may be used, with mass numbers 12 and 13, and other atoms have similar alternatives. A suitable synthesis of all the information obtained from a series of isotopic substitutions in one given molecule may sometimes be sufficient to yield internuclear distances (that is, bond lengths) and valence angles with an accuracy of 1 in 10^4. Particularly is this the case when the newer microwave techniques can be used. An accuracy of this order is embarrassingly high. For it must always be remembered that the atoms are vibrating around their mean positions: even at low temperatures the amplitudes of these residual, or zero-point, vibrations exceed the precision with which the mean bond length is known. X-ray and electron diffraction measurements seldom give an accuracy anything like so great, and seldom one better than 1 in 10^2.

In addition to the measurements of moments of inertia which have just been described, there are some more subtle, but exceedingly important, factors which help to fix the shape, or more correctly the symmetry, of a molecule. We know that a molecule of N atoms has $3N-6$ modes of internal vibration ($3N-5$ if it is a linear molecule). If the molecule has some symmetry these vibrations will reveal it. For example, a linear molecule like CO_2, in which the C atom lies symmetrically between the two O atoms, will have a total of 4 (i.e. $3 \times 3 - 5$) internal modes of vibration. Two of these can be shown to be "parallel" vibrations, in which all three atoms move along their common axis. The other two, of equal frequency, are associated with motion of the atoms "perpendicular" to this axis. In the first place it is possible from the appearance of the infrared and Raman spectra to distinguish parallel and perpendicular vibrations. This is a great aid in identifying the vibrations. And secondly it is possible to show that of the two parallel vibrations, one is symmetrical in the sense that the two O atoms move in phase towards or away from the central C atom, and the other is unsymmetrical with the corresponding motions out of phase. If it can be shown spectroscopically that there are both symmetrical and antisymmetrical modes of parallel vibration in a molecule such as CO_2, this shows that the two C=O bonds are equal. Analysis of this kind can rule out the structural formula N—O—N for N_2O, and show that it must be N—N—O. More complicated symmetries give more information. Thus C. K. Ingold and his colleagues in London have shown by combining all possible kinds of spectroscopic measurement, that benzene C_6H_6 is planar, and that the six carbon atoms lie at the corners of a regular hexagon, with the six hydrogen atoms directed radially outwards (Fig. 9). Doctors B. Stoicheff and G. Herzberg (1954) have shown, by isotopic replacement of H by D, that the carbon-carbon distance is 1.397×10^{-8} cm. The type of mathematics which is used in discussing the symmetry properties of a molecule is called Group Theory.

A few examples (to be used later) of the kind of information that is obtained in this way may be given at this stage. Thus from its pure rotation spectrum it can be shown that the H—Cl distance in hydrogen chloride gas (Fig. 4) is 1.27 x 10^{-8} cm. From the moments of inertia of water we find that the molecule is not linear, but has a valence angle (Fig. 10a) of 104.5°. From the fact that in methane the largest moment of inertia is not equal to the sum of the other two, we cut out the planar structure Fig. 8a; and by symmetry considerations we establish the tetrahedral shape of Fig. 8c. Ammonia NH_3 is not planar, but is like a pyramid

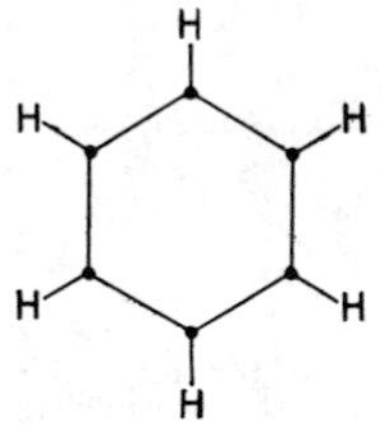

Fig. 9. A molecule of benzene. The dots denote carbon atoms arranged in a regular plane hexagonal fashion. The carbon-carbon distance is 1.397 ± 0.004 angstrom units.

(Fig. 10b) with each HNH angle equal to about 107°.

There are other ways in which information about certain parts of a molecule may be obtained. Thus in nuclear magnetic resonance we measure the energy necessary to "flip" the spin of one of the nuclei from one of its allowed orientations to another. If, for example, this nucleus is a proton as with the atom of hydrogen, and if there should happen to be a second proton in the same molecule a definite distance away from the first proton, then the energy of flip will be altered. Careful measurements of the absorption of energy in this process allow us to infer the distance apart of these two atoms, without reference to the rest of the molecule.

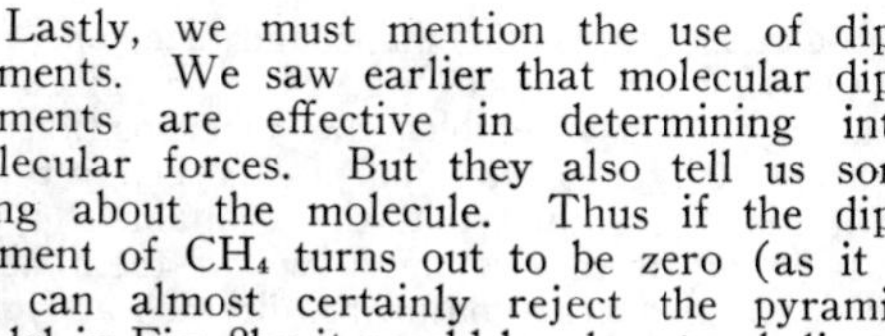

Fig. 10. (A) a water molecule H_2O, (B) an ammonia molecule NH_3.

Lastly, we must mention the use of dipole moments. We saw earlier that molecular dipole moments are effective in determining intermolecular forces. But they also tell us something about the molecule. Thus if the dipole moment of CH_4 turns out to be zero (as it is) we can almost certainly reject the pyramidal model in Fig. 8b: it would be almost unbelievable that the electrons would be attracted absolutely equally to the carbon and the hydrogens. Similarly from the facts that the dipole moment of water is not zero, and that of CO_2 is zero, we are led to the angular shape of Fig. 10a for H_2O and the linear shape for CO_2.

Theoretical Molecular Structure.—The explanation of many of the structural details just mentioned could not be seriously considered until 1927. In the early days the internal structure of an atom was unknown. (See ATOM.) How could anyone hope to know the structure of a molecule? When the electron was discovered and identified in 1897 by J. J. Thomson at the Cavendish Laboratory, Cambridge, England, it became clear that the mechanism whereby atoms exert forces on each other was essentially electronic. This led to a series of models, due to I. Langmuir and others, in which an attempt was made to locate certain electrons—the outer ones, sometimes called valence-shell electrons—at the vertices of a cube surrounding each atom. So some of the electrons would appear to "belong" to two or more atoms, and, by extrapolation from the case of the rare-gas atoms (helium, neon etc.) which appeared to be so stable as not to form compounds, and which were characterized by the presence of 8 electrons in their outer shell, it was postulated that each atom would seek to attach other atoms to itself in such a way and of such a number that it would complete its octet of electrons at the corners of the imaginary cube around it. Models of this kind, however ingenious, are unsatisfactory because a stationary electrical distribution of such a type can be shown to be unstable.

The next fundamental step was due to G. N. Lewis of California. In 1916 he made the important observation that practically all single bonds (as in H—O—H or H—Cl) could be regarded as involving two electrons. As a general rule one electron came from each of the two atoms at the ends of the bond, though in certain special cases (called donor bonds) both electrons could come from one of the atoms. These two electrons were said to be shared between the atoms. With double bonds four electrons were involved and with triple bonds six electrons. As a result of this sharing process each atom such as O, Cl, completed an octet of electrons, and H a duplet. In HCl, for example, the H atom provides just one electron, but the Cl atom has 7 electrons in its outer, valence shell (this is the M-shell). By sharing one of these 7 with H, the Cl atom acquires an interest in 8 electrons, the H atom acquires an interest in 2 electrons, and both the octet and the duplet are complete. In H—O—H the O atom has 6 valence-shell electrons, and by sharing one each with the two H atoms, it acquires its necessary total of 8. If it attempted to add on a third H atom, to form a hypothetical H_3O, it would find itself with an interest in 9 electrons, contrary to the rule. This model explains the saturation of valence, though of course it says nothing about size or shape. It is interesting to notice that in fact oxygen can attach itself to three hydrogen atoms provided that it first becomes ionized by giving up an electron. Thus the ion H_3O^+ with one net positive charge, is present very widely when an acid is dissolved in water. (See ACID). In O=C=O we preserve the octet rule for both O and C by supposing that in each bond a total of four electrons are involved. This is in agreement with their designations as double bonds.

The next important step was the introduction of wave mechanics in 1926 by Erwin Schrödinger. For the first time it became possible to say what was meant by the term electron distribution in an atom or a molecule. One result of the Uncertainty Principle of W. Heisenberg (see QUANTUM THEORY) was that on account of its small mass it was not possible to follow an electron in its orbital path, so that some new mode of description was necessary. The mode which is most common in chemical problems is that of the charge-cloud, similar in some respects to a city fog; the cloud is not equally dense everywhere, and for an atom or a molecule its density decreases as we move away from the neighborhood of the nuclei. We interpret the cloud as telling us the probability that if we could instantaneously photograph the atom or the molecule, we should find the electron in any chosen small region. The density of the cloud is proportional to the probability. The density itself is found from the wave function, which in its turn is found as the solution to the appropriate Schrödinger Wave Equation. So, in order to calculate the distribution of charge we (a) set up the appropriate wave equation, (b) solve it to get the wave function ψ, (c) write ψ^2 as the density of our charge-cloud. On the average it is as if each electron were itself smeared out into a volume distribution of electric charge, and the density of this charge is given by the square of the calculated wave function.

So far as an atom is concerned, this process gives us the charge-clouds which correspond to the distinct energy levels which are allowed for this atom. It is unfortunate that except for the one-electron problem, the wave equation is too complicated to be solved exactly. Consequently

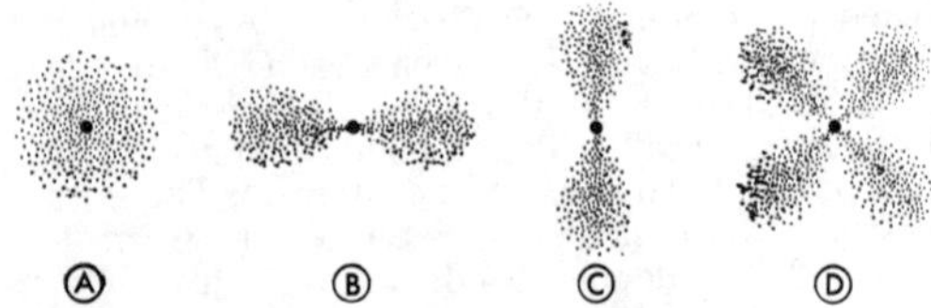

Fig. 11. Atomic orbitals, showing (A) *s*-type, with spherical symmetry, (B) and (C) *p*-type, with axial symmetry, (D) *d*-type, with four regions of high charge-cloud density. In each case the central dot denotes the position of the nucleus of the atom.

various approximations to the solution have to be obtained; and various mathematical techniques exist for getting better and better approximations. When the individual electron levels have been obtained, the Pauli Exclusion Principle is applied. This principle allows us to put not more than two electrons into each of the calculated energy levels. If we have two electrons in a charge-cloud pattern (now usually called an orbital, since it replaces the older notion of an orbital path) these two electrons must have their spins antiparallel, that is, opposed to each other. In the lowest state of the atom as a whole we simply calculate the allowed orbital energies, and then feed in electrons, two at a time, beginning with the level of lowest energy, until all our available electrons are used up.

With molecules a similar situation obtains. In the first place it is easy to show that all the inner-shell electrons of the atoms are effectively unchanged as a result of a molecule being formed. These electrons have monocentric orbitals such as those of Fig. 11. But at least some of the valence-shell electrons have orbitals which, to a high degree of accuracy, can be thought of as bicentric. Since each orbital can accommodate two electrons, with opposed spins, this shows that two electrons can have an orbital associated with a pair of adjacent atoms; these two electrons together constitute G. N. Lewis' electron-pair bond. And we can see that the deepest explanation which is possible for the existence of an electron-pair bond is in the application of the Exclusion Principle to the idea of orbitals.

In molecular hydrogen (H_2) there are only two electrons and the charge-cloud is of the form shown in Fig. 12. As the bond is due to two electrons it is a single bond, and like almost all normal single bonds the charge-cloud is axially symmetrical, that is, has cylindrical symmetry around the line of the bond.

In HCl the charge-clouds for the K- and L- shells of chlorine are just as in the isolated Cl atom. The bond is associated with two electrons whose charge-cloud pattern resembles that of Fig. 13. Other electrons in the valence-shell of chlorine have orbitals closely similar to the

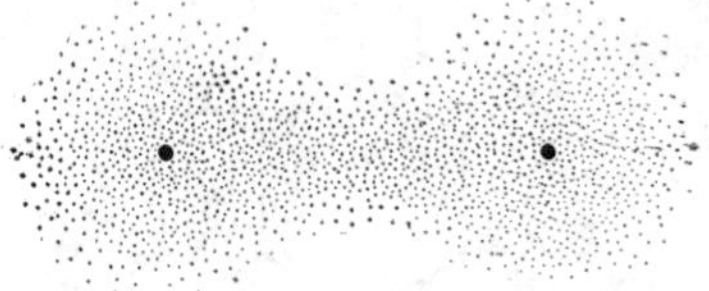

Fig. 12. Charge-cloud for molecular H_2. Thick dots denote positions of the two nuclei. Notice symmetry around the axis, and the closeness with which this diagram resembles the superposition of two diagrams such as in Fig. 11a.

isolated atom orbitals. It is of great significance that the charge-cloud for the bonding electrons is not very different from that due to a superposition of a hydrogen atomic orbital (an *s*-type orbital, see Fig. 11a) and a chlorine atomic orbital (a *p*-type orbital, see Fig. 11b). For this reason we say that the hydrogen electron has been paired with the chlorine electron to form the bond. Now the only orbitals that may be used in this way are those which are not already doubly filled. Hence the valence number of an atom is equal to the number of unpaired electrons in the atom. Nitrogen, for example, is triatomic (Fig. 10b) because there are three unpaired electrons in the outer shell of the isolated N atom.

Finally, in H_2O, we have atomic nonbonding electrons round the O atom, and their two

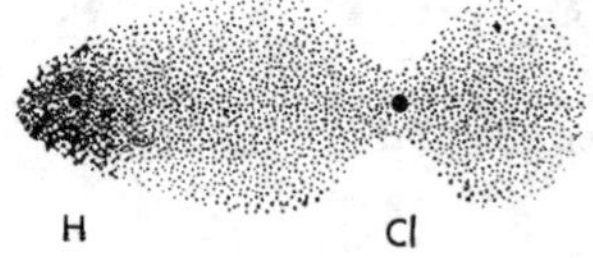

Fig. 13. Charge-cloud for molecule H-Cl. Notice symmetry around the axis, and the closeness with which this diagram resembles a superposition of diagrams such as in Figs. 11a and 11b.

charge-clouds, similar in shape and size, one for each O—H bond. (See Fig. 14.) Each separate charge-cloud resembles the superposition of a hydrogen *s*-type orbital and an oxygen *p*-type. Now it may be shown that the available *p*-type orbitals in an atom—we need two of them here for the two bonds—are naturally directed at right angles to each other. This, as Linus Pauling showed in 1931, gives us insight into the reason why the angle H—O—H is not 180°, but is nearer to 90°. Indeed the whole basis of stereochemistry lies in considerations analogous to these.

We can also see why bonds are so nearly constant, in length and energy. For if, in H_2O we replaced one H atom by another group, such as C_2H_5, to give ethyl alcohol H—O—C_2H_5,

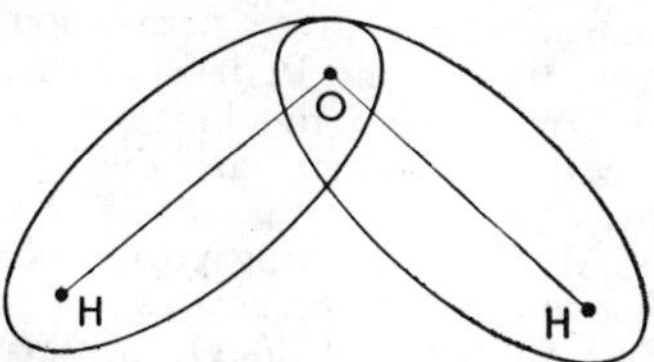

Fig. 14. Schematic representation of the two charge-clouds that represent the two O—H bonds in water H—O—H. The cloud for each bond is similar in general pattern to that shown in Fig. 13, and is almost wholly localized within the volumes obtained by rotating each closed curve around the appropriate O—H axis.

there is no particular reason why the charge-cloud for the remaining H—O region should be seriously modified. It is true that there will be some small modification, so that the O—H bond is not really identical in all molecules. But the variations from molecule to molecule are not so large that they prevent us from drawing up tables of bond properties—length, energy, force constant, dipole moment, and so on. It is also easy to see from diagrams such as those of Figs. 12–14 what is meant by the size and shape of a molecule, and the relation of all this to the van der Waals' radii mentioned earlier.

Enormous progress has been made in this field since W. Heitler and F. London first introduced some of these ideas in 1927. We can now give a fairly detailed account of most simple molecules. For details the reader is referred to the standard works listed below.

See also ELECTRON THEORY; STEREOCHEMISTRY; X-RAYS.

Bibliography.—Herzberg, Gerhard, *Molecular Spectra and Molecular Structure,* vol. 1, 2d ed. (New York 1950), vol. 2, 2d ed. (1945), vol. 3 (1966); Coulson, C. A., *Valence,* 2d ed. (New York 1961); Pullman, Bernard, *The Modern Theory of Molecular Structure* (New York 1962); Williams, Dudley, ed., *Molecular Physics,* vol. 3 (New York 1962); Ballhausen, C. J., *Molecular Orbital Theory* (New York 1964); Hirschfelder, J. O., Curtiss, C. F., and Bird, R. B., *Molecular Theory of Gases and Liquids* (New York 1964); Pauling, Linus, and Hayward, Roger, *The Architecture of Molecules* (San Francisco 1964).

C. A. COULSON,
Mathematical Institute, Oxford University, England.

MOLECULE, mŏl'ê-kūl, the smallest particle of a chemical substance capable of a separate existence. See MOLECULAR THEORY.

MOLESKIN, mōl'skĭn, originally the skin of moles used as fur, now a fabric so called from its softness like the skin of a mole, such as velveteen. It is a strong twilled cotton fabric, cropped or sheared before dyeing.

MOLESWORTH, mōlz'wûrth, **Mary Louisa** (nee STEWART; pseudonym ENNIS GRAHAM), English writer: b. Rotterdam, Netherlands, May 29, 1839; d. London, England, July 20, 1921. Her first books were sentimental novels for adults, written under the pseudonym Ennis Graham. After 1874 she used her married name as an author, achieving wide success as a writer of children's stories. Among the most popular were *Carrots* (1876) and *The Cuckoo Clock* (1877).

MOLEY, mō'lĭ, **Raymond (Charles),** American educator, editor, and author: b. Berea, Ohio, Sept. 27, 1886; d. Phoenix, Ariz., Feb. 18, 1975. He graduated from Baldwin-Wallace College in 1906, taught school, and then joined the faculty of Western Reserve University in 1916. In 1919 he was appointed director of the Cleveland Foundation, publishing the results of his work in *The Cleveland Crime Survey* (1922). Named associate professor of government at Columbia University in 1923 and professor of public law there in 1928 (retired 1954), he was research director of the New York State Crime Commission (1926–1927) and the New York State Commission on the Administration of Justice (1931–1933), the latter under Franklin D. Roosevelt, who was then governor. In March 1933, when Roosevelt became president, Moley was made assistant secretary of state and a member of the so-called "brain trust." Resigning in September, he established and edited *Today,* a weekly magazine which in 1937 was merged with *Newsweek,* Moley remaining as contributing editor. His acid criticism of the New Deal was summed up in *After Seven Years* (1939). Among his other books are *Lessons in American Citizenship . . .* (1917; 10th ed., 1930); *Our Criminal Courts* (1930); *27 Masters of Politics* (1949); and *The Republican Opportunity* (1962).

MOLFETTA, môl-fât'tä, commune and city, Italy, in Bari Province, on the Adriatic Sea, 15 miles northwest of Bari, with which it is connected by railroad. It has a magnificent Romanesque cathedral begun in the 11th century, and a well-sheltered harbor, exporting chiefly olive oil, wine, and almonds. There are variegated manufactures, as well as shipbuilding and canning industries. Just outside the town are caves of archaeological interest. Pop. of the commune (1961) 61,684.

MOLIERE, mô-lyâr' (pseudonym of JEAN BAPTISTE POQUELIN), French dramatist: b. Paris, France, bap. Jan. 15, 1622; d. there, Feb. 17, 1673. Known as the greatest French writer of comedy, he began life as an upholsterer's son and apprentice. The senior Poquelin held a position of some slight importance at the French court as *valet de chambre* and upholsterer, and he arranged for his eldest son to succeed to this office. In the meantime he sent the boy to the Jesuit college of Clermont in Paris, where he received an excellent education and made friends in the smart world—notably Armand de Bourbon, prince de Conti—who were helpful to him in later years.

Early Career in the Theater.—Molière's choice of the theater as a career was, on the face of it, a surprising one. Thanks to his father he was assured a safe position in the world; and the theater, besides being hazardous, was frowned upon by the church in which young Poquelin had been raised. His decision is generally attributed to the influence of Madeleine Béjart, daughter of a minor government official and member of a large, rather Bohemian family, interested in the theater, who had become neighbors of the Poquelins. In 1642, the year before Molière's meeting with Madeleine, the elder Poquelin had made a final attempt to get his son interested in the upholstery business. He sent the young man with Louis XIII to Narbonne, to act in his appointed role as *valet-tapissier du roi,* chiefly to make the king's bed. When the boy returned from this sojourn in the south of France, he met Madeleine, and soon persuaded his father to let him out of his contract to succeed him in office. He and Madeleine then (1643) launched the Illustre Théâtre, an attempt to establish a third playhouse in Paris. As was the fashion of the day, he took a new name, Molière.

Their efforts were unsuccessful in the capital (Molière was imprisoned briefly for debt), and in 1646 they took to the provinces. Here for 12 years they enjoyed a sufficient measure of success and got enough recognition to insure them a welcome return to the French court. In these 12 years, too, the greatness of Molière the dramatist was fashioned. As actor, producer, and business manager he learned all the tricks of the trade. As playwright, which he of necessity soon became, he was brought in close touch with his audience and was able to study at first hand the people of France. Molière's greatness rests on his knowledge of people, his understanding of human nature, and in these 12 formative years he developed this discernment.

Bettmann Archive

Molière at breakfast with Louis XIV at Versailles, from the original painting by Jean Léon Gérôme.

The repertory of plays available for itinerant actors at that time featured many tragedies. Molière's contract with his troupe stated that he was to alternate in the leading role. He was not a great tragedian, but he was an excellent comic actor. It is not surprising then to find the repertoire of Molière's company swinging to farce and Molière adapting an Italian play by Niccolò Barbieri for his first writing effort, *L'étourdi* (*The Blunderers*), produced in 1655 in Lyon. Molière, the author, always wrote roles for Molière, the actor, in which he would be sure to get laughs. The inspiration for his early plays came from the old French farces as well as the *commedia dell'arte* and, of course, from his direct experience of life. It was mostly a burlesque type of humor, with broad jokes and suggestive situations, but it evoked the basic human emotions and was very popular material. The time was becoming ripe, however, for classical comedy of the kind that Molière was soon to produce.

Return to Paris.—In 1658, Molière and his troupe returned to Paris, and on October 24 they staked their future on an appearance before the most important audience of their career: the young King Louis XIV, his brother Philippe (later duc d'Orléans), and the court, in the Guard Room of the Louvre. The vehicle in which they chose to display their talents was Pierre Corneille's tragedy *Nicomède.* Molière addressed the august assemblage with a felicitous speech and asked permission to conclude the entertainment with a little farce, one he had written for the provinces. The result was that the playwright and his company were given permission to play regularly at the royal Petit-Bourbon theater, under the patronage of the king's brother, and were thenceforth known as the *troupe de Monsieur.*

In 1659, Molière's growing power as a dramatist was shown in *Les précieuses ridicules,* q.v. (*The Affected Young Ladies*), a new comedy which satirized the social climbers of the day, their affectations and false standards. It was an immediate success and brought them the best box-office receipts of any production to date. In this, as in most of his work, Molière lashed out against the distortions in society which frustrate man's innate goodness and common sense, presenting a picture of social life in which character is shown to be more important than station. Naturally, this point of view was immensely appealing to the common people, who were able to identify themselves with his characters and to find society itself amusing.

In 1662, Molière, who was 40, married Armande Béjart, aged 18, a younger sister of Madeleine. Armande had been raised with Molière's troupe and was much loved and spoiled. She was a part of the theater from her earliest years and became a vivacious and appealing comedienne. The marriage, however, was beset with domestic difficulties. Sometimes thereafter they lived apart, and increasingly in his plays one finds themes of jealousy and unfaithfulness. Molière added fuel to the flames of gossip about his marriage by producing in 1662 a play he had written about an older man marrying a girl half his age, *L'école des femmes* (*The School for Wives*). While not one of his greatest comedies, the touch is surer, and the author is more mature than in his earlier works.

Major Comedies.—Henceforth Molière wrote and produced at an increasing pace. It was fortunate for his career that he had Louis XIV for a friend and protector; but regrettably the king encouraged him to waste his time on many divertissements for the royal festivals. In spite of many preoccupations and domestic trials, he kept on writing and acting, without taking time to polish and repolish. He had two importunate rulers to satisfy: the people and the king.

Tartuffe, one of the Molière's most famous and most controversial plays, appeared on May 12, 1664. It is the story of a hypocrite, a genuine devotee of hypocrisy, who deceives even himself. Unfortunately for the contemporary fate of the play, he is a religious hypocrite; and the storm it provoked among the ultrareligious people of Paris did not take long to break. On the fifth day of what promised to be a long and highly successful run, the king politely advised Molière to withdraw the play. For five years thereafter *Tartuffe* led a clandestine existence, having a number of readings before royalty and the aristocrats, but no public appearances. When it finally reappeared in public (after the king had composed his differences with the Holy See), it played to packed houses, much to the discomfiture of Molière's enemies; and the play has since been acclaimed one of the great masterpieces of the French theater.

Since the suppression of *Tartuffe* was a serious financial blow to Molière, he worked hurriedly to produce another play, *Don Juan, ou le festin de Pierre* (see DON JUAN), in February 1665. He yielded nothing to his caviling critics, who denounced the play as the work of an atheist.

It went uncensored, however, and in August of that year the king took him under his protection, gave him a pension of 6,000 livres, and permitted his company to be known as the *troupe du Roi.*

On June 4, 1666, Molière's greatest comedy, *Le misanthrope* (q.v.), was produced. Here he worked on a bigger canvas, painting a picture of society that is more inclusive than his former efforts at exposing particular fads and vices. In it is reflected, too, many of the domestic trials of Molière's own life. Alceste, the misanthropic young protagonist of the play, revolts against the sham and glitter of the court. He makes a strong plea for "the honest man" but argues his case so violently that one feels a neurotic, compulsive quality in his protestations. At the same time, he is deeply in love with Célimène, who is representative in many ways of the courtly vices he detests. It is difficult, therefore, to accept Alceste's arguments in favor of social sanity, right as they may be. His friend, Philinte, and Célimène's cousin, Éliante, offer the most reasoned analysis of the conflict between society, which exists on compromise, and the just man, who seeks absolute virtue. But there is no satisfactory resolution of the conflict; the audience is permitted to draw its own conclusions. In *Le misanthrope,* as in most of Molière's plays, the material is subjective in nature; the execution objective. His young wife, Armande, must have had many of the qualities of Célimène; Alceste bears many resemblances to the author. Despite the fact that it has come to be considered his greatest comedy, the play, possibly because of its subtle construction, was not a success with contemporary audiences.

Molière began work immediately on another play to increase the revenue of his troupe, and on Aug. 6, 1666, produced *Le médecin malgré lui* (*The Physician in Spite of Himself*). This famous farce pokes fun at the doctors of the day by turning a poor faggot binder, Sganarelle, into a physician in spite of himself. Molière, who was to spend the rest of his life under the care of doctors, exposes the charlatanry of the contemporary medical profession in an amusing way.

During the next year Molière underwent a most trying period; he was ill much of the time and one of the longest periods of separation from his wife was just beginning. As usual, he applied himself to new production. The following year (1668) three of his plays were produced: *Amphitryon, Georges Dandin,* and *L'avare,* q.v. (*The Miser*), of which the last was the least successful. Most of his work was being written now to satisfy Louis XIV's taste for amusement. In 1669, Molière satirized the doctors again in *M. de Pourceaugnac,* and in 1670 he produced his most successful comedy-ballet, *Le bourgeois gentilhomme* (*The Would-be Gentleman*).

Last Plays.—On Feb. 17, 1672, Madeleine Béjart died; but Molière, however much he was grieved, continued to work. On March 11 he produced *Les femmes savantes* (*The Learned Ladies,* q.v.), a much more mature comedy than *Les précieuses ridicules,* to which it is sometimes compared. His health became worse, and it was necessary to close the theater for a few days because of his inability to perform. Despite all his difficulties, he kept busy with the preparation of his last play, *Le malade imaginaire* (q.v., *The Imaginary Invalid*), the story of a man whose illnesses, unlike Molière's own, were only imaginary. On Feb. 17, 1673, the first anniversary of Madeleine's death, Molière was much worse. His friends and Armande, who had returned to their house, begged him not to go on. Molière told them he had no choice; the wages of 50 members of his troupe depended on his appearance. While he was on stage, it was observed that he was in difficulty. After the performance he complained of being cold and was carried home. When he had eaten a bit of bread and cheese, he began coughing. He called for his wife, but she was not there. He died then in the arms of two strangers who were staying at his house, without receiving the final offices of the church; and later, on these grounds, the archbishop refused him Christian burial. At Armande's request the king intervened, and burial was permitted at St. Joseph's Cemetery, but the interment was without ceremony.

During the French Revolution, Molière's supposed remains were transferred to the Panthéon, and later to the Père Lachaise Cemetery. Their identification was uncertain, however, and it is doubtful that the tomb by Alexandre Lenoir contains the actual relics of Molière.

Bibliography.—Grimarest, Jean Léonor Le Gallois, sieur de, *La vie de monsieur de Molière* (Paris 1705, reprinted 1930); Voltaire, *Ouvres de Molière* (Paris 1765); Lacroix, Paul, *Collection Molièresque* (Paris 1867–75); Despois, Eugène, ed., *Ouvres de Molière* (Paris 1873–1900); Matthews, Brander, *Molière: His Life and Works* (New York 1926); Palmer, John, *Molière: His Life and Works* (London 1930); Michaut, Gustave, *Molière, raconté par ceux qui l'ont vu* (Paris 1932); Chapman, Percy Addison, *The Spirit of Molière* (Princeton 1940); Lewis, Wyndham, *Molière: The Comic Mask* (New York 1959); Gossman, Lionel, *Men and Masks* (Baltimore 1963).

MOLINA, mō-lē'nä, **Luis,** Spanish Jesuit teacher and writer: b. Cuenca, New Castile, Spain, 1535; d. Madrid, Oct. 12, 1600. He entered the Jesuit Order in 1553, and from 1566 to 1586 taught theology at Evora, Portugal. In 1588 he published his most celebrated work, *Concordia liberi arbitrii . . .,* in Lisbon. In his teachings (Molinism), he sought to reconcile free will, divine grace, and the foreknowledge of God. If God knows, through all eternity, the righteous and the damned; if He gives His grace to all, yet requires man to be responsible for his own destiny, how is it possible to explain freedom of will, efficacy of grace, or the infallibility of God's prescience? Molina taught that grace by its very nature is always efficacious; that man's free will permits him to accept or reject it; and that God foresees throughout eternity the use each would make of the divine gift. The Jesuits supported this view, but the Dominicans hotly disputed it because they felt Molina neglected the reconciliation of free will and grace made by St. Thomas Aquinas. The controversy, referred to the Vatican in 1596, was settled satisfactorily to both sides by Pope Paul V in 1607, after Molina's death.

MOLINA, Tirso de. See TÉLLEZ, GABRIEL.

MOLINE, mō-lēn', city, Illinois, in Rock Island County, on the Mississippi River, at an altitude of 585 feet. It is served by the Chicago, Rock Island & Pacific; Chicago, Burlington & Quincy; and Chicago, Milwaukee, St. Paul and Pacific railroads, and is on many important highways. The city adjoins East Moline and Rock Island, and is directly across the river from Davenport, Iowa, about 165 miles southwest of Chicago. Moline has a fine airport, city-owned, with airline service. The immediately surrounding area is agricultural, but there are extensive coal fields near by. Together with Rock Island, the city constitutes the greatest center in the United States for the manufacture of farm implements, with such companies as Deere and International Harvester operating on a major scale. Other industrial products include electrical equipment, machinery, foundry products, machine tools, rubber products, wood products, sporting goods, and clothing. First important as a river port, Moline's industrial growth began after the decline in Mississippi steamboating in the latter part of the 19th century. It was settled about 1832, platted in 1843, and incorporated as a town in 1848 and as a city in 1872. It is governed by a mayor and council. Pop. 46,237.

MOLINET, mô-lē-nĕ′, or **MOULINET, Jean,** French poet and chronicler: b. Desvres, France, 1435; d. Valenciennes, Aug. 23, 1507. After receiving his master's degree in Paris about 1461, he served as assistant to Georges Chastellain, chronicler of the house of Burgundy, and continued Chastellain's *Chroniques* from 1474 to 1504. He was also the author of *L'art de rhétorique vulgaire* (before 1492), and a leader of the *rhétoriqueurs,* a school of Burgundian poets who favored an affected, pedantic, rhetorical style. He also wrote a prose version of the famous *Roman de la rose* (1503). A modern edition of the *Chroniques* was published, 3 vols. (1935–37); and of Molinet's *Faictz et Dictz,* 3 vols. (1936–39).

MOLINISM, mō′lĭ-nĭz'm, the teachings of Luis Molina (q.v.). The term is also sometimes used for the quietism (q.v.) taught by Miguel de Molinos (q.v.).

MOLINO DEL REY, Battle of, mô-lē′nô thĕl rē′ê, one of the bloodiest engagements of the Mexican War. It took place a few miles southwest of Mexico City on Sept. 8, 1847. Inaccurate intelligence led Gen. Winfield Scott to believe that the Mexicans at the Molino del Rey (King's Mill) were casting church bells into cannon to be used in the defense of Mexico City. He ordered the capture of the ¼-mile-long stone buildings and the Casa Mata, 500 yards to the northwest, a powder magazine. Gen. William J. Worth, in immediate command, attempted a daring daylight attack after the briefest artillery preparation. The 500 picked American attackers were quickly decimated, but reinforcements stormed the Molino and then overcame the Casa Mata. They found the powder but no evidence of cannon casting. Total American losses were 117 killed, 658 wounded, 18 missing, out of 3,447 engaged. The Mexican force was several times larger and their losses considerably more, but there are no accurate figures. Col. Ethan Allen Hitchcock referred to the battle in his diary as "a sad mistake." Little was gained for the terminal assault on Mexico City, the army's confidence was shaken, and a breach was widened between Generals Scott and Worth.

MOLINOS, mô-lē′nōs, **Miguel de,** Spanish mystic: b. near Saragossa, Spain, June 29, 1628; d. Rome, Italy, Dec. 28, 1696. He began his ecclesiastical studies early, was a parish priest in Valencia, and in 1663 was sent on a mission to Rome, where he took up permanent residence some years later. In 1675 he published his *Guida spirituale . . .* (in Italian), which bore the imprimatur of five distinguished Catholic theologians and was soon translated into a number of other languages. In 1685, however, he was arrested by the Inquisition on charges of heresy; and after a two-year trial, he pleaded guilty and was sentenced to prison for life. All Molinos' writings, printed and in manuscript (including his letters), were prohibited *in globo* and placed on the Index of literature forbidden to Catholics. His condemnation (in part instigated by a penitent Louis XIV) was based primarily on his oral teaching and his letters, rather than on his book. Molinos, whose doctrine is known as quietism (q.v.), saw Christ and the church as paths by which to approach God, but felt that man could realize God in His infinity only by divesting himself insofar as possible of all materiality. The Jesuits charged that Molinos' doctrine meant indifference to the external world and to the church and that it condoned carnal sins; Molinos himself was accused of gross personal immorality. Despite this condemnation, he received the sacraments at his death.

Consult Pierre Dudon, *Le quiétiste espagnol, Miguel de Molinos* (Paris 1921) for the Jesuit viewpoint; also John Bigelow, *Molinos the Quietist* (New York 1882).

MOLL FLANDERS, mŏl′ flăn′dẽrz (in full The Fortunes and Misfortunes of the Famous Moll Flanders), a novel by Daniel Defoe (q.v.), first published in 1722. The novel, in the form of an autobiography, tells the story of Moll Flanders' adventurous and disreputable life. Moll is born in Newgate prison. Abandoned by her mother, who is transported to America as a felon, Moll is reared by the mayor of Colchester. The novel chronicles Moll's seduction, her various liaisons, and her eventual five marriages.

Moll travels to America with one of her husbands, meets her mother, and discovers that this husband is her own brother. After leaving him, she returns to England. Destitute, Moll becomes a successful pickpocket and thief. She is caught, sentenced, and transported to America, along with one of her former husbands, a highwayman. The two become successful planters, and Moll inherits a plantation from her mother. Late in life, they return to England and live out their lives in ease and repentance.

MOLLENDO, mô-yän′dô, city, Peru, a seaport on the Pacific coast, located in the Department of Arequipa, about 50 miles southwest of Arequipa on the Pan American Highway. A railroad connects it with Puno on Lake Titicaca. Formerly the chief coastal port for southern Peru and Bolivia, it has largely been replaced by the new and safer port facilities completed in 1941 seven miles to the north at Matarani. Among its industries are textiles, flour milling, shoe and furniture manufacturing and fish canning. The chief export of the region is alpaca wool. Population: (1961) 13,574.

MÖLLENDORF, mûl′ĕn-dôrf, **Wichard Joachim Heinrich von,** Prussian general: b. Lindenberg, Germany, Jan. 7, 1724; d. Havelberg, Jan. 28, 1816. He distinguished himself in the service of Frederick II the Great during the Seven Years' War, especially in the battles of Leuthen, Hochkirk, and Torgau; and, remaining in the Prussian military service, rose to the rank of general field marshal in 1793. The next year Möllendorf commanded the Prussian Army on the Rhine and won the Battle of Kaiserslautern against the French Republic. During the Napoleonic Wars he was wounded at Auerstedt (1806) and captured, and after his release, retired from active duty. He was noted as a pioneer in seeking more humane treatment of common soldiers.

MOLLET, mô-lĕ, **Guy,** French statesman: b. Flers, Orne Department, France, Dec. 31, 1905. The son of an impoverished weaver and a concierge in a savings bank, he won a government scholarship to attend secondary school, and at 17 became a teacher in a boarding school at Le Havre. He joined the Socialist Party in 1923, and from 1932 gave his full time to politics. Wounded and captured by the Germans in June 1940, he was repatriated in February 1942, and became "M. Laboule," one of the chiefs of the resistance movement; on one occasion he was arrested by the Gestapo but released for want of evidence. Elected mayor of Arras in 1945 and secretary general of the Socialist Party in 1946, he served in Léon Blum's cabinet, and in 1949 was named French delegate to the Consultative Assembly of the Council of Europe, of which he was president in 1954–1955. On Jan. 31, 1956, he became premier of France in a left-of-center Republican Front cabinet and held office for over 16 months, until June 12, 1957, the longest tenure of any French premier to that date since World War II.

Guy Mollet

French Embassy Press and Information Division

MOLLHAUSEN, mûl'hou-zĕn, **(Heinrich) Balduin,** German traveler and writer: b. Bonn, Germany, Jan. 27, 1825; d. Berlin, May 28, 1905. The son of a Prussian army officer and engineer, Möllhausen went to the United States in 1849, and joined a scientific expedition headed by Duke Paul William of Württemberg to explore the Rocky Mountains. The expedition failed because of the hostility of the Indians, and Möllhausen experienced many hardships. He returned to America in 1853, however, and was chosen by the United States government to serve as topographer on an expedition surveying a course for a railroad to the Pacific coast. Back in Germany in 1854, he was given the post of custodian of the royal libraries in Potsdam. He visited America once more in 1857–1858, when he was sent out by the government to explore the Colorado River. He subsequently wrote some 45 full-length novels and travel books and many shorter stories, most of them dealing with American Indian and pioneer life. On the basis of these writings, he is frequently referred to as the German Cooper.

MOLLIEN, mô-lyăɴ', Comte **François Nicolas,** French statesman: b. Rouen, France, Feb. 28, 1758; d. Paris, 1850. Before the French Revolution, Mollien held various positions in the ministry of finance, including that of supervisor of the farmers-general of taxes. In 1786 he negotiated a commercial treaty with England, which abolished many restrictions on needed imports. Imprisoned for a short time during the revolution in 1794, he went to England, returning to the ministry of finance in 1799, after Napoleon's seizure of power. Recognizing his financial ability, Napoleon made him a councilor of state in 1804, and in 1806 minister of the treasury, in which capacity he assisted in reorganizing the banking system of France. During the Hundred Days he was again minister of the treasury, but although he was consulted on budgetary problems by succeeding rulers, he refused office after 1815.

MOLLISON, mŏl'ĭ-s'n, **James Allan,** British aviator: b. Lanark, Scotland, April 19, 1905; d. near London, England, Oct. 30, 1959. Commissioned in the Royal Air Force in 1923, he made many record flights, including one from Australia to England in 1931 (8 days, 19 hours, 28 minutes) and one from England to the Cape of Good Hope in 1932 (4 days, 17 hours, 5 minutes). He also made the first solo flight westward across the North Atlantic (1932) and the first England-South America flight (February 1933). In July 1933 he and his first wife, Amy Johnson, made the first England-United States crossing, and in 1934 they set an England-India record (22 hours). During World War II, Mollison was an airplane ferry pilot. He wrote two autobiographical volumes: *Death Cometh Soon or Late* (1932) and *Playboy of the Air* (1937).

MOLLN, mûln, town, Germany, in the State of Schleswig-Holstein, on the Elbe-Trave Canal, 16 miles south of Lübeck. An ancient place whose records go back to 1188, Mölln was chartered as a town in 1220, as a city in 1254, and from 1359 to 1683 was a possession of Lübeck. After World War II it was included in the German Federal Republic (West Germany). It manufactures chemicals, textiles, furniture, and mattresses, and processes food. Till Eulenspiegel, the legendary comic hero, is supposed to have died here. Pop. (1956) 13,716.

MOLLUSCA, mŏ-lŭs'kȧ, one of the great divisions or phyla of the animal kingdom, containing the oysters, clams, snails, slugs, squids, and octopus as well as the chitons and tusk shells. The class is characterized by having a mantle which secretes the shell and a radula or food-rasping organ. Both of these organs are peculiar to this group of animals. The body is primarily bilaterally symmetrical with the mouth and anus at the two ends of the body, the alimentary canal traversing it as an axis. However, the bilateral symmetry in the Gastropoda or snails is frequently obscured by a secondary change of a torsional nature. On the lower surface of the body there is developed a muscular organ, the foot, which is the organ of locomotion. This has been modified in the Cephalopoda to become the tentacles and the funnel, and in the Pelecypoda it has become a digging or plowing organ.

The outer surface of the body is encased by a pallium or mantle. This organ is attached dorsally and more or less open ventrally. The cavity between the mantle and the visceral mass is the mantle cavity in which the gills are developed. In the Pulmonata the gills disappear and a sac, the pulmonary sac, is developed in the body which is surrounded by blood vessels and functions as a lung. The outer surface of the mantle develops the shell which is present in most mollusks. This latter morphological structure exhibits an enormous number of modifications among all classes, orders, and families. Even below the family level down to the individual species, shell structure, color, and sculpture exhibit a nearly endless series of differences.

In many groups the posterior and dorsal surface of the foot bears a horny or calcareous plate, the operculum. When the animal retracts within the shell, the operculum closes the aperture. In several groups, the shell is reduced to a remnant, generally internal as in the slugs, or to a chitinized rod in the squids. It may be entirely lacking in the adults of some forms as in the nudibranchs, a group of marine mollusks.

In all mollusks, other than the bivalves, the mouth contains a remarkable structure, the radula. This consists of a band possessing a series of hooklike structures, the teeth, on its upper surface. These teeth exist in transverse rows and vary greatly in the different classes, orders, and families. The number and shape of the teeth play a very important part in the classification of the various groups, especially in the class Gastropoda. When feeding, the radula is extruded to the mouth opening and by means of strong muscles is pulled rapidly back and forth. It acts as a file in principle, rasping away particles of food, either animal or vegetable, depending upon the food requirements of the family or order to which the species may belong.

In a restricted group of the Gastropoda, the suborder Toxoglossa, the radula has become modified as a poison apparatus. The individual teeth have become elongate and spear-shaped and, in addition, associated with a poison gland. The teeth, as barbs, deliver the poison into the victim. Paralysis and death may soon follow. More than 20 deaths are known to have occurred among humans bitten by members of this group, all caused by species belonging to the family Conidae. The action of the poison is rapid, a death occurring in Queensland, Australia, only four and one half hours after the victim was bitten.

Mantle and Foot.—Typically the mantle is a paired structure, but in most groups the two halves unite in front and behind. This has its effect upon the shell, since, where the lobes are separate, there are two halves or valves to the shell, but where united there is but a single (univalve) shell. Sometimes this univalve shell is a straight cone, but, while conical, it is usually coiled in a spiral, a part of the body extending toward the apex of the cone. As the animal increases in size, the shell also increases in thickness and extent, the successive additions being usually recognizable on the external surface by lines of growth which run parallel to the free edge of the shell. When the edge of the mantle is provided with projections or lobes, these cause ridges or protuberances on the surface of the shell. When the mantle is colored (striped or spotted), the color pattern is reproduced in the shell, since pigment from the mantle is deposited along with the carbonate of lime. On the outside of the shell there is usually a thin organic cuticle and beneath this two layers of carbonate of lime. Sometimes the inner layer consists of thin lamellae parallel to the surface, the free edges of which produce diffraction spectra and thus give the inside of the shell an iridescent appearance—mother-of-pearl. (See PEARL.)

In the bivalve shell (see BIVALVES) an elastic hinge ligament connects the two valves and causes them to open. The valves are closed by muscles (the adductors), one or two in number, which extend across the body from valve to valve. In the univalves there is always a muscle attached to the inside on the axis of the shell, by the contraction of which the animal is retracted into the shell, the foot being the last part to withdraw. On the other hand, the shell is often greatly reduced and may become internal, as in the slugs and squids; or it may be entirely absent in the adult, as in the naked mollusks (nudibranchs) although it is formed in the young and then later lost.

Digestive Organs.—The alimentary canal is typically a straight tube, but in most forms it becomes convoluted to increase the amount of digestive surface. Not infrequently it is so flexed upon itself that the mouth and anus, instead of being at opposite ends of the body, are in close proximity to each other. Behind the gullet there is a large saclike stomach and closely connected with it are the ducts of the large digestive gland. The intestine is long and without enlargement.

Circulation.—The heart lies dorsal to the digestive tract enclosed in a special sac, the pericardium, which is to be regarded as the sole representative of the true body cavity or coelom. In the heart, two parts are always to be distinguished, a muscular ventricle which forces the blood through the arteries to all parts of the body, and usually two auricles which receive the blood as it comes from the gills and force it into the ventricle. The heart thus receives only oxidized blood. With the loss of the gill on one side of the body, the corresponding auricle disappears. When four gills are present, as in the genus *Nautilus,* there are four auricles.

Gills.—The gills are true ctenidia or branchial structures of various kinds. By means of cilia, water in the mantle cavity is kept in circulation. In many bivalves the gills function as marsupia, retaining the eggs until they are hatched. In addition the outer surface of the gills collects the fine food particles captured in mucus, and by means of cilia these captured food particles are led into food grooves and eventually are carried to the mouth.

Structure of the Shell.—The shell is composed usually of three layers. The outermost, the periostracum, is made up of organic material called conchiolin, which is allied to chitin. The middle layer is composed of prismatic cells of calcite, and the inner surface, the laminated or nacreous layer, is composed of aragonite. There is, however, in these two layers, a matrix of conchiolin, in which the mineral salts, mainly calcium carbonate, are impregnated.

Reproduction.—So far as known, all land pulmonates are hermaphroditic, each individual containing both sexes. However, mating generally takes place between two individuals, either as a reciprocal process or with one functioning as male and the other as a female. In most marine snails the sexes are separate. Eggs are produced either

From "American Seashells" by R. Tucker Abbott, published by D. Van Nostrand Company, Inc.

FIVE CLASSES OF MOLLUSKS: (a) *Gastropoda:* turnip whelk. (b) *Pelecypoda:* calico clam. (c) *Cephalopoda:* paper nautilus. (d) *Amphineura*: West Indian chiton. (e) *Scaphopoda:* Dall's Pacific tusk. The more recently established sixth class, *Monoplacophora*, is illustrated on the reverse side of this color plate.

Neopilina ewingi Clarke and Menzies (a), found off Peru, represents the sixth class of mollusks, *Monoplacophora*, established in 1957, x 2. Other mollusks illustrated here are found in the Western Atlantic area: (b), Juno's voluta (*Scaphella junonia* Shaw), x 3/4; (c), concentric disc clam (*Dosinia concentrica* Born), x 2/3; (d), pen shell (*Atrina seminuda* Lamark), x 1/4; (e), wentletrap shell (*Epitonium foliaceicostum* d'Orbigny), x 3; (f), western triton shell (*Cymatium occidentale* Clench and Turner), x 1/4; (g), crown shell (*Melongena corona* Gmelin), x 1 1/2; (h), angel wing (*Cyrtopleura costata* Linne), x 5/6. Enlargements or reductions are approximate.

in gelatinous masses or encapsulated within a chitinized case. In the latter, the free-swimming stage is generally passed within the capsule, the young emerging as young snails with the shell well developed. Many, if not most, of the marine bivalves give birth to their young at a very early stage, the two larval stages, the trochophore and veliger, developing in the water. These two larval or free-swimming stages have made possible a very wide dispersal, as they are subject to the movements of currents. Species with long larval life may be carried for hundreds of miles. It is for this reason that buoys, ships, and marine installations are soon covered with many kinds of mollusks as well as other organisms even when stationed far at sea. Most of the freshwater mussels have a parasitic stage, the young attaching themselves to the fins and gills of fish. Here for short or long periods of time, depending upon the species, the young derive sustenance from their fish host. At the end of their parasitic stage they drop from their host and begin to live as young bivalves in the mud and sand of lakes, ponds, and rivers.

Habits.—The mollusks are among the most adaptive of all animal groups. They are found in the great ocean deeps, in depths of over 30,000 feet (bivalves), and are known to occur up to 18,000 feet on mountain ranges (land gastropods), a vertical range of more than 9 miles. They have succeeded in occupying nearly every type of environment other than the air, and even here they have been partially successful, depending in part upon wind-blown debris to carry their eggs and even the adults over considerable territory. Their one limiting factor is lime; from this they build their shells and as there are few regions completely devoid of lime, there are few areas completely devoid of mollusks.

Most land shells are secretive in habit, hiding under leaves, boards, or other debris, particularly during dry periods. They are mainly active at night when most of their feeding is done. In many tropical areas several groups of land shells live in trees, feeding mainly upon lichens which live on the bark of the trees. With few exceptions, these tree snails are highly colored and certain of them, like the genus *Polymita* of eastern Cuba, are the most highly colored snails that exist, exceeding even the vivid coloration developed by many marine snails. Other land snails live only on limestone rocks and these, like the tree snails, feed on lichens.

Freshwater mollusks have many types of habitat, most preferring the quiet water among reeds and other aquatic plants. Others prefer the swift water of shoals and rapids, living on rocks and stones and feeding upon the algae.

Marine snails accept a very wide variety of habitats, living on and under rocks or in and around coral reefs. Others, notably the bivalves, prefer sandy and muddy bottoms where they lie buried. The depth in which they live is generally governed by the extent to which they can extend their siphons. Many others bore or drill into rocks, heavy clay, and wood. A few of the marine mollusks, particularly certain Cephalopods, are pelagic, living in the open sea hundreds of miles from any shore line. Others are to be found in the depths of the ocean, a few even at the bottom of the great deeps. The ecological area which produces the largest number of mollusks in any one region is that which extends from near low water to depths of about 50 fathoms, as this situation furnishes the optimum in protection and food. In general, tropical areas are the richest in number of species, and in these warm waters the most colorful species are also found. In colder waters, though the number of species is not so great, individuals of a few species may exist in great abundance. Most mollusks are plant feeders, living either upon live vegetation or upon decaying plant tissue. A few groups are carnivorous and feed mainly on other mollusks.

Economic Importance.—Mollusks play a very important part in the economy of man. As beneficial organisms they supply considerable food along most shore lines of the world. In addition they are a prime factor as food for many of the important food fish. Others, such as the pearl oyster, supply us with pearls and shells for various types of jewelry. Many species of fresh-water mussels are the main source of nacre for the pearl button industry. On the other hand, a few groups, like the shipworms (family Teredinidae), are among man's most destructive enemies. These are highly specialized marine clams which have become greatly modified for boring into wood, including wharf pilings and other marine structures, as well as rope and even marine cables. The financial loss from damage done to such structures and to wooden boats and vessels far exceeds the financial gain from all other beneficially-important mollusks.

Several fresh-water species and even a few land species are involved as secondary hosts for trematode worms, the blood and liver flukes which cause schistosomiasis, one of the dreaded diseases, of the tropics and some temperate regions. In the life cycle of these trematodes, usually a single, or at most only a few, species of fresh-water snails act as secondary hosts, the primary host being some vertebrate. Larvae of these parasites, leaving the snail, enter the skin and then the blood system of their primary host. Any trematode that affects mammals can usually affect man, but if the secondary host, the snail, is eliminated from a region the disease is under control.

Classification.—The Mollusca are divided into six classes based upon the modification of the foot or locomotor organ as well as the diversification of other morphological structures.

Class Monoplacophora. Deep sea mollusks having a cap-shaped shell with many structures of the soft anatomy segmented with five or more pairs of gills, nephridia, and muscles.

Class Amphineura. Chitons or coat-of-mail shells. All members of this class are marine.

1. Order Polyplacophora. This order contains most of the existing species. The shell is composed of eight plates which are covered or held together by a thick, fleshy portion of the mantle, the girdle.
2. Order Aplacophora. These are small wormlike animals without shells. The foot is reduced or lacking, and there are calcareous spicules imbedded in the mantle. They live mainly in deep water.

Class Scaphopoda. Tusk shells. All members of this class are marine. The shell and mantle together form a slightly curved tube which is open at both ends.

Class Gastropoda. Snails and slugs. Members of this class occur on land, in fresh water, and in all seas.

1. Order Prosobranchia. Nearly all members of this order are operculate. They exist on land, in fresh water, and in all seas. Most of the marine snails belong to this order.
2. Order Opisthobranchia. These are nonoperculate snails, usually without a shell or with the shell greatly reduced. All are marine.
3. Order Pulmonata. Members of this order are nonoperculate, and breathe air by means of a pulmonary sac. They constitute most of the land snails and many of the fresh-water groups.

Class Pelecypoda. Bivalves. Members of this class occur in fresh water and in all oceans.

1. Order Taxodonta. The most primitive of the bivalves, containing a series of similar teeth and sockets in each valve.

2. Order Anisomyaria. In this order the anterior adductor muscle is much reduced or wanting; the posterior adductor muscle is enlarged, and is developed near the center of the shell.

3. Order Eulamellibranchia. Most of the bivalves belong to this important order. Both adductor muscles are present and generally about the same size. The hinge plate contains but few teeth, and these may be massive or almost lacking, depending upon the group.

Class Cephalopoda. Squids and octopus. All members of this class are marine.

1. Order Dibranchia. This is by far the larger order, containing the squids, octopus, cuttlefish, and Argonauta.

2. Order Tetrabranchia. This order contains only *Nautilus* as a recent genus.

See also Ammonites; Cephalopod; Clam; Nautiloidea; Oysters; Shell.

Bibliography.—Cooke, A. K., "Molluscs," *The Cambridge Natural History*, vol. 3 (London 1895); Oldroyd, Ida S., *The Marine Shells of the West Coast of North America*, 2 vols., Stanford University Publications (Stanford 1924–27); Pilsbry, H. A., *Land Mollusca of North America*, 2 vols., The Academy of Natural Sciences (Philadelphia 1939–48); Clench, W. J., *Johnsonia, Monographs of Western Atlantic Marine Mollusks*, 2 vols. (Cambridge, Mass., 1941–53); Abbott, R. T., *American Seashells* (New York 1954); Morton, J. E., *Molluscs: An Introduction to Their Form and Functions* (New York 1960); Buchsbaum, Ralph, and Milne, Lorus J., *The Lower Animals: Living Invertebrates of the World* (New York 1960); Carter, G. S., *General Zoology of the Invertebrates*, 4th ed. (New York 1961).

William J. Clench,
Curator of Mollusks, Museum of Comparative Zoology, Harvard University.

MOLLWITZ, môl'vĭts (Pol. Malujowice), village, Poland, in Opole Province, Lower Silesia, 5 miles west of Brzeg (Brieg). Mollwitz was the scene of a famous battle (April 10, 1741) during the War of the Austrian Succession (see Succession Wars), in which Frederick II (the Great) had his first command. Frederick's cavalry was put to flight by the Austrian infantry, but Field Marshal Kurt Christoph von Schwerin finally defeated the Austrians under Field Marshal Wilhelm Reinhard von Neipperg in the battle.

MOLLY MAGUIRES, mŏl'ĭ mȧ-gwīrz', an Irish secret society formed in 1843 at Farney, County Monaghan, to intimidate bailiffs or process servers distraining for rent or impounding the cattle of tenants who were unable or unwilling to pay. In the anthracite coal-mining region of Pennsylvania in the 1850's, an inner group of the Ancient Order of Hibernians set up a similar society called by the same name, which became active on a large scale about 1865. The members, disguised in "Molly Maguire" or women's dresses, sought to intimidate officials and others, and even resorted to murder. In 1874 the Pinkerton detectives were called in by the president of the Philadelphia Coal and Iron Company to cope with the situation, and one of the detectives, James McParlan, undertook to track the murderers. Posing as a criminal, he joined the organization and became secretary of his division. After the conviction of one murderer, McParlan was under suspicion by the group, and his life was in danger. When he withdrew, his evidence served to hang the murderers, and led to the disbanding of the society in 1877.

Consult Broehl, Wayne G., Jr., *The Molly Maguires* (Cambridge, Mass., 1964).

MOLLY PITCHER. See Pitcher, Molly.

MOLNAR, môl'när, **Antal,** Hungarian musician and critic: b. Budapest, Hungary, Jan. 7, 1890. His compositions include church music, of which *Missa brevis* won the Haynald Prize in 1910; choral works; works for orchestra, piano, and organ; chamber music; and settings for songs. He played viola with various Hungarian quartets, and was teacher of composition, musical history, and solfeggio at the Municipal School of Music in Budapest (1912–1918) and at the Academy of Music from 1919. From 1933 to 1940 he also edited *Népszerü Zenefüzetek* (*Popular Musical Pamphlets*) to which many distinguished musicians contributed. As a critic he did much to further the understanding of the work of Béla Bartók, Zoltán Kodály, and other modern composers.

MOLNAR, Ferenc (originally Neumann), Hungarian playwright and novelist: b. Budapest, Hungary, Jan. 12, 1878; d. New York, N. Y., April 1, 1952. He studied law in Budapest and Geneva, became a journalist on a Budapest newspaper, and soon began to publish fiction, notably the novel *A Pál-uccai fiuk* (1907; Eng. tr., *The Paul Street Boys,* 1927). With the production of *Az ördög* (1907; Eng. tr., *The Devil,* 1908), his reputation as a playwright was established; his comedies, at once sophisticated and sentimental, continued to charm international audiences for a generation. *Liliom,* the most genuine of his plays, was presented in Budapest in 1909, and later scored a great success in the United States (1921) when Eva Le Gallienne and Joseph Schildkraut took the leading parts. It was followed by *A testör* (1910; Eng. tr., *The Guardsman*), in the New York production (1924) of which Alfred Lunt and Lynn Fontanne acted together for the first time.

During the first two years of World War I, Molnar served as a war correspondent with the Austro-German forces on the Russian front, and wrote an account of his experiences, *Haditudósitó naplója* (*A War Correspondent's Diary,* 1916). American productions of his postwar plays included *The Play's the Thing* (1927), in which Lunt and Fontanne also appeared; *The Swan* (1929); and *The Good Fairy* (1932). In 1940 he took up permanent residence in New York City, publishing his first novel with an American setting, *Farewell My Heart,* in 1945. The musical comedy *Carousel* was adapted from *Liliom* in the latter year, and *Make a Wish* from *The Good Fairy* in 1951. *Companion in Exile,* an autobiographical volume, appeared in 1950.

MOLOCH, mō'lŏk, or **MOLECH,** mō'lĕk, a pagan fire god called in the Old Testament an idol of the Ammonites, identified with the god of the Canaanites, who introduced his worship into Judah and Israel. His image was of bronze or iron, with a hollow human body, the head of a calf, and extended arms. A fire was heated in the lower part, and children were placed as sacrificial offerings in the arms, while the people danced to flutes and timbrels. Some authorities maintain that the children of the Israelites were not burned alive but sacrificed, and their bodies burned. The valley of Hinnom, or Tophet, near Jerusalem, where sacrifices of children took place, was later called Gehenna, a place of abomination.

In Leviticus 20:2-5, the Lord warns Moses against those who give their seed to Molech, and in I Kings 11:7-13, He rebukes Solomon for building a temple to Molech. Amos, Jeremiah, and Ezekiel all condemn Molech worship. In the New Testament the people are reminded (Acts

7:43) of the days when their ancestors sacrificed to Moloch.

MOLOCH or **THORNY DEVIL,** a small, harmless Australian desert lizard (*Moloch horridus*) of the family Agamidae. It is five to seven inches long, is broad and flat, and its skin is covered with irregular plates bearing thorny pointed tubercles, spines, and prickles, which are especially well developed behind the head. It lives largely on ants, which it catches on its long glutinous tongue. Although it resembles the American horned toad in its form, the moloch is brighter in color (yellowish, with brown blotches), and belongs to a different family of lizards. See also HORNED TOAD.

MOLODECHNO, mŭ-lŭ-dyĕch′nŭ, oblast, USSR, in the Belorussian SSR, just east of the Lithuanian SSR. This territory, transferred from Russia to Poland after World War I, retaken by Russia in 1939, and occupied by Germany (1941–1944), was formerly known as Vileika Oblast. It is a heavily forested region, drained by the Viliya River, and its many lakes are stocked with fish. Flax and dairy products are produced in the north, and grains and fruit in the south. The capital is the city of Molodechno, a railroad center manufacturing musical instruments, flour, and fruit and vegetable products. Pop. of oblast (1959 official est.) 810,000; of city (1931) 5,964.

MOLOKAI, mō-lô-kä′ê, island, Hawaii, located in the center of the island group and included in Maui County. This mountainous island, 259 square miles in area, is some 37 miles long and 7 to 10 miles wide. Kamakou (4,958 feet) is its highest peak. To the north, closed off from the rest of the island, is Kalaupapa, with its celebrated leper colony, founded in 1860. The colony, now a government settlement, is administered by Kalawao County, officially a district (14 miles square) subordinate to Maui County. Cattle ranches and pineapple plantations are located on the island, and there is a forest reserve, with a government forestry camp and reforestation project, and a branch of the Maui County Free Library. Pop. (1961) 5,023. See also DAMIEN DE VEUSTER, JOSEPH; DUTTON, IRA BARNES.

MOLOTOV, mô′lŭ-tôf, **Vyacheslav Mikhailovich** (original surname SKRYABIN), Russian statesman: b. Kukarka, Vyatka Province, Russia (now Sovetsk, Kirov Oblast, RSFSR, USSR), March 9, 1890. One of the leading figures in the Soviet Union from the early days of the Communist regime, Molotov began his political activity as a student in Kazan during the revolution of 1905, and joined the Bolsheviks in 1906. Three years later he was arrested and exiled to the north of Russia for a two-year term. On his release, he went to St. Petersburg (now Leningrad), where he enrolled in 1911 in the Polytechnic Institute. In 1912 he joined Joseph Stalin in founding the party newspaper *Pravda.* Exiled to Siberia in 1915, he escaped a year later and helped to plan the 1917 revolution, as a member of the Petrograd Military Revolutionary Committee; and when the Bolsheviks seized power in November 1917, he became a member of the executive committee of the Petrograd Soviet.

After the revolution, he rose rapidly in party ranks, becoming chairman of the Council of People's Commissars, equivalent to premier, in 1930. He held this office all through the difficult period of the collectivization of agriculture, the Trotskyite-Bukharinite trials, and the threat of war, until Stalin took it over in the spring of 1941, when Molotov became deputy prime minister. In 1939 he had been appointed foreign commissar (minister), and as such negotiated the nonaggression pact with Germany in August 1939. Later, after the Nazi invasion of the USSR, he attended the Allied conferences at Teheran, Yalta, and Potsdam, and the San Francisco Conference which organized the United Nations; he headed the Soviet delegation to the United Nations until 1949.

Molotov was succeeded as foreign minister by Andrei Y. Vyshinsky in 1949, but retained the post of deputy prime minister under Stalin; after the latter's death in 1953, he became foreign minister once more. He represented the USSR at the Berlin Conference of Big Four foreign ministers early in 1954, and at the Geneva Conference on Far Eastern questions later the same year. He also was a member of the Soviet delegation at the Geneva Conference of Big Four heads of state in 1955. Throughout this period he adhered to the aggressive anti-Western policy of Russia which aggravated the difficulties of the postwar years. In June 1956, allegedly at his own request, Molotov resigned as foreign minister, and in November was made minister of state control—a post comparable to that of the United States comptroller general. Bitter conflict between Molotov and Nikita S. Khrushchev (then first secretary of the Central Committee) came to a head in June 1957, and in July Khrushchev announced Molotov's dismissal from his posts as deputy prime minister and minister of state control and his expulsion from the Central Committee and the Presidium. On August 31 Molotov was appointed Soviet ambassador to the Mongolian People's Republic—a benign form of Soviet political banishment.

See also WORLD WAR II—*2. Between World Wars* (Nazi-Soviet Pact).

Consult Bromage, Bernard, *Molotov: The Story of an Era* (London 1956).

MOLTING, mōlt′ĭng, the shedding and replacement of skin or feathers by an animal. In vertebrates the molt merely serves to replace the upper layer of skin or feathers by a new covering.

Adult amphibians molt about once a month. Only the superficial layer of epidermal cells is shed, and the process takes but a few hours. The shed skin is frequently eaten by the molted animal. A molt can be elicited by the injection of the thyroid hormone, and if the thyroid gland is removed, molting ceases. The release of the thyroid hormone, in turn, is triggered by a hormone (the thyrotropic hormone) from the anterior pituitary gland.

The molt of reptiles is similar to that of amphibians. A curious feature of the molt of the rattlesnake is that some of the skin is retained by a long knob made of fused caudal vertebrae and thus becomes a section of the rattle.

Nearly all birds shed and replace their feathers during the annual molt, which usually takes place in the late summer after nesting. Some birds also have a second molt in the spring before the beginning of the breeding season. With each molt the coloring of the plumage may change, so that the bird may alternate between a summer and a winter coloring, or gradually develop the adult plumage through a series of juvenile molts. The molt of a bird takes at least several weeks, during which the bird goes into partial retirement. The feathers are dropped out a few at a time, in a definite order, so that the bird appears ragged. Bird molting is also controlled by the thyrotropic and thyroid hormones.

Arthropods must molt if they are to grow, since their rigid cuticle serves as both a covering and a skeleton. Before the molt, the animal stops feeding and withdraws to a quiet place. The molt begins when the living, cellular epidermis draws back from the overlying cuticle. The epidermis immediately begins to elaborate a new cuticle. Meanwhile the inner layers of the old cuticle are being digested by a molting fluid which is secreted from the epidermal cells into the space separating the old and the new cuticles. Finally the molting fluid is reabsorbed by the epidermis, bringing many of the digested constituents of the old cuticle back into the animal, and the remainder of the old cuticle is split along predetermined sutures and is cast off.

The new cuticle which is now revealed is still soft and pliant. The animal swallows air or water, which increases its size and stretches out the new cuticle. Within a few hours the new cuticle is hardened or tanned by chemicals secreted by the epidermal cells.

Arthropods molt all of the cuticular structures, whether on the surface or within the body. In crustaceans the molt includes the lining of the esophagus and the rectum. Insects, in addition, shed the lining of the air tubes or trachea.

Each molt may bring changes in the animal's body form. In insects the intervals between molts are called stages, and the form assumed by the insect during a particular stage is called an instar.

The molting of arthropods is also under a two-step endocrine control. The molt of a crustacean is inhibited by a hormone released by the X-organ located in the eyestalks. The withdrawal of this hormone allows a second endocrine organ, the Y-organ of the thorax, to secrete a hormone which reacts with the tissues to cause the molt.

The molt of insects is started by a hormone secreted from a group of specialized cells in the brain. This brain hormone triggers the release of a hormone by the prothoracic glands, and it is this second hormone which initiates the molt.

W. G. Van der Kloot,
Associate Professor of Zoology, Cornell University.

MOLTKE, mŏlt'kĕ, Count **Helmuth (Karl Bernhard) von,** Prussian soldier: b. Parchim, Mecklenburg-Schwerin (north Germany), Oct. 26, 1800; d. Berlin, April 24, 1891. Moltke was one of the great military strategists of the 19th century who exercised a profound influence on the growth and character of the Prussian army. He grew up on Danish soil. In 1805 his father moved to Lübeck, in Schleswig-Holstein, then ruled by the Danish king. Although the Moltke family was reduced to poverty during the Napoleonic wars, Helmuth was able to graduate from the Royal Military Academy in 1818. After several years of service in the Danish army, he transferred in 1822 to the Prussian forces. From 1836 to 1839 he served as military adviser to Mahmud II, sultan of the Ottoman Empire; but his advice was disregarded in the campaign against Ibrahim Pasha of Egypt, and his patron Mahmud II having died, he returned to Berlin, where he was assigned to the general staff. After rising through the various army grades, he was placed at the head of the general staff of the army in 1857, holding this post until 1888. His labors in reorganizing the Prussian army were of immense value to Prussia and Germany, and exerted an enormous effect on the general history of Europe. Moltke's genius for military operations was largely responsible for the defeat of Denmark in 1864, and Prussia's victory in the Austrian War (1866) can likewise be attributed to him. Then followed the Franco-Prussian War (1870–1871), for which Moltke was entirely prepared, having foreseen for some years what was likely to happen, and having prepared in advance for a campaign against France. The success of the operations was in large measure a personal triumph for Moltke, and with the capitulation of Metz he was raised to the rank of count in 1870. Following his return to Berlin in 1871 he was created field marshal and appointed for life a member of the Prussian upper house.

Consult Whitton, Frederick Ernest, *Moltke* (New York 1921).

MOLUCCAS, mō-lŭk'ăz, island group, Indonesia, formerly known as the Spice Islands and now constituting a province, Maluku, with the capital at Ambon. They comprise the eastern part of the Malay Archipelago, lying in the Molucca, Banda, Ceram (Seram), and Arafura seas between Celebes (Sulawesi) and Netherlands New Guinea (Irian). The North Moluccas include the islands of Morotai, Halmahera (the largest), Ternate, Tidore, and Makian, and the island groups of Batjan, Ovi, and Sula; the South Moluccas include the islands of Buru, Ceram, and Ambon (Amboina), the island groups of Banda, Kai, Aru, Tanimbar, Babar, and Damar, and the islands of Kisar and Wetar. The area of the islands is 33,315 square miles, and the population (1955 est.), 377,000. The inhabitants (predominantly Muslims) are mainly Javanese and other Malayan groups along the shores; inland they are transition types between Malayan, Melanesian, and Papuan.

Many of the islands, including the larger ones (Halmahera, Ceram, and Buru), are volcanic and mountainous; most of the smaller ones are of coral and are generally low. They produce spices such as nutmeg, mace, and cloves, along with copra, rice, and sago, and the larger islands export rare and valuable timber. Fishing is important. The climate is characterized by high temperatures and humidity, low winds, and heavy rains. There is a wealth of flora and fauna, including rare animals, birds, and butterflies.

Historically, civilization in the Malay Peninsula can be traced back to remote antiquity. In the Middle Ages, after spices had been introduced into Europe, the Muslims blocked the path of Europeans by land, but the Portuguese sailed around Africa and established a trading center at Ternate early in the 16th century. Thenceforward competition for the islands, and for their valuable spices, was strong. The Spaniards wrested control from the Portuguese in 1580, but were forced to yield to the Dutch and the Dutch East India Company in the 17th century. The Dutch gradually extended their influence, interrupted by brief periods of British control and by Japanese occupation of the islands in World War II. After the war the Moluccas became part of the newly formed republic of Indonesia, although the southern islands, led by Ambon, staged a revolt briefly in 1950.

MOLYBDENITE, mô-lĭb'dê-nīt; mŏl-ĭb-dē'nīt, the more important of the two commercially mined minerals containing molybdenum (q.v.), the other being wulfenite. Molybdenite corresponds chemically to molybdenum disulphide, and contains 60 per cent molybdenum and 40 per cent sulphur. The United States is the chief source of molybdenite, with Colorado the leading state. Other producing states are Utah, Arizona, New Mexico, California, and Nevada. Foreign sources include Canada, Chile, Korea, Japan, Mexico, and Norway.

Molybdenite is a soft, shiny, greasy, bluish mineral, occurring in flakes closely resembling graphite. It is produced at mines chiefly operated for molybdenum, where the molybdenite content of the raw ore is 0.4 to 3.3 per cent, and as a by-product of mines operated mainly for copper or tungsten, where the molybdenite content ranges from 0.01 to 0.08 per cent. A concentrate is produced in either case, which when shipped contains 39 to 91 per cent molybdenite, 90 per cent being considered a standard grade for price quotations. Shipments of concentrates (in pounds of contained metal) were about 92 million in 1966; they were valued at over $140 million.

The desired mineral is separated from gangue during concentration by a fine grinding and flotation employing a reagent containing pine oils, hydrocarbons, and a synthetic wetting agent. The concentrate is roasted in gas-fired furnaces to form molybdenum oxide. This oxide may be used in the steel industry without additions. Some oxide is mixed with lime to form calcium molybdate. Ferromolybdenum is prepared from the oxide by a thermite reaction. Molybdenum oxide is also the starting material for producing pure molybdenum metal. A relatively small amount of molybdenite is added directly to steel when both molybdenum and sulphur are desired.

ALVIN S. COHAN,
Scientific Design Company, Inc.

MOLYBDENUM, mô-lĭb'dê-nŭm; mŏl-ĭb-dē'nŭm, one of the most important of the refractory metals, symbol Mo, first identified as an element by Karl Wilhelm Scheele in 1778 when he differentiated molybdenite, the molybdenum sulphide mineral, from other sulphide minerals. In 1790, Peter Jacob Hjelm isolated the element by reducing molybdic oxide with carbon. Although the metal is as abundant in the earth's crust as lead, the only commercially important sources of molybdenum are molybdenite, MoS_2 and wulfenite, $PbMoO_4$ (qq.v.).

Chemical and Physical Properties.—This mechanically strong element with atomic number 42 has a melting point of 2625° C. (4757° F.), almost twice that of steel. This melting point is exceeded by only four other elements—tantalum, rhenium, tungsten, and carbon. Molybdenum has an atomic weight of 95.95 and a body-centered cubic crystal structure. With a density of 10.2 grams per cubic centimeter, molybdenum is only slightly more than half as heavy as tungsten, but is heavier than copper or iron. It has a thermal conductivity greater than that of iron or nickel and less than half that of copper. Its electrical conductivity, while one third that of copper, is higher than that of nickel, platinum, iron, and mercury.

In general, the strength and creep resistance of molybdenum and molybdenum-base alloys are higher at temperatures above 1600° F. than those of the iron-, nickel-, and cobalt-base alloys. However, molybdenum loses weight rapidly when heated above a red heat in air or any oxidizing atmosphere. Molybdenum oxide is formed, and being extremely volatile, burns off. Some progress has been made in the development of surface coatings that would prevent the oxidation of molybdenum at elevated temperatures.

Preparation.—Pure molybdenum metal is produced in two ways. Molybdic oxide can be reduced with hydrogen to form a high-purity metal powder, which is then compacted into bars and sintered by an electric current in a hydrogen atmosphere. In the other method, partially sintered bars are used as electrodes in a consumable electrode-arc melting furnace. Under vacuum, the electrode is melted into an ingot in a water-cooled copper mold.

The resulting sintered bar or melted ingot can be forged and worked into sheet, rod, wire, and tubing. Molybdenum is worked at elevated temperatures, but because of the high recrystallization temperature of the metal, and the fact that all operations are carried out below the recrystallization temperature, the metal is technically "cold worked." As the amount of deformation increases, the recrystallization temperature is lowered, and the working operations are performed at lower temperatures as the reduction in area progresses.

Alloys and Compounds.—Molybdenum is used in the production of alloy steels because it contributes to hardenability while decreasing the possibility of temper brittleness. It is economical to use and is not lost by oxidation in melting or pouring. In stainless steels containing 18 per cent chromium and 8 per cent nickel, the addition of 2 to 3 per cent molybdenum improves corrosion resistance, especially to sulphuric acid and salt water. In low- and high-alloy steels, molybdenum increases the strength and creep resistance at elevated temperatures. In steel castings, molybdenum imparts the same effects as in wrought steels. Molybdenum in gray cast iron increases strength and toughness, and produces uniformity when used in amounts up to 1 per cent. In white-iron castings, 1 per cent molybdenum improves toughness, while up to 8 per cent improves resistance to wear, corrosion, and softening at high temperatures.

Various nonferrous alloys having unusually high strength at elevated temperatures contain molybdenum. These alloys include wrought alloys of iron-chromium-nickel containing up to 6 per cent molybdenum, wrought cobalt-nickel-chromium-iron alloys containing up to 10 per cent molybdenum, wrought nickel-base alloys containing up to 10 per cent molybdenum, cast nickel-base alloys containing up to 28 per cent molybdenum, and cast cobalt-base alloys with up to 6 per cent molybdenum.

Molybdenum forms two oxides, MoO_2 and MoO_3. Only the trioxide MoO_3 is stable. Molybdenum forms compounds with all of the halogens, fluorine, chlorine, bromine, and iodine. Nitrides of molybdenum are not stable. Molybdenum reacts with carbon to form Mo_2C or MoC. Silicides are also formed; the monosilicide (MoSi) and the disilicide ($MoSi_2$) are resistant to oxidation at high temperatures. They are hard and brittle and have a metallic luster. Molybdenum also forms borides, such as Mo_3B_4, by direct combination. The most important sulphide formed is the disulfide, MoS_2, which corresponds to the mineral molybdenite. Pure molybdenum disulphide is a soft black solid with a hexagonal or triagonal structure.

Uses.—Of the molybdenum consumed in the United States (68 million pounds in 1965), the greatest quantity is used in the production of ferrous alloys. The molybdenum was added as molybdic oxide without additions, or made into briquettes, with pitch as a binder, as calcium molybdate or as ferromolybdenum.

Pure molybdenum is widely used in electronic tubes for anodes, grids, and to facilitate glass to metal tube seals. Molybdenum wire is used for heating elements in high-temperature resistance furnaces. These heating elements must be operated in a protective atmosphere because of the oxidation of molybdenum. The metal also is used for electrical contacts with silver or copper made by powder metallurgy, and for mercury-switch electrodes. The shanks of cutting tools and some types of gyroscope rotor assemblies that require acceleration to operating speeds in minimum time use molybdenum shafts to reduce vibration and twist. Molybdenum has been used successfully for electrodes in glass melting furnaces where its high melting point, strength, and good electrical conductivity are definite advantages.

Among the nonmetallic uses, molybdenum disulphide is an effective lubricant over a wide range of temperatures and under very high pressures. In the chemical industry, molybdenum compounds are used as pigment colors for printing inks, lacquers, and paints. Molybdenum is used as a catalyst, particularly in the petroleum industry. It is also used in some fertilizers.

ALVIN S. COHAN,
Scientific Design Company, Inc.

Consult Northcott, Leslie, *Molybdenum* (New York 1956); Harwood, Julius, *Metal Molybdenum* (Metals Park, Ohio, 1958); DuMond, Theodore, *Fabrication of Molybdenum* (Metals Park, Ohio, 1959); Quarrell, A. G., *Niobium, Tantalum, Molybdenum, and Tungsten* (New York 1961).

MOMBASA, mŏm-bä'sȧ, city, Kenya, capital of the Coast Province, 150 miles north of Zanzibar. Covering more than 21 square miles, it lies partly on Mombasa Island but includes 15.7 square miles on the mainland. Access to the island, which is of coral rock, about three miles long and two miles wide, is by ferries, the Nyali Bridge, and the Makupa Causeway (carrying a road, railroad, and pipeline).

As a seaport, Mombasa serves not only Kenya but also Uganda and northern Tanganyika, to both of which it is connected by rail; it handles over 7 million tons of shipping a year. Mombasa Island is separated from the mainland by Kilindini Harbor on the west, one of Africa's finest harbors, accommodating deep-draft ships, and by Mombasa Old Harbor on the east, which handles the dhows and other native craft engaged in the coastal trade that arrive and depart between December and April, the monsoon season. The anchorage connects with Port Reitz, a stretch of water three miles long by three quarters of a mile wide, on the shores of which is the airport, eight miles from Kilindini. The main exports are coffee, cotton, tea, sisal, pyrethrum, tin, soda, hides and skins, and ivory. The city's leading industries include coffee curing; marine and general engineering; a lime works; cement, glass, and soap factories; and a modern brewery.

The European section of Mombasa centers about the Kilindini and Fort Jesus roads, which cross the island. The congested Old Town, in the eastern part of the island, is Arab. Fort Jesus, built by the Arabs in 1593–1595, later a prison, was vacated in 1958 to become a historical museum. There are various mosques and temples and a Roman Catholic and an Anglican cathedral. The Institute of Muslim Education is located here, and there is a European hospital as well as clinics for the Asians, Africans, and Arabs.

Mombasa, in its long and varied history, which goes back to the pre-Christian era, has been at various times under Arab, Portuguese, and British control. In 1887 it became headquarters of the British East Africa Company, and it was capital of the East African Protectorate from 1895, when the British government took over the company's holdings, until 1907, when Nairobi replaced it. During World War II, Mombasa was a British base and naval station. A substantial percentage of the city's inhabitants are of Indian, Goan, or Arab origin. Pop. (1961) 179,575.

RICHARD E. WEBB,
Director, Reference and Library Division, British Information Services, New York, N.Y.

MOMENT, mō'mĕnt, in mechanics, the tendency, or the measurement of the tendency, of a dynamical quantity to produce motion, especially about a point or axis. For *moment of force,* see MECHANICS—*Moments or Torque.* For *moment of inertia,* see INERTIA; MECHANICS—*Energy;* MOLECULAR THEORY—*Structure of Molecules* (Experimental Molecular Structure). For *moment of momentum,* or *angular momentum,* see MOMENTUM.

By extension, the word is used in such combinations as *moment of a velocity* and *moment of an acceleration.* Such phrases correspond to nothing truly dynamic, unless we regard velocity as meaning the momentum of unit mass and acceleration as the rate of change of that momentum.

MOMENTUM, mô-mĕn'tŭm, in physics, that property possessed by an object in motion by which it tends to remain in motion as a function of its inertia (q.v.). However, while inertia is dependent only on the object's mass, momentum is equal to the product of mass and velocity and hence increases directly as either is increased or decreases as either is diminished. Where *linear momentum* (resulting from the motion of an object in a straight line) is indicated by p, the object's mass by m, and its velocity by v, then $p = mv$. In the case of *angular momentum* (resulting from the rotary motion of an object around a fixed point), where I represents the moment of inertia and ω the angular velocity of the object, the moment of momentum H is given by $H = I\omega$.

The impact (q.v.) with which a moving object strikes another object is thus not alone a function of how much mass is possessed by either or both, but how fast each is traveling. Similarly, the time required to bring a moving object to a standstill will depend both on its mass and its speed of motion. Subjected to a force *impulse* (defined as the product of the force F or torque L acting and the time t through which it acts) an object acquires an acceleration, a velocity, and through the velocity and the mass in motion it acquires momentum. These successive incremental changes (Δ) are given by $Ft = m\Delta v = \Delta p$, and $Lt = I\Delta\omega = \Delta H$. Thus impulse and angular impulse are equivalent to momentum and moment of momentum, respectively. In the various equations above, p, v, H, ω, F, and L are vector quantities which possess both a direction of action as well as a magnitude value.

FERGUS J. WOOD,
Science Editor, "The Encyclopedia Americana."

MOMMSEN, mŏm′zĕn, **Theodor,** German classical scholar and historian: b. Garding, Schleswig, Germany, Nov. 30, 1817; d. Charlottenburg, Nov. 1, 1903. He studied philology and jurisprudence at Kiel, and from 1844 to 1847 pursued archaeological studies in Italy and France. In 1848 he became professor of law at Leipzig University but, because of his liberal views during the revolutionary movement of 1848–1849, he had to resign in 1850. He was professor of law at the universities of Zurich (1852–1854) and Breslau (1854–1858), then professor of ancient history at Berlin until his death. In political life he served as a Liberal member of the Prussian House of Representatives (1873–1882). About this activity he wrote in his last will: "I have never had, nor did I aspire to, a political position and political influence." Neither in his native Germany, nor elsewhere, has there lived a scholar whose achievements in the fields of ancient Roman legal and political institutions, history and historiography, language, epigraphical and legal monuments, numismatics, and all phenomena of public life could compare with the achievements of Mommsen, working incessantly to the last day of his long life.

Mommsen's work was prodigious in quantity; there are many more than 1,000 entries in the bibliography of his writings by Zangemeister and Jacobs (see *Bibliography*), totaling 8,000 folio, 2,000 quarto, and 20,000 octavo pages. However, it is not the unbelievably enormous quantity of his writings that astonish, but rather the universality and ingeniousness of his highly scholarly literary productions, mostly pioneer works, which to this day offer starting points for further research. The extension of the domains of classical antiquity, in which he was the leading master, is immense; and the fact that later writers succeeded in supplementing or correcting some of his opinions or doctrines in no way diminishes his stature. His fanatical devotion to scientific research, his profound knowledge of all auxiliary sciences in historical studies, and the understanding of ancient texts and monuments were unique. In 1902 he received the Nobel Prize in literature.

Only a few of Mommsen's works can be mentioned here. His *Römische Geschichte* (3 vols., 1854–56, translated into English by William P. Dickson as *History of Rome,* 4 vols., 1862–75, new ed. (n.d., ?1911); a translation by Dero A. Saunders and John H. Collins, *History of Rome: An Account of Events and Persons from the Conquest of Carthage to the End of the Republic* (New York 1958) covers only material in the third volume of the original German edition; a fourth volume (to deal with Caesar's dictatorship and death) was never finished, but a fifth appeared in 1885 (translated by Dickson as *The Provinces of the Roman Empire from Caesar to Diocletian,* 2 vols., 1886; 2d ed., 1909). Two volumes on miscellaneous topics, *Römische Forschungen* (1864, 1879) complete his historical writings.

Mommsen's interest in Latin inscriptions, a knowledge and interpretation of which was essential for an understanding of the classical period, lasted throughout his lifetime. He was editor in chief of *Corpus Inscriptionum Latinarum,* the vast collection which was prepared under the auspices of the Berlin Royal Academy of Science and began to appear in 1861, and was himself entirely responsible for a number of the massive volumes. He also prepared fundamental studies of the Roman calendar and chronology, Roman coins, and the defense walls of the Roman Empire (*limes*). He wrote on Italian dialects, and brilliantly edited various classical authors. Since his death eight volumes of his collected works (1905–1913) have been published.

But Mommsen was not satisfied with these achievements. A passage from his last will (1899), which was published in the *Bullettino* dell' Istituto di Diritto Romano, 53–54: 345 (1948), shows that his greatest interest was in Roman law. His masterly editing of Justinian's *Digesta* (2 vols., 1866–70), the *Codex Theodosianus* (1905), and pre-Justinian legal sources (1861) would alone suffice to make his name immortal. His comprehensive treatment of Roman constitutional law (*Römisches Staatsrecht,* 3d ed., 1887–88, repr. 1952) and Roman criminal law (*Römisches Strafrecht,* 1899) are still inspiring mines for further research.

Bibliography.—*Theodor Mommsen als Schriftsteller,* by Karl Zangemeister and Emil Jacobs (Berlin 1905), is a bibliography of Mommsen's writings. Mommsen himself discouraged any attempt at a complete biography of his life, but the reader is referred to the following: Costa, Emilio, *Teodoro Mommsen, Discorso* (Bologna 1904); Hirschfeld, Otto, *Gedächtnisrede auf Theodor Mommsen* (Berlin 1904); Hartmann, Ludwig Moritz, *Theodor Mommsen* (Gotha 1908); Weber, Wilhelm, *Theodor Mommsen* (Stuttgart 1929); Gooch, George P., *History and Historians in the Nineteenth Century,* 2d ed., pp. 454–465 (London and New York 1935); Thompson, James W., *A History of Historical Writing,* vol. 2, pp. 502–598 (New York 1942); Heuss. Albert, *Theodor Mommsen und das 19. Jahrhundert* (Kiel 1956).

ADOLF BERGER,
City College; École Libre des Hautes Études, New York.

MOMORDICA, mō-môr′dĭ-kȧ, a genus of annual or perennial climbing herbs of the gourd family (Cucurbitaceae) with about 35 species native in tropical Africa and Asia. They are cultivated in tropical regions for their edible fruits, and sometimes elsewhere as ornamentals. The plants support themselves by tendrils, and have leaves, in the various species, varying from entire to several lobed or palmately compound. The campanulate or rotate white or yellow flowers are either male or female, with the two sexes on the same or different plants. The small fruit is oblong or spherical, contains many seeds, and in some species splits at maturity into three valves. The seeds may be flattened or curiously sculptured, the generic name referring to their appearance of having been bitten. Two species, the balsam apple (*Momordica balsamina*) and the balsam pear (*M. charantia*), are grown to a certain extent in the United States, the latter especially by Chinese, who use the fleshy arils of the seeds or the whole young fruits as food.

RICHARD M. STRAW.

MONA LISA, mō′nȧ lē′zȧ, or **MONNA LISA,** mŏn′ȧ lē′zȧ, the name given a portrait painted by Leonardo da Vinci of the second wife of Zanobi del Giocondo, a Florentine merchant. Begun in all probability in 1503, the painting remained in the artist's possession until his death, though purchased from him by Francis I of France. It now hangs in the Louvre in Paris. One of the most celebrated paintings in Occidental art, it has been praised by critics in all periods since its execution, not the least dramatic reaction having been that of an Italian painter, Vincenzo Perugia, who stole it from the museum in 1911 in a vain effort to restore it to Italian ownership. It was recovered in Florence, Italy, in 1913.

Of modest dimensions, measuring 30 inches by 20 inches, the half-length figure of *La Gioconda,* as she is often called (or *La Joconde* in France), is seated in front of a parapet, with a distant landscape in the background. Unhappily, the painting is not well preserved. Leonardo used a variety of different media, and many of the pigments have darkened, as have the coats of varnish it has received at different times. Giorgio Vasari (1511–1574) writes with particular enthusiasm of its warm and tender flesh tones with touches of red. Some faint suggestion of this quality can still be found in the hands, which were painted in a somewhat more stable medium than the face.

In addition to adaptations of the general composition, such as Raphael's portrait of Maddalena Doni and Jean Baptiste Camille Corot's *Dame à la perle,* there are a number of variant versions of the *Mona Lisa* which date back in some instances to the early 16th century. Though claims have been advanced for many of these as the original, and though some may indeed have been in part the work of Leonardo himself, most authorities accept the Louvre version as authentic and the others as studio replicas.

As a painting, the *Mona Lisa* is particularly noteworthy for the fine organization of the plastic volumes of the figure in such a way as to result in a fully realized rhythm in space. To this are added many subtle but telling touches of characterization, such as the tensed hands and the enigmatic expression of the lips and cheeks, the celebrated smile that is really no smile but the outer expression of inner life that Leonardo defines in his *Trattato* as the aim of portraiture. Achieved by the delicate gradation of modeling tone or chiaroscuro that was one of Leonardo's most significant contributions to representational painting, it has stimulated critical appreciation ranging from medical diagnosis to Walter Horatio Pater's rhapsodic essay in *The Renaissance* (1873). The likeness must have been a good one—another feminine type appears in the majority of Leonardo's paintings—but the content and expressive characterization are surely of the artist himself rather than the young Italian woman who was his subject.

Consult Clark, Sir Kenneth, *Leonardo da Vinci: An Account of His Development as an Artist* (Cambridge and New York 1939); Heydenreich, Ludwig H., *Leonardo da Vinci,* 2 vols. (New York 1955).

DAVID M. ROBB,
Professor of the History of Art, University of Pennsylvania.

MONACA, mŏn′ȧ-kȧ, borough, Pennsylvania, in Beaver County, on the Ohio River opposite the mouth of the Beaver River, 22 miles northwest of Pittsburgh. It is on a state highway, and is served by the Pittsburgh and Lake Erie Railroad. A bridge across the Ohio connects Monaca with Rochester. Among the manufactures are glass and metal products and enamelware, and there is a large atomic plant nearby. Settled in 1813, Monaca was incorporated in 1839. It has a council-manager form of government. Pop. 7,486.

MONACO, mŭ-nä′kō; mŏn′ȧ-kō; Fr. mô-nȧ-kō′, Europe's smallest sovereign principality, a hereditary monarchy. With an area of 395 acres, it borders on the Mediterranean nine miles east of Nice, and is otherwise surrounded by the Alpes-Maritimes Department of France. Famous for its natural beauty, it consists of three sections: Monaco-Ville, known also as the Rock because of its situation on a high rocky promontory extending into the Mediterranean, site of the palace, the cathedral, the government buildings, and the Oceanographic Museum; La Condamine, the section along the port; and Monte Carlo (q.v.), the principal residential and resort area, where the famous casino is located. Fontvieille, the industrial area at the foot of the Rock in La Condamine, is sometimes considered a fourth section.

The population of Monaco in 1962 was 21,783. The approximately 2,700 Monegasques are outnumbered about eight to one by people of many other nationalities. More than half of the population of Monaco is French. In addition, thousands of people who live in France depend upon Monaco for their livelihood and commute daily from neighboring towns, including four communities that formerly belonged to Monaco but were ceded to France in 1861.

About 55 per cent of Monaco's income is derived from tourists; between 25 and 30 per cent from the expanding industries—chemicals, food products, plastics, precision instruments, cosmetics, glass, ceramics, and printing; only four per cent from the casino; and the remainder from registration fees, the sale of postage stamps, and taxes on tobacco and liquor. There are no income taxes, no inheritance taxes for near relatives, and no direct personal or corporation taxes. There is no national debt, and no unemployment. Although some coins are minted in Monaco, the currency in use is French. The language spoken is French, and the ancient Monegasque patois is rarely heard.

Among the places of special interest in Monaco are the royal palace, the Cathedral of St. Nicholas, the Exotic Gardens, the Gardens of St. Martin, the Zoological Garden, the Museum of Prehistoric Anthropology, and the world-famous Oceanographic Museum. The Monte Carlo Opera House is renowned for its productions of opera and ballet. The radio station at Monte Carlo is one of the most powerful in Europe, and a television station was inaugurated in 1954.

Government.—Monaco's independence was guaranteed in a treaty made with France in 1918 and confirmed by the Versailles Treaty (1918). Under the constitution of 1911, modified in 1918, the hereditary prince was established as sovereign ruler. In addition to a judiciary and various consultative bodies, the constitution provided for a Cabinet and a Council of State to be appointed by the prince, the council to consist of a minister of state (equivalent to a premier, who must be a French citizen) and three councilors. A legislative 18-member National Council (the members elected for four-year terms by universal male suffrage) voted the budget, but the prince could initiate and veto legislation, and no direct taxes could be levied without his consent. Municipal administration, centered at Monaco-Ville, developed upon a mayor elected by the 15 members of a popularly elected Communal Council.

When the National Council refused to approve a budget in January 1959, Prince Rainier III suspended the constitution and dissolved both councils. A new constitution proclaimed in 1962 is subject to suspension only by the ruler and the National Council.

History.—The Phoenicians, who held Monaco

from the 10th to the 5th centuries B.C., were replaced by the Phocaeans. During the early Christian era it was dominated by Rome until the barbarians and Saracens erected a fort on the Rock about the 9th century. Holy Roman Emperor Otto I conferred Monaco on a Genoese prince of the House of Grimaldi in the 10th century. The first prince of Monaco was Rainier I, who ascended the throne in 1304. In 1731 the male line became extinct with Antoine I, and his daughter Louise Hippolyte succeeded to the throne. She was followed by her husband, Jacques de Goyon-Matignon, count of Thorigny, who took the name Grimaldi. In 1792 the line was deposed during the French Revolution, but was re-established in 1814 under the protection of France with Honoré I on the throne. From 1815 to 1860 Monaco was under the rule of the Kingdom of Sardinia, becoming a French protectorate in 1861.

Honoré I was succeeded by Honoré II (r. 1819–1841); Florestan I (r. 1841–1856); Charles III (r. 1856–1889); Albert I (r. 1889–1922); Louis II (r. 1922–1949); and Rainier III, 32d of the dynasty (r. 1949–), who married Grace Kelly, an American citizen of Philadelphia, Pa., in 1956.

Consult Labande, León H., *Histoire de la principauté de Monaco* (Paris 1934); Pickard, Frederick W., *Monaco and the French Riviera* (New York 1937); Playfair, Giles, and Fitz Gibbon, Constantine, *Little Tour: Andorra, Monaco, . . .* (London 1954).

MARCEL A. PALMARO,
Consul General of Monaco at New York.

MONAD, mŏn'ăd; mō'năd (from Gr. *monas,* one; alone), *in biology,* a term for the simplest organism or organic unit; *in zoology,* a primitive organism, a flagellate protozoan such as the Mastigophora; *in chemistry,* a monovalent element, radical, or atom, such as hydrogen or sodium; methyl or hydroxyl; cuprous copper or mercurous mercury. For use of the term *in philosophy,* see LEIBNIZ, BARON GOTTFRIED WILHELM VON—*Metaphysics.*

MONADNOCK, mô-năd'nŏk, or **GRAND MONADNOCK,** a mountain, 3,165 feet high, in Cheshire County, 10 miles east of Keene, N.H. A solitary peak, dominating the landscape for miles, it has an area of five miles by three. It is a typical example of resistant rock that surmounts a land surface which has been worn down almost to a plain, and the term *monadnock* is applied to any mountain of this type.

MONAGAS, mô-nä'gäs, **José Tadeo,** Venezuelan president: b. Maturín, Venezuela, Oct. 28, 1784; d. El Valle, Nov. 18, 1868. He served under Simón Bolívar in the war against Spain (1812–1821). In 1835 he supported an insurrection but later made his peace with the government. With the support of the Conservative president José Antonio Páez, he was elected president in 1847. He soon went over to the Liberal side, suppressed the Conservative Congress, and drove Páez into exile. Although he secured the presidency for his brother José Gregorio Managas in 1851, he himself retained political control of the country and again became president in 1855. His revision of the constitution in 1857, largely to perpetuate himself in power, brought about a revolt, and he was forced to flee the country in 1858. Returning, in 1868 he led a successful counterrevolution, and was again elected to the presidency, but he died before taking office.

MONAGAS, state, in northeastern Venezuela, bounded on the southeast by the Orinoco River. It has an area of 11,158 square miles, and the capital and chief trading center is Maturín. To the north are the mountains of the coastal range, south of that a tableland, with llanos still farther south and marshy land in the Orinoco delta region. The climate is tropical, with heavy rainfall. Cattle are raised, and coffee, tobacco, sugarcane, cacao, and cotton are among the crops grown on the uplands. Oilfields have been developed, and there are deposits of coal, zinc, asphalt, sulphur, and salt. The forests yield a variety of hardwoods. Pop. (1950) 175,560.

MONAGHAN, mŏn'ȧ-hăn, Ireland, an inland county in the province of Ulster, bounded on the north by Tyrone, on the east by Armagh and Louth, on the south by Meath and Cavan, and on the west by Fermanagh. Its greatest length is 40 miles and its greatest breadth is 22 miles; the area is 318,988 acres.

The name derives from the Gaelic *Muineachain* meaning "little hills." There are practically no mountains in the county, but small rolling hills are extremely numerous. The chief river is the Fane, which flows east through Inniskeen. There are many lakes, including Fea, Monalty, and Muckno. Monaghan is a county of small farmers, although linen, clothing, shoes, and potato alcohol are manufactured. The chief towns are Carrickmacross, Castleblayney, Clones, and Monaghan (the county capital). Carrickmacross is an important market town. Pop. (1956) 52,064.

PETER KAVANAGH.

MONAHANS, mŏn'ȧ-hănz, city, Texas, seat of Ward County. At an altitude of 2,615 feet in the Pecos Valley, 35 miles southwest of Odessa, it is on federal and state highways and is served by the Texas and Pacific Railroad. In a rich oil-producing, farming, and ranching area, it is a trading, shipping, and oil processing center, with plants producing chemical, metal, and cottonseed products. Nearby is Sandhills State Park. Monahans was incorporated in 1928 with a manager-council form of government. Pop. 8,333.

MONAL. See PHEASANT.

MONARCHIANISM, mô-när'kĭ-ăn-ĭz'm, a type of Christian doctrine which was current in the 2d and 3d centuries. In opposition to Gnosticism conservatives held that the Deity is not a descending series of aeons but is one sole and sovereign Eternal Being, by whose will all things exist (see APOSTLES' CREED, first sentence of the creed). The term "monarchy" (Gr. *monarchia*) referred to this sole sovereignty, as taught in the Bible (Isaiah 43–45). There were two forms of the doctrine: (1) the *dynamistic* or *adoptionist,* according to which Jesus' divine nature was either a "power" (Luke 5:17) derived from the supreme God or the rank conferred upon Him at the Resurrection (Phillippians 2:9–11); and (2) the *modalistic,* according to which the Incarnation was only a temporary "mode" of divine manifestation. Both types were eventually discarded by the church, in favor, first, of the doctrine of the Incarnate Logos, and finally that of the Eternal Trinity.

See also THIRD CENTURY—*Religion* (Christianity); TRINITY, THE.

FREDERICK C. GRANT.

MONARCHY, mŏn'ẽr-kĭ (from Gr. *monarchia,* the rule of one), a form of government in which one person is the sovereign. The Greeks, however, distinguished the legitimate one-man government of monarchy from the illegitimate one-man dictatorship of despotism or tyranny, in which latter system the ruler rules in his own interest rather than in that of the governed. In a monarchy in its pure (and original) form, the monarchical ruler combined in his person the supreme authority and power in legislation as well as in administration and adjudication. In later stages of evolution, the monarch frequently still retained his position as the supreme lawgiver, but handed over the judicial and administrative functions to specialized agencies, generally subordinate to him. Above all, the monarch was originally, and remained for a long time, the commander in chief of the armed forces of his community or nation.

In early history, as among primitive peoples to this day, the monarchical form of government was virtually the only one known and practiced. Generally, monarchy was hereditary, and the monarchical dynasty frequently claimed descent. In Asia and Africa, monarchy persisted in its autocratic form until, beginning in the 17th century, imperial expansion by European states (England, France, Holland) put an end to native monarchical autocracies, though often retaining native monarchies as instruments of more effective control of the conquered populations. Where such European imperial influence has been only short-lived—as in Ethiopia and the Arab kingdoms of Yemen and Saudi Arabia—the despotic or autocratic form of monarchy has survived to this day; in such monarchies, other institutions of absolute social domination, such as slavery, have also survived.

In Antiquity.—By contrast with the Oriental states, three peoples stood out in antiquity in their opposition to monarchy: the Greeks, Jews, and Romans. The Greeks discarded the monarchical system of government beginning in the 7th century B.C., although Sparta persisted for long in monarchical rule of an elective type. Monarchy did not fit the individualistic, rational, inquiring mentality of the Greeks, who may be said to have invented republican self-government in the Western World. Moreover, their main enemy in the 5th century B.C. was Persia, an empire which was an absolute monarchy. Monarchy thus became the symbol of external and internal servitude in ancient Greece; even after Philip and Alexander the Great subjected the Greek city-states under the Macedonian monarchy and empire, the internal institutions of self-government in the Greek city-states were carefully preserved by their Macedonian overlords.

Like the Greeks, the Jews were opposed to monarchy from very early times, as is evidenced by the vigorous and persistent attacks on monarchy in the Old Testament, particularly in the books of the prophets, such as Samuel, Isaiah, and Jeremiah. According to the classical teachings of Judaism, only God was sovereign, and no man—not even a king—could demand complete allegiance from his subjects.

Finally, the ancient Romans had their great period during their republican system of government of the last five centuries B.C. The establishment of monarchy in Rome coincided with the expansion of Rome from a relatively small city-state to a world empire; although the Roman monarchy of the imperial type served as a link between the far-flung parts of the empire, it symbolized the first phase of decay of those civic qualities in Rome that were the foundation of her greatness.

In the Middle Ages.—After the destruction of the Western Roman Empire in 476 A.D., monarchy continued in the Eastern Roman Empire which was centered in Constantinople. In the West, two types of monarchy gradually emerged. First, the bishop of Rome progressively established himself as the ruler of all Christendom, and he claimed monarchical prerogatives over all Christians in matters temporal as well as spiritual. Side by side with this essentially ecclesiastical monarchy, the German rulers sought to restore the Roman imperial monarchy under German leadership, claiming universal political allegiance throughout the Christian world. Known as the Holy Roman Empire of the Teutonic Nation, this was formally inaugurated with the coronation of Charlemagne in 800 by the pope in Rome. Legally, it lasted until 1806, when Napoleon I destroyed it, but in effect it had exercised little influence during the last few centuries of its existence.

In the Renaissance and Modern Times.—Probably the most creative contribution of monarchy to European political development was in the 16th century—the era of the birth and rise of the modern national state. The monarchy more than any other single institution was instrumental in forging the modern nation-state; in general, the main force to be overcome was the aristocracy, which was strongly opposed to increased royalist power at the center. The most important ally of the monarchies in the various nascent national states was the new middle class or *bourgeoisie,* which supplied much of the administrative personnel of the new nation-states, and was willing to allow the monarch strong central authority so long as he could maintain law and order, an efficient system of highways and other forms of communications, a stable currency, and protection against internal and external enemies.

Yet by the end of the 17th century, monarchy started to decline as a result of the growing influence of rationalism, capitalism, and individualism. England, in this century, was the first modern country to abandon the concept of absolute monarchical authority; the success of the Civil War in the 1640's culminated in the execution of King Charles I in 1649, the establishment of a republic under Oliver Cromwell, and the ascendancy of the middle classes. The monarchy was restored in 1660, but its position in English life was not clear until the Glorious or Bloodless Revolution of 1688 finally established the principle that political authority ultimately resides in Parliament. A century later, the French followed the English example, and established a republic based on the ideals of Liberty, Equality, and Fraternity. During the 19th century, monarchy was again restored in France for short periods on several occasions, but the concept of absolute monarchy deriving its authority from divine grace was dead, never to be revived again after 1870, when the Third Republic of France was set up.

Where liberalism was weak, as in Austria-Hungary, Russia, and Germany, the monarchical form of government lasted until the end of World War I. In Russia, the monarchy was destroyed in 1917, and the emperors of Germany and Austria abdicated in 1918. Today, monarchy exists in those Western nations in which it has been able to ally itself with the modern movements of democracy and liberalism, as in Great Britain, Belgium, the Netherlands, Denmark, Norway, and Sweden. The primary function of monarchy in such liberal societies is to serve as a symbol of national unity and continuity. In Britain, the monarchy has the additional important task of serving as a rallying point of unity in a commonwealth of nations diverse in background, color, religion, language, and culture.

Consult Martin, Kingsley, *The Magic of Monarchy* (New York 1937); Kern, Fritz, *Kingship and Law in the Middle Ages*, tr. from the German by S. B. Chrimes (Oxford 1939, New York 1941); Michie, Allan Andrew, *The Crown and the People* (London 1952; American title *God Save the Queen*, New York 1953); Petrie, Sir Charles, *Monarchy in the Twentieth Century* (London 1952, New York 1953).

WILLIAM EBENSTEIN,
Professor of Politics, Princeton University.

MONASHEE MOUNTAINS, mō-năsh'ē, mountain range, British Columbia, Canada, in the Rocky Mountains, west of the Selkirks, stretching about 200 miles north from the United States border. The highest peak is Hallam (10,560 feet).

MONASTERY. See MONASTICISM.

MONASTERY, The, an historical romance by Sir Walter Scott, one of the later novels of his *Waverley* series, published in 1820. The scene is mid-16th century Scotland in the last days of Catholicism, and the story concerns the noble Mary Avenel and her suitors. A losing claimant to her hand becomes a monk and other monastic characters are shown; hence the title. An apparition or spirit, the "White Lady" or "White Spirit," works outright miracles. Perhaps because Scott failed to portray the miraculous convincingly, the book was not as successful as its sequel, *The Abbot,* published the same year, which introduced Mary Queen of Scots as a character.

MONASTIC ART AND ARCHITECTURE. So great was the role played by the several monastic orders in western Europe during the thousand years after the fall of the Roman Empire that the very preservation of civilization may be credited to them. Especially was this true during the Dark Ages and through the Romanesque period of the 11th and 12th centuries. Indeed in large measure medieval art, until the Gothic period at least, was indistinguishable from monastic art. For example, the Irish monasteries in the 8th and 9th centuries produced such manuscripts as the Lindisfarne Gospels and the Book of Kells with their peculiarly northern linearism, energy, and decorative quality, surely among the great artistic triumphs of the Dark Ages. The portals of the Cluniac churches of Moissac and Vézelay are outstanding examples of Romanesque sculpture. During the later Middle Ages, the monasteries played a less dominant role and, with the growth in importance of cities and of the royal power, secular craftsmen arose to supplant them.

Similarly in architecture, the monastic churches and buildings illustrate the successive changes of style neither more nor less than do non-monastic churches or secular buildings of the same time. The differences stem from two considerations. First, a monastic establishment comprised not only a church but dormitories, refectories, infirmaries, chapter houses for formal meetings of the members, shops, and farm buildings of all sorts. The 9th century plan of the Benedictine Monastery of St. Gall in Switzerland is an early example that demonstrates the self-sufficient nature of such institutions. The monks and lay brethren of the order worked the land, did their own tanning and blacksmithing, their own brewing and baking. According to the rules of the order, hospitality was provided for travelers; guest houses were therefore required. Thus it is clear that the architectural problem of a monastery was quite similar to that of a feudal manor house, save that it was even more complicated, and revolved around the monastic church as its all important center.

A second reason that sometimes distinguishes monastic from other churches is found in the particular liturgies required by the monks. Although not unique to the monastic orders, elaborate processions played an important role in their services. In 1132, a procession of 1,212 monks was held in the Abbey of St.-Pierre at Cluny. The widespread influence of the monastic orders may be indicated by the striking similarity of five great churches built on the routes leading to Compostela (Santiago de Compostela) in northwestern Spain, those churches were St. Martial, Limoges; St. Étienne, Nevers; St. Foy, Conques; St. Sernin, Toulouse; and St. James at Compostela. Moreover, several important features of medieval architecture were essential to monasteries but might be omitted or minimized in non-monastic churches. For example, the cloister provided a sheltered walk for the monks, and often also incorporated, as at Gloucester, niches (carrels) where individuals might study or write. Since more than half of the great English cathedrals were monastic in origin, mostly Benedictine, the cloister was almost universal there, but is less often found in the French Gothic cathedrals. The cloister was, however, common in churches governed by secular canons even though they were not members of an order. The origin of the English churches also explains their setting, surrounded by the lawns and trees of the monastic grounds instead of, like the French, crowded by the houses of the towns. A second feature of monastic churches was the necessity of stalls in the choir for the individual monks. The stalls were ranged in rows facing each other. The number of rows, two or three on each side of the aisle, determined the width of the choir, and the number of seats in each row, dictated by the size of the monastery, fixed its length. Where, as was often the case in the larger churches, the laity had rights to part of the church, a screen separated the nave from the choir and preserved the latter, including the sanctuary with the high altar, for the exclusive use of members of the order. Finally some few of the monastic orders had such specific needs that they required particular types of churches. Of these, the most important was the Cistercian, founded in 1098 as an offshoot from the Benedictine Order. The typical plan had a short rectangular sanctuary without aisles. This was entered directly from the transept, also without aisles, but with its eastern wall lined with chapels. Since the rules of this order compelled manual labor, the Cistercian monks were distinguished above all others as masons. The Knights Templars and the Knights Hospitallers expressed their mission by designing their churches in a circular form inspired by the Church of the Holy Sepulchre, Jerusalem.

EVERARD M. UPJOHN.

MONASTICISM, mô-năs′tĭ-sĭz′m, a word derived from the Greek, meaning "the act or state of dwelling alone." It has been employed from early Christian times to designate a life of seclusion from the world, undertaken for religious reasons and conducted in accordance with a body of precepts called a rule. The striving for greater religious perfection by this kind of life is not exclusively Christian; monasticism is an old institution in Brahmanism, Buddhism, Judaism, and Islam. In the case of Judaism, for example, new and unexpected evidence has been furnished by the Dead Sea Scrolls (discovered 1947 ff.; see SCROLLS, THE DEAD SEA) on the life and work of a Jewish monastic community, Qumrân, in the last two centuries B.C. and the first century A.D. Since the monastic way of life, however, has had its fullest and widest significance and influence in Christianity, this article will confine itself to the rise and development of Christian monasticism. (See also BUDDHA AND BUDDHISM.)

Beginnings: In the East.—It is not necessary to look beyond the Gospel for the origin of the Christian monastic ideal; it is contained in the answer given by Jesus to the young, rich man: "If thou wilt be perfect, go, sell what thou hast, and give to the poor, and thou shalt have treasure in heaven; and come, follow me." (Matthew 19:21). Men and women soon took up these evangelical counsels, but such ascetics (for example, Origen) continued to live in the world. Hermits made their first appearance in Egypt, living in rude huts which they built on the outskirts of towns or villages, and devoting themselves to contemplation and ascetical exercises.

St. Anthony (c. 250–356) may be regarded as the founder of the ascetical life as an institution. After living as a hermit near his native village in the Faiyum, he crossed to the east bank of the Nile and for 20 years dwelt in complete isolation in an old fort at Pispir (now Deir el Memun). His reputation for holiness attracted numerous other ascetics to settle in the vicinity. He finally yielded (c. 305) to their appeals and consented to become their spiritual guide, but he did not compose or give them a rule in the strict sense. These ascetics, or anchorites, lived in separate cells, practiced continence and poverty, engaged in the study of Scripture and in spiritual conversation, and met together for liturgical services on Saturday and Sunday only. While accepting the authority of older fellow hermits, they were not bound by a common rule or by a vow of obedience. This eremitical or semieremitical form of monasticism became the norm in northern Egypt. St. Anthony has exercised a profound influence on cenobites as well as anchorites. He is honored by all, not as the author of a rule, but as a kindly spiritual father and guide, teaching above all by example.

St. Pachomius (c. 292–c. 346), as ascetic of Upper Egypt and a contemporary of St. Anthony, organized a community for the hermits in his vicinity. At Tabennisi, near Dendera, he founded the first monastery in which cenobitism (from Gr. *koinobion*), or life in common, was an essential feature. The monks were bound to obey the superior in the monastery in which they lived and to observe the rule written by Pachomius. All religious exercises were carried out in accordance with this rule, and manual labor in the form of handicrafts was also prescribed. By the time of Pachomius' death, his congregation comprised nine large monasteries for men and two convents for women. Pachomius gave monasticism its full and most characteristic form. To the practice of the virtues of continence and poverty was added that of obedience. The monk was now bound by a rule. The asceticism of the anchorites was harmoniously combined with regulated life in community. It was no longer necessary to withdraw to desert places to attain greater spiritual perfection, and monks could now engage actively in works of charity.

The anchorite and cenobital forms of monasticism spread quickly into Palestine, Syria, Asia Minor, Mesopotamia, and Armenia, and were embraced with an enthusiasm almost equal to that of Egypt. The laura (q.v.; a specialized use of the Greek word *laura,* a street or alley with shops) or semieremitical kind of ascetic life was especially favored in Palestine. Hermits lived in cells, but they were under the direction of an abbot. The center of the typical laura was a monastery which served for common liturgical services on Saturday and Sunday and as a training school for novices who wished to become hermits. St. Sabas (439–532), the most famous of these monks, founded at least seven lauras, among them the Great Laura in the valley of the Kidron (Cedron), southeast of Jerusalem. Cyril of Scythopolis (c. 523–c. 558) has left us vivid biographies of St. Euthymius, St. Sabas, St. Theodosius, and other famous monks of Palestine.

St. Pachomius founded the cenobital life, but St. Basil of Caesarea (c. 330–379) is justly regarded as the greatest figure in Eastern cenobitism. After visiting monastic centers in Egypt, Palestine, Syria, and Mesopotamia, he established a cenobital monastery on the river Iris in Pontus (modern Turkey), which soon became the model for others. For the sake of more effective control and spiritual direction, he limited the number of monks in each monastery and went much further than Pachomius in regulating the lives of the monks. Thus the hours for prayer, study, work, meals, and sleep, and even the form of dress, were all fixed in detail. Yet, strictly speaking, St. Basil did not compose a comprehensive, systematic rule. His *Longer Rules* and *Shorter Rules,* although containing detailed regulations on the monastic life, are simply parts of his *Ascetica,* or writings on the ascetic life. His *Epistle 8,* which describes the life of a monk in detail, is now recognized as a work of Evagrius Ponticus (346–399) that later found its way into collections of Basil's letters.

Monasticism has continued to be of prime importance in the Eastern and Orthodox Eastern churches down to the present time. (See ATHOS.) However, as compared with Western monasticism, it exhibits no striking changes since the 4th century. Orthodox monks revere St. Basil as their patriarch, but they do not profess a rule, nor do they belong to a definite religious order or congregation. In the strict sense, there is no Order of St. Basil. Each monastery has its own constitution, and the monastic life is of the contemplative type.

In the West.—Monasticism proper was introduced from the East into the West in the early 4th century and from that time on had a phenomenal development. Up to the Reformation, it played a major role in the cultural and spiritual life of the whole Western Church, and since that time it has continued to play such a role in the Roman Catholic Church—and, from the middle of the last century, it began to play a role in the

Anglican Communion. Among the founders of monastic life in the West should be mentioned: St. Athanasius of Alexandria who, accompanied by two Egyptian monks, spent some years in Gaul (336–337) and Italy (339–346); Martin of Tours (d. 397); Eusebius of Vercelli (d. 371); St. Ambrose (c. 339–397); St. Jerome (c. 347–419/420); St. Augustine (354–430); and John Cassian (Johannes Cassianus, c. 360–c. 435). The lives of St. Anthony and other hermits, the "rules" of Pachomius and Basil, and other Greek ascetical writings were translated into Latin. While partial "rules" were composed in the West, no comprehensive rules were written before St. Caesarius of Arles (d. 542), a contemporary of St. Benedict.

Apart from the cenobital type of life introduced for their cathedral clergy by Eusebius of Vercelli and St. Augustine among others, monasticism in the West followed its Eastern eremitical, semieremitical, and cenobital models, with some modifications based on Western temperament and experience. Early Irish monasticism exhibits a combination of Eastern and native traits. Because of its rigor it has been well described as a life of organized penance. The Irish monastic ideal of exile or pilgrimage for Christ, which led to the Irish missionary activity in the early Middle Ages, was penitential in origin.

Women, from an early date, had practiced the ascetical life in their own homes. Beginning with St. Pachomius in the 4th century the cenobital life for women spread rapidly in East and West. St. Basil, St. Ambrose, St. Jerome, and St. Augustine were all ardent promoters of the religious life for women, founded convents, or served as their spiritual directors. St. Augustine's *Letter 211* is a partial rule for a convent, and St. Caesarius of Arles composed a rule for women as well as one for men. The precepts or rules formulated for convents at this time, as later, corresponded closely to those written for men. Convents obviously had to be established in inhabited and protected areas, either in or adjacent to towns.

St. Benedict.—St. Benedict of Nursia (c. 480–c. 547) is the true father and lawgiver of Western monasticism. After long experience as a monk in an age of violence and moral decline, he finally succeeded in establishing (between 525 and 529) a monastery at Monte Cassino, Italy, about 80 miles south of Rome, and composed his rule for the monks there. Modern scholarship has shown that he drew heavily upon earlier ascetical writings, especially those of John Cassian, St. Augustine, and the Latin translations of St. Pachomius, the *Historia monachorum,* the Rules of St. Basil, and the so-called Rule of Macarius. His rule, however, bears the stamp of his own thought. It is permeated with a spirit of fatherly kindness and Christian love; at the same time, it is notable for its moderation, precision, and comprehensiveness.

The rule covers every aspect of cenobital life. In addition to the vows of poverty, chastity, and obedience, the monk is required to take a vow of stability—the most original feature of the Benedictine Rule. He is bound permanently to the monastery in which his vows are taken; the rule is intended to serve as an instrument of government and spiritual direction to groups of men living in community apart from the world and devoted entirely to the service of God. Their days are divided between prayer, spiritual reading, and manual work of various kinds. They are bound by regulations of fasting, abstinence, and other forms of austerity, but in moderation. Special emphasis is placed on corporate prayer, on community participation in the *opus Dei,* the Divine Office.

St. Benedict was not concerned with secular learning or its preservation, or with demonstrating the nobility of manual work with programs of charity outside the monastery, or even with missions among the pagans. But already under Cassiodorus (c. 485–c. 580), and especially under Pope Gregory the Great (r. 590–604), who had been a Benedictine monk himself, the Benedictines were forced by European conditions to engage in various cultural and religious activities which were not, strictly speaking, envisioned in a rule written primarily for contemplatives.

Cluniac Reform, Carthusians, Cistercians.—By the time of Emperor Charlemagne (r. 800–814), the Benedictine form of monasticism had triumphed throughout the West except in certain Spanish and Irish centers, and no essential changes were made before the Cluniac reform (910). The chief features of that reform were rigorous centralization and greater emphasis on the Divine Office, and its celebration with elaborate ritual and splendor. The abbot of Cluny exercised absolute control over all dependent monasteries, however distant. The Cluniac reform created a religious order in the strictest sense, although the term "order" was not yet employed. Excessive centralization led to the decline of the Cluniac system less than two centuries later, no reform from within being possible.

Of the other offshoots from the Benedictines proper, mention must be made of the Carthusians and especially of the Cistercians, both movements in reaction against Cluny. The Carthusians, founded (1084) by St. Bruno at the Grande Chartreuse in Dauphiné, France, marked a return to the semieremitical life. The Cistercians, or Monks of the Order of Citeaux, founded (1098) by St. Robert of Molesme, have been much more important in history. They stressed the literal observance of the Benedictine Rule, de-emphasizing Cluniac pomp and insisting on manual labor in the fields. Furthermore, the paralyzing centralization of Cluny was modified. Each monastery founded from Citeaux was regarded as an individual family under its own abbot, but all such families were under the authority of the abbot of Citeaux. The most famous of the dependent monasteries—one that in turn became the mother of 68 others—was Clairvaux, founded (1115) by St. Bernard, the greatest of all Cistercians and one of the most illustrious names in the history of the Western Church. The Cistercians, with the aid of numerous lay brothers admitted to the order, developed agriculture to a high degree and, for several centuries, played an important rôle in the economic life of Europe. In our own times the Cistercians, popularly but incorrectly called Trappists, are experiencing a remarkable growth, especially in America.

Later Orders.—Beginning in the 11th century, new orders were instituted to meet special needs or to engage in specific activities, as the Canons Regular of St. Augustine, the Templars and other military orders, the Trinitarians, the orders of mendicant friars—Franciscans, Dominicans, Carmelites, Hermits of St. Augustine—and many others. Especially from the Reformation on, new orders of priests (including the Jesuits, Oratorians, Theatines, Redemptorists, Sulpicians, and Paulists), of nuns, and of brothers have multiplied to meet special needs—pastoral duties, care of the sick and destitute, education, foreign missions—so that their number runs to several hundred; and new ones are constantly being established. But, important as the work of all such groups has been, they are not, properly speaking, monastic, since they have not made the contemplative life their primary objective nor occupied themselves solely with the monastic way of life as a spiritual discipline for the service of God.

See also RELIGIOUS ORDERS AND COMMUNITIES, and separate articles on the individual orders and founders mentioned.

MARTIN R.P. MCGUIRE
Professor of Greek and Latin
The Catholic University of America

Bibliography.—Hannah, Ian C., *Christian Monasticism: A Great Force in History* (New York 1925); Watterott, Ignaz, *Religious Life and Spirit* (St. Louis 1950); Dirks, Walter, *The Monk and the World,* tr. by Daniel Coogan (New York 1954); Bouyer, Louis, *The Meaning of the Monastic Life,* tr. by Kathleen Pond (New York 1955); Merton, Thomas, *The Silent Life* (New York 1957); Dickinson, John C., *Monastic Life in Medieval England* (New York 1962); Workman, Herbert B., *The Evolution of the Monastic Ideal* (London 1927; reprinted, Boston 1962).

MONAZITE, mon′ə-zīt, is a phosphate of cerium and other rare-earth metals, usually containing thorium. It ranges from yellowish to reddish brown, with a hardness of 5 to 5.5 and a specific gravity of 4.9 to 5.3 (higher with increasing thorium). Its formula is (Ce,La,Y, Th) PO_4. Monazite occurs as an accessory mineral in the form of tiny crystals in certain granitic and gneissic rocks, and occasionally in large crystals in pegmatites. The crystals are monoclinic. Commercial deposits are chiefly in beach or river sands formed by the weathering of the rocks in which the monazite originally occurred. The best sources are in India, Brazil, South Africa, and the United States, especially in Florida and South Carolina. Monazite yields thorium, thorium oxides, cerium metals, and rare-earth elements.

MONBODDO, Lord. See BURNETT, JAMES.

MONCK, mungk, **Sir Charles Stanley,** 4TH VISCOUNT MONCK, British administrator: b. Templemore, County Tipperary, Ireland, Oct. 10, 1819; d. County Wexford, Ireland, Nov. 29, 1894. Educated at Trinity College, Dublin, he was admitted to the Irish bar in 1841 and eight years later inherited his father's title in the Irish peerage. Returned (1852) to the House of Commons as a Liberal, he served (1855–1858) as a treasury lord under Palmerston, who named him governor general of British North America in 1861.

During the American Civil War, Monck succeeded in preventing an open break between the United States and Canada, when Confederate refugees conducted raids on the northern United States from across the Canadian border. He was also active in promoting Canadian Confederation, and after it was achieved (1867), he served for one year as the first governor general of the new Dominion of Canada. He was made a baron in the peerage of the United Kingdom in 1866.

MONCK, George. See MONK, GEORGE.

MONCTON, mungk′tən, is a city in New Brunswick, Canada, in Westmorland county, on the Petitcodiac River, 85 miles northeast of Saint John. It is on the Trans-Canadian Highway and has rail and air services. The city has railway offices, slaughterhouses, and meat-packing plants, and manufactures steel, chemicals, and woolens.

Moncton was founded in 1763 by Germans from Pennsylvania. It was known as *The Bend* until 1855, when the name was changed to *Monkton* in honor of Robert Monckton, the British general who captured nearby Fort Beauséjour from the French in 1755. In 1930 the name was officially changed to Moncton. Population: 47,891.

MOND, mond, **Ludwig,** German-British industrialist and chemist: b. Kassel, Germany, March 7, 1839; d. London, England, Dec. 11, 1909. Educated at the universities of Marburg and Heidelberg, he went to England in 1862 and became a naturalized British subject in 1880.

In 1872 he and Sir John T. Brunner started the alkali works at Winnington, Cheshire, later incorporated as Brunner, Mond & Co., which introduced into England the Solvay ammonia-soda process of manufacturing alkali. Mond also invented a means of manufacturing chlorine as a byproduct of the ammonia-soda process, and devised gas batteries, processes for manufacturing nickel based upon his discovery of nickel carbonyl, and a new method of producing gas for power and heating.

In 1896 he endowed the Davy-Faraday Research Laboratory at the Royal Institution in London. Most of his extensive art collection was bequeathed to the National Gallery, London.

MONDAY, mun′dā, is the second day of the week, following Sunday. In pagan times it was sacred to the moon. The Romans called it *lunae dies* (moon day), from which the names used in modern Romance languages (Fr. *lundi,* It. *lunedì,* Sp. *lunes*) are directly derived. The Germanic forms, including the English (from Anglo-Saxon *mōnandæg*), are translations from the Latin.

MONDRIAN, môn′drē-än, **Piet,** Dutch painter: b. Amersfoort, Netherlands, March 7, 1872; d. New York, N.Y., Feb. 1, 1944. He was the founder of neoplasticism, or de Stijl, one of the earliest and most influential schools of nonobjective art. In his neoplastic paintings, Mondrian strove for what he called "concrete universal expression"—the expression of the constant inner reality of nature, rather than its changing appearances. His work influenced architecture, furniture design, fashions and other applied arts, as well as painting.

Life. Pieter Cornelis Mondriaan (the Dutch spelling) said he was possessed by the idea of painting at a very young age. He earned diplomas from the Amsterdam Academy of Fine Arts in 1889 and 1892. Until his cubist period in Paris (1912–1914), his work was naturalistic. During World War I, he worked in Holland, seeking a purer abstract style in black and white "checkerboard" compositions. In 1917 he and Theo van Doesburg organized the magazine *de Stijl,* which presented the theories of neoplasticism. Two years later Mondrian returned to Paris, where he evolved his mature style. He lived in New York after 1940. Several of his essays are collected in *Plastic Art and Pure Plastic Art* (New York 1945).

Work. After experimenting with conventional

landscapes, symbolic works, cubism, and geometric compositions, Mondrian concluded that the "logical outgrowth of painting is the use of pure color and straight lines in rectangular opposition." In his last paintings, *Broadway Boogie-Woogie* (1943) and *Victory Boogie-Woogie* (unfinished), he utilized only the most formal elements of art: horizontal and vertical lines, shades of black, white, and gray, and the three primary colors. While he eliminated all representational elements, he avoided the static balance characteristic of geometric designs. James Johnson Sweeney, art critic and museum director, said of Mondrian's work: "the whole canvas . . . dances [as the] eye is led from one group of color notes to another." See also NEOPLASTICISM.

Consult Seuphor, Michel, *Piet Mondrian: Life and Work* (New York 1956).

MONET, mô-ne′, **Claude,** French painter: b. Paris, France, Nov. 14, 1840; d. Giverny, Dec. 5, 1926. A founder of the school of impressionism, he remained faithful to its principles throughout his long and prolific career. Monet opened a new road to landscape painting by working outdoors and applying scientific principles deduced from the laws of optics. He strove to capture fleeting visual impressions and the effects of light and air. On close inspection, an area of green foliage in a Monet canvas is found to be composed of multicolored brush strokes, but seen from a distance the freshness of the greenery appears as in nature. The painter broke down tones in the way that a prism disperses a beam of light; the eye of the beholder blends the colors.

Life. Claude Oscar Monet grew up in Le Havre, where he began to paint outdoors, encouraged by the marine artist Eugène Boudin. At 16, he exhibited his first painting in Rouen. From 1860 to 1862 he served with the French army in Algeria. On his return to France, he overrode his parents' objections and went to Paris to study art.

Monet enrolled in the studio of Charles Gleyre and became associated with a group of insurgent painters including Pissarro, Renoir, and Cézanne. Together they developed the style that came to be known as impressionism. In a scathing review of their first joint exhibition in 1874, a critic coined the term "impressionism" from a Monet canvas entitled *Impression: Sunrise.*

For the next 10 years, Monet lived, nearly starving, in the villages of Argenteuil and Vétheuil. Gradually impressionism caught on, and he became prosperous. In 1883 he moved to Giverny where he built the famous water garden that he re-created in a series of memorable paintings. He was almost blind for his last 10 years.

Work. Monet's motifs are usually simple: a haystack, some slender trees, a cluster of shrubs, or a tranquil pond. But the real subject of his paintings is light. He often treated the same subject in a series of canvases painted outdoors at various times of day. These series, showing changes in the atmosphere, reveal the history of light playing upon an object. Some of Monet's most famous paintings depict such series of scenes, notably the *Haystacks,* the *Poplars,* the *Cliffs of Étretat,* the *Mornings on the Seine,* the *Rouen Cathedrals,* the *Water Lilies,* and the *Views of the Thames.*

Monet was capable both of demonstrations of power and of displays of tender charm. His studies of the austere rocks of *Belle-Isle en Mer* show heavy waves and blinding spray dashing over granite rocks. His series of *Water Lilies* expresses the melancholy and quiet beauty of sequestered pools.

Besides his importance as a founder of impressionism, Monet ranks as one of the greatest of all landscape painters. Cézanne, who abandoned impressionism for a more abstract style in his later work, remarked that Monet was "only an eye, but my God what an eye!"

Consult Seitz, William C., *Claude Monet: Seasons and Moments* (New York 1960).

MONETA, mō-nâ′tä, **Ernesto Teodoro,** Italian journalist and peace advocate: b. Milan, Italy, Sept. 20, 1833; d. there, Feb. 10, 1918. A soldier in his youth, he became a leader of the international peace movement during the late 1800's. For his writings and organizing activities on behalf of world peace, he received the Nobel Peace Prize in 1907. The peace movement was the chief focus of the last 40 years of his life.

Early Career. When Moneta was young, Milan was under Austrian rule. He early became involved in the *Risorgimento* movement, aimed at unifying Italy. At the age of 15, he took part in the episode of the "five days," a series of demonstrations that drove the Austrians from Milan in 1848.

In 1859, during the final stage of the campaign for Italian unification, Moneta and four brothers joined the ranks of Giuseppe Garibaldi's guerrillas, known as the *cacciatori delle Alpi,* in northern Italy. The following year he took part in Garibaldi's southern expedition. He later joined the regular army of the newly founded kingdom of Italy, but resigned in 1866 to devote himself to publishing. In 1867 he became editor of the Milanese newspaper *Il secolo,* a post he held for 30 years.

Peace Activities. Moneta's military experience had the effect of turning him against war and leading him to direct his energies to the promotion of world peace. In 1878 he founded the first Italian peace society, the League of Peace and Brotherhood. In 1887, during a period of French-Italian tension, he founded an international peace society in Italy, the Lombard Peace Union, modeled on the English International Peace Society. In 1898 he started the periodical *La vita internazionale,* which published articles by prominent advocates of peace.

Moneta represented his country at various congresses organized to promote peace. At the Bern Congress of 1892, he sponsored a motion for a confederation of European states. He also served as president of the International Peace Congress that met in Milan in 1906. The following year he received the Nobel Peace Prize, which he shared with the French jurist Louis Renault.

Despite his dedication to the cause of peace, Moneta supported the war that his country waged against Turkey in 1911–1912 for the acquisition of Libya. He also favored Italy's intervention in World War I.

Writings. Moneta's writings were mainly journalistic except for his 3-volume *Le guerre, le insurrezioni, e la pace nel secolo XIX* (*War, Insurrection, and Peace in the 19th Century*) published in 1903. The work was specifically recognized in the Nobel citation.

RENÉ ALBRECHT-CARRIÉ
Professor of History
Columbia University

MONETARY CONFERENCES, mon′ə-ter-ē kon′fər-əns-ez, are meetings between nations to discuss monetary and banking problems. The first major meeting, held at Paris in 1867, was attended by delegates of 18 European nations and the United States. The principal topic was international exchange. It was decided (1) that it was wiser to adopt an existing monetary system as a standard than to devise a new one; and (2) that gold was the only standard adapted to international money. No formal agreements were made, but the way was opened to further talks.

Throughout the 19th century the struggle between gold and silver constituted a major fiscal problem, in connection with which the United States government solely or jointly initiated three international monetary conferences. The first of these, called the Second International Monetary Conference, was launched by an act of the United States Congress on Feb. 28, 1878, which directed the president to invite European nations to join in a "conference to adopt a common ratio between gold and silver for the purpose of establishing internationally the use of bimetallic money, and securing fixity of relative value between those two metals." Behind the conference lay the need to offset a potentially serious depreciation in the value of silver, caused, among other factors, by the increasingly large production of silver in the United States. Twelve nations participated in the conference, held in Paris. The United States submitted proposals calling for the unrestricted coinage of silver and its use as legal tender, and advocated a bimetallic standard on the basis of a fixed ratio between gold and silver. The attending European nations rejected the American requests by insisting that conditions within individual nations should determine the monetary functions of both silver and gold, and that the selection of either currency or both "should be governed by the special position of each state or group of states." The discussions ended without mutual agreement respecting American proposals.

In the next few years England and France met with seriously diminished gold reserves; the United States was being forced to import gold, which upset the European market; and Germany was unable to find a satisfactory means of disposing of her stocks of silver. To handle the problems posed, the French and American governments joined in calling the Third International Monetary Conference, which 19 nations attended in Paris in 1881. The nations recommended the establishment of a 15½ to 1 ratio of silver and gold and then adjourned to allow the various nations to consider the proposition before reconvening on April 12, 1882. The conference was not reassembled.

The Fourth International Monetary Conference was called by the United States to consider what measures might be taken "to increase the use of silver as money in the currency system of nations." Twenty nations were represented at sessions held in Brussels during November 1892. Lengthy discussions produced various schemes for a bimetallic standard and for the wider circulation of silver through a cooperative system. The conference finally adjourned without formal agreements, although a subsequent meeting was set for May 30, 1893, but was never held.

In 1922 another international monetary conference was held at Genoa to combat postwar inflationary trends. It accomplished little, primarily because of the effects of unstable monetary conditions in Germany. However, it was followed by a London conference, beginning on July 16, 1924, which involved 10 nations in discussions regarding monetary difficulties, particularly in Germany. The conference agreed on the so-called Dawes plan (see DAWES, CHARLES GATES), which had earlier been accepted on April 16 by Germany and was later signed on Aug. 16, 1924.

From June 12 to July 27, 1933, the famous London Monetary and Economic Conference was held, at which American Secretary of State Cordell Hull (q.v.) presided. The conference sought to reach an agreement on currency stabilization but virtually disregarded the equally important problems of war debts and reparations. On July 3, President Franklin D. Roosevelt issued his unexpected "bombshell" message, which expressed disapproval of the course of action taken by the conference. After this setback, the meetings wavered on for a few weeks, but ended in failure.

Before the conclusion of World War II, the United States, in planning to meet postwar reconstruction needs, called a monetary and financial conference which met in June 1944 at Bretton Woods, N.H. This meeting differed from earlier monetary conferences in emphasizing international banking rather than international currency agreements. Here plans were made for the creation of the International Monetary Fund and of the International Bank for Reconstruction and Development. Both were established in 1946 as autonomous intergovernmental agencies of the United Nations.

See also BANKS AND FINANCE—*18. International Bank for Reconstruction and Development;* BIMETALLISM; GOLD STANDARD—*International Gold-Bullion Standard* (International Monetary Fund); UNITED NATIONS—*2. Covenant and Charter (Intergovernmental Agencies)*.

Bibliography.—Russell, H.B., *International Monetary Conferences* (New York 1898); Whittlesey, C.R., *International Monetary Issues* (New York 1937); Halm, George N., *International Monetary Cooperation* (Chapel Hill, N.C., 1945); Morgan, Carlyle, *Bretton Woods: Clue to a Monetary Mystery* (United Nations 1945); Aufricht, Hans, *The International Monetary Fund* (New York 1964).

MONETITE, mon′ə-tīt, is a native acid phosphate of calcium, with the formula $CaHPO_4$. It occurs in massive and small triclinic crystals, in the islands of Moneta and Mona, in the West Indies. The mineral is found in limestone, beneath a deposit of guano.

MONEY, mun′ē, in an economic sense, is any medium of exchange that is widely accepted in payment for goods, services and debts without reference to the standing of the person offering it in payment.

In our highly specialized modern economy with its extreme division of labor, money is as necessary in the exchange of goods and services as language in the exchange of ideas. It is truly indispensable; in fact, if it does not function properly production, distribution, employment, and our very standard of living and well-being are directly affected. Because of this great importance, authorities in many fields have devoted much study to the nature, functioning, and phenomena of money with the result that views and definitions are legion—and vary as widely as the divergent aims and different backgrounds of their sponsors.

Some authorities maintain that use of the term *money* should be restricted to whatever serves as the standard of value; others insist that "money is what money does," therefore, they say the term should encompass all the instrumentalities, especially the obligations, which affect exchanges, such as checks, notes, drafts, mortgages, charge accounts, etc. Admittedly, it is very difficult to differentiate a complex concept such as money from all other economic and social concepts but it can be fairly said that all monetary concepts stress the aspect of standard of value, or that of medium of exchange, or both.

Relation of Money and Credit.—One of the main difficulties in getting a clear-cut concept of money is the overlapping of *money* and *credit.* Practically all modern money has an element of credit—in fact, a great deal of it is 100 per cent credit. This characteristic and the indiscriminate use of the words *cash, money,* and *credit* compound the confusion. In view of this, it is important to develop a workable (if not absolutely perfect) concept of credit, which will differentiate it from money.

The term *credit* is used in many different connections and with many different meanings. For the purpose of an understanding of money, however, credit may properly be defined as a promise to pay money. It must be immediately admitted, however, that most such promises are redeemed with credit rather than with money. This is understandable, as in an important sense credit is merely a postponed payment of money; that is, it is the term applied to a common and important use of money, namely, that of deferred payment.

Relation of Money, Credit, and Prices.—In the first half of the 20th century, the relation of money, credit, and prices was by far the most active field of economic inquiry. The "dance of the dollar," as the fluctuating price level was sarcastically characterized, became the preoccupation of economists, bankers, and politicians alike. Pressure groups were organized, books written, and political campaigns fought on different theories of eliminating the upward and downward swings of prices and business activity. The social injustice of the transfers in purchasing power from debtors to creditors, and vice versa, through changes in the price level, became generally recognized. The wide variations between *nominal* purchasing power and *real* purchasing power became more fully comprehended through the development and wider usage of index numbers. Steadily the conviction developed that the price level should be made to serve man rather than the contrary. Laws were passed and policies developed in an effort to make money a *means,* rather than an *end,* or *result,* of economic activity.

A clear idea of the terms *price* and *value* will be helpful in securing a better understanding of the relation between money and credit and price behavior. The *value* (exchange value) of a thing is its purchasing power over all other goods and services. In this sense, value is measured by the quantity of other things for which a thing can be exchanged. For example, a bushel of wheat may be exchanged for two bushels of rye, or three bushels of corn, or ten gallons of gasoline, or two hours of common labor, and so on. These and countless other ratios measure the value of wheat, in the limited sense (exchange) in which value was used above; so, the complexity of value determination—even of such simple value as exchange value—is obvious.

The price of a thing is its purchasing power over money, that is, the amount of money for which it can be exchanged. In other words, price is value expressed in terms of money. Money, therefore, has no price—it has only value. It follows that a general rise or fall in prices merely reflects a change in the value, or purchasing power, of money. The value of money falls as the general price level rises, and rises as the price level falls. This behavior pattern is summarized by the economist in this fashion: "The value of money is inverse to the level of prices."

There are many theories of the relation between money and price behavior. The boom of the 1920's, and the great depression of the 1930's, with their vast monetary experiments, conclusively demonstrated that all such theories leave much to be desired. The imponderability of the so-called human element, in fact, the perversity of human reaction, is so great that the relation between money and prices cannot be reduced to the comforting certainty of a principle or law. The explanations are still very much *theories.*

The quantity theory of money, which holds that the value of money (that is, the general price level) depends on its quantity and that *ceteris paribus* (other things being equal) prices will vary directly with the quantity of money in circulation, has the virtues of seniority, simplicity, and surface logic. It also enjoys the widest acceptance of any of the theories. Nonetheless, in its simplest form it leaves much to be desired. In particular, through the *cetcris paribus* device, it overlooks the basic importance of *demand.*

Irving Fisher's mathematical presentation of the factors which affect the general price level is a much more comprehensive and acceptable concept of monetary and price behavior. His basic formula is: $MV + M'V' = PT$. In this statement, M is the quantity of money, V is the velocity of its circulation (turnover), M′ is the total of demand deposits subject to check, V′ is the velocity of such deposits, P is the price level and T is the volume of trade.

Although frequently called the mathematical statement of the quantity theory of money, Fisher's formula is more properly *the equation of exchange.* It is, in fact, a mathematical statement of any theory of money, since it is a truism. This equation clearly indicates that an increase or decrease in velocity, or an increase or decrease in goods may affect prices just as much as a change in the quantity of money. Thus, it would be just as logical to call this the goods theory of prices or the velocity theory of prices. Moreover, it obviously does not explain why people decide to change from money to goods, in the first place—from an economic standpoint, it is an after-the-event presentation.

This overemphasis on quantity was at the bottom of the government "pump-priming" of the 1930's; but it failed, as it disregarded the basic fact that velocity (turnover) is largely controlled by the public. In fact, as the government increased the quantity, the public decreased the *velocity.*

The overemphasis on quantity inherent in the quantity theory causes people to overlook the great effect of prices on the quantity of credit (M′) in the modern economy. In fact, the amount of M′ brought into existence by the banker is determined by the price level rather than the opposite. As a practical matter, the amount of a loan (quantity) is calculated by multiplying the number of units desired by the market price of each unit. To be sure, after the credit is brought into existence, it will probably affect prices; but not necessarily: the public may commensurately slow up velocity or even increase the quantity of goods.

Kinds of Money.—Basically, there are three kinds of money: (1) commodity money, (2) credit money, and (3) fiat money.

Commodity money is money the monetary value of which approximates the value of the material it contains. Its value as a commodity is substantially the same as its value as money. Thus, with gold at $35.00 an ounce, a five-dollar gold coin containing one seventh of an ounce of pure gold would be commodity money. By the same token, with the market value of silver at seventy-five cents an ounce, a silver dollar containing one and one third ounces of silver would be commodity money.

Commodity money is usually, although not necessarily, metallic money. As a result of their widespread usage for this purpose, gold, silver, and copper are known as the monetary metals.

Because of greater convenience, and resulting public preference, commodity money usually circulates in representative form. For example, instead of a heavy silver dollar, a piece of paper giving title to the same amount of silver kept in the United States Treasury circulates. The same is true of gold if a country is on a gold basis. By means of *representative money,* commodity money circulates, it might be said, by proxy.

Many writers treat *representative money* as a distinct kind of money. In view, however, of the almost universal modern practice of keeping the monetary metal in one common pool (reserve) and having it circulate by proxy, it seems more realistic to consider representative money as the form in which commodity money generally circulates.

Credit money is the term used to designate all credit instruments widely accepted in payment for goods, services, and debts without reference to the standing of the person tendering them. Credit money, being itself a promise to pay money, presupposes the existence of another kind of money in which it may be redeemed. This money of redemption is known as standard money whereas credit money is frequently termed fiduciary money because of the element of trust.

Quick and easy redemption is the key to the general acceptability of credit money. So long as no barriers are placed in the path of redemption its value will naturally be the same as that of the money in which it can be redeemed, even though redemption never takes place. Any restriction on redemption will cause credit money to depreciate in terms of standard money to the extent of holders' estimates of the extent and duration of the limitation.

It should be noted, however, that complete loss of all faith in ultimate redemption will not necessarily mean that the inconvertible money will lose all of its value. This is because the monetary use itself creates a demand for the money and thus gives it a value. This is especially true if the quantity of credit money is controlled so that there is a scarcity of it relative to the demand for it for monetary purposes. The value of such inconvertible money is often further increased by the willingness of the government to accept it in payment of taxes at face value or some relatively high percentage of such value. In addition, the government may further bolster its value by making it *legal tender* for private debts, that is, by requiring creditors to accept the money at par in payment of all debts and claims.

Credit money is ordinarily paper money, although, as will be seen in the next section, not all paper money is credit money. Much of the paper money issued by governments and all bank notes are credit money.

It should be added that the subsidiary coins are usually made with a disproportionate weight or of a cheaper metal than the standard money so that the express, or implied, promise to redeem them contributes to their value. To the extent that their value derives from the promise rather than the silver, copper, nickel, etc. they contain, these subsidiary coins are credit money. This is true of all our minor coins (such as pennies and nickels). It is also true of our silver coins as they contain less silver by weight than the ratio of their fractional value to the unit indicates. In short, a half-dollar does not have one half as much silver as a silver dollar, nor does one quarter have one fourth as much silver as the silver dollar. This reduction of weight, of course, affects the value but the overvaluation of silver for coinage purposes causes an even greater spread between its value as a commodity and its monetary value. The reasons our coins are credit money are thus quite obvious.

Fiat money is the term used to designate money by government command. The name pointedly indicates this as the Latin word *fiat* means: let it be done. Since it becomes money only through fiat, it must be issued by government, or under the specific order and protection of sovereignty. For example, when a government takes a piece of any material and stamps or prints on it that it is so many units of money, regardless of its value as a commodity, and without making it redeemable, or convertible into other money, then forces such pieces into general circulation, that is fiat money. The essential feature of all fiat money is that its value is independent of the material from which it is made, as well as independent of any promise of redemption in other money.

Fiat money usually starts out as credit money issued under varying degrees of good faith. As redemption or maintenance of other promises becomes burdensome, increasing limitations and restrictions are introduced until repudiation is a tacit, even though not admitted, fact. Because of custom, tradition, and social inertia, such money will continue to circulate, although at a lower value. The value it will have will be affected by the extent to which it has been made legal tender and by its acceptability by the government for public dues. In addition, of course, its value will be affected by the quantity issued relative to the demand for it for monetary purposes, as that is the most important determinant in the value of all inconvertible, or fiat moneys.

Paper Money.—In its narrow, and correct, sense, paper money is merely the *form* in which most of the other kinds of money circulate. In the public mind, however, it is more closely associated with fiat than with either credit or commodity money. This may well be a folk memory, as the history of "paper money" is more interesting than reassuring!

Although paper is supposed to have been invented in China in the year 177 B.C., the Chinese did not get around to using it for money until more than a thousand years later. In the early part of the 9th century, what is thought to have been the first issue of true paper money was put out for the ostensible purpose of avoiding the difficulty of carrying around the heavy iron and copper coins used in the trade of that day. Since that time the evils, abuses, fraud, and economic dislocation flowing from the unprincipled and unwise use of paper for money have caused even more suffering than that other famous Chinese invention, gunpowder.

It is the indisputable lesson of history that sooner or later, and usually sooner, all paper money declines in quality—representative money becomes credit money, credit money becomes fiat money, and fiat money becomes the epitome of worthlessness. Even to this day, the "not worth a Continental" term which arose from the extreme depreciation of the Continental currency of revolutionary times, indicates complete lack of value. The final destruction of value, of course, comes from the excessive issue of the paper "money."

In paper money, the evil of overissue must be fought continuously. It is so tempting and so easy to print more unsupported "paper" money that it is fed into circulation in such excessive amounts that sharp depreciation, and even utter collapse of value, become inevitable. Overissue, or currency inflation, as it is commonly known, is easily recognized by those honest enough to face facts; and the remedy is well understood. But it is like a narcotic: those that should stop the inflation lose all desire to do so. The artificial economic well-being engendered by the expansion causes men to act as if the millennium had arrived until the day of reckoning descends upon them and their economic world collapses.

Some 150 years ago the French blazed such a spectacular downward trail with their *mandats* and *assignats* that it should have served to end currency tinkering for all time; but not so. Since then the nations of the world have trod this trail into a well-beaten downward road. To mention but a few outstanding cases, the Confederate money of Civil War days, and the German mark, Italian lira, French franc, and other currencies, too numerous to mention, of the post-World War I period conclusively demonstrate that it requires more than *fiat* to make *money* out of paper. Yet nations continually try to do so, even though history indicates that the ultimate consequences are foredoomed.

The great tragedy of currency inflation is that it is practically impossible to reverse the depreciation process. Once a nation sets its feet upon the economic primrose path of "easy money," it finds the descent ever steeper, the going ever more slippery, and the downward rate ever faster and faster. Because of this, paper money has been bitterly assailed as the greatest affliction ever visited on mankind. But such criticism is misdirected. It is the abuse, not the use, of paper money which causes the suffering. Properly used, paper money is undoubtedly the greatest convenience ever devised by the wit of man. It should be treasured as one of our blessings and protected from those who would misuse it, for whatever purpose.

Deposit "Money."—Demand deposits (those subject to check) are considered as money by many modern authorities. Certainly, they constitute by far the most important medium of exchange, especially in the more advanced countries. Economists estimate that more than 90 per cent of the dollar volume of all monetary transactions in the United States and Canada is through the medium of bank deposits, so they truly do a large part of the medium of exchange work of money. But it also must be admitted that checks, the form in which they do this money work, do not pass from hand to hand as does money. Checks can, of course, and do frequently, continue to pass from hand to hand by *endorsement* (they could be drawn to *bearer* and pass by delivery but this is rarely done) but generally they are deposited in a bank at the first opportunity. In fact, if not promptly presented, payment may be contested on the equitable ground of *laches* (delay in exercising rights). They not only do not circulate freely by delivery as does true money, they are also not accepted without reference to the credit standing of the issuer. Checks and bank deposits are thus credit, and not money, even though they do the major part of our exchanging and even though bank deposits constitute the largest store of liquid value in a country with a modern banking system like that of the United States or Canada.

Functions of Money.—The many services rendered by money may be grouped under four functional headings: (1) standard of value; (2) medium of exchange; (3) standard of deferred payments; and (4) store of value. Although these are basic functions, they vary greatly in relative importance from time to time and country to country. For instance, during the 1930's in the United States, it was thought necessary to restrict certain functions so that a managed money could be introduced.

In reading the following explanations of specific functions, the dynamic nature of money should be kept in mind. Money is dynamic; its functions are dynamic. This is necessarily so as the economy it serves is highly dynamic.

Standard of Value.—It is as a common denominator of value that money renders its greatest service. Without such a pecuniary language device, modern business would not be possible. Record-keeping, accounting, and finance stem from this function of money.

As can be readily seen by referring to the article on CURRENCY, man's standards of value down through the years have been legion, in fact, almost infinite. It is difficult to find anything in common usage in the past which has not served some time, some place, as the standard of value. Why a particular thing was used at a particular time is for the anthropologist and sociologist to determine; sufficient for the student of money is the fact that it was so used.

The necessity of a standard of value, even in the earliest times, is apparent because of the utter inconvenience of barter (exchange of one good for another good). The difficulty of finding the necessary double coincidence of demand and supply made it imperative to devise a separate standard so that the division of labor with its many benefits could develop.

In its earliest forms, money was a commodity with such scarcity and such utility (whether for adornment, as in the case of shells, or for further production, as in the case of the cow) that it was generally desired. The fact that some commodity became the standard of value does not mean that it did not change in value. On the contrary, crop failure, wars, and other disasters frequently caused great changes in the value of the standard itself. In addition to the changes in value flowing from physical factors, even greater changes frequently came from psychological factors. Without apparent "rhyme or reason" people sometimes just decided they did not like a thing as well as they did before. They still do this at times, so it is fair to say that there never has been, and conceivably never will be, any standard of value which will be immutable and unchangeable. At least, as long as people can change their minds, the so-called standard of value will fluctuate in purchasing power. The problem is people; not the standard.

Even though no perfect standard of value seems possible, the evils of severe or violent changes in the price level make it highly desirable to use the most stable money substance and, in addition, to do everything possible to keep upsetting psychological pressures to a minimum. Admittedly it is well-nigh impossible to keep people from acting "bullish" when they feel "bullish" and from acting "blue" when they feel "blue"; but the attempt must be made; and if it fails, the blame should be placed where it belongs.

In modern times the standard of value has often been separate and distinct from the medium of exchange. In other words, the unit used for the standard of value need not be used widely, nor even at all, as a medium of exchange. Accounts may be kept in any money specified by law or dictated by tradition. A good example of the complete separation of the "money of account" and the medium of exchange is the United States gold dollar. Other than for memorial and exposition purposes, the gold dollar has not even been coined since 1889, much less freely circulated. Nonetheless, it is the unit in which all records are kept and calculations made.

It has been said sarcastically that it is as a standard of value that money functions most poorly, yet that is the only function which has not declined markedly in importance in recent years. The evils of severe and catastrophic changes in prices are not as great as those of attempting to function without a common denominator of value. Truly, this is the indispensable function of money.

Medium of Exchange.—Through its function as the medium of exchange, money made possible the "division of labor" with its tremendous increase in production. In this respect alone, money has rendered incalculable service to mankind. In our time, as was explained above, this function has largely been taken over by checks, or "deposit money."

From the money side itself, the use of gold, or even gold certificates, as a medium of exchange in the United States was prohibited by Executive Order on April 5, 1933. This was done even though the gold dollar then, and thereafter, was declared by law to be the standard of value. In particular, the Gold Reserve Act of 1934 provided that all gold coin should be withdrawn from circulation and melted into bars and prohibited further coinage of gold in the United States except for foreign account.

Money is thus no longer *the* medium of exchange in the United States; in its true form it is no longer even *a* medium of exchange; it is, however, in its credit form a minor factor as a medium of exchange. But even though this is the case, this function should not be "written off." Economic disorganization, banking difficulties, or any other factor which reduces public confidence would make the medium of exchange services of this credit money an extremely important function again.

Standard of Deferred Payments.—Modern man differs from his ancestors in increased ability to plan ahead and increased ability to borrow. The pledge of anticipated income to secure goods and services for immediate use and enjoyment is characteristic of business and individuals. This ability of the active, enterprising members of society to command the capital and credit they need for their ventures is an outstanding advantage of our competitive capitalism. It is made possible by several factors, but the basic one is the existence of a standard of deferred payment.

Such a standard permits planning and encourages saving. All manner of contracts extending far into the future can be made in confidence if the deferred portion of the performance can be put on a standard basis. Prior to 1933, in the United States, such contracts were usually made payable in "gold dollars of the present standard of weight and fineness" and sometimes even in gold as a commodity by weight without reference to the monetary unit. Now all of this has been changed by Joint Resolution of Congress, approved June 5, 1933, which forbade the use of a "gold clause" and provided that "every obligation, heretofore or hereafter incurred," whether or not it contains a gold clause, "shall be discharged upon payment, dollar for dollar, in any coin or currency which at the time of payment is legal tender for public and private debts." This means that the money of circulation will be the money of payment in the future. The extent to which that will be a standard from one period to another period remains to be seen.

Store of Value.—The other three functions of money naturally lead to its use as a store of value. As deposit banking has developed to a high degree in many countries and as hoarding has been made illegal in most countries with positive steps taken by governments to keep it at a minimum, the store of value function has declined in importance in recent years. It has, also, declined because in most countries money no longer has commodity value, nor can it with certainty, and under all circumstances, be changed into the money commodity, or other commodities, at a specific rate.

In ordinary times, individuals keep on hand comparatively small amounts of "pocket money" for small purchases, carfare, etc. Likewise, business organizations keep small amounts on hand as petty cash and for making change. Larger amounts are needed for payroll purposes if a cash payroll is used but that usually comes directly from the bank to the payment window. Banks of course have to keep substantial amounts of money on hand to cash checks and otherwise serve their depositors.

The demand for money, or currency, varies with the swings of the business cycle, with the ups and downs of public confidence, and with the seasons. Thus, the need for additional money during the Christmas shopping season is well known. Nonetheless there really was little excuse for the wide swings and the great increase in money in circulation in the United States which characterized the period after World War II, as demand deposits were freely convertible into money and more than half of the assets back of these deposits were government bonds.

In fact, as stated earlier, bank deposits constitute the principle store of liquid purchasing power in the United States. As they ordinarily total some six times the amount of money in circulation outside of the banks and the Treasury, they have, for the reasons enumerated, largely taken over the store of value function formerly rendered by money.

Qualities of Good Money.—By definition, general acceptability is a prerequisite quality of money. Relative stability of value is also extremely important. Serious maladjustments between debtors and creditors, savers and enterprisers, pensioners and organized workers, and between the many other classes in society arise when the purchasing power of money fluctuates sharply or changes permanently. Complete stability is, of course, unattainable as that would mean that the effective supply (actual units multiplied by the turnover) would have to vary sensitively and perfectly with each change in the demand for it for monetary or any other uses to which it is put. The necessary exact adjustment between supply and demand has never been achieved in practice. Many promising theoretical plans to achieve the desired stability have been advocated but, so far, none has succeeded.

The other qualities of good money apply primarily, or solely, to coins, which are treated elsewhere, so they will only be briefly mentioned here. Portability, or relatively high value per unit, is an important quality. Divisibility, or the ability to divide the monetary commodity into exact fractions without waste or difficulty and later recombine them, is another essential quality. These divisions must be equal in all respects or *homogeneous.* (Metals such as silver and gold have the qualities of divisibility and homogeneity in high degree; cows and diamonds do not.) The money substance must be malleable enough to be shaped properly, easily recognizable, and sufficiently durable to hold its design during long periods of use.

Summarizing, the eight more important qualities of good money are: general acceptability, stability of value, portability, cognizability, divisibility, homogeneity, malleability, and durability. In practice, gold has demonstrated that it possesses these qualities in higher degree than any other substance although it must be admitted that it has proved distressingly unstable in value.

Monetary Standards.—The expression monetary standard refers to the money in which credits are ultimately redeemable in a country. If gold is the money of redemption, the country is said to be on a gold standard. *The standard money must be either commodity money or fiat money; it cannot be credit money because it is, itself, redeemable in some other kind of money.*

Although various metals have been used as standard money, the special qualities of gold and silver have made them preferred above all others since the beginning of the Christian era. In more recent times increased production and economies in its monetary use have enabled gold to far outstrip silver as a monetary base. The way in which the monetary commodity is utilized is an integral part of the monetary standard. The relative scarcity of the monetary metals has caused considerable ingenuity in their utilization. In the following explanations of the physical details of the various standards, gold will be used for the single metal standards, as it is the conventional monetary base; but it should be understood that silver, platinum, copper, or any other metal could be similarly used if public preference focused on it.

Gold Coin Standard.—The essentials of a full gold coin standard are: (1) adoption of a definite quantity of gold of a certain fineness as the unit; (2) full legal tender for the gold coins; (3) all legal tender money redeemable on demand in gold coins at par; (4) unlimited and free coinage of gold (with no more than nominal seigniorage, that is, deductions); (5) unrestricted exportation and importation of gold in any form.

Disregard or violation of any of these essentials limits the full gold coin standard by just that much. Because of the danger of public hoarding, nations in recent times have so restricted this standard that in its true form it has become merely a historical curiosity.

Gold Bullion Standard.—This monetary standard, which is the one used by most of the advanced countries, is exactly the same as the gold coin standard except that coinage is dispensed with, that is, the gold is kept in bars. In practice, however, the gold bullion standard is always modified by restrictions on the minimum amount of bullion which will be issued for other forms of money. This is often put quite high to "economize in the use of the gold"! In addition, nations usually specifically reserve the right to determine whether a particular use of the gold is in "the public interest." Thus, on the specious basis that gold is not needed by the domestic population as either a medium of exchange or a store of value, it may be released only to fill the demonstrated needs of industrial users and only for exportation. Although all such limitations constitute a departure from the full gold bullion standard, they are inherent in this standard, in practice. After all, the purpose in adopting a gold bullion standard, rather than a coin standard, is to remove all gold from internal circulation and reserve it solely for use in meeting the needs of industry and in settling international balances.

Gold Exchange Standard.—This standard is the same as the gold coin standard except that, instead of coin or bullion, gold exchange (a demand draft on a country on a gold standard) is used for the redemption of legal tender money. The gold exchange standard was quite popular among the "have not" and politically dependent nations for a while after World War I; but the wholesale departures from the international gold standard in the 1930's gave this monetary device a blow from which it will probably never fully recover.

Bimetallic Standard.—In this system the monetary standard is defined as either of two metals, a definite quantity and fineness of each being stipulated as the unit. It has the same features as the gold coin standard with respect to redemption, legal tender, free coinage, and unlimited exportation and importation. Although the bimetallic standard could be on either a coinage or a bullion basis, so far only coinage has been tried. The results have, in general, been unsatisfactory. Rather than enumerate the theoretical advantages and disadvantages, the heretofore insuperable problem in the actual operation of a bimetallic system will be explained. This fatal handicap is the tendency for cheap money to drive dearer money out of circulation. This is commonly known as Gresham's Law, after Queen Elizabeth's master of the mint, Sir Thomas

Gresham, who was one of many to call attention to the phenomenon.

In a bimetallic system Gresham's Law operates in this fashion: After the mint ratio of the two metals is fixed, any change in the world market value of one with relation to the other would cause the metal with the higher value to begin disappearing from circulation. This is so because of the obvious fact that people will hold the more valuable money and pass on the less valuable whenever they have a choice. The fixed mint ratio gives them exactly such a choice. This was conclusively demonstrated on a vast scale in the American experience with the bimetallic standard through the 19th century. One or the other of the metals was always disappearing from circulation. Thus, during the first period of legal bimetallism in the United States (1792–1834), gold went out of circulation, but in the second period (1834–1873) silver went out. Following 1873, however, the political power of the silver bloc was so great in legislative halls, that silver was usually overvalued, so it circulated while gold "did the disappearing act"!

Symmetallic Standard.—In this proposed system, the monetary standard would consist of a definite quantity of a combination of two or more metals. Redemption would be in symmetallic coins or bars, or in all of the component metals separately; likewise, issue would require presentation of definite quantities of all the component metals. Although this method would reduce the hazards of Gresham's Law to a minimum, it has so many obvious disadvantages that it has never been tried in practice.

Compensated Standard.—This new term for Irving Fisher's "stabilized dollar" is another scheme to secure more stability in the standard of value. The method proposed is that of periodically varying the quantity of metal in the unit, which would, because of this variation, be kept on a bullion basis. The proposal has the virtue of simplicity: as the unit becomes more valuable and prices decline, its metallic content would be decreased; as the unit becomes less valuable and prices rise, its metallic content would be increased.

The reduction of the gold content of the United States dollar from 25.8 grains of gold .9 fine to 15 5/21 grains .9 fine in January 1934 and the temporary permission given the president to further alter the gold content within certain limits is an instance of a passing "flirtation" with the compensated dollar idea. An important part of this "flirtation" was the gold buying activity through the Reconstruction Finance Corporation in the months *before* the approval of the Gold Reserve Act on Jan. 30, 1934. This is as near as the compensated standard has ever come to being adopted. It should be added that although the proposal has been made only in connection with gold, it would be equally adaptable to any of the other metallic standards.

Fiat Standard.—A fiat standard is whatever the government makes it. The essential difference between it and any other standard is that the monetary value must be substantially higher than that of the material contained in it and it must not be a promise to pay some other kind of money, that is, no assurance is given on redemption. In short, a substantial portion of the value of the standard must flow from the power of government. The characteristics and defects of such a monetary unit are given in the section on fiat money; those defects are likewise inherent in a fiat monetary system. In passing, it should be noted that Gresham's Law outlined in the section on bimetallism, operates in this field, too, as some fiats are worse than others.

Managed Money.—A large degree of management or control is attempted in practically all modern monetary systems. In a country like the United States, where bank deposits are freely interchangeable with money, such management is, in reality, credit management. Money behavior in this country is almost entirely corollary to developments on the credit side. The monetary authorities, therefore, concentrate their attention on credit control and, in general, permit the "chips to fall where they may" on the money side. Unfortunately, "money management" carried to the extreme, as has been the case in many countries, usually forces a country downhill to a fiat basis.

In a narrower sense, the establishment of exchange stabilization funds and similar direct government intervention may be termed money management.

Monetary System of the United States.—The unprecedented outpouring of monetary legislation and executive orders in the 1930's changed the basic character of the United States monetary system. Gold was "nationalized"; contracts calling for payment in gold were abrogated; the weight of the dollar was drastically reduced; and many other things were done with the result that it could be fairly said that a new monetary system was inaugurated.

In essence, this new monetary system is based on a highly restricted, international, administrative, gold bullion standard. Gold is no longer coined; nor is it available for domestic monetary use. Moreover, no currency is redeemed in gold for any purpose except such as the treasury may permit by regulation or special license. The Federal Reserve banks no longer own gold; they have instead "gold certificates" which in the language of the law "shall be redeemed at such times and in such amounts, as in the judgment of the Secretary of the Treasury, are necessary to maintain the equal purchasing power of every kind of currency of the United States."

The automatic regulation features of the old gold standard have thus been abandoned. In its place, there has been substituted government discretion and expediency. Inherent in such a system is the possibility, even probability, of tremendous inflation. As a practical matter, control of the monetary system has been given to the executive branch of the government instead of the central bank authorities.

RAYMOND RODGERS
Professor of Banking
New York University

Bibliography.—Johnson, Joseph F., *Money and Currency* (Boston 1921); Keynes, John M., *A Treatise on Money,* 2 vols. (New York 1930); Kemmerer, Edwin H., *Money* (New York 1935); Withers, Hartley, *The Meaning of Money,* 6th ed. (London 1937); Foster, Major Bronson, and Rodgers, Raymond, *Money and Banking,* 4th ed. (New York 1953); Day, Alan C., *The Economics of Money* (New York 1959); Dunn, Gerald T., *Monetary Decisions of the Supreme Court* (New Brunswick, N.J., 1950); Johnson, Harry, *Money, Trade, and Economic Growth* (Cambridge, Mass., 1962); Burstein, Meyer, *Money* (Cambridge, Mass., 1963).

MONEY BIRD. See BIRDS OF PARADISE.

MONEYWORT OR CREEPING JENNY. See LOOSESTRIFE.

MONGE, mônzh, **Gaspard,** French mathematician, physicist, and public official: b. Beaune, France, May 10, 1746; d. Paris, July 18, 1818. Monge made important contributions in at least three branches of mathematics. He is credited with establishing descriptive geometry on a scientific basis. In differential geometry, he made systematic investigations into the theory of curvature and its application to the central quadrics. And of equal importance was his work on the solution of partial differential equations by means of his theory of surfaces.

A child prodigy, Monge was educated in schools of the Oratorian order at Beaune and Lyon and at the school of military engineering at Mézières. At the age of 19 he taught mathematics and physics at Mézières. In 1780 he also began teaching hydraulics at the Louvre in Paris and became a member of the Académie des Sciences. In 1783 he left Mézières to become examiner of candidates for the École de Marine.

Monge was rewarded for his support of the French Revolution with the position of minister of marine, which he held in 1792–93. He was a founder of the École Polytechnique in 1794–1795 and taught there. In 1798 he accompanied his friend Napoleon Bonaparte to Egypt, where he was named president of the Cairo Institute. On his return to France, he again taught at the École Polytechnique. After Napoleon became emperor in 1804, Monge was made a senator and count of Péluse. After the downfall of Napoleon in 1815, however, Monge was deprived of his honors and expelled from his positions. Foremost among Monge's writings were *Feuilles d'analyse appliquée a la géométrie* (1795), and *Géométrie descriptive* (1799).

MONGOLIA, mong-gō'lē-ə, is a geographical region of east central Asia, lying principally between the Soviet Union and China, and including portions of those countries. Traditionally Mongolia was divided into two distinct regions, Inner Mongolia and Outer Mongolia, separated by the Gobi Desert. Inner Mongolia has been under Chinese control since the 17th century. Outer Mongolia was a Chinese province from the end of the 17th century until 1911. It was called "Outer" because, from the Chinese point of view, it was beyond—that is, outside of—Inner Mongolia.

Today the contiguous area of Mongolia is divided into the following political units: (1) the Inner Mongolian Autonomous Region, which belongs to China; (2) the Mongolian People's Republic; and (3) two political units in the Russian republic of the USSR: the Buryat and Tuva autonomous republics. The total Mongol population of these areas is about 3 million.

Mongolia is a mountainous, landlocked, arid plateau, covering some 2 million square miles of steppe, forest steppe, desert steppe, and true desert. Most of the area has a continental climate, with light precipitation and great extremes and variations of temperature.

The scattered nomadic population of Mongolia bases its economic life principally on livestock herding. Chinese immigration from the south and Russian immigration from the north are greatly extending and expanding the area's agricultural and industrial development, but they also are constricting the traditional Mongolian pastoral nomadism and significantly decreasing the total area in which the Mongols are culturally and numerically dominant.

Only in the Mongolian People's Republic do Mongols still constitute a clear majority of the population: more than 800,000 of a total population of slightly over a million in the 1960's. Russians and Ukrainians now outnumber the Mongols in the major Soviet Mongolian areas of the Buryat, Tuva, and Kalmyk Autonomous Soviet Socialist Republics.

Chinese outnumber native Mongols in the Inner Mongolian Autonomous Region, the total population of which was over 9 million in the early 1960's. The 1953 census of China reported 1,462,956 Mongols in China, mostly in the Inner Mongolian Autonomous Region.

The Kalmyk Mongols comprise a group that numbers fewer than 100,000 in European Russia. The small number of Hazara Mongols who live in central Afghanistan have lived in complete isolation from the other Mongols for centuries and constitute a unique group.

The People and Their Way of Life.—The Mongols are classic examples of the yellow, Mongoloid race. They usually possess stocky builds with short legs, and rarely exceed 5 feet 6 inches in height. The catalogue of identifying characteristics includes: round head (brachycephalic); coarse dark hair; scant beard; flat nose; slanted black or brown eyes; generally broad, flat face; and, for a brief period after birth, the "Mongolian spot" of bluish pigment in the skin of the lumbar region.

Mongolian territorial divisions include the small basic herding unit, the *bag,* ruled by an elected elder. Bags were united into *somons, khoshuns,* and *aimaks* or *banners.* Banners were sometimes joined into khanates or leagues, under hereditary princes.

The typical traditional Mongol herded livestock, lived in a wooden latticework-framed felt tent (yurt or *ger*), and moved with his herds in a fairly well-defined seasonal pattern of nomadism. The herds comprised mainly sheep, plus lesser numbers of horses, cattle, goats, and camels. Nomadic mobility depended upon the horse, which occupied a very special place in the heart of the Mongol, often reflected in song and story. Camels (the two-humped variety) served for transport, and the camel caravan was a common sight on the Mongolian steppe. Such typical Mongols drank large quantities of tea and *airak* (kumiss, or fermented mare's milk); spoke Mongolian; but rarely could read or write it; and professed Buddhist Lamaism, which included many superstitions surviving from shamanism. Widespread illiteracy, superstition, and disease characterized the Mongols. Russian and Chinese influence have affected all of these characteristics and have completely eliminated some of them.

Collectivization of the herds and concomitant settlement of the nomads eliminated pastoral nomadism among the Buryats years ago, and now threaten the *arats* (livestock-herding nomads) of the Mongolian People's Republic and Inner Mongolia. Many Buryats live in Russian log huts; some Inner Mongols live in Chinese loam huts. In the Mongolian People's Republic the yurt has changed, now often including a stove and a wooden floor and frequently electricity as well. Thousands of Mongols work in factories and live in Western-style housing. Military service, internal passports, taxes, production norms, labor laws, an extensive police system, and improved health and sanitation standards now affect the outlook and activity of the people.

Language, Literature, and Theater Arts.—The Mongols of the Mongolian People's Republic now use the Cyrillic (Russian) script. This script has been applied to the contemporary Khalkha dialect as it is spoken around the city of Ulan Bator.

The republic announced adoption of this modified Cyrillic alphabet in March 1941. From Jan. 1, 1946, all printing in the republic was done in the new alphabet, and from January 1950, use of the new alphabet became mandatory in all official business.

The People's Republic of China has announced adoption of the Latin script for Inner Mongolia. The traditional Mongolian vertical script, however, is in fact still used extensively in Inner Mongolia.

Buryats employed a Latin alphabet from 1931 to 1937, and at that time changed to Cyrillic. Differences in pronounciation, vocabulary, and grammar make Buryat sufficiently variant from Khalkha so that the two are to a large extent mutually incomprehensible. The Tuva Autonomous Republic, many of whose indigenous inhabitants formerly employed Mongolian, had been assigned its own Turkic-based language and Cyrillic alphabet. The Mongolian language belongs to the Altaic family, which also includes Turkic and Manchu-Tungusic. (See ALTAIC LANGUAGES.) Many Mongols in Buryat Mongolia and the Mongolian People's Republic speak Russian, and in Inner Mongolia many speak Chinese.

Traditional Mongolian literature was rich in epics and other oral forms, and some historical writing and legal codification developed as well; but contemporary Mongolian literature generally follows the Russian example, and much of the traditional literature has been lost completely or is known only to specialists. The Khalkha author, Tsendein Damdinsuren, and the Buryat writer, Khutsa Namsarayev, represent the new literature, based largely on Soviet models. Beginning around 1900, there had been a promising literary renaissance, especially among the Buryats, which attempted to harmonize and combine the traditional with Western literary forms and content, but most representatives of this approach lost their lives, or at least their liberty, in the great Soviet purges of 1937–1938. Tsyben Zhamtsarano, Badzar Baradin, and Solbone Tuya led this Buryat intelligentsia.

The Mongolian People's Republic has established art schools, and the State Theater of Music and Drama sponsors productions of Mongolian dramatic works. Plays of Shakespeare, Molière, Chekhov, and other classical European dramatists are also performed. After 1921 motion pictures became one of the most popular forms of entertainment. In addition to some foreign films, the republic has film studios of its own.

History.—Genghis Khan's exploits in the 13th century, the spread of Lamaism and the outbreak of Oirat-Khalkha civil war in the 17th century, and the Manchu collapse along with Japanese and Russian expansion in the 20th century constituted particularly critical developments in Mongolian history. On the Mongolian steppes there are monuments of earlier epochs, particularly of the 9th century Turks (see UIGURS), but the conquests of Genghis Khan and his immediate successors serve most conveniently as a starting point.

Between the time when Genghis Khan became emperor of the Mongols in 1206 A.D. and the fall of the Yüan (Mongol) dynasty in China in 1368, the Mongols erupted and flowed out over great areas of Asia and Europe, reaching as far as Vienna and Muscovy, and exercising control in most of China. Mongolian remnants continued even later; for example, the Khanate of the Golden Horde collected tribute in Russia until 1480. But because of their small numbers (probably not many more than 100,000 Mongols raided Europe), the relatively short period of their hegemony, and their mobile and impermanent way of life, they left surprisingly light traces of the period of their political and military supremacy. See also GENGHIS KHAN; THIRTEENTH CENTURY—*Mongol Invasions;* CHINA—*8. History* (The Yüan, 1260–1368).

Late in the 16th century there began the concentration of forces which redistributed power in central Asia. The Tibetan form of Buddhism (Lamaism), not unknown to the Mongols in earlier times, experienced a renaissance, spreading rapidly among all the Mongols and largely displacing or taking over the former shamanism. The building of the monastery of Erdeni Dzu (in north central Outer Mongolia, 250 miles west of Ulan Bator), in 1584, represented a landmark in this development, and some time later the first Jebtsun Damba Khutukhtu (Living Buddha) of Urga (b. 1623) became religious leader of a large number of the Khalkha Mongols. From that time until the 20th century, Lamaism constituted an integral part of Mongolian culture and came to absorb large numbers of the population and a large proportion of the country's wealth. A theocratic "state within a state," with its own aristocracy and its own laws, property, and customs, became a major factor in Mongolian society. In the early 20th century, lamas accounted for one third of the total male population of Outer Mongolia.

Another important development of the 17th century resulted from the great division and civil war between the western Mongols (the Oirats) and the eastern Mongols (the Khalkhas). The Manchus, who established a new dynasty in China (the Ch'ing, 1644–1912), exploited the intra-Mongol differences in order to assume dominance over most of the Mongols in three main stages: over Inner Mongolia, about 1640; over the Khalkhas of Outer Mongolia by the Diet of Dolonnor in 1691; and over the Oirats of the Kobdo district of western Outer Mongolia in 1754, when the last Oirat khan, Amursana, fled to Russian territory. Meanwhile, the Russians continued their expansion across Siberia to the Pacific, and by treaties with the Manchu emperors of China, at Nerchinsk in 1689 and at Kyakhta (Kiakhta) in 1727, they assumed control of the Buryat-Mongols. Thus by 1754 there had emerged the main outlines of the political pattern which regulated the Mongols until the 20th century: Manchu rulers of China dominated Inner and Outer Mongolia, and Russia controlled Buryat-Mongolia.

The 20th Century.—In the 20th century, the obvious weakening of Manchu control in China led to new jockeyings aimed at redrawing the lines of force in central Asia. Japan came onto the Asian mainland, and by secret treaties with Russia in 1907, 1912, and 1916, divided Mongolia into "spheres of influence" which assigned Outer Mongolia to Russia and eastern Inner Mongolia to Japan. The revolution in China and overthrow of the Manchus, plus Russian encouragement and support, led the Outer Mongols to declare "autonomy," a political condition which existed from Dec. 1, 1911, to 1919, with the eighth Jebtsun Damba Khutukhtu of Urga as head of the government. The 1915 Tripartite Treaty of Kyakhta, signed by "autonomous" Mongolia, republican China, and czarist Russia, placed Outer Mongolia in an ambiguous legal status: "autonomous," yet recognizing Chinese suzerainty, with Russia in effect controlling its foreign relations.

The Russian Bolshevik Revolution of 1917 destroyed the delicate Chinese-Russian-Mongol balance established by the Treaty of Kyakhta, and China reasserted full sovereignty over Outer Mongolia in 1919. Then, late in 1920, anti-Communist forces led by Baron Alexander von Ungern-Sternberg took refuge in Outer Mongolia as a result of the consolidation of Bolshevik control in Siberia. Red Army troops, accompanied by a small Mongolian detachment, destroyed anti-Communist forces on Outer Mongolian soil and entered Urga on July 6, 1921. Since that time, Russian influence has been paramount. The Jebtsun Damba Khutukhtu, however, remained as nominal head of the country until his death in 1924, when Outer Mongolia took the official name of Mongolian People's Republic and the city of Urga became Ulan Bator (Red Hero). Khorloin Choibalsan (1895–1952) and Sukhe Bator (1894–1923) formed and led the early Revolutionary Party, and Choibalsan served from 1939 to 1952 as premier of the republic.

Extensive economic, social, and political change occurred in the republic after 1924. Chinese economic control was broken, and social revolution became especially violent in the 1929–1932 period when an abortive attempt at collectivization of livestock resulted in mass destruction of the herds and widespread purges swept the country. At this time, the Japanese renewed active aggression on the Asian mainland, created Manchukuo, and formed an Inner Mongolian government called Meng-chiang, headed by the Mongolian prince, Te Wang. Japanese military buildup on the border of the Mongolian People's Republic in the Barga area (Manchuria) led to the Soviet-Mongolian Treaty of Mutual Assistance of 1936, and various incidents culminated in a fairly large-scale clash in which Russian troops defeated the Japanese at Nomonhan in 1939.

The Mongolian People's Revolutionary Army joined the Soviet Red Army in military operations against the Japanese in World War II in the week before Japan's surrender. A provision of the Yalta Agreement of February 1945 led to a plebiscite in the republic in October 1945, by which Mongols voted almost unanimously in favor of independence and in opposition to Chinese control (which in 1945 existed only *de jure* and not *de facto*). In January 1946, Chiang Kai-shek's Koumintang government of China officially recognized the independence of the Mongolian People's Republic, although it later withdrew that recognition. Renewed Sino-Mongolian trade relations (1952) and significant Chinese immigration (1955) followed Communist assumption of power in China in 1949.

Talks in Moscow between Premier Yumzhagiyn Tsedenbal of the Mongolian People's Republic and Soviet Leaders (May 10–15, 1957) resulted in the republic's endorsement of Soviet foreign policy, a pledge to continue economic and cultural cooperation, and an agreement for Soviet economic aid. The USSR agreed to hand over its share of Sovmongolmetal (a minerals development company) and its airport installations at Ulan Bator and Sain Shanda and to sell the Mongolneft (an oil trust) on easy terms to the republic.

After several unsuccessful applications, the Mongolian People's Republic was admitted to the United Nations as its 103d member late in 1961.

The Sino-Soviet split led to withdrawal of most Chinese influence and personnel from the Mongolian People's Republic. In 1962, however, Communist China and the Mongolian People's Republic signed a border treaty.

The republic joined the Russian-oriented economic integration unit, CEMA (Council for Economic Mutual Assistance), in 1962. In 1965 the USSR granted the republic a credit of 495 million rubles toward fulfillment of its 1966–1970 Five Year Plan and delayed Mongolia's repayment of earlier debts totaling 170 million rubles.

See also ASIA—*5. Races;* BURYAT AUTONOMOUS SOVIET SOCIALIST REPUBLIC; INNER MONGOLIA; KALMYK; TUVA AUTONOMOUS OBLAST.

Bibliography.—Cahen, Gaston, *Histoire des relations de la Russie avec le Chine sous Pierre le Grand, 1689–1730* (Paris 1912); Courant, Maurice, *L'Asie centrale aux XVII*e *et XVIII*e *siècles: empire Kalmouk ou empire Mantchou?* (Lyon 1912); Carruthers, Alexander Douglas M., *Unknown Mongolia,* 2 vols. (London 1913); Baddeley, John F., *Russia, Mongolia, China,* 2 vols. (London 1919); Korostovetz, Ivan Y., *Von Cinggis Khan zur Sowjetrepublik* (Berlin 1926); Howorth, Sir Henry H., *History of the Mongols from the 9th to the 19th Century,* 4 vols. (London 1876–1927); Huc, Evariste R., and Gabet, Joseph, *Travels in Tartary, Thibet and China, 1844–1846,* tr. by William Hazlitt, 2 vols. (London 1928); Andrews, Roy Chapman, *The New Conquest of Central Asia* (New York 1932); Riazanovskii, Valentin A., *Fundamental Principles of Mongol Law* (Tientsin 1937); Montagu, Ivor, G.S., *Land of Blue Sky* (London 1956); Bitsch, Jorgen, *Mongolia, Unknown Land* (New York 1963).

ROBERT A. RUPEN
Professor of Political Science
University of North Carolina

MONGOLIAN PEOPLE'S REPUBLIC

(OUTER MONGOLIA), an autonomous republic of east central Asia. On the west, south, and east it borders China (Sinkiang-Uigur Autonomous Region, Inner Mongolian Autonomous Region, and western Manchuria), and on the north the Soviet Union (Chita Oblast, Buryat Autonomous SSR, Tuva Autonomous Republic, and Altai Krai). It covers some 600,000 square miles, with extreme distances north to south of 782 miles (between 41° 32′ and 52° 6′ north latitude), and east to west of 1,471 miles (between 87° 47′ and 119° 54′ east longitude). While its average elevation is 5,184 feet above sea level, the republic has the general conformation of a saucer, tipped higher in the northwest and lower in the southeast.

The national flag consists of three vertical stripes of equal width: the sinister red topped by a 5-pointed gold star and beneath it the gold soyombo emblem; the center stripe of light blue; and the dexter stripe of red. The tugrik and the monggo (equivalent in value to the Russian ruble and kopeck) serve as the country's monetary units.

TABLE OF CONTENTS

For discussion of the Mongol people, their history, and their culture, see MONGOLIA.

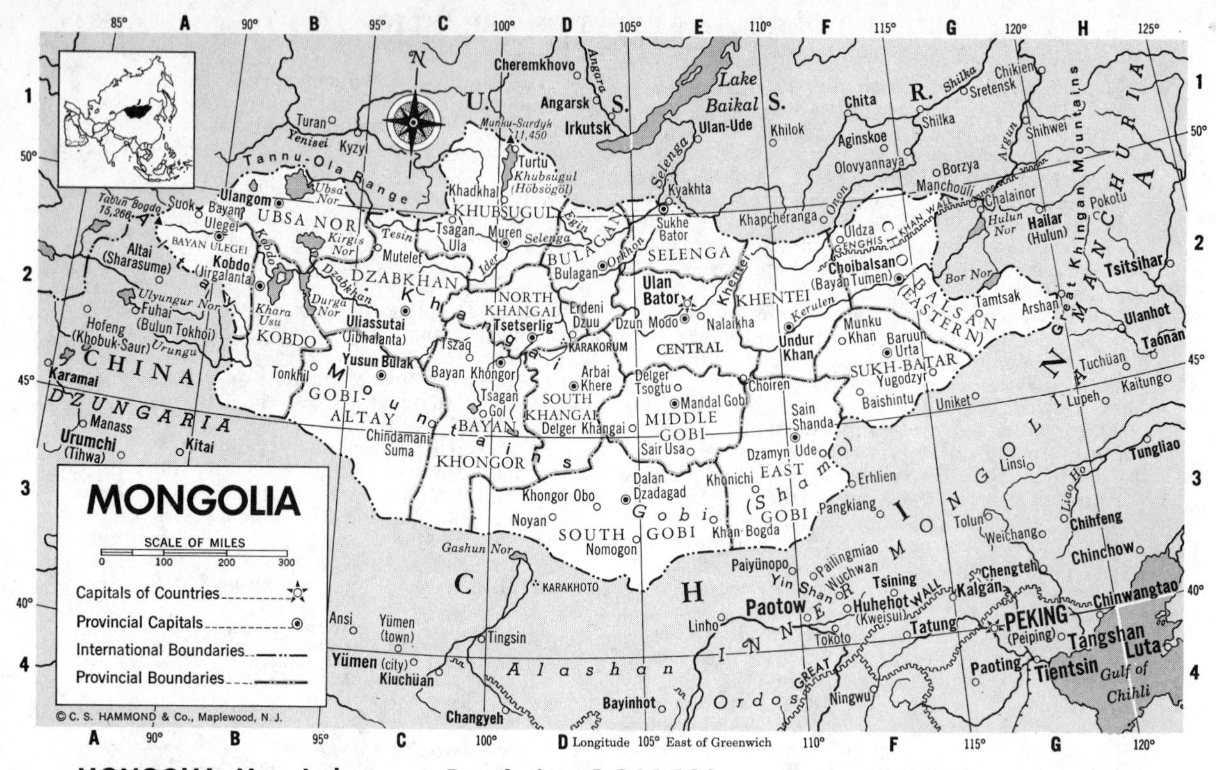

MONGOLIA Map Index

Population: 1,044,900 **Area: 600,000 square miles**

PROVINCES

Bayan Khongor, 43,600 . . . . C2
Bayan Ulegei, 45,100 . . . . A2
Bulagan, 31,200 . . D2
Central, 50,400 . . . E2
Dzabkhan, 56,800 . C2
East Gobi, 26,300 E3
Eastern, 34,300 . . G2
Gobi-Altay, 40,500 C3
Khentei, 35,400 . . E2
Khubsugul, 61,100 C1
Kobdo, 44,800 . . . . B2
Middle Gobi, 27,500 . . . . E2
North Khangai, 60,300 . . . . D2
Selenga, 43,300 . . . E2
South Gobi, 21,900 D3
South Khangai, 53,800 . . . . D2
Sukh-Batar, 30,400 F2
Ubsa Nor, 49,000 B2
Ulan Bator (municipality), 210,600 . E2

CITIES and TOWNS

Altay (Yusun Bulak), 5,300 . . C2
Arbai Khere, 3,400 D2
Baruun Urta, 3,500 F2
Bayan Khongor, 4,400 . . . . C2
Bayan Tumen (Choibalsan), 10,900 F2
Bayan Ulegei, 6,800 . . . . A2
Bulagan, 4,600 . . D2
Chindamani Suma C3
Choibalsan, 10,900 F2
Choiren E2
Dalan Dzadagad . . E3
Darkhan, 25,000 . . E2
Delger Khangai . . D2
Delger Tsogtu E2
Dzamyn Ude E3
Dzun Modo, 55,300 E2
Erdeni Dzuu D2
Jirgalanta (Kobdo), 5,800 . . . . B2
Khadkhal C1
Khan Bogda E3
Khongor Obo D3
Khonichi E3
Kobdo, 5,800 . . . . . B2
Mandal Gobi, 2,900 . . . . E2
Munku Khan F2
Muren, 7,000 . . . . . D2
Mutelet C2
Nalaikha E2
Nomogon D3
Noyan D3
Sain Shanda, 6,200 F2
Sair Usa E3
South Khangai D2
Sukhe Bator, 12,000 . . . . E2
Suok A2
Tamtsak G2
Tonkhil B2
Tsagan Gol C2
Tsagan Ula C2
Tsetserlig, 9,000 . D2
Tszaq C2
Turtu D1
Ulan Bator (cap.), 210,600 . . . . E2
Ulangom, 9,600 . . B2
Uldza F2
Uliassutai, 5,000 . C2
Undur Khan, 4,500 F2
Yugodzyr F2
Yusun Bulak, 5,300 C2

PHYSICAL FEATURES

Altay (mts.) A2
Bor Nor (lake) . . . G2
Durga Nor (lake) B2
Dzabkhan (river) . B2
Egin (river) D2
Genghis Khan (wall) F2
Gobi (desert) E3
Höbsögöl (Khubsugul) (lake) D1
Ider (river) C2
Karakorum (ruins) D2
Kerulen (river) . . . F2
Khangai (mts.) C2
Khara Usu (lake) . B2
Khentei (mts.) E2
Khubsugul (lake) . D1
Kirgis Nor (lake) . B2
Kobdo (river) B2
Munku-Sardyk (mt.) D1
Onon (river) F1
Orkhon (river) . . . D2
Selenga (river) . . . D2
Shamo (Gobi) (desert) E3
Tabun Bogdo (mt.) A2
Tannu-Ola (range) B1
Tesin (river) C2
Ubsa Nor (lake) . . B2

Population Years: Country total—1964 off. est.; capital and provinces—1962 off. est.; others—1959 off. est.

1. POLITICAL DIVISIONS, CHIEF CITIES, AND POPULATION

The Mongolian People's Republic is divided into 18 administrative divisions called *aimaks* (provinces), which are subdivided into *somon*-cooperatives (county-agricultural collectives). The *bags* (household groups) were abolished in 1959. The 1964 estimated population was 1,004,900, with 210,600 in the capital of Ulan Bator.

Cities of over 10,000 population include Choibalsan (formerly Bayan Tumen), in a coal-producing region in the eastern part of the country; Tsetserlig, located between Ulan Bator and Uliassutai; Kobdo (Jirgalanta) in the west; and the new Sukhe Bator, a transshipment point and rail depot north of Ulan Bator near the Soviet border. The smaller town of Sain Shanda, in the Gobi Desert, is significant for its airfield and its oil development.

The major portion of the population in the Mongolian People's Republic is made up of Khalkhas. Important minority population groups include 26,000 Kazakhs in the western part of the country, who occupy their own "autonomous area," the Bayan Ulegei Aimak; 22,000 Buryats who live mainly in the Selenga Valley north of Ulan Bator to the Russian border; and over 50,000 Oirats who live in the western aimaks. In the southeast, some 16,000 Mongols live in Darigangga, which once supplied camels to the Chinese Army and occupied a favored position; now it has been integrated into the regular administrative structure. Near Lake Khubsugul (Höbsögöl) in the northwest, 7,000 Darkhats still retain unique linguistic and ethnographic characteristics. The Darkhats before 1924 enjoyed a special status as persons free of taxes and were in close relationship to the Jebtsun Damba Khutukhtu (Living Buddha) of Urga. A limited number of Russians live in the republic, mainly in the capital city of Ulan Bator and other population centers, and some 10,000 Chinese are especially important in the construction industries. A few Koreans represent almost the only other population element.

2. THE LAND

The northern part of the republic includes considerable forest and mountainous terrain, as well as fertile steppe; therefore, both livestock and human population, to a large extent, concentrate in the northern third of the country. Along the northwestern border with the USSR extends the Tannu-Ola range. Northeast of Ulan Bator are the Kentei Mountains. The Khangai Mountains rise in the west central part of the country, and extending from west to southeast near the border are the Mongolian Altai and Gobi Altai. The former range rises to 15,266 feet in Tabun Bogdo, the highest peak in the Altai.

Fertile river valleys in the north, especially those of the Selenga and Orkhon, support most of the population. The valley of the Kerulen River comprises a broad highway to eastern Mongolia. Lake Khubsugul in the northwest, 83 miles long and 21 miles wide, supports a fishing industry. Many undrained salt lakes and rivers which have no outlet illustrate the fact that two thirds of the territory lies in the undrained basin of central Asia. The Selenga and the Orkhon, however, flowing into Lake Baikal in the USSR, drain ultimately to the Arctic Ocean; the Kerulen and the Onon drain toward the Pacific.

About one fourth of the country is occupied by the Gobi, the arid steppe and desert which characterizes the southern part of the republic and northern Inner Mongolia. This strip of the Gobi Desert separates the relatively densely populated and economically developed areas of the northern part of the country and southern Inner Mongolia. One of the most severe earthquakes ever recorded anywhere (11 balls on the International Scale) shifted rivers and moved mountains in the Gobi Altai region on Dec. 4, 1957. Very few people live in this area, so that only slight loss of life and limited property damage resulted. See also Gobi.

Annual precipitation, mainly in the form of summer rain, ranges in different parts of the country from 4 to 12 inches. Light snow, combined with extreme cold, results in a considerable belt of permanently frozen soil (permafrost) in the northern part of the country. The temperature range is wide; at Ulan Bator, about midway between mountains and desert, the average temperature for January is −28° C., and for July 18° C.; extremes of temperature are much greater.

3. ECONOMIC FACTORS

Agriculture.—Central planning dominates the economy of the Mongolian People's Republic, but most of the livestock continues to be privately owned despite many attempts at collectivization. The original First Five-Year Plan (1931–1935) had to be abandoned because of the nomads' extreme resistance to collectivization of their herds. A more moderate and more successful First Five-Year Plan directed development from 1948 to 1952; a Second Five-Year Plan, from 1953 to 1957; a Three-Year Plan, from 1958 to 1960; and another Five-Year Plan, from 1961 to 1965. These plans encouraged cooperation and collectivization in the livestock sector of the economy and continued to stress livestock as of primary economic importance to the republic. Most of the industry of the country relates to the handling and processing of livestock products; sheep, goats, camels, yaks, and horses are raised, providing wool, meat, and milk. In the 1960's the Soviets introduced the practice of providing fodder for winter feeding.

Mongolia's agricultural products include wheat, rye, oats, barley, corn, millet, legumes, and garden products.

Mining.—Coal production is Mongolia's chief mining industry. Coal is mined principally at Nalaikha near Ulan Bator and at Choibalsan in the eastern part of the country. In 1962, Mongolia's coal production was 860,200 tons. Oil production, which began in 1950, occurs chiefly at Sain Shanda and Dzamyn Ude in the eastern Gobi Desert. In 1962, Mongolia produced 22,600 tons of oil. Some gold, tin, lead, and copper also are mined. A new industrial center was built in the 1960's with Soviet help at Darkhan, where there are deposits of iron ore.

Trade.—Mongolia's chief exports are cattle, horses, hides, wool, meat, and butter. The nation's imports consist principally of consumer goods. In the early 1960's the Soviet Union received about 80 percent of Mongolia's total exports and supplied about 60 percent of its imports. Communist China received about 4 percent of Mongolia's exports and accounted for about 20 percent of its imports. Other nations that trade with Mongolia include Czechoslovakia and the German Democratic Republic (East Germany).

Transportation and Communications.—The Trans-Mongolian Railroad came into being after many years of discussion and in three distinct stages. First, a cutoff from the Trans-Siberian Railway reached Kyakhta in 1937; the first train operated through to Ulan Bator on Nov. 7, 1949; and the final Ulan Bator-Chining (near Kalgan, in north China) section was formally opened to traffic on Jan. 1, 1956. In 1965 the section within Chinese territory, from Erhlien to Chining, was changed from wide-gauge to standard gauge. Three other short railroad lines operate in the republic: a 20-mile wide-gauge line hauls coal from the Nalaikha mines to the factories of Ulan Bator; a spur from the Trans-Mongolian Railroad to Darkhan was completed in 1964; and a spur from the Trans-Siberian Railway at Borzya runs to Tamtsak, near the city of Choibalsan and the Barga area of Manchuria.

Conventional airplanes on the north-south international Moscow-Peking route stop at Ulan Bator and Sain Shanda. Domestic air transport connects all the aimak centers to Ulan Bator. Camels continue to carry most goods, but trucks and trains are increasingly taking over this function. Ships and barges operate on the Selenga River and on Lake Khubsugul. Few roads exist, but the Mongolian terrain generally allows cross-country driving. Many bridges have been constructed in recent years.

Radio and telephone service connect all the important centers of the country. Each of the 18 provinces publishes a newspaper. A number of periodicals are published in Ulan Bator.

4. GOVERNMENT

The constitution adopted in 1940, and amended several times since then superseded the first constitution of the republic, proclaimed in 1924. The highest organ of government is the Great People's Khural, or People's Assembly, modeled on the Supreme Soviet of the USSR and composed of deputies chosen from the urban districts, the aimaks, and the armed forces. It is elected every three years by universal suffrage of all persons, male and female, over 18 years of age, and meets at least once a year. It chooses from its number a 7-member Presidium which is in charge of state affairs during the interval between sessions of the Great Khural. The Council of Ministers, headed by a premier, or chairman, is the highest executive and administrative body of the state. The Mongolian People's Revolutionary Party represents the powerful Communist element in the republic. Justice is administered by the Supreme Court, whose members are elected by the Great Khural for a period of four years. The smaller units of government have their own khurals and courts.

All male citizens must serve in the People's Revolutionary Army, which has at times attained a strength of 80,000 men.

5. EDUCATION AND RELIGION

Nearly universal primary education in the Mongolian People's Republic has almost eliminated illiteracy and has made great inroads on superstition. In addition to secondary schools there are technical schools of agriculture, trade, and industry. The State Pedagogical Institute gives teachers' training courses, and Choibalsan University at Ulan Bator gives courses in sciences and arts to over 2,000 students. The Mongolian Committee of Sciences and Higher Education, dominant in all fields of intellectual activity, has its headquarters at Ulan Bator.

Only scattered survivals (about 100 lamas and two or three functioning temples) remain of the organized Lamaist Church in the republic. See section on *History* under MONGOLIA for the earlier church.

6. BIBLIOGRAPHY

Vladimirtsov, Boris, *Le régime social des Mongols*, tr. by Michel Carsow (Paris 1948); Friters, Gerard M., *Outer Mongolia and Its International Position* (Baltimore 1949); Lattimore, Owen, *Inner Asian Frontiers of China*, 2d ed. (Irvington-on-Hudson, N.Y., 1951); Kolarz, Walter, *Peoples of the Soviet Far East* (New York 1954); Rupen, Robert, *Mongols of the Twentieth Century*, 2 vols. (Bloomington, Ind., 1964).

ROBERT A. RUPEN
Professor of Political Science
University of North Carolina

MONGOLIAN WILD ASS. See ASS.

MONGOLOID. See MENTAL RETARDATION—*The Nature of Mental Retardation* (Classification).

MONGOLOID PEOPLES. See ANTHROPOLOGY—*Physical Anthropology;* ASIA—*5. Races; 6. Languages* (Inner Asia).

MONGOLS. See MONGOLIA.

MONGOOSE, mŏng'go͞os, any one of several genera and numerous species of small carnivores of the subfamily Herpestinae. Inhabiting Africa, southern Asia, the East Indies, and Spain, mongooses are long-bodied, long-tailed, grayish or brownish animals ranging in size from about 18 inches to 50 inches in length, including the tail. They feed on a variety of small mammals, ground-nesting birds, eggs, crayfish, and snakes. They are not, as often credited, immune to the venom of poisonous snakes. In hunting snakes, mongooses rely on their agility to dodge the snakes' strikes; also, by fluffing up their fur, they cause the snakes to misjudge striking distances.

In many places in Egypt and India mongooses are domesticated. They were introduced into the West Indies and Hawaii for rodent control, but are regarded as pests at present because of their predations on poultry.

RICHARD G. VAN GELDER.

MONHEGAN ISLAND, mŏn-hē'găn, island, Maine, about 17 miles southeast of Boothbay Harbor and politically part of Lincoln County. It is approximately two and one-half miles long and one mile in width, with an area of about two and one-half square miles. The permanent population of the island, concentrated at Monhegan Plantation, was 65 in 1960, but during the summer months an influx of visitors swells the population to about 900. Fishing and lobstering are the only regular sources of income. First popularized as an artist colony by Rockwell Kent, the steep, ragged cliffs of Monhegan and the adjacent islet Manana have provided subjects for many paintings.

The first recorded sighting of the island occurred in 1498 when it was circled by John and Sebastian Cabot. It was later visited by David Ingraham (1569); Capt. George Weymouth (1605), who gave it the name St. George's Island; and Capt. John Smith (1614). In 1626 there was a temporary settlement on the island; another settlement was established in 1654 but destroyed by the French in 1689. In 1720 it was resettled by fishermen. During the war of 1812 the American privateer *Enterprise* engaged and defeated the British brig *Boxer* on Sept. 5, 1813, offshore from Monhegan. The granite-block lighthouse, Monhegan Island Light, was erected near the center of the island in 1850, replacing a lighthouse built in 1824.

MONICA, mŏn'ĭ-kȧ, SAINT (originally MONNICA), mother of St. Augustine: b. Tagaste, North Africa (now Souk-Ahras, Algeria), c. 332; d. Ostia, Italy, 387. A Christian daughter of Christian parents, she married a pagan government official, Patricius, at the request of her parents, and devoted nearly all the remainder of her life to the conversion of her husband and her eldest son Augustine to Christianity. Her perseverance was rewarded by the baptism of Patricius in 370 and of Augustine in 387. Monica's long and devout struggle for Augustine's conversion is recorded in Book 9 of his *Confessions* (397–401), the first 10 books of which are memoirs of his life up to the time of his mother's death. Concerned by her son's wayward life, she followed him from Africa to Rome and then to Milan, where Augustine was finally converted; she died on the way back to Africa with him shortly after. She had two children besides Augustine: a second son, Navigius, and a daughter, Perpetua. The later Middle Ages saw the beginning of a cult of St. Monica, and Pope Martin V ordered the removal of her supposed remains in 1430 from Ostia to the Church of Sant'Agostino in Rome. She has frequently been named as patroness of associations of Christian wives and mothers. Her feast day is May 4.

MONIER-WILLIAMS, mŭn'ĭ-ẽr-wĭl'yămz, SIR **Monier** (originally MONIER WILLIAMS), English Sanskrit scholar: b. Bombay, India, Nov. 12, 1819; d. Cannes, France, April 11, 1899. Son of Col. Monier Williams, British surveyor general at Bombay, he was educated at Oxford under the great Sanskrit scholar Horace Hayman Wilson, and was professor of Sanskrit, Persian, and Hindustani at Haileybury, a college maintained by the East India Company in England, from 1844 until its closing in 1858 during the Indian Mutiny. In 1860 he became Boden professor of Sanskrit at Oxford, a post which he held actively until 1887. Monier-Williams was largely responsible for the establishment at Oxford of the Indian Institute, a project which he initiated in 1875 and which was finally completed in 1896. He was knighted in 1886 and added Monier to his surname the following year.

A prolific writer on Sanskrit, Hindustani, and Indian religions, Monier-Williams' *English-Sanskrit Dictionary* (1851) and *Sanskrit-English Dictionary* (1872; 2d ed., 1899) are still standard reference works. His translations from the Sanskrit were published in many editions; particularly important are his translation of the *Śakuntalā* (1853; 6th ed., 1894), and *Indian Wisdom* (1875; 4th ed., 1893), a source book representing nearly every field of classical Indian studies.

MONISM, mŏn'ĭz'm (From Gr. *monos,* single, sole, one), any philosophical theory which emphasizes unity, especially a unity among all things. It may assert that all are of the same fundamental kind or stuff, usually in conscious opposition to a dualism or "bifurcation of nature" (in Alfred North Whitehead's phrase), particularly that of mind and matter. Thus physical monism, or materialism, asserts that the world is all matter; mental monism, or idealism, that it is all mind; and "neutral monism," that it consists of events which indifferently compose things or thoughts according to how they are related. A dynamic monism, holding that the world is unified in the sense that all its parts are mutually dependent, is generally assumed by philosophers and scientists as implied in their search for systematic order.

Absolute monism, usually contrasted with pluralism, is the extreme view that strictly there is only one real individual, and that the appearance of plural and varied parts is an illusion. It is taught in the Vedantic literature (see VEDANTA) of India and was held by Parmenides in ancient Greece. Magnificent efforts to reconcile the doctrine of the World One, generally interpreted as pantheism (the Whole is God), with an admission of partial realities, including persons, have been made by Baruch Spinoza and the later absolute idealists, and by similar but less technical philosophies such as transcendentalism. Among special or limited monisms, so-called epistemological monism, or monism in the theory of knowledge, asserts that an idea or percept is one with its object and not merely a sign or copy of it. See also ABSOLUTE; DUALISM; EPISTEMOLOGY—*Perception;* IDEALISM; MATERIALISM; METAPHYSICS; PANTHEISM.

Consult Drake, Durant, *Invitation to Philosophy* (Boston 1933), or any other good introduction to philosophy.

DONALD C. WILLIAMS,
Professor of Philosophy, Harvard University.

MONITOR, mŏn'ĭ-tẽr, a type of warship so named after the spectacular battle of the *U.S.S. Monitor* and the *C.S.S. Virginia* (*Merrimac*), in Hampton Roads, Va., March 9, 1862. The essential features of the type were low freeboard, shallow draft, armor, and an armored revolving turret. Later in 1862, the Union Navy ordered 35 monitors, and in 1863, 24 more. These included 14 vessels mounting two turrets, but nearly half of the totals were never completed. After 1862, monitors gained two outstanding successes: Capt. John Rodgers in the *Weehawken* captured the ironclad *Atlanta,* south of Savannah, Ga., June 17, 1863; and Capt. George H. Perkins in the *Chickasaw,* in Mobile Bay, Aug. 5, 1864, pounded Admiral Franklin Buchanan's armored flagship *Tennessee* at close range for 90 minutes before the Confederates surrendered. The revolving turret was adopted by all navies, but the monitor type was truly important only in the American Civil War, 1861–1865. Some European navies built a few monitors later, and the United States Navy afterwards built 10, beginning in 1883. The last 4 were authorized in 1898, and 7 of these vessels were in use in 1917–1918 as submarine tenders. The British and Italian navies built and used monitors, large and small, for coastal bombardment in World War I; some of them had the hulls protected by "blisters" to lessen torpedo damage and mounted 15-inch and 18-inch guns. In World War II, Great Britain built still larger monitors, including vessels of the *Roberts* class, displacing 7,800 tons.

JOHN B. HEFFERNAN.

MONITOR AND MERRIMACK,[1] mĕr'ĭ-măk, two warships which became famous by fighting the first battle between ironclads, in Hampton Roads, Va., on March 9, 1862, during the American Civil War. The French *Gloire,* launched in 1859, and the British *Warrior* (1860) were the first ironclads to be built, but they had not met in combat. The *Monitor* gave her name to a type of warship which the United States employed successfully from 1863 to 1865 and built as late as 1898. The British Navy built monitors in the years 1914–1918 and again in 1939 (see MONITOR).

President Abraham Lincoln proclaimed a blockade of Confederate seaports on April 19, 1861, and naval officers in the North and South began to build or improvise ironclads. The Confederate ironclad ram *Manassas,* a renamed converted tug, successfully attacked Union ships in the lower Mississippi on Oct. 12, 1861, and Commodore Andrew H. Foote captured Fort Henry, Tenn., with armored Union gunboats on Feb. 6, 1862.

The Confederates planned to build one or more relatively fast, well-armed, shallow-draft armored ships, but they could not build the engines without serious delay to other vital projects. They did the best they could by reconstructing the wooden steam frigate *Merrimack,* which had been burned and scuttled when the Union Navy evacuated the Norfolk Navy Yard on April 20, 1861. The *Merrimack* had been built at the Boston Navy Yard, five years earlier. Her displacement was 3,200 tons; length, 275 feet; beam, 38½ feet; draft, 24 feet. Raised from the river mud, she was placed in drydock, her burned upper deck cut away, and an armored shield with sloping sides for 10 guns was installed. Her engines were then overhauled, a crew assembled, and the ship was renamed *Virginia.* Captain Franklin Buchanan was put in command, with Lt. Catesby ap R. Jones as his executive officer.

---

[1] EDITOR'S NOTE: Both *Merrimac* and *Merrimack* appear in contemporary documents. *Merrimack* conforms with the usage in U.S. Navy Department, *Official Records of the Union and Confederate Navies in the War of the Rebellion,* 30 vols. (Washington 1894–1922).

In the summer of 1861, Washington received many suggestions for armored vessels capable of combating the *Virginia* (*Merrimack*). A design by John Ericsson was accepted about four hours after it was officially submitted; Ericsson later proposed the name *Monitor* for the vessel. Built in record time, the ship was launched at Greenpoint, Long Island, on Jan. 30, 1862. Her displacement was 987 tons; length, 172 feet; beam, 41½ feet; draft, 10½ feet. Her two 11-inch-shell guns were mounted in a revolving armored turret. After an unsuccessful harbor trial on February 27, she put to sea on March 3, returning because of rudder trouble. Under the command of John L. Worden, with Lt. Samuel Dana Greene as executive officer, the *Monitor* departed from New York City on March 6, towed by a tug and convoyed by two steamers.

Battle of Hampton Roads.—About noon on March 8, 1862, the *Virginia,* accompanied by the gunboats *Raleigh* and *Beaufort,* started down the Elizabeth River for her first test. Captain Buchanan crossed Hampton Roads toward the anchorage off Newport News, where the sailing frigate *Congress* and sloop *Cumberland,* opened fire on him as he approached. Disregarding the gunfire, he opened a large hole in the side of the *Cumberland,* at the water line, by ramming her and summoned her to surrender. Her acting captain, Lt. George U. Morris replied, "We will sink with our colors flying." Two of the *Virginia*'s guns lost their muzzles by well-aimed shots from the *Cumberland,* and the cast-iron ram attached to the *Virginia*'s prow broke off. Leaving the sinking sloop, Buchanan shelled the *Congress* with devastating effect until she caught fire and surrendered after the death of her captain, Joseph B. Smith. Meanwhile, the steam frigates *Minnesota* and *Roanoke,* and the sailing frigate *St. Lawrence,* attempted to go to the assistance of the ships under attack, but all three ran aground. The falling tide saved them from attack, and the *Virginia* anchored off Sewall Point for the night. Captain Buchanan and other wounded were sent ashore, and Jones took command. The *Monitor* reached Hampton Roads about 9 P.M. and went alongside the grounded *Minnesota,* whose crew helped to prepare the Union ironclad for battle.

On March 9, about 8 A.M., the historic battle between the ironclads began; it lasted over four hours. The *Virginia* and the *Monitor* passed and repassed each other, firing at close range. Both crews were poorly drilled, and hits had little effect. The *Monitor* was faster, turned more easily and quickly, but could fire only one shot every seven or eight minutes. After about two hours she ran into shallow water (where the *Virginia,* because of her greater draft, could not follow) to replenish the dwindling supply of ammunition in her turret; the *Virginia* did considerable damage to the *Minnesota,* which was still aground, during the 15-minute interval. As the *Monitor* returned to the battle, the *Virginia* ran aground and had considerable difficulty in backing off, all the while being pounded by the turret guns of the *Monitor.* As soon as he was clear, Jones headed for deeper water, and the *Monitor* followed. Seizing an opportunity, Jones swung around and rammed the *Monitor,* but Worden turned to avoid the larger ship and received only a glancing blow. If the *Virginia*'s iron prow had been in place, she would have inflicted severe damage on the *Monitor.* Jones then concentrated his gunfire on the *Monitor*'s pilot house, and a direct hit drove iron splinters into Worden's eyes and dislocated the top of the house. The *Monitor* sheered into shallow water while Greene came from the turret to take command and to check steering. Jones again turned toward the *Minnesota,* but his pilots warned of the shallow water and falling tide. His ship was leaking, ammunition was low, and the engineers had kept up steam with difficulty since the *Cumberland* had riddled the smokestack. Jones headed for the navy yard at Norfolk, and the battle ended. The battle marked the close of the era of wooden fighting ships, and the *Monitor*'s revolving turret became the prototype of those in later warships.

When the Confederates evacuated Norfolk, the *Virginia* was destroyed by her own crew on May 11, 1862. The *Monitor* sank in a gale off Cape Hatteras, N.C., on Dec. 31, 1862, with a loss of 16 lives. In 1974 the remains of the vessel were identified and photographed under 220 feet of water, 15 miles south-southeast of Cape Hatteras.

Further Reading: Freeman, Fred, *Duel of the Ironclads* (Little 1969); Keeler, William F., *Aboard the USS Monitor, 1862* (Naval Inst. Press 1964); Pratt, Fletcher, *Monitor and the Merrimac* (Random House 1951).

JOHN B. HEFFERNAN,
Rear Admiral, United States Navy (Retired); Director of Naval History, Department of the Navy, 1946–1956.

MONITOR LIZARD, any of the 26 species of lizard composing the genus *Varanus* and the family Varanidae. The monitors are widely distributed in the warmer regions of the Old World, being found in southern Asia, Africa (where they are called leguaans), the East Indies, and Australia (where they are called goannas). *Leguaan, goanna,* and *guana* are regional corruptions of *iguana,* mistakenly applied by European settlers to the monitor. The genus includes the largest lizard in existence, the so-called Komodo dragon (*V. komodoensis*), which attains an approximate length of nearly 10 feet. This species is confined to three small islands, Komodo, Rintja, and Flores. Extinct species, some of which were two or three times as large as the Komodo, date back to the Eocene epoch at which time they also occurred in North America.

Monitors have several peculiarities, including a temporal arch but an incomplete postorbital arch; a parietal foramen; pleurodont dentition; scale pits; and a tongue that is smooth, long and slender, forked at the tip, and retractile into a sheath at the base, as in snakes. The monitors bear several resemblances to the snakes, although the Borneo lizard, *Lanthanotus* (family Lanthanotidae), sometimes called the "earless monitor," in some respects is closer to the ancestral stock from which the snakes are believed to have been derived.

All monitors are carnivorous, readily devouring birds, small mammals, reptiles, fishes, crustaceans, large insects, and the eggs of both reptiles and birds; sometimes they also eat carrion. While monitors may be destructive of poultry, their depredations in this respect are perhaps counterbalanced by their destruction of vermin, particularly rodents. Some species are more or less arboreal, and most of them readily take to water. The large East Indian species, *V. salvator,* has been observed swimming in the ocean some distance from land, a habit that may account for its occurrence on many islands.

The most widely distributed African species, *V. niloticus,* the largest lizard in Africa, habitually deposits its eggs in termite nests. The tunnel dug by the lizard is repaired by the termites, leaving the eggs to be incubated under the relatively uniform conditions of moisture and temperature maintained by the insects. When the young emerge from the eggs, they dig their way out of the termite nest. Similar habits have been recorded for Asiatic species.

When angered or cornered by an adversary, monitors often distend the body by filling their lungs with air, which they expel with a loud hiss. The tail becomes an effective weapon under such conditions, being used to deliver a formidable blow. The teeth may be effectively employed at close quarters. However, monitors ordinarily depend upon flight to escape their enemies. When molested many species seek safety in pools or streams, or even in the ocean. Under stress they can remain below the surface for considerable periods of time.

Monitors are eaten by natives in some regions. Dogs are trained to run them down or dig them from their burrows. Excellent leather is made from the hides of many monitors, although the skin of some species is studded with small bones (osteoderms), which render it inferior for leather.

Charles M. Bogert,
Chairman and Curator, Department of Amphibians and Reptiles, The American Museum of Natural History.

MONITOR RANGE, mountain range, Nevada, in the central part of the state, running generally north to south from the southwest end of Eureka County through north central Nye County. The range is included in Toiyabe National Forest. The highest point is Monitor Peak, which reaches an altitude of 10,856 feet. Other major elevations are Summit Mountain (10,466 feet) and Antelope Peak (10,207 feet). To the west, running parallel, is the Toquima Range.

MONITORIAL SYSTEM, an educational system in which pupils acting under the direction of a teacher, instruct other less advanced pupils. It has been known variously as the monitorial, the mutual, and the Lancastrian system of education. Dr. Andrew Bell (1753–1832), an Anglican clergyman, first published the principles of this system, based on his prior experience as a school superintendent in Madras, India, in London in 1797. Joseph Lancaster (1778–1838), a Quaker schoolmaster, opened his first monitorial school in London in 1798. Lancaster had developed his system independently, and there was long a bitter rivalry between the two men and their respective followers. These attempts to offer some elementary schooling to large numbers of the children of the poor is best understood as a part of the general movement of social reform characteristic of the age. Few trained teachers were available, but by using student teachers (monitors) a single adult teacher could have classes of 400 to 500 pupils, or even more. The adult teacher instructed his monitors who taught what they had learned to groups of less advanced pupils. In Bell's variation of the system, a monitor would teach 24 to 30 pupils. Lancaster approved of only 10 pupils per monitor.

Instruction usually took place in a single large hall with seats and desks arranged so that each monitor could teach and supervise his own group. Stations were set up along the walls with slates or sandboxes for instruction in elementary reading, writing, spelling, and arithmetic. The arrangement was most efficient. The teacher worked out detailed plans and routines. The monitors then took full charge of the instruction, grading, and promotion. Organized into a small hierarchy, they also handled the administration of the school. The system was applauded as a new "mechanical" invention in an age of industrial progress.

Monitorial schools multiplied in England and many were established in Europe and the United States, enjoying most of their success in the first half of the 19th century. When Lancaster came to the United States in 1818, he was received with great acclaim. DeWitt Clinton had already praised him as "the benefactor of the human race" and his system as "creating a new era in education."

In some cases where monitorial schools had been established they tended to delay the introduction of better schools, but because of their low cost they contributed to the growth of popular public education. The system lost favor as more funds and more adult teachers became available. Monitorial schools put great stress on the mastery of facts through memorization. There was little or no attempt to stimulate the student's capacity to reason. The monitors had little perspective on their work as they were often only one step ahead of those whom they taught. The system can be viewed as an expedient means of offering education to large numbers of students when little money and few teachers are available. Despite the shortcomings of the system, the carefully planned use of advanced students as assistant teachers frequently has educational merit even when money and trained teachers are not in short supply.

Bibliography.—The two classic statements are, Andrew Bell, *An Experiment in Education made at the Male Asylum at Madras* (London 1797) and Joseph Lancaster, *Improvements in Education* (London 1803). Ellwood P. Cubberly, *The History of Education* (Cambridge, Mass., 1920) is useful but it should be corrected in some respects by Hugh M. Pollard, *Pioneers of Popular Education* (London 1956) which is an excellent study of the European scene.

Robert S. Guttchen,
Instructor, Department of Foundations of Education, Hofstra College.

MONK or **MONCK,** mŭngk, **George,** 1st Duke of Albemarle, English general and naval commander: b. Potheridge, Devonshire, England, Dec. 6, 1608; d. Newhall, Essex, Jan. 3, 1670. He enlisted at 17, served in the Cádiz expedition under his relative Sir Richard Grenville, and about 1629 entered the Dutch Army, where he distinguished himself against the Spaniards at the siege of Breda (1637). Returning to England in 1639, he fought brilliantly against the Scots during the Second Bishop's War (1640) and led a regiment against the Irish during the rebellion which began in 1642. On the outbreak of the Civil War in England, Monk kept his commission in the king's army, but in 1644 he was captured by the Parliamentarian forces and confined in the Tower of London. After two years of imprisonment he joined his captors and served with distinction at the head of the Parliamentarian troops in Ulster from 1647 to 1649. Forced to conclude a disadvantageous truce with Owen Roe O'Neil, the Irish leader, he was recalled to England in 1649 and reprimanded at the bar of the House of Commons. At the victory of Dunbar in 1650 he did good service; a year later he was made lieutenant-general of ordinance and in Cromwell's absence was commander-in-chief of Scotland. In 1652 he was made a general of the fleet. He introduced the elements of land tactics into naval formation and administered two crushing defeats to the Dutch, Maarten Tromp being killed in the latter battle. In 1654 he again was sent to Scotland on the Royalist rising as commander of the army, and acted there with much more prudence and success. After Oliver's death and Richard Cromwell's resignation Monk set himself to effect the Stuart Restoration, quietly shifted the forces in England until all was so arranged that there was no chance of armed resistance, and then (1660) brought back Charles II—a bloodless revolution meeting with general favor. He was made Duke of Albemarle, received other high honors, maintained order and showed rare courage in London during the Plague, but with an empty treasury in 1667 could not keep the Dutch from burning the shipping in the Thames. Short, fat, fair and wrinkled, Monk was not a winning personality, being cold, prudent past a virtue and rather unprincipled; but he was a wonderfully able general, with technical skill rare in one so lacking in theoretical training. His life was written by his chaplain, Dr. Thomas Gumble (1671).

MONK. See MONASTICISM.

MONK SEAL, the hair seal of the genus *Monachus*. It is found in the Mediterranean and Caribbean seas and in the waters around Hawaii, but is now comparatively rare.

MONKBIRD, mŭngk'bûrd, an alternate name for the friarbird. See FRIARBIRD.

MONKEY BREAD. See BAOBAB.

MONKEY FLOWER, mŭng'kē, any plant of the genus *Mimulus* (figwort family), so called because the face of the foxglove-like corolla suggests that of a cheerful monkey. They are erect, tall herbs, with opposite, clasping, lanceolate dentate leaves, which bear in late summer solitary, axillary irregular blossoms of showy colors. The genus contains some 50 North American species, of which the most familiar is the square-stemmed of the Eastern and Central states (*M. ringens*). Its flower is violet. A common species in California and on the Pacific Coast (*M. guttatus*) has the corolla yellow, often blotched with red or purple.

MONKEYPOT, the fruit of a tree of the genus *Lecythis,* native to South America and Malaysia. See SAPUCAIA.

MONKEYS comprise all the tailed members of the Anthropoidea. Perhaps it should be stated here that the Anthropoidea, as a great suborder of the order Primates, is much more inclusive than the term "anthropoid apes," or the family Pongidae, as it includes all monkeys, apes and also man. It might be supposed that the monkeys would form a unified natural group; but such is not the case. The American or New World monkeys and the Old World forms constitute two separate groups, with many significant differences which are obscured by more obvious general likenesses of less diagnostic importance. The Old World monkeys are actually closer zoologically to the great apes and even to man, than they are to the American monkeys. As early as 1820, American monkeys were designated as Platyrrhina (flat nosed), in reference to the fact that their nostrils are widely separated and open laterally, while in all Old World monkeys, as in apes and man, the nostrils are closely approximated and are directed downward; hence all these forms were grouped as Catarrhina (downward nose). The terms platyrrhine and catarrhine are still in common use, but usually as descriptive terms rather than as taxonomic group names. Today all platyrrhine monkeys are grouped as a superfamily Ceboidea, while all Old World catarrhine monkeys are placed in the superfamily Cercopithecoidea. To mention a few of the features common to the two superfamilies, attention may be called to the general humanlike appearance, especially of the face, which everyone must have noticed; also the use of the hands and the habit, in most monkeys, of sitting erect; also their alertness and apparent intelligence. It may also be noted that nearly all monkeys are adapted to arboreal life. The fore and hind limbs are not greatly unequal in length. The fore feet are obviously "hands" in structure, with a more or less well-formed thumb or pollex. The pollex is reduced or lost in a few cases to be mentioned below. The hind feet have a widely divergent great toe, or hallux, which, in most cases, is capable of opposing the other toes to form a grasping foot which is functionally almost a hand, and of great service in grasping branches of trees. As this type of foot characterizes not only the monkeys, but practically all members of the order Primates except man, the nonhuman forms were grouped by Johann Friedrich Blumenbach in 1791 as Quadrumana (four-handed), while man was made the sole representative of the Bimana (two-handed). But any likeness of a monkey's grasping hind foot to a hand is functional, not structural, and "Quadrumana" and "Bimana" have long been obsolete in zoological literature. Other common features of both groups of monkeys are a single pair of mammary glands located on the thorax, a tail, often long, sometimes short, and entirely lacking in one species. There are always four incisor teeth in both upper and lower jaws, and the canines are frequently of great length, especially in the males, and, except in one family (Marmosets), there are three molars in each half of both jaws. The eyes are directed forward so that monkeys, like apes and man, have binocular vision, and careful studies of the visual mechanism and behavioral experiments on living monkeys have shown that they have true stereoscopic vision and color perception, which are lacking in other mammalian orders. The brain is surprisingly similar in both groups of monkeys. Formerly it was believed that the Old World forms were superior in intelligence to their American relatives, but experimental laboratory studies have shown the American Cebus monkey to be able to solve problems that were previously believed to be beyond the mental capacity of any animal below the manlike apes.

To contrast some of the features in which the two groups differ: in the Ceboidea, including the two families, Cebidae, the "typical" American monkeys, and the Callithricidae (Hapalidae) or the marmosets and tamarins, there are three pre-

MONKEYS

Left: The proboscis monkey, noted for its unusual nose, is a native of Borneo.

Right: The golden-headed saki from tropical South America is shy, but intelligent.

Below: The spider monkey has a useful, well-developed tail over two feet long.

(Left) Dr. B. Grzimek; (right) San Diego Zoo; (below) Zoological Society of Philadelphia

Above: The white-throated Cebus or capuchin is a circus favorite.

Below: Rhesus monkeys, from India, are very useful laboratory animals.

(Above) Zoological Society of Philadelphia; (below) Camera Press-Pix

Above: Large and strong, the hamadryas baboon has a mane of long grey hair.

Below: The night monkey, with large, sensitive eyes, makes a charming pet.

(Above and below) Dr. B. Grzimek

Below: The Philippine macaque is one of the hardiest of all monkeys.

Ernest P. Walker

molar teeth, while the superfamily Cercopithecoidea have only two. The American forms have no bony auditory meatus to the tympanic bone, while Old World monkeys have. The number of chromosomes in the cells in the two groups is also different, though it must be admitted that they have been counted in very few genera. In the rhesus monkey of India the diploid number was found to be 48 as in the chimpanzee and in man, whereas in an American Cebus it was 54. In their blood chemistry also the Old World monkeys are closer to apes and man. Old World monkeys are also essentially similar to apes and man in the menstrual function of the females. This has been studied with great care in the rhesus monkey. In the Ceboidea menstruation is usually considered to be absent, though something of the sort has been asserted to occur in some cases. Thus in all the comparisons here cited it is seen that the Asian and African monkeys have a closer likeness to the superfamily Hominoidea than to Ceboidea.

To consider first the family Cebidae, which include all American monkeys except the marmosets, they inhabit the tropical forest regions of South and Central America, and some extend into southern Mexico. Many of them spend their entire lives in the trees. In none of them is the pollex, or thumb, actually opposable to the other fingers. Some of the smaller Cebidae, such as the titis, the sakis, and night monkeys which have nonprehensile tails, feed largely on insects, birds' eggs, and small birds, in addition to fruit. The night monkeys are the only thoroughly nocturnal monkeys. The best known genus is *Cebus,* formerly familiar as the companion of itinerant organ grinders. Its tail is somewhat prehensible, though far less so than in the large howling monkeys, woolly monkeys, and spider monkeys, in which the tail is often compared functionally to an extra hand. The spider monkeys have lost the thumb. The howlers have a remarkable expansion of the hyoid bone and the thyroid cartilage of the larynx, which function as a resonance apparatus for the animal's vocalization. The diminutive marmosets and tamarins of the family Callithricidae (= Hapalidae), have sharp curved claws on all the digits except the hallux, which bears a flat nail. See also MARMOSET.

The superfamily Cercopithecoidea, the Old World monkeys, are in general larger than the Ceboidea. They are widely distributed in Asia, Africa, and the Malay Archipelago. Most of them have cheek pouches for temporary storage of food, and all have ischial callosities or seat pads on the buttocks. The tail is never prehensile. The baboons are large ground-living monkeys with elongate doglike heads, inhabiting Africa and Arabia. The Colobidae, a family represented by the langurs of Asia and the Malay Archipelago, and the guerezas of Africa, lack the cheek pouches and have sacculated stomachs, which apparently represent adaptations to leaf-eating habit. In the guerezas the thumb is reduced to a small vestige or absent entirely, thus paralleling the condition in the American spider monkeys. Noteworthy examples of the langur group are the snubnosed monkeys of northwestern China and Tibet, but the most remarkable of all is the large proboscis monkey (*Nasalis larvatus*) of Borneo, in which the nose, in adult males, attains grotesque proportions and hangs down over the mouth. The color of the face, including the proboscis, is a reddish brown flesh color.

Fossil material of monkeys is sparse and fragmentary, but there is strong reason to believe that the American and Old World groups evolved separately from tarsioid ancestors in Eocene or Paleocene time, and that the striking similarities in the two groups of monkeys represent parallel evolution. In America the oldest fossil monkeys are from the Miocene of Argentina, too late to throw light on origins, and in 1949 others were found in Colombia. In Egypt fragments of jaws and teeth from the Lower Oligocene seem to indicate that both Cercopithecoid monkeys and small anthropoid apes flourished at that time. See also BABOON; PRIMATES.

Consult DeVore, Irven, and Eimerl, Sarel, *Primates* (Morristown, N.J., 1965); Southwick, Charles H., *Primate Social Behavior* (New York 1965); Clark, W. E. LeGros, *The History of the Primates,* 5th ed. (Chicago 1966).

JAMES H. MCGREGOR,
Professor Emeritus, Department of Zoology, Columbia University.

MONKFISH, or **ANGELFISH,** a broad, flattened fish (*Squatina angelus*), closely allied to the sharks, but more like a ray in appearance, five or six feet long, having enlarged, wing-like pectoral fins which are separated from the head by a notch. It is found near the coast in the warm seas of Europe and North America; it usually stays near the bottom, is slow in motion, dull, voracious and useless, except that some shagreen may be obtained from its skin.

MONKHOUSE, mŭngk'hous, **William Cosmo,** English author, poet and art critic: b. London, March 18, 1840; d. Skegness, Lincolnshire, England, July 2, 1901. He received his education at St. Paul's School in London and in 1857 became a junior clerk in the Board of Trade office with which he was connected with advancement for the remainder of his life. Although not a great poet his work enjoys a high reputation among the works of the minor poets and as an art critic he won considerable attention. His work for the *Dictionary of National Biography* takes within its scope practically all of British art. He published *A Question of Honor,* novel (1868); *The Works of John Henry Foley* (1875); *The Italian Pre-Raphaelites* (1887); *British Contemporary Artists* (1899), etc. Among his poetical works are *A Dream of Idleness* (1865); *Corn and Poppies* (1890); *The Christ upon the Hill* (1898); and *Pasiteles the Elder,* published after his death.

MONKSHOOD. See ACONITE.

MONLUC, môɴ-lük', or **MONTLUC,** SEIGNEUR **de** (BLAISE DE LASSERAN-MASSENCOME), French marshal and military writer: b. Sainte Gemme, near Auch, 1501?; d. Estillac, near Agen, July 1577. He entered the army as an archer, fought (1525) at Pavia, accompanied the campaign of Francis I against Charles V and aided much in the outcome by improvements in tactics and in the artillery and engineering. His defense of Siena (1555) was brilliant, but he became hated, as governor of Guienne, for his severity against the Protestants. He was first to recommend the introduction of caring for the wounded and the testing of officers. His *Commentaires,* which takes in from 1521 to 1574 and Henry IV, and often called the "Soldier's Bible" have considerable value in the history of warfare. The standard edition of the *Commentaries* (*Commentaries de Messire Blaise de Montluc*) is that of the Société de l'Histoire de France, edited by A. de Ruble, 5 vols., and published in 1865–1872; another edition, with critical comments, was published by P. Courteault in 1911–1914. Both editions were published in Paris.

Consult Courteault, P., *Blaise de Montluc, historien* (Paris 1908); de Broqua, J. J., *Le Maréchal de Monluc, sa famille et son temps* (Paris 1924).

MONMOUTH, mŏn'mŭth, DUKE OF (JAMES SCOTT), royal pretender and claimant to the English throne: b. Rotterdam, Holland, April 9, 1649; d. London, England, July 15, 1685. He was the natural son of Charles II and Lucy Walters, as seems certain from the king's open recognition of him, although he so closely resembled Robert Sidney, whose mistress his mother had been, that Sidney has been supposed his father. Placed under the guardianship of Lord Crofts, he assumed the name of James Crofts and was brought up in France under the care of Henrietta Maria, the queen dowager. He was recognized and summoned to England by his father after the Restoration; was married to Anne Scott, heiress of Buccleuch, and made duke of Monmouth; and served in Holland in 1673.

His Protestant sympathies, his clemency to the Scottish covenanters whom he defeated at Bothwell Bridge (1679), and a story persistently circulated (and denied before Privy Council by the king) that Charles had secretly married his mother in Holland, made him popular with the Protestant party; and Lord Anthony Shaftesbury repeatedly urged the king to legitimatize him and ensure a peaceable Protestant succession.

After the Rye House Plot (q.v.) he escaped to Holland. Thence after the accession of James II he invaded England, possibly with the complicity of William of Orange, called the people to arms, raised a large force of Protestants, was proclaimed king at Taunton, but was defeated by the earl of Feversham (Louis Duras or Durfort) at Sedgemoor. Taken prisoner he begged for his life from the king to no purpose, and was executed at the age of 36. He was handsome, weak, fickle, and in his claims to the throne no doubt entirely under the control of political plotters. The diaries of John Evelyn and of Samuel Pepys give the setting of Monmouth's career. Consult also Roberts, G., *Life of Monmouth* (London 1844): and Fea, A., *King Monmouth* (New York 1902). The latter work outlines the popular legend that Monmouth was not executed, a substitute having taken his place, and tells how the country people long expected his return.

Consult article in *Dictionary of National Biography,* "Scott, James," vol. 17 (London 1937–38).

MONMOUTH, city, Illinois, and Warren County seat; altitude 762 feet; 14 miles west-southwest of Galesburg; 27 miles east of Burlington, Iowa. It is served by the Burlington; Rock Island Southern; and Minneapolis and St. Louis railroads, and has an airport. The surrounding country is principally agricultural, specializing in the cultivation of soybeans and grain, dairying and livestock. There are coal mines and deposits of clay nearby. The city's industrial products are pottery, sheet metal specialties, farm machinery, and furnaces. The county maintains its library here, and Monmouth is the seat of Monmouth College. First settled in 1831, Monmouth was incorporated as a town in 1836, and in 1852 as a city. It has mayor and council government. Pop. 11,022.

MONMOUTH, Battle of, in American history, a celebrated engagement between the American and British forces, the former commanded by General Washington and the latter by Sir Henry Clinton, which took place at Freehold, Monmouth County, N. J., June 28, 1778. On June 18 Sir Henry Clinton, acting under peremptory orders from the British Ministry, evacuated Philadelphia, which had been occupied by his army since the preceding September, and proceeded across New Jersey toward Brunswick, with a view of embarking on the Raritan. On hearing of this movement, Washington broke up his camp at Valley Forge, and having sent forward some light troops to harass the enemy started in pursuit. Excessive heat slowed the march of both armies.

At Allentown, Clinton turned to the right by a road leading through Freehold to Sandy Hook, to embark at the latter place; and Washington, who had hitherto been deterred by the advice of his officers, and particularly of Gen. Charles Lee, from attacking the enemy, determined at once to give him battle. The evening of the 27th found the main body of the enemy encamped on high ground near Monmouth courthouse, while the American advance, about 4,000 strong, under Lee, was posted at Englishtown, five miles distant, with the main body about three miles in the rear.

The command of the advance had originally been given to General Lafayette, with the consent of Lee; but the latter subsequently applied for and obtained it. Early on the 28th Lee engaged the rear division of the enemy, his orders being to hold it in check until the main body under Washington could come up. The Americans were at first successful, but owing to causes which have never been satisfactorily explained, the whole body soon after fell into a confusion and commenced a disorderly retreat, closely followed by the British. Washington, who was advancing hastily with the main body, received the first intimation of this movement in the crowds of fugitives who poured along the road. Exasperated at the failure of Lee to execute his orders he rode up to that general and reprimanded him. Then he re-formed them, and hastened back to bring up the main body. Lee, resuming his command, held his position with spirit until compelled to retire and brought off his troops in good order. The main body, which had meanwhile taken a favorable position on an eminence, with a morass in front and a wood in the rear, opened an effective cannonade upon the British. The latter, after an ineffectual attempt to turn the American left under Lord William (Alexander) Stirling, directed their chief efforts against the right commanded by Nathanael Greene, where Anthony Wayne, under cover of an orchard, was harassing their center by a severe fire. To dislodge him Colonel Moncton advanced with a column of royal grenadiers, but fell at the head of his troops, who were repulsed with considerable loss. The enemy at length fell back to the ground occupied by Lee in the morning, whither Washington was preparing to follow them when the approach of night and the exhaustion of his men induced him to defer the execution of his plan until the morning. During the night Clinton effected a noiseless retreat, and at daybreak was many miles away from the scene of battle. The excessive heat of the weather and the fatigued condition of the troops rendered a pursuit impracticable, and the British army proceeded unmolested to the place of embarkation. The American loss in this engagement was 69 killed and 161 wounded; the British left 249 dead. For his conduct in this battle, Lee was court-martialed and suspended for one year from his command. The story of Molly Pitcher (q.v.) is connected with this battle.

Consult Stryker, William S., *The Battle of Monmouth* (Princeton, N.J., 1927).

MONMOUTH COLLEGE, a coeducational liberal arts college in West Long Branch, N.J. Founded as Monmouth Junior College in 1933, it has been authorized since 1956 to confer B.A. and B.S. degrees, while continuing to offer to its junior college division the A.A. degree. The library contains about 40,000 volumes, and the enrollment averages over 3,200. The school colors are royal blue and white, and the varsity teams are known as the "Hawks."

MONMOUTH'S REBELLION, a rebellion by the duke of Monmouth (q.v., James Scott) against James II of England in 1685. On the death of Charles II on Feb. 6, 1685, his younger brother, the duke of York, a Roman Catholic, ascended the throne as James II. Monmouth, a Protestant, the illegitimate son of Charles II and Lucy Walters, conspired with associates to overthrow the king. From his exile in Holland he sent the earl of Argyll (Archibald Campbell, 9th earl; 1629–1685) to Scotland to stage a revolt. Monmouth himself landed at Lyme Regis, England, on June 11, attracted several thousand supporters, had himself crowned king at Taunton (June 20) but soon learned of Argyll's failure. On July 6 he led his men against the king's army encamped on Sedgemoor and was completely defeated. Captured on July 8, he was beheaded on July 15. There followed the "Bloody Assizes" (q.v.) under Judge George Jeffreys at which Monmouth's followers were mercilessly punished.

Consult Emerson, William R., *Monmouth's Rebellion* (New Haven, Conn., 1951).

MONMOUTHSHIRE, county, Great Britain on the English-Welsh border, included for some purposes in England and for others in Wales, bounded on the west and northwest by the Welsh counties of Glamorganshire and Brecknockshire, on the east by the river Wye, on the north by Herefordshire, and on the south by the estuary of the Severn. It has an area of 346,781 acres. Western Monmouthshire consists of gritstone moorland, mostly over 1,000 feet above sea level, cut by valleys, of which the best known is Ebbw Vale, running from northwest to southeast, and separated by ridges of Pennant grit. The area is part of the south Wales coalfield, and carboniferous limestone, Millstone Grit, and the coal measures dip westward in succession. A rim of carboniferus limestone on the eastern edge of the coalfield is cut by the western tributary of the river Usk at Pontypool. In the northwest resistant sandstones and Old Red Sandstone conglomerates rise to a height of 2,228 feet on the Brecknock border. Lying above Old Red Sandstone marls, the Plain of Gwent, between 100 and 400 feet, drained by the rivers Usk and Monnow, forms the central part of the county. South-east of the Usk there is a wooded area running to the river Wye which meanders through the underlying carboniferous limestone. The coastal plain between Rhymney and Portskewett is alluvial.

Agricultural production is concentrated mainly in the eastern part of the county and the coastal plain. Wheat of high quality is produced in the Usk River region, and though truck farming is important, the arable land produces chiefly fodder crops, with some oats and barley. Cider orchards are important in some areas. Over 60 percent of the land is used for grazing.

Heavy iron and steel industries flourish in the western part of the county, particularly at Pontypool, Tredegar, and Rhymney. Tinplate is produced at Abertillery, and there are chemical works, brickworks, processing of fire clay, and production of flannel cloth in the same area. Coal mining produces 10 to 15 million tons annually. Since World War II, light industries have been introduced into the county, which forms part of the South Wales Development Area. The Wye valley is a tourist area. Main railroad lines run through the county from Cardiff in Glamorganshire to Hereford, across the center of the county, and along the Severn estuary. Newport is the principal port, but the canals which converge on it are no longer in use.

The county's history has been influenced by its position on the English-Welsh border. After Roman penetration and settlements at Caerwent, Caerleon, and Monmouth in the 1st century A.D., a period of confusion, during which the county formed the kingdom of Gwent, lasted until the Norman Conquest (1066). Since the formation of the county in 1536, it has been administered as part of England, but for some purposes it is regarded as part of Wales. Newport (pop. 1961, 108,107) is the county administrative headquarters. The county seat is Monmouth (pop. 1961, 5,505). The county returns six members to Parliament.

See also WALES AND MONMOUTHSHIRE.

RICHARD E. WEBB,
Director, Reference and Library Division, British Information Services, New York, N.Y.

MONNA VANNA, mŏn'ȧ văn'ȧ a three-act drama by Maurice Maeterlinck (q.v.), first produced in Paris in 1902. Unlike his better-known dramatic experiments in impressionism, it is a romantic melodrama based on an Italian Renaissance legend. The highly rhetorical dialogue sharply contrasts with the suggestive stage "silences" of the earlier symbolistic pieces. Although the lengthy moral and philosophical debates weaken the play theatrically, the plot is inherently dramatic.

Monna Vanna, wife of the Pisan commander Guido, consents to yield her honor to the enemy commander Prinzivalle (a Byronic hero) in order to save her starving countrymen from his ruthless siege. Her husband, violently opposing her self-sacrificing decision, vehemently refuses to believe her when she returns with Prinzivalle and a triumphant account of his honorable treatment of her. Disillusioned by Guido's mistrust and outraged by his imprisonment of Prinzivalle, Monna Vanna stages a heroic and shrewd performance to save the worthier man. Pretending to want personal vengence, she acquires the keys to Prinzivalle's dungeon, and the play ends with the implication that she will later escape to a new life with him.

CHARLOTTE K. SPIVACK.

MONNET, mô-nā', **Jean,** French statesman: b. Cognac, Charente, France, Nov. 9, 1888. He left high school to join the brandy business founded by his father, and at 18 began representing it abroad. During World War I, as a liaison officer in London for the French Ministry of Commerce, he served on interallied committees to coordinate supplies and shipping. In 1919 he was named deputy secretary general of the League of Nations, but resigned in 1923 to revive his family firm. After two years he entered international banking and engaged in enterprises around the world, among them the reorganization of the Chinese railways.

When World War II began, he was chairman of the Franco-British Economic Coordination Committee. After the fall of France in 1940, he served with the British Supply Council in Washington, D.C., until 1943, when he went to Algiers as commissioner for arms, supplies, and reconstruction for the Free French government. After the war he drafted a plan to rebuild French industry, enlisting the aid of labor, management, and most political parties, and directed its operation from 1947 to 1952.

His experiences in achieving harmony among conflicting groups had led him to dream of a united Europe. With Robert Schuman, French foreign minister, he fashioned the European Coal and Steel Community (ECSC, q.v.) which pooled the coal and steel resources of six nations—France, the Federal Republic of Germany, the Netherlands, Belgium, Luxembourg, and Italy—under a supranational authority. Monnet was its president from 1952, when it began to function, until 1955. Under his inspiration, the idea was enlarged in the creation of the European Economic Community (EEC, q.v.) ratified by the Treaty of Rome in 1957, with the same members as the ECSC. Within the EEC, national trade barriers were to be eliminated by degrees, resulting eventually in an integrated mass market. Another treaty authorized an organization to promote the peaceful uses of atomic energy —the European Atomic Energy Community (EAEC, q.v.). In 1956, Monnet organized the Action Committee for a United States of Europe, a group dedicated to building political unity upon economic integration, and became its chairman.

MONNICA, SAINT. See MONICA, SAINT.

MONO INDIANS, mō'nō, a Shoshonean-speaking group living in Mono and Inyo counties and along the San Joaquin Valley range in California. Considerable confusion exists regarding the actual tribal status of these people. Some authorities feel that they are merely a subdivision of the Paiute tribe, but others believe that they constitute a part of the Uto-Aztecan linguistic group. There are two distinct dialect divisions among the Mono Indians, both related to the Paiute, Bannock, and Paviotso peoples. The meaning of the name is unknown; a common legend that it stems from the Spanish *mono* (monkey) is completely unfounded. Early United States documents often refer to them as the Mona Indians. They call themselves Nümü, meaning simply "people" or "person." The Mono live by seed gathering, fishing, and hunting. Their major art is basketry, in which their product is not unlike that of the neighboring Yokuts. The Mono population has remained more or less stable at about 1,000 persons for many years.

Consult Kroeber, A.L., *Handbook of the Indians of California,* Bureau of American Ethnology, Bulletin 78, pp. 584–589 (Washington 1925); Steward, J.H., "Ethnography of the Owens Valley Paiute," *University of California Publications,* vol. 33, no. 3, pp. 233–350 (Berkeley, Calif., 1933).

FREDERICK J. DOCKSTADER.

MONOCACY, mō̂nŏk'ȧ-sĭ, **Battle on the,** Civil War battle, July 9, 1864, on the east bank of the Monocacy River southeast of Frederick, Md., in which 14,000 Confederate troops under Lieut. Gen. Jubal A. Early defeated 6,000 Union troops under Maj. Gen. Lew Wallace. In order to divert the Army of the Potomac from its main purpose at Petersburg, Early was ordered to make a foray against Washington, D.C. Wallace's stand on the Monocacy delayed Early for a day, enabling the defenses of Washington to be strengthened.

MONOCEROS, mō̂-nŏs'ẽr-ŏs, or **UNICORN,** ū'nĭ-kôrn, a constellation, between Canis Major and Canis Minor and just to the east of Orion. Lying directly astride the Milky Way, it is a relatively inconspicuous asterism, its brightest star, α Monocerotis, being of the 4th magnitude. It is a winter constellation, and is on the meridian at 9 P.M. on February 22.

MONOCHROME, mŏn'ō̂-krōm (literally, one color), a painting or drawing in one color or different shadows of one color. More specifically, it is a technique practiced by the ancients in order to obtain a painting by filling in with a single color the outlines of a silhouette projected against a light background. This primitive type of painting was first used by the Egyptians. It then spread to the Greek world in about the 7th century B.C., and was still practiced in the time of Pliny the Elder (23–79 A.D.), who gave a description of it.

Monochromes were usually painted in red pigment, made either with cinnabar or minium, on a white ground. They were executed chiefly on terra-cotta, although a few monochromes on marble are known to have existed, such as the tablets of Herculaneum and Pompeii (now at the National Museum in Naples).

See also CHIAROSCURO; GRISAILLE.

OLGA RAGGIO.

MONOCOTYLEDONS, mŏn'ō̂-kŏt-ĭ-lē-dŭnz, a subclass (Monocotyledonae), in the plant kingdom; together with the dicotyledons (q.v.), they constitute the class Angiospermae (flowering plants). Although there is no single feature which rigidly separates monocotyledons from dicotyledons, the former constitute a fairly natural group which probably evolved from the lower dicotyledons early in the history of flowering plants. In contrast to the dicotyledons, the monocotyledons frequently have fibrous roots; simple stems without secondary thickening; simple, elongate, entire-margined, unstalked leaves with the main veins parallel; flower parts in multiples of three; and a single seed leaf or cotyledon. It is estimated that the monocotyledons comprise some 3,000 genera and 50,000 species. The orchid family, the largest in the flowering plants, includes some 500 genera and close to 20,000 species. The most important family economically of the monocotyledons and the greatest in number of individuals is the grass family, with some 6,000 species. The most vital food plants—rice, wheat, and corn—are grasses, and this family also includes rye, barley, oats, sorghum, millet, and sugarcane, as well as those plants, such as Kentucky bluegrass and timothy, on which domesticated animals graze. Similar in appearance to the grasses, but probably not too closely related, are the sedges, with some 4,000 species. Other monocotyledons are the palms—unusual in this subclass in that they are woody—the cattails, the aroids (such as Jack-in-the-pulpit, skunk cabbage, and the tropical taro, with netted venation), the lilies, the bananas, and the tiny duckweeds.

EDWIN B. MATZKE, *Columbia University.*

MONOD, mô-nō', **Jacques,** French biologist: b. Paris, Feb. 9, 1910. He collaborated with François Jacob in developing the concepts of messenger RNA (ribonucleic acid) and the operon. For this work, Monod and Jacob shared the 1965 Nobel Prize in physiology or medicine with another French biologist, André Lwoff, who studied lysogenic bacteria.

In 1961, after working with the American biologist Arthur Pardee on enzyme synthesis in mutant bacteria, Monod and Jacob began to develop their theories. They proposed that the first step in protein synthesis in the cell is the transcription of the genetic message of DNA (deoxyribonucleic acid) onto a complementary form of RNA. Since this RNA then carries the instructions for protein synthesis to the sites of synthesis in the cell (ribosomes), they named it "messenger RNA." Monod and Jacob then proposed the concept of an operon and operator gene to explain what controls the synthesis of messenger RNA. According to their theory, an operon is a group of genes that are next to one another on a chromosome and which are controlled by an operator gene. When the operator gene is not inhibited by a repressor, it directs the operon to code for a molecule of messenger RNA.

In 1953, Monod was appointed head of the department of cellular biochemistry at the Pasteur Institute in Paris, and in 1959 he was awarded a professorship on the Faculté des Sciences of the University of Paris.

MONOGAMY, mô-nŏg'à-mĭ, that form of marriage in which the husband has one wife at a time, as contrasted with bigamy and polygamy, and also with polyandry, in which a woman has two or more husbands. The possession of more than one wife is in some societies a badge of social distinction. In modern secular states polygamous marriages are illegal. See also MARRIAGE—*Monogamy.*

MONOGRAM, mŏn'ô-grăm, from the Latin *monogramma,* ultimately from Greek *monos,* single, and *gramma,* letter, is a character or cipher combining two or more letters (rarely a single letter) to represent a name. In Greek and Roman times monograms were extensively used on coins, medals, and public monuments. The most famous monogram undoubtedly is that which was incorporated in the Labarum (q.v.), that is, the intertwined letters chi and rho which are the first two letters of Greek *Christos,* Christ. In medieval times there was a proliferation of monograms, especially as used by merchants who were not entitled to display coats of arms. The commercial trading monopolies, like the Dutch East India Company, usually displayed monograms on their house flags. Perhaps the most famous of artist monograms are those of Rembrandt and Dürer. Among royal monograms may be cited those of Charlemagne, Hugues Capet, St. Louis, and the combined monogram of Henry II and Diane de Poitiers.

MONOLITH, mŏn'ô-lĭth, a stone block, usually monumental and of large dimensions. It may be an unhewn menhir; the capstone or support of a megalithic monument; a hewn obelisk; a sarcophagus; a sculptured temple; or a colossal statue. Stonehenge (q.v.) is an example of a monolithic monument. See also STONES, STANDING; MENHIR.

MONOLOGUE, mŏn'ô-lŏg, a term traditionally signifying a dramatic recitation of considerable length in a stage performance by one actor uninterrupted by other performers on the scene. The convention of the monologue, used to acquaint the audience with the situation and the meaning of the drama, is very old. Sophocles used it in his monologue of the dying Ajax, and Shakespeare supplies a famous example in Hamlet's soliloquy, "To be or not to be." Other celebrated monologues are those of Auguste in Corneille's *Cinna,* of Sosie in Molière's *Amphitryon,* and Beaumarchais' Figaro. Victor Hugo used the device in *Hernani,* showing the Emperor Charles V meditating before the tomb of Charlemagne. The monologue and the soliloquy are often synonymous. However, in an extension of the term "monologue" the word is often used with a more limited meaning, to signify a dramatic recitation by one actor who may assume several parts or leave to the listener's imagination responses of an unheard as well as unseen member of a dialogue.

MONOMACHUS, Constantine. See CONSTANTINE IX.

MONOMAKH, Vladimir. See VLADIMIR MONOMACHUS.

MONOMANIA, mŏn-ô-mā'nĭ-à (from the Gr. *monos,* single + *mania,* madness), that form of mental derangement which distinguishes itself by an abnormal conception or action on one subject only, leaving the mind sane on all other points.

MONOMETALLISM. See BIMETALLISM.

MONONA, Lake. See FOUR LAKES.

MONONGAHELA, mô-nŏn-gà-hē'là, city, Pennsylvania, in Washington County, 17 miles south of Pittsburgh on the Monongahela River. It has an airport. It lies in a coal and gas region with dairy, poultry, fruit, and truck farms. The chief manufactured products are commercial stokers, springs and axles, machinery, firebrick and other clay products, steam-producing equipment, chemicals, and costumes. Many of the inhabitants work in the large steel mills nearby at Donora and Clairton.

Joseph Parkinson settled here in 1792; and here, in August 1794 at Whiskey Point, Albert Gallatin made the speech that persuaded the men in the Whiskey Rebellion not to resist federal troops. Originally called Parkinson's Ferry, the place was incorporated in 1833 as the borough of Williamsport. Four years later the name was changed to Monongahela City. Monongahela, meaning "river with the sliding banks," is from the Indian word Menaungehilla.

The city was chartered in 1873, but in 1893 the word "City" was dropped from the official title. In 1951 it had a commission form of government. Pop. 7,113.

MONONGAHELA, river, West Virginia and Pennsylvania, which has its source in the northwestern part of West Virginia, and flows north into Pennsylvania, where it unites at Pittsburgh with the Allegheny to form the Ohio River. The headwaters of the Monongahela are in the Alleghany Mountains near the headwaters of the Potomac. The two headstreams of the Monongahela unite near Fairmont in Marion County, W. Va., and from the point of junction on the north become a swiftly flowing stream, furnishing water power for several manufacturing towns and cities. The whole course is very irregular; the length is about 300 miles. The river was made navigable about 106 miles from its mouth to Morgantown, in Monongalia County, W. Va., by a system of nine locks, and other locks above Morgantown now make the river navigable as far as Fairmont. See also PITTSBURGH.

MONONUCLEOSIS, mŏn-ō-nū-klē-ō'sĭs (also known as GLANDULAR FEVER), a disorder of unknown etiology, but probably of infectious origin. It is characterized by irregular fever, enlargement of lymph glands and spleen, and by the presence in the blood of an increased number of lymphocytes of a peculiar type. It has been recognized as a distinct disease entity only since 1935.

Occasionally it is observed in epidemic form in certain localities. The clinical picture depends somewhat upon the stage of the disease. In the prodromal period (3 to 6 days) symptoms are somewhat vague: chilliness, slight rise in temperature, sore throat, and swollen neck glands. In the middle stage (second week) cervical glandular enlargement is seen in 75 per cent of cases, with the enlarged glands somewhat tender. Soreness of the throat now becomes more pronounced, the mucous membranes being of a bright red color. The throat condition may resemble that of acute tonsillitis, Vincent's angina, or even diphtheria. The occurrence of jaundice is fairly common. After 20 days the stage of convalescence sets in, but recovery may be extremely slow. The patient is often greatly weakened, and relapses are by no means uncommon. The blood count shows a leucocytosis of from 10,000 to 15,000, the count being due to lymphocytosis. Since 1932 the most important laboratory test for this disease has been the heterophil antibody reaction, the clumping of sheep cells by the serum of infectious mononucleosis patients.

HAROLD WELLINGTON JONES, M.D.

MONOPHYSITES, mō-nŏf'ĭ-sītz (from Greek *monos,* single, and *physis,* nature), those followers of the opinion in the early Church which ascribes but one nature to Christ in contradistinction to the orthodox doctrine that he was both divine and human, true God and true man.

The Monophysites were mainly confined to the Eastern Church and obtained no footing in the West. The edict called Henoticon, issued by the Emperor Zeno in 482, was not able to quiet the long and often bloody contests incident to this controversy, and the orthodox Church, by its sentences of excommunication, occasioned a formal secession on the part of the Monophysites. This separation took place in the first half of the 6th century. Nor did they remain united among themselves. In 519 controversies arose among them respecting the question whether the body of Christ is corruptible or not.

About 560, a Monophysite, Askusnages, and after him Philoponus, a noted Alexandrian philosopher of that century, conceived the idea of styling the three persons of the Deity three Gods. These Tritheists and their adherents, even in the eyes of the Monophysites, were heretics, and were the occasion of many Monophysites turning Catholic. In Egypt, Syria and Mesopotamia the Monophysite congregations, however, remained the strongest, had patriarchs at Alexandria and Antioch, existing without interruption by the side of the imperial orthodox patriarchs. After the Syrian, Jacob Baradaeus had, about 570, established their religious constitution, they formed the independent churches of the Jacobites and Armenians, which separated from the Greeks as well as the Romans, and have for that reason been able to maintain themselves since the 7th century, even under the dominion of the Mohammedans.

Excepting their doctrine of one nature in Christ, they coincide, in the main points of belief, with the Greek Church; their worship also resembles the Greek rather than the Roman, but has, from their national character and their superstition, received variations, which are most striking in the religious constitution of the Egyptian Jacobites. See also JACOBITE CHURCH; ARMENIAN CHURCH.

MONOPLEGIA, mŏn-ō-plē'jĭ-ȧ, paralysis of a single limb, muscle, or muscle group. If it involves the face it is designated as *facial,* if the arm, *brachial,* and if the leg, *crural.* It is also termed *central* if arising from a lesion in the central nervous system, and as *peripheral* if occurring as the result of an injury to a peripheral nerve. A monoplegia of central origin is a poliomyelitis affecting the muscles of one leg. See also BRAIN; PARALYSIS.

HAROLD WELLINGTON JONES, M.D.

MONOPOLI, mō-nô'pō-lĭ, town, Italy, in the province of Bari, 26 miles east-southeast of Bari on the Adriatic Sea. Interesting for its historic remains and 12th century cathedral, it is a modern industrial center, manufacturing textiles, flour, macaroni, soap, lubricating oil, and exporting olive oil, wine, and olives. Pop. (1951) 22,600.

MONOPOLY, control by an individual, a business concern, a group or government that makes it possible to fix the prices or regulate the output of one or more articles or services. As it concerns price, monopoly means the power to fix the price of a product or a service by arbitrary methods, such as by controlling the supply. It is an exclusive right given to one or more persons to carry on some branch of trade or manufacture.

The most frequent monopolies formerly centered around the exclusive privilege to trade in certain foreign countries, to import or export certain articles, or to practice certain arts or trades. Such monopoly privileges were very common in Great Britain, particularly during the 15th and 16th centuries. Several British companies of an essentially monopolistic nature, such as the Hudson's Bay Company and the East India Company, created to exploit the resources of Great Britain's far-flung colonial empire, continued to wield considerable influence until well into the 19th century.

In general, monopolies fall into two classes: (1) public, and (2) private. Public monopolies are those undertaken by the government and would include such economic activities as the federal postal service, or the operation of toll highways by the states, or electric power plants by a municipality. Private monopolies are those held by business organizations and individuals. They may originate either from (1) a privilege granted by the government, (2) the possession of superior skill or talent, or (3) from the ownership of capital.

Thousands of private monopolies exist as the result of a privilege granted by the government in the form of a franchise, a patent, or a copyright. A franchise may confer upon a business enterprise the exclusive right to operate an electric power plant, a bus line or a railroad in a given locality. Franchises need not be exclusive; nor are they always given in perpetuity. They are granted because from the point of view of society it is considered desirable to reduce or eliminate ruinous competition in certain lines of business activity.

A patent is a right granted by the federal government (United States Patent Office) to an inventor, giving him the exclusive privilege to manufacture and market his invention for a period of 17 years. A copyright gives an author the exclusive right to his literary efforts for a period of 28 years, and may be renewed for an additional 28 years. Monopolies in the form of patents and copyrights are considered socially desirable because they promote social and economic development by stimulating new inventions and works of literature.

Certain individuals endowed with superior talent in the arts are a monopoly unto themselves. A gifted musician or a talented actor can command large sums of money for a single performance because the absence of competition creates a monopoly for those so endowed.

Quite frequently, the ownership of capital tends to result in the creation of a monopoly. Relatively few people are free to engage in the business enterprise of their choice. In most instances the selection of a business is limited both by the capital resources of the individual and the capital requirements of the enterprise. It is evident, for example, that the amount of capital necessary to organize an automobile manufacturing company or a steel company is so large that the average individual would be prevented from entering either of these lines of endeavor. Thus, the established manufacturers of automobiles and steel need not be concerned, as a rule, over the possibility of additional competition resulting from new entrants into the field. While others are not restricted largely from entering, the lack of capital gives the established firms a partial or total monopoly.

Because monopoly prices usually are higher than competitive prices, it is sometimes assumed that when a monopolist is free to fix his price, he will charge the highest price possible. But such is not always the case. In the final analysis, the motive of the monopolist is identical with that of any other business man in a capitalistic society; namely, to obtain the largest amount of net profit from the operation of his business. To achieve this objective, it may be necessary to reduce the price as a means of broadening the market for the product. Whether the monopolist decides to curtail or expand output depends upon which course of action will increase his profits. In this connection, the cost of production is a controlling factor. Under certain circumstances where the monopolist can lower total unit costs by expanding output and thus spreading his fixed costs over a larger number of units of production, he will do so. Fixed costs include such items as bond interest, real estate taxes and administrative salaries which remain constant in amount regardless of the level of production. Obviously, if production can be increased, the burden of fixed costs which must be borne by each unit of output is lowered. On the other hand, if an increase in production will be accompanied by higher fixed costs per unit, as sometimes happens, the monopolist is reluctant to expand output, unless other considerations alter his decision.

In addition to the profit motive and the cost of production, other factors which will influence the price charged by a monopolist are: (1) the development of substitutes, (2) the fear of competition, and (3) the fear of public regulation.

In addition to competition between goods of the same general type, a substantial degree of competition exists among different products which may be adapted to the same use. For example, shoes can be manufactured from a wide variety of materials other than leather. If a monopoly were to develop in the leather industry, and excessive prices were charged for the product, the consumer might be compelled to forego the purchase of leather shoes for those manufactured from other materials. Recognition of this principle of substitution would undoubtedly set a ceiling on the price that could be charged by the leather monopolist for his product.

If the monopoly is not protected by law, the fear of inviting competition might deter the monopolist from charging too high a price for his product. Potential competitors, attracted by the possibilities for large profits in the industry, might be encouraged to enter the field.

The monopolist readily recognizes the political dangers inherent in charging exorbitant prices. High prices and excessively large profits frequently are an open invitation to government control. Although the states had sought to regulate monopolistic industries earlier, the first U. S. government attempt, in 1887, was the Interstate Commerce Act. Strangely enough, the Interstate Commerce Act was not prompted by a desire to encourage competition among the railroads, but rather by a wish to eliminate the ruinous competition that threatened the solvency of the entire railroad industry. During this period it was possible to purchase a one-way coach ticket from New York to Chicago (a distance of about 900 miles) for twenty-five cents—meals included. The Sherman Antitrust Act of 1890 marked the first attempt on the part of the federal government toward blanket legislation aimed at curbing business trusts and other manifestations of monopoly. The Sherman Act declared illegal any business combination that was in restraint of trade. The Clayton Act of 1914 greatly expanded the government's authority to regulate big business practice, particularly in the banking field. The Public Utility Holding Company Act of 1935 imposed the death sentence on certain types of holding companies in the public utility field.

PATRICK DE TURO

WALT DISNEY PRODUCTIONS

A five-car monorail (*above*) takes visitors on a 2½ mile (4-km) tour of Disneyland. A suspended monorail (*right*), inaugurated in 1901, serves a 9-mile (15-km) route in Wuppertal, West Germany.

GERMAN INFORMATION CENTER

MONORAIL, a transportation system in which the vehicle travels on a single rail. There are two basic types—the suspended monorail in which the vehicle is below the rail, and the supported type with the vehicle above the rail. Existing monorail systems use steel wheels on steel rails, or rubber tires on concrete beams. The concrete beam is regarded as a rail. Monorails using air cushions and magnetic levitation as means of support are also being developed. Systems with two rails very close together, which are effectively a single support, are also classified as monorails. Normally the basic function of the monorail is to carry passengers.

Advantages and Disadvantages. Two considerations led to the development of single-rail systems. First, monorails are basically simpler than the conventional two-rail system and are therefore potentially less expensive. Second, the technical problems of a two-rail vehicle involving lurching back and forth between the rails may be solved by the use of a single rail. However, with a single rail, a major new problem of stability is introduced.

Three basic methods are used to stabilize the monorail. First, gravity stabilizes a vehicle suspended beneath the rail. Second, gyroscopes have been used to stabilize the vehicle. Generally, however, modern systems do not rely on gyroscopes. Third, straddle-type systems utilizing upper and lower horizontal wheels rolling against the side of the beam provide stability.

History. The first known monorail was built in England in 1821 by Henry Palmer. Its purpose was to carry materials. It was not until the late 19th century that passenger-carrying monorails were built. The most famous old monorail is the Schwebebahn, or "Swinging Railroad," in Wuppertal, West Germany. This 9.3-mile (15-km) line was built in 1901 and has been in use since.

The Swedish industrialist Axel L. Wenner-Gren (1881–1961) backed the development of a supported system in which the car straddles the beam. The system became known as the Alweg monorail. Since 1950, approximately 25 monorail lines have been built in Europe, the United States, and Japan, more than half utilizing the Alweg system or a derivation of it.

In addition to the Wuppertal line, the best-known monorails are the following: the one at Disneyland, Anaheim, Calif., which was completed in 1959 and measures 2.5 miles (4 km); the line constructed for the 1962 World's Fair in Seattle, Wash., which is 1 mile (1.6 km) long; the 8.2-mile (13.1-km) system built for the 1964 Olympics in Tokyo, Japan; the one constructed for Expo '70 in Osaka, Japan, totaling 2.7 miles (4.3 km); and the 3-mile (5-km) line at Walt Disney World in Orlando, Fla., completed in 1971.

Characteristics. The characteristics of the modern monorail may be illustrated by examining the system at Walt Disney World, a derivation of the straddle-type monorail pioneered by Wenner-Gren. The main line is a double-track loop that transports visitors between an amusement park, two major hotels, and a parking lot. There are ten trains, each consisting of five cars, with a capacity of 212 seated passengers per train. The cars are of aluminum honeycomb construction. They are powered by 600 volt direct current, and reach a top speed of 40 miles (64 km) per hour.

Commercial electric power is rectified to direct current at wayside, and is conveyed to the vehicle through power rails attached to the sides of the beam. Controls are automatic, but may be overriden by the operator. The cars have rubber tires that roll on top of the concrete rail beam and horizontal tires that roll against the side of the beams.

Role in Public Transit. Although monorails were originally developed to solve a technical problem, investigations have been made on utilizing the monorail in solving mass transit needs. Since a conventional elevated railroad requires a double-track structure approximately 32 feet (10 meters) wide, there are serious objections to placing such a system over city streets. Rail systems used for transit are normally placed underground in urban areas. Because their construction cost is very high, they are economical only in very high-density transportation corridors.

On the other hand, a monorail may be placed on a beam as little as 2 feet (61 cm) wide, making it acceptable as an aerial construction. The cost of such construction is about 25% that of underground construction. Thus the monorail appears to be economically viable in lower-density corridors having peak passenger travel of 10,000 to 20,000 people per hour. Many U. S. transportation corridors are within this range.

See also AIR CUSHION VEHICLE.

ROBERT F. MAST
President, ABAM Engineers Incorporated

MONOSACCHARIDE, mon-ə-sak′ə-rīd, any of a class of simple sugar molecules. Each typically consists of three to seven carbon atoms, with hydrogen and oxygen atoms in the ratio of two to one. Some naturally occurring five-carbon and six-carbon monosaccharides are especially important because they play a major role in biological processes. Other monosaccharides, some with eight, nine, or ten carbon atoms, have been synthesized. See also CARBOHYDRATES; SUGAR–*Sugar Chemistry*.

MONOSODIUM GLUTAMATE, mon-ə-sō′dē-əm glōō′tə-māt, also called MSG, is a white crystalline powder used by the food industry, restaurants, and home cooks to enhance the flavor of meat, fish, fowl, vegetables, and soups. MSG is widely used in the United States in canned, frozen, and dried foods, and it is important in Oriental cookery. Some persons develop a headache after eating foods containing MSG. This is often called the Chinese-restaurant syndrome.

MSG is the monosodium salt of glutamic acid. It was first produced in the Orient from seaweed but now is mainly derived from the gluten of wheat, corn, soybeans, or sugar beets. Its capability to enhance food flavor was discovered by the Japanese chemist Kikunae Ikeda in 1908.

MONOTHEISM, mon-ə-thē′izm, in religion, is belief in one God. The equivalent term in philosophy is theism. Monotheism is opposed to atheism, belief in no God, and to polytheism, belief in many gods. It differs from pantheism, the belief that God is inseparable from the world, in holding that God is transcendent, outside the world. At the same time it differs from deism, the belief that God has withdrawn from the world, in maintaining that he is immanent, or active in it.

The God of monotheism is, moreover, a personal being who can be imagined, although not understood, in human terms of power, wisdom, and love and who can be approached in prayer. Thus he differs from an impersonal, abstract principle, or Absolute, as in some monistic Greek (Aristotle), German (Hegel), and Hindu (Shankara) philosophy.

According to the three great monotheistic religions of the West—Judaism, Christianity, and Islam—monotheism is the highest form of religion. Some thinkers, however, consider the concept of a personal God a step toward the more sophisticated concept of an Absolute. Either way, monotheism has provided an intellectually and emotionally satisfying answer to many of man's eternal questions about the meaning of existence. It has not, however, definitely explained the presence of evil in a universe created and ruled by a benevolent, omnipotent God.

Sources of Monotheism. Jews, Christians, and Muslims traditionally have believed that monotheism was revealed by God to Adam, but that after the Fall mankind declined into polytheism. The biblical prophets and Mohammed labored mightily to remove these polluting influences and restore man's original faith.

This traditional view was challenged in the 19th century as a result of historical and anthropological research. Some scholars concluded that man's religious ideas have progressed from the animism of primitive societies through the polytheism of ancient and Eastern civilizations to culminate in the monotheism of the West. This historical view has been modified in the late 20th century. Some scholars have posited the existence of an original monotheism among primitive peoples. Others maintain that some individuals in all religions tend toward monotheism, often by way of henotheism, the worship of one great God without excluding lesser divinities.

Types of Monotheism. The major Western religions are rigidly monotheistic. In Judaism, Christianity, and Islam, God as the Creator is the all-powerful ruler of the universe, who jealously permits no rival or subordinate deities. Also just and loving, he requires trust and ethical conduct from his followers, whom he will save from sin and death. Although non-Christians have found it difficult to reconcile the doctrine of the Trinity with monotheism, Christian theologians insist that there is no contradiction. Zoroastrianism is initially dualistic, but since the good God, Ahura Mazda, defeats the evil God, Ahriman, it is ultimately monotheistic.

The major religions of the East have more or less monotheistic aspects but these shade into other views. Hindu monotheism requires loving devotion to a supreme God—Vishnu or Shiva—who will save his followers from the cycle of endless rebirths, but it permits lesser divinities. In addition, every divinity, indeed every individual human soul (atman) may be seen as sharing in The One, or Ultimate Reality, which is the creator God, Brahma, if interpreted personally, or the monistic Absolute, Brahman, if conceived of impersonally.

Sikhism, an outgrowth of Hinduism and Islam, recognizes one Supreme Being but variously interprets it monotheistically, pantheistically, or monistically. Buddhism, which also developed out of Hinduism, originally recognized no divinity but only Gautama Buddha, a man who attained enlightenment and thereby salvation from reincarnation. Gradually, however, Buddhists in Southeast Asia came to regard Gautama as if he were the supreme deity. Similarly many Japanese worship Amida Buddha as the one savior God. See also GOD; THEISM.

MONOTHELITISM, mə-noth′ə-lī-tizm, a 7th century doctrine of the nature of Christ, caused the last of the Christological controversies in the early church. The word "Monothelitism" (more correctly "Monotheletism") derives from the Greek for "single" and "will." The doctrine followed the orthodox Christian teaching that Christ has two natures, human and divine, in one person, but it held that he had only one, divine will. Such a view avoided the possibility of conflict between two wills but tended to deemphasize his human nature.

Monothelitism was proposed by Byzantine Emperor Heraclius I about 624 as a compromise with Monophysitism, the heretical doctrine that Christ has only one, divine nature. Heraclius hoped thus to win back the Monophysites, centered in Syria and Egypt, to orthodoxy and the empire endangered successively by Persian and Muslim attack. Although the patriarchs Sergius of Constantinople and Cyrus of Alexandria upheld Monothelitism, Sophronius, later patriarch of Jerusalem, objected. Sergius consulted Pope Honorius I, who wrote a letter apparently favoring Monothelitism. Heraclius then, in 638, published the *Ecthesis*, making Monothelitism official.

Later popes, however, condemned Monothelitism. Consequently, Martin I was imprisoned, tortured, and exiled by Emperor Constans II. Finally, Emperor Constantine IV in 680 called the third Council of Constantinople, which defined the orthodox view that Christ has two natures in harmony and condemned Monothelitism as heresy. This settlement increased the authority of the popes at the expense of the emperors.

MONOTREME, mon′ə-trēm, any of a small order of egg-laying mammals (Monotremata) that retain many characteristics of the reptiles from which all mammals are descended. Like other mammals monotremes have large brains, hair, and mammary glands (but no teats). Monotremes are of two families—the echidnas or spiny anteaters (Tachyglossidae) and the duck-billed platypuses (Ornithorhynchidae).

The monotremes are the only mammals whose eggs develop outside the body, like those of oviparous reptiles and birds. As in reptiles and birds, the digestive canal, the excretory duct, and the genital duct open into a common chamber—the cloaca—with a single external opening. Other reptilian features include the structure of the eye, certain skull bones, and the shoulder girdle of the skeleton. Even their stance, or carriage, resembles that of reptiles, and temperature regulation is generally poorer than in most other mammals.

MONOTYPE. See PRINTING.

MONOXIDE, mon-ok′sīd, a compound containing just one atom of oxygen in each molecule of an oxide. The term "monoxide" is used in distinguishing different oxides of the same element according to the number of oxygen atoms present in a molecule. Most commonly, it is used to distinguish carbon monoxide (CO) from carbon dioxide (CO_2). Some monoxides consist of one atom of oxygen and one atom of another element, as does carbon monoxide. Others consist of one atom of oxygen united to two atoms of another element, as does sodium monoxide (Na_2O). See also OXIDE.

MONREALE, môn-râ-ä′lā, is a town in the Sicilian province of Palermo, Italy, famous for its Norman cathedral and cloisters. It is 5 miles (8 km) southwest of Palermo. The cathedral, founded in 1174 by the Norman king William II of Sicily, combines Norman, Saracen, Byzantine, and Lombard features. The Byzantine mosaics covering the interior walls depict scenes from the Old and New Testaments. In the central apse is a half-length Christ giving his blessing. In the cloisters, pointed arches rest on decorated twin columns. Population: (1971) 23,164.

MONRO, Sir Charles Carmichael (1860–1929), British general. He was born at sea on June 15, 1860. He entered the army in 1879 and fought in India and in the South African War. When World War I began, he commanded a division and then a corps in France. He was knighted in 1915. He succeeded Sir Ian Hamilton in October 1915 as a commander in chief of the Dardanelles campaign. Under his direction the Allied troops were withdrawn from their untenable position on the Gallipoli Peninsula without appreciable loss. He was then made commander of the First Army in France (1916) and, later the same year, commander in chief in India, where he served until 1920. He was promoted to general in 1917.

From September 1923 until he retired in 1928, Monro was governor and commander in chief at Gibraltar. He was created a grand commander of the Order of the Bath in 1919 and a baronet in 1921. He died in London, England, on Dec. 7, 1929.

MONROE, Harriet (1860–1936), American poet and editor, who was the founder of *Poetry*, the most important American magazine devoted to verse. She was born in Chicago, Ill., on Dec. 23, 1860, and received her education at a private school in Georgetown in the District of Columbia. Having something of a reputation in Chicago as a poet, she was selected to write the *Columbian Ode* for the city's world's fair in 1893. In 1896 she published a biography of the architect John Wellborn Root, her brother-in-law, and in 1903 she issued five verse plays under the title *The Passing Show.* Later writings include *The Difference and Other Poems* (1923) and *A Poet's Life* (1938), an autobiography.

Harriet Monroe's poetry is generally undistinguished. Her lasting contribution was *Poetry: A Magazine of Verse,* which she founded in Chicago in 1912 and edited until her death, in Arequipa, Peru, on Sept. 26, 1936. *Poetry* provided an early outlet for new poets in the United States, including Ezra Pound, T. S. Eliot, Wallace Stevens, Elinor Wylie, Robinson Jeffers, and Marianne Moore.

JAMES MONROE

James Monroe

5th PRESIDENT OF THE UNITED STATES
IN OFFICE FROM 1817 TO 1825

BORN	April 28, 1758, in Westmoreland county, Va.
HIGHER EDUCATION	College of William and Mary (attended 1774-1776).
RELIGION	Episcopalian.
OCCUPATION	Lawyer, public official.
MARRIAGE	Feb. 16, 1786, to Elizabeth Kortright.
CHILDREN	Eliza Kortright (1786-1835); son (1799-1801); Maria Hester (1803-1850).
MILITARY SERVICE	Lieutenant to major, American Revolutionary Army.
POLITICAL PARTY	Democratic-Republican.
LEGAL RESIDENCE WHEN ELECTED	Virginia.
POSITION WHEN ELECTED	Secretary of State.
DIED	July 4, 1831, in New York City.
BURIAL PLACE	Richmond, Va.

PORTRAIT BY REMBRANDT PEALE; JAMES MONROE MUSEUM AND MEMORIAL LIBRARY

MONROE, James (1758–1831), 5th president of the United States. Monroe's public career was shaped by three great influences: the American Revolution; the principles of the Republican party, which he helped found; and his diplomatic experiences. He worked to achieve the revolutionary ideal of a representative government based on free institutions, first through the battle to defeat the Federalists and, secondly, as president, by attempting to eliminate party divisions, which he regarded as destructive of republican government.

Monroe's policies, stressing the concept of limited government and strict construction of the U. S. Constitution, were shaped in accordance with the principles of the Jeffersonian Republican party. As a result of his experiences as a diplomat, he acquired a determination to free the United States from subservience to European powers. Hence he rejected British proposals in 1823 for joint action to protect the newly won independence of the Latin American states in favor of a unilateral policy declaration later known as the Monroe Doctrine.

Unlike his close friends and political collaborators Thomas Jefferson and James Madison, Monroe was neither an intellectual nor a political innovator. His talent lay in the practical implementation of ideals and policies. Without any gifts as an orator or writer, he owed his influence and prestige both to his generally recognized integrity and honesty and to his personal charm. The latter was largely the result of an evident personal warmth, a genuine thoughtfulness, and a temperament remarkably free from vindictiveness. He was able to work with little friction with men of the most varied character and ability. A slow thinker, who carefully canvassed all alternatives before making a decision, he was praised by his contemporaries for the soundness of his judgment. In many ways his values were those of the 18th century. Therefore, it was typical of him that during his presidency this tall, raw-boned, plain-looking man still wore the knee breeches and buckled shoes of an earlier age.

EARLY CAREER

Monroe was born in Westmoreland county, Va., on April 28, 1758, the son of a modest planter. He entered William and Mary College in July 1774, but, caught up by the fervor of the revolutionary spirit, he enlisted in the Third Virginia Regiment in the spring of 1776. As a lieutenant he saw action in the battles in New York preceding Washington's retreat into New Jersey, and he distinguished himself in a vanguard action at Trenton, where he was seriously wounded. For two years he served as an aide with the rank of colonel to Gen. William Alexander (Lord Stirling). He was present during the winter of Valley Forge (1777–1778) and participated in the Battle of Monmouth.

In 1780, unable to obtain a field command, Monroe returned to Virginia to study law under Thomas Jefferson, who became a lifelong friend, patron, and major influence on his intellectual development. Monroe was elected to the Virginia House of Delegates in 1782, and his abilities and total dedication to public service won him election in 1783 to the Confederation Congress, where he sat until 1786. Here he organized the opposition to the Jay-Gardoqui proposals, by which the United States would have yielded to Spain its claim to the free navigation of the Mississippi River. He also helped lay the groundwork for territorial government embodied in the Northwest Ordinance of 1787. While in Congress, Monroe joined the advocates of a stronger government, continuing the work of his friend James Madison. Yet as a member of the Virginia ratifying convention he joined Patrick Henry and George Mason in opposing the ratification of the U. S. Constitution. He considered it defective in the excessive power granted the Senate and in authorizing direct taxes.

In 1789, now a married man, he settled in Albemarle county to be close to Jefferson. Monroe's wife, the former Elizabeth Kortright of New York, was regarded as one of the great beauties of the day. Reserved and rather cold in her manner, she was to bring to the White House a formality not always relished by Washingtonians. Here in Albemarle their two daughters, Eliza and Maria Hester, were born. A son died in infancy.

Opponent of the Federalists. Elected to the United States Senate in 1790, Monroe joined Madison (then in the House) in combating Hamilton's domestic measures, which emphasized centralization of powers in the federal government. He also opposed Washington's seemingly pro-British foreign policy. Monroe worked with Jefferson and Madison in organizing the Republican party. His contribution lay in the realm of political strategy and in establishing liaison with anti-Hamilton forces in other states. He also ably assisted Madison in defending the Republican position in the press.

In 1794, when Washington dispatched Federalist John Jay on a mission to Britain, Monroe was named minister to France in the hope that this would appease Republican critics of the administration who feared a diplomatic rupture with France. Because Monroe conceived the purpose of his mission as the preservation of Franco-American amity in the face of Washington's pro-British stance, he acted more as a Republican party spokesman than as the representative of his government. Dissatisfaction with his conduct led to his recall in 1796, engineered by Secretary of State Timothy Pickering. Monroe defended himself by publishing a harsh attack on Washington's foreign policy.

From 1799 to 1802, Monroe served as governor of Virginia, demonstrating great administrative ability and winning praise for his decisive action to suppress a slave uprising (Gabriel's Insurrection) in 1800.

Diplomat for Jefferson. President Jefferson sent Monroe to France in 1803 as a special envoy to assist Minister Robert R. Livingston in purchasing a port of deposit on the lower Mississippi River, because Spain was closing the river to American navigation in preparation for the recently negotiated retrocession of Louisiana to France. On his arrival Napoleon presented Livingston and Monroe with the choice of buying all of Louisiana or nothing. Although not authorized by their instructions they promptly accepted, a decision approved by Jefferson in spite of his doubts about the constitutionality of such an extensive territorial acquisition. Popular approval of the Louisiana Purchase established Monroe securely as a national figure, whose elevation to the presidency was but a matter of time.

From 1803 to 1807, Monroe served as minister to Britain. In 1805 he went to Madrid in a fruitless attempt to persuade Spain to acknowledge the American claim that West Florida should be included in the Louisiana Purchase. In 1806 he and William Pinkney (sent as a special envoy) negotiated a treaty providing for some relaxation of Britain's commercial restrictions. Because the treaty lacked provisions for ending the impressment of American seamen, Jefferson did not submit it to the Senate for ratification. Monroe, convinced that the treaty contained the best obtainable terms, was deeply offended.

In 1808, Monroe ran against Madison, whom he blamed for the rejection of the treaty, for the presidency in Virginia, more as a protest than as a serious candidate. He received little support, and Madison was elected president.

Member of the War Cabinet. Monroe served in the Virginia assembly in 1810 and 1811 and as governor again in 1811. In the latter year President Madison, facing a Federalist resurgence and divisions in the Republican party, appointed Monroe secretary of state. The appointment restored Monroe's friendship with Madison and Jefferson.

Admired as a practical man by younger congressmen, Monroe formed excellent working relations with Congress and obtained the cooperation of the so-called War Hawks in advancing administration programs. After the outbreak of the War of 1812 with Britain, Monroe's desire for a military command was frustrated by Secretary of War John Armstrong. The latter believed that Monroe had deprived Robert R. Livingston, Armstrong's brother-in-law, of his rightful claim to be the negotiator of the Louisiana Purchase.

In 1814, after the British invasion of Washington, which was widely laid to Armstrong's failure to mount a proper defense of the city, President Madison replaced the disgraced secretary of war with Monroe, who thus held two cabinet posts. A capable and active administrator, Monroe restored the morale of Washingtonians. The war ended, however, before the full effect of his reorganization of the War Department could be felt.

Mrs. James Monroe, by Benjamin West

JAMES MONROE MUSEUM AND MEMORIAL LIBRARY

PRESIDENCY

His service in the cabinet had made Monroe an obvious choice for president in 1816. The Republican congressional caucus chose him as the party's candidate over William H. Crawford, who had succeeded Monroe as secretary of war. The Federalist party had been badly damaged—fatally, as it turned out—by its opposition to the War of 1812. Monroe easily defeated Sen. Rufus King (N. Y.), the Federalist candidate for president, by 183 to 34 in the voting of the Electoral College.

The new president adopted a conciliatory policy toward the Federalist critics of the war. Immediately after his inauguration, Monroe toured the New England states, where there had been talk of secession during the war. The Federalists rushed to welcome him and demonstrate their loyalty. Monroe did everything he could to promote the "Era of Good Feelings"—a term first used in a Boston newspaper to refer to the mood created by his New England trip. Monroe believed that this new "era" would place free government on a solid footing by eliminating party rivalry. The experiment, however, did not outlast his second term, because sectional hostility and individual political rivalries shattered the brief unity.

Once he rejected the two-party system, Monroe could not use party loyalty as a means of advancing administration measures. Instead he had to rely on his own considerable personal contacts with congressmen and on the support of cabinet members with substantial congressional followings. He drew into his cabinet some of the most influential men of the day. The four most important were all in their posts by late 1817 and served until 1825. The secretary of the treasury, William H. Crawford, had been Monroe's rival in 1816 and was regarded as his most logical successor. The secretary of state was the experienced diplomat John Quincy Adams. The secretary of war, John C. Calhoun, had been a notable War Hawk. Attorney General William Wirt was a popular figure, famed as a lawyer and writer.

The Navy Department was headed by men of sectional rather than national influence: Benjamin Crowninshield of Massachusetts (1817–1818), Smith Thompson of New York (1818–1823), and Samuel Southard of New Jersey (1823–1825).

Acquisition of Florida. Monroe's greatest achievements as president lay in foreign affairs. Ably supported by Adams, he made substantial territorial additions and gave American policy a distinctly national orientation. Monroe welcomed an opportunity to press Spain to cede Florida and define the boundaries of Louisiana. His chance came when Gen. Andrew Jackson invaded Florida in 1818. In pursuit of hostile Indians, Jackson seized the posts of St. Marks and Pensacola, acts that many persons regarded as violations of congressional war powers. In the cabinet, Adams, an expansionist, urged Jackson's complete vindication, while Crawford and Calhoun demanded that he be reprimanded for exceeding his instructions.

Monroe chose a middle course—the posts were restored to Spain, but the administration accepted Jackson's explanation that his action had been justified by conditions in Florida. The incident led Spain to cede Florida and define, favorably to American claims, the boundary of the Louisiana Purchase in the Adams-Onís Treaty negotiated in 1819.

Election day in Philadelphia in 1816. Monroe's election led to the "Era of Good Feelings."

HISTORICAL SOCIETY OF PENNSYLVANIA

CULVER PICTURES

President Monroe and his aides discuss the Monroe Doctrine, in which the United States opposed further European colonies in the Americas and warned against European interference in the affairs of American nations.

The Monroe Doctrine. The revolutions in Spain's American colonies, which had begun in the Napoleonic era, had aroused great sympathy in the United States. Monroe, however, held back recognition, in spite of congressional pressure exerted by Henry Clay, until 1822, after Spain had ratified the Adams-Onís Treaty. The South American revolutions raised the possibility of intervention by the European powers linked in an alliance—commonly, but erroneously, known as the Holy Alliance—to suppress these revolutions as they had done in Europe. Britain, prospering from newly opened Latin American trade, opposed this move. In 1823, Foreign Minister George Canning proposed, through Richard Rush, the American minister, that the two nations jointly express their hostility to intervention. Monroe consulted Jefferson and Madison, who favored acceptance. The cabinet was divided, with only Adams strongly opposed.

Anxious to assert American independence in foreign policy, Monroe rejected the British offer, opting for a policy statement in his annual message of December 1823. In this statement, subsequently known as the Monroe Doctrine, he declared that the United States would regard any interference in the internal affairs of American states as an unfriendly act. At Adams' suggestion, Monroe included a declaration aimed at Russia that the United States considered the American continents closed to further colonization. While greeted with enthusiasm by Americans, Monroe's statement received little notice in Europe or South America, and it had no effect on European policy. England's declared opposition blocked intervention by other nations.

Domestic Controversies. In an administration committed to limited government, domestic policies received less attention. Monroe's most positive program was the construction of a network of coastal fortifications to guard against future invasions. Although extensive construction was begun, the program was drastically reduced after the Panic of 1819, when government revenues fell sharply. Monroe, interpreting the economic crisis in the narrow monetary terms then current, limited governmental action to economizing and to ensuring fiscal stability. Although he agreed to the need for improved transportation facilities, he refused to approve appropriations for internal improvements without prior amendment of the Constitution.

The calm of the Era of Good Feelings was permanently shattered by the Missouri crisis of 1819–1820, which exposed an unsuspected depth of sectional hostility. Monroe's role in the conflict was peripheral, because it was contrary to Republican doctrine for the executive to exert direct pressure on Congress. Once the compromise was worked out, Monroe gave it his full support. It admitted Maine as a free state and Missouri without restriction on slavery, barring slavery north of the 36°30′ line of latitude within the Louisiana Territory.

Monroe shared the widely held view that the effort to restrict slavery in Missouri sprang not from a selfless concern for the welfare of the slaves but from the ambitions of ex-Federalists and discontented Republicans, notably Gov. DeWitt Clinton of New York, to revive the two-party system on a sectional basis. The Missouri crisis had no effect on the presidential election of 1820. The Federalist party had disappeared as a force in national politics, and Monroe, unopposed, got all of the electoral votes but one.

Monroe's second term was rendered uncomfortable by the bitterness created by the Missouri debates and by the rivalry of the aspirants to succeed him as president. In the absence of party machinery, they sought to advance their individual candidacies by attacking administration policies. The activities of Crawford's supporters seeking to damage Secretary of State Adams caused a major setback in foreign policy in 1824, when the Senate so amended an Anglo-American agreement to suppress the international slave trade that the British government refused to ratify. As a result, hopes for an Anglo-American rapprochement were crushed. Calhoun's rivals also blocked administration efforts (Indian affairs were then under the War Department) to begin a more generous policy toward Indians.

THE RICHMOND TIMES-DISPATCH

The burial place of President and Mrs. Monroe is in Hollywood Cemetery, Richmond, Va.

RETIREMENT

Upon his retirement, Monroe lived on an estate (Oak Hill) in Loudoun county, Va. Like Jefferson, he had been left so deeply in debt by his long years of public service that it seemed he might lose all of his property. Because he had never settled his accounts (some dating from his first mission to France) with the government, he now sought reimbursement with accrued interest. While many Congressmen considered these claims not only embarrassing but excessive, President Jackson's hostility toward Monroe blocked an immediate settlement. Not until 1831 did Congress grant him $30,000 (half his claim). His last public service was as a presiding officer of the Virginia constitutional convention.

Monroe died on July 4, 1831, at his daughter's home in New York City. He was interred in New York, but was reburied in Richmond in 1858.

HARRY AMMON, *Southern Illinois University*
Author of "James Monroe: The Quest for National Identity"

Bibliography

Ammon, Harry, *James Monroe: The Quest for National Identity* (McGraw 1971).
Bemis, Samuel Flagg, *John Quincy Adams and the Foundations of American Foreign Policy* (1949; reprint, Norton 1973).
Dangerfield, George, *The Era of Good Feelings* (Harcourt 1952).
Malone, Dumas, *Jefferson and his Time,* 6 vols. (Little 1948–).
Perkins, Bradford, *Castlereagh and Adams: England and the United States, 1812–1823* (Univ. of Calif. Press 1964).
Perkins, Bradford, *The Prologue to War: England and the United States, 1805–1812* (Univ. of Calif. Press 1961).
Perkins, Dexter, *The Monroe Doctrine, 1823–1826* (Harvard Univ. Press 1927).

MONROE, Marilyn (1926–1962), American film star, whose scarred and insecure life, amid worldwide adulation, ended tragically with her suicide. She was born to unwed parents in Los Angeles, Calif., on June 1, 1926, and was called Norma Jean Baker. After an unhappy childhood spent mostly in foster homes and orphanages, she found work as a model and later as a bit player in motion pictures.

In the movies, she was touted first as a "dumb blond" and later as a "sex goddess," though with an appealing wholesomeness and vulnerability. She made motion pictures for several years but did not really claim the public's attention until she appeared in the Bette Davis vehicle *All About Eve* (1950). Her career still did not seem headed much of anywhere, however, until she played a waiflike creature in *Don't Bother to Knock* (1952). *Niagara* (1952) was an important advance, and she attained stardom in *Gentlemen Prefer Blondes* (1953).

A string of box-office successes followed: *How to Marry a Millionaire* (1953), *The Seven Year Itch* (1955), and *Bus Stop* (1956). In *Some Like It Hot* (1959), she displayed a real flair for comedy. Marilyn Monroe's last film, *The Misfits,* was released in 1961.

Ambitious to be a serious actress, Marilyn Monroe studied at the Actors Studio in New York City. She was troubled, however, by deep-seated anxieties, and her three marriages—to seaman James Daugherty, big-league baseball player Joe DiMaggio, and playwright Arthur Miller—all ended in divorce. Suspended by her studio for chronic absences and lateness, she died from an overdose of sleeping tablets in Los Angeles on Aug. 5, 1962. She immediately became a legend in the Hollywood pantheon.

Marilyn Monroe, "sex symbol" of the 1950's, was frustrated in her ambition to become a serious actress.

PICTORIAL PARADE

MONROE, a city in Connecticut, in Fairfield county, is 10 miles (16 km) north of Bridgeport on the Housatonic River. Monroe is a residential community. Vegetables, grain, and fruit are grown in the area. Monroe, settled about 1775, was incorporated in 1823. It has a council-manager form of government. Population: 12,047.

MONROE, a city in north central Georgia, is the seat of Walton county, on the Piedmont Plateau, 41 miles (65 km) east of Atlanta. Once strictly an agricultural community, Monroe now enjoys a balance as a residential, agricultural, and industrial area. Its chief industries are textiles, needlecraft, plastics, and metals.

Monroe was first settled in 1820 by residents of Virginia, South Carolina, and North Carolina, and named in honor of President James Monroe. It was incorporated in 1896 and has a mayor-council form of government. Population: 8,071.

MONROE, a city in Louisiana, is on the Ouachita River, some 35 miles (56 km) from the state's northern border and about 100 miles (160 km) east of Shreveport. Monroe is the seat of Ouachita parish (county) and is the principal trade center of northeastern Louisiana.

Cotton and soybean farming and lumbering support the economy, which also benefits from the city's location above one of the largest natural-gas fields in the United States, discovered in 1916. The chief manufactures include paper, furniture, and agricultural chemicals. Barge traffic continues along the navigable Ouachita River, competing with rail, air, and highway carriers to keep freight rates low.

Traders and trappers first settled in the area in the early 18th century, when the site was called Prairie de Canots. It became known as Fort Miro after a fort was constructed in 1791 as protection against Indians. The settlement was renamed Monroe in 1819 in honor of the *James Monroe*, the first steamboat to reach the town. In 1900, Monroe was incorporated as a city.

Monroe and West Monroe—a smaller community on the west bank of the river—are sometimes referred to as the "Twin Cities of the Ouachita." Monroe is the home of Northeastern Louisiana University. The city is governed by a commission. Population: 56,374.

MONROE, a city in Michigan, is situated in the southeastern corner of the state, 35 miles (56 km) southwest of Detroit and 17 miles (27 km) north of Toledo, Ohio. The seat of Monroe county, it is an industrial center and is Michigan's only port on Lake Erie. Manufactures include auto parts, paper, furniture, and castings.

Settled by Canadians in the 1780's, the community was called Frenchtown until renamed in honor of President Monroe in 1815. It was the site of a celebrated battle in the War of 1812. (See FRENCHTOWN, BATTLE OF.) It has council-manager government. Population: 23,894.

MONROE, a city in North Carolina, is situated in the Piedmont section, 23 miles (37 km) southeast of Charlotte. It is industrially diversified, with textile, hardware, and other manufactures and one of the nation's largest poultry-processing plants. Monroe is unusual in that it owns and operates its utilities. Incorporated in 1844, it is governed by a city manager and council. Population: 11,282.

MONROE DOCTRINE, a policy established by the United States during the administration of President James Monroe that sought to limit European political influence in the Western Hemisphere. The Monroe Doctrine was first enunciated by President Monroe in his message of Dec. 2, 1823, but it owes its origin to ideas that go back considerably further in time, and in particular to the idea that the interests and ideals of the New World are different from those of the Old. This conception is found in some of the writings of the Revolutionary period. It is implicit and explicit in George Washington's Farewell Address, which warns against close political association with European states, and again in the language of Thomas Jefferson's first inaugural. It possessed indeed a striking validity at a time when most of Europe was monarchical and reactionary, when American institutions represented new tendencies toward republicanism and democratic liberalism, and when the breadth of a great ocean made for the separateness of the United States from Europe. What may be described as American isolationism was already well developed when Monroe sent to Congress his famous message.

The Monroe Message. The message consisted of two different pronouncements. The first of these grew out of a controversy with Russia with regard to the northwest coast of America. The Russian government had in 1821 promulgated a ukase closing that coast to the commerce of other nations. This decree was contested by the United States. Secretary of State John Quincy Adams, who had long been a vigorous opponent of colonialism, declared that "the American continents, by the free and independent condition which they have assumed and maintained, are henceforth not to be considered as subjects for future colonization by any European powers." This phrase was taken over by the president and incorporated in his annual message of Dec. 2, 1823.

The second part of the message related to the former Spanish colonies in America. These colonies had revolted in the second decade of the century, and their independence had been recognized by the United States. In the summer of 1823 word arrived in Washington that the European powers might hold a congress on the colonial question, a congress that, if it followed previous European precedents, might result in armed intervention. At the same time the language of Czar Alexander I occasioned some concern. The British government had made overtures to Richard Rush, the American minister, suggesting a joint declaration on the whole problem. The matter was debated at length in the cabinet meetings of November 1823. Monroe, acting on his own initiative, drafted a statement in his message that declared, with regard to the former Spanish colonies, that "we [the United States] could not view any interposition for the purpose of oppressing them, or controlling in any other manner their destiny, by any European power, in any other light than as the manifestation of an unfriendly disposition towards the United States." The warning, we now know, was unnecessary, since no aggressive designs existed. But it needed considerable courage to pronounce it, and to do so without waiting for any understanding with Britain.

The message of December 1823 was received with much acclaim in the United States, and with natural resentment and perhaps contempt (considering the meager basis of military and naval force on which it rested) by European powers. In the years immediately following 1823, the Monroe administration resolutely refused to transform it into an alliance with any South American state, though on four occasions appeals came to do so. Moreover, when in 1826 the question of sending delegates to the so-called Panama Congress arose, a congress projected by Simón Bolívar with regard to closer cooperation between the American republics, opinion in the United States was seen to be emphatically hostile to any political understanding. For a time, indeed, Monroe's message —after all, relating to a specific and immediate problem—seemed hardly likely to become a great American diplomatic principle. It was largely ignored for almost two decades. In the 1840's the situation changed.

Its Application in the 1840's.—The intrigues of Great Britain and France to prevent the annexation of Texas to the United States, the quarrel with Great Britain over Oregon, and the fear of British purposes in California led in the 1840's to the revival of the pronouncement of 1823. President James K. Polk gave the most striking, though by no means the first, expression of this revival in the message of Dec. 2, 1845, in which he warned not only against armed intervention but also against diplomatic intervention based on the principle of the balance of power, and at the same time stressed the special applicability of the Monroe Doctrine to North America.

The Polk message was well received, but like that of 22 years before, it was not accorded congressional sanction and produced little effect abroad. In 1848 the president reiterated his statement, suggesting that the Monroe principle forbade the assumption by England or Spain of a protectorate over Yucatan, and might lead to American control of that province. Here for the first time the dogmas of 1823 became the excuse for a proposed measure of expansion. No action was taken, however.

The president's proposal with regard to Yucatan led to a great debate in which John C. Calhoun, a member of the Monroe cabinet in 1823, took strong grounds against erecting into an absolute principle what he declared was a specific declaration aimed at an immediate and present danger a quarter of a century before. This tendency to avoid commitment to a doctrine was further exemplified in the attitude of the Whig administrations of Zachary Taylor and Millard Fillmore towards the British claims of sovereignty in Central America. In the negotiations which culminated in the Clayton-Bulwer Treaty of April 19, 1850, the name of Monroe was never mentioned, though the treaty bound the British government to abstain from further colonization in the area of Central America.

The Doctrine as National Dogma.—But such a position could not be long maintained. When new controversies arose under the pact, the Democrats proceeded to invoke the Monroe Doctrine, and in the negotiations of the 1850's, which terminated in new agreements at the end of the decade, the message of Monroe was gradually elevated, not into a partisan, but into a national dogma. It is in this period that the word "doctrine" first appears; and both parties now paid tribute to it. Moreover, it began to become known abroad; and though Lord Clarendon, the British foreign secretary, refused to admit its validity when it was brought to his attention, it was dealt with more respectfully by so eminent an Englishman as Benjamin Disraeli.

The period of the Civil War saw the Monroe Doctrine sharply challenged. In the spring of 1861, Spain reasserted its sovereignty over the Dominican Republic in the Caribbean. Secretary William H. Seward at once invoked the Monroe principle in a blustering note, and received a sharp rebuff. With the victory of Northern arms, however, and with the disastrous failure of Spanish arms in the new Spanish colony, the tone of the government in Madrid changed, and evacuation took place in 1865.

Still more dramatic and fundamental was the course of events in Mexico. Taking advantage of the divided Union, the Emperor Louis Napoleon managed to set up in Mexico an imperial government under the Austrian Archduke Maximilian. In this case Seward again left no doubt of the displeasure felt by the United States. But, taught by his earlier experience, he did not invoke the Monroe Doctrine by name, and indeed maintained a rather suave opposition until the victory of the North freed his hands.

With the close of the Civil War, the sentiment for the invocation of Monroe's dogma grew by leaps and bounds. The situation might have been a ticklish one, but Secretary Seward handled it with superb address. He was aware of the opposition in France to the Mexican enterprise, and of the strain which it imposed on French finances. He was aware, too, of the heroic resistance of the Mexicans themselves. In a series of skilful diplomatic notes, he raised his tone bit by bit, and at one and the same time succeeded in preventing any rash action at home while he increased the pressure on the government in Paris. By the end of 1865 it was apparent that the French would withdraw from Mexico. There can be no question that the attitude of the United States caused the French much anxiety, and contributed in some degree to the eventual decision. To the American people the outcome of the Mexican imbroglio was the vindication of the principles of 1823.

Once rooted as national dogma the doctrine was more and more liberally interpreted, often in ways which would have seemed strange to Adams and Monroe. Before 1870 attempts had been made to link the idea of non-intervention by Europe in American affairs with the principle that territories in the New World could not be transferred from one European power to another, but this principle was most definitely asserted and most closely connected with the Monroe Doctrine in the pronouncement of President Ulysses S. Grant in 1870 when urging upon the Senate the annexation of Santo Domingo. Thereafter it was repeatedly brought forward when cessions of territory were imminent, though it appears to have passed unnoticed at the time of the cession of the little island of St. Bartholomew by Sweden to France.

In the late 1870's and early 1880's the Monroe Doctrine was frequently cited as forbidding the construction by European powers of a trans-Isthmian canal across Panama, and still more as implying that any such a canal must be under the exclusive guaranty of the United States. Presidents Rutherford B. Hayes and James A. Garfield both insisted upon this point; and in the course of time American opinion compelled the repeal of the Clayton-Bulwer Treaty of 1850 (which looked towards joint British and American control of any canal constructed) by the signing of the second Hay-Paunceforte Treaty (1901), by which Great Britain conceded the American point of view.

A still more extraordinary extension of the original doctrine was made by Grover Cleveland in his second administration when, in the name of Monroe, he demanded (1895) that the British government arbitrate a dispute with Venezuela over the boundary between that country and British Guiana, and threatened to appoint a commission to determine the line if the British did not accept his demand. This extreme position naturally provoked severe criticism across the seas, and for a time the situation was a touchy one. But on both sides of the Atlantic a more pacific sentiment prevailed, and the matter was finally settled by an arbitration agreement, the terms of which virtually conceded to Great Britain in advance much of what she claimed. It is to be noticed that in the course of this dispute Lord Salisbury, the British foreign secretary, flatly denied, in a note to the American government, that the Monroe Doctrine was, in any sense, international law.

The Venezuela Blockade of 1902.—The turn of the century saw a new and interesting development of the principles of 1823. Down to this time, these principles had never been invoked to prevent an Old World state from taking punitive action against a New World state considered guilty of wrongdoing. But in the Venezuela blockade of 1902 by Great Britain, Germany, and Italy—a blockade which, despite assertions to the contrary, may be said to have been undertaken without any thought of territorial aggrandizement—American public opinion asserted itself strongly. In the face of this public opinion British statesmen, both of the ministry and of the opposition, for the first time recognized the validity of the Monroe Doctrine. The German government was less adroit; it had to deal with its own nationalists, who were in general venomously antagonistic to the principles of 1823. It made no such obeisance as did the British, and this fact may well have had an influence over the future course of events and have helped to fix in the American mind a prejudice against the Reich which was to be a powerful factor when war broke out in 1914.

The Venezuela blockade had important effects in the United States. President Theodore Roosevelt had originally consented to the blockade by the allied powers for the purpose of collecting debts which Venezuela owed their nationals; but he became very nervous before an arrangement was made, and as a result he was soon to give a new twist to the Monroe Doctrine itself. Before commenting upon this it is worth while noting that the legend that Roosevelt compelled arbitration by threats of direct action directed against the German government has now been pretty well exploded. The dispute had hardly begun before it was put in the way of settlement.

The Roosevelt Corollary.—The area of major sensitiveness with regard to the principles of 1823 had always been the Caribbean and the Gulf of Mexico. Indeed, it is a striking fact that in every case where these principles were seriously invoked, a country in this particular area was involved. It is not strange therefore that what became known as the Roosevelt Corollary to the Monroe Doctrine was first enunciated in regard to the Dominican Republic.

This little state had been a prey to almost constant internecine strife. It also had floated various loans abroad, but had become bankrupt. There was thus a possibility that its distraught condition might provoke intervention by some European state. Anticipating such action, as early as 1904 in his annual message President Roosevelt stated that "chronic wrong-doing, or an impotence which results in a general loosening of the ties of civilized society" might, in the Western Hemisphere as elsewhere, lead to action by a strong power, and that, under the Monroe Doctrine, that power would have to be the United States.

Following out this theory, and perhaps bringing some pressure to bear upon the Dominican government, the president had negotiated an agreement for the control of the customs in the winter of 1905. The Senate balked, but Roosevelt went ahead on the basis of an executive agreement, and two years later the treaty was ratified. It set a precedent for others that were to follow.

The Roosevelt Corollary, in its first application, had resulted only in customs control. But it was soon to be carried further. The William Howard Taft administration negotiated a similar agreement and induced American bankers to make a loan to the Nicaraguan government. When its policy seemed jeopardized, marines were landed, and remained in occupation for more than a decade. In Haiti, where again American banking interests had been encouraged to take a part in the affairs of the republic, disorders and the fear of German or French action led towards intervention in 1915. In the Dominican Republic, the breakdown of government brought about American control in 1916. Thus the Roosevelt Corollary led on to direct military occupation of the territory of assumedly independent states.

The question of the Monroe Doctrine came up in connection with the drafting of the Covenant of the League of Nations at Paris in 1919. In order to placate domestic opposition President T. Woodrow Wilson found it necessary to incorporate in the Covenant itself an article declaring that nothing therein contained should affect the validity of "regional understandings" such as the Monroe Doctrine. The phrase used was a cloudy one, and it did not satisfy the president's American foes, who insisted upon further reservations to the peace treaty on the matter. That it was approved by the other signatories is, however, some indication of the increasing acceptance of the position of the United States.

The Doctrine had by this time become an object of suspicion and dislike rather than cause for gratitude in Latin America. As early as 1913, Hiram Bingham (the explorer) had suggested that it was an obsolete shibboleth. The statement was an extreme one, but it contained a germ of truth. The states of the New World were more afraid of interference on the part of the United States than they were of any action by Europe. American statesmen found themselves on the defensive in discussing the famous dogma. Secretary of State Charles Evans Hughes attempted to re-define it in terms that would remove apprehension and to justify American intervention, or interposition, as he preferred to call it, on other grounds. But the tide of opposition to American hegemony continued to swell throughout the decade of the 1920's, and it was particularly evident at the Pan American Conference of 1928. The course of events suggested a change in American policy.

The Clark Memorandum.—The withdrawal of the United States from the Dominican Republic in 1924 was a first step. But withdrawal from Nicaragua in 1925 was followed by a new intervention, and it was not until the Washington Conference on Conciliation and Arbitration in December 1928 that a really decisive move was taken in the famous Memorandum on the Monroe Doctrine (drafted by J. Reuben Clark) which definitely repudiated the Roosevelt Corollary. In January 1929 the Senate Committee on Foreign Relations, in transmitting the Kellogg-Briand pact for the outlawry of war, added a gloss, or separate report, in which the Monroe Doctrine was conservatively interpreted and based upon the principle of self-defense. In 1930 the Clark memorandum was transmitted to other governments, thus emphasizing the fact that it represented official policy.

But this was only the beginning, in a sense, for in 1933 at the conference of Montevideo, Secretary Cordell Hull put his name to a protocol which bound the United States not to intervene in the internal or external affairs of any American state. There was, indeed, a reservation to this pledge reserving the rights of the United States under international law. But in 1936 at Buenos Aires a new protocol was signed, this time without any qualification whatsoever. The connection of the principles of 1823 with a right of intervention was thus brought to an end.

The Doctrine and Collective Defense.—One hears relatively little of the Monroe Doctrine in the early 1930's. There existed in these years little danger to the status of the New World, and the prevailing tone of American policy, preoccupied as we were with internal concerns, reflected a certain indifference to questions of foreign affairs. But the rise of Adolf Hitler to power in Germany was to alter the situation materially. As a result there took place a process which has sometimes been called the internationalization of the Monroe Doctrine. The phrase is in a sense an inaccurate one, since there is no reason to believe that the American government would hesitate to assert alone and independently the principles of 1823 if it felt the necessity of so doing.

It is true, on the other hand, that measures were taken which looked to collective defense, and that these measures alter the context in which the doctrine would be invoked. Thus, for example, at the conference of Buenos Aires in 1936, an agreement was signed by the states of Latin America calling for consultation if they were threatened by any European power. In 1938, this agreement was supplemented by another, which provided for a meeting of the foreign ministers of the American states on the call of any one of them. Much more important measures were taken in 1940.

The fall of France naturally produced a strong reaction in the United States and led to the adoption of resolutions by both houses of Congress expressing opposition to the transfer of the European colonies of any power (France and Holland were of course meant) to any other power. The action of Congress was supplemented by the Conference of Havana, which drew up an elaborate scheme to meet the possible danger of any such transfer, and at the same time, going far beyond the no-transfer principle, declared that an attack on any one American power would be regarded as an attack on all. From these declarations were deduced others. At Chapultepec in 1945, the principle of collective action in case of external attack was re-stated, and various measures enumerated which would be taken in case of aggression. At Rio de Janeiro in 1947, the Inter-American Treaty of Reciprocal Assistance stated unequivocally that aggression against an American state would, on the two-thirds vote of the representatives of the states, be met with sanctions of various degrees of severity. In the meantime, between the Chapultepec and the Rio meetings, the Charter of the United Nations had established a world organization based upon the idea of common action against a law-breaking state. The original purposes of the Monroe Doctrine had thus received a far wider than national sanction.

In the World War II period the Monroe Doctrine served a useful purpose in a way hardly thought of before. The establishment of a base for American troops in Greenland, a Danish colony, in the spring of 1941, for example, was related to the principles of 1823. Monroe would certainly have been surprised at any such application of his message.

Significant Generalizations. — What significant generalizations stand out with regard to the Monroe Doctrine? Fundamentally, in 1823 the president placed his warning to Europe on grounds of national security. Yet it is not easy to see that the safety of the United States would have been jeopardized by what took place, let us say, in Patagonia or in Chile. In extending his principle so far, the president perhaps might be said to have fallen a victim to that tendency to over-generalization which not infrequently has asserted itself in American foreign policy. In a sense, future statesmen were to recognize this fact. The practical application of the doctrine, as already mentioned, was almost invariably in the region of the Caribbean, where there were security interests of the most patent kind.

Were the dangers which the doctrine was designed to prevent real dangers? As already pointed out, there seems to have been no real peril in 1823. But British acquisitive instincts in the Caribbean in the 1850's did run counter to the interests of the United States. So, too, did Napoleon III's activities in Mexico. After the American Civil War there was never a moment when there was serious danger of European aggression with an eye to conquest against an American state. European colonial ambitions were satisfied elsewhere, especially in Asia or in Africa. There were Germans, no doubt, especially German naval men, who dreamed of bases in the New World and of the extension of German influence. But the German Foreign Office was extremely cautious in the first years of the 20th century, and the danger from Germany was temporarily extinguished by the events of World War I. In the 1930's and the 1940's Adolf Hitler had objects of ambition other than Latin America.

Was the Monroe Doctrine gratefully accepted by the states to the south? To some extent, and in some specific instances, yes. It was certainly invoked by some of them when it served their interests. But, after the end of the 19th century, it was as often associated with American hegemony as with American benevolence. In this context it was an object of concern rather than a matter for admiration. Yet the principle at its base was sound, and it has been more and fully recognized in the association of the states of the New World together in the war against Hitler, and in the compacts which have followed that war. Were a real danger again to arise, in terms of actual physical aggression, it would undoubtedly once more figure prominently.

Finally, the Monroe Doctrine illustrates a general tendency that seems to inhere in American diplomacy. This tendency is towards large and sweeping generalization which captures the imagination of the mass of the people and has the advantage of being easily assimilated and of easily becoming a focus for popular support. The task of statesmanship is to relate such generalization to the actual interests of the United States. As this sketch demonstrates, the task has been well performed. In its various manifestations, the Monroe Doctrine has usually been wisely and profitably applied. It has given a broad popular and, in a sense, a broad moral basis to the specific objectives of American diplomacy.

DEXTER PERKINS
Professor Emeritus of American Civilization
Cornell University

Bibliography

Dangerfield, George, *Era of Good Feelings* (New York: Harcourt, Brace, 1952).
Donovan, Frank, *Mr. Monroe's Message: The Story of the Monroe Doctrine* (New York: Dodd, Mead, 1963).
Logan, John, *No Transfer* (New Haven: Yale University Press, 1961).
Perkins, Dexter, *History of the Monroe Doctrine,* rev. ed. (Boston: Little, Brown, 1955).
Showman, Richard, and Judson, Lyman, *The Monroe Doctrine and Growth of Western Hemisphere Solidarity* (New York: H. W. Wilson, 1941).
Whitaker, Arthur P., *The United States and the Independence of Latin America* (New York: W. W. Norton, 1964).

MONROVIA, mən-rō'vē-ə, is a city in California, in Los Angeles County, 9 miles east of Pasadena. It is on the Atchison, Topeka and Santa Fe and the Pacific Electric railways. Population: 30,015.

Although Monrovia is primarily a residential community, it has fruit-packing plants to service the orange, lemon, and avacado groves that surround it. Poultry raising and small-scale truck farming are also important in the vicinity.

Monrovia was named for W.N. Monroe, a railroad engineer who, with his associates, laid out the city in 1886. It was incorporated the following year.

MONROVIA, mən-rō'vē-ə, is the capital, largest city, and chief commercial center of Liberia, in West Africa. It is also the seat of Montserrado county. The city is situated on Cape Montserrado, just south of the mouth of the St. Paul River. Population: (1963 est.) 80,000.

Monrovia is Liberia's chief seaport, and the only free port in West Africa. Its fine deep-water harbor on Bushrod Island, which was the site of a United States submarine base during World War II, was opened in 1948. Exports include rubber, iron ore, palm kernels and oil, gold, forest products, and cassava.

Monrovia is a modern, cosmopolitan community with many new and imposing buildings, both governmental and private. The Mamba Point section of the city is a growing residential area. Most of the foreign embassies are located along United Nations Drive in this section.

The educational center of the nation, Monrovia is the seat of the University of Liberia, founded in 1863 and chartered as a university in 1950. Other schools include the College of West Africa, operated by the Methodist Church of America; Monrovia College, a Baptist institution; and St. Patrick's Catholic College.

Monrovia was founded in 1822 when the American Colonization Society chose the site for a settlement in its colony for ex-slaves from the United States. The name "Monrovia" was given originally to the whole colony, in honor of U.S. President James Monroe, who at one time had been president of the American Colonization Society. In 1824, when the colony was renamed Liberia, the name "Monrovia" was transferred to the settlement.

MONS, môNs, a town in Belgium, is the capital of the province of Hainaut. It is situated on the Trouille River, 32 miles southwest of Brussels, at the junction of the Condé-Mons Canal and the Canal du Centre. Its Flemish name is *Bergen*. Population: (1961) 26,973.

Mons is a shipping center for coal from the extensive mines of the Borinage to the southwest. It also processes sugar and produces leather goods, chemicals, and cotton and rayon textiles.

Charlemagne made Mons the capital of Hainaut in 804. In the 16th, 17th, and 18th centuries the town was repeatedly attacked and occupied by Dutch, French, and Spanish forces. During World War I it was the scene in 1914 of the first encounter between German and English forces. It was occupied by German troops in World War II, and suffered extensive damage from bombing raids in which nearly a quarter of its buildings were destroyed.

MONSIGNY, môN-sē-nyē' **Pierre Alexandre,** French composer: b. Fauquembergues, Pas-de-Calais, France, Oct. 17, 1729; d. Paris, Jan. 14, 1817. He went to Paris in 1749 and soon entered the service of Louis, duc d'Orléans, first as majordomo, and then as administrator of the duke's estates and inspector general of canals. After studying composition for a few months with Pietro Gianotti, he composed a series of 13 comic operas, the first of which, *Les aveux indiscrets,* was produced in Paris in 1759. During the French Revolution he lost his position and was impoverished, but in 1798 he was pensioned by the Opéra-Comique, and from 1800 to 1802 he served as inspector of instruction at the Conservatoire de Musique. In 1813 he became a member of the Académie des Beaux-Arts.

Monsigny was an excellent melodist, but his lack of training prevented him from being a great composer. Among his other works, all of which were highly popular, are *Le cadi dupé* (1761); *On ne s'avise jamais de tout* (1761); *Le roi et le fermier* (1762); *Le déserteur* (1769), his best opera; *Le faucon* (1772); and *Félix, ou l'enfant trouvé* (1777), his last work.

MONSON, mun'sən, **Sir Edmund John,** British diplomat: b. Seal, Kent, England, Oct. 6, 1834; d. London, Oct. 28, 1909. He was educated at Eton and at Balliol College, Oxford, receiving his B.A. degree in 1855. In 1858 he was elected a fellow of All Souls College and received his M.A. degree. Entering the diplomatic service in 1856, he held various posts as attaché, undersecretary, and consul until 1876, when he was sent on a special mission to Dalmatia and Montenegro. He served as minister to Uruguay from 1879 to 1884, to Argentina and Paraguay in 1884, and to Denmark from 1884 to 1888. Monson was appointed arbitrator of the Butterfield claims between Denmark and the United States in 1888, and decided the case in Denmark's favor in 1900; the claims had arisen out of the detention of two munitions-laden vessels, operated by the American firm of Butterfield & Co., in the Danish West Indies (Virgin Islands) in 1854. The climax of Monson's diplomatic career came in 1896–1904, when he was ambassador to France; during these years the Fashoda incident (1898; see KODOK) was settled and the Entente Cordiale (1904) was affirmed. He was knighted in 1886 and made a baronet in 1905.

MONSON, town, Massachusetts, in Hampden County, in the south central part of the state, 13 miles east of Springfield, on the Central Vermont Railway, at an altitude of 380 feet. It has woolen mills and granite quarries, with dairy and truck farms in the vicinity. Monson was settled in 1715 and incorporated as a town 45 years later. Pop. 7,355.

MONSOONS, mŏn-so͞onz′, periods of strong and often abrupt weather change which usher in and accompany a seasonal alternation of cold dry winters and hot humid summers. Known as dry (winter) and wet (summer) monsoons respectively, these climatic changes are also associated with a complete reversal in prevailing wind direction. Monsoons are produced by the seasonal march of the sun between the Northern and Southern hemispheres and the establishment of climatic regimes subject to the control of semipermanent atmospheric high and low pressure areas. (See also CLIMATE—*Air Pressure on Land and Water* and *Effects of Land and Water on Winds.*)

In summer a low pressure cell covers south central Asia, and a subtropical high pressure cell exists over the southern Indian Ocean. This produces a strong flow of warm, heavily saturated air from the ocean, with clouds and rain accompanying southwesterly winds. A typical summer monsoon thus occurs in southeastern China and over India from late April to mid-October, bringing with it a protracted period of rainfall, frequent floods, and inundation of river plains. From mid-October to April, a winter monsoon occurs over eastern Russia, China, and Japan, and southward to India; its accompanying cold, relatively dry northwesterly winds may create intense snowstorms over the mountains. The winter monsoon is created by the presence over central Siberia of a strong semipermanent high pressure cell, which in its circulation pattern produces a continuous wind flow from the dry interior of the continent. See also WINDS—*Glossary of Winds* (Monsoons).

FERGUS J. WOOD.

MONSTRANCE, mŏn′străns (from Lat. *monstrare,* to show; also called OSTENSORIUM, from Lat. *ostendere,* to display), a sacred vessel used in the Roman Catholic Church to exhibit the Eucharistic Host for public veneration. In its modern typical form, it consists of a standing frame with rays of gold or silver projecting as from a sun in all directions, in the center of which there is a glass-covered receptacle through which the Consecrated Host may be seen by the people at Benediction of the Blessed Sacrament, at Exposition of the Blessed Sacrament, and in certain solemn processions. Following the institution of the Feast of Corpus Christi (1264), the Sacred Host was at first carried in a closed ciborium. The monstrance came into common use only in the course of the 15th century. The orb and rays of the monstrance should be made of gold, or at least of silver or silver gilt. Many are set with precious stones, and those in the old cathedrals of Spain are extremely large—that of Toledo being more than 12 feet high.

Consult Thurston, Herbert, S. J., "Ostensorium," *The Catholic Encyclopedia,* vol. 11, pp. 344–346, illustrated (New York 1911); Braun, Joseph, *Das christliche Altargerät in seinem Sein und in seiner Entwicklung,* pp. 348–411 (Munich 1932).

MARTIN R. P. MCGUIRE.

MONSTRELET, môɴs-trĕ-lĕ′, **Enguerrand de,** French chronicler: b. ?1390; d. Cambrai, France, July 20, 1453. An officer in the service of the count of Luxembourg, he was present at the interview between Joan of Arc and Philip the Good, duke of Burgundy, when Joan was captured at Compiègne in 1430. Later he was provost of Cambrai and bailiff of Walincourt. He is noted as the author of the *Chronique,* in two books, concerning the years 1400–1444, a continuation of the chronicle of Jean Froissart and a valuable source of documentary information about the Hundred Years' War. A modern edition appeared in six volumes (1857–62).

MONT, mônt, **Pol de** (in full MARIA POLYDOOR KAREL DE MONT), Flemish poet and critic: b. Wambeek, Belgium, April 15, 1857; d. Berlin, Germany, June 29, 1931. Professor of literature at Antwerp from 1882, he played a prominent part in the Flemish literary renaissance in the 1880's and gained wide recognition as an impressionistic lyric poet of love and nature. Among his volumes of verse in this period were *Lentesotternijen* (1881), *Loreley* (1882), and *Fladderende vlinders* (1885). In later years he devoted himself to art criticism and history, welcoming new movements in the arts, and from 1904 to 1918 was curator of the Antwerp Museum. His major work in art history was *De schilderkunst in België van 1830 tot 1921* (1921). He also published several volumes of short stories.

MONT BLANC. See BLANC, MONT.

MONT-DE-MARSAN, mônd-mȧr-säɴ′, town and commune, France, capital of the Department of Landes, situated 70 miles south of Bordeaux, at the confluence of two small rivers, the Midou and the Douze, which here form the Midouze. The trade and shipping center of a lumbering area, the town produces furniture, pit props, turpentine, and wax, and has metalworks and meat-preserving plants. There are the ruins of a 14th century donjon. Once the seat of the viscounts of Marsan, the town became part of Béarn in 1256. It was united with the French crown in 1589, on the accession of Henry IV. Pop. (1962) town 18,059; commune 23,254.

MONT JOLI, môɴ zhô-lē′, town, Quebec, Canada, in Rimouski County, near the south bank of the St. Lawrence River, 18 miles northeast of Rimouski. It is served by the Canada & Gulf Terminal and the Canadian National railways, and has an airport. It is also the starting point and terminus of the scenic highway which runs around the Gaspé Peninsula. The distributing center for a mixed farming and lumbering district, the town has railroad shops and establishments producing aerated waters and metal, wood, and dairy products. It was founded in 1881. Population: 6,698.

MONT-LAURIER, môN lô-ryā′, town, Quebec, Canada, seat of Labelle County, situated at an altitude of 733 feet, on the Lièvre River, 80 miles north of Ottawa. The town, a railroad terminus, is a center of winter sports at the foot of Mount Sir Wilfrid in the Laurentian Highlands. There is a provincial experimental farm, and the area produces oats, hay, potatoes, and dairy cattle. Lumbering and wood products are major industries, and there is a hydroelectric station. Founded in 1915, Mont Laurier is the seat of a Roman Catholic bishopric and has a seminary. Population: 8,240.

MONT-SAINT-MICHEL, môN-săN-mē-shĕl′, islet, France, in Manche Department, Normandy, on the English Channel, 8 miles southwest of Avranches. A famous center of learning and pilgrimage as early as the 12th century, it is now an equally celebrated tourist resort. It comprises a series of medieval houses, inns, ecclesiastical buildings, and fortifications, grouped on a conical rock 256 feet high and 3 acres in area, in the Bay of St.-Michel or Mont-St.-Michel, at the mouth of the Couesnon River, which here forms the boundary between Normandy and Brittany.

Once a lofty hill in the Forest of Scissy, which was submerged in the 7th century A.D. by a tidal cataclysm, the rock in prehistoric times was crowned by a Celtic temple. The Bay of St.-Michel, 13 miles wide at its mouth and 10 miles long from north to south, is nearly dry at low water, but fills with treacherous rapidity at flood tide. In 1875 a dike nearly a mile long was built to connect the rock with the mainland.

Ramparts, towers, and bastions encircle the base of the rock, which has a circuit of about two miles, and entrance is made through a gate which opens on a single, narrow, winding street of a small village (pop. 1962, 102) built around the southern slope. The street leads by several flights of stone steps to a fortified abbey on the summit. Crowning the abbey is a church with a 12th century Romanesque nave, a Flamboyant Gothic choir built in 1450–1521, and a facade added in the 18th century. Capping its spire is a statue of St. Michael, which towers conspicuously 456 feet above the wide expanse of sandy bay and low-lying country around.

The Benedictine abbey was founded in 708 by St. Aubert, bishop of Avranches, and his first chapel, which has been restored, stands on a rocky projection on the north side of the rock. In 1203 the abbey was destroyed by King Philip II (Philip Augustus) of France and the present buildings were erected between that year and 1264. Mont-St.-Michel was a strategic fortified post during the Hundred Years' War and during the religious wars of the 16th century. It was successfully defended against all assaults by the Order of St. Michael, which was founded in the Hall of Knights of the abbey in 1469. In the 18th and first half of the 19th centuries the fortress served as a prison for political offenders.

Mont-St.-Michel is now one of the protected historical monuments of France. An elaborate process of restoration after 1863 renewed its ancient strength and beauty. Among the chief features of the Mont are the abbey church; elaborately decorated cloisters; La Merveille, the massive north wall of the abbey; the Salle des Chevaliers; the Châtelet or guardhouse; the crypts with their remarkable columns; the cellars, the dungeons, and the medieval elevator with its enormous hoisting wheel formerly operated by a donkey; and in the village, the ancient parish church, and museum. Pop. (1962) 132.

MONT-SAINT-MICHEL AND CHARTRES, shär′tr′, a historical study by Henry Brooks Adams, was privately printed in 1904 and published in 1913. In his search for a historical period which would make the sharpest contrast with the 20th century, Adams selected the century from 1150 to 1250 as the time in which man viewed himself as a unit in a unified universe. Thus *Mont-Saint-Michel and Chartres,* a study of medieval unity, is to be contrasted with its companion study of a later period, his autobiographical work, *The Education of Henry Adams,* a study of 20th century multiplicity.

Adams treats successively the simple but powerful architecture of Mont-Saint-Michel; the *Chanson de Roland;* the soaring Gothic cathedrals of the Île-de-France and surrounding regions, especially the cathedral at Chartres, and their stained glass; three remarkable women—Eleanor of Aquitaine, her daughter Mary of Champagne, and Blanche of Castile; the literature of the time; Peter Abelard; St. Francis of Assisi and the religious mystics; and finally St. Thomas Aquinas. His thesis is that the lines of force which dominated that age were unified; that there was a unity of theology, philosophy, and the arts, since the church and the universe were taken for truths. It was a coherent age marked by simple faith, energy, and a unified attitude of mind—a *universe.* For Adams its symbol was the Virgin—contrasted with the huge dynamo he saw at the Paris Exposition of 1900 and which he accepted as the symbol of the 20th century *multiverse.* Thus confronted with the complexities of his own time, Adams, like so many writers after him, felt irresistibly attracted to an age in which he saw spiritual unity and peace.

MONTAGNA, mōn-tä′nyä, **Bartolommeo,** Italian painter: b. Orzinovi, near Brescia, Italy, about 1450; d. Vicenza, Oct. 11, 1523. He settled at Vicenza in 1480 and was the first great master resident there. He also worked subsequently at Venice, Verona, and Padua. Montagna's painting in general resembles the earlier Venetian school. It is marked by distinctness, power, and severity of drawing, and has harmonious coloring in which a brown gleaming tint is noticeable. The human form is almost always shown as overmuscular. His principal works are the *Madonna and Child* at the Venice Academy, *Ecce Homo* at the Louvre (Paris), frescoes in the Church of San Nazaro at Verona, and an altarpiece in the Brera, Milan. In the Johnson Collection at Philadelphia he is represented by a *Madonna with Saints* and in the New York City Metropolitan Museum of Art by *A Lady of Rank as Saint Justina of Padua* and a *Madonna and Child.*

MONTAGNAIS INDIANS, môN-tȧ-nyĕ′ (Fr. mountaineers), loosely applied to several Amerindian tribes, but correctly and most commonly used in reference to the Algonquian people residing along the north shores of the St. Lawrence River, from St. Maurice River and interior Labrador to James Bay and the St. Lawrence

Gulf. Having driven the Eskimos from their earlier haunts, the Montagnais were in turn hounded by their inveterate foe, the Iroquois, and like the latter, gained an early reputation for cruelty. The introduction of firearms proved the undoing of the tribe, for their indiscriminate slaughter of game with the new weapon resulted in widespread famine, and they were easy prey to European disease. They are today strongly influenced by white civilization, particularly French-Canadian, and fullbloods are almost nonexistent. The Roman Catholic religion is dominant among them, but has not completely superseded traditional customs. They are a largely nomadic people, completely disinclined to an agricultural life. No reliable census is available, but their 1950 population is estimated at approximately 3,500, including their congeners, the Nascopi.

FREDERICK J. DOCKSTADER.

MONTAGNANA, mōn-tä-nyä′nä, town and commune, Italy, in Padova Province, 23 miles southwest of Padua. Its famous medieval walls, with 24 towers, were completed in the 14th century. There is also an impressive Gothic cathedral, completed about 1500, with a portal attributed to Andrea Sansovino. The modern town manufactures textile machinery and food products. Pop. (1951) town 5,884; commune 12,727.

MONTAGNARDS, môɴ-tȧ-nyär′ (also LA MONTAGNE; Eng., THE MOUNTAIN), in the French Revolution, the extreme radical party in the National Convention in the years 1792–1794; the parliamentary group of the Jacobins. The name was derived from the fact that its members occupied the highest banks of seats in the assembly. The same name was used briefly by the extreme left-wing party led by Louis Blanc during the revolution of 1848 in France.

See also FRANCE—*30. History* (The Revolutionary Era, 1789–1815); NATIONAL CONVENTION; ROBESPIERRE, MAXIMILIEN FRANÇOIS MARIE ISIDORE DE.

MONTAGU, mŏn′tȧ-gū, **Charles,** 1ST EARL OF HALIFAX, English statesman: b. Horton, Northamptonshire, England, April 16, 1661; d. London, May 19, 1715. Grandson of Henry Montagu, 1st earl of Manchester, he graduated from Trinity College, Cambridge, where he became the friend of Isaac Newton. Montagu won an early reputation as a wit for the satirical poem *The Story of the Country-Mouse and the City-Mouse* (1687), written with Matthew Prior, parodying John Dryden's *The Hind and the Panther.* An active supporter of William III's accession to the throne, he was elected to Parliament in 1689, and made a lord of the treasury three years later. His genius for public finance soon made itself evident. His bill (passed 1693) for a public loan of £1 million, to be paid off in life annuities to the subscribers, originated the national debt; and in 1694 he steered through Parliament, over stormy opposition, the law that created the Bank of England. Named chancellor of the exchequer in April 1694, he set about reforming the coinage and in 1696–1697 persuaded Parliament to call in the debased currency and authorize the issue of new coins with milled edges to prevent clipping.

Montagu became first lord of the treasury (prime minister) on May 1, 1697, but dissatisfaction was rising over King William's costly wars and intrigues on the Continent, and Montagu was forced to resign in November 1699, amid charges of personal corruption. The following year he was made Baron Halifax, and in 1701 an unsuccessful attempt was made to impeach him. He continued as a leader of the Whig junto but remained out of office until after the death of Queen Anne (1714), when he served briefly as George I's first prime minister and was elevated to the earldom.

Montagu brought his friend Newton into the mint as warden in 1696 and master in 1699. He also patronized such distinguished Whig writers as Joseph Addison and William Congreve, and served as president of the Royal Society in 1695–1698. His writings were collected in 1715, and his poems have been reprinted in various collections.

MONTAGU, Edward, 2D EARL OF MANCHESTER, English general and political leader: b. 1602; d. London, England, May 5, 1671. His father, Sir Henry Montagu (1563?–1642), as chief justice of the King's Bench, passed the death sentence on Sir Walter Raleigh in 1618 and later became one of the chief councilors of Charles I, who created him 1st earl of Manchester (1626). Edward Montagu attended Cambridge, and from 1626, when he was made a baron, was one of the leaders of the Puritan party in the House of Lords. Succeeding to the earldom on his father's death, he was given a major command in the Parliamentary Army in 1643, with Oliver Cromwell as his chief lieutenant. Manchester was in command at the Battle of Marston Moor (July 1644) but showed little inclination to fight thereafter, favoring an accommodation with the crown. Denounced by Cromwell in the House of Commons in November, he resigned his commission in April 1645, opposed the trial and execution of Charles I, and was prominent in effecting the Stuart Restoration in 1660. His grandson, CHARLES MONTAGU (1660?–1722), was created 1st duke of Manchester by George I in 1719.

MONTAGU, Elizabeth (nee ROBINSON), English society leader and author: b. York, England, Oct. 2, 1720; d. London, Aug. 25, 1800. She married (1742) Edward Montagu, grandson of the 1st earl of Sandwich, and from 1750 their house in London was the scene of a famous literary salon, to which the term "bluestocking" was first applied. Among the prominent persons who attended were George Lyttelton (1st Baron Lyttelton), Samuel Johnson, Horace Walpole, Edmund Burke, Sir Joshua Reynolds, David Garrick, Hannah More, and Fanny Burney. Mrs. Montagu wrote three of the dialogues (nos. 26–28) in Lyttelton's *Dialogues of the Dead* (1760) and was also the author of *An Essay on the Writings and Genius of Shakespear . . .* (1769), a defense of the bard against the criticism of Voltaire. Her voluminous correspondence has been published in various modern editions.

MONTAGU, John, 4TH EARL OF SANDWICH. See SANDWICH, 4TH EARL OF.

MONTAGU, LADY **Mary Wortley,** English author: b. London, England, bap. May 26, 1689; d. there, Aug. 21, 1762. Eldest daughter of Sir Evelyn Pierrepont, afterward marquess of Dorchester and 1st duke of Kingston, she married Edward Wortley Montagu, grandson of the 1st earl of Sandwich, in 1712 without her father's consent. On George I's accession, Montagu obtained the position of commissioner of the treasury, and the Montagus went to live in London, where Lady Mary's beauty, wit, and vivacity won her a wide circle of friends, among them Alexander Pope. Her *Town Eclogues* (1747) appeared in a pirated edition under the title of *Court Poems* in 1716. In the same year her husband was appointed ambassador to the Porte. Lady Mary accompanied him to Constantinople, where they remained from May 1717 to June 1718. It was during this period that her celebrated *Letters from the East* were written. In Adrianople she learned of the Turkish practice of inoculation against smallpox, and she had her son inoculated. On her return to England she introduced the practice in the face of violent opposition. Resuming her friendship with Pope, she and her husband settled in Twickenham. In 1722, however, she quarreled with the poet, who frequently satirized her thereafter, and she was also attacked by Jonathan Swift in a lampoon published in 1727. In 1739, for reasons never satisfactorily explained, Lady Mary left England to live on the Continent, chiefly in Italy, where she remained until after her husband's death in 1761. Her relations with her husband apparently remained friendly, and she corresponded frequently with her daughter, the countess of Bute. Returning to England early in 1762, she died shortly thereafter.

Lady Mary's letters are marked by wit, graphic power, keen observation, and independence of judgment. They were published in a three-volume edition in 1763. Her great-grandson, the 1st Baron Wharncliffe, edited a three-volume edition of her *Works* in 1837.

Consult Benjamin, L. S., *Lady Mary Wortley Montague: Her Life and Letters* (Boston 1925); Barry, Iris, *Portrait of Lady Mary Montague* (Indianapolis 1928); Cove, J. W., *Admirable Lady Mary; the Life and Times of Lady Mary Wortley Montague, 1689–1762* (New York 1949).

Her son, Edward Wortley Montagu (1713–1776), was a writer and traveler. He published *Reflections on the Rise and Fall of the Antient Republics. Adapted to the Present State of Great Britain* (1759).

MONTAGU, Ralph, 1st Duke of Montagu: b. about 1638; d. March 9, 1709. The son of the 2d Baron Montagu of Boughton, he obtained preferment at the court of Charles II, and in 1669 was appointed ambassador extraordinary to Louis XIV. He became a member of the Privy Council in 1672, and in 1676 was again named ambassador to Louis XIV. In this capacity he helped to arrange English neutrality in the war between the Netherlands and France. Because of political intrigues, he lost his positions in 1678, but as an early supporter of William of Orange was reappointed to the Privy Council in 1689, and in 1705 was created marquis of Monthermer and duke of Montagu.

MONTAGUE, Charles Edward, British journalist and writer: b. London, Jan. 1, 1867; d. Manchester, May 28, 1928. Of Irish parentage, he was educated at Balliol College, Oxford University (1885–1889), and in 1890 joined the staff of the Manchester *Guardian,* with which, except for his service (1914–1919) in World War I, he was affiliated until 1925. He published several novels, including *A Hind Let Loose* (1910), *Rough Justice* (1926), and *Right Off the Map* (1928); *Dramatic Values* (1911) and *Disenchantment* (1922), essays; and *Fiery Particles* (1923) and *Action* (1928), volumes of short stories.

His brother, Francis Charles Montague (b. London, Aug. 31, 1858; d. Oxford, April 8, 1935), was a historian. He served as curator of the Indian Institute, Oxford, from 1900 to 1913. His published works include *The Limits of Individual Liberty* (1885); *Life of Sir Robert Peel* (1888); *Elements of English Constitutional History* (1894); and contributions to the *Cambridge Modern History* and Longman's *Political History of England* (1907).

MONTAIGNE, môn-tĕn'y', **Michel Eyquem de,** French essayist: b. Château de Montaigne, near Bordeaux, Feb. 28, 1533; d. there, Sept. 13, 1592. As a small child he was placed under the care of a German tutor who spoke only Latin to him, and at the age of six he was sent to the Collège de Guyenne in Bordeaux. He remained in Bordeaux for seven years, and probably studied philosophy there under George Buchanan (q.v.) and Marc Antoine Muret. Thereafter he probably studied law at Bordeaux and Toulouse, and when he came of age was made a counselor of the Cour des Aides of Périgueux. This court was abolished three years later, and in 1557 Montaigne with the other members was appointed counselor of the Bordeaux Parliament, a body in which, about 1559, he made the acquaintance of Étienne de La Boétie, whose intimate friend he became. From 1561 to 1563, Montaigne was at the court of Charles IX, and he was present at the siege of Rouen in 1562. In 1565 he married Françoise de La Chassaigne, daughter of one of his fellow counselors. The deaths of his father and La Boétie in 1568 greatly lessened Montaigne's interest in public affairs. After preparing his friend's posthumous works for publication and publishing (1569) his own translation of Raymond of Sabunde's *Theologia naturalis sive Liber creaturarum,* for which he received the Order of St. Michael, he sold his post as counselor and retired to Montaigne in 1570. There in the following year he began, and in nine years completed, the first two books of his *Essais.* It is not known whether or not he intended them for publication, although their style seems to point to the fact that in their earliest form they must have been merely jottings in a commonplace book. Except for an occasional trip to Paris, Montaigne did not leave the château until 1580, when, his health having greatly deteriorated, he set out on travels through Switzerland, Germany, and Italy, meeting Torquato Tasso at Ferrara. (His *Journal* of this trip was discovered and published in 1774.) During his absence from France, and apparently against his will, he was elected mayor of Bordeaux. He served in this office from 1581 to 1583, and then was re-elected for another two-year term. His administration, which was highly successful, came to a close in 1585, and he spent the next three years in revising the first two books of the *Essais* and adding a third. In 1588 he accompanied Henry III to Rouen. His last years were spent in revising his work.

Montaigne had five daughters; only one of them, Léonor, of whom he was very fond, survived him. He was also much attached to Mlle. Marie Le Jars de Gournay, whom he called his adopted daughter, and who was fortunate enough to receive from Montaigne's widow a copy of his *Essais,* with manuscript additions and corrections, which formed the basis of an edition published in 1595.

Montaigne was the first to use the term "essay" to describe the literary form he did so much to develop. In his *Essais* he treated subjects as diverse as friendship and government, education and warfare, but his approach to them was almost always subjective. It was through the study of his own reactions, which were those of a cultivated gentleman of the Renaissance, that he developed his views of mankind. Customarily, the changes in Montaigne's philosophy are traced from an early Stoicism, through a skepticism in which he doubted that one could be certain of anything, to a final Epicureanism. His knowledge of many cultures made him basically skeptical, however, and it was this skepticism that fostered in him a spirit of tolerance in an intolerent age. Montaigne's *Essais* had great influence not only in France, but also in England, particularly on William Shakespeare and Francis Bacon.

The standard modern edition of the *Essais* is that of Fortunat Strowski (5 vols., 1906–1933). Others are those of Albert Thibaudet (1933) and Maurice Rat (3 vols., 1941–1942). The first English translation, that of John Florio, was published in 1603 and revised by William Carew Hazlitt in 1893. A later standard translation is that of Charles Cotton (1685–1693), while good modern versions include those of George B. Ives (1925), Emil J. Trechmann (1927), and Jacob Zeitlin (2 vols., 1934–1936).

See also ESSAY—*Origin of the Essay*.

Bibliography.—Emerson, Ralph W., *Representative Men* (Boston 1850); Bonnefon, Paul, *Montaigne: L'homme et l'oeuvre* (Paris 1893); Gide, André, *Essai sur Montaigne* (Paris 1929); Villey, Pierre, *Les essais de Michel de Montaigne* (Paris 1932); id., *Montaigne* (Paris 1933); Boase, Alan M., *The Fortunes of Montaigne* (London 1935); Strowski, Fortunat, *Montaigne: Sa vie publique et privée* (Paris 1938); Young, Charles L., *Emerson's Montaigne* (New York 1941); Dédéyan, Charles, *Montaigne chez ses amis anglo-saxons* (Paris 1943); Cresson, André, *Montaigne, sa vie, son oeuvre* (Paris 1947); Frame, Donald M., *Montaigne's Discovery of Man* (New York 1955).

MONTALEMBERT, môn-tà-läN-bâr′, COMTE DE (CHARLES FORBES), French journalist and politician: b. London, England, April 15, 1810; d. Paris, France, March 13, 1870. The son of an émigré, he was educated in London and Paris and at an early age identified himself with the liberal Roman Catholic movement of Félicité Robert de Lamennais and Jean Baptiste Henri Lacordaire (qq.v.). With them he founded (1830) and edited the journal *L'Avenir,* and he also joined them in advocating education outside the state system. A free Roman Catholic school which he opened with Lacordaire in 1831 was soon closed by the police. Meanwhile, the new journal had aroused opposition, and Montalembert and his colleagues went to Rome in its behalf. Nevertheless, *L'Avenir* was condemned by Pope Gregory XVI in 1832, a decision to which Montalembert submitted. In the Chamber of Peers, which Montalembert entered in 1835, in the Constituent Assembly of 1848, and in the Legislative Assembly, in which he sat from 1849 to 1857, he spoke frequently and well on ecclesiastical matters, and he became known as one of the most determined opponents of Napoleon III. Among his published works are *Histoire de Sainte Élisabeth de Hongrie, duchesse de Thuringie* (1836; Eng. tr., *The Life of Saint Elizabeth, of Hungary, Duchess of Thuringia,* 1854); *De l'avenir politique de l'Angleterre* (1855; Eng. tr., *The Political Future of England,* 1856); *L'église libre dans l'état libre* (*The Free Church in the Free State,* 1863); and *Les moines d'Occident depuis saint Benoît jusqu'à saint Bernard* (7 vols., 1860–1877; Eng. tr., *The Monks of the West, from St. Benedict to St. Bernard,* 7 vols., 1861–1879).

MONTALEMBERT, MARQUIS DE (MARC RENÉ), French military engineer: b. Angoulême, France, July 16, 1714; d. Paris, March 29, 1800. Joining the French Army at the age of 18, he saw service in the wars of the Polish and Austrian successions and then directed the construction of several forts in France. During the Seven Years' War he was a liaison officer with the Swedish Army. From his wide experience, Montalembert developed a fortification system which he offered in preference to the trace system of the marquis de Vauban, setting forth his ideas in *La fortification perpendiculaire* (*Perpendicular Fortification,* 1776–1786) and *L'art défensive supérieure à l'offensif* (*The Art of a Defense Superior to the Offensive,* 1793). His theory of achieving massed fire power by building a system of detached forts around a central stronghold was not well received in France, but it had considerable influence elsewhere, notably in Germany. Montalembert remained in France during the French Revolution, and in 1792 was appointed a general of division by Lazare Carnot. He also had some talent as a poet.

MONTALVAN, môn-täl-vän′, **Juan Pérez de,** Spanish ecclesiastic, playwright, and novelist: b. Madrid, Spain, 1602; d. there, June 25, 1638. A friend and disciple of the playwright Lope de Vega, he began writing comedies at the age of 17. After studying theology at the University of Alcalá de Henares, he was ordained a priest (1625) and later became notary to the Inquisition. He was the author of some 60 plays, most of which were collected and published in two volumes under the title *Comedias* (1635–1638). Among the best known are *Los amantes de Teruel* (*The Lovers of Teruel*) and *El segundo Séneca de España* (*The Second Seneca of Spain*), which he wrote in praise of Philip II. Several of his novels appeared in *Sucesos y prodigios de amor* (*Ordinary and Extraordinary Tales of Love,* 1625), and others in *Para todos* (*For Everyone,* 1633). His epic poem, *Orfeo en lengua castellana* (*Orpheus in Castilian,* 1624), may possibly have been written by Lope de Vega. On the death of the latter, Montalván wrote *Fama póstuma de Lope de Vega* (*Posthumous Renown of Lope de Vega,* 1636).

MONTALVO, môn-täl′vō, **García Ordóñez de** (GARCI RODRÍGUEZ DE MONTALVO), Spanish writer: fl. early 16th century. Almost nothing is known of his life, but he is remembered as the author of the first printed version of the celebrated chivalric romance *Amadís de Gaula,* q.v. (*Amadis of Gaul*), which he published in four volumes in 1508. The legend of Amadis is believed to have originated in a late 13th century Portuguese work which had come down in various Portuguese and Spanish versions, but Montalvo gave the story its classic form and was responsible for its immense popularity throughout the 16th century. The success of the book induced him to write a sequel, *Las sergas de Esplandián* (*The Deeds of Esplandian,* 1510), on Amadis' son.

MONTANA, mŏn-tăn'ȧ, Mountain state, United States, bounded on the east by North Dakota and South Dakota, on the south by Wyoming, on the southwest and west by Idaho, and on the north by the Canadian provinces of British Columbia, Alberta, and Saskatchewan. Montana averages 535 miles in length and 275 miles in width. The word *montana* is a Latin noun, in common use in Spanish-speaking countries, meaning "mountainous regions."

Known to the Indians as the Land of the Shining Mountains, Montana is the most northerly of the Rocky Mountain states. The mountains not only are the source of great mineral wealth, which with agriculture forms the basis of the state's economy, but by their beauty attract many visitors.

State flag
(Adopted Feb. 27, 1905)

Total area	147,138 square miles
Land area	145,878 square miles
Water area	1,260 square miles
Latitude	44°26'—49°N.
Longitude	104°02'—116°02'W.
Altitude (average)	3,400 feet
High point, Granite Peak	12,850 feet
Low point, near Troy	1,800 feet
Population (1970)	694,409
Capital city—Helena; population	22,730
Admitted as the 41st state	Nov. 8, 1889
State bird (adopted in 1931)	Western meadow lark
State flower (adopted in 1895)	Bitterroot
State tree (adopted in 1949)	Ponderosa or western yellow pine
State song (unofficial)	*Montana*
State motto (adopted in 1893)	*Oro y Plata* (Gold and Silver)
State nicknames	Treasure State; Bonanza State

State seal
(Officially adopted March 2, 1893)

A discussion of Montana's geography, government, social and economic life, and history is presented under the following headings:

1. PHYSICAL FEATURES

Topography.—About one fourth of Montana has an altitude of less than 3,000 feet, another fourth ranges up to 5,000 feet, while about 7 per cent, or 10,000 square miles, shows an elevation of more than 8,000 feet. Approximately two fifths of the state, lying in the central and western areas, is mountainous. The main ridge of the Rockies extends from Glacier National Park in northern Montana to Yellowstone National Park on the southern border. About two thirds of the distance south from the Canadian boundary the Continental Divide turns abruptly west to the Idaho line, where it again makes a sharp angle to the southeast. From this angle juts the Bitterroot Range, which is continued farther north by the Cabinet Mountains. Numerous small ranges, of which the Mission and the Swan are said to be the most beautiful, break the area west of the divide into fertile, well-watered valleys. Eastward from the main range, extending toward the center of the state, are the Big Belt and Little Belt Mountains; to the south and west of these are the Tobacco Root Mountains and the Bridger, Ruby, Gallatin, and Madison ranges. Extending east along the southern boundary are the lofty Absaroka Mountains and Beartooth Range, and still farther east are the Pryor and Rosebud Mountains. A number of "mountains of the plains," distinctive in their isolation, characterize the center of the state. These include the Crazy, Highwood, Big Snowy, Judith, Moccasin, Little Rocky, and Bear Paw Mountains. The northern portion of Montana east of the mountains and north of the Missouri River consists largely of a broad, glaciated plain. The eastern two fifths of the state south of the Missouri lies in the Great Plains and is characterized by sharply cut streambeds and high, arid benchlands.

Montana's numerous and extensive rivers rise in its mountains, which virtually form the apex of the continent. From Glacier National Park rivers flow north to the Saskatchewan, east to the Missouri, and west to the Columbia. East of the mountains the Missouri and its historic Three Forks tributaries of the Jefferson, Madison, and Gallatin provided an easy ingress for explorers. Its longer tributaries are the Musselshell and Montana's major international river, the Milk. The Yellowstone, largest tributary of the Missouri, is distinctive in that all of its major branches enter from the south, notably the Powder River, the Bighorn River, and Clark's Fork. The Clark Fork of the Columbia system rises on the west slope of the mountains immediately adjacent to the headwaters of the Missouri. Its tributary, the Blackfoot River, which rises near Lewis and Clark Pass, was an important artery of early travel. The Bitterroot River provides drainage from the south. To the north the Flathead River rises in British Columbia near the Montana border and flows into Flathead Lake and out again, to join the Clark Fork near Paradise. The Kootenai (in Canada, Kootenay), another international river, flows through the extreme northwestern corner of the state.

The state also has a large number of natural lakes, the biggest of which is Flathead Lake, with an area of 188 square miles, or 1,219,000 acre-feet of storage water. In addition, it has 58 man-made storage reservoirs with a capacity of 5,000 acre-feet or more. Largest of these is Fort Peck Reservoir, formed by the world's larg-

Northern Pacific Railway

The state capitol building at Helena.

est earth-fill dam, with an area of 382.8 square miles and a capacity of 19,417,000 acre-feet. Hungry Horse Reservoir has a capacity of 3,470,-000 acre-feet, and Canyon Ferry Reservoir one of 2,050,000 acre-feet.

Climate.—Montana's varied climate includes temperatures from the nation's coldest, −69.7°F. near Helena in 1954, to an occasional high of 117° in the northeast. The northern plains near the mountains lie in a chinook belt, where warm winds often quickly remove the snow cover in winter. Average annual temperatures vary from 46° in the Yellowstone Valley to 35° in the mountain valleys. The average mean temperature for the state is 42.6°. The mean annual precipitation is 15.48 inches. Growing seasons vary in length from 87 frost-free days at Philipsburg to 141 days at Roundup. See also RAINFALL.

Plant Life.—The physical characteristics of the state make a natural division of its plant life into (1) the subalpine group, which includes the small trees, shrubs, and flowers in the high mountains; (2) the montane group of coniferous trees, a large number of flowering plants, and certain types of grasses; and (3) the plains plant group, which includes an unusual number of luxuriant forage grasses, low-growing shrubs such as sagebrush, the cactus, and an additional large number of flowering plants. More than 2,000 species of wild flowers and nonflowering plants are found in Montana.

Montana range lands are classified into five types, depending on the dominant grasses of the area. The major forage grasses include blue grama, needle-and-thread grass, western wheat grass, and bluebunch wheat grass. Increasing care of the grass cover since the drought of the 1930's and the development of such new pasture grasses as crested wheat grass have resulted in a marked improvement in forage resources.

Forest lands cover almost one fourth of Montana's area, for a total of 22,400,000 acres, including 15,800,000 acres in commercial forests, 4,100,000 acres in noncommercial forests, and 2,500,000 acres in reserved forests. Among the major commercial trees are Douglas fir, larch, ponderosa pine, and western white pine, and new methods have made the large stands of lodgepole pine on the eastern approach to the mountains profitable for lumber purposes. The 11 national forests in the state—Beaverhead, Bitterroot, Custer, Deerlodge, Flathead, Gallatin, Helena, Kaniksum, Kootenai, Lewis and Clark, and Lolo—incorporate a total of 16,634,143 acres. The state forest system covers 202,960 acres.

Animal Life.—When Montana was first explored, it was heavily stocked with wild game animals, game birds, and fish. Most of these suffered severe depletion, and some became extinct. Under the supervision of federal agencies and the Montana Fish and Game Department, however, rapid recovery has been made. About 500 buffalo are maintained on the Montana National Bison Range, and about 1,000 in Yellowstone National Park, and natural increase has made it possible to establish a herd on the Crow Indian Reservation and to supplement herds in other areas. Major game animals include the mule deer, white-tailed deer, elk, moose, antelope, and bear. Management of antelope herds increased their population from less than 50,000 in 1950 to about 70,000 ten years later. Among Montana's many fur-bearing animals are beaver, mink, and muskrat.

Some 300 species of birds are found in Montana. The waterfowl species of ducks and geese and upland game birds comprise the game bird resources. Fish number over 70 species. Among those stocked from the 9 state and 4 federal hatcheries are cutthroat and rainbow trout, grayling, and red (sockeye) salmon.

Conservation.—Montana's soils reflect directly the mountain-plain character of the state. Soils of the plains and of the mountain valleys are classed as chernozem, chestnut, and brown, while the major groupings in the mountainous areas are podzol, brown podzolic, and gray wooded soils. The United States Soil Conservation Service and the Department of Agronomy and Soils of the Montana Agricultural Experiment Station in Bozeman have conducted detailed soil classifica-

MONTANA

COUNTIES

Beaverhead, 8,187 C 5
Big Horn, 10,057 J 5
Blaine, 6,727 G 2
Broadwater, 2,526 E 4
Carbon, 7,080 G 5
Carter, 1,956 M 5
Cascade, 81,804 E 3
Chouteau, 6,473 F 3
Custer, 12,174 L 4
Daniels, 3,083 L 2
Dawson, 11,269 M 3
Deer Lodge, 15,652 C 5
Fallon, 4,050 M 4
Fergus, 12,611 G 3
Flathead, 39,460 B 2
Gallatin, 32,505 E 5
Garfield, 1,796 J 3
Glacier, 10,783 C 2
Golden Valley, 931 G 4
Granite, 2,737 C 4
Hill, 17,358 F 2
Jefferson, 5,238 D 4
Judith Basin, 2,667 F 4
Lake, 14,445 B 3
Lewis and Clark, 33,281 D 3
Liberty, 2,359 E 2
Lincoln, 18,063 A 2
Madison, 5,014 D 5
McCone, 2,875 L 3
Meagher, 2,122 F 4
Mineral, 2,958 B 3
Missoula, 58,263 C 3
Musselshell, 3,734 H 4
Park, 11,197 F 5
Petroleum, 675 H 3
Phillips, 5,386 J 2
Pondera, 6,611 D 2
Powder River, 2,862 L 5
Powell, 6,660 D 4
Prairie, 1,752 L 4
Ravalli, 14,409 B 4
Richland, 9,837 M 3
Roosevelt, 10,365 L 2
Rosebud, 6,032 K 4
Sanders, 7,093 A 3
Sheridan, 5,779 M 2
Silver Bow, 41,981 D 5
Stillwater, 4,632 G 5
Sweet Grass, 2,980 G 5
Teton, 6,116 D 3
Toole, 5,839 E 2
Treasure, 1,069 J 4
Valley, 11,471 K 2
Wheatland, 2,529 G 4
Wibaux, 1,465 M 4
Yellowstone, 87,367 H 4
Yellowstone Nat'l Park, 64 F 6

CITIES and TOWNS

Absarokee, 700 G 5
Acton, 10 H 5
Alberton, 363 B 3
Albion, 1 M 5
Alder, 100 D 5
Alhambra, 50 E 4
Alzada, 28 M 5
Amsterdam, 200 E 5
Anaconda⊙, 9,771 C 4
Anceney, 10 E 5
Andes, 11 M 3
Angela, 4 K 4
Antelope, 95 M 2
Apgar, 8 B 2
Archer, 7 M 2
Arlee, 220 B 3
Armington, 62 F 3
Arrow Creek, 4 F 3
Ashland, 200 K 5
Augusta, 400 D 3
Austin, 6 D 4
Avon, 250 D 4
Babb, 50 C 2
Bainville, 217 M 2
Baker⊙, 2,584 M 4
Ballantine, 350 J 5
Bannack, 20 C 5
Barber, 2 G 4
Basin, 230 D 4
Bearcreek, 31 G 5
Bearmouth, 6 C 4
Becket, 35 G 4
Belfry, 250 H 5
Belgrade, 1,307 E 5
Belknap, 27 A 3
Belmont, 75 G 4
Belt, 656 E 3
Benchland, 100 F 3
Biddle, 83 L 5
Big Arm, 150 B 3
Bigfork, 500 C 2
Bighorn, 40 J 4
Big Sandy, 827 G 2
Big Timber⊙, 1,592 G 5
Billings⊙, 61,581 H 5
Billings, ‡87,367 H 5
Birney, 16 K 5
Black Eagle, 1,500 E 3
Blackfoot, 100 D 2
Bloomfield, 25 M 3
Bonner, 250 C 4
Boulder⊙, 1,342 E 4
Box Elder, 200 F 2
Boyd, 25 G 5
Boyes, 16 M 5
Bozeman⊙, 18,670 E 5
Brady, 230 E 2
Bridger, 717 H 5
Broadus⊙, 799 L 5
Broadview, 123 H 4
Brockton, 401 M 2
Brockway, 80 L 3
Brooks, 10 G 3
Browning, 1,700 C 2
Brusett, 2 J 3
Buffalo, 13 G 4
Busby, 600 J 5
Butte⊙, 23,368 D 5
Bynum, 30 D 3
Camas Prairie, 160 B 3
Cameron, 9 E 5
Canyon Creek, 25 D 4
Canyon Ferry, 100 E 4
Capitol, 2 M 5
Cardwell, 36 E 5
Carlyle, 20 M 4
Carter, 100 E 3
Cartersville, 140 K 4
Cascade, 714 E 3
Cat Creek, 11 H 3
Centerville, 2,284 D 4
Charlo, 150 B 3
Chester⊙, 936 E 2
Chico, 10 F 5
Chinook⊙, 1,813 G 2
Choteau⊙, 1,586 D 3
Christina, 44 G 3
Circle⊙, 964 L 3
Clancy, 550 E 4
Cleveland, 10 G 2
Clinton, 250 C 4
Clyde Park, 244 F 5
Coalridge, 21 M 2
Coalwood, 2 L 5
Coffee Creek, 79 F 3
Cohagen, 6 K 3
Collins, 7 E 3
Colstrip, 160 K 5
Columbia Falls, 2,652 B 2
Columbus⊙, 1,173 G 5
Comanche, 8 H 4
Condon, 250 C 3
Conner, 150 B 5
Conrad⊙, 2,770 D 2
Cooke City, 45 G 5
Coram, 450 C 2
Corvallis, 467 C 4
Corwin Springs, 4 F 5
Craig, 100 D 3
Crane, 152 M 3
Creston, 20 C 2
Crow Agency, 975 J 5
Culbertson, 821 M 2
Custer, 193 J 4
Cut Bank⊙, 4,004 D 2
Dagmar, 55 M 2
Danvers, 20 G 3
Darby, 538 B 4
Dayton, 60 B 3
Dean, 32 G 5
De Borgia, 95 A 3
Decker, 22 K 5
Deer Lodge⊙, 4,306 D 4
Dell, 50 D 6
Delpine, 33 F 4
Denton, 398 G 3
Devon, 33 E 2
Dillon⊙, 4,548 D 5
Divide, 105 D 5
Dixon, 300 B 3
Dodson, 196 H 2
Drummond, 494 D 4
Dupuyer, 105 D 2
Dutton, 415 E 3
East Glacier Park, 340 C 2
East Helena, 1,651 E 4
Eden, 15 E 3
Edgar, 150 H 5
Ekalaka⊙, 663 M 5
Elk Park, 53 D 4
Elliston, 300 D 4
Elmo, 150 B 3
Emigrant, 29 F 5
Enid, 7 M 3
Ennis, 501 E 5
Epsie, 60 L 5
Essex, 35 C 2
Ethridge, 19 D 2
Eureka, 1,195 B 2
Fairfield, 638 D 3
Fairview, 956 M 3
Fallon, 200 L 4
Ferdig, 14 E 2
Fergus, 2 H 3
Finch, 20 K 4
Findon, 18 F 4
Fishtail, 52 G 5
Flaxville, 185 L 2
Floral Park, 5,113 D 5
Florence, 500 B 4
Floweree, 306 E 3
Forestgrove, 90 H 3
Forsyth⊙, 1,873 K 4
Fort Belknap, 185 H 2
Fort Benton⊙, 1,863 F 3
Fortine, 250 A 2
Fort Logan, 20 E 4
Fort Peck, 975 K 2
Fort Shaw, 450 E 3
Fort Smith, 300 J 5
Four Buttes, 50 L 2
Franklin, 2 G 4
Frazer, 300 K 2
Frenchtown, 300 B 3
Fresno, 5 G 2
Froid, 330 M 2
Fromberg, 364 H 5
Galata, 48 E 2
Galen, 210 D 4
Gallatin Gateway, 200 E 5
Gardiner, 479 F 5
Garneill, 55 G 4
Garnet, 2 C 4
Garrison, 350 D 4
Garryowen, 18 J 5
Geraldine, 370 F 3
Geyser, 567 F 3
Gildford, 285 F 2
Glasgow⊙, 4,700 K 2
Glen, 100 D 5
Glendive⊙, 6,305 M 3
Glengarry, 4 G 3
Glentana, 40 K 2
Goldcreek, 76 D 4
Grant, 25 C 5
Grantsdale, 250 B 4
Grassrange, 181 H 3
Great Falls⊙, 60,091 E 3
Great Falls, ‡81,804 E 3
Greenough, 100 C 4
Greycliff, 30 G 5
Hall, 95 C 4
Hamilton⊙, 2,499 B 4
Hammond, 11 M 5
Hanover, 10 G 3
Hardin⊙, 2,733 J 5
Harlem, 1,094 H 2
Harlowton⊙, 1,375 F 4
Harrison, 275 E 5
Hathaway, 45 K 4
Haugan, 40 A 3
Havre⊙, 10,558 G 2
Hays, 950 H 2
Heart Butte, 450 C 2
Heath, 6 G 3
Hedgesville, 17 G 4
Helena (cap.)⊙, 22,730 E 4
Helmville, 76 C 4
Heron, 185 A 2
Highwood, 360 F 3
Hilger, 40 G 3
Hingham, 262 F 2
Hinsdale, 500 K 2
Hobson, 192 G 4
Hodges, 50 M 4
Hogeland, 68 H 2
Homestead, 75 M 2
Hot Springs, 664 B 3
Hungry Horse, 700 C 2
Huntley, 225 H 5
Huson, 40 B 3
Hysham⊙, 373 J 4
Ingomar, 55 J 4
Intake, 60 M 3
Inverness, 150 F 2
Ismay, 40 M 4
Jackson, 196 C 5
Jardine, 20 F 5
Jeffers, 70 E 5
Jefferson City, 99 E 4
Jefferson Island, 31 E 5
Joliet, 412 G 5
Joplin, 350 F 2
Jordan⊙, 529 J 3
Judith Gap, 160 G 4
Kalispell⊙, 10,526 B 2
Kevin, 250 D 2
Kila, 44 B 2
Kinsey, 12 L 4
Kirby, 2 J 5
Klein, 200 H 4
Knobs, 5 M 5
Knowlton, 9 L 4
Kolin, 2 G 3
Kremlin, 347 F 2
Lake McDonald, 5 B 2
Lakeside, 663 B 2
Lakeview, 13 E 6
Lambert, 141 M 3
Lame Deer, 460 K 5
Landusky, 50 H 3
Laredo, 20 G 2
Larslan, 140 K 2
Laurel, 4,454 H 5
Laurin, 60 D 5
Lavina, 169 H 4
Ledger, 15 E 2
Lennep, 4 F 4
Lewistown⊙, 6,437 G 3
Libby⊙, 3,286 A 2
Lima, 351 D 6
Limestone, 12 F 5
Lincoln, 473 D 4
Lindsay, 40 L 3
Livingston⊙, 6,883 F 5
Lloyd, 70 G 2
Locate, 49 L 4
Lockwood, 950 H 5
Lodge Grass, 806 J 5
Lodgepole, 39 H 2
Logan, 53 E 5
Lohman, 25 G 2
Lolo, 300 B 4
Lolo Hot Springs, 25 B 4
Loma, 172 F 3
Lombard, 25 E 4
Lonepine, 20 B 3
Loring, 15 J 2
Lothair, 35 E 2
Lustre, 25 K 2
Luther, 10 G 5
Madoc, 25 L 2
Malta⊙, 2,195 J 2
Manhattan, 816 E 5
Marion, 120 B 2
Marsh, 2 M 4
Martinsdale, 203 F 4
Marysville, 42 D 4

⊙ County seat. ‡ Population of metropolitan area.

All figures available from 1970 final census are supplemented by local official estimates.

MONTANA
115°
114°
113°
112°
111°
110°
Medicine Hat
Kimberley
Cranbrook
Fernie
Blairmore
Fort MacLeod
Lethbridge
Taber
Bow Island
Pincher Creek
Stirling
Conrad
Manyberries
Glenwoodville
Cardston
Whisky Gap
Coutts
Pakowki Lake
BRITISH COLUMBIA
ALBERTA
CONTINENTAL DIVIDE
49°
48°
47°
46°
45°
LINCOLN
FLATHEAD
GLACIER
TOOLE
LIBERTY
HILL
PONDERA
TETON
CHOUTEAU
SANDERS
LAKE
MINERAL
MISSOULA
LEWIS AND CLARK
CASCADE
JUDITH BASIN
POWELL
GRANITE
MEAGHER
BROADWATER
JEFFERSON
RAVALLI
DEER LODGE
SILVER BOW
GALLATIN
PARK
MADISON
BEAVERHEAD
GLACIER NATIONAL PARK
BLACKFEET INDIAN RESERVATION
FLATHEAD INDIAN RESERVATION
YELLOWSTONE NATIONAL PARK
BIG HOLE NAT'L BATTLEFIELD
BITTERROOT RANGE
Yaak
Rexford
Eureka
Troy
Libby
Whitefish
Columbia Falls
Kalispell
Polson
Browning
Cut Bank
Shelby
Chester
Havre
Conrad
Valier
Choteau
Fairfield
Great Falls
Fort Benton
Thompson Falls
Plains
Superior
Missoula
Hamilton
Stevensville
Darby
Philipsburg
Deer Lodge
Anaconda
Butte
Helena
East Helena
Townsend
Boulder
Whitehall
Three Forks
Manhattan
Belgrade
Bozeman
Livingston
White Sulphur Springs
Dillon
Virginia City
Ennis
Twin Bridges
Sheridan
West Yellowstone
Lima
Monida
Salmon
Wallace
Ashton
Dubois
Gardiner
HIGHWAYS
Limited Access
Toll Interchanges
Important Roads
Federal Route Numbers
State Route Numbers
U.S. Interstate Route Numbers
MONTANA
SCALE
0 5 10 20 40 60 80 MI.
0 5 10 20 40 60 80 KM.
State Capitals
County Seats
© C.S. HAMMOND & Co., N.Y.
Longitude

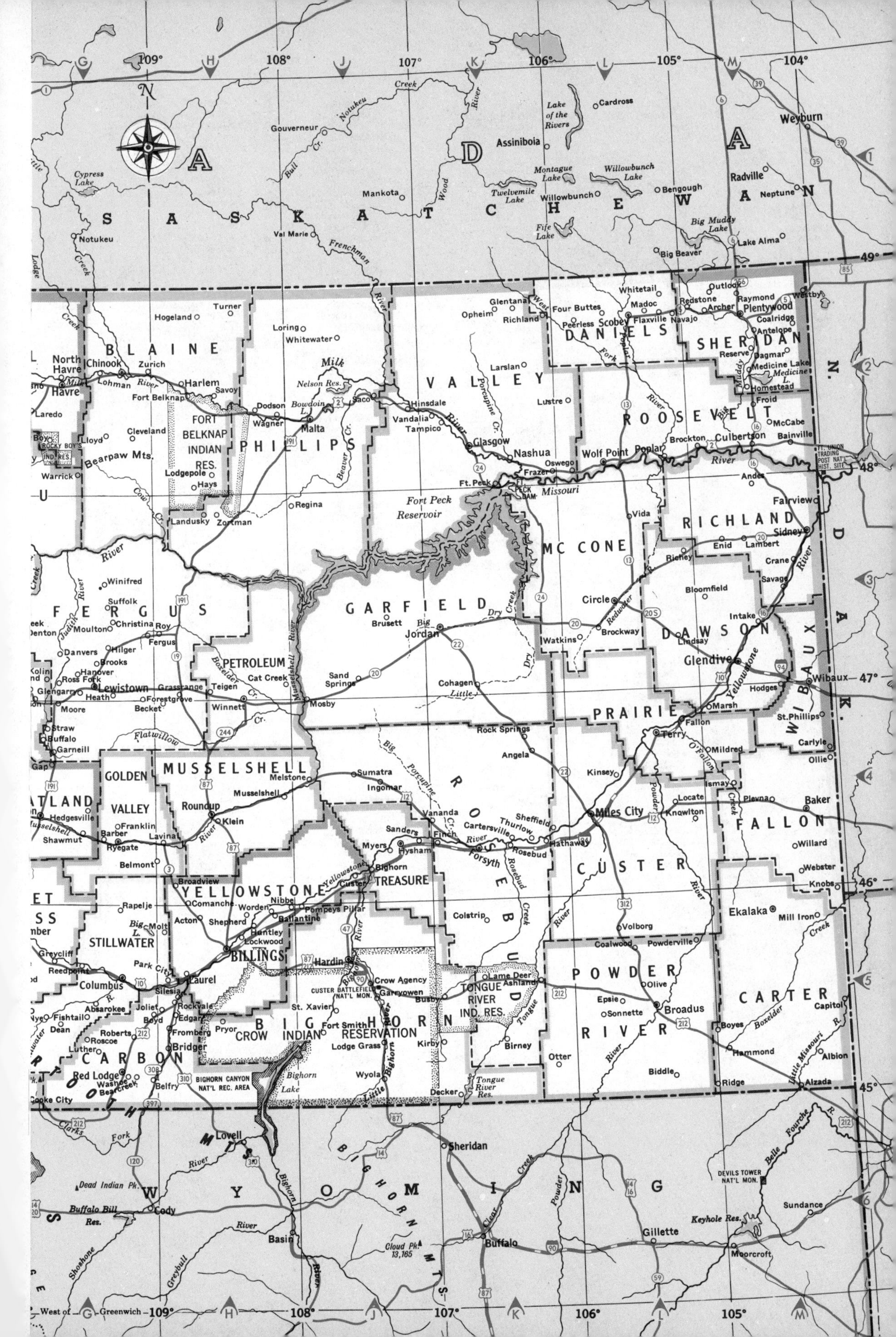
SASKATCHEWAN
Cypress Lake
Notukeu
Gouverneur
Notukeu Cr.
Bull Cr.
Mankota
Wood River
Val Marie
Frenchman River
Lake of the Rivers
Cardross
Assiniboia
Montague Lake
Willowbunch Lake
Twelvemile Lake
Willowbunch
Bengough
Fife Lake
Big Muddy Lake
Big Beaver
Weyburn
Radville
Neptune
Lake Alma
49°
109°
108°
107°
106°
105°
104°
48°
47°
46°
45°
BLAINE
North Havre
Chinook
Zurich
Havre
Milk River
Lohman
Harlem
Savoy
Fort Belknap
FORT BELKNAP INDIAN RES.
Laredo
ROCKY BOY'S IND. RES.
Lloyd
Cleveland
Bearpaw Mts.
Warrick
Lodgepole
Hays
Landusky
Zortman
Turner
Hogeland
Loring
Whitewater
PHILLIPS
Nelson Res.
Dodson
Wagner
Bowdoin L.
Malta
Saco
Beaver Cr.
Regina
VALLEY
Glentana
Opheim
Richland
Larslan
Hinsdale
Vandalia
Tampico
Glasgow
Nashua
Porcupine Cr.
Lustre
Frazer
Oswego
Ft. Peck
FT. PECK DAM
Missouri
Fort Peck Reservoir
DANIELS
Four Buttes
Peerless
Scobey
Whitetail
Madoc
Flaxville
Navajo
Poplar
SHERIDAN
Redstone
Outlook
Raymond
Westby
Archer
Plentywood
Coalridge
Antelope
Reserve
Dagmar
Medicine Lake
Homestead
ROOSEVELT
Froid
McCabe
Wolf Point
Poplar
Brockton
Culbertson
Bainville
FT. UNION TRADING POST NAT'L HIST. SITE
Andes
Vida
RICHLAND
Fairview
Sidney
Enid
Lambert
Richey
Crane
Savage
MC CONE
Circle
Bloomfield
Redwater
Brockway
Watkins
DAWSON
Intake
Lindsay
Glendive
Yellowstone
Hodges
Wibaux
WIBAUX
Marsh
Fallon
St. Phillips
Carlyle
Ollie
PRAIRIE
Terry
O'Fallon
Mildred
Ismay
FERGUS
Winifred
Suffolk
Judith River
Christina
Roy
Moulton
Denton
Fergus
Danvers
Hilger
Brooks
Hanover
Ross Fork
Lewistown
Glengarry
Heath
Grassrange
Forestgrove
Moore
Becket
Straw
Buffalo
Garneill
GARFIELD
Brusett
Big Dry
Jordan
Dry Creek
Sand Springs
Cohagen
Little Dry
PETROLEUM
Cat Creek
Teigen
Winnett
Boxelder Cr.
Musselshell River
Mosby
Flatwillow Cr.
GOLDEN VALLEY
MUSSELSHELL
Melstone
Musselshell
Roundup
Klein
Lavina
Hedgesville
Franklin
Barber
Ryegate
Shawmut
Belmont
Sumatra
Ingomar
Big Porcupine Cr.
Rock Springs
Angela
ROSEBUD
Vananda
Sanders
Myers
Hysham
Finch
Cartersville
Thurlow
Forsyth
Rosebud
Sheffield
Hathaway
Miles City
Kinsey
Locate
Knowlton
Plevna
Baker
FALLON
Willard
Webster
Knobs
Bighorn
TREASURE
Custer
CUSTER
Powder River
YELLOWSTONE
Broadview
Comanche
Worden
Nibbe
Pompeys Pillar
Ballantine
Acton
Shepherd
Huntley
Lockwood
BILLINGS
Colstrip
Volborg
Ekalaka
Mill Iron
STILLWATER
Rapelje
Molt
Big L.
Greycliff
Reedpoint
Park City
Laurel
Columbus
Silesia
Absarokee
Joliet
Rockvale
Fishtail
Dean
Boyd
Edgar
Fromberg
Roberts
Roscoe
Luther
Bridger
CARBON
Red Lodge
Washoe
Bearcreek
Belfry
Cooke City
Hardin
Crow Agency
Garryowen
CUSTER BATTLEFIELD NAT'L MON.
St. Xavier
Busby
Lame Deer
Ashland
TONGUE RIVER IND. RES.
BIG HORN
CROW INDIAN RESERVATION
Pryor
Fort Smith
Lodge Grass
Kirby
Wyola
Birney
Decker
Tongue River Res.
Bighorn Lake
BIGHORN CANYON NAT'L REC. AREA
POWDER RIVER
Coalwood
Powderville
Olive
Epsie
Sonnette
Broadus
Otter
Biddle
CARTER
Boyes
Boxelder Cr.
Capitol
Hammond
Albion
Ridge
Alzada
Little Missouri R.
NORTH DAKOTA
WYOMING
Lovell
Sheridan
Dead Indian Pk.
Cody
Buffalo Bill Res.
Basin
Greybull
Shoshone
Cloud Pk. 13,165
BIGHORN MTS.
Buffalo
Clear Creek
Powder
Gillette
Keyhole Res.
Moorcroft
Sundance
DEVILS TOWER NAT'L MON.
Belle Fourche R.
West of Greenwich

MONTANA

Place	Key
Maudlow, 75	E 4
Maxville, 44	C 4
McAllister, 62	E 5
McCabe, 18	M 2
McLeod, 7	G 5
Medicine Lake, 393	M 2
Melrose, 350	D 5
Melstone, 227	H 4
Melville, 150	F 4
Mildred, 22	M 4
Miles City⊙, 9,023	L 4
Mill Iron, 3	M 5
Milltown, 500	C 4
Miner, 12	E 5
Missoula⊙, 29,497	C 4
Moccasin, 100	F 3
Moiese, 20	B 3
Molt, 29	H 5
Monarch, 80	F 3
Monida, 10	D 6
Montague, 9	F 3
Moore, 219	G 4
Mosby, 3	J 4
Moulton, 16	G 3
Musselshell, 32	H 4
Myers, 4	J 4
Nashua, 513	K 2
Navajo, 11	M 2
Neihart, 109	F 4
Niarada, 6	B 3
Nibbe, 12	H 4
Norris, 37	E 5
North Havre, 1,073	G 2
Noxon, 250	A 3
Nyack, 31	C 2
Nye, 65	G 5
Oilmont, 75	E 2
Olive, 5	L 5
Ollie, 30	M 4
Olney, 250	B 2
Opheim, 306	K 2
Oswego, 75	L 2
Otter, 1	K 5
Outlook, 153	M 2
Ovando, 102	C 3
Pablo, 350	B 3
Paradise, 500	B 3
Park City, 400	H 5
Peerless, 100	L 2
Pendroy, 35	D 2
Perma, 25	B 3
Philipsburg⊙, 1,128	C 4
Plains, 1,046	B 3
Plentywood⊙, 2,381	M 2
Plevna, 189	M 4
Polaris, 20	C 5
Polebridge, 10	B 2
Polson⊙, 2,464	B 3
Pompeys Pillar, 69	J 5
Pony, 111	E 5
Poplar, 1,389	L 2
Potomac, 58	C 4
Powderville, 2	L 5
Power, 91	E 3
Pray, 5	F 5
Proctor, 108	B 3
Pryor, 150	H 5
Radersburg, 65	E 4
Ramsay, 140	D 4
Rapelje, 295	G 5
Ravalli, 150	B 3
Raymond, 34	M 2
Raynesford, 100	F 3
Red Lodge⊙, 1,844	G 5
Redstone, 77	M 2
Reedpoint, 125	G 5
Regina, 5	J 3
Reserve, 90	M 2
Rexford, 243	A 2
Richey, 389	L 3
Richland, 37	K 2
Ridge, 4	M 5
Ringling, 51	F 4
Roberts, 291	G 5
Rock Springs, 4	K 4
Rockvale, 10	H 5
Rocky Boy, 150	G 2
Rollins, 200	B 3
Ronan, 1,347	C 3
Roscoe, 30	G 5
Rosebud, 120	K 4
Ross Fork, 21	G 3
Roundup⊙, 2,116	H 4
Roy, 175	H 3
Rudyard, 550	F 2
Ryegate⊙, 261	G 4
Saco, 356	J 2
Saint Ignatius, 925	C 3
Saint Phillips, 10	M 4
Saint Regis, 500	A 3
Saint Xavier, 110	J 5
Saltese, 95	A 3
Sand Coulee, 500	E 3
Sanders, 50	J 4
Sand Springs, 24	J 3
Santa Rita, 125	D 2
Savage, 300	M 3
Savoy, 11	H 2
Scobey⊙, 1,486	L 2
Seeley Lake, 400	C 3
Shawmut, 60	G 4
Sheffield, 40	K 4
Shelby⊙, 3,111	E 2
Shepherd, 100	H 5
Sheridan, 636	D 5
Shonkin, 20	F 3
Sidney⊙, 4,543	M 3
Silesia, 90	H 5
Silver Bow Park, 5,524	D 4
Silver Star, 100	D 5
Simms, 299	E 3
Simpson, 70	F 2
Sixteen, 4	F 4
Somers, 950	B 2
Sonnette, 42	L 5
Southern Cross, 10	C 4
Springdale, 30	F 5
Square Butte, 48	F 3
Stanford⊙, 505	F 3
Stark, 51	B 3
Stevensville, 829	C 4
Stockett, 500	E 3
Straw, 8	G 4
Stryker, 60	B 2
Suffolk, 45	G 3
Sula, 6	B 5
Sumatra, 7	J 4
Sunburst, 604	E 2
Sun River, 190	E 3
Superior⊙, 993	B 3
Swan Lake, 200	C 3
Sweetgrass, 120	E 2
Tampico, 25	K 2
Tarkio, 25	B 4
Teigen, 20	H 3
Terry⊙, 870	L 4
Thompson Falls⊙, 1,356	A 3
Three Forks, 1,188	E 5
Thurlow, 40	K 4
Toston, 75	E 4
Townsend⊙, 1,371	E 4
Trailcreek, 10	B 2
Trego, 50	B 2
Trident, 50	E 5
Trout Creek, 200	A 3
Troy, 1,046	A 2
Turner, 175	H 2
Tuscor, 10	A 3
Twin Bridges, 613	D 5
Twodot, 118	F 4
Ulm, 450	E 3
Utica, 40	F 4
Valier, 651	D 2
Vananda, 50	K 4
Vandalia, 12	J 2
Vaughn, 345	E 3
Victor, 500	B 4
Vida, 52	L 3
Virgelle, 9	F 2
Virginia City⊙, 149	E 5
Volborg, 7	L 5
Wagner, 22	H 2
Walkerville, 1,097	D 4
Warmsprings, 1,600	D 4
Warrick, 7	G 2
Washoe, 22	G 5
Waterloo, 102	D 5
Watkins, 40	K 3
Webster, 30	M 4
Westby, 287	M 2
West Glacier, 348	C 2
West Yellowstone, 756	E 6
Whitefish, 3,349	B 2
Whitehall, 1,035	D 5
Whitepine, 50	A 3
White Sulphur Springs⊙, 1,200	E 4
Whitetail, 125	L 2
Whitewater, 100	J 2
Whitlash, 17	E 2
Wibaux⊙, 644	M 3
Wickes, 20	D 4
Willard, 5	M 4
Willow Creek, 325	E 5
Wilsall, 200	F 5
Windham, 60	F 3
Winifred, 190	G 3
Winnett⊙, 271	H 4
Winston, 115	E 4
Wisdom, 155	C 5
Wise River, 125	C 5
Wolf Creek, 200	D 3
Wolf Point⊙, 3,095	L 2
Woodside, 80	B 4
Worden, 350	H 5
Wyola, 110	J 5
Yaak, 75	A 2
Zortman, 25	H 3
Zurich, 89	G 2

OTHER FEATURES

Feature	Key
Absaroka (range)	F 5
Allen (mt.)	C 2
Arrow (creek)	F 3
Ashley (lake)	B 2
Battle (creek)	G 1
Bearhat (mt.)	C 2
Bearpaw (mts.)	G 2
Beartooth (mts.)	G 5
Beaver (creek)	J 2
Beaverhead (riv.)	D 5
Big (lake)	G 5
Big Belt (mts.)	E 4
Big Dry (creek)	K 3
Big Hole (riv.)	C 5
Big Hole Nat'l Battlefield	C 5
Bighorn (lake)	H 5
Bighorn (riv.)	J 5
Bighorn Canyon Nat'l Rec. Area	H 5
Big Muddy (riv.)	M 2
Big Porcupine (creek)	J 4
Birch (creek)	D 2
Bitterroot (range)	B 4
Bitterroot (riv.)	B 4
Blackfeet Ind. Res., 7,000	D 2
Blackfoot (riv.)	C 4
Blackmore (mt.)	F 5
Bowdoin (lake)	J 2
Boxelder (creek)	H 3
Boxelder (creek)	M 5
Bynum (res.)	D 2
Cabinet (mts.)	A 2
Canyon Ferry (lake)	E 4
Clark Fork (riv.)	A 3
Clarks Fork, Yellowstone (riv.)	G 6
Cottonwood (creek)	E 2
Cow (creek)	G 2
Crazy (peak)	F 4
Crow Ind. Res., 7,400	H 5
Custer Battlefield Nat'l Mon.	J 5
Cut Bank (creek)	D 2
Douglas (mt.)	F 5
Earthquake (lake)	E 6
Electric (peak)	F 6
Emigrant (peak)	F 5
Ennis (lake)	E 5
Flathead (lake)	C 3
Flathead (riv.)	B 3
Flathead Ind. Res., 15,494	B 3
Flatwillow (creek)	H 4
Fort Belknap Ind. Res., 1,398	H 2
Fort Peck (dam)	K 3
Fort Peck (res.)	K 3
Frenchman (riv.)	J 1
Fresno (res.)	F 2
Gallatin (peak)	E 5
Gallatin (riv.)	E 5
Georgetown (lake)	C 4
Gibson (res.)	D 3
Glacier Nat'l Park	C 2
Granite (peak)	F 5
Greenfield (lake)	D 3
Hauser (lake)	E 4
Haystack (peak)	A 3
Hebgen (dam)	E 6
Hebgen (lake)	E 6
Helena (lake)	E 4
Holter (lake)	D 4
Hungry Horse (res.)	C 2
Hurricane (mt.)	D 2
Hyalite (peak)	E 5
Jackson (mt.)	C 2
Jefferson (riv.)	D 5
Judith (riv.)	G 3
Kootenai (riv.)	A 2
Lewis (range)	C 2
Lima (res.)	D 6
Little Bighorn (riv.)	J 5
Little Bitterroot (lake)	B 2
Little Dry (creek)	K 3
Little Missouri (riv.)	M 5
Lockhart (mt.)	D 3
Lodge (creek)	G 1
Lone (mt.)	E 5
Lower Red Rock (lake)	E 6
Lower Saint Mary (lake)	C 2
Madison (riv.)	E 5
Malmstrom A.F.B., 8,374	E 3
Marias (riv.)	D 2
Mary Ronan (lake)	B 3
McDonald (lake)	B 2
McGloughlin (peak)	C 4
McGregor (lake)	B 3
Medicine (lake)	M 2
Milk (riv.)	J 2
Mission (range)	C 3
Missouri (riv.)	L 3
Musselshell (riv.)	J 3
Nelson (res.)	J 2
Ninepipe (res.)	C 3
O'Fallon (creek)	L 4
Pishkun (res.)	D 3
Poplar (riv.)	L 2
Porcupine (creek)	K 2
Powder (riv.)	L 4
Purcell (mts.)	A 2
Railley (mt.)	C 3
Red Rock (lakes)	E 6
Red Rock (riv.)	D 6
Redwater (riv.)	L 3
Rock (creek)	C 4
Rocky (mts.)	D 4
Rocky Boy's Ind. Res., 1,500	G 2
Rosebud (creek)	K 4
Sage (creek)	F 2
Saint Mary (lake)	C 2
Saint Mary (riv.)	C 1
Sandy (creek)	F 2
Sheep (mt.)	C 2
Shields (riv.)	F 4
Siyeh (mt.)	C 2
Smith (riv.)	E 3
Sphinx (mt.)	E 5
Stillwater (riv.)	G 5
Stimson (mt.)	C 2
Sun (riv.)	D 3
Swan (lake)	C 3
Swan (riv.)	C 3
Teton (riv.)	E 3
Tiber (res.)	E 2
Tongue (riv.)	K 5
Tongue River (res.)	K 5
Tongue River Ind. Res., 1,920	K 5
Upper Red Rock (lake)	E 6
Ward (peak)	A 3
Waterton-Glacier Int'l Peace Park	C 2
Whitefish (lake)	B 2
Willow (creek)	E 2
Willow Creek (res.)	D 3
Yellowstone (riv.)	M 3
Yellowstone Nat'l Park	F 6

tion and mapping studies to help determine management practices, crop potentialities, and land values. In 1968 there were 58 soil conservation districts, incorporating 90,436,476 acres, in which additional studies were being made.

Irrigation, which was begun by the Jesuit missionaries in the Bitterroot Valley in 1842, has expanded steadily. The Big Ditch, near Billings, was the most ambitious of the early private projects. The Carey Act of 1894 gave federal assistance for the Valier project, containing 68,000 acres, and for smaller areas at Billings and Big Timber. Through the National Reclamation Act of 1902 the Bureau of Reclamation had made water available for 260,307 acres by 1955. The larger projects, with their acreages, were Milk River (78,261), Sun River (76,406), Lower Yellowstone (32,591), Huntley (25,324), and Buffalo Rapids (23,052). The Bureau of Indian Affairs has promoted irrigation on Indian lands to the extent of 107,840 acres on the Flathead Indian Reservation, 44,264 acres on the Crow Indian Reservation, and 41,264 acres on the Blackfeet Indian Reservation. In 1934, under drought and depression conditions, the Montana Water Conservation Board was established; thirty years later it was servicing about 450,000 acres. In 1960, croplands consisted of a record 15,000,000 acres, irrigated lands having increased to about 1,900,000 acres. Total land devoted to grazing was in excess of 60,000,000 acres.

2. POPULATION AND POLITICAL DIVISIONS

Population Characteristics.—Of the 694,409 persons reported in Montana by the 1970 census, 663,043 were whites and 1,995 were Negroes. There are about 25,000 Indians in the state. Between 1960 and 1970, Montana gained only 2.9 per cent in population. Of the foreign-born whites, Canada, Britain, and the Scandinavian countries account for the largest numbers.

Whereas, in 1950, 43.7 per cent of the total population lived in urban communities, by 1970 the urban population represented more than 53 per cent of the total. The rural population continued to decline. Men numbered 347,005 and women 347,404 in 1970.

Political Divisions.—Montana is divided into 56 counties. There are about 130 incorporated cities and towns in the state.

Principal Cities.—Cities and towns are classified and incorporated in relation to population and taxable property valuation. First-class cities, those with populations above 10,000 at the 1970 census, include Billings, Great Falls, Missoula, Butte, Helena, Bozeman, Havre, and Kalispell. Billings, with 61,481 residents, is the most populous city.

The commission-manager form of government was adopted by Bozeman in 1921 and by Helena in 1953; other cities have governments of the mayor-council type.

At Great Falls, which takes its name from the nearby Great Falls of the Missouri, large quantities of hydroelectric power are generated to be used by factories, a huge smelter, and railways and to light a vast farming region. Butte, high on the west slope of the Rockies, was built on the copper industry, and was the smelter city of Anaconda. Billings, on the Yellowstone, is the center of a large wheat- and beet-growing and stock-raising area. Missoula, in the extreme western part of the state, is the seat of the University of Montana and the center of extensive crop, livestock, and dairying enterprises and of a great forest area. Helena, the capital, is a distributing center for a large stock-raising area. Bozeman is the center of a rich farming area and the seat of Montana State University. Kalispell is the center of a lumbering and recreational area.

Counties.—Montana's 56 counties operate as administrative units under elected three-member boards of county commissioners. The county manager system is permissible, and Petroleum County has used it since 1942. The largest county is Beaverhead, with 5,556 square miles, and the smallest is Silver Bow, with 716 square miles. The counties vary in population from Yellowstone, with 79,016 persons, to Petroleum, with 894.

GROWTH OF POPULATION SINCE 1870

Year	Population	Year	Population
1870	20,595	1940	559,456
1900	243,329	1950	591,024
1920	548,889	1960	674,767
1930	537,606	1970	694,409

Gain, 1960–1970: 2.9% (U.S. gain, 13.3%). **Density,** 1970: 4.8 persons per square mile (U.S. density, 56.2).

URBAN-RURAL DISTRIBUTION

Year	Percent urban	Percent rural
1920	31.3 (U.S., 51.2)	68.7
1930	33.7 (U.S., 56.2)	66.3
1940	37.8 (U.S., 56.6)	62.2
1950	43.7 (U.S., 64.0)	56.3
1960	50.2 (U.S., 69.9)	49.8
1970	53.4 (U.S., 73.5)	46.6

LARGEST CENTERS OF POPULATION

City or Metropolitan area[1]	1970	1960	1950
Billings (city)	61,581	52,851	31,834
Metropolitan area	87,367	...	...
Great Falls (city)	60,091	55,244	39,214
Metropolitan area	81,804	...	...
Missoula	29,497	27,090	22,485
Butte	23,368	27,877	33,251
Helena	22,730	20,227	17,581
Bozeman	18,670	13,361	11,325
Havre	10,558	10,740	8,086
Kalispell	10,526	10,151	9,737

[1] Standard metropolitan statistical area.

3. GOVERNMENT

Constitution and Elections.—Montana's constitution was formulated by a convention in 1889; of average length, it consists of 21 articles. It may be amended by a convention called by a vote of two thirds of the legislature and the approval of the people, or by referendum by a two-thirds vote of the legislature and a majority vote of the people, or by initiative. No more than three amendments may be submitted at one time. By 1967 a total of 37 amendments had been passed, and 15 proposals had been rejected.

Voters in Montana must be 18 years of age, citizens of the United States, and residents of the state for one year and of the county for 30 days immediately preceding an election. The initiative and referendum were adopted in 1906, and women suffrage was established in 1914. The political party primary election was instituted for state purposes in 1912 and for presidential nominations in 1954; the latter was repealed in 1959. Montana has two members in the United States House of Representatives. See also REFERENDUM.

Executive.—The executive department consists of the governor, lieutenant governor, secretary of state, attorney general, treasurer, auditor, and superintendent of public instruction, all of whom serve four-year terms. Of the many constitutional and appointive boards, the state Board of Examiners, consisting of the governor, secretary of state, and attorney general, is the most powerful. With the state controller, it prepares the budget and controls expenditures.

GOVERNORS OF MONTANA

TERRITORIAL		
Sidney Edgerton	Republican	1864–1865
Thomas F. Meagher (acting)	Democrat	1865–1866
Green Clay Smith	"	1866–1869
James M. Ashley	Republican	1869–1870
Benjamin F. Potts	"	1870–1883
John Schuyler Crosby	"	1883–1884
B. Platt Carpenter	"	1884–1885
Samuel T. Hauser	Democrat	1885–1887
Preston H. Leslie	"	1887–1889
Benjamin F. White	Republican	1889
STATE		
Joseph K. Toole	Democrat	1889–1893
John E. Rickards	Republican	1893–1897
Robert B. Smith	Democrat and Populist	1897–1901
Joseph K. Toole[1]	Democrat	1901–1908
Edwin L. Norris[2]	"	1908–1913
Samuel V. Stewart	"	1913–1921
Joseph M. Dixon	Republican	1921–1925
John E. Erickson[1]	Democrat	1925–1933
Frank H. Cooney[3]	"	1933–1935
W. Elmer Holt[4]	"	1935–1937
Roy E. Ayers	"	1937–1941
Samuel C. Ford	Republican	1941–1949
John W. Bonner	Democrat	1949–1953
J. Hugo Aronson	Republican	1953–1961
Donald G. Nutter	"	1961–1962
Tim M. Babcock[5]	"	1962–1969
Forrest H. Anderson	Democrat	1969–1973
Thomas L. Judge	"	1973–

[1] Resigned. [2] Succeeded from post of lieutenant governor; elected governor for term beginning in 1909. [3] Succeeded from post of lieutenant governor; died in office. [4] Succeeded from post of president of the Senate. [5] Succeeded from post of lieutenant governor; elected governor in 1964.

Legislature.—The bicameral Legislative Assembly meets in odd-numbered years for a 60-day session. Montana's 56 counties are divided into 31 districts from which candidates for the 55 seats in the Senate are elected to 4-year terms. The House of Representatives has 104 members serving 2-year terms. A 1957 law establishing a Legislative Council was approved by the courts after several years of adverse ruling on previous laws.

Judiciary.—The judicial department consists of the Senate as a court of impeachment, a Supreme Court, 18 district courts, and justices of the peace. The 5 Supreme Court judges and 28 district judges are elected for six-year terms. Justices of the peace are also elective, for two-year terms in the district in which they serve.

Taxation and Revenue.—The appointive, three-member Board of Equalization, working with the state controller, exercises general supervision over taxing policies and collections, and in a biennial report to the Legislative Assembly makes recommendations for suitable legislation. The boards of county commissioners prepare the budget in each county and lay the necessary levies.

Approximately three fifths of all revenue for state and local governmental purposes is derived from the general property tax. Counties, municipalities, and school districts depend almost entirely on this tax. There is no general sales tax in Montana, but individual income and corporation taxes have been increased. Selective sales taxes include a gasoline tax and a tax on cigarettes.

4. EDUCATION, HEALTH, AND WELFARE

Education.—The first schools in Montana were opened in 1863, and a territorial school system was established two years later. By 1868 there were 15 schools with 2,000 pupils in attendance. Free county high schools were created in 1898, and by 1900 enrollment in the state public school system totaled 39,000. Enrollment continued to increase, with some ups and downs, rising to 180,000 in the 1970's.

PUBLIC SCHOOL ENROLLMENT IN MONTANA, 1940–1970

	1940	1950	1960	1970
Elementary	75,000	80,000	109,000	121,000
Secondary	32,000	26,000	36,000	56,000

Public schools are maintained for persons between the ages of 6 and 21, and attendance is required between the ages of 8 and 16, inclusive. The system is under the state Board of Education, an appointive board of eight members created in 1893. Three additional members serve ex officio: the governor as chairman, the superintendent of public instruction as secretary, and the attorney general.

The public elementary and secondary schools are operated under a district system. Tax support comes mostly from the districts. In 1919 additional county funds were made available for poorer districts. A program of state aid, adopted in 1949, ensures more uniform support for all districts.

The state system of higher education was unified in 1913 as the University of Montana, directed by a chancellor. A council of unit presidents acting under the direct control of the Board of Education later replaced the chancellor, and in 1965 the complex became known as the Montana University System. It consists of the University of Montana, Missoula; Montana State University, Bozeman; Montana College of Mineral Science and Technology, Butte; Western Montana College, Dillon; Eastern Montana College, Billings; and Northern Montana College, Havre. Three junior colleges are associated with local high schools: Custer County, in Miles City; Dawson County, in Glendive; and Flathead Valley Community College, in Kalispell. The Roman Catholic Church operates two colleges, Carroll College in Helena and the College of Great Falls. Rocky Mountain College in Billings is sponsored by three Protestant groups, the Congregational, Methodist, and Presbyterian churches. Total enrollment in Montana's colleges and universities rose from 345 in 1900 to over 30,000 in the 1970's.

A state Board of Institutions supervises the Children's Home at Twin Bridges, the Industrial School for Boys at Miles City, a vocational school for girls at Helena, a school for the deaf and blind in Great Falls, and a school for the retarded in Boulder.

Libraries.—The larger libraries in the state are all associated with governmental or educational institutions and have special interests. At the University of Montana, the Northwest history and Law School collections are notable, while the Montana State University collection is strong in agriculture and science. The collections of the Historical Society of Montana Library and the Montana State Law Library, both in Helena, are excellent. The Montana State Library Extension Commission has a large collection for loans to local libraries. The Parmly Billings Memorial Library in Billings excels in local history and petroleum industry materials. The Great Falls, Missoula, and Kalispell libraries have good local history collections.

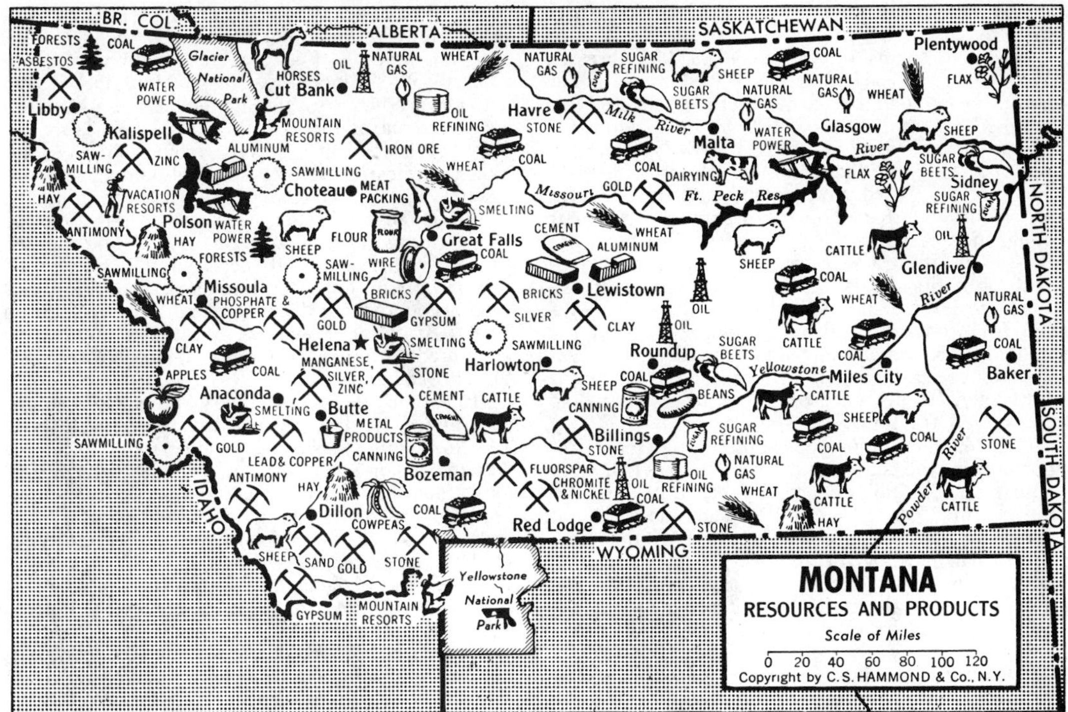

Public Health and Welfare.—The state maintains a mental hospital, a tuberculosis sanitarium, a home for the aged, and a soldiers' home, and there are federal veterans hospitals at Miles City and Helena. The major state correctional institution is the state penitentiary at Deer Lodge.

The state Board of Health, created in 1901, is in general charge of health control work, in which it cooperates with cities and counties. It early established a bacteriological laboratory for tuberculosis control, and its long-time work in sanitary engineering has been combined with water and sewage problems in an Environmental Sanitation Division. Other important divisions are Vital Statistics, established in 1907; Pure Food and Drugs, 1911; Entomology, 1913; Child Health, 1917; Industrial Health, 1939; Public Health Nursing, 1946; Health Education, 1947; Narcotics, 1949; Administration, 1963; and Public Institutions, 1963.

The Department of Public Welfare, created in 1937, coordinates federal, state, and county services. Major state services include aid to dependent children, aid to the blind, vocational rehabilitation, and silicosis benefits. The Unemployment Compensation Commission and the Industrial Accident Board assist in their respective areas.

5. ECONOMIC ACTIVITIES

From the beginning agriculture has been Montana's chief economic activity, and it still accounts for a fifth of the state's income. Mining has also been important since the 19th century, but industry became a major factor in the economy only in the mid-20th century.

Total state personal income rose from $318 million in 1940 to $957 million in 1950, and to $1,842 million in 1966. The 1966 figure represented a per capita income of $2,623, as compared with $2,963 for the nation as a whole.

Labor Force.—In 1960, Montana's total civilian labor force numbered 248,000, of whom 17.6 percent were employed in agriculture, as compared with 24.8 percent in 1950 and 31.8 percent in 1940. This shift reflected not only the increasing mechanization and efficiency of farming operations but also the rise in nonagricultural activities. Between 1950 and 1968 employment in nonagricultural establishments rose from 147,000 to 189,700, an overall increase of about 32 percent.

In 1968, mining accounted for 2.9 percent of the labor force, construction for 6.4 percent, manufacturing for 10.1 percent, transportation and utilities for 9 percent, wholesale trade for 3.2 percent, retail trade for 17.1 percent, finance and realty for 3.5 percent, services and miscellaneous activities for 17.1 percent, and government for 10.8 percent.

Despite the considerable diversity in fields of employment, trade union membership is held by some 50 percent of those employed in nonagricultural establishments. The national average is only about 35 percent.

Agriculture and Lumbering.—Over half of Montana's agricultural income is derived from crops, of which wheat, grown largely in the central, eastern, and northeastern parts of the state, is by far the most important. Montana is the third largest producer of wheat in the nation, outranked only by North Dakota and Kansas. Other crops, also cultivated mainly in the eastern and central sections, include, in the order of value, barley, sugar beets, hay, potatoes, alfalfa seed, mustard seed, flaxseed, dry edible beans, and oats. In the mountain valleys west of the Continental Divide fruit, particularly apples and cherries, is grown. Second only to wheat as a source of farm income are beef cattle and calves, most of which are raised in the eastern part of the state. Dairying and the raising of sheep and lambs rank next among the livestock industries of Montana.

Land in farms rose from 46,452,000 acres in 1940 to 65,833,760 acres in 1964. On the other hand, the number of farms in the state declined from 41,823 in 1940 to 27,020 in 1964, while the average value rose from $8,373 to $105,230 in the same period. Of the total acreage in 1954, 14 per cent was used as cropland and 76 per cent as pasturage. Most Montana farmers own their land; in 1954 only 14.5 per cent of the farm operators in the state were tenants, as compared with a national average of 24.0 per cent. In 1964 the level-of-living index (1959 = 100) was 144 for Montana rural homes, while that for the United States as a whole was 122. Electricity was used on at least 95 per cent of the farms in the state, and 92 per cent of Montana's farms had trucks and tractors.

The lumber industry is among the most important in the state, and production of lumber rose from 271 million board feet in 1939 to 833 million in 1956. Large mills, such as those at Libby and Bonner, account for half of the total. More than half of the lumber products are used within the state, largely by the railways and mines. Montana's major wood products include pulpwood, fuel wood, plyboard, posts, and timbers for mines.

Mining.—Montana's fame as a mining state was first based on metals, but since 1900 coal, petroleum, and natural gas have been produced in quantities. The total value of all minerals produced through the year 1965 is placed at $6,787,960,000. The Anaconda Copper Mining Company, which was organized in 1895 and changed its name to the Anaconda Company in 1955, provided much of the capital and leadership in mineral development. The Montana Bureau of Mines and Geology in Butte, cooperating with the United States Bureau of Mines and utilizing the facilities of the Montana School of Mines, conducts extensive survey, mapping, and statistical studies.

Gold, discovered as early as 1852, was the first mineral mined in Montana, and its placer creeks of Alder Gulch (Virginia City) and Last Chance Gulch (Helena) were among the richest in the world. The total amount of gold produced in Montana in the period 1862–1960 is estimated at 17,619,401 fine ounces, valued at $401,236,587. Silver was first mined at Argenta in 1864, and Montana ranks second among the states in its production. Associated with gold and copper lodes, the most important sources of silver have been in the mines of Philipsburg and Butte. The total amount of silver produced from 1862 through 1960 is estimated at 829,407,040 troy ounces, valued at $619,713,030. The production of both gold and silver and their values have followed economic cycles closely.

Copper took the lead among the metals with the discovery of the Anaconda lode by Marcus Daly in 1881, the building of the experimental smelter by William A. Clark, the completion of the huge reduction works at Anaconda in 1884, and the choice of Great Falls as the center for electrolytic processes in 1890. The extremely deep mines in Butte have made the production of copper increasingly expensive there, and the beginnings of open-pit mining in the Berkeley pit in 1955 opened new sources of low-cost ores. Copper is first in value in the period 1862–1960, with a production of 7,579,960 short tons valued at $2,478,799,684.

Lead has been an important byproduct of copper mining in Montana, production through 1960 reaching a total of 914,437 tons with a value of $142,600,584. Zinc, of which Montana is the leading producer in the United States, also has become a major metal, with a total value through 1960 of $503,251,056, derived from 2,661,159 tons. The American Smelting and Refining Company's smelter at East Helena processes these minerals.

Manganese reached a peak production of 200,000 tons in the state in 1918. The United States produces only 10 per cent of its needs of this militarily important mineral, and the Butte ores accounted for 99.3 per cent of this total in 1948. By 1960, however, Montana's production amounted to only 29,036 tons, about one tenth of the national total.

Enormous deposits of phosphate rock began to be utilized in 1951, when the Victor Chemical Works plant producing elemental phosphorus was opened near Butte; since 1955 about 550,000 long tons have been used annually. Large deposits of chromite ore in Stillwater and Carbon counties, which were opened during World War II, have been reopened for stock-piling purposes. In 1955 the Anaconda Aluminum Company, a subsidiary of the Anaconda Company, completed a $65 million refinery at Columbia Falls with a capacity of 120,000,000 tons annually. An aluminum rod rolling mill was constructed at Great Falls to assist in fabricating the metal.

Coal is produced in 50 of Montana's 56 counties. The principal fields are at Sand Coulee, Red Lodge, and Roundup, and the open-pit Colstrip mine has been the chief producer. Coal reserves in the state have been estimated at 222,046,940,000 tons, consisting of 2,362,610,000 tons of bituminous, 132,151,060,000 tons of subbituminous, and 87,553,270,000 tons of lignite. Production reached a peak of 4,844,000 tons in 1944, but by 1965 it had declined to only 350,000 tons.

Montana has many other minerals, including the largest vermiculite deposit in the United States, near Libby. Sapphires and garnets have been produced for use as abrasives and gems, and there are also deposits of gypsum, talc, limestone, tungsten, fluorite, and iron ore.

Interest in the commercial production of petroleum in Montana began as early as 1892, but the first significant exploitation did not take place until 1915. Major fields include Elk Basin, Kevin-Sunburst, Cat Creek, Cut Bank, the very productive Williston Basin area, and Bell Creek, which opened in 1967. With the entrance of Williston Basin into production in 1951, the state's output of petroleum rose from 8,922,000 barrels in that year to 30,240,000 barrels in 1960. Of 12 refineries in Montana, with a combined capacity of 70,350 barrels daily, the largest is that of the Carter Oil Company in Billings, which has a 20,000-barrel capacity. Major pipelines connect Montana's refineries and fields with out-of-state markets and refineries.

Natural gas, which was first used in Montana in 1915, is the fuel supply of the major cities and industrial plants. It is distributed by the Montana Power Company in the central and western part of the state and by the Montana-Dakota Utilities Company in the east. Large additional purchases have been made in Canada and Wyoming to supply the Montana market.

Manufacturing.—Montana's manufactures have been closely allied to the raw materials from

Kodachrome by Ray Atkeson © N.G.S.

Reproduced by Special Permission from "National Geographic Magazine"

Fantastic limestone architecture in Montana's famous Lewis and Clark Cavern, one of the largest in the United States.

MONTANA

Northern Pacific Railway

Autumn in the Montana Rockies.

its forests, mines, and farms. Much of its manufacturing enterprise is concerned with refining these materials in order to reduce their weight, bulk, and perishability before shipping them out of the state for the more expensive fabrication and skilled finishing. Products of this type include copper, zinc, aluminum, lead, and phosphates. Abundant electrical power and natural gas supplies, however, encourage the completion of the production process with lumber, sugar beets, wheat, and petroleum, and an expanding market provides outlets for increased dairy production, meat packing, and vegetable canning. Between 1947 and 1966, value added by manufacture rose from $91,000,000 to $245,000,000.

Of the 20,200 persons employed in the state's manufacturing plants in 1960, lumber and wood products accounted for more than 35 percent, primary metals for 18 percent, food products for 21 percent, printing and publishing for 8 percent, petroleum refining for 5 percent. Six counties—Cascade, Yellowstone, Missoula, Deer Lodge, Flathead, and Lincoln—account for two thirds of the manufacturing plants.

Power.—Electricity was first generated in Montana at Butte in 1880, and the first important hydroelectrical installation was made at Black Eagle Falls near Great Falls in 1890. The formation of the Montana Power Company in 1912 provided capital and direction for additional services, and output rose further with the construction of power plants by the federal government and the growth of the Rural Electrification Administration cooperative movement. Of the 6,040 million kilowatt-hours of electricity produced in Montana in 1960, private plants largely under the control of the three big utilities—Montana Power Company, Montana-Dakota Utilities Company, and Pacific Power and Light Company—accounted for 4,302 million, and industrial plants for 48 million. The remaining 1,690 million kilowatt-hours were produced by the federal government's plants at Canyon Ferry, Fort Peck, Hungry Horse, and Marias River.

Montana's potential hydroelectrical energy is estimated at 6,306,000 kilowatts, of which the installed capacity in 1960 totaled 1,234,950 kilowatts, or nearly 20 percent. Steam plants with a capacity of 115,800 kilowatts raised the total installed generating capacity to over 1,350,000 kilowatts. The government's Hungry Horse plant has a capacity of 285,000 kilowatts, the largest in the state; the Montana Power Company's Kerr Dam at Polson generates 168,000 kilowatts, giving it second place; and the Great Falls group of four dams, also maintained by Montana Power, has a potential of 144,000 kilowatts. See also DAMS.

Banking and Insurance.—Montana is served by about 120 commercial banks. Approximately two thirds of these are chartered by the state, the rest being national banks. There are also about 20 savings and loan associations and more than 100 credit unions.

The Western Life Insurance Company of Helena for many years was Montana's only insurance company. State-chartered companies now include Transwestern at Billings, Continental Reserve at Great Falls, Glacier Life and Capri at Missoula, and Gallatin National at Bozeman.

Trade and Tourism.—Between 1939 and 1948 the number of retail trade establishments in the state declined from 8,481 to 7,841, but total sales rose from $220,008,000 to $599,285,000. By 1958 the number of establishments was back up to 8,261, and sales had grown to $862,577,000. Four cities—Billings, Butte, Great Falls, and Missoula—accounted for 40 percent of total sales. The number of wholesale outlets remained almost the same between 1939 and 1948, rising from 1,336 to 1,338, but by 1958 it had increased to 1,606, with sales aggregating $762,943,000. Billings has the largest concentration of wholesale sales, with 20 percent of the total in 1958.

The tourist business in Montana really began in the 1850's, when wealthy persons from the East and from Europe came to hunt for big game and view the natural wonders of the region. During the 1890's it was reckoned as big business, worth $250,000 each year. By 1920 the dude ranch had been invented, and tourism was worth $1,000,000, and by 1935 an estimated 1,295,000 tourists came to spend more than $25,000,000. In 1964, about 3,500,000 visitors spent nearly $110,000,000, making the industry third in rank in the state, exceeded in value only by agriculture and mining.

For additional production statistics, see THE AMERICANA ANNUAL.

6. TRANSPORTATION AND COMMUNICATIONS

Transportation.—Historically, Montana has had excellent transportation facilities with its long rivers, low passes, early national roads, and transcontinental railroads. The first steamboat approached Fort Benton, at the head of navigation of the Missouri, in 1859. In 1880 the Utah & Northern Railroad, now part of the Union Pacific Railroad, reached Dillon, and three years later the Northern Pacific Railway was completed across the state (see also section on *History*). Of the seven railroads serving the state, five provide major connections nationally. Besides the Union Pacific and the Northern Pacific, they are the Chicago, Burlington & Quincy Railroad, the Chicago, Milwaukee, St. Paul and Pacific Railroad, and the Great Northern Railway.

The state Highway Commission was created in 1913 and received needed assistance from the Federal-Aid Road Act of 1916. The first surfaced highway in the state, a 26-mile road between Butte and Anaconda, was constructed in 1923. By 1966 there were 11,140 miles of surfaced roads, 640 of which were in the unfinished Interstate system.

Three major airlines—Northwest, Western, and Frontier—service the state. The Montana Aeronautics Commission, established in 1946, coordinates the work of the state's airports and standardizes requirements for pilots. As of 1968, there were 116 public and 325 private "flying farmer" airfields in Montana.

Communications.—The first post office in Montana was opened at Bannack in 1863, and the telegraph reached Virginia City in 1866. The *Montana Post,* originally published in Virginia City in 1864, was the first stable newspaper in Montana. Over the years a great many papers were founded, but by 1968 the total number had settled down to 15 daily, 8 Sunday, and 78 weekly papers. The Great Falls *Tribune* has the largest circulation. Among other prominent papers are the Billings *Gazette,* the *Montana Standard* of Butte, the Helena *Independent-Record,* and the *Missoulian.*

Telephone service first began as a city system in Miles City in 1881, and in Butte in 1882. By 1968 there were 316,920 telephones, of which 269,026—over 82 percent—were owned by the

Mountain States Telephone and Telegraph Company. The remainder were serviced by the Rural Electrification Administration and 19 small companies.

The first radio station in Montana was opened by KFBB in Great Falls in 1922. By 1967, 45 stations serviced the state. The first television stations were opened at Butte, Billings, Great Falls, and Missoula in 1953–1954. By 1967 there were 8 stations.

7. CULTURAL LIFE

A dramatic illustration of the interest which many of Montana's pioneers had in culture was the 200-mile midwinter trip taken in 1860 by James and Granville Stuart to secure four or five books. Some of the best actors of the day came to the mining camps, and the Langurishes in Ming's Opera House in Helena and John Maguire in the Grand Opera House in Butte continued the tradition later in the century. The frontier military forts in approved West Point fashion furnished centers where music, plays, libraries, balls, and dinners were enjoyed. Montana's early newspapers were numerous, and vigorous editorials provided intellectual stimulus. Strong churches emerged with the missionary assistance of such leaders as Father Pierre Jean De Smet, Bishop Daniel S. Tuttle, and the Rev. W. W. Van Orsdel. Montana's rapid population growth and increase in per capita wealth caused many communities to mature culturally at an early date. The establishment of a good library in Helena in 1868, followed by one in Butte in 1877, illustrates this movement. Both cities have maintained important musical organizations for many years.

Ray Manley, from Frederic Lewis

The Hillgarde Mountains near West Yellowstone.

Artists of note came early to Montana, among them George Catlin in 1832, Karl Bodmer in 1833, and John James Audubon in 1843. Edgar S. Paxson and Charles M. Russell are the best known Montana artists, and galleries in Great Falls and Helena display Russell's paintings and sculpture. Writing in Montana has been extensive, limited largely to the Western theme. Joseph Kinsey Howard's *Montana, High, Wide, and Handsome* and *Strange Empire* and A. B. Guthrie's *Big Sky* and *Way West* are probably the best known books written in the state. Interest in ceramics far beyond Montana's borders is stimulated by the Archie Bray Foundation in Helena.

The university system and the private colleges, the women's clubs, a state park movement, and a strong community museum movement all add stimulus to cultural development. The Montana Historical Society, founded in 1865, is one of the oldest in the West, and its library and museum are nationally known. Its magazine, *Montana, the Magazine of Western History,* has a nationwide circulation. The restoration of Virginia City by Charles Bovey has revived interest in pioneer life, and the Museum of the Plains Indian in Browning has focused attention on the cultural contributions of the Indians. A distinctive organization, the Montana Institute of the Arts, formed in 1948, has unified and stimulated work in a wide range of cultural interests.

8. PLACES OF INTEREST

Montana's attractions include Glacier National Park and a portion of Yellowstone National Park (qq.v.), numerous historic sites, fishing and hunting facilities, and many features typical of the West, such as rodeos, Indian ceremonials, mountain climbing, camping, and skiing. Seven Indian reservations (Blackfeet, Crow, Flathead, Fort Belknap, Fort Peck, Rocky Boy's, and Northern Cheyenne), two national monuments (Custer Battlefield and Big Hole Battlefield), the Montana National Bison Range, and a state park system, of which Morrison Cave (Lewis and Clark Cavern) State Park near Whitehall is the best known unit, form centers of interest.

There are a large number of dude ranches in the state. Annual rodeos are held at, among other places, Hardin in June; Butte, Kalispell, Lewistown, Livingston, Red Lodge, Wolf Point in July, and Cooke in August. Anaconda stages a winter carnival in January, and state fairs take place in August at Billings, Great Falls, Miles City, and Missoula. Festivals of an annual nature include the Good Friday service at St. Ignatius Mission, the Festival of the Nations at Red Lodge, and that of the Montana Institute of the Arts, which moves to various towns.

Museums of art and history include the Montana Historical Society Museum in Helena, the Charles M. Russell Gallery in Great Falls, and the Museum of the Plains Indian at Browning, headquarters of the Blackfeet Indian Reservation. The leading science museum is at the Montana College of Mineral Science in Butte. The restoration of Virginia City in Madison County has made the entire town a cultural center.

9. FAMOUS MEN AND WOMEN

Montana was settled relatively late, and many of its prominent citizens were born elsewhere. Such Montanans by adoption include the governors Sidney Edgerton (1818-1900), Samuel T. Hauser (1833–1914), Benjamin F. Potts (1836–1887), and Joseph K. Toole (1851–1929); the senators William Andrews Clark (1839–1925), Thomas J. Walsh (1859–1933), James E. Murray (1876–1961), Burton K. Wheeler (1882–), and Mike Mansfield (1903–), and the mine owners Marcus Daly (1841–1900) and Frederick A. Heinze (1869–1914). Frank Bird Linderman (1869–1938), Grace Stone Coates (1881–), and Joseph Kinsey Howard (1906–1951) won distinction in the field of letters; Harold G. Merriam (1883–), in that of education; and Edgar S. Paxson (1852–1919), Ralph De Camp (1858–1936), and Charles M. Russell (1865–1926), as painters of Indians and other Western subjects.

Among native Montanans of note are William Boyce Thompson (Virginia City, 1869–1930), miner and philanthropist; Jeannette Rankin (near Missoula, 1880–), the first woman elected to Congress; Will James (near Great Falls, 1892–1942), writer and artist; Gary Cooper (Helena, 1901–1961), actor; and Myrna Loy (Radersburg, 1905–), actress.

10. HISTORY

Access to Montana was hindered by the arid Great Plains to the east and the mountains to the west, although the great rivers provided travel routes. Probably the first white men to leave a record of their visit were the brothers François and Louis Joseph de La Vérendrye, who appear to have crossed southeastern Montana in 1742. French and Spanish traders and prospectors arrived before 1800. Following the Louisiana Purchase of 1803, the Lewis and Clark Expedition (q.v.) of 1804–1806 provided the first adequate record of the area. United States rights to the region were recognized by Great Britain in the Convention of 1818 and the Oregon Treaty of 1846.

Stabilized fur trading began at the post established by Manuel Lisa at the mouth of the Bighorn in 1807 and at those built by the British on the Kootenai in 1808. The traders of the Missouri Fur Company (Lisa, John Colter, Andrew Henry, and Pierre Menard) and the Rocky Mountain Fur Company (William Henry Ashley, Jim Bridger, Jedediah Smith, and others) mapped the trails over the area. In 1829 the Western Department of the American Fur Company established Fort Union near the mouth of the Yellowstone. This company and its successors, in which the Chouteau family of St. Louis was prominent, dominated the upper Missouri Valley until the middle of the century. Fort Benton on the Missouri and Fort Sarpy on the Yellowstone were important centers. Meanwhile, David Thompson led in the British fur trade. His North West Company, which established Salish House near Thompson Falls in 1809, was merged with the Hudson's Bay Company in 1821. Great brigades under such leaders as Alexander Ross, Peter Skene Ogden, and John Work came up the Columbia to its headwaters, but after 1846 British influence receded rapidly.

Missionary efforts were contemporaneous with the fur trade. Urged by Flatheads, Father Pierre Jean De Smet established St. Mary's Mission in the Bitterroot Valley in 1841. It was closed in 1850, however, and sold to John Owen, who operated a trading post there for 30 years. St. Ignatius Mission, built near Flathead Lake in 1854, was more successful.

After the gold rush of 1849 to California, four surveys were made by the national government for a transcontinental railroad. One of these was led by Gen. Isaac I. Stevens along the northern route in 1853. His detailed and favorable report did not then lead to a railroad, but Lt. John Mullan was instructed to build a wagon road from Fort Benton on the Missouri to Fort Walla Walla on the Columbia (1859–1863), which became an important highway.

Discoveries of gold between 1852 and 1864 produced a gold rush to Montana, and Bannack on Grasshopper Creek, Virginia City on Alder Gulch, and Helena on Last Chance Gulch soon became populous communities. Missoula, Deer Lodge, and Bozeman, located in agricultural valleys, grew as supply depots for the mining communities. For a time bandits known as road agents preyed on traveling miners who had found gold. In December 1863, however, the miners struck back by organizing as vigilantes, and they soon executed or frightened from the country the road agents. The gold rush and the resulting lawlessness made an organized government necessary, and in 1863 Idaho Territory, which included practically all of later Montana, was established. Then, on May 26, 1864, Montana Territory was formed from eastern Idaho.

Indian uprisings against the settlers began in the late 1860's. The Sioux were most implacable, and their enmity culminated on June 25, 1876, at the Battle of the Little Bighorn, in which George Armstrong Custer and his immediate command of 264 were killed. Then the Nez Percés of Idaho, seeking to escape confinement on a reservation, made a dramatic march under Chief Joseph across Montana until, on Oct. 5, 1877, they were forced to surrender.

Completion of the Northern Pacific Railway in 1883 gave impetus to farming and stock raising. The 1890's were characterized by feuds between the so-called copper kings: William A. Clark, Marcus Daly, and Frederick Augustus Heinze. These feuds involved not only control of the copper industry but state politics as well. The decade was marked also by a demand for the free coinage of silver, which was supported by miners and by debt-ridden farmers anxious for inflation.

Northern Pacific Railway

On the cattle range of western Montana.

Farming prospered after 1900, and farmers complained that the mines escaped their fair share of taxation, thus imposing an undue burden on agriculture. Eventually, in 1924, their complaints led to a license tax on mines. The decade following World War I was characterized by growing unrest among farmers and laborers. The period began conservatively when former Senator Joseph M. Dixon defeated the rising young radical leader Burton K. Wheeler for the governorship in 1920, but the people later turned toward the federal government for a solution of

Northern Pacific Railway

The city of Livingston, Montana, with the Absaroka Range of the Rockies in the background.

their problems. Senators Thomas J. Walsh and Wheeler, who was elected two years after his defeat for the governorship, both worked for federal assistance in reclamation, lower freight rates, and farm relief.

The depression that began in 1929 hit Montana heavily. Farmers received so little for their produce that they had nothing left after paying freight to market, and mass unemployment followed the closing of mines and the suspension of lumbering. Beginning in 1933, however, the federal government poured large sums into the state for relief projects, farm assistance, road building, and such reclamation and power projects as Fort Peck Dam, which was completed in 1940.

Politics, which had been liberal for two decades, became surprisingly confused in 1946, when Leif Erickson, a prominent liberal, defeated Senator Wheeler in the primary, and in turn was defeated in the general election by the more conservative Republican Zales N. Ecton. Reclamation and power development continued to be emphasized. Senator James E. Murray introduced his first Missouri Valley Authority bill in 1944, but widespread opposition to centralized control led to increased support for the state Water Conservation Board. The giant Hungry Horse Dam, completed in 1952, contributed to the development of northwestern Montana, and additional projects, such as Noxon Dam on Clark Fork and Cochrane Dam on the Missouri, were undertaken. Meanwhile, the revival of the Montana Planning Board as the state Industrial Development Board in 1955 provided a stimulus to the movement of industry to the state.

In the campaign of 1948 the Democrats carried all state offices. In 1952 they yielded the governorship to Republican J. Hugo Aronson, though they succeeded in electing Mike Mansfield to the U.S. Senate (of which he later became majority leader). Democrats remained strong at the state level until 1960, when they lost control of the state House of Representatives. Donald Nutter, a conservative Republican governor elected in 1960, was killed in an airplane crash in 1962 and was succeeded by Tim Babcock, who was reelected in 1964. Under Nutter and Babcock, spending was reduced and state budgets balanced. Babcock was defeated in the 1968 election by a Democrat, Forrest H. Anderson.

In the 1950's and 1960's, Montana was also balancing some adverse economic factors, such as troubles in agriculture and low levels of production in certain mining areas and oilfields, against the favorable factors of new industry, new oilfields, increasing population, major construction projects, particularly highways, and a notable increase in income from tourists.

11. BIBLIOGRAPHY

Dimsdale, Thomas J., *The Vigilantes of Montana* (Virginia City 1866); Leeson, Michael A., ed., *History of Montana, 1739–1885* (Chicago 1885); Chittenden, Hiram M., *The American Fur Trade of the Far West,* 3 vols. (New York 1902); Thwaites, Reuben G., ed., *Original Journals of the Lewis and Clark Expedition,* 8 vols. (New York 1904–05); Palladino, Lawrence B., *Indian and White in the North West: A History of Catholicity in Montana, 1831–1891,* 2d ed., rev. and enl. (Lancaster, Pa., 1923); Stuart, Granville, *Forty Years on the Frontier,* 2 vols., ed. by Paul C. Phillips (Cleveland 1925); Phillips, Paul C., and Dunbar, Seymour, eds., *The Journals and Letters of John Owen,* 2 vols. (Helena 1927); Raymer, Robert G., *Montana,* 3 vols. (New York 1930); Glasscock, Carl B., *The War of the Copper Kings* (New York 1935); Federal Writers' Project, *Montana, A State Guide Book* (New York 1939); Ferris, Warren A., *Life in the Rocky Mountains,* ed. by Paul C. Phillips (Denver 1940); Renne, Roland R., and Hoffmann, John W., *The Montana Citizen,* rev. ed. (Helena 1940); Burlingame, Merrill G., *The Montana Frontier* (Helena 1942); Howard, Joseph K., *Montana: High, Wide and Handsome* (New Haven 1943); Montana State University, *Montana Production, 1930–1949* (Missoula 1950); Historical Society of Montana, *Montana, The Magazine of Western History* (Helena 1951–); Kuhlman, Charles, *Legend into History* (Harrisburg, Pa., 1951); Brown, Mark H., and Felton, William R., *The Frontier Years* (New York 1955); Sharp, Paul F., *Whoop-Up Country* (Minneapolis 1955); Stewart, Edgar I., *Custer's Luck* (Norman, Okla., 1955); Brown, Mark H., and Felton, William R., *Before Barbed Wire* (New York 1956); Owings, Ralph E., *Montana Directory of Public Affairs, 1864–1955* (Hamilton, Mont., 1956); Burlingame, Merrill G., and Toole, K. Ross, *A History of Montana,* 3 vols. (New York 1957); Hamilton, James M., *From Wilderness to Statehood; A History of Montana, 1805–1900,* ed. by Merrill G. Burlingame (Portland, Oreg., 1957); Marcosson, Isaac F., *Anaconda* (New York 1957); Montana State University, *Montana Almanac* (Missoula 1957); Smurr, John W., and Toole, K. Ross, *Historical Essays on Montana and the Northwest* (Helena 1957).

MERRILL G. BURLINGAME,
Department of History and Government,
Montana State University.

MONTANA, University of, mon-tan'ə, at Missoula, Mont., a state-controlled coeducational institution, forming part of the Montana University System. It was chartered on Feb. 17, 1893, by the Montana State Legislature as the University of Montana, but in 1913, when the state's system of higher education was unified, the university's name was changed to the State University of Montana. In 1935 its name was again revised as Montana State University, and in 1965 the school's title reverted to its original form.

The main campus is situated on a 181-acre tract at the base of Mt. Sentinel and is supplemented by a 219-acre campus nearby and 400 acres atop the mountain. Other properties are a 27,000-acre forest near Greenough, some land adjoining Flathead Lake, and facilities at Fort Missoula. Enrollment, which in 1945 numbered only 2000, had passed 6,000 by the middle of the 1960's.

The university comprises a college of arts and sciences and schools of pharmacy, forestry, journalism, business administration, education, and fine arts—all giving bachelor's degrees and providing advanced study for master's degrees; a graduate professional school of law; and the graduate school, offering doctorates in philosophy and education. Other centers of specialized study are the biological station at Flathead Lake, the Forest and Conservation Experiment Station, the Lubrecht Experimental Forest, a division of extension and public service, and a wildlife research unit.

The university libraries house approximately a half million volumes, including a special Northwest historical collection, and are the regional depository for United States government documents. There is also a museum with extensive anthropological, archaeological, and other scientific collections, including one memorializing Indians of the region.

THE MONTANA UNIVERSITY SYSTEM

The University of Montana (at Missoula), Montana State University (at Bozeman), Montana College of Mineral Science and Technology (at Butte), Western Montana College (at Dillon), Eastern Montana College (at Billings), and Northern Montana College (at Havre) are land-grant institutions of higher education incorporated in a single state system, designated by statute as the Montana University System. The system was set up by the state legislature, effective July 1, 1913. General control and supervision of all six institutions is vested in the state board of education. The board is represented by an executive secretary whose office is in the state capital at Helena. Each unit of the system has its own three-man executive board and is administered by its own president.

MONTANA COLLEGE OF MINERAL SCIENCE AND TECHNOLOGY, at Butte, Mont., is a coeducational technical institution in the Montana University System. It was established in 1893, but instruction at the college level did not begin until 1900. The 12-acre campus is in the center of a major mining area and includes within its borders the state bureau of mines and geology, founded in 1919. First professional degrees are offered in mining, metallurgical, mineral-dressing, geological, and petroleum engineering. Exceptional students can pursue an honors program, and there is also a graduate school for advanced study leading to a master's degree. Regular studies are supplemented by summer fieldwork. The number of students at the college rose from just over 200 in 1945 to over 600 in the mid-1960's.

MONTANA NATIONAL BISON RANGE, near Moiese, western Montana, is between U.S. highways 93 and 10A, leading respectively to the Flathead and Thompson Falls valleys. The site, which covers 18,540 acres of grazing land and timber and has adequate water from springs and rivers, was chosen by M. J. Elrod of the University of Montana. In May 1908, Congress passed a bill authorizing establishment of the range and providing funds to buy and fence it. The American Bison Society, which had led a campaign to protect the few bison remaining in the United States, then raised more than $10,000 by popular subscription to purchase 34 bison as the nucleus of a herd to populate the area. By the mid-1960's the range was supporting about ten times its original number of bison.

The range is one of Montana's outstanding tourist attractions. A small picnic ground near range headquarters is available for public use during most of the year. In addition to the bison, deer, elk, mountain sheep, and antelope roam the range, and there are many small animals and birds.

PATRICK E. LEE

MONTANA STATE UNIVERSITY, at Bozeman, Mont., is a coeducational institution established by act of the state legislature in 1893 as the Agricultural College of the State of Montana. When it was made part of the Montana University System in 1913, the school was renamed the College of Agricultural and Mechanic Arts. In subsequent acts by the legislature the title was changed to Montana State College (1935) and, finally, to Montana State University (1965). The university's 1,170-acre campus includes an experimental farm.

There are four major units of instruction: the college of agriculture, the college of engineering, the college of letters and science, and the college of professional schools. There is also a department of continuing education and a cooperative extension service in the college of agriculture. Other major facilities are an agriculture experiment station and a digital and analog computing center. An international cooperation center offers an interdisciplinary graduate study program to prepare Americans for technical services abroad. The 165,000-volume university library contains a special collection on state agriculture. Montana State University's enrollment increased from about 2,000 in 1945 to almost 6,000 in the mid-1960's.

MONTANAN SERIES, mon-tan'ən, in geology, the Upper Cretaceous rock strata of North America, following the Coloradoan series. The series is divided into the fine-grained Pierre marine shales and the Fox Hills marine sandstone beds, in which are found coal and oil deposits as well as the remains of dinosaurs.

MONTANELLI, mōn-tä-nel'lē, **Giuseppe** (1813–1862), Italian writer and patriot. He was born in Fucecchio, Tuscany, on Jan. 21, 1813, and died there on June 17, 1862. In 1840 he was appointed professor of civil and commercial law at the University of Pisa. In 1847 he founded the newspaper *L'Italia,* and in the following year he commanded a group of Pisan volunteers in the war against Austria. Wounded at Curtatone, he was captured by the Austrians, but was released a few months later and was elected to the Tuscan Assembly. In 1849, after Grand Duke Leopold II had left Tuscany, Montanelli became, with Francesco Domenico Guerrazzi and Giuseppe Mazzoni, a member of the triumvirate governing the Florentine republic. While he was on a mission to Paris, the provisional government was overthrown and Leopold was restored to the throne. Now an exile from Tuscany, Montanelli remained in France until 1859. During these years he wrote a number of historical and political works, notably *Memorie sull'Italia e specialmente sulla Toscana dal 1814 al 1850* (*Memoirs of Italy, and Particularly of Tuscany, from 1814 to 1850;* 2 vols., 1853), as well as the dramatic poem *La tentazione* (*The Temptation;*

1856) and the tragedy *Camma* (1857). Permitted to return to Tuscany after the revolution of 1859, he became a member of the Parliament of the new Kingdom of Italy in 1861.

MONTANISM, mŏn'tȧ-nĭz'm, a religious movement which originated with Montanus, a Christian schismatic of the 2d century A.D. Converted to Christianity about 156–157 (according to some authorities, 172), he proclaimed himself to be the Paraclete (Comforter) promised by Jesus Christ (John 14:16). He soon gathered around him a group of followers who believed that he was the mouthpiece of the Holy Spirit, as were his companions Prisca (Priscilla) and Maximilla, each of whom had left her husband to join Montanus. Both these women uttered prophecies, but like Montanus claimed to be only the passive agents of the Holy Ghost. Montanus' principal tenets, apart from his belief that every believer may be the means of special revelation, were largely millenarian; in view of the approaching end of the world he enjoined asceticism, strict church discipline with the exclusion of all offending members, and the avoidance of mortal sin, which he considered the church to be unable to forgive. The activities of the Montanists in Phrygia soon aroused the opposition of the church, and Montanus and his followers were excommunicated about 175. The sect continued to flourish in Asia Minor, however, and after Montanus' death spread to the West. There its most notable convert was Tertullian (q.v.), who embraced Montanism about 207. Under his influence the asceticism of the movement was accentuated. Second marriages were condemned, stricter fasts were advocated, and flight from persecution was considered a sin. The sect died out in the West in the 3d century, but it survived in the East until the reign of Justinian (527–565), when it was suppressed.

MONTANUS. See MONTANISM.

MONTARGIS, môɴ-tȧr-zhē', town and commune, France, situated in the Department of the Loiret, 39 miles east-northeast of Orléans, on the Loing River and the Briare Canal. A market for the sheep, poultry, calves, and dairy products of the surrounding agricultural district, it also has tanneries and factories producing shoes, furniture, jewelry, and fertilizers. Montargis was once a royal residence, and it has a ruined castle as well as a church dating in part from the 12th century. The town was the setting of the semilegendary combat, said to have taken place in 1371, between the Dog of Montargis and Richard de Macaire, accused of murdering its master, Aubry de Montdidier. The dog's victory supposedly proved Macaire's guilt. During the Hundred Years' War, in 1427, the town was besieged by the English. Pop. (1962) town, 15,700; commune, 17,645.

MONTAUBAN, môɴ-tō-bäɴ', city and commune, France, capital of the Department of the Tarn-et-Garonne, situated on the Tarn and Tescou rivers, 31 miles north of Toulouse. The market of a district raising grain, table grapes, and other fruit, it has establishments processing food and producing silk and woolen textiles, pottery and porcelain, hats, and furniture. Among its many old structures are a 14th century bridge; the Church of St.-Jacques, dating in part from the 14th century; the 17th century town hall and Place Nationale; and the cathedral (1692–1739). The painter Jean Auguste Dominique Ingres (q.v.) was born in Montauban, and many of his works hang in the museum, which is housed in the former episcopal palace (1659). His *Vow of Louis XIII* is in the cathedral.

Montauban was founded in 1144 by Alphonse Jourdain, comte de Toulouse. In the 13th century it was a center of the Albigenses, and from 1360 to 1414 it was in the hands of the English. Montauban became a Huguenot stronghold in the 16th century. It was besieged in 1580 and in 1621 without success, but in 1629 was taken by Cardinal de Richelieu, who had its walls razed. After the revocation of the Edict of Nantes in 1685 the city declined greatly in importance. Pop. (1962) city, 29,716; commune, 43,401.

MONTAUK INDIANS, mŏn-tôk', members of a tribe of North American Indians of the Algonquin linguistic family formerly occupying the eastern end of Long Island, N.Y. They were among the most active participants in the manufacture of wampum. Once a powerful people, they controlled much of the island, but pestilence in the 17th century reduced their population. In 1788 the remnants went to live with the Brotherton Indians in New York. The few who remained on the island gradually declined in number, and there were only about 30 survivors in the 1950's.

MONTAUK POINT, peninsula, New York, forming the eastern extremity of Long Island. It is marked by a lighthouse authorized in 1795 and completed two years later. The structure, built of stone, is 170 feet high and has a light visible for 19 miles. Nearby is a United States Coast Guard lifesaving station. The point was the site of a receiving station and isolation hospital for soldiers who had served in the Spanish-American War. A total of 158 acres of the area is included in Montauk Point State Park. The cliffs at the edge of the point, which rise 50 to 100 feet above the ocean, are badly eroded.

MONTAUSIER, môɴ-tō-zyā', DUC DE (CHARLES DE SAINTE-MAURE), French soldier: b. Paris, France, Oct. 6, 1610; d. there, May 17, 1690. After studying at the Protestant college in Sedan, he joined the French Army. He fought with distinction in Italy and Lorraine and by 1638 had risen to the rank of *maréchal de camp*. Attracted by the beautiful Julie Lucine d'Angennes, daughter of the marquise de Rambouillet, he contributed to *La guirlande de Julie,* a celebrated garland of verse presented to her in 1641. To win her hand, Montausier became a Roman Catholic in 1645. They were married soon thereafter, and Montausier was appointed a lieutenant general and the governor of Saintonge and Angoumois. In 1663 he became governor of Normandy, and two years later he was created a duke. As guardian of the dauphin from 1668 to 1679, he supervised an edition of the classical writers *ad usum Delphini,* prepared by Jacques Bénigne Bossuet and Pierre Daniel Huet. Montausier was known for his strict moral sense and love of the truth, and he was said to have been used by Molière as the protagonist of *Le misanthrope*. Under the influence of his wife, who had been brought up in her mother's literary salon, his home became a center of the great men of letters and artists of the day, notably Jean Racine and Nicolas Boileau-Despréaux.

MONTBELIARD, môɴ-bā-lyȧr′, commune, France; in Doubs Department. It is situated 43 miles east-northeast of Besançon, on the Rhine-Rhone Canal and the Paris-Lyon railway. There is a Protestant church, St. Martin's, which was built in the 17th century; and a monument to the naturalist Georges Cuvier (1769–1832), who was born here. Montbéliard is in an industrial region, has foundries and cotton mills, manufactures clocks, and has a considerable trade in lumber, cheeses, and wine.

The town grew up around the medieval castle of the counts of Montbéliard, which was rebuilt in 1751. With the surrounding area, it became a countship of the Holy Roman Empire, passing by marriage to Württemberg in 1397. It was repeatedly occupied by the French (1674–1697, 1723–1748, and 1793–1801), becoming French territory in 1801 by the Treaty of Lunéville. Pop. (1962) commune 23,374; town 21,040.

MONTCALM DE SAINT-VERAN, môɴ-kȧlm′ dē săɴ-vā-räɴ′ (Anglicized mŏnt-käm), Marquis **Louis Joseph de,** French soldier: b. near Nimes, Feb. 29, 1712; d. Quebec, Sept. 14, 1759 He entered the army at 15, distinguished himself in the War of the Austrian Succession, and gained the rank of colonel. He was wounded at the Battle of Piacenza, Italy, in 1746, and was promoted brigadier general the next year.

In 1756 he was promoted to major general and was sent to command the French troops in Canada, where he began operations against the British with great activity and success. Fort Ontario at Oswego was carried on Aug. 14, 1756, after a well-conducted attack, and French control of the lake was restored. The next year (Aug. 9, 1757) he took Fort William Henry, at the head of Lake George, which was held by a garrison of over 2,500 men; and thus became possessed of 42 guns and large stores of ammunition and provisions. In the campaign of 1758 he occupied the strong position of Fort Carillon (Ticonderoga), made it still stronger by entrenchments, and on July 8 held it with 3,600 men against a British force of over 15,000 led by the incapable Gen. James Abercromby.

His personal bravery gained him great popularity among his soldiers; but want of energy on the part of the home government, the scarcity of food all over New France, and personal dissensions between himself and the civil governor, the marquis de Vaudreuil-Cavagnal, forbade him to look for much assistance. Montcalm expressed his conviction that in a few months the English would be masters of the French colonies in America; yet he prepared as best he could for the campaign of 1759. The English had sent strong reinforcements and were preparing for an attack on Quebec. As the success of the whole campaign and indeed the conquest of Canada depended upon the taking of that city, Montcalm concentrated his principal forces on the banks of the Montmorency River to protect it. In the first attack, July 31, the English general, James Wolfe, was repulsed; he later succeeded in landing his troops above Quebec, and on September 13 brought his whole force to the Heights of Abraham. Montcalm at once opposed his advance, but though he led the attack in person, his more numerous but inferior troops broke before the fire of the British. Wolfe fell in the moment of triumph; Montcalm was mortally wounded and died the next morning.

Consult Parkman, F., *Wolfe and Montcalm* (Boston 1884); Chapais, T., *Le marquis de Montcalm* (Quebec 1911); Lichtenberger, A., *Montcalm et la tragédie canadienne* (Paris 1934); Robitaille, G., *Montcalm et ses historiens* (Montreal 1936).

MONTCEAU-LES-MINES, môɴ-sō′lā-mēn′, commune, France; in Saône-et-Loire Department; nine miles south-southwest of Le Creusot, which it supplies with coal. It is a center of coal mining, lime burning, and copper foundries, and has hosiery factories. Pop. (1962) 29,364.

MONTCHRETIEN, môɴ-krā-tyăɴ′, **Antoine de,** French playwright and economist: b. Falaise, Calvados, about 1575; d. Tourailles, near Domfront, Orne, Oct. 8, 1621. He was at first an adventurer, and having killed his adversary in a duel, fled to England about 1605. He returned to France in 1611 and established ironworks at Ousonne-sur-Loire and later at Châtillon-sur-Loire. He was killed while taking part in a Huguenot uprising.

Among his tragedies are *Sophonisbe* (1594), *Aman* (1599), and *L'écossaise, ou Marie Stuart* (1601). His most important work was *Traicté de l'oeconomie politique* (1615; new ed. by T. Funck-Brentano, Paris 1889), a treatise on the French economy of the time. Montchrétien condemns monopolies; and advocates protection for the most important industries, freedom for the others.

MONTCLAIR, mŏnt-klâr, town, New Jersey; in Essex County; altitude 240 feet. It is situated six miles north-northwest of Newark and is served by the Delaware, Lackawanna and Western, and the Erie railroads. Montclair is a residential suburb of Newark and New York City, with an active local trade and manufactures of metal items, paints, and chemicals. It is noted for its fine homes, schools, churches, and civic and social organizations. There are three hospitals, an art museum, and a public library. New Jersey State Teachers College (founded 1908; coeducational) is in Upper Montclair, part of the town. Montclair was the home of the painter George Inness from 1878 until his death in 1894. The first settlement was made about 1666. Montclair was part of Bloomfield until 1868, when it seceded and incorporated. It has commission government. Pop. 44,043.

MONTDIDIER, môɴ-dē-dyā′, commune, France; in Somme Department; 21 miles southeast of Amiens. It is a market center for the surrounding country, has tanneries, and manufactures leather goods. There are two churches dating from the period of the 15th and 16th centuries. Montdidier dates from Merovingian times, and became a royal fief in the 12th century. During World War I it was heavily damaged in the fighting for Amiens in 1918, and again suffered in World War II. Pop. (1962) 5,778.

MONTE CARLO, mŏn′tê kär′lō, commune, Monaco, situated about a mile north of the capital of the principality; celebrated for its luxuriously appointed casino, founded in 1856, the most famous gambling establishment in the world. Monte Carlo is also noted for its scenic surroundings, its mild, healthful climate, and its attractive promenades, beautiful gardens, and elegant residences. Besides being famous as a gambling place, the town is one of the most fashionable seaside resorts on the French Riviera.

Monte Carlo is situated on an isolated escarpment (the Plateau des Spélugues), overlooking the Mediterranean Sea. The harbor below is known as La Condamine. The spot was virtually deserted until 1856, when Prince Charles III of Monaco granted a joint-stock company the right to build a casino there. Construction of the casino began in 1860, and the town grew up around it. Prince Charles named the town Monte Carlo in 1866.

The Société Anonyme des Bains de Mer et du Cercle des Étrangers, the original joint-stock company, still owns and operates the Monte Carlo gaming casino. Roulette, trente-et-quarante, and baccarat are the principal games played there. Under its present contract, which expires in 1973, the society pays the government an annual tax for the gambling concession. The tax originally covered the cost of governing Monaco, but it now yields only about 5 percent of the government's income.

In addition to the gambling rooms, the casino houses an auditorium and a famous opera house, which has staged many premiere performances of ballets by the Ballets Russes. Pop. (1963) 8,000.

MONTE CASSINO, môn'tȧ käs-sē'nō, a famous Benedictine abbey near Cassino, Italy, about 75 miles southeast of Rome. The abbey is situated at an altitude of 1,703 feet, overlooking Cassino. The monastery was founded by St. Benedict of Nursia about 529 on the site of a temple of Apollo. The original buildings were destroyed by the Lombards in the 580's and rebuilt about 720. The abbey was destroyed again in 883 by the Arabs and restored in the mid-900's.

Monte Cassino reached the zenith of its influence as a religious center in the 1000's and 1100's. Countless miracles were associated with the abbey, and it became a popular place for pilgrimages. The buildings were severely damaged by an earthquake in 1349. Reconstruction was not completed until the 1600's.

When the monasteries of Italy were disbanded by decree of the government in 1866, Monte Cassino became a national monument. It was particularly famous for its architecture and for its many works of art. The library contained many incunabula. During World War II, an Allied bombing attack in 1944 destroyed everything except a small section of the basilica and the tombs of St. Benedict and St. Scholastica. Much of the art work was destroyed at this time, but the contents of the library had been moved to Rome and remained substantially intact. Reconstruction of the buildings was largely completed by the 1960's.

MONTE ROSA. See ROSA, MONTE.

MONTECRISTO, môn-tȧ-krēs'tō, a small island in the Tyrrhenian Sea between Corsica and the coast of Italy. It lies about 25 miles south of Elba, and belongs to the Italian province of Livorno. Its area is 3.5 square miles. The terrain rises to an altitude of 2,116 feet at the center of the island.

For a short time in the late 1800's, Montecristo was a penal agricultural colony. It is now uninhabited. The island has become known chiefly through Alexandre Dumas' famous novel, *The Count of Monte Cristo.*

MONTECUCCOLI, môn-tȧ-ko͞o'kô-lē, or **MONTECUCCULI,** môn-tȧ-ko͞o'ko͞o-lē, COUNT **Raimund,** Austrian general: b. near Modena, Italy, Feb. 21, 1609; d. Linz, Austria, Oct. 16, 1680. After the French general Turenne, he was considered the greatest military commander of his time. Montecuccoli served in the Thirty Years' War and commanded the Austrian army sent against the Swedes in 1657–1660. In the conflict between Turkey and Austria for control of Hungary, he won a famous victory over the Turks at Szentgotthárd, Hungary, on Aug. 1, 1664. His book (1670) on the Turkish war was an important contribution to military history.

Later in the 1670's, Montecuccoli commanded the Austrian forces in the so-called Dutch War against Louis XIV of France. In these campaigns he effectively faced Turenne and the other great French general, Condé. For his successes, he was made a prince of the Austrian Empire and duke of Melfi in 1679.

MONTEFIASCONE, môn-tȧ-fyäs-kō'nȧ, town, Italy, in Viterbo Province, Latium, in the central part of the country. It is located on a hill overlooking Lake Bolsena, nine miles northwest of Viterbo. Montefiascone is the seat of a bishopric and has a cathedral designed by Michele Sanmicheli in 1519. Also of interest are the Church of San Flaviano (1032–1262) and the ruins of a castle of the 1500's. Pop. (1961) 12,054.

MONTEFIORE, mŏn-tē-fĭ-ō'rē, **Claude Joseph Goldsmid,** English religious leader and Biblical scholar: b. London, England, June 6, 1858; d. there, July 9, 1938. He promoted liberal reform in English Judaism and made important contributions to New Testament scholarship. Montefiore studied at Balliol College, Oxford, where he was influenced by the religious liberalism of Benjamin Jowett. In Berlin, he came to know Solomon Schechter (q.v.), whom he took to England with him in 1882. Montefiore was a founder of the Jewish Religious Union for the Advancement of Liberal Judaism (1888) and president of the Liberal Jewish synagogue in London from 1910. With Israel Abrahams he edited the *Jewish Quarterly Review* (1888–1908). His published works include *Liberal Judaism* (1903); *The Synoptic Gospels* (1909); *Judaism and St. Paul* (1914); and *Rabbinic Literature and Gospel Teachings* (1930).

MONTEFIORE, SIR **Moses Haim,** Anglo-Italian philanthropist: b. Leghorn, Italy, Oct. 24, 1784; d. Ramsgate, England, July 28, 1885. He was descended from a wealthy family of bankers; was educated in London; became a leading member of the Stock Exchange; and retired from active business in 1824. From that time he devoted himself to the service of his race, working for the removal of disabilities and oppression under which the Jews in England and elsewhere had suffered great hardship. His wife, whom he married in 1812, was Judith Cohen, a relative of the Rothschilds, and in her Montefiore found a companion who entered ardently into his philanthropic undertakings. He was for a time high sheriff of Kent, and after long exclusion and repeated re-election was legally recognized as sheriff of London in 1837. Knighted that year, he was made a baronet in 1846 in recognition of his public services. Working to ameliorate the condition of the Jews, he made a number of trips to the East and extended practical aid to them, particularly in Poland, Russia, Rumania, and the Middle East; in Bucharest he once risked his life during an anti-Jewish riot. In 1865, in memory of his wife, who died in 1862, he endowed a Jewish college on his estate near Ramsgate.

MONTEGO BAY, mŏn-tē'gō, city, Jamaica, in Cornwall county, on the Atlantic coast about 85 miles northwest of the capital, Kingston. The second-largest city in Jamaica, after Kingston, Montego Bay is a busy port and also ranks next to Kingston in commercial importance, trading in bananas, coffee, ginger, hides, rum, sugarcane, and dyewood. Manufactured products include ice, aerated water, wine cordials, and shoes; there are sugar mills nearby and oyster beds offshore. It has an excellent bathing beach and is noted as a winter resort. Columbus visited the site, then an Arawak Indian village, in 1494. Population: (1970) 42,800.

MONTEGUT, môɴ-tā-gü' **(Jean Baptiste Joseph) Émile,** French literary critic: b. Limoges, France, June 24, 1825; d. Paris, Dec. 11, 1895. Montégut began his long association with the *Revue des deux mondes* in 1847 with the publication of an article on Ralph Waldo Emerson, and was soon recognized as a sound and penetrating critic with a wide knowledge of foreign and contemporary literature. He is credited with introducing the philosophy of Emerson to France, and in 1851 published *Essais de philosophie américaine,* a translation of Emerson's *Essays.* He also published two important essays on Nathaniel Hawthorne, in 1860 and 1864. Other works include *Les Pays-Bas* (1869); *Poètes et artistes de l'Italie* (1881); *Types littéraires et fantaisies esthétiques* (1882); *Écrivains modernes de l'Angleterre,* 3 series (1885–1892); and translations of Thomas Babington Macaulay's *History of England* (185?) and the complete works of William Shakespeare (10 vols., 1873–1878).

MONTEIRO LOBATO, mōn-tā'rō lō-bä'tō, **José Bento,** Brazilian author, publisher, and businessman: b. Taubaté, Brazil, April 18, 1883; d. São Paulo, July 4, 1948. Most famous as a writer of short stories, he was a leader in the national movement in Brazilian literature, which began after World War I. In his novels, essays, and stories, he treated native Brazilian themes and social problems with both humor and compassion. He created and made famous the character of Jéca Tatú, typifying the backwoods Brazilian farmer, who appears in his first book of stories, *Urupês* (1918), and in the essays *Idéias de Jéca Tatú* (1919). The short story collections *Negrinha* (1920), *Contos leves* (1935), and *Contos pesados* (1940) are also representative of his best work. According to the novelist Erico Verissimo, they contain some of "the best pages ever written in the Portuguese language." As a publisher he launched many writers who became prominent, including Leo Vaz and Gastão Cruls. He also wrote numerous children's books.

MONTEMAYOR, môn-tâ-mä-yôr, or **MONTEMOR, Jorge de,** Portuguese-Spanish poet-novelist: b. Montemôr-o-Velho, near Coimbra, Portugal, ?1520; d. Piedmont, Italy, 1561. Little is known of his early life, but he was a chapel musician in the entourage of the Portuguese Infanta Maria on her journey to Castile for her marriage to Philip II in 1543. He was later in the service of the Infanta Juana, the Spanish wife of Prince John of Portugal, accompanied Philip II on various journeys, fought in the Netherlands, and was killed in a duel in Piedmont. Though he published a volume of poetry in 1554, he is important in literature as the author of *Diana Enamorada* (1559?), the first Spanish pastoral novel, probably inspired by the *Arcadia* (1504) of the Italian poet Jacopo Sannazaro. Mostly in Spanish, with some songs and prose passages in Portuguese, *Diana* was published in seven parts, or chapters, went through numerous editions, and was translated into English, French, Dutch, and German. Its influence was widespread, and has been traced in such works as Miguel de Cervantes' *Galatea* (1585), Sir Philip Sidney's *Arcadia* (1581, 1590), Honoré d'Urfé's *Astrée* (1607–1627), and probably in William Shakespeare's *Two Gentlemen of Verona* (1594–1595). See also DIANA.

Consult Schönherr, Gyula, *Jorge de Montemayor, sein Leben und sein Schäferroman* (Halle 1886); Rennert, Hugo A., *The Spanish Pastoral Romances* (Philadelphia 1912); Menéndez y Pelayo, Marcelino, *Orígenes de la novela* (Santander 1943); Montemayor, Jorge de, *Los siete libros de la Diana,* ed. by Francisco López Estrada (Madrid 1946).

MONTEMEZZI, mōn-tâ-mĕd'dzê, **Italo,** Italian composer: b. Vigasio, near Verona, Italy, Aug. 4, 1875; d. Verona, May 15, 1952. In addition to such works as the cantata *Cantico dei Cantici* (the first performance of which in 1900 was conducted by Arturo Toscanini) and the symphonic poems *Paolo e Virginia* (1929) and *Italia mia!* (1944), he composed a number of operas, among them *Giovanni Gallurese* (1905), *Hellera* (1909), *La nave* (1918), *La notte di Zoraima* (1930), and *L'incantesimo* (radio première in the United States 1943). His fame rests chiefly on *L'amore dei tre re* (*The Love of Three Kings*), first produced in Milan in 1913 and in New York City in 1914. Based on an effective libretto by Sem Benelli, this is recognized as one of the outstanding modern Italian operas and holds a firm place in the standard operatic repertory.

MONTENEGRO, mŏn-tĕ-nē'grō (Serb. *Crna Gora,* Black Mountain), formerly an independent kingdom; now one of the six autonomous republics which make up the Federal People's Republic of Yugoslavia. Covering 5,343 square miles and with a population of 530,361 (1971), it lies in the southwestern part of Yugoslavia, bounded on the southeast by Albania, on the southwest by the Adriatic Sea, and on the remaining sides by other regions of Yugoslavia (Dalmatia, Bosnia-Hercegovina, Serbia). There are few towns in Montenegro. Titograd, formerly Podgorica (pop. 1971, 29,217), is the capital. Cetinje was the historic capital. Other cities are Nikšić and the two ports of Bar (Antivari) and Ulčinj (Dulcigno).

The country is a succession of elevated ridges, with some lofty mountain peaks, of which the highest is Mount Durmitor (8,272 feet), and a few beautiful and verdant valleys in which the soil is tolerably fertile. The principal river is the

Morača, with its chief tributary the Zeta; it flows into the Lake of Shkodër (Scutari), which is on the Yugoslav-Albanian border. Forests of oak, ash, beech, fir, and poplar cover many of the mountainsides.

Corn, potatoes, vegetables, and several kinds of fruit are grown, but the country is a food-deficit area. Pigs, sheep, and goats are raised in considerable numbers. Agricultural methods remain primitive. Fishing, carried on principally in the Lake of Shkodër, is one of the major industries. As one of the poorer of the republics, Montenegro has had special attention in the Yugoslav government's economic plans and programs. Some new industries have been established, and the local economy has lost its purely agricultural character.

The Montenegrins belong to the Serbian branch of the South Slav peoples. Physically, they tend to be tall, well proportioned, and robust. Throughout its history, Montenegro has been known as a land of fiercely independent spirit and violence. At the same time, the people are noted for their hospitality. They speak the Serbo-Croat language, using the Cyrillic alphabet (q.v.). In religion they are mostly all of the Serbian Orthodox Church. The Communist regime is generally hostile to religion, but does not prevent the continuing practice of it.

History.—Montenegro was a part of the ancient Roman province of Illyria. During the barbarian invasions (5th century A.D.) it existed as the Serbian principality of Zeta; it later formed part of the great Serbian empire of Stephen Dushan (Stephen Nemanya IX) which for a brief period in the mid-14th century included most of the Balkan Peninsula. After the overthrow of that empire and the disastrous defeat of the Serbs by the Turks at Kosovo in 1389, Montenegro maintained in succeeding centuries a *de facto* independence. Turkish armies made many attempts to subdue the country but, because of the difficulties of the terrain and the tenacity of the people, were never more than partially successful. From 1516, Montenegro was governed by a prince-bishop, or *vladika,* first elective but after 1696 hereditary in the family of Petrović. Early in the 18th century were established the close relations with Russia which were maintained for 200 years. In 1796, Prince Peter I (r. 1782–1830) inflicted such losses on the army of the pasha of Shkodër (Scutari), who had invaded Montenegro, that for many years the Turks left the country unmolested.

Peter II (r. 1830–1851), who was a noted poet, made strenuous efforts to improve the condition of the people and to liberalize the governmental system. Peter's successor, Danilo I (actually Danilo II, r. 1851–1860), separated the princely from the ecclesiastical office, retaining only the former. His reign was marked, in 1858, by an epic victory over the Turks at Grahovo, known as the Montenegrin Marathon. Assassinated in 1860, Danilo was succeeded by Prince Nicholas, who reigned for 50 years as prince and for six more as King Nicholas I of Montenegro. In 1861, Montenegrins took part in a revolt against Turkish rule in neighboring Hercegovina, and when the revolt was put down Nicholas was compelled to agree to the occupation of a number of points in Montenegro by Turkish troops. In 1876, Montenegro and Serbia declared war on Turkey following the outbreak of a new revolt in Bosnia-Hercegovina; Russia entered the war in 1877. The Treaty of Berlin (1878), which concluded hostilities, gave Montenegro certain accessions of territory and formally recognized its independence (see BERLIN CONGRESS).

Montenegro was a member of the Balkan League of 1912 and fought against Turkey in the First Balkan War, gaining additional territory (see BALKAN WARS). Montenegro joined Serbia when World War I began in 1914 and was overrun by the German-Austrian armies in the following year. While the government proposed to resist to the end, the king attempted to make a deal with the Central Powers but could reach no agreement. When Cetinje was occupied on Jan. 13, 1916, he and his government retired to Neuilly-sur-Seine, France. After the war Nicholas tried, without success, to induce the victorious Allied powers to restore Montenegrin independence and his throne. Meanwhile, a National Assembly meeting at Podgorica on Nov. 26, 1918, declared the dynasty deposed and voted union with Serbia. Montenegro became a part of the new Kingdom of the Serbs, Croats, and Slovenes (Yugoslavia), whose independence was proclaimed on Dec. 1, 1918.

During the interwar period there was in Montenegro considerable opposition to the centralized administration run from Belgrade (Beograd), although as a compensating factor many Montenegrins were able to achieve prominence in the broader field of Yugoslav government and politics. When Yugoslavia was defeated and partitioned in 1941, Montenegro was made a protectorate of Italy, garrisoned by Italian troops; on Italian initiative it was declared independent on July 12, 1941. After the Italian surrender in September 1943, German troops occupied the key towns. During the course of the war, Montenegro was the scene of guerrilla activity on the part of both nationalist Chetniks and Communist-led Partisans. Toward the end of the war the latter got the upper hand and remained in effective control when the Germans withdrew.

Under the constitution adopted by Yugoslavia in 1945, Montenegro was given the status of a nominally autonomous "republic" with its own government, although through the centralized apparatus of the Communist Party of Yugoslavia (later renamed League of Communists) its affairs were actually controlled by Belgrade. Beginning in 1945 many Montenegrins (including Milovan Djilas) began to play important roles in the Communist movement and the national government of Tito. The population at large was not sympathetic to the Communist regime, but the latter was not seriously troubled by political disaffection in Montenegro.

Bibliography.—Denton, William, *Montenegro: Its People and Their History* (London 1877); Wyon, Reginald, and Prance, Gerald, *The Land of the Black Mountain* (London 1903); Stevenson, Francis Seymour, *A History of Montenegro* (London 1912); Bresse, Louis, *Le Monténégro inconnu* (Paris 1920); Haumant, Émile, *La formation de la Yougoslavie* (Paris 1930); West, Rebecca, *Black Lamb and Grey Falcon*, 2 vols. (New York 1941); Djilas, Milovan, *Land Without Justice* (New York 1958).

JOHN C. CAMPBELL,
Council on Foreign Relations.

MONTENERO, môn-tâ-nā′rō, mountain, Italy, second highest peak (6,171 feet) of the La Sila Mountains, 19 miles southeast of Cosenza.

MONTEPULCIANO, mōn-tâ-pōōl-chä′nō, commune and town, Italy, in Siena Province, Tuscany, 28 miles southeast of Siena. The town is picturesquely located on a height (1,950 feet) overlooking the Lake of Montepulciano. It is the trading center of a wine-producing district and has woodworking establishments. Outstanding among its many old buildings are the Palazzo Cervini, designed by the elder Antonio da Sangallo; the Palazzo Contucci, begun by Sangallo in 1519 and completed by Baldassare Peruzzi; the Palazzo Ricci, by Peruzzi; the cathedral (1532–1617), designed by Ippolito Scalza and containing a triptych (1401) by Taddeo di Bartolo; the 14th century Palazzo Communale, which has Della Robbia terra cottas; and the Church of Sant' Agostino, with a Renaissance façade by Michelozzo. At a short distance from the town is the Church of San Biago, built from 1518 to 1545 from plans by Sangallo. Montepulciano was the birthplace of Robert Cardinal Bellarmine, Pope Marcellus II, and Politian (Angelo Ambrogini). It is the seat of a bishopric and has a museum containing Etruscan antiquities. Pop. (1961) 15,820.

MONTEREAU-FAUT-YONNE, môɴ-trō'fō-yôn', town, France, situated in the Department of Seine-et-Marne, at the confluence of the Seine and Yonne Rivers, 17 miles southeast of Melun. Its numerous industrial establishments produce porcelain, pottery, mosaic tiles, bricks, electrical equipment, furniture, hosiery, and food products. It has a church dating from the 13th to 16th centuries and an equestrian statue of Napoleon I.

In Gallo-Roman times the town was known as Condate. The name of Montereau dates from the 8th century, when a monastery was dedicated to St. Martin. In 1419, John the Fearless, duke of Burgundy, was assassinated here by followers of the dauphin (later Charles VII). Nearby, on Feb. 18, 1814, Napoleon won a victory over the Allies. The town sustained some damage in World War II. Pop. (1962) 13,922.

MONTEREY, mŏn-tĕ-rā', city, California, situated in Monterey County, on Monterey Bay, 19 miles southwest of Salinas, the county seat. It is served by the Southern Pacific Railroad and by United Air Lines and Southwest Airways. The airport, 3 miles east of the city, is a regular stop between San Francisco and Los Angeles. The harbor is protected by a 1,500-foot breakwater, and the port facilities are municipally owned. Inland, back from the bay, are orchards and stock farms, and the city has fruit and vegetable canneries. Along the coast the leading industries are fishing and fish packing. The principal commercial catch is sardines (pilchards), but abalone, mackerel, albacore, tuna, shrimp, lobsters, and crabs are also taken. The processing of fish oils, fish fertilizer, and fish meal supplements this activity. Del Monte sand, a white sand used in sandblasting stone buildings, is shipped from here.

Monterey spreads over a sloping shore, with residences on the hillsides to the east and mountains farther back from the sea. It pivots on Alvarado Street, which extends from Fishermen's Wharf to the northern end of the city. There are excellent recreational facilities, a public library, and a junior college (Monterey Peninsula College). In the old customhouse (1814) and the first California theater (1844) the state maintains museums; in the former a room is devoted to a collection of manuscripts of writers associated with the area, including Robert Louis Stevenson and Ambrose Bierce. Other historic buildings include Colton Hall, where California's first constitution was framed; and the chapel (1789) of the presidio. The Presidio of Monterey, now a United States Army post, has in its grounds statues of Father Junípero Serra, who in 1770 founded the Mission San Carlos Borromeo here (it was moved shortly thereafter to Carmel), and Commodore John D. Sloat, who captured the city for the United States in 1846. Nearby are the art and literary center of Carmel-by-the-Sea and Fort Ord.

The site of Monterey was visited by Juan Rodríguez Cabrillo in 1542, and the bay was named by Sebastián Vizcaíno in 1602. The first permanent settlement, called San Carlos Borromeo, was made in 1770, when Father Serra and Gaspar de Portolá established, respectively, a mission and a presidio here. Under both Spanish (to 1822) and Mexican rule, Monterey served as the capital of Alta California. On July 7, 1846, the American flag was raised over the courthouse. Three years later a constitutional convention was held in the city, and here the first state legislature assembled. Monterey was incorporated in 1850. Government is of the city manager type. Pop. 26,302.

MONTEREY BAY, bay, California, indenting the Pacific coast in Monterey and Santa Cruz counties. It is about 26 miles across from Santa Cruz in the north to Monterey in the south and extends inland for about 10 miles. The Salinas River flows into the bay.

MONTEREY PARK, city, California, situated in Los Angeles County, 5 miles east of downtown Los Angeles, of which it is a residential suburb. It is served by the Pacific Electric Railway. There are food-processing plants and factories producing engine parts and toys. Founded in 1910, Monterey Park was incorporated in 1916. Government is of the city manager type, and the water supply system is municipally owned. Pop. 49,166.

MONTERO RIOS, môn-tā'rō rē'ōs, **Eugenio,** Spanish statesman and jurist: b. Santiago de Compostela, Nov. 13, 1832; d. Madrid, May 12, 1914. He was educated at the universities of Santiago and Madrid, and in 1864 became a professor of canon law at the latter. Elected to the Cortes in 1869, he served as minister of justice in 1870–1872 and again in 1889. He served as president of the Senate in 1894–1895, and in 1898 was president of the Spanish commission to negotiate peace after the Spanish American War. He was again president of the Senate in 1899, and in 1903 was recognized as the leader of the Liberal Party. He served as prime minister in 1905–1906, and for a third time as president of the Senate, in 1909–1914.

MONTERREY, môn-tĕr-rē'ē, city, Mexico, capital of the State of Nuevo León, on the Inter-American Highway, 440 miles north-northwest of Mexico City. With the exception of Mexico City, it is the most important manufacturing center in the republic. It is situated at an altitude of 1,624 feet on the Santa Catarina River in a fertile valley surrounded by the eastern foothills of the Sierra Madre Oriental at the northern end of the agricultural section of the state. South of the city is an extensive citrus country of mountainous valleys and rolling hills, while the arid plains of northern Nuevo León lie immediately north of it. Before its conquest by the Spaniards, the region was inhabited by nomadic Indians. These were subdued during the 1560's, and the area was quickly settled. The town was first named León, receiving its present name in 1596. In the course of the Mexican War, United States troops under Gen. Zachary Taylor stormed Monterrey during a four-day battle in 1846 (see MONTERREY, BATTLE OF). The present city combines traditional Spanish architecture, largely confined to the older residences and public buildings, with numerous outstanding examples of modern industrial and commercial construction. The basis of Monterrey's prosperity is the smelting of iron ores carried on in mills east of the city, and the manufacture of iron and steel products. There are also lead smelters, refineries of nonferrous metals, cement plants, flour and textile mills, soft drink bottling works, and some celebrated breweries. The city is also one of Mexico's leading financial centers. Close commercial ties are maintained with the United States, and the influence of the neighboring country is strong. The city is the major rail and highway center of northern Mexico. The University of Nuevo León (founded 1933) and the Monterrey Institute of Technology (1943) are here. Pop. (1960) 596,993.

MONTERREY, Battle of. In the early part of the Mexican War, Monterrey, which occupied a strong natural position and was well fortified, was held by Gen. Pedro de Ampudia with about 10,000 regular troops. In August 1846, Gen. Zachary Taylor, with a force of 6,625 men (mostly volunteers), marched from Matamoras to attack Monterrey. On September 9, he camped within 3 miles of the city. Ten days were spent in reconnoitering, and on the afternoon of September 19, Gen. William J. Worth was ordered to march with his division around the hill occupied by the bishop's palace, to take a position on the road to Saltillo, and to carry the enemy's detached works in that quarter. The main body of the army was to make a diversion against the center and left of the city by batteries erected during the night. On the following morning these batteries opened on the city, which replied with heavy fire from the citadel and other works. The lower part of the city was assaulted and entered by the Americans, and a strong Mexican work was captured after hard fighting by a brigade under Gen. John A. Quitman. Gen. William Orlando Butler entered the city at another point with the 1st Ohio Regiment. Meanwhile, General Worth carried the heights south of the river and the Saltillo road and turned the guns of the Mexican works in that quarter on the bishop's palace. The Mexicans evacuated the lower part of Monterrey during the night, and early in the morning of September 21, General Worth stormed the height overlooking the bishop's palace. By noon the palace itself was taken, and its guns turned on the Mexicans. Since the houses of the city were solidly built and the streets strongly barricaded, the Americans were forced to take each house in succession by breaking through the walls until they reached the main plaza. The conflict lasted until September 23, the Mexicans contesting every foot of ground until only the citadel remained in their possession. On the morning of September 24, General de Ampudia capitulated and with his army was permitted to march out with the honors of war. United States losses during the battle were 120 killed and 368 wounded. Mexican losses were reported to total 29 officers and 338 men.

MONTES, môn'tās, **Ismael,** Bolivian lawyer, statesman, and soldier: b. La Paz, Oct. 5, 1861; d. there, Nov. 18, 1933. He was educated at the University of La Paz and became a member of the bar in 1886. He served as a judge, and in 1890 was elected as a Liberal to the House of Deputies. In 1899 and again in 1903 he served as minister of war, and from 1904 to 1909 was president of Bolivia. During his term of office a boundary dispute with Chile was settled, and progress was made in education, agriculture, and transportation. Montes was minister to France in 1910 and minister to Great Britain in 1911. From 1913 to 1917 he served a second term as president. He was again minister to France in 1917, and from 1920 lived there in exile. Returning to Bolivia in 1928, he became head of the Liberal Party.

MONTESA, môn-tâ'sȧ, **Order of Our Lady of,** a Spanish military order established by King James II of Aragon in 1319 after the suppression of the Knights Templars (1312). It was endowed with the latter's estates. In 1587 it became united with the Spanish crown. The order was abolished in 1872, but was re-established two years later. The badge is a gold lozenge with a red cross in the field, surmounted by a trophy on a red ribbon. Knights are divided into two classes.

MONTESANO, mŏn-tĕ-sä'nō, city, Washington, seat of Grays Harbor County, situated on the Chehalis River, at the head of tidewater navigation, 10 miles east of Aberdeen. It is served by the Northern Pacific, the Union Pacific, and the Chicago, Milwaukee, St. Paul and Pacific railroads. In a farming, lumbering, and fishing region, the city produces lumber, furniture, and dairy products. First settled in 1854, it was incorporated in 1883. Pop. 2,847.

MONTESPAN, môn-tĕs-pän', MARQUISE DE (nee FRANÇOISE ATHÉNAÏS ROCHECHOUART), mistress of King Louis XIV of France: b. Tonnay-Charente, near Rochefort, 1641; d. Bourbon-l'Archambault, May 27, 1707. The second daughter of the duc de Mortemart, she was married in 1663 to Louis de Pardaillan de Gondrin, marquis de Montespan. To great beauty she added a natural liveliness and wit and a highly cultivated mind. Soon after her appearance at court in 1660, she attracted the king's attention and in 1667 became his mistress. Until 1674 she shared his favor with Louise de La Vallière. Mme. de Montespan bore eight children to the king, two of whom died in infancy. The older children were entrusted to the care of Mme. Paul Scarron (later Mme. de Maintenon). They were legitimized in 1673. Mme. de Montespan's influence over the king continued until about 1679, when a growing attachment to Mme. de Maintenon finally estranged his affections from Mme. de Montespan. She rarely appeared at court after 1684, and in 1691 she left it entirely. Her last years were spent in retirement, devoted to religious exercises, acts of benevolence, and penitence. One of her daughters by the king, Mlle. de Blois, married Philippe II, duc d'Orléans, who served as regent during Louis XV's minority.

MONTESQUIEU, môn-tĕs-kyû′, Baron **de La Brède et de** (Charles Louis de Secondat), French jurist and philosopher: b. Château de La Brède, near Bordeaux, France, Jan. 18, 1689; d. Paris, Feb. 10, 1755. The eldest son of the baron de La Brède, he attended the Oratorian College of Juilly (1700–1705) and pursued legal studies at Bordeaux (1705–1708). His next years were spent in Paris. Montesquieu's earliest writings already revealed his seriousness of purpose. His first essay (1709) praised Marcus Tullius Cicero, and his second (1711) was intended to prove that most pagans did not deserve eternal damnation. Returning home upon the death of his father in 1713, he was appointed counselor of the Parlement of Bordeaux the following year. In 1716 he inherited his uncle's title of baron de Montesquieu and his Parlement office of *président à mortier,* which he sold 10 years later.

In 1716, also, Montesquieu was elected to the Academy of Bordeaux. Among the papers he presented before it was another implied critique of Christianity, an analysis (1716) of the political use of religion by the Romans. Under his guidance the academy, of which he was several times director, turned to scientific researches. He projected a natural history of the changes of the earth (1719). His observations on natural history, delivered in 1721, indicated his great admiration for René Descartes and Sir Isaac Newton, and referred plant behavior to the general laws of matter in motion. The problem of relating his predilections for ancient ethics and politics on the one hand and modern science on the other continued to occupy him for many years.

Montesquieu was a rhetorician of the first order and an innovator of literary forms. His first major work, *Lettres persanes* (Persian Letters), was published anonymously (like all his other books) in 1721 and became a huge success. As an 18th century classic, light in vein but serious in intention, it has few equals. In some prefatory remarks Montesquieu speaks of using the epistolary form to join philosophy, politics, and ethics to a tale, and of a "secret chain" linking the whole. This reference to a hidden design and meaning introduces the reader to the principle of esoteric expression guiding all of his published writings. Here, in the guise of letters exchanged by Persians visiting France with Persians at home and with each other, he enacts the manner in which philosophy grows out of comparison and presents a penetrating critique of the beliefs, mores, fashions, and institutions of both France and Persia. The letters are given Persian dates covering a 10-year period, 5 years before and 5 years after the death of Louis XIV in 1715. The order of dates, in fact, is important for discovering the design of the work. The plot comprehends three main movements: that of the Persians in France toward deepened knowledge; that of France itself toward corruption and breakdown; and that of the wives of one of the Persians toward rebellion against the tyranny of their seraglio. These unite in a study of the forms and levels of human servitude and freedom.

Montesquieu's next major publication was *Le temple de Gnide* (1725), a paean to innocent sexual love, the precise philosophic intention of which it is difficult to discern. Early in 1728 he was admitted to the Académie Française, after some initial difficulty occasioned by a doubt in high places of the religious orthodoxy of *Lettres persanes.* The same year he set out on his travels, which took him to Vienna, Hungary, Italy, up the Rhine, and finally to London. There he remained for almost two years (1729–1731), was made a member of the Royal Society, and had ample opportunity to observe the regime on which he later based his model of the free society.

In 1734 Montesquieu published *Considérations sur les causes de la grandeur et de la décadence des Romains* (Considerations on the Causes of the Greatness and Decline of the Romans). In it he covers the period from early monarchical and republican Rome through the empire to the overrunning of the Western Empire by barbarians in the 5th century and the collapse of the Eastern Empire at a much later date. Montesquieu prefers the republic to the Western Empire, and the Western Empire to the Eastern. He admires the virtue and liberty of the republic and demonstrates that its very success in war led to the corruption of its institutions and the establishment of imperial despotism. He sees the disasters that conquest by Rome brought upon the conquered. He also realizes that forces within the empire caused its weakening long before the time of Attila (5th century A.D.). The Eastern Empire, torn with Christian strife, serves as an illustration of the improper relation of religion to political society. Montesquieu uses reflections about human nature and the foundation of political life to elucidate these matters, and he contends that general moral and physical causes rather than particular accidental causes rule the affairs of men, prescribing to individuals the degree of their freedom.

De l'esprit des lois (1748; The Spirit of the Laws) brought Montesquieu's reputation in Europe to its height. In it he attempts to demonstrate the principles that have caused the diverse development of law and custom in the nations of the world and thus to lay the basis for a modern science of politics. (For full discussion, see Spirit of Laws, The.) This work, 20 years in the making, did not escape harsh criticism, and in 1750 his rhetorically masterful *Défense de "L'esprit des lois"* answered charges of religious unorthodoxy. His last work, *Essai sur le goût dans les choses de la nature et de l'art* (Essay on Taste . . .), intended for and later printed in the *Encyclopédie,* was not completed. Its importance resides partly in his treatment of aesthetic reactions in such a way as to indicate his views concerning the good and the beautiful, views consonant with modern rather than with ancient philosophy. What his life meant to men like Jean Le Rond d'Alembert can be read in the latter's *Éloge de Monsieur de Montesquieu* (*Encyclopédie,* vol. 50).

Bibliography.—The best editions of Montesquieu's *Oeuvres complètes,* in French, are Édouard Laboulaye, ed. (Paris 1875–79); Roger Caillois, ed. (Paris 1949–51); and André Masson, ed. (Paris 1950–55), which contains the complete and highly important notebook material. David C. Cabeen, *Montesquieu* (New York 1947) is a bibliography. Works in Eng. tr. are *The Spirit of the Laws,* tr. by Thomas Nugent (New York 1949); *The Persian Letters,* tr. by J. Robert Loy (New York 1961).

Consult also Sorel, Albert, *Montesquieu* (Paris 1887); Barckhausen, Henri Auguste, *Montesquieu, ses idées et ses oeuvres d'après les papiers de la Brède* (Paris 1907); Oudin, Charles, *Le Spinozisme de Montesquieu* (Paris 1911); Dedieu, Joseph, *Montesquieu* (Paris 1913); *La pensée politique et constitutionelle de Montesquieu,* ed. by Boris Mirkine-Guetzévitch and Henri Puget (Paris 1952); Bordeaux, Bibliothèque Municipale, *Montesquieu* (Bordeaux 1955).

David Lowenthal,
Chairman, Department of Government, Wheaton College, Norton, Mass.

MONTESSORI, mon-tə-sôr′ē, **Maria** (1870–1952), Italian physician-educator, who originated the method of education that bears her name (see MONTESSORI METHOD). She was born in Chiaravelle, Ancona province, Italy, on Aug. 31, 1870. After graduating from the University of Rome—as the first woman in Italy to receive a medical degree (1896)—she worked in the university's psychiatric clinic. There she became interested in the education of retarded children, and at a state school for such children she achieved remarkable results, using methods like those developed by the French physician and teacher Jean Itard and his student Édouard Séguin.

Convinced that similar methods would be even more effective with normal children, Montessori undertook further study and research. In 1907 she opened the first Montessori school in the slums of Rome, enrolling neglected children aged 3 to 6. The mental and social development of the children in this school and others established under her direction amazed observers and soon attracted international attention. Later, she wrote voluminously about her method and conducted courses in many countries. She died in Noordwijk, the Netherlands, on May 6, 1952.

MONTESSORI METHOD, mon-tə-sôr′ē, a system of education and a philosophy of human development and learning, developed by Maria Montessori (see MONTESSORI, MARIA). Her method has had a wide influence on education, especially at the preschool and elementary levels, but its basic principle of self-motivated learning is applicable at any age. Present-day educational practices implied by such terms as ungraded school, open classroom, learning center, and programmed instruction stem in large part from Montessori's concepts. Montessori's books on her methods were first published in English as *The Montessori Method* (1912), *Dr. Montessori's Own Handbook* (1914), and *The Advanced Montessori Method* (1917).

Montessori believed that "the child of three, four, and five has one intuitive aim: self-development." To enable the child to develop his sensory, motor, and mental functions through self-teaching, a Montessori school or classroom is organized around a carefully prepared physical environment, with child-size furnishings and a variety of multisensory, manipulative, and self-correcting learning materials. A specially trained teacher prepares the environment, observes carefully, and subtly guides each child as he works with the materials at his own pace. Within this framework the child not only discovers the joy of learning for its own sake but develops the self-confidence and self-discipline that he needs to take his place in society.

Since the late 1950's, private Montessori schools and Montessori classrooms in public schools have appeared increasingly in the United States, and Montessori's major works have been republished. Her other books, related to those on the method, include *The Asborbent Mind* and *The Discovery of the Child.*

JUDITH DELMAN, *Assistant to the National Director, American Montessori Society*

Further Reading: Lillard, Paula, *Montessori: A Modern Approach* (Schocken 1972); Orem, R. C., and Stevens, George L., *American Montessori Manual* (Mafex Associates, Inc., 1970); Standing, E. Mortimer, *Maria Montessori* (1958; reprint, New Am. Lib. 1962); Wolf, Aline D., *A Parent's Guide to the Montessori Classroom* (Penn Mont Academy, Altoona, Pa., 1968).

MONTEUX, môn-tû′, **Pierre** (1875–1964), French conductor, who was one of the leading symphony orchestra conductors of the 20th century. His style was simple and restrained, and he sought to interpret the score objectively, without imposing his own personality on the music.

Monteux was born in Paris on April 4, 1875. He studied at the Paris Conservatory and became a violist. In 1911 he was named conductor of Diaghilev's Ballets Russes, in which post he won international fame for performances of new music, including Stravinsky's *Petrouchka* (1911) and *Rite of Spring* (1913). During this period he also conducted at the Paris Opera.

In 1917–1919, Monteux appeared at the Metropolitan Opera in New York, after which, until 1924, he was musical director of the Boston Symphony. He then began a ten-year association with the Concertgebouw Orchestra of Amsterdam.

Monteux returned to the United States in 1934, where he became permanent conductor of the San Francisco Symphony, which he built into one of the leading American musical organizations. After leaving San Francisco in 1952, he toured with the Boston Symphony and again appeared at the Metropolitan. In 1961 he became principal conductor of the London Symphony. An American citizen from 1942, Monteux died in Hancock, Me., on July 1, 1964.

MONTEVERDI, môn-tā-ver′dē, **Claudio** (1567–1643), Italian composer, who established opera as the leading form of musical drama. He was born in Cremona and baptized on May 15, 1567. He studied in Cremona under Marc Antonio Ingegneri, a composer and virtuoso organist. His first part-songs were published when he was 16, and the first of his many books of madrigals appeared in 1587. In 1590 he became a musician at the brilliant court of Vincenzo Gonzaga, duke of Mantua, and was named *maestro di cappella* in 1602. In Florence, in 1600, while traveling with the duke, Monteverdi probably heard the premiere performance of the opera *Euridice* by Jacopo Peri, regarded as the father of modern opera.

Monteverdi's first opera, *La favola d'Orfeo* (1607), is the earliest opera that is still performed. It was followed in 1608 by *Arianna* (score lost except for the famous *Lamento d'-Arianna*) and the ballet-opera *Il ballo delle ingrate.* After Gonzaga's death in 1612, Monteverdi settled in Venice, where he became *maestro di cappella* at St. Mark's Basilica in 1613. He continued to publish motets, madrigals, and other vocal works, and produced the dramatic scene *Il combattimento di Tancredi e Clorinda* in 1624 and the opera *Il ritorno d'Ulisse* in 1641. His crowning dramatic work, *L'incoronazione di Poppea,* was first performed in 1642. Monteverdi died in Venice on Nov. 29, 1643.

A great innovator, Monteverdi adapted various styles and harmonic devices to his purposes. He was the first to use the orchestra for color and effect and introduced string tremolo and pizzicato. Most important, perhaps, was his transformation of the recitative into arioso.

HERBERT WEINSTOCK
Coauthor of "Men of Music"

Further Reading: Arnold, Denis, *Monteverdi* (Farrar, Straus 1963); Prunières, Henri, *Monteverdi: His Life and Works*, tr. by Marie D. Mackie (Dover 1972); Schrade, Leo, *Monteverdi: Creator of Modern Music* (Norton 1969).

J. ALLAN CASH, FROM RAPHO GUILLUMETTE

In Montevideo, the fine, wide beaches and splendid summer weather attract thousands of North American tourists.

MONTEVIDEO, môn-tā-vē-thā'ō, the capital of Uruguay as well as of Montevideo department, is one of the great cities of South America. About half of Uruguay's population lives in Montevideo, giving the city unique importance in relation to the country. This situation has led an occasional writer to refer to Uruguay, at least half-seriously, as a "city-state." The city is incontestably the center of the state's political, cultural, commercial, and industrial life.

Montevideo's advantageous location has contributed greatly to its importance. It is the chief port of Uruguay, with a well-protected harbor on the northern shore of the Río de la Plata (River Plate), 130 miles (220 km) east-southeast of Buenos Aires, Argentina. Montevideo is famous for its beaches, and a string of seaside resorts stretches eastward from the city to Punta del Este, on the Atlantic Ocean.

Economy. Montevideo is the hub of the country's rail and highway systems (which connect with Argentine and Brazilian networks) and the center of air and sea routes. The interior sends its ranch products—wool, meats, hides, and grain—to the city, where they are processed and exported, and also consumed locally. Imported articles, in turn, are distributed from Montevideo to points throughout Uruguay.

Major industries include slaughtering and meat-packing, flour-milling, and clothing and textile manufacture. There are oil refineries, cement works, and power plants. Montevideo has many public employees. Others work in transportation industries, including railway shops. The city is also a major fishing port. The neighboring beaches and resorts provide a significant portion of the national income.

Aspects of the City. Montevideo is a handsome, essentially modern city, with broad streets, spacious parks, and impressive structures, some old, but for the most part new. The oldest part of Montevideo (Ciudad Vieja, or Old City) occupies a short peninsula enclosing part of the harbor. With its narrow streets, the section retains a flavor of its colonial past. The Old City is the center of financial and commercial concerns. The heart of the district is Plaza Constitución, flanked by the cathedral (consecrated 1790) and the old city hall—one of the city's outstanding remaining examples of colonial architecture.

Modern Montevideo focuses on Plaza Independencia, east of the Old City. Here are the Executive Palace and other public buildings, hotels, and apartments. Major streets converge here. The Avenida 18 de Julio, a fashionable commercial artery on which is also located the National Library, extends from this square to Battle Park. Centenary Stadium, a huge sports arena, is situated at one end of the park. Branching northward from the Avenida 18 de Julio, the broad Avenida Agraciada leads to the massive Legislative Palace (1925), a building of marble and granite.

History. By tradition, the name of the city derives from an exclamation made by a Portuguese sailor when he sighted the 500-foot- (150-meter-) high cone across the bay: "Monte vide eu!" or "I see a hill!" Montevideo was founded in 1726 by Bruno Mauricio de Zabala, the Spanish governor of Buenos Aires, to forestall Portuguese colonization of the area. For the next century it continued to be an object of contention, first between Spain and Portugal and then between Argentina and Brazil. In 1807, British forces briefly occupied it.

After 1828, when Argentina and Brazil recognized Uruguay's independence, the city began to prosper. From 1843 to 1851, during the period of civil war, combined Argentine and Uruguayan Blanco forces besieged Montevideo, which was held by Uruguayan Colorados and their Brazilian allies. Subsequently Montevideo developed rapidly, from a city of about 58,000 in 1860 to some 164,000 in 1884, and its area extended to the northwest. The city's expansion was aided by the building of railroads into the interior and a speculative building boom.

The city's modern period of growth may be said to have begun in 1903, with the election of José Batlle y Ordoñez to the presidency. The country then entered a period of greater stability than it had previously known.

J. ALLAN CASH, FROM RAPHO GUILLUMETTE

Plaza Independencia, where several major streets converge, is the hub of the modern section of Montevideo.

A dramatic event in the city's history occurred in December 1939, during World War II. The German battleship *Graf Spee,* after an encounter with British warships, entered Montevideo harbor for minor repairs. Ordered by authorities to depart, the German captain scuttled his ship outside the harbor.

Two historic meetings occurred at nearby Punta del Este in the 1960's. In August 1961 a special Organization of American States (OAS) conference established the Latin American aid program, the Alliance for Progress. And the presidents of the American nations met "at the summit" in April 1967.

Population: (1970 est.) 1,400,000.

MONTEVIDEO, University of, môn-tä-vē-thā'ō, a state-controlled institution of higher education, situated in Montevideo, Uruguay, and officially named the Universidad de la República (University of the Republic). It was formally organized as a university in 1849. To the earliest faculties, or colleges, of law (now law and social sciences) and medicine have been added faculties of agriculture, architecture, chemistry and pharmacy, dentistry, economics and business administration, engineering and surveying, humanities and science, odontology, and veterinary science. Most of the courses of study, geared to the professions, are six years in length, leading to doctoral degrees.

Institutions affiliated with the University of Montevideo include a national conservatory of music; schools of library science, social service, and fine arts; and an institute of technology and chemistry.

MONTEZ, mon'tez, **Lola** (1818–1861), British-Irish adventuress. She was born in Limerick, Ireland, the daughter of a British army officer; her original name was Marie Dolores Eliza Rosanna Gilbert. Her early marriage to an army officer was terminated in divorce in 1842. Determined to become a "Spanish" dancer, she studied a little and adopted the name Lola Montez. Her stage debut in London in 1843 was a disaster, and she never rose above mediocrity as a dancer. But she was a stunning beauty and was warmly received by audiences on the Continent. Her legendary career included a number of amorous liaisons, most notably those with the Hungarian composer Franz Liszt and the French novelist Alexandre Dumas, the elder.

Late in 1846, Lola Montez danced in Munich. King Louis I of Bavaria, exceedingly infatuated with her, made her his mistress, bestowing upon her the title countess of Landsfeld and a splendid mansion. The countess influenced the king's governmental policies, and his subjects resented her. In 1848, a year of revolutionary unrest in Europe, Louis' opponents forced his abdication, and Lola Montez had to flee.

Returning to England, she married another young army officer, whom she soon left. In 1851 she went to the United States to dance and act. After the death of her second husband she married—and later divorced—a San Francisco newspaperman. After a tour of Australia in 1855–1856, she settled in New York City, where she died on Jan. 17, 1861.

Further Reading: Holdredge, Helen, *Woman in Black: The Life of Lola Montez* (Putnam 1955).

THE METROPOLITAN MUSEUM OF ART, GIFT OF I.N. PHELPS STOKES, EDWARD S. HAWES, ALICE MARY HAWES, MARION AUGUSTA HAWES, 1937

Lola Montez, mistress of King Louis I of Bavaria.

MONTEZUMA, mon-tə-zōō'mə, is the name of two Aztec rulers of preconquest Mexico. One of the several variant forms of the name is Moctezuma.

Montezuma I (c.1390–1469) assumed the throne in 1440. He waged successful wars to extend his power and also encouraged the development of a stronger sacrificial tribal religion.

MONTEZUMA II (died 1520) was the grandson of Montezuma I. He was born in Tenochtitlán (Mexico City), possibly as early as 1466, and succeeded an uncle in 1502 or 1503. A despotic absolute monarch, Montezuma was head of state, military commander, and high priest. His incessant warfare resulted in the conquest of much territory. The Tlaxcalans, however, resisted and remained unconquered.

The tragic climax of Emperor Montezuma's reign began when the great conquistador Hernán Cortés landed in Mexico in the spring of 1519. Apparently fearing that Cortés was the god Quetzalcoatl, Montezuma sent rich gifts to keep the white stranger at a distance. But Cortés and his men proceeded inland, having with some difficulty won the help of the Tlaxcalans. Montezuma was obliged to receive the Spaniards in his splendid capital, Tenochtitlán, on Nov. 8, 1519, and he housed them in a palace. But the Spaniards seized Montezuma and held him hostage. In June 1520, after the Spaniards had angered the Aztecs by brutally suppressing a religious observance, Montezuma attempted to calm his rebellious people. They rained stones and arrows upon him. Montezuma II died shortly afterward—whether of his wounds or at the hands of the Spaniards is uncertain.

MONTEZUMA CASTLE NATIONAL MONUMENT, mon-tə-zōō′mə, preserves an area where pre-Columbian Indians lived about 1300 A.D. It is on Beaver Creek, near the Verde River, 40 miles (64 km) south of Flagstaff, Ariz. The monument, established in 1906, is administered by the National Park Service. The "castle" contains five stories with 20 rooms, and is set in a cave halfway up the face of a rock cliff. Visitors may not enter the ruin, which was named by early travelers who mistakenly believed it to be of Aztec origin. Other ruins are nearby. Montezuma Well, a limestone sinkhole, is 7 miles (11 km) north in a detached portion of the monument. For illustration, see ARIZONA.

MONTFAUCON, môɴ-fō-kôɴ′, **Bernard de** (1655–1741), French scholar and paleographer. He was born at Soulage (now in Aude department) on Jan. 13, 1655. He left a military career to join the Benedictine Congregation of St. Maur and was ordained at Toulouse in 1676. In 1687 he was sent to Paris to work on an edition of the Greek church fathers. Montfaucon's treatise *Palaeographia Graeca* (1708), based on his scrutiny of 12,000 manuscripts, established paleography as a science. His 15-volume *L'Antiquité expliquée et représentée en figures* (1719–1724) is still of value to archaeologists. His *Bibliotheca bibliothecarum* (2 vols., 1739), is a list of Greek manuscripts in European libraries. Montfaucon died in Paris on Dec. 21, 1741.

MONTFERRAT, môɴ-fe-rà′, is a historic region in Piedmont, in northwest Italy. The Italian form of the name is Monferrato. The marquisate—later a duchy—of Montferrat is associated with three dynasties: the Aleramo, Palaeologus, and Gonzaga families.

The origins of the Aleramici are poorly documented, but the family had established its control over the region by the end of the 10th century. Several of its members were crusaders in the Holy Land. The direct Aleramo male line expired early in the 14th century, and Montferrat passed, through marriage, to the Palaeologi, a powerful Byzantine family. They made Casale the capital in 1435. After the extinction of the Palaeologus male line in 1533, Charles V, the Holy Roman emperor, bestowed Montferrat upon the Gonzaga family of Mantua in 1536. The house of Savoy contested this, and Savoy in 1613 invaded Montferrat. A treaty in 1631 assigned part of Montferrat to Savoy; the rest devolved upon the French branch of the Gonzaga family. By the Peace of Utrecht (1713) this part of Montferrat also came under Savoy's jurisdiction.

MONTFORT, mont′fərt, **Simon de** (1208?–1265), Anglo-French baronial leader. He was born at Montfort in the Île-de-France, probably in 1208. His early interests were centered in the south of France, where his father, Count Simon de Montfort l'Amaury, had crusaded relentlessly and profitably against the Albigensian heretics. The younger Simon went to England in 1229 to claim his great-grandfather's estates and the earldom of Leicester and was accepted without question in the French-speaking circles of government and society. Finding favor in the eyes of King Henry III, he was at once recognized informally as earl of Leicester (formally invested April 11, 1239), and in 1238 he married the king's sister, Eleanor. In 1240 he joined a Crusade, reached Jerusalem, and returned in 1242.

Though personal antipathies quickly revealed themselves between Montfort and his royal brother-in-law, Simon remained a "king's man" and undertook in 1248 the thankless task of restoring order in English-ruled Gascony. Virtually removed from office in 1252, he bitterly resented the misgovernment at home that had denied him adequate assistance in Gascony. He insisted that the king could be irresponsible no longer but must rule with the "counsel of the magnates."

Because Montfort was by marriage near the throne, the mightiest barons gave him their support. The king, faced with bankruptcy over an abortive attempt to secure the crown of Sicily with the aid of the pope, capitulated at the Parliament of Oxford in 1258. He allowed the royal power to be exercised by a baronial committee of 15 and accepted the reform program of the Provisions of Oxford. In what occurred afterward Montfort was only occasionally concerned, for he was mainly in France, working out the terms of the Treaty of Paris (Dec. 4, 1259), by which Henry finally surrendered Normandy and Anjou and peace was established between England and France for 35 years.

The scheme of government devised in 1258 did not long survive, and Henry in 1261 was strong enough to repudiate it, with papal assent. But misgovernment and dissatisfaction still remained. In April 1263, Montfort became the acknowledged leader of the opposition and the unwavering upholder of the Provisions of Oxford. An attempt in January 1264 to avert civil war by submitting the disputes for adjudication (the Mise of Amiens) by Louis IX of France proved useless. In May 1264 the issue was decided by armed conflict in favor of Montfort's party at the Battle of Lewes.

Left with quasi-dictatorial powers, Montfort sought to rule the kingdom through an oligarchy of three electors, governing with a council of nine advisers. Recognizing that he had the backing of only a vacillating minority of the barons and that new social classes were rapidly emerging within the community, he summoned knights of the shire and, for the first time, borough representatives to Parliament in January 1265. But an oligarchy was not the answer to the question of how to create a constitutional opposition. Deserted by the 8th earl of Gloucester (Gilbert de Clare) and others, Simon de Montfort was defeated and slain in battle on Aug. 4, 1265, at Evesham, in Worcestershire.

A man of strong character, arrogant, obstinate, uncompromising, and tactless, Montfort advocated reform because he had a genuine detestation of administrative incompetence. To strengthen his position he enlisted the help of the county gentry and city burgesses. However notable this was in the history of popular representation, he made no conscious or deliberate contribution to the development of Parliament as an institution, or to the formation of a "house of commons." But Montfort was revered as a symbol of resistance to the generally unpopular English kings, and his tomb at Evesham long remained a place of pilgrimage.

GEORGE OSBORNE SAYLES, *University of London*

Further Reading: Bémont, Charles, *Simon de Montfort, Earl of Leicester, 1208–1265*, tr. by E. F. Jacob (Oxford 1930); Labarge, Margaret W., *Simon de Montfort* (Macmillan, Canada, 1962); Powicke, Frederick M., *The Thirteenth Century* (Oxford 1959); Sayles, George O., *The Medieval Foundations of England* (Methuen 1966).

MONTFORT L'AMAURY, môɴ-fôr′ lȧ-mô-rē′, **Simon de** (c.1160–1218), French count, who led the Albigensian Crusade. He was the first member of the ancient lordly family of the Île-de-France to bring the clan historic fame. Simon, through his mother, claimed the English earldom of Leicester, and for a while King John recognized him as earl. Simon's son Simon de Montfort was the great baronial leader.

Montfort L'Amaury joined the Fourth Crusade, but he ended up fighting in Syria rather than sacking Byzantine Constantinople with the main Crusader forces. Returning to France in 1207, he was eager to embark on the Crusade launched by Pope Innocent III in 1208 against the Albigenses of Languedoc, in southern France. Innocent felt that these stubbornly heretical Albigenses, or Cathari, threatened the unity of Christendom. The Crusaders from the north were motivated by greed as well as by religion, for the lands of Languedoc were rich. Simon's Crusaders perpetrated blood baths in the south, where orthodox and heretics alike resisted them.

In 1213, Simon defeated Count Raymond VI of Toulouse and his ally Peter II of Aragon at Muret. Simon's control of most of Raymond's lands received papal approval in 1215. Raymond struggled on, however, and regained some of his territories. On June 25, 1218, while besieging rebellious Toulouse, Simon was killed.

MONTGOLFIER, môɴ-gôl-fyā′, **Joseph Michel** (1740–1810) and **Jacques Étienne** (1745–1799), French inventors who built the balloon used for man's first flight. The brothers were born in Annonay, France–Joseph on Aug. 26, 1740, and Jacques on Jan. 7, 1745. While working in their father's papermaking business they kept an interest in scientific experiments. In November 1782, Joseph was inspired to design a hot-air balloon when he noted smoke and hot air rising from a fire. He immediately built a cloth balloon, filled it with hot air, and watched it rise.

In June 1783 the two brothers built a huge paper-lined linen balloon and filled it with hot air by burning wool and straw in an iron grate in the balloon's basket. The balloon rose high over Annonay. At the urging of the French Academy of Sciences, the brothers built a new balloon, which carried three animals aloft at Versailles in the presence of King Louis XVI and Marie Antoinette in September 1783. Amid mounting public excitement, Pilâtre de Rozier and the Marquis d'Arlandes volunteered to make a flight in a modified version of the balloon used at Versailles. On Nov. 21, 1783, they flew in the balloon for about 25 minutes, landing successfully about 5 miles (8 km) from their starting point at the gardens of Muette outside Paris. The brothers were honored by the academy for their work. Jacques died in Serrières on Aug. 2, 1799, and Joseph died in Balaruc-les-Bains on June 26, 1810. See also BALLOON.

MONTGOMERIE, mont-gum′rē, **Alexander** (1556?–?1610), Scottish poet, one of the last to write in Scots. He was born in Ayrshire of a landed family. After obtaining an office in the Scottish court in 1577, he became the leader of poets writing under the patronage of James VI (later James I of England) and the laureate of the court. His chief work is *The Cherrie and the Slaye* (first printed in 1597 and later enlarged). This long poem, written in 14-line stanzas, is partly a love poem and partly a moral allegory, in which the cherry represents virtue, and the sloe (blackthorn), vice. Montgomerie's other verse includes sonnets and devotional poems.

MONTGOMERY, mont-gum′rē, **Bernard Law** (1887–), British army officer. He was born on Nov. 17, 1887. Of Ulster stock, his father, Henry Montgomery, was Anglican bishop of Tasmania, where the young Montgomery spent his early years. After graduating from Sandhurst Royal Military Academy in 1908, he was commissioned a lieutenant of infantry in the Royal Warwickshire Regiment. He served in France and Belgium for three years during World War I and was twice wounded. Later, he served as a staff officer on the Rhine, in Ireland, England, and India, and in 1937 was promoted to brigadier. With the rank of major general, he commanded a division in Palestine and Transjordan during 1938–1939.

At the outbreak of World War II he went to France as acting lieutenant general in command of the 3d Division of the 2d Corps. Having evacuated his men at Dunkirk during the night of May 31–June 1, 1940, he was given command of the 5th Corps in Britain. In December 1941 he was entrusted with responsibility for the Southeastern Command, the most vital post in the defenses against possible German invasion.

On Aug. 18, 1942, Montgomery assumed command of the Eighth Army ("Army of the Nile"), which had been driven back into Egypt from Libya by German Field Marshal Erwin Rommel. In North Africa during ensuing months, "Monty" displayed the brilliant leadership that firmly established his reputation as one of the greatest generals in the war. After careful preparation, on October 23 he launched an attack upon the Germans and Italians entrenched at El Alamein in northern Egypt, and, when their lines broke, he pursued the enemy remnants into Libya. By early November, Rommel had lost more than half his forces, and Montgomery became the first of the Allied generals to inflict a decisive defeat upon a German army. In recognition of his accomplishment, on Nov. 10, 1942, he was knighted by King George VI and promoted to full general. Continuing the pursuit with the utmost vigor, he drove the surviving Germans out of Libya into Tunisia, where his Eighth Army cooperated with Gen. Dwight D. Eisenhower's forces in bringing the North African campaigns to a victorious conclusion in May 1943.

Still at the head of the Eighth Army, Montgomery participated in the Allied landing on Sicily in July 1943 and led the troops invading the Italian mainland two months later. In January 1944 he returned to Britain to command all land forces under Eisenhower preparing for the invasion of France. Toughness, common sense, and mutual respect between men and leader made it possible for him to say to the Eighth Army in farewell: "In all the battles we have fought together, we have not had one single failure."

After the successful Allied landing on the Normandy coast on June 6, 1944, Montgomery directed all land operations until August, when the great increase of American forces necessitated a reorganization of command. Montgomery took command of the Second Army Group, consisting of the Second British and First Canadian armies, which held the northern end of the Allied line in the Netherlands and Belgium. On September 1 he was promoted to the highest rank in the British Army—that of field marshal. On Dec. 17, 1944, after a German thrust through the Ardennes had split Lt. Gen. Omar Bradley's Twelfth Army Group, Montgomery was given temporary command of all British-American troops on the north side of the bulging line, with the U. S. First and Ninth armies attached to his group. On May 4, 1945, he accepted the surrender of the German troops in the Netherlands and northwest Germany. On May 22 he became chief of British forces occupying Germany and a member of the Allied Control Commission.

Raised to the peerage as Viscount Montgomery of Alamein in 1946, he was made chief of the imperial general staff. When, on Sept. 28, 1948, the Western European Union nations set up a "Permanent Defense Organization," Lord Montgomery was designated permanent military chairman. He resigned in early 1951 to accept the post of deputy supreme commander of the North Atlantic Treaty forces. He continued to serve in that capacity until he retired in 1958. Montgomery's writings include *Memoirs* (1958).

Further Reading: Lewin, Ronald, *Montgomery as Military Commander* (Stein & Day 1971).

MONTGOMERY, mont-gum'rē, **James** (1771–1854), British poet and journalist, best known for his hymns. He was born in Irvine, Scotland, on Nov. 4, 1771, the son of a Moravian clergyman, and was educated at a Moravian school near Leeds. From 1792 to 1825 he was associated with a newspaper in Sheffield. He was a competent journalist, but he gave much of his attention to poetry and attained great popularity for such books of verse as *The West Indies* (1809), exposing the evils of slavery, and *Greenland* (1819), a missionary poem. Montgomery's fame, however, rests on his hymns—*Hail to the Lord's Anointed, Forever with the Lord,* and others—which are among the finest in the English language. He died in Sheffield on April 30, 1854.

IMPERIAL WAR MUSEUM, LONDON

General Montgomery commanded the Eighth Army in its victory over the Axis at El Alamein on Nov. 5, 1942.

MONTGOMERY, mont-gum'rē, **Lucy Maud** (1874–1942), Canadian novelist, whose first book for girls, *Anne of Green Gables* (1908), brought her international recognition. She was born in Clifton, Prince Edward Island, on Nov. 30, 1874. After attending Prince of Wales College and Dalhousie University, she became a teacher, worked briefly for a newspaper, and wrote stories for magazines. Miss Montgomery was married in 1911 to Ewan MacDonald, a clergyman. She died in Toronto on April 24, 1942.

Anne of Green Gables, the story of an orphan who after a childhood of drudgery finds a satisfying home with a farm family, won great popularity among readers of all ages. It was followed by *Anne of Avonlea* (1909) and other "Anne" sequels. L. M. Montgomery, as the author signed herself, also wrote other juveniles, novels for adults, and a book of verse, *The Watchman and Other Poems* (1917).

MONTGOMERY, mont-gum'-rē, **Richard** (1738–1775), American soldier. He was born in Swords, county Dublin, Ireland, on Dec. 2, 1738. Commissioned an ensign in the British Army, he fought well at Louisburg and elsewhere in the French and Indian War. Back in England after the war, he saw less hope for promotion in peacetime, and in 1772 he left the army and returned to America. He married Robert R. Livingston's daughter and settled in Rhinebeck, N. Y.

Montgomery sympathized with the colonists in their conflict with England. In 1775 he was elected to the provincial Congress and then named a brigadier general in the colonial army. Second in command to Gen. Philip Schuyler for the Montreal expedition, he took command when Schuyler fell ill. Organizing his undisciplined troops, he took Montreal. He then joined Gen. Benedict Arnold for the siege of Quebec, in which he was killed on Dec. 31, 1775.

MONTGOMERY CHAMBER OF COMMERCE

McMONNIES FOUNTAIN (1885) marks the site of one of the oldest city wells in Montgomery, Ala.

MONTGOMERY, mont-gum′rē, the capital of Alabama and the seat of Montgomery county, is in the central part of the state on the south bank of the Alabama River. Montgomery's downtown district is situated on a bluff overlooking the river, but the city extends into the undulating hills to the south.

One of Alabama's largest cities, Montgomery is an industrial center and the market for the surrounding agricultural region. It is also an educational center and one of the state's most historically interesting cities. Because the constitution of the Confederate States was signed here on the eve of the Civil War, Montgomery is known as the cradle of the Confederacy. Later, it was the scene of important civil rights actions.

The Economy. Montgomery is situated in the heart of the Black Belt, a band of rich, dark soil that stretches across Alabama, making the city an important processing and shipping center for the cotton, dairy goods, and other farm products of the area. Its livestock market is one of the largest in the South. Montgomery is also a center for light industry, the most important being food processing, lumber, and furniture manufacturing. Textiles, bricks, chemicals, axles, and glass are also important.

The operations of the state government and the local colleges and universities also add to the city's economy. An additional boost is given by the presence of two military installations, Gunter and Maxwell Air Force bases. Maxwell has been an airfield since 1910, when it was set up and used by the Wright brothers. Air University, the top-level training command of the U. S. Air Force, is at Maxwell.

INFORMATION HIGHLIGHTS

Location: In central Alabama, on the south bank of the Alabama River, about 90 miles (145 km) south of Birmingham, 190 miles (306 km) northeast of Mobile, and 175 miles (282 km) southwest of Atlanta, Ga.
Population: The city, 133,386; the metropolitan area, 201,325.
Area: 45 square miles (117 sq km).
Elevation: Varies from 160 feet (49 meters) above sea level to 222 feet (68 meters).
Climate: Average annual temperature is 65°F (18°C), average January temperature is 49°F (9°C), and average July temperature is 82°F (28°C); average annual rainfall is 51 inches (1,295 mm).
Government: City commission, with the commission president serving as mayor.

Education, Culture, and Recreation. There are five colleges and universities in the Montgomery metropolitan area. Alabama State University, a public liberal arts college founded in 1874, is the oldest predominantly Negro college in Alabama. Auburn University at Montgomery, established by the state legislature in 1967, offers a wide variety of degree and continuing-education programs. A branch of Troy State University is open to residents of the area and servicemen from the two Air Force bases. Huntingdon College, which was founded in 1854, is a private four-year liberal arts school affiliated with the United Methodist Church. Alabama Christian College, which was established in 1942, is a liberal arts junior college affiliated with the Church of Christ.

The Montgomery Museum of the Fine Arts contains a collection of early American portraits, contemporary watercolors and drawings, prints, Indian artifacts, and Civil War items. A museum in the Alabama department of archives contains exhibits of colonial family life, costumes, decorative arts, and Indian artifacts. In addition, many of the city's historic buildings are maintained as museums.

A community concert series brings outstanding musical artists to Montgomery. The city has its own ballet company and a youth symphony. The Montgomery Little Theater and the Lamplighter Dinner Theater present plays and musicals. Horse shows, livestock exhibitions, rodeos, circuses, and the like are held at the Garrett Coliseum on the outskirts of the city. The South Alabama Fair is also held here. The city has its own professional baseball team, and the Blue-Gray college all-star football classic is held here annually.

Places of Interest. The state capitol is a Greek Revival building of stucco-covered brick situated on a beautiful landscaped hill. Its central white-domed portion was completed in 1851, and wings were added later. Some variety of rose is in bloom in the capitol gardens every month of the year. There are also a number of sculptural pieces on the grounds, including a Confederate monument, a statue of Jefferson Davis, president of the Confederacy, and a statue of the Confederate surgeon Allen Wyeth.

A frame structure, built in the early 1850's and now known as the First White House of the Confederacy, is a memorial to Jefferson Davis, who lived in it when Montgomery was the Confederate capital. The house is filled with Davis' personal belongings and with relics of the Civil War period. Davis, while he was president of the Confederacy, worshiped at St. John's Episcopal Church, built in 1836.

The Ordeman-Shaw Historic District comprises the Ordeman-Shaw House, the DeWolfe-Cooper Cottage, the Campbell-Holtzclaw Cottage, a slave quarters, and several small outbuildings. The Ordeman-Shaw House is a two-story brick and stucco building of Italianate design. The one-story Campbell-Holtzclaw Cottage has a Greek Revival portico. The DeWolfe-Cooper Cottage, which was moved to its present site in 1970, is a modified Gothic Revival house. All of the buildings were constructed in the 1840's and 1850's. In addition to these, there are numerous other antebellum houses. The Winter Building (1841), an Italianate office building with Egyptian Revival doorways, was the office of the Southern Telegraph Company, from which the order to fire on Fort Sumter was sent in 1861. Other interesting buildings include St. Peter's Roman Catholic Church (1852), of Spanish design; the Greek Revival Teague House (1848); and the Parker-Cody House (1823), a one-story town house.

History. The site of Montgomery was first settled by a few squatters in 1814. When the lands in the Territory of Alabama were opened for sale in 1817, two closely adjoining settlements—Alabama and East Alabama—were made. In 1819 these rival communities merged under the name of Montgomery, honoring the Revolutionary War hero Gen. Richard Montgomery and echoing the name of the county. The county had been named for Maj. Lemuel P. Montgomery, who had died during the decisive battle with the Creek Indians at Horseshoe Bend on the Tallapoosa River in 1814.

Within a few years Montgomery became a cotton market and distributing center for the surrounding farms. With the opening of a state bank and the beginning of construction of a railroad into western Georgia in the 1830's, the city's population and business increased. Montgomery was incorporated as a city in 1837 and designated the state capital in 1846.

By interest and by location, Montgomery was the focus of the secession movement. On Feb. 4, 1861, representatives from Alabama and five other states from the lower South that had decided to secede met in Montgomery. With Jefferson Davis as their chairman, they drafted the constitution of the Confederacy and set up the Confederate government with Montgomery as its capital. In July the capital was moved to Richmond, Va. On April 12, 1865, Maj. Gen. James Harrison Wilson led Union troops into the city and took it.

The years of Reconstruction were difficult, but the city recovered quickly. About 1900, Montgomery's possibilities as a manufacturing center were recognized, and from then on, except during the Great Depression of the 1930's, the city showed steady economic progress.

The civil rights movement scored its first great victory in Montgomery. After a black seamstress, Rosa Parks, was arrested in December 1955 for refusing to leave her seat in the section of a Montgomery city bus reserved for whites, a group of local black ministers, led by Dr. Martin Luther King, Jr., organized a boycott of the city bus lines in protest. Despite harassment, bombings, and legal actions, the blacks continued their boycott until a federal court ordered the local segregation law overthrown a year later. Through this battle, King and his policy of nonviolent resistance gained national recognition. In 1965, King led 25,000 peaceful demonstrators on a four-day march from Selma to Montgomery to petition the governor with regard to voting rights. The marchers assembled in a rally at the edge of the grounds of the capitol, where 104 years earlier the Confederacy had been formed.

In the early 1970's construction was begun on the Alabama-Coosa Waterway, which allows barge traffic from Rome, in northwest Georgia, through Montgomery, to the Gulf of Mexico at Mobile. This new waterway spurred interest in Montgomery's already prospering industrial life, and assured the city of continuing prosperity.

TThe First White House of the Confederacy was once the home of Jefferson Davis and his family.

MONTGOMERY CHAMBER OF COMMERCE

MONTGOMERY OF ALAMEIN, 1st Viscount. See MONTGOMERY, BERNARD LAW.

MONTGOMERY WARD AND COMPANY. See WARD, AARON MONTGOMERY.

MONTH. In the Gregorian calendar, universally used for civil purposes, a month is any one of the 12 periods into which the calendar year is divided. Each of these periods, called a civil or calendar month, lasts 28 civil days (February), 29 days (leap year February), 30 days (September, April, June, and November), or 31 days (January, March, May, July, August, October, and December).

In astronomy, a "month" is any of several periods of time based on the motion of the moon. The *synodic month,* 29.53059 civil days long, is the average period of revolution of the moon as measured with respect to the sun, or equivalently, the average period of time between successive new moons. The *tropical month,* 27.32158 days long, is the average period of time required by the moon to increase its longitude by 360°. The *sidereal month,* 27.32166 days long, is the average period of revolution of the moon with respect to a fixed direction in space. The *anomalistic month,* 27.55455 days long, is the average period of time between successive closest approaches of the moon to the earth. The *nodical month,* 27.21222 days long, is the average period of time between successive northward passages of the moon across the ecliptic. See also MOON—*Lunar Motion.*

MONTH IN THE COUNTRY, a five-act comedy by the Russian writer Ivan Turgenev. *A Month in the Country,* Turgenev's greatest dramatic work, was written in 1850 but not approved by the censors until 1855. It was first published in 1869 and produced in 1872.

The play deals with the disruption of a landowner's household by the arrival of a young tutor, Aleksei, with whom both the landowner's wife Natalia and her ward Vera fall in love. Natalia believes that the tutor is in love with Vera, when, in fact, he loves Natalia herself. The tutor leaves, and the household returns to its former state of boredom.

The action of the play is generally static, and much of its exposition is expressed in interior monologues. However, it effectively presents the ennui of the Russian upper classes and had a profound influence on Chekhov.

MONTHERLANT, môɴ-ter-läɴ', **Henry de** (1896–1972), French novelist, essayist, and dramatist, best known for his incisive style and his portrayal of characters who reflect some of the alternating strains of his own complex personality. Henry Marie Joseph Millon de Montherlant was born in Neuilly-sur-Seine on April 21, 1896, into an aristocratic family of Catalan origin. After attending a local Catholic college, he served in World War I. His first novels—*Le Songe* (1922; Eng. tr., *The Dream,* 1962), and *Les Bestiaires* (1926; *The Bullfighters,* 1927)—extol the masculine ideals of virility and honor that he found both in war and in sports, especially bullfighting, which he came to admire during travels in Spain.

In the 1930's, Montherlant turned to less personal subject matter. His major work of fiction, a four-part novel under the general title *Les Jeunes Filles* (1936–1939), depicts the relationship between a libertine novelist and his devoted women victims. (The four parts have appeared in English as *Young Girls, Pity for Women, The Demon of Good,* and *The Lepers.*) His other works of this period include volumes of essays expressing contempt for bourgeois democracy.

Ultimately, Montherlant found his greatest success in classically conceived, partly historical plays with opposing strains of paganism and Christianity. These include *La Reine morte* (1942; *Queen After Death, or How To Kill Women,* 1951) and *Le Maître de Santiago* (1947; *Master of Santiago,* 1951). A later novel, *Le Chaos et la nuit* (1963; *Chaos and Night,* 1964), about a Spanish anarchist, also won acclaim. Montherlant was elected to the French Academy in 1960. He committed suicide in Paris on Sept. 21, 1972.

Further Reading: Batchelor, John W., *Existence and Imagination: The Theatre of Henry de Montherlant* (Humanities Press 1967); Becker, Lucille, *Henry de Montherlant: A Critical Biography* (Southern Ill. Univ. Press 1970); Johnson, Robert B., *Henry de Montherlant* (Twayne 1968).

MONTI, mōn'tē, **Vincenzo** (1754–1828), Italian poet and prose writer, whose masterpiece is his translation (1810) of the *Iliad.* He was born in Alfonsine, near Ravenna, Italy, on Feb. 19, 1754. While a university student in the 1770's, he became known as a poet. Thereafter, at a time when the Italian states were under ever-changing foreign control, he devoted his poetic talent to extolling each government in turn. His poem *Bassvilliana* (1793), written while he was secretary to a nephew of Pope Pius VI, praised the papacy and condemned the French Revolution. When the French invaded Italy, he hailed Napoleon's victories in fulsome verse. Under Napoleon's rule, Monti became a professor at the University of Pavia, imperial poet laureate, and historiographer of the kingdom (until 1814). With the restoration of Austrian power in Italy, he praised that government. He died in Milan on Oct. 13, 1828.

A poet in the neoclassical tradition, Monti displayed a rich imagination and a mastery of language and euphony. But most of his works, including such tragedies as *Aristodemo* (1786), lack conviction.

MONTICELLI, môɴ-tē-se-lē', **Adolphe** (1824–1886), French romantic painter, who excelled in fantasy and rich, dazzling color. Monticelli was born in Marseille on Oct. 14, 1824. He studied art there and in Paris in the late 1840's, especially the work of Delacroix, whom he knew, and Titian, Rembrandt, and Watteau at the Louvre. In the 1860's, after living more than ten years in Marseille, he returned to Paris, where he painted elegant, exotic, or festive figures in dreamy parklike landscapes, as in *Réunion dans un parc* (Louvre) and *Fête champêtre* (Brooklyn Museum). His work did not have significant appeal, but it attracted some buyers, including Napoleon III. Monticelli left Paris after the Franco-Prussian War and spent the rest of his life, unrecognized and in poverty, in Marseille, where he died on June 29, 1886.

In addition to landscapes, Monticelli's work includes nudes, circus figures, portraits, and still lifes. His blazing, gleaming, vibrant color, laid on in vigorous impasto, deeply influenced Van Gogh, but it generally went unappreciated by the art world until the 20th century.

THOMAS JEFFERSON MEMORIAL FOUNDATION

Monticello, the beautiful hilltop home of Thomas Jefferson, is now a national historic landmark.

MONTICELLO, mon-tə-sel′ō, was the Virginia estate of Thomas Jefferson, the third president of the United States. The house, designed by Jefferson himself, is a classic example of late 18th century American architecture. Monticello is situated in central Virginia, in Albemarle county, about 2 miles (3 km) south of Charlottesville and the University of Virginia, which Jefferson founded. The estate is preserved as a national historic landmark.

The Site. Monticello is set on a leveled mountain 857 feet (261 meters) above sea level and 580 feet (177 meters) above ground level. The northeast base of the mountain is steep and rocky and is washed by the Rivanna River. On the southwest the mountain dips some 200 feet (60 meters) before connecting with the higher Carter's Peak. The estate is covered by a dense growth of timber, mainly hardwood deciduous trees.

The view from the summit of Monticello is majestic. To the east stretches a broad plain that Jefferson called his "sea view," because its rivers eventually flow into the Atlantic Ocean. Some 20 miles (32 km) to the west, across a gently rolling valley, tower the commanding crests of the Blue Ridge Mountains. It is a breathtaking view, which inspired Jefferson from his childhood.

The House. The entire residence is one of the finest surviving examples of the Classical Revival style, of which Jefferson was the first exponent. A three-story brick and frame building of 35 rooms (including 12 in the basement), it has the appearance of an Italian villa with a Greek portico and many features of colonial architecture. There are two major entrances, east and west. A Roman dome—inspired by that of the Hôtel de Salm in Paris—commands the west front, which opens onto the extensive gardens of the estate.

The design of the basement is one of the many examples of Jefferson's originality. Colonial estates of the time had groups of outbuildings containing the laundry, carriage house, icehouse, stables, kitchen, smokehouse, and dairy. Jefferson placed these beneath long terraces that flank the house to the north and south, where they are readily accessible but inconspicuous from the outside. Joining the terraces is an all-weather passageway containing the wine room, beer cellar, cider room, rum cellar, and wine cellar, which are also concealed from outer view.

Many other features of the structure reveal Jefferson's fecund inventiveness, amounting to what today might be considered gadgetry. A weathervane on the roof is connected with a dial on the ceiling beneath so that it can be read from the inside. Above the main entrance is a large clock with a second face visible from outside. The clock is operated by cannonball weights that are suspended on either side of the triple doorway. On each side of the mantel in the dining room are small, artfully constructed dumb-waiters, which were used to bring up bottles from the wine cellar. He believed that staircases were unattractive architectural features, so he designed inconspicuous staircases only 24 inches (61 cm) wide, resulting in an impression of interior spaciousness. The alcove beds, adapted from European models, are set into recesses in the wall. His own bed was placed in an open alcove between his bedroom and his study, and —according to tradition—could be raised by ropes when not in use.

The family burial place is southwest of the house just beyond the tree-enclosed gardens. Jefferson's tomb is surmounted by an obelisk engraved with the epitaph he composed for himself: "Here was buried Thomas Jefferson, Author of the Declaration of American Independence, of the Statute of Virginia for religious freedom, & Father of the University of Virginia."

History of Monticello. On July 19, 1735, Peter Jefferson patented the 1,000-acre (405-hectare) tract south of the Rivanna River and subsequently added 400 acres (162 hectares) for a homesite north of the Rivanna, which he acquired from a friend in exchange for Henry Wetherburn's "biggest bowl of arrack punch" and £50 in Virginia currency. Upon his death in 1757, his son Thomas inherited the property. An entry in Thomas Jefferson's manuscript garden book for Aug. 3, 1767, is the earliest known instance of his applying the name "Monticello" (Italian for "little mountain") to this property.

THOMAS JEFFERSON MEMORIAL FOUNDATION

Jefferson designed Monticello, combining features of Continental and colonial architecture. He placed his bed in an alcove between his bedroom and study. The parlor (*below*) provided views of the landscaped grounds.

THOMAS JEFFERSON MEMORIAL FOUNDATION

The leveling of the mountaintop was begun in 1768. There being no competent architect in the colonies to carry out his ideas, Jefferson studied architecture and drew his own plans, deriving his principal inspiration from the works of the 16th century Venetian architect Andrea Palladio. The residence was begun in 1769 and developed in intermittent stages as Jefferson found opportunities to return to it from his political and diplomatic activities. It was not completed until after he had left the presidency in 1809.

Jefferson began living at Monticello in February 1770, after his paternal home at Shadwell was destroyed by fire. The estate was the scene of many stirring moments. One of the most dramatic occurred in June 1781, when British dragoons dashed up the mountainside to capture Jefferson (then governor of Virginia), who narrowly escaped. In his later years, Jefferson became heavily mired in debt, and it was feared that he might have to end his life in exile from his beloved mountain. But friends assisted him, and he passed his last days there.

Ten years after Jefferson's death Monticello was purchased by a naval officer, Uriah P. Levy. Levy bequeathed it to the nation, but his will was contested and the estate passed to his heirs. One of these, New York Congressman Jefferson M. Levy, bought off the other heirs and restored the estate, which had fallen into disrepair. In 1923 the Thomas Jefferson Memorial Foundation acquired the residence with 640 acres (259 hectares) of land and dedicated it as a national shrine on July 4, 1926, the 100th anniversary of Jefferson's death. The foundation subsequently brought back many of the original furnishings, which had been widely scattered. It maintains the estate as a model of restoration.

VINCENT L. EATON*, *Former Chief Editor Information and Publications Office The Library of Congress*

MONTILLA, môn-tē'yä, is a city in southern Spain, in Córdoba province, 23 miles (37 km) south-southeast of the city of Córdoba. The pale dry sherry known as amontillado is produced here and exported to many parts of the world. The soldier Gonzalo Fernández de Córdoba (1453–1515), "the Great Captain," was born here. Population: (1960) 19,830.

MONTINI, Giovanni Battista. See PAUL VI.

MONTLUÇON, môɴ-lü-sôɴ', an industrial city in central France, is located on the Cher River and the Berry Canal, about 50 miles (80 km) north-northwest of Clermont-Ferrand. Its industrial development was spurred in the 19th century by the discovery of coal in the Commentry area and by the construction of the canal. A metallurgical center, Montluçon produces iron and steel and manufactures machinery and equipment from these metals. Other enterprises produce chemicals and fertilizer, and there are tanneries.

Montluçon, once part of the duchy of Bourbon, was fought over by the English and French in the 12th century and later. The old town is dominated by the feudal castle of the dukes of Bourbon. It also contains a Gothic church and a number of 15th and 16th century houses. Population: (1968) 57,871.

MONTMAGNY, môɴ-mà-nyē′, **Sieur de** (1583?–1653), French colonial administrator and governor of New France from 1636 to 1648. Charles Jacques Hualt de Montmagny was born in France and educated by the Jesuits. By the early 1630's he was an administrator of the Company of New France (the "Hundred Associates").

In 1636 he succeeded Samuel de Champlain as governor of the colony. He built and restored forts, including Fort St. Louis, and in 1645 arranged a truce with the Iroquois. He named the first streets in Quebec. Today his large seigneury forms Montmagny county, Quebec. In 1652, Montmagny was made governor of St. Christopher (St. Kitts), in the West Indies, where he died.

MONTMARTRE, môɴ-mär′trə, is a northern district of Paris, France, on the right bank of the Seine River. It is dominated by the Butte de Montmartre, a hill that is the city's highest point (about 330 feet, or 100 meters). Crowning the hill is the 19th century basilica of Sacré-Coeur; its Byzantine domes form a striking Parisian landmark.

Druids worshiped on the summit of the hills, followed by Romans and then by Christians (Montmartre is ultimately derived from the Latin for "hill of the martyrs"). Artists resided on the slopes of Montmartre in the 19th and early 20th centuries, giving the neighborhood a reputation for bohemianism. Today, Montmartre is known for its night life.

MONTMORENCY, môɴ-mô-räɴ-sē′, **Anne de** (1493–1567), duke, marshal, and *connétable* (high constable) of France. He was born in Chantilly, France, on March 15, 1493, to one of the country's most illustrious families.

A friend from childhood of the future king Francis I, Montmorency distinguished himself in King Francis' wars in Italy and was made marshal in 1522 and a member of the king's council. Accompanying Francis to Italy again, he was captured in the Battle of Pavia in 1525 but was released soon after. He was one of the negotiators of the Treaty of Madrid (1526), signed by Francis and Charles V of the Holy Roman Empire.

Montmorency was placed in charge of the king's household, and he also controlled the country's military and foreign affairs. He was rewarded for his many services to the crown with the office of *connétable* in 1538. But he fell from favor in 1541 and was banished from court.

Montmorency was restored to favor by Henry II on the latter's accession in 1547. In 1548 he put down a revolt in Bordeaux with considerable brutality. In 1551 he was made duke. Taken prisoner by the Spaniards at St. Quentin in 1557, he was not released until the Treaty of Cateau-Cambrésis (1559).

He did not return to court until the accession of Charles IX in 1560. Charles' mother, Catherine de Médicis, hoped Montmorency would offset the power of the Guise family. However, his antagonism to the Protestant Huguenots and to Catherine's policy of temporizing with them was such that he allied himself with François de Guise. In 1562 he was again captured while fighting the Huguenots at Dreux. After his release he drove an English army, sent to assist the Huguenots, from Le Havre (1563). Montmorency was fatally wounded in a battle at St. Denis on Nov. 10, 1567, and died in Paris two days later.

LOUIS GOLDMAN, FROM RAPHO GUILLUMETTE

The Montmartre district of Paris still attracts painters as well as tourists. In background, the Sacré-Coeur.

MONTMORENCY, môɴ-mô-räɴ-sē′, **Henri II de** (1595–1632), duke, admiral, and marshal of France. The grandson of Duke Anne, he was born in Chantilly, France, on April 30, 1595. Made an admiral when he was only 17, then governor of Languedoc, he fought actively against the Huguenots. In 1625 he defeated the Protestant fleet under Benjamin de Rohan, seigneur de Soubise, and recaptured the islands of Ré and Oléron near the Huguenot stronghold of La Rochelle. After a victory over the Spaniards in the Piedmont in 1630, Henri was made a marshal.

Two years later he joined Gaston, duke d'Orléans, the brother of King Louis XIII, in an armed rebellion against the king's minister, Cardinal Richelieu. He was captured at Castelnaudary in Languedoc. Condemned for treason, he was beheaded in Toulouse on Oct. 30, 1632. The ducal line became extinct on his death.

MONTMORENCY FALLS, mont-mə-ren′sē, a spectacular cataract near the industrial town of Montmorency, in Quebec, Canada, formed by the Montmorency River as it drops into the St. Lawrence River. The falls were named by Samuel de Champlain in honor of the Duke de Montmorency, viceroy of New France from 1619 to 1624. Dropping some 275 feet (84 meters) from a crest that is 100 feet (30 meters) wide, the falls are utilized for hydroelectric power.

MONTMORILLONITE, mont-mə-ril'ə-nīt, is a clay mineral consisting of a hydrous aluminum silicate that is found in its purest form in bentonite. The term also denotes a group of clay minerals, including montmorillonite itself, that expand when wet. See also BENTONITE; CLAY.

MONTOUR, mon-to͞or', **Esther,** American half-breed Indian of the 18th century. She had French blood in her veins and may have been descended from Louis de Buade, Count de Frontenac, governor of New France. She married Eghobund, or Eghohowin, chief of the village of Sheshequin, in New York, and her intelligence enabled her to dominate the Senecas over whom she reigned as "Queen Esther." She accompanied delegates to congresses of the Iroquois tribes in Philadelphia, where she was well received because of her pleasant manner and her beauty. In 1778 her son, fighting with the British, died in the raid on settlers in Pennsylvania's Wyoming Valley. After the colonists surrendered, the enraged Esther killed some 15 prisoners by tomahawk.

MONTPARNASSE, môɴ-pår-nås', is a section of Paris, France, on the left, or south, bank of the Seine River. The heart of the district is the intersection of Montparnasse and Raspail boulevards. Early in the 20th century Montparnasse ("Mount Parnassus") became a gathering place of artists, intellectuals, and Russian political exiles. The neighborhood retains its reputation for bohemianism—and its famous cafés. The old railroad station was replaced in the 1960's by a towering modern structure.

MONTPELIER, mont'pēl'yər, the capital of Vermont and the seat of Washington county, is in the north central part of the state, 37 miles (60 km) southeast of Burlington. The city is on the main pass through the Green Mountains. Its three principal streets follow the Winooski River and its tributary, the North Branch. The landscaped riverbanks and the heavily wooded mountains create a picturesque setting.

Montpelier's economy is based on government, insurance, and industry. The city is one of the nation's oldest insurance centers, and several life and fire insurance companies have their headquarters here. Granite, from quarries at nearby Barre, is processed in Montpelier. Other industries include printing and the manufacture of plastics, bakery products, clothespins, and sawmill machinery.

Montpelier is the home of Vermont College, a private nonsectarian institution that grants associate degrees in arts and science and bachelor of science degrees in medical technology. Founded in 1834 in Newbury, Vt., the school was moved here shortly after the Civil War. First known as Montpelier Seminary, it became Vermont Junior College in 1936 and Vermont College in 1958.

The most prominent building in Montpelier is the State House, or capitol, a granite structure in the Greek Revival style with a gold-leaf dome surmounted by a statue of Ceres, the goddess of agriculture. The Doric portico is modeled on the Temple of Theseus in Athens. The State Administration Building, formerly the national headquarters of the National Life Insurance Company, is a six-story granite structure with an interior finished in Vermont marble.

The Washington County Courthouse, built in 1832, is a red brick structure with a pillared portico and clock tower. The United Church of Christ, built in 1867, has a particularly beautiful Gothic tower, modeled on one in England. The Federal Building, housing the federal court and the post office, is a good example of the city's modern architecture. The Kellogg-Hubbard Library includes a museum that features the works of Vermont artists.

The 110-acre (45-hectare) Hubbard Park in the northwest section of the city has an unusual 50-foot (15-meter) observation tower built of stones from old stone fences. Also of interest in Montpelier are the Victorian Gothic Christ's Episcopal Church, City Hall, and the Supreme Court Building. The Pavilion Hotel, which was built in 1876, is now an office building, and it houses some state agencies.

VERMONT DEVELOPMENT DEPARTMENT

The Pavilion Office Building in Montpelier, Vt., houses the governor's office and the museum of the Vermont Historical Society.

In 1787 land for a settlement was granted to Col. Timothy Bigelow of Worcester, Mass. Col. Jacob Davis, a Revolutionary War veteran, named the settlement after the French city of Montpellier. Organized as a town in 1791, Montpelier was chartered as a city in 1805 and made the capital of the state. A wooden state house was built and used from 1808 until 1836, when a new one was completed. The second state house, a smaller version of the present one, burned in 1857. The present capitol was completed in 1859.

Montpelier has a council-manager form of government. Population: 8,609.

MONTPELLIER, môN-pe-lyā′, an ancient university city in the south of France, is on the Lez River, 6 miles (10 km) north of the Mediterranean and about 75 miles (120 km) west-northwest of Marseille. Through canalization, the Lez is connected with the Canal du Midi and the sea. The commercial center of an important wine-producing region, the city has an annual international wine fair. Agriculture flourishes in the vicinity of Montpellier, and there are food-processing plants in the city. It also manufactures a variety of metal products and equipment.

Originally a rural settlement, Montpellier, through its port of Lattes and its road system, began successfully in the 10th century to rival Marseille (not then part of France) as a center of trade. But by the end of the 15th century, with Lattes' lagoons silted up and Marseille under French control, Montpellier lost out as a commercial center. But in the meantime, Montpellier's renowned school of medicine (1221) and its university (1289) were formally established. In 1382, Montpellier came permanently under the French crown. In the 16th century, during the wars of religion, Montpellier was a Protestant stronghold. Louis XIII captured it after a long siege in 1622 but allowed the Protestants to retain their political privileges. Subsequently, Montpellier was the capital of eastern Languedoc.

Points of interest include the promenade called Le Peyrou, with terraces affording views of the sea and the mountains, the restored Gothic cathedral, and the oldest botanical garden in France (1593). Population: (1968) 161,910.

MONTPENSIER, môN-päN-syā′, **Duchess de** (1627–1693), French princess, better known as Mademoiselle or La Grande Mademoiselle. Anne Marie Louise d'Orléans was born in Paris on May 29, 1627, the daughter of Gaston, duke d'Orléans and brother of King Louis XIII, and of his wife, Marie de Bourbon, duchess de Montpensier in her own right. Through her mother, who died when Mademoiselle was a week old, she became the richest heiress in France.

Several royal marriages were considered for her, including one with Charles II of England, when he was still without a throne. Any ambitions she may have had to marry her young cousin King Louis XIV were hopelessly compromised by her ineffectual involvement in the Fronde of the Princes, during which period (1650–1653) some of France's leading princes led sporadic revolts against the king and his minister Mazarin. In March 1652, Mademoiselle entered Orléans to defy the king's forces, which threatened the city. In July she ordered the guns of the Bastille to be turned on the king's troops

MUSÉE DE VERSAILLES

The Duchess de Montpensier, "La Grande Mademoiselle."

as they entered Paris. Such futile and somewhat ridiculous gestures resulted in her exile from Paris to St. Fargeau for five years.

Upon her return to court in 1657, she fell in love with the future Duke de Lauzun. Though Lauzun was greatly beneath her in rank, the king at first agreed to their marriage in December 1670, then refused and had Lauzun imprisoned for almost ten years. Mademoiselle died on April 5, 1693.

MONTPENSIER, môN-päN-syā′, **Duke de** (1824–1890), French prince and claimant to the Spanish throne. Antoine Marie Philippe Louis d'Orléans was born in Neuilly on July 31, 1824, the fifth son of Louis Philippe, who became king of the French in 1830. Montpensier entered the army in 1842 and served in Algeria.

In 1846, Montpensier married the Spanish infanta María Luisa Fernanda, sister of Queen Isabella II of Spain and heiress presumptive since Isabella's husband was thought to be incapable of fathering children. This marriage revived British fears of the French royal house controlling the crowns of both France and Spain, and relations between Britain and France cooled.

Following the French Revolution of 1848, the couple settled in Spain. He received the title of infante in 1859. In 1868, Montpensier was suspected of plotting against Isabella and was exiled. He returned later in the year after Isabella was dethroned. He pressed his claims to the throne without success. In 1870 he killed Don Enrique, who was also a claimant to the throne, in a duel.

During the reign (1871–1873) of King Amadeus, Montpensier was exiled to the Balearic Islands. On his recall in 1873, he sided with his nephew Alfonso XII, to whom he gave one of his daughters in marriage. He died in Sanlucar de Barrameda, Spain, on Feb. 4, 1890.

DEPARTMENT OF PUBLIC RELATIONS, CITY OF MONTREAL

"Man and His World" (foreground), a permanent exposition with a geodesic dome, is part of the waterfront.

MONTREAL, mon-trē-ôl′, is the most populous city in Canada and ranks second in population to Paris among the French-speaking cities of the world. It is situated in the southwestern part of the province of Quebec, on Montreal Island in the St. Lawrence River. The city is built around a mountain, Mount Royal. The majority of its residents, who are of French-Canadian stock, use the French form of the city's name, Montréal (pronounced mōn-rā-al′).

Montreal is one of Canada's major industrial, financial, and cultural centers and its principal transportation hub. It is one of the largest inland ports in the world, lying 1,000 miles (1,600 km) up the St. Lawrence River, at the foot of the St. Lawrence Seaway, whose locks and enlarged channels have made the Great Lakes directly accessible to Atlantic Ocean shipping since 1959.

The city proper, containing about 1,250,000 people, occupies one third of Montreal Island; but in the 20th century the city limits have been virtually erased by the spread of population and industry into nearby suburbs. The Greater Montreal metropolitan area that has emerged covers all of Montreal Island as well as the island immediately to the north (Île Jésus) and many communities on the south shore of the St. Lawrence. Greater Montreal had nearly 2,750,000 residents by the early 1970's, or 45% of the population of Quebec province and considerably more than one tenth that of Canada. Some of the larger suburbs within the metropolitan area are Laval, Montréal-Nord, and Longueuil.

From the woods near the summit of Mount Royal, the tallest of many new skyscrapers in the midtown area can be seen, some of them part of an ambitious development program begun in the late 1950's and largely completed in time for the opening of Expo '67, Montreal's exceptionally successful international exposition of 1967. The program transformed nearly 100 acres (40 hectares) in the heart of the city into a complex of ultramodern hotels, office buildings, and plazas. Even more impressive, however, was the multileveled honeycomb of interconnecting corridors and shopping galleries, theaters, restaurants, and transportation facilities carved out underneath the new structures. Montrealers had acquired a unique city-within-a-city, which is always at "shirtsleeve temperatures" in a region where the average annual snowfall exceeds that in Moscow.

THE PEOPLE AND THEIR CULTURE

Montreal is a city in which two peoples and two cultures—those of French and British Canada—coexist in a troubled but long-standing union. This mixture of peoples has been enriched by the immigration after World War II of many thousands from all parts of Europe. French Canadians make up about two thirds of Montreal's

INFORMATION HIGHLIGHTS

Location: Southwestern part of the province of Quebec, Canada, on the St. Lawrence River below its junction with the Ottawa River.

Population: *City,* 1,214,352 (largest in Canada); *metropolitan area,* 2,743,208.

Area: *City,* 68 square miles (176 sq km); *metropolitan area,* 514 square miles (1,331 sq km).

Elevation: About 80 feet (25 meters) at the riverbank.

Climate: Severe winters and brief, mild summers; temperature averages 14°F (−10°C) in January, 68°F (20°C) in July.

Government: Mayor, council, and urban community council.

population, while Canadians of British ancestry make up one quarter of the total. Three out of four Montrealers are Roman Catholic. More than 20% are Protestants, with Anglicans most heavily represented.

The English-speaking Montrealers are the dominant group economically, managing and owning the largest businesses. Although many French Canadians are bilingual, the use of English as the language of business has put the French-speaking majority at a disadvantage.

Neighborhoods tend to be segregated, the English speaking families living apart from the French-speaking. In general, the less affluent neighborhoods are French-speaking. Many of these are in the so-called East End (actually northeastern Montreal). In the West End and in suburban communities in the western part of the island, middle-class, English-speaking neighborhoods are more often the rule.

The dual culture of Montreal is reflected in the city's public education and in its media. There are separate Roman Catholic and Protestant school systems. In addition there are subsystems of English- and French-speaking schools. Two of Montreal's four television stations broadcast programs in French, and two in English, and radio programming is similarly divided. Of the two daily newspapers with the largest circulations, one (the *Star*) is printed in English, and the other (*La Presse*) is printed in French.

Theatrical fare is especially varied in Montreal, where as many as a dozen theatrical groups at a time may be drawing on the riches of two literary traditions. The International Theater, an especially accomplished company, performs plays in several languages in a converted powder storehouse.

Montrealers have always been rabid sports fans. The city is the home of the Canadiens, one of the most successful of professional ice hockey teams; and the area has produced more than its share of players. Since World War II, there has been a rapidly growing following for baseball—with the Montreal Expos now representing the city in the National League. Montrealers have also taken to a modified American brand of professional football. In 1970, Montreal was selected as the site of the 1976 Olympic Games.

THE ECONOMY

Manufacturing, trade, and finance are among the principal activities that account for the economic vitality of Montreal. The Greater Montreal area generates well over half of the personal income in Quebec province and more than 60% of the value of its manufactures and retail trade. Benefiting from an ample, inexpensive supply of hydroelectric power, manufacturing industries employ about one quarter of Montreal's labor force. Other large-scale employers are the city's wholesale and retail trading establishments and financial concerns such as banks and insurance companies. Canada's first bank, the Bank of Montreal (founded in 1817), remains the nation's largest private financial institution.

Manufacturing. In its earliest years, Montreal's chief manufacture was the processing of furs. Today the range of products manufactured is enormous. The most significant industry in terms of dollars earned is petroleum refining. Second in importance is the manufacture of clothing, which employs the greatest number of workers. A few of the other important industrial enterprises are slaughtering and meat-packing, tobacco and food processing, the manufacture of locomotives and other railroad stock, pharmaceuticals, automobiles, and aircraft.

Trade and Transportation. Although rivaled by Toronto as a business and financial center, Montreal has retained its preeminent role in international trade. A key factor in the city's growth since its earliest days has been the harbor. The Port of Montreal still handles as much as a quarter of all of the tonnage passing through Canadian ports.

Montreal's harbor now extends some 12 miles (19 km) along the north bank of the St. Lawrence River. It has many modern facilities, including quays for container cargo, and serves more than 5,000 cargo ships per year. Montreal has often led world ports in the volume of grain shipments and regularly leads other Canadian ports in the value of petroleum imports.

The city can also fairly claim to be Canada's railroad capital, serving as headquarters for the two major Canadian rail corporations. It is a hub of rail connections that reach westward to Vancouver, eastward to the ports of the Maritime

DEPARTMENT OF PUBLIC RELATIONS, CITY OF MONTREAL

The Basilica-Cathedral of Mary, Queen of the World, which is on Dominion Square in midtown Montreal, is a scaled-down replica of St. Peter's in Rome.

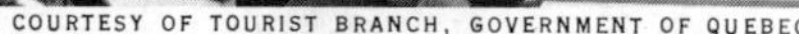

COURTESY OF TOURIST BRANCH, GOVERNMENT OF QUEBEC

CANADIAN GOVERNMENT TRAVEL BUREAU

The Métro (*above*), Montreal's subway, features beautifully decorated stations and cars with rubber-tired wheels.

Place Ville Marie (*left*) is a complex of office buildings and vaulted promenades lined with shops.

Provinces, and south to the major urban centers of the eastern United States. Major highways also radiate from Montreal. The coast-to-coast Trans-Canada Highway cuts through the downtown area via a tunnel running more than 80 feet (25 meters) below street level.

Montreal ranks second to Toronto in volume of passenger air traffic and in number of flights, but it is served by a greater number of foreign airlines and remains ahead in international air cargo. Congestion at the old Montreal International Airport, near the southwestern end of Montreal Island, led the city in the mid-1970's to begin construction of a huge new airport some 25 miles (40 km) to the north.

Tourism. Not the least of Montreal's economic mainstays is its tourist industry. Expo '67, the spectacular development of downtown Montreal, and the great increase in hotel space all added to a significant gain in tourism in the late 1960's. By the mid-1970's, the city was playing host to 4,500,000 visitors a year, or nearly three times its resident population.

THE MANY FACES OF MONTREAL

Old Montreal. Also known as Le Quartier, Old Montreal is a fairly small district, about four blocks deep and running some 14 blocks along the waterfront. It encompasses virtually all of the territory occupied by Montreal at the beginning of the 19th century.

Although modern garages, warehouses, and other recent construction have somewhat compromised the architectural integrity of the district, they have not destroyed its basic character, which is partly that of an old European city and partly that of a bohemian quarter.

On the Place d'Armes, a former market square and parade ground, is the Church of Notre Dame de Montréal. Begun in the 1820's, it is one of the finest and largest of Canada's churches, built in the Gothic Revival style with an unusual carved-wood interior. Near the church is the Seminary of St. Sulpice, the oldest structure in the city, built in 1683.

The Château de Ramezay dates from 1705. It was the residence of French, and, later, of English governors and was occupied in 1775 by invading American troops.

Montreal's oldest surviving church is Notre Dame de Bonsecours, overlooking the harbor. Built in 1772, it is called the Sailors' Church.

Midtown. As the city grew, it climbed the terraces that lie between Old Montreal and Mount Royal, to the west. Two of the principal avenues in this area are Dorchester Boulevard, along which many of the tallest skyscrapers have been erected, and Rue Ste. Catherine, the address of several large department stores that help to make the city an outstanding shopping center.

In the heart of this district is spacious, old-fashioned Dominion Square, planted with rows of shade trees. On one side of the square, dwarfed by towers of steel, concrete, and glass, stands the Basilica of Mary, Queen of the World (Marie Reine du Monde), a Roman Catholic cathedral that is a small replica of St. Peter's in Rome.

By contrast, a few blocks east of Dominion Square, is the ultramodern Place des Arts, a city-owned center of the performing arts that has been hailed as a masterpiece of integrated architecture and landscaping. Its three main structures are a theater, a recital hall, and a 3,000-seat concert hall that serves as the home of the Montreal Symphony Orchestra.

Also in the midtown area is Montreal's extraordinary underground city. It is a series of building complexes and covered promenades in or near the vicinity of Central Station, the city's principal rail terminal. The first complex, called the Place Ville Marie, is dominated by the Royal

Bank of Canada, a 48-story, 625-foot (190-meter) office tower that, because of its height and its unusual cruciform ground plan, has become one of Montreal's most distinctive landmarks. It stands beside a 4-acre (1.6-hectare) terraced plaza that covers four vaulted promenades as wide as city streets, each lined with shops, restaurants, and theaters.

Connected with the Place Ville Marie by underground passages is the Place Bonaventure, a vast structure rising 15 stories above ground. At its lower levels are subway tracks, a shopping arcade with 5 acres of shops, a huge exhibit hall, railway tracks, and a merchandise mart second in size only to that in Chicago. All of this is surmounted by a 400-room luxury hotel.

Also part of the new city are the Place Victoria, with its 47-story concrete and glass Stock Exchange Building, and the Place du Canada, with a 38-story hotel and a 28-story office building rising above a paved open-air plaza, beneath which are additional promenades.

Métro. A key element in the planning and building of the new downtown Montreal was the creation of the city's subway, the Métro, built between 1962 and 1967. Its four lines interconnect downtown. The trains, with their gleaming, well-lighted cars, run almost soundlessly on rubber-tired wheels, following each other at three-minute intervals during rush hours. The stations—each designed by a different architect—feature abstract murals, stained glass, ceramic bas-reliefs, or other ambitious decorative devices. An excellent network of connecting bus lines gives the city one of the finest urban transit systems in the Americas.

The Mountain. Mount Royal is a gently sloping, much worn-down volcanic mass, rocky and forest covered, topped by two peaks. Mount Royal proper, the higher of the two eminences, rises to 770 feet (235 meters). Chalet Lookout, near the summit, offers an extraordinary view of the old and new architecture of the downtown area that lies to the east. The view is especially impressive at dusk, when electric lighting and the setting sun combine to create a cityscape of shimmering brilliance. Westmount, a lower peak to the southwest, offers a view that is almost as spectacular.

Mount Royal Park covers most of the mountain. Near the crest is artificial Beaver Lake, on which ducks, swans, and model sailboats compete for space in summer and children and adults skate during the winter months. Horse-drawn carriage rides, outdoor concerts and plays, skiing, and sleighrides are among the activities featured at appropriate times of the year.

Canada's two best-known institutions of higher education cling to the mountainside. Far down the eastern slope are the stately old buildings of McGill University, the oldest English-language university in Canada, founded in 1821. The University of Montreal occupies a much more modern plant on the northwestern slope of the mountain. It is the country's largest French-language school, as well as the largest such university outside France.

Below Westmount is St. Joseph's Oratory, a Roman Catholic shrine whose soaring copper dome dominates the city's West End like an Old World cathedral. The imposing 20th century structure draws over 3 million visitors a year. It was built through the efforts of Brother André, a member of the Congrégation de Ste. Croix who died in 1937, to whom several miraculous cures are attributed.

Directly north of the Oratory is the Musée Historique Canadien, celebrated for waxworks that depict events in the history of Quebec.

Man and His World. On two small islands southeast of the harbor, easily accessible by subway from downtown Montreal, is the permanent exhibition *Terre des hommes,* or Man and His World, an outgrowth of Expo '67. Some of the Expo structures were preserved, among them the geodesic dome of the U. S. pavilion and the famous housing experiment called Habitat, which resembles a random pile of building blocks. However, most of the exhibits have been renewed or altered. There are museums of science and art, a marina, an aquarium, several restaurants, a midway, and many other attractions.

HISTORY

The Early Years. An Indian village of about 1,000, named Hochelaga, stood on the island site of modern Montreal when Jacques Cartier, the French discoverer of the St. Lawrence River, reached this area in 1535. Cartier climbed the mountain and gave it the name Mont Réal (Mount Royal). The village had disappeared by 1603, when Samuel de Champlain became the second-known European to visit the site. On his return in 1611, Champlain attempted to establish a manned outpost named Place Royale, but it was soon abandoned.

The first permanent European settlement was founded on the island in May 1642 by Paul de Chomedey de Maisonneuve, a former French Army officer, who brought about 50 settlers from France, including a number of Roman Catholic missionaries of the Sulpician order. A stockade was built, and the community was named Ville-Marie, a name it was to bear until after 1700.

During its first winter, Maisonneuve's settlement was almost destroyed by a flood. A 100-foot (30-meter) illuminated cross on Mount Royal commemorates this escape from disaster.

Another source of danger to the founders was the hostility of the Iroquois Indians. The first clash between the settlers and the Indians took place in 1644 on what is now the Place d'Armes.

The Montreal Canadiens, one of the world's great ice-hockey teams, plays against the Boston Bruins.

COURTESY OF TOURIST BRANCH, GOVERNMENT OF QUEBEC

DEPARTMENT OF PUBLIC RELATIONS, CITY OF MONTREAL

The Château de Ramezay, in Old Montreal, dates from 1705. Once the governor's residence, it now is a major historical museum.

Sporadic warfare was to continue until the Iroquois made peace with France in 1701.

Despite these troubles, the colony was remarkably successful, due in large part to the steadfastness of the colonists and their leaders. Jeanne Mance, one of several women among the original settlers, founded a hospital in 1645. Another remarkable woman, Marguerite Bourgeoys, who arrived in 1653, opened a school for girls and founded a secular religious order for women. In 1665 the settlement had 750 inhabitants. By the end of the century, it had more than 3,000 and had expanded beyond its stockade.

The 18th and 19th Centuries. Through the early 18th-century, the town, now known as Montréal, was the principal commercial hub of New France (French Canada), a fur-trading center, and a base for exploration of the vast interior. In 1760 it was taken by a British force commanded by Lord Jeffrey Amherst. It was ceded to Britain, with the rest of French Canada, at the end of the French and Indian War in 1763.

In November 1775, soon after the outbreak of the Revolutionary War, American troops under Gen. Richard Montgomery occupied the town. Benjamin Franklin and other American emissaries were dispatched there to enlist the support of the French-Canadian population against the British, but without success. By July 1776 the British had retaken the city. During the years that followed, the emigration of loyalist families from New England and New York state added to the small English-speaking population.

By the mid-1820's the center of the fur trade had shifted northward to Hudson's Bay, but the town's importance as a transportation crossroads was increasing. In 1825, the year in which the Erie Canal was opened far to the south, the Lachine Canal was completed in Montreal. Cutting through the heart of the city, it bypassed the treacherous Lachine Rapids, making passage between the Lower St. Lawrence and the Great Lakes considerably easier. Montreal was incorporated as a city in 1832. Its population increased from 10,000 in 1800 to 50,000 in 1850, and it served briefly (1844–1849) as the capital of the United Provinces of Canada.

During the last half of the 19th century—the era of railroads—Montreal continued to develop as a transport hub, forging rail links with Boston, New York, and Toronto. A transcontinental railroad, completed in 1885, connected Montreal with Canada's Pacific coast. Manufacturing industries sprang up on the waterfront and along the Lachine Canal, while residential building began to spill around the mountain and into remote corners of the island.

Montreal Since 1900. At the turn of the century, more than a half million people lived in Montreal and its environs. During succeeding decades, the rate of economic growth slowed, but public services, which had been lamentably underdeveloped, were much improved, and population continued to soar. The million mark was reached by midcentury, and, in the late 1950's, another era of rapid progress began with the enlargement and modernization of the harbor and the opening, in 1959, of the St. Lawrence Seaway.

Mayor Jean Drapeau promoted the midtown development program to provide a suitable setting for Expo '67. His priorities were often challenged by reformers, who charged, for example, that more was spent in 1972 to publicize Montreal's tourist attractions than was spent to rehabilitate slum housing. Few would deny, however, that Montreal had become one of North America's most interesting cities.

MONTREAL, University of, a privately controlled institution of higher education and research in Montreal, Quebec, Canada. The language of instruction is French. Since the 1950's, when it was moved from downtown Montreal, the university has occupied an impressive modern campus on the slopes of Mt. Royal, overlooking the city. The original faculties of theology, law, medicine, and arts (now arts and sciences) date from the period 1876–1887. Faculties added since that time include graduate studies; music; education sciences; social, economic, and political sciences; dental surgery; pharmacy; public health; nursing; veterinary medicine; optometry; and environmental design.

There are also more than 15 affiliated professional institutes and schools specializing in such areas as teacher training, religious studies, technical arts and applied science, and business administration. Almost all the faculties and the affiliated professional institutions offer a full range of undergraduate and graduate degrees. A doctor's degree is awarded in medicine, veterinary medicine, and dental surgery and as the highest degree for advanced study.

The university originated as a branch institution established in Montreal in 1876 by Laval University of the city of Quebec. Owing to a papal letter of instruction, the University of Montreal became virtually independent in 1889. It achieved full autonomy in 1919–1920. A new charter was granted in 1950.

MONTRÉAL-NORD, môɴ-rā-äl′ nôr′, is a city in the province of Quebec, Canada. An industrial and residential suburb of Montreal, it is situated on northeastern Montreal Island. It manufactures electrical goods and transportation equipment. Montréal-Nord was founded in 1915 and is governed by a mayor and council. Population: (1971) 89,139.

MONTREUIL, môɴ-trû′yə, **Pierre de,** French 13th century architect. Montreuil, or Montereau, was probably trained in the mason's lodge of Amiens Cathedral, near Montreuil. From 1231 he rebuilt the choir, nave, and transepts at the abbey of St. Denis. In the 1240's and 1250's he built the refectory and Lady Chapel at St. Germain des Prés, Paris, and possibly worked at the Château of St. Germain en Laye and the abbey of St. Martin des Champs. In the 1260's he constructed the facade of the south transept at Notre Dame, Paris. Montreuil emphasized large rose windows with radiating tracery, thus creating the middle, or *rayonnant* ("radiating"), stage of the Gothic style. He died about 1267.

MONTREUX, môɴ-trû′, is a town in Switzerland, in Vaud canton, on the eastern shore of Lake Geneva. It has been one of Lake Geneva's most popular resorts since the 19th century because of the beauty of its location and its exceptionally mild climate. It is sometimes referred to as the Vaud Riviera. It stretches along the lake for 3 miles (4.8 km) from the suburb of Clarens on the northwest to the castle of Chillon on the south. The land slopes up from the lake to Alpine meadows and farther inland to the Rochers de Naye, which rise to an altitude of about 6,700 feet (2,050 meters). Population: (1973 est.) 21,000.

MONTREUX CONVENTION, môɴ-trû′, an agreement signed at Montreux, Switzerland, on July 20, 1936, that restored to Turkey full control over the Turkish straits and the right to build defenses for the straits, previously denied by the Lausanne Conference of 1922–1923. Free transit was guaranteed through the straits for merchant and war vessels in peace and war, but only under carefully defined conditions.

MONTROSE, mon-trōz′, **1st Marquess of** (1612–1650), Scottish nobleman and soldier, who was an outstanding Royalist general in the English Civil War. James Graham was born in Montrose, Scotland. In 1626 he became 5th earl of Montrose. Religious strife began in Scotland in 1637 after King Charles I and Archbishop Laud attempted to change the liturgy. The Scots opposing the innovations signed the National Covenant in 1638—Montrose being prominent among the signers. Although he was soon fighting the king's forces, Montrose apparently did not regard his Covenanter's sympathies as incompatible with basic loyalty to the monarch.

In any case, Montrose joined the king in 1643. Created marquess and appointed lieutenant general in Scotland, Montrose made his way to the Highlands, virtually alone, in August 1644. Within a year he had raised an army, won six battles, through brilliant strategy, against the Lowland Presbyterians, and triumphantly entered Glasgow. But Charles was decisively defeated at Naseby on June 14, 1645. In 1646, after carrying out guerrilla activities, Montrose fled to the Continent. He returned to Scotland in 1650 to fight for Charles II, but he was betrayed, captured, and executed in Edinburgh on May 21, 1650.

Further Reading: Wedgwood, C. V., *Montrose* (Macmillan, N. Y., 1952).

MONTS, Sieur de, French explorer of Canada. See De Monts, Sieur.

MONTSERRAT, mont-sə-rat′, an island of volcanic peaks in the Leeward group in the West Indies, is a British Crown Colony. The capital is Plymouth. It is about 11 miles (18 km) long, up to 7 miles (11 km) wide, and has an area of 39 square miles (101 sq km). Montserrat has hot springs and deposits of gypsum and sulfur. The average temperature is about 78° F (23.5° C), and annual rainfall is 60 inches (1,525 mm). The chief agricultural crop is sea-island cotton. Fruits and vegetables are also grown.

The island was discovered in 1493 by Christopher Columbus and named for a Spanish mountain on which a famous monastery is located. Montserrat was colonized in 1632 by Irish settlers under Sir Thomas Warner. After brief periods of French control in 1664–1668 and 1782, it became a British possession in 1783. Montserrat was a member of the West Indies Federation from 1958 until the group was dissolved in 1962. Unlike the other islands, which became self-governing with Britain managing their external affairs and defense, Monserrat elected to remain a Crown Colony. Population: (1974) 14,800.

MONTSERRAT, mônt-ser-rät′, a mountain in northeastern Spain, in Barcelona province, Catalonia, about 30 miles (48 km) northwest of the city of Barcelona. It takes its name from the Latin *Mons Serratus*, meaning "serrated mountain." The Catalans call it Montsagrat, or "sacred mountain." Rising to about 4,070 feet (1,240 meters) above the Llobregat River, the Montserrat presents a fantastic spectacle of jagged peaks, eroded terraces and gorges, and unusually shaped boulders. A huge cleft, the Valle Malo, divides the mountain on the southeast side. According to legend, the cleft appeared at the moment of Christ's crucifixion and Montserrat became the home of the Holy Grail. A Benedictine monastery, about halfway up the eastern slope, is one of Spain's greatest shrines.

The monastery of Santa María de Montserrat is especially noted for its blackened wooden statue of the Virgin and Child set above the altar of the basilica. The shrine of Our Lady of Montserrat, the patron saint of Catalonia, attracts thousands of visitors each year, particularly newlyweds who come to receive the Virgin's blessing on the day of her nativity, September 8.

MONTT, mônt, **Jorge** (1846–1922), Chilean president. A career naval officer, he rose to become commander of the navy. In 1891, with other naval officers and members of Congress, Montt helped organize the revolt that deposed President José Manuel Balamaceda.

After serving briefly as provisional head of government, Montt was elected president and held office until 1896. Chile's armed forces were reorganized, and his administration tried to put government operations on a sound economic basis. In general, he was a weak president and lacked congressional support for his policies.

JOSEF MUENCH

In Monument Valley, the two mittens (*left*) and Merrick Butte rise nearly 1,000 feet above the plateau.

MONTT, mônt, **Manuel** (1809–1880), Chilean president. He was born in Petorca, Chile, on Sept. 5, 1809. He studied law at the National Institute in Santiago, of which he was rector from 1835 to 1840. As assistant secretary of the interior under President Joaquín Prieto, he suppressed a revolt in 1837 by soldiers protesting Chile's declaration of war against the Peru-Bolivia confederation. Montt was appointed a judge on the supreme court in 1838 and elected to the Chamber of Deputies in 1840. After serving in several cabinet posts under President Manuel Bulnes, he was elected president of Chile in 1851.

In his two terms (1851–1861) Montt, though harsh in suppressing opposition, was an able administrator. Tax reforms were introduced; the laws were reorganized and codified; education was expanded; railways and telegraph lines were built; and commerce and technology were advanced. After leaving office, Montt was president of the supreme court until his death, in Santiago, on Sept. 20, 1880.

MONTT, mônt, **Pedro** (1848–1910), Chilean president, son of Manuel Montt. He was born in Santiago, studied law at the National Institute, and in 1876 was elected to the Chamber of Deputies, of which he became president in 1885. In 1891, Montt was active in the revolutionary overthrow of President José Manuel Balmaceda by naval officers and members of Congress who opposed the president's assumption of dictatorial powers.

After serving as the new government's minister to the United States, Montt ran unsuccessfully for president in 1901. He won decisively in 1906 but did not live to complete his term. He died on Aug. 16, 1910, in Bremen, Germany, where he had gone for medical treatment.

During his term, Montt sponsored numerous domestic projects and helped reduce tensions between Chile and Argentina.

MONTVILLE, mont'vil, a city in Connecticut, in New London county, on the Thames River, is 6 miles (10 km) north of New London. Montville is in a farming area and is in part a residential community for persons employed in New London and Norwich. Textiles and paper products are manufactured. Montville is governed by a mayor. Population: 15,662.

MONUMENT VALLEY NAVAJO TRIBAL PARK is a vast scenic area within the Navajo Indian Reservation. The park, which includes Mystery and Cane valleys, comprises several thousand square miles in Arizona and Utah.

The "monuments" are the isolated monoliths of red sandstone deposited during the Permian Period that tower up to 1,000 feet (300 meters) above the valley floor. These buttes are capped by the Shinarump Conglomerate and the Moenkopi formation, which date from the Triassic Period and are more resistant to erosion. Erosion has also created unusual geological forms.

Rock paintings and artifacts confirm that pre-Columbian Indians lived in the valley. The Navajo occupation dates from the 1860's, when Chief Hoskinini led his people into the valley while Navajo elsewhere were being rounded up for removal to New Mexico. Indians living in the park today raise sheep, weave rugs, and work in nearby communities.

In the 1920's, Mr. and Mrs. Harry Goulding established Goulding's Trading Post & Lodge, and the Seventh-day Adventists later built a hospital and mission on adjacent land.

Camping and picnicking facilities are available. The park is best explored in jeeps driven by guides.

MONUMENTAL BRASSES. See BRASSES, MONUMENTAL.

MONYPENNY, mun'ē-pen-ē, **William Flavelle** (1866–1912), English journalist. He was born in Dungannon, County Tyrone, Ireland, on Aug. 7, 1866, and died in New Forest, Hampshire, England, on Nov. 23, 1912. After graduating from Dublin University he attended Balliol College, Oxford, but soon left for London, where he became a regular contributor to the *Spectator* and in 1893 joined the editorial staff of *The Times*.

In 1899 he became editor of the Johannesburg (South Africa) *Star*, which was actively supporting the Uitlanders in opposition to the policies of President Oom Paul Kruger. Monypenny soon made the *Star* a powerful political influence. At the outbreak of the South African War he enlisted in the Imperial Light Horse, fought in Natal, and went through the siege of Ladysmith. He resumed editorship of the *Star* after the war, but as he disapproved of the Chinese Labor Ordinance that permitted importation of indentured

Chinese labor, he resigned in 1903 and returned to England, where he rejoined *The Times* editorial staff and in 1908 became a director of *The Times* Publishing Company. He had published two volumes (1910–1912) of the authoritative *Life of Benjamin Disraeli, Earl of Beaconsfield* at the time of his death. George Earle Buckle completed it in four additional volumes (1914–1920).

MONZA, môn'tsä (ancient MODICIA), commune and city, Italy, in Milano Province, Lombardy, on the Lambro River, nine miles northeast of Milan. The city is a railway junction and rapidly developing industrial center, producing cotton and linen textiles. Oriental carpets, felt hats and fezzes, furniture, glass, machinery, paint, plastics, and organs. It has a motor race track where the most important Italian automobile races are held.

Monza first became important in the 6th century when Lombard kings were crowned alternately there and at Pavia, and the town's cloth trade was increasing. The Cathedral of St. John the Baptist, dating from the 13th and 14th centuries, stands on the site on the church founded about 590 by Queen Theodelinda, through whose influence the Lombards were converted from Arianism to Roman Catholicism. Her sarcophagus is in the cathedral, and the walls of the Queen Theodelinda Chapel are decorated with frescoes depicting scenes from her life, painted by the Zavattari brothers in 1444. The cathedral also possesses the famous iron crown of Lombardy, which tradition says was formed from a nail of the True Cross. (See CROWNS AND CORONETS—*Ancient and Medieval.*)

Monza also has a 13th century Gothic town hall; a royal villa built in 1777 for the Austrian Archduke Ferdinand, then governor of Lombardy, with an extensive park laid out in 1806 by order of Eugène de Beauharnais; and the Expiatory Chapel marking the spot where King Humbert I of Italy was assassinated on July 29, 1900. Pop. (1951) commune, 73,114; city, 69,263.

MONZONITE, mŏn'zō-nīt, an igneous rock of granular texture, often resembling granite in appearance. In mineral composition, however, it is intermediate between syenite and diorite, with both orthoclase and plagioclase feldspar present in about equal amounts. If quartz is present, it is called quartz monzonite.

LEWIS S. RAMSDELL.

MOOD, mōōd, or **MODE,** mōd, in grammar, the form of a verb that is used to show the manner in which a verb affirms or expresses something—whether it makes a simple statement; whether a doubt, wish, supposition, is indicated; whether a command is implied; or the like. While other languages have a number of moods to express these distinctions, in English the tendency has been to limit the moods to three: indicative, subjunctive, and imperative.

The *indicative* or *fact mood* states—or denies—a fact, or asks a direct question, as, *It is raining; That is not true; Are you ready?* In modern usage it may also express an uncertain condition, as, *If it rains tomorrow, we shall not go to the beach.*

The *subjunctive mood* does not state a fact; it represents something that exists only in the speaker's mind, and is sometimes called the mood of doubt or condition. Some grammarians divide it into the optative subjunctive, indicating something desired or intended, and the potential subjunctive, indicating something that is not actual, but is a condition contrary to fact or merely a conception of the mind. Examples of the optative subjunctive are *I move that the meeting be adjourned; Thy will be done.* Examples of the potential subjunctive are *If she had spoken up, he would be free; They are afraid lest he be captured.* The subjunctive, however, is much less used today in English than it formerly was, its place being taken by the indicative or by the imperative.

The *imperative mood* expresses command, entreaty, exhortation, or advice, or gives permission, as *Be still!; Angels and ministers of grace defend us!; Let not your heart be troubled; Assume a virtue if you have it not; Enter.*

Consult Evans, Bergen, and Evans, Cornelia, *A Dictionary of Contemporary American Usage* (New York 1957).

MOODY, mōō'dĭ, **(Arthur Edson) Blair,** American journalist and senator: b. New Haven, Conn., Feb. 13, 1902; d. Ann Arbor, Mich., July 20, 1954. After graduating from Brown University in 1922, he taught history and coached in athletics at the Moses Brown School in Providence, R.I., for a few years before joining the staff of the Detroit, Mich., *News,* an association lasting for 28 years, 17 of them as Washington correspondent. He also wrote for *Barron's Financial Weekly* and (from 1936) for the North American Newspaper Alliance, and during World War II served as war correspondent in Europe, North Africa, and the Middle East. He covered important events in Europe after the war, and in 1944–1945 was economic consultant to the Committee for Economic Development. He helped prepare Senator Arthur Hendrick Vandenberg's appeal in 1945 for bipartisan cooperation in United States foreign policy, and upon the senator's death in 1951 was appointed to fill his unexpired term of 21 months, the first active newspaper man to go directly from the press gallery to a Senate seat. Moody served as chairman of the Small Business Subcommittee, headed the inquiry into government censorship in 1952, and was chairman of the rules committee at the 1952 Democratic National Convention in Chicago. He lost his Senate seat in the Republican landslide that year. While campaigning for re-election to the Senate on the Democratic ticket in 1954 he was fatally stricken. The publisher of two suburban Detroit newspapers, he was the author of *Boom or Bust* (1941) and from 1946 was director and moderator of the radio-television program *Meet Your Congress.*

MOODY, Dan, American lawyer and public official: b. Taylor, Texas, June 1, 1893. Educated at the University of Texas, he was admitted to the bar in 1914. After serving as county attorney for Williamson County, Tex. (1920–1922) and district attorney for the 26th Judicial District (1922–1925), he became attorney general of Texas (1925–1926). He won national attention for his vigorous opposition to "Fergusonism"—the attempt to maintain the radical policies of James Edward Ferguson after he had been impeached and removed from office as governor of Texas in 1917. In her husband's place, his wife Miriam A. ("Ma") Ferguson had been elected as governor in 1924; when she sought re-election in 1926, Moody ran against her as a reform candidate, and won the election. After serving a second term as governor (1929–1931), he returned to law practice.

MOODY, Dwight Lyman, American evangelist: b. Northfield, Mass., Feb. 5, 1837; d. there, Dec. 22, 1899. Attending school until he was 13, he then worked on neighboring farms for a few years and at 17 became a clerk in his uncles' shoe store in Boston. While there he joined the Congregational Church. In 1856 he went to Chicago, became a traveling salesman for a wholesale shoe firm, and was soon making a good income. His main interest, however, was religion and human welfare, and in 1858 he organized a Sunday school in connection with which he developed a program of social welfare work. In 1860 he resigned from business to give all his time to this work. During the Civil War he served with the United States Christian Commission in their service to the troops, often working at the front. In 1863 he organized and built an undenominational church in Chicago, and in 1866 became president of the Chicago Young Men's Christian Association. For them he built Farwell Hall (sponsored by John V. Farwell), the first YMCA building in America. With the organist and singer Ira D. Sankey, Moody went to England in 1873 to conduct a remarkably successful series of revivals throughout the British Isles, in which the evangelical churches cooperated. After his return to the United States in August 1875, he made his home at Northfield, and for the next six years conducted revivals in cities from Boston to San Francisco.

Meanwhile, encouraged by Henry F. Durant, founder of Wellesley College, Moody established the Northfield Seminary (1879) for girls, and in 1881 Mount Hermon School for boys. That same year he returned to England, by invitation, to conduct a second series of evangelistic meetings which continued until June 1884. It was at one of the London meetings which closed this series that Wilfred T. Grenfell was inspired to devote his life to medical missionary work in Labrador. Moody spent the years from 1884 to 1891 in evangelistic work in the United States and Canada, in 1889 founding the Chicago Bible Institute (now called the Moody Bible Institute). University students in both Great Britain and the United States were interested in his work. In 1886 he held a conference of college students at Mount Hermon, and the following year in Northfield. At this meeting Henry Drummond gave his address on *The Greatest Thing in the World,* which has become an American classic. Held annually, these conferences stimulated the growth of the YMCA and similar student organizations in colleges. In 1891 Moody was again in England, and visited Palestine in 1892. From May to November 1893 he conducted evangelistic meetings in Chicago during the World's Fair. His sincerity and pronounced business ability gained him the confidence of responsible businessmen who supported his work. His preaching was simple, vigorous, and moving, emphasizing God's love rather than the terrors of hell. He accepted no financial profits, and all royalties from the Moody and Sankey hymnals were administered by a board of trustees chiefly for the endowment of the Northfield schools.

Consult Bradford, Gamaliel, *Dwight L. Moody, a Worker in Souls* (New York 1927), with bibliography; Erdman, Charles Rosenbury, *Dwight L. Moody, His Message for Today* (New York 1928); Moody, William Revell, *Dwight L. Moody* (New York 1930).

MOODY, Helen Wills. See WILLS, HELEN NEWINGTON.

MOODY, James, American Loyalist spy: b. New Jersey, 1744; d. Weymouth, Nova Scotia, April 6, 1809. He was a New Jersey farmer at the outbreak of the American Revolution, but in 1777 joined the British forces and soon became the most noted British spy of that period. Daring and unscrupulous, he spied on the troops of Washington, Gen. John Sullivan, and Gen. Horatio Gates. In the latter part of 1780 he was captured and imprisoned at West Point, but made his escape. Because of impaired health, he went to England in 1782, where he was given a pension of £100 a year and an award of £1,330 for his services. Obtaining a large grant of land on the Sissibou River in Nova Scotia, he settled there in 1786 and served as a colonel of militia until his death. He published an account of his adventures, called *Lieutenant James Moody's Narrative of His Exertions and Sufferings in the Cause of Government Since the Year 1776* (rev. ed. 1783).

MOODY, William Henry, American lawyer and Supreme Court justice: b. Newbury, Mass., Dec. 23, 1853; d. Haverhill, Mass., July 2, 1917. He graduated from Harvard in 1876, studied law in the office of Richard Henry Dana, author of *Two Years Before the Mast,* and began practice in Haverhill. He was city solicitor for a time, and from 1890 to 1895 was district attorney for the Eastern District of Massachusetts. He also served as a special assistant prosecutor in the Lizzie Borden murder trial. Elected to Congress by the Republicans in 1895, he was re-elected three times. He was secretary of the navy (1902–1904), succeeding John D. Long, and attorney general of the United States (1904–1906), succeeding Philander C. Knox. On Dec. 17, 1906 he was appointed an associate justice of the United States Supreme Court, but resigned in 1910 because of ill health.

MOODY, William Vaughn, American poet and playwright: b. Spencer, Ind., July 8, 1869; d. Colorado Springs, Colo., Oct. 17, 1910. After graduating from Harvard University in 1893, he became assistant in the English department there the following year. In 1895 he was appointed instructor in English at the University of Chicago and assistant professor in 1901, but he resigned in 1907 to devote all his time to writing. Besides his *Poems* (1901), he wrote the verse drama *The Masque of Judgment* (1900), and *The Fire-Bringer* (1904), a Promethean drama in verse. With Robert Morss Lovett he wrote the textbook *A First View of English Literature* (1905), the income from which enabled him to travel and write the play *A Sabine Woman,* which Margaret Anglin produced in 1906 as *The Great Divide* (q.v.). It was a pronounced success. His next play, *The Faith Healer* (1909, q.v.), had high merit but was not so successful. His *Ode in Time of Hesitation* (1900) is considered his best poem. His complete works were published in three volumes in 1912.

MOON

NASA

Central peaks and one side of crater Copernicus are seen in this picture taken by U.S. Lunar Orbiter 2 in 1969.

MOON is the only natural satellite of the earth. With a diameter more than one fourth that of the earth, it is by far the largest satellite in the solar system in relation to its primary. It moves about the earth once every lunar month in an elliptical orbit. Depending on its position in relation to the earth and sun, it appears in a number of phases from a full disk to a slender crescent. For a few days each month, at new moon, it is totally dark as seen from the earth.

The largest markings on the moon's surface—the dark areas called "seas"—are visible to the naked eye. Some 30,000 additional features, including mountains, craters, trenchlike rills, and valleys, have been identified by observers using telescopes, and detailed maps have been prepared. In addition, manned and unmanned vehicles have landed on the moon and observed fine details that cannot be seen from earth.

Many theories have been advanced to account for the existence of the moon. According to a popular hypothesis, a mass of material was flung from the surface of the primeval earth as mud is flung from a rapidly spinning wheel. This material became the moon. The theory calls attention to the moon's low specific gravity—about equal to that of the earth's surface—and to the vast cavity of the Pacific Ocean, presumed to be the scar left by the removal of the lunar material.

The activities of astronauts on the moon are described in detail and illustrated in color in the article SPACE EXPLORATION.

A second and more probable hypothesis is that the earth and moon were formed at the same time by an accretion of particles drifting about the protostar that became the sun. Theoretically, the two masses condensed near enough together to form a common system of gravity.

There is no generally accepted theory to account for the origin of the moon or, indeed, for any of the other planets or their satellites. As there are 32 natural satellites in the solar system, however, the experience that gave birth to the moon must have been common to each.

CHARACTERISTICS OF THE MOON

General Description. The moon's diameter is about 2,160 miles, or about 27 percent of the earth's. Its surface area is about 7.4 percent that of the earth, and its volume is about 2 percent that of the earth. Its density is 3.31 grams per cubic centimeter, compared with 5.52 grams per cubic centimeter for the earth. The moon's density is therefore approximately the density of rock, and the moon itself is probably a rocky mass without a metallic core. It has a surface

TABLE OF LUNAR DATA

Diameter (linear)	2,160 mi
Average apparent (angular) diameter	0.5°
Average (mean) distance from earth	238,866 mi
Least distance from earth (at *perigee*)	221,463 mi
Greatest distance from earth (at *apogee*)	252,710 mi
Average *albedo* (reflectivity of surface)	0.07
Physical constants (earth = 1):	
Mass	0.0123
Surface area	0.074
Surface gravity	0.1645
Volume	0.02
Density	0.60
Mean geocentric horizontal *parallax*	57′ 2.7″
Average daily angular motion in orbit	13°
Eccentricity of orbit	0.05490
Inclination of orbit to ecliptic plane	5° 8′
Inclination of orbit to earth's equator:	
Maximum	−28.5° to +28.5°
Minimum	−18.5° to +18.5°
Period of *sidereal* revolution and rotation—the time between two successive meridian transits of the same star	$27^d 7^h 43^m 11.5^s$
Period of *synodical* revolution—from *conjunction* to *conjunction* (approximately new moon to new moon)	$29^d 12^h 44^m 2.8^s$

gravity of about one sixth that of the earth. Accordingly, an object weighing 120 pounds on a spring scale on the earth weighs only about 20 pounds on the same scale on the moon. Escape velocity is also far less on the moon. While an initial velocity of about 6.95 miles per second is necessary for an object to escape from the earth's effective gravitational pull, an initial velocity of about 1.5 miles per second will enable an object to escape from the moon.

Since molecules of all gases will, at surface temperatures found on the sunlit moon, move faster than 1.5 miles per second, it follows that all free gases and water vapor have escaped from the surface of the moon. Gases of volcanic origin may occasionally leak from apertures in the lunar surface, and pockets of dense, inert gas may lie in some of the deeper depressions; but an atmosphere, as such, does not exist on the moon.

From this fact a number of consequences flows. Lacking a protective cover like the earth's, the moon is exposed to lethal radiations from the sun and incessant bombardment by meteorites. Furthermore, the range of heat and cold is unchecked by atmospheric insulation. Temperatures climb to about 215°F in the sunlight and plunge to about −250°F in the shade.

Because no air exists to carry dust particles and water vapor that refract and scatter sunlight, as they do on earth, the lunar sky is black both day and night. For the same reason, shadows on the moon seem totally black. Astronauts on the lunar surface reported the difficulty they had in seeing when they moved from areas of shadow to areas of sunlight.

The sun is intensely bright during the lunar day and obscures the light of stars in the sky, although under ideal viewing conditions it might be possible to see some of the brightest stars and planets. The earth, however, presents a glorious spectacle in the lunar sky; and seen from the night side of the moon, the black sky would be filled with steadily shining stars, including many that are hidden from a viewer on earth by atmospheric interference.

Through telescopes the moon's color appears as different shades of gray, but astronauts orbiting the moon and landing on its surface reported it as ranging from gray to cocoa brown. Although the surface sometimes shows slight luminescence, it shines mainly by reflecting sunlight. The moon reflects only 7 percent of the light that strikes its surface, and ranks with the planet Mercury as the poorest reflector in the solar system. It appears bright only because of its proximity to the earth. In astronomical terms, the magnitude (scale of brightness) of the full moon is −12. The brightness of the sun's light is about 400,000 times as great.

The moon at quarter phase presents half as much lighted surface as the full moon, but produces only one ninth as much light. The quarter phases reflect sunlight received at a smaller angle and, therefore, show shadows of surface irregularities that reduce the total light reflected.

Craters. According to an estimate made in 1962, there are about 300,000 craters more than a kilometer wide on the visible side of the moon. The hidden side of the moon, which does not have nearly as many of the smoother areas known as "seas" as does the side that is visible from the earth, is still more heavily marked with large, rugged craters.

The largest craters are called *walled plains*. Of these, the largest is Bailly, a pit 180 miles in diameter surrounded by mountains from 10,000 to 14,000 feet high. Clavius, a walled plain 146 miles wide, has a mountain wall from 12,000 to 17,000 feet high. Hundreds of smaller craters clutter the floors of both Bailly and Clavius. All are presumed to be the impact scars of meteorites.

Craters somewhat smaller than walled plains are called *ring plains*. Copernicus and Tycho, each about 56 miles in diameter, are the most conspicuous members of this class. Each has a cluster of mountain peaks at the center of its gorge and an extensive system of *rays* beyond its mountain walls.

Rays are associated with only a few craters, called *ray craters,* and can be seen most easily at full moon. They appear as irregular bright markings, extending radially in some cases more than 1,000 miles from the craters that are obviously their sources. They lie over mountains and valleys alike—evidence that the features underlying these rays are older than the associated ray craters.

The rays are thought to consist of materials hurled by the meteoritic explosions that produced the craters. Photographs of ray areas taken by U.S. Ranger and Lunar Orbiter space probes show secondary craters—scars of particles that were splashed over the landscape by the explosions that formed the ray craters.

Most of the large craters have either central peaks or traces of mountains on the plains within their walls. On the other hand, craters less than five miles wide generally have none. The evidence suggests that the titanic impacts responsible for the largest craters unleashed volcanic forces. These forces raised mountains that, in some cases, subsequently subsided into lava flows.

Volcanic activity also may have created the *domes* on the moon. These bell-shaped hills, rising gently from the surface, have small central pits, often hardly more than orifices. Domes are thought to be lava blisters, raised by hot

Lick Observatory

The moon's more prominent seas (maria), craters, and mountain ranges are indicated on this photograph of the full moon as it is seen through an inverting telescope.

gases as lava flows cooled and hardened.

Ranger photographs disclosed for the first time the wealth of small craters, or *craterlets,* on the moon's surface. Although many of these are undoubtedly secondary craters, some are primary craters caused by small meteorites.

The rest of the moon's craters, those called *dimple craters,* are probably not craters at all. These small holes, so deep that no bottom is visible, appear to be collapse features indicating the presence of fissures just under the surface.

Seas. There are about 30 large, irregular, dark areas on the visible side of the moon. Early telescopic observers assumed these areas consisted of water and accordingly named them oceans, seas, bays, and so on. By the time investigators learned there was no water on the moon, these names had gained common usage, and they have been retained.

The lunar seas, generally designated by the Latin word *maria* (singular, *mare*), are broad, typically flat plains. They have smoother surfaces and fewer craters than other areas of the moon. The *maria* appear darker than other parts of the moon because their smooth surfaces reflect sunlight less efficiently than the many-faceted surfaces of craters and mountains.

Several theories have been advanced to account for the flat plains, including the suggestion that they represent very ancient impacts of gigantic meteorites on the lunar surface. It is generally agreed that the plains were later formed by flooding of the areas with lava and ash, whether as a result of volcanic activity or of heat generated by radioactive decay.

LICK OBSERVATORY

Exploration of the Moon

Apollo mission landing sites are indicated on this view of the moon as seen from earth.

On July 20, 1969, Apollo 11's lunar module became the first manned craft to land on the moon. Edwin Aldrin (*below*) stands beside one landing pad of the module.

NASA

As part of the Apollo 12 lunar mission in November 1969, astronaut Alan Bean (*below, left*) walked about 600 feet (180 meters) from the landing site to inspect Surveyor 3, placed on the moon in 1967. The Apollo 14 lunar module landed in February 1970. Its astronauts encountered large boulders (*below, right*) as they walked on the surface.

NASA

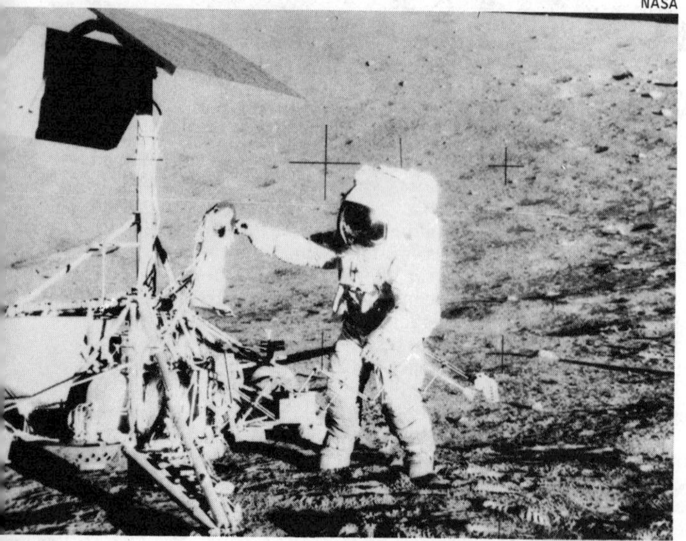

NASA

NASA

The Apollo 15 mission of July 1971 provided a magnificent live television view down the canyon of Hadley Rill.

NASA

Apollo 15 astronaut David Scott photographs the moon's surface. In his left hand he holds tongs for gathering samples of rocks. Rising in the background are the Apennine Mountains, their base about 10 miles (16 km) away.

The Apollo 16 mission of April 1972 explored a highlands area of the moon. As on the preceding mission, the vehicle known as the lunar rover (*right*) was very useful in transporting the men long distances.

Below the surface of some—but not all—of the mare regions lie concentrations of denser material known as *mascons*. The masses cause local intensifications of gravity and perturb the orbits of vehicles circling the moon. The mascons may represent rebound splashes of material following a meteorite impact, or they may be lava-flooded areas that for some reason did not later reach isostatic equilibrium.

Mountains. Of the moon's surface features, the mountains most nearly resemble familiar features of the earth. In fact, lunar mountains may have been created by the same process that produced the earth's—a folding and shrinking of the surface. Some lunar peaks tower higher than the highest mountains on earth. Epsilon, in the Leibnitz range, rises to an estimated 30,000 feet—about 1,000 feet higher than Mt. Everest. Other conspicuous lunar peaks range from 20,000 to 26,000 feet high.

The Straight Wall, which cuts across Mare Nubium, is the most prominent of several conspicuous cliffs on the moon. About 60 miles long and 1,500 feet high, it probably made its appearance along the line of a fault, when one or both rock faces of the crack slipped.

Other Features. Of all lunar formations, the *rills* or *clefts* are perhaps the strangest. These shallow trenches extend for miles. The Ariadaeus Cleft, the most conspicuous, extends for about 150 miles from the crater Ariadaeus. It is about one mile wide and about a half mile deep. Ranger photographs show several rills near the crater Alphonsus that look as though they had been gouged out by a gigantic bulldozer. Hadley Rill, explored by Apollo 15 astronauts David Scott and James Irwin in the summer of 1971, extends about 80 miles across the lunar surface and has an average depth of about 1,200 feet.

Rills and clefts are clearly collapse features, evidently caused by deep-seated fissures. The same phenomenon probably accounts for the moon's *crater chains*—strings of small craters, like or resembling dimple craters. Some of the rills appear to connect series of craterlets in chain formation.

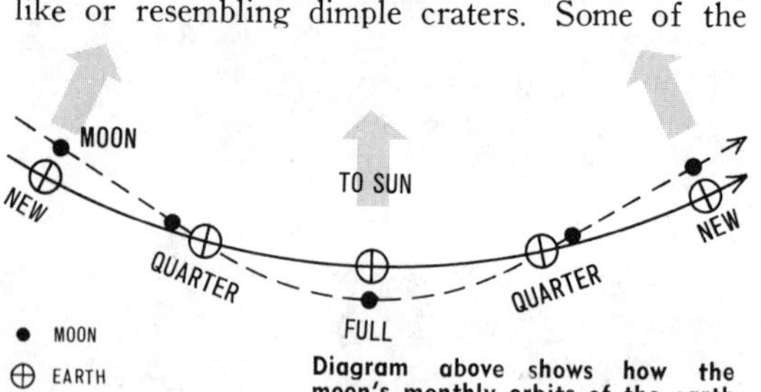

There are several prominent *valleys* in the mountain ranges on the moon. The most conspicuous is the Alpine Valley, a remarkably straight gash that runs 60 miles through the Alpine range.

Surface Materials. Unmanned probes placed on the moon in the 1960's showed that manned landings could be made safely. They revealed a lunar soil consisting of a finely granular material in which rocks of varying size are scattered, the material for the most part having a composition similar to that of basalt.

Rocks returned from the moon contained quantities of tiny glass beads such as meteorite impacts would produce, as well as particles produced by long exposure to cosmic rays. The soil yielded abundances of inert gas particles derived from the solar wind, the stream of particles flowing outward from the sun. These findings indicate that the lunar surface is ancient. In addition, some of the rocks were igneous in origin, indicating that volcanic activity has indeed taken place on the moon in the past.

MOON
NEW
TO SUN
QUARTER
FULL
QUARTER
NEW
• MOON
⊕ EARTH
MOON'S ORBIT
EARTH'S ORBIT
1
2
3

Diagram above shows how the moon's monthly orbits of the earth affect its annual journey around the sun. Below, the moon completes a revolution around the earth (from 1 to 2) during the sidereal month. The synodic month elapses between conjunctions with the sun at 1 and 3.

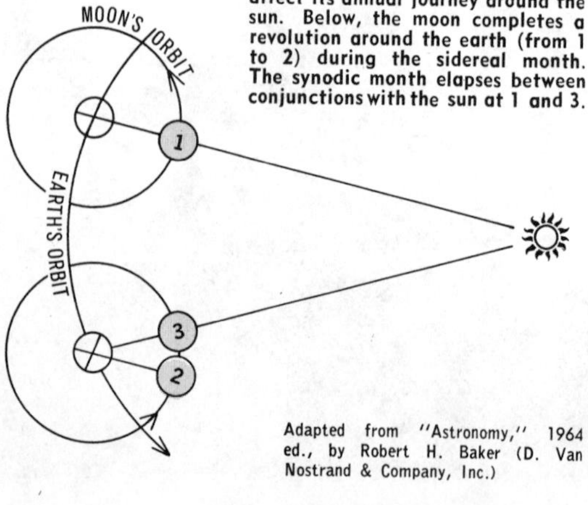

Adapted from "Astronomy," 1964 ed., by Robert H. Baker (D. Van Nostrand & Company, Inc.)

LUNAR MOTION

Revolutions. Seen from a distant vantage point, the earth-moon system would resemble the weight and counterweight of a pendulum, oscillating slowly on an invisible point. The two bodies are a binary system—bound together by each other's gravity in such a way as to describe orbits around the same center of gravity. This point, called the *barycenter,* is about 2,900 miles from the center of the earth, and about 1,000 miles beneath its surface. The location of the barycenter is dictated by the ratio between the masses of the earth and moon. Since the mass of the moon is 1/81.5 (or 1.22 percent) that of the earth, the distance between the barycenter and the moon's center is 81.5 times the distance between the barycenter and the earth's center.

The moon's distance from earth is generally given as 238,866 miles, its *mean distance.* Because the moon moves about the earth in an elliptical orbit (eccentricity=0.055), its distance varies between extremes of 221,463 miles, called *perigee,* and 252,710 miles, called *apogee.*

The apparent motion of the moon from east to west is an illusion caused by the rotation of the earth. The real motion of the moon around the earth is from west to east. The moon's average speed in orbit, 2,287 miles per hour, is sufficient to move it through an angular distance of 33′ of arc each hour—slightly more than its own apparent diameter. It traverses about 13° of arc every 24 hours. Moving at this speed, it displaces itself constantly eastward so that it rises and sets later every day. This time loss, called *retardation,* averages 50 minutes a day. Because of irregularities of the moon's motion, however, the daily retardation varies from 20 to 80 minutes.

The moon completes a revolution about the earth in an average period of 27 days, 7 hours, 43 minutes, 11.47 seconds. This period, called the *sidereal month,* varies as much as seven hours depending on the effect of certain perturbations of the moon's motion.

Because the earth moves in its orbit about the sun nearly 30 degrees while the moon is completing a revolution about the earth, the interval between new moons is slightly longer than the sidereal month. The longer interval, called the *synodic month,* averages 29 days, 12 hours, 44

LUNAR FEATURES PHOTOGRAPHED BY LUNAR ORBITER SPACECRAFT

Nearly all of the moon's surface was recorded by the cameras of the United States series of Lunar Orbiter probes launched in 1966–1967. (*Right*) The large dark crater seen in the rough terrain of the moon's hidden side is about 150 miles wide. (*Below left*) The channel-like valleys photographed by Lunar Orbiter 5 perhaps indicate volcanic eruptions and subsequent flow of fluid materials downstream to the floor of the mare, or "sea." (*Below right*) Erosion of the walls of the crater Aristarchus and of the rills in the crater's floor is clearly visible in a photograph made from a height of nearly 80 miles above the surface.

NASA

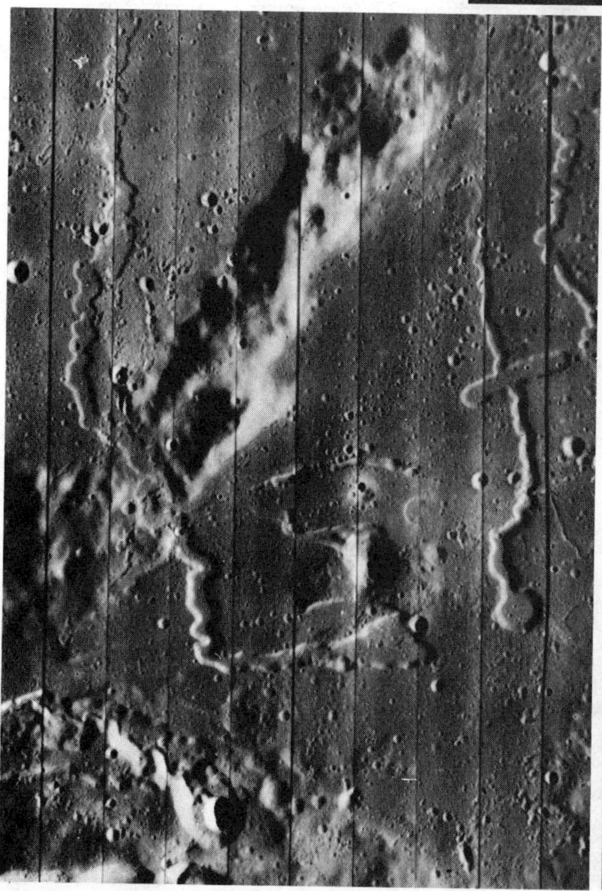

minutes, 2.78 seconds. This period may vary as much as 13 hours.

Rotation. The moon turns on its axis once during each synodic month; its rotation period exactly equals its average period of revolution. This curious coincidence of timing explains why the same side of the moon always faces the earth. The latter's gravity, although not strong enough to pull the moon out of orbit, was apparently once strong enough to lock it in a captive rotation. That the moon's diameter at a right angle to the earth is greater than the diameter in the plane of its orbit is further evidence of the earth's strong gravitational attraction.

Phases. Half of the moon, a constantly changing half, is always fully illuminated by the sun. As the moon revolves around the earth, the face turned toward earth enters and leaves the sunlight, and its appearance changes accordingly. At *new moon,* when the moon is in conjunction with the sun (approximately between the earth and sun), no sunlight strikes the visible face of the moon. The new moon, therefore, is invisible to earth.

As the moon moves eastward, the angle between it and the sun increases. A few nights after new moon, the edge of the sunlit half of the moon appears as a slender crescent for a brief period after sunset. This phase is technically the crescent after new, or *waxing crescent,* though it is popularly called the new moon. The outer edge of this crescent, the real edge of the moon's disk, is always turned toward the sun. This edge is called the moon's *limb.* The inner, concave edge is called the *terminator.* Unlike the limb, it changes shape constantly. The sharp ends of the crescent, which always point away from the sun, are called *cusps.*

The daily motion of the moon constantly increases the angle between it and the sun. Each day after new moon, therefore, more of the earthward side of the moon is illuminated and the crescent grows. In about a week, half of the moon's disk is lighted. This phase, occurring when the moon has completed one fourth of its revolution about the earth, is called *first quarter moon.*

During the following week, more and more of the moon's face comes into view, and the terminator becomes convex. The moon between first quarter and full is described as *gibbous,* a word derived from the Italian *gibboso,* meaning "hunchbacked."

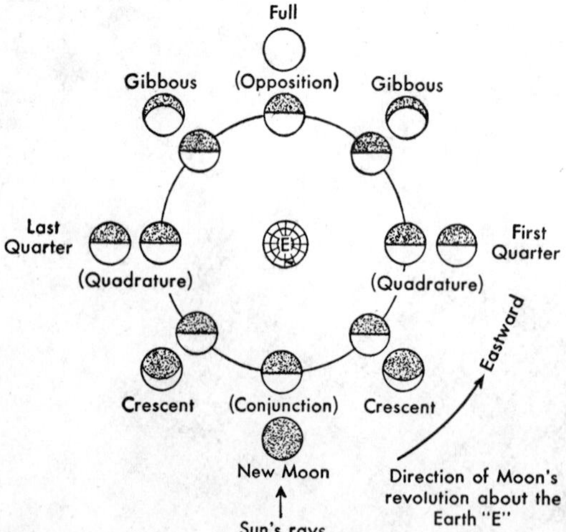

The moon's phases. Inner ring of disks shows the side of the moon always lighted. Phases as seen from the Earth (E) are shown in the outer ring of disks.

About two weeks after new moon, the moon reaches opposition, at an angle of 180° from the sun. It is then opposite the sun in the earth's sky, and its entire earthward face is lighted. This is the *full moon.* Thereafter, its motion reduces the angle between it and the sun, and the lighted face gradually disappears.

As it wanes, the moon goes through another gibbous phase, before reaching *last quarter.* At last quarter, the half of the moon's disk not seen at first quarter is visible, and the other half is dark. For about a week after last quarter, the crescent before new, or *waning crescent,* diminishes until the moon again reaches conjunction with the sun and disappears.

Occasionally during the waxing and waning crescent phases, the portion of the moon normally dark will be faintly visible. This dim light is caused by *earth-shine*—earth-reflected sunlight that is reflected back to earth from the dark part of the moon.

The moon completes its phases during the course of a single lunar day. During this time, an observer on the moon would see the sun rise slowly in the east, cross the sky in slightly less than 15 earth days, and set in the west.

On the moon's earthward side, the brilliant planet lights the lunar night. The earth remains perpetually in the lunar sky, phasing as the moon does, while stars sweep slowly from east to west beyond it. The earth's phases, however, are the opposite of the moon's. "Full earth" occurs at new moon, during the long lunar night, and "new earth" occurs at the height of the lunar day, when the sun appears to move slowly through space beyond the earth.

Librations. At any one time and from any one place, no more than 50 percent of the moon's surface may be seen from the earth. However, certain real and apparent motions of the moon enable us, in the course of time, to see somewhat more than this percentage.

Because the rotation of the moon is regular and its revolution is irregular, the earthward face of the moon is turned slightly to one side and then to the other during the course of each revolution. Brief glimpses around each limb are therefore possible. This apparent rocking of the moon from side to side is called *libration in longitude.*

The moon's orbit is inclined slightly to the earth's. Thus, in winter, when the moon is highest in the northern sky, more of its lower surface is visible. During the low moon of northern summer, more of its upper surface is visible. This apparent rocking from top to bottom is called *libration in latitude.*

The third and last libration is the only one resulting from a true irregularity of the moon's motion. Called *physical libration,* it is a barely perceptible wobble caused by the moon's aspherical shape. It permits a very limited view beyond each side of the moon during each synodic month.

Taken altogether, these extra glimpses of the moon's surface reveal about 9 percent more than can be seen at any one time (for a total of 59 percent). Forty-one percent of the moon's surface is therefore never visible to terrestrial observers.

Eclipses. As seen from earth, the sun and moon have about equal diameters—roughly 30′ of arc. Thus the disk of the moon can cover the entire disk of the sun, as periodically it does. On these occasions, called *total solar eclipses,* only the chromosphere and corona, the outer regions of the sun, may be seen.

Solar eclipses occur when the sun, moon, and earth are in line. If the moon's orbit around the earth and the earth's around the sun were in the same plane, eclipses of the sun and moon would occur every month. The plane of the moon's orbit, however, is inclined to that of the earth's by 5°8′. Thus the moon crosses the ecliptic twice each revolution, descending and ascending; and it is only at these times that total solar eclipses occur. The points of crossing are called *nodes,* the first being the *descending node* and the second the *ascending node.*

During a solar eclipse, the moon's shadow, cast into space from the side away from the sun, falls on the earth. This shadow has two parts. The central portion, the *umbra,* is a cone whose diameter at its base is the diameter of the moon. The umbra tapers to a point at a distance varying from 236,000 to 228,300 miles from the moon, depending on the distance between the sun and moon. A fainter shadow cone, the *penumbra,* surrounds the umbra. The penumbra is widest at its extreme distance from the moon and tapers from that region to the moon.

Since the mean distance from the earth to the moon is about 238,000 miles, the tip of the moon's umbra falls short of the earth in most eclipses. When the moon is at or near perigee, however, the tip forms a spot about 160 miles wide on the surface of the earth. A total eclipse of the sun may be seen by an observer standing within the shadowspot.

The motions of the earth and moon cause this spot to travel across the earth's face at more than 1,000 miles per hour. Thus the duration of totality at any location is brief. It is usually no more than two or three minutes, although it may persist slightly more than seven minutes.

Observers within 2,000 miles of the central eclipse path will see a *partial eclipse*—part of the moon's disk silhouetted against the sun. Partial eclipses occur in two other ways. When, during a central eclipse, the moon is too far away for its umbra to reach the earth, a narrow ring of the sun will be visible around the edge of the silhouette of the moon. This phenomenon is called an *annular eclipse,* from the Latin word *annulus,* meaning ring. Otherwise a partial eclipse occurs when the umbra points near the earth but not at it, and when the earth falls within the shadow of the penumbra. The maximum number of solar eclipses possible during a single year is five. Usually there are only two or three.

On less frequent occasions, the earth's shadow envelops the moon and causes a *lunar eclipse.* Total eclipses of the moon occur when the moon is full and at or near one of its nodes. The sun must be at or near the opposite node. Under these circumstances, the umbral shadow of the earth falls on the moon. This shadow cone, stretching 850,000 miles, is about 5,500 miles wide at the moon's mean distance. Since the moon moves only slightly more than its 2,160-mile diameter each hour, the average duration of an eclipse of the moon is therefore about one hour and 40 minutes.

The moon does not disappear during the so-called lunar eclipse because sunlight striking the side of the earth away from the moon is refracted and filtered by the earth's atmosphere. Although blues are absorbed, reds are transmitted around the sides of the earth, filling the earth's shadow with a red glow. This remnant of light dimly reveals the moon in a strange coppery hue, the intensity of which depends on local atmospheric conditions.

Certain variations of the positions of the earth, moon, and sun also produce partial lunar eclipses, called *penumbral eclipses.* In these, only the penumbra of the earth's shadow falls on the moon, dimming its light.

Lunar eclipses usually occur twice a year. In unusual circumstances, they occur either three times a year or not at all. See also ECLIPSE.

Tides. Both the sun and moon exert a gravitational pull on the earth. These forces, especially the moon's, produce tides in the earth's seas. At new moon and full moon, when the attractions of both bodies are working in the same plane, the ocean tides are most profoundly affected. The moon's gravitational force lifts the waters on the earth's near side. The earth itself receives a lesser pull and draws away from the waters on the far side. Consequently there are two tidal bulges, on opposite sides of the earth. Maximum high tides usually occur twice in a lunar day, when the sun and moon are in conjunction and opposition.

If the earth had no surface land, a tidal bulge would move around it directly under the moon. As it is, the continents form barriers that impede the flood and create local tide situations that differ according to the location of the land.

Tides arrive each day about 50 minutes later than the day before—a consequence of the moon's retardation. Accordingly, since the average speed of the earth's rotation is faster than the speed of the tides, the tidal movement acts as a brake on the rotation. In this way, one second is added to the earth's day about every 100,000 years. See also TIDES.

RESEARCH AND EXPLORATION

Mapping the Lunar Surface. The first man to see the moon through a telescope was Galileo, in 1609. He saw at once that some of the moon's surface features closely resemble the earth's. He drew the first map of the moon, indicating mountains, craters, and other conspicuous features. Mistakenly assuming the large, dark areas he saw were covered by water, he called them "seas" and other generic terms for bodies of water.

As telescopes improved, observers drew increasingly accurate maps. In the mid-17th century, Johannes Hewel, whose name has been Latinized to *Hevelius,* charted the principal mountains and mountain ranges. These he named after ranges on earth—Alps, Caucasus, Carpathians, and so on. A few, the d'Alembert and Leibnitz Mountains, for instance, were subsequently named for famous philosophers and scientists.

In 1651, Giovanni Riccioli charted the moon's larger craters and named them after famous astronomers and other scientists, including himself. Later selenographers adopted the custom, and the names of the craters therefore constitute a "hall of fame" of astronomers and great men in related sciences, as well as a few interlopers.

In the 20th century, the addition of cameras to telescopic equipment brought to view a world of lunar detail previously unknown. Of the maps based on photo-telescopic observations from the earth, perhaps the best is that of H. Percy Wilkins, published in 1946. It is drawn on a scale that covers the diameter of the moon in 300 inches.

The many thousands of excellent photographs sent back from the moon or its vicinity by U.S. and Soviet lunar probes and orbiters have revolutionized man's knowledge of the lunar surface. Thus, a relief chart of the visible surface of the moon has been prepared by the U.S. Air Force Aeronautical Chart and Information Center on a scale of 1:1,000,000, based on the photographs taken by the Ranger series of probes. In addition, virtually all of the surface of the hidden side of the moon also has been mapped.

Space Probes. NASA was engaged in several space programs associated with Project Apollo, the United States effort to place a team of two explorers on the moon by 1970. Before a manned landing could be attempted, possible landing sites had to be carefully surveyed and analyzed to make sure they were firm enough to support a manned landing and takeoff. The nature and appearance of these sites also had to be determined.

The first of NASA's space programs directed toward this end was the Ranger program of photoreconnaissance. NASA commissioned nine Ranger space vehicles to take and relay to earth closeups of the moon near designated target areas on its surface. Three of the Ranger missions succeeded before the program was completed in 1965, providing the first clear views of the rough surface of the lunar terrain.

The Surveyor program, the second of NASA's series of lunar probes, was designed to soft-land instrument packages on the moon. After long delays the program was successfully initiated in June 1966, with Surveyor 1. It was concluded in 1968 when Surveyor 7 was set down near the crater Tycho. All but two of the probes carried out their missions. The Surveyors were equipped with crushable footpads in order to test the strength of the lunar surface, and they carried camera systems that permitted total coverage of the landing sites. Some of the photographs, taken through light filters, were combined back on earth to provide color pictures of the moon.

Later entries in the Surveyor series had extendable metal claws that dug small trenches in the lunar soil to determine its consistency. Each of the later probes also carried a small metal box containing radioactive sources that were used to bombard the lunar surface underneath the craft with alpha particles. The particles that were scattered back to detectors on the craft from the soil provided information on the chemical content of the soil.

NASA conducted another series of lunar probes, the Lunar Orbiters, concurrently with the Surveyor program. The first entry in this series entered its preliminary orbit of the moon in August 1966; the last, Orbiter 5, was successfully placed in lunar polar orbit a year later. Each of the five Lunar Orbiters was equipped with a photographic system that could take medium- and high-resolution pictures, using two different lenses. From the several thousand high-quality photographs obtained by the Orbiters, NASA selected a number of landing sites likely to be safe for the Apollo astronauts.

Throughout the period of Ranger and Surveyor activity, astronauts destined for the moon journey were engaged in two training programs. The first of these, Project Mercury, was completed in 1963. The series of Mercury flights, made by several astronauts in single-manned vehicles, yielded important information concerning the effects of space travel on man.

In the second program, Project Gemini, two-man crews underwent training in important flight maneuvers. These exercises included rendezvous and docking of two vehicles in space and leaving and reentering the vehicles in space suits.

The Apollo mooncraft carried a three-man crew in its command module. A separate lunar module, or LM, served to carry two of the astronauts down to the moon's surface and back again. Two moon-orbital flights were made before Neil Armstrong and Edwin Aldrin of Apollo 11 became the first men to set foot on the moon, on July 20, 1969. Several other manned missions subsequently were flown to the lunar surface. For detailed accounts of man's activities on the moon, see SPACE EXPLORATION.

The Soviet Union also placed a number of probes on the moon's surface and sent unmanned craft into lunar orbit. On Oct. 7, 1959, it took the first photograph of the moon's far side, and in 1970 it returned lunar soil samples to earth by means of an automated spacecraft for the first time.

LUNAR PHENOMENA

Optical Illusions. Although the full moon appears larger when it is rising than it does at the zenith, its angular diameter, in fact, is smaller at the horizon because the moon at the zenith is about 4,000 miles nearer the observer. This deception, called *moon illusion,* probably occurs because the observer unconsciously associates the rising moon with familiar landmarks on the horizon. The risen moon, on the other hand, appears small in the great vault of the sky.

At certain times the moon appears also to linger on the horizon. It does so most conspicuously during the full moon occurring nearest the autumnal equinox in September. Then the moon's orbit is inclined to the horizon at a shallow angle, so that the disk rises in a gradual, diagonal sweep. At this time also its retardation is slight, so that it rises on several successive evenings only a few minutes later than on the night before. According to tradition, farmers used the extra hours of light at the end of the day for fall harvesting. Hence the September full moon is called the *harvest moon.* The full moon of October, repeating this phenomenon to a lesser degree, is called the *hunter's moon.*

Changing Features. From time to time observers report changes in the appearance of various surface features of the moon. Investigators believe that many of the reports result from the play of shadows moving over the face of the moon during its passage around the earth.

Certain reports, however—those concerning the crater Linné, for instance—are not so easily explained. Linné, a feature in the Mare Serenitatis, has been described at different times as large, small, bright, and dark. Occasionally it is said to have vanished Other reports describe the gradual appearance and disappearance of red spots in the region of the crater Aristarchus. Astronomers generally agree that these apparent changes are real, but whether they are caused by volcanic activity or some other agency is not known.

MYTHOLOGY AND ART

The moon held a commanding place in ancient pagan religion and mythology. The variety of its appearances and the unearthly quality of its light enchanted early man, and he attached great significance to it. The moon was depicted in all primitive hierarchies as a goddess. The Greeks cast it as Selene, the night-riding sister of Helios, god of the sun. The Romans associated it with Diana, their chaste goddess of the hunt.

The moon and imaginary flights to it have figured in fiction for nearly 2,000 years. In the 2d century a Syrian writer named Lucian wrote a fantasy, *True History,* that pretended to be the journal of a trip to the moon. Johannes Kepler, Cyrano de Bergerac, Jules Verne, H.G. Wells, and many others followed Lucian's example. Poets, painters, and musicians likewise celebrated the moon in works of art.

In folklore, the moon has several faces. In some countries, the man in the moon is taken to be a woman, even a rabbit. Strange scenes are occasionally read into the lunar markings. Interpretations may depend on the supposed influence the moon is frequently reported to have on the earth, its inhabitants, and its fruitfulness.

The word "lunatic," derived from the Latin *luna,* meaning moon, was originally applied to persons believed to have fallen under the moon's influence. Similarly, peculiarities of character were explained by a person's being *moon struck,* behaving like a *moon calf,* or *mooning about.* To counteract the supposed baleful influence of the moon, men contrived countless small ceremonies, such as that requiring a person to count his money quickly after inadvertently seeing the new moon over his left shoulder.

Superstitions about the moon abounded among farmers, who planted their crops at full moon—or new moon—to assure a full harvest. The upturned early crescent moon was taken to be a portent of wet weather. In fact, research has failed to produce any definite evidence of a connection between the moon's phases and the weather.

See also CALENDAR—*Lunar Calendars* and *Lunisolar Calendars;* MOON, BLUE.

JAMES S. PICKERING
Hayden Planetarium, New York

Bibliography

Baldwin, Ralph B., *Fundamental Survey of the Moon* (McGraw 1965).
Colby, C.B., *Moon Exploration* (Coward 1970).
Cooper, Henry S., Jr., *Moon Rocks* (Dial 1970).
Middlehurst. Barbara, and Kuiper, Gerard P., eds., *Moon, Meteorites, and Comets* (Univ. of Chicago Press 1963).
Moore, Patrick, *Survey of the Moon* (Norton 1963).
Mutch, Thomas A., *Geology of the Moon* (Princeton Univ. Press 1970).
Thomas, C. Davis, ed., *Moon: Man's Greatest Adventure* (Abrams 1970).
Wilford, John N., *We Reach the Moon* (Norton 1969).

MOON, Blue, a comparatively rare phenomenon of meteorological optics, in which the entire illuminated portion of the moon acquires a distinct blue tone. Its cause is a colloidal suspension of particles in the atmosphere. The particles, produced by volcanoes, forest fires, and other phenomena, are carried aloft by strong upward air currents. They selectively absorb red light and produce the moon's blue color.

MOON GODDESS. See MYTHOLOGY—*Myths.*

MOONEY, Edward, American cardinal: b. Mount Savage, Md., May 9, 1882; d. Rome, Italy, Oct. 25, 1958. He was the youngest child born to Thomas and Sarah Heneghan Mooney, who in 1887 established their home in Youngstown, Ohio. His classical studies were begun at St. Charles College, Ellicott City, Md., and he studied philosophy at St. Mary's Seminary, Baltimore, Md. In 1905, he entered the North American College, Rome, to begin theological training. Four years later, April 10, 1909, he was ordained by Pietro Cardinal Respighi. Returning to the United States, the future cardinal taught dogmatic theology at St. Mary's Seminary, Cleveland, Ohio. In 1916 he was named first principal of the new Cathedral Latin School, which was founded that year by Bishop Farrelly of Cleveland. Before returning to Rome in 1923 to be spiritual director of the North American College, he served for a few months as pastor of St. Patrick's Church, Youngstown, his home city.

On Jan. 8, 1926, he was consecrated archbishop of Irenopolis and appointed apostolic delegate to India by Pius XI. He served in India until Feb. 25, 1931, when he was directed by the same pope to fill a similar office in Japan. His appointment to govern the see of Rochester, N.Y., came in August 1933, and in May 1937, he was named first archbishop of Detroit, Mich. In February 1946 he returned to Rome, where on February 21 he was elevated to membership in the Sacred College of Cardinals by Pius XII. Cardinal Mooney's talents for leadership and organization were recognized by the Catholic hierarchy in the United States by his election in 1935 as chairman of the administrative board of the National Catholic Welfare Conference. During World War II he ardently defended the rights of invaded nations.

LEO DEBARRY
Former Diocesan Director
Society for the Propagation of the Faith, Detroit

MOONFISH, any of the compressed ovate highly silvery fishes of the family Carangidae, genera *Selene* and *Vomer,* including small tropical forms allied to the pompanos. One greenish species (*Vomer setipinnis*) is well known in New York Bay and markets as a pan fish, sometimes called blunt-nosed shiner. More widely recognized is the horsehead (*Selene vomer*), which reaches a length of more than a foot, and is regarded along the South Atlantic coast as one of the best of food fishes; it also occurs along the western coast of Mexico and Central America, as do certain other species.

"MOONLIGHT" SONATA, a term used popularly in Germany and England for the Beethoven *Sonata quasi una fantasia* in C sharp minor (1801). The term arose when the critic Heinrich F.L. Rellstab (1799–1860) compared the first movement to a boat gliding by moonlight on Lake Lucerne.

MOONRAT or **RAFFLE'S GYMNURUS** (*Echinosorex gymnurus*), a member of the hedgehog family (Erinaceidae) and largest living species of the mammalian order Insectivora. It is found in Malaysia, Tenasserim, southern Thailand, Sumatra, and Borneo. Anatomically, it is one of the most primitive and generalized of modern mammals. The fur is thick, coarse, and black, with a mixture of whitish hairs on upper back, shoulders, and head. Its length, from the tip of its long, pointed, shrew-like snout to the base of its tail averages about 16 inches; the bare, scaly tail is about 9½ inches long. There are five toes on each limb. The moonrat is nocturnal and feeds on insects, grubs, and small animals.

Other names for the animal include "white shrew" and, in Malayan, *Ticus bulan.* See also HEDGEHOG.

MOONSEED, a woody vine of the genera *Menispermum* and *Cocculus* of the family Menispermaceae. The Carolina moonseed is native in southeastern United States.

MOONSTONE. A translucent or transparent variety of the mineral feldspar (orthoclase, albite, or labradorite) which exhibits a delicate pearly opalescent play of colors. Used as a gem.

MOONWORT. See BOTRYCHIUM.

MOORCROFT, William, English veterinary surgeon and traveler: b. Lancashire, England, about 1765; d. Andekhui, Afghan Turkestan, Aug. 27, 1825. He studied veterinary science in France, settled in London, and made a fortune which he lost in patents, and then became veterinary surgeon (1808) to the Bengal Army. He crossed the Himalayas, explored (1811–1812) the sources of the Sutlej and Indus rivers, explored (1819–1822) Lahore and Kashmir, visited Bukhara in 1825, and died at Andekhui.

MOORE, mo͞or; mōr, **Addison Webster,** American professor of philosophy: b. Plainfield, Ind., July 30, 1866; d. London, England, Aug. 25, 1930. He was graduated at De Pauw University in 1890, taking his M.A. in 1893; Ph.D., Chicago University, 1898. He served in the University of Chicago as assistant in philosophy (1895–1897), associate (1897–1898), instructor (1898–1902), assistant professor (1902–1904), associate professor (1904–1909), and professor (1909). He lectured on philosophy at Harvard in 1918. Among his works are *Existence, Meaning and Reality* (1903), and *Pragmatism and Its Critics* (1910). He was president of the Western Philosophical Association in 1911 and of the American Philosophical Association in 1917, and he was associate author of *Creative Intelligence* (1916).

MOORE, Alfred, American jurist, son of Maurice Moore (q.v.): b. New Hanover County, N. C., May 21, 1755; d. Bladen County, Oct. 15, 1810. At 20 he became captain in a regiment of North Carolina troops, but was soon afterward obliged to resign in order to provide for his destitute relatives. When the British seized Wilmington (1781), he raised a troop of volunteers, with whom he rendered great service to the American cause. In order to alleviate the distress to which his patriotism had reduced him, the general assembly in 1782 made him attorney general. He had been licensed to practice law in 1775, and he soon attained, by hard study, a foremost rank in his profession. He was raised to the bench in 1798 and became associate justice of the Supreme Court of the United States in 1799. He resigned in 1804.

MOORE, Benjamin, American Protestant Episcopal clergyman: b. Newtown, Long Island, N. Y., Oct. 5, 1748; d. New York City, Feb. 27, 1816. He was graduated at King's (now Columbia) College in 1768, studied theology, and in May 1774 went to England to obtain orders and, in June of the same year, was ordained deacon and priest. On his return to New York he became an assistant minister of Trinity Church and succeeded to the rectorship in December 1800. In 1801 he was consecrated bishop of New York. He was also president and professor of logic in Columbia College.

MOORE, Charles Herbert, American artist: b. New York City, April 10, 1840; d. Hampshire, England, Feb. 15, 1930. He was educated in the public schools of New York City. In 1871 he became instructor in art in the Lawrence Scientific School at Harvard University. Three years later he began his career of teaching the fine arts to the Harvard undergraduates. He was made professor in 1896, a position he held until his retirement in 1909. He was curator and later director of the Fogg Art Museum (1896–1909). He published *The Development and Character of Gothic Architecture; Examples for Elementary Practice in Delineation; Character of Renaissance Architecture; Swedenborg: Servant of God;* and *Mediaeval Church Architecture of England.*

MOORE, Charles Leonard, American poet and essayist: b. Philadelphia, Pa., March 16, 1854; deceased. He was educated in the schools of his native city. In 1878–1879 he was one of the managers of the Madeira and Mamoré Railroad Construction Company and was United States consular agent at San Antonio, Brazil, the headquarters of that operation. He was afterward engaged in railroad construction in Pennsylvania. He was then secretary of one of the Disston Florida Sand companies for four years. During the next 20 years he was occupied with literary work. He was a constant contributor to *The Dial* during that time. He published *Atlas* (1881); *Poems Antique and Modern* (1883); *Book of Day Dreams* (1887); *Banquet of Palacios* (1889); *Odes* (1896); *Ghost of Rosalys* (1900); *The Red Branch Crests—a Trilogy* (1904); *Incense and Iconoclasm* (1915); and *Idols and Ideals* (1919).

MOORE, Clarence Bloomfield, American archaeologist: b. Philadelphia, Pa., Jan. 14, 1852; d. 1936. He was graduated at Harvard (1873), then traveled through most of Europe, Asia, and Egypt. He crossed the Andes and traveled down the Amazon (1876) and made a journey around the world (1878–1879). He spent more than 20 years exploring the Indian mounds of South Carolina, Georgia, Florida, Alabama, Mississippi, and Louisiana.

MOORE, Clement Clarke, American educator and poet: b. New York City, July 15, 1779; d. Newport, R.I., July 10, 1863. He was a son of Benjamin Moore (q.v.); was graduated at Columbia College in 1798; in 1823 became professor of Oriental and Greek literature at the General Theological Seminary, New York, and retired from that position in 1850. He gave to the seminary the ground on which it stands. A collection of *Poems* which he published in 1844 included *A Visit from Saint Nicholas,* better known under another title—*'Twas the Night Before Christmas*—which has long had great popularity with grown people as well as with children. Written in 1822 for his own children, these verses were printed anonymously and without Moore's knowledge in the Troy *Sentinel,* Dec. 23, 1823. He also compiled *A Compendious*

Lexicon of the Hebrew Language (1809) and wrote *George Castriot, Surnamed Scanderbeg, King of Albania* (1850).

MOORE, Clifford Herschel, American Latin professor: b. Sudbury, Mass., March 11, 1866; d. Cambridge, Mass., Aug. 31, 1931. He was graduated (1889) at Harvard University and received the Ph.D. degree (1897) at the University of Munich. He was classical master (1889–1892) at the Belmont School for Boys, Belmont, Calif., professor of Greek (1892–1894) at Phillips Academy, Andover, Mass., instructor (1894–1895), then assistant professor of Latin (1895–1898) at the University of Chicago. He then joined the faculty of Harvard University, and was assistant professor of Greek and Latin (1898–1905); professor of Latin thereafter, and dean of the faculty of arts and sciences after 1925. In 1905–1906 he was professor of Latin at the American School of Classical Studies in Rome. He edited Frederic De Forest Allen's *Medea of Euripides* (1899); Horace's *Odes and Epodes . . .* (1902); and published *The Religious Thought of the Greeks . . .* (1916, 2d ed. 1925); *Pagan Ideas of Immortality* (1918); also numerous articles on classical philology and the history of religion.

MOORE, David Hastings, American Methodist Episcopal bishop: b. Athens, Ohio, Sept. 4, 1838; d. Cincinnati, Nov. 23, 1915. He was graduated from the Ohio University in 1860 and ordained to the ministry in that year, but entered the Union Army at the outbreak of the Civil War, remaining in it till the close of the war and attaining the rank of lieutenant colonel. He was president of the Cincinnati Wesleyan Female College (1875–1880) and of the Colorado Seminary, and chancellor of the University of Denver (1880–1889). He was elected bishop in 1900 and had his episcopal residence during the three ensuing quadrennial periods in Shanghai, China, Portland, Oreg., and Cincinnati, Ohio. He retired in 1912.

MOORE, Edward, English Dante scholar: b. Cardiff, Wales, Feb. 28, 1835; d. Chagford, Devon, Eng., Sept. 2, 1916. He was educated at Pembroke College, Oxford, where he received high honors and became honorary fellow, and was principal of St. Edmund Hall, 1864–1913 and a canon of Canterbury from 1903. He is favorably known for his studies of Dante, and published *The Time References in the 'Divina Commedia'* (1887; rev. in Italian, 1900); *Contributions to the Textual Criticism of the 'Divina Commedia'* (1889); *Dante and His Early Biographers* (1890); the *Oxford Dante* (complete in one volume, 1894); and *Studies in Dante* (3 series: 1896, 1899, 1903).

MOORE, Edward, English playwright: b. Abingdon, Berkshire, England, March 22, 1712; d. Lambeth, March 1, 1757. He was, by trade, a linen draper but failed in business and took up literature. His first work was *Fables for the Female Sex* (1744), and in 1748 his *Trial of Selim the Persian* and *The Foundling* were published. He owed, no doubt, some of his success in the literary world to such prominent patrons as George Lyttelton, 1st Baron Lyttelton, and Henry Pelham. His *Gil Blas* was published in 1751 and *The Gamester* in 1753, David Garrick probably assisting him in the work. From 1753–1757 he was editor of *The World,* a satirical periodical. A collection of his works under title of *Poems, Fables and Plays* was published in 1756.

MOORE, Edward Caldwell, American theologian: b. West Chester, Pa., Sept. 1, 1857; d. Cambridge, Mass., March 26, 1943. He was graduated (1877) at Marietta College, then at Union Theological Seminary (1884). He studied (1884–1886) at the universities of Berlin, Göttingen, and Giessen, then received (1891) the Ph.D. degree at Brown University. In 1884 he was ordained to the Presbyterian ministry and served as pastor at Yonkers, N. Y. (1886–1889), and Central Congregational Church, Providence, R. I. (1889–1901). In the latter year he became Parkman professor of theology at Harvard University, and in 1915 became also Plummer professor of Christian morals in the same institution. After 1905 he was university preacher and chairman of the board of preachers at Harvard. He was lecturer at Mansfield College, Oxford, England, 1894 and 1914; at Andover Theological Seminary, 1900; at Lowell Institute, 1903; and at Yale Divinity School, 1906. He published *The New Testament in the Christian Church* (1904); *History of Christian Thought Since Kant* (1912); *The Spread of Christianity in the Modern World* (1919); *West and East* (1919); and *The Nature of Religion* (1936).

MOORE, Edward Mott, American surgeon: b. Rahway, N. J., July 15, 1814; d. Rochester, N. Y., March 3, 1902. He studied medicine in New York and Philadelphia and was graduated (1838) as M.D. at the University of Pennsylvania. He settled in Rochester in 1840. In 1842 he received a call to the chair of surgery at the Vermont Medical College in Woodstock, Vt., where he lectured for 11 years. He served then successively at Berkshire Medical College, Pittsfield, Mass. (1853–1854); Starling Medical College, Columbus, Ohio (1854–1855); then went (1858) to Buffalo Medical College, serving in the same capacity until 1882. His greatest work was done in research and experiments on the heart's action. He was president of the New York State Medical Society; a founder of the American Surgical Association, succeeding Dr. Samuel D. Gross (1883) as its president; and was president of the American Medical Association (1889–1890).

MOORE, Eliakim Hastings, American mathematician: b. Marietta, Ohio, Jan. 26, 1862; d. Chicago, Ill., Dec. 30, 1932. He was graduated (1883) at Yale, receiving the Ph.D. degree in 1885. He then studied at Berlin (1885–1886) and was appointed tutor in mathematics at Yale (1887–1889), becoming assistant professor (1889–1891) at Northwestern University and associate professor (1891–1892). In 1892 he was made professor of mathematics at the University of Chicago, becoming head of the department from 1896–1931. He edited *Transactions* of the American Mathematical Society (1899–1907) and was associate editor of the *Proceedings* of the National Academy of Sciences after 1915. His articles appeared in many mathematical periodicals.

MOORE, Frank (Horatio Franklin). See Moore, Jacob Bailey.

MOORE, George (Augustus), Irish poet, novelist, dramatist, and critic: b. Moore Hall, Ballyglass, County Mayo, Ireland, Feb. 24, 1852; d. Ebury Street, London, England, Jan. 21, 1933. He was the son of George Henry Moore (1811–1870), member of Parliament for County Mayo. Moore's talents developed slowly. As a young man, he aspired to be a painter, and in 1873 went to Paris to study art. His studies were abortive, but his stay in Paris had at least two important consequences: it introduced him to the work of the French Impressionist painters, then little known or understood, and to the writings of the naturalistic school of fiction, of which Émile Zola and the Brothers Edmond and Jules de Goncourt were leading exemplars. His first publications, however, were two volumes of somewhat derivative verse, *Flowers of Passion* (1878) and *Pagan Poems* (1881).

Moore's first novel, *A Modern Lover,* appeared in 1883, and was followed in 1884 by *A Mummer's Wife,* his first successful attempt to apply the naturalistic technique of Zola to English material. A grim study in the degradation of alcoholism, it is notable, among other things, as the book which first awakened Arnold Bennett (q.v.) to the literary possibilities of his own "Five Towns." It and *A Drama in Muslin* (1886) and *Esther Waters* (q.v., 1894) were the only books of his earlier period which Moore considered worthy of inclusion in the collected edition of his works published in the 1920's. Among the rejects, besides *A Modern Lover,* were *Spring Days* (1888), *Mike Fletcher* (1889), and *Vain Fortune* (1892). These, he used to say in later years, were not really the work of George Moore but of an inferior imitator, Amico Moorini.

In 1899 Moore associated himself with William Butler Yeats and Edward Martyn in the establishment of the Irish Literary Theatre in Dublin, for which he wrote *The Bending of the Bough,* produced in 1900. (His only other dramatic attempt, *The Strike at Arlingford,* 1893, had been rejected by all the commercial managers in London.) Full of enthusiasm for the Irish Renaissance, Moore moved to Dublin in 1901, where 4 Ely Place was his home for the next decade. Temperamental difficulties with Yeats, Lady Gregory, and the other Abbey Theatre people soon developed, and Moore's most characteristic contribution to the short-lived Renaissance was the three volumes collectively titled *Hail and Farewell* (*Ave,* 1911; *Salve,* 1912; *Vale,* 1914). These brought to its highest development a genre Moore had begun with *Confessions of a Young Man* (1888) and *Memoirs of my Dead Life* (1906)—narratives purporting to be autobiographical, but really a fictitious rearrangement on a substratum of fact. They can seldom be trusted as history, but are highly entertaining reading.

During his Dublin days Moore continued to write novels similar to those of the previous decades: *Sister Teresa* (1901), a sequel to *Evelyn Innes* (1898), and *The Lake* (1905). Thereafter he wholly abandoned his earlier techniques in favor of highly stylized retellings or reinterpretations of historical and legendary material. Most notable of these was *The Brook Kerith* (1916), a tale based on the assumption that Jesus survived His crucifixion to live thereafter as a sort of hermit, and, on meeting with St. Paul, to be horrified at what the latter had made of His teachings. Other late works are *Héloise and Abélard* (1921) and *Aphrodite in Aulis* (1930).

An authorized biography by Joseph Hone was published in 1936; other biographical and critical studies include Charles Morgan's *Epitaph on George Moore* (New York 1935); Malcom J. Brown's *George Moore: A Reconsideration* (Seattle 1956); and Nancy Cunard's *G M: Memories of George Moore* (New York 1957).

DeLancey Ferguson.

MOORE, George Edward, English philosopher: b. Upper Norwood, Surrey, England, Nov. 4, 1873; d. Cambridge, Oct. 24, 1958. Educated at Dulwich College and at Trinity College, Cambridge, he took his B.A. degree at Trinity in 1896, was fellow of Trinity (1898–1904), and lecturer at Cambridge (1911–1925), becoming professor there (1925–1939). In the United States he was from 1940 to 1944 William Allen Neilson professor at Smith College, and visiting professor at Princeton University, Mills College, Swarthmore College, and Columbia University. In 1951 the king conferred on him the Order of Merit, and in 1955 Columbia University awarded him the Butler Gold Medal for distinguished services in philosophy.

Moore's influence as an acute and original thinker made itself felt very early in Cambridge, where his *Principia Ethica* (1903) was received with enthusiasm by a group of intellectuals having such distinguished members as John Maynard Keynes, Bertrand Russell, Desmond MacCarthy, and Lytton Strachey. This book profoundly influenced the direction which subsequent ethical theory took. In epistemology and metaphysics, which occupied Moore's thought in the greater proportion of his writings, certain papers had a comparable impact on philosophical positions current at the time. Among these the most widely influential were "The Refutation of Idealism," published in *Mind,* new series, vol. 12 (Edinburgh 1903); "Professor James' 'Pragmatism,' " in *Proceedings of the Aristotelian Society,* vol. 8 (London 1907–08), also in these *Proceedings,* "The Conception of Reality," vol. 18 (1917–18), "External and Internal Relations," vol. 20 (1919–20); "The Defence of Common Sense," in *Contemporary British Philosophy,* 2d series, ed. by J. H. Muirhead (London and New York 1925); "Proof of an External World," Henrietta Hertz Lecture, in *Proceedings* of the British Academy, vol. 25 (London 1939).

Moore's distinctive technique for investigating philosophical problems, the logical analysis of concepts, provided a methodological model for a large group of philosophers, primarily in the English-speaking world. His skillful and subtle use of this method requires an intellectual sophistication standing in sharp contrast to the naïveté usually attributed to the position in defense of which he employed it—the realistic position of philosophical common sense (q.v.). That there are material bodies, spatial and temporal relations, other selves, he took to be more certain than any arguments which idealists and skeptical philosophers raise against them. A sufficient criterion for the falsity of counterclaims was that they implied the falsity or self-contradictoriness of the beliefs of common sense. Moore's employment of this criterion, together with his critical analysis of the reasoning by which common sense beliefs were attacked, resulted, by implication, in a powerful defense of ordinary language used for the expression of such beliefs. The exactitude of his attention to the philosopher's use of language, as contrasted with the ordinary use, had a far-reaching effect on the trend of subsequent philosophical investigation toward clarification and analysis rather than system building.

Chief among Moore's published works, in addition to those mentioned, are the following books and articles: *Ethics* (1912); *Philosophical Studies* (1922); *Some Main Problems of Philosophy* (1953); *Philosophical Papers,* ed. by C. D. Lewis (London and New York 1959); "The Concept of Intrinsic Value," in *Philosophical Studies;* and "Facts and Propositions" (1927), "Is Goodness a Quality?" (1932), "Imaginary Objects" (1933), "Is Existence a Predicate?" (1936), all in symposia appearing in supplementary volumes of the *Proceedings of the Aristotelian Society.*

Consult also the following by Moore: "A Reply to My Critics," in *The Philosophy of G. E. Moore,* ed. by Paul A. Schilpp, The Library of Living Philosophers, vol. 4 (Evanston 1942); "Wittgenstein's Lectures in 1930–33," *Mind,* Nos. 249, 251, 253 (Edinburgh 1954–55); "Visual Sense-Data," in *British Philosophy in the Mid-Century,* ed. by Cecil Alec Mace, (London and New York 1957).

ALICE AMBROSE,
Professor of Philosophy, Smith College.

MOORE, George Henry. See MOORE, JACOB BAILEY.

MOORE, Grace, American soprano: b. Slabtown, Cocke County, Tenn., Dec. 5, 1901; d. in an airplane crash, Copenhagen, Denmark, Jan. 26, 1947. Blonde and vivacious, Grace Moore won her way to operatic stardom by study and hard work, though her voice was not a great one and her dramatic talents were limited. When she was five years old, her family moved to Jellico, Tenn., where she sang in the First Baptist Church choir. A concert of Mary Garden's, which she attended as a student at Ward-Belmont School, Nashville, at the age of 13, fired her with the ambition to become an opera star herself. In spite of family objections to a musical career, she was allowed to study voice at the Wilson-Green Academy of Music in Chevy Chase, Md., and in 1918 she made her concert debut in Washington, D.C., on the same program with Giovanni Martinelli. This encouraged her to go to New York City where she sang in a Greenwich Village café for six months and later in a road company. Her opportunity for a Broadway debut came in 1921 when she substituted for Julia Sanderson in *Hitchy-Koo.* The next year she sang in *Up in the Clouds* and in 1923 was given the lead in Irving Berlin's *Music Box Revue,* joining the *Revue* again in 1924 and 1925. She continued her voice lessons, had several unsuccessful auditions for the Metropolitan Opera Company, and in 1926 went to Europe for 18 months of intensive work, mostly with Mary Garden's teacher Richard Barthélmy. The coveted Metropolitan contract came when the Metropolitan's impresario Giulio Gatti-Casazza heard her sing in Milan, and on Feb. 7, 1928 she made her Metropolitan debut as Mimi in *La Bohème.* Her success was immediate. Other roles in which she won great popularity were the title roles in *Manon* and *Tosca,* Juliette in *Roméo et Juliette,* Marguerite in *Faust,* Micaela in *Carmen,* and Fiora in *L'Amore dei Tre Re.* She also sang in operas at Paris, Monte Carlo, and Covent Garden.

Grace Moore scored a brilliant success as prima donna in the Metropolitan's 1939 revival of Gustave Charpentier's *Louise,* and won wide popularity in the motion picture of the opera. Her Hollywood career began in 1930 in the pictures *A Lady's Morals* and *New Moon.* While vacationing in Europe she met the Spanish film star Valentin Parera and they were married at Cannes, France, on July 15, 1931. The following year she sang in New York in the operetta *The Du Barry.* Her most popular motion picture was *One Night of Love* (1934); others in which she starred included *Love Me Forever* (1935); *The King Steps Out* (1936); *When You're in Love* (1937); and *I'll Take Romance* (1937). She sang at army hospitals and canteens in World War II and toured Europe for USO camp shows. Her autobiography *You're Only Human Once* was published in 1944. She was on a European concert tour at the time of her death. Her grave is in Chattanooga, Tenn.

MOORE, Henry, English sculptor: b. Castleford, Yorkshire, England, July 30, 1898. After serving in World War I, he studied at the Leeds School of Art and at the Royal College for Art in London. In 1925 a traveling scholarship enabled him to continue his studies in France and Italy, where he was strongly affected by the work of Masaccio, the 15th century Italian painter, and the contemporary sculpture of Pablo Picasso, Aleksandr Archipenko, and Constantin Brancuşi. He also became interested in primitive sculpture. From these influences he developed his own style. Its modeling was almost archaic in its simplicity, and he was especially interested in using heavily rounded forms in his numerous recumbent figures of women (such as the *Reclining Woman* in the Cranbrook Academy of Art). They balance a feeling of weight and repose with one of dynamic force. Another characteristic of his, piercing his figures with openings, is well illustrated in his *Recumbent Figure* in the Tate Gallery in London.

Until 1944, Moore's style tended more and more to abstraction and then, perhaps as a result of his experiences in wartime London, it became more naturalistic. He introduced the spare, massive male figure into his compositions, as in the *Family Group* at Stevenage, Hertfordshire, England. He returned to abstraction in the four figures for the Time-Life Building in London, and the *Internal and External Forms* in the Albright Gallery at Buffalo, N.Y.

Moore carved in wood, stone, and concrete, modeled in terra cotta and cast lead, and sometimes incorporated copper wire and stretched string in his compositions, as in *The Bride,* an abstraction in cast lead and copper wire in the Museum of Modern Art in New York City.

Consult Sweeney, James J., *Henry Moore* (New York 1947); Ritchie, Andrew C., *Sculpture of the Twentieth Century* (New York 1953).

MOORE, Jacob Bailey, American historian and journalist: b. Andover, N.H., Oct. 31, 1797; d. Bellows Falls, Vt., Sept. 1, 1853. After being associated with the Concord (New Hampshire) *Patriot* as author and editor (1813–1823), he helped found the New Hampshire Historical Society, of which he was librarian from 1823 to 1830 and 1837 to 1839. From 1826 to 1829 he edited the New Hampshire *Journal,* building it into a powerful political organ supporting John Quincy Adams in his second presidential campaign. Moore edited the New York *Daily Whig* (1839–1841), and was chief clerk in the Post Office Department in Washington, D.C. (1841–

1845). Librarian of the New York Historical Society (1848–1849), he resigned to establish the post office in California, and was made deputy postmaster at San Francisco. Among his publications were *A Gazetteer of the State of New Hampshire* (1823) and the first three volumes of the *Collections of the New Hampshire Historical Society* (1824–32), both in collaboration with John Farmer; *The Principles and Acts of Mr. Adams' Administration Vindicated* (1828); and *Memoirs of American Governors* (1846).

His son George Henry Moore (1823–1892) became assistant librarian of the New York Historical Society in 1841, was elected secretary of the executive board in 1848, and succeeded his father as librarian in 1849. He served as librarian until 1876 (when he resigned to administer the Lenox Library in New York City), and as secretary of the executive board until 1891. He held his post with the Lenox Library until his death. He was not only an able administrator, building up the collections of both libraries, but did much valuable research, especially in the field of American colonial and Revolutionary history.

Jacob Bailey Moore's younger son, Frank Moore (1828–1904, baptized Horatio Franklin), was known for the works he wrote and edited on the Revolutionary and Civil Wars. Among them are *Songs and Ballads of the American Revolution* (1856); *Diary of the American Revolution, from Newspapers and Original Documents* (1859–1860); *The Rebellion Record* (11 vols. and supplement, 1861–1868); *Rebel Rhymes and Rhapsodies* (1864); *The Portrait Gallery of the War* (1864); and *Women of the War* (1866). His diary, 1877–1894, 36 vols., is in the library of the New York Historical Society.

MOORE, James, American colonial governor: b. probably in Ireland c. 1640; d. Charles Town (now Charleston), S.C., 1706. Emigrating to America about 1665, he settled in Charles Town about 1675. He served on the council of the province, and in 1700 was elected governor. He was, largely through self-interest in his trading with the Indians, a leader among those who opposed the rulings of the absentee proprietary government; his political career was a stormy one, and he twice dissolved the assembly. In 1702, in the course of Queen Anne's War, he led an expedition against the Spanish in St. Augustine, besieging the city for some weeks before he had to withdraw. When he was succeeded as governor by Sir Nathaniel Johnson in 1703, on his own initiative he raised troops and headed a raid against the Apalachee Indians which considerably weakened French influence and enslaved many Indians.

His son James Moore (1667–1740) took part in his father's campaigns against the Indians. In 1713 he led a decisive expedition against the Tuscarora, and another against the Yamassees in 1715. When the proprietary government was overthrown in 1719, he was for a few months royal governor, and then attorney general. He was speaker of the assembly (1721–1725); emigrating to North Carolina about 1835, he died in a pioneer village near Cape Fear.

MOORE, James (1737–1777). See Moore, Maurice.

MOORE, John, Scottish surgeon and author: b. Stirling, Scotland, baptized Dec. 7, 1729; d. Richmond, Surrey, England, Jan. 21, 1802. He was the author of the widely read travel books *A View of Society and Manners in France, Switzerland, and Germany* (1779) and *A View of Society and Manners in Italy* (1781), and of the novel *Zeluco* (1786), from which Byron drew the inspiration for the hero of his poem *Childe Harold's Pilgrimage.* Moore's *A View of the Causes and Progress of the French Revolution* (1795), quoted by Thomas Carlyle, recounted his observations during a lengthy stay in Paris in 1792. His works were edited, with a memoir, by Robert Anderson (7 vols., 1890).

His son, Sir John Moore (1761–1809), British army officer, entered the army at the age of 15. He served in Nova Scotia (1779–1783) during the American Revolution, and was a member of Parliament from 1784 to 1790. Returning to military service, during the war against France he distinguished himself in Corsica, the West Indies, Ireland, Holland, Egypt, and Spain, proving himself an able commander and a brilliant strategist. He was knighted in 1804. In 1808–1809, at the height of his fame, he commanded the English troops supporting the Spanish against Napoleon during the Peninsular War. Forced to abandon an attack on Madrid, which Napoleon had just taken, he led a heroic 250-mile retreat to La Coruña. He inflicted heavy losses on the French while his troops were embarking, but was himself killed. Charles Wolfe's poem *The Burial of Sir John Moore at Corunna* (1817) helped greatly to make him a national hero.

MOORE, John Bassett, American jurist and diplomat: b. Smyrna, Del., Dec. 3, 1860; d. New York, N.Y., Nov. 12, 1947. An outstanding authority on international law, Moore was a graduate of the University of Virginia (1880), was admitted to the Delaware bar in 1883, and began his diplomatic career in 1885 as a law clerk in the Department of State. Appointed third assistant secretary of state in 1886, he resigned in 1891 to take the newly created chair of international law and diplomacy at Columbia University. After representing the United States on many important international commissions and in inter-American conferences, he became a member of the Permanent Court of Arbitration at The Hague in 1912, and in 1921 was appointed one of the first judges of the newly organized Permanent Court of International Justice (the World Court), serving until 1928. He resigned from the Columbia faculty in 1924 in order to edit a comprehensive digest of international adjudications throughout history, with legal commentaries. Among his major published works are *A History and Digest of International Arbitrations in Which the United States Has Been a Party* (6 vols., 1898), *A Digest of International Law* (8 vols., 1906), *Principles of American Democracy* (1918), and *Pending Neutrality Proposals* (1936). He also edited *The Works of James Buchanan* (12 vols., 1908) and *International Adjudications, Ancient and Modern* (8 vols., 1929–1936).

MOORE, Marianne Craig, American poet: b. Kirkwood, Mo., Nov. 15, 1887; d. New York City, Feb. 5, 1972. After taking an A.B. at Bryn Mawr, she returned to her home in Carlisle, Pa., where she attended business school and taught commercial subjects in the United States Indian School for four years. During World War

I she moved to New York City, settling in her Brooklyn apartment home in 1929. She worked a few years as a public library assistant and, during the final years of its publication, was editor of the *Dial,* a distinguished literary monthly.

Early poems of Miss Moore were published in British and American magazines and in the volumes *Poems* (1921), *Observations* (1924), and *Selected Poems* (1935). She has received numerous honors. *Collected Poems* (1951) won three major awards: Bollingen, National Book Award, and Pulitzer Prize. *Like a Bulwark* (1957) attests the vigor of her creative powers at 70. Other publications are her verse translations *The Fables of La Fontaine* (1954), and *Predilections* (1955), a collection of prose essays.

The titles of two of her critical essays—"Feeling and Precision" and "Humility, Concentration, Gusto"—aptly suggest distinctive qualities of her own poetry. Her style is descriptive and objective; her technique skillful in the use of sustained rhythm and intricate verse patterns and rhymes; her subject matter drawn heavily from the world of plants and animals but with overtones, symbols, and occasional moralizing of human import. Her poems are sincere, original, witty, and at times satirical. Representative examples are "The Fish," "Poetry," "A Carriage from Sweden," and "In Distrust of Merits."

WM. BRACY.

MOORE, Maurice, American jurist: b. New Hanover County, N.C., 1735; d. about April 20, 1777. While serving as an associate provincial judge in North Carolina, he published the pamphlet *The Justice and Policy of Taxing the American Colonies in Great Britain Considered* (1765), which questioned the right of Parliament to tax the colonies without granting them representation. In consequence, he was suspended as judge, but was restored in 1768 and continued to serve until suspension of the court in 1773. At first opposed to the Regulators (q.v.), he later modified his attitude, and the public letter of 1771 signed "Atticus," criticizing Governor William Tryon's severe treatment of them, has generally been attributed to him. He was the father of Alfred Moore (q.v.) and the brother of JAMES MOORE (1737–1777), who fought against the Regulators in the Battle of Alamance Creek (q.v.), but later actively supported the Revolution and served as brigadier general in command of all North Carolina forces.

MOORE, Richard Bishop, American chemist: b. Cincinnati, Ohio, May 6, 1871; d. Lafayette, Ind., Jan. 20, 1931. Taken to England by his parents in 1878, he was educated there and in Paris, and while at University College, London, 1886–1890, studied under the chemist William Ramsay (q.v.), doing special research in rare gases and radium. Returning to the United States in 1895, he attended the University of Chicago for a year, taught at the University of Missouri (1897–1905) and at Butler College (1905–1911), pioneering in the investigation of radioactive substances. He returned to England in 1907 for a year of research on the rare gaseous elements krypton and xenon. Joining the United States Department of Agriculture in 1911 as soil chemist, he transferred in 1912 to the Bureau of Mines as physiochemist in charge of the chemistry and metallurgy of rare metals, and as chief of the Division of Mineral Technology (1919–1923), organized the cryogenic laboratory and had charge of all helium work. In 1926 he received the Perkin medal for the first isolation of radium salts in the United States and for his work on mesothorium and helium, and became dean of science and head of the Department of Chemistry at Purdue University.

MOORE, Thomas, Irish national poet: b. Dublin, Ireland, May 28, 1779; d. Devizes, Wiltshire, England, Feb. 26, 1852. He graduated from Trinity College, Dublin, in 1799, and went to London, where he entered at the Middle Temple, expecting to follow a legal career. Exceptionally talented in his command of classical Greek, in 1800 he published a translation of the *Odes of Anacreon.* This was his first introduction to the London world of letters and was an immediate success. His brilliant conversational powers together with his poetical and musical gifts soon made him a favorite in fashionable society. In 1803 he was appointed registrar of the admiralty court at Bermuda; but after spending a few months there, he appointed a deputy and left for a tour of the United States, where, at Norfolk, Va., he met President Thomas Jefferson. After visiting Canada he returned to England.

In 1806 Moore published *Epistles, Odes and Other Poems,* a volume which was so roughly handled by the critic Lord Jeffrey (Francis Jeffrey) in the *Edinburgh Review* that Moore challenged him to a duel. The police appeared and put an end to the affair. Explanations followed, and the men became close friends. In consequence of a rumor that the pistols were not loaded, Byron wrote a fierce satire which caused Moore to send a challenge to him. Mutual friends interfered and a friendship was formed which lasted for life.

In 1811 Moore married the young Irish actress Bessie Dyke, to whom he was deeply devoted throughout a long and happy marriage. They lived at Kegworth in Leicestershire for some time, and moved to Mayfield Cottage, Ashbourne, Derbyshire, in 1813. His literary credit was now so high that Longmans, the publishers, signed a contract to pay £3,000 for the yet unwritten *Lalla Rookh* (q.v.). This poem was published in 1817 and brought him worldwide fame, going through many editions and being translated into many European languages. Returning from a short tour of the Continent, he went to live at Sloperton Cottage, Devizes, which remained his home until his death in 1852. His grave is in neighboring Bromham.

By the defalcation of his deputy in Bermuda, Moore was rendered liable for a debt of £6,000, which was afterward reduced to £1,000. In order to avoid the debtor's prison he was obliged to go abroad. He traveled on the Continent with friends, visited Byron in Italy in October 1819, and for three years lived in Paris, where his family joined him in 1820. Having cleared off the debt by his writings, he returned to England in 1823. That year he published *Rhymes on the Road, Fables for the Holy Alliance* (he excelled in satirical verse) and *The Loves of the Angels,* and renewed his arrangements with James Powers, the music publisher, for the continued publication of the *Irish Melodies.* These appeared in series from 1807 to 1834 and established him as the national lyrist of Ireland (see IRISH LITERATURE IN THE ENGLISH LANGUAGE—*Poetry: 19th Century Poets*). Many of the numbers, such as "The Last Rose of Summer" and "Those

Evening Bells," are generally familiar. His *National Airs* (1815) included "Oft in the Stilly Night" and the *Sacred Songs* (1816), "Sound the Loud Timbrel." In 1825 appeared his *Life of Sheridan* and *The Memoirs of Captain Rock*.

The *Life of Byron* (full title, *The Letters and Journals of Lord Byron, with Notices of his Life*), which Thomas Babington Macaulay characterized as "deserving to be classed amongst the best specimens of English prose which any age had provided," was published in 1830, and remains the most authoritative life of Byron. Byron had given Moore his memoirs in 1819 to be sold for publication after his death. Moore sold them to the publisher John Murray in 1821, but at the insistence of Byron's literary executor and close friends, bought them back and burned them.

Moore's last literary works were *The History of Ireland* in four volumes (1835–1846) and the collection of his poetical works in 10 volumes (1840–42). His later years were saddened by domestic grief, his five children all dying before him. In his old age his health and memory failed, following a seizure. His diary and correspondence, edited by Lord John Russell, were published in eight volumes (1853–56) as *Memoirs, Journal and Correspondence of Thomas Moore*.

Consult Trench, W. F., *Tom Moore* (London 1934); MacCall, S., *Thomas Moore* (London 1935); Strong, L. A. G., *Minstrel Boy* (New York 1937).

HERBERT O. MACKEY,
Author of "The Life of Thomas Moore."

MOORE, Thomas Sturge, English poet, artist, and critic: b. Hastings, Sussex, England, March 4, 1870; d. Windsor, July 18, 1944. Largely self-educated, he was deeply interested in symbolism in art and literature, and was associated with Gilbert Murray and Arthur Symons in the Masquers, a Dublin group organized to produce symbolist drama. His verse included *The Vinedresser and Other Poems* (1899); *Aphrodite Against Artemis* (1901); *The Sea is Kind* (1914); *Tragic Mothers* (1920); and *The Unknown Known . . .* (1939); his prose works include *Dürer* (1904); *Correggio* (1906); *Art and Life* (1910); *Hark to These Three* (1915); and *Armour for Aphrodite* (1929); his collected poems were published in four volumes in 1932–1933. A gifted wood engraver, he designed the cover for William Butler Yeats' *The Tower* (1928); their correspondence, 1901–1937, was published in 1953.

Consult Gwynn, F. L., *Sturge Moore and the Life of Art* (Lawrence, Kans. 1951).

MOORE, Zephaniah Swift, American educator: b. Palmer, Mass., Nov. 20, 1770; d. June 30, 1823. Graduating from Dartmouth College in 1793, he studied theology. He was pastor of First Congregational Church in Leicester, Mass., from 1797 until 1811, when he became professor of ancient languages at Dartmouth. Appointed president of Williams College in 1815, he resigned in 1820 when the legislature refused to let the college move to a more accessible location, becoming the first president of Amherst College. He was an able executive, stressing the importance of liberal studies as a preparation for a professional career.

MOORE, Lake, lake, Australia, in Western Australia, about 150 miles northeast of Perth. It is 60 miles long, salty, and frequently dry. The area is 449 square miles.

MOOREA, mō-ô-rā'ȧ (formerly EIMEO), second largest of the Windward group of the Society Islands (q.v.), French Polynesia, in the South Pacific, about 12 miles northwest of Tahiti, and governed from Papeete. It has an area of 50 square miles and is mountainous; the highest peak (3,975 feet) is Mount Tohivea. Coffee and copra are the chief crops. Cook Bay and Papetoai Bay form good harbors on the northern coast; Afareaitu is the chief town. Pop. (1956) 3,528.

MOOREHEAD, mo͝or'hĕd, **Warren King,** American archaeologist: b. Siena, Italy, of American parents, March 10, 1866; d. Boston, Mass., Jan. 5, 1939. Educated at Denison University, he spent three years at the Smithsonian Institution, and at his own expense four years investigating Indian mounds in Ohio. He had charge of archaeological work in the Ohio Valley, Utah, Colorado, and New Mexico for the Columbian Exposition, Chicago (1893), and made valuable finds. His work brought to light the important Hopewell Culture in southern Ohio (see MOUND BUILDERS AND MOUNDS—*Burial Mounds:* North America), and did much to promote public interest in American archaeology. He explored the Cahokia Mounds (Illinois) for the University of Illinois, 1920–1923 and 1927; investigated the Etowah Mounds (Georgia), 1925–1927; and as a member of the United States Board of Indian Commissioners, 1907–1933, investigated conditions in Indian reservations for the Department of the Interior. He published *The Stone Age in North America* (1910); *The American Indian in the United States, Period 1850–1914* (1914); *Stone Ornaments of the American Indians . . .* (1917); *The Hopewell Mound Group of Ohio* (1922); and, as director of the Department of Archaeology at Phillips Academy, Andover, Mass., *Archaeology of the Arkansas River Valley* (1931) and *Etowah Papers* (1932).

MOORES CREEK, mōrz or mo͝orz krēk, a short stream in Pender County, southern North Carolina, flowing into Cape Fear River. It was made famous by the Battle of Moores Creek Bridge. On Feb. 27, 1776, a force of 1,600 Loyalists led by Brig. Gen. Donald MacDonald, on the way to join Sir Henry Clinton, was intercepted about 18 miles northwest of Wilmington by a force of 1,100 North Carolina militia under Col. Richard Caswell. Within a few minutes, as they tried to cross the bridge over the creek, the Loyalists were routed with heavy losses—50 killed or wounded, and more than 800 taken prisoners. The militia lost 1 killed, 1 wounded, and captured a large amount of military supplies. Called "the Concord and Lexington of the South," the battle broke the hold of the British in North Carolina. In 1926 the battlefield of 30 acres became Moores Creek National Military Park with headquarters at the village of Currie.

MOORESTOWN, mo͝orz'toun, township, New Jersey, in Burlington County, about seven miles northeast of Camden, on the Camden-Pemberton branch of the Pennsylvania Railroad. Largely residential and the site of a Friends school, it lies in a farming area producing truck, fruit, poultry, and dairy products, and manufactures fungicides, insecticides, and wood and metal products. It was laid out in 1722 and was Hessian headquarters in 1776. It has a commission form of government. Pop. 14,179.

MOORESVILLE, mōrz'vĭl, city, North Carolina, in Iredell County, 14 miles south-southeast of Statesville, and 26 miles north of Charlotte. It is served by the Southern Railway and is on federal and state highways. It is a manufacturing town—the chief business enterprises being the manufacture of cotton, flour milling, and ironworks. Founded in 1868, it was incorporated in 1873, and has council-manager government. Pop. 8,808.

MOORHEAD, mōr'hĕd, city, Minn., and Clay County seat, altitude 929 feet, on the Red River; 249 miles northwest of Minneapolis, on the Great Northern and the Northern Pacific railroads, and on three federal highways, opposite Fargo, N. Dak. Through the airport at Fargo, it has airline service. Located in a farming region, it handles large volumes of dairy products, and poultry, also wheat and sugar beets. It has sheet-metal works, sugar mills, and makes tents, awnings, and mattresses. It is the seat of a state teachers' college and of Concordia College. The city, named for William G. Moorhead, a director of the Northern Pacific, has aldermanic government. Pop. 29,687.

MOORHEAD STATE COLLEGE, in Moorhead, Minn., is a coeducational, state-operated institution in the western part of the state. It opened in 1888 as a normal school.

Moorhead State offers a B.S. and an M.S. in education and a B.A. and an M.A. in liberal arts and in business administration. It is on the quarter system, and by attending the summer quarters a student can complete a four-year program in three years.

MOORISH ART. See ISLAMIC ART AND ARCHITECTURE.

MOORS (Lat. *Mauri;* Sp. *Moros;* Dutch, *Moors*), the people of Morocco. The Arabs who conquered the Roman Province of Mauritania in North Africa in the 7th century converted to Mohammedanism the native population, who in Europe were still called Moors, though in their own language they called themselves Berbers, while by the Arabs they were termed Moghribees, "westerners" or "men of the west." Arabic manners and customs, and in a corrupt form the Arabic language, soon prevailed in the country, the Arab conquerors freely amalgamating with their converts, who far exceeded them in numbers. In 711 an army drawn from this mixed population, under Arab leaders, crossed the straits at Gibraltar, so named from their leader, and began the conquest of the Spanish peninsula. The Spaniards and Portuguese called these invaders Moors because they came from Mauritania, and the term Moors with them soon became synonymous with Mohammedans or Moslems, as the invaders designated themselves. The Spanish writers subsequently applied the term to all the Mohammedans of northern Africa; and when, at the close of the 15th century, the Portuguese made their way around the Cape of Good Hope and encountered the Arabs on the coasts of East Africa and of Asia, they still called them Moors. See also MOROCCO.

MOOSE. The deer family (Cervidae) embraces not only all the round-horned deer, but also the caribou and moose, whose horns are flattened in a manner known as "palmation." Of this family, the American moose (*Alces americanus*) is the most colossal and also the most picturesque member. The moose of Europe and Asia, there called "elk" (q.v.), is a much smaller animal. Even in comparison with the largest American elk, the North American moose is a giant, and it is impossible to appreciate fully the great height and bulk, length of leg and size of antlers of this wonderful creature, without seeing a full-grown bull, either in his native wilds or mounted in a museum.

At nearly every point the species presents a peculiarity. The largest specimens ever shot and measured by naturalists stood from 78 to 84 inches in height at the shoulders. The body is very short in comparison with the great length of the legs, but the depth of the chest is unusually great. The end of the nose is flabby and pendulous, and overhangs the end of the chin by three or four inches. In browsing it is half prehensile, and is of great use in conveying twigs into the mouth. A moose in full winter pelage is covered by a coarse thatch of strawlike hair, from three inches in length on the body to six inches on the neck and shoulders. The color of the hair is purplish-gray, and for an animal which lives so far north, the pelage is exceptionally coarse and open

Alaska moose.

The antlers of the moose are strikingly peculiar. The upper two thirds of the beam is enormously flattened, often to a width of 12 inches or more, and the upper end of this great shovel of solid bone terminates in a row of from 6 to 12 short points. The single browtine is also well palmated, and usually terminates in three or four long points of great strength. The largest antlers known are in the Chicago Natural History Museum, and have a spread of 78 inches, greatest width of palmation 16 inches, thickness of palmation 2⅛ inches, and a total of 34 points. The weight of the antlers and skull is 93¼ pounds.

The moose is a browsing animal, and its favorite food consists of twigs of the willow, birch, hemlock, spruce, alder, aspen and maple. It also feeds upon moss, and in summer is very fond of wading in ponds and eating the stems and leaves of water-lilies. Because of their very unusual feeding-habits, moose are very difficult to rear in captivity to adult age. Moose calves are born either singly or in pairs, in May or June. At birth an average specimen stands about 32 inches in height, and is a most grotesque-looking creature. Its first coat of hair is sandy-red, like that of a buffalo calf. At 15 months, a healthy young animal is about five feet high at the shoulders. The weight of a large adult male moose is between 1,100 and 1,200 pounds, but the maximum weight for the species would probably reach 1,500 pounds.

The range of the moose extends from Nova Scotia and New Brunswick to northern Alaska, a total distance along the axis of distribution of about 4,100 miles.

The valley of the Ottawa River and its tributaries still affords good moose hunting, as does northern Manitoba. The species still exists in small numbers in northern Minnesota, and along the western slope of the Rockies as far south as the head of the Green River, Wyoming. Northward, moose are found in British Columbia, Alberta, Athabasca, Yukon, and in many parts of Alaska. Those found on the Kenai Peninsula and north of Cook Inlet have the most massive and widespreading antlers to be found, and have even been described as an independent species, under the name of *Alces gigas*.

The killing of moose is regulated by law. Open seasons are very short; the number that may be killed by each hunter is limited to one or two males, and the killing of females is forbidden.

William T. Hornaday.

MOOSE, Loyal Order of, a secret fraternal society founded in 1888 at Louisville, Ky. by Dr. J. H. Wilson. The first lodge was organized in Cincinnati, Ohio. Operating in the United States and possessions, Canada, and the British Isles, membership, restricted to the white race, totaled (1962) 1,001,518 in 3,474 units, including women's auxiliaries. The society's purpose is beneficiary; besides paying sick and death benefits to its members, it maintains a home and vocational school for orphan boys and girls at Mooseheart, near Aurora, Ill., and a home for dependent old people at Moosehaven, Orange Park, Fla. The organization publishes *Moose Magazine*.

MOOSE FACTORY, village, Ontario, Canada, on an island at the mouth of the Moose River in James Bay. It is adjacent to Moosonee on Moose River, which is a terminus of the Ontario Northland Railway. Both villages are trading posts. Two French-Canadian explorers, Pierre Esprit Radisson and Médart Chouart, Sieur de Groseilliers, were commissioned by Prince Rupert in 1668 to search for the Northwest Passage. After establishing Charles Fort and returning to England with a cargo of furs, they were sent out by the Hudson's Bay Company in 1671, and founded Moose Factory as a trading post. When war broke out between France and England, the post changed hands several times, and was destroyed at the end of the century. Rebuilt in 1730 by the company near the old site, it has retained operations to the present day. Pop. 689.

MOOSE JAW, city, Saskatchewan, Canada, situated at the junction of Moose Jaw River and Thunder Creek, 45 miles west of Regina. Divisional headquarters for the Canadian Pacific and the Canadian National railways, and for Prairie Airways Limited, it is on the route of the Trans-Canada Air Lines, and is well served by highways. Moose Jaw is located in a large agricultural area. Its industries include meat packing, milling, oil refining, electrical production, stockyards, creameries, railway terminal shops, and a woolen mill. The city has a collegiate institute and a teachers college.

The district was first settled in 1882; Moose Jaw was incorporated as a town in 1884 and as a city in 1903. The Indians called it "the place where the white man mended his cart with the jaw of a moose." Population: 31,854.

MOOSEHEAD, lake, Maine, 50 miles north of Skowhegan, at an elevation of about 1,000 feet. The largest lake in the state, its area is 120 square miles; it is 35 miles long, and 2 to 10 miles in width. The Kennebec River has its source in the lake, and an outlet leads into the Penobscot River. A lake with many islands, Moosehead is a popular resort for fishermen and hunters. Steamer service connects the shore towns, the Canadian Pacific Railroad runs along the southwestern end, and there is an airport at Greenville on the south shore, where guides and canoes are available.

MOOSEWOOD, local name in the Eastern states and Canada for the striped maple (*Acer pensylvanicum*).

MOPSUS, mŏp'sŭs, in Greek mythology, a diviner or two diviners of the same name. (1) A pre-Trojan War Mopsus, son of Ampyx and Chloris, was one of the Lapithae (q.v.) who took part in the battle with the Centaurs, and was the prophet of the Argonauts, whom he accompanied on their voyage. He died in Libya from the bite of a serpent.

(2) A post-Trojan War Mopsus was the son of Rhacius and Manto, daughter of the seer Tiresias. In a contest of divining the number of figs on a tree, he defeated Calchas, who is said to have died from mortification. Mopsus was killed in a combat with Amphilochus.

MOQUEGUA, mô-kä'gwä, department, Peru, bounded on the north by Arequipa, on the south by Tacna, on the west by the Pacific Ocean, and on the east by Puno. Its area is about 5,549 square miles. It is watered by the Tambo and Moquegua rivers, and is crossed by the Cordillera Occidental, which here has several volcanic peaks. The climate is dry—semitropical on the coast, with cooler uplands. Mainly agricultural, its irrigated lands produce wine, olives, cereals, sugarcane, and cotton, and on the mountain slopes cattle are raised.

Moquegua, capital of the department, is on the Moquegua River, 60 miles by rail from the port of Ilo, at an altitude of 4,500 feet. It is also on the Pan American Highway. Earthquakes, the latest occurring in 1868, have caused suffering to the city's industry, but it is now a processing center for olives, wine, cotton, and fruit. Pop. department (1950) 42,647; town (1940) 3,888.

MOQUELUMNAN, mō-kĕl-ŭm'năn, a name applied to a distinct language family of North American Indians, formerly included with the Costanoan in the old Powell classification, but now accorded separate status. It comprises one of the largest groups in California, occupying an area extending from the Cosumnes River south to the Fresno River, and from the Pacific Coast inland to the Sierra Nevada. The Moquelumnan are known tribally as the Miwok, of whom there are several divisions, each with an individual dialect.

MORACEAE, mô-rā'sê-ē, a family of plants in the order Urticales, composed of trees and shrubs, sometimes vines, and (rarely) herbs, related to the nettle family. The approximately 55 genera and 1,000 species grow mainly in tropical and subtropical climates. Botanical characteristics include deciduous or evergreen trees, alternate or simple leaves, and small unisexual flowers; various species have milky juice and (notably species of *Ficus*) are epiphytes. Moraceae is economically important, and its plants are grown for fruit, shade, and ornament. The most important genera are *Morus* (mulberry), including *M. alba* (white mulberry) and *M. rubra* (red mulberry); and *Ficus* (the fig), which has the most numerous species, including *F. carica* (common fig), *F. benghalensis* (banyan), and *F. elastica* (indiarubber plant). Other genera are *Maclura* (orange osage), *Artocarpus* (breadfruit), *Broussonetia* (paper mulberry), and *Brosimum* (breadnut).

MORADABAD, mo͝o-räd'ȧ-bäd, city, India, seat of Moradabad District in north central Uttar Pradesh, on the upper Ganges Plain, situated on the right bank of the Ramganga River, 90 miles east of Delhi. A railway and road junction, the city is a trade center for the wheat, rice, barley, mustard, sugar cane, and cotton which are grown in the area. Its principal industries are cotton milling and the production of lacquered brassware, for which it is noted. Moradabad was founded in 1625 by Rustam Khan, who also built the fort and splendid mosque, Jama Masjid (1631) which are its distinguishing landmarks. It was a Rohilla stronghold in the 18th century, and with its territory became part of British India in 1801. Pop. (1951) 161,854.

MORAES BARROS, mo͞o-rīs' bȧr'ro͞os, **Prudente José de,** Brazilian lawyer and political leader: b. Itú, Brazil, 1841; d. Piracicaba, Dec. 3, 1902. An ardent advocate of republicanism, Moraes Barros was a successful lawyer and in 1885 was one of three republicans to sit in the imperial parliament. After the revolution of 1889, which he was active in bringing about, he became governor of São Paulo and president of the Constituent Assembly. In 1894 he was elected president of Brazil (to 1898), the first civilian to hold the office. Although he was personally honest and an able leader, his administration was severely hampered by a series of crises resulting from the disturbed financial and political condition of the new republic.

MORAINE, mô-rān', the deposit of rock debris, composed of sand, gravel, or clay, made by a glacier. Moraines may be divided into two classes, those that exist on the ice itself and those that are formed at the edge of the ice or under it. Of the first type, the most common are the *lateral moraines.* These are ridges of debris that accumulate on the ice next to the rock wall on either side. They consist in part of material that the glacier has scraped from the valley sides and in part from avalanche debris. When two glaciers unite, two lateral moraines are brought together and form a *medial moraine.* Glaciers that result from many branches uniting may have several such medial moraines. The lower stagnant ends of many large glaciers are wholly covered with debris that was once frozen into the ice, but which has accumulated as the ice melted. Such deposits are known as *ablation moraines.* Forests grow on the ablation moraine of the Malaspina Glacier in Alaska. Moraines of the above three types seldom remain as distinct ridges after the glacier has melted way.

Of the second type, the *frontal* or *terminal moraines* are most important. These are formed at the ice front, when loss by melting just equals ice advance, and all the debris is accumulated in one ridge. In the case of valley glaciers, these form dams across the valleys, often producing lakes. In the case of continental ice sheets, the moraine may stretch across the country, as in the northern United States, at the southern margin of the glaciated region. Sometimes the ice in its retreat pauses several times, building a moraine at each pause, in which case they are called *recessional moraines.* The thin sheet of till (q.v.) that a glacier spreads over the country at large and which results chiefly from material that the ice is forced to drop from the bottom, due to overload, is called *ground moraine.* Drumlins (q.v.) are a special phase of ground moraine. Morainic debris is mostly unstratified and contains many polished and striated boulders. See also GLACIER.

MORALE, mô-ràl', the amount of zest and efficiency with which members of a social group participate in an activity. Morale may be high or low. Each member of a group learns something about the beliefs and attitudes of other members, and, to the extent that he accepts them, his morale is affected. During World War II the Morale Services Division of the United States Army sought to teach each soldier to accept with conviction these basic morale factors: faith in the cause and the future; pride and confidence in the outfit; belief in the mission; confidence in training and equipment; realistic appraisal of the job ahead; satisfaction with the job assignment; and belief in the concern of the army for an individual's welfare. The leader, as exemplar and teacher, is considered to be the principal determiner of the level of morale in any group, whether military or civilian.

American psychologists have devised many ingenious procedures for measuring the level of morale in any group. Attitude scales or personal interviews may be employed to appraise the degree of conviction with which beliefs and attitudes are accepted or rejected.

In business and industry the level of morale may be measured by such factors as absenteeism, employee turnover, accident rate, and quality of output. Many studies have been undertaken in order to maintain a high level of morale. Psychiatric diagnoses and psychological tests have been used in the hope of weeding out potential trouble-makers who might wreck the morale of a business or industrial enterprise. Paternalistic schemes have been used in the vain hope of securing high morale among workers. It seems to be the consensus that a satisfactory level of morale is achieved only when each member of a group enjoys full self-respect. The amount of job dissatisfaction in many a business or industry indicates that much research work remains to be done in the field of worker morale.

PHILIP HARRIMAN.

MORALES, mô-rä'lās, **Luis de** (called EL DIVINO), Spanish devotional painter: b. Badajoz, Spain, about 1509; d. there, May 9, 1586.

Although much of his life was spent in poverty, he was a successful artist, and his paintings were placed in churches throughout Spain. He was called to participate in decorating the Escorial (1563), but his curious style, a mixture of medieval and Renaissance elements, did not please the classically minded Philip II, and his services were not retained. However, in 1581 Philip granted the poverty-stricken artist a pension. Although Morales' style was undoubtedly influenced by foreign sources, notably in his use of North Italian chiaroscuro and in his attention to minute detail, typical of German and Flemish painting, he was purely Spanish in inspiration and feeling. His emaciated figures, elongated and melancholy, and reminiscent of Gothic representation, contain a nervous intensity and a harshness that are symbolic of the exalted mysticism pervading religion in 16th century Spain. The paintings achieved an emotional quality by his use of various mannerisms which became characteristic of his work, such as deep shadows to emphasize a sense of torment and exaltation, and Morales may be considered the founder of the manneristic school of 17th century Spanish devotional painting. In his early work he produced large canvases covered in livid unnatural colors. His color tones gradually softened, and he later painted small canvases filled with a few half-length figures. The popularity of his work created numerous imitators, mostly mediocre. Called El Divino because of his exclusive interest in religious painting, Morales concentrated on a few themes which, with slight variation, he reproduced again and again. Most typical are *Pietà, Virgin and Child, Ecce Homo* (with examples in the Prado and the New York Historical Society gallery), and *Christ Bearing the Cross.*

MORALITY PLAYS or **MORALITIES,** allegorical plays in verse, popular in the late Middle Ages. They differed from the miracle plays (q.v.), whose dramatis personae were taken from the Bible or the hierarchy of saints, while the moralities used allegorical figures personifying abstract qualities of vice and virtue, such as Charity, Wisdom, Sobriety, Folly, and Bad Habits, and generalized types such as Mankind, King, and Bishop. Basically the moralities were dramatized sermons, usually concerned with two principal themes: the struggle between forces of good and evil within man for possession of his soul, and the portrayal of man's journey through life. The latter theme is exemplified in *Everyman* (q.v.), the greatest of the English moralities. However, the moral precept in question was not always religious; it was often secular, as in *La condemnation de banquets* (c. 1507) by Nicolas de La Chesnaye, which condemns gluttony. Although they lacked dramatic action, the plays often contained much humor in the character of the Devil and his various vices, who were played realistically and with gusto. Increasing emphasis was placed on comic elements, and in time the moralities tended to merge into the comic interlude and the farce of the popular theater. Dating from the late 14th century, the morality play reached its highest development in 15th century England and France, and then declined in popularity after 1550. Noted plays include *Castell of Perseverance* (c. 1405) and *Ane Pleasant Satyre of the Thrie Estaitis . . . (Three Estates,* c. 1540). See also DRAMA—*Medieval Drama.*

MORAN, mô-răn', **Edward,** American marine painter: b. Bolton, England, Aug. 19, 1829; d. New York City, June 9, 1901. In 1844 his family emigrated to Maryland, where he worked as a weaver. Moving to Philadelphia, he studied painting with Paul Weber and James Hamilton, and by 1857 he was established there as a professional artist. He studied in England for a time (1862), and in 1872 settled in New York, where he was soon one of the city's most prominent artists. Moran's reputation rested largely on his seascapes, which show the influence of the English landscapist Joseph M. W. Turner; these include *Launching of the Life-Boat* (1865), *Relief Ship Entering Havre* (1872), and *Fishing Boats in the Irish Channel.* His outstanding achievement was a series of 13 marine paintings (completed 1899) which depict notable events in American history, such as the landing of Leif Ericson, Henry Hudson's ship entering New York harbor, and the return of the victorious American fleet after the Spanish-American War. The series was later presented to the Pennsylvania Museum of Art, Philadelphia.

PETER MORAN, his brother (b. Bolton, March 4, 1841; d. Philadelphia, Nov. 9, 1914), was noted as a painter and etcher of animal and landscape subjects. He was taught by his brothers Edward and Thomas Moran (q.v.). His works include *Pasture Land; The Pueblo of Zia, New Mexico; Santa Barbara Mission; The Stable Door; The Return of the Herd* (awarded a medal at the Centennial Exposition of 1876); and *Wolves on the Buffalo Trail.*

MORAN, Patrick Francis, Australian Roman Catholic cardinal: b. Leighlinbridge, Ireland, Sept. 16, 1830; d. Sydney, Australia, Aug. 16, 1911. Educated in Rome, he was ordained priest in 1853, became bishop of the diocese of Ossory (Ireland) in 1872, and in 1884 went to Australia as archbishop of Sydney. He was consecrated cardinal in 1885. In Australia he stirred up much controversy over religious questions, was active in Australian politics, and also supported Irish home rule. He worked energetically for educational reform, and his primacy is noted for the many schools, churches, and hospitals which he built. In addition he was a prominent scholar in Irish church history; the best known of his many writings is *History of the Catholic Archbishops of Dublin* (1864).

MORAN, Thomas, American landscape painter and etcher: b. Bolton, England, Jan. 12, 1837; d. Santa Barbara, Calif., Aug. 26, 1926. His earliest painting instructor was his brother, Edward Moran (q.v.). In 1862 the brothers went to England for further study; there Thomas was deeply influenced by the work of Joseph M. W. Turner, the English landscape painter, and in nearly all his subsequent paintings there is a Turneresque quality. He accompanied the United States Geological Expedition, headed by Ferdinand V. Hayden, to the Yellowstone River country (1871), and in 1873 went on an exploring expedition to the Colorado River. These trips resulted in his most famous landscapes, the *Grand Canyon of the Yellowstone* which was purchased by the government for the Senate Hall in the Capitol, and now on display in the Department of the Interior Building, and *Chasm of the Colorado,* purchased by Congress and placed in the Capitol. Moran went frequently to

Europe, painting a notable Venetian series (for example, *The Grand Canal, Venice; The Pearl of Venice*), as well as English rural scenes. Working in both oils and water colors, he was identified with the later period of the Hudson River School (q.v.). Despite their great popularity, Moran's vast Western canvases are regarded by many critics as being too unwieldy to be artistically effective; his best work is seen in his earlier, smaller landscapes. He also did many etchings and magazine illustrations on wood. He was elected a member of the National Academy of Design in 1884. Moran lived in Philadelphia until 1872, and subsequently in New York City and (from 1916) in Santa Barbara, Calif. Mount Moran in Wyoming and Moran Point in Arizona are named for him.

MORAND, mô-räɴ′, **Paul,** French career diplomat and author: b. Paris, France, March 13, 1889. His many experiences abroad supplied the material for most of his literary work. Originally a poet, occasionally a novelist, Morand found his true medium in short stories and travel books. During the 1920's and early 1930's, he achieved fame as the creator of a new type of exoticism: predominantly cosmopolitan in character; not lyrical, but coldly sophisticated; and relying, for its means of expression, on a skillful transposition of cinematic techniques. *Ouvert la nuit* (1922), *Fermé la nuit* (1923), *L'Europe galante* (1925), carried the reader from one metropolis to another, affording him a kaleidoscopic view of that restless period. Later on, as Morand extended his roamings to all continents, a somewhat sadder and more human note suffused his "travelogues" (*Paris-Tombouctou,* 1928; *Hiver caraïbe,* 1929; *Flèche d'Orient,* 1931; *Air indien,* 1932); his studies of various civilizations (*Bouddha vivant,* 1927; *Magie noire,* 1928; *Champions du monde,* about the United States, 1930); his panoramas of large cities (*New-York,* 1929; *London,* 1931; *Bucarest,* 1935). First sounded in 1926 (*Rien que la terre*), this note was significantly repeated in the novel which is Morand's last important effort (*L'Homme pressé,* 1941).

Consult Lemaître, G. E., *Four French Novelists,* pp. 301–392 (New York 1938); Guitard-Auviste, Ginette, *Paul Morand* (Paris 1956).

Jean-Albert Bédé.

MORANDI, mô-rän′dê, **Giorgio,** Italian painter: b. Bologna, Italy, July 20, 1890; d. there, June 18, 1964. After a brief connection with "metaphysical" painting (1918–1919), he developed a strongly independent style, influenced by Giotto, Corot, and Cezanne, but unaffected by the changing moods of 20th century painting. His works are almost all small still lifes, usually of a few bottles, cups, and other objects. They are skillfully composed and are painted in rich, muted colors. Certain elements of Morandi's work—the suffused light and concern with space—continued the metaphysical tradition and influenced the painters of the school of Rome, led by Gino Scipione and Mario Mafai.

Morandi attended the Bologna Academy of Arts and taught there from 1930 to 1956. His work won first prizes at the Venice Biennale (1948) and the São Paulo Biennal (1957).

MORATIN, mō-rä-tēn′, **Leandro Fernández de,** Spanish dramatist: b. Madrid, Spain, March 10, 1760; d. Paris, France, June 21, 1828. He was the son of Nicolás Fernández de Moratín (q.v.), who gave him most of his education and literary tastes, particularly French influences which were to characterize his work. Smallpox left him disfigured and delicate. Exceedingly timid, he revealed himself only among friends or through his work. He obtained favors of many important people, such as Count Francisco de Cabarrus, Count de Floridablanca, and the minister Manuel de Godoy. He welcomed the French occupation and abolition of the Inquisition, which had persecuted him, and accepted the post of national librarian under Joseph Bonaparte in 1811. On the return of Ferdinand VII (1814) he fled to France where he lived until his death. His literary fame is due to his renovation of the Spanish theater by the introduction of French neoclassical precepts, while insisting upon a faithful portrayal of Spanish life. He was encouraged in this by Carlo Goldoni, whom he had met in his extensive travels. Molière was his idol, but his own comedies never reached the heights of buffoonery of the French master. His first comedy, *El viejo y la niña* (1790) was a success, as were *El barón* (1804) and *La mojigata* (1804). Only two of his plays have stood the test of time: *La comedia nueva o el café* (1792), a satire of the Spanish theater, and *El sí de las niñas* (1806), probably the best Spanish play since the death of Pedro Calderón de la Barca. He also wrote neoclassical verse and *La derrota de los pedantes* (1789), a scathing prose satire on critics. His *Orígenes del teatro español* (1830) is a monument of scholarship.

Consult Umphrey, G. W., and Wilson, W. E., eds., *La comedia nueva, and El sí de las niñas* (New York 1930).

Gregory Rabassa.

MORATIN, Nicolás Fernández de, Spanish poet and dramatist: b. Madrid, Spain, July 20, 1737; d. there, May 11, 1780. He studied law at Valladolid, devoting time also to fine arts, and received a position in court after finishing his studies. He first turned to the drama, starting with the play *La Petimetra* (1762). Next came *El poeta* and the tragedy *Lucrece* in orthodox style which he held to in his later *Hormesinda* and *Guzmán el Bueno.* His last and superlative work was *Canto épico de las Naves de Cortés destruídas* (1765), one of the finest of the Spanish heroics. R. Foulché-Delbosc published his remaining works under title of *Poesías inéditas* (Madrid 1892).

MORATORIUM, mŏr′ȧ-tō′rĭ-ŭm, legal permission given by a government to debtors temporarily to postpone payment of obligations. Special moratoria have been declared for groups such as conscripted soldiers from Demosthenes' time, through the handling of Crusaders by Louis IX (St. Louis), to World War II.

General moratoria are often declared in financial crises. As early as 555 A.D., Justinian I ordered a moratorium after Italy was invaded by the Franks. The two important moratoria in United States history were those proclaimed by Presidents Herbert Hoover in 1931 and Franklin D. Roosevelt in 1933. The first was a moratorium on international debts arising from World War I, and the second took the form of a four-day bank holiday. See United States—*19. The United States in a Revolutionary Century.*

The United States Constitution, in Article I, section 10, holds that no state shall pass any law impairing the obligations of a contract. Despite this, legal opinion is divided on the constitutionality of state-declared moratoria.

WILLIAM N. KINNARD, JR.

MORAVA RIVER, mô'rá-vá (Ger. MARCH), a left-bank tributary of the Danube and the chief river of Moravia, Czechoslovakia. It rises on the south slope of the Králický Sněžnik range and takes a south-southeasterly course past Olomouc to Ostrokovice. There it bears southwest through a wide fertile valley past Uherskè Hradiště and Hodinín to the mouth of the Dyje River, then south along the Austrian border until it joins the Danube, eight miles above Bratislava. Its total length is about 227 miles, the lower 78 miles being navigable.

MORAVA RIVER (anc. MARGUS), a right-bank tributary of the Danube and the chief river of Serbia, Yugoslavia. It is formed by the confluence of the Southern Morava and the Western Morava, which receives the Ibar from the south. The Morava then flows northward for about 134 miles through a broad, fertile valley until it joins the Danube 10 miles east-northeast of Smederevo.

MORAVIA, mô-rä'vĭ-á, **Alberto** (real name ALBERTO PINCHERLE), Italian novelist: b. Rome, Italy, Nov. 28, 1907. Moravia, the most outstanding contemporary Italian writer, attracted instant attention in 1929 by his first psychological novel, *Gli indifferenti* (Eng. tr., *The Indifferent Ones,* 1932). Moravia's novel, confessional in form and realistic in methods, written by a 22-year-old unknown, marked a breakthrough in Italian literature of "art for art's sake" which condemned as sheer rhetoric all humanistic writing. The Italian critics ridiculed Moravia's work, dismissing the author as an accidental writer influenced by Fyodor Dostoyevsky. The sharp content of *The Indifferent Ones* deals with the individual faced by the relentless cruelty of life that crushes youth's aspirations of fulfilment. Unlike Dostoyevsky's characters, Moravia's heroes, Giovanni who drifts to crime and Adriana fail to attain regeneration through suffering and humility, Giovanni commits suicide. Moravia believes that great literature presumes moral significance. A prolific writer he gained insight into character and mastery of his craft from novel to novel. A series of outstanding books was widely translated and discussed abroad—*Il Conformista* (1951; Eng. tr., *The Conformist,* 1952), *Le ambizioni spagliate* (*The Wheel of Fortune,* 1937). In his short story, *The Lazy One,* the cinematographic tempo creates a surrealistic visual effect. *La Romana* (1947; Eng. tr., *The Woman of Rome,* 1952) won him world fame. The *Ciociara* (Eng. tr., *Two Women,* 1958), Moravia's most powerful novel, is a paradoxical work. It deals with the postwar disillusionment of seekers for a better world. Moravia is still in search. The *Roman Tales* (1954) extend his exploration into a new area—the slums of Rome. The Italian revaluation of Moravia's powerful and original talent went so far as to consider him a precursor of Jean-Paul Sartre, the protagonist of existentialism.

LYDIA NADEJENA.

MORAVIA, mô-rä'vĭ-á (Czech MORAVA; Ger. MÄHREN), a central region of Czechoslovakia, formerly a province, but abolished as such under a law, effective Jan. 1, 1949, sponsored by the Communist regime. Under this law, Moravia and other Czechoslovak provinces were split up into 19 smaller administrative regions. The area of Moravia (1948) was 8,219 square miles; population (1948), 2,293,773.

Geographically Moravia comprises a large basin surrounded on the north by the Sudeten Mountains, on the east by the Carpathian Mountains, and on the west by a low range of hills extending northward to the Sudetens and sloping toward a central point at the south. The climate is milder and more genial than that of most European areas of the same latitude, the mean temperature at Brno being 48° F. Moravia belongs to the Danube Basin, all the smaller streams flowing into the Morava River, a Danube tributary. Some 55 per cent of the land is arable and about 27 per cent is forest. Minerals, which include coal, iron, lignite, silver, lead, copper, graphite, and asbestos, are of considerable significance for the national economy.

Moravia is a productive and versatile agricultural area, and is highly developed industrially. Since the Communist coup of 1948, its economy, like that of the rest of Czechoslovakia, has been socialized on the Soviet model, agriculture having been extensively collectivized and industries nationalized; both have been integrated into five-year plans calling for large production increases.

The generally fertile Moravian soil produces the common cereal, leguminous, and root crops in abundance, the major crops ranging from oats, rye, flax, and potatoes in the higher regions to wheat, sugar beet, vine, malt, hops, and hemp in the lower areas; other important crops are vegetables, fruit, and tobacco. The central Hana region is noted for horse breeding. Pastures occupy a large portion of the surface, but the production of cattle has been insufficient to meet the domestic demand. On the other hand, sheep are raised in abundance and are of good quality through judicious breeding with merino strains.

Among the leading basic industries are iron and steel, centered chiefly at Ostrava and utilizing the nearby Silesian coal deposits. At Brno there are important machinery and armament plants, while Gottwaldov (formerly Zlín) is noted for its huge shoe factory. Other industries include textiles (woolens, cottons, silks), clothing, hats, beer, spirits, sugar, furniture, and lumber.

Before World War II, about 71 per cent of the Moravian population was of Slavic extraction, and some 28 per cent of German origin, most of the Germans being located in the north and south; after the war, many Germans moved into the Western and Soviet occupation zones of Germany. The people are traditionally about 90 per cent Roman Catholic. Education, as throughout Czechoslovakia, has been secularized and subordinated to the state, attendance being compulsory at elementary schools, where Russian has replaced German as the second language. There are various colleges and technical schools, and universities at Brno and Olomouc.

History.—Moravia has had a long and complex history. The Cotini (Kotins) inhabited the region about 500 B.C., various Germanic tribes entered the area about 100–500 A.D., and Slavic elements made their appearance about 500 A.D. Between 800 and 850, the Slavic kingdom of Great Moravia developed, the name Moravia being associated with the Morava River. In 1029, Moravia was united with the Kingdom of Bohemia, with which it shared the same constitution, administration, and laws. It became a margravate in 1197, with a separate court and administration. Together with Bohemia, Moravia came under the Habsburg house of Austria in 1526, Archduke Ferdinand becoming king of Bohemia. In 1849, however, Moravia was once more separated from Bohemia and became a distinct province with its capital at Brno. Subsequently, it sent 49 members to the Austrian Reichsrat in Vienna, and the provincial Diet was composed of 151 members. When the new Czechoslovak Republic was proclaimed on Oct. 28, 1918, Moravia joined with Bohemia, Slovakia, and Ruthenia to form the new state. From March 15, 1939, when Nazi Germany completed the dismemberment of Czechoslovakia following the Munich agreement of Sept. 29, 1938, until May 1945, when it was liberated at the close of World War II, Moravia, together with Bohemia, was ruled under the "Protectorate of Bohemia-Moravia," with Baron Konstantin von Neurath serving as Reich protector under Hitler. On liberation from Germany, the technical status of Moravia was briefly restored, but the Czechoslovak Republic after 1948 was brought under complete Communist control, leading to abolition of the historic provinces, and the splitting up of Moravia into Brno and Gottwaldov administrative regions, plus parts of the Jihlava, Ostrava, and Olomouc regions. See also CZECHOSLOVAKIA.

HARRY N. HOWARD,
United States Representative, United Nations Relief and Works Agency for Palestine Refugees in the Near East, Advisory Commission.

MORAVIAN CHURCHES, mô-rā'vĭ-ăn. Throughout the world there are approximately 300,000 members of the Moravian Churches, the large majority of whom are in mission stations and congregations in many nations. The Moravians are perhaps best known for their interest in foreign missions among primitive peoples.

There are two branches of the Moravian Church in America (Unitas Fratrum). The Northern Province, with headquarters in Bethlehem, Pa., has a membership of more than 36,000. The Southern Province, with headquarters in Winston-Salem, N.C., has a membership of more than 22,000. The Evangelical Unity of the Czech-Moravian Brethren in North America has over 6,000 members. A third body, the Bohemian and Moravian Brethren in Iowa, merged in 1955 with the Presbyterian Church in the United States of America, synod of Cedar Rapids.

The religious bodies named "Moravian" trace their origin to the leadership of the Bohemian martyrs Jan Hus (1371–1415) and Jerome of Prague (c. 1370–1416). The spiritual followers of Hus organized, in 1457, an association near Kunvald (Kunewald), Bohemia, for the purpose of fostering pure scriptural teaching and apostolic discipline. This association gained adherents until at the time of Martin Luther in Germany (16th century) the brethren in the organization had 400 local congregations with some 150,000 members in Bohemia and Moravia. During and after the Thirty Years' War, marked by religious dissension, the brethren lived on as a "hidden seed," but without a general organization.

There was a formal resuscitation when a small company of followers settled (1722) on the estate of Count Nikolaus Ludwig von Zinzendorf, in Saxony, where the village of Herrnhut arose. In 1735 the historic Moravian episcopate was transferred to the new group. The body began intensive evangelistic work in Europe and elsewhere. In 1736, Count Zinzendorf was banished from Saxony because of his religious zeal. After travel and labors in Europe, he came to America to preach the gospel to the Indians. The earliest Moravian settlements were made in Georgia, 1735; Pennsylvania, 1740; and North Carolina, 1753. Among the cities begun by Moravian immigrants were Bethlehem, Pa., and Salem, N.C., now part of Winston-Salem.

Bethlehem became the center of the Moravian Church in North America. Established in 1741, it was so named when Count Zinzendorf was there. In 1742 a large colony came from Europe and the Bethlehem settlement was formally organized. From then until 1762 there was a cooperative union consisting of the Moravians of Bethlehem and of nearby Nazareth. All persons worked for a common cause and received sustenance from common supplies. However, there was no surrender of private property and the participants had the right to withdraw from the cooperative organization, which was named the General Economy. The church in that period owned and operated vessels for transporting colonists from Europe.

The Moravians have no special doctrine. They call themselves simply and broadly evangelical, in accord with the general teachings of Protestants throughout the United States and the world. They accept the Old and New Testaments as containing adequate rules of faith and practice. Thus they do not have an official creed. They are known for the Christ-centered emphasis in their teaching, and this pervades their statements and discussions, their liturgy and preaching. The proceedings of their synods, the catechism, and the formal liturgy together may be said to set forth the doctrinal positions of the church.

The Moravians have a complete liturgical system of worship, with a litany used regularly on Sunday and a variety of offices for the various church seasons. In all of these, prominence is given to congregational singing. The cultivation of church music has ever been a feature of the congregational life. The Moravians are reported to have printed the first Protestant hymnal in the year 1501. Some congregations maintain trombone choirs, the members of which play sacred music on Easter Sunday morning and on other occasions. A distinctive service conducted by certain congregations is a love feast, begun in 1727, in imitation of the Agape of the Apostolic Church.

The Moravians ordain three orders of the ministry: deacons, presbyters, and bishops. The episcopacy is an office primarily for guarding sound doctrine and established order. The bishops are everywhere of equal rank and become administrators only if elected to executive offices. The other bishops serve as pastors of local churches or as teachers. The legislative authority is the synod, which consists of pastors and of elected lay delegates from the local congregations.

In the early Moravian community when there were no more than 600 members, their missionaries were already at work in 13 nations. Many non-Moravians state that Moravian historic missionary endeavor is probably without parallel in the history of Protestantism, considering the size of the group. The Moravian Church is also known as the first international Protestant church. There are branches in European nations as well as in the United States. In 1957 the general or international synod was held for the first time in the United States, when 500 years of history of the body were celebrated.

The Moravians have shown a consistent interest in movements for Christian unity, dating from Zinzendorf's efforts. He desired to diminish rather than increase denominational divisions. The Moravians thus early conducted evangelistic campaigns in Europe, turning converts into the established churches. Zinzendorf also initiated in Pennsylvania one of the earliest conferences on ways and means of merging Protestant churches.

From the days of the noted Moravian educator, John Amos Comenius (1592–1670), there has been an interest in higher education as well as in missions. Educational institutions were begun by Moravians in the United States in the 18th and early 19th centuries.

Bibliography.—Hamilton, John Taylor, *A History of the Unitas Fratrum; or the Moravian Church in the United States of America* (New York 1895); Carroll, Henry K., *The Religious Forces in the United States* (New York 1912); De Schweinitz, Paul, "History, Doctrine and Organization of the Moravian Church," *Religious Bodies, 1936*, vol. 2 (Washington 1941); *Directory of the Moravian Church* (Bethlehem, Pa., 1957).

BENSON Y. LANDIS,
Editor of the "Yearbook of American Churches."

MORAVIAN COLLEGE, an educational institution in Bethlehem, Pa., incorporating two separate academic programs: a liberal arts college, Moravian College, with separate campuses for men and women; and a graduate-professional school of theology, Moravian Theological Seminary. The institutions now represented in Moravian College in the order of their founding are Moravian Seminary and College for Women (1742) and Moravian College and Theological Seminary (1807); the present corporation was established in 1954.

Moravian Seminary and College for Women had its beginning as a seminary for young ladies in Germantown, Pa., the first boarding school for girls to be established in the 13 colonies. Founded by Countess Benigna von Zinzendorf of Saxony, daughter of Count Nikolaus Ludwig von Zinzendorf (see also MORAVIAN CHURCHES), the institution has been part of Bethlehem for more than 200 years.

Nazareth Hall, a boys school in Nazareth, Pa., was opened in 1759, soon after the establishment of Moravian communities in the Lehigh Valley, as part of the educational program of the Moravian Church. As an extension of this program, Moravian Theological Seminary was founded in 1807; its courses were those of a liberal arts college to prepare Moravian teachers and clergymen. The institution developed into Moravian College and Theological Seminary, an undergraduate college, training men for all professions, and a graduate theological seminary.

Moravian College, as a church-related institution, seeks to provide for young men and women a sound liberal education in a small college environment. The curriculum is planned around a core of the liberal arts, with various series of courses designed to help prepare students for the ministry of the church, the professions, scientific research, and business and industry.

RAYMOND S. HAUPERT,
President.

MORAVIANS. See MORAVIAN CHURCHES.

MORAVSKA OSTRAVA. See OSTRAVA.

MORAY, EARLS OF. See STUART—*James Stewart* (1499?–1544) and (1531?–1570).

MORAY, mûr′ĭ, or **MORAYSHIRE,** mûr′ĭ-shĭr; mûr′ĭ-shẽr (formerly ELGIN or ELGINSHIRE), county, northern Scotland, bounded on the north by the Moray Firth, on the west by Nairn, on the south by Inverness, and on the east by Banff. Its area is about 476 square miles. The hilly southern area, rising to over 2,000 feet and forested mostly with larch, fir, and oak, is noted for picturesque glens; northward, the country levels off across the fertile Laigh of Moray to a sandy coastline. The chief rivers are the Spey, Lossie, and Findhorn. The largest lake is Lochindorb. Salmon fishing in the rivers, sea fisheries, livestock raising, and farming are the chief occupations. Barley and oats are the chief crops. Other industries include distilling, granite, sandstone, and slate quarrying, woolen manufacture, and shipbuilding.

The chief towns are Elgin, the capital, Lossiemouth, Forres, Grantown-on-Spey, and Burghead. The county's antiquities include the cathedral at Elgin, Sweno's Stone at Forres, which was the site of Duncan's court, Kinloss Abbey, and several castles. The old province of Moray was much larger than the present county. Pop. (1961) 49,156. For the history of this area see SCOTLAND.

MORAY, mô-rā′, an eellike fish of the family Muraenidae, one distinguishing feature of which is the absence of pectoral fins, another the presence of a small, usually circular gill opening which closes as the mouth opens. There are more than 100 species ranging in size to 10 feet. They are scaleless and may be brilliantly colored, matching the coral reefs in which they live. Highly predaceous, all are equipped with powerful jaws and sharp teeth with which they can inflict fearful wounds. Unless molested, they are not pugnacious toward man, but if disturbed, they may attack viciously and can be dangerous opponents.

In certain places they are used as food, the flesh being considered delicious by some people. One species, *Muraena bellina,* was especially favored in the classical period by the Romans, who were reported to have cultivated it for food and to have kept captive specimens to which they sometimes threw recalcitrant slaves.

CHRISTOPHER W. COATES.

MORAY FIRTH, mûr′ĭ fûrth, inlet, northeastern Scotland, opening into the North Sea. In its broadest sense, it lies between Duncansby Head in Caithness County—the northeastern tip of the Scottish mainland—and Kinnairds Head in Aberdeen County (a distance of 78 miles), thus including Dornoch Firth. In its more restricted sense, it lies between Tarbat Ness in Ross and Cromarty County and Lossiemouth in Moray County; here it is entered on the north by Cromarty Firth, a deepwater inlet and site of Invergordon naval base.

MORAZAN, mō-rä-sän′, **Francisco,** Central American soldier and statesman: b. Tegucigalpa, Honduras, Oct. 3, 1792; d. San José, Costa Rica, Sept. 15, 1842. Following formation of the Central American Federation (Guatemala, Honduras, El Salvador, Nicaragua, and Costa Rica) in 1824, he became leader of the Liberals in opposition to President Manuel José Arce; when civil war ensued, Morazán defeated Arce, was himself elected president (1830), and instituted many notable reforms, including religious toleration, freedom of speech, abolition of slavery, and the fostering of education, industry, trade, and immigration. Although Morazán was reelected in 1834, his reforms had antagonized conservative elements, leading to renewed civil war and dissolution of the federation. After being elected president of El Salvador (1839), Morazán was defeated by the armies of the other Central American states, and fled to Peru. In 1842 he landed in Costa Rica, bent on re-establishing the federation; after overthrowing President Braulio

Carrillo, he himself was elected Costa Rican president, but his activities provoked a counterrevolt in which he was deposed, captured, court-martialed, and shot.

MORBIHAN, môr'bē-äN, department, France, in southern Brittany, on the Bay of Biscay. It has an area of 2,611 square miles. Part of the Armorican system, the land is hilly in the north, and has numerous granitic outcroppings, notably the desolate Landes de Lanvaux heaths. The heavily indented coast features wide estuaries and distinct peninsulas, the almost landlocked Gulf of Morbihan, from which the department gets its name, and scattered islands, including Belle-Île-en-Mer, Groix, Houat, and Hoedic. The rivers, chiefly the Scorff, Blavet, Loch, Vilaine, and Oust, flow generally southward, draining a fertile agricultural region. The climate is moist and mild.

The principal crops are buckwheat, wheat, hay, hemp, cider apples, and vegetables. The vine, figs, mulberries, aloes, and camellias flourish in such southern areas as Belle-Île-en-Mer and the Rhuis Peninsula. Other activities include cattle- and sheep-raising, beekeeping, and fishing, especially for sardine and tunny. There are numerous oyster beds. Industries comprise shipbuilding and iron foundries (chiefly at Lorient), quarrying (for kaolin, gravel, and slate), iron mining (at Gourin), sawmilling, tanning, fish canning, metalworking, and the manufacture of cloth, lace, and glassware.

Morbihan possesses France's largest legacy of megalithic monuments (about 600), chiefly at Carnac and Locmariaquer. These, the shrine at Ste.-Anne-d'Auray, and the department's bathing and scenic resorts are popular tourist attractions. The capital, Vannes, has a cathedral dating to the 13th century. Pop. (1962) 530,833.

MORDAUNT, Charles. See PETERBOROUGH, 3D EARL OF.

MORDEN, môr-dĕn', town, Province of Manitoba, Canada, on the Canadian Pacific Railway and Highway No. 3, 76 miles southwest of Winnipeg. The name is derived from Alvey Morden, an early settler. The area was visited in 1738 by Sieur de La Vérendrye on a trip to the Mandan Indians of Missouri and was later the site of Fort Pinancewaywining built by Alexander Henry in 1802. In 1883 the railway bypassed the towns of Nelson and Mountain City nearby in favor of the Dead Horse Creek area which within a year became the town of Morden and the legal and judicial center of southern Manitoba. The nearby towns became ghost towns when houses and businesses were moved to the new railway center. Much of the recent development has resulted from the building of a conservation dam by the Prairie Farm Rehabilitation Administration in 1942 making possible a modern water and sewage disposal system and attracting new industries. The town is in the center of an area of diversified agriculture which is well suited to the culture of vegetables and small fruits. On the eastern outskirts of the town is located a federal experimental farm where experimental and research work is carried on in the fields of horticulture, field crops, cattle, and poultry. The district is often referred to as the "corn and apple belt" of the prairies and is a popular tourist resort area. Nearby is produced nearly all the bentonite clay in Manitoba. Population: 3,266.

HARTWELL BOWSFIELD.

MORDENT. See MUSICAL ELEMENTS AND TERMS.

MORDVA AUTONOMOUS SOVIET SOCIALIST REPUBLIC (also called MORDOVIAN AUTONOMOUS SOVIET SOCIALIST REPUBLIC), môrd'vȧ, autonomous republic, USSR, part of the Russian SFSR, in the middle Volga Valley, south and west of the Volga. It is bordered on the southeast by the Sura River and is drained in the west by the Moksha. With an area of about 10,100 square miles, Mordva is a wooded steppe with a predominantly rural population and little industrial development except lumbering, peat mining, hemp weaving, meat packing, and the processing of dairy products. Rye, wheat, oats, beans, potatoes, and hemp are the main crops, and there are large numbers of cattle, sheep, and hogs. The population consists of Russians (57 per cent), Tatars (6 per cent), and Mordvas (37 per cent). The last-named are an ancient Finno-Ugrian nationality, now highly Russified and professing the Russian Orthodox religion. Mordva was annexed by czarist Russia in the 13th century, became a Soviet autonomous oblast in 1930, and an autonomous republic in 1934. The capital and largest city is Saransk. Pop. (1959) 999,000.

ELLSWORTH RAYMOND.

MORE, mōr, **Hannah**, English woman of letters and moralist: b. Stapleton, England, Feb. 2, 1745; d. Clifton, Sept. 7, 1833. In her 88 years of unmarried life, she was variously schoolmistress, playwright, poet and bluestocking, pamphleteer, social and educational reformer.

Hannah More was the fourth of five daughters of a charity schoolmaster, from whom she received her first lessons. In 1757, her elder sisters opened a school for girls in Bristol, in which she became first a student, then a teacher. The school was at once a success and served as a social center to attract such local luminaries as Edmund Burke. At the age of 22, she became engaged to William Turner, a wealthy squire 20 years her senior, but broke the contract after he had three times in six years postponed the ceremony. Protesting his continued affection, Turner secretly settled an annuity on her which gave her financial independence.

Her first publication, a play suitable for girls' theatricals, appeared in 1773, shortly before she went to London. There she met David Garrick, whom she won with praise of his acting in *King Lear*. His support insured the success of her plays *The Inflexible Captive* (1774) and *Percy* (1777). Through him she gained entry into the Samuel Johnson circle and the bluestockings, a group of literary ladies which included Elizabeth Montagu, Hester Thrale, and Elizabeth Vesey. In this atmosphere she wrote such verses as *Sir Eldred of the Bower* (1776), *Ode to Dragon* (1777), and *Bas Bleu* (1786).

Between Garrick's death in 1779 and the sale of the school 10 years later, Hannah More's interests turned gradually to religion. From Cowslip Green, a cottage in Wrington, the sisters, united again under Hannah's domination, carried out expeditions in philanthropy. At the urging of William Wilberforce, a leader in the Evangelical movement, she established a Sunday school at nearby Cheddar. There, as in the other schools she soon opened in the Mendip Hills, the poor were taught literacy, religion, and hygiene. Wilberforce, Zachary Macaulay (father of Thomas), and others of the "Clapham Sect" undertook to supply the newly literate with fit reading matter. The "Cheap Repository Tracts," a series of whose 114 numbers Hannah More wrote 50, presented piety in the shape of the popular literature of the day, so successfully that millions were sold at a penny each.

The "Blagdon controversy," which raged from 1800 to 1803 about her refusal to dismiss a teacher accused of "Methodism," cost her prestige and may have caused the long illness which followed. Thereafter, at Barley Wood, she devoted herself for the next 25 years to forwarding a variety of philanthropic causes. Works on the education of women, a pious novel (*Coelebs in Search of a Wife,* 1809), and didactic religious works flowed from her pen. The Bible Society, the foreign missions, and institutions to abolish slavery all received her unsparing help.

Of her vast writings, nothing remains readable today except her vivid and informative letters. She began her career as a reformer by overcoming conservative opposition; she ended it decrying the grandiose plans of her successors, whom she enjoined "to steer the middle way between the scylla of brutal ignorance and the charybdis of a literary education," for the poor.

Bibliography.—Roberts, William, *Memoirs of the Life and Correspondence of Hannah More,* 2 vols. (London 1834); *The Letters of Hannah More,* selected by R. Brimley Johnson (London 1925); Hopkins, Mary Alden, *Hannah More and her Circle* (New York 1947); Jones, M. G., *Hannah More* (Cambridge 1952).

LOUIS T. MILIC.

MORE, Henry, English philosopher: b. Grantham, England, 1614; d. Cambridge, Sept. 1, 1687. More, probably the best known of the Cambridge Platonists, was educated at Eton and Christ's College, Cambridge. He took orders, but, living mainly in Cambridge, devoted himself to study and writing. Among his friends or correspondents were his fellow Platonist Ralph Cudworth, Lady Conway and her circle, René Descartes, Jeremy Taylor, Joseph Glanvill and other fellow members of the Royal Society, and William Penn. Even as a boy at Eton More rebelled against Calvinistic predestination, and he was not satisfied by either Cambridge scholasticism or his own reading in science. He found what he needed in the Platonic tradition, from antiquity to the Florentine Marsilio Ficino, and especially in the book that had worked on Martin Luther, *Theologia Germanica.* His early illuminations were set forth in long and sometimes difficult poems (1642–1647) which owed much to Edmund Spenser. Among prose works were *An Antidote against Atheism* (1653), *Conjectura Cabbalistica* (1653), *Enthusiasmus Triumphatus* (1656), *The Immortality of the Soul* (1659), *An Explanation of the Grand Mystery of Godliness* (1660), *Enchiridion Ethicum* (1668; tr. reprinted 1930), *Divine Dialogues* (1668), *Enchiridion Metaphysicum* (1671).

Though he had a mystical (and even occult) strain in him, More was an earnest champion of the fusion of reason and faith. But this traditional aim of Christian humanism had become much more difficult because of the rise of science and the scientific rationalism of Descartes and the more radical Thomas Hobbes. At first More welcomed Descartes as a modern Plato or Plotinus, but he later reacted against Cartesian dualism and materialism. On the other hand More feared the danger to both reason and religion in some kinds of Puritan "enthusiasm." Standing firmly on the divine unity of all truth and all being, More strove to reconcile the new science with religion, to establish a modern Christian Platonism that would transcend both irreligious mechanism and religious irrationality. If this great ethical and metaphysical object was not achieved (it has not been yet), and if More was not an artist like Sir Thomas Browne whose prose remains superbly alive, still he made a noble and significant assertion of the reality of spirit in the face of disintegrating ideas. Moreover, his conception of "plastic nature," God's agent in the material world, of the "extension" of spirit, of God's omnipresence, through matter and space, affected the thought of Sir Isaac Newton; and in our own time William Butler Yeats, recoiling from the "Grey Truth" of science, acknowledged the dynamic stimulus of More's Platonism.

Bibliography.—Two modern editions are *Philosophical Poems* (Manchester, Eng., 1931), ed. by Geoffrey Bullough; and, for prose selections, *Philosophical Writings* (New York 1925), ed. by Flora Isabel MacKinnon. Richard Ward's *Life of Henry More* (London 1710; ed. by M. H. Howard, 1911) has a supplement in *The Conway Letters* (New Haven 1930), ed. by Marjorie Nicolson, who wrote several articles on More's thought (1925–1929). The fullest study is Paul R. Anderson, *Science in Defense of Liberal Religion* (New York 1933). E. A. Burtt's *Metaphysical Foundations of Modern Physical Science* (New York 1925) is of prime importance. Other discussions are in John Tulloch, *Rational Theology and Christian Philosophy in England in the Seventeenth Century,* 2d ed., 2 vols.; vol. 2, *The Cambridge Platonists,* pp. 303–409 (Edinburgh 1874), Frederick James Powicke, *The Cambridge Platonists* (London 1926); Geoffrey Philip Henry Pawson, *Cambridge Platonists and Their Place in Religious Thought* (New York 1930), and William Cecil De Pauley, *Candle of the Lord* (New York 1937).

DOUGLAS BUSH,
Gurney Professor of English, Harvard University.

MORE, Paul Elmer, American educator, editor, and critic: b. St. Louis, Mo., Dec. 12, 1864; d. Princeton, N.J., March 9, 1937. Educated at Washington University, and Harvard, he taught Sanskrit at Harvard and Sanskrit and classical literature at Bryn Mawr. Turning to journalism, he served as literary editor of the New York *Independent* and the *Evening Post* before becoming editor of *The Nation* (1909–1914). In 1914 he settled in Princeton, where he wrote and lectured until his retirement in 1934. His religious and philosophical thought, influenced by Oriental, Greek, and Christian sources, is set forth in numerous books, including *The Great Refusal* (1894), *The Religion of Plato* (1921), *Hellenistic Philosophies* (1923), *The Christ of the New Testament* (1924), *Christ the Word* (1927), *The Catholic Faith* (1931), *The Sceptical Approach to Religion* (1934). As a critic, More's reputation rests chiefly on his *Shelburne Essays,* 11 vols. (1904–1921). His humanism appears here in a reliance upon the authority of the past, distrust of an optimistic view of human nature, political conservatism, and a dualistic point of view from which man is seen apart from nature (in opposition to either romantic or naturalistic monism) and as a free moral agent. In his last years he, like his friend and fellow-humanist Irving Babbitt, became involved in the controversy over the New Humanism (q.v.), and contributed to the symposium *Humanism and America* (1930).

WALTER SUTTON.

MORE, Sir **Thomas** (also Saint Thomas More), English statesman, scholar, and man of letters: b. London, England, Feb. 7, 1478; d. there, July 6, 1535. He was the son of Sir John More (1453–1530), an eminent jurist, by his wife, Agnes Graunger. After early training at St. Anthony's School, London, Thomas More became (1491) a page in the household of John Morton, archbishop of Canterbury. Thence he went to Canterbury Hall (now Christ Church), Oxford, where he studied under Thomas Linacre and William Grocyn, champions of the New Learning of the Renaissance. Returning to London, he studied law at the Inns of Court. He considered entering the priesthood, but, finding that he had no vocation, resumed secular life and became brilliantly successful at the bar. Chosen for Parliament in 1504, he incurred the anger of Henry VII by successfully opposing the royal request for an extravagant subsidy. Thenceforth, until the accession of Henry VIII in 1509, he spent much of his time on the Continent.

During his early years in London, More widened his acquaintance among the apostles of the New Learning, notably with William Lily the grammarian, and John Colet, dean of St. Paul's. He met Erasmus on the latter's first visit to England in 1498–1499; the ensuing friendship was lifelong. On a subsequent visit, Erasmus wrote part of his *Praise of Folly* (q.v.) in More's house; its Latin title, *Encomium moriae,* is a pun on his host's name.

About 1504, More married Jane Colte, who in the seven years of their marriage bore him four children: Margaret (b. 1505; m. William Roper, 1521); Elizabeth (b. 1506; m. William Dauncy, 1525); Cecily (b. 1507; m. Giles Heron, 1525); and John (b. 1509; m. Anne Cresacre, 1529). Jane died in 1511 and a few months later More married Alice Middleton, a widow. His home life was notable for its harmony. There was no formality in his relations with his children, whose games he shared. "I have given you kisses enough," he once wrote, "but stripes hardly ever." Something of the spirit of that home can be read in the portraits which Hans Holbein made of its members.

Under Henry VIII, More rose rapidly in public service. He was undersheriff of London in 1510, and held various offices in the Inns of Court. In 1515 and 1516 he conducted diplomatic missions in France and the Netherlands, and during leisure moments on these missions wrote the famous *Utopia* (q.v.; published, in Latin, 1516; English version, by Ralph Robinson, 1551). In this work he envisaged ideals of government and society far in advance of his times. The king, who delighted in his company, gave him successive preferments: knighthood and appointment as subtreasurer to the king, 1521; high steward of Oxford University, 1524; high steward of Cambridge and chancellor of the Duchy of Lancaster, 1525. After the fall of Thomas Wolsey in 1529, he became lord chancellor of England.

In the controversies of the early Reformation period, More took the Roman Catholic side, as did Henry—at first. Like his friends Colet and Erasmus, More wanted a church purified of the accretions of the Dark Ages, but no schism. He engaged in a bitter war of pamphlets, particularly with William Tyndale, first Reformation translator of the New Testament. But Henry's insistence on divorcing Catherine of Aragon and marrying Anne Boleyn brought More to a crisis of conscience. He resigned the chancellorship in 1532 and retired to his house at Chelsea, where he continued his controversy with Tyndale.

More was willing to accept the Act of Succession which declared Anne Boleyn's children to be heirs to the throne, for that was within the temporal power of Parliament; but he would take no oath that impugned the pope's authority over the church in England or that acknowledged the justice of Henry's divorce from Catherine. He uttered no word of disloyalty, but Henry could not rest easy while the best mind in England silently condemned him. After nearly a year's imprisonment in the Tower, More was tried and condemned as a traitor, not for anything he had said or done, but for what he was supposed to have thought. He was executed by beheading.

Apart from *Utopia,* so much of More's writing was controversial that it is little read today. His most important work in English was his *History of Richard III,* not printed in full until 1557. Its substance, and much of its text, was taken over by Edward Hall and Raphael Holinshed in their chronicles. As dramatized thence by Shakespeare, More's interpretation of Richard is still the generally accepted one.

Sir Thomas More was beatified Dec. 29, 1886, by Pope Leo XIII. He was canonized by Pius XI on May 19, 1935.

Works: No complete edition exists. The most recent edition of More's Latin works was published in 1689 in Frankfurt am Main and Leipzig; his English works were collected in 1557 in London, and this edition was reproduced in facsimile in 1931 (*The English Works of Sir Thomas More* . . , ed. by William Edward Campbell with notes and introduction by Arthur William Reed, 2 vols., London 1931). A revised text, edited by Louis Mantz, is now in process at Yale University Press.

Utopia has been printed many times. The standard critical edition is still Joseph Hirst Lupton's (London 1895); that by George Sampson and Adolph C. L. Guthkelch (London 1910) includes the Latin text as well as Ralph Robinson's English. See also Jack H. Hexter's *More's Utopia: The Biography of an Idea* (Princeton 1952).

Biography: The finest contemporary source is *The Mirrour of Vertue in Worldly Greatnes; or, The Life of Sir Thomas More,* by William Roper, More's son-in-law (1496–1578). This was first printed in Paris in 1626, nearly 50 years after its author's death. The best modern biography is Raymond Wilson Chambers' *Thomas More* (London 1935). Other useful recent studies include Enid M. G. Routh's *Sir Thomas More and His Friends* (London 1934); Ernest Edwin Reynolds' *Saint Thomas More* (London 1953); and John Farrow's *The Story of Thomas More* (London 1956).

DeLancey Ferguson.

MOREA. See Peloponnesus.

MOREAS, mô-rā-ås', **Jean** (pseudonym of Iannis Papadiamantopoulos), French poet of Greek birth: b. Athens, Greece, April 15, 1856; d. Paris, France, March 30, 1910. The thoroughly French education given him as a child kindled his love for French literature. He settled in Paris at the age of 23 and joined the ranks of the symbolists whose influence pervades his first important verse (*Les Syrtes,* 1884; *Les Cantilènes,* 1886). As late as 1890, a manifesto of his, published in *Figaro* (September 18), defended symbolism against its opponents. The following year, however, *Le Pèlerin passionné* and its preface brought forth Moréas' classical propensites. Asserting that modern poetical schools had betrayed the Gallic tradition, he advocated a return to that tradition, broadly conceived as that of the Middle Ages, the Pléiade, and the 17th century. Together with a few friends, prominent among whom was Charles Maurras, he founded the so-called "École romane" and added example to precept in everything he wrote thereafter. Most typical of his definitive manner was *Les Stances,* his acknowledged masterpiece, six books of which appeared in 1899–1901, and the last, posthumously, in 1920.

Consult Raynaud, Ernest, *Jean Moréas et Les Stances* (Paris 1929); Niklaus, R., *Jean Moréas, poète lyrique* (Paris 1936).

JEAN-ALBERT BÉDÉ.

MOREAU, mô-rō′, **Gustave,** French painter: b. Paris, France, April 6, 1826; d. there April 18, 1898. He developed a romantic and symbolic style reflecting the ideas of his teacher, Théodore Chassériau, and of Eugène Delacroix and Jean Auguste Dominique Ingres. This he projected on canvas often in the form of weird, exotic renderings of Biblical and classical mythology scenes, rendered in bold, luminous color. However, he is considered a precursor of symbolism rather in the literary than the colorist sense. His chief importance, in the eyes of many critics, lies in his influence—as professor at the École des Beaux-Arts, Paris (1892–1898)—upon his pupils Henri Matisse and Georges Rouault, leaders later in the Fauve group (see FAUVISM). Financially independent and uninterested in selling his work, he left about 8,000 paintings and drawings to the city of Paris to form the Musée Gustave Moreau. Notable among his works are *Oedipus and the Sphinx* (The Metropolitan Museum, New York City); *Apparition* (Luxembourg Museum, Paris); *Salomé; The Young Man and Death.*

MOREAU, Jean Victor, French general: b. Morlaix, Finisterre, France, Feb. 14, 1763; d. Louny (Laun), Bohemia, Sept. 2, 1813. He studied law and held briefly a minor post in the justiciary at Rennes. At the beginning of the French Revolution he formed a company of the National Guard and, in 1791, was elected lieutenant colonel of the volunteer battalion of Illeet Vilaine which served under Charles François Dumouriez. He was promoted general of brigade in 1793 and general of division under Lazare Carnot in 1794. Moreau won distinction at the Battle of Turcoing and in 1795 was put at the head of the Army of the Rhine and Moselle. Several victories and a skillful retreat in the face of great odds proved him a masterly strategist. Momentarily retired because of delay in reporting Gen. Charles Pichegru's treasonable implication in a royalist plot headed by the Prince de Condé (Louis Joseph de Bourbon), Moreau was recalled to duty in 1799. After service in Italy, he was transferred to the Army of the Rhine and succeeded Barthélemy Catherine Joubert in command after that general's death. Having conducted a well-ordered retreat to Genoa, he was replaced by Jean Antoine Étienne Championnet. He supported Bonaparte in the coup d'état of 18th Brumaire and was rewarded with command of the Army of the Rhine; he defeated the Austrians in a series of engagements culminating in Hohenlinden (Dec. 3, 1800). Back in Paris, Moreau became involved with a group of royalists seeking Napoleon's ouster, although not himself royalist in sympathy. Arrested and tried, he was sentenced to two years' imprisonment, a sentence commuted by Bonaparte to exile from France. He settled at Morrisville, Pa. After Napoleon's Russian debacle, Moreau, through Jean Baptiste Jules Bernadotte of Sweden, undertook to advise the allied powers opposing the French. Amputation of both legs resulted from wounds received while conversing with Czar Alexander at the Battle of Dresden on Aug. 27, 1813. He died within the week.

Bibliography.—Beauchamp, Alphonse de, *Vie politique, militaire, et privée du général Moreau* (Paris 1814; Eng. tr. by John Philippart, London, 1814); Lapierre de Châteauneuf, Agricol-Hippolyte de, *Histoire du général Moreau* (Paris 1814); Jochmus, Karl F. L., *General Moreau—Abriss einer Geschichte seines Lebens und seiner Feldzüge* (Berlin 1814); Svin'in, Pavel P., *Some details concerning General Moreau, and His Last Moments* (London 1814); Picard, Ernest, *Bonaparte et Moreau* (Paris 1905); Daudet, Ernest, *L'exil et la mort du général Moreau* (Paris 1909); Garcot, Maurice, *Le duel Moreau-Napoléon* (Paris 1951).

JOHN J. MENG,
Hunter College, New York City.

MOREAU DE SAINT-MERY, mô-rō′ dẽ săɴ′ mā-rē′, **Médéric-Louis-Elie,** French politician: b. Fort-Royal, Martinique, Jan. 28, 1750; d. Paris, France, Jan. 28, 1819. A lawyer in his native island, then a member of the Council of Santo Domingo, he became an expert on colonial legislation (consult his *Lois et Constitutions des colonies françaises de l'Amérique sous-le-Vent,* 6 vols., 1784–1790). Having represented Martinique in the Constituent Assembly (Paris, 1789), he, a liberal monarchist, sought refuge in the United States after the fall of Louis XVI (1792). To the ensuing period, during which he operated a bookshop in Philadelphia, Pa., belong his *Description . . . de l'île de Saint-Domingue* (4 vols., 1796–1798) and a *Voyage aux Etats-Unis de l'Amérique* which remained unpublished until 1913. Upon his return to France in 1799, he enjoyed the protection of Joséphine Bonaparte, a distant relative of his, and was appointed to administrative duties in Northern Italy. After his dismissal in 1806, he retained a pension paid him by the then empress.

Consult Elicona, A. L., *Un colonial sous la Révolution en France et en Amérique: Moreau de St-Méry* (Paris 1934).

JEAN-ALBERT BÉDÉ.

MORECAMBE AND HEYSHAM, mōr′-kăm, hā′shăm, municipal borough, in northwestern Lancashire, England, comprising the seaside resort of Morecambe (incorporated in 1902) and the port of Heysham, two miles to the south, which was absorbed into the borough in 1928. On Morecambe Bay, from which it gets its name, Morecambe is, after Blackpool, a leading vacation resort of England's industrial north; it has a wide sandy beach, six miles of promenade (with Heysham), two piers, winter gardens, a *Kursaal,* a huge swimming stadium, and a good golf course. Across the bay, it commands a beautiful panorama of the Furness Fells and the lake district mountains. Heysham is a passenger port for Ireland and the Isle of Man; of ancient origin, it has cliffside ruins of a tiny pre-Norman chapel (St. Patrick's), and a parish church (St. Peter's) containing Saxon masonry in its nave and part of a Saxon cross-shaft in its churchyard. Pop. (1961) 14,495.

MOREEN. See MOIRE.

MOREHEAD, mōr′hĕd, town, Kentucky, seat of Rowan County in the northeast, at an altitude of 710 feet, on the Chesapeake and Ohio Railway and a federal highway. Morehead State College is situated here. Pop. 7,191.

MOREHEAD CITY, mōr'hĕd, town, North Carolina, in Carteret County, 33 miles southeast of New Bern. It is situated on the west shore of Beaufort Harbor at the north end of Bogue Sound, and is connected with the Atlantic Ocean by means of a four-mile channel through Beaufort Inlet. Its 1,000-foot pier is operated by the Morehead City Port Commission, and was constructed between 1935 and 1937. A new ocean terminal of the North Carolina State Ports Authority was being built in 1950, to supplement the existing shipping facilities, which, upon completion, will provide an additional 1,200-foot wharf, a transit shed, and two storage sheds.

Morehead City was founded in 1857, and incorporated three years later. Pop. 5,233.

MOREL. See FUNGUS.

MOREL-LADEUIL, mô-rĕl' lá-dû'y', **Léonard,** French sculptor and goldsmith: b. Clermont-Ferrand, France, 1824; d. Boulogne-sur-Mer, France, March 15, 1888. He studied art in Paris, and made his debut as an exhibitor at the Salon with his *Courage terrassant l'hydre de l'anarchie* in 1853. Six years later he went to Birmingham, England, where he was employed by the Messrs. Elkington, a firm of goldsmiths. Here he became known for his very beautiful *repoussé* work, and at the time of the Prince of Wales' marriage, the city of Birmingham purchased Morel-Ladeuil's plaque called *Dreams* for a wedding gift to the royal couple. Still another of his well known pieces presented to royalty, was his famous *Helicon* vase given to Queen Victoria on the occasion of her first jubilee.

MORELIA, mô-rā'lyä, city, Mexico, and capital of Michoacán state, is situated 130 miles west-northwest of Mexico City, on a fertile plateau, altitude 6,187 feet. It was founded in 1541 by the first viceroy of New Spain, Antonio de Mendoza, and was originally called Valladolid after the city of his birth in Spain. The city was renamed Morelia in 1828 in honor of José Morelos y Pavón (q.v.), priest and one of the early martyrs in Mexico's struggle for freedom from Spanish rule, who was born here. His enemy Augustín Iturbide (q.v.) was also a native.

Its chief products are corn, beans, sugar cane, fruit, and cattle. Among its industries are coffee processing, sugar refining, the extracting of vegetable oil, and the manufacture of shawls, hats, cotton goods, tobacco products, sweets, beer, chemicals, and resins.

The city is equipped with an airport, and modern radio stations. There are many fine old buildings. Pop. (1966) 133,764.

MORELL, George Webb, American soldier: b. Cooperstown, N. Y., Jan. 8, 1815; d. Scarborough, N. Y., Feb. 11, 1883. He was graduated from the West Point Military Academy in 1835, but resigned from the army two years later to become a civil engineer. He worked for three years in Michigan and in various Southern states on railroad construction, but in 1840 he settled in New York to study law. Admitted to the bar in 1842, he practiced law until 1861. During this period he served as commissioner of the United States Circuit Court for the Southern District of New York, from 1854 until the Civil War broke out, when he was made inspector general on the staff of the 1st Division, New York State Militia, and accompanied it to Washington.

He was colonel on Gen. Robert Patterson's staff during the Shenandoah campaign, and was promoted to brigadier general, then to major general, commanding the 2d Brigade, 2d Division, Army Corps, to be given next command of a division. He commanded the supports of the celebrated battery of 100 guns at Malvern Hill, and was engaged at Hanover Court House, Mechanicsville, and Gaines' Mills.

During the Chickahominy campaign, he contracted a disease that was later to prove fatal. After being mustered out of the army on Dec. 15, 1864, he retired to his farm at Scarborough, and lived there until his death.

MORELLA, mō-rā'lyä, city, Spain, is situated in the Province of Castellón, and is the principal town in the mountainous district of Maestrazgo. Originally founded by the Romans, the city became, in the Middle Ages, the stronghold of the kingdom of Valencia, and later played a prominent part in the Carlist wars.

In 1839, it was stormed by the Carlist general, Ramón Cabrera, who received for this victory the title of count of Morella. The city remained in Carlist hands until it was captured by Gen. Baldomero Espartero in 1840. Its modern industries consist of cotton textile factories, dyeing establishments, tanning, flour milling, and lumbering. It also raises cereals, almonds, and livestock. Pop. (1960) 4,162.

MORELLET, mô-rĕ-lĕ', **André,** French philosopher and writer: b. Lyon, France, March 7, 1727; d. Paris, France, Jan. 12, 1819. He studied under the Jesuits in Lyon, and then at the Sorbonne in Paris, after which he acted as tutor to a youth being sent by his family to Italy.

Morellet's growing interest in political economy was evidenced in his writings at this period in his life. They were eloquent, and possessed a keen and bitter wit rather than outstanding originality of thought. He was a personal friend of Voltaire, and a contributor to the famous *Encyclopédie* of Denis Diderot the French philosopher. He was elected to the French Academy in 1785, and seven years later, when the Academy was dissolved during the French Revolution, he managed to save its archives and the manuscript of the *Dictionnaire de l'Académie française* from the revolutionaries. He kept the valuable documents hidden until 1803 when the Academy was reorganized. It is interesting to note that 32 years afterward, Morellet was made one of the directors of this same *Dictionnaire* he had been instrumental in preserving.

MORELLI, mô-rĕ'lē, **Domenico,** Italian painter: b. Naples, Aug. 4, 1826; d. there, Aug. 13, 1901. He studied at Rome under Camillo Guerra and later was associated with the Realist leader, Filippo Palizzi.

His finest early works were *The Sicilian Vesper* and *Refugees from Aquileja.* He turned to religious subjects in 1867, of which his *Christ Walking on the Sea* and *The Descent from the Cross* are particularly well known. He painted the *Ascension of the Virgin* for the royal palace at Naples, and the results of a journey he took to the Orient were the paintings, *Street in Constantinople* and *Mohammed Before the Battle.* He was made a senator of the kingdom of Italy, and became a director of the Institute of Fine Arts and the Museum of Applied Art in Naples.

MORELLI, Giovanni (pseudonym IVAN LERMOLIEV, lyĕr-môl'yĕf), Italian art critic: b. Verona, Feb. 25, 1816; d. Milan, Feb. 28, 1891. He gained his education at Bergamo, and afterward at Aarau, Switzerland. He went next to Germany to study natural science in Munich, and while at the university there became interested in art. Returning to his native country in 1840, he associated himself whole-heartedly with the patriots who were trying to liberate Italy from Austrian domination. He took part in both the insurrection of Milan in 1848, and in that of Bergamo in 1866. He was elected deputy of the latter city (1860–1870), and in 1873 became a senator. While in this post he introduced the bill, bearing his name, which forbids the sale of works of art from public and religious institutions.

His treatises on art identification, which he usually signed with his pseudonym, were based on what were at that time new principles. He showed how paintings can be attributed to certain artists by observing the treatment of such details as hair, ears, fingers, etc. To this theory many experts—among them his main adversary, Friedrich Bode—opposed the objection that pupils of the old masters often employed the characteristics and mannerisms of their teachers. Of course, modern methods which use X-ray in examining paintings, have rendered Morelli's theories obsolete, replacing conjecture with scientific tests.

Morelli's major books are *Die Werke italienischer Meister in den Galerien von München, Dresden, und Berlin,* 3 vols. (1880), and *Kunstkritische Studien,* 3 vols. (1890–1893). The latter work was translated into English by Charles John Ffoulkes under the title *Italian Painters* (1892).

MORELOS, mô-rā'lôs, state, Mexico, lying to the south of the Federal District and the State of México. Its capital is Cuernavaca (q.v.), and it covers an area of 1,917 square miles. Situated on the south slopes of a large plateau with Popocatepetl to the northeast, the state is drained by small tributaries of the Rio de las Balsas. It is an agricultural region, producing corn, rice, sugar cane, wheat, coffee, tropical fruits and cattle. The climate ranges from semitropical to temperate. Pop. (1967) 546,000.

MORELOS Y PAVON, mō-rā'lōs ē pä-vôn', **José María,** Mexican patriot and priest: b. Morelia (then Valladolid), Michoacán, Mexico, Sept. 30, 1765; d. near Mexico City, Mexico, Dec. 22, 1815. He had some Indian ancestry, and he worked for many years as a muleteer. At the age of 30, he entered the college of Valladolid (Morelia, q.v.) and was ordained to the priesthood three years later. From 1801 to 1810 he was in charge of the parishes of Carácuaro and Nucupétaro.

He joined, in 1810, the rebellion launched by Miguel Hidalgo y Costilla, who had been rector of the college of Valladolid during Morelos' student days.

After Hidalgo's death, he kept the cause alive in the north. His few followers soon became an army, and having defeated the Spaniards in several battles, he advanced upon Mexico City. He held Cuautla for 62 days against the famous siege by the viceroy, finally effecting a skillful withdrawal of his forces. Later he captured Oaxaca (October 1812) and Acapulco (August 1813).

He was made captain general in November 1813 by the Congress convened at Chilipancingo. On Nov. 6, 1813, he proclaimed the independence of Mexico from Spain; after which he drafted a republican constitution for the newly freed country. In attempting to capture Valladolid, he was defeated by Augustín de Iturbide, and taken prisoner. He was shot as a traitor at San Cristóbal Ecatepec, and his remains now lie in the cathedral in Mexico City. The state of Morelos was so named in his honor.

MORENO, mô-rā'nō, **Alfredo Baquerizo,** bä-kâ-rē'sō, Ecuadorian president and diplomat: b. Guayaquil, Ecuador, Sept. 29, 1859; d. New York, N. Y., March 29, 1951. He was graduated in law from the University of Quito, and began to practice his profession in 1884. From 1897 to 1901 he was a member of the Superior Court of Guayaquil.

He became minister of foreign relations in 1901–1902; and a year later was elected vice president of Ecuador. He was minister to the United States during President Theodore Roosevelt's administration, and was elected president of Ecuador in 1916, serving a four-year term. Again he occupied the presidency, from 1931–1932, being deposed from office during the latter year.

He was author of *Poetas* (1882); and the novels *Titania* (1892); *El Señor Peneo* (1892); *Una Sonata en Prosa* (1894); *Evangelina* (1895); and *Luz* (1901).

MORESNET, mô-rĕz-nĕ', former neutral territory on the Belgian-German border, about 5 miles southwest of Aachen. The territory was under the protection of the signatories of the Vienna Congress (1815), and the citizens had a choice of military service with either the Belgian or the Prussian Army. Many of the inhabitants were French and Dutch, others Flemish and German.

Under the Treaty of Versailles, promulgated June 28, 1919, Belgium was awarded full sovereignty over the contested territory of Moresnet and over part of Prussian Moresnet. The territory is now part of the province of Liége.

MORET, mô-rĕ', **Alexandre,** French Egyptologist: b. Aix-les-Bains, Province of Savoie, France, Sept. 19, 1868; d. Paris, France, Feb. 2, 1938. After passing the examination for the academic title of Agrégé in history and geography in 1893, he obtained his doctorate in 1903, and became director of Egyptological studies at the *École des Hautes Etudes* at the University of Paris, where he also lectured on Oriental history. Between 1906 and 1923 he was a director of the *Musée Guimet* in Paris, and professor of Egyptology at the *Collège de France.*

MORETO Y CAVANA, mô-rā'tō e kä-vä'-nyä, **Augustín,** Spanish dramatist: b. Madrid, Spain, April 8, 1618; d. Toledo, Spain, Oct. 27, 1669. He graduated in law from the University of Alcala, and upon his return home changed his profession and began writing plays. In Madrid he found a friend and patron in Pedro Calderon de la Barca. He was very prolific, turning out drama after drama until he finally passed the 100 mark before he had reached middle age.

His popularity was immense and he was rated as the equal, if not the superior, of Lope de Vega, by his admirers, among whom were the best critics of the day. Posterity, however, while recognizing the genius of Moreto and his valuable contributions to the Spanish drama, has not sustained this high verdict of his contemporaries. One reason is that Moreto was not original in the sense that Lope de Vega was. His dramas or *Comedias de capa y espada* (cloak and sword plays), while clever in themselves and instinct with the dramatic spirit, have more than an echo of Vega and Calderón, whom he frequently borrowed from and sometimes improved upon, as in *El Desdén con el Desdén,* which is generally considered to be his masterpiece. In addition to dramas of intrigue he also produced historical dramas and wrote considerable lyrical poetry and *autos sacramentales* (religious plays).

Moreto's incursion into the field of historical drama was probably occasioned by the decree of the Royal Council and Chamber of Castile which, in 1644, ordered that, in the future, the dramatists should turn their attention to historical drama and plays based on the lives of the saints. He found a new field in recasting old plays and making them conform to the requirements of the censor, who was, in reality, controlled by the church authorities who had dictated the new move for restricting the activities of the drama and the stage. Like Shakespeare, Moreto put so much of himself into this work of reconstruction that many of the new-made dramas were more deservedly his than the work of their first creators. He excelled in depicting human passions and feelings, among them all the shades of love, including undying passion, disdain, the suffering of unrequited love, jealousy, friendship, faithfulness, unfaithfulness, intrigue in love and in the ordinary affairs of life. In this field he led the way for that true and colorful character drawing in which the Spanish drama and novel have since shown such power and realism combined with idealism.

Moreto painted people of more refined feelings and higher position in life than did Lope de Vega, probably because he was better acquainted with upper-class society than was the older dramatist. The complicated complexion of Spanish court life with its intrigues, ambitions, plots, and insincerity is well pictured in his dramas. While he lacks invention and made use, without conscience, of his predecessors, he gave the Spanish drama characterization and artistic development that it had not previously possessed, and he polished his work as no Spanish dramatist had done before his day. He thus pointed the way to the successes that have, since his time, been achieved by dramatists and novelists in Spain. What he lacked in originality of invention he made up in his knowledge of the stage and in his ability to reconstruct the scenes and thoughts of others. His plots move along with rapidity, satisfactory development and wonderful management of dialogue which is ever fluid and graceful. He presents with great skill realistic pictures of the extravagances, customs, and vices of the life of his day, and he remains the greatest of the Spanish writers of character drama. In this field he shows his deep and wide knowledge of the world and his power to analyze characters and motives, passions and prejudices. Yet, on the whole, his plays are in better taste and superior in morality to those of his contemporaries. In 1659 he entered a monastery. Among his more notable plays, besides *El Desdén con el Desdén,* are *El lindo don Diego, El valiente justiciero y ricohombre de Alcalá, El parecido en la Corte, Trampa adelante,* and *Primero es la honra.*

Consult volumes 39 and 58 of *Biblioteca de autores españoles* for articles on Moreto and the *autos sacrementales;* also Ticknor, George, *History of Spanish Literature* (New York 1849); Carrara, E., *Studio sul teatro ispano-veneto di Carlo Gozzi* (Cagliari 1901).

MORETON BAY, mōr't'n, Australia, southeast coast of Queensland, an inlet of the Pacific Ocean, 65 miles long, 20 miles wide. Moreton and Stradbroke islands form its eastern shore, and the mainland its western shore. Brisbane River flows into it.

MORETON BAY CHESTNUT, or bean tree, *Castanospermum australe,* family Leguminosae, native to Australia. It grows 40 to 60 feet high, has very long pinnate leaves, bright yellow blossoms in long clusters, and bears large brown pods each having four or five chestnut-like seeds which are edible when roasted. The timber, called black bean wood, resembles walnut but is not durable.

MORETTO, Il, ēl mô-rāt'tô (real name, ALESSANDRO BONVICINO, or BUONVICINO), Italian painter: b. Brescia, Italy, about 1498; d. there, 1554. He was a pupil of Floriano Feramola, took Titian as his model, and was also influenced by the work of Il Romanino (Girolamo Romani) and Gian Girolamo Savoldo. His pictures are distinguished for the beauty and nobility of their human figures, the serenity and balance of composition, and their color harmony, especially a silvery gray tone. The Church of St. John the Evangelist at Brescia is a veritable gallery of his pictures. Others hang in leading European galleries, and the Metropolitan Museum, New York City, has his *Christ in the Desert* and *The Entombment of Christ.*

MOREY, mō'rĭ, **Samuel,** American inventor: b. Hebron, Conn., Oct. 23, 1762; d. Fairlee, Vt., April 17, 1843. Before he was four years old, his family moved to Orford, N. H., and he attended public school there. He entered the lumbering business, but also developed his considerable talent for mechanics and engineering, and was engineer in charge of building the Connecticut River locks at Bellows Falls, Vt. He began experiments with steamboats about 1790. In 1793 he patented a steam-operated spit, and in the same year constructed a small craft propelled by a steam engine mounted on the bow, which he demonstrated on the Connecticut River at Orford. On March 25, 1795, he received a patent for a rotary steam engine. He also patented a windmill, a water wheel, and a steam pump.

In 1797, seeking capital for further experiments with steam engines, Morey went to Bordentown, N. J., where he built a side-wheel steamboat and demonstrated it successfully on the Delaware River. Failure of his financial backers, however, prevented further experiment at that time. He tried unsuccessfully to persuade Robert Fulton to adopt a model of his steamboat, and always believed that Fulton had appropriated his ideas. In 1805 and 1815 he obtained patents for steam engine improvements, and in 1820 constructed and operated on Fairlee Pond (now Lake Morey) at Fairlee, Vt., a steamboat which he called *Aunt Sally*. On April 1, 1826, he obtained one of the first American patents for an internal combustion engnie. He contributed articles on his work to *The American Journal of Science and Arts* edited by Prof. Benjamin Silliman of Yale.

MOREY, William Carey, American educator: b. North Attleboro, Mass., May 23, 1843; d. Rochester, N. Y., Jan. 21, 1925. At the outbreak of the Civil War, he left his studies at the University of Rochester to enter the Union Army as a volunteer, becoming brevet major and lieutenant colonel. Returning to the university after the war, he graduated in 1868, and in 1869 entered Rochester Theological Seminary. He was professor of history, English, and Latin at Kalamazoo College from 1870 to 1883, when he became professor of political science at the University of Rochester. He was organizer, trustee, and director of Reynolds Library there, 1884–1904. Among his many books on history and government were *Outlines of Ancient History* (1906), *The Study of Roman Law in Liberal Education* (1911), and *Ancient Peoples* (1915). He also wrote *Reminiscences of the "Pundit" Club* (1923), and numerous articles for magazines and reviews.

MOREY LETTER, The, in American political history, a forged letter used in the presidential campaign of 1880 to discredit the Republican candidate James A. Garfield. Published in the New York weekly *Truth* on Oct. 20, 1880, it purported to be a letter from Garfield to an H. L. Morey of Lynn, Mass., favoring free entry of cheap Oriental labor for work in American factories. Though instantly denounced as fraudulent, it caused Garfield the loss of five of the six electoral votes of California where the exclusion of Chinese and other Oriental labor was an issue.

MORF, môrf, **Heinrich,** Swiss philologist: b. Münchenbuchsee, Switzerland, Oct. 23, 1854; d. Thun, Jan. 23, 1921. He studied at the universities of Zurich and Strasbourg, and under Gaston Paris at the Collège de France in Paris, and at 25 was professor of Romance linguistics at Bern. He subsequently taught at Zurich (1889), Frankfort-am-Main (1901), and Berlin (1910–1921). His works include *Geschichte der französischen Literatur im Zeitalter der Renaissance* (1898), considered a masterwork; *Aus Dichtung und Sprache der Romanen* (1903–1911); *Zur sprachlichen Gliederung Frankreichs* (1913).

MORFILL, môr'fĭl, **William Richard,** English Slavonic scholar: b. Maidstone, Kent, England, Nov. 17, 1834; d. Oxford, Nov. 9, 1909. He was educated at Oriel College, Oxford, where he later became university reader in Russian and, in 1900, professor of Russian and Slavonic. He wrote extensively on Slavic languages, literature, and history, and was the author of Polish, Serbian, Bulgarian, Russian, and Czech grammars.

MORFORD, môr'fẽrd, **Henry,** American writer: b. New Monmouth, N. J., March 10, 1823; d. Aug. 4, 1881. In 1852 he founded the weekly New Jersey *Standard* at Middletown Point (now Matawan), and four years later went to New York, where he worked as a court clerk for a time and then on the editorial staff of the New York *Atlas*. He made several trips abroad, and became known for his travel books and short-trip guidebooks to Europe and America. He also published several volumes of verse and three Civil War novels, and in January 1880 founded the *Brooklyn New Monthly Magazine* which he edited and published until March 1881.

MORGAGNI, mŏr-gä'nyĕ, **Giovanni Battista** or **Giambattista,** Italian anatomist: b. Forlì, Italy, May 25, 1682; d. Padua, Dec. 5, 1771. After graduating at the age of 14 from the academy in his native town, he spent 16 years in Bologna as the student, friend, and colleague of Antonio Maria Valsalva (illustrious pupil of Marcello Malpighi), lecturer in anatomy at the university. There he took degrees in philosophy and medicine at the age of 19. In 1710 he became professor of medicine at the University of Padua, and in 1715 professor of anatomy. His famous *Adversaria Anatomica* was published in 1706, and an enlarged version, *Adversaria Omnia,* in 1741. His greatest work, published in 1761, was *De Sedibus et Causis Morborum per Anatomen Indigatis* (*The Seats and Causes of Diseases Investigated by Anatomy*), which established pathological anatomy as a science and changed the course of medical diagnosis.

MORGAN, môr'găn, **Arthur Ernest,** American civil engineer: b. Cincinnati, Ohio, June 20, 1878. He attended high school in St. Cloud, Minn., and while working for his father as a surveyor, studied engineering at night. In 1902 he went into business for himself, specializing in flood control, and in 1907–1909 was supervising engineer for the United States Government Drainage Investigations. He was president of Antioch College, 1920–1936, and was the recipient of numerous honorary degrees from other colleges and universities. In 1933–1938 he was chairman of the Tennessee Valley Authority, but was dismissed by President Franklin D. Roosevelt for refusing to provide evidence to support his charges against other members of the commission. His numerous books include *My World* (1927), *The Long Road* (1936), *Nowhere Was Somewhere* (1946), *Industries for Small Communities* (1953).

MORGAN, Charles Hill, American inventor: b. Rochester, N. Y., Jan. 8, 1831; d. Worcester, Mass., Jan. 10, 1911. He left school at the age of 12 to go to work, and at 15 became an apprentice machinist in Clinton, Mass. He attended night school, and at 21 was an expert machinist and draftsman. From 1855 to 1860 he was draftsman for Erastus B. Bigelow, carpet manufacturer, and in 1860, in partnership with his brother, he opened a paper bag factory in Philadelphia, Pa. Here he invented an automatic bag-making machine. The business was sold profitably in 1864, and Morgan joined the Washburn & Moen Company, wire makers, in Worcester, Mass. While there, he perfected a power reel (with Fred H. Daniels), a continuous rolling mill, and automatic pouring and laying reels. He established the Morgan Spring Company, Worcester, in 1881, and in 1891 organized the Morgan Construction Company to produce rolling mill machinery. From 1887 until his death he was consulting engineer for the American Steel & Wire Company, and was a trustee of Worcester Polytechnic Institute from its founding.

MORGAN, Charles Langbridge, English author: b. Kent, England, Jan. 22, 1894; d. London, Feb. 6, 1958. In 1907, he entered the Royal Navy as a cadet; he resigned in 1913, but reenlisted the following year with the outbreak of World War I. He was captured and interned in Holland—an experience which served as the basis for his best-known novel, *The Fountain* (1932). He attended Brasenose College, Oxford, from 1919 to 1921, when he joined the editorial staff of *The Times* (London), for which he was chief drama critic from 1926 to 1939. In 1923 he married Hilda Vaughan, the writer. During World War II, he served with the Admiralty.

In most of his work he dealt with moral problems. He was much concerned with the conflict between the spirit and the flesh, and his treatment of it has been characterized as mystical. In general most critics have found him to be genuinely serious, though perhaps not profound, and a thoroughly professional craftsman.

Morgan's other novels include *The Gunroom* (1919), *Portrait in a Mirror* (1929), *Sparkenbroke* (1936), *The Voyage* (1940), and *Challenge to Venus* (1957). His plays were *The Flashing Stream* (1938), *The River Line* (1952), and *The Burning Glass* (1954).

MORGAN, Conwy Lloyd (sometimes LLOYD-MORGAN), British biologist, psychologist, and philosopher: b. London, England, Feb. 6, 1852; d. Hastings, March 6, 1936. He was educated at the Royal College of Science where he was a student of Thomas H. Huxley. After teaching in South Africa for six years, he was appointed in 1884 to the chair of geology and zoology at University College, Bristol, becoming principal in 1887, and vice chancellor in 1909. He resigned from administrative work the following year, accepting appointment to the chair of psychology and ethics, which he occupied until his retirement in 1919.

Morgan saw that the psychological side of the problem of the relationship between man and the lower animals had been put in new perspective by evolutionary theory. One of the founders of animal psychology, he pioneered in the development of the experimental method. His lectures at Harvard and Clark universities played an important part in awakening psychologists in the United States to the importance of comparative psychology. In the attempt to prevent an anthropomorphic treatment of the animal mind, he enunciated his famous principle of parsimony: "In no case may we interpret an action as the outcome of the exercise of a higher psychical faculty, if it can be interpreted as the outcome of one which stands lower in the psychological scale." Mental activity he found in three evolutionary levels, ranging from a vague consciousness (in all animals) to an effective consciousness (in creatures that can profit by experience), culminating in self-consciousness (in a small number of the higher animals). Among his works of this period are *Animal Life and Intelligence* (1890), revised as *Animal Behavior* (1900), and *Introduction to Comparative Psychology* (1895).

Scientific investigation had demonstrated the facts of evolution empirically and this, Morgan believed, furnished a solid base upon which speculative thought could build a philosophical system. The principle of parsimony made it impossible for him to accept some special force, such as an *élan vital,* as the creative force in evolution in the manner of Henri Bergson (see BERGSONISM). Similarly, he rejected mechanistic explanations of novelty. Progress, he thought, was not the simple result of continuous steady advance; in organic evolution critical turning points were characterized by the appearance of new and unpredictable qualities which signified a higher stage of development. This process illustrated the concept of evolution as emergent and universally applicable throughout nature, including human nature, and both the psychic and the material worlds were mutually dependent parts of this evolution. As a scientist Morgan felt there was no need to answer the question of what caused this process, but as a philosopher, he believed that the operative power was God.

Morgan reflects the evolutionary ideas characteristic of his time, and his concern with the problem of novelty is shared by other philosophers, notably Samuel Alexander, who both influenced and was influenced by him. His Gifford lectures were published as *Emergent Evolution* (1923) and *Life, Mind, and Spirit* (1926); his other philosophical works include *Mind at the Cross-ways* (1929) and *The Emergence of Novelty* (1933). His autobiography is in *History of Psychology in Autobiography,* vol. 2 (1932), edited by Carl Allanmore Murchison.

Consult Metz, Rudolf, *A Hundred Years of British Philosophy* (London 1938).

MORGAN, Daniel, American soldier: b. Hunterdon County, N.J., 1736; d. Winchester, Va., July 6, 1802. His early life was passed in obscurity. He moved to Virginia and, in 1755, he served as a teamster on Maj. Gen. Edward Braddock's disastrous expedition. He was afterward engaged in Indian warfare and served as a lieutenant in Dunmore's War. In 1775 he was commissioned a captain and commanded a company of rifleman under George Washington. He accompanied Benedict Arnold to Quebec, and assumed command when Arnold was wounded. After initial successes, he was captured by the British and not exchanged until nearly a year afterward. He was then given command of a Virginia regiment with the rank of colonel and took a prominent part in the campaign against John Burgoyne, but as his services were not sufficiently recognized by Congress, and being in poor health, he resigned. In 1780 he returned to the service as a brigadier general under Horatio Gates, and under Nathaniel Greene, who succeeded Gates. Morgan won a brilliant victory over Sir Banastre Tarleton at the Battle of Cowpens (q.v.) on Jan. 17, 1781. His subsequent movements were of serious annoyance to the opposing general, Charles Cornwallis, but he soon resigned from the Army owing to ill health. In 1794 he returned to it as a major general and helped to crush the Whiskey Rebellion (q.v.). He was a member of Congress from 1797 to 1799.

MORGAN, Edwin Denison, American political leader: b. Washington, Mass., Feb. 8, 1811; d. New York, N.Y., Feb. 14, 1883. He entered the grocery firm of his uncle in Hartford, Conn., and two years later, at the age of 20, he became a partner in the business. He moved to New York City in 1836 and engaged in the wholesale grocery business with conspicuous success, later branching out into banking. During the cholera epidemic of 1849 he rendered devoted service, and this helped him with his political career. Elected to the state Senate in 1850 as a Whig, he continued in that office until 1856. In 1858 he became governor of the state, as a Republican, and served until 1862, providing a strong administration during the trying days of the Civil War. He was appointed to the United States Senate in 1863, and served there until 1869. He twice refused the secretaryship of the treasury, being offered it by Abraham Lincoln and Chester A. Arthur. He was connected with numerous great financial enterprises during the later years of his life, and he was a generous benefactor to education, notably to the Union Theological Seminary and Williams College.

Edwin Barber Morgan (1806–1881), his cousin, of Aurora, N.Y., was a pioneer in the express business and first president (1852) of Wells, Fargo & Company. He served in Congress (1853–1859) and, as a major stockholder of the New York *Times,* played a vital role in its exposure of the Tweed Ring (1871).

MORGAN, George Washington, American soldier and congressman: b. Washington County, Pa., Sept. 20, 1820; d. Old Point Comfort, Va., July 26, 1893. He left college in 1836 to enlist in the Texas Army and fought for the independence of that country. In 1841 he entered West Point, but left in his second year. He established a law practice at Mount Vernon, Ohio, in 1843.

When the Mexican War broke out, Morgan became a colonel and served with distinction under Gen. Winfield Scott, becoming brevet brigadier general. After the war he returned to his law practice and in 1856 was sent as United States consul to Marseille, France. In 1858 he became minister to Portugal. He entered the Army immediately upon his return to the United States in 1861, and was given a command under Maj. Gen. Don Carlos Buell, as a brigadier general. In 1862 he took command of a division of the Army of Ohio; later he was with William T. Sherman at Vicksburg. He disagreed with Sherman's policy of using Negro troops and this, in combination with illness, led to his resignation in 1863. He was a Democratic member of Congress from 1869 to 1873, where he opposed the Radical Republican reconstruction policy.

MORGAN, Sir **Henry,** Welsh buccaneer: b. Llanrhymny, Glamorganshire, Wales, about 1635; d. Jamaica, West Indies, 1688. As a boy he is said to have been kidnaped at Bristol and sold at Barbados. Just when he joined the Jamaica buccaneers is uncertain, as there were several Morgans in the marine at Jamaica at the time, but he may have commanded his own ship as early as 1663; a Captain Morgan who sailed from Jamaica in that year taking part in the sack of Vildemos, Truxillo (now Trujillo) and Granada (1665–1666). In 1666 Morgan sailed under Edward Mansfield, who had been commissioned by Sir Thomas Modyford, the governor of Jamaica, to capture Curaçao, and was chosen admiral after Mansfield's death at the hands of the Spaniards. In 1668 he captured Puerto Principe (now Camagüey) in order to get information of Spanish plans for an attack on Jamaica, which he did; he then took Porto Bello (Portobelo), Panama, after a sharp siege during which the buccaneers planted scaling ladders under the cover of captured priests and nuns, sacked the city and tortured and maltreated its inhabitants. In the end of the summer he again ravaged Cuba. The next year, 1669, saw Morgan, with a fresh commission from Modyford, attack and plunder Maracaibo. The arrival of three Spanish warships did not check Morgan's success, for he set fire to one ship, captured another, and forced the Spaniards to beach and burn the third; he killed almost all his prisoners, recovered 15,000 pieces of eight from the sunken ship, got a ransom for the city from the Spanish forces in the fort, and by a clever maneuver made his escape. Returning to Jamaica he was first reproved for exceeding his powers and then made commander in chief of the entire naval force of Jamaica, so that in 1671, with a stronger force under him than before, he approached the city of Panama, which he captured after a thrilling battle, in which the Spanish cavalry was broken by riding into a swamp, and further execution was done by a herd of cattle which the Spaniards intended should break the English ranks but which stampeded the Spanish. This attack and the capture of Panama occurred some time later than the signature of peace between England and Spain, and in consequence Morgan was ordered to England for trial in 1671. Nothing serious came of this, however, possibly because Morgan made free use of his wealth in England. In November 1674 he held a commission as lieutenant governor of Jamaica. He can hardly be called a pirate; his cruel, brutal methods were those of his enemies and England's enemies.

MORGAN, John, American physician: b. Philadelphia, Pa., June 10, 1735; d. there, Oct. 15, 1789. He served an apprenticeship in medicine with Dr. John Redmond, beginning about 1750, for six years. During this period he also attended the College of Philadelphia (now the University of Pennsylvania), graduating in 1757 with the first class. He then entered the provincial army as a surgeon, with the rank of lieutenant, resigning his commission in 1760 to continue his medical studies at London and at the University of Edinburgh, where he received the M.D. degree in 1763. The following year he studied anatomy in Paris and in Italy with Giovanni Battista Morgagni, the founder of pathological anatomy.

Upon his return to Pennsylvania in 1765, Morgan succeeded in persuading the trustees of the College of Philadelphia to open the first medical school in the colonies. His plan for the school (modeled on the lines of Edinburgh) was adopted, and he became professor of the theory and practice of medicine. In his famous commencement address of 1765, "A Discourse upon the Institution of Medical Schools in America," he urged the importance of scientific research and the teaching of science and especially medicine in the universities; however, he thought these should be based upon a broad liberal education. He also urged the establishment of specialization in American medical practice. The course of study at the college required, in addition to the lectures, one year of practice at the Pennsylvania Hospital.

In 1775, Congress appointed Morgan director general of hospitals and physician in chief of the Continental Army. His drastic reorganization of the medical department to improve the quality of the personnel and methods of treatment incurred resentment and political antagonism, which eventually led to his dismissal in January 1777. No formal charges were brought against him. George Washington and the Congress each exonerated him of any wrongdoing or neglect, but he withdrew from public life.

Morgan probably did more than any other man of his time to bring the advanced scientific medical knowledge of Europe to the colonies. He was perhaps the foremost medical educator of the pre-Revolutionary era and very likely the outstanding example of colonial medical science.

MORGAN, John Hunt, Confederate general: b. Huntsville, Ala., June 1, 1825; d. Greeneville, Tenn., Sept. 4, 1864. His family moved to Lexington, Ky., about 1830, where he was educated. In 1846, he enlisted for the Mexican War, in which he served as lieutenant of cavalry and saw action at Buena Vista. In September 1861, he left his prosperous hemp-manufacturing business in Lexington to become first a Confederate scout and then captain of a squadron. Soon discovering that he could best serve the Confederacy by adopting guerrilla methods of warfare, he began his famous series of raids. Moving with great rapidity and accompanied by his own telegraph operator, he kept himself acquainted with the plans of the enemy while he misled them regarding his own position. As the result, bridges which they expected to cross were burned, much-needed supply trains were captured, and railroad tracks were destroyed. He became a colonel in April 1862 and a brigadier general the following December. In 1863 he projected an extended raid through Kentucky, Ohio, and Indiana, but was captured on July 26 and imprisoned in the Ohio State Penitentiary, from which he escaped on November 26. In April 1864 he assumed command of the Department of Southwest Virginia, where he reorganized his forces with efficiency. However, while attempting to attack Knoxville, Tenn., he was surprised and killed at Greeneville. See Morgan's Raids into Indiana and Ohio.

Consult Swiggett, Howard, *The Rebel Raider* (Indianapolis 1934).

MORGAN, John Pierpont, American financier: b. Hartford, Conn., April 17, 1837; d. Rome, Italy, March 31, 1913. His father, Junius Spencer Morgan, was a promising Hartford merchant at the time of Morgan's birth, but by 1853 his success had caused him to be invited to London as a partner in the private banking house of Yankee dry-goods merchant George Peabody. In consequence "Pip," as Morgan was known in his youth, was taken from Boston's excellent English High School and enrolled in a private school in Switzerland and then, for a stay of less than two years, as a mathematics student at the University of Göttingen in Germany. In 1857 the tall and husky youth was installed by his father as an accountant in the New York banking firm of Duncan, Sherman & Co., Peabody's American correspondent. Four years later Morgan was set up for himself in banking. After Peabody retired in 1864, Morgan and his father joined forces with Charles H. Dabney as Dabney, Morgan & Co.; they were the New York correspondents for J. S. Morgan & Co., as Peabody's firm was henceforth known. When Dabney retired in 1871, the Morgans, together with Anthony Drexel of the Philadelphia banking family, formed a new firm, Drexel, Morgan & Co. Junius Morgan died in 1890 and Drexel in 1893 and so, beginning Jan. 1, 1895, the firm took the name of J. P. Morgan & Co. By then Morgan had been established as the "Jupiter" of American finance.

Investment banking differs considerably from everyday commercial banking, though Morgan did both. The ordinary commercial bank accepts deposits from all comers and makes short-term loans to cover the current operations of business firms. The investment bank, basically, markets the securities—the stocks and bonds—which large corporations typically use to raise their long-term capital. In Morgan's day, American big business corporations were growing very rapidly and were constantly in need of long-term funds for expansion. As the Morgan family had particularly strong connections in England, the richest capital center of the time, they could find markets for corporate securities when other bankers could not. So profitable did this business become that the Morgans themselves sometimes instigated corporate expansion, mergers, reorganizations, or other alterations in company structures which created occasions to float new securities and keep the profitable market churning.

Morgan's first spectacular coup came in 1879 when, without causing a flutter in the price, he unloaded $25 million of William H. Vanderbilt's New York Central stock in England at a profit to his firm of $3 million. Morgan, who held many proxies for these British purchasers, assumed a position of much influence as a member of the board of directors of the railroad. His greatest opportunities came after the crash of 1893 had bankrupted most of the large railroads of the United States, which promptly turned to Morgan for help—thus giving him a substantial measure of control. Perhaps even more spectacular was another phase of his business, the floating of government securities. One notable example occurred in the depths of the depression in 1895 when he acquired more than $65 million in gold for the United States government—at a considerable profit—thus saving the Treasury Department from having to suspend the redemption of its currency in coin. Morgan made history in 1901 by financing the merger out of which came the first billion dollar company, the United States Steel Corporation. In 1907, he mobilized the banking strength of New York to avert a widespread financial collapse following a Wall Street panic. But his very success in so doing showed the country how much power he wielded and prompted political action that led ultimately to the establishment of the Federal Reserve System in 1913.

Once Morgan had raised money for a company from investors who had acted largely on their confidence in him, he generally felt the necessity of protecting this investment by placing his own men on the board of directors, thereby taking a direct hand in company management. Another of the salient features of the Morgan system was the investment bankers' control over (or at least the close alliance with) the growing American institutional sources of capital. These institutions included commercial banks, trust companies that administered large estates and other properties, and the great life insurance companies. Thus the Morgan influence spread far from the financial community itself, to the heart of the big business system, and beyond that to the general population. Morgan's competitors used the same methods, but the "House of Morgan" was the kingpin of the so-called "money trust," which—according to the famous Pujo investigation in the House of Representatives in 1912—controlled the very bloodstream of the American economy. Yet, if this charge contained truth, it was essentially because the nation itself had failed to supply an alternative means of bringing order into a violently competitive economy.

Morgan was a powerful personality who was accustomed to dominating every situation. By temperament, he was an aristocrat. A man's character, he believed, was his greatest asset, and he generally avoided doing business with those whom he could not respect. He was a devout Episcopalian and a great benefactor of the church. He also gave generously to hospitals and schools. He spent many years in Europe buying art masterpieces and he was probably the greatest collector of his day. The Morgan Library in New York City became a treasury of illuminated manuscripts and books. He gave extensive financial support to many museums, and especially to The Metropolitan Museum of Art in New York City, of which he was president.

Bibliography.—John Moody, *The Masters of Capital* (New Haven 1919) is a sound popular introduction to Morgan and his times. Lewis Corey, *The House of Morgan* (New York 1930), is useful for Morgan and other members of the family. Frederick L. Allen, *The Lords of Creation* (New York 1935) is a lively supplement to Moody's work, and the same author's *The Great Pierpont Morgan* (New York 1949), while somewhat cloying in tone, is a readable biography with bibliographical references.

WILLIAM MILLER,
Editor of "Men in Business"; Author of "A New History of the United States."

MORGAN, John Pierpont, American financier: b. Irvington, N.Y., Sept. 7, 1867; d. Boca Grande, Fla., March 13, 1943. The only son of John Pierpont Morgan (1837–1913), he was educated at St. Paul School and Harvard University, graduating from the latter in 1889. After a tour at the London branch of Drexel, Morgan & Co., he entered the New York office in 1891, becoming a partner the following year. His father died when he was 45, leaving him a personal fortune in excess of $50 million. As the head of J. P. Morgan & Co., and many other enterprises, he was the major American financier of his time, though he was not able to play so dominant a role as his father had done. His greatest achievement was his financing, during World War I, of $1.5 billion of Allied military purchases in the United States. Following the stock market crash of October 1929, Morgan mobilized a banking pool of nearly $250 million to support stock prices, but he failed to match his father's success in halting the panic of 1907.

Where the historical currents had been running for the father, the tides were against the son. In his era, war profits were so great that corporations were less dependent on bankers, such as Morgan, for financing. British capital had played a major part in the previous success of the firm, but now the financial growth of the United States made Morgan's British connections less important. Moreover, the success of his father in building a great financial edifice had the effect of arousing popular feeling against so great a concentration of power, and this had led to legislation and economic regulation that significantly restricted his operations. A devout Episcopalian, like his father, he carried on the latter's work in charitable activities and as a patron of the arts.

WILLIAM MILLER.

MORGAN, Junius Spencer, American financier: b. West Springfield (now Holyoke), Mass., April 14, 1813; d. Monte Carlo, Monaco, April 8, 1890. He entered a dry-goods store when a boy and remained there until he came of age, when he was engaged for 18 months in banking in New York. He returned to the dry-goods business in Hartford, Conn., where he was junior partner in a leading firm and rapidly advanced until he formed a partnership under the name of J. M. Beebe, Morgan & Co., which became one of the largest dry-goods establishments in the United States. In 1854 he became a member of the banking house of George Peabody & Co., in London, which subsequently became J. S. Morgan & Co., and was ranked among the world's greatest banking houses. During the Civil War, the firm supported the North. It was a tribute to Morgan's standing that, in 1870, he had little difficulty in raising $50 million for France, while Paris was under siege during the Franco-Prussian War. The loan was a great success. Morgan was a generous benefactor of various public and private institutions, among them being Trinity College, Hartford, and the Hartford Orphan Asylum. He established a public library in Hartford and made valuable donations to The Metropolitan Museum of Art, Yale College, and other institutions.

MORGAN, Lewis Henry, American ethnologist: b. Aurora, N.Y., Nov. 21, 1818; d. Rochester, N.Y., Dec. 17, 1881. He graduated from Union College in 1840 and studied law for four years. Through fortunate investments, he eventually received an income which enabled him to devote himself to his researches. A Republican, he served in the New York State Assembly (1861–1868) and the state Senate (1868–1869). As a young lawyer his interest in Indians was stimulated by his friend Ely S. Parker, a Seneca Indian, who was later to be a Civil War general and United States commissioner of Indian affairs. In reward for using his legal and political abilities to defend Seneca land claims, Morgan was adopted into the tribe. He received the Indian name of Tayadaowuhkuh (One Lying Across), indicating that he lay across the boundaries dividing Indians and whites.

His first book, *League of the Ho-dé-no-sau-nee, or Iroquois* (1851), based on researches in collaboration with Parker, has been described as the first scientific description of an Indian tribe. His discoveries about the Iroquois kinship system were extended first to other tribes, and then—with the cooperation of the Smithsonian Institution and the United States Department of State—to every part of the world. Morgan had done a great deal of field work in the United States but with his pioneering use of questionnaires he was able to gather information about 139 different kinship systems, including many in Eurasia and the Pacific Islands. The results of his research were published in *Systems of Consanguinity and Affinity of the Human Family,* Smithsonian Contributions to Knowledge, no. 218, vol. 17 (1871), in which he demonstrated that peoples in various parts of the world organized their kinship relations very differently. Although his method of classifying kinship terminologies has met with criticism, more important is the fact that he was the first to grasp the sociological importance of kinship systems.

His most famous work was *Ancient Society or Researches in the Lines of Human Progress through Barbarism to Civilization* (1877). Morgan accepted the idea, current at the time, that all societies everywhere went through the same necessary stages of social development. The civilized family is the result of a series of stages beginning with complete promiscuity, through various forms of group marriage, and finally to monogamy—matriarchy being a step in the process. These institutions were given a social interpretation; for example, in certain early stages, property was held communally and political life was organized through the kinship system, but as the family developed and property increased, new forms of economic and political organization came into being. Thus *Ancient Society* constructed a speculative theory of civilization. The book was an instant source of controversy, and subsequent research has disproved some of its most important contentions; yet Morgan's ideas have played a significant part in the development of modern anthropology.

Ancient Society was at the height of its popularity when Friedrich Engels was writing *The Origins of the Family, Private Property, and the State* (1884), and Engels used much of Morgan's material. As a result the work of the Rochester lawyer and businessman has been widely popular among Marxian socialists and in the Soviet Union. A lifelong Presbyterian, he found nothing in his evolutionary theories in conflict with the essentials of his faith.

Consult Stern, Bernhard J., *Lewis Henry Morgan, Social Evolutionist* (Chicago 1931); Hays, Hoffman Reynolds, *From Ape to Angel: An Informal History of Social Anthropology* (New York 1958).

MORGAN, Sydney (LADY MORGAN, nee SYDNEY OWENSON), Irish author: b. Dublin, Ireland, about 1783; d. London, England, April 14, 1859. Her father was an actor on the Dublin stage. She was a governess for a time. Her first literary effort was a volume of poems (1801), followed by a collection of Irish songs and two novels, *Saint Clair* (1904) and the *Novice of Saint Dominick* (1805). In 1806 appeared her *Wild Irish Girl,* a novel which, avowedly nationalist in sympathy and containing good descriptive passages, established her reputation and secured for her a high position in fashionable and literary life. *The First Attack* (1807), an opera, was her only work for the stage; it had a short life. In 1812 she was married to Sir Thomas Charles Morgan, an eminent physician. In 1837 she received a civil list pension of £300 per year, the first woman author to be so rewarded. Her style was inflated and gushing; her vanity was inordinate, but she vividly depicted Irish character, and she had an eye for humorous detail. Among her other works are *O'Donnel* (1814), *Florence McCarthy* (1816), and *The O'Briens and the O'Flahertys* (1827). Two critical travel books, *France* (1817) and *Italy* (1821), brought her both warm admirers and furious opponents.

MORGAN, Thomas Hunt, American biologist: one of the chief founders of modern genetics: b. Lexington, Ky., Sept. 25, 1866; d. Pasadena, Calif., Dec. 4, 1945. His interest in biology declared itself while an undergraduate at the Kentucky College of Agriculture and Mechanical Arts (now the University of Kentucky), from which he graduated in 1886. It matured at the Johns Hopkins University, where he studied embryology under William K. Brooks, receiving the Ph.D. degree in 1891. In 1891 he became associate professor of biology at Bryn Mawr College, whence he was called to Columbia University in 1904 as professor of experimental zoology. He remained there until 1928 when he went as professor of biology to the California Institute of Technology to organize a new Division of Biology of which he became director. In 1933, Morgan was awarded the Nobel Prize in physiology and medicine, being the first to be so honored for work in genetics.

Morgan's first work was in embryology, turning soon to experimental testing of theories of how the developing egg produces a complex organism with differentiated structures. This resulted in a long series of research publications and several books on development, experimental embryology, regeneration, evolution, and adaptation.

His work in genetics began at Columbia University about 1907 and came to center on problems of the physical basis of heredity in the vinegar fly, *Drosophila melanogaster.* Soon a group of graduate students and assistants was at work in what became famous as the "fly room" in the Department of Zoology, in which the processes of inheritance in this small, rapidly breeding insect were so thoroughly analyzed that by 1915 the main outlines of the chromosome theory of heredity had been laid. The book *The Mechanism of Mendelian Heredity,* by Morgan, Alfred H. Sturtevant, Hermann J. Muller, and Calvin B. Bridges, published in 1915, contained the essential proofs that the invisible genes, the living elements responsible for the transmission of heredity, are located in linear order in the visible bodies, the chromosomes, which occur in constant numbers in the nuclei of the cells of each species of animals and plants. This, the first general theory of the transmission mechanism of heredity, was clearly the most important step in the development of the science of genetics since Mendel's publication of 1866. Morgan's masterly summary of this field, published in 1926 as *The Theory of the Gene* (rev. ed. 1928), listed the new principles added to genetics by the discoveries of his school: genes are held together in a number of linkage groups corresponding to the number of pairs of chromosomes of the species; independent assortments of genes belong to different linkage groups (a qualification of Mendel's second law); there is orderly interchange (crossing over) of genes in the same linkage group, the frequency of this being proportional to the linear distance between the genes involved. This last principle became the basis for the construction of "gene maps" showing the relative location of those genes which had been studied in this way. All subsequent work in transmission genetics has been based upon the reasoning and the evidence provided by Morgan's school.

After his departure from Columbia University, where this groundwork had been laid, Morgan's interests returned to problems of embryology, especially those involved in fertilization, while his former students and associates continued to develop his fundamental work in genetics.

Consult Sturtevant, Alfred H., "Thomas Hunt Morgan," in *Biographical Memoirs,* vol. 33, National Academy of Sciences (New York 1959).

L. C. DUNN,
Professor of Zoology, Columbia University.

MORGAN, William, American Freemason, whose death was the immediate cause of the formation of the Anti-Masonic Party; b. Culpeper County, Va., about 1774; d. possibly near Oak Orchid, N.Y., 1826. He is said to have fought in the defense of New Orleans in 1815. It is known that he was working as a mason in Batavia, N.Y., having moved there about 1823. In August 1826, he disappeared soon after a rumor had been spread that he was to reveal in a book the secrets of the Masonic Order. He was supposed to have been abducted by fellow-Masons and drowned in Lake Ontario, but his death was never proved. A corpse found near the mouth of Niagara River was stated to be his, and as such was claimed by his family, but disinterred and believed to be some one else. Much political capital was made of the alleged abduction and drowning and it was averred that Thurlow Weed, a leader in the antimasonic movement (see ANTIMASONRY), cynically said that it was "a good enough Morgan till after election," a remark that has become proverbial for campaign deceit.

Morgan's book *Illustrations of Freemasonry, by One of the Fraternity Who Has Devoted Thirty Years to the Subject* (1826) roused much less excitement than the story of his death. This book under the title *Free Masonry Exposed and Explained* was reprinted in 1912.

MORGAN. See HORSE—*Horse Breeds of the World* (table).

MORGAN CITY, city, Louisiana, in St. Mary Parish, at an altitude of six feet, situated on Berwick Bay on the navigable Atchafalaya River, 53 miles south of Baton Rouge, and served by the Southern Pacific Railway. One of the busier ports of southern Louisiana, it has water connections with the Mississippi and westward in to Texas via the Intracoastal Canal, which here joins the Plaquemine-Morgan City Waterway leading to the Gulf of Mexico. The port handles petroleum, chemicals, steel and iron products, oystershells, sulphur, and lumber. The packing of sea food provides employment for a large number of workers. Sugar cane, corn, rice, and cotton are grown in the surrounding region and are traded through the city. There is extensive fur trapping nearby, mainly of muskrat, mink, and otter, and the surrounding area is also a paradise for hunters and fishermen. The city maintains a modern library, good schools, churches, and a hospital.

History.—Settled in 1850, the city was incorporated as Brashear City in 1860, but the name was changed in 1876 in honor of Charles Morgan (1795–1878), a steamship-line owner. In 1863 the city, held by Union forces, was taken by the Confederates, but was soon abandoned by them and reoccupied by the Federals. Pop. 16,586.

MORGANATIC MARRIAGE, a marriage between a prince or noble and a woman of inferior rank in cases where a perfect marriage is not legal except with a woman of equal rank. The distinctive feature of the morganatic marriage is that the wife does not acquire the rank of the husband, and the children, legitimate though they are, do not inherit it; in some states they do not inherit entailed estates.

Morganatic marriage originated in German law and was practiced by continental European royalty and nobility until the breakdown of the old social structure after World War I. In Great Britain such marriages were made invalid in public law under the Royal Marriages Act of 1772. The Roman Catholic Church always regarded a morganatic marriage as a perfect one, and so did not permit a morganatic marriage and a regular marriage to exist at the same time.

MORGANFIELD, môr'găn-fēld, city, Kentucky, seat of Union County, at an altitude of 439 feet, 22 miles west-southwest of Henderson, and served by the Illinois Central Railroad. In an agricultural and coal mining region, there is also extensive livestock raising. The town is a railroad shipping point for tobacco, corn, wheat, and clover, and has flour mills, a seed-cleaning plant, and manufactures of furniture and metal products. There are also large oil fields nearby. St. Vincent's Academy (1820) for girls and Camp Breckinridge, an army camp active during World War II, are nearby. The waterworks are city owned and operated. Pop. 3,563.

MORGAN'S RAIDS INTO INDIANA AND OHIO. In the middle of June 1863 Gen. Braxton Bragg ordered Gen. John H. Morgan, with 2,000 picked mounted infantry and four guns to move from Tennessee into Kentucky, break up the railroad upon which Gen. William S. Rosecrans depended for supplies, capture Louisville, destroy the public works and return to Tennessee as quickly as possible. Morgan determined to exceed his orders and make a raid north of the Ohio. On July 2, with 2,460 men and four guns, he set out from Burkesville, crossed the Kentucky River in the face of Union troops guarding it, and marched northward, followed by all the Union detachments within immediate call. He passed through Columbia, after a sharp skirmish with about 300 Wolford's Kentucky cavalry, in which he lost about 40 in killed and wounded, and on the 4th reached Green River at Tebb's Bend, and demanded the surrender of Col. O. H. Moore, who, with about 300 men of the 25th Michigan, was guarding the bridge at that point. Moore replied that the Fourth of July was not a good day to surrender, and was instantly attacked with artillery and musketry. After a hard fight of three hours, in which Moore had six killed and 23 wounded, Morgan was repulsed, with a loss of 36 killed and 46 wounded, and drew off, crossing the river below the bridge. On the 5th he defeated and captured the small garrison of Lebanon and marched by Bardstown to Brandenburg, on the Ohio, where he arrived on the morning of the 8th, and seizing two steamboats began crossing his command. His passage was disputed by a gunboat and by militia with a field-piece on the Indiana shore, but by the morning of the 9th his whole command was in Indiana. Twenty-four hours later Gen. Edward H. Hobson, with 2,500 cavalry and mounted infantry and four guns, crossed the river in pursuit, and for 17 days hung upon Morgan's heels. Indiana and Ohio were aroused and turned out their militia by thousands.

After crossing the Ohio, Morgan rode north through Corydon, where he was resisted by militia, who were soon overpowered. He then pushed on to Salem, where he captured nearly 400 militia, then through Lexington and Paris to Vernon, near which place on the evening of the 11th he encountered a stiff resistance from about 1,200 militia under Colonel Love. Under cover of darkness he withdrew from Love's front, and pressing on through Dupont and Sumansville, crossed the Indiana line on the 13th to Harrison, Ohio, and concentrated his command preparatory to making his way across the Ohio into Kentucky, detaching parties to burn bridges and confuse the pursuit, and impressing fresh horses. Under cover of a feint on Hamilton he marched by night a few miles north of Cincinnati, moving directly east, closely pursued next day by Hobson, who was marching 40 miles a day, and threatened from all directions by the militia. Turning toward Berlin, where the government had a large number of animals, he was confronted by a small body of militia under Colonel Runkle, lost much precious time in threatening an attack, drew off closely followed by Runkle, and after dark of the 18th reached the banks of the Ohio, a short distance above Pomeroy, near Buffington Bar and Blennerhasset's Island, where from the first he had planned to escape. His pursuers were closing in on him from every direction. On the west Hobson was hanging on his rear; General Judah, who had been withdrawn from Kentucky, had landed his division at Portsmouth, and was marching up from the southwest; regiments were coming down the river from Parkersburg; and gunboats patroled the river and watched the fords. Early in the morning of the 19th Morgan endeavored to cross the river, but was speedily checked. He was attacked in rear by the head of Hobson's column, Judah's cavalry struck him in flank and two gunboats opened upon his front. A severe engagement cost him about 120 killed and wounded, and more than 700 of his officers and men surrendered. Morgan with the remainder escaped up the river, where he attempted to cross to Belleville by swimming his horses.

Three hundred men, under Col. B. R. Johnson, had crossed when a gunboat stopped the remainder of the column, Morgan himself returning to the Ohio shore and with about 800 men retreating inland. He had lost all his artillery and trains. He pressed on northeast through Athens and Washington, marching 35 miles a day, burning bridges behind him, with General Shackelford and 500 men close upon his rear and skirmishing with it. Near Salineville on the 26th Shackelford's advance captured 250 men, and later in the day he was intercepted near New Lisbon and Beaver Creek, and surrendered with 364 officers and men. The Union loss in the campaign July 2-26 was 19 killed, 47 wounded and 8 missing.

E. A. Carman.

MORGANTE MAGGIORE, Il, by Luigi Pulci (1432–1484), begun in 1460 and completed in 1483, is the first of the great Italian humoresque poems dealing with the material of the Old French epic, with the adventures and adventurers of the court of Charlemagne, with chivalry and deeds of valor, with Saracens, witches, and magic, with all that distinguishes men from cowards and loyalty from treachery in a world of strong arms and generous appetites, good humor and simple passions. It is a reworking of an earlier popular poem called the *Orlando,* with a few elements borrowed from another poem of the same cycle called the *Spagna.* Pulci thus obtained the traditional schematic plot of the Italian chivalric tale: the struggle between the house of Clermont and the treacherous descendants of Ganelon, resulting in the slander of Orlando, his flight to the Orient, his adventurous battles with the Saracens, his return to Paris to raise the inevitable siege by the Saracens, his reconciliation with Charlemagne, and his ultimate vengeance on his enemies at court. Pulci is more faithful to the spirit and the substance of the Carolinian tale than either of his great successors, Matteo Maria Boiardo or Ludovico Ariosto, who utilized the more fantastic and sentimental legends of the Round Table to such an extent as wholly to transform the character of chivalric romance. The earnestness of the popular legend passed over directly into the *Morgante,* to constitute the solid base for its pervasive humorism, on which the author then erects an original comic structure of his own, with not a few deliberately satiric elements. Neither Petrarchism nor classical models were strong enough in their influence on Pulci to alter or to vitiate this humorous attitude toward his subject. The reader willingly remembers three salient figures from *Il Morgante Maggiore:* that of the giant Morgante himself, whose size and corresponding appetite for food have a jolly time getting along in this world made for smaller people; that of the half-giant Margutte, liar, thief, glutton, blasphemer, and all-around rascal of perennial good-nature, the most popular personage in the rambling story; and finally that of the devil Astaroth, who treats learnedly on orthodox theology, and among whose many feats of magic the most famous and startling remains his discovery of a new Western world some years before the voyage of Columbus. Save in its best episodes, the *Morgante* is no longer much read. There is an English translation by William Roscoe.

Arthur Livingston.

MORGANTON, môr'găn-tŭn, town, North Carolina, seat of Burke County, at an altitude of 1,181 feet, 15 miles south-southwest of Lenoir, near the Catawba River, and served by the Southern Railway. The trade center for an agricultural and timber region, it manufactures leather goods, furniture, hosiery, textiles, and electrical equipment. A state school for the handicapped and a state hospital for the insane are located here.

Morganton was incorporated as a village in 1784 and as a town in 1885, and is governed by a mayor, council, and city manager. The water, power, and light systems are municipally owned. Pop. 13,625.

MORGANTOWN, môr'găn-toun, city, West Virginia, seat of Monongalia County, situated on the navigable Monongahela River, at an altitude of 960 feet, 15 miles northeast of Fairmont and 103 miles south of Pittsburgh, Pa., and served by the Baltimore and Ohio and the Monongahela railroads, state and federal highways, and an airport with scheduled air service. It is located in the midst of an area rich in oil and gas fields, bituminous coal fields, limestone quarries, and deposits of glass sand. Its principal industries are the mining and shipping of the coal and the turning of the sand into industrial and commercial glass. Rolled, plate, and pressed glasses, cut glass, wireglass, window glass, and watch crystals are made, while other industries manufacture coke, concrete blocks, and plumbing equipment. A United States ordnance works here produces chemicals from the coal and gas. The city is also the trading center for a district including a dozen small towns.

Morgantown has public and parochial schools, a city and a county hospital, over 20 churches, and is the seat of West Virginia University (q.v.). Nearby points of interest include Cooper's Rock State Forest, the largest in the state, Cheat River Canyon, Cheat Lake, and Dorsey's Knob.

History.—Although there had been earlier settlers on the site, the town was named for the brothers Zackquill and David Morgan who, in 1766, made the first successful settlement here. Morgantown was incorporated in 1785, and is governed by an elected city council and an appointed city manager. The water supply system is municipally owned. Pop. 29,431.

MORGARTEN, mōr'gär-tĕn, mountain slope, Switzerland, with an altitude of 4,084 feet, five miles north of Schwyz, on the border of Schwyz and Zug cantons, just southeast of the Lake of Aegeri. It is memorable as the scene of the battle of Nov. 15, 1315, in which a small body of Swiss mountaineers from Schwyz, Uri, and Unterwalden, ill-armed and undisciplined, totally vanquished an Austrian army of 20,000 under Duke Leopold I, sent by Frederick the Fair to avenge the seizure of the abbey of Einsiedeln the previous year. This was the first victory achieved by the Swiss in their struggle for freedom.

MORGAT, môr-gä', seaside resort, France, in Finistère Department, on Crozon Peninsula, 11 miles south of Brest. The chief occupation of the inhabitants is sardine fishing in Douarnenez Bay.

MORGENSTERN, môr'gĕn-schtĕrn, **Lina (nee Bauer),** German writer and reformer: b. Breslau, Nov. 25, 1830; d. Berlin, Germany, Dec. 16, 1909. She did much social work in Berlin after her marriage (1854) to Dr. Theodor Morgenstern. She was leader of the woman's Verein (1860–1866) in their furthering the cause of the Froebel Kindergärten, and (1866) she founded the Verein Berliner Volksküchen (public kitchens). In 1868 she started the Kinderschützverein, for the protection of children; in 1869 she founded an institute for the training of young women in the useful arts. In 1880 she established a woman's society for the rescue of immoral girls, placing them in schools to teach them housework and farming.

She wrote *Das Paradies der Kindheit* (1861); *Der Häusliche Beruf* (1875); *Die Volksküchen* (1882); *Der Beruf des Weibes* (1869); *Die Frauen des 19 Jahrhunderts* (1888–1891); *Hilfsbuch zur Gründung, Leitung und Kontrolle von Volksküchen* (1892), besides several works on the systems of economical cooking.

MORGENTHAU, môr'gĕn-tou, **Henry,** American lawyer, merchant, and ambassador: b. Mannheim, Germany, April 26, 1856; d. New York, N. Y., Nov. 25, 1946. Coming to the United States in 1865, he attended the New York public schools, the College of the City of New York, and received his LL.B. degree from the Columbia Law School. He became a partner in the law firm of Lachman, Morgenthau and Goldsmith, New York (1879–1899), was president of the Central Realty Bond and Trust Company (1899–1905), and of the Henry Morgenthau Company (1905–1913), dealers in realty. He was ambassador to Turkey (1913–1916) and at the outbreak of World War I took charge of the interests in Turkey of Great Britain, France, Italy, Russia, Belgium, Switzerland, Montenegro, and Serbia, rendering invaluable assistance to these nations. He was vice chairman of the Near East Relief, and chairman of the commission created by the League of Nations in 1923 for the settlement of the Greek refugees. In 1933 he was a delegate to the Geneva Wheat Conference—his last public service in official capacity.

He wrote *Ambassador Morgenthau's Story* (1918); and *All in a Lifetime* (1922); *My Trip Around the World* (1928); *I Was Sent to Athens* (1929).

MORGENTHAU, Henry, Jr., American public official: b. New York City, New York, May 11, 1891. He studied two years at Cornell University, and from 1922 to 1933 was publisher of the *American Agriculturist.* Under Gov. Franklin D. Roosevelt, Mr. Morgenthau served as conservation commissioner of the State of New York, also as chairman of the governor's agricultural advisory committee and member of the Taconic State Park Commission. A close friend and neighbor of the governor, the latter, after election to the presidency, appointed Mr. Morgenthau first, chairman of the Federal Farm Board, then governor of the Farm Credit Administration, and on Nov. 17, 1933, made him acting and under secretary of the treasury. He was appointed secretary of the treasury Jan. 1, 1934. Soon after the president's death, Mr. Morgenthau resigned his post (July 5, 1945) to become effective after President Truman's return from the "Big Three" conference at Berlin, being the sixth Roosevelt Cabinet appointee to resign after Mr. Truman took office. During his 11 years as head of the Treasury Department Mr. Morgenthau raised for government operations, for furtherance of the New Deal program and for war purposes, through taxation and loans $450,000,000,000, far more than all his 50 predecessors from 1789 to 1934. He died in Poughkeepsie, N. Y., on Feb. 6, 1967.

MORGHEN, môr'gân, **Raffaello,** Italian engraver: b. Florence, Italy, June 19, 1758; d. there, April 8, 1833. He received his early instruction in his art from his father, Filippo, and his uncle, Giovanni Elia, and was afterward placed as a pupil under the celebrated Volpato, whom he assisted in engraving the pictures of Raphael in the Vatican. He settled in Florence about 1793 as professor of copper-plate engraving in the Academy of Art. In 1803 he was chosen an associate of the French Institute; and in 1812 was invited to Paris by Napoleon.

Among the most remarkable of the other numerous works of Morghen may be noted *The Transfiguration* from Raphael; a *Magdalen* from Murillo; a *Head of the Savior* from Da Vinci; the *Hours* from Poussin; the *Prize of Diana* from Domenichino; the *Monument of Clement XIII* from Canova.

MORGIANA, môr-gĭ-ä'nä, a female slave figuring in "Ali Baba and the Forty Thieves," a story in the *Arabian Nights* (q.v.).

MORGUE, môrg (Old French, to look at solemnly), a place or building in large cities where the bodies of unknown persons who have perished by accident, murder or suicide are exposed, that they may be recognized by their friends. If not claimed within a certain period they are either buried or given over to medical institutions for dissection purposes. The name arose from the building in Paris, dating from the 5th century, devoted to this purpose.

MORI, Camilo, mō'rē, Chilean painter: b. Valparaiso, Chile, Sept. 24, 1896. He studied at the Academy of Fine Arts in Santiago, and in 1920 went to Europe for further training. He and other Chilean art students in Paris called themselves the Grupo Montparnasse, a title reflecting their enthusiasm for modern art. After they returned home, they held an exhibition in Santiago in 1924. Critical and public taste was not prepared for modern art, and the exhibition was generally castigated, but it proved to be an awakening stimulus for contemporary Chilean painting.

Mori served as assistant director of the Museo de Bellas Artes in Santiago (1928) and inspector of Chilean art students sent to study in Europe at government expense (1929–1930). From 1933 he was professor of drawing at the national School of Architecture in Santiago, receiving the medal of honor of the Chilean Salon Oficial in 1942. He has painted in various modernist styles.

Consult Romera, Antonio R., *Camilo Mori* (Santiago de Chile 1949).

MORIAH, mô-rī'ȧ, hill, Jerusalem, in the Muslim quarter of the Old City, now included in Jordan. Here the temples of Solomon (II Chronicles 3:1) and Herod were built, and the Mosque of Omar (also known as the Dome of the Rock) still stands. It is traditionally the mount on which Abraham was commanded to sacrifice Isaac (Genesis 22:2). Muslims revere it as the spot from which the Prophet made his famous night visit to heaven.

MORICE, mô-rēs', **Adrien Gabriel,** Canadian missionary, ethnologist, and author: b. St.-Mars, Mayenne Department, France, Aug. 27, 1859; d. St. Boniface, Manitoba, Canada, April 21, 1938. A member of the Roman Catholic Oblate Order, he was sent to British Columbia in 1880 as a missionary to the Indians and was ordained a priest two years later. Morice compiled several Indian dictionaries and grammars, including a syllabary for the important Déné language. He also made valuable maps of the Canadian Northwest. Among his many books is the authoritative *History of the Catholic Church in Western Canada* (2 vols., 1910). *Souvenirs d'un missionnaire en Colombie Britannique* (1933) is autobiographical.

MÓRICZ, mō'rĭtz, **Zsigmond,** Hungarian author, playwright, and journalist: b. Csécse, Hungary, June 30, 1879; d. Budapest, Sept. 4, 1942. He came of Transylvanian peasant stock, and as a young man was a journalist on the Budapest newspaper *Az Ujság* and an editor for various publishing houses. His first novel, *Sárarany* (1910; Golden Mud), is a realistic portrayal of Hungarian peasant life, in strong contrast to the idyllic picture of the "noble peasant" hitherto drawn by Magyar novelists. Móricz' *Fáklya* (1925; Eng. tr. by Emil Lengyel, *The Torch,* 1931) relates the frustrations of a young Calvinist minister in preaching the Gospel in a downtrodden peasant village. *Légy jó mindhalálig* (1922; Be Good Until You Die), written for children, has also won much praise, and *Erdély* (1935; Transylvania) is a well-drawn historical novel in three parts. Móricz' short stories include the realistic *Hét krajcár* (1909; Seven Pennies) and the collection *Magyarok* (1926; Hungarians). Though less successful as a playwright, he wrote some fairly effective dramas such as *Sári Biró* (1910; Judge Sari) and *Buzakalász* (1924; Sheaf of Wheat).

MORIER, mŏr'ĭ-ā, **James Justinian,** English diplomat, traveler, and author: b. Smyrna (Izmir), Turkey, ?1780; d. Brighton, England, March 19, 1849. He was the second son of Isaac Morier (1750–1817), a merchant of French Huguenot descent who became a naturalized British subject after making a fortune in Turkey. James Morier attended Harrow and in 1807 was appointed private secretary to Sir Harford Jones on a diplomatic mission to Persia. Arriving in Teheran by way of Bombay early in 1809, he was soon sent home with dispatches, making his way overland to Constantinople (İstanbul) through Armenia and Asia Minor. His account of his travels, published in 1812 as *A Journey Through Persia, Armenia, and Asia Minor to Constantinople in the Years 1808 and 1809,* at once established him as an author and became an authoritative source book. A later diplomatic journey to Persia and back in 1810–1816 resulted in another book, *A Second Journey Through Persia* (1818).

In 1817 Morier settled down to a life of letters in London, interrupted only by a special diplomatic mission to Mexico (1824–1826). His best-known novel is *The Adventures of Hajji Baba of Ispahan* (1824), about a Persian barber who rises through all manner of vicissitudes to become a diplomatic spy and a noble. Around his adventures is woven a rich tapestry of Persian life, from the bazaars to the royal court. A sequel, *The Adventures of Hajji Baba of Ispahan in England* (1828), satirizes Western life and manners through the device of the "foreign observer." Morier's later books, also mostly Oriental tales, were less successful.

MÖRIKE, mû'rĭ-kĕ, **Eduard,** German poet and novelist: b. Ludwigsburg, Württemberg, Germany, Sept. 8, 1804; d. Stuttgart, June 4, 1875. He studied theology at Urach and Tübingen and became a sort of migratory country pastor. From 1834 to 1843 he lived in the village of Cleversulzbach in Württemberg and from 1851 to 1866 was a lecturer on German literature at the Stuttgart Katharinenstift, a girl's seminary.

Mörike's love for the idyllic countryside of his native Swabia permeates his beautiful lyric poems, which were first collected in the volume *Gedichte* (1838). There is a simple folk quality about his best poems and a recurrent theme of nostalgia, along with an abundance of humor and a successful blending of realistic and imaginative details. A master of verse forms, many of them original, he used the sonnet, ottava rima, and other forms popular among poets of the romantic era, and mastered such forms of classic Greek poetry as the hexameter and the trimeter. He also wrote several narrative poems and successful ballads such as *Schön-Rohtraut* (adapted in English by George Meredith) and *Der Feuerreiter.*

Mörike's novel *Maler Nolten* (1832), a youthful and romantic work, reflects the influence of Johann Wolfgang von Goethe's *Wilhelm Meister* (1796, 1821, 1829) and shows the keen insight of a poet in the portrayal of character. Among his best-known short stories is *Mozart auf der Reise nach Prag* (1855).

Mörike's total literary output was small in quantity, but it is rich in quality. His fame spread slowly beyond Swabia. Not until Hugo Wolf set many of his finest lyrics to music did his full stature as one of Germany's greatest lyric poets become recognized.

Consult Mare, Margaret, *Edward Mörike: The Man and the Poet* (London 1957).

MORILLO, mō-rē'(l)yō, **Pablo,** CONDE DE CARTAGENA and MARQUÉS DE LA PUERTA, Spanish general: b. Zamora Province, Spain, May 5, 1778; d. Barèges, Hautes-Pyrénées Department, France, July 27, 1837. Beginning as a common soldier, he rose to the rank of general during the Napoleonic Wars and in 1815 was sent to South America to quell the revolution led by Simón Bolívar. Morillo's victory at Cartagena (Colombia), after a long siege in 1815, won him the title of conde, and the next year he took Bogotá; but his ruthless reprisals against the supporters of independence aroused much hatred. On Aug. 7, 1819, his army was decisively crushed by Bolívar at Boyacá, and the outbreak of revolution in Spain in 1820 made it necessary for him to sign an armistice. Returning home, Morillo was made a marqués in 1821; but when the absolutist regime was restored in 1823, he fell under suspicion of disloyalty and took refuge in France. He returned to Spain in 1832, was made captain general of Galicia, and led an army against the Carlists. His *Mémoires* of the South American fighting was published in French in 1826.

MORÍNIGO, mō-rē'nē-gō, **Higinio,** Paraguayan political leader: b. Paraguarí, Paraguay, Jan. 11, 1887. After serving in the Chaco War (1932–1935), he was named chief of the general staff by President Rafael Franco in 1936 and minister of war and navy by President José Félix Estigarribia in 1940. When Estigarribia was killed in an airplane accident (September 7), Morínigo became provisional president and proceeded to establish a dictatorial regime with army support. In 1943 he was elected to the presidency without opposition, but in 1947 a civil war broke out which it took Morínigo six months to suppress. He was forced to resign in June 1948, shortly before his term was to end.

MORIOKA, mō-rē-ō-kä, city, Japan, on north central Honshu Island, on the Kitakami River, 40 miles from the Pacific coast and 332.5 miles northeast of Tokyo on the Tohoku (Northeastern) Line of the Japanese National Railways. It is the capital and economic center of Iwate Prefecture, and the seat of Iwate University. The city is famous for its artistic iron kettles known as *Nambu tetsubin*. It also manufactures other iron and copper products, toys, and silk, and engages in sake brewing. It is a marketing center for fine fruits and vegetables, many originally of American origin. In the spring and fall there is a famous horse fair. Morioka was the seat and castle site of the powerful Nambu clan. About 24 miles northwest is Mount Iwate (6,740 feet), a dormant volcano, in whose crater is the Iwateyama Shrine. Pop. (1960) 157,441.

MORISCOS, mō-rĭs'kōz, a name originally applied to Spaniards who were converted to Islam after the Arab conquest of Spain in the 8th century, and later applied to the Muslims who were nominally converted to Christianity after the fall of Granada in 1492. Before 1492 the Mudejares (Muslims who had come under the rule of Christian princes in Spain) had generally been permitted to retain their customs and religion; but after the completion of the Christian reconquest, they were put under increasing pressure to adopt Christianity or leave the country. Laws to this effect were promulgated in 1501 (Castile) and 1526 (Aragon) and again by Philip II in 1567. A large proportion of the Muslims nominally accepted Christianity but continued secretly to practice Islam, and the Inquisition (installed in Spain in 1480) zealously hunted them down. In 1567–1570 a revolt of the Moriscos in Granada was crushed, and by a decree issued in 1609 they were unconditionally expelled from Spain by Philip III, in a mass deportation estimated at 500,000 over a five-year period, much to the detriment of the country's agriculture, in which they were mainly engaged.

MORISON, mŏr'ĭ-s'n, **James,** Scottish theologian: b. Bathgate, Linlithgowshire (now West Lothian), Scotland, Feb. 14, 1816; d. Glasgow, Nov. 13, 1893. Educated for the Presbyterian ministry at Edinburgh University, he found himself in disagreement with the orthodox Calvinist doctrine of election and, before he was ordained, published *The Question, "What must I do to be saved?" answered by Philanthropos* (1840), expressing the view that Christ had atoned for all men. Called to a United Secession church in Kilmarnock, Ayrshire, he was suspended from the ministry in 1841 but held the support of his congregation. In 1843 he and his father Robert Morison (also a United Secession minister), along with two others, formed the Evangelical Union (q.v.), which eventually comprised nearly 100 churches. A theological seminary, headed by Morison, was formed at the same time. In 1851 he moved to Glasgow, retiring in 1884. His followers, popularly known as Morisonians, merged with the Congregationalists after his death.

MORISON, Robert, Scottish botanist: b. Aberdeen, Scotland, 1620; d. London, England, Nov. 10, 1683. Graduated from Aberdeen University in 1638, he fought on the Royalist side in the First Bishops' War (1639) and then left Scotland for France, where he took the degree of doctor of medicine at Angers in 1648. Thereafter until 1660 Morison was one of the keepers of the garden formed at Blois by Gaston Jean Baptiste d'Orléans, duc d'Orléans, uncle of Louis XIV, who sent him all over France in search of new plants. At the Restoration in 1660, he accompanied Charles II to England and was appointed senior royal physician, king's botanist, and superintendent of all the royal gardens. From 1669 he was professor of botany at Oxford. Morison's great work was the *Plantarum historia universalis Oxoniensis* (2 vols., 1680–99; completed by Jacob Bobart), a botanical encyclopedia which sought to place the classification of plants on a scientific basis and in some respects approaches modern ideas. *Morisonia,* a genus of tropical American woody plants of the Capparidaceae family, has been named for him.

MORISON, Samuel Eliot, American historian: b. Boston, Mass., July 9, 1887. Educated at Harvard (B.A., 1908; Ph.D., 1912), he joined the faculty there in 1915 and was professor of American history from 1925 to 1955. In 1919 he was a member of the United States delegation to the Paris Peace Conference and subsequently served (1922–1925) as the first Harmsworth professor of American history at Oxford University. As a writer of history, Morison is noted for his lucid and entertaining style as well as his painstaking, impeccable scholarship. Having published *The Maritime History of Massachusetts, 1783–1860* (1921; new ed., 1941), he was chosen official historian of Harvard for its 300th anniversary celebration and in 1935–1936 brought out the first three volumes of the *Tercentennial History of Harvard College and University,* carrying the story down to the end of the 17th century. Another volume (1930), edited by Morison, covers the period 1869–1929. Meanwhile, with Henry Steele Commager, he had written *The Growth of the American Republic* (1930; 6th rev. ed., 2 vols., 1969), which became one of the most popular and respected textbooks in its field.

In 1939–1940 Morison headed the Harvard Columbus Expedition, which traced the route of the explorer back and forth across the Atlantic, and in 1942 he brought out his definitive two-volume biography of Christopher Columbus, *Admiral of the Ocean Sea,* which won a Pulitzer Prize. Named (1942) official United States naval historian for World War II, with the rank of lieutenant commander, he took part in a series of major actions in the Atlantic and Pacific and in 1947 published the first two parts of a 15-volume *History of the United States Naval Operations in World War II,* the last volume of which appeared in 1962. He retired from the Navy as a rear admiral in 1951. Among his later books is the biography *John Paul Jones* (1959), which won him a second Pulitzer Prize, *The Oxford History of the American People* (1965), and *Samuel de Champlain: Father of New France* (1972).

MORISONIANS. See MORISON, JAMES.

MORISOT, mô'rē-zō', **Berthe** (MME. EUGÈNE MANET), French painter: b. Bourges, France, Jan. 14, 1841; d. Paris, March 2, 1895. Great-granddaughter of the 18th century painter Honoré Fragonard, she broke away from her early classical training to study for a time under Jean Baptiste Camille Corot. About 1869 she met Édouard Manet, a leader of the rising impressionist school, who used her as a model in several of his paintings, and in 1874 she married his brother Eugène. After this she exhibited with the impressionists but retained her own distinctive style, characterized by lightness and transparency. Using both oils and water colors, she did many portraits of women and children, and numerous landscapes. She also made her mark in etching and lithography. Among her paintings may be mentioned *La Toilette* (Art Institute of Chicago) and *Dans la Salle à Manger* (National Gallery of Art, Washington, D.C.). Her letters and journals are valuable source material for the history of impressionism.

Consult *Correspondence of Berthe Morisot,* comp. and ed. by Denis Rouart, tr. by Betty W. Hubbard (New York 1957).

MORITZ, mō'rĭts, **Karl Philipp,** German author: b. Hameln, Germany, Sept. 15, 1757; d. Berlin, June 26, 1793. He worked his way up from a hatmaker's apprentice to a successful writer and professor at the Berlin Academy of Art. Moritz' literary fame rests mainly upon his autobiographical novel *Anton Reiser, ein psychologischer Roman* (4 vols., 1785–90). His travels in England and Italy were the subject of two other popular books: *Reisen eines Deutschen in England im Jahr 1782* (1783), widely read in English translation; and *Reisen eines Deutschen in Italien in den Jahren 1786 bis 1788* (1792–93). In Rome he became a member of Johann Wolfgang von Goethe's circle of friends and continued his association with Goethe at Weimar. His *Anton Reiser* apparently influenced Goethe's *Wilhelm Meisters Lehrjahre* (1796).

Moritz' novel *Andreas Hartkopf* (1786) also contains autobiographical elements, but it is *Anton Reiser* which has special importance in the history of German *Sturm und Drang* fiction. The hero, like the author, is born in poverty and has to work his way up from hatmaker's apprentice to a position of worldly fame, in this case success on the stage, only to suffer disillusionment in the realization that the great ideals of youth are unattainable. The book is a notable forerunner of the German biographical and psychological novel.

WILLIAM BRACY.

MORLAIX, môr-lĕ', town and commune, France, in Finistère Department, on an inlet of the English Channel, 33 miles northeast of Brest. An imposing granite railroad viaduct (752 feet long and 177 feet high, built in 1861) bisects the town by crossing the narrow valley in which it lies. Morlaix is a seaport exporting dairy and farm produce, chiefly to Great Britain and the Channel Islands. It is also an importing center for British coal, and manufactures tobacco products and paper. The town is noted for its surviving examples of Renaissance domestic architecture, and there are churches dating from the 13th and 15th centuries. It was the birthplace of Gen. Jean Victor Moreau (1763–1813) and author Émile Souvestre (1806–1854). Population: (1968) of the town 16,750.

MORLAND, môr'lănd, **George,** English painter: b. London, England, June 26, 1763; d. there, Oct. 29, 1804. His father, Henry Robert Morland (1712?–1797), was a competent artist, and the boy was apprenticed to him. The teacher was thorough but severe; the pupil, precocious but self-indulgent. Young Morland was a facile copyist of Dutch 17th century interiors, and he finally translated these genre scenes into English equivalents, which were extremely popular and sold well. A brief tour of France exposed him to the seductive art of Jean Baptiste Greuze, and his moral scenes dilute William Hogarth with Greuze and his own brand of lusciousness. Morland lived while the demand for the picturesque was at its height, and his art has been called "the very stuff of picturesque doctrine" by Thomas Sherrer Ross Boase, who notes that his "slick and sentimental country pieces . . . have never lost their hold on the heart of the public."

Morland's life is a monotonous tale of sordid pleasures and of entanglements with unscrupulous dealers and moneylenders. His marriage in 1786 resulted in a short-lived reform. In the early 1790's he was living amply at Paddington, where he kept a zoo of some variety. His powers did not flag until the end of the decade, and he went on painting until a few months before his death. He was at the height of his fame in 1790, when he exhibited *The Cottage Door,* of which Horace Walpole wrote: "As good as Gainsborough but has more harmony and better finished." In 1791 came *Inside of a Stable,* his masterpiece, now in the National Gallery, London. He was imprisoned for debt in 1799 and was not released until 1802.

Arrested again in 1804 for a tavern bill, he died in a sponging house. He had composed his own epitaph: "Here lies a drunken dog"—who had, however, painted, it is estimated, about 4,000 pictures.

WALLACE BROCKWAY.

MORLEY, môr'lĭ, **Christopher (Darlington),** American author: b. Haverford, Pa., May 5, 1890; d. Roslyn Heights, N.Y., March 28, 1957. Graduated from Haverford College (1910), he attended Oxford as a Rhodes scholar until 1913, and from 1920 to 1924 was on the staff of the New York *Evening Post.* Here he began his column "The Bowling Green," later continued in the *Saturday Review of Literature,* of which he was a contributing editor (1924–1940). Morley's first book was a volume of verse, *The Eighth Sin* (1912), and in 1917 he published his first novel, *Parnassus on Wheels,* which like *The Haunted Bookshop* (1919) reflected his pervading interest in the world of books and booksellers. His immense literary erudition and whimsically philosophical humor soon won him a wide following.

Christopher Morley

Culver Service

Two fantasies—*Where the Blue Begins* (1922), about a dog who becomes human, and *Thunder on the Left* (1925), which portrays the adult world through children's eyes—are considered by critics to be among his best works. Another highly popular book was *Kitty Foyle* (1939), the sentimental story of an office girl and a socialite youth, which was successfully filmed. Morley himself believed his most significant work was *The Trojan Horse* (1937), a reworking in modern dress of the Troilus and Cressida story.

Notable among Morley's essay collections are *Shandygaff* (1918), *Hasta la Vista* (1935), and *The Ironing Board* (1949). His numerous volumes of poetry—light, sentimental, and frequently humorous—include *The Rocking Horse* (1919), *Parson's Pleasure* (1923), *Toulemonde* (1928), and *The Ballad of New York, New York, and Other Poems, 1930–1950* (1950). He also edited, with Louella D. Everett, the 11th (1937) and 12th (1948) editions of John Bartlett's *Familiar Quotations.*

FELIX (MUSKETT) MORLEY (1894–), his brother, was editor of the Washington *Post* (1933–1940) and president of Haverford College thereafter until 1945. He won the Pulitzer Prize for editorial writing in 1936.

MORLEY, Edward Williams, American physicist and chemist: b. Newark, N.J., Jan. 29, 1838; d. Hartford, Conn., Feb. 24, 1923. Graduated from Williams College (1860) and Andover Theological Seminary (1864), he gave up an early ambition to enter the Congregationalist ministry and in 1869 became professor of natural history and chemistry at Western Reserve College, Hudson, Ohio. Morley taught at the college (which was moved to Cleveland in 1882 and renamed Western Reserve University) until 1906. In 1887 he collaborated with Albert A. Michelson in the historic Michelson-Morley experiment, designed to measure the motion of the earth through ether, the negative result of which cast doubt on the existence of ether and led to alternative speculations culminating in the relativity theory (see RELATIVITY—*Absolute Motion*). For their task, Michelson and Morley invented a new measuring instrument, the interferometer. Morley's other most distinctive contribution to science was a series of experiments (1883–1894) to determine the density of oxygen and hydrogen, and the ratio in which they combine to form water. His conclusions were published by the Smithsonian Institution in 1895.

MORLEY, Henry, English educator, editor, and literary historian: b. London, England, Sept. 15, 1822; d. Carisbrooke, Isle of Wight, May 14, 1894. Educated in Germany and at King's College, London, he began to practice as a country doctor but in 1850 returned to London, where for 15 years he assisted Charles Dickens in editing his magazine *Household Words* and its successor *All the Year Round.* In 1865 he was named professor of English literature at University College, London, and from 1878 also held the chair at Queen's College there, retiring in 1890. Morley's principal scholarly enterprise was a comprehensive literary history, *English Writers,* planned for 20 volumes but never finished; volumes 1–10 (through Shakespeare) were published in final form between 1887 and his death, and volume 11 was completed by W. Hall Griffin in 1895. Earlier versions of volumes 1 and 2 had appeared in 1864 and 1867. He also initiated and edited several important collections of literary classics in inexpensive editions, notably Morley's Universal Library (63 vols., 1883–88) and Cassell's National Library (214 vols., 1886–90).

MORLEY, John, VISCOUNT MORLEY OF BLACKBURN, English author, editor, and statesman: b. Blackburn, Lancashire, England, Dec. 24, 1838; d. Wimbledon, Sept. 23, 1923. The son of a Blackburn surgeon of modest means, he attended Lincoln College, Oxford, without graduating, and in 1860 began to work in London as a journalist. Morley soon became a friend and disciple of John Stuart Mill and in 1867 was offered the editorship of the newly established *Fortnightly Review,* which he continued to conduct until 1882. Under his direction the *Fortnightly* became a leading journal of Liberal political and economic thought, especially of the Radical wing, with many distinguished contributors. In 1878 he also began editing the English Men of Letters series, to which he contributed the life of Edmund Burke.

After two earlier unsuccessful attempts, Morley was elected to Parliament from Newcastle-upon-Tyne in 1883. He had been interested in the cause of Home Rule for Ireland since 1867; and when William Ewart Gladstone also became converted to this view, he invited Morley to serve as chief secretary for Ireland in the cabinet formed in 1886. The Home Rule bill was defeated, and the cabinet fell the same year; but Morley continued to support the principle and from 1892 to 1895 was again in office as chief secretary for Ireland. Defeated at Newcastle in the general election of 1895—largely because he had refused to vote for an eight-hour law—he was elected in the following year for the Montrose Burghs, a seat he held until his elevation to the peerage in 1908. As secretary of state for India (1905–1910), he worked with the viceroy, the 4th earl of Minto, to achieve notable legislative reforms, resigning in November 1910, but remaining in the Cabinet as lord privy seal. Because of his well-known pacifist views, he resigned from the Cabinet at the outbreak of World War I in 1914. He returned to Parliament briefly in December 1921 upon the signing of the Anglo-Irish Treaty providing for an Irish Free State.

Considered the epitome of late Victorian liberalism, Morley had a distinguished career in public affairs, but it was as a writer and editor that he made his most notable contribution. The most eminent biographer of his time, he published *Voltaire* (1872); *Rousseau* (1873); *Diderot, and the Encyclopaedists* (1878); *Burke* (1879); *Life of Richard Cobden* (1881); *Walpole* (1889); *Oliver Cromwell* (1900); and the monumental *Life of Gladstone,* 3 vols. (1903). Among his other works are several editions of *Critical Miscellanies; On Compromise* (1874); *Studies in Literature* (1891); and *Recollections,* 2 vols. (1917). A 15-volume edition of his works, with his own corrections, was published in 1921.

Consult Hirst, Francis W., *Early Life and Letters of John Morley,* 2 vols. (New York 1927); Staebler, Warren I., *The Liberal Mind of John Morley* (Princeton 1943).

MORLEY, Sylvanus Griswold, American archaeologist: b. Chester, Pa., June 7, 1883; d. Santa Fe, N.Mex., Sept. 2, 1948. He was educated at Harvard (B.A., 1907; M.A., 1908), and from 1909 to 1914 did field work in Mexico and Central America for the School of American Archaeology. From 1915 to 1940 he was associated with the Carnegie Institution of Washington, directing its project at Chichén Itzá (q.v.) from 1924. Morley became a leading authority on the ancient Maya. His published works include *An Introduction to the Study of Maya Hieroglyphs* (1915); *The Inscriptions at Copán* (1920); *Guide Book to the Ruins of Quirigua* (1935); *The Inscriptions of Petén* (5 vols., 1938); and *The Ancient Maya* (1946).

MORLEY, Thomas, English composer: b. 1557; d. October 1602. A pupil of the great William Byrd, Morley became perhaps the foremost madrigalist of his era. He took a degree in music at Oxford in July 1588, then became organist at St. Giles's, Cripplegate, and later at St. Paul's Cathedral, London. He was appointed to the Chapel Royal in 1592. In 1598, assessment rolls for the Parish of St. Helen's, Bishopsgate, show Morley's name and William Shakespeare's; it is believed that the two men were friends. A license to print songbooks and music paper having been granted to Morley in 1598, he issued his own music and many works by other composers. He is known to have married a woman named Suzan, who was granted a commission to administer his estate.

Morley won both popularity and praise during his life. His surviving compositions include, in addition to sacred music and harpsichord "lessons," two-, three-, four-, five-, and six-voice canzonets, five-voice "balletts" (lively dance airs), four- and five-voice madrigals (two of them included in *The Triumphes of Oriana,* 1601), and solo songs accompanied by lute and bass viol. Morley wrote a dialogue entitled *A Plaine and Easie Introduction to Practicall Musicke* (1597) which is valued for the light it casts on modal practices, late 16th century musical activities, and his own attractive personality.

HERBERT WEINSTOCK.

MORLEY, môr'lĭ, municipal borough, England, in Yorkshire, in the West Riding, 4 miles southwest of Leeds. Its industries are coal mining and stone quarrying, woolen milling, leather tanning, and manufacture of textile machinery, pharmaceuticals, and glass. It was besieged by the Royalists in the Civil War. Pop. (1961) 40,322.

MORMON, BOOK OF. See BOOK OF MORMON.

MORMON CRICKET, môr'mŭn, the common name of a large, black, wingless grasshopper (*Anabrus simplex*) of the Rocky Mountain states, and Canadian provinces. Its periodic migrations have caused great crop destruction, and the United States Department of Agriculture pursues an active program of control.

MORMONS, môr'mŭnz, members of the Mormon Church, properly called The Church of Jesus Christ of Latter-day Saints. The church has about 2 million members. Its headquarters are in Salt Lake City, Utah. Mormon pioneers settled Utah and that state remains the main center of Mormon life. However, "Mormon country" now extends also into all the neighboring states, especially Idaho, and as far as the Los Angeles area in California. Numerous cities in other parts of the western United States have Mormon communities, and in recent decades many Mormons have moved to metropolitan centers in the East as well. The church has had a vigorous missionary policy since its early days and has established groups in Europe, especially England, and in Oceania and Latin America.

The Book of Mormon.—The church was founded in upstate New York in 1830 by Joseph Smith (1805–1844) who claimed visions and the discovery of gold plates constituting the *Book of Mormon* (q.v.), and finally, after a period of testing, a miraculous translation of the *Book of Mormon.* This work, which resembles the English Bible, is believed by Mormons to be a document from pre-Columbian America, recording the relations of its inhabitants with God. It is regarded as the sacred history of Hebrews who came to the Western Hemisphere in three migrations and whose descendants are the Indians, whose skins have been darkened by apostasy. It is an account of divine election and rejection, of human conversion and apostasy, and—reflecting the then current concerns of western New York—it emphasizes a call to repentance.

Mormonism is the product of the intense religious turmoil of the time and its doctrines embody the optimism of those who rejected Calvinism. The *Book of Mormon* stresses free will and the importance of effort for man's salvation. Claiming communication with God, Mormonism offered reassurance and authority to men whose religious equanimity had been upset by revivalism. Today, revelation from God is believed to come through the church president (in 1959, David O. McKay, 1873–), who is the successor of the prophet-founder and is regarded as God's "prophet, seer and revelator."

Doctrine and Covenants.—The *Doctrine and Covenants* (1835; 1844; 1845; 1846, and later), a second Mormon scripture, containing revelations reported by Joseph Smith, sets forth the aim "to bring to pass the gathering of mine elect" (*Doctrine and Covenants,* sec. 29, vs. 7) and holds (sec. 28, vs. 9) that Zion or the New Jerusalem is to be built on "the borders of the Lamanites" (the *Book of Mormon* name for Indians). Implying a separated community to the west, this doctrine involved the second coming of Christ, who, it was believed, would reign from the new Zion. The Indians were to be converted and become again a "white and delightsome people" (*Book of Mormon,* II Nephi, 30:6) and share in the millennial fulfillment. Consequently, missionary concern for the Indians has remained important to the church.

Early History.—*Mormon Temples.*—From 1831 to 1846 the Mormons attempted four times to build Zion: at Kirtland, Ohio; Independence and Far West, Mo.; and Nauvoo, Ill. Independence had the strongest claim to divine appointment and remains sacred to the Mormons. Financial troubles and dissension led to failure in Kirtland, but only after construction of a temple, which remains a fine example of early American architecture and a monument to the self-sacrifice of its builders. It was the first of many temples. In Mormon temples today are performed baptism for the dead and eternal sealing of marriages. They are found throughout the West, in Hawaii, and since 1950 in Europe and New Zealand.

Expulsion from Missouri.—Mormon efforts in Missouri ended in the violent ejection of the Latter-day Saints. Their success, their religious innovations, their northern ways, their aspirations to make the region a holy land for themselves, and their favorable attitudes toward the Indians, aroused the enmity of their neighbors. Driven from Independence in the winter of 1833–1834, they went to Clay County, which in a short time they were asked to leave. At Far West, which they founded in unincorporated territory, success again led to conflict. In 1838–1839 they were expelled in a small scale "Mormon War" in which more than 40 lives were lost, all but one or two of them Mormon. Joseph Smith estimated Mormon losses in Missouri, in terms of money, at $2,000,000.

The cream-colored Mormon temple at Manti, Utah.

Josef Muench

Nauvoo.—Establishing Nauvoo on the east bank of the Mississippi in Illinois, the Mormons soon had an attractive city of 15,000 inhabitants, with temple, homes, stores, and spacious streets, as well as diverse occupations and industries. But this success issued in a second "Mormon War" which drove them out, forcing them to sell property at ridiculously low prices. External enmity was compounded with internal dissent. Polygamy had been secretly recorded as a revelation in 1843 (*Doctrine and Covenants,* sec. 132), and although it was not publicly announced until 1852 in Utah, it was practiced in Illinois. An opposition arose which rejected plural marriage and criticized church financial policy and church government, which was becoming increasingly centralized. Joseph Smith, now church president and mayor, ordered the press of the opposition Nauvoo *Expositor* destroyed by members of the Nauvoo Legion, a trained and uniformed Mormon militia. This action inflamed the already explosive gentile (non-Mormon) opposition greatly exercised over Mormon growth and participation in politics.

Death of Joseph Smith.—In the violence, Joseph Smith and his brother Hyrum (1800–1844), who were confined in the jail in Carthage, Ill., were murdered by a mob of disbanded militia and others, with the complicity of those guarding the jail. Eventually, after pressure, violence, and open fighting, the Mormons were forced to leave Nauvoo. They began their evacuation in February 1846 in sub-zero weather. This was Mormonism's great crisis and several dissenting groups withdrew.

Brigham Young and Migration to Utah.—The church was saved by the rise to leadership of Brigham Young (1801–1877), an able organizer with great determination. For weeks in a condition of great suffering, the Latter-day Saints crossed Iowa to the banks of the Missouri River, where they established Winter Quarters (now Omaha, Nebraska). After a winter of hardship and reorganization, westward migration began. The advance party of 148 left Winter Quarters on April 7, 1847, and arrived in the valley of the Great Salt Lake on July 22. Two days later, Brigham Young entered the valley after having declared, "This is the right place." In the months and years to come thousands of emigrants arrived, by wagon, by handcart, and later by train. Mormon colonization developed on a planned basis and men were "called" as a religious duty to settle throughout the intermountain region. When Brigham Young died in 1877, some 357 settlements had been established and the Mormon population was around 140,000. Settlement continued in Arizona and New Mexico, in Mexico, and even in Canada. Foreign-born as well as native converts came to the mountain Zion. From 1840 to 1900 church immigration policy brought some 90,000 Europeans, many by organized group travel, to the new settlements. Despite some attempts to preserve native cultures and languages, these immigrants were quickly assimilated to a common stock and culture.

Mormon doctrine stressed community and cooperation. In 1831 the "Law of Consecration" (*Doctrine and Covenants,* sec. 42, vss. 30–35) had been announced combining cooperative endeavor with private enterprise. Property was dedicated to the church and managed by the individual, the surplus going to the community. The "Law" was given up because of friction involved in its operation and was eventually replaced by tithing. In Nauvoo, a huge community farm was developed and later in Utah a more communal form of the "Law" was revived. During the depression of the 1930's the Church Welfare Plan used cooperative techniques to aid the needy membership. Moreover, the church concerned itself with the economic development of the region, and cooperation of various forms played an important part.

Irrigation presents the most striking monument to Mormon cooperation. In Utah only irrigation could have made farming possible, and it was ever the Mormon ideal that society be based upon agriculture. Only a group whose coherence and doctrines would make possible the discipline necessary for irrigation could have met the challenge. By 1865 there were over 1,000 miles of canals in Utah and by 1946 some 8,750 miles. Irrigation installations in 1865 were worth over $2,000,000 and in 1946 some $42,000,000.

Polygamy Renounced.—Although the Mormon Zion, now grown to imperial dimensions, prospered in Utah, conflict followed the Latter-day Saints. There was conflict with local non-Mormons, who were few; with national opinion aroused against Mormon dominance in Utah, authoritarian church polity, and especially against plural marriage; and with the federal government and its agents in the territory, who were often given to a pronounced anti-Mormon bias.

The lines were gradually drawn around the issues of Utah's admission to the Union and polygamy. The Mormons now engaged in a desperate defense of an institution which they sincerely believed to have been commanded of them by God. In 1857 President James Buchanan sent troops against them, and in 1862 Congress passed the Morrill Law, an anti-bigamy act, which was upheld by the United States Supreme Court in 1879. In 1882, the Edmunds Act and in 1887 the Edmunds-Tucker Act were passed. These were more stringent laws, the second dissolving the Mormon Church as a corporation. Sentiment was aroused to a great pitch in Utah and in the nation. With 200 Mormons in jail, the Latter-day Saints, facing defeat, gave in and in the constitutional convention of 1887 supported the definition of polygamy as a crime. In September 1890 the church president, Wilford Woodruff (1807–1898), issued a statement renouncing polygamy as effective church teaching. In 1896 Utah was admitted to the Union.

Mormon separatism had included loyalty to the United States and Utah's admission fulfilled a persistent Mormon aspiration. Yet it meant that Mormonism would henceforth have to accommodate itself to the larger gentile American community of which it was now a part.

Beliefs.—Despite the animosity the Latter-day Saints aroused in their fellow citizens, their religion is distinctively American, emphasizing

Josef Muench

Mormon temple at St. George, Utah.

optimism, self-improvement, hard work, and respect for law. Mormonism retains the Bible and much of traditional Christianity, but it has added new elements. These include the idea of human pre-existence, God as a developing being, an interpretation of Trinitarianism as tri-theism, baptism for the dead, marriage for time and eternity, and man's eternal progression toward godlike status. Mormon religious teachings affect everyday life. Health is a spiritual value and the subject of a dietary revelation banning coffee, tobacco, and liquor (*Doctrine and Covenants,* sec. 89). Recreation is given spiritual significance, and education is specially valued, a fact reflected in Utah's educational statistics. The Mormons also believe that the United States enjoys a special providential position, as does the New World as a whole.

Church Government.—Church organization is complex, with a hierarchical priesthood embracing all "worthy" males and auxiliary organizations activating women and young people. A young boy becomes a member of the Aaronic or lesser priesthood at the age of 12 and progresses through its three stages. At about 20 he becomes an elder, the first of three stages of the greater or Melchizedek priesthood. The two higher grades are seventies, to which men are advanced after mission experience, and high priest. All important Mormon Church leaders at all levels are high priests.

The local congregation is a ward, several wards composing a stake. The ward is headed by a bishop who is an unpaid pastor. Church functioning combines a high degree of central direction with tremendous rank and file participation. Most officers are unpaid. At the top of the structure is the First Presidency, made up of the president and his two counselors, and the Council of the Twelve.

It is customary for young men (and lately for some young women as well) to go on missions to various parts of the United States or to foreign countries. This is done largely at the missionary's own expense and usually for two years. From 1847 to 1947 some 51,622 missionaries went out, and in 1953 some 8,447 were at work. Converts are not made in large numbers, but missionary experience is seen as education and character building for those involved.

The church operates Brigham Young University in Provo, Utah. No collections are taken at the church services and the church is supported by tithing. See also SALT LAKE CITY; UTAH.

DISSIDENT LATTER DAY SAINT GROUPS

Reorganized Church of Jesus Christ of Latter Day Saints.—Of the groups which broke away from the Mormon Church at the time of Joseph Smith's death only five remain in existence. Of these only the Reorganized Church of Jesus Christ of Latter Day Saints is a large religious body. With its headquarters in Independence, Mo., this group had 146,076 members in 1957. It was organized by Mormons who rejected Brigham Young's leadership and many theological innovations, especially relating to polygamy and temple work. It came together in 1852 and has been recognized by the courts as the successor of the church founded by Joseph Smith, winning title to both the Kirtland Temple and the Temple Lot in Independence. Joseph Smith's widow and his immediate family adhered to this group, and his son became its president in 1860. The presidency has continued to be held by his direct descendants. The organization of the Reorganized Church is similar to that of the Utah church. Like the latter, it emphasizes a social ethic and cooperation and at an earlier time operated a large cooperative unit in southern Iowa. Many who did not go West joined this cooperative venture. The belief in contemporary revelation and its role in running church business is much more striking than in the Utah church. Also, like the latter, the Reorganized Church carries on missionary activity.

Church of Christ, Temple Lot.—This group, which lost the lot to the Reorganized Church in a lawsuit in the early 1890's, had only 3,000 members in 1956. It was founded by Granville Hedrick at the time of Joseph Smith's death, and returned to Independence in 1867. It rejects many Mormon beliefs, such as deification of men after death and polygamy.

The Church of Jesus Christ (Bickertonites).—This group, which had 2,340 members in 1957, descends from those who left the Mormon body with Sidney Rigdon (1793–1876) after the death of Joseph Smith, although it was organized by William Bickerton in 1862. Rigdon was an important leader in early Mormondom and was defeated by Brigham Young for the position of Joseph Smith's successor. This group rejects baptism for the dead, plural marriage, and other Mormon developments. It conducts missionary work among the Indians in the United States and Canada.

Church of Jesus Christ of Latter day Saints (Strangites).—This body had only 200 members in 1957; but a century earlier, James J. Strang (1813–1856), its founder and a colorful contender for Joseph Smith's position, ruled as "king" over some 3,000 followers on Mackinac Island, Mich. Strang claimed that he was Smith's personal choice for the succession. Despite the striking impression he made on Mormons outside of Nauvoo, his claims did not receive serious support. Strang also claimed revelations. In 1856 he was shot to death by two of his followers, who were hailed as heroes by antagonistic neighbors on the mainland.

Church of Jesus Christ (Cutlerites).—This is the smallest surviving group, organized by Alpheus Cutler in 1853. There were 22 members in 1957, apparently practicing community of property.

Bibliography.—Talmage, James E., *The Articles of Faith* (Salt Lake City 1899); Werner, Morris R., *Brigham Young* (New York 1925); Bennion, Lowell L., *The Religion of the Latter-day Saints* (Salt Lake City 1940); Hunter, Milton R., *Brigham Young, the Colonizer* (Salt Lake City 1941); Anderson, Nels, *Desert Saints: The Mormon Frontier in Utah* (Chicago 1942); Stegner, Wallace, *Mormon Country* (New York 1942); Brodie, Fawn M., *No Man Knows My History: The Life of Joseph Smith, the Mormon Prophet* (New York 1945), a scholarly biography of Joseph Smith, but rejected by the Mormon Church because it gives a naturalistic interpretation of his life and work; Nibley, Hugh, *No Ma'am, That's Not History* (Salt Lake City 1946), contradicting the Brodie biography; Hinckley, Gordon B., *What of the Mormons?* (Salt Lake City 1949), a brief study of the Church of Jesus Christ of Latter-day Saints, published by the church; Nelson, Lowry, *The Mormon Village* (Salt Lake City 1952); Young, Kimball, *Isn't One Wife Enough?* (New York 1954); Mulder, William, *Homeward to Zion: The Mormon Migration from Scandinavia* (Minneapolis 1957); O'Dea, Thomas F., *The Mormons* (Chicago 1957); Arrington, Leonard J., *Great Basin Kingdom: An Economic History of the Latter-day Saints 1830–1900* (Cambridge, Mass., 1958); Mulder, William, and Mortensen, A. Russell, eds., *Among the Mormons: Historic Accounts by Contemporary Observers* (New York 1958).

THOMAS F. O'DEA,
Professor of Sociology, University of Utah.

MORMYRIDAE, mô-mĭr′ĭ-dē (from Gr. *mormyros,* sea fish), a family of fishes from the Nile River and all fresh waters of tropical Africa except those of Kenya, Tanganyika, and Uganda. There are some 11 genera. The mouth is small, and the jaws are often set at the end of a tubular snout; the vertical fins are far back on a body whose greatest depth is back of the mid-line. The eyes are small and covered by a membrane. The skull structure is highly specialized, and the brain is larger in proportion to the body size than in any other fish.

Though easily recognized as members of the family, some species are fairly normal looking, but others—for example, some species of *Gnathonemus*—have elephantlike trunks from the tip of which hang fleshy filaments. Some species reach five feet in length, but most are much smaller. Their rather flat bodies weigh little for their length. They vary in color from brown, purplish, or greenish to silvery and sometimes have chalk-white bellies. Some species, perhaps all, are equipped with weak electric organs, apparently for nonvisual perception of their surroundings.

The mormyrids are mud grubbers, living in muddy streams and lakes and eating larval insects and worms. Anglers sometimes hook them. Some natives eat them, but Hugh Copley tried this and thought he was being poisoned.

Consult Boulenger, George A., *Catalogue of the Fresh-Water Fishes of Africa,* vol. 1 (London 1909); Copley, Hugh, *The Game Fishes of Africa* (London 1952).

CHRISTOPHER W. COATES,
The Aquarium, New York Zoological Society.

MORNAY, môr-nā′, **Philippe de,** SEIGNEUR DU PLESSIS-MARLY (commonly known as DUPLESSIS-MORNAY), French Huguenot leader: b. Buhy, Normandy, France, Nov. 5, 1549; d. La Forêt-sur-Sèvre, Nov. 11, 1623. He was converted to Protestantism by his mother and, after studying at Heidelberg and Pavia, joined the cause of the French Reformers. In 1572, at the time of the Massacre of St. Bartholomew, he escaped to England. Returning to France in 1573, he took up arms under Henry of Navarre, whose adviser and trusted lieutenant he later became. His influence grew steadily and he became known as "the Huguenot Pope." Mornay was appointed governor of Saumur in 1589, and he retired there in 1593 when Henry was reconciled to the papacy. At Saumur he founded a Protestant university and devoted himself to writing, remaining there until forced out of his government post in 1620 because of his Protestant views. His principal work is *De l'institution, usage, et doctrine du saint sacrement de l'eucharistie en l'église ancienne* (1598). His *Mémoires* were published posthumously in 4 volumes in 1624–1652, and in a 12-volume edition in 1824.

MORNING-GLORY, the name of a very popular twining herb, the common morning-glory (*Ipomoea purpurea*), naturalized from tropical America and widely cultivated in many named varieties, with flowers ranging from purple, red, and bluish to white and variegated forms. The name is also applied to the entire genus *Ipomoea* of the morning-glory family, Convolvulaceae (q.v.), found in all warm parts of the world. Broadly defined, *Ipomoea* includes about 400 species of (1) annual twiners, such as *I. hederacea,* whose seeds yield the medicinally useful resin pharbitisin, and *I. purpurea;* (2) perennial twiners, such as man-of-the-earth or wild potato vine (*I. pandurata*), with long, heavy tuberous roots and white flowers, found in the southern United States, and the Mexican true jalap (*I. purga* or *Exogonium purga*), with tuberous roots weighing 40 to 50 pounds (source of the drug jalap) and purplish rose flowers; and (3) evergreen twiners, often seen in greenhouses, such as the West Indian *I. Horsfalliae,* with deep rose flowers, and the blue dawn flower (*I. Learii*), with bright blue flowers that turn magenta with age. See also JALAP.

THEODOR JUST.

MORNINGSIDE COLLEGE, a coeducational institution of higher learning in Sioux City, Iowa. A nonsectarian Christian college, it was founded in 1889 and since 1894 has been affiliated with the Methodist Church. Four-year preprofessional courses are available in engineering, Christian service, law, medicine, journalism, drama, nursing, pharmacy, social work, and recreational leadership. The campus, in a suburban area of the city, contains seven buildings, including a modern library. Enrollment averages approximately 2,000.

MORNY, môr-nē', DUC **Charles Auguste Louis Joseph de,** French politician: b. Paris, France, Oct. 23, 1811; d. there, March 10, 1865. The illegitimate son of Auguste Charles Joseph, Comte de Falhaut de la Billarderie and Hortense de Beauharnais, wife of Louis Bonaparte, he was known as the Comte de Morny until 1862, when he was created a duke by his half brother, Napoleon III. From 1830 to 1838 he served with some distinction in the French Army, part of the time in Algeria, after which he combined commercial speculation with politics. Becoming a deputy in 1842, he played a major role in the coup d'état of Dec. 2, 1851, which established Napoleon III as dictator, and as minister of the interior (1851–1852) and president of the Corps Législatif (1854–1865) he exerted much influence in the Second Empire. His usually successful and probably unscrupulous commercial speculation included mining interests in Sonora, Mexico. While serving in 1857 as envoy at the coronation of Alexander II, he married Princess Sophie Trubetskoi. His political acumen, energy, and intelligence made him one of the most effective figures in the regime of Napoleon III.

MOROCCO, mō-rŏk'ō (Fr. MAROC; Sp. MARRUECOS; Arab. EL MAGHREB EL AQSA), an independent kingdom, sometimes referred to as the Sherifian Empire (from *sherif,* that is, a descendant of Mohammed). Morocco is located in northwest Africa between latitudes 28° N. and 36° N. and longitudes 1° W. and 13° W., and is bounded on the north by the Mediterranean Sea, on the west by the Atlantic Ocean, east and southeast by Algeria, and southwest by Spanish Sahara. Several "presidios" on the Mediterranean (Ceuta, Melilla, Peñón de Vélez, Alhucemas, and the Chafarinas Islands) are Spanish enclaves. Rabat is the capital.

Coat of arms

Because the boundaries of the country have not been completely delimited, no exact figure on the total area may be given, but it may be estimated at 172,045 square miles, composed of the former French Zone (150,888 square miles), the former Spanish Zone (7,589 square miles), the former International Zone of Tangier (135 square miles), the Southern Protectorate of Morocco (the Tarfaya Province) retroceded by Spain in 1958 (12,693 square miles), and the former enclave of Ifni (740 square miles) retroceded by Spain in 1969.

The total population was 11,626,000 at the 1960 census, but was over 14 million by 1968. Principal cities (with 1965 population estimates) are: Casablanca (1,085,000); Rabat-Salé (355,000); Marrakech (255,000); Fez (Fès, 235,000); Meknès (185,000); and Oujda (130,000). Although Rabat is the capital, the king has official residences also in the traditional capitals of Fez, Marrakech, and Meknès, and makes Tangier his summer capital. Arabic is the official language; French and Spanish are subsidiary languages. The dirham is the currency unit.

For the convenience of readers, this article is divided into the following sections:

1. THE LAND

Morocco may be divided roughly into four topographical areas, according to marked differences in terrain: (1) the northern coastal massif, along the Mediterranean, comprising a chain of lesser mountains known as Er Rif, part of the Tell or Maritime Atlas, and varying in elevation to about 8,000 feet; (2) the great mountain system of the Atlas, extending in three parallel ranges (Middle, High, and Anti-Atlas) from the Atlantic coast in the southwest to Algeria and the Mediterranean in the northeast; (3) the wide plateaus and lowlands lying between the mountain systems and extending westward from the foothills of the Atlas to the Atlantic; and (4) the desert Saharan region east and south of the Atlas Mountains. Both the mountain system and the Atlantic tend to moderate the tropical heat of Africa, and to provide a relatively equable temperature of between 40° and 90° F. in the northwest where the largest centers of population are located. Maximum annual rainfall of about 30 to 40 inches occurs in the northwest.

The High or Great Atlas (Fr. Grand Atlas), with an average elevation of 11,000 feet, extends from the southwestern coast between Mogador and Agadir northeastward to Algeria, and contains several of the highest peaks of North Africa, among them Mount Toubkal (13,665 feet). South of the High Atlas are the Anti-Atlas Mountains, including volcanic Mount Siroua (10,840 feet). Extending northeastward from the High Atlas chain are the Middle Atlas Mountains, with Bou Naceur (10,794 feet) the principal peak. Between the Atlas and the northern coastal mountains is the Taza corridor, providing the principal route to Algeria.

The rivers flow generally northwestward to the Atlantic, or southeastward to the Sahara; an exception is the Moulouya (Muluya), which flows northeastward from the High Atlas on a 320-mile course to the Mediterranean. Principal rivers (*oueds*) with outlets in the Atlantic are the Sebou, Bou Regreg, Oum er Rbia (Oum er Rebia), Tensift, and Sous. The River Dra flows eastward from the Atlas, turns southwestward on the Algerian border, and completes its course in the Atlantic.

2. THE PEOPLE

At the time Morocco became independent in 1956, somewhat more than half a million persons (about 5 per cent of the country's total population) were Europeans—mostly French and Spanish. By 1965 the foreign population had declined to approximately 220,000, concentrated mainly in Casablanca. The diminishing number of native Jews had declined to about 160,000. The majority of the population consists of Sunni Muslims of the Malekite rite. The main religion of the European group is Roman Catholicism (under the archbishop of Rabat).

The crude annual birthrate in Morocco is estimated at 46 per thousand of population; the death rate, 19. Life expectancy at birth is 49.6 years.

Morocco's earliest recorded inhabitants were Berber tribesmen; they continue to form the majority of the native population. Although they have embraced the Muslim faith, they are deeply attached to the maintenance of their own customs, and some of them continue to speak their particular dialects. The establishment of Arabs in Morocco dates from the conquest of Africa in the 7th century, following the hegira. These two Muslim (Moslem) groups are closely intermingled, with an admixture of Negro stock in the south. The Berbers are concentrated mainly in the mountains of Er Rif and of the Middle Atlas, in the Sous Valley, and in Casablanca. The Arabs are distributed along the Atlantic coastal plains, in the Moulouya and Sebou valleys, and in the plateaus of the Grand Atlas; they also live in the cities, where their houses are grouped in the *medinas*. Jewish communities of pre-Christian times have been augmented by Jews expelled from Europe, especially from Spain as a result of the Inquisition. These native Jews are chiefly urban dwellers grouped in particular districts, the *mellahs*.

Many of the old Moorish customs persist today, although the influence of European civilization has brought considerable change to urban areas. The proximity of the modern, well-constructed cities to the ancient walled towns with their picturesque gardens, fountains, mosques, mosaics, and narrow corridors emphasizes the curious blending of the new and the old in Morocco. In rural areas the unit of social organization remains the tribe, headed by a kaid and sometimes consisting of a number of clans.

Moorish Arabic has been spoken increasingly since the European occupation and is now the predominant language of the native population; dialects survive among some 2,000,000 tribesmen. French and Spanish, which were the official languages of the respective protected zones, are still used for administrative, educational, and economic purposes.

3. NATURAL RESOURCES

For a long time Morocco was considered to be a land essentially agricultural, but today it is becoming an industrial country, due to the discovery of important mineral resources.

Although almost annihilated by excessive felling for many centuries, forests in Morocco still spread over an important area (10,000,000 acres) and have been protected since the mid-1920's. Extensive cork oak forests are found near the Atlantic coast, and make Morocco the world's third largest producer of cork. Forests of evergreen, oak, pine, and cedar grow on the slopes of the Atlas; thuya trees from the forests near the Mediterranean yield gums and fragrant oils; date palms are cultivated in great numbers in the south; and the argan tree, peculiar to Morocco, is found in the Sous Valley. There are also large numbers of orange, lemon, almond, and olive trees. Alfa grass, used to make pulp for high-quality writing paper, is grown on the eastern steppes of the Atlas.

Since 1945, fishing has developed into a major industry. Marine products include sardines, tuna, and anchovies.

Mineral resources have been discovered and exploited only since 1920, when peace was brought by the French Protectorate. The aggregate value of mineral output has increased greatly since World War II, and it more than doubled between 1950 and 1960. Morocco ranks third among nations (behind only the United States and the Soviet Union) in production of phosphate rock; output in 1965 amounted to 9,800,000 metric tons (up from 7,500,000 tons in 1960), or 22 per cent of total world output. Iron ore production in 1965 amounted to 567,000 metric tons (iron content), down from a peak of 1,047,000 tons in 1957. Also in 1965, output (in metric tons) of

Charles May

MOROCCO: *Top:* Modern office buildings dominate the skyline of Casablanca, Morocco's chief seaport. *Bottom:* A palm-bordered plaza in the heart of the city of Tetuán.

coal was 420,000; nickel, 360,000; and manganese, 137,000. Crude oil output was 103,000 tons (150,000 in 1963), and natural gas production is about 12 million cubic meters per year. Lead, zinc, silver, salt, tin, sulphur, barite, antimony, cobalt, and copper are also produced.

Irrigation and Power.—The related hazards of drought and flood have been progressively reduced since 1930 by the construction of several large dams, among them the Sidi Saïd Machou, Kasba Zidania, Im Fout, and Daourat dams on the Oum er Rbia; the El Kansera dam on the Beth; the Cavagnac dam on the N'Fis; and the Bin el Ouidane dam on the El Abid. These works, providing water for irrigation, multiply the number of water supply points for livestock and reduce the incidence of malaria. In the far south, in the Sous and Dra valleys, modern irrigation has brought back to life farms which have been abandoned.

Hydroelectric power is of growing importance in Morocco's industrial development. The large dams contribute most of the total production of electric power, which amounted to 1.28 billion kwh. in 1965. Other sources of power are poor: coal is scarce—it is located far from the industrial towns, and its cost is high. The oil resources of Petitjean are dwindling. An Italo-Moroccan company is interested in the oil detected by prospecting in the Sous area.

4. ECONOMIC DEVELOPMENT

Agriculture.—The most important industry of Morocco is agriculture, which employs 75 per cent of the population and accounts for over 40 per cent of the national income. Therefore the government is encouraging agricultural development and supplying modern equipment in the rural areas. The amount of land under cultivation is approximately 24 million hectares (60 million acres), of which about 8 million are in pasture, 3 million are in esparto grass, 5 million are arable, 600,000 are used for vine and olive plantations, and over 5 million are in forest.

The agricultural zones are traditionally the Rharb (Gharb) plain and the Meknès area in the north, and the Chaouia and Doukkala plains, East Moulouya Valley, and South Sous Valley in the west. Other zones such as Sidi Slimane, Beni-Amir, and Haduz have been made productive by irrigation. Important works are being built to increase the irrigated areas, which already spread over 250,000 acres. Furthermore, it seems to be possible to bring under cultivation an additional 2 to 4 million acres by farming during the good climatic periods, or by extending irrigation works.

The native farmers occupy 89 per cent of the arable land, the remainder being worked by European settlers, whose large farms (average 2,000 acres) supply 15 per cent of the hard wheat, 44 per cent of the soft wheat, and 85 per cent of the citrus fruits. They also furnish 60 per cent of the aggregate agricultural exports. To help the native farmers, who were badly in need of technical education, the French introduced a policy of agricultural education and encouraged many provident societies which assist small farmers with loans. This attempt at modernization is being carried on by the Moroccan government in cooperation with the agricultural extension centers.

In 1965 major crop yields were estimated (in thousands of metric tons) as follows: wheat, 1,300; barley, 1,280; citrus fruits, 700; grapes, 490; corn, 280; potatoes, 190. Livestock include (in thousands) sheep, 12,000; goats, 9,000; cattle, 2,500; asses and mules, 1,400; horses, 325. Over 700,000 metric tons of milk and 20,000 tons of wool are produced annually. Wine production in 1965 amounted to 3,450,000 hectolitres. Hides and skins are also major products.

The United Nations index of agricultural production increased 20 per cent from the mid-1950's to the mid-1960's.

Manufactures.—In the development of industry, first priority is given to consumer goods, particularly to food production such as cheese, vinegar, chocolate, paste, sugar, oil, rice, fish preserves, flour, fruit juices, beer, and alcohol; more than 120,000 persons find employment in this industry. Flour milling is one of the most important activities of the former French zone (averaging about 250,000 metric tons, including wheat meal, annually). The fish preserving industry, after a spectacular development followed by a severe crisis, has found a normal position again. The fishing fleet, employing about 10,000 persons, had a catch of 215,000 metric tons in 1965. At the same time, building works and lime and cement factories have developed, as have marble and stone quarries and other adjuncts of the building industry. Other flourishing industries include foundries, metal works, cotton mills, repair shops, and plants producing cork goods and shoes.

The development of these modern industries has had a profound effect upon traditional Moroccan handicraft, which maintains the old-fashioned methods of production together with its artistic craftsmanship. In the old towns, 200,000 craftsmen are engaged in the making of leather goods, carpets, saddlery, basketwork, ceramics, embroidery, and jewelry. Economic planning has tried to retain the fine qualities of this traditional handicraft while at the same time encouraging its adaptation to present-day production methods.

5. BUSINESS AND TRADE

Morocco uses the current French monetary system and is a member of the French franc zone. Established in 1920, the Moroccan franc was in parity with the French metropolitan franc from 1928 to 1958. After the French devaluation of December 1958, the Moroccan franc was maintained at its former value (420 Moroccan francs = U.S. $1)[1]. The peseta, former official currency in the Spanish Zone, was withdrawn from circulation in 1958, after conversion at the rate of 10 francs to the peseta. In Tangier, a system different from the rest of the franc area prevails, which includes free exchange and a special fiscal arrangement.

In implementation of the Algeciras Act of 1906, and by a *dahir* (imperial edict) of 1946, the Banque d'État of Morocco held the exclusive right of issuing currency until 1966. But an agreement concluded between the government and the Banque d'État reassigned this right to a national establishment, the new Bank of Morocco, as of July 1, 1959. The fiduciary issue amounted to about 75 billion francs. The action led to retaliation by France, which blocked Morocco from access to the franc zone currency supply. The Moroccan government, in turn, imposed strict

[1] On Oct. 16, 1959, the Moroccan government announced that the name for its currency would be changed from Moroccan franc to derham (dirham), one derham equivalent to 100 Moroccan francs. The next day a devaluation of 20.44 per cent was announced, with official rate of exchange set at 506 Moroccan francs to the U.S. dollar.

controls over capital transfers to other countries in the franc zone.

Revenue is realized chiefly from customs duties, income from government monopolies, and taxes on agricultural products (*tertib*) and consumer goods. A biennial plan for economic expansion, begun in 1958, carried on from the two quadrennial plans (1949–1952 and 1953–1956), and was devoted to social welfare, medical research and care, agriculture, hydroelectric development, construction, and mining. Domestic resources are inadequate to meet fully the development budget, and a considerable amount of foreign aid is required. Economic development since 1920 has been financed for the most part by public and private French capital. However, French aid declined sharply following a rift in relations between the two countries in 1966, and Morocco turned increasingly to the United States, the Soviet Union, and the oil-rich Arab nations for vital assistance.

Foreign Trade.—The external trade of Morocco is subject to a permanent deficit, due to the investments required for economic development. Phosphates make up more than a fourth of the country's exports by value. Other leading exports are citrus fruits, vegetables, canned fish, manganese, and other minerals. The major imports are sugar, tea, wheat, and other foods and beverages; tobacco; petroleum products; and finished and semi-finished manufactured goods. About 40 per cent of Morocco's trade is conducted with France. West Germany, the United Kingdom, Spain, and the Benelux nations are other leading customers, and Cuba, the United States, and West Germany are major suppliers. Exports in 1966 amounted to $428 million compared with $354 million in 1960. During the same period, imports increased from $397 million to $477 million.

The balance of imports and exports is in favor of Morocco vis-à-vis the franc area, the sterling area, Germany, Spain, and the Eastern countries; but exports are exceeded by imports from the dollar area, Cuba, and China. Trade with the Common Market countries is practically balanced.

Tangier serves as an entrepôt point for the supply of the Mediterranean area. During the period 1945–1950 it was a center for black-market dealings in restricted currencies and goods, but with the recovery of western European nations the zone has lost some of its advantages as a haven for flight capital seeking safe investments. The fiscal and custom statute of Tangier, however, is still attractive for foreign trade.

6. TRANSPORTATION AND COMMUNICATIONS

Transportation.—The primitive system of trails existing before the French Protectorate has given way to a modern network of roads (about 30,000 miles, of which about 7,000 are metaled). There is also an important network of trails and forest tracks.

The railroad system, begun in 1922, consists of standard-gauge lines totaling 1,170 miles and links the main urban and economic centers. Lines connect Casablanca with Marrakech, Khourigba, and Safi; Casablanca with Rabat, Fez, and the Algerian network; Fez with Tangier; and Oujda with Colomb-Béchar, in the Sahara. About 40 per cent of the network is electrified. Morocco possesses several seaports, of which Casablanca is by far the most important, with its modern machinery and accommodations for the largest vessels. International airline service links Morocco with France, Italy, Spain, Switzerland, and other African countries. Cazes (at Casablanca), the principal airport, will be replaced as an international airport by one at nearby Nouaceur, which can accommodate jet planes; other airports are located at Salé (near Rabat), Meknès, Oujda, Marrakech, Agadir, Fez, Tetuán, and Tangier. A national air service, Royal Air Maroc, has domestic, European, and North African flights.

Communications.—The telephone service connects all towns of the former French Zone, the largest towns of the former Spanish Zone, and Tangier. Telephone communication is also maintained between Tangier and Lisbon and Madrid. Telegraph service exists in most towns, and there is cable service to France, Spain, and Gibraltar. The postal system is state managed.

Radio Maroc, the state-controlled radio, consists of a large broadcasting station whose transmission is relayed by three local stations. The government acted in 1959 to create a state monopoly over broadcasting, ordering all independent transmitters to close down by the end of the year. Morocco's first television transmitter was set up in 1954 at Casablanca. In 1967 the country had 51,000 television sets, at least 700,000 radios, and 143,000 telephones.

There are eight daily newspapers: three in Arabic, *El Islam, Et Takhir,* and *Al Ajadid;* and five in French, *Le Petit Marocain, La Vigie Marocaine, L'Echo du Maroc, La Dépêche Marocaine de Tanger,* and *Le Courrier du Maroc.*

7. EDUCATION

The native population of Morocco is still largely illiterate, the literacy rate of those aged 15 or older in 1960 being only 14 per cent. However, in 1959 a program was launched to standardize the various school systems—Koranic, French, Spanish, Jewish, and others, and education has been made compulsory for children aged 7 to 13. In 1964 there were 1,354 primary and 242 secondary and technical schools with combined teaching staffs of 37,628. There were also 15 teacher-training schools and 21 institutions of higher learning. Total enrollment increased from 410,343 in 1955 to 1,289,079 in 1964.

In the primary schools, the language of instruction for the first two years is Arabic. For the next three years French is introduced, and in secondary schools French is the language of instruction. Many French teachers serve in the Moroccan public schools.

In 1957 the Institut des Hautes Études Marocaines, at Rabat, became a full-fledged university, the Université Nationale Marocaine. It had 8,000 students in 1964. It includes faculties of science, law, and economics from two former institutions. There is also, at Casablanca, a faculty of medicine. Total enrollment in institutions of higher learning is over 10,000.

8. GOVERNMENT

Following the termination of the French and Spanish protectorates and the abolition of the international status of the Tangier Zone (see section on *History*), the kingdom of Morocco has recovered its full sovereignty. This sovereignty is vested in the king, who is theoretically an absolute monarch, holding supreme civil and religious authority, the latter in his capacity of Emir-el-Muminin, or Commander of the Faithful. He is also the chief of the armed forces. The royal title was changed on Aug. 18, 1957, and Sultan Sidi Mohammed ben Youssef (1911–1961) became King Mohammed V. On his death, his eldest son, Crown Prince Moulay Hassan (1929–), was proclaimed King Hassan II on Feb. 26, 1961.

The king presides over the Council of Ministers, which replaced the traditional Makhzen and is composed of ministers and secretaries of state who exercise authority over the various ministerial departments. In 1956 a National Advisory Assembly was established, consisting of 76 members nominated by the monarch.

On May 8, 1958, the king issued a royal charter which proclaimed his immediate aims: the organization of a constitutional monarchy based upon the principle of separate powers and the guarantee of civil liberties. On Nov. 7, 1960, a Constitutional Council created by royal order was inaugurated, consisting of 78 members representing the provinces, the political parties, the traditional institutions, and various organizations. The task of the Council is to prepare a draft constitution for popular approval by referendum.

The judiciary system is headed by the Supreme Court and consists of two separate categories of tribunals: the "modern" courts, and the traditional (or makhzen) courts. There are two appeals courts in Rabat and Tangier. Matters regarding personal and family status are dealt with by the rabbinical courts for the native Jews, and by the cadi courts for the Muslims; the latter apply the *Sharia* (Islamic law) even to the Berbers, who previously had retained their customary laws distinct from the Koranic law. There are also special military and labor courts.

The country is divided administratively into 15 provinces and 2 urban prefectures. The provinces are Agadir (including Tarfaya), Al Huceima, Chaouia (Casablanca), Fez, Ksar-es-Souk, Marrakech, Meknès, Nador, Ouarzazate, Oujda, Rabat, Tadla, Taza, Tangier, and Tetuán; the prefectures are Casablanca and Rabat-Salé. Each province is headed by a governor, and its representatives are the heads of the circles and the kaids in the rural zones and the pashas in the urban centers. Local government is developing. The first general elections were held on May 29, 1960, by universal adult suffrage for the designation of the members of the 800 municipal and rural assemblies.

A new constitution was approved by national referendum on Dec. 7, 1962. It provides for universal suffrage and for a two-chamber parliament. Members of the Chamber of Councillors are elected by local authorities and by such bodies as trade unions and chambers of commerce. The House of Representatives is elected by the people. The king, who has power to veto legislation and to dissolve the parliament, retains ultimate power through his appointed premier and cabinet. The first elections under the new constitution were held in 1963.

The Royal Armed Forces of Morocco consist of an army of approximately 40,000 men and smaller naval and air forces. Most of the officers were French and Spanish trained, but equipment of American and Soviet origin is extensively employed. By agreements made in 1959 and 1960, the United States and France evacuated all of their bases and troops from Morocco by 1963.

9. HISTORY

Morocco first appears in history as the farthest westward expansion of the Carthaginian Empire. With the fall of Carthage and the subsequent consolidation of Roman power in Africa, the provinces of Mauretania Caesariensis and Mauretania Tingitana were founded about 25 B.C. The colonies flourished until overrun, like Rome herself, by the Vandals in the 5th century. Reconquered by the Roman general Belisarius in 533–534, Mauretania remained under Roman (Byzantine) jurisdiction for another century, only to fall before Arab invaders under Okba ('Uqbah ibn-Nāfi), who swept over northern Africa after 670.

Idrīsid Dynasty.—The Berber tribes, who occupied the country from the earliest historical times, were united under the sovereignty of successive Moorish dynasties, beginning with that of Idrīs I (Idrīs ibn-'Abdullāh, or Idrīs the Elder), who was enthroned at Volubilis (north of present-day Meknès) in 788 with the title of imam, or spiritual and temporal leader of Islam. His son, Idrīs II, founded the capital city of Fez in 808. The Idrīsid dynasty lasted until 974 and was followed by the Fāṭimid dynasty (from Egypt) and Umayyad (Ommiad) dynasty (from Spain).

Almoravides.—Rising in the Sahara in the early 11th century, the powerful Muslim sect of the Almoravides (al-Murābiṭūn) extended its conquests over northern Africa and ultimately into Spain. Its chief, 'Abdallāh ibn-Yāsīn, was proclaimed ruler over Morocco in 1055, inaugurating the Berber dynasty in which his grandson, Yūsuf ibn-Tāshfīn, founder of the city of Marrakech in 1062, succeeded him.

Almohades.—The Almoravides dynasty was overthrown in 1147 by 'Abd-al-Mu'min ibn-'Ali. The new Almohades (Muwaḥḥidūn) dynasty extended its control over North Africa, including Tunis, which was captured in 1158, and over the southern part of Spain.

Marīnides and Waṭṭāsi Dynasties.—Defeated in Morocco in 1269, the Almohades gave way to the Marīnides (banu-Marīn) dynasty, which flourished until the middle of the 14th century, giving way to the Waṭṭāsi (banu-Waṭṭās) dynasty, which lasted from 1471 to 1548. During this time there was an influx of Portuguese settlers to the Atlantic coastal cities, beginning with the capture of Ceuta in 1415.

Sa'adi Dynasty.—In the 16th century a new monarchial line began with the descendants of Hasan, or Sa'adi, sherifs (nobles), who were partly of Arab stock. The Sa'adians entered Morocco from the southeast through the Dra Valley, conquered Marrakech (1520) and Fez (1548), and proceeded to force the Portuguese out of all western ports except Mazagan. The fifth of the Sa'adi dynasty, Ahmed al-Manṣūr, "the Victorious," who ruled from 1578 to 1603, captured Timbuktu (1591) and was soon master of all of Morocco. His reign is regarded as the golden age in Moroccan history; some of the structures erected by him in Marrakech still survive.

Fīlāli Dynasty: Mohammed XIV to Mohammed XVI.—The Fīlāli dynasty (also known as the Ḥassāni), of mixed Arab and Berber descent, originated among the Fīlāli sherifs of the Tafilelt oasis area of southeastern Morocco, and continued to modern times. (The present ruler, King Hassan II, is the 19th of the dynasty.) Opposing the influence of both Europeans and certain *marabouts* (Islamic hermits or saints) in North Africa, the Fīlāli expanded their power

MOROCCO: *Above:* On Sunday, market day in Tetuán, people from the surrounding mountain regions come to the city to sell their wares. *Right:* Near Meknès a peasant tramples a bag of wheat, a primitive method of threshing. *Below:* Diesel tractors hauling combines during wheat harvest in Morocco. *Lower Left:* Modern resort hotel facing the beach at Mogador, on the Atlantic coast of Morocco.

(Above) Paul Pietzsch from Black Star; (right) Burton Holmes from Ewing Galloway; (below) Ewing Galloway; (lower left) Trieschman from Black Star

Above: **View of Tangier harbor at Morocco's northwest extremity.**

Above left: **One of Marrakech's many beautiful mosques. An Arab goes to its fountain to fill his petrol tin.**

Left: **Typical Moroccan farmer with his burro going to market.**

(Above) Ross Madden from Black Star; (above left) Black Star; (left) Trieschman from Black Star; (below) A. Schiehsle from Black Star

Below: **The harbor of Casablanca with its modern installations reflects French enterprise and engineering skill.**

quickly and occupied Fez in 1649. Their first sultan, Mohammed XIV, ruled from 1649 to 1664. He was followed by Rashīd II (r. 1664–1672), who made Marrakech his capital in 1668, and by Mulai Ismā'īl "the Bloodthirsty" (r. 1672–1727), who kept Morocco strongly fortified and closely united. He also drove the Spanish from Larache, took Tangier from the English, and in 1682 established diplomatic relations with France. After his death a period of disorder followed until the accession of Mohammed XVI (r. 1757–1789), who captured Mazagan from the Portuguese (1769).

The Growth of European Influence.—Piracy and the holding of prisoners for ransom were flagrantly practiced in Morocco, in common with other Barbary states, from the 16th to the 19th centuries. Nevertheless, communication and trade with European powers, particularly the French, English, Dutch, and Spanish, became increasingly important. A treaty guaranteeing the safe movement of French ships and establishing a favored status for French consuls was signed with Louis XV in 1767. As a result of the conquest of Algeria by France in 1830, 'Abd-al-Raḥmān (r. 1822–1859) aided the Arab leader in Algeria, 'Abd-al-Qādir, and subsequently was defeated at Isly in 1844 by the French under Thomas Robert Bugeaud de la Piconnerie. At the beginning of the reign of Sidi Mohammed (Mohammed XVII, r. 1859–1873), Spain, which already possessed the presidios of Ceuta (inherited from the Portuguese) and Melilla since the end of the 15th century, invaded northern Morocco, capturing Tetuán in 1860. British intervention prevented further Spanish conquests, but in 1893, during the reign of al-Ḥasan III (r. 1873–1894), the Spanish penetrated further inland, thereby obtaining slight boundary concessions and an indemnity of some $3,000,000 by a treaty signed in 1894.

European influence in Morocco increased during the weak reign of 'Abd-al-'Azīz IV (r. 1894–1908), when insurgent tribes of northern and central Morocco were in revolt and lawlessness prevailed throughout much of the country. On May 18, 1904, Aḥmad-ibn-Muḥammad Raisūli, a Moroccan brigand, captured and held for ransom Ion Perdicaris, a United States citizen, and his stepson, a British subject. The ultimatum of United States Secretary of State John Hay, "Perdicaris alive or Raisuli dead," followed by a demonstration of United States warships and representations from European courts, compelled the sultan to comply with United States demands, and the captives were released. To safeguard her interests France arranged to police Tangier, and a French military mission proceeded to Fez.

By the Franco-British Treaty of April 8, 1904, France declared her "disinterest" in Egypt, and Britain yielded to France responsibility for seeing to "the tranquillity" of Morocco and for helping to bring about needed "administrative, financial and military reforms" there. Freedom of trade was guaranteed for 30 years in Egypt and Morocco. On Oct. 3, 1904, a Franco-Spanish agreement recognized the earlier Franco-British accord; maintained the territorial integrity of Morocco; granted the right of France to give the sultan military, economic, and financial assistance; and modified the limits of the Spanish zone of influence. The agreement was further implemented by secret clauses in 1905 and 1907.

German Intervention: The Algeciras Conference.—In the meantime, Germany began to take an active interest in the events transpiring in Morocco. By the Madrid Convention of 1880, Austria, Belgium, Denmark, Germany, France, Great Britain, Italy, Morocco, the Netherlands, Portugal, Spain, Sweden, Norway, and the United States had agreed upon the right of protection in Morocco. Germany's exclusion from the Franco-British agreements with Morocco in 1904 was interpreted as a violation of her rights under the Madrid Convention; and accordingly, on March 31, 1905, the German emperor, William II, visited Tangier and assured the sultan of his intention to uphold the integrity of the Moroccan kingdom and the equality of Germany's commercial and economic interest there.

After protracted discussions with the sultan, it was agreed that an international conference should be held at Algeciras in Spain, and delegates of the countries signatory to the Madrid Convention met there in conference on Jan. 16, 1906. After strenuous opposition and counterproposals on the part of Germany (supported only by Austria) against the French program, agreement was reached in favor of the French. The Act of Algeciras, signed on April 7, 1906, and accepted by the sultan on June 18, reiterated the principle of commercial equality in Morocco, and provided for a joint Spanish-French police force in Moroccan ports.

Establishment of the Protectorate.—The murder of Dr. Emile Mauchamp on March 19, 1907, at Marrakech resulted in the occupation of Oujda by the French. 'Abd-al-Hafiz (Mulai Hafiz) took the throne in 1908 following the deposition of his brother, 'Abd-al-'Azīz IV, but was ousted in 1912 in favor of Mulai Yusef, who reigned until Nov. 18, 1927. Meanwhile, in July 1911, Germany sent the cruiser *Panther* to Agadir to protect the concessions of German financiers, and was assured of the support of local chiefs in any resistance she might make against French paramountcy in the country. Great Britain hastened to give France her support, and a diplomatic crisis ensued among the great powers. Extended Franco-German negotiations resulted in two agreements of Nov. 4, 1911, virtually recognizing a French protectorate in Morocco but assuring German interests absolute equality in economic and commercial matters, and ceding to Germany about 100,000 square miles in the northern French Congo.

Thus the way was cleared for the Franco-Moroccan Treaty of March 30, 1912, signed at Fez, whereby the sultan recognized the establishment of what amounted to a French protectorate in Morocco. Subsequent negotiations with Spain resulted in the agreement of Nov. 27, 1912, defining Spanish rights and interests in the Spanish northern zone. In the meantime, Gen. Louis H. G. Lyautey was appointed French resident general, and he began pacification of the country which was in revolt against the sultan.

Pacification Problems and 'Abd-al-Karīm.—The pacification of the Spanish Zone was not so successful, however, as a result of troubles among the Riffs. Following a successful attack on the Spanish forces at Annual in July 1921, the Riffian leader, 'Abd-al-Karīm, conducted guerrilla operations against the Spanish, forcing them out of part of the northern zone by 1924, and creating a political crisis in Madrid. In 1925, 'Abd-al-Karīm carried the fighting into neighboring French territory, and large reinforcements of French troops were dispatched to join the Spanish in a joint campaign under Marshal Henri Philippe Pétain. 'Abd-al-Karīm surrendered on May 26, 1926, and was exiled to Réunion. Uprisings in the Grand Atlas in 1933, and in the Anti-Atlas in 1935, were put down, and peace was restored to the French Zone.

Internationalization of Tangier.—The area about Tangier remained in dispute until the convention of Dec. 18, 1923, by France, Great Britain, and Spain, providing for the demilitarization of the zone and its administration by an international Committee of Control. Urged by Benito Mussolini to make the Mediterranean an "Italian sea," the Italian Navy threatened Tangier and forced a conference at Paris in 1928, in which the Tangier Statute of 1923 was revised by the Paris Protocol of July 25, giving Italy representation on the Tangier committee.

After the fall of France in June 1940, Spanish troops occupied Tangier, international control was abolished, and the sultan's representative ejected from the zone. In 1945 the Big Four agreed to restore the international administration; Spanish occupying forces were withdrawn and on October 11 international control was restored.

World War II.—United States forces landed on the Moroccan coast on Nov. 8, 1942, preliminary to operations in the European theater. Special measures introduced in Morocco during the German occupation of France were abolished, and large detachments of Moroccan troops took part in the campaign for the liberation of France, 1944–1945. At Casablanca, President Franklin D. Roosevelt and Prime Minister Winston Churchill met secretly on Jan. 14–24, 1943, in one of the most important conferences of the war.

The Growth of Nationalism.—Growing nationalist sentiment in French Morocco came more into the open after the removal of Gen. Auguste Noguès in June 1943 and the subsequent reorganization of French administration in accordance with the more democratic policies of the Committee for National Liberation. The nationalist Istiqlal Party soon organized demonstrations in the larger cities and eventually received some support from the sultan, Sidi Mohammed ben Youssef, who had succeeded Mulai Yusef in 1927, and who now began advocating termination of the protectorate.

On Aug. 14, 1953, a conference of some 300 kaids, pashas, and Berber tribal chieftains at Marrakech, under the leadership of the pro-French pasha of Marrakech, Thami el-Mezuari el-Glaoui, decided to depose the sultan on the grounds that he had compromised his position by departing from Muslim orthodoxy and by allying himself with the nationalist Istiqlal Party. A week later, despite bloody nationalist rioting, Sidi Mohammed ben Moulay Arafa, also of the Filāli dynasty, was proclaimed the new sultan at Rabat. The French then proceeded to effect a series of administrative reforms aimed at paving the way for Moroccan self-government.

Rioting, terrorist bombings, and assassinations continued sporadically through 1954 and into 1955 as the more extreme nationalists, backed by the Arab nations, demanded the return of the deposed sultan, who had been removed by the French from Corsica to Madagascar early in 1954. Spanish officials in 1954 rejected the authority of the new sultan, declaring that the Spanish Zone would continue under the caliph appointed by ben Youssef until self-government was realized. During the summer of 1955 about 250 French and natives were killed in riots; in the mountains, patriots organized armed bands which began to be known as the National Liberation Army Forces.

Independence.—By Aug. 12, 1955, the French Cabinet had come to a decision to ask the sultan to form a government which would be representative of all elements of the Moroccan population. When this plan failed, the French government called a group of Moroccan nationalists to meet with five French Cabinet members (headed by Premier Edgar Faure) at Aix-les-Bains. The conference ended on August 27 with both sides in agreement on measures designed to restore order to Morocco and to inaugurate reforms leading to self-government.

On Oct. 29, 1955, ben Moulay Arafa (who had vacated the throne on October 1) announced his abdication, and on November 5, ben Youssef was recognized as sultan by the French government. Ben Youssef (who became King Mohammed V in 1957) made a triumphal return to Rabat on November 16, and on December 7 he installed a nationalist Cabinet headed by M'barek Bekkai. The new government opened negotiations with the French which resulted in the proclamation of independence on March 2, 1956, the same day of the signature of the Protocol of Paris, terminating the Treaty of Fez. On April 7, Spain relinquished her protectorate, and on October 29 the international status of the Tangier Zone was abolished. The southern Tarfaya Province (Southern Protectorate of Morocco) was retroceded by Spain on April 1, 1958.

Beginning in 1958, internal politics became marked by an increasing split within the Istiqlal into rightist and leftist camps. The leftists, who demanded constitutional government and economic reform, founded the National Union of Popular Forces (UNFP) in 1959. King Mohammed dismissed the leftist premier in 1960 and assumed personal conduct of the government. A year later Crown Prince Moulay Hassan came to the throne as Hassan II on his father's death.

In 1963 fighting flared up on the disputed border between Morocco and Algeria, but peace was restored through mediation of the Organization of African Unity. The kidnaping in Paris, on Oct. 28, 1965, of Moroccan leftist leader Mehdi Ben Barka led to a deep rift in relations with France, which accused the Moroccan government of instigating the act.

A political crisis in 1965 and civil disorders over unemployment and rising food prices prompted King Hassan to declare a state of emergency and assume the premiership himself. In 1967 he appointed Mohammed Benhima premier, without reducing his own power to rule through loyal ministers and technicians. Political meetings were prohibited throughout the kingdom unless sanctioned by the minister of the interior.

10. BIBLIOGRAPHY

Andrews, E. C., *Old Morocco* (New York 1923); Hardy, Georges, *Le Maroc,* vol. 3 in *Histoire des Colonies Françaises* (Paris 1931); Lyautey, Pierre, *L'empire colonial français* (Paris 1931); Maurois, André, *Lyautey* (Paris 1931); Horne, John, *Many Days in Morocco,* rev. ed. (London 1936); Thornton, Philip, *Voice of Atlas* (New York 1936); Usborne, Cecil V., *Conquest of Morocco* (London 1936); Mellor, Francis H., *Morocco Awakes* (London 1939); Guernier, Eugène, *Le Maroc* (Paris 1948); Célérier, Jean, *Le Maroc* (Paris 1948); Coindreau, Roger, and Penz, Charles, *Le Maroc* in *Collection Terres Lointaines* (Paris 1949); Landau, Rom, *Beauty of Morocco* (London 1951); Mannin, Ethel

Edith, *Moroccan Mosaic* (London 1954); La Documentation française, *Notes et Études Documentaires,* March 12, 1958 (Paris); Fodor, Eugene, ed., *Morocco,* Fodor's Modern Guides (New York 1965, rev. annually); International Bank for Reconstruction and Development, *Economic Development of Morocco* (Baltimore 1966); Bernard, Stephane, *Franco-Moroccan Conflict, 1943–1956* (New Haven 1967); Landau, Rom, *Morocco* (New York 1967).

MOROCCO, city, Morocco. See MARRAKECH.

MOROCCO, type of leather. See LEATHER AND SHOE TRADE TECHNICAL TERMS.

MORON. See MENTAL RETARDATION.

MORONI, mô-rō'nê, or **MORONE,** mô-rō'nâ, **Giambattista,** Italian painter: b. Albino, near Bergamo, Italy, ?1525; d. Brescia, Feb. 5, 1578. A member of the Brescian school, he was a pupil of Il Moretto. He painted a number of altarpieces but is best known for his portraits, which were highly regarded by Titian and are said to have influenced Sir Anthony van Dyck. Among them are a portrait of Antonio Navagero in the Brera Gallery, Milan; a self-portrait and one of Conte Secco Suardo in the Uffizi, Florence; *A Tailor,* in the National Gallery, London; *A Gentleman in Adoration Before the Madonna,* in the National Gallery, Washington; and a portrait of Bartolomeo Bongo, in the Metropolitan Museum of Art, New York.

MOROS, mō'rōz, Moslem Filipinos of Mindanao Island, where they live chiefly in the provinces of Cotabato, Lanao, and Zamboanga; the Sulu Archipelago, southwest of Mindanao; and southern Palawan Island. When the Spaniards arrived in the Philippines in the 16th century, they called the Filipinos converted to Islam Moros (Moors), meaning "Mohammedans." The name is still used popularly as a group name for Mohammedan Filipinos. According to the 1960 census, 4.9 per cent of the Filipinos are Mohammedans—a small minority in a largely Christian nation.

Some of the best-known Moro groups are the Yakans (Basilan Island); the Lanao Filipinos (divided into the Maranaos and Ilanums or Iranums); the skilled metalworkers known as Magindananos (Cotabato River Valley); who made bronze cannons (*lantaka*) before the Spaniards' arrival; and the Sulu Moros, who are noted as superb navigators. The Samals, often known as sea gypsies, are Moros who live on the immediate shore or in boats; those Moro Filipinos who dwell only on boats are called Badjaos (Bajau).

History.—The people of Sumatra were converted to Islam in the 13th century. These Mohammedanized Malays pushed northward through Borneo and Jolo into Mindanao, where Islam probably gained its first foothold in the middle of the 15th century. By the time the Spaniards appeared, there were Moro groups as far north as Mindoro and southwestern Luzon, and the explorer Miguel López de Legazpe found an estimated 80,000 of them inhabiting the shores of Manila Bay. The Spanish conquest of the Philippines stopped the spread of Islam in the islands. Mohammedanism in Mindanao might not have survived if the Spaniards had not been occupied in the early 17th century with Dutch occupation of Formosa and their attack against Manila, necessitating withdrawal to Luzon.

Soon the Spaniards and the Moros were at war—a conflict that lasted almost until the final days of Spanish sovereignty in the Philippines. Two important causes for the fighting were Spain's attempt to make Mindanao and Sulu colonies and to convert the Moros to Christianity. The Moros were organized into sultanates under the control of sultans, some of whom claimed descent from Mohammed himself. The absolutism of the sultans varied with their personal qualities. Under each sultan were *datos* (local chiefs), who assisted him in the administration of his sultanate. This political organization gave the Moros a military efficiency which was not possessed by other Filipinos.

In retaliation for Spanish expeditions against their homeland the Moros raided and sacked Christian Filipino communities in the Visayan Islands and as far north as Luzon. Travelers may still see the crumbling stone towers where Filipinos once watched to warn their people of marauding Moro fleets. With the introduction of the steamship and a better-organized military program, Spain was able to halt the Moro raids. Yet when she ceded the Philippines to the United States in 1898, her control over the Moro regions was largely ineffective.

Mindanao and Sulu were placed under a military government during the first years of American rule in the Philippines. Most Moros resisted United States attempts to govern their lands. It was during the military campaigns to pacify the Moros in 1903 that John J. Pershing gained world fame as a military leader. In 1914 civil government was established in the Moro regions, and in the following year the sultan of Sulu abdicated his rights of sovereignty, recognizing the United States (the sultanate was finally terminated in 1940). By 1922 four of the seven provinces of Mindanao and Sulu elected their own governors. Moro Filipinos have the same political rights as Christian Filipinos, and some of them are prominent national leaders. In the 1950's, however, the Philippine government had to send troops to quell some dissident Moro groups in Mindanao and Sulu.

DONN V. HART,
Social Science Foundation, University of Denver.

MOROSINI, mō-rô-sē'nê, **Francesco,** Italian general: b. Venice, Italy, 1618; d. Nauplia, Greece, Jan. 6, 1694. A member of a patrician Venetian family which included a number of doges and scholars, he joined the Venetian armed forces in 1636. From 1645, Venice was at war with the Turks, and Morosini was four times in command of the Venetian forces: 1657–1661; 1666–1669; 1684–1688; and 1693–1694. On the second occasion, in 1669, he was compelled to yield Candia, Crete, to the Turks in order to save its starving garrison, but in 1685–1687 he conquered the Peloponnesus, winning the sobriquet of Peloponnesiaco. In 1688 he became doge of Venice.

MOROTAI, mō-rô-tī', island, Indonesia, situated in the Moluccas, 15 miles northeast of Halmahera, from which it is separated by Morotai Strait. It has an area of 695 square miles, and is about 50 miles long and 25 miles wide. Chief products are timber, resin, and sago. Pop. (1961) 19,523.

MORPETH, municipal borough, England, situated in Northumberland, on the Wansbeck River, 14 miles north of Newcastle. The trading center for an agricultural region, it has establishments producing leather, woolen cloth, beer, and iron and brass products. In medieval times, Morpeth was a fortress in the warfare on the Anglo-Scottish border. The 14th century gatehouse of its castle still stands, and there are ruins of other castles nearby. The town has a church built in the 1300's, and a town hall that was designed by Sir John Vanbrugh in 1714. Pop. (1961) 17,033.

MORPHEUS, môr'fūs; popularly, môr'fē-ŭs (from Gr. *morphē,* form or shape), in Greek mythology, the god of dreams. The son of Hypnos or Somnus, the god of sleep, he is usually represented as a slumbering child. As his name implies, he shapes men's dreams.

MORPHINE, môr'fēn, an alkaloid of opium. The name is derived from the Greek god Morpheus (q.v.). Chemically, morphine is a complex derivative of phenanthrene that contains two OH groups (one phenolic, the other alcoholic) in which the hydrogen can be replaced by alkyl or acid radicals to form such substances as codeine, thebaine, and heroin. The chemical nature of these radicals modifies the effects on the body. For example, the replacement of one hydroxyl group by a methyl group (codeine) diminishes the narcotic and respiratory depressant actions but increases the convulsant action. When both OH groups are replaced by acids (diacetyl morphine), the narcotic effects are stronger than with codeine, and the convulsant action is weaker than with morphine.

Morphine was first isolated about 1805 by Friedrich W. A. Sertürner, a German pharmacist. Subsequently it was shown that most of the effect of opium is due to its morphine content. Morphine is available as morphine hydrochloride and morphine sulphate, the latter being the form commonly used medicinally. Both salts appear as white crystals or powder having a bitter taste but no odor. They darken if left exposed to light and lose water if exposed to air. The chemical formula for morphine sulphate is $(C_{17}H_{19}NO_3)_2 \cdot H_2SO_4 \cdot 5H_2O$.

Although morphine is useful medically, particularly for the relief of pain, it has undesirable properties and may cause constipation, vomiting, excitement instead of calmness, and depression of respiration. It may also cause a severe drug addiction that is difficult to control. When an overdose of the drug is taken, death may occur from respiratory failure.

Morphine has been and still is used to some extent for the control of pain in expectant mothers just before delivery. Other drugs are used to better advantage, however, and are substituted whenever possible because morphine can pass from mother to child through the placenta and cause difficulty in breathing in the newborn infant.

The manufacture and distribution of morphine, like that of all narcotic drugs, is under the Harrison Narcotic Act of 1914. Such drugs can be dispensed only by doctors holding a narcotics license, which must be renewed yearly.

See also CODEINE; OPIUM.

AUSTIN SMITH, M.D.,
Editor, "Journal of the American Medical Society."

MORPHOGENESIS, môr-fō-jĕn'ē-sĭs, has been defined by the English biochemist Joseph Needham as "the coming-into-being of characteristic and specific form in living organisms." This involves an exceedingly complex and intricately regulated sequence of events, processes, and changes (growth and differentiation), resulting in development from egg to mature form, and according to the organism's own characteristic organization. Two groups of processes are responsible for development: (1) constructive or progressive processes that contribute to building up the organism—(a) growth, or the actual increase in living matter through synthesis and storing up new protoplasm, (b) morphogenetic movements, which transport new protoplasm to places where new form appears, and (c) differentiation, which becomes increasingly apparent through differences in chemical composition detectable between stages; and (2) limiting processes, which are either external such as limited food supply, or internal such as hormones and chemical inductors that guide the expression of hereditary characters (genes). Also characteristic of development is the early appearance of polarity (apex and base), which is present even in some eggs. The orderly sequence of events and changes during development is brought about by determination, which controls the ultimate fate of all parts of an embryo.

Numerous ingenious and delicate micrurgical experiments with eggs and developing embryos, especially those of amphibians, echinoderms, worms, and other groups, involving ablation (removal), addition (implantation), exchange (transplantation), and fusion, have disclosed two quantitatively different types of eggs: (1) mosaic eggs, whose parts are clearly determined from the earliest stages; and (2) regulation eggs, in which determination begins at a later stage. The latter are particularly suitable for experimental study, for alteration of development is possible by experiment. In vertebrate eggs, best known of those studied, determination is initiated by a controlling region (primary organization center), located near the blastopore. Secondary and tertiary organization centers appear later. The ability of an embryo to develop normally or nearly so or to regenerate after experimental interference is called regulation.

The modern study of morphogenesis involves methods, data, and points of view of morphology, physiology, biochemistry, genetics, physics, and mathematics. A completely satisfactory and universally acceptable theory of morphogenesis must mold all these into a logical, consistent whole.

THEODOR JUST.

MORPHOLOGY, môr-fŏl'ō-jĭ, the division of biological science which deals with the form and structure of animals and plants. The term, which is derived from the Greek word *morphē* (form), was originated by Johann Wolfgang von Goethe. It includes anatomy and histology and, in part, embryology and cytology. For the morphology of animals, see ANATOMY, COMPARATIVE; for that of plants, see PLANTS AND PLANT SCIENCE —*1. Classification, Morphology, and Evolution; 2. Anatomy.*

MORPHY, Paul Charles, American chess player: b. New Orleans, La., June 22, 1837; d. there, July 10, 1884. He learned chess at the age of 10, and at 12 had defeated many local amateurs. He was educated at Spring Hill College and at the University of Louisiana, where he studied law for several years, occasionally playing a game. In 1857 at the first American chess congress held in New York, he had no difficulty in defeating his strongest opponents. During the next year, in England, he successfully met such players as Henry E. Bird, Boden and J. J. Löwenthal, and astonished the world of chess by playing as many as eight games simultaneously and without the board. His playing in Paris, where he won five games out of eight against Harrwitz, and exhibited his blindfold skill, was equally surprising. In 1859 he returned to the United States and here met the famous German player Adolf Anderssen, winning 7 of 11 games. Being now admitted to the bar, Morphy began to practice law in his native city; but his mental powers had been so impaired by the strain of his blind-fold chess-playing that he not only gave that up but relinquished chess entirely, and a little later abandoned all intellectual work. Morphy's skill at chess appeared to partake of the quality of genius. His brilliant achievements were not the result of long or deep deliberation, yet displayed all the elements usually observed when mental strength and quickness are sustained by profound study. Consult Löwenthal, J. J. *Morphy's Games of Chess* (London 1860).

MORRELL, Imogene Robinson, American artist: b. Attleboro, Mass.; d. Philadelphia, Nov. 22, 1908. She was married to Abram Morrell in 1869. She studied art in the United States and Europe and was a pupil of Adolf Schrodter at Düsseldorf and of Thomas Couture at Paris (1864). In 1874 she returned to America, opened a studio at Washington as a portrait and historical painter, and there established and became first president of the Washington National Academy of Fine Arts (1879). Some of her more notable paintings are *The First Battle of the Puritans; Washington Welcoming the Provision Trains at Newburgh, N. Y.; A Historical Portrait of General John A. Dix.*

MORRILL, mŏr'ĭl, **Anson Peaslee,** American politician: b. Belgrade, Maine, June 10, 1803; d. Augusta, Maine, July 4, 1887. He at first engaged in business in his native town, then in 1834 was sent to the state legislature; was sheriff of Somerset County 1839–40; and in 1850 land agent. In 1853 he was an unsuccessful candidate for governor on the Prohibition and Free-Soil tickets, but the following year he was elected as the first Republican governor of Maine, and later was a delegate to the convention which nominated John C. Frémont. In 1860 he was elected to Congress, but declined a re-election.

MORRILL, Justin Smith, American senator: b. Strafford, Vt., April 14, 1810; d. Washington, D. C., Dec. 28, 1898. He received a good primary and secondary education, was a merchant and then a farmer; was first elected to the House of Representatives in 1854. In 1867 was transferred to the Senate, in which he was long chairman of the committee of finance. With his 12 years in the lower house and 31 in the upper, he was more closely connected with Congress than any other man of his time, and was styled "The Father of the Senate." His Land-Grant College Act, approved by President Lincoln in 1862, for the creation of seats of learning in newly-settled states, has, with supplemental legislation, resulted in the erection of some 70 colleges. He introduced the war revenue tariff of 1861, commonly called the Morrill tariff, and during his later years consistently opposed the remonetization of silver. Senator Morrill wrote *The Self-Consciousness of Noted Persons* (1886).

MORRILL, Lot Myrick, American politician: b. Belgrade, Maine, May 3, 1812; d. Portland, Maine, Jan. 10, 1883. He was educated at Waterville College (now Colby University), studied law and was admitted to the bar in 1839, when he went to Augusta and established a law practice. He took an active part in politics, in 1853 was elected to the state legislature, and in 1856 was chosen president of the Senate. He was governor of his state 1858–60, and in the latter year was elected to the United States Senate, where he proved himself an indefatigable worker. He favored the resumption of specie payment and was an authority on financial, naval and Indian affairs. In 1876 he retired from the Senate to become secretary of the treasury under President Grant, and during his administration of that office constantly urged the return to specie payment. He declined an appointment to a foreign mission under President Hayes, and in 1887 became collector of customs at Portland, Maine, in which office he died.

MORRILTON, Ark., town and Conway County seat; altitude 347 feet; on the Missouri Pacific Railroad; 50 miles northwest of Little Rock. In the county, livestock and cotton are raised, and the city's industries are meat packing and the making of cottonseed oil, cloth, and cheese. Pop. 6,814.

MORRIS, Anthony, American Quaker: b. London, Aug. 23, 1654; d. Philadelphia, Pa., Oct. 23, 1721. In 1683 he settled in Burlington, West Jersey, moving three years later to Philadelphia where he acquired wealth in brewing. He was at various times alderman and mayor of the city, also served in the provincial council and the assembly. He was a founder of the William Penn Charter School.

MORRIS, Charles, English song writer: b. 1745; d. near Dorking, Surrey, July 11, 1838. In 1764 he entered the 17th Foot, with which he served in America, later exchanged into the Irish Dragoons and then into the 2d Life Guards. In 1785 he was made bard of the Beefsteak Society, and before its gatherings sang many of his wittiest efforts. He was a boon companion and associate of Charles James Fox and the Prince Regent (George IV). His humor and vivacity led John Philpot Curran to say, "Die when you will, Charles, you will die in your youth." He wrote hundreds of songs, many being political ditties for the Whigs; and a posthumous volume, *Lyra Urbanica* (1840) collected them. His *A Reason Fair to Fill my Glass* was praised by Thomas Moore and set to music by Charles Dibdin.

MORRIS, Charles, American naval officer: b. Woodstock, Conn., July 26, 1784; d. Jan. 27, 1856. Entering the navy in 1799, he participated in the war with Tripoli, was an actor in the recapture of the *Philadelphia,* in the harbor of Tripoli (1804), being the first to gain her deck when she was boarded. At the outbreak of the War of 1812 he was serving as executive officer of the *Constitution;* he was wounded in the engagement of *Old Ironsides* with the *Guerrière* (August 1812); and afterward successfully commanded the *John Adams* until, being blockaded by a British squadron in Penobscot River, he was compelled to destroy his ship to save her from being taken by the enemy. In the war with Algiers (1815) he commanded the *Congress,* and it was he who, in the *Brandywine,* carried Lafayette home to France (1825). After serving for some years as naval commissioner and as commandant of the Boston Navy Yard, he became chief of the bureau of ordnance and hydrography, which position he held until his death. He published his *Autobiography* in 1880.

MORRIS, Clara, American actress: b. Toronto, Canada, 1849; d. New Canaan, Conn., Nov. 20, 1925. She became the leading lady in Wood's Theater, Cincinnati, Ohio, and in the winter of 1869–1870, joined Augustin Daly's Fifth Avenue Company, New York. She at once achieved success in emotional roles and afterward made many tours throughout the United States. Her leading roles include *Camille;* Alixe in the *Countess de Sommerive; Mercy Merrick; Miss Multon;* Lady Macbeth; *Leah the Forsaken;* and Cora in *L'Article 47.* After her retirement from the stage she wrote much for periodicals and published in book form *A Silent Singer* (1899); *My Little Jim Crow* (1900); *A Pasteboard Crown,* fiction (1902); *Stage Confidences* (1902); *The Trouble Woman* (1904); *The Life of a Star* (1906); *Left in Charge* (1907); *New East Lynne* (1908); and *Dressing Room Receptions* (1911). She was married to F. C. Harriott in 1874. In her later years she was afflicted with blindness.

MORRIS, Sir Daniel, British colonial expert: b. Loughor, Glamorgan, May 26, 1844; d. Feb. 9, 1933. He was educated at Cheltenham, at the South Kensington Royal College of Science and at Trinity College, Dublin, where he received high honors. He was assistant director of the Royal Botanic Gardens of Ceylon in 1877; investigated and checked the coffee-leaf disease; became director of the Botanic Department of Jamaica in 1879; was commissioner in the West Indian Imperial Department 1898–1908; a member of the Canadian and West Indian Trade Commission 1909–1910; and was scientific adviser in tropical agriculture to the Colonial Office 1908–1913. He was created K. C. M. G. in 1903. Among his publications are *Cacao: How to Grow and How to Cure It* (1882); *Agricultural Resources of Saint Helena* (1884); *The Vegetable Resources of the West Indies* (1888); *Sisal Industry of the Bahamas* (1896); *Report to the West India Royal Commission on the Agricultural Resources of the West Indies* (1897); and *Forest Resources of Newfoundland* (1916).

MORRIS, Edward Joy, American author: b. Philadelphia, Pa., July 16, 1815; d. there, Dec. 31, 1881. He was graduated from Harvard in 1836 and was admitted to the bar in 1842. He was a member of the Pennsylvania legislature in 1841–1843 and of Congress in 1843–1845, and in 1850 was appointed to a mission in Naples where he remained four years. He was again in Congress as a representative of Pennsylvania in 1858–1861, and in 1861–1870 was minister to Turkey. He published *Notes of a Tour through Turkey, Greece, Egypt, Arabia Petraea to the Holy Land* (2 vols., 1842), as well as translations of works on Turkey, Norway, and Corsica, and numerous magazine and newspaper articles.

MORRIS, Esther Hobart (1814–1902), American suffragette, who was instrumental in winning women the right to vote in Wyoming. She was born Esther McQuigg in Tioga county, N. Y., on Aug. 8, 1814. She married in 1841, but was widowed four years later and moved to Illinois. Soon after she married John Morris and in 1869 went with him to Wyoming.

In Wyoming, Esther Morris became active in the struggle for women's suffrage. She led a successful effort to have the territory pass legislation granting women the right to vote in 1869. When Wyoming entered the union in 1890, it was the first state to provide for women's suffrage in its constitution.

In 1870, Morris became justice of the peace in South Pass City, the first woman to hold that post in the United States. She left Wyoming in 1874 and spent some time in New York, but she was back in 1890 in time for the statehood celebration. In 1895 she was elected as a delegate from Wyoming to the national suffrage convention in Cleveland. Esther Morris died in Cheyenne, Wyo., on April 2, 1902. Her statue represents Wyoming in Statuary Hall in the Capitol in Washington, D. C.

MORRIS, George Perry, American journalist: b. Montclair, N. J., Feb. 18, 1864; d. June 12, 1921. He was educated at Rutgers College and Johns Hopkins University, and in 1891 was associate editor of *The Congregationalist.* In 1888–90 he was on the editorial staff of the New York *Mail and Express,* on *The Congregationalist,* Boston, in 1891–1907, and on the staff of the Boston *Herald* 1907–1911. He was on the staff of the *Christian Science Monitor* (1911–1918). He published *The Norwegian Company System* (1894) and *Historic Towns of New England* (1898). He was a contributor to various magazines, especially of character studies of living notables.

MORRIS, George Pope, American journalist and poet: b. Philadelphia, Oct. 10, 1802; d. New York, July 6, 1864. With Samuel Woodworth in 1823, he helped found the New York *Mirror,* a weekly journal of literature, afterward published as the *New Mirror* and the *Evening Mirror,* in which many of the early writings of Bryant, Poe, Halleck, Willis and other American authors first appeared. In 1845 Morris established the *National Press,* which in the following year became the *Home Journal,* and which, with the assistance of Nathaniel Willis, he continued to edit almost to the end of his life. He wrote *Brier Cliff* (1826), a popular drama based on incidents of the American Revolution, and the libretto of a three-act opera, *The Maid of Saxony* (1842, music by Charles Edward Horn), based on the career of Frederick the Great. The final collection of his *Poems* (4th ed., 1860) contains *Near the Lake, My Mother's Bible, We Were Boys Together, A Long Time Ago,* and the familiar *Woodman, Spare That Tree.*

MORRIS, Gouverneur (1752–1816), American statesman and diplomat, who played an important role in the American Revolution and the writing of the Constitution. He was born in Morrisania (now part of New York City), N. Y., on Jan. 31, 1752, into a distinguished New York family. His grandfather Lewis Morris had been chief justice of New York and governor of New Jersey. Gouverneur Morris was educated at a Huguenot school in New Rochelle, N. Y., and graduated from King's College (now Columbia University) in 1768. He was admitted to the bar in 1771, at the age of 19. He lost one of his legs in an accident and wore a wooden peg leg.

American Patriot. Morris at first opposed a break between Britain and the American colonies. Like most other landed and aristocratic New Yorkers, he feared that independence would lead to social upheaval. After the Battle of Lexington (1775) he became active in the American cause, but some members of his family and a number of his associates were Loyalists. Morris represented Westchester county in the revolutionary New York provincial congress (1775–1777), where he was a strong supporter of the Continental Congress. Recognizing the need for unity, he insisted that Congress had to have power over the states. He was a member of New York's Constitutional Convention, and with John Jay and Robert R. Livingston he drafted the state's first constitution.

From 1777 to 1779, Morris was a member of the Continental Congress, where he was one of the ablest supporters of George Washington's military policies. During his term in Congress, Morris served on several important committees. He was chairman of the committee that met with British commissioners in 1778 to discuss Lord North's plan for conciliation. His report on the discussions, *Observations on the American Revolution,* was published in 1779. He drafted the instructions to Benjamin Franklin, who served as the first U. S. minister to France. Morris also prepared the instructions to be used to negotiate a peace treaty with Britain, and they formed the basis of major provisions of the Treaty of Paris (1783).

Financier. Defeated for reelection to Congress in 1779, Morris settled in Philadelphia and resumed the practice of law. His publication of a series of essays on the country's finances in the *Pennsylvania Packet* in 1780 led to his appointment the next year as assistant to Robert Morris (not a relative), superintendent of finance. Serving in that post until 1785, Gouverneur Morris drew up a plan for a decimal system of coinage that, after being modified by Thomas Jefferson and Alexander Hamilton, formed the basis for the present monetary system of the United States. Morris also invented the word "cent."

Constitutional Convention. Morris was elected a Pennsylvania delegate to the Constitutional Convention in 1787. Taking part in many debates, he advocated a strong central government, a president elected for life, and a Senate composed of members appointed for life by the president. Although his proposals failed to win approval, he accepted the compromise document and lent his literary skill to writing the final form of the Constitution.

Minister to France. In 1789 he went to France as a business agent for Robert Morris, and witnessed the outbreak of the French Revolution. His *Diary of the French Revolution,* published in 1839, is an important source of information on that period. In 1790 he went to London as a special envoy of President Washington to determine whether commercial treaties between Britain and the United States were possible. The negotiations were unsuccessful.

COURTESY OF THE NEW-YORK HISTORICAL SOCIETY

Gouverneur Morris carried out important diplomatic assignments in Britain and France for the new United States.

Morris became U. S. minister to France in 1792. He was opposed to the radical course the French Revolution had taken, and he secretly became involved in unsuccessful efforts to help King Louis XVI escape from the country. His hostility led the revolutionary government to request his recall, and he was replaced by James Madison in 1794. Morris spent the next four years traveling in Europe.

Later Career. From 1800 to 1803, Morris served as a U. S. senator from New York, filling an unexpired term. A staunch Federalist, he opposed the election of Thomas Jefferson as president in 1800 but later supported Jefferson's Louisiana Purchase. Morris had long actively promoted construction of the Erie Canal, and he became chairman of the Erie Canal Commission in 1810.

Morris became increasingly opposed to the policies of the Jefferson administration and the Republicans. He opposed the Embargo Act (1807), condemned the War of 1812, and supported the Hartford Convention. His distrust of the Republican administration led him to support extreme Federalists advocating establishment of a northern confederation during the War of 1812. At the end of his life he appeared to have lost faith in the future of the country he had helped to establish. Morris died in Morrisania, N. Y., on Nov. 6, 1816.

Further Reading: Mintz, Max M., *Gouverneur Morris & the American Revolution* (Univ. of Okla. Press 1970); Roosevelt, Theodore, *Gouverneur Morris* (1898; reprint, Scholarly Press 1971).

MORRIS, Lewis, American colonial jurist and governor: b. Morrisania (now in Bronx County), N.Y., Oct. 15, 1671; d. near Trenton, N.J., May 21, 1746. His father Richard Morris (d. 1672) and uncle Lewis Morris (d. 1691) emigrated from England to Barbados, where they prospered as merchants, and then moved to New York, where in 1670 they acquired 500 acres north of the Harlem River originally settled by Jonas Bronck. Young Morris fell heir to his uncle's estate as well as his father's, and so at the age of 20 was master of nearly 2,000 acres in New York Province and almost twice as much in Monmouth County, N.J. In 1692 he was named a judge of the Court of Common Pleas in East New Jersey and a member of the governor's council, and in 1697 his New York estate was patented as the Manor of Morrisania, of which he became first lord.

As dissatisfaction with the proprietary regime in New Jersey mounted, Morris was instrumental in securing its reconstitution as a royal colony (1702) and then, as a member of the new council, fought the corrupt and oppressive administration of the first royal governor, Viscount Cornbury (Edward Hyde), whose removal (1708) he played a major part in effecting. In 1715 he was appointed chief justice of the Province of New York, holding office until 1733, when he was dismissed after a dispute with Governor William Cosby. Since 1702, New York and New Jersey had been governed jointly, but in 1738 the administrations of the two provinces were separated and Morris was named first governor of New Jersey, which office he held until his death.

MORRIS, Lewis, American patriot, signer of the Declaration of Independence: b. Morrisania, Westchester (now Bronx) County, N.Y., April 8, 1726; d. there, Jan. 22, 1798. Grandson of Lewis Morris (1671–1746) and half brother of Gouverneur Morris (1752–1816, qq. v.), he graduated from Yale College in 1746 and inherited the family estate of Morrisania from his father Lewis Morris (1698–1762), becoming third and last lord of the manor. As relations between Great Britain and the colonies reached the breaking point in the spring of 1775, Morris led the delegation from Westchester to the New York Provincial Congress and was elected by the latter body to the Second Continental Congress, where he served on the committee to procure munitions and supplies for the Continental forces. Appointed brigadier general in command of the Westchester County militia in June 1776, he was absent from Congress when the Declaration of Independence was adopted, but signed it later in the year. Meanwhile, he took part in military action against the British, and his estate was ravaged. He sat in the New York State Senate at various times between 1777 and 1790, was a member (from 1784) of the first Board of Regents of the University of the State of New York, and strongly supported ratification of the United States Constitution at the state convention of 1788.

RICHARD VALENTINE MORRIS (1768–1815), his youngest son, became a captain in the United States Navy (1798) and in 1802 took a squadron to the Mediterranean in an attempt to conclude the war with Tripoli over the latter's demand for increased tribute for the protection of American shipping. Morris' efforts were unsuccessful, and he was ordered home in June 1803 and deprived of his commission soon after. His *Defence of the Conduct of Commodore Morris During His Command in the Mediterranean* (1804) is a valuable source of documentary information concerning American relations with the Barbary States at the time.

LEWIS RICHARD MORRIS (1760–1825), Lewis' nephew, after fighting in the American Revolution, established his residence in Springfield, Vt., in 1786 and was one of the two commissioners who negotiated Vermont's admission into the Union (1791). In 1796 he was elected to the United States House of Representatives, where he served for six years. After the indecisive presidential election of 1800, when the House was choosing between Thomas Jefferson and Aaron Burr, Morris, a Federalist, absented himself from voting on the 36th ballot, allowing his colleague to cast the state's vote for Jefferson. With similar action by the Maryland delegation and the abstention of Delaware, Jefferson's election was assured.

MORRIS, SIR Lewis, Welsh poet and educator: b. Carmarthen, Wales, Jan. 23, 1833; d. Penbryn, Nov. 12, 1907. Graduated from Jesus College, Oxford (1856), he was admitted to the bar in 1861 and practiced in London until 1880. During the later years of his life, Morris devoted his efforts largely to the promotion of higher education in Wales. From 1878 until his death he was a leading official of the University College of Wales at Aberystwyth, and in 1880–1881 he served on the committee whose report led to the foundation of the University of Wales at Cardiff in 1893. He also served as chairman of the National Eisteddfod Association, which sponsors the annual Welsh music and poetry festival, from its formation in 1880 until his death.

Morris first attracted attention as a poet with a series of three volumes of lyrics entitled *Songs of Two Worlds* (1871–75), in the style of Alfred Tennyson. These were followed by his major work, *The Epic of Hades* (1876–77), a succession of moral monologues in blank verse spoken by characters from Greek mythology. A companion work, *A Vision of Saints* (1890), followed the same plan, using Christian characters. Morris' simple, melodious, optimistic verse had a wide appeal among his contemporaries, and the *Epic* went through 45 editions; but it has failed to retain its popularity among later generations of readers.

MORRIS, Richard Brandon, American historian: b. New York, N.Y., July 24, 1904. Graduated from The City College, New York (1924), he joined the faculty there in 1927, and in 1949 was appointed professor of history at Columbia University. Morris is a leading specialist in early American legal and labor history; his major works in these areas are *Studies in the History of American Law; with Special Reference to the Seventeenth and Eighteenth Centuries* (1930) and *Government and Labor in Early America* (1946). *Fair Trial* (1952) is a popular but scholarly account of 14 famous American court cases ending with the trial of Alger Hiss. Morris also edited the *Encyclopedia of American History* (1953); *Alexander Hamilton and the Founding of the Nation* (1957); and with Henry Steele Commager, *The Spirit of Seventy-six* (2 vols., 1958). Morris received the Bancroft Prize for *The Peacemakers* (1965), and later served on the American Revolution Bicentennial Commission.

MORRIS, Robert (1734–1806), American merchant and patriot, who was the financier of the American Revolution. He was one of two men (Robert Sherman was the other) who signed all three of the country's basic documents—The Declaration of Independence, the Articles of Confederation, and the U. S. Constitution. He was born in Liverpool, England, on Jan. 31, 1734. He joined his father in America in 1747, and in 1754 he became a partner in the mercantile firm of Willing, Morris & Company of Philadelphia.

Member of Congress. Morris served as a delegate to the Continental Congress from 1775 to 1778. Hoping for a reconciliation with Britain, he refused to vote for the Declaration of Independence, although he later signed it. He quickly gained a remarkable ascendancy over the administrative and business affairs of Congress. As chairman of the Secret Committee of Trade, which handled overseas procurement of military supplies, he built up a network of partnerships and commercial affiliations that was virtually coextensive with Congress' business dealings abroad. He was the most active member of the Marine Committee, which supervised naval affairs, and also served on the Committee of Secret Correspondence, which conducted diplomatic relations.

Morris came under severe personal attack during the controversy between Silas Deane and Arthur Lee, American diplomats to France. Lee charged that Morris and Deane had conspired to defraud the United States, but the rancorous dispute eventually subsided without any clear result. After leaving Congress, with his public character impugned but intact, Morris devoted himself to private business.

Superintendent of Finance. He was recalled by a bankrupt Congress, which on Feb. 20, 1781, elected him superintendent of finance and granted him unprecedented discretionary powers. In September 1781 he was also named agent of marine. His first task was to finance the Yorktown campaign. His efforts provided the money necessary to transport Washington's army to Yorktown, Va., where the British were defeated in the last decisive battle of the war.

Morris then devoted himself to the rehabilitation of the government's finances. Aided by French and, later, Dutch loans, by revenues placed at his disposal by Pennsylvania, and by the early termination of warfare, he established the credit of his administration amid the general insolvency of the government. Disowning all past debts, which he set aside to be funded at a future time, he conserved the cash at his disposal by founding the Bank of North America, the nation's first bank. He launched an extensive circulation of "Morris's notes," which he backed with his personal fortune. He achieved significant economies, notably by introducing contracts for supplying the army. Having paid all the debts he had contracted, he resigned on Nov. 1, 1784, with a small surplus in the treasury.

Brilliantly successful as a financial administrator, Morris nevertheless devoted his main efforts while in office to a broad program of constitutional reform. He was a dedicated nationalist, who contemplated America's rise to "power, consequence and grandeur." His long-range goal was to transform Congress into an effective national government. Throughout his administration he struggled unsuccessfully to secure adoption of the impost, a proposed amendment to the Articles of Confederation granting Congress the power to collect duties on imports. Under his direction, Congress in 1782 took over responsibility for unpaid claims and securities issued during the war, even though as yet no federal revenues existed to discharge them. He thus created a national debt and endeavored to commit the country to a policy predicated on an increase in congressional powers.

COURTESY OF THE PENNSYLVANIA ACADEMY OF FINE ARTS

Robert Morris, financier of the American Revolution.

With the funding by Congress of the Revolutionary debt, Morris associated a broadly conceived reform of the country's economic institutions, which included an increase of domestic capital for business enterprise, the founding of commercial banks, and a national circulation of bank notes to provide a stable medium of exchange in lieu of state paper money. By his integration of constitutional revision with mercantile-capitalist economic reform, Morris founded the program later implemented by the adoption of the Constitution and the enactment of the Hamiltonian funding program.

Later Years. Defeated in his efforts by the end of the war, which diminished the willingness of the states to grant additional powers to Congress, Morris returned to private business, characteristically on a grand scale. In 1785 he secured a contract giving his firm a monopoly of the American tobacco trade with France. In 1789 he was one of a syndicate endeavoring to purchase the American debt owed to France and sell it to Dutch investors.

Morris attended the Constitutional Convention in 1787, was a delegate to a state convention held in 1789 to revise the constitution of Pennsylvania, and served in the U. S. Senate (1789–1795). He was a leading negotiator of the political deal in 1790 in which the location of the permanent national capital on the Potomac River was traded for Virginia votes in favor of federal assumption of state debts.

Morris, meanwhile, had turned to massive speculation in western lands. Overextended, he went bankrupt in 1797, with unpaid debts of $3 million. He was confined to debtors' prison from 1798 to 1801. After his release he lived quietly until his death in Philadelphia on May 8, 1806.

E. JAMES FERGUSON, *Queens College*

Further Reading: Ferguson, E. James, *The Power of the Purse: A History of American Public Finance, 1776–1790* (Univ. of N.C. Press 1961); Ferguson, E. James, and others, eds., *The Papers of Robert Morris*, vols. I–II (Univ. of Pittsburgh Press 1973–1975); Ver Steeg, Clarence L., *Robert Morris, Revolutionary Financier* (Univ. of Pa. Press 1954).

MORRIS, Roger (1727–1794), British soldier and Loyalist in the American Revolution. He was born in Yorkshire, England, on Jan. 28, 1727. Commissioned captain in the British Army in 1745, he fought in several engagements in America during the French and Indian War, serving as aide-de-camp to Generals Gage and Amherst. In 1758 he married Mary Philipse (1730–1825), a reigning beauty of New York society and daughter of Frederick Philipse, second lord of Philipse Manor. Her father gave her as a dowry 51,000 acres (20,600 hectares) in Putnam county. Morris' mansion in Harlem was confiscated in 1776. He died in York, England, on Sept. 13, 1794.

MORRIS, William, English poet, craftsman, and socialist: b. Walthamstow, Essex, England, March 24, 1834; d. Hammersmith, London, Oct. 3, 1896. His father was a prosperous London businessman who left his family well provided for when he died in 1847. Morris spent his boyhood on the outskirts of Epping Forest, where he acquired a lifelong love of nature. He was educated at Marlborough and Exeter College, Oxford; joined a set of pious young men styling themselves the Brotherhood; for a while he thought of taking Holy Orders and considered using his wealth to found a religious community combining asceticism with the production of sacred art. Toward the close of his undergraduate days his religious zeal was replaced by a growing interest in the arts, stimulated by vacation walking tours in northern France. His closest friend during this period, as throughout his life, was the painter Edward Burne-Jones.

Morris even as a boy had been fascinated by the Middle Ages. When he began at Oxford to write poetry it was natural he should turn to that period for inspiration. In 1856 he published a number of his poems in *The Oxford and Cambridge Magazine,* which he founded and supported for its year of existence. That same year, on leaving the university, he became a pupil in the office of G. E. Street, one of the major architects of the Gothic Revival. There he met another of his lifelong friends, Philip Webb, later a distinguished architect.

Through Burne-Jones Morris met Dante Gabriel Rossetti and was persuaded that he should also paint. He left Street's office at the end of 1856 and took a London studio with Burne-Jones. Their difficulties in finding suitable furniture led him to design much of his own, with Webb's assistance, and to join Burne-Jones and Rossetti in decorating it with medieval motifs. This was the beginning of his career in the decorative arts. He spent the summer of 1857 working with Burne-Jones and other friends, under Rossetti's direction, painting upon the walls of the newly built Oxford Union debating hall a series of pictures which, while artistically successful, soon deteriorated because of faulty technique and materials. At this time he met Jane Burden, whose pre-Raphaelite beauty made her one of Rossetti's favorite models; they were married two years later.

In 1858 Morris published his first volume of poems, *The Defence of Guenevere and Other Poems,* a moderate success. His writing was interrupted for the next few years by the building and furnishing at Upton, Kent, of Red House, designed by Webb, strong and simple in line, revealing without stucco or irrelevant trim the red bricks from which it drew its name. It was a milestone in 19th century domestic architecture. Motivated by a passionate desire to have in his house no object which was not both utilitarian and beautiful, he also joined a group of friends in founding Morris, Marshall, Faulkner, and Company, "Fine Art Workmen in Painting, Carving, Furniture, and the Metals" in April 1861. They first specialized in providing stained glass and fittings for the many new churches being built throughout England but gradually won a clientele for their domestic wares. Many of the Morris chintzes, wallpapers, tapestries, and pieces of furniture, well designed and strongly made, are still in service after almost a century of use and the designs are still copied. In 1875 Morris, who did most of the work, bought out his partners and renamed the firm Morris & Co.

After a severe illness brought on by overwork, Morris had been forced to sell Red House in 1865 and move back to London, closer to his workshops. His return to London also saw the beginning of a new poetic phase, during which he wrote *The Life and Death of Jason* (1867) and the three volumes of *The Earthly Paradise* (1868–70), a series of 25 narrative poems on classical and medieval themes whose skillfully constructed framework attests to his close study of Chaucer. These were immediately successful and established his literary reputation.

During 1870 Morris began to study and write illuminated manuscripts, producing several painted books which mark the beginning of the modern calligraphic revival. He also was learning to read Icelandic for his translations of the sagas in *The Story of Sigurd the Volsung* (1877), the poem which he considered his masterpiece. In 1871 he made his first trip to Iceland to retrace the scenes of the epics; in that same year he rented Kelmscott Manor, an early 17th century stone house whose idyllic setting among the Cotswold villages gave him great happiness during his long holidays there. In 1878 he acquired a large Georgian house on the Upper Mall at Hammersmith which he named Kelmscott House. He enjoyed thinking that both were on the banks of the same river and twice traveled the 130 miles between them by boat.

Morris' active participation in public life began in 1876 when he helped to found the Society for the Protection of Ancient Buildings, to defend the remaining early English buildings against overzealous restoration as well as actual destruction. He also became a leader of the Eastern Question Association, formed to protest Turkish treatment of Christian minorities in their European provinces. Until then a passive Liberal, he found himself speaking, circulating petitions, and writing to the press. This experience in politics turned him against Liberalism and led to a re-examination of his ideas on both art and politics; he decided that

Tate Gallery

William Morris' *La Belle Iseult* (1858).

the medieval art which he loved was indivisible from the society which had produced it and that before industrial society could produce comparable work it must be recreated and given new ideals. In 1883 he joined the Democratic Federation; for the next seven years he worked in various branches of the Socialist movement, making street addresses (which brought him into the police courts), writing, lecturing, and editing the *Commonweal,* a Socialist paper which he financed. Two prose romances of this period, *A Dream of John Ball* (1888) and *News from Nowhere* (1891) are among his finest work, rare examples of propaganda which is also art. His interest began to weaken in 1890 as the friction between the rival Socialist groups became irksome and as his health began to suffer from the severe physical and nervous stresses to which he had subjected it, but he remained a Socialist until his death. Most of his energies after 1890 were devoted to the revival of fine printing, his last major achievement.

Since Oxford, where he had admired the Bodleian manuscripts and incunabula, Morris had loved and collected handsome books. In 1871, while writing and illuminating his own manuscripts, he had planned a fine edition of his *Love Is Enough* (1873) for which he had designed initials and borders and which Burne-Jones was to illustrate. A crisis in the affairs of Morris & Co. necessitated abandonment of the original project, but his interest in typography was reawakened in 1884 when he met Emery Walker, a Hammersmith neighbor and fellow Socialist who combined a practical knowledge of printing with a great love of early books. After supervising the design and production of two of his own books without satisfactory results, he resolved to establish his own press at which he would create modern books equaling those of the 15th century. With Walker's aid he designed a type face based upon Nicolas Jenson's roman letter and early in 1891 began printing in a cottage near Kelmscott House. During the brief career of the Kelmscott Press (it closed in 1898, two years after Morris' death) it issued 53 books printed on the hand press, on handmade paper, and bound by hand, in three fonts of type designed by its proprietor. Morris also designed for it an enormous amount of decorative material. While modern taste may find the folio Chaucer, his greatest book, overdecorated and unreadable, its historical importance in bringing about the revival of fine printing and in creating new interest in book design is undeniable.

William Morris was among the most notable of the Victorians for his vitality, his range, his genius, and his enormous influence upon others. His lifelong love for the arts and crafts, his conviction that great art was the inevitable fruit of a sound society, and his idealized view of the Middle Ages coupled with an intense hatred of his own industrialized era led him inevitably to political engagement. His was a nature that could not tolerate passive acceptance of what he considered brutal or evil. He was an original and versatile designer, with a genius for adapting natural forms into pleasing decorative patterns; his love of decoration permeated his writing, his designing, his printing, all the many works to which he turned his hand. His influence has lasted; in 1955 the William Morris Society was organized to stimulate interest in his ideas and works.

JAMES M. WELLS
The Newberry Library, Chicago

Bibliography

Henderson, Philip, *William Morris* (McGraw 1967).
Mackail, John W., *The Life of William Morris* (1899; reprint, *World's Classics,* Oxford 1950).
Thompson, Edward P., *William Morris, Romantic and Revolutionary* (Lawrence 1955).
Thompson, Paul, *The Work of William Morris* (Viking 1967).
Vallance, Aymer, *The Art of William Morris* (1897).
Watkinson, Raymond, *William Morris as Designer* (Reinhold 1967).

MORRIS, Wright, American novelist, whose works, frequently using the Nebraska prairie as their locale, focus on the American character and experience. He was born in Central City, Nebr., on Jan. 6, 1910. According to his own account, his early years were spent "in the whistle stops along the Platte Valley to the west"—a childhood that was a major shaping influence on his writing. After travel in the United States, study at Pomona College in California (1930–1933), and trips to Europe, he began to write. His first novel, *My Uncle Dudley,* a picaresque account of a peripatetic journey from Los Angeles to Chicago, was published in 1942.

Generally, in his novels Morris re-creates small-town American life, perceptively depicting middle-class people through a blend of present reality and nostalgia for the past. Critics have described his penetrating, delineative style as photographic. In fact, the text of some of his books, such as the highly regarded *The Home Place* (1948), is accompanied by his own photographs to evoke mood and a sense of place.

Morris' other books include *The World in the Attic* (1949), *The Deep Sleep* (1953), *Love Among the Cannibals* (1957), and *A Life* (1973). For *The Field of Vision* (1956) he won the National Book Award for fiction.

MORRIS, city, Illinois, seat of Grundy County, 21 miles southwest of Joliet, on the Illinois River, at an altitude of 520 feet. It is served by the Chicago, Rock Island and Pacific Railroad, and is on the Lakes to Gulf Waterway and a state highway. Settled in 1834, it was laid out in 1842 and named for Isaac N. Morris, one of the Illinois and Michigan Canal commissioners who was responsible for its selection as the county seat. It was incorporated in 1853. The city is governed by a mayor and council.

Morris is a manufacturing and shipping point for the area, with coalfields nearby and clay beds used for brick and tile. Other industries include paper mills, machinery, food products, and flour mills. Dresden Nuclear Power Station, the first nuclear power plant in Illinois, was opened in Morris in 1959. Pop. 8,194.

MORRIS BROWN COLLEGE, a coeducational college of liberal arts in Atlanta, Ga., under control of the African Methodist Episcopal Church. The campus occupies 21 acres. Established in 1881 as Morris Brown University, it was chartered and first offered instruction in 1885. Its name was changed to its present form in 1932. The college is named for Bishop Morris Brown (1770–1849), a prominent free Negro religious leader in the pre-Civil War period. In addition to programs for the training of elementary and secondary school teachers, the college offers preprofessional training in law, medicine, business, the ministry, and social work.

MORRIS DANCE, English folk dance supposed to have been derived from the Moriscos in Spain and introduced into England by John of Gaunt in the latter part of the 14th century. Despite its origins, the dance is closely associated with the folk culture of the British people. Suppressed by the Puritans along with the May games, of which it was an important part, it survived and enjoyed a revival in modified form at the turn of the 20th century. Its form since its introduction has been a group of six men and a fool, a boy dressed as a woman (Maid Marian), and the Hobby Horse. All of the performers wear outlandish costumes and blackened faces and are accompanied by musicians with drum, violin, or accordion.

MORRIS ISLAND, island, South Carolina, at the south entrance to the harbor of Charleston. It is east of James Island, nearly a mile south of Fort Sumter, and about a mile and a half from Fort Moultrie. The island's guns took part in the bombardment of Fort Sumter on April 12–13, 1861, and the Confederates subsequently constructed two major emplacements there—Battery Gregg on the northern tip and the formidable Battery (Fort) Wagner to the south. After a bitter struggle lasting almost two months, the island fell to Union forces on the night of Sept. 6–7, 1863.

MORRISON, mŏr'ĭ-s'n, **Arthur,** British author: b. Kent, England, Nov. 1, 1863; d. Chalfont St. Peter, Dec. 4, 1945. He began his career as a journalist in the early 1880's in London, and worked for a time under William Ernest Henley on the *National Observer,* which first published his stories of the London slums, collected as *Tales of Mean Streets* (1894). *A Child of the Jago* (1896), a full-length novel on the same theme, contributed to the decision of the London County Council to demolish the district in which it was set. *The Hole in the Wall* (1902), another novel of London low life, was artistically perhaps his best book. Morrison also wrote a series of detective stories centered on the fictional character of Martin Hewitt, beginning with *Martin Hewitt: Investigator* (1894) and concluding with *The Green Eye of Goona* (1904). An enthusiastic collector of Oriental art, he wrote *The Painters of Japan* (2 vols., 1911), a history of art in that country from early times. His collection of Chinese and Japanese painting is in the British Museum.

MORRISON, Sir Herbert (Stanley), 1st Baron Morrison of Lambeth, British statesman: b. London, England, Jan. 3, 1888; d. Sidcup, Kent, England, March 6, 1965. He went to work at 14, and later joined the Social Democratic Federation. A conscientious objector in World War I, he became secretary of the London organization of the Labour Party in 1915 and held that post until 1947; concurrently he was a member of the London County Council (1922–1945) and its leader (1934–1940). He thus became one of the Labour Party's leading authorities on municipal affairs and was responsible for much new housing and school construction in London. When World War II began, he organized the evacuation of 1,200,000 women and children from London and other dangerous areas.

In national affairs, Morrison represented various London constituencies in Parliament in 1923–1924, 1929–1931, and continuously thereafter from 1935. When Labour took office in 1929, he was named minister of transport, resigning (1931) when Ramsay MacDonald formed a coalition with the Conservatives. During the 1930's Morrison emerged as the leader of the right-wing Labourites, opposed to united front with the Communists. In May 1940 he entered Winston Churchill's national government as minister of supply, and from October of that year to the end of World War II he held the important post of home secretary, from 1942 as a member of the inner War Cabinet.

In the Labour government formed in July 1945, Morrison became second in command to Clement Attlee, with the office of deputy prime minister and leader of the House of Commons. Like Attlee, he favored a moderate policy, and socialization was carried out in only a few sectors of the national economy. When Ernest Bevin resigned (March 1951) as foreign minister, Morrison took the post, which he held until the government left office in October. Among his books are *How London Is Governed* (1949), *The Peaceful Revolution* (1949), and *Government and Parliament: a Survey from the Inside* (1954).

MORRISON, city, Illinois, seat of Whiteside County, situated at an altitude of 670 feet, on the Chicago and North Western Railway, 12 miles east of Clinton, Iowa. The center of a dairy farming area, the city has milk-processing plants as well as factories producing refrigerators, stoves, automatic control devices, and furniture. Nearby is Unionville Mill, erected in 1858 and still grinding flour and feed. Morrison was founded in 1853 and incorporated in 1867. In 1874 the inventor James Sargent installed his first time lock on the door of the safe in the First National Bank of Morrison. The city is governed by a mayor and council. Population: 4,387.

NATIONAL PARK SERVICE PHOTO

Diorama at Morristown National Historical Park shows Washington greeting Lafayette at the Ford Mansion.

MORRISTOWN, in northern New Jersey, is a town on the Whippany River, 16 miles (26 km) northwest of Newark. It is the seat of Morris county. Although the area is primarily residential, it has important research laboratories and chemical, engineering, and paper industries.

The townsite was settled around 1710, after iron had been discovered in the vicinity. At first called New Hanover, the community was renamed in 1739 for Lewis Morris, governor of New Jersey. Morristown played a prominent part in the American Revolution. It was a Patriot military base, and its iron forges and powder mills supplied munitions to the Continental Army. At Morristown in 1837–1838, Samuel Morse and Alfred Vail developed the telegraph. Later in the century the town became the home of millionaires and celebrities.

The community's chief point of interest is Morristown National Historical Park, consisting of sites relating to the Revolutionary War. Also of interest are the Schuyler-Hamilton House (1760), where Alexander Hamilton successfully courted Elizabeth Schuyler, and the Morris Museum of Arts and Sciences.

Morristown was incorporated in 1865. It has a mayor-council form of government. Population: 17,662. See also MORRISTOWN NATIONAL HISTORICAL PARK.

MORRISTOWN, a city in east central Tennessee, is the seat of Hamblen county, about 40 miles (64 km) east-northeast of Knoxville. Its chief products are dairy products and furniture. Two junior colleges, Morristown College and Walters State Community College, are here. Crockett Tavern and Museum, a reconstruction of the tavern that was the boyhood home of David Crockett, is a landmark. Skymart, an overhead sidewalk, gives access to the second floor of all buildings on Main Street. The city was incorporated in 1855 and has a council-manager government. Population: 20,318.

MORRISTOWN NATIONAL HISTORICAL PARK, in northern New Jersey, was created in 1933 as a memorial to George Washington and the Continental Army. It consists of three units occupying 1,224 acres (496 hectares) in and near Morristown.

During the American Revolutionary War, Morristown was Washington's headquarters from January to May 1777 and from December 1779 to June 1780. With the British holding New York City, Washington used Morristown as a base from which he could move troops to the Hudson or Delaware valley, depending on which way the British marched.

Ford Mansion. General and Mrs. Washington spent the winter of 1779–1780 at the Ford Mansion in Morristown. Built in 1774, the house has authentic period furnishings. Behind it is the Historical Museum and Library, containing Washington memorabilia, displays of weapons, and documents relating to the war.

Fort Nonsense. The reconstructed earthwork known as Fort Nonsense is on a hill in Morristown. The original was probably built at Washington's orders in 1777. Its name reflects the later suspicion that it had been a make-work project for the troops encamped nearby.

Jockey Hollow. The site of the Continental Army's encampment during the winter of 1779–1780 is Jockey Hollow, 3 miles (5 km) southwest of Morristown. An area of wooded hills, streams, and flowers, it is preserved as a wildlife sanctuary. Log huts and a hospital hut like those used by the troops have been reconstructed. The Tempe Wick House, also in Jockey Hollow, is a restored farmhouse of the period.

MORRISVILLE, a borough in southeastern Pennsylvania, in Bucks county, is directly across the Delaware River from Trenton, N. J. It is mainly a residential community.

Robert Morris, one of the signers of the Declaration of Independence, had plans to make Morrisville the capital of the new nation. The government appropriated money for the purchase of land here, but in 1790, Secretary of the Treasury Alexander Hamilton threw his support to a plan to move the capital to a site on the Potomac River. As a result, Morrisville lost its bid by two votes. Morrisville was named for Robert Morris and incorporated in 1804. It has a council-manager form of government. Population: 11,309.

MORRO CASTLE, the name of two fortifications in Cuba. The first is at the east side of the entrance to Havana Harbor; built by the Spaniards in 1589–1597, it was taken by the British under Admiral Sir George Pocock in 1762, and bombarded by United States forces in the Spanish American War. The second, at Santiago de Cuba, was built soon after the first.

In Old San Juan, Puerto Rico, the massive fortress called El Morro dominates the landscape.

MORRO CASTLE DISASTER. Early on Sept. 8, 1934, the S.S. *Morro Castle,* carrying tourists from Havana to New York, caught fire and burned off the coast of New Jersey with the loss of 137 lives. The ship's captain had died of a heart attack some eight hours before the fire began. The acting captain and other officers were later charged with several counts of negligence.

MORROW, Dwight Whitney, American lawyer, banker, and diplomat: b. Huntington, W. Va., Jan. 11, 1873; d. Englewood, N. J., Oct. 5, 1931. He was educated at Amherst College, where he was a classmate of Calvin Coolidge, and from which he received his B.A. degree in 1895. Upon his graduation from Columbia Law School in 1899, he entered the employ of the law firm of Reed, Simpson, Thacher and Barnum (later Simpson, Thacher and Bartlett), of which he was made a member in 1905. He maintained this connection until 1914, when he joined the banking firm of J. P. Morgan & Co., with which he was associated until 1927. Morrow helped to frame the workmen's compensation law of New Jersey in 1911, and as a member of the New Jersey Prison Inquiry Commission (1917) and chairman of the state board of institutions and agencies (1918–1920) brought about many reforms. In 1918 he served as adviser to the Allied Maritime Transport Council. In 1927, President Coolidge appointed him ambassador to Mexico. He served in this capacity for three years, doing much to improve American-Mexican relations. Among other achievements, he succeeded in settling disputes over oil rights and aided materially in resolving the conflict between the Mexican government and the Roman Catholic Church. In 1930 he was a delegate to the London Naval Conference, and later that year was elected to the United States Senate to fill the unexpired term of Walter E. Edge.

His wife, ELIZABETH MORROW (nee CUTTER, 1873–1955), whom he married in 1903, wrote several volumes of prose and poetry and in 1939–1940 served as acting president of Smith College. Their daughter, Anne Spencer Morrow, married Charles A. Lindbergh (q.v.) in 1929.

MORROW, William W., American jurist: b. near Milton, Ind., July 15, 1843; d. San Francisco, Calif., July 24, 1929. He moved to California in 1859, was admitted to the bar in 1869, and engaged in the practice of law in San Francisco. From 1870 to 1874 he served as assistant United States district attorney, and from 1879 to 1882 he was chairman of the Republican state central committee. He was attorney of the state board of harbor commissioners (1880–1883), special attorney for the United States before the French and American Claims Commission (1881–1883), and special United States attorney in connection with the *Alabama* claims (1882–1885). From 1885 to 1891 he was a member of Congress. Morrow was a member of the federal judiciary for 32 years, serving as judge of the federal court of the northern district of California (1891–1897), and of the circuit court and circuit court of appeals (1897–1923). His decisions, many of them on important constitutional questions, are said to have totaled more than 650. He was also the author of *An Introduction to California Jurisprudence.*

MORS, môrs, or **MORSO,** môrs'û, island, Denmark, situated in Lim Fjord, Thisted County, in northwestern Jutland. The largest island in the fjord, it has an area of 142 square miles. The shores are marked by precipitous cliffs, and the interior rises to a height of 289 feet. Nykjøbing is the chief town.

MORSE, Edward Sylvester, American zoologist: b. Portland, Me., June 18, 1838; d. Salem, Mass., Dec. 20, 1925. He studied conchology for three years as a special student of Louis Agassiz at the Lawrence Scientific School, Harvard University. After teaching zoology and comparative anatomy at Bowdoin College (1871–1874), he went to Japan and taught at the Imperial University in Tokyo (1877–1880). On this and subsequent visits to the Orient, he added to his knowledge of zoology a remarkable intimacy with Chinese and Japanese art, especially ceramics, and with the folklore and archaeology of both China and Japan. His collection of Japanese pottery was acquired by the Boston Museum of Fine Arts, and he served as its curator after 1892. From 1880 until his death he was director of the Peabody Museum in Salem. Besides numerous scientific papers on zoology, ethnology, and archaeology, he was the author of *First Book of Zoölogy* (1875); *Japanese Homes and Their Surroundings* (1886); *Glimpses of China and Chinese Homes* (1902); *Mars and Its Mystery* (1906); and *Japan Day by Day* (2 vols., 1917).

MORSE, Harmon Northrop, American chemist: b. Cambridge, Vt., Oct. 15, 1848; d. Chebeague Island, Me., Sept. 8, 1920. He was graduated from Amherst College in 1873 and received his doctorate from the University of Göttingen in 1875. He was assistant in chemistry at Amherst (1875–1876), a member of the staff of the chemistry department of Johns Hopkins University (1876–1883), associate professor of chemistry there (1883–1892), professor of analytical chemistry and adjunct director of the laboratory (1892–1908), and professor of inorganic and analytical chemistry and director of the laboratory (1908–1916). He also served for a number of years as research associate of the Carnegie Institution, Washington, D.C. Morse investigated new methods of quantitative analysis, did research on permanganic acid and its salts, and accumulated data on the osmotic pressure of aqueous solutions. In addition to about 60 scientific articles, he published *Exercises in Quantitative Chemistry* (1905); and *The Osmotic Pressure of Aqueous Solutions,* Carnegie Institution Monograph No. 198 (1914).

His brother, ANSON DANIEL MORSE (1846–1916), was an educator and historian. He taught at Amherst College from 1876 to 1907 and wrote a number of studies on American political parties.

MORSE, Jedidiah, American clergyman and geographer: b. Woodstock, Conn., Aug. 23, 1761;

d. New Haven, June 9, 1826. He graduated from Yale College in 1783, remained for two more years to study theology, and was ordained in 1786. For 30 years, from 1789, he was pastor of the First Congregational Church in Charlestown, Mass. Strongly conservative in his views and opposed to Unitarianism, he founded a periodical, the *Panoplist* (1805), which set forth the orthodox point of view and deepened the split between orthodox Congregationalists and Unitarians. Morse was one of the founders of Andover Theological Seminary (1808), the New England Tract Society (1814), and the American Bible Society (1816), as well as a vigorous Federalist periodical, the *Mercury and New England Palladium* (1801). He also wrote the valuable *Compendious History of New England* (with Elijah Parish, 1804) and *Annals of the American Revolution* (1824).

Morse is remembered especially for his widely circulated geographical texts, which for the first time gave adequate attention to American geography. The first geography to be published in the United States was his *Geography Made Easy* (1784), which was followed by *The American Geography* (1789), later published as *The American Universal Geography; Elements of Geography* (1795); *The American Gazetteer* (1797); and *A New Gazetteer of the Eastern Continent* (with Elijah Parish, 1802). Samuel F. B. Morse (q.v.) was his son.

Sidney Edwards Morse (1794–1817), another son, was the founder, proprietor, and editor (1823–1858) of the Congregationalist newspaper, the *Observer,* in New York City. He collaborated with his father on *A New System of Geography* (1822), a widely popular text; and, beginning about 1835, worked out a new process of printing maps, which he called cerography and applied in various atlases issued as supplements to the *Observer.* He also published *A Geographical, Statistical and Ethical View of the American Slave-holders' Rebellion* (1863) and *Memorabilia in the Life of Jedidiah Morse* (1867).

Consult Morse, James K., *Jedidiah Morse: a Champion of New England Orthodoxy* (New York 1939).

MORSE, John Torrey, American historian: b. Boston, Mass., Jan. 9, 1840; d. Needham, March 27, 1937. Graduated from Harvard in 1860 and admitted to the bar in 1862, he practiced law until 1880 without much distinction, although his treatises *Law Relating to Banks and Banking* (1870) and *Law of Arbitration and Award* (1872) were well received. In 1879 he became a member of the Board of Overseers of Harvard, a position he held until 1891, becoming associated with Henry Cabot Lodge and Henry Adams, and with the former editing the *International Review* for four years. After publishing the biography *Alexander Hamilton* (1876), Morse initiated and arranged for the publication of the highly successful American Statesmen series of historical biographies (1882–1916). He himself served as editor and contributed biographies of Abraham Lincoln, Benjamin Franklin, Thomas Jefferson, John Adams, and John Quincy Adams. He later published lives of Oliver Wendell Holmes (1896) and Col. Henry Lee (1906).

MORSE, Samuel Finley Breese, American artist and inventor: b. Charlestown, Mass., April 27, 1791; d. New York, N.Y., April 2, 1872. The eldest son of Jedidiah Morse (q.v.), he began painting miniatures on ivory before graduating from Yale in 1810, and desired to study under Washington Allston. His parents discouraged him, but their opposition was withdrawn after a large painting, *The Landing of the Pilgrims at Plymouth,* was judged to be of great promise by Allston and Gilbert Stuart. In June 1811 Morse went to England as Allston's pupil, returning to the United States in 1815. He hoped, he said, to recapture the beauty and power of 15th century Italian painting. At that time, however, an artist in the United States could find no work except in portraiture. Morse accepted this limitation of opportunity and, after his return from Europe, worked industriously on portraits. The contemporary diarist, Philip Hone, writing in May 1833, said of him: "He is an excellent fellow and is well acquainted with the principles of his art; but he has no imagination. He makes good portraits, strong likenesses; . . . but he cannot design. There is no poetry about his paintings" (*The Diary of Philip Hone,* ed. by Allan Nevins, New York 1927, p. 93).

Samuel F. B. Morse

Bettmann Archive

In November 1825 Morse became a leader of the professional artists and students who were dissatisfied with John Trumbull's management of the American Academy of Fine Arts. On Jan. 14, 1826, the National Academy of the Arts of Design (now the National Academy of Design) was established, largely through Morse's efforts. He became its first president, holding the office until 1845 and again for a year in 1861–1862. He also gave a series of lectures on art which he believed were the first to be given in the United States. In 1832 he was appointed professor of painting and sculpture at the University of the City of New York (now New York University), becoming professor of the literature of the arts of design in 1835. The latter appointment gave him rooms in the university buildings, which enabled him to work more conveniently on the telegraph. As the buildings were not completed, portrait work was difficult; progressive concentration on the telegraph soon made the temporary interruption a final break with painting. There is only one portrait painted by Morse after 1837.

Invention of the Telegraph.—Morse's scientific and mechanical interests had appeared at an early date. With his brother Sidney Edwards Morse (see under Morse, Jedidiah), he had taken out three patents on pumps in 1817. A machine for carving marble from a model was developed in 1823, and after 1822 he showed a continuous interest in electrical experimentation.

Morse took a house in New Haven near Prof. Benjamin Silliman and was a constant visitor in Silliman's laboratory; he also developed a close friendship with Prof. James Freeman Dana of the University of the City of New York. In 1827 Morse attended a course of lectures on electricity by Dana, at which the electromagnet was demonstrated.

These interests were brought to a sharp focus by a conversation in the cabin of the ship *Sully* in October 1832, when Morse was returning from a three-year sojourn in Europe. Dr. Charles Thomas Jackson described some recent experiments with electricity in Paris, which seemed to involve little that was new. Morse, however, reacted sharply. The problem of telegraphy occupied him for the remainder of the voyage, and all the essential features of the telegraph, as constructed later, were set down in notebooks. He made a rough model soon after reaching New York City, but the work was discontinued for an interval. It was resumed late in 1835, after Morse settled in his rooms at the university. With the assistance of Prof. Leonard Dunnell Gale, he constructed a model, which he demonstrated to a few friends. The problem of long-distance transmission was clearly vital. The elements of a relay system were worked out late in 1835 or in January 1836. The work was not pushed forward with much energy in 1836, but a concentrated effort began early in 1837. The equipment was improved, and more ambitious demonstrations were given, notably on Sept. 2 and 4, 1837.

These achievements interested Alfred Vail, the son of a New Jersey ironmaster, and his brother and father. An agreement was signed for their participation in the development of the invention in return for a share in the patent. Their financial support and Alfred Vail's skill as a mechanic were essential to the presentation of the project to Congress. A caveat, looking toward an application for a patent, was acknowledged on Oct. 6, 1837, and in April 1838 a bill was introduced in Congress to grant $30,000 for the construction of a line between Washington and Baltimore. The bill was not brought to vote at this session, but a patent was applied for and was issued on June 20, 1840. Efforts to secure patents in England failed because of prior applications by Sir Charles Wheatstone and Edward Davy. The French patent could not be used, as it was not possible to construct a line in France at that time. The grant for the line to Baltimore was voted in the last hour of the session of the Senate on March 3, 1843. Despite difficulties in insulating the wires, the line was constructed with the aid of Ezra Cornell, and the first message was sent on May 24, 1844—"What hath God wrought!"

Morse and the Vails wished to sell their rights to the United States for $100,000, but the government was unwilling to take them. The Baltimore line was operated by a private company established by Morse, and new lines were soon projected. The prospects of large profits led to attempts to use the Morse system without payment of royalties, and several suits were brought, beginning with litigation in the Circuit Court of Kentucky in 1848. The court upheld Morse's patent, and in 1854 the Supreme Court sustained the decision.

Morse was largely dependent on dividends from the telegraph companies, and even in 1850 his income was small and precarious. There were no patents in Europe or in England, but 10 European countries combined in 1858 to pay him a gratuity of 400,000 francs as compensation for their use of his system. Many decorations were conferred on him in recognition of his achievement.

In 1842 Morse had demonstrated the possibility of using submarine cable, but he did little technical work on the laying of the Atlantic cable. The burden of the affairs of the telegraph companies was largely carried by Amos Kendall. Morse's last public act was the unveiling of the statue of Benjamin Franklin in Printing House Square, New York City, in January 1872. He died of pneumonia soon after.

See also TELEGRAPH.

Bibliography.—Prime, Samuel I., *Life of Samuel F. B. Morse* (New York 1875); Trowbridge, John, *Samuel Finley Breese Morse* (Boston 1901); Morse, Edward L., *Samuel F. B. Morse: His Letters and Journals,* 2 vols. (Boston 1914); Mabee, Carleton, *The American Leonardo: the Life of S. F. B. Morse* (New York 1957).

ABBOTT PAYSON USHER
Harvard University

MORSE, Wayne Lyman, American senator: b. Madison, Wis., Oct. 20, 1900; d. Portland, Oreg., July 22, 1974. After he graduated from the University of Wisconsin (1923), he took his law degree at the University of Minnesota (1928) and a doctorate in law at Columbia (1932). In 1929 he was appointed assistant professor of law at the University of Oregon, where he was full professor and dean of the Law School from 1931 to 1944. During this period Morse made a study of criminal law procedure in Oregon and became known as one of the country's leading labor arbitrators, serving as special assistant to the United States attorney general (1936–1939), Pacific Coast arbitrator of disputes between shipowners and labor unions (1938–1942), chairman of the President's Railway Emergency Board (1941), and public member of the National War Labor Board (1942–1944). In 1944 he was elected United States senator from Oregon on the Republican ticket, and was reelected in 1950. In the presidential campaign of 1952, however, he resigned from the Republican Party and gave his support to the Democratic candidate, Adlai E. Stevenson, thus losing important posts in the Senate. He became a Democrat officially in 1954, and in 1956 and 1962 was reelected to the Senate on the Democratic ticket. He was defeated for reelection in 1968. Morse had also sought, unsuccessfully, the Democratic presidential nomination in 1960.

A courageous and individualistic legislator, Morse claimed he voted "according to the merits of the issue without concern for party expediency." He was a strong proponent of labor and internationalism and one of President Eisenhower's sharpest critics. An early and vehement critic of the Vietnam War, in 1964 he was one of two members of Congress to vote against the Tonkin Gulf Resolution, which President Johnson used as a functional declaration of war. Morse opposed all appropriations bills for the war.

MORSE CODE. See SIGNALING—*Signal Lamps and Semaphore;* TELEGRAPH—*Theory and Technology.*

MORTALITY. See LIFE EXPECTANCY; POPULATION—*Growth of World Population.*

MORTAR, môr′tẽr, in armament, a complete projectile-firing weapon, rifled or smooth bore, characterized by a short barrel, low velocity, short range, and high angle of fire. An infantry mortar is a muzzle-loaded weapon, usually having a smooth bore whose diameter is less than 105 mm. An artillery mortar is a similar weapon whose bore diameter is 105 mm. or larger. Mortars are used to reach nearby targets that are protected or concealed by intervening hills or other short-range barriers.

The earliest weapons using gunpowder, developed from the ballista, might be classified as mortars; from these early mortar-type weapons, guns and howitzers were later developed. Mortars were used to a limited extent in the early period for siege purposes. Their use was revived in the latter part of the 19th century for coast defense. Ships were built with heavy side armor, but their relatively thin deck armor offered an attractive mortar target. A considerable number of 12-inch mortars were installed in harbor defenses.

In World War I, trench warfare resulted in the development of infantry and artillery mortars. At the beginning of the war the Germans used *Minenwerfer* designed and built in 1911. Both the French and British rapidly developed infantry and artillery mortars to meet the conditions imposed by trench warfare. Calibers ranged from 2 inches to 340 mm. As a result of this experience, mortars were integrated as weapons in the infantry units of all armies.

During World War II a requirement developed for close-support weapons, supplementing the artillery coverage, to prevent the enemy from manning his weapons in the interval between the lifting of the artillery barrage and attainment of the objective. Since hostile forces were normally entrenched in defensive positions, plunging fire was essential. Mortars met the need for weapons that were readily transported, capable of immediate action, and suited to fire from defilade in front-line emplacements. The mortars at the beginning of the war were the small 60 mm. and 81 mm. As the war progressed, the need for larger mortars was indicated, and weapons of medium caliber, the 105 mm. and 155 mm., were provided to blast the enemy from strong points and machine-gun bunkers. Small mortars gave maximum firepower, in terms of the ratio of weight of materiel to ammunition delivered at the target, to infantry engaged in jungle and rough terrain. Based upon experience in World War II and in Korea, infantry and artillery mortars have become an essential weapon for ground troops.

See also ARTILLERY—*Types of Artillery;* PROJECTILES—*Mortar Projectiles.*

JOHN D. BILLINGSLEY,
Professor of Ordnance, United States Military Academy.

MORTAR, in building, a mixture of lime, cement, and sand, worked with sufficient water to form a uniform paste that can be handled with a trowel and applied between bricks, stones, concrete blocks, or other materials to bind them together in masonry walls and buildings. Good mortar sticks to the surface of the bricks or stones on which it is buttered and, when properly mixed and used, hardens to lock them together, becoming part of a solid masonry structure that is weather resistant and durable. It is laid ¼- to ½-inch thick between the courses and the ends of the bricks or stones. From ¼ to ⅓ cubic yard is needed for each cubic yard of brick masonry, which requires some 500 bricks.

There are several formulas for making mortar, all using cement, lime, or a mixture of the two, with sand. That most used now in brick construction consists of one part portland cement, one part lime, and three parts sand. About 10 to 15 per cent of portland cement itself is hydrated lime, and a very strong mortar is made by using one part cement to three parts sand, but it is more easily worked if additional lime is mixed in. For some types of work, masons still prefer lime mortar, once the most commonly used. It is made by adding one part of slaked lime to three or four of sand, and mixing with water. This is the easiest to work, but it is comparatively low in strength. Plaster of paris is used in another variety, either with grout, a thin liquid mixture of lime or cement, or combined with lime and grout or with lime, sand, and grout. It sets rapidly and is useful for pointing, or patching, breaks in old mortar. Preblended commercial mortars are available, to which the user need only add water. They consist of lime, cement, sand, a waterproofer, bonding chemicals, plasticity agents, and a variety of other ingredients to make them versatile. Forms of mortar are employed in plastering (q.v.) interiors and for stucco (q.v.).

Primitive mortars were chiefly mud or a mixture of clay, water, and chopped straw, as in Egypt, Mesopotamia, and early Greece. Later Greek and early Roman stone structures were built without mortar, but the Romans eventually developed a strong cement mortar that gained favor and was used, with modifications, throughout medieval times and ever since.

FRANK DORR,
Associate Editor of "Popular Science Monthly."

MORTE DARTHUR, Le, môrt där′thẽr, a collection of Arthurian romances, the most widely read of all the works of English literature produced in the 15th century. From the closing sentence we learn that it was written by Sir Thomas Malory (q.v.), knight, and that it was completed in the ninth year of the reign of Edward IV, that is, within the 12 months ending March 3, 1470. Its composition was probably spread over many years. It was printed by England's first printer, William Caxton, in 1485 and frequently reprinted by Caxton's successors down to 1634. After a lapse of nearly two centuries it was again issued from the press in 1816 (and frequently thereafter) and thus became the inspiration for Alfred Tennyson's *Idylls of the King* and for modern treatments of individual stories by William Morris, Algeron Charles Swinburne, Matthew Arnold, James Russell Lowell, Edwin Arlington Robinson, and many others.

Until 1934 Malory's great work was known only from the text of Caxton, of which two copies have survived. Later editions were all reprints of Caxton's text, whether at first or at second hand. In 1934, however, a manuscript was discovered in the Fellows' Library of Winchester College which had not previously been recognized, presumably because it had lost several leaves both at the beginning and the end. Study revealed that, while not the copy from which Caxton printed his edition, it was in many ways more complete than Caxton's version and closer to what Malory had written. It is now evident that Caxton severely condensed Malory's text in places, divided it into books and chapters, and took other editorial liberties. A new edition based on the Winchester manuscript was published by Eugène Vinaver in 1947.

It is now apparent that the *Morte Darthur* was not a single unified work written on a previously conceived plan, but rather a collection of eight separate units not all written in the order in which they appear in the finished book. The first to be written was the "Tale of King Arthur and the Emperor Lucius" (book 5 in Caxton's edition), to which Malory prefixed the "Tale of King Arthur," the story of Arthur's birth and early life and of Merlin (Caxton, books 1–4). The remaining tales—of Lancelot, Gareth, Tristram, the Holy Grail, Lancelot and Guinevere, and the death of Arthur—were seemingly composed in the order in which they stand. The name of the work is properly applicable only to the last of the series.

Sources.—Caxton, in the introduction to his edition, tells us that Malory took his material "out of certain books of French and reduced it into English." This is in general true, but it is not a complete statement of Malory's sources. In the "Tale of King Arthur and the Emperor Lucius" he depended mainly upon an older romance in English, the *Morte Arthure* in alliterative verse. He often follows the wording of the poem closely, even preserving the alliteration, but his narrative is no slavish paraphrase. Not only does he omit a long section at the end that relates the downfall of King Arthur and the Round Table, but he eliminates all that foreshadows this final catastrophe. As a result, this section of his book is only half the length of the poem that he was following.

Malory did much the same with the long French cycle of romances in prose from which he drew much of the remaining material for his great work. There were two such prose cycles: one known as the Walter Map or, because it enjoyed the widest popularity, the Vulgate cycle; the other, derived from it, known as the Robert de Boron cycle. (In spite of the fact that both alleged authors of these cycles are well-known 12th and 13th century writers, the attributions of authorship must be rejected.) It is on the whole most likely that—except for the parts of his work which he drew from the very long prose *Lancelot* (which only the Vulgate cycle included) and the equally long prose *Tristan*—the "French book" to which Malory refers was made up of romances in the form in which they appear in the Robert de Boron cycle. Unfortunately, this cycle is preserved in French only in fragmentary form, and its contents must be inferred partly from Spanish and Portuguese translations or derivatives. Consequently, we are somewhat handicapped in studying Malory's literary methods except in those sections of his book for which we have texts much like those in the manuscript or manuscripts he was using.

Malory's Contribution.—A comparison of the *Morte Darthur* with these texts gives us considerable insight into Malory's practice. Caxton's statement that Malory "reduced" his French material into English could conceivably mean no more than that he translated it. This is not the case. He often condensed his material severely. His story of Tristram, which is one of the longer units of his work, is only one sixth the length of his original, and from the French prose *Lancelot* (which is as long as Charles Dickens' *David Copperfield*) he selected only three widely separated sections that form a fairly coherent sequence. Another of his literary practices is even more important. In the cyclical romances, episodes are constantly interlaced: an incident is related, suspended while the action of another character is introduced, resumed, interrupted again while the author takes up another thread of the story or goes off on a digression, and so on until the incident is terminated or dropped for good. While there is not a little of this medieval narrative technique in the *Morte Darthur,* it was clearly not to Malory's taste, and in many places he has brought together related incidents and arranged them in a more coherent sequence so that the result more nearly resembles the pattern of a modern novel. Finally, his art is selective. He clearly preferred the action of human characters, together with their natural impulses and motives, to the subtleties of mystical and theological interpretation. His interest is in the ideals of knighthood and chivalry, and both in his choice of incidents and in his treatment of them he is concerned with the basic virtues which constituted these ideals.

Mallory's greatest contribution in the *Morte Darthur* and the quality which, more than anything else, has kept it alive for nearly five centuries, is his narrative skill and distinguished prose style. In an age when the prose of many writers is but a chain of loosely connected clauses, Malory's sentences are crisp and businesslike. They seem to reflect his character. He gives evidence of a vigorous mind, for his thinking is logical and straightforward. Above all, he had grasped the idea of the sentence as a unit of thought. He makes much use of conversation, and his dialogue is natural and unforced. When his characters speak, what they say is so simply and directly expressed that it has the quality of inevitability. Malory was a man of action. If it is true that style is the man himself, as the comte de Buffon said, the conclusion can hardly be far wrong that Malory's prose embodies the decision and forthrightness of character suggested by the facts of his life.

It may be wondered how Malory managed to obtain the books—some of them large and costly—which he must have had in order to produce his great collection of romances. The explanation is possibly to be found in the fact that the house of the Grey Friars in London, which almost adjoined Newgate prison, is known to have had an excellent library. As we now know, Newgate was one of the prisons in which Malory was for varying periods confined. While we may regret the fact that he was forced to spend long years in confinement, it is consoling to think that imprisonment enabled him, like John Bunyan two centuries later, to produce one of the classics of English prose literature.

See also ARTHURIAN ROMANCES, THE.

The best edition of Caxton's text is that of H. Oskar Sommer, 3 vols. (London 1889–91). The Winchester manuscript is edited by Eugène Vinaver, *The Works of Sir Thomas Malory,* 3 vols. (New York and London 1947); 1 vol. ed., without commentary (Fair Lawn, N.J., and London 1954). Vinaver's *Malory* (New York and London 1929), though written before the discovery of the Winchester manuscript, is still of value.

ALBERT C. BAUGH,
Professor of English Language and Literature, University of Pennsylvania.

MORTGAGE, môr′gĭj, in law, the purported conveyance of property as security for the payment of a debt. The condition of the instrument is that, if the debt is paid according to the terms of the note, the conveyance is then void. Both real and personal property may be so mortgaged. Usually, in order to indicate the type of property involved, the conveyance of personal property to secure a debt is called a chattel mortgage (q.v.). Real estate mortgages take the form of a deed (q.v.). The borrower is called the mortgagor; the lender is called the mortgagee. Mortgages must be in writing, whatever the property secured. In order to protect innocent purchasers of a mortgaged property, mortgages must be recorded within prescribed time limits; in the United States, each of the several states sets this time limit. An unrecorded mortgage is still enforceable against the original mortgagor or any purchaser of the mortgaged property who has knowledge of its existence.

In the United States, until recently, the courts regarded a mortgage deed as in fact contemplating a conveyance of title in the event of default. If the terms of the loan were not met, foreclosure action was instituted, with the mortgagee taking possession of the property as settlement of the obligation. Title passed to the mortgagee, with little or no right of redemption on the part of the mortgagor. The recent tendency of the courts, however, has been to treat a mortgage as simply a lien against the pledged property. In the event of default on the loan, the mortgagee may institute foreclosure proceedings which in this case call for the public sale of the property to satisfy the debt. The proceeds are used, first, to pay the court and sale costs, and then the outstanding debt to the mortgagee. Any portion of the proceeds remaining goes to the mortgagor. The mortgagee may bid on the property, but without any special privilege. (See FORECLOSURE.) However, the conveyance theory is still generally applied to chattel mortgages.

More than one mortgage may be placed on a property at a given time. A first mortgage has a superior claim both as to interest income and as to principal. A second or junior mortgage receives nothing from the proceeds of the sale of a mortgaged property until the first mortgage obligation has been completely satisfied. Should the sale of a mortgaged property in foreclosure fail to realize sufficient funds to meet the full amount of debt outstanding, the debt is not extinguished; the unsatisfied portion of the loan remains an obligation of the mortgagor. The mortgagee is a general creditor of the mortgagor, with an unsecured claim against the mortgagor's assets. In many jurisdictions, the mortgagee may obtain a deficiency judgment which is an effective claim against future property holdings of the mortgagor.

Just as a mortgage must be recorded to be fully effective, so a release of mortgage (a "satisfaction piece") should be recorded to provide lasting evidence that the debt has been satisfied.

Consult Kratovil, Robert, *Real Estate Law,* 3d ed. (New York 1958); Lusk, Harold F., *Law of the Real Estate Business* (Homewood, Ill., 1958); Hoagland, Henry E., and Stone, L. D., *Real Estate Finance,* rev. ed. (Homewood, Ill., 1961).

WILLIAM N. KINNARD, JR.,
Head, Business Department, the University of Connecticut.

MORTGAGE BANKS. See BANKS AND FINANCE—*23. Mortgage Banking.*

MORTGAGE GUARANTY INSURANCE. See GUARANTY INSURANCE.

MORTIER, môr-tyā′, **Edouard Adolphe Casimir Joseph,** DUC DE TRÉVISE, French marshal: b. Cateau-Cambresis (now Le Cateau), France, Feb. 13, 1768; d. Paris, July 28, 1835. Having fought with distinction in the Napoleonic Wars, he was created marshal by the emperor (1804) and duc de Trévise (1807) after the Battle of Friedland, in which he played a major role. Mortier took part in Napoleon's Spanish and Russian campaigns, and in 1814 defended Paris against the Allies. He submitted to Louis XVIII, however, and was made a peer by the king; but his title was suspended when he refused to take part in the trial of Marshal Michel Ney late in 1815. Restored to the peerage in 1819, Mortier was minister of war and president of the council (premier) in 1834–1835. He was killed by the bomb with which Giuseppe Maria Fieschi attempted to assassinate Louis Philippe.

MORTIMER, môr′tĭ-mẽr, a family prominent in English history as earls of March and Ulster. The name was apparently assumed by ROGER (b. possibly before 990, when his father Hugh became bishop of Coutances), and was derived from the village and castle of Mortemer-en-Brai in the Pays de Caux in France, where Roger, fighting under William, duke of Normandy (later William I of England), won a victory over the forces of Henry I of France. Roger's son RALPH (I) DE MORTIMER (d.?1104) followed William to England after the Conquest, and was granted the estates forfeited by the earl of Hereford as well as other estates in Wales and England, including the town and castle of Wigmore, which became the family seat. As barons of Wigmore, the Mortimers were among the most powerful of the lords marchers and took part in the border warfare. Through advantageous marriages they increased their holdings considerably. ROGER (II) DE MORTIMER, 6TH BARON OF WIGMORE (1231?–1282), in particular was involved in conflict with Llewelyn ab Gruffydd, prince of Wales; after siding with the barons against Henry III, he became a loyal supporter of Henry and his successor Edward I.

ROGER (IV) DE MORTIMER, 8TH BARON OF WIGMORE and 1ST EARL OF MARCH (1287?–1330), grandson of Roger II, acquired through marriage additional holdings in England, Wales, and Ireland, including Ludlow, which became the family seat. He defeated (1317–1318) the attempt of Edward Bruce and his brother Robert VIII to conquer Ireland and, with the assistance of his uncle (Roger III de Mortimer, lord of Chirk, 1256?–1326), took an active part in restoring order in Wales. Opposition to the Despensers, Edward II's favorites, caused the Mortimers to be convicted and imprisoned (1322) for treason, but Roger IV made a dramatic escape (1324) from the Tower of London and fled to France. There he formed a liaison with Isabella, wife of King Edward II, assisted her in plotting against the king, and with her invaded England in 1326. They executed the Despensers, caused Edward II to be deposed and murdered (1327), and brought young Edward III to the throne. Mortimer, created 1st earl of March in

1328, virtually ruled England for a time; but his greed and cruelty, together with the "shameful peace" of 1328 which acknowledged Robert Bruce as king of Scotland, soon brought about his downfall. Edward III seized him in a midnight descent on Nottingham Castle; after being condemned without trial, he was hanged, drawn, and quartered, and his estates were forefeited.

ROGER (V) DE MORTIMER, 2D EARL OF MARCH (1327?–1360), grandson of the preceding, was gradually restored to the family estates and regained his title in 1355. He attended Edward III on his great invasion of France, took part in the abortive siege of Reims, and died while accompanying the king on his invasion of Burgundy.

EDMUND (II) DE MORTIMER, 3D EARL OF MARCH (1351–1381), son of Roger V, married Philippa, daughter of Lionel, 1st duke of Clarence, second surviving son of Edward III. Through Philippa's mother, Edmund acquired extensive estates in Ireland and assumed the title of earl of Ulster. He was marshal of England from 1369 to 1377, and lieutenant of Ireland from 1379 until his death. His daughter Elizabeth married Sir Henry Percy (Hotspur).

After the death of her father in 1368, Philippa was next in line to the throne after Edward the Black Prince and his son (later Richard II); this was the basis of the Yorkist claim to the crown that was to give rise to the Wars of the Roses in the next century (see ROSES, WARS OF THE).

ROGER (VI) DE MORTIMER, 4TH EARL OF MARCH AND 2D EARL OF ULSTER (1374–1398), son of the preceding, was proclaimed heir presumptive to the throne by Richard II in 1385, to forestall the claims of John of Gaunt (eldest surviving son of Edward III) and his descendants (house of Lancaster). Roger became lieutenant of Ireland in 1397 and was killed at the Battle of Kells. To avenge his death, Richard undertook his last disastrous campaign in Ireland.

EDMUND (IV) DE MORTIMER, 5TH EARL OF MARCH AND 3D EARL OF ULSTER (1391–1425), son of the preceding, succeeded to his father's claim to the throne but refused to plot against the Lancastrian King Henry V and served him faithfully in the French wars. Edmund died without issue, ending the male line of Mortimer. His sister Anne married Richard, earl of Cambridge, son of Edmund of Langley, 1st duke of York (fifth son of Edward III). The earldom of March passed to her son Richard, 3d duke of York, whose claim to the throne through his descent from Philippa (wife of Edmund II de Mortimer) precipitated the Wars of the Roses. When York's son ascended the throne as Edward IV in 1461, the earldom of March was merged in the crown.

MORTMAIN, môrt'mān, in law, the generic term used to describe various statutes imposing restrictions upon the donation of property by will to churches or charitable institutions. The term may also refer to statutes formerly in effect in England which prohibited corporations, whether lay or ecclesiastical, from purchasing lands without the king's license. Mortmain statutes were so named because their object was to prevent property from being possessed by a "dead hand," that is, from being permanently withdrawn from free circulation; apparently the term was derived from the fact that, in the early law, ecclesiastics were deemed civilly "dead." The early English statutes forbidding the conveyance of lands as gifts to churches were not, in general, extended to the United States. Some states, however, invalidate certain devises and bequests for charitable and religious purposes, and in others it is required that the will be executed a specified time before the death of the testator in order for such gifts to be valid. It is sometimes provided by statute that devises to charitable institutions shall not exceed a specified percentage of the testator's estate to the exclusion of his wife or descendants. It is also frequently prohibited by statute that a charity hold property above a fixed value.

RICHARD L. HIRSHBERG.

MORTON, môr't'n, 4TH EARL OF (JAMES DOUGLAS), Scottish statesman: b. about 1525; d. Edinburgh, Scotland, June 2, 1581. He inherited the earldom from his wife's father, who died in 1553. When Mary, Queen of Scots, arrived in Scotland in 1561, he was made a member of the Privy Council and in 1563 lord chancellor. In connivance with Mary's consort Henry Stewart, Lord Darnley, Morton organized the murder of her adviser David Rizzio (1566) and was forced to flee to England when Darnley perfidiously denounced him to the queen. He was soon pardoned, however, through the intervention of James Hepburn, 4th earl of Bothwell, and returned to Scotland early in 1567. Bothwell attempted to recruit him for the murder of Darnley, but Morton refused to participate; and when Mary married Bothwell on May 15, 1567, Morton took the lead in forming an alliance of the nobles against them. After Mary's abdication on July 24, he became lord chancellor again in the regency of James Stewart, earl of Moray, for the infant James VI (later James I of England); and he held a major command in the army that finally defeated Mary's forces at Langside (1568).

In 1572 Morton himself became regent. He proved to be an able and vigorous governor, working to restore order in Scotland and to improve the condition of the populace; but although he was a stanch Protestant, his preference for the Anglican church polity added the Presbyterians to his enemies, along with those who still favored Mary's cause. Finally, Esmé Stuart (Stewart), later 1st duke of Lennox, arriving from France in 1579, won the confidence of James VI and persuaded him that Morton was responsible for the murder of James' father Darnley, although his guilt was actually limited to knowledge of the plot rather than complicity in it. Morton was brought to trial, found guilty, and hastily executed.

MORTON or **MOURT,** môrt, **George,** English colonist in America: b. probably near Scrooby, Nottinghamshire, England, 1585; d. Plymouth, Mass., June 1624. Believed to have been the son of a wealthy Roman Catholic, he was converted to Puritanism at an early age and was a member of the Pilgrim colony at Leiden, Holland. From 1619 he was an agent for the Puritans in London, where he adopted the name Mourt. He is remembered as the publisher of *A Relation or Iournall of the beginning and proceedings of the English Plantation setled at Plimoth in New England* (1622), known as *Mourt's Relation,* the first account of the voyage of the *Mayflower* and the early months of Plymouth Colony. How much of this book was actually written by Morton and how much by Edward Winslow and William Bradford is not known. He emigrated to Plymouth with his family in 1623.

NATHANIEL MORTON (1613–1685), his son, was brought up by Bradford (his uncle by marriage) and from 1647 until his death was secretary of Plymouth Colony. After Bradford's death he prepared *New Englands Memoriall* (1669), based on the papers of Bradford and Winslow, which was the main authority for the history of the colony until 1855, when Bradford's *History of Plimoth Plantation* was recovered.

MORTON, John, American patriot, signer of the Declaration of Independence: b. Ridley, Pa., c. 1724; d. April 1777. He worked as a surveyor, cultivated the family farm in what is now Delaware County, Pa., and from 1756 served almost continuously as a member of the Pennnsylvania General Assembly. Morton was one of Pennsylvania's delegates to the Stamp Act Congress (1765) and a member of the Continental congresses from 1774 to 1777. In July 1776 he joined Benjamin Franklin and James Wilson in casting the votes that placed Pennsylvania on the side of independence by a slim majority of one, and he subsequently signed the Declaration. He also served as chairman of the committee to adopt the Articles of Confederation, which were ratified only after his death.

MORTON, John, English prelate: b. Dorsetshire, England, c. 1420; d. Knowle, Kent, Sept. 15, 1500. He studied law at Balliol College, Oxford, took up the practice of ecclesiastical law in London, and soon was appointed chancellor of the Duchy of Cornwall and a master in chancery. In 1450 he was made subdeacon of Lincoln and in 1458 prebendary of Salisbury and Lincoln. In the contest between the houses of York and Lancaster, Morton adhered to the latter, supporting Margaret of Anjou and Prince Edward in their exile; but after the Battle of Tewkesbury (1471) he submitted to the Yorkist Edward IV, who valued his talents sufficiently to make him master of the rolls (1473) and send him on various diplomatic missions. In 1479 Morton became bishop of Ely; but when Richard III came to the throne in 1483, he was confined in the Tower of London and then in Brecknock Castle in Wales, where he connived with Henry Stafford, 2d duke of Buckingham, to oust the king. When the plot failed, Morton managed to escape to Flanders. He has been given credit for achieving the union between the houses of York and Lancaster, effected by the marriage of Henry Tudor, earl of Richmond, to Elizabeth of York, daughter of Edward IV; and his counsel and rallying of support in England were largely responsible for the success of Richmond's invasion and his accession to the throne as Henry VII. The new king made Morton his chief counselor, and he became successively archbishop of Canterbury (1486), lord chancellor (1487), cardinal (1493), and chancellor of Oxford (1495). It is probable that the *History of Richard III,* ascribed to Sir Thomas More (who was Morton's pupil), was originally written in Latin by Morton, and translated and amplified by More.

MORTON, Julius Sterling, American agriculturist and public official: b. Adams, Jefferson County, N.Y., April 22, 1832; d. Lake Forest, Ill., April 27, 1902. He studied at the University of Michigan, moved to Nebraska in 1854, and settled at Nebraska City, where he engaged in farming. Morton served in the territorial legislature (1855–1856, 1857–1958) and as secretary of the territory (1858–1861), and continued to be active in politics as a Democrat after Nebraska became a state in 1867. He was especially interested in promoting improved agricultural methods in the state and originated the idea of setting aside a special day for tree planting. As a result, Arbor Day (q.v.) began in Nebraska in 1872 and since 1885 has been observed there on Morton's birthday. His services to agriculture and the Democratic Party were recognized when President Grover Cleveland appointed him secretary of agriculture (1893–1897). His home and land in Nebraska City are preserved as a public memorial and park.

PAUL MORTON (1857–1911), his son, after a career as an executive of the Colorado Fuel & Iron Company and the Atchison, Topeka and Santa Fe Railway, was named secretary of the navy in 1904 by President Theodore Roosevelt, but was forced to resign a year later when it was revealed that the Santa Fe had granted illegal rebates while he was its vice president. He was president of the Equitable Life Assurance Society thereafter. During his year in the cabinet, Morton was a leading "big navy" advocate.

MORTON, Levi Parsons, American banker and public official: b. Shoreham, Vt., May 16, 1824; d. Rhinebeck, N.Y., May 16, 1920. He went into business as a wholesale merchant in Boston, Mass., about 1850, and in 1855 in New York City organized Morton, Grinnell & Company, which failed when its Southern debts became uncollectable at the outbreak of the Civil War. He then established the New York banking firm of Levi P. Morton & Company (1863), which participated actively in financing the war. Reorganized as Morton, Bliss & Company (1869), it became one of the leading factors in American finance, taking part in the negotiations with Great Britain which settled the *Alabama* claims (1871–1872). Morton served in Congress as a Republican (1879–1881) and as United States minister to France (1881–1885), and was vice president of the United States (1889–1893) under Benjamin Harrison. As governor of New York State (1895–1896), he worked for civil service reform and supported measures for the consolidation of Greater New York (city). In 1899 he organized the Morton Trust Company, which merged with the Guaranty Trust Company in 1909, when he retired.

MORTON, Oliver Perry (baptized OLIVER HAZARD PERRY THROCK MORTON), American political leader: b. Salisbury, Ind., Aug. 4, 1823; d. Indianapolis, Nov. 1, 1877. He attended Miami University (Oxford, Ohio) for two years, began to practice law at Centerville, Ind., and at 29 became a circuit judge. He then attended Cincinnati College Law School for one term. Morton rose rapidly as a railroad attorney. His political interest dated from the Kansas-Nebraska Bill (1854), his opposition to which turned him to the budding Republican Party. Defeated for governor of Indiana in 1856, he accepted second place on the ticket with Henry Smith Lane four years later; when Lane went to the United States

Senate (1861), Morton was elevated to governor.

Abraham Lincoln had no abler supporter. Solidly behind the Civil War, Morton encouraged 150,000 men to enlist from Indiana. He was a militant and effective opponent of the Copperheads; and when in 1862 "peace" Democrats gained control of the Indiana legislature, Morton bypassed them by using profits from an arsenal he had started, borrowing from Washington, and privately financing the state's war effort in other ways. Although he might reasonably have been called a dictator, he was re-elected governor in 1864, this time with a Republican majority in the legislature.

Overwork afflicted Morton the following summer with a crippling paralysis. Going to France to seek medical help, he carried a message from President Andrew Johnson to Napoleon III, warning that monarch to forsake his Mexican adventure (the Maximilian affair). A man of passionate conviction, he gave no quarter to Democrats who had supported the war. In 1867 he was elected to the United States Senate and served until his death. Party influences gradually drew him away from a conciliatory reconstruction policy, and the amendment granting Negro suffrage had no more effective champion. Following the panic of 1873, he reversed his previous policy and became a "soft-money" man, an act that may have lost him the presidential nomination in 1876. A trip to Oregon to investigate bribery charges against a newly elected senator the next summer overtaxed his strength and brought on his final illness.

Bibliography.—French, William M., *Life, Speeches, State Papers and Public Services of Gov. Oliver P. Morton* (Cincinnati 1864); Foulke, William D., *Life of Oliver P. Morton,* 2 vols. (Indianapolis and Kansas City 1899); Hesseltine, William B., *Lincoln and the War Governors* (New York 1948).

EARL SCHENCK MIERS,
Author of "The General Who Marched to Hell."

MORTON, Samuel George, American physician and natural scientist: b. Philadelphia, Pa., Jan. 26, 1799; d. there, May 15, 1851. He studied medicine at the universities of Pennsylvania and Edinburgh and began to practice in Philadelphia in 1824. From 1820 he was active in the Academy of Natural Sciences there and he became its president the year before he died. Besides medicine, Morton's interests ranged to paleontology, comparative anatomy, and anthropology. In 1834 he published a study of the fossils collected on the Lewis and Clark Expedition, which laid the foundation for all future work in American paleontology. His collection of skulls, estimated at about 1,500, including some 900 human specimens, was world famous. From his studies in this area he inferred that the races of men were of diverse origin, a view which brought him into conflict with the clergy. Louis Agassiz (1807–1873) was strongly influenced by his work. Among Morton's most impressive writings were *Crania Americana* (1839), *Crania Egyptiaca* (1844), and *An Illustrated History of Human Anatomy* (1849). He was also one of the first to advocate fresh-air treatment of tuberculosis.

MORTON, Thomas, English adventurer in America: d. Agamenticus (now York), Me., 1646 or 1647. He was apparently an attorney of Clifford's Inn, London, of a somewhat doubtful reputation. He first visited New England briefly sometime between 1622 and 1624. An Anglican with little sympathy for Puritan ideals, Morton returned to America in 1625 and took over a settlement at Mount Wollaston (now Quincy, Mass.), which he renamed "Merriemounts" (Merry Mount). Here he erected a Maypole, around which wine and liquor flowed freely while his followers danced with Indian women as partners. The Puritans of Plymouth were outraged. Contrary to law, Morton had also supplied the Indians with firearms and instructed them in their use, and he was a rival of the Plymouth settlers in the fur trade. He was accordingly arrested by Capt. Miles Standish and sent back to England in 1628, and the Maypole was cut down.

In England Morton ingratiated himself with Sir Ferdinando Gorges, the proprietor of Maine, and in 1629 he was back in New England, returning to Merry Mount, setting up the Maypole again, and reopening his dealings with the Indians. Arrested and banished again in 1630, he was for a while imprisoned in Exeter, England, but was soon released to work for Gorges in his attempt to overthrow the charter of the Massachusetts Bay Company. In 1637 his *New English Canaan* was published (printed in Holland), although it had been written some years earlier. Largely satirical and highly prejudiced, it is a compendium of geographical, historical, and political observations in three parts, the first dealing with the "origin of the natives," the second with the "natural endowments of the country," and the third with "what people are planting there." It has been called "the first book of American humor," and is valuable at least as a supplementary source book for the history of the period. When he ventured back to New England in 1643, Morton was again imprisoned, in Boston, for about a year while evidence was being collected to sue him for libel against the colonies. He was finally released with a fine and repaired to Gorges' colony in Maine, where he died.

John Lothrop Motley's novels *Morton's Hope* (1839) and *Merry Mount* (1849) are based upon Thomas Morton's exploits, as are Nathaniel Hawthorne's "The Maypole of Merry Mount" (in *Mosses from an Old Manse,* 1846) and Howard Hanson's opera *Merry Mount* (1934). Morton's *New English Canaan* was reprinted, with an introduction and notes by Charles Francis Adams, in the *Publications* of the Prince Society of Boston, vol. 14 (1883).

MORTON, Thomas, English dramatist: b. Durham, England, c.1764; d. London, March 28, 1838. He was a prolific and popular playwright, whose works, ranging from comedy and drama to melodrama, farce, and musical drama, were vehicles for leading actors of the time. In his comedy *Speed the Plough* (1798) he established the character of Mrs. Grundy (who never actually appears in the play) as a highly censorious critic of manners and morals.

JOHN MADDISON MORTON (1811–1891), his son, was equally successful and even more prolific as a playwright, showing special skill in adapting French farces for the English stage. The only play of either father or son to survive today is the latter's *Box and Cox* (q.v.), still popular in amateur productions and in the adaptation *Cox and Box* (1867) for which Sir Arthur Sullivan wrote the music.

MORTON, William James, American neurologist: b. Boston, Mass., July 3, 1845; d.

Miami, Fla., March 26, 1920. The son of William Thomas Green Morton (q.v.), he studied medicine at Harvard (M.D., 1872), went to Cape Town, South Africa, as a physician for a mining company (1874–1876), and began to practice in New York City in 1878. His interest in chemistry and physics led him to develop the high frequency "static-induced" or "Morton current" which, by producing X-rays, was of great value in medicine and surgery. He edited and published the *Journal of Nervous and Mental Diseases* (1882–1886), the leading neuropsychiatric publication in the United States, and was professor of diseases of the mind and nervous system and of electrotherapeutics at the New York Post Graduate Medical School (1890–1909). Morton was one of the first to use X-rays in treating cancerous growths and skin disorders. His attempts to drive remedies into the body by electric rather than hypodermic methods contributed to the modern practice of iontophoresis, whereby ions of soluble salts are electrically introduced for therapeutic purposes.

In 1913, along with Julian Hawthorne and Josiah Quincy, Morton was convicted, as a company director, of using the mails to defraud in connection with a Canadian mining stock. Sentenced to a year and a day in prison, he was soon paroled, pardoned by President Woodrow Wilson, and, at the request of prominent citizens and physicians, restored to medical practice.

MORTON, William Thomas Green, American dental surgeon and pioneer in the use of anesthesia: b. Charlton, Mass., Aug. 9, 1819; d. New York, N.Y., July 15, 1868. He studied at the College of Dental Surgery in Baltimore and in 1842 opened a dental office in Boston with Horace Wells. Their partnership was dissolved the next year, and Wells returned to Hartford, Conn., where late in 1844 he began to use nitrous oxide (laughing gas) as an anesthetic in dentistry. Morton, meanwhile, had formed a connection with the scientist Charles Thomas Jackson, who acquainted him with the anesthetic properties of sulphuric ether. Morton used it first as a local anesthetic in July 1844 and then, after trying it out on himself and various animals, applied it as a general anesthetic (Sept. 30, 1846). The results were so successful that the distinguished surgeon John Collins Warren invited Morton to administer ether during an operation on a neck tumor. This operation, in which the anesthetic use of ether was first publicly demonstrated, took place at the Massachusetts General Hospital in Boston on Oct. 16, 1846, and was fully written up by Henry Jacob Bigelow in the *Boston Medical and Surgical Journal* (Nov. 18, 1846).

Morton at first refused to reveal the nature of his anesthetic and, disguising it with aromatic oils, named it letheon. On Nov. 12, 1846, he obtained a patent for it, with Jackson, and attempted to sell licenses for its use. Nevertheless, when the French Academy of Medicine awarded the Montyon Prize of 5,000 francs to Morton and Jackson together, Morton denied Jackson's claim and refused to take his own share. Further difficulties arose because, beginning in 1842, Crawford Williamson Long, a Georgia surgeon, had several times used ether as an anesthetic while performing operations, although he had not reported the fact until 1849. In 1852 and at two succeeding sessions of Congress, a bill appropriating $100,000 as a national testimonial to Morton for the discovery of a practical anesthetic was introduced in Congress, but it failed to pass because of the rival claims of Morton, Jackson, Long, and Wells.

Whatever the merits of their claims, Morton was certainly the most active experimenter and had assumed responsibility for the first public demonstration. His *Remarks on the Proper Mode of Administering Sulphuric Ether by Inhalation* (1847) and *On the Physiological Effects of Sulphuric Ether . . .* (1850) describe the dangers of administration, the two stages of etherization, and its effects on the central nervous system. He profited little from his work, and his later years were embittered by poverty and litigation. In 1920 he was elected to the Hall of Fame at New York University.

Consult Young, Agnes, *Scalpel*, pp. 139–155 (New York 1956).

MORTON, village, Illinois, in Tazewell County, 10 miles southeast of Peoria, at an altitude of 715 feet. It lies in an agricultural district where corn, wheat, and soybeans are grown, and cattle and poultry are raised. Bituminous coal is mined in the vicinity. Morton processes food and has some manufactures. It was incorporated as a village in 1877. Pop. 10,419.

MORTON GROVE, village, Illinois, in Cook County, 14½ miles north of Chicago, at an altitude of 625 feet. It is basically a residential suburb of Chicago, with diversified industries including pharmaceuticals, cosmetics, and heating, air conditioning, and industrial equipment. Large areas of forest preserve within the village limits offer natural recreational facilities. The village was incorporated in 1895 and named for the financier Levi Parsons Morton (q.v.), who was at that time a leading official of the Chicago, Milwaukee and St. Paul Railroad. Government is by mayor and council Pop. 26,369.

MORTUARY CUSTOMS. See Death Customs and Rites.

MORVAN, môr-väɴ', mountain range, France, in the east central section, the northernmost spur of the Massif Central (q.v.) It lies in the departments of Saône-et-Loire, Côte d'Or, Nièvre, and Yonne. The highest of its rounded peaks is Bois-du-Roi (2,959 feet). It is a scantily populated, heavily forested region with poor soil. Cattle raising, lumbering, and charcoal making are the chief industries. Several rivers, including the Yonne, originate here.

MORVI, mōr'vē, municipality, India, in Madhya Saurashtra District, Bombay State, on the Machlu River, 37 miles north of Rajkot. It is a trade center for agricultural products and has some manufacturing establishments. Morvi Technical Institute is here. The town was the capital of a former princely state of the same name (pop. 1941, 141,761; area 822 square miles), included in the Eastern Kathiawar Division of the Western India States Agency and administered by the British resident at Baroda. In 1948 it became part of the State of Saurashtra, which in 1956 was incorporated in the new State of Bombay. Pop. (1951) 40,722.

Eugene F. Irschick.

MORYSON, mŏr'ĭ-s'n, **Fynes,** English traveler and writer: b. probably in Cadeby, Lincolnshire, England, 1566; d. Feb. 12, 1630. The son of a member of Parliament, he was educated at Peterhouse, Cambridge, and spent the years 1591–1597 traveling in Europe and the Levant. In 1600 he was named secretary to Sir Charles Blount, 8th Baron Mountjoy (later earl of Devonshire), lord deputy of Ireland, and saw the final suppression of the Irish rebellion led by Hugh O'Neill, 2d earl of Tyrone. After Blount died (1606), Moryson devoted himself to writing his *Itinerary,* a detailed account of his travels, the first three parts of which were published in London in 1617. The first and third parts describe the "twelve Dominions" (including the British Isles) that he visited and are of great interest to the social historian; the second part is a valuable documented history of Tyrone's rebellion. The work was reissued in four volumes in Glasgow (1907-08). A fourth part remained in manuscript until 1903, when Charles Hughes published a large part of it as *Shakespeare's Europe: Unpublished Chapters of Fynes Moryson's Itinerary.*

MOSAIC, mō-zā'ĭk, in art, an imitation or reproduction of a painting or ornamental design, formed generally by pieces of opaque glass (tesserae) of various colors or by colored stones (especially marbles and precious or semiprecious stones) placed side by side and bedded in plaster or cement. Floor mosaics required relatively few materials and colors, though this was by no means an unbreakable rule; on the other hand, wall mosaics, which could aspire to the condition of fresco, made use of every conceivable color and shade as well as a larger range of materials.

Glass cubes have long been the normal material for most mosaic; when more sumptous effects were demanded, a thin layer of gold leaf was fused between two layers of glass, the outer one being very thin. The size of the cubes usually ranges from one quarter to three quarters of an inch; in general, they are larger and often irregular in early work, whereas in the supreme compositions of the 11th and 12th centuries they are small and shaped like true cubes. Mosaic that is to be viewed near at hand uses cubes set flat and close together, while mosaic to be viewed at a distance achieves its finest effects by irregular setting. In either instance the mosaicist works slowly against a plaster surface upon which the design has been either outlined or painstakingly painted so that all the colors and shades can be precisely matched. As many as 10,000 shades are said to be available in some of the larger mosaic studios.

Early Mosaic.—The art of mosaic originated in the Middle East, where both Egyptians and Sumerians used it as architectural decorations; the Minoans and the Egyptians of the Later Empire apparently limited its use to the minor arts. As it spread to Greece, it was at first restricted to pavements, simple patterns being succeeded by mythological subjects. In the Hellenistic age the use of mosaic became general, and materials and techniques began to catch up with the growing demand. In Rome, and later through the Roman provinces, from Britain to the Tigris-Euphrates frontier, mosaic flourished to such an extent that pavements, sometimes extremely complicated in design, remain the most eloquent evidence of the beautiful villas, town houses, and public baths which otherwise have not survived. Failure to employ the third dimension makes for inevitable monotony; thus the brief experiments with figure compositions in depth in landscape settings at Antioch on the Orontes (2d century A.D.) produce a novel impact. Unhappily, the Antioch school of mosaicists did not remain adventurous.

Byzantine Mosaic.—Mosaic as a major art is not unnaturally thought of as Byzantine or as much influenced by Byzantine traditions. Nevertheless, the most important early Christian mosaics in Rome (4th and 5th centuries) precede Byzantine models. Those surviving in the churches of Santa Costanza and Santa Pudenziana are classical in feeling. The landscape crowded with architecture derives from a type popular at Pompeii and seems to culminate in the architectural fantasies at Damascus (early 8th century) carried out by Christian mosaicists for a Muslim caliph.

At Rome, where paganism did not yield easily to the new religion, the conservative classical tradition lingered on even after the culmination of the first Byzantine style during the reign (527–565) of Justinian I. The Christ of the classicizing artists is a beardless, youthful, and altogether human figure. The Byzantine artists, more militantly Christian, usher in a bearded Christ, awesome and divine. In the conflict between the two styles, it was inevitable that the Byzantine should eventually drive out, or at least modify significantly, the classical. At no other place can the conflict be observed better than at Ravenna, where the Christ in the apse of San Vitale has been called "as beautiful as Apollo." The choir of the same church is decorated by facing groups of Justinian and Theodora with their entourages, both of hieratic splendor. In the Basilica Eufrasiana at Parenzo in Istria (now Poreč, Yugoslavia), mosaics of Justinian's age may be seen wholly extant in "the only Byzantine basilica complete in all its parts"; these include the Virgin in the apse, which is henceforth to be her favored position in a church building. Similarly, as the rules of Christian iconography crystallized, Christ Pantocrator (Almighty) was generally set in the dome, with the Evangelists near him in the four pendentives.

Early work from the eastern part of the Byzantine Empire is scanty, because much was destroyed by the iconoclastic emperors (726–843, with interruptions), who forbade picturing the human form in religious art. But some remains, notably at Salonika (Thessalonike), rival the best work at Ravenna. After the end of the iconoclastic troubles, decoration of the churches went on apace, and St. Sophia at Constantinople (Istanbul), the most magnificent of Byzantine churches, received a superb series of mosaics that stop toward the middle of the 12th century. A panel of the Virgin and Child between Emperor John II Comnenus and his wife Irene may contain true portraits of the imperial pair; the date (1118) is thus memorable in the history of the age-long quest of the speaking likeness. Here, momentarily, a highly stylized art unbends, and the subtly arranged and tinted tesserae lift the veil between the type and the individual. That Byzantine mosaic could be poetic is proved by the work (c. 1100) in the convent of Daphni near Athens; that it could be carefree is proved by

The Byzantine style of mosaics, developed in the early Christian era, is illustrated in the Church of San Vitale, Ravenna, where the Christ figure (*right*) is in the classical tradition, whereas the detail of Empress Theodora (*below*) is in full Byzantine style.

Fratelli Alinari

the decorations (early 14th century) in the Kahrieh Djami (formerly the Church of the Chora) at Constantinople, where even the purely religious scenes lose their rigor and decorative motifs are introduced solely to give pleasure. Toward the close of the Byzantine Empire, when large mosaics were too expensive to be commissioned, portable mosaics, costly but not prohibitively so to the pious, came into vogue. Made with tiny cubes set in a panel coated with wax, these may have tended to realism, as a fine example in the Opera del Duomo in Florence suggests.

It is impossible to do justice briefly to the 12th century mosaics in Sicily: those of La Martorana and the Cappella Palatina (both in Palermo), of the cathedrals at Cefalù and Monreale, and of La Zisa, a castle near Palermo. The Norman kings and officials who commissioned them bowed to Byzantine culture, and the mosaics were carried out either by Byzantine Greeks or by local artists who had been taught by the Greeks. The solemn, the grand, the hieratic—these were salient characteristics of an art summed up in the Christ Pantocrator in the tribune of Monreale or in the procession of saints in the same cathedral.

In St. Mark's Cathedral in Venice, another center of Byzantine influence, the golden ground of the mosaics glows gloriously, but the figures are often disappointingly repaired. In 12th century Rome, the Byzantine style still holds its own, but it is combined, as in the apse mosaic in Santa Maria in Trastevere, with a freedom in deploying ornamental motifs that implies that rigor is on the wane. As far as large compositions were concerned, mosaic was soon to fall from the rank of an admittedly limited but nevertheless creative art to that of an imitative technique. It seemed peculiarly made to express the mystical world view of Byzantine Christianity and be reserved for the Byzantine church building, whose vaults and domes were ideal settings for the vast heads that symbolized the theological implications of this unyielding art. Naturalism, the favorite child of the Renaissance, was alien to the mosaic, and naturalistic mosaics, though often attempted, came forth as hybrids.

Modern Mosaic.—Eventually, mosaic became a copyist's technique in the worst sense, largely used to supply durable but otherwise unsatisfactory copies of precious canvases. It had a more respectable life in jewelry, where its decorative aspect was pleasantly realized. As a major art it attained, after centuries of slavish imitation, a feeble if applauded life along with the Gothic revival of the 19th century. The busiest if not the best mosaicist of the time was Antonio Salviati (1816–1890), a Venetian whose work can be seen as far afield as London and Aachen. He had the fatal gift of slickness. Some of his contemporaries were properly content to decorate an area and at least did not aspire to Salviati's pretty-picture technique, but they followed him in seeking highly polished surfaces, with tesserae so close together as utterly to obliterate visible joints, thereby thwarting their decorative aims. More recently, however, artists have either turned to Byzantine models, or more interestingly, applied the canons of abstract art to a medium whose chief features is its inherent stylization. In neither direction has much impressive work been accomplished.

WALLACE BROCKWAY,
Author and Consultant to Bollingen Foundation.

Bibliography.—Millet, Gabriel, *Le monastère de Daphni* (Paris 1899); Wilpert, Joseph, *Die römischen Mosaiken und Malereien,* 4 vols. (Freiburg im Breisgau 1916); Dalton, Ormonde Maddock, *East Christian Art* (New York and London 1925); Diez, Ernst, and Demus, Otto, *Byzantine Mosaics in Greece* (Cambridge, Mass., 1931); Talbot Rice, David, *Byzantine Art* (New York and London 1935); Demus, Otto, *The Mosaics of Norman Sicily* (New York and London 1950); Byzantine Institute, *The Mosaics of St. Sophia at Istanbul,* ed. by T. Whittemore, 4 vols. (London 1933–1952); Caputo, G., and Driss, A., *Tunisia: Ancient Mosaics* (Paris 1962).

MOSAIC, in plant pathology, a general term applied to certain virus diseases of flowering plants. As the name suggests, the green leaves and sometimes the stems and fruits become blotched, generally with yellow or, in some cases, with white patches. Such areas are commonly composed of thinner but occasionally of thicker tissue than normal. Diseased plants may also show a twisting and curling of the leaves, and gall-like growths may be produced. Common mosaic diseases are tobacco mosaic, sugarcane mosaic, corn mosaic, cucumber mosaic, soybean mosaic, pea mosaic, tulip mosaic, and potato mosaic. In some instances, notably in tobacco and potato, serious economic losses may result from such diseases.

The tobacco mosaic virus is exceedingly infectious, and it occurs in numerous hosts other than tobacco, such as tomato, buckwheat, phlox, and snapdragon. Apparently is is usually transmitted by contact between healthy plants or seedlings and diseased plants or their remains. Aphids can carry the virus from tomato to tobacco. The best control is general sanitation. The disease is easily transmitted on the hands of field workers. In some regions resistant varieties of tobacco can be grown.

Tobacco mosaic is one of the most intensively studied of all diseases in the plant and animal kingdoms. More than 50 different strains of the virus have been described. Recent electron microscope studies show that the virus consists of rod-shaped particles 300 millimicrons $\left(\text{about } \frac{1}{100,000} \text{ inch}\right)$ long, composed of a protein sheath with a core of nucleic acid at or near the center, like a miniature candle with its wick running through the middle. The nucleic acid is essentially responsible for producing the disease symptoms, while immunological properties are determined by the protein coat.

Consult Bawden, Frederick C., *Plant Viruses and Virus Diseases,* 3d ed. (Waltham, Mass., 1952); Fraenkel-Conrat, Heinz, "Rebuilding a Virus," *Scientific American,* vol. 194, no. 6, pp. 42–47 (New York 1956); Walker, John C., *Plant Pathology,* 2d ed. (New York 1957).

EDWIN B. MATZKE.

MOSANDER, mōō-sȧn′dẽr, **Carl Gustav,** Swedish chemist and mineralogist: b. Kalmar, Sweden, Sept. 10, 1797; d. Angsholm (near Drottningholm), Oct. 15, 1858. For many years he taught chemistry and mineralogy at the Caroline Medical Institute in Stockholm, where he was closely associated with Jöns Jacob Berzelius, "the organizer of the science of chemistry." Mosander is especially noted for his work with the so-called rare-earth elements. In 1839 he discovered lanthanum; in 1842 he isolated didymium, thinking it to be a metallic element in itself, although it was later broken down into neodymium and praseodymium and in 1843 he separated oxides of terbium and erbium, which were later isolated by other scientists.

MOSASAUR, mō′sȧ-sôr, any of several Upper Cretaceous lizards of the family Mosasauridae. The family is related to the beaded lizards (Helodermatidae), monitors (Varanidae), and the Bornean earless monitor (Lanthanotidae) of the present day, and to the Lower Cretaceous families Aigialosauridae (probably the land-dwelling ancestors of mosasaurs) and Dolichosauridae. These families, with the mosasaurs, are grouped together in a superfamily, the Varanoidea or Platynota, all members of which share the development of a vertical hinge in the middle of each half of the lower jaw. In the mosasaurs this hinge reaches the highest degree of mobility, exceeded among reptiles only in some specialized snakes.

All known mosasaurs come from marine strata, and the group appears to have a worldwide distribution in the seas of the Upper Cretaceous. The largest known skeleton is about 45 feet in length, and the smallest known species probably had an adult size scarcely in excess of 2 yards. Sharp teeth point to fish-eating habits in most, but in *Globidens* the teeth are blunt, suggesting a shellfish diet.

Mosasaurs are known from many complete skeletons, and there are also fossil impressions of the skin, showing small scales like those of the living monitors (*Varanus*). Four limbs were present, but the hands and feet were modified into paddles that aided these reptiles in stabilizing their bodies in the water, while the very long and powerful tail was compressed into a sculling oar for propulsion. The name is derived from Mosa, the Latin form of Meuse (Maas), the river near whose lower course in the Netherlands remains of the reptile were first found.

See also LACERTILIA; PYTHONOMORPHA.

CHARLES M. BOGERT,
Chairman and Curator, Department of Herpetology, The American Museum of Natural History.

MOSBY, mŏz′bĭ, **John Singleton,** American lawyer and Confederate soldier: b. Edgemont, Powhatan County, Va., Dec. 6, 1833; d. Washington, D.C., May 30, 1916. Graduated from the University of Virginia (1852), he was admitted to the bar (1855) and was practicing law at Bristol, V.a., when the Civil War broke out. After service in the Confederate cavalry, he became a scout (1862) for Gen. James E. B. Stuart and in 1863 recruited an independent body of fighters, which soon became famous as Mosby's Partisan Rangers. Adopting a guerrilla style of warfare, they operated in Virginia and Maryland, cutting Union communication lines, destroying supply trains, and capturing outposts. Probably his most brilliant exploit was the capture of Brig. Gen. Edwin H. Stoughton at Fairfax, Va., in March 1863. Another of Mosby's dramatic raids resulted in the capture of Gen. Philip H. Sheridan's entire supply train near Berryville, Va., in August 1864.

After the war Mosby again took up the practice of law, settling at Warrenton, Va. He became a Republican and supported Ulysses S. Grant for the presidency. He was United States consul at Hong Kong (1878–1885), practiced law in San Francisco, Calif., for a time, and served as an assistant attorney for the Department of Justice at Washington, D.C. (1904–1910). He published *Mosby's War Reminiscences and Stuart's Cavalry Campaigns* (1887).

Consult Jones, Virgil C., *Ranger Mosby* (Chapel Hill, N.C., 1944); Mosby, John Singleton, *Memoirs,* ed. by Charles W. Russell, new ed. (Bloomington, Ind., 1959).

MOSCHELES, mŏsh′ĕ-lĕs, **Ignaz,** German pianist, composer, and teacher: b. Prague, Bohemia, May 30, 1794; d. Leipzig, Germany, March 10, 1870. He studied at the Prague Conservatory of Music, and afterward under Johann Georg Albrechtsberger and Antonio Salieri at Vienna. On the completion of his studies he made a successful professional tour in Germany, and in 1820 arrived at Paris, where he met with an exceptionally enthusiastic reception and afterward made tours of other continental capitals. In 1826 he settled in London, where he was professor of music at the Royal Academy for 21 years. Here he had Sigismund Thalberg for a pupil, as he had formerly, in Berlin, had Mendelssohn. At the latter's request he went from London to Leipzig where he was professor of music in the conservatory there from 1846 till his death. Among his finest compositions may be mentioned his Concertos Nos. 3, 4 and 5, the Concertos Fantastique and Pathétique; his great Sextette and Trio; his Sonatas Caractéristique and Mélancolique; and the duo for pianoforte, *Hommage à Händel.*

Consult *Briefe von F. Mendelssohn-Bartholdy an Ignaz und Charlotte Moscheles* (1888).

MOSCHEROSCH, môsh'ĕ-rôsh, **Johann Michael** (properly MOSENROSH; pen name PHILANDER VON SITTEWALD), German satirist: b. Willstatt, near Strasbourg, March 5, 1601; d. Worms, Germany, April 4, 1669. He was a descendant of an Aragon (Spanish) family, and was educated at Strasbourg. After various government appointments in different places, he became privy councillor to the landgravine of Hesse-Cassel.

He was admitted to the Fruchtbringende Gesellschaft in 1645 with the surname "Der Träumende" ("the Dreaming One" or "the Dreamer"). His works include: *Wunderliche und Wahrhaftige Gesichte Philanders von Sittewald,* a keen satire on the manners and customs of his time, and written in the style of Francisco Gomez de Quevedo y Villegas' *Los Sueños.* Other works are *Insomnis cura parentum, Christliches Vermachtnis eines Vaters;* and *Die Patientia,* the manuscript of which was found in the municipal library at Hamburg, Germany, in 1897.

MOSCHUS, mŏs'kŭs, Greek bucolic poet of Syracuse in Sicily, flourished about 150 B.C. Four idyls form the whole of the remains of Moschus, which exhibit great elegance of style and delicacy of conception. The Επιτάφιος βίωνος (*Lament for Bion*) was imitated by Shelley in *Adonais.*

A translation by J. M. Edmonds was published in 1912. The works of Moschus have commonly been edited with those of Bion (q.v.) and Theocritus (q.v.), and the three have been well translated by Andrew Lang (1889). See also PASTORAL.

MOSCOSO DE ALVARADO, môs-kō'sō thā äl-vä-rä'thō, **Luis de,** Spanish adventurer: b. Zafra, Badajoz, Spain, c. 1505; d. Peru, c. 1560. He served under his kinsman Pedro de Alvarado in an expedition to Guatemala in 1523–1527 and in 1534 accompanied him to Peru where he was for two years a follower of Pizarro, and then returned to Spain to live in luxury for several years on the proceeds of his services. In 1538 he attached himself to De Soto's expedition to Florida and upon the latter's death in 1542 took command and after many hardships succeeded in returning to Mexico. He was honored by the viceroy, Antonio de Mendoza, and in 1551 accompanied him to Peru where he was entrusted with important commands until his death.

MOSCOW, town, Idaho, and Latah County seat; altitude 2,564 feet; 95 miles southeast of Spokane, Washington; on the Northern Pacific; Great Northern; and Union Pacific railroads. The town is in the heart of the fertile Palouse country. White pine and mixed timber, wheat, hay, and peas are grown near by, and the town is a center for the pea industry. Other industries are concerned with lumber, seed, harvesters, creameries, flour and brick. The University of Idaho (q.v.) is here. Moscow was settled in 1879 and incorporated in 1887. Government is by a mayor and council. Pop. 14,146.

MOSCOW (Rus. MOSKVA), city and capital, USSR, located approximately in the center of European USSR, at latitude 55° 45′ N. and longitude 37° 37′ E. Though in the western part of the Soviet Union, the city lies close to the USSR center of population. Moscow is situated on both banks of the Moscow (Moskva) River, a tributary of the Oka, which in turn flows into the Volga. It is 550 feet above sea level on slightly hilly territory in the wooded steppe zone of mixed woods and meadows. In configuration, it resembles a rough circle surrounding the Kremlin, which was the original settlement in medieval times, and is today the residence of the USSR Communist rulers.

The Kremlin is one of the greatest remaining monuments of medieval Russian architecture. It is a huge citadel, a virtual little town of palaces, churches and government buildings, surrounded by stone walls 40 feet high and 12 feet thick. On top of several of the wall towers are huge red transparent stars, which are lighted at night. One side of the Kremlin faces the Moscow River. Around the other sides is the region of the "central squares," of which the most famous is Red Square, the site of Lenin's tomb and the place of the huge annual civilian and military parades. The central squares were in medieval times surrounded by the so-called Chinese Wall, most of which however has long since been torn down. Here are the main governmental buildings, the larger theaters and hotels, and the main shopping district. From this central core, wide avenues radiate out in all directions, leading toward neighboring cities, whose names they often bear. As one travels out these avenues, one crosses two boulevards, A and B, both circling the city center, some distance out. Originally both were city walls, which later were demolished as superfluous in modern times. Today city suburbs even extend far beyond boulevard B, the outermost of the two.

Moscow's climate is cool and continental. The average temperature for July is 65.6°F.; for January, 14°F. Winter temperatures as low as —44°F., however, are not uncommon. Because of its northerly location, summer days are very long, while winter daylight lasts only six hours. Rainfall is adequate, with an annual precipitation of 24.1 inches. The heaviest rains fall at the end of summer.

All the leading organizations of the Soviet regime are located in Moscow. Here can be found the headquarters of the USSR Communist Party, including its Secretariat, Presidium, Central Committee and Propaganda Administration. The Councils of Ministers (cabinets) and Supreme Soviets (legislatures) of both the USSR and the Russian Soviet Republic meet and work in Moscow. All USSR cabinet ministries are in the city, including the State Planning Committee, USSR Army and Navy headquarters, and the main offices of the Soviet secret police. As the site of the State Bank, Moscow is the financial center of the entire USSR. Other organizations of nationwide authority in the city include: the Central Council of USSR Trade Unions, the Secretariat of the Young Communist League, and the Central Council of the Voluntary Society to Aid the Army, Navy and Air Force.

Moscow is the scientific and propaganda center of the USSR. It is the seat of the USSR Academy of Science, and contains 82 colleges and universities. The largest center of book publishing in the Soviet Union, here are published the USSR's two main newspapers: *Pravda* (organ of the USSR Communist Party), and *Izvestia* (organ of the USSR government). Moscow also contains 40 stage theaters, of which two are world famous: the Bolshoi (Grand) opera and ballet theater, and the Moscow Art Theater (dramatic). In addition there are many museums, including the Tretiakov art gallery with its collections of the major works of the great Russian artists.

Moscow is also the center of railway transportation in the Soviet Union. Eleven railways radiate out of the city in all directions, not counting the belt railroad circling Moscow in the suburbs. The city is likewise the air transportation center in the USSR, airlines radiating out in all directions to the capitals of all Soviet republics, Leningrad, the Crimea, the Arctic, and even to Vladivostok. Large airports ring Moscow, some civilian but most of them military. Paved highways run from the city to Leningrad, Minsk, Ryazan, Voronezh, Gorki, and Yaroslavl. A newly completed auto road connects Moscow directly with the Crimea.

Great efforts were made during the 1930's and 1940's to improve the Moscow River port. An 80-mile canal was dug north of the city to divert Volga water into the Moscow River. This canal serves a triple purpose. First, it ensures the city an adequate supply of water. Second, hydroelectric power stations along the canal and its reservoirs help supply Moscow's enormous demands for electricity. Third, deep-draft Volga River ships can now reach the Moscow River port. By using various river systems and connecting canals, it is possible to sail from Moscow to the Baltic, White, Black, Azov, and Caspian seas, for which reason the capital is now called a "port of five seas." Nevertheless, most freight and passengers still enter and leave Moscow by rail.

Despite great decentralization of industry during the Soviet regime, Moscow today remains the largest industrial city in the Soviet Union, accounting for 15 per cent of all USSR industrial output. In czarist days, the capital was a huge center for textile industry, and was even known as the "city of calico." Today, Moscow contains almost every branch of manufacturing industry, including huge heavy industries. Most Moscow industries are those requiring technical skill, and take advantage of the large pool of skilled labor which Moscow possesses by virtue of its early industrialization. The chief branch of industry today is machinery manufacture, with concentration on complex and precision machines. In many instances, the pilot plants for new Soviet industries were first built in Moscow, which then loaned its experienced personnel to factories constructed later in other regions. The city contains the Stalin auto plant (the second largest truck factory in the USSR), and is a major center of aircraft design and manufacture. Other major products include watches, machine tools, and electrical equipment of all types. There also are large steel, synthetic dye, lumber, confectionary, baking, and sausage industries. The old czarist textile mills have been modernized and expanded under the Soviet regime, and Moscow is still one of the two leading textile centers of the USSR.

To supply all these industries with electricity, Moscow has a large number of steam electric power stations operating both in and outside the city, and using peat and lignite as fuel. Those in the city often provide heat for the houses of their district, as well as current. In addition, Moscow receives hydroelectric power from stations as far away as the upper Volga. Natural gas is piped into the city from the Saratov gas fields several hundred miles away on the lower Volga.

Moscow's huge industries require enormous quantities of raw materials which are transported to the city from all parts of European USSR, the Caucasus, and even from Asiatic USSR as far east as mid-Siberia. Altogether, 25,000,000 tons of freight flow into the city each year, the largest items being building stone, bricks, timber, coal, metal, grain and oil. Annual outgoing freight shipments are much smaller, only 5,000,000 tons, because Moscow specializes in production of machines and goods high in value but light in weight. The main items shipped out are machines, textiles and books, Moscow supplying these products to all parts of the USSR, even including the Pacific coast.

Because of its crooked narrow streets and the variegated architecture of its buildings Moscow has often been called Russia's biggest village. Since the 1930's, the Soviet regime has done much to modernize the city, widening main streets and lining them with multi-story new apartment houses and government buildings. Another improvement was the construction of the Moscow subway, with each station built of marble or granite, and decorated with mosaics of colored stone. Nevertheless, Moscow still remains a city of sharp contrasts. Turning off a broad modern boulevard, one often finds himself in a crooked lane, lined with low old buildings of almost medieval style. Even more startling is the common suburban sight of a big modern apartment house and a log cabin standing side by side. The city has an acute housing shortage, and large areas of the older sections are slums. Though the vast majority of Muscovites are Russians, members of every race in the USSR can be found in the city.

History.—Moscow was first mentioned in ancient documents in 1147, when it was a small village on the site of the present Kremlin. The city was burned down by the Mongols in 1238, but revived and by the end of the 13th century was already a separate principality. Moscow's central location in European Russia was ideal for trading, since it was on a Volga tributary, and by easy portages boats could transfer from the Volga system to all other great Russian rivers west of the Urals. Trading was also encouraged by the poor soil and unsuitable climate for good crops near Moscow. Even in medieval times, the city was an emporium for trade with the Arctic, Baltic, Ukraine, Iran, Central Asia and Siberia. Early Moscow also had a long succession of able rulers, who used their power as Mongol tax collectors to bring neighboring Russian principalities under Muscovite control. When

MOSCOW

Above: Sadovaya-Chernogryazskaya Street, a thoroughfare on the site of an old city wall.

Right: A corner on Gorki Street opposite the Moskwa Hotel.

Below: Young artists have been given this corner in the Sokolniki Park of Culture and Rest.

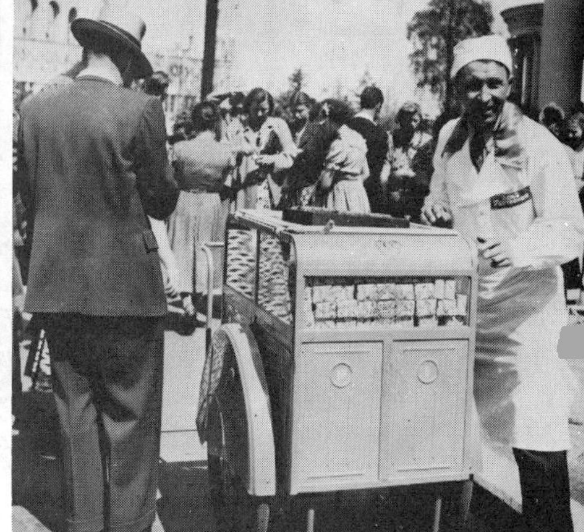

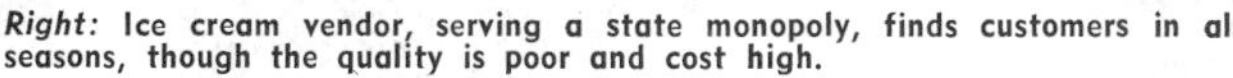

Right: Ice cream vendor, serving a state monopoly, finds customers in all seasons, though the quality is poor and cost high.

Below: Sverdlov Square in the heart of Moscow, with the famous Bolshoi Theater at the right.

(Top left, center left) Sovfoto; (top right, bottom) Van Sprang from Black Star; (center right) Edo Koenig from Black Star

Top Left: **The Cathedral of the Annunciation, with its nine golden domes, is one of three churches in the Kremlin.**

Above: **Monumental sculptural group in the Agricultural Exhibition glorifying the united efforts of the people.**

Center left: **Western-style modern concrete apartment houses are gradually replacing the charming but dilapidated wooden houses of the old city.**

Center right: **Students working in the organic chemistry laboratory of Moscow University.**

Bottom left: **A ballet performance at Moscow's Bolshoi Theater.**

Bottom right: **Platform of the Kiev Railway Terminal in Moscow.**

(Top left, right) Edo Koenig from Black Star; (center left) Van Sprang from Black Star; (center right, bottom left, right) Sovfoto

central European Russia had thus been united, Moscow broke the Mongol yoke. In 1547 Moscow's ruler Ivan the Terrible took the title of Czar (Caesar) and called the city the Third Rome. From then on, Moscow was the capital of the ever-expanding czarist state until 1711, when Peter the Great moved his residence to St. Petersburg (now Leningrad). However, Moscow remained an important commercial city, and the czars usually lived in the Kremlin part of each year. In 1812 Napoleon captured the city, but was forced to evacuate his army when Moscow burned down. The city was rebuilt, and by 1912 had a population of 1,600,000. After the Bolshevik Revolution, Lenin in 1918 moved the capital of Soviet Russia back to Moscow in order to protect the seat of government from foreign invasion. In 1941–1942 the city was besieged by German troops, but they were finally driven back, suffering their first major defeat of World War II.

Under Soviet rule, Moscow has grown tremendously. Its population has increased to more than four times the pre-Soviet level, and the city has expanded physically in all directions. Population: (1964 est.) 6,500,000.

ELLSWORTH RAYMOND
Associate Professor of Government
New York University

MOSCOW CANAL, a canal in the Russian Soviet Federated Socialist Republic, USSR, 80 miles long, completed in 1937 and until 1947 known as the Moscow-Volga Canal. It links the Volga River to the Moscow River, thus helping to establish Moscow as an inland "port of five seas." It starts in the Volga Reservoir, also known as the Sea of Moscow, 126 square miles in area, which was formed by damming up the Volga and raises the level of the river 56 feet. The water first flows through marshy terrain until it has to cross a watershed; by a system of locks and the application of electric power it surmounts the ridge to be lowered through locks and flow downhill again through some minor rivers until it reaches the Moscow River at Moscow. The canal is the main source of the city's water supply; it enables deep-draft ships to pass directly from Moscow to the Volga; and hydroelectric stations on the lower course of the canal reclaim much of the electrical energy expended on the upper course and relay it to Moscow.

MOSCOW RIVER. See MOSKVA.

MOSELEY, mōz'lĭ, **Edward Augustus,** American lawyer and public official: b. Newburyport, Mass., March 23, 1846; d. Washington, D.C., April 18, 1911. The son of a shipowner and banker, he left school at 16 and shipped as a cabin boy on one of his father's ships bound for Africa and India. At 26 he formed a lumber firm, and in 1885 and 1886 he was elected to the state legislature. After becoming secretary of the newly established Interstate Commerce Commission in 1887, Moseley studied law and was admitted to the bar so that he could work more effectively for legislation that would ensure greater safety on railroads for both employees and travelers. After 20 years of ceaseless activity he secured passage of the Safety Appliance Law, which required railroads to install block signals and other safety devices. In 1902 he went to Cuba to assist in the revision of railroad laws there.

MOSELEY, Henry, British scientist and clergyman: b. Newcastle-under-Lyme, England, July 9, 1801; d. Olveston, Gloucestershire, Jan. 20, 1872. While studying at a naval school, he wrote his first scientific paper, *On Measuring the Depth of the Cavities Seen on the Surface of the Moon* (1818). After graduating from St. John's College, Cambridge, he was ordained in the Anglican ministry, becoming a curate at West Monkton, Somersetshire, in 1828. In spite of his clerical duties he kept up his interest in mathematics and science, publishing his first book, *A Treatise on Hydrostatics and Hydrodynamics,* in 1830. He was chaplain of King's College, London (1831–1833), and professor of natural and experimental philosophy and astronomy (1831–1844), becoming an inspector of normal schools in 1844. In 1853 he was made a resident canon at Bristol Cathedral, vicar of Olveston in 1854, and chaplain in ordinary to Queen Victoria in 1855.

In a paper *On the Dynamical Stability and on the Oscillations of Floating Bodies* which appeared in the Royal Society's Philosophical Transactions for 1850, Moseley established the formulas which were adopted for determining the dynamical stability of warships. Four editions of his *Lectures on Astronomy* which were delivered at King's College were published from 1839 to 1854. His *Mechanical Principles of Engineering and Architecture* (1843) was reprinted in the United States with notes by Dennis Hart Mahan and was made a textbook at West Point. Among his other published works were *A Treatise on Mechanics, Applied to the Arts . . .* (1834), and *Astro-Theology . . .* (1847).

MOSELEY, Henry Gwyn-Jeffreys, British physicist: b. Weymouth, Dorsetshire, England, Nov. 23, 1887; d. Gallipoli Peninsula, Turkey, Aug. 10, 1915. The son of Henry Nottidge Moseley and grandson of Henry Moseley, he graduated from Trinity College, Oxford University, and became a lecturer in physics at the University of Manchester. In research work in the laboratory under Ernest Rutherford he showed great ability, particularly in the field of radioactivity. While working on X-ray spectra of the elements he made his outstanding contribution by deducing that the main properties of an element are determined, not by its atomic weight, but by a whole number defining its nuclear charge. This discovery was a landmark in the development of the periodic law of the elements and of spectrum analysis (see PERIODIC LAW; X-RAYS—*1. Physics of X-Rays:* Moseley's Atomic Numbers). When World War I broke out in 1914, Moseley enlisted as a lieutenant in the Royal Engineers. He was killed in action while taking part in the Gallipoli Campaign.

MOSELEY, Henry Nottidge, British naturalist: b. Wandsworth, Surrey, England, 1844; d. Clevedon, Somersetshire, Nov. 10, 1891. He was the son of Henry Moseley, the scientist and clergyman. Graduating from Exeter College, Oxford University, where he specialized in the natural sciences, he pursued further studies in physiology and medicine as well as in the natural sciences at Vienna, University College in London, and Leipzig. In 1871 he accompanied a government expedition to Ceylon to observe an eclipse of the sun. In 1872 he was appointed a naturalist on the scientific staff of the *Challenger* in its famous four-year voyage round the world (see CHALLENGER EXPEDITION). In 1879 he published his important *Notes by a Naturalist on the "Challenger"* (2d ed. 1892), noteworthy for its popular appeal as well as for its scientific authority. The manuscript journal that he kept of his zoological observations on this expedition is preserved in the British Museum.

After visiting the Pacific Northwest of the United States in 1877, Moseley published *Oregon: Its Resources, Climate, People, and Productions* (1878), for which he received the formal thanks of the state legislature. In 1879 he was elected a fellow of the Royal Society, and in 1881 he became Linacre professor of human and comparative anatomy at Oxford. He contributed numerous important biological memoirs to the Royal Society on corals, arthropods, and other subjects in his field.

MOSELLE, mō'zĕl, department, France, bordering Luxembourg and Germany on the north and northeast, Bas-Rhin Department on the southeast, and Meurthe-et-Moselle and Vosges departments on the west and south. The lower Vosges Mountains are in the southeast of the department, the plains of the Lorraine Plateau are in the center, and the Lorraine Basin is in the north and northeast. The climate is continental. The department has an area of 2,405 square miles and is drained by the Moselle River in the west and the Saar in the east. The Marne-Rhine Canal crosses it in the south. Metz is the capital.

Agriculturally and industrially, Moselle is one of the richest departments in France. The chief crops are fruits, tobacco, wheat, hops, and potatoes, and there are extensive vineyards along the left bank of the Moselle. There is considerable lumbering in the many forest areas, especially in the Vosges Mountains. The department is one of the richest sources of low-grade iron ore in Europe, and has large deposits of coal, salt, and kaolin. Forging and metallurgy are the chief industries of the Metz-Thionville area; other important industries are producing wine, glassmaking (including crystal and optical glass), the manufacture of earthenware and industrial porcelain, leather tanning, shoe manufacturing, brewing, woodworking, fruit and vegetable preserving.

The present Department of Moselle was included in the ancient duchy of Lorraine, of which Upper Lorraine became part of France in 1766 and was later split into four departments, Moselle being one. Moselle still has a large German-speaking population, having been annexed to Germany from 1871 to 1918 (as a result of the Franco-Prussian War) and, during World War II, from 1940 to 1944. Pop. (1962) 919,412.

MOSELLE, mô-zĕl'; Fr. mô-zĕl' (Ger. MOSEL), river, France and Germany, 320 miles long. It rises in the Vosges Mountains in southeastern Vosges Department, France; flows northwest past Remiremont, Épinal, and, in Meurthe-et-Moselle Department, past Toul; veers to the north to flow through Moselle Department past Metz and Thionville; and then northeast, leaving France a short distance beyond Thionville and forming part of the boundary between Luxembourg and Germany and then flowing through Germany to empty into the Rhine at Koblenz (Coblenz). The Saar River from the south and the Sûre (or Sauer) from the north both join it a few miles (5 and 7 respectively) west of Trier, Germany, and the Meurthe flows into it from the south at Frouard, France. It is navigable to Frouard for small boats, and is connected by canals with the Rhine, the Meuse, and the Seine. Along the steep slopes of its valley between Trier and Coblenz are grown the Riesling grapes from which the best Moselle wines are made.

MOSEN, mō'zĕn, **Julius,** German poet: b. Marieney, Vogtland, Saxony, July 8, 1803; d. Oldenburg, Oct. 10, 1867. A lawyer by profession, he became better known as a poet and dramatist, first attracting attention with his epic *Das Lied vom Ritter Wahn* (1831), which retold an old Italian legend. Like his later epic *Ahasver* (1838), this is weighted down with heavy rhetoric and philosophic reflection. His dramas, although he received an official appointment at the court theater in Oldenburg in 1844, suffer from the same faults, among them *Heinrich der Finkler* (1836), *Kaiser Otto III* (1842), and *Herzog Bernhard* (1855). He was more successful in such novels as *Der Kongress von Verona* (1842) and *Die Dresdner Gemäldegallerie* (1844), and has a still lighter touch in *Bilder im Moose* (1846), a two-volume collection. His volume of verse *Gedichte* (1836; 2d ed., 1843) contains such ballads as *Andreas Hofer, Die letzten Zehn vom vierten Regiment,* and *Der Trompeter an der Katzbach,* all of which have become German folksongs. His collected works were published in eight volumes in 1863, and in six volumes, with a biography by his son, in 1880.

MOSENROSH, Johann Michael. See MOSCHEROSCH, JOHANN MICHAEL.

MOSENTHAL, mō'zĕn-täl; -thôl, **Joseph,** German-American violinist: b. Kassel, Germany, Nov. 30, 1834; d. New York, N.Y., Jan. 6, 1896. He received his early training from his father and later from Ludwig Spohr under whom, for four years, he was leader of the second violins in the Hesse-Kassel ducal court orchestra. In 1853 he settled in New York City, where he played second violin with the Mason-Thomas Quintet from 1855 to 1868, was organist and choirmaster of Calvary (Episcopal) Church, 1860–1867, conducted the Mendelssohn Glee Club from 1867, and for 40 years was first violinist with the Philharmonic Society. He composed numerous songs, anthems, and hymns. Among his songs for male chorus were *Thanatopsis, Music of the Sea,* and *Blest Pair of Sirens.*

MOSENTHAL, Salomon Hermann, German dramatist: b. Kassel, Germany, Jan. 14, 1821; d. Vienna, Austria, Feb. 17, 1877. After attending the University of Marburg, he entered Austrian government service in 1851. Beginning in 1849, he wrote a series of sentimental, rhetorical dramas which included *Deborah* (1849), *Cäcilie von Albano* (1851), *Der Sonnenwendhof* (1856), *Die deutschen Komödianten* (1863), and *Isabella Orsini* (1870). They were well adapted to theatrical production and were popular in their time, being translated into English, Danish, Hungarian, and Italian, but are little known today. He is remembered chiefly because he wrote the librettos for such well-known operas as Karl Goldmark's *Queen of Sheba* and Otto Nicolai's *Merry Wives of Windsor.* He published a volume of verse in 1847, and his collected works were published in six volumes in 1877–1878.

MOSER, mō'zẽr, **Johann Jakob,** German jurist and publicist: b. Stuttgart, Germany, Jan. 18, 1701; d. there, Sept. 30, 1785. He received his education at the University of Tübingen, in 1720 became teacher of law there, and in 1729 was appointed to the full professorship. In 1736 he became a director of the university at Frankfurt an der Oder, but in 1739, having fallen into disfavor with Frederick William I, was compelled to resign. He then founded the academy at Hanau for the education of the young nobility in political science. He is credited with being the first to publish a systematic account of European international law. He was a prolific writer, his books numbering over 500, the most important being *Deutsches Staatsrecht,* 53 vols. (1737–54).

MOSES, mō'zẽz; mō-zĭz, religious and military chief, founder and first legislator of the Hebrew nation (c. 1350–1250 B.C.). He led Hebrew tribesmen from Egypt to the Sinaitic Peninsula (see EXODUS, BOOK OF), conferred upon them religious and political unity by means of a covenant (see BIBLE—*7. Religion and Theology of the Old Testament*), and brought them after 40 years of desert wanderings to Moab, in Transjordania (now Jordan) within sight of the land of Canaan.

Literary critics and historians tended in the 19th century to doubt the validity of the Biblical traditions concerning Moses, and they merely affirmed his historical existence. During the 20th century, by contrast, scholars have come generally to recognize a large core of historicity within the legendary character of the documentation.

Sources of Information.—The name of Moses is never mentioned in the relatively large body of Egyptian texts which have come from the 2d millennium B.C. A similar silence characterizes the Palestinian, Syro-Phoenician and Mesopotamian inscriptions of the period. This fact, however, has little significance. Archaeological documentation of the ancient Near Eastern history is marred by many lacunae. Moreover, it is doubtful that mention of Moses would have been made in the annals of the Egyptian administration or in the diplomatic letters of the Fertile Crescent ambassadors who were accredited to the Pharaonic court. The Egyptian monarchs were not prone to keep a permanent record of their military defeats. Besides, the event of the Hebrew Exodus constituted at the time a minor border incident, similar to many others. Modern historians are no longer surprised by the lack of non-Biblical evidence concerning Moses, or for that matter Abraham and the other patriarchs. The case is not unlike that of Buddha, Jesus, Mohammed or other religious figures, whose activity took place at the fringe of the political centers of civilization.

The Biblical account of Moses is found in the first five books of the Old Testament (see PENTATEUCH) and it has been thoroughly analyzed for the past 200 years; critics have been led to separate three main types of documents of various ages, provenances and historical values, which are now skillfully intermingled into an editorial whole:

(1) An early group of oral traditions, which received two different and successive editions, one in Jerusalem at the time of David and Nathan (c. 1000 B.C.) and the other in northern Israel at the time of Ahab and Elijah (c. 850 B.C.); these edited traditions are known respectively as the Yahwist account (J) and the Elohist account (E).

(2) Other traditions, especially concerned with legal matters, were gathered in northern Israel and later published in Jerusalem at the time of Josiah (621 B.C.); these traditions have been incorporated in the work of the Deuteronomist (D, so called because the laws he presented in the mouth of Moses appear now as a "second law" (Deutero-nomy) after the "first law" found now in the books of Exodus, Numbers, and Leviticus).

(3) Still other traditions, chiefly concerned with religious ritual, were gathered by the descendants of Jerusalem priests during and after the Babylonian Exile (587–538 B.C.); these are known as the work of the Priestly school (P), which is also responsible for the final editing of the earlier traditions (J, E, D) and their incorporation into the present Pentateuch. As a consequence of this analysis, historians of Moses are inclined to rely more confidently upon the earlier sources (J and E) than upon the later documents (D and P) although they recognize that even these have preserved nuggets of ancient oral traditions. Historians also point out that the figure of Moses became the object of legendary concern from about the time of the Babylonian Exile on. In the pre-Exilic period, Israel and Judah were not likely to embellish the national memories concerning Moses for they did not seem to give him the place of supreme significance which he later assumed in post-Exilic Judaism. Outside of the early sources of the Pentateuch (J and E), references and allusions to Moses are both few and sober (I Samuel 12:6, 6:4; Jeremiah 15:1).

Moses and Egypt.—The name "Moses" (in Hebrew, *Mosheh*) has been connected with the Hebrew eponym of the Levitical clan of Mushi (Numbers 26:58), although popular etymology related it to the Hebrew verb *mashah,* to draw (Exodus 2:10). Modern opinion tends to consider it as an adaptation of the Egyptian verb *msj,* to bring forth, which appears in such names as Thutmose, Rameses (Ramses), etc. If this is correct, the historical basis of the legends concerning the birth and childhood of Moses appears to be solid, and there are reasons to support the later Jewish and Christian view according to which Moses was educated in schools of Egyptian wisdom (Acts 7:22). The pharaohs of the 2d millennium B.C. trained a large body of public servants for foreign service, especially in the states of the Fertile Crescent. A number of similarities between some prescriptions of the Covenant Code (Exodus 20:21 to 23:19), which represents a nucleus of laws originating with Moses, and some Egyptian maxims may point to an Egyptian influence. It is possible that Moses also heard of the short-lived religious reform of Amenhotep IV (Akhenaton, Ikhnaton, c. 1370–1353 B.C.), but the differences which separate this example of the misnamed Egyptian "monotheism" from the Mosaic faith in Yahweh are so radical that the originality of Moses can hardly be questioned and is generally held by modern historians of comparative religions. The Egyptian god Aton, worshiped by Akhenaton, was merely a personification of a natural force, whereas the Hebraic deity, Yahweh, was clearly believed to transcend nature, even in the early days of Israel's religion.

Moses and the Midianites.—Biblical traditions tell how Moses, after the murder of an Egyptian, was compelled to flee to the Sinaitic Peninsula (Exodus 2:11–15), where he became acquainted with Midianite nomads. These were probably related to Abraham through the Ishmaelites (Genesis 25:2, 12–18; 37:28). Having married a Midianite woman (Exodus 2:16–22), Moses was exposed to his father-in-law's worship of Yahweh (Exodus 4:24–26, 28; 10–24; Numbers 10:29–32), although his own mother belonged already to a Yahwist group, as is shown by her theomorphic name, Jochebed, Yahweh-give-glory (Exodus 6:20). The revelation of the divine name at the scene of the burning bush (Exodus 3:13 fol.) indicates the specific feature of the Mosaic faith in a God who is the creator of the universe and master of history ("I cause to be whatever I cause to be," Exodus 3:14, rather than the traditional rendering, "I am that I am").

Moses and the Hebrews.—The date and route of the Exodus are still a matter of debate. According to a growing consensus, Moses led eastward from the northeastern border towns of the Nile Delta a group of Hebrew slaves and this event, which probably took place in about 1275 B.C., during the reign of Ramses II (1290–1223 B.C.), later proved to be the birth of the Hebrew nation and religion. The fugitives eluded the pursuit of an Egyptian border guard at the Sea of Reeds (a marshy region in the Isthmus of Suez) and continued southward as far as Mount Sinai (Horeb), traditionally associated with Djebel Musa, in the south of the Sinaitic Peninsula. There Moses promulgated on the behalf of the God of the Hebrew fathers, Yahweh, a covenant which bound the Hebrew tribesmen into a sociological body unique in ancient history. In them Moses instilled the sense of a universal mission (Exodus 19:4–6) which is directly responsible for the three major religions of Judaism, Christianity, and Islam. There also, Moses codified a program for national and individual morality, based upon religion, which he summarized in the "Ten Words" later developed into the traditional forms of the Decalogue (Exodus 20:1–20; Deuteronomy 5:6–21).

Moses met with recurring opposition from his own people, sometimes with open rebellion (Numbers 16), and after a protracted sojourn at the oasis of Kadesh (Ain Qedeis, northwest of the Gulf of 'Aqaba, he proceeded northward to the east of the Dead Sea. He died in the territory of Moab on Mount Nebo (Deuteronomy 34:1–8).

While later Judaism ascribed to Moses the authorship of the whole Pentateuch, including the account of his own death, modern scholarship stresses his religious and political activity. To Moses should be credited the faith which later was formulated into a monotheistic creed, by which man not only affirms the existence of one God, but also refuses to manipulate religion for individualistic or nationalistic aims and assumes total responsibility for the work of universal peace (Genesis 12:3*b*).

Bibliography.—Gressmann, H., *Mose und seine Zeit* (Göttingen 1913); Volz, P., *Mose* (Tübingen 1907), rev. ed., *Mose und sein Werk* (Tübingen 1932); Buber, M., *Moses* (Oxford 1946); Rowley, H. H., *From Joseph to Joshua* (London 1950); Hicks, G. E., *My Servant Moses* (London 1951); Auerbach, E., *Moses* (Amsterdam 1953); Griffiths, J. G., "The Egyptian derivation of the name Moses," *Journal of Near Eastern Studies*, vol. 12, pp. 225–231 (Chicago 1953); Cazelles, H., and others, *Moïse, l'Homme de l'Alliance* (Paris 1955).

NOTE: Among many works of fiction, the historical novels of Edmond Fleg (New York 1928), Louis Untermeyer (New York 1928), and Sholem Asch (New York 1951) are outstanding; on the contrary, the psychiatric essay of Sigmund Freud, *Moses and Monotheism* (New York 1939), has no historical value.

SAMUEL TERRIEN,
Auburn Professor of Old Testament, Union Theological Seminary, New York.

MOSES, Anna Mary (nee ROBERTSON; popularly GRANDMA MOSES), American painter: b. Greenwich, N.Y., Sept. 7, 1860; d. Hoosick Falls, N.Y., Dec. 13, 1961. One of ten children, a farmer's daughter with very little schooling, she became a "hired girl." In 1887 she married Thomas Salmon Moses, a farmhand. The couple rented a farm near Staunton, Va., and she took up the arduous life of a farmer's wife. In 1905 she and her husband moved to Eagle Bridge, N.Y., where he died in 1927 and she spent the rest of her long life. At the age of 78, unable to do farm work because her hands were crippled with arthritis, she began painting in oils. With no technical training, from copying Currier and Ives prints and the like she turned to painting original farm scenes and landscapes "so that people will see how we used to live." She worked from memory, not from life, but she had always been a keen observer with an instinctive feeling for color and composition. Her paintings soon attracted attention; some of them were shown at the Museum of Modern Art and she was given a "one-man show" in New York City. In all she painted more than 1,000 naive but sincere and highly individualistic pictures before her death, and she was acclaimed as an "authentic primitive" and "the grand old lady of American art."

Consult Moses, Anna Mary, *Grandma Moses: American Primitive*, ed. by Otto Kallir (New York 1946); id., *My Life's History* (New York 1951).

MOSES, Bernard, American historian and political economist: b. Burlington, Conn., Aug. 27, 1846; d. March 4, 1930. After graduating from the University of Michigan in 1870, he went to Europe for further study receiving his Ph.D. from Heidelberg in 1873. In 1875 he became professor of history at Albion College, and in 1876 professor of history at the University of California, where he pioneered in the study and teaching of Latin American history, especially the colonial period. Among his more important works are *The Establishment of Spanish Rule in America* (1898); *The Spanish Dependencies in South America* (2 vols., 1914); *Spanish Colonial Literature in South America* (1922); and *The Intellectual Background of the Revolution in South America, 1810–1814* (1926). He also served as a member of the United States Philippine Commission in 1900–1902.

MOSES, George Higgins, American diplomat and legislator: b. Lubec, Me., Feb. 9, 1869; d. Concord, N.H., Dec. 20, 1944. In 1890 he graduated at Dartmouth College. He was a leading figure in Republican political circles at Concord, N.H., where he became, in 1898, president of the Monitor and Statesman Company. During 1909–1912 he was United States minister to Greece and Montenegro. From 1918 until 1933 he was United States senator from New Hampshire; from 1925 he was president pro tempore of the Senate.

MOSHEIM, mŏs'hīm, **Johann Lorenz von,** German Protestant theologian: b. Lübeck, Oct. 9, 1694; d. Göttingen, Sept. 9, 1755. He taught at Kiel and Helmstedt prior to 1747, when he became professor and chancellor of the University of Göttingen, which he helped to found. A notable preacher and erudite theologian, he wrote several church histories, among them *Institutiones Historiae Ecclesiasticae* (1755) and *Institutiones Historiae Christianae* (1763).

MOSHER, mō'zhẽr, **Eliza Maria,** American physician: b. Cayuga County, N. Y., Oct. 2, 1846; d. New York City, Oct. 16, 1928. She graduated at the University of Michigan in 1875, studied medicine in Paris during 1879–1880, and was on the staff of the Massachusetts Reformatory for Women until 1883. For the next three years she was professor of physiology at Vassar College, and from 1886 until 1896 she practiced medicine in Brooklyn, N. Y. Thereafter she was professor of hygiene at the University of Michigan until 1902, when she resumed practice in Brooklyn.

MOSKVA, mŏs-kvȧ', Russia, an affluent of the Oka, a tributary of the Volga. Rising east of Smolensk, it flows through the city of Moscow and joins the Oka near Kolomna after a total course of 310 miles. The Battle of Borodino (q.v.) was fought near its banks.

MOSLEM SECTS. The first great schism in Islam (q.v.) was that which divided the community of believers into two opposing camps: The Sunnites and the Shi'ites. The Sunnites have always constituted the vast majority and are referred to as orthodox. The estimated number of Shi'ites and their offshoots are today some 45 million, about 15 per cent of the Moslem society, with Persia (Iran) and Iraq as their bulwark.

Shi'ites.—The Shi'ite sect did not crystallize until the Ommiad (Umayyad) period (661–750), but the underlying issue goes back to the time of Mohammed (q.v.). On his death in 632 the all-important question arose as to who should succeed him. Those who later became known as Shi'ites (partisans, that is, of Ali) maintained from the beginning that such an important office could not be left to the whims and fancies of the people, and that God had designated through Mohammed a successor (*khalīfah,* caliph) who was none other than Ali, husband of his only surviving daughter, Fatima. They further held that the office of successorship, caliphate, to which the Shi'ites prefer the term imamate, should be hereditary, limited to the progeny of Mohammed. The murder of Ali in 661 and of his two sons and successors al-Hasan (c. 669 and al-Husain (680) did not dampen the zeal of their followers. The three were immediately raised into the rank of martyrs. In their deaths they became more influential than in their lives.

In course of time the Shi'ites became more differentiated from the Sunnites. They rejected the Sunnite books of tradition (*ḥadīth*), differed in matters of law and ceremonies, did not regard participation in public worship as obligatory, and considered pilgrimage to the shrine of Ali, in Najaf, or to that of al-Husain, in Karbala, a permissible substitute for a pilgrimage to Mecca; and to the formula "No god but Allah and Mohammed is the prophet of Allah," they added "and Ali is the vicegerent (*wali*) of Allah." Having been always a minority and often subjected to persecution, they came to believe that it was lawful for a Shi'ite in time of danger to deny his Shi'ism and profess the prevailing faith (*taqīyah,* dissimulation). Shi'ites also consider it lawful to practice temporary marriage (*mut'ah*), which is frowned upon by the Sunnites.

Kharijites.—Another early but small sect which had its origin in a divergent view of the caliphate, which from our point of view is a political rather than theological issue, was the Kharijites (goers-out, seceders). Originally staunch supporters of Ali, the Kharijites broke away from him because he was willing to submit his right to the caliphate, when disputed by his rival Mu'awiyah, to arbitration. An offshoot of this sect survives today in Algeria, Zanzibar, and Oman, where primitive legal and theological views are held and intermarriage with Moslems is forbidden.

Qadarites.—The first important sect in Islam that split on theological or philosophical rather than political grounds was the Qadarites (from *qadar,* power), who maintained that man had power over his own actions. In this they went counter to the orthodox Islamic view of predestination, a corollary of God's almightiness strongly emphasized in the Koran. The Qadarite school of thought arose under the Ommiads, and claimed two of the caliphs as converts to their cause. Their interest in free will and self-determination indicates that the impulse came from contact with Greek Christian thought in Syria. The Qadarites were the precursors of the Mu'tazilites (separatists).

Rationalists.—To the Qadarite doctrine of free will the Mu'tazilites added another rational one, that of the denial of the coexistence with God of such divine attributes as wisdom and power. To the members of this school of thought, the attributes of God were not entities beside God. They further maintained that the Koran was not the "uncreated word of God" but a product of Mohammed's composition under divine influence. Their assertion of the supremacy of reason won them the title of the rationalists of Islam.

At the rise of this school its adherents were treated as heretics by the Sunnites, but when the Caliph al-Ma'mun, in the early 9th century, became himself a Mu'tazilite, its doctrine was made the official creed of the state. Al-Ma'mun even went so far as to establish an inquisition (*miḥnah*), the only one in the history of Islam. Shortly after his time orthodoxy was restored, and the sect has become practically extinct.

Twelvers.—The Shi'ites, as nonconformists, produced the largest number of sects. They first split into two: Twelvers, and Seveners. The Twelvers, also called Imamates, transmit the successorship to Mohammed (imamate) from father to son, beginning with Ali and ending with the 12th imam, Mohammed al-Muntazar (the expected one). In 878, when still a boy, Mohammed supposedly vanished in the mosque of Samarra, Iraq, and has since lived in secret, to appear on the last day as the Mahdi (rightly guided one), a sort of Messiah. Until the present the Mahdi is still in a state of occultation, and his appearance will usher in an era of universal Islam, peace, and prosperity. Since 1502 this Twelver Shi'ah has been established as the state religion of Persia, with the shah as the temporary substitute for the hidden imam. In Syria and Lebanon, a few thousand Shi'ites have survived under the name Matāwilah (friends, that is, of Ali). In Yemen, they are known as Zaydites, after a great-grandson of Ali. The Zaydites are the nearest Shi'ite faction to the Sunnites.

Seveners.—The main Seveners make the 7th imam, Isma'il (d. 760), their last and greatest one. Hence their other designation, Isma'ilites. To them, the line of "visible imams" ends in this Isma'il. In course of time the Isma'ilites deviated more and more from the body of Islam, and this resulted in a number of extreme sects considered outside the pale of Islam by the orthodox body.

As a measure of safety the Isma'ilites resorted to secrecy in the practice of their faith, and introduced initiatory practices. The number seven assumed sacred importance in their scheme, as it had done in the Pythagorean system. Though secretly organized, they inaugurated one of the most subtle and effective politico-religious propagandas ever witnessed by Islam. As emissaries (sing. *dā'i*) they employed clever teachers disguised as merchants and travelers who covered the entire area from Persia to North Africa.

In Iraq, a group closely allied to the Isma'ilites flourished under the name Qarmatians (Carmathians). The appellation comes from an Aramaic word meaning peasants. These were extreme revolutionists whose violence in the 9th to 11th centuries drenched Iraq and Syria in blood. Another closely related group was organized in northern Persia under the name Neo-Isma'ilites. These are the people known to the West under the name Assassins (*hashshāshīn,* cannabis addicts) and whose activity in the period of the Crusades resulted in the murder of many Frankish leaders. It was at that time that the word assassin was introduced into the European languages. From its birthplace in Alamut, Persia, in 1090, the Assassin movement spread into Syria. Certain elements there, dissatisfied with the local regime, were predisposed to the new doctrine. From his retreat in Syria "the old man of the mountain" terrorized the whole land. Remnants of this sect are found today in Syria, Persia, Afghanistan, and (particularly) in India, where their leader, the Aga Khan, claims descent from Ali through the Iranian founder of the order.

Fatimid Caliphate.—In North Africa, the successful Isma'ili propaganda resulted in the establishment of the caliphate (909–1171) whose members claimed descent from Fatima. This was the only Shi'ite caliphate of importance. From their capital, Cairo, the Fatimids ruled over Syria, and when the Crusaders marched against Palestine that land was a part of their domain. It was one of these caliphs, the fanatical al-Hakim (996–1021), whom the Druzes considered the final incarnation of the deity. Such a concept was a culmination of the extravagant veneration accorded Ali and his descendants by their followers.

Druzes.—The Druzes are so named after a missionary of Persian or Turkish origin, Darazi, who preached the divinity of al-Hakim among the mountaineers of Lebanon, in Syria, where he fell in battle about 1019. Darazi was the first to proclaim the divinity of al-Hakim in Egypt. The Druzes today are confined to Lebanon and Syria. In their theology and cosmogony they have retained many of the original Isma'ili doctrines. They indulge in no propaganda, accept no proselytes, keep their books secret in manuscript form, and divulge their tenets only to the initiated few called *'uqqāl* (wise), as opposed to the mass of their community, termed *juhhāl* (ignorant). They practice monogamy, ignore pilgrimage and the other pillars of Islam, and do not observe regular or congregational prayers. By the orthodox, their doctrines (and those of the Isma'ilites, Qarmatians, and Assassins) are considered extreme heterodoxies.

Nusayris.—Another ultra-Shi'ite sect which has survived in Syria is the Nusayriyah. Under the French mandate created in the 1920's the Nusayris were given a somewhat new name, Alawites (followers of Ali), and organized into a separate state with Laodicea (al-Lādhiqīyah) as capital. The Nusayris take their name from Mohammed ibn-Nusayr, a partisan of the eleventh imam al-Hasan al-Askari (d. 874). They deify Ali, practice the rites of their religion in secret, and retain clear remnants of pre-Islamic pagan beliefs. Both they and the Druzes believe in metempsychosis. Like the Druzes, the Nusayris divide their community into two groups: The multitude of the profane, who are kept in the dark so far as the tenets are concerned; and the chosen few, who are initiated into the mysteries of the cult. There are other minor sects which in their excessive veneration of Ali and his progeny raised these personages into titular deities and endowed them with superhuman power.

Three of the modern Islamic movements deserve special consideration: The Baha'is of Persia, the Wahabis of Arabia, and the Ahmadiyah of India.

Baha'is.—Baha'ism had for a forerunner another Persian sect called Babism. This was founded in 1844–1845 by Mirza Ali Mohammed and his successors, who held to the view of continuous and progressive Divine revelation. It is, therefore, an offshoot of Shi'ism. The founder claimed descent from al-Husain, the Prophet's grandson, and adopted the title of al-Bab (the gate), whence the name of his votaries. He promulgated his mission in Shiraz, where he appeared as a kind of Messiah aiming to establish the supremacy of the imamate Shi'ah over Islam. To this end he revealed a new book abrogating the Koran, and was executed by order of the Persian government at Tabriz in 1850. Some 20,000 of his followers were likewise slaughtered. In 1909 his bodily remains were transported to Haifa, on the Palestine coast.

Thirteen years after the death of al-Bab a disciple of his, another Persian, Bahaullah (splendor of God) by name, was accepted as the manifestation of the Divinity heralded by the Bab. He in turn set forth a new revelation, and addressed a series of official missives to the heads of governments in which he condemned war, preached universal peace and brotherhood, and advocated the adoption of a universal language. Fundamental in his teaching was the idea that God was unknowable except through His manifestations, the prophets, who differed outwardly but in essence were one, revealing one truth. On his death in Acre in 1892 his eldest son, Abbas Effendi, succeeded him under the title Abdul Baha (the slave of al-Baha'). Abbas Effendi resided in Acre and later in Haifa, where he died in 1921. Before World War I he visited the United States, where his followers eventually numbered several thousand, mostly in Chicago and New York.

Ahmadiyah.—Another modernist reformist sect is the Ahmadiyah, which also maintains missionary centers in the United States as well as

Britain. It is so-called after Mirza Ghulam Ahmad (d. 1908), a native of Qadian, in the Punjab. Ahmad began preaching in 1879. He taught that Christ was taken down from the cross while still alive and finally made his way into northern India, where he spent his last days. Ahmad considered himself as the person in whom the double mission of the expected Christian Messiah and Moslem Mahdi were united. He expounded the holy war (*jihād*) as striving after righteousness, a struggle in which weapons are spiritual rather than physical.

Wahabis.—Unlike these two modern movements, Wahabism sought reform by reaction rather than innovation. The founder was Mohammed ibn-Abd-al-Wahab (1703–1791), of Nejd. Unfavorably impressed by the new trends in Islamic thought and practice, ibn-Abd-al-Wahab aimed to restore Islam to the golden age of the Prophet and his early companions by stripping it of all its novel accretions. He rejected consensus of opinion as a source of authority, and condemned music and the wearing of silk and jewelry. By marriage he became allied with the ruling house of Nejd, that of Saud. In the first years of the 19th century the Wahabis had developed enough strength to impose their rule upon central and western Arabia, including the holy cities. After a long eclipse their power was reestablished by 'Abd-al-'Azīz ibn-Saud, who created Saudi Arabia in 1932 and has since been its ruler.

Sufism.—No study of Islamic sects is complete without some consideration of Sufism, which in reality is not a sect but a way of life. The word comes from an Arabic term meaning wool; early Sufis wore the material in imitation of Christian monks. Sufism is mysticism as practiced in Islam. It represents a reaction against the formalism developed in the first centuries of Islam, and is an attempt to seek direct and personal relationship with the deity. Beginning on the ascetic level, Sufism grew into a syncretic system, borrowing elements from Christian, Neo-Platonic, and Buddhist sources. From the ascetic it consequently passed on into the mystic, theosophic, and pantheistic stages.

In the 13th century Sufi fraternities or orders were organized in the different parts of the Moslem world. Earliest among these was the Qadirite, so called after a Persian, Abd-al-Qadir al-Jilani (d. 1166), who preached in Baghdad. This order now claims adherents in most Moslem lands from Algeria in the west to Java in the east. Another order, the Mawlawi, commonly known as that of the whirling dervishes, became especially strong in Ottoman Turkey. The superior of the order enjoyed the privilege of girding each new sultan-caliph with his sword. This order, together with others, was abolished by Mustafa Kemal (Kemal Atatürk).

Senusi.—One of the most recent and interesting brotherhoods is that of the Senusis (Sanusis), founded by an Algerian sheikh in 1837. It is a conservative militant order which had a wide vogue in North Africa and succeeded in establishing a theocratic state in the desert between Tripoli and Egypt. From their headquarters in the oasis of Kufra, the warlike members of this order have caused much trouble to the Italians in Libya, and to other European colonists.

Bibliography.—Haarbrücker, Theodor, *Asch-Schahrastānī's Religionspartheien und Philosophenschulen* (Halle 1850–51); Goldziher, Ignaz, *Mohammedanische Studien* (Halle 1889–90); Dussaud, René, *Histoire et religion des Nosairis* (Paris 1900); De Boer, T. J., *History of Philosophy in Islam,* tr. by E. R. Jones (London 1903); Macdonald, Duncan B., *Development of Muslim Theology, Jurisprudence, and Constitutional Theory* (New York 1903); Friedlaender, Israel, *The Heterodoxies of the Shi'ites* (New Haven 1909); Nicholson, Reynold A., *The Mystics of Islam* (London 1914); id., *Studies in Islamic Mysticism* (Cambridge 1921); Hitti, Philip K., *The Origins of the Druze People and Religion* (New York 1928); Lammens, H., *Islām: Beliefs and Institutions,* tr. by E. Denison Ross (London 1929); Donaldson, Dwight M., *The Shi'ite Religion* (London 1933); Halkin, Abraham S., *Moslem Schisms and Sects* (Tel Aviv 1935); Lewis, Bernard, *The Origins of Isma'ilism* (Cambridge 1940); Hitti, Philip K., *History of the Arabs,* 4th ed., rev. (London 1949).

PHILIP K. HITTI,
Professor of Semitic Literature, Princeton University.

MOSLER, mōz'lĕr, **Henry,** American genre painter: b. New York, June 6, 1841; d. there, April 21, 1920. He studied under James Henry Beard during 1859–1861, and in 1862–1863 he was art correspondent for *Harper's Weekly* in western campaigns of the American Civil War. The next three years were spent at schools of painting at Düsseldorf and Paris, and in 1874 he returned to Europe, first residing at Munich and from 1877 to 1894 in Paris. His *Le Retour* was the first American picture to be purchased by the French government for the Luxembourg Museum. The Metropolitan Museum of Art, New York, acquired his painting entitled *A Wedding Feast in Brittany;* and the Corcoran Art Gallery, Washington, D.C., his *Saying Grace.* Other paintings by him included *The Lost Cause; Last Sacrament; Spinning Girl; Rainy Day.*

MOSQUE, mŏsk, a Moslem house of prayer. The form of the oldest mosque was that of the Christian basilica which, however, became modified in the progress of Moslem architecture. The famous mosques of Turkey resemble the Byzantine architecture of Constantinople (Istanbul); and certain of those of India, the temples of the Jains. In course of time domes and minarets became emblematic of the more characteristic and ornate examples of Moslem art; but these are not essential, for in poor communities a bare whitewashed room may suffice for the public worship of the faithful. The mosques often include, in a quadrangular area, an immense number of columns arranged in files. In numerous instances these columns are the rich spoils of antique monuments. Mosque architecture possesses no fixed rules, lightness and elegance alone being deemed the fundamental laws of architecture. Mosques contain neither altars, nor paintings, nor images. A great quantity of lamps of various kinds form the principal interior ornament, together with some sentences from the Koran written on the white walls. The buildings are often quadrangular in plan, and have an open interior court, where are fountains for ablutions. In the southeast of the building there is a pulpit for the imām; in the direction in which Mecca lies (the *Qiblah*) there is a niche toward which the faithful look when they engage in prayer. Opposite the pulpit there is a platform surrounded by a parapet, with a desk on which is placed the Koran for the purpose of reading to the congregation. On Fridays the five daily prayers, obligatory on the faithful every day, are recited in the mosque by the whole congregation, together with additional prayers. It is not customary for women to enter the mosques, and when they do they are placed separate from the men. Several muezzins call the people to prayer. Prayers are led by an imam. The imam and the muezzins, in addition to their religious duties, generally pursue secular callings.

It is usual to cover the floor of the mosque with carpets, but there are no seats. On entering a mosque, the faithful remove their shoes. The building is never closed; and while nothing could exceed the devotion of the congregation gathered together in worship, at other times the mosques serve as convenient meeting places and abodes in which wayfarers may accommodate themselves. They also serve as schools and seats of learning. Thousands of students are regularly in attendance at the most famous of these, al-Azhar Mosque in Cairo. In addition to schools, mosques frequently have hospitals and kitchens for preparing food for the poor. The mosques are maintained for the most part by endowments in land.

See also Islamic Art and Architecture.

MOSQUERA, môs-kā'rä, **Tomás Cipriano de,** Colombian statesman: b. Popayán, Colombia, Sept. 20, 1798; d. Coconuco, Oct. 7, 1878. He fought with distinction in the war of independence and, after serving as a senator (from 1833), became president of New Granada (1845–1849). Mosquera's administration was progressive and enlightened; he reformed the monetary system, abolished the slave trade, combated clerical influence in political affairs, and advanced public education. After leaving office, he joined forces with the Liberal Party on a program of anticlericalism and decentralization of governmental power, and in 1859–1861 he led a successful Liberal revolt against the incumbent Conservative administration. Taking power as provisional president in July 1861, Mosquera proceeded to effect severe measures against the church, especially the Jesuits and monastic orders. In 1863 a new constitution was adopted, making the country a federal republic to be called the United States of Colombia, with extensive powers reserved to the states. Mosquera became the first president under the new constitution in 1863 and was elected again in 1866. But the enemies he had made by his anticlerical program and his assumption of wide personal powers brought his downfall in 1867, when he was exiled to Lima, Peru. He returned to Colombia four years later. He was the author of books on the geography of New Granada and a valuable life of Simón Bolívar (1853).

MOSQUITIA. See Mosquito Coast.

MOSQUITO, mŭs-kē'tō, a name applied to insects of the dipterous family Culicidae. The name is a diminutive of the Spanish *mosca* (fly). Throughout the world there are nearly 2,500 species grouped in about 110 genera and subgenera, among which the names *Aedes, Anopheles,* and *Culex* are the most commonly encountered. Mosquitoes are found almost everywhere in the world except in the icebound areas surrounding the poles, in extremely dry desert areas, and at elevations of over 12,000 to 14,000 feet. They have been introduced by man into many regions to which they are not native, and have often become established in such regions.

Mosquitoes are true Diptera in having only one pair of wings and a pair of halteres, or balancers. The wings and some other parts of the body (Fig. 1) are abundantly provided with scales, and the mouth parts of the female are formed into an elongated, slender, sucking tube with which she pierces the skin of her host to obtain her meals of blood. Mosquitoes are close relatives of black flies, nonbiting midges of several kinds, and of crane flies. Most of the stories about giant mosquitoes refer to the last-named insects. The wing span of most mosquito species varies between ⅜ and ½ inch, and the body, very slender and elongated, usually measures scarcely more than ¼ inch in length.

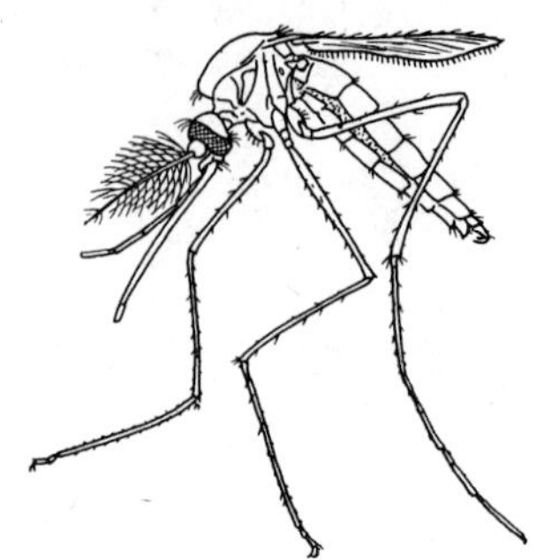

Fig. 1. Adult male mosquito (*Aedes aegypti*).

Mosquitoes are holometabolous—that is, their life history is composed of a series of stages, all quite different in form. These are the egg, larva, pupa, and adult, the first three being aquatic and the last stage invariably taking to life in the air.

Adults.—Adult mosquitoes of only a very few species are active between midnight and dawn; most species fly about, mate, and feed at other hours. Certain groups of *Aedes* and their relatives are active during the day, while most species of *Anopheles* and *Culex* are crepuscular, or nocturnal. Usually the mosquitoes that fly and bite actively in the daytime also mate and lay eggs during the day, while those that fly and bite at night are nocturnal in their mating and egg-laying habits.

Resting places are usually very important to adult mosquitoes. These locations are usually difficult to find unless the mosquito habitually enters houses to rest. Laboratory studies have shown that light, temperature, and humidity acting together at the same time are the principal factors of the environment that influence mosquito behavior. All mosquitoes have a cycle of abundance governed by seasonal changes in temperature and humidity.

Biting.—Only the female mosquito seeks the blood of man or animals for food. The female of most species requires the protein of man, animal, or bird blood to mature its eggs, but investigation continues to reveal more and more species that are autogenous —that is, forming eggs without blood meals. This is done in the female by the conversion of stored fats and proteins into materials suitable for egg formation. The mouth part components of male mosquitoes are the same as those of the female but are different in shape because of their adaptation for feeding on nectar and external moisture associated with plants. Males never suck blood.

Little is known about the factors that enable females to find sources of blood meals from great distances. At close range, temperature and humidity have some effect, and carbon dioxide transpired from the skin is even more attractive to them. Numerous tests have shown that normal skin odors, including perspiration, are not in themselves attractive to mosquitoes, but that females are extremely sensitive to a certain few of the odors that combine to produce what we recognize as skin odor. Radiant heat also appears to be a factor in attracting females.

Female mosquitoes of certain species prefer human blood, others animal blood, and still others the blood of birds. Thorough studies of the biting habits of the most important species of *Anopheles* have shown their decided preference for human blood. It is well known that in most malaria epidemics only 1 or 2 species of *Anopheles* may be infective, while 5 to 10 other species also present in the area have little or nothing to do with malaria transmission because of their preference for animals or birds, which do not carry the human parasite (see section on *Malaria*).

The mechanism by which blood is obtained by the female is shown in Fig. 2. The semirigid portion of the elongated mouth parts is inserted into the skin of the victim, and the tip is twisted and turned until it enters a capillary or "pool" of blood formed by damage to cells by the proboscis. Saliva is injected into the wound before or during the uptake of blood to prevent clotting. This is the agent responsible for the intense itching so often experienced by those who have been bitten. It is also the important factor in disease transmission, since viruses, filariae, and malaria parasites eventually find their way to the salivary glands after development within the mosquito body.

Mating.—Mating may take place between isolated pairs of adults, or it may occur within a swarm composed of extremely large numbers of males. Such swarms are usually formed, in response to light intensity, over small prominences in the landscape, such as bushes, fence posts, or even over the heads of sitting or standing people. Each male flies about in this cloud in an apparently aimless, zigzag fashion. Females in small numbers are attracted to the sound of the swarm, fly into it, are seized, and drop from the swarm with their male companions. After being fertilized, they fly to resting places to mature their eggs. The sperm received from the male is held in a small sac near the ovipositor, or egg-laying apparatus, and as each egg matures it is forced backward through the oviduct and fertilized just before being laid.

The rapid movement of the wings in flight causes the familiar buzzing sound associated with mosquitoes. The mosquito adult usually lives for about 30 days, although the life span varies widely with temperature, humidity, and other factors in the environment.

Eggs.—Some mosquitoes, especially those of the genus *Culex,* cement a large number of eggs together side by side to form a raft which floats directly on the water surface. Others, such as *Anopheles,* lay eggs singly on the water. The eggs of many species of *Aedes* are laid in nearly dry spots on vegetation growing from the water and remain viable until water inundates them to initiate hatching. Some of these eggs remain unhatched after the second, third, and even fourth drenching, thereby assuring a supply of living young insects over a long period of time. However, the duration of the egg stage usually varies from less than 1 to more than 7 days.

Mosquito eggs (Fig. 3) are laid in all kinds of water collections, but each species has its own general type of egg-laying habitat. Some species, such as *Aedes aegypti,* lay eggs in artificial containers, such as empty cans and discarded tires. Other *Aedes* species deposit their eggs only in rapidly drying collections of weed-grown water. Many *Culex* species prefer small, more or less stagnant pools. *Anopheles* mosquitoes have many types of preferred places, usually relatively large bodies of fresh water overgrown with plants, but some species prefer water at the edges of swiftly flowing streams, and some lay their eggs in pools formed in rock formations without any sign of vegetation. Some lay their eggs only in holes in trees, and a number of mosquitoes use bromeliads (parasitic plants growing in various kinds of trees), pitcher plants, and other plant receptacles.

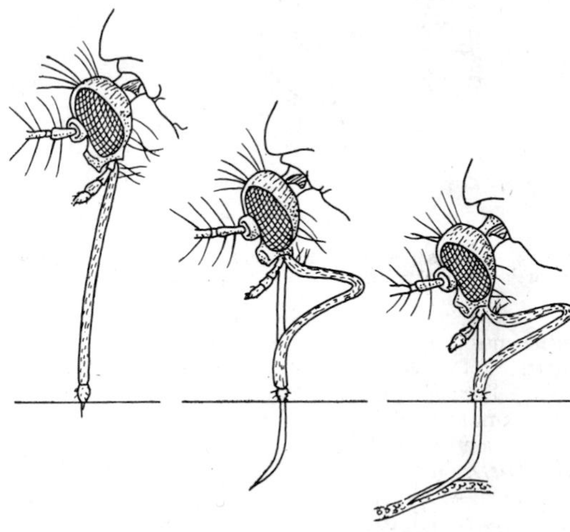

Fig. 2. Successive stages in the penetration of the sucking tube of a female mosquito feeding on blood.

Larvae.—After a sufficient incubation time has elapsed, an active, free-swimming larva hatches from the egg. It has a very well-developed head with large mouth parts, a large thorax, and an elongated abdomen, at the posterior end of which is mounted a pair of openings to the tracheal system, called the spiracles. Among

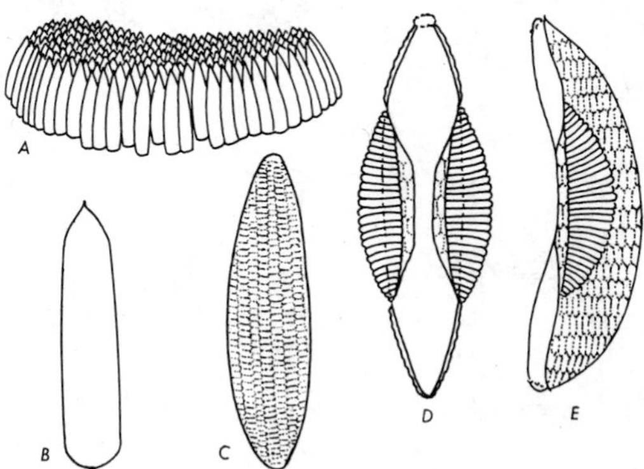

Fig. 3. Mosquito eggs. *A*, egg raft of *Culex*; *B*, single egg of *Culex*; *C*, egg of *Aedes aegypti*; *D*, egg of *Anopheles* (dorsal view); *E*, egg of *Anopheles* (lateral view).

mosquitoes there are two forms of larvae. In one of these, characteristic of *Anopheles* and its relatives, the abdominal spiracles are mounted very close to the body (Fig. 4*A*). The typical resting position of this type of larva is parallel to and at the water surface. In the other type (Fig. 4*B*), which includes most of the nonanopheline mosquitoes, the posterior spiracles are found at the end of an elongated respiratory "siphon" or tube. Larvae with a siphon hang in the water at an angle to the surface, with only the spiracles in contact with the air. In some of these non-*Anopheles* mosquitoes the tip of the siphon is provided with spines, teeth, and hooks by which it is inserted into the roots of aquatic plants for air, thus enabling the larva to live entirely submerged. In addition to the spiracles, by which oxygen is obtained directly from the air, the skin is constructed for the absorption of oxygen from the water much as in the gills of a fish. These larva can remain submerged for long periods.

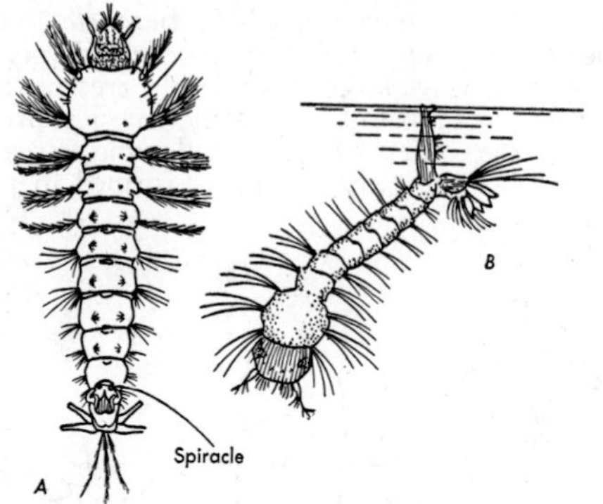

Fig. 4. *A*, dorsal view of an *Anopheles* larva; *B*, a *Culex* larva in feeding position.

Since the larval stage of the mosquito is concerned principally with growth, feeding is of utmost importance. Most mosquito larvae eat minute particles of food consisting of small bites of aquatic animal and plant life. Hence the mouth parts (Fig. 5) are usually prominent, heavy, and well muscled. Large brushes near the mouth opening create currents of water that converge at the center of the head. The incoming food particles adhere to these brushes but are scraped off by the combs and brushes of the mouth parts situated directly behind them. By a complicated series of transfers through this apparatus the food is concentrated at the mouth opening and swallowed, and the transporting water is sidetracked and expelled. The larvae of some mosquitoes are predaceous, and in these forms the mandibles are enlarged and play an important part in reducing prey to a size that can be swallowed. The usual length of larval life is 4 to 7 days, although the larvae of some species are found to live for over a month in unfavorable situations.

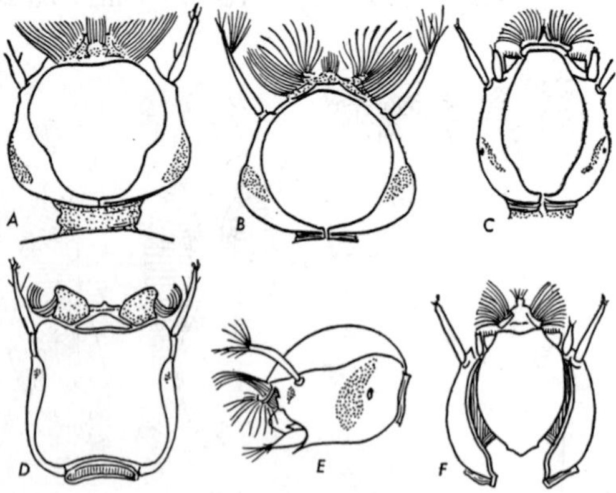

Fig. 5. Larvae heads and mouth parts. *A, Aedes aegypti; B, Culex; C, Anopheles quadrimaculatus; D, Toxorhynchites rutilus; E, Culex* (lateral view); *F, Anopheles farauti.*

Pupae.—When the larva has completed its feeding and reached full size, it sheds its skin for the last time, setting free an actively swimming pupa (Fig. 6). The pupa in most insects is a resting state within which the adult develops, but in mosquitoes the pupa swims about as freely as the larva. Its head and thorax are large and more or less fused, while the flat, elongated abdomen acts as a kind of oar to propel it through the water. Inside the pupal body a reorganization of tissues takes place. An adult mosquito gradually forms inside, and within two or three days (the length of life of the pupa of most species), the adult is fully developed and ready to emerge. This is accomplished by the adult's pulling away from the pupal skin, causing air to enter the space between the pupal skin and the mosquito. The mosquito swallows this trapped air and by swelling like a balloon splits the pupal skin along its back next to the water surface. The adult gradually pulls itself out of the skin (Fig. 7) and rests a short time to harden its tissues before flying away to start the life cycle over again.

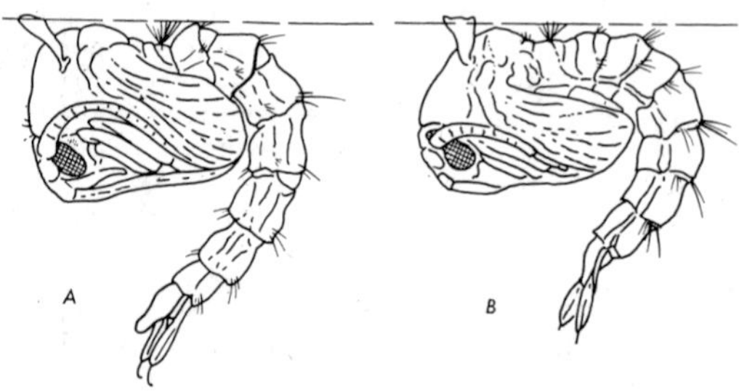

Fig. 6. Pupae in floating position at water surface. *A, Aedes atropalpus; B, Anopheles punctipennis.*

Disease Carriers.—As ordinary pests, mosquitoes are responsible in many areas of the world for the loss of valuable land, reduction in the health and productivity of livestock, and the interruption of the pleasure of many people. More important is the loss they bring as carriers of disease. No other group of insects is responsible for so much widespread human sickness.

Malaria.—Human malaria, caused by four species of parasite belonging to the genus *Plasmodium,* is prevalent around the world between latitudes 45° N. and 40° S.; it is responsible for more deaths every year than any other disease transmitted by arthropods. Only species of *Anopheles* carry malaria parasites from human to human, although other kinds of mosquitoes transmit the malarias of birds and mammals. In

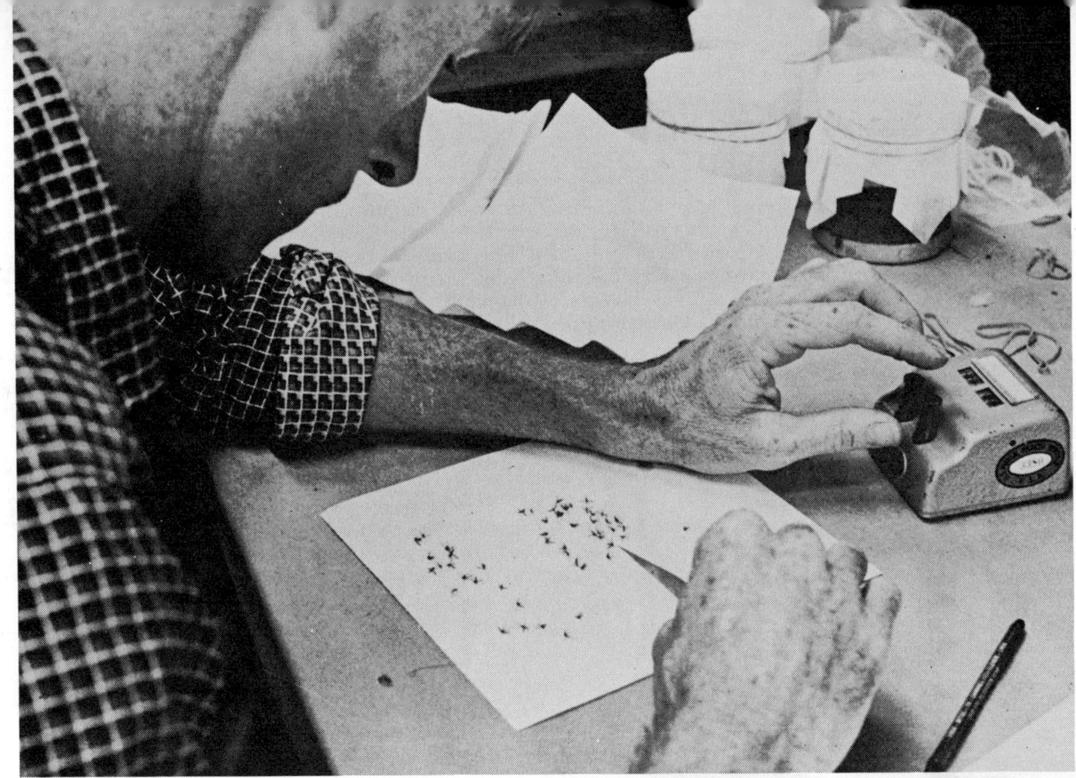

MOSQUITO

MALARIA CONTROL

Above: In a swampy island laboratory near Savannah, Ga., a United States Public Health Service communicable disease center technician tests the effects of new insecticides on mosquitoes.
Right: One drop of this West African child's blood, under microscopic examination, will reveal whether malaria parasites are present.
Below: The war against mosquitoes goes on in all latitudes; spray teams travel by all types of conveyances—including elephants, in Asia.
Bottom right: A horse is used to attract insects into a trap in Colombia, permitting a mosquito "census" to be taken of the surrounding area.

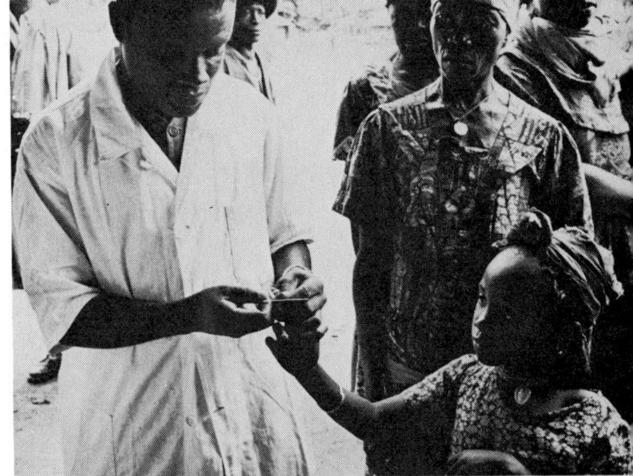

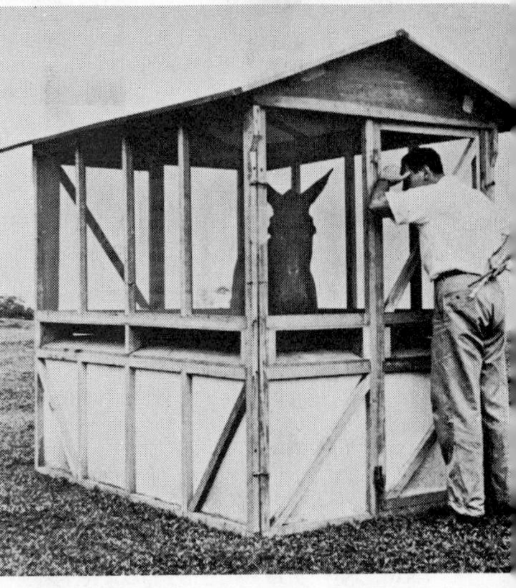

(Bottom right) Standard Oil photo; (others) World Health Organization photos

all cases the female draws up the parasites along with blood as she feeds. The parasites enter the gut of the mosquito, undergo a series of developmental stages in the gut wall, eventually pass through the gut wall, and enter the mosquito's blood stream, which carries them to the salivary glands. The life cycle of the parasite is started over when an infected mosquito discharges saliva with parasites into the blood stream of the animal or human which provides its next blood meal.

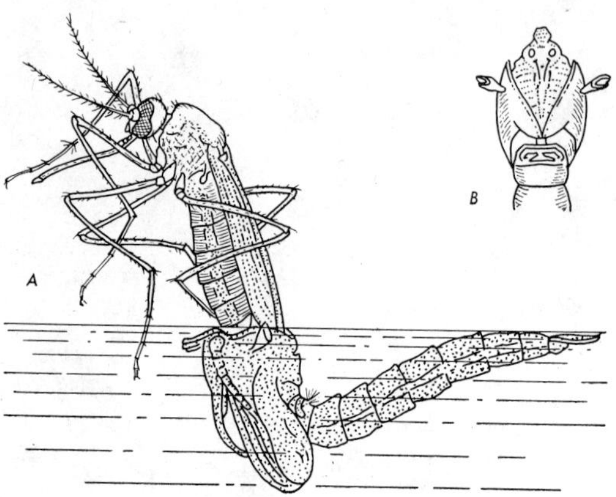

Fig. 7. *A*, an adult female of *Aedes aegypti* emerging from the submerged pupal skin; *B*, open thorax of discarded pupal skin of *Anopheles quadrimaculatus*.

Of the approximately 400 species of *Anopheles* known the world over, only about 85 or 90 have been incriminated directly or indirectly in human malaria transmission. By 1960, 6 countries had completely eradicated malaria by eradicating the species of *Anopheles* responsible for transmission, and about 70 others had eradication programs under way. See also MALARIA.

Filariasis.—Filariasis is caused by a wormlike parasite living in the blood and tissues of many different birds and mammals. In man the initial symptoms of fever, swelling, and stiffness are followed after three months to a year by swelling of the lymph passages and glands and in advanced stages of the disease by the stoppage of lymph flow by the parasites. Two species of this parasite, *Wuchereria bancrofti* and *W. malayi,* cause periodic filariasis; their numbers increase markedly in the peripheral blood of man between about 8 P.M. and 2 A.M. daily, the hours at which their mosquito hosts are most actively feeding. *W. pacifica,* a nonperiodic form, maintains comparatively even numbers of parasites in the blood stream. In both cases the adult worms live, usually in pairs, in the lymphatic vessels of the host and give rise to immature stages (microfilariae) which appear in the blood. These enter the mosquito gut at feeding time, undergo a period of development in the body of the mosquito, and migrate to her proboscis, from which they emerge and enter the intact skin or bite puncture of a new host at the next feeding. Filariasis is virtually worldwide in tropical and subtropical climates. *W. malayi* and *W. pacifica* are transmitted principally by species of *Anopheles* and *Mansonia,* while *W. bancrofti* is carried by various species of *Anopheles, Aedes*, and *Culex*. See also FILARIASIS.

Yellow Fever.—Two principal forms of yellow fever, urban and jungle, are found. Fast-disappearing urban yellow fever most often occurs in epidemics in seacoast cities in the southern part of the world where people live closely together. It is transmitted by *Aedes aegypti,* a rapidly breeding mosquito that inhabits all sorts of artificial water containers close to human habitation. Jungle yellow fever, on the other hand, is primarily a disease of forest animals, especially monkeys, and is more or less accidentally transmitted to man by species of *Haemagogus* and *Aedes* (other than *A. aegypti*) that live in forest habitats. This disease is prevalent in areas of the world having a combination of high rainfall and temperature, such as tropical rain forests of South America and Africa. The same virus is believed to cause both forms of this disease. It is picked up by the female mosquito in her blood meal and undergoes multiplication for one to three weeks in her body. Only at the end of this time is the female able to pass the virus on to other hosts by the saliva she injects at her next feeding. The mosquito remains infective for the rest of her life, but persons who have survived cases of yellow fever are thereafter immune. A mystery yet to be explained is the fact that no form of yellow fever has been recorded in the Orient, although *Aedes aegypti* is present there, sometimes in large numbers. See also YELLOW FEVER.

Dengue.—The virus of dengue is transmitted from man to man, without an animal reservoir, by *Aedes aegypti,* a worldwide mosquito; by *A. albopictus,* an inhabitant of the Pacific Islands and the Orient; and by closely related members of the so-called *A. scutellaris* group, which is confined largely to the Pacific area. However, the disease itself occurs only in various regions of the South and Southwest Pacific, India, Indonesia, New Guinea, Japan, a part of tropical Africa, the north shore of the Mediterranean, and in a few equatorial areas of the New World. Because the virus is present in the blood of man for only the first 24 hours of the infection, dengue is found only in areas where mosquitoes are present the year around. The various strains of dengue virus all produce symptoms of acute illness with fever, but immunity to any one strain lasts for the rest of a person's life. The virus is picked up by a female mosquito with a blood meal, as in the case of yellow fever, and is transmitted after about an eight-day incubation period to her next victim by saliva injection. See also DENGUE FEVER.

Other Viruses.—Various species of *Anopheles, Aedes, Culex, Psorophora,* and other genera transmit a large number of other viruses. Most important of these are the encephalitis viruses, such as Western, Eastern, and Venezuelan equine, St. Louis, California, Japanese, and Murray Valley (Australia). Because of intensified research, an increasing number of less important viruses are being made known to science. Many of these have mosquito carriers, but the method of transmission by the mosquito in many cases is not yet known. The American equine encephalitis viruses are believed to have a bird-to-mosquito-to-bird transmission cycle, man being more or less accidentally infected.

Bibliography.—Hewitt, Redginal I., *Bird Malaria,* American Journal of Hygiene Monograph No. 15 (Baltimore 1940); Bates, Marston, *The Natural History of Mosquitoes* (New York 1949); Boyd, Mark F., ed., *Malariology,* 2 vols. (Philadelphia 1949); Carpenter, Stanley J., and LaCasse, W. G., *Mosquitoes of North America* (Berkeley 1955); Horsfall, William R., *Mosquitoes; Their Bionomics and Relation to Disease* (New

York 1955); Foote, Richard H., and Cook, D. R., *Mosquitoes of Medical Importance*, U.S. Dept. of Agriculture Handbook No. 152 (Washington 1959); Snodgrass, Robert E., *The Anatomical Life of the Mosquito*, Smithsonian Miscellaneous Collections, vol. 139, no. 8 (Washington 1959); Stone, Alan, Knight, K. L., and Starcke, Helle, *A Synoptic Catalog of the Mosquitoes of the World*, Thomas Say Foundation Memoir No. 6, Entomological Society of America (College Park, Md., 1959); Christophers, Sir Samuel Rickard, *Aedes aegypti, the Yellow Fever Mosquito; Its Life History, Bionomics and Structure* (London and New York 1960).

RICHARD H. FOOTE,
Entomology Research Division, Agricultural Research Service, United States Department of Agriculture, Washington, D.C.

MOSQUITO COAST or **MOSQUITIA,** mŭs-kē′tĭ-ȧ, region, Central America, on the Caribbean coast, loosely defined as a strip about 40 miles wide extending along the entire east coast of Nicaragua and northwest along the coast of Honduras as far as the Aguán River. The area takes its name from the Mosquito (Miskito) Indians, who make up the basic population mixed with Negro and other racial elements. The region contains banana plantations and valuable hardwoods. In 1960 the World Court ruled in favor of Honduras in its dispute with Nicaragua over the land between the Coco and Patuca rivers.

MOSS, mŏs, **John Calvin,** American photoengraver: b. Washington County, Pa., Jan. 5, 1838; d. New York, N.Y., April 8, 1892. An early interest in daguerreotypes led Moss to experiment in engraving by means of photographs. With the help of his wife, Mary Bryant Moss, he established the Photoengraving Company in New York City in 1872, and when he achieved success, set up a larger company, the Moss Engraving Company. Here he trained engravers who became world famous, and although his methods were later supplanted, he was the first successful commercial photoengraver in the United States.

MOSS. See MOSSES.

MOSSADEGH, mō-sä-dĕg, **Mohammed,** Iranian statesman: b. Teheran, Iran, c. 1880; d. there, March 5, 1967. After serving in the Iranian finance ministry (1896–1900), he studied political science in Paris and law at Liège (Belgium) and Neuchâtel (Switzerland), where he took the doctorate in 1914. Returning to Iran, he was elected to the Majlis (Parliament) in 1915. When Reza Khan took control of the country (1921), Mossadegh was successively justice minister, finance minister, and foreign minister for short periods; but soon after Reza was elected shah (1925), Mossadegh broke with him and went into retirement, and subsequently was imprisoned until the shah's abdication (1941). By 1944 he was back in the Majlis, and in 1949 he emerged as leader of the militant National Front, which demanded nationalization of the British-controlled oil industry. Mossadegh was chairman of the committee that drafted the bill nationalizing the Anglo-Iranian Oil Company, and on April 29, 1951, the day after its passage, he became prime minister. Foreign consumers refused to buy oil from the nationalized industry, however, and Mossadegh was forced out of office in August 1953 by a military coup supported by the shah. He was sentenced to a prison term of three years for treason. After his release in 1956, he retired to private life. See also IRAN—*History*.

MÖSSBAUER, mûs′bou-ĕr, **Rudolf Ludwig,** a German physicist, shared the 1961 Nobel prize in physics for a research project undertaken when he was a 24-year-old graduate student. He produced gamma rays whose wavelengths were so constant that their frequencies were predictable to within one part in one hundred million million. These wavelengths provided a measuring tool of both time and space that was a thousand times more accurate than any previously known.

Born in Munich, Germany, on Jan. 31, 1929, Mössbauer received his Ph.D. in 1958 from the Munich Technische Hochschule (Institute of Technology). His Ph.D. thesis was a report on his five years of research on recoil-free gamma rays. It was largely ignored when published in 1958, but within a few years physicists recognized the many ways in which Mössbauer's gamma ray wavelengths could be used. The constant wavelengths achieved by Mössbauer became known as the *Mössbauer effect*.

Previous to Mössbauer's discovery, the gamma rays given off by atomic nuclei had fluctuating wavelengths. The fluctuation was caused by a recoil, similar to that in firing a gun. Mössbauer eliminated the recoil by enclosing the nuclei in a solid. The gamma ray wavelengths produced by this new discovery could measure the loss of one second in three million years. They were also used to verify Einstein's theory of relativity, proving that the wavelengths of light change with changes in gravity. First used mainly in nuclear physics, the Mössbauer effect has come into ever greater use as a tool in chemical physics and in solid state physics.

Mössbauer remained at the Technische Hochschule as a research fellow until 1960. The following year, he was appointed to the faculty of the California Institute of Technology in Pasadena. He began dividing his time between the two institutions in 1964.

MOSSES, mŏs′ĕz, a class, Musci, together with the liverworts, Hepaticae, constituting the Bryophyta, one of the five large groups of land plants. Mosses are worldwide in distribution, and in general inhabit the less favorable areas of this earth. Thus *Andreaea* grows on exposed rocks from the Arctic to the Antarctic, and in the tropics on high mountains. Other common rock-inhabiting forms are species of *Ulota, Orthotrichum, Grimmia,* and *Hedwigia*. These, with the lichens, initiate succession on stones, and so prepare the way for other plants. In contrast are those mosses which live in the water of running streams, such as *Hygrohypnum dilatatum, Eurhynchium rusciforme,* and especially the conspicuous water mosses in the genus *Fontinalis*. The bog moss, *Sphagnum*, is the pioneer in acid-bog succession, although it is often associated with other genera such as *Hypnum*. Still others flourish in swamps, like *Dichelyma* and the tree moss *Climacium,* which is suggestive of ground pine or a cedar tree in miniature. Many mosses, such as species of *Mnium*, form soft green carpets along the shaded banks of streams. Among the most attractive temperate-zone ferns are the mountain fern moss, *Hylocomium splendens*, which spreads like a mat on rocks and decaying logs in mountain areas and ravines; the common fern moss, *Thuidium delicatulum,* of rich woodlands, its finely branched stems suggestive of delicate fern leaves; and the plume moss, *Ptilium crista-castrensis,* of which the branches, covered with

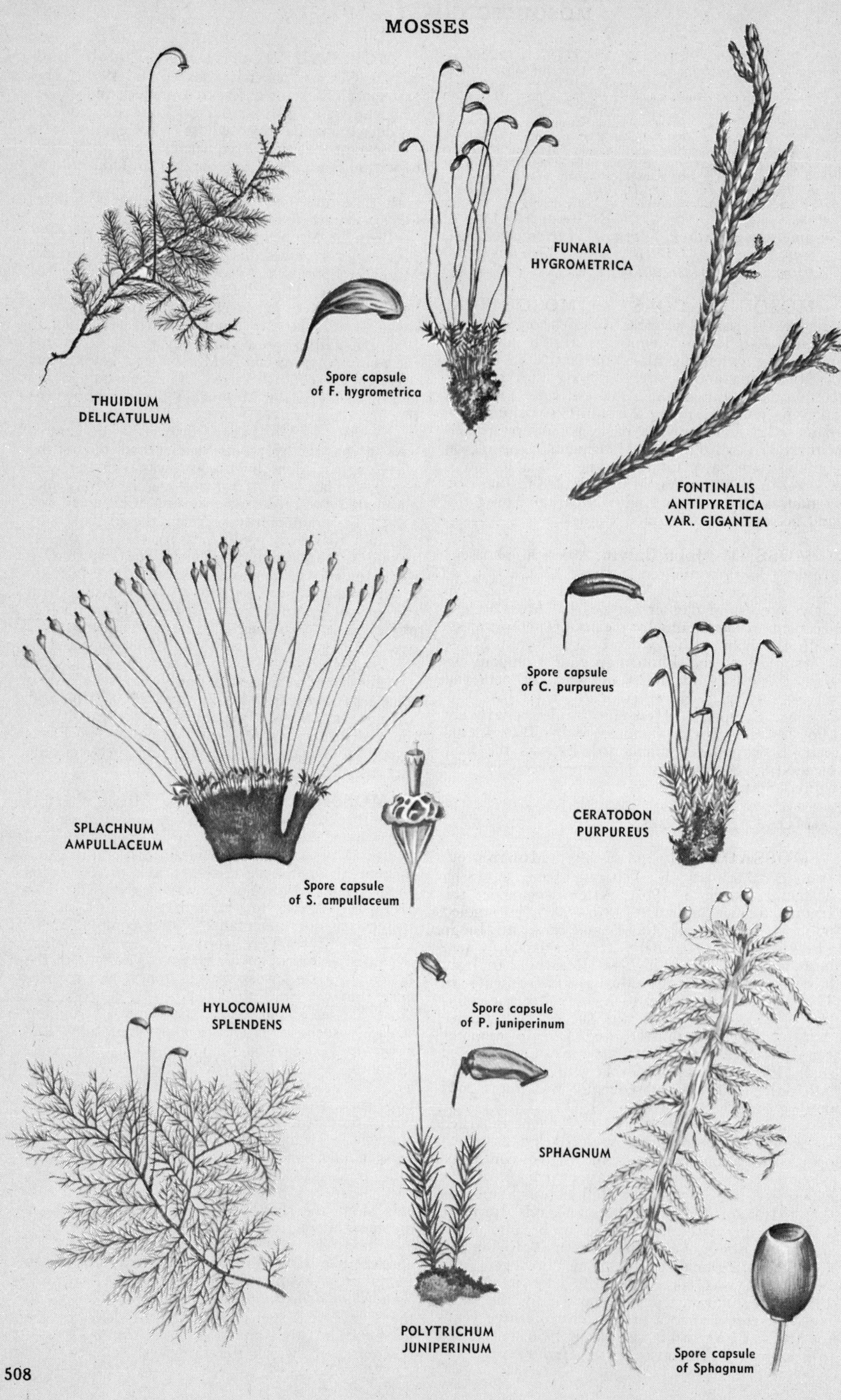
THUIDIUM
DELICATULUM
Spore capsule
of F. hygrometrica
FUNARIA
HYGROMETRICA
FONTINALIS
ANTIPYRETICA
VAR. GIGANTEA
Spore capsule
of C. purpureus
CERATODON
PURPUREUS
SPLACHNUM
AMPULLACEUM
Spore capsule
of S. ampullaceum
HYLOCOMIUM
SPLENDENS
Spore capsule
of P. juniperinum
SPHAGNUM
POLYTRICHUM
JUNIPERINUM
Spore capsule
of Sphagnum

minute, yellowish-green leaves, form feathery tufts in the cool, moist mountains of Europe, Asia, and North America. Wrapped around the bases of tree trunks the common thelia, *Thelia hirtella,* is often seen. Some species of the conspicuous hair-cap moss, *Polytrichum,* grow in damp places, such as *P. commune,* which may be over a foot high; others, like *P. piliferum,* prefer sandy habitats. Both of these occur across the Northern Hemisphere, and they are abundant in the Southern as well. Nestled in the cracks of city streets, the gray-green plants of the cosmopolitan silvery bryum, *Bryum argenteum,* may occasionally be found. Some mosses characteristically form cushions or tufts, such as the white or pincushion moss, *Leucobryum glaucum,* the widespread broom moss, *Dicranum scoparium,* and its smaller relative, *Dicranella heteromalla;* both of the latter have the leaves facing in one direction, as if brushed. *Nanomitrium,* with stems about one-tenth of a millimeter in height, and *Ephemerum,* about one millimeter high, grow on moist soil, clay and mud, and are among the smallest mosses. The twisted-stalk or cord moss, *Funaria hygrometrica,* and *Ceratodon purpureus,* both of wide distribution, grow on charred wood and bare soil, and then, like birds of passage, disappear when conditions change. Lastly there are *Splachnum,* found especially on the dung of cows, and the modest luminous moss, *Schistostega pennata,* which grows in dim caves in Europe and North America, and by focusing the light upon its chloroplasts, glows like emeralds in twilight. For structure and reproduction of mosses see also PLANTS AND PLANT SCIENCE—*1. Classification.*

EDWIN B. MATZKE.

MOSSES FROM AN OLD MANSE, title of Nathaniel Hawthorne's second collection of tales and sketches (1846). The Old Manse, Hawthorne's Concord home, is described in the opening chapter of the book. The remaining contents include many of Hawthorne's most famous short sketches, such as *The Birth-Mark, Roger Malvin's Burial,* and *The Artist of the Beautiful.* These bear witness to his love of the mysterious and the unusual; and their action passes in a world of unreality, which the genius of the author makes more visible than the world of sense.

MOSSLEY, mŏs'lĭ, municipal borough, England, in Lancashire, on the Tame River and the Huddersfield Canal. It contains woolen factories and foundries and has among its public buildings a modern Gothic church and a handsome town hall. Pop. (1961) 9,795.

MOSSORO, mo͞o-so͞o-rô', city, Brazil, in the state of Rio Grande do Norte, 150 miles west-northwest of Natal, on the Apodi River. It is a saltworking center, and a livestock and cotton market. Gypsum and marble quarries and manganese deposits are in the vicinity. Pop. (1960) 38,833.

MOST, mōst, **Johann Joseph,** German-American anarchist: b. Augsburg, Bavaria, Feb. 5, 1846; d. Cincinnati, Ohio, March 17, 1906. After working as a bookbinder, he became editor of the *Freie Presse* at Berlin, and in 1874–1878 was a member of the Reichstag for Chemnitz. Expelled from Germany, he went to London, where he founded *Die Freiheit,* an anarchist paper. In 1881 he was imprisoned for printing an article approving of the assassination of the Emperor Alexander II of Russia. Upon his release he came to the United States, and continued *Die Freiheit* in New York. In 1901 he was imprisoned for a seditious editorial on the assassination of President William McKinley.

MOST, môst (Ger. BRUX), city, Czechoslovakia, Province of Bohemia, about 48 miles northwest of Prague, to which it pipes gas from its extensive lignite fields. It is important as a mining, metallurgical, and chemical center, manufactures porcelain, and is a rail junction.

In 1938 it was claimed by Germany as part of the Sudetenland, but after World War II it was returned to the Czechs. During the war the city was badly bombed because of the nearby synthetic fuel plant. Some of its ancient churches survived. Since 1948 its industries have been controlled by the Czechoslovak People's Republic. Pop. (1957) 35,770, including suburbs.

MOSTAGANEM, môs-tȧ-gȧ-nĕm', city, Algeria, in the Department of Oran, located on the Gulf of Arzew, and on a branch of the Oran-Algiers Railway. It is situated on a steep cliff 280 feet above the Mediterranean Sea and has a deep-water harbor. The city exports wine, wool, cattle, grain, and figs. It was built on the ruins of an important city of the old Roman period and flourished in the 16th century under the Berbers, but lost its importance until the French in 1833 captured the site and built up its industries. Pop. (1960) 69,000.

MOSTAR, mō'stär, city, Bosnia and Hercegovina, Yugoslavia, former capital of Hercegovina, picturesquely situated along the cliffs in the narrow valley of the Neretva River. It is connected by rail with Sarajevo. Its industries are coal mining, aluminum and tobacco manufacture, and wine culture. It is the seat of a Roman Catholic and a Greek Orthodox bishop. Pop. (1961) 49,000.

MOSUL, mō-so͞ol', city, Iraq, capital of a province of the same name, on the west bank of the Tigris River, 220 miles north-northwest of Baghdad, and on the railroad connecting Baghdad with Syria and Turkey. Across the river is the site of ancient Nineveh, and 16 miles away is Tepe Gawra, the site of other important archaeological finds.

Mosul is an ancient Arabic town, captured by the Moslems in 636 and annexed to the Ottoman Empire in 1638. It was a place of great commercial importance on the caravan route from Persia and a cotton manufacturing center; muslin cloth was named after it. After the breakup of the Ottoman Empire, it was awarded to Iraq by the League of Nations in 1925, and has come into prominence again as a center of the oil industry in Iraq. Pop. (1947) city, 203,273; province, (1959) 740,975.

MOSZKOWSKI, môsh-kôf'skē, **Moritz,** Polish composer and pianist: b. Breslau, Germany, Aug. 23, 1854; d. Paris, France, March 9, 1925. After studying at Dresden and Berlin, he began to appear in public at the age of 19, and his success was immediate. He was a talented composer as well as performer; his opera *Boabdil* was presented at Berlin in

1892, and in New York City (in English) and Prague the following year; and he created a ballet, *Laurin* (1896), a symphonic poem, *Jeanne d'Arc,* and orchestral suites. Both his major compositions and his lighter music—two books of Spanish Dances for piano, concert waltzes, études, and miscellaneous pieces—were popular during Moszkowski's lifetime but have since been largely neglected.

MOTEL. See HOTELS—*Classification* (Motels).

MOTET, mō-tĕt', in music, a form of polyphony widely used from about 1225 to after 1750 and appearing in so many varieties that no definition can cover them all. The motet began, as its name (from the French *mot:* word) suggests, as the musical setting of a sacred text in Latin for unaccompanied chorus. Originally employed during Catholic services, it also evolved numerous secular forms, some of them in national languages and even for solo singers. Its history divides usefully into the medieval (1225–1450), Flemish (1450–1600), and baroque (1600–1750) classes. Although such later composers as Karl Philipp Emanuel Bach, Wolfgang Amadeus Mozart, Felix Mendelssohn, Robert Schumann, and Johannes Brahms—and, in France, César Franck and his disciples at the *Schola Cantorum*—have composed motets, it naturally lost its place in musical usefulness with the triumph of the preponderantly nonpolyphonic, classical-rococo style of Joseph Haydn, Mozart, and Ludwig van Beethoven.

HERBERT WEINSTOCK.

MOTH, mŏth, an insect of the order Lepidoptera, in which the wings (and some other parts of the body) are mostly clothed with scales which provide the various color patterns. The antennae are tapering, often plumose or pectinate; in contrast, the antennae of butterflies are clubbed apically, and the skipper (a butterfly of the family Hesperiidae) has a hook on the club. When at rest, moths hold their wings rooflike over the abdomen, or at right angles to the body, while butterflies "sleep" with their wings held close together over the abdomen. The vast majority of moths are nocturnal, but practically all butterflies are diurnal. Most moths are attracted to light, and many of these seem to be dazed by it and "mill" around aimlessly. This is particularly true of the noctuids or cutworm moths, and has earned for them the name "millers." However, the term is applied to other moths of similar size and habits.

Size.—Moths vary in size from tiny nepticulids, with a wing expanse little over one eighth of an inch, to the giant Atlas moth, in some forms of which the expanse exceeds 10 inches. The majority of moths are small, with a wing expanse of less than one and one-half inches, but it is the larger ones that engage our attention.

Eggs.—Eggs of moths are generally more or less spherical or oval but there still is great diversity of form: many kinds are flattened on one end and there may be depressions, rings, or tubercles. The eggs may be laid singly, in rough masses or in a regular pattern, and they may have only the protection offered by the shell itself; or they may be covered with a coating secreted by the mother. Sometimes this coating, as in the case of the white-marked tussock moth, may consist of a white froth, while, in the well-marked tussock moth, it is composed of hairs held in place by body secretions. The adults of the tent caterpillars lay their eggs about small twigs and cover them with a shellaclike substance to protect them during the winter. Most moths deposit their eggs on the plant upon which the larvae (caterpillars) are to feed, but there are some, such as the gypsy moth, that lay them in masses without apparent consideration for the welfare of their offspring: in stone walls, tin cans, or under projecting objects; in fact, anywhere that the moth may find herself at the time that the egg-laying urge comes upon her. Moths with such habits are usually very prolific, and the fact that such insects are successful in their struggle for existence is well exemplified by the destructiveness of this moth in American forests, where natural enemies are few in number. The females of the Psychidae (bagworms) are wingless and never leave the case which they build when young and enlarge as they grow. The males mate with the imprisoned female, the eggs are laid, and she shrivels and dies. The newly hatched larvae leave the case and go in search of food, building a case soon after birth.

Larvae.—The larvae, or caterpillars, of moths all conform to the same general pattern, yet they may be greatly modified to fit the varied conditions under which they live. All caterpillars have three pairs of true legs situated on the thorax (the first three segments behind the head), and, in general, most of them possess five pairs of prolegs, or stump legs. The three pairs of legs are used both for locomotion and for holding the food and directing it to the mouth; the prolegs are used for locomotion and holding the body in position while the caterpillar eats or rests, or resists attempts of enemies to dislodge it. The number of prolegs may be reduced. In some forms, there are four, three, or two pairs, the more anterior pairs being absent. In the geometrids, or measuring worms, only the two or three posterior pairs remain, and the caterpillar moves about with a deliberate, hunching motion in which the rear part of the body is carried forward until it almost meets the anchored true legs, then the body is stretched forward to full length, and the process repeated. Because of this habit, the caterpillars are called measuring worms, or inch worms, and many people believe that these caterpillars are just an inch in length. Other caterpillars have acquired rather similar habits, but none of them have developed to quite the stage of perfection attained by the geometrid larvae. Some noctuid larvae are loopers, the most notable being the cabbage looper, a serious pest of that plant.

The larvae of moths have developed various means of protection against their innumerable enemies. Some geometrid larvae cover themselves with bits of leaves, while others attach themselves to twigs or leaves with their prolegs and maintain a rigid position, themselves resembling tiny twigs. They also have the habit of dropping on a silken thread when suddenly disturbed, climbing back to the food plant when the danger is past. Others build communal silken tents in which they rest, coming out to feed, while other kinds feed within the nest, enlarging it as the food supply dwindles. Some cutworms hide in the soil during the day and feed at night. Other caterpillars conceal themselves in the crevices of bark or under debris, while still others, like the horned devil, are provided with thorns or projections of various types. They may also resemble bird droppings, or have markings of a nature that blend with the background on which they live. Some hawk moth larvae have markings in front so that they resemble the head of a snake when they assume a certain position. Many others are clothed with poisonous spines or barbed, poisonous hairs. The leaf rollers form cylinders in which to live, while the case-bearers and bagworms build protective coverings. Others mine in leaves or bore into plants.

Pupae.—The pupae are cylindrical, elongate, rounded in front and tapering behind, and show few conspicuous modifications. The pupa may be naked, in a cell in the soil, or may be enclosed in a silken cocoon. The cocoon may be flimsy or of great strength; sometimes it consists of the caterpillar's hairs, held together by silken strands or particles of leaves or debris. In the case of leaf rollers, more silken strands are added to hold the pupa in the rolled leaf. Most pupae are incapable of locomotion, but those of borers (for example, aegeriids and cossids) work their way to the exit of the cocoon and project from it, as do those of many others that live in concealed places.

Flight.—There is a great difference in the flight of adult moths. The hawk moths are streamlined and very fast flyers, being able to hover in front of flowers while they feed upon the nectar, and they are able to move backwards. The noctuids are practically all strong flyers, but most of the large moths (Cecropia, Polyphemus) and many smaller ones have an undulating flight; the hepialids are very poor flyers. While the females of many moths are wingless, and can only crawl from place to place, the females of some others (for example, the silkworm and the gypsy moth) have wings but are unable to fly.

Beneficial and Injurious Moths.—Many moths are serious pests, but there are a few that are beneficial. The best known of these is the silkworm, *Bombyx mori,* the chief source of commercial silk. Some of its relatives also produce silk, but it is of poorer quality, as is the silk of the Saturniidae. The larvae of some moths are used as food by primitive peoples, and the larvae of the pandora moth, *Coloradia pandora,* a saturniid, feeding on pine in the western mountains of the United States, were an important article of diet to Indians of the region. Man has, in a few instances, been able to utilize moths in the destruction of pest plants, a fine example being the introduction of *Cactoblastis cactorum* into Australia for the control of *Opuntia* cactus. A similar effort in South Africa has proved less successful because some native parasites destroy the larvae. And in the destruction of weeds and unwanted plants, the larvae of many moths are of considerable value.

It is impossible to mention more than a few of the more important pests. Among these are the cigar case-bearer and the pistol case-bearer, members of the family Coleophoridae, and the leaf miners of the families Gracilariidae and Lyonetiidae, the adults being very small moths. The Tineidae contain the clothes moths, which are so destructive to articles made from wool, fur, and other animal matter. The clearwing moths (Aegeriidae) are all borers in herbaceous and woody plants; the peach borer, currant borer, and squash borer do enormous damage. The Gelecheiidae contain such serious pests as the Angoumois grain moth, the peach-tree borer, the potatotuber moth, and the pink bollworm, a pest of cotton in most places where it is grown. The Oriental peach moth, the pea moth, strawberry leaf folder, grape-berry moth, bud moth, the spruce budworm, fruit-tree leaf roller, and the orange tortrix are members of the Tortricidae (including the Olethreutidae). Many of our most serious agricultural pests belong to the family Pyralidae, now divided into eight families or subfamilies. Some of these are: the European corn borer, the melon worm, the celery leaf tier, the meal moth, which feeds on damaged cereals and other seeds, the Oriental rice borer, and the sugarcane borer. The larvae of the wax moth and lesser wax moth feed on wax, even in hives containing bees, and often cause serious damage. The worst pests of such things as cereals, flour, nuts, and dried fruits are the Indian-meal moth (*Plodia interpunctella*) and the several species of *Ephestia,* including the Mediterranean flour moth. The best known of the slug moths is the saddleback caterpillar (*Sibine stimulea*), the larvae of which possess stinging hairs. The Noctuidae contain the cutworms and army worms, as well as many other pests; many of the tiger moths (Arctiidae) are pests of cultivated crops and trees, many being general feeders. The species *Datana* of the family Notodontidae, and several relatives, are gregarious and frequently injurious; the Lymantriidae contain such injurious forms as the gypsy moth, brown-tail moth, satin moth, and the tussock moths. Several of the Sphingidae (hawk moths) are injurious, the chief offenders being the tomato and tobacco worm moths, and several species feeding on grapes and apples. The tent caterpillars, of the genus *Malacosoma,* are often destructive to orchard and forest trees in America, while the lackey moth is destructive in Europe; also, members of the same family (Lasiocampidae) are the Syrian silkworm and the bibindandy of Madagascar, both important in the silk industry in the regions in which they occur. The io moth (*Automeris io*) is the only giant silkworm in North America that is rather consistently a pest; this occurs chiefly when it feeds on corn, and its stinging spines cause irritation and a nettlelike rash. The Cecropia and Promethea rarely cause serious defoliation of trees or shrubs. See also separate articles on the various families, individual moths, and pests.

Bibliography

Barnes, William, and McDunnough, James H., *Contributions to the Natural History of the Lepidoptera of North America,* 4 vols. (Decatur, Ill., 1911–24).

Comstock, John Henry, *An Introduction to Entomology,* 9th ed., rev. (Ithaca, N.Y., 1940).

Ford, E. B., *Moths* (London 1955).

Ford, R. L. E., *The Observer's Book of the Larger Moths* (New York and London, 1952).

Heinrich, Carl, *American Moths of the Subfamily Phycitidae* (Washington, D.C., 1956).

Holland, William Jacob, *The Moth Book* (New York 1949).

Imms, Augustus Daniel, *A General Textbook of Entomology,* 9th ed. (New York 1964).

Klots, Alexander B., *World of Butterflies and Moths* (New York 1958).

McDunnough, James H., *Check List of the Lepidoptera of Canada and the United States of America,* Los Angeles Museum Memoir (Los Angeles 1938–39).

Mitchell, Robert T., and Zim, Herbert S., *Butterflies and Moths* (New York 1965).

Seitz, Adolph, and other, *Macrolepidoptera of the World* (Stuttgart 1906–10).

Werner, Alfred, and Bijok, Joseph, *Butterflies and Moths* (New York 1965).

CHARLES HOWARD CURRAN,
Former Curator, Department of Insects and Spiders, The American Museum of Natural History.

MOTHER GOOSE, mŭth'ẽr gōōs, a legendary character associated with nursery rhymes (q.v.). She is mainly a heritage of folklore and was popularly associated with old wives' tales as early as the mid-17th century in France. In a poem by Jean Loret called *La muse historique* (1650) a Mother Goose tale is described as fabulous and false ("Comme un conte de la Mer-oye / Se trouvant fabuleux et faux").

It has been suggested that the mother of Charlemagne, known as Queen Goosefoot or Bertha with the great foot, was the original Mother Goose from whom this legendary "old wife" developed. But this suggestion is mere speculation, and the "old wife" as narrator of stories for children has had many names in the past. An early American tradition that the original Mother Goose or Vergoose actually lived in Boston is of course historically inaccurate apart from the fact that a Grandmother Vergoose may have been locally identified with the then popular Mother Goose legend. The history of Mother Goose as the custodian of nursery rhymes in England and America can be clearly traced.

Not until the 18th century were English nursery rhymes collected and published. John Newbery was an innovator in this new trend of publication and his *Mother Goose's Melody* (date of first edition not known, probably about 1780) was a historic collection. A reprint appeared soon afterward in America and other editions followed in England and the United States. This volume marked the beginning of the association of Mother Goose with traditional nursery rhymes.

Previously she had been associated mainly with prose tales, particularly a popular French volume of fairy tales known as *Histoires ou contes du temps passé* (1697; *Stories or Tales of Past Times*), later attributed to Pierre Perrault but now generally considered the work of his father Charles Perrault (q.v.). On the frontispiece of this volume, accompanying a scene of three children and an old woman by the fireside, was the phrase or subtitle, *Contes de ma mère l'Oye (Tales of Mother Goose).* An English translation of these tales as "told by Mother Goose" had appeared by 1729, and other editions followed. In a volume for children published about 1760 and called *The Top Book of All,* Mother Goose was listed on the title page with Nurse Lovechild, Jacky Nory, Tommy Thumb, "and other eminent Authors."

John Newbery, therefore, dispossessed Mother Goose of the popular prose fairy tales she had previously been associated with and identified her with nursery rhymes. The popularity of his *Mother Goose's Melody,* especially in the United States, established a lasting tradition. Illustrators have also contributed their part. The old woman with the high pointed hat and the magic wand, often depicted in flight upon an enormous goose, has become an inseparable part of the fabulous lore of nursery rhymes.

MOTHER-OF-PEARL (also called NACRE), the inner coating of shells of many bivalve mollusks, including pearl oysters. It resembles pearls and, like them, is composed of overlapping layers of calcium carbonate and some organic matter, particularly conchiolin. On account of its beautiful iridescence and high polish, mother-of-pearl is largely used in thin sheets to decorate articles of ornament and minor pieces of jewelry. See also PEARL.

MOTHER'S DAY, a day set aside for the purposes of honoring motherhood. Mother's Day is observed in the United States on the second Sunday in May, and in schools on the preceding Friday. The idea for the holiday is generally credited to Miss Anna M. Jarvis (1864–1948) of Philadelphia, Pa. A native of Grafton, W.Va., she went in 1904 to Philadelphia, where her mother died on May 9, 1905. On the anniversary of her mother's death she held an informal memorial meeting of friends, and in 1907 a church service was held at Grafton on the death anniversary. As a result of her efforts, Philadelphia observed the day, May 10, 1908. Miss Jarvis then became the missionary of the idea, writing thousands of letters to influential men and interviewing many public men to plead for the observance of the day. In May 1913, Pennsylvania made it a state holiday. In 1913, the United States Congress recommended that the second Sunday in May be made a national holiday honoring mothers. The first national mother's day was proclaimed by President Woodrow Wilson on May 9, 1914. It is customary for sons and daughters to wear a pink carnation if their mothers are living, white if they are dead.

MOTHERWELL, muth'ər-wel, **Robert Burns,** American painter: b. Aberdeen, Wash., Jan. 24, 1915. In his writing and teaching as well as in his painting, Motherwell made vital contributions to the abstract expressionist movement. His works, such as the monumental series *Elegy to the Spanish Republic,* often attain mural size and consist of bold, evocative figures and large flat color areas.

Motherwell obtained his bachelor's degree from Stanford University in 1937. Later, he studied at Harvard University, at the University of Grenoble in France, and at Columbia University, where at the age of 26 he decided to become a painter. Deeply influenced by the surrealists, he developed his own abstract style. In 1944, he held his first one-man show at Peggy Guggenheim's gallery Art of This Century.

His training in philosophy helped him to articulate the aims of the emerging abstract expressionist movement. In 1947, with Mark Rothko and others, he founded an art school in Greenwich Village, where highly influential discussions were held weekly by leading New York painters. He also edited a series of books *The Documents of Modern Art* (1944–52), wrote numerous essays, and taught at Black Mountain College and at Hunter College. In 1958 he married another prominent abstract expressionist, Helen Frankenthaler.

MOTION, in music, is a change of pitch in successive notes either within a single "voice" or part, or between two or more voices considered relative to one another. In the melodic progression of a single voice, *conjunct motion* proceeds by single degrees of the scale, and *disjunct motion* proceeds by leaps of more than a single degree. Several distinctions are made with respect to more than one voice: in *similar motion* the two parts move in the same direction by different intervals; in *parallel motion* they move in the same direction by the same intervals; in *contrary motion* they move in opposite directions; in *oblique motion* one remains stationary while the other moves away from it; and in *mixed motion* several voices move simultaneously in two of these types of motion.

MOTION, in physics. See MECHANICS; RELATIVITY.

MOTION PICTURES. The motion picture is the most completely explicit of the media of communication that address the eye, primary organ of perception. With its complement of sound and speech it is the most elaborately complete of the arts of recording and expression. Commonly considered apart, it is in fact much akin to all the older arts, which like it have been progressively powered by the development of tools and technologies.

The subject is dealt with in the following pages under five main headings:

- The History of Motion Pictures
- The Film Art to World War II
- Films After World War II
- Documentary Films
- Educational Films

Other aspects of the subject are discussed in the following articles: CARTOON, ANIMATED; MAKE-UP—*Motion Picture Make-Up,* and *Photographic Make-Up: Amateur and Professional;* PHOTOGRAPHY—*8. Visual Education and Documentation.*

THE HISTORY OF MOTION PICTURES

In little more than half a century the motion picture has achieved a worldwide dissemination tending to approximate that of printing. Newest of the arts, it is the first and only art to have evolved from the bottom up, born to serve the masses. All the other arts have been handed down from above. The motion picture is so expensive a medium that only mass buying power can afford it.

The motion picture has rapidly expanded its dominion in a turbulence of evolutions, characteristic of its intensive history since the last decade of the 19th century. These evolutions involve politico-economic adjustment to a changing, socially disturbed world, and internally the absorption of the electronic developments of applied science. The principal impact of applied science has been in the area of distribution, with the advent of radiographic broadcasting by television.

Television has given the motion picture the novel quality of simultaneity; the spectator is among those present at the moment of production. It also has the quality of propinquity, push-button convenience; it is the motion picture in the home, as available as running water. It is nonetheless a motion picture.

The introduction of television has inevitably caused disturbance in the production and distribution of the entertainment moving picture, the mass audience product known as the "movie," which requires going out to see. Meanwhile television has derived at least half of its presentations from motion pictures recorded on film.

Early History.—The screen achieves its ocular representatives by submitting to the eyes a rapid sequence of instantaneous, or snapshot, records of objects in phases of motion. The modern film presents 24 such phase images, or "frames" on film, per second. Those separate instants, in each of which there is no motion, are synthesized by the organs of sight into an appearance of continuous motion. The eye is not sufficiently acute to discern the lack of actual continuity.

The complex of techniques involved have behind them a long, laborious development of optics, kinetics, and photochemistry. Some of it is far back beyond record, but a relatively recent milestone came with the demonstration of the principle of the magic lantern about 1645, when Athanasius Kircher, German Jesuit and professor of mathematics, demonstrated his Magia Catoptrica, a device for projecting hand-drawn still transparency pictures on a screen in Rome. This was a beginning, but no further significant advance was made until the early decades of the 19th century.

In 1824 Peter Mark Rôget, author of the famous *Thesaurus,* having observed by looking through a Venetian blind that motion could be broken down into a series of separate phases, read a paper on the subject to the Royal Society in London. Others, like Sir John Herschel and Dr. William Henry Fitton, experimented with illusions created by rapid movement of still images, and Michael Faraday carried out investigations in the same area. Then in 1832, Dr. Joseph Antoine Ferdinand Plateau in Belgium and Dr. Simon Ritter von Stampfer in Austria simultaneously brought out devices for viewing pictures in simulated motion, the first "motion picture machines." Improved models of these devices were developed by Baron Franz von Uchatius in Austria, and William George Horner in England.

The pictures used in these machines were drawings. The next great step was the development of photography, which began with the publication of the work of Louis Jacques Mandé Daguerre in France in 1839. The first man known to have used a series of photographs to produce an illusion of movement was Coleman Sellers of Philadelphia, Pa., in 1860. By 1864 Louis Arthur Ducos du Hauron, in France, had set down on paper a substantially complete blueprint of the motion picture as we know it, and in 1870, again in Philadelphia, the first actual projection of a photographic motion picture on a screen was shown by Henry Renno Heyl.

Seven years later, in California, John D. Isaacs, an engineer retained by former governor Leland Stanford, used a battery of cameras to record the phases of motion of a running horse. It was an effective application of snapshot photography to the analysis of motion. The operator of his mechanism was Eadweard Muybridge, a local photographer who had made a previous unsuccessful effort. Muybridge became famous as a photographer, but Isaacs went back to his profession and became chief engineer of the great Harriman railway system. The pictures from California were synthesized into bits of motion in Europe by means of existing mechanisms.

Edison's Contribution.—The great step from the laboratory to the world of everyday application was nearing. In 1887 Thomas A. Edison set himself the task of doing for the eye what his phonograph was already doing for the ear. He arrived at a mechanism but lacked an adequate carrier to feed it with pictorial images. That arrived when George Eastman of Rochester brought forth a new material for the "roller photography" of his Kodak. It was film. Edison got a sample about an inch wide and 50 feet long, for $1.50. In a few weeks his peep-show Kinetoscope, the ancestor of all motion picture mechanisms, was complete and demonstrated in his laboratory. The date was Oct. 6, 1889.

Edison was little impressed. He put the machine in a corner of his library office, and there it stood gathering dust. In 1891 Thomas R. Lombard, a promoter, won Edison's consent to make a battery of ten peep-show machines for exhibition at the Columbian Exposition in Chicago, scheduled for 1892. The fair was a year late, but the Kinetoscopes did not arrive even in 1893. Edison did not care much. He had let his lawyers patent the machine in the United States in 1891. But he refused to spend $150 to patent it abroad. Many historic consequences and sundry piracies grew out of that in years ahead.

At last the Kinetoscope Parlor, with Edison's ten machines, depicting bits of prize fights and fragments of vaudeville acts, was opened at 1155 Broadway in New York City, April 14, 1894. Within months the peep-show Kinetoscope became a leading attraction in the dime-museum and penny-arcade field of showmanship. One such exhibit showing *Dolorita in the Passion Dance,* imported first for the midway of the Chicago fair, brought the films' first touch of censorship when a showing on the boardwalk in Atlantic City, N. J., was suppressed by the police.

Pressure rose rapidly in the trade for a union of the Kinetoscope with the magic lantern. One customer at a time could peer into the Kinetoscope. A magic-lantern exhibition would increase receipts and speed the turnover by entertaining a roomful of spectators simultaneously. Edison's sales department was reluctant, fearing to exhaust the novelty market. Edison himself, no entertainer, was indifferent. Concurrently, however, attempts to duplicate Edison's machine, which lacked the protection of foreign patents, had spread around the world. In the United States, Thomas Armat, of Washington, D.C., a scientifically minded real estate investor, contrived a competent projector known as the Vitascope, using Edison films, which he presented in September 1895 at the Cotton States Exposition in Atlanta, Ga. The showing made no great impression at the time, but it had a highly successful future in store for it.

In France, Louis Lumière, a photographic manufacturer, found the Kinetoscope on display in Paris and set about projection. In England exploiting importers took the Kinetoscope to Robert W. Paul, a well-known instrument maker, seeking duplicate devices. He too set to work on the problem of projecting films. A Lumière projector, the Cinématographe of historic fame, was the foundation of the French industry. It had its first commercial presentation at the end of 1895. Paul, equally successful in London, built a projector in October 1895 and demonstrated it on Feb. 28, 1896, at the Royal Institution. Named the Theatrograph, Paul's machine went into theater service to set the British development on its way.

The Lumière Cinématographe became important in the dissemination of the motion picture. It was small, portable, and uniquely capable of serving as a camera, a printing machine to make positives for projection, and a projector for public exhibition. Because of its compactness, it attained worldwide popularity.

The Nickelodeon Era.—The impetus which set the new medium of the motion picture on its way in its homeland came from a single Broadway opening, the presentation of Armat's Vitascope projecting Edison films at Koster & Bial's Music Hall in New York's Herald Square, on the evening of April 23, 1896. Thereafter the motion picture, through the Vitascope and sundry imitative devices, went into a variety show career, just as variety was becoming slightly more polite vaudeville. Films also were used as carnival "black tent" attractions and flitting exhibitions in cheap vacant storerooms. This was to last nearly a decade.

Then an Edison cameraman, Edwin S. Porter, who had been an electrician's mate in the United States Navy, ventured into experiment by making a "story picture," *The Great Train Robbery,* in 1903. By 1905 it was a hit of sensational proportions. The story picture gave the screen something to say.

In Pittsburgh, Pa., in 1905, John P. Harris, local showman, had a small idle theater on hand. For lack of other attraction, he gave it a program of motion pictures, at a five-cent admission, and called it the "Nickelodeon." In the autumn he played *The Great Train Robbery* to amazing patronage. The idea hit and imitative nickelodeons swept across the land like fire in prairie grass.

With the arrival of the primitive story picture, motion pictures, up from the penny arcade, had come upon a fecund soil of opportunity the like of which had never been presented to any art before. The United States had long been importing foreign labor from many lands, mostly from the shores of the Mediterranean. The arrivals, too poor to bring with them the arts of their homeland, found nothing but long hours in mines or steel furnaces awaiting them. The movies suddenly delivered for five cents, the cost of a tall glass of beer, entertainment and diverting information about the New World they had come to enjoy. This drew an audience whose buying power provided the foundation of the art. It also ordained the simple success-story message of the movies, which on the whole still stands unchanged.

With the nickelodeon wave the petty tradesmen of the foreign-born workers' quarters became the retail vendors of films. They were pawnbrokers and entrepreneurs from candy shops, fruit stands, bicycle-repair and cobblers' shops, secondhand clothiers, and the like. For about $150 and credit for a month's rent of an idle storeroom, with an arrangement to borrow chairs between funerals from adjacent undertakers, they became exhibitors, showmen. Humble as they were, they were to become the masters of the movies, and some of those who started so remained the masters of the movies on into the mid-century.

The upsurging business brought all manner of confusions, including piracies of product and the larcenous device of making pictures from contra-type negative, known to the trade as "duping," an abbreviation of duplicating. While at first films were purchased outright by exhibitors, very quickly the system of renting by film libraries, or exchanges, arose. There was high disorder, price cutting, duplication of service, and waste in all directions.

Other conflicts also disturbed the scene. There were endless patent infringements, many of them due to imports from Europe where Edison had failed to protect his inventions. Machines from Europe based on the Edison invention were infringements in the United States. There were copies of copies and infringements of infringements. Cutthroat competition developed in all directions.

Legal action was begun by Thomas A. Edison,

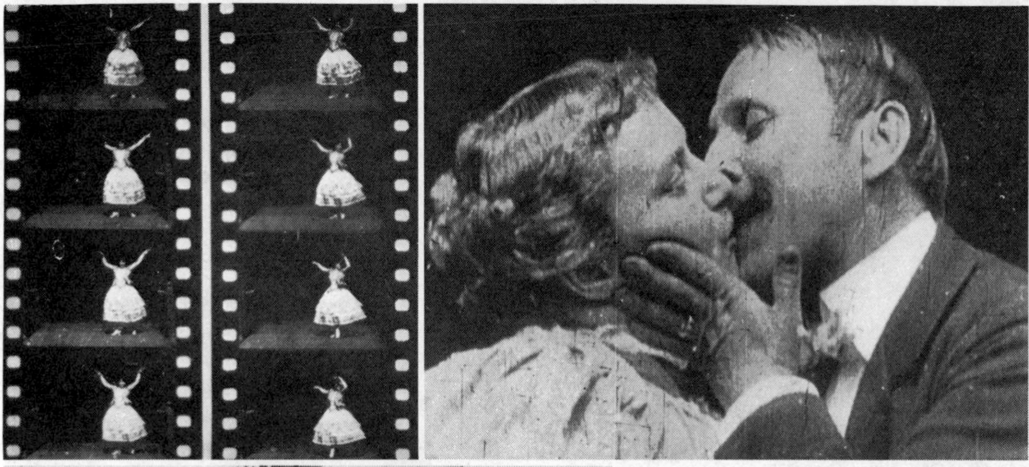

Above left: An early film strip made at Thomas A. Edison's laboratory, using the perforated film invented by George Eastman in 1888.

Above: John C. Rice and May Irwin created a sensation in 1896 in the first film kiss.

Left: Edwin S. Porter's immensely popular The Great Train Robbery (1903) was one of the earliest films to tell a story and to employ the technique of editing.

Right: The great director David Wark Griffith is shown during the shooting of Intolerance in 1916. At the camera is G. W. "Billy" Bitzer, and on the left are two of Griffith's stars, Blanche Sweet and Dorothy Gish.

Below: The first motion picture studio in the United States, the "Black Maria," built by Thomas A. Edison at West Orange, N. J. in 1893.

Photos courtesy Museum of Modern Art Film Library

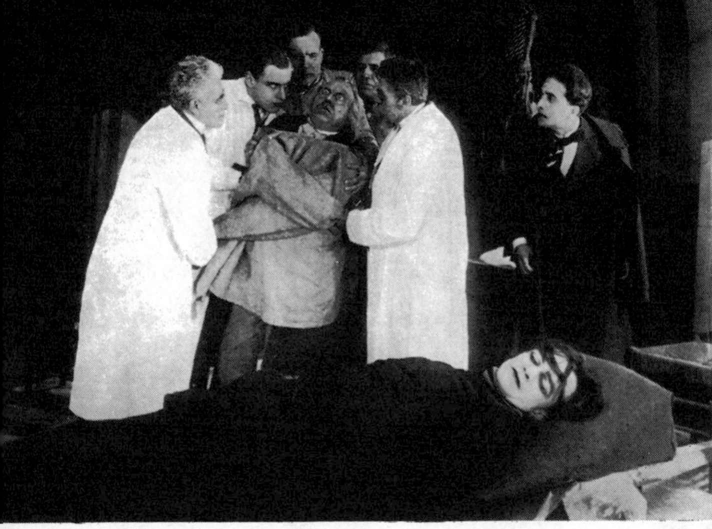

Above: The celebrated German surrealist film *The Cabinet of Dr. Caligari*, produced in 1919 by Decla Bioscop and directed by Robert Wiene.

Above: The Odessa steps massacre scene from Sergei Eisenstein's classic, *Armored Cruiser Potemkin*, produced in 1925.

Below: The Blue Angel, directed by Josef von Sternberg, introduced Marlene Dietrich to American audiences. Also starring Emil Jannings, this early sound film was produced in Germany in 1929.

Above: The screen's master comedian, Charles Chaplin, was his own producer and director in *The Gold Rush* (1925).

Below: Dublin during the Irish Revolution provided the setting for director John Ford's *The Informer*, produced in 1935 and featuring Victor McLaglen.

Photos courtesy Museum of Modern Art Film Library

Inc., against the American Mutoscope and Biograph Company in 1897. The Mutoscope, a card-wheel peep show, and the Biograph, a projector, were based on methods devised by Edison's former assistant, William Kennedy Laurie Dickson. By 1907 Biograph was in financial trouble. The Empire Trust Company of New York sent in Jeremiah J. Kennedy, a consulting engineer and executive, to liquidate the corporation. He chose rather to reform the industry, achieved a peace with Edison, and induced him to license Biograph and six other of the more competent competitors. The eight licensed producers then formed the famed Motion Picture Patents Company and its efficient marketing arm, the General Film Company. It was, during its effective period from 1909 to 1915, a richly profitable monopoly. It was to have been a complete vertical trust from film studio to theater screen, but it did not get so far as the acquisition of theaters.

That proved to be a mistake. The nickelodeon owners, humble though they were, resented their exclusion from the "trust," the focus of their resentment being a weekly license fee which all theaters were required to pay in order to use Motion Picture Patents' projectors or to secure pictures from General Film. This to them was taxation without representation. Led by exchange owner Carl Laemmle and nickelodeon magnate William Fox, they entered production and distribution in competition with the "trust." The Patents Company retaliated with strong-arm raids on their hideaway studios and suits for patent infringement, another mistake. The infringers, who became known as "independents," entered countersuits charging unlawful monopoly. The courts upheld them in the autumn of 1915, though the decision came too late for important effect. The trust had meanwhile committed suicide by its excessive conservatism.

Having achieved monopoly, the "trust" had sought to stabilize the business by enforcing conformity of product. Films were forever to be one reel long, enacted and produced by obscure nonentities; the nickelodeon public deserved no more. The "independents," closer to their audiences, knew better. Against the strict rule of the "trust" they publicized the names of players and thus released the genie of the star system from its bottle. Furthermore, to distinguish their productions from those of General Film, they expanded footage toward "feature" length.

Feature Films.—The first features came from Europe. There the development of the films followed a more conservative pattern, strongly influenced by the traditions of the stage, and inclined toward the classics and the presentation of spectacles.

By 1912 Adolph Zukor, Hungarian immigrant, up from New York's East Side, who had been successful as a furrier and then as an arcade proprietor and exhibitor, saw that there was an opportunity to make the movies into real theater, providing, like the stage, a full evening's entertainment. He imported a French-made four-reel production presenting the great Sarah Bernhardt in *Queen Elizabeth.* It had little merit but it was a moderate success. It is to be remembered as the first milestone of the modern era, not so much for what it was as for its sequel.

Significant among the features that followed was *Quo Vadis* (1913), more spectacle than drama, produced in Italy with $9,000 put up by George Kleine of Chicago. He was a distributor of foreign films, a powerful figure in the formation of the Patents Company group. In 1914 *Cabiria,* another Italian spectacle, was also shown in the United States.

But greatest of all in impact was *The Birth of a Nation,* completed in 1914–1915, a drama of the sequel to the American Civil War, inspired by the novel *The Clansman.* It was the product of David Wark Griffith, who had been an actor of no special note on the stage. He had come up through picture making for Biograph, and it was he who in 1909 had brought Miss Mary Pickford, age 16, to the screen. *The Birth of a Nation* was his major effort after he left Biograph to align himself with the independents. It cost about $100,000, an enormous gamble for that time, but it returned millions.

Meanwhile the ambitious progress of the art was demanding a more adequate home than the nickelodeon. This demand came to flower at last when the Strand Theatre was opened in New York in 1914, a challenge to the stage on "The Great White Way." It was under the direction of Samuel Lionel Rothafel, in time to emerge in fame as "Roxy." He was of the basic pattern, son of a Stillwater, Minn., showmaker, and by turns a marine with service in the Boxer Rebellion in China, a book agent, a bartender, and at first a very minor exhibitor. He brought to the Strand an atmosphere of propriety and elegance. The Marine Corps had taught him the impressiveness of uniforms, discipline, punctilio, and polished buttons, which his theater and his ushers reflected. The policy was a vast success and set the pattern for top-rank exhibition.

Along with feature-length pictures and elaborate theaters came the era of the great stars of the screen. Most important to be remembered are Mary Pickford, around whom Zukor built his film empire, and Charles Chaplin. Chaplin's star contract, signed in late 1915, for 12 two-reel comedies at a salary of $670,000 for the series, to be delivered in one year, startled the film world and started the great wave of tremendous star salaries.

In the period of the rise of the multiple-reel or feature picture, productions were made around stars and one big name was enough to sell a picture. Concurrently the American industry was enjoying what was tantamount to an automatic monopoly. World War I had forced the closing of most studios overseas and reduced production in Europe to minor propaganda efforts. American films took dominance in the world market then and held it thereafter. Coming out of the melting pot, they were inevitably international merchandise, and they were supported by a greater home market than the films of any foreign land.

The rise of the feature picture and the greater film theater, together with the expanding availability of the automobile, rapidly shrank the number of nickelodeons and strictly neighborhood theaters. A possibly overgenerous estimate claimed that at the peak of the nickelodeon days there had been 28,000 of them in the United States. The theater total by the end of the first decade of the big photoplay was probably between 18,000 and 20,000. Audiences, no longer limited to walking distance, increasingly shopped for their entertainment.

A decade of feature-picture production brought many problems to the trade, and the leading producers began to recognize that they had a common interest in solving them. This led to the employment of Will H. Hays, an able attorney and postmaster general in the cabinet of President Warren G. Harding, to organize and assume the presidency of the Motion Picture Producers and Distributors of America. He took office on March 4, 1922, and for 23 years was known as "the czar of the movies." He was succeeded by Eric A. Johnston, politically active industrialist, in September 1945. Johnston moved his headquarters from New York to Washington and renamed the organization the Motion Picture Association of America.

Color.—Color emerged from experiment half a decade after the dawn of the feature-length drama. It had been on the way from an early day. In 1896, the year the screen was born, experiments in hand-coloring Edison films were made but attracted slight interest.

Photographic color on the screen really began with Charles Urban, an American working in Great Britain. His process, known as Kinemacolor, had its first public demonstration May 1, 1908. It was a two-color process involving filters, one component red-orange, the other blue-green, used on both camera and projector. The greatest Kinemacolor production was a record of the royal visit and durbar at Delhi, a spectacle of vast Indian pomp and splendor, shown with tremendous success in England and on the Continent, starting in May 1912. The leaders of the American film industry, however, discouraged the presentation of Kinemacolor in the United States.

About the same time, an American technician, William VanDoren Kelley, began working on a two-color process by which dyes were applied to emulsions on both sides of the positive prints, substantially Kinemacolor without color filters in the projector. In 1921 his Prizma process was used in the production, in Great Britain, of an ambitious feature, *The Glorious Adventure,* starring Lady Diana Manners, the first all-color drama. The Prizma organization, however, soon collapsed because of financial difficulties.

Meanwhile, in 1915, Dr. Herbert T. Kalmus, Boston scientist with wide industrial and academic experience, had founded the Technicolor Motion Picture Corporation to pursue researches that he and some associates had initiated. They first pursued the two-color, color-in-the-film method. In 1922 Technicolor appeared on Broadway with *The Toll of the Sea.* The greatest milestone was reached 11 years later with a demonstration three-reel comedy *La Cucaracha* made in a full three-color process. Substantially natural color in complete spectrum had arrived. Technicolor thenceforth developed with a rapidly rising curve, and soon dominated major production, both at home and abroad.

Sound.—While color was becoming firmly established, the more revolutionary feature of sound arrived, bringing recorded music and speech to the screen. Edison had essayed a combination of picture and phonograph in the peepshow period, and about 1912 he had ineffectually presented projection synchronized with the phonograph. But the problem of amplifying the sound sufficiently to fill an auditorium was as yet unsolved.

Explorations in the realm of sound by the Bell Telephone Laboratories in the mid-1920's resulted in a super-phonograph, with electrical recording and amplification of sound, leading to the Vitaphone, synchronized disc and film. It was first presented to the motion picture public by Warner Brothers, entrepreneurs up from the nickelodeon, in a showing of *Don Juan* with John Barrymore in New York, Aug. 6, 1926. The disc recording method soon gave way to sound on film, a method of translating sound waves into electric impulses controlling light impingement on the "sound strip" of the films. It was powered by the photoelectric cell and radio tubes which amplified the sound as the projector amplified the visual image. The Bell Telephone or Western Electric method depended on variation in density, while the rival General Electric system, promoted through the Radio Corporation of America, used a variable area track. The patents were soon pooled and rivalry between the two methods ended. The era of the "talkies" had begun, and the silent picture was driven precipitously from the screen.

By 1953 motion picture technology was making wide use of processes of sound recording on tracks and tapes of magnetized material, and experiments were also being made in the magnetic recording of pictorial images.

See also CENSORSHIP; COMMUNICATIONS.

TERRY RAMSAYE
Author of "A Million and One Nights"

THE FILM ART TO WORLD WAR II

The film medium, "child of the laboratory and the machine," was not regarded at the time of its invention as a potential art form but as a mechanical means of reproducing works of art in the traditional media, especially the stage. Thomas A. Edison, who devised moving pictures as a complement to his phonograph, saw no further into the future of his invention than that. The ability of the film to copy the stage cheaply and disseminate copies widely and in great numbers was early apprehended, and in 1907 a company called the Film d'Art was founded in France, designed to record the performances of the Comédie Française and other eminent troupes. Joseph Jefferson, Sarah Bernhardt, Benoit Constant Coquelin, Jean Mounet-Sully, Mme. Réjane (Gabrielle Charlotte Réju), and Eleanora Duse acted for the early cameras, and Bernhardt heads the list of those who believed that the film was to be "my one chance of immortality." But, ironically, the preservation of these records has weakened reputations which might have taken their places beside the legends of Edwin Thomas Booth and Sarah Siddons. Lacking the voice, these literal photographs preserve, not the glamour of Bernhardt or the art of Duse, but the thin shadow of extinct celebrity.

This was dimly perceived even at the time. Contemporary opinion still held, what Marcel Pagnol believed as late as 1930, that "the cinema is destined to be a printing press for the drama." But the actual makers of early films—obscure, unlettered men mostly, not bound by aesthetic tradition—soon found that to make, without sound, a faithful record of a stage performance at proscenium distance from the action, resulted in nothing that would move an audience. Pre-eminently led by David Wark Griffith, they experimented toward the development of a purely visual narrative technique. They began to move the camera in close for intimate scenes and to draw it back for broad effects; to begin and end scenes in the middle of the action; and to interrupt a scene in order to introduce complementary or contrasting events occurring at a distance or at another time. A host of camera tricks, many of them discovered before 1900, were by 1912 being used as dramatic devices—the "fade," the "dissolve," "slow-motion," "stop-motion." Most important, the film makers, also by 1912, had begun to realize that they did not really "make" their films until the moment arrived when they composed all these lengths of film, taken at different times and places and at varying distances from the action, into a unified and shapely whole.

D. W. Griffith.—Since the devices described above include all the essential features of the art of the moving picture, it can be said that the elements of the art were formulated in the first decade and a half of the 20th century—but formulated in the unknown studios and shown in the shunned darkness of the nickelodeons. What was happening burst upon world consciousness with the release in 1915 of D. W. Griffith's *The Birth of a Nation.* Many factors contributed to the extraordinary success of this film, but one of its leading accomplishments was certainly the fact that it convinced the educated classes that the motion picture was not, as they had thought, merely a mechanical copy of the stage but a new, unexplored medium. With few resemblances to the theater, with some to the episodic novel, but with strong affinities to musical structure, the form of this film deeply impressed its public. Gilbert Seldes said of it, "*The Birth of a Nation* is a single picture, a unit, just as a symphony is a unit, the parts growing out of each other, growing greater because of their relation to each other . . . A dominant tone is given to the entire picture, and the subsidiary episodes are played in related keys. The cutting is perfectly done, so that interest is always kept in an episode for itself, then dispersed or concentrated elsewhere, to return to the first episode for its relation to all the others: it is cinematic counterpoint." The use of musical terms is significant. Through this film it became apparent that whatever else the moving picture might be, it was a "composition." Griffith had not only directed the action and cinematography of *The Birth of a Nation,* not only pieced it together himself in the cutting room; he had actually invented it. Elements of his story he took from two novels, but he worked without a script, arranging and accommodating the parts to each other and to the whole as he went along. (Griffith rehearsed each of his pictures in their entirety before they went before the cameras; these rehearsals constituted the actual "writing" of his films; he never, when working independently, used any form of script.) It was clear from his example that the dominant artistic intelligence in the making of a film is that of the director, who is not only the director of the actors, as on the stage, but the dramaturgist as well.

Seldes' description of *The Birth of a Nation* was written 14 years after its release. That no one knew how to describe it at the time is evidenced by the newspaper critics' use of such terms as "display" and "spectacle," obviously without being satisfied with any of them. To their assistance came a group of poets, critics, scholars, and journalists who, it suddenly appeared, had been haunting the despised nickelodeons for years. Élie Faure had published *The Art of Cineplastics* in 1912 and (Nicholas) Vachel Lindsay *The Art of the Moving Picture* in 1915. These eminent intellectuals were infatuated with the possibilities of what had been considered a plebeian, if not a pariah, medium. They were also aware that neither they nor any of their contemporaries had yet plucked out the heart of its mystery. They were not content with Faure's noun "cineplastics" nor with the National Board of Review's adjective "cinegraphic." They cautiously ventured that the medium of the moving picture appeared to be light and that its form seemed to derive from the rhythm of the varying speeds at which individual shots were passed across the screen. For the moment they said no more, but watched the rapidly developing medium for signs and portents. Meanwhile—joined in America by Seldes, in England by Iris Barry, in France by Guillaume Apollinaire—this first group of film aesthetes defended the popular art from superficial criticism: that it was vulgar, that it was mass-produced and produced for the masses, that it was machine-made. They found its vulgarity vital. They saw in the peculiar relation between the popular film and its vast audience a recrudescence of the folk art of the Middle Ages. They rejected the notion that the film was too mechanical and commercial. "Films are made by men, not machines or corporations," was the answer of Iris Barry to such critics.

The German School.—There matters rested until the appearance in 1919 of *The Cabinet of Dr. Caligari.* This famous film with its painted backdrops was redolent of the traditional arts and of art itself, and its striking use of light and shade gave credence to the belief that the film in its essential nature was a "light-play" (the German word for movie became *Lichtspiel*). Indeed, might not films be considered to be "painting in motion?" The time was ripe to think so. Léopold Survage had designed a "motion painting" as early as 1913, and cubist painters longed to add the dimension of time to their designs. In Germany and in France in the early 1920's, a film *avant-garde* sprang up composed of Hans Richter, Viking Eggeling, Francis Picabia, Fernand Léger, Man Ray, and others. Dadaist, cubist, abstract, surrealist films poured forth profusely for a while. Cheaply and obscurely made, unseen by the mass audience, they exerted little influence on professional film making but greatly affected the attitude of European and American intellectuals toward the film medium. Because they mirrored the ferment then boiling in the older arts, they had the double advantage of seeming modern while remaining comfortably traditional, inasmuch as they derived from well-known cultural movements. These films and the men who made them were leading the medium toward one of its two possible extremes: the "animated" picture, a closed world of its own. Such a film is a design recorded exactly as imagined and executed by its creator. This conception was entirely agreeable to the taste and experience of the painters who constituted this first cinematic "School of Paris," as it is to most of their descendants, the present-day film *avant-gardists* in the United States and Europe. But it seemed to leave something out of account, specifically the basic craft of film, photography itself, which in this context is reduced to the mechanical recording function it had earlier when people thought the film was properly a copy of the stage. But photography, as a medium, appears to make demands and have affinities of its own, which will be referred to below.

The influence of *Caligari* also led to another closed world, the much admired world of the German studio films of the 1920's. It was a world from which reality was rigorously excluded, but in which the aspect of reality was reproduced with a minute fidelity and skill at which film makers elsewhere marveled. The master spirit of this world was Carl Mayer, a screen writer who had never written in any other medium and the author of a long succession of famous films, beginning with *Caligari* and including *New Year's Eve, The Last Laugh,* and *Tartuffe.* Mayer dominated the films he wrote. His aim was unity of time, place, and action to heighten intensity; he pursued it by constructing in the studio vast sets through which the camera continually moved, and even flew. The moving camera, invented at least as early as 1914, had been used only occasionally. Now, Mayer discarded the American editing system with its terse assembly of many shots taken from different angles, and substituted a new, centralized and unified structure in which "cuts" were few, "takes" long, and the moving camera itself the principal stylistic feature. The result was a screen world which, like the films of the *avant-gardists,* approached "animated painting."

The American film industry, deeply impressed by German studio craftsmanship, used the moving camera to excess after 1927, and imported to Hollywood the directors Ernst Lubitsch and Fred W. Murnau, the producer Erich Pommer, Carl Mayer himself, and others. They introduced a certain sophistication of content into American films, and one American director, Josef von Sternberg, showed himself heavily under the German influence in his use of light and of the moving camera. But for the most part leading directors of the silent period (Henry King, Herbert Brenon, John S. Robertson, King Vidor, John Ford) continued and refined the editing tradition established by Griffith.

Chaplin and Others.—After Griffith, the leading creative spirit in the American film was Charles Chaplin. Known to and loved by more human beings than any other entertainer in history, he speedily achieved the capital power to produce his own films as he liked, being at once author, director, and editor as well as star. His drama *A Woman of Paris* (1923), which he wrote and directed but in which he appeared only briefly, showed his mastery of all the means of cinema, but the majority of his films, centering around the figure of "Charlie," deliberately utilize only a small segment of the total area of cinematographic means. In these films the camera is used almost solely to isolate and observe the movements and gestures of a single figure. Since Chaplin alone among film artists has controlled his own films from nearly the beginning of his career to its mature stage, it is possible to follow not only his technical and stylistic development but also the evolution of his viewpoint, from an early brutality and sentimentality through indignant social criticism to a Sophoclean irony and serenity.

Mack Sennett, Chaplin's mentor, also fathered a vein of screen comedy which used movie magic to further slapstick, and which at its best rose to irony and satire, and even to metaphysics. His principal disciples were Buster Keaton, "Fatty" Arbuckle, Harry Langdon, and Harold Lloyd, with W. C. Fields, the Marx Brothers, and Bing Crosby and Bob Hope as latter-day descendants. The enduring quality of many of their films, especially Keaton's, emphasizes how often the best screen work has come from popular entertainers unconscious of any mission other than to please, rather than from those who sought to uplift the movies or to use them as a belt line for the transmission of aesthetic values originating elsewhere.

Chaplin and Griffith aside, the only American director to approach complete control over the form and content of his films was Erich von Stroheim, though his attempts to achieve autonomy against the grain of the industry's organization eventually cost him his position as a leading director. Analyzing and then reassembling the visual elements of his films into a mosaic of detail, he strove to confer on the film the scope and psychological penetration of the novel; two of his films, the famous *Greed* (1924) and *The Wedding March* (1928), were completed in more than 40 reels. Such extravagance (more of running time than of production cost) caused his employers to remove him from control and to cut down the films to normal length. Even in this fragmentary form, these films are numbered among the masterworks of the medium.

Montage.—Rhythm, which the pioneer aesthetes had declared to be the basis of film form, was for many years neglected in film theory (though not in practice) in every film-making country except the Soviet Union. There, under state control and for political reasons, theories and experiments likely to result in more effective films were long encouraged, and a young generation of film makers set out to understand and master the medium. Sergei Mikhailovitch Eisenstein and Vsevolod Illarionovich Pudovkin in particular studied the films of all the world, but especially American films and most intensively the films of D. W. Griffith. From their study and resulting practice emerged the first fully reasoned aesthetic theory of the film medium.

They derived it principally from Griffith's *Intolerance* (1916), which Terry Ramsaye called "the only film fugue." *Intolerance* simultaneously told four stories from four different historic epochs, cutting from one to another as the progress of each demanded, and culminating in a quadruple climax in which "history itself seems to pour like a cataract across the screen." This was indeed "cinematic counterpoint," the most advanced example yet known, and too advanced for the public of 1916. Its specific revelation to the Soviet cinematographers was that the film director, as editor, could be a master juggler of time and space, juxtaposing any or all of the elements of the visible universe to produce contrast, comparison, or parallel as demanded by the theme. Pudovkin wrote, "Editing is the creative force of filmic reality," and he and his colleagues set to work to outline as precisely as possible the theory of montage.

Montage theory (the selection, cutting, and piecing together as a consecutive whole of the separate shots taken in the making of a film) asserts that everything recorded on film is but raw material for editing. Human beings are required to "behave" rather than to "act" for the camera, and are chosen rather for physical appearance than for professional skill (the "theory of typage"); their performances are actually the creation of the director-editor. All material is shot looking forward to the cutting bench, and there the creative act of film making takes place. In editing, the shots are joined together in a manner determined not by their content or narrative value, but according to a preconceived editorial pattern designed to achieve rhythmic effect. Such effects are to be secured "metrically"; sequences composed of very short shots will produce excitement or suspense; a succession of long-held shots will yield a mood of melancholy or repose; the two rhythms may also be alternated or modified to any desired degree. Montage theory holds that the assault of these measured rhythms upon human reflexes produces emotional and intellectual reactions almost independently of content.

The first fruit of the montage theory was S. M. Eisenstein's *Armored Cruiser Potemkin* (1925), with its famous Odessa steps massacre, a sequence which seemed final proof of all the assertions made about montage. After Carl Mayer saw *Potemkin,* he concluded that the German studio style he had labored to create was a blind alley, a misguided attempt to synthesize theater and painting, and that this "inspired newsreel," as *Potemkin* was often called, held the key to the future of the medium. His response was widely shared. Georg Wilhelm Pabst, who dominated the German film in the second half of the 1920's, based *The Joyless Street* (1925) and *The Love of Jeanne Ney* (1927) on montage. Film enthusiasts throughout the world saw montage as the organization and rationalization of those purely cinematic qualities which had been dimly perceived in the earlier work of Griffith and von Stroheim. The arrival in western Europe and the United States of further Soviet films—Eisenstein's *Ten Days That Shook the World* (1928), Pudovkin's *Mother* (1926) and *The End of St. Petersburg* (1927), Alexander Dovzhenko's *Arsenal* (1929)—seemed to confirm the hypothesis that montage could tell any story, dramatize any theme. The basis of film form was thought to be established.

Sound.—At this juncture the sound film arrived. Since at the beginning it was impossible either to move the camera or to edit the sound track with any freedom, the film returned to its ancient bondage to the theater and simply photographed innumerable stage plays. The art of the moving picture as an independent and unique medium seemed lost. But in 1928, before they had themselves seen a talking picture, Eisenstein and Pudovkin in a famous "manifesto" predicted that montage would apply to the sound film exactly as it had to the silent. Once the sound track could be cut (as soon it could be), dialogue, music, and "natural" sound were to be recorded and edited in counterpoint to one another as well as to the visual sequences. Sound would not reflect the visual image, nor need it have a visible source; its use would be determined thematically.

Even before it appeared, the principles enunciated in this manifesto were being applied in virtually every film-making country by veteran directors who refused to abandon the hard-won flexibility of the film and return to stage methods. King Vidor's *Hallelujah!* (1929) restored mobility to the camera and conferred it upon the microphone. Josef von Sternberg's *Morocco* (1930) reduced dialogue to a subsidiary narrative function. Particularly, the work of René Clair in *Sous les Toits de Paris* (1930), *Le Million* (1930), and *A Nous la Liberté* (1931) brilliantly revealed the potentialities of sound-image counterpoint. Since the early days of sound, complex audio-visual editing patterns have been achieved by directors working all over the world—in Lewis Milestone's *All Quiet on the Western Front* (1930), Pabst's *Kameradschaft* (1931), Fritz Lang's *M* (1932) and *Fury* (1936), Ernst Lubitsch's *The Man I Killed* (1932), John Ford's *Young Mr. Lincoln* (1939) and *The Grapes of Wrath* (1940), Frank Capra's *American Madness* (1932) and *Mr. Deeds Goes to Town* (1936), Julien Duvivier's *Poil de Carotte* (1932), Carl Theodor Dreyer's *Day of Wrath* (1944), Vincente Minelli's *The Clock* (1945), John Huston's *The Maltese Falcon* (1941) and *The Treasure of the Sierra Madre* (1947), and Fred Zinneman's *High Noon* (1951).

RICHARD GRIFFITH
Coauthor of "The Film Till Now"

FILMS AFTER WORLD WAR II

In Britain in 1946, over 30 million cinema tickets were sold every week; in the United States the number was 90 million. In 1962 the British figure had fallen to about 8 million, the American to 43 million (having reached a low point of 40 million in 1960). In the intervening years, television had come into its own, and free entertainment captured most of the mass audience.

There was an assault from another front, too. In the era immediately following the war, giant film studios everywhere found themselves facing competition from an increasing number of sources. Most important was the independent film makers, whose work had previously been exhibited chiefly in small "art" houses.

Western Europe.—The independent film makers' "revolution" began in postwar Italy. Luchino Visconti is usually credited with inventing a new cinematic form called *neorealism,* but most of his films were not seen outside Italy until long after they were made (his first international success was *Rocco and His Brothers,* 1960). It was probably Roberto Rossellini more than anyone else who was responsible for introducing neorealism internationally. His *Open City* (1945) was a new kind of film; its stars were the people and streets of Rome. Vittorio de Sica, with *Shoeshine* (1946) and *The Bicycle Thief* (1948), spoke for the underprivileged and dispossessed.

Growing out of the neorealist tradition but not part of it was the work of two giants of Italian film art—Federico Fellini and Michelangelo Antonioni. Fellini, after the moderate success of his *I Vitelloni* (1953), leapt to fame with *La Strada* (1954). He solidified his position as an important force with *La Dolce Vita* (1960), *8½* (1962), and *Juliet of the Spirits* (1965). Antonioni made uncompromising studies of guilt and betrayal: *L'Avventura* (1960), *La Notte* (1961), *The Eclipse* (1962), and the sensational *Blow-Up* (1967), which was made in Britain with an English cast.

Conventional French film making continued after the war. Two veterans of the art, René Clair and Jean Renoir, brought out new films, and they were joined, among others, by such newcomers as René Clement (*Forbidden Games,* 1952), Henri-Georges Clouzot (*Diabolique,* 1954), Robert Bresson, Jacques Demy, Claude Lelouch, and Roger Vadim.

But the most exciting development in French films was the *nouvelle vague* ("new wave"), a movement that defied conventional morality and traditional film techniques. By 1959 most of the major prizes at the film festivals were going to new-wave films. The spokesman for the movement was Jean-Luc Godard (*Breathless,* 1959; *Une femme est une femme,* 1961; *Les Carabiniers,* 1963); other important new-wave directors included François Truffaut (*The 400 Blows,* 1958; *Shoot the Piano Player,* 1960; *Jules et Jim,* 1961); Alain Resnais (*Hiroshima mon amour,* 1959; *Last Year at Marienbad,* 1961); and Marcel Camus (*Black Orpheus,* 1958).

Postwar Swedish films were dominated by Ingmar Bergman (*The Seventh Seal,* 1956; *The Magician,* 1958; *Persona,* 1966), but there also were others at work. Lars Magnus Lindgren directed *Dear John* (1966); Vilgot Sjoman delicately treated the theme of incest in *My Sister, My Love* (1967); and Bo Widerberg directed what many critics called the most beautiful picture ever made, *Elvira Madigan* (1967).

Luis Buñuel made films on two continents. His postwar pictures include the realistic *Los Olvidados* (1950), made in Mexico; the controversial *Viridiana* (1961), made in Spain; the surrealistic fantasy *The Exterminating Angel* (Mexico, 1967); and a French film made in France, *Belle de Jour* (1968).

Eastern Europe.—Postwar Soviet films had war as a recurrent theme. Those best received in the West included Sergei Bondarchuk's *Destiny of a Man* (1959), Mikhail Kalatozov's *The Cranes Are Flying* (1957), and Grigori Chukrai's *Ballad of a Soldier* (1959). Screen adaptations of literary works, long a tradition of Soviet films, reached a high point with Bondarchuk's version of Tolstoy's *War and Peace* (1963). It took several years to make, cost a reputed $100 million, and had a running time of more than six hours. Hailed by the Russians as the greatest motion picture ever produced, it was generously praised by critics when it was shown in the United States in 1968.

Until the 1960's, Czech films consisted mainly of animated cartoons and Jiři Trnka's superb puppet features. Then several imaginatively directed films, notably Milos Forman's *Loves of a Blonde* (1966), Jifi Menzel's *Closely Watched Trains* (1967), and Zbynek Bynych's *The Fifth Horseman is Fear* (1968).

Poland's first important postwar film director was Andrzej Wajda, whose trilogy consisting of *A Generation* (1954), *Kanal* (1957), and *Ashes and Diamonds* (1958) is generally conceded to have introduced Polish film art to the West. But Roman Polanski was Poland's most celebrated postwar film maker, directing motion pictures in France and the United States as well as in his own country. *Knife in the Water* (1962), made in Poland, was his first important picture; *Repulsion* (1965) was made in France with a French cast; and *Rosemary's Baby* (1968), for which he also wrote the screenplay, was made in the United States with an American cast.

Britain and the United States.—Tony Richardson dominated British film making after the war with *Look Back in Anger* (1959), *A Taste of Honey* (1961), *The Loneliness of the Long Distance Runner* (1962), and, especially, *Tom Jones* (1963). Other important British directors included David Lean (*Great Expectations,* 1946; *Lawrence of Arabia,* 1962; *Doctor Zhivago,* 1965); Joseph Losey, an American film maker working in Britain (*The Servant,* 1963; *The Accident,* 1967); Richard Lester (*A Hard Day's Night,* 1964; *Help!,* 1965; *Petulia,* 1968); John Schlesinger (*Billy Liar,* 1963; *Darling,* 1965); and Jack Clayton (*Room at the Top,* 1959; *The Pumpkin Eater,* 1964).

Some veteran American directors continued to make important films after the war—Frank Capra, George Cukor, John Ford, Alfred Hitchcock (an Englishman, but most of his career was in the United States), John Huston (an American who became an Irish citizen), Otto Preminger, Billy Wilder, William Wyler, and Fred Zinneman.

They were joined after World War II by Elia Kazan (*Viva Zapata!,* 1952; *On the Waterfront,* 1954; *A Face in the Crowd,* 1957); Joseph Mankiewicz, a screenwriter turned director (*All About Eve,* 1950; *Cleopatra,* 1963); George Stevens (*A Place in the Sun,* 1951; *The Diary of Anne Frank,* 1958); and Stanley Donen, who brought a refreshing touch to musicals (*Singin' in the Rain,* 1952; *Seven Brides for Seven Brothers,* 1954).

Jules Dassin, an American director working internationally, made the brilliant suspense film *Rififi* (1955) in France, and directed his wife, Melina Mercouri, in the immensely successful *Never on Sunday* (1961). Other outstanding American directors included Delbert Mann (*Marty,* 1955); Stanley Kubrick (*Dr. Strangelove,* 1963); Robert Wise (*The Sound of Music,* 1965); Arthur Penn (*Bonnie and Clyde,* 1967); and Mike Nichols (*Who's Afraid of Virginia Woolf?,* 1966; *The Graduate,* 1967).

Prepared by the Editors of "The Encyclopedia Americana"

DOCUMENTARY FILMS

The documentary film deals with facts and seeks to provide the spectator with information. This "film of fact" records historic and newsworthy events; preserves the customs, manners, and appearances of societies; explains and teaches scientific discoveries; and expresses controversial opinions—private and public.

Beginnings.—The earliest motion pictures made in France and England from 1895 were pictorial journalism. Itinerant photographers captured exotic scenes, and these fact films were eagerly sought after by audiences at home. In time the photographers recorded news events with a degree of regularity; these films came to be known as newsreels (*actualités*), and were first produced commercially in 1909 by Charles Pathé and Léon Franconi, in France and the United States. Previously, the Edison Company had photographed President William McKinley's inauguration in 1896. In the next few years cameramen shot miscellaneous footage in millions of feet covering such subjects as the Jeffries-Corbett prizefight, an Easter parade on Fifth Avenue, New York, the San Francisco, California, earthquake and fire, the first flight by Wilbur Wright in France, Theodore Roosevelt, and some of the exploits of Harry Houdini.

When the narrative film became the feature of the theater program, the fact film was relegated to the single reel, or to semifactual and factual features, in some of which history was re-created as well as recorded. One such short fact film was *The Horse in Action,* produced by the Pathé Company around 1911. Still a remarkable work, the film demonstrated the movements of the horse at normal and at one eighth of normal speed. An American group

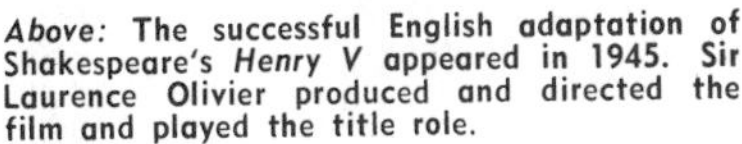

Above: The successful English adaptation of Shakespeare's *Henry V* appeared in 1945. Sir Laurence Olivier produced and directed the film and played the title role.

Below: Under Fred Zinneman's direction, the Western *High Noon* achieved a peak of dramatic tension. The film was produced by Stanley Kramer in 1952, with Gary Cooper in the leading role.

(Below) courtesy United Artists; (bottom right) Mayer-Burstyn; (others) Museum of Modern Art Film Library

Above: David O. Selznick was producer of the monumental screen version of Margaret Mitchell's Civil War novel *Gone With the Wind*. Filmed in Technicolor in 1939, it featured Clark Gable and Vivien Leigh.

Above: The Lost Weekend, directed by Billy Wilder in 1945 and starring Ray Milland, was an honest and realistic treatment of the problem of alcoholism.

Below: Culminating the emergence of Italian film art after World War II was *The Bicycle Thief* (1948), produced and directed by Vittorio De Sica and acted by a cast of nonprofessionals.

Avco Embassy

Above: Dustin Hoffman played the boy; Katharine Ross, the girl; and Anne Bancroft, her mother and his ex-mistress, in *The Graduate* (1967), Mike Nichols' black comedy about growing up in suburban America.

American International

Above: La dolce vita (1960), Federico Fellini's lush episodic account of the pleasures and wages of sin in contemporary Rome.

Rank Film Distributors of America, Inc.

Above: The Swedish director Ingmar Bergman won international fame for such elegant comedies as *Smiles of a Summer Night* (1955), as well as for the somber symbolic dramas with which he is usually identified.

Below: Playing a pair of 1930's bank robbers, Warren Beatty and Faye Dunaway crystallized nostalgia for the Depression era in *Bonnie and Clyde* (1967).

Pictorial Parade

Below: Napoleon at the Battle of Borodino, as he appears in the Russian film *War and Peace*, directed by Sergei Bondarchuk and released in the United States in 1968 in a version running for 6½ hours.

Walter Reade Organization

a little later documented the life of a typical family of Blackfoot Indians in Montana, and the communal life of birds that nested on an isolated island off the South African coast.

By 1922, the young Soviet Union had developed a powerful propaganda arm through the use of documentary film called Kino-Eye. Directed and edited by Dziga Vertov, Kino-Eye applied the peculiar resources of the cinema to develop an international film language capable of recording social and political events, and expressing approximate sensory experiences to give spectators a sense of actuality.

The Work of Robert J. Flaherty.—Robert J. Flaherty (1884–1951), an American-born and Canadian-trained mineralogical explorer, is identified as "the father of the documentary film." From 1910 to 1920, Flaherty led expeditions into the sub-Arctic regions of eastern Canada. Not satisfied simply to record his experiences of life among the Eskimos on photographs, Flaherty learned the technique of motion pictures in order that he might return to Hudson Bay and make a full film on the life of an Eskimo family. The fur merchants, Revillon Frères, whose trading posts dotted the north country, gave him financial support on condition that the completed film carry their name as its sponsor. Thus was the first sponsored documentary film born. *Nanook of the North* (1920–1921) was a saga of a primitive people's fight for existence against the pitiless weather of the sub-Arctic.

In Samoa in 1926, Flaherty produced *Moana,* recording the ritualistic practice of the tattoo and other features of island life. Subsequently, in a short unhappy association with Fred W. Murnau, a renowned German director, Flaherty participated in producing a commercially distorted motion picture of a South Sea idyl, *Tabu* (1930). In 1933–1934 Flaherty went to a rocky island off the Irish coast where he beautifully dramatized the eternal conflict of man against the sea in *Man of Aran.* After a visit to India where he produced another commercial film, *Elephant Boy* (1937), a cinematic retreat from the uncompromising standards he had previously set for himself, Flaherty entered the service of the United States Department of Agriculture (1939–1942) for which he directed *The Land,* a study of soil erosion and the dislocation of farmers by the machine. After World War II Flaherty obtained funds from the Standard Oil Company to make a romanticized feature documentary on the life of the people of the Louisiana bayou country, *Louisiana Story* (1948).

In the 1920's, films of realism were being produced all over Europe. In France, Alberto Cavalcanti caught the essential quality of metropolitan life in his film on Paris called *Rien que les heures;* others, Jean Painlevé and Jean Benoît-Lévy, for example, produced brilliant educational and nature shorts totaling hundreds of titles. Walther Ruttmann composed another "city symphony" in *Berlin* (1927), in which the actuality of city life, the contrasts of rich and poor, took on the drama of fiction.

Joris Ivens and Others.—In Joris Ivens, the world documentary movement found powerful leadership. A free-lance global cameraman-director, his work from 1927, in his native Holland, showed strong social awareness. *The Bridge* (1927) was a simple, nondramatic portrait of a Rotterdam bridge. Another of his early films was *Rain* (1929), a sort of tone poem, in which he captured the quality of a short rainstorm in the city. Later, Ivens made films for a few industrial firms in Holland. In 1932 he went to the USSR where he produced *Komsomol,* a political film that searched for contrasts in the cultural life of German and Soviet youth. With Henri Storck, a Belgian collaborator, Ivens turned his camera on the *Borinage* (1933), depicting the misery of the miners with whom the artist Vincent van Gogh had spent some of his unhappy youth. Next he directed *New Earth* (1934), a story of the dyking of the Zuider Zee, and *The Spanish Earth* (1937), a deeply felt reportage of the Civil War in Spain as seen through the eyes of the common people. This latter film he made in association with the American novelist, Ernest Hemingway. In the years to 1950, Ivens made trips throughout the world to areas of social unrest—China, Indonesia, eastern Europe—recording current history and using the motion picture as a social weapon.

In Mexico, the distinguished American still photographer, Paul Strand, found financing and governmental support for producing a classic example of the documentary, *The Wave* (1934–1935). Magnificently photographed and brilliantly scored, this featurette related a tale of the economic exploitation and revolt of a village of poor fishermen.

In England, meanwhile, film makers, scientists, poets, and teachers organized themselves into a British documentary film movement. Under the leadership of an ex-minister and publicist, John Grierson, the group produced a hundred subjects delineating the England of the transitional 1930's. Supported by industrial sponsorship and government subsidy, technicians of the highest caliber were trained, and their work influenced the incipient fact-film productions of the United States, France, and Canada. Their films covered a wide range of subjects: the work of North Sea herring fishermen, a naval survey of the Labrador coast, the survival of English village handicrafts, the social implications of the British Broadcasting Corporation (BBC), the romance of the mails, and the Ceylon tea crop.

The New Deal Era.—Concurrently, an independent American school grew out of the federal government's spectacular use of the film to rally public support for its programs of reforestation, hydroelectric power development, scientific agriculture, and human rehabilitation in the 1930's.

Pare Lorentz, a former magazine critic, in two brilliantly expressive contributions produced the most impressive work of the early New Deal film era: *The Plow That Broke the Plains* (1936), documenting the waste and exploitation of the Great Plains area which, through the overcultivation of wheat crops after World War I, had been transformed into a desert waste; and *The River* (1937), which warned of the reckless cultivation of cotton in the Mississippi River Valley, resulting in awful human and economic waste.

Out of these lyrical beginnings, Lorentz and others like Ralph Steiner, Willard van Dyke, and Alexander Hammid composed a whole series of celebrated sociological films under public and private subsidies. Probably the foremost of these latter-day essays, *The City* (1939), was a survey of community life in America, from the New England township of yesterday and the unplanned metropolis of today to the planned model city of tomorrow, decentralized and beautiful. Then came Van Dyke's *Valley Town* (1940), a view of technological unemployment in a Pennsylvania steel town; and Lorentz's *The Fight for Life* (1941), a compassionate study of poverty and the inadequate maternity care available to modern slum dwellers.

In Germany, the Nazi woman technician and ex-actress Leni Riefenstahl directed a spectacular series of pictures of the 1936 Olympic Games in Berlin. As the Germans prepared for war, Miss Riefenstahl prepared propaganda films of high brilliance to inspire their friends and terrorize their enemies: for instance, *The Triumph of the Will* (1934–1936), in which the Nazi Party functionaries were introduced to the German people; and *The Baptism of Fire* (1940), an account, of doubtful veracity, of the Nazi conquest of Poland, several versions of which were prepared and shown to officials of other governments to impress them with the irresistible might of Hitler's legions and the folly of opposing the Teutonic "wave of the future."

World War II.—A stream of documentaries flashed on the screens of the Allies from 1940 throughout World War II. Britain, under direct air attack, produced a group of outstanding films that related the human side of life during the blitz: *They Also Serve* (1940), concerning the courage of the average housewife in England; *Target for Tonight* (1941), a thrilling account of the defense of London in the blitz; and *Desert Victory* (1942–1943), a dramatic record of the British 8th Army's triumphant pursuit of Gen. Erwin Rommel's Afrika Korps across 1,300 miles of desert.

Col. Frank Capra, who had been a prominent Hollywood director, produced a series of imaginative and accurate counter-propaganda films for the United States War Department (1943–1945), realizing that good soldiers and citizens of a democracy must know and understand the nature of the enemy and the facts behind the conflict. From this premise films emerged with a most comprehensive grasp of the documentary idea, including *Prelude to War, The Nazis Strike, Divide and Conquer, The Battle of Britain, The Battle of China, The Battle of Russia,* and *War Comes to America.*

As the war reached a conclusion, an Anglo-American group produced *The True Glory* (1945), an eloquent testimony to the Allied armies that fought the war side by side. The film recorded their voices and, in millions of feet photographed by combat cameramen of the United States, Canada, France, Great Britain, Czechoslovakia, Poland, Belgium, and the Netherlands, depicted their victories and heroism.

In 1943 the Soviets made available their coverage of *One Day of War,* in which hundreds of Russian cameramen photographed happenings in a single day along their far-flung war front. *The Story of Stalingrad* was released for exhibition abroad after the war.

Postwar Period.—Even before the death of President Franklin D. Roosevelt, the United States Congress canceled major film subsidies; the balance of production underwritten by the government during the Truman administration consisted largely of films whose purpose was to interpret American political and economic policy to nations participating in foreign-aid programs.

With the formation of the United Nations, film production was blueprinted into the plan for its international information services, first under the direction of the French film maker Jean Benoît-Lévy. Unquestionably, the most distinguished documentary sponsored by UNESCO, a U.N. agency, was the joint effort by the British craftsmen Paul Rotha and Basil Wright, *World Without End* (1952–1953). By depicting economic and social reforms effected by the U.N. in two depressed regions of Mexico and Thailand, the film helped to dispel the widespread opinion that the postwar fact film had fallen on dark days.

Devotees of the documentary organized an annual festival at Edinburgh, Scotland, shortly after the war, where controversy flared over the complacency of postwar film makers, dependent upon commercial sponsorship, and the plethora of purely expositional productions. Such films were widely employed in the United States and Britain as extensions of industrial advertising programs, and they frequently lacked the inspiration and "divine discontent" of the work of earlier craftsmen like Grierson, Flaherty, and Lorentz.

However, two men had made their way to the forefront as outstanding contributors to the film document: the Englishman, Humphrey Jennings, who before his untimely death in 1950 had produced several remarkable, eclectic achievements such as the wartime studies *Listen to Britain* and *Diary for Timothy* and his final film, *Family Portrait,* commissioned by the Festival of Britain; and Arne Sucksdorff of Sweden, whose favorite theme of the conflict of good and evil in all living things was reflected first in short films like *People in the City* and *Divided World,* and then in the feature, *The Great Adventure* (1953).

The stunning, but short-lived, career of Italian "realist" films (in which nonprofessional actors dramatized their ordinary lives) had a strong counterpart in the United States (1954) with the making of a controversial, pro-labor feature, *Salt of the Earth,* performed mainly by members of the International Union of Mine, Mill and Smelter Workers in New Mexico. The film depicted an actual, violent strike against a zinc mining company that brought unity to Mexican-American and "anglo" miners and their women. Another picture with a factual flavor, Walter Wanger's *Riot in Cell Block 11,* was an offbeat Hollywood film that dealt with some deplorable aspects of American prison life, and employed real prisoners at California's Folsom State Prison as extras in mass riot scenes.

Continuing the admirable "living" biographies begun after World War II, French documentary people produced a series that by 1954 included Henri Matisse, Pablo Picasso, Georges Braque, André Gide, Colette, Paul Claudel, Arthur Honegger, and Albert Schweitzer. Documentary memorial films honored the film innovators, Louis Lumière and Georges Meliès.

JULES VICTOR SCHWERIN.

EDUCATIONAL FILMS

The tremendous potential of the film in education was appreciated by many of the pioneers in the development of the motion picture. However, the difficulties of handling the complex and heavy equipment and the fire hazard of 35mm. nitrate film kept films out of the schools until the development of the 16mm. size and its acceptance as standard for nontheatrical use in the period 1919–1923. A number of silent films made specifically for classroom use were produced in the 1920's, and the schools began to acquire 16mm. projectors. The visual education movement grew, finding enthusiastic approval from some educators, and opposition from others who feared the "mechanization of learning." The coming of sound in 1928 added a new dimension to 16mm. as well as theatrical motion pictures.

It was the Second World War, however, which helped audio-visual education to come of age. With thousands of men to be trained in new skills with a minimum expenditure in time and personnel, the armed forces turned to the 16mm. sound film and the filmstrip. New techniques and new equipment were developed. Immediately after the war, 16mm. production increased in volume and in quality, new producers joined the old ones, and in many classrooms the projector was accepted as a teaching tool like the blackboard. By 1953 more than 15,000 titles were in current distribution in the United States. Similarly, better understanding of the principles of audio-visual education and improved distribution have brought the motion picture to classrooms and informal gatherings all over the world.

Types of Educational Films.—Modern educational films use all the resources of motion picture photography and recording. Although there is still low-budget amateur production, chiefly for local use, most educational films today are produced by highly professional crews, with writers, cameramen, and editors trained in the special techniques of their field. Color is used frequently; music, sound effects, and synchronized dialogue are used as well as straight narration. All new developments in the motion picture field are scrutinized by the 16mm. producers with an eye to their possibilities in educational films. Both three-dimensional and wide-screen films are now possible in 16mm.; demonstrations were given in 1953, but the expense was still prohibitive.

The educational producer may choose from a wide variety of film types according to the needs of his particular script. Documentary films show how people live and work in various parts of the world; a number of countries have made films about their own people to send abroad, and whole series of films showing typical families of many nations have been made for geography and social studies classes. The straight demonstration film, known as the "nuts and bolts" film, is used for training in skills. Dramatization is used effectively in historical re-enactments and human relations themes and has been particularly valuable in mental health subjects.

Animated charts, diagrams, and maps have been included in educational films from the earliest days, and their value in clarifying such subjects as the circulation of the blood or the operation of the internal combustion engine is obvious. Full animation, of the Walt Disney type, is less common because of the expense, but a number of animated and semianimated films have been made. New techniques developed for non-theatrical films have included the use of static material—paintings and drawings used under the animation camera to give the illusion of movement. Another type of film developed for 16mm. use is the discussion film, which presents a problem, or two sides of an issue, and leaves the audience to reach its own conclusions through discussion.

It would be a mistake to assume that educational films are used only in the schoolroom. Industry uses films in training technicians and salesmen, and to describe its activities to the public. Governments make films to attract tourists from abroad, and to show farmers or other special groups in their own countries better methods of working. Health organizations rely on films to demonstrate good nutrition and sanitation practices to adults with little formal education. UNESCO units use films in fundamental education in underdeveloped countries. Doctors study film records of complex operations in order to improve their own knowledge and skill. And small children eagerly welcome films shown at the public libraries as another form of storytelling.

Financing and Distribution.—Unlike theatrical motion pictures, educational films are not financed by paid admissions. The producer must either sell enough prints to schools, colleges, film libraries, and other film users to pay his production costs and enough over to make the venture profitable; or the production cost must be underwritten by a sponsor who wants a particular film produced. The nonsponsored film is sold much as a book is sold, except that the unit cost is higher. Most classroom films are nonsponsored, and the producer must make sure that he wins the approval of his customers—the teachers and audio-visual directors. The sponsored film may be paid for, and of course controlled, by a government, a foundation, an industrial corporation, or an educational institution. Such prints are generally loaned to film users without charge except for shipping. The films may range from straight advertising to such classics as *Nanook* or the *The River*.

In many countries educational films are controlled and distributed by a branch of the government, usually the ministry of education. Films are then made specifically for the requirements of the department. In the United States there is no government control of films, although many government departments have produced films at various times. Most of the states have film libraries operated in connection with the state universities. In addition, many city school systems have their own film collections, as do some public libraries. Commercially operated film libraries also serve school and nonschool audiences. Religious denominations, labor unions, art galleries and museums, and many national and local organizations also have film collections for rental or loan.

While most films are distributed primarily in their country of origin, there is increasingly an international exchange of educational films. Great Britain, Canada, Australia, and the United States all use one another's productions, unhampered by language difficulties. Some western European countries have contributed to the exchange by re-recording sound tracks in several languages. India has made a large number of films, only a few of which have yet been seen in the United States. UNESCO is producing an international catalogue of film information and evaluation designed to help in sending educational films around the world.

EMILY S. JONES,
Executive Secretary, Educational Film Library Association.

Bibliography.—GENERAL HISTORY: Ramsaye, Terry, *A Million and One Nights*, 2 vols. (New York 1926); Hampton, Benjamin, *A History of the Movies* (New York 1931); Moley, Raymond, *The Hays Office* (New York 1945); Inglis, Ruth, *Freedom of the Movies: A Report on Self-Regulation* (Chicago 1947); Quigley, Martin, Jr., *Magic Shadows* (Washington 1948); Mayer, Arthur, *Merely Colossal* (New York 1953); Quigley, Martin, Jr., ed., *New Screen Techniques* (New York 1953); Houston, Penelope, *The Contemporary Cinema* (London 1963); Crowther, Bosley, *The Great Films* (New York 1967); Rotha, Paul, and Griffith, Richard, *The Film Till Now*, 2d ed. (Greenford, England, 1967).

FILM ART: Seldes, Gilbert, *The Seven Lively Arts* (New York 1924); Barry, Iris, *Let's Go to the Movies* (New York 1926); Pudovkin, Vsevolod I., *On Film Technique*, tr. by Ivor Montagu (London 1930); id., *Film Acting*, tr. by Ivor Montagu (London 1937); Barry, Iris, *D. W. Griffith: American Film Master* (New York 1940); Eisenstein, Sergei M., *The Film Sense*, tr. by Jay Leyda (New York 1942); Kracauer, Siegfried, *From Caligari to Hitler* (Princeton, N. J., 1947); Eisenstein, Sergei M., *Film Form*, ed. and tr. by Jay Leyda (New York 1949); Museum of Modern Art, *Film Notes: The Silent Era* (New York 1949); Bazin, André, *What is Cinema?*, tr. by Hugh Gray (Berkeley, Calif., 1967); Kael, Pauline, *Kiss Kiss Bang Bang* (New York 1968).

DOCUMENTARY FILMS: Waldron, Gloria, *The Information Film* (New York 1949); Manvell, Roger, *Cinema 1950* (London 1950); Griffith, Richard, *The World of Robert Flaherty* (New York 1953); Baddeley, W. Hugh, *Technique of Documentary Film Production* (New York 1963); Rotha, Paul, Road, Sinclair, and Griffith, Richard, *Documentary Films*, 3d ed. (New York 1964).

EDUCATIONAL FILMS: Dale, Edgar, *Audio-Visual Methods in Teaching*, 2d ed. (New York 1954); UNESCO, *Selected List of Catalogues for Short Films and Filmstrips* (New York 1964); Herman, Lewis, *Educational Films* (New York 1965); Groves, Peter, ed., *Film in Higher Education* (New York 1966).

MOTLEY, mot'lē, **John Lothrop**, American diplomat and historian: b. Dorchester, Mass., April 15, 1814; d. Frampton Court, near Dorchester, England, May 29, 1877. He graduated from Harvard in 1831 and then attended the universities of Göttingen and Berlin for two years. Returning to Boston, he studied law until 1841. In that year he was sent to St. Petersburg (now Leningrad), Russia, as secretary of legation, but he soon left that post and returned to the United States. His first piece of historical writing was a long article on Peter the Great (*North American Review*, October 1845). Soon after this publication he planned to study the history of the Netherlands, and William H. Prescott, then at work on his *History of Philip II*, encouraged him. Motley's *The Rise of the Dutch Republic* was published in 1856 in three volumes, at the author's expense. Although the reviews of the history were not all favorable, it quickly gained immense popularity and was subsequently translated into Dutch, French, German, and Russian.

Motley's *History of the United Netherlands* . . ., covering the late 16th and the 17th centuries, appeared in four volumes, the first two in 1860 and the last two in 1867. In 1861 he wrote two timely articles for *The Times* (London), in which he explained the causes of the Civil War in America, arguing for the benefit of the English that the United States was not a confederacy and that parts of the Union were not separable. In the same year he became U. S. minister to Austria, remaining in that position until his resignation in 1867. He accepted the post of minister to England in 1869 but was recalled the next year by President Ulysses S. Grant, apparently for political reasons. Motley continued his Dutch history with *The Life and Death of John of Barneveld . . .* (2 vols., 1874), which covered the Thirty Years' War period. It was not as popular as his previous work, but it became a major source even for Dutch historians. All his writings display a colorful style.

MOTOR, Electric, a machine that converts electrical energy to mechanical energy. When a motor is connected to a source of electrical energy, it develops a twisting effort called torque that tends to rotate the shaft of the motor. When the motor shaft is directly connected or geared or belted to a machine, that machine is driven by the motor to produce useful work.

Literally millions of motors are used in modern society. In the home, they drive the vacuum cleaner, the laundry washer, the air conditioner, the sewing machine, the blender, and other appliances. In the modern factory, the electric motor is essential for such tasks as driving lathes, milling machines, printing presses, conveyors, and grinders. Also rail and vehicular transportation systems, water-supply systems, and pumping plants are dependent on electric motors. Indeed, the electric motor—a highly efficient and compact prime mover—is used throughout a modern industrialized society.

The efficiency of a motor varies with the load placed on it and usually is highest when the motor is fully loaded. Large motors are more efficient than small ones, and, for the same horsepower rating, high-speed motors are more efficient than low-speed motors. In terms of horsepower, motors range in size from a small fraction of a horsepower to 5,000 horsepower or even larger.

Motors may be broadly classified as direct-current (dc) or alternating-current (ac) motors. In the 1880's, because the first electric power systems provided only direct current, the first motors necessarily were dc motors. After the advent of ac power systems in the 1890's, a type of ac motor called an induction motor became popular because of its simplicity. Other types of ac motors, notably the synchronous motor and the universal motor, also were developed and put to use. Even though most electrical supply systems are now ac systems, direct-current motors still play a significant role. They are used in many applications where a wide range of motor speeds is required—for instance, to drive elevators, machine tools, cranes, and conveyors.

1. Direct-Current Motors

A simplified cross-sectional view of a dc motor showing the usual construction in which

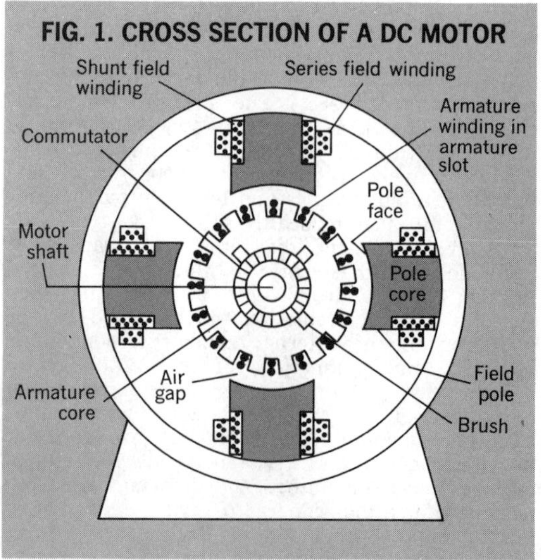
FIG. 1. CROSS SECTION OF A DC MOTOR

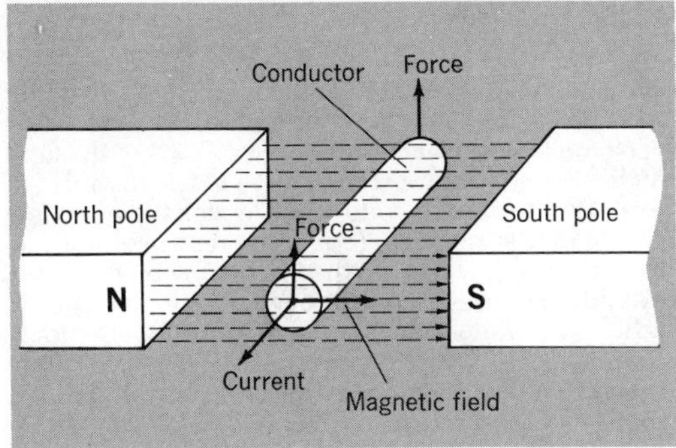

Fig. 2. Force is exerted on a current-carrying conductor when it is placed in a magnetic field.

the field poles are stationary and the armature and its windings rotate is shown in Fig. 1. Each part of a dc motor may be broadly classified as belonging either to the magnetic circuit or the electric circuit of the machine.

Magnetic-Circuit Parts. The magnetic-circuit parts of a dc motor include the armature core, the pole cores, and the field yoke. In addition to forming a part of the magnetic circuit, the field yoke provides mechanical support for end bells and bearings, which in turn position the armature and make it free to rotate past the field poles. A uniform air gap separates the armature from the field pole faces.

Electric-Circuit Parts. The electric-circuit parts of a dc motor include the field windings, the armature winding, the commutator, and the brushes. The field windings, which usually consist of insulated copper conductors, are wound around the field pole cores and are used to magnetize the magnetic-circuit parts of the motor. The armature conductors are formed into insulated coils and are placed in slots on the outer surface of the armature core. The ends of the armature coils terminate in copper segments of the commutator, and these segments are insulated from each other. Carbon brushes, held in contact with the commutator by brush holders, form a sliding contact between the commutator segments and the dc power supply to the motor.

Polarities of the Field Poles. Each field pole of a dc motor has a constant polarity while the motor is running. For example, when a 4-pole dc motor is operating, the consecutive poles would remain north, south, north, and south poles. In effect, the poles are electromagnets—they are magnetized by the direct current flowing through the field windings, and they lose most of their magnetization when the current is off.

Commutation. While the motor is running, the rotating commutator, in conjunction with the brushes riding on it, alternates the externally supplied direct current that flows in the armature conductors. The commutator reverses the current in the coil side of a conductor when it moves from under one pole to under a following opposite pole. Such a current reversal in the armature conductors is necessary to maintain uniform and continuous rotation of the armature in the same direction.

Motor Principle. The operation of a dc motor is based on a law of physics that may be stated as follows: a conductor carrying current, when placed in a magnetic field, has a force exerted on it that tends to move the conductor at right angles to the field (see Fig. 2).

With the field polarity and the current direction as shown in Fig. 2, force is exerted upward on the conductor. If either the field polarity or the direction of the current were reversed, the force on the conductor would be downward. The amount of force exerted on the conductor depends on the field strength (field flux), the amount of current flowing in the conductor, and the length of the conductor:

$$\text{Force} = \text{Field Flux} \times \text{Current} \times \text{Length}. \quad (1)$$

Motor Torque. Direct current flowing from the supply through the field windings creates a stationary magnetic field and magnetizes the pole core, field yoke, armature core, and air gap.

As shown in Fig. 3, the armature winding conductors in the armature core slots are placed at right angles to the magnetic field. When current flows from the supply through the brushes and commutator to the armature winding, the armature conductors are then carrying current in a magnetic field. As a result, a force is exerted on them in accordance with Equation (1). This force on the conductors is transmitted to the armature core, causing it to rotate as shown in Fig. 3.

The cross section of only one pole and a part of the armature are shown in Fig. 3. Actually, a dc motor has two, four, six, or more even numbers of poles, and the armature conductors are spaced uniformly about the entire circumference of the armature core.

Torque is a twisting effort defined as a force that acts on a body and tends to cause rotation of that body. The force developed in a dc motor by the interaction of the magnetic field and the armature current is called the motor torque. The amount of torque developed by a motor is proportional to the field flux and the armature current. The basic motor-torque equation may be written as

$$T = K\phi I_A \quad (2)$$

where T is the motor torque, K is a constant depending on the physical dimensions and characteristics of the particular motor, ϕ is the field flux, and I_A is the armature current.

Generator Action. In a dc generator, a motor action—torque—opposes the driving force of the prime mover turning the generator. Conversely, in a dc motor, a generator action—a generated

Fig. 3. Motor torque is developed because a force is exerted on current-carrying conductors in magnetic field.

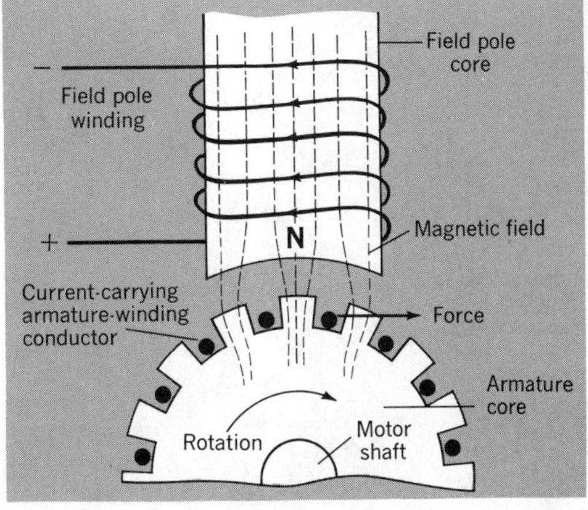

electromotive force (emf)—opposes the applied voltage of the electric supply. This generated emf, called the counter emf because it opposes the applied voltage, is proportional to the speed of the dc motor and the strength of the magnetic field. The effective voltage acting in the armature circuit of a dc motor is the difference between the applied voltage and the counter emf.

Effect of Load on Motor Speed. When a dc motor is first connected to an electric supply, there is a large inrush of current because nothing in the motor opposes the flow of current except the armature resistance, which is very low. As the motor accelerates, the counter emf increases, and this causes armature current to decrease. The current decreases as the motor accelerates until a point of equilibrium is reached where the current drawn by the motor from the supply just balances the requirement of the driven load at a constant speed.

As long as the motor-driven load remains constant, the motor speed remains constant. If the load on the motor is increased, the motor speed decreases. This decrease in speed causes a decrease in the counter emf, which in turn allows the motor to draw more current from the supply, which in turn causes the motor to develop more torque to carry the increased load at a slightly lowered speed. The end result after a load increase is that the motor speed stabilizes at a new lower speed. The end result after a decrease in the motor load is that the motor speed stabilizes at a new higher speed.

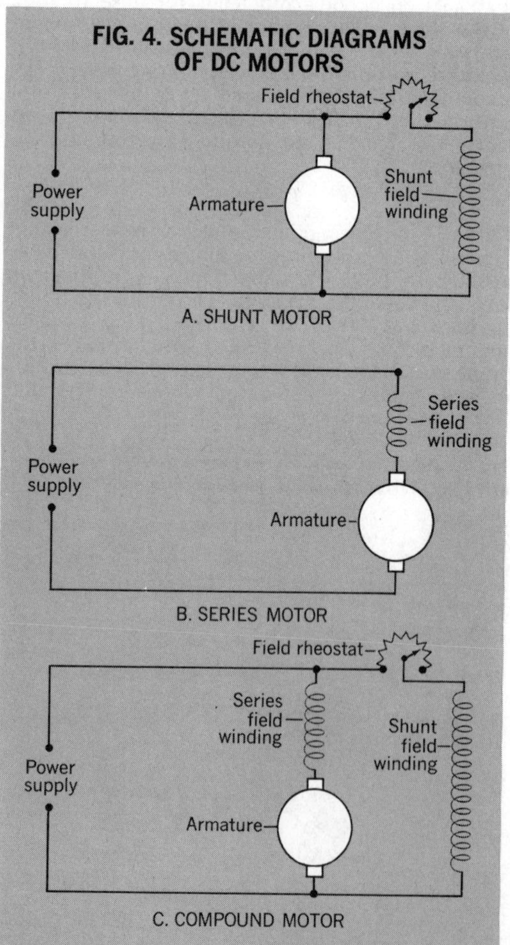

Motor Input Power. The power P in watts supplied to a dc motor from an electric supply is the motor terminal voltage E in volts multiplied by the motor current I in amperes—in equation form, $P = EI$. Most of the input power becomes available as useful output power at the motor shaft. The remainder is accounted for by heat and rotational losses in the motor.

Motor Output Power. Motor output power usually is expressed in terms of horsepower (hp). The horsepower output is proportional to both torque and speed. See also HORSEPOWER.

TYPES OF DC MOTORS

Dc motors are classified by the way their field windings are connected. There are three basic types—the shunt motor, the series motor, and the compound motor. The field winding in a shunt motor is connected in shunt (in parallel) with the armature winding, and the field winding in a series motor is connected in series with the armature winding. The compound motor has both a shunt and a series field winding. The electric circuits of the three types of dc motors are shown schematically in Fig. 4.

Shunt Motor. Because the field winding of a shunt motor is connected in parallel with the armature circuit, the field current and the field flux are relatively independent of the armature current.

The shunt motor is classed as a constant-speed motor even though its full-load speed is slightly lower than its no-load speed. However, the motor speed at any load can be varied over a wide range by adjusting the field strength. This is done by connecting a variable resistor (rheostat) in series with the motor field winding. An increase in the field strength decreases the motor speed, and a decrease in the field strength increases the motor speed. Since the speed of a shunt motor is easily adjustable, it is used for driving machine tools, fans, power shovels, and other machinery that require a wide range of speeds.

Series Motor. The field winding of a series motor is connected in series with the armature winding. Thus all motor current drawn from the supply flows through both the field winding and the armature winding. This results in a very high starting torque because both the armature current and the field strength are at their maximum values when the motor starts. As the motor accelerates and the counter emf increases, the current through the armature and field windings decreases, resulting in a lowered field strength. The speed of a series motor varies widely, depending on the amount of load being carried by the motor. At light loads, the speed is high.

The series motor is ideally suited for use as a traction motor in railway service because of its torque and speed characteristics. Because of these characteristics and because its direction of rotation is easily changed, the series motor is used to drive steel-mill equipment, cranes, and hoists.

Compound Motor. The compound motor combines the characteristics of the shunt and series motors. By varying the relative sizes of the two field windings, the motor designer can provide a compound motor that is suitable for driving irregular loads such as punch presses or reciprocating machines.

2. Alternating-Current Motors

Alternating-current motors are much more commonly used than dc motors because practically all modern electric supply systems are ac systems.

There are three general classes of alternating-current motors—polyphase induction, polyphase synchronous, and single-phase motors.

Three-phase motors are by far the most common kind of polyphase motors simply because 3-phase power systems are much more common than other polyphase systems. Three-phase motors are widely used for industrial service because 3-phase power can be generated and distributed more economically in large quantities than single-phase power. Also, a 3-phase power supply provides the simplest means for producing a rotating magnetic field, which is needed in an induction or a synchronous motor for starting or running.

Because most homes and rural areas are provided only with single-phase power, such equipment as household appliances necessarily is driven by single-phase motors. Various designs are used for single-phase motors, and their somewhat complex starting and running characteristics are more easily understood after 3-phase induction motors and 3-phase synchronous motors are discussed. Other kinds of polyphase motors, such as 2-phase motors, are not considered here.

Three-Phase Motor Principles—*Rotating Magnetic Field*. The operation of 3-phase induction motors and 3-phase synchronous motors depends on a rotating magnetic field in the air gap between the stator (stationary part) and the rotor (rotating part) of the motor.

The stator of a 3-phase motor has three individual and identical windings arranged symmetrically around its periphery. When these windings are connected to a 3-phase electric supply, three currents flow in the windings, and these currents produce what is known as a rotating magnetic field.

The currents that flow in the stator windings vary with time, as shown in Fig. 5. As shown there, the current in winding A varies sinusoidally from zero to a maximum in one direction, back to zero, to a maximum in the opposite direction, and back to zero. This is one complete cycle of current. At the same time, the currents in windings B and C also complete one cycle. Note, however, that the three currents reach their peaks one third of a cycle apart. One complete cycle of current is equal to 360 electrical degrees, so the three currents differ in phase by 120 electrical degrees. (The relationship between mechanical degrees and electrical degrees is given by $m = (2e)/p$, where m is the number of mechanical degrees, e is the number of electrical degrees, and p is the number of poles of the machine.)

As the three currents flow in the stator windings, they produce a magnetic field that in effect sweeps around the air gap at a constant speed. The speed of the rotating magnetic field is called the synchronous speed of the motor.

***Synchronous Speed*.** The synchronous speed of the motor depends on the number of magnetic poles produced by the stator winding and by the frequency of the power supply. In equation form,

$$N = (f \times 120)/p \qquad (3)$$

where N is the synchronous speed of the motor in revolutions per minute, f is the frequency of the power supply in hertz (cycles per second), and p is the number of poles produced by the stator winding.

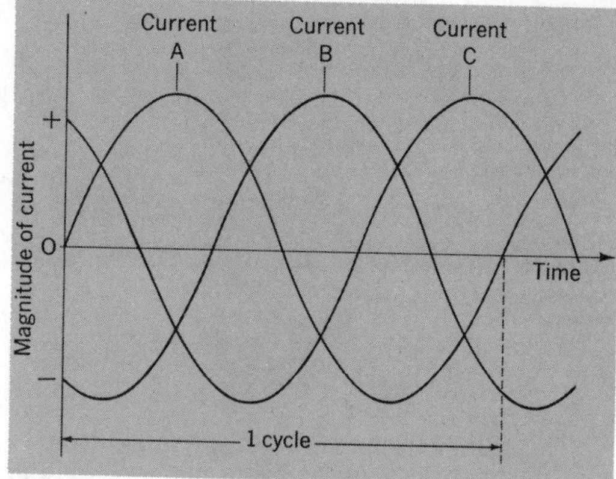

Fig. 5. Three currents in stator windings of a three-phase motor reach their peaks one third of a cycle apart and thus differ in phase by 120 electrical degrees.

A stator winding may be arranged to have two, four, six, or any other practical number of poles that is a multiple of two. For instance, if a winding were arranged to span 180° in space, it would produce two poles. If the winding were arranged to span 90° in space, it would produce four poles.

If a motor has 2-pole windings and is connected to a 60-hertz power system, the synchronous speed of the motor is 3,600 rpm, as found by using Equation (3). Similarly, if a motor has 4-pole windings and is connected to a 60-hertz system, the synchronous speed of the motor is 1,800 rpm. When a given motor is connected to a 60-hertz system or some other constant-frequency system, the synchronous speed of that motor is constant and is independent of load variations on the motor.

***Direction of Rotation*.** A 3-phase motor rotates in the same direction as the rotating magnetic field. The direction of rotation of the rotating magnetic field can be changed by interchanging any two of the three supply leads to the motor. Thus, the direction of rotation of a 3-phase motor can be reversed by interchanging any two of the three connecting leads.

***Power Factor*.** The power factor of an ac circuit is defined as the ratio of the real power to the apparent power, and it is expressed as a percentage or a decimal. A power factor as near to 100% as practicable is desirable because a low power factor decreases the efficiency of an ac system.

The term "unity power factor" means that the current wave and the voltage wave are in phase, or in step. The term "lagging power factor" means that the current wave lags behind the voltage wave. The term "leading power factor" means that the current wave leads the voltage wave.

THREE-PHASE INDUCTION MOTORS

A 3-phase induction motor has a stator containing the stator (or primary) winding and a rotor containing the rotor (or secondary) winding. The stator core and the rotor core are made of iron laminations, and the stator and rotor conductors normally are made of copper.

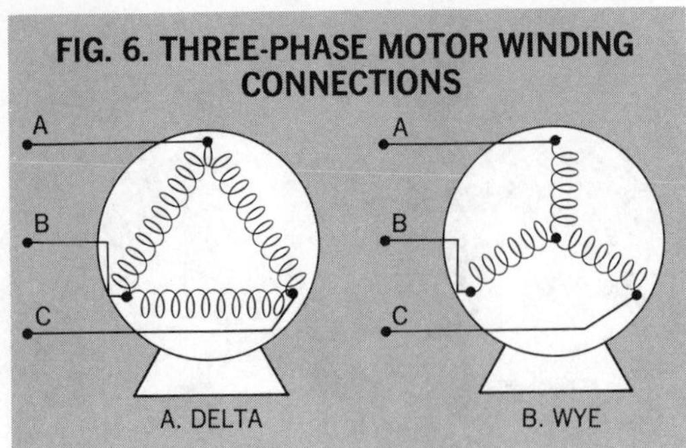

There are two main types of 3-phase induction motors—the squirrel-cage motor and the wound-rotor motor. The squirrel-cage motor is the most widely used motor of any type because of its rugged simplicity and low cost. It is used to drive such loads as fans, blowers, centrifugal pumps, and motor-generator sets. The wound-rotor motor provides greater flexibility than the squirrel-cage motor because it has an adjustable speed and a high starting torque with low starting current. It is used to drive cranes, hoists, and other loads requiring frequent starting, stopping, and reversing of the motor.

The three stator windings of a squirrel-cage motor are placed in uniformly spaced slots in the stator iron. The three windings are used to form an even number of poles, with the exact number of poles for which it is wound depending on the synchronous speed that is desired. The three windings can be interconnected by using either a wye (Y) connection or a delta (Δ) connection (see Fig. 6).

The rotor of a squirrel-cage motor has a laminated iron core with slots on its periphery. Uninsulated conductors are embedded in the slots of the cylindrical rotor core and are solidly connected to each other at each end of the rotor. The rotor winding resembles a cylindrical barred cage, hence the name "squirrel-cage" motor. (See Fig. 7.)

The stator and stator windings of a wound-rotor motor are essentially the same as those in a squirrel-cage motor. The wound-rotor motor differs from the squirrel-cage motor in that a 3-phase insulated winding, usually wye-connected, is placed in the slots on the rotor iron. Furthermore, one end of each of the three windings is terminated on a slip ring, and external connections to the windings via the slip rings are made by carbon brushes that ride on the slip rings. In this way, external resistors can be connected in series with the rotor windings, thereby providing a means for adjusting the rotor speed and the motor torque characteristics.

Fig. 7. Bare rotor conductors of a squirrel-cage motor are connected by short-circuiting end rings. With this structure, a current can be induced in the conductors.

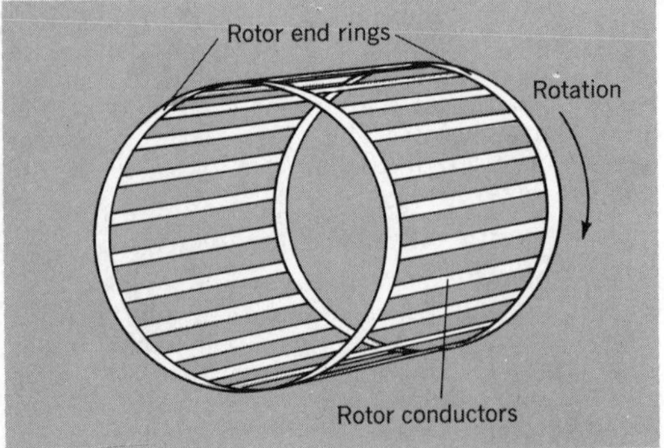

Induction-Motor Principles. In a 3-phase induction motor, as in a dc motor, motor torque is developed when conductors carrying current are placed in a magnetic field. However, in an induction motor, current is induced in the rotor winding by transformer action, whereas in a dc motor, current is conducted into the armature winding through the brushes and commutator. There is no electrical connection from the power supply to the rotor of an induction motor. The current in the rotor conductors is caused by an induced emf, which is caused by the changing magnetic field around the stator winding.

When the stator winding of an induction motor is connected to a 3-phase supply and the rotor is at a standstill, a rotating magnetic field sweeps across the stationary rotor conductors at synchronous speed. Because the rotor conductors are then in a changing magnetic field, they have an emf induced in them. This emf causes a current to flow in the short-circuited rotor winding. The amount of current that flows depends on the impedance of the motor windings. In this action, the stator winding effectively is a transformer primary winding, and the rotor winding is a short-circuited secondary winding.

The conditions necessary for motor action have thereby been established—that is, there are current-carrying conductors in a magnetic field. The current-carrying rotor conductors have a force exerted on them that tends to move them at right angles to the magnetic field of the stator. Thus the motor develops torque, and it accelerates in the same rotational direction as that of the rotating magnetic field.

In an induction motor, the rotor can never attain synchronous speed. This is so because there must be relative motion between the rotating magnetic field and the rotor in order to induce an emf in the rotor winding. If it were possible for the rotor to attain synchronous speed by some means, then the rotor would be standing still relative to the rotating magnetic field, no emf would be induced in the rotor winding, no rotor current would flow, no torque would be developed, and the rotor would slow down. In this event, the rotor speed would decrease until the rotor conductors would once again be cut by the constant-speed rotating magnetic field, emf would be induced, rotor current would flow, and torque once again would be developed to maintain the speed of the rotor. Thus, the rotor speed must always be slightly less than the synchronous speed in an induction motor.

Slip. The difference between the synchronous speed and the actual rotor speed of an induction motor is called the slip. Slip usually is expressed as a percentage of the synchronous speed:

$$\text{Slip } (\%) = \frac{\text{Synchronous speed} - \text{Rotor speed} \times 100}{\text{Synchronous speed}} \qquad (4)$$

Torque. The torque characteristic of an induction motor depends on the ratio of the rotor-circuit resistance to the rotor-circuit reactance. The torque is maximum when the resistance and the reactance are equal. Although the rotor resistance for a given rotor is nearly constant at all speeds, the rotor reactance varies with speed. Thus, the motor designer can choose a rotor with a relatively low built-in reactance for one set of torque characteristics or a rotor with a relatively high built-in reactance for another set of torque characteristics.

Speed and Torque Characteristics. The speed-torque curve of a standard induction motor is shown in Fig. 8. As shown there, the starting torque at zero rotor speed is about 125% of the full-load torque, and the slip is 100% (point A). If the rotor speed somehow became equal to the synchronous speed, the torque would be zero and the slip would be zero (point B).

The no-load speed of an induction motor is nearly equal to the synchronous speed, and the torque and slip are then very low, being only enough to overcome the motor losses. As load is added to the motor, the torque increases from nearly zero torque to the full-load torque value in almost direct proportion to the increase in slip. If load is added beyond the full-load point, a maximum or breakdown torque value is reached, beyond which the motor decelerates and stalls. As shown in Fig. 8, the breakdown torque for this standard motor occurs at about 12% slip.

Power Factor of an Induction Motor. An induction motor running at no load or at a very light load has a high lagging power factor of about 20% to 30%. As load is added, the power factor of the motor improves and is typically a lagging power factor of about 80% to 85% at full load.

Speed Control. As indicated by Equation (3), the synchronous speed of a 3-phase induction motor depends on the number of poles produced by its stator winding and the frequency of the power supply. If the frequency of the power supply is constant, as it is in a commercial power system, the only way to change the synchronous speed of an induction motor is to change the number of stator poles.

The stator winding of a 3-phase induction motor, when so designed, may be connected for different numbers of poles. This is done by using an external switch. In this way, a 2-speed motor can be produced in which the speeds have a ratio of 2 to 1. For example, a 6-pole motor can be reconnected by the switch for 12-pole operation, resulting in a change in synchronous speed from 1,200 rpm to 600 rpm. Synchronous speed ratios of induction motors for speed ratios other than 2 to 1 can be obtained by providing the stator with two separate windings. For instance a motor wound to have both a 4-pole winding and a 6-pole winding would have synchronous speeds of 1,800 rpm and 1,200 rpm, thereby providing a 2-speed motor. Moreover, each winding can be reconnected for a speed ratio of 2 to 1 by using an external switch, as mentioned previously, and thereby provide a 4-speed induction motor. A multispeed squirrel-cage induction motor can have two, three, or four synchronous speeds, but normally neither the synchronous speed nor the rotor speed is continuously adjustable between these several speeds.

The advent of the thyristor and other semiconductor devices has made it possible to develop special variable-frequency supplies for induction motors. Specially designed induction motors used with these supplies and auxiliary controls are capable of variable-speed operation because the frequency of the power supply is varied. This can be seen from Equation (3).

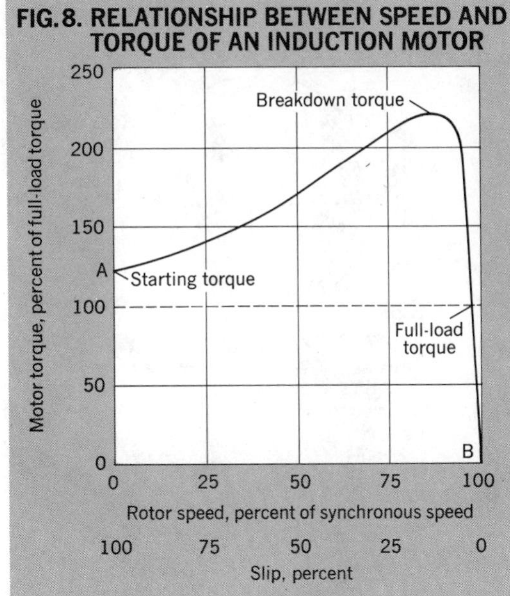

FIG. 8. RELATIONSHIP BETWEEN SPEED AND TORQUE OF AN INDUCTION MOTOR

Speed Adjustment of Wound-Rotor Motors. The rotor speed of a wound-rotor is continuously adjustable between a specified maximum and minimum limit by varying the external resistance in the rotor circuit. As resistance is added to the rotor circuit by adjusting the external resistors, the motor slip increases and the rotor speed decreases. However, if all of the external resistance is cut out by short-circuiting the three slip rings connected to the rotor winding, the wound-rotor motor takes on the same operating characteristics as a squirrel-cage motor.

Torque Adjustment of Wound-Rotor Motors. On starting a wound-rotor motor, all of the external resistance is cut into the rotor circuit, giving the motor a high starting torque with a low starting current. As the motor accelerates, the external resistance is gradually cut out of the rotor circuit, thereby providing a smooth motor acceleration under heavy load. Thus, the wound-rotor motor has good torque characteristics—high starting torque and good full-load torque. However, it costs more and is less efficient than a squirrel-cage motor.

A 200-hp, three-phase squirrel-cage induction motor.
CENTURY ELECTRIC COMPANY

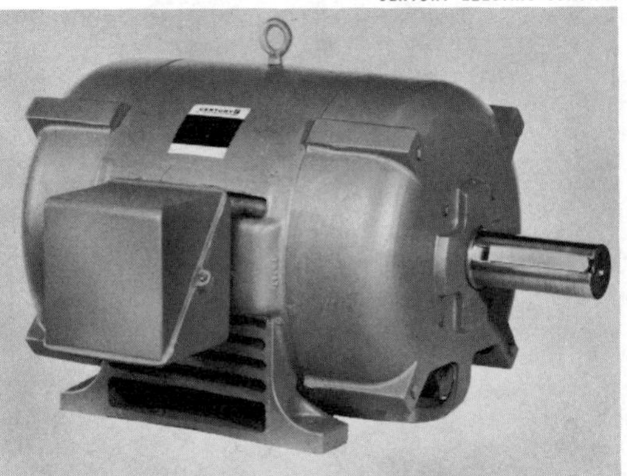

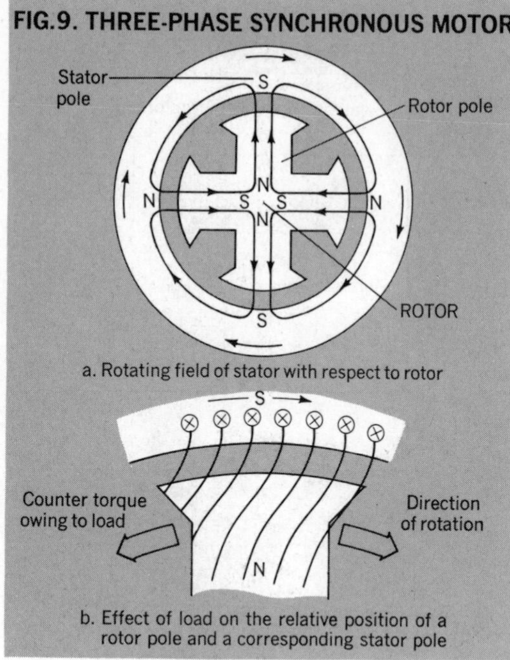

THREE-PHASE SYNCHRONOUS MOTORS

Three-phase synchronous motors are used as constant-speed, high-efficiency drives for dc and ac generators, large blowers, compressors, and centrifugal pumps. They also are used for direct-connected drives for low-speed compressors and equipment such as paper-pulp grinding mills, cement grinding mills, and metal rolling mills. In addition, they are widely used in industrial plants that require power-factor improvement.

Principles of Operation. The stator of a 3-phase synchronous motor is similar to that of a 3-phase induction motor. When the stator winding is connected to a 3-phase supply, a rotating magnetic field is produced. The speed of the rotating magnetic field is as given in Equation (3).

The rotor of a 3-phase synchronous motor usually is constructed with projecting (or salient) poles instead of having a cylindrical shape, as in an induction motor. The rotor contains the field winding, which is terminated on two slip rings so that connections can be made through brushes to a dc supply. Direct current flowing through the rotor field winding produces a fixed polarity on each of the rotor poles.

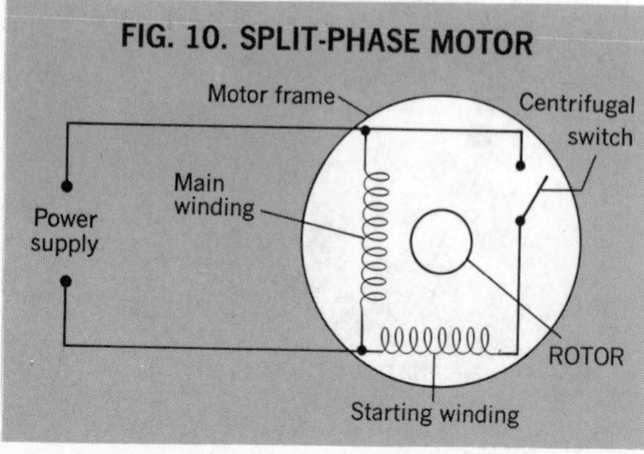

When the rotor of a 3-phase synchronous motor is brought up to synchronous speed by some means (with the stator winding connected to a 3-phase supply and the field winding connected to a dc supply), the magnetic poles of the rotor lock in step, or in synchronism, with the poles of the rotating magnetic field. The motor is able to develop torque to drive the rotor and its connected load at the same speed as that of the constant-speed rotating magnetic field.

Effect of Load. In a 3-phase synchronous motor, the motor speed is constant at all motor loads because the rotor is locked in synchronism with the rotating magnetic field, and the rotating magnetic field has a constant speed fixed by the number of poles of the motor and the frequency of the ac power supply. This can be seen from Equation (3). In contrast, in dc motors and induction motors, rotor speed decreases when the load is increased, and rotor speed increases when the load is decreased.

For the no-load condition of a synchronous motor, the center line of each rotor pole coincides very nearly with the center line of a corresponding opposite pole of the rotating magnetic field established by the stator winding. As load is added, each rotor pole drops behind its corresponding stator pole by a small amount. This angular difference in position between the two poles is called the torque angle. The load on the motor determines the amount of the torque angle, and the amount of the torque angle indirectly determines both the current drawn by the motor from the supply and the power developed by the motor. Note, however, that the rotor speed does not change as load is added. Each rotor pole position shifts slightly behind with respect to the corresponding pole of the rotating magnetic field, but the rotor continues to rotate at synchronous speed (see Fig. 9).

Synchronous Motor Starting. A 3-phase synchronous motor in itself has no starting torque because the rotating stator field passes the rotor field poles so rapidly that the rotor is unable to lock with the rotating stator field. Therefore, some means must be used to bring the rotor from standstill up, or nearly up, to synchronous speed. The usual provision for starting a synchronous motor is built into the motor in the form of a separate squirrel-cage winding on the rotor. Actually, the motor starts as an induction motor and runs as a synchronous motor.

During starting, the stator winding is connected to a 3-phase power supply, but the field winding is disconnected from the dc supply. Using the rotor squirrel-cage winding, the motor accelerates as an induction motor to its no-load speed, which is slightly less than its synchronous speed. When the motor reaches its no-load speed, the rotor dc field winding is excited with dc from the supply. If the relative polarities of the rotor poles and the rotating magnetic field poles are correct, the rotor then pulls into synchronism with the rotating magnetic field produced by the stator. The motor then runs as a synchronous motor.

The squirrel-cage winding has no effect when the motor runs as a synchronous motor. This is so because that winding is then rotating at the same speed as the rotating magnetic field, therefore has no current flowing in it, and therefore develops no torque.

Power Factor of a Synchronous Motor. The power factor of a 3-phase synchronous motor is determined not only by the load it carries but also by its dc field strength. At any given load, the synchronous motor can be made to operate at a lagging, unity, or leading power factor by adjusting the dc field strength. This advantage of a synchronous motor makes it especially useful for operation at a leading power factor to compensate for the effect of the lagging power factor of induction motors operating on the same power supply system.

SINGLE-PHASE MOTORS

Single-phase motors, which are widely used in domestic and commercial applications, generally are made in fractional horsepower sizes, such as one-half or one-third hp. A few are made in integral horsepower sizes such as 5 hp or 10 hp for use in areas where 3-phase power is not available. Single-phase motors may be classified as induction motors, synchronous motors, or commutator motors.

Induction Motors. A single-phase induction motor has a laminated iron stator core and stator windings that are connected to a single-phase supply. The rotor usually is a squirrel-cage rotor very similar to that of a 3-phase squirrel-cage induction motor. Because the rotor currents are induced, there is no need for electrical connections between the rotor and the power supply. In the foregoing respects, the single-phase induction motor is very much like the 3-phase squirrel-cage induction motor.

However, when a single-phase stator winding is connected to a single-phase power supply, the winding produces a pulsating stationary field that alternates in polarity. This field does not rotate as does the field produced by the 3-phase motor winding. A rotor placed in a pulsating stationary field is magnetized first in one direction and then in the other, and as a result no motor torque is developed. Since a single-phase motor has no starting torque, it must be started by some auxiliary means.

After a single-phase motor is started, currents are induced in the rotor, and this causes a rotor magnetic field to be produced. This field interacts with the field produced by the stator winding, resulting in a revolving field somewhat similar to that of a 3-phase motor. Torque is developed, and the motor continues to run in the direction in which it was started.

The torque developed by a single-phase induction motor is not constant but pulsates even at no load. A 3-phase induction motor has a constant torque because it has a symmetrical 3-phase winding. Consequently, a single-phase motor often is provided with a resilient mounting to prevent the transmission of objectionable noise and vibration stemming from the pulsating torque.

Single-phase induction motors are named in accordance with the type of starting method that is used. For example, split-phase, capacitor-start, and shaded-pole motors are single-phase induction motors that take their names from the starting method that is used.

Split-Phase Motor. A split-phase motor (more precisely called a split-phase resistance-start motor to distinguish it from other motors that use a split-phase method of starting) is shown schematically in Fig. 10. As indicated there, the stator coils are split into two windings—a main winding and a starting winding. These windings are placed in the stator slots so that they are 90 electrical degrees apart. The rotor has a squirrel-cage winding. Spring-loaded weights on the rotor shaft act as part of the centrifugal switch.

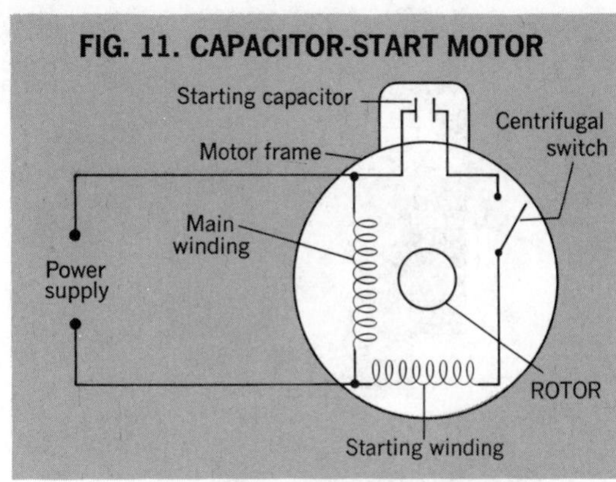

When the motor is connected to a single-phase supply and the centrifugal switch is closed, current flows in the two windings in parallel. The starting winding is wound with a few turns of small wire so that the reactance-to-resistance ratio of this winding is less than the reactance-to-resistance ratio of the main winding, which has more turns and larger wire. As a consequence, the main winding current lags behind the applied voltage more than the starting winding current lags behind the applied voltage. Because the two currents are out of phase, they produce magnetic fields that are out of phase, which in turn produce a resultant moving field that sweeps across the rotor conductors, inducing an emf in them. As a result, current flows in the rotor conductors. This current reacts with the stator field, causing the motor to develop a torque to accelerate the motor. When the motor accelerates to about 75% of its normal speed, the centrifugal switch opens, disconnecting the starting winding. Thereafter the motor continues to operate only on the main winding.

The split-phase motor has a relatively low starting torque, so it is used for driving easily started devices such as woodworking tools, grinders, and oil burners. The usual sizes of this type of motor range from 1/20 to 1/3 horsepower.

Capacitor-Start Motor. The capacitor-start motor, represented schematically in Fig. 11, has a split stator winding consisting of a main winding

This capacitor-start motor is driving an air compressor.

QUINCY INC., COMPRESSOR DIVISION, COLT INDUSTRIES

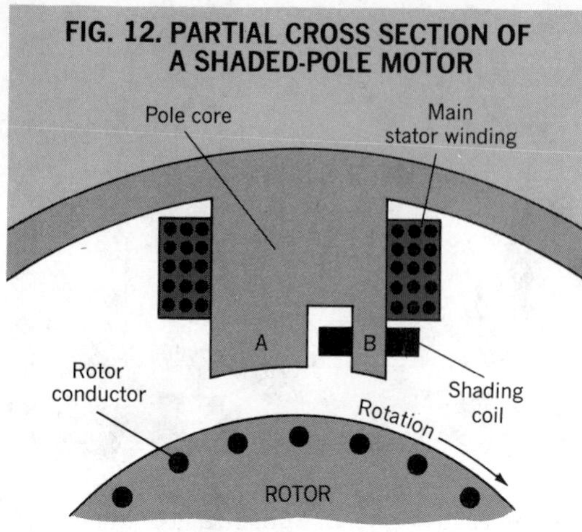

Shaded-pole motor has several poles built just like the pole shown here. The rotor has a squirrel-cage winding.

and a starting winding. The starting winding is connected in series with a capacitor and a centrifugal switch. The capacitor is used to obtain a greater phase difference between the starting winding current and the main winding current than is produced in the split-phase motor.

During the starting period of the capacitor-start motor, the currents in the main winding and the starting winding are out of phase by approximately 90 electrical degrees. Because this amount is greater than that obtained in the split-phase motor, the starting torque of the capacitor-start motor is significantly greater than that of the split-phase motor.

When the capacitor-start motor accelerates to near to its normal speed, the starting winding and the capacitor are disconnected by the centrifugal switch. Thereafter the motor continues to operate only on the main winding.

Because the capacitor-start motor has a good starting torque, it is often used for driving air compressors and other relatively hard-starting machinery.

Single-Value Capacitor Motor. A single-value capacitor motor (also called a permanent-split capacitor motor) differs from the capacitor-start motor chiefly in that the main winding, the starting winding, and the capacitor are used not only during starting but also when the motor is running. As a result, this motor has better running performance than a capacitor-start motor. However, the single-value capacitance of the capacitor used in this motor is a compromise between the best value of capacitance for starting and the best value of capacitance for running.

Two-Value Capacitor Motor. A 2-value capacitor motor (also called a capacitor-start, capacitor-run motor) differs from the single-value capacitor motor chiefly in that one value of capacitance is used for starting and a second value of capacitance is used for running. This can be achieved by using two capacitors, one of which is switched by the centrifugal switch, so that both the starting and running performances of the motor are optimized.

Shaded-Pole Motor. The shaded-pole motor is widely used in sizes of approximately 1/12 horsepower and smaller. It has the advantages of simple construction and low cost because it has no starting switch. The shaded-pole motor is often used to drive small fans.

A partial cross section of a shaded-pole motor showing the arrangement of the stator winding on one stator pole is presented in Fig. 12. The main stator winding is wound around the several stator poles and is connected to the power supply. The shading coil is a short-circuited coil that surrounds a part of the pole core. Each pole of the motor is built like the pole shown in Fig. 12. The rotor has a squirrel-cage winding.

As the magnetic field builds up in a pole core during the first half of each cycle, the field is concentrated in part A of the pole core (Fig. 12) because the inductive effect of the shading coil opposes the field increase in part B of the core. As the main field strength decreases, the field is concentrated in part B of the pole core because the shading coil opposes the decrease in field strength. Thus the changes in the field flux in part B of the pole core lag behind the changes in the field flux in part A of the core. As a result of this time lag, the magnetic field in effect moves from part A to part B of the pole. This changing field moves across the nearby rotor conductors, inducing a current in them. This current reacts with the field, causing the motor to develop a weak starting torque. The rotor rotates in the direction from the unshaded to the shaded part of a pole, as shown in Fig. 12.

Single-Phase Synchronous Motors. A single-phase synchronous motor, like a 3-phase synchronous motor, operates at an absolutely constant speed when it is supplied by a constant-frequency power system. For this reason, this kind of motor is widely used for driving clocks, timers, phonograph turntables, and tape recorders. There are two main types of single-phase synchronous motors—the reluctance motor and the hysteresis motor.

Reluctance Motor. A reluctance motor has a stator with a main winding and a starting winding to produce a rotating magnetic field. The rotor has salient iron poles and a squirrel-cage winding placed only under the salient parts of the rotor. The reluctance motor starts in the same way as the split-phase induction motor described previously. When the reluctance motor accelerates to about 75% of its synchronous speed, the starting winding is disconnected by a centrifugal switch. The motor continues to develop torque produced by its main winding until it reaches nearly synchronous speed. At that time the rotor poles are pulled into synchronism with the pulsating single-phase field of the main winding by a reluctance torque. This torque is developed because of the variation of the reluctance in the air gap, and this variation is due to the fact that flux paths near the salient poles have a lower reluctance than flux paths near the nonsalient parts of the rotor. The reluctance motor gets its name from the varying magnetic reluctance of the air gap. (Reluctance is the opposition to the production of flux in a magnetic circuit.)

Hysteresis Motor. In a hysteresis motor, the magnetic field of the stator is produced by using a split-phase method or a shaded-pole method, as described previously for single-phase induction motors. However, the cylindrical rotor of a hysteresis motor is made of hardened magnet steel, whereas the rotor of an induction motor is made of silicon steel laminations. Hardened magnet steel, which is a permanent-magnet material, is harder to magnetize and demagnetize, and thus the effect of hysteresis is greatly increased. (Hysteresis here is the lag of the magnetization of the rotor behind the change of the magnetic field applied to it.)

The stator magnetic field causes eddy currents to be induced in the rotor, and these eddy currents set up a rotor magnetic field. The reaction of the rotor magnetic field with the stator magnetic field causes the rotor to rotate. As the rotor accelerates to nearly synchronous speed, the alternations of the eddy current decrease, and the rotor develops fixed magnetic poles as a result of the magnetic characteristics of the rotor steel. The fixed poles of the rotor then lock in step with opposite poles of the revolving field, and the rotor then rotates at synchronous speed. A hysteresis motor does not require an external dc supply for magnetization of its rotor poles because its rotor is made of a permanent-magnet material.

The hysteresis motor runs more quietly and is less subject to mechanical vibrations than a reluctance motor because the former has a cylindrical rotor whereas the latter has a rotor with projecting poles. For the same fractional-horsepower output, hysteresis torque is more expensive to produce than reluctance torque. However, hysteresis torque is very steady, even under supply-voltage variations, and this makes the hysteresis motor popular for driving high-quality phonograph turntables and magnetic tape recorders.

Single-Phase Commutator Motors—*Repulsion Motor*. A simple 2-pole repulsion motor has a single stator winding distributed around the stator so as to produce two poles. The rotor has a winding like that of a dc motor armature, and the ends of the individual rotor winding coils terminate in copper segments of a commutator. Two brushes ride 180 mechanical degrees apart on the commutator. The brushes are connected together—that is, they are short-circuited.

These short-circuited brushes are placed so that the brush axis is at an angle of about 15 mechanical degrees to the main magnetic axis of the two stator poles. When this is done, the stator field induces a current in the rotor winding, and the rotor core then develops a north and a south pole. The north pole of the rotor is close to the north pole of the stator, and the south pole of the rotor is close to the south pole of the stator. The like magnetic poles repel each other, so the rotor turns—the effect that gives the repulsion motor its name. See Fig. 13.

CYLINDRICAL rotor of a hysteresis motor is made of hardened magnet steel. The larger of the two rotors shown has a fan for cooling the rotor.

ROSEMARY LEVIN

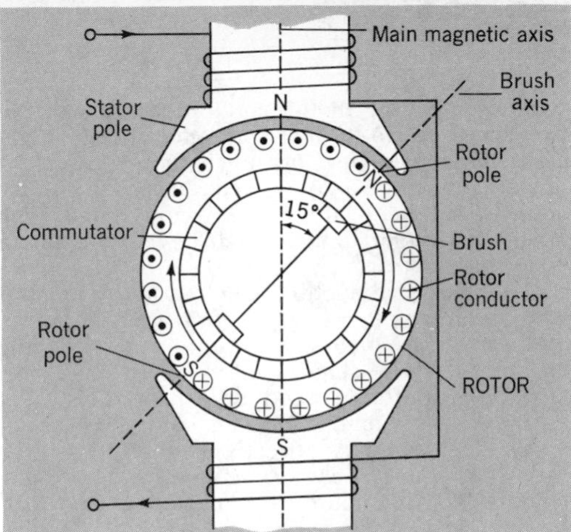

Fig. 13. Repulsion motor uses repulsion between like stator and rotor poles to turn the rotor. In the two-pole motor shown here, the angle between the main magnetic axis and the brush axis actually is about 15, although it is shown larger here for clarity.

The repulsion motor has a varying speed characteristic similar to the dc series motor and an excellent starting torque due to its use of the repulsion principle. However, owing to its disadvantages it now is little used.

***Repulsion-Start Induction Motor*.** A repulsion-start induction motor, which is basically similar in construction to a repulsion motor, starts as a repulsion motor but runs as an induction motor. When the motor reaches nearly normal speed, a centrifugal switch moves a ring that short-circuits all the commutator segments, and this makes the rotor equivalent to a squirrel-cage rotor. Thereafter, the motor runs as a single-phase induction motor. This motor, used in the size range of ½ to about 40 horsepower, combines the desirable starting characteristics of the repulsion motor with the good operating characteristics of the induction motor.

***Repulsion-Induction Motor*.** A repulsion-induction motor is basically similar in construction to a repulsion motor except that it has a squirrel-cage winding on the rotor in addition to the rotor winding connected to the commutator segments. The starting torque of this motor is produced mainly by repulsion action, as in the repulsion motor. Both windings are used at all motor speeds, so the overall performance of the motor is due to the combined effect of the repulsion winding and the squirrel-cage winding. The repulsion-induction motor is seldom used today.

***Universal Motor*.** A universal motor is designed to be supplied by either alternating current or direct current of the same voltage. Its capability for operating on an ac or dc supply makes it useful for a large market, including countries where dc is more commonly used than in the United States.

This motor is similar in construction and electrical connections to the dc series motor. In particular, its field winding is in series with its armature winding, and the coil ends of the armature winding are connected to the segments of a commutator.

The universal motor can operate at a full-load speed up to 10,000 rpm, and such a high-speed motor can develop much more power per unit weight than a low-speed motor. Also, the motor speed can vary over a wide range from high speed under light loads to low speed under heavy loads.

The universal motor, which is built in sizes from about 1/500 to 2/3 hp, is often used in household appliances such as vacuum cleaners, sewing machines, electric shavers, dishwashers, blenders, hair driers, portable hand drills, and toys. For items such as vacuum cleaners and sewing machines, the motor is directly connected to the load. For items such as blenders and portable hand drills, the motor is connected to the load through gears that reduce the speed at which the load is driven.

EUGENE C. LISTER, *Chief Electrical Engineer, Stanley Consultants, Inc.*

Bibliography

Carr, Clifford C., *Electric Machinery* (New York 1958).
Kosow, Irving, *Electric Machinery and Control* (New York 1964).
Libby, Charles C., *Motor Selection and Application* (New York 1960).
Lister, Eugene C., *Electric Circuits and Machines* (New York 1968).
Lloyd, Tom Cox, *Electric Motors and their Applications* (New York 1969).
McPartland, Joseph F., and Novak, W. J., *Electrical Equipment Manual* (New York 1965).
Millermaster, Ralph A., *Harwood's Control of Electric Motors* (New York 1970).
Siskind, Charles S., *Electrical Machines* (New York 1959).
Smeaton, Robert W., *Motor Application and Maintenance Handbook* (New York 1969).

3. History

The first commercially practical electric motor was introduced in the 1880's—more than a half century after certain fundamental discoveries in electricity and magnetism in the early 1820's. Among them were the discovery of how to make an electromagnet and that of how to produce motion from such a magnet.

Faraday demonstrated rotation of a current-carrying conductor around a magnet in 1821 (model shown).

THE SMITHSONIAN INSTITUTION

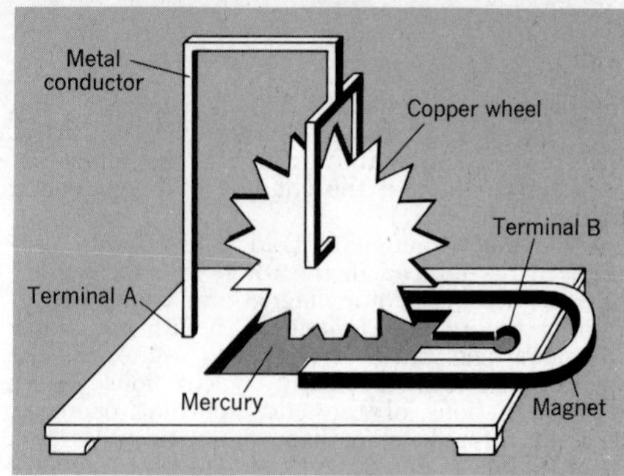

Fig. 14. Barlow obtained rotation of a star-shaped wheel in 1822. A force acts on the wheel when current from a battery (not shown) passes from terminal A, through the wheel, and through the mercury to terminal B.

In England in 1821, Michael Faraday demonstrated for the first time that continuous rotary motion could be obtained from a magnet and a movable wire. Peter Barlow modified Faraday's experiment in 1822 to show how the rotary motion of a wheel could be obtained (Fig. 14).

In the United States, Joseph Henry joined together basic components—a battery, an electromagnet, and a commutator—to build a continuously operating electric motor in 1831 (see Fig. 15). Thomas Davenport a blacksmith from Brandon, Vt., became fascinated by one of Henry's electromagnets. After several years of effort, Davenport was issued the first American patent (U. S. patent 132) on an electric motor in 1837. Davenport built many motors, and they had exceptional electrical and magnetic features for the time. Nevertheless, he spent his entire life in a fruitless effort to use electricity as a new source of motive power for commerce and industry.

Such pioneering attempts to harness electricity were in vain. One important obstacle was that the funds necessary to finance the long period of development were not available. An even more decisive factor was that the electric power was produced by batteries that required expensive metals and acids, and thus electric power could not compete commercially with the steam power produced by much cheaper coal and water.

In the 1860's and 1870's, a number of experimenters and inventors learned how the principle of self-excitation could be applied to dc generators. This development resulted in a commercially practical source of electric power. It also was learned that the dc generator was reversible in its operation—that is, it could be driven as a dc motor by another dc generator. This discovery was effectively publicized by the French engineer Hippolyte Fontaine, who noted the effects of a worker's error in connecting two generators together in 1873.

The 1880's: A Decade of Progress. During the 1880's, especially toward the end of the decade, small dc motors were beginning to be built in large quantities. They were used for driving fans, sewing machines, or dentists' drills and for other light tasks. The earliest ones were series motors, but shunt motors and compound motors were soon introduced.

The need for cheaper and cleaner urban transportation presented another potential market for electric motors. The growing cities had already turned to horsecars and cable cars to move large numbers of people to their places of work, but it began to appear possible that if horses could pull a car, then a motor should be able to do the same. One of the first practical motor-driven vehicles was devised by Werner von Siemens to carry thousands of visitors at the Berlin Exhibition in 1879.

In the United States, because of the insatiable demand for urban transportation, inventors soon were redesigning the popular Edison-Hopkinson dc generator for use as a dc motor in street railways. Frank J. Sprague devised the first modern electric street railway, for Richmond, Va., in 1887. He designed an electric motor that had a better magnetic circuit and a more rugged mechanical construction than earlier ones. Heavy sparking at the commutator was greatly reduced when Charles J. Van Depoele introduced carbon brushes instead of copper brushes in 1888.

During the 1880's, the theory of dc electromagnetic machines was advanced considerably, particularly in England. As a result, more efficient generators and motors soon were developed. Some of the more important men in this movement were R. E. B. Crompton, John Hopkinson, J. A. Ewing, Silvanus P. Thompson, and Gisbert Kapp. Because of the general recognition of the reciprocity of motor and generators, the story of dc motors henceforth was much the same as that of dc generator design.

In spite of significant advances in theory, uses for the dc motor of the mid-1880's were hampered because the distribution of direct current was limited to a few miles, and electric power was relatively expensive. However, it was gradually learned during the 1880's that alternating current could be sent economically over long distances. This advance foreshadowed the development of the ac motor.

As late as 1887, it seemed as if no practical ac motor could be designed. In 1884, John Hopkinson had demonstrated experimentally that an ac generator could be run as a motor, and probably had thereby devised the first synchronous motor. However, there still were many difficulties to overcome. In particular, the synchronous motor had no starting torque.

Unsuccessful attempts were also made to run dc motors from an ac power supply. If the motors ran at all, they sparked too much at the commutator or overheated, and they soon broke down.

Many of the advances in dc machinery had been made on the basis of crude theories or cut-and-try methods. However, because ac theory was too complex, steady advances in the design of ac machinery could not be made by such means. In 1888, Oliver B. Shallenberger did accidentally devise an ampere-hour meter, and that same year, also by chance, Elihu Thomson devised a repulsion-induction motor. While both of these were essentially induction motors, their chance discovery provided no basis for a development that would enable their discoverers to exploit them as a commercial source of power for at least a decade.

Fig. 15. Henry built a crude electric motor in 1831. An electromagnet moved like a seesaw when current was sent through electromagnet first in one direction and then in the opposite direction.

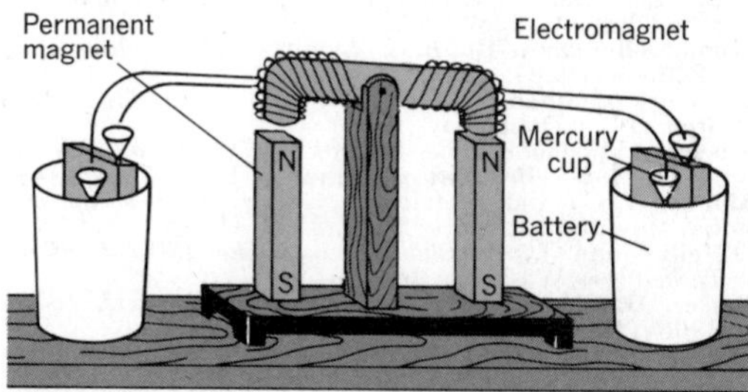

Model of motor patented by Davenport in 1837.

Induction Motor. Instead, the new kind of ac motor, the induction motor, had its origins in certain theoretical considerations. In the spring of 1888, Galileo Ferraris, a professor at a technical school in Turin, Italy, published an account of experiments he had made in the summer of 1885. From consideration of the interaction of two light waves out of phase, Ferraris had been led to the conception of a constant rotating magnetic field that was the resultant of two alternating magnetic fields 90° out of phase. He showed his students how a single current could be split into two out-of-phase currents that produced two out-of-phase magnetic fields, and he showed that the single resultant rotating magnetic field could produce rotary motion of a motor's rotor. Even though Ferraris' induction motor had a starting torque, he concluded it was only a laboratory device that could not result in a practical motor (see Fig. 16).

Independently of Ferraris, Nikola Tesla in 1887 applied for a patent on an induction motor operated by a rotating magnetic field (see Fig. 17). He also described how single-phase current could be used to run an induction motor. During the winter of 1887–1888, Tesla exhibited his single-phase induction motor, which depended on phase splitting, as did Ferraris' motor.

Also in the fall of 1887, Tesla applied for patents on a polyphase system for operating an induction motor. The patents, issued during the period from 1888 to 1896, were very comprehensive ones. Indeed, the genius of Tesla had enabled him to visualize and to patent most of the basic features of a polyphase system.

George Westinghouse, whose engineers had developed an ac system for electric lighting in 1886, bought Tesla's patents. Soon thereafter, C. F. Scott set to work with Tesla to create a commercially successful polyphase induction mo-

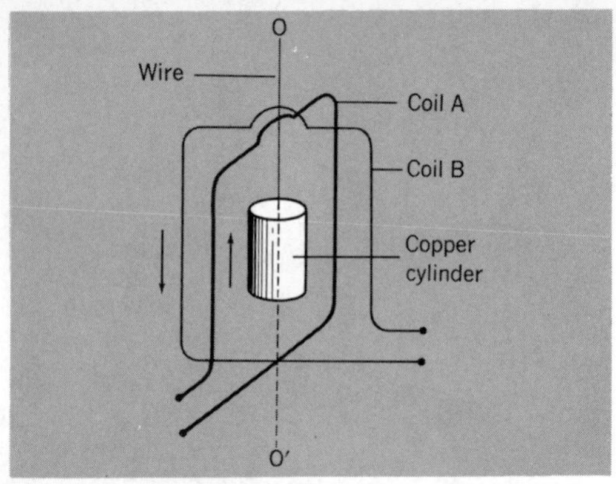

Fig. 16. Induction motor built by Ferraris in 1885 used out-of-phase currents in coils A and B to produce magnetic field that indirectly caused rotation of cylinder.

tor for Westinghouse. Unfortunately, no polyphase distribution system was in existence in 1889 to provide the power for such a motor. Moreover, even though Tesla had shown how a single-phase supply could be used for an induction motor, the relatively high frequency (about 130 cycles per second) of the single-phase system then in use for some electric lighting was a hindrance to the development of any commercial induction motor. Both of these conditions prevented the full implementation of Tesla's ideas, even though they were clear. After a year, Tesla left Westinghouse. A few Tesla motors were placed on the market, but they had only a limited success. By 1890, a financial depression forced Westinghouse to abandon temporarily further development of Tesla's induction motor.

The 1890's: A Decade of Growth for AC Motors. Tesla's patent applications in 1887 also had shown how to start a synchronous motor. In 1890 the first installation of a synchronous motor in the United States was made by the Westinghouse Company.

A number of induction and synchronous motors were shown in Germany at the Frankfurt Exhibition in 1891, where they were part of an exhibit of a high-voltage polyphase system. The Russian-born Michael von Dolivo-Dobrowolsky designed the ac motors and transformers for the system, and the Swiss-born Charles E. L. Brown designed the ac generator. Von Dolivo-Dobrowolsky showed two kinds of ac motors. One was a small induction motor with a squirrel-cage rotor, which he had invented in 1889. The other was a much larger synchronous motor that had a relatively novel dc field on the rotor. Brown improved Dolivo-Dobrowolsky's induction motor, and he had placed his own commercial versions on the market by 1893.

Fig. 17. Tesla's induction motor built in 1887 had two pairs of coils for producing a rotating magnetic field.

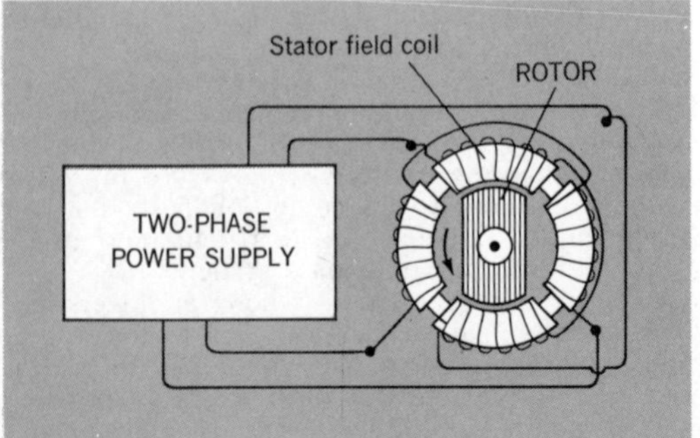

The demonstration at Frankfurt stimulated the revival of the Tesla motor by Westinghouse, and Benjamin G. Lamme turned his attention to further development of it. At the Columbian Exposition at Chicago in 1893, Westinghouse showed an even more complete polyphase system than the one at Frankfurt in 1891.

The General Electric Company, formed in 1892, had a lighting exhibit at the fair, but it showed no ac motors. However, largely due to the efforts of Elihu Thomson and Charles P. Steinmetz, the company became a formidable competitor in producing electric motors within one year.

Both Westinghouse and General Electric had successfully introduced induction and synchronous motors for industry by 1893. The financial success of their new ac motors was ensured chiefly by the completion of the Niagara Falls power plant in 1896. It not only reduced the cost of electric power but also supplied polyphase currents at the low frequency of 25 cycles per second.

Neither the single-phase induction motor nor the synchronous motor in itself has any starting torque. However, during the 1890's several means for providing a starting torque were worked out. For single-phase induction motors, the original split-phase technique of Ferraris and Tesla or the shaded-pole technique of Elihu Thomson was used. The synchronous motor was provided with a starting torque by applying induction motor techniques, such as the use of the damper windings patented by L. Hutin and M. Leblanc.

Improvements also were made in the techniques for controlling motor starting and motor speed. For example, autotransformers were used for controlling the starting of 3-phase squirrel-cage induction motors, and the Ward-Leonard system made use of an ac motor and dc generator to control the speed of a dc shunt motor. Both of these improvements were devised during the 1890's.

Developments in the 20th Century. By 1900, most of the major features of the electric motor and its associated equipment had been invented. Further refinements were made during the 20th century. For example, motors were extensively introduced in automatic control systems. However, these changes were mainly a sophistication of machinery rather than a departure from a foundation already laid.

W. James King, *Henry Ford Museum*

Bibliography

Dunsheath, Percy, *A History of Electrical Engineering* (Faber 1962).

King, W. James, *The Development of Electrical Technology in the 19th Century:* vol. 1, *The Electrochemical Cell and the Electromagnet,* U. S. National Museum, Bulletin 228, 1962.

Lamme, Benjamin G., *B. G. Lamme: An Autobiography* (Putnam 1926).

Leonard, Jonathan N., *Loki; The Life of Charles Proteus Steinmetz* (Doubleday 1929).

Maclaren, Malcolm, *The Rise of the Electrical Industry During the 19th Century* (Princeton Univ. Press 1943).

Martin, T. C., and Wetzler, J., *The Electric Motor and its Applications,* 4th ed. (Johnston 1895).

O'Neill, John J., *Prodigal Genius: The Life of Nikola Tesla* (Ives Washburn Inc. 1944).

Passer, Harold C., *The Electrical Manufacturers, 1875–1900* (Harvard Univ. Press 1953).

Thompson, Silvanus P., *Dynamo-Electric Machinery* (Spon 1882).

MOTOR APHASIA. See Aphasia.

MOTOR AREAS. See Brain—*2. Major Divisions of the Brain* (Cerebrum): Motor Functions.

MOTOR TRANSPORTATION. See Bus; Truck Transportation.

MOTORBOATS, water craft smaller than those ordinarily used as cargo ships, and propelled by internal-combustion engines (sometimes by jet engines).

History.—During the 1880's, when the weight of engines in steam launches seemed to bar further development of small power boats, a number of builders in England, France, Germany, and the United States experimented with internal-combustion engines. J. J. R. Hulme of London propelled a launch with gasoline in 1885, and a boat with an engine designed by the German Gottlieb Daimler was launched in 1886. In 1902, attempting greater speed on water, the Englishman Selwyn Francis Edge attained 19 knots with a 66-horsepower engine.

Between the turn of the century and World War I many new types of hull appeared. Designers found that if they could raise the hull partially into the air by the forward propulsion of the boat, the resistance of the water would be decreased. This discovery led to the development of the hydroplane, a boat whose hull shape, coupled with its relationship of power to weight, causes the bow to rise out of the water as the boat gathers speed. Rather than driving through the water, the hull planes over the surface. V-bottoms, round bottoms, catamarans, sea sleds, and a number of designs utilizing washboard bottoms were all tried during this period. The English naval architect Sir John Thornycroft's "skimming boat" *Tadpole* (1909) carried a web under the bow with a heart-shaped plane that lifted the bow from the water. Between 1898 and 1905, the Italian Enrico Forlanini equipped a boat with "ladder foils," and in 1907, Wilbur and Orville Wright experimented with a hydrofoil catamaran.

Marine engines have never been different in principle from internal-combustion engines for automobiles and other purposes. Except for the later air-cooled and outboard motors, they have tended to be of heavier construction, and have taken in water from beneath the hull for cooling, instead of from radiators.

Racing Motorboats.—Since the early 1900's, motorboat racers have pioneered in better engines and in new designs for hulls. In 1903 international competition was first organized when the British newspaper owner Sir Edward Harmsworth offered a cup which has since been called the Harmsworth or British International Trophy. From 1920 to 1956 this trophy was won by boats from the United States The American Power Boat Association's Gold Cup, first offered in 1904, is a coveted American trophy. World speed records are not set in the Harmsworth and American Gold Cup races because both are held on courses with bends that test the maneuverability of boats and skill of drivers as well as speed.

Under the rules of the Union of International Motor Boating, a world record may be set by making two runs of a measured mile and taking the average speed of both.

In 1939, Sir Malcolm Campbell's *Bluebird II* was timed at 141.74 mph. (miles per hour) and established a record that stood for 11 years. The hull of this boat incorporated the three-point (Apel) design, planing on two forward surfaces placed athwartship and a small area at the stern. After World War II, Campbell installed a De Haviland Goblin II jet engine, but found that his craft could not be held on course until full power was developed. In adapting motorboats to jet engines, designers faced a host of new technical problems.

The official world speed record continued to be held by a boat driven by a gasoline engine. Campbell's record was broken in 1950 when *Slo-Mo-Shun IV*, designed by Ted Jones and owned by Stanley Sayres of Seattle, Wash., went 160.3235 mph. In 1952, *Slo-Mo-Shun IV* broke its own record by going 178.497 mph. This craft was designed to avoid cavitation, which is a barrier to the development of greater speeds in propeller-driven craft; this condition occurs when the propellers turn faster than the water can close in on them, so that a partial vacuum is created. Consequently, at high speeds the propeller loses efficiency. Jones' record was surpassed in 1962 by Roy Duby, who drove his hydroplane at a speed of slightly over 200 mph. in a straightaway run of one mile.

Jet-propelled hydroplanes now hold the world's speed records on water. On Loch Ness in 1952 the English sportsman John Cobb was killed just after his jet-driven *Crusader* went 206.89 mph. for one measured mile. After completing this first run, his boat dove to the side and disintegrated. Although Cobb's one run did not constitute an official world's record, he had attained the fastest speed yet recorded on water. Donald Campbell, driving his turbojet hydroplane, *Bluebird,* set official world's records of 202.35 mph. in July 1955 and 216.02 mph. in November 1955. Later he broke his records again and again. He attained a speed of 276.33 mph. on Lake Dumbleyung in Australia in 1964.

To put motorboat racing economically within the reach of more people, the American Power Boat Association and similar organizations in other countries have drawn up rules defining various classes for competition. Motorboat racing is a thrilling and sometimes dangerous sport, with the light boats bucking wildly in each other's wakes. Spills at high speeds are not uncommon, and the rules in many classes require contestants to wear helmets and life preservers.

Classes come under the general classifications of inboard, outboard, displacement, and hydroplane, and are determined primarily by the engine's piston displacement. The size, cost, and type of hull also are often specified. There are over 35 classes in active competition in the United States. Motor and hull in the tiniest classes may cost under $1,000 while unlimited hydroplanes competing for the Gold Cup may cost $25,000 up.

Naval Motorboats.—During World War I the English designer Sir John Thornycroft invented a mono-step hull for a motor torpedo boat which was found to be faster than either a V-bottom or inverted V-bottom. The motor torpedo boat became technically the most advanced craft powered by internal combustion.

In World War II all the major naval powers had complements of motor torpedo boats, air-sea rescue boats, patrol boats, motor gunboats, and a variety of motor launches and lifeboats. Both Great Britain and the United States developed motor lifeboats that could be dropped into the sea for wrecked airmen. In addition, the United States Coast Guard had a large number of patrol boats, those over 56 feet long rated as cutters, and two types of 38 and 40 feet in length rated as pickets.

(Top) Evinrude Motors; (bottom) Chris Craft

***Above:* A 3 horsepower outboard motorboat. *Below:* A twin engine cruiser accommodating six persons.**

After World War II, France, Great Britain, Sweden, the Soviet Union, and the United States all produced motor torpedo boats that are undoubtedly the most powerful motorboats ever built. Most of these craft range between 60 and 100 feet in length, develop from 3,000 to 10,000 horsepower, and are capable of speeds from 35 to upward of 40 knots. They may be equipped with torpedo-launching devices, rocket projectors, small cannon, machine guns, and antiaircraft weapons. A typical American model was characterized in the pages of *Jane's Fighting Ships* as having "greater displacement, range, fire power and stability" than the World War II PT boats. Unlike the PT boats, built of plywood, the newer motor torpedo boats are built of aluminum.

The tactical usefulness of motor torpedo boats (MTB's) was demonstrated during the Battle of Britain in World War II. According to some naval authorities, the MTB's played a role comparable to that of the Royal Air Force in preventing invasion. The British Admiralty's summary of the war record of small motor craft states that motor torpedo boats, gunboats, and launches fought 782 actions, sank, damaged, or captured more than 500 enemy ships, and lost 176. Great Britain began World War II with 21 motor torpedo boats and ended it with 1,550.

During World War II an improved hydrofoil was developed. In this design, a stilt holds the planing surfaces under the boat so that the forward propulsion of the craft raises the hull completely out of the water. Since the resistance of the hydrofoils is not nearly so great as that of the hull, some designers expect to develop great speeds in hydrofoil craft. A number of civilian hydrofoil boats have been developed to carry passengers locally at very high speeds. Navies are continuing to produce new designs.

Motorboating for Pleasure.—After World War II, pleasure boating became a more popular recreation in the United States than it had ever been. By the mid-1960's, there were about 5 million motorboats of various types in the United States for the purpose of recreation. Something like 20 million Americans participated in motorboating; these people spent millions of dollars annually on the sport. It is true that nonmotorized boats, such as sailboats and rowboats, were also popular; but they were outnumbered by motorboats.

Most of the latter type of craft were outboards; the inboards came to less than a million. The vast increase over the years in the number and uses of motorboats was due primarily to the development of light, efficient, and relatively cheap motors, with numerous refinements making them easier to operate and to control. Plywood, aluminum, and glass fiber hulls were replacing steel and wooden types.

JOHN ASHWORTH.
Revised by the Editors.

Bibliography.—Teale, John, *Fast Boats* (New York 1962); Scharff, Robert, *Motor Boating* (New York 1963); DuCane, Peter, *High-speed Small Craft*, 3d ed. (Tuckahoe, N.Y., 1964); Solomon, Todd, and Wolf, E., *Power Boat Manual* (New York 1965); *Jane's Fighting Ships* (New York, current); American Power Boat Association, *Rule Book and Official Directory* (New York, annually).

MOTORCYCLE, mō'tẽr-sī-k'l, a two-wheeled vehicle powered by an internal-combustion engine, usually a gasoline engine. More strictly, models with small wheels are called motor scooters, and models with small, light engines mounted on light frames are called motor bicycles.

The German inventor Gottlieb Daimler (1834–1900), a pioneer in internal-combustion engines, was probably the first to design a practical motorcycle. It was built in 1885 and equipped with an air-cooled benzine engine. By the early 1900's, usable motorcycles were being produced for sale in France, Great Britain, and the United States. At first motorcycling was exclusively the sport of young and athletic men or boys. Since the engine was connected directly to either the front or rear wheel, it was necessary first to run with the machines to turn over and start the engines, and then to spring quickly into the saddles before the vehicles ran away by themselves.

The main stages in the development of the present comparatively docile machine were the placing of the engine in the center of the frame, with care to keep the center of gravity low; the use of an electric ignition instead of the old, sometimes dangerous method of preheating a gas-filled tube with a flame; and the incorporation of a chain transmission through a change-speed gear box. Also, the modern motorcycle generally has a less noisy engine, three speeds, internal expanding brakes, a comfortable saddle, springs in the front fork, and is equipped with mudguards.

Most motorcycles have air-cooled, one- or two-cylinder engines with aluminum alloy heads and other features of design to achieve maximum power with minimum weight. There have been a few European motorcycles with water-cooled engines. In Europe and the United States four-cylinder motorcycles have been manufactured.

Motorcycles have always been more popular in Europe than in North America. According to the United States Department of Transportation, Bureau of Public Roads, there were over 1¾ million motorcycles registered in the United States in 1966. This represents a tremendous increase over the numbers registered before World War II. The American Motorcycle Association makes rules for motorcycle races and otherwise encourages the use of two-wheeled vehicles. In European countries, cycle-riding is more popular; the cycle often replaces the automobile for economic and traffic reasons. After World War II, motor scooters were found to be useful in traveling bombed-out roads. The scooters have become popular in America.

The United States Army has practically replaced motorcycles with jeeps. There were about 10,000 machines for couriers in World War I, and about 5,000 at the start of World War II. The United States Army's motorcycles are used by the military police in traffic control. Other armies still use cycles for courier service.

Civilian police in American cities generally use motorcycles for the control of traffic and traffic-law enforcement. Surveys conducted by the Traffic Institute of Northwestern University and the Traffic Division of the International Association of Chiefs of Police have indicated that about 87 per cent of city police departments favored the solo motorcycle for traffic law enforcement for the following reasons: the motorcycle is maneuverable and mobile; it is cheap to operate and maintain; it has a positive psychological effect on the motorist; it is effective in parades, for sports events, and for escort details; and it occupies less space than cruising cars in congested areas.

From its first days the motorcycle has been used for racing, on tracks and cross-country. Every spring the 200-mile national championship races at Daytona Beach, Fla., attract a following from all over the United States. The National Endurance Run in Michigan is famed for the challenging qualities of its course. Other notable races are held at Laconia, N.H., Springfield, Ill., and Catalina Island, Calif. The cross-country courses commonly traverse paths, stream beds, roads that would be impassable to automobiles, and even stringers of abandoned bridges. Every year there are serious accidents in these races, and sometimes fatalities.

On September 5, 1962, at Bonneville Salt Flats, Utah, Bill Johnson of Los Angeles set an official world record of 224.57 mph. for motorcycles. Unofficial records set by him in August of the same year were still higher; they were in excess of 230 mph.

The motorcycling fraternity has always included daring spirits eager to attempt the near impossible with a machine. Hill-climbing contests are generally held on 45° slopes about 100 yards long. From a standing start, competitors mount and try to ride to the top as fast as possible. Often they strip their machines of all surplus parts to reduce weight, even sawing off the cooling fins of the engine. The rear wheels are equipped with chains. Since the earth is soon churned up and softened, the motorcycles slew wildly, and riders are often thrown. Usually the rules require that a thong be attached to the wrist of each rider so that if he is thrown, the thong yanks out of a clip connected with the ignition and "shorts" the engine. Because of this precaution, the motorcycle cannot churn about on top of the rider, or dash into the crowd.

MOTT, mot, **Frank Luther,** was an American journalist and educator who won the Pulitzer Prize in American history in 1939 for his *History of American Magazines* (3 vols., 1930–38; vol. 4, 1957). Mott was born in Keokuk County, Iowa, on April 4, 1886. After graduating from the University of Chicago in 1907, he worked on Iowa newspapers for 10 years. He then went to Columbia University for graduate study, taught English at the University of Iowa, and received a Ph.D. from Columbia in 1928. From 1927 to 1942 he was director of Iowa University's school of journalism. He then was dean of the journalism school at the University of Missouri until 1951. Mott died in Columbia, Mo., on Oct. 28, 1964.

Other books by Mott include *American Journalism . . . , 1690–1940* (1941) and *Golden Multitudes* (1947), a history of best sellers.

MOTT, James, American abolitionist: b. North Hempstead, N.Y., June 20, 1788; d. Brooklyn, N.Y., Jan. 26, 1868. He attended and taught at a Quaker boarding school in Nine Partners, N.Y., where he met Lucretia Coffin, whom he married in 1811. In 1810 he went to Philadelphia and entered his future father-in-law's business.

He was a stanch friend of William Lloyd Garrison (q.v.), assisted in the organization of the American Anti-Slavery Society in Philadelphia (1833), and with his wife attended the international antislavery convention in London in 1840. He was also a determined supporter of the cause of women's rights, and in 1848 presided over some sessions of the first woman's rights convention at Seneca Falls, N.Y. He took an active part in the establishment of Swarthmore College by the Society of Friends in 1864.

MOTT, John Raleigh, American religious and social worker: b. Livingston Manor, N.Y., May 25, 1865; d. Orlando, Fla., Jan. 31, 1955. After graduating from Cornell University in 1888, he served as chairman of the executive committee of the Student Volunteer Movement for Foreign Missions until 1920, and as student secretary (until 1915) and then general secretary (until 1931) of the International Committee of the Young Men's Christian Association (YMCA). In 1895, with Karl Fries of Sweden, he organized the World's Student Christian Federation, of which he was general secretary and later chairman until 1928. He also presided over the World Missionary Conference at Edinburgh, Scotland, in 1910, and was chairman of its Continuation Committee (to 1920) and then of the International Missionary Council, which succeeded it, until 1942.

In these various capacities, Mott played a leading role in organizing Christian youth and student movements all over the world, especially in the Far East. For his welfare work among Allied troops and prisoners of war during World War I, he was awarded the Distinguished Service Medal by the United States; and for his lifelong service in the cause of international understanding he received the Nobel Peace Prize in 1946 (with Emily Greene Balch). He was honorary president of the World Council of Churches from 1948, and author of many books on religious subjects, including *Liberating the Lay Forces of Christianity* (1932), *Five Decades and a Forward View* (1939), and *The Larger Evangelism* (1944).

MOTT, Lucretia (nee COFFIN), American abolitionist and advocate of woman's rights: b. Nantucket, Mass., Jan. 3, 1793; d. near Philadelphia, Pa., Nov. 11, 1880. At 13 she was sent to the Quaker boarding school at Nine Partners, N.Y., and there met James Mott (q.v.), whom she married in 1811 in Philadelphia. About 1818 she became an acknowledged minister of the Society of Friends and subsequently, with her husband, joined the liberal Hicksite branch of the Quakers after the schism of 1827–1828. She preached widely in the United States on reform subjects, especially slavery and woman's rights, and in 1833 helped found the American Anti-Slavery Society; but at the London world anti-slavery convention of 1840, she and a number of other women from the United States were refused recognition as official delegates. As a result of this discrimination, Mrs. Mott turned actively to the cause of woman's rights and in 1848, with Elizabeth Cady Stanton, organized the convention at Seneca Falls, N.Y., which began the feminist movement in the United States (see FEMINISM). She continued to take an active part in the anti-slavery movement, and from 1850 made her home a refuge for runaway slaves.

MOTT, Valentine, American surgeon: b. Glen Cove, N.Y., Aug. 20, 1785; d. New York, N.Y., April 26, 1865. He received his medical degree from Columbia College (1806) and then studied surgery in London and Edinburgh. In 1811 he became professor of surgery at Columbia, resigning with others in 1826 to found Rutgers Medical College. When this institution closed in 1830, he returned to Columbia, resigning in 1835 because of ill health. After six years' travel in Europe, Africa, and Asia, he joined in founding the medical department at the University of the City of New York (now New York University), and was head of the medical faculty and professor of surgery there from 1841 to 1850. From 1852 until his death he continued teaching, with the rank of professor emeritus, at Columbia.

Mott's reputation as a surgeon derives from his numerous bold and original operations, especially his vascular and osseous surgery. For the first time in medical history, he treated an aneurysm by ligating the innominate artery only two inches from the heart (1818). Other notable operations include a successful amputation at the hip joint (1824); successful ligature of the common iliac artery for aneurysm (1827); the removal of a right clavicle for malignancy (1828); and development of methods for the treatment of the jaw. He also became an authority on anesthesia in surgery after its introduction in 1846. He annotated and supervised the publication of *New Elements of Operative Surgery,* 3 vols. (1847), translated from the French of Alfred L. A. M. Velpeau; and published *Mott's Cliniques* (1860), an abstract of his later lectures.

MOTTEUX, mô-tû', **Peter Anthony** (originally PIERRE ANTOINE MOTTEUX), Franco-English translator and author: b. Rouen, France, Feb. 18, 1660; d. London, England, Feb. 18, 1718. The son of a Rouen merchant, he went to England after the revocation of the Edict of Nantes (1685) and soon turned his hand to literature. A number of his plays and operas were produced on the London stage between 1696 and 1708. He is best known for his part in the excellent translation of the works of François Rabelais (2 vols., 1693–94), which includes Sir Thomas Urquhart's rendition of the first three books (edited by Motteux) and his own translation of books 4 and 5; and for his translation (with others) of *The History of the Renowned Don Quixote de la Mancha,* 4 vols. (1700–03).

MOTTISTONE, 1ST BARON. See SEELY, JOHN EDWARD BERNARD.

MOTYCA. See MODICA.

MOUCHEZ, mōō-shĕz', **Amédée Ernest Barthélémy,** French astronomer: b. Madrid, Spain, Aug. 24, 1821; d. Wissous, France, June 25, 1892. He was educated at the French Naval Academy and remained in the navy until 1878 when he was appointed director of the Paris Observatory. He had previously distinguished himself in coast surveys of Algeria and Brazil as well as in the observation of the transit of Venus in 1874. He bent all his energies to the improvement of the observatory, and was the originator of the international photographic chart of the heavens. In 1880 he was appointed rear admiral. He wrote *La photographie astronomique à l'observatoire de Paris et la carte du ciel* (1887).

MOUFLON, mōōf'lŏn (also MOUFFLON, MUSIMON, mŭs'ĭ-mŏn), a wild sheep (*Ovis musimon*) of Corsica and Sardinia, where it wanders about the summits of the mountain ranges in small flocks. It is not certain whether this species ever existed on the mainland, but most naturalists believe that it formerly existed in Spain. The rams are about 2¼ feet tall at the withers. The males have large coiled horns, but the females are hornless. The coat is mainly rust-red above and white on the ventral surfaces. A similar mouflon inhabits Cyprus, and the aoudad (q.v.) of North Africa is often called the "ruffed mouflon."

MOUKDEN. See MUKDEN.

MOULIN, mōō-lăN', an almost vertical opening in a glacier through which a stream flowing on the surface of the ice plunges to the bottom and flows on as a subglacial stream.

MOULIN ROUGE, rōōzh (RED MILL), a noted dance hall in Paris on the right bank of the Seine, in the Montmartre district. It replaced the Jardin Mabille (1840–1875) in 1889 as the place known especially for the cancan and other gay dances. The artist Toulouse-Lautrec (q.v.) was one of the dance hall's most famous patrons, and one of his best-known lithographs is entitled *Moulin Rouge: La Goulue.* After a fire in 1915 the Moulin Rouge was converted into a music hall and then into a theater.

MOULINS, mōō-laN', commune and city, France, capital of the Department of Allier, located in the old Province of Bourbonnais, of which it was once the capital. The city is situated on the right bank of the Allier River, which is spanned here by a beautiful bridge built in the 18th century. Its Gothic cathedral (begun 1468–1508 and completed in the 19th century) contains the famous 15th century triptych of the unidentified maître de Moulins. François Augier's tomb of Duc Henri II de Montmorency (1595–1632), a masterpiece of 17th century sculpture and architecture, is in the chapel of the Lycée. Other famous monuments are the tower of the ruined ducal palace and the Renaissance pavilion of Anne de Beaujeu (1460–1522). Its industries include the manufacture of textiles, iron products, furniture, shoes, hats, and machine tools. Located on the Paris-Lyon-Mediterranean Railway, it is also a rail and commercial center and exports coal, lumber, salt, and cattle. Pop. (1962) city 23,187; commune 25,671.

MOULMEIN, mōōl-mān′, city, Burma, capital of the District of Amherst and the Tenasserim Division of Lower Burma, located on the eastern shore of the Gulf of Martaban, at the mouth of the Salween and the junction of the Gyaing and Ataran rivers, 100 miles southeast of Rangoon. It gained importance as a British administrative center after the conquest of the Tenasserim Division in the first Burmese War (1824–1826). A communications center and port, it has rail connections with Ye and Rangoon, and exports teakwood, rice, and cotton. Principal industries include distilling, shipbuilding, and the working of gold and silver. Pop. (1953) 102,777.

MOULTON, Forest Ray, American astronomer: b. Le Roy, Michigan, April 29, 1872; d. Chicago, Illinois, Dec. 7, 1952. He was graduated in 1894 at Albion College, and took the degree of Ph.D at the University of Chicago in 1899. He was appointed (1898) associate in astronomy of the University of Chicago, becoming (1900) an instructor, and (1903) assistant professor, associate professor of astronomy (1908) and professor (1912–1927). Among his many books are *New Methods in Exterior Ballistics* (1926); *Astronomy* (1931); *Consider the Heavens* (1935); *Autobiography of Science* (with J. J. Schifferes, 1945).

MOULTRIE, William, mōōl′trĭ, American soldier: b. South Carolina, 1731; d. Charleston, S. C., Sept. 27, 1805. He early allied himself with the military forces of the colonies and in the war with the Cherokees in 1761 the confidence of his fellow citizens in his ability was shown by his selection as captain of the body of troops raised to defend the frontier against the Indians. At the outbreak of the American Revolution in 1775 he was appointed colonel of the 2d colonial regiment and he also served as member of the South Carolina provincial congress in that year. He was engaged in the seizure of the public arsenals and the construction of fortifications around Charleston, and in March 1776 was ordered to construct a fort on Sullivan's Island. This he made of the only material at hand, palmetto logs, and when General Lee made an inspection he expressed his disapproval of the work, considering it totally unfit for the purpose of defense and advised its abandonment. Moultrie, however, continued the work and when an attack was made by the British Fleet under Sir Peter Parker the rude fort successfully withstood all assaults and was subsequently named for its brave commander. He was promoted to the rank of brigadier general in recognition of his services and given command of the forces in South Carolina and Georgia. So complete had been the defeat of Parker, however, that Charleston was not again attacked until 1779 when the British availed themselves of the absence of a large share of the Continental force and attacked the town. The return of General Lincoln saved the city, but in the spring of 1780 a third attack by land and sea compelled capitulation. Moultrie was held a prisoner for two years and though offered rank and money to enter the British Army remained loyal to the cause of the colonies. Release came in 1782, when he was exchanged for Burgoyne, and though promoted to the rank of major general it was too late for him again to engage in active service. He was elected governor of South Carolina in 1785 and in 1794, and published in 1802 *Memoirs of the Revolution.*

MOULTRIE, city, Georgia, and Colquitt County seat; altitude 340 feet; near the Ochlockonee River; 125 miles south of Macon; on the Atlanta, Birmingham and Coast, and Georgia and Florida railroads; has a municipal airport. Moultrie is a tobacco market and commercial center, in a section producing cotton, watermelons, and livestock.

Moultrie was incorporated in 1859 and named for Gen. William Moultrie (q.v.) of Revolutionary War fame. It has a city manager. Pop. 14,302.

MOUND BIRDS. See MEGAPODE.

MOUND BUILDERS AND MOUNDS. In the first half of the 19th century the words "Mound Builders" and mounds came into both scholastic and popular usage to refer to the great number of earth mounds discovered by European settlers in the eastern half of the United States and to their supposed builders. The term "mound" properly applies to intentional constructions, usually of earth, rarely of piled stones, erected according to a preconceived plan. Large accumulations of community refuse, also found in that region, are sometimes referred to as "mounds," but properly are called "kitchen middens."

The Indians of the opening frontier had lost much of their native culture by 1800 and had almost completely given up the practice of mound building, hence it was difficult for early students of antiquities to conceive how these disorganized societies could have provided the religious drive and supported the vast amount of nonproductive labor that must have gone into the construction of the larger earthworks. Authorities such as the Rev. Thaddeus M. Harris, Ephraim George Squier and Edwin Hamilton Davis, and Dr. Joseph Jones postulated that the mounds were constructed by an earlier race with a much higher culture which had been replaced by the more primitive Indians. Popular theories credited the Toltecs or the lost tribes of Israel.

After the Bureau of American Ethnology was established under the direction of the Smithsonian Institution, it undertook an extensive program of mound excavation, directed by Cyrus Thomas in the years 1882 to 1891, principally for the purpose of determining whether the ancestors of the historic Indians or some mysterious vanished race were the builders of the mounds. The conclusion that the structures had been made by the ancestors of the historic Indians was not accepted by all writers on the subject, and the disappearance of the more romantic theory from popular usage has been understandably slow.

The study of the archaeology of the Mississippi Valley has accelerated considerably since

1900, particularly since 1930, and numerous excavations have been made by state and national scientific organizations. Techniques of excavation, analyses of evidence, and interpretations have undergone a parallel development, and archaeologists are now able to estimate the dates of earthworks, relate them to other prehistoric cultural remains, determine their purpose, and trace developments and changes in these old cultural patterns down to the period when the various Indian tribes were first described by European explorers. Recent technical developments have provided the dendrochronological and radiocarbon methods of dating which assist greatly in assigning calendrical dates to the relative chronologies that have been developed from cultural evidence.

CLASSES OF MOUNDS

The majority of the thousands of mounds in eastern North America can be classed in one of two categories of contrasting function, form, and historical origin. These categories have been called "Burial Mounds" and "Temple Mounds." Other categories such as hill-top forts and effigy mounds, while spectacular, are not so important numerically and will be described more briefly.

BURIAL MOUNDS

Origin.—Dome-shaped or conical mounds of earth, more rarely of stone, constructed to cover central burial chambers made of logs or stone, have a general distribution in the northern hemisphere and it appears very likely that the variations of this custom are historically connected. The Egyptian pyramids, developed from earlier tomb types about 2700 B.C., and earth mounds with central stone vaults were built for the heroes of Homeric times on the European mainland. At the close of the Neolithic and in the early Bronze Age (about 2000 B.C.), the custom of burying the dead in stone chambers covered with earth mounds spread from Spain through England and western France into southern Scandinavia. In England such mounds are called "barrows." Similar burial tumuli, termed "Kurgans," were made in central Siberia in the period of the widespread Afansiev and later Andronovo Cultures of the late Neolithic, about 1700–1400 B.C. Burial mounds spread into northern China, and became a prominent mode of burial in the Choo Dynasty, about 1000 B.C.

In both the Old and New Worlds the complex of cultural traits centering around mound building shares the traits of: 1, preserving the remains of the dead—in Asia, by mummification or extracting the viscera and drying; in America, usually by drying or stripping the flesh from the bones; and 2, constructing one or more vaults for the remains at ground level or below the surface, then covering these over with conical or dome-shaped heaps of earth.

North America.—When writers have used the term "Mound Builders," they have usually had in mind first the mounds and complicated earthworks of southern Ohio, sites like the Seip Mound, Turner, the Newark earthworks, or the Hopewell Site. These sites are now assigned to the Hopewell Culture, and Carbon ^{14} time measurements indicate that the culture existed about the time of Christ. Surface remains at Hopewell sites consist of earth embankments forming geometrical figures such as squares, circles, octagons, each covering 20 to 50 acres. Several geometrical figures may occur at one site, and sometimes they are connected by extensive parallel earth ridges forming "roadways." Conical burial mounds either accompany these earthworks or occur in isolation. They range from small structures eight feet high and 100 feet in diameter to large mounds 40 feet high. The burials, usually found within log vaults, are accompanied by ornaments made of copper, pearls, bear teeth or mica; pipes carved in the form of animals sitting on platforms; pottery; and tools and weapons of polished and chipped stone.

The Adena Culture of northern Kentucky and the adjacent portion of West Virginia is related to Hopewell. The burial mounds built by the peoples of that culture were frequently large, and the Grave Creek Mound in West Virginia (70 feet high and 300 feet in diameter) is probably the largest of this type ever built in North America.

The Hopewell Culture in a somewhat simplified form is widely distributed through the Mississippi Valley. It is found in western New York State where the mounds are small. Burial mounds of this culture have been investigated in Illinois, in western Michigan and southern Wisconsin. Related remains are found extending up the valley of the Missouri River as far as Kansas City. Through Missouri the mounds tend to be small and the central burial vaults are usually made of stone. Along the Mississippi River, Hopewellian mounds were frequently placed on the edge of the bluffs that border the flood plain.

In the valley of the Tennessee River in northern Alabama, the related culture is known as "Copena." This is characterized by conical mounds of moderate size. Some contain central grave pits lined with colored clay and covered with logs and bark.

In the lower part of the Mississippi Valley the Hopewellian variant is named "Marksville." There the material culture is very similar to Hopewell but is somewhat simpler, and the variety of items made and buried with the dead is not so great. Typical sites range from single conical burial mounds to as many as eight or ten scattered about without any plan of arrangement. The largest of the southern mounds are about 100 feet in diameter at the base and 20 feet high. At several locations, such as at Marksville, Louisiana, and the Spanish Fort Site in Yazoo County in Mississippi, there is a C-shaped earth wall enclosing 10 to 20 acres placed so that the two ends touch a river. These are obviously defensive works in contrast to the apparently ceremonial geometrical earthworks of Ohio. The southern burial mounds contain central log-covered tombs or simply central deposits of bones of the dead. As many as 1,100 skeletons have been recovered from one of these deposits.

About the peripheries of its distribution the custom of building burial mounds, variations on the basic Hopewellian plan, tended to last into later times. Thus it is associated with the Weeden Island Culture of northwest Florida (700–1200 A.D.), and remnants of the custom survive until the beginning of history, about 1700 A.D. for example among the Choctaw of Mississippi. Along the Atlantic Coast and near the Great Lakes the late use of ossuaries, or large burial pits, may be a retention of the central burial vault of the Hopewellian mounds, but there no earth was heaped above the grave.

MOUND BUILDERS AND MOUNDS

Impressive reminders of vanished Indian cultures are the mounds located in the eastern half of the United States. *Above:* One of the most interesting, the Serpent Mound, more than 1,300 feet long, near Loudon, Ohio. *Right:* Representative of the conical burial mounds is this very large one near Miamisburg, Ohio. *Below:* At Ocmulgee National Monument, near Macon, Ga., is a typical mound, flattened on top for ceremonies. It was constructed by Indians of the Mississippian culture after 900 A.D.

Dache M. Reeves negatives courtesy of Smithsonian Institution

TEMPLE MOUNDS

The second numerically important category of mounds is rectangular, truncated earth pyramids, constructed to serve as bases for wooden ceremonial buildings—temples and dwellings for important politico-religious leaders Temple mounds are generally found arranged about courts one to two hundred yards in diameter, and the larger and more important tend to be at the western and eastern sides of these courts. Earth ramps with log-faced stairways frequently provided a more accessible approach to the tops of the mounds on the side toward the court. Excavations of these structures have shown that they normally contain a number of superimposed building levels. The ceremonial buildings had been intentionally destroyed at intervals, and before they were replaced a thick capping of earth was added to the entire mound surface. This renewing of the mound was an important part of the Temple Mound complex wherever it is found. Burials were occasionally made in these structures but as a secondary use and not as a primary function.

Origin of Temple Mounds.—Rectangular, flat-topped mounds of similar form, function, and construction are found in the Americas from the central part of Peru to the vicinity of the Great Lakes. The earliest temple mounds in Peru were modest earth structures that seem to date about 700–400 B.C., and from them there developed later large mud-brick pyramids which reached a height of 110 feet. In Middle America the earliest dated pyramidal structures are of about the same time. Stone rubble fill and masonry facings are characteristic. The largest of these, the Pyramid of the Sun at Teotihuacan in Mexico, measures 700 feet on a side at the base and is over 200 feet high.

At the moment there is some question as to the possibility of this temple mound-building complex having been transmitted across the Pacific to Middle America from southern Asia where a similar custom is widely distributed. A number of other cultural traits are involved in the arguments, and the question of prehistoric connections between regions is far from settled.

Temple Mounds in the Mississippi Valley.—The relatively modest earth temple mounds of the eastern United States seem to have derived from Middle America, and first appear in the lower part of the Mississippi Valley in the Troyville cultural stage about 700–900 A.D., after the decline of the major burial mound-building cultures. The temple mound building complex became incorporated into the Mississippian Culture which was developing in the central part of the Mississippi Valley from approximately 900 to 1100 A.D. After 1200 A.D. Indians carrying variations of the Mississippian Culture spread out of the Valley in all directions and their cultural influence, including temple mounds arranged about plazas, is found over a large part of the East. By 1500 this complex had reached the Atlantic Coast in Georgia and South Carolina and was on the Gulf coast of Florida. Westward it diffused into eastern Texas and Nebraska. Northward temple-mound sites are found as far as the Aztalan Site in Wisconsin. To the northeast, it extends into Ohio and eastern Kentucky. Thousands of Mississippian mound groups are found in the region outlined.

The largest pyramidal mound in the Mississippi Valley is Monks Mound near East St. Louis, Illinois. This measures 1,080 by 710 feet at the base and is 100 feet high. It was probably built about 1400–1600 A.D. and at least 60 smaller mounds, ranging up to 30 feet high are found in the bottom lands within a few miles from this largest mound of the Cahokia group. Other well known temple-mound groups are at Etowah, Georgia (highest mound, 61 feet), at Macon, Georgia (in Ocmulgee National Monument), at Moundsville, Alabama (Moundsville State Park), and the Winterville Site near Greenville, Mississippi. Some of these groups, particularly those that date late within the Mississippian Culture period (after c.1450 A.D.) are enclosed by defensive walls made of earth surmounted by a wooden palisade. This is found at such sites as Aztalan, mentioned above, at the Angel Site in southern Indiana, and at the Lake George Site near Holly Bluff, Mississippi.

If the antiquarians of the last century had read more carefully the narratives of the expedition of Hernandez de Soto, who traversed the present states of Florida, Georgia, Alabama, Mississippi, and Arkansas in the years 1541–1543, the question of a lost mound builder race need not have arisen, for these describe temple mounds being used at what must have been very nearly the highest development of Mississippian culture. Between that date and the first effective exploration and settlement of the territory west of the Appalachians about 1700 A.D., there had been a major decimation of Indian populations and disruption of their culture. Only a few tribes, such as the Natchez, Cherokee, and Creeks, retained the use of temple mounds by the beginning of the 18th century.

FORTIFICATIONS AND EFFIGY MOUNDS

Besides the two classes of mounds outlined, there are less numerous constructions which were attributed to the "mound builders." Hilltop fortifications with earth and stone walls are found from Mississippi and Georgia to New York State. They range in date from Hopewellian to Mississippian times. The Fort Ancient Site in Ohio is a well-known structure of this type. It dates in the Hopewell period.

Small mounds constructed in the form of unidentified linear figures, birds, animals, or rarely humans are particularly common in Wisconsin. The people who constructed them also built burial mounds in which the dead were placed in subfloor pits. These constructions predate the Hopewell Culture in Wisconsin.

METHOD OF MOUND CONSTRUCTION

All mounds in North America were constructed by human labor, by people carrying basket or skin loads of soil on their shoulders. Due to differences in color, individual loads frequently can be identified in the process of excavation and these weigh from 40 to 50 pounds. Sometimes the impression of a carrying basket is found enclosing a load of soil.

Bibliography.—Squier, E. G., and Davis, E. H., "Ancient Monuments of the Mississippi Valley" in *Contributions to Knowledge,* Smithsonian Institution, vol. 1, No. 1, pp. 1-306 (Washington D.C. 1848); Thomas, Cyrus, *Report of the Mound Builders* (New York 1930); Ford, J. A. and Willey, G., "An Interpretation of the Prehistory of the Eastern United States" in *American Anthropologist,* vol. 43, pp. 325-63 (Menasha, Wis., 1941); Martin, P. S., and Quimby, G. I., and Collier, D., *Indians Before Columbus* (Chicago 1947).

JAMES A. FORD,
Assistant Curator of North American Archaeology, American Museum of Natural History.

MOUND CITY GROUP NATIONAL MONUMENT, national monument, Ohio, in Ross County, on the Scioto River, four miles north of Chillicothe. The monument comprises an outstanding burial shrine of Indians of the Hopewell culture (500 B.C.–500 A.D.). Of its 67.5 acres, the mound group occupies 13 acres, with 24 mounds varying from 3 to 18 feet in height. Excavations revealed that the Indians had cremated and buried their dead in special shrines, burned the shrines, and erected earth mounds over them. Nearly 100 remains of cremated burials were found, together with objects made of marine shell, obsidian, mica, and copper; freshwater pearls; stone tobacco pipes carved in the effigy of animals and humans; a mask made from a human skull; and evidences of elaborate preparations and ceremonies. The entire burial area is surrounded by an earth wall, averaging 3½ feet in height, in the form of a square with rounded corners. The first large-scale exploration of the area was performed in 1846 by Ephraim G. Squier and Edwin H. Davis, who gave it the name of Mound City. The group became a national monument in 1923 and is under the administration of the National Park Service. There is a visitors' center. See also MOUND BUILDERS AND MOUNDS—*Burial Mounds.*

RICHARD D. FAUST.

MOUNDS VIEW, moundz, village, Minnesota, in Ramsey County, 12 miles north of St. Paul. A residential community, it was incorporated in 1958 and is governed by a mayor and council. Pop. 9,988.

MOUNDSVILLE, moundz'vĭl, city, West Virginia, seat of Marshall County, on the Ohio River, 12 miles south of Wheeling. The city is the center of a coal-producing region and manufactures glassware, enamelware, and cables. It is the site of the state penitentiary. A new City-County Public Library was erected in 1962. The city derives its name from the prehistoric Indian Grave Creek Mound, which is situated here. Moundsville was incorporated in 1865 when two small villages were merged. City manager government was instituted in 1957. Pop. 13,560.

MARTHA MYERS.

MOUNT, mount, **William Sidney,** American painter: b. Setauket, N.Y., Nov. 26, 1807; d. there, Nov. 19, 1868. He spent most of his boyhood at Stony Brook, N.Y., and in 1824 was apprenticed to his brother Henry, a sign and ornamental painter in New York City. In 1826–1827 he studied at the National Academy of Design in New York City, of which he became an associate member in 1832. His first notable painting was *Christ Raising the Daughter of Jairus* (1828), followed by a number of portraits, including those of Bishop Henry Onderdonk and Daniel Webster. Although he supported himself mainly by painting portraits, he is best remembered as a genre painter. Among his canvases are *Bargaining for a Horse* (New York Historical Society); *Raffling for the Goose* (Metropolitan Museum of Art, New York); *The Long Story* (Corcoran Gallery, Washington); and *Coming to the Point* (New York Public Library).

MOUNT AIRY, mount âr'ē, town, North Carolina, in Surry County, 38 miles north of Winston-Salem, in the foothills of the Blue Ridge Mountains. It has more than 50 industrial plants, whose products include furniture, hosiery, garments, and electrical appliances. The surrounding agricultural area produces tobacco, beef and dairy cattle, apples and peaches, and truck vegetables. The largest open-face granite quarry in the world is in Mount Airy. Settled as an overnight stage stop in the late 18th century, the town was incorporated in 1885. It adopted a council-manager form of government in 1961. Pop. 7,055.

ELIZABETH LOVILL.

MOUNT ALLISON UNIVERSITY, a coeducational institution in Sackville, New Brunswick, Canada. It is affiliated with the United Church of Canada and is governed by a Board of Regents appointed by the church and the alumni. The university developed from the Mount Allison Weslyan Academy, a school for young men (founded 1840), endowed by Charles Frederick Allison, for whom the institution is named, and a similar academy for young women (opened 1854). After degree-granting powers were conferred on it by the provincial legislature (1858), the name was changed to Mount Allison Wesleyan College, and it graduated its first class in 1863. The present name was adopted in 1913. Mount Allison was the first institution in the British Empire to confer the degree of bachelor of science on a woman (1875) and the first in Canada to grant a woman the bachelor of arts degree (1882).

Bachelor's degrees in arts, commerce, fine arts, science, home economics, education, music education, and arts with secretarial certificate are granted, as well as master's degrees in arts, science, and education and a certificate in engineering. The university library has about 110,000 volumes. College colors are garnet and gold; the alma mater song is *Mount Allison So Fair!* Average annual enrollment is about 1,200.

MOUNT ATHOS. See ATHOS.

MOUNT CARMEL, mount kär'mĕl, city, Illinois, seat of Wabash County in the southeastern part of the state, 32 miles southwest of Vincennes, Ind. Situated on bluffs that rise to an elevation of nearly 150 feet above the Wabash River, Mount Carmel is an industrial community in an oil-producing and agricultural area (wheat, corn, soybeans). Manufactures include tools, radio parts, paperboard, flour, and oil well supplies. There is a small airport. Wabash Valley Junior College was established here in 1961. Mount Carmel was founded in 1818, incorporated as a city in 1865, and has had the commission form of government since that time. Pop. 8,096.

RUTH LENGELSEN.

MOUNT CARMEL, borough, Pennsylvania, in Northumberland County, about 40 miles northwest of Reading. Anthracite coal mining is a leading industry; local plants produce clothing, chemicals, metal products, and cigars. Mount Carmel was incorporated in 1862. It is governed by a mayor and council. Pop. 9,317.

MOUNT CLEMENS, mount klĕm'enz, city, Michigan, seat of Macomb County, on the Clinton River near its outlet into Lake St. Clair, 20 miles north-northeast of Detroit. Metal products, plastics, pottery, and toys are manufactured, and there are important agricultural and floral industries. Mount Clemens was formerly well known as a mineral-springs health resort. Selfridge Air Force

Base is located nearby. Originally known as High Banks or Big Springs, Mount Clemens was platted in 1818 by Christian Clemens, after whom it was named; it was incorporated as a village in 1837 and as a city in 1879, and in 1954 adopted a commission–city administrator form of government. Pop. 20,476.

MIRIAM ALTMAN.

MOUNT DESERT ISLAND, mount dê-zûrt', island, Maine, in Hancock County, off the southeast coast of the state, 40 miles southeast of Bangor. About 14 miles long and up to 10 miles wide, with an area of about 100 square miles, it is Maine's largest island, separated from the mainland by Western Bay, Mount Desert Narrows (spanned by a vehicular bridge), and Frenchman Bay. Several indentations cut into the irregular coastline: Eastern Bay on the north; Somes Sound, a 6-mile-long fjord, on the south; and Seal Cove and Western Bay on the west. The mountainous surface rises to 1,532 feet in Cadillac Mountain, the highest point on the east coast of the United States. There are several freshwater lakes in the interior of the island. Acadia National Park, originally established as Sieur de Monts National Monument in 1916, covers about 65 square miles, most of it on Mount Desert, but also including some acreage on Schoodic Peninsula on the mainland and part of Isle au Haut to the southwest of Mount Desert. There are four towns on the island: Mount Desert, incorporated in 1789; Bar Harbor (q.v.), incorporated as Eden in 1796 and renamed in 1918; Tremont, 1848; and Southwest Harbor, set off from Tremont in 1905. The town of Cranberry Isles comprises several small islands off the shore of Mount Desert.

The island was visited and named by Samuel de Champlain in 1604, and a French Jesuit mission was established on Somes Sound in 1613. Mount Desert passed to the British in 1713, and in 1762 the first permanent settlement was made. Since the late 19th century the island has been a popular summer resort. A fire in 1947 did severe damage, but the resort areas were rebuilt.

Bar Harbor, a popular summer resort, is on Mount Desert Island, off the southeast coast of Maine.

Ewing Galloway

MOUNT EPHRAIM, mount ē'frâ-ĭm, borough, New Jersey, in Camden County, five miles south of Camden. A residential community, it was settled in the 18th century and incorporated in 1926; a commission form of government was adopted in 1935. Pop. 5,625.

MOUNT FOREST, mount fŏr'ĕst, town, Ontario, Canada, in Wellington County, on the south branch of the Saugeen River, about 40 miles northwest of Guelph. It was settled as a millsite and developed into a trading and service center for an extensive agricultural and grazing area in Wellington and Grey counties, and a shipping point for livestock and grain. It is served by both the Canadian National and Canadian Pacific railways. The surrounding area has many interesting physiographic features, including moraines, eskers, kames, kettle lakes, outwash plains, and abandoned melt-water spillways of the Pleistocene epoch. Mount Forest was incorporated as a town in 1878. Population: 3,037.

D. F. PUTNAM.

MOUNT HEALTHY, mount hĕl'thĭ, city, Ohio, situated in Hamilton County in the extreme southwestern part of the state, nine miles north of Cincinnati, of which it is a residential and industrial suburb. It produces wearing apparel, machine tools, dairy products, and flour. Founded in 1817, it is governed by a mayor and council. Pop. 7,446.

MOUNT HOLYOKE COLLEGE, mount hōl'yōk, a nondenominational, privately endowed, liberal arts college for women, situated in South Hadley, Mass. Founded by Mary Lyon (q.v.), it was chartered in 1836 and opened in 1837 as Mount Holyoke Female Seminary, and is the oldest institution of higher education for women in the United States. The name was changed to Mount Holyoke Seminary and College in 1888, and in 1893 the present name was adopted. The college offers a liberal arts curriculum consisting of two years of general education in literature, the arts, sciences, and social sciences, followed by two years of concentration in one of 24 academic departments. Under a four-college cooperative program, students may elect courses at nearby Smith or Amherst colleges or the University of Massachusetts. Degrees conferred are the bachelor of arts, master of arts, and master of arts in teaching.

Mount Holyoke College's 770-acre campus includes the Williston Memorial Library, with facilities for 300,000 volumes, and an observatory. The residence halls include special French- and Russian-language dormitories. Average undergraduate enrollment is 1,600. The school color is a medium light blue and the alma mater is *Oh Mount Holyoke We Pay Thee Devotion.*

BARBARA J. EDDY.

MOUNT KISCO, mount kĭs'kō, village, New York, 37 miles north of Grand Central Station in downtown New York City and 15 miles north of White Plains, on the Harlem Division of the New York Central Railroad. It is traversed by the Saw Mill River Parkway and four state highways. The village is a residential suburb and the trade center of upper Westchester County, with four commercial and two savings banks and some industrial activity, including copper tube manufacture, publishing, and data processing. It is the site of Northern Westchester Hospital, a voluntary, nonprofit institution. The village was founded in 1847, after the Harlem Railroad had established in this area a station called "New Castle." The name Mount Kisco, which is of Indian origin, was adopted in 1850, and incorporation took place in 1874. In 1957, by referendum, a village manager form of government was adopted. Pop. 8,172.

DAVID GOODMAN.

MOUNT LEBANON, mount lĕb′ȧ-nŭn, township, Pennsylvania, in Allegheny County, five miles southwest of Pittsburgh. It is primarily a residential community. The area was first settled about 1773 and separated from Scott Township in 1912. It is governed by commissioners and a manager. Pop. 39,596.

MOUNT McKINLEY NATIONAL PARK, mount mȧ-kĭn′lē, national park, Alaska, in the south central part of the state, in the Alaska Range, established in 1917. The area is 3,030 square miles. It is named for its principal scenic feature, Mount McKinley (20,320 feet), the highest mountain in North America. The park remains snow covered for almost nine months of the year, but during the short summer those portions below the perpetual snow line (about 6,000 feet) and free of glaciers come alive with wild flowers and nesting migratory birds. Moose, barren ground (stone) caribou, and Dall sheep are abundant, and a grizzly bear, wolf, or wolverine can occasionally be seen; these animals are able to find sufficient food and withstand the severe sub-Arctic winters, when temperatures occasionally drop to $-50°$ F. In all, some 35 species of mammals and 132 species of birds inhabit the park.

Many areas of the park are underlaid with beds of permafrost (ground that has been frozen for thousands of years); only the few inches of topsoil that thaw during the summer support plant life. White spruce is the most common tree. Scattered spruce forests are found along the streams up to 3,000 feet, sometimes with black spruce, balsam poplar, aspen, and white birch at the lower elevations. Thickets of willow and dwarf birch grow profusely on the wetter slopes, the Arctic willow extending above the timberline nearly to the perpetual snow line. Most of the streams in the park begin at the foot of glaciers and remain muddy throughout the summer, so that they are unsuitable for fish, but a few clear streams support Arctic grayling. Wonder Lake (3 miles long), a few miles from Mount McKinley, contains Mackinaw trout.

A road traverses the eastern half of the park by way of several intermountain valleys and over the drainage divides which separate them on the north slope of the Alaska Range, a distance of 90 miles, and terminates near Wonder Lake. Elevations along the road range from 1,700 feet near the east park boundary to nearly 4,000 feet at several low passes between the park's north-flowing rivers. The road connects with the Alaska road system.

See also MCKINLEY, MOUNT.

OSCAR T. DICK,
Superintendent, Mount McKinley National Park.

MOUNT MARY COLLEGE, a Roman Catholic liberal arts college for women, in Milwaukee, Wis. Founded in 1872 in Prairie du Chien as St. Mary's Institute, it became St. Mary's Academy in 1897 and St. Mary's College in 1913; the present name was adopted in 1929, when the college moved to Milwaukee. The 80-acre campus is in the northwestern part of the city, overlooking the Menomonee River. The college, which is conducted by the School Sisters of Notre Dame, awards the degrees of bachelor of arts, bachelor of science, and bachelor of science in education. The school colors are blue and white, and the school song is the *Mount Mary March.* The library has about 56,000 volumes. The average full-time enrollment is approximately 800.

SISTER MARY ELLEN.

MOUNT OLIVER, mount ŏl′ĭ-vẽr, borough, Pennsylvania, entirely surrounded by the city of Pittsburgh and situated within its southern sector, less than three miles from the downtown district. Chiefly residential, it is closely tied economically and culturally to the encompassing city, though governed independently by a mayor and council. It is named for Oliver Ormsby, who acquired patent to the land in 1800, the site having been first surveyed in 1769. In the 19th century, German immigrants gave the town its distinctive character, and their descendants constitute a major ethnic group in the present population. Mount Oliver was incorporated as a borough in 1892. Pop. 5,487.

JULIA M. CUNNINGHAM.

MOUNT PEARL, mount pûrl, town, Newfoundland, four miles west of St. John's, the provincial capital, of which it is a residential suburb. It occupies land originally granted by the British government to Sir James Pearl in 1834. In 1860, the then prince of Wales (later Edward VII) attended a horse race here. During World War I, the British admiralty erected a powerful radio station in the area, and in the late 1920's and early 1930's, Mount Pearl was the site of an airfield from which many pioneer local flights were launched. Prior to World War II, it was fast becoming a summer colony of St. John's, but the rapid population growth of the postwar period

Muldrow Glacier, the largest glacier in Alaska, is located entirely within Mount McKinley National Park.

Josef Muench

led many young people to build permanent homes. In 1955 it was incorporated as the Town of Mount Pearl Park-Glendale; it was renamed Mount Pearl in 1958. The federal government operates an experimental farm nearby. One of Newfoundland's fastest-growing communities, 80 percent of whose working population is employed in St. John's, Mount Pearl is administered by a mayor and six councillors elected every four years; these officers also control an adjacent municipal planning area of over 4,000 acres. Population: 7,211.

ALLAN M. FRASER.

MOUNT PLEASANT, city, Michigan, seat of Isabella County, on the Chippewa River, 84 miles northeast of Grand Rapids. Since the discovery of crude oil in the area in 1928, the city has been the center of Michigan's oil industry, with many producing, drilling, transportation, refining, supply, and service companies. Mount Pleasant is also the center of a prosperous cattle-, grain-, and apple-producing area. It is the site of Central Michigan University (founded 1892) and has a state home and training school for the retarded. Several bands of Chippewa Indians live on a reservation four miles east of the city—one of three federal Indian reservations east of the Mississippi River—and stage an annual pageant. There is a municipal airport. Incorporated as a village in 1875, Mount Pleasant was chartered as a home-rule city in 1889 and adopted a commission-manager form of government in 1921. Pop. 20,504.

ELSA STRUBLE.

MOUNT PLEASANT, borough, Pennsylvania, in Westmoreland County, about 30 miles southeast of Pittsburgh. Formerly an active bituminous-coal-mining center, the borough now manufactures glassware, clothing, and wood and metal products, has meat-packing, feed-processing, and dairy-products plants, and is in a flourishing agricultural area. The place developed as a stop on the Cumberland-Pittsburgh Turnpike and was incorporated as a borough in 1828. Government is by mayor and council. Pop. 5,895.

WILLIAM R. GRIFFIN.

The snow fields of Paradise Valley in Mount Rainier National Park attract skiers from autumn to spring.

Ray Atkeson

MOUNT PLEASANT, town, South Carolina, in Charleston County, across Charleston Harbor from the city of Charleston, with which it is connected by bridge. The town is the center of a truck-farming area and has a shrimping industry and shipyard. The picturesque shrimp fleet is a favorite subject for local artists. Mount Pleasant was founded in the late 18th century and incorporated in 1837. From 1882 to 1895 it was the seat of Berkeley County. Government is by mayor and council. Pop. 6,155.

MOUNT PLEASANT, city, Texas, seat of Titus County, 120 miles east of Dallas, in a region of rolling, timbered hills and valleys drained by the Sulphur River and Cypress Creek. The city is a wholesale and retail trading center, with a large oil refinery, cattle- and poultry-processing plants, and wood-manufacturing facilities. There is a municipal airport. Mount Pleasant was incorporated in 1900 and adopted a council-manager form of government in 1948. Pop. 8,877.

JOHN W. ETHEREDGE.

MOUNT PROSPECT, mount prŏs'pĕkt, village, Illinois, in Cook County, 22 miles northwest of Chicago, of which it is a residential suburb. There is also some light industry. First settled as a farming community about 1860, the area was platted in 1874; the first business building, a general store built in 1884, still stands. Mount Prospect was incorporated as a village in 1917 and adopted a village manager form of government in 1956. Pop. 34,995.

RUTH K. ANDERSON.

MOUNT RAINIER, mount rā'nēr, city, Maryland, in Prince Georges County, on the northeastern border of the District of Columbia. It is a residential community, founded in 1902 by a group of Army officers from Seattle, Wash., who named it for Mount Rainier in their home state. The city, incorporated in 1910, is governed by a mayor and council. Pop. 8,180.

ELIZABETH B. HAGE.

MOUNT RAINIER NATIONAL PARK, mount rȧ-nēr', national park, Washington, in the west central part of the state, in the Cascade Range. Of its total area of 377.8 square miles, about 25 percent is covered by towering Mount Rainier (14,410 feet), a glacier-pitted volcano. Established as a national park (the fifth in the United States) on March 2, 1899, the area is one of stark contrasts, with the mighty mountain rising nearly 2 miles above the Cascade Range, surrounded by flower meadows, alpine lakes, cascading rivers, and dark forests filled with wildlife. The mountain is covered by a mantle of ice that conceals all except the most rugged crags and ridges. There are 26 named glaciers, comprising 40 square miles of ice. Mount Rainier probably dates from the Pliocene epoch, when the volcanoes bordering the Pacific Ocean began their growth.

Trees in the park are divided into three distinct zones—transition, the lowest; Canadian; and Hudsonian, the highest, extending to the timberline. The transition zone has heavy growths of Douglas fir, western hemlock, red cedar, and a few maples, alders, western yews, and black cottonwoods. The Canadian zone contains western white pine, noble fir, spruce, Alaska cedar, and western hemlock. In the Hudsonian zone are mountain hemlocks, alpine firs, and sometimes white-barked pines. Above the timberline are found a few junipers and Arctic willows. Throughout the forest zones are luxuriant undergrowths, culminating in the flowered alpine meadows of the Hudsonian zone, where heathers, lilies, valerians, anemones, asters, lupines, and buttercups reach their most colorful growth in July and August. Among the park's wild animals are the black bear, whistling marmot, Pacific beaver, Columbian black-tailed deer, and, in the highest elevations, the white mountain goat, Rainier white-tailed ptarmigan, pipit, rosy finch, and pine siskin.

Open all year, the park has 80 miles of paved roads and numerous trails, including the Wonderland Trail, completely encircling the mountain, which takes over a week to traverse. There are skiing and other winter sports. Paradise, at 5,557 feet, was the site of a 1,000-inch snowfall in the winter of 1955–1956, heaviest on record in the United States.

See also RAINIER, MOUNT.

JOHN A. RUTTER,
Superintendent, Mount Rainier National Park.

MOUNT REVELSTOKE NATIONAL PARK, mount rĕv′'l-stōk, national park, British Columbia, Canada, in the Selkirk Mountains, about 418 miles northeast of Vancouver and 256 miles west of Calgary, Alberta. The park is accessible by the Rogers Pass section of the Trans-Canada Highway, opened in 1962, and the Canadian Pacific Railroad. Established in 1914, Mount Revelstoke National Park has an area of 100 square miles. The summit, at a general elevation of 6,400 feet, commands an imposing view of the Selkirk and Monashee ranges of the Rocky Mountain cordillera. Alpine vegetation abounds—avalanche lilies, Indian paintbrush, purple lupine, mountain rhododendron, red and white heather, and forested slopes of fir, balsam, spruce, hemlock, cedar, and pine. Picnic- and campgrounds are available, and skiing facilities are provided on the lower slopes, near the city of Revelstoke.

B. R. STYLES.

MOUNT ROYAL, mount roi′ăl, town, Quebec, Canada, on Montreal Island, west of the city of Montreal, of which it is a suburb. It is primarily a residential community but has reserved space for future industrial growth. About one fourth of the inhabitants are of French origin. The city was incorporated in 1912. Pop. 21,561.

FERNAND GRENIER.

MOUNT RUSHMORE NATIONAL MEMORIAL, mount rŭsh′mōr, national memorial, South Dakota, in the southwestern part of the state, in the Black Hills, about 25 miles southwest of Rapid City and 3 miles east of Keystone. It honors four American presidents: George Washington, Thomas Jefferson, Abraham Lincoln, and Theodore Roosevelt. Giant likenesses of the four are sculptured into the granite face of Mount Rushmore (5,725 feet), each face about 60 feet from chin to forehead, twice as high as the head of the Giza Sphinx. Suggested in 1923 by Doane Robinson, then director of the South Dakota Historical Society, the idea of the memorial was approved by the federal and South Dakota governments in 1925, and Mount Rushmore was established as a national memorial on Oct. 1, 1925. The four presidents were chosen for their roles in formulating, shaping, and strengthening American democracy.

Irving Desfor from A. Devaney

Visitors to the Mount Rushmore Memorial Museum can compare the models with the sculptures in the distance.

The work was designed by the American sculptor Gutzon Borglum (q.v.) and begun in August 1927. The first figure, that of Washington, was dedicated on July 4, 1930. After Borglum died on March 6, 1941, work on the memorial continued until October under the direction of his son Lincoln, but the last sculpture, of Roosevelt, was never quite completed. Of the 14 years between the beginning of the project and its termination, about 6½ were spent in actual work; the intervening lapses were due to unfavorable weather and to lack of funds. The total cost was just under $1 million, of which the federal government's share was about 84 percent; the rest came from private donations. The memorial, slightly less than 2 square miles in area, is a popular tourist attraction.

BURTON V. COALE,
National Park Service, United States Department of the Interior.

MOUNT SAINT JOSEPH ON THE OHIO, College of, a Roman Catholic college for women conducted by the Sisters of Charity of Cincinnati at Mount St. Joseph, Cincinnati, Ohio. Chartered in 1854, it opened as an academy; a two-year collegiate school was added in 1906, and it became a four-year college in 1920. It confers the degrees of bachelor of arts, bachelor of science, bachelor of music education, bachelor of science in nursing, and bachelor of science in elementary education. The library contains about 53,000 volumes. The college moved to a new campus in 1962. School colors are blue and gold. The average full-time enrollment is about 900 students.

MOUNT SAINT MARY'S COLLEGE, a Roman Catholic college for women, in Los Angeles, Calif., conducted by the Sisters of St. Joseph of Carondelet. The college was chartered in 1925, and the graduate school was established in 1955. Degrees awarded are the associate of arts, bachelor of arts, bachelor of science, bachelor of music, bachelor of fine arts, master of arts, master of science in education, and master of music.

MOUNT SAINT VINCENT, College of, a Roman Catholic college for women in New York City, founded in 1910 and chartered in 1911. The degree of bachelor of arts is granted in various fields, and the bachelor of science is awarded in natural sciences and commerce education. Training programs for elementary and secondary school teachers are also given.

MOUNT SAN ANTONIO COLLEGE, a coeducational public community college in Walnut, Calif. Established in 1946, it is owned, governed, and maintained by the Mount San Antonio College District, which includes the communities of Baldwin Park, Charter Oak, Covina, Diamond Bar, Industry, La Puente, La Verne, Pomona, San Dimas, Walnut, and West Covina. A two-year liberal arts transfer program and vocational accreditation are offered.

MOUNT UNION COLLEGE is a coeducational liberal arts college in Alliance, Ohio, affiliated with the Methodist Church. It was founded in 1846 as a select school, became Mount Union Seminary in 1849, and was chartered as Mount Union College in 1858. In 1911 the college was merged with Scio College in Scio, Ohio. Mount Union College was one of the first in the United States to conduct a summer school (1870). Degrees awarded are the bachelor of arts, bachelor of science, bachelor of music, and bachelor of music education.

MOUNT VERNON, a city in south central Illinois, the seat of Jefferson county, is about 80 miles (128 km) east-southeast of St. Louis. The city is both an agricultural and industrial community. The principal manufactured items are shoes, stoves, furnaces, women's wear, and auto radiators. The area's farm products include fruits, poultry, corn, and soybeans.

Mount Vernon is served by a municipal airport. In what is now the Appellate Court building, Abraham Lincoln won the Illinois Central tax case in 1859.

The city was settled mainly by Southerners and was named in honor of George Washington's estate. It became the seat of newly founded Jefferson county in 1819, was incorporated in 1837, and was chartered as city in 1872. A council-manager form of government was instituted in 1953. Population: 16,382.

MOUNT VERNON, a city in the extreme southwest corner of Indiana, is the seat of Posey county. On the Ohio River near its junction with the Wabash River, Mount Vernon is 17 miles (27 km) west of Evansville. Situated in a rich agricultural area (corn, wheat, hay, and soybeans), the city also has other industries.

Mount Vernon was founded in 1805 by Andrew McFadden, an Irish trader, and was named McFadden's Landing until 1816. Incorporated as a city in 1865, it is governed by a mayor and a council. Population: 6,770.

MOUNT VERNON is a city at the southeastern tip of New York state, in Westchester county, about 21 miles (33 km) north of midtown New York City. Served by the Penn Central railroad, the city is traversed by State Highway 22 and is near the New York State Thruway and United States Highway 1. The city is a residential suburb and an important commercial and industrial center as well. Its principal industries are apparel manufacturing, electronics, machinery, food, fabricated metals, chemicals, precious metals, and printing.

The Mount Vernon Cooperative College Center, part of the State University of New York College at Purchase, is in the city. Mount Vernon also has an extensive public library and a daily evening newspaper. For recreational activity, there is a baseball field with a seating capacity of 5,000 and a park swimming-pool complex.

The site of the present city was first settled as early as the mid-1660's and long considered a part of Eastchester. Here, in 1733, Lewis Morris was elected to the Assembly of Westchester county despite the opposition of William Cosby, the royal governor of New York. This event was reported in the New York *Weekly Journal* published by John Peter Zenger, which accused Gov. Cosby of malfeasance in office and charged that he had taken a bribe. Cosby responded by putting Zenger in jail. Zenger was charged with bringing His Majesty's Government into contempt, disturbing the peace of that government, and seditious libel. He was brought to trial in 1735, and a jury found him not guilty. His acquittal helped to establish the principle of freedom of the press in America. See also ZENGER, JOHN PETER.

During the American Revolution, several armed skirmishes took place in the Eastchester area, which was part of the "neutral ground" where guerrilla "cowboys" and "skinners" fought constantly. St. Paul's Church, begun in 1763 to serve a parish established in 1665, was used as a hospital during the war. It was restored to its revolutionary appearance in 1942, and was made a national historic site in 1943.

Mount Vernon, named after George Washington's Virginia home, began its independent existence as a planned community in 1850. In that year an association of 1,000 New York City residents, including Horace Greeley, sought to escape high rents through cooperative home building and purchased land in the town of Eastchester. Mount Vernon was incorporated as a village in 1853 and received its charter as an independent city in 1892. Over the years, good transportation and decentralization of metropolitan industry have influenced its economic growth.

Mount Vernon is governed by a mayor and a council, whose members serve four-year terms. Population: 72,778.

MOUNT VERNON, a city in central Ohio, is the seat of Knox county. It is situated on the Kokosing River, 45 miles (72 km) northeast of Columbus. It is primarily an industrial community, producing window glass and other glass products, engines, compressors, packing products, and soybean food products. The city was first settled in 1805 by pioneers from Virginia, Maryland, New Jersey, and Pennsylvania, and colonial architecture still prevails. It is the center of a productive agricultural area. The city is governed by a mayor and council. Population: 13,373.

(*Above*) The pillared east front of Mount Vernon overlooks the Potomac River. (*Right*) The west front faces on a circular drive and courtyard.

MOUNT VERNON LADIES' ASSOCIATION

MOUNT VERNON, in Virginia, about 13 miles (21 km) south of Washington, D. C., was the home of George Washington. The 500-acre (202-hectare) estate along the Potomac River is open to the public and provides an authentic glimpse of 18th century plantation life.

Description. The two-and-a-half-story Mansion House, in Georgian style, looks east over the river and west over a circular courtyard and a long bowling green flanked by formal flower beds and a kitchen garden. Along the east front extends a unique, two-story piazza designed by Washington himself to catch the river breeze. Low, curved colonnades connect the west front to the separate office, or servant's hall, and kitchen. From the office the north lane runs past a storehouse, spinning house, icehouse, and museum. The south lane from the kitchen leads past another storehouse, a smokehouse, wash house, and coach house to the stable and from there to the Washington family tomb, located according to a provision in the general's will. Beyond, on the river bank, is the wharf. The walls of the mansion and the two flanking dependencies are unusual in being made of "rusticated boards"—boards that are treated to resemble blocks of rough stone.

Inside the Mansion, the first floor is divided by a wide, cool hall running from the west to the east door. On the north are the West Parlor and the Little Parlor, or music room. Across the north end is the handsome, dark green and buff Banquet Hall, with a fine Palladian window and superb Italian marble fireplace, for the reception of Mount Vernon's many guests. South of the hall are the family dining room and the customary downstairs bedroom. At the south end are the china pantry and the library, or study, from which Washington administered the estate. Bedrooms and storerooms occupy the upper floors.

The Mansion House is decorated and filled with furniture, paintings, floor coverings, blue and white Canton china, English and American silver, and cooking utensils. As a result of careful research, they are as close as possible to those described in estate records, including the inventory taken shortly after Washington's death. Many are original estate pieces returned over the years, and others are of the period. For example, one of the Hepplewhite sideboards in the Banquet Hall was acquired to match the surviving mate of the original pair. The library now contains more than 75 of the original 884 books and several hundred duplicate volumes. The

MOUNT VERNON LADIES' ASSOCIATION

The Banquet Hall at the north end of the Mansion House is a gracious room in classical style. One of the sideboards, the mirrors, and the chairs are original.

MOUNT VERNON LADIES' ASSOCIATION

The Spinning House Quarters are on the north lane of the estate. Here the women spun and wove the wool, flax, and cotton grown on the plantation.

dimity curtains on Washington's bed were copied from a fragment of the original fabric.

History—*Early Years.* In 1674, George Washington's great-grandfather, Col. John Washington, "The Emigrant," in partnership with Nicholas Spencer, was granted 5,000 acres (2,020 hectares) lying along the Potomac River between Little Hunting Creek and Dogue Creek. Neither one lived there, but they leased acreage to tenants. In 1690 the Washington half passed to John's son Lawrence and then to Lawrence's daughter Mildred, who sold it in 1726 to her brother Augustine, father of George Washington. Augustine lived there from 1735 to 1739.

Augustine left Little Hunting Creek Plantation, as it was called, to Lawrence, his oldest son, who settled there in 1743 and renamed it Mount Vernon in honor of his commanding officer, Adm. Edward Vernon. George, half-brother of Lawrence by Augustine's second wife, spent much of his youth with Lawrence at Mount Vernon. After the death of Lawrence in 1752 and his widow's remarriage in 1754, George leased the estate for 15,000 pounds (6,800 kg) of tobacco a year. He inherited it upon her death in 1762.

Years Under George Washington. In 1754, Mount Vernon consisted of 2,126 acres (860 hectares), a few outbuildings, and a wooden cottage. This cottage had four small rooms and a central hall on the first floor. It forms the core of the present house.

Writing from Mount Vernon on Dec. 11, 1793, Washington enthusiastically described the property: "No estate in United America is more pleasantly situated than this. It lies on high, dry and healthy Country 300 miles by water from the Sea . . . on one of the finest Rivers in the world . . . situated in a latitude between the extremes of heat and cold. . . ."

For the 45 years of his ownership, the management, enlargement, and improvement of this property was one of his consuming interests. After he returned from the French and Indian War in 1758 and married the widow Martha Dandridge Custis in 1759, he spent the next 16 years at Mount Vernon peacefully pursuing his natural inclination for farming and building.

MOUNT VERNON LADIES ASSOCIATION

(*Above*) In the family dining room at Mount Vernon, the original dining table is set for dinner. (*Below*) The blue bedroom sometimes was used as a guest room. (*Right*) The central hall staircase.

HARRIS & EWING

AUTHENTICATED NEWS

Washington began early to acquire adjacent land. By 1799 the estate totaled more than 8,000 acres (3,240 hectares). It was divided into the Mansion House Farm with its gardens, lawns, and woods, and four working farms each under an overseer. Washington struggled against poor soil and inefficient labor to make the estate support, at its height, about 240 people, free and slave. Roughly 90 were attached to the main house, the rest to the four farms.

Tobacco, which wore out the soil, was all but abandoned in favor of wheat and other grains. Flour and meal, ground at a mill on Dogue Creek built in 1769, found ready markets in rapidly growing urban centers in America and the West Indies. Seasonal runs of shad and mackerel in the Potomac made seine fishing profitable. At least ten women spun, wove, and knit full time to supply the estate. In 1768 they produced more than 1,300 yards (1,190 meters) of cloth, an unusually large quantity for such an establishment. A shoemaker and a tailor were also kept busy. Like most plantations, however, Mount Vernon was not self-sufficient. Washington's frequent orders to his factors in England, Robert Cary & Co., testify to his need for imported wine, clothes, furniture, and tools, as well as for other goods.

Washington improved the Mansion in stages, drawing up his own designs and sending home precise instructions when he was absent. The first stage, begun in 1757, consisted of adding another story and redecorating. In the early 1770's, an addition was made to the south end of the house for the library and the master bedroom suite above. It was the first step in a grand design for the buildings, gardens, and lanes of the formal area.

Accomplishments during the final stage of improvements included the piazza (built 1777, paved 1786); the north addition for the Banquet Hall (completed in 1786); the office, kitchen, and connecting colonnades; and the installation on the cupola of a weathervane (1787) ornamented, according to Washington's design, with a dove of peace.

Much of this work was supervised by Lund Washington, a distant cousin, who managed the

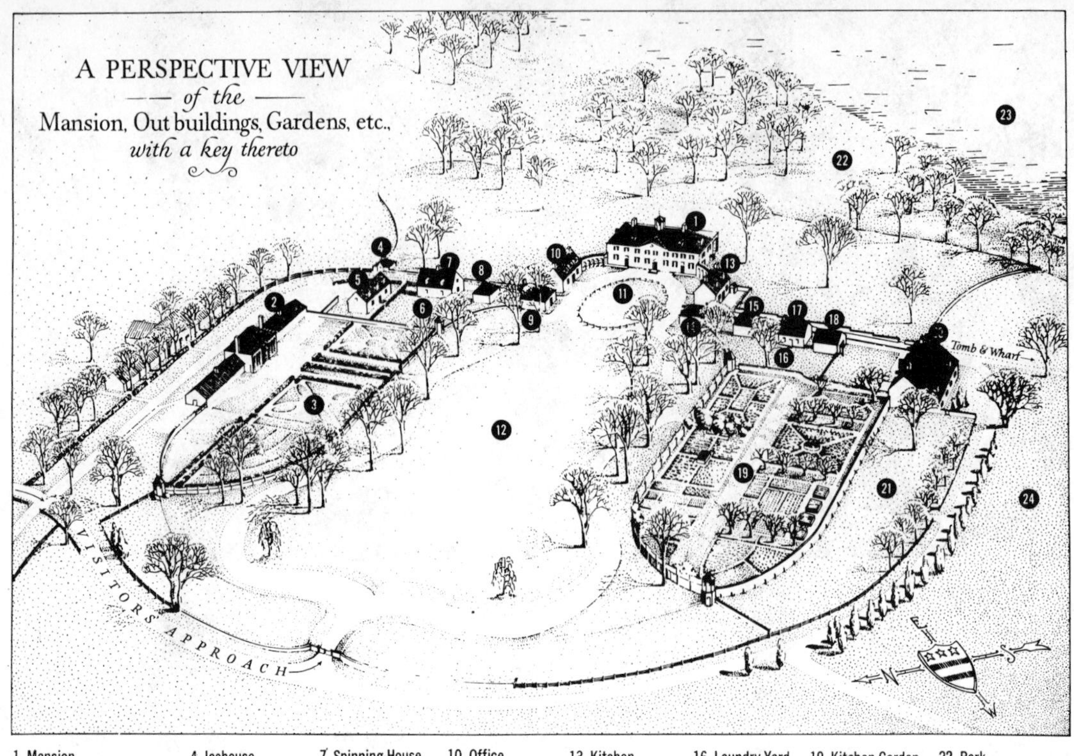

1. Mansion
2. Greenhouse and Quarters
3. Flower Garden
4. Icehouse
5. Museum
6. Botanical Garden
7. Spinning-House
8. Storehouse
9. Gardener's House
10. Office
11. Courtyard
12. Bowling Green
13. Kitchen
14. Butler's House
15. Smokehouse
16. Laundry Yard
17. Washhouse
18. Coachhouse
19. Kitchen Garden
20. Stable
21. Paddock
22. Park
23. Potomac River
24. Vineyard Enclosure

estate during the eight years its owner was away commanding the Continental Army. For the entire period of the general's absence, Lund wrote weekly letters describing the work at Mount Vernon, and the general replied, as often as possible, with detailed instructions.

Later Years. Mount Vernon passed to Washington's widow at his death in 1799. After her death in 1802 the Mansion House and 4,000 acres (1,620 hectares) went to the general's nephew Bushrod Washington, and the rest was divided among other family members. Mount Vernon descended to Bushrod's nephew John Augustine Washington in 1829 and then to his son John Augustine, Jr., the last private owner. By that time, the estate consisted of only 1,200 acres (486 hectares) of relatively unproductive farmland. Unable to maintain it, he tried unsuccessfully to sell the Mansion and 200 acres (81 hectares) to the federal and state governments.

Ann Pamela Cunningham of South Carolina in 1853 organized the Mount Vernon Ladies' Association of the Union and launched a national campaign to raise the purchase price of $200,000. In 1858 the association was granted a charter by the State of Virginia, thus saving Mount Vernon for the American people. Having gradually enlarged and restored the estate, the association continues to pursue its goal of presenting George Washington's home as it appeared at its peak in the last year of his life.

JOHN A. CASTELLANI, *Librarian*
Mount Vernon Ladies' Association

Further Reading: Fitzpatrick, John D., ed., *George Washington's Diaries*, 4 vols. (Houghton 1925); Flexner, James T., *George Washington*, 4 vols. (Little 1965–1972); Freeman, Douglas Southall, *George Washington, A Biography*, 7 vols. (Scribner 1948–1957); Johnson, Gerald W., *Mount Vernon, The Story of a Shrine* (Random House 1953).

MOUNTAIN BEAVER, also called *sewellel*, a short, stocky rodent with short, dense, brownish or grayish fur, short legs, and small eyes and ears. It is not a true beaver and does not particularly frequent mountains.

Its body is about 12 inches (30 cm) long, its tail is about 1 inch (2.5 cm) long, and it weighs about 4 pounds (2 kg). It lives in colonies in dense underbrush near water.

The mountain beaver is a good swimmer and climber. It climbs low shrubs to nip off tender shoots and small branches, and it digs tunnels through which it travels from one feeding ground to another. Mating takes place in the spring. The rodent makes its nest about 2 feet (0.6 meter) below the surface at the end of a tunnel,

Mountain beaver at the entrance to its burrow.

U. S. DEPARTMENT OF THE INTERIOR

and there usually are two or three young in a litter.

The mountain beaver, *Aplodontia rufa,* is the only surviving member of the family Aplodontidae.

MOUNTAIN BROOK, a city in north central Alabama, is in Jefferson county, on the Cahaba River, adjacent to the east of Birmingham, of which it is a residential suburb. Mountain Brook, which was incorporated as a city in 1942, covers an area of about 12 square miles (31 sq km). The city is governed by a city manager, mayor, and council. Population: 19,474.

MOUNTAIN CLIMBING, a highly active sport, is practiced in all parts of the world. It varies from making gentle ascents on easy terrain to scaling seemingly impossible crags, needles, faces, and peaks, where specialized equipment and techniques are called into play. Even where the mountain itself is comparatively easy, high altitudes, severe climatic conditions, and physical fatigue may complicate the ascent. Experience and judgment are needed to evaluate dangers such as rocks falling across otherwise easy routes, avalanches, sudden changes of weather, and lightning.

Equipment. For all climbing involving technical difficulty, the climber must be shod in special boots. Leather boots with deeply cleated rubber soles have generally replaced the heavily nailed boot used before World War II, as well as, in many cases, the lighter felt or rope-soled *Kletterschuh,* or rock-climbing shoe. A 120-foot nylon rope, 7/16 inch in diameter, is the other essential piece of equipment for climbing of any difficulty at all. Although the rope is occasionally used as a direct climbing aid, its normal function is as a safeguard to the two or three climbers who rope themselves together. If one slips, the others, with the rope well belayed, prevent his falling any great distance. Since the leader on the ascent, or the last man down on the descent, has no rope from above to safeguard him, he may fall double the distance between him and the next man. The best climber, therefore, is always placed in the lead or last position.

Rock Climbing. In rock climbing of any real difficulty, the leader climbs upward, grasping handholds mainly for balance and lifting his body mostly with his legs. The other members of the rope team belay or secure the rope, paying it out to the leader as he needs it. The rope may be belayed around the climbers' bodies, on projecting rocks, or by means of pitons. Pitons are steel spikes with an eye, which are driven solidly into a crack in the rock by a piton hammer. A snaplink or carabiner is snapped into the eye of the piton, and the rope in turn is passed through this. A piton may be on the same level of the belayer, or may be driven partway up a long lead to give the leader protection at a point well above his companions. When he reaches a secure belay point, he belays his second man as the latter climbs up to him. Only on comparatively easy rocks does the whole party climb simultaneously.

Pitons may also be used as a direct aid when holds are too small. In this rope-tension climbing, the leader drives a piton as high above him as he can and attaches the rope to it by means of a snaplink. As he leans out against the tension of the rope firmly held below, his feet adhere even to vertical faces. He climbs slowly upward, while the second man keeps taking in the rope. A stirrup may be hung from a piton to allow a climber to surmount an overhang.

Climbing down may prove to be troublesome because of the difficulty of seeing what lies below. On a steep or overhanging descent it may be necessary to rope down, or *rappel.* The middle of the rope is laid over a projecting rock, through a loop of rope or through a piton, and the two ends are allowed to drop. The climber then winds both strands around his body in such a way that he can slide in a sitting position slowly down the rope with complete control. After the last man has descended, the rope is brought down by pulling on one end of it until it passes the *rappel* point and drops down.

Snow and Ice Climbing. Snow and ice climbing may involve travel on a glacier or the ascent of steep slopes and ridges. Under all circumstances the climber must wear dark glasses to avoid snow blindness. The ice ax, which serves here as in other types of terrain as a walking stick and an aid to balance, is essential. On a glacier, especially where crevasses may lie hidden under winter snow, the ice ax is used to probe for crevasses and to test how solid the snow bridges across them are. The ice ax is also driven into the snow or ice to act as a belay point both in crevassed areas and on steep slopes. On steep slopes the leader frequently has to cut steps in the ice or hard snow in order to give good footing. Crampons are an additional aid on hard snow and ice. They are a framework of steel spikes that can be strapped onto the bottom of the boots to give additional traction. Special ice pitons or ice screws are also sometimes used.

HISTORY

Europe. Mont Blanc (15,781 feet), highest of the Alps, was the first mountain to attract climbers. Although the Genevan scientist Horace Bénédict de Saussure offered a prize in 1760 to the first person who would climb the mountain, it was not until 1786 that the physician Michel Gabriel Paccard and the peasant Jacques Balmat reached the summit. De Saussure climbed the peak the following year with Balmat and other guides. In 1800 the Grossglockner and in 1804 the Ortler were climbed. The Swiss brothers Johann Rudolph Meyer and Hieronymus Meyer reached the summit of the Jungfrau in 1811, and in 1829 the guides of Franz Joseph Hugi climbed the Finsteraarhorn, the highest peak of the Bernese Oberland.

Climbing, however, remained sporadic until Sir Alfred Wills' ascent of the Wetterhorn in 1854 opened the "golden age" of mountaineering. Peak after peak was conquered, mainly through the efforts of English climbers, who founded the Alpine Club in 1857. The highest summit of Monte Rosa was surmounted in 1855. John Tyndall and his guide, Johann Joseph Bennen, ascended the Weisshorn in 1861. The golden age was brought to a close in 1865 with the tragic ascent of the last of the great Alpine peaks, the Matterhorn, by Edward Whymper and his unfortunate companions. By 1900 nearly every Alpine summit had been climbed. Since then remarkable new routes have been ascended.

An English party under Douglas W. Freshfield explored the Caucasus for the first time in 1868 and climbed the east peak of Elbrus and Kazbek. In 1874, F. Crauford Grove, Francis

Walker, Frederick Gardiner, and the Swiss guide Peter Knubel reached the main summit of Elbrus (18,481 feet), the highest point in Europe. By 1888 the remaining principal Caucasian summits, Shkhara, Janga-Tau, Koshtan-Tau, Dykh-Tau, and the north peak of Ushba fell to English climbers.

Africa.—Africa's highest summit, Kilimanjaro (19,340 feet), was reached by the Germans Hans Meyer and Ludwig Purtscheller in 1889. More difficult Kenya (17,040 feet) fell to Sir Halford J. Mackinder's party in 1899. In 1906 Prince Luigi Amedeo of Savoy-Aosta, duke of the Abruzzi, managed to ascend Stanley (16,795 feet), highest peak of the Ruwenzori, although plagued by the incessantly bad weather which had prevented earlier parties from succeeding.

Asia.—The Himalayas have long been the goal of mountaineering expeditions. Tom G. Longstaff ascended Trisul (23,360 feet) in 1907 and held the altitude record for the highest summit yet reached (if W.W. Graham's disputed ascent of 24,002-foot Kabru is not accepted). Lenin Peak (formerly Mount Kaufmann, 23,382 feet) in the Pamirs next held the record after Eugen Allwein, Erwin Schneider, and Karl Wien climbed it in 1928. Jonsong Peak (24,340 feet), climbed by Francis S. Smythe, Gunther O. Dyhrenfurth, and others in 1930, and Kamet (25,447 feet), ascended by Smythe's party in 1931, next held the record. The next year the Americans Terris Moore and Richard L. Burdsall narrowly missed the record when they climbed Minya Konka (24,900 feet) in western China. In 1936, Noel E. Odell and H.W. Tilman of the American-British party on Nanda Devi (25,645 feet) achieved the record which was to stand for 14 years. The French Maurice Herzog and Louis Lachenal in 1950 were successful on Annapurna (26,502 feet), and held the record until Sir Edmund P. Hillary and Tenzing Norgay finally reached the crest of Mount Everest (29,028 feet) in 1953.

Early exploration of the Himalaya was carried on mainly by the British: W.W. Graham (1883) in Sikkim and Garhwal, India; Sir William Martin Conway (1892) in the Karakoram Range; Freshfield (1889) around Kanchenjunga. The Americans Dr. and Mrs. William Hunter Workman made six expeditions between 1899 and 1912. K² (28,250 feet), second highest mountain in the world, was attacked by the duke of the Abruzzi, who declared it unclimbable. Charles S. Houston and Paul Petzoldt of the 1938 American expedition reached 25,600 feet on K² before time and food ran out. Fritz Wiessner and Pasang Dawa Lama got to 27,500 feet in 1939, but unfortunately one American and three Sherpa porters were lost. In 1953 the third American K² expedition, led by Dr. Charles S. Houston, after weeks of bad weather, was driven from its camp VIII at the base of the summit pyramid to carry down seriously ill Arthur Gilkey, who was tragically lost during the descent. A strong Italian expedition led by Professor Ardito Desio finally climbed K². Following the American route, Achille Compagnoni and Lino Lacedelli reached the summit of K² on July 31, 1954. Two Bavarian expeditions led by Paul Bauer in 1929 and 1931, to Kanchenjunga (28,146 feet), third highest mountain in the world, failed on the exceedingly difficult northeast spur; their high point was 25,263 feet. The 1930 Dyhrenfurth expedition to the same mountain failed on the northwest because of avalanches. A British expedition, led by Dr. Charles Evans, successfully ascended the incredibly difficult southwest face of Kanchenjunga from the Yalung Glacier. On successive days, May 25 and 26, 1955, two separate pairs reached the summit. These were George Band with Joseph Brown, and Norman Hardie with H.R. Anthony Streather. Nanga Parbat (26,660 feet) was attacked in 1895 by Alfred F. Mummery, who disappeared with his porters, and in 1932, 1934, 1937, 1938, and 1939 by German expeditions. The lives of 14 climbers and 17 porters were lost on the mountain before Herman Buhl made his successful climb in 1953. Makalu (27,790 feet) fell to a French party in 1955. Austrians climbed Cho Oyu (26,867 feet) in 1954, Gasherbrum II (26,360 feet) in 1956, and Broad Peak (26,400 feet) in 1957. The Americans, Peter Schoening and Andrew Kauffman, ascended Hidden Peak (26,470 feet) in 1958. With the Japanese ascent of Manaslu (26,658 feet) and the international ascent of Dhaulagiri (26,810 feet) in 1960, the world's 13 highest summits had been reached by man.

Seven British attacks (1921, 1922, 1924, 1933, 1935, 1936, and 1938) on Mount Everest from the northern Tibetan side all ended in failure. In 1924, Edward F. Norton and Theodore H. Somervell reached over 28,000 feet, a point equaled, but not exceeded, by later climbers on this route. In this same year George Leigh Mallory and Andrew C. Irvine climbed into the mists high on the mountain, never to be seen again. The route to the southern Nepalese side was reconnoitered by American Dr. Charles S. Houston and British H.W. Tilman in 1950. A British expedition under Eric Shipton failed in the Khumbu icefall in 1951. The next year the Swiss successfully pioneered a route over the South Col, and Raymond Lambert and Tenzing reached a point only about 900 feet from the summit. Hillary and Tenzing made the first ascent of Everest on the same route. In 1956, four Swiss made Everest's second ascent, while two others scaled Lhotse (27,890 feet). The next person and the first American to reach Everest's summit was James Whittaker, who climbed there on May 1, 1963, with Nawang Gombu, followed on May 22 by Luther Jersted, Barry Bishop, Thomas Hornbein, and William Unsoeld. The last two ascended a new route, the difficult west ridge. Leader of this expedition was Norman Dyhrenfurth. Claims of a Chinese ascent in 1960 are generally disbelieved.

South America.—The Ecuadorian Andes received early attention. In 1872 the German Wilhelm Reiss with A.M. Escobar climbed the world's highest active volcano, 19,344-foot Cotopaxi. Eight years later Edward Whymper ascended Chimborazo (20,577 feet) and other nearby peaks. The highest mountain in the Western Hemisphere, Aconcagua (22,835 feet) in Argentina, was unsuccessfully attempted by the German Paul Güssfeldt in 1883. Mattias Zurbriggen of the Edward A. Fitzgerald expedition of 1897 made the first ascent alone. The same expedition also surmounted Tupungato (21,490 feet). Illimani, which rises to an altitude of 21,185 feet above the Bolivian capital of La Paz, was climbed in 1898 by Sir William Martin Conway. Huascarán, Peru's highest peak (22,205 feet), was first climbed by H. Bernard, P. Borchers, E. Hein, and E. Schneider in 1932. In 1911, Hiram Bingham's Yale Peruvian expedition made the first ascent of Coropuna (21,702 feet). Since World War II, Americans have again been active in the Peruvian

Above: Tenzing Norgay, Mount Everest conqueror, on a ridge at 20,000 feet.

MOUNTAIN CLIMBING

Right: Tenzing Norgay wearing an open circuit oxygen apparatus.

Below: Sir Edmund P. Hillary, after ascent, looks at the still-proud summit of Mount Everest.

(Top and bottom) British Information Services; (right) Associated Press Photo

British Information Services

Above: Camping on Everest; Hillary adjusts one of the tents. *Below:* At an altitude of 20,000 feet a member of the British 1953 Mount Everest Expedition peers into the Pit of Death, "Chrongshay."

Free-Lance Photographers Guild

Above: Fitz Roy peak in the Patagonian Andes climbed by a French party in 1952.

MOUNTAIN CLIMBING

Right: A climber in the mountains of Davos, Switzerland.

(Above) Wide World Photos; (below) Associated Press Newsphoto from Wide World; (right) Ewing Galloway

Below: K^2, the world's second highest peak, first climbed in 1954 by an Italian expedition.

Above: Kanchenjunga (28,146 feet), the world's third highest peak, on the Nepal-Sikkim border, seen from a camp of the German expedition at the 21,000-foot level, during their unsuccessful attempt in 1931. *Below:* The Italian expedition training on the Alpine Breithorn glacier for their victorious assault on the second highest peak, K^2, achieved July 31, 1954.

Wide World Photos

Andes. James C. Maxwell and David Harrah with a Harvard expedition in 1950 climbed extremely difficult Yerupaja (21,758 feet), and most of the same group joined a small French party to scale 20,550-foot Salcantay in 1952. Fitz Roy, an 11,073-foot sheer spire in Chilean Patagonia, was climbed by the French Lionel Terray and Guido Magnone in the same year.

North America.—Gigantic St. Elias, rising to 18,008 feet from tidewater, was the first peak in Alaska to attract climbers. Israel C. Russell's second expedition in 1891 reached 14,500 feet. The mountain was finally climbed in 1897 by the duke of the Abruzzi on the sixth expedition to the peak. Mount Wrangell (14,006 feet) was ascended in 1908 by Robert Dunn and William Soule, and four years later Dora Keen and G. W. Handy climbed Mount Blackburn (16,523 feet). The highest point in North America, Mount McKinley (20,320 feet), was explored by Dr. Frederick A. Cook of North Pole fame, who falsely claimed to have climbed it in 1906. In 1910 two Alaskan prospectors, Pete Anderson and Billy Taylor, climbed the north peak, some 300 feet lower than the main summit, ascending 9,000 feet from the Muldrow Glacier in one day. Belmore Browne and Herschel C. Parker reached a point only 300 feet from the summit in 1912 before being driven back by storm. The next year Archdeacon Hudson Stuck's party completed the ascent. Since World War II, various new routes have been made up Mount McKinley. The highest mountain in Canada, across the border in Yukon Territory, Mount Logan (19,850 feet) fell to a Canadian-American party under the leadership of Capt. Albert H. MacCarthy in 1924. In the 1930's a large number of Alaskan and Yukon peaks were first successfully climbed, many under the leadership of Bradford Washburn, Alaska's leading explorer-mountaineer. These included Mounts Foraker (17,395 feet), Lucania (17,150 feet), Sanford, Crillon, St. Agnes, Hayes, Bona, Fairweather, and Steele. Since World War II most of the other Alaskan and Yukon giants have been climbed, including Mounts King, Vancouver, Hubbard, and Alverstone.

After many unsuccessful earlier attempts the highest of the Canadian Rockies, 12,972-foot Mount Robson, was ascended by William W. Foster and A.H. MacCarthy with the guide Conrad Kain in 1913. This ascent has rarely been repeated. The highest summit of the interior ranges, Mount Sir Sandford (11,590 feet) in the Selkirks, was first climbed in 1912 by Edward W. D. Holway and Howard Palmer, with the Swiss guides Rudolph Aemmer and Edward Feuz. Mount Waddington (13,260 feet), the highest point in the British Columbian Coast Mountains, successfully resisted a dozen serious attempts, until William House and Fritz Wiessner forced their way to the summit of the ice-coated sheer spire in 1936.

Mountain climbing is an important sport in many of the lower ranges of the United States, such as the White and Green Mountains and the Adirondacks of the Northeast. Regions calling for more advanced technique include the Tetons and Wind River Range of Wyoming, the Colorado Rockies, the Cascades and Olympics of the Northwest, and the Sierras of California. Major mountaineering clubs are the American Alpine Club with headquarters in New York, N.Y.; Appalachian Mountain Club, Boston, Mass.; Colorado Mountain Club, Denver, Colo.; Iowa Mountaineers, Iowa City, Iowa; Mazamas, Portland, Oreg.; Mountaineers, Seattle, Wash.; Sierra Club, San Francisco, Calif.; and the Alpine Club of Canada.

Bibliography.—Irving, Robert L.G., *The Romance of Mountaineering* (New York 1935); Palmer, Howard, and Thorington, J. Monroe, *Climber's Guide to the Rocky Mountains of Canada* (New York 1940); Henderson, Kenneth A., ed. *American Alpine Club's Handbook of American Mountaineering* (Boston 1942); Young, Geoffrey W., *Mountain Craft*, 4th ed. (London 1945); Engel, Claire E., *A History of Mountaineering in the Alps* (New York 1950); Clark, R.W., *Victorian Mountaineers* (London 1953); Herzog, Maurice, *Annapurna; First Conquest of an 8,000 Meter Peak* (New York 1953); Murray, William H., *The Story of Everest* (New York 1953); Houston, C.S., and Bates, R.H., *K2: The Savage Mountain* (New York 1954); Hunt, Sir John, *Conquest of Everest* (New York 1954); Ullman, James R., *The Age of Mountaineering* (Philadelphia 1954); Hillary, Sir Edmund, *High Adventure* (New York 1955); Noyce, Wilfrid, *South Col* (New York 1955); Tenzing Norgay, *Tiger of the Snows,* written in collaboration with James R. Ullman (London and New York 1955); Lunn, Arnold, *A Century of Mountaineering 1857–1957* (London 1957); Manning, Harvey, *Mountaineering—The Freedom of the Hills* (Seattle 1960); Swiss Foundation for Alpine Research, *The Mountain World* (London and New York, nearly yearly); American Alpine Club, *American Alpine Journal* (New York, annually).

H. Adams Carter.

MOUNTAIN FINCH. See Brambling.

MOUNTAIN FLAX. See Polygala.

MOUNTAIN GOAT. See Rocky Mountain Goat.

MOUNTAIN LAUREL, a shrub or occasionally a small tree, *Kalmia latifolia,* in the heath family (Ericaceae), also called calico bush and spoonwood. It sometimes attains a height of 40 feet and a diameter of 18 inches near the base, but usually is smaller. The leaves, mostly grouped near the ends of the branches, are alternate, opposite, or in whorls of three, evergreen, leathery, dark green above, lighter below. They are two to four inches long and about one inch wide. The attractive, showy flowers are approximately an inch across, borne on glandular hairy stalks, and clustered. They are white to pink, with purplish markings inside. The 10 anthers of each flower are inserted in pouches in the fused corolla. If an insect probing for nectar touches the stamens at the base of the filaments when the flowers are mature, the anthers spring free and discharge pollen from the pores by which they open, onto the insect's body; the same effect may be produced by touching the stamens with the point of a pencil. The fruit is a thick-walled, dark, five-celled capsule. A variety of *K. latifolia* with deep pink petals, another with the petals separate, and a third with smaller leaves, have been described. Mountain laurel is native of eastern North America, where it extends from New Brunswick and Ontario to Indiana, and south through the Appalachians to Louisiana and Florida. It grows along rocky stream banks or in gravelly soil, in acid conditions, usually in shade, but also in the open if moisture is sufficient, and at times in swamps. It is often used as an ornamental in eastern North America, more sparingly in Europe. The sheep laurel, *K. angustifolia,* and the swamp laurel, *K. polifolia,* of North America, are related to the mountain laurel, but not the laurel of the classics and of poetry, which is *Laurus nobilis* of the Mediterranean region.

Edwin B. Matzke,
Professor and Chairman, Department of Botany, Columbia University.

MOUNTAIN LION, a popular name in the United States for the large American unspotted cat more generally known as puma (q.v.).

MOUNTAIN MEADOWS MASSACRE, the slaughter of a party of California-bound emigrants near Mountain Meadows, Utah, in Washington County, in September 1857. The emigrants, numbering about 137 persons from Arkansas and Missouri, were attacked by a large band of Indians, while encamped at Mountain Meadows. They held their own for three days, when they were promised safe passage by John D. Lee (q.v.), a Mormon elder and settler. Leaving the protection of their wagon barricades, they were treacherously attacked and killed by a party of Indians and whites, under the leadership of Lee. Only 17 small children were spared. The Mormons were generally blamed for the deed, although their leader, Brigham Young, had pledged his people to protect non-Mormons from Indian violence. The actual attack was probably precipitated by the lawless arrogance of the emigrants themselves, although the Mormons' fear of an impending punitive expedition by the federal government may also have been a contributing cause. The case was investigated for many years, and Lee was finally brought to trial in 1875, 18 years after the event. He was convicted and executed (1877), but a number of others accused of complicity went free.

MOUNTAIN MEN, fur trappers and traders who explored the region west of the Rocky Mountains in the 1820's and 1830's. The Western fur trade really began with the St. Louis Missouri Fur Company, chartered in 1809 under the leadership of Manuel Lisa, Pierre and Auguste P. Chouteau, and William Clark of the Lewis and Clark expedition. Later John Jacob Astor's American Fur Company entered the field. The advent of the mountain men, however, began with the company formed in 1822 by William H. Ashley (q.v.), later known as the Rocky Mountain Fur Company. Ashley meant to confine activities to trapping and trading in the familiar area of the Missouri Valley, but competition drove his trappers into the unknown regions of the Rockies, where they were forced into the way of living peculiar to the mountain men. Many of the great trappers were associated with Ashley: James Bridger, Thomas Fitzpatrick, Christopher (Kit) Carson (qq.v.), Henry Fraeb, Jedediah Smith, and the Sublette brothers, William and Milton. These men, singly or in small groups, made the first trails to Oregon and California, and the routes which they followed have become the major highways of today.

There were three types of mountain men: the hired trapper, paid an annual wage by a fur company; the skin trapper, who dealt with a single company; and the free trapper, aristocrat of the trade, who trapped and disposed of his furs as he pleased. The latter was most typical of the true mountain man. Mountain men were of various origins: French, Spanish, and American; but the stringent demands of their existence stamped out all differences, and they became a group apart, more savage than civilized.

The life of the trapper was a hazardous one; his enemies included the land, the Indian, and the rival trapper. The heyday of the Western fur trade was marked by fierce competition, and every means was used to hamper the activities of rival trappers, including the instigation of Indian attacks. The land was strange and hostile, and the trapper moved always deeper into unknown territory in his relentless search for beaver. He fought the Indians and lived with them; he adopted their way of life, their clothing, food, and shelter, and married their women. Men chose this life for adventure, for money, or as a refuge from the law, and their way of life became legendary.

Each spring the trappers gathered at a predestined spot in a mountain valley, usually in Utah or Wyoming. This meeting, known as the trappers' rendezvous, became the characteristic institution of the mountain men. To it came trappers and traders, Indians and white men, and caravans from St. Louis laden with supplies of food and luxuries to trade for furs. There the trapper disposed of his year's haul, and usually spent his earnings in a few days' riotous living, often going into debt for much of his next season's catch.

By 1840 the beaver hat was unfashionable and the price of pelts dropped radically. The fur trade declined, and the trappers became traders, Indian scouts, and guides, leading missionaries and homesteaders over the trails and routes which they had broken. See also the section on *History* in the following articles: MISSOURI; MONTANA; ST. LOUIS; WYOMING.

Consult Chittenden, Hiram M., *American Fur Trade of the Far West,* rev. ed., 2 vols. (New York 1935); Vestal, Stanley, *Mountain Men* (Boston 1937); De Voto, Bernard, *Across the Wide Missouri* (Boston 1947).

MOUNTAIN PROVINCE, province, Philippines, comprising the northern inland section of Luzon Island, between latitudes 16° and 18° N. and longitude 121° E. It is the largest province in Luzon, with an area of 5,458 square miles and a population (1948) of 278,120. The population density is 51.0 persons per square mile. The province lies mostly in mountainous terrain, and includes in its southern area all of the Cordillera Central; in the north are the eastern slopes of the same range. Mountain Province is bounded by the provinces of Cagayan, Isabela, and Nueva Vizcaya on the east, and Abra, the Ilocoas, and La Union on the west. There are many rivers: the Magat forms part of the eastern boundary, and the Chico traverses the eastern and central sections; the Agno and Abra rivers drain the south. The climate is hot and humid, and the temperate zone begins only after an altitude of over 4,000 feet is reached. The highest peaks in the province are Mounts Pulog (9,606 feet), Cauitan (8,427 feet), and Santa Tomas (7,480 feet).

Mountain Province is composed of five subprovinces: Apayao, Benguet, Bontoc, Ifugao, and Kalinga. It has 38 towns, the provincial capital being Bontoc (pop. 1948, 15,005) in Bontoc Subprovince. Baguio (pop. 1952, 31,510), 125 miles northwest of Manila, is the cultural and educational center. It is geographically located in Benguet, but has been removed from provincial jurisdiction, and is administered by the central government, of which it is the summer capital. Baguio has a mean annual temperature of 64.2°F., about 17 degrees cooler than elsewhere in the Philippines, and consequently has become a popular modern resort.

Mountain Province is an important educational center, with 415 elementary, intermediate, and secondary schools, and eight colleges. Economically the most developed area is Benguet in the south. It is also the most densely populated subprovince, with about 106 persons per square mile.

The province is largely inhabited by native tribes of Apayaos, Bontocs, Igorots, Ifugaos, and Kalingas, pagans of Malayan stock, who have developed an ingenious agricultural and irrigation system, and do very fine metalwork, wood carving and pottery making. The Banaue rice terraces in Ifugao Subprovince are world famous. Built over a period of 1,500 years by the Igorot tribes, they are an astounding feat of engineering. They extend for a distance of 1,200 miles, and rise steplike up the steep mountain sides to a height of 4,000 feet.

Economic Development.—Farming is the dominant occupation. Trinidad Valley in Benguet Subprovince is an important vegetable-growing center, and excellent tobacco is grown in Apayao. The most important crop is rice, but only enough is grown in the province to supply 50 per cent of its needs. About 25 per cent of the rice grown is used in making *tapey* (rice wine). Fruit-growing, cattle-raising, and poultry-raising projects are being systematically encouraged and developed.

Lumbering is an important factor in the economic life of the province. Luxuriant pine forests in Benguet and Apayao supply the nation's building industry with much of its raw material. In 1953 the output of the largest lumber concern ran 500,000 board feet per month, only about 25 per cent of the prewar output, but adequate for current needs.

Mining is another important factor in the province's economy. The largest copper and gold mines in the Far East are located at Mankayan, in Bontoc, about 35 miles north of Baguio. In 1952 the Lepanto-Consolidated produced 12,462 tons of copper, and four mines produced 335,403 ounces of gold and 372,415 ounces of silver.

Resources of water power, largely neglected until recently, are being rapidly developed. The Agno River Project is the biggest source of water power in Luzon. Seven plants, when completed, will develop 430,000 kilowatts, with an energy availability of 1.5 billion kilowatt hours. Six of these, with a total of 355,000 kilowatts, are to be located in Benguet. An earth dam, 450 feet high, is being built at Ambukloa in Benguet, to store 260 million cubic meters of water, and a 75,000-kilowatt power plant, under construction at Ambukloa, was scheduled to be completed in mid-1955. A single circuit 230,000-volt line will transmit inexpensive power to Manila, and a 69,000-volt line will furnish power to Baguio.

Transportation.—A north-south highway connects Mountain Province with Manila, and runs northward through Baguio and Bontoc to Tabuk in Kalinga Subprovince. Two east-west routes connect with neighboring provinces, and a railroad runs to the extreme south. Commercial air services operate between Manila and Baguio only.

History.—The region was not organized politically by the Spaniards until the mid-19th century. Under American rule Mountain Province was organized as a separate province under its present name in 1908; Baguio was incorporated and separated administratively in 1909. In 1920 the number of subprovinces was reduced from seven to five, and by 1939 the various boundaries were fixed at about their present limits.

MOUNTAIN SHEEP, a general term for wild sheep, found in Asia, North America, and a few places in the Mediterranean basin. Mountain sheep are the boldest and most active rock climbers of all land animals except wild goats and ibexes, and wherever found, they inhabit the highest, most rugged places. The haunts of the Rocky Mountain bighorn include not only the highest mountains and wild tracts of badlands, but also the rocky walls of the Grand Canyon of the Colorado. It is not strange, therefore, that the chase of wild sheep is a favorite sport with big-game hunters. The head of an old ram, adorned with massive circling horns, won by dangerous mountain climbing and fair stalking, is a trophy of which any sportsman may be proud.

The wild sheep is generally characterized by its large, spiraling horns, which often reach more than a full circle in old rams, but are much smaller in the ewes. Wild sheep are not wool bearers. Next to the skin is a coat of fine woolly hair, which serves for warmth; through this grows a coat of long, coarse hairs, large in diameter, pithy within, and easily broken, which does duty as a raincoat and gives the animal its distinctive color. In summer or late spring the old pelage is shed, and the new coat is only half an inch in length. At that season the skin is worthless as a trophy. Mountain sheep are at their best in October, November, and December, and should be hunted at no other time. The lambs are born in May, with one or two at a birth. The life span may reach 15 years, but is usually less because of disease and lack of food. Due to the difficulty of keeping captive mountain sheep of any American species alive until they reach full maturity, members of the wild species are unfamiliar to the general public in America.

Asia, Africa, and Europe.—It is probable that the first wild sheep were developed in south central Asia, in the region of the Altai Mountains in western Mongolia. Favorable conditions there have developed the Siberian argali (*Ovis ammon*), whose enormous horns are a wonder to all who behold them. A comparatively short distance southward in Tibet is the Marco Polo sheep (*O. poli*), characterized by the enormous spread of its horns. The longest horn recorded measures 75 inches in length on the great curve. South of the range of *O. poli,* in northern India, occurs the Punjab wild sheep, and the beautiful bharal or blue sheep (*Pseudois nahura*), both of them small species. Outside of Asia in the Eastern Hemisphere there are only two species of wild sheep, the small but handsomely colored mouflon (*O. musimon*) of Corsica and Sardinia, and the large Barbary wild sheep, or aoudad (*Ammotragus lervia*) of the mountains of North Africa. North of the range of the Siberian argali are the Kamchatkan sheep, a species with horns like the North American white sheep, but otherwise strongly resembling the bighorn.

North America.—North America contains a fine series of mountain-sheep species, which almost cover the mountainous regions of Alaska, and extend down the Rocky Mountain system to the region of Lake Santa María (latitude 30°) in northern Mexico. In addition a species known as Nelson's mountain sheep branches off in southwestern Nevada and extends through southern California for two thirds of its length.

There are three conspicuous and well-marked types of North American mountain sheep, as well as three offshoots, as follows:

Types	Offshoots
Bighorn (*O. canadensis*)	Nelson's sheep (*O. nelsoni*) Mexican sheep (*O. mexicanus*)
Black sheep (*O. stonei*)	
White sheep (*O. dalli*)	Fannin's sheep (*O. fannini*)

The total area of North America inhabited by mountain sheep is about 3,500 miles from north to south, and the greatest width from east to west, found in Alaska, is more than 1,000 miles.

Ovis canadensis.—The Rocky Mountain sheep or the bighorn, known since 1803, is the most widely recognized North American species, all the others being of much more recent appearance. The range of the bighorn extends from latitude 55° N and longitude 120° W to San Francisco Mountain, Arizona, embracing the whole main range of the Rockies between these points.

The bighorn is the largest and heaviest species of American mountain sheep, and carries the most massive horns. They are largest in the north, maximum development being reached in western Alberta. A large ram stands 40 inches in height at the shoulders and weighs about 300 pounds. The horns curve back, out, and up, and show yearly growth rings, which end after 8-10 years. They have been known to reach a length of 49 inches, although over 40 inches is not usual.

Ovis dalli.—The Dall sheep, or the white mountain sheep of Alaska, became known in 1884. It inhabits nearly all the mountainous regions of Alaska, except the Alaska Peninsula, the valley of the Kuskokwim, and the lower valley of the Yukon. Until recently it has been quite abundant on the Kenai Peninsula and around the head of Cook Inlet. The animal may be pure white, with a long, abundant winter pelage. It is smaller than the bighorn, and its horns are more slender. Its northern range extends almost to the Arctic Ocean, and the southern limit is found at latitude 58° N.

Ovis stonei.—The Stone sheep, or the black mountain sheep, was discovered in 1896 in northern British Columbia. Its size is the same as that of the Dall sheep. The species is characterized by the wide spread of its horns, and the very dark color of its pelage, except for the white of the rump patch and the abdomen. Its range is circumscribed to a small area in northern British Columbia.

Offshoots.—Fannin sheep, often called the "saddle-backed sheep," was discovered on the Klondike River near Dawson, in the Yukon, in 1900. It is an offshoot of the Dall sheep, and is possibly the result of crossbreeding between it and the Stone sheep. Its back, sides, and tail are bluish gray, and a brown band extends down the front of each leg; all other parts of the animal are white, and its horns are like those of the white sheep. Little is known of the range of this species.

The Mexican sheep and the Nelson bighorn sheep are both offshoots of the Rocky Mountain bighorn. They are short-haired and large-horned, and their prevailing color is pale salmon gray.

Wherever they are not fully protected by law, all species of American mountain sheep are hunted and killed, for sport and for food, while overgrazing and disease have further reduced their number. Their extinction can be prevented only by careful protection. The bighorn quickly learns the value of protection, and the herd in Yellowstone National Park has rapidly increased and become so tame that it permits visitors to approach within 30 paces.

Bibliography.—Lyddeker, Richard, *Wild Oxen, Sheep, and Goats* (London 1898); id., *The Sheep and Its Cousins* (London 1912); Morden, William J., *Across Asia's Snows and Deserts* (New York 1927); Sheldon, Charles, *The Wilderness of Denali: Explorations of a Hunter-Naturalist in Northern Alaska* (New York 1930); United States National Park Service, *Fading Trails, the Story of Endangered American Wildlife,* ed. by Charles Elliott, pp. 48-57 (New York 1942); Trippensee, Reuben E., *Wildlife Management* (New York 1948).

MOUNTAIN SICKNESS, a form of altitude sickness caused by reduced atmospheric pressure. It is common in persons reaching altitudes over 10,000 feet. Symptoms include mental dullness, nausea, vertigo, muscular weakness, euphoria, and malaise. It is also known as hypobaropathy or altitude anoxia. See also ANOXIA; AVIATION MEDICINE—*Effects of Low Air Density.*

MOUNTAIN VIEW, city, California, in Santa Clara County, 36 miles southeast of San Francisco. Electronics is the principal industry, supplemented by retail trade with the surrounding county. Moffett Field Naval Air Station is located nearby. The city was founded as a stage depot in 1852, being part of land granted to Mariano Castro by Mexican governor Juan Alvorado in 1842. In 1865, Mountain View was platted, and its growth commenced with the coming of the Southern Pacific Railroad in 1869. The city was incorporated in 1902. It has a manager-council form of government. Pop. 51,092.

JOHN O'HALLORAN.

MOUNTAINEERING. See MOUNTAIN CLIMBING.

MOUNTAINEERING IN THE SIERRA NEVADA, a book of descriptive and narrative sketches by Clarence King (q.v.), based upon personal experiences and geological fieldwork in California, published in 1872. At least half of the volume had appeared in 1871 as a series of *Atlantic Monthly* articles. He added new material, including accounts of surveying in the Yosemite region and later attempts to climb Mount Whitney. A supplement to the Whitney section was added in 1874. Numerous reprints and revised editions attest the immediate and continued popularity of the book in both England and America.

This classic of mountaineering is written in lucid and colorful prose more poetic than scientific. King describes dangers and hardships of his pioneer mountain climbing and the scenic features of the Sierras as well as his observations and speculations as a geologist. He depicts with great realism the Digger Indians, Pikes, and others who pass his way. Local-color episodes such as "The Newtys of Pike" and melodramatic narratives such as "Kaweah's Run" show him indeed, had he but chosen to pursue his literary talent, a contender with contemporary West Coast writers like Mark Twain and Bret Harte.

WILLIAM BRACY.

MOUNTAINS, the term applied to natural elevations loftier than hills. The distinction is relative, since heights termed mountains in low-lying regions would be lost among the foothills of a more rugged terrain. Single mountains are commonly called *peaks;* connected peaks, a *ridge;* an elongated ridge, a mountain *chain* or *range;* a series of ranges, often roughly parallel, a *system;* while a number of systems may be grouped in a *cordillera.*

Formation.—Mountains have their origin in widespread disturbances in the earth crust. They rear like waves whose movement is measured not in moments but in millions of years. The rigid crust is continually adjusting to an unstable interior whose rock, though solid, is rendered plastic by prolonged heat and pressure. In places the crust bends downward beneath accumulations of sediment or ice; in others, when stretched or worn thin, it bulges from interior pressure. Hence, over weakened areas, it may buckle like a crumpled table cover into great folds and hollows known as *anticlines* and *synclines* to form *fold mountains* like the Appalachians. Thus the region which centers in the Swiss Alps once covered an area perhaps a hundred and fifty miles broader than now. Such global convulsions generate enormous lateral pressures which may fracture the folds and thrust them out over neighboring strata. The Matterhorn, one of the most famous of mountains, was torn from its original base and borne some 20 miles to be upended as a gigantic rock splinter. Even the Himalayas owe something of their height to encroachments upon the unyielding strata of the Gangetic plain. In crustal breaks where one side drops or the other rises, *fault mountains* may result—common landscape features in Utah and Nevada.

Major systems have risen from elongated troughs in shallow seas called *geosynclines.* Into these troughs sediments from neighboring highlands, gathering for ages, accumulated to a depth of thousands of feet. Gradually the weakened crust gave way beneath that weight, drawing the walls ever closer until they collapsed to fill the trough with huge fragments often tilted in every direction. The Rocky Mountains rose from such a gulf which once partially bisected North America, while the loftiest of all peaks, Mount Everest, is capped with limestone strata laid down long ago in the Tethys Sea, which penetrated far into the Asian continent. Such crustal convulsions, by relieving pressure, also permitted the upwelling of molten matter which sometimes overflowed to form such intrusions of igneous rock as cover extensive areas in our Northwestern states. At other times the crustal strata merely bulged as the molten mass beneath solidified into granite formations known as *batholiths.* Mount Blanc encases such a core, whose roots penetrate far into the earth.

Periods of mountain building were succeeded by prolonged intervals of relative calm, only to be followed by later disturbances to confuse the pattern. Meanwhile, the forces of erosion continuously wore away elevated landscapes, so that the Alps now occupy scarcely a quarter of their original volume, and many peaks are but the roots of more ancient summits. Erosion even created *residual mountains* carved from a loftier terrain which has elsewhere disappeared. Mount Monadnock in New Hampshire is typical of such mountain structure.

Peaks of far different origin are *volcanoes,* mere heaps of volcanic ash or lava. Though frequently isolated, they may appear in chains which reveal arcs of weakness in the earth crust, like the backbone of Java or the Aleutian Islands. Their development is sometimes marked by violent eruptions, such as those of Vesuvius, or the terrific explosions of Krakatau in the Sunda Strait, or Katmai Volcano in Alaska. They are often symmetrical cones like Fuji in Japan.

Elsewhere, mountain peaks present a variety of forms, outlines of rare beauty like the Jungfrau, dizzy shafts like the Muztagh Tower in the Karakorums, rounded domes like Chimborazo, or flat summits like the mesas and buttes of the western United States.

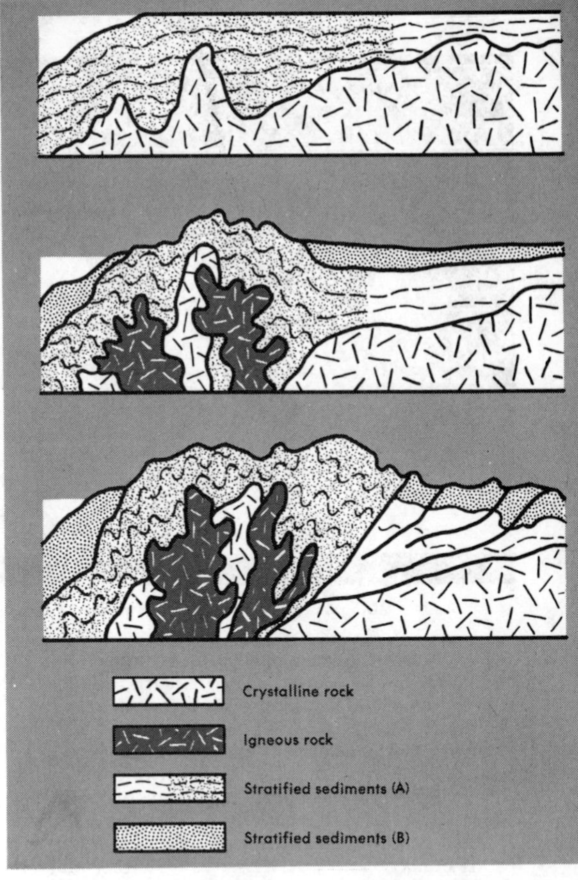

Cross-section diagrams illustrate one method of mountain formation. Sediments, gathering in ocean troughs (*top*), eventually bend and crack the substratum, releasing interior pressure which forces the rise of igneous matter (*center*) and pushes up the accumulated sedimentary material, creating mountain ridges or chains. Subsequently, additional mountains may be formed (*bottom*) as nearby sedimentary layers, deposited both before (*A*) and after (*B*) the process began, are fractured by lateral pressure.

Geological time is marked by periods of semicontinental uplift and mountain building, such as the Laramie and Hercynian revolutions. The Altai Mountains and the eroded peaks of the Brazilian and Australian highlands are immeasurably old. On the other hand, sections of the Himalayas, the Andes, and some Alaskan peaks are in a formative period and still rising. Many mountains rear from the ocean bed. Some are volcanic craters that failed to emerge above the surface. Others form great ranges like the Atlantic Ridge, which stretches north and south for some 10,000 miles from Iceland to latitude 55°S.

Effect on Climate.—Mountains have profoundly influenced global climates. In Asia the Kunlun, the Tien Shan, the Hindu Kush, and other systems, which stretch roughly from west to east, act as barricades against tempering winds and thus subject Siberia to subnormal cold, and India to excessive heat. On the other hand, North American mountain systems, which extend north and south, permit winter blasts to sweep unimpeded from the Arctic to the Gulf of Mexico. The distribution of global moisture is also disturbed so that some regions are deluged by rains, while others become deserts. In India monsoon winds recoil from the impassable ramparts of the Himalayas to flood Assam, while the southwestern United States, now semiarid, were once well wa-

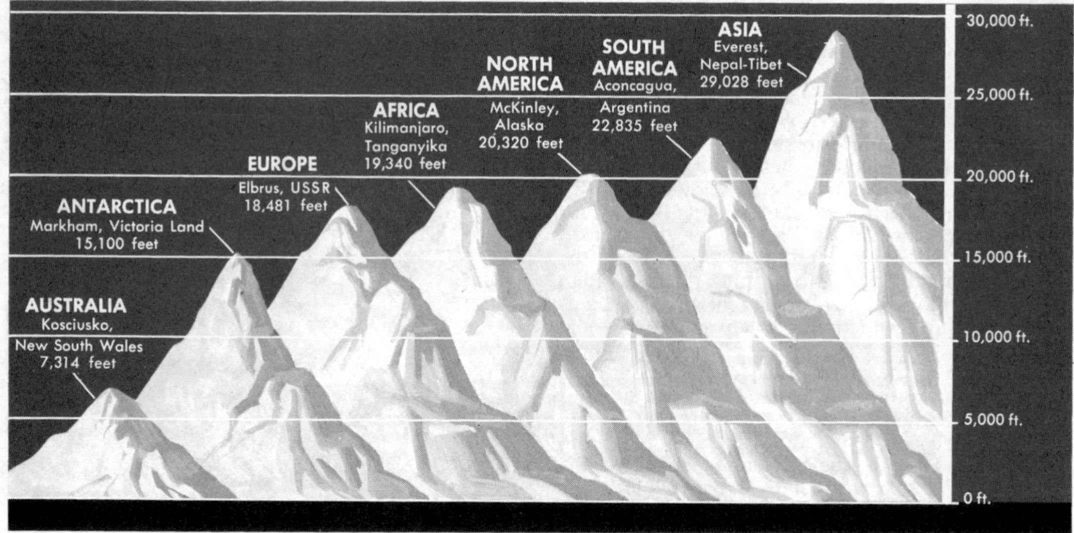

Diagram showing the loftiest peaks of each of the seven continents, ranged in order of height.

tered, until the rise of coastal ranges shut out moisture-laden winds. Even Death Valley was once a lake. Mountains are often called weather breeders, for clouds condense about their summits. Lofty peaks are capped with perpetual snow, even the Ruwenzori in equatorial Africa. Such snows, and the resultant glaciers, feed some of the world's great rivers which have their rise in mountain areas. Mountains have developed an alpine flora and fauna. The edelweiss of Switzerland, the cedars of Lebanon, and the giant sequoias of the Sierras are characteristic, as are the chamois of Europe, the yak of Asia, and the bighorn of North America.

Influence on History and Culture.—Mountains have often determined the trend of human history. They directed the drift of migratory populations from central and western Asia into Europe. Mountain barriers, by isolating the Hellenic states, prevented the cohesion which might have made Greece, instead of Rome, the dominant world power. On the other hand, mountains have provided protection, for the Alps were long regarded as the outer walls of Rome. Mountains have always given sanctuary to persecuted minorities; hence, mountaineers are proverbially independent and liberty loving. Mountains have also been prominent in art, literature, and religion. They were the legendary dwelling places of the gods, and such peaks as Olympus in Greece, Sinai in Hebrew tradition, and the lofty summits of the Himalayas became invested with a sacred character.

Mountain scenery is a lure to numberless vacationers, and mountain climbing has become so popular that the conquest of peaks like the Matterhorn, Aconcagua, and Everest have been hailed as landmarks in human achievement. (See MOUNTAIN CLIMBING.) But mountains also have more utilitarian uses. Their slopes provide summer pasturage in regions like the Pyrenees, and many are rich in timber resources. Mountain streams are harnessed to provide water power, which has been aptly termed white coal; and since mountains had their birth in major crustal disturbances, a wealth of mineral deposits has been upchurned: manganese in the Caucasus, silver and copper in the Andes, and platinum in the Urals, to mention just a few outstanding examples.

See also GEOLOGY; PHYSIOGRAPHY; VOLCANO.

PRINCIPAL MOUNTAINS OF THE WORLD

Mountain	Location	Height[1] (feet)
	AFRICA	
Kilimanjaro (Kibo)	Tanganyika	19,340
Kenya	Kenya	17,040
Stanley (Margherita)	Republic of the Congo-Uganda	16,795
Ras Dashan	Ethiopia	15,158
Meru	Tanganyika	14,979
Karisimbi	Republic of the Congo-Rwanda	14,787
Elgon	Kenya-Uganda	14,178
Guna	Ethiopia	13,881
Toubkal	Morocco	13,655
Birhan	Ethiopia	13,625
Badda	Ethiopia	13,560
Muhavura	Rwanda-Uganda	13,493
M'Goun	Morocco	13,353
Cameroon Mountain	Cameroun	13,350
Ayachi	Morocco	12,300
Teide, Pico de	Canary Islands	12,192
Thabantshonyana	Basutoland	11,425
Emi Koussi	Chad	11,204
Champagne Castle	Basutoland-South Africa	11,075
Mont-aux-Sources	Basutoland-South Africa	10,822
Kinyeti	Sudan	10,456
Gimbala	Sudan	10,073
Tahat	Algeria	9,850
Mlanje	Nyasaland	9,843
Rungwe	Tanganyika	9,713
Tsaratanana	Malagasy Republic	9,450
Cano Peak	Cape Verde Islands	9,281
Quipeio	Angola	8,563
Brandberg	South West Africa	8,550
Inyangani	Southern Rhodesia	8,517
	ANTARCTICA	
Markham		15,100
Siple		15,000
Kirkpatrick		14,603
Andrew Jackson		13,750
Lister		13,350
Erebus		13,202
Fridtjof Nansen		13,156
Sidley		12,000
Terror		10,750
	ASIA	
Everest (Chomolungma)	Nepal-Tibet	29,028
K[2]	Kashmir	28,250
Kanchenjunga	Nepal-Sikkim	28,146
Lhotse (E[1])	Nepal-Tibet	27,890
Makalu	Nepal-Tibet	27,790
Cho Oyu	Tibet	26,867

Above: A 15,000-foot-high pass near the crest of the Andes, in Peru. *Right:* Alaska's Mount Foraker rises to 17,400 feet, the third greatest elevation in the United States.

MOUNTAINS

(Top) Standard Oil Co., N.J.; (center) Adams Carter; (bottom left) French Government Tourist Office; (bottom right) Swiss National Tourist Office.

Below: A small train winds its way up the face of Mont Blanc, the highest peak in the European Alps. *Below right:* Swiss Alpine scenery in the Lake of Geneva vicinity.

Holmes, from Birnback

View of the cone of Mexico's Popocatepetl (background), a dormant volcano which towers 17,887 feet.

Dhaulagiri	Nepal	26,810
Nanga Parbat	Kashmir	26,660
Manaslu (Kutung I)	Nepal	26,658
Annapurna	Nepal	26,502
Gasherbrum I (Hidden Peak)	Kashmir	26,470
Broad Peak	Kashmir	26,414
Gosainthan	Tibet	26,291
Gyachung Kang	Nepal-Tibet	25,910
Distaghil	Kashmir	25,868
Himalchuli	Nepal	25,800
Masherbrum	Kashmir	25,660
Nanda Devi	India	25,645
Rakaposhi	Kashmir	25,550
Kamet	India	25,447
Namcha Barwa	Tibet	25,445
Ulugh Muztagh	China-Tibet	25,340
Gurla Mandhata	Tibet	25,335
Tirich Mir	Pakistan	25,263
Minya Konka	China	24,900
Communism (Stalin Peak)	USSR	24,590
Pobeda Peak	USSR-China	24,406
Muztagh Ata	China	24,388
Sad Istragh	Afghanistan	24,170
Kabru	Nepal-Sikkim	24,002
Chomo Lhari	Bhutan-Tibet	23,997
Muztagh	China	23,890
Lenin Peak	USSR	23,406
Api	Nepal	23,399
Khan Tengri	USSR	22,949
Kailas	Tibet	22,028
Hkakabo Razi	Burma	19,296
Demavend	Iran	18,600
Ararat	Turkey	16,945
Klyuchevskaya	USSR	15,912
Tabun Bogdo (Khuitun)	Mongolian People's Republic	15,266
Belukha	USSR	15,157
Kinabalu	Malaysia (North Borneo)	13,455
Yü Shan (Morrison)	Taiwan	13,259
Kerintji	Indonesia (Sumatra)	12,484
Fuji	Japan	12,397
Rindjani	Indonesia (Lombok)	12,224
Mahameru	Indonesia (Java)	12,060
Manar	Yemen	10,561
Fan Si Pan	Vietnam, North	10,308
Apo	Philippines	9,690
Bia	Laos	9,252
Hermon	Lebanon-Syria	9,232
Inthanon	Thailand	8,452
Kwanmo	Korea	8,337
Pidurtalagala	Ceylon	8,291

EUROPE

Elbrus	USSR	18,481
Dykh-Tau	USSR	17,054
Shkhara	USSR	17,037
Kazbek	USSR	16,541
Blanc	France	15,781
Ushba	USSR	15,410
Rosa (Dufourspitze)	Switzerland	15,203
Matterhorn	Switzerland	14,686
Finsteraarhorn	Switzerland	14,022
Jungfrau	Switzerland	13,642
Barre des Écrins	France	13,461
Gran Paradiso	Italy	13,323
Ortles	Italy	12,792
Grossglockner	Austria	12,460
Wetterhorn	Switzerland	12,142
Mulhacén	Spain	11,420
Aneto, Pico de	Spain	11,168
Etna	Italy	10,705
Zugspitze	Germany	9,721
Musala (Stalin Peak)	Bulgaria	9,596
Olympus	Greece	9,570
Gran Sasso d'Italia	Italy	9,560
Triglav	Yugoslavia	9,395
Korab	Albania-Yugoslavia	9,066
Gerlach (Stalin Peak)	Czechoslovakia	8,737
Negouil	Rumania	8,361
Galdhøppigen	Norway	8,097
Parnassus (Parnassós, Liákoura)	Greece	8,062
Pico	Azores	7,611
Kebnekaise	Sweden	6,965
Hvannadalshnjúkur	Iceland	6,952
Athos	Greece	6,670
Malhâo	Portugal	6,532
Ben Nevis	Scotland	4,406
Vesuvius	Italy	3,891
Snowdon	Wales	3,560

NORTH AMERICA

McKinley	Alaska	20,320
Logan	Canada	19,850
Orizaba (Citlaltépetl)	Mexico	18,700
St. Elias	Alaska-Canada	18,008
Popocatepetl	Mexico	17,887
Ixtaccihuatl	Mexico	17,671
Foraker	Alaska	17,400
Lucania	Canada	17,150
Blackburn	Alaska	16,523
Steele	Canada	16,440

Josef Muench

The east scarp of 14,495-foot Mount Whitney in California's Sierra Nevada, as seen from Owens Valley.

Bona	Alaska	16,421
Sanford	Alaska	16,208
Vancouver	Alaska	15,700
Fairweather	Alaska-Canada	15,300
Hubbard	Alaska-Canada	14,950
Whitney	California	14,495
Elbert	Colorado	14,423
Harvard	Colorado	14,420
Massive	Colorado	14,418
Rainier	Washington	14,410
Williamson	California	14,375
La Plata	Colorado	14,340
Longs Peak	Colorado	14,255
North Palisade	California	14,242
Yale	Colorado	14,196
Shasta	California	14,162
Lindsey (Old Baldy)	Colorado	14,125
Pikes Peak	Colorado	14,110
Wrangell	Alaska	14,006
Holy Cross, Mount of the	Colorado	13,986
Humphreys	California	13,972
Tajumulco	Guatemala	13,816
Gannett Peak	Wyoming	13,785
Grand Teton	Wyoming	13,766
Cook	Alaska-Canada	13,760
Kings Peak	Utah	13,498
Waddington	Canada	13,260
Wheeler Peak	New Mexico	13,160
Boundary Peak	Nevada	13,145
Robson	Canada	12,972
Granite Peak	Montana	12,799
Humphreys Peak	Arizona	12,670
Borah Peak	Idaho	12,662
Chirripó Grande	Costa Rica	12,533
Adams	Washington	12,307
Gunnbjorn	Greenland	12,139
Assiniboine	Canada	11,870
Chiriqúi	Panama	11,410
Irazú	Costa Rica	11,260
Hood	Oregon	11,245
Baker	Washington	10,750
Lassen Peak	California	10,453
Glacier Peak	Washington	10,436
Duarte, Pico (Trujillo)	Dominican Republic	10,404
Celaque	Honduras	9,400
Paricutín	Mexico	c.9,100
Guadaloupe Peak	Texas	8,751
Olympus	Washington	7,954
Harney Peak	South Dakota	7,242
Mitchell	North Carolina	6,684
Clingmans Dome	Tennessee-North Carolina	6,642
Saslaya	Nicaragua	6,500
Washington	New Hampshire	6,288
Rushmore	South Dakota	6,050
Oceania		
Carstensz	New Guinea	16,503
Wilhelmina	New Guinea	15,518
Mauna Kea	Hawaii	13,796
Mauna Loa	Hawaii	13,680
Cook	New Zealand	12,349
Balbi	Solomon Islands	10,170
Haleakala	Hawaii	10,032
Kosciusko	Australia	7,314
South America		
Aconcagua	Argentina	22,835
Ojos del Salado	Argentina-Chile	22,590
Pissis	Argentina	22,240
Huascarán	Peru	22,205
Tocorpuri	Bolivia-Chile	22,162
Llullaillaco	Argentina-Chile	22,057
Cachi	Argentina	22,047
Mercedario	Argentina	21,885
Yerupaja	Peru	21,758
Incahuasi	Argentina-Chile	21,720
Coropuna	Peru	21,696
Tupungato	Argentina-Chile	21,490
Illampu (Ancohuma)	Bolivia	21,490
Muerto, El	Argentina-Chile	21,450
Sajama	Bolivia	21,390
Nacimiento	Argentina	21,300
Illimani	Bolivia	21,185
Antofalla	Argentina	21,100
Ausangate	Peru	20,945
Chimborazo	Ecuador	20,577
Cotopaxi	Ecuador	19,347
Misti, El	Peru	19,199
Cayambe	Ecuador	19,014
Cristóbal Colón, Pico	Colombia	18,950
Huila	Colombia	18,865
Tolima	Colombia	18,438
Columna, La (Bolívar)	Venezuela	16,411
Pichincha	Ecuador	15,423
Bandeira, Pico da	Brazil	9,462

[1] Authorities differ regarding the heights of many mountain peaks. Continuing research may lead to a revision of some of the altitudes.

Bibliography.—Geikie, James, *Mountains* (New York 1914); Daly, Reginald A., *Our Mobile Earth* (New York 1926); Hobbs, W.H., *Earth Features and Their Meaning* (New York 1931); Peattie, Roderick, *Mountain Geography; a Critique and Field Study* (Cambridge, Mass., 1936); Smythe, Francis S., *Peaks and Valleys* (New

York 1938); Fenton, Carroll L., and Fenton, Mildred A., *Mountains* (New York 1942); Jeffreys, Sir Harold, *Earthquakes and Mountains* (London 1950); Lane, Ferdinand C., *The Story of Mountains* (New York 1950); Bemmelen, Reinout W. van, *Mountain Building: a Study Primarily Based on Indonesia, Region of the World's Most Active Crustal Deformations* (The Hague 1954); Huxley, Anthony, ed., *Standard Encyclopedia of the World's Mountains* (New York 1962); American Alpine Club, *The American Alpine Journal* (New York, annual); Swiss Foundation for Alpine Research, *Mountain World* (New York, annual).

FERDINAND C. LANE,
Author of "The Story of Mountains."

MOUNTAINSIDE, moun'tĭn-sīd, borough, New Jersey, in Union County, 11 miles southwest of Newark. Incorporated in 1895, Mountainside is primarily a residential area. Part of Watchung Reservation is included within its boundaries. Pop. 7,520.

MOUNTBATTEN, mount-băt"n, **Louis (Francis Albert Victor Nicholas),** 1ST EARL MOUNTBATTEN OF BURMA (formerly PRINCE LOUIS FRANCIS OF BATTENBERG), British naval leader and statesman: b. Windsor, England, June 25, 1900. The younger son of Prince Louis Alexander of Battenberg, who changed the family name to Mountbatten during World War I, and Princess Victoria, a granddaughter of Queen Victoria, he entered the Royal Navy as a cadet in 1913, and rose through the ranks to the grade of captain in 1937. He was called from the command of the aircraft carrier *Illustrious* in October 1941 to become commodore of combined operations, and from 1942 to 1943 was chief of combined operations of the British forces. During this time he was in charge of the Commandos, and directed the successful invasion of Madagascar. From 1943 to 1946 he was supreme allied commander in Southeast Asia.

Earl Mountbatten of Burma.

British Information Services

In 1947 Mountbatten was appointed viceroy of India, the last to hold that office. He then served as governor general of the Dominion of India (1947–1948), and presided over the transfer of sovereign power from Britain to the national government; he also shared responsibility for the separation of Pakistan from India. Resuming his naval career, he was made admiral (1953), and in 1955–1959 he was first sea lord of the admiralty, the position that his father had been compelled to resign in 1914 because of his Austrian birth. In 1959 he became chief of the defense staff and chairman of the chief of staff committee. He retired in 1965. Mountbatten was created viscount in 1946 and earl in 1947.

MOUNTBATTEN, Louis Alexander. See BATTENBERG, PRINCE LOUIS ALEXANDER.

MOUNTED POLICE, Royal Canadian. See ROYAL CANADIAN MOUNTED POLICE.

MOUNTLAKE TERRACE, mount'lāk, city, Washington, in Snohomish County, 15 miles north of Seattle. It is chiefly a residential section for the surrounding Puget Sound area. Manufacture of electronic equipment is the principal industry. Platted in 1949, it was incorporated in 1954. The city has a council-manager type of government. Pop. 16,600.

MOURNING. See DEATH CUSTOMS AND RITES.

MOURNING BECOMES ELECTRA, a play by Eugene Gladstone O'Neill (q.v.), subtitled *A Trilogy in Fourteen Scenes,* published in 1931. The first performance was given at the Guild Theatre in New York City, Oct. 26, 1931; the playing time was six hours with an intermission for dinner following *Homecoming,* the first play. The play ran for 145 performances and was highly successful. The trilogy includes (1) *Homecoming,* (2) *The Hunted,* and (3) *The Haunted,* treating the tragic events in the lives of the Mannon family in New England during the Civil War. (1) General Ezra Mannon, who inherited the fortune made by his father in the shipping business, has not yet returned from the war as the play opens. Living in the grim Mannon mansion are his wife, Christine, and his daughter, Lavinia. There is a terrible and obvious enmity existing between the beautiful Christine and Lavinia, her plain, stern daughter. Vinnie is in love with a romantic sea captain, Adam Brant, but comes to despise him when she discovers that not only is he the son of her father's brother and a servant girl, but that he has also become her mother's lover. Made more stern and cruel by her disillusionment, Lavinia seeks to make her mother pay for her actions by turning the family against her. When General Mannon returns, Christine, who has never loved him, poisons him, hoping to escape from the Mannon family with Adam Brant. (2) Orin, Lavinia's brother, returns from the war still deeply fond of his mother. When Vinnie tells him of Christine's unfaithfulness and the suspected murder of General Mannon, which had been made to seem a heart attack, Orin kills Adam Brant, an act which causes Christine to commit suicide. (3) Lavinia, released from the hatred of Christine, becomes more attractive and less stern and plans to marry Peter Niles, a childhood friend. Orin, driven almost to madness by the past events, tries to stop Vinnie's marriage and, sensing failure, kills himself. Peter deserts Vinnie, leaving her alone in the Mannon house to let the ghosts hound her ". . . until the curse is paid out and the last Mannon is let die."

Using the Electra (q.v.) story in Greek tragedy as the basis for a modern psychological drama, O'Neill succeeded in approximating the Greek sense of fate. By the interweaving of plot threads he conveys to an audience with no belief in supernatural retribution the inexorable ending of a twisted, ghost-ridden family.

MOURNING CLOAK, mōrn'ĭng klōk, a butterfly, *Nymphalis antiopa,* of the family Nymphalidae (brush-footed butterflies). It is found in most temperate regions of North America and Europe. Its wings are dark velvety brown, with pale yellow margins and a row of blue spots. It measures in expanse about three inches. Its caterpillars feed upon elm, willow, poplar, and other trees. In England it is known as the Camberwell Beauty.

William D. Field.

MOURNING DOVE, a wild dove, *Zenaidura macroura* of North America where it breeds from southern Canada to Mexico. It is a slim bird with a small head and measures about one foot in length. Its tail is long and pointed,

John H. Gerard from National Audubon Society

Mourning dove (*Zenaidura macroura*).

bordered with white, and the rest of the plumage is soft brown above with a few black spots on the wing; underneath it is tawny and the head and neck shows some delicate purplish reflections. The mourning dove is a gentle and usually confiding bird and its English name is probably derived from its voice. The latter is a long repeated series of monotonous coos which sound mournful to many people. Mourning doves breed in greatly varied country, from deserts and treeless plains to open woodlands and gardens, and are usually abundant, especially in the more southern parts of the United States where they are game birds. They lay two white eggs on a very flimsily built platform of sticks, usually erected in a tree.

Charles Vaurie.

MOUSE, mous, any of a large number of small rodent mammals of the family Muridae, other members of which are called rats, hamsters, voles, and lemmings. The name is also erroneously used for small forms of some of the other rodent families as, for instance, jumping mouse (Dipodidae) and pocket mouse (Heteromyidae). Usage will here, however, be restricted to the Muridae. This is the largest mammalian family in number of species, several hundred, at least, being recognized. It is also extremely widespread, almost cosmopolitan in distribution as far as wild forms are concerned, and in addition, several species, having become associated with man, are now found everywhere that man has penetrated. Though differing greatly in body size and in the form and size of the ears and limbs, all have hairy bodies and a moderately pointed head. The incisor or front teeth as in all rodents are modified to form gnawing chisels, while the canine teeth are absent and the cheek teeth reduced to the three molars above and below. The tail is usually rather long and may be either densely haired or largely covered by scales. Five toes are normally present on each hind foot, but on the front foot the pollex or thumb is greatly reduced.

The classification of the Muridae is by no means settled, but the following major divisions or subfamilies are generally recognized: Cricetinae, Lophiomyinae, Microtinae, Gerbillinae, Murinae, Dendromurinae, Otomyinae, Rhynchomyinae, and Hydromyinae.

The subfamily Cricetinae contains all of the native long-tailed mice of the Western Hemisphere together with a few Eurasian and African forms, most of which are short-tailed and called hamsters. One of the latter, the golden hamster (*Mesocricetus auratus*), has, since 1930, become well known as a pet and laboratory animal. The best known North American forms of small or mouse size are the deer and white-footed mice (*Peromyscus*) represented by numerous species, many of them living in forests and among the commonest of small mammals. Others are the American harvest mice (*Reithrodontomys*), which occur chiefly in fields and marshes, and the grasshopper mice (*Onychomys*). The latter, occurring in plains and deserts, are unusual both for their relatively short tails and their insect-eating habits. The Cricetinae are represented by a great many forms in South America, where they constitute the only subfamily of mouselike rodents.

The subfamily Lophiomyinae contains a single form, the highly peculiar African maned rat (*Lophiomys.*) The subfamily Microtinae includes the forms known as voles or field mice, and lemmings. They are confined to Eurasia and North America, inhabiting chiefly the cooler regions. Most have quite short necks, ears, and tails, and all have very complex molar teeth.

The American Museum of Natural History

Deer mouse (*Peromyscus*).

The subfamily Gerbillinae consists of a number of African and Asiatic species known as gerbils or jirds. All are desert forms, nocturnal in habit, and spending the day in burrows. The hind legs are greatly elongated, the animal hopping rather than running or walking. This type of adaptive modification is repeated in many desert rodents.

The subfamily Murinae includes a tremendous variety of forms, restricted, however, as wild native forms, to the Eastern Hemisphere, where they occur chiefly in tropical regions. All the species of Muridae which have become associated with man belong to this subfamily, however, and in this way it has become worldwide in distribution. Attention will be confined to the smaller mouse-sized forms. Some species are called field mice in Europe, but are quite distinct from North American voles called field mice. Several forms in southeastern Asia are remarkable in that the hallux or big toe is opposable like that of a monkey, and as a result the hind foot can be used for grasping small branches, thus enabling the animals to climb about the trees in which they live. The Old World harvest mice (*Micromys*) are somewhat similar, but as a result of their very small size (among the smallest of rodents), are able to climb up grass stems, around which they build small spherical nests. On the other hand, certain Australian forms (*Notomys*) show hopping desert modifications; they have large ears, a tufted tail, and greatly elongated hind legs and feet.

The best-known mouse and the form to which the name applies in its narrowest sense is the house mouse (*Mus musculus*). As a native wild animal it is confined to Eurasia and northwestern Africa, but has become cosmopolitan by accidental human introduction. As a result, the various stocks show a great deal of variation. Thus, most wild individuals have white bellies, whereas strictly commensal stock (living in human habitations) have gray bellies. The high degree of variability together with their abundance and ease of capture have caused them to be utilized to a great extent as pets and laboratory animals (particularly the all-white or albino variety, which has arisen under domestication). A great deal of medical and biological research, particularly on methods of inheritance, has been done since 1900 using house mice. As a semiwild or commensal form around houses and other buildings, however, *Mus musculus* is often a serious pest, destroying considerable quantities of stored food and other materials. In many places, on the other hand, house mice have invaded neighboring fields and open country. This has been facilitated by their high reproductive rate, several litters a year being produced by each female mouse.

The subfamily Dendromurinae includes a number of African species known as tree mice and fat mice, most forms living in tropical forest. Some species are eaten by African natives. The subfamily Otomyinae contains only the African swamp rats.

The subfamily Rhynchomyinae consists of a single species, the Philippine shrewrat (*Rhynchomys soricoides*), known only from the mountains of Luzon, where it probably feeds on worms and small insects. The fur is very soft and the teeth greatly reduced in size and number. It may be related to certain forms included in the Murinae from the Malay archipelago, particularly Celebes.

The subfamily Hydromyinae contains a number of species from Australia, New Guinea, and the Philippines. Most are called water rats, though some are more or less terrestrial and others are small enough to be called mice. Most of them are, however, aquatic, and show a reduction in the number of molar teeth.

See also Hamster; Lemming; Rat; Rodentia; Vole.

Karl F. Koopman,
American Museum of Natural History,
New York City.

Bibliography

Anderson, S., and Jones, J. K., *Recent Mammals of the World* (New York 1967).
Anthony, H. E., *Field Book of North American Mammals* (New York 1928).
Burt, W. H., and Grossenheider, R. P., *A Field Guide to Mammals* (Boston 1952).
Cahalane, Victor H., *Mammals of North America* (New York 1954).
Ellermann, J. R., *The Families and Genera of Living Rodents,* 2 vols., vol. 2 (London 1941).
Morris, Desmond, *Mammals* (New York 1965).
National Audubon Society, *Audubon Nature Encyclopedia,* 12 vols., vol. 7 (New York 1965).
Palmer, E. Laurence, *Palmer's Fieldbook of Mammals* (New York 1957).
Tate, G. H. H., *Mammals of Eastern Asia* (New York 1947).
Troughton, E., *Furred Animals of Australia* (New York 1947).
Walker, Ernest P., and others, *Mammals of the World,* 3 vols. (Baltimore, Md., 1964).

MOUSE DEER. See Chevrotain.

MOUSE OPPOSSUM. See Oppossum.

MOUSEBIRDS, a group of peculiar birds of central Africa, constituting the family Coliidae also known as colies. They are of small size, grayish colors, marked with darker tints and in some species with touches of brighter colors; have finchlike beaks, crests, short weak wings, very long tails and remarkably strong feet. They are active, but fly little, spending their lives mostly in creeping about the branches of trees in a way that with their dun colors strongly suggests the behavior of mice. They are fond of hanging head downward, and at night gather in bands that roost together in hanging postures as closely as they can crowd. Their food consists mainly of fruit; and they place their cupshaped nests in low trees and bushes.

MOUSETRAP. See Naval Terms.

MOUSSORGSKY. See Mussorgsky.

MOUSTERIAN. See Stone Age—*Middle Paleolithic.*

MOUTH, in human anatomy, the oral cavity at the beginning of the alimentary canal. It contains the tongue and the teeth and is the opening through which food is received and through which the voice issues. The mouth receives the secretions of the salivary glands. See also Alimentary Canal; Salivary Glands.

MOUTH ORGAN. See Harmonica.

MOUTH-TO-MOUTH RESPIRATION. See Artificial Respiration.

MOVIES. See Motion Pictures.

MOVING STAIRWAY. See Escalator.

MOWAT, mou'at', Sir **Oliver,** Canadian statesman: b. Kingston, Ontario, Canada, July 22, 1820; d. Toronto, April 19, 1903. Admitted to the bar, he practiced in Kingston and Toronto; was vice chancellor of Upper Canada, 1864–1872 and premier of Ontario, 1872–1896. He opposed Sir John A. Macdonald on the question of provincial autonomy, Mowat regarding the provincial legislature as sovereign within its own sphere, and his reading of the British North America Act was in this sense borne out by the

Imperial Privy Council, notably in the Ontario boundary dispute. In 1896, he entered the ministry of Sir Wilfrid Laurier (q.v.) as minister of justice and was made president of the Senate. He was appointed lieutenant governor of Ontario in 1897, and served until his death. Altogether, Mowat gave 45 years to the public service. He was given a knighthood in 1892.

MOWATT, Anna Cora. See RITCHIE, ANNA CORA OGDEN MOWATT.

MOWBRAY, mō'brā, name of an Anglo-Norman baronial house, founded at the Conquest by GEOFFREY (DE MONTBRAI), bishop of Coutances. NIGEL, his nephew, founded the second house of Mowbray; WILLIAM, 4TH BARON MOWBRAY (d. 1222?), great grandson of Nigel, was a leader in the rising against King John. JOHN DE MOWBRAY (1328?–1368) gained by marriage the earldom of Nottingham and the marshalship of England; his second son Thomas, obtained a dukedom. The line ended with JOHN, 4TH DUKE OF MOWBRAY (1444–1476), the dukedom passing to the Howard family after his daughter Anne died in 1481.

MOWBRAY, Henry Siddons, American decorative and figure painter: b. Alexandria, Egypt, Aug. 5, 1858; d. Washington, Conn., Jan. 13, 1928. After a year at the United States Military Academy, he abandoned a military career for art. In 1878 he went to Paris where he studied under Léon J. F. Bonnat. From 1886, he maintained a studio in New York where he executed many beautiful murals. He began his work as an illustrator and portrait painter but later confined himself to decorative painting in which he displayed taste in composition, perfection in draftsmanship, and warmth of tone. The frieze, *Development of the Law,* in the Appellate Court in New York City is a fine example of his work. His murals may be seen in the Congressional Library, Washington, D.C., the Federal Court, Cleveland, Ohio, Gunn Memorial Library, Washington, Conn., The Morgan Library, New York City. He was elected a national academician in 1891, and in 1903, he became the first director of the American Academy in Rome.

MOWER, mou'ẽr, **Joseph Anthony,** American soldier: b. Woodstock, Vt., Aug. 22, 1827; d. New Orleans, La., Jan. 6, 1870. After two years at Norwich University and a year working as a carpenter he enlisted in the Engineer Corps and served throughout the Mexican War. Commissioned 2d lieutenant in the regular army in 1855, he attained his captaincy in 1861. His Civil War career was one of the most distinguished. Regular army brevet commissions followed more rapid promotions in the volunteer forces. As major general of volunteers he accompanied the Missouri expedition against Price, then joined Gen. W. T. Sherman in the Atlanta campaign (November 1864) and led a division in the march to the sea. Mustered out as brevet major general in February 1866, he was recommissioned a colonel of infantry. At his death he was in command of the department of Louisiana.

MOWRER, mour'ẽr, **Edgar Ansel,** American journalist: b. Bloomington, Ill., March 8, 1892. In 1913, after study at the Sorbonne, in Paris, he graduated at the University of Michigan, and thereupon returned to France, where he became a contributor to American and English publications. On outbreak of World War I, in 1914, he joined the Paris bureau of the Chicago, Ill., *Daily News,* which was headed by his brother, and reported the campaigns in France, Belgium, and Italy. He represented his paper in Italy until 1922 when he secured transfer to the *Daily News* bureau in Berlin. His frank and critical dispatches reporting the disintegration of the Weimar Republic were republished in book form as *Germany Puts the Clock Back* (1932; rev. ed. 1939), earning him the Pulitzer Prize in journalism for the best foreign correspondence, but incurring for him the hatred of the Nazis. He was ordered to leave Germany and, in 1934, after a lecture tour in the United States, he succeeded his brother as chief of the Daily News bureau in Paris until 1940. Returning to the United States in 1940 after the German occupation of Paris, he served as deputy director of the Office of War Information in 1941–1943.

His books include: *The Dragon Awakes* (1938); *Global War* (with Martha Rajchman, 1942); and *The Nightmare of American Foreign Policy* (1948); *Challenge and Decision* (1950).

MOWRER, Paul Scott, American journalist: b. Bloomington, Ill., July 14, 1887. He became a reporter on the Chicago, Ill., *Daily News* in 1905 and, in 1910, after two years at the University of Michigan, he was made Paris correspondent for that newspaper. He reported the first Balkan War, 1912–1913, and throughout World War I he directed his newspaper's services in France. Subsequently he reported the Paris Peace Conference and postwar conferences on armaments limitation. In 1928 he won the Pulitzer Prize for best foreign correspondence. He became associate editor and chief editorial writer of the Chicago *Daily News* in 1934, and in 1935–1944 was editor of the paper. In 1945 he became European editor of the New York *Post.* He died in Beaufort, S.C., on April 4, 1971.

His books include *Balkanized Europe* (1921); *Our Foreign Affairs* (1924); and *The House of Europe* (1945). Volumes of verse included *Poems Between Wars* (1941); *And Let the Glory Go* (1955); *Twenty-one and Sixty-five* (1958); *This Teeming Earth* (1965); and *Poems* (1968).

MOYNIHAN, moi'ni-han, **Daniel Patrick** (1927–), American diplomat and educator. He was born in Tulsa, Okla., on March 16, 1927. After attending Tufts University and Fletcher School of Law and Diplomacy, he studied at the London School of Economics and Political Science (1950–1951). In 1961 he entered the Labor Department in Washington, becoming assistant secretary of labor (1963–1965). During the next four years he directed the Joint Center for Urban Studies at Massachusetts Institute of Technology and Harvard, and then taught at the Kennedy School of Government, Harvard, where he became professor of government in 1973.

Meanwhile he served as a consultant on urban affairs to President Nixon in 1971–1973, and as a delegate to the UN General Assembly in 1971. He was ambassador to India in 1973–1974, and in June 1975 was confirmed as chief U.S. representative at the United Nations. His books include *Maximum Feasible Misunderstanding* (1969) and *The Politics of a Guaranteed Income* (1973).

J. ALLAN CASH, FROM RAPHO GUILLUMETTE

Mozambique's income derives mainly from agriculture. Above, coconuts cover the ground on a copra estate.

MOZAMBIQUE, mō-zam-bēk′, is an independent country in southeastern Africa. Formerly an overseas province of Portugal known in Portuguese as Moçambique, it was granted independence on June 25, 1975. Its first president, Samora Machel, leader of the nationalist organization FRELIMO (Frente de Libertacão de Moçambique, or Mozambique Liberation Front), which had struggled for the country's independence since the early 1960's, was sworn in on that date.

Mozambique extends over 1,200 miles (1,900 km) along the southeastern coast of Africa between the Republic of Tanzania in the north and the Republic of South Africa and Swaziland in the southwest. All of Mozambique's southwestern and western neighbors, including Malawi, Zambia and Rhodesia, depend on its railway systems and deepwater ports for their outlets to the Indian Ocean.

Mozambique has experienced the longest continual European presence in sub-Saharan Africa. Since the 16th century, Portuguese traders, missionaries, and civil servants have occupied portions of the territory. But not until the beginning of the 20th century did Mozambique assume its present boundaries, governmental structure, and economic profile. Both in the past and during the 20th century, profits from the exploitation of the province's natural resources have benefited Portugal more than they have the residents of Mozambique.

1. The Land

Coastal lowland covers two fifths of the total area of Mozambique. To the west of this region is a transitional zone of hills and low plateaus ranging from 500 to 2,000 feet (150–600 meters) above sea level. Portions of western Mozambique form a third zone, with an average elevation of 3,500 feet (1,050 meters). This is an extension of the Rhodesian highlands. Included in this region are the 6,500-foot (2,000-meter) Angoni plateau in the northwest Tete district; the Namuli highlands, east of southern Malawi, with an elevation of 6,200 feet (1,900 meters); the Gorongosa highlands in central Mozambique; and the Libombo Mountain range along the southwestern frontier.

Mozambique has an extensive river network. All the rivers flow into the Indian Ocean. The major rivers from north to south are the Ruvuma, Ligonha, Lúrio, Zambezi, Save, and Limpopo. Because variations in regional rainfall make the flow of most of Mozambique's rivers irregular, their navigation on a regular basis is impossible.

Climate. Mozambique's climate is tropical, varying according to the province's topography. Each year has a wet and a dry season. Almost all of the annual rainfall occurs during the October-to-March wet season, which coincides with the Southern Hemisphere's summer. Temperatures during this period are high, varying with exposure to the rain-bearing northeast monsoon.

Temperatures along the coast range between 80° and 85° F (27°–29° C), with relative humidity around 80%. Rainfall is heavy along the central coast between Quelimane and Beira, averaging 52 inches (1,320 mm) a year. North and south of this region, annual rainfall is about 30 inches (760 mm). Precipitation and humidity drop in that part of the plain that lies inland from the coast, but rise again in the interior plateau. Mozambique's highest annual rainfall, 65 inches (1,650 mm), occurs in the mountains of northern Mozambique and along the Rhodesian frontier. Two large sections of the interior are extremely dry: the western Gaza district, where only 12 inches (300 mm) of rain fall annually; and the Zambezi Valley around Tete.

The cool, dry season, from October to May, is winter in the Southern Hemisphere. The warm Mozambique current, which flows south from the equator, gives the coast an average temperature of 67° F (19° C). This mild winter attracts many South African tourists to Mozambique's beautiful beaches.

Plant and Animal Life. Mangrove swamps and coconut and date palms occur along much of the coastline, particularly in river estuaries. Wild cashew-nut trees grow inland from the coast in the northern and southern districts. Other trees

INFORMATION HIGHLIGHTS

Official Name: People's Republic of Mozambique.
Area: 302,329 square miles (783,032 sq km).
Population: (1972 est.) 8,100,000.
Capital: Lourenço Marques.
Highest Elevation: Mt. Mlanje, on border with Malawi (9,843 feet or 3,000 meters).
Languages: Portuguese (official), Bantu languages.
Religions: Christianity, Islam, tribal religions.
Monetary Unit: Escudo (1 escudo = 100 centavos).

include cedar, ebony, ironwood, sandalwood, gum copal, and gum-yielding acacias. Bamboo and spear grass grow along riverbanks, and Landolphia rubber vines thrive in the forests. The savanna, with its flat plains, short-grass steppes, and open woodlands, dominates about three quarters of Mozambique's terrain.

The Portuguese government considers the animal life of the province to be a valuable natural resource and its conservation an important function related to that of promoting Mozambique's developing tourist industry. The rhinoceros of the northern and northeastern regions, the giraffe of the area near the South African border, and the ostrich living between the Limpopo and Save rivers are all species protected by law. Many types of antelope as well as zebra, buffalo, lion, and leopard are widely distributed throughout Mozambique. The crocodile and hippopotamus are found in the rivers and lakes.

In 1967, to implement its program of wildlife preservation, the government set aside certain regions as national parks, game preserves, and hunting concessions. The most famous of these is Gorongosa National Park, located 100 miles (160 km) northwest of Beira in the Gorongosa highlands. Game preserves include the Ruvuma Reserve in the northwest, the Gile Reserve northeast of Quelimane, the Marromeu Reserve south of the mouth of the Zambezi River for the protection of buffalo, and the Maputo Reserve in southern Mozambique for the protection of elephants. Sixteen *coutadas*, or areas of big-game concentration, have been set aside as hunting zones for tourists.

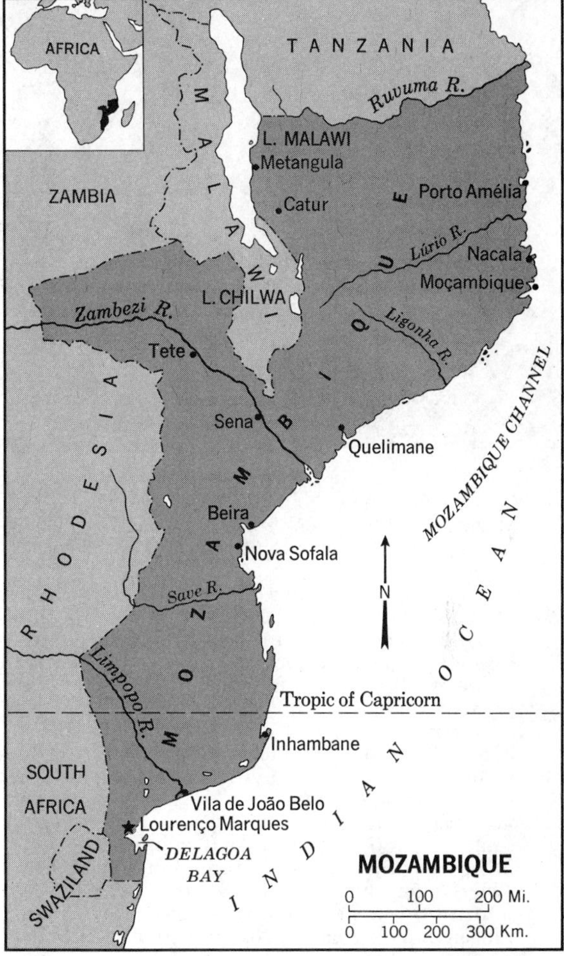

2. The People

About 98% of the population of Mozambique is African. Of the remaining 2%, over half is European. Smaller minorities include the Indian, Chinese, and *mestiço* (persons with at least one grandparent of a race different from that of the other grandparents). At least 85% of the African population lives in rural areas, and only 15% in the widely scattered towns. The towns contain about 90% of Mozambique's Chinese and about two thirds of its Europeans and Indians.

Those Europeans who live in the cities are civil servants or are engaged in industry or commerce. The Portuguese government encourages the settlement of Portuguese nationals in rural areas by providing colonists with free passage and free cleared land. Almost all of the Chinese of Mozambique engage in commerce, as do the Indians. Since the Indian merchants deal chiefly in goods destined for African consumers, many have stores in rural areas or are itinerant traders.

Mozambique is divided into nine administrative districts. Population density is highest in the fertile Zambesia and Mozambique districts in the north and along the coast in the southern district, which provides labor for the mines of the Witwatersrand in South Africa.

The African Tribes. There is considerable overlap between the African peoples of Mozambique and tribes in neighboring states. All speak Bantu languages. The major ones are Thonga in the south; Nyanja, in a variety of dialects, in the Zambezi Valley; Makua and Yao in the north; and Swahili, an Arabized Bantu language, in the northeast and along the coast.

Current tribal patterns are the result of pre-19th century migrations into the territory of peoples from the north and west and of early 19th century settlement by peoples fleeing before the Zulu armies of southern Africa. The Zambezi River is the dividing line between these two groups. A third distinct region is formed by the peoples of the Zambezi Valley itself, who were influenced by the Portuguese and Arabs who used the river as their major route into the interior.

Tribes north of the Zambezi river—the Maravi, Yao, Makua (or Macua), Lomwe (Lomue), and Makonde (Maconde)—are predominantly agriculturalists. Their society is matrilineal—that is, descent is traced through the maternal line. Over 40% of the province's African population belongs to the Makua-Lomwe linguistic family. The Makua outnumber the Lomwe by more than three to one. Most of the Swahili-speaking coastal people are of Makuan descent. Since 1900 many Lomwe have migrated to Malawi, where they now form the second-largest ethnic group.

The Makonde live on both sides of the Ruvuma River border between Mozambique and Tanzania. They have resisted the Islamization that is widespread among their Yao and Makua neighbors. Experts on African art consider Makonde sculpture, including wooden masks and statuary, to be the finest in eastern Africa.

For at least two centuries the Yao were the middlemen handling the trade between the interior and the coast. The Islamization of the tribe is so complete that the conical huts that had

INGABORG LIPPMANN

Sugarcane is cultivated for the export market on one of many large plantations in Mozambique's coastal lowland. Such estates are owned by Europeans and worked by a hired African labor force.

been common to all African inhabitants of Mozambique has been replaced among the Yao by rectangular structures built in imitation of coastal Islamic architecture.

Southern Mozambique is inhabited by tribes such as the Shona, Thonga, Chopi, and Nguni (Ngoni), who belong to the East African cattle-raising complex and are patrilineal. Cattle symbolize wealth and prestige. The *lobolo,* or bride price, is traditional among these peoples and was once paid in cattle. Today, such items as radios, bicycles, and sewing machines may be part of the *lobolo.*

The Thonga, the second-largest tribal group in Mozambique, are concentrated in the region south of the Save River. They supply 40% of the labor force migrating to the mines of South Africa. The Nguni, because of frequent intermarriage into tribes among whom they settled, are one of Mozambique's smallest distinct groups, but their impact on the province's history has been considerable. The Chopi live in the coastal areas south of the Save River. Large numbers have moved to Lourenço Marques, the capital city. Almost the entire African population of Manica e Sofala district, between the Save and Zambezi rivers, is Shona. Their numbers have grown through the migrations into Mozambique of Shona from Rhodesia and South Africa.

Class Structure. In 1930 the population of Portuguese Africa was divided by law into two categories: *indigenas* ("unassimilated" Africans) and *não indigenas* (Europeans, Asians, *mestiços,* and "assimilated" Africans). The *indigena* had to carry a passbook and was subject to labor regulations. The *não indigena* enjoyed the full rights of Portuguese citizenship.

To become an *assimilado* (an African who passed from one category to the other) the African had to measure up to stringent standards. He had to speak Portuguese, earn enough money to support himself and his family, renounce his tribal ways, pay various fees, and supply testimonials of his good character to the authorities. If the *assimilado* did not live up to what the government considered his responsibilities, his citizenship could be revoked. This system of selective assimilation tended to produce few Portuguese Africans.

In 1961 full citizenship was granted to all inhabitants of Portuguese Africa. However, the identity card each Mozambican carries classifies him according to his former status. Unassimilated Africans are restricted in their activities. They may not engage in commerce, and very few have the education to enter the professions. The majority are laborers.

Religion. Although the Constitution of Portugal guarantees all faiths the right to practice in Mozambique, Roman Catholicism is the state religion. Extensive areas of the province are Islamic, and tribal religions continue to flourish elsewhere.

The Catholic Church in Mozambique is organized into parishes (in the cities) and missions (in the countryside). The mission stations are staffed primarily by members of religious orders, who bring Catholicism and Portuguese culture to Mozambique's rural peoples. The church works with the government to promote the policy of assimilation.

Education. Education in Mozambique is the metropolitan Portuguese system adapted to local conditions. Both state-operated and officially subsidized Catholic schools have a centralized curriculum and examinations determined by government policy.

Primary education is conducted in two separate systems: *ensino de adaptação* for Africans and *ensino primário* for Europeans and assimilated Africans. *Ensinos de adaptação* serve rural areas and are operated by the Catholic Church through its local missions. The teachers are Africans, instructing their students in the Portuguese language, "the three r's," and simple technical skills. Completion of this three-year course allows the African to enter the *ensino primário,* a five-year program preparing students for entrance into either the academic or the technical high schools.

The high schools are in cities or in areas with large European populations. The academic secondary school (*liceu*) offers a seven-year program that qualifies students for entrance into an institution of higher education. In 1963 a university of general studies, offering a partial degree program, opened in Lourenço Marques, but to earn a diploma students were required to complete their education in Portugal.

A graduated tuition fee is charged throughout the educational system. It is lowest in the *ensino de adaptação* and highest in the *liceu.* This factor, together with language difficulties and low incomes, severely limits the number of Africans enrolled in schools beyond the *ensino de adaptação.*

3. The Economy

Mozambique is a predominantly agricultural country whose economic development is controlled to a large extent by Portugal. Since the late 19th century foreign capital has been a necessity for development, although investment is always subject to strict government control. Mozambique's harbors make transit trade an important part of the economy, and the exploitation of mineral resources is a potential source of great wealth. But these sectors are of minor importance when compared with the role that agriculture has played in the province's economy.

In 1961 the government initiated a 10-year plan to integrate the economies of the overseas provinces and Portugal into a single economic community. A monetary fund, the Escudo Zone, was created to facilitate interterritorial credit. All foreign exchange earned by the overseas provinces is deposited with the Bank of Portugal in Lisbon, and a corresponding amount in escudos is credited to the provincial account.

Agriculture. Agriculture is the backbone of Mozambique's economy, producing nearly four fifths of the value of total exports. Farming methods and landholding divide production into a traditional and a modern sector. European plantation agriculture and its African labor force compose the modern sector. The traditional sector is African and consists of subsistence farming (beans, peanuts, corn, manioc) and cash crops (cotton, rice, cashew nuts). The traditional African farms are the principal producers of the province's two leading export crops—cotton and cashew nuts—while the modern sector provides sugar, tea, copra, and sisal for overseas markets.

The African farmer has not been entirely free to raise what he wishes. Until 1961 a legally enforced system of compulsory cultivation required all farmers in the traditional sector of the economy, in some regions, to devote equal acreage to the production of cotton and food crops. European-operated companies had exclusive rights to the purchase of the cotton crops, in return for supervising the African growers and preparing the crop for shipment. While reforms introduced in 1961 removed the legal basis for compulsory cultivation, marketing practices remained the same.

Like the cotton crop, sugar is produced to satisfy the needs of the market in Portugal. While raw cotton is exported to Portugal to be used by the Portuguese textile industry and reexported to Mozambique as cloth, sugar is refined in the province. Until the mid-1960's cashew nuts were exported unshelled to India where they were shelled and packed for export. A sharp rise in the world market encouraged the construction of a local shelling industry in Mozambique, and by 1971 the entire cashew-nut crop was being shelled and packed for export in the province.

Manufacturing. Industry in the province at large is confined to processing agricultural products for export and beverages, tobacco, and food for local consumption. Industrial progress is expected to stem from the expansion of the existing cement, fertilizer, and steel industries in the most heavily populated cities. The development of new factories in and around Lourenço Marques and Beira has produced a boom in the construction industry in these localities. This has drawn many Africans to the cities to participate in the modern sector of the economy.

Minerals. Mining has played an insignificant role in Mozambique's economy. Gold, copper, graphite, bauxite, and other minerals have been exploited on a small scale. Deposits of diamonds, asbestos, and manganese have been discovered close to the South African border. Partially explored uranium deposits also seem promising. Beryl, columbo-tantalite, and microlite—minerals used in the manufacture of hard steel and fatigue-resisting metal alloys—have been mined only in small amounts, but they have commanded very high prices per ton, since the world's supply is extremely limited. Finally, in the course of prospecting for oil, geologists have discovered natural gas deposits near Beira.

Transportation and Tourism. Transit trade from Mozambique's neighbors, passing over the railway tracks and through the ports of the province, accounts for one fifth of all foreign-exchange earnings. The province has some 2,300 miles (3,700 km) of state-owned, state-operated railways. Each of the major ports—Lourenço Marques, Beira, and Nacala—is the terminus of a railway system. Located on Delagoa Bay, Lourenço Marques serves Swaziland, the southern part of Rhodesia, and domestic traffic from the valleys of the Limpopo and other southern rivers. Another user is South Africa, which has an agreement with the Portuguese government to use Lourenço Marques for 47.5% of the Transvaal's external trade.

The Beira network serves the Tete and Sena sugar estates and carries the major part of Zambia's imports and exports, as well as traffic from Malawi and the northern section of Rhodesia.

The northern Mozambique rail line, newest and longest in the province, has its eastern terminus at Nacala, which provides a second outlet for landlocked Malawi. This line was a key element in an ambitious agricultural development scheme of the 1970's in northern Mozambique.

The province's road network is not so well developed. It has less than 1,000 miles (1,600

Produce from small, African-owned farms is often sold in city markets such as this one in Lourenço Marques.

PAT MILLER, FROM MONKMEYER

km) of paved highway and an entire road network of less than 20,000 miles (32,000 km).

Development of the tourist trade was left to private individuals until 1959, when the Centro de Informação e Tourismo (CITM) was created to coordinate, promote, and supervise all aspects of tourism in Mozambique. In the early 1970's some 250,000 visitors annually, mostly from South Africa and Rhodesia, spent $10–$13 million a year enjoying the province's beaches and game reserves. The government hoped to attract more tourists from Europe and America through increased air service to the three international air terminals in the major ports. Air transport in the interior shuttles regularly between the many airstrips scattered throughout Mozambique.

Labor Migration. Mozambique's Africans have long traveled in great numbers to South Africa to work in its mines, a fact that favorably affects Mozambique's foreign exchange position. Large-scale migration from southern Mozambique to the South African mines was regulated initially by the Witwatersrand Native Labor Association, formed in 1901 by South African mine owners. Under an agreement with the South African government, Mozambique provided a maximum of 100,000 contract workers per year, with the wages being paid to the government of Mozambique, except for a small advance to the worker. The government deducted appropriate taxes and paid the worker in escudos when he returned to Mozambique.

Because wages in South Africa are higher than those at home, there have always been a large number of illegal migrants to the mine fields. To stop this flow, government authorities fined those who recruited workers without their permission and dismissed any officials who became involved in this activity.

4. History and Government

When the Portuguese entered the Indian Ocean in the 16th century they found its trade controlled by the Arabs. In eastern Africa, Portuguese policy centered on securing the coastal ports from the Arabs and capturing the gold and silver mines of Manica, in the mountains northwest of modern Beira.

By 1520, Quelimane, Sofala, and Moçambique, as well as ports to the north, were in Portuguese hands. The lands behind Sofala and Quelimane and the plateaus of what is now Rhodesia were occupied by the Karanga, a part of the Shona people, whose paramount chief, called the monomotapa, was the overlord of all the tribes in the region. He lived at Zimbabwe (now in Rhodesia), a collection of stone forts and buildings near the gold mines.

Penetration of the Zambezi region began in 1531 when the Portuguese founded a town at Sena, about 125 miles (200 km) up the Zambezi River, to attract the local gold trade. Sena and its upstream neighbor, Tete, brought the Portuguese into closer contact with the peoples of the monomotapa's empire, with whom they traded and eventually fought.

Missionary activity was present from the beginning, and in 1628 the monomotapa was converted to Roman Catholicism, with a resulting expansion of European influence in the interior. This was halted in 1693 when Changamire, a vassal of the monomotapa, having routed the armies of his master, turned his attention to the Portuguese settlements. Many of these had fallen by the time of his death in 1695. The 18th century was a period of decline in Mozambique, even for the uniquely Mozambican *prazo* system, which encompassed much of the Portuguese held territory in the interior.

The Prazeros. The *prazo*, or plantation system, was Portugal's response to the problem of colonizing its southern African possessions at minimum expense to the crown. It originated in the 16th century when independent merchants and soldiers ventured into the interior to make their individual fortunes as allies of the monomotapa. When they were successful he rewarded them, as he did his African vassals, with grants of land. They became "chiefs" in his kingdom, taking African wives, building armies, and expanding their holdings outside Portuguese sovereignty.

In the 17th century the Portuguese crown sought to expand its control in the interior by recognizing the validity of the monomotapa's grants to Portuguese citizens. The government further extended the concept by granting *prazos de coroa* (crown grants) to subjects who had rendered distinguished service to the crown. The *prazeros* (concessionaires) were to cultivate and colonize the land and marry European women. They seldom lived up to any of these conditions.

On his holding, the *prazero* was the absolute master, taking the powers of the traditional African chief and extending them according to European concepts of private property and forced labor. These half-caste lords of the interior were the effective government of the land behind the coast and as such came to be feared by the Portuguese authorities. The *prazo* system was outlawed in 1832, 1838, 1841, and 1854, but the law failed to eliminate the *prazeros* or the system itself as a fact of life in Mozambique.

The first serious blow to Portuguese prestige in the 19th century came from the south. In the late 1820's, Nguni groups under the leadership of Soshangane crossed the Limpopo River into Mozambique and established the empire of Gaza in the highlands near the Save River. From this base, Soshangane raided in all directions. In 1833 he massacred the garrison at Lourenço Marques. Inhambane was attacked in 1834, and Sofala was burned in 1836. Tete and Sena bought peace with annual tribute, as did the *prazos* south of the Zambezi River. The main Nguni campaigns were those conducted against African peoples, who were incorporated into the empire.

Soshangane died in 1859 leaving an empire that was to trouble the Portuguese again in 1885, when his grandson, Gungunhana, became king of Gaza. Although he nominally acknowledged Portuguese sovereignty, Gungunhana negotiated with the British and ceded the mineral rights in his kingdom to the British South Africa Company, an action that was unacceptable to the Portuguese government. In 1894, nominal vassals of Gungunhana attacked Lourenço Marques. António Enes was sent from Lisbon to deal with the king. The last of the great Bantu monarchs of southern Africa was defeated by the man whose policies were to form the basis for the modern state of Mozambique.

During the 19th century the *prazeros* were a mixed blessing to the Portuguese government. Some kept the peace in the interior, others disregarded or actively opposed Portuguese interests. From the 1860's to the 1890's, Manuel António de Sousa (known as Gouveia), a trader with control of several *prazos* south of Sena, governed central

The Zambezi River is one of the major transport arteries of East Africa. At Tete, some 250 miles (400 km) upstream, a makeshift shallow-draft ferry regularly crosses the placid river.

DICK HUFFMAN, FROM MONKMEYER

Mozambique. From 1869 he fought for the Portuguese government in the Wars of the Bongas, which constituted the second great challenge to Portuguese authority in the 19th century. (Bonga was the colloquial name of any half-caste chief of the Zambezi Valley region.) The wars were directed specifically against three generations of the da Cruz family of Massangano, the largest *prazo* on the Zambezi. The Bougas fought from 1851 to 1887 to preserve their traditional independence from government authority and were finally crushed.

The Chartered Companies. Formed for the same reasons as the *prazos,* and yet envisioned as an alternative to them, three chartered companies were capitalized between 1888 and 1896. They were to provide the administrative and financial framework within which Portuguese authority would be established throughout Mozambique. By 1900 the three companies, all of which were dominated by foreign capital, controlled two thirds of the province's land area.

Charters were for periods of 25 to 50 years and guaranteed the company the right to exploit the natural and human resources of the grant, provided that they kept the peace and paid the proper revenues. The three companies were the Moçambique Company, operating in the central region of the province; the Zambesia Company, the most profitable of the three, in the Tete and Zambesia districts; and the Niassa Company in northwest Mozambique. The companies were active well into the 20th century. The last to surrender its power to the colonial government was the Moçambique Company, which finally capitulated in 1942.

The Influence of António Enes. Britain's successful attempt to annex territory claimed by Portugal, and the resulting Anglo-Portuguese Convention of 1891, fixing the boundaries between Mozambique and its British neighbors, was a turning point in the history of Portuguese Africa. Before 1890 interest had been at a low ebb. After 1890 it quickened as Portuguese forces defeated African and *prazero* chiefs in the interior. New policies were needed to deal with new situations. It was in this capacity that António Enes and the "Generation of 1895"—men whom he trained in Mozambique and who later served there and in Angola—shaped the future of Portuguese Africa.

Enes, a journalist, former member of the Portuguese parliament, and former overseas minister, was sent to Mozambique in 1891–1892 on a special mission to prepare a program of administrative reforms for the province. His book *Mozambique,* published in 1893, helped to provide a framework for modern Portuguese colonial policy. Enes stood for a practical approach to colonial questions, based on the needs of the individual provinces and emphasizing decentralized administration and provincial autonomy. Free trade, foreign capital, forced labor for Africans, and a new administrative apparatus were his minimum requirements for the new Mozambique.

His recommendations were incorporated into the Administrative Reform Act of 1907, which fixed the basic structure of provincial government. Enes believed that as long as the African remained in his traditional environment, he could not be the equal of the Portuguese. The Native Assistance Code of 1921 defined the *assimilado* system, the means by which Africans could become Portuguese.

Enes' theories were also reflected in the Colonial Act of 1930, enacted under the sponsorship of the future prime minister and strong man of Portugal, António de Oliveira Salazar, who served very briefly as minister of colonies in that year. It provided for the centralization of administrative authority in Lisbon and the economic development of the colonies through government planning and large-scale immigration of Portuguese settlers. The object of this and subsequent legislation was to tie the colonies closer to Portugal, a goal with which Enes would have agreed.

In 1951 the colony of Mozambique was declared an overseas province of Portugal, and in

FUJIHIRA, FROM MONKMEYER

Lourenço Marques, Mozambique's political and business capital, has acquired a contemporary look due to postwar residential and commercial building. At left is a group of new apartment houses.

1972 both Mozambique and Angola became overseas states.

Nationalist Movement. With the coming of independence to Tanganyika (now Tanzania) in 1961, an African nationalist movement seeking independence for Mozambique was based in Dar es Salaam. In 1962 the separate groups combined to form the Frente de Libertacão de Moçambique, or Mozambique Liberation Front (FRELIMO) under the leadership of Dr. Eduardo Chivambo Mondlane, a U. S.-educated sociologist and the son of a Thonga chief. FRELIMO received considerable international support, notably arms and other military equipment from eastern Europe and Communist China, and financial aid from the Organization of African Unity.

Open rebellion began on Sept. 25, 1964, when guerrillas crossed the Tanzanian border into Mozambique and attacked Portuguese military installations. Fighting was confined to the northwest Niassa district in the highlands near Lake Malawi (Nyasa) and the northeast Cabo Delgado district in the Makonde plateau, with sporadic activity near the Malawi and Zambian borders. On Feb. 3, 1969, Dr. Mondlane was assassinated in Dar es Salaam, but FRELIMO activities in Mozambique continued under his successor, Samora Moises Machel. A rival liberation group, the Mozambique Revolutionary Committee (COREMO), was also active in the early 1970's but eventually disappeared.

Independence. Early in 1974 the new revolutionary government in Portugal declared its intention to grant independence to Portugal's African provinces. Thus, on June 25, 1975, 470 years of colonial rule and ten years of guerrilla warfare ended as the independent People's Republic of Mozambique came into being with FRELIMO in political control and its leader, Samora Machel, sworn in as the first president.

Machel. President Machel (pronounced mä shel') was born in 1934 in the Limpopo Valley of southern Mozambique. He attended a Roman Catholic school for six years and later became a medical assistant in a Lourenço Marques hospital. After his introduction to Eduardo Mondlane in the early 1960's, he joined the FRELIMO headquarters in Dar es Salaam, received training in guerrilla warfare in Algeria, and returned to Tanzania to lead a guerrilla force of some 3,000 men. In September 1964 he was in charge of the initial FRELIMO raid on Mozambique that marked the beginning of the Mozambican war of liberation. About a year after Mondlane's assassination in 1969, the organization's congress elected Machel president of FRELIMO.

The New Government. The new Mozambique "popular democracy," strongly Marxist in its orientation, announced a constitution of 73 clauses that specified, in addition to a president, a council of ministers and a people's assembly of 210 members, of whom some would be chosen by FRELIMO's 42-member central committee, and others would be popularly elected after they had been nominated by FRELIMO. The land and natural resources are considered to be state property, and the state will govern the exploitation of all resources. Private property is permitted, provided it does not violate the state's interests.

It became clear in the new government's first days that a Marxist-Leninist program, adapted to Africa's needs, would be followed. First would come efforts to indoctrinate the population along Communist lines, eradicate political and economic opposition, modernize some ancient beliefs and practices of tribal life, and purge FRELIMO's ranks. During the years of guerrilla warfare, trained task forces of the party had worked to indoctrinate people in some of the "liberated" northern areas. Similar task forces would now be required to work in the southern part of the country, while at the same time "dynamic groups" of party members would be established in schools, businesses, and rural areas throughout Mozambique to see that the government's policies were followed. Eventually agriculture would be collectivized, and industry and trade would be nationalized as in other Communist countries.

BARBARA DUBINS*
California State University, San José

Bibliography

Abushire, David M., and Samuels, Michael A., *Portuguese Africa: A Handbook* (Praeger 1969).
Butler, Allison Herrick, *Area Handbook for Mozambique* (U. S. Government Printing Office 1969).
Chilcote, Ronald H., *Portuguese Africa* (Prentice-Hall 1967).
Duffy, James, *Portugal in Africa* (Penguin 1963).
Mondlane, Eduardo, *The Struggle for Mozambique* (Penguin 1969).

MOZAMBIQUE (Port. MOÇAMBIQUE), seaport of the Portuguese overseas province of Mozambique, situated on a coral island a mile and a half long and a quarter of a mile wide about three miles out from the shores of Mosuril Bay. Industries include the processing of oil seed and tobacco and the manufacture of soap. Mica, timber, and agricultural products from the interior are exported. The harbor will accommodate ships with a draft of 28 feet. There is an airport at Lumba on the mainland, and a railroad runs inland from here.

The town is picturesque, with numerous buildings from the 18th century. Outstanding are the former governor's palace and three forts, the best known of which is St. Sebastian, built 1508–1511 of stone brought from Portugal in the tiny vessels of the period. The town was visited by Vasco da Gama in 1498, and was captured by the Portuguese in 1508. Although it became important as the capital of Portuguese East Africa (Mozambique), its commercial activity diminished when the capital was transferred to Lourenço Marques in 1907. There is a sizable European colony, but the inhabitants are mostly Muslims. Pop. (1960) 12,166.

MOZAMBIQUE CHANNEL, chăn'ĕl, passage between the southeast coast of Africa and the island of Madagascar, an arm of the Indian Ocean. It is over 1,000 miles long from northeast to southwest, 530 miles wide at its southern entrance, 250 miles wide in the center, and nearly 600 miles wide at the northern entrance where the Comoro Islands (Iles Comores) lie. At one period a noted resort of pirates, it is an important lane for East African shipping. On its west shore, the Portuguese overseas province of Mozambique, are a number of harbors, including those of Beira, Lourenço Marques, Mozambique, Quelimane, Nampula, and Chinde.

MOZARABS, mōz-ăr'ăbz (from Ar. *musta'rib,* through Span. *mozárabe*), term applied to Spanish Christians who in medieval times lived in districts under Muslim rule and bore the stamp of Arab culture. Particularly under the early rulers, the Umayyads, they were treated with considerable tolerance. They lived under the authority of officials they chose from among themselves who were approved by the higher authorities; they had their own taxgatherers and judges who administered the Visigothic code. Most of them spoke Arabic, and many adopted Muslim names. In turn they influenced the Muslim society amid which they lived. Especially important were the Mozarab communities of Córdoba, Seville, and Toledo, Toledo being the residence of the metropolitan under the Umayyad caliphate. They played an important role in freeing Spain from Muslim control, and for generations afterward transmitted the heritage of Islamic culture at home and abroad.

PHILIP K. HITTI.

MOZART, mō'tsärt, **(Johann Georg) Leopold,** German musician: b. Augsburg, Germany, Nov. 14, 1719; d. Salzburg, Austria, May 28, 1787. Father and teacher of Wolfgang Amadeus Mozart, he was the son of a bookbinder. Originally intending to become a priest, in 1737 he went to Salzburg to study law, but in 1743 he joined the orchestra of the prince-archbishop of Salzburg as a violinist and later was promoted to court composer and assistant conductor. He won high repute as a teacher and composer, and possessed unusually versatile interests. In 1756 he published his *Violin School,* the first attempt to established a method for playing the violin. Although he composed a good deal of religious music, symphonies and concertos, pianoforte sonatas, and the like, he is remembered chiefly for the musical education of his son and for his management of Wolfgang's career, first as a child prodigy and later as a fully fledged musician.

MOZART, Wolfgang Amadeus (christened JOHANNES CHRYSOSTOMUS WOLFGANGUS THEOPHILUS), Austrian composer: b. Salzburg, Austria, Jan. 27, 1756; d. Vienna, Dec. 5, 1791. One of the greatest geniuses in the history of music, he was the son of (Johann Georg) Leopold Mozart. A child prodigy, he began to play idly on a clavier when only three, and when five composed simple pieces which his father wrote down. His sister Maria Anna ("Nannerl"), five years his senior, also was talented as a musical performer, and in 1762 their father displayed them, first in Munich and then in Vienna, where they played for the Holy Roman emperor Francis I and Maria Theresa. In 1763 some of the boy's clavier pieces were printed, and Leopold embarked with his wonder children on a concert tour through the German states and to Brussels and Paris. On Jan. 1, 1764, the travelers were invited by Louis XV to attend supper at Versailles. In April, visiting London, the children played before George III, and Wolfgang began a close friendship with the youngest son of Johann Sebastian Bach, Johann Christian, whose gallant musical style influenced his own. By this time the eight-year-old boy was composing prolifically in many forms.

Leaving England late in the summer of 1765, the Mozarts went to Holland, where both children fell seriously ill. After two Amsterdam concerts consisting largely of Wolfgang's instrumental compositions, they went on to Belgium, Paris, Switzerland, and Munich, where they dined with the elector of Bavaria, returning to Salzburg in November. There the Prince-Archbishop Sigismund von Schrattenbach, doubting Wolfgang's reputed talent for composition, tested it by keeping him at work under surveillance for one week. In May 1767 his Latin comedy *Apollo et Hyacinthus,* K.38[1], precursor of his great operas, was performed by students at the University of Salzburg.

During a visit to Vienna in the fall of 1767, Wolfgang and Nannerl were seriously ill with smallpox. In January 1768 they were received on friendly terms by Empress Maria Theresa. Her son, Joseph II, Holy Roman emperor, ordered an *opera buffa* from the boy; *La finta semplice,* K.51, was completed that spring, but not sung until May 1, 1769. Meanwhile, for the private theater of Leopold Mozart's friend, Franz (or Friedrich) Anton Mesmer (the physician after whom mesmerism was named), Wolfgang had composed a German operetta, *Bastien und Bastienne,* K.50, probably first performed in September 1768.

From December 1769 to March 1771, Leopold and Wolfgang were in Italy, where the boy's gifts won many honors. In July 1770, Wolfgang

[1] Mozart's compositions are identified by the numbers assigned to them in the catalogue originally prepared by Ludwig von Köchel (1862).

received the Order of the Golden Spur from Pope Clement XIV. At Milan, having passed a test of his operatic ability, Wolfgang was commissioned to compose an *opera seria;* the result was *Mitridate, rè di Ponto,* K.87, first sung in Milan on Dec. 26, 1770, running for 20 nights.

Remaining in Salzburg only from March 28 to Aug. 13, 1771, father and son returned to Italy. Wolfgang's dramatic serenata *Ascanio in Alba,* K.111, was performed at Milan, Oct. 17, 1771, during the ceremonies attending the marriage of Maria Theresa's son Archduke Ferdinand. Shortly after the Mozarts' return to Salzburg, Prince-Archbishop von Schrattenbach died; he was succeeded by the less easygoing Hieronymus von Colloredo, with whom both father and son were to have serious difficulties. Now 16, Wolfgang was pouring out symphonies, religious vocal pieces, divertimentos, chamber pieces, and other music in bewildering profusion. Late in 1772, visiting Italy for a third time, he heard his opera *Lucio Silla,* K.135, sung at Milan on December 26; his familiar motet *Exsultate, jubilate,* K.165, with the popular "Alleluia," was performed there in January 1773.

In July 1773, Leopold took Wolfgang to Vienna in the hope of a court appointment for him, but Maria Theresa, though receiving them graciously, made none. The Mozarts returned to Salzburg, remaining from October 1773 to December 1774, a period during which Wolfgang composed concertos for piano and for bassoon, masses, symphonies, serenades, and much else. Leopold and Wolfgang visited Munich late in 1774; Wolfgang's *La finta giardiniera,* K.196, an *opera buffa,* was staged there on Jan. 13, 1775. Back in Salzburg, he had to compose hurriedly a dramatic festival play for a visit of Maria Theresa's son Archduke Maximilian; this was *Il rè pastore,* K.208, first heard at Salzburg on April 23. During 1775, too, he composed all five of his violin concertos.

During 1776, passed wholly in Salzburg, the Mozarts began to suffer the increasing ill will resulting from the prince-archbishop's not entirely unjustified dislike of their spending so much time in travel. To that year and 1777 belong many fine compositions, including the *"Haffner" Serenade,* K.250. Wearying of the lack of official preferment, Wolfgang again obtained leave in 1777, setting out on September 23, this time accompanied by his mother because Leopold was forced to remain in Salzburg. The goal was Paris, but after several stops en route, the travelers reached Mannheim on October 30. In that home of an orchestra famed for its virtuosity, Wolfgang, now 22, fell in love with Aloysia Weber, the soprano daughter of Fridolin Weber, an indigent musician; her first cousin, not born until 1786, was the distinguished composer Karl Maria Friedrich Ernst von Weber. Wolfgang wanted to abandon the Paris trip, but Leopold wrote angrily from home, and the travelers proceeded to Paris, arriving on March 23, 1778. The French musical world was so happily involved in the famous "war" over the rival merits of Christoph Willibald von Gluck and Niccola Piccinni that Mozart's presence created little stir. Offered a subordinate post as court organist at Versailles, he rejected it. For the great dancer Jean Georges Noverre he composed the ballet *Les petits riens,* K. App. 10, produced on June 11, 1778. Frau Mozart was taken seriously ill in June and died on July 3, leaving Wolfgang alone in Paris, where he remained without success until September, when he returned to Mannheim. The court, and the Webers with it, had removed to Munich, and Leopold soon ordered Wolfgang to return to Salzburg, where their master seemed somewhat better disposed toward him. After stopping at Munich and again courting Aloysia Weber, although she had lost interest in him, Wolfgang reached Salzburg in January 1779. To that year belong many excellent works, including the familiar *Sinfonia concertante* for violin, viola, and orchestra, K.364.

Continuing to compose and to kick against the restraints of Salzburg life, Wolfgang was at home until November 1780, when he returned to Munich, this time to compose a commissioned *opera seria*—*Idomeneo,* K.366—for staging there. Its production on Jan. 29, 1781, opened a decisive year in his life. Commanded to join the prince-archbishop in Vienna in March, Wolfgang soon quarreled violently with him and resigned from his service. Finding the Weber family in Vienna, he boarded with them, this time falling in love with Aloysia's sister Constanze, to whom he was secretly betrothed before his morally outraged father ordered him to live elsewhere. In July he began the first of his great operas, *Die Entführung aus dem Serail,* K.384.

On July 16, 1782, *Die Entführung aus dem Serail* was sung in Vienna, and on August 4, disregarding his father's vigorously expressed advice, Mozart married Constanze Weber. During that month the great Gluck requested a special singing of *Die Entführung* so that he might hear it, and invited the newly married couple to dinner. Although the success of *Die Entführung* in German cities and Prague spread Mozart's fame, he now began to suffer the financial difficulties that dogged the remaining years of his life, often finding it necessary to support himself and Constanze meagerly on the proceeds of subscription concerts. A son born to them on June 17, 1783, Raimund Leopold, lived only two months. Wishing to present Constanze to his father, Mozart took her to Salzburg (July–October 1783), then stopped at Linz, where the *"Linz" Symphony,* K.425, was composed. Poverty, evidenced by borrowing from friends and fellow Freemasons, did not dry up his inspiration: these last, most difficult years were to witness his greatest achievements. His son Karl Thomas was born in September 1784. During a visit by Leopold Mozart to Vienna in 1785, (Franz) Joseph Haydn told the proud man that his son was the greatest composer known to him. In the fall of that year, Wolfgang began to compose *Le nozze di Figaro,* K.492, to a libretto by Lorenzo Da Ponte based on Pierre Augustin Caron de Beaumarchais' play *Le mariage de Figaro.* This superb *opera buffa* was first sung at Vienna on May 1, 1786; although triumphantly successful, it was withdrawn after only nine performances.

Continuing to pour out masterworks, Mozart suffered the death of another short-lived son, Johann Thomas Leopold, in November 1786. In January 1787 he visited Prague, where the great D major *"Prague" Symphony,* K.504, was played. Having been commissioned to compose an opera for Prague, Mozart accepted Da Ponte's suggestion of Don Juan as a subject. In May he was visited by the young Ludwig van Beethoven, in search of lessons. During that month, also, Leopold died at Salzburg, aged 67. Before the year was out, Wolfgang had completed *Don Giovanni,* K.527; had composed the familiar serenade *Eine kleine Nachtmüsik,* K.525; had witnessed the triumphant premiere of *Don Giovanni* at Prague on October 29; and had been appointed chamber musician and court composer by the emperor Joseph II. Also, Constanze had a daughter, Therese, who was to live only six months. Mozart's last three great symphonies (E flat, K.543; G minor, K.550; and C major *"Jupiter,"* K.551) were completed by August 1778, composed during a period when his trivial court post required him to turn out small dance pieces for official balls.

In 1789, visiting Leipzig, Mozart discussed the neglected music of Johann Sebastian Bach with Bach's successor as cantor at the St. Thomas Church. In Berlin, in April, he was presented to Frederick William II of Prussia. Constanze was now almost constantly unwell, and Mozart was sinking more deeply into debt. Yet his magnificent Clarinet Quintet, K.581, belongs to this time, and in the fall of 1789 he began to compose, on order from Joseph II, a new *opera buffa* –*Così fan tutte*–to a Da Ponte libretto, which was sung in Vienna on Jan. 26, 1790. Another short-lived daughter, Anna, was born in November 1789. When Joseph II died in February 1790 and was succeeded by Leopold II, Mozart vainly hoped for greater official recognition. Attending Leopold's coronation ceremonies at Frankfurt am Main, he played the solo piano part in what is known as the *"Coronation" Concerto,* K.537, which had been composed in 1788.

Mozart's position in Vienna did not improve. But some time during 1790 the singer-actor-impresario Emanuel Schikaneder had suggested their collaborating on a German fairy opera *Die Zauberflöte,* K.620. Mozart worked on the score from late 1790. His son Franz Xaver Wolfgang was born on July 26, 1791, by which time he had almost completed the opera, often said to contain his most deeply moving music. During that month a stranger approached Mozart to order a Requiem Mass for an anonymous patron. Mozart also was commissioned to compose an *opera seria* –*La clemenza di Tito,* K.621–for the coronation of Leopold II as king of Bohemia. Deferring the Requiem, he went to Prague, where *La clemenza* was sung on September 6. Some days later he returned to Vienna in very bad health, but completed his masterly Clarinet Concerto, K.622, on September 28. He himself conducted the first performance of *Die Zauberflöte* two days later. Returning to the Requiem, K.626, he worked feverishly, soon experiencing fainting spells. Realizing that he could not complete the Requiem on time, he entrusted final details of it to his pupil Franz Xaver Süssmayr. On December 4, Mozart became partially paralyzed, and on the following day he died, aged 35. He was buried in an unmarked grave.

Twentieth century musical taste and judgment tend to classify Mozart with Bach and Beethoven as one of the greatest of composers, both for the variety and purity of his musical ideas and for his utter mastery in handling them. His finest achievements probably are his operas, concertos, and chamber pieces of many varieties. Mozart has few peers in the art of creating living dramatic personalities and none in his ability to combine serenely polished surfaces with rich emotional suggestiveness. And, through Haydn and Beethoven, his influence on the evolution of Western music is nearly unparalleled.

HERBERT WEINSTOCK*
Coauthor of "Men of Music"

Mozart Bibliography

Blom, Eric, *Mozart* (Macmillan 1966).
Broder, Nathan, ed., *The Great Operas of Mozart* (Norton 1964).
Davenport, Marcia, *Mozart* (Scribner 1966).
Dent, Edward J., *Mozart's Operas: A Critical Study,* 2d ed. (Oxford 1947).
Einstein, Alfred, *Mozart: His Character, His Work* (Oxford 1945).
Fischer, Hans C., and Besch, Lutz, *Life of Mozart* (St. Martins 1969).
Forman, Denis, *Mozart's Concerto Form: The First Movements of the Piano Concertos* (Praeger 1972).
Holmes, Edward, *The Life of Mozart* (Vienna House 1974).
Hughes, Spike, *Famous Mozart Operas,* rev. ed. (Dover 1972).
Hutchings, Arthur, *Companion to Mozart's Piano Concertos,* 2d ed. (Oxford 1950).
King, A. Hyatt, *Mozart Chamber Music* (Univ. of Wash. Press 1969).
King, A. Hyatt, *Mozart in Retrospect: Studies in Criticism and Bibliography* (Oxford 1955).
Lang, Paul H., ed., *Creative World of Mozart* (Norton 1963).
Levey, Michael, *Life and Death of Mozart* (Stein & Day 1971).
Raeburn, Christopher, ed., *Mozart: The Man and His Works* (Vienna House 1974).
Rosen, Charles, *The Classical Style: Haydn, Mozart, and Beethoven* (Norton 1972).
Valentin, Erich, *Mozart and His World,* rev. ed. (Viking 1970).
Weiss, David, *The Assassination of Mozart* (Morrow 1970).
Young, Percy M., *Mozart* (David White 1966).

MUAWIYA I, mo͞o-ä'wi-yə (c. 602–680), was the first caliph of the Umayyad dynasty. He was born in Mecca, the son of a rich merchant of the Umayyad clan. His predecessor as caliph and ruler of the Arab empire was Mohammed's son-in-law Ali. Though Ali had been elected by the Muslims of Medina, others contested the election, including Muawiya, at that time governor of Syria. When Ali was assassinated in 661, Muawiya succeeded him as caliph.

Muawiya moved the capital from Medina to Damascus in Syria. He transformed the Arab empire into a centralized state with a more secular emphasis. He reorganized the army, created a navy, and attempted to take Asia Minor from the Byzantines. He failed, though he threatened Constantinople twice. His armies moved east into central Asia and west into Algeria.

Muawiya introduced the hereditary principle into the caliphate by nominating his son Yazid as his successor. An astute politician, he preferred to rule by conciliation rather than force.

MUCH ADO ABOUT NOTHING is a play by William Shakespeare, generally regarded as one of his greatest comedies.

Date and Sources. *Much Ado* was entered in the Stationers' Register in August 1600 and printed later that year as acted by "the Lord Chamberlaine his servants." Speech prefixes indicate that Will Kempe played the part of Dogberry the constable. Since Kempe left the Chamberlain's Men in 1599 and *Much Ado* is not mentioned in the list of Shakespeare's plays in Francis Meres' *Palladis Tamia* in 1598, it was probably written and acted within those dates.

For the plot, Shakespeare is most indebted to a tale in Matteo Bandello's *Novelle* (1554), which was freely translated by François de Belleforest in his *Histoires tragiques* (1574). Some details are borrowed from a similar narrative in Lodovico Ariosto's *Orlando furioso* (1516), adapted by Edmund Spenser in Book II of the *Faerie Queene* (1590) and translated into English by Sir John Harrington in 1591. The confusion of the constables, the sparring and reluctant lovers, and the shift of tone from a serious and emotional story to the more detached view of high comedy are Shakespeare's own.

Technique and Characters. Although *Much Ado* is grouped in time with the romantic comedies, it is much less romantic than most. The interest is not in the valor of the battle heroes nor in the usual disguisings, surprises, and suspense that form the attraction of the romantic tale. The so-called main plot is relatively unimportant—a means to an end. The audience learns of the discovery of the intrigue between Claudio and Don Pedro long before the characters, and knows that it is only a matter of time before wrongs will be righted. The assignation of Don Pedro and Hero is not even staged because the effect on the characters is more significant than the scene itself.

To make the conventionalized Claudio a romantic hero is to make him a cad. He is attracted by a pretty girl, inquires about her inheritance and her virtue, lets Don Pedro do his wooing, contracts a typically Renaissance *mariage de convenance*, and, along with Don Pedro, denounces at the most effective time the parties of the second part when he has reason to believe that Hero is unfaithful to him. When he learns his mistake, he agrees to another marriage by way of reparation. All of this is not to say, by any means, that Claudio's marriage to Hero will not be a happy one.

But the interest does not lie in this main plot. Rather, it lies in the characters that the persons and incidents of the main plot affect. The malapropist Dogberry and his blundering crew are not romantic, but thoroughly realistic. Their scenes, deliberately alternated with serious ones, diminish the engagement of the emotions. Sentiment gives way to witty language. It is characteristic that three quarters of the play is in prose.

As for Benedick and Beatrice, not only are they not romantic, they are antiromantic. They detest the pretensions of romantic love and swing to the opposite extreme. It is the more interesting that, despite their truly believed and frequently expressed opinions, they are really in love with each other. "A star danced" when Beatrice was born, and she has "a merry heart." But she cannot refrain from introducing Benedick's name into the conversation. Benedick "cannot woo in festival terms," but from the beginning shows his vulnerability by praising Beatrice's beauty. That they are so easily tricked into declarations of love is due less to the stratagem than to the self-realization that comes from it. Their final understanding of their emotions arises when they become involved in Hero's disgrace.

That Benedick and Beatrice are the center of the play is easily demonstrated. At its presentation at Whitehall in 1613, in connection with the festivities celebrating the marriage of the Princess Elizabeth (daughter of James I) and the count palatine, it was called not *Much Ado* but *Benedicte and Betteris*.

Stage History. From the time of David Garrick's revival in 1748, with himself as Benedick and Hannah Pritchard as Beatrice, the play has been frequently on the stage. The Benedicks have included John Henderson, John Philip Kemble, Charles Kemble, William Charles Macready, Charles Kean, and Edwin Booth. Sarah Siddons, Frances Abington, Dorothea Jordan, and Helena Modjeska have been famous Beatrices. Among the most notable of later productions were Sir Henry Irving's in London in 1882, in which Ellen Terry's Beatrice excited superlatives; that at Stratford-upon-Avon in 1950, with John Gielgud and Peggy Ashcroft; and Gielgud's production in New York in 1959, with Margaret Leighton.

ROBERT HAMILTON BALL*
Queens College

Bibliography

Texts of *Much Ado* are available in editions of Shakespeare's complete works by George Lyman Kittridge (Ginn 1936) and G. B. Harrison (Harcourt 1960), and in separate form in the Arden Shakespeare (Harvard Univ. Press) and Cambridge Shakespeare (Cambridge).
Charlton, H. B., *Shakespearean Comedy* (Cambridge 1938).
Frye, Northrop, *A Natural Perspective* (Columbia Univ. Press 1965).
Muir, Kenneth, ed., *Shakespeare, the Comedies* (Prentice-Hall 1965).
Parrot, Thomas M., *Shakespearean Comedy* (Oxford 1949).

MUCKRAKERS, a group of early 20th century American journalists who wrote detailed, factual accounts of the political and economic corruption caused by the power of big business (the "Interests," the "System," the "Trusts") in the United States. They were given the name in 1906 by President Theodore Roosevelt, who borrowed it from John Bunyan's 17th century Puritan allegory *Pilgrim's Progress*. Bunyan wrote of a man "with the Muck-rake in his hand," who would rather rake filth than look upward to nobler things. Roosevelt said, "Men with the muck-rakes are often indispensable to the well-being of society; but only if they know when to stop raking the muck." He feared that the muckrakers, although they helped build public support for many of his reforms, were stirring up dangerous popular unrest.

Some of the muckrakers resented the title; others wore it proudly. All of them, however, believed they were doing something important for American society, and they were. They exerted their influence in election campaigns and played a major role in raising public support for the passage of the federal Pure Food and Drug Act, Meat Inspection Act, and Hepburn (railroad regulation) Act (all 1906). Most importantly, by combining moral indignation and hard fact, they helped prepare the American public for social reform and regulatory legislation.

The Muckraker Era. Although there had been occasional earlier exposés of graft, muckraking did not emerge as a movement until the 1900's, when a revolution in printing technology, such as the development of the halftone process, made it possible to produce inexpensive, profusely illustrated popular magazines.

Among a group of imaginative, hustling editors was S. S. McClure, who founded *McClure's Magazine* in 1893. In November 1902, *McClure's* began to publish a series of exposé articles by Ida M. Tarbell about the Standard Oil Company. In the January 1903 issue, the magazine also carried pieces on municipal and labor corruption, and, in an editorial, McClure called attention to this type of coverage. He thus sparked a movement, and soon the popular magazines were flooded with exposés. Between 1902 and 1912, the muckrake decade, more than 1,000 such articles were published. In addition to *McClure's*, the regular muckrake magazines included *Everybody's*, *Collier's*, *Cosmopolitan*, the *American*, *Hampton's*, and *Pearson's*, with occasional pieces appearing in the *Ladies' Home Journal* and *Woman's Home Companion*.

Ida Tarbell, whose Standard Oil series was published in book form as *The History of the Standard Oil Company* in 1904, was only one of the first of a distinguished roster of reform journalists. Notable among them was Lincoln Steffens, who wrote on city and state politics (*The Shame of the Cities*, 1904; *The Struggle for Self-Government*, 1906). Steffens' *Autobiography* (1931) provides an illuminating account of the muckrake philosophy.

The muckrakers treated a wide spectrum of abuses. Thomas W. Lawson wrote about insurance and stock manipulation (*Frenzied Finance*, 1905); David Graham Phillips, senatorial corruption (*The Treason of the Senate*, first published in book form in 1964); Samuel Hopkins Adams, patent medicines (*The Great American Fraud*, 1906); and Ray Stannard Baker, racial discrimination (*Following the Color Line*, 1908). The novelist Upton Sinclair also took up the muckrake and published *The Jungle* (1906), a sensational condemnation of the meat-packing industry.

Later Muckraking. The year 1912 is regarded as the end of the muckrake era. People seemed to tire of continual exposés, and many of the magazines fell under the control of financial interests that shifted them away from reform. However, muckraking did not die. Small-circulation political journals, among them the *Nation* and the *New Republic*, continued in the tradition.

More significantly, after World War II, newspapers and television revived mass-media muckraking. Syndicated columnists, such as Jack Anderson, reached nationwide audiences, and the Washington *Post*, New York *Times*, and other major newspapers created investigative reporting teams. (One was Bob Woodward and Carl Bernstein, whose articles in the *Post* helped bare the Watergate scandal.) On television, documentaries treated such subjects as the plight of migratory workers, the abuse of publicity by the Pentagon to influence public opinion, consumer problems, and environmental issues. Among the products of the "new muckraking" was Nader's Raiders, a public-interest group established by Ralph Nader, whose *Unsafe at Any Speed* (1965) forced reforms on the automobile industry. In the closing decades of the 20th century, muckraking seemed as much alive as it had in the beginning.

David M. Chalmers
Author of "The Muckrake Years"

Further Reading: Chalmers, David M., *The Muckrake Years* (Van Nostrand–Reinhold 1974); Filler, Louis, *Crusaders for American Liberalism* (Kent State Univ. Press 1964).

MUCOUS MEMBRANE. See Membrane.

MUCUS, mū'kəs, a sticky viscous fluid that serves as a lubricating and protective coating of the mucous membranes. It consists of a suspension of mucin, water, inorganic salts, and cells. Mucin is a sulfate-containing glycoprotein produced by several types of cells, known as mucous cells, which occur in mucous membranes.

Mucous cells occur from one end of the digestive tract to the other. In the mouth a large number of mucous cells are clustered on the undersurface of the tongue and in the salivary glands. Mucus produced by these cells helps soften and lubricate food to facilitate swallowing. Mucous cells are especially numerous in the stomach, where the mucus they secrete may protect the stomach from the protein-digesting enzyme pepsin. Mucous cells in the nasal passages help wash out harmful materials from inhaled air. Mucous cells do not occur in most of the mucous membrane that lines the genital and urinary tracts.

MUD DAUBER, any of several nonsocial, thread-waisted wasps (family Sphecidae) that build mud nests, usually attached to the walls of buildings or other sheltered sites. One of the most common is the yellow mud dauber (*Sceliphron cementarium*), whose nest consists of several tubular rows of cells placed side by side. Before each cell is sealed off, it is provisioned with spiders paralyzed by the wasp's sting, and an egg is laid in the cell. After hatching, the larva feeds on the paralyzed spiders.

The blue mud dauber (*Chalybion californicum*) does not build its own nests. Instead, it digs out, cleans, and restocks nests of yellow mud daubers for its own eggs. The organ-pipe mud dauber (*Trypoxylon*) builds several parallel and contiguous tubes, which somewhat resemble organ pipes.

MUD PUPPY, any of five species of salamanders found in lakes, ponds, rivers, and streams in North America. The most common species, *Necturus maculosus*, is found in southern parts of Canada and most of the United States east of the Rocky Mountains. The other four, including *N. alabamensis*, are found in southern states.

The mud puppy, sometimes called a water dog, ranges in length from 7 to 17 inches (18–43 cm). It has a somewhat doglike flattened head with purplish external gills lying just behind the head. The slimy body is brownish with darker spots, and the flat tail has an orange tint. There are four short legs, each with four toes.

Mud puppies usually stay in water near water plants and remain active the year round. They eat fish eggs and small water animals such as crayfish. The female lays eggs underwater in the spring. The young are about 1 inch (2.5 cm) long. See also Salamander.

MUD TURTLE, any of various small freshwater turtles, genus *Kinosternon*, found in the United States and in central and South America. The common mud turtle, subspecies *K. subrubrum subrubrum*, has a head with yellowish spots; a smooth unmarked brown or olive carapace, or back shell, about 4 inches (10 cm) long; and a brown or yellow plastron, or belly shell. It is found in the eastern United States from New York to Alabama. The Mississippi mud turtle, found in Arkansas, Louisiana, and adjacent states, and the Florida mud turtle of peninsular Florida, also are subspecies of *K. subrubrum*.

The yellow mud turtle, *K. flavescens flavescens*, has bright yellow markings on its head and neck. It is found in the south central states and in northern Mexico. The Sonoran mud turtle, *K. sonoriense* Le Conte, is relatively large, with a carapace up to about 5.5 inches (14 cm) long. Its head, neck, and limbs are mottled dark and light. It is found along the U. S.–Mexican border from California to southwest Texas. The striped mud turtle, *K. baurii baurii*, has three dull yellow longitudinal stripes on its carapace and two yellow stripes on each side of its head. It is found in Florida.

Mud turtles and musk turtles, genus *Sternotherus*, are in the family *Kinosternidae*.

MUDD, Samuel (1833–1883), American physician. He was born in Charles county, Md. A Confederate sympathizer, he practiced in Maryland during the Civil War. Early on the morning of April 15, 1865, the actor John Wilkes Booth came to his home and awakened him. Booth had shot President Lincoln at Ford's Theater in Washington and had broken his leg leaping to the stage from the president's box. Mudd had known Booth but later said he did not recognize him that morning. He set Booth's leg, and Booth left.

Mudd, who protested his innocence, was charged with conspiracy in the death of Lincoln—as an accessory after the fact—and convicted by a military court. He was sentenced to life in prison and sent to Fort Jefferson in the Dry Tortugas. He tried to escape and was kept in chains for two years. During a yellow fever epidemic, he saved the lives of many guards and prisoners. President Andrew Johnson pardoned him in 1869. He died in Maryland in 1883.

In later years, Mudd's grandson and others tried, with some success, to exonerate him.

Further Reading: Carter, Samuel, *The Riddle of Dr. Mudd* (Putnam 1974).

MUDSKIPPER, any of several species of gobies, fishes that spend much of their life on land. Mudskippers are about 6–8 inches (15–20 cm) long. They live in mud burrows in tidal mangrove swamps in tropical Africa, southeast Asia, and Oceania. Mudskippers spend at least three quarters of their time on shore, walking, jumping, and even climbing the roots of mangroves in search of insects to eat. They move with the aid of long, leglike pectoral fins. In many species the pelvic fins are also modified into leglike appendages.

Because the mudskipper is a fish, it needs water for breathing even when on land. It carries water for this purpose in two pulpy reservoirs above the gills. The mudskipper's large round eyes are on the end of short stalks, which may be retracted into the eye sockets. The eyes move independently and can see in all directions, as well under water as above.

Mudskippers belong to the genus *Periophthalmus*. The name mudskipper is sometimes applied to two other amphibious genera of gobies, *Boleophthalmus* and *Scartelaos*.

MUEZZIN, mū-ez′in, one who calls the Muslim faithful to prayer, usually from a minaret. The muezzin calls them to the five daily prayers and the congregational service at noon on Friday. The call of orthodox Islam, always in Arabic, consists of seven formulas: God is most great (repeated four times); I testify there is no god whatever but God (twice); I testify Mohammed is the apostle of God (twice); Come to prayer (twice); Come to salvation (twice); God is most great; there is no God whatever but God.

The main qualification of a muezzin is a melodious and far-reaching voice. The earliest muezzin was the Prophet Mohammed's Christian Abyssinian slave Bilal, who called from the roof of the humble prayer house in Medina. The muezzin has been replaced by loudspeakers in many cities today.

Philip K. Hitti
Author of "History of the Arabs"

MUFFLER, a device for reducing noise propagated by a moving stream of gas. Although mufflers are used to reduce noise from such sources as air compressors, aircraft engines, ventilating systems, and industrial plants, their most important use is the reduction of exhaust-gas noise from an internal-combustion engine in an automobile or other motor vehicle.

Every time an automobile engine fires there is an explosion. The explosions produce irregular high-pressure sound waves with peaks at various frequencies over the range from about 40 to 4,000 Hertz. These sound waves and the exhaust gases travel through the exhaust manifold and exhaust pipe to the muffler, which discharges the exhaust through a tail pipe to the atmosphere.

A typical present-day automobile muffler is shown in the cutaway diagram. Its shell is an oval steel can roughly 20 inches (50 cm) long, 10 inches (25 cm) wide, and 6 inches (15 cm) high. It contains three perforated steel tubes, two short tuning tubes, and five chambers separated by steel partitions. The combination of tubes and chambers acts as a broad-band acoustic filter that smooths sound-pressure peaks within the frequency range from 40 to 4,000 Hertz.

In the muffler illustrated most of the sound attenuation occurs in the middle chamber, where sound peaks are smoothed by causing interference of the sound waves from the perforated tubes. A single muffler reduces the sound-pressure level of the noisiest parts of the exhaust-noise spectrum roughly from 90 to 60 decibels, a thousandfold decrease. Some expensive cars have a dual exhaust and four mufflers, making the exhaust very quiet. See also Noise Control.

In this "reverse-flow" muffler, exhaust gases enter on the left, pass back and forth through the three midsection tubes, and exit on the right. Perforations (exposed in bottom cutaway) filter out the higher frequencies. Resonator sections at both ends contain short tuning tubes that reduce the lower frequencies.

MAREMONT CORP.

MUFTI, muf′tē, a Muslim official authorized to give a formal legal opinion. Normally, the opinion is offered on a question submitted by a judge or a believer. It is rendered in precise accordance with fixed precedent or as an exposition of canon law, rather than in accordance with the mufti's private judgment, and is binding on the inquirer. In the mid-19th century, as canon law became more restricted, the mufti's jurisdiction became more circumscribed.

The office of mufti frequently assumed great political importance, as in the case of Hajj Amin al-Husseini, grand mufti of Jerusalem, who resisted Jewish migration into Palestine, just before World War II, and during the war sought to ally the Arabs with the Axis powers.

MUGHUL DYNASTY, mo͝o-gul′, Muslim rulers of large parts of India. The name Mughul, or Mogul, is Persian for Mongol. The dynasty was founded in 1526 by Babur, and under his grandson Akbar (reigned 1556–1605) reached its pinnacle of greatness. Bahadur Shah II, the last Mughul emperor, was deposed in 1857.

MUGWUMP, is a term originating during the U. S. presidential campaign of 1884 between Grover Cleveland and James Blaine. The word derives from *mugquomp*, the Algonkian term for "big chief," which John Eliot used instead of "leader" when he translated the Bible for the Indians (1663). Charles Dana, editor of the New York *Sun*, applied it to those who deserted the Republican ranks to vote for Cleveland, implying that they felt themselves above party affiliations. The term is still often used for members of a party who vote for the opposing party.

MUHAMMAD. See MOHAMMED.

MUHAMMAD, mo͝o-ham′əd, **Elijah** (1897–1975), American Black Muslim leader. He was born Elijah Poole on Oct. 10, 1897, near Sandersville, Ga., one of 13 children of an itinerant Baptist preacher, and was educated to the fourth grade in the schools of rural Georgia. In 1919 he married Clara Evans, and in 1923 he took his wife and children to live in Detroit, where, for the next six years, he worked in industrial plants. From 1929 to 1931, Poole was on relief, an experience that seems to have been reflected in his later hostility toward any form of public assistance and in his emphasis on the economic program for the uplift of Black Muslims.

In 1931, Poole met Wali Farad, who as "Prophet Farad" had established the first Temple of Islam in Detroit. Poole soon became one of the most devoted followers of Farad, who eventually named him "First Minister of Islam," relieved him of his "slave name" Poole, and restored his "true Muslim name," Muhammad.

When Farad disappeared in 1934, Muhammad assumed the title of Messenger of Allah and became leader of the Nation of Islam. He was arrested in 1942 and sentenced to five years in federal prison for encouraging his followers to refuse to register for the draft during World War II. He was released in 1946, and the movement spread rapidly thereafter. He died in Chicago, Ill., on Feb. 25, 1975, and was succeeded by his son Wallace D. Muhammad. See also BLACK MUSLIMS.

C. ERIC LINCOLN
Author of "The Black Muslims in America"

MUHAMMAD AHMAD AL-MAHDI. See MOHAMMED AHMED.

MUHAMMAD ALI, viceroy of Egypt. See MOHAMMED ALI.

MUHAMMAD ALI, American boxer. See ALI, MUHAMMAD.

MUHLENBERG, mū′lən-bûrg, **Frederick Augustus Conrad** (1750–1801), American clergyman and political leader, who was the first speaker of the U. S. House of Representatives. He was born in Trappe, Pa., on Jan. 1, 1750, the second son of Heinrich Melchior Muhlenberg. After studying in Halle, Germany, he was ordained in Pennsylvania in 1770.

Muhlenberg served as pastor of Lutheran churches in Pennsylvania and New York, but his sympathy with the colonial cause soon led him to take an active part in political affairs. He was a Pennsylvania delegate to the Continental Congress (1779–1780), speaker of the state General Assembly (1780–1783), and presided over the state convention that ratified the federal Constitution (1787). A Federalist member of Congress from 1789 to 1797, he served as speaker of the House of Representatives in the first and third Congresses. He died in Lancaster, Pa., on June 4, 1801.

MUHLENBERG, mū′lən-bûrg, **Heinrich Melchior** (1711–1787), German-American clergyman, considered the founder of the Lutheran Church in America. He was born in Einbeck, Hannover, Germany, on Sept. 6, 1711. After studying theology at the universities of Göttingen and Halle, he was ordained in 1739.

Muhlenberg accepted a call in 1741 to become a missionary to the Lutheran congregations of Pennsylvania in Philadelphia, Trappe, and New Hanover. At that time the Lutherans in the United States were unorganized and without pastors, and many of their religious meetings were conducted by laymen. Muhlenberg was determined to establish union and order in the church.

Although pastor only to the three congregations that had summoned him, he preached extensively along the eastern seaboard. He visited congregations scattered from the Hudson River to the Potomac. Muhlenberg recruited new ministers from Germany and helped establish a native ministry that included several of his sons. He organized the first Lutheran synod in the United States in 1748. The synod greatly aided the growth of the Lutheran Church.

Muhlenberg's influence was felt in most of the original 13 colonies. He was instrumental in building new churches and schools and secured financial assistance from Europe. Declining health and the outbreak of the American Revolution led to his partial retirement, but he remained a prominent leader of the church. He died in Trappe, Pa., on Oct. 7, 1787.

MUHLENBERG, mū′lən-bûrg, **John Peter Gabriel** (1746–1807), American clergyman and patriot. He was born in Trappe, Pa., on Oct. 1, 1746, and died near Philadelphia on Oct. 1, 1807. The eldest son of Heinrich Melchior Muhlenberg, he studied for the ministry at Halle, Germany.

Muhlenberg became pastor of the Lutheran churches in Bedminster and New Germantown, N. J., in 1769, and in Woodstock, Va., in 1771.

Finding that, in order to enforce the payment of tithes, he had to be ordained in the Episcopal Church, he was ordained a priest in England.

Muhlenberg was chairman of the Shenandoah county committee of safety and in 1774 became a member of the Virginia House of Burgesses. At Washington's request he was made a colonel in the Continental Army. His last sermon was on the duties men owe their country; and saying, "There is a time for all things—a time to preach and a time to fight—and now is the time to fight," he stripped off his gown after the service, appeared in full uniform, called for recruits, and enrolled about 300 of the parishioners. He participated in several battles and was made brigadier general in 1777 and major general at the close of the Revolution.

After the war he moved to Pennsylvania, where he was elected a member of the supreme executive council. In 1785 he became vice president of Pennsylvania. He served as representative in Congress from 1789 to 1795 and from 1799 to 1801. In 1801 he was elected U. S. senator, but he soon resigned and was appointed supervisor of revenue for Philadelphia. From 1802 he held the office of collector of the port of Philadelphia.

MUHLENBERG, mū'lən-bûrg, **William Augustus,** American clergyman: b. Philadelphia, Pa., Sept. 16, 1796; d. New York, N. Y., April 8, 1877. He was a grandson of Frederick A. C. Muhlenberg. After graduating from the University of Pennsylvania, he was ordained a deacon of the Episcopal Church in 1817 and a priest three years later. He became assistant to the rector, Bishop White, of St. Peter's and St. James' parishes. In 1821 he went to Lancaster, Pa., becoming rector of St. James' Church, and established there the first public school in the state outside of Philadelphia.

Muhlenberg moved in 1826 to Flushing, Long Island, where in 1828 he founded a high school (later St. Paul's College). He served as its principal until 1846, when he was appointed rector of New York City's Church of the Holy Communion, built by his sister. He launched the drive to raise funds with which St. Luke's Hospital was built (1858) on 54th Street between Fifth and Sixth avenues, and he became its first superintendent and pastor. His last important accomplishments included the founding of the St. Johnland Christian industrial community on the north shore of Long Island and (1852) the organization of the first U.S. Protestant sisterhood.

Muhlenberg wrote several well-known hymns, including *I Would Not Live Alway, Like Noah's Weary Dove,* and *Shout the Glad Tidings.*

MUHLENBERG COLLEGE, mū'lən-bûrg, is a private, coeducational, liberal arts institution in Allentown, Pa., affiliated with the Lutheran Church. Established in 1848 as Allentown Seminary, it was incorporated in 1864 as Allentown Collegiate Institute and Military Academy and was given its present name in 1867 when instruction began at the college level.

Studies leading to a bachelor of arts degree are offered in languages, philosophy, physical education, and the natural and social sciences. The college has cooperative programs in engineering with Columbia University, the University of Pennsylvania, and the Massachusetts Institute of Technology, as well as in forestry with Duke University.

MÜHLHAUSEN, mül-hou'zən, is an industrial city in East Germany, in Thuringia. It is situated in a fertile district on the Unstrut River, 30 miles northwest of Erfurt. Mühlhausen has cotton and paper mills, metalworks, and dyeing and tanning plants. It also manufactures electrical equipment, shoes, and furniture.

The city has many interesting buildings, including two early churches and a 17th century town hall. The Anabaptist Thomas Münzer, a leader in the Peasants' War, had his headquarters here and was executed nearby in 1525. The town became part of Prussia in 1815. Population: (1971) 45,385.

MUIR, Edwin (1887–1959), Scottish poet. He was born in Deerness, Orkney Islands, Scotland, on May 15, 1887. After attending an Orkney school, he worked as an office clerk. In 1919 he married Willa Anderson and became a journalist in London for two years. *First Poems* was published in 1925. He later served as director of the British Institute in Rome (1949); as warden of Newbattle Abbey College, Dalkeith, Scotland (1950–1955); and as professor of poetry at Harvard (1955–1956). He died in Cambridge, England, on Jan. 3, 1959.

Muir's poems are traditional in form and strive for no innovative effects. Instead, they have a quiet naturalness that conveys Muir's personal vision, a search for a spiritual universality. Volumes include *The Labyrinth* (1949) and *Collected Poems, 1921–1951* (1952). Muir also wrote several novels and critical studies and, with his wife, translated works by Franz Kafka. An *Autobiography* appeared in 1954.

MUIR, mūr, **John,** American naturalist and explorer: b. Dunbar, Scotland, April 21, 1838; d. Los Angeles, Calif., Dec. 24, 1914. He went to the United States in 1849 with his father, who settled near Fox River, Wis. Muir entered the University of Wisconsin when he was 21 and, after a special course of four years, began a series of lonely journeys through Canada, the eastern United States, the West, and the South. In 1868, after visiting the Yosemite Valley, he made it his main central camp for six years while studying the forests and glaciers of the Sierra Nevada. He discovered 65 residual glaciers in the High Sierra.

Muir made his first trip to Alaska in 1879, discovered Glacier Bay and Muir Glacier (named after him), and explored some of the upper courses of the Yukon and Mackenzie rivers. In 1880 he accompanied the De Long search expedition to the Arctic, and in 1903–1904 he traveled in the Caucasus, Siberia, Manchuria, Japan, India, Egypt, Australia, and New Zealand.

For newspapers and periodicals, Muir wrote many articles attacking the wastage of the nation's forest resources and urging the formation of national parks. Partly as a result of his efforts, federal conservation laws were passed and both the Sequoia and Yosemite national parks were created.

Among the books that Muir wrote are *The Mountains of California* (1894); *Our National Parks* (1901); *Stickeen* (1909); *My First Summer in the Sierra* (1911); *The Yosemite* (1912); *Story of My Boyhood and Youth* (1913); and the posthumous *Travels in Alaska* (1915); *The Cruise of the Corwin* (1917); and *Steep Trails* (1918).

MUIR, Sir **William,** Scottish administrator and Arabic scholar: b. Glasgow, Scotland, April 27, 1819; d. Edinburgh, July 11, 1905. He was the brother of the Sanskrit scholar John Muir. He entered the Indian civil service at 18, became secretary of the government of the North-West Provinces, and during the Sepoy Mutiny (1857) was in charge of the intelligence department at Agra. He was lieutenant governor of the North-West Provinces from 1868 to 1874, a member of the viceroy's council from 1874 to 1876, and, after returning to England, sat on the Council of India from 1876 to 1885. He was principal of the University of Edinburg from 1885 until his death.

In addition to his career as a public servant, Muir won a wide reputation for his Islamic scholarship. He wrote a 4-volume *Life of Mahomet –History of Islam to the Era of the Hegira* (1858–1861), based on the original manuscripts of Arab historians of the 9th century A. D.

MUIR WOODS NATIONAL MONUMENT. This national monument preserves the only stand of redwoods (*Sequoia sempervirens*) in the national park system of the United States. The monument lies at an elevation of 156 feet and at the south foot of Mount Tamalpais, 3 miles inland from the Pacific Ocean and 10 miles north of the Golden Gate Bridge, and contains 491 acres of federal lands.

This area was donated to the United States in 1907 by Congressman William Kent and his wife, Elizabeth Thacher Kent. At their request, it was named in honor of John Muir, noted traveler, naturalist, and writer. The national monument was established in 1908 by presidential proclamation.

Visitors to the west coast often confuse the redwoods of the coast with the giant redwood (*Sequoia gigantea*) of the Sierra. The virgin stand of redwoods found in Muir Woods grows in this coastal region, which extends from 125 miles south to the southwest corner of Oregon.

The tallest redwood in the monument is 246 feet high, 17 feet in diameter, and its age is estimated to be 1,800 years. However, there are larger representatives of this species north of the monument. The Founders Tree in Humboldt State Park is 364 feet high, and its largest diameter is about 20 feet. This species of redwood is known to exceed 2,000 years in age.

Fred M. Martischang

MUJIBUR RAHMAN, mo͞o′jē-bər rä′män, **Sheikh** (1920–1975), first prime minister of Bangladesh. He was born in Tungipara, East Bengal, on March 17, 1920. As a teenage anti-British agitator, he suffered the first of several prison terms for political insurgency. After attending college in Calcutta, he returned to East Bengal (part of newly independent Pakistan) to study at the University of Dacca. At that time the Bengalis, the majority people of East Pakistan—in fact, of Pakistan as a whole—were dominated by the Punjabis of West Pakistan. In 1949 he was a cofounder of the Awami (People's) League, the nation's first opposition party.

By 1970, Sheikh Mujib, as he was known to his people, had become the leader of the Awami League. In that year his party, favoring the virtual independence of East Pakistan, won a majority in the National Assembly. But early in 1971, President Yahya Khan canceled the election result, imprisoned Mujib, and ordered troops to Dacca. With the defeat of Yahya Khan's army in East Pakistan in December, Yahya Khan's successor, Zulfikar Ali Bhutto, released Mujib, who had narrowly escaped execution. Mujib returned to Dacca on Jan. 10, 1972, as president of Bangladesh. Two days later he proclaimed a new, British-style constitution and resigned as president to become prime minister.

Early in 1975, Mujib amended the constitution, adopted the title of president again, instituted ,press censorship, and assumed absolute executive authority. However, on Aug. 15 he was killed in a coup d'etat in Dacca, led by a cabinet minister, Khondakar Moshtaque Ahmed.

MUKDEN, mo͝ok′den′ (Chin. Shenyang, shun′-yäng′), city, China, in Manchuria, capital of Liaoning Province, about 400 miles east-northeast of Peking, on the Hun Ho, a tributary of the Liao Ho. Mukden is one of China's largest industrial centers, situated in the southern part of the Manchurian plain, 100 miles from the Yellow Sea. It is the heart of an industrial area, including the coal and oil-shale center of Fushun (east), the coal and steel city of Penki (southeast) and the large steel center of Anshan (southwest). Mukden itself is primarily a manufacturing center for rolling stock, machine tools, electrical equipment, and chemicals. It is also the processing center for the rich farming region of southern Manchuria, which produces wheat, corn, and soybeans. Mukden is one of the cultural centers of Manchuria.

The layout of Mukden reflects the city's history. The city consists of the old Chinese town, adjoined by the arsenal district on the east and the new Japanese-built city and industrial area in the west. The old Chinese city, once surrounded by a 10-mile-long earthen wall, contains the brick-walled inner city with a former imperial palace and administrative offices. The inner city was arranged on a plan patterned after

Entrance to the Manchu tombs in Mukden

EWING GALLOWAY

Eastfoto

Plant producing heavy iron and steel machinery in Mukden.

that of Peking. The arsenal district is an old Chinese industrial area with an ordnance plant and other factories. West of the Chinese city, and extending to the main railroad station, is the new Japanese-built section of Mukden, with broad, straight thoroughfares and modern office buildings. Beyond the railroad is the West Mukden zone, a vast industrial and residential section developed under Japanese rule and housing most of the city's modern manufacturing industries. The railroad station is the hub of a large complex of marshaling yards, freight stations, and other facilities making Mukden one of the foremost railroad centers of China. It is linked by heavily traveled main lines with Harbin in northern Manchuria, Talien (Dairen) on the Liaotung Peninsula, Peking in north China proper, and with North Korea.

History.—The name Shen, which occurs in Shenyang, the city's modern Chinese name, dates from the Liao (Khitan) dynasty of the 12th century. The city was an early center of Chinese colonization in southern Manchuria until captured by the rising Manchus in the 16th century. The Manchus, who established their capital here in 1625, named the city Mukden, which is a Manchu name. After their conquest of China, the Manchus moved their capital to Peking in 1644, but many of the Manchu emperors still have their tombs in Mukden in the city's northern outskirts. The Manchus later gave the city the Chinese name Fengtien (Honored Heaven) and the title Shengking (Flourishing Capital). These names were also applied to the province of which Mukden became the capital, and which was later named Liaoning. Mukden's modern development began about 1900 when the Russians acquired railroad-building rights in Manchuria and made Mukden the hub of the newly constructed railroad system. A decisive battle was won here in 1905 by the Japanese in the Russo-Japanese War, after which Russian interests in Mukden and the rest of southern Manchuria were taken over by the Japanese. After the fall of the Manchu dynasty and the proclamation of the Chinese Republic in 1911, the city regained its ancient Chinese name, Shenyang, although foreigners continued to call it Mukden. The city became the seat of Manchurian warlords, notably Chang Tso-lin. The famous Mukden Incident, which took place at Peitaying, just northeast of the city, on Sept. 18, 1931, led to Japanese military occupation of Manchuria and establishment of the state of Manchukuo. Under the Manchukuo regime, the city regained its former Manchu Chinese name of Fengtien and was made the capital of Fengtien Province. While in Manchukuo, the city underwent a tremendous expansion, with its population rising from 421,000 in 1931 to 1,900,000 in 1945. After World War II, the city was again named Shenyang by the Chinese Nationalists, who entered Mukden in March, 1946, after Soviet troops had dismantled a large part of the city's industries. Chinese Communist forces won the city in November 1948, in their conquest of the Chinese mainland. Under the Communist regime, Mukden has again reached the industrial prosperity it had under the Japanese. Pop. (1953 census) 2,299,900.

THEODORE SHABAD,
Author, "China's Changing Map."

MULBERRY, mŭl'bĕr-ĭ, is a genus (*Morus*) of trees and shrubs, belonging to the large, economically important, mostly tropical mulberry family (Moraceae) which includes such well-known plants as the paper mulberry (*Broussonetia*), osage orange (*Maclura*), bread fruit (*Artocarpus*), fig and rubber plants (*Ficus*), hemp (*Cannabis*), and hop (*Humulus*).

There are approximately 12 highly variable species of mulberry. Two are native to the United States and two have become naturalized; the remaining species are native to temperate and warm temperate regions of the Eastern and Western hemispheres. The plants have a milky sap, scaly bark, and slender, cylindrical branches. The leaves are alternate, simple, have serrate margins, and are very variable in outline. Both simple, unlobed and deeply, irregularly lobed leaves may be found on adjacent branches or even on the same branch. The male flowers are aggregated in long cylindrical catkins, while the female flowers are in short, dense catkins. The male and female inflorescences may be borne on different branches of the same

RED MULBERRY (*Morus rubra*): details of leaves, flowers, and fruit; and tree in winter.

tree (monoecious) or on different trees (dioecious). Each ovary of the female inflorescence develops into a small, single-seeded nutlet, forming, in the aggregate, a multiple fruit.

The red mulberry (*Morus rubra* L.) is the largest tree in the genus, reaching a height of 60 feet and a diameter of 5 to 7 feet. The tree is native to eastern and central North America, reaching its largest size in the central United States. The fruit, black when mature, is eaten chiefly by animals, but the wood is valuable, being heavy, hard, and very durable when exposed to moisture. This makes it valuable for fence posts. Other uses of the wood are for furniture, interior finish, agricultural implements, and cooperage.

The Mexican mulberry (*Morus microphylla* Bucl.) is a small tree, 15 to 25 feet high, with a diameter of 10 to 15 inches. The tree, native to North America, is found in the southwestern United States and northern Mexico. The wood is used to a limited extent for carpentry work in Mexico.

The white mulberry (*Morus alba* L.) is a native of Asia, probably China. It has spread throughout Europe and has become naturalized in the eastern United States. The maximum height reached by this species is 50 feet with a trunk diameter of 2 feet. The fruit is white to pinkish and is of little value as food. The white mulberry and its varieties were introduced into both Europe and North America as food for the silkworm. It was introduced into Virginia by the London Company early in the 17th century for the purpose of establishing the silkworm industry in the New World. In Europe the roots are used to furnish a yellow dyestuff, and the wood is used for fuel and cabinet work.

The Russian mulberry (*Morus alba* var. *tatarica* L.) was introduced into North America in 1875 by Russian Mennonites. It is a very hardy, fast-growing, small, bushy tree used widely in the western United States as a shelter belt tree.

The black mulberry (*Morus nigra* L.) is a native of Asia, probably Persia, but has become naturalized in parts of Europe and the United States. It is the principal fruit-bearing species cultivated in the United States and Europe.

Frank G. Lier,
Department of Botany, Columbia University.

MULCASTER, mŭl'kăs-tẽr, **Richard,** English schoolmaster and author: b. Cumberland County, England, ?1530; d. Essex County, April 15, 1611. After completing his education at Christ Church, Oxford, he became a schoolmaster in London, where in 1561, he was appointed first headmaster of the new Merchant Taylors school. He held this post for 25 years, resigning in 1586. In 1596, he became high master of St. Paul's School, resigning in 1608. Mulcaster was renowned as a harsh disciplinarian, but as an educator had certain ideas which were ahead of his time. He gave instruction in music and singing, guiding his pupils in preparing and presenting entertainments for the royal court. He emphasized physical training and the right of girls to receive education as well as boys. He also believed that teachers should receive special training for their work. Among his books are *Positions* (1581), in which he discusses the proper measures for the physical and mental education of children, and *The Elementarie* (1582), concerned, at a time when Latin was still important, with the writing of English.

MULCH, mŭlch, a loose layer of material kept on the surface of soil for any of a variety of purposes. A mulch may be made of sawdust, planer shavings, or such plant materials as grass clippings, straw, leaves, or peat moss. The most practical mulch for large cultivated areas is a layer of the soil itself kept pulverized by frequent cultivation, especially after each rain. A mulch retards the loss of moisture by interrupting the upward movement of water by capillarity, by shading the soil, or by preventing air currents over the moist surface.

Besides conserving moisture, a mulch may prevent sudden and extreme temperature changes, diminish erosion by wind or water, retard runoff of rainfall, protect flowers, fruits, or vegetables from dirt, prevent soil puddling by breaking the impact of raindrops, retard the growth of weeds, or, on decay, add to the fertility of the soil. Around ornamental plants, a mulch may present a more pleasing appearance than that of the bare soil.

Mulches composed of coarse plant material are not practical on surfaces which are cultivated frequently during the growing season. Leaves which have not been macerated may pack down into an impervious layer, thus keeping rain water from wetting the soil. The decay of peat moss, pine needles, oak leaves, or many other materials yields acids which are injurious to some plants and beneficial to others. Some mulches may harbor injurious insects or fungi, while others may promote the growth of helpful molds or bacteria. In climates which have wide extremes of temperature or rainfall, a mulch may be harmful to perennial plants by causing the roots to grow near the surface in wet weather, where they will later be killed by freezing.

Paul Weatherwax,
Professor of Botany, Indiana University.

MULE, mūl, a term applied to any hybrid, but most commonly to the offspring of a jackass (*Equus asinus*) and a female horse (*E. caballus*). The product of a stallion and a jennet (female ass) is known as a hinny. Mules and hinnies are ordinarily sterile, and the few instances of fertile female mules have been questioned; there seem to be no records of fertile male mules. There is some variance in counts of the numbers of chromosomes in horses (33–66), asses (60–66), and mules (38–66), the more recent work indicating 66 for each; all workers seem to agree that reduction division (meiosis) in sperm production in mules is irregular, which probably accounts for the sterility. In the case of many groups of animals, when members of two different species are mated, the resulting hybrid offspring turn out to be sterile.

Mules and hinnies resemble the sire in general build and appearance, but approximate the size of the dam. A good male mule should be 15 hands high, weigh about 1,300 pounds, and should have ears that measure at least 33 inches (horizontally) from tip to tip. American breeders prefer a black color with white around the muzzle, eyes, and on the underside.

Mules have numerous advantages over horses and asses. Their size and strength make them more desirable than the latter. Compared with horses, mules are better adapted to hot weather, are less likely to overeat or overdrink, are freer from digestive ailments, and they can be fed cheaper, coarser foods. Because they are less nervous and will accept hard work, poor handling, and abuse, mules are well suited to conditions of heavy work, poor food and shelter, and inexperienced drivers. Their tough skin, strong hoofs, stamina, and surefootedness make them desirable pack animals. They can carry up to 300 pounds, but normal loads are about 200 pounds.

U.S. Department of Agriculture

A cotton mule.

Several classes of mules are employed in the United States. Draft mules are large and heavy and are used for heavy teaming, such as needed in road grading and railroad and lumber work. Farm mules are smaller and lighter than draft mules. Sugar mules, used on sugar plantations, are as large as draft mules (16 to 17 hands) but lighter, weighing from 1,150 to 1,300 pounds. Cotton mules, employed on cotton plantations, are smaller and lighter than sugar mules. Mining and pack mules are small (12 to 16 hands) and light (600 to 1,350 pounds), and good feet and a strong back are prime considerations in their selection.

The production of mules dates to pre-Biblical times, and they were valued more highly than horses. George Washington was one of the earliest advocates of mule production in the United States, importing asses for this purpose in 1785. In 1925, almost 6 million mules were in use in the United States, mostly in the South. With increased mechanization, the number of mules in the United States has declined by more than three quarters. The financial value of mules has also decreased, for the same reason.

During World War II, the United States Army reemployed mules for mountain service in Italy and Asia. Mules are still widely used where mechanical power is impractical or unavailable. They are used in Latin America, the Mediterranean region, the Middle East, and other parts of Asia and Africa. In the mid-1960's, the United Nations estimated the world's mule population at about 15 million, of which nearly 5 million were in Brazil, and over 1 million each in Mexico and in Ethiopia.

RICHARD G. VAN GELDER,
Assistant Curator of Mammals, The American Museum of Natural History, New York, N.Y.

MULE DEER (including the BLACKTAIL), a deer of the species *Dama hemionus,* occurring throughout western North America from Mexico to the southern Northwest Territories of Canada and southeastern Alaska, and from the Pacific Coast to Minnesota and Manitoba. Both the mule deer of the prairies and mountains and the blacktail deer of the coastal areas are placed by biologists in the same species. It is characterized by large ears and a dark tail with a black fringe, as opposed to the white-tailed deer which has a white-fringed tail. The mule deer of the deserts and plains frequents brushy areas, while the blacktail prefers the forest floor of the giant redwoods and western hemlocks.

Consult *The Deer of North America,* ed. by Walter P. Taylor (Washington 1956).

AUSTIN W. CAMERON.

MULHALL, mŭl'hôl, **Michael George,** Irish statistician: b. Dublin, Ireland, Sept. 29, 1836; d. there, Dec. 13, 1900. He was educated in the Irish College at Rome and in 1861 went to Buenos Aires, where he founded the *Standard,* reputedly the first English daily newspaper in South America. His *Handbook of the River Plate* (1869) was the first English book printed in Argentina. Mulhall gained a wide reputation as a statistician and in 1880 published his *Progress of the World in Arts, Agriculture, Commerce, Manufactures, Instruction, Railways, and Public Wealth.* The following year came his *Balance Sheet of the World, 1870–80* and in 1883 his *Dictionary of Statistics,* revised editions of which appeared in 1886, 1892, and 1897.

MULHEIM AN DER RUHR, mül'hīm än dẽr ro͞or', city, Germany, located in the northwestern part of the country in North Rhine-Westphalia State and lying approximately seven miles west-southwest of Essen. It is on the Ruhr River and main rail lines. The city has a variety of industries, and its products include shoes, textiles, and machinery. There are railroad shops, foundries, and blast furnaces also. Mülheim became a town in 1508. After World War II it was included in the Federal Republic of Germany (West Germany). Pop. (1965) 192,024.

MULHOUSE, mü-lo͞oz' (Ger. MÜLHAUSEN, mül-hou'zĕn), city and commune, France; located in the northeastern part of the country in the Alsace-Lorraine region and the Department of Haut-Rhin. It is 18 miles northwest of Basel, Switzerland and is on the Ill River and the Rhône-Rhine Canal. Mulhouse is an important commercial and manufacturing center, the weaving and printing of cotton textiles being one of the largest industries. The city also manufactures railway rolling stock, machinery, and chemicals. The industrial importance of Mulhouse dates from 1746, when a muslin-printing factory was established. At one time the city was famous for the workingmen's colony with model homes, established on the northwestern edges of the city by Jean Dollfus, a philanthropic member of an old Mulhouse family, in 1853.

Mulhouse was first mentioned in 717; it became an imperial free city in 1273 and in the 15th century formed an alliance with the Swiss. This ended in 1798 when the city voted to become part of France. Mulhouse was included in the cession of Alsace to Germany in 1871. It reverted to France in 1918, but again during World War II was held by the Germans. The city has been heavily damaged by military operations. Pop. (1962) city 107,946; Commune 110,735.

MULL, mul, is an island off the west coast of Scotland. The largest of the Inner Hebrides group, it is bounded on the west and south by the Atlantic Ocean, on the north and northeast by the Sound of Mull, and on the east and southeast by the Firth of Lorne. For administrative purposes, it is part of Argyll. The island is 27 miles (43 km) long and about 350 square miles (905 sq km) in area. It is irregular in shape, with sea lochs, particularly along the west coast, deeply indenting the coastline. Ulva, Gometra, Staffa, and Iona are among the islands lying in the large bay west of the island. The terrain is rugged and mountainous. Ben More, the highest mountain, rises to over 3,000 feet (914 meters) near the center of the island.

The principal community on Mull is Tobermory. Other villages include Salen and Lochbuie. Chief occupations are fishing, sheep and cattle grazing, and granite quarrying. Mull is also a summer resort noted for its picturesque scenery.

MULLEIN, mul'ən, any of a genus, *Verbascum,* of herbs of the figwort family, Scrophulariaceae, some of which are used in borders and wild gardens. About 300 species are native to Europe, northern Africa, and western and central Asia. Some species have become widely naturalized in other parts of the world. Most are annual or biennial, but a few are woody and perennial.

Mulleins vary greatly in size and shape. Most have a columnar form, are hairy or woolly, and have yellow, red, purplish, or brownish red flowers arranged in dense terminal spikes or in narrow panicles. The best-known species in the United States is the common weed *V. thapsus,* which has a stout, erect, unbranched, woolly stem, 2 to 3 feet (60–90 cm) tall, with basal leaves and a dense spike of small flowers. More than two dozen species are used, especially in Europe, as contrast plants in ornamental borders and background plantings. The common species was used in folk medicine, and the thick stem and leaf hairs were used to make lamp wicks.

RICHARD M. STRAW*, *Los Angeles State College of Applied Arts and Sciences*

MULLENS, Priscilla. See ALDEN, JOHN.

MÜLLER, mül'ər, **Adam Heinrich** (1779–1829), German political economist, whose espousal of social control was taken up by German National Socialists in the 1930's. He was born in Berlin on June 30, 1779. He studied theology and law at Göttingen and from 1806 to 1809 was tutor to Prince Bernhard of Saxe-Weimar. Through his friend Friedrich von Gentz, a political theorist associated with Metternich, Müller entered Austrian government service in 1813. His authoritarian views had proved inimical to reforming trends in Prussia. He died in Vienna on Jan. 17, 1829.

Applying Romantic philosophy to political economy, Müller found the ideal relationship between the individual and the state in medieval feudalism. He believed that the individual should be subordinate to the state and seek self-realization through integration into society. His organic view of society fostered national consciousness and rejected the materialistic, individualistic approach of Adam Smith and the classical theorists. Aside from being resurrected by the Nazis, Müller's theories influenced some nonauthoritarian socialists.

A. W. AMBLER, FROM NATIONAL AUDUBON SOCIETY

Common mullein grows wild in North America.

MÜLLER, mül'ər, **Georg Elias** (1850–1934), German psychologist, who conducted pioneer studies in psychophysics, memory and learning, and color vision.

Müller was born in Grimma, near Leipzig, Germany, on July 20, 1850, the son of a theologian. He studied history and philosophy at the universities of Leipzig and Berlin. He served in the Franco-Prussian War, after which he resumed his studies and received his Ph. D. in philosophy from the University of Göttingen in 1873. After teaching at several European universities, he returned in 1881 to Göttingen where he remained until his retirement in 1921. He died in Göttingen on Dec. 23, 1934.

In some of his earliest work, Müller performed detailed psychophysical experiments to determine how different sensory experiences are related to the physical stimuli that arouse them. One of his experiments showed how anticipation affects the discrimination of weight. Müller also did important work on memory and learning and on visual perception. His work led him to formulate psychophysical principles concerning the relation of specific neural events in the brain and corresponding events in perception. Some of these ideas were later incorporated into Gestalt psychological theories.

MULLER, mul'ər, **Hermann Joseph** (1890–1966), American biologist, who was awarded the 1946 Nobel Prize in physiology or medicine "for his discovery of the production of mutations by means of X-ray irradiation." Muller was born in New York City on Dec. 21, 1890. He studied biology at Columbia University, where, after graduation, he became a member of T. H. Morgan's genetics research group. During his career he taught at many institutions in the United States and Europe, including the University of Texas (1920–1932), where he did his prizewinning work, and the University of Indiana (1945–1964). He died in Indianapolis, Ind., on April 5, 1966.

Muller began genetics experiments in 1911 with his studies of the fruit fly (*Drosophila*). From his observations of mutations in fruit flies he was able to establish in 1926 that X rays cause genetic mutations. He demonstrated that such mutations take place as the result of changes within individual genes and of chromosome breakage.

Muller's work had several important consequences. First, since the great majority of the mutations he produced were found to be harmful, he stressed the necessity of minimizing human exposure to ionizing radiation of any kind. Second, the discovery of the mutagenic effects of X rays and other agents made it possible for scientists to create large numbers of mutations at will.

The new mutagenic agents enable researchers to make advances in genetics by facilitating, for example, the mapping of chromosomes. In biochemistry, these agents expedite the exploration of chemical changes resulting from mutations and thereby make it possible to analyze the normal synthesis of amino acids, enzymes, vitamins, and other chemical constituents of living cells. Finally, by demonstrating the existence of numerous random (nongoal-directed and nonadaptive mutations), Muller's work filled one of the last major gaps in the evidence for Darwin's theory of natural selection.

MÜLLER, Johann. See REGIOMONTANUS.

MÜLLER, mül′ər, **Johannes Peter** (1801–1858), German physician, who was one of the founders of experimental physiology. He was born in Coblenz, Germany, on July 14, 1801, the son of a shoemaker. He considered becoming a priest but soon turned to medicine and took his medical degree at Bonn in 1823 with a prize dissertation on the respiration of the fetus. An all-round medical naturalist, he taught anatomy, physiology, and pathology at Bonn and at Berlin. He died in Berlin on April 28, 1858.

In 1826, Müller enunciated his law of specific nerve energies, which states that each sense organ, when stimulated, gives rise only to its own characteristic sensation. For example, a sensation of light and nothing else is caused by electrical stimulation of the optic nerve. In 1831 he proved, by experiments on the frog, the Bell-Magendie law of the spinal-nerve roots. He produced pioneering descriptions of the microscopic anatomy of the secretory glands and of the development of the reproductive system.

Müller was one of the first pathologists to examine diseased tissues with the microscope. As a biochemist, he isolated chondrin, an important constituent of cartilage. In the later years of his life, he spent summers at the seashore studying the comparative anatomy of marine animals.

Müller's most influential work was his *Handbuch der Physiologie des Menschen* (2 vols., 1833–1840; Eng. tr., *Handbook of Human Physiology*, 1842), which was a standard textbook for two generations. It appeared at a time when European biology and medicine were still dominated by *Naturphilosophie* and other theoretical systems. Physics, chemistry, and anatomy were, however, providing new facts and methods upon which experimental physiology could be founded. With an excellent philosophical background and extensive experience in biology, Müller was ideally equipped to take the lead in this advance—through his lectures, his great textbook, and his editorship of "Muller's Archive," a journal founded in 1834.

A charming, forceful teacher, he stimulated several of the greatest German scientists of the 19th century. Through his disciples and their pupils, almost every biologist and medical scientist traces some part of his intellectual heritage to Muller.

GEORGE W. CORNER, M. D.*
Formerly, Historian, The Rockefeller Institute

Further Reading: Boring, Edwin G., *A History of Experimental Psychology*, 2d ed. (Appleton 1929); Driesch, Hans, *The History and Theory of Vitalism* (Macmillan 1914); Sigerist, Henry E., *The Great Doctors* (Norton 1933).

MÜLLER, mül′ər, **Max** (1823–1900), Anglo-German Orientalist and philologist. Friedrich Max Müller was born in Dessau, Germany, on Dec. 6, 1823, the son of the poet Wilhelm Müller. After studying Sanskrit at the University of Leipzig, he went to Berlin, where he took up Indo-European philology under the guidance of Franz Bopp. In Paris in 1845, he studied with Eugène Burnouf, who persuaded him to edit the Rig Veda. In 1846, Müller went to England, where he began work on this project, which was ultimately published as *Rig Veda with the Commentary of Sayana* (1849–1873; 2d ed., 1889–1892).

In 1850, Müller was appointed deputy Taylorian professor of modern languages at Oxford University. He became vice librarian of the Bodleian Library in 1865. In 1868 he received a chair of comparative philology. Müller retired from teaching in 1875 and devoted himself to writing and lecturing. He died in Oxford on Oct. 28, 1900.

A voluminous writer, Müller exercised considerable influence on various fields of scholarship. In comparative philology, he popularized the scientific approach to the study of linguistic phenomena in his Rede lecture *On the Stratification of Language* (1868) and *Lectures on the Science of Language* (1861–1863). His studies of comparative religion include the *Introduction to the Science of Religion* (1873) and the 50-volume *Sacred Books of the East* (1879–1899), which he edited. Invaluable to the study of Sanskrit are his *History of Ancient Sanskrit Literature* (1859) and his *Sanskrit Grammar* (1866).

MÜLLER, mül′ər, **Paul Hermann** (1899–1965), Swiss chemist, who was awarded the 1948 Nobel Prize in medicine for discovering the insect-killing powers of DDT (dichlorodiphenyltrichloroethane). He was born in Olten, Switzerland, on Jan. 12, 1899. After obtaining his doctorate in chemistry from the University of Basel in 1925, he entered the dyewood department of the J. R. Geigy Laboratories in Basel and specialized in synthetic tanning substances. In the mid-1930's he began experimenting with chemicals to protect plants against insects. By 1939 he and his staff had developed the insecticides Gesarol and Neocid, both of which contained DDT. Müller died in Basel on Oct. 12, 1965.

DDT was first used commercially in Switzerland in 1939 to combat the Colorado potato beetle. During World War II it was applied not only to controlling plant pests but also to protecting human beings from dangerous diseases carried by insects. See DDT.

The striped mullet is found in shallow water over sandy and muddy bottoms along both coasts of North America.

CALIFORNIA DEPARTMENT OF FISH & GAME

MULLET, mul′it, any of a family, Mugilidae, of food fishes found in tropical and temperate waters throughout the world. Most species are marine, but some are also found in brackish and fresh water, and other species are restricted to fresh water.

Mullets are torpedo-shaped and generally less than 2 feet (60 cm) long. The dorsal fin is separated into two parts—a front spiny-rayed portion and a hind soft-rayed portion—and the caudal fin is markedly bilobed. Mullets are usually grayish with the lateral line absent or vestigial. They prefer shallow water and usually swim in schools over sandy or muddy bottoms, where they feed on algae and decaying vegetable and animal matter.

The striped mullet (*Mugil cephalus*) is found along the Atlantic and Pacific coasts of North America as far north as Maine. It is often called black mullet in Florida. It is an unusually large species, sometimes reaching a length of 3 feet (90 cm) and a weight of 15 pounds (7 kg). It grows very fast and is frequently used in brackish and saltwater pond culture.

True mullets belong to the family Mugilidae, whereas surmullets, or goatfish, are of the family Mullidae.

MULLIGAN LETTERS, mul′i-gən, a series of letters written by the American political leader James G. Blaine in the 1860's and early 1870's to Arkansas railroader Warren Fisher, Jr. The letters, which came into the hands of James Mulligan, a former bookkeeper for Fisher, supplied a basis for charges against Blaine of questionable conduct while in office.

Mulligan disclosed the existence of the letters on May 31, 1876, while testifying before a congressional committee investigating the sale of Little Rock and Fort Smith Railroad bonds to the Union Pacific. The committee adjourned without seeing the letters.

Blaine managed, however, to obtain the correspondence from Mulligan. Refusing to release them to the committee, Blaine read them aloud on the floor of the U. S. House of Representatives on June 5, interspersed with explanations and claiming no wrongdoing. The most serious disclosure was that Blaine, while speaker of the House in 1869 and presiding over a debate on a land grant for the Little Rock and Fort Smith Railroad, had shown the promoters how to save the measure from defeat. Subsequently, Blaine obtained a favorable contract for selling securities of the railroad.

Blaine's friends considered him vindicated, but his opponents wielded the letters during his unsuccessful bids for the Republican presidential nomination in 1876 and 1880. The publication of the letters in 1884, when Blaine was the Republican presidential nominee, helped defeat him in the election.

MULLIKEN, mul′i-kən, **Robert Sanderson** (1896–), American physical chemist, who won the Nobel Prize for chemistry in 1966 for theoretical studies in which he applied the principles of quantum mechanics to extend the understanding of chemical bonding between molecules. Mulliken was born in Newburyport, Mass., on June 7, 1896. He received his B. S. from Massachusetts Institute of Technology in 1917 and his Ph. D. in physical chemistry from the University of Chicago in 1921. From 1931 to 1961 he was a professor of physics at Chicago, and remained there as a distinguished service professor of physics and chemistry.

During World War II, Mulliken directed editorial and information services in connection with the development of the atomic bomb. The work for which he won a Nobel Prize was begun before World War II and was continued after the war. In its citation on his work, the Swedish Royal Academy of Science suggested that "the future significance of the Mulliken calculations may be in synthesizing new molecules through the use of computers."

MULLITE, mul′īt, is an aluminum silicate named after the Island of Mull, Scotland, where it was first recognized as a mineral. It occasionally is found in nature where aluminum-rich rocks have been subjected to a high temperature but usually is manufactured by heating other aluminum silicates such as kyanite or andalusite. Mullite is used chiefly as a component in refractory materials for lining high-temperature furnaces and as a constituent of ceramic whitewares and porcelains. Its formula is $Al_6Si_2O_{13}$ or $3Al_2O_3 \cdot 2SiO_2$.

MULOCK, Dinah Maria. See CRAIK, DINAH MARIA MULOCK.

MULTAN, mo͝ol-tän′, is a major city in Pakistan, in southern Punjab, near the Chenab River, about 195 miles (315 km) southwest of Lahore. It is a distribution and processing center for the surrounding agricultural district as well as a fast-developing industrial city. It trades in grain, cotton, sugar, fruit, indigo, and silk. The city manufactures textiles and a variety of metal products. Pottery, leather products, ivory, and silver are also important.

Multan is a very old settled site. Tradition holds that Alexander the Great overran the settlement in the 4th century B. C. Many nations fought over the city, and the British finally conquered it from the Sikhs in 1849. It has ruined Muslim shrines, elaborate fortifications, and a Hindu temple to Vishnu. Modern buildings include institutions of higher learning. Population: (1969 est.) 596,000.

MULTATULI. See DEKKER, EDUARD DOUWES.

MULTIPLE BIRTH. In humans most pregnancies result in the birth of one child. Twins, the most common multiple birth, occur in one out of 80 to 100 pregnancies. Triplets occur once in 10,000 pregnancies and quadruplets about once in 600,000. Higher multiple births occur with much lower frequencies. An approximation of higher multiple births, known as Hellin's law, is that the frequency of triplets is approximately the square of the twinning rate, that for quadruplets it is the cube of the twinning rate, and so on. There have been a few cases of the birth of six or more infants, but in none of these cases have all of the infants survived.

Types of Multiple Births. There are two types of twins. Some are so similar that they are called *identical* twins, while others are no more similar than ordinary siblings and are called *nonidentical,* or *fraternal,* twins.

Identical twins originate from a single egg fertilized by a single sperm. One-egg, or monozygotic, twins are the result of the division of a single fertilized egg, or zygote, into two independent embryonic structures that are genetically identical, barring somatic mutation. Monozygotic twins and higher multiple births resulting from a single fertilized egg (zygote) are the only source of human beings with identical genotypes, or genetic makeup. In these cases mitosis, or cell division, provides the cells of each twin (or triplet, and so on) with descendants of the same chromosomes originally carried by the single fertilized egg, or zygote. Monozygotic twins (MZ) are always of the same sex.

Nonidentical, or fraternal, twins come from two eggs, each fertilized by a separate sperm. Two-egg, or dizygotic, twins have different genetic makeups. Dizygotic twins are of the same sex or of unlike sex in approximately equal frequency.

Using a statistical method first proposed by the French physician-statistician Adolphe Bertillon in 1874 and later by the German physician Wilhelm Weinberg in 1901, one can predict how many twins in a population are monozygotic and how many are dizygotic. The calculation is based on the fact that dizygotic twins (DZ) have an equal probability of being of like sex or of unlike sex. If n is the number of twins of unlike sex (which must be dizygotic) in a randomly selected population (P) of twins, then the same number—n—of like sex twins must be also DZ, and the remainder of twins in the population (P–2n) are monozygotic. Since the number of monozygotic twins is represented by the difference between all twins and the dizygotic twins, Weinberg's method is known as the *differential method.*

Monozygotic twins can be of any of four types. In one type, the fertilized egg, or zygote, may divide at the first cleavage, producing two independent embryonic structures. In other cases the separation into two structures may occur at a later stage of division. In some cases the single zygote may develop two inner cell masses, each of which develops into an embryo. Lastly, in some cases the division may be late or incomplete and result in conjoined, or Siamese, twins.

The developing zygote is surrounded by membranes, an inner (*amnion*) and an outer (*chorion*). Monozygotic twins may develop in four ways: (1) with separate amnions, chorions, and placentas; (2) with separate amnions and chorions but a fused placenta; (3) with separate amnions but sharing a chorion and placenta; or (4) sharing a single amnion, chorion, and placenta. In dizygotic twins, each twin has completely separate membranes, although when implantation is close together the two placentas may fuse.

Triplets, quadruplets, and other higher multiple births may all arise from different zygotes when three or more eggs are each fertilized by separate sperm, from the same zygote when a single fertilized egg divides, or from a combination of monozygotic and dizygotic multiplication. For example, triplets may arise in three ways: monozygotic triplets are derived from a single fertilized egg; dizygotic triplets from two eggs, one of which divides to form the third structure; and trizygotic triplets from three eggs.

Factors Affecting Frequency of Multiple Births. Several factors, including race, maternal age, and number of previous births affect the frequency of multiple births. The frequency of twin births, generally about 1%–1.5% of all births, shows racial variation. Japan has a low rate of twin births, about 0.7%, while Negroes have the highest rates, about 2.5% for African Negroes generally and as high as 4% for the Yorubas of Nigeria. Since monozygotic and dizygotic twins are biologically different, it is important to distinguish variation in rates between MZ and DZ twins. Twinning rates of monozygotic twins are not appreciably different from race to race. The racial difference in twinning rate is mostly due to differences in rates for dizygotic twins. In general, Negroids have the highest twinning rate, Caucasoids intermediate rates, and Mongoloids the lowest rates.

In the United States, whites have about 10 twin births per 1,000 pregnancies, about 30% of which are monozygotic twins. Nonwhites (mostly blacks) have about 13.5 twin births per 1,000 pregnancies.

Maternal age also affects the frequency of dizygotic twinning. The tendency of women to bear dizygotic twins increases from age 15 to 39 and drops after 40. The monozygotic twinning rate is fairly stable throughout the women's childbearing years. At all maternal ages, twinning rates increase steadily with birth order.

An incidence of dizygotic twinning that is higher than would be expected is observed in some families. Evidence suggests that a true increase in the dizygotic twinning rate occurs only in the female relatives of women who have had twins. This supports the hypothesis that the inheritance of a tendency to have dizygotic twins is a sex-limited genetic factor. Studies of interracial crosses show no paternal effect on the frequency of dizygotic twins.

Socioeconomic and nutritional factors may also affect the dizygotic twinning rate. In the United States and many European countries, dizygotic twinning rates have shown an unexplained decline since the 1950's.

Effect of Fertility Drugs. In the 1960's the introduction of pituitary hormones and other hormones for the treatment of some types of sterility led to striking cases of multiple births. Most of the multiple births resulting from treatment with fertility drugs were polyzygous—that is, resulting from the fertilization of more than one egg. Inexperience with the hormonal treatment, particularly with the dose levels needed, produced polyovulation, but by the 1970's increased experience resulted in fewer multiple births following fertility drug use.

Twin Studies. In 1876 the English statistician Francis Galton proposed the twin method as a means of distinguishing between the roles of environment and heredity in the determination of human variation. The concordance-discordance method (concordant when both twins possess or both are free of a trait, discordant when only one of the pair has a trait) compares the degree of similarity of monozygotic twins—that is, twins with identical genetic makeup—to that of like sex dizygotic twins—twins with different genetic makeups. It also compares the degree of similarity of monozygotic twins that have been reared together to those that have been reared apart to determine the role of environment when genetic makeup is identical. These studies depend on precise knowledge of whether the twins are monozygotic or dizygotic. Such determinations are made on the basis of placenta examination and the study of the twin's external characteristics, blood types, and other criteria.

GRACE WYSHAK
Yale University School of Medicine

MULTIPLE SCLEROSIS, sklə-rō′sis, is a chronic degenerative disease of the nervous system, the cause of which is unknown. It usually begins between the ages of 20 and 40. It is more common among whites than among blacks and seems to be more frequent in Europe, particularly in the Scandinavian countries, than in the United States. It is relatively rare in Africa and Asia. Occasionally, multiple sclerosis is seen in families, but there is no evidence that it is a genetic disorder. A variety of theories have been advanced to explain its cause, including infection by a virus or spirochete, deficiency of certain minerals or enzymes, and poisonings, but none has been proven.

Multiple sclerosis is characterized by the development of multiple lesions in the brain and spinal cord due to loss of myelin, a fatty substance that sheathes the nerve fibers. Symptoms depend on the areas of the brain or spinal cord affected.

Initially multiple sclerosis may have any of a wide variety of symptoms. There may be brief loss of vision in one eye, double vision, or a bizarre jerky movement of one or both eyes known as nystagmus. Sometimes there is difficulty with speech. Tremors, numbness, or a feeling of pins-and-needles may occur in one or more limbs, one arm or leg may be weak or hard to use, the gait may be unsteady, or there may even be loss of control of a limb.

In most cases, multiple sclerosis is slowly progressive over a period of years. The chronic relapsing form of the disease, which is the most common, often begins with one or a group of symptoms that usually disappear for a period of years until the same or frequently other symptoms appear. These too may subside after a few days or even a few hours, to be followed by another remission period with no symptoms. As time goes on, however, symptoms tend to occur more frequently and fail to subside.

In acute forms of the disease, which may run for a course of months or even weeks, symptoms develop rapidly and may remit only partially or, if completely, may be followed by a relapse in a relatively short time. In acute forms the onset is often marked by headache, vomiting, or delirium. Multiple sclerosis may also cause mental changes and convulsions. Sphincter muscles controlling bladder and bowel function are also frequently affected. Eventually there is paraplegia and increasing disability. The prognosis is variable, with some patients deteriorating rapidly but the majority living 20 or 30 years or longer before succumbing to the disease.

There is no known treatment for multiple sclerosis. It is important that the patient be given good psychological support since many become severely depressed when they are told the nature of their disease, and many of the symptoms may actually be due to psychological factors.

LOUIS J. VORHAUS, M. D.
Cornell University Medical College

MULTIPLE STARS. See BINARY STAR.

MULTIPLICATION. See ARITHMETIC—*Fundamental Operations* (Multiplication).

MULTNOMAH FALLS, mult-nō′mə, a waterfall on a small snow-fed tributary of the Columbia River, in northwestern Oregon, about 25 miles (40 km) east of Portland. The falls begin near the 4,100-foot (1,250-meter) peak of Larch Mountain, descend in a series of cascades, and then plunge 680 feet (207 meters) into a basin that empties into the Columbia River about 9 miles (14 km) west of the Bonneville Dam. Multnomah Falls was named for a tribe of Indians who lived in the region until the early 19th century, when they became extinct.

MUMFORD, mum′fərd, **Lewis** (1895–), American sociologist, writer, and critic. He wrote major studies on the history of architecture and on modern urban planning, all in the social context of human needs and aspirations. Mumford was born in Flushing, N. Y., on Oct. 19, 1895. He studied at the City College of New York, Columbia University, and the New School for Social Research but did not seek a degree because he "did not aim to be a teacher."

He was inspired by Sir Patrick Geddes, a Scottish sociologist who pioneered in civic and regional studies. In 1919, Mumford became an associate editor of the *Dial*. He contributed essays to many periodicals and in 1932 began a column of architectural criticism for the *New Yorker*. His books *Sticks and Stones* (1924) and *The Brown Decades* (1931) won critical acclaim. International renown followed for his four-volume series "Renewal of Life": *Technics and Civilization* (1934), *The Culture of Cities* (1938), *The Condition of Man* (1944), and *The Conduct of Life* (1951). Other books included *Herman Melville* (1929), *Green Memories* (1947), and *The City in History* (1961).

Although Mumford criticized the "spiritual rootlessness and loneliness of the overgrown city," he felt that its final mission is "to further man's conscious participation in the cosmic and historic process."

MUMMERS, mum′ərz, were originally bands of masked and costumed revelers in medieval Europe who took part in certain festive rites, particularly at Christmas and Whitsuntide. However, mummers were also performers in "mumming" plays, a form of drama that developed in Europe early in the 17th century. The theme of this type of play was a hero's death and reawakening, probably symbolizing the death of the earth in winter and its reawakening in spring. The word "mummer" survives as a facetious term for an actor.

Further Reading: Chambers, Edmund K., *The English Folk Play* (Oxford 1933).

MUMMY, a dead body preserved by embalming. The name arose because the skin and bones of corpses embalmed by the Egyptians of antiquity are often found to be blackened, an effect mistakenly attributed to the use of bitumen, which in Arabic is *mūmiya,* in the embalming process. The earliest indisputable evidence of attempts to preserve the body by artificial means dates to about 2600 B. C. The remarkable state of preservation of many bodies from earlier times is the result of the natural drying effect of the hot sand in which bodies were interred. Artificial embalming was developed after the use of chambered tombs and wooden coffins had introduced corpse decay, since a complete body was considered essential for the housing of the spirit in the next life.

For many centuries only the wealthy could afford mummification. Eventually cheaper methods allowed the practice to spread, but for the most part it was confined to the wealthy and to animals sacred to certain gods, such as bulls, cats, and ibises.

No description of the embalming process has been preserved from Egypt itself. The Greek authors Herodotus (*History,* II, 85–89) and Diodorus Siculus (*Bibliotheke,* I, 7) related what they were told about it, and their accounts may now be verified by the results of careful study and chemical analyses.

The essential feature of the process was thorough desiccation, effected by means of dry natron (native sodium carbonate). First, the soft internal parts of the body were removed: the brain through the nostrils; the lungs, stomach, and intestines through an incision in the left side. These organs were desiccated, wrapped in linen, and stored in the tomb in special (canopic) jars or chests. The heart and kidneys were not removed from the body. Generally the body cavities were filled with resin, resin-soaked linen, sawdust, or, occasionally, wood pitch. Then the body was dried by completely enclosing it in natron. Following the desiccation came a washing and then an anointing with oil. Finally the body was wrapped, first each digit and each limb, until the entire body was enveloped in strips of fine linen arranged in elaborate patterns. Special care was taken to prevent the nails from falling away. Models in resin-soaked linen of the external genitals were often fitted into place. In some periods a painted cartonnage mask preserved the features.

The entire process took many weeks, according to Egyptian records, 70 days elapsing between death and burial. With changes in the techniques of preparation and wrapping, the practice of embalming continued in Egypt until Christianity became the dominant religion (4th century A. D.). After that it fell into disuse.

Although archaeologists use the word "mummy" for bodies buried in Egypt and elsewhere in the world after that time, these, like the Egyptian predynastic burials, have been preserved by natural means.

See also DEATH CUSTOMS AND RITES; EGYPT, ANCIENT–*Science and Technology;* EMBALMING.

RICHARD A. PARKER
Brown University

Further Reading: Budge, Ernest A., *Mummies* (1894; reprint, Collier Bks. 1972); Lucas, Alfred, *Ancient Egyptian Materials and Industries,* 3d ed. rev. (Longmans 1948); Smith, Grafton E., and Dawson, Warren R., *Egyptian Mummies* (Dial Press 1924).

MUMPS is a contagious disease marked by painful swelling of the salivary glands. It is caused by a virus that attacks glandular and nervous tissue in particular. Mumps chiefly affects children from five to ten years of age, and approximately 85% of all infections are acquired by persons under 15 years of age. However, all ages are susceptible, males and females equally. Mumps occurs in all geographical areas. In the temperate zone, there is a concentration of cases in the winter and spring months.

A patient with mumps is usually contagious from several days before the onset of symptoms to the subsidence of salivary-gland swelling, approximately seven to ten days later. Signs of infection usually develop after an incubation period of 16 to 18 days. Approximately 30% to 40% of all exposed susceptible individuals acquire the disease in an inapparent form with no signs or symptoms of illness. The remaining 60% to 70% develop a disease of variable severity with symptoms that are dependent on the sites of infection.

Symptoms and Effects. In most cases, the mumps virus attacks the parotid, submaxillary, and sublingual salivary glands. The illness begins with fever, pain in front of the ear aggravated by chewing, and swelling of one or both parotid glands. In most cases, the symptoms of salivary-gland involvement subside without complication after a period of one to six days, depending on the severity of the infection.

Other relatively common signs of mumps are inflammation of the testes (orchitis) in the male past puberty and inflammation of the brain and spinal cord (meningoencephalitis). Orchitis is the second most common manifestation of mumps infection in the male, occurring unilaterally in 20% to 30% of males who develop the disease after puberty. Involvement of the testes is very rarely seen in boys before puberty. The common belief that mumps orchitis causes sterility has no factual basis. Mumps meningitis has been estimated to occur in about 10% of all cases. The symptoms are similar to those of nonparalytic poliomyelitis—fever, headache, vomiting, and stiff neck. In most cases, recovery is complete within a period of five to ten days. Deafness is a very rare but serious complication of mumps. In most cases it is unilateral and permanent.

Less common manifestations of mumps include involvement of the pancreas (pancreatitis), ovaries (oophoritis), breasts (mastitis), thyroid (thyroiditis), and other glands. These signs may occur singly or in combination and may precede, accompany, follow, or occur without salivary-gland involvement.

Treatment. Mumps is a self-limited generalized infection. Treatment is symptomatic and supportive. Aspirin usually controls the pain.

Prevention. The high incidence of inapparent cases and the infectivity of patients before onset of illness both combine to make isolation and quarantine of mumps patients ineffective. Mumps vaccine has been shown to be only partially effective. The protective effect of this vaccine is usually temporary. Children before puberty should not be immunized. It is not rational to delay the development of mumps in childhood, when it is generally mild, to an adult age, when it is usually more severe.

For an adult with no history of mumps, vaccine may be indicated under certain circumstances. First, a mumps skin test should be performed. A *positive* skin test indicates that the individual is immune—probably due to past inapparent or unrecognized infection. No vaccine should be given in this case. If the skin test is *negative,* it suggests lack of immunity, and vaccine would be indicated. The protection conferred by mumps vaccine is not acquired before four to six weeks. Since the incubation period of mumps is less than three weeks, the efficacy of the vaccine is obviously limited. Studies in adults, however, have suggested that mumps occurring in previously vaccinated persons seemed to be milder and associated with a lower incidence of orchitis.

SAUL KRUGMAN, M. D.
New York University College of Medicine

MUN, Thomas (1571–1641), English economist, who wrote an early exposition of mercantilist theory, stressing the importance of foreign trade. He was born in London in June 1571. For some years he was a successful merchant in the Mediterranean trade, and in 1615 he became director of the East India Company. He died in London in July 1641.

In defense of company policy of importing more from India than it was exporting there—and thus losing gold specie—Mun prepared a discourse on the East Indian trade (1621), which maintained that England's trade with any single country need not be favorable so long as its overall balance of trade was. The Indian trade was highly profitable because it brought valuable commodities into England at relatively low cost, many of which could be reexported at a profit.

Mun's major work on mercantilist theory, *England's Treasure by Foreign Trade,* published posthumously in 1664, had great influence. Its main thesis was that surplus exports lead to the accumulation of treasure, and, consequently, England could best increase its national wealth through foreign trade. See also MERCANTILISM.

MUNCH, münsh, **Charles** (1891–1968), French conductor, who was best known for his interpretation of the works of such modern French composers as Roussel, Milhaud, and Honegger—many of which he introduced. Munch was born in Strasbourg, Alsace (now France), on Sept. 26, 1891. He studied violin at the Strasbourg Conservatory and in Paris and Berlin. During World War I he served in the German Army, but as an Alsatian he became a French citizen in 1918.

Munch made his conducting debut in Paris in 1932 and conducted the orchestra of the Société des Concerts du Conservatoire from 1936 to 1946. In 1949 he succeeded Serge Koussevitzky as conductor of the Boston Symphony Orchestra and in 1951 became director of the orchestra's Berkshire Music Center. He retired from the Boston Symphony in 1962 and formed the Orchestre de Paris, with which he was on tour when he died, in Richmond, Va., on Nov. 6, 1968.

MUNCH mŏŏngk, **Edvard** (1863–1944), Norway's greatest painter and graphic artist, whose work was a major source of inspiration for modern expressionism. He was born in Løten on Dec. 12, 1863, the son of a doctor in a poor district. He studied and painted in Oslo and Paris during the 1880's and in 1892 exhibited some 50 paintings in Berlin. His works aroused so much public controversy that they were withdrawn, but German artists were deeply impressed. Munch spent most of the next 15 years in Germany. After a nervous breakdown in 1908, he returned to Norway and lived in virtual seclusion until his death at his estate, near Oslo, on Jan. 23, 1944.

MUNCH MUSEUM, OSLO

The Cry, a lithograph by Edvard Munch.

Haunted by personal anxieties—which were heightened in childhood by the death of his mother and a sister and were reinforced by a profound pessimism—Munch repudiated realistic art in order "to create living people who breathe and feel and suffer and love." The dramas of Ibsen and Strindberg and the art of Toulouse-Lautrec, Gauguin and Van Gogh influenced his work. By 1889 he had developed an existential art in which psychic realities were convincingly visualized in terms of personal symbols, powerfully undulating linear patterns, and expressively distorted color. Among his favorite themes were seduction, jealousy, and illness and death, in which woman was featured as a demonic embodiment of the life-force. Many of his best works were produced in the decade 1890–1900—paintings such as *Death in the Sick Chamber, Puberty,* and *Dance of Life* (all in the National Gallery, Oslo), as well as some of the greatest portraits of modern art. In 1894 he began to produce extremely influential works of graphic art, using in some cases the subject matter of his paintings—for example, *The Cry* (lithograph, 1895; painting, 1893).

After 1908, Munch's outlook was more affirmative and his work less tormented. In a monumental series for the University of Oslo (1910–1915), he celebrated science, history, and nature with exuberant brushwork and brilliant color.

VICTOR H. MIESEL, *Author of "Voices of German Expressionism"*

Further Reading: Hodin, Josef P., *Edvard Munch* (Praeger 1972); Langaard, Johan H., and Revo'd, Reidar, *Edvard Munch: Masterpieces from . . . the Munch Museum in Oslo* (McGraw 1964); Messer, Thomas M., *Edvard Munch* (Abrams 1972).

MUNCHEN-GLADBACH, mün'ĸĕn glät'-bäĸ, city, Germany, situated in North Rhine-Westphalia just northwest of Rheydt, its twin city, and 15 miles west of Düsseldorf. A rail junction, München-Gladbach is the center of the Rhenish cotton industry and has other manufactures as well, including textile machines, steam engines, heating and air-conditioning apparatus, armatures, and metal building materials. For years the city has been a center for male choral singing, some of its numerous choral societies being from 50 to 100 years old.

München-Gladbach's origins reach back to a Benedictine monastery, founded 972, around which grew a town. The monastery itself was rebuilt several times during the 14th to 18th centuries and is now the city hall. In 1929 the city was joined with Rheydt and Odenkirchen to form Gladbach-Reydt, but it was separated from them in 1933. In March 1945 it was captured by United States troops, being incorporated in the British occupation zone the following June. Pop. (official est. 1957) 148,400.

MUNCHHAUSEN, münĸ'hou-zĕn, BARON **Karl Friedrich Hieronymus von** (also known as BARON MUNCHAUSEN, mŭn-chô'zĭn), fabulous German storyteller: b. Bodenwerder, Hannover, Germany, May 11, 1720; d. there, Feb. 22, 1797. His fame as a storyteller was established by a small book which Rudolf Eric Raspe wrote and published in England in 1785, *Baron Munchausen's Narrative of his Marvelous Travels and Campaigns in Russia.* It was expanded by other authors in many subsequent editions and translated into German in 1786 by Gottfried A. Bürger. See also ADVENTURES OF BARON MUNCHAUSEN, THE.

MUNCHHAUSEN: A Story in Arabesques (*Münchhausen, eine Geschichte in Arabesken*), a satirical romance by Karl L. Immermann (q.v.) originally published in four volumes in Düsseldorf during 1838–1839. The eponymous hero is presented as the nephew of the famous prevaricator, while the author has also taken at least a part of his ideas from *Don Quixote* in attaching to the hero a droll serviteur who closely resembles the materialistic Sancho Panza. Other influences are traceable in the work, notably Friedrich Rückert's translation *Die Makamen des Hariri,* Jonathan Swift's *Gulliver's Travels,* and A. R. Lesage's *Gil Blas.* The story may be described as a formless mass of episodes played in Westphalian villages. The *New Münchhausen* is a traveler like Humboldt; like Gulliver he sojourns among and converses with animals; like Gil Blas he serves as kitchen boy; like Cagliostro he lives indefinitely on rejuvenating medicine. He appears in different roles and in each character successfully exploits the credulity of his audiences. As a disinterested financier and company promoter he is eminently and humorously successful. This work also contains the author's short story masterpiece *Der Oberhof.*

MUNCIE, mŭn'sĭ, city, Indiana, Delaware County seat, altitude 950 feet; on the White River, not navigable; on the Chesapeake and Ohio; the Cleveland, Cincinnati, Chicago and St. Louis; and the Indiana Railroad System, 57 miles northeast of Indianapolis. State and federal highways, an airport, and electric lines also furnish transportation facilities. The county is agricultural, with grains and hay as principal crops, although there are many dairy, fruit, and truck farms. Of the county's 250,880 acres, 237,000 are under cultivation. Among the industrial products of the city are automobile parts, boilers, glass, iron and steel wire and various wire products; metal furniture, silverware, and novelties; and various items of electrical equipment. Muncie's public school system links with the Ball State Teachers College in courses and in teaching personnel. The plant includes a building for vocational and physical education. The courthouse, city hall, post office, library, Masonic temple, and Ball Memorial Hospital are the most notable buildings. Cultural interests include a civic theater and the Ball State Art Gallery. Twelve social agencies unite in support of the Muncie Community Fund. First settled in 1827, incorporated as a town in 1847 and as a city in 1865, Muncie attained its present status as a city of the second class in 1921. Its name, fixed by act of the legislature in 1845, is derived from the name of an Indian tribe, the Munsees. The city has mayor and council, with city treasurer, auditor, clerk, and judge elected; other officers appointed. The water, light, and power systems are all privately operated. Pop. 69,080.

MUNDAY, mŭn'dĭ, **Anthony,** Elizabethan writer of plays, pageants, and pamphlets and translator of popular romances: b. London, England, 1553; d. there 1633 (buried Aug. 10 in St. Stephen's, Coleman Street). He was a draper's son, became a stationer's apprentice, traveled for a while in France and Italy, and did some acting, probably with the earl of Oxford's players.

Munday had great literary versatility but lacked originality or special creative talent. His prose pamphlets include five anti-Catholic tracts (1581–1582) based upon his observations in Rome, where he may have served as a secret political agent. About 1584 he was appointed a messenger of the queen's chamber, and between that date and 1602 he apparently had a hand in the writing of about 20 plays according to the record of Philip Henslowe's *Diary* and other evidence. Several of these were successful, but only five are now extant in which his authorship or collaboration with other authors is definitely established. They are *John a Kent and John a Cumber* (MS 1595); *Sir Thomas More* (MS c. 1596 with additions by others); *The first part . . . of Sir John Oldcastle* (1600, written 1599 in collaboration with others); and *The Downfall of . . .* and *The Death of Robert, Earle of Huntington* (1601, in collaboration with Henry Chettle).

Munday published a few volumes of verse and won some acclaim for his popular ballads, provoking Ben Jonson's satirical portrait of him as the character Balladino in *The Case is Altered* (acted 1598). His voluminous translations of popular romances were based upon French sources. In the dramatic criticism of Francis Meres' *Palladis Tamia* (1598) Munday was listed among the best writers of comedy and was considered the "best plotter." But he probably found his most successful medium as the leading writer of city pageants during the reign of James I.

Consult Turner, Celeste, *Anthony Munday, an Elizabethan Man of Letters* (Berkeley, Calif., 1928).

WILLIAM BRACY.

MUNDELEIN, mŭn'dĕ-līn, **George William,** American cardinal: b. New York, N.Y.,

July 2, 1872; d. Mundelein, Ill., Oct. 2, 1939. He was educated at St. Nicholas parochial school, De La Salle Institute, and Manhattan College, New York, N.Y., St. Vincent Seminary, Latrobe, Pa., and the Urban College of Propaganda, Rome, Italy. Ordained priest at Rome in June 1895, he returned to the United States and was named secretary to the bishop of Brooklyn. In 1897, he was made chancellor of the diocese of Brooklyn and in 1906 was named domestic prelate with the title of right reverend; he was consecrated titular bishop of Loryma and auxiliary bishop of Brooklyn on Sept. 21, 1909. Shortly afterward he became rector of the Cathedral Chapel of Queen of All Saints church, Brooklyn, where he directed an extensive building program. On Dec. 9, 1915, he was named archbishop of Chicago, and on March 24, 1924, was elevated to the Sacred College of Cardinals, becoming "The First Cardinal of the West." He was host to the 28th International Eucharistic Congress in Chicago, June 1926, and papal legate to the 8th National Eucharistic Congress in New Orleans, La., in October 1938. In the same year he presided at the beatification ceremonies of Mother Frances Xavier Cabrini in Rome, and in 1939 participated in the election of Pius XII.

During his administration of the archdiocese of Chicago for nearly 24 years, he emphasized the importance of the parochial school system in the development of Catholic and American citizenry, founded 91 parishes, and had some 600 buildings erected for religious purposes. During and after World War I he showed himself a prelate, patriot, and world citizen by his earnest support of Liberty bonds and his aid to the starving people of Europe. Always a champion of human and civil rights, he vigorously assailed the anti-Catholic and racial propaganda of the Nazi government of Germany in the years before World War II. He died of a heart attack at St. Mary of the Lake Seminary, Mundelein, Ill. In this edifice, perhaps the outstanding memorial to the cardinal in tangible form, he was buried beneath the high altar of the main chapel.

SAMUEL CARDINAL STRITCH.

MUNDELEIN, village, Illinois, in Lake County, 10 miles southwest of Waukegan and 30 miles northwest of Chicago. Situated partly in Libertyville and partly in Fremont townships, at an altitude of 676 feet, it is on a federal highway and is served by the Soo Line and Chicago North Shore and Milwaukee railroads. It is a dairying and farming center, and has shoe manufacturing. Nearby is the resort of Diamond Lake. Incorporated as Area in 1909, the village was renamed for George Cardinal Mundelein (q.v.) in 1925, and contains a small church of brick construction and colonial design named after Santa Maria del Popolo, his titular church in Rome. However, the chief memorial to Cardinal Mundelein is the Saint Mary of the Lake Seminary, containing on beautifully landscaped grounds numerous colonial-style buildings, a chapel, and the Feehan Memorial Library. In 1926, the seminary was the site of the final session of the 28th International Eucharistic Congress. Pop. 16,128.

MUNDELEIN COLLEGE, a Roman Catholic liberal arts college for women in Chicago, Ill. On the initiative of George Cardinal Mundelein, it was founded in 1930 by the Sisters of Charity of the Blessed Virgin Mary, who conduct the work, leading to a bachelor's degree, with the assistance of clerical and lay professors. The library includes a rich collection of religious works and early printed books.

MUNDT, mo͞ont, **Theodor,** German author: b. Potsdam, Prussia, Sept. 19, 1808; d. Berlin, Nov. 30, 1861. He studied at the University of Berlin, became *Privatdozent* there in 1842, and after serving as professor of literature and history at Breslau (1848–1850), returned to Berlin as university professor and librarian. He belonged to the Young German school, was considered a Radical in politics, and favored the emancipation of women. His best-known novel is *Madonna, oder Unterhaltungen mit einer Heiligen* (1835; Madonna, or Conversations with a Saint), whose central character is supposedly Charlotte Stieglitz, a Young German adherent who committed suicide in 1834 in the hope of rousing her husband to poetic greatness. He also memorialized Frau Stieglitz in *Charlotte Stieglitz, ein Denkmal* (1835). His other books include *Die Kunst der deutschen Prosa* (1837; The Art of German Prose), and numerous critical and historical works, political sketches, and travel commentaries.

Consult Draeger, Otto, *Theodor Mundt und seine Beziehungen zum Jungen Deutschland* (Marburg, Germany, 1909); Cumings, Edgar C., *Women in the Life and Work of Theodor Mundt* (Chicago 1936).

KLARA MUNDT (nee MÜLLER; pseudonym LUISE MÜHLBACH; 1814–1873), his wife, wrote many novels with social or historical themes. Her most notable work is *Friedrich der Grosse und sein Hof* (1853; Frederick the Great and His Court).

MUNERA, mū′nĕ-ră (plural of the Latin *munus,* meaning a service or duty), under the Roman Empire, the public services, charges, duties or offices which an individual was obliged to render on behalf of the state or city in which he was born or lived. Liability for *munera,* which varied from maintenance of public roads, buildings, waterworks, and riverbanks, to payment of taxes, was determined by a citizen's standing. In the case of the decurion (q.v.), or colonial or municipal councilor, the *munera* included collection of the imperial taxes, which proved to be a crushing burden, since the councilor was liable for any defaults.

MUNHALL, mŭn′hôl, an industrial borough, Pennsylvania, in Allegheny County, situated on the south bank of the Monongahela River, eight miles southeast of Pittsburgh and adjoining Homestead and West Mifflin. Its elevation is 755 feet above sea level. It has important iron and steel works of the United States Steel Corporation. Originally planned as a residential section for steel employees, it was incorporated in 1901. In 1892 it was a site of the Homestead steel strike, one of the bitterest in United States history. The borough contains the Carnegie Library of Homestead, a gift of Andrew Carnegie in 1898, equipped with a music hall, swimming pool, and other facilities. It is served by the Pennsylvania Railroad and local highways. It has a burgess and council form of government. Pop. 16,674.

MUNI, mū′nĭ, **Paul** (real name MUNI WEISENFREUND), American actor: b. Lemberg, Austria, Sept. 22, 1895; d. Santa Barbara, Calif., Aug. 25, 1967. With his parents, he emigrated to the United States in 1907, making his stage debut in Chicago in 1907 with a Yiddish company to which his parents belonged, and remaining with this group until 1914. During 1918–1926 he toured the United States and England with the Yiddish Art Theatre of New York City, and in 1926, in New York City, made his first appearance in an English-speaking role in *We Americans.* After appearing in several other plays, he scored a great success in 1931 with his portrayal of George Simon, the Jewish lawyer in *Counsellor-at-Law,* a role he revived in 1932 and 1942. Other stage vehicles included *Key Largo* (1939), *They Knew What They Wanted* (1949), and *Inherit the Wind* (1955), in which, as Clarence Darrow (Henry Drummond in the script), defense lawyer in the famous Scopes evolution trial of 1925, he gave another memorable performance, which won him the 1956 Antoinette Perry award. In London, England, he starred in *Death of a Salesman* (1949). Beginning in 1929, Muni appeared in many motion pictures, notably *Scarface, I Am a Fugitive from a Chain Gang, The Story of Louis Pasteur* (for which he won a Motion Picture Academy Award in 1936 for best performance of an actor), *The Life of Emile Zola,* and *The Last Angry Man.* He became a United States citizen in 1923.

MUNICH, mū'nĭk (Ger. MÜNCHEN, mün'-kĕn), city, Federal Republic of Germany, capital of the state of Bavaria and third largest city (after Berlin and Hamburg) of Germany. It is situated on a plateau at an elevation of 1,700 feet and on the Isar River (crossed within the city by 16 bridges), about 25 miles north of the Bavarian Alps; because of its altitude and proximity to the Alps, its climate is subject to frequent temperature changes. Munich has a tradition as one of the world's most beautiful cities, and is famous as an artistic and educational center and for its many fine buildings, churches, and parks. Although heavily bombed in World War II, when about two fifths of its buildings were totally destroyed, by 1960 it was mostly rebuilt. It is the see of the Roman Catholic archbishop and cardinal of Munich-Freising archdiocese, and of the Lutheran bishop of Bavaria. A crossroads of north-south, east-west European traffic, the city is a focal point of railroads, *Autobahn* highways, and air routes. It is an important industrial and commercial center. One of its most famous traditional products is Munich beer. Its population in 1950 was 832,000. By 1965 the population had increased to 1,210,465.

Buildings and Monuments.—Medieval Munich, built in the centuries following the founding of the city in 1158 (see section on *History*), was surrounded by ramparts and moats, and could be entered only through huge gates flanked by massive towers. Three of these old gateways, the Karlstor, Sendlinger Tor, and Isartor, have been preserved. But the dominating symbols of oldest Munich are its churches, above all the Frauenkirche (Cathedral of Our Lady, built in 1468–1488, heavily damaged in World War II but afterward largely restored), a late Gothic structure whose lofty twin towers, capped with copper domes, are the city's landmark. Of similar historic significance are the Peterskirche (St. Peter's Church, 14th century), practically demolished in the air raids, and the Theatinerkirche (Theatines' Church, 1674–1696), heavily damaged, both of which have been restored. Also dating to this period is the Residenz (city palace of the Wittelsbach dynasty), which took five centuries, from about 1400 to 1900, to build.

In the earlier part of the 19th century, the city expanded rapidly under the leadership of Louis (Ludwig) I of Bavaria (r. 1825–1848), who was responsible for the building of some of its most magnificent structures. A patron and lover of the arts, Louis and his architects, Friedrich von Gärtner (1792–1847) and Franz Karl Leo von Klenze (1784–1864), built the famous Ludwigstrasse in the Italian Renaissance style, and designed wide streets interspersed with squares and parks and adorned with fountains and monuments. The work of this period is seen in the architectural highlights of the Ludwigstrasse, including the Staatsbibliothek (State Library, 1839), the Ludwigskirche (St. Louis' Church, 1844), and the Ludwig-Maximilians-Universität (Munich University, 1840), all classicist edifices built by Gärtner, while Renaissance-style buildings designed by Klenze around 1820 are in the nearby Wittelsbacherplatz.

Munich's other notable buildings include the Altes Rathaus (Old City Hall, Gothic, 1470, destroyed in World War II but afterward restored) and the neo-Gothic Neues Rathaus (New City Hall, 1899); the Maxburg (1590), of which only the tower escaped the bombs, although the demolished palace proper was rebuilt as a modern business center; the Stadtmuseum (City Museum, 1520), Munich's largest secular Gothic building, with a spacious hall in the late Gothic style; the former Stadtschreiberei (town clerk's office, 1550), the city's best-preserved late Gothic building; the Alter Hof (Old Court, 1253), the oldest court of the rulers of Bavaria; the Gunetzrheinerhaus (baroque, 1730), mansion of Johann Gunetzrheiner (1692–1763), a great architect of that period; the Holnstein Palace (1735, now known as the archbishop's palace), built by François Cuvilliés (1695–1768), the greatest architect and decorator of the baroque age; the neoclassic Hauptmünzamt (Mint, 1809) built by Andreas Gärtner; the Feldherrnhalle (Generals' Monument, 1844), built by Friedrich Gärtner as a replica of the Loggia dei Lanzi of Florence; and the Propyläen (1864), a monumental marble structure designed by Klenze and based on the Propylaea forming the entrance to the Acropolis at Athens.

The Nymphenburg Palace on the western outskirts of Munich, a vast Italian baroque building with rococo interior decorations, is the work of many architects, decorators, and painters. The Maximilianeum (1874), one of Munich's earliest neo-Gothic structures, became the home of the Bavarian Parliament after World War II. Outstanding churches, other than those mentioned, are the Michaelskirche (St. Michael's Church, 1597), with a majestic barrel vault in Renaissance style; the church of St. Johann Nepomuk, built in 1733–1735 by the Asam brothers, Cosmas Damian (1686–1739) and Egid Quirin (1692–1750), a true gem of rococo architecture; and the ultramodern new Protestant church of St. Matthew (1955). Among the many statues is the colossal bronze figure of Bavaria, designed by Ludwig von Schwanthaler (1802–1848), from whose head a fine view of the city and the Alps is obtained.

The turn of the 19th century was particularly important, artistically, to Munich, for here there developed the *Jugendstil,* an outgrowth of the *art nouveau* movement and a major contributor to the ushering in of modern art. Outstanding architectural monuments of this movement are the state Nationalmuseum, the Künstlerhaus (Artists' House, shattered by bombs and by 1960 not yet

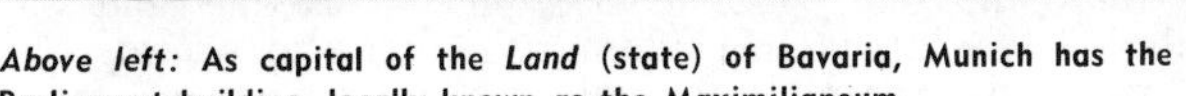

Above left: As capital of the *Land* (state) of Bavaria, Munich has the Parliament building, locally known as the Maximilianeum.

Above right: The German museum of the physical sciences and technology, founded in 1903, is the largest and most important of its kind.

Pix, Inc.

MUNICH

Above: Munich boasts that its beer is the world's finest and dates its production back to 1320.

Below: Both the Munich Frauenkirche (upper left) and the Rathaus (city hall; right) can be seen in this view of the Marienplatz.

Josef Muench

Below: Among Munich's many beer gardens, that of the Hofbräuhaus is probably the most famous.

Birnback Publishing Service

rebuilt); and the Prinzregententheater, erected for festival performances of Richard Wagner's operas. The period produced a wide variety of creative trends in literature, painting, architecture, theater, and music in Munich.

Art Collections, Theaters, Education.—Munich's art collections and theaters have traditions dating back in many cases to the 18th century. Collections belonging to the Bavarian state include that of the Glyptothek, built by Klenze in 1816–1830 (antique sculpture; building largely destroyed by bombs but being rebuilt); the Alte Pinakothek (1826–1836), a classicist building by Klenze with unique collections of Peter Paul Rubens and Albrecht Dürer (building completely gutted but being rebuilt); the Nationalmuseum (medieval, baroque, and rococo exhibits); the Neue Pinakothek and the Neue Staatsgalerie (both these buildings were destroyed in the war and have not yet been rebuilt, but their 19th and 20th century art collections were saved); and the Schack Gallery (German romantic painting). Municipal museums include the Lenbachhaus (19th century and later paintings, including 150 works by Vasili Kandinski, Russian artist, rediscovered in 1956 near Munich). Of world renown are the masterpieces of natural science and technology in the Deutsches Museum, situated on an island in the Isar.

The various Bavarian state theaters present operas at the Prinzregententheater (the traditional setting for opera, the Nationaltheater, was totally destroyed in the raids and is slowly being rebuilt); plays at the Residenztheater and, with alternating operas, at the restored Cuvilliéstheater, an outstanding sight because of the preserved rococo decorations; and operettas and musical comedies at the Gärtnerplatztheater. The city operates a playhouse (Kammerspiele im Schauspielhaus). Music is represented mostly by three symphony orchestras.

The chief center of higher education is the University of Munich (q.v.). The city's largest library is the Stadtbibliothek. There are also an institute of technology, state academies of fine arts and of music, and many vocational schools.

Parks and Festivals.—The Hofgarten in front of the Residenz and the Englischer Garten, extending for several miles throughout the city, are the principal parks (the Englischer Garten was laid out in 1789 by Benjamin Thompson, Count Rumford, q.v., a native of Woburn, Mass.). Large restaurants and beer gardens, rather than homes, are the focal points of social life; most popular is the famous Hofbräuhaus. Munich is noted for its gay and easygoing way of life. There are festivals almost the year around, beginning in January and February during the *Fasching* carnival season, when countless costume balls are held, continuing in spring with the strong-beer season, when Müncheners greet each other on the terraces and in the gardens of the city's large breweries, and progressing to the *Oktoberfest,* which attracts some 2 million visitors annually to the Theresienwiese fair grounds in downtown Munich, with their huge beer tents and endless shows and amusements. The city has a large botanical garden and one of the world's most complete zoos.

Industries.—In past centuries, Munich was a center of handicrafts, and ranked foremost in southern Germany in applied arts. While the city's world-famous breweries once played the major role in its economic life, manufacturing has been a notable feature of modern Munich. The city produces machinery, vehicles, precision and optical instruments, textiles, clothes, shoes, leather, chemicals, processed foods, and many other articles. It is an important printing and publishing center. There in a large vegetable and fruit trade. Tourism is important.

History.—The site's oldest lifeline was the road used in transporting salt from Salzburg, in the east, via Reichenhall, which led to the Isar River crossing at this place long before Munich was founded, and which followed the course of a pre-Christian Roman road. Monks from one of the nearby Benedictine abbeys started a settlement at the site called *Munichen* (a reference to monks, hence the modern name). However, the founder of Munich is considered to be Henry (called Henry the Lion; 1129–1195), duke of Saxony and Bavaria, who in 1158 built the first bridge across the river there. In the same year the town was granted market rights, and ever since its coat of arms has included the figure of a monk. In 1255 the Wittelsbach dukes established their court in Munich. Outstanding figures of this dynasty were Louis IV (called the Bavarian; ?1287–1347), Holy Roman emperor; Maximilian I, duke and elector of Bavaria (1563–1631); and Louis I, king of Bavaria (1786–1868; see section on *Buildings and Monuments*). Munich was occupied by Gustavus II (Gustavus Adolphus), of Sweden, in 1632, by the Spaniards in 1634, and by the Austrians in 1704–1714. After World War I, Munich was ruled briefly by Communists (April–May 1919). It was the birthplace in 1920 of the Nationalist Socialist (Nazi) party and was the scene in November 1923 of Adolf Hitler's unsuccessful *Putsch.* During World War II, as party headquarters, it was associated with many Nazi activities but also with the fiercest resistance which Hitler met in Germany. In 1942 Munich students tried to stage a revolt against the Nazi regime; when their plot failed, many were executed. The city was captured by the United States Seventh Army on April 30, 1945.

HERBERT HOHENEMSER.

MUNICH, University of (officially LUDWIG-MAXIMILIANS-UNIVERSITÄT), Federal Republic of Germany, a university founded at Ingolstadt, on the Danube river, in 1472 by the Bavarian duke, Ludwig the Rich; it was transferred to Landshut, on the Isar river, in 1800 by the elector Joseph Maximilian (later first king of Bavaria), deriving its official name from these two princes, and in 1826 was brought to Munich by Ludwig I. In this location it soon became a leading center of research and education, numbering among its famous professors the chemist Baron Justus von Liebig (1803–1873), the physicist Wilhelm Konrad Röntgen (1845–1923), and the surgeon Ernst Ferdinand Sauerbruch (1875–1951). The largest university in Germany, it has faculties of theology (Roman Catholic), jurisprudence, political economy, medicine, veterinary medicine, philosophy, and natural sciences. Its main buildings, executed in classical style, consist of two blocks on the Ludwigstrasse and Amalienstrasse connected by a great domed hall. During World War II about 70 per cent of its buildings were destroyed by bombing; reconstruction was undertaken after the war. Of over one million books in its prewar library, only 650,000 survived.

MUNICH CONFERENCE, a four-power conference of Great Britain, France, Germany, and Italy, held in Munich, Germany, on Sept. 29–

30, 1938, that resulted in the dismemberment of Czechoslovakia. The conference culminated a series of crises and diplomatic maneuverings provoked by the demands of Konrad Henlein, German leader in the predominantly German-speaking Czech Sudetenland, strongly supported by Adolf Hitler, chancellor of Germany. When Henlein's demands and Berlin's denunciations of Czechoslovak "atrocities" against the Sudeten Germans grew more and more extreme, Prime Minister Neville Chamberlain of Britain on August 3 sent Viscount Runciman on a six weeks' abortive mediation mission to Prague. Meanwhile, France repeatedly assured Prague that, under a treaty of 1925, she would aid Czechoslovakia in case of unprovoked German attack, although Paris was evidently reluctant to do so without British support (the Soviet Union had already pledged aid to Czechoslovakia under a 1935 treaty making such aid contingent on simultaneous French aid). Following a bellicose speech by Hitler on Sept. 12 and concentration of German troops on the Czechoslovak border, Chamberlain flew to Germany for a conference with Hitler at Berchtesgaden (Sept. 15–16), returning convinced that only cession of predominantly German-speaking Sudeten areas to Germany could save the peace. A few days later Britain and France, in effect, forced Czechoslovakia to accept Hitler's territorial demands by intimating that failure to do so would mean loss of Anglo-French aid in case of a German attack. Under the Anglo-French plan, the new frontiers were to be fixed by an international commission including Czechoslovakia. But at a second meeting with Chamberlain at Godesberg (Sept. 22–24), Hitler demanded immediate cession of the areas as the only alternative to "forcible action." Chamberlain rejected these terms; so did France and Czechoslovakia. Britain now pledged aid to France should hostilities ensue. Both governments speeded war preparations. President Franklin D. Roosevelt of the United States appealed to Hitler to continue negotiations. Chamberlain, assuring Hitler that he could "get all essentials without war and without delay," offered to attend an international conference in Berlin. Finally, on Sept. 28, Hitler agreed to the Munich conference.

The conferees—chiefly Hitler, Premier Benito Mussolini of Italy, Chamberlain, and Premier Édouard Daladier of France—met at 1 P.M. on Sept. 29 and at 1 A.M. on Sept. 30 signed the famous Munich pact. It conceded virtually all Hitler's demands for immediate territorial cessions from Czechoslovakia, the main areas to be occupied in the period Oct. 1–10 (in some areas there were to be plebiscites but these were never held). Czechoslovakia was not consulted; nor was the Soviet Union. Helpless and abandoned, the Czechoslovak government had no alternative but to capitulate. Returning to London with an Anglo-German declaration renouncing war as a means of settling their differences, Chamberlain announced he had secured "peace in our time." Within a short time, conclusion of the Munich pact led to the occupation of the Teschen area of Czechoslovakia by Poland and of parts of Slovakia, under a German-Italian award, by Hungary.

The Munich pact has been widely condemned as the pinnacle of Anglo-French appeasement of Hitler and as a key antecedent of World War II, but it has also been defended on the grounds of Anglo-French military unreadiness at the time.

See also WORLD WAR II—*2. Between World Wars;* CZECHOSLOVAKIA; SUDETENLAND.

MUNICIPAL BUDGETS. See BUDGETS, AMERICAN—*Budgets in Local Government.*

MUNICIPAL GOVERNMENT, local government of cities, towns, and other organized communities. As used in this article, the term refers primarily to the government of cities, villages, boroughs, and incorporated towns in the United States and the corresponding units in other countries. Also included are the urban communes of France and their foreign counterparts. Local governments not generally regarded as municipal are those of counties, townships, New England towns, school districts, and special districts in the United States, and such governments as those of regions, provinces, prefectures, and (usually) districts in other countries.

UNITED STATES

Distinctive features of municipal government in the United States include (1) a wide variety of municipal patterns; (2) a high degree of local self-government; and (3) a large measure of personal freedom from municipal control. Nowhere among European, Asiatic, or South American countries are these characteristics so pronounced as they are in the United States.

Historical Background.—From 1776, the year of independence, to the 1870's the history of municipal government in the United States was characterized by a gradual trend toward a system based on separation of powers and checks and balances, and by an acceptance of the democracy of Andrew Jackson, the country's seventh president. The first municipal governments, based on the British model, vested almost complete authority in a council, which served both as a plural executive and legislative body. Slowly and unevenly over the country the weak mayor-council form of government, as described below, evolved. To a large extent this form was an outgrowth of Jacksonian principles of faith in the common man and belief in elected administrative officials, short terms of office, and the spoils system.

The traditions, structures, and practices of municipal government were unequal to meet the complex urban problems accompanying the industrial development and urban growth of the latter 19th century. Most major cities became dominated by bosses, rings, and machines. Shocked at the "extravagance, corruption, and mismanagement" in city administration, James Bryce (Viscount Bryce, 1838–1922), British historian and interpreter of the American scene, concluded in 1888 that city government was "the one conspicuous failure of the United States."

The 20th century witnessed vast changes and manifold experiments in municipal government. Bossism virtually disappeared. There developed a new emphasis on responsible forms of government and efficient management.

Creation and Legal Status of Municipalities.—Municipalities are creatures of the state and legally are subject entirely to the will of the state. Each of the 50 states creates municipalities as municipal corporations primarily to meet local government needs and secondarily to serve as agents of state administration. A few states give a special charter to each municipality. Usually, however, the legislature grants a uniform charter to a class of municipalities or permits municipalities to select one of several optional charters.

Twenty-one states through constitutional provisions and four states entirely through legislative enactments have provided for a system of municipal home rule either as a substitute or alternate for the plan of special or general charters. Fundamental to home rule is the right of communities to make and later amend their own charters. This enables communities to select their governmental forms and powers consistent with the state constitution and, in some cases, the general laws of the state. The principal advantage of home rule is the flexibility it gives municipalities to adapt their governments to particular local needs.

Forms of Municipal Governments.—There are three main types of municipal government in the United States: (1) the mayor-council plan, (2) the commission plan, and (3) the council-manager plan. The mayor-council plan, in turn, may be subdivided into (a) the strong mayor-council type and (b) the weak mayor-council type. Because of many variations within each plan, generalizations concerning governmental forms should be accepted with reservations. See also CITY COUNCILS, AMERICAN.

Mayor-Council Plan.—Of the more than 17,000 municipalities in the United States, approximately 15,000 operate under mayor-council government. Every one of the 17 most populous cities (except Washington, D.C., which is under Congressional control) uses this form. Approximately half the municipalities of over 5,000 population and well over 90 per cent of those of under 5,000 population have some kind of mayor-council government.

Weak Mayor-Council Government.—The weak mayor-council form is based on the traditional American theory of separation of powers plus checks and balances. The voters elect separately a mayor and council. The mayor is usually empowered to veto ordinances and resolutions passed by the council, and the council ordinarily can override the veto by an extraordinary majority.

The administrative system lacks integration. The plan calls for the popular election of several department heads, over whom neither the mayor nor council may have any direct supervision. The council appoints certain administrative officials, and council members themselves may serve ex officio on administrative boards. A committee of the council is ordinarily responsible for formulating the budget. The mayor has only limited appointment and removal powers and lacks authority to supervise and coordinate the numerous boards and commissions found in this form. Principally because of inadequate administrative leadership afforded by weak mayor-council government, the greater number of cities have either modified the plan or abandoned it entirely.

Strong Mayor-Council Government.—In strong mayor-council government the mayor is head of the administration. There is a consolidation of related activities into a relatively small number of departments, each of which usually has a single head appointed and removable by the mayor. The mayor is responsible for the budget, and in large cities has staff and housekeeping agencies as managerial aids. An increasing, but still small, number of large cities have modified the strong mayor form to include a chief administrative officer appointed by the mayor.

The council is primarily a legislative body. Even in large cities it is likely to be small with members elected on a city-wide basis. The council does not have administrative duties.

Legally, relations between the mayor and council are much the same as in the weak mayor type. In practice, because of the importance of his position and the nature of his responsibilities, the strong mayor is more likely than the weak mayor to exert effective political leadership.

Commission Plan.—Commission government, introduced by Galveston, Texas, in 1901 and later popularized by Des Moines, Iowa, vests both lawmaking and executive powers in a commission of three to five members. Collectively the commissioners comprise both a legislative council and a plural executive. Individually each commissioner, including the mayor, heads one of the major administrative departments. The mayor presides over commission meetings and has ceremonial duties. The number of commission-governed cities declined from a peak of over 500 in 1917 to 312 by 1959. See also COMMISSION FORM OF GOVERNMENT.

Council-Manager Plan.—Council-manager government has grown in popularity. Beginning in 1908 with Staunton, Va., the council-manager plan had by late 1959 been adopted by approximately 1,600 municipalities, including between 40 and 45 per cent of all United States cities of between 10,000 and 500,000 population. More cities over 25,000 population operate under council-manager government than under any other form.

The structure of the council-manager plan is simple. The voters elect a council which in turn appoints a professional, nonpartisan manager with indefinite tenure as head of the administration. The council may remove the manager at any time. The primary duties of the mayor are to preside over council meetings and serve as ceremonial head of the municipality.

Theoretically the council makes policies and the manager merely carries them out. However, both through broad discretionary authority in administrative matters and through recommendations and advice to the council, managers are ordinarily influential in policy decisions. See also CITY MANAGER PLAN OF GOVERNMENT.

Modern Trends and Issues.—The latter part of the 20th century was expected to be a dynamic era for municipal governments. A number of major problems beset municipalities and significant trends unfolded. Solutions to the problems and precise directions to the trends, it was clear, would emerge from an interplay of contending forces and interests.

The American way of urban life calls for increasing dependence on municipal government by the city dweller for his comfort and well-being. The demand for services appears to be insatiable. A large city may perform more than 400 activities, which, if listed alphabetically, an authority has observed, might range from abattoir and airport under A to zoo under Z.

As services multiply, the tasks of municipal governments become more complex and call for technical competence and efficient management. To meet the challenge, municipalities have continued to integrate their administrative structures, to create sound systems of fiscal administration, and establish formal civil service systems.

How to finance the growing services has been an ever-present problem. The traditional source of municipal income, the general property tax, has become inadequate, and increasingly municipalities have received state authorization to broaden their tax base, especially by levying income and payroll taxes, sales taxes, and admission taxes. State aid in the form of grants-in-aid and shared taxes has increased to become second only to the general property tax as a source of municipal income.

The rapid movement of population, retail stores, and industries into urban fringe areas has had serious consequences both for the central city and the suburbs. The central city has lost a substantial part of its tax base and has become blighted with decaying sections; it has faced new parking and traffic-flow problems and has been required to furnish or subsidize services within the suburbs. Suburban residents, usually with a limited tax base, often find themselves in need of expensive services, especially water, sewerage, and schools. The entire metropolitan area—the core city and its peripheral communities—though constituting a single economic and social unit, often comprises a multiplicity of municipal governments and other political units. Only limited progress has resulted from attempts to devise satisfactory governmental arrangements for metropolitan areas.

State administrative control over municipalities has expanded to supplement the traditional control by the states through legislative enactments and judicial enforcement. The resultant issues have centered around the question as to what should be the nature and extent of administrative control. In the late 1950's state administrative supervision of municipalities was largely decentralized and fairly uncoordinated. Coercive types of administrative control, though they were increasing, were meager indeed as compared with those of continental Europe or even Great Britain.

The inability and sometimes the unwillingness of state legislatures, frequently controlled by rural elements even in predominantly urban states, to provide for urban needs has caused municipalities to turn with success to the national government for help. In some instances the national government, following the precedents set during the depression of the 1930's, has bypassed the states and given financial assistance directly to municipalities. Because of the financial resources of the national government and the sympathetic response it has generally given to urban pleas for assistance, direct national-municipal relations can be expected to continue and expand.

CANADA

With authority vested in each province to determine its local government system, Canada, like the United States, has a varied pattern of municipal government. In the greater number of provinces there are four types of municipalities: rural municipalities, villages, towns, and cities. Two provinces (Prince Edward Island and Newfoundland) do not have rural municipalities and two others, Ontario and Quebec, have a fifth type of municipality, the large county municipalities. A feature of Canadian local government is the separation of towns and cities (and frequently villages) from the surrounding county. Such separation is rare in the United States outside of Virginia, and in Great Britain is found only in the county boroughs.

The mayor-council plan is the dominant type of municipal government in Canada. The mayor may be popularly elected and a strong executive; or he may be chosen by the council from its own membership and have few special powers. In either instance the mayor (sometimes called reeve) presides over the council.

Council-manager government, as used in the United States, has increased in popularity in Canada. A few cities in Alberta and Saskatchewan use a variation of the plan calling for a plural executive.

The largest cities in Ontario and Quebec have still other forms which have some of the characteristics of cabinet government. A board or committee, on which the mayor sits, comprises an inner circle of the council and not only serves as a collegial executive but also takes the leadership in legislative policy. In some cities a board of control is popularly elected; in other cities an executive committee is appointed by the council and is assisted in its executive capacity by a chief administrative officer.

Beginning with the depression of the 1930's the trend in Canada has been toward centralized control of municipalities by the provinces. Increasingly the provinces have supervised or financed municipal activities, and in some instances they have assumed activities formerly performed by municipalities. Eight of the ten provinces have established departments of municipal affairs, with varying degrees of supervisory authority over municipalities. In spite of increasing provincial control, Canadian municipalities have a considerable amount of local autonomy.

GREAT BRITAIN, FRANCE, AND THE SOVIET UNION

The three systems of municipal government which have had the greatest worldwide influence and which have most frequently furnished the models for other countries are those of Great Britain, France, and the Soviet Union. These systems represent three contrasting traditions and philosophies as well as structures.

Great Britain.—The units for governing municipalities in Great Britain are the urban district, municipal borough, and county borough. Borough councils are composed of popularly elected councilors, aldermen selected by the councilors, and a mayor appointed by his fellow council members. Urban districts do not have aldermen and select a chairman rather than mayor as presiding officer. In all three units the council, a unicameral body, is both the legislature and the executive. Council committees supervise the various executive departments.

The tradition of local self-government is deeply rooted in Great Britain, and British municipalities still have a significant role in determining their own affairs. In modern times, however, municipalities have lost many of their functions to the national government and have been subjected to increased central control. Moreover, the trend has been for municipalities to become units for the decentralized administration of national programs rather than units for genuine local self-government.

France.—In France the commune is the unit of government for municipalities. The approximately 38,000 communes cover every square inch of French soil and may be large cities, small villages, or purely rural areas. Regardless of size or composition their governmental patterns are uniform with the exception of Paris, which, like many other capital cities, has a special status. The voters of each commune elect a council which in turn selects a mayor as its presiding officer. The mayor and his assistants execute both commune and central policies. Commune governments are subject to close supervision and control by the prefect of the department *(département)* and the Ministry of Interior. Although the degree of local self-government is less than that of Great Britain, it is far greater than that of the Soviet Union.

Soviet Union.—Municipal government in the Soviet Union follows essentially the same pattern as that used for all other government levels in that country. The voters elect a soviet (council) which appoints an executive committee as the administrative and executive organ. Legally, the executive committee is responsible to the soviet which appointed it and to the soviet at the next highest level of government. Actually, the municipal soviet is generally controlled by its executive committee, which in turn follows the dictates of party leaders. However, within the framework of basic Communist policy the soviets may review and criticize the work of the executive committees. The soviets, consisting of hundreds of members in large cities, are not policy-making bodies but rather agencies for arousing the enthusiasm and participation of large masses of people. Under the scrutiny of the executive committee, standing committees of the soviet assisted by voluntary workers direct the day-to-day administration. Each of the constituent republics of the Soviet Union exercises close control over municipal activities both directly through several ministries and indirectly through the hierarchy of local governments.

PANORAMA OF MUNICIPAL PATTERNS

Not only the structure but also the tone and spirit of municipal government vary among countries. Yet certain patterns and traditions are discernible. British traditions of personal freedom and local self-government have influenced the English-speaking world and have left varying imprints on other democratic countries. The British municipal structure, with modifications, has served as a model for municipal governments in the Commonwealth of Nations and elsewhere. In the United States and Canada, where municipal government developed to a large extent under frontier conditions conducive to improvisation and experimentation, British traditions of local democracy and decentralized control were strengthened and perpetuated.

Rejecting the Anglo-American belief in pragmatism and experimentation, the French, proceeding deductively and systematically, have established a municipal pattern characterized by symmetry and centralism. The French system has influenced much of continental Europe and also a number of countries in South America and Asia.

Municipal governments in some democratic countries do not fit readily into either the Anglo-American or French pattern. For example, Scandinavian countries and Japan, though accepting the French principle of uniformity, permit greater local autonomy than France does. German municipalities also have a somewhat higher degree of self-determination than French communes; moreover, there is a variation of municipal patterns among the German states (Länder). In Latin American municipalities, Spanish and Portuguese influences have become weaker and, except in those countries having authoritarian governments, there is a pronounced trend toward greater autonomy. Swiss municipal governments, featured by plural executives and in small communes by mass meetings of citizens for policy determination, have an outstandingly large measure of independence and self-government.

The spread of the Soviet type of municipal government has been largely a post-World War II development. The countries of eastern Europe and Communist China follow rather faithfully the municipal structure and principles of the USSR.

Bibliography.—UNITED STATES: The outstanding source of current information on United States municipal governments is *The Municipal Year Book* published annually in Chicago. The chief periodicals include the *National Civic Review* (formerly the *National Municipal Review*, New York); *Public Management* (Chicago); *American Municipal News* (Washington, D.C); *United States Municipal News* (Washington, D.C.); *American City* (New York); *Municipal Finance* (Chicago). Among the books giving general coverage to municipal government are: Adrian, Charles R., *Governing Urban America* (New York 1955); Bromage, Arthur W., *Introduction to Municipal Government and Administration* (New York 1957); Kneier, Charles M., *City Government in the United States*, 3d ed. (New York 1957). For the colonial history of United States municipal government see Griffith, Ernest S., *History of American City Government* (New York 1938). The most comprehensive legal treatise on municipal government is found in McQuillin, Eugene, *The Law of Municipal Corporations*, 3d ed., 20 vols. (Chicago 1949–1951).

CANADA: Excellent studies of Canadian municipal government can be found in Brittain, Horace L., *Local Government in Canada* (Toronto 1951); Crawford, Kenneth G., *Canadian Municipal Government* (Toronto 1954); Rowat, Donald C., *Your Local Government* (Toronto and New York 1955).

OTHER COUNTRIES: General information on municipal governments of various countries is contained in textbooks on comparative world governments, including Shotwell, James T., ed., *Governments of Continental Europe*, rev. ed. (New York 1952); Carter, Gwendolen M., and Ranney, John C., *Major Foreign Powers* (New York 1957); Zink, Harold, *Modern Governments* (Princeton 1958). A monumental book on the government and politics of selected large municipalities in every continent is that of Robson, William A., ed., *Great Cities of the World*, new ed. (New York 1957). One of the few studies in English on Latin American municipalities is that of Mouchet, Carlos, "Municipal Government," in Davis, Harold E., ed., *Government and Politics in Latin America* (New York 1958). Other references on specific countries include: Sauser-Hall, George, *The Political Institutions of Switzerland* (Zurich 1946); Arneson, Ben A., *The Democratic Monarchies of Scandinavia*, 2d ed. (Princeton 1949); Garelik, Joseph, *A Soviet City and Its People* (New York 1950); Finer, Herman, *English Local Government*, 4th ed., rev. (New York 1950); Hermans, Ferdinand A., "Local Autonomy in France and Italy," in Zurcher, Arnold J., ed., *Constitutions and Constitutional Trends Since World War II* (New York 1951); Chapman, Brian, *Introduction to French Local Government* (New York 1953); Wells, Roger H., "Local Government" in Litchfield, Edward H., and others, *Governing Postwar Germany* (Ithaca 1953); Maud, Sir John P. R., and Finer, Samuel E., *Local Government in England and Wales*, 2d ed. (New York 1953); Tinker, Hugh, *The Foundations of Local Self-Government in India, Pakistan, and Burma* (New York 1954).

GUY H. FOX,
Professor of Political Science, Michigan State University.

MUNICIPAL HOUSING. See HOUSING; CITY PLANNING IN THE UNITED STATES.

MUNICIPAL OWNERSHIP, a term applying, in a general sense, to all property owned by a municipality. More commonly, however, it is used in the United States and Canada as "municipal trading" is used in Great Britain. That is, the term refers to utility properties owned and usually operated by a municipality. A list of utilities that are municipally owned in various communities throughout the world includes water, gas, and electricity supplies, mass transportation, liquor stores, slaughterhouses, parking facilities, telephone systems, airports, harbor facilities, and sewerage and sewage disposal plants, among others.

Virtually from their beginnings, cities have operated some utilities. Although urban areas originally served primarily as centers of defense and religion, the municipal market was an early function. Other medieval municipal utilities included public baths and, in a limited way, water supplies. The scope of municipal ownership expanded over time and especially after about 1830 when technological advances in Europe and America made modern urban services possible.

In Europe the tradition of municipal provision of services has always been strong, and the idea that government should provide only those things that could not be provided by private enterprise, though sometimes presented, has never been as important as in North America. As a result, the ownership and operation of utilities by the municipality is the general practice. In the United States and Canada, on the other hand, the question of utilities policy has been a matter of debate. Historically, local utilities in these countries have been privately owned, and most of them still are. The traditional importance attached to the private enterprise idea in American culture has made private ownership seem natural, but the great amount of corruption and the low level of morality in business and government after the Civil War encouraged a subsequent reform movement having municipal ownership as one of its goals.

Advocates of municipal ownership have held that utilities should exist for service rather than profit, that municipalities can borrow money more cheaply than private companies, and that there are other advantages. Opponents say that modern management is honest, more stable, and of a higher caliber than public management, and that lack of a profit motive leads to inefficiency. Arguments pro and con have generally been emotion-packed and based on individual values rather than empirical evidence.

In some countries of Asia and Africa, utilities are likely to be supplied by state-owned corporations rather than by municipalities, or they may be privately owned as a byproduct of industrial development. Australian practice follows the European pattern, but some utilities are owned and operated by the states. Japan, South America, and Spanish-speaking North America follow generally the pattern in the United States and Canada. The communist countries make local utilities a part of state planning and control, although municipal authorities have some discretion within the policies established by the central government. In many countries with municipal ownership the principal utilities, especially water and electricity, are often under a separate board which is largely independent of the regular city government. In all countries water supply, because it is closely related to the public health, tends to be a municipal or state function.

Bibliography.—For historical background, see Mumford, Lewis, *The Culture of Cities* (New York 1938). Good case examples may be found in Robson, William A., ed., *Great Cities of the World,* new ed. (New York 1957). The most recent edition of the annual *Municipal Year Book* contains such data as are available on American municipal ownership and operation. For detailed arguments, see Bangs, C.W.H., *The Case for Public Ownership of Electric Utilities* (Chicago 1937), and Bauer, John, *The Public Utility Franchise* (Chicago 1946).

CHARLES R. ADRIAN,
Professor of Political Science, Michigan State University.

MUNICIPIUM, mū'nĭ-sĭp'ĭ-ŭm, in antiquity, an autonomous community possessing, usually, partial Roman citizenship. While such a community's municipal life was centered in a town, yet the *municipium* embraced any suburban or rural district subject to the municipality's jurisdiction. Rome required *municipia* to furnish auxiliary troops for Roman wars, to accept Roman dictation of foreign policy, and to permit periodical visits of inspection by Roman officials (prefects). Free members of a *municipium* could acquire full Roman citizenship by settling in Rome. Originally, *municipia,* which can be traced to the mid-4th century B.C., were Italian towns. Early *municipia* had only social and commercial rights (marriage and trade) with Rome and her allies. In 257 B.C., Rome began to admit as *municipia* conquered Italian communities and granted to some of them also political rights (voting and, occasionally, office holding). After 88 B.C. almost all Italian *municipia* received full rights of Roman citizenship. During the 1st century A.D. and until the mid-4th century A.D. many provincial communities in the Mediterranean area, if sufficiently Romanized, were recognized as *municipia.* While attempts to regulate this municipal organization were made at various times, yet, as several extant Roman laws reveal, no absolute uniformity in administration, in functions of local magistrates and councils, or in titles of municipal magistrates was achieved.

P. R. COLEMAN-NORTON.

MUNIN TO. See BONIN ISLANDS.

MUNISING, mū'nĭ-sĭng, city of the upper peninsula of Michigan, on Lake Superior, 43 miles southeast of Marquette. The seat of Alger County, it is 622 feet above sea level. It is served by state highways and two railroads: the Lake Superior and Ishpeming, and the Duluth, South Shore and Atlantic. Built on Munising Bay, facing Grand Island, it is picturesquely situated among wooded hills, cliffs, and waterfalls, and is a summer and winter resort. Nearby, stretching 20 miles northeast along the Lake Superior shore, are the spectacular Pictured Rocks of eroded varicolored sandstone. The city is an agricultural center and has lumbering, paper, plywood, woodenware, and furniture stock industries. Incorporated as a village in 1897 and as a city in 1915, Munising is administered under a commission-manager form of government. Pop. 3,677.

MUNITIONS. See AMMUNITION; ARTILLERY; GUN; NUCLEAR WEAPONS; SMALL ARMS.

MUNK, mo͝ongk', **Kaj,** kī, Danish clergyman and playwright: b. Maribo, Denmark, Jan. 13, 1898; d. near Silkeborg, Jan. 4, 1944. His most important work, in dramatic quality, is *Ordet* (1932, The Word), a study in both satirical and sympathetic vein of religious sectarianism; but he was also greatly successful with historical plays, usually replete with violent action, dealing with famous people, such as Herod the Great, king of the Jews, in *En Idealist* (1928, An Idealist), Henry VIII of England in *Cant* (1931), and Benito Mussolini of Italy in *Sejren* (1936, The Victory). His *Han sidder ved Smeltediglen* (1938, He Sits by the Melting Pot) recounted the successful struggle of a German professor to maintain his intellectual integrity against National Socialistic (Nazi) pressures. After the German invasion of Denmark in 1939, Munk became an outstanding spokesman against the Nazis, and his most successful historical play, *Niels Ebbesen* (1943; Eng. tr. in *Scandinavian Plays of the Twentieth Century,* Ser. 2, 1944), expresses, through the lips of a Danish hero against German oppression in the Middle Ages, his countrymen's hatred of the Nazis and all their work. For his outspokenness Munk paid with his life, for he was murdered by Nazis and their dupes.

MUNKÁCSY, mo͝on'kä-chĭ, **Mihály von** (real name MICHAEL LIEB), Hungarian painter: b. Munkács, Hungary (now Mukachevo, Ukrainian SSR), Feb. 20, 1844; d. Endenlich, near Bonn, Germany, May 1, 1900. He studied under Karl Rahl in Vienna and Ludwig Knaus in Düsseldorf, settled in Paris in 1872, and was influenced by Gustave Courbet. In Hungarian genre scenes and in historical and large, highly dramatic religious works, his style is frequently distinguished by a heavy impasto of striking colors and brilliant whites. His first important painting, done in Düsseldorf in 1868–1869, was *The Last Day of a Condemned Man* (Wilstach Collection, Philadelphia, Pa.). Other famous pictures are *Milton Dictating "Paradise Lost" to his Daughters* (1878; New York Public Library) and *Christ before Pilate* (1881; John Wanamaker Collection, Philadelphia). He is also represented in The Metropolitan Museum, the Louvre, and in museums in Chicago, Vienna, and elsewhere.

Consult Sedelmeyer, Charles, *Michael von Munkácsy* (Paris 1914).

MUNN, Orson Desaix, American publisher: b. Monson, Hampden County, Mass., June 11, 1824; d. Southampton, N.Y., Feb. 28, 1907. He was educated at the academy in Monson, was a clerk and country storekeeper there until 1846, and then bought the *Scientific American,* which he made one of the leading scientific journals of the country. Other periodicals owned by him were the *Scientific American Supplement* (1876–) and *Architects' and Builders' Edition* (1885–), now *American Homes and Gardens.* He was also head of Munn and Company, patent solicitors.

MUÑOZ MARÍN, mo͞on-yōs' mä-rēn', **Luis,** Puerto Rican political leader: b. San Juan, Puerto Rico, Feb. 18, 1898. Educated at Georgetown University in Washington, D. C., he worked as a writer and translator in New York. In 1926 he returned to San Juan to edit the daily newspaper *La Democracia* and became active in politics. Elected to the Puerto Rican Senate in 1932, he founded the Popular Democratic party six years later and subsequently rose to the presidency of the Senate. Originally a spokesman for independence, he later decided that increased autonomy in continuing association with the United States was economically more practical.

In 1948, Muñoz Marín became the first popularly elected governor of Puerto Rico. Reelected three times, he served from 1949 until 1965. He was considered the chief architect of the unique self-governing commonwealth status achieved by Puerto Rico in 1952. Recognizing the need for economic and social development, he executed a self-help program known as "Operation Bootstrap," whereby government funds were channeled toward promotion and assistance of private firms. Under his administration industry expanded dramatically, and progress was achieved in education, transportation, agriculture, health, and housing.

MUNRO, Dana Carleton, American historian: b. Bristol, R. I., June 7, 1866; d. New York City, Jan. 13, 1933. He was graduated from Brown University in 1877, then studied (1889–1890) at the universities of Strasbourg and Freiburg. He was instructor and assistant professor of Roman and medieval history at the University of Pennsylvania (1893–1902), professor of European history at the University of Wisconsin (1902–1915), and professor of medieval history at Princeton University (1915–1933); he was chairman of the department of history there (1915–1928). From 1894 to 1902 he was editor of *Translations and Reprints from Original Sources of History,* and published *Medieval History* (1902); *A Source Book of Roman History* (1904); *Syllabus of Medieval History* (1910); *German Treatment of Conquered Territory* (1918); *A Guide to the Study of Medieval History* (1931).

His son, DANA GARDNER MUNRO (1892–1942), was a historian and diplomat. He served in the Latin American division of the United States Department of State from 1921 to 1925, and in 1929 became chief of that division. He was United States minister to Haiti (1930–1932); and professor of Latin American history and affairs at Princeton University from 1932.

MUNRO, Hector Hugh, pseudonym SAKI (sä'kĭ), British author: b. Akyab, Burma, Dec. 18, 1870; d. Beaumont-Hamel, France, Nov. 13, 1916. A refreshingly imaginative satirist whose career was cut short by death in action with the Royal Fusiliers in World War I, he is best known for fictional pieces distinguished by gaiety of dialogue and narrative. Educated in grammar schools at Exmouth and Bedford, England, he returned to Burma in 1893 and was commissioned in the Burma police. The following year he reappeared in England, where he delighted readers of the *Westminster Gazette* with political sketches in the Lewis Carroll manner, issued under the name of Saki (cupbearer in the *Rubáiyát of Omar Khayyám*), and later published in 1902 as *The Westminster Alice.* From 1902 to 1908, he traveled in the Balkans, Russia, Poland, and France, as foreign correspondent for the *Morning Post.* Meanwhile, after being sidetracked into his only serious study, *The Rise of the Russian Empire* (1900), he turned to writing the short stories, published as *Reginald* (1904) and *Reginald in Russia* (1910), on which his reputation rests. These collections as well as *Chronicles of Clovis* (1911) and *Beasts and Superbeasts* (1914) reveal Saki's inviting whimsical humor and biting wit at their best. While not neglecting his penchant for political satire in these stories, he frequently portrays blithely irrepressible young men and queer and exotic animals in fantastic settings. With his fondness for flaying the pretentiously self-righteous and negatively dull, Saki reveals a flippant annoyance with adults, and a contrasting sympathy and understanding for their victims, children. Stylistically, his lack of conventional plot structure is usually more than compensated for by his fertility of invention and mastery of the unexpected phrase.

His other works include: *When William Came* (historical fantasy picturing life in Britain under German rule, 1913); *The Unbearable Bassington* (novel, 1912); *The Square Egg* (1924, with a biographical sketch by E. M. Munro); and several plays, including *The Death-Trap* and *Karl-Ludwig's Window.*

MUNRO, Wilfred Harold, American historian: b. Bristol, R. I., Aug. 20, 1849; d. Providence, R. I., Aug. 9, 1934. He was graduated (1870) at Brown University, receiving (1873) the A.M. degree. He spent 1873 in South and Central America. From 1875–1879 he was principal at Le Roy (N. Y.) Academic Institute, and was president of De Veaux College from 1881–1889. He studied at the universities of Freiburg and Heidelberg (1890–1891), when (1891–1899) he became associate professor of history and director of university extension at Brown University, and professor of European history (1899–1911), then emeritus professor. He published *Legends of Mount Hope* (1915); *Tales of an Old Seaport* (1917); *Among the Mormons in the Days of Brigham Young* (1927); editor, *Works of W. H. Prescott* (1905–1906).

MUNROE, Charles Edward, American chemist: b. Cambridge, Mass., May 24, 1849; d. Forest Glen, Md., Dec. 7, 1938. He took degrees at Harvard and George Washington universities, and taught in both institutions. He was professor of chemistry at the United States Naval Academy (1874–1876). He invented indurite, the first smokeless powder used in big guns by the United States Navy, the discovery of the formula of which he made while engaged in chemical research at the Naval Torpedo Station, Newport, R. I. (1886–1892). He also discovered the "Munroe effect," casting a new light on the nature of the detonation wave of nitroglycerine. He taught chemistry at Harvard (1871–1874); and was consulting expert to the United States Geological Survey, the United States Bureau of Mines, and the Civil Service Commission.

MUNROE, Henry Smith, American mining engineer: b. Brooklyn, N. Y., March 25,

1850; d. Litchfield, Conn., May 9, 1933. He was graduated (1869) at Columbia and received (1877) the degree Ph.D. He was (1870–1871) assistant geologist of the Ohio State Geological Survey; assistant chemist, United State Department of Agriculture (1870–1872); assistant geologist and mining engineer of the Geological Survey of Yesso, Japan (1872–1875). In 1875–1876 he was professor of mining and geology at the University of Tokio; then successively adjunct professor of surveying and practical mining (1877–1891); professor of mining (1891–1915), and emeritus professor in 1915 at Columbia University. He was also dean of the faculty of applied sciences (1897–1899) and member of the university council (1895–1915). He was manager (1881–1884), then vice president (1890–1892) of the American Institute of Mining Engineers, and was (1908–1909) president of the Mining and Metallurgical Society of America and (1909) president, Society for Promotion of Engineering Education.

MUNSEE INDIANS, an American tribe of the Delaware family, originally one of the three great divisions of that race. They were sometimes called the Wolf tribe of the Delawares. They resided along the Delaware River, and in New York, Pennsylvania and New Jersey. During the Revolution many of the Munsees removed to Canada, where at Thames, Ontario, there are some survivors. At Green Bay, Wis., is another tribal remnant and a third remnant is found in Kansas. See also DELAWARE INDIANS.

MUNSELL, Joel, American printer and antiquarian: b. Northfield, Mass., April 14, 1808; d. Albany, N. Y., Jan. 15, 1880. He established himself in Albany in 1827, and was publisher and editor of the *New York State Mechanic* from 1841 to 1843. At various times he was the publisher of the *Unionist,* the Albany *Daily State Register, Morning Express* and *Statesman,* and other journals. Munsell made a close study of the art of printing, in its history and application, and his collection of works on the subject, the largest in America, was in part purchased by the state for the New York State Library. He contributed papers to the *Transactions* of the Albany Institute, of which he was a founder, and published *Outline of the History of Printing* (1839); *The Every-Day Book of History and Chronology* (1843); *Annals of Albany,* 10 vols. (1850–1859); *A Chronology of Paper and Paper Making* (1856); and *Manual of the First Lutheran Church of Albany, 1670–1870* (1871).

MUNSEY, mŭn'sĭ, **Frank Andrew,** American editor and publisher: b. Mercer, Me., Aug. 21, 1854; d. New York, Dec. 22, 1925. He became manager of a Western Union telegraph office in Augusta, Me. He went to New York in 1882 to become editor and publisher of *The Golden Argosy,* a juvenile weekly, which he afterward changed into a monthly for adults under the style of *The Argosy. Munsey's Weekly* appeared in 1889 and after issuing this for one year he transformed it also into a monthly calling it *Munsey's Magazine.* He added other magazines, and later went into the newspaper field, buying the New York *Evening Sun, Daily News, Press, Sun, Herald, Telegram,* etc., and papers in other cities. He was a pioneer in the publication of cheap illustrated magazines, *Munsey's* being the first magazine to be sold at ten cents a copy. At one time or another he owned and published various other magazines including the *Scrap Book, Quaker, Puritan, Woman, Live Wire, Cavalier,* and *Railroad Man's Magazine.* He was the author of several books: *Afloat in a Great City* (1887); *The Boy Broker* (1888); *A Tragedy of Errors* (1889); *Under Fire* (1890); *Derringforth* (1894). He left the bulk of his fortune (estimated at the time of his death at $40,000,000) to the Metropolitan Museum of Art.

MUNSON, James Eugene, American inventor: b. Paris, N. Y., May 12, 1825; d. New York, 1906. He was educated at Amherst College, and in 1857 removed to New York, where he was court stenographer for 30 years. He invented the "Munson System" of shorthand, a machine for operating the typewriter by telegraph and a typesetting machine. He published *The Complete Phonographer* (1866); *Dictionary of Practical Phonography* (1875); *A Shorter Course in Munson Phonography* (1900); *Phonographic Dictation Book* (1904); *Munson's Pocket Dictionary of Phonography* (1906).

MUNSON, Thomas Volney, American horticulturist and plant breeder: b. Astoria, Ill., Sept. 26, 1843; d. Denison, Tex, Jan. 21, 1913. His early education was obtained in the rural district schools, followed by a course in an Academy at Lewiston. He subsequently took a course in a commercial college after which he entered the University of Kentucky, whence he was graduated in 1870. Shortly after completing his education he married and removed to the vicinity of Lincoln, Nebr. In 1873 he became interested in the improvement of the various species of the native American grapes and planned to do systematic work in the way of developing new varieties by cross-pollenation and hybridization. The experiments thus undertaken were doomed to failure because of climatic rigors and a visitation of the Rocky Mountain locusts. Undismayed, he sought a new location, settling at Denison, Tex., in 1876. There climatic conditions were much more favorable to the prosecution of such experiments and, moreover, wild grapes were more abundant and profuse. He engaged in the nursery business and in the breeding of new varieties of grapes and also growing them upon a commercial scale. During the ensuing 25-year period, he produced and experimentally fruited no less than 150,000 new varieties of grapes, many of which were far superior to those hitherto in common cultivation. Only the very best of these were selected for propagation and dissemination and so rigid and exacting was the process of elimination that but 50 varieties were retained for introduction and cultivation as a permanent addition to American viticulture. He became recognized as a botanist as well as a viticulturist, a volume entitled *Native Trees of the Southwest* having been prepared under the direction of the United States Department of Agriculture. But his specialty was always the grape and he became the recognized authority on the native wild grapes of North America. His horticultural and scientific work in hybridizing and perfecting the American grapes won recognition abroad as well as at home. In appreciation of his service in producing and introducing resistant stocks with which to restore the phylloxera-infested vineyards of France, in 1888 the French government conferred upon him the diploma and decoration of the Legion of Honor, with the title of *Chevalier du Merit Agricole*. He prepared a classification of wild grapes of North America for the United States Department of Agriculture (1890) and is remembered for his *Foundations of American Grape Culture* (1909) which embodied the practical results of more than 30 years of scientific study and research.

MUNSTER, mŭn'stẽr, province, Ireland, largest of the four provinces, bounded on the north by Connaught, on the east by Leinster, and on the west and south by the Atlantic Ocean. The province is comprised of the counties of Clare, Cork, Kerry, Limerick, Tipperary and Waterford. It contains the famous cities of Cork and Limerick, and one of the most widely renowned beauty spots in the world, Killarney. The entire west coast of the province is broken up into bays and promontories by the force of the ocean. Munster has two main communities of Irish-speaking people, in the wilds of Kerry and in the little-known Waterford hills. It is an extremely fertile province and that portion of it around Limerick and Tipperary is referred to as the "Golden Vale" on account of its fertility. Barley, corn and potatoes are grown and there are numerous dairy farms, most of which are medium-sized of about 30 to 100 acres. Coal is mined in Tipperary, Cork, and Kerry, and there are stone and marble quarries. Munster was one of the ancient kingdoms of Ireland ruled by the McCarthys and the O'Briens but after the Anglo-Norman invasion sovereignty passed to the Fitzgeralds (earls of Desmond) and the Butlers (earls of Ormond). The area of the province is 9,316.5 square miles. Pop. (1956) 877,238.

MUNSTER, mün'stẽr, city, Germany, in the state of North Rhine-Westphalia, 33 miles north of Dortmund on the Aa river and the Dortmund-Ems Canal. Prior to World War II it was the capital of the Prussian Province of Westphalia, which after the postwar British occupation became part of West Germany. Münster developed as a town in the 12th century, and was an important Hanseatic city during the 13th century. It was seized by the Anabaptists (1532–1535), and the Treaty of Westphalia, ending the Thirty Years' War was signed here October 24, 1648. The old city once bore a medieval appearance but was severely damaged by aerial bombardment and intense artillery fire during World War II. Some of its ancient buildings and industries have been restored since the war's end. Münster is the trading center of a rich agricultural area and in addition manufactures hardware, porcelain, cardboard, machinery, wire, cement, textiles and furniture. Flour milling, brewing and coal mining also flourish. Pop. (1957 est.) 160,700.

MUNSTERBERG, mün'stẽr-bĕrk, **Hugo,** German-American philosopher and psychologist: b. Danzig, Germany, July 1, 1863; d. Cambridge, Mass., Dec. 16, 1916. He taught psychology at the University of Freiburg, Baden, Germany, and was professor of psychology at Harvard University from 1892 to 1916. Münsterberg endeavored to promote good relations between the United States and Germany, but aroused opposition by his support of Germany in World War I. His earliest writings were on psychology, but his attitude was more in accord with the traditional technique of introspection than with the methods of more recent psychologists. He was concerned with the application of psychology to practical problems of industry, teaching, medical therapy, and social life. Though his work in psychology was many sided, his mentality was that of the philosopher rather than of the technical scientist. He was at Harvard during the period of Josiah Royce and William James. Münsterberg was an idealist and his philosophy was very similar to that of Josiah Royce. He criticized the pragmatism of William James mainly on the ground of its merely relativist theory of knowledge. But he was at one with James in his emphasis on the will. He was a voluntarist not only in psychology but in metaphysics as well. Under an early influence of the philosophies of Arthur Schopenhauer and Eduard von Hartmann, he regarded the fundamental nature of reality as will. He wrote: "The World-will . . . bears all existence." Central in his interests was the nature of values. He argued that the purposes of human behavior with which pragmatism was concerned were simply relative to individuals and to different times and places, often being in conflict one with another. He sought universal absolute values. These he described as in attitudes of will turned to the whole independent of individual desires. He talked of an "over-self" that is the subject of the experiences of real values. They are somehow supratemporal, "outside of time." But Münsterberg left quite unclarified the relation of the empirical experiences he studied as psychologist and those of values he asserted as philosopher. He did not discuss the relation of human wills to the "World-will," which for him was God. At times he appeared to identify them as in some forms of Hindu philosophy. Münsterberg had little enduring influence on American thought. His chief works were: *Grundzüge der Psychologie* (1900); *Der Amerikaner* (1904, rev. ed. 1912); *The Eternal Life* (1905); *Science and Idealism* (1906); *Philosophie der Werte* (1908); *The Eternal Value* (1909); *Psychology and Industrial Efficiency* (1913); *Psychology: General and Applied* (1915).

ALBAN G. WIDGERY,
Professor of Philosophy, Emeritus, Duke University.

MUNTHE, mŭn'tĕ, **Axel Martin Fredrik,** Swedish psychiatrist and writer: b. Oskarshamn, Sweden, Oct. 31, 1857; d. Stockholm, Feb. 11, 1949. He attended the University of Uppsala and obtained his medical degree in Paris. He was highly regarded as a psychiatrist and practiced for many years in Paris and in Rome. He attended Queen Victoria of Sweden for more than 30 years until her death in 1930 and spent his last years as the permanent, personal guest of King Gustav V of Sweden in the Royal Palace in Stockholm, where he died. Though he was the author of several books, his international fame as a writer came from his autobiography, *The Story of San Michele* (1929). The book was named for his former home on the island of Capri. Much of the proceeds of his writings were used to aid the poor and in the establishment of bird sanctuaries in Capri and Sweden.

MUNTJAC or **MUNTJAK,** mŭnt'jăk, a small deer (formerly *Cervulus*), which resembles the musk-deer in many points, especially in the male's having long, sharp upper canine teeth or tusks, which are effective weapons. These little deer, only about 22 inches high at the shoulder, live in hilly jungles. The bucks have lyrate, single-pronged antlers on tall pedicels; the does lack antlers. Six species are known in India (where they are called Kakars) and parts of southeast Asia. Popularly they are called barking deer from their cry of alarm. An alternate generic name is *Muntiacus.* The best known species is *M. muntjac.*

MUNZER, münt'sĕr, **Thomas,** German religious reformer and fanatic: b. Stolberg am Harz, c.1489; d. by execution, Mühlhausen, Thuringia, May 30, 1525. An Anabaptist, he joined Luther at Wittenberg in 1519 and the same year was a member of his entourage at the Leipzig debates. He soon disagreed with Luther on theology and became increasingly radical in his socio-political views as well, claiming direct communion with the Holy Spirit. While he was pastor at Zwickau (1520–1523) he tried to propagate his radical views at Wittenberg. His demagogic preachings and attempts to excite rebellion among peasants and workers through advocacy of the overthrow of the social order and establishment of a godly communist state resulted in his expulsion from Zwickau, Allstedt and Mühlhausen. At the outbreak of the Peasants' War (q.v.) Münzer returned to Mühlhausen with Heinrich Pfeiffer, another preacher, took control of the town council and established a communist theocracy. Philip, landgrave of Hesse, defeated the peasant forces at Frankenhausen, May 15, 1525, and Münzer was among the leaders executed.

MUNZINGER, mo͝ont'sĭng-ĕr, **Werner,** Swiss explorer and linguist: b. Olten, Soluthern Canton, April 21, 1832; d. Aussa district, northeastern Ethiopia, Nov. 15-16, 1875. He went to Egypt in 1852, led a trading expedition to the Red Sea (1854), settled briefly at Massawa, then made an expedition to East Africa (1855–1861). Second in command of the Heuglin expedition, on the leader's death he headed it. In 1872 he was appointed by the Khedive governor general of the eastern Sudan. On an expedition to find out whether Menelik, king of Shoa, later Menelik II (q.v.), emperor of Ethiopia, would consider an alliance with Egypt, Munzinger and his wife were killed by Galla tribesmen. He wrote grammars of native tongues and travel accounts.

MURAD, name of five Ottoman sultans:

MURAD I (1326–1389), reigning from 1362 until his death, was the first of the Ottomans to extend conquests to Europe, making Adrianople his European capital; completed organizing the Janizaries (q.v.). He took Sofia (1382) and was killed in his victory of Kossovo.

MURAD II (1403–1451), ruling from 1421–1451, patron of writers and scholars, reunited the Ottoman state, fought Hunyadi and Scanderberg and subdued the Morea (1446).

MURAD III (1546–1595), who ruled from 1574–1595, continued war with Austria, and seized (1590) large areas of the Persian Empire. The decline of the Ottoman Empire is usually dated as beginning with his reign. .

MURAD IV (1609–1640), sultan from 1623 to 1640, curtailed the power of the palace troops, and captured Baghdad from Persia (1638).

MURAD V (1840–1904) ruled for a few months in 1876. For most of his early life he was confined by a jealous uncle, Sultan Abdul Aziz. On the latter's deposition Murad acceded, but was deposed as insane (Aug. 31, 1876), and confined until his death.

MURAENA. See MORAY.

MURAL PAINTING is that branch of painting and design which is concerned with the enrichment of the walls and ceilings of buildings. Other techniques of architectural decoration used for the same purposes include mosaic, stone, or wood inlay, sgraffito, and bas-relief sculpture. Tapestry is woven material hung with similar intent.

A mural painting must always be related in design to the building of which it is a part. Its function in some instances may be only ornamental; but a fine work of mural art transcends the purposes of mere decorative embellishment: it may record the past, glorify the present, or symbolize aspirations of the future as well as playing its part in a geometric architectural unity.

Principles.—The general principles of good architectural design must govern the construction of a mural painting in its abstract, or design, elements. Architecture is concerned with the creation of hollow volumes or complexes of volumes, in materials which are suitable to the time, place, and uses of each structure. Mural decoration is only a further development, in terms of meaningful ornament, of the expression of the architectural idea in space and volume. Good ornament contributes to making the building seem psychologically suitable to its uses; the ornament may be called functional because people work and play better in appropriately decorated rooms; but a mural painting may also educate, remind, uplift, entertain, inspire fear or hope or any feeling which can be expressed in visual symbols.

Since the functions of buildings and rooms are various, it follows that many different kinds of mural painting exist. A bank, a factory, a gymnasium, a hospital, or a nursery, each has its own requirements. Mural painting may vary from the intimate to the monumental.

One of the qualities of good architecture is its relative permanence, and this affects the attitude of the mural painter as to technique, style, and subject matter. The muralist is always more concerned than is the easel painter with the lasting values of his work. He is slower to experiment with novelties, while being intensely interested in new methods which may add durability to his painting. He is the philosopher and historian among painters, and also the scientist and engineer. He is usually a deliberate, steady, and craftsmanlike worker, because a large mural demands sustained effort combined with consistency in style. A successful work must reflect calmness, co-operativeness, sympathy, and understanding for the feelings and viewpoints of many different people: the mural painter is a "public" artist, in his way a public servant.

For these reasons it is considered that a mural work using illustrative content should confine itself to truly epic subject matter. Passing or trivial events do not deserve presentation in monumental, enduring form. Perhaps the journalistic cartoon might be thought of as the proper antithesis to true mural painting. Murals whose painters have attempted to express current political fervor have seldom stood the tests of time. In dealing with history in the making, the mural painter must be something of a prophet and seer to distinguish the enduring from the temporary.

Methods of Mural Painting.—Permanence and suitability to architectural surroundings are chief factors in the mural painter's choice of the medium to be used for a particular work. This choice will otherwise be dictated by the style of painting which the artist finds most adaptable to the expression of his idea. New media develop as the artists of a period find the established methods inadequate for their needs, and for this reason they are best studied in their historical contexts.

A widening knowledge of the history of art has brought about the appreciation of many little known styles and techniques of earlier times. Prehistoric man painted on the walls of caves in Altamira and the Dordogne. Of a much later time are the Buddhist paintings done on the walls of the cave temples of Ajanta in and prior to the 7th century A.D. In early Egypt and in Crete most murals were painted using flat color and linear silhouette, the earliest known being the famous *Geese of Meidum* belonging to the Egyptian Old Kingdom (2900–2750 B.C.). Of all the ancient works studied by painters of the modern era, probably those of the Egyptians, Greeks, and Pompeians have been most influential in forming Western mural styles.

Prehistoric cave painters made their drawings directly on the rough sandstone with natural earth pigments, much as pastel is used today: in most cases preservation is due to the accidental formation of a transparent film of limestone deposited by water seepage over their surfaces. Early painters mixed adhesive gum with their pigments, probably gum acacia or gum arabic in the case of Egyptian mural works.

Cretan painting, such as that in the Palace of Knossos, c.1500 B.C., presents some of the earliest known examples of the use of fresco, which was to become one of the most important media employed in architectural decoration during many centuries. In this manner of painting the pigment is ground in water or lime water and applied to a surface of fine plaster before the plaster has become completely crystallized. The pigment is bound to the plaster surface through the interlocking of slowly forming crystals of lime carbonate, as the lime oxide returns to its original form upon exposure to the carbon dioxide of the air. An area of about a square yard is prepared and completed at a time, this being considered a day's work by the *frescanti.* Succeeding sections of plaster will show a fine indentation where they join; the indentations are planned to follow the edges of color planes in the design.

The traditional palette of the fresco painter is limited to the natural earth colors, such as yellow ochre and terra verte; the burnt earths, such as Venetian red; and a few other lime-fast colors, such as cobalt blue. Few organic dyes or synthetic colors are fast in the presence of lime. Pigments prepared by grinding potters' glazes or frit pigments found some use as early as Egyptian times. True fresco becomes more luminous with age, due to the increasing transparency of the plaster surface as the lime crystals become completely carbonated.

The process described above is that of true fresco, which requires that when a mistake has been made, the outer coat of that particular section of plaster must be removed and renewed. Retouching has sometimes been done with the use of *fresco secco,* or dry fresco, in which the binder is albumen or casein distemper; but it has seldom proved permanent. The Italians distinguish true fresco as *"buon fresco."*

True fresco and dry fresco both were practiced by the Greeks, Romans, and Pompeians, although the Roman artists preferred the harder materials of mosaic and stone inlay. True frescoes also appear in early Christian and Byzantine churches; but they rise to their greatest heights in works of the Italians of the Renaissance, beginning with the painter Cimabue. This fine fresco work followed a period in which mural painting had for a time been superseded as wall decoration by the mosaics of the Byzantines, as seen in Saint Sophia, at Ravenna, and at St. Mark's in Venice; and by the stained glass of the Gothic north.

Two great schools of art developed at this time in northern Italy, producing murals done in both fresco and tempera. These were of the school of Giotto and his followers, whose works may be seen in the lower church of St. Francis at Assisi, in the churches of Santa Croce and Santa Maria Novella at Florence, and in the Arena Chapel at Padua; and the school of Siena. Artists of both schools traveled widely and influenced art in other regions. The work of the Sienese remained essentially medieval in character, while the art of the Florentines, followers of Giotto, changed to meet the needs of the new and spreading doctrine of humanism. Masaccio's mural painting, *The Tribute Money* in the Brancacci chapel of the church of Santa Maria della Carmine at Florence, signaled a further development in style from Giottesque painting; and during the 15th century other distinctive styles developed in Umbria, Rome, and northern Italy.

As men's attention became diverted from the medieval preoccupation with extra-worldly matters to an examination of the world around them, painting kept pace with scientific observation. Artists, re-imbued with the Greek ideal of man as the center of all things, painted and anatomized the human figure, developed theories of vision which became laws of light and shade and mathematical perspective. Piero della Francesca of Umbria, in his magnificent frescoes at Arezzo depicting the *Visit of the Queen of Sheba to Solomon,* demonstrated his scientific knowledge of architectural geometry and anatomy in common with Greek idealization of the human figure, which had become the Florentine goal in painting. Luca Signorelli, in his murals of the *Last Judgment* in the Cathedral at Orvieto, exhibits knowledge of the anatomy and movement of the human figure rather than concern with religious symbolization.

Two fresco painters who emerged from the Florentine group executed works in Rome in the first half of the 16th century which may be said to have exerted more influence upon the art of the Western World than any other paintings until comparatively recent times. One of these was Raphael Sanzio, whose Umbrian studies under Perugino are thought to account for his rich use of color. Raphael's Vatican frescoes known as the *Stanze* have long been models for students of classic work. Michelangelo Buonarroti, who considered himself primarily a sculptor, became a prisoner of war in the attack of Pope Julian's forces upon the Florentine Republic and was ordered, in spite of his protest, to decorate the ceiling of the Sistine Chapel in fresco. As an

MURAL PAINTING

Courtesy Museum of Modern Art

José Clemente Orozco (Mexican, 1883–1949) at work on the six-panel fresco, *Dive Bomber and Tank*, in 1940.

Courtesy Museum of Modern Art

The completed *Dive Bomber and Tank* mural by Orozco.

architect, engineer, and sculptor, Michelangelo was in disagreement with the round-vaulted ceiling. He used his Florentine knowledge of space drawing to destroy its architectural effect. Instead we see a series of flat, bas-relief sculptural panels symbolizing the Creation, divided by painted beams, supported in turn by painted pilasters. The power and magnificence of the work is unquestioned. It remains a *tour de force* of the art of fresco, but it is also a great monument to a rebellious spirit, by which the mural painter demonstrated his refusal to approve the architecture of which his work was a part.

The style of Florentine painting was developed in terms of the use of fresco and tempera; both media encourage careful, planned work with reliance upon clearly drawn outlines, in a color range somewhat more limited than that of oil paint. The tempera medium was much used for smaller works of both Sienese and Florentine schools, executed upon wood panels first coated with gesso, a preparation of plaster and glue, employing egg yolk as a binder.

Early Flemish painters of northern Europe adopted as binding media linseed oil (oil of flaxseed) and varnishes prepared from pine pitch, in creating miniatures and small paintings to harmonize with the rich wood-paneled interiors of their region. Wall spaces which in the southern countries would call for large mural decorations here were needed for light-giving stained glass. The deep, enamel-like brilliance of underpainting and overglazing was well suited to their purposes.

It is believed that Domenico Veneziano, a Florentine traveler, introduced the northern craft of oil painting to the Florentines; but not until the sensuous Venetians rebelled against Florence's intellectual abstraction did the rich effects of oil painting become exploited in the mural decorations of Italy. Titian, a successful fresco painter early in his career in the Scuola del Santo at Padua, later became a virtuoso in the oil paint medium. His *Assumption* for the church of Santa Maria Gloriosa dei Frari, Venice, is the first oil painting to contain human figures as large as those in the biggest frescoes. Unfortunately Titian's murals for the Palace of the Doges were destroyed by fire; they were considered by contemporaries to be his greatest.

Titian's vigorous and glowing work was carried forward by Jacopo Robusti, known as Tintoretto. The careful, craftsmanlike processes which characterized the methods of the Florentines could not compete with the free, direct painting and the ease of correction of errors offered by the oil method.

Many baroque palaces of the time were richly decorated after the Venetian manner. Paolo Cagliari, known as Veronese, excelled in creating scenes of pompous splendor; his ceiling for the Doges' Palace, and various paintings for the church of San Sebastiano were typical examples of the mural work then most acceptable. Peter Paul Rubens, basing his style upon the works of Veronese, Michelangelo, and Raphael, carried the international baroque manner through all of Europe's capitals. Among his mural commissions were the decorations for the Luxembourg Palace for Marie de' Medici and the ceiling of Whitehall in England. In Spain, Domenikos Theotokopoulos, called El Greco, executed somber, emotionally intense decorations which combined Byzantine abstraction with Venetian breadth. His *Burial of the Count of Orgaz* in the Church of Santo Tomé at Toledo, is one of his best known works.

The French baroque style may be represented by the frescoes done in the Church of Val de Grace by Pierre Mignard, who headed the official French Academy under Louis XIV.

Mural painting enters a lighter phase in the rococo period which followed. Representative of his times as a mural decorator was François Boucher, whose work appears in Versailles, in the Bibliothèque Nationale at Fontainebleau and in the château of Madame de Pompadour at Bellevue.

Neither the neoclassic period nor the era of romanticism which followed were good ones for mural work; but Jacques-Louis David among neoclassicists and the romantic Théodore Chassériau, who influenced Puvis de Chavannes, left enough impression upon later muralists to deserve mention.

Mural painting in England and Germany paralleled French work to some extent and included experimentation with fresco, oil, and tempera media and also spirit-fresco, a kind of wax painting, and water-glass. In Germany the names of Peter von Cornelius, Peter von Hess, Julius Schnorr von Carolsfeld and Wilhem von Kaulbach come to the fore. In Engand a revival of mural decoration was carried forward in Victorian times by Thomas Gambier Parry, Charles West Cope, Sir Edward Poynter, and Frank Brangwyn, whose murals, executed for the San Francisco Panama-Pacific Exposition in 1915, are now set into the walls of the Veterans' Memorial Theater in San Francisco. These last are excellent examples of the influence of Impressionist light painting upon the art of the mural.

Most innovations have represented attempts to reproduce the quality of classic fresco without bowing to its limitations. Since the end of the Renaissance period, with the increasing separation in interests of painter and architect, a great majority of mural decorations have been executed for buildings already in use, making fresco inconvenient. In addition, reinforced concrete construction is chemically inimical to fresco unless elaborate precautions are taken to insulate the fresco plaster from metal or concrete. Oil paint as a medium is sensitive not only to free alkali from plaster, but also to moisture; careful priming is necessary. Also to be considered is the fact that many modern buildings are relatively impermanent; a work of art which is an integral part of the structure is difficult to save when it is torn down. It is little wonder that the French method of *marouflage* has been used by modern muralists for many years: affixing to a wall a canvas previously painted in the studio. This practice has indeed often obscured the difference between easel and mural painting; many a mural has been executed by an artist who may never have seen the building in which it would go, and who might be only vaguely aware of the color and scale of the rooms or walls involved. This is said to be true of the murals done by Puvis de Chavannes for the Boston Public Library, and of the abstractions more recently contributed by Fernand Léger to the auditorium of the United Nations building in New York City.

The first true mural paintings executed in the United States were those done by John La Farge for the Trinity Church in Boston in 1876. With the work of this painter and his group began the development of American mural painting as a consciously distinct art. Associated with La

Farge in this enterprise and others were William Morris Hunt, Edwin Austin Abbey, Henry O. Walker, Kenyon Cox, John Singer Sargent, and Edwin Blashfield. In his book, *Mural Painting in America* (1913), Blashfield stresses the debt of American mural painters to the training of Paris and the continued study of Renaissance masters, as well as modern influences like their favorite, de Chavannes.

These painters borrowed not only the style, but also the systems of symbols used by classic and European muralists. Greek and Roman deities or Biblical personages sometimes appear incongruous as symbols for forces of the modern world. Figures from American history in classic garb or in classic nudity appear in many mural paintings of the time. Only in later years did costumes of the period become acceptable in monumental works.

After admitting the neoclassic and eclectic nature of this first American school of mural painting, Blashfield goes on to say: "The style of Perugino and Pinturricchio is very beautiful, and may be used to great advantage in America, but it is not final; no style is." With public approval of the work of this group, which appeared in the 1891–1893 Columbian Exhibition in Chicago, their style became established in spite of Blashfield's wise prediction. So long as America's leading architectural firms were dominated by the official style of the French Beaux-Arts Academy, mural painting in large public buildings conformed to the classic-baroque tradition, even after most easel painters had long since discarded it.

As European styles of painting changed, so did those of America, and American mural painting responded, although slowly. Romanticism, with emphasis on emotion, is reflected in the works of John Singer Sargent. Impressionism, characterized by concern for atmosphere and light, is well represented in American mural painting by the works of the followers of the Englishman, Frank Brangwyn. But Cubism and Expressionism often involving obscure personal symbolism and formal ideas not yet understood by the public were for some time confined to the field of easel painting.

In the 1920's, attention was once more focused upon monumental mural painting by a group of artists for whom the Mexican revolution provided both theme and opportunity. The first important murals done by Diego Rivera appeared in the Mexican National Preparatory School, executed in encaustic. Here also José Clemente Orozco painted his first great frescoes. Work by David Alfaro Siqueiros, also done at this time, represented a successful attempt to combine fresco with encaustic. In spite of his unquestioned powers, Siqueiros' work displays a revolutionary violence and indifference to the accepted limitations of true mural work as to technique, form, and content.

These ambitious works were only the first of a tremendous series of monumental decorations by Mexican painters. Rivera and Orozco also executed commissions in the United States, among which are those by Orozco at Detroit and at Pomona College in California, and by Rivera in the Stock Exchange of San Francisco. Rivera's projected frescoes for Rockefeller Center in New York City were never completed because of a disagreement with his sponsors regarding a representation of Lenin in the design.

This fresh impetus given to mural painting by the work of the Mexican painters strongly influenced many artists of the United States for the duration of the government art projects set up in the 1930's under the Roosevelt administration. An unexampled flow of many kinds of art work was produced, much of which took permanent form as mural decoration in public buildings throughout the country. On the Pacific slope, notably, muralists made use of rediscovered antique methods of architectural decoration, such as mosaic in its many forms, and the unique cut stone work, or *opus sectile,* to be seen in the Alameda County Court House, Oakland, California.

The Public Works of Art Project of the Treasury awarded commissions through competitions in which a large number of competent artists participated. Among the works thus produced are the murals by Anton Refregier for the Rincon Branch of the Post Office at San Francisco. These consist of a series of casein paintings which may well be accepted as a norm of modern mural style. They present various symbols of the social progress of the State of California in a manner which is both contemporary and eclectic in the best sense.

Under the Federal Art Project of the Works Progress Administration appeared many other works, such as the highly praised murals by Philip Guston, *Maintaining America's Skills,* for the New York World's Fair.

Although government art sponsorship lasted for only eight years, by this encouragement so many artists received training in mural painting, and understanding and public demand were so increased, that opportunity for the contemporary muralist in the United States has been greatly expanded. Almost no public building of any pretensions is now planned without considering the desirability of integrated architectural decoration, whether sculpture, mosaic, inlaid stone or true mural painting.

See also AMERICAN ART; ARCHITECTURE; ART; PAINTINGS OF THE GREAT MASTERS; UNITED STATES—*38. Art and Architecture.*

Bibliography.—BOOKS: Gruner, L., *Fresco Decorations and stuccoes of the churches and palaces in Italy* (London 1844); Thomas, W. C., *Mural or Monumental Decoration* (London 1869); Crowninshield, F., *Mural Painting* (Boston 1887); Didot, G., *La Peinture Décorative en France* (Paris 1888–90); Douglas, H. G., *A Series of Architectural and Mural Decorations* (Washington 1901); Baldry, A. L., *Modern Mural Decoration* (London 1902); Westlake, N. H. J., *History of Design in Mural Painting,* 2 vols., (London 1902–05); Blashfield, E., *Mural Painting in America* (New York 1913); Crace, J. D., *The Art of Color Decoration* (London 1913); Kleinschmidt, B., *Die Basilika San Francesco in Assisi,* 3 vols. (Berlin 1915–28); Breasted, J. H., *Oriental Forerunners of Byzantine Painting* (Chicago 1924); Gusman, P., *La décoration murale à Pompéi* (Paris 1924); St. Hubert, R., *Art of Fresco Painting* (New York 1924); Allen, E. B., *Early American Wall Paintings 1710–1850* (New Haven, London 1926); McClelland, N., *Practical Book of Decorative Wall Treatments* (Philadelphia 1926); Cahill, H., *New Horizons in American Art* (New York 1936); Overmyer, G., *Government and the Arts* (New York 1939); Vanderwalker, F. N., *Interior Wall Decoration* (Chicago 1941); Hitchcock, H., *Painting toward Architecture* (New York 1948). PERIODICALS: *Museum of Modern Art,* "Murals by American Painters and Photographers" (New York 1932); *Art in Federal Buildings,* vol. 1, Bruce, E., and Watson, F., "Mural Designs 1934–1936" (Washington 1936); *M. H. de Young Memorial Museum Catalog* "Frontiers of American Art" (San Francisco 1939).

GLENN A. WESSELS, M.A.,
Professor of Art, University of California.

MURANO, Antonio da. See VIVARINI—*Antonio Vivarini.*

MURANO, mōō-rä'nô, town, Italy, one mile north of Venice on a group of islets in the Venice Lagoon. Since the 13th century it has been the center of the Venetian glass-blowing industry, specimens of which are exhibited in Murano's Museo Vetrario (see also GLASS—*Western Medieval Glass*). The town's two famous churches are the Venetian-Byzantine Church of Santi Maria e Donato, completed in the 12th century, and the Church of San Pietro Martire (rebuilt 16th century), which contains paintings by Tintoretto, Giovanni Bellini, and Paolo Veronese. Pop. (1951) 7,595.

MURAT, mû-rà', **(Charles Louis Napoléon) Achille,** French-American author: b. Paris, France, Jan. 21, 1801; d. Wascissa, near Tallahassee, Fla., April 15, 1847. He was the elder son of Joachim Murat (q.v.), French marshal, and Caroline Bonaparte, sister of Napoleon I. At the age of five, Achille became duke of Cleves and in 1808 crown prince of Naples, his father's kingdom. After the fall of Napoleon's empire and the death of Joachim in 1815, Achille and his family lived in Austria under the vigilance of the secret police. An eager student of politics and history, he became fascinated with American democracy, and in 1823 received permission from Prince Klemens von Metternich to go to the United States. He visited his uncle, Joseph Bonaparte, at Bordentown, N.J., and then journeyed southward, living first near St. Augustine, Fla. In 1825 he established a plantation near Tallahassee and in 1826 married the widow Catharine Daingerfield Gray (nee Willis), great-grandniece of George Washington.

Naturalized in 1828, Murat was admitted to the bar and became an active participant in frontier life. At the outbreak of the European revolution of 1830 he determined to use his American experience as a liberal leader abroad, but was refused permission to enter France and Italy. The last years of his life were spent in the United States in a frantic effort to gain wealth and position. He was a county judge, director of a bank, head of a canal company, and speculator in Texas lands, and also practiced law in New Orleans. Meanwhile, his Florida properties were neglected, and his debts multiplied. Never strong physically and always in emotional turmoil, he died at the age of 46, on the eve of the resurrection of his family's fortunes. Napoleon III made a settlement on Murat's American widow and received her at court with the rank of princess.

Four articles by Murat on American life were published in the *Revue trimestrielle* (Paris) in 1828 and appeared in book form as *Lettres sur les États-Unis* . . . (1830). This material also formed part of his second book, *Esquisse morale et politique des États-Unis* . . . (1832), first given English translation as *A Moral and Political Sketch of the United States of North America* (1833). His third volume was *Exposition des principes du gouvernement républicain, tel qu'il a été perfectionné en Amérique* (1833). A keen observer of United States social institutions, he was perhaps the first European to defend them against criticism then emanating from England. This defense and his graphic depiction of the Southern frontier constitute a valuable record in spite of certain weaknesses, including his defense of slavery and his strong prejudice against the North. Although the books made some stir in Europe and were translated into several languages, they failed to make an impression in the United States until 1849, when *America and the Americans,* the United States edition of *Esquisse morale et politique,* attracted some attention. Murat has continued to stand in the shade of Alexis de Tocqueville, the more learned political scientist who produced his work on American democracy a few years after Murat.

Consult Hanna, Alfred Jackson, *A Prince in Their Midst; the Adventurous Life of Achille Murat on the American Frontier* (Norman, Okla., 1946).

A. J. HANNA,
Weddell Professor of American History, Rollins College, Winter Park, Fla.

MURAT, Joachim, marshal of France and king of Naples: b. Labastide-Fortunière, Quercy (now Labastide-Murat, Lot Department), France, March 25, 1767; d. Pizzo, Italy, Oct. 13, 1815. Third son of an innkeeper, he was sent to the Lazarist Fathers' seminary at Toulouse to study for the priesthood but in February 1787 enlisted in the Chasseurs des Ardennes, a cavalry unit billeted at Toulouse. After the outbreak of the revolution, the National Guard of Montfaucon made him their representative in the Constitutional Guard of Louis XVI (1792), and by April 1793 he was a captain of the 12th Chasseurs and aide-de-camp to a general.

Napoleon's General.—The 13th Vendémiaire (Oct. 5, 1795) was a turning point in Murat's career. Young Gen. Napoleon Bonaparte gave him the mission of escorting 40 guns from an artillery park outside Paris to the Tuileries. Murat handled the task expertly, enabling the Corsican to save the National Convention from the insurgents with his "whiffs of grape." Napoleon made him his aide-de-camp in the Italian campaign (1796–1797), and Murat there first demonstrated his ability as a cavalry leader in two celebrated charges. Sent to Paris with reports of victories, he returned to Italy a brigadier general in May 1796. He performed brilliantly at Rivoli Veronese, commanded an infantry brigade in the advance on Vienna, and subsequently won high praise from Gen. André Masséna for his part in the Roman campaign (1797).

On the Egyptian expedition, Murat was made governor of Qalyubiya (Kalyubiya) Province, north of Cairo, on July 27, 1798, and subsequently commanded the cavalry in the Syrian campaign. The famous victory at Abukir (July 25, 1799), as Napoleon generously reported in his dispatch to Paris, was "mainly due to General Murat." In the same dispatch he requested Murat's promotion to general of division.

On the 19th Brumaire (Nov. 10, 1799), heading a body of grenadiers, Murat invaded the Orangerie at St.-Cloud and dispersed the Council of Five Hundred, completing the coup d'état of 18th Brumaire which marked the beginning of the Consulate. His reward was appointment as inspector of the Consular Guard and the hand of Napoleon's sister Caroline (January 1800). The Marengo campaign that summer gained him fresh laurels, and in December he was given a separate command in Italy, with the rank of lieutenant general. Recalled to Paris in January 1804 by Napoleon, he was given command of the troops of the first military division and also of the National Guard, and made governor of Paris.

On May 19, 1804, Murat received his baton as marshal of the empire, among 18 so honored. The following February he was created senator, prince, and grand admiral of France. As a reward for his services in the Austrian campaign of 1805, which included the Battle of Austerlitz, Napoleon made him (March 15, 1806) grand duke of Berg (Cleves and Berg). Thereafter the prince marshal commanded the emperor's cavalry at Jena (1806), Eylau (1807), and Friedland (1807). By this time Murat was renowned as the greatest cavalryman of the age, and on taking command of all French troops in Spain (February 1808) he expected to receive the crown of that kingdom. Spain, however, was reserved for Joseph Bonaparte, and Murat was offered Portugal or Naples. He chose the latter and was crowned king of Naples on Aug. 1, 1808.

King of Naples.—Ruling as King Joachim Napoleon, Murat was popular with the Neapolitans. He introduced the Napoleonic Code, founded military, naval, civil engineering, and polytechnic colleges, and enlarged the university faculty. Primary schools were started in every commune, and a normal school to train teachers. He also tried to improve economic conditions. His relations with the emperor, however, became strained, particularly in 1810 when his favorite project, the conquest of Sicily (where the ex-king of Naples still ruled as Ferdinand III), was frustrated by sudden withdrawal of a committed French division. When Napoleon gave him the cavalry command in the Russian campaign of 1812, the breach was temporarily healed. Murat displayed his habitual brilliance in the advance on Moscow; but when the emperor turned over to him (December 5) command of the shattered Grand Army, he showed utter incapacity. Once more he fought under Napoleon in the defeat at Leipzig (October 1813), but on Jan. 11, 1814, he signed an offensive-defensive treaty with Austria, betraying the French emperor.

After Napoleon's abdication in April 1814, Murat found himself friendless. He threw in his lot with the united Italy party and, when Napoleon escaped from Elba (March 1815), turned his army against the Austrians. His disillusioned troops refused to fight, however, and marched home in May before the Austrian advance. Murat himself fled to Cannes and offered his services to Napoleon, who contemptuously refused them. Later, at St. Helena, the exiled emperor regretted that decision, saying, "at Waterloo Murat might have given us the victory. For what did we need? To break three or four English squares. Murat was just the man for the job."

After Waterloo, with a price on his head, Murat went into hiding and then led a foolhardy attempt from Corsica to recover his kingdom, after declining Prince Klemens von Metternich's proffer of asylum at Trieste. With a few followers he landed at Pizzo, Calabria, on October 8, was immediately captured and court-martialed, and five days later was executed.

Bibliography.—Atteridge, Andrew H., *Joachim Murat* (New York and London 1911); Béchu, Marcel Ernest (Marcel Dupont), *Murat; cavalier, maréchal de France, prince et roi* (Paris 1934); Macdonell, Archibald Gordon, *Napoleon and His Marshals* (New York and London 1934); Lucas-Dubreton, Jean (Jean M. Lucas de Peslouan), *Murat* (Paris 1944); Peslouan, Hervé de, *Le roi Murat; mémoire d'épopée* (Tours 1949).

JOHN J. MENG,
President, Hunter College.

MURAT, (Napoléon) Lucien (Charles), French political leader: b. Milan, Italy, May 16, 1803; d. Paris, France, April 10, 1878. Younger son of the king of Naples, Joachim Murat (q.v.), and Caroline Bonaparte, he became prince of Pontecorvo as a child of 10. After his father's overthrow and death, he lived in Austrian exile and in 1825 went to the United States. Returning to France after the revolution of 1848, he was elected to the Constituent Assembly and the Legislative Assembly, and after the coup d'état of Louis Napoleon (1851), became a senator. When Louis Napoleon (his cousin) was proclaimed Emperor Napoleon III, Murat was given the title Prince Murat, with an annual pension. He made various unsuccessful claims to his father's throne of Naples.

MURATORI, mōō-rä-tō'rē, **Lodovico Antonio,** Italian historian and antiquarian: b. Vignola, Duchy of Modena, Oct. 21, 1672; d. Modena, Jan. 23, 1750. He studied at a Jesuit school in Modena and took his degree in law in 1694. Under the influence of Benedetto Bacchini, head of the ducal library, he turned to historical and antiquarian studies. Ordained priest in 1695, he became librarian of the Ambrosian Library at Milan the same year and in 1700 librarian and archivist to the duke of Modena. From 1716 to 1733 he was provost of Santa Maria della Pomposa in Modena.

Celebrated as the "true light of Italian learning," Muratori was a friend to scholars in all countries, especially in Italy, France, and Germany. His surviving letters number over 6,000; those of his correspondents, over 14,000. His most important work was his collection of historical sources for medieval Italy (500–1500 A.D.), *Rerum Italicarum scriptores* . . . (25 vols. in 28, 1723–51), to which he added 75 dissertations on medieval Italy in *Antiquitates Italicae medii aevi* (6 vols., 1738–42) and another on the ancient Roman liturgy (1748). In the third volume (1740) of the *Antiquitates* appeared the so-called Muratorian fragment (or canon), discovered by Muratori in the Ambrosian Library. This was an important event in the field of Biblical studies, since the fragment, dating from about 180 A.D., contains an annotated list of New Testament books, a list which reflects a decisive stage in the growth of the New Testament canon (see also BIBLE—*10. Canon of the New Testament*). Muratori also wrote a popular history of Italy to the year 1500, *Annali d'Italia* . . . (12 vols., 1744–49). His complete works were published in 36 volumes (1767–80).

Muratori was critical of certain dogmas and observances of the church, such as the veneration of the Blessed Virgin, and for a time aroused opposition. His enemies circulated the rumor that the pope, Benedict XIV, had found heresy in his works; but the pope himself came to Muratori's defense, and the rumor died down. In 1756 a biography was published by his nephew, Gian Francesco Soli Muratori.

Consult the article and bibliography by Francesco Cognasso in *Enciclopedia Cattolica,* vol. 8, cols. 1523 ff. (Vatican City 1952); also Feruccio de Carli's *Lodovico Antonio Muratori; la sua vita, la sua opera e la sua epoca* (Florence 1955). For a brief discussion of the Muratorian canon, consult Alfred Wikenhauser's *New Testament Introduction,* tr. from the German by Joseph Cunningham, pp. 37–40 (New York 1958).

FREDERICK C. GRANT,
Professor of Biblical Theology, Union Theological Seminary, New York City.

MURCHISON, mûr'chĭ-s'n, SIR **Roderick Impey,** Scottish geologist: b. Tarradale, near Muir-of-Ord, Ross and Cromarty County, Scotland, Feb. 19, 1792; d. London, England, Oct. 22, 1871. Educated at Great Marlow military college and the University of Edinburgh, he entered the army in 1807 and served in the Peninsular War against Napoleon, retiring in 1815. On the advice of Sir Humphry Davy, Murchison began to study geology and chemistry at the Royal Institution, London, in 1824 and made important observations on the volcanic origin of lava. In 1831 he began the systematic studies that were to bring him great distinction in the succeeding decade. The rocks below the Old Red Sandstone, the so-called "transition graywacke," were of unknown classification. Murchison made a comprehensive survey of these rocks in central Wales, the home of the ancient Silures, and in 1835 named them the Silurian system, publishing the classic monograph of that title (1835), later revised as *Siluria* (1854). In 1839 he also named the Devonian system, with Adam Sedgwick, on the basis of their field work in Devonshire and fossils studied by William Lonsdale. Murchison and Sedgwick, who was the originator of the Cambrian system, were in controversy for 30 years with regard to the spans of rocks that should be placed in the Silurian and Cambrian systems. The disputed beds became the Ordovician system of Charles Lapworth in 1879, after the deaths of both men.

With Philippe Édouard de Verneuil and Count Alexander Keyserling, Murchison was commissioned in 1840 by Czar Nicholas I to make a geological survey of European Russia. He was engaged in this work until 1844, publishing, with his collaborators, *The Geology of Russia in Europe and the Ural Mountains* (2 vols., 1845). In Russia he made discoveries that led to his naming the Permian system; thus he had a part in defining all but the Cambrian and Carboniferous, of the five Paleozoic systems established in his time. Knighted in 1846, he became a knight commander of the Bath in 1863 and a baronet in 1866. He was director of the Geological Survey of the British Isles from 1855 until his death.

MARSHALL KAY,
Professor of Geology, Columbia University.

MURCIA, mûr′shĭ-ȧ, Span. mōōr′thyä, province, Spain, in the southeast, bounded on the southwest by Almeria and Granada provinces, on the northwest and north by Albacete, on the northeast by Alicante, and on the southeast by 75 miles of Mediterranean shore. The modern province (area 4,369 square miles), with capital at Murcia (q.v.), was part of the former kingdom of Murcia. The climate is hot and dry, although occasional sudden rains can cause flash floods. Mountain ranges run parallel to the coast, dividing the province into valleys. The highest elevation, 5,150 feet, is in the central Sierra de Espuna. The Segura River flows southeast across the province, joining the Sangonera east of the capital, and then traverses Alicante Province to enter the sea. The coast is an alluvial plain, at the eastern end of which is located the Mar Menor, a large saltwater lagoon.

Mining and agriculture form the basis of Murcian economy. Iron, copper, lead-silver, and zinc ores are found in the uplands, and there are deposits of alum, sulphur, saltpeter, marble, gypsum, clay, and limestone. Worked since Carthaginian times, these deposits are now partly exhausted. Agriculture, carried on in the fertile *huertas,* or garden regions, relies on irrigation systems in use since Moorish times. Important food crops are truck produce, wheat, corn, pepper, olives, grapes, and some rice. Oranges are grown along the Segura; sericulture, once extensive in the capital region, is now in decline. Esparto grass and hemp, grown in the numerous sandy tracts, are a principal export. Sheep raising and beekeeping are of some importance. Industries include metalworking, in the mining districts; other products are brandy, explosives, footwear, pottery, textiles, furniture, and candy. Cartagena, the only usable port, is the center of fishing activity and also a naval base. There are hydroelectric plants on the Segura. Murcia, Cartagena, and other cities and towns are located on railway and highway networks. Among other important cities are Caravaca, Cieza, Lorca, and Yecla.

History.—The region of Murcia was first colonized by the ancient Phoenicians, Cartagena (ancient Carthago Nova) having been founded by colonists from Carthage about 225 B.C. After the Punic Wars in the 3d and 2d centuries B.C., the region became an important commercial and administrative outpost of Rome. Following Rome's fall in the 5th century A.D., Cartagena was successively conquered by the Alans and Vandals, and the region was brought under Visigothic control by King Euric (d. about 484 A.D.). Ceded to the Byzantine Empire by King Athanagild in 554 in exchange for military aid, the territory was regained for the Goths by Swinthila in 621. Moorish rule began in the 8th century, and with the fall of the Umayyad caliphate of Córdoba in 1031, Murcia became a separate entity, sometimes independent, at other times forming part of larger Moorish kingdoms. In 1243 Ferdinand III of Castile made the Moorish king in Murcia his vassal. After a Moorish revolt in Murcia was put down by James I of Aragon in 1265, the territory was returned to Castile and came under direct Castilian rule. Pop. (1960) 800,463.

GREGORY RABASSA,
Assistant Professor of Spanish and Portuguese, Columbia University.

MURCIA, city, Spain, capital of Murcia Province, situated on the Segura River, 30 miles north-northwest of Cartagena, in a rich agricultural belt or *huerta.* Vegetable canning is an important industry, and the city produces gunpowder and other varied manufactures. The Segura passes through Murcia, and along its banks are fine promenades. The old section has many narrow, winding streets, but modern buildings have been erected in the outskirts.

Murcia was first mentioned in 825, when it was supposedly founded by the Moorish emir Abder-Rahman II. Its famous cathedral, begun as a Gothic structure in the late 14th century, has a baroque façade and a tower 310 feet high. The University of Murcia was founded in 1915. Architectural monuments suffered severely during the Civil War of 1936–1939, when several churches were sacked. A museum houses many of the works of the sculptor Francisco Salzillo (1707–1783), who carved some of his finest objects for the city's famous Easter processions. Pop. (1965) 255,933.

GREGORY RABASSA.

MURDER. See HOMICIDE.

MURDOCK, mûr′dŏk, **William,** Scottish inventor: b. Lugar, near Auchinleck, Scotland, Aug. 21, 1754; b. Handsworth, England, Nov. 15,

1839. He went in 1777 to Birmingham, where he obtained employment in the famous engineering establishment of Boulton and Watt, located in the industrial suburb of Soho. A demand for Watt's pumping engines came from the Cornish mines, and Murdock was soon sent there to superintend the erection and fitting of these engines. In 1800 he was made manager of the works of Boulton and Watt, later becoming a partner.

His invention of coal-gas lighting remains his most conspicuous achievement. In 1792 he began his experiments regarding the illuminating properties of gases produced by distilling wood, peat, and coal. By 1800 he had an experimental gas apparatus in operation at Soho, and in 1802 this form of illumination was employed to celebrate the news of the Peace of Amiens. In 1803 the Boulton and Watt foundry was regularly lighted by that means.

In February 1808, Murdock read before the Royal Society a paper detailing his investigations. Gaslighting fell into the hands of promoters, and in 1809 Murdock was compelled to publish a vindication of his claims in "A Letter to a Member of Parliament." The three steam locomotives he constructed proved unworkable.

MURENA, mů-rē'nȧ, **Lucius Licinius,** Roman military commander and consul: fl. 62 B.C. Son of Lucius Licinius Murena, propraetor of Asia, who provoked the unsuccessful Second Mithridatic War (83–82 B.C.), he served as a commander (74–c. 68) in the Third Mithridatic War under Lucius Licinius Lucullus. After being praetor in Rome (65) and propraetor in Transalpine Gaul (64), he was elected consul (63). The defeated candidate, Servius Sulpicius, supported by Cato the Younger, accused Murena of bribery. He was successfully defended by Marcus Tullius Cicero, in a caustically mocking speech (*Pro Murena*) that survives, and took office in 62. Cicero was evidently motivated by political considerations, rather than by a belief in Murena's innocence.

MUREX, mū'rěks, a genus of gastropod mollusks typical of the family Muricidae, resembling the whelk; shell spiral, rough, with three or more ranges of spines simple or branched. Murices are remarkable for the beauty and variety of their spines. They were in high esteem from the earliest ages on account of the purple dye that some of them yielded. *M. pomum,* which is not so spiny as some of its congeners, is found along the coasts of the United States from Cape Hatteras to Texas. It is two to three inches long. The oyster drill (*Urosalpinx cinerea*), which uses its buccal ribbon to bore into oyster shells, is closely allied to *Murex*.

MURFREE, mûr'frē, **Mary Noailles** (pseudonym CHARLES EGBERT CRADDOCK), American short-story writer and novelist: b. near Murfreesboro, Tenn., Jan. 24, 1850; d. there, July 31, 1922. Partially crippled by a childhood illness, she passed all but a few years of her life in her native region, summering in the Cumberland Mountains, whose people became the characters of her most effective stories. Her work first appeared (1874–1875) in *Lippincott's Magazine,* and in 1878 she began to write for the *Atlantic Monthly* under the Craddock pseudonym. Her true identity was not discovered by her editors until 1885. Miss Murfree's stories of the pathos and passions of mountain life are unexcelled for authentic color, though reading is slowed by lengthy scenic descriptions and an excessive preoccupation with exact rendition of dialect. The first collection, *In the Tennessee Mountains* (1884), was followed by other books such as *The Prophet of the Great Smoky Mountains* (1885), *In the "Stranger People's" Country* (1891), and *The Young Mountaineers* (1897). She also wrote several novels of the Civil War (*Where the Battle Was Fought,* 1884; *The Storm Centre,* 1905) and of the colonial period (*The Story of Old Fort Loudon,* 1899; *The Amulet,* 1906).

Consult Parks, Edd Winfield, *Charles Egbert Craddock (Mary Noailles Murfree)* (Chapel Hill, N.C., 1941).

MURFREESBORO, mûr'frēz-bûr-ō, city, Tennessee, seat of Rutherford County, on the West Fork of Stones River, 29 miles southeast of Nashville, at an altitude of 575 feet. The city has an airport and is a shipping point for an agricultural region. Nearby are cedar forests. Chief industries are the processing of dairy products and the manufacture of hospital and heating equipment, hosiery, and wood products. Middle Tennessee State College is located here.

Murfreesboro was founded in 1766 and from 1819 to 1825 was the capital of Tennessee. An important battle of the Civil War was fought here (Dec. 31, 1862–Jan. 2, 1863) between Union Gen. William S. Rosecrans and Confederate Gen. Braxton Bragg. The battlefield is now the Stones River National Military Park. Government is by city manager. Pop. 26,360.

MÜRGER, mür-zhâr', **Henry** (original name LOUIS HENRI MURGER), French writer: b. Paris, France, March 24, 1822; d. there, Jan. 28, 1861. Son of an apartment-house janitor, he became the protégé of an academician living in the building, but was forced to leave school at 14, and worked as a law clerk and later as secretary to Count Alesksei Konstantinovich Tolstoi. At the age of 20, he was ordered by his father to leave home, and for several years he lived the impecunious Bohemian life which he later made famous. Mürger began to write poetry, until his close friend, Chamfleury, urged him to try prose. He adopted the name Henry Mürger, and in 1847 his *Scènes de la vie de Bohème* began to appear serially in *Le corsaire,* a literary review. Drawn from his Bohemian experiences—Rodolphe represents Mürger himself—these sketches were immensely popular. A dramatization, written in collaboration with Théodore Barrière and produced as *La vie de Bohème* (Nov. 22, 1849, at the Théâtre des Variétés), was an instant success. The sketches were published in book form in 1851.

In 1847 Mürger became a contributor to *L'évènement,* a review founded by Victor Hugo, and this brought him prestige. During his last years he was one of the most popular writers of the period. Because of his low birth, however, he did not receive the Legion of Honor award until 1858, and he was never accepted into the French Academy. He died of complications resulting from the malnutrition of his Bohemian years and the toxic effects of excessive coffee consumption.

Mürger's only volume of verse, *Les nuits d'hiver* (1861), culled from his notebooks, was published the day after his death. Some of these were later translated into English by Andrew Lang in *Ballads and Lyrics of Old France* (1872). The chief work for which he is remembered is the *Scènes de la vie de Bohème,* on which Giacomo

Puccini's opera *La Bohème* (1896) was based. Charming, witty, sometimes sentimental but also realistic, his work served as a bridge between the waning romantic literary tradition and the realism just coming into vogue. It introduced the term "Bohemian" into the languages of the Western World and attracted to Paris such young aspirants to the Bohemian life as the American James Abbott McNeill Whistler and the Englishman George L. P. B. du Maurier.

Consult Moss, Arthur, and Marvel, Evalyn, *The Legend of the Latin Quarter* (New York 1946).

MURGHAB RIVER or **MURGAB RIVER,** mo͝or-gäb', river, Central Asia. Rising in the western watershed of the Hindu Kush in Afghanistan, it flows generally west and northwest between the Band-i-Turkestan and Paropamisus ranges to enter the Turkmen Socialist Soviet Republic near Maruchak; it then flows in a northwesterly direction through the Mary (Merv) Oasis and, after a total course of about 530 miles, disappears by evaporation in the Kara-Kum Desert. There are several irrigation dams, including that at Tashkepristroi, where the Kushka River joins the Murghab.

MURIDAE. See MOUSE.

MURILLO, mo͞o-rē'lyô, **Bartolomé Esteban,** Spanish painter: b. Seville, Spain, bap. Jan. 1, 1618; d. there, April 3, 1682. A student of Juan del Castillo, he worked in Seville, and there is evidence of only one trip to Madrid (1658). Considered, along with Francisco de Zurbarán, to be the most important religious painter of the baroque period in Spain, he was more inclined to the expression of grace and beauty than other Spanish painters. From 1645 until his death, he was the favorite artist of the churches, convents, and monasteries of Seville, and was especially favored by the Franciscan Order. His paintings were dispersed as a result of the French invasion of Spain during the Napoleonic Wars (some of them being included in Marshal Nicolas Jean de Dieu Soult's loot) and through the decree of 1836 which deprived religious orders of all their property.

Murillo's first works can be dated about 1640 (pictures in the archbishop's palace in Seville). His style became more clearly defined in 1645 with his paintings, in brownish hues, for the Franciscan Casa Grande. These include *San Diego of Alcalá* (in the Academy of Madrid), *The Angels' Kitchen* (Louvre, Paris; 1646), and *The Death of St. Clara* (Dresden). His palette became lighter and more silvery in the decade from 1650 to 1660 in the pictures for the cathedral of Seville (*St. Isidore, St. Leander,* and *St. Anthony's Vision*). His interest in atmospheric effects (which writers of the time called the "misty style") was probably strengthened by his trip to Madrid in 1658 and his acquaintance with the late works of Diego Rodríguez de Silva y Velázquez. His masterpieces in this style are *The Birth of the Virgin* (Louvre) and the pictures in the Prado Museum (Madrid), *The Dream of the Roman Patrician* and *The Visit of the Patrician to Pope Liberius* (the last two painted for the Church of Santa María la Blanca in 1665).

With other artists, Murillo founded an academy of painting in Seville in 1660. Between 1665 and 1670 he completed his great series of paintings for the Capuchins, in which the fineness and delicacy of his technique are accentuated (including *Saints Justa and Rufina, St. Francis at the Foot of the Cross, St. Felix and the Virgin,* and *The Birth of Christ,* all in the Museum of Seville). In 1667–1668 he painted the pictures for the chapter house of the cathedral of Seville, and between 1670 and 1674 the famous series for the Hospital de la Caridad (*St. Elizabeth of Hungary Nursing the Sick, The Miracle of the Waters,* and others). In 1681 he was called upon to paint in the Capuchin convent in Cádiz, where he contracted his last illness.

Besides the various dated series which mark his chronological evolution, Murillo executed numerous paintings which are now included in the principal collections of Europe and America. The hallmarks of his work are a sweet and human expression of religion, realism, a palette of soft colors and silvery highlights, and graceful composition. As a creator of types of religious portraiture, Murillo holds a position in the Spanish baroque period comparable to that occupied by Raphael in the Renaissance. This is shown in his creation of a style of representation of the Virgin and Child, of which there are examples in the Prado Museum, the Pitti Palace (Florence), Dresden, the Wantage Collection (London), Dulwich, the Corsini Gallery (Rome), and other places. His great creation was his depiction of the Immaculate Conception, of which there are numerous, quite varied examples (in the Prado; Seville; the Louvre; Kansas City; and the Hermitage, Leningrad). Among his pictures which should be singled out for their composition are *The Flight into Egypt* (Genoa); *Betrothal of the Virgin* (Wallace Collection, London); *The Flight into Egypt* and *St. Anthony* (Leningrad). Also worthy of mention in this regard are his pictures of the *Parable of the Prodigal Son* (Beit Collection, London; National Gallery, Washington) and *The Holy Family* (Prado; National Gallery, London; Duke of Devonshire Collection, Chatsworth).

Murillo depicts Christ or St. John as children with the same charm as is seen in his famous paintings of the poor children of Seville, playing or eating fruit, which have given him his reputation as a genre painter (Munich, Cologne, Dulwich, and others). His *Women at the Window* is in the National Gallery in Washington. He was also an excellent portraitist (Prado; The Metropolitan Museum of Art, New York City; St. Louis).

Murillo was the first Spanish artist to become famous outside his own country. The German artist Joachim von Sandrart published a biographical article on him the year following his death. Murillo's pictures were highly esteemed in the art market of his time, and this appreciation increased in the following centuries. In the rococo and romantic periods much store was set by Murillo, who was the most admired of Spanish artists until the second half of the 19th century. Then his reputation diminished in contrast to the increased value put on the works of Velázquez, Francisco José de Goya, El Greco, and Zurbarán.

Bibliography.—Tubino, Francisco María, *Murillo* (Seville 1864); Curtis, Charles B., *Velazques and Murillo* (London 1883); Lefort, Paul Adolphe, *Murillo et ses élèves* (Paris 1892); Mayer, August Liebmann, *Murillo,* vol. 22 of *Klassiker der Kunst,* 2d ed. (Berlin and Leipzig 1922); Montoto de Sedas, Santiago, *Murillo* (Barcelona 1932); Muñoz, Antonio, *Murillo* (Rome 1941); Abbad Ríos, Francisco, *Las immaculadas de Murillo* (Barcelona 1948); Lafuente-Ferrari, Enrique, *Breve historia de la pintura española,* 4th ed. (Madrid 1953).

ENRIQUE LAFUENTE-FERRARI,
Museo de Arte Moderno, Madrid.

MURILLO, mōō-rē'yō, **Gerardo** (pseudonym Dr. Atl), Mexican artist: b. Guadalajara, Jalisco, Mexico, 1877. Trained in Europe, he became a pioneer in the art movement which broke away from the European tradition and developed an indigenous Mexican art. He took the Aztec name of Atl, meaning "water," and the signature Dr. Atl. Dr. Atl organized the first revolutionary labor union in Mexico, modeled on the syndicalist unions of Spain and France. He joined the Mexican revolution that broke out in 1910, and in 1914–1915 saw active service in the army of Venustiano Carranza. He died in Mexico City, Aug. 15, 1964.

Dr. Atl exerted great influence on the group of young artists, such as José Clemente Orozco, David Alfaro Siqueiros, Diego Rivera, and Jean Charlot, who were struggling to transform Mexican art forms and also the system of art education. Whereas other artists in this group drew heavily on Mexican archaeology and folklore for inspiration, Dr. Atl was a landscape painter, especially of volcanoes. Popocatepetl and Ixtaccihuatl were drawn from every aspect, and when the new volcano Paricutín appeared in a cornfield in 1943, he bought the field. Four of his numerous paintings of Paricutín were chosen by the Mexican government in 1947 as a gift to the president of the United States. In the Teatro Nacional, housed in the Palacio de Bellas Artes in Mexico City, is a glass mosaic curtain designed by Dr. Atl depicting the Valley of Mexico overlooked by the dormant volcanoes Popocatepetl and Ixtaccihuatl. Much of his work is done with special color crayons of copal resin and wax which he invented and called Atlcolors.

Consult Luna Arroyo, Antonio, *El Dr. Atl, paisajista puro* (Mexico 1952).

MURMANSK, mŏŏr-mȧnsk', oblast, USSR, in the Russian SFSR, comprising the Kola Peninsula of northern European Russia and adjacent mainland. It is bordered by the Barents Sea on the north and northeast, by the White Sea on the southeast and south, by the Karelian Autonomous SSR on the southwest, and by Finland and Norway on the west. With an area of 56,000 square miles, Murmansk Oblast is covered almost entirely with tundra in the north and by northern coniferous forest in the south. It has a six-month winter; January average temperatures range from 23° F. on the northern Murman coast, warmed by the Gulf Stream, to 12° F. in the interior, where the thermometer sometimes descends to —40° or —50°F. The oblast's economy is based largely on fishing, mining and the processing of ores, and lumbering. Agriculture is limited to dairying and greenhouse farming near the newly developed urban centers. Mink and fox pelts for export are produced on a state fur farm near the city of Murmansk. Reindeer are raised by Lapps on collective farms.

Among the oblast's mineral products are apatite and nephelite (both mined near Kirovsk, where there are ore-processing plants), copper (at Monchegorsk), nickel (mined at the town of Nikel in the Pechenga area), and iron ore (at Olenegorsk). The fishing catch, obtained with deep-sea trawlers, is 20 per cent of the Soviet total. The trawlers have their base at Murmansk, an ice-free port and capital of the oblast. Other cities are Kandalaksha, with sawmills and an aluminum plant, and Severomorsk and Polyarny, naval bases. Electric power for industry is derived mainly from hydroelectric stations along the Tuloma and Niva rivers.

The oblast was completely undeveloped as late as 1923. Most of its population migrated there from other parts of the Soviet Union during the industrialization drive; the original Lapp population numbers only about 1,800. The residents of mining towns and other urban centers account for 90 per cent of the total population, which rose from 23,000 in 1926 to 291,000 in 1939 and 474,000 in 1956. Pop. (1967 est.) 714,000.

Theodore Shabad,
Author of "Geography of the USSR."

MURMANSK, city, USSR, capital of Murmansk Oblast in the Russian SFSR, 625 miles north of Leningrad, with which it is linked by railroad. Murmansk is situated on the fjordlike Kola Gulf of the Barents Sea, about 35 miles from the open sea. It is the world's largest city north of the Arctic Circle and is an ice-free port kept open all winter by the warm Gulf Stream along the Murman coast. Murmansk is the principal Soviet base for deep-sea fishing trawlers and fishing factory ships. The fishing industry and associated enterprises (canning, freezing, smoking, and salting of fish, netmaking, and ship repair) employ half of the city's labor force. By 1960 Murmansk had also become one of the leading commercial ports of the Soviet Union. It has a merchant-marine training school, a naval repair station, and a research institute for Arctic fisheries and oceanography. The city was founded in 1915 as a port to receive Allied supplies for the Russian armies in World War I. After the Bolshevik Revolution, it was held from 1918 to 1920 by Allied interventionists. In World War II it resisted a German drive and was again used as a port for Allied lend-lease convoys. Under the impact of Soviet development of Murmansk Oblast and expansion of the city's port facilities, the population rose from 8,777 in 1926 to 117,054 in 1939, 168,000 in 1956, and 309,000 in 1970.

Theodore Shabad.

MURNER, mŏŏr'nĕr, **Thomas,** German satirist: b. Oberehnheim, Alsace, Dec. 24, 1475; d. there, before Aug. 23, 1537. He became a Franciscan monk in Strasbourg in 1490, and studied and taught in the leading European universities of his day. He translated Virgil's *Aeneid* (1515) and the *Institutes* of Justinian (1519), but is chiefly known for his brilliant, bitter satires on the social follies and ecclesiastical failing of his times. These include *Die Narrenbeschwörung* (1512), written in the manner of Sebastian Brant's satirical poem *Das Narrenschiff; Die Mühle zu Schwindelsheim* (1515); and *Geuchmatt* (1519). One of the most virulent critics of the Reformation, Murner wrote the venomous and racily witty *Von dem grossen lutherischen Narren* (1522). So violent were his diatribes against the Reformation that he was obliged to leave Alsace. After four years in Lucerne, Switzerland, where he continued his anti-Reformation activities, he was again forced to move and in 1529 returned to Oberehnheim, where he was a parish priest at the time of his death. He was perhaps the greatest Roman Catholic satirist of the 16th century.

MUROM, mōō'rŭm, city, USSR, in Vladimir Oblast of the Russian SFSR, 175 miles east of Moscow, on the Oka River. It is a railroad junction and an industrial center producing heavy machine tools, diesel locomotives, and refrigerators. The city also has textile and plywood mills.

One of the oldest centers of European Russia, Murom dates from 864 and was a major trade center in the Middle Ages on the Oka-Volga water route. Under the Soviet regime, it has had an industrial rebirth, its population rising from 22,000 in 1926 to 64,000 in 1956. Pop. (1959) 73,000.

THEODORE SHABAD.

MUROMACHI PERIOD. See PAINTING—*Eastern Art* (Japanese Painting): Muromachi Period.

MURORAN, mōō-rô-rän, city, Japan, on the southeast coast of Hokkaido, at the northern side of the entrance to Uchiura (Volcano) Bay. The port ships coal from the Yubari (Ishikari) fields, lumber, and paper, and imports supplementary iron ore for the city's iron and steel industry, which depends largely on ore from the Kutchan mines of Hokkaido. The city is connected by railroad with other towns on the south coast of the island and with those of the Ishikari River valley to the north, and by steamship with Aomori on northern Honshu and with Tokyo. Hokkaido University has a Seaweed Research Laboratory just outside the city. Pop. (1960) 145,679.

MURPHY, mûr'fĭ, **Arthur,** Irish playwright and actor: b. near Elpin, County Roscommon, Ireland, Dec. 27, 1727; d. London, England, June 18, 1805. He studied at the English Jesuit College at St. Omer, France, and later worked in a banking house in London. In October 1752 he began publishing the weekly *Gray's Inn Journal,* modeled on the *Spectator,* but in 1754, being heavily in debt and disappointed in an expected legacy, he turned to acting. On Oct. 18, 1754, he made his debut at Covent Garden as Othello. During the following season he played in David Garrick's company and wrote a farce, *The Apprentice,* which, produced at Drury Lane in 1756, was so successful that he was able to repay his debts and retire from the stage. Even more successful was his farce *The Upholsterer, or What News?* (1757).

Murphy studied law and was called to the bar in 1762, but continued writing for the stage. Some of the best known of his works were the comedies *The Way to Keep Him* (1760) and *The Old Maid* (1761); the unsuccessful *What We Must All Come To* (1764), later revived successfully as *Three Weeks After Marriage* (1776); *The School for Guardians* (1767); and *Know Your Own Mind* (1778). Of Murphy's tragedies, less successful than his comedies, the best known was *The Grecian Daughter* (1772). Murphy's plots were not original, and many of his plays were adaptations of the works of Voltaire, Molière, and other French authors. He also published an *Essay on the Life and Genius of Samuel Johnson, LL.D.* (1792), a *Life of David Garrick* (2 vols., 1801), translations of the works of Tacitus (4 vols., 1793), and a number of other translations and essays. A collection of his plays was published in seven volumes in 1786.

MURPHY, Charles Francis, American politician: b. New York, N.Y., June 20, 1858; d. there, April 25, 1924. With little formal education, he worked in a shipyard and as a horsecar driver before opening a saloon in 1878. Murphy established himself as adviser to the local workingmen and politicians, became active in Tammany Hall politics, and in 1892 he was elected leader of the 18th Assembly District. In 1898 he was appointed to his only salaried political office, that of dock commissioner. After Richard Croker retired as leader of Tammany Hall, Murphy assumed control of the organization (1902), retaining it until his death. As Tammany boss and state Democratic leader, he was a powerful force in New York City and New York State politics, but he never again sought or held public office, and he avoided publicity. He was noted for his political acumen and tact.

MURPHY, Frank, American lawyer, public official, and United States Supreme Court justice: b. Harbor Beach, Mich., April 13, 1890; d. Detroit, July 19, 1949. The son of a country lawyer, Murphy studied at the University of Michigan, receiving his law degree in 1914. During World War I he served with the infantry in France and in the army of occupation in Germany. After the war, Murphy did graduate study in law at Lincoln's Inn, London, and at Trinity College, Dublin. On returning to Michigan he was chief assistant United States attorney for eastern Michigan (1919–1920), taught law at the University of Detroit (1922–1927), and served as judge of the recorder's court in the city (1923–1930). During his term as judge he introduced the practice of naming a psychiatrist and a sociologist to the sentencing board of each case. As mayor of Detroit (1930–1933), he drastically reduced city expenses and applied half of the amount saved to feed the thousands of men made jobless by the closing of the automobile plants. He was one of the first advocates of federal relief and actively supported the Works Progress Administration (WPA) set up in the early days of President Franklin Delano Roosevelt's administration.

In 1933 Roosevelt appointed Murphy governor general of the Philippines, and when the islands received commonwealth status on Nov. 15, 1935, Murphy remained as high commissioner. While governor general he introduced woman's suffrage and the parole system. In 1936 he was elected governor of Michigan on the Democratic ticket and almost immediately was faced with the problem of a sit-down strike in one of the major automobile plants. He refused to call on the state militia to oust the strikers, fearing that the use of troops would lead to bloodshed. Although the strike was settled peacefully, Murphy was severely criticized for his stand and in 1938 was decisively defeated for re-election. He was appointed attorney general of the United States on Jan. 2, 1939; during his 13 months in office he proved a fearless opponent of official and judicial corruption, and prosecuted both business and labor for violation of the antitrust laws.

In January 1940 President Roosevelt appointed Murphy associate justice of the United States Supreme Court, and he was sworn in on Feb. 5, 1940. He soon earned a reputation as a friend of the workingman and of minority groups of all kinds. His most famous labor opinions were written in the portal-to-portal pay cases involving the Mount Clemens (Mich.) Pottery Company in 1942; The Tennessee Coal, Iron and Railroad Company in 1944; and the Jewel Ridge (Va.) Coal Corporation in 1945. The only Roman Catholic member of the Supreme Court, Murphy showed a pronounced regard for the rights of all religious sects, and many times during his court career came out strongly in defense of civil and religious liberties.

MURPHY, John Benjamin, American surgeon: b. near Appleton, Wis., Dec. 21, 1857; d. Mackinac Island, Mich., Aug. 11, 1916. He was educated at Rush Medical College, Chicago, and in Vienna and practiced in Chicago. He was professor of surgery at Rush Medical College and Northwestern University Medical School. As a teacher, researcher, and practitioner, he was regarded internationally as a leading surgeon of his time. In 1892 he devised the Murphy or Murphy's button, an appliance used to join the ends of intestines after a section had been removed, which made possible great advances in abdominal operations. By other inventions and discoveries of techniques he enlarged the knowledge of many fields of surgery, including the lungs and nervous system and bones and joints.

MURPHY, John Francis, American painter: b. Oswego, N.Y., Dec. 11, 1853; d. New York, N.Y., Jan. 30, 1921. His schooling was limited and in his art he was self-taught. He opened a studio in New York City in 1875 and his first picture to appear in the National Academy of Design was exhibited the next year. His paintings, many of which hang in American galleries, were chiefly landscapes. His *Tints of a Vanished Past* won a Hallgarten prize in 1885 and two years later he was elected to the National Academy. He received the Inness Medal in 1910.

MURPHY, William Parry, American physician: b. Stoughton, Wis., Feb. 6, 1892. He was educated at the University of Oregon and Harvard Medical School. He practiced medicine in Brookline, Mass., and was a member of the Harvard medical faculty. He engaged in research on diabetes and diseases of the blood, especially pernicious anemia, and with Dr. George R. Minot discovered that anemia could be checked by feeding quantities of liver. For this he shared the Nobel Prize in medicine in 1934 with Dr. Minot and Dr. George H. Whipple.

MURPHYSBORO, mûr'fĭz-bûr-ō, city, Illinois, seat of Jackson county, on the Big Muddy River, about 90 miles southeast of St. Louis, Mo. Formerly the center of coal-mining fields, it is a residential and industrial city in an orchard and farming region, a shipping point for apples, peaches, corn, soybeans, and wheat. Shoes, industrial labels, clothing, metal products, fertilizers and farm chemicals are manufactured. On the high school campus stands a statue of John A. Logan, Union general in the Civil War, who was born here, and a bronze plaque outside the city marks the site of the first coal mine in Illinois. The town was founded as the county seat in 1843 after fire destroyed the courthouse in Brownsville was named for a county commissioner, William Murphy. It was incorporated in 1867, and has a mayor-council government. Pop. 10,013.

MURRAY or **MORAY**, EARLS OF. See STUART.

MURRAY, mûr'ē, an English family of book publishers in London.

JOHN MURRAY (originally MACMURRAY): b. Edinburgh, Scotland, 1745; d. Nov. 6, 1793. He dropped the prefix to his name when he retired as a lieutenant of marines in 1768 and became a bookseller and publisher. He also edited the *London Mercury* and the *English Review*.

JOHN MURRAY: b. London, Nov. 27, 1778; d. June 27, 1843. On coming of age, he headed the firm and was a friend of many leading writers whose work he published, including Byron, Sir Walter Scott, Thomas Moore, Thomas Campbell, George Crabbe, and George Henry Borrow. His association with Byron was particularly close, and it was in Murray's house that the poet's controversial *Memoirs* were destroyed after his death. Murray also published some of Jane Austen's novels and Sir Charles Lyell's *Principles of Geology*. In 1809 he founded the *Quarterly Review* on Tory principles in opposition to the *Edinburgh Review*.

JOHN MURRAY: b. April 16, 1808; d. London, April 2, 1892. He was educated at the University of Edinburgh and after 1830 assisted his father, succeeding him on his death. He instituted the series of travel guidebooks which bear the firm's name. Among his significant publications was Charles Darwin's *Origin of Species* (1859).

SIR JOHN MURRAY: b. London, Dec. 18, 1851; d. Hove, Sussex, Nov. 30, 1928. He was educated at Magdalen College, Oxford, and headed the firm after his father's death. He was president of the Publishers' Association in 1898–1899 and edited Edward Gibbon's *Autobiography* (1897) and Byron's *Correspondence* (1922). He was knighted in 1926.

SIR JOHN MURRAY: b. June 12, 1884. He was educated at Magdalen and was senior director of the publishing house and editor of the *Quarterly Review*. He was knighted in 1932.

MURRAY, (George) Gilbert (Aimé), British classical scholar: b. Sydney, Australia, Jan. 2, 1866; d. Oxford, England, May 20, 1957. The son of the president of the legislative council of New South Wales, he went to England in 1877 and studied at Merchant Taylors' School, London, and St. John's College, Oxford. In 1888 he was made a fellow of New College, Oxford, and in 1889 he became professor of Greek at the University of Glasgow, where he remained until 1899. Also in 1889 he married Lady Mary Henrietta Howard, daughter of the 9th earl of Carlisle. From 1908 until his retirement in 1936 he was regius professor of Greek at Oxford.

As a scholar, he endeavored to interpret the Hellenic spirit to the modern age, notably in his English verse translations of plays of Euripides, Sophocles, Aeschylus, Aristophanes, and Menander. These were done in rhymed heroics, rather than the more conventional blank verse, in an effort to render the essential rhythmic quality of Greek poetry. Several of these were performed on the stage in the United States and England. He also produced critical editions of Euripides and Aeschylus. His other writings included *The Rise of the Greek Epic* (1907); *Five Stages of Greek Religion* (1925); *The Classical Tradition in Poetry* (1927); *Greek Studies* (1946); and *Hellenism and the Modern World* (1953).

After World War I he became engrossed in the cause of international peace and unity, and achieved among its advocates an eminence comparable to his place in scholarship. He had a part in drafting the Covenant of the League of Nations and was a promoter of the League of Nations Union, its chairman from 1923 to 1938 and copresident thereafter. In 1941 he received the Order of Merit. He was an ardent supporter of the United Nations, serving as first president of the United Nations Association general council.

Among his writings on international politics and peace were *The Problem of Foreign Policy* (1921); *Liberality and Civilization* (1938); and *From the League to the U.N.* (1947).

MURRAY, James, British soldier: b. ?1719; d. near Battle, Sussex, England, June 18, 1794. He was the fifth son of the 4th baron Elibank. He entered the British army about 1740 and commanded a brigade at the siege of Louisburg, Canada (1758) and led the army's left wing in General James Wolfe's victory on the Plains of Abraham outside Quebec (Sept. 13, 1759). As commander in Quebec, he withstood a siege by superior numbers of the French in 1760, and later that year was named governor of Quebec. In 1763 he became governor of Canada.

He adopted a conciliatory policy toward the French Canadians, which prepared the way for the Quebec Act of 1774, but British colonists accused him of favoritism and obtained his recall to England in 1766. He was cleared of all charges and in 1774 was named governor of Minorca. Here he was compelled to yield Fort St. Philip to the French and Spaniards after a harsh siege in 1782 and was court-martialed on charges by a subordinate, but was acquitted. He was made a general in 1783.

MURRAY, Sir **James Augustus Henry,** British philologist and lexicographer: b. Denholm, near Hawick, Roxburgh, Scotland, Feb. 7, 1837; d. Oxford, England, July 26, 1915. He taught in Hawick and at Mill Hill school before receiving his bachelor of arts degree at the University of London in 1873. He became known as a philologist and in 1879 was named editor of a proposed *New English Dictionary on Historical Principles,* to be published by the Clarendon Press of Oxford under the auspices of the Philological Society of London. The society had undertaken the project in 1857 and had collected much material, but the first two editors had made little progress. Murray and his staff, with thousands of volunteer assistants, broadened its scope, amassing millions of references tracing the history of English words. The first volume (*A to Ant*) was published Feb. 1, 1884; the tenth and last (T to Z) did not appear until after Murray's death. The original plan had called for completion in 10 years. The work is now known as the *Oxford English Dictionary*.

Although as editor Murray was responsible directly for only about half the work, his organizational genius guided the whole and devised the basic structure within which subsequent enlargements and refinements were accommodated. He was knighted in 1908.

MURRAY, John, American clergyman: b. Alton, Hampshire, England, Dec. 10, 1741; d. Boston, Mass., Sept. 3, 1815. His family moved to Ireland, where as a boy he was an ardent member of a Wesleyan congregation. He became attracted to the Calvinist Methodism of George Whitefield, but after moving to London was converted to the doctrines of James Relly, who preached universal redemption of all men. Excommunicated from Whitefield's group and in grave domestic trouble, he sailed in July 1770 to the Americaan colonies.

For several years he was an itinerant preacher in New Jersey and New England. His creed of the ultimate salvation of each individual found readier acceptance among the laity than the clergy, who opposed him bitterly. When he was chosen chaplain of a Rhode Island regiment in 1775, other chaplains protested, but his commission was ratified by George Washington. In 1779 he became minister of the Independent Church of Christ in Gloucester, Mass. In 1793 he was installed as pastor of a Universalist society in Boston. He is regarded as the founder of American Universalism.

See also Universalism.

MURRAY, Sir **John,** British marine zoologist and oceanographer: b. Cobourg, Ontario, Canada, March 3, 1841; d. Kirkliston, Scotland, March 16, 1914. He went to Scotland when he was 17 and studied at the University of Edinburgh. In 1868, as surgeon on a whaler, he visited Jan Mayen Island and parts of Spitsbergen, examining marine life, ocean currents, temperatures. He assisted in preparations for the voyage of the scientific exploring vessel H.M.S. *Challenger* (see Challenger Expedition) and was appointed a naturalist on its staff under Sir Charles Wyville Thomson. On the voyage (1872–1876), which circled the globe, Murray studied sea surface organisms and deposits raised from the depths. Thomson made him custodian of the collection of specimens and for nearly 20 years after the expedition's return he was absorbed in arranging and classifying these in an office in Edinburgh. After Thomson's death in 1882, Murray edited the 50-volume reports of the *Challenger*'s findings and was joint author of the narrative of the cruise. In 1897 he conducted bathymetric surveys of the freshwater lochs of Scotland and in 1910 he accompanied a group investigating the depths of the North Atlantic. Their work was summarized in *The Depths of the Sea* (1912) by Murray and Johan Hjort. Murray lost his life in a motor accident.

MURRAY, John Courtney, American Jesuit theologian: b. New York, N.Y., Sept. 12, 1904; d. there, Aug. 16, 1967. After joining the Society of Jesus, he studied at Boston College (A.B., 1926; M.A., 1927) and received the licentiate in theology from Woodstock College—the Jesuit school of theology where he later taught—and the doctorate from the Pontifical Gregorian University in Rome. In his lectures, in articles in scholarly journals, and in *We Hold These Truths* (1960) he upheld the compatibility of the church's experience of religious freedom and pluralism in the United States with the natural law tradition of Roman Catholicism.

His views, though sometimes labeled unorthodox, were vindicated when he was appointed *peritus* ("expert") to Vatican II and when many of them were incorporated in the Council's Declaration on Religious Freedom. Murray was named a consultant to the Center for the Study of Democratic Institutions and to the Vatican Secretariat for Promoting Christian Unity. He also wrote *The Problem of God* (1964) and *Problems of Religious Freedom* (1965).

MURRAY, Philip, American labor leader: b. Blantyre, Scotland, May 25, 1886; d. San Francisco, Calif., Nov. 9, 1952. He was a founder and, later, president of the CIO and first president of the United Steelworkers of America.

After going to the United States in 1902, he worked with his father in coal mines near

Pittsburgh, Pa. At 18, after protesting practices of short weight, he became embroiled in a fist fight with the check weighmen. His discharge caused a strike of several hundred men, but during the four-week walkout he was elected president of the local union of the United Mine Workers of America (UMW). He served for eight years, and then was successively elected to the union's international executive board in 1912, president of District 5 in 1916, and international vice president in 1920.

Murray became widely known as one of the chief negotiators of the miners' union. His extensive knowledge of the coal industry, his patient marshaling of facts and figures, his good humor and courtesy made him a perfect partner for the union's president, the flamboyant and aggressive John L. Lewis, alongside of whom he fought many battles.

He played an important role in November 1935 in the forming of the Committee for Industrial Organization (CIO), dedicated to unionism on an industry rather than a craft basis. He was appointed chairman of the Steel Workers' Organizing Committee in 1936, and in 1940, when Lewis retired as president of the Congress of Industrial Organizations, which had been formed in 1938, Murray succeeded him. But a break came between the two: Murray insisted on following policies he regarded as desirable and supported President Franklin D. Roosevelt for reelection, while Lewis backed the Republican Wendell L. Willkie. Lewis forced Murray out of the UMW and then led the miners' union out of the CIO. When the United Steelworkers of America was formed in 1942, Murray was elected president.

During World War II Murray was a member of the Combined Labor War Board, which Roosevelt kept informed on the war's progress. He supported President Harry S. Truman and guided the CIO through the stormy postwar period of strikes and purges of Communist unions in 1949–1950. Murray was known as a kind and considerate man, deeply religious, eloquent, and one who made few enemies. As a labor leader, he stands with Samuel Gompers and Lewis.

PHILIP TAFT,
Professor of Economics, Brown University.

MURRAY or **MORAY**, SIR **Robert**, Scottish statesman: b. about 1600; d. London, England, July 4, 1673. He was educated at the University of St. Andrews in Scotland and in France, where he fought under Louis XIII. He was knighted by Charles I of England in 1643, served with his regiment in Germany, and was entrusted with secret negotiations between Scotland and France to restore Charles, deposed in the English civil war. He devised an unsuccessful plan to free Charles from Newcastle. In 1654 he joined Charles II in his exile in Paris and returned to England with him at the Restoration in 1660, becoming a lord for the exchequer for Scotland and deputy secretary in 1663, and with the king and John Maitland, 2d earl and 1st duke of Lauderdale, governed the country until 1670. He was a founder of the Royal Society in 1660.

MURRAY, William, 1ST EARL OF MANSFIELD, British judge and parliamentary debater: b. Abbey of Scone, Perthshire, Scotland, March 2, 1705; d. Highgate, England, March 20, 1793. He was educated at Christ Church, Oxford, and was called to the bar in 1730. He became solicitor general in 1742 and entered parliament, where he was a notable speaker, especially in his opposition to William Pitt, 1st earl of Chatham, his lifelong rival. He was named attorney general in 1754 and in 1756 chief justice of the king's bench, being created Baron Mansfield of Mansfield. In 1776 he received the title Earl of Mansfield.

Although he spoke frequently in the House of Lords and held a cabinet post three times, his most noteworthy work was done on the bench, which he occupied until 1788. Cases of political delicacy came before him, and some of his judgments were unpopular, leading to attacks in the *Letters of Junius,* but he displayed courage and impartiality, as when he presided at the trial where Lord George Gordon, accused of instigating the No-Popery riots of 1780, in which Mansfield's house had been burned, was acquitted. In another case he directed that a Negro slave from Virginia, who had escaped from a ship in England, be allowed to remain free. His principal contribution to the law was modeling English commercial law into a form which fitted the needs of the age.

MURRAY, city, Kentucky, seat of Calloway County, 37 miles south-southeast of Paducah, on the east fork of Clarks River. It is situated in an agricultural region producing dark tobacco, corn, clover, and livestock. Among its manufactures are tobacco, dairy, and concrete products; lumber, popcorn, clothing, stoves, and feed. The city is the seat of Murray State College, founded in 1922. Nathan B. Stubblefield (1860–1928), whose experiments with wireless transmission are said to have antedated Guglielmo Marconi, was born and worked here. Incorporated in 1844, the community was named for John L. Murray, United States congressman from the district from 1837 to 1839. Government is by mayor and council. Pop. 13,537.

JOHN C. WATERS.

MURRAY, city, Utah, in Salt Lake County, seven miles south of Salt Lake City, on the Jordan River west of the Wasatch Range. A suburb of Salt Lake City, it is a trading center for an irrigated agricultural region yielding poultry and dairy products, sugar beets, alfalfa, and potatoes. Canned foods and textiles are produced, and it has been a smelting center for nearby lead mines. It was incorporated in 1902 and has a commission form of government. Pop. 21,206.

MURRAY RIVER, river, Australia, in New South Wales, Victoria, and South Australia. It rises in the Australian Alps, New South Wales, and flows generally westward, entering the Indian Ocean through lakes and sandbars at Encounter Bay, South Australia. It is about 1,600 miles long and for about 1,200 miles forms the border between Victoria and New South Wales. The principal river of the Murray-Darling basin, extending over 414,000 square miles, it gathers many tributaries, including the Goulburn, the Murrumbidgee, and the 1,702-mile Darling.

The Hume Dam, near Albury, where the river leaves the foothills, impounds 2 million acre-feet of water, and a series of weirs downstream helps to regulate the river flow and provide water for extensive areas where pastures, citrus fruits, and vines are grown under irrigation. Supplies have been augmented by the Snowy Mountains project. First reached in 1824, the river was named by Charles Sturt in 1830. Vast valley tracts were occupied for grazing by 1840. Steamer navigation was developed after 1853 and a fleet of paddlewheelers was operated until the 1880's, when a rail network was developed.

R.M. YOUNGER.

MURRAY STATE COLLEGE, a coeducational, multipurpose college at Murray, Ky. Founded in 1922, it occupies a 100-acre campus. Preprofessional courses are offered in dentistry, law, medicine, engineering, forestry, veterinary medicine, pharmacy, and theology. Degrees awarded include bachelor of arts, bachelor of science, bachelor of science in agriculture and home economics, bachelor of music education, bachelor of music, and master of arts in education. The school colors are royal blue and old gold; the song is *Murray State College Alma Mater;* the athletic teams are known as the Thoroughbreds. Average student enrollment is approximately 4,000.

RALPH H. WOODS.

MURRE, mûr, one of two species of sea birds of the family Alcidae which breed on the open ledges of sea cliffs on the coasts and islands of the North Atlantic, Arctic, and North Pacific oceans. The murres, or guillemots as they are called in England, vary from about 16 to 18 inches in length and are very compactly built, black above and white below, with strong and sharply pointed bills. They breed in huge and densely packed colonies, which in western Greenland have been estimated to number about one million pairs. They build no nest and lay only a single large egg on the bare rock. The egg is pear shaped and strongly tapered, which prevents it from falling from the rock; a dislodging blow will make it roll in a half circle but not roll off. About half the food of the murres consists of small fish and the rest of crustaceans, molluscs, and plankton. The two species are the common murre *(Uria aalge)* and the thick-billed or Brünnich's murre (*U. lomvia*).

CHARLES VAURIE.

MURRELET, mûr'lĕt, one of several species of the family Alcidae which inhabit the northern Pacific Ocean. Murrelets are very chunky black and white birds, about 9 inches long.

CHARLES VAURIE.

MURRI, mo͞or'rê, **Romolo,** Italian priest and social reformer: b. Monte San Pietrangeli, Ascoli Piceno province, Italy, Aug. 27, 1870; d. Rome, March 12, 1944. Father Murri interpreted Leo XIII's encyclical *Rerum Novarum* (1891) as an inspiration toward creation of a Christian Democratic movement opposing both the economics of capitalism and the ideology of socialism then emerging in Italy. In 1900 he founded in Rome an activistic movement and a review of the same name, *La cultura sociale,* dedicated to a renovation of Catholic social action.

In 1901 Leo XIII's encyclical *Graves de Communi* condemned the movement and suspended its leader *a divinis* (from ecclesiastical duties). In 1905 he organized at Bologna the *Lega democratica nazionale* (National Democratic League), emphasizing separatist, secularistic, and democratic Catholic action. Elected independently to the chamber of deputies in 1909, he was excommunicated. This led to the dissolution of the league and Murri's eclipse as a significant figure in political Catholicism. Marrying in 1912, he lived in obscurity for 30 years. Toward the end of his life, long a widower, he was reconciled with the church to whose spiritual teaching he had remained loyal. Pope Pius XII restored him to the priesthood.

A. WILLIAM SALOMONE.

MURROW, mur'ō, **Edward Roscoe,** American broadcaster and public official: b. Greensboro, N.C., April 25, 1908; d. Pawling, N.Y., April 27, 1965. A graduate of Washington State College, he worked with student and educational groups until 1935 when he became director of talks and education for the Columbia Broadcasting System.

As a CBS correspondent in World War II, Murrow became famous. His broadcasts during the German air blitz, beginning with the characteristic phrase "This . . . is London," were models of accurate and vivid reporting. After serving briefly as a CBS executive, he returned in 1947 to broadcasting, covering outstanding events. He narrated the *I Can Hear It Now* albums of recordings of recent happenings, with voices of world figures, and his television programs *See It Now* and *Person to Person* were notable. From January, 1961, until his resignation in January, 1964, he was director of the United States Information Agency.

MURRUMBIDGEE RIVER, mûr-ŭm-bĭj'ē, river, Australia, in southern New South Wales, an important tributary of the Murray. Rising in the Australian Alps, it is 981 miles long, flowing through rich pastoral and agricultural districts. The Burrinjuck dam stores water for irrigation over a 500,000-acre area producing rice, fruits, and vegetables, fodder crops, and pastures. In the 1960's the irrigated area was extended as more water became available from the Snowy Mountains project.

R.M. YOUNGER.

MURRY, mûr'ē, **John Middleton,** English critic, editor, and journalist: b. London, England, Aug. 6, 1889; d. there, March 13, 1957. He studied at Christ's Hospital, London, and Brasenose College, Oxford. In 1912 be became a journalist on the *Westminster Gazette;* and in 1915 he joined the translating and editorial staff of the British War Office, where he was made chief censor at the close of World War I. He edited *The Athenaeum* (1919–1921) and *The Adelphi* (1923–1948) and contributed to the London *Times Literary Supplement.*

Murry's writings reflect a stimulation from friendships with prominent authors such as Joyce Cary, D. H. Lawrence, T. S. Eliot, and Katherine Mansfield (whom he married in 1918). He wrote some 60 books on literature, religion, sexual psychology, economics, and current politics. They reflect quickened enthusiasms followed by rapid disillusionment and provide commentaries on Christianity, socialism, communism, democracy, and major writers such as Shakespeare, Keats, and Dostoyevsky. His autobiography *Between Two Worlds* (1935) is a fascinating document; his *Keats and Shakespeare* (1925) has continuing interest. In the United States he is best known for championing Katherine Mansfield's short stories.

Consult Lea, Frank A., *The Life of John Middleton Murry* (London 1959).

HORACE V. GREGORY.

MURTLE LAKE, mûr'tʼl, lake, British Columbia, Canada, in the Cariboo Mountains, at the southeast end of Wells Gray Provincial Park. The area is noted for its scenic beauty and is a favorite resort for hunting and fishing.

MURVIEDRO. See SAGUNTO.

MUS or **MUSH** (Turk. Muş), mōōsh, the name of a province and a town in Turkey. The province, which has an area of 2,946 square miles, is bounded on the north by Erzurum, on the east by Ağri, on the south by Bitlis, and on the west by Diyarbakir and Bingöl. It is drained by the Murat River. While wheat and tobacco are raised extensively near the town of Muş, the soil is generally poor. Most of the people are Kurds. Pop. (1955 prelim.) 136,248.

The town of Muş, capital of the province, lies 85 miles south of Erzurum on a plain 4,800 feet above sea level. An old Armenian center, it is an important agricultural market. Pop. (1955 prelim.) 10,487.

MUSA IBN-NUSAYR, mōō'sä ĭb'n nōō-sīr' (Ar. MŪSĀ IBN-NUṢAYR), Arab official and soldier: b. 640 A.D.; d. 716/717. Appointed governor of North Africa in 698 or 699, he had conquered the entire region as far as the Atlantic by 705. In 711 he sent his general Tariq on a raiding expedition to Spain. Tariq was so successful that Musa became jealous and, in the following year, headed an expedition of his own. By 713, Musa had completed the conquest of Spain. Recalled by Caliph Walid I, he left his son 'Abd-al-'Aziz in charge of the new territory and led a triumphal procession across North Africa in 714. When he arrived at Damascus, he was welcomed by Walid, but he was disgraced by the new caliph, Suleiman (r. 715–717), and ended his days in poverty.

MUSACEAE, mû-zā'sē-ē, a small tropical family of plants comprising six genera and about 150 species of the order Zingiberales (Scitaminales). It includes the banana *(Musa),* the traveler's tree *(Ravenala),* and the bird-of-paradise flower *(Strelitzia).* While most of the species are large perennial herbs with underground rhizomes, the exceptional traveler's tree develops a trunk 100 feet high. The upright portion of most forms consists of a false stem resulting from the overlapping stout leaf bases. The fact that the long, broad leaf blades have parallel pinnate veins causes them to fray in windy locations. The irregular flowers contain an inferior ovary that develops into a fleshy fruit or a three-valved capsule. The flowers are subtended by large, protective, and occasionally brilliantly colored bracts, and are frequently clustered in large inflorescences. The banana is the most prolific of all food crops, producing at least 120 times more food per unit of land area than wheat. Manila hemp, a light, tenacious fiber, is derived from the leaf bases of *Musa textilis.*

See also BANANA; MANILA HEMP; STRELITZIA; TRAVELER'S TREE.

HUGH N. MOZINGO,
University of Nevada.

MUSAEUS, mû-zē'ŭs, *in classical mythology,* a poet, priest, and seer. Ancient accounts of his parentage differ, but the most persistent versions make him the son and disciple of Orpheus (q.v.). Many legends connect him with the worship of Demeter at Eleusis. Musaeus was the reputed author of precepts addressed to his son Eumolpus, hymns, oracles, and purificatory formulas to cure diseases. Only fragments of this poetical production survive.

In Greek literature, (1) an epic poet, who flourished probably at Ephesus about 240 B.C. and composed a *Perseid* in 10 books, now lost. (2) A grammarian and epic poet, known as MUSAEUS GRAMMATICUS, of unknown origin, who lived about 500 A.D. and wrote in 343 hexameters the graceful and romantic *Hero and Leander* (q.v.), which has influenced many English poets. The best edition of the text is by Arthur Ludwich, *Musaios: Hero und Leander* (Berlin 1929).

P. R. COLEMAN-NORTON,
Princeton University.

MUSÄUS, mōō-zâ'ōōs, **Johann Karl August,** German writer: b. Jena, Germany, March 29, 1735; d. Weimar, Oct. 28, 1787. Educated at the University of Jena, he served as master of court pages at Weimar from 1763 to 1769, when he became a teacher at Weimar Gymnasium, a post he held until his death. He is best known for his parodies, of Samuel Richardson in *Grandison der Zweite* (3 vols., 1760–1762) and *Der deutsche Grandison* (2 vols., 1781–1782), and of Johann Kaspar Lavater in *Physiognomische Reisen* (4 vols., 1778–1779). Among Musäus' other works, the most popular is *Volksmärchen der Deutschen* (5 vols., 1782–1786), a collection of old German folk tales recounted in a polished, ironical manner. Three of these tales were included in Thomas Carlyle's *German Romance* (1827). An incomplete collection of stories, *Straussfedern* (1787), appeared posthumously.

MUSCA, mŭs'kȧ, the constellation of the (Southern) Fly, one of the 12 new star groups named by Johann Bayer (q.v.) in his *Uranometria* (1603). It is a very faint asterism, containing only two stars as bright as the 3d magnitude, and it lies largely within the southern branch of the Milky Way. Musca is located in right ascension 12^h40^m, declination $-72°$, and transits the upper branch of the meridian at 9 P.M. about May 14.

FERGUS J. WOOD.

MUSCAT, mŭs'kăt (also MUSKAT or MASKAT; Ar. MASQAT), town, Arabia, capital and principal port of the nominally independent Sultanate of Muscat and Oman, situated on the Gulf of Oman ('Umān), 110 miles northwest of Ras al Hadd (Ra's al-Ḥadd). The inhabitants are mostly Indians, Baluchis, and Negroes, with only a few indigenous Arabians. Because of its good natural harbor and command of the southern entrance to the Persian Gulf, Muscat has become the main center for the sultanate's exports, including dates, pomegranates, dried fruit, and fish and fish products; and also for imports, comprising rice, coffee, sugar, wheat, and cotton goods. It has a cable station and provides a port of call for small steamers, particularly those on the Bombay-Basra (al-Baṣrah) mail route. Since it lies at the foot of high hills, it directs its inland traffic, carried entirely by pack animals, through Matrah (Maṭraḥ), located three miles to the northwest by motor road.

Like other medieval Arabian towns, Muscat is a walled city with flat-roofed houses and huts and only a few lofty buildings other than minarets. It is centered on the palace of the sultan, which dates from the period of Portuguese occupation.

The residence of the British political agent and adviser to the sultan is also in Muscat, but most of the town's merchants commute to Matrah, which is more open and therefore cooler.

History.—Muscat was occupied by Afonso de Albuquerque, founder of the Portuguese empire in the East, in 1508. After the loss of Hormuz on the Persian shore in 1622, the Portuguese used Muscat as the headquarters for their fleet, making the town their chief stronghold. The Portuguese were expelled from Oman in 1650, and the town decayed until after the establishment of the present dynasty in 1744. It rose to prominence under Oman's greatest ruler, Sa'id ibn-Sultan (Sa'īd ibn-Sulṭān, r. 1804–1856), whose kingdom stretched over a large part of the Persian Gulf coast and included an East African coastal strip and some islands headed by Zanzibar. On Sa'id's death, however, the kingdom was divided between his two sons, one residing in Zanzibar and the other in Muscat. Sa'id ibn-Taimur (Sa'īd ibn-Taymūr), 13th sultan of the dynasty, succeeded to the throne in 1932. In 1951 a new treaty, confirming the traditional association begun in 1798, was negotiated by the sultan and the British government. Pop. (est. 1960) 5,500.

PHILIP K. HITTI,
Professor Emeritus of Semitic Literature, Princeton University.

MUSCAT AND OMAN, Sultanate of. See OMAN.

MUSCATEL, mŭs-kȧ-tĕl′, a sweet dessert wine made from muscat grapes in Europe and the United States. In order to conserve the sugar content, brandy is added to the must before fermentation is completed, and the alcohol content may therefore be as high as 21 per cent. Muscatel is supposed to have originated on the island of Samos. Among its most celebrated brands are those of Málaga, Sitges, and Tarragona in Spain; the Moscatel Branco of Portugal; the Frontignan and Lunel of France; and the Lachryma Christi, Canelli, and Zibibbo of Italy.

The muscatel of Montefiascone owes its unusual name of Est Est Est to an old story: the German bishop of Regensburg, Sigmund Fugger, sent his valet to taste the wines of a number of inns and mark *est* on the wall wherever he found a good wine, and *est, est* where the wine was very good. When the valet tasted the Montefiascone muscatel, he became so enthusiastic that he wrote over the inn door *est! est!! est!!!*

The climate and soil of California are suited to the growing of muscat grapes, and a good muscatel wine is produced there. Its color ranges from straw to amber.

MUSCATINE, mŭs′kȧ-tēn, city, Iowa, seat of Muscatine County, situated on the Mississippi River and U.S. Highway No. 61, at an altitude of 550 feet, 25 miles west-southwest of Davenport. It is served by the Chicago, Rock Island and Pacific and the Chicago, Milwaukee, St. Paul and Pacific railroads. The city stands on high bluffs commanding an extensive view of the river, which changes at Muscatine from a westward to a southward course. High Bridge here connects Illinois and Iowa. Just below the city is Muscatine Island, formed by a slough now partly filled in. The former island is celebrated for its watermelons, canteloupes, and sweet potatoes. Muscatine's industrial establishments process meats and canned foods, poultry, soybeans, and grains and feeds; and manufacture plastic buttons and novelties, pearl buttons and novelties, button-making machinery, lumber and cellulose products, industrial alcohol, centrifugal pumps, steel pulleys, office furniture, machine shop products, power wheelbarrows, and precision tools.

Among the city's cultural facilities are Muscatine Junior College and the P. M. Musser Public Library. Samuel Clemens (Mark Twain) lived in Muscatine for a short time, and Ellis Parker Briggs, author of *Pigs Is Pigs,* was born there. Under a charter granted originally in 1838 and revised in 1852, government is by mayor and council.

Muscatine was first settled in 1833 as a trading post. In 1836 a town site was surveyed and called Bloomington, the present name being adopted in 1849. The city served as a military post during the Civil War. After the war the lumber industry grew in importance until the 1890's, when it was outpaced by the manufacture of pearl buttons. Pop. 22,405.

MUSCI. See MOSSES.

MUSCICAPIDAE. See FLYCATCHER.

MUSCLE SHOALS, mŭs″l shōlz′, rapids, Alabama, extending for 37 miles in the Tennessee River in Lauderdale County above Florence. The foot of the rapids lies about 259 miles above the mouth of the river. The shoals are now submerged in the reservoirs of Wilson and Wheeler dams of the Tennessee Valley Authority (TVA).

A fall of 134 feet over this stretch of the Tennessee caused rapid currents which were the major, though not the sole, barrier to navigation on the river from the days of the fur traders and pioneers. In 1824, Secretary of War John C. Calhoun recommended improvement of the section as part of a route to the West. Twelve years later, in 1836, the State of Alabama, using funds from a federal land grant of 400,000 acres, completed a canal around a portion of the shoals, but the project was a failure. A more comprehensive canal system built by the federal government between 1871 and 1890 also failed to master the problem, and in 1903 President Theodore Roosevelt vetoed a congressional bill giving the dam site at the foot of the shoals to a private company.

During World War I, under the National Defense Act of 1916, the government built nitrate plants for munitions at Muscle Shoals and began construction of Wilson Dam, which was completed in 1925. Wilson Reservoir, formed by the dam, covered 15.5 miles of the shoals. Meanwhile, Muscle Shoals had become a national political issue, as Congress debated disposal of the nitrate plants and power facilities. Offers by private interests, including a proposal by Henry Ford to buy the plants and lease Wilson Dam and Wheeler Dam, which would be built upstream, were rejected by Congress. Bills for public operation, sponsored by Senator George W. Norris of Nebraska, were passed in 1928 and 1931, but both were vetoed. Finally, in 1933, the Tennessee Valley Authority Act was passed, and the dam and other properties at Muscle Shoals were transferred from the War Department to TVA. The nitrate and other chemical facilities have since been operated as a national fertilizer and munitions development center for the benefit of agriculture and industry, with emphasis on high-analysis plant nutrients.

Wheeler Dam was completed in 1936, covering what remained of the shoals, and other multiple-use dams built on the Tennessee and its tributaries finally provided a 650-mile navigation channel joining the national inland waterway system at Paducah, Ky., on the Ohio River. Because of vastly increased traffic, TVA in 1959 placed in operation a new lock with a 100-foot lift, one of the highest in the world, largely replacing three smaller existing locks at Wilson Dam.

Wilson Dam, 137 feet high and 4,535 feet long, had an installed capacity of 184,000 kilowatts in 8 generating units when it was taken over by TVA. The installation of 10 additional units in vacant stalls brought capacity to 436,000 kilowatts to take advantage of regulated water flow provided by upstream storage dams. In 1959, TVA began extension of the powerhouse to add 3 more units aggregating 162,000 kilowatts, designed to bring total installed capacity to 598,000 kilowatts.

Bibliography.—Muscle Shoals Commission, *Muscle Shoals* (Washington 1931); Blee, Clarence E., "Development of the Tennessee River Waterway," *Centennial Transactions*, American Society of Civil Engineers, pp. 1132–1146 (New York 1953); Hubbard, Preston J., "Story of Muscle Shoals," *Current History*, vol. 34, pp. 265–269 (Philadelphia 1958); King, Judson, *The Conservation Fight, from Theodore Roosevelt to the Tennessee Valley Authority* (Washington 1959).

PAUL L. EVANS,
Director of Information, Tennessee Valley Authority.

MUSCLES, mŭs″lz, the components of the muscular system, in vertebrates, that are primarily concerned with locomotion. There are three basic types of muscles in man: (1) smooth or nonstriated muscle, which deals largely with involuntary action in internal organs; (2) striated or skeletal muscle, which governs willful motion in the extremities, head, and trunk; and (3) cardiac or heart muscle, which is adapted to the continu-

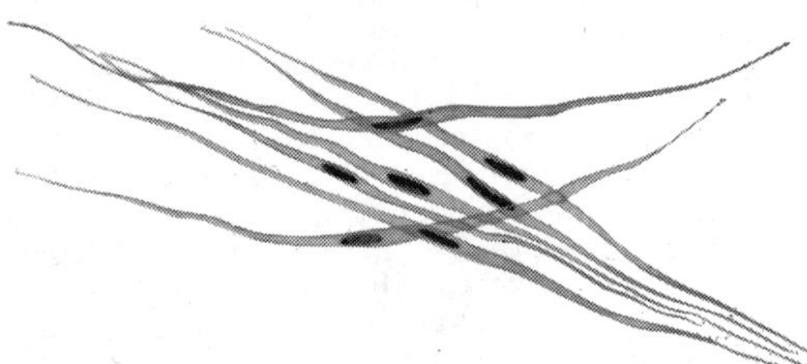

Isolated smooth muscle cells from the wall of the stomach of a cat, greatly magnified.

ous, rhythmic beat of the heart. Smooth muscle is found in the walls of the blood vessels, particularly the arteries, and in the lining walls of the respiratory, intestinal, and genitourinary tracts. Striated muscles are the red muscles which arise and insert at various strategic portions of the bony anatomy to assist in required locomotion. They are connected to bone by tendons or sinews together with fibrous sheets called ligaments. Heart muscle is endowed with its own system of continuous contraction, which is a sustained, involuntary motion. In 1939, C. L. (later Sir Charles) Evans estimated that the average human heart muscle contracts 2,600 million times in a lifetime and delivers 150,000 tons of blood from each of the two heart ventricles.

Physiology.—Enormous study has been devoted to the physiology of muscles. Myosin, the chief muscle protein, has been shown to have the ability to contract on proper stimulation even after being ground up in a tissue preparation. The origination of activity in the neuromuscular system requires a series of steps: excitation, conduction of this impulse, and response of the muscle. This can be demonstrated simply by the reflex

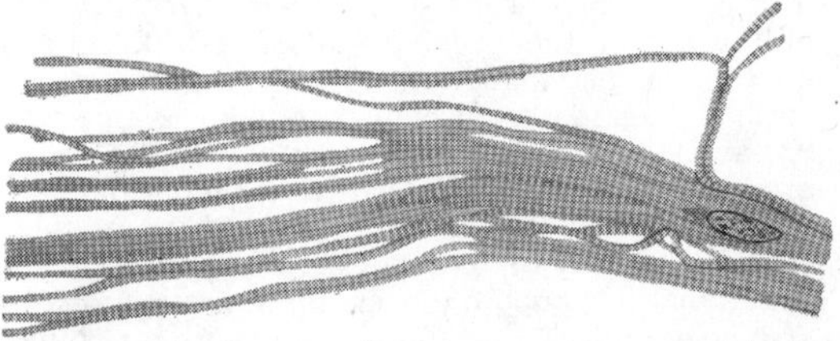

The separation of a muscle fiber of a rabbit into fibrils, greatly magnified.

arc of the spinal cord. If, for example, an area of the skin in the hand is burned, the stimulation is carried by the sensory system to the cord, which in turn sends a message to a motor nerve cell in the anterior horn. This cell promptly activates the proper muscle group in the area to remove the hand from the harmful stimulus. Among other physiological aspects of muscle is muscle metabolism, the ability of muscle to combine glycogen, its chief energy source, with the oxygen of hemoglobin and perform work. At times muscles also perform work anaerobically (without oxygen).

Muscles are endowed with a rich blood and nerve supply to accomplish their mission. The object is to induce a whole group of muscles or a bundle of muscle fibrils to contract synchronously and simultaneously. Striated muscle has been made to contract by electrical stimulation, the degree of contraction varying directly with the strength of the current. This is not true of smooth muscle and cardiac muscle, both of which contract maximally when a certain threshold stimulus is reached. According to the so-called all-or-nothing

Section of human cardiac muscle, greatly magnified.

law, the application of greater stimulation will not produce greater reaction in these groups. Once any muscle group or fiber contracts, there follows a lag period, known as the refractory period of muscle, in which no amount of stimulation will produce activity. A smoothly coordinated muscle performance is produced by the graded discharge of the motor neurons in the spinal cord; otherwise, there would be a tremor or a jerk or complete tetany in muscle action. In England in 1930, J. C. Ercles and Sir Charles Scott Sherrington found, for example, that 430 motor nerve fibers leave the spinal cord to carry directions to the gastrocnemius (calf muscle) of a cat.

Anatomy.—Microscopic study shows the unit of all muscles to be a single elongated or spindle-shaped cell with thin tapering ends and a thickened middle where the nucleus is located. Smooth muscle, the most primitive type, is found in the body in sheets of myofibrils that vary in size from 0.5 millimeter in the pregnant uterus to 15 or 20 microns in the smaller blood vessels. Microscopic strands of smooth muscle occur in the connective tissue of skin. Their action, either singly or in groups, is the reason for hair's "standing on end" and for the appearance of goose flesh from cold. Histologic study of the wall of the intestinal tract shows that the smooth muscle there is functionally arranged to assist in peristalsis, with an outer longitudinal layer and an inner circular layer.

Skeletal muscle presents quite a different picture in teased preparations under the microscope. The units appear as long muscle fibrils with cross striations and vary in length from 10 to 100 microns or more, depending on the animal. Covering the individual units is the sarcolemma, a thin, transparent membrane that also encompasses the flat individual muscle nuclei. Surrounding the myofibrils of muscle is a cytoplasmic structure called sarcoplasm. Striated muscle is gathered together in primary, secondary, and tertiary bundles surrounded by fibrous connective tissue. Microdissection has demonstrated that a collagenous structure, called the perimysium, connects the muscle bundles with the tendon, which then usually attaches itself to the periosteum of bone.

Cardiac muscle deserves special mention because of its unusual properties. The plan seems to be a network of striated muscle in which very few free endings may be discovered. This system is coordinated by a continuous sarcoplasmic network, called Purkinje fibers, which lies just below the endocardium. These fibers in turn communicate via Purkinje cells, which form the bundle of His, and the latter carries the impulse for the cardiac muscle beat. Any interference with this system may lead to heart block. In the atrioventricular conduction system, which is made up of the Purkinje fibers and the bundle of His, nature has devised a system in which all cardiac muscle fibers contract on signal in a rhythmic and automatic manner for the lifetime of the individual.

The gross anatomy of muscle shows that it connects itself to cartilage, ligaments, and skin as well as to bone. When all the muscle fibers lie on one side of a tendon like the plumes of a quill pen, the muscle is termed unipennate; when they converge on both sides of a tendon, it is bipennate. Muscles arranged in a circular manner at body orifices, such as the anus, are known as sphincters. The fixed point of muscle is commonly called the origin, while the structure point where it acts is named the insertion. The biceps muscle, for example, originates in the shoulder bones and inserts on the radius bone of the forearm, where it does its work of flexing the forearm on the upper arm. This is a lever-type muscle. Other muscles terminate in rather long tendons and have a pulleylike action. Among them is the *flexor digitorum profundus,* which flexes the fingers of the hand. Another type of muscle is one which ends in a broad, flat, tendonlike structure called the aponeurosis. Such a muscle is the external oblique muscle *(obliquus abdominis externus),* which arises in the lateral aspect of the abdominal wall and inserts in the mid-line of the aponeurosis, known as the inscription tendon. The diaphragm, the great muscle which separates the abdominal from the chest contents and assists in respiration, has a structure peculiar to itself. Its aponeurosis is a central tendon divided into right, left, and middle leaflets. The muscular parts of the diaphragm are in the periphery.

Certain basic muscle groups in the human body are worthy of mention. In the head the temporal muscle, the masseter, and the internal and external pterygoids make up the muscles of mastication. Together with many smaller muscle groups, the sternocleidomastoid muscle in front and the trapezius muscle (the diamond-shaped muscle between the neck and the shoulders) in back help to rotate the head on the trunk. Important muscles in the chest wall are the major and minor pectoral group, the *serratus anterior* and *serratus posterior* in the flanks, and the intercostals connecting the ribs. The anterior abdominal wall has three muscle layers lying laterally to the double-bellied rectus muscle in front: the external oblique, the transverse *(transversus abdominis),* and the internal oblique *(obliquus abdominis internus).* The principal muscles of the back below the trapezius are the rhomboids *(rhomboideus major* and *rhomboideus minor)* between the shoulder blades and the *latissimus dorsi* in the lateral aspects of the mid-back. The *quadratus lumborum* is the chief muscle of the lower back. The muscles of the extremities are generally divided into opposing muscle groups. The action of the biceps in flexing the forearm on the upper arm is opposed by the triceps, which extends the forearm. In a similar way, the largest muscle of the body, the *quadriceps femoris,* acts as the extensor of the upper leg, working against the *biceps femoris* in the back. In the lower leg the gastrocnemius extends the foot, and the anterior tibial muscle *(tibialis anterior)* flexes it.

Diseases.—A wide range of disorders can affect the muscular system in man. For simplicity, these diseases may be divided into three main groups, according to whether or not the central nervous system, the neuromuscular (neuromyal) junction, or the muscle itself is primarily affected. In poliomyelitis, for example, the nerve cells in the anterior horn of the spinal cord are destroyed by the virus. Muscles are then secondarily affected, and atrophy or shrivel up from disuse. Myasthenia gravis is an example of functional abnormality in the neuromyal junction. In this illness muscles, particularly the eye and facial muscles and those of swallowing and chewing, become rapidly fatigued with use. The primary muscle disorders are still poorly understood. One of them, called acute myositis (primary inflammation of muscle), is said to be a response to bacterial infection.

Other causes of muscle weakness lie outside the neuromuscular system. Psychogenic disorders, the so-called asthenias, can produce generalized muscular debility, and anemic states markedly reduce muscle ability and decrease muscle tone through disease. A search for thyroid disease and adrenal insufficiency should always be considered when muscle weakness is the chief complaint. In addition, muscle biopsy helps to distinguish these disorders from primary muscle disease.

Progressive muscular dystrophy is an inherited disease and appears to be a deficiency in the enzyme system in local muscle groups that produces muscular wasting. The childhood or pseudohypertrophic type generally affects males and is inherited

MUSCLES

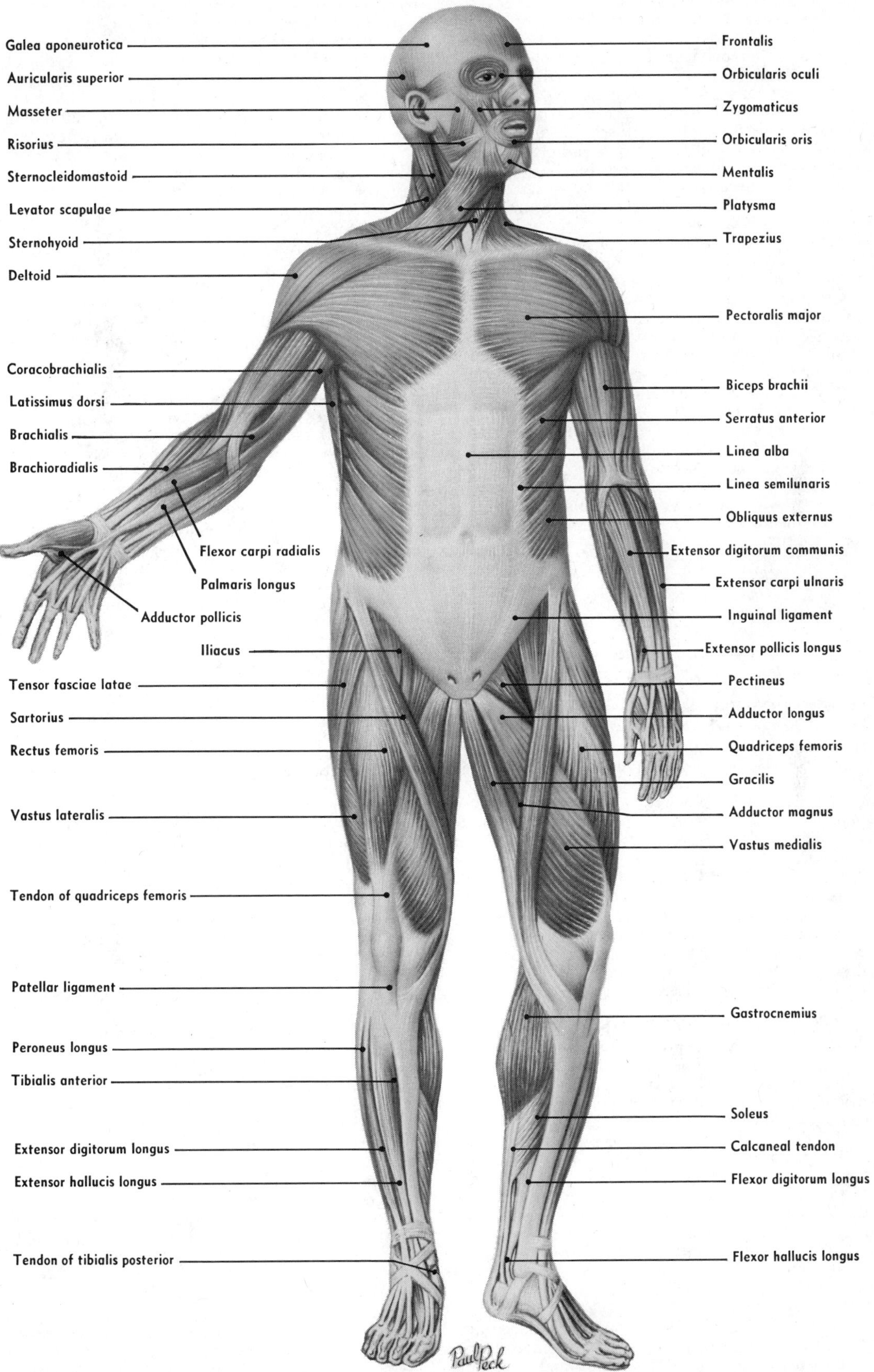
Galea aponeurotica
Auricularis superior
Masseter
Risorius
Sternocleidomastoid
Levator scapulae
Sternohyoid
Deltoid
Coracobrachialis
Latissimus dorsi
Brachialis
Brachioradialis
Flexor carpi radialis
Palmaris longus
Adductor pollicis
Iliacus
Tensor fasciae latae
Sartorius
Rectus femoris
Vastus lateralis
Tendon of quadriceps femoris
Patellar ligament
Peroneus longus
Tibialis anterior
Extensor digitorum longus
Extensor hallucis longus
Tendon of tibialis posterior
Frontalis
Orbicularis oculi
Zygomaticus
Orbicularis oris
Mentalis
Platysma
Trapezius
Pectoralis major
Biceps brachii
Serratus anterior
Linea alba
Linea semilunaris
Obliquus externus
Extensor digitorum communis
Extensor carpi ulnaris
Inguinal ligament
Extensor pollicis longus
Pectineus
Adductor longus
Quadriceps femoris
Gracilis
Adductor magnus
Vastus medialis
Gastrocnemius
Soleus
Calcaneal tendon
Flexor digitorum longus
Flexor hallucis longus
Paul Peck

as a recessive Mendelian trait. The muscles first become enlarged and then begin to atrophy. Standing, sitting, and walking powers are gradually lost, the trunk and pelvic musculature being affected first. A second type of muscular dystrophy is the adult type, inherited as Mendelian dominant in both sexes and causing muscle atrophy of the facial and pectoral girdle muscle groups. In both types inactivity and excessive weight gain are to be discouraged, and a balanced diet is important. No specific therapy is available.

An overactive thyroid gland can bring on severe muscle wasting, known as thyrotoxic myopathy. Prompt thyroid control by drugs or surgery can dramatically restore to normalcy a patient with marked muscular debility. An underactive thyroid also can cause muscle disturbance: in the myxedematous patient, muscle enlargement, cramps, and slowness of motion occur particularly in the lower legs, and the heart muscle can sometimes be affected to a point of early failure. Adequate administration of thyroid hormone is a specific remedy for this disease.

The neuromuscular system is one of enormous powers and flexibility, designed to carry out its many assignments. While many of its secrets remain unsolved, science is constantly at work, particularly with primary muscle disease.

See also ANATOMY, COMPARATIVE—*Musculature;* MUSCULAR DISTROPHY.

Consult Ham, Arthur W., *Histology,* 3d. ed. (Philadelphia 1957); Maksimov, Aleksandr A., and Bloom, William, *Textbook of Histology,* 7th ed. (Philadelphia 1957); Gray, Henry, *Anatomy of the Human Body,* 27th ed., ed. by Charles M. Gross (Philadelphia 1959).

REAUMUR S. DONNALLY, M.D.,
Washington Hospital Center, Washington, D.C.

MUSCOVITE, mŭs′kô-vīt, the name given to common or potash mica, an orthosilicate of potassium and aluminum with the general formula $KAl_3Si_3O_{10}(OH)_2$. It crystallizes in a monoclinic form and has a vitreous to pearly luster. While ordinarily colorless, it may be brown, gray, green, yellow, or, occasionally, light red. Its hardness varies from 2 to 2.5, and its specific gravity from 2.76 to 3.1. The name is derived from the term "Muscovy glass," applied to this type of mica because of its former use for windows in Russia.

Muscovite occurs in gneisses, schists, granites, and syenites in all parts of the world, but in its commercial form is most abundant in pegmatite dikes. India and the United States are the leading producers. See also MICA.

MUSCULAR DYSTROPHY, mŭs′kû-lẽr dĭs′trô-fĭ, a chronic, progressive disease of the voluntary muscles. The exact cause of muscular dystrophy is unknown, but it appears to be a deficiency in an enzyme system. The disease is not contagious or infectious.

Of the more than 200,000 persons estimated to suffer from muscular dystrophy in the United States, approximately two thirds are children. More than half of the known victims are between the ages of 3 and 13. Nevertheless, the disease may occur at any age. The first muscles affected are those of the proximal group—that is, the pelvic girdle and shoulder girdle, as opposed to the peripheral or distal muscles of the hands and feet. Ultimately, however, all of the voluntary muscles are affected. The early symptoms in children are difficulty in walking, running, or climbing stairs. Over a period of years the wasting and resultant weakening progress, eventually confining the child to a wheel chair and finally to bed. Crippling due to contractures is frequent. Although most cases have a great deal in common, four main types of the disease may be distinguished.

(1) The pseudohypertrophic type, the most prevalent form, usually commences in childhood, symptoms becoming apparent between the ages of 3 and 10. Its course is more rapid than that of any other type, and contractures appear early and may be severe. This type is hereditary in most instances and affects mainly males. Heredity is by a sex-linked recessive characteristic.

(2) The juvenile form begins in childhood or adolescence. Its progression is slower than that of the pseudohypertrophic type, and males and females are equally affected. This type is directly hereditary through a dominant genetic factor.

(3) The facioscapulohumeral type commences in early adulthood and affects first the facial muscles, shoulders, and upper arms. The clinical course usually is slow. This type is directly inherited.

(4) There are also mixed types, groups of conditions that begin between the ages of 30 and 50. Progression is variable but usually is quite rapid. These types are not inherited.

Muscular Dystrophy Associations of America, Inc., founded in 1950, sponsors a large and growing program of research dedicated to finding the cause and a cure for this disease. A program of public and professional education is among the associations' first objectives, and there is a rapidly expanding patient service and clinical program conducted in association with local chapters throughout the United States.

See also MUSCLES—*Diseases.*

ADE T. MILHOEAT, M.D.,
Chairman, Medical Advisory Board, Muscular Dystrophy Associations of America, Inc.

MUSES, mūz′ĕz, in classical mythology, goddesses of literature (particularly poetry), music, dance, and, generally, all artistic, intellectual, and scientific pursuits. They sang and danced, usually under the direction of Apollo, who in this function was surnamed Musagetes (Leader of the Muses), at festivities of greater deities and heroes. They were invariably victorious in contests with such singers as the Sirens. Their oldest seats of worship were on the slopes of Olympus, Helicon, and Parnassus, whence their cult spread throughout Hellas and then through the Graeco-Roman world. Littérateurs invoked the Muses' aid to inspire their work and to adorn it with graceful utterance and artistic embellishment.

Although the parentage, number, and names of the Muses vary in ancient accounts, the most-accepted tradition makes them virginal daughters of Zeus and Mnemosyne (Memory), nine in number, and assigns them thus: Calliope (the most distinguished Muse) to epic poetry, Clio to history, Erato to lyric and erotic poetry (sometimes also to hymns and mimicry), Euterpe to music (especially to wind instruments), Melpomene to tragic poetry, Polyhymnia to mimicry (sometimes also to hymns and lyric poetry), Terpsichore to choral poetry and dance, Thalia to comic and idyllic poetry, and Urania to astronomy.

In art the Muses appear as beautiful maidens, adorned with wreaths of palm, vine, laurel, roses, or feathers (symbolical of their victory over the Sirens), and carrying objects representative of their functions.

P. R. COLEMAN-NORTON.

MUSEUM OF MODERN ART, museum, New York, N.Y., founded in 1929 "for the purposes of encouraging and developing the study of modern arts and the application of such arts to manufacture and practical life, and furnishing popular instruction." Since 1939 it has been housed in its own modern building on West 53d Street. In addition to large permanent collections of paintings, sculptures, prints, and drawings, there are frequent special exhibitions of such works as well as of architecture, design, and photography. Circulating exhibitions are sent to towns and cities throughout the United States and Canada, and through its International Council the museum sponsors an international program which brings the art of other countries to the United States and that of the United States to countries abroad. Besides maintaining a library of works on the visual arts, the museum publishes a variety of books on art each year. An art lending service is maintained for members, and there are daily film showings from the museum's large film library. The Museum of Modern Art is supported by membership fees, contributions, admission charges, and book sales. It publishes a quarterly *Bulletin.*

MUSEUMS, mū-zē'ŭmz, institutions serving the three main functions of collection, preservation, and presentation of objects. Such objects may be specimens of nature, related to geology, astronomy, or biology; or they may illustrate the creations of man in history, art, or science. The changing emphasis in museums on one or another of these three functions reflects changes in philosophies and ways of living. Like other institutions, museums bear witness to the interests, ambitions, and attitudes of their communities.

The Origins of Museums in the Old World.—The term "museum" was applied originally in classical antiquity to a place sacred to the Muses (q.v.), with whom glorious events of the past, folk art, music and poetry, gaiety and harmony were associated. In about 280 B.C., a great research institute was founded by Ptolemy I Soter at Alexandria in Egypt, then a center of Greek learning. Known for almost seven centuries as the Museum of Alexandria, it included among its equipment statues of thinkers, votive donations, astronomical and surgical instruments, and such rare products of nature as elephant tusks and hides of uncommon animals.

While the average citizen of the ancient world or of medieval Europe had no public museums at his disposal, he enjoyed displays of paintings and statues in places of worship and in the streets. Rarities could also be viewed in the treasure chambers of temples and churches. Nevertheless, an element of awe separated the sight-seer from the objects in these places, available information was limited, and facts were interwoven with fiction.

Private Collections.—The direct forerunner of the public museum was the private collection whose owner was a famed figure in ancient Rome and Renaissance Italy. Throughout the 17th and 18th centuries, collectors, who were also known as virtuosos or aficionados, represented an international company, spreading as they did over Italy, Spain, France, Great Britain, the Netherlands, Germany, and Austria. In this multitude two types stood out: the royal or titled collector of continental Europe and the scientist collector of England, where royal collecting on a large scale ended with the execution of Charles I in 1649.

A variety of names was used to denote these private collections. Museum and gallery were two of them; among others were the cabinet and the closet, the chamber (of rarities, treasures, or otherwise), the repository, the pinacotheca, the thesaurus, and the guardaropa. Some collections were devoted to art, and some to nature study. At times decorative arts were combined with technology, and often samples of all fields of nature and human endeavor were accumulated. A common characteristic appears to have been the insatiable desire of collectors for an ever-increasing quantity of objects.

The manner of presentation varied and, together with the selection of objects, indicated the owner's prime motivation. Roman soldiers turned collectors took pride in filling their homes with booty from vanquished Greece—statuary, precious metalwork, and other crafts. Centuries later they were succeeded by military conquerors from other lands who craved possession of hoards signifying success and power. A well-stocked treasure chamber impressed visitors with a ruler's wealth and power, and in an emergency finely wrought vessels and figures of gold and silver could be coined into money and pay for the expenses of war. Although such treasure chambers, the saving vaults of a preindustrial era, might contain works of art and rarities, they were arranged in a manner befitting storage and preservation rather than presentation. When Louis XIV's collection of paintings was transferred in 1681 from his country home at Fontainebleau to the Louvre in Paris, the reporter of *Le mercure galant* wrote as follows: "Those [rooms] with the highest ceilings are adorned until the space above the cornices and the shutters are covered on both sides [with pictures]. The most precious ones are enshrined in painted cases, and one may say that one painting covers another. . . ." At times the owner would order some of his possessions to be brought to his living quarters, where their presentation not only satisfied his love of beauty and his interest in rarities, but contributed to an atmosphere of spectacular luxury.

Occasionally, a collection would proclaim the solidarity of its owner with a philosophy of life. Numerous European collections of Greek and Roman archaeology testified to the loyalty felt for many centuries to Greek ideals of beauty and Greek standards of value as well as to the greatness of the Roman Empire. The driving forces behind the formation of other private collections of the 16th, 17th, and 18th centuries were curiosity and the desire for knowledge. The Italian physician Ulisse Aldrovandi (1522–1605), for example, set himself the encyclopedic task of illustrating all nature in a private museum. Sir Hans Sloane (1660–1753), the famous British physician and naturalist, began by collecting plants related to his scientific work, but his inquisitive spirit led him far beyond his professional field. By 1733 his inventory listed 69,352 items—handwritten and printed books, instruments, pictures, vessels of precious materials, coins, medals, and objects illustrating ancient customs. In these collections of learned men, preservation rather than presentation influenced the arrangement of objects, and the quantity of items often prevented all manner of order. The owner, who knew each possession, could disregard the over-all picture, dull or confusing; the public was not generally admitted.

Public Museums.—In 1683 the Ashmolean Museum was opened as part of the School of

Desert Museum Photo by Ray Manley

Above: Animal lairs are exposed in an exhibit of the Arizona-Sonora Desert Museum near Tucson.

Below: Model of the life-sized bison group at The American Museum of Natural History in New York.

The American Museum of Natural History

I. Arons from Soviet Information Bureau

Above: Russian schoolgirls in Leningrad's State Hermitage Museum inspect a collection of 17th and 18th century Italian art.

MUSEUMS

Left: The Ashmolean Museum of Oxford University, in an engraving made soon after it was opened to the English public in 1683.

Illustration Research Service

French Embassy Press & Information Service

Above: Marionettes from Java, in the colorful garb of that island, are displayed at the Musée de l'Homme in Paris.

Royal Ontario Museum, Toronto

Above: The Royal Ontario Museum's geology gallery features a large model of the earth and its core.

Right: View of the Reading Room of the British Museum in London, frequented by students from many countries.

British Crown Copywright

Below: Visitors watch baby chicks hatching in a scientific incubator at the Chicago Museum of Science and Industry.

Chicago Museum of Science and Industry

Natural History of Oxford University and made accessible to the public, although no interpretation of its contents to the layman was attempted. The 18th century, a period of improving educational facilities for an increasing number of people, saw the transformation of numerous private collections into public museums. The British Museum was opened in London in 1759, after the purchase by the British government of Sir Hans Sloane's extensive collections, which under the terms of his will were now to serve for the "benefit of mankind." Nevertheless, persons desiring to visit the museum had to wait weeks or months for admission, which was permitted only after their credentials had been scrutinized. They were then allowed to join a conducted tour through awe-inspiring halls crowded with a confusing variety of exhibits. The traditions of the old private collections thus lingered on in the early public museums.

During the French Revolution, in 1793, the republican government declared the private collections of the kings in the Louvre in Paris to be a public museum. In 1809 a decree of Joseph Bonaparte, then king of Spain, proclaimed that the royal art collection would serve as a public museum in the Prado in Madrid, and in 1819 the Museo del Prado was duly opened by Ferdinand VII. Yet a catalogue published in 1826 still reminded the public of its debt of gratitude to the royal owner of the treasures. In the same period only those who owned a suit of the type required for court functions in Russia were admitted to the museum in the Hermitage of St. Petersburg. The French observer Louis Viardot wrote that the museum in the Belvedere Palace in Vienna was free of the disorder then characteristic of other museums. The opening in Berlin in 1830 of the Altes Museum, in a building designed for the purpose, was an important progressive step.

The Origins of Museums in the New World.—In 1773, three years before the Declaration of Independence, the first public museum in America was founded in Charleston, S.C., where it still exists as the Charleston Museum. The *South Carolina Gazette* invited the cooperation of the public "to procure . . . the natural productions of the country, either animal, vegetable, or mineral . . . together with explanations of the use of the articles in agriculture, commerce or medicine." In 1785, Philadelphia became the home of a museum which at different times was known as the American Museum, Peale's American Museum, and the Philadelphia Museum. It was to be a world in miniature, with samples of every aspect of nature and a school of "Science, Reason and Morality" that would satisfy the popular demand for polite and moral entertainment. The Tammany Society's museum in New York, established in 1790, declared welcome "any object, from whatever country it may come." The National Cabinet of Curiosities, under the authority of the Patent Office, was based on a congressional law of 1790. In addition to models, it included "specimens of compositions . . . fabrics and other manufactures and works of art." In 1799 the East India Marine Museum (now the Peabody Museum) was established in Salem, Mass., as a repository for the curiosities gathered by local ship captains in different parts of the world. Oriental sculpture and bricks with cuneiform inscriptions were brought home by American missionaries, and collections of mechanical devices were stimulated by expositions of mechanics' associations.

To John Trumbull (1756–1843), army officer and artist, goes the credit for arranging the first exhibition of European masterpieces in the United States, held in the Park Theatre in New York in 1804. Later, the New York City Hall housed a collection of casts of old sculptures and of portraits of national leaders. Geological and biological surveys of the 1830's led to the establishment of state museums—in New York in 1843, in Vermont in 1845, and in Alabama in 1848.

Financial problems beset many of the early museums and caused their closure. In its efforts to survive, Peale's Philadelphia Museum became a place of cheap entertainment, and Scudder's American Museum from 1842, under the leadership of the showman Phineas T. Barnum, included ventriloquists and educated dogs among its attractions. The same period, however, saw the beginnings of the organization that grew to be the largest compound of museums in the United States, the Smithsonian Institution. The English chemist James Smithson (1765–1829) bequeathed his property to the young republic for "the increase and diffusion of knowledge among men." Specimens brought back from the explorations of the American Southwest and the South Seas were among its early accessions. A visitor to Washington in the 1840's, Henry T. Tuckerman, wrote: "In the National Institution [which at the time took care of the collections], like nearly all of our scientific and literary establishments, as yet in embryo, sea quadrupeds from the arctic zone, birds of rare plumage, the coat in which Jackson fought at New Orleans, the rifle of an Indian chief, plants, fossils, shells and corals, mummies, trophies, busts and relics, typify inadequately natural and bold adventure." In 1841 bills were presented in the Senate for the organization of the Smithsonian Institution, which in 1846 became the governing body in charge of the national collections.

Museums of the 20th Century.—Between 1900 and 1920, 179 museums were founded in Germany, as compared with 15 new museums in the corresponding period of the 19th century, and there was a similar growth in other countries. As of 1953, the total capital investment in museums in the United States was estimated at $7 billion, and by 1959 the country was estimated to have one museum for every 43,750 persons. The rising interest in museums in the 20th century has led to the foundation of the International Museums Office in 1926 and of the International Council of Museums (ICOM) in 1946. In 1956 the ICOM sponsored an International Campaign for Museums, and 61 nations participated in an International Museum Week.

Among the significant trends of the 20th century is a tendency toward replacing the multipurpose institution that embraces various arts and sciences by more specialized museums—of natural history, science, history, archaeology, ethnology, or art. In 1957, for example, the National Museum of Canada in Ottawa was divided into a Human History Branch and a Natural History Branch. Often the field has been narrowed to health or agriculture or modern art, or to the natural history or history of a particular place. Various fields of science are illustrated in some of the large science museums, such as the Museum of Science and Industry in Chicago, the Museum of Science in Boston, the Science Museum in London, the Deutsches Museum in Munich, and the Palais de la Découverte in Paris. Specific problems of particular urgency are the fields of such smaller science museums as the American Museum of Atomic Energy in Oak Ridge, Tenn., and the Atomarium in the Tekniska Museet in Stockholm. Problems of soil and water conservation are to be dramatized in the Ghost Ranch Museum near Espanola, N.Mex. Museums illustrating the class struggle can be found in the USSR, where all types of museums serve to diffuse the ruling philosophy.

While university museums continue to stress the functions of collection and preservation, museums for the general public lay increasing emphasis on presentation. The realization of the function of the public museum as an interpreter of knowledge is primarily a contribution of the United States, where it expresses the American principle of opportunity of learning for everyone. It is related to the need of most American museums to ensure direct financial support by the public, in contrast to European institutions, which are supported mainly by tax funds. Accordingly, efforts are made to provide attractive museum buildings, well lit and ventilated, equipped with lounges and refreshment rooms. Exhibits for the layman offer summaries rather than detailed knowledge. A good exhibit is a good story. A series of arrowheads or nose ornaments may be of interest to the anthropologist with his background of knowledge, but to the layman the same exhibit seems a monotonous display or a curio providing brief amusement. The layman appreciates an introduction to the people who made or used the unfamiliar objects, to their family life and ways of making a living. In an anthropological exhibit, Man in Our Changing World, shown in the Los Angeles County Museum, stress was laid on similarities rather than differences between races. Cases filled with labeled jars containing dissected human organs are study material for the biologist, but the layman interested in health appreciates the interpretation of the human body and its functions offered to him by a large-size model of transparent plastic, as shown, for example, in the Cleveland Health Museum. In the field of geology, the Royal Ontario Museum in Toronto, Ontario, Canada, excites the layman's imagination by a large model of the planet earth and an insight into its hidden layers, presented as an introduction to a display of individual samples of rocks and minerals.

Dioramas make whole environments come alive in museums of natural history and of history. Period rooms and outdoor reconstructions of entire villages and streets bring the past close to the spectator. Figures in costumes of the period or actual men and women in costume and playing the parts of bygone farmers, craftsmen, and storekeepers enrich the visitor's experience. Outdoor museums of this kind originated in 1891 with Skansen, a department of the Nordiska Museet in Stockholm, and led to the reconstruction of Colonial Williamsburg in Virginia, Old Sturbridge Village in Massachusetts, Greenfield Village in Michigan, and Cooperstown in New York. The American Museum of Natural History in New York City uses the recorded sounds of rain and bird voices to conjure up the atmosphere of a tropical rain forest and its inhabitants. The United States National Park Service specializes in small, interpretative site museums which analyze the great outdoors around them and bring its essential features into focus.

Facilities for visitor participation are offered by many museums. Push buttons set machinery in motion, make rocks fluoresce under changing rays of light, or provide answers to questions. There are lectures and demonstrations with opportunity for discussion, workshops, and outdoor nature clubs. Special events are provided for designers, businessmen, expectant parents, old people, and blind persons. Exhibit space is offered for youth science fairs, and for exhibits of 4-H Clubs and of organizations concerned with the prevention and cure of diseases. Meeting rooms are at the disposal of congenial professional groups. The Buffalo Museum of Science and the Boston Museum of Science are known especially for their service in answering miscellaneous individual inquiries by the public. Children receive special attention in separate children's museums or in the junior departments of adult museums. Demonstrations and workshops satisfy the child's desire to touch and to handle things, to stage experiments, and to act out scenes.

Museum extension services consist of traveling exhibitions on the national and international level, presented in special trailers or packed in cases. Temporary exhibits are shown in libraries, and in store and bank windows. Loans of specimens are made to a variety of individuals and organizations, from research scientists to motion picture producers. Television takes museum resources even farther afield.

An account of museums of art and a listing of major public collections in various countries are found in the article ART GALLERIES; see also separate articles on leading museums; and sections on cultural activities in articles on cities, states, provinces, and countries.

Bibliography.—Adam, Thomas R., *The Museum and Popular Culture* (New York 1939); Coleman, Laurence V., *The Museum in America* (Washington 1939); Moore, Eleanor M., *Youth in Museums* (Philadelphia 1941); Low, Theodore L., *The Museum as a Social Instrument* (New York 1942); Wittlin, Alma S., *The Museum: Its History and Its Tasks in Education* (London 1949); American Association of Museums, *Museums Directory of the United States and Canada*, 2d ed. (Washington 1965); UNESCO, *Organization of Museums* (Paris 1967).

ALMA S. WITTLIN.

MUSHROOM, mŭsh′rōōm, the popular name given to any of the larger fleshy fungi, mostly of the class Basidiomycetes. The greatest proportion of mushrooms, comprising several hundred species, consists of gill fungi (Agaricaceae). Some authors have attempted to distinguish between mushrooms and toadstools on the basis, respectively, of their edible or poisonous qualities, but quite often the two names are used interchangeably. Like other fungi, mushrooms do not contain chlorophyll and cannot manufacture their own food. Most of them live on decaying organic matter in such forms as dead wood, humus, and manure, but a few are capable of living, at least in part, as parasites on trees. In nutritive value, mushrooms compare favorably with many fresh vegetables. They are notably rich in vitamin B but deficient in vitamins A, D, and E.

The best-known species in North America is the common edible mushroom, *Agaricus campestris*. It has a whitish cap and a stout stalk with a ring near the top. When young, the gills are pink, but later, as the spores mature, they turn brown. The wild, four-spored form is common in open grassy places. The commercial, two-spored form, which is sold fresh or canned, though very similar in appearance, is considered by some authorities to be a separate species. It is grown on a large scale in the United States, the leading state in its production being Pennsylvania. At one time it was common to grow mushrooms in caves, abandoned mines, and similar places where the proper temperature and humidity could be maintained, but with the development of the mushroom industry most mushrooms came to be grown in especially constructed houses where conditions favorable for growth might be more carefully controlled. Well-composted horse manure is still the preferred substratum for mushroom growing, but artificial manures, composed of straw and other plant residues to which organic or inorganic fertilizers have been added, are used to some extent. The amateur who wishes to grow mushrooms in his cellar may obtain further information from the United States Department of Agriculture's bulletins on mushroom growing.

In Europe several species of mushrooms are gathered in woods and fields and sold fresh or dried in the market. The same kinds usually occur commonly in the United States, and with many other edible mushrooms they would make delicious additions to the fare of anyone who would take the trouble to learn them. The great majority of mushrooms are edible, and very few cause serious poisoning. The best procedure for an amateur collector would be to learn thoroughly several common edible species and collect only those for the table. He should also learn the few very poisonous species in order to avoid them. A good field guide to the mushrooms (see *Bibliography*) would be of great assistance. There is no substitute for learning to recognize the desirable species, since there are no simple tests that may be relied upon to distinguish edible and poisonous mushrooms.

The morels, of which *Morchella esculenta* is the best-known species, are highly prized for their flavor. They have whitish stalks and conical or cylindrical, brownish to olive gray caps that are pitted or honeycombed. These easily recognized fungi should be sought in early spring in orchards and deciduous woods. The edible bolete *(Boletus edulis),* common in Europe and North America, has a reticulated stalk and a brownish cap with a separable layer of pores beneath. Other species of *Boletus* also are edible, but several have poisonous properties.

The chanterelle *(Cantherellus cibarius),* which is considered a delicacy in France, is frequent in woods and open places in much of the United States. The fruiting bodies are funnel shaped and yellow, with forked, ridgelike gills extending down the stalk. The oyster mushroom *(Pleurotus ostreatus),* so called because of its flavor, is commonly found in overlapping clusters on logs and dead or dying hardwood trees. The fruiting bodies have short, laterally attached stalks and caps that are white to ashy gray, with white gills underneath. One of the best flavored of all mushrooms, the honey agaric *(Armillaria mellea),* occurs in clusters on the ground or on old stumps and other decaying wood. Its color is light tan, honey yellow, or chestnut brown. The gills usually extend down the stalk, and the latter is provided with a ring.

The fairy-ring mushroom *(Marasmius oreades),* though rather small, is often found in abundance and is popular because of its nutty flavor and drying qualities. It is a buff-colored species that occurs chiefly in open grassy places, often in circles called fairy rings. There was once a superstition that these were rings around which fairies danced. Actually, they are caused by the outward growth of the mycelium or vegetative part of the fungus each year in an ever-broadening circle, the fungus fruiting annually in each new area of mycelial growth. Several other gill fungi, including *Agaricus campestris,* may also form fairy rings.

Species of the genus *Coprinus* are known as inky cap mushrooms because the cap and gills liquefy with age. The black color of the inky fluid is caused by the presence of numerous dark spores. The fruiting bodies, which have slender stalks and bell-shaped or cylindrical caps, commonly occur in clusters on stumps or other dead wood and on manure or manured ground. Though desirable for eating, they must be cooked soon after picking because of their deliquescent tendencies.

One of the most delicious of all mushrooms is the royal agaric or Caesar's amanita *(Amanita caesaria),* but because it occurs in a genus that contains some of the most poisonous mushrooms known, no one should collect it for eating without being thoroughly familiar with it. It is a strikingly beautiful and showy species and is easy to recognize. It has a large, smooth, reddish orange cap, which becomes lighter colored toward the striate margin, and a slender yellow stalk with a yellow ring above and a conspicuous white cup at the base. The gills are light yellow. This species was highly prized by the ancient Romans and was one of the choicest dishes served to the emperors.

None of the puffballs are known to be poisonous, although several are not eaten because of their texture. They are typically somewhat globular in shape and are found abundantly in woods and open places. Several species of *Lycoperdon* and *Calvatia* are commonly eaten. The largest of these is the giant puffball *(Calvatia gigantea),* which sometimes reaches a diameter of over four feet.

There are very few deadly poisonous mushrooms, although a number of species can cause illness. The deadliest is the destroying angel *(Amanita verna),* a gill fungus that is so easily recognized that there is little excuse for confusing it with edible mushrooms. Nevertheless, it has been estimated that 90 per cent of all deaths due to mushroom poisoning are caused by this species. The fruiting body is white throughout, with a distinct cup at the base and a well-developed ring around the stalk just beneath the cap. It has been reported that a single forkful may cause death. The first symptoms of poisoning usually do not occur before 10 to 15 hours after eating. The fly agaric of fly amanita *(Amanita muscaria)* also is poisonous, but not so deadly as the destroying angel. It has a bright red or orange cap with white scales on top and a white stalk with a bulbous base and a white ring above. The gills are white.

If mushroom poisoning is suspected, one should take an emetic and call a physician at once. A much better course is to avoid poisoning by picking and eating only well-recognized, edible species. See also FUNGI—*Class Basidiomycetes (The Club Fungi).*

Bibliography.—Güssow, Hans T., and Odell, Walter S., *Mushrooms and Toadstools* (Ottawa 1927); Krieger, Louis C. C., *A Popular Guide to the Higher Fungi (Mushrooms) of New York State* (Albany 1935); Thomas, William S., *Field Book of Common Mushrooms,* 2d enl. ed. (New York 1936); Rettew, Granville R., and Thompson, Forrest G., *Manual of Mushroom Culture,* 4th ed. (Toughkenamon, Pa., 1948); Ramsbottom, John, *Mushrooms and Toadstools* (London 1953); Smith, Alexander H., *The Mushroom Hunter's Field Guide* (Ann Arbor, Mich., 1958).

LINDSAY S. OLIVE, *Columbia University*

Top left: Lycoperdon perlatum, one of the edible species of small puffballs with white interiors.

Top center: The savory *Calvatia gigantea,* or giant puffball, may grow to a breadth of several feet.

Top right: Pleurotus ostreatus, the edible oyster mushroom, found on living and dead tree trunks.

MUSHROOMS

(Bottom left) U.S.D.A. Photograph; (all others) Roche

Right: Among the most palatable of mushrooms is the clustering honey agaric, *Armillaria mellea.*

Lower left: The poisonous *Lepiota morgani,* or green gill mushroom, in various stages of growth.

Lower right: The edible bolete, *Boletus edulis,* a common species both in America and in Europe.

MUSIAL, mū'zē-əl, **Stanley Frank,** American baseball player: b. Donora, Pa., Nov. 21, 1920. He played the outfield and first base for the St. Louis Cardinals throughout a 22-year major-league career. He set numerous batting records and, by being voted the National League's most valuable player in 1943, 1946, and 1948, he was assured of a place in the Baseball Hall of Fame. He was the first in his league to receive a yearly salary of $100,000.

Discouraged by an ailing shoulder in 1940 after two years in baseball, Musial shifted from pitcher to outfielder with such success that he was called up by the Cardinals late in 1941. A left-handed batter with a stance by which he peered at the pitcher over his right shoulder, Musial led the league in batting seven times between 1943 and 1957.

When he retired in 1963, Musial held major league slugging records for most long hits (1,377), most total bases (6,134), and most home runs hit in a doubleheader (5). Among his National League marks were most consecutive games played (895, from 1952 to 1957), most base hits (3,630), most two-base hits (725), most years batting in more than 100 runs (10), and most years leading outfielders in fielding (3). His lifetime batting average was .331 and he hit 475 home runs. Musial served as St. Louis' general manager in 1967 when the Cardinals won the World Series.

BILL BRADDOCK, *New York "Times"*

MUSIC, mū'zĭk. The ultimate origins of the art of organizing sounds are too remote in time to be determined accurately. Music in its modern Western sense has become both a fine art and a scholarly discipline. Its prime constructive elements are melody, rhythm, and harmony (qq.v.). The music of primitive peoples and of cultures (African, Amerindian, Asian, etc.) largely uninfluenced by European developments may lack harmony, and even melody as we understand it, but it is impossible to conceive of music devoid of rhythm. In Europe, music as the fine art we now recognize emerged into existence during the Middle Ages. The present article deals primarily with the history of this European and European-influenced music.

Primitive Music.—Music resulted from the merging and development of human expressive utterances. Vocal sound being one spontaneous way of displaying emotion and need, historians often assume, though without proof, that primordial music consisted of some form of song. Movements of the body being another expressive response to emotional impulses, a rhythmic form of sound organized to accompany dance or mime likewise has been cited as probably the first recognizable music. The aboriginal Veddas of Ceylon, some Patagonians, and other primitive peoples recite poems on two tones forming an interval of a second or a minor third, using these protomusical patterns as little more than carriers for words, near-melodies lacking much significance in themselves. Some Amerindians burst into cascades of shouts and wails which settle slowly into musical intervals. Still other primitives organize their calls on sounds at intervals of a fifth or a fourth, their cries in shrieking trills. Even on the most remote level available to historians of music, some structures typical of modern music are found in early stages of their evolution. The pygmies and related tribes, for example, make use of a strict polyphonic form, the canon: a leading singer and chorus begin a melody; other leading singers and choristers enter with the same melody before those who began it earlier have completed it—thus producing complex simultaneous groups of tones and forming what we now consider to be chords.

Most of the earliest known instruments—clappers, rattles, stamping tubes, and, somewhat later, drums and xylophones—are really extensions or projections of the movements of human limbs; they are rhythmic motion addressed to the ear. The relative importance of rhythm and melody differ geographically. Rhythm plays an inferior role among some peoples, whereas it dominates among others, leaving melody relatively undeveloped. One of the clearest examples of such rhythmic dominance is the polyrhythmic beating of Central African drums. These complex patterns, syncopations, and offbeats, which cannot be notated exactly, tax Western ears severely.

Music is more closely connected with the daily living of primitive peoples than with that of those in more highly evolved cultures. It occupies an important place in tribal rites concerned with birth, puberty, marriage, fertility, health, death, resurrection, rain, planting, hunting, and combat. Members of tribes commonly share in these musical activities, singing, clapping, and playing instruments. Some individuals naturally show themselves to be more gifted and skilful than others, and therefore are employed as soloists, but no real specialization as performers yet exists. Recognition of the collective, purposeful character of tribal music should not be understood to indicate that the music is merely useful or devoid of aesthetic purpose or standards. No clear line can be drawn between music at the service of ritual and music as a self-conscious art of expression and pleasure. Despite the practical intentions of tribal music, the gusto with which the singers sing and the drummers drum is remote from artless toil. The remarkable musical evolution within the confines of some tribal styles and the care bestowed upon the creation of new musical inventions parallel the individual contributions characteristic of any fine art. The most important musical element largely absent from primitive music is harmony as it has evolved in Western music since the Renaissance.

Oriental Music.—The music of the highly evolved civilizations of Asia and North Africa differs from primitive music chiefly in its well-ordered theoretical basis and in its employment of highly trained professional performers. The professional appears either as a bard (often blind) chanting the deeds of gods and kings or as a member of a group of performers attached to a court or place of worship. The profession frequently is handed down to descendants in Bachlike musical dynasties; in many areas, specialized schools provide thorough systematic musical education and training.

The Bible illustrates the musical difference between the primitive and the more civilized stages. In the books of Moses and Judges, men and women of the people sing or play upon lyres and drums at celebrations; no professionals are mentioned. Thus, when Saul requires music as an anodyne, he sends for a shepherd—David—to play for him upon the lyre. The reigns of David himself and Solomon mark the change. Levites are now selected to dedicate themselves to performing music in the Temple, and when the House of the Lord is complete, its servants include 288 music students in 24 grades "under the hands of their fathers." Such planned musical education presupposes a scientific basis, a grammar of musical elements, a theory of rhythm, and a system of modes, scales, and intervals. Under such conditions, music evolves into a methodical, conscious art and often produces a form of notation.

The music of the ancient Orient has not survived, but the cantillation of Orthodox Eastern synagogues, Eastern Christian churches, and Hindu and other Far Eastern places of worship probably preserves some of its forms. Much of the folk singing in Asia and North Africa has changed little during two or three millennia. Otherwise we must rely upon archaeology for information on the lost ancient music—studying reliefs and paintings of musical scenes, instruments dug out of tombs, supplementing these data with often controversial allusions found in ancient texts. Our sources of information are slightly richer in India, China, and Japan—where old nations and religions have survived—than in the western Orient, where Christianity and Islam put an end to the ancient civilizations. No comparable break occurred in the very Far East, and though millennia of change must be taken into consideration, mutation of musical practices has been much less drastic there.

Oriental music is richest and most sophisticated in India and Pakistan. The music of the subcontinent shows an unmatched wealth of scales, the octave being crossed in five, six, or seven finely graded steps. It also glories in an incomparable abundance of delicate grace notes and, above all, in subtly refined rhythmic patterns. These last lack the strong stresses of much Western music, and therefore seldom assume the sometimes monotonous repetitiveness of our predominating duple and triple meters. Indian melody never is entirely free; invention moves within the limitations of set patterns *(ragas)* in which a mood is related to a specific scale; it also accepts set metrical patterns *(talas)* that recur throughout a piece much as metrical feet recur in poetry.

In India, as in the rest of the Orient, music is strongly influenced by extramusical concepts. Not only scales and melodic patterns, but even single tones, stand for the cardinal points of direction, the planets, substances, humors, diseases, divisions of the calendar. Even now, when the cosmologies on which these relationships depend have been weakened, a serious Indian musician scarcely would play a morning *raga* at night. Such extramusical connotations are very noticeable in the religious music of China. The *Hymn to Confucius,* for example, must be transposed by one semitone each month because the semitones are closely related to the months. In general, East Asian music, which became strongly Mongolized, is less varied and subtle than that of India. Predominantly, it employs only two pentatonic scales—one containing two undivided major thirds and one including two major thirds alongside two semitones. Rhythm, remote from the sophisticated delicacy of Indian patterns, is almost uniformly a 2/4 beat. And whereas Indian practice tends mostly to what we should call chamber music, the Far East long ago developed large musical ensembles. Emperors of the T'ang dynasty (618–906 A.D.) supported many court orchestras, one of them consisting of more than 500 instruments, as well as an outdoor band of 1,346 men. Orchestral practices continue to be the characteristic form of Indonesian music, particularly in Bali and Java. There a *gamelan,* most often composed of well-tuned gongs, chimes, and bronze slabs, often plays a single melodic pattern slowly on the instruments of lowest pitch, faster on the middle-range instruments, and very fast on the highest ones; deep gongs mark the ends of melodic periods.

The Islamic world stretching from Morocco to Iran has a musical language closer to that of India than to the idioms of the Far East. It delights in small chamber groups playing in free, individually modified unison. It shows a wide variety of scales and rhythms, and follows the principle of compulsory melodic patterns. The contributions of individual composers are limited if compared with Western usage. The Arabic-speaking countries show a predilection for a tuning in which the two semitones within a scale each borrow a quarter-tone from their nearest lower neighbor. The result is, for example, that the interval defined by the notes DEF does not contain (as it does in Western music) a whole tone (DE) and a semitone (EF), but two equal three-quarter tones, an interval that most Westerners find it hard, if not impossible, to accept.

A notable recent development in the Orient, particularly in Japan and India, has been the rapidly increasing acceptance of performances of Western music—instrumental, vocal, and jazz. As a result, many highly trained Orientals have become expert performers and composers of music in several Western styles.

Greek Music.—Despite the unmistakable stylistic connections between the music of the Arabic-speaking peoples and that of India, Arabic theoretical writing has depended greatly upon the texts of ancient Greece. Greek musicians, scientists, and philosophers left behind them an inclusive grammar of music and extensive inquiries into the fundamentals of acoustics, aesthetics, and musical history and evolution. By these activities, as through their musical practices, the Greeks built a bridge connecting East and West, Rome, and the Middle Ages.

The Greeks acknowledged the Oriental origins of their music, even noting that none of their instruments bore a Hellenic name. Nevertheless, the indigenous culture of Crete, which they conquered about 1000 B.C., gave them one characteristic element of their musical art: choral song in praise of the gods. Hymns of this sort—to Helios, Nemesis, the Muse—survive among the musical relics notated on papyrus or engraved on stone in a letter script that can now be deciphered with considerable exactness. Rhythm usually was not strongly marked because the melodies paralleled the versification of the sung text so closely that (except at the ends of lines) a long syllable was roughly equivalent to our quarter-note, a short syllable to our eighth-note. Thus music followed text in being dactylic, trochaic, or anapaestic. Even in the rare examples showing five beats to one short syllable and two long syllables, melody follows along obediently, in the process achieving a peculiar, airy charm. In a surviving drinking song, the letter symbols above the text syllables are supplemented by dashes meant to indicate the lengths of the notes, the melodic rhythm here being somewhat independent of the text.

Like the Orientals, the Greeks used an impressive number of modes or scales. Any highly developed music without harmony seeks another sort of variety in widely varying arrangements of melodic scale steps. The oldest of the Greek modes, called enharmonic, consisted of undivided major thirds and semitones. Resembling the principal Japanese scale, this mode probably was related to it through a common ancestral culture located somewhere in Central Asia. Another mode, called chromatic, contained minor thirds and whole tones. Most later scales were, like ours, diatonic, but so multiform that we hear of 8 sizes of thirds, 7 whole tones, 13 different semitones, and 9 microtones narrower than semitones. Eventually this confusing diversity was reduced by the dropping of a majority of the older modes and by squeezing the remaining modes into a simplified "perfect system."

The melodies modeled upon these modes were interrelated with extramusical concepts in the Oriental manner. The Greeks, however, favored relationships to human qualities and moods. The ethos of a melody was its way of influencing a man's character. For this reason, music became extremely important in Greek education. Like Confucius a century earlier, Plato suggested that the ideal state should be erected on the basis of music.

Historians, misinterpreting their sources, long misrepresented Greek music as having been an entirely homophonic art in which instruments merely doubled sung melodies. We now know that this picture is false. Greek music did without true polyphony or harmony as we understand them, but Greek writers repeatedly insisted upon the beauty of simultaneous consonances and spoke of the independence of instrumental parts. The modern re-evaluation of the structural web of Greek music is important for the new light it has been shedding upon the origins of Western medieval polyphony.

Rome and the Middle Ages.—Rome, which borrowed Greek music and its theories, did little to change them, but passed them on, in both practice and commentaries, to the Middle Ages. Rome as the center of Christianity also became the center of its musical liturgy. *De Institutione Musica* of Anicius Manlius Torquatus Severinus Boethius (or Boetius, c. 480–524 A.D.), a Roman mathema tician-philosopher, was for nearly 1,000 years recognized by the Western world as the supreme authority on music. It was written long after St. Ambrose (340?–397 A.D.) had regulated Christian liturgical music and probably after the first papal *schola cantorum* had been opened.

The widespread picture of early medieval music as almost exclusively sacred is incomplete and distorted. Because almost the only people who could write were monks, who ignored the popular music outside church and abbey, only sacred music was written down and discussed. But secular music existed, and the impression that it was a later development is mistaken

The music of the Roman Church was purely vocal at first, being sung by a priest, a unison choir, and soloists: the church fathers had been opposed to the use of instruments in sacred music. This earliest music mainly served the functions of the Mass and of the daily offices from matins to vespers and complin. Its melodic idiom originally had been that of the Jewish Temple, but it must have accepted a vocabulary of melodies from the Mediterranean countries in which Christianity had taken root. St. Ambrose, bishop of Milan in the 4th century, made an effort to codify these often heterogeneous elements into a unified liturgy. Two centuries later, however, Pope Gregory I (540?–604 A.D.) imposed upon the church the somewhat different liturgical usage that became known as Gregorian chant. Except in Milan (where Ambrosian chant still is heard) and a few other locations, Gregorian chant became the exclusive form of Roman Church music. Its melodies are modal. The ecclesiastical modes that they follow differ from each other in the positions of the semitones within the octave; the principal modes can be approximated by playing on a piano the white notes between one A and the A next above it, a B and the B next above it, and so on. The melodies have not changed since the 6th century except that their original rhythms, not then written out, probably were lost as early as the 11th century, being replaced by an almost even length (of an eighth-note) for all notes.

We know extremely little about the secular music of the early Middle Ages. At the end of the 11th century, however, a courtly style of poetry began to emerge and be set to music. The courtly poets must have availed themselves of an already existing musical idiom—that of folk music and of professional minstrelsy. The many hundreds of surviving melodies show an astonishing prevalence of the modern major mode, thus differing sharply from Roman liturgical practice. This important courtly poetry-music endured from about 1100 A.D. to about 1450. It began with the *troubadours* in the south of France, resumed with the *trouvères* of northern France, and ended with the *minnesinger* of the German states (1200–1450). Not all of these poet-composers were nobles, but their attitudes were predominantly aristocratic, their texts dealing mostly with combat and death in battle, fervent religious devotion, and flowery romantic love. Their music—of which many hundreds of melodies were written out in beautiful illuminated collections—was simple and popular, but never vulgar. How much of this music was created by the poets themselves and how much by minstrels in their employ is an unanswered question.

While knightly poet-composers were riding from castle to castle to sing *rondeaux, lais, ballades,* and *virelais,* the Roman Church was evolving the first great purely Western style of music: polyphony—the ordered simultaneous sounding of two or more vocal or instrumental melodies or parts. About 1000 A.D., monastic treatises on music had begun to mention, and then to describe, *organum:* during the liturgy of church festivals, unisonal choruses alternated with soloists singing in long-drawn-out tones to the accompaniment of other soloists who pronounced the same melodic line at an interval of a fifth or a fourth below. This solemn, rather awkward, heavy form (still used in some Icelandic student songs) was altered decisively during the 11th century. Then the solo singers began to invert the two parts, placing the liturgical melody (called *cantus firmus*) below the accompaniment, which in turn became increasingly free, often consisting of two and more tones against each tone of the *cantus firmus* and thus more and more attracting the listeners' chief attention. Eventually the former accompaniment began to be regarded as the melody proper, the *cantus firmus* having become an accompanying voice or *tenor* (this word used in its literal meaning of a held voice, from the Latin *tenere,* not in the modern meaning of a vocal range). This free-melodic *organum* first reached a peak about 1150 A.D. in two French churches: St.-Martial at Limoges and Notre Dame at Paris.

Now we encounter the first composer whose name has been preserved (except for a few nonprofessional clerics of the preceding century and some courtly poets remembered for their poems rather than for their music). Master Leoninus of Notre Dame left 90 two-part *organa* for the entire church year—florid, free *colorature* soaring above the awesome drawn-out peals of the *tenor*. His successor, Perotinus, called Magnus by his contemporaries, marked the climax of this so-called *"ars antiqua,"* and about 1300 ushered in its ultimate transformation into the *"ars nova."* In his gigantic three- and even four-part *organa*, the florid *colorature* were subjected to such metrical patterns as iambs and trochees. The *tenor* droned along in still longer tones, a single tone often being held for 40 measures and more. Only in certain episodes of the *organum*, known as *clausulae*, did the *tenor* abandon its slothfulness and move along with the higher voices.

These *clausulae* at last became the nuclei of the foremost polyphonic form of the 13th century, the *motet* (not to be confused with the very different form later given that name). This took its name from the fact that it awarded a special text *(motetus)* to the upper voice or voices, a text differing from that sung by the *tenor* (the *mot*). At last, each of several voice parts sang its own text—sometimes, in fact, three or four different voices sang in as many different languages. A third polyphonic form was the *conduct*, which had a single text; its two, three, or four vocal parts moved ahead evenly, note against note (Latin *punctus contra punctum*, whence our word counterpoint), in chordal simultaneities that appear to have helped pave the way for the later harmonic conception of music.

In the realm of musical theory, experts faced the tremendous task of devising satisfactory notation for this evolving music, of codifying an accurate system of scales, and of phrasing those rules of consonance, dissonance, and rhythmic propriety without which polyphony might degenerate into chaos. The monk Guido d'Arezzo (990?–?1050) has been credited with most of these achievements, as well as with many others, but only a few of them can be traced to him authentically. His mnemonic devices for facilitating the correct performance of liturgical melodies—the Guidonian hand and solmization—were of Oriental origin, but his improvements in notation were original. Music had been written down in *neumes*, a script of dashes, dots, and hooks placed above the text syllables. These signs indicated rises and falls in the melodic line, but showed neither the actual notes nor their durations. The *neumes* sufficed only while tradition remained sufficiently strong in both Gregorian plain song and secular music. They became deficient as soon as the growing importance of polyphony made essential a degree of precision which had been unnecessary in simple melodic music. The dashes, dots, and hooks were therefore given one, two, and (probably by Guido d'Arezzo) four reference lines (this last being the staff still used in the prayerbooks of the Roman Catholic Church). The purpose of these lines was to place and relatively space the *neumes* so unmistakably that their pitches were no longer left to tradition or guesswork.

Two more centuries passed before a fundamentally metrical notation was established in which the shape of a note indicated its relative duration. This mensural notation, evolved during the 13th century, grew from a stemless *breve* and a stemmed *long* to greater complexity; it supplied the link between the unmetrical plain song notation (still used in Catholic prayerbooks) and the more recent five-line-staff system, which achieved its present form in the 17th century. But even this improved notation conveyed ambiguous values: the *longs, breves,* and *semibreves* could, without showing it, be either perfect (that is, dotted) or imperfect (not dotted), and only a careful parsing of the context could indicate which they were supposed to be.

The foremost problem of consonance-dissonance dealt with the (major) third (as CE) and its complement within the octave, the (minor) sixth (as EC). The "official" ecclesiastical music of the earlier Middle Ages had ignored these two intervals completely, but during the Gothic period they began to cross the English Channel to the Continent. As late as 1300, French musicians still found them "hard on the ear," and their final recognition and adoption as fundamentals of harmony took place only in the 15th century. The price paid for acceptance of these new consonances appears to have been the renunciation of the older "natural" third derived from the cycle of fifths, preference being given to the third provided by stopped strings (just as natural). But as the stopped-string third was slightly narrower, it consisted of two widths of whole tones, a situation intolerable in music for more than one voice or instrumental part. So, about 1300, musicians devised the earliest meantone temperament, arbitrarily dividing the narrower third into two equal, somewhat narrower whole tones.

The 14th century, period of the *"ars nova,"* ended the Middle Ages. Like most terminal eras, it was particularly rich in musical evolution. Its characterizing traits—awakening of interest in nature, man, earthly life—was faithfully reflected in the musical mirror. Sophisticated secular music rose alongside, often above, religious music; rhythm grew constantly more complex; descriptiveness and realistic intent appeared, as in painting and literature; individual contributions by admired composers began to be important per se. Two geniuses of this period stand out as powerful peers: the French Guillaume de Machaut (or Machault, 1300?–1377) and the Italian Francesco Landino (or Landini, 1325–1397). Besides many smaller works for educated singers, Machaut is renowned for having composed the earliest known complete Mass composed by a single musician, a huge non-Gregorian fabric. Landino excelled in euphonious chamber music that remarkably prefigured the chordal, harmonic developments of the future.

The chief forms of this music for vocal soloists were derived from dance-songs, as their names demonstrate: *rondeau* and *ballade* are related to "round" and "ball." Preserving vestiges of choral replies to verses sung by a leader, these had refrains. The *madrigal* (very unlike the more familiar 16th century madrigal) did not derive from a dance form; it therefore had no refrain. Another characteristic form was the *caccia* (chase), in which two voices in strict canonic imitation depicted with dash and humor scenes from ordinary life—incidents of fishing and hunting, market scenes, fire alarms, shouts, galloping hunters, barking dogs, noisy vendors, quacks, and bargaining customers.

Later Ages: 1400–1900.—Early in the 15th century, the center of musical gravity shifted northward from Italy. One center was England, with the vigorous personality of John Dunstable (1370?/1390?–1453), who accepted the latest manners from France and Italy, in return giving his

Continental colleagues the compact English style with its consonant thirds and sixths. The other center was the brilliant ducal court of Burgundy, in eastern France. There the great Guillaume Dufay (1400?–1474) flourished, a master musician of the highest skill, which he placed at the service of a serene charm not unrelated to that of his contemporary, the painter Jan van Eyck. Dufay was one of the first northern musicians to visit Italy and serve in a chapel of one of its princes. For 150 years, the leading composers from the north were to spend decades in Rome, Venice, Florence, or Mantua, while Italy, busily giving the world an entire company of great painters and sculptors, produced almost no composers of the highest rank. The atmosphere of the Italian Renaissance, which northerners drank in at the courts of the pope, the Medici, the Este, and the Sforzas, altered their traditional ways. The northern Gothic spirit, complex and angular, yielded in part to the new Italian taste for sensuous, curving lines, restful balance, limpid simplicity.

The Burgundian school lapsed about 1400. During the next century, its position was occupied by men from the Netherlands, who founded the so-called "Flemish" school. Two of the foremost names in its first generation were those of the Flemish Jean de Okeghem (or Johannes Ockeghem, 1430?–1495) and the Dutch Jacob Obrecht (1452–1505). They took over the pattern typical of Burgundian compositions: three vocal parts, with the principal melody at the top, and with a *contratenor* that filled in the tones needed to form triads along with the *cantus firmus* and the *tenor,* thus showing that harmonic preoccupation was strengthening. Okeghem and Obrecht went farther in the harmonic direction by increasing the number of voice parts to four and five and by ending many of their compositions on full triads instead of the previously usual empty fifths. They also lengthened the span of melodic lines as against the shorter sectionalizations of the Burgundians and did away with the subordinate *contratenor,* assigning roles of equal importance to all voice parts. Indeed, they stressed this equality by having the voices enter *seriatim* with the same theme, thus drawing the listeners' attention to each of them.

This "imitative" manner reached plenitude at the opening of the 16th century, in the musical generation of Josquin des Prez (1450?–1521) and Heinrich Isaak (1450?–1517), two Flemings whose rich music, built along balanced, soaring lines, seems a true counterpart of the plastic arts of the High Renaissance in the age of Bramante, Leonardo da Vinci, and Raphael. Emphasizing chords, these two great composers further signalized the impulse of harmonic feeling, the urge to move from a horizontal conception of flowing melodies to a vertical conception of interrelated chords. The older musicians had conceived their voice parts horizontally—the *tenor* first, then the *cantus firmus* and the *contratenor;* the newer men began to think vertically too, considering all the tones sounded together as consonant or dissonant chords to be ordered by the nascent rules of the new technique of harmony.

This critical change in the way of conceiving the structure of music brought about the final disappearance of the "artifices" of the Netherlanders, doomed by the fading prevalence of absolute counterpoint. These artifices, which had made their appearance in France in the 14th century, consisted chiefly in putting down a single line of notation and then deriving a polyphonic web from it by reading it first as it was, and then backwards, upside down, in mirror image, and in varying rhythms and tempos. To call such a procedure unmusical or soulless is to indulge a romantic misconception of the nature of composition. It represented the Gothic principle of building a cathedral from a small half-structural, half-ornamental nucleus as a way of achieving unity organically. No comparable effort to achieve similar unity throughout a composition appeared until the development of 20th century "twelve-tone" or "serial" procedures.

Late Gothic polyphony likewise dominated the German states, but they were deeply influenced too by the Reformation. The Protestant desire to make the congregation itself sing forced the musicians around Luther to strive for monumental simplicity and popular character. This led to the conversion of Gregorian hymns and secular songs, often with risqué texts, into solemn, vigorous *chorales.* In music, as in Bible lore, the Protestant Reformation was highly indebted to the then recent invention of printing and publishing. Owing to the activities of music printers, especially in Nürnberg, Venice, and Paris, we know more about the popular music of the early 16th century than about that of any earlier time.

Outstanding among the half-courtly, half-popular forms was the Italian *frottola,* a lyric solo song with an accompaniment either sung or played. The *frottola* mostly was set in harmonic chords rather than in contrapuntal voice parts. Out of this simple, well-wrought form, in which minor masters excelled, the major composers around 1530—Italian and Flemish—developed the most important secular musical form of 16th-century Italy, the madrigal. Idyllic or erotic, free in structure, intellectual in text and musical diction, this later madrigal was a basically vocal form of chamber music intended to be sung by cultivated amateurs seated around a table on which the voice parts were laid out. It lasted in Italy until early in the 17th century in ever-increasing harmonic sophistication. Like modern chamber music, it passed more and more into the hands of professional performers.

The French created their own variety of vocal chamber music, raising the erotic *chanson* to a climax of airy, elegant melodiousness. Paintings of the time depict such *chansons* being performed by a single singer, with instruments taking over the three other parts. In the 1560's, however, a number of French composers and poets began to write deeply passionate psalms for John Calvin's Protestants. These were intended for singing at home after dinner—again around a table—for the Huguenots admitted no musical settings in church except the sober unisons of congregational singing. Two great leaders in this effort were Claude Goudimel (1505?–1572) and Claude Le Jeune (1528–1600).

The fact that Le Jeune was called by his contemporaries "the last polyphonist" points up a momentous turn in the history of music. The age of Flemish brilliance was closing with the most brilliant and versatile of the northern masters, Orlandus Lassus (or Orlando di Lasso, 1532–1594). Born in Hainault, he lived in the Netherlands, Italy, England, France, and the German states, and was honored as no earlier musician ever had been. Knighted by Emperor Maximilian II, Orlando left a truly cosmopolitan body of works using texts in four languages—more than 2,000 pieces, among them more than 1,000 motets and 100 settings of the Magnificat, as well as

Masses, psalms, *chansons,* and German lieder.

When the Flemish supremacy ended, Italy again became the leading musical power. Italians, almost at a single blow, took possession of all the princely chapels and important cathedral organs. But before these pioneers could replace Flemish polyphony with a national idiom, an Italian summed up the transition from a Flemish to an Italian character in the very sanctum of Flemish influence, the polyphonic music of the Roman Catholic Church. This world-renowned master was Giovanni Pierluigi da Palestrina (1525?–1594). To the versatility and cosmopolitan life of Orlando di Lasso he opposed a glorious monomania and the strictest localism. He spent his whole life in Roman churches as the pope's composer, conductor, or singer, and wrote almost exclusively for the Mass and the daily offices. So doing, he created a style of solemn grandeur, celestial serenity, and mystic profundity which became the paragon of Catholic music. As a son of his increasingly baroque time, he often adopted the then recent custom of composing for two or three choruses which, now alternating and now mingling, reached the ears of listeners from different parts or levels of the church, giving them the truly baroque sensation of space.

Somewhat younger than Palestrina was his great Spanish counterpart, Tomás Luis de Victoria (1549?–1611), an ordained priest who also served in Roman churches, and who wove into otherwise somewhat Palestrina-like church music his own passionate, almost neurasthenic intensity and musical reflections of his native Spain. Victoria never composed a secular piece or used an identifiably secular theme. To modern ears, perhaps the most striking characteristic of Victoria's relatively small body of works is their hints at those harmonic and rhythmic devices which remain unmistakable hallmarks of Spanish music to this day. With Orlando and Palestrina, Victoria formed a trinity of late polyphonic religious masters of extraordinary accomplishments, the summary and valedictory of a long and remarkably fruitful period.

England approached the musical ideals of Italy more closely than they were approached by any other nation: it is not without reason that the greatest English composer of his time, William Byrd (1543–1623), has been called "the British Palestrina." Three gifted Tudor composers—the "three T's"—had just preceded him: John Taverner (1495?–1545), Christopher Tye (1500?–1573?)—a creator of the English Church anthem—and Thomas Tallis (1505?–1585). Tallis had emulated the latest Italians in a Latin motet for 40 voice parts grouped in 8 choruses. Byrd did not confine himself to religious music, though he composed for both the Roman and the English churches. He wrote "Songs of sundrie natures, some of gravitie, and others of myrth, fit for all companies." He tried his hand at English madrigals in the Italian style, thus inaugurating the extraordinary, belated flowering of the madrigal in England. He was also the father of the brilliant school of keyboard composers known as the English virginalists. Up to Byrd's time, instrumental music nowhere had matched vocal music in quality, quantity, or importance. Down to about 1600, the groups of instrumentalists who had performed at court banquets and other festivities had preferred transcriptions of vocal music—motets and madrigals—playing them now on strings, now on woodwinds or brasses. These men were, however, ripe for an idiomatic instrumental language of their own, at least for organs, virginals, viols, and lutes. Small instrumental forms had evolved from dance tunes and preludes to song accompaniments, mostly as variations on a theme. The charming character pieces and sets of variations of the Elizabethan virginalists—of Thomas Morley (1557–1602), Giles Farnaby (1560?–1640), John Bull (1563?–1628), and Orlando Gibbons (1583–1625)—were the earliest widely disseminated and successful purely instrumental compositions; additionally, they were the seeds from which modern piano music grew.

Tudor musicians also evolved the *consort,* an ensemble composed of instruments either of the same family (unbroken consort) or of various families (broken consort); this represented a polyphonic manner midway between that of chamber music and that of orchestral music. In a similar spirit, Italians began to favor instrumental groups free of vocal styles. Most daring among them was Giovanni Gabrieli (1557?–1612) at Venice. He transformed the polychoral style of Venetian state motets (settings for several simultaneous choruses) into what he called sonatas for several groups of instruments. In these, he took two new steps, carefully indicating both the exact instrumentation and the passages that should be played aloud *(forte)* and soft *(piano).*

While these changes were taking place at Venice, a group of Florentine professional and amateur musicians took another revolutionary step. In an attack on the artificial, "barbarian" Netherlandish polyphony, they availed themselves of the Renaissance's newly acquired knowledge—and misconceptions—of ancient Greek music. The generation born in the 1560's developed a speechlike, naturalistic *monody* designed to convey shifting moods and passions. This "new music" was completely free from care for counterpoint and the structures that had developed from it. This kind of monody rested on a *basso continuo* (thoroughbass), indicated by a code of added figures telling what chords should be improvised between the melody and its bass by lutes or keyboard instruments.

The new monody, ripe about 1600, at once flowered in a number of unprecedented forms. In Florence, chiefly at the hands of the so-called *"camerata"* first patronized by Giovanni Bardi, Conte di Vernio, it led almost inevitably to the *dramma per musica,* or opera (q.v.), which appeared in the 1590's in the works of Jacopo Peri (1561–1633) and Giulio Caccini (1546?–1618), but reached its first lofty peak in 1607 with the *Orfeo* of Claudio Monteverdi (1567–1643). This opera consisted essentially of naturalistic recitative full of unfolding dramatic tension, but it also included episodic dances, instrumental interludes, and choruses. For the next 40 years, operas remained rare events, being composed as courtly entertainments for princely weddings or receptions at Florence or Mantua; they were rarely repeated after their first performance. Opera kept much of this aristocratic exclusiveness until the 18th century, though in 1637 Venice, the courtless city-republic, opened the first, and for decades the only, public opera house (Teatro San Cassiano) for subscribers and those buying single admissions.

At about the time of the emergence of opera, musicians in church circles introduced a related form without stage settings, costumes, or acting: the oratorio. Named after the place of its earliest performance, the Roman oratory of San Filippo

Neri, the oratorio commonly used Old Testament texts. It was sung by soloists and a narrator, with choral and orchestral episodes, "in order," as a contemporary listener wrote, "to attract the faithful and to entertain them with spiritual profit in those hours of the night which in the fall and winter are most dangerous, above all for young people." Another monodic relative of the opera, the cantata, was of smaller size, usually consisting of lyric arias and recitatives. Both oratorio and cantata owed their first greatness to a Roman composer, Giacomo Carissimi (1605–1674).

Arias as integral parts of the cantata testify to a change in Italian taste after some 30 years of the speechlike monodic melody. Toward the middle of the 17th century, that "tedium of the recitative" to which Italian opera composers confessed, as well as the innate desire for attractive melody and balanced form, caused composers to interrupt the "unending" flow of recitative with lyric episodes in a truly melodic style and symmetrical form (a familiar example is *Ombra mai fù* from Handel's opera *Serse,* the well-known "Largo"). Many arias were given the indication *"da capo,"* meaning that after a second, contrasting section, the first section was repeated. The aria first dominated, and then domineered, at last diluting the dramatic aspects of Italian opera—to the delight of increasingly agile singers. This defection from the original Florentine ideal was abetted by the increasing influence of the stage engineers, who devised eye-filling stage pictures, transforming settings, wings, and props before delighted audiences and arranging appearances of gods and demigods—the notorious *deus ex machina*—from the skies.

The Venetian opera gradually yielded ground to the Neapolitan variety, the first important composers of which were Francesco Provenzale (1627–1704) and Alessandro Scarlatti (1660–1725), the latter writing more than 100 operas. A galaxy of brilliant composers followed, among them Nicola Porpora (1686–1768), Niccolò Jommelli (1714–1774), Tommaso Traetta (1727–1779), and Niccolò Piccinni (1728–1800). This dynasty endured into the 19th century with Giovanni Paisiello (1740–1816) and Domenico Cimarosa (1749–1801). In Neapolitan opera, the aria and the singer reigned supreme at the cost not only of recitative, chorus, and instrumental music, but also of drama, stage machinery, and acting. Except in the emerging *opera buffa,* which grew out of the *intermezzi* originally played between the acts of *opera seria,* interest in the libretto and its implications was sacrificed to melodic charm and the remarkable way of singing that came to be called *bel canto.*

The Italians also favored chamber music of intimate character, notably in sonatas for one or two violins with bass and harpsichord, really an instrumental version of vocal monody, and in *concerti grossi;* in which a small group of soloistic instruments was contrasted with the rest of the orchestra. The pioneer in this field had been Salomone Rossi, called L'Ebreo (1587–1630?); ripeness came with Arcangelo Corelli (1653–1713) and Giuseppe Torelli (1658–1709), the latter writing the earliest known concertos for solo violin and orchestra.

England again was Italy's musical next of kin. Her greatest composer in the 17th century, Henry Purcell (1659–1695), who wrote brilliant anthems and hymns, also composed violin sonatas in Corelli's manner and an opera, *Dido and Aeneas* (1689?), which differed from Italian models chiefly in the importance of the role allotted to the chorus. But the English court preferred the time-honored, balletlike *masque* and the spoken dramas of John Dryden and other poets, as well as a corrupted Shakespeare with elaborate incidental music. English opera was very slow to develop.

The opera encountered similar difficulties in France: the court clung to the semidramatic court ballet, and the first attempt to introduce a public opera house ended in bankruptcy. In the 1670's, however, an Italian-born court musician, Jean-Baptiste Lully (1632–1687), succeeded in adapting opera to French tastes and rooting it solidly in the soil of his adopted country. Lully's operas were music dramas in the original Florentine sense. He ignored the recent antidramatic preference for overdecorated lyric arias spaced out with dry recitative, employing instead an eloquent monody shaped painstakingly to the French diction of the leading actors of the Comédie Française. Respecting the French taste for correct, meaningful diction, Lully likewise responded to the national delight in dramatic and lyric aspects of nature—thunderstorms, enchanted gardens, moonlit nights. These supplied rewarding tasks for the instruments. As at all junctures of operatic history in which drama is emphasized (Monteverdi, Gluck, Verdi, Wagner), Lully's orchestra was used with the eloquent significance that most of his Italian contemporaries had neglected. Lully's counterpart in chamber music was François Couperin, called "the Great" (1668–1733). Couperin's thoroughly aristocratic concertos for strings and his numerous pieces for harpsichord adumbrated the coming formal elegance of the rococo; he also wrote sacred music, the impressiveness of which adds dimension to his figure.

Germany was as late as England and France in naturalizing the opera. A place of honor in German musical history belongs to the *lied,* which preserved an age-old tradition of intimate, tender, often popular singing, finally grafting it onto the novel Italian form of accompanied monody. Three important names must suffice here to stand for three generations: Heinrich Albert (1604–1651), Adam Krieger (1634–1666), and Johann Wolfgang Franck (1644–1710?), the last a specialist in the religious lied. These men had only national significance, but the name and works of Johann Crüger (1598–1662) spread throughout the Protestant world. His *Praxis pietatis melica,* containing many well-known hymn melodies, reached some 40 editions between 1644 and about 1744.

Long before the Germans accepted opera, they had used the new monodic style for nontheatrical purposes. Under the vigorous leadership of Heinrich Schütz (1585–1672), Protestant musicians had taken advantage of the intensity of free-flowing recitativelike melody to support scriptural texts. They had also availed themselves of the grandiose partnership of two or more simultaneous choruses, a practice that Schütz imported from Venice, where he had studied with Giovanni Gabrieli. Alongside this strong Italian influence, the Lutherans held to their own heritage, the chorale, employing its musical resources in polyphonic settings, cantatas, and organ fantasies. The three foremost masters among them were the organists Samuel Scheidt (1587–1654), Johann Pachelbel (1653–1706), and Georg Böhm (1661–1733). The church cantata for soloists, chorus, organ, and orchestra reached its loftiest pre-Bachian peak in the baroque compositions of Dietrich Buxtehude (1637–1707).

Many of the German royal, princely, and ducal

Right: Giovanni Pierluigi da Palestrina (1525?–1594), the great master of polyphonic religious music.

MUSIC

Portraits from The Bettmann Archive

Below: The musical genius, Johann Sebastian Bach (1685–1750), in a painting executed about four years before his death.

Above: In a life that spanned less than 36 years, Wolfgang Amadeus Mozart (1756–1791) composed a huge volume of work.

Left: Ludwig van Beethoven (1770–1827), in his late 40's.

Johannes Brahms (1833–1897), a mature perfectionist in the medium of symphonic orchestral composition.

Frédéric François Chopin (1810–1849), gifted pianist and composer of some of the world's finest music for the piano.

MUSIC

Richard Wagner (1813–1883), steeped in Germanic lore, drove romanticism to a powerful climax in his music dramas.

(Bottom center and bottom right) The Bettmann Archive; (others) Brown Brothers

The giant of 20th century music, Igor Stravinsky (1882–), experimented in countless modes of musical expression.

The leader of the school of composers who introduced the "twelve-tone" system, Arnold Schoenberg (1874–1951).

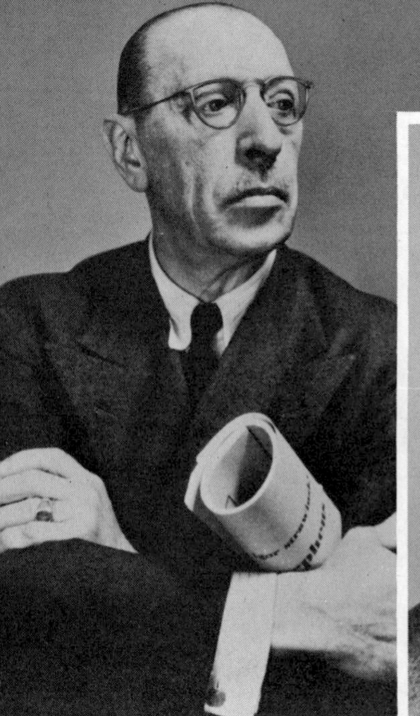

Claude Achille Debussy (1862–1918), "impressionist" master of subtle nuances and sensuous tone colors.

courts imported Italian performers in an effort to imitate the glamour of French and Italian courts; few availed themselves of native talent. Then what had occurred in Italy was repeated in Germany: the richest commercial city created a public, permanent national opera. What had happened at Venice in 1637 happened at Hamburg in 1678. The first opera heard at the newly opened opera house there was a Biblical drama by Johann Theile (1646–1724). Soon librettos were also based on distorted episodes from Greek and Roman mythology and history. Not always on a very high level, the Hamburg Opera nonetheless attracted several extremely talented composers, among them Reinhard Keiser (1674–1739), Johann Mattheson (1681–1764), and—before his Italian travels and his long years in England—George Frideric Handel (1685–1759).

These masters of the 17th and early 18th centuries—Italian, English, French, and German—built the imposing edifices of baroque music, which an extraordinary quartet of composers born in 1683 and 1685 roofed over and completed. They were Jean Philippe Rameau (1683–1764), Handel, Johann Sebastian Bach (1685–1750), and Domenico Scarlatti (1685–1757).

Rameau codified the harmonic system of the baroque in a book that had widespread, enduring influence: *Traité de l'Harmonie* (1722). A distinguished composer of instrumental and religious music, he turned to opera in his fifties. Almost at once he was acclaimed as Lully's foremost successor, eclipsing the operas of such interim men as André Campra (1660–1744) and André Destouches (1662–1749). Rameau's *Castor et Pollux* (1737) is widely regarded as the chief work of the French musical stage of his period.

The cosmopolitan Handel, though born in Germany and in part self-trained in Italy, settled in London. He had composed a German Passion and three operas to German texts, but he soon devoted himself to instrumental chamber music in Corelli's manner, to cantatas and Neapolitan-style operas to Italian texts, and to ceremonial music. His approximately 40 operas lack unifying dramatic integrity, but are storehouses of affecting, effective arias. His religious and ceremonial music shows obvious traces of Purcell's style. Handel achieved his most enduring success with his oratorios, one of which—*Messiah* (1742)—became so universally popular that it has tended to cast much of his other great music into shadow.

Bach spent his life in Saxony, now as an organist, now as a court violinist, conductor, cantor, or teacher. Deeply rooted in the polyphonic and chorale tradition, he by no means confined himself within it. He was fascinated by French orchestral music and by the baroque expressiveness of Italian homophony, most particularly in the concertos of the Venetian priest Antonio Vivaldi (1669?–1741), which he studied, transcribing some of them, until he could employ the essentials of their style for his own purposes. But the center of Bach's incomparably inclusive art was fugue, from the 48 preludes and fugues of *The Well-Tempered Clavier* through the magnificent choral fugues of the B-Minor Mass to the final summation in *Art of the Fugue,* this last incomplete. With the enormous span of his production, from violin and cello sonatas to the *St. Matthew Passion,* from the good-humored miniatures of the *Clavierbüchlein* to the mighty organ chorales and the numerous church cantatas, he composed in almost every musical genre except the two at which Handel most excelled: opera and oratorio (for Bach's so-called "Christmas Oratorio" is really six Christmas cantatas bundled together).

Domenico Scarlatti, born the same year as Handel and Bach, composed hundreds of brief harpsichord sonatas in an unprecedented nonpolyphonic style. Free in form, mercurial in their swift changes of tempo, thoroughly and exclusively native to the keyboard, they require—with their glittering arpeggios, audacious leaps, and crossed hands—the services of a virtuoso harpsichordist. With Couperin, Rameau, Handel, and Bach, Scarlatti established principles that were to become bases of music for the piano.

During the lifetimes of Rameau, Handel, Bach, and Domenico Scarlatti, a revolution in musical life occurred. Sociologically, it became manifest in a change of patronage. Up to 1700, the Catholic and Protestant churches, the courts, and the higher aristocracy had been the leading, though not the exclusive, patrons of the arts. During the 18th century, however, the rising middle class began to take over. In music, the two chief symptoms of this change were the inception of professional criticism and the development of public performances, most often for profit. Handel was the earliest important composer to dispense altogether with dependence upon clerical, royal, or noble patronage and to turn impresario in his own right, depending upon public support for the successful presentation of his operas and, particularly, his oratorios. In fact, he became a businessman, making and losing large sums of money.

The earliest critical columns dealing with music appeared in the *Mercure de France* and in two London papers, *The Tatler* (1709) and *The Spectator* (1711). Germany soon followed with musical periodicals, most of them ephemeral, but showing the increasing desire for discussion and clarification of musical aesthetics.

Public concerts were inaugurated in London in 1672 by John Banister (1630–1679), a violinist-composer. These were held in a small room with "a large raised box for the musicians, whose modesty required curtains." In Germany, the prolific composer Georg Philipp Telemann (1681–1767) followed suit with concerts in Frankfurt am Main and Hamburg; in Paris, Anne Danican Philidor (1681–1728) founded the renowned Concert Spirituel in 1725.

A change from the compositional procedures of the late baroque occurred during the early 18th century. Polyphony was scorned as stiff, pedantic, soulless, being replaced by melody with bass accompaniment. This new trend was toward the aristocratic rococo, the musical aspects of which were called *le style galant.* The rococo reacted against the graver, weightier tastes of the high baroque and the leanings of the maturing middle class, which favored simplicity and unmistakable human warmth. Polyphony was not the only victim of this revolution. Another was the traditional Italian opera, its texts dominated by mythology and Greek and Roman pseudohistory, its music dominated by nearly autonomous arias and extraordinary singers. Lampoons attacked it from the 1720's on, and in London a decisive blow was struck when the poet John Gay (1685–1732) and the musician John Christopher Pepusch (1667–1752) produced *The Beggar's Opera* (1728), a play half spoken and half sung in catchy, mostly borrowed tunes, full of wit and satire, and unafraid of vulgarity. Partly dependent upon *The Beggar's Opera* and its successors, partly descended from the *intermezzi* that long had been inserted into *opera seria,* was *opera buffa,* of which *La Serva Padrona* (1733), by Giovanni Battista Pergolesi (1710–1736), is a renowned early example. In France, the philosopher-musician Jean Jacques Rousseau (1712–1778) imitated Pergolesi's ways in *Le Devin du Village* (1752), which became very successful. In Germany, imitations of the Gay-Pepusch work at first failed, but in 1766 Johann Adam Hiller (1728–1804) laid the enduring foundations of the comic Singspiel with his *Lisuart und Dariolette.* The Singspiel, which included spoken dialogue, was to have serious as well as comic progeny, two of the most renowned works in this genre being Ludwig van Beethoven's *Fidelio* (1805) and Carl Maria von Weber's *Der Freischütz* (1821).

And yet the heroic opera was not dead. It bloomed again in the mature operas of Christoph Willibald Gluck (1714–1787). Turning—with the librettist Ranieri di Calzabigi (1714–1795)—to a reinterpretation of the original Florentine operatic ideals, Gluck attempted to reform a genre that had been dominated, as he saw it, far too long by the librettos of Metastasio (Pietro Trapassi, 1698–1782) and the extremely formalized *opera seria* that they implied. In the renowned preface to Gluck's *Alceste* (1767), we read: "I have striven to restrict music to its true office of serving poetry by means of expression and by following the situations of the story." Drastically restricting musical means, doing without *colorature,* Gluck won his most enduring success with *Orfeo ed Euridice* (1762).

The drive toward a new sort of expressiveness was accompanied by important changes in performance. The preceding centuries had made some use of contrasts between loud and soft, but usually only in contrasting *forte* and *piano* sections. The 18th century introduced greater variety in the *crescendo* and *decrescendo,* gradual increase and decrease in loudness, gradations between the two extremes. Instruments took the lead. Around 1710, the *pianoforte* with hammers was developed in Italy, France, and Germany, the earliest organ swell in England. At about the same time, orchestras in Rome started to diminish the volume of "tone little by little and then return suddenly to the full power." But another full generation passed before this new expressive means reached France and Germany. When Rameau desired to use it in his ballet *Zaïs* (1748), he was forced to describe it rather than indicate it in the score, and the German flutist-theorist Johann Joachim Quantz (1697–1773) did not even mention it in his treatise on performance (1752). The use of crescendo and decrescendo triumphed only when Niccolò Jommelli (1714–1774) introduced them to the Stuttgart court orchestra, which handed them on to the orchestra of Mannheim. The latter, under Johann Wenzel Anton Stamitz (1717–1757) and Christian Cannabich (1731–1798), became a world-famous center of orchestral performance.

Stamitz and another Mannheimer, Franz Xaver Richter (1709–1789) began to shift the symphony to the center of concert life. At about the same time, Karl Philipp Emanuel Bach (1714–1788), deserting his father's baroque structures for a German version of the rococo known as *Empfindsamkeit,* and at the same time intensifying the intimate expressiveness of writing for the piano, further assisted the rise to primacy of that orchestral form of the sonata, the symphony. A little to one side of the main stream of formal evolution, but contributing to it in much the same way, was Luigi Boccherini (1743–1805), who spent much of his life in Spain.

But the development of the symphony and its siblings, the string quartet and the piano sonata, into powerful expressions of human character was the work of Joseph Haydn (1732–1809) more than of any other single composer. In his hands, the sonata as a rule had four movements: a dramatic driving opening; an introspective, lyric second movement; a dancelike third; and a playful, happy finale. The special novelty of this form lay chiefly in the opening movement. To provide dramatic contrast to a leading theme, Italians in Pergolesi's time had introduced a second, more lyric theme. Haydn accepted this procedure and went on to elaborate the so-called development, "in which the themes, no longer treated as integers, were decomposed into characteristic fragments or motives which had enough motor power to drive ahead. The theme no longer was; it acted" (Sachs). Haydn worked out this dramatic (even operatic) procedure in his string quartets first; these, with his more than 100 symphonies, form the bulk of his enormous life work. In its increasing depth and seriousness, Haydn's music symbolized the composer's changing position. He enjoyed the patronage of wealthy aristocrats as a court composer through much of his life. But then, pensioned, he marked the momentous passage from the position of a highly respected 18th century servant to that of a free-lance 19th century artist.

Wolfgang Amadeus Mozart (1756–1791) suffered under the impact of this same socioeconomic crisis. When still young, he left the security of a court position in Salzburg; he was never able to find another source of steady income, but passed the rest of his brief existence in the shadow of poverty, in part because he lacked the steadiness of Haydn, in part because his health was never good. Still, he created an incredible wealth of music, from songs to operas, from piano pieces to concertos and symphonies. In opera alone, he covered the stylistic expanse from Italian *opera seria* and *opera buffa* to German Singspiel. He not only mastered the styles of Germany, France, and Italy, but also integrated them into a supranational style of his own. "Reconciling beauty and character, German and Italian spirit, the tragic and the comic, drama and music, voices and instruments, melos and counterpoint, he was graced in a blissful moment of history to hold the scales of style in perfect balance" (Sachs).

When Mozart died at 35, Ludwig van Beethoven (1770–1827) was 21. More than Haydn or Mozart, Beethoven was to employ music as a means of expressing both his own and mankind's struggle and suffering. But he elaborated and remodeled his compositions in a long process of transformation until they mostly left the stage of autobiography to attain that of complete aesthetic sublimation. Like Handel and Mozart, Beethoven did not, except during boyhood, find a fixed position in life. He wrote comparatively little on commission, composing instead in response to interior urges. Thus he left only a single opera as against Mozart's 20, only 9 symphonies (but several of them of unprecedented dimensions) as against Haydn's more than 100. And, for one of the first times in musical history, he composed music in an idiom beyond the comprehension of most of his contemporaries: his final string quartets had to be discovered by musicians in later years. Thus, with Beethoven, the break between "modern" composers and their audience definitely had set in.

This break helps to explain why Beethoven's immediate influence was less noticeable than might be expected. It was all but nonexistent in the operatic composers of his own time, of whom only a few of the most important can be mentioned here (see also OPERA). In Paris, André Ernest Modeste Grétry (1741–1813), Étienne Nicolas Méhul (1763–1817), and Louis Joseph Ferdinand Hérold (1791–1833) kept alive the traditions of French opera. In Paris and elsewhere, two Italians—Gaspare Spontini (1774–1851) and Luigi Cherubini (1760–1842)—followed in the wake of Gluck, but tended toward the panoply and display of "grand opera." All over Europe, and even in America, the comedic genius of Gioacchino Antonio Rossini (1792–1868) enchanted listeners. His influence showed plainly in the very different operas of Gaetano Donizetti (1797–1848) and Vincenzo Bellini (1801–1835), the latter exclusively a composer of tragic operas. In Germany, with Weber's finest works, the Teutonic variety of romantic opera became established, displaying a predilection for superhuman powers and stressing descriptive harmony and orchestration as essential elements of dramatic expression. The greatest of Weber's descendants was to be Richard Wagner.

The composer with the closest affinity to Beethoven was Franz Schubert (1797–1828), who belonged to a younger generation and therefore became a full-fledged romantic. Gifted with unparalleled melodic ease, Schubert gave small forms equal importance with large ones. To be sure, he wrote much chamber music and, like Beethoven, nine symphonies. But he gave much of his best to short piano pieces—and even from the enchantments of his trios and quartets, music lovers still return again and again to his more than 600 lieder, the greatest flood of sheer songfulness ever let loose by one man.

The first period of German romanticism ended with two composers born in 1809 and 1810. Felix Mendelssohn (1809–1847) was a full romantic in melodic-harmonic idiom, but clung to 18th century forms. He was, moreover, devoted to the music of Johann Sebastian Bach, whose *St. Matthew Passion* he revived exactly one century after its composition in 1729. His unhappy friend Robert Schumann (1810–1856) was much closer to Schubert in his lieder and his orchestral, chamber, and piano music, as he was much more Teutonically romantic in his taste for sudden change from overflowing enthusiasm to longing and sadness. Schumann's grasp of the classic procedures was not secure, and he found his best media in the lied and the brief piano piece, both of which he often linked into cycles. Exclusively pianistic was his near contemporary, the Franco-Polish Frédéric François Chopin (1810–1849), whose numerous brief pieces are so intimately related to the capabilities of the keyboard that they lose their greatness when transcribed for any other medium. Chopin's influence on the increasing deliquescence of 18th century harmony was to be marked.

In France, an intensely personal version of romanticism was the natural way of Hector Berlioz (1803–1869), whose music won its first acceptance in Germany. Berlioz composed almost nothing for the piano or chamber groups, but devoted himself to large orchestral and choral works and operas. He long had a reputation for expressing himself, and only himself, with all his nightmares, in gigantic melodramatic constructions calling for armies of performers, but recent musicians and critics have begun to value more highly his predominantly quiet oratorio *L'Enfance du Christ* (1854) and his very long, notably classic Vergilian opera *Les Troyens* (1856–1859). Berlioz was a sovereign master of instrumentation.

Romantic opera, meanwhile, evolved in three chief ways. Paris gave birth to the grand opera, of which Eugène Scribe (1791–1861) became the leading librettist and Giacomo Meyerbeer (1791–1864) the most popular composer. Brilliant and showy, with ballets, marches, enormous ensembles, and sensational deaths, it appealed as much to the eyes as—with its florid vocal lines—to the ears. In Germany, the operas of Heinrich Marschner (1795–1861), full of the weird, of cursed heroes, and of final redemption, led straight from Weber to Wagner. In Italy, where romanticism differed greatly from its German and Parisian counterparts—being best summed up, perhaps, in Alessandro Manzoni's great novel *I Promessi Sposi* (1825–1826)—the operas of Rossini, Donizetti, and Bellini maintained the Italian preference for sensuous and expressive singing.

Shortly before 1850, when the composers born about 1810 matured, romanticism entered a second, naturalistic phase. In music, this chiefly meant subordination of the purely musical to extra-musical ideas, the way a handful of powerful creators interpreted aesthetic ideals first made plain in music by Beethoven. In this sense, Richard Wagner (1813–1883) changed his style drastically midway in his life, turning aside to follow in his own way in the footsteps of the Florentine originators of opera, Gluck and Beethoven. After *Lohengrin* (1848), he abandoned the word "opera" in favor of the more ambitious "music drama" as the label for his *Gesamtkunstwerk* or synthesis of the arts. After an interim of six years, this new concept emerged with the composition of *Das Rheingold* (1854), the "foreevening" of his gigantic tetralogy, *Der Ring des Nibelungen.*

Wagner's music drama aimed at a poetically logical text lacking "closed" episodes to arrest the ceaseless flow; for the separate arias and other numbers of most earlier opera, Wagner substituted "unending," speechlike melody supported by an eloquent orchestra underlining the text and supplementing unspoken thoughts by ever-recurring symbolic themes called leitmotivs. Only in one of his mature works—his only comic opera, *Die Meistersinger von Nürnberg* (1867)—did Wagner somewhat recede from his frequently announced purposes: its text was built around a singing contest, and therefore required some return to sectional form.

Wagner's great Italian contemporary, Giuseppe Verdi (1813–1901), believed fiercely in dramatic action as the life blood of the lyric stage. Mostly content with the separate-number construction, Verdi did not accept the intellectual formulations with which Wagner was prodigal. Instead, he turned out opera after opera in substantially the old form, gradually refining his style and increasing the subtlety of his orchestra. His worldwide popularity, more immediate than Wagner's, shows no signs of diminishing. Many of his melodies are familiar to millions of people, and several characters from his operas have achieved the general familiarity of those in great novels. Few musical careers have matched his in continuing fertility: his final opera, *Falstaff* (1893), was staged 54 years after his first.

The French operas of the long Wagner-Verdi period included several that won lasting popularity but had little influence on either operatic or strictly musical developments outside France: Charles Gounod's *Faust* in 1859, the year of Wagner's *Tristan und Isolde;* Ambroise Thomas' *Mignon* (1866); Georges Bizet's *Carmen* (1875); Camille Saint-Saëns' *Samson et Dalila* (1877); and the *Manon* (1884) of the prolific Jules Massenet.

During the 19th century, too, light opera and operetta flourished, especially in France, Austria, England, and Germany. The French tradition, boasting a long lineage, was much alive in the works of Daniel François Esprit Auber (1782–1871) and, especially under the Second Empire, Jacques Offenbach (1819–1880); both men wrote one serious opera of note, Auber's *La Muette de Portici* (also called *Masaniello,* 1828) having helped to establish the manner of grand opera, Offenbach's *Les Contes d'Hoffmann* (1881) becoming a repertoire piece. In Vienna, Johann Strauss, Jr. (1825–1899), most famed as a composer of concert waltzes, revived the light opera tradition, notably in *Die Fledermaus* (1874). In England, Sir Arthur Sullivan (1842–1900), particularly when collaborating with the librettist Sir William Schwenk Gilbert (1836–1911), produced a series of comic operettas that became household fixtures throughout the English-speaking world.

Outside the lyric stage, the final, naturalistic version of musical romanticism faced some strong opposition. Two of the chief nonoperatic composers of the era were Franz Liszt (1811–1886) and Johannes Brahms (1833–1897). Around 1850, when Wagner was laboring at *Der Ring des Nibelungen,* Liszt deserted the symphony for the symphonic poem. This romantic genre in a single movement often appeared to represent literary and other extramusical ideas. Even Liszt's *Dante* and *Faust* symphonies are in fact symphonic poems in several movements: similarly, his B minor Sonata for piano is a free fantasy rather than a sonata in the older sense. Brahms, on the contrary, composed music devoid of extraneous connotations and clung to classic forms. He aimed at classical restraint and strictness in all varieties of orchestral and chamber music, but showed himself wholeheartedly romantic in his numerous lieder and short piano pieces. He never composed for the stage.

Two men, both organists, stood in age and style between the Liszt-Wagner "music of the future" group and the rich romantic classicism of Brahms. They were the Belgian César Franck (1822–1890) and the Austrian Anton Bruckner (1824–1896). Bruckner, once more with nine long symphonies, was nearer to Wagner. Franck, now remembered mainly for his only symphony, his symphonic poems, and his chamber music, stood much nearer to the Brahmsian ideology.

An active interest in folk music and its colorful vigor was a strong ingredient in the romantic naturalism of the late 19th century, a period of increasing national self-consciousness. It appeared most openly in the polemics and compositions of the Russian "Mighty Handful" or "Five," a nationalistic group that included men claiming artistic descent from Mikhail Glinka (1804–1857): Mili Balakirev (1837–1910), Aleksandr Borodin (1833–1887), César Cui (1835–1918), Modest Musorgski (1839–1881), and Nikolai Rimski-Korsakov (1844–1908). The Russian Five, however, excluded from its ranks Peter Ilich Tchaikovsky (1840–1893), who was looked upon as too "Western," but who far exceeded all other Russian composers in worldwide popularity. Tchaikovsky, especially successful in composing symphonies, concertos, symphonic poems, and operas, pointed toward 20th century developments with his elaborate and carefully constructed ballet scores. Music for ballet had fallen to low estate, from which it was rescued largely by Tchaikovsky and Léo Delibes (1836–1891).

A folk-based nationalism resembling that of the Russian Five appeared in the compositions of the Czech Bedřich Smetana (1824–1884), well known for his comic opera *The Bartered Bride* (1866) and several patriotic symphonic poems, and Antonin Dvořák (1841–1904), as well as in that of the Moravian Leoš Janáček (1854–1928). A similar penchant for regional idiom was displayed by the Norwegian Edvard Hagerup Grieg (1843–1907), the Finn Jean Sibelius (1865–1957), the Pole Stanislaw Moniuszko (1819–1872), and the Spaniards Felipe Pedrell (1841–1922), Isaac Albéniz (1860–1909), and Enrique Granados Campiña (1867–1916), as well as in several American composers, including Edward Alexander MacDowell (1861–1908). Almost every nation, often every national region, produced overtly folk-based music, the movement extending, in the United States, to levies upon Amerindian and Negroid sources.

The Modern Age.—Musical leaders of the generation active at the turn of the century struggled either to lead romanticism onward beyond its inevitable conclusion or to recognize its state of advanced decay and thus be free to substitute new conceptions. A few undiluted romanticists continued active, including Hugo Wolf (1860–1903), as exclusively a composer of lieder as Chopin had been of piano music and Gustav Mahler (1860–1911), whose completed works include nine extended symphonies and several big song cycles. Naturalism also remained viable. The sobriquet "verists" (literally truth-ists) was applied to, and finally accepted by, a group of Italian opera composers, including Pietro Mascagni (1863–1945), Ruggiero Leoncavallo (1858–1919), and the extremely popular Giacomo Puccini (1858–1924). This school had less active outriders in Germany (Eugène d'Albert or Eugen D'Albert 1864–1932) and in France (Alfred Bruneau, 1857–1934, and Gustave Charpentier, 1860–1956).

A powerful attack on the pervasive influence of Wagner arose in France in the 1890's under the aegis of the so-called "impressionists" (a term borrowed from painting), of whom by far the most important was Claude Achille Debussy (1862–1918). Fascinated by fleeting sensuous impressions, by transitory images and everything subtle and temporary, Debussy moved away from what had been regarded as functional, logical musical architecture. His most important music was produced in the two decades between 1892 (the symphonic poem *Prélude à l'Après-midi d'un faune*) and 1911 (the mystery play *Le Martyre de Saint Sébastien*), climbing to a notable summit in 1902 (his only opera, *Pelléas et Mélisande*); he also wrote very influential piano pieces, extended orchestral works, and songs. It is interesting to note that his period of greatest fertility coincided with that of the Italian verists.

Debussy's influence on melody, harmony, orchestration, and early 20th century concepts of musical form was deep and wide, though he won scarcely any orthodox followers. In France, much was owed to him by Paul Dukas (1865–1935), Albert Roussel (1869–1937), and Maurice Ravel

(1875–1937). Ravel opposed a keen sense of line to Debussy's predominant colorism, being more innately classic by nature. Non-French composers influenced to some extent by impressionism included the English-born German Frederick Delius (1862–1934); the Spanish Manuel de Falla (1876–1946), the Italian Ottorino Respighi (1879–1936), the Alsatian-American Charles Martin Loeffler (1861–1935), and the eccentric Russian Alexander Scriabin (1872–1915). As most of these composers were Debussy's close contemporaries, to call them "followers" is inexact: musical impressionism in all its manifestations belonged to a single generation.

A wry, witty reaction against the haziness and literary and other extramusical ties of Debussy's impressionism appeared in France in the music of Erik Satie (1866–1925) and in that of some members of the group known as *"Les Six,"* who began as satellites of the critic-novelist-poet-painter Jean Cocteau and of Satie himself. Several of the Six—notably Francis Poulenc (1899–1963), Arthur Honegger (1892–1955), and Darius Milhaud (1892–   )—later evolved in directions of their own, but at the hour of the group's baptism they were all audibly attracted by music-hall banalities and the most extreme antilogical literary and artistic "schools." They brought fresh air into the increasingly enclosed chamber of dying impressionism.

Already, too, Arnold Schoenberg or Schönberg (1874–1951) had begun to veer away from Wagnerian and Debussyan manners like those demonstrated in his *Verklärte Nacht* (1899) and gigantic *Gurre-Lieder* (1901–1911), turning toward expressionism (another term borrowed from painting and literature). His later compositions, most of them deserting the harmonic assumptions on which post-Renaissance Western music had rested, seemed related to inner, often subconscious visions and experiences, frequently in grotesque and distorted forms. Schoenberg's expressionistic so-called atonalism was ready in 1908, with his *Klavierstücke,* Opus 11, and reached an early peak in the melodramatic song cycle *Pierrot Lunaire* (1912), with its desertion of singing for the half-sung, half-spoken or shouted technique called *Sprechstimme.* A formidable theorist and teacher, Schoenberg became one of the most influential of 20th century musicians. Of those most immediately affected by Schoenberg's ideas, the leaders were Alban Berg (1885–1935), whose opera *Wozzeck* (1921) has held the stage, and the gnomic, all-but-dehumanized Anton von Webern (1883–1945). This Vienese group gradually evolved a theory of what is variously called "twelve-tone," "dodecaphonic," and "serial" music, the pilot work of which was Schoenberg's *Serenade,* Opus 24 (1921–1923). This exceedingly complex and controversial way of constructing all parts of a composition from a single "row" (arrangement of the 12 separate tones within an octave) has won very widespread acceptance among younger composers, but decades after its first appearance has failed almost completely to convey much delight or significance to the wide musical public.

A decade older than Schoenberg, Richard Strauss (1864–1949) began under the stars of Schumann and Brahms—even Mendelssohn—but then turned to the Liszt-Wagner ideals, finding his first personal language during the decade in which he composed seven often confessedly autobiographical tone poems (a description he preferred to "symphonic poems"), from *Don Juan* (1889) to *Ein Heldenleben* (1899). Having taxed the eloquence of nontheatrical orchestras to the utmost, Strauss had turned to opera in 1894 *(Guntram).* Then, over a period of nearly 50 years, Strauss composed 15 operas in a variety of manners stretching from the jeweled pseudo-orientalism of *Salome* (1905) and the monomaniacal expressionism of *Elektra* (1909) to the waltz-beguiled sentiment of *Der Rosenkavalier* (1911) and the elaborate mystifications of *Die Frau ohne Schatten* (1919). Strauss' tone poems and the best of his operas each have had periods of worldwide popularity, but his influence on other composers has appeared to be surprisingly small.

Igor Stravinsky (1882–   ), the Russian-born internationalist, became, with Schönberg, probably the most influential of 20th century composers. Beginning as an obvious disciple of his onetime teacher, Rimski-Korsakov, Stravinsky composed ballet scores for the impresario Serge Diaghilev (1872–1929), culminating in the mechanistically rhythmic, searingly dissonant, potent *Le Sacre du printemps* (1913). Stravinsky's later career has paralleled that of the Hispano-French painter Pablo Picasso in its frequent changes of style and direction, each one of which has aroused important echoes in the works of other composers. For a time the musical world seemed to be divided among Schönbergians, Stravinskyans, and others, some splinter groups marching under the banner of neoclassicism (a reaction from massive and autonomous complexity in the backward direction of classicizing simplicities), some under that of neoromanticism (a similar reaction, but directed toward more clearly melodic human expressiveness). Critics and many composers themselves began to hope and to call for a new synthesis.

Many of the leading composers active after World War I may be classified under one or more "isms." Early in the century, the dominating musical fact seemed to be a stormy return to naked constructive elements, often cacophonous, often noisily primitivistic, and most likely to sound anarchic to listeners still preferring 18th and 19th century music. The era's use of folk sources was not nationalistic or sentimental, but therapeutic, intended to revive rhythm, which the long concentration on counterpoint and harmony appeared to have strangled. Such a deliberate shock was the acceptance of American jazz, which was widely adopted and adapted by both American and European composers. Another came from the "Scythian" barbarisms of Stravinsky and the early music of Sergei Prokofiev (1891–1953). Still another inhered in the Magyarism of Béla Bartók (1881–1945), who significantly entitled one of his early piano pieces (1911) *Allegro barbaro.* No other era since the 16th century had so concentrated on ballet at the expense of opera: in the dance, rhythmic movement reigns supreme, for which reason ballet appealed to an era during which the classic and romantic respect for dramatic action and the demand for convincing lifelikeness found themselves relegated to minor places. Much of the most accomplished and enduring music of the period from 1910 to World War II was composed for ballet.

Another facet of later 20th century musical life has been a dislike of much 19th century music and a strong preference for the baroque and rococo styles of the 17th and 18th centuries. Such archaicism was not entirely new. Mozart and Beethoven had rediscovered the wonders of Johann Sebastian Bach's counterpoint; Haydn had composed two oratorios in admiration of Handel; Brahms and

Gabriel Fauré (1845–1924) had fed on past idioms. By 1918, when the "modern" Prokofiev composed a deliberately pastiche "Classical Symphony," however, the interest in forms of the past was becoming general among composers. Too, it effected organ building and the revival of such supposedly obsolete instruments as viols and the harpsichord; it led to the widespread presentation of series of historical concerts—and to a predilection for strict patterns like the passacaglia and other *ostinato* forms with ever-recurrent bass motives. The Brazilian composer Heitor Villa-Lobos (1887–1959) attempted to graft his highly colored native idiom onto the architecture of Bach in his *Bachianas Brasileiras.*

In the 1960's, the most "advanced" compositional modes were *musique concrète* and electronic music. These can be described as ways of organizing mechanically produced noises, in place of the sounds traditionally regarded as properly musical. The use of noisemaking appliances for naturalistic effect can be found in the music of such composers as Stravinsky, Richard Strauss, and Edgar Varèse (1885–1965). What is new in the later music is the use of noise producers (including tape recorders) as the only instruments in a composition. In the United States, John Cage (1912–), Otto Luening (1900–), and Vladimir Ussachevsky (1911–) compose electronic and other advanced music.

Of 20th century composers, some have seemed to stand aside somewhat from the chief channels of contemporary musical thought, others simply to defy classification, or even—at this close range—critical judgment. Jean Sibelius (1865–1957), who lived more than 90 years, came to loom as a noble, if receding, monument to the past, but the English Sir Edward Elgar (1857–1934) and Ralph Vaughan Williams (1872–1958), the Russian Sergei Rachmaninoff (1873–1943), the Hungarian Zoltán Kodály (1882–1967), the Swiss-American Ernest Bloch (1880–1959), and the American Charles Ives (1874–1954) have, among many others, seemed to be isolated factors of the contemporary musical scene. Then there have been the men born in the 1880's and 1890's: Prokoviev, Honegger, Milhaud; the Germans Paul Hindemith (1895–1963), once a proponent of *Gebrauchsmusik* (music for workaday uses), notable for his mastery of musical technique and theory, Carl Orff (1895–), and Kurt Weill (1900–1950), who used a distortion of American jazz for bitter satiric purposes; the Mexican Carlos Chávez (1899–); the Italians Ildebrando Pizzetti (1880–), Francesco Malipiero (1882–), and Alfredo Casella (1883–1947); and the Americans Roy Harris (1898–), Virgil Thomson (1896–), George Gershwin (1898–1937), Aaron Copland (1900–), Roger Sessions (1896–), and Wallingford Riegger (1885–1961).

Notable composers born in the 20th century include the English Sir William Walton (1902–) and Benjamin Britten (1913–); the Italian Luigi Dallapiccola (1904–) and Goffredo Petrassi (1904–); the Russian Dmitri Shostakovich (1906–); the French Olivier Messiaen (1908–); and two of the most important representatives of the European avant-garde, the French Pierre Boulez (1925–) and the German Karlheinz Stockhausen (1928–). In this brief catalogue—which obviously still will be both contracted and expanded by the action of time—mention, finally, must be made of the American Elliott Carter (1908–) and Samuel Barber (1910–), and of the Italo-American composer-librettist Gian Carlo Menotti (1911–).

See also separate articles on Jazz; Musical Elements and Terms; Opera; individual composers; the music of various countries.

Based on an article by the late Curt Sachs; edited, revised, and expanded by Herbert Weinstock.

Bibliography

Boyden, David D., *An Introduction to Music* (New York 1956).
Bukofzer, Manfred F., *Music in the Baroque Era* (New York 1947).
Einstein, Alfred, *Music in the Romantic Era* (New York 1947).
Einstein, Alfred, *A Short History of Music*, rev. ed. (New York 1947).
Ferguson, Donald N., *A History of Musical Thought*, 3d ed. (New York 1959).
Finney, Theodore M., *A History of Music*, rev. ed. (New York 1947).
Gray, Cecil, *The History of Music*, rev. ed. (New York 1931).
Grout, Donald Jay, *A History of Western Music* (New York 1960).
Lang, Paul Henry, *Music in Western Civilization* (New York 1941).
McKinney, H. D., and Anderson, W. R., *Music in History: The Evolution of an Art*, 3d ed. (Cincinnati, Ohio, 1966).
Reese, Gustave, *Music in the Middle Ages* (New York 1940).
Reese, Gustave, *Music in the Renaissance*, rev. ed. (New York 1959).
Sachs, Curt, *The Rise of Music in the Ancient World* (New York 1943).
Strunk, Oliver, *Source Readings in Music History* (New York 1950).
Weinstock, Herbert, *Music as an Art* (N.Y. 1953).
Westrup, J. A., ed., *The New Oxford History of Music*, 11 vols. (New York and London 1954–).

MUSIC APPRECIATION. A variety of musical education intended to assist musically untrained amateurs in increasing the enjoyment they can derive from listening. Music appreciation as a widespread activity has thrived especially in English-speaking countries. It has long been under attack from musicians, musicologists, and serious critics who, though sometimes willing to admit that its practitioners do some good, have insisted that it operates from false and misleading premises and produces more confusion than enlightenment.

The special difficulty presented to the musically untrained by music as an art derives from its general absence of recognizable subject matter in the sense in which the other major arts usually have such matter. It is sometimes said that, unlike the other arts, music is all art. A stimulating, imprecise figure of speech has claimed that music is "about" itself. More suggestively, though no more exactly, it could be proposed that whereas the other arts possess no form entirely separable from their contents, music possesses no narrowly specifiable contents apart from its forms.

For these reasons, composers, performers, and other trained musical people know that music itself can be discussed seriously only in its own technical terminology. The history of music must remain predominantly a collection of biographies and of the names of compositions until it can be understood in terms of the morphology of rhythmic, melodic, polyphonic, and harmonic forms and usages. More basically still, the most important facts about music cannot be discussed with, or written about for, people unable to read a score and not ready to understand the difference between, say, an ecclesiastical mode and a major or minor scale, polyphony and harmony, a suite and a sonata.

It is entirely possible to enjoy musical performances intensely without understanding them at all, just as it is possible to gain exalted pleasure from a fine sonnet without knowing what a sonnet is, or to enjoy a great painting or sculpture without knowledge of the theories and techniques by which it was produced or of its historic context and relevance. But it may be argued relevantly that what is being enjoyed under such circumstances is the materials organized by the creator rather than those specifically musical, literary, or plastic qualities of organization which constitute the object's artistic excellence.

Nor can there be much doubt that a smattering of superficial historical and biographical data concerning music and musicians has, in and for itself, considerable real value. But the fact persists that really to "appreciate" most or all of what is present to be appreciated in even a simple composition (recalling again that, as music, it cannot deal directly with the beings, ideas, and things that are most often the basic materials of literature, painting, and sculpture), a listener must acquire a complex body of technical and theoretical information. The attacks on popular music-appreciation lectures and writings have sprung from the inescapable fact that many of them attempt to substitute several sorts of peripheral and often misleading information for this essential knowledge.

People who natively enjoy music, but who are not satisfied to continue enjoying it without understanding what they are enjoying, or how it came to be what it is, can do no better than to begin at the beginning, acquiring the ability to read and understand notation. From the acquisition of that basic tool, they then can proceed to absorb a good academic history of the evolution of musical usages and forms, constantly testing their freshly acquired knowledge against performances (chiefly recorded) or scores of the music in question. For most practical purposes, such study may well begin with Gregorian chant and proceed through the stage of polyphony to harmonic music and the music of their own era.

Moving along this great road, they can acquire understanding of the constant changes in vocal and instrumental means and procedures and of the meshed relationship among music, politics, economics, national and personal characteristics, and the other arts. Determined and persistent enough, they can come to understand—really to "appreciate"—music as much as they enjoy it, and perhaps even to increase that enjoyment. But short of the willingness and ability to undertake such an extended study, they cannot acquire any very useful insight into the means, history, and condition of music as an art.

In brief, the practice of teaching music appreciation to amateurs is self-condemning if they are encouraged to believe that they need not work hard to acquire understanding of music itself. But the great value of music-appreciation techniques calculated to supply technical and theoretical knowledge to people outside of music schools, colleges, and universities is obvious. Each untrained individual attracted to music must decide for himself how much steady effort he is willing and able to put into acquiring that body of technical, theoretical, and historical information without which no real understanding of music—as distinct from the uninformed enjoyment of musical performance—can be obtained.

HERBERT WEINSTOCK, *Author of "Men of Music"*

MUSIC DRAMA. See MUSIC; MUSICAL THEATER; OPERA.

MUSIC EDUCATION. The term "music education" could apply to all aspects of the teaching of music. It has a special use, however, in the field of general education, where it refers to school programs designed to teach people to make music and to listen to music. The public schools of the United States have an outstanding program, offering music education to all students from kindergarten through grade 12.

The program of music education in U.S. schools might be viewed as the attempt of a young and vigorous society to lay the groundwork for the creation of its own musical culture. This may or may not have been the purpose of those who first advocated music in the schools. In any case, the incorporation of music into the system of universal education and the support of music education with tax funds must be viewed as a substantial form of patronage for music.

By the 1960's some form of music instruction was a part of the education of almost every American child. A survey by the research division of the National Education Association revealed that only about 0.5% of elementary schools (grades 1–6) did not allot at least 20 minutes a week to music. The median number of minutes per week in all schools in the study was 75 minutes in the lower grades and 80 minutes in grades 5 and 6. Some other countries give more time to music at this level. For example, elementary school children in Austria are required to study music two hours per week. In Australia, on the other hand, scheduling two 30-minute periods per week is common practice in infant and primary schools. Though the figures for American schools are somewhat less than the time recommended by the Music Educators National Conference and much less than the 210 minutes reported by some schools, they do indicate the ubiquitous nature of music in America's elementary schools.

ELEMENTARY SCHOOL PROGRAMS

Elementary music education seeks to provide children with many varied experiences. Singing, which was the entire music program in the 19th century, is still probably the most widely employed musical activity in the grade schools. Children are helped to find their singing voices and to learn to use them expressively. The concept that some children are "nonsingers" is much less often encountered than earlier in the century. Schools now seem to accept the responsibility of teaching everyone to sing, although the goal is far from being achieved because of lack of time for individual attention, and, frequently, the lack of a trained music specialist. Yet much beautiful singing is done by elementary school children. Part singing is generally introduced (most frequently in the 3d or 4th grade) by means of rounds and canons. By the time they are 6th graders many boys and girls are capable of singing difficult 2- and 3-part songs.

Mastery of musical notation seems to be less of an obsession than it once was with elementary school music teachers, but it still remains an important part of the program. Music reading ability is now developed through many activities rather than from singing alone.

In a well-balanced program of music education children are given opportunities to play a variety of instruments. The youngest children use very simple rhythm instruments—sometimes ones they have constructed themselves. They may invent their own notation, but they are generally led to the conventional symbolism. Many school systems use the ancient recorder (or a much simplified imitation) to provide a basic instrumental experience to all students of a certain grade, most frequently the 4th. Recorder playing in American schools does not approximate the use of the instrument in some European countries, however. The canton of Zürich in Switzerland, for example, reports that 62% of all eligible grammar school pupils voluntarily study the recorder. Tone bells and other pitch-producing percussion instruments, including those developed by the German composer Carl Orff, are also very popular in American elementary schools. The autoharp, an adaptation of the zither that permits the player to play any one of 12 chords by simply pushing the correct button, has found a home in the American schoolroom. It enables a class without access to a piano to have harmonic accompaniment to its singing or playing. Keyboard experience designed to make all students at least familiar with the piano (or organ in recent years) is another phase of elementary instrumental music that is finding ever-increasing favor in the schools. Class instrumental instruction is one of the unique contributions of American music education. Group teaching is practiced in some other countries—notably New Zealand and Israel and, to a lesser extent, Denmark, Holland, Sweden, and England where the instruction is generally outside school hours. Small groups (2 to 4 children) are a feature of the training of young people in German music schools.

Of the U.S. schools reporting in the NEA survey mentioned previously, 49% indicated that they offered their students the opportunity to have individual or group instruction in the standard instruments of the band or orchestra. In many of the schools that offer such instruction the students studying instruments are encouraged to enrich the classroom music period by playing their instruments. Most also have the opportunity to play in a band or orchestra, either in their own school or in a group representing several schools.

Listening training is often considered a major aspect of the elementary school music program, although listening is obviously an integral part of learning to sing or play an instrument. Much of what is considered "listening" was formerly called "music appreciation," now a term in some disrepute. Typically, the elementary school child is introduced to the instruments of the orchestra so that he can recognize them by sight and sound. In the larger cities symphony concerts have been part of elementary education for a number of years. One of the developments resulting from federal involvement in both the arts and education has been the extension of such opportunities to schools heretofore denied them. A few states support orchestras or opera companies that visit schools. Through records and live performances, elementary students are introduced to some of the basic musical forms and to standard items of musical literature. Music of other cultures and music related to other aspects of elementary school social studies may also be utilized as part of the listening program.

An increased interest in creating music is apparent in many elementary schools, in part the result of the Contemporary Music Project for Creativity in Music Education sponsored by the Music Educators National Conference under a grant from the Ford Foundation. Children are manipulating all types of musical materials, experimenting with electronic music, employing modal scales and polyphonic devices, and even trying their hands at 12-tone composition.

Basic to much of the musical activity in the elementary school is rhythmic bodily movement, which is regarded as essential to the development of both skills and appreciation. Folk dancing is used in both primary and intermediate schools and, in the upper grades, may involve some very intricate movements. Dances from all parts of the world are employed and frequently taught in connection with social studies as well as physical and music education. This contrasts with the concentration on local dances found in countries with a strong native tradition such as England or Austria.

JUNIOR HIGH SCHOOL PROGRAMS

The NEA survey of U.S. music education showed that about half of all students in grades 7 through 9 were enrolled in music courses. The most common practice is to require a "general music" course at some time during this 3-year period, most frequently in the 7th grade but in both 7th and 8th grades in other systems. Still another frequently encountered pattern is to alternate music with another required subject such as art, home economics, or industrial arts. The nature of this general music course is ill-defined and varies from system to system or even teacher to teacher. In fact, the "general music" course at the junior high school level is recognized as a problem area in music education. One reason is the lack of specific objectives for a "general" course. Other factors that create problems include the difficulties associated with planning music activities for a time when boys' voices are changing.

In addition to the required course, junior high schools offer a number of music electives. Most of these are performance oriented. Among the opportunities to make music in junior high school are bands, orchestras, choruses, and various small ensembles both vocal and instrumental. Group or individual instruction in wind, string, and keyboard instruments may be available for both beginning and advanced students in a school with a well-developed music program. A few junior high schools offer additional courses such as theory and harmony or music literature. Schools in other countries generally continue required music classes in the years corresponding to grades 7–9, but offer much less elective music. Performing groups in European schools are generally extracurricular and do not as frequently strive for the high playing standards reached by some U.S. groups.

SENIOR HIGH SCHOOL PROGRAMS

Music in the senior high schools has placed strong emphasis on performance. A large U.S. high school with a well-developed music program and several music teachers could be expected to offer one or two mixed choirs, boys' glee club, girls' glee club, a madrigal group, and possibly some other small ensembles such as a boys' octet or a girls' triple trio, several wind bands (marching band, concert or symphonic band, intermediate band, pep band), orchestra and possibly a string ensemble, stage band, and a variety of instrumental ensembles (string quartets, brass sextets, woodwind quintets, piano trios). Such a school requires a large amount of equipment and many special facilities for music. The NEA study indicated that 81% of American secondary schools have at least one special room for music. In Australia the figure is 73%. Some American schools have an entirely separate building devoted to music activities.

The curriculum of the performing groups has been drawn widely from the musical literature available for the various groups. Some of the material chosen for performance at concerts or festivals has been of high quality, and an extremely high degree of skill has been characteristic of the better groups in all parts of the country. Some of the music performed, however, is of questionable musical value though it may require considerable technical skill to play or sing.

An important part of the performance program of the American high school is a highly developed system of contests or festivals. Once highly competitive, culminating in the selection of a few national winners, the program now is organized within states and smaller jurisdictions and is controlled for more educational ends. In the festivals, performing groups and individuals prepare numbers from selected lists of materials and play or sing them before recognized authorities who make constructive criticisms and award ratings. Though this system must be given a great deal of the credit for the high level of accomplishment that characterizes American secondary school music education, it is also being charged with some of the shortcomings recognized in the program. Music educators are accusing themselves of having developed a system in which it is possible to be "successful" by concentrating on playing or singing well a few selections for a concert or festival while neglecting to develop true musicianship in the students. While there is no suggestion that the level of achievement in performance should be lowered, the profession is saying that experience with more and better literature, as well as analysis of the compositions, may provide even better results.

In addition to the performing groups mentioned above, musical-dramatic works are produced in many high schools. Choral and instrumental groups combine to produce musical comedies or operas. Broadway shows have become very popular as high school productions. Cooperation between music and physical education departments has resulted in performances of ballet in a few schools.

Elective course offerings in music in a comprehensive high school include several years of music theory, music literature, and music history. Some high schools have offered a major in music for many years. Generally, where this is true, arrangements are made to grant credit for outside-the-school private instruction at a local conservatory or with a professional musician in the community. New York City has long had a High School of Music and Art and the Performing Arts as part of its public school system. In recent years this idea has developed under private (Interlochen, Michigan Arts Academy) and state (North Carolina) auspices. Summer music camps have become popular in the United States as well as in France, Hungary, England, Germany, Yugoslavia, and Austria.

The emphasis on performance that has characterized American music education at the secondary level has provided well for the talented and the motivated, but has had little to offer other students. Concern for the musical education of all the students has seemed to stop at grade 6, 7, or 8. In recent years some high schools have attempted to provide musical experiences for those not interested in performance through courses with a different orientation. Two approaches have emerged. One, called "related arts," attempts to increase students' understanding of music, dance, art, architecture, poetry, and theater by concentrating on their common elements. The other approach presents music as one of the humanities along with literature, art, architecture, history, and religion. Music educators have shown a willingness to cooperate in these endeavors but insist that significant musical learning must result from them. The feeling seems to be that music must not be allotted such a small portion of the total time in the course that it would be impossible to achieve a satisfactory level of musical accomplishment.

HISTORY OF MUSIC EDUCATION

The roots of music education in the United States go back to colonial times. However, music education has grown to its present state from a humble condition in the second third of the 19th century. Adult interest in the singing schools inevitably led to calls for introduction of music into the system of public education. Lowell Mason, probably best known today for his hymn tunes such as *Olivet, Watchman,* and *Bethany,* is generally credited with introducing music into the regular curriculum of the schools; in 1838 he taught without pay for a period to demonstrate the feasibility of such instruction. The Boston School Board then hired Mason as a regular teacher of music. Boston's example was followed by Buffalo, Pittsburgh, Cincinnati, Chicago, Cleveland, San Francisco, and St. Louis in the 1840's and 1850's. The following statement from the minutes of the Cincinnati Board of Trustees and Visitors of Common Schools gives an idea of the feeling that prompted the inclusion of music as a full-fledged subject in the curriculum of America's public schools.

"Let taste and skill in this beautiful art be diffused throughout our public schools, and every family will have a new resource of pleasure, every home a new attraction. Social intercourse will be more pleasant and cheerful, and an innocent and unfailing source of amusement will be rendered accessible alike to the humblest and wealthiest members of society. A wise and benevolent Creator has placed unbounded stores of enjoyment within the reach of all, by surrounding us with an atmosphere which can be the means of producing sweet sounds capable of being combined in an endless variety, and of being made to minister in the highest degree to a refined moral and intellectual taste. Then shall not the guardians of public instruction in this city permit all the youth to have access to this fountain of pleasure."

Singing classes were first introduced in the intermediate grades, and primary school music followed in a few years. The relatively few pupils who matriculated into high school were served up a rich diet of the choruses of Handel, Haydn, Mozart, and Mendelssohn. Singing was the primary activity, but the ability to sight-read was deemed essential, and elaborate systems were developed to realize this goal. Emphasis was laid on daily drill by the classroom teachers. Music supervisors made regular visits to assist and to check the work. The evidence indicates that a remarkable degree of success was achieved. Examinations of the type used in 19th century American schools still play an important role in the systems of music education in countries such as Austria, Germany, Finland, Switzerland, and Australia.

The picture had not changed greatly at the turn of the century, although some extracurricular musical activities in the form of small orchestras began to appear in U.S. secondary schools. With the advent of a new philosophy of education, the rote song approach to singing replaced drill on exercises. At about the same time other major changes began to take place. The class piano movement has its roots in the second decade of the 20th century. Orchestras were organized in a few cities. The development of class instrumental instruction by such figures as William Mitchell in Boston provided an essential element in the educational design that was to develop following World War I. The national effort in this conflict gave an impetus to all forms of music and particularly to the instrumental variety. Many service musicians found their way into the schools as teachers in the 1920's. For a brief period orchestras were in the ascendancy, but bands soon became the popular medium for the American secondary schools. A renewed interest in strings was a phenomenon of the post-World War II period.

Early music teachers in the U.S. schools were required only to know music. Many were European-trained professional musicians. What pedagogical training they had they received on the job from the supervisor of music. The classroom teachers, on the other hand, had been to normal school and may have had an introduction to music education there. During the last half of the 19th century, new music teachers were trained at summer institutes, many of which were sponsored by the publishers of music textbooks. The first normal school for music teachers was founded by Julia Etta Crane at Potsdam, N.Y., in 1884, but it was another 40 years or more before a full collegiate course for music educators became the standard. With the advent of college-trained professional music educators (trained largely as elementary specialists, band and orchestra conductors, or choir directors) all the elements of today's program were present.

PROBLEMS AND PROSPECTS

Many of the problem areas in the field of music education were identified at the Tanglewood Symposium called by the Music Educators National Conference in the summer of 1967. There, a group of music educators met with others representing the fields of philosophy, sociology, anthropology, history, psychology, labor, religion, philanthropy, business, and educational administration to discuss the role of music in American society. Among the challenges accepted by the profession as a result of the symposium was the problem of providing musical experience for all of the students in the secondary schools rather than merely the 10 to 20% normally found in the performing organizations.

Closely linked to this problem is the matter of relating the music offered in school to the current musical scene in the country as a whole. Accused at Tanglewood of being museum keepers of 18th and 19th century music, music educators showed much interest in music of other cultures, in jazz, and in popular music, long considered unsuitable for school use. The formation of the National Association of Jazz Educators in 1968 was evidence of the seriousness of this interest. Music educators also showed more concern for their responsibility to the community at large and their role in a program of continuing education.

Related to all of these problems is the need for more and better teachers. Probably the biggest problem to be solved is that of training teachers capable of working effectively in an expanded role or reeducating those teachers already in the field. Further complicating the problem is the fact that the present undergraduate curriculum in music education is already heavier than that for other teachers. Some colleges have already moved to a 5-year program, but this does not seem economically possible for many institutions.

The question of who is to teach music in the elementary schools is yet to be resolved satisfactorily. In the 19th century, special music teachers made assignments to the grade teachers and their classes and checked on the progress. With the advent of the self-contained classroom the grade teachers were expected to carry on their own music programs, and this has been the common practice in many school systems for the past 35 years or more. However, several factors seem to demand another solution. Elementary teachers are less well trained to do their own music teaching. The state of New York, for example, no longer requires music courses in the college program of elementary teachers. In addition, the report of the Music Educators National Conference Elementary Commission, which stresses musical understanding through conceptual learning, has pointed up the need for musically trained teachers in the lower grades. These factors would seem to indicate a move in the direction of having elementary music classes taught by music specialists. This is happening in some systems, but it is doubtful whether such a change can be made rapidly across the nation because of increased expense and because of a shortage in trained elementary music specialists. It is also true that many educators are still philosophically committed to having music taught by classroom teachers. In the light of the foregoing, a recommendation of an Australian study that "the teaching of music by specialists at primary level be adopted as a principle" is interesting.

New Technology. Various new media have been employed in music education and though none have yet revolutionized practices, there are indications that the future will see many innovations. Programmed learning and teaching machines have been most widely used in teaching music theory and ear training. Some experiments have been conducted on the teaching of performance techniques by such methods. Electronic systems for group instruction in piano and organ classes have found fairly wide acceptance. Many types of music education have been offered on both educational and commercial television. The televised concert has generally been more successful as education than attempts at teaching elementary music, but even with concerts the medium has not been used to its full potential. Many excellent films and filmstrips have been developed and are widely employed in the schools. These can truly be said to be an important part of music education, in contrast to the role played by television in most school systems.

Associations. Professional associations have played an important role in the development of music education in the United States. The oldest of these is the Music Teachers National Association, founded in 1876. It was and has remained an organization of private music teachers, but, especially in its early days, has had its influence on school music. In 1884 a department of music education of the National Education Association was formed, and several more specialized or regional groups followed. One of these, the Music Supervisors National Conference (1907) became the focal organization within the profession. Renamed the Music Educators National Conference in 1934, it became the NEA's music department in 1940. The Music Educators National Conference, with over 55,000 members in 1968, has provided much direction for the establishment of America's unique system of music education. Its national and divisional meetings provide the opportunity for thousands of teachers and administrators to participate in discussions and to observe demonstrations of successful practices. Its publications program and its two journals (*Music Educators Journal* and the *Journal of Research in Music Education*) disseminate the latest thinking in the field. Fifty-one state affiliated groups provide a means of carrying new ideas to all parts of the country and seven associated organizations (American Choral Directors Association, American String Teachers Association, College Band Directors National Association, National Association of College Wind and Percussion Instructors, National Association of Jazz Educators, National Band Association, and National School Orchestra Association) offer opportunity for music educators to work in their areas of special interest.

Another influential organization is the National Association of Schools of Music. Founded in 1924 and representing then a number of independent conservatories, it had become in the 1960's an organization that accredited the degree programs of over 300 schools and departments of music in America's universities and colleges. The NASM has had a great deal to do with raising the educational standards in music at the collegiate level in the country, thus virtually eliminating the once common practice of students going to Europe for serious music study.

See also MUSIC; MUSICAL ELEMENTS AND TERMS; MUSICAL INSTRUMENTS.

CHARLES L. GARY
Music Educators National Conference

Bibliography

Bartle, Graham, *Music in Australian Schools* (Victoria, Australia, 1968).
Birge, Edward Bailey, *History of Public School Music in the United States* (Washington 1926, 1966).
Kowall, Bonnie C., ed., *Perspectives in Music Education* (Washington 1966).
Kraus, Egon, ed., *Comparative Music Education* (Mainz, Germany, 1962).
Murphy, Judith, and Sullivan, George, *Music in American Society, An Interpretive Report of the Tanglewood Symposium* (Washington 1968).
National Education Association, *Music and Art in the Public Schools* (Washington 1963).

MUSIC FESTIVALS. Music festivals can be traced at least back to the 11th century, when the French troubadours took part in the *puys,* or festivals, of the literary and musical guilds. Competitions and prizes were parts of the festivities, and the *puy d'Euvreux* was held annually from 1570 to 1614. These festivals became models for the *Sängerkriege* of the German Minnesinger and the Eisteddfod of the Welsh bards. In England, the Festival of the Sons of the Clergy was founded in 1655, and in 1724 the choral societies of Gloucester, Worcester, and Hereford joined in the Three Choirs Festival; both survived into modern times. England has had a number of other annual festivals, such as those at Norwich, Birmingham, and Leeds, as well as such irregular events as the famed Handel Festivals.

The Niederrheinische Musikfeste began in 1817, being held alternately at Cologne, Düsseldorf, and Aachen. The Tonkünstlerfeste of the Allgemeiner Deutscher Musikverein were inaugurated by Franz Liszt in 1861; they went on, in different German cities, annually until 1932. Then there have been the periodic festivals also to honor composers, often held at their birthplaces: the Beethovenfeste at Bonn, the Bachfeste at Eisenach, and the Mozartfeste at Salzburg. Wagner himself started the Bayreuther Festspiele, which have been held annually, with some interruptions, ever since.

Ross Madden from Black Star

Song recital at the music festival in Aspen, Colorado.

In America, large festivals began in Boston with one given by the Handel and Haydn Society in 1857 in that city and in Worcester during the next year. Like them special, not annual, were two festivals organized by Patrick Sarsfield Gilmore (1829–1892) in Boston; of mammoth proportions, these were single occasions of five days' concerts each. The first (1869) commemorated the end of the Civil War, the second (1872) that of the Franco-Prussian War. Among the oldest of the present-day festivals are those held annually at Worcester, Mass. (1871), and the Bach Festival at Bethlehem, Pa. (1900).

The Eastman Festival of American Music began in 1931 to present an annual week's programs of American music. From 1925 on, the Berkshire Festivals at the Library of Congress, Washington, D.C., presented annual programs of chamber music. The International Society of Contemporary Music has concerned itself with festivals of music by modern composers since 1923; these have been held in cities all over the world. The January 1961 issue of the magazine *Musical America* listed 69 summer festivals for North America, 60 for Europe, and 2 for Asia.

A few of the most notable festivals of today are: the Berkshire Festival of the Boston Symphony Orchestra, held at Tanglewood, Mass.; the Festival of Two Worlds, under the direction of the Italo-American composer-librettist Gian Carlo Menotti, held at Spoleto, Italy; the annual festival at Aspen, Colo.; the annual Pablo Casals festival, first held in southern France, but now located at San Juan, Puerto Rico; the annual season of festival opera at Glyndebourne, near Lewes, England; and—perhaps the most renowned of all contemporary festivals—that given annually at Salzburg, Austria, which has far outgrown its original purpose of commemorating Mozart, and now includes music by other composers as well.

In addition to special festivals of the sort mentioned above, many cities and other locales throughout the Western World present annual outdoor concert and operatic seasons. Festivals of jazz have proliferated, chiefly on the model of that held for several years at Newport, R. I. It has been interesting to see the festival idea reaching the Near East and the Far East, with events held at Baalbek, Lebanon, and Osaka, Japan.

Edited and enlarged by
HERBERT WEINSTOCK.

MUSICAL ELEMENTS AND TERMS.

Music is the meaningful organization of sounds. Any sound is produced by the vibration of air or of a solid body. When such vibrations are irregular, the sound is a *noise;* when they are regular, the sound is a musical *tone.* Music depends in the main on tones, but does not exclude noise (as in drums, cymbals, or clappers). Slow vibrations produce the tones and noises which we call low; faster vibrations produce higher sounds. The practical range of music extends from about 40 to about 4,000 vibrations per second, but goes beyond these limits in accessory tones, such as partials and combination tones (see ACOUSTICS).

The exact number (frequency) of vibrations or cycles gives a tone its *pitch.* In a narrower sense, we use the word pitch to refer to the standard height of the tone a′, from which all musical tones derive their pitches. It is given to all tuning forks and is played by an oboist when an orchestra tunes up. The American standard a′ is today 440 vibrations; European pitch is often somewhat lower.

The reader who wishes to make himself familiar with the elements and basic terms of music may look at a piano. On its keyboard he finds all the tones in a continuous sequence rising from the lowest (left side) to the highest (right side). The keys, white and black, alternate in a characteristic pattern seven times repeated. This consists of two easily visible groups of black keys —one of two, one of three—and of the neighboring white keys, seven in number. The white keys, in ascending order beginning to the left of each group of two black notes are called by the letters C D E F G A B.

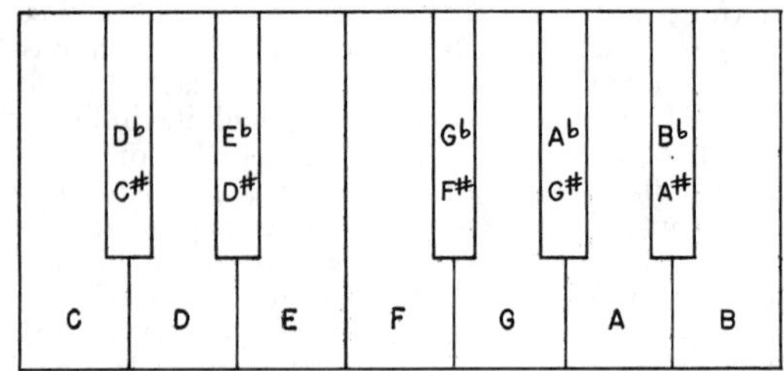

Looking at these white keys, we are under the impression that every pair of contiguous tones must be musically equidistant. But the neat arrangement deceives: while the size of a normal step, like C-D and D-E is that of a whole tone or tone, E-F and B-C form only semitones half as wide as a whole tone. The reader is here, not for the last time, confronted with an ambiguous name: tone has the two distinct meanings of an individual sound and of a whole-tone interval between two such tones. This ambiguity is probably the reason why the word *note,* originally confined to the visual symbol of an individual tone when written or printed, is often used for the tone itself.

Looking again at the keyboard, one realizes that there is no black key between those white keys which form only semitones; the black keys serve to split whole tones into semitones. Owing to their intermediate position, they alter both of their white neighbors; a black between C and D sharpens the lower neighbor by a semitone and flattens the upper neighbor by a semitone. Hence the black keys have two names each, according to their position and function within a scale or key: (1) C sharp or D flat; (2) D sharp or E flat; (3) F sharp or G flat; (4) G sharp or A flat; (5) A sharp or B flat. Abbreviating symbols are ♯ for the sharp and ♭ for the flat. Any sharp or flat is, when necessary, revoked by a natural (♮), which re-establishes the related natural tone.

Any semitone, such as E-F, is also called a minor second, and any whole tone, such as C-D, a major second. The step one semitone wider, such as C-E♭ or as D-F, is a minor third; four semitones, like C-E, form a major third. There is a perfect fourth from C to F; an augmented fourth, from C to F sharp or from F to B; a perfect fifth, from C to G; a minor sixth, from E to C; a major sixth, from D to B; a minor seventh, from C to B flat; a major seventh, from C to B; an octave, from C to C.

The word *octave* is another ambiguous term. It indicates (1) the distance enclosed between 2 tones separated by 12 semitones, which is characterized by a difference in altitude, one note being lower and one higher, but at the same time by a similarity of their essential quality, both of them being C's or D's or E's, which accounts for the repetition of the musical letter-names above and below the normal pattern indicated before; (2) the simultaneous occurrence of two such tones; (3) the sequence of tones between any tone and its octave; and (4) the same sequence without the eighth tone. It is in accordance with meaning (4) that musicians speak of octaves in different (rising) pitches as contra-, great-, small-, one-, two-, three-, four-, and five-lined octaves, the names being extended to all individual tones between C and B:

contra octave: $C_1D_1E_1F_1G_1A_1B_1$
great octave: C D E F G A B
small octave: c d e f g a b
one-lined ('middle') octave: c'd'e'f'g'a'b'
two-lined octave: c"d"e"f"g"a"b"
three-lined: $c^3d^3e^3f^3g^3a^3b^3$
four-lined: $c^4d^4e^4f^4g^4a^4b^4$

Between any C and its octave, the white keys form semitones at the third and seventh steps. But this arrangement is by no means the only one that music uses. Under the somewhat bewildering name of a *major* scale (so called because it includes a major third), it is opposed to the *minor* scale from A to A, in which a semitone, B-C, forms the second step and provides the interval of a minor third (A-C) where there is a major third in a major scale.

The other possible octave sections of the white-key row are obsolete, but survive in the ecclesiastical modes: D-D is the so-called first or Dorian mode; E-E, the third or Phrygian mode; F-F, the fifth or Lydian mode; G-G, the seventh or Mixolydian mode; A-A, the second or Hypodorian mode; B-B, the fourth or Hypophrygian mode; C-C, the sixth or Hypolydian mode; D-D, the eighth or Hypomixolydian mode (which differs from the Dorian mode in its inner structure). In all these octaves, the relative position of the semitones is the distinguishing feature.

However, these octaves are by no means confined to the white keys. With the aid of black keys, the major or the minor scale or that of an ecclesiastical mode can start on each of the 12 keys between C and B and yet preserve the characteristic position of its semitones. This is expressed by the well-known addition of tone-letters: if Beethoven's First Symphony is in C major, its basic scale is built on C, while that of his Second Symphony in D major has the same position of the semitones, but is based on a scale begun a whole tone higher. In this case the major character can be achieved only by introducing two black keys, F sharp and C sharp, without which the mode would be Dorian instead of major. In a similar way, Beethoven's Fifth Symphony in C minor needs the flatting of E, A, and B to make the C scale minor.

In order to simplify notation, the composer does not sharp or flat the notes in question each time they occur, but marks them at the beginning of each staff with the so-called key signature: one sharp for F denotes both G major and E minor; 2 sharps for F and C denote D major and B minor; 3 sharps for F, C, and G denote A major and F sharp minor; 4 sharps for F, C, G, and D denote E major and C sharp minor; 5 sharps for F, C, G, D, and A denote B major and G sharp minor; 6 sharps for F, C, G, D, A, and E denote F sharp major and D sharp minor; 7 sharps for F, C, G, D, A, E, and B denote C sharp major and A sharp minor. One flat for B, on the other hand, denotes F major and D minor; 2 flats for B and E denote B flat major and G minor; 3 flats for B, E, and A denote E flat major and C minor; 4 flats for B, E, A, and D denote A flat and F minor; 5 flats for B, E, A, D, and G denote D flat major and B flat minor; 6 flats for B, E, A, D, G, and C denote G flat major and E flat minor; 7 flats for B, E, A, D, G, C, F denote C flat major and A flat minor.

With key signatures, the reader has entered the maze of notation. Individual notes are expressed by oval *heads* placed higher up or lower down according to their position in musical space and on the keyboard. In order to make this position clear beyond doubt, the note heads are written on a *staff* of five horizontal lines, each line and each space between lines determining a definite note or tone of the scale: from below, the five lines stand for e'g'b'd"f", the four spaces for f'a'c"e", and the two places directly below the lowest and above the highest line, for d' and g". You can go beyond this narrow compass by placing additional notes, above or below the staff, on *ledger lines,* which are abbreviations of the regular lines not much wider than the note itself. But even with ledger lines (which are confusing when they exceed the number of three above each other), the one staff is not sufficient to cover the whole range of seven octaves that our music commonly uses. Hence the lower instruments, such as bassoons and double basses, and also the left hand of the pianist, avail themselves of a second staff, whose lines and spaces have a different meaning: the lines denote G B d f a, and the spaces A c e g, with corresponding ledger lines. Where too many ledger lines imperil easy reading, a dotted line, preceded by a figure 8 or 8va (*ottava*) indicates a transposition by an octave—upward if the line is drawn above the staff, downward if it is drawn below. To show the reader which of the two meanings a staff conveys, it carries one of two *clefs* right at the beginning—even before the key signature. That of the higher staff is a G, treble, or violin clef, , located on the second line from below and making it g'. That of the lower staff is an F or bass clef, , located on the fourth line from below and making it f. Besides these current two clefs, the viola has still preserved one of the otherwise extinct clefs of older times: the alto clef, , which makes the middle line a c'; the violoncello as well as the tenor trombone still cling to the tenor clef, which makes the fourth line from below a c' .

Speaking of high and low, of alto and tenor, it will be advisable to mention the principal types of musical altitude. Their terminology derives from the four or six registers of the human voice. Soprano or treble and alto or contralto belong to women and boys (although in earlier times the alto used to be a man's voice). The mezzosoprano stands between contralto and soprano. Tenor and bass or basso belong to men, with the baritone between. The instruments have taken over the vocal names: we speak of soprano cornets, alto clarinets, tenor trombones, and bass tubas.

While the staff of five lines and its clef take care of the pitches—whether a note is to be great C, small d, or anything else—the various shapes given to the notes themselves are symbols of their duration; the notes themselves show how long they shall be heard. The *head* of the note, to be sure, is always oval; and yet there are decisive differences. A plain white oval without any addition is the longest note in use, extending over four time units or *beats.* The half note, extending over two beats, is a white oval with a vertical *stem;* the quarter note, representing one beat, is a black oval with a stem. Beyond the quarter note, always dividing by two, we use a black oval with a stem and a *flag* at its end as the eighth note; with two flags, as the sixteenth; with three flags, as the thirty-second; with four flags, as the sixty-fourth; with five flags, as the one hundred and twenty-eighth. The stems, with

Whole-note Half-note Quarter Eighth Sixteenth Thirty-second

or without flags, grow upward from the right end of the head when the notes are located below the middle line of the staff. Upward from this line, the stem grows downward from the left end of the oval. In instrumental music, when two or more consecutive notes are flagged, the individual

flags are replaced by as many connecting *beams* to join them in a group; but such joining rarely exceeds the value of a quarter note; that is, it connects no more than two eighths, or four sixteenths, or eight thirty-seconds.

A dot to the right of a note adds 50 per cent to its time value: a dotted whole note measures three halves instead of two; a dotted half note, three quarters; and a dotted quarter, three eighths. Two dots behind a note add 50 plus 25 per cent: a double-dotted whole note measures $2 + 1 + \frac{1}{2}$ half notes or 7 quarters, and a double-dotted half note, $3\frac{1}{2}$ quarters or 7 eighths. A figure 3 above a group of three units indicates a triplet, which takes only the time of two such units. In a similar way, but by exception only, music uses duplets (to fill the time of three units), quadruplets (instead of three), and quintuplets (instead of four).

Often, a voice or an instrument stops for a little while in the progress of a piece. In such a case, the composer marks silence by *rests* of ade-

Whole-rest Half-rest Quarter Eighth Sixteenth Thirty-second

or

quate length. Rests, too, may be dotted or even double-dotted. A dotted half circle 𝄐, called *pause* or *fermata* (that is, stop), above an individual note lengthens it irrationally at the performer's discretion.

Music depends not only on the pitches and lengths of tones, but also on their organization in rhythmic patterns. Such organization, made visible in the well-ordered movements of the conductor, consists in the regular alternation of stressed and unstressed or less stressed time units or beats. Its symbol, the *time signature,* is usually a fraction of two figures, marked on the staff right after the key signature and not repeated on the following staffs. When the alternation of stresses is that of one beat stressed, one unstressed—we speak of two-four or 2/4 time, thus indicating that the pattern consists of two quarter notes. When, however, every stressed beat is followed by two unstressed beats, we speak of three-four or 3/4 time, thus indicating that the pattern requires the time of three quarter notes (as in the *Star-Spangled Banner* and *America,* as well as in all waltzes). When the stressed beat is followed by three unstressed beats or by one unstressed, one little stressed, and another unstressed, we speak of four-four time (as in *America the Beautiful*), with the signature 4/4 or 𝄴. When the time signature has 8 instead of 4 as the denominator, such as in 4/8, 5/8, 6/8, the unit of time is an eighth note. Inversely, the denominator 2, as in 3/2, indicates that the pattern comprises three half notes. A special case, remainder of an old, forgotten practice, is marked by 𝄵 : it is called by the archaic name *alla breve* and makes a four-four time twice as fast as it would normally be. The conductor marks only two beats within the pattern, which, though written as halves, mean actually quarters.

To facilitate playing and singing, the pattern is set between vertical bar lines running all the height of the staff. They almost always stand directly before a stressed note. The group inside the lines is called a *measure* or a *bar.* However, such a measure coincides with the rhythmical pattern only when the latter starts on the accented beat or *downbeat* (as we call it from the stressing gesture of the conductor). *God Bless America* and *My Country 'Tis of Thee* are examples. When, on the contrary, the pattern begins on the unaccented time or *upbeat* (as for example in the *Star-Spangled Banner* and *America the Beautiful*) it does not coincide with the measure.

Any deviation from the regular alternation of stressed and unstressed beats by introducing accents where normally there would be an unaccented beat—a well-known device in all forms of jazz and swing—is called syncopation.

Tempo.—Although the time signature very roughly implies a speed or tempo—a three-eight is necessarily faster than a three-four, and a three-four faster than a three-two—musical practice has better means to indicate different tempos (or, more correctly, *tempi*). In the first place, all languages use a moderate stock of terms denoting tempo and general mood. But more frequent in scores of any nationality are the internationally recognized Italian words *molto adagio,* very slow; *adagio,* slow; *largo,* broad; *larghetto,* rather broad; *andante,* not too slow; *andantino,* usually still less slow; *moderato,* moderate; *allegro,* brisk; *allegretto,* usually less brisk; *presto,* fast; *prestissimo,* as fast as possible. But these and other similar indications at the head of a piece are more or less vague, and their appropriate interpretation has often been open to discussion. A more precise direction, generally together with one of the Italian terms, is found in a short equation above the signature of the first staff of a piece. This may read, say, ♩ = MM 80. The double letter MM refers to the metronome that the mechanic Johann Nepomuk Maelzel (Mälzel) invented in 1816. It is commonly a pyramidal box with a ticking pendulum whose speed can be regulated by shifting a little weight in front of a calibrated plate: 80 means that by shifting the weight, the pendulum should be made to tick 80 times per minute and that every tick should mark a quarter note. Electric metronomes now are widely used. Changes within a piece are prescribed as *accelerando,* growing faster, and *rallentando,* growing slower. *A tempo* restores the original tempo.

Intensity.—The intensity, or volume of sound,

of an individual tone or a whole section is marked by the abbreviations pp for *pianissimo,* very soft; p for *piano,* soft; mp for *mezzopiano,* half-soft; mf for *mezzoforte,* half-loud; f for *forte,* loud; ff for *fortissimo,* very loud. Exceptionally, the extreme intensities have been exaggerated up to ppppp and fffff. Increasing intensity is called *crescendo* (growing, abbreviated *cresc.*); decreasing intensity, *decrescendo* or *diminuendo* (*decr., dim.*). Oftener, these words are replaced by graphic symbols which allow marking exactly the duration of the increase or decrease: the former one by a prone, acute angle open to the right; the latter one by a similar angle open to the left. An extraordinary accent on an individual note appears in notation as sf, for *sforzando* (strengthening), or as a short, acute angle, either prone or pointing downward.

There are finally a few signs for the correct execution of individual notes and whole groups of notes. A dot or accent above a note means *staccato* (detached), and requires a light touch and prompt release of the note, irrespective of its original time value. The opposite of staccato is *legato* (joined), which appears in notation as a shallow arc reaching from the first to the last note of the joined group. While this kind of arc is called a *slur,* the name *tie* is reserved for a similar arc that connects two notes of the same pitch whenever it is not possible or wise to write them as a whole (for instance, when a note reaches beyond a bar line or when there is no proper symbol for the time value of a note, as, let us say, for a half note plus an eighth). Second and later notes covered by a tie are not sounded anew.

Musical Forms.—The concept *form* reaches from the smallest to the largest structural units. The smallest unit is a *phrase,* generally of two or four or even eight measures, which ends in an *open cadence,* that is, a formula that leaves the listener in suspense. Only a second phrase, similar in some respect, ends in a *closed cadence* that gives a satisfactory conclusion. The two phrases, called also *antecedent* and *consequent,* form a *period.* Periods can be multiplied and grouped in a number of ways; indeed, they can be repeated without any change. When such is the case, the composer marks the repetition by a *repeat* sign: a double bar line with, toward the section to be repeated, two dots above and below the middle line of the staff. This seriation of even periods is characteristic of simple songs and of dances. In certain dances, such as the minuet which has survived in our symphonies (either in its original form or, since Beethoven, as the scherzo), the structure is ternary (threefold) or *da capo,* the first part being repeated after the second part. The composer marks this repetition either by reprinting the first part in full or by adding, after the second part, the cue *da capo* (from the beginning), to which might be added *dal fine* (to the end). But if he does this, he must print the word *fine* at the end of the first part. The second, middle section of a minuet is called *trio,* because the masters of the 17th century gave it to three solo instruments, whereas the outer sections were left to the full orchestra.

In the *rondo,* which has often been used to conclude sonatas and symphonies, the periods are arranged in a peculiar way: the sections 1,3,5,7, and so on are similar or identical, while the sections 2,4,6,8, and so on differ, both from the first one and from each other.

The slow movement of a symphony or sonata often consists in a set of *variations.* In its basic form, such a set requires a *theme,* usually in the shape of one or several periods, and a number of individual variations that disguise the theme enough to give it in all their melodic and harmonic transformations an ever new interest without effacing its general outline and character.

Preceding these typical movements of the classical symphony and sonata—the slow variations, the minuet or scherzo with its minuet, and the rondo—we most often find a first and principal movement in *sonata form.* Before describing it, two bewildering points must be clarified. In the first place, the so-called sonata form belongs not only to sonatas for piano alone or for piano and some other instrument, but also to all typical chamber music, such as trios, quartets, and quintets for three, four, and five instruments, to symphonies for full orchestra, and to concertos for some solo instrument with the accompaniment of the orchestra. In the second place, although these types of compositions have as a rule four movements (concertos have but three), only the first movement and sometimes the last have the sonata form proper. It begins with an energetic first theme in the *tonic,* that is, the principal key of the movement, and contrasts it with a more lyrical second theme in some related key. This duplex *exposition* is repeated. Then comes the *development,* during which characteristic fragments of the principal theme or of both themes are used "to fight it out" until the potentialities of the thematic material are exhausted. At this point, the exposition reappears victoriously as the *recapitulation* and ends in a decisive *coda,* or conclusion. In concertos, the coda is delayed by a *cadenza,* in which the soloist, without the orchestra, is allowed to show his bravura technique. This section is a leftover from the virtuoso times of the 18th century, and should be improvised. However, the cadenzas that we hear today are ready made and carefully studied.

There is, besides the sonata proper, a *sonatina* in smaller proportions, both as to size and as to weight. The special form of *fugue,* which may be independent or may serve as the climax of a last sonata movement, is explained in a separate article.

While all these forms are more or less strict (though all of them leave a good deal of freedom to the composer), other forms are free by definition: the *toccata,* in which chordal episodes alternate with rapid passages, the loosely written *rhapsody,* and the informal *fantasia.*

See also separate articles on musical forms.

Based on an article by the late CURT SACHS; edited and revised by HERBERT WEINSTOCK.

MUSICAL TERMS

The following glossary includes some of the terms and phrases that occur most frequently in the vocabulary of music. Important terms treated separately in this encyclopedia are designated by the reference: *See separate article.* Many English or Anglicized terms that are self-explanatory have been omitted here.

A battuta (It.).—Return to strict time after a deviation.
A cappella (It.).—Unaccompanied choral music.
Accelerando (It.).—Increasing in rapidity.
Accent. The stress or emphasis given to certain notes or passages.
Acciaccatura (It.).—In harpsichord, and sometimes in other keyboard, music, an ornament consisting of the

striking and immediate release of the lower second of a note; in slow tempos, often indicates arpeggiation.
Accidentals.—Occasional sharps, flats, and naturals placed before notes.
Accompaniment.—See separate article.
Adagio (It.).—Slowly; generally, slower than *andante* but faster than *largo.*
À deux (Fr.); **A due** (It.).—Opposite of *divisi;* indicating that two instruments are to play the same notes.
Ad libitum (Lat.).—At will or discretion, implying that the execution of a passage is left to the preference of the performer, who may include or omit a part or voice so marked or is at liberty to introduce embellishments.
Affettuoso, Affettuosamente, or **Con affetto** (It.).—With pathos and tenderness.
Agitato or **Con agitazione** (It.).—Agitatedly.
Alla breve (It.).—An indication (often 𝄵) that in common time the half-note rather than the quarter-note is to be the unit. In other words, 2/2 rather than 4/4.
Allegretto (It.).—Slower than allegro, faster than andante.
Allegro (It.).—Fast. See also separate article.
Alto (It.).—Originally a high male voice, but now a female or boy's voice of low range (also called contralto). In French and Italian, the viola.
Amoroso, Amorevole, or **Con amore** (It.).—With love or affection; tenderly.
Andante (It.).—At a very moderate tempo. See also separate article.
Andantino (It.).—Usually somewhat faster (but, confusingly, at times somewhat slower) than andante.
Animato (It.), **Animé** (Fr.).—Animated.
Anthem.—A sacred choral composition, generally as composed to a Biblical text in English.
Antiphonal.—Sung in alternating choirs, particularly in polyphonic music composed for more than one chorus.
A piacere (It.).—At the performer's pleasure.
Appassionato (It.).—Impassioned.
Appoggiatura (It.).—In modern usage, a grace note that precedes an essential tone on an accented beat.
Aria (It.).—A song or air; particularly an operatic solo. See also separate article.
Arietta (It.).—Generally a brief aria.
Arioso (It.).—A singing style between that of full aria and that of recitative.
Arpeggio (It.).—Playing the notes of a chord (in imitation of harp procedure) in rapid succession rather than simultaneously.
Ars antiqua (Lat.).—Generally, the music of the 13th century.
Ars nova (Lat.).—Generally, music of the 14th century.
A tempo (It.).—Return to normal tempo after a deviation.
Atonal Music.—See separate article.
Attacca or **Attacca subito** (It.)—Begin the next section without waiting.
Aufführungspraxis (Ger.).—The way in which early music was, and should now be, performed.
Augmentation.—Doubling the time values of notes; also, increasing the width of intervals by a semitone.

Bar.—Bar line (separating two measures), or, confusingly, a measure itself.
Baroque Music.—See separate article.
Bass.—The lowest male voice; the lowest member of many instrumental families; the lowest part or voice in a multivoiced texture. See also separate article.
Basso continuo (It.).—Thoroughbass.
Beat.—See separate article on RHYTHM.
Beats.—An acoustical effect resulting from the interference of two sound waves of differing frequencies.
Begleitung (Ger.).—Accompaniment.
Bel canto (It.).—An Italian style of singing which emphasizes agility and beauty of tone; also used to describe music intended for such singing.
Berceuse (Fr.).—A lullaby.
Binary.—A two-section form in which each section is repeated.
Bis (Fr.).—Indicating that a note or passage is to be repeated; also a synonym of encore.
Bitonality.—The use of two tonalities simultaneously.
Bolero (Span.).—See separate article.
Bouffe (Fr.).—See *buffo.*
Bow.—See separate article.
Bravura (It.).—Display of technical brilliance.
Breve.—An obsolete note equivalent to two whole notes.
Brio (It.).—Vigor, spirit, or noisiness.
Buffo (It.).—Comic.
Burletta.—See separate article.

Cabaletta (It.).—Usually, the rapid closing section of an operatic aria.
Cacophony.—Undesirable sound, disagreeable discord.
Cadence.—See separate article.
Cadenza (It.).—See separate article.
Calando (It.).—Becoming softer and slower gradually.
Calypso.—See separate article.
Canon.—See separate article.
Cantabile (It.).—In a singing manner.
Cantata (It.).—See separate article.
Canticle, Canticum (Lat.), or **Cantique** (Fr.).—Psalm-like Biblical songs outside of the Psalter of David; they include the *Benedictus, Magnificat,* and *Nunc dimittis.*
Cantillation.—Chanting in plain song style.
Cantor.—In a German Protestant church, the musical director; in Jewish services, the solo singer; in Catholic services, a soloistic choral leader.
Canzone.—See separate article.
Canzonetta (It.).—A brief or light *canzona.*
Capriccio (It.).—A brief composition of capricious nature.
Carillon (Fr.).—Bells played through a mechanism.
Carol.—Usually, a traditional Christmas song; also other devotional songs in gay or joyful style.
Castrato (It.).—A male singer whose preadolescent voice has been preserved by emasculation.
Catch.—A round, particularly of the 18th century in England.
Cavatina (It.).—In Italian opera, a vocal solo simpler, and often shorter, than an aria; often in a slow tempo and without repeated words. See also separate article.
Cembalo (It.).—The word for harpsichord in Italian and German.
Chaconne (Fr.).—A musical dance form consisting of continuous variations on a sequence of harmonically interrelated chords. See also *Passacaglia.*
Chamber Music.—Generally, instrumental music of an intimate sort, with a single player for each part.
Change Ringing.—See separate article.
Chanson (Fr.).—A song; also special song forms of the *trouvères* and the 16th century.
Chant.—See separate article.
Choir.—See separate article on CHORAL MUSIC.
Choral Music.—See separate article.
Chorale.—See separate article.
Chromaticism.—See separate article.
Clavecin (Fr.).—Harpsichord.
Clavichord.—An early stringed keyboard instrument in which the strings are set into vibration by tangents that simultaneously determine the vibrating lengths (pitches) of the strings struck.
Clef (Fr.).—See separate article.
Coda (It.).—A section added to a composition beyond the end of its natural form.
Col legno (It.).—Indicates that the strings of a violin are to be struck with the stick of the bow rather than bowed.
Coloratura (It.).—Ornamental and/or expressive runs, trills, leaps, and other virtuosic decorations, especially in 18th- and 19th-century Italian opera; by transference, a singer able to perform such decorations.
Comodo (It.).—At a convenient speed; without hurry, in a leisurely tempo.
Concertante (It.).—In the *concerto grosso* manner—that is, with parts for several soloistic instruments or for solo voices.
Concerto (It.).—See separate article.
Concerto grosso (It.).—A baroque compositional manner in which several soloistic instruments are contrasted with the full orchestral ensemble.
Concord.—See separate article on DISSONANCE.
Conducting.—See separate article.
Consonance.—See separate article on DISSONANCE.
Continuo (It.).—See *Basso continuo.*
Contralto (It.).—The lowest female singing voice.
Counterpoint.—See separate article.
Countertenor.—In modern usage, an adult male singer trained to sing soprano and contralto parts.
Crescendo (It.).—Gradually increasing in loudness.
Cyclic.—Generally, a style of composition in which several separate movements make use of some identical thematic material.

Da capo (It.).—To be repeated from the beginning.
Dal segno (It.).—To be repeated from a point indicated by the sign §.
Decrescendo (It.).—Gradually decreasing in loudness.
Development.—A characteristic compositional procedure in modern sonata form, in which thematic units are segmented and the segments subjected to various alterations, the aim being increased tension, drama, or struggle.
Diapason.—See separate article.
Diatonic.—See separate article.
Dièse (Fr.) or **Diesis** (It.).—Sharp.
Diminuendo (It.).—Gradually decreasing in loudness.
Diminution.—Halving the time values of notes; also, diminishing the width of intervals by a semitone.
Discord.—See separate article on DISSONANCE.
Dissonance.—See separate article.
Divertimento (It.).—An 18th century instrumental form, generally light in nature, midway between the suite and the symphony.
Divisi (It.).—Indicating that an instrumental group is

to be divided, each section then playing different notes.
Dolce (It.).—Sweetly, softly.
Dominant.—The fifth tone of the diatonic scale, either major or minor. In the scale of C the dominant is G, and in the scale of G the dominant is D. See separate article on HARMONY.
Dot.—Increases the time value of a note or rest by one half.
Dur (Germ.).—Major.
Durchkomponiert (Ger.).—Through-composed.
Dynamics.—Degrees of loudness and softness, indicated by signs, words, and abbreviations.
Empfindung (Ger.).—Emotion, passion.
Enharmonic.—See separate article.
Etude.—A piece intended to assist the technical training of a student of performance.
Exposition.—In a composition, the first presentation of the principal thematic material.
Falsetto (It.).—See separate article.
Fandango (Sp.).—See separate article.
Fantasia (It.) or **Fantasy.**—See separate article on FANTASIA.
Fermata (It.).—Pause.
Fifth.—See separate article; also see article on HARMONY.
Figured Bass.—See separate article on BASS.
Fioritura (It.).—Ornament, *coloratura.*
Flat.—The sign ♭ to indicate the lowering of a tone by a semitone.
Forte (It.).—Loud.
Fortissimo (It.).—Very loud.
Fourth.—The fourth tone in a scale; also an interval between a tone and the tone third above it; see also separate articles on HARMONY and SCALE.
Fugato (It.).—In fugal manner, particularly as part of a nonfugal composition.
Fugue.—See separate article.
Fundamental.—The lowest tone of a chord; also, in acoustics, the first harmonic; see also separate articles on ACOUSTICS and HARMONY.

Galop.—A hopping, rapid 19th century dance.
Gavotte.—See separate article.
Gebrauchsmusik (Ger.).—Music intended for practical use by amateurs.
Giocoso (It.).—Playful, jocose.
Giusto (It.).—Just, in exact tempo.
Glee.—See separate article.
Glissando (It. Gallicism).—In a sliding manner, usually to indicate the playing of a series of contiguous notes on a keyboard or harp by running the backs of the fingers over them.
Grace Note.—An ornamental note whose duration lessens by that much the duration of the note thus ornamented.
Grave (It.).—Solemn, slow, often low in pitch.
Gregorian Chant.—See separate article.
Ground Bass.—A recurring melodic phrase above which the upper parts or voices are varied. See also separate article.
Gusto (It.).—Taste or appropriateness.
Habanera (Sp., often incorrectly *Habañera*).—An originally Afro-Cuban dance in moderate duple time, related to the tango.
Harmonics.—See separate article; see also separate article on ACOUSTICS.
Harmony.—See separate article.
Heldentenor (Ger.).—A brilliant, powerful tenor voice adapted especially to heroic Wagnerian roles.
Hexachord.—A group of six diatonic tones, the third and fourth separated by a semitone, employed theoretically by Guido d'Arezzo.
Homophony.—A musical texture in which a principal melodic voice or part is supported chordally; opposite of polyphony.
Imitation.—A musical texture in which a melody or motive is stated by one voice or part and then, successively, in other voices or parts. See separate articles on CANON and FUGUE.
Improvisation.—Instant creation of music by the performer; also a composition giving the effect of such extemporizing.
Intermezzo (It.).—Originally a brief comic opera performed between the acts of a more serious play or opera; later an instrumental interlude or a brief independent piece.
Interval.—See separate article.
Jota (Sp.).—An Aragonese dance performed by couples, usually with castanet accompaniment.
Key.—See separate article.
Kyrie (Gr.).—See separate article on KYRIE ELEISON.
Ländler (Ger.).—A slow Austrian dance in triple time, the immediate predecessor of the waltz.
Largo (It.).—Very slow; see also separate article.
Leading Tone.—The seventh degree of a scale.
Lebhaft (Ger.).—Lively.
Legato (It.).—To be performed with no appreciable lacunae between successive tones; smooth and connected; the opposite of staccato.
Leggero, Leggiero or **Con leggerezza** (It.).—With lightness and grace, without excessive legato.
Leitmotiv (Ger. *Leitmotif*).—See separate article.
Lento (It.).—Slowly; usually faster than largo, slower than adagio.
Libretto (It.).—The literary text set in an opera or oratorio.
Lied (Ger.).—A song in German.
Lusingando (It.).—Persuasively, as with flattery.
Lustig (Ger.).—Cheerful, joyous.
Madrigal.—See separate article.
Maestoso (It.).—Majestic.
Magnificat (Lat.).—See separate article
Major.—See separate articles on HARMONY, MODES, and SCALE.
Malagueña (Sp.)—Several varieties of dances from the Spanish provinces of Malaga and Murcia.
Marcato (It.).—Marked, emphatic.
Marziale (It.).—Martial, marchlike.
Matins.—See separate article.
Mazurka (Pol.).—See separate article.
Measure.—See separate article.
Melisma (Gr.).—A vocal passage on a single text syllable.
Melodrama.—Originally a spoken play with instrumental accompaniment; see also separate article.
Melodramma (It.).—A common Italian designation for opera.
Melody.—See separate article.
Mensural Music.—See separate article.
Messa di voce (It.).—Crescendo and decrescendo during the sustaining of a single vocal tone.
Mesto (It.).—Mournful.
Metronome.—A device for regulating the exact tempo of a musical performance; see also separate article.
Mezza voce (It.).—With half voice—that is, with diminished tonal volume.
Mezzo forte (It.).—Moderately loud.
Mezzo soprano (It.).—A female vocal range between soprano and contralto.
Microtone.—An interval narrower than a semitone.
Minor.—See separate article; see also articles on HARMONY, MODES, and SCALE.
Minuet.—See separate article.
Modes.—See separate article.
Moderato (It.).—In a moderate tempo, usually between allegro and andante.
Modulation.—See separate article.
Moll (Ger.).—Minor.
Monody.—Music sung by a single person; often all accompanied solo singing.
Monophony.—Music of a single melodic line without accompaniment, in contrast to polyphony and homophony.
Mordent.—An ornament consisting of the alternation of a principal tone and the tone just below it.
Morendo (It.).—Dying away; decreasing in volume and tempo.
Mosso (It.).—With motion or movement. Thus, *più mosso,* more rapidly; *meno mosso,* slower.
Motet.—See separate article.
Motive.—The melodic germ of a theme of melody. For leading motive, see article on LEITMOTIV.
Moto (It.).—Movement or motion; thus *con moto,* lively or rapid.
Musette (Fr.).—A 17th and 18th century French bagpipe.
Music Drama.—Opera in general; more specifically, the later operas of Richard Wagner.
Musicology.—See separate article.
Mute.—A device for softening or muffling the tones of an instrument.
Nachdrücklich (Ger.).—Emphatically.
Natural.—Said of a note that is neither sharped nor flatted; also the sign ♮ indicating such a note.
Neumes.—The signs used in the plain song notation of the Middle Ages.
Nuove musiche (It.).—The musical period around 1600, which witnessed the rise of opera, oratorio, and cantata.

Obbligato (It.).—Obligatory, as designating parts or instruments that may not be omitted. Incorrectly and very confusingly, it is often used instead of *ad libitum,* which means exactly the opposite.
Octave.—See separate article.
Offertory.—See separate article.
Opera.—See separate article.
Opéra-bouffe (Fr.) or **Opera buffa** (It.).—Comic opera.
Operetta (It.).—Originally a short opera; later a musico-dramatic work of light, usually sentimental, nature.
Opus (Lat.).—Work, used to indicate the chronological position in a composer's list of works of a single composition or group of compositions.
Oratorio (It.).—See separate article.
Orchestra (Gr.).—See separate article.
Organum (Lat.).—The earliest type of polyphonic music.
Ossia (It.).—Used to indicate an alternative version of a passage, usually one less difficult to perform.
Ostinato (It.).—A melodic phrase repeated persistently and clearly throughout a composition or section; it

does not change in pitch or move from voice to voice or part to part.
Overtones.—See separate article on Acoustics.
Overture.—See separate article.

Paraphrase.—A free interpretation or elaboration.
Parlando or **Parlante** (It.).—In singing, an approximation of the tones of ordinary speech, but in a declamatory manner.
Partial.—See separate article on Acoustics.
Partita (It.).—A 17th and 18th century designation for a series of variations or a suite.
Passacaglia (fr. Spanish *pasacalle?*).—A musical dance form consisting of continuous variations on a distinguishable *ostinato,* usually in the bass, but sometimes in an upper part or voice.
Passion.—A musical setting of the Passion of Jesus Christ from one of the four Evangelists. See also separate article on Passion Music.
Pastorale.—See separate article.
Pedal Point (also **Organ Point**).—See separate article.
Perdendo (It.).—Dying away.
Pesante (It.).—Weightily, heavily, with importance.
Piacere (It.).—Pleasure; thus, *a piacere,* at the player's pleasure or fancy.
Piano (abbreviation of It. *pianoforte*).—See separate article.
Pitch.—Highness or lowness of sound.
Pizzicato (It.).—Plucked, as opposed to bowed.
Plainsong.—See separate article.
Polka.—See separate article.
Polonaise.—See separate article.
Polyphony.—See separate article.
Polyrhythm.—Simultaneous employment of contrasting rhythms.
Polytonality.—The use of two (bitonality) or more tonalities simultaneously.
Portamento (It.).—Smooth gliding from one vocal tone to another through the intervening tones.
Prelude.—See separate article.
Prestissimo (It.).—As fast as possible.
Presto (It.).—Very fast.

Rallentando (It.).—Growing gradually slower.
Recapitulation.—In sonata form, the restatement—often in altered form—of the chief subject after development.
Recitative.—See separate article.
Resolution.—The procedure of moving from a discord to a relative concord.
Rhythm.—See separate article.
Ricercar or **Ricercare** (It.).—Generally, an exercise, usually fugal, for the voice or an instrument.
Rinforzando (It.).—Practically synonymous with *sforzando,* the sudden stressing of a note or chord.
Ritardando (It.).—Gradually growing slower.
Ritenuto (It.).—A sudden decrease in tempo.
Rondeau (Fr.).—See separate article.
Rondo (It.).—See separate article on Rondeau.
Round.—See separate article.
Rubato (It.).—A performance style involving holding some tones longer than their indicated time value while curtailing others by way of compensation.

Saltarello (It.).—A 16th century Italian dance in fast triple meter.
Sanctus (Lat.).—In the Ordinary of the Mass, the fourth of the five invariable sections. See also separate article on Mass, The.
Saraband.—See separate article.
Scale.—See separate article.
Scherzando (It.).—Playful, joking, in the manner of a scherzo.
Scherzo (It.).—See separate article.
Scordatura (It.).—Abnormal tuning of a stringed instrument to make possible the playing of unusual passages.
Second.—The second tone in a scale; also an interval between a tone and the tone next above it; see also separate articles on Harmony and Scale.
Segno (It.).—A sign resembling an S and indicating the beginning or end of a section to be played or repeated.
Segue (It.).—Proceed to the following section without an intervening pause.
Seguidilla (Sp.).—A Spanish dance.
Semplice (It.).—Simple, unadorned.
Serenade.—See separate article.
Sforzando or **Sforzato** (It.).—A sudden strong emphasis of a note or chord.
Sharp.—The sign ♯ to indicate the raising of a tone by a semitone.
Siciliano (It.).—A 17th and 18th century Italian dance in dignified 6/8 or 12/8 meter, with dotted rhythms.
Signature.—The signs placed at the beginning of a composition or staff to indicate key and tempo.
Sinfonietta (It.).—A small symphony; also a small symphonic orchestra.
Singspiel (Ger.).—Opera; more specifically opera with spoken dialogue.
Slancio (It.).—Impetuosity.
Smorzando (It.).—Dying away.
Solfège (Fr.) or **Solfeggio** (It.).—The use of "sol-fa" syllables in a singing exercise.
Solmization.—Designation of the notes of the scale by syllables rather than by letters.
Sonata (It.).—See separate article.
Sonatina (It.).—See separate article on Sonata.
Soprano (It.).—The highest female voice; also the highest part in polyphonic music and the highest instrument of a family.
Sordino (It.).—The Italian word for an instrumental mute.
Sospirando (It.).—Sighing.
Sostenuto or **Sostenendo** (It.).—Sustaining a tone; also diminishing a tempo.
Sprechstimme (Ger.).—The oratorical type of speech used in the melodrama.
Stabat Mater (Lat.).—See separate article.
Staccato (It.).—To be played in a detached, brief, manner; the opposite of legato.
Staff.—See separate article.
Strepitoso (It.).—Noisy.
Stretto (It.).—See separate article on Fugue.
Stringendo (It.).—Increasing in tempo.
Subdominant.—The fourth degree of a scale; see also separate articles on Harmony and Scale.
Suite.—In instrumental music, a composition made up of independent sections, often of dances or of sections of opera and ballet.
Symphonic Poem.—A one-movement orchestral composition usually related to extramusical ideas or subject matter.
Symphony.—See separate article.
Syncopation.—A modification of musical rhythm caused by stressing the weak beat.

Tamtam.—A gong, not to be confused with tom-tom.
Tango.—See separate article.
Tarantella (It.).—See separate article.
Tempo.—See separate article.
Teneramente (It.).—Tenderly.
Tenor.—See separate article.
Tenuto (It.).—To be held or sustained.
Ternary.—A three-section form (ABA), in which, after a second section, the first section is repeated.
Tessitura (It.).—The prevalent range of a vocal part.
Theme.—A melodic subject of an entire musical composition or of a movement.
Third.—The third tone in a scale; also an interval between a tone and the tone second above it; see also separate articles on Harmony and Scale.
Thoroughbass (old spelling of through, plus bass).—Indication of an accompaniment by bass notes only, with figures indicating chords and intervals to be added above them (figured bass), actually a form of shorthand.
Through-composed (fr. Ger. *durchkomponiert*).—Said of a song in which each stanza has its own music.
Timbre (Fr.).—The quality or color of tone.
Time.—In music, a term with several meanings: meter, tempo, and the duration of a note or chord.
Toccata (It.).—Literally, touched, a piece for a keyboard instrument, generally in brilliant style; now often a similar composition for orchestra.
Tonality.—See separate article.
Tone.—See separate article.
Tone Poem.—Richard Strauss' term for a symphonic poem.
Tonic.—The keynote, or the tone from which the prevailing tonality of a piece is derived. See separate article on Key.
Transcription.—Renotation of music to be played or sung by voices or instruments other than those for which it was composed (arrangement).
Transposition.—A shift in key.
Treble.—The highest natural human voice, particularly that of preadolescent boys; also the highest part of a choral composition and the upper parts in concerted instrumental music.
Tremolo (It.).—A vibrating, tremulous effect produced by the human voice and some instruments, often confused with vibrato (q.v.).
Triad.—See separate article.
Trill.—See separate article.
Trio.—See separate article.
Triplet.—See separate article.
Tritone.—The interval of the augmented fourth, three whole tones wide.
Turn.—An ornament made up of four or five notes—the principal note and the notes removed from it by a semitone.
Tutti (It.).—In concertos and other orchestral pieces, the sections scored for the entire orchestra.
Twelve-tone Music.—The so-called "atonal" music as developed by Arnold Schönberg and others into a system in which a composition is evolved from an arrangement of the twelve chromatic tones, called a tone-row or series.

Upbeat.—Notes occurring as parts of a melody preceding the first bar line.
Variations.—Modifications of a musical motive or theme.
Veloce (It.).—Fast.
Vibrato (It.).—On stringed instruments played with a bow, the slight, rapid alterations of pitch achieved by rapid oscilation of the finger pressing a string; in singing, a tremulous effect achieved by rapid interruptions of tone (often confused with tremolo, q.v.).
Vivace.—Lively, quick.
Vorspiel (Ger.).—Overture, prelude.
Whole tone.—The interval of the major second.
Zapateado (Sp.).—A Spanish solo dance in triple time with stamping of the heels, often in syncopation.
Zarzuela (Sp.).—A Spanish variety of opera or operetta with spoken dialogue.

MUSICAL INSTRUMENTS were not "invented." They developed slowly and comparatively late. They developed from rhythmically moving limbs, from stamping feet, and slapping hands; later, hands and feet were replaced by more effective devices—wooden clapper sticks or pounding bamboos—or the ground to be stamped upon yielded to some covered pit in the earth or to a felled and dug-out tree. Such simple contrivances and the rattles that shook from the dancers' ankles or in women's hands were the beginnings of the first large class of instruments, which scientific classification calls the idiophones, or instruments of materials sonorous by nature without needing any artificially induced tension. Most of them are struck; but a good many are pounded, shaken, scraped, plucked, and even rubbed.

As a second class, primitive tribes created the aerophones, so named from the air that constitutes their main vibrating agent. A minority of them are "free"; that is, some contraption like a propeller stirs the open air. Such is the widely spread "bull-roarer," a slab of wood whirled around the player's head on a thread. The majority, however, are wind instruments in the common sense, with the air vibrating inside a slender tube.

Most wind instruments belong to the families of flutes and of trumpets, though only in a general way. The flutes are often mere whistles of bone or reed without fingerholes, capable only of a single, screaming note; and the trumpets, roughly made of hollow stems or branches, are often used as megaphones, to be spoken, shouted, or wailed into, or to mask the player's natural voice. Such masking of the natural voice is one of the strongest indications that the instruments of the primitive peoples were not so much tools of music in the sense that we give this word as rather magical charms. Tied into a complicated network of cosmological ideas and symbols, of sun and moon, of male and female, of fire and water, they were supposed to help, with their characteristic sounds and shapes, in driving away malevolent demons and in creating life, growth, and bliss.

The densest network of such connotations surrounds the instruments of the third class, the membranophones or drums, in which a bladder or skin, to be struck or rubbed, is tightly stretched across an opening. Many are kept as sacred idols and receive veneration and sacrifices. Their outer forms are numberless and betray, in all their variety, the derivation from two principal sources: the carved and hollowed tree and a lathed earthenware pot. (Our modern military drums are ultimate offspring of the tree, our kettledrums of the earthenware pot.) Apart from them, the frame drums (popularly called tambourines) have no actual bodies, but only hoops to serve as frames for the skins.

The fourth class, chordophones or stringed instruments, reach, in the primitive world, only preparatory stages. Most of them share their forms with the hunter's bow, a few with the shapes of swinging traps for big game (in which a flexible rod in the ground stretches a rope descending from its loose end to a covered pit). Other forms of stringed instruments among modern primitives seem to be degenerated types sunk down from higher civilizations rather than early developments.

In the high civilizations of the ancient Orient, the magic connotations grow weaker, but by no means disappear. Instead, a real instrumental music, quite rudimentary in primitive cultures, becomes independent and increasingly important. The two classes of idiophones and membranophones yield a good deal of their earlier preponderance to strings and wind instruments capable of playing melodies. The wind instruments form sets of tubes (panpipes), one for each note, or, the player produces different tones by stopping the fingerholes of one single tube. The stringed instruments, in a similar way, have one string for each tone required. They are called open strings. In other cases, the players produce these tones by stopping one single string at different places.

The earliest of the new, resourceful stringed instruments were the harp and the lyre. The harp, deriving from the musical bow, had, as its scientific definition reads, the plane of the strings vertical on the plane of the soundboard. The neck emerged from the end of the body, bent forward, and sent the strings down to the soundboard (instead of emerging straight from the body, as in the violin, and dismissing the strings almost parallel to the soundboard). The lyre, on the contrary, had a yoke with arms and crossbar instead of a neck to hold the strings. The harp spread from ancient Egypt to China and was evidently the only stringed instrument in India. The lyre, on the other hand, did not penetrate either to China or to India, but was confined to the Mediterranean and the neighboring corner of Asia. It became the principal instrument in ancient Israel (David's "harp" as a translation of Hebrew *kinnor* is a misnomer) and later in Greece, Etruria, and Rome. The *kithara* of the Greeks was the heavy, carefully joined instrument of professionals; their *lyra* was a lighter variety for the benefit of beginners and amateurs. East Asia never saw the lyre; nor did it assign any important role to the harp. Instead, it devised a zither (or neckless stringed instrument) in a lengthy rectangular form with silken strings to be tuned by triangular shiftable bridges. It is still alive and highly esteemed as the *ch'e* of China and the *koto* of Japan.

Around 2000 B.C., some country in or near Asia Minor produced the lute, consisting of a resonance body with a neck on which the various notes of the melody were "stopped" by pressing the fingers down at the proper places on one string or two. This family, from which derive the lutes found all over the central belt, from Japan to Spain, became particularly important because it led to the discovery of an exact mathematical measurement of musical intervals: the octave had to be stopped right in the middle of the string (ratio 2:1); the perfect fifth at two thirds (3:2); the perfect fourth at three quarters (4:3); the major third at four fifths (5:4); and the minor third at five sixths (6:5), and so forth. Hence the name *kanon* or rule that the Greeks bestowed on it.

Almost all the stringed instruments were

plucked, either with bare fingers or with an artificial plectron of some kind. Bowing, which probably started in central Asia, became known only thousands of years later; the earliest evidences date from the end of the first millennium of our era, and the legend that Nero "fiddled" has no historical backing.

Wind instruments played a minor role in the ancient Orient. But while the various types of flutes were known all over the world, reed pipes became the almost exclusive property of the Mediterranean and the southwest of Asia, including India. They were either clarinets, with single reeds to interrupt the player's wind, or oboes, with double reeds as the mouthpiece. Both kinds were usually blown in pairs with the two mouthpieces between the player's lips at the same time. Mostly, one pipe seems to have played the melody, and the other pipe a sustained "drone" or pedal note, as do our bagpipes. Those double pipes were indeed quite closely related to our bagpipes. For the player's mouth, like that of a glass blower, was kept independent from regular respiration and used as a wind chamber or bag, while the nose took care of breathing in and out and of feeding the mouth as much as necessary. Later, some types of reed instruments, for example, the Indian snake charmers' pipes, facilitated this method by inserting the tubes in a calabash to serve as an artificial wind chamber, and still later, some instruments replaced the rigid calabash by a flexible bladder or skin and became bagpipes. The translation of the word *sumponiah* in the Book of Daniel by "bagpipe" is erroneous: our earliest evidences of bagpipes date from the Christian era.

Horns and trumpets had two manufacturing centers: one was Mongolia, which fed all Asia, and later Europe; the other was Etruria, which fed the Grecian world and Rome, especially the Roman Army.

The idiophones developed, in east Asia, an important family of chimes, or sets of well-tuned sonorous bodies, of bamboo tubes or wooden slabs (xylophones), of porcelain bowls, of metal slabs (metallophones—from which our modern celesta stems), or gongs (gong chimes), and of bells (bell chimes or carillons). Several of them have found their way to the West.

Even drums, at least in Burma, have been united to form chimes within a trellis around the drummer, who performs complicated pieces with incredible dexterity. For the rest, the changes in drums have been, in the Orient, in size rather than in quality.

In musical instruments more than in any other field, Europe was a peninsula of Asia. We do not know how the harps and lyres prevalent in the north were imported—through northern Asia or via the Atlantic. All other instruments were imported either through Byzantium, the gateway of the East, or after the Mohammedan conquest of Spain in 711. Among them were the ancestors of all our modern instruments: violins, lutes, and guitars; zithers, from which, much later, the stringed keyboard instruments derived; flutes, oboes, and clarinets; trumpets, horns, and kettledrums. Among them was also the organ. It had been invented in antiquity at a time unknown—the famous model of a hydraulic organ by the Alexandrian, Ktesibios, was, obviously, only the invention of a certain type of organ, not of the organ itself. The clergy opposed it in early Christian times, but accepted it long before 1000 A.D. By this time, it had so much increased in size that the organ of the monastery at Winchester, England, in 980 had no less than 26 bellows and 400 pipes, and required two players. But one should not fancy these organs to have had keyboards in a modern way or register stops to change intensity and color. They all were so-called mixture organs, in which every note was automatically accompanied by higher octaves and fifths—by 10 of them in Winchester, and, in later organs, up to 20. Only in the 14th century did the organ change its principle: it was given several keyboards and even pedals, modern keys, and solo stops of different tone colors. Rightfully the greatest composer of the time, Guillaume de Machaut, could call it the king of instruments.

In the same century, we hear for the first time of stringed keyboard instruments, such as clavichords and virginals (qq.v.). Their invention was indicative of a growing trend toward chords. A little later, the short-necked lute, introduced many centuries before from Persia, came of age as a Western instrument: its technique, which had been strictly melodic in the Orient, changed to the playing of several strings at a time in chords as well as in counterpoint. With this new technique, the lute was able to render, with more or less accuracy, all compositions written for voices or instrumental ensembles, and thus attained in the home a dominant position comparable to that more recently held by the piano.

The 15th century departed from the medieval habit of compressing high and low voices into a medium range that allowed all of them to participate wherever they wanted. The new style of combining high, medium, and low voices in their proper ranges and at fixed distances from each other led to an extension of musical space upward and downward and, consequently, to the construction of musical instruments of high, medium, and low tessitura. From the 15th century on, the more important instruments were built in complete families of sopranos, altos, tenors, and basses, such as soprano recorders, alto cromornes, tenor flutes, and bass viols. Indeed, in 1493, Spanish musicians wondered at viols as tall as men which they had seen in Rome; they were double basses.

The 16th century delighted in creating as many different and contrasting tone colors as possible—many more than we use or know today. This resulted in an astonishing number of instruments built in whole families, from sopranos down to bass and double-bass sizes, and, particularly, of flutes and double-reed instruments such as bassoons, cromornes, shawms, *rauschpfeifen,* rankets, and others. The most curious among them were the rankets, very short, thick cylinders of wood or ivory in which the wind canal was led through 10 alternately ascending and descending bores. Most of these reed instruments had wooden caps to conceal the reeds and make them inaccessible to the lips. They served as wind chambers similar to the bags of bagpipes. As a consequence, they were not able to overblow into higher octaves or to change from forte to piano.

We are indebted to the 16th century, also, for having created, out of a confusing crowd of sizes, types, and shapes, the two most important families of bowed instruments: the *viole da braccio* or violins and the *viole da gamba.* (In English usage, viola—the singular of viole—means today the alto size of the violin family, while the members of the now rare gamba family are referred

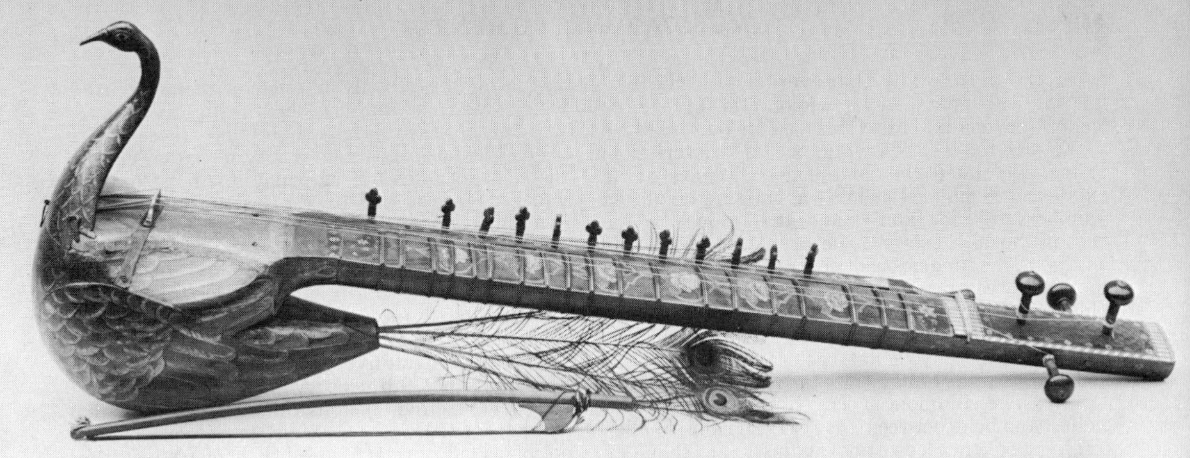

MUSICAL INSTRUMENTS

Above: Stringed type, a long-neck lute from India, where it is called a *mayuri.*

Right: Woodwinds, flutes of bamboo, made and played by Cuna Indians of Panama.

Below: Percussion type, a somewhat primitive marimba from Africa.

The Metropolitan Museum of Art

Radio Corporation of America

Above: The Electronic Music Synthesizer, developed by RCA, for which is claimed the capacity to create almost unlimited tone variations and rhythms.

to as the viols.) The characteristics of the violin family—violin, viola, violoncello or simply 'cello, and double bass (this last in part really a viol)—are too well known to need a redescription. It may be stated that in the first decades of its existence the highest string was missing on all the members of the family, and that, down to the end of the 18th century, the neck was about half an inch, the fingerboard several inches, shorter than they became in the 19th century. (All the older specimens still in use have been changed to the present lengths.) The viols, basically similar, had a deeper body, a flat back, and six or seven strings essentially thinner than those of the violin family. The commonest size, close to that of the 'cello, was held between the legs, and the smaller sizes, upon the legs, not against the shoulder (whence the name viola da gamba or leg fiddle). Unlike the bowing of violins and their next of kin, the bowing was done with the palm of the hand upward and with the accented beats played toward the pointed end of the bow. The tone itself was cool, silvery, and reserved. These traits account for the long-lasting discrimination between the two families, the viols being considered aristocratic chamber instruments, and the violins vulgar dance instruments. Only Italy, homeland of the violin and its greatest makers, decided, as early as about 1600, in favor of the new family and discarded the other bowed instruments almost entirely.

The 17th century also neglected the wind instruments, mainly because their windcaps hindered them from being flexible enough for the novel emotional style of the time. The violin family reigned supreme. Only at the end of the century did the wind instruments begin to be popular. Still, the violin family remained unchallenged as the kernel of the orchestra and of chamber music down to the 20th century, and it has preserved this central position essentially to the present.

The rehabilitation of wind instruments as the characterizing elements of the score, as opposed to the more neutral tints of the strings, came from France in Jean-Baptiste Lully's time (c. 1660). The military fife, the military shawm, and the hunter's horn were transformed into the flute, the oboe, and the French horn, and obtained seats in the orchestra. One generation later, a German master, Johann Christoph Denner, made the clarinet out of a rarely used folk pipe.

The trumpet was late in joining the orchestra, partly because the self-styled "knightly" guild in which the trumpeters were organized precluded, or at least discouraged, any cooperation with ordinary musicians. Whenever composers insisted on calling them in, the customary group of three trumpeters and one kettledrummer were kept apart, often above the orchestra, and entrusted with special festive passages without merging with the orchestra proper. However, the guilds were doomed, and the orchestra needed, more and more, the collaboration of brass instruments. As far as was proper and possible, composers used trombones, which, owing to their gliding mechanism, could instantaneously change the length of the tube and, hence, produce a complete chromatic scale. But the trumpets and French horns were capable only of the few additional tones that overblowing provided. Substitutions were tried; thus, we find in Johann Sebastian Bach's scores a slide trumpet, which, by the use of a tube sliding in trombone fashion, allowed for the chromatic notes unobtainable on ordinary trumpets; and, also, the already obsolete *cornetto* or *zink,* which was a rather short, slightly curved wooden horn with fingerholes like those of an oboe. The hornists found a way to flatten at least the skeletal notes by "stopping" their fist into the widened end or bell of the instrument; but the notes thus obtained proved to be inferior in tone quality. Hornists and trumpeters also tried out a fingerhole and key system similar to that of the *zinken* (key horns, key trumpets). But the interruption of the otherwise homogeneous metal tube was not satisfactory either. The solution of the problem, definitive so far, came in the second decade of the 19th century with the invention of the valves (either pistons or rotary valves), that is, additional lengths of tube, to be connected or disconnected with the speed of a piano key, thus transforming the original length of the instrument into any length necessary for producing a full chromatic range. This new versatility allowed the trumpets and horns to merge with the rest of the orchestra and to give it color and intensity unheard before; modern orchestration scores as many brass instruments as woodwinds, or even more.

The 19th century added a few more families of brass instruments to the trumpets, horns, and trombones: the cornet, developed from the old postilion's horn; its relatives, the alto horn, the baritone, the euphonium, and the tuba; and, as a rare supplement for solemn passages, the Wagner tubas, hybrids between the French horn and the ordinary tuba.

The woodwinds, too, in the 19th century were built in whole families reminiscent of those of the 16th century: the flutes were given altos and basses; the oboes, English horns (altos) and baritones; the clarinets, altos, basses, and double basses; the bassoons, double bassoons. The new basses and double basses posed new problems; the fingerholes were spaced beyond the reach of the fingers and needed a complicated key mechanism with double levers. However, the whole conception of fingerholes and keys was entering a new stage, best known from Theobald Boehm's construction in 1832 of the modern flute, in which the fingerholes were not placed at the convenience of the hands, but according to acoustical laws, while easy fingering was safeguarded by an ingenious system of keys.

Not much later, a resourceful instrument maker in Brussels and, thereafter, in Paris, Adolphe Sax, in about 1840 added a new family under the name of saxophones (q.v.) : brass clarinets with wide parabolical tubes and with bent-up bells in all sizes except the straight soprano.

Sax also improved an impressive number of other wind instruments, both wood and brass, and built a new family of brasses, known as the saxhorns, (see HORN), which are more or less the cornets and the tubas fused in one complete, homogeneous set.

Another Frenchman, the bandmaster, Sarrus, followed, around 1860, with the sarrusophones: a complete family of metal oboes, stronger and fuller than the orchestral oboes and bassoons. They are forgotten except for the double bass, which sometimes replaces the weaker double bassoon.

While Sax was working at his inventions, the organ builders developed a cheaper home and chapel surrogate, with reeds instead of pipes: the harmonium. The organ itself got rid of the fragile mechanical action that connected key and pipe by wooden trackers and stickers and adopted the British invention of a pneumatic action (Joseph Booth 1827 and Charles S. Barker 1832) which, among other advantages, made it possible to separate the keyboards from the pipework and to place them wherever the organist could be seated best. Later on, a part of this pneumatic action was even electrified (Barker 1868).

The harp, too, underwent its decisive and so far definitive improvement. Its seven pedals had been able to sharp its seven strings per octave by a semitone each and thus, theoretically, to make a complete chromatic scale available. Practically, they did not allow for playing in flat tonalities. Sébastien Érard in Paris, who gave the piano its modern action, transformed the single action into a double action in 1810: each of the seven pedals can be stopped midway to sharp the string by a semitone, and pushed all the way down to sharp the string by a whole tone. In more recent times, so-called chromatic harps have been designed, for example, by Lyon and Healy in Chicago, all of them with a complete chromatic range of strings and without pedals, but none of these has won enduring acceptance.

The present condition of the traditional musical instruments is about this: the members of the violin family have not changed; the piano remains essentially as it was more than a century ago; the woodwinds and brasses have been altered very little.

Meanwhile, a new fifth class of sound-producing instruments has been created: the electrophones or electronic instruments. In them, tone is produced by electric circuits that are switched on and interrupted in several ways. Notable among them have been the *Theremin* (1924), its frequencies and volume both controlled by movements of the player's hands; the *Ondes Martenot* (1928), for which Darius Milhaud, André Jolivet, and Olivier Messiaen have composed special music; the Hammond Organ and the Novachord, both inventions of Laurens Hammond (1895–). Both the photoelectric sound track originally developed for motion pictures and the tape recorder—essentially reproductive instruments—have been utilized as direct instrumental means, notably in the mixing and organization of sounds (including noises) for compositional purposes. The once vigorously stated confidence of proponents of electronic musical instruments that they would gradually replace the traditional ones has not to date been proved justified: except for the reproduction of music performed by the traditional means, electric and electronic musical instruments thus far have failed to establish themselves in the concert and recital hall and in the opera house. They have, however, played a considerable role in the performance of several varieties of jazz.

Revised by HERBERT WEINSTOCK.

Consult Sachs, Curt, *The History of Musical Instruments* (New York 1940); Edgerly, Beatrice, *From the Hunter's Bow: The History and Romance of Musical Instruments,* ed. by Boris Erich Nelson (New York 1942); Geiringer, Karl, *Musical Instruments: Their History in Western Culture from the Stone Age to the Present* (New York 1945); Baines, Anthony, *European and American Musical Instruments* (New York 1966).

MUSICAL THEATER. Music played an important role in the earliest known protodramatic and proto-theatrical performances, both those of a religious nature and those intended as secular amusement. Indeed, the appearance of plays entirely dispensing with musical accompaniment appears to have been made relatively late. Alongside the spoken play in verse or prose, multifarious, overlapping forms of musical theater have evolved. These include wordless mimed and danced forms, pantomime, melodrama, opera, operetta, minstrel shows, burlesque, musical comedy, vaudeville, and the revue or extravaganza. The varieties of theatrical entertainment with music greatly outnumber those without it.

During recent centuries, the chief sort of wordless musical theatrical art and entertainment has been ballet (q.v.). The music of the *Ballet Comique de la Royne,* which was performed during the celebration of a royal marriage at Versailles in 1581, has survived. During the reign of Louis XIV—who himself often danced in court entertainments—ballet music was cultivated intensively by Jean-Baptiste Lully (1632–1687), who collaborated with Molière to produce *comédie-ballet,* a mixture of drama and dance, of which a renowned exemplar is *Le Bourgeois-gentilhomme* (1670). Lully and his successors, including Jean-Philippe Rameau (1683–1764) also introduced ballets into their operas, thus setting a usage that has persisted in France and spread elsewhere.

In England, meanwhile, the nobility had come to favor an imported, adapted form of musical theater known as masque, a mélange of spoken poetry, acting, dance, and vocal and instrumental music often staged lavishly. Ben Jonson (1572–1637) wrote notable masque texts; leading composers of masque scores included Thomas Campion (1567–1620) and Henry Lawes (1596–1662), the latter having composed the music to John Milton's *Comus* (1634). After the Restoration in 1660, Italian opera began to supersede the masque in England.

From the late 17th century to the end of the 19th, ballet threw up a large group of great dancers and choreographers. Outstanding among them were Marie Camargo (1710–1770), Jean-Georges Noverre (1727–1809), Auguste Vestris (1760–1842), Carlotta Grisi (1821–1899), Marius Petipa (1822–1910), Marie Taglioni (1804–1884), and Fanny Elssler (1810–1884). Much of the music to which they worked has been lost, but some ballet scores by great composers of the 18th and early 19th centuries survive, including Gluck's *Don Juan* (1761) and Beethoven's *Die Geschöpfe des Prometheus* (1801). Schools of ballet using different techniques toward different ends developed in several European countries, most notably in Italy, France, Russia, and Denmark.

During the 19th century, ballet music was mostly the work of inferior composers, a condition from which it was rescued chiefly by Léo Délibes (*Coppélia,* 1870; *Sylvia,* 1876) and Peter Ilich Tchaikovsky (*The Swan Lake,* 1876; *The Sleeping Beauty,* 1889; *The Nutcracker,* 1892). The Ballets Russes of Serge Diaghilev (1872–1929), bursting on Western Europe in 1909, influenced not only all ballet, but also composition, painting, stage design, and even literature. In London, earlier ballet companies finally evolved into the world-famed Sadler's Wells Ballet (later renamed Royal Ballet). In New York, where other troupes had developed a large public, the New York City Ballet became outstanding. Since the first ballet score that Igor Stravinsky (1882–) composed for Diaghilev (*The Firebird,* 1910), a large portion of the most distinguished 20th century music has been composed for dancing.

Paralleling the modern aspects of ballet has been the so-called "modern dance," which, however, has largely dispensed with traditional ballet

Leonard McCombe

A scene from one of the musical theater's most popular productions, *My Fair Lady*, based on Shaw's *Pygmalion*.

techniques. Related to expressionism and largely of Central European origin, it has failed to equal the popularity of ballet. In its persistent American forms, leading dancer-choreographers have been Martha Graham, Doris Humphrey, and Charles Edward Weidman. Other theatrical dancing has included adapted folk forms, so-called "ballroom dancing," tap, softshoe, and related varieties often included in minstrel shows, vaudeville, musical comedy, revue, and related motion pictures.

The most enduring sort of serious musical theater with text has been opera (q.v.), which emerged in Italy about 1600 and has enlisted the services of most great composers (Johann Sebastian Bach and Johannes Brahms being noted exceptions) ever since. Related to opera are the play with incidental music, either instrumental or vocal or both, and the melodrama, in which the text is spoken to musical accompaniment.

Operetta, originally a short opera, flourished in France, Germany, and Austria, somewhat later in England and the United States, tending to become constantly lighter and more sentimental. Noted composers of operetta and closely related forms of light opera have included: in France, Daniel François Esprit Auber (1782–1871), Jacques Offenbach (1819–1880), Charles Lecocq (1832–1918), and André Messager (1853–1929); in Austria, Hungary, and Germany, Franz von Suppé (1819–1895), Johann Strauss, Jr. (1825–1899), Karl Millöcker (1842–1899), Franz Lehár (1870–1948), Oscar Straus (1870–1954), Leo Fall (1873–1925), Emmerich Kálmán (1882–1953), and Robert Stolz (1882–   ); in England, Sir Arthur Sullivan (1842–1900), working with his famed librettist, Sir William Schwenk Gilbert (1836–1911). In the United States, the first outstanding composer of operetta was Victor Herbert (1859–1924), soon followed by other immigrants from Europe, including Rudolf Friml (1879–   ) and Sigmund Romberg (1887–1951). In the works of many of these later composers, the thin line dividing operetta from musical comedy all but vanished.

The 19th century American minstrel show, presenting a sentimentalized and comically distorted version of southern Negro life, but played by white men "in blackface," consisted of jokes, dances, songs, and impersonations. Much of its vitality was passed on to vaudeville and musical comedy. Related to the minstrel show, but appearing later in the 19th century, was burlesque. A mixture of very broad, usually risqué, humor, travesties, dance, imitations and songs, burlesque evolved one form of its own, the strip tease. Frowned upon by moralists, burlesque frequently fell foul of the police; it has now largely passed into sentimentalized history.

Much of the vitality of both the minstrel show and burlesque was absorbed by the variety show (usually so called in England) somewhat misleadingly called vaudeville in America. (The French word *vaudeville* originally meant a type of topical song, later a short theatrical sketch including such songs.) Developing after the Civil War, American vaudeville flourished with ever-increasing strength from 1833, when the Keith-Albee Vaudeville Circuit was formed under the joint managership of Edward F. Albee (1857–1930) and Benjamin Franklin Keith (1846–1914). The acts under their aegis, often playing in theaters owned by them, included song, dance of many sorts, acrobatic feats, trained animals, comic and other sketches, and many so-called "specialty" acts. Vaudeville often recruited stars from the legitimate stage, opera, and ballet, usually on a temporary basis. The acts moved about the country on long circuits, of which the Orpheum and Pantages were well known. Performers in the "two-a-day," becoming top-billed stars, frequently left the circuits to perform in musical comedy, revue, and spoken plays; many of them were later stars of radio and television. Vaudeville in its most vivid and familiar form gradually died out, killed off by the motion picture, radio, and television.

A genre of musical theater which has become perhaps the leading American contribution to the stage is musical comedy. Deriving clearly from comic opera and operetta, less obviously from the minstrel show and vaudeville, it became a recognized separate form chiefly after 1900. Typically hung on a slender thread of plot, it consists largely of sung and danced musical numbers interspersed with jokes. Quickly developing traditions of its own and a group of highly expert performers, it also evoked a notable line of popular composers and that staple of American popular music, the show song. Only a few of the many successful composers of musical-comedy scores can be mentioned here: Jerome Kern (1885–1945), Irving Berlin (1888–   ), Cole Porter (1893–   ), George Gershwin (1898–1937), Vincent Youmans (1898–1946), Richard Rodgers (1902–   ), and Frederick Loewe (1904–   ). In more recent years, formal ballets have increasingly become integral parts of musical comedy, particularly as it has tended to recede from the sophistication it displayed in the 1920's and 1930's, becoming more and more operettalike, particularly in the very successful shows with librettos by Oscar Hammerstein II (1895–1960), beginning with *Oklahoma!* (1943).

Closely connected with both vaudeville and musical comedy has been the extravaganza known as the revue. Dispensing with plot, it has been in effect an elaborate vaudeville show. To this genre belong such renowned series as the *Ziegfeld Follies, George White's Scandals*, and *Earl Carroll's Vanities*. Like vaudeville and musical comedy, the revue has had some place in motion pictures since the advent of sound. Its most recent recognizable descendant has been the occasional television "spectacular."

The most internationally renowned of all American musicotheatrical works undoubtedly has been Gershwin's *Porgy and Bess* (1935), to a text derived from DuBose Heyward's novel *Porgy* (and a dramatized version thereof). Called an opera, *Porgy and Bess* is in reality a musical comedy with operatic leanings. It represents a tendency toward musicodramatic treatment of serious themes in the American popular theater, a tendency that has produced works of many shadings, from musical-comedy versions of pathetic, even tragic, plays to the proto-operas of Gian-Carlo Menotti.

Among the longest-running musicals in New York stage history have been *The Threepenny Opera,* by Weill and Blitzstein; *My Fair Lady,* by Lerner and Loewe; *Hello, Dolly!,* by Stewart and Herman; *Fiddler on the Roof,* by Bock and Harnick; and the record-breaking *The Fantasticks,* by Jones and Schmidt.

HERBERT WEINSTOCK
Coauthor of "Men of Music"

Neil Fujita from Rapho-Guillumette

The off-Broadway hit *Threepenny Opera* was composed by Kurt Weill, with lyrics by Bertold Brecht, in 1928.

MUSICOLOGY, mū′zĭ-kŏl′ô-jĭ, the organized scientific study of music. Many of its activities have a very long history, but as a separate academic discipline it emerged in Germany and Austria after the middle of the 19th century. Its important pioneers emphasized "that musical studies, particularly those in the field of history, should be raised to the same level of seriousness and accuracy which had long been adopted in the other fields of knowledge, natural sciences as well as humanities" (*Harvard Dictionary of Music*).

The musicological curriculum first proposed was to include notation, history, acoustics, melody, rhythm, harmony, counterpoint, philosophical speculation, and general research. The inclusiveness of this claim aroused opposition, and musicology more recently has come to deal chiefly with research, tending to remain aloof from (though naturally parallel with) traditional academic studies of theory, counterpoint, harmony, and form and the teaching of music history. Thus, *Webster's New International Dictionary* defines musicology as "a branch of knowledge of field of investigation; esp., historical study of musical documents, investigation of sources, gathering and organization of neglected data, etc." An American musicologist, Otto Kinkeldey (1878–   ) has written: "It distinguishes carefully between the actual work of the musician, the artist (creative or reproductive), and the work of the scholar or of the scientific observer and investigator." Recognized university courses in musicology, some of them advanced graduate study leading to the Ph.D. degree, naturally have evoked textbooks of its procedures. Particularly useful in acquiring understanding of its scope and methods is Glenn Haydon's *Introduction to Musicology,* published in several revised editions since its first appearance in 1941.

HERBERT WEINSTOCK.

MUSK DEER, mŭsk dēr, *Moschus moschiferus,* a small deerlike animal which differs so greatly from other members of the deer family or Cervidae that it is placed in a special subfamily, the Moschinae. The distinguishing features include, among others, the presence of a gall bladder, a relatively unconvoluted brain and complete lack of antlers in both sexes. Other features, found in the males only, are a pair of long canine tusks in the upper jaw and a musk gland on the abdomen.

The musk deer is only 20 to 22 inches high at the shoulder, somewhat higher in the hind quarters. The legs are rather heavy and the feet are remarkable for the great development of the lateral toes, the hoofs of which touch the ground. The ears are long and the tail very short. The color is brown, more or less mottled with lighter patches, and the young are spotted. The pelage consists partly of coarse, bristly hairs with which are mingled shorter hairs of a woolly texture.

The musk deer is widely distributed throughout central and eastern Asia, and several local races or subspecies have been recognized. In the mountains, notably in the Himalayas, it is commonly found, in summer, at elevations of 8,000 to 12,000 feet. It extends westward into Kashmir, northward to Kansu, China, and also occurs in Mongolia, parts of Siberia, and even Sakhalin Island. A subspecies is found in Korea, and a southern one inhabits Assam and Upper Burma and extends into French Indochina. In habit the musk deer is solitary, extremely wary, agile, and fleet footed. It frequents thickets of birch, juniper, and rhododendron in the daytime, feeding chiefly at morning and evening twilight and at night on grass, moss, and leaves. Mating occurs in January and the young are born in June. The males are said to fight fiercely during the mating season, using as weapons the canine tusks in the upper jaw, which sometimes exceed three inches in length.

The feature to which the animal owes its popular fame is a saccular cutaneous gland called the musk pod, found in the male only. Located on the abdomen with an opening in front of the preputial aperture, the gland attains about the size of a hen's egg in the adult. The secretion in the pouch forms a semisolid mass of dark brown color and strong odor which, when dried and processed, yields the highly valued musk of commerce, used as a base for many perfumes. The animals are so persistently and ruthlessly hunted for musk that they are in danger of extinction in some regions. See also DEER; PERFUMES AND PERFUMERY; RUMINANTS.

Consult Flower, W. H., and Lydekker, R., *Mammals, Living and Extinct* (London 1891); Harper, F., *Extinct and Vanishing Mammals of the Old World* (New York 1945); Tate, G. H. H., *Mammals of Eastern Asia* (New York 1947).

MUSK OX, *Ovibos moschatus,* a remarkable member of the Bovidae (q.v.), is found only in Arctic regions of North America, including a number of the Arctic islands, and the northern coastal region of Greenland; but fossil remains show that during the Pleistocene ice age it extended as far southward as Kansas and Kentucky, and inhabited northern Europe and parts of Siberia. Regarding its zoological affinities, some mammalogists consider it most closely related to the bison, while others regard it as more nearly allied to the antelopes, goats, and sheep. The name *Ovibos* signifies "sheep ox."

The animal resembles a small ox with extremely long, shaggy hair which on the sides may hang almost to the feet. Mingled with the long hair is a dense woolly undercoat which is shed in the spring. The color is dark brown in general, paler on the back, and the feet are white. The horns are extremely broad at the base, especially in adult males, in which they almost meet in the midline, forming a heavy frontlet. They curve downward at the sides of the head, then upward and forward at the tips. There is only one species; but three races or subspecies, differing in minor features, are recognized. The musky odor is commonly considered to be a general emanation, though it has been suggested that the suborbital gland may be its source.

The musk ox feeds on grass, moss, sedge, and shoots and leaves of the dwarf willow, scraping the snow away with its hoofs when necessary. It is commonly found in herds of 10 to 30 animals. Though it wanders locally in search of food it is in no sense migratory. When attacked the herd quickly forms a compact circle with the young ones in the center and the horned adults facing outward. This affords adequate defense against wolves, the chief natural enemy, but against men armed with rifles it merely renders easy the annihilation of the herd. Continual ruthless slaughter by Eskimos, explorers, and sportsmen has greatly diminished the number of musk oxen and even exterminated them in many regions, so that the species is doomed unless efficient protective measures are enforced. The Canadian government has forbidden the killing of musk oxen and has established a sanctuary of 15,000 square miles northeast of Great Slave Lake. In 1930 the United States introduced a number of the Greenland subspecies into Alaska where the musk ox, formerly present, has been extinct since the middle of the 19th century. In 1942 the introduced animals, transferred meanwhile to Nunivak Island off the Alaska coast, had almost tripled their original number.

Consult Flower, W. H., and Lydekker, R., *Mammals, Living and Extinct* (London 1891); Hone, E., *The Present Status of the Muskox in Arctic North America and Greenland,* Special Publication, American Committee for International Wild Life Protection, Vol. 1, No. 5 (Cambridge 1934); Allen, G. M., *Extinct and Vanishing Mammals of the Western Hemisphere* (New York 1942); Cahalane, V. H., *Mammals of North America* (New York 1947).

MUSK PLANT, a popular name for several unrelated plants. The one most common to the United States is *Mimulus moschatus,* of the family Scrophulariaceae, a native of the Western states. In Europe the name is most applied to *Erodium moschatum* of the family order Geraniaceae, a native of the Mediterranean region. The name is applied in the West Indies to *Guarea grandifolia,* a mahogany-like tree which is also known as muskwood; and to *Trichilia moschata,* also called musk tree. This name is also applied to a Tasmanian tree, *Olearia argophylla.* An East Indian plant, *Ferula sumbul,* is known as musk root. Its starchy roots are used as a substitute for musk in perfumery.

MUSK SHREW. See SHREW.

MUSK TURTLE, or **STINKPOT.** See TURTLES, TORTOISES AND TERRAPINS.

MUSK WOOD, a tree, *Guarea grandifolia,* of the family Meliaceae, so called in the West Indies because the bark smells so strongly of musk that it may be used as a perfume. Although the tree attains timber size the wood contains a bitter resinous substance which unfits it for many purposes.

MUSKEGON, mŭs-kē'gŭn, city, Michigan, Muskegon County seat, altitude 590 feet, is located on Lake Michigan, at the mouth of Muskegon River, 35 miles northwest of Grand Rapids, on the Pennsylvania; Chesapeake and Ohio; and Grand Trunk railroads. It is a port of entry, and has water transportation on the Great Lakes, car ferry service to Milwaukee, Wis., and airline service. Among its manufactured products are airplane and automobile engines, billiard and bowling equipment, piston rings, motor castings, filing devices, gasoline pumps, and knit goods. It is one of the great oil refining centers of Michigan. Many of its buildings and civic institutions have been provided through the benefactions of Charles H. Hackley, wealthy lumberman and philanthropist.

The name Muskegon is of Indian origin, meaning "river with marshes." It was first settled as a trading post in 1810, was incorporated as a village in 1861, and re-incorporated as a city in 1869. The city has commission-manager form of government. Pop. 44,631.

MUSKEGON HEIGHTS, city, Michigan, Muskegon County, is located just south of Muskegon, on the Chesapeake and Ohio; Grand Trunk; and Pennsylvania railroads. It is a residential suburb of Muskegon, but shares in the industrial activity of the larger community. Pop. 17,304.

MUSKELLUNGE, mŭs'kĕ-lŭnj, the great pike, *Esox masquinongy,* of the lakes of the interior of North America. See PIKE, PICKEREL.

MUSKET, a hand firearm with which infantry soldiers were formerly armed. When first introduced, early in the 16th century, it was discharged by means of a lighted match, and was so heavy that it had to be laid across a staff to be fired. To make use of it the soldier was required to carry a slow-burning match with him which was apt to be extinguished in wet weather. The wheel lock followed, the chief feature of which was a wheel made to revolve by means of a spring and to cause sparks by friction against a flint. The next improvement was the flintlock proper (about 1625), in which sparks were produced by one impact of a piece of flint on the steel above the priming powder. Musketeers were soon introduced into all armies. In the beginning of the 17th century infantry consisted of pikemen and musketeers, and all changes in regard to the relative proportion of the two arms were always in favor of the latter. The flintlock musket was introduced into the British Army toward the end of the 17th century, and was the British musket of the days of the Peninsular War and Waterloo, known familiarly as "Brown Bess." It was superseded by the percussion musket in 1842, this musket being in turn superseded by the rifle.

MUSKIE, mus'kē, **Edmund Sixtus,** American political leader, governor, and U.S. senator: b. Rumford, Me., March 28, 1914. His father was a Polish immigrant whose name originally was *Marciszewski.* Muskie graduated from Bates College (B.A., 1936) and Cornell Law School (LL.B., 1939) and then began to practice law in Waterville, Me. During World War II he was a naval officer.

After the war Muskie returned to his law practice and entered Democratic politics. He served in the Maine House of Representatives and helped build the weak state Democratic party. Nominated for governor in 1954, he campaigned on economic issues and won. The Republican legislature approved most of his program.

In 1958, Muskie was elected to the U.S. Senate, where he gained recognition as an authority on problems of air and water pollution. In 1968 he was the unsuccessful Democratic nominee for vice president. After the election, he became a critic of the Vietnam War, which he had generally supported.

Muskie's judicious manner appealed to many voters, and he became a favorite for the 1972 Democratic presidential nomination. But support eroded during his cautious primary campaign, and his cause was undermined by a series of "dirty tricks" financed by aides to President Richard Nixon, who was seeking reelection. After being falsely accused in a published letter of condoning a slur on Americans of French-Canadian descent, Muskie showed public anger. Later, he virtually abandoned his campaign.

MUSKMELON. See MELON.

MUSKOGEE, mus-kō'gē, city, Oklahoma, 47 miles southeast of Tulsa. It is the seat of Muskogee county.

Natural resources of the surrounding region include cotton and deposits of lime, together with oil and natural gas; and the zinc fields are near enough to support the manufacture of zinc and lead products. The city deals extensively in dairy products, such as butter and cheese. Its industrial establishments make road machinery, cottonseed products, oil-well equipment, batteries, castings, aircraft, automobile parts, tools, furniture, radios and phonographs, and paper and leather products.

Muskogee is the seat of a state school for the blind, and of a veterans hospital. There is a public library, an art gallery, a city museum, a city hospital and the Eastern Oklahoma Hospital.

The city was settled about 1810, incorporated as a village in 1861, and chartered as a city in 1898. Government is by mayor and council. Pop. 37,331.

MUSKOKA, mŭs-kō'kȧ, district, Canada; in Ontario, bordering Georgian Bay; the name also being borne by a beautiful lake and river, and comprehensively applied to the extensive region, 4,000 square miles in extent, lying between Georgian Bay on the west, Lake Nipissing on the north, Ottawa River on the east and Lake Simcoe on the south. The capital of the district is Bracebridge, on the Canadian National Railway. The region is a paradise for sportsmen, with between 800 and 1,000 lakes and smaller bodies of water, chief of which are Muskoka, Rosseau and Joseph lakes, all abounding in fish and studded with beautiful islands; several rivers and picturesque waterfalls, notably High Falls and South Falls on the Muskoka River and Bridal Veil Falls on the Shadow River; and extensive forests filled with game. It is one of the most popular summer resorts in Canada, and is visited annually by thousands of people. During the summer, steamboats ply on the principal lakes, connecting with the Canadian National Railway and the Canadian Pacific Railway. Area of Muskoka District: 1,585 square miles.

MUSKRAT, an aquatic rodent (*Ondatra zibethicus* or *Fiber zibethicus*) numerous throughout North America, and yielding a valuable fur. It is a member of the rat family (Muridae), and is, in effect, a gigantic vole or meadow-mouse, with a tail flattened sideways into a powerful swimming instrument, and fringed with stiff hairs. The hind feet are set obliquely to the leg; the ears are very small and buried in fur; the muzzle is blunt and furry; the palms and soles are naked and fringed with hairs. The average total length is about 21 inches, of which the tail is more than a third, measuring as long as the body without the head. The color varies above from almost black to pale brown; sides of head and body, chestnut-brown; under-fur, bluish gray; feet, dark brown; tail, black. Those of the Rocky Mountain region are smaller and paler than Eastern ones. The musky odor of these animals is due to a thick fluid secreted in two small glands near the generative organs, which imparts a taint to the flesh that makes it unpalatable to most persons.

These animals live along small streams, and in swampy places generally; being most abundant around Chesapeake Bay and in the marshy lakes of the upper Mississippi region and northward to Hudson Bay. Where the banks have some elevation they form extensive burrows, which have entrances below the surface of the water, and gradually ascend till they terminate in a chamber above the level of high water. These burrows are most frequently made under the roots of trees, or in other situations of difficult access. The excavations are of great injury to artificial embankments along canals and rivers, by permitting the water to undermine and to make large breaches in them, and in some parts of the country they do serious damage to canal embankments and river-dikes. When, however, these animals inhabit low and marshy situations, they construct conical houses usually surrounded by water, not unlike those of the beaver but smaller, composed of reeds, etc., mixed with clay. These houses have subterranean passages leading to them, and are inhabited by many individuals during the winter; but in the warm weather they desert them entirely, and dwell in pairs in a bank burrow while they rear their young. The houses contain a large, smooth-walled chamber, above the water line, and when frozen are sufficiently solid to form a protection against all but the largest carnivora; but they are usually destroyed and swept away in the spring floods, so that a new house is erected every season.

The muskrat feeds mainly upon aquatic vegetation, especially the rootstocks and basal parts of stems, and is especially fond of pond lilies. These it brings to the shore to eat, almost always during the night, for it is essentially nocturnal, although often seen abroad in the daytime. It is very fond of mussels, and brings great quantities of these ashore, always, when possible, at the same place, so that piles of their shells accumulate to indicate favorite feeding spots. In summer the muskrats feed on shore herbage somewhat, and frequently go some distance to get a meal of growing corn, garden vegetables, or fallen fruit. They are accused also of occasional fish-catching, and are unwelcome in waters devoted to fish culture. Because of the commercial value of its fur and its destructiveness in some places, the muskrat is incessantly persecuted by man. It is also preyed upon by many natural enemies—minks, wolverines, foxes, wildcats, badgers, wolves, birds of prey, water moccasins, snapping turtles, pike, and others, which capture many young and some adults. Nevertheless muskrats are so secretive and so prolific, and have found so many advantages in civilized areas, that they are likely to maintain their numbers indefinitely. They produce from three to 12 young at a birth, and often breed three to five times a year.

Muskrats are taken by shooting, spearing in winter (through their houses or through the ice), or, most numerously, by trapping. In certain districts, as along Chesapeake Bay, men make a regular business of trapping muskrats in winter.

Consult Hodgson, Robert G., *Successful Muskrat Farming*, 6th ed. (Toronto 1930); Elliman, J. R., *Families and Genera of Living Rodents*, 2 vols. (London 1940–41).

MUSLIM or **MOSLEM.** See ISLAM; MOSLEM SECTS.

MUSLIN, mŭz'lĭn, a name used for various fabrics of cotton or silk, of different degrees of fineness. The word is derived from the city of Mosul on the Tigris River, now in Iraq, where the cloth is thought to have been originally made. Marco Polo describes muslins of silk and gold which he saw at Mosul in the late 13th century. The finest cottons so named, however, came in ancient times from India, especially Madras and Dacca, whose fabrics were spoken of as "woven air and running water" because of their fineness; they were not infrequently adorned with gold. Modern muslins range from fine crisp fabrics, often dotted or figured, used for women's clothes, to coarser materials used for bed linens. Silk muslins, often called by the French name *mousselines,* are also still produced.

MUSORGSKI or **MOUSSORGSKY,** mo͝o-sôrg'skû-ĭ, **Modest Petrovich**, Russian composer: b. Karevo, Pskov Government, Russia, March 21, 1839; d. St. Petersburg, March 28, 1881. The composer's father was a wealthy landowner, his paternal grandmother a peasant. Even as a small child he showed a tendency to compose spontaneously, inspired by the fairy tales he heard from his nurse. His mother began his musical education early, and he gave his first piano recital before an audience of family and friends at nine. Later he had formal instruction, but there always remained something amateurish and self-taught in his technique. At 13 he was sent to the Cadet School in St. Petersburg, where he took an interest in history while, on the musical side, the choirmaster urged him to study church music. As an officer in St. Petersburg (1856–1858), he became acquainted with Mili A. Balakirev, Aleksandr P. Borodin, César A. Cui, and Nikolai A. Rimski-Korsakov, who, together with Musorgski, later became known as the Mighty Five, founders of a new school of realistic national music in Russia. Musorgski quit the army in 1858, but financial losses resulting from the freeing of the serfs in 1861 forced him to become a civil servant. From 1858 he suffered from nervous ailments and alcoholism.

His songs, choral and piano music had already won him a reputation when, in 1868, he began to compose *Boris Godunov,* the libretto based on Aleksander Pushkin's historical play. The opera is suffused with Musorgski's feeling for the Russian past, his popular sympathies, and his ability to hit off character sharply with sparse and simple musical touches. Dramatic power saves *Boris* from being a sprawling panorama, which was a danger in view of its scope and relative plotlessness. Though the producers had twice rejected it, this masterwork was warmly received at its world premiere in the Maryinsky Theatre in St. Petersburg, Feb. 8, 1874. Musorgski was already working on his second major opera, *Khovanshchina,* basing it on the turbulent beginnings of Peter the Great's reign; but he never completed it, and after 1874, the year of his piano suite *Pictures from an Exhibition,* his powers declined as his health failed. After Musorgski's death, Rimski-Korsakov finished *Khovanshchina,* and also edited Musorgski's other works with such a free hand that for many years much music known as Musorgski's was in essentials Rimski's. Objections by critics and public finally forced restoration of the scores as originally composed, and in 1928 the Soviet government began to print a monumental edition of the original texts. See also BORIS GODUNOV, grand opera; RUSSIAN LANGUAGE AND CULTURAL LIFE—*4. Music*.

Consult Calvocoressi, Michel D., *Mussorgsky* (London 1946); Seroc, Victor I., *The Mighty Five* (New York 1948).

MUSSELBURGH, mŭs''l-bŭ-rŭ, burgh and seaport, Scotland, in Midlothian, on the Firth of Forth, six miles east of Edinburgh, of which it is gradually becoming a suburb. The river Esk divides it into Musselburgh proper and Fisherrow, the port. It has noted golf links, and a curious old jail built in 1590 of stones from the shrine and chapel of Loretto. Prince Charles Edward, the Young Pretender, slept in Pinkie House, a Jacobean mansion, the night after the Battle of Prestonpans (1745). Loretto School, one of Scotland's best public schools, is in Musselburgh. Industries include papermaking, brewing, and the manufacture of twine products. Coal is mined in the vicinity and there are a number of market gardens. There is a large fishing population located in Fisherrow. Pop. (1961) 17,273.

MUSSELS, mŭs''lz, a term generally applied to most of the fresh-water bivalves in the families

Unionidae, Margaritanidae, and Mutelidae, and to a limited number of marine bivalves, most of these latter being in the family Mytilidae.

Fresh-water Forms.—The family Unionidae is widespread in Central and North America, Europe, and Asia. The Margaritanidae, limited to North America, Europe, and Asia, comprises very few species. They are similar in their habits to the Unionidae, differing only in minor anatomical details. The Mutelidae are distributed mainly in South America, Africa, and Australia. Nearly all of the Unionidae are parasitic on fish during their early laval stages. After fertilization the young are held in the gills where additional growth takes place. Upon developing a small bivalve shell, usually with two tiny hooks on the ventral margin, they are ready to be extruded. At this stage they are known as glochidia. A violent contraction of the two valves of the female mussel ruptures the glochidial membrane, and the young glochidia are expelled through the exhalant siphon. The few that may directly contact a fish host fasten themselves to the gills or fins. Here they become encysted for shorter or longer periods of time, depending entirely upon the fluids of their host for sustenance. Upon the maturity of this second larval stage, the encystment sloughs away, and the still minute mussel leaves its host and begins its own existence on the stream or lake bottom. There is considerable variation in the duration of the parasitic stage and in the selection of the fish host among the many species of fresh-water clams. In general, the most widely distributed species of mussels have a wide selection of fish hosts.

In North America their greatest development has occurred in the Ohio River system and in the Alabama-Coosa river system. Shells of these mussels were in considerable demand for making pearl buttons, but the development of plastics has lessened this demand somewhat. Primitive man used these various mussels for food, as attested by the numerous shell heaps which are found along many river margins where these animals were abundant. Pearls of considerable value have been found in certain species of mussels but their occurrence is rare, at least as smooth, rounded pearls of commercial value.

Marine Mussels.—Most of the marine species that are called "mussels" belong to a single family, Mytilidae. They occur in nearly all temperate and tropical seas of the world. They frequent the intertidal zone, clinging to rocks, other shells, wharf structures, and even to each other. The valves are generally elongate, pointed at one end and smoothly rounded at the other. In Europe they are an important food item, but are much less so in New England where they are equally abundant. Their minor value as an item of food is offset by the damage they do as fouling organisms, clinging to the bottom of ships, buoys, intake tunnels, and many other marine structures. This necessitates frequent cleaning and scraping of such structures, and adds enormously to maintenance costs. See also BIVALVES; MOLLUSCA.

WILLIAM J. CLENCH.

MUSSET, mü-sĕ′ **(Louis Charles) Alfred de,** French poet and playwright: b. Paris, France, Dec. 11, 1810; d. there, May 2, 1857. He was born into cultured, comfortable circumstances, and educated at the Collège Henri IV, where his first compositions won high praise. He hesitated at first among several professions, but by his 20th year, when he published the volume of verse entitled *Contes d'Espagne et d'Italie,* he had definitely chosen letters. For the next few years Musset's poems and plays showed the influence of Lord Byron, especially in their satirical quality and sense of doom. His start in the theater, with *La nuit vénitienne* (1830), was not happy.

The winter of 1833–1834 marked the crisis of Musset's life—his connection with George Sand (q.v.), and their Italian journey. With little real sympathy save a joint consciousness of genius, the two could not hope for enduring happiness; but the affair preluded two years (1834–1836) of intense literary creation by Musset. During these years he wrote the *Nuits* (see NUIT DE MAI) and various other love poems, which have won him the title of the greatest French love poet. *Stances à la Malibran* was also composed at this time. For the theater he wrote, among other pieces, *On ne badine pas avec l'amour* (1834, q.v.), *Lorenzaccio* (1834), and *Il ne faut jurer de rien* (1836). It is a tribute to his dramatic power that although many of his plays were not intended for production, he is perhaps the only playwright among the romantics who holds the stage today. In prose he wrote *La confession d'un enfant du siècle* (1836, q.v.), an account of his life with Sand, which is also a political testament and the evocation of an era. Shortly thereafter he broke with romanticism in the *Lettres de Dupuis et de Cotonet* (1836–1837).

After 1840 Musset's creativity began to decline, a not illogical development in view of his precocious beginning, his pessimism, and dissipation; but he did publish the patriotic song *Le Rhin allemand,* an answer to Nikolaus Becker's *Rheinlied;* and the popular comedy, *Il faut qu'une porte soit ouverte ou fermée* (1845). Over conservative opposition he was elected to the French Academy in 1852. His collected works were published in France (1933–1938).

Consult Musset, Paul de, *Biographie d'Alfred de Musset* (Paris 1877); Sedgwick, Henry D., *Alfred de Musset* (Indianapolis 1931).

MUSSOLINI, mōōs-sô-lē′nē, **Benito,** Italian premier and dictator: b. Dovia di Predappio, Forlì Province, Italy, July 29, 1883; d. Dongo, Como Province, April 28, 1945. Mussolini's father Alessandro was a blacksmith with socialistic leanings, who named his son for the Mexican liberator Benito Juárez. At great sacrifice, the family procured Benito an education, first at parochial school and then at a normal school; at various times he was an elementary school teacher. The chief events of Mussolini's early life were his sojourn in Switzerland, where he went in 1902 and became associated with a group of revolutionaries, finally being expelled from the country for his activities; his stay in the Austrian Trentino in 1908–1909, which aroused his nationalistic feelings; and his reading of Friedrich Wilhelm Nietzsche and Georges Sorel, philosophers of force. By the outbreak of World War I in 1914, Mussolini was Forlì's leading Socialist and the trenchant editor of the party's official newspaper *Avanti!*

After hesitating for some weeks, Mussolini espoused the Allied cause in the war, perhaps motivated by French bribes. The Italian Socialists as a group remained pacifist, and Mussolini was forced from the party and his editorship (Oct. 20, 1914). On November 14 of that year, he founded his own *Il Popolo d'Italia* in Milan, justifying Italian entry into the war by saying it would promote the proletarian cause throughout Europe. He himself was drafted as a private and severely wounded in a training accident (Feb. 23, 1917), eventually returning to his newspaper. By this time his break with socialism was complete.

Rise to Power.—Postwar conditions suited Mussolini's policy of cynical opportunism. To gain backing, he played on fears of the sizable Communist movement, and appealed to the growing patriotic discontent with Italy's share in the postwar settlement. On March 23, 1919 in Milan, he founded the first of the *Fasci di combattimento,* a political grouping whose program mixed syndicalist and nationalist catchwords. He backed Gabriele D'Annunzio's seizure of Fiume, which in its illegality and use of bluff was typical of his own future foreign policy. Mussolini used his bands of blackshirted *squadristi* against strikers, Communists, and Socialists in the turbulent years 1919–1922, as Fascist affiliates continued to spring up in northern Italy. His claim to be Italy's savior from communism was born in these years, but cannot be accepted; by 1920 the Communist threat had receded.

In the 1921 elections, 22 Fascists were returned to Parliament, and the party was organized nationally, Mussolini being known as *Il Duce,* the leader, a title later copied by Hitler and others. In 1922 a prolonged general strike was broken by the *squadristi,* clearing the way for the carefully planned march on Rome (Oct. 28, 1922). During this crisis Mussolini himself stayed in Milan, until the vacillating King Victor Emmanuel III, ignoring the advisers who would have arrested Mussolini, called upon him to form a cabinet (October 31).

Dictatorship.—Once in power, Mussolini moved step by step to establish a dictatorial regime. A new electoral law, adopted in 1923, guaranteed the Fascist Party a two-thirds majority in Parliament; five years later elections were reduced to the registration of a yes or no vote on a list of candidates prepared by the Fascist Grand Council, whose members were appointed by Mussolini. Finally, in 1938, the Chamber of Deputies was abolished in favor of a Chamber of Fasci and Corporations, with an entirely appointive membership. To insure his personal rule further, the dictator always reserved several cabinet portfolios for himself. Any attempt to oppose the regime was smashed by the secret police and the armed Fascist militia.

Encouraged by the apparent weakness of the democratic powers during the years of economic depression, Mussolini embarked on an aggressive foreign program, beginning with the invasion of Ethiopia (October 1935). When the League of Nations imposed sanctions, he defied the world organization, and finally in December 1937 withdrew Italy from membership. In the summer of 1936, in cooperation with the German dictator Adolf Hitler, he intervened openly in the Spanish Civil War on the side of Gen. Francisco Franco, sending tens of thousands of Italian troops and large numbers of planes to fight in Spain during the next three years. In October 1936 the Rome-Berlin Axis was formed by a secret agreement, which became an open military alliance in May 1939. In April of the latter year Italy annexed Albania.

Downfall.—Expecting to score an easy victory after Hitler's initial successes, Mussolini led Italy into World War II in June 1940. But repeated defeats in the field and the threatened invasion of Italy by the Allies led to his downfall only three years later. He was turned out by the Fascist Grand Council itself on July 25, 1943, and taken into custody, from which he was freed by German paratroopers on September 12. Carried off to northern Italy, which was under German occupation, he headed a puppet regime there until the final German collapse. He attempted to flee Italy in disguise, but was seized by partisans on his way to Switzerland, and shot with his mistress, Clara Petacci. His body, defiled by the Milanese populace, was later sequestered by the Italian government, which feared that his grave might become a shrine for the Fascist remnant.

By marriage to Rachele Guidi, Mussolini had five children, of whom his favorite was the eldest daughter, Edda, wife of Count Galeazzo Ciano (q.v.). Besides his extensive political writings and speeches, he was the author of a book on John Huss (1913; Eng. tr., 1929); a novel (Eng. tr., *The Cardinal's Mistress,* 1928); a play, with Giovacchino Forzano (Eng. tr., *Napoleon: the Hundred Days,* 1932); and two volumes of autobiography (Eng. tr., *My Autobiography,* 1928, 1939; *The Fall of Mussolini,* 1948).

See also FASCISM; ITALY—*3. History* (Modern Italy): The Rise and Fall of Fascism.

MUSTAFA KEMAL. See KEMAL ATATURK.

MUSTANG. See HORSE—*Types of Riding Horses* (Mustang).

MUSTARD, mŭs′tẽrd, any of about 100 plants of the genus *Brassica* (family Brassicaceae, q.v.) with yellow flowers and linear or oblong pods. Several species are grown for their seeds, especially *B. alba* and *B. nigra.*

MUSTARD GAS. See CHEMICAL WARFARE; SULPHUR COMPOUNDS.

MUSTELIDAE, mŭs-tĕl′ĭ-dē, a family of carnivorous mammals related to the dogs, bears, and raccoons and traceable to early Oligocene times. A special characteristic of the family is the presence of only one molar tooth on each side of the upper jaw. In general, the dentition resembles that of the cats. The family includes five subfamilies: weasels (Mustelinae), skunks (Mephitinae), badgers (Melinae), ratels (Mellivorinae), and otters (Lutrinae), thus including the ermine, stoat, mink, ferret, polecat, marten, sable, fisher, and wolverine. The habitat is worldwide outside Australasia and Madagascar, but it is in the subarctic and temperate regions of the Northern Hemisphere that the Mustelidae are numerous and produce the most valuable fur.

MUT, mo͞ot, in Egyptian religion, one of the chief goddesses, wife of Ammon (Amon, Amen), and mother of Khonsu; especially worshiped at Thebes. Her name signifies "mother."

MUTANABBI, al-, ăl-mo͝o-tă-năb′bĭ (real name ABU-AL-ṬAYYIB AḤMAD IBN-ḤUSAYN), Arabian poet: b. Al Kufa (now in Iraq), 915; d. near Baghdad, 965. The sobriquet al-Mutanabbi', meaning "prophecy claimant," was conferred upon him in his youth. His most important work, *Diwān,* comprising 289 poems, shows great talent and national spirit besides richness of language, but there are defects of exaggeration in poor taste and certain flattery that is lowering to the general dignity of the verses.

The thousandth anniversary of his death was commemorated in 1935 in Syria, Lebanon, and other lands.

The *Dīwān* was edited by Friedrich Heinrich Dieterici (1861) and Nāṣīf al-Yāziji (1882), and a translation was made by Joseph von Hammer-Purgstall (1824).

See also ARABIC LITERATURE—*The 'Abbāsid Period.*

MUTATIONS, mû-tā'shŭnz, in biology, a relatively abrupt alteration of some heritable character of a living organism (gene, chromosome), resulting in new varieties, as when a purple-flowered sweet pea gives rise to a white-flowered variety. An example of a mutation early observed in animals was the short-legged, or Ancon, breed of sheep which arose as a mutant in a flock of sheep in 1791. About 1900, the Dutch botanist Hugo de Vries attracted attention to the mutation theory by his observations on the evening primrose, *Oenothera lamarckiana,* in which he observed exceptional plants differing from their parents in conspicuous ways (in flower size, in shape of leaves, etc.), but we now know that *O. lamarckiana* is a peculiar kind of hybrid (a "constant" or true-breeding hybrid) and that the exceptional offspring were actually the result of hybridity. However, since 1910, actual mutations have been observed in pure material, and especially in the small fruit fly *Drosophila,* a favorite object for mutation studies because of the ease with which it can be bred on a large scale in the laboratory, and because of its well-known genetic background. It has been found (originally in Thomas Hunt Morgan's laboratory at Columbia University and confirmed in the laboratories of the world) that occasionally the pure wild type gives rise to an aberrant individual. For example, a mutant *Drosophila* may have white eyes instead of the normal red, or short wings instead of long, black body instead of gray, and so forth. Any mutation is comparatively rare, in the sense that it involves only one fly in about a half million. But from the mutant a new race may be derived, such as a mutant with white eyes, or short wings.

Thus, mutations are the building blocks of evolution. However, mutations are random variations in the sense that they are of all sorts—mostly bad, in fact. In the evolution of the horse, for example, most mutations influencing speed would have led to decreased speed. Only very exceptionally would one have led to increased speed. The great speed of the thoroughbred race horse undoubtedly is due to selection by the breeder of such fortunate mutations. In a state of nature, under the competitive conditions of overproduction (as applies to all species in nature), the speedier type would have survived and displaced the less speedy. The natural selection of the speedier individual arising from mutation in a sense exemplifies Darwin's survival of the fittest, or natural selection. Thus evolution would come about through the natural selection of beneficial mutations.

Generally a mutation does not cause a very conspicuous change. In *Drosophila,* the eyes, for example, can be made only slightly less red than those of the normal, the bristles slightly shorter, and so forth. Earlier observers, including de Vries, gained the impression that mutations were always large changes, undoubtedly because the large ones were conspicuous and were the first to attract attention. However, the small mutations are far more important for evolution than are the large ones, for they exert their effect late in the development of the individual and so are less apt to disturb this development radically than are the large mutations. A very common type of large mutations is one, known as a lethal, that exerts its effect early in development and that causes the death of the developing embryo.

Mutations may be caused by physical and chemical factors. In 1927 Hermann Joseph Muller showed that mutations can be produced artificially by means of X-rays. The mutagenic effects of X-rays are due to ionization. In addition to X-rays, all other ionizing radiation is mutagenic, including gamma radiation, alpha particles, protons, neutrons, and electrons. The proportion of mutations produced depends on the dose of the ionizing agent, and in general varies directly as the dose. The Hiroshima bomb, because of its ionizing radiations, undoubtedly produced a large number of mutations in the bombed population, but most of its mutagenic effects will become apparent only in distantly future generations. It has more recently been found that mustard gas, peroxides, and a number of other chemical agents are mutagenic. There may be some connection between mutations and cancer; for the more potent mutagens are carcinogenic.

See also CROSS-FERTILIZATION—*Mutation and Recombination;* EUGENICS—*Experimental Eugenics* (Mutation); EVOLUTION, ORGANIC GENES; GENETICS; HEREDITY; PLANTS AND PLANT SCIENCE—*6. Plant Breeding, Genetics, and Cytogenetics* (The Gene); VARIATION.

EDGAR ALTENBURG,
Professor Emeritus of Biology, Rice University.

MU'TAZILITES. See MOSLEM SECTS—*Rationalists.*

MUTINY, mū'tĭ-nĭ, a revolt against constituted authority in army, navy, or air forces, or in any ship at sea. Mutiny implies a conspiracy, although not necessarily premeditated. While it is possible to charge one person with mutiny, such an offense has usually been held as insubordination or disobedience of orders. Sedition differs from mutiny in that it is a revolt against the government itself rather than merely against officers representing the government. The Articles of War of the United States punishes by death or such other punishment as a court-martial may direct any person subject to military law who attempts to create or who begins, excites, causes, or joins in any mutiny or sedition, or who withholds information about a mutiny, or who does not aid in suppressing mutiny or sedition. In the early 19th century a death sentence was mandatory in the navy.

The right to strike of civilian seamen who are members of a labor union has been a subject of controversy. It is generally conceded that a strike in port is not a mutiny. The right to strike at sea is less clearly defined.

In England from 1689 to 1879 the annual law of Parliament providing for the army was known as the Mutiny Act. When Dumbarton's Scottish regiment mutinied shortly after the Revolution of 1688 it was questioned whether soldiers could be punished for mutiny or desertion in time of peace.

Thereafter Parliament provided for such punishment, but only from year to year, to ensure parliamentary control of the army. In 1879 the Mutiny Act was combined with the Articles of War in a new military code, called the Army Discipline and Regulation Act (thereafter the Army Act), and eventually the Army and Air Force Act.

The Sepoy Mutiny (1857–1858), a revolt of native Sepoy troops in India, was the most extensive in British army history. Much has been written about the mutiny on the naval ship *Bounty* in 1789. The mutineers put Capt. William Bligh and 19 men in an open boat which they sailed 4,000 miles from near the Friendly (Tonga) Islands to Timor. Three mutineers were tried and put to death, but ten of them settled on Pitcairn Island, where some of their descendants remain. (See also MUTINY ON THE BOUNTY.) A mutiny at the Nore in 1797 blocked shipping on the Thames for 17 days. Richard Parker, the leader, was hanged.

In the American Revolution, six regiments of the Pennsylvania Line mutinied at Morristown, N.J., on Jan. 2, 1781, but returned to duty. Three New Jersey regiments mutinied on Jan. 20, 1781. Two ringleaders were hanged. A mutiny of Pennsylvania recruits who marched on the Continental Congress was suppressed in June 1783. In the War of 1812 there were mutinies of the 23d Infantry at Manlius, N.Y.; of the 5th Infantry at Utica, N.Y.; and of a militia company at Buffalo, N.Y. Six men of a Tennessee militia regiment were put to death for a mutiny that occurred at Fort Jackson, Ala., in 1814. This became a campaign issue when the commanding general, Andrew Jackson, was candidate for president. A naval mutiny on the brig *Somers* in 1842 resulted in the hanging of Midshipman Philip Spencer, son of the Secretary of War, John Canfield Spencer, and two sailors.

In World War I the Russian Navy mutinied at Kronstadt in 1917, the Austrian Navy mutinied at Cattaro in 1918, and the German Navy at Kiel, resulting in the sinking of the German battle fleet.

DON RUSSELL.

MUTINY ON THE BOUNTY, a historical novel by Charles Nordhoff and James Norman Hall, published in 1932. It is the first volume of a trilogy, completed by *Men Against the Sea* (1934) and *Pitcairn Island* (1934).

The book might best be described as fictionalized history. The story of the *Bounty* is fully recorded in contemporary documents, including the courts-martial of the mutineers who were captured. The vessel, under the command of William Bligh, had been sent to Tahiti to fetch breadfruit plants to the British West Indies. On the return voyage, Bligh's tyrannical conduct provoked a mutiny, led by the ship's third in command, Fletcher Christian. Bligh and the loyal members of the crew were set adrift in an open boat, and finally, after a desperate voyage, reached the Dutch settlements on Timor. Christian and eight of the mutineers, with their Polynesian wives, established themselves on the then uncharted Pitcairn Island, where their descendants still live.

Nordhoff and Hall closely follow the facts of history, merely adding to the ship's company a fictitious midshipman, Roger Byam, to serve as narrator. Inasmuch as both authors had been resident in the South Seas for 12 years, they brought to the Polynesian chapters a sympathetic understanding of native life surpassed, perhaps, only by Robert Louis Stevenson. Equally noteworthy is the double portrayal of Bligh, first as the tyrant of the *Bounty,* and then as the heroic leader of the open-boat voyage to Timor. He is recognizably the same in each volume: the very toughness which made him unbearable in everyday life was the quality which carried him, and with him his crew, through an ordeal seldom matched in the annals of the sea.

MUTISM. See DEAFNESS.

MUTSUHITO. See MEIJI TENNO.

MUTTONBIRD, mŭt″n-bûrd, an Australasian name of uncertain origin for sea birds of the family Procellariidae used as human food and yielding valuable oil and feathers. The short-tailed shearwater (*Puffinus tenuirostris* or *P. brevicaudus*) is the common muttonbird of Australia and Tasmania and the sooty shearwater (*Puffinus griseus*) that of New Zealand. Other species to which the name is applied are the great-winged (*Pterodroma macroptera*), Kermadec (*Pterodroma neglecta* or *P. phillippii*), and white-headed (*Pterodroma lessoni*) petrels. See also SHEARWATER.

H. T. PORTER.

MUTUAL FUNDS are open-end investment companies that invest shareholders' money in a portfolio of securities. They are "open end" in that they normally offer new shares to the public on a continuing basis and promise to redeem outstanding shares on any business day. Mutual fund investors thus are always able to sell their shares back to the fund at net asset value—that is, the present market value of the portfolio behind each outstanding share. American mutual funds, the first of which was formed in Boston in 1924, began to be a major force in the nation's securities markets in the 1960's. These funds pursue a great variety of investment objectives. For more detailed information, see INVESTMENT COMPANY—*Mutual Funds;* INVESTMENTS.

MUTUAL SAVINGS BANKS. See BANKS AND BANKING—*Mutual Savings Banks.*

MWERU, Lake, mwā'rōō (Fr. MOERO), lake, Africa, on the border between Zambia and Katanga province, Zaire. The lake is situated at an altitude of 3,025 feet. It is about 70 miles long and 30 miles wide, with an area of 1,700 square miles; the Luapula River flows northward through it. Small steamboats ply the lake, its chief ports being Kilwa and Pweto, Congo. There are extensive fisheries. The lake was discovered by the Portuguese traveler Francisco José de Lacerda e Almeida in 1798, visited by David Livingstone in 1867, and first explored by Sir Alfred Sharpe in 1890.

MY ÁNTONIA, ȧn'tô-nyȧ, a novel by Willa Cather, published in 1918. It is the third and best of the stories based on the author's memories of her girlhood in Nebraska in the 1880's.

The Shimerdas are a Bohemian (Czech) family who take up a homestead on the Nebraska prairie. The parents are unfit for pioneering; the father, in loneliness and despair, at last commits suicide. The strongest and most resilient of the family is Ántonia, about 12 years old when the story opens. Driven by her tyrannical elder brother, Ambrosch, she does a man's work on the farm in her early teens. Later, like other immigrant girls, she goes into domestic service in the nearby town of Black Hawk. Seduced by Larry Donovan, a worthless railroader, she returns to the farm, bears a child, and later marries Anton Cuzak. We last see her as mother of a big family and mistress of a prosperous farm.

The story is told episodically by Jim Burden, a neighbor who has known Ántonia from childhood. The narrative includes a cross section of Midwestern prairie society in an era of change. Some of the comments on the narrowness of small-town life anticipate Sinclair Lewis' *Main Street,* published two years later.

DeLancey Ferguson
Formerly, Brooklyn College

MY COUNTRY! 'TIS OF THEE. See America.

MYASTHENIA GRAVIS, mī-əs-thē'nē-ə gra'vəs, is a disease that causes voluntary muscles to become weak and to tire easily. It most prominently affects the muscles of the head, particularly those of the eyes and the back of the throat, and the muscles of the larynx and respiratory tract. Women are affected twice as frequently as men, with the incidence highest between the ages of 20 and 40.

The first sign of myasthenia gravis is often weakness of one eye muscle, which may cause double vision or drooping of an eyelid. Sometimes weakness of one part of the face causes an unnatural smile or the mouth to droop to one side. A victim of the disease may be unable to swallow a whole glass of water, without resting, because the muscles in the back of the throat become fatigued. The symptoms disappear with rest.

All symptoms of myasthenia gravis are aggravated by fatigue, insufficient sleep, excessive alcohol intake, emotional stress, or infection, particularly of the respiratory tract. The disease sometimes develops acutely, but most often it begins slowly. Symptoms advance irregularly, getting worse for a while, then remaining the same or even getting better, but over a period of years there is gradual worsening. The major danger associated with myasthenia gravis arises from progressive paralysis or infection, particularly that involving the respiratory tract.

The cause of myasthenia gravis is not known, but it is known that the symptoms are produced by an imbalance in two chemicals—acetylcholine and cholinesterase—that are necessary for normal neuromuscular function. The disease is treated by drugs that antagonize cholinesterase. Some patients have tumors of the thymus gland, and in some of these patients removal of the thymus results in remission of symptoms.

Louis J. Vorhaus, M. D.
Cornell University Medical College

MYCENAE, mī-sē'nē, an ancient city in Greece, was situated in the area of the modern nome (department) of Argolis, about 9 miles (15 km) north of the Gulf of Argolis. Set on a rocky formation in the northeastern part of the Argive plain, Mycenae was chiefly a citadel controlling the road from the Peloponnesus to Corinth.

Mycenae was founded by non-Greeks about 2900 B. C. It was destroyed about 1150 B. C. by Greek invaders from the north; reoccupied by Dorians about 1100; and destroyed again, by Argives, about 470 B. C. The city was revived in the 4th century B. C., but by the 2d century A. D. it was in ruins.

The acme of Mycenaean civilization was reached during 1400–1150 B. C., the era of its great cultural achievements. Toward the end of this era, Mycenae was the scene of the dramatic tragedies of the house of Atreus, portrayed by Aeschylus in his *Oresteia* trilogy of the mid-5th century B. C.

The first excavations at Mycenae, by Heinrich Schliemann in 1876–1878, uncovered an acropolis, a palace, massive walls, many tombs, the so-called Treasury of Atreus, the Gate of Lions, and objects of art such as golden masks and ornaments, inlaid weapons, and ceramics.

See also Aeschylus—*The Oresteian Trilogy;* Atreus; Atreus, Treasury of; Greece—*History of Greece to 330 A. D.*

P. R. Coleman-Norton
Formerly, Princeton University

Further Reading: Cottrell, Leonard, *Lion Gate: A Journey in Search of the Mycenaeans* (Fernhill 1964); Desborough, Vincent R., *The Last Myceanaeans and Their Successors* (Oxford 1964); Mylonas, George E., *Mycenae and the Mycenaean Age* (Princeton Univ. Press 1966).

MYCENAEAN CIVILIZATION. See Aegean Civilization; Greece—*History of Greece to 330 A. D.* and *Archaeology.*

MYCOPLASMA, mī'kō-plaz-mə, are a group of microorganisms that are intermediate between viruses and bacteria. This group of microorganisms is usually referred to as the *pleuropneumonialike organisms,* or PPLO. Unlike viruses, PPLO do not require a host cell in which to grow and multiply. Although the classification of PPLO, or mycoplasma, is still somewhat controversial, many microbiologists now classify them as the genus *Mycoplasma* of the bacteria class Schizomycetes. Many species of mycoplasma are known to cause disease. In man, "virus pneumonia" is caused by *M. pneumoniae,* and a type of arthritis known as Reiter's syndrome is thought to be caused by a PPLO.

The PPLO are an unusual group of microorganisms. Their most outstanding characteristic is the absence of a cell wall. Each PPLO cell is bounded only by a thin cell membrane. Some forms are very small and pass through filters that retain bacteria and allow only viruses and rickettsia to pass. PPLO range from 0.125 to 0.250 microns in diameter. Some require steroids, such as cholesterol, for growth.

Under certain environmental conditions true bacteria, such as *Proteus* and *Salmonella,* can form stages that lack a cell wall and are very similar to PPLO. These bacterial forms are known as *L forms.* The loss of the cell wall in these bacteria may be induced in a number of ways. The most common cause is exposure to an antibiotic, such as penicillin, or to a toxic substance, such as lithium chloride. One major difference between L forms of bacteria and PPLO is that some types of L forms (called L phase cells) may revert to the original bacterial type. Also, it has not yet been shown that L forms are the causative agents of any disease.

Mycoplasma were first recognized in 1898 by the French biologists Edmond Nocard and Pierre Roux, who found the organisms in the pleural fluid of cattle suffering from pleuropneumonia. They called the microorganisms *pleuropneumonia organisms,* or PPO. When similar organisms were found in other animals, they were called PPLO, a term that is now used to include all members of this group. In addition to infecting humans and cattle, PPLO are known to cause disease in goats, swine, sheep, and chickens.

DAVID A. OTTO
Stephens College

MYCORHIZA or **MYCORRHIZA,** mī-kō-rī'zȧ, the combination of a fungus and a root acting as a single organ, in which the relationship is mutually beneficial. The significance of this relationship was discovered by Albert Bernard Frank during the latter part of the 19th century. At the request of the Prussian government, Frank had begun studies on the possibility of breeding truffles (which are also mycorhizal fungi) when he became sidetracked onto the broader subject of mycorhizal associations. He defined two types of such fungi: *ectotrophic fungi,* which form sheaths around the roots, and *endotrophic fungi,* whose hyphae are found primarily within the root cells. In the former type, some hyphae penetrate between the root cells, and some may even enter the cells.

Mycorhizal roots typically lack root hairs, the fungus replacing entirely or in large part the absorptive functions of the hairs in securing minerals and water. The fungus, in return, receives at least part of its food from the root. The relationship might be considered a special type of parasitism, but one in which each partner benefits from the other's presence. All roots of a given plant are not necessarily mycorhizal; many of the roots may be free of the fungus. Although mycorhizae are found mostly in woody plants, nonwoody plants such as orchids, Indian pipe, and others also have them. Some authorities believe that all species of woody plants, at least in some environments, have mycorhizae. It is noteworthy that mycorhizae generally develop best in soils deficient in mineral nutrients, the plant apparently being able to obtain needed elements from the soil more efficiently when the fungus is present in its roots. Mycorhizal roots are generally different in appearance from normal ones. Besides lacking hairs, they are frequently thicker than normal, sometimes dichotomously branched, and usually yellowish brown to dark brown in color, although they may be white, yellow, pink, bluish, violet, or black.

The Indian pipe, a small, whitish, relative of *Rhododendron,* lacks chlorophyll and is therefore unable to manufacture its own food. It has become entirely dependent upon a mycorhizal fungus for its food. Since the seeds do not contain the fungus, in order to survive they must fall on ground where the fungus is present. Most orchids have fungi in their roots and appear unable to survive in nature without them, nor can their tiny seeds germinate in nature unless the appropriate fungus is present. This explains why orchid growers plant seeds in soil obtained from around established orchids. The coralroot orchid (*Corallorhiza*), like the Indian pipe, lacks chlorophyll and depends upon a fungus for its food. In this case, the fungus lives mostly within the roots, being particularly concentrated in the outermost root cells.

Most mycorhizal fungi are club fungi (Basidiomycetes). A particular species of mycorhizal fungus is often associated with only a few (sometimes only one) species of woody plants. This explains why fruiting bodies of some fungi appear only under certain trees. For example, mushrooms such as *Boletus elegans,* which has a mycorhizal relationship with larch, occur only under larch trees, whereas the fly agaric (*Amanita muscaria*) is found primarily under birch and pine, with which it is associated in similar relationship.

LINDSAY S. OLIVE,
Professor of Botany, Columbia University.

MYCOSES, mī-kō'sēz, diseases due to the infection of any part of the body by fungi. The yeast- and moldlike fungi that infect man and animals are microscopic in size. Fortunately, of the thousands of known species of yeasts and molds, only about 100 produce disease in plants, less than 50 are capable of infecting animals and man, and less than 15 cause fatal disease in man.

Fungus Diseases of the Skin, Hair, and Nails.—The fungi that grow in the superficial layers of the skin or in the hair or nails of the fingers and toes are called dermatophytes, and the diseases that they cause are known as dermatomycoses. These fungi cannot live in the deeper layers of the skin or in the internal organisms of the body.

Fungus infections of the hair and skin of man were discovered years before the first pathogenic bacteria were found. In 1839 Johann Lukas Schoenlein of Germany described a fungus in the hair of children in a disease called favus, and in 1846 another German, Karl Ferdinand Eichstedt, found a second type of fungus in a disease of the skin called pityriasis versicolor. Thirty years later, in 1876, Robert Koch of Germany discovered the anthrax bacillus, which caused fatal disease in animals and man.

The lesions produced by the dermatophytes were known to physicians for hundreds of years before the fungal etiology was established. The lesions on the skin often grew in a ringlike manner, and those in the hair caused circular or ringlike areas of baldness. Not knowing of the existence of microscopic organisms, physicians assumed that the disease was caused by a worm and called the disease ringworm. This name is still used by many people and some doctors, but it should be emphasized that ringworm of the hair, skin, and nails is caused by fungi and not by a worm.

Tinea pedis, ringworm of the feet, or athlete's foot, is the most common fungus infection of man. The estimates of human infection vary from 60 to 80 per cent. The fungus can be found by examining scrapings of the skin from between the toes in many individuals who have never had any evidence of disease. It is mildly contagious and is believed to be spread by infected individuals walking on wooden floors or wooden slats in shower baths in gymnasiums. This is undoubtedly the origin of the name "athlete's foot." Careful washing of the feet and the daily use of clean dry socks are the best protection against infection. In World War II, particularly in the tropics, where soldiers could not keep their feet clean and dry, tinea pedis became one of the chief causes of disability. Several different fungi will produce athlete's foot. The most common type is *Trichophyton mentagrophytes,* but the disease may be caused by various species of *Trichophyton* and occasionally by

Epidermophyton floccosum and species of *Microsporum* or *Candida albicans.* Severe infections are very disabling and should be treated by a physician specializing in dermatology or diseases of the skin.

Tinea unguium is the name applied to fungus infection of the nails of the hands or feet. The affected nails become lusterless, discolored, thickened, brittle, and finally erode away. Two different species of fungi infect the nails. The most common and destructive is *Trichophyton rubrum,* whose activity is confined to the nail itself. The less common type of infection is with *Candida albicans,* which not only invades the nail but produces inflammation of the soft tissues about the nails. The process of infection is very slow, requiring months to years to destroy the nails completely. Spontaneous cures do not occur, but treatment by a competent dermatologist usually effects a restoration of the nail.

Tinea cruris, also known as ringworm of the groin, or jockey itch, is caused by *Epidermophyton floccosum* and certain species of *Trichophyton.* This infection is found in all parts of the world but is more common in tropical countries and in athletes, as suggested by the common name "jockey itch." The skin becomes red and scaly, and itches. If neglected, the disease may progress to vesicles and vesiculopustules, but it is readily cured if treated promptly.

Tinea corporis, often called tinea circinata, or ringworm of the body, is caused by various species of *Trichophyton* or *Microsporum.* This disease occurs in both tropical and temperate countries. The infection starts as a small scaly path of skin surrounded by a circle of crusting vesicles and pustules. The peripheral zone invades the normal surrounding skin, producing larger and larger rings; this peculiar method of spread resulted in the original name "ringworm of the skin." Tinea corporis responds readily to treatment, but a tropical variety called tinea imbricata is very resistant to treatment.

Tinea barbae, ringworm of the beard or barber's itch, is caused by several species of *Trichophyton* and *Microsporum.* This disease is frequently seen in Europe but is rare in the United States. It was originally spread from man to man by barbers' tools, hence the name "barber's itch." The disease has appeared in the United States in cattle-raising and feeding areas, where infection is spread from cattle to man without the assistance of the barber. If the mild lesions are neglected, they may develop into boggy, granulomatous masses that are not only unsightly and painful but will require many months to heal even with the best treatment.

Tinea capitis, or ringworm of the scalp, is an infection of the hairs of the head. The fungi invade the hairs, causing them to break off near the scalp and leave circular areas of baldness. There are four different species of fungi that produce ringworm of the scalp, and each is sometimes different in its method of infection. *Microsporum canis* and *M. gypseum* infect cats and dogs and spread from these animals to young children. *M. audouini* is a natural parasite of children. It was common in Europe but rare in the United States until World War II, when large epidemics appeared among school children in the United States and Canada. The fourth type, previously rare in the United States, is called black-dotted ringworm and is caused by *Trichophyton tonsurans.* This type of infection, which has become prevalent, was introduced into New York City from Puerto Rico and into Texas from Mexico. The fungus attacks the hair of both children and adults. Hairs infected by the first three species give a greenish fluorescence when exposed to ultraviolet light, while the fourth species does not show this peculiarity. Infections caused by *M. audouini* and *T. tonsurans* are much more difficult to treat than those caused by *M. canis* and *M. gypseum,* but all can be cured by persistent treatment.

Tinea favosa, or honeycomb ringworm, is caused by *Trichophyton schoenleini, T. violaceum,* or *M. gypseum* and is chronic and difficult to treat. Yellowish cup-shaped crusts with a peculiar "mousy" odor appear over the scalp. The hair bulbs may be completely destroyed, leaving partial or complete baldness. This disease is most common in Russia, Poland, the Balkans, Egypt, and about the Mediterranean area. It is rare in England, the United States, and Canada.

Fungus Infections of the Deeper Layers of the Skin.—Larger and more destructive lesions appear when the fungus has the ability to invade the deeper layers of the skin and the subcutaneous tissues.

Chromoblastomycosis is caused by a group of related fungi, including such species as *Phialophora verrucosa, Hormodendrum pedrosoi,* and *H. compactum.* The lesions begin as small wartlike growths, which grow slowly and spread slowly over a period of months or years. These lesions may finally cover the feet and legs with papillary vegetation. The lesions are not painful, and the general health of the individual is not affected. This type of fungus has been isolated from wood pulp, and many patients give a history of a slight wound with a splinter or stick before the onset of the disease. This infection does not spread from man to man. The early small lesions can be cured by surgical removal. The larger, more chronic ones may respond to treatment with the antibiotic, amphotericin B.

Maduromycosis, also known as Madura foot, or mycetoma, begins as an infection of the skin or subcutaneous tissues but progresses to invade the muscle and even the bones. The feet are most often invaded, as suggested by the name "Madura foot." The disease is most common in tropical countries and in the southern United States, where the practice of going about the fields and woods barefooted invites the introduction of fungi into cuts and abrasions. The most common cause is the fungus *Allescheria boydii,* followed by various species of *Nocardia,* but some 25 species belonging to 10 different genera are known to produce this type of infection. There are specific drug treatments for some types, but none for others; in the latter, the foot and leg have to be amputated to prevent spread of secondary bacterial infection from the local lesion to the internal organs of the body. This infection does not spread from man to man.

Sporotrichosis is caused by a single species of fungus, *Sporotrichum schenckii,* which is worldwide in distribution. It may be a parasite of plants but also has been found growing on deadwood and mosses. Horticulturists, florists, and farmers are most often infected, but anyone can acquire the disease. The lesions are usually confined to the skin and subcutaneous tissues but may invade the bones, lungs, and other organs. A black necrotic lesion appears at the point of infection, which is frequently on the hand or on other exposed areas of the body. A chain of subcutaneous nodules develops along the lymph channels that drain the site of infection, and these may break out through the skin to give a chain of ulcers. The disease responds to treatment in a period of months but will persist for years if not treated. Sporotrichosis does not spread from man to man.

Fungus Diseases of the Mucous Membranes.—Rhinosporidiosis, caused by *Rhinosporidium seeberi,* is an infection of the mucous membranes of the nose, eyes, ears, and larynx. The most characteristic lesions are in the nose, out of which long fleshy, polyplike masses grow. This disease occurs most often in India and Ceylon and other parts of the tropics, but a number of cases have been found in the United States. The infection seems to be acquired while swimming, diving, or working in stagnant water. The early small lesions can be cured by surgical excision, but there is no very effective treatment for the advanced cases. This infection does not spread from man to man.

Thrush is characterized by the development of soft white patches on the mucous membranes of the mouth and vagina. Thrush of the mouth was formerly very common in infants and young children but is now relatively rare. Thrush of the vagina is not uncommon, particularly in women with diabetes. *Candida albicans* is the most frequent cause of thrush, but some cases are caused by *Geotrichum candidum.*

C. albicans does not limit itself to the mucous membranes but may infect the nails of the finger, the superficial layer of the skin, the intestinal tract, the bronchi and lungs, and occasionally the bones and brain. The local lesions respond well to local treatment, but the generalized infections may be fatal.

Infection of the Lungs and Internal Organs.—Most of the fungus infections that kill patients belong in this group. The symptoms are not unlike those of tuberculosis, and the death rate may be even higher than found in tuberculosis.

Actinomycosis and nocardiosis are caused by organisms that are the connecting link between bacteria and fungi, although they are classified as fungi. Actinomycosis is caused by an anaerobic, gram-positive branching fungus called *Actinomyces bovis,* and nocardiosis by an aerobic gram-positive branching fungus called *Nocardia asteroides. A. bovis* lives normally in the gums and about decaying and neglected teeth, while *Nocardia* lives in the soil and infects a variety of animals as well as man. Both types of fungi produce disease of the lungs, bones, and internal organs and frequently burrow to the surface of the body, producing draining sinuses. Penicillin is a specific drug for actinomycosis, but it does not cure nocardial infections. These are treated with the sulfonamides.

North American blastomycosis is caused by *Blastomyces dermatitidis.* This disease occurs naturally in North America, as the name suggests, and is most common in the Mississippi Valley and southeastern United States. Apparently the soil is the source of the infection, and the fungus has been isolated from this source. Dogs become infected, as well as man, but the disease does not spread from dogs to man or from man to man. Occasionally, the infection is limited to the skin, where it produces verrucous or ulcerating lesions, which are chronic and last for many years. The more severe infections are in the lungs, bones, and other organs. Most patients are cured in a period of months by treatment with the chemical hydroxystilbamidine or the antibiotic amphotericin B.

South American blastomycosis is caused by a related species of *Blastomyces* called *B. brasiliensis* and is confined to South America. The mucous membranes and glands are more often involved in the South American disease. This infection responds partially to sulfonamides but seems to resist hydroxystilbamidine. It is now being treated with amphotericin B.

Cryptococcosis or European blastomycosis is caused by a yeastlike fungus called *Cryptococcus neoformans.* This disease occurs throughout the world, and the organism has been isolated from soil and from deposits of chicken and pigeon manure. Cows, dogs, horses, leopards, and other animals may be infected. The disease does not spread from animal to man or from man to man. Occasionally, the disease begins in the skin, and sometimes tumorlike masses are produced in the subcutaneous tissue, but the lungs, brain, and bones are most often involved. The brain infections were almost always fatal before treatment with amphotericin B was discovered.

Histoplasmosis is caused by *Histoplasma capsulatum.* This disease occurs in localized areas scattered over the world, but the largest endemic area is in the central part of the United States. The fungus has been isolated from soil and from pigeon, chicken, and bat manure. It is most often breathed into the lungs in dust but may produce local mucosal lesions in the nose, ears, mouth, larynx, and intestines. Most infections are mild and do not produce symptoms, but leave behind calcified areas in the lungs. Horses have infection without symptoms. Dogs may have mild infection or may die of the disease, but the organisms do not spread from animals to man or from man to man. Some of the pulmonary and most of the generalized infections resulted in death before the new treatment with amphotericin B.

Coccidiodomycosis is caused by *Coccidiodes immitis.* This disease occurs in the dry southwestern part of the United States, in Mexico, and in the western third of South America. The organism has been isolated from the soil and is apparently inhaled with dust. The skin is rarely infected. Most infections do not produce symptoms, or produce mild symptoms which resemble a cold or the grippe. In the more severe infections it continues to spread in the lungs and then invades the other organs of the body including the bones and brain. Horses, cows, and sheep acquire the disease in the endemic areas, but the infections do not spread from animal to man or from man to man. There was no specific treatment before the introduction of amphotericin B.

Bibliography.—Conant, Norman F., Smith, D. T., Baker, R. D., Callaway, J. L., and Martin, D. S., *Manual of Clinical Mycology,* 2d ed. (Philadelphia 1954); Pillsbury, Donald M., Shelley, W. B., and Kligman, A. M., *Dermatology* (Philadelphia 1956); Dubos, René J., *Bacterial and Mycotic Infections of Man,* 3d ed. (Philadelphia 1958); Lewis, George M., Hopper, M. E., Weilson, J. W., and Plunkett, O. A., *An Introduction to Medical Mycology,* 4th ed. (Chicago 1958).

DAVID T. SMITH, M.D.,
Professor of Microbiology, Associate Professor of Medicine, Duke University School of Medicine.

MYDDELTON or **MIDDLETON,** mĭd'-'l-tŭn, SIR **Hugh,** British contractor: b. Galch

Hill, Denbigh, Wales, c. 1560; d. London, Dec. 10, 1631. A goldsmith, banker, clothmaker, and member of Parliament (1603–1628), he was chiefly noted as contractor for the New River project to augment London's insufficient water supply by building a canal from springs at Chadwell and Amwell, Hertfordshire, to London. Constructed in 1609–1613 with the aid of funds from James I, who paid half the cost in return for half the profits, the canal was 38¾ miles long, 10 feet wide, and about 4 feet deep. It was financially unsuccessful in Myddelton's lifetime but became highly profitable afterward. He was made a baronet in 1622.

MYELITIS, mī-ĕ-lī′tĭs, any disease of the spinal cord characterized by inflammation. Myelitis is an extremely serious medical condition. Its effects are variable combinations of paralysis of movement and impairment of sensation, the severity depending upon the location and extent of the disease. If the whole cross-sectional extent of the cord becomes involved at any level, all power of voluntary movement and all sensation are lost below the affected level (*transverse myelitis*).

Myelitis may be the result of infection of the spinal cord by any of a considerable number of microorganisms. *Poliomyelitis,* for example, is due to infection of the nerve cells in the gray matter of the cord by a particular form of filterable virus; the crippling effects of this disease are due to the fact that the cells most severely attacked are those which supply the nerve impulses needed for voluntary movements of the muscles. The familiar illness called *shingles* (herpes zoster) is another variety of myelitis caused by a virus. In this, the cells attacked are chiefly those having to do with sensation rather than movement. Other forms of virus-induced myelitis are much rarer.

The causative organisms of syphilis and tuberculosis occasionally infect the spinal cord. There generally is accompanying inflammation of the coverings (meninges) of the cord, so that it is more usual to speak of *meningomyelitis* in connection with these diseases. The common pus-producing bacteria may at times invade the spinal cord, producing an abscess of the cord (*suppurative myelitis*), but this is extremely rare, because the cord apparently has considerable resistance to direct infection of this sort. Even rarer are cases of myelitis resulting from infection by disease-producing fungi.

In another large and important group of myelitis cases, evidence of inflammation of the cord is present, but no infection or other causative agent can be found. Although some cases follow upon many sorts of common respiratory, gastrointestinal, or more generalized infections, all available evidence indicates that the myelitis is not produced directly by the infecting organism, which acts at most as a precipitating rather than a causative factor. In this group, the disease process may vary in severity from affection of a small portion of the cord to involvement of the entire brain and spinal cord at all levels (*encephalomyelitis*). This variety of disease is the subject of much research, but the causes and mechanisms of disease production remain unexplained.

Treatment must be aimed at eradicating the cause of the disease, if known, and preventing complications from paralysis or loss of sensation. In many cases, considerable improvement can be expected with appropriate treatment.

EDWARD P. RICHARDSON, JR., M.D.,
Massachusetts General Hospital, Boston.

MYERS, mī′ẽrz, **Charles Samuel,** British psychologist: b. London, England, March 13, 1873; d. Winsford, Cheshire, Oct. 12, 1946. Educated at Cambridge, he taught physiology and psychology there from 1902 to 1922 and was chiefly responsible for the establishment of the first English laboratory of experimental psychology, opened at the university in 1912. As consultant psychologist to the British armed forces in France during World War I, he pioneered in the treatment of shell shock. In 1921, with Henry J. Welch, Myers founded the National Institute of Industrial Psychology, which played a major role in the development of that branch of science in Britain. He was editor of the *British Journal of Psychology* (1911–1924) and author of the notable *Textbook of Experimental Psychology* (1909), *Industrial Psychology in Great Britain* (1926), and other books.

MYERS, Gustavus, American social historian: b. Trenton, N.J., March 20, 1872; d. New York, N.Y., Dec. 7, 1942. Brother of the painter Jerome Myers (q.v.), he was brought up in poverty, with little formal education, but succeeded in gaining a foothold as a newspaper man in New York City in his early 20's. In 1900 he published his first significant book, *History of Public Franchises in New York City,* a "muckraking" exposé of corruption in municipal government and business. This was followed by *History of Tammany Hall* (1901; rev. ed., 1917) and his most famous work, *History of the Great American Fortunes* (3 vols., 1910; rev. ed., 1 vol., 1936), which attained the status of a near classic. Though undoubtedly marked by the author's bias, it is a monument of exhaustive research and played an influential part in awakening the public conscience to abuses in the nation's economic life. Among Myers' later books were *History of the Supreme Court of the United States* (1912) and *History of Bigotry in the United States* (1943).

MYERS, Jerome, American painter: b. Petersburg, Va., March 20, 1867; d. New York, N.Y., June 19, 1940. He studied at Cooper Union and the Art Students League in New York City and began to work as a painter of signs and stage sets. Soon he was painting the New York City street scenes for which he became famous, depicting everyday life, such as housewives marketing or gossiping, old-clothes men, fish markets, and street merry-go-rounds, in a bright, lyric style. Myers was one of the organizers of the famous Armory Show in New York (1913). Typical of his work in museums throughout the United States are *The Night Mission* (Metropolitan Museum of Art, New York City) and *The End of the Street* (Art Institute of Chicago). He published an autobiography, *Artist in Manhattan* (1940).

MYGALOMORPH SPIDERS. See SPIDERS—*The Kinds of Spiders* (Mygalomorph Spiders).

MYITKYINA, myĭ′chē′nä, town, Burma, capital of Kachin State and Myitkyina District in Upper Burma, on the right bank of the upper Irrawaddy River, about 50 miles (80 km) from the Chinese border. It is the head of the railroad running south to Mandalay (about 260 miles, or 420 km) and beyond, and the head of navigation for steamers plying the Irrawaddy during the low-water season. The town is a market and trading center, with jade mines nearby.

During World War II the Japanese captured Myitkyina (May 1942) in their campaign to cut the Burma Road, and turned it into a military base with a key airfield. In May 1944, American and Chinese forces seized the airfield, and on Aug. 3, 1944, captured the town. Afterward the Ledo (Stilwell) Road was extended to Myitkyina from India, and southward to Bhamo and beyond, to link up with the Burma Road. A road links Myitkyina with Tengchung, China.

MYKONOS, mē′kô-nôs, is one of the Greek Cyclades islands, in the Aegean Sea. It lies just northeast of the smaller—but historically more significant—island of Delos. Mykonos is 9 miles (14 km) long, 6 miles (10 km) wide, and has an area of about 33 square miles (85 sq km). The terrain is rocky and mountainous, rising to an altitude of 1,195 feet (365 meters). The chief town is Mykonos.

Fishing is important economically, and wine, honey, olive oil, and cheese are produced. The island's sunshine and sea breezes, in addition to its landscape and picturesque setting, combine to make Mykonos a popular tourist attraction. Population: (1961) 3,633.

MYLITTA, mi-lit′ə, was the Babylonian goddess of fertility, associated with the Greek Aphrodite and the Assyrian Ishtar. Custom required every Babylonian woman, once in her life, to sit in Mylitta's temple until a stranger threw a coin into her lap and offered to have intercourse with her. Upon consummation of the sexual act, the woman was released from her obligation.

MYNAH BIRD, mī′nə, any of several species of starlings that are able to mimic many sounds and are popular as cage birds. Mynahs are native to southeastern Asia and usually inhabit forests or open regions. Heavily built birds, the mynahs vary from 10 to 15 inches (25–38 cm) in length and generally have powerful bills and big feet.

The best-known species is probably the talking mynah, or hill mynah (*Gracula religiosa*). It has black plumage glossed with purple and green, relieved by bold white patches in the wing and curious bright yellow wattles below the eye and on the nape. The bill is orange and the legs yellow. A handsome and very self-confident bird, the hill mynah can be taught to whistle and to talk remarkably well. It feeds entirely on fruit.

Other species of mynah birds are white or various shades of gray and brown. Some have long graceful crests. Mynahs have been introduced as pets in many countries. Some have escaped and breed freely, such as the crested mynah (*Acridotheres cristatellus*) found near Vancouver, British Columbia.

Charles Vaurie*
The American Museum of Natural History

MYOPIA. See Eye—*How the Eye Functions;* Nearsightedness.

MYRDAL, mĕr′däl, **Gunnar Karl** (1898–), Swedish economist, political leader, and United Nations administrator, who wrote an influential study highlighting the tremendous differences between ideals and realities in the treatment of Negroes in the United States. Myrdal was born in Gustafs, Dalarna (Dalecarlia) province, Sweden, on Dec. 6, 1898. He graduated from the law school of the University of Stockholm and obtained a doctorate of jurisprudence in economics in 1927. He was a professor of political economy from 1933 to 1950. A leader of the Swedish Social Democratic party, he served in the First Chamber (Senate) of the Riksdag in 1935–1938 and 1944–1945 and was minister of trade and commerce in 1945–1947. In 1938–1942 in the United States, he conducted a study on the status of Negroes under the auspices of the Carnegie Corporation, and published the findings in *An American Dilemma: The Negro Problem and Modern Democracy* (1944). In 1947–1957 he was executive secretary of the UN Economic Commission for Europe. He was co-winner of the 1974 Nobel Memorial Prize in economic science.

Myrdal contributed to general economic theory in *Monetary Equilibrium* (1939), *The Political Element in the Development of Economic Theory* (1953), and *Value in Social Theory* (1958) and also wrote extensively on the economic problems of developing countries in *An International Economy: Problems and Prospects* (1956), *Beyond the Welfare State* (1960), and *Asian Drama: An Inquiry into the Poverty of Nations* (1968). In 1960 he was appointed to the new chair of international economics at Stockholm.

Alva Reiner Myrdal (1902–), his wife, an educator and sociologist, was director of the Department of Social Sciences of the United Nations Educational, Scientific and Cultural Organization (UNESCO) from 1951 until 1955. She then became Sweden's envoy to India.

William Ebenstein
University of California, Santa Barbara

MYRIAPODA, mir-ē-ap′ə-də, is the name sometimes given to a group of arthropods that includes the millipedes and the centipedes as well as several small, uncommon, and not easily differentiated groups (Pauropoda and Symphyla). Although the name myriapod (or myriopod) is still occasionally used, most zoologists now classify the millipedes as class Diplopoda and the centipedes as class Chilopoda.

All myriapods have elongate, wormlike bodies made up of numerous, similar leg-bearing segments. Unlike most other arthropods, these animals do not have the body divided into a thorax and abdomen. All myriapods lay eggs, and the young are born as larvae, with three legs in the Diplopoda and six in the Chilopoda.

All myriapods are terrestrial animals with the exception of two that are considered semiaquatic because they live in the intertidal areas along the seacoasts. The terrestrial myriapods like damp dark places under logs and stones, in the bark of trees, in caves, and in and around decaying vegetation.

In the Diplopoda, or millipedes, the body is elongate and rounded. Each segment has two pairs of legs, except the first two or three segments and the last segment, each of which has only one pair. The millipede's head has a single pair of antennae that are short and usually seven-jointed. An upper lip and a lower lip form the mouth. The segments of the body vary in number from 9 in the Pauropoda to nearly 200 in some other species. The reproductive organs lie ventral to the intestine, with the external openings a little behind the head. The Diplopoda are sluggish animals depending largely on their thick hard body walls for protection. They frequently curl up to protect the soft underside when disturbed. Decaying vegetable and animal matter is their principal food, but a few feed on living roots and tender plants, sometimes proving destructive in gardens. Most, however, are somewhat beneficial in reducing vegetable matter to humus. See also MILLEPEDE.

In the Chilopoda or centipedes, the body is elongate and flattened, with only one pair of legs to each segment. The number of segments varies from 15 to 173. The antennae are long and at least 12 jointed. The mouth parts are composed of two pairs of maxillae and one pair of hooklike jaws, called maxillipeds, which project forward beneath the head, and each of which is provided with a poison gland. Centipedes are quick and ferocious in attacking animals with their poison fangs. Some in the tropics are large enough to be troublesome to man. See also CENTIPEDE.

Myriapods are found throughout the world except in the extreme polar regions. The earliest fossil remains are from the Devonian period.

JOHN C. PALLISTER,
The American Museum of Natural History.

MYRMEX, mûr′mĕks, in classical mythology, an Athenian maid, whom Athena, goddess of wisdom and patroness of Athens, metamorphosed into an ant, because Myrmex professed that she had discovered the plow, which Athena herself had invented.

P. R. COLEMAN-NORTON.

MYRMIDONS, mûr′mĭ-dŏnz, in classical mythology, a people of Thessaly, Greece. Their chief claim to fame is that the warriors of this tribe accompanied Achilles, the Thessalian hero, to the Trojan War (1194–1184 B.C.). Their eponymous ancestor was Myrmidon, the son of Zeus and Eurymedusa, whom Zeus, disguised as an ant, seduced. For this reason—the Greek word *myrmex* means "ant"—their son was called Myrmidon. Another legend relates that Zeus made his son Aeacus king of Thessaly and, since this region was not then inhabited by human beings, metamorphosed all its ants into people, who thence were called Myrmidons. A third tale tells that Zeus transformed the ants of the Aegean island of Aegina into the Myrmidons, who then emigrated into Thessaly under the leadership of Peleus, the father of Achilles.

In modern times the term sometimes is applied to subordinates who execute their superiors' commands pitilessly and without protest. Hence court officials, such as sheriffs, process servers, and even policemen, occasionally are called myrmidons of the law.

P. R. COLEMAN-NORTON.

MYRON, mī′rŏn, Greek sculptor and engraver: b. Eleutherae, Boeotia, Greece, c. 480 B.C.; d. after 425 B.C. In the generation preceding him, a new process of casting in bronze was discovered, facilitating the creation of a wide variety of new compositions. It is the merit of Myron, who worked at Athens, that he took advantage of this innovation and made use chiefly of bronze, in which he proved himself a versatile and masterly artist. Ancient authors unanimously praise his statues of deities, heroes, athletes, and animals, of which many were commissioned by city-states as well as by wealthy individuals throughout the Hellenic world from Asia Minor to Magna Graecia.

Myron's most celebrated sculptures were the *Cow, Athena and Marsyas,* and the *Discobolus* (Discus Thrower). The *Cow,* designed for Athens, was taken in the 1st century B.C. to Rome, where it was still to be seen in the 6th century A.D. It inspired almost 40 epigrams in the *Greek Anthology*. Of the numerous copies of *Athena and Marsyas* the best two are divided: *Athena* in the Liebieghaus at Frankfurt am Main, Germany, and *Marsyas* in the Museo Laterano in Rome, Italy. A small copy of the group is in the Museum of Fine Arts, Boston. One of the best marble copies of Myron's lost bronze *Discobolus* is in the National Museum, Rome. Critics have credited Myron with some 20 statues, but have rejected about 20 others attributed to him. The consensus of scholars of art is that he was intensely individual style, but adhered to anatomical accuracy in capturing difficult and transitory attitudes of the human figure, and that he carved not only beautiful but also distinctive faces.

Bibliography.—Gardner, Ernest A., *Six Greek Sculptors,* pp. 56–78 (New York 1910); id., *A Handbook of Greek Sculpture,* pp. 265–275, 2d ed. (London 1915); Mirone, Salvatore, *Mirone d'Eleutere* (Catania 1921); Klöter, Hermann, *Myron im Licht neuerer Forschungen* (Giessen 1933); Arias, Paolo E., *Mirone* (Florence 1940).

P. R. COLEMAN-NORTON,
Princeton University.

MYRRH, mûr, a gum resin obtained from the tree *Commiphora abyssinica* and from other species of the genus *Commiphora,* such as *C. myrrha,* of the family Burseraceae, found in East Africa and Arabia. As exuded from the tree stem, it is a yellowish, oily liquid; on solidifying, it forms into yellowish brown to reddish brown granules with a pleasing balsamic odor and lasting, bitter, aromatic taste. In ancient times myrrh was used in making incense and other perfumes, in embalming, and as a medical application. Along with gold and frankincense, it was one of the gifts of the wise men to the Christ child (Matthew 2:11). However, the myrrh of the Bible is thought by some authorities to have been often a mixture of substances, perhaps of myrrh and labdanum, an oleoresin derived from various species of *Cistus,* or rockrose. In modern times myrrh is used in making such products as dentifrices and perfumes; in medicine it has been used in tonics, as a carminative and ingredient in cathartic tablets, and, in tincture form, in treating diseases of the oral cavity.

MYRRH, the common name of a perennial herb, *Myrrhis odorata,* a member of the parsley family, known in Europe as sweet cicely. It has sweet-scented herbage and is sometimes cultivated as a flavoring for salads and other dishes, or as a border for its fragrant white flowers.

MYRRHA, mĭr′ȧ, in classical mythology, the mother of Adonis (q.v.), who was one of the mortals beloved by Aphrodite, goddess of love. It appears that Myrrha's name originally was either Zmyrna or Smyrna, for whom the city of Smyrna in Asia Minor (now İzmir in Asiatic

Turkey) was named. The commonest form of the myth relates that Zmyrna scorned the cult of Aphrodite, who thereupon punished her by inspiring in her an incestuous passion for her father Cinyras, king of Cyprus (or Theias, king of Assyria). Aided by her nurse, Zmyrna disguised her identity, shared her father's bed, and satisfied her unnatural love. After the details of her pregnancy had been discovered, Cinyras attempted to kill Zmyrna. She fled and, about to be overtaken, besought divine aid to become invisible. Through pity the deities transformed her into the myrrh tree (see MYRRH), whence her later name. In due time the tree trunk burst and bore Adonis.

Gaius Helvius Cinna (q.v.), a Roman poet of the mid-1st century B.C., took this theme for his poem (now fragmentary) entitled *Zmyrna*.

P. R. COLEMAN-NORTON.

MYRTLE, mûr't'l, the name of various plants, especially those in the genus *Myrtus,* family Myrtaceae. *Myrtus* includes some 100 species, mostly indigenous to warmer parts of South America and Australia. The best known is *M. communis,* the myrtle of classical literature, sacred to Venus; it is native of Mediterranean regions and Asia Minor, and widely grown in cultivation. It is an evergreen shrub with opposite, leathery, aromatic, oval, entire leaves, and white or pink-tinged flowers less than an inch across. The flowers, developed singly, have four or five sepals, four or five petals, numerous stamens, and a two- or three-chambered ovary with numerous ovules. The berry is bluish black or, sometimes, white. As in other plants long in cultivation, numerous varieties exist, differing mostly in size, shape, texture, and variegation of the leaves. Myrtle has been used since ancient times for wreaths and decorations in religious and civil ceremonies. Myrtle oil, distilled from the leaves, is used medicinally in parts of southern Europe and Asia Minor, and in perfumes. The berries of a white-fruited variety are eaten in Greece, while the dried fruits serve as condiments. The hard, elastic wood, of unusual grain, is utilized locally for furniture and in turnery.

Other plants called myrtle include the running myrtle or periwinkle, *Vinca minor;* the crape myrtle, *Lagerstroemia indica;* the sand myrtle, *Leiophyllum buxifolium;* the wax myrtle, *Myrica cerifera;* and the Oregon myrtle or California laurel, *Umbellularia californica.*

EDWIN B. MATZKE.

MYRTLE BEACH, town, South Carolina, in Horry County, 14 miles southeast of Conway. Named for its thick growth of myrtles, the town, with its equable climate and fine beach, is a year-round resort. Myrtle Beach State Park and the Socastee yacht basin, on the Intracoastal Waterway, are nearby. Incorporated in 1938, the town has a mayor-council form of government. Pop. 8,536.

MYRTLE WARBLER, wôr'blẽr, a small songbird (*Dendroica coronata*), the most abundant of the American wood warblers. It is a little over five inches in size with a black, yellow, and white plumage; adults and young can be easily identified in the field by their bright yellow rumps. Male and female are similar in appearance, but the male is brighter, more boldly patterned, with purer, deeper black and richer yellow. The breeding range is enormous, extending from the northern limits of the trees in Alaska and Canada, south to the Great Lakes and northern New York; the winter range is from Oregon, Kansas, the Great Lakes, and New England to Panama and the West Indies. The name is derived from the bird's fondness for bayberries, the fruit of the wax myrtle (*Myrica cerifera*), its chief winter food.

Allan D. Cruickshank from National Audubon Society

Male myrtle warbler.

CHARLES VAURIE.

MYSIA, mĭsh'ĭ-ȧ, ancient region of northwest Asia Minor, bounded, with variations from time to time, on the west by the Aegean Sea, on the north by the Hellespont and the Propontis (Sea of Marmara), on the northeast and east by Bithynia and Phrygia respectively, and on the south by Lydia. The boundaries with Bithynia and Phrygia were vague and changed from time to time while, in the northwest, the Troas area of Troy and its environment was not always considered part of the region. In the period of ancient Greek city-states, the Mysian coast was dotted with Greek cities, among the most important being Adramyttium (modern Edremit), Cyzicus (Kapidaği Peninsula), Pergamum (Bergama), and Lampsacus (Lâpseki). Mysia was ruled successively by Lydia, Persia, Macedon, and Syria. After the defeat of Antiochus III (the Great) of Syria by the Romans in 190 B.C., it was assigned by Rome to the kingdom of Pergamum, and in 130 B.C. it became part of the Roman province of Asia. In modern times it is part of Turkey.

The Mysians, according to ancient historians, were a distinct people who spoke a language resembling Lydian and Phrygian. The historian Strabo held that they were of Thracian origin and linked them with the inhabitants of Moesia, a Roman province extending to the Danube and Black Sea. Homer, in the *Iliad,* mentions the Mysians as allies of the Trojans. In Biblical history, St. Paul passed through Mysia on his second missionary journey (Acts 16:7, 8) and took ship at Adramyttium (Acts 27:2) on his way to Rome.

MYSORE, mī-sōr', or **MAISUR,** mī-so͞or', state, India, in the southwest, bounded by the Arabian Sea on the west and by the states of

Bombay on the north, Andhra Pradesh on the east, Madras on the southwest, and Kerala on the south. As constituted on Nov. 1, 1956, at the time of the general reorganization of Indian states, it consists of the old landlocked State of Mysore, the old State of Coorg, parts of Bombay and Madras states (including coastal areas giving it a seaboard of approximately 200 miles), and parts of Hyderabad. Its area is 74,326 square miles, or more than twice that of the old state. Its population in 1961, based on that year's census, was 23,586,772; its estimated population in 1968 was between 25 and 26 million. The population is overwhelmingly Hindu, consisting in the old state of 91 per cent Hindus, 6 per cent Muslims, and 1 per cent each of Christians and Jains. The predominant language is Kannada (Kanarese), followed by Telugu and Hindustani. The capital of Mysore State is Bangalore (1966 population: 972,419).

Physical Features and Resources.—Mysore is traversed by the Western Ghats near the coast and the Eastern Ghats in the east, while the Nilgiri Hills are in the south. Physically, the state falls into two distinct areas: the hilly country in the west, very wet, with lofty mountains and evergreen forests; and the plains country, with an elevation of 2,000 to 3,000 feet, in the east, relatively dry and constituting the major part of the inhabited area. The climate is equable and tropical, with an average minimum temperature of 60° F. in December and an average maximum of 90° F. in May. The chief rivers include the Kaveri (Cauvery) in the south, the Tungabhadra in the north, and the Penner and Ponnaiyar (southern Penner) in the east, all draining eastward; and the Sharavati, in the northwest, draining westward. An extensive hydroelectric power system includes the station near Sivasamudram Island, in the Kaveri River, the Mahatma Gandhi works on the Sharavati, and the newer Sharavati River Valley Project (largest in India), near Jog, with an ultimate 891,000-kilowatt capacity, begun in 1958. Numerous dams support widespread irrigation in the east. Among forest products, Mysore's teak, ebony, and cedar are famous for their strength and beauty; bamboo and sandalwood are other products. About 95 per cent of India's gold output comes from the Kolar Gold Fields mines in eastern Mysore; the state is also rich in other minerals including manganese, iron ore, and chromite. The fauna include tigers, leopards, panthers, wild boars, bears, spotted deer, and elephants. There are large coastal fisheries.

Economic Life.—In both agriculture and industry Mysore is one of India's advanced states. The chief agricultural products are rice, millet, pulses, sugarcane, cotton, coconut, coffee, tea, cardamons, and pepper. Cattle, buffalo, sheep, and goats are raised. Major industries include textiles (silk, cotton, wool) at Bangalore, Davangere, and elsewhere, iron and steel (chiefly at Bhadravati), metals, chemicals, paper and printing, soap, porcelain, and processing of agricultural products. The state government controls numerous industrial enterprises, while the federal government owns large machine-tool, electronics, aircraft, and telephone industries at Bangalore. The chief cottage industries are leatherwork, ornaments, pottery, weaving, carpentry, sandalwood and ivory work, and beekeeping.

There are good railroad, highway, and airways systems, radiating chiefly from Bangalore. With its many natural beauty spots and architectural monuments, the state is a paradise for tourists. Among its most famous attractions are Gersoppa Falls (Jog Falls) near Jog, on the Sharavati River; Brindavan Gardens, at Krishnarajasagara, near Mysore; and many temples.

Government and Education.—The government of Mysore consists of a governor aided by a council of ministers responsible to the state legislature. The legislature comprises two houses: the Legislative Assembly, with 208 popularly elected members, and the Legislative Council, with 63 members, partly nominated and partly elected by specified electoral groups. Administratively, the state is divided into four divisions (Bangalore, Mysore, Belgaum, and Gulbarga) and 19 districts.

Higher education is provided chiefly by the University of Mysore (founded 1916) at Mysore and Bangalore, and Karnatak University (founded 1949) at Dharwar, which have many regional affiliated colleges. There is an Indian Institute of Science (founded 1911) at Bangalore. The state has a large number of primary and secondary schools. The literacy rate in 1951, based on that year's census, was 19.29 per cent (males, 29.08 per cent; females, 9.16 per cent).

History.—After the invasion of India (327–325 B.C.) by Alexander the Great, Mysore formed part of the Mauryan Empire, and later came under the rule of the kings of the Satavahana dynasty, continuing to about 225 A.D. Frequently warring local princes were dominant until the 14th century, when a powerful new Hindu dynasty, the Vijayanagar, asserted its control for more than two centuries. The Vijayanagar army was defeated by Muslims in 1565 at the Battle of Talikota, paving the way for the founding of the kingdom of Mysore in 1612 by Raja Oedyar, a Hindu leader. This dynasty was overthrown in

A sparkling cascade in lovely Brindavan Gardens at Krishnarajasagara, near the city of Mysore.

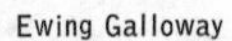
Ewing Galloway

the mid-18th century by the Muslim general Hyder Ali (q.v.), who warred against the Marathas and the British; he was followed in office by his son, Tipu Sahib (q.v.), who continued to oppose the British until they defeated and killed him at the siege of Seringapatam in 1799. The British restored the former dynasty, but later took over administration of Mysore directly from 1831 to 1881, when rule by the hereditary maharaja was again restored, although under British paramountcy. After the end of British rule in 1947, the maharaja became a constitutional administrative head with the title of *rajpramukh,* the actual administration being entrusted to civil ministers. With the reorganization of the states on Nov. 1, 1956, the institution of *rajpramukh* was abolished and replaced by the office of governor.

BIMLA PRASAD.

MYSORE or **MAISUR,** city, India, in southern Mysore State, headquarters of Mysore Division and Mysore District. Situated 85 miles southwest of Bangalore, it adjoins Chamundi

Marilyn Silverstone from Nancy Palmer

Atop Chamundi Hill, a great stone bull overlooks Mysore.

Hill, noted for its park, Hindu temple, and fine views of the city, especially striking at night. Called sometimes the "garden city" of southern India because of its many parks and wide streets, Mysore contains some magnificent buildings, the foremost being the maharaja's palace, a modern structure (completed 1897) in Hindu and Saracenic styles, containing a famous ivory and gold throne. At the annual Dashahara festival (September–October), signifying the victory of good over evil, the palace, illuminated at night, serves as a center for huge processions. Other notable buildings include the Jaganmohan Palace, with its museum and art gallery, and Lalitha Mahal Palace. The city is one of the two chief seats (the other being Bangalore) of the University of Mysore, founded in 1916. There are large-scale silk-weaving and sandalwood-oil factories, as well as cotton-textile and other industries and various handicrafts. Founded in the 16th century, Mysore became the dynastic capital of Mysore State in 1799 and retained that status until 1956 when, under the States Reorganization Act, the princely dynasties were abolished. Pop. (1951) 244,323.

BIMLA PRASAD.

MYSTERIES OF UDOLPHO, The, mĭs′-tẽr-ĭz, ü-dŏl′fō, a novel, published in 1794, by the English writer Ann Radcliffe. An outstanding example of the Gothic school of literature, it tells the story of Emily St. Aubert, an aristocratic French girl who is held by a scoundrel, Montoni, in the gloomy medieval castle, Udolpho, in the Apennines. Emily suffers many mystifying and terrifying experiences at Udolpho and elsewhere before finally finding happiness with her fiancé, Valancourt. Ghosts, as well as bandits and other villains, are involved in Emily's adventures, but the mysteries always turn out to have natural explanations. The characters are stilted and melodramatic, but the novel has power in its elements of suspense and its vivid descriptions of nature and scenery in the rugged Pyrenees and Apennines.

MYSTERIOUS STRANGER, The, mĭs-tẽr′ĭ-ŭs strān′jẽr, a story by Mark Twain, written mostly in Vienna in 1898 and published posthumously in 1916. His last important creative writing, it dramatizes the concepts expounded in his philosophical essay, *What Is Man?*

The time of the story is 1590; the place, an Austrian village, Eseldorf (Donkeytown). The narrator is Theodor Fischer, a lad akin to Tom Sawyer or Huckleberry Finn; his chums are Seppi Wohlmeyer and Nikolaus Bauman. The ruling powers in the village are an astrologer and the priest, Father Adolf, symbolizing bigotry and fraud. Both persecute another priest, Father Peter, who has been suspended for allegedly doubting eternal damnation.

To the boys appears a handsome youth, the "mysterious stranger," who identifies himself as Satan, a nephew of his famous namesake. He amazes the lads by modeling miniature people and animals and bringing them to life, then horrifies them by callously destroying his own creations. He also performs miracles in the village, especially by providing succor for Father Peter and his niece, Marget. This leads to charges of theft and black magic. Satan contrives Father Peter's acquittal; then, having promised the boys that the old man shall thenceforth live happily, he fulfills the promise by making him insane, for only a madman can long be happy in this world.

At intervals, too, Satan takes the boys on journeys in time and space, showing them the folly, cruelty, and stupidity of mankind. Only man, he tells them, has the moral sense; only man inflicts pain for the pleasure of inflicting it. A man's every act, moreover, is ordained by circumstances and environment: "nothing can change the order of [his] life after the first event has determined it."

Last of all, Satan tells Theodor that life itself is only a vision, a dream— "a grotesque and foolish dream. Nothing exists but you. And you are but a *thought*—a vagrant thought, a useless thought, a homeless thought, wandering forlorn among the empty eternities!"

Mark Twain told William Dean Howells that in *The Mysterious Stranger* he did what he had always wanted to do—"write a book without reserves.... I believe I can make it tell what I think of Man." When he read the opening chapters to his wife, she said, "It is perfectly horrible—and perfectly beautiful!" He agreed.

DeLancey Ferguson.

MYSTERY CULTS, mĭs′tĕr-ĭ kŭltz, or **MYSTERIES,** rites conducted under conditions of secrecy. No one is admitted to take part without a more or less elaborate preliminary initiation and without accepting an obligation never to reveal to the uninitiated what he has seen or heard. The name "mystery" derives from Greek *myein,* "to close the eyes or lips." Mysteries in this sense are to be sharply distinguished from mysticism, which is a philosophical or religious attitude, and they have nothing to do with the medieval mystery plays (see Miracle and Mystery Plays), properly written "mistery," which derive their name from Low Latin *ministerium* (trade guild), because such guilds commonly produced them.

Suggested Origins.—It is common enough to exclude certain classes of persons from religious rites. There are, for example, ceremonies in many parts of the world which are performed by one sex only, the other being kept at a distance. Well-known examples from history are the Thesmophoria (q.v.) in classical Greece and the Roman rites of Bona Dea (q.v.), both performed by women only; and again in ancient Rome, the proclamation regularly made before certain ceremonies bidding "foreigner, fettered person, woman and girl" to keep away ("... *hostis vinctus mulier virgo exesto...,*" from Sextus Pompeius Festus, *De verborum significatu,* ed. by Wallace M. Lindsay, p. 72, l. 11, Leipzig 1933). Women are rigidly excluded from the initiations of adolescent boys among many uncivilized peoples, as are young children and uninitiated men. Exclusion of persons not in a state of ritual purity is very common. But these things are not properly mysteries, for evidently a sex disability cannot be got rid of by any initiation, and ritual uncleanness is generally to be disposed of by quite simple processes, such as bathing or abstaining from some kind of food for a time.

The example most nearly in point is the business of what Arnold van Gennep (see *Bibliography*) called *rites de passage* (threshold rites), ceremonies which mark the passage from one stage of existence to another (childhood to adolescence or maturity, unmarried to married, maturity to old age, finally life to death). In numerous stages of culture, but mostly below the level of civilization, a considerable amount of ritual attends all these, and often quite elaborate instruction goes with it. For example, a girl, on showing the first symptoms of adolescence, is often secluded and instructed by the older women in her future duties. Such seclusion and all that attends it might quite easily develop into a rite reserved for certain persons and kept secret from the rest of the community. Indeed, secret societies with their initiatory rites and other practices, sometimes wild and extraordinary, that are the exclusive privilege of their members, are a not uncommon feature of several savage and barbarian societies—for example, the Indians in former times on the Pacific coast of North America. It is likely that some of these at least are developments from the more normal threshold rites. It is, however, to be noticed that ritual of this kind does not fully explain what went on in certain mystery cults known to have existed.

Another suggestion is that mysteries, or some of them, result from the suppression of the religion of a conquered people by their conquerors. There are, of course, abundant cases of a persecuted religion being carried on in secret; the best-known example is found in the early history of Christianity. If we look at the evidence from classical Greece, we have the remarkable statement of Diodorus Siculus (*Bibliotheke,* book 5, chap. 77, sect. 3) that in Crete the ritual of two of the most famous mystery cults, those of Eleusis and Samothrace, went on quite openly. If there is any truth in this, it might mean that the Greek-speaking invaders did not try to suppress the native cult in Crete, but did so in some other parts of their sphere of influence. But polytheism is a very tolerant system as a rule, and generally invaders respect the gods of the invaded and their rites, especially if they intend to live in the territory they are conquering; for how can they look for prosperity there unless they maintain correct relations with the supernatural powers? Friendly relations with these are often made easier by identifying the local deities with their own, or at least associating them in some way, as in Greece the native goddess Hera was made the sister and wife of the invaders' Zeus.

As to the threshold rites mentioned, there is at least one marked difficulty in supposing them to have originated such mystery cults as the most famous of all, that of Eleusis. Savage initiations belong to certain periods of human life, and their object is to fit the initiate for the next stage of their careers; but the Eleusinian ritual was seasonal and initiates might be of any age from childhood on.

On the whole, perhaps it is most plausible to suppose that mysteries are originally extreme examples of the care taken to exclude from any religious ceremonies felt to be highly important all hostile influences, such as the presence of profane and defiled persons or foreigners, who are potential enemies and may, if they learn the proper method of approach to the local gods, entice them away or otherwise secure their favor for themselves. This, if correct, explains only the origin and primary meaning of mysteries, not their later developments.

Eleusis.—There is archaeological evidence that the place, about 14 miles northwest of Athens, where the Eleusinian mysteries were celebrated, had been holy from prehistoric times. Its secrets were well kept, and we have no detailed knowledge of what went on in the Hall of Initiation (Telesterion); but we are tolerably well informed about such parts of the ritual as were performed openly. Furthermore, certain hints and half revelations allow us to make at least intelligent guesses at the secret proceedings. We also know the associated myth. Hades-Pluto, a combination of the god of the dead (Hades) and the giver of the wealth of the soil (Pluto), desired a wife and, with the connivance of Zeus, carried off Kore (literally, the Maiden), otherwise known as Persephone, to use the commonest form of a name plainly not Greek and appearing in a variety of shapes. Again we have a conflation of a goddess of the dead with the "corn maiden," the young crops. Her mother Demeter, goddess of the fruits of the earth, sought her long and vainly. Finding out that Kore was in the underworld, Demeter took the form of an old woman and wandered over the earth, which all this while lay desolate, because she was too grief stricken to perform her function of making it fertile. At last, being hospitably received by the royal household of Eleusis, she revealed herself and her rites to the people of that place, after some subsidiary incidents, and bade them celebrate these rites and build her a temple.

The season of the mysteries is the latter half of the month Boedromion, which is in late summer. This is the most desolate-looking time of year in Greece; the harvest, much earlier than in more northerly climates, is all in, and Kore is literally underground, for the new corn was stored in underground silos. The fields lie apparently waste under the sun, since it is a very dry time of year. It is therefore clearly advisable to make sure that when the autumn rains begin and plowing and sowing are possible, Kore will come again—in other words, there will be another harvest. We know that after several days of preliminary rites, including a ritual bath in the sea by all initiates and a formal address which warned away certain classes of persons ritually impure or unable to understand Greek, the celebrants set out from Athens to go to Eleusis, some four hours' journey on foot, on the 19th day of the month. Arriving at the holy place that evening, the worshipers entered the Telesterion, and there the actual celebration of the mysteries took place. It seems very probable that whatever else was done, there was some kind of representation, perhaps in a sort of sacred ballet, of the rape of Kore-Persephone; and there is an interesting scrap of evidence from St. Hippolytus (*Philosophumena sive omnium haeresium refutatio*, book 5, chap. 1, sect. 8), late indeed and isolated but in itself perfectly credible, that at the climax of the whole ritual an ear of reaped corn was shown in silence to the congregation. Hippolytus indicates, truly or falsely, that this sight was reserved for *epoptai,* those who, being already initiated, came again for a second revelation.

If this showing of the corn is true, its significance is clear enough: the Corn Maiden does not stay underground but comes again with each new harvest. In other words, the performance, however much elaborated in later times when it had been taken over by Athens from Eleusis, was to begin with an ancient ceremony, perhaps quite as much magical as religious, for ensuring the continued supply of corn to the community, and therefore the continued communal existence. We may be certain that the hopes of a blessed future for the initiates, which are expressed as early as the "Homeric" *Hymn to Demeter* (perhaps 7th century B.C.) and which continue to be heard of until quite late times, are based on no positive teaching, eschatological or other, from the presiding clergy. All references to what was done indicate that the initiates were shown certain holy sights and apparently themselves performed certain simple symbolic actions. It is significant that the word used for betraying the mysteries to the uninitiated means literally to "dance out" (*exorcheisthai*) the rites. What those present read into the ritual was their own affair, and probably to begin with amounted to no more than a hope that Demeter and her daughter, pleased with the initiates' observance of their prescribed ritual, would use their influence with the powers of the underworld, to which they themselves belonged, though not primarily as goddesses of the dead.

Samothrace.—Less is known of the famous mysteries on the island of Samothrace in honor of the "Great Gods," to use the local name. They were commonly identified with the Kab(e)iroi (Cabeiri, Cabiri), somewhat vague deities whose name indicates that they were not of Greek origin, for it seems to be identical with the Semitic word *kabirim* (mighty ones), of which their common Greek title *dynatoi* (powerful) would appear to be a translation. There is, however, little likelihood that their cult was of Semitic origin; possibly the name was given them by Phoenician sailors, since they were regarded as special protectors of seafarers. So far as we know, they formed a group of older and younger figures, both male and female, and had but little mythology. Such groups are found over a wide area in and near the Greek world and pass under a variety of names. The Samothracian cult became famous, though not early (about the end of the 5th century B.C.) in the Greek world, and a little is known of it from mentions in ancient authors and from the discovery of remains of its buildings. One outstanding feature has its parallels in many parts of the world. A requisite for admission to the mysteries was confession of sins. This was, at least originally, a form of purification, akin to the washings, purgings, and so forth, which are part of many early rites. To mention the sins in due form and before the proper authorities was, as it were, to spit them out and so to be rid of them. The process was rather quasimechanical than moral (consult Raffaele Pettazzoni, *La confessione dei peccati,* vol. 3, pp. 163–185, Bologna 1936). Though little is known of the procedure in these mysteries, they may serve as an example of the sort of cults that prevailed in the eastern Mediterranean region probably from a date previous to Greek civilization.

Late Antiquity.—The Graeco-Roman world from about the beginning of the Roman Empire (31 B.C.) grew increasingly familiar with mystery cults not attached to any state. These were of Eastern origin, modified to at least the extent of adopting a Western language, generally Greek. Outstanding examples were firstly, the rites of the Egyptian Isis and Osiris. The native ritual of the latter contained elements which at least to a Greek suggested mystery cults (Herodotus, book 2, chaps. 170, 171). But outside Egypt there developed a highly elaborate and impressive ceremonial, including, after a period of preparation for the initiate, an initiation in which the latter was supposed to visit the world of the dead, return to earth, and finally appear glorified as an incarnate sun-god (Lucius Apuleius, *Metamorphoses,* book 11, sects. 23, 24). This, however, was connected with Isis, the initiation to Osiris being apparently of considerable, but somewhat less, importance.

There was also the worship of the Persian Mithras, whose rites were for men only and included an elaborate system of seven ascending grades. This was especially popular in the Roman army, and the artificial caves (Mithraea), in which it was carried on, have been discovered in many parts of the Roman world where garrisons existed. Several cults with ceremonies more or less of mystery type came from the Near East, such as those of the Great Mother (Cybele) and her attendant Attis, and of the Phrygian god Sabazius. Finally, mysteries of Dionysus were popular, especially in Italy, where they seem to have varied from serious religious sects to chiefly social associations. Most of, if not all, these cults seem to have involved a belief that the initiate, having been more or less assimilated to a deity who had suffered and emerged triumphant, would not only enjoy the deity's favor in this life but be assured of a blissful lot in the next.

Christianity. It is not uncommon to find the term "mysteries" used of those Christian ceremonies, especially the Eucharist, to which only baptized believers were admitted. For instance, St. Cyril of Jerusalem uses it thus and also of baptism. The line is not always easy to draw between this meaning and the common one of a doctrine not generally revealed or needing a prepared audience. Heretical and Gnostic sects are often said to have had their own mysteries.

H. J. Rose
Author of "Ancient Roman Religion"

Bibliography

Cumont, Franz, *Oriental Religions in Roman Paganism* (1911; Eng. tr., Dover 1957).
Farnell, Lewis R., *The Cults of the Greek States,* vol. 3 (Oxford Univ. Press 1907).
Gennep, Arnold van, *The Rites of Passage* (1909; Eng. tr., Univ. of Chicago Press 1960).
Harrison, Jane E., *Prolegomena to the Study of the Greek Religion* (Macmillan 1921).
Nilsson, Martin P., *A History of the Greek Religion* (1955; Eng. tr., Norton 1964).

MYSTERY OF EDWIN DROOD, an unfinished novel by the English author Charles Dickens. Published serially, *The Mystery of Edwin Drood* had been completed through its sixth installment by the time of Dickens' death in 1870.

The mystery is: who killed Edwin Drood, if indeed he was killed? The melodramatic characters and events oscillate between Cloisterham (Rochester) and London, with lurid scenes in London opium dens and in weird corners of Cloisterham Cathedral. The characters include John Jasper, evil choirmaster of the cathedral, his nephew Edwin Drood, and the heroine Rosa Bud. Rosa, engaged to Edwin, becomes the object of Jasper's undeclared passion. Edwin disappears, leaving not a trace behind, although circumstances point to foul play. When it comes out that Edwin and Rosa had secretly broken their engagement by mutual consent, Jasper displays such strong emotion that people suspect him of Edwin's murder.

Dickens increases the suspense by pointing the finger of suspicion at some of the other characters, and he introduces a mysterious detective named Datchery, believed by some critics to be the missing Edwin. According to this theory, Edwin had escaped a murder trap laid by Jasper and is now bent on exposing the villain. However, Dickens' intended ending is unknown.

Felix Grendon
Author of "Anglo-Saxon Charms"

MYSTERY PLAYS. See Miracle and Mystery Plays.

MYSTERY STORIES. The mystery story may loosely be described as that kind of fiction having as its chief objective the mystification of the reader and the creation of uncertainty and suspense. If mystery fiction, like all prose fiction, is regarded as a continuum, with one type, or genre, merging seamlessly with others, it is apparent that difficulties are raised with regard to precise definition and classification. Such fiction nearly always deals with crime–real, imagined, or threatened–and some critics prefer the term "crime fiction" to identify the form.

Within the field, three main types are recognized: Gothic novels, detective stories, and criminal fiction. From these, variants have arisen, including spy stories, police procedurals, and suspense fiction.

Gothic Novels. The Gothic novel is a melodramatic romance, heavily laced with horror and supernatural influences. The setting is important –an ancient castle, for example, with hidden doors and passageways, a dungeon, and dark, forbidding recesses. Some evil lurks, creating unaccountable sounds and portentous happenings. Hinges creak; lightning, thunder, and rain are standard weather; and mysterious winds ruffle curtains and extinguish candles. The victim, whose sanity or life is threatened, is usually a young woman of unspotted virtue.

The first Gothic novelist is said to be Horace Walpole, with *The Castle of Otranto* (1764), followed by Mrs. Ann Radcliffe (*The Mysteries of Udolpho,* 1794). The tradition was continued by Mary Shelley (*Frankenstein,* 1817), Joseph Le Fanu (In a Glass Darkly, 1872), and Bram Stoker (*Dracula,* 1897). In the middle of the 19th century, a large number of sensational novels, called "penny dreadfuls" and published in interminable weekly parts, carried on the Gothic form, usually at a subliterary level.

In the latter half of the 19th century the popularity of Gothic novels declined. However, the genre was revived in the 20th century, shorn of its supernatural trappings. It was largely an American specialty, written by women for women, beginning with Mary Roberts Rinehart (*The Circular Staircase,* 1908). She was followed by other prolific writers, including Leslie Ford, pen name of Zenith Brown; Mignon Eberhart; and Mabel Seeley. In England, Daphne du Maurier (*Rebecca,* 1938) and others wrote in the Gothic tradition.

In 20th century Gothic fiction, the heroine often acts foolishly, failing to reveal important clues and taking on perilous independent investigations. Novels of this type have mockingly been called "Had-I-but-Known" fiction.

There was a steady output of "Gothics" until the mid-1960's, when an avalanche took place, generally of paperback originals that, for the most part, slavishly copied proven formulas. The 1970's marked a return to the supernatural, reflecting widespread interest in the occult.

Detective Stories. In the middle of the 19th century a new type of mystery was developed–the detective story, in which a character of amazing deductive intellect follows a trail of clues to solve a puzzle involving crime, usually murder. The recognized inventor of the genre is Edgar Allan Poe, American poet and student of the macabre, who termed such stories tales of ratiocination. In *The Murders of the Rue Morgue* (1841), Poe introduced the amateur French investigator C. Auguste Dupin, who became the prototype for the astute heroes of endless detective stories. Just as significantly, in but three short stories, Poe supplied an extraordinary number of the ploys and devices that have been standard fare in such fiction ever since.

Strangely, the ground that was so well sown by Poe lay fallow for decades in the United States. Not until Anna Katharine Green published *The Leavenworth Case* (1878) did the detective story achieve widespread currency in America, particularly in dime novels and other cheap-edition formats.

In Europe, however, the situation was different. The French quickly realized the possibilities inherent in detective fiction, and in 1866, Émile Gaboriau published *L'Affaire Lerouge,* introducing the police detective Monsieur Lecoq. Gaboriau was quickly followed by Fortuné du Boisgobey and, later, by Gaston Leroux.

In England, also, the detective story gained widespread popularity. In *The Woman in White* (1860), Wilkie Collins moved close to the form, and his *The Moonstone* (1868) is squarely within the genre. Even Charles Dickens ventured into the field, and his *The Mystery of Edwin Drood* might have been a great detective novel had it not remained unfinished at his death.

But it was a struggling Scottish physician, driven to writing by the poverty of his practice, who gave the detective story its undying popularity. The writer was Arthur Conan Doyle, whose creation Sherlock Holmes, first presented in the novel *A Study in Scarlet* (1887), became the amateur detective of unrivaled perspicacity. With his bumbling friend Dr. Watson, Holmes solved the most dastardly and baffling crimes, in *The Sign of the Four* (1890), *The Hound of the Baskervilles* (1902), and *The Valley of Fear* (1915) and in numerous short stories. Holmes' public would not let Doyle kill him off, and he is still commemorated today.

With Holmes came the deluge. Among the important early figures were R. Austin Freeman, whose Dr. Thorndyke was one of the first detectives to use forensic medicine. Freeman also created the "inverted" detective story, in which the identity of the guilty party is quickly known to the reader, with the interest deriving from the detective's efforts to identify him. Baroness Orczy, author of the Scarlet Pimpernel adventures, provided one of the first "armchair" detectives with her Old Man in the Corner. A. E. W. Mason created Monsieur Hanaud; G. K. Chesterton, the cleric-detective Father Brown; E. C. Bentley, Philip Trent; and Ernest Bramah, the blind sleuth Max Carrados. In the United States, Jacques Futrelle provided readers with Professor Augustus S. F. X. Van Dusen; Carolyn Wells, Fleming Stone; and Melville Davisson Post, Uncle Abner.

The "pure" detective story reached its "golden age" between World Wars I and II. Such stories are highly formalized as an intellectual contest between the reader and the writer (and his fictional detective). They require strict fair play with the reader in that he has the same exposure to the clues as the detective and an equal opportunity to reach the solution.

In the United States, the "golden age" was launched by S. S. Van Dine, pen name of Willard Huntington Wright, with his erudite sleuth Philo Vance. He was followed by Ellery Queen (both writer and detective), the joint pen name of Frederic Dannay and Manfred B. Lee; and Rex Stout, who created the gargantuan "armchair" investigator Nero Wolfe.

England produced a longer roster. Most famous is Agatha Christie, who invented both Hercule Poirot and Miss Marple. Others include Freeman Wills Crofts (Inspector French); H. C. Bailey (Reginald Fortune); Anthony Berkeley, pen name of A. B. Cox (Roger Sheringham); the American-born John Dickson Carr (Dr. Fell), who also used the pen name Carter Dickson (Sir Henry Merrivale); and Dorothy Sayers (Lord Peter Wimsey).

Since 1940 there has been less emphasis on fair play. Writers of note of this era include the Americans Erle Stanley Gardner, with his redoubtable lawyer-detective Perry Mason; the husband-and-wife team Frances and Richard Lockridge, who wrote about the husband-and-wife detectives Mr. and Mrs. North; and Emma Lathen, joint pen name of Mary J. Latis and Martha Hennisart, who created the Wall Street banker-detective John Putnam Thatcher. In England, leading writers include Josephine Tey, pen name of Elizabeth Mackintosh (Inspector Grant), and Edmund Crispin, pen name of Robert Bruce Montgomery (Gervase Fen). New Zealand produced Ngaio Marsh (Roderick Alleyn); Australia, Arthur W. Upfield (Inspector Napoleon Bonaparte); and France, Georges Simenon (Inspecteur Maigret).

In the 1920's, in the United States, there was a reaction against traditional detective fiction, and the "hard-boiled" school emerged. The hard-boiled detective—the so-called private eye—talks and acts tough, taking his knocks and returning them in kind, far removed from the likes of the sophisticated Norths or the gentlemanly Lord Peter Wimsey. Dashiell Hammett led the field, and his Sam Spade (*The Maltese Falcon,* 1930) and Continental Op stories were the inspiration of many writers, notably Raymond Chandler (Philip Marlowe) and Ross Macdonald, pen name of Kenneth Millar (Lew Archer).

The hard-boiled school reached its commercial zenith with the Mike Hammer novels of Mickey Spillane, beginning with *I, The Jury* (1947). Spillane concentrated on more-explicit sex and sex-oriented violence. His influence continued to be felt in the 1970's with its numerous superhero paperback books. It is sometimes difficult to tell which are parodies and which are serious efforts. In any case, hard-boiled fiction has been carried to the edge of pornography.

Criminal Fiction. In fiction about criminals, the reader tends to identify with the criminal, not his pursuers. Interest in the lives and exploits of criminals began in the 17th century, with the reports of rogues, highwaymen, and swindlers, whose activities were frequently romanticized and fictionalized. A specialist in the field was Daniel Defoe, whose *Moll Flanders* and *Colonel Jack,* both published in 1722, are first-person narratives in which a criminal attempts to raise sympathy for his behavior.

In the 19th century, in France, fiction about criminals was published by Eugène Sue (*Les Mystères de Paris,* 1842–1843) and Honoré de Balzac. In England, Edward Bulwer Lytton brought out *Paul Clifford* (1830) and *Eugene Aram* (1832), and Dickens, in *Oliver Twist* (1837–1839), provided one of literature's most penetrating portraits of the criminal underworld. In a later era, Marie Belloc Lowndes wrote *The Lodger* (1913), a novel about Jack the Ripper.

Contemporaneously, the "gentleman crook" was introduced in France by Maurice Leblanc, with Arsène Lupin, and in England by Ernest W. Hornung, with Raffles.

With the rise of the detective story, criminal fiction declined, and even during the gangster era of the 1920's and 1930's little was written about the underworld. In the late 1950's, however, a revival took place with the paperback novels of Richard Stark, pen name of Donald E. Westlake. Stark's tales of professional criminal entrepreneurs resulted in a subgenre of criminal stories, the "caper" novels, in which audacious criminals plan and execute complex robberies, usually coming a cropper because of a seemingly small and unforeseen complication.

In the realm of organized crime, Mario Puzo's *The Godfather* (1969) unleashed a flood of fiction about the Mafia and similar syndicates that continued into the 1970's. Some were intended as serious narrative studies of the "organization" and its activities and place in American society. Others were sex-and-violence paperback thrillers, in which indestructible superheroes wage one-man wars against the organization and its minions.

A bypath of criminal fiction is stories about rogues-turned-investigators. These heroes, modern Robin Hoods who began as engaging scoundrels, turn their talents to championing the underdog by unconventional or illegal means, so as to bring to ground miscreants apparently beyond the law. The novels of England's Leslie Charteris, creator of The Saint, best typify this fiction. He was followed by John Creasey with his "Baron" and "Toff" novels.

Spy Stories. The spy story, or tale of international intrigue, is mainly a 20th century phenomenon, although earlier examples, such as James Fenimore Cooper's *The Spy* (1821), can be found. Early in the 20th century, the Englishman E. Phillips Oppenheim wrote more than 100 novels dealing, as he said, "with the shadowy and mysterious world of diplomacy." Equally prolific was his countryman William Le Queux, and another Englishman, Erskine Childers, wrote the famous *The Riddle of the Sands* (1903).

Such writers established spy fiction as a predominantly English genre. Subsequently, there were John Buchan and his Richard Hannay books, notably *The Thirty-Nine Steps* (1915); W. Somerset Maugham (*Ashenden*, 1928); Eric Ambler (*The Mask of Dimitrios*, 1939); and Graham Greene (*The Confidential Agent*, 1939). During World War II, Manning Coles, the joint pen name of Adelaide Frances Oke Manning and Cyril Henry Coles, began a series of lighthearted spy novels, and Helen MacInnes published the first of her bestsellers, *Above Suspicion* (1941).

After the war, Ian Fleming's James Bond stories, beginning with *Casino Royale* (1953; in the U. S., 1954) brought on a flood of spy and espionage fiction. Some of these books were realistic, such as *The Spy Who Came in from the Cold* (1963) by John Le Carré, pen name of David Cornwell, and *The Ipcress File* (1963) by Len Deighton. Others were parodies, such as John Gardner's farcical Boysie Oakes stories, the misadventures of a bumbling, cowardly spy. In the 1970's the spy and hard-boiled forms clearly overlapped, with the spy tending to become little more than a private eye operating on an international stage.

Police Procedurals. The police procedural novel is identified as the day-to-day account of police force activities. The type, which attempts to provide a relatively high degree of realism, is usually traced to the 1940's, with the work of Lawrence Treat (*H as in Hunted*, 1946; *T as in Trapped*, 1947). But its roots extend to the 19th century, with fictional and semifictional police "reminiscences," and to Freeman Wills Croft's Inspector French and Georges Simenon's Inspecteur Maigret. In *Murder for Pleasure*, critic Howard Haycraft used the term "police procedural" to classify Helen Reilly's books about Inspector McKee, which first appeared in 1930. The high points of later police procedurals include the 87th precinct stories of Ed McBain, pen name of Evan Hunter; John Creasey's Commander Gideon novels; the California-locale fiction of Elizabeth Linington (Detective Maddox, Lieutenant Mendoza, and Sergeant Clock); and the Martin Beck books by Sweden's Maj Sjöwall and Per Wahlöö.

Suspense Fiction. The suspense story has a strong psychological interest and is concerned with the exploration of character, emotion, and motivation in a context of crime and pursuit. Important writers include Dorothy B. Hughes, Cornell Woolrich, Julian Symons, and Dick Francis.

ALLEN J. HUBIN
Editor of "Best Detective Stories of the Year"

Bibliography

Barzun, Jacques, and Taylor, Wendell Hertig, *A Catalogue of Crime* (Harper 1971).
Butler, William Vivian, *The Durable Desperadoes* (Macmillan, London, 1973).
Haycraft, Howard, *Murder for Pleasure* (Appleton 1941).
Symons, Julian, *Mortal Consequences* (Harper 1972).
Thomson, H. Douglas, *Masters of Mystery* (Collins 1931).

MYSTIC is an unincorporated village in southeastern Connecticut, in New London county, about 7 miles (11 km) east of New London. Situated on the Mystic River, which flows south into Long Island Sound, it is part of the towns of Groton and Stonington. Historically a shipbuilding center, it is now the home of Mystic Seaport, a maritime museum.

History. The site of Mystic was an area within the English Warwick Patent of 1631, and was secured for colonization by the Pequot War of 1637. The name is an anglicized contraction of the Algonquin words "missi" (great tidal) and "tuk" (river). Farming, fishing, and small-craft construction were the chief occupations of the early settlers, who received land grants beginning in 1650. By the end of the century, sloops and schooners were being built in the Mystic area for the coastal and West Indies trades.

At the beginning of the 19th century there were three small settlements in the valley—Mystic at the head of the river and two at the narrows downstream. The latter two were later grouped under the name of Mystic. The settlement at the head of the river was thereafter known as Old Mystic.

Fishing and whaling became important in the 19th century. A few highly profitable sealing voyages provided the capital for venturing into the whaling industry. From 1822 to 1862, 28 vessels from Mystic completed 103 voyages, bringing back cargoes of whale oil and bone.

At the same time, wooden shipbuilding reached its peak, and Mystic shipyards produced some of the fastest clippers ever built. In the 19th century 800 vessels, from smacks to full-rigged ships, were launched on the Mystic River.

MYSTIC SEAPORT PHOTOGRAPH, MYSTIC, CT.

The last wooden whaler, the *Charles W. Morgan,* is now a floating exhibit at the maritime museum in Mystic, Conn. Built in 1841 in New Bedford, Mass., she hunted whales for more than 80 years and earned more money than any other whaler on record.

The demand for larger hulls of iron and steel led to a decline in wooden shipbuilding, and during the 1870's most yards in Mystic were forced to close. Available capital was redirected into knitting mills and light industry, but most of these facilities had disappeared by the mid-20th century. Mystic became a resort town as the popularity of Mystic Seaport grew. It is also a center for boating and fishing enthusiasts.

Mystic Seaport. From a modest beginning in 1929 as an association to collect and display marine memorabilia, Mystic Seaport has developed into a major outdoor museum covering some 40 acres (16 hectares). The refurbished village, complete with cobblestoned streets, features more than 60 historic buildings of the coastal region from New York to Maine and some 200 ships and boats, all assembled to recreate the atmosphere of a mid-19th century seafaring community.

Life in the age of sail is shown by numerous working exhibits. Skilled craftsmen demonstrate maritime trades in such exhibits as the sail loft, rigging loft, shipsmith shop, weave shop, and shipcarver's shop. Other buildings in the Village Area include the bank, shipping office, print shop, chapel, schoolhouse, apothecary shop, tavern, and ship chandlery.

Virtually all types of American small craft have been collected at Mystic. Three major vessels may be boarded by visitors. They are the *Charles W. Morgan,* the only surviving whaling bark, which has been declared a national historic landmark; the *Joseph Conrad,* a square-rigged training ship; and the *L. A. Dunton,* a Grand Banks fishing schooner. Smaller vessels at Mystic include the blockade runner *Australia* and the smack *Erma C. Berry.*

Formal museum buildings, an art gallery, a children's museum, a planetarium, and a research library are among the attractions of Mystic Seaport. There is also a preservation shipyard engaged in the restoration of wooden vessels.

DONALD R. JUDGE
Librarian, Mystic Seaport, Inc.

Further Reading: Anderson, Virginia B., *Maritime Mystic* (Marine Historical Assn. 1962).

MYSTIC SHRINE. See SHRINERS.

MYSTICISM. The essence of all mystical experience is that it is the direct apprehension of a Unity, a oneness, or a One, which is without internal divisions or distinctions, without internal multiplicity. But this is reached in two different ways, giving rise to two types of mystical experience, the extrovertive and the introvertive.

The extrovertive mystic perceives physical objects as "all One" and as permeated by the One or the Divine. Thus Meister Eckhart (Johannes Eckhart, 1260?–1327) says "all blades of grass, wood, and stone, are one." And Jakob Böhme (1575–1624) says: "In this light my spirit saw through all things and I recognized God in grass and plants." This type of experience tends to philosophical pantheism.

But of far greater importance in the history of religion has been the introvertive type of mystical experience. In all cultures this is normally reached by turning the mind in upon itself and plunging down below all layers of superficial experience to the very foundation of the mystic's own mind. All sensations, images, thoughts, desires, and volitions—the entire empirical content of consciousness—have to be suppressed. What is then left is not, as one might expect, unconsciousness, but rather the bare unity of the self, empty of all content, the pure ego.

Perhaps the earliest description of this completely paradoxical experience is found in the Mandukya Upanishad. It is there said to be "pure unitary consciousness wherein awareness of the world and of multiplicity is completely obliterated. It is ineffable peace. It is the supreme good. It is One without a second. It is the Self." The essence of the experience is this undifferentiated unity. In the Upanishads this is first interpreted as the unity of the finite mind of the individual, and then as being identical with the unity of the cosmic One, the Universal Self, Brahman. The last word of the quotation, the word "Self," means both the individual self and the Universal Self, which are identical. Experiences descriptively indistinguishable from this appear in other cultures and are interpreted in terms of the religious concepts characteristic of those cultures. For instance, Jan van Ruysbroeck (1293–1381), the Flemish Christian mystic, writes of "the God-seeing man" that his spirit "is undifferentiated and without distinction, and therefore it feels nothing but the unity." Plainly this is the same as the undifferentiated unity of the Upanishad, though some Christian writers may say that the latter must be something inferior.

Mysticism in Religion and Philosophy. Mysticism in religion and philosophy must ultimately be based upon someone's mystical experience. But mystical experience itself makes no statements of any kind. Although nonsensuous, it is in this respect like sense experience. The color red says nothing. It simply is. Only intellectual interpretations of sense experience give rise to propositions. One must make a corresponding distinction between mystical experience and its interpretations. Mystical statements in religion or philosophy can only be interpretations of mystical experience.

There is a further point. The same physical sensation may be the basis of divergent interpretations. For instance, a white something glimmering in the night may be taken by one person as a ghost, by another as a sheet hung on a clothesline, by a third as a white-painted rock. Analogously, descriptively indistinguishable mystical experiences may be interpreted by a Christian as union with the Christian God, by a Muslim as union with Allah, by a Buddhist as a glimpse of Nirvana, by a Hindu as union with Brahman.

The statement just made is admittedly extremely controversial. Some Christians will maintain that since all non-Christian religions are inferior to Christianity, or even wholly false, the mystical experiences at the basis of Hindu or Buddhist ideas must be different from, and inferior to, the experiences of Christian mystics—although they generally admit that there are common elements.

Mysticism is no doubt in a broad sense a religious phenomenon, but it does not favor one religion over another. The Christian, Muslim, Hindu, and Buddhist mystics all fit their experiences into the frameworks of their pre-existing creeds and interpret them in terms of those creeds. For instance, since undifferentiated unity is empty of all content, vacant, void, nothingness (note the paradox), it is interpreted by Eckhart and Ruysbroeck as being the Godhead prior to its self-differentiation into the three Persons of the Trinity; as the impersonal One by Plotinus (205?–270); and simply as the Void (*śūnya*) by Mahayana Buddhists. It also follows that mysticism can exist by itself without being embodied in any creed or connected with any organized religion.

Analogously, mysticism can combine with almost any metaphysics. Vedantic mysticism produced idealistic acosmism. Christian mysticism usually goes with a realistic world view. The mysticism of Plotinus was fitted by him into the framework of a modified Platonism. He also teaches that a series of emanations descending from the One constitute the universe. To this downward way corresponds the upward way which is the ascent of the soul back to union with the One from which it came.

Certain philosophical systems in the West are sometimes termed "mystical," for instance those of Georg W. Hegel, Friedrich von Schelling, Arthur Schopenhauer, and Francis Herbert Bradley. What this generally means is not that these philosophers were themselves mystics, but rather that they adopted ideas which originated as interpretations of someone's mystical experiences and which then floated off into general literature and culture, whence they were picked up by these authors. For instance, the proposition that time is mere appearance must have originated in the minds of mystics whose timeless experience—what is undifferentiated is necessarily timeless—impressed them as being the only "true" reality. But philosophers who never had that experience have believed that proposition.

Christian Mysticism. Dionysius the Areopagite (pseudonym of an unknown individual who lived probably in the 5th century), undoubtedly on the basis of his own experience, stressed the *via negativa.* The undifferentiated Godhead, being empty, can have no positive characters and can be spoken of only in negatives. "It is not immovable nor in motion, or at rest, and has no power, and does not live and is not life; nor does is belong to the category of nonexistence or that of existence." Later Christian mystics also stressed the negative divine which is frequently conveyed by metaphors such as darkness and silence.

Something has been said previously regarding Eckhart and Ruysbroeck. The most famous of the Spanish school of mystics were St. Teresa of Ávila (1515–1582) and St. John of the Cross (1542–1591). St. Teresa's writings give descriptions of her ecstasies. She was highly emotional and uncritical. Her language is always that of simple piety. Hence she describes her mystical experience simply as "union with God" without any attempt at distinguishing the experienced unity from the concept of God in terms of which she interprets it. She and St. John of the Cross joined forces in reforming and founding Carmelite monasteries. St. John is famous for his book *Noche oscura del alma* (Eng. tr., *The Dark Night of the Soul*). He uses the word "darkness" as a metaphor for the obliteration of sensations, images, and thoughts, which the introvertive experience involves, and also for the long periods of "aridity" in which the mystic finds himself unable to achieve union and tends to feel himself abandoned.

The word "union" in mystical literature is ambiguous. Whereas in Vedantic literature the finite self, when in the mystical consciousness, realizes its literal identity with the divine being, such a claim is thought in Christianity, Islam, and Judaism to amount to blasphemy or at least to the "heresy" of pantheism. Hence when Christian mystics speak of union with God, they do not usually mean identity. They insist that the creature always remains distinct from the Creator. According to St. John, the union occurs "when the two wills, the will of God and the will of the soul, are conformed together, neither desiring aught repugnant to the other." Nevertheless mystics everywhere tend toward the idea of pantheistic identity. This results in tension between the mystics and the orthodox authorities. Meister Eckhart was accused of pantheistic utterances and prepared an elaborate defense, but died before the issue came to trial.

Islamic Mysticism. Otherwise referred to as Sufism, Islamic mysticism flourished chiefly in the Arab countries and Persia. It makes its appearance in the 8th century, but its golden age centers in the 11th to the 13th centuries. As in Christianity, mystical experience is interpreted as union with God, but here also tension arose between the mystics and the orthodox theologians regarding the meaning of union. In 922 al-Hallaj was crucified in Baghdad for words which seemed to amount to a claim of being identical with God. Characteristic of Sufism is this saying of al-Bistami (d. about 875): "I went from God to God until they cried unto me in me 'O Thou I.'" Famous among Sufi poets were Farid al-Din 'Attar (d. about 1220) and Jalal al-Din Rumi (1207–1273). The outstanding philosopher of Sufism was the great al-Ghazzali (1058–1111). Trained as a theologian and lawyer, he became professor of divinity in Baghdad, but gave up his professorship to live the Sufi life. In his writings he endeavored to weld Sufism and Muslim orthodoxy into a consistent body of thought. His position in Islam has been compared to that of St. Augustine in Christianity.

Hindu Mysticism. The Upanishads are among the sublimest mystical writings of the world. They are believed to have been composed by unknown "forest sages" between 1000 and 400 B. C. The passage from the Mandukya quoted previously describes the basic experience that is interpreted in a number of remarkable doctrines. He who attains this experience realizes his identity with Brahman, the Universal Self. This is expressed in the formula "That art thou." He obtains release from reincarnation and ultimate absorption in the Divine. According to the philosophy of Shankara (fl. about 800 A. D.), the distinctionless Unity, Brahman, is the sole reality, all else being illusion. Several other philosophies, divergent from that of Shankara, were also founded on the same basic mystical experience.

Buddhist Mysticism. Buddhism is based on the "enlightenment" experience of the Buddha (563?–?483 B. C.) which, there is good reason to suppose, is identical with the introvertive experience of the Mandukya Upanishad. Buddhism centers on the mystical concept of Nirvana. Nirvana is the ultimate goal achieved by following the "Noble Eightfold Path," the final term of which is mystical contemplation. He who achieves this goal is freed from reincarnation. What happens to him then? The common Western idea that Nirvana is annihilation is undoubtedly false. The individual ceases to be a finite individual. What is annihilated are the common empirical conditions—sensations, images, thoughts, desires, volitions—which constitute the finite or individual personality of the particular man.

Jewish Mysticism. The Jewish tradition is not rich in mysticism defined as including union. This is because Judaism as a religion belongs generally to the prophetic or objective type, in which the notion of union with God is not encouraged. Gershom G. Scholem, a leading authority, affirms that union is not a necessary element in Jewish mysticism. For instance, what in that tradition is called "Throne-Mysticism" consists in a vision of God seated on the Throne. But in Christianity, Islam, Hinduism, and Buddhism, visions and voices are excluded from the class of mystical experiences because the latter must be formless and nonsensuous, whereas a vision involves sensuous forms or images. The notion of *devekut*, that is, adhesion or direct contact with God, tends in the Jewish tradition to take the place of union. Nevertheless, there have been exceptions. Abraham ben Samuel Abulafia, born in 1241, believed that he experienced union. Many of the 18th and 19th century Hasidim were also genuine mystics in this sense. Characteristic of the Jewish attitude to mystical union is that of Martin Buber (1878–1965), who experienced the undifferentiated unity of the classical introvertive type. He at first interpreted it as union but later repudiated this view and insisted that what is encountered is not God but only the basic unity of the individual's private self. He no longer believed that union with God is possible in this life.

WALTER T. STACE
Author of "Mysticism and Philosophy"

Bibliography

Jones, Rufus M., *New Studies in Mystical Religion* (1927; reprint, Gordon Press).

Marquette, Jacques de, *Introduction to Comparative Mysticism* (Philosophical Lib. 1949).

Mukerjee, Radhakamal, *The Theory and Art of Mysticism* (Asia Pub. 1960).

Nicholson, Reynold A., *The Mystics of Islam* (1913; Dufour 1965).

Otto, Rudolf, *Mysticism East and West* (1932; Eng. tr., Meridian 1957).

Scholem, Gershom G., *Major Trends of Jewish Mysticism,* 3d rev. ed. (Schocken 1954).

Spencer, Sidney, *Mysticism in World Religion* (Barnes, A. S. 1966).

Stace, Walter T., *Mysticism and Philosophy* (Lippincott 1960).

Suzuki, Daisetz T., *Mysticism: Christian and Buddhist* (Harper 1957).

Underhill, Evelyn, *Mysticism* (1911; Harper 1957).

Zaehner, Robert C., *Hindu and Muslim Mysticism* (Oxford Univ. Press 1961).

MYTH. See MYTHOLOGY; FOLKLORE.

MYTHOLOGY, in the literal sense, is the telling of stories. Specifically, it is the body of traditional tales, or the study of them, either of mankind in general or of some particular people such as the Babylonians, Indians, Chinese, or Greeks. Most peoples have or have had tales of this kind, though this is not true of all peoples; the Romans, for instance, appear to have been almost without any such traditions. In many cases the tales go back to very early days, earlier than the invention or adoption of writing; thus, a very large number of such legends have been collected from the mouths of illiterate savage and barbarous peoples by modern investigators.

Classification. Mythological stories may be divided into three classes: myths proper; sagas, or legends; and folktales, or *Märchen*.

Myths. Myths are a kind of imaginative precursor of scientific investigation. Early man sought explanations of the phenomena of nature. As far back as we can trace human development, he also possessed customs and habits, especially religious rites, and more or less definite beliefs of some kind, which he sought to explain to himself. He found the explanations in imaginative pictures, often wildly grotesque but not infrequently full of rudely poetical images and incidents. For people with little factual knowledge and none of the elaborate apparatus and means of recording results which modern scientists possess, these imaginative pictures gave satisfactory explanations, for example, of how the world came to have its present form, why day and night succeed each other regularly, why this or that custom prevails, and so forth.

Often, though by no means universally, these stories are recited regularly at certain seasons of the year and hours of the day or night, or in many cases were acted out in a primitive kind of drama, because such performances are thought to be efficacious in maintaining the present state of things. For instance, the local myth explaining the origin of the sun is believed to have power to prevent the world from slipping back into a supposed primeval state in which all was dark. One of the most famous tales, with a distribution from Greece to New Zealand (intermediate stages are being gradually discovered), tells how heaven and earth, thought of as husband and wife, used to be close together until they were separated by their children, who were cramped for room between them. When not part of ritual, these myths are still, or have been in the past, much valued as explanations pure and simple, and therefore are known as *etiological myths.*

Sagas or Legends.—These have behind them real events, such as a war or other noteworthy happening. Probably the most famous is the Troy saga, which goes back originally to a real war between the inhabitants of Greece proper and a thriving settlement of the same or a kindred people inhabiting the Troad, a region on the Asiatic short of the Dardanelles. Traditionally, this took place early in the 12th century B.C.; our earliest account of it is in Homer, several centuries later, and the tale has been embroidered with all manner of accretions, including divine interventions, the exploits of individual fighters, and so forth.

An English example is the *Ballad of Chevy Chase,* which is a very distorted account of the historical Battle of Otterburn (1388) between the English under Sir Henry Percy (Hotspur) and the Scots under the 2d earl of Douglas. In this case, we can check the extent to which the ballad maker has deviated from the real facts; in the case of Troy we can only conjecture, with the help of archaeology, what really happened, and certainly cannot write a factual account of the war on the basis of Homer and later tellers of the saga.

Folk Tales or Märchen.—These are pure fiction and seem to have no other origin than a desire to amuse and interest. Modern investigations have proved that a number of themes or motifs are common to all or most of the large groups of such tales, which have been collected from nations all over the world. Thus in the late 19th century 345 variants of the story of Cinderella and other tales having some or all of its main incidents were collected by Marian R. Cox (*Cinderella,* London 1893), and many more have come to light since. It would seem that once such a tale becomes popular in its place of origin, it can spread indefinitely, overleaping barriers of language and geographical distance. Thus the tale of the one-eyed giant (Cyclops) is to be found in Homer and also among the Lapps and in the *Arabian Nights.*

Tales of Mixed Elements.—In any given story of sufficient length and elaboration, elements of more than one kind of traditional tale, or of all three, may be found. Thus, the long and complicated history of the Argonauts, preserved in several Greek and Latin authors, contains elements of pure folk tale, is probably a saga to begin with, and has here and there an episode which is etiological myth (consult Janet Bacon, *The Voyage of the Argonauts,* Boston 1924?). A popular god or hero, such as Krishna or Hercules, gathers about him quantities of traditional material with which originally he had nothing to do; and folk tales often take the shape of anecdotes concerning some famous man, which are told and retold of one well-known figure after another, with variations of detail.

Types of Myths.—The myth may be of several kinds. One of the most important, which is widespread but not universal, is the creation myth. Some of the most famous examples of this are Semitic, especially the Babylonian and the Hebrew. Often the existing world is represented as having been made by a god out of strange material, sometimes the body of a primeval monster, such as the dragon Tiamat, with details explaining what parts of the immense carcass were used for the various parts of the world, sky, earth, sea, and so forth. Not uncommonly, the primal material is an enormous egg, which splits open, giving birth to a god of some sort, and half its shell is used to form the dome of the sky, the rest making the earth. A well-known instance of this is contained in that strange complex of doctrines, theological and cosmological, which was produced in Greece from about the 6th century B.C. onward and is known collectively as Orphism, from the literary fiction by which its writings were commonly attributed to the legendary musician Orpheus (consult William K. C. Guthrie, *Orpheus and Greek Religion,* pp. 92 ff., London 1935). A very common feature of creation myths is the presence alongside the Creator, who is usually though not always the supreme god, of a second figure, commonly critical of or even hostile to him and his works. An outstanding example is Coyote in Amerindian traditions; the whole matter is ably dealt with by Ugo Bianchi (*Il dualismo religioso,* Rome 1958; consult also Raffaele Pettazzoni, *The All-Knowing God,* pp. 369 ff., 454, and note 69, London 1956).

It should be noted that several peoples, both savage and civilized, have no account of the creation of the world by any supernatural beings, although their gods may originate some features of it, such as particular food plants. This is true, for example, of Greek tradition, the concept of a Creator being philosophical (as in the *Timaeus* of Plato) and not popular; even in philosophy it is not postulated by all schools, the Epicureans, for instance, totally denying it. Especially, the creation of man is by no means always attributed to a god, the presence of humanity in the world being accounted for in various and often grotesque ways.

Closely related to the creation myths are those which deal with a worldwide deluge; it must be remembered that the "world" of the original framers of such myths was but a small, and often a very small, fraction of the earth's surface. This has been fully dealt with by Sir James G. Frazer (*Folk-lore in the Old Testament,* vol. 1, London 1919). But it may be noted, firstly, that such a story is not always necessarily a myth proper, but may rest upon some extensive local inundation. Thus the stories of Utnapishtim in Sumerian and Babylonian tradition and of Noah in Genesis seem based on a real flood known to have occurred in Mesopotamia and to have overwhelmed the city of Ur. The Hebrew account even gives (Genesis 7:20) the depth of the floodwater—15 cubits (about 26 feet), which agrees pretty exactly with the archeological evidence (consult Sir Leonard Woolley in Glyn E. Daniel and others, *Myth or Legend?* pp. 39–47, New York 1955). Secondly, whatever the origin of any particular form of story, it is often associated with a kind of secondary creation. Either the floodwaters cover everything and there is no dry land until some animal or supernatural being dives and fetches up a little earth, which is then expanded into the world by magical means; or men are cared for by various creatures until the waters recede, and the men then adopt these hosts as totems. This is, of course, pure etiological myth and is naturally confined to regions where totemism exists.

Another widespread form of myth deals with the love affairs and marriages of gods and goddesses. Some of these probably amount to no more than genealogical inventions. Hecataeus, for example, in Herodotus (book 2, chap. 143) was not unique when he traced his ancestry through 15 human generations and then claimed a god as his 16th ancestor—that is to say, he could go back no further by any reliable tradition. But a large number are cosmic. The sky is commonly thought of as a male, the earth as a female, and they are husband and wife; hence a good proportion of the stories of a sky-god's affairs, whether with goddesses or with mortal women, are really variants of the immemorial statement: "Father Sky wedded Mother Earth, and that is why she has so many children," that is, vegetation of all sorts. This theme, however, is far from being universal; for example, the sky-deity in Egypt is the goddess Nut, who obviously cannot be anyone's father or husband. There are other cosmic marriages of lesser, but still wide, results in the constitution of the world. Thus, in Greek tradition, Oceanus (not what we mean by the ocean, but a river supposed to encircle the earth) and his consort Tethys are the father and mother of all rivers, besides other offspring.

Types of Sagas.—Since sagas go back to real events, it is clearly impossible to make any brief classification of them or their themes. It should, however, be noticed that they regularly include the exploits of noteworthy men, less commonly women, such as the Greeks styled "heroes" (properly and originally nobles, persons of good family). They had a regular cult of such personages, normally at their supposed burial places, from which they were thought still to exercise at least a local and limited influence. In European tradition—Greek, Celtic, Slav, or Germanic—they are regularly warriors, but the leading figures of Finnish sagas tend rather to be notable magicians. There is also a very widespread type, the culture hero, that is, the legendary originator of the customs and industries of his people, or of some of them. He, however, is often a purely imaginary being, and so belongs rather to the realm of myth than to saga proper.

Sagas are a long-lived form of traditional tale, and traces of them are still to be found in the unhistorical and often unwritten popular accounts of prominent persons, including some as recent as the 1st Earl Kitchener, the fact of whose death was by no means universally accepted; indeed, he showed some signs of joining the company of those saga figures who do not die but mysteriously disappear. They include persons as diverse as the Roman Emperor Nero, the British King Arthur, and the Holy Roman Emperor Frederick I Barbarossa.

Types of Folk Tales.—A large number of folk tales fall into one general category, most plausibly accounted for by the fact that such tales are the production of the lower orders of society, such as peasants, for the most part. They are not composed for the delight of persons of distinguished ancestry who would listen to the exploits of their great forebears and other such themes of saga. In these folk tales it is very common to see success attending the most unlikely characters. The youngest and supposedly most foolish son or daughter succeeds where the older ones fail; the weak and unwarlike little man overcomes giants and other formidable creatures by his cunning; a child discovers the truth where adults are at fault, and so on. This is the imaginative compensation of people who feel themselves inferior or oppressed, a kind of daydream or wishful thinking.

Another characteristic is that folk tales are generally moral, but of a narrow morality. For example, the successful hero or heroine is regularly kind, but on the other hand may be a prodigious and unashamed liar. Objection to lying seems to have originated among the stronger and more highly placed, who despised it, not as morally wrong, but as the resource of the weak, who could not vindicate their conduct by force if it was questioned. It is noteworthy that the earliest expression of such a sentiment in European literature comes from the almost invincible hero Achilles (Homer, *Iliad,* book 9, lines 312–313), while the weaker Odysseus (who, by the way, is partly a figure of folk tale) lies elaborately and ingeniously on occasion.

The marvels which are so common a feature of folk tales are often reflections of real beliefs. For instance, witchcraft is still believed in here and there, and individuals who practice it still exist; a malignant or occasionally a benevolent witch is one of the regular characters in thousands of folk tales. Supernatural beings, such as fairies, jinn, and so forth, are usually of a kind that is still believed in or has been till recently. The widespread idea that the dead retain an interest in and sometimes can influence the fortunes of the living is one which survives despite the teachings of the higher religions and often in contradiction to them. Thus a folk tale may be a sociological document of some importance.

See also EGYPTIAN RELIGION; FOLK TALES AND MYTHS OF THE AMERICAN INDIANS; FOLKLORE; GREECE—*12. Greek Mythology;* NATURE WORSHIP; PERSIAN MYTHOLOGY; ROMAN RELIGION; SCANDINAVIAN MYTHOLOGY; SLAV MYTHOLOGY.

Bibliography.—Handbooks on particular mythologies are common. H. J. Rose, *A Handbook of Greek Mythology,* 6th ed. (New York and London 1958) contains an introductory chapter on the classification and explanation of traditional tales; consult also Robert Graves, *The Greek Myths,* 2 vols. (Baltimore 1955). For a study with psychological presuppositions, consult Carl G. Jung and Károly Kerényi, *Introduction to a Science of Mythology.* There is a large collection of material in Raffaele Pettazzoni, *Miti e leggende,* 2 vols (Turin 1948–53). The standard work on folk tales is Stith Thompson, *Motif-Index of Folk-Literature,* rev and enl. ed., 6 vols. (Bloomington, Ind., 1955–58); shorter works include John A. Macculloch, *The Childhood of Fiction* (London 1905), and Alexander Haggerty Krappe *The Science of Folk-Lore* (London 1930). Consult also Leach, Maria, ed., *Funk & Wagnalls Standard Dictionary of Folklore, Mythology and Legend,* 2 vols. (New York 1949–50); Frazer, Sir James G., *The Golden Bough: a Study in Magic and Religion,* 3d ed., rev. and enl., 13 vols. (New York 1958), abr. ed., 1 vol., reissue (New York 1960); G.-H. Luquet and others, *Larousse Encyclopedia of Mythology,* with an introduction by Robert Graves (New York 1959); Bulfinch, Thomas, *Mythology* (any ed.).

H. J. ROSE,
Late Professor of Greek, University of St. Andrews, Scotland.

MYTILENE. See LESBOS.

MYXEDEMA, mĭk-sê-dē′mȧ, a disease first described by Sir William Gull in 1873, and named because of mucoid substance accumulating especially in the subcutaneous tissue and making it simulate edema. It results from a deficiency of thyroid hormone, which may stem from too complete excision of thyroid tissue or from defective control of the thyroid by a pituitary hormone. Most commonly, however, myxedema appears spontaneously without obvious cause. In general, the thyroid gland suffers atrophy, with lost glandular tissue being replaced by fibrous tissue.

The disease occurs most commonly in individuals 30 to 60 years old, and is five times more frequent in females than in males. The appearance of an adult patient is characteristic: the expression is dull and apathetic; eyelids are puffy; outer third of eyebrows may be missing; tongue is swollen; hair is thin, coarse, and dry; skin is cool, thick, dry, scaly, and frequently yellowish. The patient notes a slowing down, weakness, and muscular aches; his movements, reflexes, and thinking are slowed; speech is halting, slurred, and hoarse; there is usually constipation, anemia, and marked intolerance to cold; menses increase in duration and amount; metabolic rate is low. The juvenile type has essentially the same symptoms, although they may be less marked. Additional features are retarded growth and sometimes delayed dentition.

The disease is slowly progressive; all degrees of severity exist, depending on the extent of thyroid failure. Medication consists of desiccated thyroid substance, taken orally. Relief of symptoms is prompt and dramatic, but changes in physical appearance may not be noticed for several months.

See also CRETINISM.

LESLIE B. AREY.

MYXOPHYCEAE, mĭk-sô-fĭs′ê-ē (known also as CYANOPHYCEAE or SCHIZOPHYCEAE), the botanical class that includes the "blue-green algae"; it is the sole class in the division Cyanophyta (see ALGAE). The typical blue-green color of many of the genera is the result of masking of the chlorophyll α and β-carotene with the phycobilin pigments phycocyanin (blue) and phycoerythrin (red). Because of variation in the abundance of the phycobilins, the plants may be decidedly reddish or almost black in macroscopic appearance. Their color may also be affected by the presence of pigmented, gelatinous surface coatings which surround the cells. The pigments of Myxophyceae, unlike those of all other algae, are not localized in sharply delimited plastids, but instead are dispersed as droplets in the more peripheral cytoplasm, the chromoplasm. The cells are bounded by cellulose walls and frequently, in addition, by the pectic sheaths already mentioned; the latter may be firm or diffluent and are often stratified. The cells of Myxophyceae differ further from those of other plants in their lack of prominent aqueous vacuoles, in the storage form of their photosnythate, namely, "cyanophycean starch," and in the organization of the nuclear material. The latter is not delimited clearly from the cytoplasm by a membrane, and a nucleolus is absent. Division of the nuclear material simulates mitosis in a few genera but seems to be passive and effected by cell division in others. The possible relation of the Myxophyceae to bacteria has frequently been suggested, but the evidence hardly supports such a view.

The plant bodies of Myxophyceae may be unicellular, colonial, or filamentous. Filamentous genera may be unbranched, branched, or falsely branched, the latter because of rupture of unbranched filaments through their sheaths. Reproduction of unicellular forms is by cell division. The colonial and filamentous genera multiply by fragmentation. Fragments of filamentous genera are known as hormogonia; these may grow into new plants under favorable circumstances. Hormogonia may arise through the death of cells in the filament (*Oscillatoria*) or between heterocysts (*Nostoc* and *Anabaena*). Heterocysts, which are transparent cells with nodular wall thickenings at their poles, are resistant and sporelike; they are capable of germination into vegetative filaments. Akinetes, also thick-walled dormant cells, are granular and filled with reserve photosnythates; they also may germinate into vegetative phases. A few genera form spores (endospores) endogenously. Sexuality has not been observed among Myxophyceae.

Regarding the nutritional and photosynthetic activities of Myxophyceae, study of a number of genera in bacteria-free culture has revealed that they are entirely autotrophic, although they may utilize organic supplements in culture media. Use of radioactive isotopes has firmly established the fact that certain Myxophyceae (*Nostoc* sp. and *Anabaena* sp.) have the capacity to fix gaseous nitrogen.

The Myxophyceae are found everywhere on and in moist soil, tree bark, stones, and timber; on the leaves of mosses; and on and within liveworts and other plants (*Nostoc* in *Anthoceros, Anabaena* in *Cycas* and *Azolla*). They are abundant in both fresh and salt water and may be benthic or planktonic. *Polycystis* and *Anabaena,* among others, are genera which frequently appear in water blooms. A rather specialized group of Myxophyceae is present in hot springs in temperatures ranging up to 85°C. A number of these Myxophyceae precipitate rocklike deposits known as travertine (q.v.).

Consult Smith, Gilbert M., *Fresh-water Algae of the United States* (New York 1950); id., ed., *Manual of Phycology* (Waltham, Mass., 1951).

HAROLD C. BOLD,
Vanderbilt University.

MYXOSPORIDIA, mĭk-sô-spô-rĭd′ĭ-ȧ, an order of Sporozoa (q.v.)' having its growing phase amoebic and reproducing constantly by spore formation during this period. They are chiefly parasitic on fish and amphibians but may occur in invertebrates; epidemics among fish and even silkworms are caused by members of this order.

MYXOSPORIUM, mĭk-sô-spō′rĭ-ŭm, a genus of imperfect fungi of the order Melanconiales, resembling those of the genus *Gloeosporium.* They grow on bark, and one species *M. corticolum,* causes a mild canker on apples and pears.

MZAB, m′zäb′, region, Algeria, comprising a group of oases in the Sahara, about 100 miles southeast of Laghouat. The main center is Ghardaia. The region is inhabited by a Berber people known as the Mzab, a heretical Islamic sect expelled from the coast early in the Middle Ages.

National Park Service photo by George A. Grant

NATIONAL PARKS: Midway Geyser Basin and Firehole River in Yellowstone National Park.

N. The sequence *l, m, n* in the order of the letters of the alphabet is extremely ancient, and preserved with great regularity. Even in those scripts in which the old Semitic arrangement has been disturbed, these three tend to stay together; for example, Arabic (23, 24, 25). Ethiopic is an exception, having *n* 12th; *l* and *m* 2d and 4th respectively, with *ḥ* interpolated. The view has even been advanced, and widely accepted, that the Latin *elementum* (-*a*) meanting alphabet (and hence elementary) is nothing but the names of these three letters (given as *el, em, en* by Latin grammarians)—supposedly the first three in a second row of letters, just as alphabet (that is, *a, b*) or *abecedarium* (first attested about the beginning of the 6th century) arose from the first two (or three) letters.

Be that as it may, and it must be admitted that the theory lacks proof, the form of the letter *n*, like that of *m* and *l*, has not varied greatly throughout the long history of the scripts derived from the North Semitic. It appears that the letter *m* is a differentiation of the labial from the dental nasal *n;* and in fact, in the final position, the alternation *m* and *n*, demanded in part by assimilation to the initial consonant of a following word (the Sanskrit *sandhi*), is frequent. Thus Greek, Celtic, Germanic, Balto-Slavonic all substituted -*n* for Indo-European *m;* Moabite, Aramäic, and Arabic have a plural in -*n*, where Hebrew shows -*m*. Assimilation also affects the place of articulation of a nasal medially. The participle of Latin *sumo* (classical *sumptus*, with -*p*- inserted as a glide) shows up in Italian as *sunto;* Gothic has *fimf* corresponding to Latin *quinque*, the former with a labial nasal (before *f*), the latter with a velar nasal (before *qu*).

But palatal and velar nasals are not commonly distinguished in the writing, though Sanskrit writes the cerebral, palatal, and velar nasals by symbols distinct from that of the dental *n*, and in Greek the practice arose of writing γ as a palatal nasal before κ, γ, χ. This came about from the fact that in the group *gn* the *g* passed into a palatal nasal, thus giving the symbol an additional value. A similar change took place in Latin (compare the pronunciation *signe, segno* in French and Italian), occasionally so written (*singnifer*), and English has to be content to use *ng* with this phonetic value (the technical symbol is ŋ), e.g. in *king*, as well as for -*ngg*- (as in *longer, finger*), and similarly *nk* for -*ngk*- (as in *lynx, monkey*). Fundamentally this variation is a matter of syllabic division (*ng*, when *g* belongs to the same syllable as *n;* -*ng-g*- when *g* belongs to the following syllable). However, some of the northern English dialects have -*ng*- not -*ng-g*- in the medial position, and conversely the Midlands often have -*ng-g*- instead of -*ng*- in words like *singing*. In present participles (ending in -*ng*) the dental nasal *n* superseded -*ng* in early modern English, as is clearly shown by the spelling *standyn* for standing (*fardin* for *farthing*), and this utterance is still widespread and found among educated speakers. Conversely -*ng* has been substituted analogically for *n* (*chicking, gudging* for *chicken, gudgeon*), but this practice is mostly confined to the less well educated. Final -*n* is not heard after -*m* (*autumn* beside *autumnal, damn* beside *damnation*); *handicap* stands for *hand-in-cap*, and the loss of -*n* in unaccented monosyllables is responsible for the pairs *a* and *an, i'* and *in, o'* and *on*, and (with syntactical differentiation) *my* and *mine, no* and *none*. Misdivision is responsible for *a newt* (for *an ewt*, Middle English *ewte*) and other words (*nick-name, adder, apron, auger*) that have taken on or lost *n*-, as the case may be. This proves that the difference of juncture heard in *an aim, a name* is not stable.

As for the form of the symbol (the 14th letter of the North Semitic original script), in Cretan we find ⟨ʅ⟩ and in Sinaitic ⟨〰⟩. But already Phoenician and Moabite have 𐤍 or 𐤍, and the Greek Ν and Latin **N** are readily traced back to this. The Slavonic Н (Cyrillic N) is a slight and obvious modification of **N**. The Semitic name of the letter is *nūn* (whence Greek *nū*), and its meaning is said to be "fish." Actually a fishlike symbol does appear, apparently with the *n*-value, in some Sinaitic inscriptions.

A syllabic -*n* (compare the article M) is heard in *mutton, heaven*, and a syllabic -*n* is occasionally substituted for it (in rapid speech after -*k*- as in *spoken, bacon*). Breathed *n* and *ng* (written *nh, ngh*) occur in Welsh as the result of mutation; in English, a partial assimilation to preceding *s* (in *snow*) has the effect of depriving *n* of some element of voice, but the combination is often unstable and in Latin it was the *s* that disappeared (*niuem* [acc.] is cognate, compare the treatment of *sm* described in the article M). Nasalization of vowels is often inadequately written by the symbol *n*, that is in French, where it is a strong nasal resonance (*vin, cent*). It usually affects a preceding vowel even when *n* remains a consonant (contrast the *a*, with a slight "nasal twang," in *man* with that of *bad*); and in many parts of North America nasalization may pervade the entire utterance.

Parallel to *mį* before *ū* is *nį* (written *n*), the standard pronunciation in words like *new,* though again in many parts of North America the consonantal *į* element is lacking. For bibliography see ALPHABET.

JOSHUA WHATMOUGH.

NABATAEANS, nab-ə-tē'ənz, an Arab people whose kingdom at one time extended as far north as Damascus. Around the end of the 4th century B.C. they were established in Petra (in the present kingdom of Jordan), which they made their capital, and thereafter their sway was greatly extended. They forced the Edomites up into southern Judah. The location of Petra on the route of commerce from southern Arabia to Syria is credited with the prosperity of the kingdom in the 1st and 2d centuries B.C. and the 1st century A.D. The Nabataeans guarded their trade routes and grew wealthy by imposing customs' duties. At its height under Aretas IV (9 B.C.–40 A.D.) the kingdom reached to Damascus. The Nabataean kingdom was conquered by Trajan in 105 A.D., and became a Roman province.

Consult Glueck, Nelson, *Deities and Dolphins* (New York 1965).

NABLUS, nab'ləs (ancient SHECHEM; later NEAPOLIS), town, Jordan, located in the northwestern region, between Mounts Ebal and Gerizim, 30 miles north of Jerusalem. It is a busy trading and industrial center, producing soap and olive oil, and is the seat of a Greek bishop. Shechem was important in patriarchal times, and has the traditional sites of the tombs of Joshua and Joseph and Jacob's Well. Abimelech ruled it, then destroyed it; Jeroboam I ruled as king of Israel from Shechem. The name of Neapolis, of which Nablus is the Arabic corruption, was bestowed by Vespasian. The town figured conspicuously during the Crusades. It was a religious center of the Samaritans, some of whose descendants still live here. The bulk of the population, however, is Muslim. Population: (1961) 45,768.

NABOB, nā'bob (from Hind. *navvāb,* colloquial *nabāb*), the title applied to a native ruler in India. It also designated a provincial governor of the Mogul Empire. Europeans returning wealthy from the East had the word applied to them, and, by semantic widening, *nabob* came to be used to designate any very wealthy man.

NABOKOV, nə-bô'kəf, **Vladimir,** Russian-American author: b. St. Petersburg (now Leningrad), Russia, April 23, 1899. One of the most original mid-20th century writers in English, Nabokov became noted for his experimental style and satiric wit. He was relatively unknown until he published *Lolita* (1958), a novel dealing with the passion of a middle-aged intellectual for a 12-year-old "nymphet." *Lolita,* an immediate best seller that was made into a successful film, was both praised as a modern classic and condemned as a work of "highbrow pornography."

The son of a well-to-do St. Petersburg family, Nabokov came in contact with English influences at an early age and, through his tutors and governesses, learned English before he could read Russian. In 1919, two years after the Bolsheviks came to power, Nabokov went to England, where he received his B.A. from Trinity College, Cambridge, in 1922. About this time he began publishing poems, stories, and essays in Russian under the pseudonym "V. Sirin."

In 1940, Nabokov emigrated to the United States, where he became a citizen in 1945. He held positions at several American colleges and universities, including Wellesley, Cornell, and Harvard, and at the same time wrote and published in American magazines. A lifelong interest in the study of moths and butterflies brought him recognition as a lepidopterist. In 1959 he gave up his teaching career to devote his full time to writing, and he and his family settled in Switzerland.

Nabokov's first novel in English was *The Real Life of Sebastian Knight* (1941). Later books in English include *Conclusive Evidence* (1951), an evocative remembrance of his childhood in Russia, which brought him comparisons with Proust; *Pnin* (1957), a satire about a Russian émigré professor in America; *Nabokov's Dozen* (1958), a collection of 13 stories; and *Pale Fire* (1962), a satire on academic life. Nabokov also published an English translation of Pushkin's *Eugene Onegin* (1963), which he describes as "the great work of my life," and, with the assistance of his son Dmitri, translations of many of his early Russian stories and novels.

NABONIDUS, nab-ō-nī'dəs (Assyrian *Nabū-na'id*), Babylonian king: d. about 538 B.C. He was the last of the Chaldean dynasty to reign at Babylon (556–c.538 B.C.). Not a member of the family of Nebuchadnezzar II, he may have usurped the throne. He seems to have performed religious duties zealously, and to have restored various ancient shrines, but his neglect of the gods Marduk (Merodach) and Nebo (Nabu) brought him into conflict with the priestly class. His antiquarian interests, so strongly indicated by his inscriptions, are thought to have occupied him to such an extent that they were responsible for his disregarding the state's defense. He spent several years of his reign in the oasis Teima, in northern Arabia, during which period, it is believed, his son Belshazzar actually governed at Babylon. According to Eusebius, after Babylon had fallen Nabonidus fortified himself at Borsippa, only to be captured there by Cyrus the Great, who nevertheless treated him with kindness and permitted him exile in Carmania (now Kerman). A cuneiform record of Cyrus, however, indicates that Nabonidus was delivered over to Gobryas, Cyrus' general, and died in mysterious circumstances. See also BELSHAZZAR.

NABOTH, nā'both, an Israelite, owner of a vineyard in Jezreel, during the reign of Ahab, king of Israel (1 Kings 21). The palace of Ahab immediately adjoined this vineyard, which became an object of the king's desire and he offered to purchase it or give another in exchange for it. When Naboth refused to part with the "inheritance of his fathers," Ahab was bitterly disappointed, but his wife, Jezebel, sent letters in Ahab's name, sealed them with his signet and caused Naboth to be tried for blasphemy and treason on the testimony of two suborned witnesses and stoned to death. This crime brought down the curse of Elijah upon the guilty couple (2–26), which was fulfilled soon after in the fate of both. See AHAB.

NABU or **NEBO.** See PISGAH.

NACHTIGAL, näKH'ti-gäl, **Gustav,** German explorer in Africa: b. Eichstedt, Germany, Feb. 23, 1834; d. at sea near Cape Palmas, April 19, 1885. After studying medicine, he became a military surgeon, then went to Africa in search of health. In 1869 the king of Prussia sent him with gifts to the sultan of Bornu, in recognition of kindness shown to German explorers. His journey through Fezzan and Tibesti was over country hitherto untraversed by a European. He arrived at Kuka in 1870, thence explored Borku, Kanem, and the country south of Bornu, and on his way back to Cairo passed through Wadai. The years from 1875 to 1882 he spent in Germany arousing national interest in German colonization. He entered the consular service in 1882, becoming consul to Tunis, and in 1884 was German commissioner for the annexation of Togoland, Kamerun, and Lüderitzland. He died on his way back to Europe. Nachtigal's work marked a distinct era in the exploration of northern Africa and even more notably in German colonial policy.

NACOGDOCHES, nak-ə-dō'chəz, city, Texas, seat of Nacogdoches County, 130 miles northeast of Houston. The region produces beef cattle, milk, and poultry. The chief manufactures are lumber, feed, fertilizers, cottonseed oil, filter clays, and clothing. Stephen F. Austin State College is located here.

Nacogdoches was named for a chief of the Tejas Indians. It was visited by de Soto, then by La Salle, and was first settled by Spaniards in 1716, when they set up a mission for the Indians. It was on the old Spanish highway called El Camino Real. From 1819 on it was the center of Texan revolutionary efforts, and Sam Houston lived here. The Old Stone Fort, built in 1779 and torn down in 1901, was re-erected in 1923. The city has a commission government. Pop. 22,544.

NAD, or nicotinamide adenine dinucleotide, is a coenzyme involved in the oxidation of foodstuffs in the cell. It is also known as *diphosphopyridine nucleotide* (*DPN*) or *Coenzyme I.* Coenzymes are molecules that are necessary for the functioning of enzymes.

NAD is found in most plant and animal cells together with a similar coenzyme, nicotinamide adenine dinucleotide phosphate (NADP), which differs from NAD in having an extra phosphate molecule. NADP is also known as *triphosphopyridine nucleotide* (*TPN*). NAD and NADP, which have similar functions, are the active forms of niacin, one of the water-soluble B vitamins.

The initial reactions in cellular oxidation of food involve the removal of hydrogen from metabolic intermediates. These reactions are catalyzed by enzymes called *dehydrogenases,* which remove the hydrogen and transfer it to the nicotinamide group of NAD, thereby producing reduced NAD (NADH). This reaction is reversible, and thus the coenzyme function of NAD is to act as a hydrogen carrier by undergoing reversible oxidation-reduction of the nicotinamide ring. These changes can be readily observed even in intact cells because NADH, but not NAD, has a light-absorption peak at 340 millimicrons, and it also has characteristic fluorescence properties.

Because of its role in oxidation-reduction reactions, NAD is found to be mainly, but not exclusively, in the mitochondria of the cell, where it is associated with the dehydrogenases of the citric acid cycle and the NADH oxidase system of the respiratory chain. See also COENZYME; CITRIC ACID CYCLE.

DAVID GRIFFITHS, *University of Warwick*

NADER, nā'dər, **Ralph,** American lawyer and writer, who led a crusade for automobile safety and consumer protection: b. Winsted, Conn., Feb. 27, 1934. He graduated from Princeton in 1955 and received his law degree at Harvard in 1958. While working on automobile accident cases in Hartford legal practice, Nader became appalled at the number of fatalities. He sought to alert the public to the need for safer cars by lecturing, lobbying in Washington, and by writing magazine articles and a book, *Unsafe at Any Speed* (1965), which became a best seller. In the book he detailed defects in American cars and criticized manufacturers for concentrating on speed and style instead of passenger safety.

Public interest was aroused, and Nader was called to testify at Senate hearings. His efforts were instrumental in securing enactment of the 1966 Traffic Safety Act, which empowered the federal government to set safety standards for all cars sold in the United States. Nader charged that a General Motors investigator had spied on him, and he won a $425,000 settlement.

Nader became a leader of the consumer movement. He formed the Center for the Study of Responsive Law, Public Citizen Inc., the Center for Auto Safety, and other groups. During school vacations hundreds of young people known as "Nader's Raiders" joined him. He and his associates published reports on many subjects. Nader criticized the executive branch, Congress, and federal regulatory agencies for being more responsive to special interests than to private citizens. He warned of radiation dangers from color television sets, X rays, and atomic energy plants. He cited hazards in food and drugs and criticized nonenforcement of job safety standards. He gave data to sympathetic congressmen who worked to pass laws reflecting his points of view.

NADIR, nā'dər, in astronomy, that point of the heavens which is diametrically opposite to the zenith or point directly over our heads. The zenith and nadir are the two poles of the horizon; the zenith, nadir, and center of the earth are in one straight line.

NADIR SHAH, nä'dər shä (TAHMASP KULI KHAN), king of Persia: b. Khurasan, 1688; d. June 20, 1747. He was of Turkish blood and poor family. He early showed his cunning by his attempts, while in the service of different governors of Khurasan, to take over that province, but was unsuccessful. Putting himself at the head of a band of robbers, he got possession of several strongholds in Khurasan. In 1726 he entered the service of Tahmasp II, for whom he checked the Afghans and defeated the Turks, and from whom he received four provinces. When Tahmasp was defeated at Hamadan by the pasha of Baghdad and was forced to cede the provinces on the Araxes to the Turks and to make a disgraceful peace, Nadir dethroned him (1732), put Tahmasp's son Abbas III in his place, and took the regency upon himself. The lost provinces were won back from the Turks, and in 1736, upon the death of Abbas, Nadir came to the throne. He invaded Afghanistan and conquered it in 1737–1738. He then seized most of India from

Mohammed Shah, the Mogul emperor. In 1739 he captured Delhi and pillaged it, the treasure he carried away including the Koh-i-noor diamond and the Peacock Throne. He subjugated Bukhara (Bokhara) and Khwarizm (Khiva), and so extended his empire that it reached from the Indus and the Oxus to the Euphrates and the Caspian. From 1743 to 1746 he was engaged in war with the Turks. Officers of his guard, weary of his brutal cruelty, assassinated him.

NAEVIUS, nē′vĭ-ŭs, **Gnaeus,** Roman poet and dramatist: b. probably Rome, c. 270 B.C.; d. Utica, Africa, c. 201 B.C. After service in the First Punic War (264–241 B.C.), he embarked on a literary career in 235. He wrote epic and satire, but won his fame in drama; his work survives mostly in quotations in later Latin writers. Naevius was a plebeian, and his rancorous attacks on aristocrats, particularly Scipio Africanus and the Metelli, caused his imprisonment for libel in 206 B.C. After apologies in two plays written in prison, he was released; but renewed aspersions resulted in his exile to Utica. There he composed the *Bellum Poenicum* (*Bellum Punicum*), which treated the First Punic War and the early history of Rome and Carthage. It was the earliest Latin national epic in Saturnian verse (q.v.), the native Italian meter; some 65 verses survive. Naevius' epic verse strongly influenced Quintus Ennius and Virgil, and his plays were admired by Titus Maccius Plautus and Terence (Publius Terentius Afer). He invented the *fabula praetexta,* the Roman historical drama.

For Latin text with Eng. tr., consult Warmington, Eric H., *Remains of Old Latin,* vol. 2, pp. 46–156 (Cambridge, Mass., 1957).

P. R. COLEMAN-NORTON.

NAGA, nä′gȧ, a people who inhabit the Naga Hills of Assam in India and the Upper Chindwin River region of north Burma. Physically the Naga show some Mongoloid characteristics. They speak a Tibeto-Burmese language closely related to those of the neighboring Kachin and Kuki-Chin peoples. There are a number of Naga tribes: the Angami, Ao, Konyak, Lhota, Rengma, and Sema Naga. They dwell on hilltops in villages fortified by bamboo hedges and pits against enemy attack. The Angami Naga build wooden houses, often ornamented with carving, while the Ao and Lhota Naga dwell in houses of bamboo raised on piles. Many of the tribes practice rude cultivation in burnt-over forest clearings, but the Angami and Sema Naga grow rice on irrigated terraces along the lower hill slopes. The Sema Naga have hereditary chiefs served by debtor slaves who sometimes number half the community. The Angami and Lhota Naga are governed by a council of elders and an elected chief. Among some tribes an individual can raise his status by giving a series of feasts. The Ao Naga have a system in which boys are assigned special duties according to age. The Naga were formerly head-hunters; the capture of an enemy head brought status to a man and prosperity and fertility to his village. Head-hunting was suppressed under the British in the early 20th century, but recurred during and after World War II.

The Naga of Burma are gradually being assimilated by their Shan and Kachin (Jhingpaw) neighbors. Those in Assam have tended to retain their tribal identity, and around 1947 some of the more sophisticated Naga organized with the objective of achieving a Naga state independent of the Indian government. There followed several years of fighting between the Naga and the Indian troops sent to bring them under control. In 1957 the semiautonomous territory occupied by the Naga was organized as the Naga Hills Tuensang Area, administered by the president of the Republic of India through the governor of Assam. This led to a renewed struggle by the Naga nationalists, and in 1960 Prime Minister Jawaharlal Nehru of India agreed to the establishment of a separate Naga state (Nagaland), the smallest in the Indian union, with an area of about 6,000 square miles and a population of 350,000 to 400,000. See also NAGA HILLS.

Bibliography.—Hutton, John Henry, *The Angami Nagas* (London 1921); id., *The Sema Nagas* (London 1922); Mills, James Philip, *The Lhota Nagas* (London 1922); Smith, William Carlson, *The Ao Naga Tribe of Assam* (London 1925); Mills, James Philip, *The Ao Nagas* (London 1926).

ELIZABETH E. BACON.

NAGA, nä′gä, city, the Philippines, capital of Camarines Sur Province, in southeast Luzon, on the Bicol River, five miles south of San Miguel Bay. The region was visited by the Spaniards in 1573, and the Spanish town of Nueva Caceres was shortly built on the site of the former native village of Naga. It served as the capital of the united Camarines provinces, and when they were divided in 1919 into Camarines Norte and Camarines Sur, Naga was made capital of the latter. The city produces cement, and the surrounding area raises corn, rice, and hemp. Pop. (1948) 56,238.

NAGA, nä′gȧ (Sanskrit *nāga*), a mythical race of serpent-associated creatures found widely in the literature and art of India, whether Hindu, Buddhist, or Jain. The naga may be represented simply as a great serpent, usually many-headed, or as a creature with a serpent tail and a human torso and head surmounted by a crown or halo of expanded cobra hoods. More usually it is a man or woman wearing a crown of cobra heads arching from behind, forming a kind of protective umbrella. This headgear may stand for a crown worn in ancient times by the pre-Aryan rulers of India.

The naga king, far from being fierce, is usually represented as a patron of fertility, peace, health, wealth, justice, and spiritual enlightenment. In Buddhist stories, nagas give the Enlightened One his first bath, shelter him from a seven-day storm raised by enemies to prevent his Enlightenment, obtain a share in his relics, and restore to men the famous lost sutra known as the *Prajñāpāramitā.* Jainism has a cobra-crowned savior, Parshvanatha (Pārśvanātha), said to have lived about 250 years before the Buddha and credited with having introduced into India the now popular doctrine of ahimsa (nonviolence).

RODERICK MARSHALL.

NAGA HILLS, a mountain chain extending along the border between Assam (India) and Burma, between the Brahmaputra and upper Chindwin rivers. A part of the Arakan-Yoma mountain system, the Naga Hills comprise three main ranges, the Barail, the Naga, and the Patkai. The highest peaks are Saramati (12,553 feet) in the Patkai Range and Japvo (9,890 feet) in the Barail Range. These rugged, forested hills, which form a barrier between Assam and upper Burma, are the home of the Naga (q.v.) tribes.

NAGANO, nä-gä-nô, city, Japan, capital of Nagano Prefecture, in central Honshu, on a branch of the Shinano River, 110 miles northwest of Tokyo. A major center of the silk industry before World War II, it is now mainly an agricultural market, especially for apples. There are also manufactures of woolens and other textiles. In Nagano is the great Zenkoji Temple (7th century), visited each year by large numbers of Buddhist pilgrims. Pop. (1960) 160,522.

NAGAOKA, nä-gä-ô-kä, city, Japan, in Niigata Prefecture, in central Honshu, on the Shinano River, 35 miles south of Niigata. It is one of Japan's principal oil-production centers, and also produces machine tools and textiles. Pop. (1960) 148,254.

NAGASAKI, nä-gä-sä-kê, city, Japan, capital of Nagasaki Prefecture, on the northwest coast of Kyushu, on Nagasaki Peninsula, a projection of Hizen Peninsula. Its beautiful natural harbor (2½ miles long) is protected at the entrance by islands, and the city rises in terraces on the surrounding hills. Nagasaki is a major port and shipbuilding center; it also produces electric goods and is noted for its tortoise-shell ware. The Suwa Shrine, in the northeastern part of the city adjoining Suwa Park, is the center of a colorful festival (the Okunchi Festival) held annually (October 7–9). The Chinese-styled Sofukuji Temple (17th century) is also of great interest.

Nagasaki was first visited by the Portuguese in 1571 and became the earliest center of Christianity in Japan. From 1641, after foreigners had been excluded from the rest of Japan, Nagasaki alone remained open, to the Dutch and Chinese. Finally, by the treaty of 1854, United States commerce was admitted to the port, and other Western countries began trading there soon after. On Aug. 9, 1945, the second atomic bomb dropped on Japan by the United States destroyed over a third of Nagasaki and killed or injured about 75,000 people. The devastation included the largest Roman Catholic cathedral in Japan. Restoration of the city and its commerce was rapid. Pop. (1960) 344,153.

NAGAUR, nȧ-gour′, town, India, capital of Nagaur District, in central Rajasthan State. The district, on the edge of the Thar Desert, was formerly part of the princely state of Jodhpur (Marwar). Like the rest of the desert subregion of Rajputana, it is a great sandy plain with several streams that empty into the Luni. Despite a low average yearly rainfall, some cotton, wheat, and barley is grown, mostly in the southern part, and Nagaur cattle are world famous.

The town of Nagaur, 75 miles northeast of Jodhpur, is the center of a handicrafts industry, providing mainly brass utensils, ivory toys, and cotton cloth. It is thought to have been founded by the Naga Rajputs, and was held by a Ghurid chief and later by a Rathor clan of Rajputs under the Mogul emperor Shah Jahan (r. 1628–1658). A thick wall, built in the 12th or 13th century, surrounds the town, which contains two Hindu temples, a five-domed mosque, and an imposing fort. Pop. (1961) 24,296.

EUGENE F. IRSCHICK.

NAGEL, nä′gĕl, **Charles,** American lawyer and cabinet officer: b. Colorado County, Texas, Aug. 9, 1849; d. St. Louis, Mo., Jan. 5, 1940. After attending the St. Louis Law School, he studied Roman law and political economy at the University of Berlin and in 1873 was admitted to the Missouri bar. From 1893 to 1897 he served as president of the city council of St. Louis, and in 1908 he was named a member of the Republican National Committee. He was secretary of commerce and labor in the cabinet of President William Howard Taft from 1909 to 1913.

NÄGELI or **NAEGELI,** nâ′gĕ-lê, **Karl Wilhelm von,** Swiss botanist: b. Kilchberg, near Zurich, Switzerland, March 27, 1817; d. Munich, Germany, May 10, 1891. Professor of botany at the University of Munich from 1858, he investigated the living matter and nuclei of cells and the mode of cell growth. He is credited with the discovery of the antheridia and spermatozoids of ferns, and also originated the micellar theory on the structure of ultramicroscopic particles.

NAGORNO-KARABAKH AUTONOMOUS OBLAST, nŭ-gôr′nŭ kȧ-rŭ-bȧk′, administrative division, USSR, in the Azerbaidzhan SSR, in Transcaucasia. The oblast, whose name means "Mountainous Karabakh," is on the northeast slopes of the Lesser Caucasus, and has an area of 1,700 square miles. The population is 90 per cent Armenian. Fruit, wine, tobacco, woolens, rugs, and silk are produced, and livestock graze the mountain pastures, where Karabakh (Karabagh) horses used to be bred. The capital, Stepanakert (pop., 1959 census, 19,600), and Shusha (pop., 1959 census, 6,100) are the principal towns. The area was under Turkish and Persian rule in the 17th and 18th centuries, passing to Russia in 1813. Karabakh was ravaged during the Russian Civil War (1918–1920). Because of its Armenian majority, it was declared an autonomous oblast within the Azerbaidzhan Republic in 1923. Pop. (1959) 130,600.

THEODORE SHABAD.

NAGOYA, nä-gô-yä, city, Japan, capital of Aichi Prefecture, in central Honshu, on Ise Bay. The third largest city in Japan and a major port, industrial, and rail center, Nagoya has been known since the 13th century for its pottery and porcelain, and today also produces textiles, machine tools, automobiles, metalwork, and chemicals. Notable points of interest are the Higashi-Honganji Temple (Buddhist), the Atsuta Shrine (Shinto), and the Nittaiji Temple (Buddhist). Historic Nagoya Castle (1612) was destroyed in an air raid in 1945. Nagoya University (given university status in 1949) is situated in the city. Pop. (1960) 1,591,935.

NAGPUR, näg′po͝or, city, India, capital of Nagpur District, 420 miles northeast of Bombay. From 1743 it was the capital of the Maratha kingdom of Nagpur, and under British rule was capital of the Central Provinces (from 1861) and of the Central Provinces and Berar (from 1903). Under the Republic of India it was the capital of Madhya Pradesh State until 1956, when a reorganization transferred it to Bombay. Nagpur, 1,000 feet above sea level, is built around Sitabaldi Hill, where in 1817 a Maratha army of 18,000 was repulsed by a British garrison numbering 1,350. Nagpur is an important railroad center. Besides numerous cotton and woolen mills, there is an important hand-weaving industry. Nagpur University was founded in 1923; there are also technical and industrial schools in the city. Pop. (1968) 729,712.

NAGUIB, nȧ-gēb′, **Mohammed,** Egyptian army officer: b. Khartoum, Egypt, 1901. Commissioned a 2d lieutenant at the age of 19 from Cairo's Royal Military Academy, he later attended Fuad I University, and in 1948 fought as a brigadier in the Israeli-Arab War. On July 23, 1952, in a virtually bloodless coup d'état, the Egyptian Army seized control of the regime, forced King Farouk's abdication, and in September installed General Naguib as premier and president. The real power, however, was in the hands of Gamal Abd el-Nasser, who assumed the post of deputy premier. By 1954 an intense rivalry had developed between Naguib and Nasser. Naguib was temporarily removed from office, then restored, and finally was forced into retirement on a pension.

NAGUILIAN, nä-gê-lē′än, municipality, Philippine Islands, on Luzon in the center of the Province of La Union, 9 miles southeast of San Fernando. Pop. (1960) 19,872.

NAGY, nôdj, **Imre,** Hungarian statesman: b. Kaposvár, Hungary, 1896; d. in USSR or Hungary, prior to June 17, 1958. Born of poor peasant parents, Nagy became a Communist at an early age and after the failure of the short-lived Communist regime of Béla Kun in 1919 emigrated to Soviet Russia. His main interests lay in agriculture and economics. He returned to Hungary in the wake of the Russian occupation in 1945, and served as minister of agriculture in the first postwar cabinet. Soon there were signs that Nagy was disconcerted with the ruthless exploitation of his native country and by the complete subservience of his fellow-Communist rulers to dictation from Moscow.

After the death of Stalin, in June 1953, he was appointed premier. He soon made himself relatively popular through measures of liberalization, especially in the field of agriculture. In 1955 he was removed by his enemy Mátyás Rákosi. From retirement he was called upon to lead the nation during the night that followed the outbreak of the Hungarian revolution on Oct. 23, 1956. After some hesitation he sided with the overwhelming majority of the Hungarian people and opposed Russian efforts to reestablish Communism in Hungary by force. On November 4, when strong Soviet forces attacked Budapest, Nagy made a dramatic radio appeal to the free world. He then found asylum at the Yugoslav embassy, from where Soviet forces had guaranteed his safe passage home. This promise was broken on November 22 when he, with some of his friends, was forcibly abducted by Russian troops. He was first detained in Rumania, then brought to secret trial, where he courageously refused to admit any guilt. His execution was announced by the Hungarian News Agency on June 17, 1958, on behalf of the Hungarian Ministry of Justice.

NAHA, nä-hä or **NAWA,** nä-wä (formerly NAFA), seaport at the southern tip of Okinawa, the largest of the Ryukyu Islands. Until 1945 it was the capital of the Okinawa Prefecture. In August of that year, after heavy fighting which virtually destroyed the city it became the headquarters of the United States military governor of the Ryukyus. Its chief products are textiles, Panama hats, sugar, lacquerware, and pottery. Pop. (1958) 188,002.

NAHANT, nȧ-hȧnt′, town, Massachusetts, in Essex County 9 miles east-northeast of Boston. It is on a long narrow peninsula which extends into the Massachusetts Bay four miles south from Lynn. There are two small villages, one Nahant, the other Little Nahant. The whole peninsula is a residential section; many of the dwellings are summer homes. Though settled in 1630, the peninsula was not purchased from the Indians until a century later, when a Lynn farmer obtained a deed from Chief Poquanum for a suit of clothes, two stone pestles and a jew's-harp. A tavern, erected in 1802, and steamboat service to Boston in 1817 popularized it. Pop. 4,119.

NAHANT BAY, an inlet of Massachusetts Bay, in the northeast corner of Massachusetts on the south shore of Essex County. The peninsula on which Nahant is located separates it from Lynn Harbor.

NAHUEL HUAPI, Lake, nä-wĕl′ wä-pē′, lake, Argentina, in the territories of Neuquén and Río Negro on the east slope of the Andes; area 300 square miles; depth 1,000 feet. Surrounded by forests and snow-capped mountains it is one of the favorite resort areas in the Argentinian Andes. The region was established as a national park in 1934. Victoria Island, in the center of the lake, is equipped with a forestry research station.

NAHUM, nā′hŭm (Hebrew for "rich in God's comfort"), one of the 12 minor Hebrew prophets of the Old Testament, whose only record is the book, attributed to 607–606 B.C., that bears his name, a reference in Nehemiah 7:7, as "Rehum" being a copyist's error. Nahum is described as "The Elkoshite," either the son of a man named Elkosh, or native of a village of that name in Galilee, the location of which is uncertain. St. Jerome states that the village in Galilee which bore the name of Elkesi in the 4th century A.D. was the prophet's birthplace, and the Galilean village Capernaum, signifying the "village of Nahum," has also been vaguely speculated upon. The tomb of the prophet is pointed out at Alkush near Mosul—ancient Nineveh—and his life has been associated with the great city, the destruction of which he prophesied. His book entitled *The Burden of Nineveh. The Book of the Vision of Nahum the Elkoshite,* should be compared with that of Jonah which illustrates the remission of God's judgments, while Nahum describes their execution, in a style full of animation, fancy and originality, and at the same time clear and rounded. His language throughout is classical and in the purest Hebrew, belonging to the second half of Hezekiah's reign, or to the time immediately following the defeat of Sennacherib before Jerusalem. Nineveh was at that time the capital of the great and flourishing Assyrian Empire. It was a city of vast extent and population; the center of the principal commerce of the world. Its wealth, however, was not altogether derived from trade. The prophet denounced it as a "bloody city . . . full of lies and robbery" (Nahum 3:1), and compared it, in its plundering of neighboring nations, to the lion that "filled his holes with prey, and his dens with ravin" (Nahum 2:12). It was strongly fortified, its colossal walls, 100 feet high, with their 1,500 towers, bidding defiance to all enemies. Yet so totally was it destroyed that by the 2d century A.D. not a vestige of it remained; even its site was for centuries a matter of doubt and uncertainty.

The Book of Nahum consists of a single poem which opens with a superb vision of God's coming to judge the nations (Nahum 1:2–8); then follows an address to the Assyrians describing their confusion and overthrow (1:9–11, 14), verses 12–13 parenthetically consoling the Israelites with promises of future rest and relief from oppression. Chapter 2 depicts vividly the siege and capture of Nineveh (612 B.C.) by its foes, the Medes and Chaldeans, and the consternation of the inhabitants. Chapter 3 describes the utter ruin of the great city and the various contributing causes. Its fall is compared to that of No-Ammon, Thebes in Egypt, about a half century before (3:8–10) to illustrate the punishment coming upon the Assyrian Empire and the deliverance and restoration of Israel. With a wide view of the working of Providence and an avoidance of all moralistic or homiletic utterances, this powerful prophecy advances with majestic unity from its noble proem to its close.

Consult Davidson, Andrew Bruce, *Nahum, Habbakuk and Zephaniah* in Cambridge Bible series (London 1896); Smith, George Adam, *The Book of the Twelve Prophets,* rev. ed., vol. 2 (New York 1929).

NAIADS, nā′ădz, in classical mythology, female minor spirits classed among nymphs (q.v.), who inhabited all forms of fresh water, such as fountains, springs, wells, rivers and lakes. They were worshiped widely throughout the Graeco-Roman world because of the folk belief that many of them, as benevolent patronesses, presided over waters of either curative or prophetic powers.

P. R. COLEMAN-NORTON.

NAIDU, nä′ĭ-do͞o, **Sarojini** (nee CHATTOPADHYAY), Indian poet and political leader: b. Hyderabad, India, Feb. 13, 1879; d. Lucknow, March 2, 1949. Her father, Dr. Aghorenath Chattopadhyay, was a Bengali Brahmin, founder and principal of Nizam College. She was educated at Madras University and in England at King's College, London, and Girton College, Cambridge, and in 1898 married Dr. M. G. Naidu, chief medical officer to the nizam of Hyderabad. Known for her mastery of English (she was elected a fellow of the Royal Society of Literature in 1914), she published three volumes of poetry in that language—*The Golden Threshold* (1905), *The Bird of Time* (1912), *The Broken Wing* (1915)—all widely translated throughout India and Europe. Though written in English, they are Indian in subject and background. Arthur Symons wrote the preface to the first volume, and Edmund Gosse to the second. Mme. Naidu ranks next to Rabindranath Tagore as India's best-known modern poet.

Mme. Naidu worked for many years to improve the status of Indian women. Her active public career in politics and social reform began in 1905, when she addressed the All-India Social Conference at Calcutta. She received the British decoration, the Kaiser-i-Hind gold medal, in 1908 for her organization of flood-relief work in Hyderabad. In 1919 she became a follower of Mohandas K. Gandhi, was jailed several times for civil disobedience, and in 1925 was elected the first woman president of the Indian National Congress. She conducted a famous salon for many years at the Taj Mahal Hotel in Bombay. During World War II she supported Gandhi's antiwar position and was again imprisoned (1942–1943) by the British. After India attained dominion status in 1947, she served as governor of the United Provinces until her death.

NAIL. See SKIN AND SKIN DISEASES—*Anatomy of the Skin* (Nails).

NAILS, nālz, slender lengths of metal used in fastening together two or more pieces of wood or other material. They are driven through the first piece or pieces into the last. Most have heads to take the hammer blow and are pointed for penetration. They are classified as wire nails, cut nails, and handmade (or wrought or forged) nails. Their use goes back to Biblical times, in which nails, probably iron, were used in construction as early as 1100 B.C.

In the United States, in colonial times, nail making was a household industry in which whole families engaged in the evening after completion of chores and on winter days when outdoor work was impossible. Nail rods in widths of the length of the nails required were obtained from a merchant or ironmaker. These rods were heated over small home forges and sheared into blanks. Heads were put on by hammering blanks in a die or vise. The finished nails were then traded to merchants for supplies.

The first process of cutting nails from unheated iron nail rod was devised in 1777 by Jeremiah Wilkinson of Cumberland, R.I. In the next 50 years, patents were issued for some 120 nail-cutting machines, but only one was thoroughly practical—the machine patented by Ezekiel Reed of Massachusetts in 1786, from which modern nail-making machines have been developed. The first patent in England was granted to John Clifford in 1790.

Wire nails came into use first in France in 1834. The first wire-nail machine in the United States was built in New York City in 1851 by Thomas Morton. It was kept in operation until 1902 and was then placed in a museum. Cut nails continue in use, but those made from steel wire far outnumber them in manufacture, amounting to more than 500,000 tons annually. It has been estimated, for example, that 67,000 nails weighing 390 pounds may be needed for building a 5-room frame house.

Manufacture.—In making nails, the wire is first straightened by being drawn through a series of smooth rolls. It is then wound into coils from which it is fed into the machines in a series of jerks, each jerk putting sufficient wire into a gripper die to form one nail. These grippers are actually two dies, which clamp together to make an anvil. Enough wire is left projecting for the head, which is formed automatically by the stroke of a hammer that may be driven either by a powerful spring or a cam. The gripper dies then spring apart, the hammer cocks again, the headed nail moves forward, and two cutters, or knives, bite it off to finished size and at the same time shape its point. Adjustment of these knives determines the length of the nail and the kind of point put on it. The marks on the nail below the head are made by the grippers. By changing these gripper dies and the hammer, any type of head can be put on: flat, oval, round, countersunk, corrugated, numbered, or bossed. Short nails can be barbed by special gripper dies; longer ones by barbing rolls on the machine. For strong holding power, some nails are made with annular- or helical-threaded shanks.

Modern nail makers are driven at 700 rpm. (revolutions per minute) by individual electric motors. They have tungsten carbide gripper dies, cutters, hammers, and feed-grip insets, and are rated at 700 nails per minute in any size within a machine range. They normally produce about 5 pounds of 8d (eightpenny) common nails per minute, or 24 kegs or boxes holding 100 pounds each for every 8-hour shift. The machines may be adjusted to handle wire sizes from 15 to 10¼ gage and to turn out nails from 1 to 2½ inches long. Because of precision adjustments and the use of tungsten carbide tools, they make nails to closer tolerances and with sharper points over a longer continuous operating time than had been considered possible. Each machine has automatic safety devices to stop it if any malfunction occurs. Oil is supplied under pressure or by gravity to moving parts, and a magnetic belt carries the nails to nail buggies.

As the nails stream from the machines, they are rough, whiskered, and burred, and have to be cleaned and polished in rotating drums, called tumblers, which hold from 1,000 to 5,000 pounds each. Into the tumblers with the nails go sawdust to pick up little slivers and oil and grease from the machines. The nails remain in the rotating tumblers from 45 minutes to an hour, after which the sawdust is sifted out and the nails are bright and clean. Those requiring fine points cannot be tumbled, so special care is exercised in their manufacture to prevent deposits of oil and grease.

When other than this bright finish is required, the nails undergo further treatment. They may be galvanized to retard rust, tinned, blued or "sterilized," or cement coated. The last process consists of dipping them in a resin mixture which fuses slightly under the heat generated when the nail is driven, and forms a bond between it and the wood.

Standard stock sizes of common wire nails follow:

Size	2d	3d	4d	5d	6d	7d	8d	9d	10d	12d	16d	20d	30d	40d	50d	60d
Length	1″	$1\frac{1}{4}''$	$1\frac{1}{2}''$	$1\frac{3}{4}''$	2″	$2\frac{1}{4}''$	$2\frac{1}{2}''$	$2\frac{3}{4}''$	3″	$3\frac{1}{4}''$	$3\frac{1}{2}''$	4″	$4\frac{1}{2}''$	5″	$5\frac{1}{2}''$	6″
Gage	15	14	$12\frac{1}{2}$	$12\frac{1}{2}$	$11\frac{1}{2}$	$11\frac{1}{2}$	$10\frac{1}{4}$	$10\frac{1}{4}$	9	9	8	6	5	4	3	2
Head diameter	$\frac{11}{64}''$	$\frac{13}{64}''$	$\frac{1}{4}''$	$\frac{1}{4}''$	$\frac{17}{64}''$	$\frac{17}{64}''$	$\frac{9}{32}''$	$\frac{9}{32}''$	$\frac{5}{16}''$	$\frac{5}{16}''$	$\frac{11}{32}''$	$\frac{13}{32}''$	$\frac{7}{16}''$	$\frac{15}{32}''$	$\frac{1}{2}''$	$\frac{17}{32}''$
Quantity per pound	845	540	290	250	165	150	100	90	65	60	45	30	20	17	13	10

The penny system of sizing nails, designated by the letter "d," originated in England, where "d" is the symbol for penny or pence. One explanation is that 100 nails of 4d, 6d, 10d size, and so on, cost 4, 6, or 10 pence. Another is that 1,000 10d nails weighed 10 pounds, and so on, assuming that "d" was a corruption of the symbol for pound, a theory not generally accepted by etymologists.

FRANK DORR,
Associate Editor of "Popular Science Monthly."

NAIMAN, nī′mȧn, a pastoral nomadic people of Central Asia. At the beginning of the 13th century, the Naiman were a Mongol-speaking tribe dwelling in far western Mongolia north of the Altai Mountains. Conquered at that time by Genghis Khan, they were incorporated into the Mongol nation, but unlike many Mongol tribes, which became scattered in the course of imperial conquest, the main body of Naiman remained in their Altai homeland. Later they adopted Turkic speech and became part of the Kazakh (Kazak) nation which took form on the western steppes in the 15th century. In the earlier 20th century the Naiman remained an important Kazakh tribe, wintering along the Irtysh River and moving with their flocks into the high valleys of the Altai during the summer.

ELIZABETH E. BACON.

NAIRN, nârn, or **NAIRNSHIRE,** nârn′shĭr, county, Scotland, in the northeast, on the south coast of Moray Firth, bounded on the east by Morayshire and on the south and west by Inverness. Except for the coastal strip (about 10 miles long) the area of 162.9 square miles is hilly, rising to an altitude of 2,162 feet. The county is drained by the Nairn and Findhorn rivers, both rising in Inverness and flowing northeast into Moray Firth. Nearly one fifth of the area is in woodland. Sheep and cattle raising are principal occupations, and oats, barley, and potatoes are the chief crops. Fishing, once important, has declined, except for some salmon fishing.

Nairn, the county town (population, 1961, 4,899), on Moray Firth at the mouth of the Nairn River, is a popular golf and bathing resort. Five miles southwest is Cawdor Castle (15th century), anachronistically used by Shakespeare as the scene of the murder of King Duncan by Macbeth (11th century). Population: (1961) 8,423.

NAIRNE, nârn, **Carolina** (nee OLIPHANT), BARONESS NAIRNE, Scottish lyric poet: b. Gask, Perthshire, Scotland, Aug. 16, 1766; d. there, Oct. 26, 1845. An early admirer of Robert Burns, she followed his example in writing songs to old Scottish tunes, beginning with *The Pleuchman* (plowman) in 1792 and her celebrated song of homesickness, *Land o' the Leal* (1798; also known by its opening words "I'm wearin' awa'"). In 1806 she married her cousin Major William Murray Nairne, who became Baron Nairne in 1824 when the titles of Scottish Jacobites were restored. Lady Nairne kept her writing a complete secret, even from her husband, publishing anonymously or with the pseudonym Mrs. Bogan of Bogan (B.B.). Some of her songs approached those of Burns in lyric quality. Among her best-known pieces are the humorous ballad *The Laird o' Cockpen* and the Jacobite songs *The Hundred Pipers, Charlie Is My Darling,* and *Will Ye No Come Back Again?* Her works were collected posthumously as *Lays from Strathearn* (1846) and later by Charles Rogers (1869; new ed., 1886).

NAIROBI, nī-rō′bē, is the capital of the republic of Kenya, in East Africa. It is Kenya's largest city, its transportation hub, and its cultural center. Administratively, Nairobi is a separate federal district of Kenya, outside the country's provincial structure. Population: (1962) 266,794.

Nairobi's area of 264 square miles lies on the Kikuyu Plateau of south central Kenya, 70 miles southwest of Mount Kenya and 175 miles northwest of Mount Kilimanjaro. Situated at an altitude of 5,452 feet, Nairobi has an equable climate, with a mean temperature of 67°F and an annual rainfall of 34 inches. Its cool season extends from June through August.

Nairobi is the headquarters of the East African Railways and Harbours system, which links it to the hinterland and to the Indian Ocean port of Mombasa, 280 miles to the southeast. Scheduled flights from its airport connect with international air services. Coffee, cotton, tea, pyrethrum, and sisal are shipped through the city for export. Cattle raising is a major occupation in the vicinity. Nairobi's industries include meat packing and canning, flour milling, fruit preserving, and various kinds of light manufacturing. The city is also an outfitting center for hunting and photographic safaris.

Nairobi began as a camp for workers on the Mombasa-Uganda railroad in 1899. In 1920 the area was drained, and Nairobi was rebuilt as a modern town. It was chartered as a city in 1950. Among its major cultural institutions are the Coryndon Memorial Museum (founded 1929), with notable wildlife and anthropological exhibits; the McMillan Memorial Library (1931); and the University College of Nairobi (1956), a division of the University of East Africa. Nairobi National Park (1946), on the outskirts, is a 40-square-mile wildlife reserve stocked with East African animal species.

NAISMITH, nā'smith, **James,** Canadian-American physical education director who originated the game of basketball: b. Almonte, Ontario, Canada, Nov. 6, 1861; d. Lawrence, Kans., Nov. 28, 1939. He worked briefly in a logging camp before entering McGill University, where he graduated in 1887. He then went to Presbyterian College in Montreal to study for the ministry. At the same time he became director of physical education at McGill. His success as a physical education director prompted him to choose this as his life work. In 1890 he entered the Young Men's Christian Association Training School at Springfield, Mass., where he remained as director of physical education until 1895. In 1898 he received a degree in medicine at Gross Medical College in Denver, Colo. (later the medical school of the University of Colorado). From that time until his retirement in 1937, he served as professor of physical education at the University of Kansas, in Lawrence.

In 1891, while still a student at the YMCA school in Springfield, Naismith invented basketball. Luther Halsey Gulick, superintendent of physical education at the school, had asked his students to devise a game that could be played indoors during the winter months. Using a soccer ball, and two peach baskets as goals, Naismith developed a tossing game by mounting the baskets at either end of the gymnasium, on the edge of an elevated running track. The track was 10 feet above the floor, and this height became standard for the baskets. Nearly all of his original rules are still in force. In 1936, when basketball was first named an Olympic sport, Naismith was honored internationally as its inventor, and the National Association of Basketball Coaches sent him to Berlin as their guest to witness its Olympic debut. See also BASKETBALL.

NAIVASHA, Lake, nī-vä'shə, is in Kenya, East Africa, about 40 miles northwest of the city of Nairobi, in the eastern branch of the Great Rift Valley, at an altitude of 6,200 feet. It is 12 miles long, 9 miles wide, up to 60 feet deep, and has no outlet. The water is fresh and drinkable, but slightly alkaline. The lake is stocked with black bass and is frequented by hippopotamuses, flamingos, and pelicans. Volcanic Crescent Island, formerly wholly within the lake, is now joined to the southern shore. On the northeast shore is the town of Naivasha, market center for the surrounding cattle- and sheep-raising area and a popular resort for boating, fishing, and duck hunting. Lake Naivasha was discovered in 1883 by the German explorer Gustav Adolf Fischer.

NAJARA, na-jä'rä, **Israel ben Moses,** Palestinian Hebrew poet: b. Safad (Safed), Palestine, 1555; d. Gaza, 1628. The most significant Hebrew poet of his day, he lived most of his life in Safad. Najara wrote both secular and religious poems, songs, prayers, elegies, and hymns. Many of them were incorporated into Oriental Jewish liturgy and had widespread influence on Jewish literature. Extremely sensuous in their imagery but permeated by strong religious feeling, they are deeply emotional and mystical. Some of the more pious Jews regarded them as too much like love songs for inclusion in the prayer book. Many were set to Arabic, Spanish, and Turkish popular tunes. Najara wrote more than 1,000 songs. A collection, *Zemirot Israel* (Songs of Israel), was published in 1587. At his death he was rabbi in Gaza.

NAKED AND THE DEAD, The, a novel by Norman Mailer, published in 1948. Long and detailed, it was hailed as a notable portrayal of the South Pacific fighting by a typical body of American troops in World War II.

The campaign it describes dates, by internal evidence, between September 1944 and March 1945; the scene is the imaginary island of Anopopei; the main characters are Gen. Edward Cummings, commanding the invasion, his staff, and the members of an infantry platoon led by Sgt. Sam Croft. Details of the fighting derive in part from the Marines' struggle at Cape Gloucester and from such later stages of the Solomons campaign as Bougainville and Munda. The narrative technique resembles John Dos Passos' in *U.S.A.* (1937): direct action is interspersed with "time machine" flashbacks of the characters' previous careers, as Dos Passos used "newsreels" to synchronize his fictitious events with the life of his period.

Liaison between staff and platoon is supplied by 2d Lt. Robert Hearn, a somewhat muddled idealist, at first Cummings' pet and later the butt of his cold sadism. Sent by the general on a desperate reconnaisance with Croft's platoon, Hearn dies because his sergeants resent his authority and, by withholding vital information, maneuver him into a Japanese field of fire. Standard irony is provided when the reconnaisance proves needless—Japanese resistance has collapsed before the remnants of the patrol get back.

Nearly every character suffers a neurosis of some kind, or is a fugitive from something in his past. After a while this becomes tiresome. The author attempts to differentiate the men by their speech, but only half succeeds, for the vocabulary is always the same, whether it is spelled to look like Georgia or like South Boston. As a study of men in battle, *The Naked and the Dead* does not measure up to such an earlier work as Stephen Crane's *The Red Badge of Courage* (1895).

DeLancey Ferguson.

NAKHICHEVAN, nä-ĸē-chĕ-vän′, city, USSR, capital of the Nakhichevan Autonomous SSR. It is situated 80 miles southeast of Yerevan, Armenia, on the right bank of the Nakhichevan River, a tributary of the Aras, which forms the Iranian border nearby. An ancient town, it still preserves two richly ornamented mausoleums dating from the 12th century. Nakhichevan was annexed to Russia in 1828 and served as a trade center on the caravan route linking Tbilisi (Tiflis) and Tabriz. Pop. (1970 est.) 33,000.

Theodore Shabad.

NAKHICHEVAN AUTONOMOUS SOVIET SOCIALIST REPUBLIC, political-administrative division, USSR, in Transcaucasia, on the Iranian border. The Nakhichevan Autonomous SSR is part of the Azerbaidzhan SSR, but is separated from the main body of Azerbaidzhan by Soviet Armenia. With an area of 2,100 square miles, the Nakhichevan republic is situated on the southern slopes of the Zangezur Mountains, on the left bank of the Aras River, which forms the border with Iran. The climate is semiarid, with precipitation ranging from 8 to 20 inches. Cotton and wheat are grown in irrigated fields in the valley; orchards, vineyards, tobacco, and sericulture predominate on the mountain slopes; and sheep are raised in the mountains. Salt, lead, and molybdenum are the principal mineral products. The republic, with its capital at Nakhichevan, is served by highways and by a railroad along the Aras River, connecting at Dzhulfa with the Iranian railroad system. The population is mainly of Azerbaidzhani-Turkish origin. The republic was formed in 1924. Pop. (1970 est.) 202,000.

Theodore Shabad.

NALCHIK, näl′chĭk, city, USSR, capital of the Kabardian-Balkar Autonomous Soviet Socialist Republic of the Russian SFSR, 50 miles southeast of Pyatigorsk, with which it is linked by highway. Nalchik is situated in the northern foothills of the Caucasus, on the left bank of the little Nalchik River, at an elevation of about 1,500 feet. Served by a railroad spur of the Rostov-Baku main line, the city's industries include meat-packing, machine-building, and furniture factories. Nalchik also has a molybdenum smelter, processing ore from the Tyrny-Auz mine in the Caucasus. Nalchik's pleasant climate, parks, and tree-shaded streets make it a popular resort town. The city has a teachers college and several research institutes, including an experimental farm. Nalchik was founded in 1818 as a fortified Russian post. It has been the Kabardian-Balkar capital since 1922. Population: (1970) 146,000.

NAMANGAN, nä-mäng-gän′, oblast, USSR, in the Uzbek SSR, in the Fergana Valley of Central Asia. With an area of 2,700 square miles, Namangan Oblast occupies the northeast third of the Fergana Valley and is watered by the Naryn and Syr Darya rivers along its southern border. Cotton, silk, and fruit growing and dairy farming are the principal economic activities in the irrigated areas along the two rivers. Grain (mainly wheat) is grown and livestock is grazed on the mountain slopes in the northern part of the oblast. Cotton-ginning, oilseed-pressing, textile-manufacturing, and food-processing industries are concentrated at Namangan, the oblast capital, and at Chust. The oblast was formed in 1941. Pop. (1959) 594,000.

Theodore Shabad.

NAMANGAN, city, USSR, capital of Namangan Oblast in the Uzbek SSR. Located 130 miles east-southeast of Tashkent, on the river Namangan-sai, a tributary of the Syr Darya, Namangan is the center of an oasis in the northeastern part of the Fergana Valley of Central Asia. It serves the surrounding cotton-, silk-, and fruit-growing district and processes its products. There are cotton gins, oilseed presses, textile, and food-processing plants. Namangan is served by a railroad from Tashkent. The city developed long before the Russians' arrival in Central Asia in the 19th century. Pop. (1970 est.) 175,000.

Theodore Shabad.

NAMAQUALAND, nȧ-mä′kwȧ-lănd, or **NAMALAND,** nä′mȧ-lănd, region, South Africa, on the west coast, extending from 22° 43′ to 31° south latitude, with an eastern boundary varying between 80 to 350 miles inland from the coast. The lower reaches of the Orange River cross Namaqualand. The area to the north of the river in South West Africa is known as Great Namaqualand; that to the south, in Cape Province, Union of South Africa, is known as Little Namaqualand, with Springbok as its capital. The whole region lies in a belt receiving less than 15 inches of rainfall per year, but wheat is grown in favorable localities in Little Namaqualand. Elsewhere the land is devoted to the pasturing of cattle and sheep. Karakul is a major export. Rich diamond deposits occur in the alluvial gravels of both Great and Little Namaqualand. Copper is mined in Little Namaqualand. The region is named after its inhabitants, the Namaquas or Namas.

NAMATH, nā′məth, **Joe Willie,** American football player: b. Beaver Falls, Pa., May 31, 1943. Coached by Paul (Bear) Bryant, Namath was a great quarterback for the University of Alabama from 1962 to 1964. He then joined the professional New York Jets of the American Football League (AFL), and his popularity and achievements on the field helped bring about a merger of the AFL and the older National Football League (NFL). In 1969, in the third Super Bowl game between the AFL and NFL champions, Namath passed the Jets to victory, 16–7, over the Baltimore Colts in one of football's big upsets.

Frequent injuries to his knees affected Namath's career. A daring and resourceful quarterback, he threw long, accurate passes, which he released swiftly and often to his receivers. By 1972 he had completed more than 100 touchdown passes and had accounted for 18,000 total yards gained. His reputation as a high-living bachelor contributed to Namath's popularity. His autobiography, *I Can't Wait Until Tomorrow...'Cause I Get Better Looking Every Day,* was published in 1969.

NAMATJIRA, näm-ät-jē′rȧ, **Albert,** Australian aboriginal painter: b. Hermannsburg,

Northern Territory, Australia, July 28, 1902; d. Alice Springs, Aug. 8, 1959. A member of the Aranda (Arunta) tribe, he was educated at the Hermannsburg Mission School, then worked as a stockman and ranch hand. After seeing watercolor paintings in an exhibition at the mission in 1934, he attempted drawings and poker-work designs of animals on wood. He had his first lessons in painting in 1936, and two years later an exhibition of his landscapes was held in Melbourne, where it attracted some attention. This was followed in 1939 by an exhibition in Adelaide. In 1944 another group of his paintings was exhibited in Melbourne, followed the next year by a Sydney showing. By this time Namatjira had gained a considerable following. Reproductions of his work were sold widely, a documentary film was done on him (1946), and he became an associate of the Royal South Australian Society of Arts; but he continued to live among members of his tribe.

His paintings are conventional in style but have a striking vitality, capturing the brilliant colors of the landscapes of the central Australian area where he lived and worked. He painted about 2,000 watercolors in all. Before his death, four of his sons and at least twelve members of his tribe had taken up painting.

R. M. YOUNGER.

NAMIBIA, nä-mib′ē-ə, is the name given to South West Africa by the United Nations and African liberation groups. See SOUTH WEST AFRICA.

NAMPA, năm′pȧ, city, Idaho, in Canyon County, in the Boise River valley, 20 miles west of Boise, at an altitude of 2,492 feet. Nampa is on the Union Pacific Railroad and state and federal highways, and has a municipal airport. Situated in a diversified agricultural area noted especially for its dairy products, the city is an important freight terminal and also has beet-sugar refineries, meat-packing, and other food-processing plants. Among the newer industries is a trailer factory.

Nampa began in October 1883 as a watering point on the railroad. Irrigation of the surrounding area, begun in 1885, brought increased settlement, and in 1890 the town was incorporated as Nampa, named for Nampuh (bigfoot), an Indian chief of huge size. Educational facilities include Northwest Nazarene College (1915). There is also a stadium seating 10,000, where the Snake River Stampede, one of the largest rodeos in the West, is held annually in July. City government is by mayor and council. Pop. 20,768.

NAMUR, nä-mo͝or′, Fr. nȧ-mür′ (Du. NAMEN), province, Belgium, bordered by France on the South, approximately 1,413 square miles. A Roman outpost in the land of the Aduatics, it became a county under the reign of Charlemagne. Its boundaries remained without change until the end of the 18th century. Under the French regime, it was enlarged and became the Department of Sambre-et-Meuse (1795–1814). It received its present still larger shape under William I of Orange, who added to the territory parts of Brabant, Liège, and France. Namur is the only unilingual French-speaking province of Belgium.

Since the Middle Ages, Namur was the seat of an important metallurgical industry. The exploitation of iron ore lasted until the early 19th century. At present, it is a center of the glass and plate-glass industry. Raw materials for industrial use, granite, dolomite, sandstone, marble, and China clay (kaolin) are exploited. The age-old traditional copper industry has survived and has been modernized: it produces artistic brasswares of the finest quality.

Although highly industrialized, the landscape retains its beauty and attraction for tourists. Namur remains one of Belgium's most popular resort regions on account of its beautiful and romantic scenery: rivers wind through rocky gorges; there are many spectacular underground caves; and, reminiscent of feudal times, a great number of old castles crown the hills. Pop. (1958) 368,750.

JAN-ALBERT GORIS.

NAMUR, city, Belgium, capital of Namur Province. It is located 35 miles southeast of Brussels, at the confluence of the Meuse and Sambre rivers, a strategic position which decided the Romans to establish the military base Namurcum Castrum here. Since that time, it has been a stronghold commanding an extensive region. Its citadel has been repeatedly rebuilt, the last time in 1817 during the short reunion of Holland and Belgium. The town and its castle were often besieged. Louis XIV of France captured Namur in 1692 and had the event celebrated by the poet Jean Baptiste Racine. It took the king a week to occupy the town, and the citadel held out for 22 days. In 1695, William III of England besieged and took Namur with 80,000 men. The last siege was in 1914, when the city fell to the Germans after a short but spirited resistance.

Namur is famous for its chorals and for an often re-enacted medieval custom, the battle of the *échasseurs,* or stilt walkers. Its origin goes back to the 13th century when the local count, against whom the Namurois had revolted, refused to see them if they came to him either on foot, on horseback, or by boat. When they presented themselves on stilts, the count pardoned their offenses.

Besides the citadel, the outstanding monuments are the cathedral (18th century), the Convent of Notre Dame, and the Church of St. Loup (1621), a baroque building which was referred to by Victor Hugo as the masterpiece of Jesuit architecture. The Musée Diocésain has a fine collection of 1,300 objects of old religious art. Namur is a natural gateway for tourists to the picturesque region of the Meuse and the Sambre. Industrially, it has tanneries, flour mills, and cutlery and machine manufacturing. Pop. (1958) 33,062.

JAN-ALBERT GORIS,
Belgian Government Information Center, New York City.

NANA, nä′nä, a novel by Émile Zola published in 1880, the 9th in a series of 20 related novels issued (1871–1893) under the general title *Les Rougon-Macquart.* Nana, the beautiful daughter of the drunkard Coupeau and the laundress Gervaise (characters in *L'assommoir,* another of the series), becomes the mistress of a shady banker and later of an actor who finally deserts her. The product of an evil heritage, morally moronic, and embittered by the early disappointments of her courtesan career, Nana uses her beauty as a lethal lure to bring all her lovers to ruin. Her victims include a captain, who steals from his regimental funds for her, and his brother, who commits suicide. In the end she suffers a horrible death by smallpox. A brutal but powerful story of social decadence in France during the regime of Napoleon III, the novel illustrates the corrosive effect of evil and the degradation and ruin to which men are driven by the dual lash of lust and greed.

NANA SAHIB, nä'nä sä'hĭb (real name DANDHU PANTH), Indian leader: b. near Cawnpore (Kanpur), India, ?1825; d. probably in Nepal, ?1860. He was the adopted son of Baji Rao II, last Maratha peshwa, deposed by the British in 1818. The Nana Sahib inherited his father's great wealth but was denied (1853) the pension paid by the British to Baji Rao during his lifetime. When the Indian Mutiny broke out in 1857, the Nana Sahib encouraged it. Early in June he laid siege to Cawnpore, where the British garrison finally surrendered on June 27. The Nana Sahib promised them safe conduct to Allahabad; but as they were embarking on barges in the Ganges with their women and children, he opened a withering fire. One boat got away but was overtaken three days later, and all but four men were eventually killed. The 211 women and children surviving were herded into a building in the city and on July 15 were massacred, their bodies being thrown into a well. The Nana Sahib was pursued by the British, and his forces were repeatedly defeated until, in 1859, he disappeared into the jungle of Nepal, where he presumably perished.

NANAIMO, nȧ-nī'mō, city, British Columbia, Canada, on the east coast of Vancouver Island, on the Strait of Georgia, 55 miles northwest of Victoria and 40 miles west of the mainland city of Vancouver. Nanaimo is a major distribution center linking Vancouver Island with the mainland, having railroad connections with Victoria and air and ferry services across the strait. Lumbering is the main industry of the surrounding area, which also has dairy, fruit, and other farms. In the city are sawmills and shipyards, and a major sulphate pulp plant is nearby. Nanaimo is also an active fishing port. Founded as a trading post of the Hudson's Bay Company in 1849, it developed as a coal-mining center and was incorporated as a city in 1874. Coal-mining operations in the area ended in 1953. Population: 14,948.

NANAK, nä'nȧk (called GURU, teacher), Indian religious leader, founder of Sikhism: b. Talwandi (modern Nankana Sahib), near Lahore, India, 1469; d. Kartarpur, ?1539. Son of a farmer and village land steward, he left school before he was 12 and spent much of his time among the mendicant ascetics in the desert near his home. Soon after he was 17, Nanak entered government service in Sultanpur as a storekeeper. A few years later, as the result of a vision, he left his work to become a wandering teacher of what he saw as the true religion, a combination of Hinduism and Islam without their ritualism and formalism.

He was much influenced by the poet-mystic Kabir, and revived the monotheism of the Upanishads. In addition to the worship of one god, he taught tolerance for all religions and the necessity for selflessness, sincerity, purity, and truth. His teachings are contained in the Granth Sahib, the sacred book of the Sikhs, which was compiled in 1604. Before his death he named his disciple Angad as his successor, and returned to his family in Kartarpur. See also INDIA—*13. Religion and Philosophy* (Sikhism); SIKHS

NANCHANG, nän'chäng, city, China, capital of Kiangsi Province, on the right bank of the Kan Kiang, at the head of the river's delta on Poyang Lake. Nanchang is the economic and transportation center of the province, situated 160 miles southeast of Wuhan. It is the junction of the Nanchang-Kiukiang and Chekiang-Kiangsi railroads. Its industries include cotton milling, paper and matchmaking, machine building (machine tools and farm implements), food processing (mainly vegetable oils), pharmaceuticals, and pesticides for agriculture. Most of the industries are concentrated in the left-bank suburb, which is served by the Kiukiang railroad terminus. Nanchang's ancient city wall, dating from the Sung dynasty (12th century), has been razed to make way for the city's reconstruction. The city's main street, the bridge across the Kan Kiang, and other features are named for August 1, the day in 1927 when 30,000 Communist-led troops revolted here against the Kuomintang forces of Chiang Kai-shek. The day is marked each year in Communist China as Army Day. Nanchang was occupied by the Japanese in World War II from 1939 to 1945. Pop. (1959) 600,000.

NANCRÈDE, näɴ-krĕd', **Paul Joseph Guérard de,** French-American teacher and publisher: b. Héricy, near Fontainebleau, France, March 16, 1761; d. Paris, Dec. 15, 1841. He went to America (1780) as a volunteer in the French Army that aided the Revolution, and later settled in Boston. Nancrède taught French at Harvard College (1787–1798) and compiled what is believed to have been the first American college French text, *L'abeille françoise* (1792), comprising excerpts from famous authors of the Enlightenment. In 1796 he established a printing and publishing business in Boston, pioneering in the issue of French works. After eight years in France, he founded a similar business in Philadelphia in 1812.

CHARLES BEYLARD GUÉRARD DE NANCRÈDE (1847–1921), his grandson, was a distinguished Philadelphia surgeon, noted for abdominal and brain operations. From 1889 until his death he was professor of surgery at the University of Michigan.

NANCY, näɴ-sē', city, France, prefecture of the Meurthe-et-Moselle Department, 219 miles by rail east of Paris on the Paris-Strasbourg line; on the left bank of the Meurthe River six miles above its juncture with the Moselle, and of the Marne-Rhine Canal; altitude 660 feet.

The ancient capital of Lorraine, Nancy is famed for its 18th century parks, squares, and public and private buildings of surpassing elegance, many of them designed by Emmanuel Héré (1705–1763), the architect commissioned by Stanislas I Leszczynski, duke of Lorraine (1737–1766) and former king of Poland, to continue the work of embellishment of his predecessors. The gemlike Place Stanislas, a public square constructed in 1752–1756 and the town's focal point, is the masterwork of Héré. Fronting it from the south is the Town Hall, and on its west side the Fine Arts Museum with collections of Italian and Spanish as well as French schools of painting, glassware, and Jacques Callot's engravings. Ending the short Rue Héré, north of the square, is the triumphal arch erected by Stanislas to honor his son-in-law, King Louis XV. Beyond it extends the long Place de la Carrière, flanked by

18th century houses, at the end of which is the Government Palace, another of Héré's works (1760). East of this building is the 57-acre Promenade de la Pépinière, a park laid out in 1765. Adjoining the Government Palace on the west is the Ducal Palace (1502–1544) occupied by the Lorraine Historical Museum.

Among notable churches are the Church of the Cordeliers, a 15th century structure, burial place of the dukes of Lorraine, and site of many interesting effigies; the Church of Notre-Dame de Bonsecours (1740) containing the tombs of its builder, King Stanislas, and his queen; and the cathedral, a fine 18th century edifice.

The University of Nancy has faculties of law, letters, sciences, medicine, and pharmacy. There are also schools of agriculture and mining, a colonial institute, and an institute for deaf mutes and the blind.

Industries include a state tobacco factory, potteries, art glass works, printing, shoe manufacture, bronze and forged-iron works, breweries (there is also a brewing school), cloth manufactures, and biscuit factories.

In the 12th century the dukes of Lorraine made Nancy their capital. Charles the Bold of Burgundy was killed in battle under the city walls in 1477. Louis XIII seized the duchy in 1633, but in 1697 France yielded it to Duke Leopold. King Stanislas was the last sovereign duke; after his death in 1766 Lorraine and its capital were reincorporated in France. Pop. (1962) 127,729.

NANDU. See RHEA.

NANINO, nä-nē′nō, **Giovanni Maria** (sometimes NANINI), Italian composer: b. Tivoli, Italy, c. 1545; d. Rome, March 11, 1607. A pupil of Giovanni Palestrina, he became choirmaster at the Church of Santa Maria Maggiore in Rome in 1571, resigning after four years to found a public school of music, the first such school to be established in Rome by an Italian. Nanino was assisted at the school, which was highly successful, by Palestrina and his own younger brother Giovanni Bernardino Nanino (c. 1550–1623), also a gifted composer. The elder Nanino became a singer in the papal chapel in 1577, and in 1604 was named choirmaster of the Sistine Chapel, where his motet for six voices, *Hodie nobis coelorum rex,* is still sung on Christmas morning. He is highly regarded as a composer not only of religious but also of secular music. Among his publications are a notable volume of motets (1586), and several books of madrigals and canzonets. Many of his compositions appear in other collections, and much of his work remains in manuscript in the Vatican archives and private collections.

NANKING, năn′kĭng′, city, China, capital of Kiangsu Province, on the Yangtze River and 170 miles west of Shanghai, with which it is linked by railroad. Nanking is a former capital of China and the country's traditional literary center. It is situated on the right bank of the Yangtze River, 150 miles from the river's mouth, and at the junction of railroads leading to Shanghai, Tientsin and Wuhu. The city's traditional industries are silk goods, satin, and cotton cloth. Nankeen, a durable cotton cloth, was originally made here. Under Communist rule, after 1949, the city acquired new heavy industrial plants, producing fluorescent lights, radios, telephones, movie projectors, cameras, microscopes and steam-turbine generators. Many of the city's industries, including large chemical plants, are located in the left-bank suburb of Pukow, terminus of the railroad from Tientsin.

Nanking is an important cultural and educational center, with Nanking University and eight other institutions of higher learning, several scientific research institutes, and the astronomical observatory of Tzu-chin Shan (Purple Mountain). Nanking is surrounded by the remains of a circuitous 26-mile-long wall that encloses not only the built-up city area, but also farming suburbs. The wall extends to Nanking's riverside suburb of Siakwan (opposite Pukow), where shipping and commercial activities are concentrated. In the hills northeast of the city, just outside the wall, on the slopes of Tzu-chin Shan, are the tombs of the early Ming emperors and a memorial and mausoleum of Sun Yat-sen, founder of modern China. Although the present city dates from 1368, its site has been occupied since the Han dynasty (2d century B.C.) by cities variously known as Chienyeh, Chienyang, Shengchow, and Kiangning. The city first became a capital of China under the Sun kingdom (222–280) and under the Eastern Chin (Tsin) dynasty (317–420). While barbarians ruled northern China, Nanking remained the capital of the southern dynasties (the Sung, Chi, Liang, and Chen) from 420 to 589. The city was first named Yingtien by the first Ming emperors, who made it their southern capital in 1368 and then gave the city its modern name (Nanking means "southern capital"). It continued to function as one of the twin capitals of the Mings, even after they moved their seat to Peking (northern capital) in 1421. The Treaty of Nanking (1842), which ended the Opium War, opened five major Chinese ports to foreign trade. During the Taiping rebellion, the city, temporarily renamed Tienching (Heavenly Capital), was the capital of the rebels from 1853 to 1864. Nanking itself was opened to foreign trade in 1899. During the Chinese revolution, Nanking was captured by the insurgents in 1911 and served briefly as the seat of Sun Yat-sen's provisional presidency. In March 1927, the city fell to the Nationalist unification forces, and in 1928 it became the capital of the Nationalist government of Chiang Kai-shek, supplanting Peking (which was renamed Peiping). In the Sino-Japanese War, Nanking fell to the Japanese in December 1937, shortly after the national capital had been moved to Chungking. The ensuing looting and atrocities (the "rape of Nanking") shocked the world. The Japanese surrender in China was signed in Nanking in September 1945, and the Nationalist capital was returned here from Chungking. The city fell in April 1949 to the Communists, who once again restored the national seat of government to Peking. Pop. (1957) 1,419,000.

NANNA, nän′nä, in Scandinavian mythology, wife of Balder and goddess of purity and vegetation. Her name means "blossom," and she was the daughter of Nip, which means "bud." In the myth of the death of Balder, Nanna falls dead by the side of her husband and is placed upon his bier so that she may accompany him in death. When Balder's brother Hermod visits the land of the dead to gain Balder's freedom, he finds Nanna ministering to him as he lies sick and pale on a couch. Balder wishes Hermod to take Nanna back with him, but she refuses to leave her husband. Balder is the personification of life-giving light, and his wife,

Nanna, is the personification of vegetation which dies when the great light giver, the sun, goes on his winter journey to the south. Balder is generally called the radiant god of sunshine; and his wife, like the classical Proserpina, goes down into the underworld.

NANNING (YUNGNING), an important city in southwest Kwangsi Province, China, is on the north bank of the Yukiang, chief southern tributary of the Sikiang. Linked by rail with French Indochina and by road and river with Kweilin, capital of Kwangsi, and with Canton, it is a trading center for rice, hemp, tobacco, and cotton cloth. Pop. (1953) 194,600.

NANSEN, Fridtjof, frēt'yŏf nän'sĕn, Norwegian Arctic explorer, zoologist, statesman, and humanitarian: b. Fröen, Norway, Oct. 10, 1861; d. Oslo, May 13, 1930. He studied zoology at the University of Christiania (now Oslo), and in 1882 made an Arctic voyage in a sealing vessel for the purpose of studying animal life in the higher latitudes. On his return he was appointed curator of the Museum of Natural History, Bergen. In 1888, he led an expedition across Greenland a little north of latitude 64°N., an account of this journey being published in England in 1891, under the title *Across Greenland.* He returned to Norway the following year and was appointed curator of the Museum of Comparative Anatomy at the University of Christiania. In 1893, he sailed aboard a specially built steamer, the *Fram,* in the expectation that, entering the polar ice in the neighborhood of the New Siberian Islands, the ship would drift eastward south of the pole and come out on the east side of Greenland. This expectation was based on the fact that articles belonging to the *Jeannette,* an Arctic expedition vessel lost in 1881 (see JEANNETTE EXPEDITION), had drifted in about three years from Bering Strait across the polar regions to Greenland. After being carried to latitude 83°59′N., he left the *Fram* and, with a single companion, Lieut. F. H. Johansen, took to the ice, equipped with sledges, dogs, and kayaks. In this way he reached a higher latitude than any previously attained, 86°14′N. (April 8, 1895), and then turned southwestward to Franz Josef Land (now Fridtjof Nansen Land), where he spent the winter of 1895–1896. On June 17, 1896, he fell in with members of the Jackson-Harmsworth Expedition (see JACKSON, FREDERICK GEORGE), with whom he returned by ship to Vardö, Norway. The *Fram* (under Capt. O. N. Sverdrup), which had reached latitude 85°57′N., arrived in Norway eight days later via the west coast of Spitzbergen (Svalbard).

Numerous honors were conferred upon Nansen, including a professorship of zoology at the University of Christiania. In 1900, he joined an expedition to explore the North Atlantic, and in the following year became director of the International Commission for Study of the Sea. He was strongly favorable to the separation of Norway from Sweden (1905), and served as the first Norwegian minister to Great Britain (1906–1908). He resigned his diplomatic post in 1908 to become professor of oceanography at the University of Christiania. Between 1910 and 1914, he made four oceanographic expeditions in the North Atlantic and Arctic oceans. At the close of World War I, he was placed in charge of the repatriation of about 500,000 prisoners of war from Siberia, China, and other parts of the world. Under the sponsorship of 12 governments and 48 national Red Cross societies, he directed the administration of relief to sufferers from famine in Russia (1921–1923). He also served as League of Nations high commissioner for relief work among Russian, Armenian, and Greek refugees. For these activities, he was awarded the Nobel Peace Prize for 1921–1922. A strong supporter of the League of Nations, Nansen subsequently served as Norwegian delegate to the League. In 1925, he was chosen rector of St. Andrews University, Scotland. Among his published works are *Eskimo Life* (1891), *Farthest North* (1897), *Norway and the Union with Sweden* (1905), *Through Siberia* (1914), *Armenia and the Near East* (1928), and numerous scientific books, including reports of his various expeditions.

NANSEN, Hans, Danish statesman: b. Flensburg, Schleswig-Holstein, Nov. 28, 1598; d. Copenhagen (København), Nov. 12, 1667. As mayor of Copenhagen, Nansen was the leader of the antiaristocratic party whose influence resulted in the abolition of the privileges of the nobility and the institution by Frederick III of the absolute monarchy in Denmark (1660).

NANTERRE, näɴ-târ′, France, town in the Department of Seine, located at the foot of Mount Valérien, eight miles west of Paris. Its chief industry is the manufacture of chemicals. It is the traditional birthplace of St. Geneviève (q.v.), patron of Paris. Pop. (1962) 83,155.

NANTES, näɴt, France, capital of the Department of Loire-Atlantique and an important commercial port situated on the right bank of the Loire at its confluence with the Erdre, 248 miles by rail west-southwest of Paris. The usefulness of the port was enhanced by the construction of a ship canal in 1891 to St. Nazaire, 40 miles to the west at the mouth of the Loire, and by extensive harbor improvements undertaken after 1914. The city is the see of a bishop; it has courts of first resort and of commerce, a chamber of commerce and an exchange, a college, a seminary, a secondary ecclesiastical school, a secondary school of medicine, and a hydrographic school. Among its products are blankets, textiles, ship machinery and supplies, cordage, chemicals, glue, and various food products, including biscuits, sugar, sardines, and preserved meats. There are also cotton mills, iron works, glass works, and important shipbuilding docks. Nantes carries on an extensive trade with the French Union and with foreign countries. Among the more interesting public buildings are the cathedral, in flamboyant Gothic style, which was begun in the 15th century and completed in the 19th; the ducal castle, which dates back to the 9th or 10th century and was rebuilt in the 15th century, flanked with massive round towers; the Palais des Beaux Arts (1900), which contains a fine collection of paintings.

Before the conquest of Gaul by the Romans, Nantes was the principal town of the Namnetes, a leading Gallic tribe of Brittainy. During the 9th century it was thrice taken by Norse raiders and almost entirely ruined. In 1118, when it had again become prosperous, a fire reduced the greater part of the town to ashes. During the Hundred Years' War, it suffered much, repeatedly falling into the hands of the opposite parties. For a long time it formed one of the most valuable possessions of the dukes of Brittany, but when Anne of Brittany, heiress of the dukedom and a native of Nantes, married Louis XII in 1499, it passed with the rest of her possessions to the crown of France. The most memorable event connected with the history of Nantes was the famous edict (see EDICT OF NANTES) issued by Henry IV, April 13, 1598, securing the Protestants in the free exercise of their religion. The *noyades* (drownings) of the monster Jean Baptiste Carrier (q.v.) during the revolution were perpetrated here. Pop. (1962) commune 246,227.

NANTES, Edict of. See EDICT OF NANTES.

NANTEUIL, nän-tû'y', **Robert,** French copperplate engraver: b. Reims, France, 1618/1630; d. Paris, Dec. 9, 1678. After completing his thesis for a degree in philosophy, he studied engraving under Nicolas Regnesson and in 1647 went to Paris, where his work was so well received that Louis XIV appointed him designer and engraver to the king. Nanteuil generally used pastel crayons in drawing the designs for his engravings. His portraits, of which 243 plates survive in the Bibliothèque Nationale, including particularly fine ones of Jules Cardinal Mazarin, Louis XIV, the Vicomte de Turenne, and Anne of Austria, are noted for their skilled simplicity and lifelike drawing.

NANTICOKE, năn'tĭ-kōk (Nentigo, "tidewater people"), a former American Indian tribe speaking an Algonquian language closely related to that of the Delaware Indians. When first discovered by Europeans in 1608 they resided on the east shore of the Nanticoke River, where their principal village, also called Nanticoke, was situated. They lived by fishing and hunting, and had a reputation among neighboring tribes for their skill in witchcraft. In 1642 the Nanticoke were declared enemies of the Maryland colony, but in 1678 a peace treaty brought an end to hostilities and in 1698 reservations were set apart for them. About 1725 most of them began to move northward, gradually going up the Susquehanna River and finally settling at Owego, Chugnut, and Chenango in southern New York State. Those who remained behind in Maryland, under the name of Wiwash, numbered only 30 in 1792. Some of those in New York State amalgamated with the Iroquois, but a majority migrated west about 1784 and joined the Delawares in Ohio and Indiana, where they lost their identity as a separate people.

NANTICOKE, city, Pennsylvania, in Luzerne County; altitude 538 feet; 7 miles southwest of Wilkes-Barre on the Susquehanna River, on the site of a former Nanticoke Indian village. Nanticoke is situated in one of the richest anthracite coal regions in the world, and a considerable part of its population is employed in nearby coal mines. It is a center for the manufacture of rayon and nylon, and also has a large cigar factory. The city owes its origin to Nanticoke Falls, which furnish the water power for local mills and factories. The Jersey Central and the Pennsylvania railroads provide freight service. Across the Susquehanna from Nanticoke is the village of West Nanticoke; on the nearby hill known as Tillsbury Knob is found the only tract remaining from the original land grant made to William Penn still in the possession of his descendants. Nanticoke was surveyed and platted in 1793 and incorporated as a borough in 1874. In 1926 it was granted a city charter. The government is administered by a mayor and council. Pop. 14,632.

NANTUCKET ISLAND, năn-tŭk'ĕt, island, Massachusetts, is situated about 25 miles south of Cape Cod across Nantucket Sound. To the west Muskeget Channel separates it from Martha's Vineyard. Extending 14 miles in an east-west direction, Nantucket, with two small islands off its western extremity, Muskeget and Tuckernuck, constitute Nantucket County (area 46 square miles); the county and Nantucket town are coextensive. The island is flat and sandy, with cranberries, heather, and wild roses growing on its moors. The village of Nantucket, located on a good harbor on the north shore, is the county seat and chief trading center; it has steamer connections with Wood's Hole on Cape Cod.

The town has a public library (the Athenaeum), the Jethro Coffin house (1686), an old mill, and a fine whaling museum occupying an old sperm-candle factory. Its historic houses built by whaling captains from the profits of voyages to the Pacific islands and the Orient and its natural facilities for boating and bathing have made it a popular summer resort and artists' colony. Smaller communities on the island are Siasconset on the east coast, Wauwinet, Quidnet, and Squam Head.

Visited by Bartholomew Gosnold in 1602, it was first settled in 1659 by Quaker families from Salisbury, Mass., led by Thomas Macy. The town was incorporated in 1687 and the county formed in 1695. In the 18th century it became a famous whaling port, and it continued a center of the industry until the mid-19th century. There are regular town meetings and officials are elected annually. Population: village, 2,461; town, 3,774.

NANTUNG, nän'tŏŏng', city, China, in Kiangsu Province, on the north bank of the Yangtze River, 65 miles northwest of Shanghai. Center of a major cotton-growing area, it has important cotton mills. Pop. (1953) 260,400.

NAOROJI, nou-rō'jē, **Dadabhai,** first Indian member of the British Parliament: b. Bombay, Sept. 4, 1825; d. there, July 2, 1917. The son of a Parsi priest, he was educated at the Elphinstone Institution (later Elphinstone School and College) in Bombay, where in 1854 he became the first native professor of mathematics and natural philosophy (1854). In 1855 he went to England, where he resided for many years. Through his efforts the Indian Civil Service was opened to native Indians in 1870, and he did much for the improvement of Indian business and industry. He served as prime minister to the prince of Baroda in 1874; from 1875 to 1887 he held important government positions in Bombay; and in 1886, 1893, and 1906 he was president of the Indian National Congress. For many years he was president of the London Indian Society. From 1892 to 1895 he was Liberal Party member for Central Finsbury in the House of Commons, and in the latter year was made a member of the Royal Commission on Indian Expenditure. His numerous publications include *England's Duties to India* (1867); *The Wants and Means of*

India (1870); *Poverty and Un-British Rule in India* (1901); and *The Rights of Labour* (1906).

NAPA, năp'ȧ, city, California, the seat of Napa County, 49 miles northeast of San Francisco; at an altitude of 20 feet. It is the trade and shipping center for the fertile Napa Valley, celebrated for its vineyards, wineries, and fruit orchards. The city produces canned and dried fruit, dairy products, and leather goods. Nearby tourist attractions are a petrified forest, mineral springs, and the Napa redwoods. Also in the vicinity are Pacific Union College (Seventh Day Adventist), and the Napa State Hospital for the Insane. Napa is served by the Southern Pacific railroad, a multilane highway leading to Oakland and San Francisco, and an airport, and it is the terminus of barge navigation on the Napa River. Settled in 1840, the city was incorporated in 1872 and reincorporated in 1915. It is governed by a council manager. Pop. 35,978.

ELLA W. MILLER.

NAPALM, nā'päm, is an aluminum soap that makes gasoline thicken (gel), and it is also the thickened gasoline itself. In warfare, this sticky substance is used as a burning agent hurled by flamethrowers or dropped from the air in fire bombs. "Napalm" is an acronym formed from the *na*phthenic and *palm*itic acids from which it is made. It was developed during World War II by Harvard University scientists and the U.S. Army Chemical Warfare Service.

Because napalm adheres to whatever it hits and burns hotly, it has been used extensively against protected military targets, such as troops behind bunkers. Napalm bombs caused great damage in Japanese cities in World War II and destroyed many villages in the Vietnam War.

NAPERVILLE, nā'pẽr-vĭl, city, Illinois, in Du Page County, on the Du Page River, 28 miles west of Chicago. The town is served by the Chicago, Burlington & Quincy Railroad, and is linked with Chicago and Aurora by a multiple lane highway and a tollway. In an agricultural and dairying district, Naperville produces ice cream, furniture, cotton and burlap bags, building blocks, and boilers. It is the seat of the coeducational North Central College and its affiliate, the Evangelical Theological Seminary. First settled in 1831, the town was named for Joseph Naper, who plotted the townsite in 1832 and erected a sawmill. It was incorporated as a village in 1857 and as a city in 1890. The city is governed by a commission. Pop. 23,885.

MIRIAM B. FRY.

NAPHTALI, năf'tȧ-lī, the sixth son of the Biblical patriarch, Jacob; his mother was Bilhah, Rachel's maid (Genesis 30:7–8). Little is known of Naphtali except that he was one of the 12 sons of Jacob, the traditional ancestors of the Hebrew tribes. The territory of the descendants of Naphtali lay north and west of the sea of Galilee, from the Lebanon Mountains to the southern tip of the Sea of Galilee, and thus included the rich and fertile area adjoining the upper reaches of the Jordan River and the western shore of the sea (Deuteronomy 33:23; Joshua 19:32–39). As a frontier tribe it was exposed to invasions from the north and east. The ancient Song of Deborah celebrates the heroes of Naphtali who "jeoparded their lives unto the death" in the war against Jabin, the Canaanite king (Judges 5:18). When Tiglath-pileser III overran northern Palestine in 733 B.C. he carried off the population to Assyria; Naphtali disappears from history at this time. Later the district became famous as "Galilee of the Gentiles" (Matthew 4:15), the home of Jesus Christ and most of his disciples, and the scene of his ministry.

FREDERICK C. GRANT.

NAPHTHA, năf'thȧ, a term applied to low-boiling liquids produced by fractionation of crude petroleum or by thermal or catalytic cracking of petroleum products. It comprises complex mixtures of hydrocarbons boiling at temperatures in the range of about 40° to 150° C., with molecules containing 5 to 9 carbon atoms. The densities of naphthas normally range from 0.67 to 0.72; products with high aromatic contents, however, have somewhat greater densities. Naphthas are used principally for solvents, dry cleaning fluids, and fuels. As a solvent, its applications include the preparation of rubber solutions, wood preservatives, and varnishes. Naphthas are also used to extract oils, including some essential oils used in the preparation of perfumes and essences, from certain seeds and flowers. The first use was for fuel in lamps.

Originally, the term naphtha was applied to the volatile products of asphalts and bitumens found issuing from the ground in the Caspian Sea region of Russia and Persia (Iran). For many years the word has been associated with inflammable liquid hydrocarbons which evaporate fairly readily upon exposure to air. Currently, the term is seldom used commercially or scientificially without a distinctive prefix indicating the product's origin. Thus, the terms petroleum or mineral naphtha, crude or coal tar naphtha, shale naphtha, and wood naphtha (methyl alcohol), refer to the distillate fractions obtained from petroleum, coal tar, shale, and wood, respectively.

See also HYDROCARBONS.

F. W. BANES.

NAPHTHALENE, năf'thȧ-lēn, an aromatic hydrocarbon compound with the chemical composition $C_{10}H_8$. The compound contains two condensed benzene rings capable of the resonating structures shown in Fig. 1. (For the theory of structural resonance, see the article BOND, in Chemistry.)

I II III

Fig. 1

The empirical chemical composition of naphthalene was first determined by Michael Faraday (1791–1867) in 1826. A two-ring form (structure II) was proposed for the compound in 1866 by Emil Erlenmeyer (1825–1909), in accordance with the structure of the benzene molecule proposed by Kekulé in 1865 (Friedrich August Kekulé von Stradonitz, 1829–1896). That two rings, sharing a pair of adjacent carbon atoms, are present in the naphthalene molecule has been proved definitely by identification of products formed by the oxidation of naphthalene and certain of its derivatives having monosubstituents on one or both rings. This is demonstrated by the oxidation of nitro- and aminonaphthalenes, shown in Fig. 2. Also, in catalytic hydrogenation, the naphthalene molecule takes up 10 atoms of hydrogen to form a compound with the chemical composition $C_{10}H_{18}$.

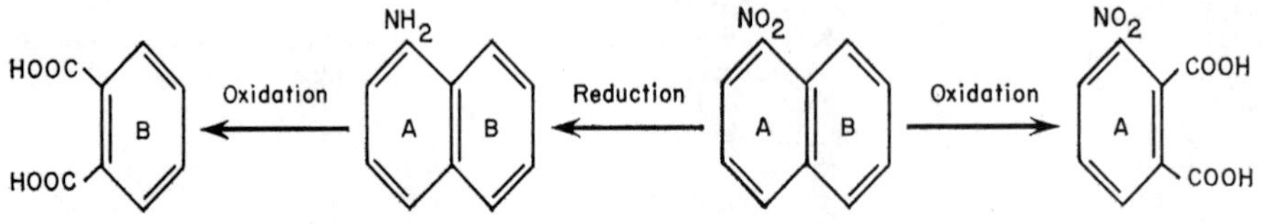

Fig. 2

Otto Linné Erdmann (1804–1869) proposed that structures I and III were equivalent forms of the structure proposed by Erlenmeyer. This proposal has been supported by the work of Linus Pauling (1901–), which indicated that the three structures have approximately the same energy and molecular configuration. Resonance between the structures should stabilize the naphthalene molecule to a greater extent than the Kekulé resonance of benzene, which involves only two equivalent states. Actual data indicate that the resonance energy of naphthalene is about 25 kilogram calories per mole higher than that of benzene. In its reactions, however, naphthalene behaves as if the double bonds were "frozen" in the pattern of structure II; that is, naphthalene reacts as a double aromatic ring.

The eight hydrogen atoms of naphthalene are located at the positions shown in Fig. 3. These atoms are not equivalent; in many cases, the four

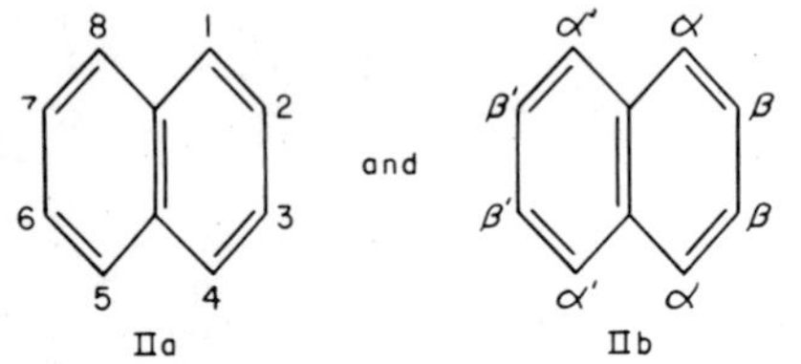

Fig. 3

in positions 1, 4, 5, and 8 (the α positions) show differences in reactivity from those in positions 2, 3, 6, and 7 (the β positions). In benzene, the substitution for a single hydrogen atom gives only one product, since the benzene molecule is chemically symmetrical, its hydrogen atoms being all similarly related to one another and to the carbon atoms. In naphthalene, on the other hand, two different kinds of monosubstitution are possible, depending on the position (α or β) of the hydrogen atom displaced, for the α hydrogen atoms are always more directly associated with the central pair of carbon atoms than are the β atoms.

Disubstitution on two adjacent carbon atoms in the naphthalene molecule corresponds to disubstitution at the *ortho* positions of molecules in the benzene series. The 1,8 and 4,5 positions, called *peri* positions, are also similar to the *ortho*-substituted benzene compounds. Thus, both naphthylene 1,8-dicarboxylic acid (naphthalic acid) and 2,3-dicarboxylic acid (phthalic acid) readily form anhydrides. As a result of the various locations of pairs of hydrogen atoms on the naphthalene nucleus, a large number of derivatives can be obtained by disubstitution. Ten isomers of disubstituted naphthalenes are possible if the two substituent groups are identical; and if the two groups are different, 14 distinct isomers can be produced. The locations of substituents on the naphthalene nucleus are designated according to the numerical positions shown in structure IIa. The positions of disubstituents are also indicated by special terms: thus, 1,2 are *ortho* positions; 1,3, *meta;* 1,4, *para;* 1,5, *ana;* 1,6, *epi;* 1,7, *kata;* 1,8, *peri;* 2,6, *amphi;* and 2,7, *pros.*

Naphthalene displays the general characteristics of the aromatic hydrocarbons. With chlorine, bromine, nitric acid, and sulphuric acid it reacts (similarly to, but somewhat more readily than, benzene) to form chlorides, bromides, nitrates, and sulphonates. Reaction with the halogens tends to produce α-monosubstituted products, while reaction with sulphuric acid forms a mixture of α- and β-sulphonic acids. In certain cases where reactions are subject to steric hindrance, the substituents tend to go into the less-hindered β positions to a degree which depends on the reaction temperature as well as on the nature of the reagents and solvents. Thus, naphthalene sulphonates predominate at the α position when the reaction is carried out at low temperatures, but at higher temperatures (160°–170° C.) the β-substituted product is more frequently formed.

The derivatives of naphthalene containing amino, hydroxyl, and sulphonic groups in various combinations provide the raw materials for the production of a wide variety of dyestuffs. Especially important dyes, including the various azo dyes and Congo red, are produced by coupling the sulphonic acid derivatives of naphthalene with diazonium compounds. Other dyes are prepared from phthalic anhydride derivatives, including indigo (from anthranilic acid) and fast vat dyes (from anthraquinone).

Oxidation products of naphthalene vary with the reaction conditions and with the type of oxidation agent employed. Thus, oxidation with chromic acid in an acetic acid solution produces 1,4-naphthoquinone, while phthalic acid is the chief product formed by oxidation with potassium dichromate in an acidic medium. Phthalic acid, a particularly important product of naphthalene, is produced commercially by vapor-phase catalytic oxidation with air, using a vanadium pentoxide catalyst; the acid dehydrates to phthalic anhydride, which sublimes and collects on the cooled surfaces of a condenser.

In addition reactions, also, naphthalene shows somewhat greater reactivity than benzene. It is reduced by sodium and ethyl alcohol to produce 1,4-dihydronaphthalene, while benzene shows no reaction with these reagents. Again, benzene does not react with sodium and amyl alcohol, but naphthalene is converted to 1,2,3,4-tetrahydronaphthalene (tetralin). The reaction stops with the addition of four atoms of hydrogen, since tetralin is a substituted benzene compound and is therefore unreactive to the reagents. This derivative is an important solvent for fats, resins, varnishes, lacquers, and other organic products. The completely hydrogenated product, decalin ($C_{10}H_{18}$), is also used for certain solvent applications.

Naphthalene is formed in the pyrolysis of many organic compounds. In modern petroleum processing, high-temperature catalytic cracking produces some naphthalene by the condensation of unsaturated cracked products, including butadiene, acetylene, and cyclohexene. The most important source of naphthalene is coal tar, the viscous aromatic product obtained by destructive distillation of bituminous coal at high temperatures. Naphthalene crystallizes out of the "middle oil" fraction of coal tar, this middle fraction boiling in the range of 170° to 230° C. Phenol also distills over in this boiling range, and must be removed from the crude solid naphthalene. Separation is accomplished by centrifuging the crude naphthalene, pressing it to remove residual oils, warming it, treating it with hot caustic soda, and washing it to remove neutralized phenol derivatives. The washed product is then sublimed or distilled to produce white rhombic leaflets, which melt at 80.3° C. (boiling point, 218° C.). Naphthalene has an unpleasant penetrating odor, and a burning taste. It burns with a sooty flame and a pitchy odor. Although it is insoluble in cold water and only slightly soluble in hot water, it is readily soluble in hot alcohol or in ether.

The major commercial use for naphthalene is in the production of phthalic anhydride. This material is esterified with alcohols to produce plasticizers for various resinous products, particularly vinyl chloride resins; and it is esterified with a polyhydroxy compound such as glycerol to form alkyd resins, essential ingredients of many surface-coating compounds.

F. W. Banes.

NAPHTHENES, năf′thēnz, a series of saturated cyclic hydrocarbon compounds of the general formula, C_nH_{2n}, also called cycloalkanes and cycloparaffins. The term refers primarily to alkyl derivatives of cyclopentane, such as methyl cyclopentane and 1,1-dimethyl cyclopentane, and to a lesser extent to cyclohexane and its alkylated derivatives, including the mono-, di-, and trimethyl cyclohexanes. Among the higher molecular-weight naphthenes are alkyl derivatives of bicyclopentane and decahydronaphthylene.

Straight-run gasoline and other light petroleum fractions contain naphthene in concentrations characteristic of the crude petroleum from which they are distilled. The light fractions of some California, Texas, and Pennsylvania crudes contain as much as 20 to 40 per cent naphthenes.

Besides being important components of motor gasolines, naphthenes serve as raw materials from which toluene, xylenes, adipic acid, caprolactam, and other important petrochemicals are derived.

F. W. Banes.

NAPHTHENIC ACIDS, năf-thēn′ĭk, a class of monocarboxylic acid compounds found in crude oils. Most of the naphthenic acids are derivatives of cyclopentane or its homologues, but some are derivatives of bicyclic cyclopentane compounds or alkylated cyclohexanes. In naphthenic acids of commercial interest the carboxyl group is usually attached to the alkyl chain, as in the case of an important member of the naphthenic acid group, cyclopentane acetic acid:

```
   CH2—CH2
  /     |
CH2     |
  \     |
   CH2—CH—CH2—COOH
```

The proof that the naphthenic acids are characterized by this type of structure was worked out in the late 19th century; at the same time it was shown that the carboxyl group (COOH) is rarely linked directly to the cyclopentane ring. Cyclohexane derivatives, with structures analogous to those shown above, are found in only very small quantities.

Naphthenic acids are found in all crude petroleums, but only a few naphthenic and asphaltic crudes (including those of Russia, Venezuela, and California, which contain acids in concentrations as high as 1 to 2 per cent) have concentrations great enough to make recovery profitable. The acids are recovered from straight-run distillates (primarily kerosene and gas oil cuts) by caustic scrubbing and acidification.

Naphthenic acids are viscous liquids with high stability to oxidation. When freshly distilled they are colorless and odorless, but both color and odor develop upon storage. In common with other carboxylic acids, they form esters and metal salts, and can be reduced to the corresponding alcohols.

The acids as such are used in only small quantities in the production of oil-emulsion breakers, cleaning compounds, and rubber-reclaiming oils, but the metallic derivatives of naphthenic acids are of considerable commercial importance. These derivatives include lead, cobalt, manganese, and zinc salts (paint driers), which take up over 50 per cent of all naphthenic acid production; lead and aluminum salts (used in lubricants); copper and zinc salts (fungicides); and sodium, potassium, and ammonium salts (emulsifiers and demulsifiers). During World War II large quantities of naphthenic acids were used in the manufacture of the incendiary, napalm.

F. W. Banes.

NAPIER, nā′pĭ-ẽr, Sir **Charles James**, British army officer and military administrator: b. London, England, Aug. 10, 1782; d. Portsmouth, Aug. 29, 1853. He entered the British Army as an ensign at the age of 12; served with distinction in the Peninsular War from 1808 to 1811; commanded a brigade in the War of 1812; and served as British military administrator of the Greek island of Cephalonia (1822–1830), where he instituted numerous reforms and built a network of roads.

Napier's most famous achievement was his conquest of Sind (now part of West Pakistan). Before the first Anglo-Afghan War (1839–1842) the British had established treaty relations with the Baluchi amirs of Hyderabad (lower Sind), Khairpur (upper Sind), and Mirpur (east central Sind), and British reverses in Afghanistan determined the British governor general of India to strengthen control of Sind. Napier, who had gone to India in 1841 and been posted to Hyderabad in 1842, believed that "the annexation of Sind would be a very beneficient piece of rascality," and acted accordingly. The Battle of

Miani near Hyderabad (Feb. 17, 1843), in which his small force vanquished a much larger Baluchi army, brought most of the amirs to terms, and his defeat of the amir of Mirpur at Dabo on March 24 paved the way for the formal annexation of Sind in August 1843. While head of the civil and military administration of Sind Napier led a campaign against the northwest tribes (1844–1845) and commanded an army in the first Sikh war (1846). In 1849–1850 he served as commander in chief of the British Indian Army.

Sir William Francis Patrick Napier (1785–1860), his brother, joined the army at the age of 14, served in the expedition against Copenhagen, Denmark, in 1807, and played an outstanding role in the Peninsular War from 1808 to 1814. He is best known as the author of *History of the War in the Peninsula* (6 vols., 1828–1840), which has been called "the finest military history in English."

NAPIER, John, 8th Laird of Merchiston, Scottish mathematician: b. Merchiston Castle, near Edinburgh, Scotland, 1550; d. there, April 4, 1617. Little is known of Napier's early life. He studied for a session or two at St. Andrew's University, beginning at the age of 13, and probably continued his education in Europe. On his marriage in 1572, he was invested with an estate by his father, Sir Archibald Napier (1534–1608), and passed the remainder of his life as a landed proprietor, devoting his leisure to theology, invention, and mathematics. He conducted agricultural experiments and devised a hydraulic screw to remove water from flooded coal pits. Perhaps inspired by the Spanish Armada (1588) he made "Secret Inventions, profitable and necessary in these Days for Defence of this Island, and withstanding of Strangers, Enemies of God's Truth and Religion," which included two "burning glasses" (mirrors) for firing hostile ships, an artillery piece, and an armored chariot.

Napier's permanent fame, however, rests upon his contributions to mathematics. By 1594 he had formulated the general principles of logarithms; he devoted the next 20 years to working out the theory of logarithms, devising methods for their calculation, and making laborious computations for the first canon or table of logarithms. His *Mirifici logarithmorum canonis descriptio* (1614; *Description of the Marvelous Canon of Logarithms*) contained, in addition to the table, an explanation of the theory of logarithms and their use in arithmetical and trigonometrical calculations. The further development of logarithm tables by Napier, Henry Briggs (1561-1630), and others, vastly simplified the computational tasks imposed by rapidly widening scientific interests, especially in the field of astronomy.

Napier's mathematical inventions included a primitive calculating machine; a system for multiplying, dividing, and extracting roots of numbers by moving counters on a chessboard; and a device for the performance of multiplication and division known as Napier's bones, which consisted of 10 mutually adjustable calculating rods with multiplication tables marked on them.

NAPIER, Robert Cornelis, 1st Baron Napier of Magdala, British soldier: b. Colombo, Ceylon, Dec. 6, 1810; d. London, England, Jan. 14, 1890. Commissioned a 2d lieutenant in the Bengal engineers of the East India Company in December 1826, at the age of 16, he served with distinction in the Sikh wars (1845–1846 and 1848–1849), played an important part in the suppression of the Indian Mutiny (1857–1859), and in 1860, during the Taiping Rebellion, commanded a division in the British expedition to China.

Napier gained worldwide fame in 1868, when he led an expedition to Abyssinia (modern Ethiopia) to force the release of Englishmen held captive by Emperor Theodore. His force landed on the coast of Eritrea in northeast Africa on Jan. 2, 1868. Having supervised the construction of a 12-mile-long supply railway to his inland base, he set out with his army on January 25 on a 420-mile journey into the interior of Abyssinia. On April 10, Napier reached the plateau of Magdala, where he defeated Theodore's troops. On April 13, he stormed Magdala, Theodore's capital, where the emperor was found dead by his own hand. For the dashing brilliance of Napier's rescue of the British prisoners he was created Baron Napier of Magdala on July 17, 1868. Subsequently he served as commander in chief of the British Indian Army (1870–1876), as governor of Gibraltar (1876–1883), and as constable of the Tower of London (1886–1890).

NAPIER OF MAGDALA. See Napier, Robert Cornelis.

NAPIER, borough, New Zealand, the capital of Hawke's Bay Provincial District, situated on the south shore of Hawke Bay on the eastern side of North Island, 170 miles northeast of Wellington. The commercial center of a grazing district, Napier exports wool, hides, frozen meats, and dairy products through its harbor, Port Ahuriri. Manufactures include woolen textiles, fertilizers, and tobacco. A popular winter resort, it has air, rail, and highway connections with Wellington, Gisborne, and other New Zealand cities. Laid out in 1865 and constituted a borough in 1874, Napier was completely rebuilt after its destruction by earthquake in 1931. Pop. (1956) 27,507.

NAPLES, nā'p'lz (It. Napoli, nä'pô-lē; anc. Neapolis), commune and city of Italy, the capital of the province of the same name and of the region Campania, is situated on the north shore of the Bay of Naples, 120 miles southeast of Rome. For centuries the capital of the Kingdom of Naples (see Naples, Kingdom of) and of that of the Two Sicilies (see Sicilies, Kingdom of The Two), it is still the commercial and cultural center of southern Italy. It ranks as the country's third largest city in population and is, after Genoa, its busiest port. The incomparable natural beauties and balmy climate have charmed visitors from all over the world, starting with Virgil, who is buried in nearby Posillipo, down to Johann Wolfgang von Goethe, Percy Bysshe Shelley, Giacomo Leopardi and the innumerable tourists who visit it every year.

Naples occupies a fan-shaped area extending about five miles along the bay and stretching inland up the slopes of the surrounding hills. The older quarters and the business districts lie near the coast and on the lower slopes, while the more modern residential sections extend well up the hills, especially the Vomero. Along the waterfront, from Castel Nuovo to the little fishermen's inlet of Mergellina, runs a broad thoroughfare; here is the picturesque little port of Santa Lucia. Beyond Mergellina, the road winds up the hill to Posilipo, famous for the beauty of its villas. Along with such fine residential areas, Naples has crowded slums that developed during the city's period of rapid growth after 1861. Extensive measures have been taken to eradicate these blighted areas.

Commerce and Industry. Naples is southern Italy's most important center of trade. Its fine natural harbor has undergone steady improvement since the 1200's, and today the city has excellent port facilities, equipped to handle large oceangoing vessels.

In spite of Naples' commercial importance, its industry has developed slowly. In and around the city are food-processing establishments, railroad shops, shipyards, iron and steel works, oil refineries, leather goods factories, and chemical plants. Since Naples is near many points of interest, including Pompeii, the islands of Capri and Ischia, and the Amalfi Drive, tourism is one of the city's chief sources of income.

Historic Buildings. Naples has several imposing medieval castles. Castel dell'Ovo (12th century) sits on a rocky islet off Santa Lucia; Castel Nuovo (13th century), with a sculptured Renaissance triumphal arch, dominates the main harbor; and Castel Sant'Elmo (14th century) overlooks the city from the Vomero.

Naples has more than 200 churches, many of which date from the 13th and 14th centuries. During the Neapolitan baroque era of the 17th and 18th centuries, most of the old churches were restyled, and many new ones were built. Santa Chiara, formerly the church of the royal family, was severely damaged during World War II, but has since been restored to its original Gothic architecture. The Church of Monteoliveto, also damaged during the war, is rich in Renaissance sculpture. The city's cathedral, built between 1272 and 1323, includes the chapel of San Gennaro (St. Januarius), Naples' patron saint. The chapel, an excellent example of 17th century Neapolitan art, contains relics of the saint (see JANUARIUS). Other important churches include San Giovanni a Carbonara, built in 1343; San Domenico Maggiore, a Gothic building begun in 1289; and Santi Severino e Sosio, with 17th century decorations. On the Vomero, the monastery of San Martino, founded in the 14th century and rebuilt in the 17th century, commands an imposing view of the Bay of Naples and the surrounding area.

Cultural Life. Naples has a rich cultural heritage. In the 1600's a local school of painting flourished. In the 1600's and 1700's, Neapolitan composers, including the Scarlattis, Paisiello, Cimarosa, and Pergolesi, were among the best in Italy. The San Carlo Opera House, founded in 1737, is the largest in Italy. The university, dating from 1224, is southern Italy's chief institution of higher learning. The National Library, housed in the 17th century royal palace, has more than 1,300,000 volumes.

The National Museum and the National Gallery contain Naples' most important art collections. The former has classical sculpture and other treasures from the destroyed cities of Pompeii and Herculaneum. The latter, located in the royal palace of Capodimonte, has one of Italy's foremost collections of paintings. The monastery of San Martino houses a collection of items about the history of Naples.

History. Naples, which derives its name from *Neapolis,* meaning "new city," is built on the site of *Parthenope,* an ancient Rhodian outpost. The present city was founded in the 600's B.C. by settlers from the Greek colony of Cumae. Under Roman rule, beginning in 327 B.C., the city was a resort. After the fall of the Roman Empire in the 5th century A.D., it was occupied successively by the Ostrogoths, Lombards, and Byzantines.

Naples was ruled by its own dukes from 736 to 1139. It was then incorporated in the kingdom of the Two Sicilies, of which it was made the capital. In 1266 the Two Sicilies were captured by Charles I of Anjou. Charles lost the island of Sicily 16 years later, and the mainland territories that he retained became the kingdom of Naples. In 1443, Naples and Sicily were reunited under Alfonso V of Aragon. In 1485, France seized the city, but under the Treaties of Blois (1504–1505) both Naples and Sicily were ceded to Spain. The Peace of Utrecht in 1713 awarded the Two Sicilies to Austria. Austria's return of the territory to Spain in 1734 marked the beginning of the Spanish Bourbon monarchy in Naples.

During the Napoleonic Wars, France held Naples from 1806 until 1815, when the Congress of Vienna restored the Two Sicilies to the Bourbons. In 1860 the last Bourbon king, Francis II, was defeated by the Italian nationalist leader Giuseppe Garibaldi. The next year, Naples became part of the united kingdom of Italy.

After the unification of Italy, Naples, together with Genoa, became one of the country's two leading seaports. Naples suffered heavy damage during World War II before its capture by the Allies in 1943. After the war it underwent rapid expansion. Population: (1961) 1,182,815.

See also NAPLES, KINGDOM OF; PARTHENOPEAN REPUBLIC; SICILIES, KINGDOM OF THE TWO.

NAPLES, nā'pəlz, **Bay of,** is a semicircular inlet of the Tyrrhenian Sea, on the west coast of the Italian peninsula, between Cape Miseno and Punta Campanella. It is about 20 miles long and 10 miles wide. It takes its name from its chief city. Surrounded by hills and dominated by Mount Vesuvius (see VESUVIUS), the bay is famed for its beauty. Its coastline is dotted with small towns and resorts, among them Pozzuoli, Portici, Torre Annunziata, Castellammare di Stabia, and Sorrento. The resort islands of Capri, Ischia, and Procida stand at the entrance to the bay.

NAPLES, nā'pəlz, **Kingdom of,** was a former state in Italy, in the southern part of the peninsula, south of the Papal States. Although it existed at times as a separate entity, it was long united with Sicily to form the kingdom of the Two Sicilies, of which the city of Naples was the capital. (See SICILIES, KINGDOM OF THE TWO.)

After the 12th century, southern Italy was part of the Kingdom of Sicily founded by the Normans. When Charles I of Anjou (q.v.), who was invested with the crown in 1266, lost Sicily following the Sicilian Vespers (1282), the mainland territories left under his rule became known as the kingdom of Naples. The Angevin claim to Sicily, now ruled by the Aragonese, caused a series of wars, until Queen Joanna I of Naples gave up her claims in 1372. Long and bloody dynastic struggles within the kingdom of Naples among the Houses of Anjou, Durazzo, and later Aragon, ended only in 1443, when Alphonso V of Aragon won the throne of Naples by defeating René I of Anjou (q.v.). However, the Angevin claim, which had passed to the

French crown, led Charles VIII and Louis XII of France to invade Naples; the last Aragonese king was deposed in 1501. After the defeat of Louis, the Treaty of Blois assigned both Naples and Sicily to Spain, which ruled jointly the two kingdoms through viceroys from 1504 until 1707. This was a period of decay: Spanish officials exploited the countries, the creation of large estates depressed agriculture, no commercial nor cultural progress was made. Poverty, ignorance, and superstition reigned supreme. A popular revolt in Naples (1647) led by Masaniello (q.v.) was violently suppressed. During the War of the Spanish Succession the kingdom was conquered by Austria, but Charles of Bourbon (later Charles III of Spain, q.v.) succeeded in recapturing both Naples and Sicily in 1734. The direct rule by the cadet line of the Spanish branch of the Bourbons did not improve the situation. Some reforms were occasionally made, only to be revoked as soon as conditions permitted. In 1799 the liberal revolution in Naples, supported by French arms, resulted in the creation of the short-lived Parthenopean Republic (q.v.). Finally in 1805 King Ferdinand IV was forced by the French to flee to Sicily, which remained under his rule throughout the Napoleonic period. Napoleon placed on the throne of Naples first his brother Joseph, then his brother-in-law Joachim Murat (q.v.). After the fall of Napoleon, Ferdinand, who had hitherto borne the titles of Ferdinand IV of Naples and Ferdinand II of Sicily, returned to Naples and formally merged the two kingdoms (1816), styling himself Ferdinand I of the Two Sicilies.

NAPLES YELLOW (ANTIMONY YELLOW or NEAPOLITAN YELLOW) is a very poisonous lead antimonate pigment, varying in color from orange-yellow to sulphur-yellow. Although seldom used in paints, it has been applied in ceramics since ancient times. Because various substitute mixtures such as Venetian red with zinc white and cadmium yellow are called by the same name, it has come to identify a general shade of yellow rather than a specific pigment or chemical compound.

NAPO, nä'pō, river, Ecuador, an affluent of the Amazon, which rises on the north side of Cotopaxi, and after a southeasterly course, forming for a considerable distance the boundary between Colombia and Ecuador, joins the Amazon just beyond the eastern boundary of Peru. It is navigable for nearly 500 miles for steamers; it flows through a region rich in mineral and vegetable wealth.

NAPOLEON I, nȧ-pō-lē'ŭn (full French name NAPOLÉON BONAPARTE; Ital. NAPOLEONE BUONAPARTE; called LE PETIT CAPORAL and THE CORSICAN), emperor of the French: b. Ajaccio, Corsica, Aug. 15, 1769; d. Longwood, St. Helena, May 5, 1821. His father, Carlo Maria Buonaparte, a lawyer, claimed nobility, and his claim was accepted by the French authorities, although the grand dukes of Tuscany had never recognized the pretentions of the Corsican Buonapartes to kinship with the noble Florentine family of the same name. Carlo, in 1764, at 18, had married Maria Letizia Ramolino. Eight of their 13 children survived, and were destined to live illustrious lives: JOSEPH (1768–1844), the future king of Naples; NAPOLEON (1769–1821, the emperor; this first name had been adopted from an old Corsican family, the Bozzis, with whom the Buonapartes were allied; their first child, b. and d. 1765, had already been named Napoleon); LUCIEN (1775–1840); MARIE ANNA ELISA (1777–1820); LOUIS (1778–1846, king of Holland, the father of Charles-Louis-Napoleon who was to reign as Napoleon III); MARIA PAULINA (originally CARLOTTA, 1780–1825, married first to Gen. Emmanuel Leclerc, later to Prince Camillo Borghese); MARIA ANNUNCIATA, later CAROLINA (1782–1839, married Joachim Murat, king of Naples); and JÉRÔME (1784–1860, king of Westphalia). The father died in 1785, and thenceforth Napoleon, the strongest-willed of them all, was head of the family. During all his life he showed a kind of clannish loyalty which made him shower honors and riches on all members of the tribe, and extend his generosities to the protectors of his youth. For parentage and family relationships see BONAPARTE articles.

Corsica had been acquired by the French from Genoa in 1768, and secured just before the birth of Napoleon, after the defeat at Ponte Novo of the forces of resistance led by Pasquale di Paoli, who fled to England. Carlo Buonaparte had first fought the French, but he quickly rallied to their side and befriended the governor, Gen. L. C. R. de Marbeuf; in January 1779, he went to France with his two older sons, placed them in the college at Autun, in east central France, and secured a king's scholarship for Napoleon at the Military Academy at Brienne, 25 miles from Troyes. The boy was not yet ten when he entered this school (March 23, 1779), where he was to stay until October 1784. His school years were neither particularly happy nor brilliant; he seems to have made few real friends, except for L. A. F. de Bourrienne (q.v.) and to have felt like a stranger among the French boys. He had a very perceptible Italian accent, yearned for the liberation of Corsica, and still looked up to Paoli as his hero. His marks were not outstanding except in mathematics, and at the final examination, he placed 42d out of 58. Upon being graduated as a second lieutenant in September 1785, he was assigned to an artillery regiment, and was stationed in turn at Valence, Lyon, Douai, Auxonne, and again at Valence (1791) as a first lieutenant. Having no liking for garrison life in provincial towns, he obtained numerous lengthy leaves which he spent in Ajaccio and Paris. During the period 1785–1793 he managed to spend 59 months on more or less regular furloughs.

As a son of the Enlightenment Napoleon had welcomed the dawn of the revolution, from July 1789 on, and after Corsica had been incorporated into France in November, and Paoli allowed to return, he took advantage of the opportunity to play a role in the politics of his native island. He was elected lieutenant colonel in the Corsican national guard. A rift had developed between Paoli and Count Carlo Andrea Pozzo di Borgo on one side and the Buonaparte clan on the other, and Napoleon used such violent methods against the faction of Pozzo di Borgo in the spring of 1792 that he had to go back to Paris to justify himself. He was reinstated in the regular army as a captain in July. In Paris, he witnessed the bloody events of June 20 and August 10, which gave him a healthy scorn for mob violence as well as for the vacillations of Louis XVI. In January 1793, he took part in the abortive invasion of the Sardinian island of Maddalena. When England entered the war against France, Paoli, whose pro-English sympathies were well known, was denounced as an English agent, and his arrest was ordered by the Convention. The break between Paoli and the French became open, and the Buonaparte family had to flee the island and take refuge in Marseille. Corsica was taken over by the British Navy, which was to keep it until the fall of 1796. Thus was Napoleon finally compelled to renounce his Corsican dreams and to turn to France for his destiny.

During his garrison years, he had equipped himself with a considerable amount of knowledge, reading voraciously anything at hand and taking abundant notes, on Voltaire, Rousseau, the writers of the Enlightenment, a host of history books, and especially manuals on tactics, like the *Essai de tactique générale* (1772) of Count J. A. H. de Guibert, which brought to his attention the need for speedy offensive, for a lightening of striking columns, for a concentration of forces: all the principles he would later apply in such masterly fashion. He even published in July 1793 a short political pamphlet in dialogue form, the *Souper de Beaucaire,* in which the weaknesses of the federalist movement of the Girondins are analyzed; it constitutes an unequivocal profession of the tenets of the centralist Parisian group called the Mountain. At the end of August, Toulon and the French Fleet were delivered to the British by rebellious federalist and royalist groups. The Army of Italy was entrusted with the task of recapturing the harbor, and here we find the first real opportunity for Napoleon. Thanks to his Corsican friend, A. C. Saliceti, he was placed in command of the artillery of the besieging forces and given a free hand to put into effect his plan of concentrating the attack on the fort of Eguillette, which dominated the roadstead. After violent action, in which Napoleon was twice wounded, the fort fell on Dec. 17, 1793, and the British retired, leaving a good part of the French Fleet and the port installations intact. Two months later, Napoleon Buonaparte was promoted to brigadier general.

The upheaval of 9 Thermidor (July 27, 1794) threatened to put a stop to his progress; he had come to be identified with the Robespierre faction, and was arrested and detained some time at Antibes. But at the beginning of 1795, he was entrusted with the preparation of a new expedition against Corsica which, however, came to naught. Then he received an order to rejoin the Army of the West, to campaign against the insurgent Vendéens. This he refused to do and was struck off the list of active officers.

Marriage and the Italian Campaigns.—The crisis of Vendemiaire (October 1795) offered him his second decisive opportunity. The Convention was confronted by an incipient insurrection of monarchist forces gathered around the St. Roch Church. One of its members, Vicomte Paul François Jean Nicolas de Barras, remembering Napoleon at the siege of Toulon, called upon him to save the Convention, which he did by having Joachim Murat bring in artillery from the Camp des Sablons, thus checkmating the insurgents. His stature having grown considerably, he was a few months later named by the succeeding government, the Directory, to the command of the Army of Italy (March 2, 1796). This promotion was perfectly proper since he had been connected before with this army and had drafted strategic plans for it, but it was helped by his new friendship with Barras and the elegant circles he was now frequenting. He had fallen violently in love with one of the queens of fashion of the time, Joséphine de Beauharnais, whose husband, an erstwhile commander of the Army of the Rhine, had been guillotined in 1793, and whose languid charm (she was born in Martinique) fascinated him. Despite the difference in age—she was 33, he 27—despite the fact that she had two children, Eugène and Hortense, and had no financial resources, they regularized their situation and were married on March 9, 1796. All through the years, in spite of her infidelities, of the barrenness of their union, even of his repudiation of her in 1810, he always kept for her a deep and warm feeling, tinged with passionate romanticism. Her death in May 1814 caused him genuine sorrow.

At the time of his marriage Napoleon changed his name from Buonaparte to Bonaparte. He arrived at his headquarters in Nice on March 27, 1796, and soon afterwards initiated the series of Italian campaigns which were to last 20 months, until November 1797, and which were destined to reveal his military genius and provide an unequalled classic to students of strategy. He had under his command an army of 38,000 fairly good troops and he was opposed by Gen. J. P. de Beaulieu with 30,000 Austrians, and Gen. Michele Colli with about 25,000 Piedmontese. In a few days, Bonaparte defeated Beaulieu at Montenotte, west of Genoa, Colli at Mondovì, and signed with the latter an armistice at Cherasco (April 28, 1796). Pursuing Beaulieu, he crossed the Adda at Lodi, after a brilliant action—about which he would write at St. Helena, "It made me conceive the ambition of performing great things"—and entered Milan on May 14. Beaulieu had retreated towards the Mincio and Mantua. Bonaparte beat him again and laid siege to Mantua.

Italy, however, was only a secondary theater of war, the main one being on the Rhine, where Gen. J. V. Moreau had about 200,000 troops facing a similar force of Austrians. But the enemy, with interior lines of communications, was freer to shift troops from one theater to the other, which he did, thanks to Moreau's inaction, at the end of July. Count D. S. von Wurmser, succeeding Beaulieu, descended into Italy on both banks of Lake Garda, with 45,000 men in three columns. Abandoning the siege of Mantua, Napoleon established himself south of Lake Garda, and struck successively at Wurmser's columns at Lonato (July 31) and Castiglione (August 5). While Wurmser was re-establishing himself on the Brenta, Napoleon advanced up the Adige to take Trent, then came down on Wurmser's rear, forcing him to retreat to Mantua, where he was surrounded. A new Austrian commander, Josef Alvinczy, descended into Italy through the Brenner Pass with 50,000 men. Napoleon, having established himself at Verona, advanced 15 miles to Arcole to meet him; three days of hard fighting ensued (November 15–17) in the course of which Napoleon personally led an assault on the bridge across the Alpone River, administering a severe defeat on the new Austrian commander.

At that time, the Directory decided to make Italy a more important theater of war at the beginning of 1797 and to send Napoleon 40,000 reinforcements; but they did not arrive until

March, after the main battles had been fought. Alvinczy, having been ordered to try once again to relieve Mantua, advanced from Roveredo in three columns. Napoleon smashed the main one at Rivoli (Jan. 14, 1797), then hastened back to Mantua to block a relief column coming from Padua. On February 2, Wurmser was forced by famine to surrender Mantua, and on the same day Napoleon ended his armistice with the pope and occupied the Papal States. Final victory was now in sight. Napoleon had about 80,000 men with whom he pushed via the Trieste route into the Tirol, pursuing the Archduke Charles to Klagenfurt, then to Leoben, where, on April 18, he signed peace preliminaries.

The personal policy of Bonaparte was now everywhere in evidence: his excessive requisitions; the occupation of Venice; the organization of the Cispadane Republic (q.v.) in 1796, merged a year later into the Cisalpine Republic (q.v.); his direct negotiations with the pope—everything shows the civilian power of the Directory consistently neglected, and compelled to follow the initiatives of the victorious general. The Treaty of Campoformio (Oct. 17, 1797) gave to France Belgium, the Ionian Islands, the promise of the left bank of the Rhine, and recognized the Cisalpine Republic, while Austria received Venice, with her territories up to the Adige.

Egypt.—In December 1797, Napoleon, back in Paris, was acclaimed a triumphant hero. But England had not disarmed, and the Directory proposed an expedition across the English Channel, naming Bonaparte commander of the Army of England. An inspection of the Channel bases, however, convinced him of the impracticability of the project. Another idea already had taken root in his mind, and was being nurtured by Talleyrand: strike at England by cutting her Mediterranean commercial route to India. That meant an expedition to Egypt. Rapidly organized (March–May 1798) in the harbors of Toulon, Genoa, and Civitavecchia, and on Corsica, the expedition comprised 280 transports, protected by more than 55 war vessels, and carrying 38,000 troops, 1,200 horses, and 171 guns. Moreover, it was to transport a mission of almost 200 scientists including archaeologists. A contribution of 3 million francs levied upon Switzerland had helped finance the enterprise. The fleet sailed on May 19, concentrated off Sardinia, then took over Malta with little difficulty. The British were still uncertain of its destination, but Horatio Nelson sailed towards Alexandria, where he arrived two days before the French, then returned to Sicily.

The French expedition disembarked at Adjmir on July 1 and occupied Alexandria the next day. Then the advance began to Cairo, across a desert and up the Nile's left bank. Napoleon expected a popular uprising against the feudal Mamelukes, but this failed to materialize. After a preliminary clash with the Mameluke cavalry on July 13, he defeated them on July 21, near the Pyramids, forming his infantry in squares to repel their charges. Entering Cairo, he established his headquarters there and attempted to gain the good will of the Egyptians. However, on August 1, Nelson surprised the French Fleet at Aboukir and annihilated it, except for two ships.

Thus marooned in Egypt, Napoleon spent the rest of the year establishing his domination over the country, trying vainly to discover ways of pushing on to India, and participating in the work of the scientific mission, which in particular was preparing the first draft of what was to become the Suez Canal. At the beginning of 1799 he had to forestall an attack on Egypt by invading Syria and taking Jaffa, infested by the plague (March 6). But he failed before Acre (May 20), defended by Commodore William Sidney Smith and Colonel A. Le Ricard de Philippeaux, an émigré whom he had known at Brienne. Back in Egypt, he annihilated a Turkish force which had landed at Aboukir (July 25). The Directory had tried to re-establish communications with Egypt by sending Admiral E. E. Bruix into the Mediterranean, but to no avail. It also had authorized Bonaparte to return; these instructions never reached him, but he had decided on his own to sail back, upon learning disquieting political and military news from France. He left secretly August 24, managed to escape, with great luck, the British blockade and landed at Fréjus October 9.

The Consulate.—He was acclaimed by the populace. The Second Coalition had inflicted severe reverses upon France and Italy had been lost. Gen. André Masséna, it is true, by his victory at Zürich had begun to re-establish the situation; but internally, the Directory could only govern by alternate illegal blows on the right and on the left. Inflation was rampant, the capitalist bourgeoisie was fearful, the troops extremely dissatisfied, and many people were thinking of a change in the constitution and looking around for a savior. Bonaparte allied himself with one of the five directors, Abbé Sieyès, and a coup d'état was engineered: on November 9 (18 Brumaire) the transfer of the two assemblies, the Ancients and the Five Hundred, to a Paris suburb, St. Cloud, was voted, and Napoleon received command of the Paris garrison. The next day, after a great deal of floundering, and when he had been saved from possible physical violence and outlawing only by the presence of mind of his brother Lucien, who was president of the Five Hundred, Napoleon finally sent in Murat's grenadiers to expel the deputies. During the evening the Ancients named three provisional consuls—Sieyès, (Pierre) Roger Ducos, and Napoleon.

Sieyès had expected to be able to keep Napoleon in secondary position; but it soon became apparent who would be the master. The admirably coordinated physical and mental abilities of Napoleon proclaimed his superiority. He was endowed with an amazing capacity for work, an astonishing speed of judgment, and an extraordinary power of assimilation, capped by untiring imagination. He possessed, moreover, a great deal of charm, and a natural authority based on a wide gamut of attitudes, from calculated simplicity to a skillful use of violence. Having climbed almost to the top, he was playing a sharp and prudent game to reach the pinnacle of power.

Now he came near to assuming the garb of an intellectual, and expressed the sentiments of a middle-of-the-roader. He proclaimed his desire for internal security and social order, and for the peace which he knew France craved. While thus cultivating popularity, he carried on discussions on the draft of a new constitution, which was to be a compromise between the ideas of Sieyès and his own authoritarian tendencies. The provision of a list of notabilities from which eligible candidates must be chosen effectively smothered democratic suffrage. The legislative power was broken down into four assemblies: the Tribunate, the Legislative Body, the Council of State, and the Senate. The executive was in the hands of three Consuls, of whom the First Consul had the widest executive powers, together with the power of initiating laws. Sieyès, on the invitation of Napoleon, designated as Consuls the minister of justice, J. J. R. de Cambacérès and Charles François Lebrun, Napoleon himself to be First Consul. A plebiscite ratified the constitution by 3,011,007 ayes against 1,562 noes (February 1800).

Now in the saddle, Napoleon began to consolidate his power and to pursue the two policies which were expected of him: peace and the establishment of internal order. Taking command of the Army of Reserve, he crossed the Alps at the Grand St. Bernard (May 15, 1800) and entered Milan on June 2. In the Piedmont plain, his army unexpectedly met a much stronger Austrian force at Marengo on June 14. The French troops were retreating in disorder, when the arrival of Gen. L. C. A. Desaix de Veygoux and a strong charge by François Christophe Kellerman saved the day. The first couriers had brought to Paris reports of a defeat, which caused rejoicing among the First Consul's enemies. But news of the victory supervening silenced the opposition and, as a royalist agent said at the time, "Marengo was the christening of Napoleon's personal power." The peace with Austria was secured only after the success of Jean Victor Moreau at Hohenlinden December 3, and was signed at Lunéville (Feb. 9, 1801), giving France the left bank of the Rhine, extending the Cisalpine Republic to the Adige and generally confirming the clauses of the Treaty of Campoformio. As for England, faced by an economic crisis and by the dissolution of the Coalition, she signed a peace treaty at Amiens (March 25, 1802), keeping Ceylon and Trinidad, but giving up Egypt, Minorca, Elba, and Malta, the last of which was supposed to be evacuated inside of three months. That peace, however precarious, was the first general peace in Europe in a decade.

At the same time Napoleon was reorganizing France and giving her a body of institutions which were to last through the 19th century and to a certain extent still form the basis of her present structure: he maintained the administrative divisions created by the revolution (departments, etc.) but put at their head appointed functionaries (prefects, etc.) and generally emphasized centralization. He reorganized justice and took an active part, although more modest than has been believed, in framing the Civil Code (see CODE—*Code Napoléon*), which reaffirms the judicial conquests of the revolution: personal liberty, freedom of conscience and of work, property rights, equality. Consecrating the ruin of legalized privilege, the code was to serve as a model for many European and American states during the 19th century. It is the main basis for Napoleon's claim that he was the heir and savior of the revolution.

Napoleon also made important reforms in government financing. The assessment and collection of taxes were thenceforth reserved to functionaries of the central power, and collectors were required to make a deposit in advance of their collections. He established the Bank of France and fixed the relation of 15.5 between gold and silver and the value of the gram of gold at 3 francs 10 centimes; that standard was to last until 1926. He was much interested in education, as a way of controlling the minds of men, and as a means of training military officers and civil servants. After several years of discussion he created the Université de France, really a ministry of education to license teachers, set the program of studies and control the examinations. This centralized and near-monopolistic conception of education has prevailed in France to the present time. In this work of reorganization, he lacked the omniscience which has sometimes been attributed to him, but he had the good sense to make use of the best experts, regardless of their political inclinations and of their past. Napoleon may be said to have consolidated the conquests made during the revolution by the bourgeoisie, and to have solidified the French civil service, for better or for worse, into the form it still retains.

Despite the victory of Marengo, opposition to the First Consul was not immediately disarmed. The royalists were agitating in Vendée and, in Paris, Georges Cadoudal exploded an infernal machine which killed 22 people but missed Bonaparte. He retaliated against both the right and the left, transporting republicans to Guiana, and executing some monarchists. To undermine the royalist party, he decided on a rapprochement with the church: this was attained by the Concordat (July 15, 1801), which recognized Catholicism as the religion of the majority of Frenchmen. The First Consul would nominate the bishops, the pope give them the spiritual investiture; the clergy would be paid by the government. The *Organic Articles,* a law regulating public worship comprising 77 articles relating to Catholicism and 44 to Protestantism, were combined with the Concordat and both ratified on April 8, 1802. Not accepted by the pope, the *Organic Articles* made the church more subservient to state authority. The Concordat and *Organic Articles* were to govern the relations of church and state in France for more than a century until their abrogation in 1905 by the law of separation. The other cults, Protestant and Jewish, were similarly reorganized. Some opposition to these clerical measures continuing in the Tribunate, he broke it by skillful manipulation of the procedure for renewal of members. He also had his police disperse the opposition which gathered in Mme. de Staël's salon and kept her in semiexile 60 miles from Paris. His aim to achieve absolute power was now unmistakable. On Aug. 4, 1802, a new constitution made him Consul for life, and subordinated the Assemblies to him.

Emperor.—The final break with the royalists came after another plot by Cadoudal was discovered, and its organizer shot. On the night of March 15, 1804, Napoleon had his troops kidnap the duke of Enghien (Louis Antoine Henri de Bourbon-Condé) at Ettenheim, Baden, and had him shot summarily at Vincennes; thus he proclaimed himself an accomplice of the regicides of 1792. After further manipulation of public opinion, the question arose of giving Bonaparte supreme powers. On May 18, 1804, the Senate declared that "it was of the highest interest of the French people to entrust the government of the Republic to an hereditary Emperor," and established the order of succession by male primogeniture. A plebiscite accepted the proposal by 3,572,-329 ayes against 2,579 noes.

The pope was induced to come to Paris and preside at coronation ceremonies held in the Cathedral of Notre Dame on Dec. 2, 1804. Napoleon, however, made a point of crowning himself to avoid any quarrel over investiture; he also crowned Josephine. Catholic France was now obliged to acquiesce in Bonaparte's elevation. To give the new dynasty a prestige comparable to the monarchy's a court was organized; some émigrés were induced to return, while a new nobility was created, based on military exploits or civilian services, which has survived to this day. This new imperial court never attained the elegant nonchalance of the *ancien régime;* it was too military, sometimes vulgar, and could never shake off the memories of its origins. But it helped establish the imperial domination, which asserted itself also through a servile press, a subservient literature, an efficient police, a regimented university system, and even a controlled church. The institution of the Legion of Honor (1802), with its ranks (*grand officier, commandeur, officier, chevalier*), and the selection of its members reserved to Napoleon, was another means of gaining the loyalty of a new hierarchy of talents. The master supervised everything, from the building of strategic highways in the Alps, to the Sèvres manufacture of porcelain. In 1812, in Moscow, just before the retreat, he gave the Comédie-Française a statute which is still in force in its general lines. Napoleon's authority, much tighter than the Bourbons', smacked of enlightened despotism; it foreshadowed modern totalitarianism.

The Peace of Amiens (March 25, 1802) was short-lived. English businessmen were disappointed by French tariff restrictions which hampered trade. France, with her purchase of Louisiana from Spain (1800) and the San Domingo expedition of 1802, seemed bent on acquiring another colonial empire. Moreover, early in 1802 Bonaparte intervened in Switzerland to have the Valais canton constituted an independent republic (later annexed to France); and in August of the same year he annexed Elba, then Piedmont in September, and Parma in October. By the Act of Mediation (Feb. 19, 1803) he restored the Swiss confederation, re-establishing the cantonal system. In the same month he suppressed free cities and ecclesiastical principalities in Germany. England seized upon these aggressions as a reason for declining to evacuate Malta. It is idle to speculate on the responsibilities for the renewal of the war. The fact is that French continental dynamism and English ambition for sea domination simply could not coexist peacefully. On April 26, 1803, an English ultimatum left no alternative but war. Early in May, France sold Louisiana to the United States, Napoleon realizing that the vast province, so difficult to defend, would be a liability, and American gold an asset in the coming conflict.

The war started slowly, for lack of a convenient theater. Napoleon had already begun before 1802 to assemble a barge flotilla as a threat to invade England. It was considerably enlarged in 1803 and 1804 and the decision for an invasion was finally made in the latter year. An expeditionary force was concentrated at Boulogne and a plan was devised to obtain French control of the English Channel for a period long enough to ensure the safe convoy of the troops. Vice Admiral P. C. J. B. S. de Villeneuve was ordered to sail for the West Indies, in order to attract Nelson's English Fleet there, and then to return in haste to cover the Channel crossing. The plan started well enough, Villeneuve sailing from Toulon on Jan. 18, 1805. He succeeded in luring the English Fleet to the Antilles, but due to a combination of bad luck, poor orders and incompetence, he found himself on the return voyage blockaded in Cádiz by Nelson's superior fleet. The invasion was doomed and Napoleon abandoned it on August 24. Upon orders to sail for Naples, Villeneuve sallied forth and was caught off Trafalgar by Nelson, who attacked his line of 33 ships with two columns, ruptured it and annihilated the center and rear guard (Oct. 21, 1805). Though Nelson was killed at Trafalgar, thenceforth command of the sea was assured to England and Napoleon was forced to limit his ambitions to continental conquests.

A new coalition, the third, had already been formed (Aug. 9, 1805), between England, Russia, and Austria, which had been affronted by the transformation of the Republic of Italy into an hereditary kingdom, with Napoleon as king, and his stepson Eugène as viceroy. Napoleon shifted his army from Boulogne to the Rhine, the Main and the Danube, there to surround the forces of the Austrian general, Karl Mack von Leiberich at Ulm (October 18), to take Linz and Vienna and, shifting north, to meet the Russians and Austrians at Austerlitz (December 2). Although outnumbered, 65,000 to 82,500, Napoleon succeeded by a feint on his right in throwing the enemy center out of balance, then breaking through, he put the allied troops to flight across frozen marshes, where French artillery decimated them. The French suffered 6,800 casualties and inflicted 27,200 (including 12,200 killed and wounded and 15,000 prisoners). Austerlitz is surely the most brilliant and most decisive of Napoleon's victories. It has become the mainstay of his military glory. Austria, by the Treaty of Pressburg (Bratislava, Dec. 26, 1805), gave up Venetia and recognized Bavaria, Württemberg, and Baden as independent kingdoms, thus excluding herself from southern Germany.

Prussia had stayed out of the third coalition. But during the summer of 1806, she became annoyed and worried by the double-dealing diplomatic maneuvers about Hannover and by the formation of the Confederation of the Rhine (July 12), which excluded her from western and southern Germany. A Prussian ultimatum demanded that the French withdraw behind the Rhine (Oct. 1, 1806). Upon its rejection, the fourth coalition was organized, grouping England, Russia, and Prussia. The Prussians had an army of 130,000 men, steeped in the tradition of Frederick the Great, and enjoying a high military reputation, but cumbersome, slow-moving, and unable to cope with the newer, lightning-like strategy of the emperor. Napoleon had concentrated his army, roughly equal to the Prussian force, along the Main Valley. Each army tried to cut the other's communications on the left, but the slower Prussians were forced to retreat and Napoleon with 95,000 troops met the corps of Gen. Friedrich Ludwig Hohenlohe, 40,000 strong, at Jena, while Louis Nicolas Davout, with 26,000 men, contained and finally routed the main Prussian corps at Auerstedt (Oct. 14, 1806). Twelve days later Napoleon was in Berlin, having shattered the myth of Prussian invincibility, and determined to punish Prussia through heavy contributions and requisitions. To strike at the Russians, he pushed east, met them in hard and indecisive clashes, the most celebrated of which was the bloody battle at Eylau (Feb. 8, 1807), and in the spring won a decisive victory at Friedland (June 13), which led to the Treaty of Tilsit (July 7) and to a kind of reversal of alliances. Czar Alexander I, irritated by British delays in sending forces to the Continent, and seduced by the blandishments of Napoleon, whom he met on a raft on the Niemen (Neman) and who unfolded before his eyes a project of co-domination of the Continent, not only renounced the British alliance, but promised to take an active part in the Continental System. This moment may be considered the apogee of Napoleon's power.

The Continental System had been devised to stifle British economy, based on credit and exports, and by the decrees of Berlin (Nov. 21, 1806), Fontainebleau (Oct. 13, 1807), and Milan, it prohibited the importation of British goods. There was no thought that it would starve Britain into submission (at that time she imported less than 20 per cent of her wheat); but it did create a serious economic crisis in England, despite the fact that it soon became inefficient through a huge amount of contraband and a system of licenses by which Napoleon authorized trade with England for a fee. The system helped France develop her industries and some agricultural products, like sugar beets, but created in Europe an enormous amount of ill-will against French economic imperialism.

The empire extended from Hamburg to Rome, comprised 130 departments and was surrounded by kingdoms given to members of Napoleon's family: Naples to Joseph, later king of Spain; Holland to Louis; Westphalia to Jérôme; Cleves (Cleve) to Murat, Caroline's husband, and so on. In 1810, 7 kingdoms and 30 principalities were vassals of France. Even Sweden called upon a French marshal, Jean Baptiste Jules Bernadotte, to be heir to her childless king. Only Russia kept her independence. And everywhere the Civil Code, religious tolerance, and the revolutionary principles in Napoleonic garb followed French arms.

But Portugal, for a century under British influence, was a big loophole in the Continental System. In agreement with Manuel de Godoy, the corrupt favorite of the queen and the real ruler of Spain, Napoleon sent an expedition to subdue Portugal and left enough troops in Spain to dominate the country. But an insurrection in Madrid compelled the French to a ferocious repression. Guerrillas then attacked the French armies and inflicted on them their first resounding defeat in the capitulation of Gen. Pierre A. Dupont de l'Etang at Baílen (July 23, 1808). Napoleon tried to secure his rear by a spectacular but inconclusive meeting with Czar Alexander at Erfurt (September-October). He then invaded Spain, entered Madrid, took revolutionary measures in favor of the peasantry, in order to break the power of the clergy, but to no avail; and the holy war continued against the French, pushing them back slowly with the help of the duke of Wellington, whom Masséna had been unable to dislodge from his lines at Torres Vedras.

Napoleon still dreamed of universal monarchy on the Roman pattern while nationalisms were awakening everywhere, particularly in Germany, Italy, and Austria. In 1809, Austria again challenged Napoleon, who succeeded in entering Vienna, was held in check at Essling (May 22), but won at Wagram (July 5), and imposed the treaty of Schönbrunn (October 14) which gave him the Illyrian provinces. But the French forces were showing signs of strain, and Napoleon noted a new spirit of resistance in Austria. He wanted now to establish a legitimate dynasty, and since Josephine could not give him an heir, he decided to divorce her. He could not marry his great love, the Polish Countess Marie Walewska, who, however, would bear him a son (May 4, 1810). He requested the hand of the 18-year-old Archduchess Marie-Louise of Austria and married her by proxy on March 11, and formally on April 2, 1810. The desired legitimate son, named even before his birth king of Rome, was born March 20, 1811.

Invasion of Russia, and the Abdication.— The Napoleonic regime seemed for the moment more secure than ever. But Russia had abandoned the Continental System which was making the czar unpopular, and was almost openly preparing for war. In France, military classes were being mobilized in anticipation, a severe economic crisis was creating unemployment, taxes were growing heavier, and definite signs of lassitude and disaffection were appearing. The break with Russia came in June 1812. The czar had contrived to sign an alliance with Bernadotte of Sweden and a peace treaty with the Turks, while Napoleon was heavily engaged in Spain. Even so, Napoleon had a 3 to 1 numerical superiority against the Russians when he crossed the Niemen (Neman) on June 22. But his strategy, suited to the narrow confines of the northern Italian plains, was ineffective in the vast open spaces of Russia; his supply system, always poor, since his troops lived on the country during his short, sharp campaigns, collapsed when the Russians applied the scorched earth policy; the medical system, never too brilliant, disintegrated. Napoleon pursued the retreating Russians with a speed unequalled even in our day: Vilna, June 26; Vitebsk, July 24; Smolensk, August 16. At Borodino the Russians made a stand and a bloody battle ensued (September 7). Napoleon entered Moscow on September 14. But the city was on fire the next day, and since the czar refused to negotiate, and lack of supplies made it unfeasible to spend the winter in the city, there seemed no choice but to lead the victorious army home. The retreat began October 19. Starvation, defections, harassment by the Cossacks, the early and bitter cold, the fighting (crossing of the Berezina, Nov. 26-28), ravaged the Grand Army. When it reached the Niemen (December 14), it comprised only about 30,000 survivors; more than 500,000 men had disappeared in Russia.

It was clearly the beginning of the end, and Europe sensed it. Napoleon had left the army on December 5, leaving Murat in command, and hurried back to France, concerned over a plot of Gen. Claude François de Malet against his regime. Arriving in Paris on the 18th, he succeeded in raising another army; but officers were lacking, the generals suffered from war fatigue, and he was now overextended, with commitments from Spain to Poland and a great number of fortresses to garrison. In spite of victories at Lützen (May 2, 1813), and at Bautzen (May 21), peace negotiations came to naught, and after his setback in the Battle of Leipzig (October 16-19), Napoleon had to retreat behind the Rhine. The Allies pressed their advantage in the early months of 1814 and France was invaded. Napoleon showed his old tactical genius in that campaign, by beating one after the other the Allied columns converging upon Paris (Montmirail, Champaubert, Feb. 10-11, 1814). But the jig was up for the balance of numbers was now irretrievably on the side of the Allies. On March 22 the English government announced that it would never treat with Napoleon, and eight days later the Allies entered Paris. On April 6 Napoleon agreed to an unconditional abdication. We know now with certainty (since the publication of Armand A. de Caulaincourt's *Mémoirs* in 1933) that he unsuccessfully attempted suicide by poison during the night of April 12. On the 20th, he bade farewell to his troops in the courtyard of Fontainebleau.

Elba, the Hundred Days and Waterloo.—The Allies had granted him sovereignty over the island of Elba. On the trip south he encountered hostile manifestations around Avignon, and had to disguise himself in an Austrian uniform. At Elba, he showed his old activity, reforming and reorganizing the island, but only his mother, his sister Paulina Borghese, and Marie Walewska with their son came to see him. Marie-Louise refused to come (he had seen her and their son for the last time on Jan. 24, 1814). Knowing that France was restive and dissatisfied, he escaped from Elba and on March 1, 1815, landed in France near Antibes, to begin that brief adventure known as the Hundred Days. His trip to Paris, by way of the Alpine road and Grenoble, was an incredible, exhilarating, romantic triumph. The government of Louis XVIII fled. Napoleon tried to assume the posture of the liberal heir of the revolution and of the peaceful sovereign. But Europe would not relent, nor forget her ten years of fear. War was necessary again. Napoleon invaded Belgium with the hope of defeating the Anglo-Prussian armies. When, after a few days of secondary skirmishes, he came in contact with Wellington at Mont-Saint-Jean, near Waterloo, he was unable to break the English lines and after the arrival of Prussian reinforcements, the French troops broke and could not be reorganized before Laon (June 18).

Defeated, Napoleon hurried back to Paris. Unable to gain support for further resistance, he abdicated in favor of his son. But this proposal was ignored and on July 8, Louis XVIII reentered Paris. Napoleon now decided to place himself under the protection of his greatest enemies. He boarded the British warship *Bellerophon.* "I come, like Themistocles, to claim a seat by the hearth of the British people," he wrote the prince regent. It was decided that he should be sent to St. Helena and held there a prisoner for the rest of his life. He was transferred to the *Northumberland* with his small retinue for the three months' voyage. Upon his arrival, he was at first lodged with an English family, and the episode of his good-natured friendship with their 13-year-old daughter, Betsy Balcombe, casts light on the human side of his nature. Transferred to the estate of Longwood, under the petty surveillance of Sir Hudson Lowe, he spent the time reminiscing for the benefit of his followers (Comte Henry Gratien Bertrand; Comte Charles Tristan de Montholon; Baron Gaspard Gourgaud; Comte Emmanuel A. D. de Las Cases; his valet Marchand), writing his *Mémoirs,* and in general building up the Napoleonic legend. From the end of 1819 on, he suffered from a stomach disease, now diagnosed as a gastric ulcer, from which he died May 5, 1821.

The prodigious adventures of Napoleon, giving a preview of the rise and fall of the modern dictators, created a legend which presented him as the champion of liberalism and nationalism, and as an architect of the United States of Europe. Surrounded by an enormous aura of military glory, it was to become for the next generations a deep nostalgia which found its first expression when Napoleon's body was brought back triumphantly in 1840 and which explains the astounding success of the plebiscite of his nephew, Napoleon III, in 1851.

JEAN BOORSCH, *Yale University.*

Bibliography.—*Mémoires pour servir à l'histoire de France sous Napoléon* (Paris 1823); *Correspondence of Napoleon* (Paris 1858–69); Masson, Frédéric, *Napoléon et sa famille,* 13 vols. (Paris 1897–1919); Driault, Edouard, *Napoléon et l'Europe,* 5 vols. (Paris 1910–27); *Memoirs of Queen Hortense* (New York 1927); Driault, Edouard, *La vraie figure de Napoléon* (Paris 1928); Driault, Edouard, *La Vie fulgurante de Napoléon* (Paris 1930); Kircheisen, Friedrich Max, *Napoleon* (New York 1932); Caulaincourt, Armand Augustin Louis, Marquis de, *Mémoires* (Paris 1933); Lefebvre, Georges, *Napoléon* (Paris 1947); Marchand, Louis Joseph, *Mémoires* (Paris 1952); Thompson, James Matthew, *Napoleon Bonaparte, His Rise and Fall* (Oxford 1952); Savant, Jean, *Napoleon in His Time* (London 1958); Korngold, Ralph, *Last Years of Napoleon* (New York 1960); Markham, Felix M. H., *Napoleon* (New York 1964).

NAPOLEON II, son of Napoleon I. See REICHSTADT, DUKE OF.

NAPOLEON III (known as LOUIS NAPOLEON; full name CHARLES LOUIS NAPOLEON BONAPARTE), emperor of the French, nephew of Napoleon I; b. Paris, France, April 20, 1808; d. Chislehurst, England, Jan. 9, 1873. He was the third son of Louis Bonaparte, younger brother of Napoleon I, and Hortense de Beauharnais, daughter of Josephine, first wife of Napoleon I. After the final exile of Napoleon I to St. Helena (1815), Hortense took refuge at Constance, then Augsburg, and finally, in 1819, in Arenenberg Castle on Lake Constance in the Swiss canton of Thurgau. Separated from her husband, she had received custody of Louis Napoleon who, at the Augsburg Gymnasium, received an essentially German education. At 23, in 1831, he took part in an insurrection against the pope in Romagna, fell sick and was saved from the Austrians by his mother, who took him to Paris, to England, then back to Arenenberg Castle. The death of his older brother Napoleon Louis (1804–1831) in the Romagna insurrection, and of the duke of Reichstadt (q.v.), Napoleon I's only son, a year later, left him as the chief representative of the Napoleonic tradition and heir presumptive to the imperial crown. For five years he devoted himself to writing. The works of this period include *Rêveries Politiques, Considérations Politiques et Militaires sur la Suisse,* and an artillery manual. He was made an honorary Swiss citizen and an artillery captain in the Bern regiment. On Oct. 30, 1836, he attempted a *Putsch* at Strasbourg; it failed and he was arrested and deported. After briefly visiting the United States in 1837, he returned to Switzerland, which he left for England in 1838 to avoid a Franco-Swiss incident over his presence.

The return of the body of Napoleon I from St. Helena in 1840 caused an upsurge of the Napoleonic popularity. Louis Napoleon tried to use this popularity by fomenting another rising at Boulogne (August 5), which failed miserably. He was condemned to perpetual imprisonment and was detained for six years in the fortress of Ham in Picardy. There he read widely and wrote such books as *Fragments historiques,* and

L'extinction du paupérisme (1844). The latter reveals a socialistic utopian turn of mind; it advocates the resettlement of underprivileged families on parcels of land in order to make them self-sufficient. On May 25, 1846, he escaped by donning the clothes of a workman while the fortress was under repairs and fled to London. Three days after the outbreak of the Revolution of 1848 he returned to France, but he was requested to leave the country. On June 4 he was returned by four constituencies, but declined the election when still declared under the law exiling the Bonapartes. On September 17 he was elected in five departments and could not therefore be kept out; he took his place in the National Assembly on the 26th. During the discussions on the new constitution it was decided, upon the insistence of Alphonse M. L. de Lamartine, to have the president elected directly by the people (October 9). An amendment which would have barred Napoleon's candidacy was thought unnecessary after his lamentable, stammering defense at the tribune. But soon his propaganda was in full swing and his election came as a thunderbolt when he polled 5,400,000 votes, against 1,400,000 for Louis Eugène Cavaignac, 370,000 for the socialist, Alexandre Auguste Ledru-Rollin, and 17,000 for Lamartine——the provinces had asserted themselves and had followed the call of the Napoleonic legend.

Louis Napoleon always considered his amazing triumph as a direct, popular, democratic mandate to put an end to social unrest and parliamentarian prattling and to establish an authoritarian democracy. He took every opportunity to recall the "origins of his power." But the elections of May 13, 1849, returned a strong majority of conservative monarchists who soon opposed the president, and he became hopelessly entangled in the Roman question. The latter dated back to March 1849, when the Constituent Assembly voted to safeguard the liberal institutions established in Rome by the uprising of February 9th against attempts of the Austrians and Pope Pius IX to destroy them. But the objectives of the expedition, sent according to that vote under Gen. Nicolas Charles Victor Oudinot, were completely reversed when Oudinot's troops were fired upon by the Romans. After a month's siege the French Army captured Rome on July 3, suppressed the new-born republic, and restored the temporal power of Pius IX. Thus Napoleon was trapped for 21 years into supporting a government inimical to his own democratic ideals, and later into preventing the Italians from making Rome the capital of their kingdom. Pope Pius IX, the most conservative of pontiffs, refused to be reconciled with "progress, liberalism, and modern civilization," ideas he detested, but which were the ostensible mottoes of Louis Napoleon's regime.

Through fear of the left, he was forced to lean towards the conservative Catholics, and that uneasy alliance has cast a shadow of misunderstanding upon every act of the regime. A leftist insurrection on June 13, protesting the Roman imbroglio, was easily crushed. Special elections on March 10, 1850 having returned 21 out of 31 invalidated Red deputies, a new, undemocratic electoral law was passed. Napoleon made a triumphant tour of the country, proclaiming his intentions of "saving, through order, the great principles of the French Revolution." He requested that a constitutional provision forbidding a second term be repealed, and that the electoral law be abrogated; but both motions were rejected. Finally, on Dec. 2, 1851, a coup d'état dissolved the National Assembly, reestablished universal suffrage, and appealed to the people to support the president. There was little popular resistance, except on the 4th, when troops had to storm a few barricades. The plebiscite gave 7,400,000 ayes, 600,000 noes. The new constitution gave the chief executive a term of 10 years, authority over the ministers, and created two assemblies. The empire was restored by another plebiscite, 7,800,000 for, 250,000 against (Nov. 21, 1852). Napoleon assumed the name of Napoleon III since the king of Rome had been formally, even if ephemerally, recognized as Napoleon II. See REICHSTADT, DUKE OF.

The Second Empire.—Politically, the empire was to evolve, in the following 18 years, from an authoritarian to a liberal (1860), then to a parliamentary form (April 1870), while the opposition grew ever stronger. Economically, it was a period of expansion, fostered by the dynamism of the St. Simonians and the social interest of the emperor. Credit institutions were developed (Crédit Foncier, 1852; Mobilier, 1852; Industriel, 1859; Lyonnais, 1863; Société Générale, 1864). The railroad network was actively pushed (13,000 kilometers in the first 6 years). The capitalistic and industrial structure of France then assumed its modern form. Paris was transformed by Baron Georges Eugène Haussmann. Universal Expositions in 1855 and 1867 proclaimed the eminence of French industry and its progressive outlook. After ten years of work, a French company opened the Suez Canal on Nov. 17, 1869. Prosperity was generally high, unionism was getting its start; the rate of economic expansion of the Second Empire is possibly the fastest of French history.

Napoleon III on Jan. 30, 1853 married a Spanish beauty, Eugénie de Montijo, who gave him a son (March 16, 1856). The tone of the court was at the same time brilliant and family-like. The empress was pious, charitable, but in the later years of the empire, she exerted a dangerous influence on foreign policy. Externally, the empire was marked first by the Crimean War (March 18, 1854-March 30, 1856), in which France and England defeated Russia. Then came the Italian campaign (April 20-Nov. 11, 1859), by which Austria was compelled to cede Lombardy to Italy and France received Savoy and Nice. The expedition to Mexico began as a common Anglo-Franco-Spanish venture (October 1861) to secure the payment of public debts; but England and Spain soon withdrew their troops and only France kept an army in the country. French troops were used to support the Archduke Maximilian of Austria as emperor of Mexico from the moment of his arrival at Veracruz in May 1864. When they withdrew, his tottering regime fell under the blows of the Juaristas, and he was captured and shot at Querétaro (June 19, 1867). This expedition was a considerable strain on the French Army, and a totally futile expenditure of blood and money. A showdown with Prussia was brewing since her victory at Sadowa (July 3, 1866) against Austria. War came suddenly (July 19, 1870) as an aftermath of the Hohenzollern candidacy to the Spanish throne, and as a result of the doctoring by Bismarck of the Ems Dispatch (q.v.). The French Army was poorly led, followed obsolete tactics, suffered many reverses

(Wissembourg, Forbach), and was finally trapped with Achille François Bazaine at Metz and Napoleon at Sedan. The emperor capitulated on September 1st. On the 4th the empress fled Paris and the republic was proclaimed. Napoleon remained a prisoner of war until March 19, 1871, when he went to Camden Place, Chislehurst, where he died on Jan. 9, 1873. During the last years of his reign his sufferings from a kidney stone had broken his spirit. Eugénie survived until July 11, 1920.

Perhaps no other sovereign has been as maligned and misrepresented by political passion as Napoleon III, a victim of the fiery diatribes of Victor Hugo. But the time has come for a cool reappraisal of his aims and realizations as a Caesarian democrat and a social planner. Besides the works quoted above, see also his *History of Julius Caesar* (1865); *Letters to Prince Napoleon* (1927); *Lettres à Mme Cornu* (1937).

Consult Rheinhardt, E. A., *Napoleon and Eugénie* (New York 1931); Baco, F., *Napoléon III Inconnu* (Paris 1932); La Gorce, P. F., *Napoléon III et sa politique* (Paris 1933); Guériot, P., *Napoléon III* (Paris 1939); Guérard, A., *Napoléon III* (Cambridge, Mass. 1943); Berl, H., *Napoleon III, Demokratie u. Diktatur* (Munich 1946); Palm, F. C., *England and Napoleon III* (Durham, N.C. 1948); Guillemin, H., *Le coup du 2 décembre* (Paris 1951).

JEAN BOORSCH.

NAPOLEON, Eugène Louis Jean Joseph (known as PRINCE IMPERIAL), only son of Napoleon III: b. Paris, France, March 16, 1856; d. Zululand, South Africa, June 1, 1879. After the fall of the empire, he went to England with the empress and entered the military school at Woolwich. He volunteered for service in Zululand, where he was killed in an ambush.

Consult Martinet, A., *Le Prince Impérial* (Paris 1895); Filon, A., *Le Prince Impérial* (Paris 1912); Praviel, A., *La fin tragique du Prince Impérial* (Paris 1928).

NAPOLEON, PRINCE. See BONAPARTE, JÉRÔME.

NAPOLEON, city, Ohio, county seat of Henry County, on the Maumee River, 36 miles southwest of Toledo. It is served by two railroads, the Wabash and the Detroit, Toledo, and Ironton and is a marketing center for the agricultural products grown in the area. Industries include food and dairy products, metal products, tile and brick. The government is by mayor and council. Pop. 7,791.

NAPOLEON, a former piece of French money valued at about $4 or 20 francs. See LOUIS D'OR.

NAPOLEON LE PETIT (*Napoleon the Little*), the title of Victor Hugo's savage satire on Napoleon III (Brussels 1852).

NAPOLEON'S TOMB, the burial place of Napoleon Bonaparte under the dome of the Invalides in Paris. It has the form of a circular crypt 20 feet deep and 36 in diameter, open at the top. The tomb was designed by Ludovico Tullio Visconti, and on the walls are 10 marble reliefs by Pierre Charles Simart. The sarcophagus is 13 feet long, 6½ feet wide, 14½ feet high, cut from a single block of red porphyry, 67 tons in weight, surrounded by 12 victories by James Pradier. The inscription above the entrance to the crypt is taken from Napoleon's will: "I desire that my ashes shall rest on the banks of the Seine, in the midst of the French people that I have loved so well." Two adjoining tombs are those of the emperor's friend, Géraud Christophe Michel Duroc, and his companion, Henri Gratien Bertrand. Napoleon's remains were brought here in 1840 from St. Helena. In December 1940 the Germans reburied his son, the king of Rome (1811–1832), in an adjoining chapel.

NAQUET, nȧ'kā', **Alfred Joseph,** French chemist and social reformer: b. Carpentras, France, Oct. 6, 1834; d. Paris, Nov. 10, 1916. In 1867 he lost his professorship in the faculty of medicine in Paris and was condemned to 15 months' imprisonment for his share in the activities of a secret revolutionary society. In 1869 he fled to Spain after the publication of his book, *Religion, propriété, famille.* He returned to France in September 1870 and in the revolution became secretary of national defense. Soon after he was elected to the Chamber of Deputies and began agitation against the French marriage laws. His agitation for the re-establishment of divorce resulted in the law of 1884, and in 1886, through his continued efforts, divorce became legal after three years of definite separation, on the demand of one of the parties concerned. He was the author of a number of books on chemistry, the divorce question, and economic and political problems.

NARAKA, nŭr'ȧ-kȧ, in Hindu theology, a term equivalent to the English word hell. In Naraka there are 28 divisions, in which sinners of as many different classes are confined and subjected to tortures corresponding to the gravity of their offenses.

NARBADA, nẽr-bŭd'ȧ, or **NERBUDDA** (ancient NAMADOS), river in central India, about 775 miles long, rising in the mountains near the border of Madhya Pradesh and Vindhya Pradesh. It flows generally west and west-southwest across north Bombay Province and enters the Gulf of Cambay below Broach. Only about 60 miles of its lower course are navigable. The river is sacred to the Hindus, who make pilgrimages to its banks at Suklatirtha, Marble Rocks, Nemawar, and Amarkantak.

NARBONNE, när-bŏn', France, the chief town of an arrondissement in the Department of Aude, in a beautiful hill-girt plain, eight miles from the Mediterranean and 31 miles east of Carcassonne, commanding the entrance into Spain by the southwest. It is of historical interest as the Roman Narbo Martius, reputedly the earliest Roman colony (118 B.C.) beyond the Alps. About 309 A.D. it became the capital of Gallia Narbonensis, and had its capitol, forum, theater, aqueducts, and triumphal arches, of which there are few remains. In 412 (A.D.) it was taken by the Visigoths, and in 719 by the Saracens, from whom it was recovered by Pepin in 759. During the 11th and 12th centuries it was a prosperous manufacturing city, but subsequently deteriorated owing to the silting of its harbor. Its port, La Nouvelle, is 13 miles distant by canal. The principal edifices are the 12th and 13th century Romanesque church of Saint Paul Serge; the unfinished cathedral of Saint Just (13th-15th century); and the former archbishop's palace, now the city hall, in which are a good museum and a picture gallery.

A seminary and hydrographical school are among its educational institutions. The white-heather honey of Narbonne maintains its ancient celebrity; wine is produced, chiefly for blending purposes. The manufacture of bricks and tiles, sulphur refining, cooperage, and the distillation of brandy are among its industries. Pop. (1946) 26,301.

NARCISSISM, när-sĭs'iz'm, in orthodox psychoanalysis, an intense degree of self-love. The sexual instinct is directed towards one's own body or psychological attributes. By corollary, the narcissist is indifferent to other persons, unless by attracting their favorable attention his self-admiration is proportionately enhanced. The libido (sexual energy) is directed solely upon the self, or. in psychoanalytic terms, is "cathected" to the self. Narcissism is the primitive counterpart of egotism. It is contrasted with libidinal cathexis towards other persons. The psychoanalyst believes that a narcissistic individual is incapable of bestowing love upon anyone other than himself. In certain forms of mental disorders extreme narcissism is said to occur, and a mild degree of self-love is said to be present in many psychological functions.

Psychoanalysts differentiate between primary and secondary narcissism. Primary narcissism is normal among young infants, who find autoerotic gratifications in their own bodies. Secondary narcissism Freud defined as that which occurs when love-objects are taken away or when the libido is redirected from the external objects or persons toward which it has been flowing. Various psychopathologies eventuate from the latter type of narcissism.

Consult Healy, William, and others, *Structure and Meaning of Psychoanalysis* (New York 1930); Hendricks, Ives, *Facts and Theories of Psychoanalysis* (New York 1939).

PHILIP HARRIMAN.

NARCISSUS, när-sĭs'ŭs, in Greek mythology, the son of the river god Cephissus. Narcissus was of surpassing beauty, but excessively vain and inaccessible to the feeling of love. Echo pined away to a mere voice because her love for him found no return. Nemesis determined to punish him for his coldness of heart, and caused him to drink at a certain fountain, wherein he saw his own image, and was seized with a passion for himself. As a result, he pined away, and the gods transformed him into the flower which still bears his name. See also ECHO.

NARCISSUS, a genus of plants of the family Amaryllidaceae (q.v.). The species, numbering from 16 to about 50, according to different authors, have bulbous roots, narrow grass-like leaves, and generally white or yellow flowers borne singly or in small clusters and protruding from a dry spathe at the summit of a leafless scape. Because of their hardiness, ease of cultivation, habit of blooming in early spring, beauty and fragrance, many of the species and their numerous hybrids and varieties have been general garden favorites for centuries. Some are useful for winter forcing, especially the polyanthus narcissus (*N. tazetta*) with its popular forms the paper white and the Chinese sacred lily. In general, the garden species succeed best in well-drained garden soil of medium texture and richness. The bulbs should be planted in autumn about five inches deep and three inches apart, and should not be disturbed until they appear to be failing, perhaps after three years. Then when the foliage has died down the clumps may be dug, the bulbs divided, cleaned and stored in a cool dry place until planting time. Among the most popular species are the poet's narcissus (*N. poeticus*), also known as pheasant's eye, the jonquil (*N. jonquilla*), and *N. tazetta* mentioned above. The Lenten lily (*N. pseudo-narcissus*), or daffodil, is also one of the most widespread and hardy. See also DAFFODIL.

NARCOSIS, när-kō'sĭs, a state of profound stupor, unconsciousness, or arrested activity. The condition is produced by the action of one or more of a large list of drugs known as *narcotics.*

NARCOSYNTHESIS, när-kô-sĭn'thê-sĭs, a form of treatment used in psychoaneuroses, especially in what is known as the war neuroses. One of the sleep-inducing drugs is injected intravenously into the patient, to produce stupor or arrested activity. In successful cases this brings forth emotionally charged conversation in which the patient unburdens his mind. The discussion ensuing is known as *synthesis.*

NARCOTIC, a drug that dulls the senses, relieves pain, induces sleep, and can produce addiction in varying degrees.

Opium, known as a narcotic through the ages, consists of the dried gum of the unripe pod of the Oriental poppy (*Papaver somniferum*). In 1803 morphine was successfully extracted from opium, and later codeine and other alkaloids also were isolated. Heroin is morphine treated with concentrated acetic acid. In more recent years, synthetic substances that have a narcotic effect have been produced. These include methadone (Dolophine), meperidine (Demerol), and pentazocine (Talwin). The importation, manufacture, sale, and distribution of all narcotics in the United States is under strict federal control. Some narcotics, such as morphine and meperidine, are valuable pain relievers and are frequently used in medicine. Heroin, on the other hand, is no longer used medicinally in the United States, but it is sold illegally.

Incidence of Narcotic Addiction. Since World War II there has been a steady increase in the incidence of opiate addiction in the United States, of which heroin addiction accounted for 90%. The slum areas of large cities had been the traditional foci of narcotic addiction, but during the late 1960's and early 1970's increasing numbers of middle- and upper-class young people became involved with narcotics. In addition, younger children, some of grade school age, became addicted. The U.S. Bureau of Narcotics and Dangerous Drugs reported 68,000 narcotic addicts in the United States in 1969, but the actual number was much greater and estimates of 200,000 to 250,000 may not be excessive.

Characteristics of Narcotic Addiction. Narcotics vary in their ability to produce addiction, with heroin highly addictive as compared with pentazocine. The characteristics of addiction are tolerance, craving, and withdrawal. Tolerance is the body's ability to adapt to the drug so that larger and larger amounts of the drug become necessary to produce the same effect obtained initially with a smaller dose. Tolerance to one narcotic often produces tolerance to other related narcotics. Opiate tolerance can develop so completely that a dose that ordinarily would be lethal will not be felt by a person who has built up a tolerance to high doses. Craving is the psychological desire to reexperience the drug's effects or to avoid the withdrawal sickness. When a narcotic is suddenly stopped, the ensuing abstinence syndrome consists of such symptoms as vomiting, muscle pains and jerks, diarrhea, runny nose, tearing, gooseflesh, fever, and delirium.

Dangers of Narcotic Addiction. The greatest danger of addiction is the possibility of an overdose. An overdose can result when the addict receives an unusually potent supply of narcotic or when he loses his tolerance—for example, after being in jail or a hospital—and then resumes taking the high dose to which he had been accustomed. In addition, there are several diseases that occur frequently among addicts. Many of these, such as hepatitis, abscesses, and blood stream infections, result from the use of contaminated needles and syringes. See also DRUG ADDICTION; HEROIN; MORPHINE; METHADONE.

SIDNEY COHEN, M.D.
Director, Division of Narcotic Addiction and Drug Abuse, National Institute of Mental Health

NARCOTICS TRAFFIC AND CONTROL.

NARCOTICS TRAFFIC AND CONTROL. The corpse of a 15-year-old boy, found slumped against a wall in an alley of a New York slum, proved from the autopsy examination to be riddled with numerous needle-jab marks in the fleshy part of the left arm. Tests indicated a heavy saturation of an opium-derivative in the body. The verdict of the medical examiner, after an examination of the victim's vital organs, was "OD"—overdose—or death from an injection of heroin of greater strength than the body could tolerate.

The first link in the chain that led to the death in the New York alley may have taken place as long as a year before in a remote field in rural Turkey, where the seed that would blossom into opium was planted. The process of opium production begins when the petals drop from the poppy blossom, leaving the pod. The pod is slit, and the milky liquid that oozes out is allowed to harden and then is scraped off. The harvested material, known as gum opium, goes through a number of processing stages and then is surreptitiously slipped past customs inspectors into the United States. Thereafter, it moves through the city distribution web—from the higher-ups, the men who "deal in weight," through the small-time peddlers, themselves most often addicts, who "push" (sell) 3-ounce glassine bags of heavily diluted heroin for $2 or $3 apiece.

NARCOTICS SUPPLY

Growing Opium. At the start of the 1970's more than 80% of the supply of heroin, the drug of choice among narcotic addicts, was entering the United States from routes beginning in the poppy fields of Lebanon and Turkey, where opium is grown as a cash crop. Other principal places where the poppy plant is cultivated are Mexico and the "golden triangle" of southeast Asia: the northern portions of Burma, Thailand, and Laos.

The United States has attempted to bring pressure on Turkey to restrict the growing of poppy plants. In 1968, as a result of a $3 million loan from the United States to Turkey for opium eradication and for conversion to other crops, the number of provinces in which it is legally permitted to grow opium poppies was reduced from 17 to 9. The immediate outcome of this effort, however, was an almost doubled Turkish opium production, the result of more intensive cultivation in legal areas and a sharp rise in illegal plantings. About 100,000 peasant farmers engage in opium production in Turkey, and enforcement officials have to take into account the farmers' potential influence at election time.

In Lebanon, some farmers have been persuaded to turn to sunflower plants instead of opium for marketing, but the diverse political characteristics of countries producing opium make total control of poppy cultivation unlikely. There is considerable production in mainland China, North Korea, and North Vietnam, for instance, and, since these countries do not belong to the United Nations, the UN's efforts at international narcotics control tend to have little effect in these places.

Manufacturing Heroin. Raw opium is first converted into a so-called morphine base, and then it is refined by a chemical process into heroin, the most potent of the opium derivatives. For the American market, most of this work is done in clandestine laboratories in southern France, particularly in the Marseille region. These laboratories need not be large and complex, so they are readily concealed behind the walls of respectable-appearing villas.

Smuggling Heroin. Efforts to cope with the smuggling of narcotics into the United States have been compared by a narcotics agent to those of "a blind goalie in a hockey game." Another agent has observed: "We can harass them and make it harder, but we're never going to win this smuggling war."

The problem evolves from the fact that heroin worth thousands of dollars can be carried in small quantities into the United States by numerous routes. Caches have been found in hollowed-out ski poles, false-bottomed wine bottles, oscilloscopes, and car bodies. One woman was caught at an airport with five kilos (11 pounds) of heroin strapped to her body under a bulging maternity dress. Diplomats can make excellent smugglers, since their status precludes examination of their luggage at international border points.

Most arrests for smuggling result not from the patrol of entry spots into the United States but rather from information supplied to narcotics agents. Much of this information arrives from merchants selling heroin abroad, who benefit not only from their original sale but also from rewards for tipping off border guards. Federal narcotics agents stationed abroad also maintain surveillance over sites where large drug transactions occur. Traffickers, for their part, attempt to avoid apprehension by transferring their purchase to another person, one not involved in the original transaction, who can then easily bring the drug into the country.

More than 140 kilos (300 pounds) of heroin was seized by federal agents in one year, but this accounts for only a small percentage of the smuggling total. The logistics of law enforcement can be appreciated from the fact that, not counting seamen and airline personnel, some 200 million persons enter the United States yearly.

The Bureau of Narcotics and Dangerous

Drugs, established in the Department of Justice, which is responsible for enforcement of federal narcotics laws, has more than 800 agents. The vulnerability of this staff to temptations of huge profits from drug sales is evidenced by the fact that in one year 14 federal agents were themselves indicted for trafficking in narcotics. The U.S. Bureau of Customs maintains only 15 special agents to monitor drug traffic into New York City's airports and along its waterfront, and its forces are even sparser at other entry points.

See also INTERNATIONAL CRIMINAL POLICE ORGANIZATION.

Marketing Heroin. The economics of the heroin market go a long way toward explaining the willingness of many persons to take the risks involved in trading in the drug. One kilogram (2.2 lb) of morphine-base is worth about $350 in Turkey. When the same amount is refined in France, its value rises to $3,500. By the time the drug is unloaded in New York City, the kilogram can be sold for $18,000.

In New York, the first step is to dilute the pure product into a mixture with only 25% heroin, the rest usually being milk sugar or quinine. The mixture is then divided into one-ounce (28.3-gram) lots, which sell for $500 each. Later, these are cut into packets containing only 5% heroin that can be purchased for $5, the so-called nickel bags. All told, by the time the heroin available for $350 in Turkey has been marketed in New York, its worth has increased to approximately $225,000.

Heroin transactions take place with great stealth. One New York dealer recited the following routine for receiving a shipment from a courier. The dealer has a man park a car in a downtown lot. The man leaves the parking ticket stub at the desk of the hotel where the courier is registered. The courier takes the car out of the lot, removes the money hidden in the trunk, puts the heroin in its place, and then parks the car in another lot and leaves the stub at a prearranged drop.

Drug transactions between small-time sellers and addicts are not nearly as elaborate, though diligent efforts are made to avoid apprehension by the police. Most usually, narcotics squad officers employ an addict, who had been arrested earlier, to make additional purchases with marked money. For this service the informant may receive more lenient treatment, a compromise justified by law enforcement officers on the ground that it permits them to arrest persons higher in the drug trade. To avoid being caught with drugs in their possession, some traffickers exchange heroin packets mouth-to-mouth, with a kind of kissing maneuver. If the police intervene, the person holding the drug will swallow the packet.

After public agitation about drugs began to mount in the late 1960's, the tendency was for organized criminals to move out of drug traffic. According to William J. Durkin, a regional director of the Bureau of Narcotics and Dangerous Drugs, "There is no Mr. Big who controls everything in one city or even in one neighborhood."

CONTROL EFFORTS

International Cooperation. The first international effort to control drug traffic took place with the calling of the Opium Convention at The Hague in 1912. In 1946 the UN assumed control of narcotics regulation. In 1916 treaties among nations were grouped under "A Single Convention of Narcotics Drugs," and an International Control Board was established in Geneva. Sixty-six nations had signed the convention by 1970, but the powers of the board tend to be more those of moral suasion than effective supervision.

U.S. Legislation. As a result of the 1912 meeting in The Hague, the U.S. Congress in 1914 passed the Harrison Act, still the country's basic narcotics legislation. The Harrison Act is essentially a revenue measure, imposing a tax on transactions in narcotics. Presumably the law was not intended to interfere with medical treatment of addicts, but a number of U.S. Supreme Court decisions, as these were interpreted by the Federal Bureau of Narcotics, frightened physicians out of the treatment field from fear of criminal prosecution.

Under the Harrison Act, failure to pay the requisite tax could result in a maximum sentence of 10 years. The act made no mention of either addicts or addiction. In 1951 the Boggs Amendment substantially raised the penalty for possession of narcotics—including both heroin and marihuana—and these penalties were again increased in 1951 by the Narcotic Drug Control Act.

That act provides a mandatory 5-to-10-year sentence for a second offense of narcotics possession and a 10-to-40-year sentence for a third offense. That such penalties accord with public sentiment was evident from a 1970 Gallup Poll, which found that almost half of the American people believed that sentences of more than 10 years should be imposed on heroin and marihuana traffickers.

Attempts have been made, however, to remove marihuana from the Narcotic Drug Control Act and to lessen sentences for offenses connected with it. Twenty-seven states changed marihuana possession from a felony to a misdemeanor in 1970, but the lack of consensus became apparent as New Hampshire made possession of marihuana a felony rather than a misdemeanor.

Civil Commitment. The *Robinson* v. *California* decision by the U.S. Supreme Court in 1962 altered methods for dealing with addicts by declaring that addiction could not constitutionally be regarded as a crime but must be treated as an illness. The decision resulted in the inauguration of civil commitment programs in the larger jurisdictions and in the passage of the federal Narcotic Addict Rehabilitation Act of 1966.

Civil commitment procedures soon came under strong attack, however, on three major grounds: (1) that addicts no longer have the same protections guaranteed accused criminals; (2) that under the guise of treatment, addicts are put into institutions that are called hospitals but do not differ from prisons; and (3) that civil commitment programs show no greater success than the earlier penal approaches.

In part because of such ineffectiveness and in part because of ideology, there are advocates of the view that drug transactions ought to be removed from both criminal and civil commitment sanctions. Thus in 1970 the American Civil Liberties Union resolved that "compulsory treatment or incarceration of drug users is a violation of civil liberties" and maintained that "an individual has a right to use his own body as he wishes and this right includes the use and possession of narcotics."

The British Program. Other reformers have looked to Britain for a model narcotics program. Although drug use has escalated rapidly in Britain, London, a city about the size of New York, had only 3,000 addicts—about 3% of the total found in New York—at the start of the 1970's. Until 1968, all British physicians were able to prescribe drugs to anyone. Since then, however, Britain has licensed a corps of 500 doctors, who work in government-approved clinics, to handle addicts. Early reports indicated that persons seeking treatment—most of the doctors are psychiatrists who attempt to wean the addict from his narcotic dependence—tend to fare well. There were also reports, however, of a considerable rise in illicit trafficking in narcotics, possibly because of the drying up of legal prescription sources.

See also DRUG ADDICTION AND ABUSE; HEROIN; MARIHUANA; NARCOTIC; OPIUM.

GILBERT GEIS
California State College, Los Angeles
Coauthor of "Man, Crime, and Society"

Further Reading: Anslinger, Harry J., and Tompkins, William F., *Traffic in Narcotics* (New York 1953); Eldridge, William B., *Narcotics and the Law* (Chicago 1967); Lindesmith, Alfred R., *The Addict and the Law* (Bloomington, Ind., 1965).

NARCOTINE, när'kō-tēn, an alkaloid of opium. It is present in opium to the extent of 0.5–10 per cent, according to the source, and is isolated after the morphine and codeine have been removed. It has the formula $C_{22}H_{23}NO_7$ and belongs to the isoquinoline types; it is closely related to hydrastine, differing only by an additional methoxyl (OCH_3) group. The principal use of narcotine is in the preparation of cotarnine, which is formed when the molecule is split by oxidative hydrolysis. Cotarnine, in the form of its salts, is of considerable value as a styptic agent.

NARDINI, när-dē'nē, **Pietro,** Italian violinist and composer: b. Livorno, Italy, April 12, 1722; d. Florence, May 7, 1793. He studied the violin first in Leghorn, then in Padua with Giuseppe Tartini, becoming his teacher's most successful pupil. In 1753 he was chosen for the post of solo violinist at the court of the duke of Württemberg in Stuttgart, where he remained until 1767. After his return to Italy, he became in 1770 musical director at the court of Grand-duke Leopold of Tuscany in Florence. Nardini was not only a great performer, admired for the exceptional purity of his tone, but also a gifted composer of chamber music. He wrote six concertos for violin and orchestra, 15 sonatas for violin and bass, six string quartets, six duets for two violins, and six trios with the flute. Some of his sonatas are still included in the repertory of great violinists. The sonatas were re-edited by J. D. Alard and by Ferdinand David.

NARES, nârz, SIR **George Strong,** British naval officer and explorer: b. Aberdeen, Scotland, April 24, 1831; d. Surbiton, England, Jan. 15, 1915. Son of a naval officer, he attended the Royal Naval College at New Cross and entered the service at 14. In 1852–1854 he served on one of the expeditions searching for the lost party of Sir John Franklin in the Canadian Arctic. Specializing in oceanographic research, Nares was named captain of the *Challenger,* which in 1872–1874 made a notable voyage of exploration in the South Atlantic and South Pacific, being the first steamship to cross the Antarctic Circle (see CHALLENGER EXPEDITION). He was then transferred to the *Alert,* on which he led an expedition (1875–1876) to reach the North Pole from Grant Land (Ellesmere Island, Canada). Though the pole was not attained, Sir Albert Hastings Markham, a member of the party, reached 83° 20′ 26″ north latitude, breaking previous records; another member, Lt. Pelham Aldrich, discovered and rounded Cape Columbia, the northernmost point in Canada. Nares was knighted in 1876 and became a vice admiral in 1892. Cape Nares on Ellesmere Island and Nares Land in Greenland are named for him.

NARES LAND, a region of Greenland, on the northwest coast of the island, constituting the western portion of Peary Land, along Victoria Fjord. It is named for Sir George Strong Nares (q.v.).

NAREW RIVER, nä'rĕf, river, Poland and USSR, a major tributary of the Western Bug. The Narew rises a few miles across the Polish border in the Soviet republic of Belorussia, flows west into Poland north of the famous Bialowieza Forest (once the home of the European bison, the wisent), west northwest to Lomza, then southwest to its confluence with the Western Bug, which it joins about 20 miles north of Warsaw. (From its confluence with the Narew to its junction with the Vistula, the Bug is sometimes called the Bug-Narew.) About 270 miles long, the Narew is navigable below the mouth of its tributary, the Biebrza.

NARIÑO, nä-rē'nyō, **Antonio,** Colombian soldier and political leader: b. Santa Fe (Bogotá), New Granada (Colombia), April 9, 1765; d. Leiva, Colombia, Dec. 13, 1823. While employed by the Spanish administration in New Granada, Nariño published translations of French and United States political writings (including Thomas Paine's *Rights of Man*), and agitated with much effect for independence from Spain. Because of these activities he was deported to Spain in 1795. After escaping in 1797, he returned to New Granada to resume the struggle for independence and was twice imprisoned. In September 1811, following the Revolution of 1810, he was elected president of Cundinamarca, the province in which Bogotá lies. In 1814, following the restoration of Ferdinand VII to the Spanish throne, Nariño was defeated by Don Pablo Morillo, who had been dispatched from Spain to regain the rebellious colonies, and was again transported to Spain where he was imprisoned until 1820. In 1821, following his return to Colombia, he was named vice president by Simón Bolívar but resigned after two months. Nariño was an ardent advocate of a strongly centralized government for the former Spanish colonies (including New Granada and Venezuela). Largely because of his intellectual influence, Nariño is regarded as a major figure in Colombia's struggle for independence.

NARRAGANSETT BAY, inlet of the Atlantic Ocean, extending into the State of Rhode Island about 30 miles. Conanicut Island and Rhode Island, situated at the mouth of the bay, divide the entrance into three passages. The three principal arms of the bay are Greenwich Bay, on the northeast; Providence River (an estuary), in the north; and Mount Hope Bay, on the northwest. An important shipping center in colonial times, the bay sustains an active fishing industry and numerous resorts, of which the most famous is Newport on Rhode Island.

NARRAGANSETT INDIANS, a tribe of the Algonquian linguistic family, related to the Niantic Indians (q.v.). The Narragansett, whose name means "people of the small point," migrated into the Rhode Island region from the southwest, and eventually became the most powerful tribe in southern New England. It was largely due to their influence that Roger Williams (1603?–1683) was able to lay the foundations for the present State of Rhode Island. For the most part they were friendly to the colonists until King Philip's War (q.v.) in 1675–1676. Following tremendous losses in the famous Great Swamp Fight of that war, the surviving Narragansett took refuge with other New England tribes, and were never again an important group. From a maximum population of perhaps 5,000, they shrank to about 25 in 1900. In the early 1960's about 250 individuals were members of the Narragansett Association of Rhode Island, and were seeking by this means to establish a tribal entity once again. However, it is questionable whether any of these individuals could be classed as fullblood Narragansett. See also CANONICUS.

FREDERICK J. DOCKSTADER.

NARRATIVE POETRY, năr′ȧ-tĭv pō′ĕ-trĭ, a kind of poetry devoted to storytelling. Stories can be told in lyric or pastoral poetry and of course in verse drama, as they have been from Hesiod and Theocritus and the Greek dramatists onwards, but the poetic forms peculiarly appropriate to narrative are the unpretentious ballad and the stately epic, whether of the heroic or romantic type. It may be that heroic epic evolved from ballad, as romantic epic certainly evolved from heroic. See also LITERARY FORMS.

Ballad.—The ballad is a widespread and ancient poetic form. It has been thought that early Israelite and Roman history, as presented in Judges and in the first books of Livy's *History of Rome,* is based on ballad material. Some 300 English and Scottish ballads are known, many dating from the 14th century. The transmission of ballads is oral and they are therefore susceptible to alteration, but though their authorship is unknown they were certainly composed (in substantially their present form) by individual poets, and are not mere accretions. Their subjects are mainly historical, supernatural, or romantic. They are in stanzaic form, with many set phrases and repetitions, and are intended to be sung. They show little literary sophistication or ethical profundity. The ballad form has also been used by serious modern poets, as in Samuel Taylor Coleridge's *Rime of the Ancient Mariner* or Oscar Wilde's *Ballad of Reading Gaol.* See also BALLAD.

Heroic Epic.—Epic is spacious in scope, lofty in style, and elaborate in structure. The metrical unit of the epic is the line rather than the stanza, and it is meant to be recited rather than sung. Even the earliest examples show mature reflection on relationships among men and between man and the supernatural; usually the serious epic sets forth the ethical ideals and aspirations of the society out of which it grows and for which it speaks. Its matter derives from history or what is accepted as such; this may be dealt with imaginatively but not fancifully. Usually its theme is some great war or the genesis of central human institutions or a quest for some significant goal. The epic hero is a self-sufficient individual who asserts himself against hostile forces, human or supernatural, not by magic but by his own prowess. He is concerned for his own satisfaction and glory, but by transcending ordinary limitations he pushes back the boundaries of what is possible for men and serves as an exemplar to his whole society. The greater epics have enjoyed an almost scriptural authority among the peoples that cherished them, and so have substantially shaped their characters. In classical antiquity and again in the humanist age authorship of a successful epic was the greatest distinction to which a mortal could aspire.

Heroic epics of disparate societies show remarkable similarities—not only in the basic premises of the heroic career, but even in such details as the use of formulaic language and the descriptions of fighting or feasting, arrivals and departures, and dressing and undressing. These similarities are probably to be explained as a common strain in human nature, but they may be due to literary influence. The *Gilgamesh Epic* may have been the ultimate inspiration for the epics of India in the East and of Greece in the West. The Greek poems were certainly the models for the "literary" epics of Europe, and may have influenced the "natural" epics also.

Oral and Written Composition.—There are obvious differences between such epics as the *Iliad, Song of Roland,* and *Nibelungenlied,* on the one hand, and the *Aeneid, Lusiads,* and *Paradise Lost,* on the other. In the former group the author is anonymous or so detached as to convey the impression that the poems are timeless natural phenomena, not the work of individual poets. The narrative proceeds in clear sunlight and expects of its audience an understanding heart, not bookish erudition. In the latter group the conscious artistry of the individual poet is evident. He expects a sophisticated audience which will appreciate literary virtuosity and recognize literary allusions. It has been customary to distinguish the two kinds by such terms as "natural" and "literary." But the so-called natural epic also reveals the hand of an artist, and a better distinction is that between oral and written composition. The oral composer carries in his mind a mass of verbal formulas (proper names with an assortment of epithets, for example) which will fill various metrical requirements within a line. These he can insert automatically, and thereby free himself to find the words which context and meter require to fill his line. Oral composition explains the character of Yugoslav, Russian, Spanish, and other epics, as well as that of Homer's *Iliad* and *Odyssey.* Homer's poems may well have been composed in writing, but they followed the techniques of oral composition.

Written composition allows greater freedom to manipulate lines in order to gain subtlety, but the patterns of epithets, formulae, similes, and the like, established by the exigencies of oral composition, are retained. The high seriousness and responsibility are also retained; nothing could be more earnest than Virgil's *Aeneid* or John Milton's *Paradise Lost.* But forms survive for their aesthetic value after their serious burden has faded, and then sometimes acquire a new burden of seriousness. Thus, heroic epic is reduced to mere prettiness in Apollonius of Rhodes' *Argonautica* (3d century B.C.), and then acquires new seriousness in the *Aeneid* (1st century B.C.). In Ariosto's highly artistic but utterly playful *Orlando Furioso* (early 16th century), epic is emptied of all seriousness, but Spenser gives a similarly playful fantasy weighty allegorical significance in his *Faerie Queene* (late 16th century). If epic implies high seriousness, the long romantic poems should not be classed as epics.

Gilgamesh Epic.—Twelve tablets containing the major portion of the Assyrian version of the *Gilgamesh Epic* were found in the library of Ashurbanipal (7th century B.C.) in Nineveh, and these were subsequently supplemented by fragments of the Sumerian version dating from the 3d millennium B.C. The hero asserts his individuality against hostile forces of nature and barbarism and even against gods. He is distressed and frightened when his bosom friend Enkidu dies, and goes on a dangerous quest to Utnapishtim (the Babylonian Noah) to fetch the secret of immortality. The quest fails, and Gilgamesh reconciles himself to mortality. Gilgamesh himself is a powerful and proud and at the same time thoughtful and sensitive hero. By reason of its long hold on the civilizations of the Near and Middle East, its manifest influence upon Genesis, and its possible influence upon Indian and Greek epic, the *Gilgamesh Epic* may be directly or indirectly the most influential poem in the world.

Iliad and Odyssey.—The *Iliad* provides Europe's gage for epic, as the rich but tragic figure of Achilles best exemplifies the tragic hero. Achilles, who had chosen a short but glorious instead of a long but commonplace life, finds himself cheated even of glory when Agamemnon takes his prize, the girl Briseis. No blame attaches to such a hero when he withdraws from fighting, though his comrades need his help. The death of his friend Patroclus brings him back to the fight; and he kills Hector, though he knows his own death will follow. Although his whole being is bent on abusing Hector's body, he consents to return it to Hector's father Priam, and so wins through to his highest nobility. It is Achilles' overpowering concern with his own glory that glorifies all humanity. The *Iliad* was learned by heart by Greek schoolboys, and contributed much to the Greek passion for achieving excellence in all fields.

The classical Greeks believed that Homer, whom tradition placed in the 9th or 8th century B.C., was the author of the *Iliad* and the *Odyssey.* This opinion was accepted until the 19th century; but in the 19th and early 20th centuries it was thought that these epics must be late patchworks of numerous short lays, because it was believed both that the early Greeks could not write and that so long a poem must have been written. During the same period it was thought that a number of inconsistencies within the poems could best be explained by multiple authorship. But in the 1930's it was proved that long poems could be composed orally, and in the 1950's the decipherment of the Minoan Linear B script proved that Greeks could write hundreds of years before the 8th century B.C. The inconsistencies are not serious in a long work intended for recitation in parts. On the contrary, modern critics are agreed that only a single masterful artist could conceive and execute such unified and consistently excellent works as the *Iliad* and *Odyssey.* See also HIEROGLYPHICS, HITTITE AND CRETAN—*Cretan Hieroglyphics.*

Where the warrior's prowess is the mark of excellence in the *Iliad,* in the *Odyssey* it is ingenuity and resourcefulness together with great wealth and stately mansions. Evil has raised its head, as in the case of the suitors of Penelope and of Odysseus' shipmates who open his bag of winds. The epic's structure, too, is more sophisticated. Odysseus' adventures during the early years of his homeward journey are told in a flashback in the middle of the poem, and the remainder of the work describes his return and vengeance directly. The early books are in effect an account of the education of Odysseus' son Telemachus—not, significantly, to be a great warrior, but to be a courteous and responsible landed gentleman. Because of the different social and ethical presuppositions of the two works, many critics hold that the *Odyssey* and the *Iliad* are not by the same author; but most critics explain the differences on the grounds that the *Odyssey* is a poem of peace, while the *Iliad* is a poem of war.

A number of other epics dealing with the heroes of Troy and of Thebes, all later than the *Iliad* and *Odyssey,* are known to have existed, but none have survived.

Alexandrian Epic.—In the Hellenistic age (3d to 1st centuries B.C.) literature moved from the deep earnestness of the classical period to mere belles-lettres, learned, polished, and generally superficial. Characteristic of the period is the *Argonautica* of Apollonius of Rhodes (3d century B.C.), an account of the quest for the Golden Fleece and of the loves of Jason and Medea. Apollonius wrote his poem in part to disprove the contention of Callimachus (c. 305–c. 240), an Alexandrian scholar, that epic could no longer be written, for all Alexandrian art favored the dainty miniature. The *Argonautica* is in fact a series of elaborately wrought episodes lacking sweep and profundity. Jason is a curiously helpless hero effective only in the field of love. The best portion is the love story in book 3; this is Europe's first psychological study of a girl in love, and was Virgil's model for his Dido episode in the *Aeneid.* Callimachus himself and other Alexandrians wrote a number of epyllia or miniature epics, as did some of their Roman imitators. See also ARGONAUTS.

Posthomerica, Dionysiaca, Hero and Leander.—Episodes of the Trojan War after the funeral of Hector (where the *Iliad* ends) are recounted, in Homeric style but with un-Homeric sentimentality, in the 14-book *Posthomerica* of Quintus of Smyrna, probably of the 4th century A.D. The *Dionysiaca* of Nonnus (5th century A.D.) recounts the career of Dionysus, and especially his conquests of eastern lands, in 48 books of torrential language and fantastic imagery. Verse romance foreshadows its later development most clearly in the *Hero and Leander* of Musaeus (5th century A.D.).

Roman Epic.—In form, and in much of its substance, Latin literature imitated the Greek. It is significant that the first work of Latin literature was a translation of the *Odyssey* by Livius Andronicus (c. 284–c. 204 B.C.). We know of two other early Latin epics, the *Annales* of Quintus Ennius (239–169 B.C.) and the *Bellum Punicum* of Gnaeus Naevius (c. 270–c. 201 B.C.).

Aeneid.—Virgil (70–19 B.C.) is second only to Homer. The first six books of the *Aeneid* are modeled upon the *Odyssey* and the latter six upon the *Iliad,* and there are countless borrowings in detail from these and other Greek poems; but Virgil has transformed the whole into a personal and thoroughly Roman book, setting forth the divinely ordained origin and mission of the Roman people. Aeneas is no self-willed hero like Achilles or Odysseus, but a disciplined instrument of destiny who suppresses his own desires (as in the Dido episode) for the sake of the task destiny has assigned him. In effect the *Aeneid* presented both a justification and a program for the Roman Empire. Because it was read and revered continuously, and did not need to be resurrected at the Renaissance, it affected not only subsequent European poetry but also European political theory.

Metamorphoses.—The 15-book masterpiece, *Metamorphoses,* of Ovid (43 B.C.–?17 A.D.) is not epic except in the sense that it makes the establishment of the Roman Empire the culmination of the cosmic order. The poem contains a long series of stories, disparate but artfully connected with one another, all involving changes of shape, from the transformation of chaos into order after the flood to that of Julius Caesar into a star. This great storehouse of myth has been quarried by hundreds of artists and poets, among them Geoffrey Chaucer and William Shakespeare.

Later Latin Epic.—The influence of Virgil is notable in four epic poets of the latter half of the 1st century A.D.: Lucan (39–65), Publius Statius (45?–?96), Valerius Flaccus (dates unknown), and Silius Italicus (26–101). The best of their poems is Lucan's *Civil War,* sometimes called *Pharsalia,* which tells of the conflict between Caesar and Pompey. Lucan is turgid and sometimes ghoulish, but he shows great energy and Stoic convictions. There are no convictions in Statius' *Thebais* but only a polished narrative of the war between Eteocles and Polynices, the sons of Oedipus. Statius also began but did not live to finish an *Achilleis.* Valerius Flaccus' *Argonautica* is an adaptation of and improvement upon the *Argonautica* of Apollonius of Rhodes. Silius Italicus, who was a retired lawyer, versified an account of the Hannibalic War (the Second Punic War), in 17 dull and tasteless books. In the late 4th century, Claudian, who was probably born in Egypt, wrote a series of spirited epics on the wars of the Emperor Honorius and his general Stilicho.

Pre-Renaissance European Epic.—A number of non-Mediterranean epics written almost two millenniums after Homer reflect cultural and artistic conditions no more advanced than Homer's. The oldest English epic is *Beowulf,* which was written near Northumbria in the 8th century. The poem, which shows a curious fusion of pagan and Christian elements, celebrates the hero's defense and extension of civilization over monstrous forces hostile to it, first over the brutish Grendel and his uncanny mother, and then over a firedrake.

The *Song of Roland,* probably of the 11th century, is far the most refined and artistic of the group. The basis of the story is the annihilation of Charlemagne's rear guard at Roncesvalles in the Pyrenees in 778, but the poem transforms the defeat into a moral victory. Roland is a perfect epic hero, self-sufficient like Achilles and concerned for his own glory at the risk of his cause, but his allegiance is to God and his heroism is on behalf of Christendom and against the paynims; at his death he reaches his gauntlet to the archangel Michael, who accepts it. The friendship of Roland and Oliver recalls that of Achilles and Patroclus, or Gilgamesh and Enkidu.

The *Nibelungenlied* (12th century) shows several strands. The first portion, of which the scene is Worms, the capital of Burgundy, tells how Siegfried wooed Kriemhild, sister of King Gunther; how he won Brunhild to be Gunther's wife; and how Siegfried was treacherously killed by Gunther's vassal, Hagen, to secure the Nibelungen hoard for Gunther. In the second portion, the widowed Kriemhild marries the pagan Etzel (Attila the Hun) and later invites the Burgundians to a feast in order to take vengeance upon them. The poem ends with a general slaughter. Siegfried's falling in love with a lady he has never seen (Kriemhild) shows the influence of romance; on the other hand, the real hero of the poem is the stark and terrifying Hagen. The story rests on an adaptation of the *Poetic Edda,* which Richard Wagner (1813–1883) used directly for his *Ring of the Nibelungs.* The art of the *Nibelungenlied* is crude as compared with *Roland;* yet the poem has exerted great influence in German-speaking countries.

The *Cid,* of the 12th century, celebrates the Spanish hero Rodrigo Díaz de Vivar (or Bivar), who died in 1099. This is virtually the success story of a great and proud warrior whose energy wins him wealth, recall from banishment, and vengeance upon highborn enemies who had affronted him.

The *Kalevala,* which the Finns regard as their national epic, was pieced together out of old lays by Elias Lönnrot (1802–1884) in the 19th century, when scholars believed all oral epics had been so constituted. The heroes of the *Kalevala* are not truly epic because their reliance is on magic rather than their own prowess. The meter and much of the substance of the *Kalevala* is imitated in Henry Wadsworth Longfellow's *Song of Hiawatha* (1855).

Verse Romances.—The rebirth of epic as of other literary genres began with direct imitation of the ancients. Thus, Petrarch (1304–1374) wrote a Latin epic entitled *Africa;* while by precept in his *Ars Poetica* and by example in his *Christiad,* Marco Girolamo Vida (d. 1566) taught that the proper model for epic is Virgil. But artistic independence asserted itself and produced a series of scintillating and highly finished romances. Luigi Pulci (1432–1484) wrote the ebullient *Morgante Maggiore;* Matteo Maria Boiardo (1434–1494), the sophisticated *Orlando Innamorato;* and Lodovico Ariosto (1474–1533), the richly tapestried *Orlando Furioso,* which is the finest of all. Under the influence of the Counter Reformation, but using Ariosto's techniques, Torquato Tasso (1544–1595) produced his serious and flawless *Jerusalem Delivered,* whose theme is the First Crusade. In Portugal, Luiz de Camões (1524–1580) wrote his patriotic *Lusiads,* which does for Portugal and Christendom what the *Aeneid* did for Rome and the empire. The theme of the *Lusiads* is Vasco da Gama's heroic voyage to India around the Cape of Good Hope. In England, Edmund Spenser (1552?–1599) glorified Queen Elizabeth in *The Faerie Queene,* which is like Ariosto's work in form but is given serious allegorical meaning;

and John Milton (1608–1674) in his *Paradise Lost* dealt with the loftiest theme of all, the justification of the ways of God to man.

In the 18th century, production of narrative poetry (but with none of Milton's earnestness) was enormous; Richard Blackmore alone wrote 85 books, based mainly on Arthurian legend. The movement continued in the 19th century with better results at the hands of Walter Scott, Robert Southey, George Gordon Byron, Alfred Tennyson, William Morris, and Matthew Arnold. In the United States, Stephen Vincent Benét's exact and illuminating treatment of the Civil War in *John Brown's Body* (1928) returns to a serious, patriotic theme.

See also ARTHURIAN ROMANCES, THE; BIBLE; CHAUCER, GEOFFREY—*Works;* DANTE ALIGHIERI; MAHABHARATA; RAMAYANA; ROMANCE; SHAH NAMEH; TRISTAN; and separate articles on works and authors cited.

MOSES HADAS,
Jay Professor of Greek, Columbia University.

Bibliography.—Bowra, Cecil M., *From Virgil to Milton* (London 1945); Van Doren, Mark, *The Noble Voice* (New York 1946); Hadas, Moses, *History of Greek Literature* (New York 1950); Bowra, Cecil M., *Heroic Poetry* (London 1952); Tillyard, Eustace M. W., *The English Epic and Its Background* (London 1954); Kroeber, Karl, *Romantic Narrative Art* (Madison, Wis., 1960).

NARROWS, The, năr'ōz, strait, in New York Bay, separating Staten Island from the Brooklyn, N.Y., shore of Long Island. About three miles long and one mile wide (at its narrowest point), the Narrows joins the upper and lower New York bays. In 1964 the Verrazano-Narrows Bridge, a cable-suspension bridge with the world's longest main span (4,260 feet), was opened across the Narrows.

NARSES, när'sēz, Byzantine administrator and general: b. ?478; d. Rome, Italy, ?573. A eunuch in the Byzantine imperial household in Constantinople, Narses gained the favor of the emperor and empress, Justinian and Theodora, and was quickly promoted to high court offices, including those of chamberlain, *comes sacri cubiculi* (head of the imperial household), and prefect of the treasury. He displayed outstanding ability in 537 when he was sent to Alexandria to restore the peace, which had been disturbed by religious conflicts. In 538 he was sent by Justinian to assist, and perhaps to reduce the power of, the famous general Belisarius, who was then engaged in ousting the Ostrogoths from Italy. After the recall of Belisarius in 548, Narses (then about 70 years old) was given command in Italy with the task of repelling the Ostrogoths, led by the vigorous and chivalrous Totila, who had again won control of the Italian Peninsula. In a brilliant campaign he defeated the Gothic army at Taginae (near modern Gubbio) in the Apennines in 552, killing Totila; and in 553 he brought the Gothic power in Italy to an end with the defeat and death of Teias, Totila's successor, in a battle west of Salerno. In 554 he repelled an invasion of Alamannic hordes, and in the succeeding years the last isolated remnants of Gothic opposition were crushed. From 554 until his dismissal by Justin II in 567 (perhaps because of avarice in his administration), Narses was prefect of Italy. By training an able if unscrupulous administrator, the eunuch Narses became in his old age one of the Byzantine Empire's great generals. Some sources state that he died in 568 on the eve of the Lombard invasion of Italy.

NARTHEX, när'thĕks (Gr. *narthēx,* reed), a long narrow arcaded porch placed at the entrance of early Christian churches, sometimes separated from the nave by a screen or low wall. Catechumens, penitents, and others not allowed to enter the church proper were permitted within the narthex. In basilican churches, the narthex was at the west end of the nave, within the atrium. Byzantine churches frequently had two narthexes: an outer, so-called exonarthex; and an inner narthex, forming part of the church's main structure. Although the ritual function of the narthex has disappeared, the term is still used as a synonym for a porch or vestibule at a church entrance.

NARUSZEWICZ, nä-rōō-shĕ'vĕch, **Adam Stanislaw,** Polish ecclesiastic, historian, and poet: b. Pinsk (now in the USSR), Oct. 20, 1733; d. Janow Podlaski, Poland, July 6, 1797. He became a Jesuit in 1748, and taught in Jesuit schools at Vilnyus and Warsaw in Poland. After the suppression of the Jesuit order he became bishop of Smolensk (1788) and of Lutsk (1790). His poetry, consisting largely of translations and paraphrases of Greek and Latin authors, was first published in 1778. Because of his most celebrated work, the *History of the Polish Nation* (6 vols., 1780–1786), covering the history of his country down to the unification of the Polish and Lithuanian crowns in 1386, he has been called the Polish Tacitus. Despite the fact that it is largely a chronology of Polish reigns, Naruszewicz' history is distinguished by its critical use of a large number of sources as well as by the excellence of its style.

NARVA, när'vȧ, city, USSR, in northeastern Estonian SSR, about 85 miles southwest of Leningrad, on the high left bank of the Narva River. An important cotton-milling town, Narva contains the Kreenholm Cotton Mill, founded in 1857 and once one of the largest in Europe. Other industries in Narva are sawmilling, furniture making, meat packing, and dairying. Since World War II, Narva has become an important producer of electric power, which is transmitted by high-voltage lines to Leningrad and the rest of Estonia. The power producers are a 50,000-kilowatt hydroelectric station on the Narva River, built in 1955, and a 300,000-kilowatt thermal power plant, which opened in 1959. The thermal power plant, located in the western outskirts of Narva, is fueled with oil shale from nearby mines.

First mentioned in chronicles dating from 1256, Narva was founded by Danes in 1223 and developed as an early trading center of the Hanseatic League on the border of the realm of Novgorod. It was in Narva that goods shipped by river from Novgorod were transferred to Baltic Sea vessels. Narva became a fortress of the Teutonic Order in the mid-14th century. In 1543, Ivan the Terrible founded the Russian fortress of Ivangorod on the right bank of the Narva River opposite Narva, but as a result of Russian defeats in the Livonian War (1558–1583), Narva passed to Swedish control. Peter the Great finally won Narva for Russia in 1704. In the 19th century Narva developed as a major textile center with a population of 45,000, employing more than half of Estonia's industrial workers by 1900. The importance of Narva's industries declined in independent Estonia between the two world wars because of lack of markets. Under Soviet rule (after 1940), Narva's development was set back by heavy destruction in World War II. Among the few historic sites remaining (after the virtual razing of the old town of Narva in World War II) are memorials to the Russian soldiers who stormed Narva in 1704 and 1944. Ivangorod, formerly the right-bank section of Narva, passed from Estonia to the Leningrad Oblast of the Russian SFSR in 1947. Pop. (1956 est.) 21,300.

THEODORE SHABAD,
Author of "Geography of the USSR."

NARVA, Battle of, an engagement at Narva on the Gulf of Finland, fought on Nov. 20, 1700, between Russian troops under Prince Carl Eugen de Croy and Swedish troops under the young Charles XII. On Oct. 4, 1700, Narva, then under Swedish control, was besieged by an army of 40,000 Russians led by Peter the Great. When a Swedish relief army of 8,000 men led by Charles unexpectedly appeared near Narva on November 19, Peter took panic, gave over the command to Prince de Croy, and fled. On the following day the outnumbered Swedes utterly routed the Russian army in a daring attack.

NARVA RIVER, river, USSR, on the border between the Estonian SSR and the Russian SFSR. The 48-mile-long Narva is the outlet of Lake Peipus and flows north past the city of Narva to the Gulf of Finland of the Baltic Sea. The Estonian beach resort of Narva-Joesuu is situated at the river's mouth. Rapids at Narva, 10 miles from the sea, are the site of a 50,000-kilowatt hydroelectric station, built in 1955. The power dam forms a reservoir of 75 square miles, south of the city of Narva. The river is not navigable but is used for floating logs to the sawmills of Narva. Formerly the river was also called the Narova.

THEODORE SHABAD.

NARVÁEZ, när-vä'äth, **Pánfilo de,** Spanish soldier: b. Valladolid, Spain, c. 1470; d. at sea, November 1528. One of the first of the Spanish conquistadors, Narváez played an important role under Diego Velázquez (1465?–?1524) in the reduction of Cuba to a Spanish colony. In 1520 he was sent by Velázquez on a punitive expedition against Hernán Cortés (q.v.) in Mexico. The expedition was a complete failure; Narváez was defeated in battle by Cortés, his troops defected, he lost an eye in the fighting, and he was taken captive. His most celebrated undertaking was his expedition to Florida to carry out the patent granted him by Charles V in 1526 to subjugate and exploit the region. In April 1528, Narváez landed near Tampa Bay on the west coast of Florida with several hundred men and began a vain search for the region's reputed wealth. Turned back by hostile Indians and by lack of food, Narváez and his men after much suffering reached the coast at Apalachee Bay, near the present town of St. Marks. Since the expedition had lost contact with its ships, it was forced to construct five crude flatboats and attempt to work its way along the Gulf Coast to the nearest Spanish settlement, on the Pánuco River in Mexico. Near Matagorda Bay on the Texas coast, Narváez and two of his men were swept to sea in a sudden storm and were presumed lost. Previously, three other boats had been wrecked or had foundered at sea. Four survivors of the expedition, led by Cabeza de Vaca (second in command to Narváez), eventually crossed Texas on foot and made their way south through western Mexico to the Spanish settlement of Culiacán in 1536.

Consult Lowery, Woodbury, *Spanish Settlements Within the Present Limits of the United States, 1513–1561* (New York 1901); Brebner, John B., *Explorers of North America, 1492–1806* (New York 1933).

NARVÁEZ, Ramón María, DUKE OF VALENCIA, Spanish general and statesman: b. Loja, Spain, Aug. 5, 1800; d. Madrid, April 23, 1868. A conservative supporter of Isabella II, Narváez fought against the Carlists in Catalonia from 1834 to 1836, defeating Gen. Miguel Gómez in the latter year. In 1840 he led an unsuccessful insurrection against Gen. Baldomero Espartero, the chief of Spain's liberal government. After the fall of Espartero, Narváez played a major role in the government of Isabella, but his increasingly reactionary policies proved unable to maintain her tottering throne.

NARVIK, när'vĭk, city, Norway, near the head of Ofot Fjord. Narvik's port is ice-free the year round and is a major transshipment point for iron ore shipped by rail from Kiruna and Gallivare in Sweden. When the port site was chosen in 1887, it was named Victoriahavn; it was renamed Narvik in 1898, four years before being opened for shipping. During World War II, Narvik was one of the key points seized by Germany to launch her invasion of Norway. See also WORLD WAR II—*3. Early Campaigns* (Norway and Denmark). Pop. (1957) 12,325.

NARWHAL, när'hwăl, a large porpoise (*Monodon monoceros* Linnaeus) which inhabits northern Arctic seas. The narwhal belongs to the zoological family Delphinidae, and with the beluga or white whale forms the separate subfamily Delphinapterinae, characterized by the free cervical or neck vertebrae. The narwhal and beluga are probably of more ancient origin than other porpoises, in which these vertebrae become fused together. When full-grown the narwhal has a length of about 16 feet. The head is rounded, the back has a low ridge instead of a fin, and the pectoral fins are short and broad. The color of the body is gray above and white below, everywhere mottled with black. The young are darker colored, while old individuals are often nearly all white.

The narwhal's most striking characteristic is a very long, spirally grooved tusk which projects forward from the left side of the upper jaw of the male. The corresponding tusk or maxillary tooth of the right side remains concealed in the gum throughout the animal's life, although occasionally both tusks are developed. In the female neither tusk is visible. The largest tusks are about 8 feet long. It has been suggested that the narwhal makes use of its tusk to break the ice, to transfix its prey, or in combat, but these suggestions lack confirmation. When the tusks were first introduced into Europe, their true origin was not known, and they were supposed to be the horns of the mythical unicorn.

Narwhals occur in herds among the loose ice of the Arctic north of latitude 65° N. They migrate to higher latitudes as the ice recedes, and return in the fall. Their food includes polar cod, crustaceans, and Greenland halibut. Very rarely, individual narwhals have strayed southward along the coast of Europe as far as the Thames estuary in England. The polar Eskimos, living in the settlements around Thule, in northwest Greenland, depend largely on the narwhal for dog food and leather. Formerly it was a major source of oil and food for the Eskimos themselves.

DAVID E. SERGEANT,
Arctic Unit, Canadian Fisheries Research Board.

NASBY, Petroleum V. See LOCKE, DAVID ROSS.

NASH, năsh, **Abner,** American politician: b. Amelia County, Va., Aug. 8, 1740?; d. Philadelphia, Pa., Dec. 2, 1786. He studied law and removed to New Bern, N. C., where he practiced successfully and in 1774 he was a member of the first provincial congress of North Carolina. He served as member of the council which framed the state constitution in 1776 and was speaker of the senate in 1779. He was governor of the state from 1779–1781 and in 1782–1786 sat in the Continental Congress. His brother Francis, a brigadier general in the Continental Army, was mortally wounded in the battle of Germantown.

NASH, John, English architect: b. London, 1752; d. East Cowes Castle, Isle of Wight, May 13, 1835. He studied and practiced architecture under Sir Robert Taylor; then retired from business until 1793; and upon his re-entry into the profession gained much royal and noble patronage. He laid out Regent's Park and the street leading up to the park, now called Regent Street; remodeled Buckingham Palace and altered the Brighton Pavilion. He was particularly fond of single façades, of projecting colonnades and of a plentiful use of plaster and stucco. The use of cast iron girders was principally introduced by Nash, who patented several varieties.

NASH, Ogden (1902–1971), American poet, noted especially for his humorous verse. Nash was born on Aug. 19, 1902, in Rye, N. Y. His family originally came from the South, and one of his ancestors had been governor of North Carolina. Nash was raised in Savannah, Ga. He was educated at St. George's School in Rhode Island and, briefly, at Harvard University.

After trying for several years to adapt himself to the business world in New York, as a bond salesman and an advertising man, Nash finally discovered his genius for witty verse and improbable rhymes. His first poem accepted for publication by *The New Yorker* magazine in 1930 began: "I sit in an office at 244 Madison Avenue / And say to myself, You have a responsible job, havenue?" The next year one of his most popular verses, titled *Reflection on Ice-Breaking,* advised shy suitors that "Candy is dandy / But liquor is quicker."

Besides publishing 19 books of poetry, Nash collaborated in 1943 with humorist S. J. Perelman and composer Kurt Weill on a musical comedy, *One Touch of Venus,* that was highly successful. While living principally in New York at this time, Nash continued to write amusing verses and give poetry readings and lectures. His permanent home, however, became Baltimore, Md., where he died on May 19, 1971.

NASH, Richard (called BEAU NASH), English leader of fashion: b. Swansea, Wales, Oct. 18, 1674; d. Feb. 3, 1762. He studied at Jesus College, Oxford, was for a time in the army, but finding military discipline not to his liking, entered at the Inner Temple. In 1705 his skill in gaming took him to Bath, which in 1703 had become a much frequented watering-place. He determined to improve the provincial character of the spa, and soon became a self-appointed but arbitrary master of ceremonies. He was known as the "King of Bath" and his rule was celebrated in prose and verse. His code included the prohibition of swords within his realm, a restriction which tended toward that consideration for the public peace which was then growing in England. His vanity grew with his power; he appeared in a monstrous cream-colored beaver and invariably journeyed by post-chariot with three span of grays, footmen and outriders. Gambling was prohibited by law in 1740, and Nash, by 1745, had lost his trade. The town granted him an annuity of £10 a month. Goldsmith wrote his life (1762).

NASH, or **NASHE, Thomas,** English satirist and dramatist: b. Lowestoft, Suffolk, 1567; d. 1601. He studied at Cambridge in 1586, spent some time on the Continent, and before 1588 came to London. In 1589 he published his *Anatomie of Absurdities.* In the literary warfare carried on between the Puritans and bishops Nash took an active part in behalf of the latter. Under the pseudonym PASQUIL he published the tracts *A Countercuffe Given to Martin Junior* (1589) and *Pasquil's Apologie* (1590). In 1592 he issued his powerful satire on contemporary society, *Pierce Pennilesse, His Supplication to the Divell.* His *Christes Teares over Jerusalem* (1593) followed in repentant mood, and he affected to dismiss satire, in which, he said, he had "prodigally conspired against good houres." His notable work of picaresque fiction, *The Unfortunate Traveller, or the Life of Jack Wilton* (1594), to a certain extent anticipated Defoe. Involved in a paper war with Gabriel Harvey, who had boasted of having put him to silence, he thereupon published *Have with You to Saffron-Walden, or Gabriel Harvays Hunt Is Up* (1596), brimming with scorn. Nash also wrote plays, in whole or in part. He completed, unsatisfactorily (1594), Marlowe's *Dido.* His *Summers Last Will and Testament* (1593), comedy, was first published in 1600. A play, *The Isle of Dogs,* led to his imprisonment for attacks contained in it. He died having, as one epitaph put it, "never in his life paid shoemaker or tailor." Nash's personality was somewhat unique in Elizabethan literature. His prose was vigorous and his verses were at times those of a poet. His works were edited by Grosart (1883–1885).

NASHUA, năsh'ū-ȧ, city, New Hampshire, one of Hillsborough County's seats; altitude 152 feet; on the Nashua and Merrimack rivers; 34 miles southeast of Concord; on the Boston and Maine Railroad; has a municipal airport. Nashua is the second largest city in the state, with well diversified industries. In 1823 the Nashua Manufacturing Company, the oldest industry in the city, was formed; it is known chiefly for its woolen blankets, although it manufactures other textile products. Machine tools and lathes were developed here in 1838–1852. Elias Howe (q.v.)

perfected the sewing machine in 1844–1846. The first watches were made by machinery about 1860. The first waxed wrappers for bread were made here in 1908. Major factory products now are: textiles including blankets, paper box machinery, shoes, gummed and coated paper, asbestos products, shears, navigational equipment, electronic equipment, and refrigerators. A United States fish hatchery here has huge rearing ponds. Various other points of interest in the city include Greeley Park (125 acres), a gift to the city for recreation purposes; Holman Stadium, seating 5,300; Colonial House, built in 1803, an architectural gem; and Marsh Tavern, a well known stagecoach hostelry, dating from 1804. Originally a fur-trading post known as Watanic, the site was settled in 1656, became Dunstable town in 1673 and Nashua in 1803. It was incorporated as a city in 1853. Pop. 55,820.

NASHVILLE, city, Tennessee, state capital, seat of Davidson County, and a port of entry, is situated on both banks of the Cumberland River (connected by bridges), and covers an area of more than 22 square miles. The city's average altitude is 500 feet. Nashville lies in the north central part of the state, 138 miles northwest of Chattanooga and 184 miles southwest of Louisville (highway mileage), in the Tennessee Basin, and is surrounded by a fertile agricultural area in which are raised cotton, tobacco, grains, livestock, fruits, and other products. The city is served by the Nashville, Chattanooga and St. Louis, the Louisville and Nashville, and the Tennessee Central railroads. On each side of the river is a municipal airport (the Berry and the Cumberland), which together provide Nashville with passenger transport, charter, and private airplane facilities. About 14 miles southeast of the city is the Sewart Air Force Base. A network of federal and state highways converges on Nashville for motorbus and truck transportation. There is river transport service also, the Cumberland at this point having a 9-foot channel. Although Nashville is a modern city, it has "a serene, Athenian quality," as Hodding Carter puts it.

Commerce and Industry.—Nashville is an important commercial center, with a thriving wholesale and retail trade; and six banking institutions, including a branch of the Atlanta Federal Reserve Bank. The city is also an important printing and publishing center, having two daily newspapers and more than 50 periodicals, most of them issued by religious or professional groups. It has railroad shops, limestone quarries, foundries, meat packing plants, and establishments which produce butter, spices, coffee, and other foods, rayon and cellophane, woven and knit clothing, shoes and boots, tobacco products, boats and barges, bridges, stoves, brick, and other products.

Educational and Cultural Institutions.—Nashville is one of the South's most important educational centers. Besides its public school system, it has private and parochial academic schools, business schools, a junior college for girls, and eight coeducational institutions of higher learning. Of these last there are, for white students, George Peabody College for Teachers—the largest teacher training center in the South—and Vanderbilt University (both institutions are private and nonsectarian); Trevecca Nazarene College (Nazarene); David Lipscomb College (Church of Christ); and Scarritt College for Christian Workers (Methodist). For Negro students, there are Fisk University (which dates from 1865) and the Meharry Medical College (both of which are private and nonsectarian), and the Tennessee Agricultural and Industrial State College, one of the largest educational institutions for Negroes in the world. Each of Nashville's colleges and universities has its own library facilities, and the city's public library has a collection of about 436,000 volumes, in addition to files of Nashville's newspapers dating from 1818. In the War Memorial Building are housed the State Archives and two state historical museums containing relics of wars in which Tennesseeans have fought. Vanderbilt University owns the Thurston Collection of Antiquities and Minerals which includes numerous artifacts of the Moundbuilders. In the Nashville Art Museum are rare collections of European ceramics and the works of American painters. Fisk University has an art gallery with unusually fine examples of modern art, including paintings by Paul Cezanne, Pablo Picasso, Diego Rivera, and Georgia O'Keeffe. Housed in the Parthenon in the city's Centennial Park is the Gowan Collection of paintings by American artists, dating from the colonial period. The Hermitage Hotel displays a score of Civil War scenes by the American artist William Gaul. Nashville has its own symphony orchestra and other musical organizations, among which are the world-renowned Jubilee Singers of Fisk University.

Notable Buildings and Other Points of Interest.—Near the heart of Nashville, on an eminence once known as Cedar Knob, is the State Capitol. Completed in 1855, it was patterned after an Ionic temple and built of fossilized Tennessee limestone blocks. Near its east portico is a bronze, equestrian statue of Andrew Jackson, 7th president of the United States, who as a young man, had his law office in Nashville; and whose beautiful old home, The Hermitage (1835), just a few miles northeast of the city, is maintained as a memorial to him. On the grounds of the capitol is the tomb of his friend, James K. Polk, one of Tennessee's governors and 11th United States president. Nearby is another building of classic design, the War Memorial, containing the historical museums already mentioned, and an auditorium with a seating capacity of 2,200. Perhaps Nashville's most beautiful public building is the replica of the Athenian Parthenon, with its 46 magnificent columns and its classical statuary. This modern structure of steel and concrete replaces an earlier replica in plaster, opened to the public in 1897.

Reminders of Nashville before the Civil War are the spacious private dwellings, built of bricks that were made by slaves, which can still be seen in the older parts of the city. A number of the city's churches also antedate the Civil War. Among these are First Lutheran Church (1838), St. Mary's Roman Catholic Church (1847), First Presbyterian Church (third on the site since 1816, and the cornerstone of which was laid in 1849), Holy Trinity Protestant Episcopal Church (built in the 1850's and given to its Negro parishioners in 1908), and First Christian Science Church (built 1856–1881 for an Episcopal congregation). Noted for the beauty of their architecture among the newer places of worship is the Roman Catholic Cathedral of the Incarnation, patterned after the church of San Martino ai

Monti in Rome; the Vine Street Temple (Jewish Reformed), designed in Byzantine style; and Christ Episcopal Church, in Victorian Gothic.

The city has a number of public parks containing playgrounds, swimming pools, lakes, tennis courts, municipal golf courses, driveways, bridle paths, and other recreational facilities. An unusually large variety of trees grows on its public and private grounds. Gardening is a popular hobby among Nashville denizens, and the city is famous for its iris which attracts visitors during the April Iris Festival when the flower blooms in parks and gardens.

Government.—The city's government is of the mayor-councilmanic type. Nashville's welfare program includes slum clearance and housing projects. As the capital of Tennessee, state government operations occupy a large place in the life of the city, and determine many aspects of its character. The federal government maintains in Nashville a customhouse and offices of several of its other agencies.

History.—Moundbuilders were the earliest human beings known to have inhabited the site of Nashville, but Shawnee Indians were the first ever seen by white explorers. In 1780 a white man's settlement was made at what was then called French Lick or Big Salt Lick, on the Cumberland River. As agent for the Transylvania Company, James Robertson had already explored the area and, late in 1779, led the first band of migrants overland from their homes in the Wautauga Settlement. They arrived at their destination on New Year's Day of 1780. In the spring they were joined by a second group, led by Col. John Donelson who came by flatboat, arriving after a harrowing thousand-mile river journey during which 33 of the group perished. (Among the survivors was Colonel Donelson's daughter Rachael, who later married Andrew Jackson.) The same year (1780), the Cumberland Compact was drawn up under which the little community of about 300 made provisions for its government and security. Seven crude forts were erected along the river, the most important of which was named Fort Nashborough in honor of Gen. Francis Nash, Revolutionary hero who had died at the Battle of Germantown. In 1784 Nashville became the official name of the settlement and was incorporated as a town. It grew rapidly, particularly after the admission of Tennessee into the Union in 1796. In 1806 it was chartered as a city and had a mayor-aldermanic government. Nashville was already a trading center with flour and cotton mills, foundries and smithies. With the inauguration of steamboat service about 1819, and the completion of the first bridge over the Cumberland, Nashville became an important river port for the shipment of cotton down the Ohio and Mississippi. By this time, the city was also a fashionable center for the schooling of the daughters of wealthy Tennesseans. Except for 10 years, the state legislature met there during all the period between 1812 and 1843, when Nashville was officially designated the state's capital. Two years later, the Nashville and Chattanooga Railroad (now the Nashville, Chattanooga and St. Louis) was chartered, the first railroad in the state to be completed (1854). This not only contributed to the development of Nashville as a railroad center but also gave the city better commercial connections with the Middle West.

On the question of slavery the city was divided, but after the state seceded from the Union in 1861, Nashville became one of the Confederacy's military headquarters, and home guards for the city were organized. In 1862, under threat of attack, the capital was temporarily moved to Memphis. A few days later Nashville surrendered to Union forces, and martial law was soon proclaimed. In 1864, in an attempt by a Confederate force to capture the city, a battle was fought in its environs. (See NASHVILLE, CAMPAIGN AND BATTLE OF.) The attempt proved disastrous, and Nashville remained in Union hands. Its suffering following the war was severe until, in 1868, a move for investigation instituted by its citizens released it from carpetbag rule. Recovery was slow until the middle of the 1870's, but the period 1870–1880 saw the population increase from 25,865 to 43,350, and reach 76,168 by 1890. The modern commercial, industrial, and educational center of today was beginning to emerge. When Tennessee celebrated its 100th year as a state, more than 6,000,000 visitors saw its Centennial Exposition at Nashville, opened officially by President McKinley. The growth of industries in the 1900's continued but at a slower pace until World War II, when extensive expansion took place.

Population.—Nashville is the second most populous city in the state, being exceeded only by Memphis. Its foreign-born population is small; its Negro population represents about 28 per cent of the total. The following figures indicate the population growth during the 20th century: (1900) 80,865; (1910) 110,364; (1920) 118,342; (1930) 153,866; (1940) 167,402; (1950) 174,307; (1960) 170,874; (1970) 447,877.

NASHVILLE, the name of a Confederate privateer that left Charleston in 1861 on a cruise to England and captured booty to the amount of $3,000,000. In February 1863 she was sunk by a Federal ironclad in the Savannah River.

NASHVILLE, Campaign and Battle of. When General Sherman's picked army of 62,000 left Atlanta Nov. 15, 1864 for the March to the Sea, the Confederate Army under Gen. John Bell Hood, strengthened by Gen. Nathan B. Forrest's cavalry, was on the Tennessee River in the vicinity of Tuscumbia and Decatur, with Stephen Dile Lee's corps across the river and in advance of Florence. Active preparations were making for a move on Nashville with the Ohio as a possible objective. Gen. George Henry Thomas had been sent to Nashville six weeks before to organize a force to resist Hood. Toward the last of October the Twenty-third Corps (Gen. John McAllister Schofield's) and the Fourth Corps (D. S. Stanley's) were ordered to General Thomas, who sent them under General Schofield to Pulaski, with orders to delay Hood as long as possible to allow of the needed concentration and organization at Nashville.

General Thomas was working most energetically at Nashville to organize an army to meet Hood, while General Schofield, with his inferior force, was holding against him with the utmost stubbornness to gain time for Thomas.

Hood was baffled in his attempt to intercept General Schofield at Pulaski and Columbia, Schofield reaching the latter place, forming solidly before Hood, who arrived November 27, and holding him there to the limits of possibility. Again, by skillful work, Schofield reached

Franklin in advance of Hood, marching his troops at night within rifle-shot of the enemy's lines at Spring Hill. Here Hood threw his army *en masse* upon Schofield, who had taken position around the town. The attack was delivered at 4 P.M., and lasted into the night. It was one of the most desperate assaults of the Confederates on any field, and most depressing for them in its results, five general officers being killed, six wounded and one captured. (See FRANKLIN, BATTLE OF.) The night of the 30th Schofield withdrew to Nashville, and the morning of December 1 Thomas' army was united.

A part of Andrew Jackson Smith's veteran division arrived at Nashville during the battle of Franklin, but not in time to be sent to General Schofield. The rest of his division, and General James Blair Steedman's division from Chattanooga also arrived December 1.

Hood advanced the day after the battle of Franklin and established his lines in front of Nashville December 2. Not until Hood appeared before Columbia with the entire army that had confronted the three armies under Sherman, re-enforced with Forrest's 10,000 cavalry, and the fact appeared that Schofield was fighting a gallant, almost desperate game to hold him back while Thomas was working energetically to organize his forces, did the authorities at Washington and City Point realize that Thomas had been left with inadequate means.

This created a feeling at Washington and City Point approaching a panic. It was feared that Hood might avoid Thomas, cross the Cumberland and carry out President Davis' plan to have him push on to the Ohio. This fear was redoubled when the necessity appeared for Schofield to retire from Franklin. It was not so clearly seen that his stubborn holding against Hood had saved the situation which Sherman created. Instead of leaving Thomas, who up to that time had never lost a movement or a battle, to deal with Hood as his full knowledge of the situation might suggest, it was insisted that he should at once attack. The straits of the situation were recognized at City Point, and the day after Schofield's arrival Grant telegraphed: "Arm and put in your trenches your quartermaster's employees, citizens, etc." The fourth day Thomas was peremptorily ordered to attack. He calmly went on with his energetic preparations to deal a final blow to Hood. His despatches, clearly showing his situation and his active work, were ridiculed by Edwin M. Stanton and Henry W. Halleck, and Grant repeated his orders to attack, and next directed Halleck to relieve him, first with Schofield, and next with Logan, and Grant himself started to take general direction, although Thomas had explained that while he had the troops ready to attack, a sleet-storm had covered the country with a sheet of ice upon which neither men nor horses could move, but that the moment it melted he would attack. When John Alexander Logan reached Louisville he was met with the news of an overwhelming victory. The two-days' battle, December 15 and 16, was remarkable for its perfection of plan, and for the fact that in its progress to the end this plan was closely followed.

The Confederate main and advanced lines were intrenched on bold hills about two miles from the city. Their advanced salient was established within three eighths of a mile of the Union center. The Union lines extended from the river above the city to the river below it. The Confederate lines were compact between the Murfreesboro Railroad at their right and the Hillsborough Turnpike, which ran south from the center of the city, across the Union center. Thus the Confederate lines covered less than half of the Union position. Benjamin Franklin Cheatham's corps was on the right, Lee's corps formed the center, and Alexander Peter Stewart's corps the left.

More than half the inner line was held by quartermasters' employees under Quartermaster-General Donaldson, and the rest of that line by new troops under Gen. J. F. Miller. Gen. A. J. Smith's corps held the right of the advanced Union line, Gen. T. J. Wood's line the center and General Schofield the left. General Steedman's division was in echelon to the front on the left. The night before the battle General Schofield's corps was moved to the left and front of Wood's line, and prepared to take prominent part in turning the Confederate left. The morning of the 15th fog veiled the rapid formation of Union forces in front of their works.

The battle began at 8 o'clock by a successful attack by General Steedman's division upon the earthworks commanding the extreme left. This attracted the enemy's attention to that quarter. About 10 o'clock Smith's corps moved against Hood's left, and James Harrison Wilson's cavalry corps of 9,000 horsemen and 3,500 dismounted men swung off in its wide circuit against the left and rear of the Confederate works, one division extending to the river below the city, and forcing back Hood's cavalry reserve under Gen. James Ronald Chalmers. Forrest's main body had been sent to attack Murfreesboro. Smith's corps moved obliquely against the Confederate left flank and took it in reverse. Schofield by a wide detour penetrated still further to the rear. At the same time Wood assaulted in front. Wilson's troopers carried earthworks, captured 27 guns and swept squarely into the rear of the Confederate left. These movements compelled its withdrawal for two miles. The next afternoon the same tactics were continued by Smith, Schofield and Wilson, while Wood on the Union center, and Steedman on the left, pushed forward to Hood's new line. This had been reformed with Benjamin Franklin Cheatham on the left, Stewart in the center and Lee on the right. The Union lines began the attack upon Hood's position at 3 o'clock with an unsuccessful assault by two brigades from Wood and one from Steedman upon the Confederate right. Soon after 4 o'clock Smith and Wood's corps on the front, with Schofield operating on their right and against the Confederate left flank, attacked in force, soon carrying the entire line. This attack and its results General Hood thus described in his official report: "The position gained by the enemy being such as to enfilade our line caused in a few moments our entire line to give way, and our troops to retreat down the pike in the direction of Franklin, most of them, I regret to say, in great confusion, all efforts to reform them being fruitless." Here 54 guns in position were captured. There was immediate and hot pursuit for nine days, led by Wilson's cavalry, when the remnant of Hood's forces crossed the Tennessee, having suffered a loss during his campaign of over 13,500 prisoners and 72 guns, and here the Union pursuit ended. Over 2,000 deserters came into the Union lines.

The result vindicated Thomas' insisting upon waiting for the remounting of his cavalry, since Wilson with his troopers formed an essential and controlling element in the battle and in a pursuit which were designed to disintegrate an army.

The records do not show the number of men with which Hood reached Tupelo. He claims that there were 18,500 left there after 3,000 were furloughed. He further says that of 14,000 that left Tupelo to join Gen. J. E. Johnston in North Carolina, 9,000 deserted. General Johnston's reports show that when Hood's forces reached him they numbered 3,953 officers and men. Thus, after Nashville, Hood's splendid force of Confederate fighters did not again appear as an army on the theater of war.

Even this complete victory, defeating the contemplated advance of the Confederate Army to the Ohio, did not fully allay the panic at Washington lest Sherman's movement to the sea should prove to have left the central West without sufficient protection, and while every possible effort in pursuit was being put forth in horrible weather, General Halleck thus telegraphed Thomas:

> Permit me, General, to urge the vast importance of a hot pursuit of Hood's army. Every possible sacrifice should be made, and your men for a few days will submit to any hardships and privations to accomplish the great result. If you can capture or destroy Hood's army General Sherman can entirely crush out the rebel military force in all the Southern States. He begins a new campaign about the first of January, which will have the most important results if Hood's army can now be used up. A most vigorous pursuit on your part is, therefore, of vital importance to General Sherman's plans. No sacrifice must be spared to obtain so important a result.

General Thomas, nagged beyond endurance, put an end to this style of despatches by the following reply:

> Your despatch of 12 M., this day, is received. General Hood's army is being pursued as rapidly and as vigorously as it is possible for one army to pursue another. We can not control the elements, and you must remember that, to resist Hood's advance into Tennessee, I had to reorganize and almost thoroughly equip the force now under my command. I fought the battle of the 15th and 16th instant with the troops but partially equipped; and, notwithstanding the inclemency of the weather and the partial equipment, have been enabled to drive the enemy beyond Duck River, crossing two streams with my troops, and driving the enemy from position to position without the aid of pontoons, and with but little transportation to bring up supplies of provisions and ammunition. I am doing all in my power to crush Hood's army, and, if it be possible, will destroy it. But pursuing an enemy through an exhausted country, over mud roads completely sogged with heavy rains, is no child's play, and can not be accomplished as quickly as thought of. I hope, in urging me to push the enemy, the department remembers that General Sherman took with him the complete organization of the Military Division of the Mississippi, well equipped in every respect, as regards ammunition, supplies, and transportation, leaving me only two corps, partially stripped of their transportation to accommodate the force taken with him, to oppose the advance into Tennessee of that army which had resisted the advance of the army of the Military Division of the Mississippi on Atlanta, from the commencement of the campaign till its close, and which is now, in addition, aided by Forrest's cavalry. Although my progress may appear slow, I feel assured that Hood's army can be driven from Tennessee, and eventually driven to the wall by the force under my command. But too much must not be expected of troops which have to be reorganized, especially when they have the task of destroying a force, in a winter's campaign, which was able to make an obstinate resistance to twice its numbers in spring and summer. In conclusion, I can safely state that this army is willing to submit to any sacrifice to crush Hood's army, or to strike any other blow which may contribute to the destruction of the rebellion.

This changed the tone of despatches from Washington and City Point. Grant and Stanton sent congratulations, and Grant, in his official report, after setting forth his impatience and apprehensions that Hood would go north, said of Thomas: "But his final defeat of Hood was so complete, that it will be accepted as a vindication of that distinguished officer's judgment."

H. V. BOYNTON.

NASHVILLE, CHATTANOOGA AND SAINT LOUIS RAILWAY, The. The first railroad completed in the State of Tennessee. It was first advocated by Dr. James Overton who, in 1843, offered himself as a candidate for the legislature. He based his canvass on his railroad project which he believed would permit control of the large cotton trade of Georgia and Alabama. He was defeated, and his plan was deemed impracticable by the people who dubbed him "Old Chattanooga." Two years after his defeat, however, the necessity for other outlets from Nashville besides the Cumberland River brought the subject of railroads under agitation again. Through the pressure of many influential citizens the legislature passed an act on Dec. 11, 1845, incorporating a railroad from Nashville to Chattanooga. This act was amended in 1847 to permit the town of Nashville to subscribe $500,000 for the benefit of the road, and "to raise money on loans by pledging the faith of the corporation; by pledging a portion of its taxes; by mortgage or otherwise to an amount not exceeding what might be demanded for the calls on the stock." Other major subscriptions were: from Murfreesboro, Tenn., $30,000; Charleston, S. C., $500,000; the Georgia Railroad and Banking Company of Augusta, Ga., $250,000. The shares of stock then had a par value of $25. In many instances the subscriber paid for his stock by actual work on the line, or in materials furnished. The state also gave material assistance by lending its endorsement to the bonds of the company issued from time to time on completed miles of railroad. The first train ran from Nashville to Antioch, 11 miles, on April 13, 1851, and when, on July 4, of the same year, a train arrived at Murfreesboro, the event was the occasion of a great celebration. People from all the surrounding country were on hand to celebrate this mark of progress. By May 1853, the road had reached Bridgeport, Ala., on the Tennessee River whence communication was established with Chattanooga by steamboat; but the entire line, 151 miles in length, was not completed until Feb. 1854. The iron track rail used was purchased in England, and delivered at Nashville for about $45 per ton. In November 1871, the company purchased from the State of Tennessee the railroad properties of the Nashville and Northwestern Railroad Company, a line extending from Nashville, Tenn., to Hickman, Ky. In 1873 the name of the corporation was changed to its present name. The Western and Atlantic Railroad, extending from Chattanooga, Tenn., to Atlanta, Ga., was leased from Dec. 27, 1890, to Dec. 27, 1919, and later extended for an additional 50 years to Dec. 27, 1969. The Paducah and Memphis division is leased from the Louisville and Nashville Railroad Company for 99 years from Dec. 14, 1895. The several branches of the present system were built under separate charters, some of them by independent corporations. The parent company operates its present mileage under the charters granted originally to the various corporations which have been merged from time to time into its line. The main line extends from Memphis, Tenn., through Nashville and Chattanooga to

Atlanta, Ga. Its various branches extend to Union City, Tenn., and Paducah, Ky.; Sparta, Pikeville, Hohenwald and Lewisburg, Tenn.; and Gadsden, Ala. From most of these terminals the road has connections with other railroads to all parts of the country. During the Civil War the line was in charge of the Federal military authorities from March 1862 to Sept. 1865. The railway suffered many losses in equipment and through distruction during the Civil War and did not emerge from its difficulties until the early 1890's. But it has never passed through any form of reorganization, nor has it compromised or failed to pay any obligation.

NASHVILLE CONVENTION, in American history, a convention of delegates from the Southern states held at Nashville, Tenn., June 10, 1850, called to consider the slavery question and the encroachments of Northern abolitionists. The Wilmot Proviso and the Missouri Compromise were disapproved, but resolutions of open resistance advanced by Texas, South Carolina and Mississippi were voted down. The convention, which was never generally popular, met again in November and again moderate resolutions were adopted. For text of the resolutions adopted at both meetings consult Harper's *Encyclopedia of United States History,* vol. 8 (New York 1915).

NASIK, nä'sĭk, or **NASSICK,** India, headquarters of a district of the same name in the State of Bombay; on the Godavari River, 30 miles from its source, and 107 miles northeast of Bombay. Nasik town is situated 5 miles northwest of Nasik Road, a station on the Great Indian Peninsula Railway. Due to the sanctity of the river Godavari, and to the belief that Rama, hero of the Ramayana, lived here for some time with his wife Sita, and his brother Lakshman, Hindus consider Nasik to be of special interest and holiness. On both sides of the river, but chiefly on its southeastern bank, lies the town of Nasik. Its buildings, covering an area of about 2 square miles, are divided into two parts—the new town to the north and the old town to the south. Though a place of great antiquity, the old town of Nasik has no ruins or buildings of any age, except the mosque on the site of the old fort. Nasik is the Nasica of Ptolemy, and was anciently a Mahratta capital. It is noted for its manufactures of brass and copper products, paper, and cotton. Interesting relics of the ancient religion were excavated in the 2d or 3d century A.D. Pop. (1966) 149,268.

NASMITH, nā'smĭth, SIR **Martin Eric Dunbar,** British naval officer: b. 1883; d. 1965. As commander of submarine E 11 in World War I, he destroyed 96 Turkish vessels in the Sea of Marmora, an effort for which he was awarded the Victoria Cross. In 1928 he was promoted rear admiral; in 1932, vice admiral; and 1932–1934 he was commander in chief of the East Indies station. While serving as lord commissioner of the admiralty and chief of naval personnel (1935–1938) he was promoted admiral (1936). Vice admiral of the United Kingdom and lieutenant of the Admiralty in 1945, since 1948 he has been vice chairman of the Imperial War Graves Commission.

NASMYTH, nāz'mĭth, **Alexander,** Scottish painter: b. Edinburgh, Scotland, Sept. 9, 1758; d. there, April 10, 1840. Portrait painting was his specialty. He became pupil, and subsequently assistant, to Allan Ramsay, Jr., and accompanied that artist to London. He returned to Edinburgh (1779); and traveled in Italy (1782), where he devoted himself to landscape and historical painting. He was intimate with Robert Burns, and painted his portrait which is in the London National Gallery. Other of his notable works are: the large *River Scene* owned by the Society of Arts; *The Port of Leith* (1824); and *The Lawn Market* (1824). In 1822 he published 16 scenes described by Sir Walter Scott. Simple in style, his landscapes are finely composed and very impressive although as a painter he is considered inferior to his son Patrick (q.v.). Somewhat weak in coloring, his execution is neat and detailed rather than vigorous in character. The Nasmyths were an artistic family of whom, between 1829 and 1866, no less than six women painters exhibited in London.

NASMYTH, James, Scottish engineer: b. Edinburgh, Scotland, Aug. 19, 1808; d. South Kensington, England, May 7, 1890. He was the son of Alexander Nasmyth (q.v.). After study at Edinburgh University, he went to London in 1829, offered his services to Henry Maudslay, founder of a well-known engineering firm, and was appointed assistant in his private workshop. There he remained until 1831, when he returned to Edinburgh and constructed a set of machine tools with which he began business in 1834 at Manchester. Here he was so successful that he had soon to erect a large new workshop at Patricroft near Manchester, where he became famous as a machine constructor and inventor. Chief among his inventions was the steam hammer, designed in 1839, and in 1842 patented in an improved form. The first hammer was constructed from a view of Nasmyth's sketches by Joseph Schneider at Creusot, in France, about 1841; but the first British one was erected by Nasmyth at Patricroft in 1843. Among Nasmyth's further inventions are a nut-shaping machine, a hydraulic punching-machine and a flexible shaft for driving small drills. In 1856 he retired from the firm of Nasmyth, Gaskell and Company, which he had founded, and devoted himself to the study of astronomy. He was the first to observe the mottled appearance of the sun's surface known as "willow-leaves" or "rice grains" (1860). He is author of *Remarks on Tools and Machinery* in Sir Benjamin Baker's *Elements of Mechanism* (1858); *The Moon Considered as a Planet, a World and Satellite* (1874), with James Carpenter, and an autobiography edited by Dr. S. Smiles (1883, new ed. 1895).

NASMYTH, Patrick Milner, Scottish painter: b. Edinburgh, Scotland, Jan. 7, 1787; d. Lambeth, London, England, Aug. 17, 1831. He studied under his father, Alexander, and developed great talent for landscape in spite of ill health and a crippled right hand which necessitated the use of the left in painting. He went to London in his 20th year and established his reputation in 1809 by his first picture *A View of Loch Katrine* which was exhibited at the Royal Academy. He invariably painted *en plein air;* in his last sickness he was raised on his bed to watch through the window a violent thunder-storm that was raging, during which he expired. His pictures are highly valued; his *View in Surrey* sold in 1892 for $13,125.

NASO. See Ovid.

NASR-AL-DIN, nä'sər-al-dēn', shah of Persia: b. April 24, 1831; d. May 1, 1896. Although he was not the heir apparent, his mother induced his father, Mohammed Shah, to proclaim him heir. His accession in 1848 was disputed by ʿAli Mohammed, known as the Báb, who had founded a pantheistic sect whose doctrine forbade concubinage and polygamy. Nasr-al-Din crushed this opposition immediately and put down several insurrections later.

During his reign, in which he was assisted by his vizier, Taqi Khan, he emerged as one of Persia's ablest rulers. He began his rule with reform measures and proved himself a master of finance. Later in his reign, telegraph services were established in Persia, connecting Europe and India. On the international scene, by his occupation of Herat in 1856, he provoked a war with Britain that resulted in Persia's evacuation of Afghanistan in 1857. In 1873–1878 and in 1889, he visited western Europe and tried to establish friendly relations with Britain. Later he turned to Russia, which was vying with Britain for influence in Persia. He favored Western civilization so long as it did not conflict with his power. Nasr-al-Din was assassinated. His son Muzaffar-al-Din succeeded him.

NASSAU, nas'ô, **Robert Hamill,** American missionary in West Africa; b. near Norristown, Pa., Oct. 11, 1835; d. May 6, 1921. After teaching in Lawrenceville, N.J., he studied three years in the Princeton Theological Seminary (1856–1859). Later, he studied medicine at the University of Pennsylvania. His linguistic ability, intimate knowledge of African native thought, customs and languages, and his skill in managing African tribesmen, made him an effective missionary. In the last eleven years of his life in Ambler, Pa., he wrote several books, the most notable of which was *Fetichism in West Africa.*

NASSAU, nas'ô, is the capital and chief commercial center of the Bahama Islands, a British colony in the Atlantic Ocean off the coast of Florida. Nassau is situated on New Providence, the most important island in the Bahamas. The city is built on rising coral ground at the northeastern end of the island. It is served by an international airport, and its excellent harbor permits entry to large steamships.

Nassau has fine public buildings and numerous points of historical, scenic, or architectural interest. The western entrance to the harbor is dominated by historic Fort Charlotte, named after Queen Charlotte, consort of King George III. The fort has many dungeons, corridors, and underground stairways. The Sea Gardens, at the eastern end of the harbor, attract many visitors who, through a glass-bottomed boat, may view a submarine coral garden with fish of many colors, sizes, and shapes. Nassau has a mild and healthful climate, and is a popular winter resort for Americans and West Indians.

Nassau was founded by the English in the 1600's. It was destroyed by the French and Spanish in 1703 and rebuilt in 1718. Twenty years later, it was fortified and opened to free trade. Population: (1962) 57,858.

NASSAU, nas'ô, Ger. näs'ou, is a historic region in West Germany, covering the western part of Hesse state and the Montabaur district of Rhineland-Palatinate. Situated north and east of the Rhine River, Nassau is a hilly, forested area intersected by the Taunus Mountains and the Lahn River. The valleys produce wine, fruit, and grains. There are mineral deposits and mineral springs. Wiesbaden is the chief city. The seat of the House of Nassau, Nassau was an independent duchy in the Confederation of the Rhine from 1806 to 1866, when it was annexed by Prussia and included in the province of Hesse-Nassau.

NASSAU, House of, nas'ô, Ger. näs'ou, was a princely family whose duchy was located on the east bank of the Rhine. The title was taken by Walram I, count of Nassau (d. 1198), a descendant of one Drutwin (d. 1076), generally regarded as the founder of the house of Nassau. Walram placed his lands under the suzerainty of the king of Germany. The duchy increased considerably in size. About the year 1255 their patrimony was divided into two branches of the house of Nassau by Walram's grandsons, Walram II and Otto I. The estates of the elder German line, founded by Walram II, were in the southern part on the left bank of the Lahn River where Wiesbaden became the ducal residence. Adolf of Nassau, son of Walram II, became king of Germany (1292–1298). The German line was later partitioned into several branches, but Walram's share of Nassau was united with Nassau-Weilburg (1816). When Duke Adolf (1817–1905) took sides with Austria (1866), Nassau was absorbed into the kingdom of Prussia.

The younger Dutch line, founded by Otto I (d. about 1292), occupied the northern part of the region on the right bank of the river, and was closely identified with the history of the Netherlands. Its capital was Siegen. It was later divided among Otto's three sons. From this division arose: (1) The Engelbert I, of Nassau-Dillenburg branch, which acquired lands in the Low Countries (1404). A descendant, Henry III, later inherited both German and Dutch possessions. His son, René, inherited from his father the principality of Orange. At his death (1544), his titles and estates passed to his cousin, William I, count of Nassau, later surnamed William the Silent (d. 1584), the famous stadholder of the Netherlands, whose descendants were known as princes of Orange-Nassau. One of them was William III who became William III of England, that line becoming extinct in 1702.

(2) John VI, count of Nassau, a younger brother of Henry III, ruled Nassau-Dillenburg until 1606, when his four sons founded new branches, two of which were extinct by 1739. The Nassau-Siegen branch, founded by the eldest son, Count Johann Moritz (1604–1679) became extinct in 1743; but the Nassau-Dietz line, founded by the third son, Ernest Casimir, has survived to the present. One of Ernest Casimir's descendants, John William Friso, inherited the Orange possessions in the Netherlands, and the latter's son, William IV, after reuniting all the Orange estates (1743), became hereditary stadholder of the Netherlands in 1747. The title was lost by his son William V in 1795 when he was expelled by the French republicans. Upon his death in 1806, the latter's son William VI succeeded to the duchy of Nassau. The new duke, refusing to adhere to the Confederation of

the Rhine (q.v., the league of German states formed by Napoleon), joined the Prussian Army, was captured at Jena (Oct. 14, 1806), and all his possessions confiscated. However, when the Congress of Vienna constituted the kingdom of the Netherlands, to include Belgium and Holland, he was chosen the first sovereign and was proclaimed King William I on Mar. 16, 1815. In recompense for his hereditary estates, given to Prussia and Nassau, he received the grand duchy of Luxembourg. The now royal house of ORANGE (sometimes still called Orange-Nassau) continues to rule over the Netherlands.

NASSER, nä'sẽr, **Gamal Abdel** (Arab. JAMAL ABD AL-NASIR), Egyptian statesman: b. Beni Mor, Upper Egypt, Jan. 15, 1918; d. Cairo, Sept. 28, 1970. A prominent figure on the world political stage for nearly two decades, Nasser stood as the symbol of Arab nationalism from the Atlantic to the Persian Gulf. Despite numerous political and military setbacks, he retained enormous prestige among the Arab masses, and he skillfully used this power base to capitalize on the intensified East-West rivalry in the Middle East.

The son of a postal clerk, young Nasser was educated at a secondary school in Cairo, and at the age of 20 was graduated from the Royal Military Academy. After being wounded in the Arab-Israeli war of 1948, he led other army officers in conspiring to overthrow the government of King Faruk—a plot that succeeded on July 23, 1952. The dominant force in the Revolutionary Command Council that seized power, Nasser assumed the office of prime minister in 1954 and of president in 1956.

Nasser's early years in power were devoted to helping the workers and peasants through land-reform measures, to ending British occupation of the Suez Canal, and to constructing the High Dam south of Aswan. One of his greatest successes came in the 1954 pact calling for withdrawal of British troops from Suez. Two years later, however, the United States cancelled plans to assist in building the High Dam and Nasser countered by nationalizing the Suez Canal. In November 1956, Britain, France, and Israel invaded Egypt, but their forces soon withdrew in the face of strong United Nations pressure. Nasser's break with the West was consolidated when the Soviets supplied the necessary assistance to launch the Aswan project. In 1958 he moved to implement his ambition of leading a unified Arab world with the merger of Egypt and Syria as the United Arab Republic. But the secession of Syria in 1961 proved a sharp blow to these hopes.

Nasser's most humiliating defeat came in the June 1967 war with Israel, a conflict that he helped precipitate. Surprisingly, in the wake of Israel's military triumph, Nasser's leadership among the Arabs was enhanced as Jordan's King Hussein and other moderate heads of state rallied to his cause. At the same time, the Soviet Union undertook a massive replenishment of Egypt's armed forces, as well as installing its own military presence in the country.

By 1970 the pace of events had quickened. Egyptian and Israeli forces were in daily combat on the Suez front when Nasser suddenly accepted a U.S. peace initiative and cease-fire. Before the talks could begin, civil war erupted in Jordan, but Nasser brought the two sides together in Cairo to sign a peace agreement the day before his sudden death of a heart attack.

NAST, năst, **Condé,** American publisher: b. New York, N.Y., March 26, 1874; d. there, Sept. 19, 1942. The son of a German father and French mother, he obtained the B.A. and M.A. degrees at Georgetown University and in 1898 took a law degree at Washington University (St. Louis, Mo.). From 1900 to 1907 he was successively advertising and business manager of Collier's publications, and meanwhile, in 1904, he organized his own firm, the Home Pattern Company. In 1909 he bought *Vogue* magazine, which under his direction became one of the world's leading fashion periodicals. He later acquired *House and Garden* and *Vanity Fair,* the latter merging with *Vogue* in 1935. The Condé Nast Publications, which he organized in 1922, was very successful.

NAST, Thomas, American illustrator and cartoonist: b. Landau, Bavaria, Sept 27, 1840; d. Guayaquil, Ecuador, Dec. 7, 1902. Brought to the United States as a child, he studied at the National Academy of Design, New York. At the age of 15 he became a news illustrator for *Frank Leslie's Illustrated Magazine,* and on the staff he received further technical training. He was sent to England in 1860 by the *New York Illustrated News* and also covered the revolt of Giuseppe Garibaldi in Italy. Having contributed satirical drawings to *Harper's Weekly* since 1859, he joined the magazine's staff in 1862. At Harper's he was encouraged to use his gift for caricature and to produce drawings with ideas instead of mere pictures of events. In a short time he became the most influential and famous cartoonist in the country. Eliminating unnecessary pictorial detail and shortening captions, he furthered the development of the modern political cartoon and made it more forceful.

For about 20 years, Nast's cartoons strongly influenced contemporary journalism, politics, and public opinion. During the Civil War, Abraham Lincoln called him "our best recruiting sargeant." Relentless in his attacks on injustice and on corruption in government, he is best known for his series of cartoons (1869–1871) attacking Tammany Hall and its boss William M. Tweed (q.v.). Outstanding among them were *Who Stole the People's Money?* (Aug. 19, 1871) and *The Tammany Tiger Let Loose* (Nov. 11, 1871). Through this work, he was largely responsible for the overthrow of the Tweed Ring. He popularized the tiger as a symbol of Tammany, contributed to the American concept of the appearance of Santa Claus, and invented the donkey and elephant emblems of the Democratic and Republican parties. Besides publishing briefly *Nast's Weekly* (1892–1893), he illustrated a number of books and did some painting in oil. In May 1902, he was appointed consul at Guayaquil, Ecuador, where he died. See also CARICATURE; CARTOON.

Consult Paine, Albert Bigelow, *Thomas Nast: His Period and His Pictures.*

NASTURTIUM, năs-tûr'shŭm, any of several species of plants of the genus *Tropaeolum,* some of which are grown for their attractive orange, yellow, or red flowers. *Tropaeolum majus,* the common garden nasturtium, is an annual that has given rise to many varieties differing in stature and in color of flowers. *Tropaeolum minus* is similar to *T. majus,* though smaller. The leaves and flowers of these two species can be eaten in salads, and the young fruits can be pickled and used like capers. *Tropaeolum tuberosum,* the añu or edible nasturtium, is cultivated in Andean highlands for its tubers that are used for food.

JOHN W. THIERET.

NAT TURNER'S REBELLION. See TURNER, NAT.

NATAL, nȧ-täl′, city, Brazil, seaport and capital of the state of Rio Grande do Norte; situated about 260 miles southeast of Fortaleza on the right bank of the Potengi River a short distance from the sea. The principal industries are cotton spinning, weaving, and, especially, salt refining, the state refining 90 per cent of all Brazilian salt. Chief exports are sugar, cotton, salt, hides, and carnauba wax. There are rail connections with Recife and Maceió to the south. Natal is also served by weekly coastal steamers. Eight miles from town an airport serves aviation companies in the transatlantic trade. Pop. (1966 est.) 204,000.

NATAL, nə-tal′, province, Republic of South Africa, bounded on the east by the Indian Ocean, on the south by Cape of Good Hope Province, on the west by Lesotho and by the Orange Free State, and on the north by Transvaal, Swaziland, and Mozambique. One of the four original provinces of the Union, it is the smallest of them, with an area of 33,578 square miles, including 10,362 square miles for Zululand. The population at the 1960 census was 2,979,920. The capital is Pietermaritzburg (pop. 1960, 91,178). The largest city in Natal is Durban (pop. 1960, 560,010; of metropolitan area, 681,492). Durban is the second largest city in the Republic of South Africa (after Johannesburg), and it is the country's most important port.

Physical Features.—The coast, about 375 miles long, is the outlet of many rocky, unnavigable streams but contains no important inlets except the landlocked bay embraced by Durban. From the narrow, fertile coastal plain, which broadens considerably in the northern area occupied by Zululand, the terrain rises rapidly into a central area of hills and ridges covered with coarse grass or woodlands. This region, ranging from 2,000 to 4,000 feet above sea level, ascends in the west to the foothills of the Drakensberg mountains, forming the province's western boundary. The chief rivers include the Pongola, along the northern border, the Tugela, in the central region, and the Umzimkulu and Umtamvuna, along the Cape Province border.

The coastal climate, warmed by the southerly Mozambique Current, is subtropical, giving Durban a mean annual temperature of 70.5° F.; the colder climate inland becomes bracing with rising elevations. Rainfall is plentiful, Natal being the best watered of the provinces; mean annual rainfall on the coast is over 39 inches, being heaviest in the summer rainy season (October–March).

Fauna and Flora.—Many of the larger animals once found in Natal, such as the elephant, hippopotamus, and buffalo, have disappeared, but smaller wildlife, including the leopard, ant bear, fox, otter, crocodile, hyena, zebra, and many kinds of antelopes and monkeys, are found. Notable among game reserves are Giant's Castle, in the Drakensberg region, containing many eland, and Hluhluwe Reserve, Zululand (white rhinoceros). Snakes include the mamba, python, cobra, and puff adder. Birds include eagles, vultures, and the secretary bird. Forests of indigenous trees have dwindled under clearing or exploitation. In the midland and mountain forest areas, the *podocarpus* (yellowwood) is perhaps the best known of many species.

The People.—Of the total 1960 population of 2,979,920, only 340,235 (approximately 11 per cent) were whites. Of the non-white population, 394,854 were Asiatics (chiefly Indians), 45,253 Coloreds (people of mixed blood), and 2,199,578 were Africans of Zulu and other Bantu stock. The Indian population, stemming from workers brought into Natal in 1860 to work the sugar plantations, is far larger than the Indian communities in all three other provinces combined. The bulk of the whites are of British extraction, Natal being traditionally the most British province; however, the Dutch are strongly represented in some of the northern districts, and there are small numbers of Germans, Scandinavians, and others.

Religion.—Among the whites the principal religious groups are the Anglican, Dutch Reformed, Methodist, Roman Catholic, and Presbyterian, in that order. The largest number of nonwhite Christians attend native separatist churches; after these the chief groups are the Roman Catholic, Methodist, Anglican, and Lutheran. About half the nonwhites are pagans. The Indians are mostly Hindus, the number of Muslims being relatively small.

Government.—Like the other provinces, Natal is governed according to the South Africa Constitution Act of 1961. The provincial administrator is appointed by the state president of the republic for a term of five years. Members of the provincial council, which has the power to deal with such internal matters as elementary and secondary education, hospitals, roads, and finance, are elected for five years. The central government controls higher and technical education. Laws passed by the provincial council may be vetoed by the state president. Natal has 10 members (8 elected and 2 appointed by the state president) in the Senate and 18 members (all elected) in the House of Assembly of South Africa.

Education.—There are separate schools for each race. Primary and secondary schooling are free for Colored, Asiatic, and Bantu pupils; excepting certain schools, they are also free for white children. Attendance is compulsory for white and Colored children between ages 7 and 15. The chief higher education institution is the University of Natal (q.v.).

Transportation.—The main railroad system includes 1,546 miles of government-owned lines, about one eighth of the South African Railways network; the tracks between Durban and Volksrust, on the Transvaal border, are electrified. The national government also operates bus and truck routes in Natal. Durban is a key point in the state-owned South African Airways system.

Economy.—***Agriculture.***—The chief product is sugar from the Zululand and coastal strip cane fields. The industry dates back to the 1840's, when the first sugar was produced—from imported cane—in a primitive mill at Umhlali, north of Durban. A century later over 340,000 acres were devoted to sugarcane, and with production of sugar showing sharp expansion since mid-century, Natal has provided all of the country's needs, plus a large export surplus. Tobacco, tea, cotton, fruits, and other subtropical plants grow in the coastal areas. Other products include maize, wheat, kaffir corn, and potatoes. There are stock raising and dairy industries. Large inland areas are devoted to cultivation of the black wattle, the bark and extract of which (used in tanning) are important exports.

Mining.—Second after the Transvaal as a coal producer, Natal produces the Union's best-quality coal, with annual output, chiefly from the inland Klip River, Vryheid, and Utrecht fields, exceeding 5.5 million tons. The province has small deposits of gold, copper, chrome, manganese, titanium, and other metals.

Fisheries.—Due to the rocky sea bottom, there is no trawl fishing in Natal waters, but many large fish, including the barracuda or Spanish mackerel, kingfish, salmon bass, and mussel-cracker, are taken in sea angling. Trout and bass abound in the rivers. Durban is a center for both offshore and Antarctic whaling.

Manufactures.—Durban has railroad, sugar-refining, automobile assembly, and brewing industries. Its manufactures include metalware, furniture, rubber, wattle extract, and many miscellaneous products. Pietermaritzburg is a center of the wattle bark industry.

History.—Natal owes its name to Vasco da Gama (q.v.), who sighted its coast on Christmas Day 1497 and named it Terra Natalis. The first British settlement was made at Durban (then called Port Natal) in 1824. In 1837 Voortrekkers on the Great Trek of 1834–1837 reached Natal, and on Dec. 16, 1838, they decisively defeated Dingaan, the Zulu chief, at the battle of the Blood River (Dec. 16, Dingaan's Day, is celebrated annually as one of the Union's chief national holidays). The same year the Voortrekkers founded Pietermaritzburg, and in 1840 the republic of Natalia. However, this state foundered with the annexation of Natal by Great Britain in 1843. Natal was made part of Cape Colony the following year, and in 1856 it became a separate colony. During the Zulu war of 1879 (see ZULULAND), notable battles were fought at Isandhlwana and Ulundi, while in 1881 the Boers defeated the British at Majuba Hill. In 1897 Zululand was annexed to Natal. During the South African War (q.v.), Natal was the scene of numerous engagements, including the siege of Ladysmith (Nov. 2, 1899–Feb. 28, 1900). In 1903 the districts of Utrecht and Vryheid were added to Natal. In 1910 Natal joined Cape Colony, the Orange Free State, and Transvaal in forming the Union of South Africa. Restrictive measures against South Africa's Indian community, chiefly concentrated in Natal, have caused recurrent friction between the Union, on the one hand, and India and Pakistan, on the other.

See also SOUTH AFRICA, REPUBLIC OF.

Consult Hattersley, Alan F., *Portrait of a Colony* (New York 1940); id., *The British Settlement of Natal* (New York 1950).

ROLAND C. GASK,
Staff Editor, "The Encyclopedia Americana."

NATAL, University of, an institution of higher education at Pietermaritzburg and Durban, in Natal Province, Union of South Africa. Established on March 15, 1949, the university dates its beginnings to two older institutions: Durban Technical Institute (later Natal Technical College), founded in 1907; and Natal University College, which opened in Pietermaritzburg in 1910. University work began in 1922, when Natal University College assumed sponsorship for engineering and commerce classes at the university level conducted at Natal Technical College.

The following degree courses are offered: at Pietermaritzburg—arts, fine arts, science, law, education, agriculture (also first-year courses in medicine, dentistry, engineering, and veterinary science); at Durban—arts, social science, science, engineering, survey, architecture, commerce and administration, education, and law. Certain degree courses may be taken on a part-time basis. Courses for nonwhites are given in separate centers in Durban, and there is a medical college confined to nonwhites.

NATAL GRASS (also called RUBY GRASS or ROSE GRASS), common name for *Tricholaena repens (T. rosea)* of the grass family (Gramineae, tribe Paniceae). An upright, slender, perennial grass, native to Africa, it has been introduced to the sandy soils of Florida and has become an important forage plant. It reaches a height of 2 to 4 feet and has 4- to 10-inch-long purple panicles and a general light purple to pink or wine color. Since it will not withstand freezing, it is usually cultivated as an annual. The genus includes about 15 species, most of which are African.

RICHARD M. STRAW.

NATAL PLUM, a common name for *Carissa grandiflora,* a spiny shrub in the dogbane family (Apocynaceae), native to Natal, South Africa. The spreading, densely branched plant reaches 6 to 15 feet in height, and bears bifurcate spines in the axils of its opposite, broadly ovate, leathery leaves. The fragrant white flowers mature to ovoid scarlet berries up to two inches long, which are edible but of no special importance as fruit. The shrubs withstand light frost and some drought, and make excellent hedges. They are grown in warmer parts of California and Florida.

RICHARD M. STRAW.

NATCHEZ, năch'ĕz, city, Mississippi, the county seat of Adams County, on the Mississippi River, at an altitude of 215 feet, about 100 miles (by road) southwest of Jackson and 168 miles northwest of New Orleans. There is a free bridge across the Mississippi from Vidalia, La., to Natchez. It is a trade and shipping center for a region which produces livestock, timber, and cotton. Industrial activity includes meat packing, pecan shelling, and the manufacture of automobile tires and tubes, furniture, boxes, wallboard, rayon pulp, and other wood products. The 400 producing oil wells in the county also affect the economy of Natchez, which has two recycling plants. The city has industrial port facilities, including a grain elevator. On state and federal highways, it has freight service by the Illinois Central, Mississippi Central, Missouri Pacific, and Natchez and Southern railroads, and its airport is served by the Southern and Trans-Texas airlines.

A center of pre-Civil War culture, Natchez is famous for having preserved its Old South atmosphere. During the Pilgrimage, an annual festival held in March when the azalea and camellia gardens are in bloom, hostesses in costumes of the 1860's welcome visitors to 30 ante-bellum mansions. These include Elgin, Linden, and Airlie (all built before 1790); The Briars (1812), where Varina Howell married Jefferson Davis; Gloucester (c. 1800), the home of Winthrop Sargent, the first territorial governor of Mississippi; Monmouth (1818), the home of General John Quitman of Mexican War fame; and Rosalie (1820) on the site of Fort Rosalie. Connelly's Tavern (1795) and Stanton Hall (1851) are open all year.

The main part of the city is on high bluffs, and Silver Street along the river front is the only remaining part of "Natchez-Under-the-Hill," a waterfront section which was notorious during much of the 19th century. Three esplanades overlooking the Mississippi River are a relic of the drilling grounds used by Spanish soldiers. Parks include Confederate Memorial Park and Duncan Park. The latter was once the grounds of Auburn, an ante-bellum mansion, but is now open to the public and includes a swimming pool, golf course, and other recreational facilities.

The city was incorporated in 1803. Municipal government (private charter, 1846) is of the mayor-council type, with a mayor, elected for four years, and a 12-man board of aldermen, elected for four years on overlapping terms.

The first settlement on this site was Fort Rosalie, erected on the bluffs in 1716 by Sieur de Bienville (Jean Baptiste le Moyne). It was destroyed in 1729 by the Natchez Indians for whom the surrounding country was named. In 1763, Great Britain obtained possession of the settlement, and it was captured in 1779 by Bernardo de Gálvez, the Spanish governor of Louisiana. The United States acquired Natchez from Spain by treaty in 1795, but did not take official possession until 1798.

With the opening of the Mississippi River, Natchez gained importance as a supply depot and river port. At the southern terminal of the Natchez Trace (q.v.), the city experienced a sudden growth in population in the early 19th century as waves of immigrants came down the Trace to share the prosperity of an economy based on cotton. This economy produced large plantations, great fortunes, and a luxurious way of life, and made Natchez an aristocratic community whose political and cultural influence was felt throughout the Mississippi Valley. The steamboat era, beginning in 1811, made Natchez one of the great cotton ports of the world and initiated its period of greatest wealth, when most of the famous mansions were built. The capital of the Territory of Mississippi (1798–1802) and of the state of Mississippi (1817–1821), Natchez lost prestige when the capital was moved to Jackson. However, it was still a commercial and cultural center of the South until it was occupied (1863) by federal troops during the Civil War. Population: 19,704.

Consult Marshall, Theodora B., and Evans, G. C., *They Found It in Natchez* (New Orleans 1939); Kane, Harnett T., *Natchez on the Mississippi* (New York 1947); Cooper, J. Wesley, *Natchez, a Treasure of Ante-Bellum Homes* (Natchez 1957); Moore, Edith W., *Natchez Under-the-Hill* (Natchez 1958); Pishel, Robert G., *Natchez, Museum City of the Old South*, rev. ed. (Tulsa, Okla., 1959).

ELENORA GRALOW,
Librarian, Fisk Public Library, Natchez, Miss.

NATCHEZ INDIANS, năch′ĕz, nä-chā′ (meaning unknown), an important American Indian tribe (now extinct) of the Muskhogean language family, living in the vicinity of the city of Natchez, Miss., which was named after this remarkable tribe. At one time the largest and most powerful group of the lower Mississippi area, the Natchez held sway until defeated in a war with the French and their Choctaw allies in 1729–1730. Together with two related subtribes, the Taënsa and the Avoyel, the Natchez were forced to disperse. Some 400 were shipped as slaves to Santo Domingo, and the balance broke into three refugee bands. One fled to South Carolina and joined the Cherokee, another went to live with the Chickasaw of northern Mississippi, and the largest remnant settled with the Creek on Tallahassee River.

Some of their interesting features included the high quality of their textiles and pottery, the practice of head-flattening to an unusual extent, and a highly developed caste system. The position of the chief, or "Great Sun" was akin to that of an actual god; at his death, his wives were expected to join him, and parents often sacrificed their children. The religious customs of the Natchez have been described at some length, for they were unique in North American Indian culture. The tribe was a true theocracy, somewhat monotheistic in nature, with an extreme degree of sun worship with a most complicated ritual. Large temples were erected on top of high mounds, and the colorful costumes and elaborate ceremonies astonished the early explorers. Yet today there are no identifiable Natchez artifacts known to exist, so complete was the destruction of this tribe.

Although the Natchez tribe is extinct today, there are a few persons who can claim a small percentage of Natchez blood, thanks to the widespread scattering of survivors; and as late as 1940 there were at least two individuals who could still speak the language. No accurate population figures exist, but at their maximum the tribe probably numbered about 4,000 persons.

FREDERICK J. DOCKSTADER,
Director, Museum of the American Indian.

NATCHEZ TRACE, The, a road from Natchez, Miss., to Nashville, Tenn., a vital route during the late 18th and early 19th centuries.

The president of the United States in 1801 authorized the Army to clear out a road from Nashville to Natchez to assure direct communication between the recently created Mississippi Territory and the Northeast. The fewer than 9,000 people of the territory then occupied the east bank of the Mississippi near Natchez. Nearly 500 miles of wilderness, belonging to the Chickasaw and Choctaw Indians, separated this distant American outpost from the nearest settlement, Nashville, which in turn was separated by 200 miles of wilderness from the settlements of eastern Tennessee.

The task of opening the road, which consisted of removing trees and brush from a narrow strip, was entrusted to the commander of Regular Army troops, Gen. James Wilkinson. He easily secured the consent of the Indians and had the clearing done during the next two years. The route selected generally followed that of a well-known Indian trail which had been used for generations.

For the next two decades it was an important part of the most widely used route of travel between the lower Mississippi country and the Northeast. Frontiersmen taking their products in flatboats down river to New Orleans or Natchez, finding it difficult to row upstream, preferred to walk over the Trace to Nashville, and from there return to their homes. It was also a most significant post route. In time of war, either with the Indians or with Great Britain in 1812–1815, troops and supplies passed over it to the troubled areas. It continued in use until the appearance of the steamboat provided a faster way of travel between the lower South and the rest of the country.

In 1938, Congress authorized the construction of the Natchez Trace Parkway to commemorate this historic road. The parkway, a unit of the National Park System, more than a third completed by 1960, resembles a park more than a highway because, by means of exhibits, wayside markers, museums, and sections of the old road in its right-of-way, it tells the story of the old Natchez Trace and the region it traversed.

DAWSON A. PHELPS,
Historian, National Park Service.

NATCHITOCHES, nă'kĭ-tŏsh, city, Louisiana, the seat of Natchitoches Parish, in the north central part of the state, on the Cane River and near the Red River, about 55 miles by road southeast of Shreveport, at an altitude of 105 feet. It is a trade and shipping center for a cotton-producing region. Industrial activity includes processing cotton and its byproducts and the manufacture of brick and tile. Northwestern State College of Louisiana and a United States fish hatchery are located there. Other points of interest include many houses dating from the French and Spanish colonial periods. Said to be the oldest city in the state, it was founded about 1714 as a French trading post and came under United States control in 1803. Its location on vital land and water routes gave Natchitoches commercial and military importance until the Red River changed its course in 1832, depriving the town of its position as a transportation center. The name derives from the Natchitoch Indians, an extinct tribe of the Caddo confederacy, who were friendly to the settlers. Incorporated in 1819 and reincorporated in 1872, it has the commission form of municipal government. Pop. 15,974.

NATHAN, nā'thăn, a Hebrew prophet in the time of David and Solomon. He was a descendant of the school of prophets under Samuel, and was David's confidential adviser. Thus, guided by a revelation, he forbade David to build the temple in Jerusalem. When the king desired to take Bathsheba as his wife, and ordered her husband Uriah the Hittite to be treacherously slain in battle so that he might carry out his plan, the prophet rebuked him by telling the story of the ewe lamb (II Samuel 12:1–4). When the king became angry at the tale of injustice, the prophet turned on him and said, "You are the man." (The parable is echoed even in the Koran, in sura 38:20–24.) The whole situation reflects the semi-barbarous society from which ancient Israel was emerging, and the moral conditions that surrounded the Hebrew people. The point of the story is the ethical advance made under the leadership of the prophets.

Eventually, Nathan rendered another great service to David by frustrating the treasonable plans of Adonijah (I Kings 1) and thus assuring the succession to Solomon. Finally, he wrote a record of the reign of David which probably underlies the account in the Old Testament (see I Chronicles 29:29). His sons held high posts in the court, one as "the king's friend," a recognized title of great importance in the ancient Oriental world, and another having charge of the supply of provisions for the royal household (I Kings 4:1–6). Some scholars have seen in the organization of the ritual of Solomon's temple and in the music of the Levites the final achievement of Nathan, but this is questionable.

FREDERICK C. GRANT.

NATHAN, George Jean, American editor, author, and drama critic: b. Fort Wayne, Ind., Feb. 14, 1882; d. New York, N.Y., April 8, 1958. Educated at Cornell University, from which he received his A.B. degree in 1904, he attended the University of Bologna in 1905. He entered journalism on the editorial staff of the New York *Herald* (1905–1906) and then became dramatic critic and associate editor of *Bohemian* magazine and *Outing* (1906–1908). He wrote on theater for *Harper's Weekly* (1908–1910); Associated Sunday Magazines (1908–1914); and for a national syndicate of newspapers (1912–1929). In addition, he was drama critic on *Puck* (1915–1916); *Judge* (1922–1935); *Life* (1935–1936); and also on *The Smart Set,* which he edited from 1914 to 1923 with H. L. Mencken (q.v.). Together they founded in 1924 *The American Mercury* with which he was associated until 1941. From 1943 until shortly before his death, he conducted a weekly column of drama criticism on the New York *Journal-American.*

Nathan was an extremely learned and well-informed critic, and his articles were lively and highly controversial, interlarded with many references to little-known Middle European dramas. Many of his enemies, who had felt the cut of his sharp pen, suspected him of inventing some of the titles for his own private amusement, but if taxed, he could always supply documentation. He was the Thersites of American dramatic critics and had a strong influence on such playwrights as Eugene O'Neill, William Saroyan, and Arthur Miller. A prolific author, he wrote over 30 volumes of dramatic criticism and comment, including a series entitled *The Theatre Book of the Year* (published annually 1943–1951). Long a bachelor, he married the actress Julie Haydon in 1955.

Consult Frick, Constance, *The Dramatic Criticism of George Jean Nathan* (Ithaca, N.Y., 1943); Angoff, Charles, ed., *The World of George Jean Nathan* (New York 1952).

GEORGE FREEDLEY,
Curator, Theater Collection, New York Public Library.

NATHAN, Robert, American novelist: b. New York, N.Y., Jan. 2, 1894. Educated in private schools and at Harvard University, he published *Peter Kindred,* his first novel, in 1919. In such works as *The Puppet Master* (1923) and *The Bishop's Wife* (1928) he developed the blend of fantasy, bittersweet humor, and satiric style that is his hallmark. He became famous with *One More Spring* (1933), a novel about the depression. Most of his more than 30 subsequent novels were delicately wrought fables or gentle love stories. They included *Road of Ages* (1935), on displaced Jews in Europe; *Journey of Tapiola* (1938), a parable with animal characters; and *Portrait of Jennie* (1940), perhaps his best novel, about a young artist and a girl who materializes from the past. Outside the main currents of American literature, he continued to write in this vein, and his books were all popular. While some critics have dismissed his works as pallid or cloyingly sentimental, none have denied his technical dexterity and gift for style. He published several volumes of poetry, collecting in *The Green Leaf* (1950) that which he considered his best. Among his later novels are *The Innocent Eve*

(1951); *So Love Returns* (1958); and *The Color of Evening* (1960).

NATHAN THE WISE (Ger. NATHAN DER WEISE), drama by Gotthold Ephraim Lessing (q.v.), published in 1779. Lessing wrote the play after he was prevented by censorship from continuing to publish a series of essays on controversial religious questions. Thus, although it is also a great artistic achievement, it is primarily a presentation of Lessing's concepts of religious tolerance and the brotherhood of good men. Nathan, a Jew living in Jerusalem during the time of the Crusades, sums up this message eloquently in the famous parable of the three rings: no religion can offer absolute proofs for the reliability of its sacred narratives, whereas ethical teaching in all major religions is identical and complies with rational (that is, absolute) laws for human conduct. Therefore, adherents of all religions should cease forcing their beliefs on others and expend their energies in developing what they have in common, namely, virtue.

It is implied in the drama that the old religions should be superseded by a new religion of reason. This consists simply of trust in the benevolence of Providence, acceptance of trials, and virtuous conduct. Nathan is the prophet of this religion. He did not despair when his flourishing family was wiped out by Christians, but gratefully accepted a Christian foster child, Recha, as a substitute. God's love is shown when Recha is rescued from a fire almost miraculously by a Christian Knight Templar. It is a trial for Nathan when the Templar, frustrated in his desire to marry Recha, denounces him to authorities who could execute him for rearing a Christian in ignorance of her religion. But everything ends happily when Nathan proves that the young people are actually brother and sister and long-lost relatives of Saladin, the ruler of Jerusalem. Now Christian, Jew, and Mohammedan are united in one loving family, all confessing the new religion of reason. The drama is an 18th-century version of Job, in which Nathan is made to understand God rather than to fear him; or of *Oedipus,* in which an incestuous marriage is gently avoided, not fatalistically enforced.

Nathan was the first important German play in blank verse, thereafter the accepted meter for German classical drama. It is one of the most popular plays in the standard repertory of German and Austrian theaters.

Consult Lessing, Gotthold E., *Nathan the Wise,* tr. by William A. Steel, Everyman's Library (London and New York 1949); Garland, Henry B., *Lessing, the Founder of Modern German Literature* (Cambridge, England, 1949).

ROBERT R. HEITNER,
Professor of Germanic Languages, University of California at Los Angeles.

NATHANAEL, nȧ-thăn'ā-ĕl, one of the earliest of Jesus' disciples, according to the Gospel of John, but not the other three. He was a native of Cana in Galilee, not far from Nazareth (John 21:2), and at first followed John the Baptist. Becoming convinced of Jesus' supernatural insight, he followed him (John 1:46–49). Some have identified him with the Bartholomew (meaning "son of Tolmai") named in the other Gospels, but the evidence is not convincing. Others have conjectured that he was the bridegroom at the wedding in Cana (John 2), but this is only conjecture. Much more probable is his identification with the group named in John 21:2, who were the first to see the risen Christ in Galilee. See also BARTHOLOMEW, SAINT.

FREDERICK C. GRANT.

NATICK, nā'tĭk, town, Massachusetts, in Middlesex County, on the Charles River, at an altitude of 160 feet, 18 miles (by road) west-southwest of Boston. It is a manufacturing center, producing shoes, saws and edge tools, boxes, baseballs, preserves and jellies, housecoats and dusters, electronic equipment, organs, metal stampings, and aluminum and magnesium sand castings. Agriculture in the vicinity is devoted mostly to truck farming and raising apples and peaches.

Natick was founded in 1651 by John Eliot (q.v.), "Apostle to the Indians," as a special settlement for Indian converts to Christianity. It was for the most part an Indian town until after the Revolutionary War, when white men began to crowd out the Indians and to take control of the government. There is a monument to Eliot in South Natick. A boulder memorial on the Natick Common marks the Henry Wilson Tree, planted by "the Natick cobbler," who became vice president of the United States (1873–1875). Harriet Beecher Stowe wrote of the town in her novel *Oldtown Folks* (1869), which she based on her husband's accounts of his childhood there. Horatio Alger spent his last years there and died there in 1899. Incorporated as a town in 1781, Natick adopted the representative town meeting form of government in 1953. Pop. 31,057.

ELIZABETH H. PARTRIDGE.

NATION, nā'shŭn, **Carry** (nee CARRY AMELIA MOORE), American temperance agitator: b. Garrard County, Ky., Nov. 25, 1846; d. Leavenworth, Kans., June 9, 1911. After attending the Missouri State Normal School, she married Dr. Charles Gloyd in 1867. He was an alcoholic, which made married life unhappy and permanently embittered her against intoxicating liquor. She left Gloyd, who died six months later, and in 1877 married David Nation, a lawyer and minister. While living in Medicine Lodge, Kans., in the 1890's, she began her famous campaign against the saloons which flourished illegally in that prohibition state. She eventually resorted to violent tactics and entered the establishments, destroying stocks of liquor and wrecking furniture and fixtures with iron bars or stones. Extending her activities to other cities in Kansas, she first used a hatchet, which became her symbol, while wrecking a saloon in Wichita in 1901. In that year her husband divorced her for desertion.

Mrs. Nation went on with her "hatchetations" of "joints," as she called these exploits, in such cities as San Francisco, Washington, and New York, and was arrested about 30 times. She lectured, spoke between the acts of carnivals, and sold souvenir hatchets, making enough money to pay her fines and to build a home for drunkards' wives in Kansas City. In 1904 she published a rambling autobiography, *The Use and Need of the Life of Carry A. Nation.*

A very tall woman of unusual strength and energy, she was given to mystic seizures and appears to have suffered from hereditary paranoia—her mother was a psychotic who believed herself to be Queen Victoria. While her greatest wrath was directed toward alcohol, she also inveighed against such things as corsets, shortened skirts, and smoking. She was an active suffragette, but received little support from national women's suffrage organizations or temperance movements. There were few immediate results of her activities; however, she did help to establish the climate of public opinion which made constitutional prohibition possible in 1920.

Consult Asbury, Herbert, *Carry Nation* (New York 1929).

NATIONAL ACADEMY OF DESIGN, an American association devoted to the fine arts, academician membership in which is limited to 125 painters, 50 sculptors, 25 architects, 25 graphic artists, and 25 aquarellists; associate membership is unlimited in the five classes. The Society of American Artists merged with the academy in 1906. The School of Fine Arts, conducted since 1825, is located at 5 East 89th Street, New York, N.Y. Classes in oil and water-color painting, drawing, sculpture, and a mural workshop with members of the academy instructing are held from September to May. In addition there is a summer session from June 1 to August 15. The home and exhibition building of the society is at 1083 Fifth Avenue, New York, N.Y. The governing council of the organization is made up of the officers and six academicians. First known as the New York Drawing Association, a secession in 1825 of young artists from the first Academy of Arts in New York founded in 1802, the present name was adopted in 1828.

NATIONAL ACADEMY OF SCIENCES, an organization of distinguished scientists, dedicated to the furtherance of science and its use for the general welfare. Although not a government agency, the academy has long enjoyed close relations with the federal government, and its headquarters are located in Washington, D.C. Its Congressional Charter of March 3, 1863, approved by President Abraham Lincoln, specifies that ". . . the Academy shall, whenever called upon by any department of the Government, investigate, examine, experiment, and report upon any subject of science or art, the actual expense of such investigations, examinations, experiments, and reports, to be paid from appropriations which may be made for the purpose, but the Academy shall receive no compensation whatever for any service to the Government of the United States."

In 1916, the National Research Council was organized by the academy to facilitate the participation of a broader representation of scientists and technologists in the aims of the academy as a measure of national preparedness. The Research Council was perpetuated by the academy on April 29, 1919, in response to a further request from President Woodrow Wilson.

The National Academy of Sciences comprises 14 sections: mathematics, astronomy, physics, engineering, chemistry, geology, botany, zoology and anatomy, physiology, pathology and microbiology, anthropology, psychology, geophysics, and biochemistry. A maximum of 35 members, who must be United States citizens, and 4 foreign associates are elected annually by the current membership in recognition of continuing achievement in scientific or technological research.

The members of the National Research Council, numbering about 280, are appointed by the president of the academy from academic, industrial, and government organizations throughout the country, following nomination of the various groups. The council is organized into the following divisions: anthropology and psychology, biology and agriculture, chemistry and chemical technology, earth sciences, engineering and industrial research, mathematics, medical sciences, and physical sciences. Full legal responsibility for all the activities of the National Research Council is vested in the academy.

The over-all Academy-Research Council organization brings together in appropriate groups the most competent scientists and engineers in the country to deal broadly with scientific problems and to exchange information in the furtherance of research. The undertakings of the Academy-Research Council vary widely in nature and in the duration and type of effort required; the patterns of organization are kept flexible to permit each problem to be approached in a suitable manner. Work is carried on through permanent boards and institutes, committees, subcommittees and panels, as well as *ad hoc* groups for special purposes. Most of these units are assigned to one or another of the eight divisions of the Academy-Research Council and receive general guidance from the appropriate division chairman. An Office of Scientific Personnel, an Office of International Relations, and an Office of Documentation deal with problems in those areas common to all the sciences.

The Academy-Research Council does not maintain laboratories of its own but seeks to stimulate and further the work of individual scientists and to coordinate investigations dealing with broad problems in research, both nationally and internationally. These purposes are carried out through a wide variety of means, including conferences, technical committees, surveys, collection and collation of scientific and technical data, the sponsorship of scientific publications and research organizations, and the administration of public and private funds for research projects and fellowships.

Publications of the Academy-Research Council include an *Annual Report* to the United States Congress, the monthly *Proceedings of the National Academy of Sciences,* the bimonthly *News Report,* an irregular series of scientific and technical reports, and its *Biographical Memoirs,* published annually to honor deceased members of the academy.

NATIONAL AERONAUTICS AND SPACE ADMINISTRATION, a U.S. government agency responsible for civilian aeronautical and space research programs. NASA was established by the National Aeronautics and Space Act of 1958 and began operating on October 1 of that year with personnel and facilities of the National Advisory Committee for Aeronautics (NACA), which it replaced.

Facilities. Five NACA laboratories became NASA installations: Langley Research Center and Wallops Station, in Virginia; Ames Research Center and Flight Research Center, in California; and Lewis Research Center, in Ohio. Transferred from Department of Defense space activities to NASA were the Army's Jet Propulsion Laboratory, operated by the California Institute of Technology, and a division of the Army Ballistic Missile Agency, in Alabama, which became the George C. Marshall Space Flight Center.

As space activity expanded, NASA added the Goddard Space Flight Center, in Maryland; a launch operations complex at Cape Canaveral—

later named the John F. Kennedy Space Center—in Florida; the Manned Spacecraft Center, in Texas; and the Electronic Research Center (ERC), in Massachusetts. The ERC became a facility of the Department of Transportation in 1970 and was renamed the Transportation Systems Center.

Offices and Functions. NASA is headed by an administrator responsible for all functions and authorities assigned to the agency. Program offices direct NASA's research and development programs, functional offices furnish support and guidance to the administrator and other headquarters offices, and field centers are responsible for execution of the programs.

The Office of Manned Space Flight directs the development of large launch vehicles and spacecraft and related systems for manned space missions. It manages the Manned Spacecraft Center, the Marshall Space Flight Center, and the Kennedy Space Center. The office was responsible for the Mercury, Gemini, and Apollo projects that achieved the goal of landing men on the moon and returning them safely to earth. Its responsibilities now also include space station (Skylab) and space shuttle programs.

The Office of Space Science and Applications—at one time two separate offices—is responsible for scientific explorations of space, the planets, and the moon, and for such applications of space technology as meteorology and communications. It developed Ranger, Lunar Orbiter, and Surveyor spacecraft to investigate the moon, and Mariner spacecraft to study and photograph Venus and Mars. Its Syncom and Relay communications satellites were the basis for the Intelsat satellites operated by the Communications Satellite Corporation. For meteorological studies it developed Tiros—now ESSA—satellites, Applications Technology Satellites (ATS's), and Nimbus satellites. Its installations are Goddard Space Flight Center, the Jet Propulsion Laboratory, and Wallops Station.

The Office of Advanced Research and Technology establishes the scientific and technological base for future aeronautical and space flight, through a broad program of research on aircraft, spacecraft, launch vehicles, nuclear and other propulsion systems, electronics, and biotechnology. It has management responsibilities for the Ames, Flight, Langley, and Lewis research centers, and for the joint NASA-Atomic Energy Commission's Space Nuclear Propulsion Office. Its projects include research on the supersonic transport (SST), lifting bodies, vertical and short take-off and landing airplanes (V/STOL), fatigue and stress in metals, computer applications, fibers and plastics, high-strength alloys, miniaturization of instruments, fuel cells, lubricants, noise suppression, aircraft safety, and other areas of study.

The Office of Tracking and Data Acquisition develops and operates facilities and related equipment for tracking spacecraft and receiving and processing data. It also manages NASA's long-line communications systems. Three worldwide networks exist. The Space Tracking and Data Acquisition network services scientific, communications, and meteorological satellites, the Deep Space Network tracks and communicates with lunar and interplanetary spacecraft, and the Manned Space Flight Network performs the same services for manned spacecraft.

George B. DeGennaro
National Aeronautics and Space Administration

NATIONAL ARCHIVES AND RECORDS SERVICE. See General Services Administration, the.

NATIONAL ASSOCIATION FOR THE ADVANCEMENT OF COLORED PEOPLE, an American civil rights organization. The NAACP was preceded by the Niagara Movement (1905) of Negro militants, led by W.E.B. Du Bois (q.v.). A bloody race riot in Springfield, Ill., in 1908 prompted a group of prominent white liberals to join forces in 1909 with the Niagara Movement. The NAACP was incorporated in 1910, and Du Bois became editor of its publication, *Crisis.*

To achieve its goal of social, political, and economic equality for Negroes, the NAACP has focused on litigation, legislation, and education. It has won numerous victories in federal courts, including Supreme Court decisions protecting the Negro's franchise (1915), abolishing municipal housing-segregation ordinances (1917), and—the most epochal—striking down the "separate but equal" schooling formula (1954). The 1954 ruling unequivocally forbade segregation in public schools.

Under Roy Wilkins (q.v.), who became executive secretary of the NAACP in 1955, total membership in all 50 states reached about 500,000. Once considered radical, the NAACP yielded this reputation to younger groups in the 1950's and 1960's. See also Civil Rights Movement.

NATIONAL ASSOCIATION OF MANUFACTURERS, The (N.A.M.). A convention, consisting of several hundred representative American manufacturers, met in Cincinnati, Ohio, Jan. 22, 1895, and provided for the organization of a national association of manufacturers. At the first annual convention of the association held in Chicago Jan. 21, 1896, the name "The National Association of Manufacturers of the United States of America" was adopted, a preamble setting forth the objects of the association was published, and a constitution was adopted.

> The general objects for which the association works are: (1) the promotion of the industrial interests of the United States; (2) the fostering of the domestic and foreign commerce of the United States; (3) the betterment of the relations between employers and their employees; (4) the protection of the individual liberty and rights of employer and employee; (5) the dissemination of information among the public with respect to the principles of individual liberty and ownership of property; (6) the support of legislation in furtherance of those principles and opposition to legislation in derogation thereof.

The association has standing committees on the following subjects: agricultural cooperation; economic policy; economic security; educational cooperation; employment relations; government finance; healthful working conditions; industrial economics; industrial financing; industrial practices; national defense and industrial mobilization; patents and trademarks; public relations; relations of government to industry; scientific research study of depressions; tariff and transportation.

To advise the standing committees in their deliberations, the association has a number of advisory groups. In addition, the association has been sponsoring the most widespread and complete program ever undertaken by organized industry to tell its story to the public through the National Industrial Information Committee.

The membership of the association consists of individuals, firms, and corporations engaged in manufacturing. Dues are based on capitalization, and the income is expended in the interests of the members. There are branch offices in Washington, D.C., and San Francisco, Calif.

NOEL SARGENT, *Secretary*

NATIONAL CEMETERIES, burial grounds on United States soil, established by various acts of Congress for the interment of any member or former member of the United States armed forces whose last service terminated honorably. The veteran's husband or wife may be buried in a national cemetery; and their minor children or adult children who are dependent by reason of physical or mental disability may be interred in the grave of one of the parents. There is no cost for the grave site.

National cemeteries had their inception shortly after the American Civil War. Of the total interments about 10,700 are those of Confederates, being mainly in the national cemeteries of Arlington, Camp Butler, City Point, Cypress Hills, Finn's Point, Fort Smith, Hampton, Jefferson Barracks, Little Rock, Philadelphia, Springfield, and Woodlawn. In the 1960's over 800,000 veterans and members of the families rested in 98 national cemeteries. Of these cemeteries, 85 were under the Department of Defense and were supervised by the Army's quartermaster general; the remaining 13 cemeteries were under the Department of the Interior. The following is a list of the national cemeteries by name and location:

Alexandria, Pineville, La.
Alexandria, Va.
Alton, Ill.
Andersonville, Ga.
*Andrew Johnson, Greeneville, Tenn.
Annapolis, Md.
*†Antietam, Sharpsburg, Md.
Arlington, Va.
Balls Bluff, Leesburg, Va.
Baltimore, Md.
Barrancas, Warrington, Fla.
Baton Rouge, La.
*† Battleground, Washington, D.C.
Beaufort, S.C.
Beverly, N.J.
Black Hills, Sturgis, S.Dak.
Camp Butler, Springfield, Ill.
Camp Nelson, Nicholasville, Ky.
Cave Hill, Louisville, Ky.
*†Chalmette National Cemetery, Arabi, La.
Chattanooga, Tenn.
City Point, Hopewell, Va.
Cold Harbor, Richmond, Va.
Corinth, Miss.
Crown Hill, Indianapolis, Ind.
Culpeper, Va.
*Custer Battlefield, Crow Agency, Mont.
Cypress Hills, Brooklyn, N.Y.
Danville, Ky.
Danville, Va.
Fayetteville, Ark.
Finn's Point, Salem, N.J.
Florence, S.C.
Fort Bliss, Texas
*†Fort Donelson, Dover, Tenn.
Fort Gibson, Okla.
Fort Harrison, Richmond, Va.
Fort Leavenworth, Kans.
Fort Logan, Denver, Col.
Fort McPherson, Maxwell, Nebr.
Fort Rosecrans, San Diego, Calif.
Fort Sam Houston, Texas
Fort Scott, Kans.
Fort Smith, Ark.
Fort Snelling, Minneapolis, Minn.
*†Fredericksburg, Va.
*†Gettysburg, Pa.
Glendale, Va.
Golden Gate, San Bruno, Calif.
Grafton, W.Va.
Hampton, Va.
Jefferson Barracks, St. Louis, Mo.
Jefferson City, Mo.
Keokuk, Iowa
Knoxville, Tenn.
Lebanon, Ky.
Lexington, Ky.
Little Rock, Ark.
Long Island, Farmingdale, L.I., N.Y.
Loudon Park, Baltimore, Md.
Marietta, Ga.
Memorial of the Pacific, Honolulu, Hawaii
Memphis, Tenn.
Mill Springs, West Somerset, Ky.
Mobile, Ala.
Mound City, Ill.
Nashville, Madison, Tenn.
Natchez, Miss.
New Albany, Ind.
New Bern, N.C.
Perryville, Ky.
Philadelphia, Pa.
*†Poplar Grove, Petersburg, Va.
Port Hudson, Zachary, La.
Puerto Rico, San Juan, Puerto Rico
Quincy, Ill.
Raleigh, N.C.
Richmond, Va.
Rock Island, Ill.
Saint Augustine, Fla.
Salisbury, N.C.
San Antonio, Texas
San Francisco, Calif.
Santa Fe, N.Mex.
Seven Pines, Sandston, Va.
*†Shiloh, Pittsburg Landing, Tenn.
Sitka, Alaska
Soldiers' Home, Washington, D.C.
Springfield, Mo.
Staunton, Va.
*†Stones River, Murfreesboro, Tenn.
*†Vicksburg, Miss.
Willamette, Portland, Oreg.
Wilmington, N.C.
Winchester, Va.
Woodlawn, Elmira, N.Y.
*†Yorktown, Va.
Zachary Taylor, Louisville, Ky.

* Under the Department of the Interior.

† Administered by the National Park Service; it also administers the military cemetery which is part of the Chalmette National Historical Park, La.

JAMES G. HATTOX, *Colonel, U.S. Army, Department of the Army, Memorial Division.*

The government has established abroad 22 permanent military cemeteries for the burial of deceased military personnel of World War I and World War II whose next of kin had requested that final interment be made outside the continental limits of the United States. The American Battle Monuments Commission has erected memorials to the war dead at these overseas cemeteries. The commission also maintains a cemetery in Mexico City where the remains of 750 Americans who died in the Mexican War are buried.

AMERICAN OVERSEAS MILITARY CEMETERIES

(Under the American Battle Monuments Commission)

Name	Location	Number of acres	Number of interments
World War I			
Aisne-Marne	Belleau, France	42½	2,288
Brookwood	England	4½	468
Flanders Field	Waregem, Belgium	6	368
Meuse-Argonne	Romagne, France	130½	14,246
Oise-Aisne	Fère, France	36½	6,012
Saint Mihiel	Thiaucourt, France	40½	4,152
Somme	Bony, France	14	1,837
Suresnes	Paris, France	7½	1,565*
Total		282	30,936
World War II			
Ardennes	Neuville, Belgium	50½	5,250
Brittany	St. James, France	28	4,410
Cambridge	England	30½	3,811
Epinal	France	48	5,255
Florence	Italy	70	4,402
Henri-Chapelle	Belgium	57	7,989
Lorraine	St.-Avold, France	113½	10,489
Luxembourg	Luxembourg	50½	5,076
Manila	Philippines	152	17,182
Netherlands	Margraten, Holland	65½	8,301
Normandy	St. Laurent, France	172½	9,386
North Africa	Carthage, Tunisia	27	2,840
Rhône	Draguignan, France	12	861
Sicily-Rome	Nettuno, Italy	77	7,862
Total		954	93,114
Grand Total		1,236	124,050

* Including 24 unknown dead of World War II.

WILLIAM A. WALKER, *Colonel, U.S. Army, The American Battle Monuments Commission.*

NATIONAL CITY, city, California, in San Diego County, on San Diego Bay just south of the city of San Diego and 10 miles from the Mexican border. It is the site of a United States naval station, and it has ship repair facilities. Industries include machine shops, furniture manufacturing, and food-processing plants. It is also the hope of the Maytime Band Review. National City was settled in 1868 and incorporated in 1887. Its government is by city manager and five councilmen. Pop. 43,184.

NATIONAL CONFERENCE OF CATHOLIC BISHOPS, the organization of all the Roman Catholic bishops of the United States for the joint exercise of their pastoral office. It was established on Nov. 14, 1966, in response to Vatican II's Decree on the Bishops' Pastoral

Office, to succeed the pastoral meetings of the former National Catholic Welfare Conference. The social-action secretariat of the NCWC is continued in the U.S. Catholic Conference, Inc.

NATIONAL CONFERENCE ON SOCIAL WELFARE was organized in 1874 as the Conference of Boards of Public Charities, and was later known as the National Conference of Charities and Correction and also as the National Conference of Social Work until acquiring its present name in 1956. It is a voluntary association of about 6,500 individuals and organization members who support the program with their dues and participation. There are no membership requirements. Its purpose is to provide an annual forum for the critical examination of basic social welfare problems and issues, held in the spring in a selected city. Its function is extended by the publication in four or more volumes of the papers presented at the annual forum; by the distribution of *Social Welfare Forum,* the proceedings of the forum; and by publication of other special volumes. The National Conference on Social Welfare also publishes a quarterly *Bulletin.* Headquarters are maintained at Columbus, Ohio, and there is a branch office in New York City.

NATIONAL CONSUMERS' LEAGUE, The, an organization formed in 1899 by a group of men and women who were deeply concerned about the depressing labor conditions under which goods which Americans bought were manufactured and distributed. Its purposes were to awaken the interest of consumers in their responsibility for labor conditions and to promote fair labor standards by the methods of investigation, education, and legislation. The organization's first general secretary was the dynamic reformer Florence Kelley.

In the early 1900's the league investigated working conditions in some major consumer industries and brought the facts about those conditions before the public. It issued consumer labels—at first in the women's and children's cotton underwear industry—to those firms which met the league's labor standards. At about the same time, it began to press for legislation to ban the evils of sweatshops, child labor, and other appalling labor conditions. It published in 1904 the first handbook on child labor laws and prepared a model child labor code for the states. The league worked vigorously for the establishment of the federal Children's Bureau to protect child health and welfare. When federal legislation to curb child labor was challenged in the courts, it fought, with a battery of well-known lawyers representing it, to preserve this legislation. When the law was declared unconstitutional, it sought ratification of a child labor amendment to the United States Constitution. Similarly, the league fought for a quarter of a century to improve the miserable conditions under which women were obliged to work—publishing facts concerning the effects of long hours and industrial strains on women to prove to the public the need for regulation by law. Its efforts helped to establish the Women's Bureau in the Department of Labor.

The National Consumers' League helped to introduce minimum wage legislation in the United States. It sought the enactment of state minimum wage laws and undertook legal battles in their defense. When early state legislation was declared unconstitutional, it drafted in 1933 a new minimum wage bill to meet the Supreme Court's objections to the old ones. This bill was quickly passed by seven state legislatures and in 1937 the Supreme Court upheld its constitutionality. Enactment of the federal Fair Labor Standards Act in 1938 was the historical culmination of the league's efforts in this field. It has vigorously fought for improvements in the act since its passage.

One of the major and earliest champions of social security, unemployment compensation, and workmen's compensation legislation, the National Consumers' League played a vital role in the enactment of these laws and has worked continuously for their improvement. The league has been one of the pioneers in calling attention to the need to improve labor conditions on large farms and to sponsor projects to help migrant farm workers and their families. Activity in support of protective legislation for agricultural workers now forms an important part of the league's work. The organization's headquarters are in Washington, D.C.

VERA WALTMAN MAYER,
General Secretary, National Consumers' League.

NATIONAL CONVENTION, a French revolutionary assembly which met from Sept. 21, 1792, to Oct. 26, 1795, as a constitutional and legislative body. The third assembly of the deputies elected by the French people after 1789 decreed the suspension of the king on Aug. 10, 1792, and voted the election of the National Convention, which was constituted primarily to make a republican constitution but actually became a supreme governing body. The convention met in the hall of the Tuileries on Sept. 20, 1792, and was installed the following day. The history of this body is divided into three periods.

In the first period (Sept. 21, 1792–June 2, 1793), its first act was to make France a republic on Sept. 22, 1792, by abolishing the throne. This was followed by the trial of Louis XVI on Jan. 15, 1793, his sentence to death the following day, and his execution on Jan. 21, 1793. Internal dissension between the leftist party, the Mountain (so called because of its position high up in the convention amphitheater), whose members were known as Montagnards, and the more moderate revolutionary party, the Girondists, resulted in the overthrow of the latter through the pressure exerted on the convention by the Parisian mob on June 2, 1793.

During the second period (June 2, 1793–July 27, 1794), the convention, under the dictatorship of Maximilien Robespierre who in turn was influenced by the Jacobins, created the Revolutionary Tribunal in October 1793 which sent thousands of its political opponents to the guillotine in what was known as the Reign of Terror (q.v.). However, the Montagnards were divided into three factions, one with Robespierre as the leader, and rival groups which were led by Jacques René Hébert and Georges Jacques Danton, both of whom were executed in the spring of 1794. The National Convention largely lost its power in this period to its own creations, the Committee of Public Safety, which virtually ruled France as an independent executive, and the Committee of General Security, which controlled the revolutionary police.

In the last period, the moderate party, which

was known as the Thermidoreans, ultimately triumphed with the execution of Robespierre on July 28, 1794, and a regime of reaction began. The Convention dissolved on Oct. 26, 1795. See also FRENCH REVOLUTION.

NATIONAL COUNCIL OF THE CHURCHES OF CHRIST IN THE UNITED STATES OF AMERICA, The. The National Council is a fellowship of 34 nationwide communions (27 Protestant and 7 Eastern Orthodox) with more than 37,850,000 members who desire to cooperate in their common tasks.

The Council was established at Cleveland, Ohio, on Nov. 29, 1950. This was made possible by the decision of eight interdenominational agencies to combine their forces. These agencies, which by their official action transferred their functions and responsibilities to the National Council, were:

Federal Council of the Churches of Christ in America
Foreign Missions Conference of North America
Home Missions Council of North America
International Council of Religious Education
Missionary Education Movement of the United States and Canada
National Protestant Council on Higher Education
United Council of Church Women
United Stewardship Council

Five additional agencies later decided to merge their interests in the National Council:

Church World Service
Inter-seminary Committee
Protestant Film Commission
Protestant Radio Commission
Student Volunteer Movement

The National Council is the direct creation of the churches themselves. Its constitution was ratified by the highest authority of each of the member denominations. The council is directly responsible to the denominations as represented at the General Assembly which meets biennially, and the General Board, which meets bimonthly.

The National Council encourages Christian churches to cooperate with one another and to maintain close working relations with more than 900 state and local councils of churches and a still larger number of state and local councils of church women and over 2,000 interdenominational ministerial associations throughout the nation.

Nonmember communions which share the basic faith in Jesus Christ as Divine Lord and Saviour may become members of the National Council under the provisions outlined in the constitution.

The National Council of Churches is an incorporated body, pursuant to the Membership Corporation Law of the State of New York, with its principal offices located in New York, N.Y.

J. QUINTER MILLER,
Assistant General Secretary.

NATIONAL COVENANT. See COVENANTERS.

NATIONAL EDUCATION ASSOCIATION OF THE UNITED STATES. The National Education Association of the United States (NEA) is the inclusive organization for teachers of all grade levels in both public and private schools. Organized at Philadelphia, Pa., in 1857 as the National Teachers' Association "to elevate the character and advance the interests of the profession of teaching, and to promote the cause of popular education in the United States," it became a federation of teachers, administrators, and normal schools in 1870 and changed its name to the National Educational Association. With a charter from Congress the association assumed its present name in 1907.

Official Structure.—The association is governed by a representative assembly of delegates chosen by more than 5,000 state and local affiliates. The president is the actual and ceremonial, but non-salaried, head of the organization. While he serves for only one year, he is vested with great appointive powers and is the chairman of several important committees. The business of the association is conducted by a board of directors, an executive committee, and a board of trustees. The major administrator of the association, however, is the executive secretary. He directs the execution of the association's policies and supervises the headquarters staff of about 500 persons. The headquarters staff is divided into 13 divisions, such as legislation, press and radio, publications, travel, and research. In addition to the work of the staff, important phases of the educational program are in the hands of commissions on policies, legislation, teacher welfare, safety, professional standards, and retirement. Special and standing committees deal with citizenship teaching, professional ethics, international relations, and other functions.

Departments.—Parallel to this structure and quite independent of it, are the association's 30 departments, which are semi-independent organizations with constitutions, officers, and educational programs. The departments are organized on (1) an administrative basis, such as principals, deans, superintendents; (2) on a curricular basis, such as physical education, social studies, music; (3) on a group or class basis, such as higher education, rural schools, exceptional children; (4) on a service basis, such as research, audio-visual instruction, retired teachers. Each of the principal departments maintains a full-time secretary and a staff in the headquarters building at Washington, D.C.

Joint Committees.—In addition to the official structure and the departments, the association utilizes several joint committees, commissions, and councils which cooperate with organizations that are outside the educational profession. For several years the association has maintained joint committees with the American Legion, the American Medical Association, the American Library Association, the National Congress of Parents and Teachers, and other organizations. In 1952 it helped to form the World Confederation of Organizations of the Teaching Profession.

Policies.—The association has consistently espoused a selected number of policies. It has endorsed the federal Office of Education; it has favored various kinds of federal aid to education; it has demanded the complete separation of public schools and churches; it has vigorously promoted the welfare, status, and freedom of teachers; it has called for steadily rising standards for teachers.

To execute its policies the association sponsors several regional and national conventions, the largest of which is the summer meeting of the teachers and the legislative assembly.

Publications.—To effect its purposes the association also conducts a gigantic publication program. It publishes a monthly journal sent to every member, an annual volume of proceedings, a handbook, research reports, and scores of bulletins; and the departments also issue yearbooks, magazines, surveys, and studies in enormous quantities. In addition to conventions and publications, the association issues news releases, sponsors radio and television programs, and directs petitions, protests, inquiries, and surveys.

History.—The history of the association falls into three periods.

During the first period, 1857 to 1870, the organization was small and weak. Its one great achievement was its part in securing the establishment of the federal Department of Education.

During the second period, 1870–1917, the association grew slowly, but steadily, in size, influence, and aggressiveness. The meeting of 1884 at Madison, Wis., is often cited as the turning point in the association's fortunes. The presidencies of such outstanding men as Nicholas Murray Butler (1895), Charles William Eliot (1903), and David Starr Jordan (1915) contributed to the organization's dignity and status. The creation of a committee on salaries and tenure marked in 1903 the beginning of a change in policy, one that was concerned with teacher welfare. And finally the election of a woman, Ella Flagg Young, as president in 1910 signified a definite trend toward democratic control and popular growth.

The third period, 1917 to the present, has been characterized by an enormous growth in membership, by an increased concern for teacher welfare, and by continued agitation for federal aid to public education. In 1917 the association established headquarters in Washington, D.C. In 1918 one of its committees issued the famous and influential statement concerning the seven cardinal principles of secondary education. Even more important and significant was the creation, at Salt Lake City in 1920, of the representative assembly, whereby the association secured continuity and guaranteed national rather than local control. In 1921 it started the *NEA Journal.*

During the 1930's the association upheld teacher standards. It has become the aggressive defender of teachers whose tenure or prerogatives are threatened. The association's status and influence are indicated by its growth from 10,000 members in 1918 to over 1 million in the late 1960's and by the contrast between its first quarters in a private home and its present multimillion dollar headquarters in Washington.

EDGAR B. WESLEY, *University of Michigan.*

Bibliography.—The principal sources for the history of the association are its annual *Proceedings,* 1857 to date, and the *Journal.* Mildred S. Fenner's *NEA History* (Washington 1945) is a small, readable account. The most comprehensive secondary account is by Edgar B. Wesley, *NEA: The First Hundred Years* (New York 1957); American Association of School Administrators, *National Educational Assessment: Pro and Con* (Washington, D.C., 1966).

NATIONAL FORESTS, the forests of the United States under the administration of the federal government in the public interest, managed by the Forest Service, a bureau of the United States Department of Agriculture. The Forest Service was established within the Department of Agriculture by act of Congress in 1905. It inherited the functions of the Bureau of Forestry and the administration of the forest reserves, now called national forests. The forest reserves under the Department of the Interior had been set aside from public domain lands by presidential proclamations between 1891 and 1905.

The major responsibilities of the Forest Service are: management of national forests and grasslands; promotion of good forest management among private landowners through cooperative programs with the states; and research in managing, protecting, and developing forest resources and products. In 1905 there were 60 forest reserves, covering 56 million acres. Some 20 million acres were acquired under the Weeks Law of 1911, which provided for purchase of land to protect headwaters of navigable streams. These lands are largely in 48 national forests in the eastern part of the country. In 1953 about 4 million acres in the Great Plains were placed under Forest Service administration. These lands, the dust bowls of the 1930's, are now the green expanses of the national grasslands. There are now 154 national forests, 19 national grasslands, and other minor acreages managed by the Forest Service, for a total of about 187 million acres in 44 states, Puerto Rico, and the Virgin Islands. For the purpose of administering the national forests, the Forest Service, with national headquarters in Washington, D. C., has 9 regional offices. Within each region are several national forests, which in turn are divided into ranger districts. See also FORESTRY.

Forest Service Functions.—Conservation and scientific forestry practices have come a long way since the first forest reserve in 1891. Lands once locked up to preserve their resources are now used and managed for the benefit of each American. The Forest Service permits timber cutting, grazing of livestock, hunting, fishing, and other recreation in the national forests. All lands within the national forest systems, including national grasslands, are managed under two guiding principles: (1) multiple use, managing the lands to make each area yield the combination of uses best suited to the public needs; (2) sustained yield, maintaining a continuous supply of all forest resources.

National forest lands which supply water for agriculture, industry, recreation, and domestic use are managed to prevent erosion and help control floods. Yet there may also be camping, skiing, and timber cutting on the same land. Timber resources are managed to provide a continuous supply of lumber and other forest products, to demonstrate good scientific forestry practices, and to improve cover and food supplies for wildlife. The timber harvest is handled so that it does not spoil other values on the same land, such as fishing streams, trails for hiking and riding, or scenic roads. National forest ranges are managed to provide a sustained supply of forage and browse for livestock and game animals. Many range areas are also key watersheds, and grazing is coordinated with the water use. Wildlife, too, is managed as a renewable crop to keep animal numbers in balance with available food and shelter.

The scenic beauty found in the national forests yearly draws millions of visitors to these areas. Visits reached over 160 million visitor-days of use in 1969, almost six times the amount of use recorded in 1951. National forests offer hunting, fishing, hiking, swimming, picnicking, camping, and skiing facilities, boating, riding, and wilderness or primitive areas for pack trips and rustic enjoyment, far from the crowding, noise, and dirt of cities.

National Forests.—The following list gives the names of the national forests by state, indicating some of the outstanding features and the area of each forest.

Above: **A pack train in a wilderness area of the Wallowa-Whitman National Forest, Oregon.** ***Right:*** **Skiing at the Squaw Valley winter sports center in the Tahoe National Forest, California.** ***Bottom of page:*** **Cattle graze on a national grassland in Oregon. Grasslands, reclaimed from dust bowls, also nourish wildlife, protect watersheds, and provide space for hunting and other recreation.**

(Top left and right) Ray Atkeson; (bottom) United States Forest Service

ALABAMA

William B. Bankhead.—Limestone gorges; deer, turkey, and squirrel hunting; 178,736 acres.

Conecuh.—Fishing, small-game hunting, and swimming; 83,752 acres.

Talladega.—Scenic drives, camping, picnicking, small-game hunting, and fishing; 357,526 acres.

Tuskegee.—Fishing, hunting, picnicking, and camping; 10,777 acres.

ALASKA

Chugach.—Remote Aleut villages; glaciers; winter sports area; hunting for moose, Alaskan brown bear, mountain goats, ducks, and grouse; 4,726,081 acres.

Tongass.—*North Division:* Indian villages, museum; hundreds of islands, fjords, and snow-capped mountains; wilderness trails; winter sports; boating; *South Division:* Totems, Indian villages, fjords, winter sports; 16,015,904 acres.

ARIZONA

Apache.—Partly in New Mexico. Scenic trail and drive; prehistoric Blue River cliff dwellings; Blue Range Wilderness Area; 1,732,531 acres.

Coconino.—Sycamore Canyon Wild Area; San Francisco Peaks (12,655 feet); scenic and photographic opportunities; 1,800,786 acres.

Coronado.—Partly in New Mexico. Rugged mountains, cactus to fir trees, swimming to skiing, all within an hour's drive; wild area; Desert Museum; miniature Beaver National Forest demonstration area; 1,792,263 acres.

Kaibab.—National game preserve, deer and wild buffalo herds, Supai Indian village, and geological formations; 1,718,803 acres.

Prescott.—Nation's largest ghost town, rugged back country, horse trails, and dude ranches; 1,247,593 acres.

Sitgreaves.—Pueblo ruins, large elk herd, saddle and pack trips; 771,095 acres.

Tonto.—Elevations 1,500 to 7,300 feet, Superstition Mountains, 30,000 acres of man-made lakes; saddle and pack trips, skin diving, and water skiing; 2,894,278 acres.

ARKANSAS

Ouachita.—Partly in Oklahoma. Historic Indian lands, medicinal springs, mountains, and artificial lakes; 1,546,731 acres.

Ozark.—Oak forests, rock cliffs, and pools; 1,064,993 acres.

St. Francis.—Former submarginal farmlands now producing valuable timber; 20,611 acres.

CALIFORNIA

Angeles.—San Antonio Peak (10,000 feet), chaparral forest, wild area; skiing, boating, and swimming; 648,739 acres.

Calveras Bigtree.—Smallest national forest; 379 acres.

Cleveland.—World's largest telescope at Mount Palomar Observatory on Mount Palomar; wild area; 391,316 acres.

Eldorado.—Partly in Nevada. Rugged mountains in the Sierra Nevada; spectacular Lake Tahoe; California gold rush country, site of Sutter's Mill; 642,052 acres.

Inyo.—Partly in Nevada. High Sierra Wilderness Area; Palisade glacier; Mount Whitney (14,495 feet), highest point in the continental United States; bristlecone pine trees—among oldest living things; 1,834,812 acres.

Klamath.—Partly in Oregon. Wilderness areas, mountain lakes and streams; 1,697,609 acres.

Lassen.—Hot springs, volcanic lava-flow tubes, Indian pictographs and hieroglyphics, and old immigrant trails; 1,045,194 acres.

Los Padres.—Home of rare California condor; rugged country with elevations to 9,000 feet; oceanside camping; 1,749,285 acres.

Mendocino.—Beautiful lake country, wilderness area; 867,433 acres.

Modoc.—Migratory bird refuge; scene of Modoc Indian

Upper left: **An angler greets a logger in a North Carolina national forest. Wise management permits both recreational and economic use of resources.** *Above:* **A family enjoys the wilderness at a campground.** *Lower left:* **Visitors meet wildlife in forest refuges.**

United States Forest Service

wars; lava flows; 1,688,235 acres.

Plumas.—Feather Falls, one of the highest (640-foot drop) and most picturesque falls in the United States; historic gold-mining areas; limestone caves; 1,147,394 acres.

San Bernardino.—Historic landmarks; highest mountains in southern California; 614,586 acres.

Sequoia.—Giant sequoia "big trees," High Sierra Wilderness Area, game refuge; 1,118,594 acres.

Shasta-Trinity.—Mount Shasta (14,162 feet), lava beds, Glass Mountain, Castle Crags, limestone and lava caves; 2,037,746 acres.

Sierra.—Giant sequoia, Central Sierra section of the John Muir Trail, wilderness and wild areas; 1,295,745 acres.

Six Rivers.—Giant redwood; 935,267 acres.

Stanislaus.—High mountain country; 895,840 acres.

Tahoe.—Squaw Valley—site of 1960 Winter Olympics; fine winter sports facilities; 696,834 acres.

COLORADO

Arapaho.—Ghost towns, gold-silver mining; scenic drive on peak-to-peak highway; 984,489 acres.

Grand Mesa-Uncompahgre.—Two forests; Grand Mesa Plateau (10,500 feet); 250 lakes and reservoirs; 1,317,-967 acres.

Gunnison.—Ghost towns, wild area, 27 peaks of over 12,000 feet; 1,660,050 acres.

Pike.—Pike's Peak (14,110 feet), with highway to summit; 1,084,815 acres.

Rio Grande.—Wild areas, rugged country; 1,798,539 acres.

Roosevelt.—Rugged Continental Divide; many alpine lakes; canyons and glaciers; 771,473 acres.

Routt.—Continental Divide, with perpetual ice and snow; 1,144,772 acres.

San Isabel.—Highest average elevation of any national forest; 1,103,859 acres.

San Juan.—Cataracts, peculiar geological formations, archaeological ruins, and historic mines; 1,849,612 acres.

White River.—Glenwood Canyon, Hanging Lake, mineral hot springs; source of marble for Lincoln Memorial and Tomb of the Unknown Soldier; 1,960,931 acres.

FLORIDA

Apalachicola.—Old Fort Gadsden; pine-hardwood forests; 556,496 acres.

Ocala.—Botanical features, subtropical wilderness; 361,-252 acres.

Osceola.—State game breeding ground, cypress swamps; 157,233 acres.

GEORGIA

Chattahoochee.—Southern end of Appalachian Trail, Blue Ridge Mountains; 680,097 acres.

Oconee.—Archaeological remains, Piedmont wildlife refuge; 95,838 acres.

IDAHO

Boise.—Portion of Sawtooth Wilderness Area; scenes of Indian camps and massacres; abandoned mines and ghost towns; virgin stands of ponderosa pine; 2,632,492 acres.

Caribou.—Partly in Utah and Wyoming. Historic markers and trails, natural soda springs, and wilderness country; 978,032 acres.

Challis.—Majestic mountains and wilderness; Lost River Range, with Mount Borah (12,655 feet); 2,447,206 acres.

Clearwater.—Selway-Bitterroot Wilderness Area; stands of virgin white pine; 1,676,753 acres.

Coeur d'Alene.—Coeur d'Alene Lake, with over 100 miles of shoreline; Cataldo Mission, built in 1848; 723,408 acres.

Kaniksu.—Partly in Montana and Washington. Ancient grove of cedars; Cabinet Mountains Wild Area; Chimney Rock; 1,626,220 acres.

Nezperce.—Wilderness big-game hunting; hot springs; historic Elk City; 2,196,037 acres.

Payette.—Deepest gorge in the United States; Payette Lakes Recreational Area; Idaho Wilderness Area; 2,-307,150 acres.

St. Joe.—Rugged Bitterroot Range of Idaho-Montana divide; 868,650 acres.

Salmon.—Historic Lewis and Clark Trail; 1,768,100 acres

Sawtooth.—Partly in Utah. "Silent City of Rocks"—fantastic formations worn by wind and water; developed hot springs; 1,802,680 acres.

Targhee.—Partly in Wyoming; Grand Canyon of the Snake River and the Teton and Snake ranges; 1,663,249 acres.

ILLINOIS

Shawnee.—Prehistoric stone forest and Indian mounds; rock formations; 211,021 acres.

INDIANA

Hoosier.—Pioneer Mothers Memorial Forest, containing nation's outstanding specimen of black walnut; 120,381 acres.

KENTUCKY

Daniel Boone.—Sandstone cliffs 100 feet high; natural rock arches, limestone caves, and mineral springs; 464,683 acres.

LOUISIANA

Kisatchie.—Natchitoches, oldest town in Louisiana, on Old San Antonio Road; one of the largest pine nurseries in the world; 591,409 acres.

MICHIGAN

Hiawatha.—Upper Peninsula woodlands and Great Lakes shorelines; 832,641 acres.
Huron.—Lumberman's Monument; 413,838 acres.
Manistee.—Winter sports areas; lake beaches; 449,443 acres.
Ottawa.—Numerous falls, lakes, and streams; 862,405 acres.

MINNESOTA

Chippewa.—Headwaters of the Mississippi; 641,266 acres.
Superior.—Five thousand lakes; 1,959,353 acres.

MISSISSIPPI

Bienville.—Numerous forest-management demonstration areas; 175,648 acres.
Delta.—Deer hunting, fishing, virgin bottomland hardwood; 58,956 acres.
DeSoto.—Site of South Mississippi Gun and Dog Club field trials; 500,408 acres.
Holly Springs.—Intensive erosion-control projects; 143,461 acres.
Homochitto.—One of the finest natural timber-growing sites in the United States; forest-management demonstration areas; 189,072 acres.
Tombigbee.—Indian mounds; lakes; 65,232 acres.

MISSOURI

Clark.—Big springs; Ozark Mountains covered with oak and pine forests; brilliant fall coloring and spring bloom; 901,290 acres.
Mark Twain.—Ozark Mountains; numerous caves, rock cairns, and springs; 451,493 acres.

MONTANA

Beaverhead.—Wilderness; Big Hole Battlefield Monument; Sacajewea Memorial Area; Bannack, the first capital of Montana Territory; 2,130,936 acres.
Bitterroot.—Partly in Idaho. Ancient Indian hieroglyphics; St. Mary's Mission and Fort Owen; spectacular Bitterroot Mountains; 1,574,626 acres.
Custer.—Partly in South Dakota. Granite Peak (12,799 feet); hundreds of lakes; glaciers, ice caverns, and fossil beds; Indian hieroglyphics and burial grounds; 1,171,491 acres.
Deerlodge.—Alpine lakes; wilderness area; 1,134,556 acres.
Flathead.—Geological formations, including massive Chinese Wall; jagged Mission Mountains; 2,336,400 acres.
Gallatin.—Thousands of miles of trout streams; 11 outstanding waterfalls; 1,700,139 acres.
Helena.—Old Fort Logan blockhouse; ghost towns; boat trip through "Gates of the Mountains" Wild Area on Missouri River; 966,614 acres.
Kootenai.—Partly in Idaho. Cabinet Mountains Wild Area; limestone canyons; 1,818,394 acres.
Lewis and Clark.—Bob Marshall Wilderness, Chinese Wall, scenic limestone canyons, many open parks; 1,862,018 acres.
Lolo.—Partly in Idaho. Selway-Bitterroot Wilderness Area; foot trails to 100 lakes and peaks; 2,502,698 acres.

NEBRASKA

Nebraska.—Entire forest in game refuge; nesting ground of great blue heron; 245,409 acres.

NEVADA

Humboldt.—Spectacular canyons and colorful cliffs; historic mining camps; 2,507,829 acres.
Toiyabe.—Partly in California. Ghost towns, rugged High Sierra country; 3,118,869 acres.

NEW HAMPSHIRE

White Mountain.—Partly in Maine. Major part of the White Mountains; Presidential Range; spring skiing in Tuckerman Ravine, on Mount Washington (6,288 feet); 715,731 acres.

NEW MEXICO

Carson.—Sangre de Cristo Mountains; Wheeler Peak (13,160 feet); Taos, home and burial place of Kit Carson, and Taos Indian pueblo; 1,318,289 acres.
Cibola.—Bighorn sheep; Pueblo Indian villages; prehistoric ruins; ancient "sky city" of Acoma; 1,660,648 acres.
Gila.—Prehistoric ruins; semidesert to alpine country; 2,694,744 acres.
Lincoln.—White Mountain (12,000 feet)—summit in Apache Indian Reservation; 1,086,311 acres.
Santa Fe.—Truchas peaks (13,000 feet); wilderness and wild areas; 1,231,630 acres.

NORTH CAROLINA

Croatan.—Historic New Bern, settled 1710; 152,351 acres.
Nantahala.—Lakes and waterfalls; Joyce Kilmer Memorial Forest; 447,570 acres.
Pisgah.—Mount Mitchell (6,684 feet —highest point east of Mississippi; spring rhododendron bloom; 479,722 acres.
Uwharrie.—43,391 acres.

OHIO

Wayne.—Beautiful fall coloring of hardwoods; 108,822 acres.

OREGON

Deschutes.—Snow-clad peaks, ice caves, waterfalls; over 300 lakes; lava caves; wilderness area; 1,587,707 acres.
Fremont.—Indian paintings and writings; protected herds of antelope; 1,208,378 acres.
Malheur.—Fossil beds of prehistoric plants and animals; extensive ponderosa pine stands; 1,204,835 acres.
Mount Hood.—Hot springs, glaciers, flower-filled meadows, wild areas; 1,115,428 acres.
Ochoco.—Fort Watson and Camp Maury, frontier-day Army posts; scenes of early range wars; 845,880 acres.
Rogue River.—Partly in California. Table Rock, site of bloody war with Rogue River Indians; sugar pine and Douglas fir forests; 621,027 acres.
Siskiyou.—Partly in California. Oregon coast; rare plants and animals; 1,078,951 acres.
Siuslaw.—Bordered by Pacific Ocean; 34 miles of public beach; 622,809 acres.
Umatilla.—Partly in Washington. Skyline trip along summit of Blue Mountains; hot sulfur springs; 1,389,697 acres.
Umpqua.—Spectacular cataracts; unique stands of incense cedar; 983,991 acres.
Wallowa-Whitman.—Two national forests. Glaciers, lakes, rare wild flowers, spectacular scenery; 2,490,892 acres.
Willamette.—Most heavily timbered national forest in the United States; extensive volcanic formations; 1,665,835 acres.
Winema.—Formerly Indian lands; 908,985 acres.

PENNSYLVANIA

Allegheny.—Allegheny Plateau country; virgin timber stands; 471,081 acres.

SOUTH CAROLINA

Francis Marion.—Ruins and remains of early colonial settlements and plantations; 245,619 acres.
Sumter.—Piedmont and Blue Ridge Mountains; 341,597 acres.

SOUTH DAKOTA

Black Hills.—Partly in Wyoming. Crystal caves, canyons, and waterfalls; historic gold rush area where famed frontier characters lived and were buried; famous Homestake Mine; 1,219,896 acres.

TENNESSEE

Cherokee.—Partly in North Carolina. Rugged mountain country; 595,097 acres.

TEXAS

Angelina.—Rolling sandy hills with longleaf-pine–hardwood forest along river bottomland; 154,392 acres.
Davy Crockett.—Timber-management demonstration area; 161,556 acres.
Sabine.—Southern pine and hardwood forest; 183,844 acres.
Sam Houston.—Flatlands; "Big Thicket" area; 158,205 acres.

UTAH

Ashley.—Kings Peak (13,498 feet); exposed geological formations a billion years old; 1,282,829 acres.
Cache.—Partly in Idaho. Rugged mountains; skiing; 657,351 acres.
Dixie.—Table Cliff Point, with view of four states (Colorado, Arizona, Nevada, and Utah); spectacularly colored cliffs; 1,851,341 acres.
Fishlake.—Petrified Wood Scenic Area; 1,415,666 acres.
Manti-La Sal.—Partly in Colorado. Unique geology; Indian hieroglyphics and cliff dwellings; world's largest aspen trees; 1,263,760 acres.
Uinta.—Timpanogos Cave; alpine scenic highway; 774,903 acres.
Wasatch.—Partly in Wyoming. Mountains on the doorstep of Salt Lake City; 859,077 acres.

VERMONT

Green Mountain.—New England villages; Champlain Valley and historic battlegrounds of Revolutionary and French and Indian wars; skiing; 232,134 acres.

VIRGINIA

George Washington.—Partly in West Virginia. Limestone caverns; unusual geological sites; Civil War iron furnaces; rugged mountain terrain; 1,003,278 acres.
Jefferson.—Partly in Kentucky. Transitional zone between southern and northern flora; Appalachian Trail; Civil War iron furnaces; 543,970 acres.

WASHINGTON

Colville.—Grand Coulee Dam, largest masonry structure

in the world; old mission near Kettle Falls; noted for deer hunting; 928,292 acres.
Gifford Pinchot.—Lakes, snowcapped peaks; historic Indian huckleberry fields; mineral springs; 1,263,300 acres.
Mount Baker.—Glaciers; alpine lakes; Douglas firs as tall as 200 feet; 1,818,294 acres.
Okanogan.—North Cascade Wilderness Area; 2,042,213 acres.
Olympic.—Dense rain forests; scores of lakes and streams; 621,756 acres.
Snoqualmie.—Snoqualmie Falls (270 feet high); giant Douglas firs; 1,207,774 acres.
Wenatchee.—Lake Chelan, 50 miles long, between precipitous mountain ranges; 1,205,397 acres.

WEST VIRGINIA

Monongahela.—Spectacular Seneca Rocks on Seneca Indian trail; limestone caves; 805,734 acres.

WISCONSIN

Chequamegon.—Hundreds of large and small lakes; 827,067 acres.
Nicolet.—Northern Wisconsin lake region; 640,528 acres.

WYOMING

Bighorn.—Prehistoric Indian Medicine Wheel on Medicine Mountain; Indian battlefields; snowcapped peaks and glaciers; 1,113,768 acres.
Bridger.—Bridger Wilderness Area; glaciers; 1,699,838 acres.
Medicine Bow.—Scenic mountains; 1,069,083 acres.
Shoshone.—Snow-topped Wind River Range; largest glaciers in the Rocky Mountains; 2,426,118 acres.
Teton.—Unspoiled scenic backcountry, famous for big-game herds; Continental Divide; 1,700,766 acres.

PUERTO RICO

Caribbean.—Scenic drive through tropical rain forest; trails to waterfalls and to peaks of the rugged Sierra de Luquillo mountains; swimming; views of offshore islands; 27,889 acres.

CLINT DAVIS,
Forest Service, United States Department of Agriculture.

NATIONAL GALLERY, The, England's national art gallery, in Trafalgar Square, London, housing the greatest collection of paintings in Great Britain, a collection widely representative of all aspects of European painting. It was founded in 1824, when the House of Commons voted sufficient money to buy the collection of 38 pictures owned by John Julius Angerstein. The continuing growth of the collection has depended on a combination of private patronage and financial and legislative aid from the government. The gallery has been on its present site since 1838. The façade was designed by William Wilkins; as a result of additions, there are now 35 exhibition rooms, a reference section, and modern rooms for the conservation studios and scientific department.

The collection of about 2,000 pictures, mainly concerned with European painting, ranges from the 13th to the early 20th century. It contains masterpieces by many famous artists. Outstanding among the Tuscan paintings of the Renaissance are the three works by Piero della Francesca and the *Battle of San Romano,* one of a series of three by Paolo Uccello; in Leonardo da Vinci's *Virgin of the Rocks* (a later version than that at the Louvre in Paris) and in Michelangelo's *Entombment,* the gallery possesses a fitting climax to this period. Of the Venetians, the 8 Giovanni Bellinis are only equaled by the 10 works by his pupil, Titian, which includes his *Bacchus and Ariadne.* The Arnolfini double portrait by Jan van Eyck shows in a unique way this artist's contribution to the northern Renaissance. The gallery is strong in Dutch 17th century pictures, with two Vermeers and masterpieces by the leading genre, landscape, and marine artists. Significantly there are 19 Rembrandts, of which his *Equestrian Portrait* is unique in this artist's oeuvre. The power of Rubens is displayed in his *Château de Steen* and in his portrait of his second wife's sister, called *Le Chapeau de Paille.* Two portraits of Philip IV show this aspect of Velázquez' work at its best, while his *"Rokeby Venus"* is his only surviving female nude. The 17th and 19th century French schools are also well represented, and the gallery is able to give a representative display of the masters of English painting.

GREGORY MARTIN,
Assistant Keeper, The National Gallery.

The National Gallery in Trafalgar Square, London.

London Daily Express

NATIONAL GALLERY OF ART. See SMITHSONIAN INSTITUTION, THE.

NATIONAL GEOGRAPHIC SOCIETY, a society chartered as a nonprofit scientific and educational organization "for the increase and diffusion of geographic knowledge." Established in 1888 in Washington, D.C., it is still headquartered there. It promotes research and exploration in geography and allied sciences and publishes color-illustrated articles of broad geographic interest in its monthly *National Geographic Magazine.* The circulation of the magazine to the society's members and to schools, libraries, and other institutions exceeds 3 million copies an issue. Through the years the society has sponsored, often in cooperation with other institutions, 200 expeditions and research projects that have reached to the earth's poles, extended man's frontiers on land, in the air, and on and under the sea, and probed a million light-years into interstellar space.

The society's prized Hubbard Medal and Special Gold medals honor explorers and scientists for outstanding contributions to geography. Member dues also support the work of a staff of writers, photographers, and cartographers who travel extensively and provide much of the magazine's contents. The cartographic staff prepares

Above: **Engineers of the District of Columbia National Guard construct a panel bridge.** ***Top right:*** **Their truck breasting flood waters, Kansas National Guardsmen answer emergency duty summons.** ***Lower right:*** **Shells are loaded into a tank during Tennessee National Guard field training at Fort Stewart, Ga.**

(Above) District of Columbia National Guard; (top right and lower right) The National Guardsman

large, 10-color map supplements, 21 million copies of which are distributed annually, and other special maps. The school service division produces the *National Geographic School Bulletin,* distributed weekly, during the school year, to 130,000 teachers and students; and the book service prepares frequent authoritative, illustrated volumes on geography-related subjects.

MELVILLE BELL GROSVENOR,
President and Editor, National Geographic Society.

NATIONAL GUARD, the generic term for the state-organized units of the Army and Air Force of the United States, composed of citizens who undergo a minimum required training and are available for service in national or local emergencies. National Guard units are subject to the call of the governor of their state or territory except when ordered into federal service by the president of the United States. Equipment is furnished by the federal government, and units must maintain certain standards to be federally recognized. Forty-eight hours of drill and two weeks of active training are required each year, for which drill pay is received. Regular officers serve as instructors and inspectors. The National Guard is distinct from the Organized Reserve, which is directly administered by the armed services without state connections. The Navy and Marine Corps have no National Guard units.

Organization.—On June 30, 1963, the Army National Guard was composed of 361,080 officers and men, organized into approximately 4,000 combat, support, and service units in 2,500 communities. There were 17 infantry division, 4 brigades and 7 battle groups, 7 armored divisions, 27 tank battalions, 78 artillery battalions, 42 air defense battalions, and 16 special forces units, plus 34 Nike-Ajax and 30 Nike-Hercules missile batteries. The Air National Guard had a strength of 74,325 personnel and 1,658 aircraft organized into squadrons as follows: fighter interceptor, 27; tactical reconnaissance, 11; air transport, 17; air refueling, 4; aeromedical, 92; ground communications, 106; and troop carrier, 4. Approximately 25 percent of Air National Guard personnel are kept on full-time status for equipment maintenance; missile battalions, 30 percent; and other Army units, 4 percent.

History.—The National Guard has evolved from the militia of colonial days when almost every settlement had to have miiltary protection. After the American Revolution, a militia organized on the Swiss pattern was planned for national defense, and the Uniform Militia Law of 1792 made every "free, able-bodied, white male citizen of the respective states" between 18 and 45 a potential soldier who, when called, would provide his own arms and equipment for a period of up to three months. Congress, however, took no steps to enforce this law, so state-organized, elite units of citizen soldiers evolved during the first half of the 19th century. The Seventh Regiment of the New York State Militia assumed the title of "National Guards" in 1824 while providing escort for the Marquis de Lafayette. The term became popular and, with the founding of the National Guard Association of the United States in 1878, the organized militia of the various states came to be designated generally as the National Guard.

These poorly trained militia units proved unsuitable for the types of war in which the United States engaged. Their periods of service were too short and, in both the War of 1812 and the Spanish-American War, some refused to serve outside of the United States. Regulars fought the wars against the Indians, regulars with volunteers the

Mexican War, and during the Civil War the armies on both sides were composed of volunteers and conscripts.

The Spanish-American War disclosed grave weaknesses in the Army establishment, and Elihu Root, secretary of war from 1899 to 1904, undertook a reform, basing it on Gen. Emory Upton's *The Military Policy of the United States,* written more than 20 years before. Upton had recommended a regular army, a national volunteer force similar in concept to the present Organized Reserve, and a militia supported exclusively by the states and used only as intended by the Constitution to execute the laws, suppress insurrection, and repel invasion. This was opposed by Representative Charles W.F. Dick of Ohio, a militia officer who sponsored the Dick Act of 1903, which made the National Guard the country's reserve force, federally equipped but remaining under state control. Not until the Hay (or National Defense) Act of 1916 was the National Guard made subject to a federal call.

Conscription was resorted to early in World War I, but the National Guard furnished 17 out of the 42 divisions organized. Guard units received new designations and, since most had been infantry and cavalry, many of these had to be formed into machine-gun, artillery, and service elements. In World War II, the integrity of the National Guard was not maintained and, after that war, the Department of Defense tried without success to get a single national service. With the establishment of the United States Air Force in 1947, the Air National Guard became a separate institution. During the Korean War, 8 divisions, 12 regimental combat teams, and 22 air wings were called to active duty. These comprised one third of the Army National Guard and 80 percent of the Air National Guard.

Problems.—The Reserve Forces Act of 1955 was the first corrective legislation applied to the National Guard after 1916. This act required enlistees in all reserve forces to serve for eight years, the first six months of which would be on active duty training with regular forces. Reserve units were thereby freed of responsibility for basic training, and emphasis in unit training shifted from the night drill to the full-time weekend. The annual training period remained a problem, good leadership personnel usually finding it difficult to spare two weeks from businesses or professions, and the services considering this period too short for proper training.

Although the politically powerful National Guard Association has opposed a civil defense role for this force, nevertheless, in the event of nuclear attack, the National Guard, with its geographic distribution and tradition of responding to emergencies, would no doubt provide key elements in recovery, especially through its signal, medical, military-police, engineer, and transportation units.

The militia clauses in the United States Constitution (Art. I, sect. 8) have given to the National Guard a dual status which has enhanced its political power sometimes at the expense of military effectiveness. Its control rests in both federal and state authority. Moreover, it is one of two reserve forces available to the nation and often competes with the Organized Reserve for funds. On the other hand, the Army National Guard has demonstrated that it can maintain higher levels of troop strength and training than the Army Reserve, and the Guard's long history, its local roots, and the state and community support which give it high morale provide evidence for its claim that it is the proper way for citizens of the United States to discharge their age-old militia responsibilities.

Berlin Call-Up.—The call-up for one year of certain National Guard units during the Berlin crisis of 1961 demonstrated that some corrective action was still needed to enable reserve forces to respond to a partial as well as total mobilization. The problem is basically that of readiness, priority, and equity in call-up of units. The National Guard is now included in the reorganization and reshaping of divisions program of the Regular Army known as ROAD (Reorganization Objectives of Army Divisions). The 6 divisions designated for a priority call-up in national emergencies have had their troop organization strength raised from 70 to 80 percent. During the Berlin crisis, the United States, for the first time in its history, was able to use its reserve forces to support foreign policy. Chancellor Konrad Adenauer of West Germany claimed that the major factor in the mitigation of Soviet demands was the rapid buildup of American armed forces.

See also ARMY, DEPARTMENT OF THE—*Army Staff;* CONSCRIPTION; MILITIA—*United States;* UNITED STATES—*31. Army* and *33. Air Force.*

Consult Millis, Walter, *Arms and Men: A Study in American Military History* (New York 1956); Eliot, George Fielding, *Reserve Forces and the Kennedy Strategy* (Harrisburg, Pa., 1962).

JOHN D. HAYES,
Rear Admiral, United States Navy, Retired.

NATIONAL INCOME. See INCOME; WEALTH.

NATIONAL INDUSTRIAL CONFERENCE BOARD, INCORPORATED (NICB), an independent and nonprofit institution in New York City for business and industrial fact-finding through scientific research. Founded in 1916, the board conducts research in the fields of economics, business management, and human relations. Facts, experiences, and opinions in these fields are collected and analyzed, and this information is disseminated through published reports, press releases, and correspondence.

Supplementing the NICB's published research is its conference, seminar, and educational activity. The board holds five open conferences annually in New York City and in other principal United States and Canadian cities, bringing together authorities from business, labor, education, and government to discuss timely business subjects. The board also conducts several seminars and courses each year, focusing on personnel problems, economics, and business policies.

The work of the board is made possible through the support of more than 3,700 subscribing associates, including business organizations, trade associations, labor unions, libraries, government bureaus, individuals, and colleges and universities.

H. BRUCE PALMER,
President, National Industrial Conference Board, Inc.

NATIONAL INSTITUTE OF ARTS AND LETTERS, The, an honorary institution for the furtherance of literature and the fine arts in the United States, founded in 1898 by the American Social Science Association. It was incorporated by an act of Congress. Its membership is limited to 250 native or naturalized citizens qualified by notable achievements in art, literature, or music. Election to the institute, located in New York City, is an honor conferred by working artists of distinction on their peers.

The institute confers certain awards and honors for work of excellence. It awards *The Gold Medal* annually for distinguished achievement in each of two categories of literature and the arts, with a rotation of 10 categories designated in the bylaws. In conjunction with the American Academy of Arts and Letters, founded by the institute in 1904 and consisting of a group of 50 persons chosen exclusively from the institute membership for special distinction, the institute makes annual grants of $2,500 each to 18 artists, writers, and composers for work of outstanding merit. It likewise confers an annual $1,000 prize in architecture, the Arnold W. Brunner Memorial. Other awards, made possible through the generosity of independent donors, are the $1,000 Loines Award for Poetry, the Marjorie Peabody Waite Award of $1,500 to an older person for continuing achievement in his art, and the Richard and Hinda Rosenthal Foundation awards of $2,000, one for an American novel which, though not a commercial success, is a considerable literary achievement, and the other to a younger American painter of great distinction who has not yet been accorded due recognition. None of the money prizes may be given to a member of the institute. In special instances, the institute also presents an Award for Distinguished Service to the Arts.

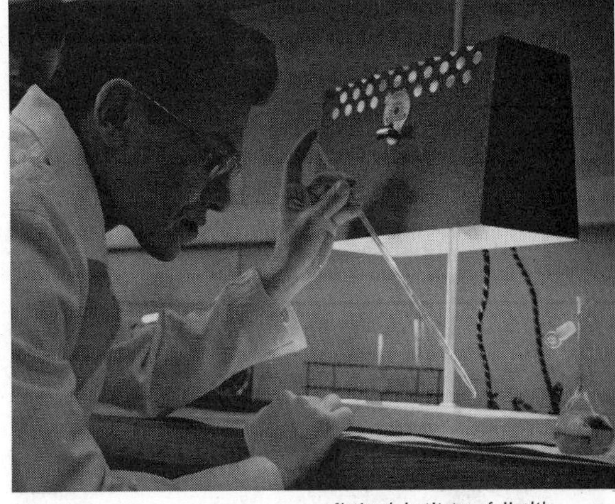

National Institutes of Health

In the Laboratory of Chemical Pharmacology at the National Cancer Institute, a researcher works under an infrared lamp on a process measuring precursor chemicals in the constituents of mouse tissues. Such analyses aid the study of the biochemical action of antitumor drugs.

Obverse and reverse of the Gold Medal of the National Insitute of Arts and Letters.

See also American Academy of Arts and Letters.

Felicia Geffen,
Assistant Secretary-Treasurer, The National Institute of Arts and Letters.

NATIONAL INSTITUTES OF HEALTH (NIH), the major federal agency supporting medical research in the United States. It is the principal research arm of the Public Health Service of the United States Department of Health, Education, and Welfare, and it is primarily concerned with the extension of basic knowledge about human health problems.

As infectious diseases such as tuberculosis, smallpox, pneumonia, and diphtheria have been been brought under control in the United States, cancer, heart disease, mental illness, and other chronic diseases have become the main concerns of medical research. Accordingly, the National Institutes of Health, through the programs of its nine institutes, four divisions, and clinical center, supports and conducts research on cancer, heart disease, mental illness, arthritis, metabolic diseases, neurological diseases, blindness, dental diseases, allergies and infectious diseases, child health and human development, and the basic biological sciences.

The total NIH research budget for 1963 exceeded $890 million, about 43 percent of the total national medical research support. About 80 percent of NIH-supported research is conducted in medical and dental schools, universities, and other nonfederal institutions, through research project grants; research training grants, traineeships, and fellowships; and grants to assist in the construction of research facilities. Advisory groups composed of leading nonfederal scientists and citizens review all NIH grants before they receive final approval. In January 1963, the National Institutes of Health in Bethesda, Md., employed approximately 10,000 full-time workers, including about 1,500 with doctoral degrees.

The Public Health Service's role in medical research began in 1887 with the establishment of the Laboratory of Bacteriology—the parent organization of the National Institutes of Health—on Staten Island, N.Y. Research programs grew rapidly after World War II, when the rising interest in science created a demand for progress in the medical sciences. Since that time, research and the application of new knowledge derived from research have contributed to improved health levels generally and to reduction of a number of specific disease problems, including: improved techniques in repairing defects of the blood vessels and arteries; accepted use of corrective heart surgery; discovery of the cause, leading to the control of, a disease blinding newborn infants; synthesis and practical use of a pain-killing drug more powerful than morphine; discovery of a drug effective for periods of over five years against a rare type of cancer found in young mothers; and partial deciphering of the code of chemicals that set the genetic or hereditary pattern.

James A. Shannon, M.D.,
Director, The National Institutes of Health.

NATIONAL JEWISH WELFARE BOARD (JWB), an agency founded in 1917 and authorized by the United States Department of Defense to provide for the religious, morale, and welfare needs of Jewish military personnel and their dependents; through a merger in 1921 it also became the national association of Jewish Community Centers and the Young Men's and Young Women's Hebrew Associations (YM-YWHA's). Through its Commission on Jewish Chaplaincy, JWB recruits, ecclesiastically endorses, and serves all Jewish military chaplains, of whom there were 358 at the end of 1962, and it is the only Jewish member agency of the United Service Organization (USO). JWB provides consultative and administrative services for the cultural, recreational, and athletic programs of the center and camp units affiilated with the Jewish Community Centers and YM-YWHA's, of which there were 437 in 279 communities in 1962. National headquarters of JWB are in New York City.

A founder and the American member of the World Federation of YMHA's, JWB has played a major role in the federation's establishment and sponsorship of the Jerusalem YMHA and in introducing the Jewish community center movement in 34 countries abroad. JWB also sponsors the Jewish Book Council of America, the National Jewish Music Council, a Jewish Center Lecture Bureau, and the annual Jewish Youth Week. It gives annual national merit fellowships for training in social work and three annual Frank L. Weil awards for outstanding contributions in its three fields of work: service in the Jewish community center field, welfare and religious work for the armed forces, and advancement of Jewish culture.

SANFORD SOLENDER,
Executive Vice President, National Jewish Welfare Board.

NATIONAL LABOR RELATIONS BOARD (NLRB), a body created by the Congress of the United States to administer the provisions of the National Labor Relations (or Wagner) Act, governing the labor-management relations of firms in interstate commerce, except transportation. Enacted by Congress in 1935, the National Labor Relations Act declared it to be the public policy of the United States "to eliminate the causes of certain substantial obstructions to the free flow of commerce and to mitigate and eliminate these obstructions when they have occurred by encouraging the practice and procedure of collective bargaining and by protecting the exercise by workers of full freedom of association, self-organization, and designation of representatives of their own choosing for the purpose of negotiating the terms and conditions of their employment or other mutual aid or protection."

Certain acts of employers were defined as unfair labor practices under the act and the National Labor Relations Board of three members was authorized to prevent, upon complaint, acts interfering with the rights of employees to establish unions of their own choosing for purposes of collective bargaining and to hold elections to determine representatives of employees.

The Labor-Management Relations Act of 1947 (known as the Taft-Hartley Act) amended the original act, retaining the definition of employer unfair labor practices, enumerating a set of acts by unions which were designated as unfair labor practices, and creating the independent Federal Mediation and Conciliation Service. As a result of its increased responsibilities, the board was enlarged to five members by Congress. The 1947 amendments also provided for a general counsel of the board with final authority to handle charges of unfair labor practices and to prosecute complaints.

The board has 28 regional offices, each headed by a regional director, and it also operates subregional offices. The board does not initiate action against employers or unions. It considers complaints by private parties of unfair labor practices against emloyers, unions, or both, and petitions for representative elections. In both instances, the initial request must be made to one of the regional offices. If the regional director finds the charge valid and the board has jurisdiction, he will direct a complaint and schedule a hearing before an examiner. Witnesses can testify at hearings and can be subpoenaed. Parties have the right to appear in person, by counsel, or by other representatives, to examine and cross-examine witnesses, and to present other evidence. In the hearing, the rules of evidence are controlling as far as practicable.

At the conclusion of the hearing, the trial examiner prepares an intermediate report containing an analysis of the evidence and recommendations to the board. If no exceptions to the trial examiner's recommendations are filed, the board may adopt the report on its own, or it may set aside or modify the report. The board can order affirmative action in the case of unfair labor practices, such as reinstatement of improperly discharged workers with back pay, or any other action which will effectuate the purposes of the law. Those aggrieved by an order of the board may appeal to the United States Circuit Court of Appeals, which has the authority to affirm, deny, or modify orders of the board. In cases where compliance is refused, the board can ask the Circuit Court of Appeals for the enforcement.

In 1961, under the Landrum-Griffin Act of 1959, amending the 1947 act, the board delegated its powers to determine election cases to the regional directors, who were given power to determine whether a question of representation exists, the appropriate bargaining unit, and challenges on the casting and counting of votes subject to discretionary review by the board. The board is also required to seek injunctive relief in jurisdictional disputes or in the maintenance of secondary boycotts.

The great majority of unfair labor practices cases that come before the board are settled by voluntary agreement of the parties. In 1962, 24,848 new cases were filed, including 13,479 unfair labor practice cases and 11,286 representation cases. Most were settled, withdrawn, or found without merit. This is evident in that while 13,479 cases of unfair labor practices cases were handled to a conclusion, formal complaints were issued only in 1,470 instances.

See also LABOR LEGISLATION—*1. Labor Legislation in the United States;* NATIONAL MEDIATION BOARD.

PHILIP TAFT,
Professor of Economics, Brown University.

NATIONAL MEDIATION BOARD, an independent federal agency created as the United States Board of Mediation under the Railway Labor Act, approved May 20, 1926, and made the National Mediation Board by amendment of June 21, 1934. Air carriers were included by an amendment of April 10, 1936, and the negotiation of union shop agreements permitted by a further amendment of Jan. 10, 1951. The general purpose of the act is to avoid interruption to interstate commerce on rail and air carriers engaged therein; to provide for prompt settlement of disputes involving rates of pay, rules, and working conditions; and to provide for prompt settlement of representation disputes between rail and air carriers and their employees. The board consists of three members appointed for three-year terms by the president, subject to confirmation by the Senate; an executive secretary; and a limited number of field mediators and office employees. See also Mediation.

Eugene C. Thompson,
Executive Secretary, National Mediation Board.

NATIONAL MONUMENTS. See National Parks and Monuments.

NATIONAL MUSEUM. See United States National Museum.

NATIONAL PARKS AND MONUMENTS. In the United States, national parks are spacious land areas, essentially of primitive or wilderness character, that contain scenery and natural wonders so outstanding in quality that their preservation intact for the benefit and enjoyment of the people has become a national concern. National parks can be established only by acts of Congress. National monuments are those lands that have been reserved for the protection and perpetuation of the historic, prehistoric, or scientific objects or features they contain. Some national monuments, such as the Petrified Forest and Grand Canyon, have been reestablished as national parks by acts of Congress. National parks, monuments, and memorials, and many national historical and military parks and sites, are administered by the National Park Service of the United States Department of the Interior.

Origin and History of National Parks.—The original concept of preserving the nation's scenic and historic treasury can be traced to a group of farsighted expeditionaries. Members of the Washburn-Langford-Doane Expedition had traveled for weeks in 1870 through the lofty country of northwestern Wyoming. On the night of September 19, they sat talking around a campfire, reflecting on this enchanted land with its vast, dense forests, high waterfalls thundering into rocky canyons, mighty geysers spouting steam and water high into the air, towering columns of lava rock, and abundance of wildlife.

The group discussed what could be done with this land of natural marvels. Cornelius Hedges, a Montana judge, thought that there should be no private ownership of any part of this region, but that it should be set aside as a great park to be protected in its natural state for the use and enjoyment of all people. Here at this campfire, then, was born the idea of our national parks. Subsequently, on March 1, 1872, President Grant signed a bill that created Yellowstone National Park—first in the nation and in the world.

Through the inspiration of John Muir and other conservationists, Congress, in 1890, established General Grant (now part of Kings Canyon National Park), Sequoia, and Yosemite national parks in California. Nine years later, Mount Rainier in the State of Washington was added. Today, the revelations of nature and history can be enjoyed in 36 national parks.

National Monuments.—The Antiquities Act, approved by Congress on June 8, 1906, gave the president authority to declare by public proclamation the establishment of national monuments. Under this authority, Devils Tower in Wyoming, an 865-foot tower of columnar rock formed by volcanic intrusion, was designated as the first national monument on Sept. 24, 1906. Since that time, the number of national monuments has grown to 84.

National Park Service.—Spurred by the concentrated campaign waged by Stephen T. Mather, then assistant to the secretary of the Interior, Congress in 1916 established the National Park Service and Mather was appointed its first director. He was instructed by Congress "to conserve the scenery and the natural and historic objects and wildlife (in the parks) and to provide for their enjoyment in such a manner and by such means as will leave them unimpaired for the enjoyment of future generations." This basic principle remains the underlying policy by which units of the national park system are administered.

In 1932, the Waterton-Glacier International Peace Park was established to commemorate the goodwill that exists between the United States and Canada. Its boundaries are formed by Glacier National Park, Mont., on the American side, and The Waterton Lakes National Park, in the Province of Alberta, on the Canadian side.

The Reorganization Act of 1933 prompted the national park system's most rapid growth. It gave the National Park Service the responsibility for administering all national parks and monuments, national military parks, national battlefield parks and sites, national memorials, the national capital park system, and certain national cemeteries.

National Historical and Military Parks.—National historical, military, and battlefield parks are distinguished from those national monuments that protect historic objects only in that they derive their legal status from acts of Congress rather than from proclamations of the president. National memorials and inactive national cemeteries, the significance of both of which derives from human association, also can be established only by acts of Congress.

In August 1935, the Historic Sites Act was approved to provide for the establishment of national historic sites and for the protection and administration of historic areas of national interest. National historic sites may be designated by the secretary of the interior, pursuant to the 1935 act, but most are chosen by Congress.

National Parkways.—To review park, parkway, and recreational area programs at every level of government, Congress authorized an important survey with the Park, Parkway, and Recreational Area Study Act of 1936. This directive, which required a survey of lands that are chiefly valuable for recreational purposes, has resulted in the service acquiring national parkways. Established only by acts of Congress, national parkways are federally owned, restricted motor roads within a wide parklike right-of-way, designed for pleasure travel and embracing scenic and recreational features or historic sites.

National Seashores and Other Areas.—Other recreational areas administered by the National Park Service include national seashores, lakeshores, scenic riverways, a national scenic trail, and national recreational areas.

Cape Hatteras National Seashore, established in 1953, was the first national seashore administered by the park service. Others were established at Cape Cod, Mass., Padre Island, Texas, Point Reyes, Calif., Fire Island, N.Y., Assateague Island, Md.-Va., Cape Lookout, N.C., and Gulf Islands, Fla.-Miss.

Park System Administration.—In addition to a headquarters staff, a design and construction office, a service center, and a National Capital Parks office in Washington, D.C., the National Park Service has a service center in San Francisco and regional offices in Omaha, Philadelphia, Richmond, San Francisco, Seattle, and Santa Fe. The majority of the units in the system have resident superintendents.

Private concessionaires are permitted to operate restaurants, cabins, motels, hotels, and lodges in various scenic, scientific, and historic units of the national park system. The National Park Service maintains in 83 areas 552 campgrounds that are available to the public at a modest charge. The service also conducts free guided hikes and campfire and lecture programs.

All national parks are wildlife sanctuaries. Hunting is prohibited, but fishing is permitted, with state licenses required in some areas.

Park Service Program and Areas.—The national park system attracts about 170 million visits annually, including visits to the White House. Types of areas in the system are shown below.

NATIONAL PARK SYSTEM

Type of area	Number	Acres
National parks	36	14,683,352.65
National historical parks	14	64,449.28
National monuments	84	10,218,335.32
National military parks	11	31,906.83
National memorial park	1	70,436.00
National battlefields	6	5,946.50
National battlefield parks	3	7,156.40
National battlefield sites	3	785.87
National historic sites	53	10,233.21
National memorials	19	5,747.42
National cemeteries	10	220.13
National seashores	8	518,205.23
Parkways	5	150,350.19
National lakeshores	4	189,614.85
National scenic riverways	3	145,364.22
National capital park[1]	1	7,832.86
White House	1	18.07
Parks (other)[2]	5	25,605.97
National recreation areas	13	3,809,004.00
International park	1	2,721.50
National scientific reserve	1	32,500.00
Trail	1	50,000.00
Total	283	30,029,786.50

[1] Comprises 706 units within the District of Columbia.
[2] Parks without national designation and Theodore Roosevelt Island.

In the late 1960's there was a dawning realization by the general public that the quality of life in the United States was deteriorating because of pollution of air and water and desecration of natural areas. In addition to the National Park Service and the Forest Service, many other federal and state agencies, corporations, and individuals began working in the 1970's for more parks and improved environment.

Following are brief descriptions of the major areas administered by the National Park Service, grouped according to their major functions as parks, monuments, and recreation areas; historical parks, sites, and memorials, and military parks and battlefields. Also given is the state in which each area is located, the year of establishment of the area's current status under the National Park Service (in parentheses), and its approximate acreage in federal land.

PARKS, MONUMENTS, AND RECREATION AREAS

National Parks.—In the United States and its territories, certain areas administered by the National Park Service have been designated as national parks.

Acadia, Me. (1919).—Rugged coastal area on Mount Desert Island; also picturesque Schoodic Peninsula on mainland and half of Isle au Haut, exhibiting spectacular cliffs; 31,644 acres.

Big Bend, Texas (1944).—Spectacular mountain and desert scenery enclosed in the great bend of the Rio Grande; variety of geological structures; 700,221 acres.

Bryce Canyon, Utah (1928).—Amphitheaters filled with a countless array of fantastically eroded pinnacles of vivid coloring; 36,010 acres.

Canyonlands, Utah (1964).—Erosion-scarred area including natural arches, chasms, standing rocks, and mesas rising over 7,800 feet; 257,640 acres.

Carlsbad Caverns, N. Mex. (1930).—Beautifully decorated limestone caverns, largest underground chambers yet discovered; 45,846 acres.

Crater Lake, Oreg. (1902).—Vividly blue lake of exceptional depth and clearness in crater of extinct volcano; 160,290 acres.

Everglades, Fla. (1947).—Only subtropical park on U.S. mainland; extensive watercourses, vast mangrove forests and sawgrass prairies; abundant wildlife; rare and colorful birds; 1,400,533 acres.

Glacier, Mont. (1910).—A region of picturesque peaks, gigantic precipices, and numerous lakes and glaciers. Forms part of the Waterton-Glacier International Peace Park established in 1932; 1,009,159 acres.

Grand Canyon, Ariz. (1919).—Most spectacular part of the Colorado River's greatest canyon, which is 217 miles long; 673,203 acres.

Grand Teton, Wyo. (1929).—Series of peaks comprising the most impressive part of the Teton Range; also portion of Jackson Hole; 302,443 acres.

Great Smoky Mountains, N.C.-Tenn. (1930).—Includes portion of the Great Smokies, loftiest range east of the Black Hills, S. Dak.; luxuriant vegetation at lower elevations; 509,184 acres.

Guadalupe Mountains, Texas (1966).—Mountain range of Trans-Pecos Texas, including highest peaks in the state; features world's largest known fossil reef; 77,518 acres.

Haleakala, Maui, Hawaii (1961).—Dormant volcano with colorful crater; interesting birdlife; 17,130 acres.

Hawaii Volcanoes, Hawaii (1916).—Impressive, active volcanic areas on the island of Hawaii; rare plants and birds; 178,911 acres.

Hot Springs, Ark. (1921).—Has 47 hot mineral springs used in treating certain ailments; 3,535 acres.

Isle Royale, Mich (1940).—Forested island, the largest in Lake Superior, distinguished for its wilderness character; great moose herd; pre-Columbian copper mines; 539,339 acres.

Kings Canyon, Calif. (1940).—Mountain wilderness dominated by the two enormous canyons of the Kings River and by the summit peaks of the High Sierra; the former General Grant National Park, with its giant sequoias, is a detached section of the park; 453,768 acres.

Lassen Volcanic, Calif. (1916).—Contains Lassen Peak, only recently active volcano (1914–1921) in coterminous United States; 106,934 acres.

Mammoth Cave, Ky. (1936).—Interesting caverns, including spectacular cave onyx formations and river 360 feet below surface; 51,351 acres.

Mesa Verde, Colo. (1906).—Most notable and best preserved prehistoric cliff dwellings in the United States; 51,018 acres.

Mount McKinley, Alaska (1917).—Mount McKinley, highest mountain in North America; large glaciers of the Alaska Range; abundant wildlife; 1,939,359 acres.

Mount Rainier, Wash. (1899).—Includes Mount Rainier (14,410 feet), with the greatest glacial system of any peak in the United States proper; dense forests and flowered meadows; 241,571 acres.

North Cascades, Wash. (1968).—Wild region of mountains and lakes; 505,000 acres.

Olympic, Wash. (1938).—A rain-forest wilderness, with snow-capped peaks, mountain lakes, forests of unusual density, and bands of the rare Roosevelt elk; 888,-558 acres.

Petrified Forest, Ariz. (1906).—Display of petrified wood; Indian ruins; part of the Painted Desert; 94,190 acres.

Platt, Okla. (1906).—Contains springs with distinctive mineral properties; 912 acres.

Redwood, Calif. (1968).—Coast redwood forests, including the world's tallest tree; 57,094 acres.

Rocky Mountain, Colo. (1915).—Includes heart of the Rockies; 65 named peaks 10,000 to 14,255 feet high; many glacial lakes; 256,620 acres.

Sequoia, Calif. (1890).—Contains great groves of giant

NATIONAL PARKS

Above: More than 140 inches of rain falls annually on Olympic National Park in Washington to produce a rich coniferous forest.

Right: Wind and sand erosion has sculptured these strangely beautiful rock forms in the Joshua Tree National Monument, California.

Below: Glistening gypsum sand dunes up to 45 feet high are characteristic of the landscape of the White Sands National Monument in New Mexico.

(Center) Fred H. Ragsdale from Alpha; (top) Bruce Nelson, (bottom) Carlos Elmer, from Shostal

Left: **In Virginia's Shenandoah National Park, about 330 square miles of America's first frontier are preserved in their wild and quiet beauty.**

Thomas Hollyman from Photo Researchers

NATIONAL PARKS

Right: **Cape Cod National Seashore in Massachusetts is a normally peaceful world of sand dunes and sunny skies.**

Below: **The eternal contest between wave and granite is a chief attraction in Maine's Acadia National Park.**

(Right) M. Woodbridge Williams, National Park Service; (bottom) Robert Holland from Shostal

Great Northern Railway

Upper St. Mary Lake, one of the numerous crystal-clear lakes (notice the rocky lake bed, lower left) in Glacier National Park, Montana. The lake, originally believed by the Indians to be unfathomable, is at its deepest 200 feet. On the left, overshadowing the lake are Red Eagle (8,800 feet) and Little Chief (9,542 feet) mountains. The single pinnacle in the center is Mount Jackson (10,023 feet).

NATIONAL PARKS

Above: An informal campfire talk by a National Park Service ranger-naturalist at Olympic National Park.

Below: Workers build retaining wall at an overlook commanding a view of the lake at Crater Lake National Park.

Above: To track the movements of bears in Yellowstone National Park they are trapped, daubed with a spot of color, and released from the trap as shown here.

Bottom left: A ranger catches a poacher in the Everglades National Park. Craft are propeller-driven airboats.

Below: In the vast wildernesses of many national parks communication is often a problem. Here a ranger in the Everglades Park uses a radiotelephone system.

National Park Service photographs

Right: **A "rescue" on a precipitous cliff at Crater Lake National Park—an example of the training given to park rangers. Sunlit lake surface is 1,200 feet below.**

Above: **Rangers on patrol in Yosemite National Park. Their duties include fire and pest control, search and rescue, wildlife management, and law enforcement.**

NATIONAL PARKS

Below: **Rescue of a young bear whose head was trapped in a milk can in the Yosemite Park. To free the animal, a worker cut off the neck of the can with a chisel.**

National Park Service photographs

Above: Devils Postpile National Monument in California. A lava flow ages ago hardened into basalt columns.

Right: Fort Laramie National Historic Site, Wyoming. The Army post once protected wagon trails. Restored quarters appear at right.

NATIONAL MONUMENTS AND HISTORIC SITES

Left: Casa Grande National Monument, Arizona; an adobe tower built in the 14th century by the Indians. A metal roof now shields it from the weather. *Below:* Aztec Ruins National Monument, New Mexico; remains of a 12th century Indian pueblo of masonry and timber, which once contained 500 rooms. The circular kiva, or ceremonial chamber (*center foreground*), is a restoration.

(Top left and right) Union Pacific Railroad; (center left and bottom) Josef Muench

sequoias, world's largest trees and among the oldest living things; also Mount Whitney (14,495 feet), loftiest peak in United States outside of Alaska; 385,419 acres.

Shenandoah, Va. (1935).—Includes outstanding portions of the Blue Ridge Mountains, with Skyline Drive; 193,445 acres.

Virgin Islands, Virgin Islands (1956).—Tropical island area rich in plant and animal life; prehistoric Carib Indian relics; ruins of sugar mills; 14,418 acres.

Voyageurs, Minn. (authorized 1971).—Woods and waters; canoeing, fishing, hiking; 219,431 acres.

Wind Cave, S. Dak. (1903).—Beautiful limestone caverns with crystal formations; elk, bison; 28,059 acres.

Yellowstone, Wyo.-Mont.-Idaho (1872). — Contains more geysers than are found in all of the rest of the world; hot springs, mud volcanoes, petrified forests, beautifully colored canyon, abundant wildlife; 2,213,207 acres.

Yosemite, Calif. (1890).—Includes magnificent Yosemite Valley, spectacular waterfalls, High Sierra country, three groves of giant sequoias; 758,112 acres.

Zion, Utah (1919).—Contains colorful Zion Canyon, an outstanding example of a deep, narrow, vertically walled chasm; former volcanic activity; 132,470 acres.

National Monuments.—The national monuments in the United States are preserved as nationally significant landmarks, or as structures or areas of scientific, historic, or prehistoric interest.

Andrew Johnson, Tenn. (1942).—The president's home, tailor shop, and grave; 16 acres.

Arches, Utah (1929).—Extraordinary examples of erosion in arches, windows, and pinnacles; 33,690 acres.

Aztec Ruins, N. Mex. (1921).—Ruins of 12th century American Indian town; 27 acres.

Badlands, S. Dak. (1939).—Eroded layers of sedimentary deposits, containing many prehistoric animal fossils; 99,986 acres.

Bandelier, N. Mex. (1916).—Prehistoric Indian houses of the later Pueblo period; 30,649 acres.

Black Canyon of the Gunnison, Colo. (1933).—Deep, sheer-sided canyon of geologic interest; 13,034 acres.

Booker T. Washington, Va. (1957).—Site of birthplace and childhood home of Negro leader and educator; 200 acres.

Buck Island Reef, Virgin Islands (1961).—Fine Caribbean marine garden; island rookery of frigate birds and pelicans; 850 acres.

Cabrillo, Calif. (1913).—Memorial to Juan Rodríguez Cabrillo, discoverer of San Diego Bay, 1542; 81 acres.

Canyon de Chelly, Ariz. (1931).—Prehistoric Indian ruins at the base of red cliffs, or in canyon caves; modern Navajo farms; 83,840 acres.

Capitol Reef, Utah (1937).—Long, colorful, buttressed sandstone cliffs of Gothic appearance; 36,116 acres.

Capulin Mountain, N. Mex. (1916).—Huge cinder cone, a recently (geologically speaking) extinct volcano; 680 acres.

Casa Grande, Ariz. (1918).—Prehistoric adobe tower built by Indians; 473 acres.

Castillo de San Marcos, Fla. (1924).—Oldest masonry fort in the United States, started by Spanish in 1672, to protect St. Augustine; 19 acres.

Castle Clinton, N.Y. (1950).—Built 1808–1811, served successively as fort, entertainment center, and immigrant landing depot; 1 acre.

Cedar Breaks, Utah (1933).—Great amphitheater eroded into the colorful Pink Cliffs; 6,155 acres.

Chaco Canyon, N. Mex. (1907).—Thirteen major prehistoric Indian ruins, representing highest point of Pueblo civilization; hundreds of smaller ruins; 20,939 acres.

Channel Islands, Calif. (1938).—Large rookery of sea lions; unique plants and animals; includes Santa Barbara and Anacapa Islands; 18,167 (land area 1,120) acres.

Chesapeake and Ohio Canal, Md.-W.Va. (1961).—One of the older, least-altered American canals; 4,475 acres.

Chiricahua, Ariz. (1924).—Wilderness of unusual rock shapes; 10,481 acres.

Colorado, Colo. (1911).—Eroded sandstone formations, sheer-walled canyons; 17,607 acres.

Craters of the Moon, Idaho (1924).—Volcanic cones, craters, lava flows, and other volcanic phenomena; 48,004 acres.

Custer Battlefield, Mont. (1946).—Site of the Battle of the Little Bighorn River, June 25, 1876; 765 acres.

Death Valley, Calif.-Nev. (1933).—Vast desert, weird formations, salt and borax beds; includes the lowest point in the Western Hemisphere, 282 feet below sea level; 1,879,088 acres.

Devils Postpile, Calif. (1911).—Symmetrical blue-gray columns rising to 60 feet; an old basaltic lava flow; 798 acres.

Devils Tower, Wyo. (1906).—Tower of columnar volcanic rocks rising 865 feet; the first national monument; 1,267 acres.

Dinosaur, Utah-Colo. (1915).—Spectacular canyons and a fossil quarry; 184,648 acres.

Effigy Mounds, Iowa (1949).—Indian mounds in shapes of birds and animals; 1,382 acres.

El Morro, N. Mex. (1906).—Inscription Rock of soft sandstone, in which are many old carvings, including prehistoric inscriptions and those of early Spanish explorers and American settlers; 881 acres.

Fort Frederica, Ga. (1945).—Built by British colonizer, Gen. James E. Oglethorpe, in 1736–1748; 210 acres.

Fort Jefferson, Fla. (1935).—Fort built in 1846 to control Florida Straits; a military prison; bird refuge; 47,125 acres.

Fort McHenry National Monument and Historic Shrine, Md. (1939).—Fort, the defense of which in 1814 inspired the writing of *The Star-Spangled Banner*; 43 acres.

Fort Matanzas, Fla. (1924).—Spanish fort, 1737; 228 acres.

Fort Pulaski, Ga. (1924).—Early 19th century fort; 5,364 acres.

Fort Sumter, S.C. (1948).—Site of engagement beginning the Civil War; 2 acres.

Fort Union, N. Mex. (1956).—Key fort on Santa Fe Trail in opening of the Southwest; 721 acres.

George Washington Birthplace, Va. (1930).—House and gardens on site of Washington's birthplace; 394 acres.

George Washington Carver, Mo. (1951).—Site of birthplace and childhood home of the famous Negro scientist and educator; 210 acres.

Gila Cliff Dwellings, N. Mex. (1907).—Well-preserved cliff dwellings in natural cavities; 160 acres.

Glacier Bay, Alaska (1925).—Tidewater glaciers, rare species of wildlife; 2,274,248 acres.

Gran Quivira, N. Mex. (1909).—Site of 17th century Spanish mission, mission buildings, and Pueblo Indian house mounds; 611 acres.

Grand Canyon, Ariz. (1932).—Part of the famous, many-colored canyon of the Colorado River; 193,040 acres.

Grand Portage, Minn. (1960).—Nine-mile portage and reconstructed trading post on principal route into the Northwest; 315 acres.

Grand Sand Dunes, Colo. (1932).—Shifting dunes; 34,980 acres.

Homestead National Monument of America, Nebr. (1939).—Site of the first claims under the Homestead Act of 1862; 163 acres.

Hovenweep, Utah-Colo. (1923).—Prehistoric towers, pueblos, and cliff dwellings; 505 acres.

Jewel Cave, S. Dak. (1908).—Limestone caverns, calcite crystal formations; 1,275 acres.

Joshua Tree, Calif. (1936).—Desert flora and fauna, with stand of Joshua trees; 505,082 acres.

Katmai, Alaska (1918).—Dying volcanic region, including the Valley of Ten Thousand Smokes; 2,697,590 acres.

Lava Beds, Calif. (1925).—Principal theater of Modoc Indian War, 1873; volcanic phenomena; 46,239 acres.

Lehman Caves, Nev. (1922).—A complex of limestone caverns; 640 acres.

Montezuma Castle, Ariz. (1906).—Well-preserved cliff dwellings; 783 acres.

Mound City Group, Ohio (1923); Group of prehistoric Indian mounds; 68 acres.

Muir Woods, Calif. (1908).—Stand of coast redwoods; 485 acres.

Natural Bridges, Utah (1908).—Three natural sandstone bridges, highest rising 222 feet above stream bed and spanning 261 feet; 2,650 acres.

Navajo, Ariz. (1909).—Three famous cliff dwellings; 360 acres.

Ocmulgee, Ga. (1936).—Remains of prehistoric mounds and towns; 683 acres.

Oregon Caves, Oreg. (1909).—Limestone caves; 480 acres.

Organ Pipe Cactus, Ariz. (1937).—Traces of the Camino del Diablo, old Spanish route; unique desert plants; 328,691 acres.

Perry's Victory and International Peace Memorial, Ohio (1936).—Shaft at Put-in-Bay commemorating Commodore Oliver Perry's victory in Battle of Lake Erie, 1813, and a century of peace between Canada and the United States; 14 acres.

Pinnacles, Calif. (1908).—Spirelike rock formations 500–1,200 feet high, and other volcanic phenomena; 13,618 acres.

Pipe Spring, Ariz. (1923).—Historic Mormon fort; 40 acres.

Pipestone, Minn. (1937).—Indian quarry, source of material used in making peace pipes; 276 acres.

Rainbow Bridge, Utah (1910).—Salmon-pink sandstone natural bridge, arching 309 feet above the gorge bottom; 160 acres.

Russell Cave, Ala. (1961).—Cave whose archaeological record indicates almost continuous human habitation from 6000 B.C. to about 1650 A.D.; 310 acres.

Saguaro, Ariz. (1933).—Cactus forest; 76,188 acres.

Scotts Bluff, Nebr. (1919).—Oregon Trail landmark; 2,199 acres.

Sitka, Alaska (1910).—Site of stockade where Indians made their last stand against Russian settlers; totem poles; 54 acres.

Statue of Liberty, N.Y. (1924).—Huge copper statue on Bedloe's Island in New York Harbor; commemorates Franco-American alliance in American Revolution; universal symbol of freedom and democracy; 10 acres.

Sunset Crater, Ariz. (1930).—Volcanic cone, highly colored on the upper part; lava flows; 3,040 acres.

Timpanogos Cave, Utah (1922).—Limestone cave on side of Mount Timpanogos; 250 acres.

Tonto, Ariz. (1907).—14th century Pueblo cliff dwellings; 1,120 acres.

Tumacacori, Ariz. (1908).—Historic Spanish mission; 10 acres.

Tuzigoot, Ariz. (1939).—Excavated ruins of a pueblo which flourished between 1000 and 1400 A.D.; 43 acres.

Walnut Canyon, Ariz. (1915).—Cliff dwellings in caves under ledges of limestone; 1,642 acres.

White Sands, N. Mex. (1933).—White gypsum dunes; 140,247 acres.

Wupatki, Ariz. (1924).—Prehistoric pueblos of red sandstone; 34,585 acres.

Yucca House, Colo. (1919).—Unexcavated ruins of prehistoric Indian pueblo; not open to the public, 100 acres.

National Parkways.—The national parkways are elongated parks; they feature roads designed for pleasure travel and contain historic, scenic, or recreational features of national significance.

Blue Ridge Parkway, Va.-N.C. (1936).—Follows the Blue Ridge Mountains at an average elevation of 3,000 feet; preserves mountain folk culture and offers large recreational areas; estimated length, when completed, 469 miles; 64,051 acres.

George Washington Memorial Parkway, Va.-Md. (acquisition enacted 1930).—When completed, will extend about 49 miles along both sides of the Potomac River, from Great Falls to Mount Vernon and Fort Washington; features many landmarks associated with the life of George Washington; 4,594 acres.

Natchez Trace Parkway, Miss.-Tenn.-Ala. (1938).—Road follows an old Indian trail between Nashville and Natchez, known as the Natchez Trace, a vital route in early travel; estimated length, 450 miles when completed; 26,803 acres.

National Capital Parks.—The National Capital Parks include 724 units in the District of Columbia, Virginia, and Maryland, comprising the park system of the nation's capital. The system was initiated in 1790 by act of Congress and transferred to the National Park Service in 1933. Its 7,024 acres contain part of the Chesapeake and Ohio Canal and the many parks of the District of Columbia. Now listed independently are Prince William Forest Park, Va.; Catoctin Mountain Park, Md.; and the Baltimore-Washington Parkway, Md. In 1961, Congress authorized the 1,059-acre Piscataway Park, in order to preserve the Maryland Potomac River shoreline, which contains the view from Mount Vernon, the George Washington Memorial Parkway, and Fort Washington.

National Scenic Trail.—First of this category, established in 1968, is the Appalachian Trail, 2,000 miles from Maine to Georgia.

National Recreation Areas.—These are federal reservations to conserve and develop, for public enjoyment, recreational resources of national significance, including places of scenic, natural, or historic interest and their wildlife. The National Park Service administers them.

Amistad, Texas (1965).—Contains U.S. part of the Amistad Reservoir on the Rio Grande; 65,000 acres.

Arbuckle, Okla. (1965).—Surrounds the Arbuckle Reservoir; 8,851 acres.

Bighorn Canyon, Wyo.-Mont. (1966).—Surrounds a 71-mile reservoir; 47 miles of Bighorn Canyon; 122,623 acres.

Coulee Dam, Wash. (1946).—Franklin D. Roosevelt Lake, formed by Grand Coulee Dam; 98,500 acres.

Curecanti, Colo. (1965).—Blue Mesa, Morrow Point, and Crystal reservoirs; 41,103 acres.

Delaware Water Gap, N.J.-Pa. (1965).—Scenic area along Delaware River; 37-mile-long Tocks Island Reservoir to be constructed; 68,826 acres.

Glen Canyon, Ariz.-Utah (1958).—Contains Lake Powell, formed by Glen Canyon Dam; 1,196,545 acres.

Lake Chelan, Wash. (1968).—Beautiful Stehekin Valley; part of fjord-like lake; 62,000 acres.

Lake Mead, Ariz.-Nev. (1936 and 1947).—Lake Mead, formed by Hoover Dam, and Lake Mohave, formed by Davis Dam, both on the Colorado River; 1,936,978 acres.

Ross Lake, Wash. (1968).—Mountain-ringed reservoirs in Skagit River Canyon; 107,000 acres.

Sanford, Texas (1965).—Surrounds Sanford Reservoir on the Canadian River; 39,792 acres.

Shadow Mountain, Colo. (1952).—Shadow Mountain Lake and Lake Granby; 18,240 acres.

Whiskeytown-Shasta-Trinity, Calif. (1965).—Whiskeytown Reservoir, Lake Shasta, Trinity Mountains; 41,987 acres.

HISTORICAL PARKS, SITES, AND MEMORIALS

National Historical Parks.—The national historical parks administered by the National Park Service feature areas or structures of great historical significance.

Appomattox Court House, Va. (1954).—At this place, on April 9, 1865, Gen. Robert E. Lee surrendered his Confederate Army to the Federal Army under Gen. Ulysses S. Grant; 937 acres.

Chalmette, La. (1939).—The scene of part of the Battle of New Orleans, an American victory in the War of 1812; contains a military cemetery; 83 acres.

City of Refuge, Hawaii (1961).—Sacred ground which provided refuge for defeated Hawaiian warriors, noncombatants, and taboo breakers until 1819; situated on the coast; features prehistoric house sites, royal fishponds, and coconut groves; 181 acres.

Colonial, Va. (1936).—Cape Henry Memorial marks approximate site of first landing of colonists who made first permanent English settlement in America on Jamestown Island; also includes Yorktown, where culminating battle of the American Revolution was fought; 7,065 acres.

Cumberland Gap, Ky.-Tenn.-Va. (1955).—Mountain pass of the Wilderness Road, explored by Daniel Boone and carrying great trans-Allegheny migration to the frontiers; 20,184 acres.

Harpers Ferry, W. Va. (1963).—Scenic and historic area in Blue Ridge Mountains, site of colonial events and the John Brown raid of 1859; 469 acres.

Independence, Pa. (1956).—Structures and properties associated with the American Revolution in Philadephia, including Independence Hall, Congress Hall, Old City Hall, and Independence Square, as well as the Deshler-Morris House in Germantown; 16 acres.

Minute Man, Mass. (1959).—Tract containing original stone walls, boulders, and other features of the natural setting where, on April 19, 1775, the opening day of the American Revolution, the British troops retreating from the battles of Lexington and Concord were fired on by the colonial minute men; 86 acres.

Morristown, N.J. (1933).—Sites of important military encampments during American Revolution. George Washington's headquarters, 1779–1780; 958 acres.

Saratoga, N.Y. (1948).—Scene of American victory over British in 1777; turning point of the American Revolution and one of the decisive battles of world history; 2,432 acres.

National Historic Sites.—The national historic sites owned by the federal government are historic areas, buildings, or objects preserved because of their great national significance.

Abraham Lincoln Birthplace, Ky. (1959).—Traditional birthplace cabin of Lincoln, enclosed in a memorial building on the site of the birthplace; 117 acres.

Adams, Mass. (1946).—The mansion which was the home of presidents John Adams and John Quincy Adams, as well as later distinguished family descendants; 5 acres.

Bent's Old Fort, Colo. (1963).—The fort was built by William and Charles Bent and Ceran St. Vrain, possibly as early as 1833, as a frontier trading post. It was one of the great centers of the fur-trading enterprise during the height of its activity in the Rocky Mountains. John Frémont used the fort as a base of his operations for his expedition in 1845; 178 acres.

Christiansted, Virgin Islands (1952).—Commemorates the Danish colonial history of the Virgin Islands, including Fort Christiansvaern and public buildings on the Christiansted, St. Croix, waterfront; 8 acres.

Edison Home, N.J. (1955).—The furnished, late-Victorian-style home of Thomas A. Edison and his family; 14 acres.

Fort Davis, Texas (1963).—Named after Secretary of War Jefferson Davis, who later became the first and only president of the Confederacy, the fort was constructed in the Davis Mountains north of the big bend of the Rio Grande, to guard principal crossings. Following the Civil War, the fort, surrendered to Confederate troops in 1861, was reactivated and reconstructed; 447 acres.

Fort Laramie, Wyo. (1960).—Site of the fur-trading post and surviving buildings of the military post guarding the covered-wagon trails to Oregon, Utah, and California; 192 acres.

Fort Raleigh, N.C. (1941).—Site of the first attempted English settlement within the confines of what is now United States territory, 1585–1587; 19 acres.

Fort Smith, Ark. (1961).—This bastion of the Southwestern frontier from 1817 to 1827 became the center of law enforcement and judicial activity for the Indian Territory between 1872 and 1890. Fort Smith was garrisoned until 1871, when the United States Criminal Court of the Western District was moved there and housed in one of the fort buildings; 14 acres.

Fort Vancouver, Wash. (1961).—Early trading center and seat of political and military authority in the Pacific Northwest as headquarters of the Hudson's Bay Company from 1825 to 1849; a United States military reservation for 100 years thereafter; 75 acres.

Hampton, Md. (1948).—A great Georgian-style mansion built during the latter part of the 18th century; 45 acres.

Home of Franklin D. Roosevelt, N.Y. (1945).—Birthplace, home, and "Summer White House" of President Franklin D. Roosevelt at Hyde Park; 94 acres.

Hopewell Village, Pa. (1938).—Ruins of a furnace and other structures of an 18th century and early 19th century American ironmaking village; 848 acres.

Jefferson National Expansion Memorial, Mo. (1935).—Commemorates the notable persons and events connected with United States territorial expansion; 85 acres.

St. Thomas, Virgin Islands (1961).—Contains Fort Christian, completed by the Danes in 1680, the oldest standing structure in the Islands; 2 acres.

Sagamore Hill, N.Y. (1963).—The Victorian-style mansion on Long Island was the Theodore Roosevelt home from 1887 until his death in 1919. When Roosevelt became president, it served as the summer White House; 85 acres.

Salem Maritime, Mass. (1938).—Wharf, Old Custom House, and other houses associated with New England's maritime, architectural, and literary history; 9 acres.

San Juan, Puerto Rico (1949).—Oldest fortifications within the present territorial limits of the United States, begun by the Spanish in the 16th century; 40 acres.

Theodore Roosevelt Birthplace. N.Y. (1963).—It was the home of the Roosevelt family when Theodore Roosevelt was born on Oct. 27, 1858. He spent 14 years of his childhood there.

Vanderbilt Mansion, N.Y. (1940).—Palatial American residence of the late 19th century; 212 acres.

A number of other national historical sites have the same national status but are owned by private organizations rather than by the federal government, though the organizations are assisted administratively by the National Park Service. The years in parentheses indicate when these sites were designated as national historical sites.

Chicago Portage, Ill. (1952).—A part of the portage used by French and American pioneers between Lake Michigan and the Mississippi system; 91 acres.

Chimney Rock, Nebr. (1956).—A famous landmark and campsite on the Oregon Trail, rising 500 feet above the North Platte River valley; 83 acres.

Dorchester Heights, Mass. (1951).—The site on which the American batteries were placed which helped to force the British to evacuate Boston on March 17, 1776; 5 acres.

Gloria dei (Old Swedes') Church, Pa. (1942).—The second-oldest Swedish church in the United States, founded in 1677; present structure erected about 1700; 3 acres.

Golden Spike, Utah (1957).—Site of the driving of a golden spike on May 10, 1869, to complete the first transcontinental railroad; 7 acres.

Jamestown, Va. (1940).—Part of the site of the first permanent English settlement in North America, on the upper end of Jamestown Island; 22 acres.

McLoughlin House, Oreg. (1941).—The home (1846–1857) of Dr. John McLoughlin, important in the early development of the Pacific Northwest; less than 1 acre.

St. Paul's Church, N.Y. (1943).—An imposing 18th century church significant in early American history; 6 acres.

San Jose Mission, Texas (1941).—Established in 1720, an outstanding example of the frontier Spanish mission; 4 acres.

Touro Synagogue, R.I. (1946).—One of the finest surviving examples of American colonial religious architecture; less than 1 acre.

National Memorials.—Listed below are a number of structures or areas designated national memorials by acts of Congress, to commemorate ideas, events, or personages of national significance. In 1962, Congress also authorized the Lincoln Boyhood National Memorial, in Indiana, and the Hamilton Grange National Memorial, to preserve the home of Alexander Hamilton in New York City.

Arkansas Post, Ark. (1960).—Scene of significant events connected with exploration and settlement of the lower Mississippi Valley. Arkansas Post was the first white settlement of semipermanent character in the lower Mississippi Valley. It was established in 1686 as a fur-trading post by Henri de Tonty, a lieutenant of the famed explorer, the sieur La Salle; 740 acres.

Coronado, Ariz. (1952).—Commemorates Francisco Coronado's exploration of the Southwest (1540–1542); 2,745 acres.

Custis-Lee Mansion, Va. (1959).—Antebellum home of the Custis and Lee families and a memorial to Gen. Robert E. Lee; 3 acres.

De Soto, Fla. (1949).—Commemorates the landing of Hernando De Soto in Florida in 1539 and his exploration of the southern part of the United States; 25 acres.

Federal Hall, N.Y. (1939).—The site of the old city hall, renamed Federal Hall, the first seat (1789) of the new federal government, in New York City; less than 1 acre.

Fort Caroline, Fla. (1953).—Overlooks the site of René Goulaine de Laudonnière's colony, where the French attempted (1564) to settle within the present United States; 120 acres.

Fort Clatsop, Oreg. (authorized 1958).—The site of the winter encampment (1805–1806) of the Lewis and Clark Expedition; 106 acres.

General Grant, N.Y. (1959).—Memorial to Ulysses S. Grant, victorious Civil War general of the Union armies, and the tomb of General and Mrs. Grant; less than 1 acre.

House Where Lincoln Died, Washington, D.C. (authorized 1896).—House where President Abraham Lincoln died on April 15, 1865, refurnished as a typical home of the 1860's; less than 1 acre.

Lincoln Memorial, Washington, D.C. (authorized 1911).—Seated figure of Lincoln in a classical memorial structure of great beauty; less than 1 acre.

Lincoln Museum, Washington, D.C. (purchase provided for in 1866).—Collection of Lincolniana in the building which was once Ford's Theater, in which Lincoln was shot; less than 1 acre.

Mount Rushmore, S.Dak. (1925).—Colossal figures of Presidents George Washington, Thomas Jefferson, Abraham Lincoln, and Theodore Roosevelt, carved on the face of Mount Rushmore by the sculptor, Gutzon Borglum; 1,228 acres.

Thomas Jefferson, Washington, D.C. (1934).—Classical-style, colonnaded rotunda, with quotations from Jefferson's writings inscribed on the interior walls; 1 acre.

Washington Monument, Washington, D.C. (authorized 1848).—An obelisk 555 feet high, in commemoration of George Washington; less than 1 acre.

Wright Brothers, N.C. (1933).—Site of first sustained flights (1903) by Wilbur and Orville Wright in a heavier-than-air machine; 324 acres.

National Memorial Park.—The only national memorial park is situated in North Dakota and is dedicated to and named for Theodore Roosevelt. Established in 1947, it embraces badlands along the Little Missouri River and a part of the former president's Elkhorn Ranch; it covers 69,024 acres.

MILITARY PARKS AND BATTLEFIELDS

National Military Parks.—A number of national military parks were transferred from the jurisdiction of the War Department to that of the National Park Service in 1933. Horseshoe Bend and Oak Ridge, established in 1959 and 1960 respectively, were placed directly under Park Service administration. The dates in parentheses in the following list represent the years in which the parks were originally established.

Chickamauga and Chattanooga, Ga.-Tenn. (1890).—Sites of the Civil War battlefields of Chickamauga, Orchard Knob, Lookout Mountain, and Missionary Ridge, occurring in operations around Chattanooga during 1863; 8,190 acres.

Fort Donelson, Tenn. (1928).—Fort controlling the upper Cumberland River, captured by Gen. Grant in 1862; 119 acres.

Fredericksburg and Spotsylvania County Battlefields Memorial, Va. (1927).—Portions of the battlefields of Fredericksburg, Chancellorsville, the Wilderness, and Spotsylvania Court House, fought over between 1862 and 1864; 2,514 acres.

Gettysburg, Pa. (1895).—Battlefield marking the turning point of the Civil War (1863); burial ground dedicated by President Lincoln in his Gettysburg Address; 2,804 acres.

Guilford Courthouse, N.C. (1917).—Commemorates Revolutionary battle of March 15, 1781; 151 acres.

Horseshoe Bend, Ala. (1959).—Site of victory of Gen. Andrew Jackson over the Creek Indian Confederacy on March 27, 1814, opening Alabama and other parts of the old Southwest to settlement; 2,040 acres.

Kings Mountain, S.C. (1931).—Site of an American frontier victory on Oct. 7, 1780, at a critical point in the Revolutionary War; 3,950 acres.

Moores Creek, N.C. (1926)—Site of the victory on Feb. 27, 1776, of the North Carolina Patriots over the Loyalists, advancing the Revolutionary cause in the South; 42 acres.

Pea Ridge, Ark. (1960).—Scene, on March 7–8, 1862, of one of the biggest engagements of the Civil War west of the Mississippi; 4,211 acres.

Shiloh, Tenn. (1894).—Scene of the Battle of Shiloh in 1862, preparing the way for Grant's successful siege of Vicksburg; also, well-preserved Indian mounds; 3,557 acres.

Vicksburg, Miss. (1899).—Well-preserved fortifications manned during the 47-day siege of Vicksburg in 1863; 1,375 acres.

National Battlefield Parks.—The following Civil War battlefields are preserved as national battlefield parks:

Kennesaw Mountain, Ga. (1947).—Site, on June 27, 1864, of one of the heavy assaults made by Gen. William T. Sherman on Confederate positions during the Atlanta campaign; 2,883 acres.

Manassas, Va. (1940).—Scene of the first and second battles of Manassas or Bull Run, on July 21, 1861, and August 29–30, 1862; 2,039 acres.

Richmond, Va. (1944).—Scene of several Civil War battles in defense of Richmond; 745 acres.

National Battlefields.—Certain battlefields of historical importance are preserved, in part or in whole, as national battlefields:

Big Hole, Mont. (1910).—Site of battle during retreat of Chief Joseph and the Nez Percé Indians, 1877; 200 acres.

Fort Necessity, Pa. (1961).—Scene of the first major battle of the French and Indian War, fought on July 3, 1754, between Colonial troops led by George Washington and French troops assisted by Indian allies; 2 acres.

Petersburg, Va. (1962).—Well-preserved earthworks used during the Civil War Battle of the Crater and the longest siege in the history of the United States, 1864–1865; 1,504 acres.

Stones River, Tenn. (1960).—Scene of the midwinter battle (Dec. 31, 1862–Jan. 2, 1863) which opened the Federal offensive to trisect the Confederacy; 324 acres.

Tupelo, Miss. (1961).—Commemorates the Civil War Battle of Tupelo, July 13–14, 1864; 1 acre.

National Battlefield Sites.—Several other battlefields have been officially maintained as national battlefield sites:

Antietam, Md. (1890).—Scene of the battle which ended Gen. Lee's first invasion of the North in 1862; 184 acres.

Brices Cross Roads, Miss. (1929).—Scene of the Civil War battle of June 10, 1864; 1 acre.

Cowpens, S.C. (1929).—Site of Daniel Morgan's victory over the British under Banastre Tarleton on Jan. 17, 1781; 1 acre.

National Cemeteries.—Ten national cemeteries established by acts of Congress were transferred from the War Department to the administration of the National Park Service on Aug. 10, 1933. All but four of these are inactive. In addition, the Andrew Johnson and Custer Battlefield national monuments contain active cemetery sections, and Chalmette National Historical Park contains an inactive cemetery section. See NATIONAL CEMETERIES.

See also PARKS—*County, State, and National Systems* and separate articles about many of the parks, monuments, and sites listed in the foregoing account. For a discussion of national parks in Canada, see CANADA—*25. National Parks.*

GEORGE B. HARTZOG, JR.,
Director, National Park Service, United States Department of the Interior.

NATIONAL PORTRAIT GALLERY, museum, London, England, on St. Martin's Place, behind the National Gallery. It was founded by Parliament in 1856 to collect and exhibit the best authentic contemporary portraits of past British men and women of fame. The gallery contains over 4,000 portraits, including paintings, drawings, miniatures, busts, medallions, and works in other media, dating mainly from 1505 to the present day. Portraits of living persons (other than the sovereign and consort) are not exhibited, except when likenesses of such persons appear in group portraits which include one or more deceased subjects. Among the treasures of the gallery are the full-length cartoon of Henry VIII by Hans Holbein the Younger; several miniatures by Nicholas Hilliard, Isaac Oliver, and Samuel Cooper; and a number of portraits painted by Sir Joshua Reynolds, Thomas Gainsborough, George Romney, Sir Thomas Lawrence, George Frederic Watts, and John Singer Sargent. In some cases, notably those of Percy Bysshe Shelley and Jane Austen, the only known portrait from life is preserved. The library is rich in photographs and engravings of portraits that are housed elsewhere, and of photographs from life.

National Portrait Gallery
The National Portrait Gallery in London.

J. F. KERSLAKE,
Assistant Keeper, National Portrait Gallery.

NATIONAL RECOVERY ADMINISTRATION (NRA), a former federal agency which was set up under the National Industrial Recovery Act, approved June 16, 1933, and which was dissolved by order of the president on Jan. 1, 1936, after the United States Supreme Court on May 27, 1935, in a unanimous decision, had declared Section 3 of Title I of the act, its most important provision, unconstitutional.

The National Industrial Recovery Act and its companion measure, the original Agricultural Adjustment Act (declared unconstitutional by the Supreme Court, Jan. 6, 1936), were the two most important legislative measures enacted during the early days of the Roosevelt (New Deal) administration for the purpose of combating the economic depression which began in the fall of 1929, and in 1933 was at about its worst. The National Industrial Recovery Act was designed to relieve industrial unemployment (then very widespread) by shortening hours of labor, increasing wages, and eliminating unfair trade practices as well as destructive price cutting through the enforcement of such codes of fair competition as might be adopted under Section 3 and Title I of the act and approved by the president. The code-making authority was the vital feature of the act, and when the Supreme Court ruled that the making of codes was a legislative function which Congress could not delegate, even to the president, it cut the heart out of the law. Thereafter there was little reason for keeping the NRA alive, and it was kept alive only long enough to correlate and summarize such information as it had collected and could collect with respect to the effect on industry of code administration and the discontinuance thereof.

Immediately after approving the Industrial Recovery Act, President Roosevelt appointed Brig. Gen. Hugh S. Johnson, who had resigned from the army in 1919, to administer the provisions of Title I. He at once embarked upon the task of establishing codes of fair competition. By Jan. 1, 1935 it was stated that approximately 98 per cent of all American industry represented by 541 codes and 177 supplementary codes was operating under the industrial self-government program contemplated by the Recovery Act. Other accomplishments, according to a report, included: (1) The elimination of child labor and the curtailment of industrial housework; (2) the establishment of the principle of a limited work week and minimum rates of pay; (3) the decrease of industrial unemployment; and (4) the curtailment of wage-cutting in price competition.

General Johnson resigned as administrator Sept. 24, 1934, and three days later President Roosevelt, by executive order, created the National Industrial Recovery Board to carry on the work begun by General Johnson, and vested it with all of the powers which had been conferred upon him. Following the Supreme Court's decision, the president, on June 14, 1935, approved a joint resolution of Congress extending the provisions of Title I of the act, in greatly modified form, to April 1, 1936. The following day the National Industrial Recovery Board was abolished by an executive order which re-created the Office of Administrator, abolished when General Johnson resigned Under the new regime, James L. O'Neill was appointed acting administrator, an assistant to the administrator to represent labor was created, an Advisory Council was set up, and a Division of Review and a Division of Business Co-operation were created. The executive order decreeing the dissolution of the NRA on Jan. 1, 1936, was issued by the president on Dec. 23, 1935. The same order abolished the Office of Administrator and transferred to the Department of Commerce the Advisory Council and the divisions of Review and of Business Co-operation to function therein until April 1, 1936.

While General Johnson was at the helm, NRA was front page news almost daily. He was a picturesque character with a remarkable flair for the dramatic. Throughout the country he made speeches threatening to "crack down" on those industrialists who balked at going his way. He adopted the "Blue Eagle" as NRA's emblem; insisted that it be used as a mark of identification on all goods manufactured under code provisions, and that all householders display replicas of it in their windows as evidence of their loyalty to the country and as a guarantee that they would purchase only products bearing the insignia. Among the public there was much criticism of the codes. Some contended that their effect was to give an undue advantage to big business; that they abolished competition; and that they were formulated by and for the benefit of the leaders in the respective industries without regard to the rights of small industrialists. No one accused General Johnson of undue partiality toward big business. His job was to see that the various industries adopted codes, while for the most part the codes were written by the industries themselves. The general impression now is that the NRA attempted entirely too much. It insisted upon the codification of all industries, big and little, even adopting codes for barbers and pants pressers, which, like some of the other codes, increased prices without improving workmanship or quality.

NRA

Decision.—Two principal questions were involved in the case which resulted in the final dissolution of the NRA. One was whether Congress had the right to delegate its legislative power, and the other was whether Congress had the power to fix the hours and wages of employees engaged in the internal commerce of a state because such wages and hours may have an indirect effect on interstate commerce. The answer of the Supreme Court to both questions was an emphatic "No." The facts in the case were briefly these: the A. L. A. Schecter Poultry Corporation and the Schecter Live Poultry Market; Joseph Schecter, operator of the latter and financial backer of the former; and Martin, Alex and Aaron Schecter, operators of the Poultry Corporation, conducted a wholesale poultry business in Brooklyn, N. Y., and had been convicted in a Federal District Court of violating in numerous ways the Live Poultry Code which had been promulgated under Section 3 of the National Industrial Recovery Act. Before the Supreme Court, to which the case was taken on appeal, attorneys for the government insisted that the provisions of the act authorizing the adoption of codes should be viewed in the light of the "grave national crisis with which Congress was confronted" when the law was enacted. To this contention the Supreme Court, in an opinion by Chief Justice Hughes, said:

"Extraordinary conditions may call for extraordinary remedies. . . . Extraordinary conditions do not create or enlarge constitutional power. . . . Section 3 of the Recovery Act is without precedent. It supplies no standards for any trade, industry or activity. It does not undertake to prescribe rules of conduct to be applied to particular states of fact determined by appropriate administrative procedure. Instead of prescribing rules of conduct, it authorizes the making of codes to prescribe them. For that legislative undertaking Section 3 sets up no standards, aside from the statement of the general aims of rehabilitation, correction, and expansion described in Section 1. In view of the scope of that broad declaration, and of the nature of the few restrictions that are imposed, the discretion of the President in approving or prescribing codes, and thus enacting laws for the government of trade and industry throughout the country, is virtually unfettered. We think the code-making authority thus conferred is an unconstitutional delegation of legislative power. Congress cannot delegate legislative power."

With respect to the right of the government to fix the wages and hours of labor, the court said: "We are of the opinion that the attempt through provisions of the code to fix the hours and wages of employes of the defendants in their intrastate business was not a valid exercise of Federal Power. . . . On both the grounds we have discussed, the attempted delegation of legislative power, and the attempted regulation of intrastate transactions which affect interstate commerce only indirectly, we hold the code provisions here in question to be invalid, and that the judgment of conviction must be reversed."

NATIONAL RESEARCH COUNCIL. A scientific body in the United States, organized, at the request of President Wilson in 1916, by the National Academy of Sciences under its congressional charter for the purposes of promoting research in the natural sciences and encouraging the application and dissemination of scientific knowledge. As the principal operating agency of the academy, the council fosters research projects and furnishes professional advice to governmental and private organizations; it also administers funds entrusted to it for research and fellowship programs.

The membership is composed of representatives of nearly 100 scientific and technical societies, research institutions, or government agencies; and also of members-at-large appointed by the council. There are about 225 members. In addition to its general committees, the council has eight divisions: international relations; mathematical and physical sciences, including astronomy; engineering and industrial research; chemistry and chemical technology; geology and geography; medical sciences; biology and agriculture; and anthropology and psychology.

The work of the council is carried on largely through its approximately 400 committees, boards, and panels, which have as members more than 2,000 distinguished scientists. The council does not maintain its own scientific laboratories; its chief concern is the cooperation and integration of research activities.

The council receives no government appropriation. The administrative expenses are defrayed by the income from a permanent endowment established from a gift of the Carnegie Corporation of New York, a portion of which was used to erect the Academy-Council Building in Washington, D.C. Financial support of scientific projects and fellowships is obtained from contracts with governmental or private agencies and from special grants from foundations, societies, and individuals. This support amounts to about $3,000,000 annually. Almost half of this sum goes to support the advanced study of more than 400 fellows appointed under the 15 predoctoral and postdoctoral fellowship programs which the council administers for various organizations.

The publications of the National Research Council are: *Bulletins* consisting mainly of monographic reports on the work of council committees; *Reprint and Circular Series*, shorter papers of current scientific interest; *Highway Research Abstracts; Mathematical Tables and Other Aids to Computation; Prevention of Deterioration Abstracts;* and numerous miscellaneous reports, bulletins, and bibliographies.

RAYMUND L. ZWEMER,
Executive Secretary, National Research Council.

NATIONAL RETAIL DRY GOODS ASSOCIATION (NRDGA), a retail trade group with a membership of more than 7,000 retail stores located in every state in the United States, in Canada, and in 10 foreign countries, is incorporated under the laws of the State of New York. Its board of directors is chosen from the executives of member stores, and its purpose is to aid in developing increased efficiency in every phase of retail operating procedures.

It is a nonprofit, voluntary membership organization, with administrative headquarters in its own New York, N. Y., office building, and with branch offices in Washington, D.C., and in San Francisco, Calif.

The NRDGA is regarded as one of the leading trade associations in the world, functioning in all areas in which the interests of the retail trade are at stake. Its actions are particularly directed to matters which, except for association action, individual stores could not accomplish alone, or could not do so as economically as their association.

The NRDGA is subdivided into ten major groups and divisions, each staffed by experts in their particular field of retailing and each functioning under the supervision of its own board of directors, consisting of member-store executives in their special field of retail activity. These groups and divisions are:

The Controllers' Congress
The Merchandising Division
The Store Management Group
The Personnel Group
The Sales Promotion Division
The Credit Management Division
The Traffic Group
The Delivery Group
The Ready-to-Wear Group
The Smaller Stores Division

The association has back of it more than 40 years of experience and exhaustive research, upon which it draws to provide for member stores technical assistance and advice on every phase of retailing, and store operating problems.

One important aspect of NRDGA activity consists of the interesting and mutually helpful ideas on retailing exchanged by merchants who attend the association's yearly meetings of its groups and divisions and its annual convention. The value of such exchanges of information is evidenced by the fact that more than 20,000 store executives gather each year for these sessions.

NRDGA activities—its policies and functions—are entirely governed by the vote of member stores.

NATIONAL SAFETY COUNCIL. This noncommercial, nonprofit association, hub of the safety movement in the United States, was established in 1913. The membership, totaling about 7,500, includes industrial and transportation members employing more than 9,000,000 persons, service or professional organizations which may control or influence safety work in hundreds of branches or units, and community or state safety organizations which carry on extensive programs of safety in their territories. There is a staff of 275 persons at the headquarters office in Chicago. Regional offices are maintained in New York and San Francisco. Approximately 1,000 men and women serve without pay as council officers and committeemen. The work of the National Safety Council is financed largely through membership dues.

The principal activities are of three sorts:

1. **Printed Material.**—Published material is of three kinds: (a) nine monthly magazines, reviewing current happenings in every kind of

safety work; (b) several hundred technical pamphlets and memos, providing standard information on safe equipment and safe methods; (c) a constant flow of inspirational and interest-maintaining safety material, such as posters, newspaper publicity, radio releases, newsletters, and calendars.

2. **Conventions and Conferences.**—An annual, five-day, national convention is held, with an average attendance of 12,000 persons and comprising 125 sessions. Help is also given in the organizing of numerous regional safety conferences.

3. **Field Service.**—States and cities are given assistance in forming safety organizations, in improving traffic control measures, and in related problems. Some 75 community and state safety organizations are affiliated with the National Safety Council.

R. L. Forney,
General Secretary, National Safety Council.

NATIONAL SCIENCE FOUNDATION, The, is a federal agency, established by Congress in 1950 "to promote the progress of science; to advance the national health, prosperity and welfare; to secure the national defense; and for other purposes."

The foundation has the responsibility of developing and encouraging the pursuit of a national policy for the promotion of basic research and education in the sciences; for initiating and supporting basic scientific research in the mathematical, physical, medical, biological, engineering, and other sciences, and for appraising the impact of research upon industrial development and upon the national welfare.

In carrying out these broad objectives, the foundation supports research and education through grants and fellowships, fosters the exchange of scientific information among scientists in the United States and foreign countries, and surveys the nature and extent of scientific research and development activities in the United States. In view of the magnitude of the over-all federal research and development program, which in the mid-1950's was more than two billion dollars, an especially important function of the foundation is the study of the federal program in support of scientific research, the role of the federal government in support of science, and the correlation of the foundation's scientific research program with those of other groups, both private and public. With the cooperation and participation of the scientific societies of America, the foundation maintains a register of scientific and technical personnel and provides a central clearinghouse of information covering scientific and technical personnel in the United States.

Organizationally, the foundation consists of the 24-member National Science Board, chosen by the president of the United States from among persons eminent in the fields of the basic sciences, medical science, engineering, agriculture, education, and public affairs; and a director chosen by the president to serve for a term of six years. The principal operating divisions are: Biological and Medical Research; Mathematical, Physical, and Engineering Sciences; and Scientific Personnel and Education, which is concerned with the award of scholarships and graduate fellowships and problems relating to education in the sciences.

Lee Anna Embrey.

NATIONAL SECURITY ORGANIZATION. The National Security Act of 1947 including the 1949 Amendments and Reorganization Plans 3 and 6 of 1953 forms the basis for the National Security Organization within the United States. The legislation provides for the determination of integrated policies and procedures for the departments, agencies, and functions of the federal government having to do with national security. It establishes three separately administered military departments: the Army, the Navy, and the Air Force, and provides for the coordination and unified direction of the military departments under the civilian control of the Secretary of Defense.

History and Nature of National Security Act.—The movement which finally led to the passage of this act originated shortly after World War I with certain proponents of air power who believed that greater autonomy and importance should be given to the United States Army Air Force. It was argued that this could best be brought about by a merger of the War and Navy Departments, with all air activities segregated in a single division of the merged departments. The proposed arrangement was not adopted because it would have deprived the Navy of essential control over its aviation activities. The early plans also contemplated absorption of the Marine Corps by the Army.

Drawing upon World War II experience, and the demonstrated value of certain inter-service procedures, the law, as passed on July 26, 1947, did not merge the armed services but set up a separate Air Force and attempted an integration of all of the forces and resources needed for waging modern warfare. Civilian control over the military forces was retained in accordance with the political philosophy of the Constitution of the United States, expressed in making the President Commander in Chief of the Army and Navy. James Forrestal became the first Secretary of Defense on Sept. 17, 1947.

Following recommendations made by the Hoover Commission, the National Security Act was amended in 1949. The military establishment became one executive department, the Department of Defense, and the former executive departments of the Army, the Navy, and the Air Force were designated as military departments, but the Secretaries of these three Departments ceased to have cabinet rank. The position of Chairman of the Joint Chiefs of Staff, which had existed informally since World War II, was made statutory.

Another reorganization of the National Security Organization took place in 1953 (Reorganization Plans 3 and 6) based on the report of the Rockefeller Committee. The National Security Resources Board, the Munitions Board, and the Research and Development Board were abolished; at the same time an Office of Defense Mobilization was formed and appointment of additional Assistant Secretaries of Defense were authorized.

The National Security Act is organized under four titles; Title I—Coordination for National Security; Title II—The Department of Defense; Title III—Miscellaneous provisions having to do with salaries of personnel, definitions, funds, and other such matters; Title IV—Promotion of Economy and Efficiency Through Establishment of Uniform Budgetary and Fiscal Procedures and Organizations.

TITLE I: COORDINATION FOR NATIONAL SECURITY

By this title, three activities are created: a National Security Council which recognizes the need for close and continued coordination on a high level within the federal government of the domestic, military, and foreign policies of the country; a Central Intelligence Agency which correlates, evaluates, and disseminates intelligence having a bearing on national security; and an Office of Defense Mobilization for improved and systematized planning in regard to the control and use, in the event of an emergency, of the country's manpower, natural resources, and industrial facilities.

National Security Council.—The function of the council is to advise the president with respect to the integration of the nation's domestic, foreign, and military policies, so as to enable the armed services and other departments of the government to discharge effectively their responsibilities with respect to national security. Specifically, it is the duty of the council to assess and appraise the objectives, commitments, and risks of the United States in relation to the country's actual and potential military power.

The council is composed of the president, who presides at its meetings; the vice president; the secretary of State; the secretary of Defense; the director of the Office of Defense Mobilization; and the director of the Foreign Operations Administration, as permanent members. Secretaries and under secretaries of other executive departments and the military departments may be appointed to the council by the president. No military officers are members of the council although they may be called on for advice and recommendation on any subject under consideration by the Council.

Central Intelligence Agency.—This agency is established under the National Security Council and makes its reports and recommendations to the council. The duties of the agency are to coordinate in the interest of national security the intelligence activities of the several government departments with a view to avoiding duplication of effort and working at cross purposes; with correlating and evaluating intelligence gathered by the intelligence activities of the several government departments and agencies; and with disseminating such intelligence within the government, using existing agencies and facilities where appropriate.

Office of Defense Mobilization.—This office took the place of the National Security Resources Board and was created by Reorganization Plan No. 3 of 1953 to advise and assist the president concerning the coordination of military, industrial, and civilian mobilization for the national defense, including policies and programs for vital material stockpiling, manpower, and production.

TITLE II: THE DEPARTMENT OF DEFENSE

The Department of Defense is an executive department of the government headed by a secretary of Defense who is the principal assistant to the president on all matters relating to the department. Within the Department of Defense are the three military departments of the Army, the Navy, and the Air Force.

Secretary of Defense.—The secretary of Defense is appointed from civilian life by the president with the consent of the Senate. He exercises direction, control, and authority over the Department of Defense. The secretary is assisted by a deputy secretary of Defense who coordinates the activities of the Department of Defense as directed by the secretary, and who exercises the powers of the secretary during his absence or disability. There are nine assistant secretaries of Defense with specific duties prescribed by the secretary as follows: comptroller; manpower and personnel; legislative and public affairs; international security; research and development; supply and logistics; properties and installations; health and medical; military applications engineering. Provision is also made for a general counsel, with the rank of assistant secretary, to act as chief legal adviser of the Department of Defense.

Officers of the armed services may be detailed to duty as assistants and personal aides to the secretary of Defense, but he is specifically enjoined from establishing a military staff.

The Armed Services.—The military departments of the Army, the Navy, and Air Force replaced the former executive departments of War and Navy. Each military department is separately administered by its civilian secretary under the direction, authority, and control of the secretary of Defense. Each has an under secretary and several assistant secretaries.

Department of the Army.—The term is construed by the act to mean the Department of the Army at the seat of government and all field headquarters, forces, reserve components, installations, activities, and functions under the control and supervision of this department. The head of the department has the title secretary of the Army. The United States Army, within the Department of the Army, includes land combat and service forces, and such aviation and water transportation as may be organic therein. The army is to be organized, trained, and equipped primarily for prompt and sustained combat incident to operations on land.

Department of the Navy.—No change was made in the name of this department, nor in the title of the secretary of the Navy. The term is construed by the act to mean the Department of the Navy at the seat of government; the headquarters, United States Marine Corps; the entire operating forces of the United States Navy, including naval aviation, and of the United States Marine Corps; all field activities, headquarters, forces, bases, installations, activities, and functions under the control and supervision of the Department of the Navy; and of the United States Coast Guard when it operates as part of the Navy in time of war. Naval aviation is integrated with the naval service within the Department of the Navy.

The act stipulates that the United States Navy is to be organized, trained, and equipped primarily for prompt and sustained combat incident to operations at sea, and that it shall be generally responsible for naval reconnaissance, anti-submarine warfare, and the protection of shipping.

In order to leave no question as to the status of the United States Marine Corps, the act stipulates that the Marine Corps shall be organized, trained, and equipped to provide fleet marine forces, together with supporting air components, for service with the fleet in the seizure or defense of advanced naval bases and for the conduct of such land operations as may be essential to the prosecution of a naval campaign.

Department of the Air Force.—This newest of the military departments is headed by the secretary of the Air Force. The term is construed to mean the Department of the Air Force at the seat of government and all field headquarters, forces, reserve components, installations, activities, and functions under the control of the Air Force. The Air Force is to be organized, trained and equipped primarily for prompt and sustained offensive and defensive air operations, and shall be responsible for the preparation of the air forces necessary for the effective prosecution of war except as otherwise assigned.

Armed Forces Policy Council.—The council was formed to advise the secretary of Defense on matters of broad policy relating to the armed forces. Membership of the council consists of the secretary of Defense, chairman; deputy secretary of Defense; secretary of the Army; secretary of the Navy; secretary of the Air Force; chairman of the Joint Chiefs of Staff; chief of Staff, United States Army; chief of Naval Operations; chief of Staff, United States Air Force; and commandant, United States Marine Corps (only on Marine Corps matters).

Joint Chiefs of Staff.—The Joint Chiefs of Staff comprising a chairman, without voting rights; the chief of Staff, United States Army; chief of Naval Operations; and the chief of Staff, United States Air Force; plus the commandant of the Marine Corps when any matter under consideration directly concerns the Marine Corps, are the principal military advisers to the president, the National Security Council, and the secretary of Defense. The principal duties of the Joint Chiefs of Staff are: (1) to prepare strategic plans and to provide for the strategic direction of the military forces, including the unification, where appropriate, of commands in strategic areas; (2) to review major material and personnel requirements of the military forces, and to prepare joint logistic plans and responsibilities in accordance therewith; (3) to formulate policies for the education and training of the military forces, and (4) to provide United States representation on the military staff committee of the United Nations.

Joint Staff.—The Joint Chiefs of Staff are authorized to have a staff of not more than 210 officers composed of approximately an equal number from each of the three armed services.

WILLIAM J. MORGAN,
Division of Naval History, United States Navy Department.

NATIONAL SECURITY RESOURCES BOARD, an agency of the federal government, established by the National Security Act of 1947 (Public Law 253, 80th Congress, 1st Session, July 26, 1947). Its functions are set forth in Title I, Section 103, of that act, as follows:

(a) There is hereby established a National Security Resources Board (hereinafter in this section referred to as the "Board") to be composed of the Chairman of the Board and such heads or representatives of the various executive departments and independent agencies as may from time to time be designated by the President to be members of the Board. The Chairman of the Board shall be appointed from civilian life by the President, by and with the advice and consent of the Senate.

(b) The Chairman of the Board, subject to the direction of the President, is authorized, subject to the civil-service laws and the Classification Act of 1923, as amended, to appoint and fix the compensation of such personnel as may be necessary to assist the Board in carrying out its functions.

(c) It shall be the function of the Board to advise the President concerning the coordination of military, industrial, and civilian mobilization, including: (1) policies concerning industrial and civilian mobilization in order to assure the most effective mobilization and maximum utilization of the Nation's manpower in the event of war; (2) programs for the effective use in time of war of the Nation's natural and industrial resources for military and civilian needs, for the maintenance and stabilization of the civilian economy in time of war, and for the adjustment of such economy to war needs and conditions; (3) policies for unifying, in time of war, the activities of Federal agencies and departments engaged in or concerned with production, procurement, distribution, or transportation of military or civilian supplies, materials, and products; (4) the relationship between potential supplies of, and potential requirements for, manpower, resources, and productive facilities in time of war; (5) policies for establishing adequate reserves of strategic and critical material, and for the conservation of these reserves; (6) the strategic relocation of industries, services, government, and economic activities, the continuous operation of which is essential to the Nation's security.

(d) In performing its functions, the Board shall utilize to the maximum extent the facilities and resources of the departments and agencies of the Government.

The board also has continuing statutory functions in connection with the disposal of government-owned rubber producing facilities under the Rubber Act of 1948, in connection with the mandatory authority for the procurement of articles or materials needed for the armed forces or the Atomic Energy Commission under the Selective Service Act of 1948, and in connection with the need for improved highways for the national defense under the Federal-Aid Highway Act of 1948. Moreover, the chairman of the board is a statutory member of the National Security Council, and a member of the Defense Mobilization Board (Executive Order 10200, Jan. 3, 1951).

Following the establishment of the board in 1947, the president designated as its membership the chairman of the National Security Resources Board, the secretary of the treasury, the secretary of defense, the secretary of the interior, the secretary of agriculture, the secretary of commerce, and the secretary of labor. The secretary of state was added to the board's membership on Feb. 19, 1948.

Arthur Middleton Hill served as first chairman of the NSRB from Aug. 29, 1947, to Dec. 15, 1948. On Dec. 16, 1948, Dr. John R. Steelman succeeded him, as acting chairman, until April 26, 1950, when W. Stuart Symington, first secretary of the air force, took the oath of office as chairman, a post in which he served until May 4, 1951. The president then named as acting chairman Jack O. Gorrie who had served as the executive assistant to both Dr. Steelman and Mr. Symington.

During the years of its existence, the board, in cooperation with other agencies of the federal government, with the state governments, and representatives of industry, labor, and agriculture, has made a variety of studies on the nation's resources, prepared draft emergency legislation, laid the foundations for the establishment of the emergency defense agencies, participated in the work of the National Security Council, and advised the president on alternative mobilization plans and national security "readiness measures" involving the nation's human and material resources in the event of war.

In addition to its statutory functions, the board has exercised other responsibilities relating to the national security, executive orders, and other presidential directives.

To assist the president to coordinate emergency defense production activities under the Defense Production Act of 1950, the chairman of the

NSRB was directed by Executive Order 10161, Sept. 9, 1950, to resolve interagency issues, prescribe approved policy and program objectives, and advise the president on the progress of the defense production program.

While the board's mobilization planning proved useful in the nation's partial mobilization precipitated by the North Korean aggression in 1950, the board continues its primary concern with broad national policy which affects the nation's resources potential in the event of all-out war.

NATIONAL SOCIALIST (NAZI) PARTY. The National Socialist movement in Germany grew out of the economic dislocations, humiliations, and frustrations of the German people after defeat in World War I and the imposition of the Versailles Treaty. Loss of territories, abatement of military prestige, reparations burdens, and monetary inflation with resultant destruction of the independent middle class, created psychological conditions favoring acceptance of Nazi theories. These included repudiation of war guilt, assertion that the war had not been lost on the battlefield but on the home front by the treachery of non-German elements (particularly the Jews), contempt for democratic procedures, the need of a leader to raise Germany to her rightful place of world dominance, and the subordination of the individual to the state. The Nazi Party originated in the mildly radical German Workers' Party, founded in 1918, which Adolf Hitler and his friends renamed National Socialist German Workers' Party (Nazionalsozialistische Deutsche Arbeiterpartei). At a party congress held in 1920 Hitler announced a 25-point program including both radical and conservative features. It won him the support of all important elements of the population, including the military, white-collar, and industrialist classes. The party dissolved on Germany's defeat in 1945. See also HITLER, ADOLF; GERMANY—*The Third Reich, 1933–1945.*

NATIONAL SOCIETY OF COLONIAL DAMES OF AMERICA, The. An ancestral and patriotic organization of American women, founded May 19, 1892, and composed of one Colonial Society from each of the 13 original states, one society from the District of Columbia, and one associate society from each of the 27 noncolonial states. To be eligible for membership, a woman must be descended from some worthy ancestor who rendered valuable service to the colonies and who became a resident of America previous to 1750. Membership is by invitation only. The membership in 1954 was about 13,200. The objects of the society are: to preserve colonial history, traditions, manuscripts, records, relics, and buildings, to perpetuate the brave deeds and glorious memory of the colonists, and to encourage patriotism.

Churches and colonial houses of historical importance have been restored, historical sites marked, and prizes awarded for essays on patriotic subjects to pupils of schools and colleges. Forty-four historical museums are maintained by 27 state societies.

Indian nurses have been trained by scholarships and returned to work among their own people.

Large sums of money were raised for relief during the Spanish-American War. In World War I over $100,000 was supplied to hospital ships in the United States Navy. In World War II many ambulances were purchased, Red Cross rooms maintained, USO branches at Ketchikan, Alaska, completely supported, and in the Korean War aid sent to the U.S.S. *Gunston Hall,* and to airbases at Keflavik, Iceland. Colors were presented to the First Marine Corps Women's Reserve in honor of Col. Ruth Cheney Streeter, member of the society; later, in her honor, a recreation area was equipped and presented to the Headquarters Detachment of the Women Marines in Washington, D.C.

A large endowment fund was raised for the restoration and support of Sulgrave Manor, the English home of the ancestors of George Washington.

Gunston Hall, home of George Mason, author of the Virginia Declaration of Rights, owned by the State of Virginia, is managed by a Board of Regents nominated by the National Society and appointed by the governor of Virginia.

Headquarters of the National Society is at Dumbarton House, Washington, D.C.

ELIZABETH C. KENT,
Recording Secretary.

NATIONAL SOCIETY OF UNITED STATES DAUGHTERS OF 1812, an organization founded for the purpose of memorializing historical events from the close of the war of the American Revolution to the formation of the United States (as such) and till the close of the second war with Great Britain in 1815.

This present society is the outcome of the "General Society United States Daughters 1812," founded by Flora Adams Darling in 1892, on the anniversary of the battle of New Orleans, January 8. Its work begins where that of the Revolutionary commemorative societies leaves off, namely, when the treaty of peace was ratified by the Congress in session on Jan. 14, 1784. The qualifications for membership are: Any white woman over 18 years of age, of good character and a lineal descendant of an ancestor who rendered civil, military or naval service during the War of 1812, or the period of the causes which led to that war (subsequent to the War of the Revolution), Jan. 14, 1784, to Nov. 2, 1815, may be eligible to membership, provided the applicant be acceptable to the society. The society was incorporated under federal laws in 1901.

NATIONAL URBAN LEAGUE, an interracial group founded in New York City in 1910 as a professional community service voluntary agency to secure equal opportunity for Negro citizens in the fields of education, employment, housing, health, and welfare. By the early 1970's approximately 100 affiliated chapters were active throughout the United States. League policies are set up by an interracial board of trustees; the league's program is carried out by a professional staff of more than 1,200 employees, and by thousands of volunteers. Donations from individuals and civic, industrial, and philanthropic groups support the national headquarters in New York City; the United Fund assists local affiliates. The league expanded under the leadership of Whitney M. Young, Jr., its executive secretary from 1961 until his death in 1971. Vernon E. Jordan, Jr., succeeded Young.

NATIONAL WEALTH. See WEALTH—*National Wealth.*

NATIONALISM AND INTERNATIONALISM. Nationalism is a state or condition of mind characteristic of certain peoples with a homogeneous culture, living together in close association on a given territory, and sharing a belief in a distinctive existence and a common destiny. Such persons have a deep sense of belonging, a keen feeling of loyalty to the in-group, and a desire to contribute to its welfare. These sentiments lead to like-mindedness, conformity, and even exclusiveness, which find their expression in group action designed to add to the liberty, prestige, prosperity and power of the nation. Nationalism connotes a loyalty to the group entity superior to all other loyalties, a pride in its achievements, and a belief in its excellence, or even superiority over all other similar entities, and thus readily leads to aggressiveness. As such, while its greatest impulsion has come from intellectual circles, it makes its greatest appeal to the masses. This state of mind may change substantially in intensity and depth, depending upon conditions of time and place. It varies all the way from the healthy patriotism of the Swiss nation to the fanatical intolerance of Nazi Germany.

Nationality.—Loyalty to the in-group, the core of nationalism, is of a type with similar feelings of attachment to tribe, clan, caste, or city. But eventually the sights are raised, and the focus is the larger group entity, the nation or the state. Nation and state may be one and the same, as in the case of the United States; indeed, most of the states of the world today are of the nature of nation-states. But an entity may be classed as a nation because it has attained a high degree of cultural homogeneity, although it is under the domination of another power, as in the case of Poland after its partition.

The nation is an aggregate of individuals united by certain ties—political, racial, religious, cultural (including language), and historical, notably a common origin or at least a belief therein. In any particular case, it may be that not all these bonds are present. Switzerland is a strongly integrated nation, although in each of its three separate divisions a different tongue is spoken. Race is also a powerful bond of unity, but there are strong nations which seem able to get along despite the presence of several races within their frontiers. The same is true of religion. In the usual case, religion is a strong bulwark of nationhood, although some strong nations have within their borders two or more religious faiths. The most important consideration in this matter is a corporate will: a sufficiently powerful determination to live and work together. For, as Giuseppe Mazzini once said, nationalism is "the consciousness of a mission to be fulfilled for the sake of mankind. It does not depend upon race or descent, but upon a common thought and a common goal."

BASIS OF NATIONHOOD

Having defined nationalism and nationality, we may proceed now to a discussion of the basic foundations of nationhood—the factors of language, race, national character, religion, territory, political institutions, and economic integration.

Language.—The factor of national language is of the utmost importance; it can be considered the major distinguishing mark of nationality. People speaking the same language obviously can understand one another, and this fact alone contributes to a sense of belonging, a sentiment of solidarity. Most men really feel at home only in their own tongue. Furthermore, possession of means of mutual communication permits the development of a national literature. Its earliest manifestations usually take the form of patriotic ballads and sagas, glorifying heroes and military victories in the nation's history. Thus is group loyalty inseminated. It is significant that after the Norman Conquest, English nationality had little chance to emerge before the fusion of Anglo-Saxon with Norman French to form a single English language. As the nation evolves, a writer of great eminence and force may emerge to contribute further to the creation of group consciousness, both because of the influence of his work, and because the masses, by honoring him, honor the country from which he sprang. Such a role was played in England by Chaucer and Shakespeare, in Spain by Cervantes, in Italy by Dante. It is thus evident that nothing makes a larger contribution to the emergence of a distinctive culture and way of life than the national language. The invention of printing was a milestone in this movement. The cheap newspaper which was the result of this epochal invention made possible the propaganda of the French Revolution, described below. Without the cheap printing press the emergence of the "nation in arms" in 1792 is almost inconceivable. Further proof of the close relationship between language and nationalism is found in the efforts of extremely nationalistic states to suppress rival languages and to exalt and propagate their own. In this connection should be noted the tendency of newly emancipated states to revive their ancient script, and to take extreme measures to obliterate the use of the language formerly current, especially if it is that of a hated former ruler.

It is not implied that the possession of a single national language is absolutely essential to the creation of group consciousness. In Belgium, Canada, and South Africa more than one official language is in use. The case of Switzerland has already been mentioned. But rival languages are undoubtedly a serious handicap which can be overcome only if other factors, for instance the fear of attack from abroad, are able to engender a sufficient degree of national unity.

Race.—Among the foundations of nationalism the factor of language, just discussed, is closely allied with the matter of race. When a given people is fired by a profound belief—whether true or false—that they are of common or even exclusive racial stock, they are well on their way to that group consciousness and pride which are the soul of nationalism and which sometimes develop into a belief that they are superior to all others. Many leaders have fostered the idea that their people are "God's chosen." Joseph Chamberlain wrote, "The Anglo-Saxon race is infallibly destined to be the predominant race in the history and civilization of the world." Other writers, like Hippolyte Adolphe Taine, confusing language and race, have contrived to create the myth of a peculiar Aryan race represented as superior to all others. Adolf Hitler, making wide use of the writings of Heinrich von Treitschke, Joseph Arthur de Gobineau, Adam Heinrich Müller, Houston Stewart Chamberlain, and that official spokesman for Nazi supremacy, Hans Günther, forced on the Germans that poisonous doctrine—an intolerant belief in the purity and supremacy of the blond Nordic. This concept was invoked to justify the extermination of millions of Jews and the aggressive annexation of Austria, the Sudetenland, and Alsace-Lorraine. But while some of the worst manifestations of racialism were found in Nazi Germany and Japan, no great power has been entirely free from similar aberrations. Even small powers have given way to the temptations of racial prejudice and bigotry.

The dynamic forces of racialism are actually based on myth, but they are nonetheless potent and dangerous—since what counts in this matter is not so much what is true, but what one believes to be true. It should never be forgotten, however, that modern scholarship has demonstrated, first, that there is no such thing as a pure race and, second, that no race can be proved to be superior. This is particularly true of the Nazi concept of a distinct Nordic race, denied by all reputable anthropologists throughout the world. In fact, what is known as race is really a mere matter of environment, and race prejudice an artificial phenomenon, the creation of accident and the product of teaching and propaganda. Nevertheless, all peoples seem to be particularly susceptible to incitements through press, platform, and personal influence designed to arouse and stimulate pride of race. In fact, so great is the temptation for every nation to erect about itself high walls of race prejudice and exclusivism, that one of the first steps toward the creation of an effective international organization would have to be to break through these walls and work to promote a higher form of loyalty, namely, loyalty to the whole human race.

National Character.—A most significant factor in the evolution of modern nationalism is found in the growth of national character. That nations possess peculiar traits and distinct characteristics is generally admitted by scholars, although the latter deny that these are attributable to factors of race or origin. The explanation is found rather in the influence of environment—the effect of living together for generations under the same type of laws and government, in given conditions of economic life, territory, geography, climate, and world position, which produce a relative conformity and constancy of attitude. But national character is not completely constant or unchangeable; in the 17th century the Germans were generally indolent and peaceful, the British rebellious and turbulent. And the Americans, for so long isolationist in foreign affairs and in their relations with Europeans, curiously subject to an inferiority complex, show few signs of either of these traits today. Nevertheless, national character, and particularly a belief therein, plays an important role in the development of national consciousness. A peculiar pattern of institutions, customs and beliefs, including a distinctive development of the art forms, gives dignity to group life and a certain sense of belonging which are the very essence of the national spirit.

One important aspect of the culture pattern is a tendency to cherish historical traditions, notably by purposeful commemoration of historical events such as national independence and great military victories. Beloved national heroes of both peace and war are glorified and their praises sung. Pilgrimages to battlefields and the birthplaces of great men of the past are fostered. Such tendencies have been particularly apparent in Soviet Russia during the years after World War II, leading many authorities to believe that Russian nationalism, rather than the propagation of world revolution, is now the chief motive force in the Kremlin.

Religion.—Religion has always played a major role in the march of nationalism, and in fact in its primitive manifestations nationalism was really a religious phenomenon. This, however, has not continued to be the case; most religions today extend across a number of frontiers, as is the case with Christianity, Buddhism, Confucianism, Judaism, Hinduism, and Mohammedanism. And in some strong nations—the United States, for instance—freedom of religion has prevailed and numerous cults have flourished. Religious differences within a given nation have hindered or postponed the spread of nationalism, and the existence of a single powerful national church has been a potent nationalistic factor. This is particularly true when adherence to a given church is shared by the larger part of the population, and even more so where the church is "national" in the sense of belonging exclusively to one state, giving the people the sense of possessing something peculiarly sacred which is all their own. That there is a deep-rooted relationship between religion and the cult of the nation is shown by the canonization of Joan of Arc, and the tendency of some peoples to revere their national heroes as saints. The extent to which religion and nationalism may go hand in hand is shown by the role of Roman Catholicism in Ireland and in Prussian Poland; in both cases the church was largely instrumental in keeping the national spirit alive in the face of foreign domination. A similar role was played by the Scottish kirk after the 17th century; it differentiated the Scots sharply from the English and fed the flame of national sentiment as probably nothing else in the circumstances could have done. Coming to modern times, Nazi Germany and Soviet Russia showed their respect for the power of the church over the emotions of the people by taking the most extreme measures to mold it according to the needs of the national myth. It is interesting, too, that at the present time it is customary for the church, even in the freest countries, to preach the necessity of loyalty to the flag and obedience to secular authority. This is undoubtedly a prudent policy, since nowhere in our present-day world is the church in a position to challenge the power of the state to hold the loyalty and fidelity of the ordinary citizen.

Territory.—The fact that a given people is conscious of living within definite frontiers on a given portion of the world's surface constitutes an important element in the acquisition of nationhood. This is true despite the cases of those nations—the Poles in Russia, the Czechs in Austria-Hungary, and the Scots in Britain—which successfully maintained an intense group loyalty and patriotism while mere subdivisions of the larger entity by which they had been subjugated. Some nations have actually been formed precisely because they were a geographic-political entity with definite frontiers. At times the acquisition of too great an expanse of national domain has weakened the hold of group consciousness; but today, due to rapidity of modern modes of travel and the existence of remarkable methods of mass indoctrination—cheap newspapers, the cinema, radio, and television—it is possible to tighten and maintain the bonds of national unity even to the remotest corner of the widest realm. In fact, the existence of such modern methods holds out hope that some day it may be possible to inculcate a sense of group loyalty and a feeling of mutual understanding throughout the entire globe.

Political Institutions.—There is a close connection between the emergence of political institutions in a given area and the intensification of the national sentiment. Consciousness of group solidarity—to put it more simply, the ability to live together smoothly and peacefully—is undoubtedly a prerequisite to the successful operation of common agencies and procedures of government. If the integration comes about by agreement, as in the case of the 13 British colonies that joined to form the United States, such sociological-psychological solidarity may be absolutely essential. But even where unification comes about by force, unless there is a certain degree of group understanding and loyalty, the union may not be able to endure. On the other hand, the existence of common political institutions—notably a strong central government—may itself exert a commanding influence in engendering and consolidating the national sentiment of a given people. Germany's unification was finally consummated only after Bismarck had imposed on the many local and rival sovereigns of that divided country the authority of a powerful central government. In the United States, without the centralizing influence of the federal government, acting under the firm authority of a Constitution whose integrity was guaranteed by that extraordinary institution, the Supreme Court, it is difficult to conceive how national solidarity could ever have been achieved; the disastrous experience of the new republic under the Articles of Confederation shows that this assertion is not based on mere speculation. A strong government is the focus of loyalty. It is depended upon for the most vital services to the people—the public order and the general welfare at home, and security against invasion from abroad. In fact it is the supreme agency for the pursuit of unfulfilled national aspirations. As it meets these responsibilities, it is loved and respected, its leaders revered and honored. Even more, once the government has been established, it has at its disposal remarkably effective means for the spread of patriotic loyalty among the masses; it may create it by education and propaganda, or even impose it by force of law.

Economic Factors.—The division of the world into strong nations is explainable in part by economic factors. At the close of the Middle Ages, the growth of great national states proceeded hand in hand with a remarkable commercial and economic expansion. The rivalry between states was tremendously stimulated by the great discoveries and by the colonizations that followed and facilitated the acquisition by each state of a distinctive national character. Furthermore, under the influence of mercantilism, the economic life of the nation, hitherto almost purely local, took on a national character, as commerce and trade came under the control of strong centralized governments. This process was greatly stimulated by improvements in means of travel and communication. The predominant influence of mercantilism served to strengthen the hold of the government over every aspect of the economic activity of the nation. Every effort was made to render the state self-sufficient. Thus exports were stimulated, imports discouraged, and the colonies integrated with the economic home front. This extraordinary economic expansion was buttressed by military power, notably by the building of great navies designed to protect the far-flung interests of the metropolis. In the process vast fortunes were amassed, and new heroes emerged, thus creating a new, influential class of persons, those most interested in inculcating among the masses a spirit of national exclusiveness. Furthermore, this class possessed the most potent agencies of propaganda to accomplish this purpose.

Coming to modern times, the close connection between economic factors and nationhood is quite evident. International competition for markets, rivalry for scarce raw materials, the tendency of the government to replace the individual in buying and selling in the international field, and even in banking, the frantic exclusiveness induced by depression and inflation, have led to a bewildering maze of measures of autarchy—quotas, subsidies, exchange controls, high tariffs, and other restrictions—and have served to heighten national feeling and hamper the growth of international understanding. Economic nationalism seems to be most prevalent in those countries least able to stand the pressure of international competition. The weak power is the first to suffer unrest and disunity, to demand a strong government to repress "subversion," and to set in motion the defensive and offensive measures deemed necessary to meet the emergency; but even the strongest powers have not been free from similar phenomena.

GROWTH OF NATIONALISM

Although nationalism is distinctly a modern development, its roots lie in the period when prehistoric men first organized themselves into tribes. For the tribe, with its intense religious loyalty, fierce clannishness, local pride, and hatred of the "barbarian," shows many of the traits of present-day nationalism. In tribal society, the struggle for the preservation and extension of group solidarity was waged intensively. On the other hand, the main bond among tribesmen was that of blood kinship, while relations within the tribe were personal rather than political. Moreover, at this period in man's development there was little trace of patriotism, or love of homeland; the sense of attachment to a particular territory developed later.

City-States.—The first signs of patriotism appear with the rise of the early city-states, when for various reasons—considerations of defense, economic advantages, religious values—men began to group themselves about certain vantage points. Here the growth of commerce at home and of foreign trade abroad led to the first breakup of the tribal system, and brought the first traces of the modern political system. A typical example of the early city-state—and the most famous—is provided by the story of Athens. Here was developed a strong sense of group solidarity. The citizen was conscious of a common origin, a distinctive cultural pattern, and an assumed common destiny. Cultural homogeneity was further enhanced by religious rites glorifying the national heroes and reinforcing a sense of superiority with respect to the foreigner or "barbarian." Furthermore, the citizens had become attached to a given territory. Thus in Athens we find many of the elements of modern nationalism.

But the city-states gave way to the patriarchal empires, a process brought about by the expansion of one city-state or its conquest by a rival power on the rise. Such expansion augmented the national pride of the conquering power, kindling further the national spirit, and at the same time served to intensify the group loyalty of the submerged or conquered minority. The best example of such an entity is the great Roman Empire. In its aggressive, unprincipled and hypocritical foreign policy it reminds us of the integral nationalism practiced by Hitler and Mussolini. But it lacked the cultural homogeneity, the intense feeling of patriotism, and the overall sense of loyalty to a state or sovereign characteristic of nationalism as we know it today.

Middle Ages.—If, in the city-state and the patriarchal empire, the historian can find many of the typical features of present-day nationalism, the same cannot be said of the period of the Middle Ages. The basic unit of political organization, the feudal domain, did not lend itself to the development of group solidarity, nor permit the growth of any national sentiment. Mankind in general lived in groups too isolated, too poor and small, too provincial, to feel any sense of attachment to a national or cultural entity. Medieval towns, in general, were so separated from one another and so dominated by a spirit of localism that they could not serve as the basis for any larger group loyalty. Furthermore, there existed a measure of universal solidarity which was incompatible with the separatism characteristic of nationalism. The church was a major focus of individual loyalty, and its sway was almost universal. The Holy Roman Empire, too, despite its weakness, exercised for a considerable time a cosmopolitan influence. In this matter it is significant that nationalism evolved most rapidly in those lands, notably in France and England, where the imperial power was most remote and its influence weakest. Another factor was the existence of a fierce parochialism within each entity later to become a nation; thus where Scottish clan hated its neighbor clan there was little chance, except perhaps in time of great peril, that all the clans together could feel a national spirit of solidarity as against England or even France. It was necessary to await the consolidation of the king's authority over the realm before the nation could emerge. Here the work of Henry IV in France and of Henry VII and Henry VIII in England is most significant. This crucial task accomplished by the monarch was made possible by a great commercial revolution, enabling a new middle class to emerge, which allied itself with the king and gave him the support required to overcome the anarchy and decentralization of the feudal system. It is also worth noting that national consolidation was accomplished earliest where the geographical situation was most favorable, as in England, isolated as she was from the Continent, and in France, where the king could operate from the strongly fortified bastion built about Paris, in the region known as the Ile de France. The process of consolidation went on in England, Spain, France, Russia, and Poland, with the result that by the middle of the 18th century national states had emerged in most of Europe. In the Balkans, however, and in Germany and Italy, this movement was postponed for another hundred years.

As powerful monarchs were gradually establishing their authority and laying the foundation for separate statehood, other important influences were at work. One was the slow but sure development of national languages, already discussed. This came about hand in hand with the weakening of Latin as the language of universal use for education, literature, and diplomacy. As a consequence national literatures emerged, permitting the dissemination among the masses of works which kindled the national spirit and engendered a consciousness of separate existence. Another result was the weakening of the church's hold over education, which gradually became more and more secular and at the same time less universal in outlook.

The Reformation, the rise of Protestantism, and the growing emphasis upon national churches all contributed to the consolidation of separate, exclusive states. For instance, Presbyterianism in Scotland served to quicken the parochial spirit of its people and give them a sense of national exclusiveness. In Germany, the effect of Martin Luther's famous addresses was the amalgamation of religion and patriotism into a militant national faith.

Another influence favorable to the emergence of modern nationalism was offered by the great discoveries and the ensuing economic expansion of Europe. The bitter rivalries thus engendered fed the national spirit, the glorious deeds of discovery fired the national pride, and the great wars which followed had a dynamic and lasting effect in this same direction. Finally the traders, bankers, and shippers, a new class representing vast wealth and wielding great influence, were not slow to feed the flame, for they realized the necessity of gaining the support of the citizens, from whom they had to enlist the sailors and the fighters if the nation was to keep pace with its rivals. In this connection the role of mercantilism must not be neglected—the narrow commercial policies adopted in most states after 1500. This system operated to promote interstate rivalry and jealousies, intensify national pride, and promote international friction. It was therefore a heady stimulant to the pride and arrogance of nations.

The major role played by the monarch in laying the basis for the modern national state has already been mentioned. The local sway of the feudal lords and barons gradually had to give way before the emerging power of the king, permitting the development of national instrumentalities of government and the establishment of the "law of the realm." This was particularly true in England, where the common law finally consolidated its hold over the entire country, contributing immeasurably to the consciousness of the citizens that they were set apart from the rest of the world. In some states the appearance of democratic government was a further step in this direction.

The French Revolution.—It is impossible to fix a date for the beginning of modern nationalism. The underlying social, economic, political, and intellectual forces accomplished their work only gradually, and at a different rate in each region depending upon the peculiar circumstances of the particular case. Some authorities place the actual origins of modern nationalism at the time of the Reformation; others date it from the Peace of Westphalia in 1648, which ushered in the modern system of independent sovereign states. Still other authorities, and they represent the majority, insist that nationalism as we know it began with the French Revolution. But, as we have seen, the way had already been opened by the emergence of a system of strong, well-integrated states, the work of powerful monarchs. Also, the minds of men had been prepared for the spirit of nationalism by the teachings of the Enlightenment in the 18th century. The great apostle of modern nationalism was Jean Jacques Rousseau. He stressed the value of the moral unity of the masses, who are bound together in pursuit of a common purpose—the good of the whole. Furthermore, he insisted that the community should be governed by laws issuing from the people themselves, and not from a divine-right monarch standing above the law. He emphasized the necessity of a supreme loyalty to *la patrie* (the fatherland), a duty so sacred as almost to become an article of religious faith. He decried any idea of fidelity to something higher, for instance world society or the entire human race. In short, he sought to arouse the masses to a belief in a common heritage and a common destiny, claiming for men a status of democratic equalitarianism, and for nations a right of self-determination. It was for the men of 1789 to put these principles into practice, at least for a time.

At first professing absolute fidelity to the doctrines of popular sovereignty, individual liberty, social equality and fraternity, the Jacobins, under the stress of rebellion at home and attack from abroad, soon allowed the movement to deteriorate. Force and militarism took precedence over humanitarianism and fraternal love. The movement became fanatical. Soon there began to emerge those remarkable instrumentalities of nationalism which have been so widely employed ever since, notably by totalitarian dictatorships, but which have not been neglected by the most advanced democracies. The concept of the "nation in arms," universal conscription, emotional appeals for flag and country, the composition of a national anthem, the glorification of national heroes, the establishment of a system of public education grounded in the vernacular and dedicated to spreading revolutionary doctrines, insistence on the universal use of the French language, invention of a new kind of popular journalism and, finally, the organization of impressive rituals in the form of national ceremonies—all were employed as part of a vast scheme to create and intensify a national cult.

The doctrines of the revolution were professed to be universal—not designed for Frenchmen alone—but before long the Jacobins were thinking in terms of selfish national interest. They embarked on expansion and conquest. Nationalism, then as always, feeds on war. As the sansculottes marched to do battle abroad, they took their doctrines with them, and they spread their nationalism much faster than their democracy. This was true even before the rise of Napoleon, but when the Little Corporal assumed power he greatly intensified the development already under way. Fortified by supreme power and an admirable political organization and system of laws, he made excellent use of all the Jacobin paraphernalia of nationalism, employing it to the limit of his own keen shrewdness. Thus he was able to indoctrinate a whole generation of Frenchmen with the concepts of "glory." He taught lessons in this field which later governments, especially in other countries, have never forgotten. Everywhere he awakened submerged peoples to a sense of their own destiny, and thus did much to start Italy and Germany on that march for unity which they were to achieve several generations later. In fact Napoleon, who was actually destroyed by the dynamic national spirit he did so much to create, initiated the upheaval which ultimately transformed the continent, dividing it into separate entities inspired by the fervor of nationalism.

The metamorphosis of French nationalism after 1792, transformed as it was from a liberal, universalist movement into one marked by reaction and conquest, illustrates a point already made, namely, that nationalism is always a creature of environment, subject to change. It can be democratic, liberal, or fascist, according to circumstances. At times it may not exceed the bounds of a healthy patriotism, at others it will be the cause or the result, or even both at once, of expansionism and war. The story of nationalism since 1815 will bear out this assertion.

The 19th Century.—The 19th century has been called by some authors the great age of nationalism. During most of the century, after the aberrations of the Jacobins and Napoleon Bonaparte, what has been called "liberal nationalism" was revived and became predominant. This is a type of group consciousness characterized by intense patriotism and loyalty but faithful to the doctrines of individual and national freedom, in other words, espousing human rights and the right of self-determination of peoples. It tends to be high-minded and altruistic, universalistic and pacific. One of the greatest movements to be inspired by this spirit was the American War of Independence. This revolution was liberal and humanitarian, fought in the name of the great liberal principles dating back to John Locke and the Puritan Revolution, so admirably reformulated by Thomas Jefferson and Thomas Paine, and immortalized in the Declaration of Independence. In Britain, under the influence above all of Jeremy Bentham, liberal nationalism reached its highest point in the 19th century. As an intellectual movement it spread throughout western and central Europe. Based mainly on the middle classes, highly tinged with romanticism, and preaching the doctrine of free trade, this school of thought adopted certain typically Jacobin ideas, namely free popular education, universal military service, and popular journalism. These ideas were disseminated with great force and effect by Mazzini, who, as spiritual leader of the movement for unity and independence in Italy, became the most influential apostle of liberal nationalism in the entire century. Other leading philosophers of this movement were Giuseppe Garibaldi in Italy, Victor Hugo in France, and William Ewart Gladstone in England.

A major factor in the extraordinary emergence of nationalism during the 19th century was the first Industrial Revolution. By this is meant in general the amazing series of mechanical inventions ushered in by the invention of the flying shuttle in 1733 by John Kay. In modern states industry and commerce, and eventually society as a whole, were actually transformed by the developments made possible by the work of Thomas Savery, Thomas Newcomen, and James Watt in steam power, Sir Richard Arkwright and Samuel Crompton in textile manufacture, the Abraham Darbys and Henry Cort in coal and iron,

Sir Henry Bessemer in steel, and other pioneers. The consequences were incalculable. Mass production was introduced, great factory cities created, a working class or proletariat developed. Also, a new middle class was engendered, and the ranks of the capitalist class greatly augmented, from which the "empire builders," the keenest nationalists, emerged. The power of states to produce and to expand increased immeasurably. Demand for outlets for the investment of capital, and the need for raw materials to feed the hungry new factories led to the search for new possessions in distant regions—or gave empire builders the pretext to undertake such a search—and this meant a new wave of colonialism and imperialism. Exploits of adventurers and military geniuses like Robert Clive and Cecil John Rhodes were both a cause and a consequence of a new, intense kind of national pride. Another result was the development of modern methods for the communication of intelligence—through rail, telegraph, telephone, and cheap newspapers.

Major events of the 19th century owe their impulsion to the irresistible forces of nationalism. Greece and Belgium won nationhood early in this period. Nationalistic fervor inspired the great uprisings of 1830 and 1848. Across the Atlantic nationalism inoculated the Spanish and Portuguese colonies in Central and South America, which were able to win their independence, inspired and led by heroes such as Simon Bolívar and José de San Martín. During the two decades after 1855 both Germany and Italy belatedly won their unity through the genius of Prince Otto von Bismarck and Conte Camillo Benso di Cavour, respectively. Serbia, Rumania, and Montenegro won their liberty in 1878. Bulgaria was separated from Turkey. On the other hand, the Poles, Finns, Letts, Czechs, and Croats, among others, continued to be persecuted and oppressed, but this only served to solidify their national loyalty and to push them toward the independence they were later to win and—in some cases—to lose once again. Late in the century Japan, inspired by a high degree of national aspiration, became a world power. Since most of these events occurred through rebellion or war, it is evident that the pacifist slogans of liberal nationalism were often more honored in the breach than in the observance. Furthermore, as has so often been demonstrated, movements initially high-minded and altruistic readily deteriorated into expansionism, aggression, and war.

One may cite as examples Napoleon III and Bismarck, whose policies, originally professing fidelity to the doctrines of liberalism, eventually became reactionary and aggressive. Bismarck's unification of Germany was conservative and authoritarian, but Germany's annexation of Alsace-Lorraine in 1871 was accomplished in violation of the tenets of self-determination.

Toward the end of the 19th century came a remarkable intensification of nationalism, due in great part to a new industrial revolution. This caused Europe to burst its economic bonds and spread its power and influence throughout the world. New markets were sought in far-off China and Africa. A new wave of expansionism was initiated, as France spread further into Africa, encouraged by Bismarck after the debacle of 1871, and the British obtained control of Suez and embarked on new adventures in colonialism. Germany, too, seeking a "place in the sun," sought to extend her sway from Berlin to Baghdad. Even the United States was caught up in the current, and after a successful war with Spain found herself ensconced in Puerto Rico and the Philippines. New rivalries and frictions resulted, with new dangers of war, narrowly averted, as France and England clashed over Fashoda (now Kodok), Germany and France over Morocco, Russia and England over Persia. Grandiose schemes of expansion were dreamed up, mutual fears exacerbated, and a great armaments race launched. Some started new powerful navies, others augmented their existing naval power, compulsory military service was established in many lands, and in general the atmosphere was prepared for that great turning point in history, the explosion at Sarajevo.

The 20th Century.—As already remarked, the 19th century has been called the age of liberal nationalism, although it must be admitted that both at the beginning and at the end of that period, nationalism of an extreme variety was current. But if the 19th can be considered the century of liberal nationalism, certainly the 20th is the period of integral or fascist nationalism. The first decade, it is true, was relatively calm, and great hopes were held out for peace and security by optimists who reflected the spirit of the two Hague Conferences of 1899 and 1907. But these hopes were shattered in 1914. The nationalist and imperialist rivalries prior to 1914 undoubtedly contributed to the outbreak of World War I. In fact, nationalism was both a cause and a result of that conflict.

Since World War I the most dynamic manifestations of nationalism have occurred in authoritarian states, notably in Nazi Germany, the new Japan, Fascist Italy, and Soviet Russia. Some smaller states, too, have fallen under its sway—Juan Domingo Perón's Argentina, Francisco Franco's Spain, Antonio de Oliveira Salazar's Portugal, and Tito's Yugoslavia. Yet the Treaty of Versailles had been signed in an atmosphere of liberal nationalism. Woodrow Wilson's Fourteen Points were an expression of this philosophy, and the peace settlements were inspired in principle by the tenets of national self-determination, as shown by the establishment of the mandates scheme of the League of Nations, the creation of a free Poland, and the breaking up of the Austro-Hungarian empire into states based on national integrity. Unfortunately, however, many of the solutions adopted in 1919 ran counter to the Wilsonian ideal, for the American president was unable to obtain acceptance throughout for the formulas contained in his Fourteen Points. In defiance of the explosive verities of self-determination, new grievances were perpetrated. A status quo in which one finds a Fiume (now Rijeka), Shantung, or South Tirol, not to mention the Saar and the Polish Corridor, could hardly be expected to endure. In fact the eventual breakdown of the Versailles settlement, as well as the demise of the League of Nations, can be traced in large part to the injustices perpetrated in 1919 in violation of basic concepts of liberalism and self-determination. For one major cause of international disputes and resulting wars is simply unjust treatment meted out to helpless states, especially if they eventually become powerful enough to threaten the status quo.

Except for a brief period of comparative peace and optimistic hopes, extending roughly from

1920 to 1929, the world since World War I has been in almost constant turmoil. One of the major characteristics of the period—both a cause and a result of its cataclysms—has been the manifestation of extreme nationalism. No state has been free from this phenomenon, but in certain authoritarian powers nationalism has reached a pitch of frenzy never before seen, not even in the wildest days of Jacobin fanaticism. Thus Benito Mussolini, a follower of Niccòlo Machiavelli, Auguste Maurice Barrès and Georges Sorel (the apostle of violence) rather than of his liberal compatriot, Mazzini, indoctrinated a generation of Italians with the most extreme type of nationalism. Japan, already strongly nationalist, destroyed its democratic trappings in the early 1930's and became more and more rigorously fascist at home and expansionist abroad until it finally broke completely with the family of nations and embarked on total war. In fact, some authorities, contrasting Japan's meticulous compliance with international law during the Russo-Japanese War (1904–1905) with its incredible atrocities in World War II, ascribe this change to the purposeful inculcation among the masses of new doctrines of extreme, fanatical nationalism. The expansion which began in Manchuria finally overran Singapore and New Guinea. Hitler, destroying the democracy of the Weimar Republic, imposed a ruthless dictatorial regime on his people, broke the chains of Versailles, rearmed the nation, and marched into the Rhineland, Vienna, and later Prague. He took the final step when he attacked Poland in 1939. By his violent racial doctrines, his anti-Semitism, his bitter, intolerant, violent demand for absolute fidelity to a mystical and all-powerful Reich, and his control of the German mind through the corruption of press, platform, radio, the schools, and the universities, Adolf Hitler made himself the god of modern integral nationalism. He outdid Robespierre and Napoleon, and surpassed Barrès, Sorel, and Houston Stewart Chamberlain.

While the actual origins of great wars are difficult to determine, Hitler's aggressive imperialism and fanatical expansionism, seconded by a Mussolini already well schooled in such doctrines and with hands still bloody from his Ethiopian conquest, undoubtedly were major causes of World War II. Characteristic of this spirit is a negation of all humanitarian values, an uncompromising rejection of liberal and progressive principles, a total subjection of the individual to the domination of an all-powerful state, whose worship is postulated as a sacred, almost religious duty, and a devotion to the devastating doctrine that, in the pursuit of the national interest, any means is justified by the end in view. In a world imbued with this spirit, war is almost inevitable, and free nations can only conserve their liberty by constant vigilance and a determination to keep their powder dry.

Since World War II, nationalism has continued to play a major role throughout the world. The Hitlerian techniques were developed still further by Joseph Stalin, who proved himself an apt pupil of fascist nationalism. In Soviet Russia nationalism, stealing the show from the universalist doctrines of world communism, has inspired an expansion as rapid and as extensive as any in the history of the world. Many of the nations liberated after World Wars I and II have been subjugated anew, again as a result of a spirit of nationalism, but this time of a very different kind. This is true of Poland, Rumania, Czechoslovakia, Hungary, and China, although Yugoslavia, again due to the force of nationalism under a stubborn leader, Tito, has thus far escaped. Nor should we forget the fate of the once-free states, liberated as a result of World War I—Estonia, Latvia, and Lithuania. Elsewhere, however, the effect of nationalism has been to liberate certain regions from colonial rule. Thus India and Burma have separated from Britain, and Indonesia from the Dutch, while Indochina, Morocco, Tunis, and even Algeria strain at the leash of French sovereignty. In fact the slogan so often heard, "Colonialism is dead," is merely a general recognition of the liberating force of nationalism in the world today.

MAIN CHARACTERISTICS OF NATIONALISM

A brief description of the basic features of nationalism may serve to explain the nature of its dangers to individual states and to world peace.

Relativity.—As already suggested, the exact character of any particular case of nationalism is largely determined by environment. The state of mind of a given people may be entirely transformed according to changes in time and circumstance. Nationalism in the United States itself has shown significant variations explainable by factors of changing environment. Thus, while the Revolution was fought in a spirit of liberal nationalism which Locke and Rousseau would have applauded, the Spanish-American War was initiated in a wave of imperialist emotion. And the retreat from Europe and the League of Nations after 1920 was a clear manifestation of exclusive, isolationist nationalism. In World War I the general sentiment of the masses, even after American intervention in the conflict, remained basically isolationist. This is in sharp contrast with public opinion throughout World War II, at least after Pearl Harbor, for despite a national patriotism that reached a high pitch of intensity, Americans never faltered in their hopes for a new international organization which, it was confidently expected, would serve to ensure peace and security once the victory had been won. It has only been because of the disillusionments of the peace, and particularly since the outbreak of the "Cold War," that American nationalism has tended to become once again to some degree self-centered and isolationist, with some unmistakable signs of exclusiveness and intolerance.

Artificiality.—If nationalism is environmental, it is also to a large extent artificial. It is not a harmonious, natural growth, but the result of a long process which reaches its climax only after a given people has spent a long period of living and working together. This process can be greatly accelerated, however, by various methods, today only too familiar, of purposeful stimulation. In other words, nationalism is a state of mind which can be, and often is, induced by governmental and private propaganda. It can be the creature of ambitious leaders who wish to form certain patterns of opinion which they expect to use, for their own purposes perhaps, or for ends they consider to be in the public interest.

The most volcanic degrees of nationalism have been consciously and insidiously contrived. The fanatical propaganda of the French Revolution, the press-radio-platform paraphernalia of Joseph Paul Goebbels, the "brain washing" technique peculiar to communism, are striking examples of such methods. In this process, the youth of the nation is singled out as most impressionable and most easily molded. The effort is begun among the youngest children, and includes attempts to enlist the active support of family and school. The Germans under Hitler, and the Russian Communists today, have developed their techniques in this matter to the pitch of perfection. No age-group, no portion of the population, is neglected. The nationalist organizations take the form of clubs, cells, societies, or parties, and all cooperate to augment the fanaticism of the masses to the greater glory of the state. Glorify the nation, exaggerate its accomplishments, convince the masses that they constitute "God's chosen people," spread broadcast the slogan, "My country right or wrong," or, even more lethal, "My country always right," establish a conviction that the fatherland is in imminent danger of attack (whether this be true or false) and, over it all, obliterate all sense of measure, any vestige of objectivity, and one has all the ingredients for concocting a high degree of extreme nationalism. In this matter the most effective formula appears to be a close cooperation of thinker and actor; someone must furnish the doctrine, but someone else must be ready to propagate it among the masses. Lazare Carnot and Bertrand Barère provided the philosophy, Robespierre and Napoleon put it into practice. Alfred Rosenberg wrote the doctrines (acquired abroad from Sorel, Charles Maurras and others, but with valuable assistance at home from Georg Wilhelm Friedrich Hegel and Treitschke), while Goebbels gave these doctrines violent application.

Irrationality.—The ability of governmental and civic leaders to spread the ferment of nationalism among the masses is greatly facilitated by its highly irrational character. The extreme patriot is largely impervious to rational argument. Even in free countries, he may never hear the truth, especially if he reads only tendentious newspapers or tunes in his radio to biased, chauvinistic commentators. Moreover, it is difficult to see how adults can consider the international problems facing their nation with any degree of objectivity if as young children their minds were formed by history books that were one-sided and biased.

Intolerance and Exclusivism.—In early times, man's supreme loyalty was centered on his religion. Today this place has been taken by the nation. As the most despised of antisocial individuals within the state, the traitor has displaced the heretic. This supreme loyalty is not only self-centered and exclusive; it has likewise a curious negative element. It thrives on anti-foreign sentiment, especially when this can be focused on a particular country, the object of special disdain. Thus the nationalism of the United States has been traditionally anti-British, that of England has been anti-French, that of France anti-German, while Polish nationalism (probably the most intense of all) has been anti-Russian and anti-German. A striking contemporaneous illustration of this phenomenon is found in the case of the USSR, whose integral nationalism is so violently anticapitalist. Given the atmosphere of exclusivism in which it flourishes, together with its negative character, nationalism is both a cause and a consequence of intolerance. Intolerance of all criticism of one's own government or its policies may result in the total suppression of free speech. Intolerance of foreigners, both as individuals and in the mass, and refusal to examine calmly and objectively the policies of a foreign government, tend to create an attitude favorable to international dispute and war; or it may take the form of arrogance toward the immigrant, an attitude which may go all the way from social discrimination to the passage of laws denying the foreigner comparable economic opportunities in particular or, in general, equal protection of the laws. Nationalistic intolerance finds expression in many countries, in various methods of oppression directed against devotees of religions having an international character, national minorities, members of so-called "inferior races," and persons espousing economic and social doctrines of foreign origin.

INTERNATIONALISM

Various meanings are attached to that elusive term, internationalism. To some it is a method of international cooperation, comprising a complex of instrumentalities of interstate organization—League of Nations, International Labour Organization, the International Court of Justice, World Bank, United Nations—and includes in its purview their origin, evolution and activities. To others the term means, in common with nationalism itself, a certain condition of mind, and it is in this sense that it is used here. Thus interpreted, internationalism means a consciousness of membership in a global society, or community of the peoples of the world, and a willingness to allow one's particular nation to join the existing organizations established by and for this community. It also includes a disposition to surrender to world institutions a greater or less degree of sovereignty, depending on the intensity of one's faith in the available methods of international cooperation. The "minimalist" would be willing to grant to a global institution only those powers considered essential for the maintenance and enforcement of international security. The "maximalist" is a partisan of some form of actual world government. The former champions the present United Nations; the latter will be found in the ranks of the world federalists. Between the two extremes one will find varying degrees of internationalism. This attitude or state of mind is unlike cosmopolitanism in that it does not imply an abandonment of one's loyalty to his particular state or nation, or a disposition to substitute for his attachment to the latter a higher relationship to the whole world, regarded as the only true fatherland.

It was only following World War I that internationalism as just defined reached the stage of practical experimentation. True, the way had been prepared for centuries, as advanced thinkers —Henry IV's great minister, the duc de Sully, Immanuel Kant, William Penn, and many others —formulated utopian plans for world organization designed to end war and maintain peace. But little came of these plans until 1919. Considerable progress had already been made, to be sure, in the field of international law, especially since 1648, and international arbitration had come into fairly frequent use during the 19th century. Two Hague Conferences, in 1899 and 1907 respectively, had spread the hope—too optimistic, so it turned out—for the codification of international law and the settlement of international disputes by peaceful means. But the actual birth of internationalism did not occur until the founding of the League of Nations in 1919. The growth of internationalism from this point on is discussed in other articles. See INTERNATIONAL COURT OF JUSTICE; INTERNATIONAL LABOR ORGANIZATION; INTERNATIONAL LAW; LEAGUE OF NATIONS; UNITED NATIONS, THE.

There is no incompatibility between liberal nationalism and a spirit of internationalism. If kept within reasonable limits, a healthy patriotism is a great spiritual force. In fact, it is a prerequisite to the spirit of fidelity, faith, and determination among the citizen body which is the soul of nationhood. Unless its people possess a high degree of loyalty and solidarity, no nation can endure in the present competitive world. But nationalism that is narrow or egotistical is incompatible with any degree of progress toward internationalism and will, as history demonstrates, become a lethal weapon of discord and conflict.

JOHN B. WHITTON,
Princeton University.

Bibliography.—Hayes, Carlton J. H., *Essays on Nationalism* (New York 1926); Barker, Sir Ernest, *National Character and the Factors in its Formation* (London 1927); Baron, Salo W., *Modern Nationalism and Religion* (New York 1927); Meinecke, Friedrich, *Weltbuergertum und Nationalstaat,* 7th ed. (Munich and Berlin 1928); Beard, Charles A., *The Idea of National Interest: An Analytical Study of American Foreign Policy* (New York 1934); Pinson, Koppel S., *A Bibliographical Introduction to Nationalism* (New York 1935); Carr, Edward H., chairman, *Nationalism: A Report by a Study Group of Members of the Royal Institute of International Affairs* (London 1939); Kohn, Hans, *World Order in Historical Perspective* (Cambridge, Mass., 1941); Wright, Quincy, *A Study of War,* 2 vols. (Chicago 1942); Hertz, Friedrich O., *Nationality in History and Politics: A Study of the Psychology and Sociology of National Sentiment and Character* (London 1944); Kohn, Hans, *The Idea of Nationalism: A Study in Its Origins and Background* (New York 1944); Carr, Edward H., *Nationalism and After* (New York 1945); Janowsky, Oscar I., *Nationalities and National Minorities,* with special reference to east-central Europe (New York 1945); Kohn, Hans, *Prophets and Peoples: Studies in Nineteenth Century Nationalism* (New York 1946); Sturzo, Luigi, *Nationalism and Internationalism* (New York 1946); Hayes, Carlton J. H., *The Historical Evolution of Modern Nationalism* (New York 1948); Earle, Edward Mead, ed., *Nationalism and Internationalism: Essays Inscribed to Carlton J. H. Hayes* (New York 1950); Znaniecki, Florian, *Modern Nationalities: A Sociological Study* (Urbana, Ill., 1952); Deutsch, Karl W., *Nationalism and Social Communication: An Inquiry into the Foundations of Nationality* (Troy and New York 1953); Rustow, Dankwart A., *A World of Nations* (Washington 1967); Tung, William L., *International Law in an Organizing World* (New York 1968).

NATIONALITY, năsh-ŭn-ăl'ĭ-tĭ, a term used in both cultural and legal senses. As a cultural term, nationality has reference to the cultural, racial, linguistic, and ideological status of an individual or group. Thus an individual may be said to be German, Polish, Italian, or Greek without regard to his citizenship, domicile, or legal nationality. Because the application of different criteria may lead to different results, it is frequently difficult to determine the cultural nationality of a person or the limits of a national minority.

In the cultural sense of the term, especially if the linguistic criterion of nationality is applied, there are multinational states, such as Switzerland, the Soviet Union, the United States, and India, and there are nationalities extending to several states. The French nationality, by the linguistic criterion, includes not only the people of France but also some of those in Belgium and Switzerland; and the German nationality includes not only the people of East and West Germany but also most of those of Austria and many of those of Switzerland. Such situations have given rise to the problem (dealt with in many treaties) of protecting racial, linguistic, and religious minorities, as well as to political demands for the transfer of irredentas, for the self-determination of peoples by plebiscite, or for the transfer of populations. Such arrangements, which have assumed major political importance in international politics since World War I, indicate wide acceptance of the theory of Giuseppe Mazzini and other nationalists of the mid-19th century that the boundaries of each state should conform to the boundaries of a nationality. This theory stimulated the unifications of Italy and Germany at that time, and the disintegration of the Habsburg empire after World War I.

International Law.—As a term in international law, nationality refers to the relation (of an individual to a state) such that the state may extend its law to the individual and protect him when he is in the territory of another state. Nationality is not synonymous with citizenship, a term of municipal law implying reciprocal obligations of allegiance and protection between the state and the citizen. The inhabitants of protectorates and other dependencies of a state are usually nationals of the state but not citizens because they are not entitled to constitutional guarantees of civil rights.

Legal nationality is determined primarily by the municipal law of states, but international law imposes some limitations on municipal law in this respect. Thus the nationality of individuals at birth can be determined only by the principles *jus soli* (referring to place of birth) and *jus sanguinis* (referring to the nationality of the parents). A state may adopt either or both of these principles in its legislation, thus giving rise to the possibility of either multiple nationality or statelessness. Multiple nationality may exist at birth if the individual acquires one nationality *jus soli* and others *jus sanguinis.* Again, an individual's father and mother may have different nationalities, and each may have multiple nationalities; he may thereby acquire two or more nationalities *jus sanguinis.* In a state which applies only the *jus sanguinis,* a child may be born stateless if his parents are aliens whose country applies only the *jus soli.* The United States, the United Kingdom, France, and most other states apply both principles, but some of the Swiss cantons apply only the *jus sanguinis* and some of the Scandinavian states only the *jus soli.*

Nationality can be changed after birth by the process of naturalization. National laws usually provide for naturalization of aliens, after a prescribed period of residence, upon application to a specified authority. Naturalization results in dual nationality if the country of origin adheres to the principle of permanent allegiance. There has been a tendency, however, for states to accept the principle, long professed by the United States, that naturalization results automatically in expatriation from the state of origin. The International Court of Justice held in the Nottebohm case that naturalization, even though in accord with a state's law, is not effective internationally if the individual had no genuine connection with the naturalizing state.

Naturalization is presumed to extend automatically to all permanent residents of ceded territories who have the nationality of the ceding state. Treaties of cession, however, often give such persons an option to retain their original nationalities by declaration or by migration from the ceded territories during a specified period of time.

Under the laws of some states the naturalization of a woman may be effected by marriage to an alien or by the naturalization of her husband; and the naturalization of children, by the naturalization of their parents. Thus by marrying an alien, a woman may acquire his nationality under the law of his state, while retaining her original nationality under the law of her own state. She may become stateless, however, if the law of her husband's state recognizes the independent status of women, while the law of her state of origin, recognizing the unity of the family, considers that her marriage has resulted in her expatriation. Efforts have been made by international conventions under the auspices of the League of Nations and the United Nations to eliminate the possibility of multiple nationality or of statelessness at birth, by naturalization, or by marriage, but no convention has been generally accepted.

The term nationality is applied to ships and corporations as well as to individuals. A ship is presumed to have the nationality of the state whose flag it is entitled to fly (the state in which it is registered), but this presumption may be rebutted, especially in times of war, if the owners of the ship have a different nationality from that of the ship. Similarly, a corporation is presumed to have the nationality of the state which incorporated it, but this presumption may be rebutted if the nationality of the majority of the directors or stockholders, or the principle seat of business of the corporation, indicates that the concern's major connection is with another state.

See also ALLEGIANCE; CITIZENSHIP; NATIONALISM AND INTERNATIONALISM; NATURALIZATION.

QUINCY WRIGHT,
Professor of Foreign Affairs, Woodrow Wilson Department of Foreign Affairs, University of Virginia.

NATIONALIZATION, năsh-ŭn-ăl-ĭ-zā'-shŭn, the acquisition and operation by a national government of business enterprises formerly owned and operated by private individuals or corporations. Most states have nationalized their postal and telegraphic systems, and many have nationalized railways and other means of transportation. It is the policy of socialism to nationalize all productive industry and agriculture; this policy has been carried out in the Soviet Union and other communist states. Great Britain, under the Labour government, nationalized many important industries, but the nationalization was effected as a matter of expediency in each particular case rather than in pursuance of socialist doctrine. There has been, in fact, a tendency in all countries to depart from the laissez-faire policies of the 19th century, and to sanction extensive governmental intervention in social and economic matters in the interests of the underprivileged, the general welfare, the conservation of natural resources, national security, economic planning, or socialistic doctrines. Thus many countries have nationalized large businesses and industries, including banks and insurance companies; mining concerns; power, communication, and transportation systems; and other industries of military importance.

It has been a common practice to compensate the owners, at least in part, for such expropriations. The constitutions of the United States and many other states require that compensation be paid if property is taken by the government for public purposes. Communist states, however, oppose the private ownership of capital in principle, and have not given such compensation. States of eastern Europe, Latin America, and Asia have usually given inadequate compensation to expropriated private interests when instituting agrarian reforms or asserting the state's ownership of subsurface mineral resources.

Foreign-Owned Property.—The practice of nationalization has been a subject of international interest when foreign properties or concessions have been nationalized. Apart from fruitless protests when the Soviet Union and other communist states nationalized foreign property in their territories, there have been protests against nationalization in underdeveloped countries where many of the large-scale enterprises were owned by foreign corporations.

In the 1920's, the United States objected to the nationalization of subsurface oil properties of American corporations in Mexico; and Greece objected when the Mavrommatis Palestine concession to exploit the power resources of the Jordan was nationalized by Great Britain as the League of Nations mandatory. Great Britain objected to the nationalization of the Anglo-Iranian Oil Company by Iran in the 1940's. Great Britain and France objected to the nationalization of the Universal Suez Canal Company by Egypt in 1956. The Netherlands objected to the extensive nationalization of Dutch properties in Indonesia in 1958. Many of these cases, which originally aroused vigorous protests, have been settled by international negotiation or adjudication.

The Asian-African group in the United Nations has insisted that the right to nationalize natural resources is implied by the principle of self-determination recognized by the United Nations Charter. The group's position was supported by a large majority of the United Nations General Assembly in 1952 in a resolution passed over the opposition of the United States, the United Kingdom, and other states which believed that the duty to compensate private owners was not sufficiently recognized in the resolution.

It appears that under international law the right of eminent domain is an attribute of sovereignty, but that the exercise of this right against the property of foreign individuals or corporations is a denial of justice, violating an international obligation, if there is no public purpose or if adequate compensation is refused.

It has been argued that concessions to foreign corporations constitute a contractual obligation whose impairment is forbidden by international law, unless it is required by a grave exigency involving national security. However, the International Court of Justice (United Nations) in the Anglo-Iranian Oil Company case (I.C.J. Reports, 1952, p. 93) indicated that a concession made by a state with a foreign corporation is not an international agreement and is subject to the municipal law of the conceding state—a position asserted by the Calvo doctrine that investors must assume the risk of adverse legislation in the country in which they invest.

Such concessions are, therefore, subject to the proper exercise of eminent domain, unless the conceding state has agreed to respect them by explicit treaty with the state of the concessionaire. This was held by the Permanent Court of International Justice (League of Nations) to be the situation in the Mavrommatis Palestine concession, because the mandatory (Great Britain) had by the terms of the mandate, an international instrument, accepted an obligation to respect pre-existing concessions in the territory (Publications of the Court, series A, nos. 2, 5, 11). In the case of the Universal Suez Canal Company, Great Britain and France sought to prove that the concession of the company was given treaty status, on the ground that it was referred to in the Constantinople Convention of 1888 assuring freedom of navigation in the canal. Egypt and other countries, however, refused to accept this construction, and the nationalization of the canal seems to have been recognized on the understanding that Egypt would compensate the company and maintain freedom of navigation through the canal as required by the treaty of 1888.

Consult Friedman, Samy, *Expropriation in International Law* (London 1953); Gould, Wesley L., *An Introduction to International Law,* pp. 465 ff. (New York 1957); Thayer, Philip, ed., *Tensions in the Middle East* (Baltimore 1958).

QUINCY WRIGHT.

NATIONS, League of. See LEAGUE OF NATIONS.

NATO. See NORTH ATLANTIC TREATY AND WESTERN EUROPEAN UNION.

NATOIRE, nȧ-twȧr′, **Charles Joseph,** French painter and etcher: b. Nîmes, France, March 3, 1700; d. Castel Gandolfo, Italy, August 29, 1777. A student of François Lemoyne, Natoire is best known for rococo allegorical paintings which show the influence of his contemporary, François Boucher. Some of the best examples of his work decorate the Hôtel de Soubise, the Cabinet des Médailles, and the Bibliothèque Nationale, in Paris, and the former royal palace at Versailles.

NATORP, nä′tôrp, **Paul,** German philosopher: b. Düsseldorf, Germany, January 24, 1854; d. Marburg, August 17, 1924. Appointed professor at Marburg University in 1885, Natorp was (with Hermann Cohen) a leader of the so-called Marburg school of neo-Kantian philosophy, one of whose tenets was the drastic subordination of the individual to society. He was the author of numerous works in pedagogy, the theory of knowledge, and the history of philosophy. See also NEO-KANTIANISM.

NATROLITE, nă′trô-līt (also called NEEDLE ZEOLITE), an alumino-silicate mineral belonging to the general class of fibrous zeolites. Natrolite has the general formula $Na_2(Al_2Si_3O_{10})\cdot 2H_2O$. It crystallizes in slender prisms belonging to the orthorhombic system. Its three refractive indices are: alpha, 1.480; beta, 1.482; and gamma, 1.493. It has a specific gravity of 2.25 and a hardness of 5.0 to 5.5. The structure of natrolite resembles that of feldspar, but is more open and contains water. This may be driven off and taken up again, or it may be replaced by other compounds. Because the positive sodium ions in zeolite molecules are readily exchanged for other positive ions, including the calcium and magnesium ions characteristic of hard water, the zeolites make excellent water softeners. Natrolite is not used for water conditioning, however, since natural zeolites have been superseded by synthetic ion-exchange minerals and resins. Natrolite occurs in cavities in basalts, and in seams in some other rocks. In the United States, it is found in Connecticut, New Jersey, Arkansas, and in the Lake Superior region; it also occurs in Nova Scotia, Canada. Natrolite has been used as a gem stone, since it takes a good polish; it has a whitish luster, ranging from translucent to transparent.

W. T. READ.

NATRON, nā′trŏn, crude sodium carbonate decahydrate ($Na_2CO_3\cdot 10H_2O$). It usually occurs mixed with other sodium compounds in deposits formed by the evaporation of surface waters. Natron occurs abundantly in arid regions; it has been mined and used for many centuries in Egypt (see also NATRUN, WADI EL). Sodium carbonate is one of the more important raw materials used by the chemical industry; since the natural deposits are usually distant from industrial markets, however, natron has been displaced in great part by soda ash (Na_2CO_3) made from common salt.

W. T. READ.

NATRONA, nȧ-trō′nȧ, village, Pennsylvania, in Allegheny County, 25 miles northeast of Pittsburgh by state highway; altitude, 800 feet. Situated in Harrison Township on the Allegheny River, Natrona is served by the Pennsylvania Railroad. The village was named after the natron (native sodium carbonate) formerly produced from local brine wells. Production of this salt, begun as early as 1853, has been discontinued; the former saltworks house a small chemical industry.

NATRUN, Wadi el, nät′rōōn (from Arab. *naṭrun,* natron), valley, Egypt, about 65 miles west northwest of Cairo. Wadi el Natrun is a desert depression (as much as 25 feet below sea level) about 30 miles long and 4 miles wide. It contains a series of small lakes, sometimes called the Natron Lakes, whose waters are rich in salts. The annual evaporation of the lake waters during the long dry season has deposited a 10-to-27-foot-thick crust of natron and common salt on the lake beds. The deposits have been worked since ancient times.

Also called Nitria or the Nitrian Desert, the Wadi el Natrun region was formerly a major center of Christian monasticism following the establishment of a huge colony of hermits in the second half of the 4th century. Of the nearly 100 Coptic monasteries that once flourished there, only a few remain.

NATSUME KINNOSUKE, nät-tsōō-mĕ kĭn-nō-sōō-kĕ (pseudonym NATSUME SŌSEKI), Japanese writer: b. Edo (modern Tokyo), Japan, Jan. 5, 1867; d. there, Dec. 9, 1916. After a career largely devoted to studying and teaching English, Natsume gained quick recognition as a writer following the publication of his first novels, including *Waga hai wa neko de aru* (1905–1906; Eng. tr., *I Am a Cat,* 1909), *Botchan* (1906; Eng. tr., *Botchan, Master Darling,* 1918, and *Botchan,* 1953), and *Kusamakura* (1906; Eng. tr., *Pillow of Grass,* 1927, and *Unhuman Tour,* 1927). *Waga hai wa neko de aru* is a witty social critique written from the viewpoint of a cat. At a time when melodrama and naturalism were the rule in Japanese novels, Natsume's relaxed, classical style along with his profound psychological insights and realistic observations gained him a wide audience. His subsequent influence on the Japanese novel has been considerable.

NATTIER, nà'tyā, **Jean Marc,** French portrait painter: b. Paris, France, March 17, 1685; d. there, Sept. 7, 1766. The son of a portrait painter, he probably studied under Jean Jouvenet and won first prize at the French Academy at the age of 15. During the course of Peter the Great's European travels, Nattier was summoned by him to Antwerp in 1715 to paint his portrait, his wife Catherine I, and prominent members of his entourage. Nattier's *Petrification of Phineus and His Companions* led to his election to the Academy in 1718. He turned from mythological and historical subjects to portrait painting and soon became one of the most fashionable portraitists of his time. He received numerous royal commissions from Louis XV to paint the ladies of his court, including Marie Leszczynska and Madame de Pompadour.

His graceful, elegant portraits were characteristic of the period. Elegance and tact overcame faithful characterization in them. He usually treated his subjects as mythological themes portrayed in soft, rounded lines and light colors, especially a bright blue. Nattier is well represented in European museums and his portrait of the *Princesse de Condé as Diana* is at the Metropolitan Museum of Art in New York City.

NATTY BUMPPO, bŭmp'ō, the central character in James Fenimore Cooper's *Leatherstocking Tales* (q.v.).

NATU LA (NATHU LA), nä'tōō lä, Himalayan pass, Sikkim, Protectorate of India, on the Sikkim-Tibet border, at an altitude of about 14,000 feet, 15 miles northeast of Gangtok. This much-traveled pass is on the main road which leads from Sikkim into the Chumbi Valley, Tibet, and connects with the main India-Tibet trade route. When snow closes the Jelep La six miles southeast, Natu La often is used as an alternative.

NATURAL BRIDGE, village, New York, in Jefferson County, eight miles northeast of Carthage. This tourist resort has a natural bridge and caverns carved out of limestone by the Indian River. The caverns extend about 1,000 feet underground.

NATURAL BRIDGE, village, Virginia, in Rockbridge County, 16 miles south of Lexington, near the James River, at the entrance to Jefferson National Forest. A famous natural bridge over Cedar Creek, one of the natural wonders of America, is located just west of the village. This limestone arch is about 215 feet high, 50 to 100 feet wide, and has a span of about 90 feet. It was once part of a cave roof or the roof of an underground tunnel through which the creek flowed. Thomas Jefferson owned the bridge at one time and a public highway now passes over it. There also are magnesia and lithia springs and a saltpeter cave in the village.

NATURAL BRIDGES NATIONAL MONUMENT, Utah, in the southeastern part of the state, San Juan County, about 30 miles west of Blanding, with an area of 2,649.7 acres. It consists of three natural bridges, spectacularly carved out of sandstone by erosion. The bridges cross canyons as much as 2,500 feet deep in a 6,000-foot high plateau. Sipapu Bridge, the largest, is 222 feet high with a span of 261 feet. Its name, taken from Hopi legends, refers to the gateway through which men's souls emerge from the underworld and finally return to it. Kachina Bridge is next in size with a height of 205 feet and a span of 186 feet. Its name is a Hopi word for "sacred dance" and it was chosen because Hopi dance symbols were found carved on the bridge. Owachomo (Hopi "flatrock mound") is 108 feet high, has a span of 194 feet, and is considered to be the oldest (at least 10 million years old). The colors of the bridges range from salmon pink to deep violet.

Cliff dwellers originally inhabited the area and a series of their dwellings and caves remain in the canyon walls. Ute and Paiute Indians displaced them at least 500 years ago. The first known white visitor was a man called Cass Hite who explored the region in the 1880's. In 1908 they were set aside as a national monument.

NATURAL GAS. See GAS, FUEL; PETROLEUM.

NATURAL HISTORY, American Museum of. See AMERICAN MUSEUM OF NATURAL HISTORY.

NATURAL HISTORY, in its widest sense, that department of knowledge which comprehends the sciences of zoology and botany, chemistry, natural philosophy or physics, geology, palaeontology and mineralogy. It is now, however, commonly used to denote collectively the sciences of botany and zoology, or these together with geology, mineralogy and palaeontology, exclusive of physics and chemistry, and it is sometimes restricted to denote the science of zoology alone.

NATURAL HISTORY OF SELBORNE, The, a celebrated work by Gilbert White (q.v.), published in 1789. Its material consists of White's letters to Daines Barrington and Thomas Pennant, in which the writer describes outdoor life in the little Hampshire village which his works made famous and interesting alike to students of nature and to lovers of good books, among which the *Natural History* ranks as a classic of science and of letters.

NATURAL LAW. For more than two millenniums the idea of natural law or the law of nature has played a prominent part in philosophical thought and political theory. It has been applied in each field as a criterion of contemporary ideas and institutions and thus has served to justify either conservatism or change. However, since the words *nature* and *natural* have many meanings, the modern attempt to extend a consideration of natural law beyond ethics and politics to natural sciences has created ambiguities and has caused the doctrine of the law of nature to be challenged by materialists since the mid-18th century.

Although there has been much difference of opinion about the contents of the law of nature, yet almost all admit the existence of such a law. Many definitions of natural law have been given by Greek philosophers, Roman jurists, patristic theologians, medieval scholastics, and modern savants. But generally, throughout most of mankind's western history, the notion of natural law has been conceived as the ultimate norm of right and wrong, as the ideal pattern of the life according to Nature, as the law discernible to reason and distinct from what positive law has been contained in codes established by the state or the church.

Probably the most influential *description* of natural law is that formulated by the Eastern Roman Emperor Justinian the Great in 533 A.D. when in his *Institutiones* (I.2.11), he declares: "The laws of nature, which are observed equally among all nations, established—as it were—by divine providence, remain ever firm and immutable." Perhaps the best *definition* of natural law is that furnished by St. Thomas Aquinas in 1269 when in his *Summa Theologica* (I-II.91.2) he writes: "The function of the natural law" is to "discern what is good and what is evil. . . . The natural law is nothing else than the rational creature's participation of the eternal law."

If we combine the above description and definition, we can consider that natural law is (1) that part of morality which provides universal rules for governing man's external acts; (2) the code dictated by conscience. It is not a law deduced from human education and experience, but a law regulating man's general rights and duties in relation to God's or Nature's moral government and man's moral capacity and accountability. From these considerations we find that the law of nature has three characteristics: (1) universality, because its precepts are always the same in all times and among all peoples; (2) necessity, because it is a demand upon man's rational nature; (3) immutability, because it is independent of all human authority.

The conception of natural law appears early among historical conceptions of justice. The opinions of Marcus Tullius Cicero (106–43 B.C.) perhaps have had the most influence of several opinions current before the Christian era. Influenced by Greek Stoicism, Cicero repeatedly and eloquently exalts the natural law which he calls "the supreme law, which was born in all the ages before any law had been written or any state had been established" (*De Legibus,* I.6.19). He claims that "True law is right reason in agreement with nature; it is universal, unchanging, everlasting; it summons to duty by its commands; it averts from injury by its prohibitions" (*De Republica,* III.22.33.). But Roman jurists eventually identified the characteristic concept of natural law (*jus naturale*) with the law of nations (*jus gentium*), a system of positive law which incorporates principles found in the laws of all nations, which points to a similarity in the ideas of all peoples, and which is common to the whole human race (Justinian, *Institutiones,* I.2.2).

During the Middle Ages natural law was conceived mostly in its humanistic aspect, that is, in its application to particular conditions. Because of the dominant religious trend of those troubled times, the law of nature was identified with the law of God. Gratian, the codifier of canon law (*jus canonicum*), considered natural law as what is contained in the Law and the Gospel whereby everyone is commanded to do to another what he wishes to be done to himself, and is forbidden to inflict upon another what he does not wish to be done to himself. In other words, natural law became identified with the so-called golden rule of Matthew 7:12 and Luke 6:31 (*Concordia Discordantium Canonum,* I. D. 1, praef.).

After the Protestant Reformation the theories and doctrines of natural law were prominent in discussions both on international law (*jus inter gentes*) and on general jurisprudence. International law was, in fact, built on natural law by Hugo Grotius (1583–1645) who held that human laws can establish nothing contrary to nature (*De Jure Belli et Pacis,* II.3.6). In general jurisprudence, Sir William Blackstone (1723–1780) maintained that no human laws are valid if they are contrary to the law of nature and that such of them as are valid derive all their force and all their authority from the natural law (*Commentaries on the Laws of England,* introd., sect. 2, p. 41). In politics and in political economy the liberal rationalists of the 17th and 18th centuries, notably John Locke and Jean Jacques Rousseau, adopted natural law to assert man's claim to the natural rights of life, liberty, and the pursuit of happiness. These natural rights are recognized in the American Declaration of Independence (1776) and in the French Declaration of the Rights of Man and of the Citizen (1789), both instruments born of political revolution.

Despite the attacks of totalitarian foes, the concept of natural law has survived into the 20th century to reassert mankind's natural rights—notably in the Universal Declaration of Human Rights (1948) promulgated by the General Assembly of the United Nations.

Bibliography.—Rachel, Samuel, *De Jure Naturae et Gentium Dissertationes* (Kiel 1676), tr. by J. P. Bate as *Dissertations on the Law of Nature and of Nations* (Washington 1916); Haines, Charles G., *The Revival of Natural Law Concepts* (Cambridge, Eng., 1930); Pufendorf, Samuel, *De Jure Naturae et Gentium Libri Octo,* 3d ed. (Amsterdam 1688), photographic reproduction of 1688 ed. with tr. by C. H. and W. A. Oldfather as *On the Law of Nature and Nations* (London 1934); Maritain, Jacques, *The Rights of Man and Natural Law* (London 1945); Natural Law Institute, University of Notre Dame, *Proceedings* (Notre Dame 1947–); Le Boutillier, Cornelia T., *American Democracy and Natural Law* (New York 1950); D'Entrèves, Alessandro P., *Natural Law: An Introduction to Legal Philosophy* (London 1951); Gerhart, Eugene C., *American Liberty and Natural Law* (Boston 1953).

P. R. Coleman-Norton,
Princeton University.

NATURAL RESOURCES. See individual countries.

NATURAL RIGHTS. See Natural Law.

NATURAL SELECTION, the theory proposed by Charles R. Darwin and Alfred Russel Wallace in 1858 to explain the vast diversification of species in the plant and animal kingdoms, with their multitudes of distinct types adjusted to meet almost every possibility of self-maintenance in the variety of conditions set by the external world. Natural selection bears upon the phenomena of evolution in general. The facts in nature from which the theory of natural selection is argued are the great diversity of individual organisms; the heritability of variant characters; the enormous overproduction of plant spores and seeds and of animal eggs and young; and the consequently inevitable "struggle for existence." Parallel to the artificial selection of variants by man in breeding domestic animals, it is inferred that there is a natural selection in nature favoring advantageous variants and tending to eliminate disadvantageous ones. Modern interpretation emphasizes selection of groups rather than selection at the individual level. Progressive divergence of plant and animal populations is regarded as arising from the greater breeding potential of members of each generation that vary in the direction of better adjustment to their environment—to some particular feature of it, to environmental changes, or to newly-invaded, different environments. Less favorable variations have a correspondingly lessened probability of survival, and accordingly are progressively eliminated. Adaptation is, therefore, the basis for selection. Continuous structural modifications, in line with a constantly changing environment, lead to the origin of new species. Darwin also stressed sexual selection, which is a factor in developing courtship adornments of animals and other sex differences.

Improved adjustment to the environment may be physiological, anatomical, or behavioral. It may consist of improvements in internal physiology—capacity to digest special foods, greater resistance to heat or cold, or improved internal controls of body functions (homeostasis). Adaptation also may involve varied mechanical adjustments of body parts to opportunities offered by the environment such as locomotion above or below the ground, in trees, or in the air. Special habits of food getting, mating, and reproduction, or self-defense likewise may cause similar adaptations. It is very striking that improved or changed adjustments may lie wholly in changes of behavior, without discernible changes of structure. A good example is found in the nest-building instincts of animals, which are inherited just as are their color, form, and physiological changes.

One of the principal objections to the theory of natural selection is that the incipient variation would be of too little advantage to be favored. This does not seem to be the case with variations in behaviour. In the development of *acquired* (physical) characters, special behavior sets the stage for preserving any incipient *heritable* variation, either structural or behavioral. This is referred to as the "Baldwin principle" by George G. Simpson (1953) and Conrad H. Waddington (1953). Geographic isolation explains another difficulty in establishing the origin of new forms. This factor was underemphasized by Darwin according to Moritz F. Wagner (1868), Ernest Mayr (1942), Warder C. Allee and others (1949). There are many instances in which a character that has become established and distinctive under conditions of isolation is preserved in a distinct species when parent form and derived form are brought together again.

A specific objection formerly was raised against the interpretation that natural selection is the operative factor in producing the slight differences that appear to be adaptive. A good example is wild mice's coat color, which varies and tends to blend with the color of their native terrain. Francis B. Sumner was able to demonstrate by breeding experiments in 1932 that minor differences in the color of the hair of white-footed mice (the most abundant and ubiquitous of North American wild mice) are inherited. Lee R. Dice devised another set of experiments in 1947 to meet the further objection that such color differences and resemblances to soil could not afford effective protection to the mice because they are nocturnal. He used owls as the natural predator and simulated the conditions of terrain and light in laboratory cages. Statistical analysis of the results showed that the differential in the number of mice captured from a natural background, as against one to which their color was not adjusted, was such that rapid evolution by selection would take place.

The effectiveness of natural selection in relation to predation was tested by Sumner in 1935 in an ingenious experiment with small fishes that have the capacity for color change. A considerable number of such fishes were placed in two tanks, one painted black on the inside and the other white. In a few weeks the color of the fish matched their respective tanks. When two small penguins were introduced as typical predators into each tank with an equal number of black and white fishes the penguins ate the fishes voraciously. After the two penguins were removed, three-fourths of the fishes eaten in the black tank were white, whereas in the white tank the majority eaten were black. This differential certainly makes possible effective selection for either background resemblance or for the capacity to adjust to background by color change. Further experiments by Dwight Isely in 1938 with protectively-colored grasshoppers and chickens as predators fully confirm Sumner's results.

The rapid development of insect strains immune to DDT and other insecticides (Henry J. Quayle, 1943) and rusts capable of attacking rust-resistant strains of wheat and other cereal grains (Helen Hart, 1944) indicate a *selection pressure* affecting all organisms in their flow from generation to generation.

Paleontologists, ecologists, and geneticists have contributed to the interpretation of the natural selection theory. The fact that cooperation may be a characteristic of "survival value" throws much light on the evolution of societies and on the evolution of man, according to authors Julian S. Huxley (1942), George G. Simpson (1944, 1949, 1953), Warder C. Allee and others (1949). See EVOLUTION, ORGANIC; DARWINIAN THEORY; GENETICS; and HEREDITY.

Consult Huxley, Julian S., *Evolution, the Modern Synthesis* (New York 1942); Allee, W. C., Park, Orlando, Park, Thomas, Emerson, A. E., and Schmidt, Karl P., *Principles of Animal Ecology* (Philadelphia 1949); Simpson, George Gaylord, *Major Features of Evolution* (New York 1953).

KARL P. SCHMIDT,
Chief Curator, Department of Zoology, Chicago Natural History Museum.

NATURAL TONES are tones produced by the natural alteration of nodal points in wind instruments by pressure only. See also HARMONICS.

NATURALISM, in the fine arts, is a representation of nature closely approximating its appearance, but without either photographic fidelity or attempt at illusion. Opposed to *idealism* and implying less crudeness than *realism* naturalism is the mean between the two.

In literature, naturalism is a style of fiction writing which aims at scientific objectivity in the portrayal of characters conceived of as motivated primarily by impersonal biological, economic, and social forces. Thus the social environment, rather than individual character, is the driving force affecting plot development. The forerunners of naturalism in France were Stendhal and Balzac. Flaubert, acclaimed a leader of the school, rejected both the terms "naturalism" and "realism" as not applicable to his work. The Goncourts and Alphonse Daudet, usually regarded as of this school, might better be termed impressionistic than naturalistic writers. Émile Zola defined the naturalistic method and is popularly regarded as the exemplar of the type; but the novelist of that late 19th century epoch best deserving the title is Guy de Maupassant.

From France naturalism spread to other countries. George Gissing and George Moore were leading British novelists who adopted the method, while in the United States Stephen Crane and Frank Norris were prominent early followers of a movement that soon became worldwide.

NATURALISM. In philosophy, this term stands (1) for a certain type of philosophy in general or (2) for a certain kind of ethical theory. In the former usage naturalism is sometimes defined as a particular way or method of approaching philosophical problems and sometimes as a particular set of conclusions arrived at as answers to these problems. Thus many naturalists describe naturalism, not as a theory of the nature of reality, but as a specific temper of mind, namely, a confidence in the empirical, experimental, or scientific method as the only reliable method of reaching the truth about man and the world, or of guiding action; and a rejection of faith, revelation, authority, tradition, a priori reasoning, and intuition as sources of truth or guidance. For it all meaning originates in experience, and all beliefs must be tested by experience in accordance with the general canons of scientific method. In this sense, then, naturalism is roughly equivalent to empiricism.

On other occasions naturalism is described primarily as consisting of certain philosophical conclusions which are opposed in general to the characteristic doctrines of religion, supernaturalism, and idealism. The main tenets thus ascribed to naturalism are the following. (a) Every state of the world or event in it can be explained causally or mechanically by reference to previous states or events, or else is the result of chance. Teleological or purposive explanations are not necessary or even possible, and no cosmic purpose is involved in the world process. (b) No God or other supernatural being or kind of entity (such as Plato's Ideas) is required to explain the world, and, indeed, no such beings exist at all. The natural world of objects and events in space and time is all that is real, and it is self-existent and self-explanatory or else is simply inexplicable. (c) Man is wholly a part of this natural world in space and time, both as to body and mind and as to origin and destiny. No element of his being is immortal, and he is only an incidental product of the world process, whether considered as an individual or as a species. (d) There are no absolute values or transcendental norms, known to us in non-empirical ways. All values and norms are in some sense a function of human attitudes, interests, needs, satisfactions, individual or social, or at least of natural processes and regularities. They have no support of a supernatural, nonnatural, or cosmic nature, even if they have some sort of universal validity.

It is not clear that all of these doctrines are essential to naturalism. For example, Bertrand Russell's essay *A Free Man's Worship* expresses a naturalistic view of the world, and yet he was at that time an absolutist in ethics. But at any rate, these doctrines are typical of naturalism.

The relation of naturalism (in the sense of a set of conclusions) to monism, materialism, and determinism requires comment. Naturalism is often represented as denying any dualism of mind and matter and as affirming some monistic view of their nature, and in general this is true. But, again, Russell in *Mysticism and Logic* was a naturalist and a dualist, so that monism hardly seems essential. More specifically, naturalism is frequently identified with materialism, both by opponents and by proponents. And indeed, materialists are usually naturalists, for example, Democritus and Roy Wood Sellars (though not always, for example, the Stoics). But the reverse cannot be said to be true, since many naturalists, like John Dewey and his followers, decline to call themselves materialists. Determinism likewise is said to be a part of naturalism, but there have been naturalists who were not determinists, namely, Epicurus, Lucretius, and Dewey. Naturalists commonly do hold that nature is a realm of causal law, but it is not necessary for them to do so. They may, for instance, be indeterminists in their interpretation of quantum mechanics.

We may, then, describe naturalism either as a certain view about method or as a certain set of conclusions. We should, however, not regard a man who holds this view about method as a naturalist unless he also holds this set of conclusions; nor should we call a man who holds these conclusions a naturalist unless he has arrived at them by this method. The point seems to be that, whether there is a strict logical connection between the method and the conclusions or not, in practice naturalism is a combination of the two. The naturalist adopts and generalizes the scientific approach, and following this scientific method he feels forced to accept the conclusions indicated.

In a narrower sense, the term "naturalism" is used in 20th century ethical discussions for a certain kind of ethical theory. This use of the term is due to George Edward Moore. Here "naturalism" stands for the view that ethical concepts or properties can be defined in terms of nonethical concepts or properties of the sort that appear in empirical or scientific judgments of fact. For example, if one holds that "good" means "desired" or "satisfying," or that "right" means "dictated by society" or "conducive to the general happiness," and that similar definitions can be given for all other ethical terms, then he is a naturalist in this sense. It follows on such a view that moral and other value judgments are true or false and can be established by empirical observation—in fact, ethics becomes a branch of some empirical science like psychology or sociology.

It is obvious that a naturalist in the more general sense will often be a naturalist in this narrower sense when he comes to deal with ethics and values. But one may be an ethical naturalist without being a naturalist in one's general philosophical position; one may believe, for example, that all ethical terms can be defined by reference to desire and satisfaction, and yet be a supernaturalist. One may also, however, be a naturalist in the wider sense without being an ethical naturalist, if one holds, as some do, that value judgments are not assertions which are true or false but expressions of emotion, attitude, and so forth.

WILLIAM K. FRANKENA,
Professor of Philosophy, University of Michigan.

NATURALIZATION, any process by which a state confers its nationality or its citizenship upon a person after birth. Persons acquire the original nationality of the state in whose territory they are born (*jus soli*), or the state of the parents' nationality (*jus sanguinis*), or both, according to the law of the respective states. This original nationality may change by a transfer of territory, which normally changes the nationality of permanent residents who had the nationality of the transferring state; by marriage to an alien, which under the law of some states changes the nationality of the wife; by special legislative grant of nationality to an individual or a group; or by emigration and voluntary acceptance of the nationality of the state of immigration in accordance with its laws.

While all these modes of transfer of nationality constitute naturalization in the broad sense, the term is often applied in a narrower sense only to the last method. Nearly all states now have general laws declaring the conditions under which individual naturalization may be effected. Qualifications in respect to length of residence, age of the applicant, and moral character are usually prescribed, and qualifications as to literacy, wealth, health, beliefs, culture, and race must sometimes be complied with. Naturalization is often treated as an executive process, sometimes as a legislative or judicial process. Formal application (first papers) usually has to be made some time before naturalization (second papers) is finally granted. Sometimes the latter is celebrated by a formal ceremony involving the taking of an oath of allegiance. In the interval between formal application and the final grant, the applicant sometimes has to submit to certain tests and investigations to make sure that he conforms to the requirements of the law.

Limitations of International Law upon Naturalization.—Nationality, as a legal status, is to be distinguished from citizenship (q.v.). The latter is a status under the law of a state which confers certain legal advantages and imposes certain obligations upon the individual. Nationality, on the other hand, is a status under international law giving a state the right to legislate for and protect its nationals, even in foreign countries. While, in general, nationality is derived from citizenship and both from the law of the state, international law imposes certain general limitations upon the capacity of the state to confer nationality and treaties may impose special limitations. (Tunis Nationality Decrees, P.C.I.J., Ad. Op. No. 4; Acquisition of Polish Nationality, P.C.I.J., Ad. Op. No. 7, World Court Reports, vol. 1, pp. 156, 245.) International law may also consider a person a national of a state even though that state had not conferred citizenship upon him. Thus, in the United States, Indians in the tribal condition and the native inhabitants of the insular possessions were originally nationals of the United States but not citizens; however, special legislation since 1924 has conferred citizenship upon the Indians and upon persons born in the islands since their acquisition by the United States.

While international law permits a state to impose nationality at birth upon individuals according to the law of the soil (*jus soli*), or the law of the blood (*jus sanguinis*), or both, it does not in general permit a state to naturalize persons without their consent. (*Mackenzie* v. *Hare,* 239 U.S. 299.) Thus, efforts of a state to escape international responsibility for injuries to resident aliens by passing laws (so-called Calvo clauses) declaring that such persons who acquire land or concessions are to be regarded as its nationals in respect to such interests have been held invalid by arbitral tribunals. (*North American Dredging Co.* v. *Mexico,* U.S.-Mexico Claims Commission, Opinions, 1927, p. 21.)

International practice has permitted the imposition of nationality upon wives and minor children of men who naturalize, but the modern tendency has been to permit a married woman to retain her original nationality. The inconvenience which often follows from the division of the family on nationality lines has induced some states to create a presumption that all members of the family have the nationality of the husband and father, to be overruled only by express declaration of an intention to retain the original nationality.

In transfers of territory, the practice permitting imposition of the new nationality upon permanent residents of the territory who have the transferring state's nationality has often been mitigated by treaties giving such persons the option to retain their original nationality by declaration within a stated period of time. (*Schwartzkopf* v. *Uhl,* 1943, 137 F. 2nd 898.) In the treaty of peace between the United States and Spain in 1898, this option was given to natives of Spain resident in the ceded islands, but not to natives of the islands. The United States treaties acquiring California (1848) and Alaska (1867) included similar provisions, but no such option was permitted in the treaties for the annexation of Louisiana (1803) and Florida (1819). Treaties ending the world wars of the 20th century have generally given the inhabitants of transferred territory an option to retain their original nationality by suitable declaration, at least if they spoke the language of the ceding state.

In individual naturalization, international law requires that it be a voluntary act of the applicant, open only to persons clearly connected with the naturalizing state by permanent residence or service in a civil or military capacity. In the absence of such conditions, the state of alleged naturalization cannot protect the individual against another state. (*Nottebohm* case, *Liechtenstein* v. *Guatemala,* I.C.J., 1955.)

Dual Nationality and Statelessness.—Although international law imposes limitations upon the capacity of states to make naturalization laws, yet within these limitations states have wide discretion, and a difference in the laws of states may create conditions of dual or multiple nationality or of statelessness. Efforts have been made to develop international law by treaties to avoid such conditions. The Conference for the Codification of International Law, called by the League of Nations in 1930, drew up three conventions at its session at The Hague, based upon its conviction "that it is in the general interest of the international community to secure that all its members should recognize that every person should have a nationality and should have one nationality only."

Dual or multiple nationality may exist at birth when a person acquires the nationality of one state by the *jus soli* and of other states by the *jus sanguinis,* which is sometimes applicable both to the father and the mother if they have different nationalities. One of the Hague conventions of 1930 sought to avoid this by permitting the individual to choose, and by requiring third states to recognize that he had only the nationality of the state with which he was most closely connected.

A person may be born stateless if the state in whose territory he was born applies only the *jus sanguinis* and the state of his parents' nationality applies only the *jus soli.* To avoid this, one of the Hague conventions provided that states accord their nationality to persons born in their territory who would not otherwise acquire any nationality, provided the mother was a national.

Dual nationality may also arise from the refusal of the state of origin to recognize naturalization as effecting expatriation. The common law maintained the principle of permanent allegiance, and Great Britain's refusal to recognize the naturalization of British subjects in the United States was a contributing factor to the War of 1812. Strangely, while the United States was insisting through its diplomats that naturalized persons had expatriated themselves and could not be impressed into the British naval service, American courts continued to support the common law doctrine of permanent allegiance until 1868, when Congress declared that "the right of expatriation is a natural and inherent right of all people," that any order or decision of any officer of the United States to the contrary was invalid, and that "all naturalized citizens of the United States while in foreign countries are entitled to and shall receive from the government the same protection of person and property which is accorded to native born citizens." The United States has made a number of treaties since that time providing for expatriation by naturalization. Great Britain abandoned the principle of permanent allegiance, by statute, in 1870.

Married women may have dual nationality or be stateless because of a conflict of laws concerning the effect of marriage to an alien or the naturalization of the husband upon the nationality of the wife. If the law of the husband's state recognizes the unity of the family under his nationality and that of the wife's state recognizes individual nationality, the wife will have dual nationality. But if the situation is reversed, the wife will be stateless. One of the Hague conventions provided that the wife shall not lose nationality by marriage to an alien or by the naturalization of her husband unless she acquires his nationality, and the naturalization of the husband shall not change the wife's nationality without her consent.

NATURALIZATION LAWS

Although nationality is a fundamental relationship in both international and national law, national laws governing the matter vary greatly among states and in most modern states have been subject to frequent and radical changes. The general character of naturalization laws depends in considerable measure on the country's situation regarding immigration and emigration. Young, sparsely populated, and rapidly developing countries, such as those of the Americas, have generally welcomed immigration and have consequently provided by law for easy naturalization, resulting in loss of previous allegiance. Old, more densely populated, and less rapidly developing countries, such as those of Europe, have had little immigration and have often sought to discourage emigration, to make naturalization difficult, and to recognize expatriation only if the government consents. Countries generally tend to take this position in time of war.

The United States shifted its position after World War I from one of welcoming immigration and naturalization to one of imposing rigorous restraints on economic, cultural, and political grounds. Restrictions based on national origin, literacy, health, moral character, and ideology have created serious obstacles to immigration and naturalization. On the other hand, the human rights movement, which demands equality for women, equality of races and economic opportunity, and freedom of movement, has tended toward the elimination of arbitrary racial and other discriminations, and toward the relaxation of restrictions in favor of refugees. These diverse pressures have led to numerous special laws and regulations in the field of immigration and naturalization, especially in the period after World War II. The same factors have been operative, though in less degree, in other countries, and naturalization laws have become increasingly fluid.

United States.—The Constitution authorizes Congress "to establish an uniform rule of naturalization" (Article I, section 8, clause 4), and an act of 1790 provided that the children of citizens of the United States born abroad should be considered "natural born citizens" provided the father had been at some time resident in the United States. An act of 1855 eliminated the term "natural born" and made it clear that nationality could be conferred *jure sanguinis* only by the father. The act of 1790 also provided for the naturalization of "free white persons" who had resided in the United States for at least two years. This period was raised to five years in 1795, to 14 years by the notorious alien acts of 1798, and restored to five years by an act of 1802, which also provided for the automatic naturalization of minor children upon the naturalization of the father.

After the Civil War, an act of 1870 extended the naturalization act to "aliens of African nativity and to persons of African descent." An act of 1882 forbade the naturalization of Chinese. A series of judicial decisions held that Chinese (before the act of 1882), Japanese, Hindus, Afghans, Filipinos, Koreans, and Hawaiians were not "white persons," but that Syrians, Armenians, and Mexicans (even though largely of Indian blood) were. Thus Asiatics east of Persia could not naturalize and, as immigration was made contingent upon capacity to naturalize, could not migrate to the United States. These discriminations were eliminated with respect to the Chinese by an act of 1940 and the treaty of 1943 with China. The McCarran-Walter Act of June 27, 1952, eliminated explicit Asiatic discriminations, putting all Asiatics and Africans on the national origins quota first introduced for Europeans by the act of 1924. In accordance with this principle, the total permitted immigration (154,000 a year as of 1955) is apportioned among all countries in proportion to the estimated contribution of that country to the American population as it was in 1920. Asiatics and Africans are limited to a quota of 100 from each country. Eastern Europeans have very small quotas, while the British, Irish, Germans, and Scandinavians have the largest.

The act of 1855 provided for the first time that women eligible for naturalization became citizens automatically on marriage to a citizen. This was repeated in the law of 1907, with the addition that an American woman would lose her nationality on marrying a foreigner but could resume citizenship at the termination of the marital status if she registered in an American consulate or returned to the United States.

The 14th Amendment, which went into force in 1868, gave constitutional validity to a principle which had been accepted in a law of 1866, by providing that "All persons born or naturalized in the United States, and subject to the jurisdiction thereof [thus excluding tribal Indians, children of foreign ambassadors, and natives of unincorporated territories of the United States], are citizens of the United States and the State wherein they reside." Previously, citizenship had been primarily a state matter, federal citizenship being a derivative. It was held that even Chinese and other persons ineligible to naturalization were citizens if born in the United States. (*United States* v. *Wong Kim Ark,* 1898, 169 U.S. 649.)

The act of 1868, already noted, provided for expatriation upon naturalization and the act of 1907 created a presumption of expatriation of naturalized citizens who resided for two years in the country of origin or five years in any other country without registering at a United States consulate.

Comprehensive regulations for naturalization were provided for the first time by an act of 1906. It gave federal district courts and state courts of record jurisdiction in naturalization; established a Bureau of Immigration and Naturalization, changed in 1933 to the Immigration and Naturalization Service in the Department of Labor; and provided in detail for naturalization procedures. Five years' residence was required and a declaration of intention (first papers) had to be made at least two years before final naturalization. As amended in 1918 and 1926, this law provided that persons who had served in the United States armed services were excused from the residence requirement; and enemy aliens, deserters, anarchists, polygamists, persons not of good moral character, and persons not attached to the principles of the Constitution were excluded. Conscientious objectors were held to be in the latter category in the cases of Mme. Rosika Schwimmer, a Hungarian pacifist (*United States* v. *Schwimmer,* 1929, 279 U.S. 644, 652), and Professor McIntosh, a Canadian conscientious objector in the Yale Divinity School (*United States* v. *McIntosh,* 1931, 283 U.S. 605, 626).

The Cable Act of 1922 modified the act of 1907 by providing for individual naturalization of women married to citizens, with a reduction of the residence requirement, and for retention of citizenship by American women marrying foreigners in the absence of an express renunciation of citizenship. An act of 1934 further equalized the status of men and women by permitting acquisition of nationality *jure sanguinis* through the mother as well as the father, and permitting a reduction of the residence required for the naturalization of an alien marrying an American woman.

An act of 1940 codified the law of nationality, and permitted the naturalization of Chinese, Indians, and Filipinos. By the Alien Registration Act of 1940, all aliens living in the United States for 30 days or more were required to be registered and fingerprinted. Over 5 million registered during the next year. The Internal Security Act of 1950 required the annual reporting of all alien residents. Some 2 million reported in 1951, of which two thirds were Mexicans (324,000), Italians (229,000), Canadians (217,000), Poles (213,000), British (193,000), Russians (126,000), and Germans (118,000).

The entire field of immigration and nationality was again codified by the McCarran-Walter Act of 1952, passed over President Harry S. Truman's veto. It occupies 118 pages in the statutes and repeals 48 acts previously in force on the subject. The act made all Asiatics eligible for naturalization and immigration, extended the quota system to Asian countries, gave a preference to immigrants with special skills and with family connections in the United States, and introduced new qualifications for immigration and naturalization designed to exclude the ill, indigent, illiterate, immoral, and seditious, including Communists. The design was to facilitate the rapid naturalization of aliens lawfully in the United States. Declarations of intention two years before naturalization were no longer required and naturalization could be effected 30 days after petition and rigorous examination. The act also provided for cancellation of naturalization by discovery of fraud, by seditious behavior, or by prolonged residence abroad. The administration of the law was entrusted to the attorney general and the secretary of state.

The number of annual naturalizations has varied greatly. It reached a peak of 442,000 in 1944 and a low point of 55,000 in 1951, rising to 118,000 in 1954. Of this number, about two thirds originated in nine countries: Great Britain (16,565), Canada (13,062), Germany (11,679), Italy (10,926), Poland (8,342), Japan (6,750), Ireland (5,324), Soviet Union (3,832), Mexico (3,710). The large number of Japanese reflects their eligibility resulting from the act of 1952.

Great Britain and the Commonwealth.—The British Nationality and Status of Aliens Act of 1914 repealed earlier legislation and for the first time dealt with the subject comprehensively. It defined natural born British subjects as including "any person born within His Majesty's Dominions and allegiance" or born in a British ship even in a foreign port, and "any person born out of His Majesty's Dominions whose father was at the time of that person's birth a British subject." The secretary of state was authorized to grant certificates of naturalization to aliens who had resided in British territory for five years or had served the crown for that length of time, provided they were of good character, had "an adequate knowledge of the English language," intended to continue British residence or service, and took an oath of allegiance. The act also provided for revocation of naturalization obtained by false representation or in case evidence emerged of trading with an enemy, of continued allegiance to an enemy, of serious crime within five years of naturalization, of bad character at the date of naturalization, or of seven years' residence abroad other than in British service or in the service of a British business or institution. The act gave governments of British possessions similar powers to issue certificates of naturalization, provided that, in a self-governing dominion, the legislature had conferred such powers.

This act provided that the wife of a British subject should be deemed a British subject and the wife of an alien should be deemed an alien. An amendment of 1933, however, provided that a woman would not lose British nationality by marriage to an alien or by the naturalization of her husband unless she acquired her husband's nationality. Provision was also made for a British woman who married an alien to retain British nationality by declaration. Furthermore, the naturalization of an alien would not naturalize his wife unless she consented by declaration.

The Nationality Act of 1948 re-enacted most of the earlier legislation, but provided that "British subjects" should include "citizens" of the United Kingdom and of the scheduled dominions. It also provided for acquisition of United Kingdom "citizenship" by birth and by naturalization.

The British Dominions in general adopted the British legislation of 1914. In principle there is a common allegiance of the crown, and therefore, as provided in the act of 1948, nationals of all British Dominions have a common status of "subjects," which can be acquired by naturalization under authority of any government of the Commonwealth. Prior to this act of 1948, the Dominions might create a local citizenship or nationality not in conformity with the British Nationality Act of 1914 and, therefore, not making the individual a subject of the crown in the general sense.

The Irish Free State, by the Constitution of 1922, provided for the status of "citizen of the Irish Free State," not precisely conforming to the status of British subject. Ireland has subsequently ceased to be a member of the Commonwealth, and India, though it continues to be a member of the Commonwealth, has not, since it achieved independence, considered its nationals subjects of the crown.

Other Countries.—The variety of the laws in effect in other countries can be illustrated by statistics for 71 countries, based upon those prepared for the Harvard Research in International Law in 1929. Nationality at birth is acquired solely by the *jus sanguinis* in 17 countries, including the Soviet Union, Germany, Austria, Hungary, Switzerland, China, Japan, and most of the countries of Eastern Europe; primarily by the *jus soli,* but with limited provision for *jus sanguinis,* in 27 countries, including the United States, Great Britain, the British Dominions, and most Latin American states; by both systems, with primary emphasis on the *jus sanguinis,* in 27 countries, including France, Spain, the Scandinavian countries, Italy, Turkey, and most Western European and Middle Eastern states.

The age required for naturalization varies from 18 to 25 years and the period of residence required from one to ten years, with five years the commonest. Most states provide for a shortening of the period of residence for persons married to a national or employed in the state's military or civil service. Nearly all countries provide for automatic naturalization of minor children on the naturalization of the father.

The naturalized citizen enjoys an equal status with the native-born citizen in 10 countries, including Great Britain and Canada. In other countries, the naturalized citizen is under certain disabilities, especially ineligibility for certain offices, as in the United States, or subject to expatriation by prolonged foreign residence. Thirty-seven countries, including the United States, Great Britain, Germany, and Japan, recognize automatic expatriation by naturalization abroad; 24, including France, the Scandinavian countries, and China, require the consent of the country of origin, in most cases to assure fulfillment of the military service obligation. Seventeen countries regard foreign military or civil service as automatically resulting in expatriation, and 13 recognize such a result conditionally. Twenty-nine countries, including the United States, provide for expatriation of manifestations of disloyalty or bad character; 19, by extended residence abroad.

In the 19th century, nearly all countries provided for the naturalization of alien wives by marriage to a national or by the naturalization of the husband, but since the United States Cable Act of 1922, a large number of countries, including Argentina, Uruguay, and the Soviet Union, have eliminated one or both of these rules. Similarly, in the 19th century most countries provided for the expatriation of women on marriage to an alien or on the naturalization of the husband, but since World War I the United States, Great Britain, the British Dominions, France, Germany, Italy, Japan, the Scandinavian countries, and many others have eliminated this rule.

Naturalization laws have fluctuated between the principles of family solidarity, national solidarity, and individual freedom of choice. While the latter principle has in the main prevailed since World War I, the principle of national solidarity has not disappeared and has even been strengthened in some countries since World War II as a consequence of radical ideological cleavages. See also ALIEN; CITIZENSHIP.

QUINCY WRIGHT.

Bibliography.—Flournoy, Richard W., and Hudson, Manley O., eds., *A Collection of Nationality Laws of Various Countries, as Contained in Constitutions, Statutes and Treaties* (New York 1929); Harvard Research in International Law, Richard W. Flournoy, reporter, "Draft Code on Nationality," *American Journal of International Law,* supplement (1929); Gettys, Cora Luella, *The Law of Citizenship in the United States* (Chicago 1934); Briggs, Herbert W. ed., *The Law of Nations,* 2d ed., pp. 452–516 (New York 1952); U. S. Immigration and Naturalization Service, *Gateway to Citizenship* (Washington 1962); American Council for Nationalities Service, *How to Become a Citizen* (Dobbs Ferry, N.Y., 1963).

NATURE STUDY, the study of our natural surroundings. This means the near and the far away, the very small and the extremely huge, the visible and that which is invisible. It means trees, birds, bacteria, clouds, wind, rocks, and stars. It also includes sounds we can hear, heat that we can feel, gravity that pulls us to the earth, and a number of radiations that, like radio, require special instruments to detect. In short, it includes everything and anything that is natural as well as man-made gadgets that depend upon natural materials and forces for their operation.

In the early history of mankind the natural environment was the source for food and shelter. Natural materials were used to fashion tools and natural fires were tamed to provide heat and light. The calls of animals could indicate danger or mere contentment and man learned to know the difference because life depended in large part upon such knowledge. Lightning and thunder were frightening until their nature was understood. Man was curious about his surroundings and tried to find out just how ordinary rocks or minerals might be changed to precious metals such as gold and silver. Much of what was in part observed and in part imagined became folklore, and various sayings, especially sayings about the weather, were passed from person to person and from generation to generation. When a written language was developed much of what had been passed by word of mouth became a written record and many aspects of nature were included in such writings. Here one can find the observations and thoughts of the great philosophers. The great religious leaders found that the use of commonplace knowledge about nature could be made the basis of their moral and ethical lessons. Such ideas were taught as parables and many of these have meaning to people today because accurate observations and reports of natural events have an element of permanence that depends very largely upon the accuracy of the observer and the honesty and care of the reporter. Thus we can say that nature study is as old as man himself.

Nature study is commonly a part of elementary school work but it is often carried on rather informally. Just as children must have asked questions about the wind, stars, insects, and birds of John Amos Comenius (1592–1670), so they ask questions about natural things and their environment today. Comenius is credited with preparing the first schoolbook with pictures so we have reasons to think that he began the trend toward our illustrated books of today. He taught that the beginning of knowledge was with the seeing and hearing and other sense impressions of things. He argued that the beginning of teaching should also be with actual things—real and useful things that could be noted by the senses. After having observed real things there would be opportunities to tell about them and to develop a written record. The ideas of Comenius were developed by Jean Jacques Rousseau (1712–1778) and were given wide acceptance through Johann Heinrich Pestalozzi (1746–1827) who emphasized the need for studying the child and taught that sense impressions of nature were the true foundations of instruction and the only true bases of human knowledge. Since these early recorded ideas concerning nature study were promoted on the European continent, one is impressed with the greatness of Benjamin Franklin (1706–1790) who was advocating the study of nature when Pestalozzi was only three years old. In this connection it is with a sense of pride that we can read from *Franklin's Proposals Relating to the Education of Youth in Pennsylvania* that " . . . Children are capable of studying nature, for they have eyes, and don't want curiosity; they ask questions, and love to be informed; and here we need only awaken and keep up in them the desire for learning and knowing, which is natural in all mankind."

North America was a relatively new continent in the time of Franklin and this newness brought a host of explorers many of whom were serious students of nature. They also prepared written and often artistic records of the natural environment. A host of such persons can be named and their contributions to nature study cited. Such persons as John Bartram (1699–1777), André Michaux (1746–1802), Alexander Wilson (1766–1813), Benjamin Silliman (1779–1864), Asa Gray (1810–1888), Louis Agassiz (1807–1873) and many others have left a heritage of nature study in America that has been carried forward by a growing number of persons who have studied natural materials and events and who, through their work, have also influenced the education of youth.

Nature study as a part of educational practices in our schools was given its great initial beginnings by such persons as Edward Austin Sheldon (1823–1897), William Torrey Harris (1835–1909), and Wilbur Samuel Jackman (1855–1907). Sheldon is often looked upon as the person who introduced the nature study idea into the United States through his enthusiasm for, and development of, the object study method. He came to this idea at a training institute held in Toronto in 1859 where he saw collections of things and their educational values in an exhibit developed by Pestalozzian workers in England. He brought these ideas into the Oswego (New York) Primary Teachers' Training School where teachers from many parts of the United States came to study. His book *Lessons on Objects,* published in 1865, also helped to extend the idea. Harris became superintendent of schools in St. Louis and later United States Commissioner of Education. His work in developing a syllabus in nature study for the St. Louis schools in 1871 did much to introduce nature study into schools of the United States. Jackman grew up in Pennsylvania and became head of the teacher training work at the University of Chicago. He put his ideas about nature study in several textbooks and in 1903 presented his ideas in the 3d *Yearbook of The National Society for the Study of Education.* Much of the nature study emphasis in education is due to the efforts of the educators and scientists that have been mentioned in the foregoing discussion.

When we discuss nature study we associate many of the ideas and developments with the work of Anna Botsford Comstock (1854–1930) and E. Laurence Palmer (1888–), and with Cornell University where they carried on much of their work. The nature study emphasis in New York State grew out of the great agricultural depression of the period 1891–1893. This depression caused youth from the farms to flock to the cities where they could not find work. The New York State Legislature, upon the recommendation of a state-wide committee, made an appropriation in part to foster the teaching of nature study in the rural schools. This was done with the idea that if youth came to know and enjoy the natural environment, they would decide to remain on the farm. The development of the program was assigned to Liberty Hyde Bailey and in 1896 he wrote the first leaflet on nature study for teachers. Bailey's book, entitled *The Nature Study Idea,* published in 1903, justified nature study to meet the objections of educators, teachers, and scientists. He gave arguments in support of the importance of early studies of nature as a means of attracting youth into an area where they may wish to do serious studies later. He answered the educators who reasoned that there should be increased stress on the classics rather than studies of toads. He reasoned with the teachers who felt that nature study could not be added to an already crowded curriculum by showing them that nature study was not anything new but only something that would make the regular school program more interesting and educational. He justified the notion that studying nature for oneself was better than to read or to be told about natural events.

Bailey emphasized that nature study was primarily a process of seeing the things that one looks at and the drawing of proper conclusions from what one sees. He felt that it was possible to educate a child in terms of the environment and in the process make life fuller and richer. He wanted the study of the environment to be careful and thoughtful so that the ideas gained would be accurate and meaningful. Mrs. Comstock and her many associates at Cornell University developed these ideas and much of her thinking was brought together in a book, *The Handbook of Nature Study,* published in 1911. Palmer carried forward the nature study leadership at Cornell from 1919 to 1952. His extensive writing, speaking, and teaching helped both to develop and extend the emphasis on nature study as a school activity as well as its relationship to hobbies, writing, and the wise use of natural resources.

Nature study in the 1950's was a major part of the science work in our elementary schools. Much of it continues to be incidental and depends upon the questions of children about natural things and events. Curriculum leaders interested in science are giving increased attention to a planned science program which encourages youth to study many aspects of their natural environment. In almost all such programs one finds attention given to animals, plants, rocks, winds, shadows, weather, heat, stars, and other aspects of the natural environment. A real nature study curriculum leader will stress real experiences with the animals, plants, and other natural things in the immediate environment. Other leaders in elementary program planning will often stress the unusual that most children may experience only in a zoo or a botanic garden. With a stress on the unusual there is great dependence on illustrations and the accompanying text with whatever inaccuracies and unplanned distortions that the published materials may have included. This introduces the danger that nature study may become something to be learned from books alone without opportunity for the eager and direct study of natural materials and forces with all the joys of a discoverer. This danger has been of deep concern to members of the American Nature Study Society since its organization in 1908.

Some people have assumed that nature study is limited to a study of living animals and plants. Such was not the case with the leaders of the nature study movement nor is it the point of view of nature study leaders today. While their own preparation often stressed the biological aspects of nature they encourage and help the teachers with the study of rocks and minerals, the candle flame, toys of the home, electricity and magnetism and their uses, and other aspects of the physical world.

The nature study emphasis is not uncommon in our junior and senior high schools. More attention would be given to this emphasis if the teachers had had opportunities to learn from nature while making their preparation for teaching. The nature study approach is given much prominence in the methods and materials studied in many science courses in our colleges. Thus it can be said that the nature study idea has permeated and added richness to the educational process from nursery school into post-graduate work. More than that, nature study has become a hobby for millions of people who love to collect and study rocks, shells, nature photographs, and ideas for conversation or writing.

For some people nature study is an occupation and for some a profession. There are many persons who study nature and write about their observations in such interesting ways that their books are sought by people who frequent the booksellers and by librarians who seek materials for public and for school libraries. Some persons find a profession in the study of nature by means of photographic and sound equipment. They find a ready market for their photographic and related records in the moving picture industry, through illustrated lectures, and through publications.

More and more the people of the United States are growing aware of the dwindling of our natural resources. The complete disappearance of the once abundant passenger pigeon and the near disappearance of the whooping crane brings to all the challenge of learning to live with our natural surroundings. Thus there is added impetus for the study of nature with the hope that an understanding and love of nature will bring about a public opinion that will safeguard and conserve our resources so that our children and our children's children may find much to study and enjoy in our natural environment.

Bibliography.—Comstock, Anna B., *Handbook of Nature Study,* 24th ed. (New York 1939); Palmer, E. Laurence, *Fieldbook of Natural History* (New York 1949); Hillcourt, William, *Field Book of Nature Activities and Conservation* (New York 1961); Krutch, Joseph Wood, *The Twelve Seasons* (New York 1961); Teale, Edwin Way, *Adventures in Nature* (New York 1961); Dale, Alan, *Observations and Experiments in Natural History* (New York 1962); Headstrom, Richard, *Adventures with a Hand Lens* (Philadelphia 1962); Stone, R. H., *Tropical Nature Study* (New York 1964); Carson, Rachel, *The Sense of Wonder* (New York 1965); Hylander, Clarence J., *Wildlife Communities; From the Tundra to the Tropics in North America* (Boston 1966); Kieran, John, *An Introduction to Nature. Birds—Wild Flowers—Trees* (New York 1966).

PHILIP G. JOHNSON,
Chairman, Section on Nature, Science and Conservation Education, Rural Education Department, New York State College of Agriculture, Cornell University.

NATURE WORSHIP. The worship of the heavens, the planets, the elements, the manifestation of all forms of life, vegetable and animal, including the personified life attributed to inanimate objects. Nature worship, though probably everywhere occasioned by the natural impulse of man to fear the terrific manifestations of nature and to show great respect for the powerful and the mysterious, has taken many different bypaths in the development of the various human races and families. The early investigators into the phenomena of natural religions failed to recognize this diversity of development, and they proceeded to build universal theories on divergent growths. Hence all of their theories have either partially or completely fallen by the wayside, or have survived the test of time only as a diminutive part of the original whole. Yet the work of the early investigator has not been done in vain; for, inasmuch as he has thought deeply he has set others thinking. Concerning no part of the extensive field of mythology have more divergent theories been advanced than nature worship. By various writers the origin of worship has been traced to ancestor deification, to the fructification engendered by earth and sky, to the fear inspired in primitive man by the lightning, storms and winds, to the fearful ravages of mysterious all-powerful beings who brought diseases and death. Others claim that the first worship of man was given to powerful and cunning animals and especially to the serpent. Still other writers have maintained that man's first gods were his own ancestors; while others see him worshiping the glory and majesty of the sun and the mystic beauty and mysterious healing powers of the moon. Others have traced his first religious ideas to the rains and the mists and have placed his primitive gods on the mountains amid the sources of the streams or in the clouds, the home of the rains.

To these early mythological investigators it never seemed to occur that man's early conceptions of this nature were not at all religious in the modern acceptation of the terms; that they grew out of fear and mysterious dread. This primitive religious conception continued one of the strong features of man's worship far down into the monotheistic age of religion. Metaphorically the Jehovah of the Hebrews was a god of mysterious might who rode upon the winds and planted his footsteps upon the storm. At the sound of the horns of the priests of Israel walled cities fell down, just as the forests of old fell before the whistles of the wind gods. The fervid poetry of the greatest of the Hebrew poets is fairly alive with images borrowed from the polytheistic nature worshipers who surrounded them or with whom the race came into contact during its periods of exile. In this Hebrew poetry every phase of nature seems alive, as it is in the Greek and Roman, Egyptian, Babylonian and Indian poetry. In primitive Hindu literature and in the poetic imagery of China and Japan nature appears as one great whole deified in different yet, in many respects, suggestively similar ways. Among the American Indians the deification of the more striking forms of nature is everywhere evident. These primitive ideas became conventionalized, elaborated, amalgamated with other ideas and they long continued to act upon and to be reacted upon by society. A primitive belief was that people were drowned because spirits hidden in the depths dragged them down. The wind was supposed to cry like a lost child. The combination of the two made the Llorona of Spanish lands in Europe and America, who, crying like a lost child, leads the unwary, after nightfall, into a pool or bog where she or her attendants catches him by the legs and drags him down to death. Many primitive nature myths and unions of myths have become much more complicated than the Llorona. In fact little in nature worship even among the most primitive races now existing is to be found in anything like its original form. Hence the analysis of nature myths is a very complex and difficult matter. Yet the general conception of how primitive man thought is not difficult to understand.

Society and Nature Worship.— Although apparently simple, all modern manifestations of worship, however primitive, are in reality very complex; for society and its beliefs have, for long ages, been continually acting and reacting upon one another. In the more primitive society existing to-day, the medicine-men are universally believed to possess spiritual or magical powers. They are generally the medium between the people and the powers of the material universe and of the future world. They thus bear, in a sense, a divine character which belongs to them through the natural logic of their official position. Here we see, in the early stage of its development, one of the powerful factors in the organization of primitive beliefs of the nature worshipers into organized and complicated mythology. The governing class, consisting of priests or medicine-men, chiefs and leading warriors, early learned to claim descent from their nature gods, about whom they began to invent and relate the stories which we now call myths. The sun became the great ancestor of the Peruvian priests and nobility, of the Mixteca warrior class, as of the ruling body of other great races, the most noted of which was the Egyptian. Once this relationship had been attained the glorification of the sun became the glorification of the ruling powers and the consequent subjugation of the masses to them. Ritual, ceremony, a highly organized and disciplined priesthood and religious society followed; and of this the governing class soon became the head. Among the Toltecs in Mexico, Quetzalcoatl the wind god became the ruling deity and his superior priests, who were always chosen from the nobility, were believed to be his representatives upon earth and his lineal, blood descendants. The royal family and the nobles also represented themselves as god-born. Very frequently the king was also high priest of the nation and as such he was known as *the* Quetzalcoatl, or the chief of the gods. The principal races of Chiapas and Yucatan also believed themselves to be descended from the wind god, while the Mixtecas and several tribes of Guatemala called themselves «Children of the Sun.» The latter wore upon their breasts and backs the yellow symbol of the sun. In Persia and Egypt the complicated court life centred on the belief of the classes and the masses in the divine origin of the priesthood and the nobility and their descent from Re, the sun god. Thus the relation of religious primitive belief to the rulers of the people developed a complicated religio-political condition that finally became very complex in its nature. Out of this condition grew the acknowledged relationship of the hierarchy of the gods. This was the birth of the great religious systems of Persia, Babylonia and Egypt, which continued to grow more complex until their ultimate decline and disappearance. This, too, is more or less the path followed by the great religions of antiquity, all of which bear plainly the marks of primitive nature worship. The development of a religious theocracy gave very specified functions to the most prominent of the deities. Thus Thoth, the Egyptian wind god, being the original messenger god, became the carrier of souls; and the moon goddess, Isis, the mother of medicine and the healing art. Thoth, as the bearer of moisture and rains and the generator of growth, became the culture god, the patron of learning and the judge of good and evil in men's lives. All these conventionalized ideas of Thoth and Isis are very far removed from primitive man's conception of the wind and the moon as factors in his life. The great changes that took place were due to the peculiar organization of Egyptian society and the antiquity of her civilization.

Animism.— Primitive man undoubtedly held beliefs that we can scarcely comprehend to-day. One of these has been termed animism, a designation that appears to mean different things to different investigators and writers using it. It has been variously defined as belief in souls, spirits and magic power.

All recent investigation tends to show that primitive man made practically no distinction as to animation or life, between himself and the active elements of nature around him. The sun, moon, stars, winds, clouds, thunder and lightning were beings like himself who had at their command very superior magic power. The stories of all Indo-Europeans and the American Indians are filled with myths depicting the contests in magic that took place between their deities and nature heroes. The Indian stories especially present characters essentially human, so human indeed that they are frequently deceived and duped not only by man himself but also by the lower animals and even at times by inanimate things. These hero characters are neither divinities, nor souls, nor spirits in the modern acceptation of the terms. They are simply the wielders of magic power. Therefore, when certain writers on mythology talk glibly about the religious emotion in the presence of nature giving birth to animism, they are speaking about the past in terms of to-day, forgetful of two facts. The first of these is that even races as far advanced in civilization as the Indians of southeastern Canada and the United States seem to exhibit no appreciation of the beauties of nature, as nature itself. The second is, that religious emotion is the result of the teachings of organized religion, exercised consciously or unconsciously to stir up such feelings. Fear and terror of any object inspired respect in all ages of the past as they do to-day. Out of these primal elemental feelings combined with that of admiration, ancient religious beliefs and systems were built up slowly from primitive nature beliefs. The belief in souls and spirits, as things apart from the existence of humanity, came very much later in the religious development of humanity.

Transmigration.—Intimately connected with animation is the belief in transmigration. In fact the one presupposes the other; and both seem to belong to certain stages in the social development of all society. The wind was a most powerful agent of destruction, the mysterious beings hidden in the clouds shouted with their thunderous voices and shot forth their darts of fire. Other beings sent forth the rain from the heavens and the mountains. Yet they all remained invisible as did the spirits that moved the trees and the water; therefore, they must possess the power of rendering themselves invisible, reasoned the nature worshipper. The same mode of reasoning accounted for spirits in everything and endowed the personified elements, planets and phases of nature with the magical power of taking upon themselves other bodily forms at will. Out of this idea of transmigration grew the Hindu belief in reincarnation, which, in the case of Vishnu (q.v.), was carried to an almost unlimited number of bodily changes, each one bringing with it a new existence upon earth. Among many fairly civilized races there still exist in the masses at least a belief in spirits that inhabit trees, rocks, lakes, rivers, mountains, hills, clouds, caves and winds; and this belief teaches us how nature worship grew up and long continued to claim the unquestioned faith of humanity. The belief that human souls may be transmigrated into the bodies of animals, and vice versa, is still held by many races and peoples, and the ghost or disembodied spirit has but recently retreated from the stronghold of science; and so recent is its departure that a goodly body of so-called scientists are gravely experimenting with and seeking data as to its existence and habits.

Another development of animism and transmigration was the belief in guardian spirits which seems to have been almost universal. Very early in his social development man is found attempting to subject to his will and his uses, by his magic, the various mysterious powers of nature. Dances, charms, incantations, amulets, magic potions and other primitive means were made use of to this end. Amulets, believed to be powerful, were carried about on the body for self-protection and the wearer made efforts to get some supernatural being to become his protector. Often this being was supposed to reside in the fetish he carried upon his person. These developed by a complexed society became, in the course of time, household gods, probably through totems. Later society made patron saints to replace the grosser conceptions of heathenism. But all hail back to nature worship with its belief in transmigrating spirits, which has been father to ghosts, fairies, pigmies and a host of good and of evil-disposed supernatural beings.

Taboo.— Connected with these supernatural beings, which later became classed as gods, demigods, ghosts, or non-natural beings, were many tabooes or restrictions on the actions of humanity with respect to these nature spirits. The taboo might be a restriction from doing a certain thing at a certain time or under a certain condition; or it might enjoin the performance of a certain act or ceremony under like conditions. The custom of observing tabooes added, in the course of time, a species of veneration and of sacredness to the act and to the object of the taboo. Thus acts intended originally for the protection of the tribe, through continued repetition, grew to be part of the most sacred ceremonies. Thus the tabooes of the nature worshipers seem to have played a very prominent part in the building up of their most revered religious rituals. The taboo was closely associated with the tribal totems and with tree and other worship.

Through long years of association with nature worship particular places, days, epochs, trees, streams and persons were looked upon as sacred and, as such, subject to taboo. The emperors of the Aztecs and the Peruvians, at the time of the discovery of America, were believed by their people to be so sacred as to be almost gods; and around them clustered as many ceremonial tabooes as about the temples of their most revered deities. But in each case these tabooes reacted upon the ruler himself, placing many restrictions upon his actions in public and in private. Moctezuma II might not place his foot upon the bare earth lest his divine character be thus soiled. So he was carried about in a palanquin by official royal bearers, while other attendants spread before him a gorgeous carpet to protect his imperial feet from contamination when he left the palanquin. He might wear a suit of clothes but once, and if state or other reasons required a change of apparel a dozen times a day, it also demanded a completely new outfit. But while to wear a suit of clothes twice would defile the emperor, the representative of the gods, it was likely to bring special heavenly blessings to anyone of noble birth wearing it. So Moctezuma's cast-off clothing was eagerly sought and proudly worn by the highest nobility in the empire. In Peru it was taboo to make the vessels of the temple of the sun in the capital of any other material than gold whose shining color represented the radiant face of the deity; while all the furnishings of the moon goddess were required to be of silver. This latter example well illustrates the extreme growth of naturalistic ideas from commonplace, natural associations to taboo of the most rigid sacred character. About these nature tabooes grew up many legends to account for them or to explain them. The Peruvians asserted that gold was formed from the tears of the sun god; the Mixtecas declared that it was the sacred excrement from his shining body. The Colombian Indians in the neighborhood of Bogotá inaugurated their new emperor into office by painting his naked body completely with gold dust, thus symbolizing that he was the direct representative of the sun, the great racial father upon earth. Such complicated ceremonies with their rigid, uncompromising tabooes, imply a long-developed civilization or culture built upon nature worship.

The Nature Gods.— Nature worship, which, as has already been said, had its origin in the fear of the destructive forces of nature and a desire to placate them, or in respect for virile qualities in the same, grew in time, as man became more civil in his habits, to be a very complicated institution. Under the Aztecs, Mayas, Quiches, Zapotecas, Mixtecas, Pueblo Indians and Peruvians in America and among the great civilized nations of Europe, northern Africa and southern and western Asia, in the pre-Christian era, nature worship had become organized, in each case, into a most complicated religio-philosophical system which defined the attributes and sphere of action of each of the deities and explained his relationship to the gods as a whole, to the state, to the priesthood, to the nobility and to the masses. This called for an extensive classification and cataloguing of the nature deities. This had already taken place in the religious systems of all the great civilized nations in pre-Christian days. Naturally, under such a system, where almost every phase of animate nature was represented by its special deity, the list of the gods became very great. Yet they all came under a few primary divisions. The upper religions were occupied by the sun, moon and other planets, by the dawn and the darkness, the clouds, the thunder and the lightning, the winds of the four quarters of the heavens and their accompanying night spirits or wind spirits. In most nature religions these regions were divided into the upper heavens, inhabited by the sun, moon, planets and gods of dawn and darkness; and the lower heavens, the home of the clouds, winds, rain gods and other deities of the elements. The earth was the home of the deities of growth and fertility and the general habitat of the household penates and guardian spirits; while the regions within the earth or beyond the borders of the natural world, that is out on the great elemental ocean which, in most mythologies, surrounded the earth, were the regions of death and decay. Within the earth, too, quite frequently were the regions of birth. These ideas and divisions sprang naturally out of nature worship. At death all things go back into the earth; at birth all the vegetable kingdom evidently comes out of it. This was one of the patent facts that first appealed to the imagination of myth-making primitive man. There was a tendency to divide the deities of these divine regions into beneficent and malevolent beings. Thus arose the idea of the warring of the nature gods.

The Functions of the Gods.— Nature worship, originating independently, as it undoubtedly did, in different quarters of the world, naturally developed along different lines among people racially and linguistically different. But as the origin of the pantheistic conceptions that distinguished it were essentially the same, there is a striking similarity in the functions and attributes of the nature gods everywhere. The earth, which gives birth to all things, is the universal mother; the sky, which sends the fructifying rains, is the husband of the earth and the great nature father. The sun, with his vivifying rays is the father of growth. The winds, with their ceaseless movements and their great speed, become the messengers of the gods, the bringers of culture and the purifiers or healers. But there are beneficent winds and harmful winds, gentle winds and destructive winds. Those working in the interest of man are represented as in a constant struggle with those seeking to harm him. This feature of nature worship is strongly evident in many myths. In the Mexican mythology Quetzalcoatl, the beneficent east wind is represented as the culture hero struggling with Tetzcatlipoca, the black spirit of the night, or the night wind. Hiawatha fought and defeated the Great Pearl Feather, the wind that broods over the pestilential marshes; and he fought his own father Mudjikierwis, the west wind and the father of all the winds of heaven, who finally shares his kingdom with him, making him the Keewatin, the northwest wind, the home wind.

The Serpent in Nature Worship.— Everywhere the serpent drags its tortuous length through the habitat of the nature gods. Many explanations of its presence there have been presented by students of mythology, but most of these explanations have been unfortunately fanciful or manufactured to fit preconceived theories. The serpent is inseparably associated with the wind gods. Sometimes, he is a kindly deity; at others he is the spirit of malevolence. This is a natural development of nature and in no way demands a supernatural explanation since it fits in with the nature of the winds. Quetzalcoatl (q.v.), the great culture hero of Mexico, Yucatan and Guatemala, was represented as a plumed serpent, and the serpent formed the most conspicuous decoration of his temples. Yet others of the Mexican wind gods also bore the sign of the serpent. The robe of the mother of the gods was represented as consisting of interwoven snakes. The serpent was frequently intimately connected with the deities of fruition and birth, probably because the wind gods were also thus connected. But the destroying force was also represented as a winged serpent in many parts of the world. This is but another form of the evil wind. This latter conception gave birth to the dragons of destruction bearing with them fire or lightning as their destroying agents. From this conception to that of the evil one, the old serpent, the personified force of evil as found in the Persian and other related religions, is but a step. Christianity and the Hebrew faith borrowing the imagery of the nature religions have made it vividly familiar to us.

In Roman and Greek mythologies, the gods of healing are associated with the serpent and not the least of these is Apollo. This association of the serpent with the gods of birth and healing explains their relationship to public worship which has produced so much discussion and investigation and has given birth to the so-called theory of serpent worship. With the Chinese, as with the Toltecs, the wind god (in the case of the Chinese in the shape of a dragon) became a sort of world divinity, the great wisdom, the universal benefactor. As the fructifying rain bringer, the serpent represented kindly forces; as the rain preventer his tendencies were evil.

The Cross in Mythology.— Throughout all primitive America and in many of the mythologies of the eastern hemisphere the world was divided into four quarters over which ruled one of the winds, all of which were frequently represented as so many serpents or dragons. Quetzalcoatl, the Toltec culture god, sailed away to the unknown land on a raft of snakes, or in a boat moved by supernatural serpents, which were at once symbolical of his origin as a wind god and his office as the greatest culture hero of the American races and the symbol of divine wisdom and earthly progress. Being the symbol of fertility, the serpent naturally became that of the so-called pallic worship which was also symbolized by the cross, as the representative of the four quarters of the earth in which lived the winds and the rain gods. In pre-Columbian times the cross was the symbolical representation of the activity of the winds as the bearers of fertility throughout Mexico, most of Central America and the Pueblo and some other Indians of the United States. In the form of the swastika (the four-footed cross with the ends bent, generally at right angles), the cross became the symbol of good fortune and (among the American Indians) of generation. The Cretan mother goddess, the great deity of fertility, is represented, in her surviving statues, with snakes coiled about her waist and arms; and she was worshiped in the temple of the sacred cross. Throughout Crete, where her worship seems to have had a very important place, the cross was looked upon as a sacred symbol. Like the rain gods of Mexico and Central America, the mother god of Crete was worshiped on the tops of the hills and the high places from whence descended the fructifying waters. Like the tlalocks and other gods of the rain cross she was connected with death and life, more especially the latter. In the course of time the cross, especially in America, came to form a very important part of the decoration of temples and sacred places in pre-Columbian days. The trail of the cross, like the trail of the serpent, runs across Mexico and Central America and a very considerable part of the United States.

Fire.— Along with sunshine, rain, air in motion and regeneration, fire early became for man one of the sacred elements. To him it symbolized (among many races) the sun, the great generator and the source of all heat. By the use of fire it was possible for him to greatly enlarge his range of diet, to fell the huge forest trees and shape his canoes from them.

It enabled him to shatter great masses of rock and to shape them roughly to his ends. Later on it enabled him to smelt metals and to attach them to his car of progress. As it was hurled from the cloud it became symbolical of the power that hurled it. As it was vomited forth from the volcanoes, it came to signify the titanic forces of the underworld and became inseparably connected with punishment for offenses connected with the infernal regions, in various mythologies. From these primitive beliefs later religious systems borrowed much of their systematized ideas of the nature of future punishment.

The Future Life.—As the beneficent beings who brought their favors to the earth occupied the upper air; and as there, too, is the home of the sun, the moon and the planets which were supposed to strongly influence human life for good or evil, very many races looked upon these regions as the home of their future life. Some beliefs held that the souls of the dead went to the sun, others to the moon, still others to the great cloud land, a mid-region between the earth and the home of the superior deities. Some races placed the future world in the far north or northwest, in the region of the northern lights, whose brilliancy probably suggested the idea. Among many Indian tribes the rainbow was believed to be the bridge that spanned the great gulf separating the earth ocean and the sky ocean. Numerous other American tribes believed that the dead went to some great underground region. But all the nature religions presented the future life as essentially the same as that upon earth though surrounded by happier, because more fortunate conditions. Communication was not only possible between the earth and the future world but the rainbow bridge had been climbed or the great gulf had been frequently crossed in the magic stone canoe by the mortal heroes of nearly every United States Indian tribe. Some legends depict the tribal hero as scaling the heights of heaven on the back of a great bird, or in the wicker-car of the star or sun-maidens or in numerous other manners; for to the nature worshiper the universe was one great whole, the parts of which were not essentially different from one another.

Theories of Nature Worship.—At the head of the early naturalistic school is Max Müller. He maintains, with the disciples of his school, that the worship of nature was the primary religious efforts of man; and he attempts to prove his position by means of comparative mythology. His theory, which applied only to the Indo-European races, was carried to an absurd limit by many of his school. E. B. Tylor looks upon the worship of the dead as the earliest of human cults and Herbert Spencer takes the same ground. The latter derives from this source all other forms of worship. Tylor traces the history of the so-called animistic faith, while Spencer displays its evolution. Wundt maintains that religion finds its origin in the primitive belief in human souls and in an early animism out of which a belief in magic and fetishism grew. Dunkheim believes that the totemic principle, or belief in mysterious power (the mana or magic power) is the source of all religion. All of these investigators have hit upon certain important truths, but no one of them has been able to grasp the significance of the wide field of mythology, for thev all have made categorical statements upon which they have built up elaborate theories.

Bibliography.—Fergusson, J., *Rude Stone Monuments* (London 1872); Spencer, Herbert, *Principles of Sociology* (London 1876); Lang, Andrew, *Custom and Myth* (London 1884); Chantepie de la Saussaye, P. D., *Lehrbuch der Religionsgeschichte* (Freiburg 1887); Buckland, A. W., *Anthropological Studies* (London 1891); Goblet d'Alviella, E., *La Migration des symboles* (Paris 1891); Lefevre, A., *La religion* (Paris 1892); Moorehead, W. K., *Primitive Man in Ohio* (New York 1892); Brinton, D. G., *Myths of the New World* (Philadelphia 1896); Crooke, W., *Popular Religion and Folklore of Northern India* (London 1896); Jastrow, M., *Religion of Babylonia and Assyria* (Boston 1898); Müller, M., *Natural Religion* (London 1898); Lang, A., *Myth, Ritual and Religion* (New York 1899); Sayce, A. H., *Religion of Ancient Egypt and Babylonia* (Edinburgh 1902); Taylor, E. B., *Primitive Culture* (Boston 1903); Lang, A., *The Making of Religion* (London 1898; New York 1909); Durkheim, Emile, *La vie religieuse* (Paris 1912); Frazer, J. G., *The Golden Bough* (London 1907–13); id., *Worship of Nature* (New York 1926).

JOHN HUBERT CORNYN,
Birmingham Southern College.

NAUCRATIS, nô'kră-tĭs, Egypt, an ancient Greek colony, the remains of which are 50 miles by rail southeast of Alexandria. It existed as early as the beginning of the 7th century B.C., and was approached by a navigable canal in the western part of the delta, near the Canopic branch of the Nile. Its chief period of splendor was during the reign of Amasis II, 570–520 B.C., under whom it was recognized as the official capital of the Greeks in Egypt. Its site was rediscovered in 1884 by Professor Flinders Petrie. Subsequent excavations have uncovered the remains of buildings described by Herodotus, the Hellenium, temples to Apollo, Aphrodite, the Dioscuri, and others; and there have been valuable finds of early Greek pottery and other archaeological treasures.

Consult Petrie, W. M. F., *Naukratis* (London 1886); Gardner, E. A., "Naukratis II," *Publications,* Egyptian Exploration Fund, Vols. 3, 6 (London 1886–88); Hogarth, D. G., "Naukratis, 1903," *Journal of Hellenic Studies,* Vol. 25 (London 1905).

NAUCYDES, nô-sĭ'dēz, Greek sculptor. He flourished in the first quarter of the 4th century B.C. His birthplace was Argos, and he was the pupil of the elder Polyclitus of the Peloponnesian school of sculpture. He carved a gold and ivory statue of Hebe for the temple of Hecate at Argos; a bronze statue of Hecate; a Hermes; several statues of Victory; a portrait of the poetess Erinna; *Phryxus Sacrificing the Ram* (for the Acropolis at Athens); and a discus thrower. The younger Polyclitus was his pupil.

NAUEN, nou'ĕn, town, East Germany, in Brandenburg, is located 25 miles northwest of Berlin. Its manufactures include machinery, soap, and food products. A powerful radio station here was dismantled in 1945–1947. The town was first mentioned in 981, and was chartered in 1292. Pop. (1957) 12,828.

NAUGATUCK, nô'gȧ-tŭk, town and borough, Connecticut, New Haven County, is located on the Naugatuck River, 5 miles south of Waterbury, on the New York, New Haven and Hartford Railroad. The chief industry is the manufacture of rubber footwear and chemicals, and there is a huge rubber regenerating mill. Other manufactured products are cosmetic containers, plastics, safety pins, chocolate bars, airplane instruments, glass, mirrors, copper floats, chains, metal stampings, tools, and screw machine products. Charles Goodyear, discoverer of rubber vulcanization, lived here and established a factory here in 1843. Two early buildings of historic interest are Porter Tavern, built about 1752, and Collins Tavern, built in 1810.

Naugatuck is an Indian phrase meaning "one tree." In 1679, while still a part of Mattatuck (now Waterbury), the community was referred to as Judd's Meadows. In 1773 a new ecclesiastical society was created under the name of Salem Society, and somewhat later the area came to be called Salem Bridge. It was incorporated in 1844 as Naugatuck, the name by which the town had been more generally called since the opening of a post office there in 1834. The borough was incorporated in 1893. The government is vested in a warden and board of burgesses who hold office two years and who appoint many of the administrative officials. Pop. 23,034.

NAUGATUCK, a river in Connecticut. It rises in the northern part of Litchfield County, flows south through a hilly part of the state, and enters the Housatonic River at Derby. It supplies water power to many mills and factories. Waterbury is the chief city on its banks.

NAUGHTY MARIETTA, nô'tĭ mâr-ĭ-ĕt'ȧ, a light opera by the Irish-American composer, Victor Herbert (1859–1924), produced in New York in 1910. Several of its songs are still widely popular and are frequently heard. Among them are *Italian Street Song, Ah! Sweet Mystery of Life, I'm Falling in Love with Someone.* Herbert composed some 40 light operas.

NAUHEIM or **BAD NAUHEIM**, bät' nou'hīm, town, West Germany, in the state of Hesse (1945), is located 17 miles northeast of Frankfurt, on the northeastern slope of the Taunus Mountains. It is a well-known health resort noted for its warm carbonated mineral springs which are highly saline. It became a town in 1854. Napoleon Bonaparte gave it to Marshal Louis Davout, but from 1815–1866 it belonged to the electorate of Hesse-Cassel. It was ceded to the grand duchy of Hesse-Darmstadt in 1866. Pop. (1956) 13,062.

NAULETTE, nô-lĕt', a limestone cave in Belgium, on the Lesse River, near Dinant, where in 1866 an imperfect human lower jaw was found together with bones of the mammoth, rhinoceros, and reindeer. The jaw, now in the Brussels Museum of Natural History, was assigned to the Mousterian period.

NAUMACHIA, nô-mā'kĭ-ȧ, or **NAUMACHY**, nô'mȧ-kĭ (from the Greek *naus,* ship, and *machē,* battle), among the Romans a public spectacle, representing a naval action. Julius Caesar was the first who exhibited a spectacle of this sort, which soon became the favorite amusement of the Roman people. Buildings were erected by the emperors, specially adapted for the purpose. They resembled the amphitheaters, and like them were at first built of wood. Domitian erected one of stone. A *naumachia,* built by Augustus, was 1,800 feet long and 200 feet wide, and was capable of containing 50 ships with three banks of oars, besides many small vessels. They were flooded by means of subterranean canals, so that the ships were raised from the dry floor before the eyes of the spectators. These sea-fights were exhibited with the same splendor and reckless disregard of human life which characterized the gladiatorial combats. Titus exhibited a sea fight in which 3,000 men were engaged and ships almost equal in number to two real fleets were shown in combat by Domitian. The crews generally consisted of gladiators, prisoners, or condemned criminals.

NAUMANN, Friedrich (in full, JOSEPH FRIEDRICH), German politician: b. Störmthal, near Leipzig, Germany, March 25, 1860; d. Travemünde, Germany, Aug. 24, 1919. He left the Lutheran ministry in 1894 to enter politics. In 1896, together with others, he founded the National Socialist Party, of which he became the first president. In his book *Mitteleuropa* (1915) he outlined a plan for a central European German empire. After the November Revolution in 1918, he became one of the founders of the German Democratic Party.

NAUPLIA, nô'plē-ə, is a city in Greece, at the northern end of the Gulf of Argolis, about 25 miles South of Corinth. It is the capital of the nome (province) of Argolis. Its name is spelled *Návplion* in Greek.

A seaport since ancient times, Nauplia was occupied by the Venetians during the Middle Ages, and later by the Turks. From 1830 to 1834 it was the capital of Greece. Population: (1961) 8,918.

NAURU, nä-o͞o'ro͞o, is an island republic in the southwestern Pacific Ocean. Formerly a United Nations Trust Territory under Australian administration, Nauru achieved independence on Jan. 31, 1968. The island's income is dependent on its extensive phosphate deposits.

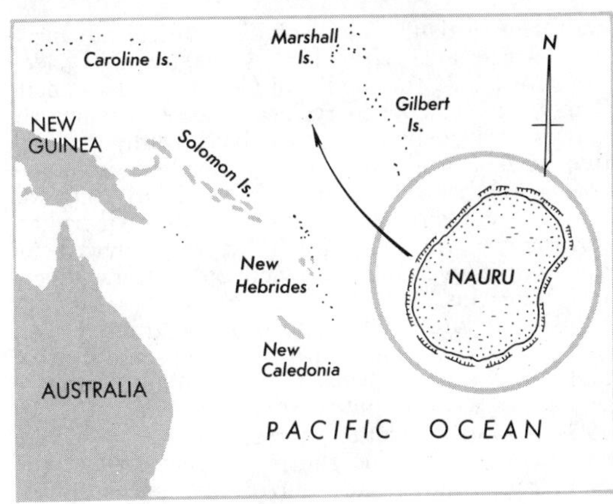

Land. Nauru lies 26 miles (42 km) below the equator, at longitude 166° 56′ E. It is an oval-shaped island approximately 12 miles (19 km) in circumference and covers an area of 5,263 acres (2,129 hectares). An encircling coral reef is exposed at low tide, and there is no anchorage.

Between the sandy beach and the coral cliffs is a fertile strip ranging in width from 150 to 300 yards (140–270 meters), where most of Nauru's people live. Beyond this lies a more or less barren plateau containing extensive phosphate deposits, the island's major economic resource. The removal of the phosphate exposes a rugged terrain consisting of coral pinnacles that rise some 50 feet (15 meters) above the old coral formation.

The island's hot climate is tempered by cooling sea breezes. Temperatures range between 76° and 93° F (24° and 34° C), with medium to high humidity. Average annual rainfall is over 80 inches (200 cm), much of it occurring during the westerly monsoon season (November to February).

People. When Nauru became independent in 1968 the total population barely exceeded 6,000, making it the smallest among nations. The indigenous Nauruans, who number just over 3,000, are related to the Micronesian peoples to the northeast. Other peoples on the island include about 1,800 Gilbert and Ellice Islanders and 900 Chinese, who work the phosphate. There are also about 500 Europeans in Nauru.

The Nauruans have adopted Christianity. Education is compulsory for Nauruans between the ages of 5 and 17. The curriculum is taken from the Australian system, with instruction in English.

Land tenure is governed by traditional customs, and apart from small allotments held by the government and missions the entire island is owned by individuals. The Nauruans live along the fertile rim, which is traversed by a 16-foot-wide (5-meter) road from which paths and tracks lead to the settlements.

Economy. Throughout the 20th century, Nauru's economy has been built around the phosphate industry and royalties arising from it. A light railroad carries the phosphate to the coast, where it is conveyed along a cantilever trestle across the reef for loading directly into ships' holds. Phosphate shipments exceed 1,500,000 tons annually, and are primarily to Australia and New Zealand. The island's revenue (in excess of $10 million annually) greatly exceeds the cost of imports, chiefly hardware, machinery, food supplies, and motor vehicles. Some food products are grown; hogs and poultry are raised.

A radio system, including radiotelephone service, operates between Nauru and Australia, with circuits to other South Pacific islands. Freighters operate to Australia and New Zealand. A small airfield is located in the southwestern part of the island.

History. The island was first sighted by outsiders in 1798, from the American whaling vessel *Hunter* under the command of Captain Fearn, who named it Pleasant Island. It was formally annexed by Germany in 1888 and from then on was known by its native name, Nauru. Phosphate was discovered in the late 1890's, and exploitation began in 1901. German control of Nauru ended in 1914, when the Australian Expeditionary Force took over the island during World War I.

The League of Nations placed the island under the joint administration of Britain, Australia, and New Zealand as a mandated territory in 1920. Control of the phosphate industry was vested in the 3-government British Phosphate Commission.

Nauru suffered severely during World War II. It was shelled by a German raider in December 1940 and bombed by the Japanese before they occupied the island in August 1942. It was then bombed by Allied aircraft, and with Japanese food ships hampered, food supplies ran short. The Japanese deported 1,200 Nauruans for forced labor on Truk; the 737 survivors returned to Nauru after the Australians reoccupied the island in 1945.

In 1947, Nauru became a UN Trust Territory administered by Australia on behalf of the joint administering authority of Australia, Britain, and New Zealand. The island's political advancement accelerated after 1951, when the first elections were held for the Local Government Council. The 9-member council replaced the old Council of Chiefs, a largely hereditary body without effective power. Full powers of legislation, administration, and jurisdiction remained with the administrator, who was appointed by the Australian government, but henceforth he was advised by the Local Government Council on matters affecting Nauruans.

By the late 1960's, phosphate extraction had destroyed about one third of the island's area, and it was estimated that the remaining phosphate would be worked out within three decades. In 1967 it was agreed that, through purchase of the capital assets of the phosphate commission, the Nauruans would take control of the phosphate industry in 1970.

After Australia and the other administering powers agreed to grant Nauru independence, a constitutional convention chose Jan. 31, 1968, as the date for the transfer of power. The constitution provides for a president and a cabinet of six drawn from the 18-member Legislative Assembly, which is elected by adult franchise.

R. M. YOUNGER,
Author of "Australia and the Australians"

NAUSICAA, ancient Greek heroine mentioned in the *Odyssey.* She was the daughter of Alcinous, king of the Phaeacians, who befriended the shipwrecked Odysseus.

NAUTCH, nâch (Hind. *nāc*), in India, a dance performed by the dancing girls attached to the temples, called Nautch girls, who are brought up and trained in the art.

NAUTILOIDEA, nô-tĭ-loi′dê-ȧ, one of three subclasses in the Cephalopoda. The genus *Nautilus,* which contains the chambered nautilus, is the last surviving member of this once large and varied group of Cephalopods.

The earliest fossil nautiloid shells appeared in the Upper Cambrian Period and became greatly differentiated and very abundant in the Ordovician and Devonian. By the Cretaceous Period they had diminished to but a single order or group, the Nautilida, and by mid-tertiary had almost completely disappeared. Since then they have persisted only as a single genus, *Nautilus,* which occurs in the tropical portions of the western Pacific and Indian oceans. Over 300 genera and 2,500 fossil species have been described in this subclass. The large number of genera are grouped into 14 orders.

The study of this group as well as other fossil cephalopods is exceedingly complex and relationships between the various orders are far from being understood. A vast number of terms have been employed to describe the complex morphology of the shell structure.

Consult Flower, R. H., and Kümmel, B., "A Classification of Nautiloidea," *Journal of Paleontology,* 24:604-616 (1950); Shrock, R. R. and Twenhofel, W. H., *Principles of Invertebrate Paleontology* (New York 1953).

WILLIAM CLENCH.

NAUTILUS, nô′tĭ-lŭs, a genus of Cephalopods in the subclass Nautiloidea. Only three or four living species are known, of which *Nautilus pompilius* is the most abundant. These various species occur in the tropical portions of the Indian and western Pacific oceans. They live on the ocean floor in depths ranging from four to as much as 700 meters, and they are captured mainly in fish traps. Little is known regarding their life history. The shell they produce is quite remarkable as it is septate, that is, it contain a series of chambers, the animal itself occupying the outer or last chamber produced. As the animal grows larger, the outer wall of the shell is built forward, and the animal moves forward and then seals off the vacated area with a thin partition or septum. All of the septa are perforated in the middle by a single, narrow tube, or siphuncle, which is a slender tubular prolongation of the visceral hump. All of the vacated chambers contain a gas similar to air, except for having a little less oxygen and somewhat more nitrogen. This gas increases materially the buoyancy of the shell, and makes it easier for the animal to swim.

A thin mantle covers the entire animal and, in addition, adheres to the shell. The head contains a pair of lateral eyes which lack crystalline lens. The tentacles, which may number up to 90, form two circles about the mouth. There are a pair of horny or calcareous jaws, a radula, and a tongue. There is a short tubular esophagus which connects with the stomach, and behind the stomach there is a large liver and other digestive glands. A simple tubular intestine is coiled backward and ends at the anus, which empties into the anal chamber or mantle cavity. There are four gills and no ink sac. The heart lies ventral of the intestine and posterior to the gills.

There is a much thickened area over the head known as the hood, which acts as an operculum when the animal withdraws into the shell.

WILLIAM CLENCH.

NAUTILUS, in hydraulic engineering, a diving bell (q.v.) requiring no suspension. Water admitted through the cock into pipes flows into the exterior chambers, causing the apparatus to sink. The workmen enter through an aperture at the top, closed by an airtight cover, and can in still water move the machine in any required direction by stepping on the ground and pushing. Air is condensed in a reservoir at the surface to a degree somewhat greater than the condensation due to the depth, and passes through a pipe into the chambers, rendering the machine specifically lighter than water and enabling it to lift stones or other objects below. A gauge indicates the amount of lifting power attained as the air is admitted into the chambers.

NAUTILUS, The U.S.S., a submarine embodying some principles of the fictional archetype for which it was named, described in 1870 by Jules Verne in his classic tale of scientific adventure, *Twenty Thousand Leagues Under the Sea.* But where the power plant of the fictional Captain Nemo's *Nautilus* was electric (like the real submarines the French Navy began building only 16 years later), the U.S.S. *Nautilus* is powered by an atomic pile. The keel of this first atomic-powered submersible was laid in June 1952, and she was launched in January 1954. The engineering plant consists of a reactor in which the terrific power of uranium is harnessed to a "slow" chain reaction. The uranium, consumed at the rate of about one pound per month, requires replenishment only once a year. Situated behind the control room is the reactor. Heavily lead-shielded for protection against radiation, it converts water into superheated steam which, in turn, operating through a heat exchanger, converts other water into steam that drives a turbine. Thus, the *Nautilus* is not only the first atomic but also the first steam submarine.

During a memorable 8,146-mile voyage, begun at Pearl Harbor, Hawaii, on July 23, 1958, the 3,000-ton *Nautilus* became the first ship to make a transpolar crossing. Equipped with an inertial guidance system in addition to other navigational devices, it went under the polar ice cap near Point Barrow, Alaska, on August 1, and traveled 1,830 miles in 96 hours, at depths exceeding 400 feet, before surfacing between Greenland and Svalbard (Spitsbergen). The vessel made its historic passage beneath the North Pole on August 3 at 11:15 P.M. (EDT). Besides adding to man's knowledge of the Arctic Ocean subsurface and attaching new military significance to Arctic waters, the voyage pioneered the shortest known sea route between the Pacific Ocean and Europe.

NAUVOO, nô-vōō'; nô'vōō, city, Illinois, in Hancock County, 10 miles south of Fort Madison, Iowa, on a promontory on the Mississippi River and served by the Atchison, Topeka, and Santa Fe Railroad at East Fort Madison, Ill. It is situated at an altitude of 620 feet in a fruit-growing region and its principal industries are connected with the manufacture of wine and blue cheese.

Settled in 1830 as Commerce, its name was changed to Nauvoo when Joseph Smith and his followers of the Church of Jesus Christ of Latter-day Saints (Mormons, q.v.), settled there in 1839. The Illinois legislature granted the Mormons a charter and a militia called the Nauvoo Legion. Smith was mayor and commander in chief of the legion. By 1845 Nauvoo was the largest city in Illinois, with a population of 20,000. A temple was begun on a hill, but it was burnt and demolished later. After a riot in which Smith and his brother Hyrum were murdered, the Mormons left the settlement. From 1849 to 1856 the Icarians, a French communistic group under Étienne Cabet (q.v.) had a settlement there but internal disagreements split the community some going to St. Louis and others to Corning, Iowa. Later, Irish and German immigrants rebuilt Nauvoo. Grape growing was introduced and wine making prospered. In 1920 the making of blue cheese was begun. There is an annual Grape Festival attended by thousands. The Joseph Smith homestead, the Brigham Young house, and other old buildings are historic shrines. Pop. 1,047.

NAVAJO CHURCH, năv'à-hō. This name is given to a remarkable spire of white sandstone rising from the top of the red cliffs just west of the Continental Divide a short distance east of Gallup, N. Mex. It is visible for several miles from the Atchison, Topeka, and Santa Fe Railroad near Wingate station. Navajo Church is an object of veneration for the Navajo Indians of the vicinity. Its rock formations have several large caves.

NAVAJO or **NAVAHO INDIANS,**[1] an important tribe of the Athapascan stock of Indians, in 1955 on four reservations aggregating 15,364,828 acres in northeastern Arizona, northwestern New Mexico, and southeastern Utah, at an average elevation of 6,000 feet above sea level. According to Fray Alonso Benavides (1630), who referred to the tribe as "Apaches de Navajó," the word "Navajo" meaning "great planted fields," the name was never applied to the Navajo by themselves, their own tribal designation being "Diné" (people).

There is no evidence that the Navajo were seen by the Spanish explorers of the Southwest in the 16th century, although the latter passed through the present Navajo country in 1540, 1583, and 1598. It is therefore believed that at this early period they were an insignificant agricultural tribe, but gradually increased in population largely through the adoption of natives of both allied and other stocks during succeeding years. Their territory is entirely within the arid region and their lands are chiefly desert; but in the canyons and about the bases of the mesas that abound in their territory, horticulture is practiced through deep planting in the sandy soil, while in the valley of the Rio San Juan, which is the largest stream in their country,

Herbert from Frederic Lewis

Navajo mother preparing a meal in front of her summer hogan.

farming is carried on to a greater extent, in 1950 the total acreage planted in vegetal crops totaling 38,064.

Agriculture, however, forms but a meager part of Navajo subsistence, his livelihood being gained principally from the flocks and herds, of which in 1953 there were 423,406 sheep, 2,284 beef and dairy cattle, and 63,879 goats, the sheep, besides furnishing the chief food supply, netting a large sum in wool and blankets. These blankets, which are celebrated, are woven by the women on simple looms and in pleasing and sometimes intricate designs of various colors. Formerly native dyes of rare delicacy of tone were employed, but these have given way to glaring aniline colors, and the decorative patterns have also been largely modified to meet the demands of the white man. The Navajo also weave belts, garters and saddle girths, and make a few basket trays, for ceremonial use. Some of the men are expert silversmiths.

Although more closely related to the Apache than to any other tribe, the Navajo are con-

[1] Modern authorities prefer Nava*h*o spelling.

siderably mixed, embodying elements of Pueblo, Shoshonean, Yuman, and even of Spanish blood; hence there is perhaps a greater variety in their physical features than among many Indian tribes.

The typical Navajo dwelling is a dome-shaped framework of logs or sticks covered with brush, bark or grass, and earth, with a smoke hole at the apex and a doorway in one side. Rude shelters with open fronts are erected for use in summer. If a person dies in a house the dwelling is believed to become haunted and is destroyed.

Dr. Washington Matthews (q.v. 1843–1905), one of the foremost students of the Navajo, discovered the existence of 51 clans, grouped into about a dozen phratries, which are probably not homogeneous organizations as among some Indians. A Navajo belongs to the clan of his mother, and a man may not marry a woman belonging to his own clan, or, as a rule, one of his own phratry. The religion of the Navajo is elaborate and complicated. They have a great many ceremonies, most of which are performed for healing the sick, but others are conducted to ensure success in planting, harvesting, building, war, nubility, marriage, travel, and for bringing rain. Sacrifice, elaborate dry paintings with sand and pigments, masquerade, dancing, prayer, and song are the elements of the ceremonies, the gods being personated by the masked performers.

History.—Almost from the beginning of the 17th century the Navajo were enemies of the sedentary tribes and of the Spanish colonists, and although they were never so predatory and warlike as their Apache cousins, the Spanish villages and Pueblo settlements suffered almost continuously from their raids up to the time of the conquest of New Mexico by American forces in 1846, followed by the establishment of military posts throughout the Southwest. Treaties were made with the tribe in 1846, 1848, and 1849, but they were of no avail in keeping in check their depredations, which continued at intervals until 1858, although expeditions were led against them. In 1849, after the Navajo killed a Negro servant at Fort Defiance, it became necessary to wage warfare against the Indians from August until December, when 50 Navajo were killed and a large number of sheep and other stock were lost. Another treaty was signed, but during 1860 the depredations continued, and another expedition was led against them, but without success. In April the natives boldly attacked Fort Defiance, but were repulsed. In the winter of 1860–1861 an active campaign was made against them, and although practically their only loss was in sheep, they were compelled to sue for peace in February 1861, when an armistice of a year was agreed to, during which the troops were withdrawn. In a dispute over a horse race at Fort Fauntleroy (near the present Fort Wingate), New Mexico, a dozen Navajo were brutally killed.

Emboldened by the withdrawal of the troops on account of the Civil War, the Indians resumed their raids, which they continued almost uninterruptedly until 1863, when Col. Christopher (Kit) Carson began operations against them and a plan was formulated to transfer the Navajo from their old haunts to Fort Sumner, at the Bosque Redondo, on the Pecos River, in eastern New Mexico. All who refused to go after July 20, 1863, were to be regarded as hostile and be treated accordingly, yet by the close of the year only 200 prisoners were at Fort Sumner or on the way there. Early in 1864 Carson made a campaign to the Canyon de Chelly in the heart of the Navajo country in northeastern Arizona, where he killed 23 and captured more than 200 of the Indians. As a result, by the close of 1864 more than 7,000 of the tribe were held as prisoners at the Bosque Redondo. By 1865 there were 8,491, but it was supposed this number represented only half of the tribe. The experiment, however, proved a failure, so that after the death of about a thousand of the Indians, the escape of others, and an expenditure of a million dollars in their support in a region ill-adapted to their progress, the remainder, numbering 7,304, were removed to their old country in July 1868, an appropriation of $422,000 having been made in that year to give them a new start.

Since that time the Navajo have been peaceable and industrious. They make good laborers and are slowly developing agricultural pursuits, which the government has assisted by increasing the amount of water for irrigation, domestic, and stock purposes. The internal government of the Navajo, which has met much success, is conducted by a tribal council whose numbers come from various parts of the reservation. The Navajo population in the 1960's was estimated at 90,000, more than that for any other tribe in the United States.

See also INDIANS, AMERICAN—*North American Culture Areas* (Cultures): Southwestern; INDIANS, EDUCATION OF THE.

Bibliography.—Navajo literature has increased so greatly during recent years that only a list of the more important later titles are here included. For earlier publications consult *A Bibliography of the Navaho Indians* by C. Kluckhohn and K. Spencer (New York 1940).

For later publications: Elmore, Francis H., *Ethnobotany of the Navajo* (Albuquerque, N. Mex. 1943); Watkins, Frances E., *The Navaho* (Los Angeles 1943); Adair, John, *The Navajo and Pueblo Silversmiths* (Norman, Okla. 1944); Leighton, Alexander H., and Dorothea, *The Navaho Door* (Cambridge, Mass. 1944); Hannum, Alberta, *Spin a Silver Dollar* (New York 1945); Haile, Berard, (1) *The Navaho Fire Dance, or Corral Dance;* (2) *The Navaho War Dance* (both St. Michael's, Ariz. 1946); Kluckhohn, Clyde, and Leighton, Dorothea, *The Navaho* (Cambridge, Mass. 1946); Wheelwright, Mary C., *Hail Chant and Water Chant* (Santa Fe, N. Mex. 1946); Leighton, D., and Kluckhohn, C., *Children of the People* (Cambridge, Mass. 1947); Amsden, Charles A., *Navaho Weaving, its Technic and History* (Albuquerque, N. Mex. 1949); Wheelwright, Mary C., *Emergence Myth According to the Hanelthnayhe or Upward-Reaching Rite,* recorded by Berard Haile (Santa Fe, N. Mex. 1946); Babington, Suren H., *Navajos, Gods, and Tom-toms* (New York 1950); Reichard, Gladys A., *Navajo Religion* (New York 1950); Waters, Frank, *Masked Gods* (Albuquerque, N. Mex. 1950); McCombe, Leonard, *Navaho Means People* (Cambridge, Mass. 1951); Miller, Joseph, *Monument Valley and the Navajo Country, Arizona and Utah* (New York 1951); Ward, Elizabeth, *No Dudes, Few Women* (Albuquerque, N. Mex. 1951); Underhill, Ruth, *Here Come the Navaho!* (Lawrence, Kan. 1953).

F. W. HODGE,
Southwest Museum, Los Angeles.

NAVAJO MOUNTAIN, peak, Utah, rising high above the Arizona Plateau in the extreme southern part of San Juan County, Utah, at an altitude of 10,416 feet. It has rarely been ascended by white men; there are no motor roads to it, and it can only be visited by pack-trips from Goulding's Trading Post. From its summit, a short distance south of the rim of Glen Canyon of the Colorado River, a great view is obtained of the upper part of the Grand Canyon region, the Henry Mountains, the Vermilion Cliffs, and other features of the high plateaus.

Left: **A Navajo silversmith fashioning a piece of the silver and turquoise jewelry for which the tribe is famous. This worker is on a reservation in northern Arizona.**

American Airlines

NAVAJO

Right: **Navajo weaver at Roughrock on the reservation between Canyon de Chelly and Monument Valley, displaying another Navajo hand skill.**

Left: **A mother carries her child in traditional Indian fashion—lashed to a cradleboard.**

NAVAJO INDIANS

Below: **Worker in natural gas plant on the vast tristate (Arizona-New Mexico-Utah) Navajo Reservation.**

Left: **Navajos hold their own elections for tribal officers and council delegates.**

Below: **Navajo courts deal with all except major crimes committed on the reservation.**

Above: **A desk sergeant of the Navajo Reservation police talks with patrol cars by radio.**

(Top left) Andre de Dienes; all other photographs, Bureau of Indian Affairs

The mountain is forest clad, several springs issue from its sides, and in its northern slope are the Great Rainbow and Owl natural bridges. A dome-shaped uplift of the sedimentary rocks created the mountain, and its top is capped by Dakota sandstone.

NAVAJOITE, năv-ȧ-hō′īte, a rare mineral of dark-brown color, fibrous structure, silky luster, and probable monoclinic symmetry; chemically hydrated vanadium pentoxide, $V_2O_5 \cdot 3H_2O$; found in vanadiferous uranium ore in the Monument No. 2 mine on the Navajo Indian Reservation, Apache County, Arizona, and named in honor of the Navajo Indians on whose reservation it was discovered in 1951.

NAVAL ACADEMY, United States. See UNITED STATES NAVAL ACADEMY.

NAVAL ARCHITECTS AND MARINE ENGINEERS, Society of, a society organized under the laws of New York State on May 10, 1893, its object being the promotion of the art of shipbuilding, both commercial and naval. Classes of membership, which in 1955 numbered 6,200, consist of members, associates, juniors, honorary members and associates, benefactors, and permanent members.

NAVAL ARCHITECTURE, the science and art of designing ships to give them the nautical and structural qualities needed to accomplish their commercial, military, or recreational purposes. The construction of ships belongs to the subject of shipbuilding and will be touched upon in this article only in so far as the problems of construction influence the design of ships. Naval architecture as an art dates back to the earliest efforts of man to improve his means of locomotion and transportation. The primitive canoe probably antedated the wheel, but the promotion of naval architecture to the realm of the sciences did not take place until the 19th century. It lagged behind some of the other sciences largely because it is not an exact science, susceptible to precise mathematical treatment as, for example, astronomy or electricity. Naval architecture must in fact be viewed as an art with scientific foundations, rather than as a science.

During the 18th century European mathematicians developed various theories concerning floating bodies, some of which they considered applicable to ships. Their aim was to express the underwater form of ships mathematically with the hope of arriving at forms that would offer the minimum resistance to passage through the water. In 1721 Emanuel Swedenborg, the Swedish philosopher and mathematician, wrote a treatise on the subject entitled *A Mode of Discovering the Powers of Vessels by the Application of Mechanical Principles.* The most notable scientific contributions to naval architecture during that century were those made by Fredrik Henrik Chapman (1721–1808), a Swedish naval officer who was for many years in charge of Sweden's dockyards. He began the practice of passing on his knowledge of the subject through published papers. The French also contributed much in that way. The more common practice in such matters until the 19th century was for master builders to guard as valuable secrets what had been handed down to them and what they learned from their own experience.

During the first half of the 19th century the advent of iron for shipbuilding and steam for propulsion necessitated a more scientific approach to naval architecture. The advances made in all of the physical sciences during that period also contributed to the development of naval architecture as a science. By the end of the 19th century, existing knowledge in this field was well disseminated and all of the leading shipbuilding countries of the world had schools for teaching naval architecture.

Just as in the past, the primary purpose of practically all ships today is to serve as vehicles for the transportation of men and materials. This is as true of the humble tramp ship carrying in cargo twice the weight of its hull, machinery, and outfit, as it is of the luxury liner carrying a comparatively small amount of cargo, a large amount of fuel to enable it to make high speed, and with its space devoted largely to accommodations for passengers. In the case of warships the things carried consist of ammunition, consumable stores, and fuel, besides weapons, a large crew to man the weapons, and protection against enemy weapons.

Design Requirements.—The naval architect is faced with two fundamental requirements in designing a ship: the ship must be able to go from place to place at a speed appropriate to its service, and it must be able to do so with safety under all reasonable conditions of sea, weather, and loading. The measures that are at his disposal to meet these requirements are, however, circumscribed by the fact that the thing he is designing is a floating object. The weight he can devote to any one element of the design, whether part of the ship itself or to its cargo, is limited by the consideration that a floating body can weigh no more than the water it displaces. Weight devoted to one feature of the design ceases to be available for other features. Thus, every pound of weight entering into the construction and equipment of the ship must serve a useful purpose if it is to stand critical scrutiny. The architect of a structure on land is confronted with no such problems and limitations. One of the chief preoccupations of the naval architect is, therefore, the judicious use of the weight at his disposal and as a corollary the continuous search for lighter materials and equipment and for weight-saving methods in constructing ships.

Nevertheless, by the nature of the problem the characteristics given to any particular ship must always be a compromise of its many important features. This is less so for merchant ships than for warships because the service for which the merchant ship is designed is known with some degree of certainty, whereas there is always considerable uncertainty as to the conditions under which the warship will be called upon to fight, and hence as to the relative importance of its various characteristics. See WARSHIPS for a more complete discussion of this subject.

Classification Societies.—It is at this point appropriate to describe briefly the part that the marine insurance business plays in naval architecture. Marine insurance affects importantly the design of merchant ships because the merchant ship is a commercial proposition that must be able to compete with other ships in the same trade. Its construction must, therefore, be such that the owner will not be at a disadvantage with his competitors in obtaining insurance at reasonable rates. In order to underwrite such risks the marine insurance companies must have some guide as to the quality of the ship they are requested to insure. This is furnished by classification societies that have been established in a number of maritime countries: Lloyd's Register of Shipping combined with the British Corporation Register in Great Britain; the American Bureau of Shipping in the United States; the Bureau Veritas in France, and others. These societies set standards of design, construction, and equipment for merchant ships, many backed by laws and international agreements.

Normally all ships other than warships are built in accordance with the standards and under the supervision of one of these societies or the ship can be built without such supervision, surveyed afterward, and then granted classification if it meets the society's requirements. A classed ship must be surveyed from time to time in order to retain its classification. So long as the ship's classification remains in effect the owner can obtain insurance at prevailing normal rates. The principal features that are covered by classification are reserve buoyancy as implemented by load line regulations, watertight subdivision, communication and other equipment stipulations, minimum requirements as to quality, disposition, and dimensions of materials used in the construction of ships, and regulations with regard to tonnage measurements. Classification thus acts in the common interests of the owner, the insurance underwriters, the shipper, and the traveling public. There is divided opinion whether such associations have been a stimulus to the development of naval architecture, or whether they have been a retarding influence due to their normal conservatism.

Buoyancy.—When a ship is floating in still water the weight of water it displaces is exactly equal to the weight of the ship and its contents. The volume of the enveloping surface of the ship must, however, be greater than the volume of water displaced, otherwise the slightest additional weight would cause it to sink. For safety there must, therefore, be a margin or reserve of buoyancy over and above the buoyancy required for floatation. The percentage of reserve buoyancy provided in a design depends on the kind of vessel in question, ranging from close to zero for a submarine when in diving condition, and about 25 per cent when running on the surface to 100 per cent or more for passenger vessels with watertight upper decks and high sides. Certain types of warships, such as large cruisers and airplane carriers, also have large reserve buoyancy.

Reserve buoyancy fluctuates with the loading of ships. The actual amount considered necessary in merchant ships varies with the size and type of vessel, with the season of the year, and with the geographical area in which the ship will operate. Vessels engaged in winter service in the North Atlantic Ocean are considered to need a greater margin of safety in this respect than in any other service. Because reserve buoyancy can be easily visualized and checked by measuring and controlling the draft and freeboard of ships, load line regulations have become the standard method of controlling reserve buoyancy.

Great Britain, acting through the government Board of Trade in conjunction with Lloyd's classification society and the associations of naval architects, was the first to give legal status to such requirements. So far as merchant ships operating under the American flag are concerned, the first act of Congress requiring compulsory load line markings was passed in 1929 and became effective on Sept. 2, 1930. It applied only to American ships engaged in foreign trade. A Coastwise Load Line Act was passed by Congress in August 1935, covering also vessels operating on the Great Lakes. Broadly speaking, the objects aimed at in load line requirements are to permit the deepest possible loading of the vessel compatible with safety under all conditions of weather and areas of operation, after making provision for minor casualties that might jeopardize the reserve of buoyancy.

Stability.—In addition to adequate buoyancy ships must also have the necessary stability to resist the capsizing effect of wind, waves, unequal load distribution, and flooding to at least a limited extent. Meeting the requirements of stability are unique to naval architecture and present problems encountered in no other engineering profession. The general principles underlying stability are comparatively simple and may be readily understood by analyzing what happens when a ship floating in still water is given a small inclination from the upright as shown in the accompanying figure.

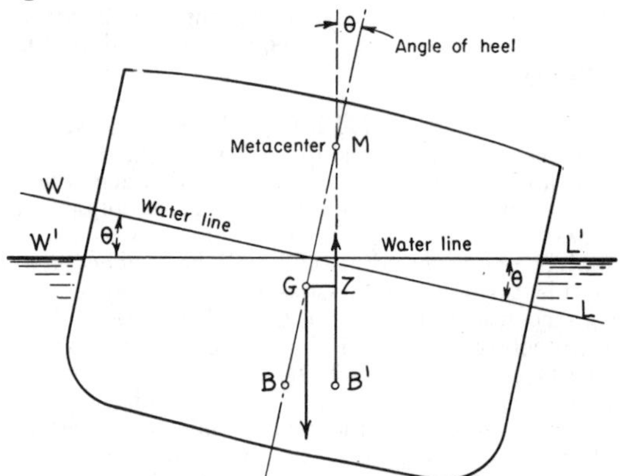

Fig. 1. *W'L'* is water line when ship is upright. *WL* is water line when ship is inclined at angle θ.

The elementary rules of hydrostatics apply to ships under such circumstances. These are that the weight of the ship equals the weight of the water displaced and that with the ship upright the center of gravity *G* of the ship and the center of gravity of the water displaced, known as the center of buoyancy *B,* lie in the same vertical line. When the ship is inclined, the center of buoyancy *B* moves to *B'* because of the change in the shape of the displaced water. The force of buoyancy then acts vertically upward through B^1. If this line cuts the center line of the ship at a point *M* above the center of gravity *G,* the two forces produce a couple tending to rotate the ship back to the upright and the ship is said to be in stable equilibrium. If the vertical through *B'* cuts the center line below *G* the couple that is formed rotates the ship further away from the upright and the ship is said to be in unstable equilibrium. The point *M* is called the transverse metacenter. It is not a fixed point except for small angles of inclination, up to about 15° for ships of normal underwater form. The distance *GM* is called the transverse metacentric height or simply the metacentric height of the ship. It is the criterion used for visualizing broadly a ship's initial stability and behavior when inclined from the upright and for comparing one ship with another in respect to initial stability. Longitudinal stability lends itself to similar analysis with rotation taking place around the athwartship axis of the ship, but as such stability is never critical in ships of normal form and use, no further discussion of this aspect of stability is necessary in this article.

For larger angles of inclination the position of the metacenter *M* moves downward until an angle of heel is reached where it falls below the center of gravity. The ship is then unstable and any further inclination will lead to capsizing. Calculations are made to determine the righting moments at the various angles of inclination. These are plotted as ordinates in terms of righting arms (*GZ* in the diagram) against angles of inclination as abscissae, thus producing a curve which shows the full range of stability of the ship and the inclination at which the righting moment (actually the righting arm *GZ*) is at its maximum and finally becomes zero. The description of the calculations necessary for producing this curve is too complicated and space consuming for inclusion in an article of this kind.

Many factors affect the actual stability and the range of stability of ships such as the location of the center of gravity; draft and form of underwater hull; loading, and freeboard. For example, ships with a high freeboard have a long range of stability through which they can be inclined without danger of capsizing. The range of stability is seldom made less than 50° and for vessels with high freeboard may be as much as 100°. It is the business of the naval architect to provide such stability in the design that the vessel will be safe and seaworthy in all weather if handled with ordinary skill and if the loading is as prescribed.

For safety alone it is not necessary for the metacenter to be above the center of gravity when the ship is upright. A ship can be so designed that with the metacenter slightly below the center of gravity it will list a few degrees to one side or the other until it reaches an inclination at which the metacenter arises above the center of gravity. The ship will remain in the slightly listed position if in still water and if no change in the distribution of weights on board is made. If the vessel has a high freeboard and a long range of stability such a vessel may be entirely safe and seaworthy. Atlantic liners were at one time deliberately designed with little or no initial metacentric height in order to give them an easy and slow rolling motion.

Structural Strength.—In addition to making provision for adequate buoyancy and stability the naval architect must also design ships with sufficient strength to withstand all of the stresses to which they may be subjected in service. The greatest stresses are those which result from the interaction of the forces of gravity and buoyancy causing the ship to bend as a beam. The distribution of the weight of the ship and its contents and the support of buoyancy along its length are not uniform even in still water. When the ship encounters waves at sea the uneven distribution of weight and buoyancy is accentuated many fold.

Under these circumstances two extreme situations may arise: one with the ship supported at mid-length on the crest of a wave; the other with the ends supported on the crests of waves and with the trough of the waves amidship. An assumption must then be made as to the height of the waves because upon this are dependent the bending stresses to which the ship will be subjected. Some naval architects assume that under the most adverse circumstances the height of the waves will not be greater than $\frac{1}{20}$th of their length, the maximum length of storm waves being pretty well known; others assume a height equal to $1.1 \sqrt{\text{wave length}}$. It is, however, impossible to foresee all combinations and contours of waves that may be encountered in a storm, thus there is always some uncertainty as to the magnitude of the forces that may be involved. The actual calculations follow the same lines as those for loaded beams under various conditions of support. In addition to the girder stresses to which ships are subjected there are transverse and panting stresses; concentrated stresses due to heavy local weights such as machinery, armor, and guns; the battering effect of waves, and the stresses that are imposed on the structure in docking or grounding.

Practical experience must come to the aid of theory in deciding on the structural strength needed to resist these forces, because of uncertainty as to their magnitude in many cases. In general, if the design under consideration is not too dissimilar from previous designs that have shown no weakness in service the naval architect can feel reasonably certain of the adequacy of the new design. The accumulated experience of navies and of the merchant service is of great value in confirming or modifying the theoretical considerations, but when novel types or sizes of ships beyond precedent are involved, the skill and judgment of the architect are taxed to the utmost in estimating the various stresses that may be encountered. The normal reaction of the classification societies and marine underwriters is to go slow and to play safe in departing from standard practice. Naval architects, shipbuilders, and ship owners are more likely to be interested in progress and improvements. A long period of discussion is likely to ensue when novel designs or changes in practices are proposed, but with the accumulation of experience the doubtful questions adjust themselves.

Rolling and Pitching.—The action of waves set up rolling, pitching, and other oscillations of a complex nature in ships at sea. Of these, rolling is normally the most important. All such motions are related in a large measure to the stability characteristics of the ship. When a vessel is floating in disturbed water the location of the center of buoyancy is changing constantly, thus causing the vessel to depart from the upright. The force of gravity operating through the center of gravity of the ship is at the same time acting to return the ship to the upright. In the process the ship acquires angular velocity and swings beyond the upright, then a righting moment in the opposite direction comes into play to restore the ship again to the upright, thus rolling begins. In the absence of waves or other disturbances the friction of the water quickly brings a rolling ship to rest.

There are a number of factors that influence rolling. In general, vessels of large metacentric height roll quickly, those of small metacentric height have a sluggish rolling motion. When floating among waves which are large as compared to the vessel, the ship of great metacentric height tends to float like a board, keeping its deck practically parallel to the surface of the waves. The vessel of small metacentric height will, under such circumstances, at times roll toward the wave crest instead of away from it, a very undesirable condition with low freeboard vessels. In practice, vessels vary widely in their periods of oscillation. For large vessels the shortest period from the extreme on one side to the extreme on the other is of the order of three seconds and is encountered in low freeboard warships such as monitors; this because such ships have a large metacentric height. A large vessel of small metacentric height may take as much as ten seconds for a single roll from side to side.

For small angles less than about 15° rolling is practically isochronous, that is, the time taken for a complete roll varies little with the angle. This ceases to be true when larger angles are reached. If there were nothing to retard rolling, ships that are otherwise perfectly seaworthy might reach capsizing angles when among waves whose period coincides with that of the ship because each passing wave would add a little to the amplitude of roll, just as large oscillations can be imparted to a swinging weight by applying to it small but properly timed impulses. The skilled seaman can do much to limit excessive rolling by changing course sufficiently to break up synchronism. The risk of capsizing due to rolling alone is, therefore, not very great.

Rolling even when not excessive is objectionable for a number of reasons. For one thing, the traveling public objects to rolling because it causes seasickness. Next to the common cold, seasickness is probably responsible for more human misery than any other of man's minor ailments. Heavy rolling may result in damage to the ship and to the cargo, as well as injury to the personnel on board. In warships, heavy rolling interferes with accurate gunfire. In all ships rolling of any magnitude is objectionable because it is an operating handicap. For these reasons naval architects have given much thought to antirolling devices. The devices that are or have been employed either in actual service or experimentally to reduce rolling are (1) bilge keels; (2) antirolling tanks; (3) gyroscopic stabilizers; (4) moving weights, and (5) stabilizing fins.

Bilge keels are fins attached to the bottom of the ship at the turn of the bilge. Their longitudinal extent varies from 25 to 75 per cent of the length of the ship and their depth from approximately 1 foot to 3 feet depending on the size and type of ship. Ever since their effectiveness in reducing rolling was first demonstrated, around 1870, bilge keels have been fitted to nearly all ocean-going vessels, both commercial and naval. If properly proportioned and fitted, they reduce the maximum angle of roll to less than one-half of what it would be without them. They also slow down the period of rolling. Their effectiveness increases with the speed of the ship.

The earliest installation of antirolling tanks was made in about 1874. Broadly speaking, this device consists of tanks opposite each other at the sides of the ship, connected at the bottom by a tunnel, or large pipe, through which water flows from side to side as the ship rolls. In some installations the shifting of the water is accelerated and controlled by pumps. Such installations are particularly suited to icebreakers, as bilge keels cannot be used on such ships. In all cases the shifting of water or other liquids from side to side if properly timed resists the righting moment of the ship and thereby dampens the rolling. Gyroscopic stabilizers have advantages as well as disadvantages compared to other devices. Some of the disadvantages are high cost, weight, delicacy of adjustment, and the power required for their operation. Gyroscopic stabilizers have been installed on many yachts and on some large ships, the largest being a ship of about 41,000 tons displacement. The experience on this ship was that it reduced the angle of roll about 44 per cent when the free roll away from the vertical was as much as 5°. The weight of the installation came to about 700 tons. Retractable stabilizing fins that can be moved in and out at will and controlled from within the ship are recent antirolling devices. They have achieved a considerable degree of popularity, both for certain types of warships and for passenger ships.

Speed and Resistance.—To the layman the most interesting fact about ships is usually their speed. The keen interest taken by the general public in the speed records of transatlantic passenger liners illustrates this point. The methods in use at present for determining the power required to drive ships at desired speeds and the underwater forms best suited to economical propulsion are comparatively recent developments in naval architecture. They are based on the scientific research during the last half of the 19th century of William Froude, an English engineer, and of his son R. E. Froude. These methods were later carried to a high state of perfection in the model basin at Washington, D.C., by the late Rear Admiral David W. Taylor, Construction Corps, United States Navy.

The principles underlying these methods are that the resistance of a ship in moving through water at a given speed is made up of three factors, first, the skin friction between water and the surface of the ship. This is dependent only on the nature of the surface as to smoothness, the wetted area, and the speed of the ship. It varies slightly with variations in the form of the ship because such variations affect the velocity of the water over the hull, but in general this variation is too slight to be of importance in practice. The second element is wave-making resistance, and is due to the waves that are formed by a ship moving through the water. Power is required to produce these waves and must come from the power driving the ship. The third element is eddy-making resistance, and is due to the eddies formed in the water behind square corners of the hull and attachments, such as sternposts or propeller struts.

The skin friction component can be calculated with considerable accuracy from experiments on the frictional resistance of plane surfaces towed through water at known speeds. Froude demonstrated that the remaining resistance (wave and eddy-making) of a full-sized ship could be calculated with considerable accuracy from careful determination of similar resistance of a small model of the ship when towed at a speed corresponding to the desired speed of the ship, the corresponding speeds of model and ship being in the ratio of the square roots of their linear dimensions. For a ship 500 feet long, for example, and a model 20 feet long, the ratio of linear dimensions is 25; so that the actual speed of the model corresponding to 20 knots for the ship, would be $20 \div \sqrt{25}$, or four knots. Model experiments lend themselves to comparatively inexpensive and rapid investigations of the effect on speed and power due to changes in shape and dimensions which would be impracticable if attempted on full-sized ships. The principles followed in passing from models to full-sized ships can also be applied in passing from one full-sized ship to another, provided the two ships are similar, or nearly so.

Model Basins.—Model basins thus became the principal tools of the naval architect in designing ships. They are found in practically all shipbuilding countries of the world. There are at present some thirty-five model-testing stations with a total of forty-eight basins. The first model basin was built by William Froude, in Torquay, England, in 1872. One of the earliest and the most advanced basin for its time was the one designed and built by Naval Constructor David W. Taylor for the United States Navy in Washington, D.C. in 1899. A new station was completed and put in operation by the U. S. Navy in 1940 at Carderock, Maryland, a few miles outside of Washington. It was named the David Taylor Model Basin to commemorate Rear Admiral Taylor's world renowned work in this field. This station has four separate basins —one for the normal testing of ship models in deep water, a second for testing models of ferryboats, towboats and barges in shallow water, a third for testing models of high-speed craft, such as motorboats, patrol boats and coastal torpedo boats, and a fourth for testing special models and for conducting extended research which cannot be worked into the normal busy schedule of the large basins.

The main basin was originally 963 feet long but was extended in 1945 and 1946 to a length of 2,775 feet. Its width is 51 feet and its depth 22 feet. Two model towing carriages span this basin having speeds of 15 and 18 knots respectively. Models up to 32 feet in length and displacement up to 10,000 pounds may be towed in this basin; the standard model length is about 20 feet. The shallow water basin is about 250 feet long and 51 feet wide. Its depth can be varied to suit the test being conducted, from a maximum of 10 feet down to a minimum of a few inches. A turning basin formed like the letter J at one end of the shallow water basin makes it possible to study the behavior of models up to 20 feet long when making turns up to about 180°.

The high-speed model basin is 2,968 feet long. It has two carriages capable of being operated at 40 and 60 knots respectively. It is 21 feet wide, 10 feet deep, for a length of 1,160 feet, and 16 feet deep for the remaining length. The small model basin is 142 feet long, 10 feet wide, and 5 feet 6 inches deep. Models in this basin have a length not exceeding 5 or 6 feet. They are towed by what is known as a gravity dynamometer, actuated by a falling weight, or by a special device, depending upon the test. There is at Carderock a circulating water channel built for flow studies and special investigations on ship models, in which the model floats stationary in a moving stream of water. This channel is 22 feet wide, 9 feet deep, and the moving water in it has a maximum speed of 10 knots.

The towing models in the cold weather countries of northern Europe are generally made of paraffin wax, which is cast in a mold roughly representing the shape and scaled-down dimensions of the hull of the ship. In the warmer countries of Europe, such as Italy, and in the United States, the towing models are normally made of wood. Recently a wax compound has been developed that will retain its shape under higher temperatures. Both the wax and the wood models are roughed to shape in special machines and are then finished by hand. All large model basins, both in the United States and abroad, are equipped with self-propulsion dynamometers, for fitting in or on the model, by which the ship models are made to drive themselves along the model basin. An electric motor, combined with devices to measure thrust, torque, and revolutions, is connected by a shaft passing through the model to a small propeller representing the design proposed for the ship.

Using the data obtained from the towing and the self-propulsion tests of the model, it is possible to determine not only the effective horsepower necessary to tow the full-sized ship but the horsepower which the propelling machinery must develop, taking into account the mechanical friction losses between the engine and the propeller, as well as the hydraulic loss in the propeller itself. The ratio between the effective horsepower as defined above and the horsepower developed by the propelling machinery (indicated horsepower for reciprocating engines, brake horsepower for Diesel engines, and shaft horsepower for turbines) is called the propulsion coefficient. It ranges from about .6 to .8 and depends on the friction in the machinery and shaft bearings, on the efficiency of the propellers, on the shape of the stern of the ship, on the flow of water to the propellers, but mainly on the number of propellers used to drive the ship.

With four propellers driving the ship the propulsive coefficient is about .6, with two propellers it is about .7, and with a single propeller the coefficient is about .8. This range of values represents fair, average practice obtained in well-designed modern vessels. Lower values than these are usually due to difficult service requirements, inefficient hull design, unsuitable propellers, or a poor selection of machinery. While single screw ships show the highest propulsive efficiency, the limit of power which can be developed by a single screw is constantly being increased. In addition, there are other reasons for preferring multiple screws to a single screw—such as greater security against complete breakdown at sea, better maneuverability, and the advantage of being able to subdivide the propelling machinery between several compartments—this being particularly important in warships to guard against complete disablement from a single lucky hit.

Influence of Materials.—As naval architecture has been largely influenced by the materials used in ship construction, brief allusion to these materials seems appropriate. The material used in the construction of ships underwent, broadly speaking, two changes during the 19th century: a change from wood to iron, which dates from approximately the middle of the century, and a change from iron to steel, which dates from about 1880. Wood is still used as the principal material for building small vessels, such as yachts, motorboats, small tugs, and barges.

The material now generally used for ship construction is a plain carbon steel, frequently called medium steel, which in a standard test specimen exhibits an ultimate tensile (or breaking) strength of approximately 60,000 pounds per square inch of cross-sectional area and an elongation (or stretch) of 25 per cent of the original length of the test section of the specimen. Such steel was not produced in the United States in commercial quantities until 1883 when it was specified for the ships of what was then called the New Navy. With the demand for weight saving in warship construction as well as in the construction of high-speed passenger liners, steels of higher tensile strength and better all-round properties than medium steel have been dveloped. Such steels are more expensive than medium steel, but have made it possible for the naval architect to produce ship designs that would not have been practical with medium steel. However, medium steel is still the most extensively used grade for hull construction except when more strength for the same weight, or the same strength for less weight, is desired, especially in warships, in which case higher strength steels are used in the most highly stressed locations, such as the upper decks, the sheer strakes, the flat keel, and certain other portions of the hull plating and structure.

The high tensile steel most commonly used in warship construction is one having an ultimate tensile strength of 70,000 to 90,000 pounds per square inch and an elongation of 22 per cent. This steel contains not over .18 per cent carbon and up to 1.30 per cent manganese (as compared with .31 per cent maximum carbon and .75 per cent maximum manganese in medium steel), and usually contains small percentages of silicon, vanadium, and titanium. This alloy, and various other alloys offered commercially as high tensile steels, are often used in the construction of merchant ships.

In warship construction, a steel known as special treatment steel (STS), which is specially heat treated during manufacture, was developed for its ballistic qualities and has been used as armor protection. This steel usually contains about 3 per cent nickel, or equivalent alloying elements, and, in addition to its ballistic properties, exhibits a tensile strength above 100,000 pounds per square inch and over 27 per cent elongation. STS is being used in increasing quantities in warship construction in the dual role of hull plating or decking and for its ballistic protection, but has not been used extensively for merchant ship construction. A steel known as HY8O containing about 2 per cent nickel has come into use for merchant ships where strength and weight saving are of particular importance.

Aluminum alloys are used extensively on warships as well as merchant ships for upper works, stateroom bulkheads, furniture, and certain doors, because of the great weight saving that can be effected thereby. Chromium-nickel stainless steels are used where strength or corrosion resistance, or both, are governing considerations. This latter kind of steel must, however, be used with caution because under certain conditions of exposure to salt water it is no more corrosion resistant than medium steel.

Welding.—The progress of welding has had a marked effect on naval architecture both in the design of ships and in the selection of materials. The use of welding, in place of riveting, in hull construction has effected considerable weight savings by eliminating plate overlaps, butt straps and rivetheads. It also effects savings in time and often in cost. The problem of achieving water and oil tightness has been greatly simplified. As a consequence, 100 per cent welded hulls in merchant ships and the smaller classes of warships (destroyers and smaller) are becoming the rule rather than the exception, and welding is displacing riveting more and more in the largest warships and merchant ships. Welding is also being used in other parts of ships. Piping is extensively welded, and many parts, such as stems, sternposts, shaft struts, and machinery foundations, formerly made as castings or forgings, are being fabricated by welding together formed plates or shapes, sometimes combined with smaller forgings or castings. Welding has made it possible for the naval architect to place the metal where it does the most good.

While welding has many advantages, it has also introduced new problems or focused attention on old, sometimes unrecognized problems. To realize the full benefits of welding, the design must be such as to take advantage of prefabrication of subassemblies and so that erection will take place in the proper sequence to avoid distortion and locked up stresses. Design must also allow adequate access to all joints for proper welding, and must be governed by the properties of the materials which it is necessary to use to ensure weldability. In most instances the materials best suited to ship construction can be utilized. Weldability can be assured by specifying more closely the carbon and other composition limits of the material.

Two closely related and important factors on which welding has focused attention are notches and notch-sensitivity of structural materials. Welded ship design must pay more careful attention to the avoidance of sharp corners or other abrupt changes in section, which constitute notches and disturb the uniform distribution of stresses, than was necessary in riveted designs. Provision must also be made for the exclusion of notch-sensitive materials, since such materials do not readily stretch and deform to redistribute concentrated stresses, but instead often start to crack at a notch even when the external loads are little more than normal. Notch-sensitivity is intensified by low temperatures.

The replacement of wood by iron and other metals as shipbuilding materials and the substitution of steam for sail to drive ships exercised a particularly great influence on naval architecture because these changes made it possible to increase the size of ships. These developments necessitated also the use of scientific methods wherever possible in designing ships. The tendency toward an increase in size has been very marked since 1885, so that now ships have reached dimensions which are limited only by the draft of water in channels and in harbors, by the docking and wharf facilities available in the ports to which they trade, by the size of drydocks in which they must be placed for painting and repairs, and by the width of canal locks through which they must pass.

Subdivision.—In the field of naval architecture as distinguished from shipbuilding, one of the most important advances has been the improvement in the design of merchant ships, particularly in passenger ships, to make them less vulnerable to sinking or capsizing after sustaining collision or war damage. Providing protection against the hazards of sinking or capsizing as the result of battle damage has always been a major consideration in the design of warships, but the problem there has been somewhat different from that of merchant ships because the question of cost is secondary in the case of warships, and earning a return on the investment is not involved.

If the underwater shell of a ship is torn open by a collision, or other cause, that portion of the ship to which the sea has access will fill with water to the level of the sea outside. The effect on the ship as a whole will be twofold: (1) The ship will settle bodily into the water by an amount which will depend on the quantity of water entering the ship. At the same time, unless the flooded compartments are located amidship, the ship will trim by the head or by the stern, as the case may be. The effect will be to reduce the distance above water of the deck to which the watertight bulkheads are carried. If the sinkage is such as to bring this deck below the level of the sea, water will enter adjacent undamaged compartments by flowing along this deck and will cause progressive flooding until the ship founders through loss of buoyancy. (2) The flooding of one or more compartments will, in general, change the transverse stability of the ship. The mathematical proof of this statement is too lengthy for an article of this kind. Suffice it to say that the net effect of flooding one or more compartments may be either a gain or a loss in metacentric height, depending on the proportions of the ship and the length of the flooded spaces. If there is a loss of metacentric height, the ship may become unstable and take a severe list or even capsize.

The foundering of a ship, owing to sinkage and trim, is usually a relatively slow process, often taking several hours, but capsizing, owing to instability, if it occurs, is likely to be sudden. For example, the S.S. *Titanic,* after sideswiping an iceberg, remained afloat for about three hours, although the starboard side was torn open for a distance of about 300 feet. On the other hand, the S.S. *Empress of Ireland* capsized and sank in 15 minutes, and the S.S. *Lusitania* capsized and sank in 20 minutes. If war damage, instead of collision damage, is sustained, loss of the vessel may follow the damage by only a few minutes, whether from foundering or capsizing. In both World Wars there were, however, instances of ships remaining afloat many hours and even days after being hit by torpedoes. This was the experience especially during World War II with ships built under the sponsorship of the Maritime Commission.

The prevention of either foundering or capsizing lies in fitting transverse bulkheads so spaced that (1) leakage water will be confined to an amount which will not sink or trim the ship sufficiently to immerse the tops of watertight bulkheads, and (2) the lost water plane will be confined to an extent which will not cause sufficient loss of metacentric height to result in an excessive angle of heel.

Naval architects in all countries recognized at an early date that ships could and should, by appropriate watertight subdivision, be made safer against sinking than was the current practice, but as shipping is internationally a highly competitive business, no nation by itself could require radical departures along these lines in the design of its ships without detriment to its shipowners, because from the operating point of view, closely spaced bulkheads interfere with cargo handling and stowage, with passenger accommodations, and with machinery arrangements, not to mention a higher original investment because of the greater cost of building such ships. In the extreme case, if bulkheads were spaced very closely together, the ship might be rendered entirely useless as a commercial investment. On the other hand, a ship with no transverse bulkheads would be unable to survive any leakage beyond that which could be handled by the pumps. Somewhere between these two extremes lies the best design. The history of improvement in the watertight subdivision of merchant ships is an interesting study. It is the history of marine disasters and of the repercussions of such disasters on the public and on the legislative bodies of governments. These have finally required shipowners to provide certain minimum watertight subdivision in ships carrying passengers beyond 12 in number.

The classification societies and marine underwriters at an early date required the fitting of a peak or collision bulkhead. Regulations with regard to loading and reserve buoyancy were also established many years ago and have already been mentioned. When screw propellers replaced paddle wheels, an afterpeak bulkhead became an obvious necessity to prevent leakage through the stern tubes from flooding the ship. The fitting of a double bottom in larger ships, that is, an inner skin in the way of the large compartments, such as machinery spaces and cargo holds, was soon adopted as the best way of protecting ships against the effects of flooding caused by striking submerged objects or by grounding. There was, however, considerable reluctance on the part of shipowners to add anything more in the way of transverse bulkheads, except as needed for strength and other structural reasons, because of the operating disadvantages mentioned above.

In 1866, the British passenger ship S.S. *London* sank with a loss of 233 persons. After investigation of the accident, the British Institution of Naval Architects recommended that all ships should be so constructed that they would remain afloat with one compartment open to the sea, and that passenger ships should remain afloat with two adjacent compartments open to the sea. This society had, however, no powers to place its recommendations into effect. In 1882, Lloyd's *Register of Shipping* incorporated subdivision requirements in its rules for the first time, and specified that ships more than 280 feet long were to have transverse watertight bulkheads, the number required increasing with the length of the ship. In 1890, the British Board of Trade suggested the first scientific approach to the question of spacing transverse bulkheads by calling attention to the fact that a curve of floodable length could be plotted for each ship, which would make it possible to determine, by making certain assumptions, the maximum length of the ship which could be flooded without causing the ship to sink when damaged at any particular point. In 1895, the German steamship *Elbe* sank with the loss of 335 passengers, which fact led the Society of German Shipowners to issue subdivision regulations based on floodable length. These regulations divided merchant ships into two classes: primarily passenger ships and primarily cargo ships. The regulations called for different degrees of subdivisions for the two classes, but there was no general acceptance of these regulations.

The disaster which finally impressed on the public, on shipowners, on insurance societies, and on governments the necessity for better subdivision of ships was the sinking in the north Atlantic, on her maiden voyage in April 1912, of the S.S. *Titanic,* with the loss of 1,513 lives. After a preliminary investigation of the disaster by the British Board of Trade, the British government invited an International Conference on Safety of Life at Sea to meet in London in 1913. The conference agreed on certain fundamentals and on curves for defining the minimum and maximum subdivision for the two extreme classes of ships mentioned above. The convention was signed in January 1914, but owing to the World War, which started in July 1914, none of the signatory nations put the regulations fully into effect. After the war, British shipowners engaged in replacing war losses, contended that the subdivision requirements of the 1914 conference for ships primarily of the cargo type and carrying few passengers were too severe and requested relaxation of the rules by the Board of Trade. After a conference between British and American representatives in Washington in 1920, it was agreed to relax the requirements for the cargo type of ship. At an international conference in 1929 agreement was reached on many of the moot questions. After the loss of the S.S. *Morro Castle* by fire in 1934 and the S.S. *Mohawk* by collision in 1935 the United States Senate appointed a committee to investigate ship safety for United States vessels. This committee recommended in Senate Report 184, 1937, higher standards for subdivision, fire protection, stability in damaged condition, and other matters affecting the safety of ships at sea. The International Conference on Safety at Sea held in London in 1948 adopted a convention to replace the 1929 convention which includes some of the recommendations of the senate report. Ships flying the American flag and, therefore, subject to United States Coast Guard inspection are required to meet standards that are actually higher than called for by the 1948 convention as they include many of the requirements of Senate Report 184.

The decision as to the number and spacing of watertight bulkheads to insure the maximum chance of survival of a ship in case of collision would, on first thought, seem to be a simple one. Actually, it is very complicated and becomes, in the last analysis, a compromise as have so many other decisions in naval architecture. There are two opposed points of view in this matter: one is that the bulkheads should be spaced as far apart as is possible while still permitting the flooding of the predetermined number of compartments; the other is that the closer the bulkheads are spaced, the safer the ship (leaving out of consideration the operating disadvantages in close spacing already mentioned above). At the international conference, the latter point of view prevailed; namely, that there is continually increasing safety with decreased bulkhead spacing. Instead, however, of prescribing one-, two-, or three-compartment subdivisions with the bulkheads spaced as far apart as possible within each grade or subdivision, the convention gave a permissible length of compartment, which is obtained by multiplying the floodable length by a factor less than unity or as a limit equal to unity, called the *factor of subdivision.* In order to describe briefly the subdivisional characteristics of ships, the terms *one-compartment* ship, *two-compartment* ship, *three-compartment* ship, etc., were adopted, meaning that when any two adjacent compartments of a ship can be flooded without submerging the vessel below the margin line (a line 3 inches below the uppermost deck to which the transverse bulkheads are carried), it is termed a two-compartment ship; when three adjacent compartments can be so flooded, it is termed a three-compartment ship, etc. Obviously, the maximum flooding is coupled with the minimum damage when such damage occurs where a bulkhead meets the side of the ship. If the damage does not come at a bulkhead, then the greater the distance between bulkheads, the greater the permissible damage which will flood only one compartment.

For the reasons already stated, these standards were not made compulsory on ship operators, but, in the case of the United States, the Bureau of Marine Inspection and Navigation of the federal government, which has jurisdiction over such matters, adopted many of them, especially the ones having to do with fire prevention and extinction. The Maritime Commission went a step further in its designs by exceeding many of the requirements of the international agreements. For example, all new cargo vessels under its jurisdiction, such as the Liberty ships, were required to have not less than a one-compartment standard of subdivision. A vessel is said to be a one-compartment ship when it can survive flooding of any one of its main compartments, throughout a large part of its operating range under normal loading conditions.

It is difficult to evaluate the exact effect which design policies and practices have on any complicated engineering product such as a ship, but the following data are interesting as indicative of at least the broad general influence of the "safer ships" design policy adopted by the Maritime Commission. During World War II, 758 merchant vessels operating under the War Shipping Administration suffered war damage. Of this number 467 did not have Maritime Commission sponsorship in design. Of these 467 ships, 80 per cent sank as the result of the damage received. Of the 291 ships which were built in accordance with Maritime Commission subdivision and other safety at sea practices, only 53 per cent sank as the result of damage received. There were at least six of these ships whose survival can be ascribed definitely to the compartmentation policy adopted by the Maritime Commission. It was clearly established also that ships built to these standards remained afloat longer than ships not so designed even when they sank eventually, thus providing more time for the personnel to abandon ship.

The whole problem of bulkhead spacing is also complicated by the kind of cargo which happens to be in the compartment at the time of flooding. To arrive at any conclusion in the matter, an assumption must be made as to the permeability of each compartment. By *permeability* is meant the extent to which leakage water can permeate flooded spaces. It is expressed as a percentage of the total volume of the space under consideration. For example, an empty hold can take nearly its entire volume of seawater. The permeability of such a space is, therefore, about 98 per cent. On the other hand, a ballast tank already entirely filled with water can take no more water; therefore, its permeability is zero. Spaces used for various purposes may have any degree of permeability between these two extremes. A hold filled with canned goods in cases has a permeability of about 30 per cent; one filled with furniture in boxes, about 80 per cent. It will be seen that the effect on the ship, as a whole, of flooding a given space will depend on the amount of water which enters this space, which in turn will depend on its permeability. Hence, before the effects of flooding can be calculated, definite values for the permeability of the spaces involved must be assumed, but the actual permeability in service cannot be known by the naval architect for all conditions, as it may vary considerably from voyage to voyage, depending on the amount and kind of cargo carried. In the last analysis, mathematics can take the naval architect only part way in arriving at the best solution for the subdivision of ships, after which, judgment and a suitable compromise of the conflicting considerations must do the rest. See also Ship; Shipping and Shipbuilding Terms; Submarine—*3. The Modern Submarine.*

Bibliography.—Rossell, Henry E., and Chapman, L. B., eds., *Principles of Naval Architecture,* 2 vols. (New York 1939); Hovgaard, William, *Structural Design of Warships,* 2d ed. rev. (Annapolis, Md., 1940); Manning, George C., *Manual of Ship Construction* (New York 1942); Rabl, Samuel S., *Practical Principles of Naval Architecture,* 2d ed. rev. (New York 1942); Taylor, David W., *The Speed and Power of Ships,* 2d ed. rev. (Washington, D.C., 1943); Comstock, John P., *Introduction to Naval Architecture,* 2d ed. (New York 1944); Van Lammeren, W. P. A., Troost, L., and Koning, J. G., *Resistance, Propulsion and Steering of Ships* (Amsterdam 1948); Adair, Jamie, and Gillmer, T. C., *Fundamentals of Naval Construction and Damage Control* (Annapolis, Md., 1951); Attwood, Edward L., Pengelly, Herbert S., and Sims, Alfred J., *Theoretical Naval Architecture* (New York 1953); Baker, Elijah, *Introduction to Steel Shipbuilding,* 2d ed. (New York 1953); Barnaby, Kenneth C., *Basic Naval Architecture,* 5th ed. (Tuckahoe, N.Y., 1967).

J. A. Furer,
Rear Admiral, United States Navy (Retired).

NAVAL AVIATION, a term embracing the aviation forces, afloat or ashore, which are organic parts of a navy, including aircraft carriers and seaplane tenders with their complements of aircraft, naval air stations, and training and support facilities.

The military airplane developed rapidly during the early part of the 20th century, and provided a new, lethal weapon in sea and land warfare. Recognizing its potential, almost all of the world's navies were quick to adopt the airplane to help carry out their individual missions. In the case of several modern navies the airplane has become the dominant instrument of naval power, playing a wide variety of roles which cover the complete spectrum of naval operations. In other navies the airplane has been assigned important, but nevertheless subordinate, naval tasks; Russia, for example, tends to pattern her naval structure after that of pre-World War II Germany, using the submarine as the basic component of her navy.

The character and importance of a naval air force depend upon the tasks assigned to the navy of which it is a part. Is the navy required to ensure the day-to-day freedom of the seas and to promote, protect, and support its country's interests on and beyond the seas? Is it to be employed mainly to stop its enemies from communicating through the seas with each other? Or does its mission lie somewhere between these two extremes? The answers to these questions determine the role of airplanes—and indeed the very design of the aircraft themselves—in any given navy; thus, the character of a nation's navy and its air component is determined by basic national policy. The fundamental military policy of a nation, in turn, is determined in great part by geographical and economic factors, including access to critical raw materials, dependence upon sea lines of communications with overseas allies and suppliers, and the ability of the nation's economy to support military expenditures.

The navies of the United States and of the Union of Socialist Soviet Republics, a maritime nation on the one hand and a land power on the other, provide classic examples of the effects of national policy on the character of naval aviation. In peacetime United States naval forces must ensure the day-to-day freedom of the seas for herself and her allies; and in time of war they must control critical sea areas so that the country may have access to strategic raw materials, so that she may project her military power overseas wherever required, and so that she may deny these advantages to enemies. Accordingly United States naval aviation relies primarily upon strategically mobile, carrier-based aircraft designed to carry out a wide variety of tasks in peace as well as in war. On the other hand, the naval forces of the USSR, a land power dominating the Eurasian land mass without prime dependence on the seas, have been developed (as would be expected) primarily to sever sea lines of communications and thereby to isolate the various maritime nations from each other. Consequently, the naval air forces of the Soviet Union consist primarily of strategically immobile, land-based bombers whose primary mission is to search out and attack transport and fighting ships within range of Soviet bases.

The air forces of the other navies of the world fall between these two extremes, with their characters strongly influenced by national economic capacities as well as by geography. In the case of Japan, a maritime nation historically dependent upon sea lines of communication for her economic survival, the major efforts toward reconstituting her defense forces in the post-World War II years have been directed at reestablishing the navy she lost as a result of the war; but as a result of economic limitations the Japanese Navy is of a purely defensive character, designed for antisubmarine warfare and for escort of shipping vessels. Accordingly, the country's naval aircraft are limited to land-based patrol aircraft. In another part of the world, the Royal Netherlands Navy is also limited in size and defensive in posture, because the Dutch economy cannot support a large navy, no matter how desirable such an institution might be from a national point of view. Because of the maritime geography of the widespread Netherlands interests, the country's primary requirement is a strategically mobile force capable of protecting any part of its extended sea communications. As a result, the Dutch Navy relies heavily on carrier-based antisubmarine aircraft.

EVOLUTION OF NAVAL AVIATION

Early Naval Aircraft.—The major navies of the world became interested in the airplane as an adjunct of naval power in the first decade of the 20th century. Early experiments were crude and progress was relatively slow, yet the United States, England, France, Japan, Holland, Germany, Italy, and Russia all concluded that heavier-than-air aircraft could make contributions to their navies. Germany, in addition, acquired some rigid airships, and Italy experimented with semirigid lighter-than-air craft. An Italian naval officer, Lt. Mario Calderara, received flight instruction in March, 1909, from Orville Wright, thereby becoming the first known military pilot in history.

Italy, during its war with Turkey in 1911–1912, became the first country to conduct air warfare operations of even a limited sort. The Italian Navy participated in the operations to the extent that the airships used were manned jointly by army and navy crews.

Several early experiments indicated the future role that the airplane would play in the United States Navy. In November 1910 a civilian pilot, Eugene Ely, took off from a platform installed on the bow of the cruiser U.S.S. *Birmingham,* lying at anchor in Hampton Roads, Va., and successfully landed ashore. In January 1911, Ely took off from a field at San Francisco and landed aboard the U.S.S. *Pennsylvania* on a crudely constructed flight deck. His plane was brought to a halt by means of hooks, mounted on the landing gear, which picked up lines fastened to sandbags on the deck. The plane was then turned around, and Ely flew it off the platform and returned to the shore. Before the month was out, Glenn Curtiss, following a line of development in which a Frenchman, Henri Fabre, had achieved partial success the preceding summer, took off from the water and landed again, thereby marking the advent of the practical hydroplane. In February 1911, Curtiss flew from the shore to the U.S.S. *Pennsylvania,* landed his hydroplane alongside the ship, and was hoisted aboard; his aircraft was then placed back in the water, and he flew to shore to complete the circuit. Further experiments were conducted with great vigor in the United States and England, and firms in both countries were soon manufacturing practical flying boats.

In early 1913, American naval aviators based ashore at Guantanamo Bay, Cuba, participated in fleet maneuvers in which they flew scouting missions, spotted mines, searched for submarines, and experimented with aerial photography and bombing; and in July 1913, British seaplanes also took part in fleet maneuvers, operating with the H.M.S. *Hermes.* One of the first military actions in which naval aircraft played a role occurred during the deployment of United States naval forces at Tampico and Veracruz, Mexico, in early 1914, when Lt. (j.g.) P. N. L. Bellinger made successful reconnaissance flights over the enemy lines at Veracruz. These early tests established the capability of aircraft to operate with the fleet under wartime conditions.

World War I.—The outbreak of World War I, a few months after the Veracruz action, provided the first real test of naval aviation. Great Britain used naval airplanes with considerable effectiveness in a number of missions: in the Dardanelles campaign seaplanes based aboard the *Ark Royal* and the *Ben-My-Chree* spotted for naval gunfire, flew reconnaissance missions, searched for mines, bombed enemy troops, attacked railway lines between Constantinople and Europe, and attacked enemy shipping with both bombs and crude torpedoes; and in other theaters the British used naval aircraft to attack isolated German ships and to assist in the defense of the British Isles against German airplane and zeppelin raids. By the end of the war the chief duties of the Royal Naval Air Service had become reconnaissance for the fleet, and searching for and attacking U-boats.

Throughout the war British naval aircraft consisted primarily of seaplanes; but the Royal Navy continued to experiment with landplanes, and in 1916 selected the cruiser *Furious* for conversion to a carrier with flight decks both forward and aft of the bridge superstructure. Landplanes could be launched from this ship, but because of the obstruction of the bridge, could not be regularly recovered. Despite this severe shortcoming, planes from the *Furious* attacked dirigible sheds at Tønder, Denmark, on July 19, 1918. The conversion of the *Argus* to a flush-deck carrier had been started in 1917, marking the advent of the modern aircraft carrier.

The Germans used naval aircraft in their blockade of England, attacking allied merchant vessels with bombs and torpedoes and, on occasion, alighting near merchant ships to place boarding parties aboard; and airplanes operating from the raider *Wolf* herded merchant ships toward the raider by the threat of bombing. Naval zeppelins attacked Allied shipping, raided London, and performed reconnaissance missions against Allied naval forces and shipping.

Both Italy and the Austro-Hungarian Empire used aircraft in their naval operations against each other in the Adriatic Sea—for reconnaissance, for aerial defense, and for bombing cities. The Italian Navy's principal use of aircraft, however, was in the protection of shipping, particularly against submarines. For this purpose seaplane stations were constructed ringing the Italian Peninsula, and at Homs and Tripoli in Libya on the Mediterranean coast of Africa. In an effort to free themselves from complete dependence upon fixed bases, the Italians also converted two ships to seaplane carriers.

The major mission of United States naval aviation in World War I was antisubmarine warfare, including bombing attacks against Germany's submarine bases which set the pattern for the "attack at source" concept of later years. In France, England, Ireland, Italy, and on the coasts of the United States, bases were established from which flying boats and nonrigid airships operated. Although aircraft were crude by present standards and lacked effective weapons and searching devices, Navy pilots attacked 25 submarines and sank or damaged 12 of them. Because of the urgency of antisubmarine patrol during World War I, the United States Navy virtually suspended its experiments with ship-based aircraft.

The flying boat was the principal naval combat aircraft in World War I, being used primarily for antisubmarine warfare. At the end of the war, the already well-established capabilities of flying boats were dramatically demonstrated when the first transatlantic flight was made by the United States Navy's *NC-4* in May 1919.

Between the Wars.—From its successful utilization in World War I it was apparent that aviation had become a permanent and significant addition to naval warfare, but the emergence of the aircraft as a major component of naval power occurred only as the result of the persistent application of aeronautical technology to naval needs in postwar years. Many avenues were explored in attempts to adapt the airplane to naval usage, and from the more successful efforts evolved the aircraft carrier, specialized carrier aircraft, ship-based observation seaplanes, and large patrol aircraft (both land-based and sea-based).

Following the lead of Great Britain, the United States and Japan undertook serious development of aircraft carriers and their tactical employment in the early 1920's. The first United States carrier, the *Langley,* was converted from the collier *Jupiter* and commissioned in March 1922. A small Japanese carrier, *Hosyo,* was commissioned in late 1922, the first carrier designed as such from the keel up. A number of problems were resolved on these early carriers: arresting techniques were worked out, refueling and rearming facilities were developed, and the necessity of a bridge structure on one side of the flight deck for the purpose of conning the ship and controlling air operations was demonstrated. Some of these features have been retained in modern aircraft carriers.

The Washington Naval Treaty of 1922 set a limit on the total carrier tonnage of each signatory nation; and it limited the displacement of individual new carriers to 27,000 tons, although it allowed the construction of a restricted number of larger carriers through the completion of vessels whose keels had been laid and through the conversion of existing ships. Under the terms of the treaty the United States ultimately converted two battle cruiser hulls laid down in 1920 and 1921 to the carriers *Saratoga* and *Lexington;* the Japanese converted a battle cruiser and a battleship; the British completed the *Eagle,* reworked the *Furious* to an aircraft carrier, and also converted two of its sister ships; France turned the battleship *Normandie* into the carrier *Béarn.* Through new construction during the 1920's and early 1930's, the signatory nations attempted to gain the maximum possible number of carriers within their overall tonnage limitations. As a result, a class of light fleet carriers of less than 20,000 tons was developed as the best compromise between small hull size and effective complement of aircraft. In the United States Navy these included the *Ranger,* the *Enterprise,* the *Yorktown,* and the *Wasp.* Although by 1939 most of the Washington Treaty signatories were no longer seriously abiding by treaty provisions, the 27,000-ton provision had a particular influence on the United States carrier program, and the famed *Essex* class ships of World War II were designed within this tonnage limitation. (See also NAVAL CONFERENCES—*Washington Conference.*)

The development of carrier aircraft themselves was strongly influenced by tactical considerations and technological limitations. At the close of World War I the primary tactical applications of naval aircraft consisted of level-flight bombing and torpedo attacks, aerial combat with machine guns, and reconnaissance and scouting. During the early 1920's the United States Navy developed the technique of diving at the target when releasing bombs. This was refined into an almost vertical dive maneuver and came to be known as dive bombing. It is generally believed that the Germans and Japanese, who adopted dive bombing as a primary tactic in their own air forces, first observed the technique in demonstrations by United States Navy and Marine Corps pilots at air shows.

To get the most effective results from the aircraft embarked in a single carrier, capabilities for several different missions were incorporated in the design of each type of aircraft. A number of combinations were attempted, and by the beginning of World War II the categories of carrier aircraft (particularly in the United States Navy) had become fairly well defined: torpedo attack and horizontal bombing were performed by large airplanes; dive bombing and scouting were conducted by smaller and faster aircraft; and air combat was done by small fighter aircraft designed for maximum performance and maximum firepower, but with only marginal ability to deliver bombs.

Although aircraft carriers and carrier aircraft undoubtedly constituted the most important naval air weapon developments between World War I and World War II, considerable effort was devoted by most naval powers to operating aircraft from cruisers and battleships. Less successful experiments were conducted with destroyer- and submarine-based aircraft. The United States, in 1919, and the Japanese, in 1920, again following the example of the British Navy, experimented with platforms on top of battleship turrets from which light planes were launched under their own power. In 1922 the United States Navy successfully launched float planes from the U.S.S. *Maryland* with a compressed-air catapult mounted on a turntable. At the end of their flights the planes landed alongside the ship to be hoisted aboard, following the method developed by Glenn Curtiss in 1911. Quickly installed on other United States battleships and cruisers, catapults were also adopted by other navies. Aircraft based on battleships and cruisers were used for scouting purposes and to spot the fall of shot from the ships' big guns. In response to the need for aerial defense, some efforts were made to fit these ships with fighters, but these met with little success because of the inherent lack of fighter performance available in float planes.

Between the wars the flying boat developed into a large aircraft, more heavily armed, with a substantial increase in range. The employment of the flying boat in this era tended more toward long-range search and patrol tasks, rather than toward training for antisubmarine warefare.

In the 1920's both the United States and the British navies, influenced by the technical successes of the Germans in World War I with lighter-than-air craft, acquired huge rigid dirigibles. In the United States Navy these large airships were intended primarily for use as scouting auxiliaries, but fleet exercises demonstrated a serious vulnerability to carrier-based aircraft and the susceptibility of dirigibles to storm damage was emphasized by a series of disasters. After four major crashes the Navy abandoned large dirigibles in favor of smaller, less expensive, nonrigid lighter-than-air craft, and these were used thereafter for off-shore antisubmarine patrols with great success.

World War II.—In contrast with World War I, World War II emphasized aviation's organic and dominant role in naval warfare. In 1918 the British had combined their Royal Naval Air Service and Royal Flying Corps to form the independent Royal Air Force, but prior to the outbreak of World War II control of the sea-going units then comprising the Fleet Air Arm was returned to the Admiralty. The Admiralty also was given control of the Coastal Command, which consisted of shore-based aircraft for off-shore patrol. In Japan, too, naval aviation forces (which had been developed as the major component of the Japanese Navy) were under the direct control of the navy.

Germany, on the other hand, continued to submerge naval aviation missions in its regular air force. This failure to provide the World War II German Navy with its own organic aviation forces is thought by many military analysts to have been a serious blunder by Nazi leaders.

The German submarine campaign in the Atlantic Ocean during the early days of World War II was the major threat to the tenuous sea lanes of communication between the Allies. The Allies responded by establishing naval aviation bases throughout the North and South Atlantic areas to protect vital shipping from U-boat attacks. Large landplanes were distinctly favored for these patrol tasks because of their superior performance; however, the ability of flying boats to operate from almost any protected body of water gave them such mobility that they were used throughout the war by the British and United States navies. America's fleet of nonrigid airships was greatly expanded and performed yeoman service in coastal antisubmarine patrol and in protecting merchant convoys. The Allied campaign against the German submarines was finally won when many small, mobile, aircraft carriers became available for intensive antisubmarine operations in the open Atlantic Ocean.

In the Pacific Ocean in late 1941, two decisive events conclusively established the importance of aviation as a part of modern naval power: the successful Japanese attack on Pearl Harbor by carrier-based aircraft on Dec. 7, 1941; and, several days later, the sinking by Japanese bombers of the British battleships *Prince of Wales* and *Repulse,* cruising without air cover off the coast of Malaya. The latter episode demonstrated that air cover was essential for naval forces operating within range of enemy aircraft. As the war progressed, aircraft carriers (which supplied their own air cover) proved that they could repel attacks by land-based aircraft. See also WORLD WAR II—*10. War in the Central and Northern Pacific* (Pearl Harbor); *11. War In Eastern Asia* (Japanese Advance in Southeast Asia: 1941–1942).

Under the unique conditions of combat imposed by the geography of the Pacific theater, the only means of carrying the United States offensive to the enemy lay in the fast carrier striking forces of the Pacific Fleet. Although in 1942 the country possessed a mere handful of effective aircraft carriers, by late 1943 its carrier forces in the Pacific had three or four (and in 1945 as many as five) fast carriers operating in every task group, accompanied by supporting battleships and cruisers and surrounded by destroyers. These tactical dispositions resulted in an improved mutual defense for the participating ships in each group and in a powerful, concentrated, offensive power. By operating several such groups in proximity it was possible to bring a force of 1,000 carrier-based aircraft to bear against a single Japanese objective. New logistic techniques permitted these task forces to be resupplied while underway in the forward operating areas. Largely independent of fixed bases, the fast carriers attained a degree of mobility and staying power which enabled them to sweep vast areas clear of Japanese aircraft and open the way for devastating air attacks on Japanese shore installations. The Navy's prewar trend toward multipurpose capabilities in naval aircraft was accelerated: fighters and torpedo planes were both used to deliver bombs in diving attacks, and some efforts were made to adapt bombers to torpedo dropping.

To augment its burgeoning program of large carrier construction, the United States Navy in 1941 began installing flight decks on merchant vessels as an expedient to provide escort carriers for the protection of slow shipping. These so-called jeep carriers proved invaluable for escorting convoys, for operating with destroyers in hunter-killer operations against submarines, and in supporting amphibious operations.

After serious losses in carriers to United States fast carrier task forces at the Battle of Midway in June 1942, the Japanese made desperate efforts to recover their carrier strength by putting flight decks on capital ships as well as by rushing construction of new carriers, but they could not match the rapidly increasing naval air power of the United States.

After World War II.—In the decade following World War II, United States naval aviation continued to expand its capabilities at a rapid rate, largely as a result of technological advances conceived or initiated during the war. The U.S.S. *Midway,* the first of a large class of carriers, joined the fleet in 1945. With a design displacement of about 45,000 tons, the *Midway* class ships embodied radical departures from the *Essex* class carriers, incorporating in their design armored flight decks, the elimination of gun batteries on flight deck level, and other innovations. The size of these ships reflected the demand for more flight deck space to accommodate the bigger and faster naval aircraft, particularly jet aircraft, which were becoming available. The performance of carrier aircraft continued to improve with advances in aeronautical technology, and by 1950, at the outbreak of the Korean War, the United States and British navies were flying jet aircraft and helicopters from carriers in routine operations.

Naval aviation was one of the decisive factors in the Korean War. Operating from fields in South Korea and from carriers in the Sea of Japan and the Yellow Sea, United States Navy and Marine aircraft attacked enemy supply lines, provided close air support for ground troops, and furnished air and antisubmarine defense for the United Nations' naval forces blockading North Korea.

A new generation of carrier aircraft, greatly

improved in combat performance, appeared several years after the Korean War. In order to accommodate the large engines required for supersonic speeds, the quantity of fuel demanded by extended flight ranges, and the elaborate electronic systems needed for combat under all weather conditions, these aircraft were radically larger than their predecessors. Fighters averaged 30,000 pounds; and jet attack planes, when fully loaded for bombing missions, grossed over 60,000 pounds. Guided missiles, both air-to-air and air-to-ground, were added to aircraft armament systems.

To handle these larger, faster, and heavier aircraft, a huge new attack carrier, the U.S.S. *Forrestal,* was completed for the United States Navy in 1955. With a design displacement of 60,000 tons and a deck length of more than 1,000 feet, this was the first attack carrier to be built from the hull up with an angled deck, steam catapults, and the mirror landing system—British technical innovations which made possible the expeditious and safe handling of large, high-speed aircraft. Three other ships of the same class (the *Saratoga,* the *Ranger,* and the *Independence*) were completed shortly after the *Forrestal,* and two more (the *Constellation* and the *Kitty Hawk*) were completed in 1961.

The attack carrier *Enterprise* was the first to be powered by atomic energy. This powerful vessel was commissioned in 1961; it is over 1,000 feet in length, displaces 75,700 tons, and is powered by eight nuclear reactors, which can run something like five years without refueling. The maximum speed is 35 knots. The *Enterprise* carries a crew of 4,000 men and over 70 aircraft.

In 1955 the tactical atomic bomb became available to the United States Navy. The striking power of a single carrier, with 60 per cent of its complement of aircraft capable of delivering nuclear weapons, has attained proportions hardly measurable in conventional terms.

Since the Korean War, France, the Netherlands, Canada, and Australia have increased the size of their naval forces; Great Britain has continued to modernize her carriers and aircraft and has added atomic weapons to the armament of her carrier-based aircraft; and Japan, now aligned with the Western nations, has re-established shore-based naval aviation units as part of her home defense forces. The navy of the USSR operates thousands of shore-based planes.

Two naval links in America's early warning system: the Lockheed-built WV-2 and a radar picket escort vessel.

Official U.S. Navy Photograph

UNITED STATES NAVAL AVIATION

In the United States Navy, aviation pervades all aspects of fleet operations. In the attack carrier striking forces, carrier-based aircraft with performance generally equivalent, and often superior, to land-based counterparts, provide the Navy's primary offensive weapon, providing the mobility and versatility which is the basic source of United States naval power. In the antisubmarine forces, aviation again plays an important role. The antisubmarine carriers of the fleets, with their complements of specialized aircraft, form the core of the famed hunter-killer groups. These tactical units, consisting of one carrier and a number of destroyers, have the job of hunting down and destroying marauding enemy submarines in the open seas. Large land- and sea-based patrol aircraft, capable of both detecting and destroying undersea craft, are also part of the Navy's antisubmarine forces.

A unique example of the integration which characterizes aviation within the Navy is found in the United States Marine Corps. The Marines have their own organic air force to ensure maximum effectiveness in the performance of their assigned functions, which are generally associated with amphibious warfare; however, the Marine Corps is actually an organizational category of the Naval Establishment and for many purposes its aviation forces are used interchangeably with those of the Navy proper.

The renowned tactical mobility of the United States fleets at sea, and their relative independence from shore bases in forward areas, is realized through mobile logistic support forces which provide them with fuel, ammunition, and other supplies even when they are engaged in combat operations. Such far-ranging support is made possible primarily by carrier-based aircraft which protect the supply ships from hostile airplanes and submarines.

The Navy produces its own pilots in the Naval Air Training Command, and naval combat aircraft are specifically designed for their particular tasks. Naval aviators exercise commands, not only in exclusively aeronautical areas, but also in fleets and at the highest levels in the Navy Department.

ROBERT E. DIXON, *Rear Admiral, USN*
Chief, Bureau of Aeronautics

Bibliography.—Brodie, Bernard, *Seapower in the Machine Age* (Princeton 1941); Saunders, Hilary A., St. George, *Per Ardua; the Rise of British Air Power, 1911–1939* (London 1945); Buchanan, A. Russell, ed., *The Navy's Air War* (New York 1946); Lee, Asher, *The German Air Force* (London 1946); U.S., Navy, Office of the Chief of Naval Operations, *United States Naval Aviation in the Pacific* (Washington 1947); Turnbull, Archibald D., and Lord, Clifford L., *History of United States Naval Aviation* (New Haven 1949); U.S. Naval Institute, *Air Operations in Naval Warfare,* reading supplement (Annapolis 1957); *Jane's All the World Aircraft* (New York, current).

NAVAL COMMUNICATIONS, a term referring in one sense to the dissemination and exchange of information pertaining to the naval establishment and its functions, and designating radio, teletype, and other systems for communicating information and orders. In the United States the communications division of the Navy maintains and operates the shore facilities and services required to provide communications for the operating forces, the Navy Department, and

Above: The F8U "Crusader," here being catapulted from the deck of the *Forrestal*, is capable of speeds of over 1,000 miles per hour.

Above right: Test flight of the Grumman S2F-3. The plane houses advanced antisubmarine electronic equipment and armaments.

Official U.S. Navy Photographs

NAVAL AVIATION

Right: Transport helicopters, part of a modern amphibious striking force, stand ready for take-off on the flight deck of the *Boxer*.

Below: The United States Navy's largest carrier-based aircraft in the late 1950's was the A3D "Skywarrior," a twin-jet attack bomber.

(Right) Official U.S. Marine Corps Photo; (below) Official U.S. Navy Photograph

Right: A mirror, part of the landing system of the carrier *Saratoga*, reflects the image of a plane which has just touched down.

Below: A pilot's view of the British carrier H.M.S. *Victorious*. The angled deck extends 41 feet outward from the port side.

(Right) Official U.S. Navy Photograph; (below) Official British Admiralty Photograph

the shore establishment. Its chief means of transmission are twenty powerful radio stations strategically located throughout the world. Five of these stations—designated primary communication centers—furnish complete radio coverage for the major portions of the earth's most important ocean areas. The primary communication centers are at Washington, D.C.; San Francisco, Calif.; Pearl Harbor, Hawaii; Guam; and Port Lyautey, Morocco. Cable and wireless services utilized for naval communications include telephony and telegraphy, and teletypewriter, facsimile, and television systems. Other means of communication used by the Navy include flashing lights and other visual signals; sound signals such as bells and sirens; and conventional mail and messenger services. (See also SIGNALS AND SIGNALING; TELEGRAPHY —*Military and Naval Telegraph.*)

In a broader sense of the term, naval communications include all marine strategic communications: the system of routes and transport for moving men and supplies between bases and to and from theaters of operations. The primary wartime mission of a navy is to control the sea and thereby to maintain the sea communications of its homeland, while disrupting those of the enemy. For this purpose it is essential first to seek out and destroy the enemy's naval forces, and second to impose a naval blockade to prevent the movement of enemy transport ships carrying troops and matériel.

Until the coming of air power the problems and techniques of achieving and maintaining control of the sea involved only the world's oceans and the relatively narrow littoral areas which could be brought under the fire of naval guns—rarely deeper than twenty miles inland. With the development of aviation, however, the inland distance which might feel a navy's striking power was increased several hundred miles; and conversely sea communications could be threatened seriously by land-based aircraft. The development of military and naval missiles has so far extended the range of both land- and sea-based air power that the problems of sea communications can no longer be sharply distinguished from those of land and air strategic communications.

In his numerous works on seapower the great American naval historian, Alfred Thayer Mahan (1840–1914), dealt extensively with the theme of strategic communications, and in his *Naval Strategy* (1911) he made the now classic statement that "Communications dominate war." History is replete with illustrations of Mahan's axiom. One of the earliest examples occurred in the Greco-Persian Wars (499–479 B.C.) when Persia's King Xerxes directed his military forces to attack Greece via the land route north of the Aegean Sea. After the Persian Army crossed the Hellespont (the modern Dardanelles) it was supplied by fleets of supply ships which in turn were protected by hundreds of fighting ships. The Persian armies conquered their way into Greece, seizing and destroying all before them, including Athens itself, but their continued success was contingent upon the ability of Persian naval forces to maintain supply routes across the Aegean Sea. Then, in 480 B.C., the Greek fleet, led by the Spartan Eurybiades but generally directed and inspired by the Athenian Themistocles, met and overwhelmed Xerxes' fleet at the Battle of Salamis, a short distance from Athens. This victory disastrously reduced the naval strength by which the extended Persian lines of communication were maintained. Within a year the decisiveness of Salamis became evident when the weakened remnants of the once invincible Persian Army were destroyed at the Battle of Plataea (479 B.C.), and soon thereafter a Greek thrust across the Aegean to Asia Minor destroyed most of Xerxes' remaining naval forces.

An outstanding example of the significance of naval communications is found in the history of the rise of England, a rise based to a high degree on the country's seapower. Her geographical location contributed much to making England a seafaring nation, and when the commercial revolution of the 14th and 15th centuries shifted the world's major trade routes so that many of them passed a short distance from England's shores the enterprising English grasped the opportunity to control those vital sea communications. To possess distant colonies, as did the Spanish, Portuguese, and Dutch, was profitable only if the goods and riches of the colonies could reach the homelands. During the Tudor era (16th century) England harassed the sea communications between Spain and her colonies, and during the third quarter of the 17th century she effectively challenged the Dutch monopoly of the carrying trade into northwestern Europe. After three Anglo-Dutch wars, despite the brilliant naval tactics of such Dutch admirals as Maarten Tromp and Michel de Ruyter, the English wrung from the Dutch at the Treaty of Westminster (1674) the concession that all Dutch ships were obliged to salute the flag of England whenever Dutch and English ships should meet in the waters between northwestern Spain and southern Norway—a clear demonstration of England's growing control over those "Narrow Seas" through which passed the vital trade routes to northwestern Europe.

The lengthy Anglo-French struggle from 1688 to 1815, sometimes referred to as the Second Hundred Years' War, contained many examples of the vital importance of naval communications. Several times Britain was threatened by invasion from the Continent, but each time the French were halted by their inability to gain control of the English Channel separating the British Isles from Europe. The offensive phases of Britain's efforts demonstrated further the decisiveness of naval communications. By dominating the principal ocean routes involved, Britain was able to project her own power overseas while denying the same opportunity to her enemies, and her judicious use of seapower was one of the major reasons for Britain's conquest of Canada and India during the Seven Years' War (1756–1763). Only once during this series of wars did Britain lose control of the sea at a time when her enemies were in a position to capitalize on her unfavorable situation. In the autumn of 1781, during the American Revolution, a French fleet prevented British succor from reaching General Charles Cornwallis, beleaguered on the peninsula between the James and York rivers in Tidewater Virginia; as a result Cornwallis was forced to surrender, and the British lost the war. This decisive defeat was a humiliating demonstration to Britain of the need to control her sea communications if she would maintain her hold on her far-flung empire.

One of the major uses of seapower by the Union during the American Civil War was to blockade the South, thereby severing communications between the Confederacy and Europe.

The spectacular but ultimately futile commerce raiding carried out by the *Alabama* and other Confederate warships was intended to disrupt Union sea communications throughout the world, as well as to weaken the Union's blockading forces. Had the Union succumbed to the temptation to detach ships from the blockade to hunt down the marauders the effectiveness of Confederate commerce raiding would have been far more pronounced.

During the Spanish-American War in 1898 the principal roles of America's navy in the Caribbean area was to transport troops and equipment to Cuba and to cut Spanish sea communications with the island. These activities, combined with the American naval victory over Admiral Pascual Cevera at Santiago, Cuba, in July 1898, contributed greatly to the defeat of the Spanish in Cuba.

During World War I, Britain's navies effectively blockaded Germany and protected British sea communications throughout the world, and following the entry of the United States into the war in April 1917 ships of the American Navy were similarly employed. In both world wars German naval power was used primarily for the purpose of cutting British sea communications. The World War I U-boat strikes almost succeeded in bringing defeat to Britain, demonstrating again the country's absolute dependence on imports of food and other materials. In World War II the vigor with which German seapower attacked Allied naval communications caused Prime Minister Winston Churchill to state that the Battle of the Atlantic, as the U-boat war was called, caused him more concern than any other single factor in the war.

In the Pacific area, too, naval communications dominated World War II. Japan's crippling strike against the United States fleet at Pearl Harbor in December 1941 prevented America from challenging the Japanese thrust into Southeastern Asia; and Japan's invasion of the Solomon Islands in May 1942 as well as her plans to occupy the Fiji and Samoan groups were for the dual purpose of establishing an outer defense perimeter in the South Central Pacific and an offensive position from which to sever naval communications linking the United States, Australia, and New Zealand. In August 1942 the Allied forces invaded Guadalcanal in the Solomons in an offensive-defensive thrust to repel the Japanese from this strategic position.

The United States Navy's offensive against the Japanese had begun in the early days of the war when American submarines were ordered to strike at ships plying the routes between the Japanese home islands and the newly conquered areas from which Japan was drawing much-needed raw materials, particularly oil, and throughout the war in the Pacific the Navy continued to attack this "jugular vein" of the Japanese war machine —the sea communications between Japan and resource-rich Southeastern Asia. Once that objective had been achieved (early in 1945) the Japanese fleet, lacking fuel oil for its ships, was rendered incapable of action, and Japan had long since lost her ability effectively to challenge Allied naval communications.

In the Korean War (1950–1953) the United States Navy's control over its sea communications was virtually undisputed. The vital supply lines which it maintained in that war stretched from Korea and Japan across the Pacific to the United States and through the Indian Ocean to the oil-producing region of the Persian Gulf.

ROBERT M. LANGDON,
Associate Professor of History and Government, United States Naval Academy.
CHARLES M. QUINN,
Commander, United States Navy Signal Corps.

NAVAL CONFERENCES. For nearly 15 years between World Wars I and II, the major naval powers agreed voluntarily, in a series of naval disarmament conferences, to certain limitations on their navies. Several developments at the close of World War I helped to bring on these efforts. When the smoke cleared away late in 1918, the British felt a sense of naval disillusionment. The German High Seas Fleet, against which they had strained every effort since 1900, was captive at Scapa Flow and would soon sink beneath its waters. The British, war-weary and heavily in debt, had looked forward to relief from their crushing naval expenditures. To their dismay, they found an intensification, rather than a relaxation, in the naval programs of the Americans and the Japanese, whose war experience had been less exacting. That struck at one of the cardinal points of British policy. With their prosperity and safety dependent upon control of long and vital sea lanes, they had come to feel that they had a right to a stronger navy than anyone else. One of the prime causes of misunderstanding in the situation was that the United States Navy was primarily concerned with offsetting Japan's increasing influence in the Pacific. The difficulty was that any American naval force strong enough to deter the Japanese would also be strong enough, in the eyes of Britons, to be a challenge to British maritime security.

There was also the beginning of a doubt as to the formerly unquestioned supremacy of the battleship, around which naval rivalry had centered for years. The battle cruiser, in which armor was sacrificed for extra speed, had been pretty much discredited by the experience of the Battle of Jutland (1916); but the battleship, capable of absorbing the same punishment as it dealt out, still held a strong first place in most professional naval opinion. (See WARSHIPS, MODERN—*Battleships.*) The aviators, however, were beginning to claim that aerial bombs could end the battleship's long-touted role as a nation's "first line of defense." The cost of battleships had been rising steadily, and in lay minds the sudden sweeping obsolescence resulting from the all big-gun *Dreadnought* (built by the British in 1905–1906) had been impressive. If the battle fleets could be frozen at existing strength, a repetition of the costly prewar rivalry might be avoided.

Finally, there was the determined effort on the part of the new Republican administration in the United States, which came into power in March 1921, to do something tangible about disarmament. The initiative came primarily from Charles Evans Hughes, the secretary of state. With its small Army and Air Force, no significant steps could be taken by the United States toward disarmament in those directions; the obvious sacrificial victims were the powerful new superdreadnoughts under construction.

Washington Conference (1921–1922).—With this point in mind, invitations were issued by the United States in August 1921 to a conference in Washington to discuss naval limitations and also some Pacific and Far Eastern problems. It was hoped, among other things, to prevent renewal of the Anglo-Japanese Alliance and to check the advances made by Japan in China while the other powers were preoccupied in war. For the naval limitations discussion, Great Britain, Japan, France, and Italy were invited; for the discussion of general Far Eastern questions, bids also went to Belgium, the Netherlands, Portugal, and China.

It was significant, but not unnatural, that the initiative in the whole naval disarmament movement came almost entirely from civilian statesmen and was opposed by most professional naval officers. During the preliminaries in the United States, matters were almost entirely in the hands of Hughes and Assistant Secretary of the Navy Theodore Roosevelt, Jr., neither of whom had had any direct experience in either foreign relations or naval matters. The General Board, the Navy's advisory group of "elder statesmen," was strongly opposed to the proposed drastic cut in naval strength, but it was kept in the dark as to the startling American proposals.

There was a profound sensation when Secretary Hughes, at the opening session of the Washington Conference in November 1921, announced the general proposal of a naval holiday, "freezing" the navies at a strength of 525,000 tons for Britain and the United States, 315,000 for Japan, and 175,000 each for France and Italy. As an evidence of its sincerity, the United States would scrap a considerable part of its huge new fleet under construction. It was hoped that the proposed 5-5-3 ratio would extend to all categories of warships, but exceptions immediately appeared. In the matter of cruisers, the British, headed by Arthur James Balfour, agreed as to fleet cruisers but said that the matter of patrol cruisers—the bulk of the force—would have to be left to the experts, where nothing happened. The British and Americans both wanted to eliminate submarines, but the French and Italians insisted upon retaining them, as the weapon of the weaker powers. That left the capital ships to sustain the impact. A limit of 35,000 tons was placed upon these, except for Britain's 42,100-ton battle cruiser *Hood* under construction. The United States, having only one minor aircraft carrier, was permitted to convert the projected battle cruisers *Lexington* and *Saratoga*. There was to be a 10-year "naval holiday" with no new construction in capital ships except to maintain the ratios.

The United States removed more than 200 vessels from its Navy List by sinking, scrapping, or, in a few cases, demilitarization. Two old battleships were given to the Army to be sunk by its bombers; numerous other predreadnoughts were broken up for scrap. Most of the new superdreadnoughts were scrapped in the shipyard, but two of them, already launched, were almost three quarters completed. One, the 31,800-ton *West Virginia,* was spared, and would fight in World War II; but her sister ship, the *Washington,* representing the last word in naval architecture, was taken out beyond the Virginia capes one November day in 1924 to be sunk before she was ever commissioned. Her tough hull withstood the impact of two torpedoes and four one-ton bombs exploded close by. Not until 14 heavy shells were smashed into her by naval gunfire did she finally sink, one of the most spectacular sacrifices to the hope for world peace. Had all those new ships been completed, the United States would have had by far the mightiest navy afloat.

These partly completed vessels were not the only sacrifices. The Japanese were unwilling to accept their 60 per cent quota of British and United States battle strength until these nations agreed not to strengthen any of their existing defenses in the western Pacific. This left the Philippines, Guam, and Hong Kong as virtual hostages to the Japanese, with no powerful British or American bases closer than Pearl Harbor and Singapore.

In addition to these various naval agreements embodied in a treaty on Feb. 6, 1922, the conference produced a Four-Power Treaty (Dec. 13, 1921) of the United States, Britain, Japan, and France, supplanting the old Anglo-Japanese Alliance of 1902. In the Four-Power Treaty, the signatories agreed to respect each others' insular possessions and to consult if these should be threatened. In addition, with Italy, Belgium, the Netherlands, Portugal, and China, they agreed to a Nine-Power Treaty (Feb. 6, 1922) guaranteeing the territorial integrity and administrative independence of China and repeating the Open Door principle.

None of the nations came away from Washington really satisfied. The Americans had gained recognition of parity with Britain and had broken up the Anglo-Japanese Alliance, but had scrapped ships that would have given them an adequate deterrent to Japan. The British had prevented the richer Americans from outbuilding them, but for the first time they had formally agreed that another navy might be as strong as theirs. The Japanese had prevented the others from building up powerful bases within striking distance of Japan, but had sacrificed some national pride in agreeing to the short end of the 5-5-3 ratio. France and Italy had agreed to an even weaker relative strength, but had prevented the abolition of the submarine.

Geneva Conference (1927).—With capital ships frozen, the competition quickly shifted to cruisers, which were not included in the Washington terms. This led quickly to serious misunderstandings between the British and Americans. Not having commissioned a single new cruiser between 1908 and 1923, the United States was faced with a long, stern chase. By 1926, England had 40 modern cruisers, Japan 19, and the United States only 10; including additions which were on the way, the respective totals were 54, 25, and 15. Consequently, since England was unlikely to cut down her surplus, the United States would need some 200,000 tons of cruisers to catch up.

The real crux of the Anglo-American troubles lay in the opposing preferences for "light" cruisers of about 7,500 tons with 6-inch guns as against "heavy" 10,000-ton ships with 8-inch guns. The Americans wanted to use most of their tonnage in heavy ships with longer cruising radius. The British, needing large numbers of cruisers to guard their lengthy sea lanes, and having numerous bases for refueling, not only preferred light cruisers for themselves, but also wanted to limit the Americans as far as possible to that type.

These opposing viewpoints of the "eight-inch admirals" and "six-inch admirals" burst out in full force in the second naval limitation conference, summoned through President Calvin Coolidge's initiative, at Geneva in 1927. The French and Italians did not attend. The Americans sought to extend the 5-5-3 principle to all naval categories, but the British were determined not to lose their primacy. The professional naval officers had more to say at this conference than at the others, and were far less ready than the civilians to concede things which they considered essential to naval strength. The conference therefore failed to reach any tangible results.

First London Conference (1930).—Three years after Geneva, with the civilians once more running things, it was a different story. President Herbert Hoover, who had very negative views about naval expenditures, discussed the matter with England's new Labour prime minister, Ramsay MacDonald, when he came to America. The upshot was a third naval limitation conference at London early in 1930, with Secretary of State Henry L. Stimson at the head of the United States delegation.

The British cut their "irreducible" cruiser needs from 70 to 50, with a total tonnage of 339,000, but they held the Americans to 18 8-inch cruisers, the rest to be 6-inch. The Japanese, taking full advantage of the Anglo-American friction, managed to secure a 10-10-7 ratio in cruisers and parity with the United States and Britain in submarines, each having a 52,700-ton limit. Since France and Italy had once again refused to participate, the conference agreed to certain "escape" provisions to meet possible competition from nonsignatories. Finally, the 10-year building holiday agreed upon at Washington was extended to 1936. The American heavy cruiser advocates waged a bitter fight against the treaty, but it was finally ratified.

The negative attitude of President Hoover, combined with the serious economic depression, checked American naval construction almost completely, and the United States fell far behind the quotas permitted by the conference agreements. The tide turned in 1934 when, under the influence of President Franklin D. Roosevelt and Carl Vinson, chairman of the House Naval Affairs Committee, naval construction, aimed at parity with Britain, was revived.

By the mid-1930's, the naval limitation system was beginning to crack up. A general disarmament conference at Geneva in 1932–1933 failed completely. In 1934, Adolf Hitler's Germany denounced the disarmament terms of the Versailles Treaty and secured England's agreement to equality in submarines and 35 per cent of over-all British naval strength. France and Italy were also increasing their navies.

Second London Conference (1935).—Late in 1935, the fourth and final naval limitation conference met at London in the vain hope of continuing the principle of treaty limitation. Italy refused to participate. Japan demanded full parity with the United States and Britain in all categories of ships. When the Americans objected, Japan withdrew from the conference and announced that it would no longer participate in limitation terms after 1936. The atmosphere of frustration and uncertainty was strong when, on March 25, 1936, the United States, Britain, and France signed a treaty giving recognition to the general principles of limitation, but containing so many "escalator clauses" to meet outside rivalry that it really marked the end of the 15-year effort. The limitation agreements technically came to an end on Dec. 31, 1936. In the meantime, Britain announced its heaviest building program since 1921, and quickly laid down its *Prince of Wales* class of battleships, which were completed early in World War II. The United States did likewise; its new *Washington* and her sister ships were faster and much more costly than the earlier *Washington*.

Though the movement ended in failure, it had accomplished something. It had probably saved millions, if not billions, of dollars at a time when the economic depression made that important. It had probably saved Britain and the United States from more serious misunderstandings than their differences over cruisers. And it had at least given the world a tangible example of voluntary limitation. On the other hand, it may have contributed to troubles in the Pacific and Far East by reducing American naval strength which might otherwise have been an effective deterrent to Japanese ambitions.

See also DISARMAMENT; FAR EASTERN AFFAIRS.

Bibliography.—Davis, George T., *A Navy Second to None* (New York 1940); Sprout, Harold H., and Margaret T., *Toward a New Order of Sea Power* (Princeton 1940); Mitchell, Donald W., *History of the Modern Amerian Navy from 1883 through Pearl Harbor* (New York 1946); Tate, Merze, *The United States and Armaments* (Cambridge, Mass., 1948); O'Connor, Raymond G., *Perilous Equilibrium: the United States and the London Naval Conference of 1930* (Lawrence, Kans., 1962).

ROBERT G. ALBION,
Gardiner Professor of Oceanic History and Affairs, Harvard University.

NAVAL DISTRICTS. The geographical limits of the United States naval districts and their headquarters are as follows:

District No.	Geographical limits	Headquarters
1	Maine, New Hampshire, Vermont, Massachusetts, and Rhode Island (including Block Island).	Boston, Mass.
2	There is no second naval district.	
3	Connecticut, New York, northern part of New Jersey including counties of Monmouth, Middlesex, Somerset, Hunterdon, and all counties north thereof; also the Nantucket Shoals Lightship.	New York, N.Y.
4	Pennsylvania; southern part of New Jersey including counties of Mercer, Burlington, Ocean, and all counties south thereof; Delaware, including Winter Quarter Shoal Light Vessel; Ohio.	Philadelphia, Pa.
5	Maryland less Anne Arundel, Prince Georges, Montgomery, St. Marys, Calvert, and Charles counties; West Virginia; Virginia less Arlington, Fairfax, Stafford, King George, Prince William, and Westmoreland counties, and the city of Alexandria; also all waters of Chesapeake Bay including its arms and tributaries except waters within the fourth naval district and the counties comprising the Potomac River and Severn River naval commands west of a line extending from Smith Point to Point Lookout thence following the general contour of the shoreline of St. Marys, Calvert, and Anne Arundel counties, as faired by straight lines from headland to headland across rivers and estuaries; Kentucky and the counties of Currituck, Camden, Pasquotank, Gates, Perquimans, Chowan, Dare, Tyrrell, Washington, Hyde, Beaufort, Pamlico, Craven, Carteret, Jones, and Onslow, North Carolina.	Norfolk, Va.
6	South Carolina; Georgia; North Carolina except the counties of Currituck, Camden, Pasquotank, Gates, Perquimans, Chowan, Tyrrell, Washington, Hyde, Beaufort, Pamlico, Craven, Jones, Carteret, Onslow, and Dare; Florida; Alabama; Tennessee; and Mississippi.	Charleston, S.C.

7	There is no seventh naval district.	
8	Louisiana; Oklahoma; Texas; Arkansas; New Mexico.	New Orleans, La.
9	Michigan; Indiana; Illinois; Wisconsin; Minnesota; Iowa; Missouri; North Dakota; South Dakota; Nebraska; Kansas; Colorado; and Wyoming.	Great Lakes, Ill.
10	The Island of Puerto Rico, other U.S. islands in the Caribbean Sea, the Caribbean Sea itself, and to limits as defined by the Navy Department.	San Juan, Puerto Rico
11	Arizona; Clark County, Nevada; southern part of California, including counties of Santa Barbara, Kern, and San Bernardino, and all counties south thereof.	San Diego, Calif.
12	Utah; Nevada (except Clark County); northern part of California, including counties of San Luis Obispo, Kings, Tulare, Inyo, and all counties north thereof.	San Francisco, Calif.
13	Washington; Oregon; Idaho; and Montana.	Seattle, Wash.
14	Hawaiian Islands and islands to the westward and southward, including Midway, Wake, Kure, Johnston and Palmyra Islands, Kingman Reef, and Kwajalein Atoll (Marshall Islands).	Pearl Harbor, Hawaii
15	Panama Canal Zone	Balboa, C.Z.
16	There is no sixteenth naval district.	
17	Alaska and Aleutian Islands	Kodiak, Alaska

Each naval district is commanded by a designated commandant who is the direct representative of the Navy Department and its bureaus. In the administration of the affairs of the district, the commandant does not personally supervise the management of the several groups or units under him, but transacts the necessary business with the officer commanding the group or unit. The responsibility for the organization and efficient operation of administrative units within his command, such as, United States naval bases, recruiting stations, submarine bases, schools, inspection activities, navy shipbuilding activities at private plants, etc., rest with the officer in command of each unit. Communications relating entirely to the technical work of these establishments are carried on direct with the bureau or station concerned. Communications of any administrative unit, which involve questions of military policy or which affect the operation of any other unit in the district, are forwarded through the commandant of the naval district for recommendation or other appropriate action.

The most important groups under certain of the naval districts are the "United States naval bases," formerly known as navy yards, located at Portsmouth, N.H.; Boston, Mass.; Brooklyn, N.Y.; Philadelphia, Pa.; Norfolk, Va.; Charleston, S.C.; Bremerton, Wash.; Mare Island, Calif.; and Pearl Harbor, Hawaii. The mission of a naval base is to furnish direct service to the operating forces. A naval base is defined as that agency in a given locality which comprises and integrates all naval activities which are capable of contributing to its mission. A component of the naval base is the "United States naval shipyard" under which are integrated all departments and divisions of the former navy yard organizations which contribute directly or indirectly to the building, repairing, overhauling, docking, altering, converting, and outfitting ships; and to related or special manufacturing. In addition to the shipyard, the naval base may, and, in the case of practically all naval districts does, contain other activities, such as a naval supply depot, a naval hospital, a naval ammunition depot, a naval net depot, a naval receiving station, a marine barracks, etc. All of the component activities of the naval base, including the shipyard as a component activity, are under the military command and coordination control of an officer designated commandant of the naval base, who is directly responsible to the commandant of the naval district in which the base is located. The command relationship of the commandant of the naval base to the several component activities parallels that of a division flag officer to the ships of the division under his command, in that the commanding officer of each component activity exercises autonomy within his command and must produce results which contribute to the effectiveness of the naval base as a whole.

Each of the component activities of a naval base, including each shipyard as one component activity, is under the direct control of a commanding officer. Each such commanding officer is under the supervision of the commandant of the naval base for matters of internal security, defense, administration of military personnel, and for coordination of his activity with other components of the naval base in providing logistic services to the operating forces. For all other matters, including assignment of work, allotment of funds, assignment of personnel, establishment of operating methods, procedures, organization, etc., each such commanding officer is under the direct supervision of the cognizant agency of the Navy Department, except when such control is specifically delegated to the district commandant by the Navy Department.

The officer ordered to command of a United States naval shipyard must be technically trained in the building and repair of ships and must have had substantial previous experience in the technical and management phases of such work, both in United States naval shipyards and in the Navy Department. Such commanding officer may have been designated for engineering duty only. It is the duty of the commanding officer of a naval shipyard to supervise and direct all of the work of the shipyard; to assume full responsibility for the quality and quantity of work produced; and to assure the efficient and economical performance of the work of the shipyard.

J. A. Furer,
Rear Admiral, United States Navy (Retired).

NAVAL EDUCATION. Technological and social changes within the navies of the world have had profound effects upon naval education and training. The transition from sail to steam, accompanied by the institution of more humane methods of discipline to replace older methods including flogging, provided marked stimulation for the education of naval personnel. The two world wars of the 20th century and the recent dawn of the nuclear age have resulted in even more dramatic changes.

UNITED STATES

In the days of sail, enlisted men and officers received most of their training aboard ship. Student officers (midshipmen) were given some formal schooling in mathematics and astronomy to enable them to navigate scientifically. As steam engines and rifled guns replaced sail and smooth bores, it became apparent that officers would need at least a basic general and technical education. The founding of the United States Naval Academy at Annapolis, Md., in 1845 was an expression of this need. In addition, officers who specialized in the design of warships and their armament required advanced technical education. The Royal Naval College at Greenwich, England, the École d'Application Maritime, Paris, France, and the University of Glasgow in Scotland, pioneered in engineering training for naval officers. Until about 1900 United States Naval officers were sent abroad to European schools for postgraduate education. In 1901, however, courses in ship construction for naval officers were established at the Massachusetts Institute of Technology. This was soon followed by courses at other universities for postgraduate training in naval engineering and naval ordnance.

Until World War I enlisted men continued to receive all their training aboard ship. The advent of radio and complex gunfire control systems in warships during the first two decades of this century made some formal schooling ashore of enlisted men necessary.

Aims of Naval Education.—Although navy instructional techniques follow many of the approved practices in public education, the learning atmosphere has certain significant differences. There is an environment that reflects the customs and traditions basic to the navy. The individual is placed in an atmosphere where he is continually stimulated to make these customs, traditions, and ideals a part of his life. He develops a sense of belonging to a fighting service essential to national security. The navy recognizes that gains in education and training demand:

(1) Adoption of technological and tactical improvements without delay.

(2) Utilization of significant advances in civilian education, psychology, and other sciences.

(3) Objective appraisal of all education and training programs of the Reserve and Regular forces.

(4) Integration—where feasible and advantageous to naval training programs with the training and educational activities of the other United States military services.

Responsibility for Education and Training.—The education and training responsibility of the chief of naval personnel is defined in *United States Navy Regulations* (1948) as ". . . recruit, basic, technical training and education of all personnel of the Navy including the Naval Reserve and the Naval Reserve Officers' Training Corps, as individuals, except such types of training as are assigned to other bureaus, offices or commands. . . ." The exceptions are aviation training and professional education, and technical training of medical personnel.

The education and training programs for which the chief of naval personnel is completely responsible may be grouped under five headings: enlisted, officer, functional, officer candidate and Naval Reserve.

Whereas the chief of naval personnel is responsible for the training of individuals (except as noted above) the chief of naval operations is responsible for training which is frequently identified as "team" or "group" training.

Fleet operational training includes the training of ships afloat, either singly or in groups, as well as the training of personnel as units of a ship's company. Training is provided in all forms of gunnery, damage control, engineering, combat information center (CIC), communications, and in tactical exercises. In addition, several shore-based schools, controlled by the fleet, have been established to fulfill particular needs. Among these are Fleet Sonar schools, CIC Team Training Centers, Fleet Gunnery and Torpedo schools, Fleet Training centers, and Naval Amphibious Training units.

The deputy chief of naval operations for air is responsible for the coordination of the aviation training program, both afloat and ashore. The shore-based program is administered by the chief of naval air training.

The chief of the Bureau of Medicine and Surgery (the surgeon general of the navy) is responsible for providing the professional education and training of the Medical, Dental, Medical Service, Nurse, and Hospital Corps. He establishes professional standards and policies, and trains personnel at naval hospitals or civilian installations, if the navy does not have the facilities. In the organization of the Graduate Medical Training Program, the general is assisted by a civilian Board of Consultants to insure that Medical Corps personnel meet the highest professional standards in the country.

In the execution of his assigned training responsibility, the commandant of the Marine Corps provides individual training for enlisted and officer personnel of the Marine Corps. The mission of conducting basic individual training of recruits has been assigned to the commanding generals of the Marine Corps Recruit depots. Training in basic subjects for all other enlisted men is the responsibility of each commanding officer. Primary responsibility for the basic training of newly commissioned officers has been assigned to the commandant, Marine Corps Schools, Quantico, Va.

The naval technical assistants to the secretary of the navy are: the chiefs of the bureaus; the chief of naval research and the chief of naval material; the judge advocate general; and the commandant of the Marine Corps. As we have seen, specific training responsibility has been assigned to certain of these assistants. *United States Navy Regulations* (1948) further provides that the other naval technical assistants shall make recommendations to the chief of naval personnel relative to the training and education of naval personnel who are assigned, or are intended for assignment, to duties in the field over which each technical assistant has authority. For this reason, the chiefs of the bureaus of Aeronautics, Ordnance, Ships, Supplies and Accounts, Yards and Docks; the judge advocate general, and the chief of naval research have considerable voice in the training of their own specialists. Likewise, certain branches of the Office of the Chief of Naval Operations—such as Naval Communications, the Hydrographic Office, and Naval Intelligence, determine training requirements of their own highly specialized personnel.

Education of Officer Candidates.—Naval officers are educated in a variety of ways. Some begin their naval education as midshipmen at the United States Naval Academy or at one of the Naval Reserve Officers Training Corps (NROTC) units; others become officers after years of service as enlisted men.

United States Naval Academy.—Although chaplains and schoolmasters were carried aboard navy ships in the early days, young officers received only rudimentary and haphazard instruction. This deficiency, and the development of steam-driven ships requiring officers with engineering training, led to the establishment of the United States Naval Academy in the year 1845. Today the four-year program at the academy emphasizes the humanities and the sciences along with the basic knowledge required of the naval profession. The emphasis is on a broad base of fundamentals rather than on specialization.

Midshipmen are indoctrinated through precept and example with ideals of duty, honor, and loyalty in order that the naval service may be provided with junior officers capable of assuming high responsibilities of military leadership and citizenship. For information on methods of admission to the academy and other pertinent matters see UNITED STATES NAVAL ACADEMY.

Naval Reserve Officers Training Corps (NROTC).—The purpose of the NROTC is to provide junior officers with a sound basic education for the Naval and Marine Corps Reserve. The NROTC grew from the first six units established in 1926 to a total of 27 units by the beginning of World War II (1941) when it became a part of the United States Navy's V-12 college training program.

In 1946, Congress authorized a new program within the NROTC for the training of officer candidates for the Regular Navy and Marine Corps (Public Law 729). As now established, the NROTC has the following mission: "To provide, by a permanent system of training and instruction in essential Naval subjects at civilian educational institutions, a source from which qualified officers may be obtained for the Navy and Marine Corps, and the Naval Reserve and Marine Corps Reserve."

By 1957 there were 53 NROTC units located in colleges and universities throughout the United States. These units are administered by professors of naval science who are captains, United States Navy, or colonels, United States Marine Corps, and are staffed by officers and enlisted personnel of the United States Navy and United States Marine Corps.

There are two types of NROTC students—regular and contract. Regular students are selected by means of a nation-wide annual competitive examination, personal interviews, and other selection procedures, and are appointed midshipmen in the United States Naval Reserve. The annual quota, as determined by the needs of the service, is divided equitably among all the states and territories. With the exception of refundable fees, regular students receive all their academic educational expenses, as well as retainer pay, for a period of not more than four academic years, and are commissoned in the regular service. After three years of service they must choose between a permanent commission or further service and transfer to the Reserve inactive service until they have fulfilled their eight-year obligation. Contract students, unlike the regular students, do not enter the program through nationwide competition, but are selected locally by the professor of naval science from interested students in the entering freshman class. They have the status of civilians who have entered into a contract with the navy. They are not entitled to the compensation paid regular students but are furnished commutation of subsistence during their third and fourth years of training. They do not receive educational expenses. Contract students are in training for reserve commissions.

Regular NROTC students may take almost any desired college course (premedical and predental being the major exceptions) leading to a baccalaurate or higher degree, but must include therein 24 semester hours of naval science (the curriculum for which is provided by the chief of naval personnel), one year of college physics, mathematics through trigonometry, and English of sufficient scope to develop proficiency in oral and written expression. Contract students are not restricted in their choice of curriculum except that they must meet the naval science, English, and mathematics requirements. It is contemplated that in the future approximately one half of the line officers of the navy will be NROTC graduates. See also NAVAL RESERVE—*Reserve Officer Procurement* (Naval Reserve Officers Training Corps).

Merchant Marine and State Maritime Academies.—There are five maritime academies: the United States Merchant Marine Academy at Kings Point, N.Y., operated by the United States Maritime Commission; and four academies under state auspices—the California Maritime Academy at Vallejo; the Maine Maritime Academy at Castine; the Massachusetts Maritime Academy at Hyannis; and the New York State Maritime College at Ft. Schuyler in New York, N.Y. The mission of each of these schools is to prepare selected candidates for careers as officers in the United States Merchant Marine Service.

The navy is interested in commissioning the graduates of these academies as ensigns, United States Naval Reserve, in order to build up the Merchant Marine Reserve and to this end maintains a Department of Naval Science at each academy. The navy provides naval personnel and equipment, textbooks and instructional material, and conducts the course in Naval Science which is required for each Merchant Marine cadet who aspires to a commission in the Naval Reserve.

The Officer Candidate School, Newport, R.I.—The mission of this school is to instruct and indoctrinate enlisted candidates for commissions in the Naval Reserve. During the 16-week course, instruction is provided in seamanship, communications, navigation, naval weapons, naval machinery, damage control, military justice, and leadership. Candidates must be college graduates and meet the age, citizenship, mental, moral, and physical requirements. Candidates may be civilians, inactive reservists, or active duty personnel. Successful candidates receive commissions in the restricted and unrestricted line or staff corps of the Naval Reserve. Training of women officers of the regular navy came about with the passage of Public Law 625 of June 1948. This act authorized enlistment and appointment of women in the regular navy and Naval Reserve.

The officer candidates attend an eight-week indoctrination session prior to their commissioning as officers in the Naval Reserve. This permits further screening after the initial selection and permits those unsuited to military life to be disenrolled before going into the second phase of the program provided for training of junior officers and results in a stronger and more select program for all chosen to continue training.

The program gives identical indoctrination to college graduates, enlisted women who are selected for the program, and college women who are accepted for training during their junior year. Junior officers, upon completion of their training, are immediately assigned to active duty.

Education for Officers.—After the successful candidate becomes a United States Marine Corps or United States Navy officer, his education continues on a more advanced basis.

Periods of Training.—Normally the further

education of an officer falls into the four periods described below.

Basic Period. An ensign's first assignment is normally in a ship of the fleet, where he receives intensive training under the supervision of more experienced officers. His duties may include: on-the-job training, short courses ashore related to his afloat assignments, courses through the navy correspondence courses center and the United States Armed Forces Institute, and required reading. He is rotated through the various departments on the ship and during his first six years, acquires a basic foundation of varied experience.

During this period, an officer may request a type of duty such as submarine or aviation duty. Officers applying for such assignments are selected on the basis of physical and mental qualifications and past record. Some officers are transferred to such specialties as civil engineering or supply corps duty.

Technical Period. The technical period typically occurs between the 6th and 12th years of commissioned service. During the first part of this period a line officer becomes eligible for his first shore duty. One year of this duty must be spent in the General Line School. Officers may apply for assignment to postgraduate courses conducted by the United States Naval Postgraduate School at Monterey, Calif., or at certain associated civilian colleges and universities. Applicants for the postgraduate instruction are selected by boards of officers appointed by the chief of naval personnel.

The Command and Staff Period.—The command and staff period includes the 12th to 30th years of an officer's career in the grades of lieutenant commander through captain. Normally after 12 years of service an officer has completed his first tour of shore duty which may have included one or more years of postgraduate study and a second tour at sea. He has completed his basic and his technical education. His sea and shore experience has prepared him for the advanced training of the command and staff period. His job becomes increasingly less one of operation and more one of leadership with greater responsibility and authority. Each officer is encouraged to request assignments which will further advance his training.

Special and Technical Schools for Officers.—Schools in this classification are maintained for the purpose of providing technical and refresher instruction in a variety of subjects as required to meet the needs of the many technical specialties. These courses, normally attended by junior officers, range from one week to 12 months in length. They are conducted at 16 schools and include instruction in the following categories: public works for Civil Engineering Corps (CEC) officers; atomic, biological and chemical warfare defense; damage control and fire-fighting; electronics; public information; ordnance and gunnery; basic Supply Corps training; freight transportation and cargo handling; naval justice; photography interpretation; and, when required, indoctrination training for chaplains.

The Five-Term College Program (Academic Education).—In 1946 Rear Admiral James L. Holloway, Jr. (1898–), as head of a navy board concerned with the proper education of officers, proposed a broader basis of acceptable training for prospective naval officers. The "Holloway Plan," approved by the secretary of the navy and implemented by Public Law 729, assured Reserve and United States Navy temporary officers accepted for transfer to the regular navy that they would have equal opportunity in the postwar navy with their contemporaries who were graduates of the Naval Academy. To this end the curriculum of the Naval Academy was reviewed to include approximately 2½ years of academic education and 1½ years of professional naval education. Arrangements were made to bring the education and training of all officers transferred to the Regular Navy to this minimum level of achievement. The five-term college program was inaugurated to furnish the required academic education for these officers.

Postgraduate Training.—The navy requires commissioned officers with advanced general and technical training to meet operational and logistic requirements for the maintenance and development of national seapower in peacetime and for rapid expansion in emergencies. Postgraduate education of commissioned officers, both men and women, in many fields is part of the fundamental naval personnel planning policy. Some, but not all, officers are selected for postgraduate education.

Advanced education in a technical specialty forms an important part of the preparation of officers who are later selected for special duty designations such as engineering. In the navy program, officers are usually given postgraduate education after they have served several years in the fleet. In this way, the advantages of maturity and broad viewpoint are realized.

The United States Naval Postgraduate School located at Monterey, Calif., is concerned with the graduate technical and professional education of naval officers. The instruction is conducted partly at the school itself and partly at various civilian institutions in order to utilize the best available resources in each field. Some instruction is conducted entirely at Monterey and some entirely at civilian schools; some courses include study at civilian schools after a year or more at Monterey. Naval intelligence postgraduate instruction is conducted at the Naval Intelligence School, Washington, D.C., which is a subcommand of the Naval Postgraduate School.

The establishment at Monterey comprises three distinct components—the General Line School, the Management School, and the Engineering School. The mission of the 9½ month General Line course is to broaden the mental outlook and increase the professional knowledge of line officers in such a manner as to enable them to meet the duties, responsibilities, and complexities of higher rank, thereby improving the efficiency and combat readiness of the navy. The general policy, insofar as practicable, is for all career line naval officers to attend the General Line School after five to seven years of commissioned service. This will be the first education period.

The Armed Forces Staff College at Norfolk, Va., is under the technical direction and supervision of the Joint Chiefs of Staff. The chief of naval operations is responsible for the operation and maintenance of the facilities used by the college, and administrative control is delegated to the chief of naval personnel. The mission of the school is to train selected officers of the armed forces in joint operations.

The Industrial College of the Armed Forces, Washington, D.C., is also a joint educational institution operated under the jurisdiction of the

Joint Chiefs of Staff. The Department of the Army is responsible for budget and maintenance. The mission of the college is to prepare selected officers of the armed forces for important command, staff, and planning assignments in the Department of Defense, and to prepare selected civilians for industrial mobilization planning assignments in any government agency, by:

(1) Conducting a course of study in all phases of our national economy and interrelating the economic factors with political, military, and psychological factors.

(2) Conducting a course of study in all aspects of joint logistic planning and the interrelation of this planning to joint strategic planning and to the national policy planning.

(3) Conducting a course of study of peacetime and potential wartime governmental organizations and the most effective wartime controls..

The National War College, at Washington, D.C., is a joint college under the technical direction and supervision of the Joint Chiefs of Staff. The Department of the Army has budgetary and maintenance responsibility.

The mission of this 10-month course is: (1) to prepare selected personnel of the armed forces and other governmental departments for the exercise of joint high-level policy command and staff functions, and for the performance of strategic planning duties in their respective departments; (2) to promote the development of understanding of those agencies of government and those factors of power potential which are an essential part of a national war effort.

The Naval War College at Newport, R.I., is under the supervision of the chief of naval operations. Fiscal, logistics support, and personnel matters are administered by the chief of naval personnel.

The mission of the college is to further an understanding of the fundamentals of warfare, international relations, and interservice operations, with emphasis on their applicability to future naval warfare, in order to prepare officers for higher command.

The Enlisted Training Program.—The prime objective of the navy's enlisted training program is to develop the civilian enlistee into a petty officer skilled in the technical requirements of his rating, aware of his responsibilities as a leader, informed of his duties as a citizen of the United States.

In addition to formal or school training, the enlisted man is trained throughout his naval career while on the job. The navy also provides opportunities for self-study through training courses, which prepare him for advancement, and through self-study and correspondence courses offered by the Navy Correspondence Courses Center and the United States Armed Forces Institute, which provide a valuable supplement to any phase of training.

A successful enlisted career normally terminates with transfer to Fleet Reserve after 20 years or more of active duty. Yet some enlisted men take advantage of the several opportunities offered during their normal careers to advance themselves to the status of warrant officers, commissioned warrant officers, or commissioned officers.

Recruit Training.—It is in recruit training that the individual receives his early impressions of the navy. Such impressions are likely to be the lasting ones, and it is here that the transition from civilian to military life must be accomplished. Recruits must be prepared mentally and physically for usefulness at sea. The manner in which this preparation is accomplished has a lasting effect upon the navy, for from these men come the petty officers, warrant officers, and some of the commissioned officers of the navy of the future. The kind of start these men get, the attitudes toward themselves and the Navy that are developed, the fundamental knowledges and understandings with which they must be equipped, are of such importance that recruit training cannot be over-emphasized.

Recruit training is conducted in a 10- to 14-week training period at the training centers at Great Lakes, Ill., and San Diego, Calif. Of the 14 weeks, 10 are devoted to the regularly scheduled training of recruits; one week, or its equivalent to service (mess cooking, work details, watches); two weeks to recruit leave; and one week to the retraining period and out-processing. From recruit training the recruit is channeled toward the rating group best suited to his qualifications, or transferred to the operating units of the navy where he can learn more about the navy and thus exercise better judgment in planning his service career.

Service Schools.—The service schools, planned, administered, and supported by the chief of naval personnel, are designed to provide technical training for individuals at successively higher levels. Class A schools are designed to cover the groundwork for general service ratings, the curricula including all the technical qualifications required for petty officer third and second class. Class B schools provide formal training in technical qualifications for advancement to first class and chief petty officers, while Class C schools provide formal training in a particular job qualification or skill which is closely related to the man's rating. Class C schools are subdivided into Class C-1 and Class C-2 schools. The C-1 schools are located in naval establishments, while C-2 schools are special schools, recognized by the chief of naval personnel, but operated in civilian manufacturing plants.

Functional Training.—Traditionally, formalized navy schools fell into two general categories: schools for officers and schools for enlisted personnel. As the normal duties of enlisted personnel differed widely from those of officers, the technical qualifications likewise differed materially. However, during World War II an extensive need was found for another type of training which did not fit readily into either category. A new type of training in which both officers and enlisted personnel learned to function together in the coordinated performance of an operational task aboard ship was inaugurated. This type of training is often called "team" or "group" training.

The Naval Schools, Mine Warfare will partially illustrate functional training. These schools provide numerous courses of instruction using facilities both afloat and ashore, for both officers and enlisted personnel. They give a basic course for officers and in this they are not unlike officers' technical schools. They also give technical courses for minemen and in these they resemble enlisted schools. But these same schools also give an operational course in which officers and enlisted personnel obtain instruction designed to enable them to work together as a team in readying mines for operational usage. These schools also provide an indoctrination course for the prospective skippers of mine vessels, specialized courses in aviation mines, courses for submarine officers and enlisted personnel, and specialized aspects of minesweeping for rated electricians and boatswains mates. Thus, these schools, concentrated at one location, provide instruction in all areas of mine warfare for all types of personnel who are concerned with the specialization.

United States Marine Corps.—The United States Marine Corps, which is an independent service within the Department of the Navy, shares in navy educational programs. The United States Naval Academy at Annapolis serves the Marine Corps: there are Marine Corps units in the NROTC; and Marine Corps officers receive advanced training in Navy schools. In accordance with the amphibious character of the Marine Corps and its traditions, the basic training of enlisted men is a combination of land training and naval training. This is conducted at the two Marine Corps Recruit depots at Parris Island, S.C., and San Diego, Calif. For advanced training, enlisted men participate in the schools of the United States Navy. Many marines also take correspondence courses through the Marine Corps Institute and the United States Armed Forces Institute.

Summary.—The United States Navy's training program for enlisted personnel is an essential part of the growth and development of the individual and is a foundation stone on which a career in the service must be built. The backbone of the naval service is the enlisted man. Through enlisted training he must be indoctrinated into the service from civilian life; he must be given the fundamental tools of skill and knowledge that will make him of use to the naval service; he must be trained in the technology of his specialty in accordance with his aptitude and ability; he must be taught to work smoothly and efficiently with others as a part of a team, he must be afforded the opportunity and the media for learning by doing, under competent direction and leadership; he must be enabled to grow professionally and as a member of a military force, through training and experience; and he must be advanced in accordance with his competence and effectiveness.

CANADA

The Royal Canadian Navy (RCN) was established in 1910 during a period of growing awareness that the naval strength of Germany represented a threat to British control of the seas.

Officers.—The education and training of officers for RCN began before the inception of the navy itself. An old naval hospital in the dockyard at Halifax, N.S., was converted for use as a naval college and was opened on Jan. 11, 1910. Two old British cruisers, H.M.S. *Niobe* and *Rainbow,* were also used as training ships. Even before this, the first group of young men had begun their training as officers in the Canadian government ship *Canada.*

Boys between the ages of 14 and 16 were entered and given a two-year course to be followed by a year's cruiser training. Later, the course was lengthened to three years and the curriculum broadened so as to include preparation for other than naval careers. In 1915, the subjects taught included mathematics, navigation, physics, engineering, seamanship, geography, history, English, French, and German.

The Halifax explosion in 1917 rendered the naval college building uninhabitable and the staff and cadets were moved to Kingston, Ontario, where accommodation was provided by the Royal Military College. In September 1918, the Naval College was transferred to Esquimalt. Before a permanent location for the college was found, postwar retrenchment changed the picture and in 1922 it was closed. From this time until World War II, the training of cadets was carried out in ships and establishments of the British Royal Navy. Officers were also sent to the British Royal Navy for advanced and specialized courses.

In 1942, Royal Roads at Esquimalt, B.C., was opened as a training establishment for regular officers. In 1949, the establishment was incorporated in a tri-service scheme known as the Canadian Services College and army, navy, and air force officers received a common academic and military training.

In general, prospective officers have at least a secondary school education and are enrolled as cadets. Their education in the service is designed to bring them to second-year-university level or, in the specialist branches, to degree standard. Officers may be entered in one of the following plans: (1) Regular Officers Training Plan; (2) College Training Plan; (3) Venture Training Plan; (4) Upper Yardmen; (5) Branch Officers.

Enlisted men may become officers, meeting some of the necessary requirements of taking a set of Canadian educational tests established on the college level, including some which have their parallel in the work of a technical institute. Each officer candidate from the "lower deck" must pass three or four of these higher tests, the choice depending upon his branch of the service and anticipated avenue of advancement.

Enlisted Men.—The minimum educational requirement for entry into the Royal Canadian Navy is completion of the eighth year of elementary school. The newly enlisted recruit receives very little further academic schooling during his initial training period of 21 weeks, which is devoted largely to professional training. He does, however, get about 16 lectures, treating in an elementary manner a variety of topics. These lectures include two on the significance of guided missiles and atomic energy in modern warfare.

Located at the Educational Training School in Royal Canadian Navy Barracks, Esquimalt, is the preparatory school. This is a school designed to give eight months of advanced educational training to men selected by fleet selection boards for eventual promotion to officer status. These men have been under special quarterly report for a year or more, have shown officerlike qualities, met certain professional standards and have qualified educationally as mentioned above. In the preparatory school they pass the higher educational tests required for promotion, and in some cases, one or two additional.

Preparatory school men are in different avenues of promotion, depending on their age, scholastic ability and branch. A few of the youngest and most gifted are made ready to enter a university course leading to a degree in engineering, honors physics and mathematics, or to the bachelor of commerce degree, the latter being open only to men of the supply branch. A few others, also superior students, but older (24–29), are designated upper yardmen and will become general list officers after about two years of professional training following graduation from the preparatory school. The majority of the students are older men (30 or more) destined to become Branch Officers. These are limited-career officers qualified only in the field in which they specialized while on the "Lower Deck." Upon graduation and completion of a short course of further professional training they are promoted to the ranks of Commissioned Boatswain, Commissioned Electrical Officer, Commissioned Supply Officer, etc. The best of them will, after a few years, be given an opportunity to qualify as officers of the General List.

After new entry (recruit) training and (normally) an interval at sea; professional or trade training is continued in one of the RCN training schools. Among the most important of these are: the Torpedo-Anti-Submarine School, the Gunnery School, the Electrical School, the Mechanical Training establishments, the Naval Air Maintenance School, the Ordnance School, the Navigation Direction School. In each of these schools, instruction in mathematics and science is included at each level. In the Supply and Secretariat School, science and mathematics give place to bookkeeping, English, and accounting.

There is also a large educational program outside the professional and trade schools. It is based on a system of correspondence courses and voluntary school classes. This Royal Canadian Navy Correspondence Course system is designed to help men to pass RCN educational tests. There are two basic educational tests, one in arithmetic, the other in English, established on approximately the level of the eighth grade of elementary school. Both of these elementary tests must be passed for qualification as a petty officer second class in a technical branch or petty officer first class in a nontechnical branch. There are also tests in English, French, mathematics, physics, chemistry, bookkeeping, and navigation; these are known in the RCN as Canadian intermediate educational tests.

The above outline does not exhaust all the educational opportunities open to enlisted men of the RCN. They may compete, for example, on equal terms with civilians for acceptance in the Regular Officer Training Plan and the Venture Plan. There are also opportunities for men who wish to prepare for re-establishment in civil life. They may take, at public expense, various correspondence courses made available through the Department of Veterans Affairs.

Education of enlisted men is carried on largely by officers of the Instructor Branch of the RCN. These officers have degrees in the arts, science, or engineering, and are, with few exceptions, licensed as secondary school teachers. See also MILITARY EDUCATION AND TRAINING, and sections on defense in articles on individual countries.

JOHN V. NOEL, JR.,
Captain, United States Navy; Bureau of Naval Personnel, Department of the Navy.

NAVAL GUNS. See GUNS.

NAVAL INSTITUTE, United States, a private, non-profit professional society founded in 1873 at Annapolis, Md., by officers on duty at the United States Naval Academy. Its objectives are the advancement of professional, literary, and scientific knowledge in the Navy. It publishes the *Proceedings* which has reflected the best current and advanced professional thinking of officers and men in the Navy.

Two prize essay contests annually, one for officers and one for enlisted men, stimulate articles on professional subjects. The *Proceedings* also specializes in the publication of historical material by foreign Naval officers.

The Naval Institute acts as the university press for the Naval Academy, publishing texts used throughout the Navy in professional education and training. It also publishes books of general interest dealing with naval history.

The institute membership is composed of most of the senior officers of the Navy and a large number of civilians throughout the world who are interested in naval matters. Associate membership is open to the public. The members elect annually a Board of Control which governs all institute activities, including the selection of articles for the *Proceedings.* A permanent staff under the Board of Control is headed by a secretary treasurer who is always a senior officer on active duty at the Naval Academy. While physically situated on the grounds of the Naval Academy at Annapolis, the institute is an independent, non-government, self-supporting professional society.

NAVAL INTELLIGENCE is the term applied to the collection, evaluation, recording, and assembling in usable form, of naval information which may be useful to the Department of the Navy in time of war, as well as in peace. It is usually thought of as information concerning foreign governments, and especially foreign navies, maritime capabilities, industrial potential, etc., but it includes much information about our own country. Special emphasis is placed on obtaining knowledge of the naval strength, resources, dispositions and intentions of foreign powers. An Office of Naval Intelligence was established by the United States Navy on March 23, 1882, while the British and German navies organized similar agencies in 1885 and 1891, respectively. Long before this period navies had made intermittent attempts to gather information but upon establishment of the Office of Naval Intelligence (ONI), a systematic compilation of data was begun on docking facilities of the ports of the world; foreign navies; naval personnel, numbers, recruitment, training; naval maneuvers; fueling stations; new inventions and patents; submarine cables and telegraph lines; engineering resources of the United States; manufactures of material suitable for naval use; commerce and trade routes; merchant vessels suitable for naval auxiliary use; harbor fortifications; suppliers of maps and charts. The publication of data on professional and technical subjects of special interest began in 1883 and has continued.

The first director of Naval Intelligence was Lt. T.B.M. Mason, USN, who served three years. The first United States naval attaché sent abroad was Lt. Comdr. French E. Chadwick, accredited to London, Oct. 28, 1882. He distinguished himself there and later served as chief of staff to Admiral William Thomas Sampson in the war with Spain. Afterwards he was president of the Naval War College and wrote the standard history of the Spanish-American War. In November 1885, an attaché was accredited to three capitals, Paris, St. Petersburg, and Berlin. In November 1888 one was accredited to Rome and Vienna, and in Feb. 1895 one to Tokyo and Peking. In February 1897, one was sent to Madrid, thus before the Spanish-American War we had five naval attachés abroad. In 1910 an attaché was accredited to Buenos Aires, Rio de Janeiro, and Santiago de Chile, our first to South America. On the eve of World War I in 1914 the United States Navy had six officers abroad accredited as naval attachés in 10 capitals. At the same time Great Britain had 9 officers serving as naval attachés. In wartime, 1914–1918, the United States Navy established 12 additional naval attachés in as many capitals and added assistants. World War II again increased the attaché staffs. In May 1954 the United States Navy had naval attachés accredited in 45 foreign capitals. The naval attaché in London was a rear admiral with 10 assistants, while the attachés in Paris, Rome, and Taipei, Formosa, each had five or more assistants. At the same time 39 foreign nations had naval attachés in Washington.

Although the basic duties and purposes of ONI have not changed since 1882 the drastic changes in ship construction, the introduction of naval aviation, the multiplication of types of weapons, the astonishing developments in electronics, the improvements in navigational instruments, and aids to navigation, have added to the complexity of the problems involved in collecting, compiling, recording and correcting information. The first head of ONI organized the work along functional lines rather than according to geographical areas from which it originated. Thus all data on navigation were brought together, studied and evaluated, as was done also for data on shipbuilding, marine engines, fuel, guns, ammunition, airplane design, aviation engines, seaplane development, aircraft carriers, bombs, ship supply, etc. This basic organization was essentially unchanged in 1954, but the far greater number of subjects on which data were collected had required some changes in method. In supplying the technical bureaus of the Department of the Navy with data everything was still brought together on each subject, as, for example, radio. Each technical bureau—Ships, Ordnance, Aeronautics, Yards and Docks—has all foreign information collated for its use. Likewise, the planning divisions of the Office of Naval Operations could apply to ONI for all information or any specific information concerning a particular country and be given an evaluation of the available data on that country, the data on one country being put together in what ONI calls the monograph for that nation.

In the collection of information ONI has never relied entirely on naval attachés. Other sources of information are consular reports; reports of ambassadors and ministers to the State Department; reports of intelligence officers of ships of the Navy which visit foreign ports; reports from tourists, businessmen, newspaper correspondents, and commercial travellers; commercial reports of business firms; newspapers and periodicals; books of travel, guide books, geographies published at home and abroad; and agents. The United States Army has had an Intelligence Office since 1885, and the Air Force has had one since it was established as a separate department in 1947. These agencies and the Intelligence divisions of other government departments cooperate in their work and exchange information. On July 26, 1947, the Congress provided for a Central Intelligence Agency (CIA) which functions by collecting, collating and evaluating intelligence assembled by the State Department, the Defense Department, or other government agencies, and its own service. While this CIA is the principal intelligence advisor for the president, the National Security Council, and the Congress, it has in no sense changed or lessened the duties or importance of ONI. On the contrary, its existence has served to emphasize the necessity for an efficient and effective ONI.

Each naval district has an intelligence officer who functions under the Commandant along general lines prescribed by ONI. Each naval vessel visiting a foreign port has an intelligence officer to make certain reports. There is an intelligence officer on the staff of each principal naval command.

ONI became a part of the Bureau of Navigation when first established, but it has been a part of the Office of the Chief of Naval Operations since the creation of this organization in 1915.

ONI has always preferred to operate without self-advertising in war and in peace. In spite of various newspaper stories of exploits of Intelligence officers, the tradition has been one of official silence.

When the United States declared war in 1917 ONI was assigned many duties not usually considered as being related to Intelligence. For example, much of the work in what has since been called "economic warfare" fell to the lot of the Intelligence officers. ONI had planned to take over the inspection of neutral merchant vessels in our ports, and from this duty was derived the task of checking on the quantity and type of maritime supplies which such ships proposed to purchase supposedly for their own use.

ONI organized also a counterintelligence service and a system for protection against sabotage. With the cooperation of the United States Coast Guard, then operating under the Navy Department, our ports and their installations were guarded against misuse or sabotage, and all industrial plants and commercial shipyards were protected. This sabotage detail gave special attention to fire-prevention.

When the United States entered World War I in 1917, there were 8 officers and 18 civil service clerks in ONI in Washington, D.C. On Armistice Day 1918 this total of 26 had grown by 306.

Between the two wars the personnel assigned to ONI was sharply curtailed. The peacetime complement abroad and in Washington was only slightly larger than it had been in 1914. After the outbreak of war in Europe in 1939 there was a rapid expansion, and by Dec. 1, 1941, there were 230 officers, 175 enlisted men, and 300 civilians in the Washington office, while in the naval districts there were well over 1,000 more. In foreign posts there were then 133 officers and 200 enlisted men. During World War II the numbers in Intelligence work in the districts reached a peak in 1943, with 2,597 officers, 3,091 enlisted men, and a considerable number of civilians. ONI in Washington reached a peak in numbers in 1944, with 426 officers, about 600 enlisted men, and 358 civilians. In foreign posts there were then 270 officers and about 300 enlisted men.

In May 1954 the director of Naval Intelligence was a rear admiral and his assistant held the same rank. The Naval Intelligence Division had three principal subdivisions: (1) Security Branch, with a Censorship Section, an Investigations Section, a Commerce and Travel Section, and a Security Control Section. This branch dealt with all problems of security and loyalty of individuals for the Department of the Navy. (2) Intelligence Branch, with sections named Foreign, Collection and Dissemination, Staff, Air, and Operational Intelligence. (3) Administrative Branch.

JOHN B. HEFFERNAN,
Rear Admiral, United States Navy (Retired).

NAVAL LAW. See MARITIME LAW; MILITARY LAW.

NAVAL MANEUVERS. See ARMY, NAVY, AND AIR FORCE MANEUVERS.

NAVAL MILITIA. See NAVAL RESERVE.

NAVAL MINES. See SUBMARINE MINES, MINELAYING, AND MINE COUNTERMEASURES.

NAVAL OBSERVATORY. See OBSERVATORY—*North American Observatories.*

NAVAL RANK. See INSIGNIA OF RANK, ARMED FORCES.